PREFACE

This 121st edition of *Wisden* has presented in its compilation the usual pleasure and the customary problems. Of the latter, much the most ticklish has been how best to make the space needed to accommodate the ever-increasing amount of Test and one-day international cricket. This has had to be done without enlarging the almanack or, as some have suggested, making two volumes of it, one for domestic cricket, the other for cricket overseas.

In the last year alone, Sri Lanka have played inaugural Test matches against India, New Zealand and Australia, all of which require, as they now always will, their own section. Thirty years ago the Test cricket records occupied 21 pages; now, based on a broadly similar selection, they take up over 80.

Some pruning, therefore, has been necessary. Although the scores of the three major one-day county competitions are still shown in full, only the later rounds of the Benson and Hedges Cup and the NatWest Bank Trophy are accompanied by match reports. University Blues before 1947 have gone, though they are all, of course, listed in earlier *Wisdens*. A key as to where to find them appears on page 636.

The index has also been rearranged. A detailed index was first used in *Wisden* in 1938, the same year, as it happens, that Women's Cricket first gained recognition. Each entry has always had a separate line. Now, as a means of saving space, the entries are run on. I am indebted to E. M. Wellings for the help he gave in implementing the change.

The choice of the Five Cricketers of the Year gave more scope than is sometimes the case. In the previous season, for example, four out of the five more or less selected themselves. This time only John Emburey did so. Mike Gatting makes a second member of the successful Middlesex side. That Essex are unrepresented is only because Ken McEwan and John Lever were ineligible for having already appeared. The same applied to Richard Hadlee of the touring New Zealanders and to Kapil Dev who led India to success in the Prudential World Cup. Instead, Jeremy Coney represents New Zealand, as being typical of the determination they bring to their cricket, and Mohinder Amarnath is included for the remarkable successes he enjoyed on his return to the Indian side, culminating in the leading part he played in the semi-finals and final of the World Cup. Chris Smith of Natal, Hampshire and England finds a place as the batsman who made the greatest advance in the 1983 English season.

From Australia comes an article by R. J. Parish, tracing the events of the last five years which have so altered the structure of the game there. The author having been Chairman, at the time, of the Australian Cricket Board, Mr Parish's first account of the war and peace with Packer is of definitive interest. David Green, cricketer turned journalist, writes on Zaheer Abbas, the twentieth batsman and the first Pakistani to complete 100 first-class hundreds. Stephen Green, Curator of MCC, picks out some significant centenaries; Marcus Williams links two of his great interests, cricket and stamps, to make a collectors' piece, and Matthew Engel covers the main political story of the sporting year, the attempt made by a number of members of MCC to force the committee of the club to send a side to South Africa in the winter of 1983-84.

My thanks are due to these and many other correspondents and contributors. As will be seen from the list on the following page, there are the best part of 100 of them. Nor does that list include the countless secretaries, especially of counties and schools, who so willingly give their help. Leslie Smith, who assisted Wilfred H. Brookes, Haddon Whitaker, Hubert Preston and Norman Preston when they edited *Wisden*, re-emerged to read the proofs of this one, for which I am very grateful. Richard Streeton held the fort for me in Australia until I was able to get there for the third Test match.

As "keepers", respectively, of the record section, the books, the obituaries and Births and Deaths, Barry McCaully, John Arlott, Bob Arrowsmith and Robert Brooke attended between them to over 200 pages, all of which are indispensable to the character of the book. The printers have worked indefatigably and Christine Forrest with an allegiance and an eye for detail which have been the editor's greatest standbys. As consultant and technician Graeme Wright was again the all-rounder of the team.

JOHN WOODCOCK

Longparish,
Hampshire.

★ ★ ★ ★ ★

From the 1985 edition, WISDEN *will be published by John Wisden & Co. Ltd, the owners of the copyright. Correspondence should be addressed to: Wisden Cricketers' Almanack, John Wisden & Co. Ltd, Benson Street, Cambridge CB4 3QL.*

LIST OF CONTRIBUTORS

The Editor acknowledges with gratitude the assistance afforded in the preparation of the Almanack by the following:

H. E. Abel (Surrey)
Jack Arlidge (Sussex)
John Arlott (Book Reviews)
David Armstrong (Minor Counties)
Robert L. Arrowsmith
Chris Aspen
Diane Back
Alex Bannister
Jack Bannister (Warwickshire)
Brian Bearshaw (Lancashire)
Scyld Berry
J. Watson Blair (Scotland)
Dick Brittenden
Robert Brooke
Sue Bullen
Kenneth R. Bullock (Canada)
C. R. Buttery (New Zealand)
John Callaghan (Yorkshire)
Michael Carey
Terry Cooper
Geoffrey Copinger
Tony Cozier (West Indies)
Brian Croudy
Patrick Eagar
Matthew Engel
Paton Fenton (Oxford University)
Charles Fortune
Bill Frindall
Nigel Fuller (Essex)
Mike Gear
David Green
Stephen Green
David Hallett (Cambridge University)
Les Hatton
Brian Hayward (Hampshire)
Brian Heald
Murray Hedgecock
Eric Hill (Somerset)
Grenville Holland (UAU)
Ken Ingman (ESCA)

V. H. Isaacs (Limited-overs records)
Martin Johnson (Leicestershire)
Ken Kelly
Brian Langley
Stephanie Lawrence
John Lawson (Nottinghamshire)
Peter Lush
Barry McCaully
Peter Mackinnon (Australia)
Michael Melford
John Minshull-Fogg
Chris Moore (Worcestershire)
Dudley Moore (Kent)
Gerald Mortimer (Derbyshire)
Mike Neasom
Don Neely
R. J. Parish
A. L. A. Pichanick (Zimbabwe)
Qamar Ahmed (Pakistan)
Findlay Rea
Netta Rheinberg
Geoffrey Saulez
Peter Sichel (South Africa)
Derek Scott (Ireland)
Bill Smith
Leslie Smith
F. S. Speakman (Northamptonshire)
Richard Streeton
P. N. Sundaresan (India)
E. W. Swanton
John Thicknesse (Middlesex)
J. B. G. Thomas (Glamorgan)
Gerry Vaidyasekera (Sri Lanka)
D. R. Walsh (HMC Schools)
E. M. Wellings
Geoff Wheeler (Gloucestershire)
Phil Wilkins
Marcus Williams
A. S. R. Winlaw
Wilfred Wooller

CONTENTS

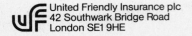

INDEX

Note: For reasons of space, certain entries which appear in alphabetical order in sections of the Almanack are not included in this index. These include names that appear in Test Cricketers, Births and Deaths of Cricketers, Individual batting and bowling performances in the 1983 first-class season, and Oxford and Cambridge Blues.

c. = catches; d. = dismissals; p'ship = partnership; r. = runs; w. = wickets.

* Signifies not out or an unbroken partnership

A

Aamer Malik (Lahore):– 2 hundreds on début, *130.*

Abdul Kadir (Pak.):– Test p'ship record, *225.*

Abdul Qadir (Pak.):– 103 w. in Pakistan season, *155;* 10 w. or more in Test (1), *225.*

Abel, R. (Eng.):– 33,124 r., *133;* 3,309 r. in season, *144;* Highest for Surrey, *129;* 74 hundreds, *130;* 357* v Somerset, *127, 129;* Hundreds v Gents, *248;* 2 Test hundreds, *189, 198;* Carrying bat in Test, *172;* 379 for 1st wkt, *139.*

Adcock, N. A. T. (SA):– 104 w. in Tests, *178;* 26 w. in series, *201;* Test p'ship record, *227.*

Addresses of representative bodies, *319-20.*

Adhikari, H. R. (Ind.):– Test captain, *230;* 1 Test hundred, *231;* Test p'ship records, *223, 240.*

Afaq Hussain (Pak.):– Test p'ship record, *227.*

Aftab Baloch (Pak.):– Test début at 16, *184;* 428 v Baluchistan, *127.*

Agha Zahid (HBL):– 2 hundreds in match (2), *131.*

Ahad Khan (Pak. Rlwys):– 9 w. for 7 r., *151.*

Alabaster, J. C. (NZ):– Test p'ship records, *229, 236.*

Alderman, T. M. (Aust.):– 42 w. in series, *181, 195;* Test p'ship record, *225.*

Alexander, F. C. M. (WI):– Test captain, *201, 230, 232;* 1 Test hundred, *218;* 23 d. in series, *182;* 5 c. in Test innings, *183.*

Alim-ud-Din (Pak.):– 2 Test hundreds, *212, 240;* Test p'ship record, *212.*

Allan, P. J. (Aust.):– 10 w. in innings, *150.*

Allcott, C. F. W. (NZ):– 301 for 2nd wkt, *141;* 190* for 8th wkt, *142;* Test p'ship record, *227.*

Allen, D. A. (Eng.):– 122 w. in Tests, *177;* Test p'ship records, *212.*

Allen, G. O. (Eng.):– Test captain, *188, 201, 208;* Test cricket at 45, *185;* 1 Test hundred, *206;* 81 w. in Tests, *177;* 10 w. in innings, *150;* 10 w. or more in Test (1), *210;* Test p'ship record, *207.*

Alletson, E. B. (Notts):– Fast scoring, *136;* 34 r. in over, *137.*

Alley, W. E. (Som.):– 3,019 r. in season, *144.*

Allom, M. J. C. (Eng.):– Test hat-trick, *181, 207.*

Allott, P. J. W. (Eng.):– Test p'ship record, *210.*

Altaf Shah (HBFC):– 355 for 5th wkt, *141.*

Amarnath, L. (Ind.):– Test captain, *221, 230, 239;* Hundred on Test début, *171, 209;* 410 for 3rd wkt, *141.*

Amarnath, M. (Ind.):– Cricketer of the Year, *55;* 2,648 r. in Tests, *168;* 7 Test hundreds, *222, 231, 239;* 2,234 r. in season, *145;* Test p'ship records, *223, 232, 240.*

Amarnath, S. (Ind.):– Hundred on Test début, *171, 235;* Test p'ship record, *236.*

Ames, L. E. G. (Kent):– 37,248 r., *132;* 2,434 r. in Tests, *167;* 1,000 r. (17), *134;* 3,058 r. in season, *144;* 102 hundeds, *130;* 8 Test hundreds, *189, 198, 202, 206;* 2 hundreds in match, *131;* Double-hundred v Gents, *248;* 1,113 d., *159;* 127 d. in season, *159;* 8 d. in Test, *182;* 2,482 r. and 100 d. in season, *1,919 r. and 121 d. in season, 1,795 r. and 127 d. in season, 157;* Test p'ship records, *199, 207.*

Amin Lakhani (Pak. Univs):– Double hat-trick, *148.*

Amir Elahi (Ind. and Pak.):– Test p'ship record, *240.*

Amiss, D. L. (Eng.):– 36,879 r., *132;* 3,612 r. in Tests, *166;* 2,000 r. (2), *144;* 1,000 r. (20), *134;* 85 hundreds, *131;* 11 Test hundreds, *202, 206, 209, 211;*

C

E

Eady, C. J. (Tas.):– 566 v Wellington, *129*.

Edgar, B. A. (NZ):– 3 Test hundreds, *220, 229, 237;* Slow scoring, *174;* Test p'ship record, *220*.

Edmonds, P. H. (Eng.):– Test p'ship record, *210*.

Edrich, J. H. (Eng.):– Test captain, *188;* 39,790 r., *132;* 5,138 r. in Tests, *166;* 2,644 r. v Australia, *196;* 2,000 r. (2), *144;* 1,000 r. (21), *134;* 103 hundreds, *130;* 12 Test hundreds, *189, 202, 206, 209;* 2 hundreds in match (4), *131;* 310* v New Zealand, *127, 170, 206;* 57 boundaries in innings, *137;* 1st wkt hundreds, *139;* Test p'ship records, *207, 210*.

Edrich, W. J. (Eng.):– 36,965 r., *132;* 3,539 r. in season, *143, 145;* 2,440 r. in Tests, *166;* 1,010 r. (April 30/May 31), *146;* 1,000 r. (15), *134;* 86 hundreds, *130;* 6 Test hundreds, *189, 198, 206;* Avge of 80.43 in English season, *145;* 424* for 3rd wkt, *141;* Test p'ship records, *199*.

Edwards, R. (Aust.):– 2 Test hundreds, *191*.

Elliott, G. (Vic.):– 9 w. for 2 r., *151*.

Elliott, H. (Eng.):– 1,206 d., *159;* 10 d. in match, *159*.

Emburey, J. E. (Eng.):– Cricketer of the Year, *59;* 100 w. (1), *153*.

Emmett, G. M. (Eng.):– 2 hundreds in match (2), *131*.

Emmett, T. (Eng.):– 16 w. in day, *151*.

Endean, W. R. (SA):– 3 Test hundreds, *199, 215, 227;* Test p'ship records, *216, 227*.

Engineer, F. M. (Ind.):– 2,611 r. in Tests, *168;* 2 Test hundreds, *209, 231;* Test p'ship records, *210, 236*.

England:– B & H World Series Cup, *978-90;* Definition of first-class matches, *339, 1245;* England in Test cricket (*see p. 126*); England v Rest of the World, *246;* Highest individual Test innings, *169;* Highest Test innings, *169;* Leading batsmen in Tests, *166;* Leading bowlers in Tests, *177;* Lowest Test innings, *169;* Most consecutive Test appearances, *185;* Most Test appearances, *122;* Most Test appearances as captain, *123;* Oldest Test player, *185;* Representative body, *319;* Summary of Tests, *185;* Test cricketers (1877-1983), *83-95;* Youngest and oldest on Test début, *184*.

England in Australia and New Zealand, 1982-83, *879-903*.

England v New Zealand, 1983, *271-92*.

English Schools Cricket Association:– Address, *320;* 1983 season, *828-30*.

English Industrial Estates Trophy, *786*.

Errata in *Wisden*, 1983, *1103*.

Essex:– *335, 355-70;* Highest score, *161;* Highest individual score, *128;* Lowest score, *162*.

Essex II, *801, 802, 804*.

Esso Scholarships, *600*.

Eton v Harrow, *327-8*.

Evans, T. G. (Eng.):– 2,439 r. in Tests, *166;* 2 Test hundreds, *202, 209;* 1,060 d., *159;* 219 d. in Tests, *182;* 75 d. v Australia, *195;* 20 d. in series, *182*.

F

Fagg, A. E. (Eng.):– 27,291 r., *133;* 58 hundreds, *130;* 2 double hundreds, *132;* 2 hundreds in match (2), *131*.

Fairbairn, A. (Middx):– hundred on début, *129*.

Family connections, *243-5*.

Fane, F. L. (Eng.):– Test captain, *188, 197;* 1 Test hundred, *198*.

Farnes, K. (Eng.):– 10 w. or more in Test (1), *194*.

Farrimond, W. (Eng.):– 7 d. in innings, *160*.

Faulkner, G. A. (SA):– 4 Test hundreds, *199, 215;* 82 w. in Tests, *178*.

Favell, L. E. (Aust.):– 1 Test hundred, *222;* 2 hundreds in match (2), *131*.

Fazal Mahmood (Pak.):– Test captain, *223, 232, 239;* 139 w. in Tests, *179;* 10 w. or more in Test (3), *213, 225, 234*.

Features of 1983, *253-6*.

Fender, P. G. H. (Eng.):– All-round, *157;* Hundred in 35 minutes, *135*.

Ferguson, W. (WI):– 10 w. or more in Test (1), *205*.

Fernandes, M. P. (WI):– Test captain, *201*.

Fernando, E. R. N. S. (SL):– Test p'ship record, *243*.

Ferris, G. J. F. (Leics.):– Hat-trick in 1983, *254*.

Ferris, J. J. (Aust. and Eng.):– 10 w. or more in Test (1), *200*.

H

O

P

PACO Cup (Pak.), *1130-9.*

Page, M. L. (NZ):– Test captain, *205, 226;* 1 Test hundred, *206;* Test p'ship record, *207.*

Pairaudeau, B. H. (WI):– Hundred on Test début, *171, 231;* Test p'ship record, *232.*

Pakistan:– Definition of first-class matches, *1245-6;* Domestic season 1982-83, *1123-39;* Highest individual Test innings, *169;* Highest Test innings, *169;* Leading batsmen in Tests, *168;* Leading bowlers in Tests, *179;* Lowest Test innings, *169;* Most Test appearances, *122;* Most Test appearances as captain, *123;* Oldest Test player, *185;* Pakistan in Test cricket *(see p. 126);* Representative body, *319;* Summary of Tests, *187;* Test cricketers (1952-83), *119-22;* Youngest and oldest on Test début, *184.*

Pakistan v Australia, 1982-83, *904-17.*

Pakistan v India, 1982-83, *923-37.*

Pakistan in India, 1983-84, *917.*

Palm, A. W. (SA):– 244* for 6th wkt, *142.*

Palmer, G. E. (Aust.):– 78 w. in Tests, *178;* 10 w. or more in Test (2), *195.*

Parfitt, P. H. (Eng.):– 26,924 r., *132;* 1,000 r. (15), *134;* 58 hundreds, *130;* 7 Test hundreds, *198, 206, 209, 212;* 2 hundreds in match (2), *131;* Test p'ship records, *207, 212.*

Parkar, G. A. (Ind.):– 421 for 1st wkt, *139.*

Parkar, Z. A. (Bombay):– 10 d. in match, *160.*

Parker, C. W. L. (Glos.):– 3,278 w., *154;* 200 w. (5), *152;* 100 w. (16), *155;* 100 w. by June 12, *153;* 17 w. in match, *150;* 10 w. in innings, *149;* 6 hat-tricks, *148;* Double hat-trick, *148.*

Parker, J. M. (NZ):– Test-captain, *236;* 3 Test hundreds, *206, 220, 235;* Test p'ship records, *220.*

Parker, P. W. G. (Eng.):– 32 r. in over, *137.*

Parkhouse, W. G. A. (Eng.):– 1,000 r. (15), *134.*

Parkin, C. H. (Eng.):– 200 w. (2), *152.*

Parks, J. H. (Eng.):– All-round, *156;* 3,003 r. in season, *144.*

Parks, J. M. (Eng.):– 36,673 r., *132;* 1,000 r. (20), *134;* 51 hundreds, *130;* 2 Test hundreds, *198, 203;* 1,182 d., *159;* 114 d. in Tests, *182;* 8 c. in Test, *182;* Test p'ship records, *199, 204.*

Parks, R. J. (Hants):– 10 d. in match, *160.*

Partnerships:– Highest for each country, *140-3;* Highest in Tests, *176-7.*

Pascoe, L. S. (Aust.):– Test p'ship record, *220.*

Passailaigue, C. C. (WI):– 487* for 6th wkt, *138, 142.*

Pataudi (Sen.), Nawab of (Eng. and Ind.):– Test captain, *208;* 4 successive hundreds, *135;* Hundred on Test début, *171, 190.*

Pataudi (Jun.), Nawab of (Ind.):– Test captain, *123, 208, 221, 230, 234;* 2,793 r. in Tests, *168;* 6 Test hundreds, *209, 222, 235;* 2 hundreds in match (2), *131;* Test p'ship record, *210.*

Patel, B. P. (Ind.):– 1 Test hundred, *231;* Test p'ship records, *232, 236.*

Patel, D. N. (Worcs.):– All-round, *158.*

Patel, J. M. (Ind.):– 14 w. in Test, *180, 223;* 9 w. in Test innings, *180, 223.*

Patil, S. M. (Ind.):– 3 Test hundreds, *209, 222, 241;* Test p'ship record, *240.*

Paynter, E. (Eng.):– 653 r. in series, *200;* 4 Test hundreds, *190, 198;* 2 hundreds in match (2), *131;* 2 hundreds in same Test, *172, 198;* 322 v Sussex, *127;* Test avge of 59.23, *170;* Test p'ship records, *203.*

Peach, H. A. (Surrey):– Fast scoring, *136;* 4 w. with consecutive balls, *147.*

Pearse, D. K. (Natal):– Out handled the ball, *146.*

Pearson, A. J. G. (CUCC and Som.):– 10 w. in innings, *150.*

Peate, E. (Eng.):– 214 w. in season, *152;* 8 w. for 5 r., *151.*

Peel, R. (Eng.):– 1,754 w., *154;* 102 w. in Tests, *177;* 100 w. (8), *155;* 10 w. or more in Test (2), *194;* 292 for 8th wkt, *142.*

Pegler, S. J. (SA):– Test p'ship record, *216.*

Pellew, C. E. (Aust.):– 2 Test hundreds, *192.*

Perks, R. T. D. (Worcs.):– 2,233 w., *154;* 100 w. (16), *155.*

Perrin, P. A. (Essex):– Highest for Essex, *128;* 29,709 r., *133;* 1,000 r. (18), *134;* 66 hundreds, *130;* 2 hundreds in match (4), *131;* 343* v Derbyshire, *127, 128;* 68 boundaries in innings, *137.*

T

NOTES BY THE EDITOR

The summer of 1983 was so long in coming that when May went out the country was still awash after one of the wettest springs anyone could remember. There was talk of counties facing financial ruin. In the first five weeks of the season Lord's lost fourteen whole days' play and 89 hours of scheduled cricket. "Our groundstaff", wrote the secretary of Worcestershire, "are both physically and mentally exhausted . . . for moving wet and heavy flat sheets holding gallons of water is both a depressing and tiring procedure". Even by June 3, Gloucestershire, in their home fixtures, had not managed a single full day's cricket.

Yet in September, when stumps were finally drawn, those who play the game for a living or watch it as a pastime were deeply tanned. After that awful start the sun had played a long and brilliant innings. As if by providence, it came out as soon as the competing countries began to arrive in England for the third Prudential World Cup, which started on June 9, and for the next three months it hardly went in.

Rather than the losses which had begun to seem inevitable, several counties finished by returning profits. Thanks to what they described as "careful budgeting", Gloucestershire were one. As a result of "strenuous efforts to contain expenditure", Lancashire have made ends meet, in spite of having experienced in 1982 the worst financial year in their long and famous history. As soon as the season was over work got under way at Old Trafford which will improve the facilities there, though not, unfortunately, for the press. There are few grounds in the world, surprising though it may seem, where less is done for those who write about the game. At the expense of an ominous if salutary reduction in their playing staff, Nottinghamshire turned a deficit of £50,000 in 1982 into a small profit. In the less prosperous counties, relief that a disaster had been averted rather than confidence that a corner had been turned was the prevailing emotion. In some, as much as 40 per cent of their annual revenue comes, via Lord's, from major sponsorships, gate receipts from representative games, and fees from radio and television. In 1983 none received less than £138,000. Those which had staged Test matches drew up to £180,000. The Test and County Cricket Board's total allocation exceeded £3,000,000.

India win the World Cup

The World Cup was a great success and India's victory a splendid surprise. They brought warmth and excitement in the place of dampness and depression. In the early years of limited-overs cricket no-one, themselves included, took India seriously. Their strength lay much more in waging battles of attrition. Now, on pitches which had had no time to quicken up after all the rain, their lack of fast bowling was not the hindrance it might have been. Three of their batsmen could also bowl, which was vital for the way it shortened their tail. When, after beating West Indies in the final at Lord's, they flew home, it was to be fêted through the length and breadth of India. Not six months later they were being pilloried for having "capitulated" to the same West Indian side. Indian crowds, like the game itself, can be unmercifully fickle.

Australia, beaten by Zimbabwe on the opening day, made little impact on the competition. Defeat by Sri Lanka cost New Zealand a place in the semi-finals and was another result which confounded expectations. England's performance was an improvement on their mostly dismal play in Australia and New Zealand in the winter of 1982-83. At the end of June, when the visiting teams went their separate ways, they were asked to tender, should they wish to, for the next World Cup. First to show an interest were India and Pakistan, who were exploring the idea of staging it jointly.

New Zealand's Historic Victory

India were not alone in having as captain a charismatic figure. Theirs, recently appointed, was Kapil Dev. Pakistan had Imran Khan, who inspired them to sweeping victories at home over Australia and India. England stood by Bob Willis, a man of indomitable spirit though no tactician, and their series against New Zealand maintained quite successfully the enthusiasm generated by the World Cup. One of the reasons for this was New Zealand's victory in the second Test at Headingley, their first over England in England. With a considerable all-rounder in Richard Hadlee, a wide spread of experience, a discerning captain in Geoff Howarth and an unsophisticated sense of mission, the New Zealanders had a good tour.

New Ideas for First-Class Cricket

New Zealand's displeasure at the way in which the first-class counties rested some of their leading players against them was understandable. For some time now a TCCB working party has been considering how the first-class game in England might with advantage be reorganised. Among suggestions put to them has been one which could involve touring teams in some sort of domestic competition, as a spur to their opponents. The idea of forming, one day, two divisions in the Championship, each consisting of nine sides, is also being considered. Perhaps with this in mind, and knowing that if it were to happen the existence of an eighteenth county could be useful, Shropshire, and, as a combined force, Durham and Northumberland have expressed an interest in joining the Championship. The last county to be granted first-class status was Glamorgan in 1921. But as 1983 ended the TCCB announced that no changes would be made in the present Championship format (24 three-day matches) until 1986 at the earliest.

A Rare Bird

When the England selectors came to pick their side to tour Fiji (for the first time, though only for a few days), New Zealand and Pakistan in early 1984, the problems they faced were much the same as they had been a year earlier. Of the most successful county players many were either ineligible, through being foreign, or unavailable, for having played together in South Africa. The bowlers who were chosen occupied 19th, 29th, 38th, 41st, 78th and 85th places in the averages. In years gone by they would have come from the first ten or twelve. In 34th place was a unique species – a Dane now playing for Derbyshire. Ole Mortensen's nationality, incidentally, entitles him for purposes of registration to be classified as a "home" player. When considering whether it was right that it should, the TCCB, using their discretionary powers, took into account Denmark's membership of the European Economic Community. In Australia, ethnic groups from many European countries are making their mark on the game. Such names as Hilzinger and Zampatti, Nordstrom and Zablica, Kroschel and Olsen, and Yagmich and Dedopulos are commonplace in Grade cricket in Adelaide, Melbourne and Sydney, many of them being Kims, Gregs, Rodneys and Waynes.

Umpiring Problems

At the annual dinner of MCC, held in the Banqueting Suite at Lord's, the Archbishop of Canterbury spoke of cricket as "a game to be played, not a battle to be won". Well, the game did have a better year in the way it was treated by its players. One lamentable exception occurred in the Cricketer Cup when the old boys of two great schools, Malvern and Repton, allowed themselves to be carried away by an inordinate desire to win. More often, when feelings ran high umpiring was the cause. In a series between Pakistan and India the Indian manager flew home to discuss it. When West Indies visited India the West Indian captain spoke out against it. In Australia, during the England tour, it became a controversy inflamed by the constant use of slow-motion replays.

Sir Donald Bradman, no less, thinks the time has come for electronic assistance to be made available to umpires in Test matches, for use in certain types of dismissal (run-outs, stumpings and occasionally catches). If it had been, an absurdly bad run-out decision, in the first over of the match, would not have cast a shadow across the fifth Test in January between England and Australia in Sydney. On the other hand, the tempo of the game would be further slowed down and the umpire's supremacy undermined. Umpires themselves, while acknowledging their fallibility, prefer things as they are. So, for the moment, do I.

Excessive Use of Short-Pitched Bowling

I am less in sympathy with umpires for the way they have allowed fast bowlers to resort ever more frequently to the thuggery of the bouncer. This has got so badly out of hand that for all but a few highly talented batsmen it is now madness not to have a helmet handy. The viciousness of much of today's fast bowling is changing the very nature of the game. A day's play in West Indies, when the West Indians are in the field, may be expected to consist of the minimum requirement of overs, if there is one, and as many as three bouncers an over (perhaps 250 a day), so long as the pitch has anything in it. To add to their menace, many of them are bowled from round the wicket. I am not saying the West Indians are the only offenders, but they are the worst. The TCCB's decision, taken at their December meeting, to dispense with the agreement allowing only one bouncer an over in domestic English first-class cricket, was a setback to those who see intimidatory bowling as a curse of the modern game. Already each season ends with more broken fingers and cracked ribs than the one before. One day, a white line may have to be drawn across the pitch, as a warning mark to bowlers.

An Appealing Continuity

A proposal at the beginning of 1983 to alter the rules governing appealing was rejected, though it was a close call. Had it been implemented it would have meant the first real change of its kind since 1744. The Laws for the Umpires for that year stated that they were "not to order any man out unless appeal'd to by any one of ye players". The present law states that "the Umpires shall not give a batsman out unless appealed to by the other side". It would have been a pity to have had to alter so ancient a decree. There is more to be said, I think, for reverting to the old no-ball rule, based on the back foot, rather than as it is now on the front foot. Since the switch to the front foot the number of no-balls bowled has increased hugely, yet because they have to be called later than when the back-foot rule applied the batsman has virtually no time in which to take advantage of them. Towards the end of 1983, in more than one Test series, wides and no-balls, with obvious logic though for the first time, were debited to the bowlers.

South African Repercussions

The year did not pass, inevitably, without much talk and thought of South Africa. The Australian government began it by banning from entry into that country all cricketers who had toured South Africa with unofficial sides. Predictably enough, such a boycott was found to be impracticable. West Indies were the next to be drawn into the South African vortex, their Board of Control instructing Clive Lloyd's team, who were already assembled in England for the World Cup, not to play against Yorkshire in a warm-up match at Hull if Boycott and Sidebottom, both with South African connections, were chosen to oppose them. The future of the 1984 tour by West Indies to England was at once thrown into doubt, with the English counties being resolutely opposed to any such political interference. In the end the West Indian Board, like the Australian government, weakened. However, the reaction of certain West Indian governments to the likely presence of South Africans in the next England side to visit the Caribbean is already causing anxiety.

Still on South Africa, there was a protracted debate at Lord's, prompted by a special resolution calling on MCC to send a side to South Africa in the winter of 1983-84. Despite the club's official view that such a tour would not be in their own best interests nor those of the game as a whole, a sizeable proportion of the MCC membership, when balloted, supported the resolution. Passions were roused. Mercifully, though, no friends were lost, as happened during the Packer affair. In the end, too, the committee's view prevailed. Many members found themselves in a dilemma, being opposed to apartheid yet at the same time jealous of their own freedom of movement.

Spotting the Wrong-'Un at Lord's

This was not the only tight corner in which MCC found themselves. In August wide publicity was given to the claim that some of the oil paintings hanging at

Lord's, mostly in the Memorial Gallery, were fakes. Started in 1864 by Sir Spencer Ponsonby-Fane, the MCC Collection contains a wide variety of pictures, of which something like 300 were, at the time, on display. Of these, some 150 were oils. Those of doubtful origin formed a part of a valuable bequest made in the 1940s by Sir Jeremiah Colman. For many years MCC have presented the game and its history by exhibiting the most comprehensive display of cricketing memorabilia in the world. Fourteen of their pictures have now been taken out of circulation.

A Change of Chairman

To deter English first-class cricketers from going to South Africa with any sort of representative side, the TCCB thought at one time of writing "loyalty" clauses into the contracts of the England team. No-one was more opposed to this than the players themselves, whose influence, through the Cricketers' Association, grows little by little. When, at the start of October, George Mann retired as Chairman of the Board, having served in that capacity for five years, he must have heaved a sigh of relief. Once something of a sinecure, the job is now endlessly demanding. The former Middlesex and England captain brought to it a disarming blend of integrity, conscientiousness and charm. It would be nice to think that circumstances will allow his successor, Charles Palmer, another former England cricketer and county captain, more time in which to ease the tensions which undoubtedly exist between MCC and the TCCB. As a past President of one and now Chairman of the other, Mr Palmer will be familiar with the conflict.

His first duty was the agreeable one of welcoming into the fold a new sponsor, Texaco, an American oil company who will in future be associated with one-day Internationals and also the World Cup should it be held in England in 1987. Texaco have taken the place of the Prudential Assurance Company. Another major sponsorship changed hands soon afterwards when it was announced that the County Championship (sponsored by Schweppes since 1977) had been taken on by the Britannic Assurance Company. Between them these two sponsorships are worth something like £500,000 a year. Yet the support of the many smaller firms and private individuals who pay for such essentials as match balls (£30 each) or the players' lunches is just as much an integral part of the scene. Cricket is not alone in being so beholden to its sponsors. From the most humble Point to Point, for example, to Derby Day at Epsom it is the same story. It is a trend which puts a heavy strain on the marketing men of cricket, whether at Lord's or round the counties.

Essex Overtake Middlesex

The 1983 County Championship produced a battle royal between Essex, the eventual winners, and Middlesex, the long-time leaders. One of the effects of the TCCB's ban on the fifteen Englishmen who played together in South Africa in March 1982 is that by their uninterrupted presence they provide their own counties with an ironic advantage. Essex, for example, would have been less likely to become champions had Graham Gooch and John Lever been slipping away to play for England. For all that, theirs was a fine success. No team has a better spirit than Essex, and their captain, Keith Fletcher, in his outwardly crestfallen way, stands no nonsense from them. In the South African, Ken McEwan, they also had the outstanding batsman of the 1983 season.

Essex's Championship victory avenged their earlier defeat at the hands of Middlesex in a desperately close finish in the Benson and Hedges Cup final. Somerset made up for a disappointing Championship season by winning the NatWest Bank Trophy, their victory over Middlesex in the semi-final having produced from Ian Botham one of the outstanding innings of the summer. In the John Player Sunday League Somerset were runners-up to Yorkshire, whose first victory this was in any of the four major competitions since they took the Gillette Cup in 1969. It was followed, sadly but all too predictably, by another of those acrimonious but very public disputes in which Yorkshire seem to specialise.

To the chagrin and bewilderment of his supporters, Boycott was given the sack within a few weeks of being awarded a testimonial for 1984. He had just moved into the top ten run-getters of all time, and in August he had scored nearly 1,000 first-class runs for Yorkshire. The reason given for his dismissal – that youth must be served – hardly rang true. Taciturn he may be; recalcitrant too. In Yorkshire, though, he is something of a folk hero. Through their last few barren years he alone has given them anything to boast about. To pension him off, when he was still so prolific, seemed to be asking for trouble, and so it proved. The time came, I am afraid, when an unwieldy committee looked to be fighting not so much for Yorkshire as among themselves.

Two Outstanding Achievements

Perhaps the outstanding individual performance of the year was Imran Khan's in taking 53 wickets in nine Test matches against Australia and India, all of them in Pakistan on pitches which, as a rule, make fast bowlers wish they had stayed at home. Just how much Imran's presence meant to Pakistan became startlingly evident in November when they had to do without him in Australia. By then, in India, Sunil Gavaskar had equalled Bradman's record of 29 Test hundreds. Soon afterwards he passed it. The tribute which Gavaskar must have valued most of all came from Bradman himself when he referred to him as "a great little player".

Wholesale Collusion

The English season was one in which contrivance, not to say connivance, played an unsatisfactorily prominent part. The regulations no longer preclude it as they did, so that during May, when it was so wet, innings were being regularly forfeited, usually by mutual agreement between the captains. The century in 35 minutes which Steve O'Shaughnessy scored on the last day of Lancashire's last match was meaningless. "I would rather have had to work hard for a fifty", said O'Shaughnessy. The long hops and full tosses being served up at the time, in an effort to procure a declaration, reduced the game to a farce. Then, too, rain had caused much loss of play, and the players, or most of them, had had just about enough. It is not that they play more than they did. They play less, in fact, than they sometimes have. What so exhausts them, I think, is the surfeit of one-day cricket – with all the dashing about, both on and off the field, which that involves, the close finishes which it produces and the nervous energy which it consumes.

Quality and Quantity

If the game is more stereotyped than it was, owing to the emphasis on fast and medium-paced bowling and the corresponding lack of spin, there is still a lot of wonderfully good cricket to be seen in the course of an English season. Much of the bowling is ruthlessly ungenerous; there is some very fine batting and any amount of brilliant fielding. As the overseas influence wanes there may be less, but the England team should eventually become stronger. The wider use of artificial pitches can only be for the good. Conversely, it is worrying how many fewer state schools now include cricket in their curriculum. Physical education advisers have tended to move away from traditional sports and to concentrate more on peripheral activities. In the planning of today's housing estates, recreational facilities seem seldom to have been a high priority.

Yet if proof is needed of the extent of general cricket interest, the extraordinary number of books being published on the game provides it. One must assume they sell. So far as the newspaper offerings of top players are concerned, these need careful watching. However vigilant the censors are at Lord's and Melbourne, mud is occasionally being thrown. For the most part, though, such writings as Willis's on his innermost thoughts, as they appear in print, or Mike Brearley's when as a player he revealed them, point to first-class cricket, however competitive it has become, as being still a proudly chivalrous game.

FIVE CRICKETERS OF THE YEAR

MOHINDER AMARNATH

On May 3, 1983, Mohinder Amarnath reached his 1,000 Test runs for the year. No-one has achieved that target by so early a date, and while it has to be admitted that he was enabled to do this feat by playing a plethora of Test cricket, it should be acknowledged that he could hardly have triumphed in more adverse circumstances than on Indian tours of Pakistan and the West Indies. Moreover, during the 1982-83 season Amarnath hit more runs – 2,355 at an average of 81 – than anyone else has ever done in a first-class season outside England. Still on the crest of a wave, he followed up by winning man-of-the-match awards in the World Cup semi-final against England and in the final against West Indies, when India achieved one of the game's most unexpected victories.

Yet Amarnath, and India, merely had walk-on parts during the first two World Cup tournaments. And in England he had an even lower profile than elsewhere, since he had played only two Test matches there, both in 1979 and without distinction. So the half-year or so of personal success that the Indian enjoyed, as triumphant as any cricketer can have known, came as a surprise to most followers of the game in England.

MOHINDER AMARNATH BHARDWAJ, or "Jimmy" as he prefers to be known, was born in Patiala on September 24, 1950. His father, "Lala" Amarnath, who scored India's first Test century, was employed in the retinue of the sports-loving Maharajah of Patiala to encourage the development of cricket within his north Indian state.

From the start "Lala" was an influence upon his three sons, all of whom played first-class cricket (the oldest of them, Surinder, going on to represent India as a left-handed batsman). The father, renowned as something of a martinet, taught Mohinder to love cricket to the exclusion of all other games. Another paternal instruction was that any short ball was there to be hooked.

Although Mohinder made his Test début as a medium-pace in-swing bowler (like his father) against Australia in 1969, batting soon became his chief concern and the hook his forte. The stroke helped him to his first major success in Australia in 1977-78 during the World Series controversy, and again when India toured Pakistan and the Caribbean last winter. But the hook has been the reason behind not only his ups but his downs.

Early in 1979, in a Test match against Australia in Bombay, Amarnath emerged in a solar topee (again in imitation of his father), tried to hook Rodney Hogg and fell on his wicket. Later that year, during India's tour of England, he was hit on the head half a dozen times and kept refusing to wear a helmet. The culmination came when he failed to pick up a ball from Richard Hadlee out of a dark background at Trent Bridge: he missed the ball and it fractured his skull. It was several months before Amarnath could play again; and then he found that the injury had damaged his eyesight. So as a temporary measure he wore spectacles, and as a permanent one he adopted an open-chested, crouched stance after the style of Jim Parks or the late Ken Barrington. But his courage had in no way been impaired.

It was some time, however, before India's selectors called on Amarnath again. When England toured there in 1981-82 he was not chosen for any Test match, nor for India's return tour in the summer of 1982. Amarnath was then playing in Lancashire League cricket for Crompton (after four seasons with Lowerhouse) and, seeing that India's batting line-up had one or two vacancies, felt a renewed determination to prove himself at international level. He duly did so during India's visit to Pakistan in 1982-83. While Imran Khan harassed his colleagues, taking 40 wickets in the six-match series for fewer than 14 runs each, Amarnath scored three centuries and three fifties in his ten innings.

In the West Indies immediately afterwards he carried on against Roberts, Marshall, Holding and Garner from where he had left off against Imran and Sarfraz. He was selected as the player of the series on either side after hitting 598 runs in his nine innings. The hook shot stood him in good stead while his team-mates tried vainly to contend with the imitation of body-line which Malcolm Marshall delivered from round the wicket. Few batsmen can claim to have withstood the four-man West Indian pace attack as it has been constituted in recent years: Geoff Boycott and the Australian Bruce Laird have succeeded defensively, Graham Gooch and Amarnath by aggressive means.

This purple patch continued into the World Cup, where Amarnath scored 237 runs in eight innings (twice run out), and was an effective reserve seamer even though his run-up had dwindled to an amble. Since the competition followed a month after India's series in the Caribbean, he was by then well attuned to West Indian pace. Indeed this familiarity with the West Indies bowling is one reason that Amarnath gives for India's winning of the cup. The presence of good fielders and stroke-makers, not all that common in Indian sides of the past, was another factor, along with the slow pitches that prevailed.

His bowling at Old Trafford, where the pitch had "no grass and was very uneven" was as important as his 46 (run out) when India chased a modest England total. In the final he stood firm while the West Indian bowling was at its most hostile and Srikkanth went for his ebullient shots at the other end. Together they shared the highest partnership of the match. Finally his amiable, almost apologetic medium pace finished off three of the last four wickets for 12 runs.

However, and sadly, the man whom Imran Khan amongst others called the best player of fast bowling in contemporary cricket was brought down to earth during the latter half of the year. In the home series against Pakistan and in the first two Tests against West Indies, he was unable to reach double figures. Whether the reason was delayed shell shock or related to that inexplicable phenomenon known as form, the Indian god was found to have feet of clay. – S.B.

J. V. CONEY

Being vulnerable in ways that "full-time" teams are not, New Zealand rely heavily on attitude and team-work. The major cricketing nations of the world are in business every day, with the result that one of their super-stars is usually in form. New Zealand's balloon floats only when the gases are mixed just right and everyone is fresh, willing and ambitious. They are a team fashioned out of a positive attitude to contest every run, whether batting or bowling. To perform well, every man must do the basic things better than their opponents. In this way they work as a unit.

JEREMY VERNON CONEY, born in Wellington on June 21, 1952, epitomises this attitude. As a child of the 1960s he still grants majesty to athletes and innocence to games. Sports are fun. For him, playing for New Zealand matters most. So long as the majority of the New Zealand team feel this way they are aware that miracles may occur.

In many ways Coney represents all that is best in New Zealand cricket. He becomes more determined and motivated when playing for his country. The excitement of Test cricket brings a new dimension to his game. He is able to concentrate on concentrating, as national pride lifts his performance. When questioned at the end of an innings that has helped his side to victory, the word "pride" usually figures in his phrases.

Coney made his first-class début – for a New Zealand Under-23 XI against Auckland – when he was eighteen, a tall, gangling youth who dressed as the "flower-power children" did at that time. His shoulder-length hair prevented him from being selected for Wellington in one age-group team. When he arrived in Australia as a replacement for an injured Glenn Turner in December 1973, his cricket gear consisted of a yellowing and heavily plastered bat, which bore the name of his club, "Onslow", in large letters on the back. The team manager, R. A. Vance, now Chairman of the New Zealand Cricket Council, gave Coney some money and told him to go and buy a new bat. Some hours later Coney returned with a guitar and made do with other players' cast-offs. His love of music is still with him and he frequently enlivens bus tours by playing his guitar. Today his hair style has changed markedly and his only problem with cricket clothing is that the trousers are not always long enough.

Coney made his mark in his first Test when he scored 45 against Australia at Sydney. He stood firm against an Australian attack for 135 minutes with a composure which belied his 21 years and relative inexperience. He also held three catches at slip in Australia's first innings. Throughout his career he has possessed sharp hands and been an asset in the slips.

In his apprenticeship years Coney played to stay in. Occupation of the crease was his prime objective. As his confidence has developed he has realised that a half-volley is a gift to be driven with widened shoulders and swirling bat, and he is now adept in driving in the classic, old-fashioned way wide of mid-on.

After a promising beginning, which included taking part in New Zealand's first victory over Australia, Coney was in the wilderness for five years, emerging for the series against Pakistan in New Zealand in 1979, when Bevan Congdon, also a medium-paced all-rounder, retired. He made his return a striking one, scoring 6, 36, 69, 82 and 49 in his first five innings. It seemed as if the Test-match atmosphere gave an edge to his batting that was not always apparent when he was playing more mundane first-class matches.

This was the time when crowd involvement in cricket was coming to the fore in New Zealand. The louder the roar of the crowd the straighter Coney played. During this series against Pakistan, he utilised his skills learnt from volley-ball matches to counter the rising deliveries of Imran Khan. To protect his ribs he leapt in the air to come down on the ball and eliminate catches to close-in fielders. The first few times he did it, patrons at the ground laughed, as did the Pakistanis; but by the end of the series critics were conscious that he had found a new way of handling lifting deliveries. Since then he has used the same technique to good effect, as against Bob Willis in England in 1983.

Throughout cricket history there have been quality batsmen who have had great difficulty in breaking the barrier imposed by scoring a Test century. By the end of New Zealand's tour of England in 1983 Coney had played 42 Test innings and made ten half-centuries without going on to three figures. Bobby Simpson scored his first 100 for Australia only in his 30th Test.

When Coney made his début for Wellington, in 1971-72, one-day cricket was just being introduced to New Zealand. He is now the product of having played the limited-overs game for all his career. From its outset he has benefited from the knack of successfully pacing a game towards the end of an innings. He is, however, a cricketer who is not going to appear high in the averages at the end of his career. Until statistics can indicate such factors as courage and refusal to surrender they will not adequately convey the mettle of such innings as Coney played in 1983 in the Prudential World Cup.

At Edgbaston, chasing 235, New Zealand were in trouble against England when Willis quickly disposed of Turner and Edgar. Coney shared partnerships of 71 with Howarth and 70 with Hadlee which took New Zealand close to victory. Keeping calm in the eye of the storm he was 66 not out when the winning run was struck off the penultimate ball. In the last few seasons Coney has gained a reputation for being New Zealand's "bits and pieces" man. On the third day of the first Test in England last year, when England sought quick runs, Coney bowled 27 overs of seemingly innocuous medium-pace and conceded only 39 runs. His bowling also played a vital part in New Zealand's historic victory in the second Test at Headingley. When England batted a second time, 152 runs in arrears, Coney bowled Lamb for 28 and had Botham caught soon afterwards.

To spectators in New Zealand Coney is in some ways a mystery. Until the last few seasons his cricket record was more promising than impressive. Now, after several spine-tingling finishes, his efforts have brought recognition as well as success. Unlike many of his contemporaries he regards international cricket as an experience unparalleled in joy and excitement – D.N.

JOHN EMBUREY

A bowler's first experience of taking 100 wickets in a season would normally be cause for unqualified delight. But great as was JOHN ERNEST EMBUREY's satisfaction in fulfilling that ambition, he would happily have traded it for the seventeen extra points that would have enabled Middlesex to retain the County Championship. And with the possible exception of John Lever, whose wickets for Essex were taken at the breakneck speed of one every five and a half overs, no player in either of the top two teams contributed more than Middlesex's 6 feet 2 inches off-spinning all-rounder.

One of their four "ever-presents" by dint of his England suspension, he not only took 96 wickets in the Championship and scored 772 runs, but as acting-captain in eight games, while Mike Gatting was away, he led the side to five of their eleven victories, four of them successively during the World Cup. Though he had a number of outstanding games, notably against Leicestershire at Lord's (match-figures of eight for 22 in 21.2 overs and scores of 47 and 73 not out), the keynote of his season was consistency. Only once did he take more than five wickets in an innings – six for 13 against Kent at Dartford. But on eighteen other occasions he took three or more, and but for a combination of wet weather and unhelpful pitches in the last four matches, when in common with his fellow-spinner, Phil Edmonds, he had to be content with seven costly wickets, he could be counted on for an analysis that would have won Middlesex an extra vital victory.

Though he relies less on variations of flight than most great off-spinners, Emburey's high arm, poise in the delivery stride, and extreme closeness to the stumps when he lets the ball go, make him in other respects a classic bowler of his type. A big spinner when conditions call for it, his wicket-to-wicket line of flight, allied to steady length and drift from leg to off, earn him many successes, either bowled off-stump or caught at slip or at the wicket, against batsmen playing for the ball to turn. His habit of hugging the stumps is a valuable asset. But from time to time he plants his front foot so far across – outside off-stump at the non-striker's end – that it lets him down by obscuring the umpire's view for an lbw decision. Let batsmen be warned, however: he was working on the fault for Western Province in South Africa last winter.

Mike Gunton, Emburey's cricket master at Peckham Manor School in South London, was the first influence on his bowling, when at the age of eleven he changed him from a medium-pacer (he once took eight for 8) into an off-spinner. But as a youngster on Middlesex's staff, his main influence was Fred Titmus. "To start with, I just learned from watching him: it wasn't his way to press opinions on young players", remembers Emburey. "But he wasn't backward when I did approach him – he hardly drew breath! The best advice he gave me was: 'Just keep it tight – eventually they'll get themselves out.' Fred used the air a lot himself – I was amazed how slowly he bowled when we played together in a benefit game a year or two ago – but it's because of that advice that I tend to bowl flatter than most off-spinners." It was to Emburey's own distant medium-pacer days, however, that he traces his command of the off-spinner's out-swinging arm-ball. "Nowadays, I grip the ball the same way as for an off-break", he said, then added regretfully, "but there are still a good many batsmen who know when it's coming!"

His own batting has improved so much in the past two English seasons that from being looked on as little more than an obdurate tail-ender, he has ambitions to complete the double of 100 wickets and 1,000 runs (until 1982, his aggregate topped 300 only once). "I got fed up being regarded as someone who could just stay there and decided to be more aggressive. Having such a short backlift, I had to come *to* the ball, and from going down the pitch found the bowlers' length was suffering: a fair number of my sixteen 6s last year were with the pull when they dropped short. If things go as I hope, though, and I get back into the England side when my suspension ends, my best chance of the double may be in 1984."

Emburey has mixed feelings about the venture to South Africa in 1982. "The obvious attraction was a lump sum in the bank; but I'd have thought twice about going if I'd known the ban would last three years – that stunned all of us. Assuming I would have been chosen for England's tours, and played my share of Tests at home, I have lost financially. I missed playing very much in 1982, but last year I was resigned to it. The only times I missed it then were when England were struggling and I thought I might have helped."

He was born at Peckham on August 20, 1952 and the discovery that his mother's brother had had Surrey trials stirred Emburey's interest, so that at thirteen, under the tutelage of Mr Gunton, he first thought of making cricket his career. But setbacks lay ahead that twice made him temporarily abandon the idea. The first came in 1971, when after three years with Surrey Young Amateurs and Young Cricketers, including a tour of Canada on which Bob Willis and Geoff Howarth were among his team-mates, he learned that for financial reasons the club could not take him on their staff. Disappointed enough not to act on their advice to write to Middlesex, he owed it to Arthur McIntyre, then Surrey's coach, that Don Bennett, McIntyre's counterpart at Lord's, took the initiative and got in touch with him. After taking 22 wickets for their Second XI, he signed a three-month contract for Middlesex in July 1971 and in 1973 made his Championship début for them against Derbyshire at Burton upon Trent, taking three for 50 in the second innings.

But though Mike Brearley, among others, quickly recognised his promise, Titmus's undiminished skill so limited his chances that, when at the end of 1976 he had made no more than seventeen appearances, he decided for the second time to seek a livelihood outside the game. Luckily for Emburey, however, Titmus left Middlesex that autumn to succeed McIntyre as Surrey's coach, and the frustrated, not to say impatient, youngster returned joyfully to Lord's. First-choice off-spinner at last, he won his county cap at once, taking 81 wickets in his first full season, and by 1978 was in the England team at Lord's, dismissing Bruce Edgar of New Zealand with his fourth ball in a Test. Had it not been for the lure of financial security offered by the South African venture, prompted too, by concern about the durability of an often painful back, he would almost certainly by now have added many to his 22 Test caps. As it is, for John Emburey 1985 can't come too soon. – J.D.T.

MIKE GATTING

As Middlesex reeled off their titles and trophies between 1976 and 1982, it began to occur to Lord's loyalists that somebody, one day, would have to succeed Mike Brearley, the architect of victory. Clive Radley, Phil Edmonds, then John Emburey were all candidates in the years preceding Brearley's retirement, before Mike Gatting was finally placed in charge of a team of many talents. He was expected to extend Middlesex's "golden age" by presenting their somewhat fickle supporters with a trophy. He did so, too, and it was the first one available. He revealed the Brearley touch by forcing the Essex batsmen to panic as Middlesex, losers all day, pinched a cliff-hanging victory in the Benson and Hedges Cup final. Most acceptable as the B & H was, Gatting spent the rest of the summer insisting, "We've got to get that Championship. We've got to hang on. It's not over yet", even when Middlesex had a handsome lead.

It is never pleasant to be omitted, marginally, from Test selection, but, shrugging off the rejection, Gatting devoted his energies and batsmanship to Middlesex. As if to show that he has not yet acquired Brearley's full range of luck, when he was required for the last two Tests, Roland Butcher and Wilf Slack were extracted from the side by injury. There were other strokes of bad luck, some self-confessed "unprofessional cricket", and in the end Essex took the title.

Gatting does not review 1983 as a chance irrevocably missed. "We are good enough to win the Championship next time. The incentive is now stronger than ever." His England recall reminded Gatting of two ambitions – a Test century and a regular place in the England side. The century looked odds-on at Lord's in the third Test, but a mistimed hook ended a brilliant innings and two over-ambitious shots at Nottingham meant that his tour place was again in doubt. He had lost a similar debate in 1982, but, to the relief of his many admirers, he was chosen now.

He does get out playing challenging strokes. When criticised for this, he gives the cricketer's reply: "That's the way I play and make my runs", and if you enjoy his dismissive hook, riveting square-cut and eagerness to loft the ball, you don't complain at assorted modes of dismissal. In 1983, for the third consecutive year, he became the highest qualified Englishman in the batting averages. Since the selectors constantly ask, "Where are the batsmen? They are all from overseas", Gatting may have been hard done by recently. Either that or his approach did not appeal to those who matter. In terms of ability he should have been competing consistently with David Gower, Derek Randall and Allan Lamb for the positions from three to five. His strokeplay is in their class, but the Nottingham Test was his 24th, compared with Gower's 53rd and Randall's 40th. However, the others have made centuries and, as yet, Gatting has not.

MICHAEL WILLIAM GATTING was born on June 6, 1957 in the London suburb of Kingsbury. His family moved to Willesden, nearer the centre of London, when he was two. He and his younger brother, Steve, had a do-it-yourself grounding in their main sports, playing cricket and football endlessly alongside the family garage. His schools were Wykeham Primary and John Kelly. The unlocking of the door to serious cricket came through an advertisement placed by the Brondesbury club when Mike was twelve. There the coach to the colts, Peter Farara, and Ted Jackson moulded his power.

In the close-knit world of North London club cricket, his talents became well known from the time he was fourteen. Jackson let the Middlesex coach, Don Bennett, know all about the hard-hitting boy at Brondesbury and Bennett was impressed enough to send for him in May 1972, to fill a gap in the county Second XI. Still only fourteen, Gatting was unfortunate enough to encounter a Test bowler, Kent's John Shepherd, who dismissed him first ball. The highlight of the next two summers was helping Middlesex to their third consecutive Under-25 title in 1974. His football was also good enough to take him near to the top; he played at junior level for Queen's Park Rangers. "They said I was overweight for a goalkeeper", he recalls. "I played for Watford's South-East Counties' side as a full-back. They offered me an apprentice's contract. I'd also thought of teaching PE after passing O-levels." But by this time it was clear where he was going to succeed. His brother became the footballer – for Arsenal and Brighton.

Mike, now concentrating on cricket, was given his chance in the Middlesex first side shortly after his eighteenth birthday in 1975, the first year of the Middlesex revival. In his first innings he was caught on the boundary off Worcestershire's Ted Hemsley for 10. Two more unsuccessful county games followed, but he scored heavily for the seconds and finished the season set for 1976. His contribution in the first half of that Championship year matched expectations before he went with England's Young Cricketers to West Indies, where he topped the batting averages and also took most wickets.

When twenty, he went to Pakistan and New Zealand, making his Test début at Karachi after Brearley, the tour captain, had broken his arm. Gatting was chosen ahead of Ian Botham. In contrast to later, bolder dismissals he was lbw playing no stroke to Abdul Qadir's googly and lbw to a full toss from Iqbal Qasim, for 5 and 6, and, six weeks later, against New Zealand in Auckland, he was bowled by Boock for 0. That was that, in Test terms, for over two years. He was included in the Prudential Cup squad in 1979, but without getting a game.

His first home Tests came against West Indies in 1980, when he was in the side that drew the last four matches, making a solid 56 at Old Trafford. In the same summer he made another half-century in the Centenary Test against Australia at Lord's. In the 1981 Ashes series, when he scored four more fifties, he and Boycott were the only batting specialists chosen for every match. In between these home series he went to West Indies with Botham's side, but his only Test chance was at Bridgetown, a match of profound unhappiness in which Ken Barrington died and Mike made a "pair". In India, in 1981-82, under Keith Fletcher, despite averaging 55 and scoring fast in the zonal matches, he batted at number seven or eight in three of the Tests, usually having to try to press on after much slow early play. Back at home in 1982, as in 1983, he was the most commanding English batsman at county level, but then, too, he had to wait until half-way through the summer for the call from the selectors which he describes as "send for Gatts". He married Elaine in 1980 and in the same year opened a sports shop in Radlett. – T.C.

CHRIS SMITH

When CHRISTOPHER LYALL SMITH first arrived in Southampton in the late spring of 1980, Hampshire supporters found themselves weighing up a powerfully built, fair-haired 21-year-old whose square shoulders were matched by the determined set of his jaw. Ever since, this elder son of a Walsall-raised father and Scottish mother, born in Durban on October 15, 1958, has been proving that for once first impressions were very accurate. In his first summer Smith held together a Hampshire side that was in the early stages of re-building, after the fruitful days of Richards and Roberts, and one deprived of the services of Greenidge and Marshall by a West Indian tour.

In this maiden season, Smith was the only Hampshire batsman to reach 1,000 runs, a feat achieved mainly from a position in the order which he did not relish – number two. Two summers followed which equally demonstrated the strength of will which his whole being suggests.

He wanted to play county cricket unshackled by the strictures of overseas regulations. This meant satisfying the requirements of qualification. So for two summers he had to be content with occasional first-team appearances, spending the rest of his time in the Second XI where, even for someone of his temperament, boredom threatened. But this two-year exile served one very real purpose – it increased Smith's steely determination to become, as he had set out to do in 1979, the successor to Barry Richards in the Hampshire dressing-room. He has never made any bones about his ambitions. "I want to be known as a good batsman. . . My ambition is to score as many runs as I can . . . I would be quite happy to bat for two days if there was a century at the end of it." Within a few weeks his textbook technique, iron will and unshakable concentration had convinced even the most sceptical that his targets were well within his scope.

By the later stages of 1980, when his 1,000-run landmark was within sight, Smith was prepared to admit that acceptance as a good player was really only a rung on a ladder of ambition which had carried him through a daunting coaching schedule since he was a boy of ten. Before returning to Natal that winter, he confided that his sights were firmly set on following Tony Greig into the England side. It was that which steeled Smith during his two frustrating summers of qualification and which fired him when, early in the 1983 season, he became, in cricketing terms, "English". That spring, once the weather had relented, he quickly began to make up for lost time.

His secret ambition was to score 1,500 runs and to play his way into the selectors' awareness, perhaps even to stake some claim to a place on England's winter tour. In his first innings of the summer he scored an unbeaten 129 at Leicester – and that set the pattern. His 1,000 came up in only his nineteenth innings, against Gloucestershire in late June. It contained two other centuries – a career-best 193 at Derby and exactly 100 off Lancashire in the next match at Bournemouth. In that same innings at Bournemouth his nineteen-year-old brother, Robin, scored a century on his first-class début in England.

Chris's effort drew this appraisal from Jack Simmons, who had laboured long and hard on Lancashire's behalf to contain the brotherly onslaught: "He reminds me a bit of Boycott, but with more shots." Many other bowlers were to draw a similar parallel before the summer ended.

Smith is the first to admit that he has not the exceptional natural gifts of his younger brother; but he has proved beyond all doubt that practice can be a passport to success. Even as a young boy he would spend half an hour every morning in the net in the garden of his family home; every Sunday, summer and winter, he was in the nets by eight o'clock in the morning, working with a former Natal player, Grayson Heath, the coach his father brought in to channel youthful enthusiasm.

What Heath's coaching and Smith's natural ambition have fashioned is a player of textbook correctness, unshakable application and with the patience to apply the maxim of play the good ball and wait to hit the bad. He admits that he is still vulnerable against really fast, short-pitched deliveries, although his investment of £1,000 in a bowling machine, which was exported to Durban and set up in the family net to fire bouncers at him in the winter of 1982-83, has improved his technique.

In the end it came as no surprise to most people when he was selected for the third Test against New Zealand in 1983. But it stunned the likeable Smith. When Hadlee had him leg-before first ball, he plumbed the depths of personal misery and self-doubt. That was, he admits, the worst moment of his life, followed by the most depressing two days he has spent. But his temperament pulled him through, and his second-innings 43 is one of his two outstanding memories of a spectacular season. The other was his 163 against the ultimate champions, Essex, at Southend, when Hampshire became the first side since the war to score 400 in the fourth innings of a Championship match and win it.

So the summer of 1983 ended with Smith having scored more runs in all competitions than anyone else in England, and having achieved another rung on his personal ladder. The next one is to be accepted as a Test batsman of genuine quality. Past experience suggests that "Kippy" Smith (thus known because of his fondness for sleeping in dressing-rooms) has the will, the drive and the technique to manage it. – M.N.

[*Patrick Eagar*

Kapil Dev, watched by Mohinder Amarnath (Man of the Match), holds up the Prudential
World Cup, Lord's, June 25.

SELECTORS AT WORK

[*Ken Kelly*]

R. G. D. Willis (*captain*), P. J. Sharpe, P. B. H. May (*chairman*), A. C. Smith, and A. V. Bedser discussing the final choice of an England team.

ENGLAND'S TEAM v NEW ZEALAND AT THE OVAL

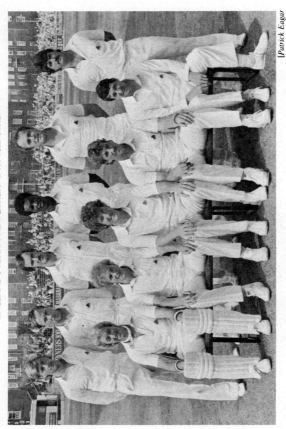

Back row: G. Fowler, V. J. Marks, C. J. Tavaré, N. G. Cowans, P. H. Edmonds, A. J. Lamb. *Front row:* R. W. Taylor, D. I. Gower, R. G. D. Willis (*captain*), I. T. Botham, D. W. Randall.

[*Patrick Eagar*

[*Ken Kelly*

Above: Jeremy Coney, having just hit the winning run, hails New Zealand's first Test victory in England. *Below:* Geoff Howarth and his side celebrate it.

[Ken Kelly

Alan Jones of Glamorgan, who retired at the end of the 1983 season to become his county's coach, with over 36,000 first-class runs to his credit.

VIOLENCE IN THE OUTFIELD

[Patrick Eagar]

Ground invasions are increasingly becoming the concern of cricket administrators. Here Terry Alderman, the Australian bowler, is carried off the field at Perth after clashing with a spectator during the first Test match between England and Australia in November 1982. Alderman, whose shoulder was badly damaged, did not play again for several months.

THE FIRST-CLASS UMPIRES, 1983

[*Sport and General*

Back row: J. Birkenshaw, D. R. Shepherd, D. J. Constant, R. A. White, B. Leadbeater, C. T. Spencer, N. T. Plews, R. Palmer, J. H. Harris, K. Ibadulla, M. J. Kitchen, P. J. Eele, A. G. T. Whitehead, D. O. Oslear, J. W. Holder. *Front row*: P. B. Wight, K. E. Palmer, W. E. Alley, H. D. Bird, A. Jepson, C. Cook, R. Julian, J. van Geloven, B. J. Meyer, D. G. L. Evans.

[*Patrick Eagar*

M. W. GATTING (Middlesex and England)

[*Patrick Eagar*

C. L. SMITH (Hampshire and England)

[*Patrick Eagar*

M. AMARNATH (India)

[*Ken Kelly*

J. V. CONEY (New Zealand)

[Ken Kelly

J. E. EMBUREY (Middlesex and England)

MCC AND SOUTH AFRICA

By MATTHEW ENGEL

The summer of 1983 will mainly be remembered as a time when cricket people could forget their troubles and enjoy the game and the sunshine, if only temporarily. The problem of South Africa was never that far away from anyone's consciousness. But its prime manifestation came in a manner that left little damage, and was even rather quaint.

On July 13, the members of the Marylebone Cricket Club voted to support their committee and reject a proposal to send a touring team of their own to South Africa. In the history of one of sport's most intractable crises, it will probably not be regarded as one of the most momentous decisions; in the history of one of sport's most famous and most powerful clubs, it may well have been.

The idea of trying to use MCC as a locomotive to pull South Africa back into world cricket had been conceived a year earlier at a meeting of the six-man executive of the right-wing pressure group, Freedom in Sport: the Conservative MP John Carlisle, Jeff Butterfield, Tommie Campbell, John Reason, Edward Grayson and Lord Chalfont. All except Mr Campbell also happened to be members of MCC. The club had not been directly involved in the issue since 1968. On that occasion the committee, in spite of the cancellation of the 1968-69 tour over South Africa's refusal to admit Basil D'Oliveira, was still defending, though with growing unease, the principle of continuing cricketing links. It beat off liberal opposition, led by two of the less conventional men to captain the England team, the Rev. David Sheppard and Michael Brearley, by a margin of more than three to one.

In the fifteen intervening years very little had changed in South Africa's general political outlook. But a great deal had changed in cricket since the formation of the multi-racial South African Cricket Union in 1977. The game was integrated in theory, and sometimes in practice. There was a better case for playing South Africa in the eighties than there ever had been in the totally segregated sixties. But even more had changed in the rest of the world: attitudes had hardened and the sports boycott had become a weapon with a wider purpose.

Something else had changed: MCC no longer had that much authority to do anything about it. 1968 was also the year when it surrendered its role as the ruling body of English cricket and moved into a nebulous position of influence without anything like the same direct power – the house of Lord's in this sense being like the House of Lords. It was associated with the policies made elsewhere in cricket, without being able to change them. As far as the boycott went, cricket was in any case forced largely to comply with policies made elsewhere.

None the less, MCC seemed ideal for Freedom in Sport's purposes. Its supporters could get nowhere with any of cricket's ruling bodies, national or international. But, under Rule 43, it takes only 50 members to demand a special general meeting. Finding 50 was not a problem for Mr Carlisle and his friends. They set up their own committee including the evocative names of Denis Compton and Bill Edrich. There were brief but hopeless

[*Press Association*

Lord's, March 16, 1983. Accompanied by Denis Compton and W. J. Edrich, John Carlisle, MP, hands a petition to J. A. Bailey, secretary of MCC, calling for a Special General Meeting to discuss the South African resolution.

talks with the real committee to see if an accommodation could be reached. In April, Jack Bailey, the secretary of MCC, stood at the Grace Gates and received a petition proposing "that the members of MCC Committee implement the selection of a touring party to tour South Africa in 1983-84". He has been seen looking happier.

The problem Mr Bailey – and cricket – now faced was a curious one. MCC, in theory, had become merely a private club. Plenty of private clubs had been touring South Africa and dispensing discreet aid and comfort throughout the years of supposed isolation. It quickly became clear, because of the sanctions that would almost certainly be applied to any current first-class players who might make the tour, that, if forced to send a team, the committee would have to despatch players not far above customary club level – the men who habitually raise the flag for Marylebone and cricket in places like Bangladesh or the United States. But the very initials MCC have a special power. Few people with a casual involvement in cricket at home and even fewer overseas have cottoned on to the club's diminished role. The last Test-playing tour party to be called MCC had been in 1976-77. After six years the change had still not permeated the consciousness of much of the world's cricketing public. Thus one of the great dangers of the tour would have been mistaken identity. Indeed the most worried man I met before the vote was one of the likely tourists, who thought South Africa might get it wrong and unleash their fastest bowlers at him.

The case put by the 50 members and sent out on their behalf by MCC was that a tour would recognise the progress made by SACU, "halt the slide of international sport towards total political influence and possible disintegration, and allow long-suffering sports people to get on with sport". MCC's rebuttal acknowledged that the resolution would appeal to many members and talked about "hypocrisy and double standards" among South Africa's opponents. But it then argued that such a tour would achieve nothing in cricketing terms, breach the Gleneagles Agreement, which the British Government was pledged to support, and endanger the club's remaining positions in the game; as custodian of the Laws, as owner of Lord's, which the black countries might refuse to visit, and in ICC, for which MCC still automatically provided the president and secretary. Since a number of overseas officials regarded this as an anachronism anyway, Mr Bailey and the incumbent president, Sir Anthony Tuke, were aware that they might be the first casualties.

The meeting was fixed for the night prior to the first Test – well after the World Cup and the annual ICC meeting. The World Cup was conducted amid constant rumours that the South Africans, having bought their own teams of English and West Indian rebels in successive years, were now trying to sign anything that moved. A SACU delegation, led by Joe Pamensky, paid its annual, now ritualised visit to the ICC which in an equally ritualised way refused to see them. Mr Pamensky's visit was very public but he said little about the impending MCC vote, beyond saying that any team it sent would be very welcome.

The postal votes began to pile up at MCC's solicitors in the City. There were rumours about these too, most of them saying that the proponents were not far short of the two-thirds majority they would need to carry the motion and well above the simple majority that would be regarded as a huge moral victory and a humiliation for the club's establishment. Everyone Mr Carlisle met at Lord's, he said later, told him they were voting for him. Since his majority at Luton West had gone up from 200 to 12,000 at the June General Election, he may well have been feeling invulnerable. His only moment of discomfort came when the Prime Minister (ineligible to join MCC owing to her sex) came out against the tour in the Commons.

The evening of July 13 turned out to be one of almost unbearable heat. The committee had hired Central Hall, Westminster, the largest available, in the expectation that around 2,000 of the 18,000 members would wish to come. But it was no night for attending meetings voluntarily. Only 1,000 turned up. The meeting was also a little overshadowed. By coincidence, a few hundred yards across Parliament Square, the newly elected House of Commons was debating whether or not to bring back hanging. Some thought that MCC was debating whether or not to hang itself.

Mr Carlisle proposed the motion. His speech – cogent and well received – made much of the argument that it was unfair to treat sporting and business links differently. He was seconded by John Pashley, a former Yorkshire League cricketer, who emphasised the importance of not being pushed around in a speech that was passionate and effective until, for a hot evening, it went on too long.

The motion was opposed by Hubert Doggart, a former President of MCC, who, as in the committee's written argument, conceded part of the case before putting over the official view of the realities of the situation and implying that Mr Carlisle's motives were political rather than sporting. He was seconded, in similar vein, by Colin Cowdrey who, fifteen years earlier, had been prominent in the "bridge-building" school of thought. Both went down well, assisted by their known love for the game and their gentle demeanour which enabled them to disguise some sharp debating points. The floor speakers included another Conservative MP Andrew Hunter, Denis Compton and Brian Johnston (a popular BBC commentator), all for the motion; the antis included two churchmen – David Sheppard, now Bishop of Liverpool, and John Stacey.

But the debate did not matter. As Mr Bailey knew (though he says he did not tell a soul) the Carlisle forces were already beaten. They had lost the postal vote 6,069 to 3,935; they lost the vote in the hall 535 to 409 – an overall total of 6,604 to 4,344 against the resolution, or 60.3 per cent to 39.7.

The expectations that had built up in the past few days now worked heavily against Mr Carlisle and his supporters. The focus was on the committee victory rather than on the perhaps more remarkable fact that 40 per cent of those who voted and almost a quarter of MCC's traditionally docile membership had repudiated the committee on a matter on which it had fought furiously to enforce its point of view. This suggested that MCC's rulers might have many more uncomfortable nights, over all kinds of issues, in the years to come.

Mr Carlisle felt later, in view of what everyone had told him beforehand, that he must have been defeated by the votes of people who never go to Lord's. He thought too that it had been a mistake to pin down the committee by putting a date to the tour, when the important thing was winning the principle. Mr Bailey thought the exercise had cleared the air and enhanced the reputation of the club. Everyone agreed that, whether or not MCC debated the matter again, cricket was not going to be able to forget South Africa.

AUSTRALIA – A NEW ERA

By R. J. PARISH

The Australian season of 1983-84 completed the fifth year of the agreement between the Australian Cricket Board and World Series Cricket. It was in May 1977 that World Series Cricket burst upon the cricketing world and in May 1979 that agreement was reached between the two factions; after two years of trauma, disastrous law suits and internecine disputes.

Much has been written as to the reasons why a private promoter entered the field of the commercial promotion of international cricket. It is not my intention to recapitulate those reasons or to attempt to justify arguments one way or the other. However, it would be wrong of me not to take this opportunity to clarify the Australian Board's motive and method in reaching the agreement it did. The Board has been, and is still, concerned that its action has not been fully understood.

In June 1977, at a special meeting of the International Cricket Conference, the effect of the private promotion of international cricket was fully discussed and it was unanimously agreed that there should be no unilateral attempts to reach a compromise or solution. ICC set up a sub-committee to pursue negotiations with WSC with a view to achieving an agreement eagerly sought by several of the Test-match-playing countries. By late 1978 it was becoming more and more apparent that, if a solution were to be reached, it would depend on the attitude and initiative of the Australian Board.

In January 1979 the Chairman of ICC gave written authorisation to the Australian Board to hold unilateral talks with WSC. Both the Chairman and Secretary of ICC were informed in February 1979 that continuing talks raised hopes of achieving a solution. Detailed negotiations continued, and on April 24, 1979, the Board announced that it had accepted, in principle, an offer from PBL Sports Pty Ltd. On April 27 a telex was sent to the Secretary of ICC setting out the relevant details as they affected other countries. It was made clear that Australia had not committed and would not commit ICC or other countries but could only use their best endeavours to implement what had been agreed.

The non-disclosure of the financial conditions caused some consternation. However, it has always been the Australian Board's policy not to make public the financial conditions relating to television fees and sponsorships. ICC was assured that the agreement provided no bonanza for the Australian Board, and whether or not the agreement was financially successful would depend on the ability of the promoters to encourage attendance at the programme of matches. The Board had acted honourably and entered into the agreement in the best interests, as they saw them, of international cricket.

Now, what has happened over the past five years? It was understandable that, in arriving at a solution, the promoters of WSC should want a combination of what they saw as the best of their own cricket with the best of the traditional game. So, out of the negotiations came a mixture of traditional Test cricket with one-day Internationals.

The control of the game reverted to the Australian Board while PBL undertook, with their considerable expertise, to promote the programme. This provided for two visiting Test-playing countries to be involved each season. Initially it was agreed that each visiting country would play three Tests against Australia. Interspersed would be a total of fifteen one-day Internationals with a final the best of five matches. Test cricket would maintain its traditional red ball and white clothing. The one-day competition would use a white ball, coloured clothing and play a number of day/night matches.

By agreement, the first participants in this "new era" were England and West Indies in 1979-80. India who had been invited to tour Australia in that season agreed to transfer to 1980-81 and to combine with New Zealand. West Indies and Pakistan agreed to tour together in 1981-82. The 1979-80 joint tour was not easy to arrange. England were not happy about the number of one-day internationals, finally agreeing to play a total of eight preliminary games, four each against West Indies and Australia and a final the best-of-three. Coloured clothing was unacceptable, even though it was considered essential for night games. England were also apprehensive about using the white ball in one-day daylight matches, though one of the reasons for using the white ball in both day and day/night matches was to differentiate between traditional Test cricket and the series of one-day internationals. Finally, after weeks of discussion, the joint tour by England and West Indies was confirmed, though England were not agreeable to their three-match Test series being for the Ashes. Australia also agreed with England that after the first three years of this type of programme the Board would give consideration to reverting to the traditional Ashes programme for England's 1982-83 tour of Australia.

The 1979-80 season was successful. A total of 228,936 attended the three Tests against England and 216,659 the three against West Indies. Australia failed to qualify for the final of the Benson and Hedges World Series Cup, and one preliminary match, England against West Indies, scheduled to be played at Melbourne, was completely abandoned because of rain. Nevertheless, a total of 258,825 attended the eleven preliminary and two final matches. The total attendance for the international season in Australia of 703,420 compared favourably with previous figures.

A survey taken during the season showed that support for Test cricket and the limited-overs games was more or less equally divided. A majority supported the use of coloured clothing in one-day games. It became apparent during the season that the mixing of Test cricket and one-day Internationals was somewhat confusing to the public and difficult for the players. Some of the players found it hard to adapt from normal Test cricket to the hustle and bustle of the interspersed limited-overs games. Nevertheless, a similar type of programme as that provided in the original agreement was confirmed for the seasons 1980-81 (India and New Zealand) and 1981-82 (West Indies and Pakistan).

In 1980-81 the world attendance record for a one-day game was broken in Melbourne when 52,990 attended the first final between New Zealand and Australia. In 1981-82, again in Melbourne, a West Indies-Australia preliminary one-day match attracted 78,142 spectators. Financially, the three seasons 1979-80, 1980-81, and 1981-82 were successful, especially when compared with 1977-78 and 1978-79, the seasons of the rift, both of which had shown substantial losses.

With the experience of the three previous seasons and in the light of the assurance given to England in 1979-80 to review the type of programme for their 1982-83 tour, it was decided to revert to the traditional five-Test tour for the Ashes series and to play the Tests first, followed by fifteen one-day games and a best-of-three final. The result was a success. At a preliminary match, between England and Australia in Melbourne, a new record attendance for one-day limited-overs matches of 84,360 was established. The overall attendance at international cricket in 1982-83 totalled almost 1,100,000 – a substantial increase over the total for 1979-80.

It has to be remembered that only two-thirds of the Australian population are now of Anglo-Saxon origin. The other third, principally European, has never been exposed to cricket. But it is pleasing to note the increasing interest in cricket from members of ethnic groups.

Cricket is a players' game. Test cricket is the game preferred by the players, the one for which they have been trained. However, they appreciate the financial need to play a combination of traditional and limited-overs cricket. Administrators must judge the success of a players' game by the number of participants. In Australia there are more players than ever before. A public opinion poll conducted in June 1983 showed that the most popular sport in Australia is cricket. Long may that continue.

PHILATELIC CRICKET

By MARCUS WILLIAMS

In view of the antiquity of cricket and stamps it was for long a disappointment to those interested in both fields that, while Olympic Games, football and other sporting issues abounded from the world's post offices, stamps depicting cricket were absent – although to fill the void some ingenious collectors suggested that Apollo was displaying his talents as a bowler rather than a discus thrower on a Greek stamp of 1906, and cited other stamps which showed sports with resemblances to cricket.

Honour was eventually satisfied on January 18, 1962 from an unlikely source – the Cape Verde Islands, a Portuguese colony 500 miles off the west African coast whose cricket activity is largely confined to chirping in the hearth. Later the same year Pakistan issued two more stamps with cricketing links and some 30 other countries have followed suit, to the point where stamps are probably as popular as any branch of cricketana.

The total of stamps issued actually to illustrate a facet of cricket or incidentally associated in some way with the game is now well into three figures and continually growing through new issues. Nor does this take into account the possibility of further retrospective discoveries of the type that have recently unearthed, years after their issue, stamps and other philatelic material found to have connections with cricket. It is through these that the beginnings of cricket philately have gradually been taken back far beyond Cape Verde – and even Apollo – to the latter part of the nineteenth century.

The oldest of these items known to me at the time of writing are three envelopes with the name of the Young America CC of Germantown, Philadelphia printed in the top left corner and postmarked 1886, during the flourishing of the game in that part of the United States before the First World War. The club was in existence for 34 years, from its foundation in 1855 to its merger with the Germantown CC in 1889. It must have been at its zenith, at least in its own opinion, around 1879, when it took on Richard Daft's touring English professionals on level terms. Daft's team won by an innings.

Envelopes bearing the name of a cricket club or organization and carried through the mail come within the scope of a comprehensive stamp collection, as do the popular souvenir envelopes – sometimes autographed by leading players or personalities – which accompany new stamp issues and important matches or anniversaries. The stamps on these envelopes usually receive by hand a specially designed postmark, unique to the event and available for one day only. There are a few lucky collectors who also have some far earlier cricket postmarks, which bear the names of cricket grounds and date from around the turn of the century. The postmarks were used at temporary post offices set up at the grounds for the despatch of press reports and other urgent messages. They were almost certainly not applied to mail but only to cancel stamps affixed to telegram application forms to pay the transmission fee. It is only through the breaching of Post Office regulations that the handful of actually used examples have survived (although samples can be found in

[*Mike Scott*

Top row: Antigua 1975, Cape Verde 1962, Great Britain 1973. *Second row:* Pakistan 1962 (shows Ayub Trophy), Barbados 1983. *Bottom left:* Sri Lanka 1982, Grenada 1969. *Bottom right:* Nuremburg pre-World War I.

Post Office records): it was policy that all telegram forms should be destroyed once the message was sent, but some evidently slipped through the net.

The first recorded postmark was produced for Bramall Lane, Sheffield, in July 1887 for a match between Yorkshire and Surrey, and another was made for the same ground when it staged its only Test match (England v Australia) in July 1902. Other grounds covered over a period of more than twenty years include Trent Bridge, Taunton, Edgbaston, Bradford, Leyton and, for the match between MCC and South Africa in June 1901, Lord's. Although a wide variety of cricketing subjects has been featured on stamps – the detailing of them all is regrettably beyond the scope of this article – Lord's itself has not yet appeared. There are hopes, however, of that being rectified if the British Post Office decides to commemorate the bicentenary of Lord's and MCC in 1987.

Many aspects of cricket history have already been represented on stamps, notably the Centenary Test at Melbourne (a delightful set of six from Australia in 1977) and the centenary of the first Test in England (GB 1980); the centenary of the Ashes (a pre-stamped envelope from Australia in 1982); the inaugural Test match in Sri Lanka (also 1982); West Indies' winning of the first Prudential World Cup (twelve different Caribbean territories issued stamps in 1975 and 1976); the centenary of cricket in Fiji (1974); and the 75th anniversary of Bermuda's Cup Match (1976).

Of the game's great players to have featured on stamps, there are almost enough to form an eleven, immensely strong in batting. The first to be honoured was Sir Garfield Sobers, on a Barbados independence issue of 1966, and he subsequently appeared on two stamps of 1977 which showed the ceremony at Bridgetown Racecourse where he was knighted by the Queen. To join him he has W. G. Grace (GB 1973), K. S. Ranjitsinhji (India 1973), Vivian Richards (Antigua 1975 and 1976, Barbuda 1975), Sir Donald Bradman (anonymously on a South African stamp of 1976), Sir Frank Worrell (Turks and Caicos Islands 1980, but misspelt 'Worrel') and Victor Trumper (Australia 1981), with middle-order support Sir William Milton (Rhodesia 1969), captain of South Africa in two of her early Test matches and subsequently administrator of Southern Rhodesia.

Andy Roberts, featured at the same times as Richards, would spearhead the attack, supported by Sobers, Grace, Worrell and Richards. To make up the side, with a wicket-keeper a priority, they might call on the unnamed Indian Test players on a 1971 stamp or some likely-looking performers from Grenada (1969). As umpire they could summon Sir Edmund Barton (Australia 1951 and 1969), the country's first prime minister and the only one to have stood in first-class matches.

Unlikely, however, to make the World Stamp XI is the batsman on the Cape Verde stamp, for although his left toes are cocked in the best W. G. Grace fashion, his grip would make orthodox, and most unorthodox, strokeplay impossible. The batsman, too, on the oldest known cricket stamp of any kind, a perforated publicity label from the Nuremberg Football Club in southern Germany before the First World War, would rule himself out of such august company by wearing only one pad and no gloves, while the baseballer's stance of the batsman from Sharjah (1972), now a flourishing desert outpost of cricket, leaves him prey to the yorker.

Our selected eleven could tour the world to parade their talents on, I suppose, universally sticky wickets. Stamps of Liberia (1956) and Romania (1979) illustrate Melbourne Cricket Ground, albeit in its guise as the main stadium for the 1956 Olympics; a Barbados issue (1983) shows Kensington Oval, Bridgetown, and one of Ceylon (1967) the Esplanade ground in Galle, which was chosen for a Test match in March 1984. Then there are the pleasant, though humbler, settings of Albert Park, Suva (Fiji 1942 and 1954), and Warner Park, St Kitts (1952 and 1954). They might also venture to some of the remote cricketing areas of the South Pacific which have found their way on to stamps, there to take part in the 150-or-more-a-side inter-village games in Samoa (1971) and Tokelau (1979), or the Bounty holiday match on Norfolk Island (1981). They would, however, be disbarred from the all-women contests of New Caledonia (1975) except as umpires and scorers.

A final illustration of the links between cricket and stamps: funds for the construction of a recreation ground in Basseterre, the capital of St Kitts, were provided by the sale of stamps issued in 1923 which marked the colony's tercentenary; the island's first governor, after whom the ground was named, was Sir Thomas Warner – an ancestor of Sir Pelham's!

ZAHEER ABBAS – A FLOURISHING TALENT

TWENTIETH BATSMAN TO REACH 100 HUNDREDS

By DAVID GREEN

Zaheer Abbas burst upon the world of cricket in 1971 at the age of 23. In the opening match of Pakistan's tour of England that year, at Worcester, he made a rapid 100 and continued in prolific form, scoring 731 runs in May. The first Test match started at Edgbaston on June 3 and by June 4 Zaheer, during the course of a magnificent innings of 274, had completed 1,000 for the season.

Opponents, press and public were struck by the slender, bespectacled newcomer's mastery over an England attack which included Peter Lever, Ray Illingworth and Derek Underwood and had, only the previous winter, proved too strong for the Australians on their own pitches. His elegance, timing and powers of concentration (he batted for over nine hours and hit 38 4s) were acclaimed. Nevertheless, some reservations were expressed. England, having omitted the out-of-sorts John Snow, had had no bowler of high pace to test this young man with the full and curiously looped backlift, and the Edgbaston pitch had been dead. Would the languid-looking Zaheer succeed on quicker wickets or when the ball seamed and swung? One who did not hedge his bets was Ted Dexter, who noted in a broadcast that up to the start of the tour Zaheer had made nine hundreds in only 45 first-class innings. "You must", said Dexter, "be some batsman if you can score a century every five knocks you have".

In the event, Zaheer, or "Zed" as he has been almost universally known since his association with Gloucestershire began in 1972, has mocked the doubters. He has already made well over 30,000 runs at an average of comfortably more than 50, and on December 12, 1982, his 215 for Pakistan against India at Lahore was his 100th first-class hundred. By September 1983 he had made a century in each innings of a match on eight occasions, and on four of them one of the centuries was a "double"; both are feats unparalleled in the annals of the game. In Test matches he had scored his 4,000th run and was averaging 46.81.

This bald statistical recital gives the impression that all went smoothly for Zaheer after that remarkable performance in what was only his second Test match – his first had been against New Zealand in 1969 – but this is far from being the case. Zaheer's impressive Test figures mask some inconsistencies. After his triumph at Edgbaston he had to wait three years for his next Test century, which was again a big one and against England – 240 in The Oval Test of 1974. There was another long gap before his third, which was against Australia at Adelaide in 1976-77. Prosperous series against India and New Zealand in 1978-79 brought him three hundreds, yet in his next 23 Test innings he made only 528 runs. Then came some marvellous batting in Pakistan in 1982-83 against Australia and India, a veritable run-glut which included five Test centuries, the 215 at Lahore among them.

These ups and downs are mentioned less as criticism than as an illustration of the character which Zaheer, a man whose *persona* is quiet to the point of diffidence, has frequently shown in overcoming adversity. Poor form, for him, is a more serious matter than for most players, for apart from his wife, Najma, their daughters, Rudaba and Roshana, and the immediate circle of his family, cricket and more particularly batting is the breath of life to him. Where such dedication exists, failure is not easily shrugged off, and introspection and worry can compound a player's difficulties.

Technical faults have sometimes been advanced to explain Zaheer's extremes of form, but this seems to me to be nonsense. He has scored a century on every six and a half visits to the crease. Leaving aside the phenomenal Sir Donald Bradman, whose ratio of centuries to innings was one to 2.8, Zaheer's striking-rate, among those who have made 100 hundreds, is excellent. Batsmen who have made a comparable number of runs with a higher career average can be counted on the fingers of one hand. No one with a "faulty" method could perform at Zaheer's level over fourteen seasons, winter and summer, and to attempt to explain his failures in this way is to misunderstand the man and the nature of his art.

Zaheer's love of batting is manifested not through mere sterile occupation of the crease, with runs being scored at a rate dictated by the level of the bowler's competence, but rather through a will to dominate bowlers, almost irrespective of their skill or of the condition of the pitch. This is a characteristic he shares with his great contemporary, Vivian Richards. The shortish ball just outside off stump, which a player more prudent or less talented might studiously ignore, is to him there to be hit, and the same can apply to the straight, good-length ball, from which he scores with an ease and frequency which only Richards and perhaps Greg Chappell have matched in recent years.

Such an ambitious approach carries its own penalties. Inevitably, attacking strokes aimed at good balls leave little margin for error. Zaheer, therefore, more than most, can be affected by slight loss of form; the flowing cover-drive, if edged, carries to slip in a way that the careful defensive prod does not. On balance, however, his attitude is fully justified by his record. The spectator must expect the occasional early dismissal, but in compensation he sees, when Zaheer is going well, strokeplay of a beauty which illuminates a utilitarian age.

Like all great players, he has an uncomplicated method. It is based first on correct footwork, so that he is positioned advantageously in relation to the length and line of each delivery. Secondly, though his backswing may not please the purist, the bat's downward path, which is much more important, is so strictly vertical as to satisfy the most pernickety geometrician. His power is derived from a high backlift, sweet timing and wristy acceleration of the blade at the moment of impact. It is this wristiness, together with the consequent free follow-through, that gives his batting its seductive bloom. When watching him, I am constantly reminded of Beldham's photographic studies of the heroes of cricket's Golden Age – of Fry, Trumper, Ranji and MacLaren.

He has no favoured area of scoring, striking the ball as firmly off the back foot as the front and despatching it with the same certainty through mid-wicket as past mid-off or wide of cover point. Such all-round mastery makes him at times impossible to contain, for no matter where the bowler

[*Patrick Eagar*

Zaheer Abbas – twentieth batsman to reach 100 hundreds.

directs his attack, Zaheer, his intentions almost invariably aggressive, can fashion a scoring stroke. He is still only 36, so that cricket-lovers (though perhaps not bowlers) will hope to be delighted by his artistry for several seasons yet.

ZAHEER ABBAS'S 100 HUNDREDS

197	Karachi v East Pakistan at Karachi, 1968-69
103*	PIA v Bahawalpur at Bahawalpur, 1969-70
136*	PIA v Karachi B at Karachi, 1969-70
136	PIA v Karachi A at Karachi, 1969-70
118	PIA A v East Pakistan Greens at Dacca, 1970-71
196	PIA A v East Pakistan Whites at Dacca, 1970-71
161	PIA A v Bahawalpur at Karachi, 1970-71
111	PIA A v Punjab University at Lahore, 1970-71
202	PIA A v Karachi Blues at Karachi, 1970-71
110	Pakistanis v Worcestershire at Worcester, 1971
138	Pakistanis v Kent at Gravesend, 1971
274	Pakistan v England at Birmingham, 1971
100*	Pakistanis v Lancashire at Manchester, 1971
112	World XI v Western Australia at Perth, 1971-72
106	World XI v Tasmania Combined XI at Hobart, 1971-72
143	Pakistanis v Western Australia at Perth, 1972-73
113	Pakistanis v Tasmania at Hobart, 1972-73
105	Pakistanis v Central Districts at Wanganui, 1972-73
170	Pakistanis v Wellington at Wellington, 1972-73
110	PIA v Karachi at Karachi, 1972-73
153*	Gloucestershire v Surrey at The Oval, 1973
103	Gloucestershire v Somerset at Bristol, 1973
145	Pakistan XI v World XI at Karachi, 1973-74
129	Pakistan XI v World XI at Lahore, 1973-74
112	PIA v Pakistan Railways at Lahore, 1973-74
112	PIA v Punjab at Lahore, 1973-74
174	PIA v Sind at Lahore, 1973-74
112	Gloucestershire v Cambridge University at Cambridge, 1974
137	Pakistanis v Minor Counties at Jesmond, 1974
104	Pakistanis v Glamorgan at Swansea, 1974
240	Pakistan v England at The Oval, 1974
117	Pakistanis v Sussex at Hove, 1974
131	PIA v Pakistan Railways at Lahore, 1974-75
157	PIA v National Bank at Lahore, 1974-75
111	Gloucestershire v Kent at Cheltenham, 1975
123	Gloucestershire v Nottinghamshire at Nottingham, 1975
170	Dawood Industries v PIA at Lahore, 1975-76
155	Sind A v Pakistan Universities at Lahore, 1975-76
188	Gloucestershire v Yorkshire at Leeds, 1976
141	Gloucestershire v Somerset at Taunton, 1976
216* / 156*	Gloucestershire v Surrey at The Oval, 1976
104	Gloucestershire v Sussex at Gloucester, 1976
153	Gloucestershire v Essex at Cheltenham, 1976
177	Gloucestershire v Glamorgan at Cardiff, 1976
177	Gloucestershire v Leicestershire at Leicester, 1976
230* / 104*	Gloucestershire v Kent at Canterbury, 1976
106	Gloucestershire v Worcestershire at Worcester, 1976
101	Pakistan v Australia at Adelaide, 1976-77
104	Gloucestershire v Sussex at Hove, 1977
105	Gloucestershire v Somerset at Bristol, 1977

205* 108* }	Gloucestershire v Sussex at Cheltenham, 1977
100*	Gloucestershire v Hampshire at Southampton, 1977
100	Gloucestershire v Cambridge University at Cambridge, 1978
140	Gloucestershire v Somerset at Taunton, 1978
213	Gloucestershire v Sussex at Hove, 1978
104	Gloucestershire v Derbyshire at Gloucester, 1978
121	Gloucestershire v New Zealanders at Bristol, 1978
132	Gloucestershire v Hampshire at Basingstoke, 1978
176	Pakistan v India at Faisalabad, 1978-79
235*	Pakistan v India at Lahore, 1978-79
135	Pakistan v New Zealand at Auckland, 1978-79
126	Pakistanis v South Australia at Adelaide, 1978-79
101	Gloucestershire v Glamorgan at Cardiff, 1979
147	Gloucestershire v Somerset at Taunton, 1979
151*	Gloucestershire v Warwickshire at Bristol, 1979
111	PIA v Lahore at Lahore, 1979-80
170	PIA v Pakistan Railways at Lahore, 1979-80
114	Pakistanis v West Zone at Pune, 1979-80
104	Gloucestershire v Northamptonshire at Bristol, 1980
173	Gloucestershire v Somerset at Taunton, 1980
110*	PIA v Karachi at Karachi, 1980-81
138	PIA v MCB at Karachi, 1980-81
154*	PIA v National Bank at Lahore, 1980-81
100* 100* }	PIA v Pakistan Railways at Lahore, 1980-81
215* 150* }	Gloucestershire v Somerset at Bath, 1981
101*	Gloucestershire v Hampshire at Southampton, 1981
100	Gloucestershire v Warwickshire at Gloucester, 1981
135* 128 }	Gloucestershire v Northamptonshire at Northampton, 1981
145	Gloucestershire v Sussex at Hove, 1981
159	Gloucestershire v Glamorgan at Bristol, 1981
136*	Gloucestershire v Kent at Cheltenham, 1981
103*	Gloucestershire v Worcestershire at Worcester, 1981
117	Pakistanis v South Australia at Adelaide, 1981-82
134	Pakistan v Sri Lanka at Lahore, 1981-82
144	Gloucestershire v Oxford University at Oxford, 1982
162* 107 }	Gloucestershire v Lancashire at Gloucester, 1982
147	Pakistanis v Worcestershire at Worcester, 1982
148*	Pakistanis v Derbyshire at Chesterfield, 1982
126	Pakistan v Australia at Faisalabad, 1982-83
125 101 }	PIA v Karachi at Karachi, 1982-83
108	BCCP Patron's XI v Indians at Rawalpindi, 1982-83
215	Pakistan v India at Lahore, 1982-83

Of Zaheer's 100 hundreds, 54 were scored in England, 34 in Pakistan, eight in Australia, three in New Zealand and one in India.

1884 – A YEAR TO REMEMBER

By STEPHEN GREEN (MCC Curator)

As a result of George Orwell's seminal work, most of us will have entered 1984 with some sense of foreboding. As a consequence, the year will probably prove to be something of an anticlimax; it may even be uneventful. By contrast, 1884 was a significant year, not least in cricket history. In his book *Lord's 1787-1945* Sir Pelham Warner said: "Looking back, it seems to me that the season of 1884 marked something like the beginning of international cricket as we understand it today."

Among the cricketing visitors to England were the first touring team from Philadelphia. This historic city has always been a great centre of American cricket and the late nineteenth century witnessed some fine performances by Philadelphian players. In addition to the American tourists, 1884 saw an Australian visit. As can be seen from a study of photographs of the touring side, 1884 was a transitional period for cricket dress. At this period coloured shirts were disappearing and white ones were becoming customary. White buckskin boots were first worn in 1882. Sweaters were also beginning to appear, and Shaw and Shrewsbury's team which visited Australia in 1884-85 had quite a modern appearance with matching blazers and caps. The wearing of ties on the field was not so common as it had been, but small bow ties were in fashion.

Even in those seemingly golden days, not everyone was content. In Lillywhite's *Cricketers' Annual* there was an article by "Incog" entitled "Cricket in 1884". It includes these ever-topical words: "Some hypercritical persons, no doubt sensitive and solicitous for the highest interest of the game, are apt to decry everything which savours of the commercial element in connection with our national sport." Even then there was a feeling that there were too many and too-frequent tours.

Until 1884 Test matches in England had all been played at Kennington Oval, owing to the pioneering influence of the Surrey Secretary, C. W. Alcock. The famous Test match of 1882 and the following series down under in 1882-83 had generated much interest in the international game, and for the first time three Test matches were allocated for the 1884 season. Old Trafford and Lord's thus became Test grounds.

The Old Trafford match was due to start on July 10, but the Manchester weather ran true to form and no play was possible on the first day. The weather ensured that the match was drawn, but Australia had the better of it. Old Trafford looked different in those days. The present pavilion dates from 1894, but its predecessor was quite a handsome edifice. In 1856 the Manchester Cricket Club had had to move from their home in the Chester Road, to make way for an Art Treasures' Exhibition. Less than a mile away they found eight acres of good, level, sandy land. The pavilion was described as being "a great ornament to the ground". Not the least of its amenities was "an excellent wine cellar, no unimportant acquisition in a cricket pavilion".

England were victorious in the Lord's Test by an innings and 5 runs. The headquarters of cricket also looked very different from the way it does today. The area adjacent to the Wellington Road was occupied by

Henderson's Nursery; next door to that was the Clergy Orphanage. The Tennis Court stood where the Mound Stand is now, and the pavilion, erected after the fire of 1825, still had five years to run before it was demolished to make way for Verity's present structure.

At Lord's, 1884 was a busy year off the field as well as on it. MCC commissioned the 1884 Code of the Laws of Cricket, a conservative revision which remained in force until 1947. Directed towards clarification of existing legislation rather than radical change, it laid down how many players could take part in a game and the number of innings there should be. The ways runs could be scored and how the result of a match could be decided were listed. There was a separate section containing the laws for one-day matches. In these games six-ball overs were legalised, though in first-class cricket the over still consisted of four balls. There were definitions for such terms as "dead ball", "byes" and "wicket down"; the thickness of the bails was specified; boundaries were mentioned for the first time. The most radical change, initiated by Lord Harris, was an alteration to Law 48 concerning no-balls and read: "If the umpire at the bowler's end be not satisfied of the absolute fairness of the delivery of any ball, he shall call 'No-ball'." This was an attempt to eradicate an epidemic of throwing.

The only President of MCC ever to die during his period of office, the Hon. Robert Grimston, passed away on April 7, 1884. Two days earlier John Wisden had also died, of cancer, at the age of 57. He was a splendid all-round cricketer who seems to have been universally respected. Although the centenary of his birth (in Brighton) in 1926 was not specially noted by *Wisden*, the jubilee issue of 1913 contained many tributes to him, including one from Sir Kenelm Digby who had been in the Harrow XI when Wisden was coach there. Sir Kenelm wrote: "I have the pleasantest recollection of his quiet, modest and unassuming character, his unfailing good temper, his keenness in and enjoyment of his work, his genial disposition which made him a great favourite with all the present and former members of the school with whom he came in contact." Sir Spencer Ponsonby-Fane wrote in a similar vein: "He was a very fine and accurate bowler, perfect length. He was a fast medium, but I think he was classed as a fast bowler. . . He was a good field, and an excellent bat, which was rather exceptional for a bowler at that time."

Wisden was known as the Little Wonder on account of his small physique and cricketing prowess. He was only 5 feet 4½ inches in height and in his prime he weighed but 7 stones. His outstanding feat on the field of play occurred in the North v South match of 1850 when he clean bowled all his opponents in their second innings. In 1852 he joined forces with James Dean to found the United All England XI. Three years later, with Frederick Lillywhite, he established the cricket outfitting business which he managed for a good number of years. In 1857 he was appointed Secretary of the Cricketers' Fund Friendly Society, an office he held until his death. In 1859 he went with George Parr's pioneering team to Canada and the United States, and in 1864 he set the seal on his distinguished career by issuing the first number of *Wisden*, called then simply *The Cricketer's Almanack*. Though a pale shadow of its later self, it proved to be "the Book of Genesis in the Cricketers' Bible".

TEST CRICKETERS

FULL LIST FROM 1877 TO SEPTEMBER 1, 1983

These lists have been compiled on a home and abroad basis, appearances abroad being printed in *italics*.

Abbreviations. E: England. A: Australia. SA: South Africa. WI: West Indies. NZ: New Zealand. In: India. P: Pakistan. SL: Sri Lanka.

All appearances are placed in this order of seniority. Hence, any England cricketer playing against Australia in England has that achievement recorded first and the remainder of his appearances at home (if any) set down before passing to matches abroad. Although the distinction between amateur and professional was abolished in 1963, initials of English professionals before that date are still given in brackets. The figures immediately following each name represent the total number of appearances in *all* Tests.

Where the season embraces two different years, the first year is given; i.e. 1876 indicates 1876-77.

When South Africa left the British Commonwealth in 1961 they ceased membership of the Imperial Cricket Conference, which in 1965 was renamed the International Cricket Conference. The rules of membership were changed then so that, although Pakistan have left the Commonwealth, they remain members of ICC.

ENGLAND

Number of Test cricketers: 503

Abel (R.) 13: v A 1888 (3) 1896 (3) 1902 (2); *v A 1891 (3); v SA 1888 (2)*

Absolom, C.A. 1: *v A 1878*

Allen (D. A.) 39: v A 1961 (4) 1964 (1); v SA 1960 (2); v WI 1963 (2) 1966 (1); v P 1962 (4); *v A 1962 (1) 1965 (4); v SA 1964 (4); v WI 1959 (5); v NZ 1965 (3); v In 1961 (5); v P 1961 (3)*

Allen, G. O. 25: v A 1930 (1) 1934 (2); v WI 1933 (1); v NZ 1931 (3); v In 1936 (3); *v A 1932 (5) 1936 (5); v WI 1947 (3); v NZ 1932 (2)*

Allom, M. J. C. 5: *v SA 1930 (1); v NZ 1929 (4)*

Allott, P. J. W. 5: v A 1981 (1); v In 1982 (2); *v In 1981 (1); v SL 1981 (1)*

Ames (L. E. G.) 47: v A 1934 (5) 1938 (2); v SA 1929 (1) 1935 (4); v WI 1933 (3); v NZ 1931 (3) 1937 (3); v In 1932 (1); *v A 1932 (5) 1936 (5); v SA 1938 (5); v WI 1929 (4) 1934 (4); v NZ 1932 (2)*

Amiss, D. L. 50: v A 1968 (1) 1975 (2) 1977 (2); v WI 1966 (1) 1973 (3) 1976 (1); v NZ 1973 (3); v In 1967 (2) 1971 (1) 1974 (3); v P 1967 (1) 1971 (3) 1974 (3); *v A 1974 (5) 1976 (1); v WI 1973 (5) v NZ 1974 (2); v In 1972 (3) 1976 (5); v P 1972 (3)*

Andrew (K. V.) 2: v WI 1963 (1); *v A 1954 (1)*

Appleyard (R.) 9: v A 1956 (1); v SA 1955 (1); v P 1954 (1); *v A 1954 (4); v NZ 1954 (2)*

Archer, A. G. 1: *v SA 1898*

Armitage (T.) 2: *v A 1876 (2)*

Arnold (E. G.) 10: v A 1905 (4); v SA 1907 (2); *v A 1903 (4)*

Arnold, G. G. 34: v A 1972 (3) 1975 (1); v WI 1973 (3); v NZ 1969 (1) 1973 (3); v In 1974 (2); v P 1967 (2) 1974 (3); *v A 1974 (4); v WI 1973 (3); v NZ 1974 (2); v In 1972 (4); v P 1972 (3)*

Arnold (J.) 1: v NZ 1931

Astill (W. E.) 9: *v SA 1927 (5); v WI 1929 (4)*

Athey, C. W. J. 3: v A 1980 (1); *v WI 1980 (2)*

Attewell (W.) 10: v A 1890 (1); *v A 1884 (5) 1887 (1) 1891 (3)*

Bailey, T. E. 61: v A 1953 (5) 1956 (4); v SA 1951 (2) 1955 (5); v WI 1950 (2) 1957 (4); v NZ 1949 (4) 1958 (4); v P 1954 (3); *v A 1950 (4) 1954 (5) 1958 (5); v SA 1956 (5); v WI 1953 (5); v NZ 1950 (2) 1954 (2)*

Bairstow, D. L. 4: v A 1980 (1); v WI 1980 (1); v In 1979 (1); *v WI 1980 (1)*

Bakewell (A. H.) 6: v SA 1935 (2); v WI 1933 (1); v NZ 1931 (2); *v In 1933 (1)*

Balderstone J. C. 2: v WI 1976 (2)

Barber, R. W. 28: v A 1964 (1) 1968 (1); v SA 1960 (1) 1965 (3); v WI 1966 (2); v NZ 1965 (3); *v A 1965 (5); v SA 1964 (4); v In 1961 (5); v P 1961 (3)*

Barber (W.) 2: v SA 1935 (2)

Barlow, G. D. 3: v A 1977 (1); *v In 1976 (2)*

Barlow (R. G.) 17: v A 1882 (1) 1884 (3) 1886 (3); *v A 1881 (4) 1882 (4) 1886 (2)*

Barnes (S. F.) 27: v A 1902 (1) 1909 (3) 1912 (3); v SA 1912 (3); *v A 1901 (3) 1907 (5) 1911 (5); v SA 1913 (4)*

Barnes (W.) 21: v A 1880 (1) 1882 (1) 1884 (2) 1886 (2) 1888 (3) 1890 (2); *v A 1882 (4) 1884 (5) 1886 (1)*

Barnett (C. J.) 20: v A 1938 (3) 1948 (1); v SA 1947 (3); v WI 1933 (1); v NZ 1937 (3); v In 1936 (1); *v A 1936 (5); v In 1933 (3)*

Barratt (F.) 5: v SA 1929 (1); *v NZ 1929 (4)*

Barrington (K. F.) 82: v A 1961 (5) 1964 (5) 1968 (3); v SA 1955 (2) 1960 (4) 1965 (3); v WI 1963 (5) 1966 (2); v NZ 1965 (2); v In 1959 (5) 1967 (3); v P 1962 (4) 1967 (3); *v A 1962 (5) 1965 (5); v SA 1964 (5); v WI 1959 (5) 1967 (5); v NZ 1962 (3); v In 1961 (5) 1963 (1); v P 1961 (2)*

Barton (V. A.) 1: *v SA 1891*

Bates (W.) 15: *v A 1881 (4) 1882 (4) 1884 (5) 1886 (2)*

Bean (G.) 3: *v A 1891 (3)*

Bedser (A. V.) 51: v A 1948 (5) 1953 (5); v SA 1947 (2) 1951 (2) 1955 (1); v WI 1950 (3); v NZ 1949 (2); v In 1946 (3) 1952 (4); v P 1954 (2); *v A 1946 (5) 1950 (5) 1954 (1); v SA 1948 (5); v NZ 1946 (1) 1950 (2)*

Berry (R.) 2: v WI 1950 (2)

Binks, J. G. 2: v In 1963 (2)

Bird M. C. 10: *v SA 1909 (5) 1913 (5)*

Birkenshaw J. 5: *v WI 1973 (2); v In 1972 (2); v P 1972 (1)*

Bligh, Hon. I. F. W. 4: *v A 1882 (4)*

Blythe (C.) 19: v A 1905 (1) 1909 (2); v SA 1907 (3); *v A 1901 (5) 1907 (1); v SA 1905 (5) 1909 (2)*

Board (J. H.) 6: *v SA 1898 (2) 1905 (4)*

Bolus, J. B. 7: v WI 1963 (2); v In 1963 (5)

Booth (M. W.) 2: *v SA 1913 (2)*

Bosanquet, B. J. T. 7: v A 1905 (3); *v A 1903 (4)*

Botham, I. T. 63: v A 1977 (2) 1980 (1) 1981 (6); v WI 1980 (5); v NZ 1978 (3) 1983 (4); v In 1979 (4) 1982 (3); v P 1978 (3) 1982 (3); *v A 1978 (6) 1979 (3) 1982 (5); v WI 1980 (4); v NZ 1977 (3); v In 1979 (1) 1981 (6); v SL 1981 (1)*

Bowden, M. P. 2: *v SA 1888 (2)*

Bowes (W. E.) 15: v A 1934 (3) 1938 (2); v SA 1935 (4); v WI 1939 (2); v In 1932 (1) 1946 (1); *v A 1932 (1); v NZ 1932 (1)*

Bowley (E. H.) 5: v SA 1929 (2); *v NZ 1929 (3)*

Boycott, G. 108: v A 1964 (4) 1968 (3) 1972 (2) 1977 (3) 1980 (1) 1981 (6); v SA 1965 (2); v WI 1966 (4) 1969 (3) 1973 (3) 1980 (5); v NZ 1965 (2) 1969 (3) 1973 (3) 1978 (2); v In 1967 (2) 1971 (1) 1974 (1) 1979 (4); v P 1967 (1) 1971 (2); *v A 1965 (5) 1970 (5) 1978 (6) 1979 (3); v SA 1964 (5); v WI 1967 (5) 1973 (5) 1980 (4); v NZ 1965 (2) 1977 (3); v In 1979 (1) 1981 (4); v P 1977 (3)*

Bradley, W. M. 2: v A 1899 (2)

Braund (L. C.) 23: v A 1902 (5); v SA 1907 (3); *v A 1901 (5) 1903 (5) 1907 (5)*

Brearley, J. M. 39: v A 1977 (5) 1981 (4); v WI 1976 (2); v NZ 1978 (3); v In 1979 (4); v P 1978 (3); *v A 1976 (1) 1978 (6) 1979 (3); v In 1976 (5) 1979 (1); v P 1977 (2)*

Brearley, W. 4: v A 1905 (2) 1909 (1); v SA 1912 (1)

Brennan, D. V. 2: v SA 1951 (2)

Briggs (John) 33: v A 1886 (3) 1888 (3) 1893 (2) 1896 (1) 1899 (1); *v A 1884 (5) 1886 (2) 1887 (1) 1891 (3) 1894 (5) 1897 (5); v SA 1888 (2)*

Brockwell (W.) 7: v A 1893 (1) 1899 (1); *v A 1894 (5)*

Bromley-Davenport, H. R. 4: *v SA 1895 (3) 1898 (1)*

Brookes (D.) 1: v WI 1947
Brown (A.) 2: v In 1961 (1); v P 1961 (1)
Brown, D. J. 26: v A 1968 (4); v SA 1965 (2); v WI 1966 (1) 1969 (3); v NZ 1969 (1); v In 1967 (2): v A 1965 (4); v WI 1967 (4); v NZ 1965 (2); v P 1968 (3)
Brown, F. R. 22: v A 1953 (1); v SA 1951 (5); v WI 1950 (1); v NZ 1931 (2) 1937 (1) 1949 (2); v In 1932 (1); v A 1950 (5); v NZ 1932 (2) 1950 (2)
Brown (G.) 7: v A 1921 (3); v SA 1922 (4)
Brown (J. T.) 8: v A 1896 (2) 1899 (1); v A 1894 (5)
Buckenham (C. P.) 4: v SA 1909 (4)
Butcher, A. R. 1: v In 1979
Butcher, R. O. 3: v WI 1980 (3)
Butler (H. J.) 2: v SA 1947 (1); v WI 1947 (1)
Butt (H. R.) 3: v SA 1895 (3)

Calthorpe, Hon. F. S. G. 4: v WI 1929 (4)
Carr, A. W. 11: v A 1926 (4); v SA 1929 (2); v SA 1922 (5)
Carr, D. B. 2: v In 1951 (2)
Carr, D. W. 1: v A 1909
Cartwright, T. W. 5: v A 1964 (2); v SA 1965 (1); v NZ 1965 (1); v SA 1964 (1)
Chapman, A. P. F. 26: v A 1926 (4) 1930 (4); v SA 1924 (2); v WI 1928 (3); v A 1924 (4) 1928 (4); v SA 1930 (5)
Charlwood (H. R. J.) 2: v A 1876 (2)
Chatterton (W.) 1: v SA 1891
Christopherson, S. 1: v A 1884
Clark (E. W.) 8: v A 1934 (2); v SA 1929 (1); v WI 1933 (2); v In 1933 (3)
Clay, J. C. 1: v SA 1935
Close (D. B.) 22: v A 1961 (1); v SA 1955 (1); v WI 1957 (2) 1963 (5) 1966 (1) 1976 (3); v NZ 1949 (1); v In 1959 (1) 1967 (3); v P 1967 (3); v A 1950 (1)
Coldwell (L. J.) 7: v A 1964 (2); v P 1962 (2); v A 1962 (2); v NZ 1962 (1)
Compton (D. C. S.) 78: v A 1938 (4) 1948 (5) 1953 (2) 1956 (1); v SA 1947 (5) 1951 (4) 1955 (5); v WI 1939 (3) 1950 (1); v NZ 1937 (1) 1949 (4); v In 1946 (3) 1952 (2); v P 1954 (4); v A 1946 (5) 1950 (4) 1954 (4); v SA 1948 (5) 1956 (5); v WI 1953 (5); v NZ 1946 (1) 1950 (2)
Cook (C.) 1: v SA 1947
Cook, G. 7: v In 1982 (3); v A 1982 (3); v SL 1981 (1)
Cook, N. G. B. 2: v NZ 1983 (2).
Cope, G. A. 3: v P 1977 (3)
Copson (W. H.) 3: v SA 1947 (1); v WI 1939 (2)
Cornford (W. L.) 4: v NZ 1929 (4)
Cottam, R. M. H. 4: v In 1972 (2); v P 1968 (2)
Coventry, Hon. C. J. 2: v SA 1888 (2)
Cowans, N. G. 8: v NZ 1983 (4); v A 1982 (4)
Cowdrey, M. C. 114: v A 1956 (5) 1961 (4) 1964 (3) 1968 (4); v SA 1955 (1) 1960 (5) 1965 (3); v WI 1957 (5) 1963 (2) 1966 (4); v NZ 1958 (4) 1965 (3); v In 1959 (5); v P 1962 (4) 1967 (2) 1971 (1); v A 1954 (5) 1958 (5) 1962 (5) 1965 (4) 1970 (3) 1974 (5); v SA 1956 (5); v WI 1959 (5) 1967 (5); v NZ 1954 (2) 1958 (2) 1962 (3) 1965 (3) 1970 (1); v In 1963 (3); v P 1968 (3)
Coxon (A.) 1: v A 1948
Cranston, J. 1: v A 1890
Cranston, K. 8: v A 1948 (1); v SA 1947 (3); v WI 1947 (4)
Crapp (J. F.) 7: v A 1948 (3); v SA 1948 (4)
Crawford J. N. 12: v SA 1907 (2); v A 1907 (5); v SA 1905 (5)
Cuttell (W. R.) 2: v SA 1898 (2)

Dawson, E. W. 5: v SA 1927 (1); v NZ 1929 (4)
Dean (H.) 3: v A 1912 (2); v SA 1912 (1)
Denness, M. H. 28: v A 1975 (1); v NZ 1969 (1); v In 1974 (3); v P 1974 (3); v A 1974 (5); v WI 1973 (5); v NZ 1974 (2); v In 1972 (5); v P 1972 (3)
Denton (D.) 11: v A 1905 (1); v SA 1905 (5) 1909 (5)
Dewes, J. G. 5: v A 1948 (1); v WI 1950 (2); v A 1950 (2)

Dexter, E. R. 62: v A 1961 (5) 1964 (5) 1968 (2); v SA 1960 (5); v WI 1963 (5); v NZ 1958 (1) 1965 (2); v In 1959 (2); v P 1962 (5); *v A 1958 (2) 1962 (5); v SA 1964 (5); v WI 1959 (5); v NZ 1958 (2) 1962 (3); v In 1961 (5); v P 1961 (3)*

Dilley, G. R. 17: v A 1981 (3); v WI 1980 (3); v NZ 1983 (1); *v A 1979 (2); v WI 1980 (4); v In 1981 (4)*

Dipper (A. E.) 1: v A 1921

Doggart, G. H. G. 2: v WI 1950 (2)

D'Oliveira, B. L. 44: v A 1968 (2) 1972 (5); v WI 1966 (4) 1969 (3); v NZ 1969 (3); v In 1967 (2) 1971 (3); v P 1967 (3) 1971 (3); *v A 1970 (6); v WI 1967 (5); v NZ 1970 (2); v P 1968 (3)*

Dollery (H. E.) 4: v A 1948 (2); v SA 1947 (1); v WI 1950 (1)

Dolphin (A.) 1: *v A 1920*

Douglas, J. W. H. T. 23: v A 1912 (1) 1921 (5); v SA 1924 (1); *v A 1911 (5) 1920 (5) 1924 (1); v SA 1913 (5)*

Downton, P. R. 4: v A 1981 (1); *v WI 1980 (3)*

Druce, N. F. 5: *v A 1897 (5)*

Ducat (A.) 1: v A 1921

Duckworth (G.) 24: v A 1930 (5); v SA 1924 (1) 1929 (4) 1935 (1); v WI 1928 (1); v In 1936 (3); *v A 1928 (5); v SA 1930 (3); v NZ 1932 (1)*

Duleepsinhji, K. S. 12: v A 1930 (4); v SA 1929 (1); v NZ 1931 (3); *v NZ 1929 (4)*

Durston (F. J.) 1: v A 1921

Edmonds, P. H. 23: v A 1975 (2); v NZ 1978 (3) 1983 (2); v In 1979 (4) 1982 (3); v P 1978 (3); *v A 1978 (1); v NZ 1977 (3); v P 1977 (2)*

Edrich, J. H. 77: v A 1964 (3) 1968 (5) 1972 (5) 1975 (4); v SA 1965 (1); v WI 1963 (3) 1966 (1) 1969 (3) 1976 (2); v NZ 1965 (1) 1969 (3); v In 1967 (2) 1971 (3) 1974 (3); v P 1971 (3) 1974 (3); *v A 1965 (5) 1970 (6) 1974 (4); v WI 1967 (5); v NZ 1965 (3) 1970 (2) 1974 (2); v In 1963 (2); v P 1968 (3)*

Edrich, W. J. 39: v A 1938 (4) 1948 (5) 1953 (3); v SA 1947 (4); v WI 1950 (2); v NZ 1949 (4); v In 1946 (1); v P 1954 (1); *v A 1946 (5) 1954 (4); v SA 1938 (5); v NZ 1946 (1)*

Elliott (H.) 4: v WI 1928 (1); *v SA 1927 (1); v In 1933 (2)*

Emburey, J. E. 22: v A 1980 (1) 1981 (4); v WI 1980 (3); v NZ 1978 (1); *v A 1978 (4); v WI 1980 (4); v In 1979 (1) 1981 (3); v SL 1981 (1)*

Emmett (G. M.) 1: v A 1948

Emmett (T.) 7: *v A 1876 (2) 1878 (1) 1881 (4)*

Evans, A. J. 1: v A 1921

Evans (T. G.) 91: v A 1948 (5) 1953 (5) 1956 (5); v SA 1947 (5) 1951 (3) 1955 (3); v WI 1950 (3) 1957 (5); v NZ 1949 (4) 1958 (5); v In 1946 (3) 1952 (4) 1959 (2); v P 1954 (4); *v A 1946 (4) 1950 (5) 1954 (4) 1958 (3); v SA 1948 (3) 1956 (5); v WI 1947 (4) 1953 (4); v NZ 1946 (1) 1950 (2) 1954 (2)*

Fagg (A. E.) 5: v WI 1939 (1); v In 1936 (2); *v A 1936 (2)*

Fane, F. L. 14: *v A 1907 (4); v SA 1905 (5) 1909 (5)*

Farnes, K. 15: v A 1934 (2) 1938 (4); *v A 1936 (2); v SA 1938 (5); v WI 1934 (2)*

Farrimond (W.) 4: v SA 1935 (1); *v SA 1930 (2); v WI 1934 (1)*

Fender, P. G. H. 13: v A 1921 (2); v SA 1924 (1) 1929 (1); *v A 1920 (3); v SA 1922 (5)*

Ferris, J. J. 1: *v SA 1891*

Fielder (A.) 6: *v A 1903 (2) 1907 (4)*

Fishlock (L. B.) 4: v In 1936 (2) 1946 (1); *v A 1946 (1)*

Flavell (J. A.) 4: v A 1961 (2) 1964 (2)

Fletcher, K. W. R. 59: v A 1968 (1) 1972 (1) 1975 (2); v WI 1973 (3); v NZ 1969 (2) 1973 (3); v In 1971 (2) 1974 (3); v P 1974 (3); *v A 1970 (5) 1974 (5) 1976 (1); v WI 1973 (4); v NZ 1970 (1) 1974 (2); v In 1972 (5) 1976 (3) 1981 (6); v P 1968 (3) 1972 (3); v SL 1981 (1)*

Flowers (W.) 8: v A 1893 (1); *v A 1884 (5) 1886 (2)*

Ford, F. G. J. 5: *v A 1894 (5)*

Foster, F. R. 11: v A 1912 (3); v SA 1912 (3); *v A 1911 (5)*

Foster, N. A. 1: v NZ 1983

Foster, R. E. 8: v SA 1907 (3); *v A 1903 (5)*

Fothergill (A. J.) 2: *v SA 1888 (2)*

Fowler, G. 6: v NZ 1983 (2); v P 1982 (1); *v A 1982 (3)*

Freeman (A. P.) 12: v SA 1929 (3); v WI 1928 (3); *v A 1924 (2); v SA 1927 (4)*

Fry, C. B. 26: v A 1899 (5) 1902 (3) 1905 (4) 1909 (3) 1912 (3); v SA 1907 (3) 1912 (3); *v SA 1895 (2)*

Gatting, M. W. 24: v A 1980 (1) 1981 (6); v WI 1980 (4); v NZ 1983 (2); v P 1982 (3); *v WI 1980 (1); v NZ 1977 (1); v In 1981 (5); v P 1977 (1)*
Gay, L. H. 1: *v A 1894*
Geary (G.) 14: v A 1926 (2) 1930 (1) 1934 (2); v SA 1924 (1) 1929 (3); *v A 1928 (4); v SA 1927 (2)*
Gibb, P. A. 8: v In 1946 (2); *v A 1946 (1); v SA 1938 (5)*
Gifford, N. 15: v A 1964 (2) 1972 (3); v NZ 1973 (2); v In 1971 (2); v P 1971 (2); *v In 1972 (2); v P 1972 (2)*
Gilligan, A. E. R. 11: v SA 1924 (4); *v A 1924 (5); v SA 1922 (2)*
Gilligan, A. H. H. 4: *v NZ 1929 (4)*
Gimblett (H.) 3: v WI 1939 (1); v In 1936 (2)
Gladwin (C.) 8: v SA 1947 (2); v NZ 1949 (1); *v SA 1948 (5)*
Goddard (T. W.) 8: v A 1930 (1); v WI 1939 (2); v NZ 1937 (2); *v SA 1938 (3)*
Gooch, G. A. 42: v A 1975 (2) 1980 (1) 1981 (5); v WI 1980 (5); v NZ 1978 (3); v In 1979 (4); v P 1978 (2); *v A 1978 (6) 1979 (2); v WI 1980 (4); v In 1979 (1) 1981 (6); v SL 1981 (1)*
Gover (A. R.) 4: v NZ 1937 (2); v In 1936 (1) 1946 (1)
Gower, D. I. 53: v A 1980 (1) 1981 (5); v WI 1980 (1); v NZ 1978 (3) 1983 (4); v In 1979 (4) 1982 (3); v P 1978 (3) 1982 (3); *v A 1978 (6) 1979 (3) 1982 (5); v WI 1980 (4); v In 1979 (1) 1981 (6); v SL 1981 (1)*
Grace, E. M. 1: v A 1880
Grace, G. F. 1: v A 1880
Grace, W. G. 22: v A 1880 (1) 1882 (1) 1884 (3) 1886 (3) 1888 (3) 1890 (2) 1893 (2) 1896 (3) 1899 (1); *v A 1891 (3)*
Graveney (T. W.) 79: v A 1953 (5) 1956 (2) 1968 (5); v SA 1951 (1) 1955 (5); v WI 1957 (4) 1966 (4) 1969 (1); v NZ 1958 (4); v In 1952 (4) 1967 (3); v P 1954 (3) 1962 (4) 1967 (3); *v A 1954 (2) 1958 (5) 1962 (3); v WI 1953 (5) 1967 (5); v NZ 1954 (2) 1958 (2); v In 1951 (4); v P 1968 (3)*
Greenhough (T.) 4: v SA 1960 (1); v In 1959 (3)
Greenwood (A.) 2: *v A 1876 (2)*
Greig, A. W. 58: v A 1972 (5) 1975 (4) 1977 (5); v WI 1973 (3) 1976 (5); v NZ 1973 (3); v In 1974 (3); v P 1974 (3); *v A 1974 (6) 1976 (1); v WI 1973 (5); v NZ 1974 (2); v In 1972 (5) 1976 (5); v P 1972 (3)*
Greig, I. A. 2: v P 1982 (2)
Grieve, B. A. F. 2: *v SA 1888 (2)*
Griffith, S. C. 3: *v SA 1948 (2); v WI 1947 (1)*
Gunn (G.) 15: v A 1909 (1); *v A 1907 (5) 1911 (5); v WI 1929 (4)*
Gunn (J.) 6: v A 1905 (1); *v A 1901 (5)*
Gunn (W.) 11: v A 1888 (2) 1890 (2) 1893 (3) 1896 (1) 1899 (1); *v A 1886 (2)*

Haig, N. E. 5: v A 1921 (1); *v WI 1929 (4)*
Haigh (S.) 11: v A 1905 (2) 1909 (1) 1912 (1); *v SA 1898 (2) 1905 (5)*
Hallows (C.) 2: v A 1921 (1); v WI 1928 (1)
Hammond, W. R. 85: v A 1930 (5) 1934 (5) 1938 (4); v SA 1929 (4) 1935 (5); v WI 1928 (3) 1933 (3) 1939 (3); v NZ 1931 (3) 1937 (3); v In 1932 (1) 1936 (2) 1946 (3); *v A 1928 (5) 1932 (5) 1936 (5) 1946 (4); v SA 1927 (5) 1930 (5) 1938 (5); v WI 1934 (4); v NZ 1932 (2) 1946 (1)*
Hampshire, J. H. 8: v A 1972 (1) 1975 (1); v WI 1969 (2); *v A 1970 (2); v NZ 1970 (2)*
Hardinge (H. T. W.) 1: v A 1921
Hardstaff (J.) 5: *v A 1907 (5)*
Hardstaff (J. jun.) 23: v A 1938 (2) 1948 (1); v SA 1935 (1); v WI 1939 (3); v NZ 1937 (3); v In 1936 (2) 1946 (2); *v A 1936 (1); v WI 1947 (3)*
Harris, Lord 4: v A 1880 (1) 1884 (2); *v A 1878 (1)*
Hartley, J. C. 2: *v SA 1905 (2)*
Hawke, Lord 5: *v SA 1895 (3) 1898 (2)*
Hayes (E. G.) 5: v A 1909 (1); v SA 1912 (1); *v SA 1905 (3)*
Hayes, F. C. 9: v WI 1973 (3) 1976 (2); *v WI 1973 (4)*

Hayward (T. W.) 35: v A 1896 (2) 1899 (5) 1902 (1) 1905 (5) 1909 (1); v SA 1907 (3); *v A 1897 (5) 1901 (5) 1903 (5); v SA 1895 (3)*

Hearne (A.) 1: *v SA 1891*

Hearne (F.) 2: *v SA 1888 (2)*

Hearne (G. G.) 1: *v SA 1891*

Hearne (J. T.) 12: v A 1896 (3) 1899 (3); *v A 1897 (5); v SA 1891 (1)*

Hearne (J. W.) 24: v A 1912 (3) 1921 (1) 1926 (1); v SA 1912 (2) 1924 (3); *v A 1911 (5) 1920 (2) 1924 (4); v SA 1913 (3)*

Hemmings, E. E. 5: v P 1982 (2); *v A 1982 (3)*

Hendren (E. H.) 51: v A 1921 (2) 1926 (5) 1930 (2) 1934 (4); v SA 1924 (5) 1929 (4); v WI 1928 (1); *v A 1920 (5) 1924 (5) 1928 (5); v SA 1930 (5); v WI 1929 (4) 1934 (4)*

Hendrick, M. 30: v A 1977 (3) 1980 (1) 1981 (2); v WI 1976 (2) 1980 (2); v NZ 1978 (3); v In 1974 (3) 1979 (4); v P 1974 (2); *v A 1974 (2) 1978 (5); v NZ 1974 (1) 1977 (1)*

Heseltine, C. 2: v SA 1895 (2)

Higgs, K. 15: v A 1968 (1); v WI 1966 (5); v SA 1965 (1); v In 1967 (1); v P 1967 (3); *v A 1965 (1); v NZ 1965 (3)*

Hill (A.) 2: *v A 1876 (2)*

Hill, A. J. L. 3: *v SA 1895 (3)*

Hilton (M. J.) 4: v SA 1951 (1); v WI 1950 (1); *v In 1951 (2)*

Hirst (G. H.) 24: v A 1899 (1) 1902 (4) 1905 (3) 1909 (4); v SA 1907 (3); *v A 1897 (4) 1903 (5)*

Hitch (J. W.) 7: v A 1912 (1) 1921 (1); v SA 1912 (1); *v A 1911 (3) 1920 (1)*

Hobbs (J. B.) 61: v A 1909 (3) 1912 (3) 1921 (1) 1926 (5) 1930 (5); v SA 1912 (2) 1924 (4) 1929 (1); v WI 1928 (2); *v A 1907 (4) 1911 (5) 1920 (5) 1924 (5) 1928 (5); v SA 1909 (5) 1913 (5)*

Hobbs, R. N. S. 7: v In 1967 (3); v P 1967 (1) 1971 (1); *v WI 1967 (1); v P 1968 (1)*

Hollies (W. E.) 13: v A 1948 (1); v SA 1947 (3); v WI 1950 (2); v NZ 1949 (4); *v WI 1934 (3)*

Holmes, E. R. T. 5: v SA 1935 (1); *v WI 1934 (4)*

Holmes (P.) 7: v A 1921 (1); v In 1932 (1); *v SA 1927 (5)*

Hone, L. 1: *v A 1878*

Hopwood (J. L.) 2: v A 1934 (2)

Hornby, A. N. 3: v A 1882 (1) 1884 (1); *v A 1878 (1)*

Horton (M. J.) 2: v In 1959 (2)

Howard, N. D. 4: *v In 1951 (4)*

Howell (H.) 5: v A 1921 (1); v SA 1924 (1); *v A 1920 (3)*

Howorth (R.) 5: v SA 1947 (1); *v WI 1947 (4)*

Humphries (J.) 3: *v A 1907 (3)*

Hunter (J.) 5: *v A 1884 (5)*

Hutchings, K. L. 7: v A 1909 (2); *v A 1907 (5)*

Hutton (L.) 79: v A 1938 (3) 1948 (4) 1953 (5); v SA 1947 (5) 1951 (5); v WI 1939 (3) 1950 (3); v NZ 1937 (3) 1949 (4); v In 1946 (3) 1952 (4); v P 1954 (2); *v A 1946 (5) 1950 (5) 1954 (5); v SA 1938 (4) 1948 (5); v WI 1947 (2) 1953 (5); v NZ 1950 (2) 1954 (2)*

Hutton, R. A. 5: v In 1971 (3); v P 1971 (2)

Iddon (J.) 5: v SA 1935 (1); *v WI 1934 (4)*

Ikin (J. T.) 18: v SA 1951 (3) 1955 (1); v In 1946 (2) 1952 (2); *v A 1946 (5); v NZ 1946 (1); v WI 1947 (4)*

Illingworth (R.) 61: v A 1961 (2) 1968 (3) 1972 (5); v SA 1960 (4); v WI 1966 (2) 1969 (3) 1973 (3); v NZ 1958 (1) 1965 (1) 1969 (3) 1973 (3); v In 1959 (2) 1967 (3) 1971 (3); v P 1962 (1) 1967 (1) 1971 (3); *v A 1962 (2) 1970 (6); v WI 1959 (5); v NZ 1962 (3) 1970 (2)*

Insole, D. J. 9: v A 1956 (1); v SA 1955 (1); v WI 1950 (1) 1957 (1); *v SA 1956 (5)*

Jackman, R. D. 4: v P 1982 (2); *v WI 1980 (2)*

Jackson, F. S. 20: v A 1893 (2) 1896 (3) 1899 (5) 1902 (5) 1905 (5)

Jackson (H. L.) 2: v A 1961 (1); v NZ 1949 (1)

Jameson, J. A. 4: v In 1971 (2); *v WI 1973 (2)*

Jardine, D. R. 22: v WI 1928 (2) 1933 (2); v NZ 1931 (3); v In 1932 (1); *v A 1928 (5) 1932 (5); v NZ 1932 (1); v In 1933 (3)*

Jenkins (R. O.) 9: v WI 1950 (2); v In 1952 (2); *v SA 1948 (5)*

Jessop, G. L. 18: v A 1899 (1) 1902 (4) 1905 (3) 1909 (2); v SA 1907 (3) 1912 (2); *v A 1901 (5)*

Jones, A. O. 12: v A 1899 (1) 1905 (2) 1909 (2); *v A 1901 (5) 1907 (2)*
Jones, I. J. 15: v WI 1966 (2); *v A 1965 (4); v WI 1967 (5); v NZ 1965 (3); v In 1963 (1)*
Jupp (H.) 2: *v A 1876 (2)*
Jupp, V. W. C. 8: v A 1921 (2); v WI 1928 (2); *v SA 1922 (4)*

Keeton (W. W.) 2: v A 1934 (1); v WI 1939 (1)
Kennedy (A. S.) 5: *v SA 1922 (5)*
Kenyon (D.) 8: v A 1953 (2); v SA 1955 (3); *v In 1951 (3)*
Killick, E. T. 2: v SA 1929 (2)
Kilner (R.) 9: v A 1926 (4); v SA 1924 (2); *v A 1924 (3)*
King (J. H.) 1: v A 1909
Kinneir (S. P.) 1: *v A 1911*
Knight (A. E.) 3: *v A 1903 (3)*
Knight (B. R.) 29: v A 1968 (2); v WI 1966 (1) 1969 (3); v NZ 1969 (2); v P 1962 (2); *v A 1962 (1) 1965 (2); v NZ 1962 (3) 1965 (2); v In 1961 (4) 1963 (5); v P 1961 (2)*
Knight, D. J. 2: v A 1921 (2)
Knott, A. P. E. 95: v A 1968 (5) 1972 (5) 1975 (4) 1977 (5) 1981 (2); v WI 1969 (3) 1973 (3) 1976 (5) 1980 (4); v NZ 1969 (3) 1973 (3); v In 1971 (3) 1974 (3); v P 1967 (2) 1971 (3) 1974 (3); *v A 1970 (6) 1974 (6) 1976 (1); v WI 1967 (2) 1973 (3); v NZ 1970 (1) 1974 (2); v In 1972 (5) 1976 (5); v P 1968 (3) 1972 (3)*
Knox, N. A. 2: v SA 1907 (2)

Laker (J. C.) 46: v A 1948 (3) 1953 (3) 1956 (5); v SA 1951 (2) 1955 (1); v WI 1950 (1) 1957 (4); v NZ 1949 (1) 1958 (4); v In 1952 (4); v P 1954 (1); *v A 1958 (4); v SA 1956 (5); v WI 1947 (4) 1953 (4)*
Lamb, A. J. 15: v NZ 1983 (4); v In 1982 (3); v P 1982 (3); *v A 1982 (5)*
Langridge (James) 8: v SA 1935 (1); v WI 1933 (2); v In 1936 (1) 1946 (1); *v In 1933 (3)*
Larkins, A. W. 6: v A 1981 (1); v WI 1980 (3); *v A 1979 (1); v In 1979 (1)*
Larter (J. D. F.) 10: v SA 1965 (2); v NZ 1965 (1); v P 1962 (1); *v NZ 1962 (3); v In 1963 (3)*
Larwood (H.) 21: v A 1926 (2) 1930 (3); v SA 1929 (3); v WI 1928 (2); v NZ 1931 (1); *v A 1928 (5) 1932 (5)*
Leadbeater (E.) 2: *v In 1951 (2)*
Lee (H. W.) 1: *v SA 1930*
Lees (W. S.) 5: *v SA 1905 (5)*
Legge G. B. 5: *v SA 1927 (1); v NZ 1929 (4)*
Leslie, C. F. H. 4: *v A 1882 (4)*
Lever, J. K. 20: v A 1977 (3); v WI 1980 (1); v In 1979 (1); *v A 1976 (1) 1978 (1) 1979 (1); v NZ 1977 (1); v In 1976 (5) 1979 (1) 1981 (2); v P 1977 (3)*
Lever, P. 17: v A 1972 (1) 1975 (1); v In 1971 (1); v P 1971 (3); *v A 1970 (5) 1974 (2); v NZ 1970 (2) 1974 (2)*
Leveson Gower, H. D. G. 3: *v SA 1909 (3)*
Levett, W. H. V. 1: *v In 1933*
Lewis, A. R. 9: v NZ 1973 (1); *v In 1972 (5); v P 1972 (3)*
Leyland (M.) 41: v A 1930 (3) 1934 (5) 1938 (1); v SA 1929 (5) 1935 (4); v WI 1928 (1) 1933 (1); v In 1936 (2); *v A 1928 (1) 1932 (5) 1936 (5); v SA 1930 (5); v WI 1934 (3)*
Lilley (A. A.) 35: v A 1896 (3) 1899 (4) 1902 (5) 1905 (5) 1909 (5); v SA 1907 (3); *v A 1901 (5) 1903 (5)*
Lillywhite (James jun.) 2: *v A 1876 (2)*
Lloyd, D. 9: v In 1974 (2); v P 1974 (3); *v A 1974 (4)*
Loader (P. J.) 13: v SA 1955 (1); v WI 1957 (2); v NZ 1958 (3); v P 1954 (1); *v A 1958 (2); v SA 1956 (4)*
Lock (G. A. R.) 49: v A 1953 (2) 1956 (4) 1961 (3); v SA 1955 (3); v WI 1957 (3) 1963 (3); v NZ 1958 (5); v In 1952 (2); v P 1962 (3); *v A 1958 (4); v SA 1956 (1); v WI 1953 (5) 1967 (2); v NZ 1958 (2); v In 1961 (5); v P 1961 (2)*
Lockwood (W. H.) 12: v A 1893 (2) 1899 (1) 1902 (4); *v A 1894 (5)*
Lohmann (G. A.) 18: v A 1886 (3) 1888 (3) 1890 (2) 1896 (1); *v A 1886 (2) 1887 (1) 1891 (3); v SA 1895 (3)*
Lowson (F. A.) 7: v SA 1951 (2) 1955 (1); *v In 1951 (4)*
Lucas, A. P. 5: v A 1880 (1) 1882 (1) 1884 (2); *v A 1878 (1)*
Luckhurst, B. W. 21: v A 1972 (4); v WI 1973 (2); v In 1971 (3); v P 1971 (3); *v A 1970 (5); 1974 (2); v NZ 1970 (2)*
Lyttelton, Hon. A. 4: v A 1880 (1) 1882 (1) 1884 (2)

Macaulay (G. G.) 8: v A 1926 (1); v SA 1924 (1); v WI 1933 (2); *v SA 1922 (4)*
MacBryan, J. C. W. 1: v SA 1924
McConnon (J. E.) 2: v P 1954 (2)
McGahey, C. P. 2: *v A 1901 (2)*
MacGregor, G. 8: v A 1890 (2) 1893 (3); *v A 1891 (3)*
McIntyre (A. J. W.) 3: v SA 1955 (1); v WI 1950 (1); *v A 1950 (1)*
MacKinnon, F. A. 1: *v A 1878*
MacLaren, A. C. 35: v A 1896 (2) 1899 (4) 1902 (5) 1905 (4) 1909 (5); *v A 1894 (5) 1897 (5) 1901 (5)*
McMaster, J. E. P. 1: *v SA 1888*
Makepeace (H.) 4: *v A 1920 (4)*
Mann, F. G. 7: v NZ 1949 (2); *v SA 1948 (5)*
Mann, F. T. 5: *v SA 1922 (5)*
Marks, V. J. 2: v NZ 1983 (1); v P 1982 (1)
Marriott, C. S. 1: v WI 1933
Martin (F.) 2: v A 1890 (1); *v SA 1891 (1)*
Martin, J. W. 1: v SA 1947
Mason, J. R. 5: *v A 1897 (5)*
Matthews (A. D. G.) 1: v NZ 1937
May, P. B. H. 66: v A 1953 (2) 1956 (5) 1961 (4); v SA 1951 (2) 1955 (5); v WI 1957 (5); v NZ 1958 (5); v In 1952 (4) 1959 (3); v P 1954 (4); *v A 1954 (5) 1958 (5); v SA 1956 (5); v WI 1953 (5) 1959 (3); v NZ 1954 (2) 1958 (2)*
Mead (C. P.) 17: v A 1921 (2); *v A 1911 (4) 1928 (1); v SA 1913 (5) 1922 (5)*
Mead (W.) 1: v A 1899
Midwinter (W. E.) 4: *v A 1881 (4)*
Milburn, C. 9: v A 1968 (2); v WI 1966 (4); v In 1967 (1); v P 1967 (1); *v P 1968 (1)*
Miller, A. M. 1: *v SA 1895*
Miller, G. 32: v A 1977 (2); v WI 1976 (1); v NZ 1978 (2); v In 1979 (3) 1982 (1); v P 1978 (3) 1982 (1); *v A 1978 (6) 1979 (1) 1982 (5); v WI 1980 (1); v NZ 1977 (3); v P 1977 (3)*
Milligan, F. W. 2: *v SA 1898 (2)*
Millman (G.) 6: v P 1962 (2); *v In 1961 (2); v P 1961 (2)*
Milton (C. A.) 6: v NZ 1958 (2); v In 1959 (2); *v A 1958 (2)*
Mitchell (A.) 6: v SA 1935 (2); v In 1936 (1); *v In 1933 (3)*
Mitchell, F. 2: *v SA 1898 (2)*
Mitchell (T. B.) 5: v A 1934 (2); v SA 1935 (1); *v A 1932 (1); v NZ 1932 (1)*
Mitchell-Innes, N. S. 1: v SA 1935
Mold (A. W.) 3: v A 1893 (3)
Moon, L. J. 4: *v SA 1905 (4)*
Morley (F.) 4: v A 1880 (1); *v A 1882 (3)*
Mortimore (J. B.) 9: v A 1964 (1); v In 1959 (2); *v A 1958 (1); v NZ 1958 (2); v In 1963 (3)*
Moss (A. E.) 9: v A 1956 (1); v SA 1960 (2); v In 1959 (3); *v WI 1953 (1) 1959 (2)*
Murdoch, W. L. 1: *v SA 1891*
Murray, J. T. 21: v A 1961 (5); v WI 1966 (1); v In 1967 (3); v P 1962 (3) 1967 (1); *v A 1962 (1); v SA 1964 (1); v NZ 1962 (1) 1965 (1); v In 1961 (3); v P 1961 (1)*

Newham (W.) 1: *v A 1887*
Nichols (M. S.) 14: v A 1930 (1); v SA 1935 (4); v WI 1933 (1) 1939 (1); *v NZ 1929 (4); v In 1933 (3)*

Oakman (A. S. M.) 2: v A 1956 (2)
O'Brien, T. C. 5: v A 1884 (1) 1888 (1); *v SA 1895 (3)*
O'Connor (J.) 4: v SA 1929 (1); *v WI 1929 (3)*
Old, C. M. 46: v A 1975 (3) 1977 (2) 1980 (1) 1981 (2); v WI 1973 (1) 1976 (2) 1980 (1); v NZ 1973 (2) 1978 (1); v In 1974 (3); v P 1974 (3) 1978 (3); *v A 1974 (2) 1976 (1) 1978 (1); v WI 1973 (4) 1980 (1); v NZ 1974 (1) 1977 (2); v In 1972 (4) 1976 (4); v P 1972 (1) 1977 (1)*
Oldfield (N.) 1: v WI 1939

Padgett (D. E. V.) 2: v SA 1960 (2)
Paine (G. A. E.) 4: *v WI 1934 (4)*
Palairet, L. C. H. 2: v A 1902 (2)
Palmer, C. H. 1: *v WI 1953*
Palmer, K. E. 1: *v SA 1964*

Parfitt (P. H.) 37: v A 1964 (4) 1972 (3); v SA 1965 (2); v WI 1969 (1); v NZ 1965 (2); v P 1962 (5); *v A 1962 (2); v SA 1964 (5); v NZ 1962 (3) 1965 (3); v In 1961 (2) 1963 (3); v P 1961 (2)*

Parker (C. W. L.) 1: v A 1921

Parker, P. W. G. 1: v A 1981

Parkhouse (W. G. A.) 7: v WI 1950 (2); v In 1959 (2); *v A 1950 (2); v NZ 1950 (1)*

Parkin (C. H.) 10: v A 1921 (4); v SA 1924 (1); *v A 1920 (5)*

Parks (J. H.) 1: v NZ 1937

Parks (J. M.) 46: v A 1964 (4) 1972 (3); v SA 1960 (5) 1965 (3); v WI 1963 (4) 1966 (4); v NZ 1965 (3); v P 1954 (1); *v A 1965 (5); v SA 1964 (5); v WI 1959 (1) 1967 (3); v NZ 1965 (2); v In 1963 (5)*

Pataudi, Nawab of, 3: v A 1934 (1); *v A 1932 (2)*

Paynter (E.) 20: v A 1938 (4); v WI 1939 (2); v NZ 1931 (1) 1937 (2); v In 1932 (1); *v A 1932 (3); v SA 1938 (5); v NZ 1932 (2)*

Peate (E.) 9: v A 1882 (1) 1884 (3) 1886 (1); *v A 1881 (4)*

Peebles, I. A. R. 13: v A 1930 (2); v NZ 1931 (3); *v SA 1927 (4) 1930 (3)*

Peel (R.) 20: v A 1888 (3) 1890 (1) 1893 (1) 1896 (1); *v A 1884 (5) 1887 (1) 1891 (3) 1894 (5)*

Penn, F. 1: v A 1880

Perks (R. T. D.) 2: v WI 1939 (1); *v SA 1938 (1)*

Philipson, H. 5: *v A 1891 (1) 1894 (4)*

Pilling (R.) 8: v A 1884 (1) 1886 (1) 1888 (1); *v A 1881 (4) 1887 (1)*

Place (W.) 3: *v WI 1947 (3)*

Pocock, P. I. 17: v A 1968 (1); v WI 1976 (2); *v WI 1967 (2) 1973 (4); v In 1972 (4); v P 1968 (1) 1972 (3)*

Pollard (R.) 4: v A 1948 (2); v In 1946 (1); *v NZ 1946 (1)*

Poole (C. J.) 3: *v In 1951 (3)*

Pope (G. H.) 1: v SA 1947

Pougher (A. D.) 1: *v SA 1891*

Price, J. S. E. 15: v A 1964 (2) 1972 (1); v In 1971 (3); v P 1971 (1); *v SA 1964 (4); v In 1963 (4)*

Price (W. F. F.) 1: v A 1938

Prideaux, R. M. 3: v A 1968 (1); *v P 1968 (2)*

Pringle, D. R. 7: v In 1982 (3); v P 1982 (1); *v A 1982 (3)*

Pullar (G.) 28: v A 1961 (5); v SA 1960 (3); v In 1959 (3); v P 1962 (2); *v A 1962 (4); v WI 1959 (5); v In 1961 (3); v P 1961 (3)*

Quaife (Wm) 7: v A 1899 (2); *v A 1901 (5)*

Radley, C. T. 8: v NZ 1978 (3); v P 1978 (3); *v NZ 1977 (2)*

Randall, D. W. 40: v A 1977 (5); v NZ 1983 (3) 1982 (3); v P 1982 (3); *v A 1976 (1) 1978 (6) 1979 (2) 1982 (4); v NZ 1977 (3); v In 1976 (4); v P 1977 (3)*

Ranjitsinhji, K. S. 15: v A 1896 (2) 1899 (5) 1902 (3); *v A 1897 (5)*

Read, H. D. 1: v SA 1935

Read (J. M.) 17: v A 1882 (1) 1890 (2) 1893 (1); *v A 1884 (5) 1886 (2) 1887 (1) 1891 (3); v SA 1888 (2)*

Read, W. W. 18: v A 1884 (2) 1886 (3) 1888 (3) 1890 (2) 1893 (2); *v A 1882 (4) 1887 (1); v SA 1891 (1)*

Relf (A. E.) 13: v A 1909 (1); *v A 1903 (2); v SA 1905 (5) 1913 (5)*

Rhodes (H. J.) 2: v In 1959 (2)

Rhodes (W.) 58: v A 1899 (3) 1902 (5) 1905 (4) 1909 (4) 1912 (3) 1921 (1) 1926 (1); v SA 1912 (3); *v A 1903 (5) 1907 (5) 1911 (5) 1920 (5); v SA 1909 (5) 1913 (5); v WI 1929 (4)*

Richardson (D. W.) 1: v WI 1957

Richardson (P. E.) 34: v A 1956 (5); v WI 1957 (5) 1963 (1); v NZ 1958 (4); *v A 1958 (4); v SA 1956 (5); v NZ 1958 (2); v In 1961 (5); v P 1961 (3)*

Richardson (T.) 14: v A 1893 (1) 1896 (3); *v A 1894 (5) 1897 (5)*

Richmond (T. L.) 1: v A 1921

Ridgway (F.) 5: *v In 1951 (5)*

Robertson (J. D.) 11: v SA 1947 (1); v NZ 1949 (1); *v WI 1947 (4); v In 1951 (5)*

Robins, R. W. V. 19: v A 1930 (2); v SA 1929 (1) 1935 (3); v WI 1933 (2); v NZ 1931 (1) 1937 (3); v In 1932 (1) 1936 (2); *v A 1936 (4)*

Roope, G. R. J. 21: v A 1975 (1) 1977 (2); v WI 1973 (1); v NZ 1973 (3) 1978 (1); v P 1978 (3); *v NZ 1977 (3); v In 1972 (2); v P 1972 (2) 1977 (3)*

Root (C. F.) 3: v A 1926 (3)
Rose, B. C. 9: v WI 1980 (3); *v WI 1980 (1); v NZ 1977 (2); v P 1977 (3)*
Royle, V. P. F. A. 1: *v A 1878*
Rumsey, F. E. 5: v A 1964 (1); v SA 1965 (1); v NZ 1965 (3)
Russell (A. C.) 10: v A 1921 (2); *v A 1920 (4); v SA 1922 (4)*
Russell, W. E. 10: v SA 1965 (1); v WI 1966 (2); v P 1967 (1); *v A 1965 (1); v NZ 1965 (3); v In 1961 (1); v P 1961 (1)*

Sandham (A.) 14: v A 1921 (1); v SA 1924 (2); *v A 1924 (2); v SA 1922 (5); v WI 1929 (4)*
Schultz, S. S. 1: *v A 1878*
Scotton (W. H.) 15: v A 1884 (1) 1886 (3); *v A 1881 (4) 1884 (5) 1886 (2)*
Selby (J.) 6: *v A 1876 (2) 1881 (4)*
Selvey, M. W. W. 3: v WI 1976 (2); *v In 1976 (1)*
Shackleton (D.) 7: v SA 1951 (1); v WI 1950 (1) 1963 (4); *v In 1951 (1)*
Sharp (J.) 3: v A 1909 (3)
Sharpe (J. W.) 3: v A 1890 (1); *v A 1891 (2)*
Sharpe, P. J. 12: v A 1964 (2); v WI 1963 (3) 1969 (3); v NZ 1969 (3); *v In 1963 (1)*
Shaw (A.) 7: v A 1880 (1); *v A 1876 (2) 1881 (4)*
Sheppard, Rev. D. S. 22: v A 1956 (2); v WI 1950 (1) 1957 (2); v In 1952 (1); v P 1954 (2) 1962 (2); *v A 1950 (2) 1962 (5); v NZ 1950 (1) 1963 (3)*
Sherwin (M.) 3: v A 1888 (1); *v A 1886 (2)*
Shrewsbury (A.) 23: v A 1884 (2) 1886 (3) 1890 (2) 1893 (3); *v A 1881 (4) 1884 (5) 1886 (2) 1887 (1)*
Shuter, J. 1: v A 1888
Shuttleworth, K. 5: v P 1971 (1); *v A 1970 (2); v NZ 1970 (2)*
Simpson, R. T. 27: v A 1953 (3); v SA 1951 (3); v WI 1950 (3); v NZ 1949 (2); v In 1952 (2); v P 1954 (3); *v A 1950 (5) 1954 (1); v SA 1948 (1); v NZ 1950 (2) 1954 (2)*
Simpson-Hayward, G. H. 5: *v SA 1909 (5)*
Sims (J. M.) 4: v SA 1935 (1); v In 1936 (1); *v A 1936 (2)*
Sinfield (R. A.) 1: v A 1938
Smailes (T. F.) 1: v In 1946
Smith, A. C. 6: *v A 1962 (4); v NZ 1962 (2)*
Smith, C. A. 1: *v SA 1888*
Smith (C. I. J.) 5: v NZ 1937 (1); *v WI 1934 (4)*
Smith, C. L. 2: v NZ 1983 (2)
Smith (D.) 2: v SA 1935 (2)
Smith (D. R.) 5: *v In 1961 (5)*
Smith (D. V.) 3: v WI 1957 (3)
Smith (E. J.) 11: v A 1912 (3); v SA 1912 (3); *v A 1911 (4); v SA 1913 (1)*
Smith (H.) 1: v WI 1928
Smith, M. J. K. 50: v A 1961 (1) 1972 (3); v SA 1960 (4) 1965 (3); v WI 1966 (1); v NZ 1958 (3) 1965 (3); v In 1959 (2); *v A 1965 (5); v SA 1964 (5); v WI 1959 (5); v NZ 1965 (3); v In 1961 (4) 1963 (5); v P 1961 (3)*
Smith (T. P. B.) 4: v In 1946 (1); *v A 1946 (2); v NZ 1946 (1)*
Smithson (G. A.) 2: *v WI 1947 (2)*
Snow, J. A. 49: v A 1968 (5) 1972 (5) 1975 (4); v SA 1965 (1); v WI 1966 (3) 1969 (3) 1973 (1) 1976 (3); v NZ 1965 (1) 1969 (2) 1973 (3); v In 1967 (3) 1971 (2); v P 1967 (1); *v A 1970 (6); v WI 1967 (4); v P 1968 (2)*
Southerton (J.) 2: *v A 1876 (2)*
Spooner, R. H. 10: v A 1905 (2) 1909 (2) 1912 (3); v SA 1912 (3)
Spooner (R. T.) 7: v SA 1955 (1); *v In 1951 (5); v WI 1953 (1)*
Stanyforth, R. T. 4: *v SA 1927 (4)*
Staples (S. J.) 3: *v SA 1927 (3)*
Statham (J. B.) 70: v A 1953 (1) 1956 (3) 1961 (4); v SA 1951 (2) 1955 (4) 1960 (5) 1965 (1); v WI 1957 (3) 1963 (2); v NZ 1958 (2); v In 1959 (3); v P 1954 (4) 1962 (3); *v A 1954 (5) 1958 (4) 1962 (5); v SA 1956 (4); v WI 1953 (4) 1959 (3); v NZ 1950 (1) 1954 (2); v In 1951 (5)*
Steel, A. G. 13: v A 1880 (1) 1882 (1) 1884 (3) 1886 (3) 1888 (1); *v A 1882 (4)*
Steele, D. S. 8: v A 1975 (3); v WI 1976 (5)
Stevens, G. T. S. 10: v A 1926 (2); *v SA 1922 (1) 1927 (5); v WI 1929 (2)*
Stevenson, G. B. 2: *v WI 1980 (1); v In 1979 (1)*

Stewart (M. J.) 8: v WI 1963 (4); v P 1962 (2); *v In 1963 (2)*

Stoddart, A. E. 16: v A 1893 (3) 1896 (2); *v A 1887 (1) 1891 (3) 1894 (5) 1897 (2)*

Storer (W.) 6: v A 1899 (1); *v A 1897 (5)*

Street (G. B.) 1: *v SA 1922*

Strudwick (H.) 28: v A 1921 (2) 1926 (5); v SA 1924 (1); *v A 1911 (1) 1920 (4) 1924 (5); v SA 1909 (5) 1913 (5)*

Studd, C. T. 5: v A 1882 (1); *v A 1882 (4)*

Studd, G. B. 4: *v A 1882 (4)*

Subba Row, R. 13: v A 1961 (5); v SA 1960 (4); v NZ 1958 (1); v In 1959 (1); *v WI 1959 (2)*

Sugg (F. H.) 2: v A 1888 (2)

Sutcliffe (H.) 54: v A 1926 (5) 1930 (4) 1934 (4); v SA 1924 (5) 1929 (5) 1935 (2); v WI 1928 (3) 1933 (2); v NZ 1931 (2); v In 1932 (1); *v A 1924 (5) 1928 (4) 1932 (5); v SA 1927 (5); v NZ 1932 (2)*

Swetman (R.) 11: v In 1959 (3); *v A 1958 (2); v WI 1959 (4); v NZ 1958 (2)*

Tate (F. W.) 1: v A 1902

Tate (M. W.) 39: v A 1926 (5) 1930 (5); v SA 1924 (5) 1929 (5) 1935 (1); v WI 1928 (3); v NZ 1931 (1); *v A 1924 (5) 1928 (5); v SA 1930 (5); v NZ 1932 (1)*

Tattersall (R.) 16: v A 1953 (1); v SA 1951 (5); v P 1954 (1); *v A 1950 (2); v NZ 1950 (2); v In 1951 (5)*

Tavaré, C. J. 26: v A 1981 (2); v WI 1980 (2); v NZ 1983 (4); v In 1982 (3); v P 1982 (3); *v A 1982 (5); v In 1981 (6); v SL 1981 (1)*

Taylor (K.) 3: v A 1964 (1); v In 1959 (2)

Taylor, R. W. 51: v A 1981 (3); v NZ 1978 (3) 1983 (4); v In 1979 (3) 1982 (3); v P 1978 (3) 1982 (3); *v A 1978 (6) 1979 (3) 1982 (5); v NZ 1970 (1) 1977 (3); v In 1979 (1) 1981 (6); v P 1977 (3); v SL 1981 (1)*

Tennyson, Hon. L. H. 9: v A 1921 (4); *v SA 1913 (5)*

Thompson (G. J.) 6: v A 1909 (1); *v SA 1909 (5)*

Thomson, N. I. 5: *v SA 1964 (5)*

Titmus (F. J.) 53: v A 1964 (5); v SA 1955 (2) 1965 (3); v WI 1963 (4) 1966 (3); v NZ 1965 (3); v P 1962 (2) 1967 (2); *v A 1962 (5) 1965 (5) 1974 (4); v SA 1964 (5); v WI 1967 (2); v NZ 1962 (3); v In 1963 (5)*

Tolchard, R. W. 4: *v In 1976 (4)*

Townsend, C. L. 2: v A 1899 (2)

Townsend, D. C. H. 3: *v WI 1934 (3)*

Townsend (L. F.) 4: *v WI 1929 (1); v In 1933 (3)*

Tremlett (M. F.) 3: *v WI 1947 (3)*

Trott (A. E.) 2: *v SA 1898 (2)*

Trueman (F. S.) 67: v A 1953 (1) 1956 (2) 1961 (4) 1964 (4); v SA 1955 (1) 1960 (5); v WI 1957 (5) 1963 (5); v NZ 1958 (5) 1965 (2); v In 1952 (4) 1959 (5); v P 1962 (4); *v A 1958 (3) 1962 (5); v WI 1953 (3) 1959 (5); v NZ 1958 (2) 1962 (2)*

Tufnell, N. C. 1: *v SA 1909*

Turnbull, M. J. 9: v WI 1933 (2); v In 1936 (1); *v SA 1930 (5); v NZ 1929 (1)*

Tyldesley (E.) 14: v A 1921 (3) 1926 (1); v SA 1924 (1); v WI 1928 (3); *v A 1928 (1): v SA 1927 (5)*

Tyldesley (J. T.) 31: v A 1899 (2) 1902 (5) 1905 (5) 1909 (4); v SA 1907 (3); *v A 1901 (5) 1903 (5); v SA 1898 (2)*

Tyldesley (R. K.) 7: v A 1930 (2); v SA 1924 (4); *v A 1924 (1)*

Tylecote, E. F. S. 6: v A 1886 (2); *v A 1882 (4)*

Tyler (E. J.) 1: *v SA 1895*

Tyson (F. H.) 17: v A 1956 (1); v SA 1955 (2); v P 1954 (1); *v A 1954 (5) 1958 (2); v SA 1956 (2); v NZ 1954 (2) 1958 (2)*

Ulyett (G.) 25: v A 1882 (1) 1884 (3) 1886 (3) 1888 (2) 1890 (1); *v A 1876 (2) 1878 (1) 1881 (4) 1884 (5) 1887 (1); v SA 1888 (2)*

Underwood, D. L. 86: v A 1968 (4) 1972 (2) 1975 (4) 1977 (5); v WI 1966 (2) 1969 (2) 1973 (3) 1976 (5) 1980 (1); v NZ 1969 (3) 1973 (1); v In 1971 (1) 1974 (3); v P 1967 (2) 1971 (1) 1974 (3); *v A 1970 (5) 1974 (5) 1976 (1) 1979 (3); v WI 1973 (4); v NZ 1970 (2) 1974 (2); v In 1972 (4) 1976 (5) 1979 (1) 1981 (6); v P 1968 (3) 1972 (2); v SL 1981 (1)*

Valentine, B. H. 7: *v SA 1938 (5); v In 1933 (2)*

Verity (H.) 40: v A 1934 (5) 1938 (4); v SA 1935 (4); v WI 1933 (2) 1939 (1); v NZ 1931 (2) 1937 (1); v In 1936 (3); *v A 1932 (4) 1936 (5); v SA 1938 (5); v NZ 1932 (1); v In 1933 (1)*

Vernon, G. F. 1: *v A 1882*

Vine (J.) 2: *v A 1911 (2)*

Voce (W.) 27: v NZ 1931 (1) 1937 (1); v In 1932 (1) 1936 (1) 1946 (1); *v A 1932 (4) 1936 (5) 1946 (2); v SA 1930 (5); v WI 1929 (4); v NZ 1932 (2)*

Waddington (A.) 2: *v A 1920 (2)*

Wainwright (E.) 5: v A 1893 (1); *v A 1897 (4)*

Walker (P. M.) 3: v SA 1960 (3)

Walters, C. F. 11: v A 1934 (5); v WI 1933 (3); *v In 1933 (3)*

Ward (A.) 7: v A 1893 (2); *v A 1894 (5)*

Ward, A. 5: v WI 1976 (1); v NZ 1969 (3); v P 1971 (1)

Wardle (J. H.) 28: v A 1953 (3) 1956 (1); v SA 1951 (2) 1955 (3); v WI 1950 (1) 1957 (1); v P 1954 (4); *v A 1954 (4); v SA 1956 (4); v WI 1947 (1) 1953 (2); v NZ 1954 (2)*

Warner, P. F. 15: v A 1909 (1) 1912 (1); v SA 1912 (1); *v A 1903 (5); v SA 1898 (2) 1905 (5)*

Warr, J. J. 2: *v A 1950 (2)*

Warren (A. R.) 1: v A 1905

Washbrook (C.) 37: v A 1948 (4) 1956 (3); v SA 1947 (5); v WI 1950 (2); v NZ 1937 (1) 1949 (2); v In 1946 (3); *v A 1946 (5) 1950 (5); v SA 1948 (5); v NZ 1946 (1) 1950 (1)*

Watkins (A. J.) 15: v A 1948 (1); v NZ 1949 (1); v In 1952 (3); *v SA 1948 (5); v In 1951 (5)*

Watson (W.) 23: v A 1953 (3) 1956 (2); v SA 1951 (5) 1955 (1); v NZ 1958 (2); v In 1952 (1); *v A 1958 (2); v WI 1953 (5); v NZ 1958 (2)*

Webbe, A. J. 1: *v A 1878*

Wellard (A. W.) 2: v A 1938 (1); v NZ 1937 (1)

Wharton (A.) 1: v NZ 1949

White, J. C. 15: v A 1921 (1) 1930 (1); v SA 1929 (3); v WI 1928 (1); *v A 1928 (5); v SA 1930 (4)*

White (D. W.) 2: *v P 1961 (2)*

Whysall (W. W.) 4: v A 1930 (1); *v A 1924 (3)*

Wilkinson (L. L.) 3: *v SA 1938 (3)*

Willey, P. 20: v A 1980 (1) 1981 (4); v WI 1976 (2) 1980 (5); v In 1979 (1); *v A 1979 (3); v WI 1980 (4)*

Willis, R. G. D. 83: v A 1977 (5) 1981 (6); v WI 1973 (1) 1976 (2) 1980 (4); v NZ 1978 (3) 1983 (4); v In 1974 (1) 1979 (3) 1982 (3); v P 1974 (1) 1978 (3) 1982 (2); *v A 1970 (4) 1974 (5) 1976 (1) 1978 (6) 1979 (3) 1982 (5); v WI 1973 (3); v NZ 1970 (1) 1977 (5) 1981 (5); v In 1976 (5) 1981 (5); v P 1977 (3); v SL 1981 (1)*

Wilson, C. E. M. 2: *v SA 1898 (2)*

Wilson, D. 6: *v NZ 1970 (1); v In 1963 (5)*

Wilson, E. R. 1: *v A 1920*

Wood (A.) 4: v A 1938 (1); v WI 1939 (3)

Wood, B. 12: v A 1972 (1) 1975 (3); v WI 1976 (1); v P 1978 (1); *v NZ 1974 (2); v In 1972 (3); v P 1972 (1)*

Wood, G. E. C. 3: v SA 1924 (3)

Wood (H.) 4: v A 1888 (1); *v SA 1888 (2) 1891 (1)*

Wood (R.) 1: *v A 1886*

Woods S. M. J. 3: *v SA 1895 (3)*

Woolley (F. E.) 64: v A 1909 (1) 1912 (3) 1921 (5) 1926 (5) 1930 (2) 1934 (1); v SA 1912 (3) 1924 (5) 1929 (3); v NZ 1931 (1); v In 1932 (1); *v A 1911 (5) 1920 (5) 1924 (5); v SA 1909 (5) 1913 (5) 1922 (5); v NZ 1929 (4)*

Woolmer, R. A. 19: v A 1975 (2) 1977 (5) 1981 (2); v WI 1976 (1) 1980 (2); *v A 1976 (1); v In 1976 (2)*

Worthington (T. S.) 9: v In 1936 (2); *v A 1936 (3); v NZ 1929 (4)*

Wright, C. W. 3: *v SA 1895 (3)*

Wright (D. V. P.) 34: v A 1938 (3) 1948 (1); v SA 1947 (4); v WI 1939 (3) 1950 (1); v NZ 1949 (1); v In 1946 (2); *v A 1946 (5) 1950 (5); v SA 1938 (3) 1948 (3); v NZ 1946 (1) 1950 (2)*

Wyatt, R. E. S. 40: v A 1930 (1) 1934 (4); v SA 1929 (2) 1935 (5); v WI 1933 (2); v In 1936 (1); *v A 1932 (5) 1936 (2); v SA 1927 (5) 1930 (5); v WI 1929 (2) 1934 (4); v NZ 1932 (2)*
Wynyard, E. G. 3: v A 1896 (1); *v SA 1905 (2)*

Yardley, N. W. D. 20: v A 1948 (5); v SA 1947 (5); v WI 1950 (3); *v A 1946 (5); v SA 1938 (1); v NZ 1946 (1)*
Young (H. I.) 2: v A 1899 (2)
Young (J. A.) 8: v A 1948 (3); v SA 1947 (1); v NZ 1949 (2); *v SA 1948 (2)*
Young, R. A. 2: *v A 1907 (2)*

AUSTRALIA

Number of Test cricketers: 319

A'Beckett, E. L. 4: v E 1928 (2); v SA 1931 (1); *v E 1930 (1)*
Alderman, T. M. 16: v E 1982 (1); v WI 1981 (2); v P 1981 (3); *v E 1981 (6); v NZ 1981 (3); v P 1982 (1)*
Alexander, G. 2: v E 1884 (1); *v E 1880 (1)*
Alexander, H. H. 1: v E 1932
Allan, F. E. 1: v E 1878
Allan, P. J. 1: v E 1965
Allen, R. C. 1: v E 1886
Andrews, T. J. E. 16: v E 1924 (3); *v E 1921 (5) 1926 (5); v SA 1921 (3)*
Archer, K. A. 5: v E 1950 (3); v WI 1951 (2)
Archer, R. G. 19: v E 1954 (4); v SA 1952 (1); *v E 1953 (3) 1956 (5); v WI 1954 (5); v P 1956 (1)*
Armstrong, W. W. 50: v E 1901 (4) 1903 (3) 1907 (5) 1911 (5) 1920 (5); v SA 1910 (5); *v E 1902 (5) 1905 (5) 1909 (5) 1921 (5); v SA 1902 (3)*

Badcock, C. L. 7: v E 1936 (3); *v E 1938 (4)*
Bannerman, A. C. 28: v E 1878 (1) 1881 (3) 1882 (4) 1884 (4) 1886 (1) 1887 (1) 1891 (3); *v E 1880 (1) 1882 (1) 1884 (3) 1888 (3) 1893 (3)*
Bannerman, C. 3: v E 1876 (2) 1878 (1)
Bardsley, W. 41: v E 1911 (4) 1920 (5) 1924 (3); v SA 1910 (5); *v E 1909 (5) 1912 (3) 1921 (5) 1926 (5); v SA 1912 (3) 1921 (3)*
Barnes, S. G. 13: v E 1946 (4); v In 1947 (5); *v E 1938 (1) 1948 (4); v NZ 1945 (1)*
Barnett, B. A. 4: *v E 1938 (4)*
Barrett, J. E. 2: *v E 1890 (2)*
Beard, G. R. 3: *v P 1979 (3)*
Benaud, J. 3: v P 1972 (2); *v WI 1972 (1)*
Benaud, R. 63: v E 1954 (5) 1958 (5) 1962 (5); v SA 1952 (4) 1963 (4); v WI 1951 (1) 1960 (5); *v E 1953 (3) 1956 (5) 1961 (4); v SA 1957 (5); v WI 1954 (5); v In 1956 (3) 1959 (5); v P 1956 (1) 1959 (3)*
Blackham, J. McC. 35: v E 1876 (2) 1878 (1) 1881 (4) 1882 (4) 1884 (2) 1886 (1) 1887 (1) 1891 (3) 1894 (1); *v E 1880 (1) 1882 (1) 1884 (3) 1886 (3) 1888 (3) 1890 (2) 1893 (3)*
Blackie, D. D. 3: v E 1928 (3)
Bonnor, G. J. 17: v E 1882 (4) 1884 (3); *v E 1880 (1) 1882 (1) 1884 (3) 1886 (2) 1888 (3)*
Booth, B. C. 29: v E 1962 (5) 1965 (3); v SA 1963 (4); v P 1964 (1); *v E 1961 (2) 1964 (5); v WI 1964 (5); v In 1964 (3); v P 1964 (1)*
Border, A. R. 51: v E 1978 (3) 1979 (3) 1982 (5); v WI 1979 (3) 1981 (3); v In 1980 (3); v NZ 1980 (3); v P 1978 (2) 1981 (3); *v E 1980 (1) 1981 (6); v NZ 1981 (3); v In 1979 (6); v P 1979 (3) 1982 (3); v SL 1982 (1)*
Boyle, H. F. 12: v E 1878 (1) 1881 (4) 1882 (1) 1884 (1); *v E 1880 (1) 1882 (1) 1884 (3)*
Bradman, D. G. 52: v E 1928 (4) 1932 (4) 1936 (5) 1946 (5); v SA 1931 (5); v WI 1930 (5); v In 1947 (5); *v E 1930 (5) 1934 (5) 1938 (4) 1948 (5)*
Bright, R. J. 16: v E 1979 (1); v WI 1979 (1); *v E 1977 (3) 1980 (1) 1981 (5); v P 1979 (3) 1982 (2)*
Bromley, E. H. 2: v E 1932 (1); *v E 1934 (1)*

Brown, W. A. 22: v E 1936 (2); v In 1947 (3); *v E 1934 (5) 1938 (4) 1948 (2); v SA 1935 (5); v NZ 1945 (1)*

Bruce, W. 14: v E 1884 (2) 1891 (3) 1894 (4); *v E 1886 (2) 1893 (3)*

Burge, P. J. 42: v E 1954 (1) 1958 (1) 1962 (3) 1965 (4); v SA 1963 (5); v WI 1960 (2); *v E 1956 (3) 1961 (5) 1964 (5); v SA 1957 (1); v WI 1954 (1); v In 1956 (3) 1959 (2) 1964 (3); v P 1959 (2) 1964 (1)*

Burke, J. W. 24: v E 1950 (2) 1954 (2) 1958 (5); v WI 1951 (1); *v E 1956 (5); v SA 1957 (5); v In 1956 (3); v P 1956 (1)*

Burn, K. E. 2: *v E 1890 (2)*

Burton, F. J. 2: v E 1886 (1) 1887 (1)

Callaway, S. T. 3: v E 1891 (2) 1894 (1)

Callen, I. W. 1: v In 1977

Carkeek, W. 6: *v E 1912 (3); v SA 1912 (3)*

Carlson, P. H. 2: v E 1978 (2)

Carter, H. 28: v E 1907 (5) 1911 (5) 1920 (2); v SA 1910 (5); *v E 1909 (5) 1921 (4); v SA 1921 (2)*

Chappell, G. S. 82: v E 1970 (5) 1974 (6) 1976 (1) 1979 (3) 1982 (5); v WI 1975 (6) 1979 (3) 1981 (3); v NZ 1973 (3) 1980 (3); v In 1980 (3); v P 1972 (3) 1976 (3) 1981 (3); *v E 1972 (5) 1975 (4) 1977 (5) 1980 (1); v WI 1972 (5); v NZ 1973 (3) 1976 (2) 1981 (3); v P 1979 (3); v SL 1982 (1)*

Chappell, I. M. 75: v E 1965 (2) 1970 (6) 1974 (6) 1979 (2); v WI 1968 (5) 1975 (6) 1979 (1); v NZ 1973 (3); v In 1967 (4); v P 1964 (1) 1972 (3); *v E 1968 (5) 1972 (5) 1975 (4); v SA 1966 (5) 1969 (4); v WI 1972 (5); v NZ 1973 (3); v In 1969 (5)*

Chappell, T. M. 3: *v E 1981 (3)*

Charlton, P. C. 2: *v E 1890 (2)*

Chipperfield, A. G. 14: v E 1936 (3); *v E 1934 (5) 1938 (1); v SA 1935 (5)*

Clark, W. M. 10: v In 1977 (5); v P 1978 (1); *v WI 1977 (4)*

Colley, D. J. 3: *v E 1972 (3)*

Collins, H. L. 19: v E 1920 (5) 1924 (5); *v E 1921 (3) 1926 (3); v SA 1921 (3)*

Coningham, A. 1: v E 1894

Connolly, A. N. 29: v E 1965 (1) 1970 (1); v SA 1963 (3); v WI 1968 (5); v In 1967 (3); *v E 1968 (5); v SA 1969 (4); v In 1964 (2); 1969 (5)*

Cooper, B. B. 1: v E 1876

Cooper, W. H. 2: v E 1881 (1) 1884 (1)

Corling, G. E. 5: *v E 1964 (5)*

Cosier, G. J. 18: v E 1976 (1) 1978 (2); v WI 1975 (3); v In 1977 (4); v P 1976 (3); *v WI 1977 (3); v NZ 1976 (2)*

Cottam, W. J. 1: v E 1886

Cotter, A. 21: v E 1903 (2) 1907 (2) 1911 (4); v SA 1910 (5); *v E 1905 (3) 1909 (5)*

Coultard, G. 1: v E 1881

Cowper, R. M. 27: v E 1965 (4); v In 1967 (4); v P 1964 (1); *v E 1964 (1) 1968 (4); v SA 1966 (5); v WI 1964 (5); v In 1964 (2); v P 1964 (1)*

Craig, I. D. 11: v SA 1952 (1); *v E 1956 (2); v SA 1957 (5); v In 1956 (2); v P 1956 (1)*

Crawford, W. P. A. 4: *v E 1956 (1); v In 1956 (3)*

Darling, J. 34: v E 1894 (5) 1897 (5) 1901 (3); *v E 1896 (3) 1899 (5) 1902 (5) 1905 (5); v SA 1902 (3)*

Darling, L. S. 12: v E 1932 (2) 1936 (1); *v E 1934 (4): v SA 1935 (5)*

Darling, W. M. 14: v E 1978 (4); v In 1977 (1); v P 1978 (1); *v WI 1977 (3); v In 1979 (5)*

Davidson, A. K. 44: v E 1954 (3) 1958 (5) 1962 (5); v WI 1960 (4); *v E 1953 (5) 1956 (2) 1961 (5); v SA 1957 (5); v In 1956 (1) 1959 (5); v P 1956 (1) 1959 (3)*

Davis, I. C. 15: v E 1976 (1); v NZ 1973 (3); v P 1976 (3); *v E 1977 (3); v NZ 1973 (3) 1976 (2)*

De Courcy, J. H. 3: *v E 1953 (3)*

Dell, A. R. 2: v E 1970 (1); v NZ 1973 (1)

Donnan, H. 5: v E 1891 (2); *v E 1896 (3)*

Dooland, B. 3: v E 1946 (2); v In 1947 (1)

Duff, R. A. 22: v E 1901 (4) 1903 (5); *v E 1902 (5) 1905 (5); v SA 1902 (3)*

Duncan, J. R. F. 1: v E 1970

Dymock, G. 21: v E 1974 (1) 1978 (3) 1979 (3); v WI 1979 (2); v NZ 1973 (1); v P 1978 (1); *v NZ 1973 (2); v In 1979 (5); v P 1979 (3)*
Dyson, J. 27: v E 1982 (5); v WI 1981 (2); v NZ 1980 (3); v In 1977 (3) 1980 (3); *v E 1981 (5); v NZ 1981 (3); v P 1982 (3)*

Eady, C. J. 2: v E 1901 (1); *v E 1896 (1)*
Eastwood, K. H. 1: v E 1970
Ebeling, H. I. 1: *v E 1934*
Edwards, J. D. 3: *v E 1888 (3)*
Edwards, R. 20: v E 1974 (5); v P 1972 (2); *v E 1972 (4) 1975 (4); v WI 1972 (5)*
Edwards, W. J. 3: v E 1974 (3)
Emery, S. H. 4: *v E 1912 (2); v SA 1912 (2)*
Evans, E. 6: v E 1881 (2) 1882 (1) 1884 (1); *v E 1886 (2)*

Fairfax, A. G. 10: v E 1928 (1); v WI 1930 (5); *v E 1930 (4)*
Favell, L. E. 19: v E 1954 (4) 1958 (2); v WI 1960 (4); *v WI 1954 (2); v In 1959 (4); v P 1959 (3)*
Ferris, J. J. 8: v E 1886 (2) 1887 (1); *v E 1888 (3) 1890 (2)*
Fingleton, J. H. 18: v E 1932 (3) 1936 (5); v SA 1931 (1); *v E 1938 (4); v SA 1935 (5)*
Fleetwood-Smith, L. O'B. 10: v E 1936 (3); *v E 1938 (4); v SA 1935 (3)*
Francis, B. C. 3: *v E 1972 (3)*
Freeman, E. W. 11: v WI 1968 (4); v In 1967 (2); *v E 1968 (2); v SA 1969 (2); v In 1969 (1)*
Freer, F. W. 1: v E 1946

Gannon, J. B. 3: v In 1977 (3)
Garrett, T. W. 19: v E 1876 (2) 1878 (1) 1881 (3) 1882 (3) 1884 (3) 1886 (2) 1887 (1); *v E 1882 (1) 1886 (3)*
Gaunt, R. A. 3: v SA 1963 (1); *v E 1961 (1); v SA 1957 (1)*
Gehrs, D. R. A. 6: v E 1903 (1); v SA 1910 (4); *v E 1905 (1)*
Giffen, G. 31: v E 1881 (3) 1882 (4) 1884 (3) 1891 (3) 1894 (5); *v E 1882 (1) 1884 (3) 1886 (3) 1893 (3) 1896 (3)*
Giffen, W. F. 3: v E 1886 (1) 1891 (2)
Gilmour, G. J. 15: v E 1976 (1); v WI 1975 (5); v NZ 1973 (2); v P 1976 (3); *v E 1975 (1); v NZ 1973 (1) 1976 (2)*
Gleeson, J. W. 29: v E 1970 (5); v WI 1968 (5); v In 1967 (4); *v E 1968 (5) 1972 (3); v SA 1969 (4); v In 1969 (3)*
Graham, H. 6: v E 1894 (2); *v E 1893 (3) 1896 (1)*
Gregory, D. W. 3: v E 1876 (2) 1878 (1)
Gregory, E. J. 1: v E 1876
Gregory, J. M. 24: v E 1920 (5) 1924 (5) 1928 (1); *v E 1921 (5) 1926 (5); v SA 1921 (3)*
Gregory, R. G. 2: v E 1936 (2)
Gregory, S. E. 58: v E 1891 (5) 1894 (5) 1897 (5) 1901 (5) 1903 (4) 1907 (2) 1911 (1); *v E 1890 (2) 1893 (3) 1896 (3) 1899 (5) 1902 (5) 1905 (3) 1909 (5) 1912 (3); v SA 1902 (3) 1912 (3)*
Grimmett, C. V. 37: v E 1924 (1) 1928 (5) 1932 (3); v SA 1931 (5); v WI 1930 (5); *v E 1926 (3) 1930 (5) 1934 (5); v SA 1935 (5)*
Groube, T. U. 1: *v E 1880*
Grout, A. T. W. 51: v E 1958 (5) 1962 (2) 1965 (5); v SA 1963 (5); v WI 1960 (5); *v E 1961 (5) 1964 (5); v SA 1957 (5); v WI 1964 (5); v In 1959 (4) 1964 (1); v P 1959 (3) 1964 (1)*
Guest, C. E. J. 1: v E 1962

Hamence, R. A. 3: v E 1946 (1); v In 1947 (2)
Hammond, J. R. 5: *v WI 1972 (5)*
Harry, J. 1: v E 1894
Hartigan, R. J. 2: v E 1907 (2)
Hartkopf, A. E. V. 1: v E 1924
Harvey, M. R. 1: v E 1946
Harvey, R. N. 79: v E 1950 (5) 1954 (5) 1958 (5) 1962 (5); v SA 1952 (5); v WI 1951 (5) 1960 (4); v In 1947 (2); *v E 1948 (2) 1953 (5) 1956 (5) 1961 (5); v SA 1949 (5) 1957 (4); v WI 1954 (5); v In 1956 (3) 1959 (5); v P 1956 (1) 1959 (3)*
Hassett, A. L. 43: v E 1946 (5) 1950 (5); v SA 1952 (5); v WI 1951 (4); v In 1947 (4); *v E 1938 (4) 1948 (5) 1953 (5); v SA 1949 (5); v NZ 1945 (1)*

Hawke, N. J. N. 27: v E 1962 (1) 1965 (4); v SA 1963 (4); v In 1967 (1); v P 1964 (1); *v E 1964 (5) 1968 (2); v SA 1966 (2); v WI 1964 (5); v In 1964 (1); v P 1964 (1)*

Hazlitt, G. R. 9: v E 1907 (2) 1911 (1); *v E 1912 (3); v SA 1912 (3)*

Hendry, H. S. T. L. 11: v E 1924 (1) 1928 (4); *v E 1921 (4); v SA 1921 (2)*

Hibbert, P. A. 1: v In 1977

Higgs, J. D. 22: v E 1978 (5) 1979 (1); v WI 1979 (1); v NZ 1980 (3); v In 1980 (2); *v WI 1977 (4); v In 1979 (6)*

Hilditch, A. M. J. 9: v E 1978 (1); v P 1978 (2); *v In 1979 (6)*

Hill, C. 49: v E 1897 (5) 1901 (5) 1903 (5) 1907 (5) 1911 (5); v SA 1910 (5); *v E 1896 (3) 1899 (3) 1902 (5) 1905 (5); v SA 1902 (3)*

Hill, J. C. 3: *v E 1953 (2); v WI 1954 (1)*

Hoare, D. E. 1: v WI 1960

Hodges, J. H. 2: v E 1876 (2)

Hogan, T. G. 1: *v SL 1982*

Hogg, R. M. 26: v E 1978 (6) 1982 (3); v WI 1979 (2); v NZ 1980 (2); v In 1980 (2); v P 1978 (2); *v E 1981 (2); v In 1979 (6); v SL 1982 (1)*

Hole, G. B. 18: v E 1950 (1) 1954 (3); v SA 1952 (4); v WI 1951 (5); *v E 1953 (5)*

Hookes, D. W. 14: v E 1976 (1) 1982 (5); v WI 1979 (1); *v E 1977 (5); v P 1979 (1); v SL 1982 (1)*

Hopkins, A. J. Y. 20: v E 1901 (2) 1903 (5); *v E 1902 (5) 1905 (3) 1909 (2); v SA 1902 (3)*

Horan, T. P. 15: v E 1876 (1) 1878 (1) 1881 (4) 1882 (4) 1884 (4); *v E 1882 (1)*

Hordern, H. V. 7: v E 1911 (5): v SA 1910 (2)

Hornibrook, P. M. 6: v E 1928 (1); *v E 1930 (5)*

Howell, W. P. 18: v E 1897 (3) 1901 (4) 1903 (3); *v E 1899 (5) 1902 (1); v SA 1902 (2)*

Hughes, K. J. 56: v E 1978 (6) 1979 (3) 1982 (5); v WI 1979 (3) 1981 (3); v NZ 1980 (3); v In 1977 (2) 1980 (3); v P 1978 (2) 1981 (3); *v E 1977 (1) 1980 (1) 1981 (6); v NZ 1981 (3); v In 1979 (6); v P 1979 (2) 1982 (3)*

Hunt, W. A. 1: v SA 1931

Hurst, A. G. 12: v E 1978 (6); v NZ 1973 (1); v In 1977 (1); v P 1978 (2); *v In 1979 (2)*

Hurwood, A. 2: v WI 1930 (2)

Inverarity, R. J. 6: v WI 1968 (1); *v E 1968 (2) 1972 (3)*

Iredale, F. A. 14: v E 1894 (5) 1897 (4); *v E 1896 (2) 1899 (3)*

Ironmonger, H. 14: v E 1928 (2) 1932 (4); v SA 1931 (4); v WI 1930 (4)

Iverson, J. B. 5: v E 1950 (5)

Jackson, A. 8: v E 1928 (2); v WI 1930 (4); *v E 1930 (2)*

Jarman, B. N. 19: v E 1962 (3); v WI 1968 (4); v In 1967 (4); v P 1964 (1); *v E 1968 (4); v In 1959 (1); 1964 (2)*

Jarvis, A. H. 11: v E 1884 (3) 1894 (4); *v E 1886 (2) 1888 (2)*

Jenner, T. J. 9: v E 1970 (2) 1974 (2); v WI 1975 (1); *v WI 1972 (4)*

Jennings, C. B. 6: *v E 1912 (3); v SA 1912 (3)*

Johnson I. W. 45: v E 1946 (4) 1950 (5) 1954 (4); v SA 1952 (1); v WI 1951 (5); v In 1947 (4); *v E 1948 (4) 1956 (5); v SA 1949 (5); v WI 1954 (5); v NZ 1945 (1); v In 1956 (2); v P 1956 (1)*

Johnson, L. J. 1: v In 1947

Johnston W. A. 40: v E 1950 (5) 1954 (4); v SA 1952 (5); v WI 1951 (5); v In 1947 (4); *v E 1948 (5) 1953 (3); v SA 1949 (5); v WI 1954 (4)*

Jones, E. 19: v E 1894 (1) 1897 (5) 1901 (2); *v E 1896 (3) 1899 (5) 1902 (2); v SA 1902 (1)*

Jones, S. P. 12: v E 1881 (2) 1884 (4) 1886 (1) 1887 (1); *v E 1882 (1) 1886 (3)*

Joslin, L. R. 1: v In 1967

Kelleway, C. 26: v E 1911 (4) 1920 (5) 1924 (5) 1928 (1); v SA 1910 (5); *v E 1912 (3); v SA 1912 (3)*

Kelly, J. J. 36: v E 1897 (5) 1901 (5) 1903 (5); *v E 1896 (3) 1899 (5) 1902 (5) 1905 (5); v SA 1902 (3)*

Kelly, T. J. D. 2: v E 1876 (1) 1878 (1)

Kendall, T. 2: v E 1876 (2)

Kent, M. F. 3: *v E 1981 (3)*

Kippax, A. F. 22: v E 1924 (1) 1928 (5) 1932 (1); v SA 1931 (4); v WI 1930 (5); *v E 1930 (5) 1934 (1)*

Kline L. F. 13: v E 1958 (2); v WI 1960 (2); *v SA 1957 (5); v In 1959 (3); v P 1959 (1)*

Laird, B. M. 21: v E 1979 (2); v WI 1979 (3) 1981 (3); v P 1981 (3); *v E 1980 (1) 1981 (3); v P 1979 (3) 1982 (3)*

Langley, G. R. A. 26: v E 1954 (2); v SA 1952 (5); v WI 1951 (5); *v E 1953 (4) 1956 (3); v WI 1954 (4); v In 1956 (2); v P 1956 (1)*

Laughlin, T. J. 3: v E 1978 (1); *v WI 1977 (2)*

Laver, F. 15: v E 1901 (1) 1903 (1); *v E 1899 (4) 1905 (5) 1909 (4)*

Lawry, W. M. 67: v E 1962 (5) 1965 (5) 1970 (5); v WI 1968 (5); v In 1967 (4); v P 1964 (1); *v E 1961 (5) 1964 (5) 1968 (4); v SA 1966 (5) 1969 (4); v WI 1964 (5); v In 1964 (3) 1969 (5); v P 1964 (1)*

Lawson, G. F. 13: v E 1982 (5); v WI 1981 (1); v NZ 1980 (1); *v E 1981 (3); v P 1982 (3)*

Lee, P. K. 2: v E 1932 (1); v SA 1931 (1)

Lillee, D. K. 65: v E 1970 (2) 1974 (6) 1976 (1) 1979 (3) 1982 (1); v WI 1975 (5) 1979 (3) 1981 (3); v NZ 1980 (3); v In 1980 (3); v P 1972 (3) 1976 (3) 1981 (3); *v E 1972 (5) 1975 (4) 1980 (1) 1981 (6); v WI 1972 (1); v NZ 1976 (2) 1981 (3); v P 1979 (3); v SL 1982 (1)*

Lindwall, R. R. 61: v E 1946 (4) 1950 (5) 1954 (4) 1958 (2); v SA 1952 (4); v WI 1951 (5); v In 1947 (5); *v E 1948 (5) 1953 (5) 1956 (4); v SA 1949 (4); v WI 1954 (5); v NZ 1945 (1); v In 1956 (3) 1959 (2); v P 1956 (1) 1959 (2)*

Love, H. S. B. 1: v E 1932

Loxton, S. J. E. 12: v E 1950 (3); v In 1947 (1); *v E 1948 (3); v SA 1949 (5)*

Lyons, J. J. 14: v E 1886 (1) 1891 (3) 1894 (3) 1897 (1); *v E 1888 (1) 1890 (2) 1893 (3)*

McAlister, P. A. 8: v E 1903 (2) 1907 (4); *v E 1909 (2)*

Macartney, C. G. 35: v E 1907 (5) 1911 (1) 1920 (2); v SA 1910 (4); *v E 1909 (5) 1912 (3) 1921 (5) 1926 (5); v SA 1912 (3) 1921 (2)*

McCabe, S. J. 39: v E 1932 (5) 1936 (5); v SA 1931 (5); v WI 1930 (5); *v E 1930 (5) 1934 (5) 1938 (4); v SA 1935 (5)*

McCool, C. L. 14: v E 1946 (5); v In 1947 (3); *v SA 1949 (5) v NZ 1945 (1)*

McCormick, E. L. 12: v E 1936 (4); *v E 1938 (3); v SA 1935 (5)*

McCosker, R. B. 25: v E 1974 (3) 1976 (1) 1979 (2); v WI 1975 (4) 1979 (1); v P 1976 (3); *v E 1975 (4) 1977 (5); v NZ 1976 (2)*

McDonald, C. C. 47: v E 1954 (2) 1958 (5); v SA 1952 (5); v WI 1951 (1) 1960 (5); *v E 1956 (5) 1961 (3); v SA 1957 (5); v WI 1954 (5); v In 1956 (2) 1959 (5); v P 1956 (1) 1959 (3)*

McDonald, E. A. 11: v E 1920 (3); *v E 1921 (5); v SA 1921 (3)*

McDonnell, P. S. 19: v E 1881 (4) 1882 (3) 1884 (2) 1886 (2) 1887 (1); *v E 1880 (1) 1884 (3) 1888 (3)*

McIlwraith, J. 1: *v E 1886*

Mackay K. D. 37: v E 1958 (5) 1962 (3); v WI 1960 (5); *v E 1956 (3) 1961 (5); v SA 1957 (5); v In 1956 (3) 1959 (5); v P 1959 (3)*

McKenzie, G. D. 60: v E 1962 (5) 1965 (4) 1970 (3); v SA 1963 (5); v WI 1968 (5); v In 1967 (2); v P 1964 (1); *v E 1961 (3) 1964 (5) 1968 (5); v SA 1966 (5) 1969 (3); v WI 1964 (5); v In 1964 (3) 1969 (5); v P 1964 (1)*

McKibbin, T. R. 5: v E 1894 (1) 1897 (2); *v E 1896 (2)*

McLaren, J. W. 1: v E 1911

Maclean, J. A. 4: v E 1978 (4)

McLeod, C. E. 17: v E 1894 (1) 1897 (5) 1901 (2) 1903 (3); *v E 1899 (1) 1905 (5)*

McLeod, R. W. 6: v E 1891 (3); *v E 1893 (3)*

McShane, P. G. 3: v E 1884 (1) 1886 (1) 1887 (1)

Maddocks, L. V. 7: v E 1954 (3); *v E 1956 (2); v WI 1954 (1); v In 1956 (1)*

Mailey, A. A. 21: v E 1920 (5) 1924 (5); *v E 1921 (3) 1926 (5); v SA 1921 (3)*

Mallett, A. A. 38: v E 1970 (2) 1974 (5) 1979 (1); v WI 1968 (1) 1975 (6) 1979 (1); v NZ 1973 (3); v P 1972 (2); *v E 1968 (1) 1972 (2) 1975 (4) 1980 (1); v SA 1969 (3); v NZ 1973 (3); v In 1969 (5)*

Malone, M. F. 1: *v E 1977*

Mann, A. L. 4: v In 1977 (4)

Marr, A. P. 1: v E 1884

Marsh, R. W. 91: v E 1970 (6) 1974 (6) 1976 (1) 1979 (3) 1982 (5); v WI 1975 (6) 1979 (3) 1981 (3); v NZ 1973 (3) 1980 (3); v In 1980 (3); v P 1972 (3) 1976 (3) 1981 (3); *v E 1972 (5) 1975 (4) 1977 (5) 1980 (1) 1981 (6); v WI 1972 (3); v NZ 1973 (3) 1981 (3); v P 1979 (3) 1982 (3)*

Martin, J. W. 8: v SA 1963 (1); v WI 1960 (3); *v SA 1966 (1); v In 1964 (2); v P 1964 (1)*

Massie, H. H. 9: v E 1881 (4) 1882 (3) 1884 (1); *v E 1882 (1)*

Massie, R. A. L. 6: v P 1972 (2); *v E 1972 (4)*

Matthews, T. J. 8: v E 1911 (2); *v E 1912 (3); v SA 1912 (3)*

Mayne, E. R. 4: *v E 1912 (1); v SA 1912 (1) 1921 (2)*

Mayne, L. C. 6: *v SA 1969 (2); v WI 1964 (3); v In 1969 (1)*

Meckiff, I. 18: v E 1958 (4); v SA 1963 (1); v WI 1960 (2); *v SA 1957 (4); v In 1959 (5); v P 1959 (2)*

Meuleman, K. D. 1: *v NZ 1945*

Midwinter, W. E. 8: v E 1876 (2) 1882 (1) 1886 (2); *v E 1884 (3)*

Miller, K. R. 55: v E 1946 (5) 1950 (5) 1954 (4); v SA 1952 (4); v WI 1951 (5); v In 1947 (5); *v E 1948 (5) 1953 (5) 1956 (5); v SA 1949 (5); v WI 1954 (5); v NZ 1945 (1); v P 1956 (1)*

Minnett, R. B. 9: v E 1911 (5); *v E 1912 (1); v SA 1912 (3)*

Misson, F. M. 5: v WI 1960 (3); *v E 1961 (2)*

Moroney, J. R. 7: v E 1950 (1); v WI 1951 (1); *v SA 1949 (5)*

Morris, A. R. 46: v E 1946 (5) 1950 (5) 1954 (4); v SA 1952 (5); v WI 1951 (4); v In 1947 (4); *v E 1948 (5) 1953 (5); v SA 1949 (5); v WI 1954 (4)*

Morris, S. 1: v E 1884

Moses, H. 6: v E 1886 (2) 1887 (1) 1891 (2) 1894 (1)

Moss, J. K. 1: v P 1978

Moule, W. H. 1: *v E 1880*

Murdoch, W. L. 18: v E 1876 (1) 1878 (1) 1881 (4) 1882 (4) 1884 (1); *v E 1880 (1) 1882 (1) 1884 (3) 1890 (2)*

Musgrove, H. 1: v E 1884

Nagel, L. E. 1: v E 1932

Nash, L. J. 2: v E 1936 (1); v SA 1931 (1)

Nitschke, H. C. 2: v SA 1931 (2)

Noble, M. A. 42: v E 1897 (4) 1901 (5) 1903 (5) 1907 (5); *v E 1899 (5) 1902 (5) 1905 (5) 1909 (5); v SA 1902 (3)*

Noblet, G. 3: v SA 1952 (1); v WI 1951 (1); *v SA 1949 (1)*

Nothling, O. E. 1: v E 1928

O'Brien, L. P. J. 5: v E 1932 (2) 1936 (1); *v SA 1935 (2)*

O'Connor, J. D. A. 4: v E 1907 (3); *v E 1909 (1)*

Ogilvie, A. D. 5: v In 1977 (3); *v WI 1977 (2)*

O'Keeffe, K. J. 24: v E 1970 (2) 1976 (1); v NZ 1973 (3); v P 1972 (2) 1976 (3); *v E 1977 (3); v WI 1972 (5); v NZ 1973 (3) 1976 (2)*

Oldfield, W. A. 54: v E 1920 (3) 1924 (5) 1928 (5) 1932 (4) 1936 (5); v SA 1931 (5); v WI 1930 (5); *v E 1921 (1) 1926 (5) 1930 (5) 1934 (5); v SA 1921 (1) 1935 (5)*

O'Neill, N. C. 42: v E 1958 (5) 1962 (5); v SA 1963 (4); v WI 1960 (5); *v E 1961 (5) 1964 (4); v In 1959 (5) 1964 (2); v P 1959 (3)*

O'Reilly, W. J. 27: v E 1932 (5) 1936 (5); v SA 1931 (2); *v E 1934 (5) 1938 (4); v SA 1935 (5); v NZ 1945 (1)*

Oxenham, R. K. 7: v E 1928 (3); v SA 1931 (1); v WI 1930 (3)

Palmer, G. E. 17: v E 1881 (4) 1882 (4) 1884 (2); *v E 1880 (1) 1884 (3) 1886 (3)*

Park, R. L. 1: v E 1920

Pascoe, L. S. 14: v E 1979 (2); v WI 1979 (1) 1981 (1); v NZ 1980 (3); v In 1980 (3); *v E 1977 (3) 1980 (1)*

Pellew, C. E. 10: v E 1920 (4); *v E 1921 (5); v SA 1921 (1)*

Philpott, P. I. 8: v E 1965 (3); *v WI 1964 (5)*

Ponsford, W. H. 29: v E 1924 (5) 1928 (2) 1932 (3); v SA 1931 (4); v WI 1930 (5); *v E 1926 (2) 1930 (4) 1934 (4)*

Pope, R. J. 1: v E 1884

Rackemann, C. G. 1: v E 1982

Ransford, V. S. 20: v E 1907 (5) 1911 (5); v SA 1910 (5); *v E 1909 (5)*

Redpath, I. R. 66: v E 1965 (1) 1970 (6) 1974 (6); v SA 1963 (1); v WI 1968 (5) 1975 (6); v In 1967 (3); v P 1972 (3); *v E 1964 (5) 1968 (5); v SA 1966 (5) 1969 (4); v WI 1972 (5); v NZ 1973 (3); v In 1964 (2) 1969 (5); v P 1964 (1)*

Reedman, J. C. 1: v E 1894

Renneberg, D. A. 8: v In 1967 (3); *v SA 1966 (5)*

Richardson, A. J. 9: v E 1924 (4); *v E 1926 (5)*
Richardson, V. Y. 19: v E 1924 (3) 1928 (2) 1932 (5); *v E 1930 (4); v SA 1935 (5)*
Rigg, K. E. 8: v E 1936 (3); v SA 1931 (4); v WI 1930 (1)
Ring, D. T. 13: v SA 1952 (5); v WI 1951 (5); v In 1947 (1); *v E 1948 (1) 1953 (1)*
Ritchie, G. M. 3: *v P 1982 (3)*
Rixon, S. J. 10: v In 1977 (5); *v WI 1977 (5)*
Robertson, W. R. 1: v E 1884
Robinson, R. D. 3: *v E 1977 (3)*
Robinson, R. H. 1: v E 1936
Rorke, G. F. 4: v E 1958 (2); *v In 1959 (2)*
Rutherford, J. W. 1: *v In 1956*
Ryder, J. 20: v E 1920 (5) 1924 (3) 1928 (5); *v E 1926 (4); v SA 1921 (3)*

Saggers, R. A. 6: *v E 1948 (1); v SA 1949 (5)*
Saunders, J. V. 14: v E 1901 (1) 1903 (2) 1907 (5); *v E 1902 (4); v SA 1902 (2)*
Scott, H. J. H. 8: v E 1884 (2); *v E 1884 (3) 1886 (3)*
Sellers, R. H. D. 1: *v In 1964*
Serjeant, C. S. 12: v In 1977 (4); *v E 1977 (3); v WI 1977 (5)*
Sheahan, A. P. 31: v E 1970 (2); v WI 1968 (5); v NZ 1973 (2); v In 1967 (4); v P 1972 (2); *v E 1968 (5) 1972 (2); v SA 1969 (4); v In 1969 (5)*
Shepherd, B. K. 9: v E 1962 (2); v SA 1963 (4); v P 1964 (1); *v WI 1964 (2)*
Sievers, M. W. 3: v E 1936 (3)
Simpson, R. B. 62: v E 1958 (1) 1962 (5) 1965 (3); v SA 1963 (5); v WI 1960 (5); v In 1967 (3) 1977 (5); v P 1964 (1); *v E 1961 (5) 1964 (5); v SA 1957 (5) 1966 (5); v WI 1964 (5) 1977 (5); v In 1964 (3); v P 1964 (1)*
Sincock, D. J. 3: v E 1965 (1); v P 1964 (1); *v WI 1964 (1)*
Slater, K. N. 1: v E 1958
Sleep, P. R. 4: v P 1978 (1); *v In 1979 (2); v P 1982 (1)*
Slight, J. 1: *v E 1880*
Smith, D. B. M. 2: *v E 1912 (2)*
Spofforth, F. R. 18: v E 1876 (1) 1878 (1) 1881 (1) 1882 (4) 1884 (3) 1886 (1); *v E 1882 (1) 1884 (3) 1886 (3)*
Stackpole, K. R. 43: v E 1965 (2) 1970 (6); v WI 1968 (5); v NZ 1973 (3); v P 1972 (1); *v E 1972 (5); v SA 1966 (5) 1969 (4); v WI 1972 (4); v NZ 1973 (3); v In 1969 (5)*
Stevens, G. B. 4: *v In 1959 (2); v P 1959 (2)*

Taber, H. B. 16: v WI 1968 (1); *v E 1968 (1); v SA 1966 (5); 1969 (4); v In 1969 (5)*
Tallon, D. 21: v E 1946 (5) 1950 (5); v In 1947 (5); *v E 1948 (4) 1953 (1); v NZ 1945 (1)*
Taylor, J. M. 20: v E 1920 (5) 1924 (5); *v E 1921 (5) 1926 (3); v SA 1921 (2)*
Thomas, G. 8: v E 1965 (3); *v WI 1964 (5)*
Thompson, N. 2: v E 1876 (2)
Thoms, G. R. 1: v WI 1951
Thomson, A. L. 4: v E 1970 (4)
Thomson, J. R. 49: v E 1974 (5) 1979 (1) 1982 (4); v WI 1975 (6) 1979 (1) 1981 (2); v In 1977 (5); v P 1972 (1) 1976 (1) 1981 (3); *v E 1975 (4) 1977 (5); v WI 1977 (5); v NZ 1981 (3); v P 1982 (3)*
Thurlow, H. M. 1: v SA 1931
Toohey, P. M. 15: v E 1978 (5) 1979 (1); v WI 1979 (1); v In 1977 (5); *v WI 1977 (3)*
Toshack, E. R. H. 12: v E 1946 (5); v In 1947 (2); *v E 1948 (4); v NZ 1945 (1)*
Travers, J. P. F. 1: v E 1901
Tribe, G. E. 3: v E 1946 (3)
Trott, A. E. 3: v E 1894 (3)
Trott, G. H. S. 24: v E 1891 (3) 1894 (5) 1897 (5); *v E 1888 (3) 1890 (2) 1893 (3) 1896 (3)*
Trumble, H. 32: v E 1894 (1) 1897 (5) 1901 (5) 1903 (4); *v E 1890 (2) 1893 (3) 1896 (3) 1899 (5) 1902 (3); v SA 1902 (1)*
Trumble, J. W. 7: v E 1884 (4); *v E 1886 (3)*
Trumper, V. T. 48: v E 1901 (5) 1903 (5) 1907 (5) 1911 (5); v SA 1910 (5); *v E 1899 (5) 1902 (5) 1905 (5) 1909 (5); v SA 1902 (3)*
Turner, A. 14: v WI 1975 (6); v P 1976 (3); *v E 1975 (3); v NZ 1976 (2)*
Turner, C. T. B. 17: v E 1886 (2) 1887 (1) 1891 (3) 1894 (3); *v E 1888 (3) 1890 (2) 1893 (3)*

Veivers, T. R. 21: v E 1965 (4); v SA 1963 (3); v P 1964 (1); *v E 1964 (5); v SA 1966 (4); v In 1964 (3); v P 1964 (1)*

Waite, M. G. 2: *v E 1938 (2)*
Walker, M. H. N. 34: v E 1974 (6); 1976 (1); v WI 1975 (3); v NZ 1973 (1); v P 1972 (2) 1976 (2); *v E 1975 (4); 1977 (5); v WI 1972 (5); v NZ 1973 (3) 1976 (2)*
Wall, T. W. 18: v E 1928 (1) 1932 (4); v SA 1931 (3); v WI 1930 (1); *v E 1930 (5) 1934 (4)*
Walters, F. H. 1: v E 1884
Walters, K. D. 74: v E 1965 (5) 1970 (6) 1974 (6) 1976 (1); v WI 1968 (4); v NZ 1973 (3) 1980 (3); v In 1967 (2) 1980 (3); v P 1972 (1) 1976 (3); *v E 1968 (5) 1972 (4) 1975 (4) 1977 (5); v SA 1969 (4); v WI 1972 (5); v NZ 1973 (3) 1976 (2); v In 1969 (5)*
Ward, F. A. 4: v E 1936 (3); *v E 1938 (1)*
Watkins, J. R. 1: v P 1972
Watson, G. D. 5: *v E 1972 (2); v SA 1966 (3)*
Watson, W. 4: v E 1954 (1); *v WI 1954 (3)*
Wellham, D. M. 4: v WI 1981 (1); v P 1981 (2); *v E 1981 (1)*
Wessels, K. C. 5: v E 1982 (4); *v SL 1982 (1)*
Whatmore, D. F. 7: v P 1978 (2); *v In 1979 (5)*
Whitney, M. R. 2: *v E 1981 (2)*
Whitty, W. J. 14: v E 1911 (2); v SA 1910 (5); *v E 1909 (1) 1912 (3); v SA 1912 (3)*
Wiener, J. M. 6: v E 1979 (2); v WI 1979 (2); *v P 1979 (2)*
Wilson, J. W. 1: *v In 1956*
Wood, G. M. 42: v E 1978 (6) 1982 (1); v WI 1981 (3); v NZ 1980 (3); v In 1977 (1) 1980 (3); v P 1978 (1) 1981 (3); *v E 1980 (1) 1981 (6); v WI 1977 (5); v NZ 1981 (3); v In 1979 (2); v P 1982 (3); v SL 1982 (1)*
Woodcock, A. J. 1: v NZ 1973
Woodfull, W. M. 35: v E 1928 (5) 1932 (5); v SA 1931 (5); v WI 1930 (5); *v E 1926 (5) 1930 (5) 1934 (5)*
Woods, S. M. J. 3: *v E 1888 (3)*
Woolley, R. D. 1: *v SL 1982*
Worrall, J. 11: v E 1884 (1) 1887 (1) 1894 (1) 1897 (1); *v E 1888 (3) 1899 (4)*
Wright, K. J. 10: v E 1978 (2); v P 1978 (2); *v In 1979 (6)*

Yallop, G. N. 33: v E 1978 (6); v WI 1975 (3); v In 1977 (1); v P 1978 (1) 1981 (1); *v E 1980 (1) 1981 (6); v WI 1977 (4); v In 1979 (6); v P 1979 (3); v SL 1982 (1)*
Yardley, B. 33: v E 1978 (4) 1982 (5); v WI 1981 (3); v In 1977 (1) 1980 (2); v P 1978 (1) 1981 (3); *v WI 1977 (5); v NZ 1981 (3); v In 1979 (3); v P 1982 (2); v SL 1982 (1)*

SOUTH AFRICA

Number of Test cricketers: 235

Adcock, N. A. T. 26: v E 1956 (5); v A 1957 (5); v NZ 1953 (5) 1961 (2); *v E 1955 (4) 1960 (5)*
Anderson, J. H. 1: v A 1902
Ashley, W. H. 1: v E 1888

Bacher, A. 12: v A 1966 (5) 1969 (4); *v E 1965 (3)*
Balaskas, X. C. 9: v E 1930 (2) 1938 (1); v A 1935 (3); *v E 1935 (1); v NZ 1931 (2)*
Barlow, E. J. 30: v E 1964 (5); v A 1966 (5) 1969 (4); v NZ 1961 (5); *v E 1965 (3); v A 1963 (5); v NZ 1963 (3)*
Baumgartner, H. V. 1: v E 1913
Beaumont, R. 5: v E 1913 (2); *v E 1912 (1); v A 1912 (2)*
Begbie, D. W. 5: v E 1948 (3); v A 1949 (2)
Bell, A. J. 16: v E 1930 (3); *v E 1929 (3) 1935 (3); v A 1931 (5); v NZ 1931 (2)*
Bisset, M. 3: v E 1898 (2) 1909 (1)
Bissett, G. F. 4: v E 1927 (4)
Blanckenberg, J. M. 18: v E 1913 (5) 1922 (5); v A 1921 (3); *v E 1924 (5)*
Bland, K. C. 21: v E 1964 (5); v A 1966 (1); v NZ 1961 (5); *v E 1965 (3); v A 1963 (4); v NZ 1963 (3)*
Bock, E. G. 1: v A 1935
Bond, G. E. 1: v E 1938
Botten, J. T. 3: *v E 1965 (3)*

Brann, W. H. 3: v E 1922 (3)
Briscoe, A. W. 2: v E 1938 (1); v A 1935 (1)
Bromfield, H. D. 9: v E 1964 (3); v NZ 1961 (5); *v E 1965 (1)*
Brown, L. S. 2: *v A 1931 (1); v NZ 1931 (1)*
Burger, C. G. de V. 2: v A 1957 (2)
Burke, S. F. 2: v E 1964 (1); v NZ 1961 (1)
Buys, I. D. 1: v E 1922

Cameron, H. B. 26: v E 1927 (5) 1930 (5); *v E 1929 (4) 1935 (5); v A 1931 (5); v NZ 1931 (2)*
Campbell, T. 5: v E 1909 (4); *v E 1912 (1)*
Carlstein, P. R. 8: v A 1957 (1); *v E 1960 (5); v A 1963 (2)*
Carter, C. P. 10: v E 1913 (2); v A 1921 (3); *v E 1912 (2) 1924 (3)*
Catterall, R. H. 24: v E 1922 (5) 1927 (5) 1930 (4); *v E 1924 (5) 1929 (5)*
Chapman, H. W. 2: v E 1913 (1); v A 1921 (1)
Cheetham, J. E. 24: v E 1948 (1); v A 1949 (3); v NZ 1953 (5); *v E 1951 (5) 1955 (3); v A 1952 (5); v NZ 1952 (2)*
Chevalier, G. A. 1: v A 1969
Christy, J. A. J. 10: v E 1930 (1); *v E 1929 (2); v A 1931 (5); v NZ 1931 (2)*
Chubb, G. W. A. 5: *v E 1951 (5)*
Cochran, J. A. K. 1: v E 1930
Coen, S. K. 2: v E 1927 (2)
Commaille, J. M. M. 12: v E 1909 (5) 1927 (2); *v E 1924 (5)*
Conyngham, D. P. 1: v E 1922
Cook, F. J. 1: v E 1895
Cooper, A. H. C. 1: v E 1913
Cox, J. L. 3: v E 1913 (3)
Cripps, G. 1: v E 1891
Crisp, R. J. 9: v A 1935 (4); *v E 1935 (5)*
Curnow, S. H. 7: v E 1930 (3); *v A 1931 (4)*

Dalton, E. L. 15: v E 1930 (1) 1938 (4); v A 1935 (1); *v E 1929 (1) 1935 (4); v A 1931 (2); v NZ 1931 (2)*
Davies, E. Q. 5: v E 1938 (3); v A 1935 (2)
Dawson, O. C. 9: v E 1948 (4); *v E 1947 (5)*
Deane, H. G. 17: v E 1927 (5) 1930 (2); *v E 1924 (5) 1929 (5)*
Dixon, C. D. 1: v E 1913
Dower, R. R. 1: v E 1898
Draper, R. G. 2: v A 1949 (2)
Duckworth, C. A. R. 2: v E 1956 (2)
Dumbrill, R. 5: v A 1966 (2); *v E 1965 (3)*
Duminy, J. P. 3: v E 1927 (2); *v E 1929 (1)*
Dunell, O. R. 2: v E 1888 (2)
Du Preez, J. H. 2: v A 1966 (2)
Du Toit, J. F. 1: v E 1891
Dyer, D. V. 3: *v E 1947 (3)*

Elgie, M. K. 3: v NZ 1961 (3)
Endean, W. R. 28: v E 1956 (5); v A 1957 (5); v NZ 1953 (5); *v E 1951 (1) 1955 (5); v A 1952 (5); v NZ 1952 (2)*

Farrer, W. S. 6: v NZ 1961 (3); *v NZ 1963 (3)*
Faulkner, G. A. 25: v E 1905 (5) 1909 (5); *v E 1907 (3) 1912 (3) 1924 (1); v A 1910 (5) 1912 (3)*
Fellows-Smith, J. P. 4: *v E 1960 (4)*
Fichardt, C. G. 2: v E 1891 (1) 1895 (1)
Finlason, C. E. 1: v E 1888
Floquet, C. E. 1: v E 1909
Francis, H. H. 2: v E 1898 (2)
Francois, C. M. 5: v E 1922 (5)
Frank, C. N. 3: v A 1921 (3)
Frank, W. H. B. 1: v E 1895

Fuller, E. R. H. 7: v A 1957 (1); *v E 1955 (2); v A 1952 (2); v NZ 1952 (2)*
Fullerton, G. M. 7: v A 1949 (2); *v E 1947 (2) 1951 (3)*
Funston, K. J. 18: v E 1956 (3); v A 1957 (5); v NZ 1953 (3); *v A 1952 (5); v NZ 1952 (2)*

Gamsy, D. 2: v A 1969 (2)
Gleeson, R. A. 1: v E 1895
Glover, G. K. 1: v E 1895
Goddard, T. L. 41: v E 1956 (5) 1964 (5); v A 1957 (5) 1966 (5) 1969 (3); *v E 1955 (5) 1960 (5); v A 1963 (5); v NZ 1963 (3)*
Gordon, N. 5: v E 1938 (5)
Graham, R. 2: v E 1898 (2)
Grieveson, R. E. 2: v E 1938 (2)
Griffin, G. M. 2: *v E 1960 (2)*

Hall, A. E. 7: v E 1922 (4) 1927 (2) 1930 (1)
Hall, G. G. 1: v E 1964
Halliwell, E. A. 8: v E 1891 (1) 1895 (3) 1898 (1); v A 1902 (3)
Halse, C. G. 3: *v A 1963 (3)*
Hands, P. A. M. 7: v E 1913 (5); v A 1921 (1); *v E 1924 (1)*
Hands, R. H. M. 1: v E 1913
Hanley, M. A. 1: v E 1948
Harris, T. A. 3: v E 1948 (1); *v E 1947 (2)*
Hartigan, G. P. D. 5: v E 1913 (3); *v E 1912 (1); v A 1912 (1)*
Harvey, R. L. 2: v A 1935 (2)
Hathorn, C. M. H. 12: v E 1905 (5); v A 1902 (3); *v E 1907 (3); v A 1910 (1)*
Hearne, F. 4: v E 1891 (1) 1895 (3)
Hearne, G. A. L. 3: v E 1922 (2); *v E 1924 (1)*
Heine, P. S. 14: v E 1956 (5); v A 1957 (4); v NZ 1961 (1); *v E 1955 (4)*
Hime, C. F. W. 1: v E 1895
Hutchinson, P. 2: v E 1888 (2)

Ironside, D. E. J. 3: v NZ 1953 (3)
Irvine, B. L. 4: v A 1969 (4)

Johnson, C. L. 1: v E 1895
Jones, P. S. T. 1: v A 1902

Keith, H. J. 8: v E 1956 (3); *v E 1955 (4); v A 1952 (1)*
Kempis, G. A. 1: v E 1888
Kotze, J. J. 3: v A 1902 (2); *v E 1907 (1)*
Kuys, F. 1: v E 1898

Lance, H. R. 13: v A 1966 (5) 1969 (3); v NZ 1961 (2); *v E 1965 (3)*
Langton, A. B. C. 15: v E 1938 (5); v A 1935 (5); *v E 1935 (5)*
Lawrence, G. B. 5: v NZ 1961 (5)
Le Roux, F. le S. 1: v E 1913
Lewis, P. T. 1: v E 1913
Lindsay, D. T. 19: v E 1964 (3); v A 1966 (5) 1969 (2); *v E 1965 (3); v A 1963 (3); v NZ 1963 (3)*
Lindsay, J. D. 3: *v E 1947 (3)*
Lindsay, N. V. 1: v A 1921
Ling, W. V. S. 6: v E 1922 (3); v A 1921 (3)
Llewellyn, C. B. 15: v E 1895 (1) 1898 (1); v A 1902 (3); *v E 1912 (3); v A 1910 (5) 1912 (2)*
Lundie, E. B. 1: v E 1913

Macaulay, M. J. 1: v E 1964
McCarthy, C. N. 15: v E 1948 (5); v A 1949 (5); *v E 1951 (5)*
McGlew, D. J. 34: v E 1956 (1); v A 1957 (5); v NZ 1953 (5) 1961 (5); *v E 1951 (2) 1955 (5) 1960 (5); v A 1952 (4); v NZ 1952 (2)*
McKinnon, A. H. 8: v E 1964 (2); v A 1966 (2); v NZ 1961 (1); *v E 1960 (1) 1965 (2)*
McLean, R. A. 40: v E 1956 (5) 1964 (2); v A 1957 (4); v NZ 1953 (4) 1961 (5); *v E 1951 (3) 1955 (5) 1960 (5); v A 1952 (5); v NZ 1952 (2)*

McMillan, Q. 13: v E 1930 (5); *v E 1929 (2); v A 1931 (4); v NZ 1931 (2)*
Mann, N. B. F. 19: v E 1948 (5); v A 1949 (5); *v E 1947 (5) 1951 (4)*
Mansell, P. N. F. 13: *v E 1951 (2) 1955 (4); v A 1952 (5); v NZ 1952 (2)*
Markham, L. A. 1: v E 1948
Marx, W. F. E. 3: v A 1921 (3)
Meintjes, D. J. 2: v E 1922 (2)
Melle, M. G. 7: v A 1949 (2); *v E 1951 (1); v A 1952 (4)*
Melville, A. 11: v E 1938 (5) 1948 (1); *v E 1947 (5)*
Middleton, J. 6: v E 1895 (2) 1898 (2); v A 1902 (2)
Mills, C. 1: v E 1891
Milton, W. H. 3: v E 1888 (2) 1891 (1)
Mitchell, B. 42: v E 1930 (5) 1938 (5) 1948 (5); v A 1935 (5); *v E 1929 (5) 1935 (5) 1947 (5);*
   v A 1931 (5); v NZ 1931 (2)
Mitchell, F. 3: *v E 1912 (1); v A 1912 (2)*
Morkel, D. P. B. 16: v E 1927 (5); *v E 1929 (5); v A 1931 (5); v NZ 1931 (1)*
Murray, A. R. A. 10: v NZ 1953 (4); *v A 1952 (4); v NZ 1952 (2)*

Nel, J. D. 6: v A 1949 (5) 1957 (1)
Newberry, C. 4: v E 1913 (4)
Newson, E. S. 3: v E 1930 (1) 1938 (2)
Nicholson, F. 4: v A 1935 (4)
Nicolson, J. F. W. 3: v E 1927 (3)
Norton, N. O. 1: v E 1909
Nourse, A. D. 34: v E 1938 (5) 1948 (5); v A 1935 (5) 1949 (5); *v E 1935 (4) 1947 (5)*
   1951 (5)
Nourse, A. W. 45: v E 1905 (5) 1909 (5) 1913 (5) 1922 (5); v A 1902 (3) 1921 (3); *v E 1907*
   (3) 1912 (3) 1924 (5); v A 1910 (5) 1912 (3)
Nupen, E. P. 17: v E 1922 (4) 1927 (5) 1930 (3); v A 1921 (2) 1935 (1); *v E 1924 (2)*

Ochse, A. E. 2: v E 1888 (2)
Ochse, A. L. 3: v E 1927 (1); *v E 1929 (2)*
O'Linn, S. 7: v NZ 1961 (2); *v E 1960 (5)*
Owen-Smith, H. G. 5: *v E 1929 (5)*

Palm, A. W. 1: v E 1927
Parker, G. M. 2: *v E 1924 (2)*
Parkin, D. C. 1: v E 1891
Partridge, J. T. 11: v E 1964 (3); *v A 1963 (5); v NZ 1963 (3)*
Pearse, O. C. 3: *v A 1910 (3)*
Pegler, S. J. 16: v E 1909 (1); *v E 1912 (3) 1924 (5); v A 1910 (4) 1912 (3)*
Pithey, A. J. 17: v E 1956 (3) 1964 (5); *v E 1960 (2); v A 1963 (4); v NZ 1963 (3)*
Pithey, D. B. 8: v A 1966 (2); *v A 1963 (3); v NZ 1963 (3)*
Plimsoll, J. B. 1: *v E 1947*
Pollock, P. M. 28: v E 1964 (5); v A 1966 (5) 1969 (4); v NZ 1961 (3); *v E 1965 (3); v A 1963*
   (5); v NZ 1963 (3)
Pollock, R. G. 23: v E 1964 (5); v A 1966 (5) 1969 (4); *v E 1965 (3); v A 1963 (5); v NZ*
   1963 (1)
Poore, R. M. 3: v E 1895 (3)
Pothecary, J. E. 3: *v E 1960 (3)*
Powell, A. W. 1: v E 1898
Prince, C. F. H. 1: v E 1898
Procter, M. J. 7: v A 1966 (3) 1969 (4)
Promnitz, H. L. E. 2: v E 1927 (2)

Quinn, N. A. 12: v E 1930 (1); *v E 1929 (4); v A 1931 (5); v NZ 1931 (2)*

Reid, N. 1: v A 1921
Richards, A. R. 1: v E 1895
Richards, B. A. 4: v A 1969 (4)
Richards, W. H. 1: v E 1888
Robertson, J. B. 3: v A 1935 (3)
Rose-Innes, A. 2: v E 1888 (2)

Routledge, T. W. 4: v E 1891 (1) 1895 (3)
Rowan, A. M. B. 15: v E 1948 (5); *v E 1947 (5) 1951 (5)*
Rowan, E. A. B. 26: v E 1938 (4) 1948 (4); v A 1935 (3); 1949 (5); *v E 1935 (5) 1951 (5)*
Rowe, G. A. 5: v E 1895 (2) 1898 (2); v A 1902 (1)

Samuelson, S. V. 1: v E 1909
Schwarz, R. O. 20: v E 1905 (5) 1909 (4); *v E 1907 (3) 1912 (1); v A 1910 (5) 1912 (2)*
Seccull, A. W. 1: v E 1895
Seymour, M. A. 7: v E 1964 (2); v A 1969 (1); *v A 1963 (4)*
Shalders, W. A. 12: v E 1898 (1) 1905 (5); v A 1902 (3); *v E 1907 (3)*
Shepstone, G. H. 2: v E 1895 (1) 1898 (1)
Sherwell, P. W. 13: v E 1905 (5); *v E 1907 (3); v A 1910 (5)*
Siedle, I. J. 18: v E 1927 (1) 1930 (5); v A 1935 (5); *v E 1929 (3) 1935 (4)*
Sinclair, J. H. 25: v E 1895 (3) 1898 (2) 1905 (5) 1909 (4); v A 1902 (3); *v E 1907 (3); v A 1910 (5)*
Smith, C. J. E. 3: v A 1902 (3)
Smith, F. W. 3: v E 1888 (2) 1895 (1)
Smith, V. I. 9: v A 1949 (3) 1957 (1); *v E 1947 (4) 1955 (1)*
Snooke, S. D. 1: *v E 1907*
Snooke, S. J. 26: v E 1905 (5) 1909 (5) 1922 (3); *v E 1907 (3) 1912 (3); v A 1910 (5) 1912 (2)*
Solomon, W. R. 1: v E 1898
Stewart, R. B. 1: v E 1888
Stricker, L. A. 13: v E 1909 (4); *v E 1912 (2); v A 1910 (5) 1912 (2)*
Susskind, M. J. 5: *v E 1924 (5)*

Taberer, H. M. 1: v A 1902
Tancred, A. B. 2: v E 1888 (2)
Tancred, L. J. 14: v E 1905 (5) 1913 (1); v A 1902 (3); *v E 1907 (1) 1912 (2); v A 1912 (2)*
Tancred, V. M. 1: v E 1898
Tapscott, G. L. 1: v E 1913
Tapscott, L. E. 2: v E 1922 (2)
Tayfield, H. J. 37: v E 1956 (5); v A 1949 (5) 1957 (5); v NZ 1953 (5); *v E 1955 (5) 1960 (5); v A 1952 (5); v NZ 1952 (2)*
Taylor, A. I. 1: v E 1956
Taylor, D. 2: v E 1913 (2)
Taylor, H. W. 42: v E 1913 (5) 1922 (5) 1927 (5) 1930 (4); v A 1921 (3); *v E 1912 (3) 1924 (5) 1929 (3); v A 1912 (3) 1931 (5); v NZ 1931 (1)*
Theunissen, N. H. G. de J. 1: v E 1888
Thornton, P. G. 1: v A 1902
Tomlinson, D. S. 1: *v E 1935*
Traicos, A. J. 3: v A 1969 (3)
Trimborn, P. H. J. 4: v A 1966 (3) 1969 (1)
Tuckett, L. 9: v E 1948 (4); *v E 1947 (5)*
Tuckett, L. R. 1: v E 1913

van der Bijl, P. G. V. 5: v E 1938 (5)
Van der Merwe, E. A. 2: v A 1935 (1); *v E 1929 (1)*
Van der Merwe, P. L. 15: v E 1964 (2); v A 1966 (5); *v E 1965 (3); v A 1963 (3); v NZ 1963 (2)*
Van Ryneveld, C. B. 19: v E 1956 (5); v A 1957 (4); v NZ 1953 (5); *v E 1951 (5)*
Varnals, G. D. 3: v E 1964 (3)
Viljoen, K. G. 27: v E 1930 (3) 1938 (4) 1948 (2); v A 1935 (4); *v E 1935 (4) 1947 (5); v A 1931 (4); v NZ 1931 (1)*
Vincent, C. L. 25: v E 1927 (5) 1930 (5); *v E 1929 (4) 1935 (4); v A 1931 (5); v NZ 1931 (2)*
Vintcent, C. H. 3: v E 1888 (2) 1891 (1)
Vogler, A. E. E. 15: v E 1905 (5) 1909 (5); *v E 1907 (3); v A 1910 (2)*

Wade, H. F. 10: v A 1935 (5); *v E 1935 (5)*
Wade, W. W. 11: v E 1938 (3) 1948 (5); v A 1949 (3)
Waite, J. H. B. 50: v E 1956 (5); 1964 (2); v A 1957 (5); v NZ 1953 (5) 1961 (5); *v E 1951 (4) 1955 (5) 1960 (5); v A 1952 (5) 1963 (4); v NZ 1952 (2) 1963 (3)*

Walter, K. A. 2: v NZ 1961 (2)
Ward, T. A. 23: v E 1913 (5) 1922 (5); v A 1921 (3); *v E 1912 (2) 1924 (5); v A 1912 (3)*
Watkins, J. C. 15: v E 1956 (2); v A 1949 (3); v NZ 1953 (3); *v A 1952 (5); v NZ 1952 (2)*
Wesley, C. 3: *v E 1960 (3)*
Westcott, R. J. 5: v A 1957 (2); v NZ 1953 (3)
White, G. C. 17: v E 1905 (5) 1909 (4); *v E 1907 (3) 1912 (2); v A 1912 (3)*
Willoughby, J. T. I. 2: v E 1895 (2)
Wimble, C. S. 1: v E 1891
Winslow, P. L. 5: v A 1949 (2); *v E 1955 (3)*
Wynne, O. E. 6: v E 1948 (3); v A 1949 (3)

Zulch, J. W. 16: v E 1909 (5) 1913 (3); v A 1921 (3); *v A 1910 (5)*

WEST INDIES

Number of Test cricketers: 178

Achong, E. 6: v E 1929 (1) 1934 (2); *v E 1933 (3)*
Alexander, F. C. M. 25: v E 1959 (5); v P 1957 (5); *v E 1957 (2); v A 1960 (5); v In 1958 (5); v P 1958 (3)*
Ali, Imtiaz 1: v In 1975
Ali, Inshan 12: v E 1973 (2); v A 1972 (3); v In 1970 (1); v P 1976 (1); v NZ 1971 (3); *v E 1973 (1); v A 1975 (1)*
Allan, D. W. 5: v A 1964 (1); v In 1961 (2); *v E 1966 (2)*
Asgarali, N. 2: *v E 1957 (2)*
Atkinson, D. St E. 22: v E 1953 (4); v A 1954 (4); v P 1957 (1); *v E 1957 (2); v A 1951 (2); v NZ 1951 (1) 1955 (4); v In 1948 (4)*
Atkinson, E. St E. 8: v P 1957 (3); *v In 1958 (3); v P 1958 (2)*
Austin, R. A. 2: v A 1977 (2)

Bacchus, S. F. A. 19: v A 1977 (2); *v E 1980 (5); v A 1981 (2); v In 1978 (6); v P 1980 (4)*
Baichan, L. 3: *v A 1975 (1); v P 1974 (2)*
Barrow, I. 11: v E 1929 (1) 1934 (1); *v E 1933 (3) 1939 (1); v A 1930 (5)*
Barrett, A. G. 6: v E 1973 (2); v In 1970 (2); *v In 1974 (2)*
Bartlett, E. L. 5: *v E 1928 (1); v A 1930 (4)*
Betancourt, N. 1: v E 1929
Binns, A. P. 5: v A 1954 (1); v In 1952 (1); *v NZ 1955 (3)*
Birkett, L. S. 4 *v A 1930 (4)*
Boyce, K. D. 21: v E 1973 (4); v A 1972 (4); v In 1970 (1); *v E 1973 (3); v A 1975 (4); v In 1974 (3); v P 1974 (2)*
Browne, C. R. 4: v E 1929 (2); *v E 1928 (2)*
Butcher, B. F. 44: v E 1959 (2) 1967 (5); v A 1964 (5); *v E 1963 (5) 1966 (5) 1969 (3); v A 1968 (5); v NZ 1968 (3); v In 1958 (5) 1966 (3); v P 1958 (3)*
Butler, L. 1: v A 1954
Bynoe, M. R. 4: *v In 1966 (3); v P 1958 (1)*

Camacho, G. S. 11: v E 1967 (5); v In 1970 (2); *v E 1969 (2); v A 1968 (2)*
Cameron, F. J. 5: *v In 1948 (5)*
Cameron, J. H. 2: *v E 1939 (2)*
Carew, G. M. 4: v E 1934 (1) 1947 (2); *v In 1948 (1)*
Carew, M. C. 19: v E 1967 (1); v NZ 1971 (3); v In 1970 (3); *v E 1963 (2) 1966 (1) 1969 (1); v A 1968 (5); v NZ 1968 (3)*
Challenor, G. 3: *v E 1928 (3)*
Chang, H. S. 1: *v In 1978*
Christiani, C. M. 4: v E 1934 (4)
Christiani, R. J. 22: v E 1947 (4) 1953 (1); v In 1952 (2); *v E 1950 (4); v A 1951 (5); v NZ 1951 (1); v In 1948 (5)*
Clarke, C. B. 3: *v E 1939 (3)*
Clarke, S. T. 11: v A 1977 (1); *v A 1981 (1); v In 1978 (5); v P 1980 (4)*

Constantine, L. N. 18: v E 1929 (3) 1934 (3); *v E 1928 (3) 1933 (1) 1939 (3); v A 1930 (5)*
Croft, C. E. H. 27: v E 1980 (4); v A 1977 (2); v P 1976 (5); *v E 1980 (3); v A 1979 (3) 1981 (3); v NZ 1979 (3); v P 1980 (4)*

Da Costa, O. C. 5: v E 1929 (1) 1934 (1); *v E 1933 (3)*
Daniel, W. W. 5: v In 1975 (1); *v E 1976 (4)*
Davis, B. A. 4: v A 1964 (4)
Davis, C. A. 15: v A 1972 (2); v NZ 1971 (5); v In 1970 (4); *v E 1969 (3); v A 1968 (1)*
Davis, W. W. 1: v In 1982
De Caires, F. I. 3: v E 1929 (3)
Depeiza, C. C. 5: v A 1954 (3); *v NZ 1955 (2)*
Dewdney, T. 9: v A 1954 (2); v P 1957 (3); *v E 1957 (1); v NZ 1955 (3)*
Dowe, U. G. 4: v A 1972 (1); v NZ 1971 (1); v In 1970 (2)
Dujon, P. J. 8: v In 1982 (5); *v A 1981 (3)*

Edwards, R. M. 5: *v A 1968 (2); v NZ 1968 (3)*

Ferguson, W. 8: v E 1947 (4) 1953 (1); *v In 1948 (3)*
Fernandes, M. P. 2: v E 1929 (1); *v E 1928 (1)*
Findlay, T. M. 10: v A 1972 (1); v NZ 1971 (5); v In 1970 (2); *v E 1969 (2)*
Foster, M. L. C. 14: v E 1973 (1); v A 1972 (4) 1977 (1); v NZ 1971 (3); v In 1970 (2); v P 1976 (1); *v E 1969 (1) 1973 (1)*
Francis, G. N. 10: v E 1929 (1); *v E 1928 (3) 1933 (1); v A 1930 (5)*
Frederick, M. C. 1: v E 1953
Fredericks, R. C. 59: v E 1973 (5); v A 1972 (5); v NZ 1971 (5); v In 1970 (4) 1975 (4); v P 1976 (5); *v E 1969 (3) 1973 (3) 1976 (5); v A 1968 (4) 1975 (6); v NZ 1968 (3); v In 1974 (5); v P 1974 (2)*
Fuller, R. L. 1: v E 1934
Furlonge, H. A. 3: v A 1954 (1); *v NZ 1955 (2)*

Ganteaume, A. G. 1: v E 1947
Garner, J. 32: v E 1980 (4); v A 1977 (2); v In 1982 (4); v P 1976 (5); *v E 1980 (5); v A 1979 (3) 1981 (3); v NZ 1979 (3); v P 1980 (3)*
Gaskin, B. B. M. 2: v E 1947 (2)
Gibbs, G. L. R. 1: v A 1954
Gibbs, L. R. 79: v E 1967 (5) 1973 (5); v A 1964 (5) 1972 (5); v NZ 1971 (2); v In 1961 (5) 1970 (1); v P 1957 (4); *v E 1963 (5) 1966 (5) 1969 (3) 1973 (3); v A 1960 (3) 1968 (5) 1975 (6); v In 1958 (1) 1966 (3) 1974 (5); v P 1958 (3) 1974 (2)*
Gilchrist, R. 13: v P 1957 (5); *v E 1957 (4); v In 1958 (4)*
Gladstone, G. 1: v E 1929
Goddard, J. D. C. 27: v E 1947 (4); *v E 1950 (4) 1957 (5); v A 1951 (4); v NZ 1951 (2) 1955 (3); v In 1948 (5)*
Gomes, H. A. 27: v E 1980 (4); v A 1977 (3); v In 1982 (5); *v E 1976 (2); v A 1981 (3); v In 1978 (6); v P 1980 (4)*
Gomez, G. E. 29: v E 1947 (4) 1953 (4); v In 1952 (4); *v E 1939 (2) 1950 (4); v A 1951 (5); v NZ 1951 (1); v In 1948 (5)*
Grant, G. C. 12: v E 1934 (4); *v E 1933 (3); v A 1930 (5)*
Grant, R. S. 7: v E 1934 (4); *v E 1939 (3)*
Greenidge, A. E. 6: v A 1977 (2); *v In 1978 (4)*
Greenidge, C. G. 41: v E 1980 (4); v A 1977 (2); v In 1982 (5); v P 1976 (5); *v E 1976 (5) 1980 (5); v A 1975 (2) 1979 (3) 1981 (2); v NZ 1979 (3); v In 1974 (5)*
Greenidge, G. A. 5: v A 1972 (3); v NZ 1971 (2)
Grell, M. G. 1: v E 1929
Griffith, C. C. 28: v E 1959 (1) 1967 (4); v A 1964 (5); *v E 1963 (5) 1966 (5); v A 1968 (3); v NZ 1968 (2); v In 1966 (3)*
Griffith, H. C. 13: v E 1929 (3); *v E 1928 (3) 1933 (2); v A 1930 (5)*
Guillen, S. C. 5: *v A 1951 (3); v NZ 1951 (2)*

Hall, W. W. 48: v E 1959 (5) 1967 (4); v A 1964 (5); v In 1961 (5); *v E 1963 (5) 1966 (5); v A 1960 (5) 1968 (2); v NZ 1958 (3) 1966 (3); v P 1958 (3)*
Haynes, D. L. 29: v E 1980 (4); v A 1977 (2); v In 1982 (5); *v E 1980 (5); v A 1979 (3) 1981 (3); v NZ 1979 (3); v P 1980 (4)*

Headley, G. A. 22: v E 1929 (4) 1934 (4) 1947 (1) 1953 (1); *v E 1933 (3) 1939 (3); v A 1930 (5); v In 1948 (1)*
Headley, R. G. A. 2: *v E 1973 (2)*
Hendriks, J. L. 20: v A 1964 (4); v In 1961 (1); *v E 1966 (3) 1969 (1); v A 1968 (5); v NZ 1968 (3); v In 1966 (3)*
Hoad, E. L. G. 4: v E 1929 (1); *v E 1928 (1) 1933 (2)*
Holder, V. A. 40: v E 1973 (1); v A 1972 (3) 1977 (3); v NZ 1971 (4); v In 1970 (3) 1975 (1); v P 1976 (1); *v E 1969 (3) 1973 (2) 1976 (4); v A 1975 (3); v In 1974 (4) 1978 (6); v P 1974 (2)*
Holding, M. A. 36: v E 1980 (4); v In 1975 (4) 1982 (5); *v E 1976 (4) 1980 (5); v A 1975 (5) 1979 (3) 1981 (3); v NZ 1979 (3)*
Holford, D. A. J. 24: v E 1967 (4); v NZ 1971 (5); v In 1970 (1) 1975 (2); v P 1976 (1); *v E 1966 (5); v A 1968 (2); v NZ 1968 (3); v In 1966 (1)*
Holt, J. K. 17: v E 1953 (5); v A 1954 (5); *v In 1958 (5); v P 1958 (2)*
Howard, A. B. 1: v NZ 1971
Hunte, C. C. 44: v E 1959 (5); v A 1964 (5); v In 1961 (5); v P 1957 (5); *v E 1963 (5) 1966 (5); v A 1960 (5); v In 1958 (5) 1966 (3); v P 1958 (1)*
Hunte, E. A. C. 3: v E 1929 (3)
Hylton, L. G. 6: v E 1934 (4); *v E 1939 (2)*

Johnson, H. H. H. 3: v E 1947 (1); *v E 1950 (2)*
Johnson, T. F. 1: *v E 1939*
Jones, C. M. 4: v E 1929 (1) 1934 (3)
Jones, P. E. 9: v E 1947 (1); *v E 1950 (2); v A 1951 (1); v In 1948 (5)*
Julien, B. D. 24: v E 1973 (5); v In 1975 (4); v P 1976 (1); *v E 1973 (3) 1976 (2); v A 1975 (3); v In 1974 (4); v P 1974 (2)*
Jumadeen, R. R. 12: v A 1972 (1) 1977 (2); v NZ 1971 (1); v In 1975 (4); v P 1976 (1); *v E 1976 (1); v In 1978 (2)*

Kallicharran, A. I. 66: v E 1973 (5); v A 1972 (5) 1977 (5); v NZ 1971 (2); v In 1975 (4); v P 1976 (5); *v E 1973 (3) 1976 (3) 1980 (5); v A 1975 (6) 1979 (3); v NZ 1979 (3); v In 1974 (5) 1978 (6); v P 1974 (2) 1980 (4)*
Kanhai, R. B. 79: v E 1959 (5) 1967 (5) 1973 (5); v A 1964 (5) 1972 (5); v In 1961 (5) 1970 (5); v P 1957 (5); *v E 1957 (5) 1963 (5) 1966 (5) 1973 (3); v A 1960 (5) 1968 (5); v In 1958 (5) 1966 (3); v P 1958 (3)*
Kentish, E. S. M. 2: v E 1947 (1) 1953 (1)
King, C. L. 9: v P 1976 (1); *v E 1976 (3) 1980 (1); v A 1979 (1); v NZ 1979 (3)*
King, F. M. 14: v E 1953 (3); v A 1954 (4); v In 1952 (5); *v NZ 1955 (2)*
King, L. A. 2: v E 1967 (1); v In 1961 (1)

Lashley, P. D. 4: *v E 1966 (2); v A 1960 (2)*
Legall, R. 4: v In 1952 (4)
Lewis, D. M. 3: v In 1970 (3)
Lloyd, C. H. 90: v E 1967 (5) 1973 (5) 1980 (4); v A 1972 (3) 1977 (2); v NZ 1971 (2); v In 1970 (5) 1975 (4) 1982 (5); v P 1976 (5); *v E 1969 (3) 1973 (3) 1976 (5) 1980 (4); v A 1968 (4) 1975 (6) 1979 (2) 1981 (3); v NZ 1968 (3) 1979 (3); v In 1966 (3) 1974 (5); v P 1974 (2) 1980 (4)*
Logie, A. L. 5: v In 1982 (5)

McMorris, E. D. A. 13: v E 1959 (4); v In 1961 (4); v P 1957 (1); *v E 1963 (2) 1966 (2)*
McWatt, C. A. 6: v E 1953 (5); v A 1954 (1)
Madray, I. S. 2: v P 1957 (2)
Marshall, M. D. 17: v E 1980 (1); v In 1982 (5); *v E 1980 (4); v In 1978 (3); v P 1980 (4)*
Marshall, N. E. 1: v A 1954
Marshall, R. E. 4: *v A 1951 (2); v NZ 1951 (2)*
Martin, F. R. 9: v E 1929 (1); *v E 1928 (3); v A 1930 (5)*
Martindale, E. A. 10: v E 1934 (4); *v E 1933 (3) 1939 (3)*
Mattis, E. H. 4: v E 1980 (4)
Mendonca, I. L. 2: v In 1961 (2)
Merry, C. A. 2: *v E 1933 (2)*
Miller, R. 1: v In 1952
Moodie, G. H. 1: v E 1934

Murray, D. A. 19: v E 1980 (4); v A 1977 (3); *v A 1981 (2); v In 1978 (6); v P 1980 (4)*
Murray, D. L. 62: v E 1967 (5) 1973 (5); v A 1972 (4) 1977 (2); v In 1975 (4); v P 1976 (5); *v E 1963 (5) 1973 (3) 1976 (5) 1980 (5); v A 1975 (6) 1979 (3); v NZ 1979 (3); v In 1974 (5); v P 1974 (2)*

Nanan, R. 1: *v P 1980*
Neblett, J. M. 1: v E 1934
Noreiga, J. M. 4: v In 1970 (4)
Nunes, R. K. 4: v E 1929 (1); *v E 1928 (3)*
Nurse, S. M. 29: v E 1959 (1) 1967 (5); v A 1964 (4); v In 1961 (1); *v E 1966 (5); v A 1960 (3) 1968 (5); v NZ 1968 (3); v In 1966 (2)*

Padmore, A. L. 2: v In 1975 (1); *v E 1976 (1)*
Pairaudeau, B. H. 13: v E 1953 (2); v In 1952 (5): *v E 1957 (2); v NZ 1955 (4)*
Parry, D. R. 12: v A 1977 (5); *v NZ 1979 (1); v In 1978 (6)*
Passailaigue, C. C. 1: v E 1929
Phillip, N. 9: v A 1977 (3); *v In 1978 (6)*
Pierre, L. R. 1: v E 1947

Rae, A. F. 15: v In 1952 (2); *v E 1950 (4); v A 1951 (3); v NZ 1951 (1); v In 1948 (5)*
Ramadhin, S. 43: v E 1953 (5) 1959 (4); v A 1954 (4); v In 1952 (4); *v E 1950 (4) 1957 (5); v A 1951 (5) 1960 (2); v NZ 1951 (2) 1955 (4); v In 1958 (2); v P 1958 (2)*
Richards, I. V. A. 52: v E 1980 (4); v A 1977 (2); v In 1975 (4) 1982 (5); v P 1976 (5); *v E 1976 (4) 1980 (5); v A 1975 (6) 1979 (3) 1981 (3); v In 1974 (5); v P 1974 (2) 1980 (4)*
Rickards, K. R. 2: v E 1947 (1); *v A 1951 (1)*
Roach, C. A. 16: v E 1929 (4) 1934 (1); *v E 1928 (3) 1933 (3); v A 1930 (5)*
Roberts, A. M. E. 45: v E 1973 (1) 1980 (3); v A 1977 (2); v In 1975 (2) 1982 (5); v P 1976 (5); *v E 1976 (5) 1980 (3); v A 1975 (5) 1979 (3) 1981 (2); v NZ 1979 (2); v In 1974 (5); v P 1974 (2)*
Roberts, A. T. 1: *v NZ 1955*
Rodriguez, W. V. 5: v E 1967 (1); v A 1964 (1); v In 1961 (2); *v E 1963 (1)*
Rowe, L. G. 30: v E 1973 (5); v A 1972 (3); v NZ 1971 (4); v In 1975 (4); *v E 1976 (2); v A 1975 (6) 1979 (3); v NZ 1979 (3)*

St Hill, E. L. 2: v E 1929 (2)
St Hill, W. H. 3: v E 1929 (1); *v E 1928 (2)*
Scarlett, R. O. 3: v E 1959 (3)
Scott, A. P. H. 1: v In 1952
Scott, O. C. 8: v E 1929 (1); *v E 1928 (2); v A 1930 (5)*
Sealey, B. J. 1: *v E 1933*
Sealy, J. E. D. 11: v E 1929 (2) 1934 (4); *v E 1939 (3); v A 1930 (2)*
Shepherd, J. N. 5: v In 1970 (2); *v E 1969 (3)*
Shillingford, G. C. 7: v NZ 1971 (2); v In 1970 (3); *v E 1969 (2)*
Shillingford, I. T. 4: v A 1977 (1); *v P 1976 (3)*
Shivnarine, S. 8: v A 1977 (3); *v In 1978 (5)*
Singh, C. K. 2: v E 1959 (2)
Small, J. A. 3: v E 1929 (1); *v E 1928 (2)*
Smith, C. W. 5: v In 1961 (1); *v A 1960 (4)*
Smith, O. G. 26: v A 1954 (4); v P 1957 (5); *v E 1957 (5); v NZ 1955 (4); v In 1958 (5); v P 1958 (3)*
Sobers, G. S. 93: v E 1953 (1) 1959 (5) 1967 (5) 1973 (4); v A 1954 (4) 1964 (5); v NZ 1971 (5); v In 1961 (5); 1970 (5); v P 1957 (5); *v E 1957 (5) 1963 (5) 1966 (5) 1969 (3) 1973 (3); v A 1960 (5) 1968 (5); v NZ 1955 (4) 1968 (3); v In 1958 (5) 1966 (3); v P 1958 (3)*
Solomon, J. S. 27: v E 1959 (2); v A 1964 (4); v In 1961 (4); *v E 1963 (5); v A 1960 (5); v In 1958 (4); v P 1958 (3)*
Stayers, S. C. 4: v In 1961 (4)
Stollmeyer, J. B. 32: v E 1947 (2) 1953 (5); v A 1954 (2); v In 1952 (5); *v E 1939 (3) 1950 (4); v A 1951 (5); v NZ 1951 (2); v In 1948 (4)*
Stollmeyer, V. H. 1: *v E 1939*

Taylor, J. 3: v P 1957 (1); *v In 1958 (1); v P 1958 (1)*

Trim, J. 4: v E 1947 (1); *v A 1951 (1); v In 1948 (2)*

Valentine, A. L. 36: v E 1953 (3); v A 1954 (3); v In 1952 (5) 1961 (2); v P 1957 (1); *v E 1950 (4) 1957 (2); v A 1951 (5) 1960 (5); v NZ 1951 (2) 1955 (4)*
Valentine, V. A. 2: *v E 1933 (2)*

Walcott, C. L. 44: v E 1947 (4) 1953 (5) 1959 (2); v A 1954 (5); v In 1952 (5); v P 1957 (4); *v E 1950 (4) 1957 (5); v A 1951 (3); v NZ 1951 (2); v In 1948 (5)*
Walcott, L. A. 1: v E 1929
Watson, C. 7: v E 1959 (5); v In 1961 (1); *v A 1960 (1)*
Weekes, E. D. 48: v E 1947 (4) 1953 (4); v A 1954 (5) v In 1952 (5); v P 1957 (5); *v E 1950 (4) 1957 (5); v A 1951 (5); v NZ 1951 (2) 1955 (4); v In 1948 (5)*
Weekes, K. H. 2: *v E 1939 (2)*
White, W. A. 2: v A 1964 (2)
Wight, C. V. 2: v E 1929 (1); *v E 1928 (1)*
Wight, G. L. 1: v In 1952
Wiles, C. A. 1: *v E 1933*
Willett, E. T. 5: v A 1972 (3); *v In 1974 (2)*
Williams, A. B. 7: v A 1977 (3); *v In 1978 (4)*
Williams, E. A. V. 4: v E 1947 (3); *v E 1939 (1)*
Wishart, K. L. 1: v E 1934
Worrell, F. M. M. 51: v E 1947 (3) 1953 (4) 1959 (4); v A 1954 (4); v In 1952 (5) 1961 (5); *v E 1950 (4) 1957 (5) 1963 (5); v A 1951 (5) 1960 (5); v NZ 1951 (2)*

NEW ZEALAND

Number of Test cricketers: 153

Alabaster, J. C. 21: v E 1962 (2); v WI 1955 (1); v In 1967 (4); *v E 1958 (2); v SA 1961 (5); v WI 1971 (2); v In 1955 (4); v P 1955 (1)*
Allcott, C. F. W. 6: v E 1929 (2); v SA 1931 (1); *v E 1931 (3)*
Anderson, R. W. 9: v E 1977 (3); *v E 1978 (3); v P 1976 (3)*
Anderson, W. M. 1: v A 1945
Andrews, B. 2: *v A 1973 (2)*

Badcock, F. T. 7: v E 1929 (3) 1932 (2); v SA 1931 (2)
Barber, R. T. 1: v WI 1955
Bartlett, G. A. 10: v E 1965 (2); v In 1967 (2); v P 1964 (1); *v SA 1961 (5)*
Barton, P. T. 7: v E 1962 (3); *v SA 1961 (4)*
Beard, D. D. 4: v WI 1951 (2) 1955 (2)
Beck, J. E. F. 8: v WI 1955 (4); *v SA 1953 (4)*
Bell, W. 2: *v SA 1953 (2)*
Bilby, G. P. 2: v E 1965 (2)
Blair, R. W. 19: v E 1954 (1) 1958 (2) 1962 (2); v SA 1952 (2) 1963 (3); v WI 1955 (2) *v E 1958 (3); v SA 1953 (4)*
Blunt, R. C. 9: v E 1929 (4); v SA 1931 (2); *v E 1931 (3)*
Bolton, B. A. 2: v E 1958 (2)
Boock, S. L. 12: v E 1977 (3); v WI 1979 (3); v P 1978 (3); *v E 1978 (3)*
Bracewell, B. P. 5: v P 1978 (1); *v E 1978 (3); v A 1980 (1)*
Bracewell, J. G. 8: v In 1980 (1); *v E 1983 (4); v A 1980 (3)*
Bradburn, W. P. 2: v SA 1963 (2)
Burgess, M. G. 50: v E 1970 (1) 1977 (3); v A 1973 (1) 1976 (2); v WI 1968 (2); v In 1967 (4) 1975 (3); v P 1972 (3) 1978 (3); *v E 1969 (2) 1973 (3) 1978 (3); v A 1980 (3); v WI 1971 (5); v In 1969 (3) 1976 (3); v P 1969 (3) 1976 (3)*
Burke, C. 1: v A 1945
Burtt, T. B. 10: v E 1946 (1) 1950 (2); v SA 1952 (1); v WI 1951 (2); *v E 1949 (4)*
Butterfield, L. A. 1: v A 1945

Cairns, B. L. 32: v E 1974 (2) 1977 (1); v A 1976 (1) 1981 (3); v WI 1979 (3); v In 1975 (1) 1980 (3); v P 1978 (3); v SL 1982 (2); *v E 1978 (2) 1983 (4); v A 1973 (1) 1980 (3); v In 1976 (2); v P 1976 (2)*

Cameron, F. J. 19: v E 1962 (3); v SA 1963 (3); v P 1964 (3); *v E 1965 (2); v SA 1961 (5); v In 1964 (1); v P 1964 (2)*

Cave, H. B. 19: v E 1954 (2); v WI 1955 (3); *v E 1949 (4) 1958 (2); v In 1955 (5); v P 1955 (3)*

Chapple, M. E. 14: v E 1954 (1) 1965 (1); v SA 1952 (1) 1963 (3); v WI 1955 (1); *v SA 1953 (5) 1961 (2)*

Chatfield, E. J. 10: v E 1974 (1) 1977 (1); v A 1976 (2) 1981 (1); v SL 1982 (2); *v E 1983 (3)*

Cleverley, D. C. 2: v SA 1931 (1); v A 1945 (1)

Collinge, R. O. 35: v E 1970 (2) 1974 (2) 1977 (3); v A 1973 (3); v In 1967 (2) 1975 (3); v P 1964 (3) 1972 (2);*v E 1965 (3) 1969 (1) 1973 (3) 1978 (1); v In 1964 (2) 1976 (1); v P 1964 (2) 1976 (2)*

Colquhoun, I. A. 2: v E 1954 (2)

Coney, J. V. 24: v A 1973 (2) 1981 (3); v WI 1979 (3); v In 1980 (3); v P 1978 (3); v SL 1982 (2); *v E 1983 (4); v A 1973 (2); 1980 (2)*

Congdon, B. E. 61: v E 1965 (3) 1970 (2) 1974 (2) 1977 (3); v A 1973 (3) 1976 (2); v WI 1968 (3); v In 1967 (4) 1975 (3); v P 1964 (3) 1972 (3); *v E 1965 (3) 1969 (3) 1973 (3) 1978 (3); v A 1973 (3); v WI 1971 (5); v In 1964 (3) 1969 (3); v P 1964 (1) 1969 (3)*

Cowie, J. 9: v E 1946 (1); v A 1945 (1); *v E 1937 (3) 1949 (4)*

Cresswell G. F. 3: v E 1950 (2); *v E 1949 (1)*

Cromb, I. B. 5: v SA 1931 (2); *v E 1931 (3)*

Crowe, J. J. 4: v SL 1982 (2); *v E 1983 (2)*

Crowe, M. D. 7: v A 1981 (3); *v E 1983 (4)*

Cunis R. S. 20: v E 1965 (3) 1970 (2); v SA 1963 (1); v WI 1968 (3); *v E 1969 (1); v WI 1971 (5); v In 1969 (3); v P 1969 (2)*

D'Arcy, J. W. 5: *v E 1958 (5)*

Dempster, C. S. 10: v E 1929 (4) 1932 (2); v SA 1931 (2); *v E 1931 (2)*

Dempster, E. W. 5: v SA 1952 (1); *v SA 1953 (4)*

Dick, A. E. 17: v E 1962 (3); v SA 1963 (2); v P 1964 (2); *v E 1965 (2); v SA 1961 (5); v P 1964 (3)*

Dickinson, G. R. 3: v E 1929 (2); v SA 1931 (1)

Donnelly, M. P. 7: *v E 1937 (3) 1949 (4)*

Dowling, G. T. 39: v E 1962 (3) 1970 (2); v In 1967 (4); v SA 1963 (1); v WI 1968 (3); v P 1964 (2); *v E 1965 (3) 1969 (3); v SA 1961 (4); v WI 1971 (2); v In 1964 (4) 1969 (3); v P 1964 (2) 1969 (3)*

Dunning, J. A. 4: v E 1932 (1); *v E 1937 (3)*

Edgar, B. A. 24: v A 1981 (3); v WI 1979 (3); v In 1980 (3); v P 1978 (3); v SL 1982 (2); *v E 1978 (3) 1983 (4); v A 1980 (3)*

Edwards, G. N. 8: v E 1977 (1); v A 1976 (2); v In 1980 (3); *v E 1978 (2)*

Emery, R. W. G. 2: v WI 1951 (2)

Fisher, F. E. 1: v SA 1952

Foley, H. 1: v E 1929

Franklin, T. J. 1: *v E 1983*

Freeman, D. L. 2: v E 1932 (2)

Gallichan, N. 1: *v E 1937*

Gedye, S. G. 4: v SA 1963 (3); v P 1964 (1)

Gray, E. J. 2: *v E 1983 (2)*

Guillen, S. C. 3: v WI 1955 (3)

Guy, J. W. 12: v E 1958 (2); v WI 1955 (2); *v SA 1961 (2); v In 1955 (5); v P 1955 (1)*

Hadlee, D. R. 26: v E 1974 (2) 1977 (1); v A 1973 (3) 1976 (1); v In 1975 (3); v P 1972 (2); *v E 1969 (2) 1973 (3); v A 1973 (3); v In 1969 (3); v P 1969 (3)*

Hadlee, R. J. 44: v E 1977 (3); v A 1973 (3) 1976 (2) 1981 (3); v WI 1979 (3); v In 1975 (2) 1980 (3); v P 1972 (1) 1978 (3); v SL 1982 (2); *v E 1973 (1) 1978 (3) 1983 (4); v A 1973 (3) 1980 (3); v In 1976 (3); v P 1976 (3)*

Hadlee, W. A. 11: v E 1946 (1) 1950 (2); v A 1945 (1); *v E 1937 (3) 1949 (4)*

Harford, N. S. 8: *v E 1958 (4); v In 1955 (2); v P 1955 (2)*

Harford, R. I. 3: v In 1967 (3)

Harris, P. G. Z. 9: v P 1964 (1); *v SA 1961 (5); v In 1955 (1); v P 1955 (2)*

Harris, R. M. 2: v E 1958 (2)

Hastings, B. F. 31: v E 1974 (2); v A 1973 (3); v WI 1968 (3); v In 1975 (1); v P 1972 (3); *v E 1969 (3) 1973 (3); v A 1973 (3); v WI 1971 (5); v In 1969 (2); v P 1969 (3)*

Hayes, J. A. 15: v E 1950 (2) 1954 (1); v WI 1951 (2); *v E 1958 (4); v In 1955 (5); v P 1955 (1)*

Henderson, M. 1: v E 1929

Hough, K. W. 2: v E 1958 (2)

Howarth, G. P. 34: v E 1974 (2) 1977 (3); v A 1976 (2) 1981 (3); v WI 1979 (3); v In 1980 (3); v P 1978 (3); v SL 1982 (2); *v E 1978 (3) 1983 (4); v A 1980 (2); v In 1976 (2); v P 1976 (2)*

Howarth, H. J. 30: v E 1970 (2) 1974 (2); v A 1973 (3) 1976 (2); v In 1975 (2); v P 1972 (3); *v E 1969 (3) 1973 (2); v WI 1971 (5); v In 1969 (3); v P 1969 (3)*

James, K. C. 11: v E 1929 (4) 1932 (2); v SA 1931 (2); *v E 1931 (3)*

Jarvis, T. W. 13: v E 1965 (1); v P 1972 (3); *v WI 1971 (4); v In 1964 (2); v P 1964 (3)*

Kerr, J. L. 7: v E 1932 (2); v SA 1931 (1); *v E 1931 (2) 1937 (2)*

Lees, W. K. 21: v E 1977 (2); v A 1976 (1); v WI 1979 (3); v P 1978 (3); v SL 1982 (2); *v E 1983 (2); v A 1980 (2); v In 1976 (3); v P 1976 (3)*

Leggat, I. B. 1: *v SA 1953*

Leggat, J. G. 9: v E 1954 (1); v SA 1952 (1); v WI 1951 (1) 1955 (1); *v In 1955 (3); v P 1955 (2)*

Lissette, A. F. 2: v WI 1955 (2)

Lowry, T. C. 7: v E 1929 (4); *v E 1931 (3)*

MacGibbon, A. R. 26: v E 1950 (2) 1954 (2); v SA 1952 (1); v WI 1955 (3); *v E 1958 (5); v SA 1953 (5); v In 1955 (5); v P 1955 (3)*

McEwan, P. E. 3: v WI 1979 (1); *v A 1980 (2)*

McGirr, H. M. 2: v E 1929 (2)

McGregor, S. N. 25: v E 1954 (2) 1958 (2); v SA 1963 (3); v WI 1955 (4); v P 1964 (2); *v SA 1961 (5); v In 1955 (4); v P 1955 (3)*

McLeod E. G. 1: v E 1929

McMahon T. G. 5: v WI 1955 (1); *v In 1955 (3); v P 1955 (1)*

McRae, D. A. N. 1: v A 1945

Matheson, A. M. 2: v E 1929 (1); *v E 1931 (1)*

Meale, T. 2: *v E 1958 (2)*

Merritt, W. E. 6: v E 1929 (4); *v E 1931 (2)*

Meuli, E. M. 1: v SA 1952

Milburn, B. D. 3: v WI 1968 (3)

Miller, L. S. M. 13: v SA 1952 (2); v WI 1955 (3); *v E 1958 (4); v SA 1953 (4)*

Mills, J. E. 7: v E 1929 (3) 1932 (1); *v E 1931 (3)*

Moir, A. M. 17: v E 1950 (2) 1954 (2) 1958 (2); v SA 1952 (1); v WI 1951 (2) 1955 (1); *v E 1958 (2); v In 1955 (2); v P 1955 (3)*

Moloney D. A. R. 3: *v E 1937 (3)*

Mooney, F. L. H. 14: v E 1950 (2); v SA 1952 (2); v WI 1951 (2); *v E 1949 (3); v SA 1953 (5)*

Morgan, R. W. 20: v E 1965 (2) 1970 (2); v WI 1968 (1); v P 1964 (2); *v E 1965 (3); v WI 1971 (3); v In 1964 (4); v P 1964 (3)*

Morrison, B. D. 1: v E 1962

Morrison, J. F. M. 17: v E 1974 (2); v A 1973 (3) 1981 (3); v In 1975 (3); *v A 1973 (3); v In 1976 (1); v P 1976 (2)*

Motz, R. C. 32: v E 1962 (2) 1965 (3); v SA 1963 (2); v WI 1968 (3); v In 1967 (4); v P 1964 (3); *v E 1965 (3) 1969 (3); v SA 1961 (5); v In 1964 (3); v P 1964 (1)*

Murray, B. A. G. 13: v E 1970 (1); v In 1967 (4); *v E 1969 (2); v In 1969 (3); v P 1969 (3)*

Newman J. 3: v E 1932 (2); v SA 1931 (1)

O'Sullivan, D. R. 11: v In 1975 (1); v P 1972 (1); *v A 1973 (3); v In 1976 (3); v P 1976 (3)*

Overton, G. W. F. 3: *v SA 1953 (3)*

Page, M. L. 14: v E 1929 (4) 1932 (2); v SA 1931 (2); *v E 1931 (3) 1937 (3)*

Parker, J. M. 36: v E 1974 (2) 1977 (3); v A 1973 (3) 1976 (2); v WI 1979 (3); v In 1975 (3); v P 1972 (1) 1978 (2); *v E 1973 (3) 1978 (2); v A 1973 (3) 1980 (3); v In 1976 (3); v P 1976 (3)*

Parker, N. M. 3: *v In 1976 (2); v P 1976 (1)*

Petherick, P. J. 6: v A 1976 (1); *v In 1976 (3); v P 1976 (2)*

Petrie, E. C. 14: v E 1958 (2) 1965 (3); *v E 1958 (5); v In 1955 (2); v P 1955 (2)*

Playle, W. R. 8: v E 1962 (3); *v E 1958 (5)*

Pollard, V. 32: v E 1965 (3) 1970 (1); v WI 1968 (3); v In 1967 (4); v P 1972 (1); *v E 1965 (3) 1969 (3) 1973 (3); v In 1964 (4) 1969 (1); v P 1964 (3) 1969 (3)*

Poore, M. B. 14: v E 1954 (1); v SA 1952 (1); *v SA 1953 (5); v In 1955 (4); v P 1955 (3)*

Puna, N. 3: v E 1965 (3)

Rabone, G. O. 12: v E 1954 (2); v SA 1952 (1); v WI 1951 (2); *v E 1949 (4); v SA 1953 (3)*

Redmond, R. E. 1: v P 1972

Reid, J. F. 4: v In 1980 (3); v P 1978 (1)

Reid, J. R. 58: v E 1950 (2) 1954 (2) 1958 (2) 1962 (3); v SA 1952 (2) 1963 (3); v WI 1951 (2) 1955 (4); v P 1964 (3); *v E 1949 (2) 1958 (5) 1965 (3); v SA 1953 (5) 1961 (5); v In 1955 (5) 1964 (4); v P 1955 (3) 1964 (3)*

Roberts, A. D. G. 7: v In 1975 (2); *v In 1976 (3); v P 1976 (2)*

Roberts, A. W. 5: v E 1929 (1); v SA 1931 (2); *v E 1937 (2)*

Rowe, C. G. 1: v A 1945

Scott, R. H. 1: v E 1946

Scott, V. J. 10: v E 1946 (1) 1950 (2); v A 1945 (1); v WI 1951 (2); *v E 1949 (4)*

Shrimpton, M. J. F. 10: v E 1962 (2) 1965 (3) 1970 (2); v SA 1963 (1); *v A 1973 (2)*

Sinclair, B. W. 21: v E 1962 (3) 1965 (3); v SA 1963 (3); v In 1967 (2); v P 1964 (2); *v E 1965 (3); v In 1964 (2); v P 1964 (3)*

Sinclair, I. M. 2: v WI 1955 (2)

Smith, F. B. 4: v E 1946 (1); v WI 1951 (1); *v E 1949 (2)*

Smith, H. D. 1: v E 1932

Smith, I. D. S. 9: v A 1981 (3); v In 1980 (3); v SL 1982 (2); *v E 1983 (2); v A 1980 (1)*

Snedden, C. A. 1: v E 1946

Snedden, M. C. 9: v A 1981 (3); v In 1980 (3); v SL 1982 (2); *v E 1983 (1)*

Sparling, J. T. 11: v E 1958 (2) 1962 (1); v SA 1963 (2); *v E 1958 (3); v SA 1961 (3)*

Sutcliffe, B. 42: v E 1946 (1) 1950 (2) 1954 (2) 1958 (2); v SA 1952 (2); v WI 1951 (2) 1955 (2); *v E 1949 (4) 1958 (4) 1965 (1); v SA 1953 (5); v In 1955 (5) 1964 (4); v P 1955 (3) 1964 (3)*

Taylor, B. R. 30: v E 1965 (1); v WI 1968 (3); v In 1967 (3); v P 1972 (3); *v E 1965 (2) 1969 (2) 1973 (3); v WI 1971 (4); v In 1964 (3) 1969 (2); v P 1964 (3) 1969 (1)*

Taylor, D. D. 3: v E 1946 (1); v WI 1955 (2)

Thomson, K. 2: v In 1967 (2)

Tindill, E. W. T. 5: v E 1946 (1); v A 1945 (1); *v E 1937 (3)*

Troup, G. B. 12: v A 1981 (2); v WI 1979 (3); v In 1980 (2); v P 1978 (2); *v A 1980 (2); v In 1976 (1)*

Truscott, P. B. 1: v P 1964

Turner, G. M. 41: v E 1970 (2) 1974 (2); v A 1973 (3) 1976 (2); v WI 1968 (3); v In 1975 (3); v P 1972 (3); v SL 1982 (2); *v E 1969 (2) 1973 (3); v A 1973 (2); v WI 1971 (5); v In 1969 (3) 1976 (3); v P 1969 (1) 1976 (2)*

Vivian, G. E. 5: *v WI 1971 (4); v In 1964 (1)*

Vivian, H. G. 7: v E 1932 (1); v SA 1931 (1); *v E 1931 (2) 1937 (3)*

Wadsworth, K. J. 33: v E 1970 (2) 1974 (2); v A 1973 (3); v In 1975 (3); v P 1972 (3); *v E 1969 (3) 1973 (3); v A 1973 (3); v WI 1971 (5); v In 1969 (3); v P 1969 (3)*

Wallace, W. M. 13: v E 1946 (1) 1950 (2); v A 1945 (1); v SA 1952 (2); *v E 1937 (3) 1949 (4)*

Ward, J. T. 8: v SA 1963 (1); v In 1967 (1); v P 1964 (1); *v E 1965 (1); v In 1964 (4)*

Watt, L. 1: v E 1954

Webb, M. G. 3: v E 1970 (1); v A 1973 (1); *v WI 1971 (1)*

Webb, P. N. 2: v WI 1979 (2)

Weir, G. L. 11: v E 1929 (3) 1932 (2); v SA 1931 (2); *v E 1931 (3) 1937 (1)*

Whitelaw, P. E. 2: v E 1932 (2)
Wright, J. G. 25: v E 1977 (3); v A 1981 (3); v WI 1979 (3); v In 1980 (3); v P 1978 (3); v SL 1982 (2); *v E 1978 (2) 1983 (3); v A 1980 (3)*

Yuile, B. W. 17: v E 1962 (2); v WI 1968 (3); v In 1967 (1); v P 1964 (3); *v E 1965 (1); v In 1964 (3) 1969 (1); v P 1964 (1) 1969 (2)*

INDIA

Number of Test cricketers: 164

Adhikari, H. R. 21: v E 1951 (3); v A 1956 (2); v WI 1948 (5) 1958 (1); v P 1952 (2); *v E 1952 (3); v A 1947 (5)*
Ali, S. Abid, 29: v E 1972 (4); v A 1969 (1); v WI 1974 (2); v NZ 1969 (3); *v E 1971 (3) 1974 (3); v A 1967 (4); v WI 1970 (5); v NZ 1967 (4)*
Ali, S. Nazir, 2: v E 1933 (1); *v E 1932 (1)*
Ali, S. Wazir, 7: v E 1933 (3); *v E 1932 (1) 1936 (3)*
Amarnath, L. 24: v E 1933 (3) 1951 (3); v WI 1948 (5); v P 1952 (5); *v E 1946 (3); v A 1947 (5)*
Amarnath, M. 37: v E 1976 (2); v A 1969 (1) 1979 (1); v WI 1978 (2); v NZ 1976 (3); *v E 1979 (2); v A 1977 (5); v WI 1975 (4) 1982 (5); v NZ 1975 (3); v P 1978 (3) 1982 (6)*
Amarnath, S. 10: v E 1976 (2): *v WI 1975 (2); v NZ 1975 (3); v P 1978 (3)*
Amar Singh 7: v E 1933 (3); *v E 1932 (1) 1936 (3)*
Amir Elahi 1: *v A 1947*
Apte, A. L. 1: *v E 1959*
Apte, M. L. 7: v P 1952 (2); *v WI 1952 (5)*
Arun Lal 4: v SL 1982 (1); *v P 1982 (3)*
Azad, K. B. J. 4: v E 1981 (3); *v NZ 1980 (1)*

Baig, A. A. 10: v A 1959 (3); v WI 1966 (2); v P 1960 (3); *v E 1959 (2)*
Banerjee, S. A. 1: v WI 1948
Banerjee, S. N. 1: v WI 1948
Bedi, B. S. 67: v E 1972 (5) 1976 (5); v A 1969 (3); v WI 1966 (2) 1974 (4) 1978 (3); v NZ 1969 (3) 1976 (3); *v E 1967 (3) 1971 (3) 1974 (3) 1979 (3); v A 1967 (2) 1977 (5); v WI 1970 (5) 1975 (4); v NZ 1967 (4) 1975 (2); v P 1978 (3)*
Bhandari, P. 3: v A 1956 (1); v NZ 1955 (1); *v P 1954 (1)*
Binny, R. M. H. 9: v E 1979 (1); v P 1979 (6); *v A 1980 (1); v NZ 1980 (1)*
Borde, C. G. 55: v E 1961 (5) 1963 (5); v A 1959 (5) 1964 (3) 1969 (1); v WI 1958 (4) 1966 (3); v NZ 1964 (4); v P 1960 (5); *v E 1959 (4) 1967 (3); v A 1967 (4); v WI 1961 (5); v NZ 1967 (4)*

Chandrasekhar, B. S. 58: v E 1963 (4) 1972 (5) 1976 (5); v A 1964 (2); v WI 1966 (3) 1974 (4) 1978 (4); v NZ 1964 (2) 1976 (3); *v E 1967 (3) 1971 (3) 1974 (2) 1979 (1); v A 1967 (2) 1977 (5); v WI 1975 (4); v NZ 1975 (3); v P 1978 (3)*
Chauhan, C. P. S. 40: v E 1972 (2); v A 1969 (1) 1979 (6); v WI 1978 (6); v NZ 1969 (2); v P 1979 (6); *v E 1979 (4); v A 1977 (4) 1980 (3); v NZ 1980 (3); v P 1978 (3)*
Chowdhury, N. R. 2: v E 1951 (1); v WI 1948 (1)
Colah, S. H. M. 2: v E 1933 (1); *v E 1932 (1)*
Contractor, N. J. 31: v E 1961 (5); v A 1956 (1) 1959 (5); v WI 1958 (5); v NZ 1955 (4); v P 1960 (5); *v E 1959 (4); v WI 1961 (2)*

Dani, H. T. 1: v P 1952
Desai, R. B. 28: v E 1961 (4) 1963 (2); v A 1959 (3); v WI 1958 (1); v NZ 1964 (3); v P 1960 (5); *v E 1959 (5); v A 1967 (1); v WI 1961 (3); v NZ 1967 (1)*
Dilawar Hussain 3: v E 1933 (2); *v E 1936 (1)*
Divecha, R. V. 5: v E 1951 (2); v P 1952 (1); *v E 1952 (2)*
Doshi, D. R. 32: v E 1979 (1) 1981 (6); v A 1979 (6); v P 1979 (6); v SL 1982 (1); *v E 1982 (3); v A 1980 (3); v NZ 1980 (2); v P 1982 (4)*
Durani, S. A. 29: v E 1961 (5) 1963 (5) 1972 (3); v A 1959 (1) 1964 (3); v WI 1966 (1); v NZ 1964 (3); *v WI 1961 (5) 1970 (3)*

Engineer, F. M. 46: v E 1961 (4) 1972 (5); v A 1969 (5); v WI 1966 (1) 1974 (5); v NZ 1964 (4) 1969 (2); *v E 1967 (3) 1971 (3) 1974 (3); v A 1967 (4); v WI 1961 (3); v NZ 1967 (4)*

Gadkari, C. V. 6: *v WI 1952 (3); v P 1954 (3)*
Gaekwad, A. D. 26: v E 1976 (4); v WI 1974 (3) 1978 (5); v NZ 1976 (3); *v E 1979 (2); v A 1977 (1); v WI 1975 (3) 1982 (5)*
Gaekwad, D. K. 11: v WI 1958 (1); v P 1952 (2) 1960 (1); *v E 1952 (1) 1959 (4); v WI 1952 (2)*
Gaekwad, H. G. 1: v P 1952
Gandotra, A. 2: v A 1969 (1); v NZ 1969 (1)
Gavaskar, S. M. 90: v E 1972 (5) 1976 (5) 1979 (1) 1981 (6); v A 1979 (6); v WI 1974 (2) 1978 (6); v NZ 1976 (3); v P 1979 (6); v SL 1982 (1); *v E 1971 (3) 1974 (3) 1979 (4) 1982 (3); v A 1977 (5) 1980 (3); v WI 1970 (4) 1975 (4) 1982 (5); v NZ 1975 (3) 1980 (3); v P 1978 (3) 1982 (6)*
Ghavri, K. D. 39: v E 1976 (3) 1979 (1); v A 1979 (6); v WI 1974 (3) 1978 (6); v NZ 1976 (2); v P 1979 (6); *v E 1979 (4); v A 1977 (3) 1980 (3); v NZ 1980 (1); v P 1978 (1)*
Ghorpade, J. M. 8: v A 1956 (1); v WI 1958 (1); v NZ 1955 (1); *v E 1959 (3); v WI 1952 (2)*
Ghulam Ahmed 22: v E 1951 (2); v A 1956 (2); v WI 1948 (3) 1958 (2); v NZ 1955 (1); v P 1952 (4); *v E 1952 (4); v P 1954 (4)*
Gopalan, M. J. 1: v E 1933
Gopinath, C. D. 8: v E 1951 (3); v A 1959 (1); v P 1952 (1); *v E 1952 (1); v P 1954 (2)*
Guard, G. M. 2: v A 1959 (1); v WI 1958 (1)
Guha, S. 4: v A 1969 (3); *v E 1967 (1)*
Gul Mahomed 8: v P 1952 (2); *v E 1946 (1); v A 1947 (5)*
Gupte, B. P. 3: v E 1963 (1); v NZ 1964 (1); v P 1960 (1)
Gupte, S. P. 36: v E 1951 (1) 1961 (2); v A 1956 (3); v WI 1958 (5); v NZ 1955 (5); v P 1952 (2) 1960 (3); *v E 1959 (5); v WI 1952 (5); v P 1954 (5)*

Hafeez, A. 3: *v E 1946 (3)*
Hanumant Singh 14: v E 1963 (2); v A 1964 (3); v WI 1966 (2); v NZ 1964 (4) 1969 (1); *v E 1967 (2)*
Hardikar, M. S. 2: v WI 1958 (2)
Hazare, V. S. 30: v E 1951 (5); v WI 1948 (5); v P 1952 (3); *v E 1946 (3) 1952 (4); v A 1947 (5); v WI 1952 (5)*
Hindlekar, D. D. 4: *v E 1936 (1) 1946 (3)*

Ibrahim, K. C. 4: v WI 1948 (4)
Indrajitsinhji, K. S. 4: v A 1964 (3); v NZ 1969 (1)
Irani, J. K. 2: *v A 1947 (2)*

Jai, L. P. 1: v E 1933
Jaisimha, M. L. 39: v E 1961 (5) 1963 (5); v A 1959 (1) 1964 (3); v WI 1966 (2); v NZ 1964 (4) 1969 (1); v P 1960 (4); *v E 1959 (1); v A 1967 (2); v WI 1961 (4) 1970 (3); v NZ 1967 (4)*
Jamshedji, R. J. 1: v E 1933
Jayantilal, K. 1: *v WI 1970*
Jilani, M. Baqa 1: *v E 1936*
Joshi, P. G. 12: v E 1951 (2); v A 1959 (1); v WI 1958 (1); v P 1952 (1) 1960 (1); *v E 1959 (3); v WI 1952 (3)*

Kanitkar, H. S. 2: v WI 1974 (2)
Kapil Dev 53: v E 1979 (1) 1981 (6); v A 1979 (6); v WI 1978 (6); v P 1979 (6); v SL 1982 (1); *v E 1979 (4) 1982 (3); v A 1980 (3); v WI 1982 (5); v NZ 1980 (3); v P 1978 (3) 1982 (6)*
Kardar, A. H. (*see* Hafeez)
Kenny, R. B. 5: v A 1959 (4); v WI 1958 (1)
Khan, M. Jahangir, 4: *v E 1932 (1) 1936 (3)*
Kirmani, S. M. H. 69: v E 1976 (5) 1979 (1) 1981 (6); v A 1979 (6); v WI 1978 (6); v NZ 1976 (3); v P 1979 (6); v SL 1982 (1); *v E 1982 (3); v A 1977 (5) 1980 (3); v WI 1975 (4) 1982 (5); v NZ 1975 (3) 1980 (3); v P 1978 (3) 1982 (6)*
Kischenchand, G. 5: v P 1952 (1); *v A 1947 (4)*

Kripal Singh, A. G. 14: v E 1961 (3) 1963 (2); v A 1956 (2) 1964 (1); v WI 1958 (1); v NZ 1955 (4); *v E 1959 (1)*
Krishnamurthy, P. 5: *v WI 1970 (5)*
Kulkarni, U. N. 4: *v A 1967 (3); v NZ 1967 (1)*
Kumar, V. V. 2: v E 1961 (1); v P 1960 (1)
Kunderan, B. K. 18: v E 1961 (1) 1963 (5); v A 1959 (3); v WI 1966 (2); v NZ 1964 (1); v P 1960 (2); *v E 1967 (2); v WI 1961 (2)*

Lall Singh 1: *v E 1932*

Madan Lal 31: v E 1976 (2) 1981 (6); v WI 1974 (2); v NZ 1976 (1); v SL 1982 (1); *v E 1974 (2) 1982 (3); v A 1977 (2); v WI 1975 (4) 1982 (2); v NZ 1975 (3); v P 1982 (3)*
Maka, E. S. 2: v P 1952 (1); *v WI 1952 (1)*
Malhotra, A. 3: v E 1981 (2); *v E 1982 (1)*
Maninder Singh 8: *v WI 1982 (3); v P 1982 (5)*
Manjrekar, V. L. 55: v E 1951 (2) 1961 (5) 1963 (4); v A 1956 (3) 1964 (3); v WI 1958 (4); v NZ 1955 (5) 1964 (1); v P 1952 (3) 1960 (5); *v E 1952 (4) 1959 (2); v WI 1952 (4) 1961 (5); v P 1954 (5)*
Mankad, A. V. 21: v E 1976 (1); v A 1969 (5); v WI 1974 (1) 1976 (1); v NZ 1969 (2); *v E 1971 (3) 1974 (1); v A 1977 (3); v WI 1970 (3)*
Mankad, V. 44: v E 1951 (5); v A 1956 (3); v WI 1948 (5) 1958 (2); v NZ 1955 (4); v P 1952 (4); *v E 1946 (3) 1952 (3); v A 1947 (5); v WI 1952 (5); v P 1954 (5)*
Mansur Ali Khan (*see* Pataudi)
Mantri, M. K. 4: v E 1951 (1); *v E 1952 (2); v P 1954 (1)*
Meherhomji, K. R. 1: *v E 1936*
Mehra, V. L. 8: v E 1961 (1) 1963 (2); v NZ 1955 (2); *v WI 1961 (3)*
Merchant, V. M. 10: v E 1933 (3) 1951 (1); *v E 1936 (3) 1946 (3)*
Milkha Singh, A. G. 4: v E 1961 (1); v A 1959 (1); v P 1960 (2)
Modi, R. S. 10: v E 1951 (1); v WI 1948 (5); v P 1952 (1); *v E 1946 (3)*
Muddiah, V. M. 2: v A 1959 (1); v P 1960 (1)
Mushtaq Ali 11: v E 1933 (2); 1951 (1); v WI 1948 (3); *v E 1936 (3) 1946 (2)*

Nadkarni, R. G. 41: v E 1961 (1) 1963 (5); v A 1959 (5) 1964 (3); v WI 1958 (1) 1966 (1); v NZ 1955 (1) 1964 (4); v P 1960 (4); *v E 1959 (4); v A 1967 (3); v WI 1961 (5); v NZ 1967 (4)*
Naik, S. S. 3: v WI 1974 (2); *v E 1974 (1)*
Naoomal Jeoomal 3: v E 1933 (2); *v E 1932 (1)*
Narasimha Rao, M. V. 4: v A 1979 (2); v WI 1978 (2)
Navle, J. G. 2: v E 1933 (1); *v E 1932 (1)*
Nayak, S. V. 2: *v E 1982 (2)*
Nayudu, C. K. 7: v E 1933 (3); *v E 1932 (1) 1936 (3)*
Nayudu, C. S. 11: v E 1933 (2) 1951 (1); *v E 1936 (2) 1946 (2); v A 1947 (4)*
Nissar, Mahomed 6: v E 1933 (2); *v E 1932 (1) 1936 (3)*
Nyalchand, K. 1: v P 1952

Pai, A. M. 1: v NZ 1969
Palia, P. E. 2: *v E 1932 (1) 1936 (1)*
Parkar, G. A. 1: *v E 1982*
Parkar, R. D. 2: v E 1972 (2)
Parsana, D. D. 2: v WI 1978 (2)
Patankar, C. T. 1: v NZ 1955
Pataudi sen., Nawab of, 3: *v E 1946 (3)*
Pataudi jun., Nawab of (now Mansur Ali Khan) 46: v E 1961 (3) 1963 (5) 1972 (3); v A 1964 (3) 1969 (5); v WI 1966 (3) 1974 (4); v NZ 1964 (4) 1969 (3); *v E 1967 (3); v A 1967 (3); v WI 1961 (3); v NZ 1967 (4)*
Patel, B. P. 21: v E 1976 (5); v WI 1974 (3); v NZ 1976 (3); *v E 1974 (2); v A 1977 (2); v WI 1975 (3); v NZ 1975 (3)*
Patel, J. M. 7: v A 1956 (2) 1959 (3); v NZ 1955 (1); *v P 1954 (1)*
Patil, S. M. 20: v E 1979 (1) 1981 (4); v P 1979 (2); v SL 1982 (1); *v E 1982 (2); v A 1980 (3); v NZ 1980 (3); v P 1982 (4)*
Patil, S. R. 1: v NZ 1955
Patiala, Yuvraj of, 1: v E 1933
Phadkar, D. G. 31: v E 1951 (4); v A 1956 (1); v WI 1948 (4) 1958 (1); v NZ 1955 (4); v P 1952 (2); *v E 1952 (4); v A 1947 (4); v WI 1952 (4); v P 1954 (3)*

Prasanna, E. A. S. 49: v E 1961 (1) 1972 (3) 1976 (4); v A 1969 (5); v WI 1966 (1) 1974 (5); v NZ 1969 (3); *v E 1967 (3) 1974 (2); v A 1967 (4) 1977 (4); v WI 1961 (1) 1970 (3) 1975 (1); v NZ 1967 (4) 1975 (3); v P 1978 (2)*
Punjabi, P. H. 5: *v P 1954 (5)*

Rai Singh, K. 1: *v A 1947*
Rajinder Pal 1: v E 1963
Rajindernath, V. 1: v P 1952
Ramaswami, C. 2: *v E 1936 (2)*
Ramchand, G. S. 33: v A 1956 (3) 1959 (5); v WI 1958 (3); v NZ 1955 (5); v P 1952 (3); *v E 1952 (4); v WI 1952 (5); v P 1954 (5)*
Ramji, L. 1: v E 1933
Rangachari, C. R. 4: v WI 1948 (2); *v A 1947 (2)*
Rangnekar, K. M. 3: *v A 1947 (3)*
Ranjane, V. B. 7: v E 1961 (3) 1963 (1); v A 1964 (1); v WI 1958 (1); *v WI 1961 (1)*
Reddy, B. 4: *v E 1979 (4)*
Rege, M. R. 1: v WI 1948
Roy, A. 4: v A 1969 (2); v NZ 1969 (2)
Roy, Pankaj 43: v E 1951 (5); v A 1956 (3) 1959 (5); v WI 1958 (5); v NZ 1955 (3); v P 1952 (3) 1960 (1); *v E 1952 (4) 1959 (5); v WI 1952 (4); v P 1954 (5)*
Roy, Pranab 2: v E 1981 (2)

Sandhu, B. S. 7: *v WI 1982 (4); v P 1982 (3)*
Sardesai, D. N. 30: v E 1961 (1) 1963 (5) 1972 (1); v A 1964 (3) 1969 (1); v WI 1966 (2); v NZ 1964 (3); *v E 1967 (1) 1971 (3); v A 1967 (2); v WI 1961 (3) 1970 (5)*
Sarwate, C. T. 9: v E 1951 (1); v WI 1948 (2); *v E 1946 (1); v A 1947 (5)*
Saxena, R. C. 1: *v E 1967*
Sekhar, T. A. 2: *v P 1982 (2)*
Sen, P. 14: v E 1951 (2); v WI 1948 (5); v P 1952 (2); *v E 1952 (2); v A 1947 (3)*
Sengupta, A. K. 1: v WI 1958
Sharma, P. 5: v E 1976 (2); v WI 1974 (2); *v WI 1975 (1)*
Shastri, R. J. 19: v E 1981 (6); *v E 1982 (3); v WI 1982 (5); v NZ 1980 (3); v P 1982 (2)*
Shinde, S. G. 7: v E 1951 (3); v WI 1948 (1); *v E 1946 (1) 1952 (2)*
Shodhan, D. H. 3: v P 1952 (1); *v WI 1952 (2)*
Shukla, R. C. 1: v SL 1982
Sivaramakrishnan, L. 1: *v WI 1982*
Sohoni, S. W. 4: v E 1951 (1); *v E 1946 (2); v A 1947 (1)*
Solkar, E. D. 27: v E 1972 (5) 1976 (1); v A 1969 (4); v WI 1974 (4); v NZ 1969 (1); *v E 1971 (3) 1974 (3); v WI 1970 (5) 1975 (1)*
Sood, M. M. 1: v A 1959
Srikkanth, K. 6: v E 1981 (4); *v P 1982 (2)*
Srinivasan, T. E. 1: *v NZ 1980*
Subramanya, V. 9: v WI 1966 (2); v NZ 1964 (1); *v E 1967 (2); v A 1967 (2); v NZ 1967 (2)*
Sunderram, G. 2: v NZ 1955 (2)
Surendranath, R. 11: v A 1959 (2); v WI 1958 (2); v P 1960 (2); *v E 1959 (5)*
Surti, R. F. 26: v E 1963 (1); v A 1964 (2) 1969 (1); v WI 1966 (2); v NZ 1964 (1) 1969 (2); v P 1960 (2); *v E 1967 (2); v A 1967 (4); v WI 1961 (5); v NZ 1967 (4)*
Swamy, V. N. 1: v NZ 1955

Tamhane, N. S. 21: v A 1956 (3) 1959 (1); v WI 1958 (4); v NZ 1955 (4); v P 1960 (2); *v E 1959 (2); v P 1954 (5)*
Tarapore, K. K. 1: v WI 1948

Umrigar, P. R. 59: v E 1951 (5) 1961 (4); v A 1956 (3) 1959 (3); v WI 1948 (1) 1958 (5); v NZ 1955 (5); v P 1952 (5) 1960 (5); *v E 1952 (4) 1959 (4); v WI 1952 (5) 1961 (5); v P 1954 (5)*

Vengsarkar, D. B. 63: v E 1976 (1) 1979 (1) 1981 (6); v A 1979 (6); v WI 1978 (6); v P 1979 (5); v SL 1982 (1); *v E 1979 (4) 1982 (3); v A 1977 (5) 1980 (3); v WI 1975 (2) 1982 (5); v NZ 1975 (3) 1980 (3); v P 1978 (3) 1982 (6)*

Venkataraghavan, S. 55: v E 1972 (2) 1976 (1); v A 1969 (5) 1979 (3); v WI 1966 (2) 1974 (2) 1978 (6); v NZ 1964 (4) 1969 (2) 1976 (3); *v E 1967 (1) 1971 (3) 1974 (2) 1979 (4); v A 1977 (1); v WI 1970 (5) 1975 (3) 1982 (5); v NZ 1975 (1)*

Viswanath, G. R. 91: v E 1972 (5) 1976 (5) 1979 (1) 1981 (6); v A 1969 (4) 1979 (6); v WI 1974 (5) 1978 (6); v NZ 1976 (3); v SL 1982 (1); v P 1979 (6); *v E 1971 (3) 1974 (3) 1979 (4) 1982 (3); v A 1977 (5) 1980 (3); v WI 1970 (3) 1975 (4); v NZ 1975 (3) 1980 (3); v P 1978 (3) 1982 (6)*

Vizianagram, Maharaj Sir Vijaya 3: *v E 1936 (3)*

Wadekar, A. L. 37: v E 1972 (5); v A 1969 (5); v WI 1966 (2); v NZ 1969 (3); *v E 1967 (3) 1971 (3) 1974 (3); v A 1967 (4); v WI 1970 (5); v NZ 1967 (4)*

Yadav, N. S. 15: v E 1979 (1) 1981 (1); v A 1979 (5); v P 1979 (5); *v A 1980 (2); v NZ 1980 (1)*

Yajurvindra Singh 4: v E 1976 (2); v A 1979 (1); *v E 1979 (1)*

Yashpal Sharma 33: v E 1979 (1) 1981 (2); v A 1979 (6); v P 1979 (6); v SL 1982 (1); *v E 1979 (3) 1982 (3); v A 1980 (3); v WI 1982 (5); v NZ 1980 (1); v P 1982 (2)*

Yograj Singh 1: *v NZ 1980*

Note: Hafeez, on going later to Oxford University, took his correct name, Kardar.

PAKISTAN

Number of Test cricketers: 94

Abdul Kadir 4: v A 1964 (1); *v A 1964 (1); v NZ 1964 (2)*

Abdul Qadir 14: v E 1977 (3); v A 1982 (3); v WI 1980 (2); v In 1982 (5); *v E 1982 (3); v In 1979 (3)*

Afaq Hussain 2: v E 1961 (1); *v A 1964 (1)*

Aftab Baloch 2: v WI 1974 (1); v NZ 1969 (1)

Aftab Gul 6: v E 1968 (2); v NZ 1969 (1); *v E 1971 (3)*

Agha Saadat Ali 1: v NZ 1955

Agha Zahid 1: v WI 1974

Alim-ud-Din 25: v E 1961 (2); v A 1956 (1) 1959 (1); v WI 1958 (1); v NZ 1955 (3); v In 1954 (5); *v E 1954 (3) 1962 (3); v WI 1957 (5); v In 1960 (1)*

Amir Elahi 5: *v In 1952 (5)*

Anwar Hussain 4: *v In 1952 (4)*

Anwar Khan 1: *v NZ 1978*

Arif Butt 3: *v A 1964 (1); v NZ 1964 (2)*

Ashraf Ali 2: v SL 1981 (2)

Asif Iqbal 58: v E 1968 (3) 1972 (3); v A 1964 (1); v WI 1974 (2); v NZ 1964 (3) 1969 (3) 1976 (3); v In 1978 (3); *v E 1967 (3) 1971 (3) 1974 (3); v A 1964 (1) 1972 (3) 1976 (3) 1978 (2); v WI 1976 (5); v NZ 1964 (3) 1972 (3) 1978 (2); v In 1979 (6)*

Asif Masood 16: v E 1968 (2) 1972 (1); v WI 1974 (2); v NZ 1969 (1); *v E 1971 (3) 1974 (3); v A 1972 (3) 1976 (1)*

Azhar Khan 1: v A 1979

Azmat Rana 1: v A 1979

Burki, J. 25: v E 1961 (3); v A 1964 (1); v NZ 1964 (3) 1969 (1); *v E 1962 (5) 1967 (3); v A 1964 (1); v NZ 1964 (3); v In 1960 (5)*

D'Souza, A. 6: v E 1961 (2); v WI 1958 (1); *v E 1962 (3)*

Ehtesham-ud-Din 5: v A 1979 (1); *v E 1982 (1); v In 1979 (3)*

Farooq Hamid 1: *v A 1964*

Farrukh Zaman 1: v NZ 1976

Fazal Mahmood 34: v E 1961 (1); v A 1956 (1) 1959 (2); v WI 1958 (3); v NZ 1955 (2); v In 1954 (4); *v E 1954 (4) 1962 (2); v WI 1957 (5); v In 1952 (5) 1960 (5)*

Ghazali, M. E. Z. 2: *v E 1954 (2)*
Ghulam Abbas 1: *v E 1967*
Gul Mahomed 1: v A 1956

Hanif Mohammad 55: v E 1961 (3) 1968 (3); v A 1956 (1) 1959 (3) 1964 (1); v WI 1958 (1);
    v NZ 1955 (3) 1964 (3) 1969 (1); v In 1954 (5); *v E 1954 (4) 1962 (5) 1967 (3); v A 1964
    (1); v WI 1957 (5); v NZ 1964 (3); v In 1952 (5) 1960 (5)*
Haroon Rashid 23: v E 1977 (3); v A 1979 (2) 1982 (3); v In 1982 (1); v SL 1981 (2); *v E
    1978 (3) 1982 (1); v A 1976 (1) 1978 (1); v WI 1976 (5); v NZ 1978 (1)*
Haseeb Ahsan 12: v E 1961 (2); v A 1959 (1); v WI 1958 (1); *v In 1960 (5)*

Ibadulla, K. 4: v A 1964 (1); *v E 1967 (2); v NZ 1964 (1)*
Ijaz Butt 8: v A 1959 (2); v WI 1958 (3); *v E 1962 (3)*
Ijaz Faqih 2: v WI 1980 (1); *v A 1981 (1)*
Imran Khan 49: v A 1979 (2) 1982 (3); v WI 1980 (4); v NZ 1976 (3); v In 1978 (3) 1982 (6);
    v SL 1981 (1); *v E 1971 (1) 1974 (3) 1982 (3); v A 1976 (3) 1978 (2) 1981 (3); v WI 1976
    (5); v NZ 1978 (2); v In 1979 (5)*
Imtiaz Ahmed 41: v E 1961 (3); v A 1956 (1) 1959 (3); v WI 1958 (3); v NZ 1955 (3);
    v In 1954 (5); *v E 1954 (4) 1962 (4); v WI 1957 (5); v In 1952 (5) 1960 (5)*
Intikhab Alam 47: v E 1961 (2) 1968 (3) 1972 (3); v A 1959 (1) 1964 (1); v WI 1974 (2); v
    NZ 1964 (3) 1969 (3) 1976 (3); *v E 1962 (3) 1967 (3) 1971 (3) 1974 (3); v A 1964 (1)
    1972 (3); v WI 1976 (1); v NZ 1964 (3) 1972 (3); v In 1960 (3)*
Iqbal Qasim 36: v E 1977 (3); v A 1979 (3) 1982 (2); v WI 1980 (4); v In 1978 (3) 1982 (2);
    v SL 1981 (3); *v E 1978 (3); v A 1976 (3) 1981 (2); v WI 1976 (2); v In 1979 (6)*
Israr Ali 4: v A 1959 (2); *v In 1952 (2)*

Jalal-ud-Din 3: v A 1982 (1); v In 1982 (2)
Javed Akhtar 1: *v E 1962*
Javed Miandad 52: v E 1977 (3); v A 1979 (3) 1982 (3); v WI 1980 (4); v NZ 1976 (3); v In
    1978 (3) 1982 (6); v SL 1981 (3); *v E 1978 (3) 1982 (3); v A 1976 (3) 1978 (2) 1981 (3);
    v WI 1976 (1); v NZ 1978 (3); v In 1979 (6)*

Kardar, A. H. 23: v A 1956 (1); v NZ 1955 (3); v In 1954 (5); *v E 1954 (4); v WI 1957 (5);
    v In 1952 (5)*
Khalid Hassan 1: *v E 1954*
Khalid Wazir 2: *v E 1954 (2)*
Khan Mohammad 13: v A 1956 (1); v NZ 1955 (3); v In 1954 (4); *v E 1954 (2); v WI
    1957 (2); v In 1952 (1)*

Liaqat Ali 5: v E 1977 (2); v WI 1974 (1); *v E 1978 (2)*

Mahmood Hussain 27: v E 1961 (1); v WI 1958 (3); v NZ 1955 (1); v In 1954 (5); *v E 1954(2)
    1962 (3); v WI 1957 (3); v In 1952 (4) 1960 (5)*
Majid J. Khan 63: v E 1968 (3) 1972 (3); v A 1964 (1) 1979 (3); v WI 1974 (2) 1980 (4);
    v NZ 1964 (3) 1976 (3); v In 1978 (3) 1982 (1); v SL 1981 (1); *v E 1967 (3) 1971 (2) 1974 (3)
    1982 (1); v A 1972 (3) 1976 (3) 1978 (2) 1981 (3); v WI 1976 (5); v NZ 1972 (3) 1978 (2);
    v In 1979 (6)*
Mansoor Akhtar 13: v A 1982 (3); v WI 1980 (2); v In 1982 (3); v SL 1981 (1); *v E 1982
    (3); v A 1981 (1)*
Maqsood Ahmed 16: v NZ 1955 (2); v In 1954 (5); *v E 1954 (4); v In 1952 (5)*
Mathias, Wallis 21: v E 1961 (1); v A 1956 (1) 1959 (2); v WI 1958 (3); v NZ 1955 (1); *v E
    1962 (3); v WI 1957 (5); v In 1960 (5)*
Miran Bux 2: v In 1954 (2)
Mohammad Aslam 1: *v E 1954*
Mohammad Farooq 7: v NZ 1964 (3); *v E 1962 (2); v In 1960 (2)*
Mohammad Ilyas 10: v A 1968 (2); v NZ 1964 (3); *v E 1967 (1); v A 1964 (1); v NZ 1964 (3)*
Mohammad Munaf 4: v E 1961 (2); v A 1959 (2)
Mohammad Nazir 8: v E 1972 (1); v WI 1980 (4); v NZ 1969 (3)
Mohsin Khan 22: v E 1977 (1); v A 1982 (3); v In 1982 (6); v SL 1981 (2); *v E 1978 (3) 1982
    (3); v A 1978 (1) 1981 (2); v NZ 1978 (1)*

Mudassar Nazar 35: v E 1977 (3); v A 1979 (3) 1982 (3); v In 1978 (2) 1982 (6); v SL 1981 (1); *v E 1978 (3) 1982 (3); v A 1976 (1) 1978 (1) 1981 (3); v NZ 1978 (1); v In 1979 (5)*
Mufasir-ul-Haq 1: *v NZ 1964*
Munir Malik 3: v A 1959 (1); *v E 1962 (2)*
Mushtaq Mohammad 57: v E 1961 (3) 1968 (3) 1972 (3); v WI 1958 (1) 1974 (2); v NZ 1969 (2) 1976 (3); v In 1978 (3); *v E 1962 (5) 1967 (3) 1971 (3) 1974 (3); v A 1972 (3) 1976 (3) 1978 (2); v WI 1976 (5); v NZ 1972 (2) 1978 (3); v In 1960 (5)*

Nasim-ul-Ghani 29: v E 1961 (2); v A 1959 (2) 1964 (1); v WI 1958 (3); *v E 1962 (5) 1967 (2); v A 1964 (1) 1972 (1); v WI 1957 (5); v NZ 1964 (3); v In 1960 (4)*
Naushad Ali 6: v NZ 1964 (3); *v NZ 1964 (3)*
Nazar Mohammad 5: *v In 1952 (5)*
Nazir Junior (*see* Mohammad Nazir)
Niaz Ahmed 2: v E 1968 (1); *v E 1967 (1)*

Pervez Sajjad 19: v E 1968 (1) 1972 (2); v A 1964 (1); v NZ 1964 (3) 1969 (3); *v E 1971 (3); v NZ 1964 (3) 1972 (3)*

Rashid Khan 2: v SL 1981 (2)
Rehman, S. F. 1: *v WI 1957*
Rizwan-uz-Zaman 3: v SL 1981 (2); *v A 1981 (1)*

Sadiq Mohammad 41: v E 1972 (3) 1977 (2); v WI 1974 (1) 1980 (3); v NZ 1969 (3) 1976 (3); v In 1978 (1); *v E 1971 (3) 1974 (3) 1978 (3); v A 1972 (3) 1976 (2); v WI 1976 (5); v NZ 1972 (3); v In 1979 (3)*
Saeed Ahmed 41: v E 1961 (3) 1968 (3); v A 1959 (3) 1964 (1); v WI 1958 (3); v NZ 1964 (3); *v E 1962 (5) 1967 (3) 1971 (1); v A 1964 (1) 1972 (2); v WI 1957 (5); v NZ 1964 (3); v In 1960 (5)*
Salah-ud-Din 5: v E 1968 (1); v NZ 1964 (3) 1969 (1)
Saleem Altaf 21: v E 1972 (3); v NZ 1969 (2); v In 1978 (1); *v E 1967 (2) 1971 (2); v A 1972 (3) 1976 (2); v WI 1976 (3); v NZ 1972 (3)*
Salim Malik 8: v In 1982 (6); v SL 1981 (2)
Salim Yousuf 1: v SL 1981
Sarfraz Nawaz 49: v E 1968 (1) 1972 (2) 1977 (2); v A 1979 (3); v WI 1974 (2) 1980 (2); v NZ 1976 (3); v In 1978 (3) 1982 (6); *v E 1974 (3) 1978 (2) 1982 (1); v A 1972 (2) 1976 (2) 1978 (2) 1981 (3); v WI 1976 (4); v NZ 1972 (3) 1978 (3)*
Shafiq Ahmad 6: v E 1977 (3); v WI 1980 (2); *v E 1974 (1)*
Shafqat Rana 5: v E 1968 (2); v A 1964 (1); v NZ 1969 (2)
Shahid Israr 1: v NZ 1976
Shahid Mahmood 1: *v E 1962*
Sharpe, D. 3: v A 1959 (3)
Shuja-ud-Din 19: v E 1961 (2); v A 1959 (3); v WI 1958 (3); v NZ 1955 (3); v In 1954 (5); *v E 1954 (3)*
Sikander Bakht 26: v E 1977 (2); v WI 1980 (1); v NZ 1976 (1); v In 1978 (2) 1982 (1); *v E 1978 (3) 1982 (2); v A 1978 (2) 1981 (3); v WI 1976 (1); v NZ 1978 (3); v In 1979 (5)*

Tahir Naqqash 10: v A 1982 (3); v In 1982 (2); v SL 1981 (3); *v E 1982 (2)*
Talat Ali 10: v E 1972 (3); *v E 1978 (2); v A 1972 (1); v NZ 1972 (1) 1978 (2)*
Taslim Arif 6: v A 1979 (3); v WI 1980 (2); *v In 1979 (1)*
Tauseef Ahmed 6: v A 1979 (3); v SL 1981 (3)

Waqar Hassan 21: v A 1956 (1) 1959 (1); v WI 1958 (1); v NZ 1955 (3); v In 1954 (5); *v E 1954 (4); v WI 1957 (1); v In 1952 (5)*
Wasim Bari 73: v E 1968 (3) 1972 (3) 1977 (3); v A 1982 (3); v WI 1974 (2) 1980 (2); v NZ 1969 (3) 1976 (2); v In 1978 (3) 1982 (6); *v E 1967 (3) 1971 (3) 1974 (3) 1978 (3) 1982 (3); v A 1972 (3) 1976 (3) 1978 (2) 1981 (3); v WI 1976 (5); v NZ 1972 (3) 1978 (3); v In 1979 (6)*
Wasim Raja 45: v E 1972 (1) 1977 (3); v A 1979 (3); v WI 1974 (2) 1980 (4); v NZ 1976 (1); v In 1982 (1); v SL 1981 (3); *v E 1974 (2) 1978 (3) 1982 (1); v A 1978 (1) 1981 (3); v WI 1976 (5); v NZ 1972 (3) 1978 (3); v In 1979 (6)*
Wazir Mohammad 20: v A 1956 (1) 1959 (1); v WI 1958 (3); v NZ 1955 (3); v In 1954 (5); *v E 1954 (2); v WI 1957 (5); v In 1952 (1)*

Younis Ahmed 2: v NZ 1969 (2)

Zaheer Abbas 58: v E 1972 (2); v A 1979 (2) 1982 (3); v WI 1974 (2) 1980 (3); v NZ 1969 (1) 1976 (3); v In 1978 (3) 1982 (6); v SL 1981 (1); *v E 1971 (3) 1974 (3) 1982 (3); v A 1972 (3) 1976 (3) 1978 (2) 1982 (2); v WI 1976 (3); v NZ 1972 (3) 1978 (2); v In 1979 (5)*
Zulfiqar Ahmed 9: v A 1956 (1); v NZ 1955 (3); *v E 1954 (2); v In 1952 (3)*

SRI LANKA

Number of Test cricketers: 24

de Alwis, R. G. 2: v A 1982 (1); *v NZ 1982 (1)*
de Mel, A. L. F. 6: v E 1981 (1); v A 1982 (1); *v In 1982 (1); v P 1981 (3)*
de Silva, D. S. 8: v E 1981 (1); v A 1982 (1); *v NZ 1982 (2); v In 1982 (1); v P 1981 (3)*
de Silva, G. R. A. 4: v E 1981 (1); *v In 1982 (1); v P 1981 (2)*
Dias, R. L. 6: v E 1981 (1); v A 1982 (1); *v In 1982 (1); v P 1981 (3)*

Fernando, E. R. N. S. 3: v A 1982 (1); *v NZ 1982 (2)*

Goonatillake, H. M. 5: v E 1981 (1); *v In 1982 (1); v P 1981 (3)*
Gunasekera, Y. 2: *v NZ 1982 (2)*
Guneratne, R. P. W. 1: v A 1982

Jayasekera, R. S. A. 1: *v P 1981*
Jeganathan, S. 2: *v NZ 1982 (2)*
John, V. B. 2: *v NZ 1982 (2)*

Kaluperuma, L. W. 2: v E 1981 (1); *v P 1981 (1)*

Madugalle, R. S. 8: v E 1981 (1); v A 1982 (1); *v NZ 1982 (2); v In 1982 (1); v P 1981 (3)*
Mendis, L. R. D. 6: v E 1981 (1); v A 1982 (1); *v In 1982 (1); v P 1981 (3)*

Ranasinghe, A. N. 2: *v In 1982 (1); v P 1981 (1)*
Ranatunga, A. 5: v E 1981 (1); v A 1982 (1); *v In 1982 (1); v P 1981 (2)*
Ratnayake, R. J. 3: v A 1982 (1); *v NZ 1982 (2)*
Ratnayeke, J. R. 5: *v NZ 1982 (2); v In 1982 (1); v P 1981 (2)*

Silva, S. A. R. 1: *v NZ 1982*

Warnapura, B. 4: v E 1981 (1); *v In 1982 (1); v P 1981 (2)*
Wettimuny, M. D. 2: *v NZ 1982 (2)*
Wettimuny, S. 7: v E 1981 (1); v A 1982 (1); *v NZ 1982 (2); v P 1981 (3)*
Wijesuriya, R. G. C. E. 1: *v P 1981*

TWO COUNTRIES

Twelve cricketers have appeared for two countries in Test matches, namely:

Amir Elahi, *India and Pakistan.*
J. J. Ferris, *Australia and England.*
S. C. Guillen, *West Indies and NZ.*
Gul Mahomed, *India and Pakistan.*
F. Hearne, *England and South Africa.*
A. H. Kardar, *India and Pakistan.*

W. E. Midwinter, *England and Australia.*
F. Mitchell, *England and South Africa.*
W. L. Murdoch, *Australia and England.*
Nawab of Pataudi, sen., *England and India.*
A. E. Trott, *Australia and England.*
S. M. J. Woods, *Australia and England.*

MOST TEST APPEARANCES FOR EACH COUNTRY

England: M. C. Cowdrey 114.
Australia: R. W. Marsh 91.
South Africa: J. H. B. Waite 50.
West Indies: G. S. Sobers 93.

New Zealand: B. E. Congdon 61.
India: G. R. Viswanath 91.
Pakistan: Wasim Bari 73.

MOST TEST APPEARANCES AS CAPTAIN
FOR EACH COUNTRY

England: P. B. H. May 41.
Australia: R. B. Simpson 39.
South Africa: H. W. Taylor 18.
West Indies: C. H. Lloyd 54.

New Zealand: J. R. Reid 34.
India: Nawab of Pataudi, jun., 40.
Pakistan: A. H. Kardar 23.

ENGLAND v REST OF THE WORLD

The following were awarded England caps for playing against the Rest of the World in England in 1970, although the five matches played are now generally considered not to have rated as full Tests: D. L. Amiss (1). G. Boycott (2), D. J. Brown (2), M. C. Cowdrey (4), M. H. Denness (1), B. L. D'Oliveira (4), J. H. Edrich (2), K. W. R. Fletcher (4), A. W. Greig (3), R. Illingworth (5), A. Jones (1), A. P. E. Knott (5), P. Lever (1), B. W. Luckhurst (5), C. M. Old (2), P. J. Sharpe (1), K. Shuttleworth (1), J. A. Snow (5), D. L. Underwood (3), A. Ward (1), D. Wilson (2).

CRICKET RECORDS

Amended by BARRY McCAULLY to end of 1983 season in England

Unless stated to be of a minor character, all records apply only to first-class cricket including some performances in the distant past which have always been recognised as of exceptional merit.

*Denotes not out or an unbroken partnership.

(A), (SA), (WI), (NZ), (I), (P) or (SL) indicates either the nationality of the player, or the country in which the record was made.

INDEX

BATTING

BOWLING AND FIELDING

ALL-ROUND CRICKET

THE SIDES

TEST MATCH RECORDS

MISCELLANEOUS

BATTING RECORDS

INDIVIDUAL SCORES OF 300 OR MORE

499	Hanif Mohammad	Karachi v Bahawalpur at Karachi	1958-59
452*	D. G. Bradman	NSW v Queensland at Sydney	1929-30
443*	B. B. Nimbalkar	Maharashtra v Kathiawar at Poona	1948-49
437	W. H. Ponsford	Victoria v Queensland at Melbourne..................	1927-28

429	W. H. Ponsford	Victoria v Tasmania at Melbourne	1922-23
428	Aftab Baloch	Sind v Baluchistan at Karachi	1973-74
424	A. C. MacLaren	Lancashire v Somerset at Taunton	1895
385	B. Sutcliffe	Otago v Canterbury at Christchurch	1952-53
383	C. W. Gregory	NSW v Queensland at Brisbane	1906-07
369	D. G. Bradman	South Australia v Tasmania at Adelaide	1935-36
365*	C. Hill	South Australia v NSW at Adelaide	1900-01
365*	G. S. Sobers	West Indies v Pakistan at Kingston	1957-58
364	L. Hutton	England v Australia at The Oval	1938
359*	V. M. Merchant	Bombay v Maharashtra at Bombay	1943-44
359	R. B. Simpson	NSW v Queensland at Brisbane	1963-64
357*	R. Abel	Surrey v Somerset at The Oval	1899
357	D. G. Bradman	South Australia v Victoria at Melbourne	1935-36
356	B. A. Richards	South Australia v W. Australia at Perth	1970-71
355	B. Sutcliffe	Otago v Auckland at Dunedin	1949-50
352	W. H. Ponsford	Victoria v NSW at Melbourne	1926-27
350	Rashid Israr	Habib Bank v National Bank at Lahore	1976-77
345	C. G. Macartney	Australians v Nottinghamshire at Nottingham	1921
344*	G. A. Headley	Jamaica v Lord Tennyson's XI at Kingston	1931-32
344	W. G. Grace	MCC v Kent at Canterbury	1876
343*	P. A. Perrin	Essex v Derbyshire at Chesterfield	1904
341	G. H. Hirst	Yorkshire v Leicestershire at Leicester	1905
340*	D. G. Bradman	NSW v Victoria at Sydney	1928-29
340	S. M. Gavaskar	Bombay v Bengal at Bombay	1981-82
338*	R. C. Blunt	Otago v Canterbury at Christchurch	1931-32
338	W. W. Read	Surrey v Oxford University at The Oval	1888
337*	Pervez Akhtar	Railways v Dera Ismail Khan at Lahore	1964-65
337†	Hanif Mohammad	Pakistan v West Indies at Bridgetown	1957-58
336*	W. R. Hammond	England v New Zealand at Auckland	1932-33
336	W. H. Ponsford	Victoria v South Australia at Melbourne	1927-28
334	D. G. Bradman	Australia v England at Leeds	1930
333	K. S. Duleepsinhji	Sussex v Northamptonshire at Hove	1930
332	W. H. Ashdown	Kent v Essex at Brentwood	1934
331*	J. D. Robertson	Middlesex v Worcestershire at Worcester	1949
325*	H. S. T. L. Hendry	Victoria v New Zealanders at Melbourne	1925-26
325	C. L. Badcock	South Australia v Victoria at Adelaide	1935-36
325	A. Sandham	England v West Indies at Kingston	1929-30
324	J. B. Stollmeyer	Trinidad v British Guiana at Port-of-Spain	1946-47
324	Waheed Mirza	Karachi Whites v Quetta at Karachi	1976-77
323	A. L. Wadekar	Bombay v Mysore at Bombay	1966-67
322	E. Paynter	Lancashire v Sussex at Hove	1937
321	W. L. Murdoch	NSW v Victoria at Sydney	1881-82
319	Gul Mahomed	Baroda v Holkar at Baroda	1946-47
318*	W. G. Grace	Gloucestershire v Yorkshire at Cheltenham	1876
317	W. R. Hammond	Gloucestershire v Nottinghamshire at Gloucester.	1936
316*	V. S. Hazare	Maharashtra v Baroda at Poona	1939-40
316*	J. B. Hobbs	Surrey v Middlesex at Lord's	1926
316	R. H. Moore	Hampshire v Warwickshire at Bournemouth	1937
315*	T. W. Hayward	Surrey v Lancashire at The Oval	1898
315*	P. Holmes	Yorkshire v Middlesex at Lord's	1925
315*	A. F. Kippax	NSW v Queensland at Sydney	1927-28
314*	C. L. Walcott	Barbados v Trinidad at Port-of-Spain	1945-46
313	H. Sutcliffe	Yorkshire v Essex at Leyton	1932
312*	W. W. Keeton	Nottinghamshire v Middlesex at The Oval	1939
312*	J. M. Brearley	MCC Under 25 v North Zone at Peshawar	1966-67
311*	G. M. Turner	Worcestershire v Warwickshire at Worcester	1982
311	J. T. Brown	Yorkshire v Sussex at Sheffield	1897
311	R. B. Simpson	Australia v England at Manchester	1964
311	Javed Miandad	Karachi Whites v National Bank at Karachi	1974-75
310*	J. H. Edrich	England v New Zealand at Leeds	1965
310	H. Gimblett	Somerset v Sussex at Eastbourne	1948

309	V. S. Hazare	The Rest v Hindus at Bombay	1943-44
308*	F. M. M. Worrell	Barbados v Trinidad at Bridgetown	1943-44
307	M. C. Cowdrey	MCC v South Australia at Adelaide	1962-63
307	R. M. Cowper	Australia v England at Melbourne	1965-66
306*	A. Ducat	Surrey v Oxford University at The Oval	1919
306*	E. A. B. Rowan	Transvaal v Natal at Johannesburg	1939-40
305*	F. E. Woolley	MCC v Tasmania at Hobart	1911-12
305*	F. R. Foster	Warwickshire v Worcestershire at Dudley	1914
305*	W. H. Ashdown	Kent v Derbyshire at Dover	1935
304*	P. H. Tarilton	Barbados v Trinidad at Bridgetown	1919-20
304*	A. W. Nourse	Natal v Transvaal at Johannesburg	1919-20
304*	E. D. Weekes	West Indians v Cambridge University at Cambridge	1950
304	R. M. Poore	Hampshire v Somerset at Taunton	1899
304	D. G. Bradman	Australia v England at Leeds	1934
303*	W. W. Armstrong	Australians v Somerset at Bath	1905
303*	Mushtaq Mohammad	Karachi Blues v Karachi University at Karachi	1967-68
302*	P. Holmes	Yorkshire v Hampshire at Portsmouth	1920
302*	W. R. Hammond	Gloucestershire v Glamorgan at Bristol	1934
302	W. R. Hammond	Gloucestershire v Glamorgan at Newport	1939
302	L. G. Rowe	West Indians v England at Bridgetown	1973-74
301*	E. H. Hendren	Middlesex v Worcestershire at Dudley	1933
301	W. G. Grace	Gloucestershire v Sussex at Bristol	1896
300*	V. T. Trumper	Australians v Sussex at Hove	1899
300*	F. B. Watson	Lancashire v Surrey at Manchester	1928
300*	Imtiaz Ahmed	PM's XI v Commonwealth XI at Bombay	1950-51
300	J. T. Brown	Yorkshire v Derbyshire at Chesterfield	1898
300	D. C. S. Compton	MCC v N. E. Transvaal at Benoni	1948-49
300	R. Subba Row	Northamptonshire v Surrey at The Oval	1958

† *Hanif Mohammad batted for 16 hours 10 minutes – the longest innings in first-class cricket.*

HIGHEST INDIVIDUAL SCORES FOR TEAMS

For English Teams in Australia

307	M. C. Cowdrey	MCC v South Australia at Adelaide	1962-63
287	R. E. Foster	England v Australia at Sydney	1903-04

Against Australians in England

364	L. Hutton	England v Australia at The Oval	1938
219	A. Sandham	Surrey at The Oval (record for any county)	1934

For Australian Teams in England

345	C. G. Macartney	v Nottinghamshire at Nottingham	1921
334	D. G. Bradman	Australia v England at Leeds	1930

Against English Teams in Australia

307	R. M. Cowper	Australia v England at Melbourne	1965-66
280	A. J. Richardson	South Australia v MCC at Adelaide	1922-23

For Each First-Class County

Derbyshire	274	G. Davidson v Lancashire at Manchester	1896
Essex	343*	P. A. Perrin v Derbyshire at Chesterfield	1904
Glamorgan	287*	D. E. Davies v Gloucestershire at Newport	1939
Gloucestershire	318*	W. G. Grace v Yorkshire at Cheltenham	1876
Hampshire	316	R. H. Moore v Warwickshire at Bournemouth	1937
Kent	332	W. H. Ashdown v Essex at Brentwood	1934
Lancashire	424	A. C. MacLaren v Somerset at Taunton	1895
Leicestershire	252*	S. Coe v Northamptonshire at Leicester	1914
Middlesex	331*	J. D. Robertson v Worcestershire at Worcester	1949

Northamptonshire..	300	R. Subba Row v Surrey at The Oval	1958
Nottinghamshire..	312*	W. W. Keeton v Middlesex at The Oval†	1939
Somerset	310	H. Gimblett v Sussex at Eastbourne	1948
Surrey	357*	R. Abel v Somerset at The Oval	1899
Sussex	333	K. S. Duleepsinhji v Northamptonshire at Hove	1930
Warwickshire	305*	F. R. Foster v Worcestershire at Dudley	1914
Worcestershire	311*	G. M. Turner v Warwickshire at Worcester	1982
Yorkshire	341	G. H. Hirst v Leicestershire at Leicester	1905

† *On this date Eton played Harrow at Lord's*

HIGHEST IN A MINOR COUNTY MATCH

| 323* | F. E. Lacey | Hampshire v Norfolk at Southampton | 1887 |

HIGHEST IN MINOR COUNTIES CHAMPIONSHIP

282	E. Garnett	Berkshire v Wiltshire at Reading	1908
254	H. E. Morgan	Glamorgan v Monmouthshire at Cardiff	1901
253*	G. J. Whittaker	Surrey II v Gloucestershire II at The Oval	1950
253	A. Booth	Lancashire II v Lincolnshire at Grimsby	1950
252	J. A. Deed	Kent II v Surrey II at The Oval (on début)	1924

HIGHEST FOR ENGLISH PUBLIC SCHOOL

| 278 | J. L. Guise | Winchester v Eton at Eton | 1921 |

HIGHEST IN OTHER MATCHES

628*	A. E. J. Collins, Clark's House v North Town at Clifton College. (A Junior House match. His innings of 6 hours 50 minutes was spread over four afternoons.)	1899
566	C. J. Eady, Break-o'-Day v Wellington at Hobart	1901-02
515	D. R. Havewalla, B.B. and C.I. Rly v St Xavier's at Bombay	1933-34
506*	J. C. Sharp, Melbourne GS v Geelong College at Melbourne	1914-15
502*	Chaman Lal, Mehandra Coll., Patiala v Government Coll., Rupar at Patiala .	1956-57
485	A. E. Stoddart, Hampstead v Stoics at Hampstead	1886
475*	Mohammad Iqbal, Muslim Model HS v Islamia HS, Sialkot at Lahore	1958-59
466*	G. T. S. Stevens, Beta v Lambda (University College School House match) at Neasden	1919
459	J. A. Prout, Wesley College v Geelong College at Geelong	1908-09

HUNDRED ON DEBUT IN ENGLAND

(The following list does not include instances of players who have previously appeared in first-class cricket outside England or who performed the feat before 1946. Particulars of the latter are in *Wisdens* prior to 1984.)

114	F. W. Stocks	Nottinghamshire v Kent at Nottingham	1946
108	A. Fairbairn	Middlesex v Somerset at Taunton	†‡1947
124	P. Hearn	Kent v Warwickshire at Gillingham	1947
215*	G. H. G. Doggart	Cambridge University v Lancashire at Cambridge	1948
107*	G. Barker	Essex v Canadians at Clacton	†1954
135	J. K. E. Slack	Cambridge University v Middlesex at Cambridge	1954
100*	E. A. Clark	Middlesex v Cambridge University at Cambridge	1959
113	G. J. Chidgey	Free Foresters v Cambridge University at Cambridge	1962

108	D. R. Shepherd	Gloucestershire v Oxford University at Oxford	1965
110*	A. J. Harvey-Walker	Derbyshire v Oxford University at Burton upon Trent	†1971
173	J. Whitehouse	Warwickshire v Oxford University at Oxford	1971
106	J. B. Turner	Minor Counties v Pakistanis at Jesmond	1974
112	J. A. Claughton	Oxford University v Gloucestershire at Oxford	†1976
100*	A. W. Lilley	Essex v Nottinghamshire at Nottingham	1978
146*	J. S. Johnson	Minor Counties v Indians at Wellington	1979
110	N. R. Taylor	Kent v Sri Lankans at Canterbury	1979
146*	D. G. Aslett	Kent v Hampshire at Bournemouth	1981
116	M. D. Moxon	Yorkshire v Essex at Leeds	†1981
100	D. A. Banks	Worcestershire v Oxford University at Oxford	1983
122	A. A. Metcalfe	Yorkshire v Nottinghamshire at Bradford	1983

† *In second innings.*
‡ *A. Fairbairn (Middlesex) in 1947 scored hundreds in the second innings of his first two matches in first-class cricket: 108 as above, 110* Middlesex v Nottinghamshire at Nottingham.*

* * * * *

Notes: A number of players abroad have also made a hundred on a first appearance.

The highest innings on début was hit by W. F. E. Marx when he made 240 for Transvaal against Griqualand West at Johannesburg in 1920-21.

There are three instances of a cricketer making two separate hundreds on début: A. R. Morris, New South Wales, 148 and 111 against Queensland in 1940-41, N. J. Contractor, Gujarat, 152 and 102* against Baroda in 1952-53, and Aamer Malik, Lahore "A", 132* and 110* against Railways in 1979-80.

J. S. Solomon, British Guiana, scored a hundred in each of his first three innings in first-class cricket: 114* v Jamaica; 108 v Barbados in 1956-57; 121 v Pakistanis in 1957-58.

R. Watson-Smith, Border, scored 310 runs before he was dismissed in first-class cricket, including not-out centuries in his first two innings: 183* v Orange Free State and 125* v Griqualand West in 1969-70.

G. R. Viswanath and D. M. Wellham alone have scored 100 on both their début in first-class cricket and in Test cricket. Viswanath scored 230 for Mysore v Andhra in 1967-68 and 137 for India v Australia in 1969-70. Wellham scored 100 for New South Wales v Victoria in 1980-81 and 103 for Australia v England in 1981.

MOST INDIVIDUAL HUNDREDS

(50 or More)

	Hundreds Total	Hundreds Abroad	100th 100		Hundreds Total	Hundreds Abroad	100th 100
J. B. Hobbs	197	22	1923	T. W. Graveney	122	31	1964
E. H. Hendren	170	19	1928	D. G. Bradman	117	41†	1947
W. R. Hammond	167	33	1935	M. C. Cowdrey	107	27	1973
C. P. Mead	153	8	1927	A. Sandham	107	20	1935
H. Sutcliffe	149	14	1932	Zaheer Abbas	105	47	1982-83
F. E. Woolley	145	10	1929	T. W. Hayward	104	4	1913
G. Boycott	139	27	1977	J. H. Edrich	103	13	1977
L. Hutton	129	24	1951	G. M. Turner	103	25	1982
W. G. Grace	126	1	1895	L. E. G. Ames	102	13	1950
D. C. S. Compton	123	31	1952	E. Tyldesley	102	8	1934

† *Scored outside Australia.*

J. W. Hearne 96	A. C. Russell 71	C. A. Milton 56
C. B. Fry 94	D. Denton 69	R. G. Pollock 56
W. J. Edrich 86	I. V. A. Richards 69	C. Hallows 55
G. S. Sobers 86	M. J. K. Smith 69	Hanif Mohammad....... 55
J. T. Tyldesley 86	S. M. Gavaskar 68	W. Watson 55
D. L. Amiss 85	R. E. Marshall 68	C. G. Greenidge 54
P. B. H. May 85	R. N. Harvey 67	D. J. Insole 54
R. E. S. Wyatt........... 85	P. Holmes 67	W. W. Keeton 54
J. Hardstaff, jun. 83	J. D. Robertson 67	W. Bardsley.............. 53
R. B. Kanhai 83	P. A. Perrin 66	A. E. Dipper 53
M. Leyland............... 80	A. I. Kallicharran 65	G. L. Jessop 53
B. A. Richards........... 80	R. T. Simpson 64	K. S. McEwan 53
K. F. Barrington......... 76	G. Gunn 62	James Seymour 53
J. G. Langridge.......... 76	G. H. Hirst 60	E. H. Bowley............. 52
C. Washbrook............ 76	R. B. Simpson 60	D. B. Close 52
H. T. W. Hardinge 75	P. F. Warner 60	A. Ducat................. 52
R. Abel 74	I. M. Chappell 59	E. R. Dexter 51
D. Kenyon 74	K. W. R. Fletcher 59	Javed Miandad........... 51
C. H. Lloyd.............. 74	A. L. Hassett............ 59	J. M. Parks.............. 51
Majid J. Khan........... 73	V. S. Hazare 59	W. W. Whysall........... 51
Mushtaq Mohammad..... 72	A. Shrewsbury 59	G. Cox, jun. 50
J. O'Connor 72	A. E. Fagg 58	H. E. Dollery 50
Wm. Quaife.............. 72	P. H. Parfitt 58	K. S. Duleepsinhji 50
K. S. Ranjitsinhji....... 72	W. Rhodes 58	H. Gimblett.............. 50
D. Brookes 71	L. B. Fishlock 56	W. M. Lawry............. 50
G. S. Chappell 71	A. Jones 56	F. B. Watson 50

TWO SEPARATE HUNDREDS IN A MATCH

Eight times: Zaheer Abbas.
Seven times: W. R. Hammond.
Six times: J. B. Hobbs, G. M. Turner.
Five times: C. B. Fry.
Four times: D. G. Bradman, G. S. Chappell, J. H. Edrich, L. B. Fishlock, T. W. Graveney, H. T. W. Hardinge, E. H. Hendren, G. L. Jessop, P. A. Perrin, B. Sutcliffe, H. Sutcliffe.
Three times: L. E. G. Ames, G. Boycott, I. M. Chappell, D. C. S. Compton, M. C. Cowdrey, D. Denton, K. S. Duleepsinhji, R. E. Foster, R. C. Fredericks, S. M. Gavaskar, W. G. Grace, C. G. Greenidge, G. Gunn, M. R. Hallam, Hanif Mohammad, M. J. Harris, T. W. Hayward, V. S. Hazare, D. W. Hookes, L. Hutton, Javed Miandad, A. Jones, R. B. McCosker, P. B. H. May, C. P. Mead, A. C. Russell, Sadiq Mohammad, J. T. Tyldesley.
Twice: Agha Zahid, D. L. Amiss, B. J. T. Bosanquet, R. J. Boyd-Moss, C. C. R. Dacre, G. M. Emmett, A. E. Fagg, L. E. Favell, H. Gimblett, C. Hallows, R. A. Hamence, A. L. Hassett, G. A. Headley, J. H. King, A. F. Kippax, P. N. Kirsten, J. G. Langridge, H. W. Lee, E. Lester, C. B. Llewellyn, C. G. Macartney, C. A. Milton, A. R. Morris, P. H. Parfitt, Nawab of Pataudi jun., E. Paynter, C. Pinch, R. G. Pollock, R. M. Prideaux, Qasim Omar, W. Rhodes, B. A. Richards, Pankaj Roy, James Seymour, R. B. Simpson, G. S. Sobers, E. Tyldesley, C. L. Walcott, W. W. Whysall.

Notes: W. Lambert scored 107 and 157 for Sussex v Epsom at Lord's in 1817 and it was not until W. G. Grace made 130 and 102* for South of the Thames v North of the Thames at Canterbury in 1868 that the feat was repeated.

T. W. Hayward (Surrey) set up a unique record in 1906 when in one week – six days – he hit four successive hundreds, 144 and 100 v Nottinghamshire at Nottingham and 143 and 125 v Leicestershire at Leicester.

D. W. Hookes (South Australia) scored four successive hundreds in eleven days at Adelaide in 1976-77: 185 and 105 v Queensland (tied match) and 135 and 156 v New South Wales.

A. E. Fagg alone has scored two double-hundreds in the same match: 244 and 202* for Kent v Essex at Colchester, 1938.

L. G. Rowe is alone in scoring hundreds in each innings on his first appearance in Test cricket: 214 and 100* for West Indies v New Zealand at Kingston in 1971-72.

Zaheer Abbas (Gloucestershire) set a unique record in 1976 by twice scoring a double hundred and a hundred in the same match without being dismissed: 216* and 156* v Surrey at The Oval and 230* and 104* v Kent at Canterbury. In 1977 he achieved this feat for a third time, scoring 205* and 108* v Sussex at Cheltenham, and in 1981 for a fourth time, scoring 215* and 150* v Somerset at Bath.

M. R. Hallam (Leicestershire), opening the batting each time, achieved the following treble: 210* and 157 v Glamorgan at Leicester, 1959; 203* and 143* v Sussex at Worthing, 1961; 107* and 149* v Worcestershire at Leicester, 1965. In the last two matches he was on the field the whole time, as was C. J. B. Wood when he scored 107* and 117* for Leicestershire against Yorkshire at Bradford, 1911.

W. L. Foster, 140 and 172*, and R. E. Foster, 134 and 101*, for Worcestershire v Hampshire at Worcester in July 1899, were the first brothers each to score two separate hundreds in the same first-class match.

The brothers I. M. Chappell, 145 and 121, and G. S. Chappell, 247* and 133, for Australia v New Zealand at Wellington in 1973-74, became the first players on the same side each to score a hundred in each innings of a Test match.

G. Gunn, 183, and G. V. Gunn, 100*, for Nottinghamshire v Warwickshire at Birmingham in 1931, provide the only instance of father and son each hitting a century in the same innings of a first-class match.

BATSMEN WHO HAVE SCORED 25,000 RUNS

	Career	R	I	NO	HI	100s	Avge
J. B. Hobbs	1905-34	61,237	1,315	106	316*	197	50.65
F. E. Woolley...........	1906-38	58,969	1,532	85	305*	145	40.75
E. H. Hendren	1907-38	57,611	1,300	166	301*	170	50.80
C. P. Mead	1905-36	55,061	1,340	185	280*	153	47.67
†W. G. Grace	1865-1908	54,896	1,493	105	344	126	39.55
W. R. Hammond	1920-51	50,551	1,005	104	336*	167	56.10
H. Sutcliffe	1919-45	50,138	1,088	123	313	149	51.95
T. W. Graveney........	1948-72	47,793	1,223	159	258	122	44.91
G. Boycott...............	1962-83	44,210	925	139	261*	139	56.24
T. W. Hayward	1893-1914	43,551	1,138	96	315*	104	41.79
M. C. Cowdrey.........	1950-76	42,719	1,130	134	307	107	42.89
A. Sandham.............	1911-38	41,284	1,000	79	325	107	44.82
L. Hutton	1934-60	40,140	814	91	364	129	55.51
M. J. K. Smith	1951-75	39,832	1,091	139	204	69	41.84
W. Rhodes...............	1898-1930	39,802	1,528	237	267*	58	30.83
J. H. Edrich	1956-78	39,790	979	104	310*	103	45.47
R. E. S. Wyatt	1923-57	39,405	1,141	157	232	85	40.04
D. C. S. Compton	1936-64	38,942	839	88	300	123	51.85
E. Tyldesley............	1909-36	38,874	961	106	256*	102	45.46
J. T. Tyldesley........	1895-1923	37,897	994	62	295*	86	40.60
J. W. Hearne	1909-36	37,252	1,025	116	285*	96	40.98
L. E. G. Ames	1926-51	37,248	951	95	295	102	43.51
D. Kenyon...............	1946-67	37,002	1,159	59	259	74	33.63
W. J. Edrich	1934-58	36,965	964	92	267*	86	42.39
D. L. Amiss	1960-83	36,879	954	102	262*	85	43.28
J. M. Parks..............	1949-76	36,673	1,227	172	205*	51	34.76
D. Denton	1894-1920	36,479	1,163	70	221	69	33.37
G. H. Hirst...............	1891-1929	36,323	1,215	151	341	60	34.13
A. Jones.................	1957-83	36,049	1,168	72	204*	56	32.89
Wm. Quaife.............	1894-1928	36,012	1,203	186	255*	72	35.38
R. E. Marshall..........	1945-72	35,725	1,053	59	228*	68	35.94

	Career	R	I	NO	HI	100s	Avge
G. Gunn..................	1902-32	35,208	1,061	82	220	62	35.96
D. B. Close..............	1949-83	34,911	1,220	170	198	52	33.24
J. G. Langridge	1928-55	34,380	984	66	250*	76	37.45
G. M Turner	1964-83	34,346	792	101	311*	103	49.70
C. Washbrook	1933-64	34,101	906	107	251*	76	42.67
K. W. R. Fletcher	1962-83	33,957	1,025	146	228*	59	38.63
M. Leyland	1920-48	33,659	932	101	263	80	40.50
H. T. W. Hardinge....	1902-33	33,519	1,021	103	263*	75	36.51
R. Abel..................	1881-1904	33,124	1,007	73	357*	74	35.46
Zaheer Abbas...........	1965-83	32,307	682	80	274	105	53.66
C. A. Milton	1948-74	32,150	1,078	125	170	56	33.73
J. D. Robertson.......	1937-59	31,914	897	46	331*	67	37.50
J. Hardstaff, jun.	1930-55	31,847	812	94	266	83	44.35
James Langridge.......	1924-53	31,716	1,058	157	167	42	35.20
K. F. Barrington	1953-68	31,714	831	136	256	76	45.63
Mushtaq Mohammad .	1957-83	31,044	840	104	303*	72	42.17
C. B. Fry	1892-1921	30,886	658	43	258*	94	50.22
D. Brookes	1934-59	30,874	925	70	257	71	36.10
P. Holmes	1913-35	30,574	810	84	315*	67	42.11
R. T. Simpson	1944-63	30,546	852	55	259	64	38.32
L. G. Berry	1924-51	30,225	1,056	57	232	45	30.25
K. G. Suttle	1949-71	30,225	1,064	92	204*	49	31.09
P. A. Perrin	1896-1928	29,709	918	91	343*	66	35.92
P. F. Warner	1894-1929	29,028	875	75	244	60	36.28
J. O'Connor	1921-39	28,875	906	80	248	72	34.95
T. E. Bailey	1945-67	28,642	1,072	215	205	28	33.42
R. B. Kanhai...........	1955-77	28,639	663	82	256	83	49.29
E. H. Bowley	1912-34	28,378	859	47	283	52	34.94
B. A. Richards	1964-83	28,358	576	58	356	80	54.74
G. S. Sobers............	1953-74	28,315	609	93	365*	86	54.87
C. H. Lloyd	1963-83	28,660	674	87	242*	74	48.82
A. E. Dipper	1908-32	28,075	865	69	252*	53	35.27
D. G. Bradman	1927-49	28,067	338	43	452*	117	95.14
P. B. H. May	1948-63	27,592	618	77	285*	85	51.00
A. C. Russell	1908-30	27,545	719	59	273	71	41.73
Majid J. Khan	1961-83	27,328	697	60	241	73	42.90
E. G. Hayes	1896-1926	27,318	896	48	276	48	32.21
A. E. Fagg..............	1932-57	27,291	803	46	269*	58	36.05
J. H. Hampshire	1961-83	27,267	892	108	183*	42	34.77
James Seymour.........	1900-26	27,238	911	62	218*	53	32.08
P. H. Parfitt............	1956-74	26,924	845	104	200*	58	36.33
G. L. Jessop...........	1894-1914	26,698	855	37	286	53	32.63
D. E. Davies	1924-54	26,566	1,033	79	287*	32	27.84
M. J. Stewart	1954-72	26,492	898	93	227*	49	32.90
A. Shrewsbury..........	1875-1902	26,439	811	90	267	59	36.66
P. E. Richardson.......	1949-65	26,055	794	41	185	44	34.60
M. H. Denness	1959-80	25,886	838	65	195	33	33.48
H. Makepeace..........	1906-30	25,799	778	66	203	43	36.23
W. Gunn...............	1880-1904	25,791	850	72	273	48	33.15
W. Watson..............	1939-64	25,670	753	109	257	55	39.86
G. Brown	1908-33	25,649	1,012	52	232*	37	26.71
G. M. Emmett...........	1936-59	25,602	865	50	188	37	31.41
J. B. Bolus..............	1956-75	25,598	833	81	202*	39	34.03
W. E. Russell...........	1956-72	25,525	796	64	193	41	34.87
C. J. Barnett...........	1927-54	25,389	821	45	259	48	32.71
L. B. Fishlock..........	1931-52	25,376	699	54	253	56	39.34
A. I. Kallicharran......	1966-83	25,240	624	66	243*	65	45.23
D. J. Insole............	1947-63	25,237	743	72	219*	54	37.61
J. M. Brearley	1961-83	25,185	768	102	312*	45	37.81
J. Vine....................	1896-1922	25,171	920	79	202	34	29.92

	Career	R	I	NO	HI	100s	Avge
R. M. Prideaux.........	1958-75	25,136	808	75	202*	41	34.29
J. H. King	1895-1926	25,122	988	69	227*	34	27.34

†*In recent years some statisticians have removed from W. G. Grace's record a number of matches which they consider not to have been first-class. The above figures are those which became universally accepted upon appearance in W. G. Grace's obituary in the* Wisden *of 1916. Some works of reference give his career record as being '54,211–1,478–104–344–124–39.45. These figures also appeared in the 1981 edition of* Wisden.

Note: K. S. Ranjitsinhji (1893-1920) had career figures of 24,692–500–62–285*–72–56.37.

1,000 RUNS IN A SEASON

(Includes Overseas Tours and Seasons)

28 times: W. G. Grace 2,000 (6); F. E. Woolley 3,000 (1), 2,000 (12).

27 times: M. C. Cowdrey 2,000 (2); C. P. Mead 3,000 (2), 2,000 (9).

26 times: J. B. Hobbs 3,000 (1), 2,000 (16).

25 times: E. H. Hendren 3,000 (3), 2,000 (12).

24 times: G. Boycott 2,000 (3); Wm. Quaife 2,000 (1); H. Sutcliffe 3,000 (3), 2,000 (12).

23 times: A. Jones.

22 times: T. W. Graveney 2,000 (7); W. R. Hammond 3,000 (3), 2,000 (9).

21 times: D. Denton 2,000 (5); J. H. Edrich 2,000 (6); W. Rhodes 2,000 (2).

20 times: D. L. Amiss 2,000 (2); D. B. Close; G. Gunn; T. W. Hayward 3,000 (2), 2,000 (8); James Langridge 2,000 (1); J. M. Parks 2,000 (3); A. Sandham 2,000 (8); M. J. K. Smith 3,000 (1), 2,000 (5); C. Washbrook 2,000 (2).

19 times: K. W. R. Fletcher; J. W. Hearne 2,000 (4); G. H. Hirst 2,000 (3); D. Kenyon 2,000 (7); E. Tyldesley 3,000 (1), 2,000 (5); J. T. Tyldesley 3,000 (1), 2,000 (4).

18 times: L. G. Berry 2,000 (1); H. T. W. Hardinge 2,000 (5); R. E. Marshall 2,000 (6); P. A. Perrin; G. M. Turner 2,000 (3); R. E. S. Wyatt 2,000 (5).

17 times: L. E. G. Ames 3,000 (1), 2,000 (5); T. E. Bailey 2,000 (1); D. Brookes 2,000 (6); D. C. S. Compton 3,000 (1), 2,000 (5); L. Hutton 3,000 (1), 2,000 (8); J. G. Langridge 2,000 (11); M. Leyland 2,000 (3); K. G. Suttle 2,000 (1), Zaheer Abbas 2,000 (2).

16 times: D. G. Bradman 2,000 (4); D. E. Davies 2,000 (1); E. G. Hayes 2,000 (2); C. A. Milton 2,000 (1); J. O'Connor 2,000 (4); James Seymour 2,000 (1).

15 times: G. Barker; K. F. Barrington 2,000 (3); E. H. Bowley 2,000 (4); M. H. Denness; A. E. Dipper 2,000 (5); H. E. Dollery 2,000 (2); W. J. Edrich 3,000 (1), 2,000 (8); J. H. Hampshire; P. Holmes 2,000 (7); Mushtaq Mohammad; R. B. Nicholls 2,000 (1); P. H. Parfitt 2,000 (3); W. G. A. Parkhouse 2,000 (1); B. A. Richards 2,000 (1); J. D. Robertson 2,000 (9); G. S. Sobers; M. J. Stewart 2,000 (1).

Notes: F. E. Woolley reached 1,000 runs in 28 consecutive seasons (1907-1938). C. P. Mead did so 27 seasons in succession (1906-1936).

Outside England, 1,000 runs in a season has been reached most times by D. G. Bradman (in 12 seasons in Australia).

Three batsmen have scored 1,000 runs in a season in each of four different countries: G. S. Sobers in West Indies, England, India and Australia; M. C. Cowdrey and G. Boycott in England, South Africa, West Indies and Australia.

FOUR HUNDREDS OR MORE IN SUCCESSION

Six in succession: C. B. Fry 1901; D. G. Bradman 1938-39; M. J. Procter 1970-71.
Five in succession: E. D. Weekes 1955-56.

Four in succession: D. G. Bradman 1931-32, 1948-49; D. C. S. Compton 1946-47; N. J. Contractor 1957-58; K. S. Duleepsinhji 1931; C. B. Fry 1911; W. R. Hammond 1936-37, 1945-46; H. T. W. Hardinge 1913; T. W. Hayward 1906; J. B. Hobbs 1920, 1925; D. W. Hookes 1976-77; P. N. Kirsten 1976-77; J. G. Langridge 1949; C. G. Macartney 1921; K. S. McEwan 1977; P. B. H. May 1956-57; V. M. Merchant 1941-42; A. Mitchell 1933; Nawab of Pataudi sen. 1931; L. G. Rowe 1971-72; P. Roy 1962-63; Sadiq Mohammad 1976; Saeed Ahmed 1961-62; H. Sutcliffe 1931, 1939; E. Tyldesley 1926; W. W. Whysall 1930; F. E. Woolley 1929; Zaheer Abbas 1970-71, 1982-83.

MOST HUNDREDS IN A SEASON

Eighteen: D. C. S. Compton in 1947. These included six hundreds against the South Africans in which matches his average was 84.78. His aggregate for the season was 3,816, also a record.

Sixteen: J. B. Hobbs in 1925, when aged 42, played 16 three-figure innings in first-class matches. It was during this season that he exceeded the number of hundreds obtained in first-class cricket by W. G. Grace.

Fifteen: W. R. Hammond in 1938.

Fourteen: H. Sutcliffe in 1932.

Thirteen: G. Boycott in 1971, D. G. Bradman in 1938, C. B. Fry in 1901, W. R. Hammond in 1933 and 1937, T. W. Hayward in 1906, E. H. Hendren in 1923, 1927 and 1928, C. P. Mead in 1928, and H. Sutcliffe in 1928 and 1931.

FAST FIFTIES

Minutes

8† C. C. Inman (57)	Leicestershire v Nottinghamshire at Nottingham.....	1965
11 C. I. J. Smith (66)	Middlesex v Gloucestershire at Bristol..................	1938
14 S. J. Pegler (50)	South Africans v Tasmania at Launceston.............	1910-11
14 F. T. Mann (53)	Middlesex v Nottinghamshire at Lord's................	1921
14 H. B. Cameron (56)	Transvaal v Orange Free State at Johannesburg	1934-35
14 C. I. J. Smith (52)	Middlesex v Kent at Maidstone...........................	1935

† *Full tosses were bowled to expedite a declaration.*

FAST HUNDREDS

Minutes

35 P. G. H. Fender (113*)	Surrey v Northamptonshire at Northampton	1920
35† S. J. O'Shaughnessy (105)	Lancashire v Leicestershire at Manchester............	1983
37 C. M. Old (107)	Yorkshire v Warwickshire at Birmingham.............	1977
40 G. L. Jessop (101)	Gloucestershire v Yorkshire at Harrogate	1897
41 N. F. M. Popplewell (143)	Somerset v Gloucestershire at Bath	1983
42 G. L. Jessop (191)	Gentlemen of South v Players of South at Hastings	1907
43 A. H. Hornby (106)	Lancashire v Somerset at Manchester...................	1905
43 D. W. Hookes (107)	South Australia v Victoria at Adelaide	1982-83
44 R. N. S. Hobbs (100)	Essex v Australians at Chelmsford......................	1975

Note: The fastest known hundred in terms of balls received is off 34 balls by D. W. Hookes (above). P. G. H. Fender is calculated to have made his hundred off not fewer than 40 balls and not more than 46.

† *Scored on the last day of the season against a deliberate succession of long hops and full tosses bowled by D. I. Gower and J. J. Whitaker in the hope they might expedite a declaration.*

FAST DOUBLE-HUNDREDS

Minutes

120	G. L. Jessop (286)	Gloucestershire v Sussex at Hove	1903
120	C. H. Lloyd (201*)	West Indians v Glamorgan at Swansea	1976
130	G. L. Jessop (234)	Gloucestershire v Somerset at Bristol	1905
131	V. T. Trumper (293)	Australians v Canterbury at Christchurch	1913-14

FAST TRIPLE-HUNDREDS

Minutes

181	D. C. S. Compton (300)	MCC v N. E. Transvaal at Benoni	1948-49
205	F. E. Woolley (305*)	MCC v Tasmania at Hobart	1911-12
205	C. G. Macartney (345)	Australians v Nottinghamshire at Nottingham	1921
213	D. G. Bradman (369)	South Australia v Tasmania at Adelaide	1935-36

FAST SCORING

P. G. H. Fender, for Surrey v Northamptonshire at Northampton in 1920, scored 113* out of 171 in forty-two minutes. He reached 50 in nineteen minutes and 100 in thirty-five minutes. Fender and H. A. Peach added 171 (unfinished) in forty-two minutes for the sixth wicket.

E. B. Alletson, for Nottinghamshire v Sussex at Hove in 1911, scored 189 out of 227 runs obtained while at the wicket in ninety minutes. He went from 50 to 189 in thirty minutes.

For Auckland v Otago at Dunedin in 1936-37, P. E. Whitelaw and W. N. Carson added 445 runs for the third wicket in 268 minutes – a world record.

H. Sutcliffe (194) and M. Leyland (45) hit 102 off six consecutive overs for Yorkshire v Essex at Scarborough, 1932.

RECORD HIT

The Rev. W. Fellows, while at practice on the Christ Church ground at Oxford in 1856, drove a ball bowled by Charles Rogers 175 yards from hit to pitch.

MOST PERSONAL SIXES IN AN INNINGS

15	J. R. Reid (296)	Wellington v N. Districts at Wellington	1962-63
13	Majid J. Khan (147*)	Pakistanis v Glamorgan at Swansea	1967
13	C. G. Greenidge (273*)	D. H. Robins' XI v Pakistanis at Eastbourne	1974
13	C. G. Greenidge (259)	Hampshire v Sussex at Southampton	1975
13	G. W. Humpage (254)	Warwickshire v Lancashire at Southport	1982
12	Gulfraz Khan (207)	Railways v Universities at Lahore	1976-77
11	C. K. Nayudu (153)	Hindus v MCC at Bombay	1926-27
11	C. J. Barnett (194)	Gloucestershire v Somerset at Bath	1934
11	R. Benaud (135)	Australians v T. N. Pearce's XI at Scarborough	1953

Note: W. J. Stewart (Warwickshire) hit seventeen 6s in the match v Lancashire, at Blackpool, 1959; ten in his first innings of 155 and seven in his second innings of 125.

MOST PERSONAL BOUNDARIES IN AN INNINGS

68	P. A. Perrin (343*)	Essex v Derbyshire at Chesterfield	1904
65	A. C. MacLaren (424)	Lancashire v Somerset at Taunton	1895
64	Hanif Mohammad (499)	Karachi v Bahawalpur at Karachi	1958-59
57	J. H. Edrich (310*)	England v New Zealand at Leeds	1965
55	C. W. Gregory (383)	NSW v Queensland at Brisbane	1906-07
54	G. H. Hirst (341)	Yorkshire v Leicestershire at Leicester	1905
53	A. W. Nourse (304*)	Natal v Transvaal at Johannesburg	1919-20
51	W. G. Grace (344)	MCC v Kent at Canterbury	1876
51	C. G. Macartney (345)	Australians v Nottinghamshire at Nottingham	1921
50	D. G. Bradman (369)	South Australia v Tasmania at Adelaide	1935-36
50	A. Ducat (306*)	Surrey v Oxford University at The Oval	1919
50	B. B. Nimbalkar (443*)	Maharashtra v Kathiawar at Poona	1948-49
50	J. R. Reid (296)	Wellington v N. Districts at Wellington	1962-63

Note: Boundaries include sixes.

MOST RUNS SCORED OFF ONE OVER

(All instances refer to six-ball overs)

36	G. S. Sobers	off M. A. Nash, Nottinghamshire v Glamorgan at Swansea (six 6s)	1968
34	F. C. Hayes	off M. A. Nash, Lancashire v Glamorgan at Swansea (646666)	1977
34	E. B. Alletson	off E. H. Killick, Nottinghamshire v Sussex at Hove (46604446; including two no-balls)	1911
32	C. C. Inman	off N. W. Hill, Leicestershire v Nottinghamshire at Nottingham (466664; full tosses were provided for him to hit)	1965
32	C. C. Smart	off G. Hill, Glamorgan v Hampshire at Cardiff (664664)	1935
32	I. R. Redpath	off N. Rosendorff, Australians v Orange Free State at Bloemfontein (666644)	1969-70
32	P. W. G. Parker	off A. I. Kallicharran, Sussex v Warwickshire at Birmingham (466664)	1982
31	A. W. Wellard	off F. E. Woolley, Somerset v Kent at Wells (666661)	1938
31	M. H. Bowditch (1) and M. J. Procter (30)	off A. A. Mallett, Western Province v Australians at Cape Town (Procter hit five 6s)	1969-70
30	I. T. Botham	off P. A. Smith, Somerset v Warwickshire at Taunton (4466460 including one no-ball)	1982
30	D. G. Bradman	off A. P. Freeman, Australians v England XI at Folkestone (466464)	1934
30	H. B. Cameron	off H. Verity, South Africans v Yorkshire at Sheffield (444666)	1935
30	D. T. Lindsay	off W. T. Greensmith, South African Fezela XI v Essex at Chelmsford (066666 to win the match)	1961
30	A. J. Lamb	off A. I. Kallicharran, Northamptonshire v Warwickshire at Birmingham (644664)	1982
30	Majid J. Khan	off R. C. Davis, Pakistanis v Glamorgan at Swansea (606666)	1967
30	A. W. Wellard	off T. R. Armstrong, Somerset v Derbyshire at Wells (066666)	1936

30	D. Wilson	off R. N. S. Hobbs, Yorkshire v MCC at Scarborough (466266)	1966
30	P. L. Winslow	off J. T. Ikin, South Africans v Lancashire at Manchester (446646)	1955
30	Zaheer Abbas	off D. Breakwell, Gloucestershire v Somerset at Taunton (466626)	1979

Note: The greatest number of runs scored off an eight-ball over is 34 (40446664) by R. M. Edwards off M. C. Carew, Governor-General's XI v West Indians at Auckland, 1968-69.

300 RUNS IN ONE DAY

345	C. G. Macartney	Australians v Nottinghamshire at Nottingham	1921
334	W. H. Ponsford	Victoria v New South Wales at Melbourne	1926-27
333	K. S. Duleepsinhji	Sussex v Northamptonshire at Hove	1930
331*	J. D. Robertson	Middlesex v Worcestershire at Worcester	1949
325*	B. A. Richards	S. Australia v W. Australia at Perth	1970-71
322†	E. Paynter	Lancashire v Sussex at Hove	1937
318	C. W. Gregory	New South Wales v Queensland at Brisbane	1906-07
316†	R. H. Moore	Hampshire v Warwickshire at Bournemouth	1937
315*	R. C. Blunt	Otago v Canterbury at Christchurch	1931-32
312*	J. M. Brearley	MCC Under 25 v North Zone at Peshawar	1966-67
311*	G. M. Turner	Worcestershire v Warwickshire at Worcester	1982
309*	D. G. Bradman	Australia v England at Leeds	1930
307*	W. H. Ashdown	Kent v Essex at Brentwood	1934
306*	A. Ducat	Surrey v Oxford University at The Oval	1919
305*	F. R. Foster	Warwickshire v Worcestershire at Dudley	1914

† *E. Paynter's 322 and R. H. Moore's 316 were scored on the same day: July 28, 1937.*

HIGHEST PARTNERSHIPS

577	V. S. Hazare (288) and Gul Mahomed (319), fourth wicket, Baroda v Holkar at Baroda	1946-47
574*	F. M. M. Worrell (255*) and C. L. Walcott (314*), fourth wicket, Barbados v Trinidad at Port-of-Spain	1945-46
561	Waheed Mirza (324) and Mansoor Akhtar (224*), first wicket, Karachi Whites v Quetta at Karachi	1976-77
555	P. Holmes (224*) and H. Sutcliffe (313), first wicket, Yorkshire v Essex at Leyton	1932
554	J. T. Brown (300) and J. Tunnicliffe (243), first wicket, Yorkshire v Derbyshire at Chesterfield	1898
502*	F. M. M. Worrell (308*) and J. D. C. Goddard (218*), fourth wicket, Barbados v Trinidad at Bridgetown	1943-44
490	E. H. Bowley (283) and J. G. Langridge (195), first wicket, Sussex v Middlesex at Hove	1933
487*	G. A. Headley (344*) and C. C. Passailaigue (261*), sixth wicket, Jamaica v Lord Tennyson's XI at Kingston	1931-32
470	A. I. Kallicharran (230*) and G. W. Humpage (254), fourth wicket, Warwickshire v Lancashire at Southport	1982
465*	J. A. Jameson (240*) and R. B. Kanhai (213*), second wicket, Warwickshire v Gloucestershire at Birmingham	1974
456	W. H. Ponsford (248) and E. R. Mayne (209), first wicket, Victoria v Queensland at Melbourne	1923-24
456	Khalid Irtiza (290) and Aslam Ali (236), third wicket, United Bank v Multan at Karachi	1975-76
455	B. B. Nimbalkar (443*) and K. V. Bhandarkar (205), second wicket, Maharashtra v Kathiawar at Poona	1948-49
451	D. G. Bradman (244) and W. H. Ponsford (266), second wicket, Australia v England, Fifth Test, at The Oval	1934
451*	S. Desai (218*) and R. M. H. Binny (211*), first wicket, Karnataka v Kerala at Chikmagalur	1977-78
451	Mudassar Nazar (231) and Javed Miandad (280*), third wicket, Pakistan v India at Hyderabad	1982-83

PARTNERSHIPS FOR FIRST WICKET

561	Waheed Mirza and Mansoor Akhtar, Karachi Whites v Quetta at Karachi..	1976-77
555	P. Holmes and H. Sutcliffe, Yorkshire v Essex at Leyton	1932
554	J. T. Brown and J. Tunnicliffe, Yorkshire v Derbyshire at Chesterfield	1898
490	E. H. Bowley and J. G. Langridge, Sussex v Middlesex at Hove	1933
456	E. R. Mayne and W. H. Ponsford, Victoria v Queensland at Melbourne....	1923-24
451*	S. Desai and R. M. H. Binney, Karnataka v Kerala at Chikmagalur	1977-78
428	J. B Hobbs and A. Sandham, Surrey v Oxford University at The Oval	1926
424	J. F. W. Nicholson and I. J. Siedle, Natal v Orange Free State at Bloemfontein	1926-27
421	S. M. Gavaskar and G. A. Parkar, Bombay v Bengal at Bombay	1981-82
418	Kamal Najamuddin and Khalid Alvi, Karachi v Railways at Karachi	1980-81
413	V. Mankad and P. Roy, India v New Zealand at Madras (world Test record)	1955-56
405	C. P. S. Chauhan and M. S. Gupte, Maharashtra v Vidarbha at Poona	1972-73
395	D. M. Young and R. B. Nicholls, Gloucestershire v Oxford University at Oxford	1962
391	A. O. Jones and A. Shrewsbury, Nottinghamshire v Gloucestershire at Bristol.	1899
390	G. L. Wight and G. L. R. Gibbs, B. Guiana v Barbados at Georgetown....	1951-52
390	B. Dudleston and J. F. Steele, Leicestershire v Derbyshire at Leicester	1979
389	Majid J. Khan and Shafiq Ahmed, Punjab A v Sind A at Karachi	1974-75
389	Mudassar Nazar and Mansoor Akhtar, United Bank v Rawalpindi at Lahore	1981-82
387	G. M. Turner and T. W. Jarvis, New Zealand v West Indies at Georgetown.	1971-72
382	R. B. Simpson and W. M. Lawry, Australia v West Indies at Bridgetown ..	1964-65
380	H. Whitehead and C. J. B. Wood, Leicestershire v Worcestershire at Worcester	1906
379	R. Abel and W. Brockwell, Surrey v Hampshire at The Oval	1897
378	J. T. Brown and J. Tunnicliffe, Yorkshire v Sussex at Sheffield	1897
377*	N. F. Horner and Khalid Ibadulla, Warwickshire v Surrey at The Oval	1960
375	W. H. Ponsford and W. M. Woodfull, Victoria v New South Wales at Melbourne	1926-27

FIRST-WICKET HUNDREDS IN BOTH INNINGS

B. Sutcliffe and D. D. Taylor, for Auckland v Canterbury in 1948-49, scored for the first wicket 220 in the first innings and 286 in the second innings. This is the only instance of two double-century opening stands in the same match.

T. W. Hayward and J. B. Hobbs in 1907 accomplished a performance without parallel by scoring over 100 together for Surrey's first wicket four times in one week: 106 and 125 v Cambridge University at The Oval, and 147 and 105 v Middlesex at Lord's.

L. Hutton and C. Washbrook, in three consecutive Test match innings which they opened together for England v Australia in 1946-47, made 138 in the second innings at Melbourne, and 137 and 100 at Adelaide. They also opened with 168 and 129 at Leeds in 1948.

J. B. Hobbs and H. Sutcliffe, in three consecutive Test match innings which they opened together for England v Australia in 1924-25, made 157 and 110 at Sydney and 283 at Melbourne. On 26 occasions – 15 times in Test matches – Hobbs and Sutcliffe took part in a three-figure first-wicket partnership. Seven of these stands exceeded 200.

G. Boycott and J. H. Edrich, in three consecutive Test match innings which they opened together for England v Australia in 1970-71, made 161* in the second innings at Melbourne, and 107 and 103 at Adelaide.

In 1971 R. G. A. Headley and P. J. Stimpson of Worcestershire shared in first-wicket hundred partnerships on each of the first four occasions they opened the innings together: 125 and 147 v Northamptonshire at Worcester, 102 and 128* v Warwickshire at Birmingham.

J. B. Hobbs during his career, which extended from 1905 to 1934, helped to make 100 or more for the first wicket in first-class cricket 166 times – 15 of them in 1926, when in consecutive innings he helped to make 428, 182, 106 and 123 before a wicket fell. As many as 117 of the 166 stands were made for Surrey. In all first-class matches Hobbs and A. Sandham shared 66 first-wicket partnerships of 100 or more runs.

P. Holmes and H. Sutcliffe made 100 or more runs for the first wicket of Yorkshire on 69 occasions; J. B. Hobbs and A. Sandham for Surrey on 63 occasions; W. W. Keeton and C. B. Harris of Nottinghamshire on 46; T. W. Hayward and J. B. Hobbs of Surrey on 40; G. Gunn and W. W. Whysall of Nottinghamshire on 40; J. D. Robertson and S. M. Brown of Middlesex on 34; C. B. Fry and J. Vine of Sussex on 33; R. E. Marshall and J. R. Gray of Hampshire on 33; D. E. Davies and A. H. Dyson of Glamorgan on 32; and G. Boycott and R. G. Lumb of Yorkshire on 27.

J. Douglas and A. E. Stoddart in 1896 scored over 150 runs for the Middlesex first wicket three times within a fortnight. In 1901, J. Iremonger and A. O. Jones obtained over 100 for the Nottinghamshire first wicket four times within eight days, scoring 134 and 144* v Surrey at The Oval, 238 v Essex at Leyton, and 119 v Derbyshire at Welbeck.

J. W. Lee and F. S. Lee, brothers, for Somerset in 1934, scored over 100 runs thrice in succession in the County Championship.

W. G. Grace and A. E. Stoddart, in three consecutive innings against the Australians in 1893, made over 100 runs for each opening partnership.

C. Hallows and F. B. Watson, in consecutive innings for Lancashire in 1928, opened with 200, 202, 107, 118; reached three figures twelve times, 200 four times.

H. Sutcliffe, in the period 1919-1939 inclusive, shared in 145 first-wicket partnerships of 100 runs or more.

There were four first-wicket hundred partnerships in the match between Somerset and Cambridge University at Taunton in 1960. G. Atkinson and R. T. Virgin scored 172 and 112 for Somerset and R. M. Prideaux and A. R. Lewis 198 and 137 for Cambridge University.

PARTNERSHIP RECORDS FOR ALL COUNTRIES

Best First-Wicket Stands

Pakistan	561	Waheed Mirza (324) and Mansoor Akhtar (224*), Karachi Whites v Quetta at Karachi	1976-77
English	555	P. Holmes (224*) and H. Sutcliffe (313), Yorkshire v Essex at Leyton	1932
Australian	456	W. H. Ponsford (248) and E. R. Mayne (209), Victoria v Queensland at Melbourne	1923-24
Indian	451*	S. Desai (218*) and R. M. H. Binny (211*), Karnataka v Kerala at Chikmagalur	1977-78
South African	424	J. F. W. Nicolson (252*) and I. J. Siedle (174), Natal v Orange Free State at Bloemfontein	1926-27
West Indian	390	G. L. Wight (262*) and G. L. R. Gibbs (216), British Guiana v Barbados at Georgetown	1951-52
New Zealand	387	G. M. Turner (259) and T. W. Jarvis (182), New Zealand v West Indies at Georgetown	1971-72

Best Second-Wicket Stands

English	465*	J. A. Jameson (240*) and R. B. Kanhai (213*), Warwickshire v Gloucestershire at Birmingham	1974
Indian	455	B. B. Nimbalkar (443*) and K. V. Bhandarkar (205), Maharashtra v Kathiawar at Poona	1948-49

Australian	451	W. H. Ponsford (266) and D. G. Bradman (244), Australia v England at The Oval	1934
West Indian	446	C. C. Hunte (260) and G. S. Sobers (365*), West Indies v Pakistan at Kingston	1957-58
Pakistan	426	Arshad Pervez (220) and Mohsin Khan (220), Habib Bank v Income Tax Dept at Lahore	1977-78
South African	305	S. K. Coen (165) and J. M. M Commaille (186), Orange Free State v Natal at Bloemfontein	1926-27
New Zealand	301	C. S. Dempster (180) and C. F. W. Allcott (131), New Zealanders v Warwickshire at Birmingham	1927

Best Third-Wicket Stands

Pakistan	456	Khalid Irtiza (290) and Aslam Ali (236), United Bank v Multan at Karachi	1975-76
New Zealand	445	P. E. Whitelaw (195) and W. N. Carson (290), Auckland v Otago at Dunedin	1936-37
West Indian	434	J. B. Stollmeyer (324) and G. E. Gomez (190), Trinidad v British Guiana at Port-of-Spain	1946-47
English	424*	W. J. Edrich (168*) and D. C. S. Compton (252*), Middlesex v Somerset at Lord's	1948
Indian	410†	L. Amarnath (262) and R. S. Modi (156), India in England v The Rest at Calcutta	1946-47
Australian	390*	J. M. Wiener (221*) and J. K. Moss (200*), Victoria v Western Australia at Melbourne	1981-82
South African	341	E. J. Barlow (201) and R. G. Pollock (175), South Africa v Australia at Adelaide	1963-64

† *415 runs were added for this wicket for India v England at Madras in 1981-82 in two separate partnerships. See Highest Test Wicket Partnerships for details.*

Best Fourth-Wicket Stands

Indian	577	V. S. Hazare (288) and Gul Mahomed (319), Baroda v Holkar at Baroda	1946-47
West Indian	574*	C. L. Walcott (314*) and F. M. M. Worrell (255*), Barbados v Trinidad at Port-of-Spain	1945-46
English	470	A. I. Kallicharran (230*) and G. W. Humpage (254), Warwickshire v Lancashire at Southport	1982
Australian	424	I. S. Lee (258) and S. O. Quin (210), Victoria v Tasmania at Melbourne	1933-34
Pakistan	350	Mushtaq Mohammad (201) and Asif Iqbal (175), Pakistan v New Zealand at Dunedin	1972-73
South African	342	E. A. B. Rowan (196) and P. J. M. Gibb (203), Transvaal v N. E. Transvaal at Johannesburg	1952-53
New Zealand	324	J. R. Reid (188*) and W. M. Wallace (197), New Zealanders v Cambridge University at Cambridge	1949

Best Fifth-Wicket Stands

Australian	405	S. G. Barnes (234) and D. G. Bradman (234), Australia v England at Sydney	1946-47
English	393	E. G. Arnold (200*) and W. B. Burns (196), Worcestershire v Warwickshire at Birmingham	1909
Indian	360	Uday Merchant (217) and M. N. Raiji (170), Bombay v Hyderabad at Bombay	1947-48
Pakistan	355	Altaf Shah (276) and Tariq Bashir (196), House Building Finance Corporation v Multan at Multan	1976-77
South African	338	R. G. Pollock (194) and A. L. Wilmot (152), Eastern Province v Natal at Port Elizabeth	1975-76

West Indian .... 335 B. F. Butcher (151) and C. H. Lloyd (201*), West Indians
v Glamorgan at Swansea.. 1969

New Zealand... 266 B. Sutcliffe (355) and W. S. Haig (67), Otago v Auckland
at Dunedin... 1949-50

Best Sixth-Wicket Stands

West Indian .... 487* G. A. Headley (344*) and C. C. Passailaigue (261*),
Jamaica v Lord Tennyson's XI at Kingston 1931-32

Australian...... 428 M. A. Noble (284) and W. W. Armstrong (172*),
Australians v Sussex at Hove.................................... 1902

English........... 411 R. M. Poore (304) and E. G. Wynyard (225), Hampshire
v Somerset at Taunton 1899

Indian .... 371 V. M. Merchant (359*) and R. S. Modi (168), Bombay v
Maharashtra at Bombay 1943-44

Pakistan .... 353 Salah-ud-Din (256) and Zaheer Abbas (197), Karachi v
East Pakistan at Karachi.. 1968-69

South African.. 244* J. M. M. Commaille (132*) and A. W. Palm (106*),
Western Province v Griqualand West at Johannesburg .. 1923-24

New Zealand... 226 E. J. Gray (126) and R. W. Ormiston (93), Wellington v
Central Districts at Wellington.................................. 1981-82

Best Seventh-Wicket Stands

West Indian .... 347 D. St E. Atkinson (219) and C. C. Depeiza (122), West
Indies v Australia at Bridgetown 1954-55

English........... 344 K. S. Ranjitsinhji (230) and W. Newham (153), Sussex v
Essex at Leyton 1902

Australian...... 335 C. W. Andrews (253) and E. C. Bensted (155), Queensland
v New South Wales at Sydney 1934-35

Pakistan .... 308 Waqar Hassan (189) and Imtiaz Ahmed (209), Pakistan v
New Zealand at Lahore 1955-56

South African.. 299 B. Mitchell (159) and A. Melville (153), Transvaal v
Griqualand West at Kimberley.................................. 1946-47

Indian .... 274 K. C. Ibrahim (250) and K. M. Rangnekar (138),
Bijapur XI v Bengal XI at Bombay 1942-43

New Zealand... 265 J. L. Powell (164) and N. Dorreen (105*), Canterbury v
Otago at Christchurch 1929-30

Best Eighth-Wicket Stands

Australian...... 433 A. Sims (184*) and V. T. Trumper (293), An Australian
XI v Canterbury at Christchurch 1913-14

English........... 292 R. Peel (210*) and Lord Hawke (166), Yorkshire v
Warwickshire at Birmingham.................................... 1896

West Indian .... 255 E. A. V. Williams (131*) and E. A. Martindale (134),
Barbados v Trinidad at Bridgetown 1935-36

Pakistan .... 240 Gulfraz Khan (207) and Raja Sarfraz (102), Railways v
Universities at Lahore 1976-77

Indian .... 236 C. T. Sarwate (235) and R. P. Singh (88), Holkar v Delhi
and District at Delhi 1949-50

South African.. 222 D. P. B. Morkel (114) and S. S. L. Steyn (261*), Western
Province v Border at Cape Town 1929-30

New Zealand... 190* J. E. Mills (104*) and C. F. W. Allcott (102*), New
Zealanders v Civil Service at Chiswick 1927

Best Ninth-Wicket Stands

English........... 283   A. Warren (123) and J. Chapman (165), Derbyshire v
Warwickshire at Blackwell 1910

Indian 245   V. S. Hazare (316*) and N. D. Nagarwalla (98),
Maharashtra v Baroda at Poona 1939-40

New Zealand... 239   H. B. Cave (118) and I. B. Leggat (142*), Central Districts
v Otago at Dunedin 1952-53

Australian....... 232   C. Hill (365*) and E. Walkley (53), South Australia v New
South Wales at Adelaide 1900-01

South African.. 221   N. V. Lindsay (160*) and G. R. McCubbin (97), Transvaal
v Rhodesia at Bulawayo 1922-23

Pakistan 190   Asif Iqbal (146) and Intikhab Alam (51), Pakistan v
England at The Oval... 1967

West Indian .... 155*†A. Persaud (85) and K. C. Glasgow (102), Demerara v
Berbice at Rose Hall.. 1976-77

† *201 runs were added for this wicket in two separate partnerships; K. C. Glasgow retired
hurt and was replaced by C. E. H. Croft when 155 had been added.*

Best Tenth-Wicket Stands

Australian....... 307   A. F. Kippax (260*), and J. E. H. Hooker (62), New South
Wales v Victoria at Melbourne 1928-29

Indian 249   C. T. Sarwate (124*) and S. N. Banerjee (121), Indians v
Surrey at The Oval.. 1946

English 235   F. E. Woolley (185) and A. Fielder (112*), Kent v
Worcestershire at Stourbridge....................................... 1909

Pakistan .... 196* Nadeem Yousuf (202*) and Maqsood Kundi (109*) Muslim
Commercial Bank v National Bank at Lahore 1981-82

New Zealand... 184   R. C. Blunt (338*) and W. Hawkesworth (21), Otago v
Canterbury at Christchurch 1931-32

South African.. 174   H. R. Lance (168) and D. Mackay-Coghill (57*), Transvaal
v Natal at Johannesburg 1965-66

West Indian 138   E. L. G. Hoad (149*) and H. C. Griffith (84), West
Indians v Sussex at Hove 1933

Note: All the English record wicket partnerships were made in the County Championship.

HIGHEST AGGREGATES IN A SEASON: OVER 3,000

	Season	I	NO	R	HI	100s	Avge
D. C. S. Compton	1947	50	8	3,816	246	18	90.85
W. J. Edrich	1947	52	8	3,539	267*	12	80.43
T. W. Hayward........	1906	61	8	3,518	219	13	66.37
L. Hutton	1949	56	6	3,429	269*	12	68.58
F. E. Woolley...........	1928	59	4	3,352	198	12	60.94
H. Sutcliffe	1932	52	7	3,336	313	14	74.13
W. R. Hammond	1933	54	5	3,323	264	13	67.81
E. H. Hendren	1928	54	7	3,311	209*	13	70.44
R. Abel....................	1901	68	8	3,309	247	7	55.15
W. R. Hammond.......	1937	55	5	3,252	217	13	65.04
M. J. K. Smith	1959	67	11	3,245	200*	8	57.94
E. H. Hendren	1933	65	9	3,186	301*	11	56.89
C. P. Mead..............	1921	52	6	3,179	280*	10	69.10
T. W. Hayward........	1904	63	5	3,170	203	11	54.65
K. S. Ranjitsinhji......	1899	58	8	3,159	197	8	63.18
C. B. Fry.................	1901	43	3	3,147	244	13	78.67
K. S. Ranjitsinhji......	1900	40	5	3,065	275	11	87.57

	Season	I	NO	R	HI	100s	Avge
L. E. G. Ames	1933	57	5	3,058	295	9	58.80
J. T. Tyldesley	1901	60	5	3,041	221	9	55.29
C. P. Mead	1928	50	10	3,027	180	13	75.67
J. B. Hobbs	1925	48	5	3,024	266*	16	70.32
E. Tyldesley	1928	48	10	3,024	242	10	79.57
W. E. Alley	1961	64	11	3,019	221*	11	56.96
W. R. Hammond	1938	42	2	3,011	271	15	75.27
E. H. Hendren	1923	51	12	3,010	200*	13	77.17
H. Sutcliffe	1931	42	11	3,006	230	13	96.96
J. H. Parks	1937	63	4	3,003	168	11	50.89
H. Sutcliffe	1928	44	5	3,002	228	13	76.97

Note: W. G. Grace scored 2,739 runs in 1871 – the first batsman to reach 2,000 runs in a season. He made ten hundreds and twice exceeded 200, with an average of 78.25 in all first-class matches. At the time, the over consisted of four balls.

HIGHEST AGGREGATES IN A SEASON: OVER 2,000

Since Reduction of Championship Matches in 1969

	Season	I	NO	R	HI	100s	Avge
Zaheer Abbas	1976	39	5	2,554	230*	11	75.11
G. Boycott	1971	30	5	2,503	233	13	100.12
G. M. Turner	1973	44	8	2,416	153*	10	67.11
G. M. Turner	1970	46	7	2,379	154*	10	61.00
Zaheer Abbas	1981	36	10	2,306	215*	10	88.69
J. H. Edrich	1969	39	7	2,238	181	8	69.93
M. J. Harris	1971	45	1	2,238	177	9	50.86
R. T. Virgin	1970	47	0	2,223	178	7	47.29
K. S. McEwan	1983	39	5	2,176	189*	8	64.00
I. V. A. Richards	1977	35	2	2,161	241*	7	65.48
J. B. Bolus	1970	53	9	2,143	147*	2	48.70
A. I. Kallicharran	1982	37	5	2,120	235	8	66.25
D. L. Amiss	1976	38	6	2,110	203	8	65.93
G. M. Turner	1981	42	4	2,101	168	9	55.28
Javed Miandad	1981	37	7	2,083	200*	8	69.43
Majid J. Khan	1972	38	4	2,074	204	8	61.00
G. Boycott	1970	42	5	2,051	260*	4	55.43
A. J. Lamb	1981	43	9	2,049	162	5	60.26
J. H. Edrich	1971	44	1	2,031	195*	6	47.23
D. L. Amiss	1978	41	3	2,030	162	7	53.42

Note: The feat was not achieved in 1974, 1975, 1979 or 1980.

HIGHEST BATTING AVERAGES IN AN ENGLISH SEASON

(Qualification: 12 innings)

	Season	I	NO	R	HI	100s	Avge
D. G. Bradman	1938	26	5	2,429	278	13	115.66
G. Boycott	1979	20	5	1,538	175*	6	102.53
W. A. Johnston	1953	17	16	102	28*	0	102.00
G. Boycott	1971	30	5	2,503	233	13	100.12
D. G. Bradman	1930	36	6	2,960	334	10	98.66
H. Sutcliffe	1931	42	11	3,006	230	13	96.96
R. M. Poore	1899	21	4	1,551	304	7	91.23
D. R. Jardine	1927	14	3	1,002	147	5	91.09
D. C. S. Compton	1947	50	8	3,816	246	18	90.85
G. M. Turner	1982	16	3	1,171	311*	5	90.07

	Season	I	NO	R	HI	100s	Avge
D. G. Bradman	1948	31	4	2,428	187	11	89.92
Zaheer Abbas............	1981	36	10	2,306	215*	10	88.69
K. S. Ranjitsinhji......	1900	40	5	3,065	275	11	87.57
D. R. Jardine	1928	17	4	1,133	193	3	87.15
W. R. Hammond	1946	26	5	1,783	214	7	84.90
D. G. Bradman	1934	27	3	2,020	304	7	84.16
R. B. Kanhai............	1975	22	9	1,073	178*	3	82.53
Mudassar Nazar........	1982	16	6	825	211*	4	82.50
J. B. Hobbs	1928	38	7	2,542	200*	12	82.00
C. B. Fry	1903	40	7	2,683	234	9	81.30
W. J. Edrich	1947	52	8	3,539	267*	12	80.43

HIGHEST AGGREGATES OUTSIDE ENGLAND

	Season	I	NO	R	HI	100s	Avge
In Australia							
D. G. Bradman	1928-29	24	6	1,690	340*	7	93.88
In South Africa							
J. R. Reid	1961-62	30	2	1,915	203	7	68.39
In West Indies							
E. H. Hendren	1929-30	18	5	1,765	254*	6	135.76
In New Zealand							
G. M. Turner	1975-76	20	4	1,244	177*	5	77.75
In India							
C. G. Borde.............	1964-65	28	3	1,604	168	6	64.16
In Pakistan							
Zaheer Abbas...........	1973-74	24	5	1,597	174	5	84.05

Note: In more than one country, the following aggregates of over 2,000 runs have been recorded.

M. Amarnath (P/I/WI)	1982-83	34	6	2,234	207	9	79.78
S. M. Gavaskar (I/P)..	1978-79	30	6	2,121	205	10	88.37
J. R. Reid (SA/A/NZ)	1961-62	36	2	2,083	203	7	61.26
R. B. Simpson							
(I/P/A/WI)	1964-65	34	4	2,063	201	8	68.76

1,000 RUNS IN MAY

Three batsmen have scored 1,000 runs in May, and four others – D. G. Bradman twice – have made 1,000 runs before June. Their innings-by-innings records are as follows:

W. G. Grace, May 9 to May 30, 1895 (22 days):

	Runs	Avge
13, 103, 18, 25, 288, 52, 257, 73*, 18, 169	1,016	112.88

"W.G." was within two months of completing his 47th year.

W. R. Hammond, May 7 to May 31, 1927 (25 days):

27, 135, 108, 128, 17, 11, 99, 187, 4, 30, 83, 7, 192, 14	1,042	74.42

Hammond scored his 1,000th run on May 28, thus equalling "W.G.'s" record of 22 days.

C. Hallows, May 5 to May 31, 1928 (27 days):

100, 101, 51*, 123, 101*, 22, 74, 104, 58, 34*, 232	1,000	125.00

Cricket Records

		Runs	Avge
T. W. Hayward, April 16 to May 31, 1900:			
120*, 55, 108, 131*, 55, 193, 120, 5, 6, 3, 40, 146, 92		1,074	97.63
D. G. Bradman, April 30 to May 31, 1930:			
236, 185*, 78, 9, 48*, 66, 4, 44, 252*, 32, 47*		1,001	143.00
On April 30 Bradman scored 75 not out.			
D. G. Bradman, April 30 to May 31, 1938:			
258, 58, 137, 278, 2, 143, 145*, 5, 30*		1,056	150.85
Bradman scored 258 on April 30, and his 1,000th run on May 27.			
W. J. Edrich, April 30 to May 31, 1938:			
104, 37, 115, 63, 20*, 182, 71, 31, 53*, 45, 15, 245, 0, 9, 20*		1,010	84.16
Edrich scored 21 not out on April 30. All his runs were scored at Lord's.			
G. M. Turner, April 24 to May 31, 1973:			
41, 151*, 143, 85, 7, 8, 17*, 81, 13, 53, 44, 153*, 3, 2, 66*, 30, 10*, 111		1,018	78.30

1,000 RUNS IN TWO SEPARATE MONTHS

Only four batsmen, C. B. Fry, K. S. Ranjitsinhji, H. Sutcliffe and L. Hutton, have scored over 1,000 runs in each of two months in the same season. L. Hutton, by scoring 1,294 in June 1949, made more runs in a single month than anyone else. He also made 1,050 in August 1949.

OUT HANDLED THE BALL

J. Grundy	MCC v Kent at Lord's	1857
G. Bennett	Kent v Sussex at Hove	1872
W. H. Scotton	Smokers v Non-Smokers at East Melbourne	1886-87
C. W. Wright	Nottinghamshire v Gloucestershire at Bristol	1893
E. Jones	South Australia v Victoria at Melbourne	1894-95
A. W. Nourse	South Africans v Sussex at Hove	1907
E. T. Benson	MCC v Auckland at Auckland	1929-30
A. W. Gilbertson	Otago v Auckland at Auckland	1952-53
W. R. Endean	South Africa v England at Cape Town	1956-57
P. J. Burge	Queensland v New South Wales at Sydney	1958-59
Dildar Awan	Services v Lahore at Lahore	1959-60
Mahmood-ul-Hasan	Karachi University v Railways-Quetta at Karachi	1960-61
Ali Raza	Karachi Greens v Hyderabad at Karachi	1961-62
Mohammad Yusuf	Rawalpindi v Peshawar at Peshawar	1962-63
A. Rees	Glamorgan v Middlesex at Lord's	1965
Pervez Akhtar	Multan v Karachi Greens at Sahiwal	1971-72
Javed Mirza	Railways v Punjab at Lahore	1972-73
R. G. Pollock	Eastern Province v Western Province at Cape Town	1973-74
C. I. Dey	Northern Transvaal v Orange Free State at Bloemfontein	1973-74
Nasir Valika	Karachi Whites v National Bank at Karachi	1974-75
Haji Yusuf	National Bank v Railways at Lahore	1974-75
Masood-ul-Hasan	PIA v National Bank 'B' at Lyallpur	1975-76
D. K. Pearse	Natal v Western Province at Cape Town	1978-79
A. M. J. Hilditch	Australia v Pakistan at Perth	1978-79
Musleh-ud-Din	Railways v Lahore at Lahore	1979-80
Mohsin Khan	Pakistan v Australia at Karachi	1982-83

OUT OBSTRUCTING THE FIELD

C. A. Absolom	Cambridge University v Surrey at The Oval	1868
T. Straw	Worcestershire v Warwickshire at Worcester	1899
T. Straw	Worcestershire v Warwickshire at Birmingham	1901
J. P. Whiteside	Leicestershire v Lancashire at Leicester	1901
L. Hutton	England v South Africa at The Oval	1951
J. A. Hayes	Canterbury v Central Districts at Christchurch	1954-55
D. D. Deshpande	Madhya Pradesh v Uttar Pradesh at Benares	1956-57
M. Mehra	Railways v Delhi at Delhi	1959-60
K. Ibadulla	Warwickshire v Hampshire at Coventry	1963
Kaiser	Dera Ismail Khan v Railways at Lahore	1964-65
Qasim Feroze	Bahawalpur v Universities at Lahore	1974-75
T. Quirk	Northern Transvaal v Border at East London	1978-79

Note: This method of dismissal has occurred twice in the *John Player League:*

R. W. Tolchard	Leicestershire v Middlesex at Lord's	1972
D. J. S. Taylor	Somerset v Warwickshire at Birmingham	1980

OUT HIT THE BALL TWICE

H. E. Bull	MCC v Oxford University at Lord's	1864
H. R. J. Charlwood	Sussex v Surrey at Hove	1872
R. G. Barlow	North v South at Lord's	1878
P. S. Wimble	Transvaal v Griqualand West at Kimberley	1892-93
G. B. Nicholls	Somerset v Gloucestershire at Bristol	1896
A. A. Lilley	Warwickshire v Yorkshire at Birmingham	1897
J. H. King	Leicestershire v Surrey at The Oval	1906
A. P. Binns	Jamaica v British Guiana at Georgetown	1956-57
K. Bavanna	Andhra v Mysore at Guntur	1963-64
Zaheer Abbas	PIA 'A' v Karachi Blues at Karachi	1969-70

BOWLING AND FIELDING RECORDS

FOUR WICKETS WITH CONSECUTIVE BALLS

J. Wells	Kent v Sussex at Brighton	1862
G. Ulyett	Lord Harris's XI v New South Wales at Sydney	1878-79
G. Nash	Lancashire v Somerset at Manchester	1882
J. B. Hide	Sussex v MCC and Ground at Lord's	1890
F. J. Shacklock	Nottinghamshire v Somerset at Nottingham	1893
A. D. Downes	Otago v Auckland at Dunedin	1893-94
F. Martin	MCC and Ground v Derbyshire at Lord's	1895
A. W. Mold	Lancashire v Nottinghamshire at Nottingham	1895
W. Brearley†	Lancashire v Somerset at Manchester	1905
S. Haigh	MCC v Army XI at Pretoria	1905-06
A. E. Trott‡	Middlesex v Somerset at Lord's	1907
F. A. Tarrant	Middlesex v Gloucestershire at Bristol	1907
A. Drake	Yorkshire v Derbyshire at Chesterfield	1914
S. G. Smith	Northamptonshire v Warwickshire at Birmingham	1914
H. A. Peach	Surrey v Sussex at The Oval	1924
A. F. Borland	Natal v Griqualand West at Kimberley	1926-27
J. E. H. Hooker†	New South Wales v Victoria at Sydney	1928-29

R. K. Tyldesley†	Lancashire v Derbyshire at Derby	1929
R. J. Crisp	Western Province v Griqualand West at Johannesburg	1931-32
R. J. Crisp	Western Province v Natal at Durban	1933-34
A. R. Gover	Surrey v Worcestershire at Worcester	1935
W. H. Copson	Derbyshire v Warwickshire at Derby	1937
W. A. Henderson	N.E. Transvaal v Orange Free State at Bloemfontein	1937-38
F. Ridgway	Kent v Derbyshire at Folkestone	1951
A. K. Walker §	Nottinghamshire v Leicestershire at Leicester	1956
S. N. Mohol	Board of Control President's XI v Minister for Small Savings' XI at Poona	1965-66
P. I. Pocock	Surrey v Sussex at Eastbourne	1972

† *Not all in the same innings.*
‡ *Trott achieved another hat-trick in the same innings of this, his benefit match.*
§ *Walker dismissed Firth with the last ball of the first innings and Lester, Tompkin and Smithson with the first three balls of the second innings, a feat without parallel.*

Notes: In their match with England at The Oval in 1863, Surrey lost four wickets in the course of a four-ball over from G. Bennett.

Sussex lost five wickets in the course of the final (six-ball) over of their match with Surrey at Eastbourne in 1972. P. I. Pocock, who had taken three wickets in his previous over, captured four more, taking in all seven wickets with eleven balls, a feat unique in first-class matches. (The eighth wicket fell to a run-out.)

P. G. H. Fender (Surrey) took six Middlesex wickets with eleven balls (including five with seven) at Lord's in 1927.

HAT-TRICKS

Double Hat-Trick

Besides Trott's performance, which is given in the preceding section, the following instances are recorded of players having performed the hat-trick twice in the same match, Rao doing so in the same innings.

A. Shaw	Nottinghamshire v Gloucestershire at Nottingham	1884
T. J. Matthews	Australia v South Africa at Manchester	1912
C. W. L. Parker	Gloucestershire v Middlesex at Bristol	1924
R. O. Jenkins	Worcestershire v Surrey at Worcester	1949
J. S. Rao	Services v Northern Punjab at Amritsar	1963-64
Amin Lakhani	Combined XI v Indians at Multan	1978-79

Five Wickets with Six Consecutive Balls

W. H. Copson	Derbyshire v Warwickshire at Derby	1937
W. A. Henderson	N.E. Transvaal v Orange Free State at Bloemfontein	1937-38
P. I. Pocock	Surrey v Sussex at Eastbourne	1972

Most Hat-Tricks

Seven times: D. V. P. Wright.
Six times: T. W. Goddard, C. W. L. Parker.
Five times: S. Haigh, V. W. C. Jupp, A. E. G. Rhodes, F. A. Tarrant.
Four times: R. G. Barlow, J. T. Hearne, J. C. Laker, G. A. R. Lock, G. G. Macaulay, T. J. Matthews, M. J. Procter, T. Richardson, F. R. Spofforth, F. S. Trueman.
Three times: W. M. Bradley, H. J. Butler, W. H. Copson, R. J. Crisp, J. W. H. T. Douglas, J. A. Flavell, A. P. Freeman, G. Giffen, K. Higgs, A. Hill, W. A. Humphries, R. D. Jackman, R. O. Jenkins, A. S. Kennedy, W. H. Lockwood, E. A. McDonald, T. L. Pritchard, J. S. Rao, A. Shaw, J. B. Statham, M. W. Tate, H. Trumble, D. Wilson, G. A. Wilson.

Unusual Hat-Tricks

All "Stumped":   by W. H. Brain off C. L. Townsend, Gloucestershire v
Somerset at Cheltenham... 1893

All "Caught":   by G. J. Thompson off S. G. Smith, Northamptonshire v
Warwickshire at Birmingham................................. 1914

by Cyril White off R. Beesly, Border v Griqualand West at
Queenstown.. 1946-47

by G. O. Dawkes (wicket-keeper) off H. L. Jackson,
Derbyshire v Worcestershire at Kidderminster 1958

All "LBW":   H. Fisher, Yorkshire v Somerset at Sheffield.................. 1932

J. A. Flavell, Worcestershire v Lancashire at Manchester . 1963

M. J. Procter, Gloucestershire v Essex at Westcliff.......... 1972

B. J. Ikin, Griqualand West v OFS at Kimberley 1973-74

M. J. Procter, Gloucestershire v Yorkshire at Cheltenham . 1979

TEN WICKETS IN ONE INNINGS

	O	M	R		
E. Hinkly (Kent)				v England at Lord's	1848
J. Wisden (North)...............				v South at Lord's	1850
V. E. Walker (England)........	43	17	74	v Surrey at The Oval	1859
E. M. Grace (MCC)............	32.2	7	69	v Gents of Kent at Canterbury.	1862
V. E. Walker (Middlesex).....	44.2		104	v Lancashire at Manchester.....	1865
G. Wootton (All England)	31.3	9	54	v Yorkshire at Sheffield.........	1865
W. Hickton (Lancashire)......	36.2	19	46	v Hampshire at Manchester.....	1870
S. E. Butler (Oxford)	24.1	11	38	v Cambridge at Lord's............	1871
James Lillywhite (South)......	60.2	22	129	v North at Canterbury...........	1872
W. G. Grace (MCC)............	46.1	15	92	v Kent at Canterbury	1873
A. Shaw (MCC).................	36.2	8	73	v North at Lord's...............	1874
E. Barratt (Players)............	29	11	43	v Australians at The Oval	1878
G. Giffen (Australian XI)	26	10	66	v The Rest at Sydney.............	1883-84
W. G. Grace (MCC)............	36.2	17	49	v Oxford University at Oxford .	1886
G. Burton (Middlesex)	52.3	25	59	v Surrey at The Oval	1888
†A. E. Moss (Canterbury).....	21.3	10	28	v Wellington at Christchurch ..	1889-90
S. M. J. Woods (Cambridge U.)	31	6	69	v Thornton's XI at Cambridge .	1890
T. Richardson (Surrey)........	15.3	3	45	v Essex at The Oval...............	1894
H. Pickett (Essex)..............	27	11	32	v Leicestershire at Leyton	1895
E. J. Tyler (Somerset)	34.3	15	49	v Surrey at Taunton	1895
W. P. Howell (Australians)	23.2	14	28	v Surrey at The Oval	1899
C. H. G. Bland (Sussex)	25.2	0	48	v Kent at Tonbridge	1899
J. Briggs (Lancashire)..........	28.5	7	55	v Worcestershire at Manchester	1900
A. E. Trott (Middlesex)........	14.2	5	42	v Somerset at Taunton	1900
F. Hinds (A. B. St Hill's XI) .	19.1	6	36	v Trinidad at Port-of-Spain.....	1900-01
A. Fielder (Players)	24.5	1	90	v Gentlemen at Lord's	1906
E. G. Dennett (Gloucestershire)	19.4	7	40	v Essex at Bristol	1906
A. E. E. Vogler (E. Province)	12	2	26	v Griqualand West at Johannes-burg...............................	1906-07
C. Blythe (Kent)	16	7	30	v Northamptonshire at North-ampton............................	1907
A. Drake (Yorkshire)...........	8.5	0	35	v Somerset at Weston-super-Mare...............................	1914
F. A. Tarrant (Maharaja of Cooch Behar's XI)............	35.4	4	90	v Lord Willingdon's XI at Poona	1918-19
W. Bestwick (Derbyshire).....	19	2	40	v Glamorgan at Cardiff.........	1921
A. A. Mailey (Australians).....	28.4	5	66	v Gloucestershire at Cheltenham	1921
C. W. L. Parker (Glos.)........	40.3	13	79	v Somerset at Bristol.............	1921
T. Rushby (Surrey)	17.5	4	43	v Somerset at Taunton	1921
J. C. White (Somerset)	42.2	11	76	v Worcestershire at Worcester .	1921

	O	M	R		
G. C. Collins (Kent)	19.3	4	65	v Nottinghamshire at Dover	1922
H. Howell (Warwickshire)	25.1	5	51	v Yorkshire at Birmingham	1923
A. S. Kennedy (Players)	22.4	10	37	v Gentlemen at The Oval	1927
G. O. Allen (Middlesex)	25.3	10	40	v Lancashire at Lord's............	1929
A. P. Freeman (Kent)	42	9	131	v Lancashire at Maidstone	1929
G. Geary (Leicestershire)	16.2	8	18	v Glamorgan at Pontypridd	1929
C. V. Grimmett (Australians)	22.3	8	37	v Yorkshire at Sheffield	1930
A. P. Freeman (Kent)	30.4	8	53	v Essex at Southend................	1930
H. Verity (Yorkshire)	18.4	6	36	v Warwickshire at Leeds	1931
A. P. Freeman (Kent)	36.1	9	79	v Lancashire at Manchester	1931
V. W. C. Jupp (Northants)	39	6	127	v Kent at Tunbridge Wells	1932
H. Verity (Yorkshire)	19.4	16	10	v Nottinghamshire at Leeds......	1932
T. W. Wall (South Australia)	12.4	2	36	v New South Wales at Sydney ..	1932-33
T. B. Mitchell (Derbyshire) ...	19.1	4	64	v Leicestershire at Leicester	1935
J. Mercer (Glamorgan)	26	10	51	v Worcestershire at Worcester .	1936
T. W. Goddard (Glos.)	28.4	4	113	v Worcestershire at Cheltenham	1937
T. F. Smailes (Yorkshire)	17.1	5	47	v Derbyshire at Sheffield	1939
E. A. Watts (Surrey)	24.1	8	67	v Warwickshire at Birmingham	1939
W. E. Hollies (Warwickshire)	20.4	4	49	v Nottinghamshire at Birmingham......................	1946
J. M. Sims (East)	18.4	2	90	v West at Kingston	1948
T. E. Bailey (Essex)	39.4	9	90	v Lancashire at Clacton	1949
J. K. R. Graveney (Glos.)	18.4	2	66	v Derbyshire at Chesterfield	1949
R. Berry (Lancashire)	36.2	9	102	v Worcestershire at Blackpool ..	1953
S. P. Gupte (Bombay)	24.2	7	78	v Combined XI at Bombay	1954-55
J. C. Laker (Surrey)	46	18	88	v Australians at The Oval	1956
J. C. Laker (England)	51.2	23	53	v Australia at Manchester	1956
G. A. R. Lock (Surrey)	29.1	18	54	v Kent at Blackheath	1956
K. Smales (Nottinghamshire) .	41.3	20	66	v Gloucestershire at Stroud	1956
P. Chatterjee (Bengal)	19	11	20	v Assam at Jorhat	1956-57
J. D. Bannister (Warwickshire)	23.3	11	41	v Comb. Services at Birmingham	1959
A. J. G. Pearson (Cambridge University)	30.3	8	78	v Leicestershire at Loughborough......................	1961
N. I. Thomson (Sussex)	34.2	19	49	v Warwickshire at Worthing	1964
P. J. Allan (Queensland)	15.6	3	61	v Victoria at Melbourne	1965-66
I. J. Brayshaw (W. Australia)	17.6	4	44	v Victoria at Perth	1967-68
Shahid Mahmood (Karachi Whites)	25	8	58	v Khairpur at Karachi	1969-70
E. E. Hemmings (International XI)	49.3	14	175	v West Indies XI at Kingston...	1982-83

† *On début in first-class cricket.*

MOST WICKETS IN A MATCH

19-90	J. C. Laker	England v Australia at Manchester	1956
17-48	C. Blythe	Kent v Northamptonshire at Northampton	1907
17-50	C. T. B. Turner	Australians v England XI at Hastings	1888
17-54	W. P. Howell	Australians v Western Province at Cape Town	1902-03
17-56	C. W. L. Parker	Gloucestershire v Essex at Gloucester	1925
17-67	A. P. Freeman	Kent v Sussex at Hove	1922
17-89	W. G. Grace	Gloucestershire v Nottinghamshire at Cheltenham ..	1877
17-89	F. C. L. Matthews	Nottinghamshire v Northants at Nottingham	1923
17-91	H. Dean	Lancashire v Yorkshire at Liverpool	1913
17-91	H. Verity	Yorkshire v Essex at Leyton	1933
17-92	A. P. Freeman	Kent v Warwickshire at Folkestone	1932
17-103	W. Mycroft	Derbyshire v Hampshire at Southampton..............	1876
17-106	G. R. Cox	Sussex v Warwickshire at Horsham......................	1926
17-106	T. W. Goddard	Gloucestershire v Kent at Bristol.........................	1939

17-119	W. Mead	Essex v Hampshire at Southampton	1895
17-137	W. Brearley	Lancashire v Somerset at Manchester	1905
17-159	S. F. Barnes	England v South Africa at Johannesburg	1913-14
17-201	G. Giffen	South Australia v Victoria at Adelaide	1885-86
17-212	J. C. Clay	Glamorgan v Worcestershire at Swansea	1937

Notes: H. A. Arkwright took eighteen wickets for 96 runs in a 12-a-side match for Gentlemen of MCC v Gentlemen of Kent at Canterbury in 1861.

W. Mead took seventeen wickets for 205 runs for Essex v Australians at Leyton in 1893, the year before Essex were raised to first-class status.

F. P. Fenner took seventeen wickets for Cambridge Town Club v University of Cambridge at Cambridge in 1844.

OUTSTANDING ANALYSES

(Also see Ten Wickets in One Innings)

	O	M	R	W		
H. Verity (Yorkshire)	19.4	16	10	10	v Nottinghamshire at Leeds ...	1932
G. Elliott (Victoria)	19	17	2	9	v Tasmania at Launceston	1857-58
Ahad Khan (Railways)	6.3	4	7	9	v Dera Ismail Khan at Lahore	1964-65
J. C. Laker (England)	14	12	2	8	v The Rest at Bradford	1950
D. Shackleton (Hampshire)	11.1	7	4	8	v Somerset at Weston-super-Mare	1955
E. Peate (Yorkshire)	16	11	5	8	v Surrey at Holbeck	1883
F. R. Spofforth (Australians)	8.3	6	3	7	v England XI at Birmingham .	1884
W. A. Henderson (N.E. Transvaal)	9.3	7	4	7	v Orange Free State at Bloemfontein	1937-38
Rajinder Goel (Haryana)	7	4	4	7	v Jammu and Kashmir at Chandigarh	1977-78
V. I. Smith (South Africans)	4.5	3	1	6	v Derbyshire at Derby	1947
S. Cosstick (Victoria)	21.1	20	1	6	v Tasmania at Melbourne	1868-69
Israr Ali (Bahawalpur)	11	10	1	6	v Dacca U. at Bahawalpur	1957-58
A. D. Pougher (MCC)	3	3	0	5	v Australians at Lord's	1896
G. R. Cox (Sussex)	6	6	0	5	v Somerset at Weston-super-Mare	1921
R. K. Tyldesley (Lancashire)	5	5	0	5	v Leicestershire at Manchester	1924
P. T. Mills (Gloucestershire)	6.4	6	0	5	v Somerset at Bristol	1928

SIXTEEN OR MORE WICKETS IN A DAY

17-48	C. Blythe	Kent v Northamptonshire at Northampton	1907
17-91	H. Verity	Yorkshire v Essex at Leyton	1933
17-106	T. W. Goddard	Gloucestershire v Kent at Bristol	1939
16-38	T. Emmett	Yorkshire v Cambridgeshire at Hunslet	1869
16-52	J. Southerton	South v North at Lord's	1875
16-69	T. G. Wass	Nottinghamshire v Lancashire at Liverpool	1906
16-38	A. E. E. Vogler	E. Province v Griqualand West at Johannesburg	1906-07
16-103	T. G. Wass	Nottinghamshire v Essex at Nottingham	1908
16-83	J. C. White	Somerset v Worcestershire at Bath	1919

200 OR MORE WICKETS IN A SEASON

	Season	O	M	R	W	Avge
A. P. Freeman........	1928	1,976.1	423	5,489	304	18.05
A. P. Freeman........	1933	2,039	651	4,549	298	15.26
T. Richardson........	1895‡	1,690.1	463	4,170	290	14.37
C. T. B. Turner**....	1888†	2,427.2	1,127	3,307	283	11.68
A. P. Freeman........	1931	1,618	360	4,307	276	15.60
A. P. Freeman........	1930	1,914.3	472	4,632	275	16.84
T. Richardson........	1897‡	1,603.4	495	3,945	273	14.45
A. P. Freeman........	1929	1,670.5	381	4,879	267	18.27
W. Rhodes..............	1900	1,553	455	3,606	261	13.81
J. T. Hearne...........	1896‡	2,003.1	818	3,670	257	14.28
A. P. Freeman........	1932	1,565.5	404	4,149	253	16.39
W. Rhodes..............	1901	1,565	505	3,797	251	15.12
T. W. Goddard.......	1937	1,478.1	359	4,158	248	16.76
W. C. Smith............	1910	1,423.3	420	3,225	247	13.05
T. Richardson........	1896‡	1,656.2	526	4,015	246	16.32
A. E. Trott.............	1899‡	1,772.4	587	4,086	239	17.09
T. W. Goddard.......	1947	1,451.2	344	4,119	238	17.30
M. W. Tate	1925	1,694.3	472	3,415	228	14.97
J. T. Hearne...........	1898‡	1,802.2	781	3,120	222	14.05
C. W. L. Parker	1925	1,512.3	478	3,311	222	14.91
G. A. Lohmann	1890‡	1,759.1	737	2,998	220	13.62
M. W. Tate	1923	1,608.5	331	3,061	219	13.97
C. F. Root	1925	1,493.2	416	3,770	219	17.21
C. W. L. Parker	1931	1,320.4	386	3,125	219	14.26
H. Verity	1936	1,289.3	463	2,847	216	13.18
G. A. R. Lock........	1955	1,408.4	497	3,109	216	14.39
C. Blythe	1909	1,273.5	343	3,128	215	14.54
E. Peate................	1882†	1,853.1	868	2,466	214	11.52
A. W. Mold............	1895‡	1,629	598	3,400	213	15.96
W. Rhodes..............	1902	1,306.3	405	2,801	213	13.15
C. W. L. Parker	1926	1,739.5	556	3,920	213	18.40
J. T. Hearne...........	1893‡	1,741.4	667	3,492	212	16.47
A. P. Freeman........	1935	1,503.2	320	4,562	212	21.51
G. A. R. Lock........	1957	1,194.1	449	2,550	212	12.02
A. E. Trott.............	1900	1,547.1	363	4,923	211	23.33
G. G. Macaulay	1925	1,338.2	307	3,268	211	15.48
H. Verity	1935	1,279.2	453	3,032	211	14.36
J. Southerton	1870†	1,876.5	709	3,074	210	14.63
G. A. Lohmann	1888†	1,649.1	783	2,280	209	10.90
C. H. Parkin...........	1923	1,356.2	356	3,543	209	16.94
G. H. Hirst	1906	1,306.1	271	3,434	208	16.50
F. R. Spofforth	1884†	1,577	653	2,774	207	13.25
A. W. Mold............	1894‡	1,288.3	456	2,548	207	12.30
C. W. L Parker	1922	1,294.5	445	2,712	206	13.16
A. S. Kennedy	1922	1,346.4	366	3,444	205	16.80
M. W. Tate	1924	1,469.5	465	2,818	205	13.74
E. A. McDonald	1925	1,249.4	282	3,828	205	18.67
A. P. Freeman........	1934	1,744.4	440	4,753	205	23.18
C. W. L. Parker	1924	1,303.5	411	2,913	204	14.27
G. A. Lohmann	1889‡	1,614.1	646	2,714	202	13.43
H. Verity	1937	1,386.2	487	3,168	202	15.68
A. Shaw.................	1878†	2,630	1,586	2,203	201	10.96
E. G. Dennett.........	1907	1,216.2	305	3,227	201	16.05
A. R. Gover...........	1937	1,219.4	191	3,816	201	18.98
C. H. Parkin...........	1924	1,162.5	357	2,735	200	13.67
T. W. Goddard	1935	1,553	384	4,073	200	20.36
A. R. Gover...........	1936	1,159.2	185	3,547	200	17.73

	Season	O	M	R	W	Avge
T. W. Goddard	1939§	819	139	2,973	200	14.86
R. Appleyard	1951	1,313.2	391	2,829	200	14.14

† *Indicates 4-ball overs; ‡ 5-ball overs. All others were 6-ball overs except § 8-ball overs.*
** *Exclusive of matches not reckoned as first-class.*

Notes: In four consecutive seasons (1928-31), A. P. Freeman took 1,122 wickets, and in eight consecutive seasons (1928-35), 2,090 wickets. In each of these eight seasons he took over 200 wickets.

T. Richardson took 1,005 wickets in four consecutive seasons (1894-97).

In 1896, J. T. Hearne took his 100th wicket as early as June 12. In 1931, C. W. L. Parker did the same and A. P. Freeman obtained his 100th wicket a day later.

C. T. B. Turner is the only bowler to take over 100 wickets in first-class matches in a season in Australia – 106 wickets in twelve matches, 1887-88.

100 OR MORE WICKETS IN A SEASON

Since Reduction of Championship Matches in 1969

	Season	O	M	R	W	Avge
M. D. Marshall	1982	822	225	2,108	134	15.73
L. R. Gibbs	1971	1,024.1	295	2,475	131	18.89
R. D. Jackman	1980	746.2	220	1,864	121	15.40
A. M. E. Roberts	1974	727.4	198	1,621	119	13.62
B. S. Bedi	1974	1,085.3	307	2,760	112	24.64
P. G. Lee	1975	799.5	199	2,067	112	18.45
D. L. Underwood	1978	815.1	359	1,594	110	14.49
R. M. H. Cottam	1969	989.1	252	2,294	109	21.04
M. J. Procter	1977	777.3	226	1,967	109	18.04
T. W. Cartwright	1969	880.5	373	1,748	108	16.18
M. J. Procter	1969	639.3	160	1,623	108	15.02
P. J. Sainsbury	1971	845.5	332	1,874	107	17.51
D. J. Shepherd	1970	1,123.3	420	2,031	106	19.16
J. K. Lever	1978	681.1	160	1,610	106	15.18
J. K. Lever	1979	700	166	1,834	106	17.30
J. K. Lever	1983	569	137	1,726	106	16.28
D. L. Underwood	1979	799.2	335	1,575	106	14.85
D. L. Underwood	1983	936.3	358	2,044	106	19.28
N. Gifford	1970	965.5	331	2,092	105	19.92
F. J. Titmus	1970	1,106.3	320	2,804	105	26.70
B. S. Bedi	1973	864.2	307	1,884	105	17.94
R. J. Hadlee	1981	708.4	231	1,564	105	14.89
T. W. Cartwright	1971	976.4	407	1,852	104	17.80
Intikhab Alam	1971	1,097.4	244	2,950	104	28.36
F. J. Titmus	1971	1,065.1	341	2,355	104	22.64
N. Gifford	1983	1,043.4	346	2,393	104	23.00
J. E. Emburey	1983	935	328	1,842	103	17.88
D. Wilson	1969	964.1	384	1,772	102	17.37
R. N. S. Hobbs	1970	736	178	2,183	102	21.40
D. L. Underwood	1971	945.5	368	1,986	102	19.47
D. L. Underwood	1969	808.3	355	1,561	101	15.45
P. G. Lee	1973	740.3	181	1,901	101	18.82
Sarfraz Nawaz.........	1975	728.4	175	2,051	101	20.30
M. W. W. Selvey	1978	743.5	199	1,929	101	19.09
D. R. Doshi	1980	961.2	268	2,700	101	26.73
I. T. Botham	1978	605.2	143	1,640	100	16.40

Note: The feat was not achieved in 1972 or 1976.

1,500 WICKETS OR MORE IN A CAREER

	Career	*W*	*R*	*Avge*
W. Rhodes	1898-1930	4,187	69,993	16.71
A. P. Freeman	1914-36	3,776	69,577	18.42
C. W. L. Parker	1903-35	3,278	63,821	19.46
J. T. Hearne	1888-1923	3,061	54,342	17.75
T. W. Goddard	1922-52	2,979	59,116	19.84
†W. G. Grace	1865-1908	2,876	51,545	17.92
A. S. Kennedy	1907-36	2,874	61,044	21.24
D. Shackleton	1948-69	2,857	53,303	18.65
G. A. R. Lock	1946-71	2,844	54,710	19.23
F. J. Titmus	1949-82	2,830	63,313	22.37
M. W. Tate	1912-37	2,784	50,567	18.16
G. H. Hirst	1891-1929	2,739	51,300	18.72
C. Blythe	1899-1914	2,506	42,136	16.81
W. E. Astill	1906-39	2,431	57,781	23.76
J. C. White	1909-37	2,356	43,759	18.57
W. E. Hollies	1932-57	2,323	48,656	20.94
F. S. Trueman	1949-69	2,304	42,154	18.29
J. B. Statham	1950-68	2,260	36,995	16.36
R. T. D. Perks	1930-55	2,233	53,770	24.07
D. L. Underwood	1963-83	2,224	44,014	19.79
J. Briggs	1879-1900	2,221	35,390	15.93
D. J. Shepherd	1950-72	2,218	47,298	21.32
E. G. Dennett	1903-26	2,147	42,568	19.82
T. Richardson	1892-1905	2,105	38,794	18.42
T. E. Bailey	1945-67	2,082	48,170	23.13
R. Illingworth	1951-83	2,072	42,023	20.28
F. E. Woolley	1906-38	2,068	41,066	19.85
G. Geary	1912-38	2,063	41,339	20.03
D. V. P. Wright	1932-57	2,056	49,305	23.98
J. Newman	1906-30	2,032	51,211	25.20
A. Shaw	1864-97	2,021	24,496	12.12
S. Haigh	1895-1913	2,012	32,091	15.94
H. Verity	1930-39	1,956	29,146	14.90
J. C. Laker	1946-65	1,944	35,789	18.40
W. Attewell	1881-1900	1,932	29,745	15.39
A. V. Bedser	1939-60	1,924	39,281	20.41
W. Mead	1892-1913	1,916	36,388	18.99
A. E. Relf	1900-21	1,897	39,724	20.94
P. G. H. Fender	1910-36	1,894	47,457	25.05
J. W. H. T. Douglas	1901-30	1,893	44,159	23.32
J. H. Wardle	1946-58	1,846	35,027	18.97
G. R. Cox	1895-1928	1,843	42,138	22.86
M. S. Nichols	1924-39	1,841	39,845	21.64
J. W. Hearne	1909-36	1,839	44,927	24.43
G. G. Macaulay	1920-35	1,837	32,440	17.65
N. Gifford	1960-83	1,824	41,637	22.82
J. B. Mortimore	1950-75	1,807	41,904	23.18
G. A. Lohmann	1884-98	1,805	25,110	13.91
C. Cook	1946-64	1,782	36,578	20.52
R. Peel	1882-99	1,754	28,446	16.21
H. L. Jackson	1947-63	1,733	30,101	17.36
T. P. B. Smith	1929-52	1,697	45,059	26.55
J. Southerton	1854-79	1,680	24,257	14.43
A. E. Trott	1892-1911	1,674	35,316	21.09
A. W. Mold	1889-1901	1,673	26,012	15.54
T. G. Wass	1896-1920	1,666	34,091	20.46
V. W. C. Jupp	1909-38	1,658	38,166	23.01
C. Gladwin	1939-58	1,653	30,265	18.30

	Career	W	R	Avge
W. E. Bowes	1928-47	1,639	27,470	16.76
A. W. Wellard	1927-50	1,614	39,302	24.35
N. I. Thomson	1952-72	1,597	32,866	20.57
J. Mercer	1919-47	1,593	37,302	23.41
G. J. Thompson	1897-1922	1,591	30,060	18.89
T. Emmett	1866-88	1,582	21,147	13.36
J. M. Sims.................	1929-53	1,582	39,401	24.90
Intikhab Alam...........	1957-82	1,571	43,472	27.67
W. Voce	1927-52	1,558	35,961	23.08
A. R. Gover..............	1928-48	1,555	36,753	23.63
B. S. Bedi	1961-81	1,547	33,478	21.64
T. W. Cartwright........	1952-77	1,536	29,357	19.11
K. Higgs	1958-82	1,531	36,196	23.64
James Langridge........	1924-53	1,530	34,524	22.56
J. A. Flavell	1949-67	1,529	32,847	21.48
C. F. Root	1910-33	1,512	31,933	21.11
R. K. Tyldesley..........	1919-35	1,509	25,980	17.21

†*In recent years some statisticians have removed from W. G. Grace's record a number of matches which they consider not to have been first-class. The above figures are those which became universally accepted upon appearance in W. G. Grace's obituary in the* Wisden *of 1916. Some works of reference give his career record as being 2,809–50,999–18.15. These figures also appeared in the 1981 edition of* Wisden.

100 WICKETS IN AN ENGLISH SEASON EIGHT TIMES OR MORE

23 times: W. Rhodes 200 wkts (3).

20 times: D. Shackleton.

17 times: A. P. Freeman 300 wkts (1), 200 wkts (7).

16 times: T. W. Goddard 200 wkts (4), C. W. L. Parker 200 wkts (5), R. T. D. Perks, F. J. Titmus.

15 times: J. T. Hearne 200 wkts (3), G. H. Hirst 200 wkts (1), A. S. Kennedy 200 wkts (1).

14 times: C. Blythe 200 wkts (1), W. E. Hollies, G. A. R. Lock 200 wkts (2), M. W. Tate 200 wkts (3), J. C White.

13 times: J. B. Statham.

12 times: J. Briggs, E. G. Dennett 200 wkts (1), C. Gladwin, D. J. Shepherd, N. I. Thomson, F. S. Trueman.

11 times: A. V. Bedser, G. Geary, S. Haigh, J. C. Laker, M. S. Nichols, A. E. Relf.

10 times: W. Attewell, W. G. Grace, R. Illingworth, H. L. Jackson, V. W. C. Jupp, G. G. Macaulay 200 wkts (1), W. Mead, T. B. Mitchell, T. Richardson 200 wkts (3), R. K. Tyldesley, D. L. Underwood, J. H. Wardle, T. G. Wass, D. V. P. Wright.

9 times: W. E. Astill, T. E. Bailey, W. E. Bowes, C. Cook, H. Howorth, J. Mercer, A. W. Mold 200 wkts (2), J. Newman, C. F. Root 200 wkts (1), A. Shaw 200 wkts (1), J. Southerton 200 wkts (1), H. Verity 200 wkts (3).

8 times: T. W. Cartwright, H. Dean, J. A. Flavell, A. R. Gover 200 wkts (2), H. Larwood, G. A. Lohmann 200 wkts (3), R. Peel, J. M. Sims, F. A. Tarrant, R. Tattersall, G. J. Thompson, G. E. Tribe, A. W. Wellard, F. E. Woolley, J. A. Young.

100 WICKETS IN A SEASON OVERSEAS

W		Season	R	Avge
116	M. W. Tate	1926-27 (I)	1,599	13.78
106	C. T. B. Turner..................	1887-88 (A)	1,441	13.59
106	R. Benaud........................	1957-58 (SA)	2,056	19.39
104	S. F. Barnes	1913-14 (SA)	1,117	10.74
103	Abdul Qadir	1982-83 (P)	2,367	22.98

ALL-ROUND CRICKET

20,000 RUNS AND 2,000 WICKETS IN A CAREER

	Career	R	Avge	W	Avge	'Doubles'
W. E. Astill	1906-39	22,726	22.54	2,431	23.76	9
T. E. Bailey	1945-67	28,642	33.42	2,082	23.13	8
W. G. Grace	1865-1908	54,896	39.55	2,876	17.99	8
G. H. Hirst	1891-1929	36,323	34.13	2,739	18.72	14
R. Illingworth	1951-83	24,134	28.06	2,072	20.28	6
W. Rhodes	1898-1930	39,802	30.83	4,187	16.71	16
M. W. Tate	1912-37	21,717	25.01	2,784	18.16	8
F. J. Titmus	1949-82	21,588	23.11	2,830	22.37	8
F. E. Woolley	1906-38	58,969	40.75	2,068	19.85	8

THE DOUBLE

2,000 RUNS AND 200 WICKETS IN A SEASON

1906	G. H. Hirst	2,385 runs and 208 wickets

3,000 RUNS AND 100 WICKETS IN A SEASON

1937	J. H. Parks	3,003 runs and 101 wickets

2,000 RUNS AND 100 WICKETS IN A SEASON

	Season	R	W		Season	R	W
W. G. Grace	1873	2,139	106	F. E. Woolley	1914	2,272	125
W. G. Grace	1876	2,622	129	J. W. Hearne	1920	2,148	142
C. L. Townsend	1899	2,440	101	V. W. C. Jupp	1921	2,169	121
G. L. Jessop	1900	2,210	104	F. E. Woolley	1921	2,101	167
G. H. Hirst	1904	2,501	132	F. E. Woolley	1922	2,022	163
G. H. Hirst	1905	2,266	110	F. E. Woolley	1923	2,091	101
W. Rhodes	1909	2,094	141	L. F. Townsend	1933	2,268	100
W. Rhodes	1911	2,261	117	D. E. Davies	1937	2,012	103
F. A. Tarrant	1911	2,030	111	James Langridge	1937	2,082	101
J. W. Hearne	1913	2,036	124	T. E Bailey	1959	2,011	100
J. W. Hearne	1914	2,116	123				

1,000 RUNS AND 200 WICKETS IN A SEASON

	Season	R	W		Season	R	W
A. E. Trott	1899	1,175	239	M. W. Tate	1923	1,168	219
A. E. Trott	1900	1,337	211	M. W. Tate	1924	1,419	205
A. S. Kennedy	1922	1,129	205	M. W. Tate	1925	1,290	228

The double feat of scoring 1,000 runs and taking 100 wickets in one season of first-class cricket has been accomplished as follows, the last instance being by F. J. Titmus in 1967:

Sixteen times: W. Rhodes.
Fourteen times: G. H. Hirst.
Ten times: V. W. C. Jupp.
Nine times: W. E. Astill.
Eight times: T. E. Bailey, W. G. Grace, M. S. Nichols, A. E. Relf, F. A. Tarrant, M. W. Tate, F. J. Titmus, F. E. Woolley.
Seven times: G. E. Tribe.
Six times: P. G. H. Fender, R. Illingworth, James Langridge.
Five times: J. W. H. T. Douglas, J. W. Hearne, A. S. Kennedy, J. Newman.
Four times: E. G. Arnold, J. Gunn, R. Kilner, B. R. Knight.
Three times: W. W. Armstrong (Australians), L. C. Braund, G. Giffen (Australians), N. E. Haig, R. Howorth, C. B. Llewellyn, J. B. Mortimore, Ray Smith, S. G. Smith, L. F. Townsend, A. W. Wellard.

Note: A complete list of those performing the feat once or twice will be found on p.202 of the 1982 *Wisden*.

WICKET-KEEPER'S DOUBLE

	Season	R	D
L. E. G. Ames	1928	1,919	121
L. E. G. Ames	1929	1,795	127
L. E. G. Ames	1932	2,482	100
J. T. Murray	1957	1,025	104

1,000 RUNS AND 50 WICKETS IN A SEASON

Since Reduction of Championship Matches in 1969

Season		R	Avge	W	Avge
1969	A. W. Greig	1,130	27.56	69	23.60
	Mushtaq Mohammad	1,831	59.06	78	24.38
	G. S. Sobers	1,023	42.62	54	24.42
1970	A. W. Greig	1,008	24.00	59	27.69
	Mushtaq Mohammad	1,482	36.14	58	28.50
	G. S. Sobers	1,742	75.73	64	24.06
	P. M. Walker	1,049	24.39	60	26.65
1971	M. A. Buss	1,337	31.83	62	26.59
	A. W. Greig	1,242	27.00	77	29.07
	R. A. Hutton	1,009	31.53	80	20.35
	Mushtaq Mohammad	1,660	33.87	52	27.25
	M. J. Procter	1,786	45.79	65	18.95
	G. S. Sobers	1,485	46.40	53	30.96
1972	K. D. Boyce	1,023	30.08	82	20.20
	Mushtaq Mohammad	1,949	59.06	57	19.82
	M. J. Procter	1,219	40.63	58	16.55
1974	Imran Khan	1,016	36.28	60	30.13
1975	A. W. Greig	1,699	47.19	56	33.41
	C. E. B. Rice	1,155	33.00	53	25.98
1976	I. T. Botham	1,022	34.06	66	28.48
	Imran Khan	1,092	40.44	65	23.41
	M. J. Procter	1,209	34.54	68	28.05
1977	C. E. B. Rice	1,300	35.13	50	22.26
1978	M. J. Procter	1,655	50.15	69	23.89
1979	J. R. T. Barclay	1,093	32.14	52	24.03
	M. J. Procter	1,241	38.78	81	18.91
	C. E. B. Rice	1,297	41.83	58	19.63
	P. Willey	1,109	41.07	52	32.63

Season		R	Avge	W	Avge
1980	M. J. Procter	1,081	34.87	51	18.25
1981	C. E. B. Rice	1,462	56.23	65	19.20
1982	I. T. Botham	1,241	44.32	66	22.98
	R. C. Ontong	1,204	31.68	64	32.17
	D. N. Patel	1,104	26.92	50	30.62
	P. Willey	1,783	50.94	51	26.88
1983	R. C. Ontong	1,310	38.52	56	36.66
	J. N. Shepherd	1,025	36.60	67	30.55

HUNDRED AND HAT-TRICK

W. G. Grace, MCC v Kent at Canterbury; 123, five for 82, and six for 47 including hat-trick (12-a-side)	1874
G. Giffen, Australians v Lancashire at Manchester; 13, 113, and six for 55 including hat-trick	1884
W. E. Roller, Surrey v Sussex at The Oval; 204, four for 28 including hat-trick, and two for 16. (Unique instance of 200 and hat-trick)	1885
W. B. Burns, Worcestershire v Gloucestershire at Worcester; 102*, three for 56, including hat-trick, and two for 21	1913
V. W. C. Jupp, Sussex v Essex at Colchester; 102, six for 61, including hat-trick, and six for 78	1921
R. E. S. Wyatt, MCC v Ceylon at Colombo; 124 and five for 39 including hat-trick.	1926-27
L. N. Constantine, West Indians v Northamptonshire at Northampton; seven for 45, including hat-trick, 107 (five 6s), and six for 67	1928
D. E Davies, Glamorgan v Leicestershire at Leicester; 139, four for 27, and three for 31 including hat-trick	1937
V. M. Merchant, Dr C. R. Pereira's XI v Sir Homi Mehta's XI at Bombay; 1, 142, three for 31 including hat-trick, and no wicket for 17	1946-47
M. J. Procter, Gloucestershire v Essex at Westcliff-on-Sea; 51, 102, three for 43, and five for 30 including hat-trick (all lbw)	1972
M. J. Procter, Gloucestershire v Leicestershire at Bristol; 122, no wkt for 32, and seven for 26 including hat-trick	1979

HUNDRED AND TEN WICKETS IN ONE INNINGS

V. E. Walker, England v Surrey at The Oval; ten for 74, four for 17, 20* and 108.	1859
E. M. Grace, MCC v Gentlemen of Kent at Canterbury; five for 77, ten for 69, and 192*	1862
W. G. Grace, MCC v Oxford University at Oxford; two for 60, ten for 49, and 104.	1886
F. A. Tarrant, Maharaja of Cooch Behar's XI v Lord Willingdon's XI at Poona; ten for 90, one for 22, 182* and 8*	1918-19

HUNDRED IN EACH INNINGS AND FIVE WICKETS TWICE

G. H. Hirst, Yorkshire v Somerset at Bath; six for 70, five for 45, 111 and 117*.	1906

WICKET-KEEPING RECORDS

MOST DISMISSALS IN A CAREER

	Ct	St	Total
R. W. Taylor (1960-83)	1,424	170	1,594
J. T. Murray (1952-75)	1,270	257	1,527
H. Strudwick (1902-27)	1,215	253	1,468

	Ct	St	Total
F. H. Huish (1895-1914)	952	376	1,328
D. Hunter (1889-1909)	955	372	1,327
B. Taylor (1949-73)	1,082	212	1,294
H. R. Butt (1890-1912)	971	291	1,262
A. P. E. Knott (1965-83)	1,130	131	1,261
J. H. Board (1891-1915)	852	354	1,206
H. Elliott (1920-47)	904	302	1,206
J. M. Parks (1949-76)	1,089	93	1,182
R. Booth (1951-70)	946	176	1,122
L. E. G. Ames (1926-51)	698	415	1,113
G. Duckworth (1923-47)	751	339	1,090
H. W. Stephenson (1948-64)	752	332	1,084
J. G. Binks (1955-75)	895	176	1,071
T. G. Evans (1939-69)	811	249	1,060
A. Long (1960-80)	922	124	1,046
G. O. Dawkes (1937-61)	896	146	1,042
R. W. Tolchard (1965-83)	912	125	1,037
W. L. Cornford (1921-47)	656	344	1,000

100 OR MORE DISMISSALS IN A SEASON

127 (79ct, 48st)	L. E. G. Ames, Kent	1929
121 (69ct, 52st)	L. E. G. Ames, Kent	1928
110 (62ct, 48st)	H. Yarnold, Worcestershire	1949
107 (77ct, 30st)	G. Duckworth, Lancashire	1928
107 (96ct, 11st)	J. G. Binks, Yorkshire	1960
104 (82ct, 22st)	J. T. Murray, Middlesex	1957
102 (70ct, 32st)	F. H. Huish, Kent	1913
102 (95ct, 7st)	J. T. Murray, Middlesex	1960
101 (85ct, 16st)	R. Booth, Worcestershire	1960
100 (62ct, 38st)	F. H. Huish, Kent	1911
100 (36ct, 64st)	L. E. G. Ames, Kent	1932
100 (91ct, 9st)	R. Booth, Worcestershire	1964

TEN OR MORE DISMISSALS IN A MATCH

12 (8ct, 4st)	E. Pooley	Surrey v Sussex at The Oval	1868
12 (9ct, 3st)	D. Tallon	Queensland v New South Wales at Sydney	1938-39
12 (9ct, 3st)	H. B. Taber	New South Wales v South Australia at Adelaide	1968-69
11 (all ct)	A. Long	Surrey v Sussex at Hove	1964
11 (all ct)	R. W. Marsh	Western Australia v Victoria at Perth	1975-76
11 (all ct)	D. L. Bairstow	Yorkshire v Derbyshire at Scarborough	1982
10 (5ct, 5st)	H. Phillips	Sussex v Surrey at The Oval	1872
10 (2ct, 8st)	E. Pooley	Surrey v Kent at The Oval	1878
10 (9ct, 1st)	T. W. Oates	Nottinghamshire v Middlesex at Nottingham	1906
10 (1ct, 9st)	F. H. Huish	Kent v Surrey at The Oval	1911
10 (9ct, 1st)	J. C. Hubble	Kent v Gloucestershire at Cheltenham	1923
10 (8ct, 2st)	H. Elliott	Derbyshire v Lancashire at Manchester	1935
10 (7ct, 3st)	P. Corrall	Leicestershire v Sussex at Hove	1936
10 (9ct, 1st)	R. A. Saggers	New South Wales v Combined XI at Brisbane	1940-41
10 (all ct)	A. E. Wilson	Gloucestershire v Hampshire at Portsmouth	1953
10 (7ct, 3st)	B. N. Jarman	South Australia v New South Wales at Adelaide	1961-62
10 (all ct)	L. A. Johnson	Northamptonshire v Sussex at Worthing	1963
10 (all ct)	R. W. Taylor	Derbyshire v Hampshire at Chesterfield	1963
10 (8ct, 2st)	L. A. Johnson	Northamptonshire v Warwickshire at Birmingham	1965
10 (9ct, 1st)	R. C. Jordon	Victoria v South Australia at Melbourne	1970-71

10 (all ct)	R. W. Marsh†	Western Australia v South Australia at Perth	1976-77
10 (6ct, 4st)	Taslim Arif	National Bank v Punjab at Lahore	1978-79
10 (9ct, 1st)	Arif-ud-Din	United Bank v Karachi 'B' at Karachi	1978-79
10 (all ct)	R. W. Taylor	England v India at Bombay	1979-80
10 (all ct)	R. J. Parks	Hampshire v Derbyshire at Portsmouth	1981
10 (9ct, 1st)	A. Ghosh	Bihar v Assam at Bhagalpur	1981-82
10 (8ct, 2st)	Z. A. Parkar	Bombay v Maharashtra at Bombay	1981-82
10 (9ct, 1st)	Kamal Najamuddin	Karachi v Lahore at Multan	1982-83

† *Marsh also scored a hundred (104), a unique "double".*

SEVEN OR MORE DISMISSALS IN AN INNINGS

8 (all ct)	A. T. W. Grout	Queensland v Western Australia at Brisbane	1959-60
7 (4ct, 3st)	E. J. Smith	Warwickshire v Derbyshire at Birmingham	1926
7 (6ct, 1st)	W. Farrimond	Lancashire v Kent at Manchester	1930
7 (all ct)	W. F. F. Price	Middlesex v Yorkshire at Lord's	1937
7 (3ct, 4st)	D. Tallon	Queensland v Victoria at Brisbane	1938-39
7 (all ct)	R. A. Saggers	New South Wales v Combined XI at Brisbane	1940-41
7 (1ct, 6st)	H. Yarnold	Worcestershire v Scotland at Dundee	1951
7 (4ct, 3st)	J. W. Brown	Scotland v Ireland at Dublin	1957
7 (6ct, 1st)	N. Kirsten	Border v Rhodesia at East London	1959-60
7 (all ct)	M. S. Smith	Natal v Border at East London	1959-60
7 (all ct)	K. V. Andrew	Northamptonshire v Lancashire at Manchester	1962
7 (all ct)	A. Long	Surrey v Sussex at Hove	1964
7 (all ct)	R. M. Schofield	Central Districts v Wellington at Wellington	1964-65
7 (all ct)	R. W. Taylor	Derbyshire v Glamorgan at Derby	1966
7 (6ct, 1st)	H. B. Taber	New South Wales v South Australia at Adelaide	1968-69
7 (6ct, 1st)	E. W. Jones	Glamorgan v Cambridge University at Cambridge	1970
7 (6ct, 1st)	S. Benjamin	Central Zone v North Zone at Bombay	1973-74
7 (all ct)	R. W. Taylor	Derbyshire v Yorkshire at Chesterfield	1975
7 (6ct, 1st)	Shahid Israr	Karachi Whites v Quetta at Karachi	1976-77
7 (all ct)	J. A. Maclean	Queensland v Victoria at Melbourne	1977-78
7 (5ct, 2st)	Taslim Arif	National Bank v Punjab at Lahore	1978-79
7 (all ct)	Wasim Bari	Pakistan v New Zealand at Auckland	1978-79
7 (all ct)	R. W. Taylor	England v India at Bombay	1979-80
7 (all ct)	D. L. Bairstow	Yorkshire v Derbyshire at Scarborough	1982
7 (6ct, 1st)	R. B. Phillips	Queensland v New Zealanders at Brisbane	1982-83
7 (3ct, 4st)	Masood Iqbal	Habib Bank v Lahore at Lahore	1982-83

WICKET-KEEPERS' HAT-TRICKS

W. H. Brain, Gloucestershire v Somerset at Cheltenham, 1893 – three stumpings off successive balls from C. L. Townsend.

G. O. Dawkes, Derbyshire v Worcestershire at Kidderminster, 1958 – three catches off successive balls from H. L. Jackson.

MOST CATCHES – EXCLUDING WICKET-KEEPERS

In a Career

1,018	F. E. Woolley (1906-38)	811	D. B. Close (1949-83)
877	W. G. Grace (1865-1908)	786	J. G. Langridge (1928-55)
830	G. A. R. Lock (1946-71)	755	E. H. Hendren (1907-38)
819	W. R. Hammond (1920-51)	755	C. A. Milton (1948-74)

In a Season

78	W. R. Hammond	1928		65	W. R. Hammond	1925
77	M. J. Stewart	1957		65	P. M. Walker	1959
73	P. M. Walker	1961		65	D. W. Richardson	1961
71	P. J. Sharpe	1962		64	J. Tunnicliffe	1904
70	J. Tunnicliffe	1901		64	K. F. Barrington	1957
69	J. G. Langridge	1955		64	G. A. R. Lock	1957
69	P. M. Walker	1960		63	K. J. Grieves	1950
65	J. Tunnicliffe	1895		63	C. A. Milton	1956

In a Match

10	W. R. Hammond	Gloucestershire v Surrey at Cheltenham		1928
8	W. B. Burns	Worcestershire v Yorkshire at Bradford		1907
8	A. H. Bakewell	Northamptonshire v Essex at Leyton		1928
8	W. R. Hammond	Gloucestershire v Worcestershire at Cheltenham		1932
8	K. J. Grieves	Lancashire v Sussex at Manchester		1951
8	C. A. Milton	Gloucestershire v Sussex at Hove		1952
8	G. A. R. Lock	Surrey v Warwickshire at The Oval		1957
8	J. M. Prodger	Kent v Gloucestershire at Cheltenham		1961
8	P. M. Walker	Glamorgan v Derbyshire at Swansea		1970
8	Javed Miandad	Habib Bank v Universities at Lahore		1977-78

In an Innings

7	M. J. Stewart	Surrey v Northamptonshire at Northampton	1957
7	A. S. Brown	Gloucestershire v Nottinghamshire at Nottingham	1966

THE SIDES

HIGHEST TOTALS

1,107	Victoria v New South Wales at Melbourne	1926-27
1,059	Victoria v Tasmania at Melbourne	1922-23
951-7 dec.	Sind v Baluchistan at Karachi	1973-74
918	New South Wales v South Australia at Sydney	1900-01
912-8 dec.	Holkar v Mysore at Indore	1945-46
910-6 dec.	Railways v Dera Ismail Khan at Lahore	1964-65
903-7 dec.	England v Australia at The Oval	1938
887	Yorkshire v Warwickshire at Birmingham	1896
849	England v West Indies at Kingston	1929-30
843	Australians v Oxford and Cambridge Universities Past and Present at Portsmouth	1893

HIGHEST FOR EACH FIRST-CLASS COUNTY

Derbyshire	645	v Hampshire at Derby	1898
Essex	692	v Somerset at Taunton	1895
Glamorgan	587-8	v Derbyshire at Cardiff	1951
Gloucestershire	653-6	v Glamorgan at Bristol	1928
Hampshire	672-7	v Somerset at Taunton	1899
Kent	803-4	v Essex at Brentwood	1934
Lancashire	801	v Somerset at Taunton	1895

Leicestershire	701-4	v Worcestershire at Worcester	1906
Middlesex	642-3	v Hampshire at Southampton	1923
Northamptonshire	557-6	v Sussex at Hove	1914
Nottinghamshire	739-7	v Leicestershire at Nottingham	1903
Somerset	675-9	v Hampshire at Bath	1924
Surrey	811	v Somerset at The Oval	1899
Sussex	705-8	v Surrey at Hastings	1902
Warwickshire	657-6	v Hampshire at Birmingham	1899
Worcestershire	633	v Warwickshire at Worcester	1906
Yorkshire	887	v Warwickshire at Birmingham	1896

LOWEST TOTALS

12	Oxford University v MCC and Ground at Oxford	†1877
12	Northamptonshire v Gloucestershire at Gloucester	1907
13	Auckland v Canterbury at Auckland	1877-78
13	Nottinghamshire v Yorkshire at Nottingham	1901
14	Surrey v Essex at Chelmsford	1983
15	MCC v Surrey at Lord's	1839
15	Victoria v MCC at Melbourne	†1903-04
15	Northamptonshire v Yorkshire at Northampton	†1908
15	Hampshire v Warwickshire at Birmingham	1922
	(Following on, Hampshire scored 521 and won by 155 runs.)	
16	MCC and Ground v Surrey at Lord's	1872
16	Derbyshire v Nottinghamshire at Nottingham	1879
16	Surrey v Nottinghamshire at The Oval	1880
16	Warwickshire v Kent at Tonbridge	1913
16	Trinidad v Barbados at Bridgetown	1941-42
16	Border v Natal at East London (first innings)	1959-60
17	Gentlemen of Kent v Gentlemen of England at Lord's	1850
17	Gloucestershire v Australians at Cheltenham	1896
18	The 'B's v England at Lord's	1831
18	Kent v Sussex at Gravesend	†1867
18	Tasmania v Victoria at Melbourne	1868-69
18	Australians v MCC and Ground at Lord's	†1896
18	Border v Natal at East London (second innings)	1959-60
19	Sussex v Surrey at Godalming	1830
19	Sussex v Nottinghamshire at Hove	†1873
19	MCC and Ground v Australians at Lord's	1878
19	Wellington v Nelson at Nelson	1885-86

† *Signifies that one man was absent.*

Note: At Lord's in 1810, The 'B's, with one man absent, were dismissed by England for 6.

LOWEST TOTAL IN A MATCH

| 34 | (16 and 18) Border v Natal at East London | 1959-60 |
| 42 | (27 and 15) Northamptonshire v Yorkshire at Northampton | 1908 |

Note: Northamptonshire batted one man short in each innings.

LOWEST FOR EACH FIRST-CLASS COUNTY

Derbyshire	16	v Nottinghamshire at Nottingham	1879
Essex	30	v Yorkshire at Leyton	1901
Glamorgan	22	v Lancashire at Liverpool	1924
Gloucestershire	17	v Australians at Cheltenham	1896
Hampshire	15	v Warwickshire at Birmingham	1922

Kent	18	v Sussex at Gravesend	1867
Lancashire	25	v Derbyshire at Manchester	1871
Leicestershire	25	v Kent at Leicester	1912
Middlesex	20	v MCC at Lord's	1864
Northamptonshire	12	v Gloucestershire at Gloucester	1907
Nottinghamshire	13	v Yorkshire at Nottingham	1901
Somerset	25	v Gloucestershire at Bristol	1947
Surrey	14	v Essex at Chelmsford	1983
Sussex	19	v Nottinghamshire at Hove	1873
Warwickshire	16	v Kent at Tonbridge	1913
Worcestershire	24	v Yorkshire at Huddersfield	1903
Yorkshire	23	v Hampshire at Middlesbrough	1965

HIGHEST MATCH AGGREGATES

2,376 for 38 wickets	Maharashtra v Bombay at Poona	1948-49
2,078 for 40 wickets	Bombay v Holkar at Bombay	1944-45
1,981 for 35 wickets	England v South Africa at Durban	1938-39
1,929 for 39 wickets	New South Wales v South Australia at Sydney	1925-26
1,911 for 34 wickets	New South Wales v Victoria at Sydney	1908-09
1,905 for 40 wickets	Otago v Wellington at Dunedin	1923-24

In England

1,723 for 31 wickets	England v Australia at Leeds	1948
1,601 for 29 wickets	England v Australia at Lord's	1930
1,507 for 28 wickets	England v West Indies at The Oval	1976
1,502 for 28 wickets	MCC v New Zealanders at Lord's	1927
1,499 for 31 wickets	T. N. Pearce's XI v Australians at Scarborough	1961
1,496 for 24 wickets	England v Australia at Nottingham	1938
1,494 for 37 wickets	England v Australia at The Oval	1934

LOWEST MATCH AGGREGATE

105 for 31 wickets	MCC v Australians at Lord's	1878

Note: The lowest aggregate since 1900 is 158 for 22 wickets, Surrey v Worcestershire at The Oval, 1954.

HIGHEST FOURTH INNINGS TOTALS

(Unless otherwise stated, the side making the runs won the match.)

654-5	England v South Africa at Durban	1938-39
	(After being set 696 to win. The match was left drawn on the tenth day.)	
604	Maharashtra v Bombay at Poona	1948-49
	(After being set 959 to win.)	
576-8	Trinidad v Barbados at Port-of-Spain	1945-46
	(After being set 672 to win. Match drawn on fifth day.)	
572	New South Wales v South Australia at Sydney	1907-08
	(After being set 593 to win.)	
529-9	Combined XI v South Africans at Perth	1963-64
	(After being set 579 to win. Match drawn on fourth day.)	

518	Victoria v Queensland at Brisbane	1926-27
	(After being set 753 to win.)	
507-7	Cambridge University v MCC and Ground at Lord's	1896
502-6	Middlesex v Nottinghamshire at Nottingham	1925
	(Game won by an unfinished stand of 271; a county record.)	
502-8	Players v Gentlemen at Lord's	1900
500-7	South African Universities v Western Province at Stellenbosch	1978-79

LARGEST VICTORIES

Largest Innings Victories

Inns and 851 runs:	Railways (910-6 dec.) v Dera Ismail Khan (Lahore)	1964-65
Inns and 666 runs:	Victoria (1,059) v Tasmania (Melbourne)	1922-23
Inns and 656 runs:	Victoria (1,107) v New South Wales (Melbourne)	1926-27
Inns and 605 runs:	New South Wales (918) v South Australia (Sydney)	1900-01
Inns and 579 runs:	England (903-7 dec.) v Australia (The Oval)	1938
Inns and 575 runs:	Sind (951-7 dec.) v Baluchistan (Karachi)	1973-74
Inns and 527 runs:	New South Wales (713) v South Australia (Adelaide)	1908-09
Inns and 517 runs:	Australians (675) v Nottinghamshire (Nottingham)	1921

Largest Victories by Runs Margin

685 runs:	New South Wales (235 and 761-8 dec.) v Queensland (Sydney)	1929-30
675 runs:	England (521 and 342-8 dec.) v Australia (Brisbane)	1928-29
638 runs:	New South Wales (304 and 770) v South Australia (Adelaide)	1920-21
625 runs:	Sargodha (376 and 416) v Lahore Municipal Corporation (Faisalabad).	1978-79
609 runs:	Muslim Commercial Bank (575 and 282-0 dec.) v WAPDA (Lahore).	1977-78
571 runs:	Victoria (304 and 649) v South Australia (Adelaide)	1926-27
562 runs:	Australia (701 and 327) v England (The Oval)	1934

Victory Without Losing a Wicket

Lancashire (166-0 dec. and 66-0) beat Leicestershire by ten wickets (Manchester).	1956
Karachi 'A' (277-0 dec.) beat Sind 'A' by an innings and 77 runs (Karachi)	1957-58
Railways (236-0 dec. and 16-0) beat Jammu and Kashmir by ten wickets (Srinagar)..	1960-61
Karnataka (451-0 dec.) beat Kerala by an innings and 186 runs (Chikmagalur)....	1977-78

TIED MATCHES IN FIRST-CLASS CRICKET

There have been 28 tied matches since the First World War.

Somerset v Sussex at Taunton	1919
(The last Sussex batsman not allowed to bat under Law 45 [subsequently Law 17 and now Law 31])	
Orange Free State v Eastern Province at Bloemfontein	1925-26
(Eastern Province had two wickets to fall.)	
Essex v Somerset at Chelmsford	1926
(Although Essex had one man to go in, MCC ruled that the game should rank as a tie. The ninth wicket fell half a minute before time.)	
Gloucestershire v Australians at Bristol	1930
Victoria v MCC at Melbourne	1932-33
(Victoria's third wicket fell to the last ball of the match when one run was needed to win.)	
Worcestershire v Somerset at Kidderminster	1939

Southern Punjab v Baroda at Patiala	1945-46
Essex v Northamptonshire at Ilford	1947
Hampshire v Lancashire at Bournemouth	1947
D. G. Bradman's XI v A. L. Hassett's XI at Melbourne	1948-49
Hampshire v Kent at Southampton	1950
Sussex v Warwickshire at Hove	1952
Essex v Lancashire at Brentwood	1952
Northamptonshire v Middlesex at Peterborough	1953
Yorkshire v Leicestershire at Huddersfield	1954
Sussex v Hampshire at Eastbourne	1955
Victoria v New South Wales at Melbourne	1956-57
T. N. Pearce's XI v New Zealanders at Scarborough	1958
Essex v Gloucestershire at Leyton	1959
Australia v West Indies (First Test) at Brisbane	1960-61
Bahawalpur v Lahore 'B' at Bahawalpur	1961-62
Hampshire v Middlesex at Portsmouth	1967
England XI v England Under 25 XI at Scarborough	1968
Yorkshire v Middlesex at Bradford	1973
Sussex v Essex at Hove	1974
South Australia v Queensland at Adelaide	1976-77
Central Districts v England XI at New Plymouth	1977-78
Peshawar v Allied Bank at Peshawar	1979-80
Victoria v New Zealanders at Melbourne	1982-83

Note: Since 1948 a tie has been recognised only when the scores are level with all the wickets down in the fourth innings. This ruling applies to all grades of cricket, and in the case of a one-day match to the second innings, provided that the match has not been brought to a further conclusion.

MATCHES BEGUN AND FINISHED IN ONE DAY

Since 1900. A fuller list may be found in the Wisden *of 1981 and preceding editions.*

Yorkshire v Worcestershire at Bradford, May 7	1900
MCC and Ground v London County at Lord's, May 20	1903
Transvaal v Orange Free State at Johannesburg, December 30	1906
Middlesex v Gentlemen of Philadelphia at Lord's, July 20	1908
Gloucestershire v Middlesex at Bristol, August 26	1909
Eastern Province v Orange Free State at Port Elizabeth, December 26	1912
Kent v Sussex at Tonbridge, June 21	1919
Lancashire v Somerset at Manchester, May 21	1925
Madras v Mysore at Madras, November 4	1934
Ireland v New Zealanders at Dublin, September 11	1937
Derbyshire v Somerset at Chesterfield, June 11	1947
Lancashire v Sussex at Manchester, July 12	1950
Surrey v Warwickshire at The Oval, May 16	1953
Somerset v Lancashire at Bath, June 6 (H. T. F. Buse's benefit)	1953
Kent v Worcestershire at Tunbridge Wells, June 15	1960

TEST MATCH RECORDS

SCORERS OF 2,000 RUNS IN TESTS

FOR ENGLAND

	T	I	NO	R	HI	100s	Avge
G. Boycott	108	193	23	8,114	246*	22	47.72
M. C. Cowdrey	114	188	15	7,624	182	22	44.06
W. R. Hammond	85	140	16	7,249	336*	22	58.45
L. Hutton	79	138	15	6,971	364	19	56.67
K. F. Barrington	82	131	15	6,806	256	20	58.67
D. C. S. Compton	78	131	15	5,807	278	17	50.06
J. B. Hobbs	61	102	7	5,410	211	15	56.94
J. H. Edrich	77	127	9	5,138	310*	12	43.54
T. W. Graveney	79	123	13	4,882	258	11	44.38
H. Sutcliffe	54	84	9	4,555	194	16	60.73
P. B. H. May	66	106	9	4,537	285*	13	46.77
E. R. Dexter	62	102	8	4,502	205	9	47.89
A. P. E. Knott	95	149	15	4,389	135	5	32.75
D. I. Gower	53	93	8	3,742	200*	7	44.02
D. L. Amiss	50	88	10	3,612	262*	11	46.30
A. W. Greig	58	93	4	3,599	148	8	40.43
I. T. Botham	63	100	3	3,548	208	12	36.57
E. H. Hendren	51	83	9	3,525	205*	7	47.63
F. E. Woolley	64	98	7	3,283	154	5	36.07
K. W. R. Fletcher	59	96	14	3,272	216	7	39.90
M. Leyland	41	65	5	2,764	187	9	46.06
C. Washbrook	37	66	6	2,569	195	6	42.81
G. A. Gooch	42	75	4	2,540	153	4	35.77
B. L. D'Oliveira	44	70	8	2,484	158	5	40.06
W. J. Edrich	39	63	2	2,440	219	6	40.00
T. G. Evans	91	133	14	2,439	104	2	20.49
L. E. G. Ames	47	72	12	2,434	149	8	40.56
W. Rhodes	58	98	21	2,325	179	2	30.19
T. E. Bailey	61	91	14	2,290	134*	1	29.74
M. J. K. Smith	50	78	6	2,278	121	3	31.63
D. W. Randall	40	68	5	2,073	174	5	32.90
P. E. Richardson	34	56	1	2,061	126	5	37.47

FOR AUSTRALIA

	T	I	NO	R	HI	100s	Avge
D. G. Bradman	52	80	10	6,996	334	29	99.94
G. S. Chappell	82	145	18	6,746	247*	22	53.11
R. N. Harvey	79	137	10	6,149	205	21	48.41
K. D. Walters	74	125	14	5,357	250	15	48.26
I. M. Chappell	75	136	10	5,345	196	14	42.42
W. M. Lawry	67	123	12	5,234	210	13	47.15
R. B. Simpson	62	111	7	4,869	311	10	46.81
I. R. Redpath	66	120	11	4,737	171	8	43.45
K. J. Hughes	56	100	6	3,744	213	8	39.82
R. W. Marsh	91	144	11	3,558	132	3	26.75
A. R. Border	51	91	16	3,539	162	9	47.18
A. R. Morris	46	79	3	3,533	206	12	46.48
C. Hill	49	89	2	3,412	191	7	39.21
V. T. Trumper	48	89	8	3,163	214*	8	39.04

	T	I	NO	R	HI	100s	Avge
C. C. McDonald	47	83	4	3,107	170	5	39.32
A. L. Hassett	43	69	3	3,073	198*	10	46.56
K. R. Miller	55	87	7	2,958	147	7	36.97
W. W. Armstrong	50	84	10	2,863	159*	6	38.68
K. R. Stackpole	43	80	5	2,807	207	7	37.42
N. C. O'Neill	42	69	8	2,779	181	6	45.55
S. J. McCabe	39	62	5	2,748	232	6	48.21
G. M. Wood	42	81	5	2,554	126	7	33.60
W. Bardsley	41	66	5	2,469	193*	6	40.47
W. M. Woodfull	35	54	4	2,300	161	7	46.00
P. J. Burge	42	68	8	2,290	181	4	38.16
S. E. Gregory	58	100	7	2,282	201	4	24.53
R. Benaud	63	97	7	2,201	122	3	24.45
G. N. Yallop	33	62	3	2,199	172	6	37.27
C. G. Macartney	35	55	4	2,131	170	7	41.78
W. H. Ponsford	29	48	4	2,122	266	7	48.22
R. M. Cowper	27	46	2	2,061	307	5	46.84

FOR SOUTH AFRICA

	T	I	NO	R	HI	100s	Avge
B. Mitchell	42	80	9	3,471	189*	8	48.88
A. D. Nourse	34	62	7	2,960	231	9	53.81
H. W. Taylor	42	76	4	2,936	176	7	40.77
E. J. Barlow	30	57	2	2,516	201	6	45.74
T. L. Goddard	41	78	5	2,516	112	1	34.46
D. J. McGlew	34	64	6	2,440	255*	7	42.06
J. H. B. Waite	50	86	7	2,405	134	4	30.44
R. G. Pollock	23	41	4	2,256	274	7	60.97
A. W. Nourse	45	83	8	2,234	111	1	29.78
R. A. McLean	40	73	3	2,120	142	5	30.28

FOR WEST INDIES

	T	I	NO	R	HI	100s	Avge
G. S. Sobers	93	160	21	8,032	365*	26	57.78
C. H. Lloyd	90	149	10	6,238	242*	16	44.87
R. B. Kanhai	79	137	6	6,227	256	15	47.53
E. D. Weekes	48	81	5	4,455	207	15	58.61
I. V. A. Richards	52	80	4	4,411	291	14	58.03
A. I. Kallicharran	66	109	10	4,399	187	12	44.43
R. C. Fredericks	59	109	7	4,334	169	8	42.49
F. M. M. Worrell	51	87	9	3,860	261	9	49.48
C. L. Walcott	44	74	7	3,798	220	15	56.68
C. C. Hunte	44	78	6	3,245	260	8	45.06
B. F. Butcher	44	78	6	3,104	209*	7	43.11
C. G. Greenidge	41	70	5	2,962	154	6	45.56
S. M. Nurse	29	54	1	2,523	258	6	47.60
G. A. Headley	22	40	4	2,190	270*	10	60.83
J. B. Stollmeyer	32	56	5	2,159	160	4	42.33
L. G. Rowe	30	49	2	2,047	302	7	43.55

FOR NEW ZEALAND

	T	I	NO	R	HI	100s	Avge
B. E. Congdon	61	114	7	3,448	176	7	32.22
J. R. Reid	58	108	5	3,428	142	6	33.28
G. M. Turner	41	73	6	2,991	259	7	44.64
B. Sutcliffe	42	76	8	2,727	230*	5	40.10
M. G. Burgess	50	92	6	2,684	119*	5	31.20
G. T. Dowling	39	77	3	2,306	239	3	31.16
G. P. Howarth	34	62	5	2,014	147	6	35.33

FOR INDIA

	T	I	NO	R	HI	100s	Avge
S. M. Gavaskar	90	158	12	7,625	221	27	52.22
G. R. Viswanath	91	155	10	6,080	222	14	41.93
P. R. Umrigar	59	94	8	3,631	223	12	42.22
D. B. Vengsarkar	63	103	10	3,484	157*	6	37.46
V. L. Manjrekar	55	92	10	3,208	189*	7	39.12
C. G. Borde	55	97	11	3,061	177*	5	35.59
Nawab of Pataudi jun. ..	46	83	3	2,793	203*	6	34.91
M. Amarnath	37	64	5	2,648	120	7	44.88
F. M. Engineer	46	87	3	2,611	121	2	31.08
Pankaj Roy	43	79	4	2,442	173	5	32.56
Kapil Dev	53	77	8	2,253	126*	3	32.65
V. S. Hazare	30	52	6	2,192	164*	7	47.65
A. L. Wadekar	37	71	3	2,113	143	1	31.07
V. Mankad	44	72	5	2,109	231	5	31.47
S. M. H. Kirmani	69	99	14	2,100	101*	1	24.70
C. P. S. Chauhan	40	68	2	2,084	97	0	31.57
M. L. Jaisimha	39	71	4	2,056	129	3 ·	30.68
D. N. Sardesai	30	55	4	2,001	212	5	39.23

FOR PAKISTAN

	T	I	NO	R	HI	100s	Avge
Zaheer Abbas	58	94	7	4,073	274	11	46.81
Javed Miandad	52	83	14	3,992	280*	10	57.85
Majid J. Khan	63	106	5	3,931	167	8	38.92
Hanif Mohammad	55	97	8	3,915	337	12	43.98
Mushtaq Mohammad	57	100	7	3,643	201	10	39.17
Asif Iqbal	58	99	7	3,575	175	11	38.85
Saeed Ahmed	41	78	4	2,991	172	5	40.41
Sadiq Mohammad	41	74	2	2,579	166	5	35.81
Wasim Raja	45	74	12	2,321	117*	2	37.43
Mudassar Nazar	35	54	5	2,138	231	6	43.63
Imtiaz Ahmed	41	72	1	2,079	209	3	29.28

HIGHEST INNINGS TOTALS IN TESTS

903-7 dec.	England v Australia at The Oval	1938
849	England v West Indies at Kingston	1929-30
790-3 dec.	West Indies v Pakistan at Kingston	1957-58
758-8 dec.	Australia v West Indies at Kingston	1954-55
729-6 dec.	Australia v England at Lord's	1930
701	Australia v England at The Oval	1934
695	Australia v England at The Oval	1930
687-8 dec.	West Indies v England at The Oval	1976
681-8 dec.	West Indies v England at Port-of-Spain	1953-54
674	Australia v India at Adelaide	1947-48
668	Australia v West Indies at Bridgetown	1954-55
659-8 dec.	Australia v England at Sydney	1946-47
658-8 dec.	England v Australia at Nottingham	1938
657-8 dec.	Pakistan v West Indies at Bridgetown	1957-58
656-8 dec.	Australia v England at Manchester	1964
654-5	England v South Africa at Durban	1938-39
652-8 dec.	West Indies v England at Lord's	1973
652	Pakistan v India at Faisalabad	1982-83
650-6 dec.	Australia v West Indies at Bridgetown	1964-65

The highest innings for the countries not mentioned above are:

644-7 dec.	India v West Indies at Kanpur	1978-79
622-9 dec.	South Africa v Australia at Durban	1969-70
551-9 dec.	New Zealand v England at Lord's	1973
454	Sri Lanka v Pakistan at Faisalabad	1981-82

LOWEST INNINGS TOTALS IN TESTS

26	New Zealand v England at Auckland	1954-55
30	South Africa v England at Port Elizabeth	1895-96
30	South Africa v England at Birmingham	1924
35	South Africa v England at Cape Town	1898-99
36	Australia v England at Birmingham	1902
36	South Africa v Australia at Melbourne	1931-32
42	Australia v England at Sydney	1887-88
42	New Zealand v Australia at Wellington	1945-46
42†	India v England at Lord's	1974
43	South Africa v England at Cape Town	1888-89
44	Australia v England at The Oval	1896
45	England v Australia at Sydney	1886-87
45	South Africa v Australia at Melbourne	1931-32
47	South Africa v England at Cape Town	1888-89
47	New Zealand v England at Lord's	1958

The lowest innings for the countries not mentioned above are:

76	West Indies v Pakistan at Dacca	1958-59
62	Pakistan v Australia at Perth	1981-82
93	Sri Lanka v New Zealand at Wellington	1982-83

† *Batted one man short.*

HIGHEST INDIVIDUAL TEST INNINGS

365*	G. S. Sobers, West Indies v Pakistan at Kingston	1957-58
364	L. Hutton, England v Australia at The Oval	1938
337	Hanif Mohammad, Pakistan v West Indies at Bridgetown	1957-58
336*	W. R. Hammond, England v New Zealand at Auckland	1932-33

334	D. G. Bradman, Australia v England at Leeds	1930
325	A. Sandham, England v West Indies at Kingston	1929-30
311	R. B. Simpson, Australia v England at Manchester	1964
310*	J. H. Edrich, England v New Zealand at Leeds	1965
307	R. M. Cowper, Australia v England at Melbourne	1965-66
304	D. G. Bradman, Australia v England at Leeds	1934
302	L. G. Rowe, West Indies v England at Bridgetown	1973-74
299*	D. G. Bradman, Australia v South Africa at Adelaide	1931-32
291	I. V. A. Richards, West Indies v England at The Oval	1976
287	R. E. Foster, England v Australia at Sydney	1903-04
285*	P. B. H. May, England v West Indies at Birmingham	1957
280*	Javed Miandad, Pakistan v India at Hyderabad	1982-83
278	D. C. S. Compton, England v Pakistan at Nottingham	1954
274	R. G. Pollock, South Africa v Australia at Durban	1969-70
274	Zaheer Abbas, Pakistan v England at Birmingham	1971
270*	G. A. Headley, West Indies v England at Kingston	1934-35
270	D. G. Bradman, Australia v England at Melbourne	1936-37
266	W. H. Ponsford, Australia v England at The Oval	1934
262*	D. L. Amiss, England v West Indies at Kingston	1973-74
261	F. M. M. Worrell, West Indies v England at Nottingham	1950
260	C. C. Hunte, West Indies v Pakistan at Kingston	1957-58
259	G. M. Turner, New Zealand v West Indies at Georgetown	1971-72
258	T. W. Graveney, England v West Indies at Nottingham	1957
258	S. M. Nurse, West Indies v New Zealand at Christchurch	1968-69
256	R. B. Kanhai, West Indies v India at Calcutta	1958-59
256	K. F. Barrington, England v Australia at Manchester	1964
255*	D. J. McGlew, South Africa v New Zealand at Wellington	1952-53
254	D. G. Bradman, Australia v England at Leeds	1930
251	W. R. Hammond, England v Australia at Sydney	1928-29
250	K. D. Walters, Australia v New Zealand at Christchurch	1976-77
250	S. F. A. Bacchus, West Indies v India at Kanpur	1978-79

The highest individual innings for other countries are:

231	V. Mankad, India v New Zealand at Madras	1955-56
157	S. Wettimuny, Sri Lanka v Pakistan at Faisalabad	1981-82

TEST BATTING AVERAGE OVER 50
(Qualification: 20 innings)

Avge		T	I	NO	R	HI	100s
99.94	D. G. Bradman (*A*)	52	80	10	6,996	334	29
60.97	R. G. Pollock (*SA*)	23	41	4	2,256	274	7
60.83	G. A. Headley (*WI*)	22	40	4	2,190	270*	10
60.73	H. Sutcliffe (*E*)	54	84	9	4,555	194	16
59.23	E. Paynter (*E*)	20	31	5	1,540	243	4
58.67	K. F. Barrington (*E*)	82	131	5	6,806	256	20
58.61	E. D. Weekes (*WI*)	48	81	5	4,455	207	15
58.45	W. R. Hammond (*E*)	85	140	16	7,249	336*	22
58.03	I. V. A. Richards (*WI*)	52	80	4	4,411	291	14
57.85	Javed Miandad (*P*)	52	83	14	3,992	280*	10
57.78	G. S. Sobers (*WI*)	93	160	21	8,032	365*	26
56.94	J. B. Hobbs (*E*)	61	102	7	5,410	211	15
56.68	C. L. Walcott (*WI*)	44	74	7	3,798	220	15
56.67	L. Hutton (*E*)	79	138	15	6,971	364	19
55.00	E. Tyldesley (*E*)	14	20	2	990	122	3
54.20	C. A. Davis (*WI*)	15	29	5	1,301	183	4
53.81	A. D. Nourse (*SA*)	34	62	7	2,960	231	9
53.11	G. S. Chappell (*A*)	82	145	18	6,746	247*	22
52.22	S. M. Gavaskar (*I*)	90	158	12	7,625	221	27
51.62	J. Ryder (*A*)	20	32	5	1,394	201*	3
50.06	D. C. S. Compton (*E*)	78	131	15	5,807	278	17

HUNDRED ON TEST DEBUT

C. Bannerman (165*)	Australia v England at Melbourne	1876-77
W. G. Grace (152)	England v Australia at The Oval	1880
H. Graham (107)	Australia v England at Lord's	1893
K. S. Ranjitsinhji (154*)...	England v Australia at Manchester	1896
P. F. Warner (132*).........	England v South Africa at Johannesburg	1898-99
R. A. Duff (104).............	Australia v England at Melbourne	1901-02
R. E. Foster (287)	England v Australia at Sydney	1903-04
G. Gunn (119)..............	England v Australia at Sydney	1907-08
R. J. Hartigan (116)	Australia v England at Adelaide	1907-08
H. L. Collins (104)	Australia v England at Sydney	1920-21
W. H. Ponsford (110)	Australia v England at Sydney	1924-25
A. Jackson (164)	Australia v England at Adelaide	1928-29
G. A. Headley (176)........	West Indies v England at Bridgetown	1929-30
J. E. Mills (117)...........	New Zealand v England at Wellington	1929-30
Nawab of Pataudi (102)	England v Australia at Sydney	1932-33
B. H. Valentine (136)	England v India at Bombay	1933-34
L. Amarnath (118)	India v England at Bombay	1933-34
P. A. Gibb (106)	England v South Africa at Johannesburg	1938-39
S. C. Griffith (140)	England v West Indies at Port-of-Spain	1947-48
A. G. Ganteaume (112)	West Indies v England at Port-of-Spain	1947-48
J. W. Burke (101*)..........	Australia v England at Adelaide	1950-51
P. B. H. May (138)	England v South Africa at Leeds	1951
D. H. Shodhan (110)	India v Pakistan at Calcutta................................	1952-53
B. H. Pairaudeau (115)	West Indies v India at Port-of-Spain	1952-53
O. G. Smith (104)	West Indies v Australia at Kingston	1954-55
A. G. Kripal Singh (100*) ..	India v New Zealand at Hyderabad	1955-56
C. C. Hunte (142)	West Indies v Pakistan at Bridgetown	1957-58
C. A. Milton (104*).........	England v New Zealand at Leeds	1958
A. A. Baig (112)...........	India v England at Manchester	1959
Hanumant Singh (105)	India v England at Delhi	1963-64
Khalid Ibadulla (166)	Pakistan v Australia at Karachi...........................	1964-65
B. R. Taylor (105)..........	New Zealand v India at Calcutta	1964-65
K. D. Walters (155).........	Australia v England at Brisbane	1965-66
J. H. Hampshire (107)	England v West Indies at Lord's	1969
G. R. Viswanath (137)	India v Australia at Kanpur...............................	1969-70
G. S. Chappell (108)........	Australia v England at Perth	1970-71
†L. G. Rowe (214, 100*) ..	West Indies v New Zealand at Kingston	1971-72
A. I. Kallicharran (100*) ..	West Indies v New Zealand at Georgetown	1971-72
R. E. Redmond (107)	New Zealand v Pakistan at Auckland	1972-73
F. C. Hayes (106*)	England v West Indies at The Oval	1973
C. G. Greenidge (107)	West Indies v India at Bangalore.........................	1974-75
L. Baichan (105*)...........	West Indies v Pakistan at Lahore	1974-75
G. J. Cosier (109)	Australia v West Indies at Melbourne	1975-76
S. Amarnath (124)	India v New Zealand at Auckland	1975-76
Javed Miandad (163)........	Pakistan v New Zealand at Lahore	1976-77
A. B. Williams (100)........	West Indies v Australia at Georgetown	1977-78
D. M. Wellham (103).......	Australia v England at The Oval	1981
Salim Malik (100*)..........	Pakistan v Sri Lanka at Karachi.........................	1981-82
K. C. Wessels (162)	Australia v England at Brisbane	1982-83

† *L. G. Rowe is the only batsman to score a hundred in each innings on début.*

300 RUNS IN FIRST TEST MATCH

314	L. G. Rowe (214, 100*)	West Indies v New Zealand at Kingston	1971-72
306	R. E. Foster (287, 19)	England v Australia at Sydney......................	1903-04

HUNDRED AND TEN WICKETS IN A TEST MATCH

I. T. Botham	114 and thirteen for 106	England v India at Bombay...........	1979-80
Imran Khan	117 and eleven for 180	Pakistan v India at Faisalabad........	1982-83

TWO SEPARATE HUNDREDS IN A TEST MATCH

Three times: S. M. Gavaskar v West Indies (1970-71), v Pakistan (1978-79), v West Indies (1978-79).

Twice in one series: C. L. Walcott v Australia (1954-55).

Twice: H. Sutcliffe v Australia (1924-25), v South Africa (1929); G. A. Headley v England (1929-30 and 1939); G. S. Chappell v New Zealand (1973-74), v West Indies (1975-76).

Once: W. Bardsley v England (1909); A. C. Russell v South Africa (1922-23); W. R. Hammond v Australia (1928-29); E. Paynter v South Africa (1938-39); D. C. S. Compton v Australia (1946-47); A. R. Morris v Australia (1946-47); A. Melville v England (1947); B. Mitchell v England (1947); D. G. Bradman v India (1947-48); V. S. Hazare v Australia (1947-48); E. D. Weekes v India (1948-49); J. Moroney v South Africa (1949-50); G. S. Sobers v Pakistan (1957-58); R. B. Kanhai v Australia (1960-61); Hanif Mohammad v England (1961-62); R. B. Simpson v Pakistan (1964-65); K. D. Walters v West Indies (1968-69); †L. G. Rowe v New Zealand (1971-72); I. M. Chappell v New Zealand (1973-74); G. M. Turner v Australia (1973-74); C. G. Greenidge v England (1976); G. P. Howarth v England (1977-78); ‡A. R. Border v Pakistan (1979-80); L. R. D. Mendis v India (1982-83).

  † *L. G. Rowe's two hundreds were on his Test début.*

  ‡ *A. R. Border scored 150* ad 153 to become the first batsman to score 150 in each innings of a Test match.*

HUNDRED AND DOUBLE-HUNDRED IN SAME TEST

K. D. Walters (Australia)	242 and 103 v West Indies (Sydney)	1968-69
S. M. Gavaskar (India)	124 and 220 v West Indies (Port-of-Spain)	1970-71
†L. G. Rowe (West Indies)	214 and 100* v New Zealand (Kingston)	1971-72
G. S. Chappell (Australia)	247* and 133 v New Zealand (Wellington)	1973-74

  † *On Test début*

MOST RUNS IN A TEST SERIES

	T	I	NO	R	HI	100s	Avge		
D. G. Bradman	5	7	0	974	334	4	139.14	A v E	1930
W. R. Hammond ...	5	9	1	905	251	4	113.12	E v A	1928-29
R. N. Harvey	5	9	0	834	205	4	92.66	A v SA	1952-53
I. V. A. Richards...	4	7	0	829	291	3	118.42	WI v E	1976
C. L. Walcott	5	10	0	827	155	5	82.70	WI v A	1954-55
G. S. Sobers	5	8	2	824	365*	3	137.33	WI v P	1957-58
D. G. Bradman	5	9	0	810	270	4	90.00	A v E	1936-37
D. G. Bradman	5	5	1	806	299*	4	201.50	A v SA	1931-32
E. D. Weekes........	5	7	0	779	194	4	111.28	WI v I	1948-49
†S. M. Gavaskar	4	8	3	774	220	4	154.80	I v WI	1970-71
Mudassar Nazar ...	6	8	2	761	231	4	126.83	P v I	1982-83
D. G. Bradman	5	8	0	758	304	2	94.75	A v E	1934
D. C. S. Compton ..	5	8	0	753	208	4	94.12	E v SA	1947

  † *Gavaskar's aggregate was achieved in his first Test series.*

CARRYING BAT THROUGH TEST INNINGS

(Figures in brackets show side's total)

A. B. Tancred	26*	(47)	South Africa v England (Cape Town)	1888-89
J. E. Barrett..........	67*	(176)	Australia v England (Lord's)	1890
R. Abel................	132*	(307)	England v Australia (Sydney)	1891-92
P. F. Warner........	132*	(237)	England v South Africa (Johannesburg)	1898-99
W. W. Armstrong ..	159*	(309)	Australia v South Africa (Johannesburg)	1902-03
J. W. Zulch..........	43*	(103)	South Africa v England (Cape Town)	1909-10

W. Bardsley	193*	(383)	Australia v England (Lord's)	1926
W. M. Woodfull	30*	(66)‡	Australia v England (Brisbane)	1928-29
W. M. Woodfull	73*	(193)†	Australia v England (Adelaide)	1932-33
W. A. Brown	206*	(422)	Australia v England (Lord's)	1938
L. Hutton	202*	(344)	England v West Indies (The Oval)	1950
L. Hutton	156*	(272)	England v Australia (Adelaide)	1950-51
Nazar Mohammad	124*	(331)	Pakistan v India (Lucknow)	1952-53
F. M. M. Worrell	191*	(372)	West Indies v England (Nottingham)	1957
T. L. Goddard	56*	(99)	South Africa v Australia (Cape Town)	1957-58
D. J. McGlew	127*	(292)	South Africa v New Zealand (Durban)	1961-62
C. C. Hunte	60*	(131)	West Indies v Australia (Port-of-Spain)	1964-65
G. M. Turner	43*	(131)	New Zealand v England (Lord's)	1969
W. M. Lawry	49*	(107)	Australia v India (Delhi)	1969-70
W. M. Lawry	60*	(116)†	Australia v England (Sydney)	1970-71
G. M. Turner	223*	(386)	New Zealand v West Indies (Kingston)	1971-72
I. R. Redpath	159*	(346)	Australia v New Zealand (Auckland)	1973-74
G. Boycott	99*	(215)	England v Australia (Perth)	1979-80
S. M. Gavaskar	127*	(286)	India v Pakistan (Faisalabad)	1982-83
Mudassar Nazar	152*	(323)	Pakistan v India (Lahore)	1982-83
S. Wettimuny	63*	(144)	Sri Lanka v New Zealand (Christchurch)	1982-83

† *One man absent.*   ‡ *Two men absent.*

Notes: G. M. Turner (223*) holds the record for the highest score by a player carrying his bat through a Test innings. He is also the youngest player to do so, being 22 years 63 days old when he first achieved the feat (1969).

D. L. Amiss (262*) batted throughout England's second innings of 432 for nine v West Indies at Kingston, 1973-74, the tenth wicket adding 40, unbroken, in fifty-three minutes.

D. L. Haynes (55 and 105) opened the batting and was last man out in each innings for West Indies v New Zealand at Dunedin, 1979-80.

FASTEST TEST FIFTIES

Minutes

28	J. T. Brown	England v Australia at Melbourne	1894-95
29	S. A. Durani	India v England at Kanpur	1963-64
30	E. A. V. Williams	West Indies v England at Bridgetown	1947-48
30	B. R. Taylor	New Zealand v West Indies at Auckland	1968-69
33	C. A. Roach	West Indies v England at The Oval	1933
34	C. R. Browne	West Indies v England at Georgetown	1929-30

FASTEST TEST HUNDREDS

Minutes

70	J. M. Gregory	Australia v South Africa at Johannesburg	1921-22
75	G. L. Jessop	England v Australia at The Oval	1902
78	R. Benaud	Australia v West Indies at Kingston	1954-55
80	J. H. Sinclair	South Africa v Australia at Cape Town	1902-03
86	B. R. Taylor	New Zealand v West Indies at Auckland	1968-69

Note: The fastest known hundred in a Test match in terms of balls received is off 67 balls by J. M. Gregory for Australia v South Africa at Johannesburg, 1921-22. R. C. Fredericks, for West Indies v Australia at Perth, 1975-76, reached his hundred off 71 balls. I. T. Botham, for England v Australia in 1981, reached three figures off 87 balls in the third Test match and off 86 balls in the fifth.

FASTEST TEST DOUBLE-HUNDREDS

Minutes

214	D. G. Bradman	Australia v England at Leeds	1930
223	S. J. McCabe	Australia v England at Nottingham	1938
226	V. T. Trumper	Australia v South Africa at Adelaide	1910-11
234	D. G. Bradman	Australia v England at Lord's	1930
240	W. R. Hammond	England v New Zealand at Auckland	1932-33
241	S. E. Gregory	Australia v England at Sydney	1894-95
245	D. C. S. Compton	England v Pakistan at Nottingham	1954

FASTEST TEST TRIPLE-HUNDREDS

Minutes
287	W. R. Hammond..	England v New Zealand at Auckland	1932-33
336	D. G. Bradman....	Australia v England at Leeds	1930

MOST RUNS IN A DAY BY A BATSMAN

309	D. G. Bradman....	Australia v England at Leeds	1930
295	W. R. Hammond..	England v New Zealand at Auckland	1932-33
273	D. C. S. Compton	England v Pakistan at Nottingham	1954
271	D. G. Bradman....	Australia v England at Leeds	1934

MOST RUNS IN A DAY (BOTH SIDES)

588	England (398 for six), India (190 for no wkt) at Manchester	1936
522	England (503 for two), South Africa (19 for no wkt) at Lord's	1924
508	England (221 for two), South Africa (287 for six) at The Oval	1935

MOST RUNS IN A DAY (ONE SIDE)

503	England (503 for two) v South Africa at Lord's	1924
494	Australia (494 for six) v South Africa at Sydney	1910-11
475	Australia (475 for two) v England at The Oval	1934
471	England (471 for eight) v India at The Oval	1936
458	Australia (458 for three) v England at Leeds	1930
455	Australia (455 for one) v England at Leeds	1934

SLOWEST INDIVIDUAL TEST BATTING

2* in 80 minutes	C. E. H. Croft, West Indies v Australia at Brisbane	1979-80
3* in 100 minutes	J. T. Murray, England v Australia at Sydney	1962-63
5 in 102 minutes	M. A. K. Pataudi, India v England at Bombay	1972-73
8 in 120 minutes	T. E. Bailey, England v South Africa at Leeds	1955
9 in 120 minutes	W. Newham, England v Australia at Sydney	1887-88
9 in 125 minutes	T. W. Jarvis, New Zealand v India at Madras	1964-65
10* in 133 minutes	T. G. Evans, England v Australia at Adelaide	1946-47
18 in 194 minutes	W. R. Playle, New Zealand v England at Leeds	1958
20 in 195 minutes	Hanif Mohammad, Pakistan v England at Lord's	1954
21 in 210 minutes	P. G. Z. Harris, New Zealand v Pakistan at Karachi	1955-56
28* in 250 minutes	J. W. Burke, Australia v England at Brisbane	1958-59
31 in 264 minutes	K. D. Mackay, Australia v England at Lord's	1956
35 in 332 minutes	C. J. Tavaré, England v India at Madras	1981-82
40 in 289 minutes	H. L. Collins, Australia v England at Manchester	1921
45 in 318 minutes	Shuja-ud-Din, Pakistan v Australia at Lahore	1959-60
55 in 336 minutes	B. A. Edgar, New Zealand v Australia at Wellington	1981-82
57 in 346 minutes	G. S. Camacho, West Indies v England at Bridgetown	1967-68
58 in 367 minutes	Ijaz Butt, Pakistan v Australia at Karachi	1959-60
68 in 458 minutes	T. E. Bailey, England v Australia at Brisbane	1958-59
99 in 505 minutes	M. L. Jaisimha, India v Pakistan at Kanpur	1960-61
105 in 575 minutes	D. J. McGlew, South Africa v Australia at Durban	1957-58
114 in 591 minutes	Mudassar Nazar, Pakistan v England at Lahore	1977-78
197* in 682 minutes	F. M. M. Worrell, West Indies v England at Bridgetown .	1959-60
259 in 705 minutes	G. M. Turner, New Zealand v West Indies at Georgetown .	1971-72
337 in 970 minutes	Hanif Mohammad, Pakistan v West Indies at Bridgetown .	1957-58

Note: C. J. Tavaré scored 147 in 710 minutes in two innings (69 in 287 minutes and 78 in 423 minutes) for England v Australia at Manchester, 1981.

SLOWEST TEST HUNDREDS

557 minutes Mudassar Nazar, Pakistan v England at Lahore 1977-78
545 minutes D. J. McGlew, South Africa v Australia at Durban 1957-58
488 minutes P. E. Richardson, England v South Africa at Johannesburg........... 1956-57

Note: The slowest for any Test in England is 458 minutes by K. W. R. Fletcher, England v Pakistan, The Oval, 1974.

LOWEST TEST SCORES IN FULL DAY'S PLAY

 95 At Karachi, October 11, 1956. Australia 80 all out; Pakistan 15 for two (first day, 5½ hours).
104 At Karachi, December 8, 1959. Pakistan 0 for no wicket to 104 for five v Australia (fourth day, 5½ hours).
106 At Brisbane, December 9, 1958. England 92 for two to 198 all out v Australia (fourth day, 5 hours). *England were dismissed five minutes before the close of play, leaving no time for Australia to start their second innings.*
112 At Karachi, October 15, 1956. Australia 138 for six to 187 all out; Pakistan 63 for one (fourth day, 5½ hours).
117 At Madras, October 19, 1956. India 117 for five v Australia (first day, 5½ hours).
122 At Port Elizabeth, March 4, 1957. England's last wicket fell after the first twenty minutes without addition. South Africa then made 122 for seven in five and a half hours (third day, 6 hours).
122 At Brisbane, December 8, 1958. Australia 156 for six to 186 all out; England 92 for two (third day, 5 hours).
122 At Melbourne, January 3, 1959. Australia 282 for seven to 308 all out and 9 for one; England 87 all out (fourth day, 5 hours). *There were two intervals between innings, amounting to twenty minutes.*
122 At Melbourne, December 30, 1978. Australia 243 for four to 258 all out; England 107 for eight (second day, 6 hours).
123 At Hyderabad, January 4, 1978. England 123 for two to 191 all out; Pakistan 55 for one (third day, 5½ hours).
124 At Dacca, November 17, 1959. Pakistan 74 for four to 134 all out; Australia 64 for one (fourth day, 5½ hours).
124 At Kanpur, December 23, 1959. India 226 for six to 291 all out; Australia 59 for two (fourth day, 5½ hours).
128 At Bridgetown, February 9, 1954. England 53 for two to 181 for nine v West Indies (third day, 5 hours).

In England

151 At Lord's, August 26, 1978. England 175 for two to 289 all out; New Zealand 37 for seven (third day, 6 hours).
159 At Leeds, July 10, 1971. Pakistan 208 for four to 350 all out; England 17 for one (third day, 6 hours).

HIGHEST MATCH AGGREGATES

Runs	Wkts			Days played
1,981	35	South Africa v England at Durban	1938-39	10†
1,815	34	West Indies v England at Kingston......................	1929-30	9‡
1,764	39	Australia v West Indies at Adelaide.....................	1968-69	5
1,753	40	Australia v England at Adelaide	1920-21	6

Runs	Wkts			Days played
1,723	31	England v Australia at Leeds..............................	1948	5
1,661	36	West Indies v Australia at Bridgetown	1954-55	6

† *No play on one day.*   ‡ *No play on two days.*

LOWEST MATCH AGGREGATES

(For a completed match)

Runs	Wkts			Days played
234	29	Australia v South Africa at Melbourne	1931-32	3†
291	40	England v Australia at Lord's...............................	1888	2
295	28	New Zealand v Australia at Wellington...................	1945-46	2
309	29	West Indies v England at Bridgetown....................	1934-35	3
323	30	England v Australia at Manchester......................	1888	2

† *No play on one day.*

HIGHEST FOURTH INNINGS TOTALS

To win

406-4	India v West Indies at Port-of-Spain...	1975-76
404-3	Australia v England at Leeds...	1948

To draw

654-5	England (needing 696 to win) v South Africa at Durban......................	1938-39
429-8	India (needing 438 to win) v England at The Oval	1979

To lose

445	India (lost by 47 runs) v Australia at Adelaide	1977-78
440	New Zealand (lost by 38 runs) v England at Nottingham......................	1973

HIGHEST TEST WICKET PARTNERSHIPS

413 for 1st	V. Mankad (231) and P. Roy (173) for India v New Zealand at Madras..	1955-56
451 for 2nd	W. H. Ponsford (266) and D. G. Bradman (244) for Australia v England at The Oval..	1934
451 for 3rd	Mudassar Nazar (231) and Javed Miandad (280*) for Pakistan v India at Hyderabad...	1982-83
411 for 4th	P. B. H. May (285*) and M. C. Cowdrey (154) for England v West Indies at Birmingham...	1957

405 for 5th	S. G. Barnes (234) and D. G. Bradman (234) for Australia v England at Sydney	1946-47
346 for 6th	J. H. W. Fingleton (136) and D. G. Bradman (270) for Australia v England at Melbourne	1936-37
347 for 7th	D. St E. Atkinson (219) and C. C. Depeiza (122) for West Indies v Australia at Bridgetown	1954-55
246 for 8th	L. E. G. Ames (137) and G. O. Allen (122) for England v New Zealand at Lord's	1931
190 for 9th	Asif Iqbal (146) and Intikhab Alam (51) for Pakistan v England at The Oval	1967
151 for 10th	B. F. Hastings (110) and R. O. Collinge (68*) for New Zealand v Pakistan at Auckland	1972-73

BOWLERS WITH 75 WICKETS IN TESTS

FOR ENGLAND

	T	Balls	R	W	Avge	5 W/i	10 W/m
F. S. Trueman	67	15,178	6,625	307	21.57	17	3
R. G. D. Willis	83	16,042	7,471	305	24.49	16	—
D. L. Underwood	86	21,862	7,674	297	25.83	17	6
I. T. Botham	63	14,727	6,876	277	24.82	20	4
J. B. Statham	70	16,056	6,261	252	24.84	9	1
A. V. Bedser	51	15,918	5,876	236	24.89	15	5
J. A. Snow	49	12,021	5,387	202	26.66	8	1
J. C. Laker	46	12,027	4,101	193	21.24	9	3
S. F. Barnes	27	7,873	3,106	189	16.43	24	7
G. A. R. Lock	49	13,147	4,451	174	25.58	9	3
M. W. Tate	39	12,523	4,055	155	26.16	7	1
F. J. Titmus	53	15,118	4,931	153	32.22	7	—
H. Verity	40	11,143	3,510	144	24.37	5	2
C. M. Old	46	8,858	4,020	143	28.11	4	—
A. W. Greig	58	9,802	4,541	141	32.20	6	2
T. E. Bailey	61	9,712	3,856	132	29.21	5	1
W. Rhodes	58	8,220	3,425	127	26.96	6	1
D. A. Allen	39	11,297	3,779	122	30.97	4	—
R. Illingworth	61	11,934	3,807	122	31.20	3	—
J. Briggs	33	5,332	2,094	118	17.74	9	4
G. G. Arnold	34	7,650	3,254	115	28.29	6	—
G. A. Lohmann	18	3,821	1,205	112	10.75	9	5
D. V. P. Wright	34	8,135	4,224	108	39.11	6	1
R. Peel	20	5,216	1,715	102	16.81	6	2
J. H. Wardle	28	6,597	2,080	102	20.39	5	1
C. Blythe	19	4,438	1,863	100	18.63	9	4
W. Voce	27	6,360	2,733	98	27.88	3	2
T. Richardson	14	4,485	2,220	88	25.22	11	4
M. Hendrick	30	6,208	2,248	87	25.83	—	—
W. R. Hammond	85	7,967	3,138	83	37.80	2	—
F. E. Woolley	64	6,495	2,815	83	33.91	4	1
G. O. Allen	25	4,390	2,379	81	29.37	5	1
D. J. Brown	26	5,098	2,237	79	28.31	2	—
H. Larwood	21	4,969	2,212	78	28.35	4	1
F. H. Tyson	17	3,452	1,411	76	18.56	4	1

FOR AUSTRALIA

	T	Balls	R	W	Avge	5 W/i	10 W/m
D. K. Lillee	65	17,084	7,860	335	23.46	22	7
R. Benaud	63	19,108	6,704	248	27.03	16	1
G. D. McKenzie	60	17,681	7,328	246	29.78	16	3
R. R. Lindwall	61	13,650	5,251	228	23.03	12	—
C. V. Grimmett	37	14,573	5,231	216	24.21	21	7
J. R. Thomson	49	10,199	5,326	197	27.03	8	—
A. K. Davidson	44	11,587	3,819	186	20.53	14	2
K. R. Miller	55	10,461	3,906	170	22.97	7	1
W. A. Johnston	40	11,048	3,826	160	23.91	7	—
W. J. O'Reilly	27	10,024	3,254	144	22.59	11	3
H. Trumble	32	8,099	3,072	141	21.78	9	3
M. H. N. Walker	34	10,094	3,792	138	27.47	6	—
A. A. Mallett	38	9,990	3,940	132	29.84	6	1
B. Yardley	33	8,909	3,986	126	31.63	6	1
M. A. Noble	42	7,109	3,025	121	25.00	9	2
I. W. Johnson	45	8,780	3,182	109	29.19	3	—
G. Giffen	31	6,325	2,791	103	27.09	7	1
A. N. Connolly	29	7,818	2,981	102	29.22	4	—
C. T. B. Turner	17	5,195	1,670	101	16.53	11	2
A. A. Mailey	21	6,117	3,358	99	33.91	6	2
F. R. Spofforth	18	4,185	1,731	94	18.41	7	4
R. M. Hogg	26	5,387	2,277	94	24.22	5	2
J. W. Gleeson	29	8,857	3,367	93	36.20	3	—
N. J. N. Hawke	27	6,974	2,677	91	29.41	6	1
A. Cotter	21	4,633	2,549	89	28.64	7	—
W. W. Armstrong	50	8,052	2,923	87	33.59	3	—
J. M. Gregory	24	5,581	2,648	85	31.15	4	—
J. V. Saunders	14	3,565	1,796	79	22.73	6	—
G. Dymock	21	5,545	2,116	78	27.12	5	1
G. E. Palmer	17	4,519	1,678	78	21.51	6	2

FOR SOUTH AFRICA

	T	Balls	R	W	Avge	5 W/i	10 W/m
H. J. Tayfield	37	13,568	4,405	170	25.91	14	2
T. L. Goddard	41	11,736	3,226	123	26.22	5	—
P. M. Pollock	28	6,522	2,806	116	24.18	9	1
N. A. T. Adcock	26	6,391	2,195	104	21.10	5	—
C. L. Vincent	25	5,863	2,631	84	31.32	3	—
G. A. Faulkner	25	4,227	2,180	82	26.58	4	—

FOR WEST INDIES

	T	Balls	R	W	Avge	5 W/i	10 W/m
L. R. Gibbs	79	27,115	8,989	309	29.09	18	2
G. S. Sobers	93	21,599	7,999	235	34.03	6	—
A. M. E. Roberts	45	10,801	5,026	197	25.51	11	2
W. W. Hall	48	10,421	5,066	192	26.38	9	1
S. Ramadhin	43	13,939	4,579	158	28.98	10	1
M. A. Holding	36	8,134	3,694	151	24.46	10	2
A. L. Valentine	36	12,953	4,215	139	30.32	8	2
J. Garner	32	7,326	2,861	131	21.83	2	—
C. E. H. Croft	27	6,165	2,913	125	23.30	3	—
V. A. Holder	40	9,095	3,627	109	33.27	3	—
C. C. Griffith	28	5,631	2,683	94	28.54	5	—

FOR NEW ZEALAND

	T	Balls	R	W	Avge	5 W/i	10 W/m
R. J. Hadlee	44	11,355	5,164	200	25.82	15	3
R. O. Collinge...........	35	7,689	3,393	116	29.25	3	—
B. R. Taylor	30	6,334	2,953	111	26.60	4	—
R. C. Motz..............	32	7,034	3,148	100	31.48	5	—
B. L. Cairns.............	32	8,005	3,096	97	31.91	5	1
H. J. Howarth..........	30	8,833	3,178	86	36.95	2	—
J. R. Reid	58	7,725	2,835	85	33.35	1	—

FOR INDIA

	T	Balls	R	W	Avge	5 W/i	10 W/m
B. S. Bedi...............	67	21,364	7,637	266	28.71	14	1
B. S. Chandrasekhar..	58	15,963	7,199	242	29.74	16	2
Kapil Dev..............	53	11,573	6,082	206	29.52	15	1
E. A. S. Prasanna.....	49	14,353	5,742	189	30.38	10	2
V. Mankad	44	14,686	5,236	162	32.32	8	2
S. Venkataraghavan...	55	14,582	5,530	155	35.67	3	1
S. P. Gupte..............	36	11,284	4,403	149	29.55	12	1
D. R. Doshi.............	32	9,202	3,450	113	30.53	6	—
K. D. Ghavri............	39	7,042	3,656	109	33.54	4	—
R. G. Nadkarni	41	9,165	2,559	88	29.07	4	1
S. A. Durani	29	6,446	2,657	75	35.42	3	1

FOR PAKISTAN

	T	Balls	R	W	Avge	5 W/i	10 W/m
Imran Khan	49	12,552	5,318	232	22.92	16	4
Sarfraz Nawaz	49	12,028	5,020	155	32.38	4	1
Fazal Mahmood........	34	9,834	3,434	139	24.70	13	4
Intikhab Alam..........	47	10,474	4,494	125	35.95	5	2
Iqbal Qasim.............	36	9,294	3,426	115	29.79	4	2
Mushtaq Mohammad.	57	5,260	2,309	79	29.22	3	—

Note: Only G. S. Sobers (West Indies), R. Benaud (Australia), I. T. Botham (England) and Kapil Dev (India) have scored 2,000 runs and taken 200 wickets.

MOST WICKETS IN A TEST MATCH

19-90	J. C. Laker.........	England v Australia at Manchester...............	1956
17-159	S. F. Barnes	England v South Africa at Johannesburg.......	1913-14
16-137†	R. A. L. Massie ...	Australia v England at Lord's	1972
15-28	J. Briggs	England v South Africa at Cape Town..........	1888-89
15-45	G. A. Lohmann ...	England v South Africa at Port Elizabeth......	1895-96
15-99	C. Blythe	England v South Africa at Leeds	1907
15-104	H. Verity	England v Australia at Lord's	1934
15-124	W. Rhodes	England v Australia at Melbourne	1903-04
14-90	F. R. Spofforth	Australia v England at The Oval	1882

MOST WICKETS IN A TEST MATCH

14-99	A. V. Bedser	England v Australia at Nottingham	1953
14-102	W. Bates	England v Australia at Melbourne	1882-83
14-116	Imran Khan	Pakistan v Sri Lanka at Lahore	1981-82
14-124	J. M. Patel	India v Australia at Kanpur	1959-60
14-144	S. F. Barnes	England v South Africa at Durban	1913-14
14-149	M. A. Holding	West Indies v England at The Oval	1976
14-199	C. V. Grimmett	Australia v South Africa at Adelaide	1931-32

† *On Test début.*

Notes: The best for South Africa is 13-165 by H. J. Tayfield against Australia at Melbourne, 1952-53.

The best for New Zealand is 11-58 by R. J. Hadlee against India at Wellington, 1975-76.

MOST WICKETS IN A TEST INNINGS

10-53	J. C. Laker	England v Australia at Manchester	1956
9-28	G. A. Lohmann	England v South Africa at Johannesburg	1895-96
9-37	J. C. Laker	England v Australia at Manchester	1956
9-69	J. M. Patel	India v Australia at Kanpur	1959-60
9-86	Sarfraz Nawaz	Pakistan v Australia at Melbourne	1978-79
9-95	J. M. Noreiga	West Indies v India at Port-of-Spain	1970-71
9-102	S. P. Gupte	India v West Indies at Kanpur	1958-59
9-103	S. F. Barnes	England v South Africa at Johannesburg	1913-14
9-113	H. J. Tayfield	South Africa v England at Johannesburg	1956-57
9-121	A. A. Mailey	Australia v England at Melbourne	1920-21
8-7	G. A. Lohmann	England v South Africa at Port Elizabeth	1895-96
8-11	J. Briggs	England v South Africa at Cape Town	1888-89
8-29	S. F. Barnes	England v South Africa at The Oval	1912
8-29	C. E. H. Croft	West Indies v Pakistan at Port-of-Spain	1976-77
8-31	F. Laver	Australia v England at Manchester	1909
8-31	F. S. Trueman	England v India at Manchester	1952
8-34	I. T. Botham	England v Pakistan at Lord's	1978
8-35	G. A. Lohmann	England v Australia at Sydney	1886-87
8-38	L. R. Gibbs	West Indies v India at Bridgetown	1961-62
8-43†	A. E. Trott	Australia v England at Adelaide	1894-95
8-43	H. Verity	England v Australia at Lord's	1934
8-43	R. G. D. Willis	England v Australia at Leeds	1981
8-51	D. L. Underwood	England v Pakistan at Lord's	1974
8-52	V. Mankad	India v Pakistan at Delhi	1952-53
8-53	G. B. Lawrence	South Africa v New Zealand at Johannesburg	1961-62
8-53†	R. A. L. Massie	Australia v England at Lord's	1972
8-55	V. Mankad	India v England at Madras	1951-52
8-56	S. F. Barnes	England v South Africa at Johannesburg	1913-14
8-58	G. A. Lohmann	England v Australia at Sydney	1891-92
8-58	Imran Khan	Pakistan v Sri Lanka at Lahore	1981-82
8-59	C. Blythe	England v South Africa at Leeds	1907
8-59	A. A. Mallett	Australia v Pakistan at Adelaide	1972-73
8-60	Imran Khan	Pakistan v India at Karachi	1982-83
8-65	H. Trumble	Australia v England at The Oval	1902
8-68	W. Rhodes	England v Australia at Melbourne	1903-04
8-69	H. J. Tayfield	South Africa v England at Durban	1956-57
8-69	Sikander Bakht	Pakistan v India at Delhi	1979-80
8-70	S. J. Snooke	South Africa v England at Johannesburg	1905-06
8-71	G. D. McKenzie	Australia v West Indies at Melbourne	1968-69
8-72	S. Venkataraghavan	India v New Zealand at Delhi	1964-65
8-76	E. A. S. Prasanna	India v New Zealand at Auckland	1975-76
8-79	B. S. Chandrasekhar	India v England at Delhi	1972-73
8-81	L. C. Braund	England v Australia at Melbourne	1903-04
8-84†	R. A. L. Massie	Australia v England at Lord's	1972
8-85	Kapil Dev	India v Pakistan at Lahore	1982-83

8-86	A. W. Greig........	England v West Indies at Port-of-Spain.........	1973-74
8-92	M. A. Holding	West Indies v England at The Oval..............	1976
8-94	T. Richardson......	England v Australia at Sydney	1897-98
8-104†	A. L. Valentine...	West Indies v England at Manchester	1950
8-107	B. J. T. Bosanquet	England v Australia at Nottingham	1905
8-126	J. C. White........	England v Australia at Adelaide	1928-29
8-143	M. H. N. Walker..	Australia v England at Melbourne	1974-75

† *On Test début.*

Note: The best for New Zealand is 7-23 by R. J. Hadlee against India at Wellington, 1975-76.

MOST WICKETS IN A TEST SERIES

	T	R	W	Avge		
S. F. Barnes	4	536	49	10.93	England v South Africa...	1913-14
J. C. Laker.............	5	442	46	9.60	England v Australia	1956
C. V. Grimmett......	5	642	44	14.59	Australia v South Africa .	1935-36
T. M. Alderman......	6	893	42	21.26	Australia v England	1981
R. M. Hogg..........	6	527	41	12.85	Australia v England	1978-79
Imran Khan............	6	558	40	13.95	Pakistan v India.............	1982-83
A. V. Bedser..........	5	682	39	17.48	England v Australia	1953
D. K. Lillee..........	6	870	39	22.30	Australia v England	1981
M. W. Tate	5	881	38	23.18	England v Australia	1924-25
W. J. Whitty.........	5	632	37	17.08	Australia v South Africa .	1910-11
H. J. Tayfield	5	636	37	17.18	South Africa v England...	1956-57
A. E. E. Vogler	5	783	36	21.75	South Africa v England...	1909-10
A. A. Mailey........	5	946	36	26.27	Australia v England	1920-21
G. A. Lohmann	3	203	35	5.80	England v South Africa...	1895-96
B. S. Chandrasekhar	5	662	35	18.91	India v England.............	1972-73

TEST HAT-TRICKS

F. R. Spofforth......	Australia v England at Melbourne.................................	1878-79
W. Bates..............	England v Australia at Melbourne.................................	1882-83
J. Briggs.............	England v Australia at Sydney.....................................	1891-92
G. A. Lohmann.....	England v South Africa at Port Elizabeth	1895-96
J. T. Hearne..........	England v Australia at Leeds.......................................	1899
H. Trumble..........	Australia v England at Melbourne.................................	1901-02
H. Trumble..........	Australia v England at Melbourne.................................	1903-04
T. J. Matthews†.... } T. J. Matthews ..... }	Australia v South Africa at Manchester	1912
M. J. C. Allom‡	England v New Zealand at Christchurch........................	1929-30
T. W. Goddard.....	England v South Africa at Johannesburg.......................	1938-39
P. J. Loader.........	England v West Indies at Leeds...................................	1957
L. F. Kline..........	Australia v South Africa at Cape Town	1957-58
W. W. Hall..........	West Indies v Pakistan at Lahore	1958-59
G. M. Griffin.......	South Africa v England at Lord's.................................	1960
L. R. Gibbs	West Indies v Australia at Adelaide	1960-61
P. J. Petherick‡	New Zealand v Pakistan at Lahore	1976-77

† *T. J. Matthews did the hat-trick in each innings of the same match.*

‡ *On Test début.*

MOST BALLS BOWLED IN A TEST MATCH

S. Ramadhin (West Indies) sent down 774 balls in 129 overs against England at Birmingham, 1957. It was the most delivered by any bowler in a Test, beating H. Verity's 766 for England against South Africa at Durban, 1938-39. In this match Ramadhin also bowled the most balls (588) in any single first-class innings, including Tests.

It should be noted that six balls were bowled to the over in the Australia v England Test series of 1928-29 and 1932-33, when the eight-ball over was otherwise in force in Australia.

WICKET-KEEPING RECORDS

Most Dismissals in a Test Career

	T	Ct	St	Total
R. W. Marsh (Australia)	91	322	12	334
A. P. E. Knott (England)	95	250	19	269
T. G. Evans (England).................	91	173	46	219
Wasim Bari (Pakistan)	73	175	26	201
D. L. Murray (West Indies)	62	181	8	189
A. T. W. Grout (Australia)..........	51	163	24	187
R. W. Taylor (England)	51	155	7	162
S. M. H. Kirmani (India).............	69	128	32	160
J. H. B. Waite (South Africa)	50	124	17	141
W. A. Oldfield (Australia)............	54	78	52	130
J. M. Parks (England)†	46	103	11	114

† *J. M. Parks's figures include two catches taken in three Tests in which he did not keep wicket.*

Note: K. J. Wadsworth (92ct, 4st) made most dismissals for New Zealand.

Most Dismissals in a Test Series

28 (28 ct)	R. W. Marsh............	Australia v England	1982-83
26 (26ct)	R. W. Marsh............	Australia v West Indies (6 Tests)...........	1975-76
26 (23ct, 3st)	J. H. B. Waite............	South Africa v New Zealand	1961-62
24 (21ct, 3st)	A. P. E. Knott	England v Australia (6 Tests)	1970-71
24 (24ct)	D. T. Lindsay...........	South Africa v Australia	1966-67
24 (22ct, 2st)	D. L. Murray...........	West Indies v England	1963
23 (22ct, 1st)	F. C. M. Alexander...	West Indies v England	1959-60
23 (21ct, 2st)	A. E. Dick............	New Zealand v South Africa	1961-62
23 (20ct, 3st)	A. T. W. Grout	Australia v West Indies	1960-61
23 (22ct, 1st)	A. P. E. Knott	England v Australia (6 Tests)	1974-75
23 (21ct, 2st)	R. W. Marsh............	Australia v England	1972
23 (23ct)	R. W. Marsh............	Australia v England (6 Tests)	1981
23 (16ct, 7st)	J. H. B. Waite............	South Africa v New Zealand	1953-54
22 (22ct)	S. J. Rixon............	Australia v India	1977-78
21 (20ct, 1st)	A. T. W. Grout	Australia v England	1961
21 (16ct, 5st)	G. R. A. Langley........	Australia v West Indies	1951-52
21 (13ct, 8st)	R. A. Saggers...........	Australia v South Africa	1949-50
21 (15ct, 6st)	H Strudwick	England v South Africa	1913-14
20 (18ct, 2st)	T. G. Evans	England v South Africa	1956-57
20 (17ct, 3st)	A. T. W. Grout	Australia v England	1958-59
20 (16ct, 4st)	G. R. A. Langley........	Australia v West Indies	1954-55
20 (19ct, 1st)	H. B. Taber............	Australia v South Africa	1966-67
20 (16ct, 4st)	D. Tallon............	Australia v England	1946-47
20 (18ct, 2st)	R. W. Taylor............	England v Australia (6 Tests)	1978-79

Most Dismissals in One Test

10 (all ct)	R. W. Taylor.........	England v India at Bombay	1979-80
9 (8ct, 1st)	G. R. A. Langley...	Australia v England at Lord's	1956
9 (all ct)	D. A. Murray........	West Indies v Australia at Melbourne	1981-82
8 (6ct, 2st)	L. E. G. Ames	England v West Indies at The Oval	1933
8 (6ct, 2st)	A. T. W. Grout ...	Australia v Pakistan at Lahore	1959-60
8 (all ct)	A. T. W. Grout ...	Australia v England at Lord's	1961
8 (all ct)	J. J. Kelly	Australia v England at Sydney	1901-02
8 (all ct)	G. R. A. Langley...	Australia v West Indies at Kingston	1954-55
8 (all ct)	J. M. Parks	England v New Zealand at Christchurch	1965-66

8 (all ct)	D. T. Lindsay........	South Africa v Australia at Johannesburg...	1966-67
8 (7ct, 1st)	H. B. Taber	Australia v South Africa at Johannesburg...	1966-67
8 (all ct)	Wasim Bari.........	Pakistan v England at Leeds....................	1971
8 (all ct)	R. W. Marsh........	Australia v West Indies at Melbourne	1975-76
8 (all ct)	R. W. Marsh........	Australia v New Zealand at Christchurch ...	1976-77
8 (all ct)	W. K. Lees...........	New Zealand v Sri Lanka at Wellington.....	1982-83

Most Dismissals in a Test Innings

7 (all ct)	Wasim Bari..........	Pakistan v New Zealand at Auckland..........	1978-79
7 (all ct)	R. W. Taylor..........	England v India at Bombay....................	1979-80
6 (all ct)	A. T. W. Grout	Australia v South Africa at Johannesburg	1957-58
6 (all ct)	D. T. Lindsay	South Africa v Australia at Johannesburg	1966-67
6 (all ct)	J. T. Murray	England v India at Lord's	1967
6 (5ct, 1st)	S. M. H. Kirmani...	India v New Zealand at Christchurch	1975-76

MOST CATCHES – EXCLUDING WICKET-KEEPERS

In a Test Career

M. C. Cowdrey (England).............	120 in 114 matches
G. S. Chappell (Australia).............	114 in 82 matches
R. B. Simpson (Australia).............	110 in 62 matches
W. R. Hammond (England)............	110 in 85 matches
G. S. Sobers (West Indies)	109 in 93 matches
I. M. Chappell (Australia).............	105 in 75 matches

In a Test Series

15	J. M. Gregory	Australia v England	1920-21
14	G. S. Chappell..........	Australia v England (6 Tests)	1974-75
13	R. B. Simpson	Australia v South Africa	1957-58
13	R. B. Simpson	Australia v West Indies	1960-61

In One Test

7	G. S. Chappell..............	Australia v England at Perth.....................	1974-75
7	Yajurvindra Singh	India v England at Bangalore	1976-77
6	A. Shrewsbury.............	England v Australia at Sydney	1887-88
6	A. E. E. Vogler............	South Africa v England at Durban	1909-10
6	F. E. Woolley.............	England v Australia at Sydney	1911-12
6	J. M. Gregory.............	Australia v England at Sydney	1920-21
6	B. Mitchell..............	South Africa v Australia at Melbourne	1931-32
6	V. Y. Richardson........	Australia v South Africa at Durban................	1935-36
6	R. N. Harvey..........	Australia v England at Sydney	1962-63
6	M. C. Cowdrey..........	England v West Indies at Lord's	1963
6	E. D. Solkar	India v West Indies at Port-of-Spain	1970-71
6	G. S. Sobers	West Indies v England at Lord's	1973
6	I. M. Chappell..........	Australia v New Zealand at Adelaide	1973-74
6	A. W. Greig............	England v Pakistan at Leeds	1974
6	D. F. Whatmore	Australia v India at Kanpur	1979-80
6	A. J. Lamb	England v New Zealand at Lord's...................	1983

In a Test Innings

5	V. Y. Richardson.........	Australia v South Africa at Durban....................	1935-36
5	Yajurvindra Singh	India v England at Bangalore.............................	1976-77

YOUNGEST TEST PLAYERS

Years	Days			
15	124	Mushtaq Mohammad .	Pakistan v West Indies at Lahore	1958-59
16	191	Aftab Baloch............	Pakistan v New Zealand at Dacca	1969-70
16	248	Nasim-ul-Ghani.........	Pakistan v West Indies at Bridgetown ...	1957-58
16	352	Khalid Hassan	Pakistan v England at Nottingham	1954
17	118	L. Sivaramakrishnan ..	India v West Indies at Antigua	1982-83
17	122	J. E. D. Sealy...........	West Indies v England at Bridgetown.....	1929-30
17	193	Maninder Singh	India v Pakistan at Karachi	1982-83
17	239	I. D. Craig................	Australia v South Africa at Melbourne ..	1952-53
17	245	G. S. Sobers.............	West Indies v England at Kingston	1953-54
17	265	V. L. Mehra.............	India v New Zealand at Bombay	1955-56
17	300	Hanif Mohammad	Pakistan v India at Delhi	1952-53
17	341	Intikhab Alam	Pakistan v Australia at Karachi............	1959-60

Note: The youngest Test players for countries not mentioned above are: England – D. B. Close, 18 years 149 days, v New Zealand at Manchester, 1949; New Zealand – D. L. Freeman, 18 years 197 days, v England at Christchurch, 1932-33; South Africa – A. E. Ochse, 19 years 1 day, v England at Port Elizabeth, 1888-89; Sri Lanka – A. Ranatunga, 18 years 78 days, v England at Colombo, 1981-82.

OLDEST PLAYERS ON TEST DEBUT

Years	Days			
49	119	J. Southerton............	England v Australia at Melbourne........	1876-77
47	284	Miran Bux	Pakistan v India at Lahore	1954-55
46	253	D. D. Blackie............	Australia v England at Sydney	1928-29
46	237	H. Ironmonger	Australia v England at Brisbane............	1928-29
42	242	N. Betancourt............	West Indies v England at Port-of-Spain .	1929-30
41	337	E. R. Wilson	England v Australia at Sydney	1920-21
41	27	R. J. D. Jamshedji ...	India v England at Bombay.................	1933-34
40	345	C. A. Wiles..............	West Indies v England at Manchester....	1933
40	251	D. S. de Silva	Sri Lanka v England at Colombo	1981-82
40	216	S. P. Kinneir	England v Australia at Sydney	1911-12
40	110	H. W. Lee	England v South Africa at Johannesburg	1930-31
40	56	G. W. A. Chubb.......	South Africa v England at Nottingham ..	1951
40	37	C. Ramaswami	India v England at Manchester	1936

Note: The oldest Test player on début for New Zealand was H. M. McGirr, 38 years 101 days, v England at Auckland, 1929-30.

OLDEST TEST PLAYERS

(Age on final day of their last Test match)

Years	Days			
52	165	W. Rhodes	England v West Indies at Kingston	1929-30
50	327	H. Ironmonger	Australia v England at Sydney	1932-33
50	320	W. G. Grace	England v Australia at Nottingham	1899
50	303	G. Gunn	England v West Indies at Kingston	1929-30
49	139	J. Southerton	England v Australia at Melbourne	1876-77
47	302	Miran Bux	Pakistan v India at Peshawar	1954-55
47	249	J. B. Hobbs	England v Australia at The Oval	1930
47	87	F. E. Woolley	England v Australia at The Oval	1934
46	309	D. D. Blackie	Australia v England at Adelaide	1928-29
46	206	A. W. Nourse	South Africa v England at The Oval	1924
46	202	H. Strudwick	England v Australia at The Oval	1926
46	41	E. H. Hendren	England v West Indies at Kingston	1934-35
45	245	G. O. Allen	England v West Indies at Kingston	1947-48
45	215	P. Holmes	England v India at Lord's	1932
45	140	D. B. Close	England v West Indies at Manchester	1976

MOST CONSECUTIVE TEST APPEARANCES

87	G. R. Viswanath, India	Georgetown 1970-71 to Karachi 1982-83
85	G. S. Sobers, West Indies	Port-of-Spain 1954-55 to Port-of-Spain 1971-72
74	S. M. Gavaskar, India	Bombay 1974-75 to Antigua 1982-83
71	I. M. Chappell, Australia	Adelaide 1965-66 to Melbourne 1975-76
65	A. P. E. Knott, England	Auckland 1970-71 to The Oval 1977
61	R. B. Kanhai, West Indies	Birmingham 1957 to Sydney 1968-69
61	I. T. Botham, England	Wellington 1977-78 to Nottingham 1983
58†	A. W. Greig, England	Manchester 1972 to The Oval 1977
58†	J. R. Reid, New Zealand	Manchester 1949 to Leeds 1965
54	Kapil Dev, India	Faisalabad 1978-79 to Antigua 1982-83
53	K. J. Hughes, Australia	Brisbane 1978-79 to Sydney 1982-83
52	R. W. Marsh, Australia	Brisbane 1970-71 to The Oval 1977
52	P. B. H. May, England	The Oval 1953 to Leeds 1959
52	F. E. Woolley, England	The Oval 1909 to The Oval 1926
51	G. S. Chappell, Australia	Perth 1970-71 to The Oval 1977

† *Indicates complete Test career.*

SUMMARY OF ALL TEST MATCHES

To end of 1983 season in England

ENGLAND

Against	W		L		D		T		Total
Australia	83	..	95	..	73	..	0	..	251
South Africa	46	..	18	..	38	..	0	..	102
West Indies	21	..	25	..	34	..	0	..	80
New Zealand	30	..	2	..	25	..	0	..	57
India	28	..	8	..	31	..	0	..	67
Pakistan	13	..	2	..	21	..	0	..	36
Sri Lanka	1	..	0	..	0	..	0	..	1
Totals	222	..	150	..	222	..	0	..	594

AUSTRALIA

Against	W		L		D		T		Total
England	95	..	83	..	73	..	0	..	251
South Africa	29	..	11	..	13	..	0	..	53
West Indies	26	..	13	..	12	..	1	..	52
New Zealand	8	..	2	..	5	..	0	..	15
India	20	..	8	..	11	..	0	..	39
Pakistan	9	..	8	..	6	..	0	..	23
Sri Lanka	1	..	0	..	0	..	0	..	1
Totals	188	..	125	..	120	..	1	..	434

SOUTH AFRICA

Against	W		L		D		T		Total
England	18	..	46	..	38	..	0	..	102
Australia	11	..	29	..	13	..	0	..	53
New Zealand	9	..	2	..	6	..	0	..	17
Totals	38	..	77	..	57	..	0	..	172

WEST INDIES

Against	W		L		D		T		Total
England	25	..	21	..	34	..	0	..	80
Australia	13	..	26	..	12	..	1	..	52
New Zealand	5	..	3	..	9	..	0	..	17
India	19	..	5	..	24	..	0	..	48
Pakistan	7	..	4	..	8	..	0	..	19
Totals	69	..	59	..	87	..	1	.	216

NEW ZEALAND

Against	W		L		D		T		Total
England	2	..	30	..	25	..	0	..	57
Australia	2	..	8	..	5	..	0	..	15
South Africa	2	..	9	..	6	..	0	..	17
West Indies	3	..	5	..	9	..	0	..	17
India	4	..	10	..	11	..	0	..	25
Pakistan	1	..	8	..	12	..	0	..	21
Sri Lanka	2	..	0	..	0	..	0	..	2
Totals	16	..	70	..	68	..	0	..	154

INDIA

Against	W		L		D		T		Total
England	8	..	28	..	31	..	0	..	67
Australia	8	..	20	..	11	..	0	..	39
West Indies	5	..	19	..	24	..	0	..	48
New Zealand	10	..	4	..	11	..	0	..	25
Pakistan	4	..	6	..	20	..	0	..	30
Sri Lanka	0	..	0	..	1	..	0	..	1
Totals	35	..	77	..	98	..	0	..	210

PAKISTAN

Against	W		L		D		T		Total
England............	2	..	13	..	21	..	0	..	36
Australia	8	..	8	..	7	..	0	..	23
West Indies........	4	..	7	..	8	..	0	..	19
New Zealand......	8	..	1	..	12	..	0	..	21
India................	6	..	4	..	20	..	0	..	30
Sri Lanka...........	2	..	0	..	1	..	0	..	3
Totals	30	..	33	..	69	..	0	..	132

SRI LANKA

Against	W		L		D		T		Total
England............	0	..	1	..	0	..	0	..	1
Australia	0	..	1	..	0	..	0	..	1
New Zealand......	0	..	2	..	0	..	0	..	2
India................	0	..	0	..	1	..	0	..	1
Pakistan	0	..	2	..	1	..	0	..	3
Totals	0	..	6	..	2	..	0	..	8

ENGLAND v AUSTRALIA

Season	England	Australia	T	E	A	D
	Captains					
1876-77	James Lillywhite	D. W. Gregory	2	1	1	0
1878-79	Lord Harris	D. W. Gregory	1	0	1	0
1880	Lord Harris	W. L. Murdoch	1	1	0	0
1881-82	A. Shaw	W. L. Murdoch	4	0	2	2
1882	A. N. Hornby	W. L. Murdoch	1	0	1	0

THE ASHES

Season	England	Australia	T	E	A	D	Held by
	Captains						
1882-83	Hon. Ivo Bligh	W. L. Murdoch	4*	2	2	0	E
1884	Lord Harris[1]	W. L. Murdoch	3	1	0	2	E
1884-85	A. Shrewsbury	T. Horan[2]	5	3	2	0	E
1886	A. G. Steel	H. J. H. Scott	3	3	0	0	E
1886-87	A. Shrewsbury	P. S. McDonnell	2	2	0	0	E
1887-88	W. W. Read	P. S. McDonnell	1	1	0	0	E
1888	W. G. Grace[3]	P. S. McDonnell	3	2	1	0	E
1890†	W. G. Grace	W. L. Murdoch	2	2	0	0	E
1891-92	W. G. Grace	J. McC. Blackham	3	1	2	0	A
1893	W. G. Grace[4]	J. McC. Blackham	3	1	0	2	E
1894-95	A. E. Stoddart	G. Giffen[5]	5	3	2	0	E
1896	W. G. Grace	G. H. S. Trott	3	2	1	0	E
1897-98	A. E. Stoddart[6]	G. H. S. Trott	5	1	4	0	A
1899	A. C. MacLaren[7]	J. Darling	5	0	1	4	A
1901-02	A. C. MacLaren	J. Darling[8]	5	1	4	0	A
1902	A. C. MacLaren	J. Darling	5	1	2	2	A
1903-04	P. F. Warner	M. A. Noble	5	3	2	0	E
1905	Hon. F. S. Jackson	J. Darling	5	2	0	3	E
1907-08	A. O. Jones[9]	M. A. Noble	5	1	4	0	A

Captains

Season	England	Australia	T	E	A	D	Held by
1909	A. C. MacLaren	M. A. Noble	5	1	2	2	A
1911-12	J. W. H. T. Douglas	C. Hill	5	4	1	0	E
1912	C. B. Fry	S. E. Gregory	3	1	0	2	E
1920-21	J. W. H. T. Douglas	W. W. Armstrong	5	0	5	0	A
1921	Hon. L. H. Tennyson[10]	W. W. Armstrong	5	0	3	2	A
1924-25	A. E. R. Gilligan	H. L. Collins	5	1	4	0	A
1926	A. W. Carr[11]	H. L. Collins[12]	5	1	0	4	A
1928-29	A. P. F. Chapman[13]	J. Ryder	5	4	1	0	E
1930	A. P. F. Chapman[14]	W. M. Woodfull	5	1	2	2	A
1932-33	D. R. Jardine	W. M. Woodfull	5	4	1	0	E
1934	R. E. S. Wyatt[15]	W. M. Woodfull	5	1	2	2	A
1936-37	G. O. Allen	D. G. Bradman	5	2	3	0	A
1938†	W. R. Hammond	D. G. Bradman	4	1	1	2	A
1946-47	W. R. Hammond[16]	D. G. Bradman	5	0	3	2	A
1948	N. W. D. Yardley	D. G. Bradman	5	0	4	1	A
1950-51	F. R. Brown	A. L. Hassett	5	1	4	0	A
1953	L. Hutton	A. L. Hassett	5	1	0	4	E
1954-55	L. Hutton	I. W. Johnson[17]	5	3	1	1	E
1956	P. B. H. May	I. W. Johnson	5	2	1	2	E
1958-59	P. B. H. May	R. Benaud	5	0	4	1	A
1961	P. B. H. May[18]	R. Benaud[19]	5	1	2	2	A
1962-63	E. R. Dexter	R. Benaud	5	1	1	3	A
1964	E. R. Dexter	R. B. Simpson	5	0	1	4	A
1965-66	M. J. K. Smith	R. B. Simpson[20]	5	1	1	3	A
1968	M. C. Cowdrey[21]	W. M. Lawry[22]	5	1	1	3	A
1970-71†	R. Illingworth	W. M. Lawry[23]	6	2	0	4	E
1972	R. Illingworth	I. M. Chappell	5	2	2	1	E
1974-75	M. H. Denness[24]	I. M. Chappell	6	1	4	1	A
1975	A. W. Greig[25]	I. M. Chappell	4	0	1	3	A
1976-77‡	A. W. Greig	G. S. Chappell	1	0	1	0	—
1977	J. M. Brearley	G. S. Chappell	5	3	0	2	E
1978-79	J. M. Brearley	G. N. Yallop	6	5	1	0	E
1979-80‡	J. M. Brearley	G. S. Chappell	3	0	3	0	—
1980‡	I. T. Botham	G. S. Chappell	1	0	0	1	—
1981	J. M. Brearley[26]	K. J. Hughes	6	3	1	2	E
1982-83	R. G. D. Willis	G. S. Chappell	5	1	2	2	A

In Australia..........................			134	49	66	19	
In England..........................			117	34	29	54	
Totals..................................			251	83	95	73	

* *The Ashes were awarded in 1882-83 after a series of three matches which England won 2-1. A fourth unofficial match was played, each innings being played on a different pitch, and this was won by Australia.*

† *The matches at Manchester in 1890 and 1938 and at Melbourne (Third Test) in 1970-71 were abandoned without a ball being bowled and are excluded.*

‡ *The Ashes were not at stake in these series.*

Notes: The following deputised for the official touring captain or were appointed by the home authority for only a minor proportion of the series:

[1] A. N. Hornby (First). [2] W. L. Murdoch (First), H. H. Massie (Third), J. McC. Blackham (Fourth). [3] A. G. Steel (First). [4] A. E. Stoddart (First). [5] J. McC. Blackham (First). [6] A. C. MacLaren (First, Second and Fifth). [7] W. G. Grace (First). [8] H. Trumble (Fourth and Fifth). [9] F. L. Fane (First, Second and Third). [10] J. W. H. T. Douglas (First and Second). [11] A. P. F. Chapman (Fifth). [12] W. Bardsley (Third and Fourth). [13] J. C. White (Fifth). [14] R. E. S. Wyatt (Fifth). [15] C. F. Walters (First). [16] N. W. D. Yardley (Fifth). [17] A. R. Morris (Second). [18] M. C. Cowdrey (First and Second). [19] R. N. Harvey (Second). [20] B. C. Booth (First and Third). [21] T. W. Graveney (Fourth). [22] B. N. Jarman (Fourth). [23] I. M. Chappell (Seventh). [24] J. H. Edrich (Fourth). [25] M. H. Denness (First). [26] I. T. Botham (First and Second).

HIGHEST INNINGS TOTALS

For England in England: 903-7 dec. at The Oval, 1938
　　　　　in Australia: 636 at Sydney, 1928-29

For Australia in England: 729-6 dec. at Lord's, 1930
　　　　　in Australia: 659-8 dec. at Sydney, 1946-47

LOWEST INNINGS TOTALS

For England in England: 52 at The Oval, 1948
　　　　　in Australia: 45 at Sydney, 1886-87

For Australia in England: 36 at Birmingham, 1902
　　　　　in Australia: 42 at Sydney, 1887-88

INDIVIDUAL HUNDREDS IN THE MATCHES 1876-77–1982-83

For England (171)

132*	R. Abel, Sydney	1891-92
120	L. E. G. Ames, Lord's	1934
185	R. W. Barber, Sydney	1965-66
134	W. Barnes, Adelaide	1884-85
129	C. J. Barnett, Adelaide	1936-37
126	C. J. Barnett, Nottingham	1938
132*	K. F. Barrington, Adelaide	1962-63
101	K. F. Barrington, Sydney	1962-63
256	K. F. Barrington, Manchester	1964
102	K. F. Barrington, Adelaide	1965-66
115	K. F. Barrington, Melbourne	1965-66
119*	I. T. Botham, Melbourne	1979-80
149*	I. T. Botham, Leeds	1981
118	I. T. Botham, Manchester	1981
113	G. Boycott, The Oval	1964
142*	G. Boycott, Sydney	1970-71
119*	G. Boycott, Adelaide	1970-71
107	G. Boycott, Nottingham	1977
191	G. Boycott, Leeds	1977
128*	G. Boycott, Lord's	1980
137	G. Boycott, The Oval	1981
103*	L. C. Braund, Adelaide	1901-02
102	L. C. Braund, Sydney	1903-04
121	J. Briggs, Melbourne	1884-85
140	J. T. Brown, Melbourne	1894-95
121	A. P. F. Chapman, Lord's	1930
102†	D. C. S. Compton, Nottingham	1938
147 103*	} D. C. S. Compton, Adelaide	1946-47
184	D. C. S. Compton, Nottingham	1948
145*	D. C. S. Compton, Manchester	1948

102	M. C. Cowdrey, Melbourne	1954-55
100*	M. C. Cowdrey, Sydney	1958-59
113	M. C. Cowdrey, Melbourne	1962-63
104	M. C. Cowdrey, Melbourne	1965-66
104	M. C. Cowdrey, Birmingham	1968
188	M. H. Denness, Melbourne	1974-75
180	E. R. Dexter, Birmingham	1961
174	E. R. Dexter, Manchester.	1964
158	B. L. D'Oliveira, The Oval	1968
117	B. L. D'Oliveira, Melbourne	1970-71
173†	K. S. Duleepsinhji, Lord's	1930
120†	J. H. Edrich, Lord's	1964
109	J. H. Edrich, Melbourne	1965-66
103	J. H. Edrich, Sydney	1965-66
164	J. H. Edrich, The Oval	1968
115*	J. H. Edrich, Perth	1970-71
130	J. H. Edrich, Adelaide	1970-71
175	J. H. Edrich, Lord's	1975
119	W. J. Edrich, Sydney	1946-47
111	W. J. Edrich, Leeds	1948
146	K. W. R. Fletcher, Melbourne	1974-75
287†	R. E. Foster, Sydney	1903-04
144	C. B. Fry, The Oval	1905
102	D. I. Gower, Perth	1978-79
114	D. I. Gower, Adelaide	1982-83
152*	W. G. Grace, The Oval	1880
170	W. G. Grace, The Oval	1886
111	T. W. Graveney, Sydney	1954-55
110	A. W. Greig, Brisbane	1974-75
119†	G. Gunn, Sydney	1907-08
122*	G. Gunn, Sydney	1907-08

102*	W. Gunn, Manchester......	1893
251	W. R. Hammond, Sydney.	1928-29
200	W. R. Hammond, Melbourne	1928-29
119* 177 }	W. R. Hammond, Adelaide	1928-29
113	W. R. Hammond, Leeds ..	1930
112	W. R. Hammond, Sydney.	1932-33
101	W. R. Hammond, Sydney.	1932-33
231*	W. R. Hammond, Sydney.	1936-37
240	W. R. Hammond, Lord's..	1938
169*	J. Hardstaff jun., The Oval..	1938
130	T. W. Hayward, Manchester	1899
137	T. W. Hayward, The Oval	1899
114	J. W. Hearne, Manchester.	1911-12
127*	E. H. Hendren, Lord's.....	1926
169	E. H. Hendren, Brisbane..	1928-29
132	E. H. Hendren, Manchester	1934
126*	J. B. Hobbs, Melbourne ...	1911-12
187	J. B. Hobbs, Adelaide	1911-12
178	J. B. Hobbs, Melbourne ...	1911-12
107	J. B. Hobbs, Lord's.........	1912
122	J. B. Hobbs, Melbourne ...	1920-21
123	J. B. Hobbs, Adelaide	1920-21
115	J. B. Hobbs, Sydney........	1924-25
154	J. B. Hobbs, Melbourne ...	1924-25
119	J. B. Hobbs, Adelaide	1924-25
119	J. B. Hobbs, Lord's.........	1926
100	J. B. Hobbs, The Oval.....	1926
142	J. B. Hobbs, Melbourne ...	1928-29
126	K. L. Hutchings, Melbourne	1907-08
100†	L. Hutton, Nottingham ...	1938
364	L. Hutton, The Oval........	1938
122*	L. Hutton, Sydney...........	1946-47
156*	L. Hutton, Adelaide	1950-51
145	L. Hutton, Lord's............	1953
103	Hon. F. S. Jackson, The Oval	1893
118	Hon. F. S. Jackson, The Oval	1899
128	Hon. F. S. Jackson, Manchester	1902
144*	Hon. F. S. Jackson, Leeds	1905
113	Hon. F. S. Jackson, Manchester	1905
104	G. L. Jessop, The Oval....	1902
106*	A. P. E. Knott, Adelaide .	1974-75
135	A. P. E. Knott, Nottingham	1977
137†	M. Leyland, Melbourne....	1928-29
109	M. Leyland, Lord's..........	1934
153	M. Leyland, Manchester...	1934
110	M. Leyland, The Oval......	1934
126	M. Leyland, Brisbane	1936-37
111*	M. Leyland, Melbourne....	1936-37
187	M. Leyland, The Oval......	1938
131	B. W. Luckhurst, Perth	1970-71
109	B. W. Luckhurst, Melbourne	1970-71

120	A. C. MacLaren, Melbourne	1894-95
109	A. C. MacLaren, Sydney..	1897-98
124	A. C. MacLaren, Adelaide	1897-98
116	A. C. MacLaren, Sydney..	1901-02
140	A. C. MacLaren, Nottingham	1905
117	H. Makepeace, Melbourne	1920-21
104	P. B. H. May, Sydney......	1954-55
101	P. B. H. May, Leeds	1956
113	P. B. H. May, Melbourne.	1958-59
182*	C. P. Mead, The Oval......	1921
102†	Nawab of Pataudi, Sydney	1932-33
216*	E. Paynter, Nottingham....	1938
174†	D. W. Randall, Melbourne	1976-77
150	D. W. Randall, Sydney	1978-79
115	D. W. Randall, Perth.......	1982-83
154*†	K. S. Ranjitsinhji, Manchester	1896
175	K. S. Ranjitsinhji, Sydney.	1897-98
117	W. W. Read, The Oval	1884
179	W. Rhodes, Melbourne ...	1911-12
104	P. E. Richardson, Manchester	1956
135*	A. C. Russell, Adelaide ...	1920-21
101	A. C. Russell, Manchester	1921
102*	A. C. Russell, The Oval....	1921
105	J. Sharp, The Oval..........	1909
113	Rev. D. S. Sheppard, Manchester	1956
113	Rev. D. S. Sheppard, Melbourne	1962-63
105*	A. Shrewsbury, Melbourne	1884-85
164	A. Shrewsbury, Lord's	1886
106	A. Shrewsbury, Lord's	1893
156*	R. T. Simpson, Melbourne	1950-51
135*	A. G. Steel, Sydney.........	1882-83
148	A. G. Steel, Lord's..........	1884
134	A. E. Stoddart, Adelaide..	1891-92
173	A. E. Stoddart, Melbourne	1894-95
112†	R. Subba Row, Birmingham	1961
137	R. Subba Row, The Oval .	1961
115†	H. Sutcliffe, Sydney........	1924-25
176 127 }	H. Sutcliffe, Melbourne ...	1924-25
143	H. Sutcliffe, Melbourne ...	1924-25
161	H. Sutcliffe, The Oval......	1926
135	H. Sutcliffe, Melbourne ...	1928-29
161	H. Sutcliffe, The Oval......	1930
194	H. Sutcliffe, Sydney........	1932-33
138	J. T. Tyldesley, Birmingham	1902
100	J. T. Tyldesley, Leeds	1905
112*	J. T. Tyldesley, The Oval .	1905
149	G. Ulyett, Melbourne	1881-82
117	A. Ward, Sydney............	1894-95
112	C. Washbrook, Melbourne	1946-47
143	C. Washbrook, Leeds	1948

109†	W. Watson, Lord's	1953	120	R. A. Woolmer, Lord's	1977
133*	F. E. Woolley, Sydney	1911-12	137	R. A. Woolmer, Manchester	1977
123	F. E. Woolley, Sydney	1924-25			
149	R. A. Woolmer, The Oval	1975			

† *Signifies hundred on first appearance in England–Australia Tests.*

Note: In consecutive innings in 1928-29, W. R. Hammond scored 251 at Sydney, 200 and 32 at Melbourne, and 119* and 177 at Adelaide.

For Australia (193)

133*	W. W. Armstrong, Melbourne	1907-08
158	W. W. Armstrong, Sydney	1920-21
121	W. W. Armstrong, Adelaide	1920-21
123*	W. W. Armstrong, Melbourne	1920-21
118	C. L. Badcock, Melbourne	1936-37
165*†	C. Bannerman, Melbourne	1876-77
136 130 }	W. Bardsley, The Oval.....	1909
193*	W. Bardsley, Lord's.........	1926
234	S. G. Barnes, Sydney	1946-47
141	S. G. Barnes, Lord's........	1948
128	G. J. Bonnor, Sydney	1884-85
112	B. C. Booth, Brisbane	1962-63
103	B. C. Booth, Melbourne....	1962-63
115	A. R. Border, Perth	1979-80
123*	A. R. Border, Manchester	1981
106*	A. R. Border, The Oval ...	1981
112	D. G. Bradman, Melbourne	1928-29
123	D. G. Bradman, Melbourne	1928-29
131	D. G. Bradman, Nottingham	1930
254	D. G. Bradman, Lord's.....	1930
334	D. G. Bradman, Leeds.....	1930
232	D. G. Bradman, The Oval	1930
103*	D. G. Bradman, Melbourne	1932-33
304	D. G. Bradman, Leeds.....	1934
244	D. G. Bradman, The Oval	1934
270	D. G. Bradman, Melbourne	1936-37
212	D. G. Bradman, Adelaide	1936-37
169	D. G. Bradman, Melbourne	1936-37
144*	D. G. Bradman, Nottingham...........	1938
102*	D. G. Bradman, Lord's....	1938
103	D. G. Bradman, Leeds.....	1938
187	D. G. Bradman, Brisbane.	1946-47
234	D. G. Bradman, Sydney ...	1946-47
138	D. G. Bradman, Nottingham...........	1948
173*	D. G. Bradman, Leeds.....	1948
105	W. A. Brown, Lord's.......	1934
133	W. A. Brown, Nottingham	1938
206*	W. A. Brown, Lord's.......	1938
181	P. J. Burge, The Oval......	1961
103	P. J. Burge, Sydney........	1962-63
160	P. J. Burge, Leeds...........	1964
120	P. J. Burge, Melbourne.....	1965-66
101*†	J. W. Burke, Adelaide	1950-51
108†	G. S. Chappell, Perth	1970-71
131	G. S. Chappell, Lord's......	1972
113	G. S. Chappell, The Oval .	1972
144	G. S. Chappell, Sydney	1974-75
102	G. S. Chappell, Melbourne	1974-75
112	G. S. Chappell, Manchester	1977
114	G. S. Chappell, Melbourne	1979-80
117	G. S. Chappell, Perth	1982-83
115	G. S. Chappell, Adelaide..	1982-83
111	I. M. Chappell, Melbourne	1970-71
104	I. M. Chappell, Adelaide...	1970-71
118	I. M. Chappell, The Oval .	1972
192	I. M. Chappell, The Oval .	1975
104†	H. L. Collins, Sydney	1920-21
162	H. L. Collins, Adelaide....	1920-21
114	H. L. Collins, Sydney	1924-25
307	R. M. Cowper, Melbourne	1965-66
101	J. Darling, Sydney...........	1897-98
178	J. Darling, Adelaide........	1897-98
160	J. Darling, Sydney...........	1897-98
104†	R. A. Duff, Melbourne	1901-02
146	R. A. Duff, The Oval	1905
102	J. Dyson, Leeds..............	1981
170*	R. Edwards, Nottingham..	1972
115	R. Edwards, Perth...........	1974-75
100	J. H. Fingleton, Brisbane..	1936-37
136	J. H. Fingleton, Melbourne	1936-37
161	G. Giffen, Sydney	1894-95
107†	H. Graham, Lord's..........	1893
105	H. Graham, Sydney.........	1894-95
100	J. M. Gregory, Melbourne	1920-21
201	S. E. Gregory, Sydney	1894-95
103	S. E. Gregory, Lord's.......	1896
117	S. E. Gregory, The Oval ..	1899
112	S. E. Gregory, Adelaide....	1903-04
116†	R. J. Hartigan, Adelaide ..	1907-08
112†	R. N. Harvey, Leeds	1948
122	R. N. Harvey, Manchester	1953
162	R. N. Harvey, Brisbane....	1954-55

167	R. N. Harvey, Melbourne.	1958-59	182	A. R. Morris, Leeds........		1948
114	R. N. Harvey, Birmingham	1961	196	A. R. Morris, The Oval ...		1948
154	R. N. Harvey, Adelaide ...	1962-63	206	A. R. Morris, Adelaide....		1950-51
128	A. L. Hassett, Brisbane...	1946-47	153	A. R. Morris, Brisbane....		1954-55
137	A. L. Hassett, Nottingham	1948	153*	W. L. Murdoch, The Oval		1880
115	A. L. Hassett, Nottingham	1953	211	W. L. Murdoch, The Oval		1884
104	A. L. Hassett, Lord's......	1953	133	M. A. Noble, Sydney......		1903-04
112	H. S. T. L. Hendry, Sydney	1928-29	117	N. C. O'Neill, The Oval...		1961
188	C. Hill, Melbourne..........	1897-98	100	N. C. O'Neill, Adelaide ...		1962-63
135	C. Hill, Lord's........	1899	116	C. E. Pellew, Melbourne ...		1920-21
119	C. Hill, Sheffield..........	1902	104	C. E. Pellew, Adelaide......		1920-21
160	C. Hill, Adelaide..........	1907-08	110†	W. H. Ponsford, Sydney...		1924-25
124	T. P. Horan, Melbourne...	1881-82	128	W. H. Ponsford, Melbourne		1924-25
129	K. J. Hughes, Brisbane ...	1978-79	110	W. H. Ponsford, The Oval.		1930
117	K. J. Hughes, Lord's	1980	181	W. H. Ponsford, Leeds....		1934
137	K. J. Hughes, Sydney ...	1982-83	266	W. H. Ponsford, The Oval		1934
140	F. A. Iredale, Adelaide...	1894-95	143*	V. S. Ransford, Lord's.....		1909
108	F. A. Iredale, Manchester.	1896	171	I. R. Redpath, Perth........		1970-71
164†	A. Jackson, Adelaide......	1928-29	105	I. R. Redpath, Sydney ...		1974-75
147	C. Kelleway, Adelaide ...	1920-21	100	A. J. Richardson, Leeds....		1926
100	A. F. Kippax, Melbourne .	1928-29	138	V. Y. Richardson, Melbourne		1924-25
130	W. M. Lawry, Lord's......	1961	201*	J. Ryder, Adelaide..........		1924-25
102	W. M. Lawry, Manchester	1961	112	J. Ryder, Melbourne........		1928-29
106	W. M. Lawry, Manchester	1964	102	H. J. H. Scott, The Oval ..		1884
166	W. M. Lawry, Brisbane....	1965-66	311	R. B. Simpson, Manchester		1964
119	W. M. Lawry, Adelaide ...	1965-66	225	R. B. Simpson, Adelaide..		1965-66
108	W. M. Lawry, Melbourne .	1965-66	207	K. R. Stackpole, Brisbane		1970-71
135	W. M. Lawry, The Oval...	1968	136	K. R. Stackpole, Adelaide		1970-71
100	R. R. Lindwall, Melbourne	1946-47	114	K. R. Stackpole, Nottingham		1972
134	J. J. Lyons, Sydney	1891-92	108	J. M. Taylor, Sydney		1924-25
170	C. G. Macartney, Sydney .	1920-21	143	G. H. S. Trott, Lord's......		1896
115	C. G. Macartney, Leeds ...	1921	135*	V. T. Trumper, Lord's		1899
133*	C. G. Macartney, Lord's .	1926	104	V. T. Trumper, Manchester		1902
151	C. G. Macartney, Leeds ...	1926	185*	V. T. Trumper, Sydney ...		1903-04
109	C. G. Macartney, Manchester	1926	113	V. T. Trumper, Adelaide..		1903-04
187*	S. J. McCabe, Sydney	1932-33	166	V. T. Trumper, Sydney		1907-08
137	S. J. McCabe, Manchester	1934	113	V. T. Trumper, Sydney		1911-12
112	S. J. McCabe, Melbourne .	1936-37	155†	K. D. Walters, Brisbane...		1965-66
232	S. J. McCabe, Nottingham	1938	115	K. D. Walters, Melbourne		1965-66
104*	C. L. McCool, Melbourne	1946-47	112	K. D. Walters, Brisbane ...		1970-71
127	R. B. McCosker, The Oval	1975	103	K. D. Walters, Perth........		1974-75
107	R. B. McCosker, Nottingham	1977	103†	D. M. Wellham, The Oval		1981
170	C. C. McDonald, Adelaide	1958-59	162†	K. C. Wessels, Brisbane ..		1982-83
133	C. C. McDonald, Melbourne	1958-59	100	G. M. Wood, Melbourne..		1978-79
147	P. S. McDonnell, Sydney..	1881-82	112	G. M. Wood, Lord's........		1980
103	P. S. McDonnell, The Oval	1884	141	W. M. Woodfull, Leeds....		1926
124	P. S. McDonnell, Adelaide	1884-85	117	W. M. Woodfull, Manchester		1926
112	C. E. McLeod, Melbourne	1897-98	111	W. M. Woodfull, Sydney ..		1928-29
110*	R. W. Marsh, Melbourne .	1976-77	107	W. M. Woodfull, Melbourne		1928-29
141*	K. R. Miller, Adelaide ...	1946-47	102	W. M. Woodfull, Melbourne		1928-29
145*	K. R. Miller, Sydney	1950-51	155	W. M. Woodfull, Lord's...		1930
109	K. R. Miller, Lord's	1953	102†	G. N. Yallop, Brisbane		1978-79
155	A. R. Morris, Melbourne	1946-47	121	G. N. Yallop, Sydney		1978-79
122 } 124* }	A. R. Morris, Adelaide....	1946-47	114	G. N. Yallop, Manchester.		1981
105	A. R. Morris, Lord's	1948				

† *Signifies hundred on first appearance in England–Australia Tests.*

Notes: D. G. Bradman's scores in 1930 were 8 and 131 at Nottingham, 254 and 1 at Lord's, 334 at Leeds, 14 at Manchester, and 232 at The Oval.

D. G. Bradman scored a hundred in eight successive Tests against England in which he batted – three in 1936-37, three in 1938 and two in 1946-47. He was injured and unable to bat at The Oval in 1938.

W. H. Ponsford and K. D. Walters each hit hundreds in their first two Tests.

C. Bannerman and H. Graham each scored their maiden hundred in first-class cricket in their first Test.

No right-handed batsman has obtained two hundreds for Australia in a Test match against England, and no left-handed batsman for England against Australia.

H. Sutcliffe, in his first two games for England, scored 59 and 115 at Sydney and 176 and 127 at Melbourne in 1924-25. In the latter match, which lasted into the seventh day, he was on the field throughout except for 86 minutes, namely 27 hours and 52 minutes.

C. Hill made 98 and 97 at Adelaide in 1901-02, and F. E. Woolley 95 and 93 at Lord's in 1921.

H. Sutcliffe in 1924-25, C. G. Macartney in 1926 and A. R. Morris in 1946-47 made three hundreds in consecutive innings.

J. B. Hobbs and H. Sutcliffe shared eleven first-wicket three-figure partnerships.

L. Hutton and C. Washbrook twice made three-figure stands in each innings, at Adelaide in 1946-47 and at Leeds in 1948.

H. Sutcliffe, during his highest score of 194, v Australia in 1932-33, took part in three stands each exceeding 100, viz. 112 with R. E. S. Wyatt for the first wicket, 188 with W. R. Hammond for the second wicket, and 123 with the Nawab of Pataudi for the third wicket. In 1903-04 R. E. Foster, in his historic innings of 287, added 192 for the fifth wicket with L. C. Braund, 115 for the ninth with A. E. Relf, and 130 for the tenth wicket with W. Rhodes.

When L. Hutton scored 364 at The Oval in 1938 he added 382 for the second wicket with M. Leyland, 135 for the third wicket with W. R. Hammond and 215 for the sixth wicket with J. Hardstaff jun.

D. C. S. Compton and A. R. Morris at Adelaide in 1946-47 provide the only instance of a player on each side hitting two separate hundreds in a Test match.

G. S. and I. M. Chappell at The Oval in 1972 provide the first instance in Test matches of brothers each scoring hundreds in the same innings.

G. Boycott (191 at Leeds, 1977) is the only batsman to score his hundredth first-class century in a Test match.

RECORD PARTNERSHIPS FOR EACH WICKET

For England

323 for 1st	J. B. Hobbs and W. Rhodes at Melbourne	1911-12
382 for 2nd†	L. Hutton and M. Leyland at The Oval	1938
262 for 3rd	W. R. Hammond and D. R. Jardine at Adelaide	1928-29
222 for 4th	W. R. Hammond and E. Paynter at Lord's	1938
206 for 5th	E. Paynter and D. C. S. Compton at Nottingham	1938
215 for 6th {	L. Hutton and J. Hardstaff jun. at The Oval	1938
	G. Boycott and A. P. E. Knott at Nottingham	1977
143 for 7th	F. E. Woolley and J. Vine at Sydney	1911-12
124 for 8th	E. H. Hendren and H. Larwood at Brisbane	1928-29
151 for 9th	W. H. Scotton and W. W. Read at The Oval	1884
130 for 10th†	R. E. Foster and W. Rhodes at Sydney	1903-04

For Australia

244 for 1st	R. B. Simpson and W. M. Lawry at Adelaide	1965-66
451 for 2nd†	W. H. Ponsford and D. G. Bradman at The Oval	1934
276 for 3rd	D. G. Bradman and A. L. Hassett at Brisbane	1946-47
388 for 4th†	W. H. Ponsford and D. G. Bradman at Leeds	1934
405 for 5th†	S. G. Barnes and D. G. Bradman at Sydney	1946-47
346 for 6th†	J. H. Fingleton and D. G. Bradman at Melbourne	1936-37
165 for 7th	C. Hill and H. Trumble at Melbourne	1897-98

243 for 8th†	R. J. Hartigan and C. Hill at Adelaide	1907-08
154 for 9th†	S. E. Gregory and J. McC. Blackham at Sydney	1894-95
127 for 10th†	J. M. Taylor and A. A. Mailey at Sydney	1924-25

† *Denotes record partnership against all countries.*

MOST RUNS IN A SERIES

England in England	562 (average 62.44)	D. C. S. Compton	1948
England in Australia	905 (average 113.12)	W. R. Hammond	1928-29
Australia in England	974 (average 139.14)	D. G. Bradman	1930
Australia in Australia	810 (average 90.00)	D. G. Bradman	1936-37

TEN WICKETS OR MORE IN A MATCH

For England (36)

13-163 (6-42, 7-121)	S. F. Barnes, Melbourne	1901-02
14-102 (7-28, 7-74)	W. Bates, Melbourne	1882-83
10-105 (5-46, 5-59)	A. V. Bedser, Melbourne	1950-51
14-99 (7-55, 7-44)	A. V. Bedser, Nottingham	1953
11-102 (6-44, 5-58)	C. Blythe, Birmingham	1909
11-176 (6-78, 5-98)	I. T. Botham, Perth	1979-80
10-253 (6-125, 4-128)	I. T. Botham, The Oval	1981
11-74 (5-29, 6-45)	J. Briggs, Lord's	1886
12-136 (6-49, 6-87)	J. Briggs, Adelaide	1891-92
10-148 (5-34, 5-114)	J. Briggs, The Oval	1893
10-179 (5-102, 5-77)†	K. Farnes, Nottingham	1934
10-60 (6-41, 4-19)	J. T. Hearne, The Oval	1896
11-113 (5-58, 6-55)	J. C. Laker, Leeds	1956
19-90 (9-37, 10-53)	J. C. Laker, Manchester	1956
10-124 (5-96, 5-28)	H. Larwood, Sydney	1932-33
11-76 (6-48, 5-28)	W. H. Lockwood, Manchester	1902
12-104 (7-36, 5-68)	G. A. Lohmann, The Oval	1886
10-87 (8-35, 2-52)	G. A. Lohmann, Sydney	1886-87
10-142 (8-58, 2-84)	G. A. Lohmann, Sydney	1891-92
12-102 (6-50, 6-52)†	F. Martin, The Oval	1890
10-58 (5-18, 5-40)	R. Peel, Sydney	1887-88
11-68 (7-31, 4-37)	R. Peel, Manchester	1888
15-124 (7-56, 8-68)	W. Rhodes, Melbourne	1903-04
10-156 (5-49, 5-107)†	T. Richardson, Manchester	1893
11-173 (6-39, 5-134)	T. Richardson, Lord's	1896
13-244 (7-168, 6-76)	T. Richardson, Manchester	1896
10-204 (8-94, 2-110)	T. Richardson, Sydney	1897-98
11-228 (6-130, 5-98)†	M. W. Tate, Sydney	1924-25
11-88 (5-58, 6-30)	F. S. Trueman, Leeds	1961
10-130 (4-45, 6-85)	F. H. Tyson, Sydney	1954-55
10-82 (4-37, 6-45)	D. L. Underwood, Leeds	1972
11-215 (7-113, 4-102)	D. L. Underwood, Adelaide	1974-75
15-104 (7-61, 8-43)	H. Verity, Lord's	1934
10-57 (6-41, 4-16)	W. Voce, Brisbane	1936-37
13-256 (5-130, 8-126)	J. C. White, Adelaide	1928-29
10-49 (5-29, 5-20)	F. E. Woolley, The Oval	1912

For Australia (35)

10-239 (4-129, 6-110)	L. O'B. Fleetwood-Smith, Adelaide	1936-37
10-160 (4-88, 6-72)	G. Giffen, Sydney	1891-92
11-82 (5-45, 6-37)†	C. V. Grimmett, Sydney	1924-25
10-201 (5-107, 5-94)	C. V. Grimmett, Nottingham	1930
10-122 (5-65, 5-57)	R. M. Hogg, Perth	1978-79
10-66 (5-30, 5-36)	R. M. Hogg, Melbourne	1978-79
12-175 (5-85, 7-90)†	H. V. Hordern, Sydney	1911-12
10-161 (5-95, 5-66)	H. V. Hordern, Sydney	1911-12
10-164 (7-88, 3-76)	E. Jones, Lord's	1899
11-134 (6-47, 5-87)	G. F. Lawson, Brisbane	1982-83
10-181 (5-58, 5-123)	D. K. Lillee, The Oval	1972
11-165 (6-26, 5-139)	D. K. Lillee, Melbourne	1976-77
11-138 (6-60, 5-78)	D. K. Lillee, Melbourne	1979-80
11-159 (7-89, 4-70)	D. K. Lillee, The Oval	1981
11-85 (7-58, 4-27)	C. G. Macartney, Leeds	1909
10-302 (5-160, 5-142)	A. A. Mailey, Adelaide	1920-21
13-236 (4-115, 9-121)	A. A. Mailey, Melbourne	1920-21
16-137 (8-84, 8-53)†	R. A. L. Massie, Lord's	1972
10-152 (5-72, 5-80)	K. R. Miller, Lord's	1956
13-77 (7-17, 6-60)	M. A. Noble, Melbourne	1901-02
11-103 (5-51, 6-52)	M. A. Noble, Sheffield	1902
10-129 (5-63, 5-66)	W. J. O'Reilly, Melbourne	1932-33
11-129 (4-75, 7-54)	W. J. O'Reilly, Nottingham	1934
10-122 (5-66, 5-56)	W. J. O'Reilly, Leeds	1938
11-165 (7-68, 4-97)	G. E. Palmer, Sydney	1881-82
10-126 (7-65, 3-61)	G. E. Palmer, Melbourne	1882-83
13-110 (6-48, 7-62)	F. R. Spofforth, Melbourne	1878-79
14-90 (7-46, 7-44)	F. R. Spofforth, The Oval	1882
11-117 (4-73, 7-44)	F. R. Spofforth, Sydney	1882-83
10-144 (4-54, 6-90)	F. R. Spofforth, Sydney	1884-85
12-89 (6-59, 6-30)	H. Trumble, The Oval	1896
10-128 (4-75, 6-53)	H. Trumble, Manchester	1902
12-173 (8-65, 4-108)	H. Trumble, The Oval	1902
12-87 (5-44, 7-43)	C. T. B. Turner, Sydney	1887-88
10-63 (5-27, 5-36)	C. T. B. Turner, Lord's	1888

† *Signifies ten wickets or more on first appearance in England-Australia Tests.*

Note: J. Briggs, J. C. Laker, T. Richardson in 1896, R. M. Hogg, A. A. Mailey, H. Trumble and C. T. B. Turner took ten wickets or more in successive Tests. J. Briggs was omitted, however, from the England team for the first Test match in 1893.

MOST WICKETS IN A SERIES

England in England	46 (average 9.60)	J. C. Laker	1956
England in Australia	38 (average 23.18)	M. W. Tate	1924-25
Australia in England	42 (average 21.26)	T. M. Alderman (6 Tests)	1981
Australia in Australia	41 (average 12.85)	R. M. Hogg (6 Tests)	1978-79

WICKET-KEEPING – MOST DISMISSALS

	M	Ct	St	Total
†R. W. Marsh (Australia)	42	141	7	148
A. P. E. Knott (England)	34	97	8	105
†W. A. Oldfield (Australia)	38	59	31	90
A. A. Lilley (England)	32	65	19	84
A. T. W. Grout (Australia)	22	69	7	76
T. G. Evans (England)	31	63	12	75

† *The number of catches by R. W. Marsh (141) and stumpings by W. A. Oldfield (31) are respective records in England–Australia Tests.*

SCORERS OF OVER 2,000 RUNS

	T	I	NO	R	HI	Avge
D. G. Bradman	37	63	7	5,028	334	89.78
J. B. Hobbs	41	71	4	3,636	187	54.26
G. Boycott	38	71	9	2,945	191	47.50
W. R. Hammond	31	58	3	2,852	251	51.85
H. Sutcliffe	27	46	5	2,741	194	66.85
C. Hill	41	76	1	2,660	188	35.46
J. H. Edrich	32	57	3	2,644	175	48.96
G. S. Chappell	35	65	8	2,619	144	45.94
M. C. Cowdrey	43	75	4	2,433	113	34.26
L. Hutton	27	49	6	2,428	364	56.46
R. N. Harvey	37	68	5	2,416	167	38.34
V. T. Trumper	40	74	5	2,263	185*	32.79
W. M. Lawry	29	51	5	2,233	166	48.54
S. E. Gregory	52	92	7	2,193	201	25.80
W. W. Armstrong	42	71	9	2,172	158	35.03
I. M. Chappell	30	56	4	2,138	192	41.11
K. F. Barrington	23	39	6	2,111	256	63.96
A. R. Morris	24	43	2	2,080	206	50.73

BOWLERS WITH 100 WICKETS

	T	Balls	R	W	5 W/i	Avge
D. K. Lillee	29	8,516	3,507	167	11	21.00
H. Trumble	31	7,895	2,945	141	9	20.88
R. G. D. Willis	35	7,294	3,346	128	7	26.14
M. A. Noble	39	6,845	2,860	115	9	24.86
R. R. Lindwall	29	6,728	2,559	114	6	22.44
W. Rhodes	41	5,791	2,616	109	6	24.00
S. F. Barnes	20	5,749	2,288	106	12	21.58
C. V. Grimmett	22	9,224	3,439	106	11	32.44
I. T. Botham	23	5,851	2,701	105	8	25.72
D. L. Underwood	29	8,000	2,770	105	4	26.38
A. V. Bedser	21	7,065	2,859	104	7	27.49
G. Giffen	31	6,325	2,791	103	7	27.09
W. J. O'Reilly	19	7,864	2,587	102	8	25.36
R. Peel	20	5,216	1,715	102	6	16.81
C. T. B. Turner	17	5,195	1,670	101	11	16.53

ENGLAND v SOUTH AFRICA

Season	England	South Africa	T	E	SA	D
		Captains				
1888-89	C. A. Smith[1]	O. R. Dunell[2]	2	2	0	0
1891-92	W. W. Read	W. H. Milton	1	1	0	0
1895-96	Lord Hawke[3]	E. A. Halliwell[4]	3	3	0	0
1898-99	Lord Hawke	M. Bisset	2	2	0	0
1905-06	P. F. Warner	P. W. Sherwell	5	1	4	0
1907	R. E. Foster	P. W. Sherwell	3	1	0	2
1909-10	H. D. G. Leveson Gower[5]	S. J. Snooke	5	2	3	0
1912	C. B. Fry	F. Mitchell[6]	3	3	0	0
1913-14	J. W. H. T. Douglas	H. W. Taylor	5	4	0	1

Captains

Season	England	South Africa	T	E	SA	D
1922-23	F. T. Mann	H. W. Taylor	5	2	1	2
1924	A. E. R. Gilligan[7]	H. W. Taylor	5	3	0	2
1927-28	R. T. Stanyforth[8]	H. G. Deane	5	2	2	1
1929	J. C. White[9]	H. G. Deane	5	2	0	3
1930-31	A. P. F. Chapman	H. G. Deane[10]	5	0	1	4
1935	R. E. S. Wyatt	H. F. Wade	5	0	1	4
1938-39	W. R. Hammond	A. Melville	5	1	0	4
1947	N. W. D. Yardley	A. Melville	5	3	0	2
1948-49	F. G. Mann	A. D. Nourse	5	2	0	3
1951	F. R. Brown	A. D. Nourse	5	3	1	1
1955	P. B. H. May	J. E. Cheetham[11]	5	3	2	0
1956-57	P. B. H. May	C. B. van Ryneveld[12]	5	2	2	1
1960	M. C. Cowdrey	D. J. McGlew	5	3	0	2
1964-65	M. J. K. Smith	T. L. Goddard	5	1	0	4
1965	M. J. K. Smith	P. L. van der Merwe	3	0	1	2

In South Africa	58	25	13	20
In England	44	21	5	18
Totals......................................	102	46	18	38

Notes: The following deputised for the official touring captain or were appointed by the home authority for only a minor proportion of the series:

[1] M. P. Bowden (Second). [2] W. H. Milton (Second). [3] Sir T. C. O'Brien (First). [4] A. R. Richards (Third). [5] F. L. Fane (Fourth and Fifth). [6] L. J. Tancred (Second and Third). [7] J. W. H. T. Douglas (Fourth). [8] G. T. S. Stevens (Fifth). [9] A. W. Carr (Fourth and Fifth). [10] E. P. Nupen (First), H. B. Cameron (Fourth and Fifth). [11] D. J. McGlew (Third and Fourth). [12] D. J. McGlew (Second).

HIGHEST INNINGS TOTALS

For England in England: 554-8 dec. at Lord's, 1947
in South Africa: 654-5 at Durban, 1938-39

For South Africa in England: 538 at Leeds, 1951
in South Africa: 530 at Durban, 1938-39

LOWEST INNINGS TOTALS

For England in England: 76 at Leeds, 1907
in South Africa: 92 at Cape Town, 1898-99

For South Africa in England: 30 at Birmingham, 1924
in South Africa: 30 at Port Elizabeth, 1895-96

INDIVIDUAL HUNDREDS IN THE MATCHES 1888-89–1965

For England (87)

120	R. Abel, Cape Town	1888-89		158	L. Hutton, Johannesburg..	1948-49
148*	L. E. G. Ames, The Oval.	1935		123	L. Hutton, Johannesburg..	1948-49
115	L. E. G. Ames, Cape Town	1938-39		100	L. Hutton, Leeds	1951
148*	K. F. Barrington, Durban .	1964-65		110*	D. J. Insole, Durban........	1956-57
121	K. F. Barrington, Johannesburg	1964-65		102	M. Leyland, Lord's..........	1929
				161	M. Leyland, The Oval......	1935
117	G. Boycott, Port Elizabeth	1964-65		136*	F. G. Mann, Port Elizabeth	1948-49
104†	L. C. Braund, Lord's	1907		138†	P. B. H. May, Leeds	1951
208	D. C. S. Compton, Lord's	1947		112	P. B. H. May, Lord's.......	1955
163†	D. C. S. Compton, Nottingham......................	1947		117	P. B. H. May, Manchester	1955
				102	C. P. Mead, Johannesburg	1913-14
115	D. C. S. Compton, Manchester	1947		117	C. P. Mead, Port Elizabeth	1913-14
				181	C. P. Mead, Durban	1922-23
113	D. C. S. Compton, The Oval	1947		122*	P. H. Parfitt, Johannesburg	1964-65
				108*	J. M. Parks, Durban........	1964-65
114	D. C. S. Compton, Johannesburg	1948-49		117† 100 }	E. Paynter, Johannesburg .	1938-39
112	D. C. S. Compton, Nottingham......................	1951		243	E. Paynter, Durban	1938-39
				175	G. Pullar, The Oval.........	1960
158	D. C. S. Compton, Manchester	1955		152	W. Rhodes, Johannesburg	1913-14
101	M. C. Cowdrey, Cape Town	1956-57		117†	P. E. Richardson, Johannesburg	1956-57
155	M. C. Cowdrey, The Oval	1960		108	R. W. V. Robins, Manchester	1935
105	M. C. Cowdrey, Nottingham........................	1965		140 111 }	A. C. Russell, Durban	1922-23
104	D. Denton, Johannesburg .	1909-10				
172	E. R. Dexter, Johannesburg	1964-65		137	R. T. Simpson, Nottingham	1951
				121	M. J. K. Smith, Cape Town	1964-65
119†	J. W. H. T. Douglas, Durban	1913-14		119†	R. H. Spooner, Lord's	1912
				122	H. Sutcliffe, Lord's	1924
219	W. J. Edrich, Durban	1938-39		102	H. Sutcliffe, Johannesburg	1927-28
191	W. J. Edrich, Manchester .	1947		114	H. Sutcliffe, Birmingham..	1929
189	W. J. Edrich, Lord's........	1947		100	H. Sutcliffe, Lord's	1929
143	F. L. Fane, Johannesburg .	1905-06		104 109* }	H. Sutcliffe, The Oval......	1929
129	C. B. Fry, The Oval	1907				
106†	P. A. Gibb, Johannesburg	1938-39		100*	M. W. Tate, Lord's	1929
120	P. A. Gibb, Durban	1938-39		122†	E. Tyldesley, Johannesburg	1927-28
138*	W. R. Hammond, Birmingham	1929		100	E. Tyldesley, Durban........	1927-28
				112	J. T. Tyldesley, Cape Town	1898-99
101*	W. R. Hammond, The Oval	1929		112	B. H. Valentine, Cape Town	1938-39
136*	W. R. Hammond, Durban	1930-31				
181	W. R. Hammond, Cape Town	1938-39		132*†	P. F. Warner, Johannesburg	1898-99
				195	C. Washbrook, Johannesburg	1948-49
120	W. R. Hammond, Durban	1938-39				
140	W. R. Hammond, Durban	1938-39		111	A. J. Watkins, Johannesburg	1948-49
122	T. W. Hayward, Johannesburg	1895-96		134*	H. Wood, Cape Town	1891-92
132	E. H. Hendren, Leeds	1924		115*	F. E. Woolley, Johannesburg	1922-23
142	E. H. Hendren, The Oval.	1924		134*	F. E. Woolley, Lord's	1924
124	A. J. L. Hill, Cape Town .	1895-96		154	F. E. Woolley, Manchester	1929
187	J. B. Hobbs, Cape Town ..	1909-10		113	R. E. S. Wyatt, Manchester	1929
211	J. B. Hobbs, Lord's.........	1924		149	R. E. S. Wyatt, Nottingham	1935
100	L. Hutton, Leeds	1947				

For South Africa (58)

138	E. J. Barlow, Cape Town .	1964-65		127	K. C. Bland, The Oval.....	1965
144*	K. C. Bland, Johannesburg	1964-65		120	R. H. Catterall, Birmingham	1924

120	R. H. Catterall, Lord's.....	1924	112	A. D. Nourse, Cape Town	1948-49
119	R. H. Catterall, Durban ...	1927-28	208	A. D. Nourse, Nottingham	1951
117	E. L. Dalton, The Oval....	1935	129	H. G. Owen-Smith, Leeds	1929
102	E. L. Dalton, Johannesburg	1938-39	154	A. J. Pithey, Cape Town ..	1964-65
116*	W. R. Endean, Leeds	1955	137	R. G. Pollock, Port Elizabeth	1964-65
123	G. A. Faulkner, Johannesburg	1909-10	125	R. G. Pollock, Nottingham	1965
112	T. L. Goddard, Johannesburg	1964-65	156*	E. A. B. Rowan, Johannesburg	1948-49
102	C. M. H. Hathorn, Johannesburg	1905-06	236	E. A. B. Rowan, Leeds....	1951
			115	P. W. Sherwell, Lord's.....	1907
104*	D. J. McGlew, Manchester	1955	141	I. J. Siedle, Cape Town...	1930-31
133	D. J. McGlew, Leeds.......	1955	106	J. H. Sinclair, Cape Town.	1898-99
142	R. A. McLean, Lord's	1955	109	H. W. Taylor, Durban	1913-14
100	R. A. McLean, Durban....	1956-57	176	H. W. Taylor, Johannesburg.........................	1922-23
109	R. A. McLean, Manchester	1960			
103	A. Melville, Durban	1938-39	101	H. W. Taylor, Johannesburg.........................	1922-23
189 104* }	A. Melville, Nottingham...	1947	102	H. W. Taylor, Durban	1922-23
117	A. Melville, Lord's..........	1947	101	H. W. Taylor, Johannesburg.........................	1927-28
123	B. Mitchell, Cape Town ...	1930-31	121	H. W. Taylor, The Oval...	1929
164*	B. Mitchell, Lord's..........	1935	117	H. W. Taylor, Cape Town	1930-31
128	B. Mitchell, The Oval......	1935	125	P. G. V. van der Bijl, Durban	1938-39
109	B. Mitchell, Durban	1938-39			
120 189* }	B. Mitchell, The Oval......	1947	124	K. G. Viljoen, Manchester	1935
120	B. Mitchell, Cape Town ...	1948-49	125	W. W. Wade, Port Elizabeth	1948-49
120	A. D. Nourse, Cape Town	1938-39			
103	A. D. Nourse, Durban.....	1938-39	113	J. H. B. Waite, Manchester	1955
149	A. D. Nourse, Nottingham	1947			
115	A. D. Nourse, Manchester	1947	147	G. C. White, Johannesburg	1905-06
129*	A. D. Nourse, Johannesburg	1948-49	118	G. C. White, Durban.......	1909-10
			108	P. L. Winslow, Manchester	1955

† *Signifies hundred on first appearance in England–South Africa Tests.*

Notes: P. F. Warner carried his bat through the second innings.

The highest score by a South African batsman on début is 93* by A. W. Nourse at Johannesburg in 1905-06.

P. N. F. Mansell made 90 at Leeds in 1951, the best on début in England.

A. Melville's four hundreds were made in successive Test innings.

RECORD PARTNERSHIP FOR EACH WICKET

For England

359 for 1st†	L. Hutton and C. Washbrook at Johannesburg	1948-49
280 for 2nd	P. A. Gibb and W. J. Edrich at Durban	1938-39
370 for 3rd†	W. J. Edrich and D. C. S. Compton at Lord's......................	1947
197 for 4th	W. R. Hammond and L. E. G. Ames at Cape Town	1938-39
237 for 5th	D. C. S. Compton and N. W. D. Yardley at Nottingham...........	1947
206* for 6th	K. F. Barrington and J. M. Parks at Durban	1964-65
115 for 7th	M. C. Bird and J. W. H. T. Douglas at Durban...................	1913-14
154 for 8th	C. W. Wright and H. R. Bromley-Davenport at Johannesburg..	1895-96
71 for 9th	H. Wood and J. T. Hearne at Cape Town	1891-92
92 for 10th	A. C. Russell and A. E. R. Gilligan at Durban	1922-23

For South Africa

260 for 1st†	I. J. Siedle and B. Mitchell at Cape Town	1930-31
198 for 2nd†	E. A. B. Rowan and C. B. van Ryneveld at Leeds..................	1951
319 for 3rd	A. Melville and A. D. Nourse at Nottingham.......................	1947

214 for 4th†	H. W. Taylor and H. G. Deane at The Oval	1929
157 for 5th†	A. J. Pithey and J. H. B. Waite at Johannesburg	1964-65
171 for 6th	J. H. B. Waite and P. L. Winslow at Manchester	1955
123 for 7th	H. G. Deane and E. P. Nupen at Durban	1927-28
109* for 8th	B. Mitchell and L. Tuckett at The Oval	1947
137 for 9th†	E. L. Dalton and A. B. C. Langton at The Oval	1935
103 for 10th†	H. G. Owen-Smith and A. J. Bell at Leeds	1929

† *Denotes record partnership against all countries.*

MOST RUNS IN A SERIES

England in England	753 (average 94.12)	D. C. S. Compton	1947
England in South Africa	653 (average 81.62)	E. Paynter	1938-39
South Africa in England	621 (average 69.00)	A. D. Nourse	1947
South Africa in South Africa	582 (average 64.66)	H. W. Taylor	1922-23

TEN WICKETS OR MORE IN A MATCH

For England (23)

11-110 (5-25, 6-85)†	S. F. Barnes, Lord's	1912
10-115 (6-52, 4-63)	S. F. Barnes, Leeds	1912
13-57 (5-28, 8-29)	S. F. Barnes, The Oval	1912
10-105 (5-57, 5-48)	S. F. Barnes, Durban	1913-14
17-159 (8-56, 9-103)	S. F. Barnes, Johannesburg	1913-14
14-144 (7-56, 7-88)	S. F. Barnes, Durban	1913-14
12-112 (7-58, 5-54)	A. V. Bedser, Manchester	1951
11-118 (6-68, 5-50)	C. Blythe, Cape Town	1905-06
15-99 (8-59, 7-40)	C. Blythe, Leeds	1907
10-104 (7-46, 3-58)	C. Blythe, Cape Town	1909-10
15-28 (7-17, 8-11)	J. Briggs, Cape Town	1888-89
13-91 (6-54, 7-37)†	J. J. Ferris, Cape Town	1891-92
10-207 (7-115, 3-92)	A. P. Freeman, Leeds	1929
12-171 (7-71, 5-100)	A. P. Freeman, Manchester	1929
12-130 (7-70, 5-60)	G. Geary, Johannesburg	1927-28
11-90 (6-7, 5-83)	A. E. R. Gilligan, Birmingham	1924
10-119 (4-64, 6-55)	J. C. Laker, The Oval	1951
15-45 (7-38, 8-7)†	G. A. Lohmann, Port Elizabeth	1895-96
12-71 (9-28, 3-43)	G. A. Lohmann, Johannesburg	1895-96
11-97 (6-63, 5-34)	J. B. Statham, Lord's	1960
12-101 (7-52, 5-49)	R. Tattersall, Lord's	1951
12-89 (5-53, 7-36)	J. H. Wardle, Cape Town	1956-57
10-175 (5-95, 5-80)	D. V. P. Wright, Lord's	1947

For South Africa (6)

11-112 (4-49, 7-63)†	A. E. Hall, Cape Town	1922-23
11-150 (5-63, 6-87)	E. P. Nupen, Johannesburg	1930-31
10-87 (5-53, 5-34)	P. M. Pollock, Nottingham	1965
12-127 (4-57, 8-70)	S. J. Snooke, Johannesburg	1905-06
13-192 (4-79, 9-113)	H. J. Tayfield, Johannesburg	1956-57
12-181 (5-87, 7-94)	A. E. E. Vogler, Johannesburg	1909-10

† *Signifies ten wickets or more on first appearance in England–South Africa Tests.*

Note: S. F. Barnes took ten wickets or more in his first five Tests v South Africa and in six of his seven Tests v South Africa. A. P. Freeman and G. A. Lohmann took ten wickets or more in successive matches.

MOST WICKETS IN A SERIES

England in England	34 (average 8.29)	S. F. Barnes	1912
England in South Africa	49 (average 10.93)	S. F. Barnes	1913-14
South Africa in England	26 (average 21.84)	H. J. Tayfield	1955
South Africa in England	26 (average 22.57)	N. A. T. Adcock	1960
South Africa in South Africa	37 (average 17.18)	H. J. Tayfield	1956-57

ENGLAND v WEST INDIES

	Captains					
Season	England	West Indies	T	E	WI	D
1928	A. P. F. Chapman	R. K. Nunes	3	3	0	0
1929-30	Hon. F. S. G. Calthorpe	E. L. G. Hoad[1]	4	1	1	2
1933	D. R. Jardine[2]	G. C. Grant	3	2	0	1
1934-35	R. E. S. Wyatt	G. C. Grant	4	1	2	1
1939	W. R. Hammond	R. S. Grant	3	1	0	2
1947-48	G. O. Allen[3]	J. D. C. Goddard[4]	4	0	2	2
1950	N. W. D. Yardley[5]	J. D. C. Goddard	4	1	3	0
1953-54	L. Hutton	J. B. Stollmeyer	5	2	2	1
1957	P. B. H. May	J. D. C. Goddard	5	3	0	2
1959-60	P. B. H. May[6]	F. C. M. Alexander	5	1	0	4

THE WISDEN TROPHY

	Captains						
Season	England	West Indies	T	E	WI	D	Held by
1963	E. R. Dexter	F. M. Worrell	5	1	3	1	WI
1966	M. C. Cowdrey[7]	G. S. Sobers	5	1	3	1	WI
1967-68	M. C. Cowdrey	G. S. Sobers	5	1	0	4	E
1969	R. Illingworth	G. S. Sobers	3	2	0	1	E
1973	R. Illingworth	R. B. Kanhai	3	0	2	1	WI
1973-74	M. H. Denness	R. B. Kanhai	5	1	1	3	WI
1976	A. W. Greig	C. H. Lloyd	5	0	3	2	WI
1980	I. T. Botham	C. H. Lloyd[8]	5	0	1	4	WI
1980-81†	I. T. Botham	C. H. Lloyd	4	0	2	2	WI
	In England........................		44	14	15	15	
	In West Indies....................		36	7	10	19	
	Totals..............................		80	21	25	34	

† *The Test match at Georgetown, scheduled as the second of the series, was cancelled owing to political pressure.*

Notes: The following deputised for the official touring captain or were appointed by the home authority for only a minor proportion of the series:
[1]N. Betancourt (Second), M. P. Fernandes (Third), R. K. Nunes (Fourth). [2]R. E. S. Wyatt (Third). [3]K. Cranston (First). [4]G. A. Headley (First), G. E. Gomez (Second). [5]F. R. Brown (Fourth). [6]M. C. Cowdrey (Fourth and Fifth). [7]M. J. K. Smith (First), D. B. Close (Fifth). [8]I. V. A. Richards (Fifth).

HIGHEST INNINGS TOTALS

For England in England: 619-6 dec. at Nottingham, 1957
    in West Indies: 849 at Kingston, 1929-30

For West Indies in England: 687-8 dec. at The Oval, 1976
    in West Indies: 681-8 dec. at Port-of-Spain, 1953-54

LOWEST INNINGS TOTALS

For England in England: 71 at Manchester, 1976
    in West Indies: 103 at Kingston, 1934-35

For West Indies in England: 86 at The Oval, 1957
    in West Indies: 102 at Barbados, 1934-35

INDIVIDUAL HUNDREDS IN THE MATCHES 1928–1980-81

For England (77)

105	L. E. G. Ames, Port-of-Spain	1929-30
149	L. E. G. Ames, Kingston .	1929-30
126	L. E. G. Ames, Kingston .	1934-35
174	D. L. Amiss, Port-of-Spain	1973-74
262*	D. L. Amiss, Kingston	1973-74
118	D. L. Amiss, Georgetown.	1973-74
203	D. L. Amiss, The Oval	1976
107†	A. H. Bakewell, The Oval	1933
128†	K. F. Barrington, Bridgetown	1959-60
121	K. F. Barrington, Port-of-Spain	1959-60
143	K. F. Barrington, Port-of-Spain	1967-68
116	G. Boycott, Georgetown ..	1967-68
128	G. Boycott, Manchester ...	1969
106	G. Boycott, Lord's	1969
112	G. Boycott, Port-of-Spain .	1973-74
104*	G. Boycott, St John's.......	1980-81
120†	D. C. S. Compton, Lord's	1939
133	D. C. S. Compton, Port-of-Spain	1953-54
154†	M. C. Cowdrey, Birmingham	1957
152	M. C. Cowdrey, Lord's ...	1957
114	M. C. Cowdrey, Kingston .	1959-60
119	M. C. Cowdrey, Port-of-Spain	1959-60
101	M. C. Cowdrey, Kingston .	1967-68
148	M. C. Cowdrey, Port-of-Spain	1967-68
136*†	E. R. Dexter, Bridgetown.	1959-60
110	E. R. Dexter, Georgetown	1959-60
146	J. H. Edrich, Bridgetown..	1967-68
104	T. G. Evans, Manchester..	1950
129*	K. W. R. Fletcher, Bridgetown	1973-74
123	G. A. Gooch, Lord's	1980
116	G. A. Gooch, Bridgetown	1980-81
153	G. A. Gooch, Kingston	1980-81
154*	D. I. Gower, Kingston	1980-81
258	T. W. Graveney, Nottingham	1957
164	T. W. Graveney, The Oval	1957
109	T. W. Graveney, Nottingham	1966
165	T. W. Graveney, The Oval	1966
118	T. W. Graveney, Port-of-Spain	1967-68
148	A. W. Greig, Bridgetown .	1973-74
121	A. W. Greig, Georgetown	1973-74
116	A. W. Greig, Leeds..........	1976
140†	S. C. Griffith, Port-of-Spain	1947-48
138	W. R. Hammond, The Oval	1939
107†	J. H. Hampshire, Lord's ..	1969
106*†	F. C. Hayes, The Oval.....	1973
205*	E. H. Hendren, Port-of-Spain	1929-30
123	E. H. Hendren, Georgetown	1929-30

159	J. B. Hobbs, The Oval	1928	107	P. E. Richardson, The Oval	1957
196†	L. Hutton, Lord's............	1939	133	J. D. Robertson, Port-of-Spain	1947-48
165*	L. Hutton, The Oval........	1939	152†	A. Sandham, Bridgetown..	1929-30
202*	L. Hutton, The Oval........	1950	325	A. Sandham, Kingston	1929-30
169	L. Hutton, Georgetown ..	1953-54	108	M. J. K. Smith, Port-of-Spain	1959-60
205	L. Hutton, Kingston	1953-54	106†	D. S. Steele, Nottingham..	1976
113	R. Illingworth, Lord's ...	1969	100†	R. Subba Row, Georgetown	1959-60
127	D. R. Jardine, Manchester	1933	122†	E. Tyldesley, Lord's	1928
116	A. P. E. Knott, Leeds......	1976	114†	C. Washbrook, Lord's......	1950
135	P. B. H. May, Port-of-Spain	1953-54	102	C. Washbrook, Nottingham	1950
285*	P. B. H. May, Birmingham	1957	116†	W. Watson, Kingston	1953-54
104	P. B. H. May, Nottingham	1957	100*	P. Willey, The Oval........	1980
126*	C. Milburn, Lord's	1966	102*	P. Willey, St John's	1980-81
112†	J. T. Murray, The Oval....	1966			
101*†	J. M. Parks, Port-of-Spain	1959-60			
107	W. Place, Kingston..........	1947-48			
126	P. E. Richardson, Nottingham	1957			

For West Indies (80)

105	I. Barrow, Manchester	1933	113*	C. H. Lloyd, Bridgetown..	1967-68
133	B. F. Butcher, Lord's......	1963	132	C. H. Lloyd, The Oval.....	1973
209*	B. F. Butcher, Nottingham	1966	101	C. H. Lloyd, Manchester ..	1980
107	G. M. Carew, Port-of-Spain	1947-48	100	C. H. Lloyd, Bridgetown ..	1980-81
103	C. A. Davis, Lord's........	1969	137	S. M. Nurse, Leeds	1966
150	R. C. Fredericks, Birmingham	1973	136	S. M. Nurse, Port-of-Spain	1967-68
138	R. C. Fredericks, Lord's...	1976	106	A. F. Rae, Lord's	1950
109	R. C. Fredericks, Leeds ...	1976	109	A. F. Rae, The Oval	1950
112†	A. G. Ganteaume, Port-of-Spain	1947-48	232†	I. V. A. Richards, Nottingham	1976
134	}C. G. Greenidge, Manchester	1976	135	I. V. A. Richards, Manchester	1976
101	}		291	I. V. A. Richards, The Oval	1976
115	C. G. Greenidge, Leeds ...	1976	145	I. V. A. Richards, Lord's .	1980
184	D. L. Haynes, Lord's.......	1980	182*	I. V. A. Richards, Bridgetown	1980-81
176†	G. A. Headley, Bridgetown	1929-30	114	I. V. A. Richards, St John's	1980-81
114	}G. A. Headley, Georgetown	1929-30	122	C. A. Roach, Bridgetown .	1929-30
112	}		209	C. A. Roach, Georgetown	1929-30
223	G. A. Headley, Kingston..	1929-30	120	L. G. Rowe, Kingston......	1973-74
169*	G. A. Headley, Manchester	1933	302	L. G. Rowe, Bridgetown ...	1973-74
270*	G. A. Headley, Kingston..	1934-35	123	L. G. Rowe, Port-of-Spain	1973-74
106	}G. A. Headley, Lord's	1939	161†	O. G. Smith, Birmingham.	1957
107	}		168	O. G. Smith, Nottingham .	1957
105*	D. A. J. Holford, Lord's ..	1966	226	G. S. Sobers, Bridgetown .	1959-60
166	J. K. Holt, Bridgetown.....	1953-54	147	G. S. Sobers, Kingston.....	1959-60
182	C. C. Hunte, Manchester..	1963	145	G. S. Sobers, Georgetown	1959-60
108*	C. C. Hunte, The Oval	1963	102	G. S. Sobers, Leeds.........	1963
135	C. C. Hunte, Manchester..	1966	161	G. S. Sobers, Manchester .	1966
121	B. D. Julien, Lord's.........	1973	163*	G. S. Sobers, Lord's	1966
158	A. I. Kallicharran, Port-of-Spain	1973-74	174	G. S. Sobers, Leeds	1966
119	A. I. Kallicharran, Bridgetown	1973-74	113*	G. S. Sobers, Kingston....	1967-68
110	R. B. Kanhai, Port-of-Spain	1959-60	152	G. S. Sobers, Georgetown	1967-68
104	R. B. Kanhai, The Oval ...	1966	150*	G. S. Sobers, Lord's	1973
153	R. B. Kanhai, Port-of-Spain	1967-68	168*	C. L. Walcott, Lord's.......	1950
150	R. B. Kanhai, Georgetown	1967-68	220	C. L. Walcott, Bridgetown	1953-54
157	R. B. Kanhai, Lord's	1973	124	C. L. Walcott, Port-of-Spain	1953-54
118†	C. H. Lloyd, Port-of-Spain	1967-68	116	C. L. Walcott, Kingston ...	1953-54

141	E. D. Weekes, Kingston... 1947-48	138	F. M. M. Worrell, The Oval 1950
129	E. D. Weekes, Nottingham 1950	167	F. M. M. Worrell, Port-of-
206	E. D. Weekes, Port-of-		Spain 1953-54
	Spain 1953-54	191*	F. M. M. Worrell, Notting-
137	K. H. Weekes, The Oval.. 1939		ham 1957
131*	F. M. M. Worrell, George-	197*	F. M. M. Worrell, Bridge-
	town 1947-48		town 1959-60
261	F. M. M. Worrell, Notting-		
	ham 1950		

† *Signifies hundred on first appearance in England–West Indies Tests. S. C. Griffith pro-*
vides the only instance for England of a player hitting his maiden century in first-class cricket
in his first Test.

RECORD PARTNERSHIPS FOR EACH WICKET

For England

212 for 1st	C. Washbrook and R. T. Simpson at Nottingham	1950
266 for 2nd	P. E. Richardson and T. W. Graveney at Nottingham	1957
264 for 3rd	L. Hutton and W. R. Hammond at The Oval	1939
411 for 4th†	P. B. H. May and M. C. Cowdrey at Birmingham	1957
130* for 5th	C. Milburn and T. W. Graveney at Lord's	1966
163 for 6th	A. W. Greig and A. P. E. Knott at Bridgetown	1973-74
197 for 7th†	M. J. K. Smith and J. M. Parks at Port-of-Spain	1959-60
217 for 8th	T. W. Graveney and J. T. Murray at The Oval...................	1966
109 for 9th	G. A. R. Lock and P. I. Pocock at Georgetown	1967-68
128 for 10th	K. Higgs and J. A. Snow at The Oval	1966

For West Indies

206 for 1st	R. C. Fredericks and L. G. Rowe at Kingston	1973-74
249 for 2nd	L. G. Rowe and A. I. Kallicharran at Bridgetown	1973-74
338 for 3rd†	E. D. Weekes and F. M. M. Worrell at Port-of-Spain	1953-54
399 for 4th†	G. S. Sobers and F. M. M. Worrell at Bridgetown	1959-60
265 for 5th†	S. M. Nurse and G. S. Sobers at Leeds	1966
274* for 6th†	G. S. Sobers and D. A. J. Holford at Lord's	1966
155* for 7th‡	G. S. Sobers and B. D. Julien at Lord's	1973
99 for 8th	C. A. McWatt and J. K. Holt at Georgetown	1953-54
63* for 9th	G. S. Sobers and W. W. Hall at Port-of-Spain	1967-68
67* for 10th	M. A. Holding and C. E. H. Croft at St John's	1980-81

† *Denotes record partnership against all countries.*
‡ *231 runs were added for this wicket in two separate partnerships: G. S. Sobers retired ill*
and was replaced by K. D. Boyce when 155 had been added.

TEN WICKETS OR MORE IN A MATCH

For England (10)

11-98 (7-44, 4-54)	T. E. Bailey, Lord's...	1957
10-93 (5-54, 5-39)	A. P. Freeman, Manchester	1928
13-156 (8-86, 5-70)	A. W. Greig, Port-of-Spain	1973-74
11-48 (5-28, 6-20)	G. A. R. Lock, The Oval	1957
11-96 (5-37, 6-59)†	C. S. Marriott, The Oval	1933
10-142 (4-82, 6-60)	J. A. Snow, Georgetown	1967-68
10-195 (5-105, 5-90)†	G. T. S. Stevens, Bridgetown	1929-30
11-152 (6-100, 5-52)	F. S. Trueman, Lord's..	1963
12-119 (5-75, 7-44)	F. S. Trueman, Birmingham......................................	1963
11-149 (4-79, 7-70)	W. Voce, Port-of-Spain...	1929-30

For West Indies (10)

11-147 (5-70, 6-77)†	K. D. Boyce, The Oval	1973
11-229 (5-137, 6-92)	W. Ferguson, Port-of-Spain	1947-48
11-157 (5-59, 6-98)†	L. R. Gibbs, Manchester	1963
10-106 (5-37, 5-69)	L. R. Gibbs, Manchester	1966
14-149 (8-92, 6-57)	M. A. Holding, The Oval	1976
10-96 (5-41, 5-55)†	H. H. H. Johnson, Kingston	1947-48
11-152 (5-66, 6-86)	S. Ramadhin, Lord's	1950
10-123 (5-60, 5-63)	A. M. E. Roberts, Lord's	1976
11-204 (8-104, 3-100)†	A. L. Valentine, Manchester	1950
10-160 (4-121, 6-39)	A. L. Valentine, The Oval	1950

† *Signifies ten wickets or more on first appearance in England–West Indies Tests.*

Note: F. S. Trueman took ten wickets or more in successive matches.

ENGLAND v NEW ZEALAND

	Captains					
Season	England	New Zealand	T	E	NZ	D
1929-30	A. H. H. Gilligan	T. C. Lowry	4	1	0	3
1931	D. R. Jardine	T. C. Lowry	3	1	0	2
1932-33	D. R. Jardine[1]	M. L. Page	2	0	0	2
1937	R. W. V. Robins	M. L. Page	3	1	0	2
1946-47	W. R. Hammond	W. A. Hadlee	1	0	0	1
1949	F. G. Mann[2]	W. A. Hadlee	4	0	0	4
1950-51	F. R. Brown	W. A. Hadlee	2	1	0	1
1954-55	L. Hutton	G. O. Rabone	2	2	0	0
1958	P. B. H. May	J. R. Reid	5	4	0	1
1958-59	P. B. H. May	J. R. Reid	2	1	0	1
1962-63	E. R. Dexter	J. R. Reid	3	3	0	0
1965	M. J. K. Smith	J. R. Reid	3	3	0	0
1965-66	M. J. K. Smith	B. W. Sinclair[3]	3	0	0	3
1969	R. Illingworth	G. T. Dowling	3	2	0	1
1970-71	R. Illingworth	G. T. Dowling	2	1	0	1
1973	R. Illingworth	B. E. Congdon	3	2	0	1
1974-75	M. H. Denness	B. E. Congdon	2	1	0	1
1977-78	G. Boycott	M. G. Burgess	3	1	1	1
1978	J. M. Brearley	M. G. Burgess	3	3	0	0
1983	R. G. D. Willis	G. P. Howarth	4	3	1	0
	In New Zealand		26	11	1	14
	In England		31	19	1	11
	Totals		57	30	2	25

Notes: The following deputised for the official touring captain or were appointed by the home authority for only a minor proportion of the series:
[1]R. E. S. Wyatt (Second). [2]F. R. Brown (Third and Fourth). [3]M. E. Chapple (First).

HIGHEST INNINGS TOTALS

For England in England: 546-4 dec. at Leeds, 1965
          in New Zealand: 593-6 dec. at Auckland, 1974-75

For New Zealand in England: 551-9 dec. at Lord's, 1973
          in New Zealand: 440 at Wellington, 1929-30

LOWEST INNINGS TOTALS

For England in England: 187 at Manchester, 1937
in New Zealand: 64 at Wellington, 1977-78

For New Zealand in England: 47 at Lord's, 1958
in New Zealand: 26 at Auckland, 1954-55

INDIVIDUAL HUNDREDS IN THE MATCHES 1929-30–1983

For England (62)

122†	G. O. Allen, Lord's.........	1931
137†	L. E. G. Ames, Lord's.....	1931
103	L. E. G. Ames, Christchurch......................	1932-33
138*†	D. L. Amiss, Nottingham .	1973
164*	D. L. Amiss, Christchurch	1974-75
134*	T. E. Bailey, Christchurch	1950-51
126†	K. F. Barrington, Auckland	1962-63
163	K. F. Barrington, Leeds ...	1965
137	K. F. Barrington, Birmingham..........................	1965
103	I. T. Botham, Christchurch	1977-78
103	I. T. Botham, Nottingham	1983
109	E. H. Bowley, Auckland ..	1929-30
115	G. Boycott, Leeds...........	1973
131	G. Boycott, Nottingham ..	1978
114	D. C. S. Compton, Leeds .	1949
116	D. C. S. Compton, Lord's	1949
128*	M. C. Cowdrey, Wellington	1962-63
119	M. C. Cowdrey, Lord's	1965
181	M. H. Denness, Auckland	1974-75
141	E. R. Dexter, Christchurch	1958-59
100	B. L. D'Oliveira, Christchurch......................	1970-71
117	K. S. Duleepsinhji, Auckland..........................	1929-30
109	K. S. Duleepsinhji, The Oval	1931
310*†	J. H. Edrich, Leeds	1965
155	J. H. Edrich, Lord's	1969
115	J. H. Edrich, Nottingham .	1969
100	W. J. Edrich, The Oval....	1949
178	K. W. R. Fletcher, Lord's.	1973
216	K. W. R. Fletcher, Auckland..........................	1974-75
105†	G. Fowler, The Oval	1983

111†	D. I. Gower, The Oval	1978
112*	D. I. Gower, Leeds	1983
108	D. I. Gower, Lord's	1983
139†	A. W. Greig, Nottingham .	1973
100*	W. R. Hammond, The Oval	1931
227	W. R. Hammond, Christchurch......................	1932-33
336*	W. R. Hammond, Auckland..........................	1932-33
140	W. R. Hammond, Lord's..	1937
114†	J. Hardstaff jun., Lord's...	1937
103	J. Hardstaff jun., The Oval	1937
100	L. Hutton, Manchester	1937
101	L. Hutton, Leeds	1949
206	L. Hutton, The Oval........	1949
125†	B. R. Knight, Auckland ...	1962-63
101	A. P. E. Knott, Auckland.	1970-71
102*†	A. J. Lamb, The Oval......	1983
137*	A. J. Lamb, Nottingham ..	1983
196	G. B. Legge, Auckland	1929-30
113*	P. B. H. May, Leeds	1958
101	P. B. H. May, Manchester	1958
124*	P. B. H. May, Auckland ..	1958-59
104*†	C. A. Milton, Leeds	1958
131*†	P. H. Parfitt, Auckland ...	1962-63
158	C. T. Radley, Auckland ...	1977-78
100†	P. E. Richardson, Birmingham..........................	1958
121†	J. D. Robertson, Lord's ...	1949
111	P. J. Sharpe, Nottingham..	1969
103†	R. T. Simpson, Manchester	1949
117†	H. Sutcliffe, The Oval......	1931
109*	H. Sutcliffe, Manchester...	1931
109†	C. J. Tavaré, The Oval	1983
103*	C. Washbrook, Leeds	1949

For New Zealand (21)

104	M. G. Burgess, Auckland	1970-71
105	M. G. Burgess, Lord's.....	1973
104	B. E. Congdon, Christchurch......................	1965-66
176	B. E. Congdon, Nottingham	1973
175	B. E. Congdon, Lord's	1973
136	C. S. Dempster, Wellington	1929-30
120	C. S. Dempster, Lord's....	1931
206	M. P. Donnelly, Lord's....	1949
116	W. A. Hadlee, Christchurch......................	1946-47

122	G. P. Howarth, Auckland	1977-78
102	G. P. Howarth, Auckland	1977-78
123	G. P. Howarth, Lord's.....	1978
117†	J. E. Mills, Wellington ...	1929-30
104	M. L. Page, Lord's..........	1931
121	J. M. Parker, Auckland ...	1974-75
116	V. Pollard, Nottingham ...	1973
105*	V. Pollard, Lord's	1973
100	J. R. Reid, Christchurch ..	1962-63
114	B. W. Sinclair, Auckland..	1965-66
101	B. Sutcliffe, Manchester...	1949
116	B. Sutcliffe, Christchurch.	1950-51

† *Signifies hundred on first appearance in England–New Zealand Tests.*

RECORD PARTNERSHIPS FOR EACH WICKET

For England

223 for 1st	G. Fowler and C. J. Tavaré at The Oval	1983
369 for 2nd	J. H. Edrich and K. F. Barrington at Leeds	1965
245 for 3rd	W. R. Hammond and J. Hardstaff jun. at Lord's	1937
266 for 4th	M. H. Denness and K. W. R. Fletcher at Auckland	1974-75
242 for 5th	W. R. Hammond and L. E. G. Ames at Christchurch	1932-33
240 for 6th†	P. H. Parfitt and B. R. Knight at Auckland	1962-63
149 for 7th	A. P. E. Knott and P. Lever at Auckland	1970-71
246 for 8th†	L. E. G. Ames and G. O. Allen at Lord's	1931
163* for 9th†	M. C. Cowdrey and A. C. Smith at Wellington.....................	1962-63
59 for 10th	A. P. E. Knott and N. Gifford at Nottingham	1973

For New Zealand

276 for 1st	C. S. Dempster and J. E. Mills at Wellington	1929-30
131 for 2nd	B. Sutcliffe and J. R. Reid at Christchurch	1950-51
190 for 3rd	B. E. Congdon and B. F. Hastings at Lord's	1973
142 for 4th	M. L. Page and R. C. Blunt at Lord's.................................	1931
177 for 5th	B. E. Congdon and V. Pollard at Nottingham	1973
117 for 6th	M. G. Burgess and V. Pollard at Lord's	1973
104 for 7th	B. Sutcliffe and V. Pollard at Birmingham	1965
104 for 8th	A. W. Roberts and D. A. R. Moloney at Lord's	1937
64 for 9th	J. Cowie and T. B. Burtt at Christchurch............................	1946-47
57 for 10th	F. L. H. Mooney and J. Cowie at Leeds..............................	1949

† *Denotes record partnership against all countries.*

TEN WICKETS OR MORE IN A MATCH

For England (7)

11-140 (6-101, 5-39)	I. T. Botham, Lord's	1978
10-149 (5-98, 5-51)	A. W. Greig, Auckland..	1974-75
11-65 (4-14, 7-51)	G. A. R. Lock, Leeds...	1958
11-84 (5-31, 6-53)	G. A. R. Lock, Christchurch....................................	1958-59
11-70 (4-38, 7-32)†	D. L. Underwood, Lord's..	1969
12-101 (6-41, 6-60)	D. L. Underwood, The Oval.....................................	1969
12-97 (6-12, 6-85)	D. L. Underwood, Christchurch................................	1970-71

For New Zealand (3)

10-144 (7-74, 3-70)	B. L. Cairns, Leeds	1983
10-140 (4-73, 6-67)	J. Cowie, Manchester...	1937
10-100 (4-74, 6-26)	R. J. Hadlee, Wellington...	1977-78

† *Signifies ten wickets or more on first appearance in England–New Zealand Tests.*

Note: D. L. Underwood took twelve wickets in successive matches against New Zealand in 1969 and 1970-71.

HAT-TRICK AND FOUR WICKETS IN FIVE BALLS

M. J. C. Allom, in his first Test match, v New Zealand at Christchurch in 1929-30, dismissed C. S. Dempster, T. C. Lowry, K. C. James, and F. T. Badcock to take four wickets in five balls (w-www).

ENGLAND v INDIA

Season	England	*Captains* India	T	E	I	D
1932	D. R. Jardine	C. K. Nayudu	1	1	0	0
1933-34	D. R. Jardine	C. K. Nayudu	3	2	0	1
1936	G. O. Allen	Maharaj of Vizianagram	3	2	0	1
1946	W. R. Hammond	Nawab of Pataudi sen.	3	1	0	2
1951-52	N. D. Howard[1]	V. S. Hazare	5	1	1	3
1952	L. Hutton	V. S. Hazare	4	3	0	1
1959	P. B. H. May[2]	D. K. Gaekwad[3]	5	5	0	0
1961-62	E. R. Dexter	N. J. Contractor	5	0	2	3
1963-64	M. J. K. Smith	Nawab of Pataudi jun.	5	0	0	5
1967	D. B. Close	Nawab of Pataudi jun.	3	3	0	0
1971	R. Illingworth	A. L. Wadekar	3	0	1	2
1972-73	A. R. Lewis	A. L. Wadekar	5	1	2	2
1974	M. H. Denness	A. L. Wadekar	3	3	0	0
1976-77	A. W. Greig	B. S. Bedi	5	3	1	1
1979	J. M. Brearley	S. Venkataraghavan	4	1	0	3
1979-80	J. M. Brearley	G. R. Viswanath	1	1	0	0
1981-82	K. W. R. Fletcher	S. M. Gavaskar	6	0	1	5
1982	R. G. D. Willis	S. M. Gavaskar	3	1	0	2
	In England......................		32	20	1	11
	In India..........................		35	8	7	20
	Totals.............................		67	28	8	31

Notes: The 1932 Indian touring team was captained by the Maharaj of Porbandar but he did not play in the Test match.

The following deputised for the official touring captain or were appointed by the home authority for only a minor proportion of the series:

[1]D. B. Carr (Fifth). [2]M. C. Cowdrey (Fourth and Fifth). [3]P. Roy (Second).

HIGHEST INNINGS TOTALS

For England in England: 633-5 dec. at Birmingham, 1979
    in India: 559-8 dec. at Kanpur, 1963-64

For India in England: 510 at Leeds, 1967
    in India: 487 at Delhi, 1981-82

LOWEST INNINGS TOTALS

For England in England: 101 at The Oval, 1971
    in India: 102 at Bombay, 1981-82

For India in England: 42 at Lord's, 1974
    in India: 83 at Madras, 1976-77

INDIVIDUAL HUNDREDS IN THE MATCHES 1932–1982

For England (55)

188	D. L. Amiss, Lord's	1974
179	D. L. Amiss, Delhi..........	1976-77
151*	K. F. Barrington, Bombay	1961-62
172	K. F. Barrington, Kanpur .	1961-62
113*	K. F. Barrington, Delhi....	1961-62
137	I. T. Botham, Leeds	1979
114	I. T. Botham, Bombay	1979-80
142	I. T. Botham, Kanpur	1981-82
128	I. T. Botham, Manchester .	1982
208	I. T. Botham, The Oval ...	1982
246*†	G. Boycott, Leeds	1967
155	G. Boycott, Birmingham ..	1979
125	G. Boycott, The Oval	1979
105	G. Boycott, Delhi	1981-82
160	M. C. Cowdrey, Leeds	1959
107	M. C. Cowdrey, Calcutta..	1963-64
151	M. C. Cowdrey, Delhi	1963-64
118	M. H. Denness, Lord's.....	1974
100	M. H. Denness, Birmingham..............	1974
126*	E. R. Dexter, Kanpur	1961-62
109†	B. L. D'Oliveira, Leeds....	1967
100*	J. H. Edrich, Manchester..	1974
104	T. G. Evans, Lord's	1952
113	K. W. R. Fletcher, Bombay	1972-73
123*	K. W. R. Fletcher, Manchester.................	1974
129	G. A. Gooch, Madras	1981-82
200*†	D. I. Gower, Birmingham.	1979
175†	T. W. Graveney, Bombay.	1951-52

151	T. W. Graveney, Lord's ...	1967
148	A. W. Greig, Bombay......	1972-73
106	A. W. Greig, Lord's	1974
103	A. W. Greig, Calcutta......	1976-77
167	W. R. Hammond, Manchester	1936
217	W. R. Hammond, The Oval	1936
205*	J. Hardstaff jun., Lord's ...	1946
150	L. Hutton, Lord's............	1952
104	L. Hutton, Manchester	1952
107	R. Illingworth, Manchester	1971
127	B. R. Knight, Kanpur	1963-64
107	A. J. Lamb, The Oval......	1982
125	A. R. Lewis, Kanpur	1972-73
214*	D. Lloyd, Birmingham	1974
101	B. W. Luckhurst, Manchester	1971
106	P. B. H. May, Nottingham	1959
121	P. H. Parfitt, Kanpur	1963-64
131	G. Pullar, Manchester......	1959
119	G. Pullar, Kanpur	1961-62
126	D. W. Randall, Lord's	1982
119	D. S. Sheppard, The Oval	1952
100†	M. J. K. Smith, Manchester	1959
149*	C. J. Tavaré, Delhi..........	1981-82
136†	B. H. Valentine, Bombay .	1933-34
102	C. F. Walters, Madras......	1933-34
137*†	A. J. Watkins, Delhi........	1951-52
128	T. S. Worthington, The Oval	1936

For India (41)

118†	L. Amarnath, Bombay	1933-34
112†	A. A. Baig, Manchester ...	1959
121	F. M. Engineer, Bombay..	1972-73
101	S. M. Gavaskar, Manchester	1974
108	S. M. Gavaskar, Bombay..	1976-77
221	S. M. Gavaskar, The Oval	1979
172	S. M. Gavaskar, Bangalore	1981-82
105†	Hanumant Singh, Delhi	1963-64
164*	V. S. Hazare, Delhi.........	1951-52
155	V. S. Hazare, Bombay	1951-52
127	M. L. Jaisimha, Delhi	1961-62
129	M. L. Jaisimha, Calcutta..	1963-64
116	Kapil Dev, Kanpur	1981-82
192	B. K. Kunderan, Madras ..	1963-64
100	B. K. Kunderan, Delhi.....	1963-64
133	V. L. Manjrekar, Leeds ...	1952
189*	V. L. Manjrekar, Delhi.....	1961-62
108	V. L. Manjrekar, Madras ..	1963-64
184	V. Mankad, Lord's	1952
114	V. M. Merchant, Manchester	1936
128	V. M. Merchant, The Oval	1946

154	V. M. Merchant, Delhi	1951-52
112	Mushtaq Ali, Manchester..	1936
122*	R. G. Nadkarni, Kanpur ..	1963-64
103	Nawab of Pataudi jun., Madras......................	1961-62
203*	Nawab of Pataudi jun., Delhi........................	1963-64
148	Nawab of Pataudi jun., Leeds........................	1967
129*	S. M. Patil, Manchester....	1982
115	D. G. Phadkar, Calcutta...	1951-52
140	P. Roy, Bombay	1951-52
111	P. Roy, Madras	1951-52
130*	P. R. Umrigar, Madras	1951-52
118	P. R. Umrigar, Manchester	1959
147*	P. R. Umrigar, Kanpur	1961-62
103	D. B. Vengsarkar, Lord's ..	1979
157	D. B. Vengsarkar, Lord's .	1982
113	G. R. Viswanath, Bombay	1972-73
113	G. R. Viswanath, Lord's ..	1979
107	G. R. Viswanath, Delhi....	1981-82
222	G. R. Viswanath, Madras .	1981-82
140	Yashpal Sharma, Madras..	1981-82

† *Signifies hundred on first appearance in England–India Tests.*

RECORD PARTNERSHIPS FOR EACH WICKET

For England

159 for 1st	P. E. Richardson and G. Pullar at Bombay	1961-62
221 for 2nd	D. L. Amiss and J. H. Edrich at Lord's	1974
169 for 3rd	R. Subba Row and M. J. K. Smith at The Oval	1959
266 for 4th	W. R. Hammond and T. S. Worthington at The Oval	1936
254 for 5th†	K. W. R. Fletcher and A. W. Greig at Bombay	1972-73
171 for 6th	I. T. Botham and R. W. Taylor at Bombay	1979-80
125 for 7th	D. W. Randall and P. H. Edmonds at Lord's	1982
168 for 8th	R. Illingworth and P. Lever at Manchester	1971
83 for 9th	K. W. R. Fletcher and N. Gifford at Madras	1972-73
70 for 10th	P. J. W. Allott and R. G. D. Willis at Lord's	1982

For India

213 for 1st	S. M. Gavaskar and C. P. S. Chauhan at The Oval	1979
192 for 2nd	F. M. Engineer and A. L. Wadekar at Bombay	1972-73
316 for 3rd†‡	G. R. Viswanath and Yashpal Sharma at Madras	1981-82
222 for 4th†	V. S. Hazare and V. L. Manjrekar at Leeds	1952
190* for 5th	Nawab of Pataudi jun. and C. G. Borde at Delhi	1963-64
130 for 6th	S. M. H. Kirmani and Kapil Dev at The Oval	1982
169 for 7th	Kapil Dev and Yashpal Sharma at Kanpur	1981-82
128 for 8th	R. J. Shastri and S. M. H. Kirmani at Delhi	1981-82
104 for 9th	R. J. Shastri and Madan Lal at Delhi	1981-82
51 for 10th	R. G. Nadkarni and B. S. Chandrasekhar at Calcutta	1963-64

† *Denotes record partnership against all countries.*

‡ *415 runs were added between the fall of the 2nd and 3rd wickets: D. B. Vengsarkar retired hurt when he and Viswanath had added 99 runs.*

TEN WICKETS OR MORE IN A MATCH

For England (6)

10-78 (5-35, 5-43)†	G. O. Allen, Lord's	1936
11-145 (7-49, 4-96)†	A. V. Bedser, Lord's	1946
11-93 (4-41, 7-52)	A. V. Bedser, Manchester	1946
13-106 (6-58, 7-48)	I. T. Botham, Bombay	1979-80
10-70 (7-46, 3-24)†	J. K. Lever, Delhi	1976-77
11-153 (7-49, 4-104)	H. Verity, Madras	1933-34

For India (2)

10-177 (6-105, 4-72)	S. A. Durani, Madras	1961-62
12-108 (8-55, 4-53)	V. Mankad, Madras	1951-52

† *Signifies ten wickets or more on first appearance in England–India Tests.*

Note: A. V. Bedser took eleven wickets in a match in the first two Tests of his career.

ENGLAND v PAKISTAN

Season	England	Captains Pakistan	T	E	P	D
1954	L. Hutton[1]	A. H. Kardar	4	1	1	2
1961-62	E. R. Dexter	Imtiaz Ahmed	3	1	0	2
1962	E. R. Dexter[2]	Javed Burki	5	4	0	1
1967	D. B. Close	Hanif Mohammad	3	2	0	1
1968-69	M. C. Cowdrey	Saeed Ahmed	3	0	0	3
1971	R. Illingworth	Intikhab Alam	3	1	0	2
1972-73	A. R. Lewis	Majid J. Khan	3	0	0	3
1974	M. H. Denness	Intikhab Alam	3	0	0	3
1977-78	J. M. Brearley[3]	Wasim Bari	3	0	0	3
1978	J. M. Brearley	Wasim Bari	3	2	0	1
1982	R. G. D. Willis[4]	Imran Khan	3	2	1	0
	In England		24	12	2	10
	In Pakistan		12	1	0	11
	Totals		36	13	2	21

Notes: [1]D. S. Sheppard captained in Second and Third Tests. [2]M. C. Cowdrey captained in Third Test. [3]G. Boycott captained in Third Test. [4]D. I. Gower captained in Second Test.

HIGHEST INNINGS TOTALS

For England in England: 558-6 dec. at Nottingham, 1954
        in Pakistan: 507 at Karachi, 1961-62

For Pakistan in England: 608-7 dec. at Birmingham, 1971
        in Pakistan: 569-9 dec. at Hyderabad, 1972-73

LOWEST INNINGS TOTALS

For England in England: 130 at The Oval, 1954
        in Pakistan: 191 at Hyderabad, 1977-78

For Pakistan in England: 87 at Lord's, 1954
        in Pakistan: 199 at Karachi, 1972-73

INDIVIDUAL HUNDREDS IN THE MATCHES 1954–1982

For England (34)

112	D. L. Amiss, Lahore	1972-73
158	D. L. Amiss, Hyderabad ..	1972-73
183	D. L. Amiss, The Oval	1974
139†	K. F. Barrington, Lahore..	1961-62
148	K. F. Barrington, Lord's...	1967
109*	K. F. Barrington, Nottingham......................	1967
142	K. F. Barrington, The Oval	1967
100†	I. T. Botham, Birmingham	1978

108	I. T. Botham, Lord's	1978
121*	G. Boycott, Lord's	1971
112	G. Boycott, Leeds	1971
100*	G. Boycott, Hyderabad	1977-78
278	D. C. S. Compton, Nottingham......................	1954
159†	M. C. Cowdrey, Birmingham......................	1962
182	M. C. Cowdrey, The Oval	1962

100	M. C. Cowdrey, Lahore ...	1968-69
205	E. R. Dexter, Karachi......	1961-62
172	E. R. Dexter, The Oval ...	1962
114*	B. L. D'Oliveira, Dacca ...	1968-69
122	K. W. R. Fletcher, The Oval	1974
153	T. W. Graveney, Lord's ...	1962
114	T. W. Graveney, Nottingham	1962
105	T. W. Graveney, Karachi .	1968-69
116	A. P. E. Knott, Birmingham	1971

108*†	B. W. Luckhurst, Birmingham	1971
139	C. Milburn, Karachi	1968-69
111	P. H. Parfitt, Karachi	1961-62
101*	P. H. Parfitt, Birmingham.	1962
119	P. H. Parfitt, Leeds	1962
101*	P. H. Parfitt, Nottingham .	1962
165	G. Pullar, Dacca	1961-62
106†	C. T. Radley, Birmingham	1978
105	D. W. Randall, Birmingham	1982
101	R. T. Simpson, Nottingham	1954

For Pakistan (22)

109	Alim-ud-Din, Karachi	1961-62
146	Asif Iqbal, The Oval........	1967
104*	Asif Iqbal, Birmingham	1971
102	Asif Iqbal, Lahore...........	1972-73
138†	Javed Burki, Lahore	1961-62
140	Javed Burki, Dacca	1961-62
101	Javed Burki, Lord's	1962
111 104	} Hanif Mohammad, Dacca .	1961-62
187*	Hanif Mohammad, Lord's.	1967
122†	Haroon Rashid, Lahore	1977-78
108	Haroon Rashid, Hyderabad	1977-78

138	Intikhab Alam, Hyderabad	1972-73
200	Mohsin Khan, Lord's	1982
114†	Mudassar Nazar, Lahore...	1977-78
100*	Mushtaq Mohammad, Nottingham	1962
100	Mushtaq Mohammad, Birmingham	1971
157	Mushtaq Mohammad, Hyderabad	1972-73
101	Nasim-ul-Ghani, Lord's	1962
119	Sadiq Mohammad, Lahore	1972-73
274†	Zaheer Abbas, Birmingham	1971
240	Zaheer Abbas, The Oval ..	1974

† *Signifies hundred on first appearance in England–Pakistan Tests.*

Note: Three batsmen – Majid J. Khan, Mushtaq Mohammad and D. L. Amiss – were dismissed for 99 at Karachi, 1972-73: the only instance in Test matches.

RECORD PARTNERSHIPS FOR EACH WICKET

For England

198 for 1st	G. Pullar and R. W. Barber at Dacca	1961-62
248 for 2nd	M. C. Cowdrey and E. R. Dexter at The Oval	1962
201 for 3rd	K. F. Barrington and T. W. Graveney at Lord's	1967
188 for 4th	E. R. Dexter and P. H. Parfitt at Karachi	1961-62
192 for 5th	D. C. S. Compton and T. E. Bailey at Nottingham	1954
153* for 6th	P. H. Parfitt and D. A. Allen at Birmingham	1962
159 for 7th	A. P. E. Knott and P. Lever at Birmingham	1971
99 for 8th	P. H. Parfitt and D. A. Allen at Leeds	1962
76 for 9th	T. W. Graveney and F. S. Trueman at Lord's	1962
79 for 10th	R. W. Taylor and R. G. D. Willis at Birmingham	1982

For Pakistan

122 for 1st	Hanif Mohammad and Alim-ud-Din at Dacca.....................	1961-62
291 for 2nd†	Zaheer Abbas and Mushtaq Mohammad at Birmingham	1971
180 for 3rd	Mudassar Nazar and Haroon Rashid at Lahore	1977-78
153 for 4th	{ Javed Burki and Mushtaq Mohammad at Lahore	1961-62
	Mohsin Khan and Zaheer Abbas at Lord's	1982
197 for 5th	Javed Burki and Nasim-ul-Ghani at Lord's	1962
145 for 6th	Mushtaq Mohammad and Intikhab Alam at Hyderabad	1972-73
51 for 7th	Saeed Ahmed and Nasim-ul-Ghani at Nottingham	1962
130 for 8th†	Hanif Mohammad and Asif Iqbal at Lord's.........................	1967
190 for 9th†	Asif Iqbal and Intikhab Alam at The Oval	1967
62 for 10th	Sarfraz Nawaz and Asif Masood at Leeds	1974

† *Denotes record partnership against all countries.*

TEN WICKETS OR MORE IN A MATCH

For England (1)

13-71 (5-20, 8-51)   D. L. Underwood, Lord's.. 1974

For Pakistan (1)

12-99 (6-53, 6-46)   Fazal Mahmood, The Oval.. 1954

FOUR WICKETS IN FIVE BALLS

C. M. Old, v Pakistan at Birmingham in 1978, dismissed Wasim Raja, Wasim Bari, Iqbal Qasim and Sikander Bakht to take four wickets in five balls (ww-ww).

ENGLAND v SRI LANKA

Captains

Season	England	Sri Lanka	T	E	SL	D
1981-82	K. W. R. Fletcher	B. Warnapura	1	1	0	0

The only match played, at Colombo, produced no individual centuries or century partnerships. The best performances were as follows:

Highest score for England: 89 by D. I. Gower.
Sri Lanka: 77 by R. L. Dias.

Best bowling in an innings for England: 6-33 by J. E. Emburey.
Sri Lanka: 4-70 by A. L. F. de Mel.

Best match bowling for England: 8-95 by D. L. Underwood.
Sri Lanka: 5-103 by A. L. F. de Mel.

Best wicket partnership for England: 83 for the 3rd by C. J. Tavaré and D. I. Gower.
Sri Lanka: 99 for the 5th by R. S. Madugalle and A. Ranatunga.

AUSTRALIA v SOUTH AFRICA

Captains

Season	Australia	South Africa	T	A	SA	D
1902-03S	J. Darling	H. M. Taberer[1]	3	2	0	1
1910-11A	C. Hill	P. W. Sherwell	5	4	1	0
1912E	S. E. Gregory	F. Mitchell[2]	3	2	0	1
1921-22S	H. L. Collins	H. W. Taylor	3	1	0	2
1931-32A	W. M. Woodfull	H. B. Cameron	5	5	0	0
1935-36S	V. Y. Richardson	H. F. Wade	5	4	0	1
1949-50S	A. L. Hassett	A. D. Nourse	5	4	0	1
1952-53A	A. L. Hassett	J. E. Cheetham	5	2	2	1
1957-58S	I. D. Craig	C. B. van Ryneveld[3]	5	3	0	2
1963-64A	R. B. Simpson[4]	T. L. Goddard	5	1	1	3
1966-67S	R. B. Simpson	P. L. van der Merwe	5	1	3	1
1969-70S	W. M. Lawry	A. Bacher	4	0	4	0
	In South Africa.....................		30	15	7	8
	In Australia...........................		20	12	4	4
	In England............................		3	2	0	1
	Totals...................................		53	29	11	13

S Played in South Africa.   A Played in Australia.   E Played in England.

Notes: The following deputised for the official touring captain or were appointed by the home authority for only a minor proportion of the series:
[1]J. H. Anderson (Second), E. A. Halliwell (Third). [2]L. J. Tancred (Third). [3]D. J. McGlew (First). [4]R. Benaud (First).

HIGHEST INNINGS TOTALS

For Australia in Australia: 578 at Melbourne, 1910-11
 in South Africa: 549-7 dec. at Port Elizabeth, 1949-50

For South Africa in Australia: 595 at Adelaide, 1963-64
 in South Africa: 622-9 dec. at Durban, 1969-70

LOWEST INNINGS TOTALS

For Australia in Australia: 153 at Melbourne, 1931-32
 in South Africa: 75 at Durban, 1949-50

For South Africa in Australia: 36† at Melbourne, 1931-32
 in South Africa: 85 at Johannesburg, 1902-03

 † *Scored 45 in the second innings giving the smallest aggregate of 81 (12 extras) in Test cricket.*

INDIVIDUAL HUNDREDS IN THE MATCHES 1902-03—1969-70

For Australia (55)

159*	W. W. Armstrong, Johannesburg	1902-03	151*	R. N. Harvey, Durban	1949-50
132	W. W. Armstrong, Melbourne	1910-11	116	R. N. Harvey, Port Elizabeth	1949-50
132†	W. Bardsley, Sydney	1910-11	100	R. N. Harvey, Johannesburg	1949-50
121	W. Bardsley, Manchester	1912	109	R. N. Harvey, Brisbane	1952-53
164	W. Bardsley, Lord's	1912	190	R. N. Harvey, Sydney	1952-53
122	R. Benaud, Johannesburg	1957-58	116	R. N. Harvey, Adelaide	1952-53
100	R. Benaud, Johannesburg	1957-58	205	R. N. Harvey, Melbourne	1952-53
169†	B. C. Booth, Brisbane	1963-64	112†	A. L. Hassett, Johannesburg	1949-50
102*	B. C. Booth, Sydney	1963-64	167	A. L. Hassett, Port Elizabeth	1949-50
226†	D. G. Bradman, Brisbane	1931-32			
112	D. G. Bradman, Sydney	1931-32	163	A. L. Hassett, Adelaide	1952-53
167	D. G. Bradman, Melbourne	1931-32	142†	C. Hill, Johannesburg	1902-03
299*	D. G. Bradman, Adelaide	1931-32	191	C. Hill, Sydney	1910-11
121	W. A. Brown, Cape Town	1935-36	100	C. Hill, Melbourne	1910-11
189	J. W. Burke, Cape Town	1957-58	114	C. Kelleway, Manchester	1912
109†	A. G. Chipperfield, Durban	1935-36	102	C. Kelleway, Lord's	1912
203	H. L. Collins, Johannesburg	1921-22	157	W. M. Lawry, Melbourne	1963-64
112	J. H. Fingleton, Cape Town	1935-36	101†	S. J. E. Loxton, Johannesburg	1949-50
108	J. H. Fingleton, Johannesburg	1935-36			
			137	C. G. Macartney, Sydney	1910-11
118	J. H. Fingleton, Durban	1935-36	116	C. G. Macartney, Durban	1921-22
119	J. M. Gregory, Johannesburg	1921-22	149	S. J. McCabe, Durban	1935-36
178	R. N. Harvey, Cape Town	1949-50	189*	S. J. McCabe, Johannesburg	1935-36

154	C. C. McDonald, Adelaide	1952-53
118 101* }	J. Moroney, Johannesburg	1949-50
111	A. R. Morris, Johannesburg	1949-50
157	A. R. Morris, Port Elizabeth	1949-50
127†	K. E. Rigg, Sydney	1931-32
142	J. Ryder, Cape Town	1921-22

153	R. B. Simpson, Cape Town	1966-67
134	K. R. Stackpole, Cape Town	1966-67
159	V. T. Trumper, Melbourne	1910-11
214*	V. T. Trumper, Adelaide..	1910-11
161	W. M. Woodfull, Melbourne	1931-32

For South Africa (36)

114†	E. J. Barlow, Brisbane	1963-64
109	E. J. Barlow, Melbourne ..	1963-64
201	E. J. Barlow, Adelaide	1963-64
127	E. J. Barlow, Cape Town .	1969-70
110	E. J. Barlow, Johannesburg	1969-70
126	K. C. Bland, Sydney	1963-64
162*	W. R. Endean, Melbourne	1952-53
204	G. A. Faulkner, Melbourne	1910-11
115	G. A. Faulkner, Adelaide	1910-11
122*	G. A. Faulkner, Manchester	1912
152	C. N. Frank, Johannesburg	1921-22
102	B. L. Irvine, Port Elizabeth	1969-70
182	D. T. Lindsay, Johannesburg	1966-67
137	D. T. Lindsay, Durban.....	1966-67
131	D. T. Lindsay, Johannesburg	1966-67
108	D. J. McGlew, Johannesburg	1957-58
105	D. J. McGlew, Durban	1957-58
231	A. D. Nourse, Johannesburg	1935-36

114	A. D. Nourse, Cape Town	1949-50
111	A. W. Nourse, Johannesburg	1921-22
122	R. G. Pollock, Sydney	1963-64
175	R. G. Pollock, Adelaide ...	1963-64
209	R. G. Pollock, Cape Town	1966-67
105	R. G. Pollock, Port Elizabeth	1966-67
274	R. G. Pollock, Durban....	1969-70
140	B. A. Richards, Durban	1969-70
126	B. A. Richards, Port Elizabeth	1969-70
143	E. A. B. Rowan, Durban .	1949-50
101	J. H. Sinclair, Johannesburg	1902-03
104	J. H. Sinclair, Cape Town	1902-03
103	S. J. Snooke, Adelaide.....	1910-11
111	K. G. Viljoen, Melbourne	1931-32
115	J. H. B. Waite, Johannesburg	1957-58
134	J. H. B. Waite, Durban....	1957-58
105	J. W. Zulch, Adelaide......	1910-11
150	J. W. Zulch, Sydney	1910-11

† *Signifies hundred on first appearance in Australia–South Africa Tests.*

RECORD PARTNERSHIPS FOR EACH WICKET

For Australia

233 for 1st	J. H. Fingleton and W. A. Brown at Cape Town	1935-36
275 for 2nd	C. C. McDonald and A. L. Hassett at Adelaide	1952-53
242 for 3rd	C. Kelleway and W. Bardsley at Lord's	1912
168 for 4th	R. N. Harvey and K. R. Miller at Sydney	1952-53
143 for 5th	W. W. Armstrong and V. T. Trumper at Melbourne	1910-11
107 for 6th	C. Kelleway and V. S. Ransford at Melbourne	1910-11
160 for 7th	R. Benaud and G. D. McKenzie at Sydney	1963-64
83 for 8th	A. G. Chipperfield and C. V. Grimmett at Durban	1935-36
78 for 9th {	D. G. Bradman and W. J. O'Reilly at Adelaide	1931-32
{	K. D. Mackay and I. Meckiff at Johannesburg	1957-58
82 for 10th	V. S. Ransford and J. W. Whitty at Melbourne	1910-11

For South Africa

176 for 1st	D. J. McGlew and T. L. Goddard at Johannesburg	1957-58
173 for 2nd	L. J. Tancred and C. B. Llewellyn at Johannesburg	1902-03
341 for 3rd†	E. J. Barlow and R. G. Pollock at Adelaide	1963-64

206 for 4th	C. N. Frank and A. W. Nourse at Johannesburg	1921-22
129 for 5th	J. H. B. Waite and W. R. Endean at Johannesburg	1957-58
200 for 6th†	R. G. Pollock and H. R. Lance at Durban	1969-70
221 for 7th	D. T. Lindsay and P. L. van der Merwe at Johannesburg	1966-67
124 for 8th†	A. W. Nourse and E. A. Halliwell at Johannesburg	1902-03
85 for 9th	R. G. Pollock and P. M. Pollock at Cape Town	1966-67
53 for 10th	L. A. Stricker and S. J. Pegler at Adelaide	1910-11

† *Denotes record partnership against all countries.*

TEN WICKETS OR MORE IN A MATCH

For Australia (5)

14-199 (7-116, 7-83)	C. V. Grimmett, Adelaide	1931-32
10-88 (5-32, 5-56)	C. V. Grimmett, Cape Town	1935-36
10-110 (3-70, 7-40)	C. V. Grimmett, Johannesburg	1935-36
13-173 (7-100, 6-73)	C. V. Grimmett, Durban	1935-36
11-24 (5-6, 6-18)	H. Ironmonger, Melbourne	1931-32

For South Africa (2)

| 10-116 (5-43, 5-73) | C. B. Llewellyn, Johannesburg | 1902-03 |
| 13-165 (6-84, 7-81) | H. J. Tayfield, Melbourne | 1952-53 |

Note: C. V. Grimmett took ten wickets or more in three consecutive matches in 1935-36.

AUSTRALIA v WEST INDIES

| | | Captains | | | | | | |
Season	Australia	West Indies	T	A	WI	T	D
1930-31A	W. M. Woodfull	G. C. Grant	5	4	1	0	0
1951-52A	A. L. Hassett[1]	J. D. C. Goddard[2]	5	4	1	0	0
1954-55W	I. W. Johnson	D. S. Atkinson[3]	5	3	0	0	2
1960-61A	R. Benaud	F. M. M. Worrell	5†	2	1	1	1

THE FRANK WORRELL TROPHY

| | | Captains | | | | | | |
Season	Australia	West Indies	T	A	WI	T	D	Held by
1964-65W	R. B. Simpson	G. S. Sobers	5	1	2	0	2	WI
1968-69A	W. M. Lawry	G. S. Sobers	5	3	1	0	1	A
1972-73W	I. M. Chappell	R. B. Kanhai	5	2	0	0	3	A
1975-76A	G. S. Chappell	C. H. Lloyd	6	5	1	0	0	A
1977-78A	R. B. Simpson	A. I. Kallicharran[4]	5	1	3	0	1	WI
1979-80A	G. S. Chappell	C. H. Lloyd[5]	3	0	2	0	1	WI
1981-82A	G. S. Chappell	C. H. Lloyd	3	1	1	0	1	WI
	In Australia		32	19	8	1	4	
	In West Indies		20	7	5	0	8	
	Totals		52	26	13	1	12	

† *The First Test at Brisbane resulted in a tie. This is the only instance of a Test match resulting in a tie.*

A Played in Australia. W Played in West Indies.

Notes: The following deputised for the official touring captain or were appointed by the home authority for only a minor proportion of the series:
[1] A. R. Morris (Third). [2] J. B. Stollmeyer (Fifth). [3] J. B. Stollmeyer (Second and Third). [4] C. H. Lloyd (First and Second). [5] D. L. Murray (First).

HIGHEST INNINGS TOTALS

For Australia in Australia: 619 at Sydney, 1968-69
          in West Indies: 758-8 dec. at Kingston, 1954-55

For West Indies in Australia: 616 at Adelaide, 1968-69
          in West Indies: 573 at Bridgetown, 1964-65

LOWEST INNINGS TOTALS

For Australia in Australia: 82 at Adelaide, 1951-52
          in West Indies: 90 at Port-of-Spain, 1977-78

For West Indies in Australia: 78 at Sydney, 1951-52
          in West Indies: 109 at Georgetown, 1972-73

INDIVIDUAL HUNDREDS IN THE MATCHES 1930-31–1981-82

For Australia (60)

128	R. G. Archer, Kingston....	1954-55
121	R. Benaud, Kingston	1954-55
117	B. C. Booth, Port-of-Spain	1964-65
126	A. R. Border, Adelaide ...	1981-82
223	D. G. Bradman, Brisbane .	1930-31
152	D. G. Bradman, Melbourne	1930-31
106	G. S. Chappell, Bridgetown	1972-73
123 }
109* }	‡G. S. Chappell, Brisbane	1975-76
182*	G. S. Chappell, Sydney	1975-76
124	G. S. Chappell, Brisbane ..	1979-80
117†	I. M. Chappell, Brisbane ..	1968-69
165	I. M. Chappell, Melbourne	1968-69
106*	I. M. Chappell, Bridgetown	1972-73
109	I. M. Chappell, George-town	1972-73
156	I. M. Chappell, Perth.......	1975-76
109†	G. J. Cosier, Melbourne...	1975-76
143	R. M. Cowper, Port-of-Spain	1964-65
102	R. M. Cowper, Bridgetown	1964-65
127*†	J. Dyson, Sydney	1981-82
133	R. N. Harvey, Kingston	1954-55
133	R. N. Harvey, Port-of-Spain	1954-55
204	R. N. Harvey, Kingston ...	1954-55
132	A. L. Hassett, Sydney......	1951-52
102	A. L. Hassett, Melbourne .	1951-52
130*†	K. J. Hughes, Brisbane	1979-80
100*	K. J. Hughes, Melbourne .	1981-82
146†	A. F. Kippax, Adelaide....	1930-31
210	W. M. Lawry, Bridgetown	1964-65
105	W. M. Lawry, Brisbane....	1968-69
205	W. M. Lawry, Melbourne .	1968-69
151	W. M. Lawry, Sydney	1968-69
118	R. R. Lindwall, Bridge-town	1954-55
109*	R. B. McCosker, Mel-bourne	1975-76
110	C. C. McDonald, Port-of-Spain	1954-55
127	C. C. McDonald, Kingston	1954-55
129	K. R. Miller, Sydney	1951-52
147	K. R. Miller, Kingston	1954-55
137	K. R. Miller, Bridgetown..	1954-55
109	K. R. Miller, Kingston	1954-55
111	A. R. Morris, Port-of-Spain	1954-55
181†	N. C. O'Neill, Brisbane....	1960-61
183	W. H. Ponsford, Sydney...	1930-31
109	W. H. Ponsford, Brisbane	1930-31
132	I. R. Redpath, Sydney	1968-69
102	I. R. Redpath, Melbourne	1975-76
103	I. R. Redpath, Adelaide...	1975-76
101	I. R. Redpath, Melbourne	1975-76
124	C. S. Serjeant, George-town	1977-78
201	R. B. Simpson, Bridgetown	1964-65
142	K. R. Stackpole, Kingston	1972-73
122	P. M. Toohey, Kingston ...	1977-78
136	A. Turner, Adelaide	1975-76
118	K. D. Walters, Sydney	1968-69
110	K. D. Walters, Adelaide...	1968-69
242 }
103 }	K. D. Walters, Sydney	1968-69
102*	K. D. Walters, Bridgetown	1972-73
112	K. D. Walters, Port-of-Spain	1972-73
126	G. M. Wood, Georgetown	1977-78

‡ *G. S. Chappell is the only player to score hundreds in both innings of his first Test as captain.*

For West Indies (49)

108	F. C. M. Alexander, Sydney	1960-61	178	C. H. Lloyd, Georgetown.	1972-73
219	D. S. Atkinson, Bridgetown	1954-55	149	C. H. Lloyd, Perth	1975-76
117	B. F. Butcher, Port-of-Spain	1964-65	102	C. H. Lloyd, Melbourne....	1975-76
101	B. F. Butcher, Sydney......	1968-69	121	C. H. Lloyd, Adelaide	1979-80
118	B. F. Butcher, Adelaide ...	1968-69	123*	F. R. Martin, Sydney.......	1930-31
122	C. C. Depeiza, Bridgetown	1954-55	201	S. M. Nurse, Bridgetown ..	1964-65
125†	M. L. C. Foster, Kingston	1972-73	137	S. M. Nurse, Sydney........	1968-69
169	R. C. Fredericks, Perth	1975-76	101	I. V. A. Richards, Adelaide	1975-76
101†	H. A. Gomes, Georgetown	1977-78	140	I. V. A. Richards, Brisbane	1979-80
115	H. A. Gomes, Kingston ...	1977-78	107	L. G. Rowe, Brisbane.......	1975-76
126	H. A. Gomes, Sydney.......	1981-82	104†	O. G. Smith, Kingston	1954-55
124*	H. A. Gomes, Adelaide ...	1981-82	132	G. S. Sobers, Brisbane	1960-61
102*	G. A. Headley, Brisbane..	1930-31	168	G. S. Sobers, Sydney........	1960-61
105	G. A. Headley, Sydney	1930-31	110	G. S. Sobers, Adelaide.....	1968-69
110	C. C. Hunte, Melbourne ..	1960-61	113	G. S. Sobers, Sydney........	1968-69
101	A. I. Kallicharran, Brisbane	1975-76	104	J. B. Stollmeyer, Sydney ...	1951-52
127	A. I. Kallicharran, Port-of-		108	C. L. Walcott, Kingston ...	1954-55
	Spain	1977-78	126	C. L. Walcott, Port-of-	
126	A. I. Kallicharran, King-		110	Spain	1954-55
	ston	1977-78	155		
106	A. I. Kallicharran, Adelaide	1979-80	110	C. L. Walcott, Kingston ...	1954-55
117	} R. B. Kanhai, Adelaide....	1960-61	139	E. D. Weekes, Port-of-	
115				Spain	1954-55
129	R. B. Kanhai, Bridgetown	1964-65	100†	A. B. Williams, George-	
121	R. B. Kanhai, Port-of-Spain	1964-65		town	1977-78
105	R. B. Kanhai, Bridgetown	1972-73	108	F. M. M. Worrell, Mel-	
129†	C. H. Lloyd, Brisbane......	1968-69		bourne	1951-52

† *Signifies hundred on first appearance in Australia–West Indies Tests.*
Note: F. C. M. Alexander hit the only hundred of his career in a Test match.

RECORD PARTNERSHIPS FOR EACH WICKET

For Australia

382 for 1st†	W. M. Lawry and R. B. Simpson at Bridgetown	1964-65
298 for 2nd	W. M. Lawry and I. M. Chappell at Melbourne......................	1968-69
295 for 3rd†	C. C. McDonald and R. N. Harvey at Kingston.....................	1954-55
336 for 4th	W. M. Lawry and K. D. Walters at Sydney..........................	1968-69
220 for 5th	K. R. Miller and R. G. Archer at Kingston...........................	1954-55
206 for 6th	K. R. Miller and R. G. Archer at Bridgetown	1954-55
134 for 7th	A. K. Davidson and R. Benaud at Brisbane	1960-61
137 for 8th	R. Benaud and I. W. Johnson at Kingston	1954-55
97 for 9th	K. D. Mackay and J. W. Martin at Melbourne	1960-61
73 for 10th	J. W. Gleeson and A. N. Connolly at Sydney	1968-69

For West Indies

145 for 1st	C. C. Hunte and B. A. Davis at Bridgetown	1964-65
165 for 2nd	M. C. Carew and R. B. Kanhai at Brisbane	1968-69
242 for 3rd	C. L. Walcott and E. D. Weekes at Port-of-Spain	1954-55
198 for 4th	L. G. Rowe and A. I. Kallicharran at Brisbane	1975-76
210 for 5th	R. B. Kanhai and M. L. C. Foster at Kingston	1972-73
165 for 6th	R. B. Kanhai and D. L. Murray at Bridgetown	1972-73
347 for 7th†‡	D. St E. Atkinson and C. C. Depeiza at Bridgetown	1954-55
82 for 8th	H. A. Gomes and A. M. E. Roberts at Adelaide	1981-82
122 for 9th†	D. A. J. Holford and J. L. Hendriks at Adelaide	1968-69
56 for 10th	J. Garner and C. E. H. Croft at Brisbane	1979-80

† *Denotes record partnership against all countries.*
‡ *The 347 partnership for the 7th wicket is the highest for this wicket in first-class cricket.*

TEN WICKETS OR MORE IN A MATCH

For Australia (7)

11-222 (5-135, 6-87)†	A. K. Davidson, Brisbane	1960-61
11-183 (7-87, 4-96)†	C. V. Grimmett, Adelaide	1930-31
10-115 (6-72, 4-43)	N. J. N. Hawke, Georgetown	1964-65
11-79 (7-23, 4-56)	H. Ironmonger, Melbourne	1930-31
10-127 (7-83, 3-44)	D. K. Lillee, Melbourne	1981-82
10-159 (8-71, 2-88)	G. D. McKenzie, Melbourne	1968-69
10-185 (3-87, 7-98)	B. Yardley, Sydney	1981-82

For West Indies (2)

10-113 (7-55, 3-58)	G. E. Gomez, Sydney	1951-52
11-107 (5-45, 6-62)	M. A. Holding, Melbourne	1981-82

† *Signifies ten wickets or more on first appearance in Australia–West Indies Tests.*

AUSTRALIA v NEW ZEALAND

Season	Australia	*Captains* New Zealand	T	A	NZ	D
1945-46N	W. A. Brown	W. A. Hadlee	1	1	0	0
1973-74A	I. M. Chappell	B. E. Congdon	3	2	0	1
1973-74N	I. M. Chappell	B. E. Congdon	3	1	1	1
1976-77N	G. S. Chappell	G. M. Turner	2	1	0	1
1980-81A	G. S. Chappell	G. P. Howarth[1]	3	2	0	1
1981-82N	G. S. Chappell	G. P. Howarth	3	1	1	1
	In Australia		6	4	0	2
	In New Zealand		9	4	2	3
	Totals		15	8	2	5

A Played in Australia. N Played in New Zealand.

Note: The following deputised for the official touring captain: [1]M. G. Burgess (Second).

HIGHEST INNINGS TOTALS

For Australia in Australia: 477 at Adelaide, 1973-74
        in New Zealand: 552 at Christchurch, 1976-77

For New Zealand in Australia: 312 at Sydney, 1973-74
        in New Zealand: 484 at Wellington, 1973-74

LOWEST INNINGS TOTALS

For Australia in Australia: 162 at Sydney, 1973-74
        in New Zealand: 210 at Auckland, 1981-82

For New Zealand in Australia: 200 at Melbourne, 1973-74
        in New Zealand: 42 at Wellington, 1945-46

INDIVIDUAL HUNDREDS IN THE MATCHES 1945-46–1981-82

For Australia (14)

247* 133	}G. S. Chappell, Wellington	1973-74	122†	K. R. Stackpole, Melbourne		1973-74
176	G. S. Chappell, Christchurch	1981-82	104*	K. D. Walters, Auckland..		1973-74
145 121	}I. M. Chappell, Wellington	1973-74	250	K. D. Walters, Christchurch		1976-77
101	G. J. Gilmour, Christchurch	1976-77	107	K. D. Walters, Melbourne		1980-81
132	R. W. Marsh, Adelaide....	1973-74	111†	G. M. Wood, Brisbane.....		1980-81
159*	I. R. Redpath, Auckland..	1973-74	100	G. M. Wood, Auckland ...		1981-82

For New Zealand (9)

132	B. E. Congdon, Wellington	1973-74	117	J. F. M. Morrison, Sydney	1973-74
107*	B. E. Congdon, Christchurch	1976-77	108	J. M. Parker, Sydney.......	1973-74
161	B. A. Edgar, Auckland....	1981-82	101 110*	}G. M. Turner, Christchurch	1973-74
101	B. F. Hastings, Wellington	1973-74	141	J. G. Wright, Christchurch	1981-82

† *Signifies hundred on first appearance in Australia–New Zealand Tests.*

Notes: G. S. and I. M. Chappell at Wellington in 1973-74 provide the only instance in Test matches of brothers both scoring a hundred in each innings and in the same Test.

G. S. Chappell's match aggregate of 380 (247* and 133) for Australia at Wellington in 1973-74 is the record in Test matches.

RECORD PARTNERSHIPS FOR EACH WICKET

For Australia

106 for 1st	G. M. Wood and B. M. Laird at Auckland		1981-82
141 for 2nd	I. R. Redpath and I. M. Chappell at Wellington		1973-74
264 for 3rd	I. M. Chappell and G. S. Chappell at Wellington		1973-74
106 for 4th	I. R. Redpath and I. C. Davis at Christchurch		1973-74
93 for 5th	G. S. Chappell and K. D. Walters at Christchurch		1976-77
92 for 6th	G. S. Chappell and R. W. Marsh at Christchurch		1981-82
217 for 7th†	K. D. Walters and G. J. Gilmour at Christchurch		1976-77
93 for 8th	G. J. Gilmour and K. J. O'Keeffe at Auckland		1976-77
57 for 9th	R. W. Marsh and L. S. Pascoe at Perth		1980-81
60 for 10th	K. D. Walters and J. D. Higgs at Melbourne		1980-81

For New Zealand

107 for 1st	G. M. Turner and J. M. Parker at Auckland		1973-74
108 for 2nd	G. M. Turner and J. F. M. Morrison at Wellington		1973-74
125 for 3rd	G. P. Howarth and J. M. Parker at Melbourne		1980-81
229 for 4th†	B. E. Congdon and B. F. Hastings at Wellington		1973-74
88 for 5th	J. V. Coney and M. G. Burgess at Perth		1980-81
105 for 6th	M. G. Burgess and R. J. Hadlee at Auckland		1976-77
66 for 7th	K. J. Wadsworth and D. R. Hadlee at Adelaide		1973-74
53 for 8th	B. A. Edgar and R. J. Hadlee at Brisbane		1980-81
73 for 9th	H. J. Howarth and D. R. Hadlee at Christchurch		1976-77
47 for 10th	H. J. Howarth and M. G. Webb at Wellington		1973-74

† *Denotes record partnership against all countries.*

TEN WICKETS OR MORE IN A MATCH

For Australia (1)

11-123 (5-51, 6-72)   D. K. Lillee, Auckland 1976-77

Note: The best match figures by a New Zealand bowler are 9-166 (5-82, 4-84), R. O. Collinge at Auckland, 1973-74, and 9-146 (3-89, 6-57), R. J. Hadlee at Melbourne, 1980-81.

AUSTRALIA v INDIA

Season	Australia	*Captains* India	T	A	I	D
1947-48*A*	D. G. Bradman	L. Amarnath	5	4	0	1
1956-57*I*	I. W. Johnson[1]	P. R. Umrigar	3	2	0	1
1959-60*I*	R. Benaud	G. S. Ramchand	5	2	1	2
1964-65*I*	R. B. Simpson	Nawab of Pataudi jun.	3	1	1	1
1967-68*A*	R. B. Simpson[2]	Nawab of Pataudi jun.[3]	4	4	0	0
1969-70*I*	W. M. Lawry	Nawab of Pataudi jun.	5	3	1	1
1977-78*A*	R. B. Simpson	B. S. Bedi	5	3	2	0
1979-80*I*	K. J. Hughes	S. M. Gavaskar	6	0	2	4
1980-81*A*	G. S. Chappell	S. M. Gavaskar	3	1	1	1
	In Australia......................		17	12	3	2
	In India............................		22	8	5	9
	Totals		39	20	8	11

A Played in Australia.   I Played in India.

Notes: The following deputised for the official touring captain or were appointed by the home authority for only a minor proportion of the series:
[1]R. R. Lindwall (Second). [2]W. M. Lawry (Third and Fourth). [3]C. G. Borde (First).

HIGHEST INNINGS TOTALS

For Australia in Australia: 674 at Adelaide, 1947-48
in India: 523-7 dec. at Bombay, 1956-57

For India in Australia: 445 at Adelaide, 1977-78
in India: 510-7 dec. at Delhi, 1979-80

LOWEST INNINGS TOTALS

For Australia in Australia: 83 at Melbourne, 1980-81
in India: 105 at Kanpur, 1959-60

For India in Australia: 58 at Brisbane, 1947-48
in India: 135 at Delhi, 1959-60

INDIVIDUAL HUNDREDS IN THE MATCHES 1947-48–1980-81

For Australia (36)

112	S. G. Barnes, Adelaide	1947-48	198*	A. L. Hassett, Adelaide ...	1947-48
162†	A. R. Border, Madras......	1979-80	100	K. J. Hughes, Madras	1979-80
124	A. R. Border, Melbourne .	1980-81	213	K. J. Hughes, Adelaide....	1980-81
185†	D. G. Bradman, Brisbane.	1947-48	100	W. M. Lawry, Melbourne .	1967-68
132	} D. G. Bradman, Melbourne	1947-48	105	A. L. Mann, Perth	1977-78
127*			100*	A. R. Morris, Melbourne .	1947-48
201	D. G. Bradman, Adelaide	1947-48	163	N. C. O'Neill, Bombay	1959-60
161	J. W. Burke, Bombay	1956-57	113	N. C. O'Neill, Calcutta	1959-60
204†	G. S. Chappell, Sydney	1980-81	114	A. P. Sheahan, Kanpur	1969-70
151	I. M. Chappell, Melbourne	1967-68	103	R. B. Simpson, Adelaide....	1967-68
138	I. M. Chappell, Delhi	1969-70	109	R. B. Simpson, Melbourne	1967-68
108	R. M. Cowper, Adelaide ...	1967-68	176	R. B. Simpson, Perth........	1977-78
165	R. M. Cowper, Sydney	1967-68	100	R. B. Simpson, Adelaide....	1977-78
101	L. E. Favell, Madras........	1959-60	103†	K. R. Stackpole, Bombay .	1969-70
153	R. N. Harvey, Melbourne .	1947-48	102	K. D. Walters, Madras......	1969-70
140	R. N. Harvey, Bombay	1956-57	125	G. M. Wood, Adelaide	1980-81
114	R. N. Harvey, Delhi........	1959-60	121†	G. N. Yallop, Adelaide	1977-78
102	R. N. Harvey, Bombay	1959-60	167	G. N. Yallop, Calcutta	1979-80

For India (23)

100	M. Amarnath, Perth	1977-78	128*†	Nawab of Pataudi, Madras	1964-65
108	N. J. Contractor, Bombay.	1959-60	174	S. M. Patil, Adelaide........	1980-81
113†	S. M. Gavaskar, Brisbane .	1977-78	123	D. G. Phadkar, Adelaide....	1947-48
127	S. M. Gavaskar, Perth	1977-78	109	G. S. Ramchand, Bombay	1956-57
118	S. M. Gavaskar, Melbourne	1977-78	112	D. B. Vengsarkar, Banga-	
115	S. M. Gavaskar, Delhi	1979-80		lore	1979-80
123	S. M. Gavaskar, Bombay..	1979-80	137†	G. R. Viswanath, Kanpur.	1969-70
116	} V. S. Hazare, Adelaide	1947-48	161*	G. R. Viswanath, Banga-	
145				lore	1979-80
101	M. L. Jaisimha, Brisbane..	1967-68	131	G. R. Viswanath, Delhi.....	1979-80
101*	S. M. H. Kirmani, Bombay	1979-80	114	G. R. Viswanath, Mel-	
116	V. Mankad, Melbourne	1947-48		bourne	1980-81
111	V. Mankad, Melbourne	1947-48	100*	Yashpal Sharma, Delhi.....	1979-80

† Signifies hundred on first appearance in Australia–India Tests.

RECORD PARTNERSHIPS FOR EACH WICKET

For Australia

191 for 1st	R. B. Simpson and W. M. Lawry at Melbourne	1967-68
236 for 2nd	S. G. Barnes and D. G. Bradman at Adelaide	1947-48
222 for 3rd	A. R. Border and K. J. Hughes at Madras................................	1979-80
159 for 4th	R. N. Harvey and S. J. E. Loxton at Melbourne	1947-48
223* for 5th	A. R. Morris and D. G. Bradman at Melbourne	1947-48
151 for 6th	T. R. Veivers and B. N. Jarman at Bombay..............................	1964-65
64 for 7th	T. R. Veivers and J. W. Martin at Madras................................	1964-65
73 for 8th	T. R. Veivers and G. D. McKenzie at Madras..........................	1964-65
87 for 9th	I. W. Johnson and W. P. A. Crawford at Madras.....................	1956-57
52 for 10th	K. J. Wright and J. D. Higgs at Delhi.......................................	1979-80

For India

192 for 1st	S. M. Gavaskar and C. P. S. Chauhan at Bombay..................	1979-80
193 for 2nd	S. M. Gavaskar and M. Amarnath at Perth............................	1977-78
159 for 3rd	S. M. Gavaskar and G. R. Viswanath at Delhi......................	1979-80
159 for 4th	D. B. Vengsarkar and G. R. Viswanath at Bangalore	1979-80
109 for 5th	A. A. Baig and R. B. Kenny at Bombay...............................	1959-60
188 for 6th	V. S. Hazare and D. G. Phadkar at Adelaide........................	1947-48
132 for 7th	V. S. Hazare and H. R. Adhikari at Adelaide	1947-48
127 for 8th	S. M. H. Kirmani and K. D. Ghavri at Bombay	1979-80
57 for 9th	S. M. H. Kirmani and K. D. Ghavri at Sydney	1980-81
39 for 10th	C. G. Borde and B. S. Chandrasekhar at Calcutta..................	1964-65

TEN WICKETS OR MORE IN A MATCH

For Australia (7)

11-105 (6-52, 5-53)	R. Benaud, Calcutta...	1956-57
12-124 (5-31, 7-93)	A. K. Davidson, Kanpur	1959-60
11-166 (5-99, 7-67)	G. Dymock, Kanpur..	1979-80
10-91 (6-58, 4-33)†	G. D. McKenzie, Madras..	1964-65
10-151 (7-66, 3-85)	G. D. McKenzie, Melbourne..	1967-68
10-144 (5-91, 5-53)	A. A. Mallett, Madras	1969-70
11-31 (5-2, 6-29)†	E. R. H. Toshack, Brisbane...	1947-48

For India (6)

10-194 (5-89, 5-105)	B. S. Bedi, Perth	1977-78
12-104 (6-52, 6-52)	B. S. Chandrasekhar, Melbourne	1977-78
10-130 (7-49, 3-81)	Ghulam Ahmed, Calcutta..	1956-57
11-122 (5-31, 6-91)	R. G. Nadkarni, Madras...	1964-65
14-124 (9-69, 5-55)	J. M. Patel, Kanpur..	1959-60
10-174 (4-100, 6-74)	E. A. S. Prasanna, Madras	1969-70

† *Signifies ten wickets or more on first appearance in Australia–India Tests.*

AUSTRALIA v PAKISTAN

	Captains					
Season	*Australia*	*Pakistan*	*T*	*A*	*P*	*D*
1956-57P	I. W. Johnson	A. H. Kardar	1	0	1	0
1959-60P	R. Benaud	Fazal Mahmood[1]	3	2	0	1
1964-65P	R. B. Simpson	Hanif Mohammad	1	0	0	1
1964-65A	R. B. Simpson	Hanif Mohammad	1	0	0	1
1972-73A	I. M. Chappell	Intikhab Alam	3	3	0	0
1976-77A	G. S. Chappell	Mushtaq Mohammad	3	1	1	1
1978-79A	G. N. Yallop[2]	Mushtaq Mohammad	2	1	1	0
1979-80P	G. S. Chappell	Javed Miandad	3	0	1	2
1981-82A	G. S. Chappell	Javed Miandad	3	2	1	0
1982-83P	K. J. Hughes	Imran Khan	3	0	3	0
	In Pakistan......................		11	2	5	4
	In Australia....................		12	7	3	2
	Totals		23	9	8	6

A Played in Australia.   P Played in Pakistan.

Notes: [1]Imtiaz Ahmed captained in Second Test. [2]K. J. Hughes captained in Second Test.

HIGHEST INNINGS TOTALS

For Australia in Australia: 585 at Adelaide, 1972-73
in Pakistan: 617 at Faisalabad, 1979-80

For Pakistan in Australia: 574-8 dec. at Melbourne, 1972-73
in Pakistan: 501-6 dec. at Faisalabad, 1982-83

LOWEST INNINGS TOTALS

For Australia in Australia: 125 at Melbourne, 1981-82
in Pakistan: 80 at Karachi, 1956-57

For Pakistan in Australia: 62 at Perth, 1981-82
in Pakistan: 134 at Dacca, 1959-60

INDIVIDUAL HUNDREDS IN THE MATCHES 1956-57–1982-83

For Australia (23)

142	J. Benaud, Melbourne	1972-73
105†	A. R. Border, Melbourne	1978-79
150* 153	} A. R. Border, Lahore	1979-80
116*	G. S. Chappell, Melbourne	1972-73
121	G. S. Chappell, Melbourne	1976-77
235	G. S. Chappell, Faisalabad	1979-80
201	G. S. Chappell, Brisbane	1981-82
196	I. M. Chappell, Adelaide	1972-73
168	G. J. Cosier, Melbourne	1976-77
105†	I. C. Davis, Adelaide	1976-77
106	K. J. Hughes, Perth	1981-82
105	R. B. McCosker, Melbourne	1976-77
118†	R. W. Marsh, Adelaide	1972-73
134	N. C. O'Neill, Lahore	1959-60
135	I. R. Redpath, Melbourne	1972-73
106*	G. M. Ritchie, Faisalabad	1982-83
127	A. P. Sheahan, Melbourne	1972-73
153† 115	} R. B. Simpson, Karachi	1964-65
107	K. D. Walters, Adelaide	1976-77
100	G. M. Wood, Melbourne	1981-82
172	G. N. Yallop, Faisalabad	1979-80

For Pakistan (21)

152*	Asif Iqbal, Adelaide	1976-77
120	Asif Iqbal, Sydney	1976-77
134*	Asif Iqbal, Perth	1978-79
101*	Hanif Mohammad, Karachi	1959-60
104	Hanif Mohammad, Melbourne	1964-65
129*	Javed Miandad, Perth	1978-79
106*	Javed Miandad, Faisalabad	1979-80
138	Javed Miandad, Lahore	1982-83
166†	Khalid Ibadulla, Karachi	1964-65
158	Majid J. Khan, Melbourne	1972-73
108	Majid J. Khan, Melbourne	1978-79
110*	Majid J. Khan, Lahore	1979-80
111	Mansoor Akhtar, Faisalabad	1982-83
135	Mohsin Khan, Lahore	1982-83
121	Mushtaq Mohammad, Sydney	1972-73
137	Sadiq Mohammad, Melbourne	1972-73
105	Sadiq Mohammad, Melbourne	1976-77
166	Saeed Ahmed, Lahore	1959-60
210*	Taslim Arif, Faisalabad	1979-80
101	Zaheer Abbas, Adelaide	1976-77
126	Zaheer Abbas, Faisalabad	1982-83

† *Signifies hundred on first appearance in Australia–Pakistan Tests.*

RECORD PARTNERSHIPS FOR EACH WICKET

For Australia

134 for 1st	I. C. Davis and A. Turner at Melbourne	1976-77
233 for 2nd	A. P. Sheahan and J. Benaud at Melbourne	1972-73
179 for 3rd	K. J. Hughes and G. S. Chappell at Faisalabad......................	1979-80
217 for 4th	G. S. Chappell and G. N. Yallop at Faisalabad......................	1979-80
171 for 5th	G. S. Chappell and G. J. Cosier at Melbourne	1976-77
139 for 6th	R. M. Cowper and T. R. Veivers at Melbourne	1964-65
134 for 7th	A. R. Border and G. R. Beard at Lahore	1979-80
117 for 8th	G. J. Cosier and K. J. O'Keeffe at Melbourne	1976-77
83 for 9th	J. R. Watkins and R. A. L. Massie at Sydney	1972-73
52 for 10th	{ D. K. Lillee and M. H. N. Walker at Sydney	1976-77
	{ G. F. Lawson and T. M. Alderman at Lahore	1982-83

For Pakistan

249 for 1st†	Khalid Ibadulla and Abdul Kadir at Karachi	1964-65
195 for 2nd	Sadiq Mohammad and Majid J. Khan at Melbourne	1972-73
223* for 3rd†	Taslim Arif and Javed Miandad at Faisalabad........................	1979-80
155 for 4th	Mansoor Akhtar and Zaheer Abbas at Faisalabad	1982-83
139 for 5th	Mushtaq Mohammad and Asif Iqbal at Sydney	1972-73
115 for 6th	Asif Iqbal and Javed Miandad at Sydney	1976-77
104 for 7th	Intikhab Alam and Wasim Bari at Adelaide	1972-73
111 for 8th	Majid J. Khan and Imran Khan at Lahore	1979-80
56 for 9th	Intikhab Alam and Afaq Hussain at Melbourne	1964-65
87 for 10th	Asif Iqbal and Iqbal Qasim at Adelaide................................	1976-77

† *Denotes record partnership against all countries.*

TEN WICKETS OR MORE IN A MATCH

For Australia (2)

10-111 (7-87, 3-24)†	R. J. Bright, Karachi..	1979-80
10-135 (6-82, 4-53)	D. K. Lillee, Melbourne...	1976-77

For Pakistan (5)

11-218 (4-76, 7-142)	Abdul Qadir, Faisalabad..	1982-83
13-114 (6-34, 7-80)†	Fazal Mahmood, Karachi.......................................	1956-57
12-165 (6-102, 6-63)	Imran Khan, Sydney...	1976-77
11-118 (4-69, 7-49)	Iqbal Qasim, Karachi...	1979-80
11-125 (2-39, 9-86)	Sarfraz Nawaz, Melbourne......................................	1978-79

† *Signifies ten wickets or more on first appearance in Australia–Pakistan Tests.*

AUSTRALIA v SRI LANKA

	Captains					
Season	Australia	Sri Lanka	T	A	SL	D
1982-83SL	G. S. Chappell	L. R. D. Mendis	1	1	0	0

SL Played in Sri Lanka.

The only match played was at Kandy.

INDIVIDUAL HUNDREDS

For Australia (2)

143* D. W. Hookes, Kandy ..... 1982-83 | 141 K. C. Wessels, Kandy 1982-83

Highest score for Sri Lanka: 96 by S. Wettimuny

Best bowling in an innings for Australia: 5-66 by T. G. Hogan
Sri Lanka: 2-113 by A. L. F. de Mel

Best partnerships for Australia: 170 for the 2nd wicket by K. C. Wessels and D. W. Hookes
155* for the 5th wicket by D. W. Hookes and A. R. Border
Sri Lanka: 96 for the 5th wicket by L. R. D. Mendis and A. Ranatunga

Highest total for Australia: 514-4 dec.
Sri Lanka: 271

SOUTH AFRICA v NEW ZEALAND

Season	South Africa	*Captains* New Zealand	T	SA	NZ	D
1931-32N	H. B. Cameron	M. L. Page	2	2	0	0
1952-53N	J. E. Cheetham	W. M. Wallace	2	1	0	1
1953-54S	J. E. Cheetham	G. O. Rabone[1]	5	4	0	1
1961-62S	D. J. McGlew	J. R. Reid	5	2	2	1
1963-64N	T. L. Goddard	J. R. Reid	3	0	0	3
	In New Zealand		7	3	0	4
	In South Africa		10	6	2	2
	Totals		17	9	2	6

N Played in New Zealand. S Played in South Africa.

Note: [1]B. Sutcliffe captained in Fourth and Fifth Tests.

HIGHEST INNINGS TOTALS

For South Africa in South Africa: 464 at Johannesburg, 1961-62
in New Zealand: 524-8 at Wellington, 1952-53

For New Zealand in South Africa: 505 at Cape Town, 1953-54
in New Zealand: 364 at Wellington, 1931-32

LOWEST INNINGS TOTALS

For South Africa in South Africa: 148 at Johannesburg, 1953-54
in New Zealand: 223 at Dunedin, 1963-64

For New Zealand in South Africa: 79 at Johannesburg, 1953-54
in New Zealand: 138 at Dunedin, 1963-64

INDIVIDUAL HUNDREDS IN THE MATCHES 1931-32–1963-64

For South Africa (11)

122*	X. C. Balaskas, Wellington	1931-32	101 R. A. McLean, Durban.... 1953-54
103†	J. A. J. Christy, Christchurch......................	1931-32	113 R. A. McLean, Cape Town.......................... 1961-62
116	W. R. Endean, Auckland.	1952-53	113† B. Mitchell, Christchurch.. 1931-32
255*†	D. J. McGlew, Wellington	1952-53	109† A. R. A. Murray, Wellington...................... 1952-53
127*	D. J. McGlew, Durban	1961-62	
120	D. J. McGlew, Johannesburg..........................	1961-62	101 J. H. B. Waite, Johannesburg.......................... 1961-62

For New Zealand (7)

109	P. T. Barton, Port Elizabeth..........................	1961-62	135 J. R. Reid, Cape Town 1953-54
101	P. G. Z. Harris, Cape Town......................	1961-62	142 J. R. Reid, Johannesburg.......................... 1961-62
107	G. O. Rabone, Durban	1953-54	138 B. W. Sinclair, Auckland.. 1963-64
			100† H. G. Vivian, Wellington . 1931-32

† *Signifies hundred on first appearance in South Africa–New Zealand Tests.*

RECORD PARTNERSHIPS FOR EACH WICKET

For South Africa

196 for 1st	J. A. J. Christy and B. Mitchell at Christchurch......................	1931-32
76 for 2nd	J. A. J. Christy and H. B. Cameron at Wellington	1931-32
112 for 3rd	D. J. McGlew and R. A. McLean at Johannesburg	1961-62
135 for 4th	K. J. Funston and R. A. McLean at Durban	1953-54
130 for 5th	W. R. Endean and J. E. Cheetham at Auckland	1952-53
83 for 6th	K. C. Bland and D. T. Lindsay at Auckland	1963-64
246 for 7th†	D. J. McGlew and A. R. A. Murray at Wellington..................	1952-53
95 for 8th	J. E. Cheetham and H. J. Tayfield at Cape Town	1953-54
60 for 9th	P. M. Pollock and N. A. T. Adcock at Port Elizabeth	1961-62
47 for 10th	D. J. McGlew and H. D. Bromfield at Port Elizabeth..............	1961-62

For New Zealand

126 for 1st	G. O. Rabone and M. E. Chapple at Cape Town......................	1953-54
51 for 2nd	W. P. Bradburn and B. W. Sinclair at Dunedin	1963-64
94 for 3rd	M. B. Poore and B. Sutcliffe at Cape Town	1953-54
171 for 4th	B. W. Sinclair and S. N. McGregor at Auckland	1963-64
174 for 5th	J. R. Reid and J. E. F. Beck at Cape Town	1953-54
100 for 6th	H. G. Vivian and F. T. Badcock at Wellington	1931-32
84 for 7th	J. R. Reid and G. A. Bartlett at Johannesburg	1961-62
73 for 8th	P. G. Z. Harris and G. A. Bartlett at Durban	1961-62
69 for 9th	C. F. W. Allcott and I. B. Cromb at Wellington	1931-32
49* for 10th	A. E. Dick and F. J. Cameron at Cape Town..........................	1961-62

† *Denotes record partnership against all countries.*

TEN WICKETS OR MORE IN A MATCH

For South Africa (1)

11-196 (6-128, 5-68)†	S. F. Burke, Cape Town...	1961-62

† *Signifies ten wickets or more on first appearance in South Africa–New Zealand Tests.*

Note: The best match figures by a New Zealand bowler are 8-180 (4-61, 4-119), J. C. Alabaster at Cape Town, 1961-62.

WEST INDIES v NEW ZEALAND

	Captains					
Season	West Indies	New Zealand	T	WI	NZ	D
1951-52N	J. D. C. Goddard	B. Sutcliffe	2	1	0	1
1955-56N	D. St E. Atkinson	J. R. Reid[1]	4	3	1	0
1968-69N	G. S. Sobers	G. T. Dowling	3	1	1	1
1971-72W	G. S. Sobers	G. T. Dowling[2]	5	0	0	5
1979-80N	C. H. Lloyd	G. P. Howarth	3	0	1	2
	In New Zealand......................		12	5	3	4
	In West Indies........................		5	0	0	5
	Totals..................................		17	5	3	9

N Played in New Zealand. W Played in West Indies.

Notes: The following deputised for the official touring captain or were appointed by the home authority for only a minor proportion of the series:
[1] H. B. Cave (First). [2] B. E. Congdon (Third, Fourth and Fifth).

HIGHEST INNINGS TOTALS

For West Indies in West Indies: 564-8 at Bridgetown, 1971-72
in New Zealand: 546-6 dec. at Auckland, 1951-52

For New Zealand in West Indies: 543-3 dec. at Georgetown, 1971-72
in New Zealand: 460 at Christchurch, 1979-80

LOWEST INNINGS TOTALS

For West Indies in West Indies: 133 at Bridgetown, 1971-72
in New Zealand: 77 at Auckland, 1955-56

For New Zealand in West Indies: 162 at Port-of-Spain, 1971-72
in New Zealand: 74 at Dunedin, 1955-56

INDIVIDUAL HUNDREDS IN THE MATCHES 1951-52–1979-80

By West Indies (20)

109†	M. C. Carew, Auckland ...	1968-69	258	S. M. Nurse, Christchurch	1968-69
183	C. A. Davis, Bridgetown ..	1971-72	214†	L. G. Rowe, Kingston......	1971-72
163	R. C. Fredericks, Kingston	1971-72	100*⎰		
105†	D. L. Haynes, Dunedin....	1979-80	100	L. G. Rowe, Christchurch.	1979-80
122	D. L. Haynes, Christchurch......................	1979-80	142	G. S. Sobers, Bridgetown .	1971-72
			152	J. B. Stollmeyer, Auckland	1951-52
100*†	A. I. Kallicharran, Georgetown......................	1971-72	115	C. L. Walcott, Auckland ..	1951-52
			123	E. D. Weekes, Dunedin ...	1955-56
101	A. I. Kallicharran, Port-of-Spain......................	1971-72	103	E. D. Weekes, Christchurch	1955-56
			156	E. D. Weekes, Wellington	1955-56
100*	C. L. King, Christchurch ..	1979-80	100	F. M. M. Worrell, Auckland......................	1951-52
168†	S. M. Nurse, Auckland	1968-69			

By New Zealand (12)

101	M. G. Burgess, Kingston	1971-72
166*	B. E. Congdon, Port-of-Spain	1971-72
126	B. E. Congdon, Bridgetown	1971-72
127	B. A. Edgar, Auckland	1979-80
103	R. J. Hadlee, Christchurch	1979-80
117*	B. F. Hastings, Christchurch	1968-69
105	B. F. Hastings, Bridgetown	1971-72
147	G. P. Howarth, Christchurch	1979-80
182	T. W. Jarvis, Georgetown	1971-72
124†	B. R. Taylor, Auckland	1968-69
223*	G. M. Turner, Kingston	1971-72
259	G. M. Turner, Georgetown	1971-72

† *Signifies hundred on first appearance in West Indies–New Zealand Tests.*

Notes: E. D. Weekes in 1955-56 made three hundreds in consecutive innings.

L. G. Rowe and A. I. Kallicharran each scored hundreds in their first two innings in Test cricket, Rowe being the only batsman to do so in his first match.

RECORD PARTNERSHIPS FOR EACH WICKET

For West Indies

225 for 1st	C. G. Greenidge and D. L. Haynes at Christchurch	1979-80
269 for 2nd	R. C. Fredericks and L. G. Rowe at Kingston	1971-72
174 for 3rd	S. M. Nurse and B. F. Butcher at Auckland	1968-69
162 for 4th	⎰ E. D. Weekes and O. G. Smith at Dunedin	1955-56
	⎱ C. G. Greenidge and A. I. Kallicharran at Christchurch	1979-80
189 for 5th	F. M. M. Worrell and C. L. Walcott at Auckland	1951-52
254 for 6th	C. A. Davis and G. S. Sobers at Bridgetown	1971-72
143 for 7th	D. St E. Atkinson and J. D. C. Goddard at Christchurch	1955-56
75 for 8th	J. D. C. Goddard and S. Ramadhin at Dunedin	1955-56
56 for 9th	D. A. J. Holford and V. A. Holder at Port-of-Spain	1971-72
31 for 10th	T. M. Findlay and G. C. Shillingford at Bridgetown	1971-72

For New Zealand

387 for 1st†	G. M. Turner and T. W. Jarvis at Georgetown	1971-72
139 for 2nd	G. M. Turner and B. E. Congdon at Port-of-Spain	1971-72
75 for 3rd	B. E. Congdon and B. F. Hastings at Christchurch	1968-69
175 for 4th	B. E. Congdon and B. F. Hastings at Bridgetown	1971-72
110 for 5th	B. F. Hastings and V. Pollard at Christchurch	1968-69
220 for 6th†	G. M. Turner and K. J. Wadsworth at Kingston	1971-72
98 for 7th	J. V. Coney and R. J. Hadlee at Christchurch	1979-80
136 for 8th†	B. E. Congdon and R. S. Cunis at Port-of-Spain	1971-72
62* for 9th	V. Pollard and R. S. Cunis at Auckland	1968-69
41 for 10th	B. E. Congdon and J. C. Alabaster at Port-of-Spain	1971-72

† *Denotes record partnership against all countries.*

TEN WICKETS OR MORE IN A MATCH

For New Zealand (2)

11-102 (5-34, 6-68)†	R. J. Hadlee, Dunedin	1979-80
10-166 (4-71, 6-95)	G. B. Troup, Auckland	1979-80

† *Signifies ten wickets or more on first appearance in West Indies–New Zealand Tests.*

Note: The best match figures by a West Indian bowler are 9-125 (5-86, 4-39), S. Ramadhin at Christchurch, 1951-52, and 9-81 (6-23, 3-58), S. Ramadhin at Dunedin, 1955-56.

WEST INDIES v INDIA

	Captains					
Season	West Indies	India	T	WI	I	D
1948-49*I*	J. D. C. Goddard	L. Amarnath	5	1	0	4
1952-53*W*	J. B. Stollmeyer	V. S. Hazare	5	1	0	4
1958-59*I*	F. C. M. Alexander	Ghulam Ahmed[1]	5	3	0	2
1961-62*W*	F. M. M. Worrell	N. J. Contractor[2]	5	5	0	0
1966-67*I*	G. S. Sobers	Nawab of Pataudi jun.	3	2	0	1
1970-71*W*	G. S. Sobers	A. L. Wadekar	5	0	1	4
1974-75*I*	C. H. Lloyd	Nawab of Pataudi jun.[3]	5	3	2	0
1975-76*W*	C. H. Lloyd	B. S. Bedi	4	2	1	1
1978-79*I*	A. I. Kallicharran	S. M. Gavaskar	6	0	1	5
1982-83*W*	C. H. Lloyd	Kapil Dev	5	2	0	3
	In India............................		24	9	3	12
	In West Indies......................		24	10	2	12
	Totals....................		48	19	5	24

I Played in India.　W Played in West Indies.

Notes: The following deputised for the official touring captain or were appointed by the home authority for only a minor proportion of the series:
[1]P. R. Umrigar (First), V. Mankad (Fourth), H. R. Adhikari (Fifth). [2]Nawab of Pataudi jun. (Third, Fourth and Fifth). [3]S. Venkataraghavan (Second).

HIGHEST INNINGS TOTALS

For West Indies in West Indies: 631-8 dec. at Kingston, 1961-62
in India: 644-8 dec. at Delhi, 1958-59

For India in West Indies: 469-7 at Port-of-Spain, 1982-83
in India: 644-7 dec. at Kanpur, 1978-79

LOWEST INNINGS TOTALS

For West Indies in West Indies: 214 at Port-of-Spain, 1970-71
in India: 151 at Madras, 1978-79

For India in West Indies: 97† at Kingston, 1975-76
in India: 118 at Bangalore, 1974-75

† *Five men absent hurt.*

INDIVIDUAL HUNDREDS IN THE MATCHES 1948-49–1982-83

For West Indies (63)

250	S. F. A. Bacchus, Kanpur	1978-79
103	B. F. Butcher, Calcutta	1958-59
142	B. F. Butcher, Madras	1958-59
107†	R. J. Christiani, Delhi......	1948-49
125*	C. A. Davis, Georgetown	1970-71
105	C. A. Davis, Port-of-Spain	1970-71
110	P. J. Dujon, Antigua	1982-83
100	R. C. Fredericks, Calcutta	1974-75
104	R. C. Fredericks, Bombay	1974-75
123	H. A. Gomes, Port-of-Spain	1982-83

101†	G. E. Gomez, Delhi........	1948-49
107†	C. G. Greenidge, Bangalore	1974-75
154*	C. G. Greenidge, Antigua	1982-83
136	D. L. Haynes, Antigua.....	1982-83
123	J. K. Holt, Delhi	1958-59
101	C. C. Hunte, Bombay	1966-67
124†	A. I. Kallicharran, Bangalore	1974-75
103*	A. I. Kallicharran, Port-of-Spain	1975-76

187	A. I. Kallicharran, Bombay	1978-79
256	R. B. Kanhai, Calcutta....	1958-59
138	R. B. Kanhai, Kingston...	1961-62
139	R. B. Kanhai, Port-of-Spain	1961-62
158*	R. B. Kanhai, Kingston...	1970-71
163	C. H. Lloyd, Bangalore.....	1974-75
242*	C. H. Lloyd, Bombay......	1974-75
102	C. H. Lloyd, Bridgetown...	1975-76
143	C. H. Lloyd, Port-of-Spain	1982-83
106	C. H. Lloyd, Antigua......	1982-83
130	A. L. Logie, Bridgetown ..	1982-83
125†	E. D. A. McMorris, Kingston..................	1961-62
115†	B. H. Pairaudeau, Port-of-Spain	1952-53
104	A. F. Rae, Bombay	1948-49
109	A. F. Rae, Madras	1948-49
192*	I. V. A. Richards, Delhi...	1974-75
142	I. V. A. Richards, Bridge-town	1975-76
130	I. V. A. Richards, Port-of-Spain	1975-76
177	I. V. A. Richards, Port-of-Spain	1975-76
109	I. V. A. Richards, George-town	1982-83
100	O. G. Smith, Delhi..........	1958-59

142*†	G. S. Sobers, Bombay......	1958-59
198	G. S. Sobers, Kanpur......	1958-59
106*	G. S. Sobers, Calcutta.....	1958-59
153	G. S. Sobers, Kingston...	1961-62
104	G. S. Sobers, Kingston...	1961-62
108*	G. S. Sobers, Georgetown	1970-71
178*	G. S. Sobers, Bridgetown .	1970-71
132	G. S. Sobers, Port-of-Spain	1970-71
100*	J. S. Solomon, Delhi........	1958-59
160	J. B. Stollmeyer, Madras ..	1948-49
104*	J. B. Stollmeyer, Port-of-Spain	1952-53
152†	C. L. Walcott, Delhi........	1948-49
108	C. L. Walcott, Calcutta...	1948-49
125	C. L. Walcott, Georgetown	1952-53
118	C. L. Walcott, Kingston...	1952-53
128†	E. D. Weekes, Delhi........	1948-49
194	E. D. Weekes, Bombay....	1948-49
162 101	} E. D. Weekes, Calcutta....	1948-49
207	E. D. Weekes, Port-of-Spain	1952-53
161	E. D. Weekes, Port-of-Spain	1952-53
109	E. D. Weekes, Kingston...	1952-53
111	A. B. Williams, Calcutta ..	1978-79
237	F. M. M. Worrell, Kingston	1952-53

For India (45)

114*†	H. R. Adhikari, Delhi......	1948-49
101*	M. Amarnath, Kanpur	1978-79
117	M. Amarnath, Port-of-Spain	1982-83
116	M. Amarnath, Antigua.....	1982-83
163*	M. L. Apte, Port-of-Spain	1952-53
109	C. G. Borde, Delhi	1958-59
121	C. G. Borde, Bombay......	1966-67
125	C. G. Borde, Madras........	1966-67
104	S. A. Durani, Port-of-Spain	1961-62
109	F. M. Engineer, Madras ...	1966-67
102	A. D. Gaekwad, Kanpur ..	1978-79
116	S. M. Gavaskar, George-town	1970-71
117*	S. M. Gavaskar, Bridge-town	1970-71
124 220	} S. M. Gavaskar, Port-of-Spain	1970-71
156	S. M. Gavaskar, Port-of-Spain	1975-76
102	S. M. Gavaskar, Port-of-Spain	1975-76
205	S. M. Gavaskar, Bombay..	1978-79
107 182*	} S. M. Gavaskar, Calcutta..	1978-79
120	S. M. Gavaskar, Delhi	1978-79
147*	S. M. Gavaskar, George-town	1982-83

134*	V. S. Hazare, Bombay	1948-49
122	V. S. Hazare, Bombay	1948-49
126*	Kapil Dev, Delhi	1978-79
100*	Kapil Dev, Port-of-Spain ..	1982-83
118	V. L. Manjrekar, Kingston	1952-53
112	R. S. Modi, Bombay........	1948-49
106†	Mushtaq Ali, Calcutta......	1948-49
115*	B. P. Patel, Port-of-Spain .	1975-76
150	P. Roy, Kingston	1952-53
212	D. N. Sardesai, Kingston ..	1970-71
112	D. N. Sardesai, Port-of-Spain	1970-71
150	D. N. Sardesai, Bridgetown	1970-71
102	R. J. Shastri, Antigua	1982-83
102	E. D. Solkar, Bombay	1974-75
130	P. R. Umrigar, Port-of-Spain	1952-53
117	P. R. Umrigar, Kingston ..	1952-53
172*	P. R. Umrigar, Port-of-Spain	1961-62
157*	D. B. Vengsarkar, Calcutta	1978-79
109	D. B. Vengsarkar, Delhi ..	1978-79
139	G. R. Viswanath, Calcutta	1974-75
112	G. R. Viswanath, Port-of-Spain	1975-76
124	G. R. Viswanath, Madras .	1978-79
179	G. R. Viswanath, Kanpur .	1978-79

† *Signifies hundred on first appearance in West Indies–India Tests.*

RECORD PARTNERSHIPS FOR EACH WICKET

For West Indies

296 for 1st†	C. G. Greenidge and D. L. Haynes at Antigua.........................	1982-83
255 for 2nd	E. D. A. McMorris and R. B. Kanhai at Kingston.......................	1961-62
220 for 3rd	I. V. A. Richards and A. I. Kallicharran at Bridgetown	1975-76
267 for 4th	C. L. Walcott and G. E. Gomez at Delhi.............................	1948-49
219 for 5th	E. D. Weekes and B. H. Pairaudeau at Port-of-Spain	1952-53
250 for 6th	C. H. Lloyd and D. L. Murray at Bombay.............................	1974-75
127 for 7th	G. S. Sobers and I. L. Mendonca at Kingston	1961-62
124 for 8th†	I. V. A. Richards and K. D. Boyce at Delhi	1974-75
106 for 9th	R. J. Christiani and D. St E. Atkinson at Delhi	1948-49
98* for 10th†	F. M. M. Worrell and W. W. Hall at Port-of-Spain	1961-62

For India

153 for 1st	S. M. Gavaskar and C. P. S. Chauhan at Bombay	1978-79
344* for 2nd†	S. M. Gavaskar and D. B. Vengsarkar at Calcutta	1978-79
159 for 3rd	M. Amarnath and G. R. Viswanath at Port-of-Spain..............	1975-76
172 for 4th	G. R. Viswanath and A. D. Gaekwad at Kanpur	1978-79
204 for 5th†	S. M. Gavaskar and B. P. Patel at Port-of-Spain..................	1975-76
137 for 6th	D. N. Sardesai and E. D. Solkar at Kingston	1970-71
186 for 7th†	D. N. Sardesai and E. D. Solkar at Bridgetown	1970-71
107 for 8th	Yashpal Sharma and B. S. Sandhu at Kingston	1982-83
122 for 9th	D. N. Sardesai and E. A. S. Prasanna at Kingston	1970-71
62 for 10th	D. N. Sardesai and B. S. Bedi at Bridgetown	1970-71

† *Denotes record partnership against all countries.*

TEN WICKETS OR MORE IN A MATCH

For West Indies (2)

11-126 (6-50, 5-76)	W. W. Hall, Kanpur..	1958-59
12-121 (7-64, 5-57)	A. M. E. Roberts, Madras...	1974-75

For India (2)

11-235 (7-157, 4-78)†	B. S. Chandrasekhar, Bombay....................................	1966-67
10-223 (9-102, 1-121)	S. P. Gupte, Kanpur..	1958-59

† *Signifies ten wickets or more on first appearance in West Indies–India Tests.*

WEST INDIES v PAKISTAN

	Captains					
Season	West Indies	Pakistan	T	WI	P	D
1957-58W	F. C. M. Alexander	A. H. Kardar	5	3	1	1
1958-59P	F. C. M. Alexander	Fazal Mahmood	3	1	2	0
1974-75P	C. H. Lloyd	Intikhab Alam	2	0	0	2
1976-77W	C. H. Lloyd	Mushtaq Mohammad	5	2	0	3
1980-81P	C. H. Lloyd	Javed Miandad	4	1	0	3
	In West Indies.........................		10	5	2	3
	In Pakistan.............................		9	2	2	5
	Totals....................		19	7	4	8

P Played in Pakistan. W Played in West Indies.

HIGHEST INNINGS TOTALS

For West Indies in West Indies: 790-3 dec. at Kingston, 1957-58
in Pakistan: 493 at Karachi, 1974-75

For Pakistan in West Indies: 657-8 dec. at Bridgetown, 1957-58
in Pakistan: 406-8 dec. at Karachi, 1974-75

LOWEST INNINGS TOTALS

For West Indies in West Indies: 154 at Port-of-Spain, 1976-77
in Pakistan: 76 at Dacca, 1958-59

For Pakistan in West Indies: 106 at Bridgetown, 1957-58
in Pakistan: 104 at Lahore, 1958-59

INDIVIDUAL HUNDREDS IN THE MATCHES 1957-58–1980-81

For West Indies (17)

105*†	L. Baichan, Lahore	1974-75
120	R. C. Fredericks, Port-of-Spain	1976-77
100	C. G. Greenidge, Kingston	1976-77
142†	C. C. Hunte, Bridgetown	1957-58
260	C. C. Hunte, Kingston	1957-58
114	C. C. Hunte, Georgetown	1957-58
101	B. D. Julien, Karachi	1974-75
115	A. I. Kallicharran, Karachi	1974-75
217	R. B. Kanhai, Lahore	1958-59
157	C. H. Lloyd, Bridgetown	1976-77
120*	I. V. A. Richards, Multan	1980-81
120	I. T. Shillingford, Georgetown	1976-77
365*	G. S. Sobers, Kingston	1957-58
125	G. S. Sobers, Georgetown	1957-58
109*	G. S. Sobers, Georgetown	1957-58
145	C. L. Walcott, Georgetown	1957-58
197†	E. D. Weekes, Bridgetown	1957-58

Pakistan (14)

135	Asif Iqbal, Kingston	1976-77
337†	Hanif Mohammad, Bridgetown	1957-58
103	Hanif Mohammad, Karachi	1958-59
122	Imtiaz Ahmed, Kingston	1957-58
123	Imran Khan, Lahore	1980-81
100	Majid J. Khan, Karachi	1974-75
167	Majid J. Khan, Georgetown	1976-77
123	Mushtaq Mohammad, Lahore	1974-75
121	Mushtaq Mohammad, Port-of-Spain	1976-77
150	Saeed Ahmed, Georgetown	1957-58
107*	Wasim Raja, Karachi	1974-75
117*	Wasim Raja, Bridgetown	1976-77
106	Wazir Mohammad, Kingston	1957-58
189	Wazir Mohammad, Port-of-Spain	1957-58

† *Signifies hundred on first appearance in West Indies–Pakistan Tests.*

RECORD PARTNERSHIPS FOR EACH WICKET

For West Indies

182 for 1st	R. C. Fredericks and C. G. Greenidge at Kingston	1976-77
446 for 2nd†	C. C. Hunte and G. S. Sobers at Kingston	1957-58
162 for 3rd	R. B. Kanhai and G. S. Sobers at Lahore	1958-59
188* for 4th	G. S. Sobers and C. L. Walcott at Kingston	1957-58
185 for 5th	E. D. Weekes and O. G. Smith at Bridgetown	1957-58
151 for 6th	C. H. Lloyd and D. L. Murray at Bridgetown	1976-77
70 for 7th	C. H. Lloyd and J. Garner at Bridgetown	1976-77
50 for 8th	B. D. Julien and V. A. Holder at Karachi	1974-75
46 for 9th	J. Garner and C. E. H. Croft at Port-of-Spain	1976-77
44 for 10th	R. Nanan and S. T. Clarke at Faisalabad	1980-81

For Pakistan

159 for 1st‡	Majid J. Khan and Zaheer Abbas at Georgetown	1976-77
178 for 2nd	Hanif Mohammad and Saeed Ahmed at Karachi	1958-59
169 for 3rd	Saeed Ahmed and Wazir Mohammad at Port-of-Spain	1957-58
154 for 4th	Wazir Mohammad and Hanif Mohammad at Port-of-Spain	1957-58
87 for 5th	Mushtaq Mohammad and Asif Iqbal at Kingston	1976-77
166 for 6th	Wazir Mohammad and A. H. Kardar at Kingston	1957-58
128 for 7th	Wasim Raja and Wasim Bari at Karachi	1974-75
73 for 8th	Imran Khan and Sarfraz Nawaz at Port-of-Spain	1976-77
73 for 9th	Wasim Raja and Sarfraz Nawaz at Bridgetown	1976-77
133 for 10th†	Wasim Raja and Wasim Bari at Bridgetown	1976-77

† Denotes record partnership against all countries.

‡ 219 runs were added for this wicket in two separate partnerships: Sadiq Mohammad retired hurt and was replaced by Zaheer Abbas when 60 had been added. The highest partnership by two opening batsmen is 152 by Hanif Mohammad and Imtiaz Ahmed at Bridgetown, 1957-58.

TEN WICKETS OR MORE IN A MATCH

For Pakistan (1)

12-100 (6-34, 6-66)	Fazal Mahmood, Dacca	1958-59

Note: The best match figures by a West Indian bowler are 9-187 (5-66, 4-121), A. M. E. Roberts at Lahore, 1974-75, and 9-95 (8-29, 1-66), C. E. H. Croft at Port-of-Spain, 1976-77.

NEW ZEALAND v INDIA

	Captains					
Season	New Zealand	India	T	NZ	I	D
1955-56I	H. B. Cave	P. R. Umrigar[1]	5	0	2	3
1964-65I	J. R. Reid	Nawab of Pataudi jun.[2]	4	0	1	3
1967-68N	G. T. Dowling	Nawab of Pataudi jun.	4	1	3	0
1969-70I	G. T. Dowling	Nawab of Pataudi jun.	3	1	1	1
1975-76N	G. M. Turner	B. S. Bedi[3]	3	1	1	1
1976-77I	G. M. Turner	B. S. Bedi	3	0	2	1
1980-81N	G. P. Howarth	S. M. Gavaskar	3	1	0	2
	In India		15	1	6	8
	In New Zealand		10	3	4	3
	Totals		25	4	10	11

I Played in India.   N Played in New Zealand.

Notes: [1] Ghulam Ahmed captained in First Test. [2] B. W. Sinclair captained in First Test. [3] S. M. Gavaskar captained in First Test.

HIGHEST INNINGS TOTALS

For New Zealand in New Zealand: 502 at Christchurch, 1967-68
in India: 462-9 dec. at Calcutta, 1964-65
450-2 dec. at Delhi, 1955-56

For India in New Zealand: 414 at Auckland, 1975-76
in India: 537-3 dec. at Madras, 1955-56

LOWEST INNINGS TOTALS

For New Zealand in New Zealand: 100 at Wellington, 1980-81
in India: 127 at Bombay, 1969-70

For India in New Zealand: 81 at Wellington, 1975-76
in India: 88 at Bombay, 1964-65

INDIVIDUAL HUNDREDS IN THE MATCHES 1955-56–1980-81

For New Zealand (16)

120	G. T. Dowling, Bombay...	1964-65	119*	J. R. Reid, Delhi	1955-56
143	G. T. Dowling, Dunedin ..	1967-68	137*†	B. Sutcliffe, Hyderabad....	1955-56
239	G. T. Dowling, Christ-		230*	B. Sutcliffe, Delhi	1955-56
	church......................	1967-68	151*	B. Sutcliffe, Calcutta........	1955-56
102†	J. W. Guy, Hyderabad.....	1955-56	105†	B. R. Taylor, Calcutta	1964-65
137*	G. P. Howarth, Wellington	1980-81	117	G. M. Turner, Christ-	
104	J. M. Parker, Bombay.....	1976-77		church......................	1975-76
123*	J. F. Reid, Christchurch ...	1980-81	113	G. M. Turner, Kanpur.....	1976-77
120	J. R. Reid, Calcutta	1955-56	110	J. G. Wright, Auckland....	1980-81

For India (20)

124†	S. Amarnath, Auckland....	1975-76	153	Nawab of Pataudi jun.,	
109	C. G. Borde, Bombay......	1964-65		Calcutta......................	1964-65
116†	S. M. Gavaskar, Auckland	1975-76	113	Nawab of Pataudi jun.,	
119	S. M. Gavaskar, Bombay..	1976-77		Delhi	1964-65
100*†	A. G. Kripal Singh, Hy-		106*	G. S. Ramchand, Calcutta	1955-56
	derabad......................	1955-56	173	P. Roy, Madras	1955-56
177	V. L. Manjrekar, Delhi....	1955-56	100	P. Roy, Calcutta	1955-56
118†	V. L. Manjrekar, Hydera-		200*	D. N. Sardesai, Bombay...	1964-65
	bad...........................	1955-56	106	D. N. Sardesai, Delhi	1964-65
102*	V. L. Manjrekar, Madras .	1964-65	223†	P. R. Umrigar, Hyderabad	1955-56
231	V. Mankad, Madras........	1955-56	103*	G. R. Viswanath, Kanpur	1976-77
223	V. Mankad, Bombay	1955-56	143	A. L. Wadekar, Wellington	1967-68

† *Signifies hundred on first appearance in New Zealand–India Tests. B. R. Taylor provides the only instance for New Zealand of a player scoring his maiden hundred in first-class cricket in his first Test.*

RECORD PARTNERSHIPS FOR EACH WICKET

For New Zealand

126 for 1st	B. A. G. Murray and G. T. Dowling at Christchurch	1967-68
155 for 2nd	G. T. Dowling and B. E. Congdon at Dunedin	1967-68
222* for 3rd†	B. Sutcliffe and J. R. Reid at Delhi	1955-56
103 for 4th	G. T. Dowling and M. G. Burgess at Christchurch	1967-68
119 for 5th	G. T. Dowling and K. Thomson at Christchurch	1967-68
87 for 6th	J. W. Guy and A. R. MacGibbon at Hyderabad	1955-56
163 for 7th	B. Sutcliffe and B. R. Taylor at Calcutta	1964-65
81 for 8th	V. Pollard and G. E. Vivian at Calcutta	1964-65
69 for 9th	M. G. Burgess and J. C. Alabaster at Dunedin	1967-68
61 for 10th	J. T. Ward and R. O. Collinge at Madras	1964-65

For India

413 for 1st†	V. Mankad and P. Roy at Madras	1955-56
204 for 2nd	S. M. Gavaskar and S. Amarnath at Auckland	1975-76
238 for 3rd	P. R. Umrigar and V. L. Manjrekar at Hyderabad	1955-56
171 for 4th	P. R. Umrigar and A. G. Kripal Singh at Hyderabad	1955-56
127 for 5th	V. L. Manjrekar and G. S. Ramchand at Delhi	1955-56
193* for 6th†	D. N. Sardesai and Hanumant Singh at Bombay	1964-65
116 for 7th	B. P. Patel and S. M. H. Kirmani at Wellington	1975-76
143 for 8th†	R. G. Nadkarni and F. M. Engineer at Madras	1964-65
105 for 9th {	S. M. H. Kirmani and B. S. Bedi at Bombay	1976-77
	S. M. H. Kirmani and N. S. Yadav at Auckland	1980-81
57 for 10th	R. B. Desai and B. S. Bedi at Dunedin	1967-68

† *Denotes record partnership against all countries.*

TEN WICKETS OR MORE IN A MATCH

For New Zealand (1)

11-58 (4-35, 7-23)	R. J. Hadlee, Wellington	1975-76

For India (2)

11-140 (3-64, 8-76)	E. A. S. Prasanna, Auckland	1975-76
12-152 (8-72, 4-80)	S. Venkataraghavan, Delhi	1964-65

NEW ZEALAND v PAKISTAN

		Captains				
Season	New Zealand	Pakistan	T	NZ	P	D
1955-56P	H. B. Cave	A. H. Kardar	3	0	2	1
1964-65N	J. R. Reid	Hanif Mohammad	3	0	0	3
1964-65P	J. R. Reid	Hanif Mohammad	3	0	2	1
1969-70P	G. T. Dowling	Intikhab Alam	3	1	0	2
1972-73N	B. E. Congdon	Intikhab Alam	3	0	1	2
1976-77P	G. M. Turner[1]	Mushtaq Mohammad	3	0	2	1
1978-79N	M. G. Burgess	Mushtaq Mohammad	3	0	1	2
	In Pakistan		12	1	6	5
	In New Zealand		9	0	2	7
	Totals		21	1	8	12

N Played in New Zealand.   P Played in Pakistan.
Note: [1] J. M. Parker captained in Third Test.

HIGHEST INNINGS TOTALS

For New Zealand in New Zealand $\begin{cases} \text{402 at Auckland, 1972-73} \\ \text{402 at Napier, 1978-79} \end{cases}$
in Pakistan: 482-6 dec. at Lahore, 1964-65

For Pakistan in New Zealand: 507-6 dec. at Dunedin, 1972-73
in Pakistan: 565-9 dec. at Karachi, 1976-77
561 at Lahore, 1955-56

LOWEST INNINGS TOTALS

For New Zealand in New Zealand: 156 at Dunedin, 1972-73
in Pakistan: 70 at Dacca, 1955-56

For Pakistan in New Zealand: 187 at Wellington, 1964-65
in Pakistan: 114 at Lahore, 1969-70

INDIVIDUAL HUNDREDS IN THE MATCHES 1955-56–1978-79

For New Zealand (11)

119*	M. G. Burgess, Dacca...... 1969-70	111	S. N. McGregor, Lahore .. 1955-56
111	M. G. Burgess, Lahore 1976-77	107†	R. E. Redmond, Auckland 1972-73
129†	B. A. Edgar, Christchurch 1978-79	128	J. R. Reid, Karachi 1964-65
110	B. F. Hastings, Auckland . 1972-73	130	B. W. Sinclair, Lahore 1964-65
114	G. P. Howarth, Napier..... 1978-79	110†	G. M. Turner, Dacca....... 1969-70
152	W. K. Lees, Karachi........ 1976-77		

For Pakistan (22)

175	Asif Iqbal, Dunedin......... 1972-73	126	Mohammad Ilyas, Karachi 1964-65
166	Asif Iqbal, Lahore........... 1976-77	201	Mushtaq Mohammad, Dunedin 1972-73
104	Asif Iqbal, Napier 1978-79	101	Mushtaq Mohammad, Hyderabad..................... 1976-77
103	Hanif Mohammad, Dacca 1955-56		
100*	Hanif Mohammad, Christchurch...................... 1964-65	107	Mushtaq Mohammad, Karachi.................... 1976-77
203*	Hanif Mohammad, Lahore 1964-65	166	Sadiq Mohammad, Wellington 1972-73
209	Imtiaz Ahmed, Lahore 1955-56		
163†	Javed Miandad, Lahore 1976-77	103*	Sadiq Mohammad, Hyderabad..................... 1976-77
206	Javed Miandad, Karachi ... 1976-77		
160*	Javed Miandad, Christchurch...................... 1978-79	172	Saeed Ahmed, Karachi..... 1964-65
		189	Waqar Hassan, Lahore..... 1955-56
110	Majid J. Khan, Auckland . 1972-73	135	Zaheer Abbas, Auckland.. 1978-79
112	Majid J. Khan, Karachi.... 1976-77		
119*	Majid J. Khan, Napier 1978-79		

† *Signifies hundred on first appearance in New Zealand–Pakistan Tests.*

Note: Mushtaq and Sadiq Mohammad, at Hyderabad in 1976-77, provide the fourth instance in Test matches, after the Chappells (thrice), of brothers each scoring hundreds in the same innings.

RECORD PARTNERSHIPS FOR EACH WICKET

For New Zealand

159 for 1st	R. E. Redmond and G. M. Turner at Auckland	1972-73
195 for 2nd†	J. G. Wright and G. P. Howarth at Napier	1978-79
178 for 3rd	B. W. Sinclair and J. R. Reid at Lahore...............................	1964-65
128 for 4th	B. F. Hastings and M. G. Burgess at Wellington....................	1972-73
183 for 5th†	M. G. Burgess and R. W. Anderson at Lahore........................	1976-77
91 for 6th	M. G. Burgess and W. K. Lees at Karachi............................	1976-77
186 for 7th†	W. K. Lees and R. J. Hadlee at Karachi..............................	1976-77
100 for 8th	B. W. Yuile and D. R. Hadlee at Karachi	1969-70
96 for 9th†	M. G. Burgess and R. S. Cunis at Dacca	1969-70
151 for 10th†	B. F. Hastings and R. O. Collinge at Auckland	1972-73

For Pakistan

147 for 1st‡	Sadiq Mohammad and Majid J. Khan at Karachi	1976-77
114 for 2nd	Mohammad Ilyas and Saeed Ahmed at Rawalpindi..................	1964-65
171 for 3rd	Sadiq Mohammad and Majid J. Khan at Wellington	1972-73
350 for 4th†	Mushtaq Mohammad and Asif Iqbal at Dunedin	1972-73
281 for 5th†	Javed Miandad and Asif Iqbal at Lahore	1976-77
217 for 6th†	Hanif Mohammad and Majid J. Khan at Lahore	1964-65
308 for 7th†	Waqar Hassan and Imtiaz Ahmed at Lahore	1955-56
72 for 8th	Asif Iqbal and Imran Khan at Lahore	1976-77
52 for 9th	Intikhab Alam and Arif Butt at Auckland............................	1964-65
65 for 10th	Salah-ud-Din and Mohammad Farooq at Rawalpindi	1964-65

† *Denotes record partnership against all countries.*
‡ *In the preceding Test of this series, at Hyderabad, 164 runs were added for this wicket by Sadiq Mohammad, Majid J. Khan and Zaheer Abbas. Sadiq Mohammad retired hurt after 136 had been scored.*

TEN WICKETS OR MORE IN A MATCH

For Pakistan (3)

10-182 (5-91, 5-91)	Intikhab Alam, Dacca...	1969-70
11-130 (7-52, 4-78)	Intikhab Alam, Dunedin..	1972-73
11-79 (5-37, 6-42)†	Zulfiqar Ahmed, Karachi...	1955-56

† *Signifies ten wickets or more on first appearance in New Zealand–Pakistan Tests.*

Note: The best match figures by a New Zealand bowler are 9-70 (4-36, 5-34), F. J. Cameron at Auckland, 1964-65.

NEW ZEALAND v SRI LANKA

	Captains					
Season	*New Zealand*	*Sri Lanka*	*T*	*NZ*	*SL*	*D*
1982-83N	G. P. Howarth	D. S. de Silva	2	2	0	0

N Played in New Zealand.

Highest total for New Zealand: 344 at Christchurch.
              Sri Lanka: 240 at Wellington.

Lowest total for New Zealand: 201 at Wellington.
              Sri Lanka: 93 at Wellington.

Highest individual innings for New Zealand: 89 by W. K. Lees at Christchurch.
              Sri Lanka: 79 by R. S. Madugalle at Wellington.

Best innings bowling for New Zealand: 4-33 by R. J. Hadlee at Wellington.
Sri Lanka: 5-60 by V. B. John at Wellington.

Best partnership for New Zealand: 79 for the 8th wicket by J. V. Coney and W. K. Lees at
Christchurch.
Sri Lanka: 130 for the 5th wicket by R. S. Madugalle and D. S. de Silva
at Wellington.

INDIA v PAKISTAN

Season	India	Captains Pakistan	T	I	P	D
1952-53*I*	L. Amarnath	A. H. Kardar	5	2	1	2
1954-55*P*	V. Mankad	A. H. Kardar	5	0	0	5
1960-61*I*	N. J. Contractor	Fazal Mahmood	5	0	0	5
1978-79*P*	B. S. Bedi	Mushtaq Mohammad	3	0	2	1
1979-80*I*	S. M. Gavaskar[1]	Asif Iqbal	6	2	0	4
1982-83*P*	S. M. Gavaskar	Imran Khan	6	0	3	3
	In India..................................		16	4	1	11
	In Pakistan............................		14	0	5	9
Totals...			30	4	6	20

I Played in India.   P Played in Pakistan.

Note: [1]G. R. Viswanath captained in Sixth Test.

HIGHEST INNINGS TOTALS

For India in India: 539-9 dec. at Madras, 1960-61
in Pakistan: 465 at Lahore, 1978-79

For Pakistan in India: 448-8 dec. at Madras, 1960-61
in Pakistan: 652 at Faisalabad, 1982-83

LOWEST INNINGS TOTALS

For India in India: 106 at Lucknow, 1952-53
in Pakistan: 145 at Karachi, 1954-55

For Pakistan in India: 150 at Delhi, 1952-53
in Pakistan: 158 at Dacca, 1954-55

INDIVIDUAL HUNDREDS IN THE MATCHES 1952-53–1982-83

For India (18)

109*	M. Amarnath, Lahore......	1982-83	127*‡	S. M. Gavaskar, Faisalabad	1982-83
120	M. Amarnath, Lahore......	1982-83	146*	V. S. Hazare, Bombay.....	1952-53
103*	M. Amarnath, Karachi.....	1982-83	128	R. J. Shastri, Karachi.......	1982-83
177*	C. G. Borde, Madras.......	1960-61	110†	D. H. Shodhan, Calcutta...	1952-53
111 137 }	S. M. Gavaskar, Karachi ..	1978-79	102	P. R. Umrigar, Bombay ...	1952-53
			108	P. R. Umrigar, Peshawar..	1954-55
166	S. M. Gavaskar, Madras...	1979-80	115	P. R. Umrigar, Kanpur	1960-61

‡ *Carried his bat.*

117	P. R. Umrigar, Madras	1960-61	145†	G. R. Viswanath, Faisala-	
112	P. R. Umrigar, Delhi.......	1960-61		bad...........................	1978-79
146*	D. B. Vengsarkar, Delhi ..	1979-80			

For Pakistan (26)

103*	Alim-ud-Din, Karachi	1954-55	231	Mudassar Nazar, Hydera-	
104†	Asif Iqbal, Faisalabad	1978-79		bad...........................	1982-83
142	Hanif Mohammad, Baha-		152*‡	Mudassar Nazar, Lahore...	1982-83
	walpur.......................	1954-55	152	Mudassar Nazar, Karachi..	1982-83
160	Hanif Mohammad, Bombay	1960-61	101	Mushtaq Mohammad,	
135	Imtiaz Ahmed, Madras.....	1960-61		Delhi........................	1960-61
117	Imran Khan, Faisalabad ...	1982-83	124*	Nazar Mohammad, Luck-	
154*†	Javed Miandad, Faisalabad	1978-79		now	1952-53
100	Javed Miandad, Karachi ...	1978-79	121†	Saeed Ahmed, Bombay	1960-61
126	Javed Miandad, Faisala-		103	Saeed Ahmed, Madras	1960-61
	bad...........................	1982-83	107	Salim Malik, Faisalabad ...	1982-83
280*	Javed Miandad, Hydera-		176†	Zaheer Abbas, Faisalabad	1978-79
	bad...........................	1982-83	235*	Zaheer Abbas, Lahore	1978-79
101*	Mohsin Khan, Lahore	1982-83	215	Zaheer Abbas, Lahore	1982-83
126	Mudassar Nazar, Bangalore	1979-80	186	Zaheer Abbas, Karachi	1982-83
119	Mudassar Nazar, Karachi...	1982-83	168	Zaheer Abbas, Faisalabad.	1982-83

† *Signifies hundred on first appearance in India–Pakistan Tests.*

‡ *Carried his bat.*

RECORD PARTNERSHIPS FOR EACH WICKET

For India

192 for 1st	S. M. Gavaskar and C. P. S. Chauhan at Lahore	1978-79
125 for 2nd	S. M. Gavaskar and M. Amarnath at Hyderabad	1982-83
190 for 3rd	M. Amarnath and Yashpal Sharma at Lahore......................	1982-83
183 for 4th	V. S. Hazare and P. R. Umrigar at Bombay	1952-53
177 for 5th	P. R. Umrigar and C. G. Borde at Madras	1960-61
98 for 6th	S. M. Patil and Kapil Dev at Faisalabad	1982-83
95 for 7th	S. M. H. Kirmani and Kapil Dev at Bombay	1979-80
122 for 8th	S. M. H. Kirmani and Madan Lal at Faisalabad	1982-83
149 for 9th†	P. G. Joshi and R. B. Desai at Bombay	1960-61
109 for 10th†	H. R. Adhikari and Ghulam Ahmed at Delhi......................	1952-53

For Pakistan

162 for 1st	Hanif Mohammad and Imtiaz Ahmed at Madras	1960-61
246 for 2nd	Hanif Mohammad and Saeed Ahmed at Bombay	1960-61
451 for 3rd†	Mudassar Nazar and Javed Miandad at Hyderabad	1982-83
287 for 4th	Javed Miandad and Zaheer Abbas at Faisalabad	1982-83
213 for 5th	Zaheer Abbas and Mudassar Nazar at Karachi	1982-83
207 for 6th	Salim Malik and Imran Khan at Faisalabad	1982-83
88 for 7th	Mushtaq Mohammad and Intikhab Alam at Calcutta	1960-61
82 for 8th	Wasim Raja and Iqbal Qasim at Kanpur............................	1979-80
60 for 9th	Wasim Bari and Iqbal Qasim at Bangalore	1979-80
104 for 10th	Zulfiqar Ahmed and Amir Elahi at Madras........................	1952-53

† *Denotes record partnership against all countries.*

TEN WICKETS OR MORE IN A MATCH

For India (2)

11-146 (4-90, 7-56)	Kapil Dev, Madras	1979-80
13-131 (8-52, 5-79)†	V. Mankad, Delhi	1952-53

For Pakistan (5)

12-94 (5-52, 7-42)	Fazal Mahmood, Lucknow	1952-53
11-79 (3-19, 8-60)	Imran Khan, Karachi	1982-83
11-180 (6-98, 5-82)	Imran Khan, Faisalabad	1982-83
10-175 (4-135, 6-40)	Iqbal Qasim, Bombay	1979-80
11-190 (8-69, 3-121)	Sikander Bakht, Delhi...	1979-80

† *Signifies ten wickets or more on first appearance in India–Pakistan Tests.*

INDIA v SRI LANKA

Season	India		Sri Lanka	T	I	SL	D
		Captains					
1982-83*I*	S. M. Gavaskar		B. Warnapura	1	0	0	1

I Played in India.

One match was played at Madras.

INDIVIDUAL HUNDREDS

For India (2)

155 S. M. Gavaskar
114* S. M. Patil

For Sri Lanka (2)

105⎫
105⎭ L. R. D. Mendis

HIGHEST INNINGS TOTALS

For India: 566-6 dec.
For Sri Lanka: 394.

BEST INNINGS BOWLING

For India: 5-85 by D. R. Doshi.
For Sri Lanka: 5-68 by A. L. F. de Mel.

BEST WICKET PARTNERSHIPS

For India: 173 for the 2nd wicket by S. M. Gavaskar and D. B. Vengsarkar.
For Sri Lanka: 153 for the 3rd wicket by R. L. Dias and L. R. D. Mendis.

PAKISTAN v SRI LANKA

Captains

Season	Pakistan	Sri Lanka	T	P	SL	D
1981-82P	Javed Miandad	B. Warnapura[1]	3	2	0	1

P Played in Pakistan.

Note: [1]L. R. D. Mendis deputised for the official touring captain in the Second Test.

HIGHEST INNINGS TOTALS

For Pakistan: 500-7 dec. at Lahore, 1981-82.
For Sri Lanka: 454 at Faisalabad, 1981-82.

LOWEST INNINGS TOTALS

For Pakistan: 270 at Faisalabad, 1981-82.
For Sri Lanka: 149 at Karachi, 1981-82.

INDIVIDUAL HUNDREDS IN THE MATCHES 1981-82

For Pakistan (4)

153†	Haroon Rashid, Karachi ...	1981-82	100*† Salim Malik, Karachi	1981-82
129	Mohsin Khan, Lahore	1981-82	134† Zaheer Abbas, Lahore	1981-82

For Sri Lanka (2)

109   R. L. Dias, Lahore .... 1981-82 | 157   S. Wettimuny, Faisalabad . 1981-82

† *Signifies hundred on first appearance in Pakistan–Sri Lanka Tests.*

RECORD WICKET PARTNERSHIPS

For Pakistan: 161 for the 4th wicket by Salim Malik and Javed Miandad at Karachi.
For Sri Lanka: 217 for the 2nd wicket by S. Wettimuny and R. L. Dias at Faisalabad.

TEN WICKETS OR MORE IN A MATCH

For Pakistan (1)

14-116 (8-58, 6-58)   Imran Khan, Lahore... 1981-82

Note: The best match figures by a Sri Lankan bowler are 9-162 (4-103, 5-59) by D. S. de Silva at Faisalabad, 1981-82.

SRI LANKAN RECORD PARTNERSHIPS FOR EACH WICKET

77 for 1st	S. Wettimuny and H. M. Goonatillake v Pakistan at Faisalabad..	1981-82
217 for 2nd	S. Wettimuny and R. L. Dias v Pakistan at Faisalabad	1981-82
153 for 3rd	R. L. Dias and L. R. D. Mendis v India at Madras	1982-83
49 for 4th	⎰ S. Wettimuny and R. S. Madugalle first innings v New Zealand at Christchurch	1982-83
	⎱ E. R. N. S. Fernando and R. S. Madugalle second innings v New Zealand at Christchurch	1982-83
130 for 5th	R. S. Madugalle and D. S. de Silva v New Zealand at Wellington	1982-83
89 for 6th	L. R. D. Mendis and A. N. Ranasinghe v India at Madras	1982-83
77 for 7th	A. N. Ranasinghe and D. S. de Silva v India at Madras	1982-83
61 for 8th	R. S. Madugalle and D. S. de Silva v Pakistan at Faisalabad	1981-82
42 for 9th	J. R. Ratnayeke and A. L. F. de Mel v India at Madras	1982-83
32 for 10th	A. L. F. de Mel and G. R. A. de Silva v India at Madras	1982-83

MISCELLANEOUS

RELATIONS IN TEST CRICKET

FATHERS AND SONS

England
J. Hardstaff (5 Tests, 1907-08) and J. Hardstaff jun. (23 Tests, 1935–1948).
Sir L. Hutton (79 Tests, 1937–1954-55) and R. A. Hutton (5 Tests, 1971).
F. T. Mann (5 Tests, 1922-23) and F. G. Mann (7 Tests, 1948-49–1949).
J. H. Parks (1 Test, 1937) and J. M. Parks (46 Tests, 1954–1967-68).
F. W. Tate (1 Test, 1902) and M. W. Tate (39 Tests, 1924–1935).
C. L. Townsend (2 Tests, 1899) and D. C. H. Townsend (3 Tests, 1934-35).

Australia
E. J. Gregory (1 Test, 1876-77) and S. E. Gregory (58 Tests, 1890–1912).

South Africa
F. Hearne (4 Tests, 1891-92–1895-96) and G. A. L. Hearne (3 Tests, 1922-23–1924).
    F. Hearne also played 2 Tests for England in 1888-89.
J. D. Lindsay (3 Tests, 1947) and D. T. Lindsay (19 Tests, 1963-64–1969-70).
A. W. Nourse (45 Tests, 1902-03–1924) and A. D. Nourse (34 Tests, 1935–1951).
L. R. Tuckett (1 Test, 1913-14) and L. Tuckett (9 Tests, 1947–1948-49).

West Indies
G. A. Headley (22 Tests, 1929-30–1953-54) and R. G. A. Headley (2 Tests, 1973).
O. C. Scott (8 Tests, 1928–1930-31) and A. P. H. Scott (1 Test, 1952-53).

New Zealand
W. M. Anderson (1 Test, 1945-46) and R. W. Anderson (9 Tests, 1976-77–1978).
W. A. Hadlee (11 Tests, 1937–1950-51) and D. R. Hadlee (26 Tests, 1969–1977-78); R. J. Hadlee (44 Tests, 1972-73–1983).
H. G. Vivian (7 Tests, 1931–1937) and G. E. Vivian (5 Tests, 1964-65–1971-72).

India
L. Amarnath (24 Tests, 1933-34–1952-53) and M. Amarnath (37 Tests, 1969-70–1982-83); S. Amarnath (10 Tests, 1975-76–1978-79).
D. K. Gaekwad (11 Tests, 1952–1960-61) and A. D. Gaekwad (26 Tests, 1974-75–1982-83).
Nawab of Pataudi (Iftikhar Ali Khan) (3 Tests, 1946) and Nawab of Pataudi (Mansur Ali Khan) (46 Tests, 1961-62–1974-75).
    Nawab of Pataudi sen. also played 3 Tests for England, 1932-33–1934.
V. Mankad (44 Tests, 1946–1958-59) and A. V. Mankad (22 Tests, 1969-70–1977-78).
Pankaj Roy (43 Tests, 1951-52–1960-61) and Pranab Roy (2 Tests, 1981-82).

India and Pakistan
M. Jahangir Khan (4 Tests, 1932–1936) and Majid J. Khan (63 Tests, 1964-65–1982-83).
S. Wazir Ali (7 Tests, 1932–1936) and Khalid Wazir (2 Tests, 1954).

Pakistan
Nazar Mohammad (5 Tests, 1952-53) and Mudassar Nazar (35 Tests, 1976-77–1982-83).

GRANDFATHERS AND GRANDSONS

Australia
V. Y. Richardson (19 Tests, 1924-25–1935-36) and G. S. Chappell (82 Tests, 1970-71–1982-83);
   I. M. Chappell (75 Tests, 1964-65–1979-80); T. M. Chappell (3 Tests, 1981).

GREAT-GRANDFATHER AND GREAT-GRANDSON

Australia
W. H. Cooper (2 Tests, 1881-82 and 1884-85) and A. P. Sheahan (31 Tests, 1967-68–1973-74).

BROTHERS IN SAME TEST TEAM

England
E. M., G. F. and W. G. Grace: 1 Test, 1880.
C. T. and G. B. Studd: 4 Tests, 1882-83.
A. and G. G. Hearne: 1 Test, 1891-92.
   F. Hearne, their brother, played in this match for South Africa.
D. W. and P. E. Richardson: 1 Test, 1957.

Australia
E. J. and D. W. Gregory: 1 Test, 1876-77.
C. and A. C. Bannerman: 1 Test, 1878-79.
G. and W. F. Giffen: 2 Tests, 1891-92.
G. H. S. and A. E. Trott: 3 Tests, 1894-95.
I. M. and G. S. Chappell: 43 Tests, 1970-71–1979-80.

South Africa
S. J. and S. D. Snooke: 1 Test, 1907.
R. H. M. and P. A. M. Hands: 1 Test, 1913-14.
E. A. B. and A. M. B. Rowan: 9 Tests, 1948-49–1951.
P. M. and R. G. Pollock: 23 Tests, 1963-64–1969-70.
A. J. and D. B. Pithey: 5 Tests, 1963-64.

West Indies
G. C. and R. S. Grant: 4 Tests, 1934-35.
J. B. and V. H. Stollmeyer: 1 Test, 1939.
D. St E. and E. St E. Atkinson: 1 Test, 1957-58.

New Zealand
J. J. and M. D. Crowe: 2 Tests, 1983.
D. R. and R. J. Hadlee: 10 Tests, 1973–1977-78.
H. J. and G. P. Howarth: 4 Tests, 1974-75–1976-77.
J. M. and N. M. Parker: 3 Tests, 1976-77.
B. P. and J. G. Bracewell: 1 Test, 1980-81.

India
S. Wazir Ali and S. Nazir Ali: 2 Tests, 1932–1933-34.
L. Ramji and Amar Singh: 1 Test, 1933-34.
C. K. and C. S. Nayudu: 4 Tests, 1933-34–1936.
A. G. Kripal Singh and A. G. Milkha Singh: 1 Test, 1961-62.
S. and M. Amarnath: 8 Tests, 1975-76–1978-79.

Pakistan
Wazir and Hanif Mohammad: 18 Tests, 1952-53–1959-60.
Wazir and Mushtaq Mohammad: 1 Test, 1958-59.
Hanif and Mushtaq Mohammad: 19 Tests, 1960-61–1969-70.
Hanif, Mushtaq and Sadiq Mohammad: 1 Test, 1969-70.
Mushtaq and Sadiq Mohammad: 26 Tests, 1969-70–1978–79.

Sri Lanka
M. D. and S. Wettimuny: 2 Tests, 1982-83.

TEST MATCH GROUNDS

In Chronological Sequence

	City and Ground	Date of First Test	Match
1.	Melbourne, Melbourne Cricket Ground	March 15, 1877	Australia v England
2.	London, Kennington Oval	September 6, 1880	England v Australia
3.	Sydney, Sydney Cricket Ground (No. 1)	February 17, 1882	Australia v England
4.	Manchester, Old Trafford	July 11, 1884	England v Australia

This match was due to have started on July 10, but rain prevented any play.

	City and Ground	Date of First Test	Match
5.	London, Lord's	July 21, 1884	England v Australia
6.	Adelaide, Adelaide Oval	December 12, 1884	Australia v England
7.	Port Elizabeth, St George's Park	March 12, 1889	South Africa v England
8.	Cape Town, Newlands	March 25, 1889	South Africa v England
9.	Johannesburg, Old Wanderers*	March 2, 1896	South Africa v England
10.	Nottingham, Trent Bridge	June 1, 1899	England v Australia
11.	Leeds, Headingley	June 29, 1899	England v Australia
12.	Birmingham, Edgbaston	May 29, 1902	England v Australia
13.	Sheffield, Bramall Lane*	July 3, 1902	England v Australia
14.	Durban, Lord's*	January 1, 1910	South Africa v England
15.	Durban, Kingsmead	January 18,1923	South Africa v England
16.	Brisbane, Exhibition Ground*	November 30, 1928	Australia v England
17.	Christchurch, Lancaster Park	January 10, 1930	New Zealand v England
18.	Bridgetown, Kensington Oval	January 11, 1930	West Indies v England
19.	Wellington, Basin Reserve	January 24, 1930	New Zealand v England
20.	Port-of-Spain, Queen's Park Oval	February 1, 1930	West Indies v England
21.	Auckland, Eden Park	February 17, 1930	New Zealand v England

This match was due to have started on February 14, but rain prevented any play on the first two days. February 16 was a Sunday.

	City and Ground	Date of First Test	Match
22.	Georgetown, Bourda	February 21, 1930	West Indies v England
23.	Kingston, Sabina Park	April 3, 1930	West Indies v England
24.	Brisbane, Woolloongabba	November 27, 1931	Australia v South Africa
25.	Bombay, Gymkhana Ground*	December 15, 1933	India v England
26.	Calcutta, Eden Gardens	January 5, 1934	India v England
27.	Madras, Chepauk	February 10, 1934	India v England
28.	Delhi, Feroz Shah Kotla	November 10, 1948	India v West Indies
29.	Bombay, Brabourne Stadium*	December 9, 1948	India v West Indies
30.	Johannesburg, Ellis Park*	December 27, 1948	South Africa v England
31.	Kanpur, Green Park (Modi Stadium)	January 12, 1952	India v England
32.	Lucknow, University Ground*	October 25, 1952	India v Pakistan
33.	Dacca, Dacca Stadium*	January 1, 1955	Pakistan v India
34.	Bahawalpur, Dring Stadium	January 15, 1955	Pakistan v India
35.	Lahore, Lawrence Gardens (Bagh-i-Jinnah)*	January 29, 1955	Pakistan v India
36.	Peshawar, Gymkhana Ground	February 13, 1955	Pakistan v India
37.	Karachi, National Stadium	February 26, 1955	Pakistan v India

	City and Ground	Date of First Test	Match
38.	Dunedin, Carisbrook	March 11, 1955	New Zealand v England
39.	Hyderabad, Fateh Maidan		
	(Lal Bahadur Stadium)	November 19, 1955	India v New Zealand
40.	Madras Corporation Stadium*	January 6, 1956	India v New Zealand
41.	Johannesburg, New Wanderers	December 24, 1956	South Africa v England
42.	Lahore, Gaddafi Stadium	November 21, 1959	Pakistan v Australia
43.	Rawalpindi, Rawalpindi Club Ground	March 27, 1965	Pakistan v New Zealand
44.	Nagpur, Vidarbha Cricket		
	Association Ground	October 3, 1969	India v New Zealand
45.	Perth, Western Australian		
	Cricket Association Ground	December 11, 1970	Australia v England
46.	Hyderabad, Niaz Stadium	March 16, 1973	Pakistan v England
47.	Bangalore, Karnataka		
	Cricket Association Ground	November 22, 1974	India v West Indies
48.	Bombay, Wankhede Stadium	January 23, 1975	India v West Indies
49.	Faisalabad, Iqbal Park	October 16, 1978	Pakistan v India
50.	Napier, McLean Park	February 16, 1979	New Zealand v Pakistan
51.	Multan, Ibn-e-Qasim Bagh Stadium	December 30, 1980	Pakistan v West Indies
52.	St John's (Antigua), Recreation Ground	March 27, 1981	West Indies v England
53.	Colombo, Saravanamuttu Oval	February 17, 1982	Sri Lanka v England
54.	Kandy, Asgiriya Stadium	April 22, 1983	Sri Lanka v Australia

Denotes no longer used for Test matches. In some instances the ground is no longer in existence.

ENGLAND v REST OF THE WORLD

In 1970, owing to the cancellation of the South African tour to England, a series of matches was arranged, with the trappings of a full Test series, between England and the Rest of the World. It was played for the Guinness Trophy.

	Captains				
England	Rest		M	E	R
R. Illingworth	G. S. Sobers		5	1	4

HIGHEST TOTALS FOR AN INNINGS

By England		**By Rest of the World**
409 at Birmingham		563-9 at Birmingham

LOWEST TOTALS FOR AN INNINGS

By England		**By Rest of the World**
127 at Lord's		276 at Nottingham

INDIVIDUAL HUNDREDS IN THE MATCHES

For England (3)

157	G. Boycott, The Oval	113*	B. W. Luckhurst, Nottingham
110	B. L. D'Oliveira, Birmingham		

For Rest of the World (8)

119	E. J. Barlow, Lord's		101	C. H. Lloyd, Birmingham
142	E. J. Barlow, Nottingham		114	R. G. Pollock, The Oval
100	R. B. Kanhai, The Oval		183	G. S. Sobers, Lord's
114*	C. H. Lloyd, Nottingham		114	G. S. Sobers, Leeds

TEN WICKETS OR MORE IN A MATCH

For Rest of the World (1)

12-142 (7-64, 5-78) E. J. Barlow, Leeds.

Note: The best match figures by an England bowler were 7-106 (4-43, 3-63), B. L. D'Oliveira, Nottingham; 7-130 (4-59, 3-71), A. W. Greig, Nottingham; and 7-117 (7-83, 0-34), P. Lever, The Oval.

HAT-TRICK AND FOUR WICKETS IN FIVE BALLS

E. J. Barlow (Rest of the World), Leeds.

APPEARANCES FOR REST OF THE WORLD

E. J. Barlow (5), F. M. Engineer (2), L. R. Gibbs (4), Intikhab Alam (5), R. B. Kanhai (5), C. H. Lloyd (5), G. D. McKenzie (3), D. L. Murray (3), Mushtaq Mohammad (2), P. M. Pollock (1), R. G. Pollock (5), M. J. Procter (5), B. A. Richards (5), G. S. Sobers (5).

Note: A list of those players who appeared for England in these matches may be found on page 123.

GENTLEMEN v PLAYERS

The highest individual scores were:

266*	J. B. Hobbs	Scarborough.	1925	215	W. G. Grace	The Oval.....	1870
247	R. Abel	The Oval.....	1901	203	T. W. Hayward	The Oval.....	1904
241	L. Hutton	Scarborough.	1953	201	L. E. G. Ames	Folkestone..	1933
232*	C. B. Fry	Lord's.........	1903	195	R. Abel	The Oval.....	1899
223	C. P. Mead	Scarborough.	1911	194*	E. H. Hendren	The Oval.....	1932
217	W. G. Grace	Hove	1871				

Notes: W. G. Grace made no fewer than fifteen hundreds for Gentlemen v Players. On his 58th birthday – at The Oval in July 1906 – he scored 74.

J. B. Hobbs in all matches under this title scored sixteen hundreds, and had an aggregate of 4,052 runs with an average of 54.75.

The match, first played in 1806, has not been contested since 1962, owing to the abolition of the amateur status in first-class cricket.

There were 137 matches played at Lord's from 1806; Players won 68, Gentlemen won 41, and 28 were drawn. Individual hundreds and results since 1919 appeared in *Wisden* 1963, page 358.

LARGE ATTENDANCES

Test Series

943,000	Australia v England (5 Tests)	1936-37
In England		
549,650	England v Australia (5 Tests)	1953

Test Match

†350,534	Australia v England, Melbourne (Third Test)	1936-37
325,000+	India v England, Calcutta (Second Test)..................................	1972-73
In England		
158,000+	England v Australia, Leeds (Fourth Test)	1948
137,915	England v Australia, Lord's (Second Test)	1953

Test Match Day

90,800	Australia v West Indies, Melbourne (Fifth Test, 2nd day)	1960-61

Other First-Class Matches in England

80,000+	Surrey v Yorkshire, The Oval (3 days)	1906
78,792	Yorkshire v Lancashire, Leeds (3 days)	1904
76,617	Lancashire v Yorkshire, Manchester (3 days)............................	1926

One-day International

84,153	Australia v England, Melbourne	1982-83

† *Although no official figures are available, the attendance at the Fourth Test between India and England at Calcutta, 1981-82, was thought to have exceeded this figure.*

LORD'S CRICKET GROUND

Lord's and the MCC were founded in 1787. The Club has enjoyed an uninterrupted career since that date, but there have been three grounds known as Lord's. The first (1787-1810) was situated where Dorset Square now is; the second (1809-13), at North Bank, had to be abandoned owing to the cutting of the Regent's Canal; and the third, opened in 1814, is the present one at St John's Wood. It was not until 1866 that the freehold of Lord's was secured by the MCC. The present pavilion was erected in 1890 at a cost of £21,000.

HIGHEST INDIVIDUAL SCORES MADE AT LORD'S

316*	J. B. Hobbs	Surrey v Middlesex..............................	1926
315*	P. Holmes..........	Yorkshire v Middlesex	1925
281*	W. H. Ponsford ..	Australians v MCC	1934
278	W. Ward	MCC v Norfolk (with E. H. Budd, T. Vigne and F. Ladbroke)..................................	1820
278	D. G. Bradman ..	Australians v MCC..............................	1938
277*	E. H. Hendren ...	Middlesex v Kent	1922

HIGHEST TOTALS OBTAINED AT LORD'S

First-Class Matches

729-6	Australia v England	1930
665	West Indians v Middlesex	1939
652-8	West Indies v England	1973
629	England v India	1974
612-8	Middlesex v Nottinghamshire..	1921

610-5	Australians v Gentlemen	1948
609-8	Cambridge University v MCC and Ground	1913
608-7	Middlesex v Hampshire	1919
607	MCC and Ground v Cambridge University	1902

Minor Match

| 735-9 | MCC and Ground v Wiltshire | 1888 |

BIGGEST HIT AT LORD'S

The only known instance of a batsman hitting a ball over the present pavilion at Lord's occurred when A. E. Trott, appearing for MCC against Australians on July 31, August 1, 2, 1899, drove M. A. Noble so far and high that the ball struck a chimney pot and fell behind the building.

THROWING THE CRICKET BALL

140 yards 2 feet, Robert Percival, on the Durham Sands, Co. Durham Racecourse .. 1884
   (There is evidence which suggests that this may have been in 1882.)
140 yards 9 inches, Ross Mackenzie, at Toronto... 1872

Notes: W. F. Forbes, on March 16, 1876, threw 132 yards at the Eton College Sports. He was then 18 years of age.

William Yardley, while a boy at Rugby, threw 100 yards with his right hand and 78 yards with his left .

Charles Arnold, of Cambridge, once threw 112 yards with the wind and 108 against. W. H. Game, at The Oval in 1875, threw the ball 111 yards and then back the same distance. W. G. Grace threw 109 yards one way and back 105, and George Millyard 108 with the wind and 103 against. At The Oval in 1868, W. G. Grace made three successive throws of 116, 117 and 118 yards, and then threw back over 100 yards. D. G. Foster (Warwickshire) threw 133 yards, and in 1930 he made a Danish record with 120.1 metres – about 130 yards.

DATES OF FORMATION OF COUNTY CLUBS NOW FIRST-CLASS

County	First known county organisation	Present Club Original date	Reorganisation, if substantial
Derbyshire	November 4, 1870	November 4, 1870	—
Essex	By May, 1790	January 14, 1876	—
Glamorgan	1863	July 6, 1888	—
Gloucestershire	November 3, 1863	1871	—
Hampshire	April 3, 1849	August 12, 1863	July, 1879
Kent	August 6, 1842	March 1, 1859	December 6, 1870
Lancashire	January 12, 1864	January 12, 1864	—
Leicestershire	By August, 1820	March 25, 1879	—
Middlesex	December 15, 1863	February 2, 1864	—
Northamptonshire	1820	1820	July 31, 1878
Nottinghamshire	March/April, 1841	March/April, 1841	December 11, 1866
Somerset	October 15, 1864	August 18, 1875	—
Surrey	August 22, 1845	August 22, 1845	—
Sussex	June 16, 1836	March 1, 1839	August, 1857
Warwickshire	May, 1826	1882	—
Worcestershire	1844	March 5, 1865	—
Yorkshire	March 7, 1861	January 8, 1863	December 10, 1891

DATES OF FORMATION OF CLUBS IN THE
CURRENT MINOR COUNTIES CHAMPIONSHIP

County	First known county organisation	Present Club
Bedfordshire	May, 1847	November 3, 1899
Berkshire	By May, 1841	March 17, 1895
Buckinghamshire	November, 1864	January 15, 1891
Cambridgeshire	March 13, 1844	June 6, 1891
Cheshire	1819	September 29, 1908
Cornwall	1813	November 12, 1894
Cumberland	January 2, 1884	April 10, 1948
Devon	1824	November 26, 1899
Dorset	1862 *or* 1871	February 5, 1896
Durham	January 24, 1874	May 10, 1882
Hertfordshire	1838	March 8, 1876
Lincolnshire	1853	September 28, 1906
Norfolk	January 11, 1827	October 14, 1876
Northumberland	1834	December, 1895
Oxfordshire	1787	December 14, 1921
Shropshire	1819 *or* 1829	June 28, 1956
Staffordshire	November 24, 1871	November 24, 1871
Suffolk	July 27, 1864	August, 1932
Wiltshire	February 24, 1881	January, 1893

CONSTITUTION OF COUNTY CHAMPIONSHIP

There are references in the sporting press to a champion county as early as 1825, but the list is not continuous and in some years only two counties contested the title. The earliest reference in any cricket publication is from 1864, and at this time there were eight leading counties who have come to be regarded as first-class from that date – Cambridgeshire, Hampshire, Kent, Middlesex, Nottinghamshire, Surrey, Sussex and Yorkshire. The newly formed Lancashire club began playing inter-county matches in 1865, Gloucestershire in 1870 and Derbyshire in 1871, and they are therefore regarded as first-class from these respective dates. Cambridgeshire dropped out after 1871, Hampshire, who had not played inter-county matches in certain seasons, after 1885, and Derbyshire after 1887. Somerset, who had played matches against the first-class counties since 1879, were regarded as first-class from 1882 to 1885, and were admitted formally to the Championship in 1891. In 1894, Derbyshire, Essex, Leicestershire and Warwickshire were granted first-class status, but did not compete in the Championship until 1895 when Hampshire returned. Worcestershire, Northamptonshire and Glamorgan were admitted to the Championship in 1899, 1905 and 1921 respectively and are regarded as first-class from these dates. An invitation in 1921 to Buckinghamshire to enter the Championship was declined, owing to the lack of necessary playing facilities, and an application by Devon in 1948 was unsuccessful.

MOST COUNTY CHAMPIONSHIP APPEARANCES

763	W. Rhodes	Yorkshire	1898-1930
707	F. E. Woolley	Kent	1906-38
665	C. P. Mead	Hampshire	1906-36

MOST CONSECUTIVE COUNTY CHAMPIONSHIP APPEARANCES

423	K. G. Suttle	Sussex	1954-69
412	J. G. Binks	Yorkshire	1955-69
399	J. Vine	Sussex	1899-1914
344	E. H. Killick	Sussex	1898-1912
326	C. N. Woolley	Northamptonshire	1913-31
305	A. H. Dyson	Glamorgan	1930-47
301	B. Taylor	Essex	1961-72

Notes: J. Vine made 417 consecutive appearances for Sussex in *all* first-class matches between July 1900 and September 1914.

J. G. Binks did not miss a Championship match for Yorkshire between making his début in June 1955 and retiring at the end of the 1969 season.

CHAMPION COUNTY SINCE 1864

Note: The earliest county champions were decided usually by the fewest matches lost, but in 1888 an unofficial points system was introduced. In 1890, the Championship was constituted officially. Since 1977, it has been sponsored by Schweppes.

1864	Surrey	1898	Yorkshire	1948	Glamorgan
1865	Nottinghamshire	1899	Surrey	1949	{ Middlesex
1866	Middlesex	1900	Yorkshire		{ Yorkshire
1867	Yorkshire	1901	Yorkshire	1950	{ Lancashire
1868	Nottinghamshire	1902	Yorkshire		{ Surrey
1869	{ Nottinghamshire	1903	Middlesex	1951	Warwickshire
	{ Yorkshire	1904	Lancashire	1952	Surrey
1870	Yorkshire	1905	Yorkshire	1953	Surrey
1871	Nottinghamshire	1906	Kent	1954	Surrey
1872	Nottinghamshire	1907	Nottinghamshire	1955	Surrey
1873	{ Gloucestershire	1908	Yorkshire	1956	Surrey
	{ Nottinghamshire	1909	Kent	1957	Surrey
1874	Gloucestershire	1910	Kent	1958	Surrey
1875	Nottinghamshire	1911	Warwickshire	1959	Yorkshire
1876	Gloucestershire	1912	Yorkshire	1960	Yorkshire
1877	Gloucestershire	1913	Kent	1961	Hampshire
1878	Undecided	1914	Surrey	1962	Yorkshire
1879	{ Nottinghamshire	1919	Yorkshire	1963	Yorkshire
	{ Lancashire	1920	Middlesex	1964	Worcestershire
1880	Nottinghamshire	1921	Middlesex	1965	Worcestershire
1881	Lancashire	1922	Yorkshire	1966	Yorkshire
1882	{ Nottinghamshire	1923	Yorkshire	1967	Yorkshire
	{ Lancashire	1924	Yorkshire	1968	Yorkshire
1883	Nottinghamshire	1925	Yorkshire	1969	Glamorgan
1884	Nottinghamshire	1926	Lancashire	1970	Kent
1885	Nottinghamshire	1927	Lancashire	1971	Surrey
1886	Nottinghamshire	1928	Lancashire	1972	Warwickshire
1887	Surrey	1929	Nottinghamshire	1973	Hampshire
1888	Surrey	1930	Lancashire	1974	Worcestershire
1889	{ Surrey	1931	Yorkshire	1975	Leicestershire
	{ Lancashire	1932	Yorkshire	1976	Middlesex
	{ Nottinghamshire	1933	Yorkshire	1977	{ Middlesex
1890	Surrey	1934	Lancashire		{ Kent
1891	Surrey	1935	Yorkshire	1978	Kent
1892	Surrey	1936	Derbyshire	1979	Essex
1893	Yorkshire	1937	Yorkshire	1980	Middlesex
1894	Surrey	1938	Yorkshire	1981	Nottinghamshire
1895	Surrey	1939	Yorkshire	1982	Middlesex
1896	Yorkshire	1946	Yorkshire	1983	Essex
1897	Lancashire	1947	Middlesex		

Notes: The title has been won outright as follows: Yorkshire 31 times, Surrey 18, Nottinghamshire 13, Lancashire 8, Middlesex 8, Kent 6, Gloucestershire 3, Warwickshire 3, Worcestershire 3, Glamorgan 2, Hampshire 2, Essex 2, Derbyshire 1, Leicestershire 1.

Eight times the title has been shared as follows: Nottinghamshire 5, Lancashire 4, Middlesex 2, Surrey 2, Yorkshire 2, Gloucestershire 1.

The earliest date the Championship has been won in any season since it was expanded in 1895 was August 12, 1910, by Kent.

THE MINOR COUNTIES CHAMPIONS

1895	Norfolk	1924	Berkshire	1958	Yorkshire II
	Durham	1925	Buckinghamshire	1959	Warwickshire II
	Worcestershire	1926	Durham	1960	Lancashire II
1896	Worcestershire	1927	Staffordshire	1961	Somerset II
1897	Worcestershire	1928	Berkshire	1962	Warwickshire II
1898	Worcestershire	1929	Oxfordshire	1963	Cambridgeshire
1899	Northamptonshire	1930	Durham	1964	Lancashire II
	Buckinghamshire	1931	Leicestershire II	1965	Somerset II
	Glamorgan	1932	Buckinghamshire	1966	Lincolnshire
1900	Durham	1933	Undecided	1967	Cheshire
	Northamptonshire	1934	Lancashire II	1968	Yorkshire II
1901	Durham	1935	Middlesex II	1969	Buckinghamshire
1902	Wiltshire	1936	Hertfordshire	1970	Bedfordshire
1903	Northamptonshire	1937	Lancashire II	1971	Yorkshire II
1904	Northamptonshire	1938	Buckinghamshire	1972	Bedfordshire
1905	Norfolk	1939	Surrey II	1973	Shropshire
1906	Staffordshire	1946	Suffolk	1974	Oxfordshire
1907	Lancashire II	1947	Yorkshire II	1975	Hertfordshire
1908	Staffordshire	1948	Lancashire II	1976	Durham
1909	Wiltshire	1949	Lancashire II	1977	Suffolk
1910	Norfolk	1950	Surrey II	1978	Devon
1911	Staffordshire	1951	Kent II	1979	Suffolk
1912	In abeyance	1952	Buckinghamshire	1980	Durham
1913	Norfolk	1953	Berkshire	1981	Durham
1920	Staffordshire	1954	Surrey II	1982	Oxfordshire
1921	Staffordshire	1955	Surrey II	1983	Hertfordshire
1922	Buckinghamshire	1956	Kent II		
1923	Buckinghamshire	1957	Yorkshire II		

SECOND ELEVEN CHAMPIONS

1959	Gloucestershire	1968	Surrey	1977	Yorkshire
1960	Northamptonshire	1969	Kent	1978	Sussex
1961	Kent	1970	Kent	1979	Warwickshire
1962	Worcestershire	1971	Hampshire	1980	Glamorgan
1963	Worcestershire	1972	Nottinghamshire	1981	Hampshire
1964	Lancashire	1973	Essex	1982	Worcestershire
1965	Glamorgan	1974	Middlesex	1983	Leicestershire
1966	Surrey	1975	Surrey		
1967	Hampshire	1976	Kent		

FEATURES OF 1983

Double-Hundreds

252	W. Larkins	Northamptonshire v Glamorgan at Cardiff.
243*	A. I. Kallicharran	Warwickshire v Glamorgan at Birmingham.
236	W. Larkins	Northamptonshire v Derbyshire at Derby.
216	M. W. Gatting	Middlesex v New Zealanders at Lord's.
216	I. V. A. Richards	Somerset v Leicestershire at Leicester.
214*	G. Boycott	Yorkshire v Nottinghamshire at Worksop.
209*	A. I. Kallicharran	Warwickshire v Lancashire at Birmingham.
208*	T. A. Lloyd	Warwickshire v Gloucestershire at Birmingham.
207	R. T. Robinson	Nottinghamshire v Warwickshire at Nottingham.
201*	N. E. Briers	Leicestershire v Warwickshire at Birmingham.

Hundred in Each Innings of a Match

168	119	D. G. Aslett	Kent v Derbyshire at Chesterfield.
102	152*	M. R. Benson	Kent v Warwickshire at Birmingham.
163	141*	G. Boycott	Yorkshire v Nottinghamshire at Bradford.
139	124	R. J. Boyd-Moss .	Cambridge University v Oxford University at Lord's.
104	100*	C. G. Greenidge .	Hampshire v Lancashire at Liverpool.
152	118*	A. I. Kallicharran.	Warwickshire v Sussex at Birmingham.

Fastest Hundreds

35 minutes: S. J. O'Shaughnessy for Lancashire v Leicestershire at Manchester.
41 minutes: N. F. M. Popplewell for Somerset v Gloucestershire at Bath.

Hundred Before Lunch

G. Boycott, Yorkshire v Nottinghamshire at Bradford (3rd day).
G. A. Gooch, Essex v Cambridge University at Cambridge (1st day).
W. Larkins, Northamptonshire v Glamorgan at Cardiff (1st day; he also scored 100 between lunch and tea).

Hundred on Début

100 D. A. Banks for Worcestershire v Oxford University at Oxford.
122 A. A. Metcalfe for Yorkshire v Nottinghamshire at Bradford.

First to 1,000 Runs

K. S. McEwan (Essex) on June 22.

First to 2,000 Runs

K. S. McEwan (Essex) on August 25.

Carrying Bat Through Completed Innings

J. C. Balderstone (100* out of 198), Leicestershire v Worcestershire at Hereford.
G. D. Barlow (44* out of 83), Middlesex v Essex at Chelmsford.
G. Boycott (112* out of 233), Yorkshire v Derbyshire at Sheffield.
R. G. P. Ellis (103* out of 161), Oxford University v Glamorgan at Oxford.
J. A. Hopkins (109* out of 240), Glamorgan v Derbyshire at Swansea.
T. A. Lloyd (124* out of 230), Warwickshire v Surrey at The Oval.
J. A. Ormrod (63* out of 136), Worcestershire v Derbyshire at Derby.

Partnerships of 250 and over

342 (2nd wicket) W. Larkins (187) and P. Willey (147*), Northamptonshire v Lancashire at Northampton – county record.
321 (3rd wicket) C. L. Smith (193) and T. E. Jesty (187), Hampshire v Derbyshire at Derby.
318 (3rd wicket) C. T. Radley (119) and M. W. Gatting (216), Middlesex v New Zealanders at Lord's.
308 (2nd wicket) T. A. Lloyd (123) and A. I. Kallicharran (243*), Warwickshire v Glamorgan at Birmingham.
293 (2nd wicket) T. A. Lloyd (126) and A. I. Kallicharran (209*), Warwickshire v Lancashire at Birmingham.
290 (2nd wicket) D. R. Turner (122*) and M. C. J. Nicholas (158), Hampshire v Oxford University at Oxford.
289 (2nd wicket) T. A. Lloyd (208*) and D. L. Amiss (142), Warwickshire v Gloucestershire at Birmingham.
268 (5th wicket) M. W. Gatting (160) and J. E. Emburey (133), Middlesex v Essex at Chelmsford.
268 (6th wicket) J. N. Shepherd (168) and D. A. Graveney (94), Gloucestershire v Warwickshire at Birmingham.
263 (1st wicket) G. A. Gooch (174) and B. R. Hardie (129), Essex v Cambridge University at Cambridge.

First-Wicket Hundred in Both Innings of a Match

158	132	C. L. Smith and V. P. Terry, Hampshire v Lancashire at Bournemouth.
180	118	G. D. Barlow and A. J. T. Miller, Middlesex v Northamptonshire at Lord's.

Eight Wickets in an Innings

Eight for 42 S. R. Barwick........ Glamorgan v Worcestershire at Worcester.
Eight for 46 S. T. Jefferies........ Lancashire v Nottinghamshire at Nottingham.

Thirteen or More Wickets in a Match

Fourteen for 158 (7-103 and 7-55) D. L. Underwood .. Kent v Worcestershire at Canterbury.
Thirteen for 161 (7-88 and 6-73) D. L. Underwood .. Kent v Nottinghamshire at Nottingham.

Hat-tricks

G. J. F. Ferris .... Leicestershire v Northamptonshire at Leicester.
D. A. Graveney..... Gloucestershire v Leicestershire at Leicester (in a sequence of four wickets in five balls).
Imran Khan .... Sussex v Warwickshire at Birmingham.
M. D. Marshall...... Hampshire v Somerset at Taunton (in a sequence of four wickets in five balls).
N. Phillip.............. Essex v Northamptonshire at Wellingborough.

Outstanding Analyses

4.1–1–6–6 Imran Khan Sussex v Warwickshire at Birmingham (including the hat-trick).
7.3–4–4–6 N. Phillip.... Essex v Surrey at Chelmsford.

First to 100 Wickets

J. E. Emburey (Middlesex) on September 1.

1,000 Runs and 50 Wickets

R. C. Ontong (Glamorgan) .... 1,310 runs and 56 wickets.
J. N. Shepherd (Gloucestershire) ... 1,025 runs and 67 wickets.

100 Wickets and 500 Runs

J. E. Emburey (Middlesex) .... 103 wickets and 782 runs.

Eight or More Dismissals in a Match by a Wicket-keeper

Nine   D. E. East (all ct) .... Essex v Sussex at Hove.
Eight R. J. Parks (all ct)........ Hampshire v Somerset at Bournemouth.

Six Dismissals in an Innings by a Wicket-keeper

D. E. East (all ct) .... Essex v Sussex at Hove.
C. Maynard (all ct)....... Lancashire v Glamorgan at Swansea.
R. W. Taylor (all ct)..... Derbyshire v Yorkshire at Sheffield.

Highest Innings Totals

634 for seven declared: Middlesex v Essex at Chelmsford.
544 for nine declared: New Zealanders v Somerset at Taunton.
529 for eight declared: Northamptonshire v Glamorgan at Cardiff.
528: Somerset v Leicestershire at Leicester.
470 for eight declared: Kent v Warwickshire at Folkestone.
462: Somerset v Kent at Taunton.
454 for seven declared: Hampshire v Derbyshire at Derby.
451 for nine declared: Surrey v Worcestershire at Worcester.

Lowest Innings Totals

14: Surrey v Essex at Chelmsford.
53: Nottinghamshire v Derbyshire at Derby.
65: Lancashire v Nottinghamshire at Nottingham.
69: Worcestershire v Nottinghamshire at Worcester.
74: Middlesex v Warwickshire at Birmingham.

Innings Total Under 100 in Each Innings

74 and 78: Middlesex v Warwickshire at Birmingham.

Over 50 Extras in an Innings

52 (B 7, l-b 16, w 7, n-b 22): Leicestershire v Northamptonshire at Leicester.
50 (B 4, l-b 12, n-b 34): Warwickshire v Kent at Folkestone.

Variations in Side's Totals

551 Middlesex (83 and 634 for seven declared) v Essex at Chelmsford.

Career Aggregate Milestones

35,000 runs:	A. Jones.
25,000 runs:	A. I. Kallicharran.
15,000 runs:	J. C. Balderstone, G. Cook, G. P. Howarth, D. W. Randall, R. W. Tolchard, P. Willey, G. A. Gooch, R. A. Woolmer.
10,000 runs:	I. T. Botham, A. R. Butcher, M. W. Gatting.
50 hundreds:	K. S. McEwan.
1,000 wickets:	R. E. East, C. M. Old.
500 wickets:	S. T. Clarke, G. W. Johnson, D. S. Steele.
500 catches:	D. S. Steele.
1,000 dismissals:	R. W. Tolchard.

County Caps Awarded in 1983

Essex	N. E. Foster.
Glamorgan	A. L. Jones, C. J. C. Rowe, M. W. W. Selvey.
Gloucestershire	D. R. Shepherd, P. W. Romaines.
Hampshire	V. P. Terry, T. M. Tremlett.
Kent	D. G. Aslett, E. A. E. Baptiste, R. M. Ellison.
Middlesex	K. P. Tomlins.
Nottinghamshire	R. T. Robinson.
Somerset	T. Gard, N. F. M. Popplewell.
Warwickshire	A. M. Ferreira, N. Gifford.
Yorkshire	S. J. Dennis.

No caps were awarded by Derbyshire, Lancashire, Leicestershire, Northamptonshire, Surrey, Sussex and Worcestershire.

FIRST-CLASS AVERAGES, 1983

BATTING

(Qualification: 8 innings, average 10.00)

* Signifies not out.   † Denotes a left-handed batsman.

	I	NO	R	HI	100s	Avge
I. V. A. Richards (*Somerset*)	20	4	1,204	216	5	75.25
C. G. Greenidge (*Hampshire*)	27	5	1,438	154	4	65.36
M. W. Gatting (*Middlesex*)	28	5	1,494	216	6	64.95
J. A. Carse (*Northamptonshire*)	10	8	129	36*	0	64.50
K. S. McEwan (*Essex*)	39	5	2,176	189*	8	64.00
Imran Khan (*Sussex*)	25	3	1,260	124*	2	57.27
C. S. Cowdrey (*Kent*)	34	10	1,364	123	5	56.83
A. J. Lamb (*Northamptonshire*)	29	7	1,232	137*	5	56.00
G. Boycott (*Yorkshire*)	40	5	1,941	214*	7	55.45
†A. I. Kallicharran (*Warwickshire*)	34	4	1,637	243*	6	54.56
M. A. Lynch (*Surrey*)	39	10	1,558	119	3	53.72
C. L. Smith (*Hampshire*)	39	3	1,923	193	6	53.41
†G. Fowler (*Lancashire*)	30	3	1,403	156*	5	51.96
P. Willey (*Northamptonshire*)	40	8	1,546	175*	4	48.31
†G. D. Barlow (*Middlesex*)	39	7	1,545	132	4	48.28
R. A. Smith (*Hampshire*)	12	3	434	104*	3	48.22
D. K. Standing (*Sussex*)	8	3	240	60	0	48.00
R. A. Woolmer (*Kent*)	22	1	994	129	4	47.33
M. D. Marshall (*Hampshire*)	16	4	563	112	2	46.91
†D. M. Smith (*Surrey*)	20	4	748	131*	2	46.75
†J. G. Wright (*Derbyshire and New Zealanders*)	13	0	605	136	1	46.53
†D. I. Gower (*Leicestershire*)	32	5	1,253	140	5	46.40
†R. J. Hadlee (*Nottinghamshire and New Zealanders*)	15	2	596	103	1	45.84
Zaheer Abbas (*Gloucestershire*)	19	0	867	116	3	45.63
†T. A. Lloyd (*Warwickshire*)	41	4	1,673	208*	5	45.21
R. P. Moulding (*Oxford University*)	13	3	448	80*	0	44.80
†M. R. Benson (*Kent*)	37	3	1,515	152*	4	44.55
D. L. Amiss (*Warwickshire*)	43	4	1,721	164	3	44.12
Kapil Dev (*Northamptonshire*)	10	2	349	120	1	43.62
†A. J. T. Miller (*Middlesex and Oxford University*)	26	3	1,002	127*	1	43.56
D. G. Aslett (*Kent*)	36	3	1,437	168	3	43.54
R. G. Williams (*Northamptonshire*)	40	10	1,305	104*	1	43.50
†W. N. Slack (*Middlesex*)	28	4	1,034	140	3	43.08
C. J. Tavaré (*Kent*)	24	0	1,030	109	1	42.91
T. E. Jesty (*Hampshire*)	30	5	1,072	187	1	42.88
A. W. Stovold (*Gloucestershire*)	42	3	1,671	181	4	42.84
†D. R. Turner (*Hampshire*)	17	3	598	122*	1	42.71
†B. C. Broad (*Gloucestershire*)	27	2	1,061	145	3	42.44
†D. Lloyd (*Lancashire*)	15	3	507	123	1	42.25
W. Larkins (*Northamptonshire*)	42	0	1,774	252	5	42.23
D. B. Pauline (*Surrey*)	21	2	796	115	1	41.89
P. A. Neale (*Worcestershire*)	40	3	1,521	139	2	41.10
R. O. Butcher (*Middlesex*)	19	3	657	179	2	41.06
R. T. Robinson (*Nottinghamshire*)	41	3	1,545	207	2	40.65
G. D. Mendis (*Sussex*)	46	6	1,624	133*	4	40.60
V. P. Terry (*Hampshire*)	33	6	1,096	115	3	40.59
I. T. Botham (*Somerset*)	21	0	852	152	3	40.57

	I	NO	R	HI	100s	Avge
B. F. Davison (*Leicestershire*)	41	6	1,417	123*	3	40.48
A. J. Stewart (*Surrey*)	17	4	525	118*	1	40.38
A. P. E. Knott (*Kent*)	30	9	848	92*	0	40.38
N. E. Briers (*Leicestershire*)	38	6	1,289	201*	1	40.28
G. A. Gooch (*Essex*)	38	1	1,481	174	4	40.02
J. C. Balderstone (*Leicestershire*)	41	4	1,478	112	3	39.94
G. Cook (*Northamptonshire*)	41	3	1,510	128	1	39.73
†J. Abrahams (*Lancashire*)	39	7	1,261	178	3	39.40
G. P. Howarth (*Surrey and New Zealanders*)	23	2	820	144	1	39.04
N. R. Taylor (*Kent*)	39	6	1,275	155*	5	38.63
†R. D. V. Knight (*Surrey*)	38	6	1,235	101*	1	38.59
R. C. Ontong (*Glamorgan*)	43	9	1,310	112	3	38.52
K. J. Barnett (*Derbyshire*)	40	3	1,423	121	3	38.45
D. N. Patel (*Worcestershire*)	44	2	1,615	112	3	38.45
D. L. Bairstow (*Yorkshire*)	35	6	1,102	100*	1	38.00
A. Hill (*Derbyshire*)	40	5	1,311	137*	4	37.45
P. M. Roebuck (*Somerset*)	38	5	1,235	106*	1	37.42
I. S. Anderson (*Derbyshire*)	37	4	1,233	112	1	37.36
M. C. J. Nicholas (*Hampshire*)	43	5	1,418	158	3	37.31
C. E. B. Rice (*Nottinghamshire*)	30	2	1,026	101*	2	36.64
J. N. Shepherd (*Gloucestershire*)	34	6	1,025	168	2	36.60
†N. H. Fairbrother (*Lancashire*)	26	5	759	94*	0	36.14
†D. J. Thomas (*Surrey*)	31	5	937	119	2	36.03
I. A. Greig (*Sussex*)	10	1	324	147*	1	36.00
E. A. E. Baptiste (*Kent*)	26	5	755	136*	2	35.95
J. G. Wyatt (*Somerset*)	12	2	352	82*	0	35.20
R. J. Boyd-Moss (*Northamptonshire and Cambridge University*)	43	2	1,437	139	3	35.04
A. Sidebottom (*Yorkshire*)	21	7	490	78	0	35.00
L. L. McFarlane (*Lancashire*)	9	8	35	12*	0	35.00
K. R. Pont (*Essex*)	27	4	802	125*	2	34.86
P. W. Romaines (*Gloucestershire*)	41	4	1,286	135	3	34.75
D. R. Pringle (*Essex*)	21	4	586	102*	1	34.47
†N. A. Felton (*Somerset*)	12	1	376	173*	1	34.18
M. D. Moxon (*Yorkshire*)	23	0	780	153	1	33.91
A. J. Hignell (*Gloucestershire*)	37	6	1,044	109*	2	33.67
†C. Gladwin (*Essex*)	14	0	470	89	0	33.57
I. P. Butcher (*Leicestershire*)	30	1	973	139	3	33.55
G. Sharp (*Northamptonshire*)	24	8	536	98	0	33.50
J. D. Love (*Yorkshire*)	38	7	1,020	76*	0	32.90
†A. R. Butcher (*Surrey*)	44	3	1,349	128	3	32.90
P. A. Smith (*Warwickshire*)	17	3	458	114	1	32.71
K. W. R. Fletcher (*Essex*)	36	3	1,077	151*	2	32.63
†S. T. Jefferies (*Lancashire*)	12	4	260	75*	0	32.50
P. B. Clift (*Leicestershire*)	33	7	843	100*	1	32.42
F. C. Hayes (*Lancashire*)	28	1	866	149	3	32.07
J. H. Hampshire (*Derbyshire*)	21	2	601	85	0	31.63
†A. L. Jones (*Glamorgan*)	40	7	1,036	99	0	31.39
G. W. Humpage (*Warwickshire*)	42	6	1,116	141*	2	31.00
K. P. Tomlins (*Middlesex*)	27	5	670	132*	1	30.45
G. Miller (*Derbyshire*)	30	7	699	84	0	30.39
†A. Jones (*Glamorgan*)	37	2	1,059	105	1	30.25
D. A. Banks (*Worcestershire*)	13	1	363	100	1	30.25
J. D. Birch (*Nottinghamshire*)	38	2	1,086	95	0	30.16
D. W. Randall (*Nottinghamshire*)	28	2	777	94	0	29.88
†K. Sharp (*Yorkshire*)	21	1	597	139	2	29.85
†C. H. Lloyd (*Lancashire*)	16	1	447	86	0	29.80
B. R. Hardie (*Essex*)	37	2	1,042	129	1	29.77
M. S. Scott (*Worcestershire*)	12	2	297	76	0	29.70

	I	NO	R	HI	100s	Avge
P. Bainbridge (*Gloucestershire*)	43	2	1,217	146	1	29.68
K. D. Smith (*Warwickshire*)	47	4	1,272	109	2	29.58
C. T. Radley (*Middlesex*)	38	6	943	119	1	29.46
P. Carrick (*Yorkshire*)	32	8	697	83	0	29.04
D. J. Capel (*Northamptonshire*)	24	5	534	109*	1	28.10
N. E. J. Pocock (*Hampshire*)	35	8	755	60*	0	27.96
J. E. Emburey (*Middlesex*)	33	5	782	133	1	27.92
†I. J. Gould (*Sussex*)	23	6	474	59*	0	27.88
C. J. Richards (*Surrey*)	35	8	751	85*	0	27.81
A. P. Wells (*Sussex*)	28	4	665	92	0	27.70
M. J. Bamber (*Northamptonshire*)	14	1	360	77	0	27.69
R. W. Tolchard (*Leicestershire*)	35	7	775	80*	0	27.67
T. S. Curtis (*Worcestershire and Cambridge University*)	37	5	880	92	0	27.50
R. G. P. Ellis (*Middlesex and Oxford University*)	26	2	658	103*	1	27.41
S. J. O'Shaughnessy (*Lancashire*)	28	3	685	105	2	27.40
J. A. Hopkins (*Glamorgan*)	43	2	1,123	116	2	27.39
†S. P. Henderson (*Glamorgan and Cambridge University*)	35	5	820	135*	1	27.33
†J. W. Lloyds (*Somerset*)	35	2	901	100	1	27.30
†K. I. Hodgson (*Cambridge University*)	15	5	272	47	0	27.20
R. J. Doughty (*Gloucestershire*)	11	6	135	32*	0	27.00
B. Hassan (*Nottinghamshire*)	34	1	890	112	1	26.96
J. G. Varey (*Oxford University*)	10	3	187	69*	0	26.71
D. A. Francis (*Glamorgan*)	39	5	903	89*	0	26.55
J. Garner (*Somerset*)	16	6	265	44	0	26.50
D. B. D'Oliveira (*Worcestershire*)	39	2	972	102	1	26.27
†R. L. Ollis (*Somerset*)	22	2	517	99*	0	25.85
A. M. Ferreira (*Warwickshire*)	24	6	465	66	0	25.83
J. A. Ormrod (*Worcestershire*)	41	3	967	84	0	25.44
J. J. Whitaker (*Leicestershire*)	16	4	305	56*	0	25.41
A. J. Wright (*Gloucestershire*)	17	2	380	56*	0	25.33
†S. G. Hinks (*Kent*)	10	0	253	87	0	25.30
C. M. Wells (*Sussex*)	40	6	857	71	0	25.20
G. S. le Roux (*Sussex*)	17	1	401	80	0	25.06
†S. J. G. Doggart (*Cambridge University*)	18	5	323	70	0	24.84
W. P. Fowler (*Derbyshire*)	26	2	591	91	0	24.62
N. F. M. Popplewell (*Somerset*)	39	3	886	143	1	24.61
†R. M. Ellison (*Kent*)	21	7	343	63	0	24.50
C. W. J. Athey (*Yorkshire*)	32	1	758	90	0	24.45
G. W. Johnson (*Kent*)	30	13	413	79*	0	24.29
I. R. Payne (*Surrey*)	11	4	167	43	0	23.85
T. Davies (*Glamorgan*)	15	4	260	69*	0	23.63
P. Johnson (*Nottinghamshire*)	28	2	612	125	1	23.53
†K. D. James (*Middlesex*)	8	2	141	34	0	23.50
L. Potter (*Kent*)	11	0	258	50	0	23.45
R. G. Lumb (*Yorkshire*)	15	1	328	60	0	23.42
J. Simmons (*Lancashire*)	31	2	679	104	2	23.41
M. J. Weston (*Worcestershire*)	38	1	862	115	1	23.29
C. J. C. Rowe (*Glamorgan*)	33	2	721	82	0	23.25
†G. S. Clinton (*Surrey*)	22	3	439	105	1	23.10
†P. W. Denning (*Somerset*)	36	3	758	99	0	22.96
Asif Din (*Warwickshire*)	21	3	411	65	0	22.83
M. S. A. McEvoy (*Worcestershire*)	26	1	569	103	1	22.76
D. S. Steele (*Northamptonshire*)	31	6	569	60	0	22.76
D. E. East (*Essex*)	32	4	635	91	0	22.67
N. F. Williams (*Middlesex*)	25	7	407	63	0	22.61
G. Monkhouse (*Surrey*)	18	5	291	46	0	22.38

	I	NO	R	HI	100s	Avge
P. R. Downton (*Middlesex*)	30	7	508	87	0	22.08
V. J. Marks (*Somerset*)	27	3	530	44*	0	22.08
†R. C. Russell (*Gloucestershire*)	32	9	507	64*	0	22.04
G. Pathmanathan (*Cambridge University*)	13	1	263	64	0	21.91
J. R. T. Barclay (*Sussex*)	37	3	743	65	0	21.85
†D. J. Humphries (*Worcestershire*)	30	4	560	59	0	21.53
Nasir Zaidi (*Lancashire*)	16	6	215	51	0	21.50
D. A. Graveney (*Gloucestershire*)	28	8	427	94	0	21.35
†J. R. P. Heath (*Sussex*)	18	2	335	39	0	20.93
L. B. Taylor (*Leicestershire*)	18	6	250	47	0	20.83
I. Cockbain (*Lancashire*)	15	1	291	52	0	20.78
†H. Morris (*Glamorgan*)	14	3	228	34	0	20.72
P. W. G. Parker (*Sussex*)	27	2	512	79	0	20.48
†B. C. Rose (*Somerset*)	9	0	184	52	0	20.44
R. I. H. B. Dyer (*Warwickshire*)	15	3	242	93	0	20.16
D. P. Hughes (*Lancashire*)	28	2	522	153	1	20.07
A. M. Green (*Sussex*)	30	2	552	53	0	19.71
E. W. Jones (*Glamorgan*)	18	5	256	39	0	19.69
P. J. Heseltine (*Oxford University*)	10	1	176	40	0	19.55
N. G. Cowley (*Hampshire*)	27	9	351	29	0	19.50
A. C. S. Pigott (*Sussex*)	29	8	408	63	0	19.42
N. A. Foster (*Essex*)	16	4	232	40*	0	19.33
J. F. Steele (*Leicestershire*)	26	9	327	50	0	19.23
R. E. East (*Essex*)	27	5	420	80*	0	19.09
J. E. Morris (*Derbyshire*)	20	1	361	58	0	19.00
†C. M. Old (*Warwickshire*)	25	4	396	62	0	18.85
T. M. Tremlett (*Hampshire*)	19	5	263	59	0	18.78
G. A. Tedstone (*Warwickshire*)	16	3	243	67*	0	18.69
B. N. French (*Nottinghamshire*)	38	4	630	91	0	18.52
C. J. Tunnicliffe (*Derbyshire*)	25	0	461	91	0	18.44
J. W. Southern (*Hampshire*)	13	5	146	45*	0	18.25
I. Folley (*Lancashire*)	9	4	91	25	0	18.20
D. W. Varey (*Cambridge University*)	20	1	342	65	0	18.00
†D. J. Wild (*Northamptonshire*)	9	0	162	48	0	18.00
N. A. Mallender (*Northamptonshire*)	27	9	320	71*	0	17.77
R. J. Finney (*Derbyshire*)	35	2	578	71	0	17.51
C. Maynard (*Lancashire*)	27	3	417	61*	0	17.37
†G. J. Parsons (*Leicestershire*)	15	3	207	56	0	17.25
J. D. Inchmore (*Worcestershire*)	26	4	377	51	0	17.13
R. G. D. Willis (*Warwickshire*)	20	9	183	37	0	16.63
G. B. Stevenson (*Yorkshire*)	25	1	396	52	0	16.50
P. J. W. Allott (*Lancashire*)	18	4	225	41	0	16.07
R. W. Taylor (*Derbyshire*)	30	7	366	41*	0	15.91
N. Phillip (*Essex*)	26	0	413	80	0	15.88
T. Gard (*Somerset*)	33	4	457	51	0	15.75
A. H. Wilkins (*Gloucestershire*)	15	3	185	54	0	15.41
R. S. Cowan (*Sussex*)	10	0	154	50	0	15.40
P. Moores (*Worcestershire*)	11	1	154	30	0	15.40
J. K. Lever (*Essex*)	17	3	211	44	0	15.07
W. W. Davis (*Glamorgan*)	18	9	135	39*	0	15.00
B. J. M. Maher (*Derbyshire*)	12	2	150	52	0	15.00
P. H. L. Wilson (*Somerset*)	11	7	60	25	0	15.00
P. A. Slocombe (*Somerset*)	17	2	224	66	0	14.93
S. N. Hartley (*Yorkshire*)	19	1	261	69	0	14.50
S. T. Clarke (*Surrey*)	24	4	285	43	0	14.25
†G. R. Dilley (*Kent*)	9	1	114	29	0	14.25
†C. H. Dredge (*Somerset*)	26	5	296	50	0	14.09
†R. A. Pick (*Nottinghamshire*)	8	2	84	25*	0	14.00
R. J. Parks (*Hampshire*)	15	2	180	52	0	13.84

	I	NO	R	HI	100s	Avge
K. A. Hayes (*Lancashire and Oxford University*)	12	0	165	45	0	13.75
S. Oldham (*Derbyshire*)	17	4	177	39	0	13.61
B. J. Lloyd (*Glamorgan*)	12	2	135	38	0	13.50
†N. Gifford (*Worcestershire*)	21	6	201	39	0	13.40
A. E. Warner (*Worcestershire*)	15	5	131	26*	0	13.10
P. H. Edmonds (*Middlesex*)	20	4	208	65	0	13.00
E. E. Hemmings (*Nottinghamshire*)	32	3	377	38	0	13.00
H. T. Rawlinson (*Oxford University*)	9	2	91	24	0	13.00
K. Stevenson (*Hampshire*)	9	3	77	25	0	12.83
D. A. Reeve (*Sussex*)	20	5	192	42*	0	12.80
†K. E. Cooper (*Nottinghamshire*)	27	7	254	30*	0	12.70
D. G. Moir (*Derbyshire*)	21	3	224	53	0	12.44
G. C. Small (*Warwickshire*)	8	3	62	31	0	12.40
M. K. Bore (*Nottinghamshire*)	16	5	135	24	0	12.27
J. G. Thomas (*Glamorgan*)	9	1	96	23	0	12.00
M. W. W. Selvey (*Glamorgan*)	24	3	250	63	0	11.90
J. D. Carr (*Middlesex and Oxford University*)	10	4	67	18	0	11.16
R. A. Cobb (*Leicestershire*)	10	0	110	28	0	11.00
R. M. Ellcock (*Worcestershire*)	18	4	154	36	0	11.00
K. Saxelby (*Nottinghamshire*)	28	3	274	35	0	10.96
G. V. Palmer (*Somerset*)	13	2	119	78	0	10.81
N. G. B. Cook (*Leicestershire*)	24	5	201	32	0	10.57
M. Watkinson (*Lancashire*)	20	4	168	29	0	10.50
†M. R. Davis (*Somerset*)	17	5	125	20*	0	10.41
S. Turner (*Essex*)	19	2	177	30	0	10.41
M. A. Fell (*Nottinghamshire*)	9	0	93	41	0	10.33
D. L. Underwood (*Kent*)	20	6	142	26*	0	10.14

BOWLING

(Qualification: 10 wickets in 10 innings)

† *Denotes left-arm bowler.*

	O	M	R	W	Avge	BB
Imran Khan (*Sussex*)	46.2	12	86	12	7.16	6-6
†J. K. Lever (*Essex*)	569	137	1,726	106	16.28	7-55
M. D. Marshall (*Hampshire*)	532.5	144	1,327	80	16.58	7-29
M. Hendrick (*Nottinghamshire*)	552.1	190	1,122	66	17.00	6-17
R. A. Woolmer (*Kent*)	86	29	170	10	17.00	3-13
J. E. Emburey (*Middlesex*)	935	328	1,842	103	17.88	6-13
P. B. Clift (*Leicestershire*)	619.4	167	1,592	83	19.18	5-20
†D. L. Underwood (*Kent*)	936.3	358	2,044	106	19.28	7-55
K. D. James (*Middlesex*)	89	20	217	11	19.72	5-28
T. M. Lamb (*Northamptonshire*)	188.2	57	416	21	19.80	4-27
L. B. Taylor (*Leicestershire*)	529.5	151	1,381	69	20.01	7-73
J. Garner (*Somerset*)	277	74	708	35	20.22	6-37
N. Phillip (*Essex*)	477.2	87	1,409	69	20.42	6-4
T. M. Tremlett (*Hampshire*)	600.2	198	1,346	63	21.36	6-82
†P. H. Edmonds (*Middlesex*)	820.3	230	1,974	92	21.45	6-38
†D. S. Steele (*Northamptonshire*)	678	255	1,460	68	21.47	5-48
M. A. Holding (*Derbyshire*)	169	41	451	21	21.47	5-48
R. J. Hadlee (*Nottinghamshire and New Zealanders*)	431.3	123	1,065	49	21.73	6-53
G. R. Dilley (*Kent*)	275.3	73	681	31	21.96	5-70
R. G. Williams (*Northamptonshire*)	434.1	148	1,036	47	22.04	4-18

	O	M	R	W	Avge	BB
G. Monkhouse (*Surrey*)	373.3	97	1,040	47	22.12	7-51
S. T. Clarke (*Surrey*)	693.1	183	1,773	79	22.44	7-53
A. E. Warner (*Worcestershire*)	210.3	39	608	27	22.51	4-72
D. R. Pringle (*Essex*)	288.4	53	928	41	22.63	7-32
G. J. F. Ferris (*Leicestershire*)	360	74	1,205	53	22.73	7-42
†N. Gifford (*Warwickshire*)	1,043.4	346	2,393	104	23.00	6-22
W. W. Daniel (*Middlesex*)	324.3	51	1,106	48	23.04	7-61
S. Turner (*Essex*)	282.1	76	624	27	23.11	5-30
N. A. Foster (*Essex*)	417	78	1,216	52	23.38	6-46
†D. Lloyd (*Lancashire*)	199	60	400	17	23.52	5-22
E. A. E. Baptiste (*Kent*)	376.3	88	1,187	50	23.74	5-39
Kapil Dev (*Northamptonshire*)	161	47	385	16	24.06	4-24
O. H. Mortensen (*Derbyshire*)	518.3	108	1,605	66	24.31	6-27
A. Needham (*Surrey*)	164	50	470	19	24.73	6-30
†S. T. Jefferies (*Lancashire*)	278.1	74	797	32	24.90	8-46
G. B. Stevenson (*Yorkshire*)	460.1	103	1,400	56	25.00	5-35
S. P. Hughes (*Middlesex*)	268.3	61	910	36	25.27	6-32
†N. G. B. Cook (*Leicestershire*)	878.1	321	1,859	73	25.46	5-35
G. S. le Roux (*Sussex*)	362.3	92	950	37	25.67	5-17
N. G. Cowley (*Hampshire*)	440.3	147	1,053	41	25.68	4-10
R. G. D. Willis (*Warwickshire*)	376.5	98	1,058	41	25.80	5-35
P. I. Pocock (*Surrey*)	681.2	200	1,774	68	26.08	7-79
A. C. S. Pigott (*Sussex*)	582.5	98	1,889	72	26.23	6-22
A. Walker (*Northamptonshire*)	165.4	30	578	22	26.27	4-61
N. F. Williams (*Middlesex*)	532.2	114	1,659	63	26.33	5-77
M. Watkinson (*Lancashire*)	319.3	69	929	35	26.54	6-51
J. Simmons (*Lancashire*)	744	214	1,807	68	26.57	7-73
W. W. Davis (*Glamorgan*)	452.4	110	1,389	52	26.71	7-70
K. Saxelby (*Nottinghamshire*)	410.2	95	1,337	50	26.74	5-52
A. P. Pridgeon (*Worcestershire*)	700	166	1,978	72	27.47	5-21
C. H. Dredge (*Somerset*)	492.3	127	1,323	48	27.56	5-51
A. Sidebottom (*Yorkshire*)	361	81	1,080	39	27.69	5-6
J. G. Thomas (*Glamorgan*)	144.5	34	529	19	27.84	5-78
†P. Carrick (*Yorkshire*)	848.1	303	1,750	62	28.22	7-44
K. E. Cooper (*Nottinghamshire*)	579	164	1,610	57	28.24	7-33
G. J. Parsons (*Leicestershire*)	269	73	823	29	28.37	5-51
D. L. Acfield (*Essex*)	497.1	140	1,222	43	28.41	7-100
B. J. Griffiths (*Northamptonshire*)	536.2	130	1,424	50	28.48	6-92
M. C. J. Nicholas (*Hampshire*)	277.2	74	774	27	28.66	5-45
J. D. Inchmore (*Worcestershire*)	488.3	104	1,369	47	29.12	5-45
R. M. Ellison (*Kent*)	598.4	167	1,491	51	29.23	5-73
N. A. Mallender (*Northamptonshire*)	525.2	112	1,642	56	29.32	6-48
D. A. Reeve (*Sussex*)	472.1	131	1,233	42	29.35	4-15
C. M. Old (*Warwickshire*)	656.3	152	1,824	62	29.41	5-50
R. Illingworth (*Yorkshire*)	411.5	137	951	32	29.71	4-48
N. G. Cowans (*Middlesex*)	286	60	912	30	30.40	5-43
J. N. Shepherd (*Gloucestershire*)	776.1	209	2,047	67	30.55	7-50
W. Hogg (*Warwickshire*)	384.4	74	1,198	39	30.71	5-63
†S. J. Dennis (*Yorkshire*)	525.2	119	1,600	52	30.76	4-32
J. W. Lloyds (*Somerset*)	358.1	98	1,079	35	30.82	5-120
P. Willey (*Northamptonshire*)	483.5	159	991	32	30.96	4-51
P. J. W. Allott (*Lancashire*)	457.4	131	1,178	38	31.00	5-45
K. Stevenson (*Hampshire*)	187.5	39	656	21	31.23	5-81
†D. J. Thomas (*Surrey*)	547	113	1,781	57	31.24	4-22
G. V. Palmer (*Somerset*)	208.3	39	630	20	31.50	5-38
A. M. Ferreira (*Warwickshire*)	502.4	131	1,277	40	31.92	5-19
†J. F. Steele (*Leicestershire*)	520.1	161	1,280	40	32.00	4-3
V. J. Marks (*Somerset*)	615.3	199	1,698	53	32.03	6-79
C. L. Smith (*Hampshire*)	167	44	547	17	32.17	3-35
M. W. W. Selvey (*Glamorgan*)	629.4	138	2,003	62	32.30	6-47

	O	M	R	W	Avge	BB
†R. J. Finney (*Derbyshire*)	281.5	43	970	30	32.33	5-58
†D. A. Graveney (*Gloucestershire*)	512.1	156	1,198	37	32.37	6-88
G. W. Johnson (*Kent*)	631.1	166	1,652	51	32.39	7-76
J. A. Carse (*Northamptonshire*)	238.5	50	722	22	32.81	5-43
I. T. Botham (*Somerset*)	232.2	55	728	22	33.09	5-38
Nasir Zaidi (*Lancashire*)	191.3	48	530	16	33.12	3-27
S. J. O'Shaughnessy (*Lancashire*)	236.2	44	830	25	33.20	4-73
†G. E. Sainsbury (*Gloucestershire*)	625.4	150	1,937	58	33.39	6-66
P. H. L. Wilson (*Somerset*)	248.3	45	837	25	33.48	4-77
E. E. Hemmings (*Nottinghamshire*)	710.4	195	2,000	59	33.89	7-23
N. F. M. Popplewell (*Somerset*)	232	38	786	23	34.17	4-69
G. Miller (*Derbyshire*)	492.5	132	1,278	37	34.54	5-71
†D. G. Moir (*Derbyshire*)	462.5	121	1,385	40	34.62	5-44
†M. R. Davis (*Somerset*)	240.4	43	873	25	34.92	4-34
†C. J. Tunnicliffe (*Derbyshire*)	428.4	94	1,372	39	35.17	4-30
†C. E. Waller (*Sussex*)	754	223	1,873	53	35.33	6-126
C. M. Wells (*Sussex*)	376.3	82	1,135	32	35.46	4-69
†R. E. East (*Essex*)	338	96	889	25	35.56	5-45
A. J. Pollock (*Cambridge University*)	230.2	49	750	21	35.71	5-107
†J. W. Southern (*Hampshire*)	369.5	115	966	27	35.77	5-60
S. Oldham (*Derbyshire*)	387.2	85	1,120	31	36.12	4-56
R. C. Ontong (*Glamorgan*)	645	131	2,053	56	36.66	6-64
†J. H. Childs (*Gloucestershire*)	664.5	200	1,761	48	36.68	6-81
D. N. Patel (*Worcestershire*)	685.5	204	1,799	49	36.71	5-52
R. M. Ellcock (*Worcestershire*)	244	39	931	25	37.24	4-70
S. J. Malone (*Hampshire*)	547.1	123	1,797	48	37.43	4-39
I. R. Payne (*Surrey*)	158.5	41	450	12	37.50	5-13
†R. K. Illingworth (*Worcestershire*)	664.5	172	1,830	48	38.12	5-26
T. E. Jesty (*Hampshire*)	256.5	70	804	21	38.28	3-48
P. M. Such (*Nottinghamshire*)	214	44	767	20	38.35	6-123
I. V. A. Richards (*Somerset*)	188	61	462	12	38.50	3-56
†M. K. Bore (*Nottinghamshire*)	370.1	99	1,040	27	38.51	4-29
P. Bainbridge (*Gloucestershire*)	416.4	106	1,199	30	39.96	4-67
I. A. Greig (*Sussex*)	185	26	681	17	40.05	4-42
P. A. Smith (*Warwickshire*)	218	29	844	21	40.19	3-56
†S. C. Booth (*Somerset*)	296.2	85	849	21	40.42	4-26
J. P. Agnew (*Leicestershire*)	248	42	930	23	40.43	3-34
†I. J. Curtis (*Surrey*)	269	82	690	17	40.58	6-28
C. J. C. Rowe (*Glamorgan*)	473.4	91	1,572	38	41.36	4-29
B. J. Lloyd (*Glamorgan*)	288.5	47	876	21	41.71	4-93
†T. A. Cotterell (*Cambridge University*)	273	67	758	17	44.58	5-89
H. T. Rawlinson (*Oxford University*)	154.5	31	626	14	44.71	5-123
R. D. V. Knight (*Surrey*)	236	60	677	15	45.13	3-58
J. R. T. Barclay (*Sussex*)	231.3	59	774	17	45.52	3-30
S. R. Barwick (*Glamorgan*)	129.3	21	532	11	48.36	8-42
L. L. McFarlane (*Lancashire*)	216.4	38	742	15	49.46	3-53
J. Abrahams (*Lancashire*)	216	41	658	13	50.61	3-83
G. A. Gooch (*Essex*)	212	46	572	11	52.00	3-40
K. B. S. Jarvis (*Kent*)	500.5	95	1,579	30	52.63	3-32
S. P. Perryman (*Worcestershire*)	253.5	54	750	14	53.57	4-91
C. S. Cowdrey (*Kent*)	220.2	34	733	12	61.08	3-80
M. D. Petchey (*Oxford University*)	206.2	36	804	12	67.00	2-70
†A. H. Wilkins (*Gloucestershire*)	205	24	820	12	68.33	2-25
S. J. G. Doggart (*Cambridge University*)	285.2	60	844	12	70.33	3-3
K. I. Hodgson (*Cambridge University*)	297	75	871	12	72.58	4-58

The following bowlers took ten wickets but bowled in fewer than ten innings:

	O	M	R	W	Avge	BB
F. D. Stephenson (*Gloucestershire*)	74.4	18	230	14	16.42	5-56
S. R. Tracy (*New Zealanders and Gloucestershire*)	54.1	10	170	10	17.00	5-29

	O	M	R	W	Avge	BB
A. M. E. Roberts (*Leicestershire*)	101.2	19	294	16	18.37	5-26
N. S. Taylor (*Yorkshire*)	111.1	23	427	14	30.50	5-49
G. C. Small (*Warwickshire*)	110.5	19	349	10	34.90	3-13
J. R. Turnbull (*Oxford University*)	130	34	424	12	35.33	4-51

FIELDING IN 1983

68	D. E. East (63ct, 5st)
63	R. C. Russell (46ct, 17st)
60	R. J. Parks (51ct, 9st)
59	P. R. Downton (54ct, 5st)
58	C. J. Richards (51ct, 7st, including 3ct in the field)
55	D. L. Bairstow (47ct, 8st)
53	R. W. Tolchard (44ct, 9st)
52	B. N. French (49ct, 3st)
51	R. W. Taylor (49ct, 2st)
50	T. Gard (42ct, 8st)
47	A. P. E. Knott (39ct, 8st)
46	G. Sharp (41ct, 5st)
45	I. J. Gould (32ct, 13st)
37	R. O. Butcher
36	D. J. Humphries (27ct, 9st)
35	G. Cook (including 5ct, 3st as wicket-keeper)
35	G. A. Gooch
30	B. R. Hardie
30	N. E. J. Pocock
30	J. F. Steele

29	G. W. Johnson
29	C. Maynard (27ct, 2st)
29	D. S. Steele
28	G. W. Humpage (23ct, 5st, including 7ct in the field)
28	R. D. V. Knight
27	C. S. Cowdrey
27	G. A. Tedstone (23ct, 4st)
26	M. C. J. Nicholas
25	E. W. Jones (24ct, 1st)
23	I. S. Anderson
23	J. E. Emburey
22	D. L. Amiss
22	G. D. Barlow
22	C. T. Radley
22	K. P. Tomlins
21	C. G. Greenidge
21	N. F. M. Popplewell (including 2ct as wicket-keeper)
20	J. D. Birch
20	T. Davies (18ct, 2st)
20	D. W. Randall

INDIVIDUAL SCORES OF 100 AND OVER

There were 262 three-figure innings in first-class cricket in 1983, nineteen fewer than in 1982. The list includes 225 hit in the County Championship and 31 in other first-class games, but not the six hit by the New Zealand touring team, which can be found in the New Zealand tour section.

* *Signifies not out.*

K. S. McEwan (8)
189* Essex v Worcs., Colchester
181 Essex v Glos., Colchester
174 Essex v Derby., Derby
151 Essex v Leics., Leicester
142 Essex v Kent, Tunbridge Wells
142 Essex v Hants, Southend
107 Essex v Glam., Cardiff
104 Essex v Glam., Southend

G. Boycott (7)
214* Yorks. v Notts., Worksop
169* Yorks. v Derby., Chesterfield
163 } Yorks. v Notts., Bradford
141* }
140* Yorks. v Glos., Cheltenham
112* Yorks. v Derby., Sheffield
101 Yorks. v Kent, Sheffield

M. W. Gatting (6)
216 Middx v New Zealanders, Lord's
160 Middx v Essex, Chelmsford
118 Middx v Sussex, Lord's
116 Middx v Warw., Lord's
105 Middx v Somerset, Lord's
100* Middx v Yorks., Leeds

A. I. Kallicharran (6)
243* Warw. v Glam., Birmingham
209* Warw. v Lancs., Birmingham
173* Warw. v Surrey, The Oval
152 } Warw. v Sussex, Birmingham
118* }
111 Warw. v Kent, Folkestone

C. L. Smith (6)
193 Hants v Derby., Derby
163 Hants v Essex, Southend
129* Hants v Leics., Leicester
125 Hants v Glos., Portsmouth
118 Hants v Lancs., Liverpool
100 Hants v Lancs., Bournemouth

C. S. Cowdrey (5)
123 Kent v Leics., Folkestone
113 Kent v Yorks., Sheffield
103* Kent v Cambridge U., Cambridge
103* Kent v Somerset, Taunton
101* Kent v Lancs., Maidstone

G. Fowler (5)
156* Lancs. v Yorks., Manchester
133 Lancs. v Glam., Manchester
107 Lancs. v Northants, Northampton
105 England v New Zealand, The Oval
100 Lancs. v Leics., Manchester

D. I. Gower (5)
140 Leics. v Sussex, Hove
124 Leics. v Cambridge U., Cambridge
112* Leics. v Glam., Leeds
108* Leics. v Glam., Hinckley
108 England v New Zealand, Lord's

A. J. Lamb (5)
137* England v New Zealand, Nottingham
119 Northants v Glam., Cardiff
108 Northants v Surrey, The Oval
107* Northants v Yorks., Northampton
102* England v New Zealand, The Oval

W. Larkins (5)
252 Northants v Glam., Cardiff
236 Northants v Derby., Derby
145 Northants v Glam., Northampton
137 Northants v Lancs., Northampton
100 Northants v Middx, Lord's

T. A. Lloyd (5)
208* Warw. v Glos., Birmingham
126 Warw. v Lancs., Birmingham
124* Warw. v Surrey, The Oval
123 Warw. v Glam., Birmingham
112 Warw. v Somerset, Taunton

I. V. A. Richards (5)
216 Somerset v Leics., Leicester
142* Somerset v Surrey, Taunton
128* Somerset v Northants, Weston-super-Mare
117* Somerset v Northants, Northampton
103 Somerset v Kent, Taunton

N. R. Taylor (5)
155* Kent v Glam., Cardiff
116* Kent v Essex, Tunbridge Wells
114 Kent v Cambridge U., Cambridge
111 Kent v Leics., Leicester
104 Kent v Somerset, Taunton

G. D. Barlow (4)
132 Middx v Essex, Chelmsford
128 Middx v Lancs., Lord's
113 Middx v Surrey, Lord's
105 Middx v Hants, Uxbridge

M. R. Benson (4)
102⎫
152*⎬ Kent v Warw., Birmingham
111 Kent v Glam., Cardiff
105 Kent v Cambridge U., Cambridge

G. A. Gooch (4)
174 Essex v Cambridge U., Cambridge
111 Essex v Yorks., Chelmsford
110 Essex v Leics., Chelmsford
103 Essex v Worcs., Colchester

C. G. Greenidge (4)
154 Hants v Surrey, Southampton
116 Hants v Worcs., Southampton
104⎫
100*⎬ Hants v Lancs., Liverpool

A. Hill (4)
137* Derby. v Worcs., Derby
121 Derby. v Warw., Nuneaton
111 Derby. v Surrey, The Oval
106 Derby. v Lancs., Blackpool

G. D. Mendis (4)
133* Sussex v Worcs., Worcester
132 Sussex v Worcs., Hove
121* Sussex v Northants, Hove
105 Sussex v Middx, Hove

A. W. Stovold (4)
181 Glos. v Derby., Derby
164* Glos. v Warw., Cheltenham
122 Glos. v Surrey, Bristol
106 Glos. v Hants, Portsmouth

P. Willey (4)
175* Northants v Hants, Northampton
147* Northants v Lancs., Northampton
117* Northants v Worcs., Northampton
108 Northants v Notts., Nottingham

R. A. Woolmer (4)
129 Kent v Lancs., Maidstone
120 Kent v Surrey, Canterbury
118 Kent v Middx, Dartford
110 Kent v Somerset, Maidstone

J. Abrahams (3)
178 Lancs. v Worcs., Manchester
117* Lancs. v Hants, Bournemouth
105 Lancs. v Kent, Maidstone

D. L. Amiss (3)
164 Warw. v Kent, Folkestone
142 Warw. v Glos., Birmingham
111 Warw. v Essex, Nuneaton

D. G. Aslett (3)
168⎫
119⎬ Kent v Derby., Chesterfield
111 Kent v Sussex, Hove

J. C. Balderstone (3)
112 Leics. v Kent, Leicester
108 Leics. v Notts., Nottingham
100* Leics. v Worcs., Hereford

K. J. Barnett (3)
121 Derby. v Surrey, The Oval
106 Derby. v Kent, Chesterfield
103 Derby. v Northants, Derby

I. T. Botham (3)
152 Somerset v Leics., Leicester
107 Somerset v Worcs., Worcester
103 England v New Zealand, Nottingham

R. J. Boyd-Moss (3)
139⎫
124⎬ Cambridge U. v Oxford U., Lord's
101 Northants v Leics., Leicester

B. C. Broad (3)
145 Glos. v Notts., Bristol
109 Glos. v Essex, Colchester
100 Glos. v Yorks., Cheltenham

A. R. Butcher (3)
128 Surrey v Glam., Swansea
122 Surrey v Worcs., Guildford
100 Surrey v Lancs., The Oval

I. P. Butcher (3)
139 Leics. v Notts., Leicester
107 Leics. v Northants, Leicester
103 Leics. v Glos., Leicester

B. F. Davison (3)
123* Leics. v New Zealanders, Leicester
106 Leics. v Essex, Chelmsford
101 Leics. v Glam., Hinckley

F. C. Hayes (3)
149 Lancs. v Sussex, Horsham
127* Lancs. v Derby., Blackpool
116 Lancs. v Yorks., Manchester

M. A. Lynch (3)
119 Surrey v Hants, Southampton
112 Surrey v Worcs., Worcester
101* Surrey v Sussex, Hove

M. C. J. Nicholas (3)
158　Hants v Oxford U., Oxford
110　Hants v Glos., Bristol
100*　Hants v Derby., Portsmouth

R. C. Ontong (3)
112　Glam. v Yorks., Middlesbrough
109　Glam. v Surrey, Swansea
105*　Glam. v Kent, Cardiff

D. N. Patel (3)
112　Worcs. v Warw., Birmingham
111　Worcs. v Glos., Worcester
105　Worcs. v Surrey, Guildford

P. W. Romaines (3)
135　Glos. v Kent, Bristol
121　Glos. v Worcs., Bristol
100*　Glos. v Yorks., Cheltenham

W. N. Slack (3)
140　Middx v Glam., Lord's
138*　Middx v Cambridge U., Cambridge
107　Middx v Surrey, The Oval

R. A. Smith (3)
104*　Hants v Sussex, Basingstoke
100*　Hants v Lancs., Bournemouth
100　Hants v Glos., Bristol

V. P. Terry (3)
115　Hants v Sussex, Eastbourne
114　Hants v Lancs., Bournemouth
106*　Hants v Notts., Bournemouth

Zaheer Abbas (3)
116　Glos. v Glam., Swansea
112　Glos. v Lancs., Southport
109　Glos. v Warw., Cheltenham

E. A. E. Baptiste (2)
136*　Kent v Yorks., Sheffield
102*　Kent v Sussex, Hove

R. O. Butcher (2)
179　Middx v Derby., Uxbridge
110　Middx v Kent, Dartford

K. W. R. Fletcher (2)
151*　Essex v Glam., Cardiff
110　Essex v Surrey, Chelmsford

A. J. Hignell (2)
109*　Glos. v Hants, Bristol
103　Glos. v Somerset, Bath

J. A. Hopkins (2)
116　Glam. v Glos., Swansea
109　Glam. v Derby., Swansea

G. W. Humpage (2)
141*　Warw. v Yorks., Birmingham
105　Warw. v Kent, Birmingham

Imran Khan (2)
124*　Sussex v Surrey, The Oval
101　Sussex v Hants, Eastbourne

M. D. Marshall (2)
112　Hants v Kent, Bournemouth
100*　Hants v Surrey, Southampton

P. A. Neale (2)
139　Worcs. v Lancs., Manchester
135　Worcs. v Glam., Abergavenny

S. J. O'Shaughnessy (2)
105　Lancs. v Leics., Manchester
100*　Lancs. v Yorks., Leeds

K. R. Pont (2)
125*　Essex v Glam., Southend
105　Essex v Kent, Chelmsford

C. E. B. Rice (2)
101*　Notts. v Middx, Nottingham
100*　Notts. v Glos., Bristol

R. T. Robinson (2)
207　Notts. v Warw., Nottingham
110　Notts. v Worcs., Worcester

K. Sharp (2)
139　Yorks. v Surrey, Scarborough
121　Yorks. v Glos., Cheltenham

J. N. Shepherd (2)
168　Glos. v Warw., Birmingham
112　Glos. v Kent, Bristol

J. Simmons (2)
104　Lancs. v Glam., Swansea
101*　Lancs. v Derby., Blackpool

D. M. Smith (2)
131*　Surrey v Glam., Swansea
106*　Surrey v Middx, The Oval

K. D. Smith (2)
109　Warw. v Glos., Cheltenham
103　Warw. v Middx, Lord's

D. J. Thomas (2)
119　Surrey v Notts., The Oval
103*　Surrey v Sussex, Hove

The following each played one three-figure innings:

I. S. Anderson, 112, Derby v Kent, Chesterfield.
P. Bainbridge, 146, Glos. v New Zealanders, Bristol; D. L. Bairstow, 100*, Yorks. v Middx, Leeds; D. A. Banks, 100, Worcs. v Oxford U., Oxford; N. E. Briers, 201*, Leics. v Warw., Birmingham.
D. J. Capel, 109*, Northants v Somerset, Northampton; P. B. Clift, 100*, Leics. v Sussex, Hove; G. S. Clinton, 105, Surrey v Glos., Bristol; G. Cook, 128, Northants v Kent, Canterbury.
D. B. D'Oliveira, 102, Worcs. v Middx, Worcester.
R. G. P. Ellis, 103*, Oxford U. v Glam., Oxford; J. E. Emburey, 135, Middx v Essex, Chelmsford.
N. A. Felton, 173*, Somerset v Kent, Taunton.
I. A. Greig, 147*, Sussex v Oxford U., Oxford.
R. J. Hadlee, 103, Notts. v Sussex, Hove; B. R. Hardie, 129, Essex v Cambridge U., Cambridge; B. Hassan, 112, Notts. v Essex, Chelmsford; S. P. Henderson, 135*, Glam. v Warw., Birmingham; D. P. Hughes, 153, Lancs. v Glam., Manchester.
T. E. Jesty, 187, Hants v Derby., Derby; P. Johnson, 125, Notts. v Glos., Bristol; A. Jones, 105, Glam. v Sussex, Cardiff.
Kapil Dev, 120, Northants v Somerset, Weston-super-Mare; C. L. King, 123, Worcs. v Somerset, Worcester; R. D. V. Knight, 101*, Surrey v Essex, Chelmsford.
D. Lloyd, 123, Lancs. v Northants, Northampton; J. W. Lloyds, 100, Somerset v Northants, Northampton.
M. S. A. McEvoy, 103, Worcs. v Warw., Birmingham; A. A. Metcalfe, 122, Yorks. v Notts., Bradford; A. J. T. Miller, 127*, Oxford U. v Hants, Oxford; M. D. Moxon, 153, Yorks. v Lancs., Leeds.
D. B. Pauline, 115, Surrey v Sussex, The Oval; N. F. M. Popplewell, 143, Somerset v Glos., Bath; D. R. Pringle, 102*, Essex v Hants, Southend.
T. B. Racionzer, 115, Scotland v Ireland, Downpatrick; C. T. Radley, 119, Middx v New Zealanders, Lord's; P. M. Roebuck, 106*, Somerset v Hants, Taunton.
D. M. Smith, 100*, Warw. v Oxford U., Birmingham; P. A. Smith, 114, Warw. v Oxford U., Birmingham; A. J. Stewart, 118*, Surrey v Oxford U., The Oval.
C. J. Tavaré, 109, England v New Zealand, The Oval; K. P. Tomlins, 132*, Middx v Sussex, Hove; D. R. Turner, 122*, Hampshire v Oxford U., Oxford.
M. J. Weston, 115, Worcs. v Sussex, Hove; R. G. Williams, 104*, Northants v Yorks., Bradford; S. H. Wootton, 104, Warw. v Cambridge U., Cambridge.

TEN WICKETS IN A MATCH

There were 23 instances of bowlers taking ten or more wickets in a match in first-class cricket in 1983, one fewer than in 1982. The list includes 22 in the County Championship and one by the New Zealand touring side.

J. K. Lever (3)
12-95   Essex v Sussex, Hove
11-95   Essex v Northants, Ilford
11-163   Essex v Yorks., Chelmsford

D. L. Underwood (3)
14-158   Kent v Worcs., Canterbury
13-161   Kent v Notts., Nottingham
10-124   Kent v Middx, Dartford

P. H. Edmonds (2)
10-72   Middx v Warw., Birmingham
10-161   Middx v Surrey, The Oval

N. Gifford (2)
10-176   Warw. v Surrey, The Oval
10-196   Warw. v Kent, Folkestone

The following each took ten wickets in a match on one occasion:
D. L. Acfield, 10-140, Essex v Lancs., Manchester.
B. L. Cairns, 10-144, New Zealand v England, Leeds; P. Carrick, 12-89, Yorks. v Derby., Sheffield; S. T. Clarke, 11-111, Surrey v Essex, The Oval.
W. W. Daniel, 10-107, Middx v Glos., Bristol.
G. J. F. Ferris, 10-104, Leics. v Glam., Hinckley.

E. E. Hemmings, 11-77, Notts. v Lancs., Nottingham.
S. T. Jefferies, 11-95, Lancs. v Notts., Nottingham; G. W. Johnson, 10-172, Kent v Northants, Canterbury.
M. D. Marshall, 10-124, Hants v Essex, Southend; O. H. Mortensen, 11-89, Derby. v Yorks., Sheffield.
J. Simmons, 12-133, Lancs. v Glos., Southport.
L. B. Taylor, 11-102, Leics. v Notts., Leicester.

SIX WICKETS IN AN INNINGS

There were 81 instances of bowlers taking six or more wickets in an innings in first-class cricket in 1983, eleven fewer than in 1982. The list includes 69 in the County Championship, five by the New Zealand touring side, and seven in other first-class matches.

D. L. Underwood (6)
7-55 Kent v Worcs., Canterbury
7-55 Kent v Leics., Folkestone
7-88 Kent v Notts., Nottingham
7-103 Kent v Worcs., Canterbury
6-44 Kent v Middx, Dartford
6-73 Kent v Notts., Nottingham

N. Gifford (5)
6-22 Warw. v Middx, Birmingham
6-77 Warw. v Derby., Birmingham
6-85 Warw. v Kent, Folkestone
6-92 Warw. v Lancs., Birmingham
6-94 Warw. v Surrey, The Oval

P. H. Edmonds (4)
6-38 Middx v Derby., Chesterfield
6-49 Middx v Cambridge U., Cambridge
6-87 Middx v Surrey, The Oval
6-93 Middx v New Zealanders, Lord's

J. K. Lever (4)
7-55 Essex v Sussex, Hove
7-63 Essex v Cambridge U., Cambridge
7-78 Essex v Yorks., Chelmsford
6-36 Essex v Northants, Ilford

M. D. Marshall (4)
7-29 Hants v Somerset, Bournemouth
6-46 Hants v Somerset, Taunton
6-58 Hants v Worcs., Southampton
6-73 Hants v Essex, Southend

N. Phillip (4)
6-4   Essex v Surrey, Chelmsford
6-19 Essex v Glos., Colchester
6-38 Essex v Worcs., Colchester
6-92 Essex v Leics., Chelmsford

D. L. Acfield (2)
7-100 Essex v Lancs., Manchester
6-34 Essex v Somerset, Taunton

B. L. Cairns (2)
7-46 New Zealanders v Warw., Birmingham
7-74 New Zealand v England, Leeds

S. T. Clarke (2)
7-53 Surrey v Warw., The Oval
6-48 Surrey v Essex, The Oval

K. E. Cooper (2)
7-33 Notts. v Worcs., Worcester
6-89 Notts. v Leics., Nottingham

G. J. F. Ferris (2)
7-42 Leics. v Glam., Hinckley
6-43 Leics. v Essex, Chelmsford

M. Hendrick (2)
6-17 Notts. v Leics., Nottingham
6-55 Notts. v Lancs., Nottingham

A. C. S. Pigott (2)
6-22 Sussex v Derby., Eastbourne
6-74 Sussex v Worcs., Hove

P. I. Pocock (2)
7-79 Surrey v Somerset, Taunton
6-74 Surrey v Notts., The Oval

J. N. Shepherd (2)
7-50 Glos. v Warw., Birmingham
7-64 Glos. v Glam., Cheltenham

M. Watkinson (2)
6-51 Lancs. v Sussex, Horsham
6-69 Lancs. v Glam., Swansea

The following each took six wickets in an innings on one occasion:

S. R. Barwick, 8-42, Glam. v Worcs., Worcester; B. P. Bracewell, 6-111, New Zealanders v Essex, Chelmsford.

E. J. Chatfield, 6-40, New Zealanders v Glos., Bristol; J. H. Childs, 6-81, Glos. v Derby., Bristol; P. Carrick, 7-44, Yorks. v Derby., Sheffield; I. J. Curtis, 6-28, Surrey v Oxford U., The Oval.

W. W. Daniel, 7-61, Middx v Glos., Bristol; W. W. Davis, 7-70, Glam. v Notts., Ebbw Vale.

J. E. Emburey, 6-13, Middx v Kent, Dartford.

N. A. Foster, 6-46, Essex v Sussex, Ilford.

J. Garner, 6-37, Somerset v Kent, Maidstone; D. A. Graveney, 6-88, Glos. v Northants, Northampton; B. J. Griffiths, 6-92, Northants v Essex, Ilford.

R. J. Hadlee, 6-53, New Zealand v England, The Oval; K. A. Hayes, 6-58, Oxford U. v Warw., Birmingham; E. E. Hemmings, 7-23, Notts. v Lancs., Nottingham; S. P. Hughes, 6-32, Middx v Glos., Bristol.

Imran Khan, 6-6, Sussex v Warw., Birmingham.

S. T. Jefferies, 8-46, Lancs. v Notts., Nottingham; G. W. Johnson, 7-76, Kent v Northants, Canterbury.

N. A. Mallender, 6-48, Northants v Worcs., Northampton; V. J. Marks, 6-79, Somerset v Yorks., Weston-super-Mare; G. Monkhouse, 7-51, Surrey v Notts., The Oval; O. H. Mortensen, 6-27, Derby. v Yorks., Sheffield.

A. Needham, 6-30, Surrey v Oxford U., The Oval.

R. C. Ontong, 6-64, Glam. v Leics., Hinckley.

D. R. Pringle, 7-32, Essex v Middx, Chelmsford.

G. E. Sainsbury, 6-66, Glos. v Worcs., Worcester; M. W. W. Selvey, 6-47, Glam. v Oxford U., Oxford; J. Simmons, 7-73, Lancs. v Glos., Southport; P. M. Such, 6-123, Notts. v Kent, Nottingham.

L. B. Taylor, 7-73, Leics. v Notts., Leicester; T. M. Tremlett, 6-82, Hants v Derby., Portsmouth.

C. E. Waller, 6-126, Sussex v Essex, Hove.

HONOURS' LIST

In 1983, the following were decorated for services to cricket.

New Year's Honours: I. W. Johnson (Australia) (for services to sports' administration, particularly to cricket) CBE; F. G. Mann (England) CBE; R. A. Vance (New Zealand) (for services to cricket and the community) CBE; B. A. Johnston (England) (for services to broadcasting and cricket) OBE.

Queen's Birthday Honours: C. S. Elliott (England) MBE; C. F. Collins (New Zealand) OBE.

THE NEW ZEALANDERS IN ENGLAND, 1983

After 52 years, and at the 29th attempt, New Zealand beat England in a Test match in England. For that victory the tenth New Zealand side to England will hold a lasting place in its country's cricket history. Unbeaten outside the Test matches, Geoff Howarth's team may be regarded alongside its most eminent predecessors, although in some respects it failed to fulfil expectations. The other three Tests were lost by convincing margins, two of them in four days, and New Zealand failed to reach the semi-finals of the Prudential Cup, which occupied the team's interest in June before the first-class tour began.

The problems of choosing a team to cope with a programme of limited-overs and first-class cricket have in the past been presented as one reason for the poor performance of touring sides facing dual commitments, but this could not be applied to the 1983 New Zealanders. They represented the core of New Zealand's recent successes in both forms of the game. Howarth, Richard Hadlee and John Wright (as well as Glenn Turner in the Prudential Cup squad) knew English conditions from regular county cricket, while Lance Cairns, Martin Crowe and Evan Gray had recently played league cricket in England. Jeff Crowe had played for South Australia in the Sheffield Shield for five years. No previous New Zealand side to England could boast such experience.

Following the final Test, Willis, the England captain, said there was a need for New Zealand to find some fast bowlers, and certainly, Hadlee apart, the New Zealand attack had held few fears for England's batsmen. Neither Ewen Chatfield nor Martin Snedden, the candidates to share the new ball with Hadlee, was better than a useful fast-medium, with Snedden the quicker of the two and the 33-year-old Chatfield the more accurate. It speaks volumes, perhaps, that Chatfield's five for 95 in sympathetic conditions at Headingley was a personal best in Test cricket. Although surprising batsmen occasionally with unexpected lift and away movement, he lacked that decisive edge to open a Test attack. Snedden failed to do himself justice. Hit for 105 in twelve overs on his first appearance in England (v England in the World Cup at The Oval), he took time to find an "English length" and had too few weapons on a good wicket.

The medium-paced Cairns, whose big hitting frequently provided brief entertainment, also began the tour out of sorts but regained form with eight wickets against Warwickshire on the eve of the second Test. With ten wickets he played the major role in that historic Headingley victory. In addition to swing he had at his disposal an excellent leg-cutter, a useful slower ball and even a leg-spinner. Martin Crowe, at medium-fast pace, joined the seam brigade later in the tour and could develop into a fine all-rounder. During the tour the New Zealanders gave two games to the twenty-year-old Auckland fast bowler, Sean Tracy, with Gloucestershire on a cricket scholarship. His performance against Brian Close's XI gave promise that he might answer some of New Zealand's bowling problems in the future.

Chosen as Man of the Series, Hadlee always lived up to his reputation and his own high standards. His bowling, off a shortened run-up, was a model for an aspiring fast bowler, full of variation, control and hostility. At 33 he remained one of the world's leading fast bowlers, as well as strengthening his claims to a place among the top all-rounders. His left-handed batting had few frills but his approach was undeniably effective. His 21 wickets were a record for a New

Zealand bowler against England, surpassing Tony MacGibbon's 20 in the five-Test series of 1958.

Of the two spinners, the tall off-spinner, John Bracewell, enjoyed greater opportunity and success, finishing the tour as leading wicket-taker. He was less effective in the Test matches, but at 25 he was still a novice. It is to be hoped New Zealand continue to encourage his development. Gray, slow left-arm and right-hand middle-order batsman, enjoyed an afternoon of success in his début Test at Lord's.

If their bowling was always going to handicap the New Zealanders, the failure of their recognised batsmen to provide match-winning or match-saving innings in the Test matches was a serious setback. No one reached three figures in the series. Bruce Edgar and Wright, both accomplished left-handed openers, only once provided a first-wicket stand of more than 20 – at Headingley – although each enjoyed individual success. When Wright, whose calling of a run was dismal for a professional cricketer, suffered a broken toe against Leicestershire, his place in the final Test was taken by the tall, upright Auckland opener, Trevor Franklin, who discovered that a run of high scores against the counties meant little when it came to Test cricket.

The great pity was that Glenn Turner, in England for the Prudential Cup only, could not be persuaded to remain with the touring side. His experience and class batsmanship would have strengthened New Zealand's early order considerably. Howarth, twice the victim of run-out mix-ups with Wright, had an unlucky tour, only occasionally providing evidence of his true ability. His captaincy was never less than adequate and he led a popular, well-mannered side which made a big contribution to a happy summer's cricket. The twenty-year-old Martin Crowe, while still getting the feel of Test cricket, did enough to show that he should be the bulwark of his country's batting for years to come.

An appreciation of Jeremy Coney's contribution will be found in the Five Cricketers of the Year section. The epitome of the New Zealand cricketer who makes the transition from Saturday afternoon club cricket to Test cricket with only limited first-class experience, often under-rated, he was vital to the side, either shoring up the innings or containing opposing batsmen with his deceptively mild swing bowling.

Of the two wicket-keepers, Warren Lees and Ian Smith, the latter inspired the greater confidence with tidy, undemonstrative displays, regaining his Test place after Lees had an erratic first Test at The Oval. A broken finger put Smith out of consideration for the fourth Test.

During the tour Howarth spoke out about the attitude of counties in respect of the opposition they provided touring sides, a criticism which was later echoed by the team's manager, Sir Allan Wright, and has been made by other tourists. Howarth's reaction came after his side's early and easy victory over a second-strength Hampshire eleven at a time when New Zealand were in need of a good work-out before the third Test. The TCCB could do worse than look to the hospitality it affords its visitors in this respect. – G.A.W.

THE NEW ZEALANDERS IN ENGLAND, 1983

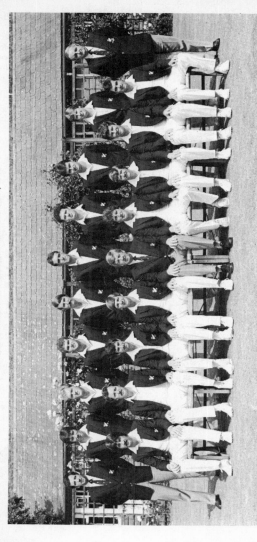

[*Patrick Eagar*

Back row: P. A. Borrie (*doctor*), M. C. Snedden, J. J. Crowe, M. D. Crowe, E. J. Chatfield, T. J. Franklin, J. G. Bracewell, E. J. Gray, I. D. S. Smith, J. J. O'Sullivan (*scorer*). *Front row:* W. K. Lees, J. V. Coney, R. J. Hadlee, G. P. Howarth (*captain*), Sir Allan Wright (*manager*), J. G. Wright, G. M. Turner, B. L. Cairns, B. A. Edgar. (Note: G. M. Turner returned to New Zealand after the World Cup.)

NEW ZEALAND TOUR RESULTS

Test matches – Played 4: Won 1, Lost 3.

First-class matches – Played 13: Won 7, Lost 3, Drawn 3.

Wins – England, Essex, Hampshire, Leicestershire, Warwickshire, Worcestershire, D. B. Close's XI.

Losses – England (3).

Draws – Gloucestershire, Middlesex, Somerset.

Non first-class matches – Played 2: Won 1, Drawn 1. *Win* – Surrey. *Draw* – Combined Services.

TEST MATCH AVERAGES

ENGLAND – BATTING

	T	I	NO	R	HI	100s	Avge
A. J. Lamb	4	8	2	392	137*	2	65.33
D. I. Gower	4	8	1	404	112*	2	57.71
C. J. Tavaré	4	8	0	330	109	1	41.25
D. W. Randall	3	6	1	194	83	0	38.80
I. T. Botham	4	8	0	282	103	1	35.25
G. Fowler	2	4	0	134	105	1	33.50
M. W. Gatting	2	4	0	121	81	0	30.25
P. H. Edmonds	2	4	1	63	43*	0	21.00
C. L. Smith	2	4	0	78	43	0	19.50
R. G. D. Willis	4	7	2	67	25*	0	13.40
N. G. B. Cook	2	4	0	51	26	0	12.75
R. W. Taylor	4	7	1	63	21	0	10.50
N. G. Cowans	4	7	1	22	10	0	3.66

Played in one Test: G. R. Dilley 0, 15; N. A. Foster 10, 3; V. J. Marks 4, 2.

*Signifies not out.

BOWLING

	O	M	R	W	Avge	BB
R. G. D. Willis	123.3	38	273	20	13.65	5-35
N. G. B. Cook	135.2	56	275	17	16.17	5-35
I. T. Botham	112.5	27	340	10	34.00	4-50
N. G. Cowans	125	25	447	12	37.25	3-74

Also bowled: G. R. Dilley 25–6–52–0; P. H. Edmonds 87.1–30–221–4; N. A. Foster 28–5–75–1; M. W. Gatting 7–3–13–0; V. J. Marks 43–20–78–3; C. L. Smith 12–2–31–2.

NEW ZEALAND – BATTING

	T	I	NO	R	HI	100s	Avge
R. J. Hadlee	4	8	2	301	92*	0	50.16
B. A. Edgar	4	8	0	336	84	0	42.00
J. G. Wright	3	6	0	230	93	0	38.33
J. V. Coney	4	8	1	238	68	0	34.00
G. P. Howarth	4	8	0	189	67	0	23.62
M. D. Crowe	4	8	0	163	46	0	20.37
B. L. Cairns	4	7	1	116	32	0	19.33
W. K. Lees	2	4	1	47	31*	0	15.66
I. D. S. Smith	2	3	1	22	17*	0	11.00
E. J. Gray	2	4	0	38	17	0	9.50
J. G. Bracewell	4	7	1	56	28	0	9.33
E. J. Chatfield	3	5	2	17	10*	0	5.66
J. J. Crowe	2	4	0	22	13	0	5.50

Played in one Test: T. J. Franklin 2, 7; M. C. Snedden 9, 12.

*Signifies not out.

BOWLING

	O	M	R	W	Avge	BB
J. V. Coney	63	26	115	5	23.00	2-21
R. J. Hadlee	232	65	559	21	26.61	6-53
B. L. Cairns	184	52	461	16	28.81	7-74
J. G. Bracewell	123	28	364	10	36.40	4-108
E. J. Chatfield	153	37	440	11	40.00	5-95

Also bowled: M. D. Crowe 21-1-58-2; E. J. Gray 48-12-128-4; G. P. Howarth 3-2-1-0; M. C. Snedden 36-8-109-4.

NEW ZEALAND TOUR AVERAGES – FIRST-CLASS MATCHES

BATTING

	M	I	NO	R	HI	100s	Avge
M. D. Crowe	11	19	5	819	134*	3	58.50
R. J. Hadlee	8	11	2	477	92*	0	53.00
J. G. Wright	7	10	0	498	136	1	49.80
G. P. Howarth	11	18	1	697	144	1	41.00
B. A. Edgar	11	21	2	742	100	1	39.05
T. J. Franklin	9	18	3	539	98*	0	35.93
J. V. Coney	9	17	3	437	68	0	31.21
J. J. Crowe	11	19	2	470	79	0	27.64
W. K. Lees	6	9	4	136	42*	0	27.20
E. J. Gray	9	15	3	280	72	0	23.33
B. L. Cairns	11	14	2	254	60	0	21.16
M. C. Snedden	10	9	0	154	35	0	17.11
J. G. Bracewell	11	16	3	183	38	0	14.07
I. D. S. Smith	8	12	3	104	32*	0	11.55
E. J. Chatfield	9	8	4	45	13*	0	11.25
S. R. Tracy	2	2	0	4	4	0	2.00

* Signifies not out.

BOWLING

	O	M	R	W	Avge	BB
M. D. Crowe	76	12	284	12	23.66	3-21
R. J. Hadlee	345.1	95	855	36	23.75	6-53
J. V. Coney	124.5	40	339	14	24.21	3-19
E. J. Gray	143	40	398	16	24.87	4-24
J. G. Bracewell	325.5	73	1,095	41	26.70	6-111
B. L. Cairns	341.1	101	877	32	27.40	7-46
M. C. Snedden	236.2	37	845	30	28.16	5-68
E. J. Chatfield	303.3	79	818	28	29.21	6-40

Also bowled: B. A. Edgar 5–0–17–1; G. P. Howarth 17–4–41–1; S. R. Tracy 33.1–5–115–8.

FIELDING

I. D. S. Smith 21 (19ct, 2st), J. V. Coney 14, J. J. Crowe 13, M. D. Crowe 13, G. P. Howarth 12, W. K. Lees 12, J. G. Bracewell 10, E. J. Gray 7, B. L. Cairns 6, B. A. Edgar 6, T. J. Franklin 6, J. G. Wright 6, R. J. Hadlee 3, E. J. Chatfield 1.

†At Portsmouth, June 30, July 1. Drawn. Combined Services 100 for five dec. (J. G. Bracewell three for 26) and 105 for nine (J. G. Bracewell four for 31); New Zealanders 221 for five dec. (T. J. Franklin 108 retired, E. J. Gray 61 not out).

SOMERSET v NEW ZEALANDERS

At Taunton, July 2, 3, 4. Drawn. After a speculative start, Wright, missed when 0, and Howarth launched a big first innings, culminating in Cairns hitting 60 from 29 balls with four 6s and seven 4s. They batted until the second lunchtime. Then a good start and a third-wicket partnership of 126 in 43 overs between Lloyds and Slocombe, both surviving early chances, gave way to a collapse against the spinners. The New Zealanders did not enforce the follow-on, and for 70 minutes added to their lead, eventually setting Somerset 324 to win in 220 minutes. Denning provided a lively start; but he lacked support and after Garner had hit Bracewell for 26 in an over Davis and Wilson were left to survive the final six overs.

New Zealanders

T. J. Franklin c Garner b Wilson	0	– not out	34
B. A. Edgar lbw b Marks	34	– not out	11
J. G. Wright c Wyatt b Wilson	85		
*G. P. Howarth c Gard b Lloyds	88		
J. J. Crowe c Gard b Davis	27		
E. J. Gray lbw b Garner	72		
R. J. Hadlee c Gard b Wilson	82		
J. G. Bracewell c and b Davis	38		
†W. K. Lees not out	46		
B. L. Cairns c Gard b Wilson	60		
B 1, l-b 12, w 1, n-b 2	16	L-b 1	1

1/1 2/100 3/143 4/237 （9 wkts dec.) 544　　　　　　　(no wkt dec.) 46
5/243 6/399 7/399 8/464 9/544

M. C. Snedden did not bat.

Bowling: *First Innings*—Garner 15–6–32–1; Wilson 29–6–109–4; Davis 26–2–123–2; Popplewell 7–1–50–0; Marks 35–10–125–1; Lloyds 16–2–89–1. *Second Innings*—Garner 6–1–17–0; Wilson 6–2–11–0; Davis 2–1–4–0; Marks 2.5–0–7–0; Rose 1–0–6–0.

Somerset

J. W. Lloyds c Lees b Bracewell	84	– (6) c Lees b Bracewell	14
*B. C. Rose b Cairns	34	– c Cairns b Snedden	12
P. W. Denning c Bracewell b Cairns	0	– (1) b Gray	99
P. A. Slocombe b Bracewell	66	– (5) b Bracewell	13
†T. Gard c Wright b Bracewell	5	– (8) c Crowe b Bracewell	12
M. R. Davis b Gray	0	– (9) not out	20
N. F. M. Popplewell c Edgar b Gray	7	– (3) c Bracewell b Snedden	0
J. G. Wyatt c Howarth b Bracewell	0	– (7) c Gray b Bracewell	14
V. J. Marks not out	26	– (4) c Lees b Snedden	0
J. Garner c Franklin b Gray	16	– c Wright b Bracewell	26
P. H. L. Wilson c Wright b Gray	12	– not out	3
B 7, l-b 7, w 1, n-b 2	17	B 4, l-b 2, w 1, n-b 1	8

1/57 2/67 3/193 4/196   267 1/38 2/52 3/52 4/81   (9 wkts) 221
5/205 6/209 7/210 8/230 9/252   5/133 6/157 7/161 8/176 9/215

Bowling: *First Innings*—Hadlee 16–3–49–0; Snedden 14–5–50–0; Cairns 19–9–36–2; Bracewell 28–9–91–4; Gray 13–8–24–4. *Second Innings*—Hadlee 10–1–40–0; Snedden 8–3–29–3; Cairns 7–2–19–0; Bracewell 23–9–73–5; Gray 20–6–48–1; Howarth 3–2–4–0.

Umpires: B. J. Meyer and D. J. Constant.

GLOUCESTERSHIRE v NEW ZEALANDERS

At Bristol, July 6, 7, 8. Drawn. Gloucestershire batted throughout the final day to force the draw, mainly through the efforts of Bainbridge whose 146 was a career-best. Lacking Broad, Zaheer and Shepherd, Gloucestershire were easy meat for the New Zealand pace bowlers on the first day. Wright's 136, which included a 6 and 22 4s, enabled the touring team to build a lead of 218 by the end of the second day. Only Sean Tracy, a twenty-year-old New Zealand pace bowler on a cricket scholarship, and Graveney presented much challenge. When Gloucestershire lost their first five second-innings wickets for 141, a New Zealand victory looked very likely. But by then the pitch was playing easily and Bainbridge was well set. Russell and Graveney gave valuable support in lengthy partnerships and by the time Bainbridge was seventh out, having hit twenty boundaries in four and a half hours, the match was virtually saved.

Gloucestershire

A. W. Stovold c Bracewell b Chatfield	58	– c J. J. Crowe b Hadlee	21
P. W. Romaines lbw b Hadlee	23	– run out	30
P. Bainbridge c M. D. Crowe b Chatfield	3	– lb b Hadlee	146
A. J. Hignell hit wkt b Coney	10	– b Snedden	0
A. J. Wright c Howarth b Chatfield	0	– c Wright b Bracewell	26
R. J. Doughty c Coney b Hadlee	10	– c Howarth b Bracewell	2
*D. A. Graveney c Coney b Hadlee	3	– (8) not out	27
†R. C. Russell b Chatfield	8	– (7) c Edgar b Bracewell	30
J. H. Childs not out	0	– c Hadlee b Snedden	3
G. E. Sainsbury b Chatfield	1	– not out	8
S. R. Tracy c Coney b Chatfield	0		
B 1, l-b 3	4	B 4, l-b 5, w 1, n-b 2	12

1/37 2/48 3/79 4/82   120 1/24 2/68 3/72   (8 wkts) 305
5/99 6/102 7/117 8/119 9/120   4/133 5/141 6/225 7/286 8/295

Bowling: *First Innings*—Hadlee 14–7–25–3; Snedden 8–0–42–0; Chatfield 17.3–6–40–6; Coney 4–1–9–1. *Second Innings*—Hadlee 20–9–31–2; Snedden 20–2–74–2; Chatfield 18–4–51–0; Bracewell 29–4–87–3; Coney 11–1–50–0.

New Zealanders

J. G. Wright c Hignell b Doughty	136	J. G. Bracewell b Graveney	0
B. A. Edgar b Tracy	39	†I. D. S. Smith not out	19
J. J. Crowe c Russell b Tracy	8	B 1, l-b 8, w 3, n-b 3	15
*G. P. Howarth c Hignell b Graveney	60		
M. D. Crowe not out	61	1/122 2/136 3/218 (6 wkts dec.) 338	
J. V. Coney b Bainbridge	0	4/270 5/272 6/275	

M. C. Snedden, R. J. Hadlee and E. J. Chatfield did not bat.

Bowling: Tracy 21–5–55–2; Sainsbury 23–8–55–0; Bainbridge 16–6–39–1; Doughty 13–0–66–1; Childs 17–6–70–0; Graveney 14–3–38–2.

Umpires: H. D. Bird and D. G. L. Evans.

MIDDLESEX v NEW ZEALANDERS

At Lord's, July 9, 10, 11. Drawn. For the first time on their tour the New Zealanders played a county whose announced aim was to beat them, the realisation dawning on Middlesex that their sole post-war win over a touring side had been against the 1976 West Indians. After two and a half days of purposeful cricket, Middlesex were within sight of their objective. After winning the toss, Gatting made the most of four lives – the first two, a stumping at 34 and a catch behind at 56, were in the "sitter" class – to score his first double-hundred. The chances notwithstanding, it was a brilliant innings, containing four 6s and 28 4s in 241 minutes. Radley, content to play second fiddle in a stand of 318, went on to score 119 in 258 minutes. On the second day Edmonds and Emburey, helped by some careless batting, spun the tourists out 152 behind, a deficit that had been exactly cancelled out when Martin Crowe and Gray began a saving partnership of 135 on the final afternoon. Crowe batted for 283 minutes.

Middlesex

K. P. Tomlins b Cairns	9	J. E. Emburey not out	10
W. N. Slack lbw b Chatfield	22	L-b 2, n-b 3	5
C. T. Radley c J. J. Crowe b Coney	119		
*M. W. Gatting c J. J. Crowe b Coney	216	1/19 2/46 (4 wkts dec.) 386	
R. O. Butcher not out	5	3/364 4/376	

†P. R. Downton, P. H. Edmonds, N. F. Williams, N. G. Cowans and W. W. Daniel did not bat.

Bowling: Snedden 7–1–18–0; Chatfield 24–3–69–1; Cairns 26–5–78–1; Gray 13–1–78–0; Bracewell 19–3–82–0; Coney 17–4–56–2.

New Zealanders

T. J. Franklin lbw b Edmonds	45	– c sub b Williams	12
J. J. Crowe c sub b Emburey	8	– b Emburey	34
*G. P. Howarth b Emburey	72	– (5) c Radley b Edmonds	11
M. D. Crowe st Downton b Edmonds	10	– not out	134
J. V. Coney c sub b Emburey	3	– (3) c and b Edmonds	38
E. J. Gray c Tomlins b Edmonds	5	– lbw b Slack	42
J. G. Bracewell c Radley b Edmonds	23	– not out	3
†W. K. Lees not out	35		
B. L. Cairns c Radley b Edmonds	0		
M. C. Snedden lbw b Edmonds	11		
E. J. Chatfield b Daniel	13		
B 1, l-b 4, n-b 4	9	B 8, l-b 6, n-b 14	28

1/93 2/111 3/128 4/139	234	1/24 2/83 3/122 (5 wkts) 302	
5/149 6/159 7/180 8/180 9/196		4/152 5/287	

Bowling: *First Innings*—Cowans 6–2–10–0; Daniel 9.1–1–36–1; Williams 3–0–20–0; Emburey 43–16–66–3; Edmonds 44–11–93–6. *Second Innings*—Williams 8–2–15–1; Daniel 8–2–30–0; Edmonds 39–6–118–2; Emburey 30–6–77–1; Gatting 1–0–8–0; Slack 8–2–13–1; Butcher 2–0–11–0; Radley 1–0–2–0.

Umpires: D. R. Shepherd and C. T. Spencer.

ENGLAND v NEW ZEALAND

First Cornhill Test

At The Oval, July 14, 15, 16, 17, 18. England won by 189 runs. England triumphed comprehensively, despite being bowled out for only 209 on a good pitch in their first innings and being jeered from the field after making only 194 runs from 98 overs in a whole day's play in their second. They succeeded, however, in putting the game out of reach of their opponents who, required to bat for some ten hours to save it, lost their last seven wickets for only 73 runs in 23 overs.

With Dilley unfit, England opted to play two spinners and omitted Foster, of Essex, who, with only sixteen first-class games and 55 wickets to his name, had been standing by. After winning the toss, England batted unevenly against bowlers who found the ball would swing on a cloudless but sultry first day, Hadlee finishing with six for 53 after an intelligent display of sustained accuracy and variations of pace. Randall, after much playing and missing at the start, was left unbeaten with 75.

Willis, however, then bowled with great life and hostility to remove Wright and Jeff Crowe without conceding a run. This pattern continued on the second morning when New Zealand were reduced to 41 for five (Willis four for 10 in twelve overs) before Hadlee and Coney added 84 together in only fifteen overs by making the most of the variable quality of England's second-line bowling.

Hadlee, driving powerfully off the front foot, took 16 runs from one over from Botham, whose first three overs cost 28, and with Coney batting sensibly it needed an athletic piece of fielding at mid-on by Willis, rounded off by a direct hit, to run out Coney. Hadlee had made 84 from 78 balls when Botham, finishing more happily than he had started, caught and bowled him.

England, helped by two escapes by Fowler before he had reached 50, then built on their slender lead in perfect conditions for batting. With Tavaré playing impressive strokes all round the wicket, the pair put on 223, only the eleventh double-century opening partnership in England's history. Fowler reached his maiden Test century, and Tavaré his second, the first time since 1960 that both England openers had made three figures in the same innings. Their dismissal, in quick succession, led to England losing the initiative on the third day against accurate bowling, thoughtfully handled by Howarth. After the crowd had vented their displeasure at that, only 5,600 turned up on the Sunday to see Lamb, struggling to recapture his form, complete an unbeaten 102 after five hours, the first time since 1974 that an England innings had contained three century-makers.

Willis's declaration asked New Zealand to make 460 for victory, a fourth-innings total exceeded only by England's 654 for five in the Durban timeless Test of 1939. The England captain, again bowling very fast, quickly reduced them to 26 for two, but Wright and Howarth added 120 for the third wicket, coping with the problems of spinners bowling into the rough and suggesting that the game might be saved if they could survive the pre-lunch session on the last day. Wright, however, was run out in only the seventh over after a stay of four hours and eventually Marks and Edmonds, operating virtually unchanged, worked their way through some modest batting, leaving New Zealand with the consolation only of the Man of the Match award, deservedly won by Hadlee. The total attendance was 34,043 and receipts £168,240. – M.J.C.

England

G. Fowler lbw b Hadlee	1	– run out	105
C. J. Tavaré run out	45	– c Howarth b Bracewell	109
D. I. Gower b Hadlee	11	– c Howarth b Hadlee	25
A. J. Lamb b Cairns	24	– not out	102
I. T. Botham b Hadlee	15	– run out	26
D. W. Randall not out	75	– c Coney b Hadlee	3
V. J. Marks c Lees b Hadlee	4	– c M. D. Crowe b Bracewell	2
P. H. Edmonds c and b Bracewell	12	– not out	43
†R. W. Taylor lbw b Hadlee	0		
*R. G. D. Willis c J. J. Crowe b Bracewell	4		
N. G. Cowans b Hadlee	3		
B 6, l-b 6, n-b 3	15	B 8, l-b 23	31

1/2 2/18 3/67 4/104   209   1/223 2/225 3/269 (6 wkts dec.) 446
5/116 6/154 7/184 8/191 9/202   4/322 5/329 6/336

Bowling: *First Innings*—Hadlee 23.4–6–53–6; Chatfield 17–3–48–0; Cairns 17–3–63–1; Bracewell 8–4–16–2; M. D. Crowe 5–0–14–0. *Second Innings*—Hadlee 37.2–7–99–2; Cairns 30–7–67–0; Chatfield 35–9–85–0; M. D. Crowe 3–0–9–0; Bracewell 54–13–115–2; Coney 27–11–39–0; Howarth 3–2–1–0.

New Zealand

J. G. Wright c Gower b Willis	0	– (2) run out	88
B. A. Edgar c Taylor b Willis	12	– (1) c Taylor b Willis	3
J. J. Crowe c Randall b Willis	0	– c Lamb b Willis	9
*G. P. Howarth b Cowans	4	– c Taylor b Edmonds	67
M. D. Crowe b Willis	0	– c Taylor b Edmonds	33
J. V. Coney run out	44	– lbw b Marks	2
R. J. Hadlee c and b Botham	84	– c Taylor b Marks	11
J. G. Bracewell c and b Botham	7	– (9) c Gower b Marks	0
†W. K. Lees not out	31	– (8) not out	8
B. L. Cairns c Lamb b Botham	2	– c Willis b Edmonds	32
E. J. Chatfield c Willis b Botham	0	– not out	10
L-b 6, n-b 6	12	B 3, l-b 1, n-b 3	7

1/0 2/1 3/10 4/17   196   1/10 2/26 3/146 4/197   270
5/41 6/125 7/149 8/182 9/188   5/202 6/210 7/228 8/228 9/228

Bowling: *First Innings*—Willis 20–8–43–4; Cowans 19–3–60–1; Botham 16–2–62–4; Edmonds 2–0–19–0. *Second Innings*—Willis 12–3–26–2; Cowans 11–2–41–0; Botham 4–0–17–0; Marks 43–20–78–3; Edmonds 40.1–16–101–3.

Umpires: H. D. Bird and D. G. L. Evans.

WORCESTERSHIRE v NEW ZEALANDERS

At Worcester, July 20, 21, 22. New Zealanders won by 100 runs. The New Zealanders' first win brought qualified satisfaction. The visitors' acting-captain, Richard Hadlee, severely criticised the pitch, which he labelled "not fit for first-class or club cricket". Inchmore and Pridgeon reduced the New Zealanders to 71 for seven on the opening morning, but Martin Crowe and Hadlee pulled them round with an eighth-wicket stand of 122. D'Oliveira, who had the grille of his helmet broken by a lifter from Hadlee, hit a sparkling 77 in Worcestershire's reply, with McEvoy lending good support in compiling his maiden half-century for the county. The touring side, with a first-innings lead of 46, left the home side a target of 257 in four hours, but took only 35.3 overs to bowl them out for 156.

New Zealanders

T. J. Franklin c McEvoy b Pridgeon	2	– c Humphries b Pridgeon	35
B. A. Edgar c Perryman b Inchmore	13	– c McEvoy b Inchmore	36
J. V. Coney lbw b Inchmore	1	– c McEvoy b Perryman	2
J. J. Crowe lbw b Pridgeon	4	– not out	41
M. D. Crowe c McEvoy b Inchmore	65		
E. J. Gray c D'Oliveira b Inchmore	7	– lbw b Inchmore	7
†I. D. S. Smith c Humphries b Inchmore	0	– c D'Oliveira b Perryman	4
J. G. Bracewell c Banks b Perryman	20	– not out	30
*R. J. Hadlee c McEvoy b Perryman	68		
M. C. Snedden c Patel b Pridgeon	14	– (5) c Inchmore b Pridgeon	29
B. L. Cairns not out	29		
B 5, l-b 9, w 5, n-b 4	23	B 5, l-b 15, w 3, n-b 3	26

1/12 2/13 3/26 4/29   246   1/59 2/76 3/82   (6 wkts dec.) 210
5/38 6/38 7/71 8/193 9/210   4/129 5/143 6/151

Bowling: *First Innings*—Pridgeon 27.4–9–65–3; Inchmore 25–8–82–5; Perryman 23–6–48–2; Patel 7–2–14–0; Weston 8–1–14–0. *Second Innings*—Pridgeon 23–5–83–2; Inchmore 20–8–31–2; Perryman 19–7–58–2; Patel 3–0–12–0.

Worcestershire

M. S. A. McEvoy c J. J. Crowe b Hadlee	54	– lbw b Hadlee	24
M. J. Weston lbw b Snedden	0	– c Cairns b Hadlee	0
T. S. Curtis lbw b Bracewell	11	– (11) absent hurt	
*D. N. Patel c Coney b Snedden	2	– (3) c Smith b Snedden	6
D. B. D'Oliveira c Hadlee b Coney	77	– (4) c Smith b Hadlee	0
D. A. Banks lbw b Hadlee	0	– (5) b Coney	36
†D. J. Humphries b Hadlee	3	– (6) c J. J. Crowe b Hadlee	41
R. K. Illingworth c Franklin b Coney	11	– (7) b Coney	0
J. D. Inchmore c J. J. Crowe b Bracewell	4	– (8) c M. D. Crowe b Cairns	24
S. P. Perryman c J. J. Crowe b Coney	7	– (9) c Bracewell b Cairns	8
A. P. Pridgeon not out	2	– not out	2
B 4, l-b 10, w 1, n-b 4	19	B 2, l-b 4, w 2, n-b 7	15

1/29 2/65 3/112 4/112   200   1/1 2/29 3/29 4/44   156
5/122 6/173 7/182 8/183 9/194   5/88 6/88 7/143 8/145 9/156

Bowling: *First Innings*—Hadlee 16–2–53–3; Cairns 16–6–44–0; Snedden 15–3–47–2; Bracewell 8–2–18–2; Coney 6.5–2–19–3. *Second Innings*—Hadlee 13–3–42–4; Cairns 8.3–3–28–2; M. D. Crowe 4–1–19–0; Snedden 5–0–21–1; Coney 5–1–31–2.

Umpires: P. B. Wight and D. O. Oslear.

WARWICKSHIRE v NEW ZEALANDERS

At Birmingham, July 23, 25, 26. New Zealanders won by 172 runs, thanks to a best-ever return for his country by Cairns of seven for 46. The opening bowler had been warned about his Test place before the match and his second-innings performance gave the perfect answer. All the New Zealand batsmen got runs with Jeff Crowe playing well in both innings and Edgar batting in the match for 63 overs for an equivalent number of runs. After the loss of two hours to rain on the first day, Warwickshire declared when 140 behind, to open up the game, but the bowling of Cairns was too much for an indeterminate batting display by the home team.

New Zealanders

T. J. Franklin b P. A. Smith	33	– b Hogg	17
B. A. Edgar lbw b Ferreira	17	– not out	46
J. G. Wright lbw b P. A. Smith	15		
J. J. Crowe b Gifford	63	– (3) c and b Gifford	79
J. V. Coney lbw b P. A. Smith	68	– not out	0
*G. P. Howarth b Gifford	55		
E. J. Gray not out	28		
†I. D. S. Smith not out	32		
B. L. Cairns (did not bat)		– (4) b Gifford	7
L-b 13, w 1, n-b 10	24	B 7, w 1, n-b 1	9

1/41 2/67 3/76 4/208   (6 wkts dec.) 335 1/27 2/142 3/150 (3 wkts dec.) 158
5/230 6/278

M. C. Snedden and E. J. Chatfield did not bat.

Bowling: *First Innings*—Willis 6–2–13–0; Hogg 17–4–39–0; Small 15–7–28–0; P. A. Smith 20–2–90–3; Gifford 28–4–101–2; Ferreira 17–3–40–1. *Second Innings*—Small 6–0–22–0; Hogg 6–0–17–1; Gifford 13–3–50–2; P. A. Smith 6–1–32–0; Lloyd 7–1–28–0.

Warwickshire

K. D. Smith c Smith b Chatfield	10	– (2) lbw b Cairns	39
T. A. Lloyd lbw b Chatfield	13	– (1) c Howarth b Chatfield	1
D. L. Amiss c and b Gray	78	– b Cairns	9
G. W. Humpage run out	16	– b Cairns	10
P. A. Smith lbw b Cairns	4	– st Smith b Gray	5
A. M. Ferreira not out	55	– not out	11
†G. A. Tedstone not out	3	– c Coney b Cairns	0
G. C. Small (did not bat)		– lbw b Cairns	3
N. Gifford (did not bat)		– b Cairns	0
*R. G. D. Willis (did not bat)		– b Cairns	37
W. Hogg (did not bat)		– b Snedden	1
L-b 8, w 1, n-b 7	16	B 4, l-b 2, w 1, n-b 3	10

1/16 2/30 3/48 4/65   (5 wkts dec.) 195 1/6 2/35 3/49 4/67   126
5/187   5/71 6/71 7/75 8/79 9/124

Bowling: *First Innings*—Snedden 14–1–52–0; Chatfield 19–4–60–2; Cairns 17–5–41–1; Coney 6–0–22–0; Gray 9–5–4–1. *Second Innings*—Snedden 10.2–0–45–1; Chatfield 6–2–13–1; Cairns 17–5–46–7; Coney 7–4–9–0; Gray 3–1–3–1.

Umpires: M. J. Kitchen and N. T. Plews.

ENGLAND v NEW ZEALAND

Second Cornhill Test

At Leeds, July 28, 29, 30, August 1. New Zealand won by five wickets. New Zealand's first victory in a Test in England, following seventeen defeats and eleven draws, arrived shortly after tea on the fourth day when Coney completed their task of scoring 101 with a leg-side 4 off Botham – the first ball of the only over Willis permitted Botham, so unintelligently had he bowled in New Zealand's first innings. Because England were in almost as hopeless a position after three days as they had been two years earlier in the Test against Australia upon which Botham made such an imperishable impact, only about 3,000 spectators saw the winning hit. But more than 30,000 had watched the game develop and all knew New Zealand's groundwork was well laid. For England, only Willis, who took the nine wickets he needed to become the fourth man to reach 300 in Test cricket, and Gower, with a handsome but unavailing 112 not out in the second innings, had reason to remember it with satisfaction. The toss was admittedly important, enabling Howarth to give his bowlers first use of a pitch that started damp to make it last; but in matters of skill, not excluding team selection, they proved themselves the better side.

It was happy, too, that the man who made the winning hit should have a sense of history: with Willis, charging down the slope at the end from which he took his eight for 43 against Australia in 1981, New Zealand hearts were fluttering when the lanky Coney walked in to bat at 61 for four. Nerves had let them down before in similar positions. A fifth wicket fell, all five to Willis, at 83. But Coney kept a steady head and with Hadlee, watched by father Walter, steered New Zealand home. Later, asked what was in his mind as Willis imperilled what had looked a fairly simple victory, Coney modestly tipped his cap to history by saying: "The main feeling was thinking of all the New Zealand players who have been coming here for 52 years, better players than myself, and making sure that their sweat and effort had not been in vain."

But despite Coney's contribution, and workmanlike efforts by Wright and Edgar in New Zealand's first innings, backed up by a punishing 75 from Hadlee, the match was essentially decided by the performances of the opposing sets of bowlers. In Cairns and Chatfield New Zealand had two whose speed was better suited to conditions than their faster England rivals. By bowling a full length they also gave the ball a better chance to swing. The 33-year-old Cairns, who won the Man of the Match award with his first bag of ten wickets in a Test, and Chatfield, who took five for 95 in England's second innings, were New Zealand's obvious heroes. But no miscarriage of justice would have been required for Hadlee to emerge with comparable figures. Accurate and businesslike off his spry clipped run, he beat the bat innumerable times. His control was exceptional and, generated by a high arm and strong body action, his pace sufficient.

Coney, with slow-medium swing, took three good wickets, including the vital one of Lamb when England were within 36 of clearing a deficit of 152 with eight second-innings wickets standing, and Howarth handled his bowlers adroitly. An injury to Dilley's heel in his second over, combined with Botham's lack of control, gave Willis extra problems. But considering the strength of the breeze that blew from west to east across the ground all match, he took too long deciding at which end Cowans, in particular, was better suited, and never gave the impression of searching for the most telling combination.

Although conditions helped the seam bowlers, New Zealand could be satisfied to bowl England out half an hour before the close on the first day, in view of the fact that shortly before tea there were eight wickets still to fall. The turning-point was a brilliant diving catch by Martin Crowe, left-handed at square leg, which ended a threatening innings by Lamb from a stroke that looked sure to go for 4. Tavaré, eighth out, propped up the innings for 295 minutes, while Botham briefly revived memories of 1981 by hitting a 6 and six 4s in 37 minutes. Cairns's seven for 74 was the first instance of a New Zealander taking seven wickets in an innings against England in a Test.

Edgar, hit by Botham on the thigh, was forced to retire hurt after 50 minutes on the second day, returning at the fall of the fifth wicket to partner Hadlee for the final 50 minutes as the score reached 252 for five. Wright, batting 288 minutes, was New Zealand's mainstay, but two run-outs marred his innings. At 52, changing his mind about an off-side single, he left Howarth stranded for Lamb to close in and hit the bowler's stumps. Three hours later, when Cowans had Martin Crowe lbw, another indecisive call by Wright led to the running out of Jeff Crowe by Cowans from long-leg. When Wright, unsettled, left next over, miscuing to mid-off, three wickets had been lost for 1 run in twelve minutes. Hadlee, first with Coney, then Edgar, stopped the rot.

England might still have evened up the game with wickets early on the third day, but Hadlee and Edgar carried their stand to 84, guaranteeing a substantial lead. Hadlee hit eight 4s in 185 minutes and Edgar had batted 282 minutes in two visits to the crease when he was ninth out. England, starting their second innings 50 minutes after lunch with a deficit of 152, looked to have the makings of a recovery when Lamb helped Gower take the score to 116 for two. Then Coney bowled Lamb and by close of play England were 154 for six. Gower's hundred, his first in a home Test since his 200 not out against India four years before, lasted 281 minutes and contained fourteen 4s. The total attendance was 36,050 and receipts totalled £150,000. – J.D.T.

England

G. Fowler c Smith b Chatfield	9	– c Smith b Chatfield	19
C. J. Tavaré c Smith b Coney	69	– b Chatfield	23
D. I. Gower c Coney b Cairns	9	– not out	112
A. J. Lamb c M. D. Crowe b Cairns	58	– b Coney	28
I. T. Botham c Howarth b Cairns	38	– c Howarth b Coney	4
D. W. Randall c Coney b Cairns	4	– c Smith b Chatfield	16
P. H. Edmonds c Smith b Cairns	8	– c Smith b Chatfield	0
G. R. Dilley b Cairns	0	– c Smith b Chatfield	15
†R. W. Taylor not out	10	– b Cairns	9
*R. G. D. Willis c J. J. Crowe b Coney	9	– c Coney b Cairns	4
N. G. Cowans c Bracewell b Cairns	0	– c M. D. Crowe b Cairns	10
B 4, l-b 7	11	B 8, l-b 3, w 1	12

1/18 2/35 3/135 4/175   225   1/39 2/44 3/116 4/126   252
5/185 6/205 7/205 8/209 9/225   5/142 6/142 7/190 8/217 9/221

Bowling: *First Innings*—Hadlee 12–9–44–0; Chatfield 22–8–67–1; Cairns 33.2–14–74–7; Coney 12–3–21–2; Bracewell 1–0–8–0. *Second Innings*—Hadlee 26–9–45–0; Chatfield 29–5–95–5; Cairns 24–2–70–3; Coney 8–1–30–2.

New Zealand

J. G. Wright c Willis b Cowans	93	– c Randall b Willis	26
B. A. Edgar b Willis	84	– c Edmonds b Willis	2
*G. P. Howarth run out	13	– c Randall b Willis	20
M. D. Crowe lbw b Cowans	37	– c Lamb b Willis	1
J. J. Crowe run out	0	– b Willis	13
J. V. Coney c Gower b Willis	19	– not out	10
R. J. Hadlee b Cowans	75	– not out	6
J. G. Bracewell c Dilley b Edmonds	16		
†I. D. S. Smith c Tavaré b Willis	2		
B. L. Cairns not out	24		
E. J. Chatfield lbw b Willis	0		
B 1, l-b 4, w 1, n-b 8	14	B 8, l-b 7, n-b 10	25

1/52 2/168 3/169 4/169   377   1/11 2/42 3/60 4/61   (5 wkts) 103
5/218 6/304 7/348 8/351 9/377   5/83

Bowling: *First Innings*—Willis 23.3–6–57–4; Dilley 17–4–36–0; Botham 26–9–81–0; Cowans 28–8–88–3; Edmonds 45–14–101–1. *Second Innings*—Willis 14–5–35–5; Cowans 5–0–23–0; Dilley 8–2–16–0; Botham 0.1–0–4–0.

Umpires: B. J. Meyer and D. J. Constant.

†At The Oval, August 4. New Zealanders won by 56 runs. New Zealanders 222 for nine (60 overs) (J. V. Coney 51, E. J. Gray 47, B. L. Cairns 34; S. T. Clarke three for 28); Surrey 166 (46.2 overs) (D. M. Smith 37; M. C. Snedden three for 33).

HAMPSHIRE v NEW ZEALANDERS

At Bournemouth, August 6, 7, 8. New Zealanders won by nine wickets. Hampshire rested Greenidge, Marshall and Parks which led to the county being accused by Howarth of "cheating the public". On a seaming pitch, Hampshire were dismissed cheaply, giving the New Zealanders an advantage which they never released. The tourists were particularly indebted to Martin Crowe, who shared a fifth-wicket stand of 76 in 97 minutes with Gray. Hampshire batted without resolution in their second innings, although Jesty showed spirit. The match only just lasted into the third day.

Hampshire

V. P. Terry lbw b Snedden	20	– c Lees b Snedden	1
C. L. Smith c Gray b Chatfield	9	– c Lees b M. D. Crowe	5
M. C. J. Nicholas b Chatfield	5	– c Edgar b Chatfield	18
T. E. Jesty c M. D. Crowe b Snedden	29	– b M. D. Crowe	24
R. A. Smith lbw b Snedden	12	– c Bracewell b Snedden	7
*N. E. J. Pocock run out	21	– b Bracewell	24
N. G. Cowley lbw b M. D. Crowe	16	– b M. D. Crowe	13
T. M. Tremlett b Tracy	10	– c Lees b Gray	24
K. Stevenson c Chatfield b M. D. Crowe	4	– lbw b Bracewell	22
†C. F. E. Goldie c Gray b Tracy	6	– not out	0
S. J. Malone not out	1	– run out	0
L-b 11, n-b 5	16	B 10, n-b 6	16

1/12 2/25 3/67 4/68   149   1/2 2/25 3/41 4/45   154
5/90 6/115 7/128 8/142 9/142   5/67 6/94 7/107 8/151 9/153

Bowling: First Innings—Snedden 17–1–53–3; Chatfield 20–9–42–2; Tracy 10.4–3–29–2; M. D. Crowe 5–2–9–2. *Second Innings*—Snedden 11–1–51–2; Chatfield 6–4–3–1; M. D. Crowe 6–2–21–3; Tracy 8–1–36–0; Bracewell 8.1–1–26–2; Gray 2–1–1–1.

New Zealanders

B. A. Edgar c Goldie b Stevenson	12	– lbw b Nicholas	8
T. J. Franklin c Jesty b Malone	22	– not out	25
*G. P. Howarth lbw b Cowley	26		
M. D. Crowe lbw b Cowley	70		
J. J. Crowe st Goldie b Cowley	11	– (3) not out	24
E. J. Gray c Pocock b Nicholas	38		
J. G. Bracewell c Pocock b Nicholas	1		
†W. K. Lees c Stevenson b Nicholas	0		
M. C. Snedden c Goldie b Malone	35		
E. J. Chatfield not out	13		
S. R. Tracy c Nicholas b Stevenson	4		
B 5, l-b 4, w 3	12	B 1, l-b 1, w 1	3

1/19 2/69 3/69 4/101   244   1/18   (1 wkt) 60
5/177 6/186 7/186 8/195 9/237

Bowling: First Innings—Malone 24–5–50–2; Stevenson 23–2–95–2; Tremlett 4–1–7–0; Cowley 31–13–55–3; Nicholas 14–4–21–3; C. L. Smith 1–0–4–0. *Second Innings*—Malone 5–1–23–0; Stevenson 2–0–7–0; Nicholas 4–0–27–1.

Umpires: P. J. Eele and R. Julian.

ENGLAND v NEW ZEALAND

Third Cornhill Test

At Lord's, August 11, 12, 13, 15. England won by 127 runs to take a 2-1 lead in the four-match series. Three changes had been made to the team that lost at Headingley, the selectors introducing Smith of Hampshire and Foster of Essex for Fowler and Dilley, who were not fit, and later calling up the Leicestershire left-arm spinner, Cook, from a Championship game at Chelmsford when Edmonds ricked his back getting out of his car the day before the Test. It was the first time since 1959, in the first Test against India, that England had fielded three new players in a home Test. New Zealand gave a first cap to Gray, replacing Jeff Crowe, though it was not immediately clear whether he was in the side for his batting or his left-arm slow bowling. Howarth, who won the toss and gave England first use of a pitch that favoured the bowlers more as the game developed, bowled neither Gray nor the off-spinner, Bracewell, in England's first innings. Willis, conversely, had Cook on after nineteen overs of New Zealand's first innings.

A policy of inserting the opposition expects wickets before lunch, and with the last ball of his first over Hadlee provided that of the hapless Smith, lbw on the back leg to his first ball in Test cricket. A second wicket should have been Gower's. In consecutive overs, when 21 and 25, he was twice let off by Cairns: the first an easy chance from a mistimed hook off Crowe to square-leg, the ball hanging in the air for a long time; the second a flier off Chatfield through Cairns's left hand at third slip. Thereafter the morning was England's as Gower, graceful in the drive and assured on the leg side, and the patient Tavaré, picking up runs in the oft-vacated third-man area, laid the innings' foundations. Hadlee, controlled and hostile off his economical run, often beat the bat, but his fellow seam bowlers pitched too short to utilise the wicket's vagaries. Both batsmen reached 50 soon after lunch, Tavaré with the only boundary of his 206-minute innings. Gower's 228-minute 108, on the other hand, featured sixteen 4s. His dismissal to a ball that kept low, and Lamb's to one that lifted surprisingly, increased doubts about the pitch and put pressure on Gatting and Botham to ensure that England's position was not eroded. Botham never looked secure, but Gatting, after some uncertainty, flowered on his home ground, off-driving handsomely with a full follow-through and savagely despatching anything short to the boundary. His 50, off 73 balls, included nine 4s; his unbeaten 74 in England's first-day score of 279 for five was his highest in Test cricket and should have been taken to three figures next morning. Instead, hooking unwisely, he top-edged Hadlee to square-leg, so opening the tail for the New Zealand fast bowler.

New Zealand's innings owed everything to Edgar (238 minutes) and Crowe (116 minutes) and was undermined in the afternoon by Cook, intelligently employing the old-fashioned virtues of flight and spin. He was well supported by the keen England fielding. Brought back for his second spell at 5.25, when New Zealand were 158 for three, he removed the resolute Edgar with his third ball and with two later wickets in three balls reduced New Zealand to 176 for six by the close. First thing on Saturday he had Hadlee caught at slip with his arm ball to register five wickets in his first Test. The remainder of the innings fell to Botham, not straining for speed but getting movement and bounce.

When England batted again the large crowd, enjoying a sunny Lord's Test Saturday after several dismal years, sat nervously for nineteen minutes until Smith got off the mark with a working to fine-leg, a stroke with which they became familiar as his innings wore on. Gower, in full command of his talents, quickly outscored Smith, posting 33 of their 50 partnership, but walking forward to drive Gray he was marvellously caught by Crowe, diving forward to take one-handed a ball that had turned sufficiently to find the inside edge. Gray next removed Lamb with a beautiful delivery which floated into him, turned and jumped from the bat, and when he bowled the advancing Gatting the slow left-armer's figures since lunch were 15.3–4–29–3. Hadlee, too, restricted England's progress, so that when Botham joined Smith (35 not out) in the 50th over, England's lead of 254 still left New Zealand with a chance. Hadlee, in a splendid over, improved that chance with a brute of a ball which Smith, protecting his face, could only fend to slip. However, Botham, having picked up ones and twos with quiet assurance, began to unleash his powerful strokes, hitting seven 4s in his 61, and when he was caught at point shortly before the close of a finely contested day's play a satisfied crowd rose in appreciation of their favourite's return to form. England's 206 for seven at stumps meant a lead of 341, though when their last three wickets fell for only 5 more runs on Monday morning New Zealand's victory target allowed two minutes for every run.

A lunch score of 43 for two, however, showed the hopelessness of their task. In the fourth over Wright, after enjoying several long-hops from Botham, gave Taylor his 150th Test catch, and in the seventh Howarth, nursing a face injury from morning nets, nudged a rising ball from Willis to the wicket-keeper. In the afternoon Lamb, adding two catches to his four in the first innings, became the fifth player to share the England record of six catches in a Test match by a non-wicket-keeper, and Willis, Cowans and Cook worked their way methodically through the Kiwis' batting. Some lively hitting by Hadlee and Cairns brightened the closing stages, as well as tarnishing Cook's figures, while Coney held out for two and a half hours before becoming Foster's first wicket in Test cricket. At 5.13, Cook parried Chatfield's drive in the air and running back caught the ball right-handed to complete a memorable début and a comfortable victory for England with a day to spare.

The match was attended by 70,831 people, the receipts being £344,050. – G.A.W.

England

C. J. Tavaré b M. D. Crowe	51	– c M. D. Crowe b Hadlee	16
C. L. Smith lbw b Hadlee	0	– c Coney b Hadlee	43
D. I. Gower lbw b M. D. Crowe	108	– c M. D. Crowe b Gray	34
A. J. Lamb c sub (J. J. Crowe) b Chatfield	17	– c Hadlee b Gray	4
M. W. Gatting c Wright b Hadlee	81	– b Gray	15
I. T. Botham lbw b Cairns	8	– c Coney b Chatfield	61
†R. W. Taylor b Hadlee	16	– c and b Coney	7
N. A. Foster c Smith b Hadlee	10	– c Wright b Coney	3
N. G. B. Cook b Chatfield	16	– c Bracewell b Chatfield	5
*R. G. D. Willis c Smith b Hadlee	7	– not out	2
N. G. Cowans not out	1	– c Smith b Chatfield	1
B 3, l-b 3, w 2, n-b 3	11	B 5, l-b 6, w 9	20

1/3 2/152 3/174 4/191   326   1/26 2/79 3/87 4/119   211
5/218 6/288 7/290 8/303 9/318   5/147 6/195 7/199 8/208 9/210

Bowling: *First Innings*—Hadlee 40–15–93–5; Cairns 23–8–65–1; Chatfield 36.3–8–116–2; M. D. Crowe 13–1–35–2; Coney 8–7–6–0. *Second Innings*—Hadlee 26–7–42–3; Chatfield 13.3–4–29–3; Cairns 3–0–9–0; Bracewell 11–4–29–0; Gray 30–8–73–3; Coney 6–4–9–1.

New Zealand

J. G. Wright c Lamb b Willis	11	– c Taylor b Botham	12
B. A. Edgar c Willis b Cook	70	– c Lamb b Cowans	27
*G. P. Howarth b Cook	25	– c Taylor b Willis	0
M. D. Crowe b Botham	46	– c Foster b Cowans	12
J. V. Coney b Cook	7	– c Gatting b Foster	68
E. J. Gray c Lamb b Botham	11	– c Lamb b Cook	17
J. G. Bracewell c Gower b Cook	0	– (8) lbw b Willis	4
R. J. Hadlee c Botham b Cook	5	– (7) b Willis	30
B. L. Cairns c Lamb b Botham	5	– b Cook	16
†I. D. S. Smith c Lamb b Botham	3	– not out	17
E. J. Chatfield not out	5	– c and b Cook	2
L-b 5, n-b 3	8	B 3, l-b 4, n-b 7	14

1/18 2/49 3/147 4/159   191   1/15 2/17 3/57 4/61   219
5/176 6/176 7/176 8/183 9/184   5/108 6/154 7/158 8/190 9/206

Bowling: *First Innings*—Willis 13–6–28–1; Foster 16–5–40–0; Cowans 9–1–30–0; Botham 20.4–6–50–4; Cook 26–11–35–5. *Second Innings*—Willis 12–5–24–3; Botham 7–2–20–1; Cowans 11–1–36–2; Cook 27.2–9–90–3; Foster 12–0–35–1.

Umpires: D. J. Constant and D. G. L. Evans.

ESSEX v NEW ZEALANDERS

At Chelmsford, August 17, 18, 19. New Zealanders won by 48 runs. The New Zealanders took advantage of an easy-paced pitch and a weakened attack to run up a formidable first-innings total after winning the toss. Howarth and Martin Crowe both hit centuries and shared in a stand of 210 in only two and a half hours. Despite a forceful contribution from Pont, which contained a 6 and thirteen 4s, Essex trailed by 88 and the tourists built steadily upon their advantage before Essex were left with a target of 309 in four hours. Gooch answered the challenge with a flowing half-century while Gladwin also impressed with some fierce driving until he was caught on the boundary. In the end, however, Bracewell inspired a New Zealand victory, even though he proved expensive.

New Zealanders

*G. P. Howarth c Lilley b Pont	144 – (10) c Lilley b Phillip	7
T. J. Franklin b Hughes	41 – (1) c Gooch b R. E. East	47
J. J. Crowe lbw b Hughes	0 – c D. E. East b R. E. East	42
M. D. Crowe not out	116 – (9) b Hughes	13
E. J. Gray retired hurt	0 – (11) not out	3
I. D. S. Smith b Golding	10 – (4) b Golding	5
†W. K. Lees not out	0 – (5) c Gladwin b Hughes	12
J. G. Bracewell (did not bat)	– (2) c Hardie b Hughes	12
M. C. Snedden (did not bat)	– (6) c Hardie b Gooch	21
B. L. Cairns (did not bat)	– (7) c Phillip b Hughes	25
R. J. Hadlee (did not bat)	– (8) c McEwan b Gooch	26
L-b 3, n-b 7	10	B 3, l-b 1, n-b 3	7

1/60 2/60 3/270 4/319 (4 wkts dec.) 321 1/24 2/95 3/110 4/110 220
5/132 6/158 7/189 8/202 9/211

Bowling: *First Innings*—Phillip 12–1–36–0; Hughes 16–0–91–2; Gooch 8–4–19–0; Golding 14–2–44–1; Pont 18–2–77–1; R. E. East 7–0–44–0. *Second Innings*—Phillip 11–2–35–1; Hughes 15.2–0–71–4; Golding 14–1–53–1; R. E. East 16–5–37–2; Gooch 7–0–17–2.

Essex

*G. A. Gooch b Snedden	26 – b Cairns	54
C. Gladwin c Cairns b Hadlee	6 – c J. J. Crowe b Bracewell	89
B. R. Hardie lbw b Snedden	4 – (4) c Howarth b Bracewell	13
K. S. McEwan c and b M. D. Crowe	26 – (3) b Cairns	5
K. R. Pont b Snedden	81 – c Smith b Bracewell	32
A. W. Lilley c and b Bracewell	7 – lbw b M. D. Crowe	0
N. Phillip lbw b Hadlee	4 – b Bracewell	3
†D. E. East c Franklin b Snedden	36 – b Bracewell	16
R. E. East b Snedden	19 – c Smith b Bracewell	23
A. K. Golding not out	2 – not out	6
M. G. Hughes c Lees b Bracewell	10 – c Lees b Hadlee	0
B 1, l-b 7, n-b 4	12	B 6, l-b 8, n-b 5	19

1/29 2/39 3/47 4/102 233 1/84 2/92 3/129 4/174 260
5/131 6/146 7/169 8/217 9/220 5/180 6/191 7/220 8/245 9/256

Bowling: *First Innings*—Hadlee 14–2–30–2; Snedden 19–3–68–5; M. D. Crowe 6–1–37–1; Cairns 8–3–18–0; Bracewell 22.4–3–68–2. *Second Innings*—Hadlee 10.1–3–26–1; Snedden 10–4–38–0; Cairns 15–3–41–2; Bracewell 15–1–111–6; M. D. Crowe 5–1–25–1.

Umpires: R. Palmer and J. van Geloven.

LEICESTERSHIRE v NEW ZEALANDERS

At Leicester, August 20, 21, 22. New Zealanders won by eight wickets. The tourists completed their fifth consecutive first-class victory over county sides, but at a high cost. Wright suffered a broken toe, after being hit while batting by Agnew, and wicket-keeper Smith broke a finger when dropping Gower. Both missed the fourth Test match, but the good form shown by Franklin was some compensation. Davison batted superbly on the first day, hitting a 6 and nineteen 4s, and the tourists' target of 215 in 210 minutes was made to look simple, Leicestershire's spinners bowling ineffectively on a turning pitch.

Leicestershire

J. C. Balderstone lbw b Snedden	0	– c sub b Coney	18
J. P. Addison b Chatfield	51	– c Franklin b Bracewell	16
N. E. Briers c M. D. Crowe b Bracewell	57	– (4) c Cairns b Snedden	2
D. I. Gower c Coney b Bracewell	6	– (5) c Coney b Bracewell	17
B. F. Davison not out	123	– (6) b Bracewell	16
P. B. Clift c Smith b Chatfield	12	– (7) c sub b Chatfield	22
*†R. W. Tolchard not out	17	– (8) b Bracewell	26
N. G. B. Cook (did not bat)		– (3) b Bracewell	0
J. F. Steele (did not bat)		– c M. D. Crowe b Chatfield	6
J. P. Agnew (did not bat)		– b Cairns	26
L. B. Taylor (did not bat)		– not out	37
B 9, l-b 4, n-b 2	15	L-b 6, n-b 6	12

1/0 2/98 3/106 4/193 (5 wkts dec.) 281   1/39 2/39 3/39 4/45 198
5/225   5/63 6/102 7/102 8/128 9/134

Bowling: *First Innings*—Snedden 10–2–39–1; Chatfield 20–5–48–2; Cairns 20–8–55–0;
M. D. Crowe 4–0–7–0; Bracewell 26–6–95–2; Coney 2–0–22–0. *Second Innings*—Snedden
12–0–46–1; Chatfield 14–2–44–2; Bracewell 24–7–80–5; Coney 3–1–6–1; Cairns 3.4–0–10–1.

New Zealanders

T. J. Franklin c Tolchard b Balderstone	61	– not out	98
B. A. Edgar lbw b Clift	54	– st Tolchard b Steele	33
*J. G. Wright lbw b Agnew	32		
J. V. Coney c Clift b Agnew	37	– not out	50
J. J. Crowe lbw b Agnew	22		
M. D. Crowe not out	25	– (3) b Cook	22
†I. D. S. Smith c Steele b Clift	9		
J. G. Bracewell c and b Clift	0		
M. C. Snedden c Steele b Clift	4		
B 4, l-b 5, w 2, n-b 10	21	L-b 12, n-b 1	13

1/122 2/130 3/174 4/224 (8 wkts dec.) 265   1/73 2/101 (2 wkts) 216
5/225 6/246 7/250 8/265

B. L. Cairns and E. J. Chatfield did not bat.

Bowling: *First Innings*—Taylor 20–8–43–0; Agnew 28–2–83–3; Clift 18.1–7–35–4; Cook
5–2–13–0; Steele 14–3–42–0; Balderstone 10–4–28–1. *Second Innings*—Agnew 11–1–35–0;
Clift 5–0–20–0; Cook 17–5–55–1; Steele 16–4–53–1; Balderstone 7–0–31–0; Briers 1.5–0–9–0.

Umpires: M. J. Kitchen and A. G. T. Whitehead.

ENGLAND v NEW ZEALAND

Fourth Cornhill Test

At Nottingham, August 25, 26, 27, 28, 29. England won by 165 runs and took the series by
three matches to one. New Zealand were never masters of their own destiny once England
had pulled themselves together after the unconvincing first two sessions. A partnership of
186 in 32 overs on the first evening between Botham and Randall took England clear, and
in fine, warm weather the result was more or less assured by the end of the second day.

England omitted Thomas of Surrey from their chosen twelve. New Zealand gave Franklin a first cap, Wright being injured; Lees returned for Smith, who was also injured, and Snedden replaced Chatfield. Snedden disposed of Tavaré in his first over, Cairns scooping up a very good, low slip catch. Smith and Gower stabilised the innings without dominating. Gower continued to bat without a helmet after receiving a crack on the back of the head from a ball by Hadlee.

New Zealand did not bowl straight enough, and their fortunes declined to a low point when Crowe, fielding at short leg, had a finger dislocated. However, their prospects improved sharply in mid-afternoon when Gower was yorked, Smith and Lamb gave close-in catches and Gatting played a reckless sweep. But England's decision to include an extra batsman in preference to a bowler proved crucial. Botham and Randall followed reconnaissance by providing the rare sight of two English batsmen attacking spectacularly at both ends. Botham, after more than a year below his best, rediscovered the sort of violent strokeplay that makes good-length bowling irrelevant. Bracewell's spin was hit for 31 in two overs and as Hadlee hopefully propelled the new ball it was hammered for 26 in two overs. Randall was an equal partner, carving the ball through the off side with increasing audacity. Botham hit three 6s and fourteen 4s. His century took 99 balls, his second 50 a mere 26.

Randall and Botham were both out before the close, which meant a prosaic second morning. In the afternoon Edgar and Howarth profited against a pace trio which had assorted problems, including a final warning for Willis for following through on the pitch. Cook was a splendid stand-by for his captain, settling into a long, nagging spell. He had Howarth, playing early, but the innings really disintegrated in the final session with a series of mistimings against Cook, whose 24 consecutive overs brought him four for 34.

Willis sent his batsmen in again. His chief reasons for not making New Zealand follow on were the lack both of a fifth bowler and a rest day. The move also eliminated, to all intents and purposes, New Zealand's chance of squaring the series. Much of England's batting was casual, reflecting their advantageous position. Lamb, however, appreciated the fact that runs were available without any pressure and he played with authority. Hadlee introduced a notable personal finale by setting a New Zealand record of 21 wickets in England and becoming the first New Zealander – the nineteenth in all – to reach 200 Test wickets.

Needing an impossible 511 in eleven hours, New Zealand made a fight of it. Edgar continued his excellent series. Howarth again succumbed after doing the hard work; Crowe's unlucky game ended when he received one of the nastiest balls of the match, and England's last-day task was eased when Edgar was dug out near the close of the fourth day after 266 minutes of resolute defence. Coney batted for ten minutes longer and Hadlee fired off a succession of typically ferocious drives. He cracked fourteen 4s and took the match just beyond the half-way point of the final day. Hadlee's fine entertainment confirmed his status as Cornhill's Man of the Series. The total attendance was 34,763 and the takings were £161,300. – T.C.

England

C. J. Tavaré c Cairns b Snedden	4	– c sub (J. J. Crowe) b Bracewell	13
C. L. Smith c Howarth b Bracewell	31	– c Howarth b Snedden	4
D. I. Gower b Cairns	72	– c Lees b Bracewell	33
A. J. Lamb c Howarth b Bracewell	22	– not out	137
M. W. Gatting lbw b Bracewell	14	– c Lees b Cairns	11
I. T. Botham lbw b Snedden	103	– c Edgar b Gray	27
D. W. Randall c Edgar b Hadlee	83	– b Hadlee	13
†R. W. Taylor b Bracewell	21	– b Hadlee	0
N. G. B. Cook c Lees b Snedden	4	– c Lees b Cairns	26
*R. G. D. Willis not out	25	– b Hadlee	16
N. G. Cowans c Bracewell b Cairns	7	– b Hadlee	0
B 11, l-b 14, n-b 9	34	B 6, l-b 10, w 1	17

1/5 2/94 3/136 4/156   420   1/5 2/58 3/61 4/92   297
5/169 6/355 7/356 8/379 9/407   5/149 6/188 7/188 8/252 9/297

Bowling: *First Innings*—Hadlee 30–7–98–1; Snedden 28–7–69–3; Cairns 33.4–9–77–2; Bracewell 28–5–108–4; Coney 2–0–10–0; Gray 3–0–24–0. *Second Innings*—Hadlee 28–5–85–4; Snedden 8–1–40–1; Bracewell 21–2–88–2; Cairns 20–9–36–2; Gray 15–4–31–1.

New Zealand

T. J. Franklin c Smith b Botham	2	– b Willis	7
B. A. Edgar c Smith b Cook	62	– c Gower b Cook	76
*G. P. Howarth c and b Cook	36	– c Tavaré b Cowans	24
J. V. Coney c Gatting b Cook	20	– (5) c Taylor b Cook	68
E. J. Gray run out	3	– (6) c Gatting b Smith	3
R. J. Hadlee c Smith b Cowans	7	– (3) not out	92
†W. K. Lees lbw b Cook	1	– c Lamb c Cowans	7
M. D. Crowe c and b Cook	34	– (4) c Taylor b Cowans	0
M. C. Snedden b Cowans	9	– c Taylor b Cook	12
B. L. Cairns c Gower b Cowans	26	– b Cook	11
J. G. Bracewell not out	1	– c Taylor b Smith	28
L-b 5, n-b 1	6	B 2, w 1, n-b 14	17

1/4 2/80 3/124 4/127   207   1/67 2/67 3/71 4/156   345
5/131 6/135 7/135 8/157 9/201   5/161 6/184 7/228 8/264 9/290

Bowling: *First Innings*—Botham 14–4–33–1; Willis 10–2–23–0; Cowans 21–8–74–3; Cook 32–14–63–5; Gatting 5–2–8–0. *Second Innings*—Willis 19–3–37–1; Botham 25–4–73–0; Cook 50–22–87–4; Cowans 21–2–95–3; Gatting 2–1–5–0; Smith 12–2–31–2.

Umpires: H. D. Bird and B. J. Meyer.

D. B. CLOSE'S XI v NEW ZEALANDERS

At Scarborough, August 31, September 1, 2. New Zealanders won by 119 runs, to remain unbeaten outside the Test series. Edgar, with sixteen boundaries in his hundred, and Franklin put on a century opening stand in 26 overs, before being parted by the young West Indian, Harper. On the second day, Close led a rearguard action to save the follow-on as Tracy, in his second match of the tour, took five for 29. When New Zealand batted again, Martin Crowe made his third century of the tour (eighteen 4s) and put on 151 in 32 overs with his brother, whose 65 included three 6s and seven 4s. Set to make 385 in 395 minutes, Close's XI quickly lost Azad to a fine catch in the gully by Gray. On the last day, gale force winds caused hot drinks to be brought out and the use of the bails to be abandoned, but the conditions did not prevent the home side being bowled out again.

New Zealanders

B. A. Edgar c Whitney b Mushtaq	100	– c Azad b Stephenson	3
T. J. Franklin c Agnew b Harper	43	– b Whitney	15
J. J. Crowe lbw b Harper	20	– c Sadiq b Harper	65
M. D. Crowe c Taylor b Agnew	30	– not out	110
*G. P. Howarth c Mushtaq b Azad	34	– (8) not out	11
E. J. Gray lbw b Harper	30	– (5) b Harper	10
†I. D. S. Smith c Whitney b Stephenson	2	– c and b Azad	1
B. L. Cairns c Sadiq b Stephenson	0	– (6) c King b Agnew	17
M. C. Snedden b Whitney	19		
E. J. Chatfield not out	2		
S. R. Tracy c King b Close	0		
L-b 9, w 1, n-b 2	12	B 7, l-b 4, w 1, n-b 3	15

1/100 2/141 3/196 4/200   292   1/11 2/27 3/178   (6 wkts dec.) 247
5/252 6/263 7/263 8/272 9/291   4/199 5/217 6/235

Bowling: *First Innings*—Stephenson 11–3–31–2; Whitney 11–1–48–1; Agnew 10–1–33–1; King 3–0–18–0; Mushtaq 16–1–58–1; Harper 14–5–36–3; Azad 13–3–51–1; Close 1.4–0–5–1. *Second Innings*—Stephenson 11–2–59–1; Whitney 7–3–12–1; Mushtaq 8–0–38–0; Agnew 10–0–58–1; Harper 14–3–45–2; Azad 6–2–20–1.

D. B. Close's XI

Sadiq Mohammad c Gray b Snedden	0	– b Tracy ... 35
K. B. J. Azad b Tracy	15	– c Gray b Snedden ... 1
J. H. Hampshire c J. J. Crowe b Snedden	31	– (5) c Edgar b M. D. Crowe ... 85
C. L. King lbw b Tracy	0	– c M. D. Crowe b Howarth ... 26
Mushtaq Mohammad c Smith b Snedden	10	– (6) not out ... 60
R. A. Harper c Smith b Tracy	7	– (7) lbw b M. D. Crowe ... 5
*D. B. Close b Tracy	51	– (8) c and b Gray ... 1
F. D. Stephenson c J. J. Crowe b Snedden	1	– (9) c M. D. Crowe b Edgar ... 19
†R. W. Taylor st Smith b Gray	14	– (3) b M. D. Crowe ... 22
M. R. Whitney not out	5	– (11) c Franklin b Gray ... 1
J. P. Agnew b Tracy	4	– (10) c Franklin b Gray ... 1
B 4, l-b 6, w 2, n-b 5	17	L-b 4, n-b 5 ... 9

1/0 2/19 3/19 4/37   **155**   1/5 2/58 3/64 4/118   **265**
5/46 6/88 7/92 8/127 9/151   5/202 6/218 7/221 8/248 9/261

Bowling: *First Innings*—Snedden 11–1–41–4; Tracy 6.3–0–29–5; Gray 8–1–24–1; M. D. Crowe 9–2–36–0; Chatfield 6–3–8–0. *Second Innings*—Snedden 9–2–22–1; Tracy 8–1–21–1; Gray 27–5–88–3; Howarth 11–0–36–1; M. D. Crowe 16–2–72–3; Edgar 5–0–17–1.

Umpires: J. van Geloven and B. Leadbeater.

LORDS AND COMMONS CRICKET, 1983

No fewer than seven fixtures were casualties of the General Election campaign in June and its immediate aftermath. In fact bat was not put to ball until the new charity fixture on June 26 against Old England, when, in an enjoyable day's cricket, more than 450 runs were scored. Basil D'Oliveira's 72 was top score for Old England; for Lords and Commons Michael Rawlinson, son of a former Attorney General, made 96.

Matches cancelled owing to the General Election were those against St Paul's School, ACAS, Diplomatic Service, Westminster School, The Mandarins, Conservative Agents and BBC.

Old England 244 for eight; Lords and Commons 209 for five. Old England won by 35 runs.
Guards CC 245 for nine dec.; Lords and Commons 217. Guards CC won by 28 runs.
Dutch Parliament 252 for seven; Lords and Commons 150. Dutch Parliament won by 102 runs.
MCC 208 for five dec.; Lords and Commons 96. MCC won by 112 runs.
Eton Ramblers 200; Lords and Commons 158. Eton Ramblers won by 42 runs.
Old Westminster 262; Lords and Commons 200. Old Westminster won by 62 runs.
Department of Energy 150 for seven dec.; Lords and Commons 118 for nine. Drawn.
Lords and Commons 168 for six dec.; Law Society CC 124 for seven. Drawn.
Harrow Wanderers – match abandoned owing to rain.

THE PRUDENTIAL WORLD CUP, 1983

The third World Cup, the last to be sponsored by the Prudential Assurance Company, began with two fine surprises, when India beat West Indies and Zimbabwe beat Australia in the opening round of matches, and ended with the greatest surprise of all, when India beat West Indies again, this time in the final at Lord's. None of the eight sides had to make do without a victory.

The competition differed from its two predecessors in that in the preliminary groups the sides played each other not once but twice. This was partly to increase revenue but also to lessen the chances of a side being eliminated through having greater misfortune with the weather than its rivals. In the event, no sooner had the sides started to arrive in England for the 1983 World Cup than the rain, which had made the month of May one of the wettest on record, cleared away.

Of the 27 matches played, only three were not begun and finished in a day. Many were played in warm sunshine, and throughout the competition, from June 9-25, interest ran high. After losing their opening match, West Indies carried all before them until failing, for the first time, to win the final. Australia had a disappointing fortnight, and with Imran Khan unfit to bowl for them, Pakistan were a shadow of the side which had trounced India and Australia in the previous winter.

New Zealand's main batting provided them with insufficient runs for a consistent challenge, while Sri Lanka, though they won their return match against New Zealand, were too short of bowling to be a serious threat. Zimbabwe, playing for the first time, having qualified as winners of the ICC Trophy in 1982, made a welcome contribution. Their side included several players with first-class experience, acquired when, as Rhodesia, their country played in the Currie Cup. Apart from beating Australia they gave West Indies a run for their money at Worcester.

India's unexpected success (they were quoted at 66 to 1 before the competition began) came under a young and relatively new captain (Kapil Dev) and owed much to the presence in their side of three all-rounders (Kapil Dev, Roger Binny and Mohinder Amarnath) who, at critical moments, found enough in the conditions to help form an effective attack. Who would ever have thought before a ball was bowled that the leading wicket-takers in the competition would be the Sri Lankan de Mel and Binny, with his gentle medium-pace?

Each side received 60 overs. No bowler was allowed more than twelve overs per innings and, to prevent negative bowling, the umpires applied a stricter interpretation than in first-class cricket in regard to wides and bumpers.

The total amount of the Prudential Assurance Company's sponsorship was £500,000, and the gate receipts came to £1,195,712. The aggregate attendance was 232,081, compared with 160,000 in 1975 and 132,000 in 1979. The surplus, distributed to full and associate members of the International Cricket Conference, was in excess of £1,000,000, this being over and above the prior payments of £53,900 to each of the seven full members and one of £30,200 to Zimbabwe.

In addition to the Trophy and silver-gilt medals for each player, India received £20,000 for their victory. As runners-up West Indies won £8,000. The losing semi-finalists, England and Pakistan, each won £4,000. There were also

THE INDIAN WORLD CUP PARTY

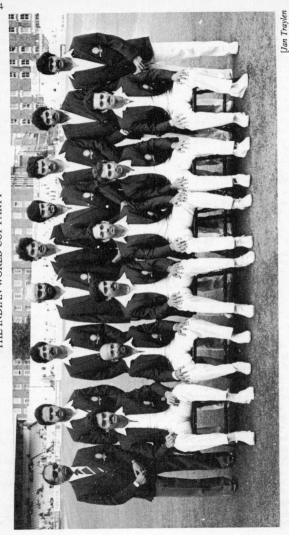

[*Jan Traylen*

Back row: P. R. Man Singh (*manager*), Yashpal Sharma, K. Srikkanth, B. S. Sandhu, R. J. Shastri, S. M. Patil. R. M. H. Binny, K. B. J. Azad, S. Valson. *Front row:* D. B. Vengsarkar, S. M. H. Kirmani, Kapil Dev (*captain*). M. Amarnath, S. M. Gavaskar, Madan Lal.

awards of £1,000 to the group winners, plus Man of the Match awards (£200 for the group matches, £400 for the semi-finals and £600 for the final).

At their meeting which followed the World Cup, the ICC asked for tenders, to be submitted by the end of 1983, from countries wishing to stage the competition when next it is held.

FINAL GROUP TABLES

	Played	Won	Lost	Points	Runs per Over
Group A					
ENGLAND	6	5	1	20	4.67
PAKISTAN	6	3	3	12	4.01
New Zealand	6	3	3	12	3.93
Sri Lanka	6	1	5	4	3.75
Group B					
WEST INDIES	6	5	1	20	4.31
INDIA	6	4	2	16	3.87
Australia	6	2	4	8	3.81
Zimbabwe	6	1	5	4	3.49

The top two countries in each section qualified for the semi-finals.
Where two countries finished with the same number of points, the position in the group was determined by their scoring-rate.

ENGLAND v NEW ZEALAND

At The Oval, June 9. England won by 106 runs, a convincing victory over a New Zealand side who had beaten them five times during the winter. Once Lamb and Gatting, coming together at 117 for three, had made 115 in sixteen overs, there was no doubt that England would score enough runs. Lamb's 102 was made off only 103 balls and the last 25 overs produced 203 runs. New Zealand's disappointing bowling was followed by a poor start to their innings of 62 for four, and although Crowe made 97 before being last out, they had lost sight of victory long before.

Man of the Match: A. J. Lamb.

England

G. Fowler c Coney b Cairns	8	†I. J. Gould not out	14
C. J. Tavaré c Edgar b Chatfield	45	G. R. Dilley not out	31
D. I. Gower c Edgar b Coney	39	L-b 12, w 1, n-b 5	18
A. J. Lamb b Snedden	102		
M. W. Gatting b Snedden	43	1/13 2/79 3/117 (6 wkts, 60 overs) 322
I. T. Botham c Lees b Hadlee	22	4/232 5/271 6/278

V. J. Marks, P. J. W. Allott and *R. G. D. Willis did not bat.

Bowling: Hadlee 12–4–26–1; Cairns 12–4–57–1; Snedden 12–1–105–2; Chatfield 12–1–45–1; Coney 6–1–20–1; Crowe 6–0–51–0.

New Zealand

G. M. Turner lbw b Willis	14	B. L. Cairns lbw b Botham		1
B. A. Edgar c Gould b Willis	3	M. C. Snedden c Gould b Gatting		21
J. G. Wright c Botham b Dilley	10	E. J. Chatfield not out		9
*G. P. Howarth c Lamb b Marks	18	B 2, l-b 4, w 4, n-b 1		11
J. V. Coney run out	23			
M. D. Crowe run out	97	1/3 2/28 3/31	(59 overs)	216
†W. K. Lees b Botham	8	4/62 5/85 6/123		
R. J. Hadlee c Lamb b Marks	1	7/136 8/138 9/190		

Bowling: Willis 7–2–9–2; Dilley 8–0–33–1; Botham 12–0–42–2; Allott 12–1–47–0; Marks 12–1–39–2; Gatting 8–1–35–1.

Umpires: B. J. Meyer and D. O. Oslear.

PAKISTAN v SRI LANKA

At Swansea, June 9. Pakistan won by 50 runs. Though put in on a damp pitch, Pakistan had no difficulty in making a score which always looked certain to be out of Sri Lanka's reach. An opening stand of 88 between Mudassar and Mohsin was followed by a fine innings of 82 by Zaheer and a violent assault on the medium-paced bowling by Miandad and Imran. Sri Lanka were always behind the required scoring-rate and Pakistan did not miss Imran's bowling.

Man of the Match: Mohsin Khan.

Pakistan

Mudassar Nazar c de Silva		Ijaz Faqih run out		2
b Ratnayake	36	Tahir Naqqash not out		0
Mohsin Khan b John	82	B 4, l-b 4		8
Zaheer Abbas c Kuruppu b de Mel	82			
Javed Miandad lbw b de Mel	72	1/88 2/156	(5 wkts, 60 overs)	338
*Imran Khan not out	56	3/229 4/325 5/332		

†Wasim Bari, Rashid Khan, Shahid Mahboob and Sarfraz Nawaz did not bat.

Bowling: de Mel 12–2–69–2; John 12–2–58–1; Ratnayake 12–0–65–1; Ranatunga 9–0–53–0; de Silva 10–0–52–0; Samarasekera 5–0–33–0.

Sri Lanka

S. Wettimuny c Rashid b Sarfraz	12	†R. G. de Alwis not out		59
B. Kuruppu run out	72	R. J. Ratnayake c Mudassar b Sarfraz		13
R. L. Dias b Rashid	5	V. B. John not out		12
*L. R. D. Mendis b Tahir	16	L-b 8, w 10, n-b 4		22
A. Ranatunga c and b Mudassar	31			
M. A. R. Samarasekera run out	0	1/34 2/58 3/85	(9 wkts, 60 overs)	288
D. S. de Silva c Wasim Bari b Sarfraz	35	4/142 5/143 6/157		
A. L. F. de Mel c Tahir b Shahid	11	7/180 8/234 9/262		

Bowling: Sarfraz 12–1–40–3; Shahid 11–0–48–1; Tahir 8–0–49–1; Rashid 12–1–55–1; Ijaz 12–1–52–0; Mudassar 4–0–18–1; Zaheer 1–0–4–0.

Umpires: K. E. Palmer and D. R. Shepherd.

AUSTRALIA v ZIMBABWE

At Nottingham, June 9. Zimbabwe won by 13 runs. In their first appearance in the competition, the amateurs of Zimbabwe brought off a bigger surprise than any in the previous two World Cups. The Australian captain described his side as being "outplayed".

Having been put in, Zimbabwe made no more than a steady start, but from 94 for five their captain, Duncan Fletcher, who was once a professional with Rishton in the Lancashire League, led an acceleration, adding 70 in fifteen overs with Curran and 75 in twelve overs with Butchart. Australia missed five catches, bowled moderately and, though Wood and Wessels gave their innings an adequate start, they slipped behind the required rate against Fletcher's four for 42 and some fine fielding and catching.

Man of the Match: D. A. G. Fletcher.

Zimbabwe

A. H. Shah c Marsh b Lillee	16	K. M. Curran c Hookes b Hogg	27
G. A. Paterson c Hookes b Lillee	27	I. P. Butchart not out	34
J. G. Heron c Marsh b Yallop	14	L-b 18, w 7, n-b 6	31
A. J. Pycroft b Border	21		—
†D. L. Houghton c Marsh b Yallop	0	1/55 2/55 3/86 (6 wkts, 60 overs)	239
*D. A. G. Fletcher not out	69	4/86 5/94 6/164	

P. W. E. Rawson, A. J. Traicos and V. R. Hogg did not bat.

Bowling: Lawson 11–2–33–0; Hogg 12–3–43–1; Lillee 12–1–47–2; Thomson 11–1–46–0; Yallop 9–0–28–2; Border 5–0–11–1.

Australia

G. M. Wood c Houghton b Fletcher	31	G. F. Lawson b Butchart	0
K. C. Wessels run out	76	R. M. Hogg not out	19
*K. J. Hughes c Shah b Fletcher	0	B 2, l-b 7, w 2	11
D. W. Hookes c Traicos b Fletcher	20		—
G. N. Yallop c Pycroft b Fletcher	2	1/61 2/63 3/114 (7 wkts, 60 overs)	226
A. R. Border c Pycroft b Curran	17	4/133 5/138	
†R. W. Marsh not out	50	6/168 7/176	

D. K. Lillee and J. R. Thomson did not bat.

Bowling: Hogg 6–2–15–0; Rawson 12–1–54–0; Butchart 10–0–39–1; Fletcher 11–1–42–4; Traicos 12–2–27–0; Curran 9–0–38–1.

Umpires: D. J. Constant and M. J. Kitchen.

INDIA v WEST INDIES

At Manchester, June 9, 10. India won by 34 runs. India began with a well-earned victory over the holders. Put in after a delayed start, they struggled in damp conditions and poor light to make 79 for three in 22 overs, but a splendid innings of 89 by Yashpal led them on to their highest score in three World Cups. Greenidge and Haynes made a confident start, scoring 49 before Haynes was run out in the fourteenth over. From this moment India began to take a grip on the game, and when play ended for the day West Indies were 67 for two in 22 overs. Richards was out early next day and West Indies declined so swiftly that by the 47th over they were 157 for nine. A last-wicket stand of 71 between Roberts and Garner was beginning to cause India serious concern when a smart stumping by Kirmani brought them victory. They had won only one previous Prudential Cup match, against East Africa in 1975.

Man of the Match: Yashpal Sharma.

India

S. M. Gavaskar c Dujon b Marshall	19	Madan Lal not out	21
K. Srikkanth c Dujon b Holding	14	†S. M. H. Kirmani run out	1
M. Amarnath c Dujon b Garner	21	R. J. Shastri not out	5
S. M. Patil b Gomes	36	B 4, l-b 10, w 1, n-b 8	23
Yashpal Sharma b Holding	89		—
*Kapil Dev c Richards b Gomes	6	1/21 2/46 3/76 4/125 (8 wkts, 60 overs)	262
R. M. H. Binny lbw b Marshall	27	5/141 6/214 7/243 8/246	

B. S. Sandhu did not bat.

Bowling: Holding 12–3–32–2; Roberts 12–1–51–0; Marshall 12–1–48–2; Garner 12–1–49–1; Richards 2–0–13–0; Gomes 10–0–46–2.

West Indies

C. G. Greenidge b Sandhu	24	A. M. E. Roberts not out	37
D. L. Haynes run out	24	M. A. Holding b Shastri	8
I. V. A. Richards c Kirmani b Binny	17	J. Garner st Kirmani b Shastri	37
S. F. A. Bacchus b Madan Lal	14	B 4, l-b 17, w 4	25
*C. H. Lloyd b Binny	25		
†P. J. Dujon c Sandhu b Binny	7	1/49 2/56 3/76	(54.1 overs) 228
H. A. Gomes run out	8	4/96 5/107 6/124	
M. D. Marshall st Kirmani b Shastri	2	7/126 8/130 9/157	

Bowling: Kapil Dev 10–0–34–0; Sandhu 12–1–36–1; Madan Lal 12–1–34–1; Binny 12–1–48–3; Shastri 5.1–0–26–3; Patil 3–0–25–0.

Umpires: B. Leadbeater and A. G. T. Whitehead.

ENGLAND v SRI LANKA

At Taunton, June 11. England won by 47 runs, giving another confident batting performance. This time it was Gower who played the outstanding innings, hitting five 6s and twelve 4s in 130, which made the loss through run-outs of Gatting and Botham less costly than it might have been. Though batting with spirit, Sri Lanka were never in sight of making the 334 they needed.

Man of the Match: D. I. Gower.

England

G. Fowler b John	22	G. R. Dilley b de Mel	29
C. J. Tavaré c de Alwis b Ranatunga	32	V. J. Marks run out	5
D. I. Gower b de Mel	130	P. J. W. Allott not out	0
A. J. Lamb b Ratnayake	53	L-b 11, w 9	20
M. W. Gatting run out	7		
I. T. Botham run out	0	1/49 2/78 3/174	(9 wkts, 60 overs) 333
†I. J. Gould c Ranatunga b Ratnayake	35	4/193 5/194 6/292 7/298 8/333 9/333	

*R. G. D. Willis did not bat.

Bowling: de Mel 12–3–62–2; John 12–0–55–1; Ratnayake 12–0–66–2; Ranatunga 12–0–65–1; de Silva 12–0–65–0.

Sri Lanka

S. Wettimuny lbw b Marks	33	A. L. F. de Mel c Dilley b Allott	27
B. Kuruppu c Gatting b Dilley	4	R. J. Ratnayake c Lamb b Dilley	15
R. L. Dias c Botham b Dilley	2	V. B. John b Dilley	0
*L. R. D. Mendis c Willis b Marks	56	L-b 12, w 2, n-b 3	17
R. S. Madugalle c Tavaré b Marks	12		
A. Ranatunga c Lamb b Marks	34	1/11 2/17 3/92	(58 overs) 286
D. S. de Silva st Gould b Marks	28	4/108 5/117 6/168	
†R. G. de Alwis not out	58	7/192 8/246 9/281	

Bowling: Willis 11–3–43–0; Dilley 11–0–45–4; Allott 12–1–82–1; Botham 12–0–60–0; Marks 12–3–39–5.

Umpires: M. J. Kitchen and K. E. Palmer.

NEW ZEALAND v PAKISTAN

At Birmingham, June 11, 12. New Zealand won by 52 runs. Put in when play started at 1.45, New Zealand were reduced to 120 for five by the fine leg-spin bowling of Qadir, but recovered during an interrupted afternoon to finish the day with 211 for eight in 56 overs. Next morning they added 27 runs before, in the first eight balls from Hadlee and Cairns, Mohsin, Mudassar and Zaheer were dismissed for no score. From this remarkable start Pakistan never recovered against accurate bowling by Coney, Hadlee and Cairns.

Man of the Match: Abdul Qadir.

New Zealand

G. M. Turner c Bari b Rashid	27		J. G. Bracewell lbw b Rashid	3
B. A. Edgar c Imran b Qadir	44		†W. K. Lees not out	24
J. G. Wright c Bari b Qadir	9		E. J. Chatfield not out	6
B. L. Cairns b Qadir	4		L-b 20, w 4, n-b 1	25
*G. P. Howarth st Bari b Qadir	16			
J. V. Coney c Ijaz b Shahid	33		1/57 2/68 3/80	(9 wkts, 60 overs) 238
M. D. Crowe c Mohsin b Rashid	34		4/109 5/120 6/166	
R. J. Hadlee c Bari b Sarfraz	13		7/197 8/202 9/223	

Bowling: Sarfraz 11–1–49–1; Shahid 10–2–38–1; Rashid 11–0–47–3; Mudassar 12–1–40–0; Qadir 12–4–21–4; Ijaz 1–0–6–0; Zaheer 3–0–12–0.

Pakistan

Mohsin Khan lbw b Hadlee	0		Abdul Qadir not out	41
Mudassar Nazar c Lees b Cairns	0		Sarfraz Nawaz c Crowe b Chatfield	13
Zaheer Abbas b Hadlee	0		Rashid Khan c and b Cairns	9
Javed Miandad lbw b Chatfield	35		B 5, l-b 6, w 3, n-b 2	16
*Imran Khan c Chatfield b Hadlee	9			
Ijaz Faqih c Edgar b Coney	12		1/0 2/0 3/0	(55.2 overs) 186
Shahid Mahboob c Wright b Coney	17		4/22 5/54 6/60	
†Wasim Bari c Edgar b Coney	34		7/102 8/131 9/158	

Bowling: Hadlee 9–2–20–3; Cairns 9.2–3–21–2; Chatfield 12–0–50–2; Crowe 2–0–12–0; Coney 12–3–28–3; Bracewell 11–2–39–0.

Umpires: H. D. Bird and B. Leadbeater.

AUSTRALIA v WEST INDIES

At Leeds, June 11, 12. West Indies won by 101 runs. Though West Indies, put in when play started on a damp day at 3.30, lost three wickets for 32 in nine overs to Lawson and Hogg, they were comfortably placed when the day's play ended at 160 for five after 42 overs, a stand of 76 between Gomes and Bacchus having won back the initiative. Next morning West Indies extended their score to 252 for nine, after which Australia's batsmen were soon in trouble. A ball from Holding lifted sharply from an unpredictable pitch, which was criticised by both captains, and came back to hit Wood on the side of the head. He was taken to hospital with severe concussion. Wessels and Hughes were out for 55, and though Hookes and Yallop took Australia swiftly to 114 for two, adding 59 in eight overs, Australia collapsed to a new, young fast bowler, Winston Davis. One of the replacements for the injured Garner and Marshall, Davis took six of the last seven wickets at a personal cost of 14 runs.

Man of the Match: W. W. Davis.

West Indies

C. G. Greenidge c Wood b Hogg	4	A. M. E. Roberts c Marsh b Lillee	5
D. L. Haynes c Marsh b Lawson	13	M. A. Holding run out	20
I. V. A. Richards b Lawson	7	W. W. Daniel not out	16
H. A. Gomes c Marsh b Lillee	78	B 1, l-b 9, w 10, n-b 11	31
*C. H. Lloyd lbw b MacLeay	19		
S. F. A. Bacchus c Wessels b Yallop	47	1/7 2/25 3/32 4/78 (9 wkts, 60 overs) 252
†P. J. Dujon lbw b Lawson	12	5/154 6/192 7/208 8/211 9/252

W. W. Davis did not bat.

Bowling: Lawson 12–3–29–3; Hogg 12–1–49–1; MacLeay 12–1–31–1; Lillee 12–0–55–2; Yallop 5–0–26–1; Border 7–0–31–0.

Australia

G. M. Wood retired hurt	2	G. F. Lawson c Dujon b Davis	2
K. C. Wessels b Roberts	11	R. M. Hogg not out	0
*K. J. Hughes c Lloyd b Davis	18	D. K. Lillee b Davis	0
D. W. Hookes c Dujon b Davis	45	B 1, l-b 4, w 5, n-b 8	18
G. N. Yallop c Holding b Davis	29		
A. R. Border c Lloyd b Davis	17	1/18 2/55 3/114 (30.3 overs) 151
K. H. MacLeay c Haynes b Davis	1	4/116 5/126 6/114
†R. W. Marsh c Haynes b Holding	8	7/141 8/150 9/151

Bowling: Roberts 7–0–14–1; Holding 8–2–23–1; Davis 10.3–0–51–7; Daniel 3–0–35–0; Gomes 2–0–10–0.

Umpires: D. J. Constant and D. G. L. Evans.

INDIA v ZIMBABWE

At Leicester, June 11. India won by five wickets. Zimbabwe, put in after a start delayed by drizzle until after lunch, showed little of their form of two days earlier and were unsettled by the amount of swing and bounce obtained by the Indian bowlers, especially Madan Lal. The Indian fielding was fallible, but Kirmani took five catches – a wicket-keeping record in the competition. India made the 156 they required comfortably.

Man of the Match: Madan Lal.

Zimbabwe

A. H. Shah c Kirmani b Sandhu	8	R. D. Brown c Kirmani b Shastri	6
G. A. Paterson lbw b Madan Lal	22	P. W. E. Rawson c Kirmani b Binny	3
J. G. Heron c Kirmani b Madan Lal	18	A. J. Traicos run out	2
A. J. Pycroft c Shastri b Binny	14	L-b 9, w 9	18
†D. L. Houghton c Kirmani b Madan Lal	21		
*D. A. G. Fletcher b Kapil Dev	13	1/13 2/55 3/56 (51.4 overs) 155
K. M. Curran run out	8	4/71 5/106 6/114
I. P. Butchart not out	22	7/115 8/139 9/148

Bowling: Kapil Dev 9–3–18–1; Sandhu 9–1–29–1; Madan Lal 10.4–0–27–3; Binny 11–2–25–2; Shastri 12–1–38–1.

India

K. Srikkanth c Butchart b Rawson	20	*Kapil Dev not out	2
S. M. Gavaskar c Heron b Rawson	4		
M. Amarnath c sub b Traicos	44	W 2	2
S. M. Patil b Fletcher	50		
R. J. Shastri c Brown b Shah	17	1/13 2/32 (5 wkts, 37.3 overs) 157
Yashpal Sharma not out	18	3/101 4/128 5/148

R. M. H. Binny, Madan Lal, †S. M. H. Kirmani and B. S. Sandhu did not bat.

Bowling: Rawson 5.1–1–11–2; Curran 6.5–1–33–0; Butchart 5–1–21–0; Traicos 11–1–41–1; Fletcher 6–1–32–1; Shah 3.3–0–17–1.

Umpires: J. Birkenshaw and R. Palmer.

ENGLAND v PAKISTAN

At Lord's, June 13. England won by eight wickets. Having started badly when Willis, in a fine opening spell, removed Mohsin and Mansoor, Pakistan's innings never promised to produce enough runs to trouble England. Under Zaheer's influence 64 runs were scored in the last ten overs, but England, with Gower and Lamb batting boldly again and Fowler holding the other end with gradually increasing confidence, won in the 51st over.

Man of the Match: Zaheer Abbas.

Pakistan

Mohsin Khan c Tavaré b Willis	3	Abdul Qadir run out	0
Mudassar Nazar c Gould b Allott	26	Sarfraz Nawaz c and b Botham	11
Mansoor Akhtar c Gould b Willis	3	†Wasim Bari not out	18
Javed Miandad c Gould b Botham	14	B 5, l-b 8, w 3, n-b 3	19
Zaheer Abbas not out	83		
*Imran Khan run out	7	1/29 2/33 3/49 4/67 (8 wkts, 60 overs) 193	
Wasim Raja c Botham b Marks	9	5/96 6/112 7/118 8/154	

Rashid Khan did not bat.

Bowling: Willis 12–4–24–2; Dilley 12–1–33–0; Allott 12–2–48–1; Botham 12–3–36–2; Marks 12–1–33–1.

England

G. Fowler not out	78
C. J. Tavaré lbw b Rashid	8
D. I. Gower c Sarfraz b Mansoor	48
A. J. Lamb not out	48
B 1, l-b 12, w 2, n-b 2	17

1/15 2/93   (2 wkts, 50.4 overs) 199

M. W. Gatting, I. T. Botham, †I. J. Gould, V. J. Marks, G. R. Dilley, P. J. W. Allott and *R. G. D. Willis did not bat.

Bowling: Rashid 7–2–19–1; Sarfraz 11–5–22–0; Raja 3–0–14–0; Mudassar 8–0–30–0; Qadir 9.4–0–53–0; Mansoor 12–2–44–1.

Umpires: B. J. Meyer and A. G. T. Whitehead.

NEW ZEALAND v SRI LANKA

At Bristol, June 13. New Zealand won by five wickets. After being put in, Sri Lanka lost an early wicket to Hadlee, but during a fourth-wicket stand of 71 in twenty overs between Mendis and Madugalle they still looked capable of making a fair score. However, Hadlee returned to break the stand and later prevented any flourish by the tailenders. Turner and Wright made 89 for New Zealand's first wicket in only eighteen overs, and with a handsome innings by their captain, Howarth, New Zealand cruised home with more than twenty overs to spare.

Man of the Match: R. J. Hadlee.

Sri Lanka

S. Wettimuny lbw b Hadlee	7	A. L. F. de Mel c and b Hadlee		1
B. Kuruppu c Hadlee b Chatfield	26	R. J. Ratnayake b Hadlee		5
R. L. Dias b Chatfield	25	V. B. John not out		2
*L. R. D. Mendis b Hadlee	43	L-b 6, w 1, n-b 1		8
R. S. Madugalle c Snedden b Coney	60			
A. Ranatunga lbw b Hadlee	0	1/16 2/56 3/73	(56.1 overs)	206
D. S. de Silva b Coney	13	4/144 5/144 6/171		
†R. G. de Alwis c Howarth b Snedden..	16	7/196 8/199 9/199		

Bowling: Hadlee 10.1–4–25–5; Snedden 10–1–38–1; Chatfield 12–4–24–2; Cairns 7–0–35–0; Coney 12–0–44–2; M. D. Crowe 5–0–32–0.

New Zealand

G. M. Turner c Mendis b de Silva	50	J. V. Coney not out		2
J. G. Wright lbw b de Mel	45	†I. D. S. Smith not out		4
*G. P. Howarth c Madugalle		L-b 6, w 3		9
b de Mel.	76			
M. D. Crowe c de Alwis b de Mel	0	1/89 2/99	(5 wkts, 39.2 overs)	209
J. J. Crowe lbw b John	23	3/110 4/176 5/205		

R. J. Hadlee, B. L. Cairns, M. C. Snedden and E. J. Chatfield did not bat.

Bowling: de Mel 9–2–35–3; John 8.2–0–49–1; Ratnayake 11–0–55–0; de Silva 9–0–39–1; Ranatunga 2–0–22–0.

Umpires: H. D. Bird and D. R. Shepherd.

INDIA v AUSTRALIA

At Nottingham, June 13. Australia won by 162 runs. Though Kapil Dev took an early wicket and subsequently ran through the later batting, the other Indian bowlers caused few problems. Chappell's 110 was made off 131 balls and his partnership of 144 in 29 overs with Hughes took Australia on their way to an unassailable position early in the day, Yallop carrying on when Chappell was out at 206 for four. India were without Gavaskar, and Australia had rested Lillee in favour of the left-arm spinner, Hogan. However, it was the young fast-medium bowler, MacLeay, with six wickets, who did most damage to India.
Man of the Match: T. M. Chappell.

Australia

K. C. Wessels b Kapil Dev	5	K. H. MacLeay c and b Kapil Dev		4
T. M. Chappell c Srikkanth		T. G. Hogan b Kapil Dev		11
b Amarnath.	110	G. F. Lawson c Srikkanth		
*K. J. Hughes b Madan Lal	52	b Kapil Dev.		6
D. W. Hookes c Kapil Dev		R. M. Hogg not out		2
b Madan Lal.	1	B 1, l-b 14, w 8, n-b 2		25
G. N. Yallop not out	66			
A. R. Border c Yashpal Sharma		1/11 2/155 3/159	(9 wkts, 60 overs)	320
b Binny.	26	4/206 5/254 6/277		
†R. W. Marsh c Sandhu b Kapil Dev ..	12	7/289 8/301 9/307		

Bowling: Kapil Dev 12–2–43–5; Sandhu 12–1–52–0; Binny 12–0–52–1; Shastri 2–0–16–0; Madan Lal 12–0–69–2; Patil 6–0–36–0; Amarnath 4–0–27–1.

India

R. J. Shastri lbw b Lawson	11	R. M. H. Binny lbw b MacLeay	0
K. Srikkanth c Border b Hogan	39	†S. M. H. Kirmani b MacLeay	12
M. Amarnath run out	2	B. S. Sandhu not out	9
D. B. Vengsarkar lbw b MacLeay	5	B 1, l-b 4, w 3, n-b 2	10
S. M. Patil b MacLeay	0		
Yashpal Sharma c and b MacLeay	3	1/38 2/43 3/57 (37.5 overs) 158	
*Kapil Dev b Hogan	40	4/57 5/64 6/66	
Madan Lal c Hogan b MacLeay	27	7/124 8/126 9/136	

Bowling: Lawson 5–1–25–1; Hogg 7–2–23–0; Hogan 12–1–48–2; MacLeay 11.5–3–39–6; Border 2–0–13–0.

Umpires: D. O. Oslear and R. Palmer.

WEST INDIES v ZIMBABWE

At Worcester, June 13. West Indies won by eight wickets. As in their famous win over Australia, Zimbabwe owed much to Fletcher who, coming in at 65 for four, added 92 with Houghton. Momentarily, when Rawson removed Haynes and Richards and West Indies were 23 for two, another sensation was just conceivable, but between stoppages for bad light Greenidge and Gomes soon killed Zimbabwe's hopes.

Man of the Match: C. G. Greenidge.

Zimbabwe

A. H. Shah b Roberts	2	I. P. Butchart lbw b Holding	0
G. A. Paterson c Dujon b Holding	4	G. E. Peckover not out	16
J. G. Heron st Dujon b Gomes	12	B 1, l-b 23, w 7, n-b 7	38
A. J. Pycroft run out	13		
†D. L. Houghton c Dujon b Roberts	54	1/7 2/7 (7 wkts, 60 overs) 217	
*D. A. G. Fletcher not out	71	3/35 4/65	
K. M. Curran b Roberts	7	5/157 6/181 7/183	

P. W. E. Rawson and A. J. Traicos did not bat.

Bowling: Roberts 12–4–36–3; Holding 12–2–33–2; Daniel 12–4–21–0; Davis 12–2–34–0; Gomes 8–0–42–1; Richards 4–1–13–0.

West Indies

C. G. Greenidge not out	105
D. L. Haynes c Houghton b Rawson	2
I. V. A. Richards lbw b Rawson	16
H. A. Gomes not out	75
B 1, l-b 8, w 9, n-b 2	20

1/3 2/23 (2 wkts, 48.3 overs) 218

S. F. A. Bacchus, *C. H. Lloyd, †P. J. Dujon, W. W. Daniel, A. M. E. Roberts, M. A. Holding and W. W. Davis did not bat.

Bowling: Rawson 12–1–39–2; Curran 10.3–1–37–0; Butchart 9–1–40–0; Fletcher 4–0–22–0; Traicos 9–0–37–0; Shah 4–0–23–0.

Umpires: D. G. L. Evans and J. Birkenshaw.

ENGLAND v NEW ZEALAND

At Birmingham, June 15. New Zealand won by two wickets. Such a result seemed unlikely when England, early in the day, were making a confident start, but the pitch was not entirely consistent in bounce and an experiment with Botham at No. 3 proved unsuccessful. Only Gower, with an immaculate 92 not out from 96 balls, contributed much after an opening stand of 63 between Fowler and Tavaré, and he could not stop the loss of the last three wickets for 1 run with 4.4 overs unused. England's score seemed adequate when Willis removed Turner and Edgar with only 3 runs scored, and at 75 for four New Zealand were still fighting an uphill battle. But while Coney held one end, his partners, especially Hadlee, gave him support which kept New Zealand close to the required scoring-rate. With two wickets left, they needed 4 runs off the last over, or 3 if they still had a wicket intact. Off the fifth ball, with the scores level, Bracewell struck a 4 to settle the issue.

Man of the Match: J. V. Coney.

England

G. Fowler c J. J. Crowe b Chatfield	69	G. R. Dilley b Hadlee	10
C. J. Tavaré c Cairns b Coney	18	P. J. W. Allott c Smith b Hadlee	0
I. T. Botham c and b Bracewell	12	*R. G. D. Willis lbw b Chatfield	0
D. I. Gower not out	92	B 4, l-b 10, w 1	15
A. J. Lamb c J. J. Crowe b Cairns	8		
M. W. Gatting b Cairns	1	1/63 2/77 3/117 (55.2 overs) 234
†I. J. Gould lbw b Cairns	4	4/143 5/154 6/162
V. J. Marks b Hadlee	5	7/203 8/233 9/233

Bowling: Hadlee 10–3–32–3; Cairns 11–0–44–3; Coney 12–2–27–1; Bracewell 12–0–66–1; Chatfield 10.2–0–50–2.

New Zealand

G. M. Turner lbw b Willis	2	R. J. Hadlee b Willis	31
B. A. Edgar c Gould b Willis	1	B. L. Cairns lbw b Willis	5
*G. P. Howarth run out	60	J. G. Bracewell not out	4
J. J. Crowe b Allott	17	B 2, l-b 22, w 1, n-b 3	28
M. D. Crowe b Marks	20		
J. V. Coney not out	66	1/2 2/3 3/47 4/75 (8 wkts, 59.5 overs) 238
†I. D. S. Smith b Botham	4	5/146 6/151 7/221 8/231

E. J. Chatfield did not bat.

Bowling: Willis 12–1–42–4; Dilley 12–1–43–0; Botham 12–1–47–1; Allott 11.5–2–44–1; Marks 12–1–34–1.

Umpires: K. E. Palmer and J. Birkenshaw.

WEST INDIES v INDIA

At The Oval, June 15. West Indies won by 66 runs. West Indies' batting was sustained by a relatively subdued Richards in an innings of only seven 4s. His stands of 101 with Haynes and 80 in fourteen overs with Lloyd brought West Indies to 198 for three, and though he was out in the 52nd over, India were given a stiff task. For a time, after a start of 21 for two, Amarnath and Vengsarkar raised hopes of a strong Indian challenge, reaching 89 for two after only 21 overs, but Vengsarkar was then struck in the mouth by a lifting ball from Marshall. Despite a vigorous innings by Kapil Dev, the effort faded away.

Man of the Match: I. V. A. Richards.

West Indies

C. G. Greenidge c Vengsarkar		H. A. Gomes not out	27
b Kapil Dev.	9	A. M. E. Roberts c Patil b Binny	7
D. L. Haynes c Kapil Dev		M. D. Marshall run out	4
b Amarnath.	38	M. A. Holding c sub b Madan Lal	2
I. V. A. Richards c Kirmani		W. W. Davis not out	0
b Sandhu.	119	L-b 13, w 5	18
*C. H. Lloyd run out	41		
S. F. A. Bacchus b Binny	8	1/17 2/118 3/198 (9 wkts, 60 overs)	282
†P. J. Dujon c Shastri b Binny	9	4/213 5/239 6/240 7/257 8/270 9/280	

Bowling: Kapil Dev 12–0–46–1; Sandhu 12–2–42–1; Binny 12–0–71–3; Amarnath 12–0–58–1; Madan Lal 12–0–47–1.

India

K. Srikkanth c Dujon b Roberts	2	Madan Lal not out	8
R. J. Shastri c Dujon b Roberts	6	†S. M. H. Kirmani b Marshall	0
M. Amarnath c Lloyd b Holding	80	B. S. Sandhu run out	0
D. B. Vengsarkar retired hurt	32	B 3, l-b 13, n-b 5	21
S. M. Patil c b Gomes	21		
Yashpal Sharma run out	9	1/2 2/21 3/130 (53.1 overs)	216
*Kapil Dev c Haynes b Holding	36	4/143 5/193 6/195	
R. M. H. Binny lbw b Holding	1	7/212 8/214 9/216	

Bowling: Roberts 9–1–29–2; Holding 9.1–0–40–3; Marshall 11–3–20–1; Davis 12–2–51–0; Gomes 12–1–55–1.

Umpires: B. J. Meyer and D. R. Shepherd.

PAKISTAN v SRI LANKA

At Leeds, June 16. Pakistan won by 11 runs. Twice during the day Sri Lanka seemed within sight of victory – in the morning when Pakistan, having been put in, found the ball moving about disconcertingly and were 43 for five, and again in the evening when the Sri Lankan third-wicket pair were moving steadily to within 74 runs of the required score. Pakistan were saved first by Imran's 102 not out and his sixth-wicket stand of 144 with Shahid, and later by the leg-spinner Qadir who took three wickets in eight balls as Sri Lanka were gathering themselves for a final dash for victory. Seven wickets fell for 37 runs and a last-wicket stand of 25 by de Mel and John, who needed 37 in the last six overs, merely emphasised Sri Lanka's lost opportunity.

Man of the Match: Abdul Qadir.

Pakistan

Mohsin Khan c Ranatunga b de Mel	3	Sarfraz Nawaz c Madugalle b de Mel	9
Mansoor Akhtar c de Alwis b de Mel	6	Abdul Qadir not out	5
Zaheer Abbas c Dias b de Mel	15	B 1, l-b 4, w 4, n-b 2	11
Javed Miandad lbw b Ratnayake	7		
*Imran Khan not out	102	1/6 2/25 (7 wkts, 60 overs)	235
Ijaz Faqih lbw b Ratnayake	0	3/30 4/43	
Shahid Mahboob c de Silva b de Mel	77	5/43 6/187 7/204	

†Wasim Bari and Rashid Khan did not bat.

Bowling: de Mel 12–1–39–5; John 12–1–48–0; Ratnayake 12–2–42–2; Ranatunga 11–0–49–0; de Silva 12–1–42–0; Wettimuny 1–0–4–0.

Sri Lanka

S. Wettimuny c Shahid b Rashid	50	†R. G. de Alwis c Miandad b Qadir	4
B. Kuruppu b Rashid	12	A. L. F. de Mel c Imran b Sarfraz	17
R. L. Dias st Bari b Qadir	47	V. B. John not out	6
*L. R. D. Mendis c Bari b Qadir	33	L-b 8, w 17, n-b 2	27
R. J. Ratnayake st Bari b Qadir	1		
R. S. Madugalle c Qadir b Shahid	26	1/22 2/101 3/162 (58.3 overs)	224
A. Ranatunga c Zaheer b Qadir	0	4/162 5/166 6/166	
D. S. de Silva run out	1	7/171 8/193 9/199	

Bowling: Rashid 12–4–31–2; Sarfraz 11.3–2–25–1; Shahid 10–1–62–1; Mansoor 1–0–8–0; Ijaz 12–0–27–0; Qadir 12–1–44–5.

Umpires: D. O. Oslear and A. G. T. Whitehead.

AUSTRALIA v ZIMBABWE

At Southampton, June 16. Australia won by 32 runs. Though their off-spinner, Traicos, who played for South Africa in 1970, again bowled economically, Zimbabwe could not stop Australia from making 272 for seven which, when Zimbabwe were 109 for five and falling below the required rate, seemed ample. However, Houghton added 103 in seventeen overs with Curran and was batting well enough to suggest that the final 61 in eight overs was within his side's powers. At that point Chappell and Hogg took four wickets for 1 run.

Man of the Match: D. L. Houghton.

Australia

G. M. Wood c Rawson b Traicos	73	K. H. MacLeay c Rawson b Butchart	9
T. M. Chappell c Traicos b Rawson	22	T. G. Hogan not out	5
*K. J. Hughes b Traicos	31	L-b 16, w 2, n-b 6	24
D. W. Hookes c Brown b Fletcher	10		
G. N. Yallop c Houghton b Curran	20	1/46 2/124 (7 wkts, 60 overs)	272
A. R. Border b Butchart	43	3/150 4/150	
†R. W. Marsh not out	35	5/219 6/231 7/249	

D. K. Lillee and R. M. Hogg did not bat.

Bowling: Hogg 9–2–34–0; Rawson 9–0–50–1; Fletcher 9–1–27–1; Butchart 10–0–52–2; Traicos 12–1–28–2; Curran 11–0–57–1.

Zimbabwe

R. D. Brown c Marsh b Hogan	38	I. P. Butchart lbw b Hogg	0
G. A. Paterson lbw b Hogg	17	P. W. E. Rawson lbw b Hogg	0
J. G. Heron run out	3	A. J. Traicos b Chappell	19
A. J. Pycroft run out	13	V. R. Hogg not out	7
†D. L. Houghton c Hughes b Chappell	84	B 1, l-b 10, w 1, n-b 10	22
*D. A. G. Fletcher b Hogan	2	1/48 2/53 3/79 4/97 (59.5 overs)	240
K. M. Curran lbw b Chappell	35	5/109 6/212 7/213 8/213 9/21	

Bowling: Hogg 12–0–40–3; Lillee 9–1–23–0; Hogan 12–0–33–2; MacLeay 9–0–45–0; Border 9–1–30–0; Chappell 8.5–0–47–3.

Umpires: D. G. L. Evans and R. Palmer.

ENGLAND v PAKISTAN

At Manchester, June 18. England won by seven wickets. England qualified for the semi-final with a comfortable victory over Pakistan, whose 232 for eight never seemed likely to be enough on a pitch of mild pace. Efficient bowling and fielding pinned down the early Pakistan batsmen, and just as Miandad was promising an acceleration, a fine throw from Botham ran him out. Fowler and Tavaré launched England's innings with the minimum of disquiet, and by the time Fowler was first out at 115 he had set England on the path to victory.

Man of the Match: G. Fowler.

Pakistan

Mohsin Khan c Marks b Allott	32
Mudassar Nazar c Gould b Dilley	18
Zaheer Abbas c Gould b Dilley	0
Javed Miandad run out	67
*Imran Khan c Willis b Marks	13
Wasim Raja c Willis b Marks	15
Ijaz Faqih not out	42

Rashid Khan did not bat.

Sarfraz Nawaz b Willis	17
Abdul Qadir run out	6
†Wasim Bari not out	2
B 3, l-b 14, w 2, n-b 1	20
1/33 2/34 3/87 4/116 (8 wkts, 60 overs)	232
5/144 6/169 7/204 8/221	

Bowling: Willis 12–3–37–1; Dilley 12–2–46–2; Allott 12–1–33–1; Botham 12–1–51–0; Marks 12–0–45–2.

England

G. Fowler c Miandad b Mudassar	69
C. J. Tavaré c Raja b Zaheer	58
D. I. Gower c Zaheer b Mudassar	31
A. J. Lamb not out	38

M. W. Gatting not out	14
B 1, l-b 15, w 7	23
1/115 2/165 3/181 (3 wkts, 57.2 overs)	233

I. T. Botham, †I. J. Gould, V. J. Marks, G. R. Dilley, P. J. W. Allott and *R. G. D. Willis did not bat.

Bowling: Rashid 11–1–58–0; Sarfraz 10.2–2–22–0; Qadir 11–0–51–0; Ijaz 6–0–19–0; Mudassar 12–2–34–2; Zaheer 7–0–26–1.

Umpires: H. D. Bird and D. O. Oslear.

NEW ZEALAND v SRI LANKA

At Derby, June 18. Sri Lanka won by three wickets. After their win over England, New Zealand came down with a bump and were always struggling against Sri Lanka, who eventually won their first victory of the tournament. At one time New Zealand, having been put in on a lively pitch, were 116 for nine before a last-wicket stand of 65 between Snedden and Chatfield restored a gleam of hope. Two good innings by Kuruppu and Dias all but extinguished that, but from 129 for two Sri Lanka's middle batting faltered nervously and it needed the stiffening influence of Dias to see them home after five wickets had fallen for 32 runs.

Man of the Match: A. L. F. de Mel.

New Zealand

G. M. Turner c Dias b de Mel	6
J. G. Wright c de Alwis b de Mel	0
*G. P. Howarth b Ratnayake	15
M. D. Crowe lbw b Ratnayake	8
B. A. Edgar c Samarasekera b de Silva	27
J. V. Coney c sub b de Silva	22
R. J. Hadlee c Madugalle b de Mel	15
†W. K. Lees c Ranatunga b de Mel	2

B. L. Cairns c Dias b de Mel	6
M. C. Snedden run out	40
E. J. Chatfield not out	19
B 4, l-b 5, w 11, n-b 1	21
1/8 2/8 3/32 (58.2 overs)	181
4/47 5/88 6/91	
7/105 8/115 9/116	

Bowling: de Mel 12–4–32–5; Ratnayake 11–4–18–2; Ranatunga 10–2–50–0; de Silva 12–5–11–2; Samarasekera 11.2–2–38–0; Wettimuny 2–0–11–0.

Sri Lanka

S. Wettimuny b Cairns	4	D. S. de Silva run out	2
B. Kuruppu c and b Snedden	62	†R. G. de Alwis not out	11
A. Ranatunga b Crowe	15		
R. L. Dias not out	64	B 1, l-b 4, w 10	15
*L. R. D. Mendis lbw b Chatfield	0		
R. S. Madugalle c Lees b Snedden	6	1/15 2/49	(7 wkts, 52.5 overs) 184
M. A. R. Samarasekera c Lees b Hadlee	5	3/129 4/130	
		5/139 6/151 7/161	

A. L. F. de Mel and R. J. Ratnayake did not bat.

Bowling: Hadlee 12–3–16–1; Cairns 10–2–35–1; Snedden 10.5–1–58–2; Chatfield 12–3–23–1; Crowe 4–2–15–1; Coney 4–1–22–0.

Umpires: D. J. Constant and B. Leadbeater.

INDIA v ZIMBABWE

At Tunbridge Wells, June 18. India won by 31 runs. A remarkable match contained one of the most spectacular innings played in this form of cricket. India, who had chosen to bat on a pitch from which the ball moved a lot, were 9 for four – soon to be 17 for five – when their captain, Kapil Dev, came in. No-one could foresee then that a week later India would be winning the whole tournament; indeed, qualification for the semi-final was in grave doubt. With Binny and Madan Lal, Kapil Dev took the score to 140 for eight and by then was in full flow. Kirmani provided sensible support in an unbroken ninth-wicket stand of 126 in sixteen overs while Kapil Dev, with six 6s and sixteen 4s in all, reached 175, beating the previous highest for the tournament, Glenn Turner's 170 for New Zealand against East Africa at Edgbaston in 1975. The match was still not firmly in India's hands, for Curran, who with Rawson had been responsible for India's early disasters, played a dashing innings of 73, and it was not until he was ninth out at 230 in the 56th over that India were safe.

Man of the Match: Kapil Dev.

India

S. M. Gavaskar lbw b Rawson	0	R. J. Shastri c Pycroft b Fletcher	1
K. Srikkanth c Butchart b Curran	0	Madan Lal c Houghton b Curran	17
M. Amarnath c Houghton b Rawson	5	†S. M. H. Kirmani not out	24
S. M. Patil c Houghton b Curran	1	L-b 9, w 3	12
Yashpal Sharma c Houghton b Rawson	9		
*Kapil Dev not out	175	1/0 2/6 3/6 4/9	(8 wkts, 60 overs) 266
R. M. H. Binny lbw b Traicos	22	5/17 6/77 7/78 8/140	

B. S. Sandhu did not bat.

Bowling: Rawson 12–4–47–3; Curran 12–1–65–3; Butchart 12–2–38–0; Fletcher 12–2–59–1; Traicos 12–0–45–1.

Zimbabwe

R. D. Brown run out	35	I. P. Butchart b Binny	18
G. A. Paterson lbw b Binny	23	G. E. Peckover c Yashpal b Madan Lal	14
J. G. Heron run out	3	P. W. E. Rawson not out	2
A. J. Pycroft c Kirmani b Sandhu	6	A. J. Traicos c and b Kapil Dev	3
†D. L. Houghton lbw b Madan Lal	17	L-b 17, w 7, n-b 4	28
*D. A. G. Fletcher c Kapil Dev b Amarnath	13	1/44 2/48 3/61 4/86	(57 overs) 235
K. M. Curran c Shastri b Madan Lal	73	5/103 6/113 7/168 8/189 9/230	

Bowling: Kapil Dev 11–1–32–1; Sandhu 11–2–44–1; Binny 11–2–45–2; Madan Lal 11–2–42–3; Amarnath 12–1–37–1; Shastri 1–0–7–0.

Umpires: M. J. Kitchen and B. J. Meyer.

WEST INDIES v AUSTRALIA

At Lord's, June 18. West Indies won by seven wickets. From a start of 37 for two, Australia's innings prospered while Hughes and Hookes were adding 101, and for a time something over 300 seemed possible. In the end it needed some robust blows from Marsh for them to reach 273 for six, and it soon became clear that this was well within the reach of the West Indian batsmen on a good pitch. Haynes played on at 79, but Greenidge and Richards took the score past 200 at a pace which ensured that no undue haste would be needed thereafter.

Man of the Match: I. V. A. Richards.

Australia

G. M. Wood b Marshall	17		†R. W. Marsh c Haynes b Holding	37
T. M. Chappell c Dujon b Marshall	5		T. G. Hogan not out	0
*K. J. Hughes b Gomes	69		B 1, l-b 18, w 6, n-b 1	26
D. W. Hookes c Greenidge b Davis	56			—
G. N. Yallop not out	52		1/10 2/37 3/138 (6 wkts, 60 overs) 273	
A. R. Border c and b Gomes	11		4/176 5/202 6/266	

J. R. Thomson, D. K. Lillee and R. M. Hogg did not bat.

Bowling: Roberts 12–0–51–0; Marshall 12–0–36–2; Davis 12–0–57–1; Holding 12–1–56–1; Gomes 12–0–47–2.

West Indies

C. G. Greenidge c Hughes b Hogg	90		*C. H. Lloyd not out	19
D. L. Haynes b Hogan	33		B 3, l-b 18, w 1, n-b 2	24
I. V. A. Richards not out	95			—
H. A. Gomes b Chappell	15		1/79 2/203 3/238 (3 wkts, 57.5 overs) 276	

S. F. A. Bacchus, †P. J. Dujon, M. D. Marshall, A. M. E. Roberts, M. A. Holding and W. W. Davis did not bat.

Bowling: Hogg 12–0–25–1; Thomson 11–0–64–0; Hogan 12–0–60–1; Lillee 12–0–52–0; Chappell 10.5–0–51–1.

Umpires: K. E. Palmer and A. G. T. Whitehead.

ENGLAND v SRI LANKA

At Leeds, June 20. England won by nine wickets. Making their only change of the competition, Cowans for the injured Dilley, England won the shortest match in it very easily. On a pitch which gave the bowlers a little help, Sri Lanka were always struggling, with Willis doing much to set their innings on its unhappy course. Fowler, with Tavaré and then Gower, made the 137 needed in only 24.1 overs.

Man of the Match: R. G. D. Willis.

Sri Lanka

S. Wettimuny lbw b Botham	22	A. L. F. de Mel c Lamb b Marks	10
B. Kuruppu c Gatting b Willis	6	R. J. Ratnayake not out	20
A. Ranatunga c Lamb b Botham	0	V. B. John c Cowans b Allott	15
R. L. Dias c Gould b Cowans	7	B 5, l-b 2, w 3, n-b 2	12
*L. R. D. Mendis b Allott	10		
R. S. Madugalle c Gould b Allott	0	1/25 2/30 3/32	(50.4 overs) 136
D. S. de Silva c Gower b Marks	15	4/40 5/43 6/54	
†R. G. de Alwis c Marks b Cowans	19	7/81 8/97 9/103	

Bowling: Willis 9–4–9–1; Cowans 12–3–31–2; Botham 9–4–12–2; Allott 10.4–0–41–3; Gatting 4–2–13–0; Marks 6–2–18–2.

England

G. Fowler not out	81
C. J. Tavaré c de Alwis b de Mel	19
D. I. Gower not out	27
B 1, l-b 3, w 3, n-b 3	10

1/68　　　　　(1 wkt, 24.1 overs) 137

A. J. Lamb, M. W. Gatting, I. T. Botham, †I. J. Gould, V. J. Marks, P. J. W. Allott, *R. G. D. Willis and N. G. Cowans did not bat.

Bowling: de Mel 10–1–33–1; Ratnayake 5–0–23–0; John 6–0–41–0; de Silva 3–0–29–0; Ranatunga 0.1–0–1–0.

Umpires: B. Leadbeater and R. Palmer.

NEW ZEALAND v PAKISTAN

At Nottingham, June 20. Pakistan won by 11 runs. To qualify for the semi-final, Pakistan needed not only to beat New Zealand but to make enough runs in their 60 overs to give them a better scoring-rate throughout the tournament. They met this second requirement, achieving an overall scoring-rate of 4.01 against New Zealand's 3.94, through an unbroken fourth-wicket stand of 147 in 75 minutes between Zaheer and Imran, during which they made 47 off Hadlee's last five overs. New Zealand were soon in trouble against Sarfraz, Mudassar and Qadir and it was not until Coney led the last three wickets in a sterling attempt at making 85 off the final ten overs that Pakistan had any uneasy moments. Bracewell helped him to add 59 in five overs and 13 were needed off the last over, but Coney, attempting a second run, was run out off the first ball from Imran's throw.

Man of the Match: Imran Khan.

Pakistan

Mohsin Khan c Cairns b Coney	33	*Imran Khan not out	79
Mudassar Nazar b Coney	15	B 1, l-b 2, w 2, n-b 1	6
Javed Miandad b Hadlee	25		
Zaheer Abbas not out	103	1/48 2/54 3/114	(3 wkts, 60 overs) 261

Ijaz Faqih, Shahid Mahboob, Sarfraz Nawaz, Abdul Qadir, †Wasim Bari and Rashid Khan did not bat.

Bowling: Hadlee 12–1–61–1; Cairns 12–1–45–0; Chatfield 12–0–57–0; Coney 12–0–42–2; Bracewell 12–0–50–0.

New Zealand

G. M. Turner c Bari b Sarfraz	4	†W. K. Lees c sub b Mudassar	26
J. G. Wright c Imran b Qadir	19	J. G. Bracewell c Mohsin b Sarfraz	34
*G. P. Howarth c Miandad b Zaheer	39	E. J. Chatfield not out	3
M. D. Crowe b Mudassar	43	L-b 8, w 5, n-b 1	14
B. A. Edgar lbw b Shahid	6		
J. V. Coney run out	51	1/13 2/44 3/85	(59.1 overs) 250
R. J. Hadlee c Mohsin b Mudassar	11	4/102 5/130 6/150	
B. L. Cairns c Imran b Qadir	0	7/152 8/187 9/246	

Bowling: Rashid 6–1–24–0; Sarfraz 9.1–1–50–2; Qadir 12–0–53–2; Ijaz 6–1–21–0; Shahid 10–0–37–1; Mudassar 12–0–43–3; Zaheer 4–1–8–1.

Umpires: D. G. L. Evans and M. J. Kitchen.

AUSTRALIA v INDIA

At Chelmsford, June 20. India won by 118 runs. Australia would have qualified for the semi-final if they had won here, having a faster overall scoring-rate than India, but they gave a poor performance. India's innings was slow to develop, and for some time after the third wicket fell at 65 it was not certain that they would muster enough runs. But the later batsmen all made useful contributions and the Australian bowlers helped with fifteen no-balls and nine wides. In an innings of 247, extras provided the second-highest score. In the absence of Hughes, injured in the previous match, Hookes captained Australia and was one of the victims of Binny, who came on in the sixteenth over, swung the ball a little and, with an able partner in Madan Lal, quickly reduced Australia from 46 for one to 78 for seven.
Man of the Match: R. M. H. Binny.

India

S. M. Gavaskar c Chappell b Hogg	9	Madan Lal not out	12
K. Srikkanth c Border b Thomson	24	†S. M. H. Kirmani lbw b Hogg	10
M. Amarnath c Marsh b Thomson	13	B. S. Sandhu b Thomson	8
Yashpal Sharma c Hogg b Hogan	40	L-b 13, w 9, n-b 15	37
S. M. Patil c Hogan b MacLeay	30		
*Kapil Dev c Hookes b Hogg	28	1/27 2/54 3/65	(55.5 overs) 247
K. B. J. Azad c Border b Lawson	15	4/118 5/157 6/174	
R. M. H. Binny run out	21	7/207 8/215 9/232	

Bowling: Lawson 10–1–40–1; Hogg 12–2–40–3; Hogan 11–1–31–1; Thomson 10.5–0–51–3; MacLeay 12–2–48–1.

Australia

T. M. Chappell c Madan Lal b Sandhu	2	T. G. Hogan c Srikkanth b Binny	8
G. M. Wood c Kirmani b Binny	21	G. F. Lawson b Sandhu	16
G. N. Yallop c and b Binny	18	R. M. Hogg not out	8
*D. W. Hookes b Binny	1	J. R. Thomson b Madan Lal	0
A. R. Border b Madan Lal	36	L-b 5, w 5, n-b 4	14
†R. W. Marsh lbw b Madan Lal	0		
K. H. MacLeay c Gavaskar b Madan Lal	5	1/3 2/46 3/48 4/52	(38.2 overs) 129
		5/52 6/69 7/78 8/115 9/129	

Bowling: Kapil Dev 8–2–16–0; Sandhu 10–1–26–2; Madan Lal 8.2–3–20–4; Binny 8–2–29–4; Amarnath 2–0–17–0; Azad 2–0–7–0.

Umpires: J. Birkenshaw and D. R. Shepherd.

WEST INDIES v ZIMBABWE

At Birmingham, June 20. West Indies won by ten wickets. Zimbabwe's 171 represented a recovery. Before a bold innings of 62 by Curran they were 42 for five, having had no answer to the pace and hostility of Marshall and Garner. The medium-paced Zimbabwean bowlers could do little to worry Haynes and Bacchus on a mild pitch, and though Traicos, the off-spinner, bowled his twelve overs for only 24 runs, West Indies cruised home with nearly fifteen overs to spare.

Man of the Match: S. F. A. Bacchus.

Zimbabwe

R. D. Brown c Lloyd b Marshall	14	G. E. Peckover c and b Richards	3
G. A. Paterson c Richards b Garner	6	P. W. E. Rawson b Daniel	19
J. G. Heron c Dujon b Garner	0	A. J. Traicos not out	1
A. J. Pycroft c Dujon b Marshall	4	B 4, l-b 13, w 7, n-b 7	31
†D. L. Houghton c Lloyd b Daniel	0		
*D. A. G. Fletcher b Richards	23	1/17 2/17 3/41 (60 overs) 171	
K. M. Curran b Daniel	62	4/42 5/42 6/79	
I. P. Butchart c Haynes b Richards	8	7/104 8/115 9/170	

Bowling: Marshall 12–3–19–2; Garner 7–4–13–2; Davis 8–2–13–0; Daniel 9–2–28–3; Gomes 12–2–26–0; Richards 12–1–41–3.

West Indies

D. L. Haynes not out	88
S. F. A. Bacchus not out	80
L-b 1, w 3	4

(no wkt, 45.1 overs) 172

A. L. Logie, I. V. A. Richards, H. A. Gomes, *C. H. Lloyd, †P. J. Dujon, J. Garner, M. D. Marshall, W. W. Daniel and W. W. Davis did not bat.

Bowling: Rawson 12–3–38–0; Butchart 4–0–23–0; Traicos 12–2–24–0; Curran 9–0–44–0; Fletcher 8.1–0–39–0.

Umpires: H. D. Bird and D. J. Constant.

SEMI-FINALS

ENGLAND v INDIA

At Manchester, June 22. India won by six wickets. Though England made a brisk and promising start, this was a pitch similar to those on which India are so hard to beat at home. Binny, Azad and Amarnath had only to bowl a steady length to reduce the England batsmen, as they sought to attack, to mistimings and countless uses of the bat's edge. The fact that the faster Kapil Dev had been no great menace while Fowler and Tavaré were making 69 at 4 an over was an indication that the faster England bowlers would not pose the same problems to the Indian batsmen, who have plenty of experience of slow pitches of low bounce. Two run-outs – of Lamb and Gould – made a recovery of the initiative even more unlikely. For more than an hour not a 4 was hit, and it needed a few rough, mostly edged strokes by Dilley to lift the score above 200. India, with little need to hurry, duly found the going easier against bowling which came on to the bat more readily. Though Gavaskar and Srikkanth were out for 50, Amarnath and Yashpal added 92 with increasing belligerence and Patil and Yashpal hurried the match to its close, at one time making 63 off nine overs.

Man of the Match: M. Amarnath.

England

G. Fowler b Binny	33	G. R. Dilley not out		20
C. J. Tavaré c Kirmani b Binny	32	P. J. W. Allott c Patil b Kapil Dev		8
D. I. Gower c Kirmani b Amarnath	17	*R. G. D. Willis b Kapil Dev		0
A. J. Lamb run out	29	B 1, l-b 17, w 7, n-b 4		29
M. W. Gatting b Amarnath	18			
I. T. Botham b Azad	6	1/69 2/84 3/107	(60 overs)	213
†I. J. Gould run out	13	4/141 5/150 6/160		
V. J. Marks b Kapil Dev	8	7/175 8/177 9/202		

Bowling: Kapil Dev 11–1–35–3; Sandhu 8–1–36–0; Binny 12–1–43–2; Madan Lal 5–0–15–0; Azad 12–1–28–1; Amarnath 12–1–27–2.

India

S. M. Gavaskar c Gould b Allott	25	*Kapil Dev not out		1
K. Srikkanth c Willis b Botham	19	B 5, l-b 6, w 1, n-b 2		14
M. Amarnath run out	46			
Yashpal Sharma c Allott b Willis	61	1/46 2/50	(4 wkts, 54.4 overs)	217
S. M. Patil not out	51	3/142 4/205		

K. B. J. Azad, R. M. H. Binny, Madan Lal, †S. M. H. Kirmani and B. S. Sandhu did not bat.

Bowling: Willis 10.4–2–42–1; Dilley 11–0–43–0; Allott 10–3–40–1; Botham 11–4–40–1; Marks 12–1–38–0.

Umpires: D. O. Oslear and D. G. L. Evans.

WEST INDIES v PAKISTAN

At The Oval, June 22. West Indies won by eight wickets. Though Mohsin held one end until only three of Pakistan's 60 overs remained, their innings never promised to produce enough runs to bother West Indies. On a good, firm pitch the Pakistan batsmen, from whom Miandad was missing through influenza, struggled to such an extent that the boundary was reached only twice. Even though Mohsin and Zaheer made 54 in a third-wicket stand, the score had reached just 88 when Zaheer played on to Gomes from some way down the pitch in the last over before lunch. This was during a spell when Gomes and Richards were using up the fifth bowler's allotment economically. Greenidge and Haynes made an unspectacular start for West Indies, but Richards and Gomes finished the match with an unbroken stand of 132 and more than eleven overs to spare.

Man of the Match: I. V. A. Richards.

Pakistan

Mohsin Khan b Roberts	70	Sarfraz Nawaz c Holding b Roberts		3
Mudassar Nazar c and b Garner	11	Abdul Qadir not out		10
Ijaz Faqih c Dujon b Holding	5	†Wasim Bari not out		4
Zaheer Abbas b Gomes	30	B 6, l-b 13, w 4, n-b 5		28
*Imran Khan c Dujon b Marshall	17			
Wasim Raja lbw b Marshall	0	1/23 2/34 3/88	(8 wkts, 60 overs)	184
Shahid Mahboob c Richards b Marshall	6	4/139 5/139 6/159 7/164 8/171		

Rashid Khan did not bat.

Bowling: Roberts 12–3–25–2; Garner 12–1–31–1; Marshall 12–2–28–3; Holding 12–1–25–1; Gomes 7–0–29–1; Richards 5–0–18–0.

West Indies

C. G. Greenidge lbw b Rashid 17
D. L. Haynes b Qadir 29
I. V. A. Richards not out.................. 80
H. A. Gomes not out 50
B 2, l-b 6, w 4........................ 12

1/34 2/56   (2 wkts, 48.4 overs) 188

*C. H. Lloyd, S. F. A. Bacchus, †P. J. Dujon, A. M. E. Roberts, M. D. Marshall, J. Garner and M. A. Holding did not bat.

Bowling: Rashid 12–2–32–1; Sarfraz 8–0–23–0; Qadir 11–1–42–1; Mahboob 11–1–43–0; Raja 1–0–9–0; Zaheer 4.4–1–24–0; Mohsin 1–0–3–0.

Umpires: D. J. Constant and A. G. T. Whitehead.

FINAL

INDIA v WEST INDIES

At Lord's, June 25. India defeated on merit the firm favourites, winning a low-scoring match by 43 runs. It was an absorbing game of increasing drama and finally of much emotion. The result, as surprising as, on the day, it was convincing, had much to do with the mental pressures of containment in limited-overs cricket.

Amarnath was named Man of the Match by Mike Brearley for a stabilising innings of 26 against hostile fast bowling after the early loss of Gavaskar, followed by his taking three late West Indian wickets, Dujon's being especially important. Dujon and Marshall had lifted West Indies, needing 184 to win, from 76 for six to 119 for six, a recovery based on the calm application of sound batting principles and one which was threatening to achieve after all the result which everyone had expected.

Lord's, groomed like a high-born lady, bathed in sunshine and packed to capacity, was at its best when Lloyd won the toss and invited India to bat: a distinct advantage, it seemed, for his battery of fast bowlers. The Lord's wicket often inclines to extravagant morning life. Now it never lost this capacity to allow movement off the seam, sufficient to be of much significance later in the day for the medium-paced attack of Madan Lal and Sandhu, who removed the cream of the West Indian batting, and for the seemingly inoffensive Binny, who accounted for the dangerous Lloyd.

There was an explosive start to the match, Garner hurling the ball down, chest-high on the line of the off stump. Roberts, fast but flatter, had Gavaskar caught at the wicket in his third over. To score off such an attack was a problem, but Srikkanth showed how: he hooked Roberts for 4, pulled him for 6 and square drove him to the Tavern boundary like a pistol shot. Yashpal, released from the constraints of speed, drove the slow spin of Gomes high and wide to the off, but straight to cover point. At lunch India were 100 for four. Afterwards Kapil Dev perished at deep long-on and Patil lost concentration. Madan Lal, Kirmani and Sandhu added 31 late runs, but India's total of 183 seemed many too few.

West Indies started badly. Greenidge padded up to the deceptive Sandhu and was bowled. Richards, however, swept the total swiftly and effortlessly to 50. Then, when 33, he mistimed a hook and Kapil Dev took a fine catch over his shoulder, running back towards the mid-wicket boundary. Madan Lal followed with two more quick wickets, those of Haynes and Gomes. All three fell for 6 runs in nineteen balls. Lloyd drove Binny to mid-off and immediately after tea Bacchus was caught at the wicket. It remained for Amarnath to break the partnership between Dujon and Marshall which, just in time, he did. India were an entertaining and well-drilled team, learning and improving as they progressed towards the final. – W.W.

The attendance was 24,609, including members.

India

S. M. Gavaskar c Dujon b Roberts	2	Madan Lal b Marshall	17
K. Srikkanth lbw b Marshall	38	†S. M. H. Kirmani b Holding	14
M. Amarnath b Holding	26	B. S. Sandhu not out	11
Yashpal Sharma c sub b Gomes	11	B 5, l-b 5, w 9, n-b 1	20
S. M. Patil c Gomes b Garner	27		
*Kapil Dev c Holding b Gomes	15	1/2 2/59 3/90 (54.4 overs)	183
K. B. J. Azad c Garner b Roberts	0	4/92 5/110 6/111	
R. M. H. Binny c Garner b Roberts	2	7/130 8/153 9/161	

Bowling: Roberts 10–3–32–3; Garner 12–4–24–1; Marshall 11–1–24–2; Holding 9.4–2–26–2; Gomes 11–1–49–2; Richards 1–0–8–0.

West Indies

C. G. Greenidge b Sandhu	1	M. D. Marshall c Gavaskar b Amarnath	18
D. L. Haynes c Binny b Madan Lal	13	A. M. E. Roberts lbw b Kapil Dev	4
I. V. A. Richards c Kapil Dev b Madan Lal	33	J. Garner not out	5
*C. H. Lloyd c Kapil Dev b Binny	8	M. A. Holding lbw b Amarnath	6
H. A. Gomes c Gavaskar b Madan Lal	5	L-b 4, w 10	14
S. F. A. Bacchus c Kirmani b Sandhu	8	1/5 2/50 3/57 4/66 (52 overs)	140
†P. J. Dujon b Amarnath	25	5/66 6/76 7/119 8/124 9/126	

Bowling: Kapil Dev 11–4–21–1; Sandhu 9–1–32–2; Madan Lal 12–2–31–3; Binny 10–1–23–1; Amarnath 7–0–12–3; Azad 3–0–7–0.

Umpires: H. D. Bird and B. J. Meyer.

WORLD CUP RECORDS

Batting

Highest individual score: 175* – Kapil Dev, India v Zimbabwe (Tunbridge Wells), 1983.

Hundred before lunch: 101 – A. Turner, Australia v Sri Lanka (The Oval), 1975.

Highest total: 338 for five – Pakistan v Sri Lanka (Swansea), 1983.

Highest total – batting second: 288 for nine – Sri Lanka v Pakistan (Swansea), 1983.

Lowest total: 45 – Canada v England (Manchester), 1979.

Highest match aggregate: 626 – Pakistan v Sri Lanka (Swansea), 1983.

Lowest match aggregate: 91 – Canada v England (Manchester), 1979.

Biggest victories: Ten wickets – India beat East Africa (Leeds), 1975.
Ten wickets – West Indies beat Zimbabwe (Birmingham), 1983.
202 runs – England beat India (Lord's), 1975.

Narrowest victories: One wicket – West Indies beat Pakistan with 2 balls to spare (Birmingham), 1975.
9 runs – England beat New Zealand (Manchester), 1979.

Record partnerships for each wicket

182 for 1st	R. B. McCosker and A. Turner, Australia v Sri Lanka at The Oval	1975
176 for 2nd	D. L. Amiss and K. W. R. Fletcher, England v India at Lord's	1975
195* for 3rd	C. G. Greenidge and H. A. Gomes, West Indies v Zimbabwe at Worcester	1983
149 for 4th	R. B. Kanhai and C. H. Lloyd, West Indies v Australia at Lord's	1975
139 for 5th	I. V. A. Richards and C. L. King, West Indies v England at Lord's	1979
144 for 6th	Imran Khan and Shahid Mahboob, Pakistan v Sri Lanka at Leeds	1983
75* for 7th	J. A. G. Fletcher and I. P. Butchart, Zimbabwe v Australia at Nottingham	1983
54 for 8th	D. S. de Silva and R. G. de Alwis, Sri Lanka v Pakistan at Swansea	1983
	R. G. de Alwis and A. L. F. de Mel, Sri Lanka v England at Taunton	1983
126* for 9th	Kapil Dev and S. M. H. Kirmani, India v Zimbabwe at Tunbridge Wells	1983
71 for 10th	A. M. E. Roberts and J. Garner, West Indies v India at Manchester	1983

Bowling and Fielding

Best analysis: seven for 51 – W. W. Davis, West Indies v Australia (Leeds), 1983

Most economical analysis: 12–8–6–1 – B. S. Bedi, India v East Africa (Leeds), 1975

Most expensive analysis: 12–1–105–2 – M. C. Snedden, New Zealand v England (The Oval), 1983

Wicket-keeping – most dismissals: 5 – S. M. H. Kirmani, India v Zimbabwe (Leicester), 1983

Fielding – most catches: 3 – C. H. Lloyd, West Indies v Sri Lanka (Manchester), 1975

WORLD CUP NATIONAL RECORDS

Australia
Highest total: 328 for five v Sri Lanka (The Oval), 1975
Lowest total: 129 v India (Chelmsford), 1983
Highest score: 110 – T. M. Chappell v India (Nottingham), 1983
Best bowling: six for 14 – G. J. Gilmour v England (Leeds), 1975

England
Highest total: 334 for four v India (Lord's), 1975
Lowest total: 93 v Australia (Leeds), 1975
Highest score: 137 – D. L. Amiss v India (Lord's), 1975
Best bowling: five for 39 – V. J. Marks v Sri Lanka (Taunton), 1983

India
Highest total: 262 for eight v West Indies (Manchester), 1983
Lowest total: 132 for three v England (Lord's), 1975
Highest score: 175* – Kapil Dev v Zimbabwe (Tunbridge Wells), 1983
Best bowling: five for 43 – Kapil Dev v Australia (Nottingham), 1983

New Zealand
Highest total: 309 for five v East Africa (Birmingham), 1975
Lowest total: 158 v West Indies (The Oval), 1975
Highest score: 171* – G. M. Turner v East Africa (Birmingham), 1975
Best bowling: five for 25 – R. J. Hadlee v Sri Lanka (Bristol), 1983

Pakistan
Highest total: 338 for five v Sri Lanka (Swansea), 1983
Lowest total: 151 v England (Leeds), 1979
Highest score: 103* – Zaheer Abbas v New Zealand (Nottingham), 1983
Best bowling: five for 44 – Abdul Qadir v Sri Lanka (Leeds), 1983

Sri Lanka
Highest total: 288 for nine v Pakistan (Swansea), 1983
Lowest total: 86 v West Indies (Manchester), 1975
Highest score: 72 – B. Kuruppu v Pakistan (Swansea), 1983
Best bowling: five for 32 – A. L. F. de Mel v New Zealand (Derby), 1983

West Indies
Highest total: 293 for six v Pakistan (The Oval), 1979
Lowest total: 140 v India (Lord's), 1983
Highest score: 138* – I. V. A. Richards v England (Lord's), 1979
Best bowling: seven for 51 – W. W. Davis v Australia (Leeds), 1983

Zimbabwe
Highest total: 240 v Australia (Southampton), 1983
Lowest total: 155 v India (Leicester), 1983
Highest score: 84 – D. L. Houghton v Australia (Southampton), 1983
Best bowling: four for 42 – D. A. G. Fletcher v Australia (Nottingham), 1983

PREVIOUS WINNERS

1975 WEST INDIES beat Australia by 17 runs
1979 WEST INDIES beat England by 92 runs

THE ASHES

The Ashes were originated in 1882 when, on August 29, Australia defeated the full strength of England on English soil for the first time. The Australians won by the narrow margin of 7 runs and the following day the *Sporting Times* printed a mock obituary notice, written by Shirley Brooks, son of an editor of *Punch*, which read:

"In affectionate remembrance of English Cricket which died at The Oval, 29th August, 1882. Deeply lamented by a large circle of sorrowing friends and acquaintances, R.I.P. N.B. The body will be cremated and the Ashes taken to Australia."

The following winter the Hon. Ivo Bligh, afterwards Lord Darnley, set out to Australia to recover these mythical Ashes. Australia won the first match by nine wickets, but England won the next two, and the real ashes came into being when some Melbourne women burnt a bail used in the third game and presented the ashes in an urn to Ivo Bligh.

When Lord Darnley died in 1927, the urn, by a bequest in his will, was given to MCC, and it held a place of honour in the Long Room at Lord's until 1953 when, with other cricket treasures, it was moved to the newly built Imperial Cricket Memorial near the pavilion. There it stands permanently, together with the velvet bag in which the urn was originally given to Lord Darnley and the scorecard of the 1882 match.

★　★　★　★

Note: At the time of the 1982 centenary of The Oval Test match, evidence was provided that the Ashes were the remains of a ball, that they were presented to the Hon. Ivo Bligh around Christmas 1882, and that they were handed over to the England captain by Sir William Clarke. This account does not tally with the version by Florence, Countess of Darnley (the Hon. Ivo Bligh's widow) and by members of her family. Possibly more than one presentation of some ashes took place on the 1882-83 tour in view of the great interest shown in Australia towards Ivo Bligh and his cricketing mission.

THE CRICKET COUNCIL

The Cricket Council, which was set up in 1968 and reconstituted in 1974 and January 1983, acts as the governing body for cricket in the British Isles. It is composed of the following, the officers listed being those for January-September 1983.

Chairman: F. G. Mann.
Vice-Chairman: J. D. Robson.
8 Representatives of Test and County Cricket Board: F. G. Mann, C. R. M. Atkinson, D. J. Insole, C. H. Palmer, C. S. Rhoades, A. C. Smith, F. M. Turner, A. G. Waterman.
5 Representatives of National Cricket Association: J. D. Robson, F. R. Brown, F. H. Elliott, J. Lane, J. G. Overy.
3 Representatives of Marylebone Cricket Club: D. G. Clark, J. G. W. Davies, C. G. A. Paris.
1 Representative (non-voting) of Minor Counties Cricket Association: G. L. B. August.
1 Representative (non-voting) of Irish Cricket Union: D. Scott.
1 Representative (non-voting) of Scottish Cricket Union: R. W. Barclay.
Secretary – D. B. Carr.

The following were the officers from October 1, 1982–January 25, 1983.

President: Sir Anthony Tuke.
Chairman: C. H. Palmer.
Chairman of Public Relations and Promotion Sub-Committee: F. M. Turner.
5 Representatives of Test and County Cricket Board: F. G. Mann, D. J. Insole, C. S. Rhoades, A. C. Smith, A. G. Waterman.
5 Representatives of National Cricket Association: J. D. Robson, F. R. Brown, F. H. Elliott, J. Lane, J. G. Overy.
5 Representatives of Marylebone Cricket Club: D. G. Clark (Vice-Chairman), G. O. Allen (resigned October 26, 1982), J. G. W. Davies, C. G. A. Paris, W. H. Webster.
1 Representative of Minor Counties Cricket Association: R. A. C. Forrester.
1 Representative (non-voting) of Irish Cricket Union: D. Scott.
1 Representative (non-voting) of Scottish Cricket Union: R. W. Barclay.
Secretary – D. B. Carr; *Deputy Secretary –* J. A. Bailey; *Secretary, PR and Promotion –* P. M. Lush.

THE TEST AND COUNTY CRICKET BOARD

The TCCB was set up in 1968 to be responsible for Test matches, official tours, and First-Class and Minor Counties competitions. It is composed of representatives from seventeen First-Class counties; Marylebone Cricket Club; Minor Counties Cricket Association; Oxford University Cricket Club, Cambridge University Cricket Club, the Irish Cricket Union and the Scottish Cricket Union.

Officers 1982-83

Chairman: F. G. Mann.

Chairman of Committees: F. G. Mann (Adjudication, Executive); F. R. Brown (County Pitches); D. J. Insole (Cricket, Overseas Tours); C. R. M. Atkinson (Discipline); A. G. Waterman (Finance and General Purposes); B. Coleman (PR and Marketing); D. R. W. Silk (Registration); P. B. H. May (Selection); D. B. Carr (Umpires); M. D. Vockins (Under 25 and Second XI Competitions).

Secretary – D. B. Carr; *Assistant Secretary (Admin.) –* B. Langley; *Assistant Secretary (Cricket) –* M. E. Gear; *PR and Marketing Manager –* P. M. Lush; *Promotions Officer –* R. J. Roe.

THE NATIONAL CRICKET ASSOCIATION

With the setting up of the Cricket Council in 1968 it was necessary to form a separate organisation to represent the interests of all cricket below the first-class game, and it is the National Cricket Association that carries out this function. It comprises – Representatives from 50 County Cricket Associations and Representatives from 16 national cricketing organisations.

Officers 1982-83

President: F. R. Brown.
Chairman: J. D. Robson.
Secretary: B. J. Aspital.

Director of Coaching: K. V. Andrew.
Hon. Treasurer: D. A. Jackson.
Assistant Secretary: P. G. M. August.

ADDRESSES OF REPRESENTATIVE BODIES

INTERNATIONAL CRICKET CONFERENCE: J. A. Bailey, Lord's Ground, London NW8 8QN.
ENGLAND: Cricket Council, D. B. Carr, Lord's Ground, London NW8 8QN.
AUSTRALIA: Australian Cricket Board, D. L. Richards, 70 Jolimont Street, Jolimont, Victoria 3002.
SOUTH AFRICA: South African Cricket Union, Charles Fortune, PO Box 55009, Northlands 2116, Transvaal.
WEST INDIES: West Indies Cricket Board of Control, G. S. Camacho, 8B Caledonia Avenue, Kingston 5, Jamaica.
INDIA: Board of Control for Cricket in India, A. W. Kanmadikar, E-4 Radio Colony, Indore (MP).
NEW ZEALAND: New Zealand Cricket Council, G. T. Dowling, PO Box 958, Christchurch.
PAKISTAN: Board of Control for Cricket in Pakistan, A. A. K. Abbasi, Gaddafi Stadium, Lahore.
SRI LANKA: Board of Control for Cricket in Sri Lanka, Nuski Mohamed, 35 Maitland Place, Colombo 7.
ARGENTINA: Argentine Cricket Association, R. H. Gooding, c/o The English Club, 25 de Mayo 586, 1002 Buenos Aires.

BANGLADESH: Bangladesh Cricket Control Board, Syed Ashraful Huq, The Stadium, Dacca.

BERMUDA: Bermuda Cricket Board of Control, Wilton L. Smith, PO Box 992, Hamilton.

CANADA: Canadian Cricket Association, K. D. Wilson, 1306–1261 Nelson Street, Vancouver, British Columbia.

DENMARK: Danish Cricket Association, Peter S. Hargreaves, Lykkesborg Alle 7, 2860 Soborg.

EAST AFRICA: East African Cricket Conference, A. E. Dudhia, PO Box 1198, Lusaka, Zambia.

FIJI: Fiji Cricket Association, P. I. Knight, PO Box 300, Suva.

GIBRALTAR: Gibraltar Cricket Association, T. J. Finlayson, 21 Sandpits House, Withams Road.

HONG KONG: Hong Kong Cricket Association, S. K. Sipahimalani, Centre for Media Resources, University of Hong Kong, Knowles Bldg, Pokfulam Road.

ISRAEL: Israel Cricket Association, G. Kandeli, 35/7 Minz Street, Petach Tiqua.

KENYA: Kenya Cricket Association, K. G. Purohit, PO Box 46480, Nairobi.

MALAYSIA: Malaysian Cricket Association, Daljit Singh Gill, c/o High Court (Mahkamah Tinggi), Kuala Lumpur.

NETHERLANDS: Royal Netherlands Cricket Association, P. J. Trijzelaar, Willem de Zwijgerlaan 96A, The Hague.

PAPUA NEW GUINEA: Papua New Guinea Cricket Board of Control, N. R. Agonia, PO Box 812, Port Moresby.

SINGAPORE: Singapore Cricket Association, R. Sivasubramaniam, 5000-D Marine Parade Road 22-16, Laguna Park, Singapore 1544.

USA: United States Cricket Association, Naseeruddin Khan, 2361 Hickory Road, Plymouth Meeting, Pennsylvania 19462.

WEST AFRICA: West Africa Cricket Conference, Lt-Col. W. A. Jibunch, c/o Cricket Secretariat, National Sports Commission, PO Box 145, Lagos, Nigeria.

ZIMBABWE: Zimbabwe Cricket Union, A. L. A. Pichanick, PO Box 452, Harare.

BRITISH UNIVERSITIES SPORTS FEDERATION: 28 Woburn Square, London WC1.

CLUB CRICKET CONFERENCE: D. J. Annetts, 353 West Barnes Lane, New Malden, Surrey, KT3 6JF.

ENGLAND SCHOOLS' CRICKET ASSOCIATION: C. J. Cooper, 68 Hatherley Road, Winchester, Hampshire SO22 6RR.

IRISH CRICKET UNION: D. Scott, 45 Foxrock Park, Foxrock, Co. Dublin.

MINOR COUNTIES CRICKET ASSOCIATION: D. J. M. Armstrong, Thorpe Cottage, Mill Common, Ridlington, North Walsham.

NATIONAL CRICKET ASSOCIATION: B. J. Aspital, Lord's Ground, London, NW8 8QN.

SCARBOROUGH FESTIVAL: Lt Cdr H. C. Wood, North Marine Road, Scarborough, Yorkshire.

SCOTTISH CRICKET UNION: R. W. Barclay, Admin. Office, 18 Ainslie Place, Edinburgh, EH3 6AU.

THE SPORTS COUNCIL: Emlyn B. Jones, 16 Upper Woburn Place, London WC1.

ASSOCIATION OF CRICKET UMPIRES: L. J. Cheeseman, 16 Ruden Way, Epsom Downs, Surrey, KT17 3LN.

WOMEN'S CRICKET ASSOCIATION: 16 Upper Woburn Place, London WC1.

The addresses of MCC, the First-Class Counties, and Minor Counties are given at the head of each separate section.

THE MARYLEBONE CRICKET CLUB, 1983

Patron – HER MAJESTY THE QUEEN

President – SIR ANTHONY TUKE

President Designate – A. H. A. DIBBS

Life Vice-President – G. O. ALLEN

Treasurer – D. G. CLARK

Chairman of Finance – E. W. PHILLIPS

Secretary – J. A. BAILEY

(Lord's Cricket Ground, St John's Wood, NW8 8QN)

Assistant Secretaries – LT COL. L. G. JAMES (Administration), LT-COL. J. R. STEPHENSON (Cricket), WG-CDR V. J. W. M. LAWRENCE (Chief Accountant)

Curator – S. E. A. GREEN

MCC Committee for 1982-83: Sir Anthony Tuke (President), R. Aird, G. O. Allen, A. V. Bedser, F. R. Brown, A. N. S. Burnett, Lord Caccia, D. G. Clark, E. A. Clark, N. J. Cosh, M. C. Cowdrey, J. G. W. Davies, G. H. G. Doggart, J. T. Faber, S. C. Griffith, J. S. O. Haslewood, A. C. D. Ingleby-Mackenzie, D. J. Insole, P. B. H. May, M. E. L. Melluish, F. W. Millett, C. G. A. Paris, E. W. Phillips, Sir Oliver Popplewell, D. R. W. Silk, R. A. Sligh, C. Stansfield Smith, E. W. Swanton, A. G. Waterman.

At the 196th Annual Meeting of MCC, held at Lord's on May 4, 1983, C. G. A. Paris was appointed a Trustee of the club, the vacancy arising from the death of G. C. Newman. Sir Oliver Popplewell was nominated to serve as a Trustee from October 1, 1983, when R. Aird was due to retire. Sir Anthony Tuke was nominated to become Chairman of Finance upon the retirement of E. W. Phillips on September 30, 1983. Consideration was given to an Interim Report of the MCC Special Working Party set up, under the chairmanship of D. G. Clark, as a result of the Special General Meeting held in July 1982 at which approximately 30 per cent of those voting expressed support for changes in the existing structure of the Committee. The terms of reference of the Working Party were to "scrutinize the role of MCC", to "look at Lord's" and to "review the Rules of the Club (with special reference to the structure of the Committee and Sub-Committees)".

A deficit after taxation of £108,313 was reported, this being largely due to the expenditure of £216,221 on an extensive programme of maintenance and ground improvements. It was also estimated that the Special General Meetings held in July and August 1982 incurred a total of £12,881 in direct costs. Good increases were announced in income from match receipts, particularly Box Hire. It was stated that the development scheme for the Tennis and Squash Courts area, on which it had been planned to start work in October 1982, had been postponed, owing partly to a number of objections lodged by members. A reappraisal of the situation was to be carried out. The membership of the club on

December 31, 1982, when there were 8,408 candidates on the waiting list, was 18,170. In 1982, 233 members died, there were 209 resignations and 145 lapsed memberships.

Among notable personalities connected with the game whose deaths were reported were General Sir Ronald Adam, Adjutant General to the Forces for much of the Second World War and President of MCC in 1946, G. C. Newman, a Trustee of MCC from 1969 and a former President of Middlesex, R. L. O. Bridgeman, a member of the Tennis and Squash Sub-Committee, G. W. A. Chubb, a former South African Test player and twice President of the South African Cricket Association, H. P. Crabtree, for some years MCC's enthusiastic Coaching Adviser for youth, F. S. Lee, an Honorary Life Member of the club and renowned, when his playing days with Somerset were over, as an outstanding first-class umpire, W. G. L. F. Lowndes, who captained Hampshire in the 1930s, K. D. Mackay, a cricketer of distinctive mannerisms who played 37 times for Australia, B. L. Muncer, formerly chief coach at Lord's, T. A. Pearce, President of Kent in 1978 and welcoming host to many cricketers in Hong Kong, and A. Sandham, scorer of 41,284 first-class runs and the "complete Surrey cricketer".

A. H. A. Dibbs was nominated by Sir Anthony Tuke to succeed him as President of MCC on October 1, 1983. Aged 64, Alex Dibbs has held high office in both the National Westminster Bank and British Airways and had a lifelong interest in all sports.

A Special General Meeting of MCC, requisitioned in accordance with Rule 43 by 118 members of the Club, was held in Central Hall, Westminster, on July 13, 1983, with the President in the chair, the object being to vote on a resolution, put forward by J. R. Carlisle, MP for Luton West, that "the members of MCC Committee implement the selection of an MCC touring party to tour South Africa in 1983-84". At the club's Annual Meeting on May 4 discussion of the South African issue had been cut short at the President's behest, in view of this pending Special General Meeting. At the end of a debate lasting three hours, at which some 1,200 members were present, the Committee's adjuration that the resolution be rejected was quite comfortably carried. In a postal ballot held in advance of the Special General Meeting (though the result of it was not known until after the debate) 6,069 members voted against the Resolution and 3,935 for it. Of those who waited to vote in the Hall, 535 were against the Resolution and 409 in favour of it. The Resolution, proposed by Mr Carlisle, was seconded by J. P. Pashley. G. H. G. Doggart, President of MCC in 1982, and M. C. Cowdrey acted as the Committee's official spokesmen. An account of the meeting and events leading up to it may be found on page 65.

MCC v MIDDLESEX

At Lord's, April 27, 28, 29. Abandoned.

At Cambridge, May 11, 12, 13. MCC drew with CAMBRIDGE UNIVERSITY (See Cambridge University section).

At Oxford, May 25, 26, 27. MCC drew with OXFORD UNIVERSITY (See Oxford University section).

†At Lord's, July 14. MCC Young Cricketers won by eight wickets. MCC 233 for five dec. (M. E. Gear 78, R. D. V. Knight 60, A. Needham 40 not out); MCC Young Cricketers 239 for two (I. M. Clough 106, R. T. Hart 85 not out, R. N. Berry 33 not out).

At Titwood, Glasgow, August 17, 18, 19. MCC lost to SCOTLAND by five wickets (See Other Matches, 1983).

†At Roehampton, August 24, 25. MCC won by nine wickets. MCC 220 for two dec. (R. E. Hayward 100 not out, R. T. Hart 84 not out) and 40 for one; Ireland 49 (A. J. Pollock six for 18, D. Wilson three for 3) and 207 (R. T. Wills 100, G. D. Harrison 32; A. J. Pollock five for 69, D. Wilson three for 79).

At Swansea, August 24, 25, 26. MCC drew with WALES (See Other Matches, 1983).

MCC ENGLAND HONORARY CRICKET MEMBERS

C. J. Barnett	P. B. H. May, CBE	P. H. Parfitt
W. E. Bowes	W. Watson	F. H. Tyson
H. Larwood	P. E. Richardson	M. C. Cowdrey, CBE
W. Voce	T. E. Bailey	J. T. Murray, MBE
L. E. G. Ames, CBE	M. J. K. Smith, OBE	J. M. Parks
Sir Leonard Hutton	J. Hardstaff	D. B. Close, CBE
D. C. S. Compton, CBE	J. B. Statham, CBE	B. L. D'Oliveira, OBE
D. V. P. Wright	F. S. Trueman	R. Illingworth, CBE
J. T. Ikin	T. W. Graveney, OBE	G. Pullar
T. G. Evans, CBE	G. A. R. Lock	F. J. Titmus, MBE
C. Washbrook	C. Milburn	J. H. Wardle
A. V. Bedser, CBE	D. A. Allen	D. J. Brown
W. J. Edrich, DFC	R. W. Barber	M. H. Denness
J. C. Laker	E. R. Dexter	J. M. Brearley, OBE

OTHER MATCHES AT LORD'S, 1983

June 13. ENGLAND beat PAKISTAN by eight wickets (See Prudential World Cup section).

June 18. WEST INDIES beat AUSTRALIA by seven wickets (See Prudential World Cup section).

June 25. Prudential World Cup final. INDIA beat WEST INDIES by 43 runs (See Prudential World Cup section).

OXFORD UNIVERSITY v CAMBRIDGE UNIVERSITY

June 29, 30, July 1. Drawn. Three declarations were not enough to produce a result to the 139th University match. Little time was wasted, however, in the search for one, and for Boyd-Moss the occasion brought rare distinction. He became the first batsman ever to have scored two separate hundreds in the same University match and the first in the history of the fixture to have scored three successive hundreds, having made exactly 100 when Cambridge were making the 272 they had been set to win in 1982. He also passed, by 12, M. J. K. Smith's record aggregate for the match of 477 runs, and took seven Oxford wickets for 68 with his orthodox left-arm spin. Being the better, more confident side, Cambridge held the initiative almost throughout, scoring at a lively rate and being threatened with defeat only briefly, when Ellis was making 83 as his side attempted to score 304 in 265 minutes to win the match. There was a twin brother on each side, John Varey of Oxford and David of Cambridge.

Cambridge University

T. S. Curtis (*Worcester RGS and Magdalene*) b Petchey	75	– b Hayes	0
D. W. Varey (*Birkenhead and Pembroke*) c Cullinan b Hayes	6	– b Carr	32
R. J. Boyd-Moss (*Bedford and Magdalene*) c Carr b Petchey	139	– c Heseltine b Petchey	124
*S. P. Henderson (*Downside and Magdalene*) not out	51	– retired hurt	8
G. Pathmanathan (*Colombo Coll. and Darwin*) b Carr	5	– c Carr b Rawlinson	64
S. J. G. Doggart (*Winchester and Magdalene*) not out	31	– b Carr	18
K. I. Hodgson (*Oundle and Downing*) (did not bat)		– not out	6
T. A. Cotterell (*Downside and Peterhouse*) (did not bat)		– c Heseltine b Rawlinson	4
B 4, l-b 4, w 2, n-b 5	15	L-b 4, w 2, n-b 2	8

1/12 2/227 3/240 4/250   (4 wkts dec.) 322   1/10 2/83 3/195   (6 wkts dec.) 264
                                                    4/252 5/254 6/264

A. J. Pollock (*Shrewsbury and Trinity*), C. C. Ellison (*Tonbridge and Peterhouse*) and †S. G. P. Hewitt (*Bradford GS and Peterhouse*) did not bat.

Bowling: *First Innings*—Petchey 26–3–127–2; Hayes 9.5–1–57–1; Varey 9–1–37–0; Rawlinson 11–3–43–0; Carr 25–7–43–1. *Second Innings*—Petchey 25–3–129–1; Hayes 6–3–9–1; Carr 28–7–84–2; Rawlinson 9–1–32–2; Moulding 1–0–2–0.

Oxford University

R. G. P. Ellis (*Haileybury and St Edmund Hall*) b Hodgson	18 – c Curtis b Cotterell	83
A. J. T. Miller (*Haileybury and St Edmund Hall*) c Ellison b Boyd-Moss	62 – b Boyd-Moss	48
P. G. Heseltine (*Holgate GS and Keble*) lbw b Doggart	13 – c Pollock b Boyd-Moss	29
*G. J. Toogood (*N. Bromsgrove HS and Lincoln*) c Doggart b Boyd-Moss	14 – lbw b Hodgson	5
K. A. Hayes (*QEGS, Blackburn and Merton*) c Varey b Cotterell	45 – b Hodgson	11
R. P. Moulding (*Haberdashers' Aske's and Christ Church*) lbw b Cotterell	66 – c Ellison b Boyd-Moss	27
J. G. Varey (*Birkenhead and St Edmund Hall*) not out	40 – c Doggart b Boyd-Moss	0
J. D. Carr (*Repton and Worcester*) not out	16 – lbw b Boyd-Moss	0
H. T. Rawlinson (*Eton and Christ Church*) (did not bat)	– not out	18
†M. R. Cullinan (*Hilton Coll. SA and Worcester*) (did not bat)	– not out	2
B 1, l-b 7, w 1	9	L-b 7, w 1, n-b 5	13

1/34 2/71 3/100 4/117   (6 wkts dec.) 283   1/123 2/143 3/152   (8 wkts) 236
5/182 6/248   4/166 5/194 6/205 7/205 8/221

M. D. Petchey (*Latymer Upper and Christ Church*) did not bat.

Bowling: *First Innings*—Hodgson 15–2–61–1; Pollock 7.2–1–24–0; Ellison 3–2–6–0; Doggart 35–11–74–1; Cotterell 23–7–57–2; Boyd-Moss 20–9–41–2; Curtis 1–0–11–0. *Second Innings*—Pollock 4–1–6–0; Hodgson 26–5–64–2; Ellison 6–0–26–0; Doggart 14–4–48–0; Cotterell 16–4–43–1; Boyd-Moss 12–4–27–5; Curtis 6–2–9–0.

Umpires: D. G. L. Evans and B. J. Meyer.

OXFORD v CAMBRIDGE, RESULTS AND HUNDREDS

The University match dates back to 1827. Altogether there have been 139 official matches, Cambridge winning 53 and Oxford 45, with 41 drawn. Results since 1950:

1950	Drawn	1968	Drawn
1951	Oxford won by 21 runs	1969	Drawn
1952	Drawn	1970	Drawn
1953	Cambridge won by two wickets	1971	Drawn
1954	Drawn	1972	Cambridge won by an innings and
1955	Drawn		25 runs
1956	Drawn	1973	Drawn
1957	Cambridge won by an innings and	1974	Drawn
	186 runs	1975	Drawn
1958	Cambridge won by 99 runs	1976	Oxford won by ten wickets
1959	Oxford won by 85 runs	1977	Drawn
1960	Drawn	1978	Drawn
1961	Drawn	1979	Cambridge won by an innings and
1962	Drawn		52 runs
1963	Drawn	1980	Drawn
1964	Drawn	1981	Drawn
1965	Drawn	1982	Cambridge won by seven wickets
1966	Oxford won by an innings and 9 runs	1983	Drawn
1967	Drawn		

Seventy-five three-figure innings have been played in the University matches. For those scored before 1919 see 1940 *Wisden*. Those subsequent to 1919 include the six highest, as shown here:

238*	Nawab of Pataudi	1931 Oxford		119	J. M. Brearley	1964 Cam.
211	G. Goonesena	1957 Cam.		118	H. Ashton	1921 Cam.
201*	M. J. K. Smith	1954 Oxford		118	D. R. W. Silk	1954 Cam.
201	A. Ratcliffe	1931 Cam.		117	M. J. K. Smith	1956 Oxford
200	Majid J. Khan	1970 Oxford		116*	D. R. W. Silk	1953 Cam.
193	D. C. H. Townsend	1934 Oxford		116	M. C. Cowdrey	1953 Oxford
170	M. Howell	1919 Oxford		115	A. W. Allen	1934 Cam.
167	B. W. Hone	1932 Oxford		114*	D. R. Owen-Thomas	1972 Cam.
158	P. M. Roebuck	1975 Cam.		114	J. F. Pretlove	1955 Cam.
157	D. R. Wilcox	1932 Cam.		113*	J. M. Brearley	1962 Cam.
155	F. S. Goldstein	1968 Oxford		113	E. R. T. Holmes	1927 Oxford
149	J. T. Morgan	1929 Cam.		112*	E. D. Fursdon	1975 Oxford
146	R. O'Brien	1956 Cam.		111*	G. W. Cook	1957 Cam.
146	D. R. Owen-Thomas	1971 Cam.		109	C. H. Taylor	1923 Oxford
145*	H. E. Webb	1948 Oxford		108	F. G. H. Chalk	1934 Oxford
145	D. P. Toft	1967 Oxford		106	Nawab of Pataudi	1929 Oxford
142	M. P. Donnelly	1946 Oxford		105	E. J. Craig	1961 Cam.
139	R. J. Boyd-Moss	1983 Cam.		104	H. J. Enthoven	1924 Cam.
136	E. T. Killick	1930 Cam.		104	M. J. K. Smith	1955 Oxford
135	H. A. Pawson	1947 Oxford		103*	A. R. Lewis	1962 Cam.
131	Nawab of Pataudi	1960 Oxford		103*	D. R. Pringle	1979 Cam.
129	H. J. Enthoven	1925 Cam.		102*	A. P. F. Chapman	1922 Cam.
127	D. S. Sheppard	1952 Cam.		101*	R. W. V. Robins	1928 Cam.
124	R. J. Boyd-Moss	1983 Cam.		101	N. W. D. Yardley	1937 Cam.
124	A. K. Judd	1927 Cam.		100*	M. Manasseh	1964 Oxford
124	A. Ratcliffe	1932 Cam.		100	P. J. Dickinson	1939 Cam.
122	P. A. Gibb	1938 Cam.		100	N. J. Cosh	1967 Cam.
121	J. N. Grover	1937 Oxford		100	R. J. Boyd-Moss	1982 Cam.

* *Signifies not out.*

Highest Totals

503	Oxford	1900	432-9	Cambridge	1936
457	Oxford	1947	431	Cambridge	1932
453-8	Oxford	1931	425	Cambridge	1938

Lowest Totals

32	Oxford	1878	42	Oxford	1890
39	Cambridge	1858	47	Cambridge	1838

Notes: A. P. F. Chapman and M. P. Donnelly enjoy the following distinction: Chapman scored a century at Lord's in the University match (102*, 1922); for Gentlemen v Players (160, 1922), (108, 1926); and for England v Australia (121, 1930). M. P. Donnelly scored a century at Lord's in the University match (142, 1946); for Gentlemen v Players (162*, 1947); and for New Zealand v England (206, 1949).

A. Ratcliffe's 201 for Cambridge remained a record for the match for only one day, being beaten by the Nawab of Pataudi's 238* for Oxford next day.

M. J. K. Smith (Oxford) and R. J. Boyd-Moss (Cambridge) are the only players who have scored three hundreds. Smith scored 201* in 1954, 104 in 1955, and 117 in 1956; Boyd-Moss scored 100 in 1982 and 139 and 124 in 1983. His aggregate of 489 surpassed Smith's previous record of 477.

The following players have scored two hundreds: W. Yardley (Cambridge) 100 in 1870 and 130 in 1872; H. J. Enthoven (Cambridge) 104 in 1924 and 129 in 1925; Nawab of Pataudi (Oxford) 106 in 1929 and 238* in 1931; A. Ratcliffe (Cambridge) 201 in 1931 and 124 in 1932; D. R. W. Silk (Cambridge) 116* in 1953 and 118 in 1954; J. M. Brearley

(Cambridge) 113* in 1962 and 119 in 1964; D. R. Owen-Thomas (Cambridge) 146 in 1971 and 114* in 1972.

F. C. Cobden, in the Oxford v Cambridge match in 1870, performed the hat-trick by taking the last three wickets and won an extraordinary game for Cambridge by two runs. The feat is without parallel in first-class cricket. Cobden obtained the last three Oxford wickets in each innings – a curious coincidence. Other hat-tricks, all for Cambridge, have been credited to A. G. Steel (1879), P. H. Morton (1880), J. F. Ireland (1911), and R. G. H. Lowe (1926).

S. E. Butler, in the 1871 match, took all the wickets in the Cambridge first innings. The feat is unique in University matches. He bowled 24.1 overs. In the follow-on he took five wickets for 57, making fifteen for 95 runs in the match.

P. R. Le Couteur scored 160 and took eleven Cambridge wickets for 66 runs in 1910 – the best all-round performance in the history of the match.

D. W. Jarrett (Oxford 1975, Cambridge 1976), S. M. Wookey (Cambridge 1975-76, Oxford 1978) and G. Pathmanathan (Oxford 1975-78, Cambridge 1983) are alone in gaining cricket Blues for both Universities.

ETON v HARROW

July 2. Drawn. The 148th Eton and Harrow match produced an evenly contested draw in its second year as a one-day fixture. There was some determined batting for Harrow by Ford and Peel-Yates, while Marsland defended stubbornly for Eton. For the most part the medium-paced bowlers held the initiative. Luke, Buckland, Berry and Redmayne restricted most Harrovian thoughts of aggression until Lloyd-Jones attacked merrily. Harrow's opening bowlers, in their turn, were constrictingly accurate.

Harrow

*J. W. S. Raper c Inkin b Pettifer	8	†R. G. Robinson run out	0
W. D. Peel-Yates b Redmayne	45	J. D. Prior not out	12
J. M. H. Ford c Greenwood b Berry	73	B 9, l-b 14, w 2	25
D. J. Nirmalalingam lbw b Pettifer	16		
S. A. James c Russell b Redmayne	3	1/18 2/141 3/145 4/161 (6 wkts dec.) 214	
A. T. C. Lloyd-Jones not out	32	5/167 6/171	

J. E. J. Booth, D. B. M. Fox and C. A. S. Swan did not bat.

Bowling: Pettifer 29–3–85–2; Luke 11–4–17–0; Buckland 6–1–17–0; Greenwood 8–1–23–0; Berry 8–1–19–1; Redmayne 9–3–28–2.

Eton

F. P. E. Marsland b Fox	49	S. H. Greenwood c Robinson b Booth	2
R. V. Watson c Peel-Yates b Fox	9	†P. A. D. Inkin not out	0
M. H. Brooks b Raper	24		
J. P. Berry c and b Nirmalalingam	29	B 3, l-b 13, n-b 5	21
*W. A. B. Russell b Nirmalalingam	2		
C. G. M. Redmayne c James b Raper	14	1/22 2/59 3/105 4/111 (7 wkts) 150	
C. E. Pettifer not out	0	5/135 6/145 7/147	

R. J. F. Luke and W. L. C. Buckland did not bat.

Bowling: Fox 12–4–31–2; Raper 12–3–31–2; Booth 9–3–21–1; Swan 4–2–4–0; James 4–0–9–0; Nirmalalingam 5–1–33–2.

Umpires: D. B. Harman and A. E. D. Smith.

ETON v HARROW, RESULTS AND HUNDREDS

Of the 148 matches played Eton have won 49, Harrow 44 and 55 have been drawn. This is the generally published record, but Harrow men object strongly to the first game in 1805 being treated as a regular contest between the two schools, contending that it is no more correct to count that one than the fixture of 1857 which has been rejected.

The matches played during the war years 1915-18 and 1940-45 are not reckoned as belonging to the regular series.

Results since 1950:

1950	Drawn	1967	Drawn
1951	Drawn	1968	Harrow won by seven wickets
1952	Harrow won by seven wickets	1969	Drawn
1953	Eton won by ten wickets	1970	Eton won by 97 runs
1954	Harrow won by nine wickets	1971	Drawn
1955	Eton won by 38 runs	1972	Drawn
1956	Drawn	1973	Drawn
1957	Drawn	1974	Harrow won by eight wickets
1958	Drawn	1975	Harrow won by an innings and 151 runs
1959	Drawn		
1960	Harrow won by 124 runs	1976	Drawn
1961	Harrow won by an innings and 12 runs	1977	Eton won by six wickets
		1978	Drawn
1962	Drawn	1979	Drawn
1963	Drawn	1980	Drawn
1964	Eton won by eight wickets	1981	Drawn
1965	Harrow won by 48 runs	1982	Drawn
1966	Drawn	1983	Drawn

Forty-five three-figure innings have been played in matches between these two schools. Those since 1918:

161*	M. K. Fosh	1975	Harrow	106	D. M. Smith	1966	Eton
159	E. W. Dawson	1923	Eton	104	R. Pulbrook	1932	Harrow
158	I. S. Akers-Douglas	1928	Eton	103	L. G. Crawley	1921	Harrow
153	N. S. Hotchkin	1931	Eton	103	T. Hare	1947	Eton
151	R. M. Tindall	1976	Harrow	102*	P. H. Stewart-Brown	1923	Harrow
135	J. C. Atkinson-Clark	1930	Eton	102	R. V. C. Robins	1953	Eton
115	E. Crutchley	1939	Harrow	100	R. H. Cobbold	1923	Eton
112	A. W. Allen	1931	Eton	100*	P. V. F. Cazalet	1926	Eton
112*	T. M. H. James	1978	Harrow	100	A. N. A. Boyd	1934	Eton
111	R. A. A. Holt	1937	Harrow	100*	P. M. Studd	1935	Harrow
109	K. F. H. Hale	1929	Eton	100	S. D. D. Sainsbury	1947	Eton
109	N. S Hotchkin	1932	Eton	100	M. J. J. Faber	1968	Eton
107	W. N. Coles	1946	Eton				

* *Signifies not out.*

In 1904, D. C. Boles of Eton, making 183, set up a new record for the match, beating the 152 obtained for Eton in 1841 by Emilius Bayley, afterwards the Rev. Sir John Robert Laurie Emilius Bayley Laurie. M. C. Bird, Harrow, in 1907, scored 100 not out and 131, the only batsman who has made two 100s in the match. N. S. Hotchkin, Eton, played the following innings: 1931, 153; 1932, 109 and 96; 1933, 88 and 12.

July 23. Benson and Hedges Cup final. MIDDLESEX beat ESSEX by 4 runs (See Benson and Hedges Cup section).

MCC SCHOOLS v NATIONAL ASSOCIATION OF YOUNG CRICKETERS

July 27, 28. Drawn. At the end of a good first day MCC Schools held an advantage, Medlycott, slow left-arm, having taken six for 52 in NAYC's first innings. Pepper and Fordham then shared an unbroken fifth-wicket stand of 78 in only 38 minutes to give MCC Schools an overnight lead of 25. Redfarn's declaration at this score conceded the initiative, Hicks hitting 162 in 200 minutes and putting NAYC in control. Cox's declaration set MCC Schools 264 in approximately three hours. Whitmore and Lenham made 120 together for their third wicket, but they finished 47 short.

National Association of Young Cricketers

A. J. Squire (*Suffolk*) run out 20		
N. Hicks (*Surrey*) c Lenham b Burton 25	– (1) c Whitmore b Lenham 162
S. Goldsmith (*Kent*) c Whitmore b Medlycott ... 27	– (2) b Stephenson 33
D. Fitton (*Lancashire*) b Smith........................ 0	– (3) not out.............................. 37
A. R. Harwood (*Buckinghamshire*) c Lenham	– (4) b Smith............................. 36
b Medlycott. 26	
*I. Cox (*Somerset*) c Fordham b Medlycott....... 8	
S. A. J. Kippax (*Yorkshire*) b Medlycott 43	
K. Patel (*Staffordshire*) c Lenham b Medlycott .. 8	
L. Roll (*Gloucestershire*) c and b Medlycott...... 4	
†A. J. Storr (*Yorkshire*) not out 4	
B 9, l-b 2, w 1, n-b 3 15	B 3, l-b 7, w 7, n-b 3 20

1/28 2/73 3/73 4/85   (9 wkts dec.) 180   1/77 2/184 3/288   (3 wkts dec.) 288
5/109 6/120 7/130 8/160 9/180

I. S. Bishop (*Gloucestershire*) did not bat.

Bowling: *First Innings*—Whitehouse 6–3–21–0; Burton 7–1–14–1; Lenham 5–0–22–0; Medlycott 25.1–10–52–6; Smith 21–5–56–1; Stephenson 1–1–0–0. *Second Innings*—Whitehouse 4–1–14–0; Burton 9–2–46–0; Lenham 6.5–0–44–1; Medlycott 19–3–88–0; Smith 11–3–26–1; Stephenson 9–1–50–1.

MCC Schools

R. M. Pepper (*Dover GS*) not out 88	– c Storr b Harwood 18
J. P. Stephenson (*Felsted*) b Harwood 2	– b Harwood 9
M. Whitmore (*Lutterworth GS*) c Cox b Roll ... 17	– b Kippax 62
N. J. Lenham (*Brighton*) b Patel 33	– st Storr b Kippax 63
*P. A. Redfarn (*Cambridge College*)	– c Goldsmith b Kippax............. 2
c and b Patel. 4	
A. Fordham (*Bedford Modern*) not out............ 51	– not out 18
K. T. Medlycott (*Wandsworth CS*)	– c Harwood b Kippax 23
(did not bat).	
W. Smith (*Colston's*) (did not bat)	– not out 12
J. N. Whitehouse (*Sir William Turner*)	– (9) c Cox b Roll 0
(did not bat).	
B 3, l-b 5, w 2....................................... 10	B 2, l-b 7, n-b 1.............. 10

1/12 2/46 3/111 4/127   (4 wkts dec.) 205   1/24 2/35 3/155 4/160   (7 wkts) 217
                                         5/161 6/196 7/196

R. J. P. Burton (*Shrewsbury*) and †J. M. Robinson (*Solihull*) did not bat.

Bowling: *First Innings*—Bishop 7–1–21–0; Harwood 11–1–39–1; Roll 15–4–45–1; Kippax 9–3–23–0; Patel 9–1–31–2; Goldsmith 2–0–10–0; Fitton 3–0–26–0. *Second Innings*—Bishop 5–0–21–0; Harwood 9–2–33–2; Roll 20–3–51–1; Kippax 25–5–94–4; Goldsmith 1–0–8–0.

Umpires: D. E. E. Collins and G. E. Loveland.

July 29. NCA Young Cricketers won by seven wickets. Combined Services 189 for seven (55 overs) (M. J. Robinson 79); NCA Young Cricketers 191 for three (54 overs) (R. C. W. Mason 100 not out, G. D. Rose 55 not out, B. G. Evans 33).

August 5. Australian Young Cricketers beat England Young Cricketers by seven wickets (See Australian Young Cricketers tour section).

August 11, 12, 13, 15. Third Cornhill Test. ENGLAND beat NEW ZEALAND by 127 runs (See New Zealand tour section).

WILLIAM YOUNGER CUP FINAL

August 27. Shrewsbury won by 2 runs, amidst great excitement. Hastings, at the start of their 45th and last over, were 189 for seven, needing 3 for victory. But Tudor rose to the occasion, taking all three wickets without conceding a run, two of them to outstanding catches by Hutchinson. The second of these, a skier from Duval, was reckoned to be in the air long enough for the batsmen to have crossed twice. For Shrewsbury, who were put in, Gale scored a patient 53. T. D. Booth Jones, once of Sussex, made 85 for Hastings, leaving them seemingly near to victory at 163 for four. Richard and Robin Burnett, who each took three wickets for Hastings, are the grandsons of the late Frank Woolley. Shrewsbury received £1,000 and Hastings and St Leonards Priory £600. Both sides were appearing in their first final and had female scorers, Miss Nicola Mulhearn for Shrewsbury and Mrs Judith Thwaites for Hastings. In an earlier round J. Hitchmough of Liverpool had made a record score for the competition of 178 not out.

Shrewsbury

J. Foster c Wren b Coles	22	R. T. Tudor b R. B. Burnett	5
D. Williamson		D. C. Perry b R. S. F. Burnett	10
lbw b A. C. Booth Jones	10	J. Pollard not out	3
*S. C. Gale c Coles		A. S. Barnard not out	6
b R. S. F. Burnett	53		
I. J. F. Hutchinson b R. B. Burnett	36	B 7, l-b 2, w 10, n-b 2	21
†K. J. Mulhearn run out	7		
D. C. Parry b R. B. Burnett	18	1/31 2/40 3/112 (45 overs, 9 wkts) 191
H. D. Banks c Wren		4/123 5/145 6/149
b R. S. F. Burnett	0	7/158 8/177 9/185

Bowling: A. C. Booth Jones 9–2–14–1; Coles 9–1–42–1; Duval 9–1–28–0; R. S. F. Burnett 9–2–48–3; R. B. Burnett 9–1–38–3.

Hastings and St Leonards Priory

T. D. Booth Jones c Mulhearn		J. Coles run out	2
b Williamson	85	R. S. F. Burnett not out	6
J. Lawson c Mulhearn b Tudor	3	†P. Wren c Hutchinson b Tudor	0
I. Gillespie lbw b Pollard	22	C. P. Duval c Hutchinson b Tudor	0
K. Turk c Banks b Williamson	21		
*A. C. Booth Jones c Pollard		B 1, l-b 6, w 4, n-b 1	12
b Williamson	23		
G. Gill c Gale b Tudor	0	1/11 2/44 3/122 4/163 (44.5 overs) 189
R. B. Burnett b Tudor	15	5/164 6/172 7/174 8/189 9/189

Bowling: Tudor 8.5–1–41–5; Perry 4–1–17–0; Barnard 9–0–29–0; Pollard 9–1–22–1; Williamson 9–0–33–3; Banks 5–0–35–0.

Umpires: R. P. Cross and K. W. Nicholson.

NATIONAL CLUB CRICKET CHAMPIONSHIP WINNERS
1969-1983

D. H. Robins Trophy

1969   HAMPSTEAD beat Pocklington Pixies by 14 runs.
1970   CHELTENHAM beat Stockport by three wickets.
1971   BLACKHEATH beat Ealing by eight wickets.
1972   SCARBOROUGH beat Brentham by six wickets.
1973   WOLVERHAMPTON beat The Mote by five wickets.
1974   SUNBURY beat Tunbridge Wells by seven wickets.
1975   YORK beat Blackpool by six wickets.

John Haig Trophy

1976   SCARBOROUGH beat Dulwich by five wickets.
1977   SOUTHGATE beat Bowdon by six wickets.
1978   CHELTENHAM beat Bishop's Stortford by 15 runs.
1979   SCARBOROUGH beat Reading by two wickets.
1980   MOSELEY beat Gosport Borough by nine wickets.
1981   SCARBOROUGH beat Blackheath by 57 runs.
1982   SCARBOROUGH beat Finchley by 4 runs.

William Younger Cup

1983   SHREWSBURY beat Hastings and St Leonards Priory by 2 runs.

WHITBREAD NATIONAL VILLAGE CHAMPIONSHIP FINAL

August 28. Quarndon of Derbyshire won the village championship for the first time when they beat Troon, victors three times previously, by eight wickets when Hibberd, a bank clerk, hit the last two balls of the final over to the long-leg boundary for 4. Troon, put in, were restricted to 155 for six, Quarndon using left-arm spin from both ends for much of the innings. Taylor, a police constable, and Butcher, a postal engineer, had five wickets between them for 52 runs. When Quarndon batted, Farmer, a Rolls Royce engineer, joined Hibberd at 53 for two and their unbroken third-wicket partnership of 104 saw them home.

Man of the Match: D. Hibberd.

Troon

*T. Carter c Underwood b Butcher	15	P. Johns b Taylor	1
J. Spry b Butcher	23	I. Williams not out	22
B. Carter not out	55	B 5, l-b 6, w 1, n-b 1	13
S. Kitchen c Hollis b Taylor	19		
S. Pedlar c Underwood b Taylor	6	1/39 2/44 3/95 (6 wkts, 40 overs) 155	
J. Warren lbw b Morris	1	4/103 5/116 6/117	

†G. James, H. James and P. Cook did not bat.

Bowling: Underwood 4–0–12–0; Tunaley 9–0–28–0; Butcher 9–3–21–2; Taylor 8–1–31–3; Morris 8–0–34–1; Acton 2–0–16–0.

Quarndon

S. A. Underwood b Kitchen	36
J. Morris c Spry b Kitchen	14
I. Farmer not out	38
D. Hibberd not out	53
B 2, l-b 9, w 2, n-b 3	16

1/52 2/53   (2 wkts, 39.2 overs) 157

*R. Crossley, A. Acton, †S. Hollis, C. Richardson, R. Taylor, F. Butcher and M. J. Tunaley did not bat.

Bowling: H. James 6.2–2–29–0; Cook 9–0–39–0; Kitchen 9–3–27–2; Johns 9–0–33–0; Pedlar 6–1–13–0.

Umpires: E. Johnston and J. O'Neill.

VILLAGE CRICKET CHAMPIONSHIP WINNERS 1972-83

Sponsored by John Haig Ltd

1972 TROON (Cornwall) beat Astwood Bank (Worcestershire) by seven wickets.
1973 TROON (Cornwall) beat Gowerton (Glamorgan) by 12 runs.
1974 BOMARSUND (Northumberland) beat Collingham (Nottinghamshire) by three wickets. (*Played at Edgbaston after being rained off at Lord's*)
1975 GOWERTON (Glamorgan) beat Isleham (Cambridgeshire) by six wickets.
1976 TROON (Cornwall) beat Sessay (Yorkshire) by 18 runs.
1977 COOKLEY (Worcestershire) beat Lindal Moor (Cumbria) by 28 runs.

Sponsored by *The Cricketer*

1978 LINTON PARK (Kent) beat Toft (Cheshire) by four wickets.

Sponsored by Samuel Whitbread and Co. Ltd

1979 EAST BIERLEY (Yorkshire) beat Ynysygerwyn (Glamorgan) by 92 runs.
1980 MARCHWIEL (Clwyd) beat Longparish (Hampshire) by 79 runs.
1981 ST FAGANS (Glamorgan) beat Broad Oak (Yorkshire) by 22 runs.
1982 ST FAGANS (Glamorgan) beat Collingham (Nottinghamshire) by six wickets.
1983 QUARNDON (Derbyshire) beat Troon (Cornwall) by eight wickets.

September 3. NatWest Bank Trophy final. SOMERSET beat KENT by 24 runs (See NatWest Bank Trophy section).

QUALIFICATION AND REGISTRATION

Regulations Governing the Qualification and Registration of Cricketers in Test and Competitive County Cricket

1. QUALIFICATIONS FOR ENGLAND

Subject to the overriding discretion of the Test and County Cricket Board, acting with the consent of the International Cricket Conference, the qualifications for playing for England shall be:

(a) That the cricketer was born in the British Isles; or

(b) That the cricketer's father or mother was born in the British Isles and that he himself is residing and has been resident therein during the preceding four consecutive years; or

(c) That the cricketer is residing and has been resident in the British Isles during the preceding ten years; or

(d) That the cricketer is residing and has been resident in the British Isles during the preceding four consecutive years and since the day before his fourteenth birthday.

All these qualifications apply only if the cricketer has not played for any other country in a Test match or (if the Board so decides) any other international match during the specified period of residence or in the case of (a) during the previous four years.

It is also required that the player shall have made a declaration in writing to the Board that it is his desire and intention to play for England and in (b), (c) and (d) that he shall be a British or Irish citizen.

2. QUALIFICATIONS FOR REGISTRATION FOR COMPETITIVE COUNTY CRICKET

(a) A cricketer qualified for England shall only be qualified for registration for:

(i) The county of his birth.
(ii) The county in which he is residing and has been resident for the previous twelve consecutive months.
(iii) The county for which his father regularly played.

(b) In addition, a cricketer qualified for England shall be qualified for registration for a county if:

(i) He has none of the above qualifications for any county and is not registered for one; or
(ii) Although qualified and/or registered by one or more counties, the county or counties concerned have confirmed in writing that they do not wish to register him or retain his registration.

This paragraph (b), however, will not permit registration of a player who has been under contract to a county for the previous season and has failed to accept the offer of a new contract for the new season. It does not prevent his application for a Special Registration.

3. REGISTRATION

Normally new registrations take place during the close season, but in exceptional circumstances a county may apply to register a player in the course of a season.

No cricketer may be registered for more than one county at any one time or, subject to the overriding discretion of the Board, for more than one county during any one season. However, this shall not prevent a player qualified to play for England, and already registered for a minor county, from being registered for a first-class county with the consent of the minor county concerned, who will not lose his registration.

Except with the Board's approval no county may have registered for it more than 35 cricketers at any one time.

4. SPECIAL REGISTRATION

The qualification for county cricket may be wholly or partially waived by the Board and a cricketer qualified to play for England may be "specially registered" should the Board conclude that it would be in the best interests of competitive county cricket as a whole. For this purpose the Board shall have regard to the interests of the cricketer concerned and any other material considerations affecting the county concerned including, if applicable, the cricketer's age and the other Special Registrations of the county in previous years.

No application for Special Registration will be entertained in respect of a cricketer who has a contract of employment with another county in the absence of that county's consent, except during the period between January 1 and the start of the new season, if the cricketer's contract is due to expire in that period.

5. CRICKETERS NOT QUALIFIED TO PLAY FOR ENGLAND

No county shall be entitled to play more than one unqualified cricketer in any competitive match, except where two unqualified cricketers were registered for the county on November 28, 1978 or if *bona fide* negotiations had been begun before that date and were completed before the 1979 season.

The player must have remained registered without a break and had a contract of employment with the county since the start of the 1979 season, except in any season during which he was a member of an official touring team to the British Isles.

If a registered overseas player is invited to play for his country for the whole or part of a tour of the British Isles, his county must release him and, except with the prior consent of the Board, may not play him during that tour.

6. NEGOTIATIONS BETWEEN COUNTIES AND CRICKETERS

No county may approach or be involved in discussions with any unregistered cricketer who is not qualified for that county with a view to offering him a trial or registering him:

(i) During the currency of a season without having given not less than fourteen days' previous notice in writing; or

(ii) During the close season without having given notice in writing

to any county for which he is qualified for registration by virtue of birth or residence before making any such approach or engaging in any such discussions.

No county may approach or be involved in discussions with any cricketer under the age of sixteen on April 15 in the current year, unless the cricketer is qualified for registration by that county or is not qualified for registration by any other first-class county.

7. RESIDENCE

A player does not interrupt his qualifying period of residence by undertaking government service or occasional winter work for business reasons outside the county in which his residence is situated. Nor is it interrupted by his playing official matches for his country, provided that the Board's permission is obtained.

The qualifying period cannot run while the cricketer has a contract with or is registered by another county.

8. INELIGIBILITY FOR ENGLAND

Players qualified for England who formed a team to play representative matches in South Africa in March 1982 will be ineligible for selection for England for three years from April 15, 1982. The same ineligibility applies to any other cricketers who joined any part of the same tour of South Africa.

SCHWEPPES COUNTY CHAMPIONSHIP, 1983

The seventh and last Schweppes-sponsored Championship saw a battle royal between Middlesex, who settled into top place in June with six successive victories, and Essex, who then took advantage of a gradual Middlesex fade-out, and under the inspiration of Lever – quite seriously ill in mid-season – took over the lead in late August and maintained top place to win the £14,000 first prize. Middlesex, whose faint hopes of retaining the title were destroyed by rain on the last day of the season, had to be content with the runners-up prize of £7,500.

Hampshire, the early pace-setters, felt the loss of their World Cup stars, but rallied to finish third for the second successive season. They won £3,500, while Leicestershire, who were always among the top teams, had to be content with the £1,750 for fourth position, a slight decline from their runners-up spot in 1982. Fifth place went to Warwickshire, the surprise team of the season. Wooden spoonists in 1981 and 1982, they again struggled in the first month of the season, but a remarkable run of seven successive wins took them to third place in July and they remained thereabouts for the rest of the season.

Northamptonshire, Kent and Surrey never looked likely to mount a challenge, remaining in mid-table for most of the season, but Derbyshire, after a bad start, improved encouragingly under the captaincy of the youthful Kim Barnett. They finished in ninth place, one ahead of Somerset, who had a curiously undistinguished Championship season. Sussex, so promising in 1981, continued their decline of 1982, while

SCHWEPPES CHAMPIONSHIP TABLE

Win = 16 points*	Played	Won	Lost	Drawn	Bonus points Batting	Bonus points Bowling	Points
1 – Essex (7)	24	11	5	8	69	79	324
2 – Middlesex (1)	23	11	4	8	60	72	308
3 – Hampshire (3)	24	10	2	12	62	71	289
4 – Leicestershire (2)	24	9	3	12	52	81	277
5 – Warwickshire (17)	24	10	3	11	52	64	276
6 – Northamptonshire (9)	24	7	4	13	63	77	252
7 – Kent (13)	24	7	4	13	68	70	250
8 – Surrey (5)	24	7	4	13	65	70	247
9 – Derbyshire (11)	24	7	5	12	46	65	219
10 – Somerset (6)	24	3	7	14	57	75	180
11 – Sussex (8)	23	3	10	10	50	72	170
12 – Gloucestershire (15)	23	3	8	12	56	61	165
12 – Lancashire (12)	24	3	4	17	56	61	165
14 – Nottinghamshire (4)	24	3	10	11	39	62	149
15 – Glamorgan (16)	24	2	10	12	45	64	141
16 – Worcestershire (14)	24	2	11	11	43	54	129
17 – Yorkshire (10)	23	1	5	17	45	64	125

1982 positions in brackets.

Hampshire and Derbyshire totals each include 12 points for a win in a match reduced to one innings.

The following two matches were abandoned and are not included in the above table: May 11, 12, 13 – Gloucestershire v Sussex at Gloucester and Middlesex v Yorkshire at Lord's.

Gloucestershire, despite a good start, and Lancashire, in the lower reaches throughout, have still to see their rebuilding programmes bear fruit.

Nottinghamshire, champions in 1981, had a bad year, while Glamorgan and Worcestershire, both trying, in different ways, to rebuild their fortunes, must have been disappointed. Finally, what of Yorkshire? Never higher than fifteenth, they finished last for the first time ever, the troubles within the club showing no signs of abating. – R.W.B.

REGULATIONS FOR SCHWEPPES CHAMPIONSHIP

(As applied in 1983)

1. Prize-money

First (Essex)	£14,000
Second (Middlesex)	£7,500
Third (Hampshire)	£3,500
Fourth (Leicestershire)	£1,750
Winner of each match	£150
Each bonus point	£5

2. Scoring of Points

(a) For a win. 16 points, plus any points scored in the first innings.

(b) In a tie, each side to score eight points, plus any points scored in the first innings.

(c) If the scores are equal in a drawn match, the side batting in the fourth innings to score eight points, plus any points scored in the first innings.

(d) **First Innings Points** (awarded only for performances **in the first 100 overs** of each first innings and retained whatever the result of the match).

    (i) A maximum of four batting points to be available as under:
        150 to 199 runs – 1 point; 200 to 249 runs – 2 points; 250 to 299 runs – 3 points; 300 runs or over – 4 points.

    (ii) A maximum of four bowling points to be available as under:
        3 to 4 wickets taken – 1 point; 5 to 6 wickets taken – 2 points; 7 to 8 wickets taken – 3 points; 9 to 10 wickets taken – 4 points.

(e) If play starts when less than eight hours playing time remains and a one innings match is played, no first innings points shall be scored. The side winning on the one innings to score 12 points.

(f) The side which has the highest aggregate of points gained at the end of the season shall be the Champion County. Should any sides in the Schweppes Championship table be equal on points the side with most wins will have priority.

3. Hours of Play

1st and 2nd days .... 11.00 a.m. to 6.30 p.m. (12 noon to 7.30 p.m. on Sundays)
3rd day .... 11.00 a.m. to 6.00 p.m.

Play may cease on the last day up to 30 minutes earlier than the scheduled time for cessation of play by mutual agreement of the captains.

The captains may agree or, in the event of disagreement the umpires may decide to play 30 minutes (or minimum ten overs) extra time at the end of the first and/or second day's play if, in their opinion, it would bring about a definite result on that day.

Intervals

Lunch: 1.15 p.m. to 1.55 p.m. (1st and 2nd days) 2.15 p.m to 2.55 p.m. on Sundays
      1.00 p.m. to 1.40 p.m. (3rd day)

Tea: 4.10 p.m. to 4.30 p.m. (1st and 2nd days) 5.10 p.m. to 5.30 p.m. on Sundays
      3.40 p.m. to 4.00 p.m. (3rd day)

4. Substitutes

A substitute shall be allowed as of right in the event of a cricketer currently playing in a
Schweppes Championship match being required to join the England team for a Test
match (or one-day International). Such substitutes may be permitted to bat or bowl in that
match, subject to the approval of the TCCB.

5. New ball

The captain of the fielding side shall have the choice of taking the new ball after 100 overs
have been bowled with the old one.

6. Covering of Pitches

The whole pitch shall be covered:
  (i) The night before a match and, if necessary, until the first ball is bowled.
 (ii) On each night of a match and, if necessary, throughout Sunday.
(iii) In the event of play being suspended on account of bad light or rain during the
     specified hours of play.

7. Declarations

Law 14 will apply, but, in addition, a captain may also forfeit his first innings, subject to
the provisions set out in Law 14.2. If, owing to weather conditions, the match has not
started when less than eight hours playing time remains, the first innings of each side shall
automatically be forfeited and a one-innings match played.

8. Over-rate Fines

In 1983, the minimum over-rate to be achieved by counties, before a financial penalty was
imposed, was 19.00 overs per hour. In assessing any fines, of which counties paid half and
players half, the season was divided into two parts (11 matches) and fines graded on the
following basis per half season:
Under 19.00 overs per hour – £1,000
Under 18.50 overs per hour – £1,500
Under 18.00 overs per hour – £2,000
Under 17.50 overs per hour – £2,500

(Additional £500 penalty for each 0.5 o.p.h. below these rates.)

When calculating the over-rate, an allowance of two minutes was made for each wicket
taken. In the event of a player from either side being seriously injured and having to leave
the field, any such time, additional to the two minutes, was also a deductable allowance.
The contribution to be made by each player to any fine was to be decided by the county
concerned.

OVER-RATE AND RUN-RATE IN SCHWEPPES CHAMPIONSHIP, 1983

| | Over-rate per hour | | | Run-rate per |
	1st half	2nd half	Total	100 balls
Derbyshire (9)	*17.98	‡18.50	18.24 (17)	48.15 (12)
Essex (1)	‡18.54	†18.24	18.37 (16)	54.29 (2)
Glamorgan (15)	19.00	‡18.78	18.68 (12)	45.28 (17)
Gloucestershire (12)	19.03	19.31	19.18 (6)	53.30 (5)
Hampshire (3)	‡18.81	†18.45	18.61 (13)	53.21 (6)
Kent (7)	19.10	19.26	19.18 (6)	58.09 (1)
Lancashire (12)	†18.25	19.25	18.77 (11)	47.02 (15)
Leicestershire (4)	19.41	19.82	19.62 (2)	52.54 (7)
Middlesex (2)	20.01	‡18.90	19.38 (4)	52.11 (8)
Northamptonshire (6)	‡18.76	19.06	18.92 (9)	51.77 (9)
Nottinghamshire (14)	‡18.99	†18.07	18.45 (15)	47.23 (14)
Somerset (10)	19.20	19.35	19.27 (5)	47.42 (13)
Surrey (8)	‡18.52	†18.51	18.52 (14)	54.28 (3)
Sussex (11)	‡18.66	19.00	18.83 (10)	50.16 (10)
Warwickshire (5)	19.45	19.49	19.47 (3)	53.88 (4)
Worcestershire (16)	19.11	19.09	19.10 (8)	48.32 (11)
Yorkshire (17)	19.91	19.66	19.77 (1)	46.07 (16)

1983 average rate			18.96	50.68
1982 average rate			19.06	51.38
1981 average rate			18.62	50.86
1980 average rate			18.95	50.47
1979 average rate			19.36	48.37
1978 average rate			19.45	47.53

* £2,000 fine.   †£1,500 fine.   ‡£1,000 fine.

1983 Championship positions are shown in parentheses after name of county.

SCHWEPPES CHAMPIONSHIP STATISTICS FOR 1983

	For			Against		
County	Runs	Wickets	Average	Runs	Wickets	Average
Derbyshire	8,940	325	27.50	9,609	283	33.95
Essex	9,341	294	31.77	8,981	362	24.80
Glamorgan	9,091	329	27.63	10,587	266	39.80
Gloucestershire	10,174	310	32.81	10,002	281	28.13
Hampshire	10,159	251	40.47	9,521	336	28.33
Kent	10,655	285	37.38	10,696	347	30.82
Lancashire	9,508	318	29.89	9,108	268	33.98
Leicestershire	9,075	289	31.40	9,250	358	25.83
Middlesex	8,834	270	32.71	8,413	352	23.90
Northamptonshire	10,492	295	35.56	9,063	320	28.32
Nottinghamshire	8,134	333	24.42	8,833	289	30.56
Somerset	9,347	329	28.41	9,598	310	30.96
Surrey	9,728	293	33.20	9,794	307	31.90
Sussex	9,301	331	28.09	9,877	300	32.92
Warwickshire	10,180	300	33.93	9,815	299	32.82
Worcestershire	9,217	360	25.60	9,414	251	37.50
Yorkshire	9,321	304	30.66	8,936	287	31.13
	161,497	5,216	30.96	161,497	5,216	30.96

COUNTY CHAMPIONSHIP – MATCH RESULTS 1864-1983

County	Years of Play	Played	Won	Lost	Tied	Drawn
Derbyshire	1871-87; 1895-1983	1,950	483	728	–	739
Essex..................	1895-1983	1,914	523	572	5	814
Glamorgan	1921-1983	1,448	324	512	–	612
Gloucestershire	1870-1983	2,190	656	818	1	715
Hampshire...........	1864-85; 1895-1983	2,023	530	712	4	777
Kent...................	1864-1983	2,310	860	710	2	738
Lancashire...........	1865-1983	2,389	913	477	3	996
Leicestershire.......	1895-1983	1,880	402	728	1	749
Middlesex...........	1864-1983	2,091	794	536	5	756
Northamptonshire.	1905-1983	1,647	391	599	2	655
Nottinghamshire ...	1864-1983	2,221	673	594	–	954
Somerset.............	1882-85; 1891-1983	1,921	461	811	3	646
Surrey	1864-1983	2,467	1,001	538	4	924
Sussex	1864-1983	2,362	674	824	4	860
Warwickshire	1895-1983	1,894	503	557	1	833
Worcestershire	1899-1983	1,835	442	676	1	716
Yorkshire...........	1864-1983	2,491	1,163	401	2	925
Cambridgeshire	1864-69; 1871	19	8	8	–	3
		35,052	10,801	10,801	38	13,412

STATUS OF MATCHES IN THE UK

(a) Automatic First-Class Matches

The following matches of three or more days duration should automatically be considered first-class:

(i) County Championship matches.

(ii) Official representative tourist matches from ICC full member countries, unless specifically excluded.

(iii) MCC v any first-class county.

(iv) Oxford v Cambridge and either University against first-class counties.

(v) Scotland v Ireland.

(b) Excluded from First-Class Status

The following matches of three or more days duration should not normally be accorded first-class status:

(i) County "friendly" matches.

(ii) Matches played by Scotland or Ireland, other than their annual match against each other.

(iii) Unofficial tourist matches, unless circumstances are exceptional.

(iv) MCC v Oxford/Cambridge.

(v) Matches involving privately raised teams, unless included officially in a touring team's itinerary.

(c) Consideration of Doubtful Status

Matches played by unofficial touring teams of exceptional ability can be considered in advance and decisions taken accordingly.

Certain other matches comprising 22 recognised first-class cricketers might also be considered in advance.

DERBYSHIRE

President: The Duke of Devonshire
Chairman: D. C. Robinson
Chairman, Cricket Committee: C. S. Elliott
Secretary/Chief Executive: R. Pearman
    County Ground, Nottingham Road, Derby
    DE2 6DA (Telephone: 0332-683211)
Captain: 1983 – B. Wood and K. J. Barnett;
    1984 – K. J. Barnett
Coach: P. E. Russell

For the fifth time in nine years, a change of captaincy was forced upon Derbyshire during a season. Barry Wood, over whose reappointment there had been much debate eight months earlier, stepped down in the first week of May. "I find it too demanding", said Wood, "to captain the team and maintain the standards I have set myself during my career as an opening batsman and as a bowler". Geoff Miller, whom Wood had succeeded during the 1981 season, stood in until the committee made the brave decision to appoint Kim Barnett, at 22 the youngest captain in the county's history.

Barnett proved to be an excellent choice and came through the disruption caused by Wood's withdrawal and injuries to John Hampshire, Paul Newman and Miller to lead Derbyshire to seven victories in the Schweppes County Championship, a total bettered only once, under Derek Morgan in 1966, in twenty seasons. They were on their way out of the Benson and Hedges Cup before Barnett took control and lost to Middlesex in the second round of the NatWest Bank Trophy, but they rose six places in the John Player League. While Barnett gained in stature, Wood's career disintegrated unhappily. Three consecutive Championship defeats at the beginning of June gave some substance to Wood's claim that it was an insult for him to be omitted, a remark for which he was disciplined. When later he refused to give a pledge of support to the captain and administration, it was clear that Wood would not again play for Derbyshire and his contract was terminated by mutual consent in July. It was a sad ending for a player who had represented England in twelve Tests. The controversy did not ease Barnett's task, but the new captain smiled his way through it and revealed strength of character in the way he created a happy dressing-room atmosphere.

Barnett's batting flourished, especially when he began to open the innings with Iain Anderson, and he was one of two people who did most to transform moderate expectations into a successful and enjoyable season. The other was Ole Mortensen, a fast bowler from Denmark who took 84 wickets in all competitions. This was an extraordinary story. Mortensen gave up a job in a tax office and came to England to pursue his dream of becoming the first Dane to succeed in county cricket. He arrived as an unknown quantity and soon became an automatic choice, being accurate, hostile and, above all, a bowler of unquenchable spirit. The pity was that he could not be joined earlier by Michael Holding, who bowled beautifully in the closing weeks of the season. The West Indian was injured during the crowd invasion at the end of the World Cup final and could not play with any regularity until mid-August. He had been engaged because the South African, Peter Kirsten, was taking a summer off and John Wright was on the New Zealand tour of England. Derbyshire had to satisfy the Test and County Cricket Board that Holding would play county cricket for two seasons before the registration was approved and it was announced in September that Kirsten would not be returning.

The season turned for Derbyshire in June after they had been completely outplayed, in successive matches, by Middlesex, Leicestershire and Essex. Morale was improved by Roger Finney's 71 against Essex which, while insufficient to avert an innings defeat, indicated that the younger players nurtured in the second team by Philip Russell were making progress. Derbyshire won three of their next four Championship matches, including, on a bad pitch at Abbeydale Park, their first victory over Yorkshire since 1957. Finney, Bill Fowler and John Morris, virtually unknown at the start of the season, helped the maturing Anderson and the experienced Alan Hill to give backbone to the team. As they grew together, so Derbyshire became more formidable opponents, with Barnett insisting on a positive approach.

Barnett and Anderson completed 1,000 runs for the first time and Hill, often too readily discarded in the past, rewarded faith in him with four hundreds and the highest aggregate of his career. The tail often contributed and Colin Tunnicliffe was only 9 short of a maiden century after a rousing innings against Hampshire at Portsmouth. Tunnicliffe and Steve Oldham, diligent and enthusiastic medium-paced bowlers, were released at the end of the season and will be missed, especially as the spinners were disappointing. Miller, troubled by a back injury, had an uneven season and Dallas Moir, who returned after initially announcing his retirement, could not reproduce his 1982 form.

Bob Taylor, in his 23rd season, maintained his remarkable consistency and won his 50th England cap during the series against New Zealand. Taylor's standards never flagged even in Derbyshire's darkest years and he enjoyed the success of the younger players more than most. His keenest pleasure came from the Championship victory over Yorkshire, the first during his career, and he continued to improve the world record for dismissals which he had taken off John Murray at the start of the previous winter's tour of Australia. Everybody, including even his talented deputy Bernard Maher, will be sad when Taylor's outstanding career comes to an end.

Derbyshire's hopes of winning the Sunday League disappeared in August when they lost three games out of four. Barnett said that his side was not ready to win a major competition and acknowledged that the success of 1983, when nobody expected much, has set a standard for the future. The captain, young, English and ambitious, has the temperament to cope with any pressures. – J.G.M.

DERBYSHIRE 1983

[*Bill Smith*]

Back row: I. S. Anderson, S. Oldham, O. H. Mortensen, D. G. Moir, R. J. Finney, J. E. Morris. *Front row*: G. Miller, C. J. Tunnicliffe, K. J. Barnett (*captain*), R. W. Taylor, A. Hill. *Inset*: P. G. Newman, J. H. Hampshire.

DERBYSHIRE RESULTS

All first-class matches – Played 24: Won 7, Lost 5, Drawn 12.

County Championship matches – Played 24: Won 7, Lost 5, Drawn 12.

Bonus points – Batting 46, Bowling 65.

Competition placings – Schweppes County Championship, 9th; NatWest Bank Trophy, 2nd round; Benson and Hedges Cup, 4th in Group B; John Player League, 6th eq.

COUNTY CHAMPIONSHIP AVERAGES

BATTING

	Birthplace	M	I	NO	R	HI	Avge
K. J. Barnettc	Stoke-on-Trent	24	40	3	1,423	121	38.45
A. Hillc	Buxworth	24	40	5	1,311	137*	37.45
I. S. Anderson	Derby	21	37	4	1,233	112	37.36
G. Millerc	Chesterfield	21	30	7	699	84	30.39
J. H. Hampshirec	Thurnscoe	14	19	2	485	84	28.52
W. P. Fowler	St Helens	17	26	2	591	91	24.62
M. A. Holding	Kingston, Jamaica	6	5	1	90	63	22.50
J. E. Morris............	Crewe	10	20	1	361	58	19.00
C. J. Tunnicliffec	Derby	17	25	0	461	91	18.44
R. W. Taylorc	Stoke-on-Trent	16	21	6	267	41*	17.80
R. J. Finney	Darley Dale	20	35	2	578	71	17.51
B. J. M. Maher	Hillingdon	8	12	2	150	52	15.00
S. Oldhamc	Sheffield	15	17	4	177	39	13.61
D. G. Moir.............	Mtarfa, Malta	17	21	3	224	53	12.44
O. H. Mortensen	Jutland, Denmark	18	23	15	76	14*	9.50
P. G. Newman	Leicester	7	5	0	14	12	2.80

Also batted: A. Watts (*Chapeltown*) (2 matches) 6, 33*; B. Woodc (*Ossett*) (3 matches) 18, 4; J. G. Wrightc (*Darfield, NZ*) (4 matches) 60, 6, 41.

*Signifies not out.   cDenotes county cap.

BOWLING

	O	M	R	W	Avge	BB
M. A. Holding	169	41	451	21	12.47	5-48
O. H. Mortensen	518.3	108	1,605	66	24.31	6-27
R. J. Finney	281.5	43	970	30	32.33	5-58
G. Miller	492.5	132	1,278	37	34.54	5-71
D. G. Moir.............	462.5	121	1,385	40	34.62	5-44
C. J. Tunnicliffe	428.4	94	1,372	39	35.17	4-30
S. Oldham.............	387.2	85	1,120	31	36.12	4-56

Also bowled: I. S. Anderson 28-4-146-1; K. J. Barnett 3-0-13-0; W. P. Fowler 60-13-214-2; J. H. Hampshire 2-0-4-0; A. Hill 6.2-3-15-0; J. E. Morris 2-2-0-0; P. G. Newman 88.5-20-321-7; A. Watts 22-4-87-1; B. Wood 20-4-74-0.

The following played a total of eight three-figure innings for Derbyshire in County Championship matches – A. Hill 4, K. J. Barnett 3, I. S. Anderson 1.

DERBYSHIRE v GLOUCESTERSHIRE

At Derby, April 30, May 1, 2. Drawn. Gloucestershire 3 pts. Play was possible only on the first day. Wood put Gloucestershire in and Stovold batted for 380 minutes, sharing century stands with Broad and Zaheer (154 in 35 overs).

Gloucestershire

B. C. Broad c Tunnicliffe b Miller	24	A. J. Hignell not out...................... 4
A. W. Stovold b Oldham	181	B 3, l-b 2, n-b 8...................... 13
P. Bainbridge lbw b Miller	34	
Zaheer Abbas lbw b Oldham	82	1/62 2/179 (4 wkts) 343
P. W. Romaines not out	5	3/333 4/338

*D. A. Graveney, J. N. Shepherd, †R. C. Russell, G. E. Sainsbury and J. H. Childs did not bat.

Bonus points – Gloucestershire 3 (Score at 100 overs: 270-2).

Bowling: Oldham 20–5–46–2; Tunnicliffe 21–3–62–0; Moir 22–4–61–0; Wood 15–4–39–0; Newman 17–2–70–0; Miller 21–6–52–2.

Derbyshire

*B. Wood, J. G. Wright, K. J. Barnett, J. H. Hampshire, G. Miller, A. Hill, S. Oldham, P. G. Newman, C. J. Tunnicliffe, †R. W. Taylor and D. G. Moir.

Umpires: H. D. Bird and D. O. Oslear.

At Leicester, May 4, 5, 6. DERBYSHIRE drew with LEICESTERSHIRE.

DERBYSHIRE v LANCASHIRE

At Chesterfield, May 11, 12, 13. Drawn. Derbyshire were under the temporary leadership of Miller between Wood's resignation and the appointment of Barnett. Lancashire won the toss but the only play possible was in the final 90 minutes of the first day.

Derbyshire

B. Wood b Watkinson	4
J. G. Wright lbw b Folley.................	6
A. Hill not out...............................	14
K. J. Barnett not out.......................	21
L-b 2, n-b 4	6

1/7 2/61 (2 wkts) 51

J. H. Hampshire, *G. Miller, S. Oldham, P. G. Newman, C. J. Tunnicliffe, †R. W. Taylor and D. G. Moir did not bat.

Bowling: Allott 9–5–16–0; Folley 6–4–8–1; Watkinson 5–1–12–1; Simmons 4–2–9–0; O'Shaughnessy 1–1–0–0.

Lancashire

G. Fowler, M. Watkinson, S. J. O'Shaughnessy, D. P. Hughes, F. C. Hayes, *C. H. Lloyd, J. Abrahams, J. Simmons, †C. Maynard, P. J. W. Allott and I. Folley.

Umpires: J. van Geloven and B. J. Meyer.

At Nottingham, May 28, 30, 31. DERBYSHIRE beat NOTTINGHAMSHIRE by six wickets.

DERBYSHIRE v HAMPSHIRE

At Derby, June 4, 6, 7. Drawn. Derbyshire 1 pt, Hampshire 8 pts. Derbyshire decided to bat first on a drying pitch and, with greater acccuracy, Southern could have improved on his five for 60, only Miller looking comfortable. Jesty and Smith passed their previous best scores in a partnership of 321 which threatened the Hampshire third-wicket record. Jesty, in dazzling style, hit 25 4s in 289 minutes: Smith (one 6 and 21 4s) maintained a steely concentration for 443 minutes. Derbyshire, left with seven hours and twenty minutes, were sustained by Barnett's example and a timely stand between Miller and Taylor.

Derbyshire

I. S. Anderson c Jesty b Southern	15	– c Parks b Southern	59
J. E. Morris c Jesty b Southern	20	– c Smith b Nicholas	27
A. Hill b Southern	0	– lbw b Smith	46
*K. J. Barnett c Tremlett b Southern	4	– st Parks b Southern	68
R. J. Finney c Tremlett b Cowley	30	– lbw b Tremlett	3
G. Miller c Smith b Tremlett	58	– not out	22
P. G. Newman c Smith b Cowley	0	– b Southern	1
†R. W. Taylor lbw b Cowley	3	– not out	41
D. G. Moir b Tremlett	17		
S. Oldham c Parks b Southern	9		
O. H. Mortensen not out	6		
B 3, l-b 1, w 2, n-b 2	8	B 4, l-b 8, w 11, n-b 9	32

1/18 2/18 3/24 4/49   170   1/56 2/137 3/192   (6 wkts) 299
5/96 6/102 7/115 8/153 9/161   4/216 5/235 6/243

Bonus points – Derbyshire 1, Hampshire 4.

Bowling: *First Innings*—Malone 3–0–11–0; Emery 2–0–6–0; Southern 43–20–60–5; Cowley 32–10–63–3; Tremlett 10–1–22–2. *Second Innings*—Malone 21–6–59–0; Emery 16–7–20–0; Nicholas 15–6–22–1; Jesty 6–2–19–0; Southern 38–15–84–3; Cowley 14–9–10–0; Tremlett 11–4–14–1; Smith 14–4–39–1.

Hampshire

C. L. Smith c Moir b Oldham	193	N. G. Cowley st Taylor b Moir	18
T. M. Tremlett c Taylor b Mortensen	4	J. W. Southern not out	11
D. R. Turner b Mortensen	1	B 10, l-b 14, w 1, n-b 5	30
T. E. Jesty b Mortensen	187		
M. C. J. Nicholas b Mortensen	1	1/14 2/16 3/337 (7 wkts dec.) 454
*N. E. J. Pocock lbw b Finney	9	4/343 5/370 6/432 7/454	

†R. J. Parks, K. St J. D. Emery and S. J. Malone did not bat.

Bonus points – Hampshire 4 (Score at 100 overs: 305-2).

Bowling: Newman 10–1–32–0; Mortensen 22–6–59–4; Moir 38–13–106–1; Oldham 30.3–5–105–1; Miller 7–1–32–0; Anderson 12–2–36–0; Finney 12–1–54–1.

Umpires: J. van Geloven and D. J. Constant.

At Uxbridge, June 8, 9, 10. DERBYSHIRE lost to MIDDLESEX by nine wickets.

DERBYSHIRE v LEICESTERSHIRE

At Derby, June 11, 13, 14. Leicestershire won by an innings and 4 runs. Leicestershire 23 pts, Derbyshire 4 pts. Leicestershire won the toss and, on a shortened first day, were struggling at 48 for five. The last five wickets added 203, with Tolchard and Steele the key figures and Taylor, merrily, almost doubling his previous best. Derbyshire's batting was dreadful and Ferris, an eighteen-year-old fast bowler from Antigua making his Championship début, enjoyed match figures of eight for 73. Derbyshire were weakened by injuries and Anderson's illness, but offered little resistance.

Leicestershire

I. P. Butcher c Anderson		
b Tunnicliffe.	1	
J. C. Balderstone c Maher		
b Tunnicliffe.	4	
N. E. Briers b Oldham	22	
B. F. Davison lbw b Tunnicliffe	20	
T. J. Boon lbw b Mortensen	0	
*†R. W. Tolchard lbw b Finney	30	
P. B. Clift c Maher b Finney	31	

J. F. Steele not out 38
N. G. B. Cook c Moir b Oldham........ 32
L. B. Taylor b Mortensen 47
G. J. F. Ferris not out 0
    B 2, l-b 11, w 1, n-b 12 26

1/2 2/28 3/28   (9 wkts dec.) 251
4/48 5/48 6/123
7/128 8/179 9/248

Bonus points – Leicestershire 3, Derbyshire 4.

Bowling: Mortensen 24–2–72–2; Tunnicliffe 27–7–77–3; Oldham 16–5–47–2; Finney 9–3–22–2; Moir 3.2–0–7–0.

Derbyshire

A. Hill b Ferris		3 – b Ferris	0
J. E. Morris lbw b Taylor		4 – b Steele	29
*K. J. Barnett b Clift	17	– c Davison b Clift	25
R. J. Finney c Tolchard b Taylor	8	– b Clift	39
W. P. Fowler b Ferris	5	– c Clift b Cook	12
C. J. Tunnicliffe c Steele b Clift	8	– (7) c Tolchard b Clift	11
†B. J. M. Maher lbw b Ferris	2	– (6) lbw b Clift	4
D. G. Moir c Clift b Ferris	2	– c Briers b Ferris	20
S. Oldham b Ferris	8	– b Ferris	15
O. H. Mortensen lbw b Clift	1	– not out	4
I. S. Anderson not out	2	– absent ill	
B 5, l-b 7, w 3, n-b 4	19	B 1, w 2, n-b 6	9

1/6 2/15 3/41 4/52   79   1/0 2/46 3/62 4/104   168
5/54 6/56 7/62 8/66 9/71   5/110 6/114 7/125 8/149 9/168

Bonus points – Leicestershire 4.

Bowling: *First Innings*—Taylor 9–5–22–2; Ferris 17.5–8–29–5; Clift 12–4–9–3. *Second Innings*—Ferris 13.5–3–44–3; Clift 21–5–58–4; Cook 20–7–39–1; Steele 8–1–18–1.

Umpires: P. J. Eele and K. Ibadulla.

DERBYSHIRE v ESSEX

At Derby, June 15, 16. Essex won by an innings and 25 runs. Essex 24 pts, Derbyshire 4 pts. After winning the toss, Derbyshire were soon heading for their third consecutive Championship defeat when they were hustled out before lunch by Lever, Foster and Pringle. McEwan then shredded Derbyshire's attack in a savage display, scoring 178 in 201 minutes with five 6s and 27 4s. Essex declared at lunch on the second day and, importantly for Barnett's young and inexperienced side, Finney scored a purposeful 71. Pride was restored, even if Finney could not avert a two-day defeat by an infinitely superior team.

Derbyshire

I. S. Anderson c Hardie b Lever	4	– c D. E. East b Foster ... 10
J. E. Morris c D. E. East b Lever	6	– lbw b Lever ... 14
A. Hill lbw b Foster	3	– b Lever ... 1
*K. J. Barnett c D. E. East b Lever	1	– c McEwan b Lever ... 0
R. J. Finney c D. E. East b Pringle	14	– c Pringle b Foster ... 71
W. P. Fowler c Pringle b Lever	0	– c Foster b Lever ... 28
C. J. Tunnicliffe c McEwan b Foster	28	– c D. E. East b Pringle ... 29
†R. W. Taylor c Gooch b Pringle	5	– lbw b Acfield ... 31
D. G. Moir c D. E. East b Foster	3	– c Pringle b Foster ... 34
S. Oldham c Lever b Pringle	6	– c D. E. East b Foster ... 0
O. H. Mortensen not out	4	– not out ... 4
L-b 10, n-b 8	18	L-b 7, n-b 14 ... 21

1/4 2/11 3/13 4/16   92   1/23 2/27 3/27 4/27   243
5/16 6/48 7/72 8/79 9/87   5/68 6/120 7/183 8/233 9/234

Bonus points – Essex 4.

Bowling: *First Innings*—Lever 11–2–42–4; Foster 13–4–24–3; Pringle 8–5–8–3. *Second Innings*—Lever 18–4–76–4; Foster 27.3–3–90–4; Pringle 16–4–47–1; Acfield 3–0–9–1.

Essex

G. A. Gooch b Oldham	83	R. E. East b Mortensen ... 14
B. R. Hardie c Fowler b Tunnicliffe	2	J. K. Lever not out ... 8
*K. W. R. Fletcher lbw b Oldham	7	N. A. Foster c and b Tunnicliffe ... 0
K. S. McEwan c Fowler b Mortensen	178	L-b 2, w 2, n-b 22 ... 26
K. R. Pont c Barnett b Moir	7	
D. R. Pringle c Anderson b Mortensen	9	
†D. E. East b Tunnicliffe	26	

D. L. Acfield did not bat.

1/12 2/32 3/213   (9 wkts dec.) 360
4/252 5/302 6/302
7/335 8/354 9/360

Bonus points – Essex 4, Derbyshire 4.

Bowling: Mortensen 24–3–103–3; Tunnicliffe 18.3–4–78–3; Oldham 19–2–62–2; Finney 5–1–23–0; Moir 15–2–68–1.

Umpires: P. J. Eele and K. Ibadulla.

At Bath, June 18, 20, 21. DERBYSHIRE beat SOMERSET by 123 runs.

At Sheffield, June 22, 23, 24. DERBYSHIRE beat YORKSHIRE by 22 runs.

DERBYSHIRE v MIDDLESEX

At Chesterfield, June 25, 27. Middlesex won by nine wickets. Middlesex 22 pts, Derbyshire 5 pts. The pitch began to encourage spin on the first day after Gatting had put Derbyshire in. The all-round strength of the Middlesex attack restricted Derbyshire to 151 and, although three wickets fell in the last half-hour on Saturday, Middlesex were only 10 behind at 141 for five. Lively batting by Williams, missed twice, took the Middlesex lead to 90, giving Edmonds and Emburey the scope to ensure a sixth consecutive Championship victory with a lovely exhibition of spin bowling. They were backed by excellent catching.

Derbyshire

J. E. Morris c Gatting b Cowans	0	– c Slack b Emburey	33
I. S. Anderson c Gatting b Williams	3	– b Edmonds	27
A. Hill c Gatting b Emburey	36	– c Slack b Emburey	12
*K. J. Barnett c Downton b Gatting	22	– c Butcher b Edmonds	18
R. J. Finney c Downton b Gatting	6	– c Barlow b Edmonds	1
G. Miller c Butcher b Edmonds	35	– c Barlow b Emburey	3
W. P. Fowler b Edmonds	25	– c Butcher b Edmonds	0
C. J. Tunnicliffe c Butcher b Edmonds	0	– c Emburey b Edmonds	2
†R. W. Taylor c Gatting b Emburey	0	– st Downton b Edmonds	22
D. G. Moir not out	4	– c Slack b Emburey	12
S. Oldham c Slack b Emburey	7	– not out	3
B 1, l-b 4, w 1, n-b 7	13	B 3, n-b 1	4

1/4 2/4 3/33 4/49   151   1/50 2/67 3/82 4/84   137
5/106 6/124 7/125 8/132 9/136   5/98 6/98 7/98 8/114 9/129

Bonus points – Derbyshire 1, Middlesex 4.

Bowling: *First Innings*—Cowans 9–5–14–1; Williams 9–4–27–1; Hughes 6–1–22–0; Gatting 9–1–26–2; Edmonds 15–3–32–3; Emburey 11.1–4–17–3. *Second Innings*—Cowans 7–1–28–0; Edmonds 21.5–11–38–6; Williams 6–1–17–0; Emburey 21–5–50–4.

Middlesex

G. D. Barlow run out	21	– retired hurt	18
W. N. Slack lbw b Finney	23	– c Anderson b Moir	7
C. T. Radley c Barnett b Oldham	32	– not out	9
*M. W. Gatting c Miller b Moir	49	– not out	11
†P. R. Downton c Miller b Moir	1		
R. O. Butcher c Anderson b Oldham	10		
J. E. Emburey lbw b Oldham	0		
P. H. Edmonds c Miller b Oldham	32		
N. F. Williams not out	50		
S. P. Hughes c Barnett b Finney	2		
N. G. Cowans b Finney	10		
L-b 5, w 1, n-b 5	11	L-b 3	3

1/49 2/49 3/131 4/131   241   1/18   (1 wkt) 48
5/141 6/143 7/164 8/204 9/229

Bonus points – Middlesex 2, Derbyshire 4.

Bowling: *First Innings*—Tunnicliffe 16–4–49–0; Oldham 33–6–72–4; Finney 11.5–2–31–3; Miller 12–2–28–0; Moir 18–7–50–2. *Second Innings*—Miller 8–3–15–0; Moir 9.5–5–20–1; Fowler 2–0–10–0.

Umpires: R. Julian and B. Leadbeater.

DERBYSHIRE v WORCESTERSHIRE

At Derby, July 2, 4, 5. Derbyshire won by eight wickets. Derbyshire 24 pts, Worcestershire 3 pts. Derbyshire, slipping to 36 for four after being put in, were rescued by Hill's unbeaten century. He shared stands of 85 and 121 with Miller and Fowler respectively, enabling Derbyshire to declare. Worcestershire collapsed inexplicably on a good pitch and followed on 208 behind. Led by Neale and Patel, Worcestershire showed greater resolution in their second innings and, when they were all out, left Derbyshire 55 minutes and twenty overs in which to score 200. With Anderson batting particularly well, Derbyshire won their third victory in four matches with eight balls to spare.

Derbyshire

I. S. Anderson c Ellcock b Warner	18	– c Patel b Warner	85
J. E. Morris lbw b Ellcock	1	– c Weston b Pridgeon	35
A. Hill not out	137	– not out	47
*K. J. Barnett hit wkt b Warner	4	– not out	12
R. J. Finney b Warner	0		
G. Miller c Moores b Warner	49		
W. P. Fowler c Patel b D'Oliveira	63		
C. J. Tunnicliffe c Ormrod b Illingworth	18		
†R. W. Taylor b Ellcock	21		
S. Oldham not out	9		
B 2, l-b 12, w 3, n-b 7	24	B 3, l-b 11, n-b 10	24

1/2 2/29 3/36 4/36   (8 wkts dec.) 344   1/64 2/183   (2 wkts) 203
5/121 6/242 7/290 8/327

O. H. Mortensen did not bat.

Bonus points – Derbyshire 4, Worcestershire 3 (Score at 100 overs: 306-7).

Bowling: *First Innings*—Ellcock 16–2–55–2; Warner 25–6–72–4; Pridgeon 23–5–63–0; Illingworth 31–6–73–1; Patel 7–2–26–0; D'Oliveira 9–1–31–1. *Second Innings*—Ellcock 9–0–46–0; Warner 5.4–1–32–1; Illingworth 8–0–47–0; Pridgeon 5–0–25–1; Patel 4–0–29–0.

Worcestershire

J. A. Ormrod not out	63	– c Anderson b Miller	31
M. J. Weston lbw b Tunnicliffe	6	– c Mortensen b Oldham	37
A. P. Pridgeon b Mortensen	5	– (11) c Taylor b Finney	1
*P. A. Neale c Taylor b Oldham	15	– (3) lbw b Oldham	83
D. N. Patel lbw b Tunnicliffe	32	– (4) c Taylor b Tunnicliffe	98
D. B. D'Oliveira c Taylor b Oldham	1	– (5) c Taylor b Miller	16
M. S. Scott lbw b Tunnicliffe	0	– (6) not out	57
†P. Moores b Mortensen	0	– (7) c Taylor b Oldham	23
R. K. Illingworth lbw b Mortensen	0	– (8) c Miller b Mortensen	8
A. E. Warner c Morris b Mortensen	0	– (9) c Taylor b Tunnicliffe	8
R. M. Ellcock b Tunnicliffe	8	– (10) b Miller	18
L-b 3, n-b 5	8	B 2, l-b 10, w 2, n-b 13	27

1/9 2/26 3/51 4/101   136   1/67 2/93 3/248 4/271   407
5/104 6/119 7/120 8/135 9/135   5/293 6/334 7/348 8/360 9/406

Bonus points – Derbyshire 4.

Bowling: *First Innings*—Mortensen 13–1–46–4; Tunnicliffe 16.2–7–30–4; Oldham 10–3–23–2; Finney 6–0–29–0. *Second Innings*—Mortensen 27–5–73–1; Tunnicliffe 25–3–88–2; Oldham 27–6–84–3; Finney 7.3–2–17–1; Miller 33–9–91–3; Fowler 7–2–27–0.

Umpires: J. W. Holder and P. B. Wight.

At Bristol, July 9, 11, 12. DERBYSHIRE drew with GLOUCESTERSHIRE.

At Birmingham, July 13, 14, 15. DERBYSHIRE beat WARWICKSHIRE by ten wickets.

DERBYSHIRE v NORTHAMPTONSHIRE

At Derby, July 16, 17, 18. Drawn. Derbyshire 3 pts, Northamptonshire 8 pts. Larkins took full advantage of Barnett's decision to put Northamptonshire in, giving a magnificent display in scoring the first double-century of his career, which came in 330 minutes with two 6s and 31 4s, before Northamptonshire declared at their highest-ever total against Derbyshire. The home side were then in trouble at 91 for seven, but Barnett played well in adversity, reaching his first century of the season with two straight 6s off Steele after batting for 208 minutes. A combination of Anderson's careful innings and a storm, which cut 100 minutes out of the final afternoon, ensured Derbyshire's survival after they had followed on.

Northamptonshire

*G. Cook c Anderson b Oldham	6	Kapil Dev not out	13
W. Larkins b Fowler	236	B 1, l-b 10, w 3, n-b 2	16
P. Willey c Moir b Mortensen	15		
R. J. Boyd-Moss b Moir	80	1/13 2/62	(4 wkts dec.) 439
R. G. Williams not out	73	3/273 4/416	

D. S. Steele, †G. Sharp, B. J. Griffiths, T. M. Lamb and A. Walker did not bat.

Bonus points – Northamptonshire 4, Derbyshire 1.

Bowling: Mortensen 16–1–71–1; Oldham 23–2–96–1; Finney 15–4–41–0; Watts 10–2–43–0; Moir 24–4–97–1; Fowler 7–0–49–1; Anderson 3–0–26–0.

Derbyshire

J. E. Morris run out	6	– c sub b Griffiths	4
I. S. Anderson c Cook b Lamb	28	– c Steele b Larkins	91
D. G. Moir c Cook b Walker	19		
A. Hill c Sharp b Walker	4	– (3) c Sharp b Lamb	23
*K. J. Barnett b Williams	103	– (4) not out	53
R. J. Finney c Cook b Lamb	0	– (5) not out	3
W. P. Fowler c Steele b Griffiths	6		
†B. J. M. Maher c Cook b Lamb	0		
S. Oldham c Larkins b Willey	39		
A. Watts not out	33		
O. H. Mortensen c Steele b Griffiths	4		
B 1, l-b 6, n-b 2	9	B 11, l-b 6, w 5	22
1/13 2/50 3/54 4/83	251	1/26 2/105 3/193	(3 wkts) 196
5/83 6/90 7/91 8/189 9/219			

Bonus points – Derbyshire 2, Northamptonshire 4.

Bowling: *First Innings*—Griffiths 21.5–3–54–2; Walker 15–5–49–2; Willey 25–11–27–1; Lamb 23–7–41–3; Steele 14–4–35–0; Kapil Dev 7–1–23–0; Williams 5–2–13–1. *Second Innings*—Walker 9–4–21–0; Griffiths 18–5–49–1; Lamb 16–5–38–1; Williams 10–3–20–0; Willey 9–6–10–0; Steele 8–3–12–0; Kapil Dev 1–0–3–0; Larkins 7–0–21–1.

Umpires: C. Cook and A. G. T. Whitehead.

At Portsmouth, July 27, 28, 29. DERBYSHIRE lost to HAMPSHIRE by six wickets.

DERBYSHIRE v KENT

At Chesterfield, July 30, August 1, 2. Drawn. Derbyshire 7 pts, Kent 8 pts. Batsmen dominated on a good pitch, Aslett being particularly impressive as he emulated Benson's feat in Kent's previous match by scoring two hundreds, the first passing his previous best.

Holding, making his Championship début for Derbyshire, did not bowl again after tea on the first day. Barnett and Anderson scored contrasting hundreds and shared opening partnerships of 158 and 109. Kent set Derbyshire 331 to win in 154 minutes and twenty overs and there was some shoddy cricket when, at one stage, they tried to encourage the chase by bowling slow full tosses and making no effort in the field.

Kent

R. A. Woolmer c Maher b Holding	5	– c Miller b Mortensen	32
N. R. Taylor c Maher b Mortensen	12	– c Maher b Mortensen	1
D. G. Aslett c sub b Miller	168	– c Hill b Miller	119
M. R. Benson b Miller	66	– c Barnett b Finney	46
*C. S. Cowdrey c Miller b Mortensen	2	– not out	42
E. A. E. Baptiste c Mortensen b Tunnicliffe	63	– not out	14
†A. P. E. Knott b Mortensen	30		
G. W. Johnson c Miller b Mortensen	4		
R. M. Ellison c Barnett b Moir	63		
D. L. Underwood not out	5		
B 8, l-b 6, w 2, n-b 3	19	L-b 3, n-b 4	7

1/18 2/23 3/132 4/151   (9 wkts dec.) 437   1/5 2/75   (4 wkts dec.) 261
5/256 6/299 7/315 8/414 9/437   3/193 4/215

K. B. S. Jarvis did not bat.

Bonus points – Kent 4, Derbyshire 3 (Score at 100 overs: 433-8).

Bowling: *First Innings*—Holding 11–1–49–1; Mortensen 16–2–73–4; Finney 10–0–63–0; Tunnicliffe 12–2–51–1; Miller 39–7–117–2; Moir 13–0–65–1. *Second Innings*—Mortensen 13–2–54–2; Tunnicliffe 12–0–60–0; Moir 4–0–33–0; Miller 11–0–56–1; Finney 7–0–51–1.

Derbyshire

I. S. Anderson lbw b Ellison	112	– st Knott b Underwood	48
*K. J. Barnett c Knott b Ellison	106	– b Johnson	68
A. Hill b Johnson	5	– run out	8
J. H. Hampshire c Johnson b Jarvis	11	– c Jarvis b Aslett	3
R. J. Finney c Aslett b Baptiste	19	– c Woolmer b Johnson	68
G. Miller c Knott b Baptiste	5	– not out	24
C. J. Tunnicliffe c Baptiste b Jarvis	42	– c Cowdrey b Underwood	1
†B. J. M. Maher not out	28	– not out	13
D. G. Moir b Ellison	16	– not out	2
M. A. Holding b Baptiste	1		
O. H. Mortensen not out	1		
B 1, l-b 14, n-b 7	22	B 4, l-b 8, w 4, n-b 4	20

1/158 2/167 3/189 4/234   (9 wkts dec.) 368   1/109 2/139 3/143   (7 wkts) 255
5/240 6/292 7/321 8/356 9/361   4/143 5/234 6/236 7/252

Bonus points – Derbyshire 4, Kent 4.

Bowling: *First Innings*—Jarvis 28–0–109–2; Baptiste 23–1–112–3; Underwood 7–2–13–0; Ellison 28–5–72–3; Johnson 6–0–19–1; Woolmer 8–0–21–0. *Second Innings*—Jarvis 8–1–22–0; Baptiste 6–0–30–0; Underwood 21–0–38–2; Johnson 12–4–33–2; Ellison 11.4–2–22–0; Aslett 7–2–66–1; Taylor 2–0–24–0.

Umpires: D. R. Shepherd and D. O. Oslear.

At Eastbourne, August 6, 8, 9. DERBYSHIRE drew with SUSSEX.

DERBYSHIRE v SOMERSET

At Derby, August 13, 15, 16. Drawn. Derbyshire 4 pts, Somerset 7 pts. Somerset batted steadily, if unexcitingly, after winning the toss, having most trouble with Miller, who took five wickets for the first time in the summer. Derbyshire were held together only by a stand of 125 between Hill and Hampshire after Davis had taken three early wickets. Roebuck's declaration left Derbyshire to score 308 in 243 minutes but they were already well below the required rate before rain washed out all but three balls of the last twenty overs.

Somerset

*P. M. Roebuck c Maher b Oldham	13	– b Tunnicliffe 94
J. W. Lloyds lbw b Mortensen	55	– lbw b Oldham 41
P. W. Denning lbw b Oldham	11	– c Anderson b Miller 5
N. F. M. Popplewell c Oldham b Mortensen	9	– run out 35
R. L. Ollis st Maher b Miller	50	
P. A. Slocombe c Maher b Oldham	31	– not out 5
V. J. Marks b Miller	27	– (5) b Mortensen 40
†T. Gard c Finney b Miller	50	
J. Garner lbw b Miller	8	– (7) not out 2
M. R. Davis c Tunnicliffe b Miller	7	
C. H. Dredge not out	0	
B 4, l-b 1, n-b 7	12	B 4, l-b 4, n-b 3 11

1/31 2/75 3/87 4/100   **273**   1/73 2/86 3/131   (5 wkts dec.) **233**
5/147 6/185 7/236 8/252 9/272   4/224 5/230

Bonus points – Somerset 3, Derbyshire 3 (Score at 100 overs: 262-8).

Bowling: *First Innings*—Mortensen 20-8-35-2; Tunnicliffe 17-7-49-0; Oldham 26-7-71-3; Finney 15-3-35-0; Miller 25.4-9-71-5. *Second Innings*—Mortensen 16-3-70-1; Tunnicliffe 7-0-34-1; Oldham 18-6-36-1; Finney 6-0-21-0; Miller 21-5-61-1.

Derbyshire

I. S. Anderson lbw b Davis	1	– (3) lbw b Garner 33
†B. J. M. Maher c Popplewell b Davis	11	– (1) c Gard b Marks 52
*K. J. Barnett c Garner b Davis	0	– (2) c Roebuck b Marks 47
A. Hill b Lloyds	56	– not out 36
J. H. Hampshire lbw b Dredge	74	
R. J. Finney c Roebuck b Lloyds	12	– (5) c Garner b Popplewell 7
G. Miller c Garner b Lloyds	4	– (6) not out 0
W. P. Fowler c Roebuck b Garner	3	
C. J. Tunnicliffe c Marks b Davis	28	
S. Oldham not out	0	
O. H. Mortensen lbw b Garner	0	
L-b 5, n-b 5	10	L-b 10, n-b 1 11

1/12 2/12 3/12 4/137   **199**   1/95 2/116   (4 wkts) **186**
5/164 6/165 7/168 8/199 9/199   3/165 4/186

Bonus points – Derbyshire 1, Somerset 4.

Bowling: *First Innings*—Garner 16.3-7-28-2; Marks 18-7-34-0; Lloyds 7-2-23-3; Davis 11-3-34-4; Dredge 13-3-39-1; Popplewell 10-2-31-0. *Second Innings*—Garner 7-1-19-1; Davis 13-2-37-0; Dredge 11-0-38-0; Marks 16-1-53-2; Popplewell 4.3-1-20-1; Lloyds 2-0-8-0.

Umpires: W. E. Alley and N. T. Plews.

At Swansea, August 20, 22, 23. DERBYSHIRE beat GLAMORGAN by two wickets.

At Blackpool, August 24, 25, 26. DERBYSHIRE drew with LANCASHIRE.

DERBYSHIRE v YORKSHIRE

At Chesterfield, August 27, 29, 30. Drawn. Derbyshire 7 pts, Yorkshire 4 pts. A lively innings by Fowler and a last-wicket stand of 66 between Moir and Mortensen helped to stretch Derbyshire's innings after they had won the toss. Carrick bowled steadily but Barnett's decision to bat into Monday was justified by Holding's fine performance. On a pitch which gave him no assistance, he was too fast and hostile for Yorkshire, who followed on 208 behind. The situation was made for Boycott, who batted 487 minutes and hit fifteen 4s in a display of sustained concentration and immaculate technique. He gave only one chance, off Miller at 88.

Derbyshire

*K. J. Barnett b Stevenson	6	M. A. Holding b Stevenson	8
I. S. Anderson run out	62	D. G. Moir b Dennis	53
A. Hill st Bairstow b Carrick	64	O. H. Mortensen not out	14
J. H. Hampshire c Boycott b Carrick	32		
G. Miller c Moxon b Carrick	0	L-b 3, w 2, n-b 10	15
R. J. Finney c Bairstow b Carrick	17		
W. P. Fowler run out	91	1/9 2/140 3/141 4/144	368
†B. J. M. Maher lbw b Carrick	6	5/172 6/203 7/236 8/273 9/302	

Bonus points – Derbyshire 3, Yorkshire 3 (Score at 100 overs: 261-7).

Bowling: Dennis 21.2-3-68-1; Stevenson 18-6-41-2; Moxon 12-1-43-0; Sidebottom 15-3-50-0; Carrick 47-12-122-5; Illingworth 13-2-29-0.

Yorkshire

G. Boycott c Maher b Holding		1 – not out	169
A. Sidebottom c Moir b Miller	61	(7) not out	44
K. Sharp b Mortensen	1	b Mortensen	27
J. D. Love c Anderson b Holding	4	c Anderson b Miller	49
†D. L. Bairstow c Holding b Mortensen	5	b Finney	42
P. Carrick b Holding	7	c Anderson b Miller	0
M. D. Moxon c Hampshire b Holding	25	(2) st Maher b Moir	42
G. B. Stevenson c Finney b Miller	51		
S. J. Dennis b Holding	0		
*R. Illingworth not out	3		
C. W. J. Athey absent injured			
W 1, n-b 1	2	B 9, l-b 6, w 4, n-b 4	23
1/2 2/3 3/16 4/33	160	1/75 2/140 3/218 (5 wkts)	396
5/64 6/85 7/151 8/157 9/160		4/313 5/316	

Bonus points – Yorkshire 1, Derbyshire 4.

Bowling: *First Innings*—Holding 16.3-3-48-5; Mortensen 7-2-26-2; Moir 15-7-32-0; Miller 8-0-38-2; Finney 6-2-14-0. *Second Innings*—Holding 26-8-54-0; Finney 14-2-48-1; Miller 51-19-104-2; Moir 27-8-57-1; Mortensen 18-8-28-1; Fowler 8-3-24-0; Anderson 6-1-31-0; Hill 4-1-11-0; Barnett 2-0-12-0; Hampshire 2-0-4-0.

Umpires: D. R. Shepherd and R. A. White.

DERBYSHIRE v NOTTINGHAMSHIRE

At Derby, September 7, 8, 9. Derbyshire won by 100 runs. Derbyshire 20 pts, Nottinghamshire 4 pts. Derbyshire were put in on a green and lively pitch, only Barnett and

Miller looking comfortable. Nottinghamshire had no answer to Holding, Mortensen and Newman, playing together for the first time in the Championship, and conceded a first-innings advantage of 84 with their lowest-ever total against Derbyshire. More than four hours were lost on the second day, but Miller's 63 in 69 minutes set up a Derbyshire declaration. Holding took the first five wickets and only Robinson, forced to retire for a time after a blow on the arm from Holding, offered any lengthy resistance to Derbyshire's fast bowlers.

Derbyshire

*K. J. Barnett c Rice b Cooper	47	– b Cooper 63
I. S. Anderson c Randall b Hendrick	7	
A. Hill c French b Cooper	5	– (2) b Hendrick 31
J. H. Hampshire c French b Cooper	1	– (3) not out 31
G. Miller lbw b Hendrick	23	– (4) c Johnson b Pick 63
R. J. Finney c Birch b Cooper	19	– (5) not out 5
W. P. Fowler c French b Hendrick	6	
P. G. Newman c French b Hendrick	1	
†R. W. Taylor c Hemmings b Pick	9	
M. A. Holding c French b Cooper	0	
O. H. Mortensen not out	12	
B 1, n-b 6	7	B 1, l-b 2, w 1, n-b 5 9

1/15 2/40 3/42 4/85   137   1/88 2/100 3/191   (3 wkts dec.) 202
5/88 6/102 7/113 8/115 9/115

Bonus points – Nottinghamshire 4.

Bowling: *First Innings*—Hendrick 20–13–20–4; Saxelby 7–1–40–0; Cooper 20–9–32–5; Pick 10.2–1–37–1; Hemmings 1–0–1–0. *Second Innings*—Hendrick 25–11–46–1; Pick 8–1–49–1; Cooper 28–8–88–1; Saxelby 3–1–10–0.

Nottinghamshire

P. Johnson c Taylor b Holding	10	– b Holding 0
R. T. Robinson c Taylor b Mortensen	0	– lbw b Mortensen 79
D. W. Randall b Mortensen	0	– c Taylor b Holding 1
*C. E. B. Rice c Hampshire b Newman	20	– c Taylor b Holding 2
J. D. Birch lbw b Holding	0	– c and b Holding 46
†B. N. French b Newman	13	– lbw b Holding 4
E. E. Hemmings b Mortensen	0	– c Taylor b Mortensen 6
K. Saxelby not out	1	– c Barnett b Finney 7
R. A. Pick run out	0	– not out 25
K. E. Cooper c and b Newman	0	– run out 0
M. Hendrick b Mortensen	4	– c Taylor b Mortensen 5
B 1, l-b 2, w 1, n-b 1	5	L-b 2, n-b 9 11

1/4 2/4 3/25 4/25   53   1/0 2/12 3/47 4/84   186
5/45 6/48 7/48 8/48 9/48   5/94 6/126 7/140 8/163 9/164

Bonus points – Derbyshire 4.

Bowling: *First Innings*—Holding 9–3–23–2; Mortensen 11–3–25–4; Newman 2–2–0–3. *Second Innings*—Holding 15–3–53–5; Mortensen 7.5–1–28–3; Newman 12–0–67–0; Finney 6–0–27–1.

Umpires: R. Palmer and K. Ibadulla.

At The Oval, September 10, 12, 13. DERBYSHIRE drew with SURREY.

ESSEX

President: T. N. Pearce
Chairman: A. G. Waterman
Chairman, Cricket Committee: D. J. Insole
Secretary/General Manager: P. J. Edwards
  County Ground, New Writtle Street,
  Chelmsford CM2 0PG
  (Telephone: 0245-354533)
Captain: K. W. R. Fletcher

In carrying off their second Schweppes County Championship title within the space of five years, Essex demonstrated the ability to come from behind and conquer acute disappointment. The end of July arrived with their character to overcome adversity being questioned. They had managed to lose the Benson and Hedges Cup Final against Middlesex by 4 runs from a position where it had seemed easier to win; they had lost by the same margin and in similar fashion to Kent in the second round of the NatWest Bank Trophy; and they found themselves with considerable ground to make up in the title race. Yet, like worthy champions, they recovered their form and confidence to overtake Middlesex and win the Championship by sixteen points.

Inevitably there were those quick to point out that they were lucky not to be weakened by excessive Test calls. With Graham Gooch and John Lever still banned because of their South African "safari" and Derek Pringle falling out of favour with the selectors, Neil Foster was the only Essex player called up by England. Yet the county faced with several injury problems before claiming the game's most coveted prize. For several matches they were forced to soldier on without their strongest pace attack. Foster missed the last seven Championship games, following an operation to remove two six-inch metal plates from his back, while Lever missed the same number of matches, first with a broken toe and then after undergoing an operation for a serious abdominal condition. Pringle, too, missed a third of the programme through one injury or another.

The summer was a personal triumph for Ken McEwan, this year's beneficiary, who underlined in thrilling style that he is a world-class batsman. He confirmed the point with eight Championship centuries and became the first Essex player for 28 years to top 2,000 runs in a season. Gooch, although having to wait until the last month of the season to score the first of his three Championship hundreds, supported him well. Before this late burst of Championship runs, Gooch was at his most awesome in limited-overs battles. Against Glamorgan, for example, in a John Player League match – Essex finished seventh in that competition – he set a new individual record of 176. In between the skilful manipulation of his forces, Keith Fletcher weighed in with his customary 1,000 first-class runs, as did Brian Hardie.

Yet the key to Essex's Championship success was provided by the resilient and popular Lever. To miss a third of the season and still finish with 106 wickets was a remarkable feat. Foster, before his date with the surgeon, also confirmed his promise: he won his first Test cap and selection for England's winter tour of Fiji, Pakistan and New Zealand. Norbert Phillip, too, performed with distinction. The West Indian lost his place in mid-season, but when the absence of Lever and Foster resulted in his recall, he responded magnificently. Six of his 69 wickets came at the cost of just 4 runs – his Championship best – when Surrey suffered the humiliation of being bowled out for 14 in their first innings at Chelmsford in May, the third-lowest score ever recorded at first-class level. Pringle, plagued with a no-balling problem and, at times, costly, nevertheless provided telling support to a pace and seam attack which resulted in Ray East and David Acfield undertaking much less work than they might have expected.

Pringle also produced many useful performances with the bat, as did David East. But it was as wicket-keeper that the latter excelled, finishing with more first-class victims than anyone else in the country. Like Pringle and Foster, he has youth on his side and should help inspire the county to a rewarding future. The same can be said of Chris Gladwin, a well-built left-handed batsman who opened the innings during the final exciting weeks of the summer. He has the confidence and ability to go for his strokes, much as Gooch does, although his natural inclination to attack the bowling tended to bring about his downfall in the 30s. Once he injects a little more self-discipline to go with his obvious talent, there is every reason to believe he will succeed at the highest level.

With their blend of youth and experience, possessed in depth, Essex can look forward confidently to 1984. Their dressing-room will not be quite the same, however, in the months head. That is because Ray East, "Clown Prince" of the county circuit, will be coaching and captaining the Second XI in succession to Mike Denness, who has left to concentrate on a business career. East, who took his 1,000th first-class wicket in 1983, will be available for first-team duty if required, but his major task will be to give youngsters the benefit of his experience and good humour. – N.F.

ESSEX 1983

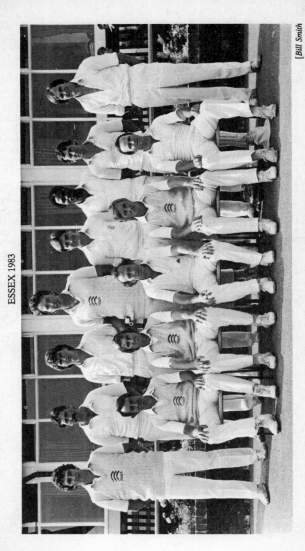

[*Bill Smith*]

Back row: B. R. Hardie, G. A. Gooch, K. R. Pont, D. R. Pringle, C. Gladwin, N. Phillip, D. E. East, R. E. East. *Front row*: D. L. Acfield, J. K. Lever, K. W. R. Fletcher (*captain*), S. Turner, K. S. McEwan.

ESSEX RESULTS

All first-class matches – Played 26: Won 11, Lost 6, Drawn 9.

County Championship matches – Played 24: Won 11, Lost 5, Drawn 8.

Bonus points – Batting 69, Bowling 79.

Competition placings – Schweppes County Championship, winners; NatWest Bank Trophy, 2nd round; Benson and Hedges Cup, r/u; John Player League, 6th eq.

COUNTY CHAMPIONSHIP AVERAGES

BATTING

	Birthplace	M	I	NO	R	HI	Avge
K. S. McEwanc.......	Bedford, SA	24	35	5	2,051	189*	68.36
G. A. Goochc.........	Leytonstone	24	35	1	1,227	111	36.08
K. W. R. Fletcherc..	Worcester	24	34	3	1,026	151*	33.09
K. R. Pontc..........	Wanstead	19	23	3	658	125*	32.90
D. R. Pringlec	Nairobi, Kenya	16	20	4	503	102*	31.43
C. Gladwin............	East Ham	8	12	0	375	61	31.25
B. R. Hardiec	Stenhousemuir	23	34	2	896	69	28.00
D. E. Eastc	Clapton	24	29	4	565	91	22.60
N. A. Fosterc	Colchester	12	14	4	219	40*	21.90
R. E. Eastc	Manningtree	19	24	4	355	80*	17.75
N. Phillipc...........	Bioche, Dominica	18	24	0	406	80	16.91
J. K. Leverc	Stepney	17	16	3	207	44	15.92
S. Turnerc...........	Chester	14	18	2	161	30	10.06
D. L. Acfieldc	Chelmsford	21	21	12	66	16	7.33

Also batted: A. W. Lilley (*Ilford*) (1 match) 2, 61.

* *Signifies not out.*   c*Denotes county cap.*

BOWLING

	O	M	R	W	Avge	BB
J. K. Lever............	541	127	1,647	98	16.80	7-55
N. Phillip	454.2	84	1,338	68	19.67	6-4
D. R. Pringle..........	267.4	47	872	40	21.80	7-32
N. A. Foster...........	389	73	1,141	51	22.37	6-46
S. Turner	260	69	583	24	24.29	5-30
D. L. Acfield..........	482.1	132	1,201	43	27.93	7-100
R. E. East..............	292.2	70	777	22	35.31	5-45

Also bowled: K. W. R. Fletcher 8.3–0–57–0; C. Gladwin 3–0–11–0; G. A. Gooch 187–37–514–8; K. S. McEwan 7–0–28–1; K. R. Pont 56–15–134–4.

The following played a total of sixteen three-figure innings for Essex in County Championship matches – K. S. McEwan 8, G. A. Gooch 3, K. W. R. Fletcher 2, K. R. Pont 2, D. R. Pringle 1.

At Cambridge, April 27, 28, 29. ESSEX drew with CAMBRIDGE UNIVERSITY.

At Lord's, April 30, May 2, 3. ESSEX drew with MIDDLESEX.

At Cardiff, May 4, 5, 6. ESSEX drew with GLAMORGAN.

ESSEX v KENT

At Chelmsford, May 11, 12, 13. Kent won by six wickets. Kent 19 pts, Essex 3 pts. After Gooch had departed to Dilley's first ball of the match, Pont collected his first Championship century for five years, his innings including two 6s and eleven 4s. Fletcher batted well before he, like Pont, was removed by the hostile Dilley. When rain washed out the second day's play, both sides decided to forfeit an innings to force a positive result. Thanks to the fluency of Tavaré, Woolmer and Benson, not to mention several no-balls from Pringle, Kent won with nine balls of the final twenty overs to spare.

Essex

G. A. Gooch b Dilley	0	R. E. East c Tavaré b Underwood	2
B. R. Hardie c Knott b Ellison	15	J. K. Lever b Dilley	26
*K. W. R. Fletcher b Dilley	55	D. L. Acfield not out	0
K. S. McEwan b Ellison	29	B 1, l-b 13, n-b 3	17
K. R. Pont b Dilley	105		
D. R. Pringle c and b Underwood	19	1/0 2/41 3/91	320
N. Phillip c Cowdrey b Woolmer	40	4/108 5/168 6/269	
†D. E. East b Dilley	12	7/288 8/291 9/299	

Bonus points – Essex 3, Kent 3 (Score at 100 overs: 299-8).

Bowling: Dilley 21.4–3–70–5; Jarvis 18–4–53–0; Ellison 26–5–74–2; Underwood 22–8–66–2; Woolmer 9–3–26–1; Johnson 8–1–14–0.

Essex forfeited their second innings.

Kent

N. R. Taylor (did not bat)		– lbw b Pringle	16
R. A. Woolmer (did not bat)		– lbw b Phillip	63
*C. J. Tavaré (did not bat)		– b Lever	94
M. R. Benson (did not bat)		– c D. E. East b Pringle	78
C. S. Cowdrey (did not bat)		– not out	31
†A. P. E. Knott (did not bat)		– not out	11
		B 1, l-b 14, w 1, n-b 12	28

1/55 2/114 3/247 4/283 (4 wkts) 321

G. W. Johnson, R. M. Ellison, G. R. Dilley, D. L. Underwood and K. B. S. Jarvis did not bat.

Bowling: Lever 19.3–1–84–1; Phillip 12–1–40–1; Pringle 20–1–81–2; Gooch 3–1–12–0; R. E. East 8–2–27–0; Acfield 12–0–49–0.

Kent forfeited their first innings.

Umpires: D. O. Oslear and R. A. White.

At Leicester, May 25, 26, 27. ESSEX lost to LEICESTERSHIRE by four wickets.

ESSEX v SURREY

At Chelmsford, May 28, 30, 31. Drawn. Essex 7 pts, Surrey 4 pts. On the second afternoon Surrey were skittled out for the lowest score in their history, their first innings lasting a mere 14.3 overs. Phillip and Foster, making the ball swing in the humid atmosphere, were their tormentors and only a boundary from Clark, the sole one of the innings, spared them the humiliation of recording the lowest-ever first-class score. Five wickets fell with the total on 8. The next day a fine century from Knight, well supported by Clinton, enabled Surrey to win back some self-respect. After a barren opening day because of rain, Fletcher showed that there was nothing wrong with the pitch with a century full of grace and elegance after Knight had gambled on putting the home side in to bat.

Essex

G. A. Gooch b Thomas	1	R. E. East c Lynch b Clarke	19
B. R. Hardie b Clarke	16	†D. E. East c Butcher b Pocock	17
*K. W. R. Fletcher c Lynch		N. A. Foster not out	19
b Monkhouse	110	D. L. Acfield run out	0
K. S. McEwan c Lynch b Knight	45	B 4, l-b 10, n-b 6	20
K. R. Pont b Pocock	12		—
N. Phillip b Pocock	8		287
S. Turner c and b Knight	20		

1/1 2/27 3/113 4/156
5/179 6/222 7/238 8/252 9/276

Bonus points – Essex 3, Surrey 4.

Bowling: Clarke 20–3–58–2; Thomas 20–2–78–1; Monkhouse 13–2–49–1; Knight 17–6–33–2; Pocock 19.5–6–49–3.

Surrey

A. R. Butcher c D. E. East b Phillip	2	c Gooch b Foster	5
G. S. Clinton c D. E. East b Foster	6	not out	61
A. Needham b Foster	0	lbw b Phillip	4
*R. D. V. Knight lbw b Phillip	0	not out	101
M. A. Lynch lbw b Phillip	0		
†C. J. Richards c Turner b Phillip	0		
D. J. Thomas lbw b Foster	0		
I. R. Payne b Phillip	0		
G. Monkhouse lbw b Phillip	2		
S. T. Clarke b Foster	4		
P. I. Pocock not out	0		
		B 1, l-b 8, w 2, n-b 3	14

1/2 2/5 3/6 4/8 5/8 6/8 7/8 8/8 9/14   14   1/11 2/18   (2 wkts) 185

Bonus points – Essex 4.

Bowling: *First Innings*—Phillip 7.3–4–4–6; Foster 7–3–10–4. *Second Innings*—Phillip 13–2–39–1; Foster 13–2–33–1; Turner 7–3–16–0; Gooch 22–6–45–0; Acfield 17–7–23–0; R. E. East 1–0–5–0; Pont 5–1–10–0.

Umpires: W. E. Alley and J. W. Holder.

At Taunton, June 4, 6, 7. ESSEX beat SOMERSET by 141 runs.

ESSEX v NOTTINGHAMSHIRE

At Chelmsford, June 8, 9, 10. Essex won by eight wickets. Essex 23 pts, Nottinghamshire 3 pts. Essex won with thirteen balls to spare after Hassan had defied them for just over six hours. He eventually fell to Ray East, the left-arm spinner going on to his best figures of the season as he wrapped up the tail. On the opening day, only teenager Johnson looked at ease after Nottinghamshire had been put in. Fletcher and McEwan continued their fine form as Essex built a lead of 180, and Pont batted with resolution rather than fluency following their departure.

Nottinghamshire

B. Hassan c Hardie b Phillip	11	– c Phillip b R. E. East 112
R. T. Robinson c Fletcher b Foster	14	– lbw b Acfield 13
*J. D. Birch b Phillip	31	– b Foster 56
P. Johnson c Fletcher b Foster	54	– lbw b Foster 1
†B. N. French c Hardie b Phillip	0	– b R. E. East 15
M. A. Fell c Gooch b Acfield	4	– lbw b Turner 32
E. E. Hemmings st D. E. East b Acfield	18	– b Foster 13
K. Saxelby lbw b Acfield	4	– c D. E. East b R. E. East 1
K. E. Cooper not out	18	– c Hardie b R. E. East 5
M. Hendrick c Acfield b Foster	2	– not out 2
P. M. Such lbw b Acfield	0	– c Fletcher b R. E. East............ 1
B 4, l-b 11	15	B 2, l-b 18, w 2, n-b 5 27

1/18 2/43 3/76 4/82   171   1/27 2/147 3/149 4/184   278
5/90 6/126 7/138 8/148 9/170   5/250 6/256 7/262 8/271 9/277

Bonus points – Nottinghamshire 1, Essex 4.

Bowling: *First Innings*—Phillip 13–2–52–3; Foster 18–4–57–3; Turner 5–2–23–0; Acfield 15–2–24–4. *Second Innings*—Phillip 12–3–25–0; Foster 30–9–69–3; Acfield 47–18–79–1; R. E. East 31.2–14–45–5; Turner 18–5–33–1.

Essex

G. A. Gooch c Birch b Cooper	13	– st French b Cooper 31
B. R. Hardie c Hendrick b Saxelby	42	– b Saxelby 20
*K. W. R. Fletcher b Cooper	76	– (4) not out........................ 16
K. S. McEwan b Hemmings	79	– (3) not out........................ 27
K. R. Pont c Cooper b Hemmings	62	
N. Phillip b Cooper	20	
S. Turner c Such b Hemmings	3	
†D. E. East c sub b Saxelby	17	
R. E. East b Such	19	
N. A. Foster lbw b Hemmings	11	
D. L. Acfield not out	0	
B 2, l-b 6, n-b 1	9	L-b 9, n-b 1 10

1/33 2/69 3/212 4/214   351   1/51 2/71   (2 wkts) 104
5/244 6/253 7/281 8/325 9/340

Bonus points – Essex 3, Nottinghamshire 2 (Score at 100 overs: 263-6).

Bowling: *First Innings*—Hendrick 15–3–45–0; Saxelby 21–9–52–2; Cooper 32–7–95–3; Hemmings 45.3–14–107–4; Such 18–7–43–1. *Second Innings*—Hendrick 5–0–19–0; Cooper 10–1–36–1; Saxelby 7–0–30–1; Such 1.5–0–9–0.

Umpires: B. Dudleston and J. H. Harris.

At Tunbridge Wells, June 11, 13, 14. ESSEX drew with KENT.

At Derby, June 15, 16. ESSEX beat DERBYSHIRE by an innings and 25 runs.

ESSEX v NORTHAMPTONSHIRE

At Ilford, June 22, 23, 24. Essex won by an innings and 51 runs. Essex 24 pts, Northamptonshire 4 pts. This match ended after only an hour's play on the final day, during which Lever and Foster captured Northamptonshire's last six wickets for a mere 24 runs. Northamptonshire had also struggled for runs in their first innings, the accuracy and hostility of Lever being instrumental in their downfall on a pitch offering encouraging bounce. Hardie and McEwan both batted attractively for Essex, while a responsible effort from Ray East ensured maximum bonus points, despite the stout-hearted efforts of Griffiths.

Northamptonshire

*G. Cook c McEwan b Lever	12	11 – lbw b Lever	12
W. Larkins lbw b Lever	1	14 – c and b Phillip	1
P. Willey c Gooch b Lever	49	– c Gooch b Foster	21
D. J. Wild b Lever	0	– c D. E. East b Lever	5
R. G. Williams c Fletcher b R. E. East	40	– c Phillip b Foster	10
M. J. Bamber not out	35	– c Hardie b Lever	17
D. S. Steele lbw b Foster	17	– lbw b Lever	0
†G. Sharp lbw b Phillip	6	– not out	6
N. A. Mallender c D. E. East b Foster	1	– c Hardie b Foster	3
T. M. Lamb lbw b Foster	0	– c Gooch b Foster	0
B. J. Griffiths b Lever	15	– b Lever	0
L-b 8, n-b 1	9	B 4, n-b 2	6

1/12 2/35 3/35 4/122   197   1/4 2/19 3/26 4/38   81
5/122 6/146 7/157 8/158 9/158   5/70 6/72 7/72 8/79 9/80

Bonus points – Northamptonshire 1, Essex 4.

Bowling: *First Innings*—Lever 21.2–5–59–5; Phillip 14–2–38–1; Foster 17–4–48–3; Acfield 5–0–15–0; R. E. East 13–4–26–1; Gooch 2–1–2–0. *Second Innings*—Lever 15.4–4–36–6; Phillip 10–1–16–1; Foster 13–3–23–3.

Essex

G. A. Gooch lbw b Griffiths	15	J. K. Lever c Williams b Steele	12
B. R. Hardie c Cook b Griffiths	51	N. A. Foster b Mallender	22
*K. W. R. Fletcher c Cook b Griffiths	33	D. L. Acfield c Larkins b Mallender	2
K. S. McEwan c Sharp b Griffiths	69		
K. R. Pont c Cook b Griffiths	22	B 11, l-b 5, w 1, n-b 6	23
N. Phillip b Griffiths	0		
†D. E. East lbw b Willey	0	1/43 2/81 3/173 4/184	329
R. E. East not out	80	5/184 6/185 7/229 8/283 9/318	

Bonus points – Essex 4, Northamptonshire 3 (Score at 100 overs: 318-8).

Bowling: Mallender 21.4–1–108–2; Griffiths 39–10–92–6; Lamb 3–0–9–0; Wild 3–2–10–0; Steele 7–0–46–1; Willey 30–11–40–1; Williams 1–0–1–0.

Umpires: J. Birkenshaw and N. T. Plews.

ESSEX v SUSSEX

At Ilford, June 25, 27. Essex won by nine wickets. Essex 23 pts, Sussex 4 pts. Fletcher was at his best as he stroked twelve boundaries to help Essex overcome the early loss of Gooch. Pringle later held the innings together with his best Championship score to date and then Foster, making good use of the uneven bounce, collected career-best figures as Sussex disintegrated. The visitors put up more resistance in their second innings, but Essex coasted to their third successive Championship victory with a day to spare. Their only disappointment was an injury to Hardie, forced to retire with a broken nose after a ball from Colin Wells had hit him in the face.

Essex

G. A. Gooch b le Roux	11	– b Reeve	13
B. R. Hardie c and b Pigott	41	– retired hurt	27
*K. W. R. Fletcher lbw b Reeve	79		
K. S. McEwan b le Roux	7	– not out	11
K. R. Pont run out	25		
D. R. Pringle not out	68		
†D. E. East b Barclay	2	– (3) not out	14
R. E. East c Heath b Waller	15		
J. K. Lever c Mendis b Waller	9		
N. A. Foster st Gould b Waller	2		
D. L. Acfield lbw b C. M. Wells	1		
B 1, l-b 10, w 6, n-b 4	21	B 4	4

1/14 2/123 3/139 4/156   281 1/38   (1 wkt) 69
5/216 6/219 7/241 8/267 9/276

Bonus points – Essex 3, Sussex 4.

Bowling: *First Innings*—le Roux 21–2–76–2; Pigott 15–1–62–1; Reeve 15–5–30–1; C. M. Wells 5.3–1–13–1; Waller 29–12–55–3; Barclay 7–0–24–1. *Second Innings*—le Roux 4–0–18–0; Pigott 1–0–2–0; C. M. Wells 6–2–17–0; Reeve 5–0–14–1; Parker 1.2–0–14–0.

Sussex

G. D. Mendis c Gooch b Foster	0	– b Foster	1
J. R. P. Heath c D. E. East b Foster	25	– lbw b Lever	25
*J. R. T. Barclay c Hardie b Lever	9	– b Pringle	49
C. M. Wells c D. E. East b Pringle	11	– c R. E. East b Lever	16
P. W. G. Parker c Hardie b Foster	22	– c Pringle b Foster	17
D. A. Reeve lbw b Lever	1	– (9) c Acfield b Foster	31
A. P. Wells lbw b Pringle	10	– (6) c Pringle b Acfield	23
G. S. le Roux c Hardie b Foster	0	– (7) c Acfield b Pringle	25
†I. J. Gould b Foster	16	– (8) c Hardie b Acfield	29
A. C. S. Pigott c Fletcher b Foster	6	– c Hardie b Lever	8
C. E. Waller not out	0	– not out	0
		B 5, l-b 10, n-b 10	25

1/1 2/32 3/38 4/47   100 1/7 2/54 3/91 4/109   249
5/48 6/73 7/73 8/93 9/99   5/138 6/172 7/173 8/217 9/245

Bonus points – Essex 4.

Bowling: *First Innings*—Lever 15–3–46–2; Foster 14.1–2–46–6; Pringle 4–0–7–2; R. E. East 1–0–1–0. *Second Innings*—Lever 17–2–53–3; Foster 16.1–2–64–3; Pringle 12–1–46–2; Acfield 24–5–61–2.

Umpires: J. Birkenshaw and N. T. Plews.

At Nottingham, July 2, 4, 5. ESSEX beat NOTTINGHAMSHIRE by 201 runs.

At Nuneaton, July 9, 11, 12. ESSEX lost to WARWICKSHIRE by ten wickets.

ESSEX v HAMPSHIRE

At Southend, July 13, 14, 15. Hampshire won by four wickets. Hampshire 20 pts, Essex 6 pts. Hampshire achieved the rare distinction of scoring over 400 runs in the fourth innings to achieve a remarkable win with eleven balls to spare. Smith was the architect of their triumph after his side had been set 407 to win in nearly six and a half hours. His 163 included 28 4s on a pitch which became easier as the match wore on. The hostility of Marshall and accuracy of Tremlett forced Essex to struggle in their first innings, while Turner and Pringle destroyed Hampshire in theirs. But then McEwan, with two 6s and 22 4s in his 142, and Pringle, with his first century for Essex, saw to it that Hampshire were left a huge task.

Essex

G. A. Gooch c Pocock b Tremlett	25	– b Marshall	39
B. R. Hardie c Nicholas b Marshall	67	– c Parks b Marshall	7
*K. W. R. Fletcher c Pocock b Tremlett	39	– b Marshall	12
K. S. McEwan c Nicholas b Marshall	0	– c Nicholas b Southern	142
K. R. Pont c and b Marshall	1	– c Greenidge b Marshall	3
D. R. Pringle c Greenidge b Tremlett	14	– not out	102
N. Phillip c Pocock b Marshall	6	– c Pocock b Cowley	9
S. Turner c Parks b Tremlett	14	– not out	2
†D. E. East not out	18		
R. E. East c Pocock b Marshall	4		
D. L. Acfield c Terry b Marshall	0		
L-b 12, w 1, n-b 1	14	B 8, l-b 9, w 5, n-b 2	24

1/68 2/137 3/137 4/143   202   1/17 2/37 3/115   (6 wkts dec.) 340
5/147 6/165 7/175 8/181 9/202   4/127 5/267 6/323

Bonus points – Essex 2, Hampshire 4.

Bowling: First Innings—Marshall 28.2–6–73–6; Malone 7–0–39–0; Tremlett 28–7–65–4; Nicholas 3–1–11–0. *Second Innings*—Marshall 17–4–51–4; Malone 12–3–28–0; Tremlett 11–0–33–0; Southern 22–2–78–1; Nicholas 12–1–52–0; Cowley 15.5–4–74–1.

Hampshire

C. G. Greenidge b Pringle	34	– lbw b Turner	45
C. L. Smith lbw b Turner	3	– c McEwan b Pringle	163
M. C. J. Nicholas c Gooch b Turner	4	– b R. E. East	72
V. P. Terry c Pringle b Turner	0	– c Acfield b Phillip	41
*N. E. J. Pocock c D. E. East b Turner	0	– (6) c Turner b R. E. East	52
M. D. Marshall c R. E. East b Turner	6	– (7) not out	4
N. G. Cowley lbw b Pringle	0	– (8) not out	0
T. M. Tremlett c Gooch b Pringle	15		
†R. J. Parks c Turner b Pringle	9		
J. W. Southern b Pringle	37	– (5) b R. E. East	0
S. J. Malone not out	4		
L-b 2, w 1, n-b 21	24	B 2, l-b 11, n-b 20	33

1/31 2/46 3/55 4/55   136   1/67 2/255 3/324   (6 wkts) 410
5/59 6/59 7/61 8/79 9/103   4/324 5/405 6/405

Bonus points – Essex 4.

Bowling: First Innings—Phillip 5–2–16–0; Pringle 17.2–4–66–5; Turner 17–7–30–5. *Second Innings*—Phillip 13–2–42–1; Pringle 21–2–92–1; R. E. East 40.1–6–161–3; Turner 19–6–41–1; Gooch 2–0–13–0; Acfield 11–4–28–0.

Umpires: B. J. Meyer and D. R. Shepherd.

ESSEX v GLAMORGAN

At Southend, July 16, 18, 19. Essex won by an innings and 3 runs. Essex 24 pts, Glamorgan 4 pts. Following early alarms, McEwan snatched the initiative for Essex with his sixth Championship hundred of the season, his effort containing twelve 4s during a stay of 135 minutes. Afterwards, Pont stroked his way to a career-best score with the help of one 6 and seventeen 4s as he resisted for nearly six hours before running out of partners. Glamorgan were forced to follow on, 243 behind, after collapsing to Foster and Pringle, and although Ontong enabled them to achieve a measure of self-respect during their second innings, only a stubborn last-wicket stand carried the match into its final day.

Essex

G. A. Gooch c Morris b Davis	16	R. E. East c E. W. Jones b Rowe	4
B. R. Hardie b Thomas	12	N. A. Foster c A. Jones b Rowe	29
*K. W. R. Fletcher c Morris b Selvey	8	D. L. Acfield c Rowe b Selvey	12
K. S. McEwan c E. W. Jones b Selvey	104	B 7, l-b 8, w 8, n-b 2	25
K. R. Pont not out	125		—
D. R. Pringle b Davis	17	1/30 2/30 3/61	359
S. Turner c E. W. Jones b Davis	7	4/179 5/223 6/242	
†D. E. East c A. L. Jones b Rowe	0	7/243 8/261 9/316	

Bonus points – Essex 4, Glamorgan 4 (Score at 100 overs: 357-9).

Bowling: Davis 30–9–81–3; Thomas 15–3–61–1; Selvey 18.2–2–56–3; Ontong 4–0–17–0; Rowe 33–7–119–3.

Glamorgan

A. Jones c D. E. East b Gooch	20	– lbw b Foster	2
J. A. Hopkins lbw b Foster	1	– c Hardie b Pringle	2
*M. W. W. Selvey c Turner b Foster	4	– (10) c Pringle b Gooch	6
R. C. Ontong b Turner	12	– (3) c McEwan b Acfield	79
A. L. Jones c McEwan b Pringle	17	– (4) lbw b Foster	0
H. Morris c Gooch b Pringle	13	– (5) c D. E. East b Acfield	29
D. A. Francis c Hardie b Pringle	1	– (6) lbw b Foster	27
C. J. C. Rowe c Hardie b Pringle	3	– (7) b Pringle	33
J. G. Thomas c McEwan b Foster	18	– (8) c Pont b Gooch	7
†E. W. Jones c D. E. East b Foster	6	– (9) b Gooch	0
W. W. Davis not out	1	– not out	39
L-b 4, n-b 16	20	B 2, l-b 6, n-b 8	16

1/5 2/15 3/47 4/51	116
5/72 6/78 7/87 8/94 9/115	

1/4 2/16 3/16 4/123	240
5/128 6/165 7/175 8/175 9/181	

Bonus points – Essex 4.

Bowling: *First Innings*—Foster 17.5–6–32–4; Pringle 18–7–22–4; Gooch 8–2–14–1; Turner 12–2–28–1. *Second Innings*—Foster 11.5–2–50–3; Pringle 11–1–49–2; Turner 3–0–9–0; Gooch 11–1–40–3; Acfield 21–7–50–2; R. E. East 6–2–16–0; Fletcher 1–0–10–0.

Umpires: B. J. Meyer and D. R. Shepherd.

At Hove, July 27, 28, 29. ESSEX beat SUSSEX by an innings and 53 runs.

ESSEX v MIDDLESEX

At Chelmsford, August 6, 8, 9. Drawn. Essex 7 pts, Middlesex 4 pts. In saving the match after being bowled out on the first morning for only 83, Middlesex recorded the biggest total in the Championship since 1947, falling only 8 short of their all-time record compiled 60 years earlier. The recovery was spearheaded by Barlow, whose 330 minutes' effort contained sixteen 4s, and carried on by Gatting (two 6s and eighteen 4s) and Emburey with a career-best score. On the opening day, Barlow carried his bat as Middlesex were routed on a green pitch, Pringle's ability to swing the ball causing the chief damage. Gladwin, a powerfully built left-hander making his first appearance of the season, caught the eye as Essex built up a first-innings lead of 206. In the first hour after tea on the last day, Pont and Gooch bowled 48 overs as Essex concentrated on improving their over-rate and thus avoiding a statutory fine.

Middlesex

G. D. Barlow not out	44	– st East b Acfield	132
W. N. Slack c East b Lever	0	– lbw b Lever	24
C. T. Radley lbw b Lever	7	– c East b Lever	67
*M. W. Gatting c East b Pringle	12	– c Acfield b Pont	160
R. G. P. Ellis lbw b Pringle	0	– c Foster b Lever	5
J. E. Emburey c McEwan b Pringle	1	– c sub b Gooch	133
†P. R. Downton b Pringle	0	– c Gooch b McEwan	67
P. H. Edmonds c Hardie b Pringle	0	– not out	6
N. F. Williams c Gooch b Foster	10	– not out	1
W. W. Daniel c Lever b Pringle	2		
N. G. Cowans c East b Pringle	0		
B 1, n-b 6	7	B 10, l-b 12, w 6, n-b 11	39
	83	(7 wkts dec.)	634

1/1 2/9 3/41 4/41
5/49 6/53 7/53 8/65 9/80

1/44 2/254 3/256
4/263 5/531 6/605 7/633

Bonus points – Essex 4.

Bowling: *First Innings*—Lever 7–2–17–2; Foster 11–4–27–1; Pringle 9.5–1–32–7. *Second Innings*—Lever 40–12–94–3; Foster 33–7–86–0; Pringle 10–0–49–0; Gooch 56–9–173–1; Acfield 38–19–88–1; Pont 26–6–71–1; Fletcher 3–0–15–0; Gladwin 3–0–11–0; McEwan 2–0–8–1.

Essex

G. A. Gooch c Slack b Daniel	12	J. K. Lever c Emburey b Cowans	1
C. Gladwin c Downton b Cowans	61	N. A. Foster c Daniel b Williams	29
*K. W. R. Fletcher b Cowans	32	D. L. Acfield not out	4
K. S. McEwan c Ellis b Daniel	17	B 1, l-b 9, w 3, n-b 19	32
B. R. Hardie c Emburey b Williams	38		
D. R. Pringle lbw b Cowans	15		289
K. R. Pont c Downton b Williams	5		
†D. E. East b Daniel	43		

1/14 2/94 3/124
4/166 5/192 6/198
7/204 8/205 9/262

Bonus points – Essex 3, Middlesex 4.

Bowling: Daniel 16.5–1–64–3; Cowans 24–4–72–4; Williams 20–5–59–3; Edmonds 9–2–33–0; Gatting 8–3–13–0; Emburey 7–1–16–0; Slack 1–1–0–0.

Umpires: M. J. Kitchen and B. Leadbeater.

ESSEX v LEICESTERSHIRE

At Chelmsford, August 10, 11, 12. Drawn. Essex 4 pts, Leicestershire 7 pts. Davison, whose century in 223 minutes contained twelve boundaries, provided the backbone of the Leicestershire innings after they had won the toss. In the end, he perished against Phillip, who bowled with commendable hostility. Replying, Essex never came to terms with Ferris and Agnew (the latter joined the action after Cook had been summoned to join the England Test party), and were forced to follow on. Thanks to Gooch's first Championship hundred of the season, one which took him over five hours, and consistent support down the order, Essex comfortably saved the match.

Leicestershire

J. C. Balderstone lbw b Phillip	25	N. G. B. Cook b Phillip	14
I. P. Butcher lbw b Lever	1	L. B. Taylor b R. E. East	22
N. E. Briers lbw b Phillip	58	G. J. F. Ferris not out	10
B. F. Davison b Phillip	106	B 1, l-b 17, n-b 12	30
J. J. Whitaker c D. E. East b Phillip	0		
P. B. Clift lbw b Phillip	2		301
*†R. W. Tolchard c R. E. East b Turner	20		
J. F. Steele c Hardie b Acfield	13		

1/2 2/73 3/106
4/106 5/122 6/157
7/222 8/261 9/272

Bonus points – Leicestershire 3, Essex 4 (Score at 100 overs: 282-9).

Bowling: Lever 13–3–34–1; Phillip 33–9–92–6; Turner 20–3–48–1; R. E. East 9.4–2–27–1; Acfield 28–9–70–1.

Essex

G. A. Gooch c Butcher b Ferris	9	lbw b Balderstone	110
C. Gladwin b Clift	35	c Briers b Taylor	25
*K. W. R. Fletcher lbw b Ferris	0	lbw b Taylor	49
K. S. McEwan b Agnew	32	c Whitaker b Steele	51
B. R. Hardie c Steele b Ferris	18	c Butcher b Clift	45
N. Phillip b Agnew	6	c Tolchard b Ferris	20
S. Turner lbw b Agnew	0	lbw b Agnew	8
†D. E. East c Steele b Ferris	1	run out	11
R. E. East c Butcher b Ferris	8	b Butcher	25
J. K. Lever lbw b Ferris	1	c Agnew b Balderstone	28
D. L. Acfield not out	1	not out	1
L-b 7, w 1, n-b 10	18	L-b 6, w 1, n-b 14	21

1/16 2/16 3/78 4/84
5/99 6/99 7/107 8/126 9/128
129

1/43 2/144 3/245 4/257
5/294 6/309 7/333 8/346 9/390
394

Bonus points – Leicestershire 4.

Bowling: *First Innings*—Taylor 8–3–20–0; Ferris 12.5–3–43–6; Clift 10–6–14–1; Agnew 15–6–34–3. *Second Innings*—Taylor 25–8–50–2; Ferris 21–2–83–1; Clift 35–15–68–1; Agnew 16–3–60–1; Balderstone 21–11–26–2; Steele 36–12–83–1; Briers 1–1–0–0; Whitaker 2–1–1–0; Butcher 2–0–2–1.

Umpires: D. O. Oslear and M. J. Kitchen.

At Wellingborough, August 13, 15, 16. ESSEX beat NORTHAMPTONSHIRE by 128 runs.

At Chelmsford, August 17, 18, 19. ESSEX lost to NEW ZEALANDERS by 48 runs (See New Zealand tour section).

ESSEX v GLOUCESTERSHIRE

At Colchester, August 20, 22. Essex won by an innings and 37 runs. Essex 24 pts, Gloucestershire 2 pts. The visitors were soon left regretting their decision to bat on a lively strip as the Essex pace and seam attack, spearheaded by Phillip, routed them in fewer than 40 overs. Then the brilliant McEwan put them to the sword with a thrilling exhibition of strokeplay which brought him 32 4s in a shade over four hours. Broad resisted soundly when Gloucestershire went in again, but once he was gone Essex quickly brought their resistance to a close, winning with a day to spare.

Gloucestershire

A. W. Stovold c Hardie b Phillip	2	– c Pont b Lever 26
B. C. Broad c Gooch b Lever	0	– c D. E. East b Lever 109
P. Bainbridge c Fletcher b Phillip	11	– c Hardie b Acfield 29
P. W. Romaines c Phillip b Lever	12	– c Hardie b Lever 32
A. J. Wright c Fletcher b Phillip	29	– c Fletcher b Acfield 22
A. J. Hignell c Hardie b Phillip	0	– c Hardie b Lever 0
J. N. Shepherd lbw b Turner	1	– b Phillip 14
*D. A. Graveney c D. E. East b Phillip	8	– c Gladwin b Phillip 1
†R. C. Russell c D. E. East b Phillip	4	– not out 15
J. H. Childs b Lever	5	– c Lever b Phillip 0
G. E. Sainsbury not out	4	– c Gooch b Acfield.................... 6
L-b 5, n-b 1	6	L-b 10, n-b 1................ 11

1/3 2/3 3/22 4/34	82	1/52 2/125 3/200 4/211 265
5/34 6/35 7/52 8/64 9/73		5/211 6/233 7/243 8/244 9/244

Bonus points – Essex 4.

Bowling: First Innings—Lever 14.3–4–41–3; Phillip 15–4–19–6; Turner 10–3–16–1. *Second Innings*—Lever 22–2–90–4; Phillip 18–2–68–3; Acfield 34.5–11–67–3; Turner 10–3–29–0.

Essex

G. A. Gooch c Shepherd b Sainsbury .. 7	N. Phillip st Russell b Childs............. 0
C. Gladwin c Russell b Bainbridge 35	S. Turner not out............................ 14
B. R. Hardie c Stovold b Graveney..... 62	
K. S. McEwan b Bainbridge 181	B 1, l-b 2, n-b 3...................... 6
*K. W. R. Fletcher c Russell b Bainbridge. 1	1/16 2/67 3/168 (6 wkts dec.) 384
K. R. Pont not out........................... 78	4/169 5/347 6/348

†D. E. East, J. K. Lever and D. L. Acfield did not bat.

Bonus points – Essex 4, Gloucestershire 2.

Bowling: Sainsbury 18–4–67–1; Shepherd 12–1–84–0; Bainbridge 26.5–6–110–3; Childs 19–0–81–1; Graveney 20–8–36–1.

Umpires: W. E. Alley and C. T. Spencer.

ESSEX v WORCESTERSHIRE

At Colchester, August 24, 25. Essex won by an innings and 58 runs. Essex 24 pts, Worcestershire 3 pts. McEwan once more underlined his brilliance in becoming the first Essex player to exceed 2,000 runs in a season since D. J. Insole in 1955. He also became the first batsman of the summer to reach this milestone as he plundered two 6s and 25 4s in 288 minutes. Gooch also scored a century, in just over three hours, after Worcestershire, put in, had crumbled against Lever and Phillip. The visitors showed much greater fight in their second innings, owing chiefly to Patel whose 95, made in 65 balls, contained two 6s and fourteen 4s.

Worcestershire

M. S. A. McEvoy c East b Phillip	15	– c Gladwin b Turner	13
M. S. Scott b Lever	23	– (5) b Phillip	21
J. A. Ormrod b Lever	3	– c East b Lever	1
*D. N. Patel b Phillip	3	– b Phillip	95
T. S. Curtis c Gooch b Phillip	4	– lbw b Lever	0
M. J. Weston c Gooch b Phillip	28	– (2) b Lever	18
†D. J. Humphries c McEwan b Phillip	0	– lbw b Acfield	34
J. D. Inchmore b Lever	0	– b Acfield	51
R. M. Ellcock c Hardie b Phillip	0	– c Fletcher b Phillip	12
S. P. Perryman c East b Lever	3	– not out	4
A. P. Pridgeon not out	2	– lbw b Acfield	10
L-b 1, n-b 2	3	L-b 4, n-b 8	12

1/36 2/41 3/46 4/50   84   1/34 2/34 3/38 4/38   271
5/50 6/50 7/59 8/62 9/76   5/146 6/153 7/215 8/250 9/256

Bonus points – Essex 4.

Bowling: *First Innings*—Lever 17–7–43–4; Phillip 16.5–3–38–6. *Second Innings*—Lever 13–2–80–3; Phillip 15–2–69–3; Turner 6–1–22–1; Acfield 16–0–88–3.

Essex

G. A. Gooch lbw b Patel	103	S. Turner c Curtis b Patel	30
C. Gladwin lbw b Ellcock	20	†D. E. East run out	2
B. R. Hardie lbw b Inchmore	13		
K. S. McEwan not out	189	B 1, l-b 5, n-b 1	7
*K. W. R. Fletcher b Patel	2		
K. R. Pont c and b Inchmore	29	1/41 2/65 3/226 4/248 (8 wkts dec.) 413
N. Phillip c Pridgeon b Perryman	18	5/327 6/352 7/398 8/413

J. K. Lever and D. L. Acfield did not bat.

Bonus points – Essex 4, Worcestershire 3.

Bowling: Ellcock 7–0–51–1; Pridgeon 22–1–90–0; Inchmore 18–1–73–2; Perryman 19.5–1–93–1; Patel 29–7–99–3.

Umpires: C. T. Spencer and B. Leadbeater.

At The Oval, August 27, 29, 30. ESSEX lost to SURREY by seven wickets.

At Manchester, August 31, September 1, 2. ESSEX drew with LANCASHIRE.

ESSEX v YORKSHIRE

At Chelmsford, September 10, 12, 13. Drawn. Essex 7 pts, Yorkshire 6 pts. Fletcher had no hesitation in inserting his rivals on what proved to be a green and spiteful pitch. Boycott and Moxon batted with great determination, but once they were out only Love offered any real resistance against an attack magnificently spearheaded by Lever, who, during Yorkshire's first innings, reached 100 wickets for the season. Gooch, despite a broken finger which forced him to retire hurt before he had scored, returned at No. 6 to perform with great authority in an innings lasting 152 minutes and containing a 6 and fifteen 4s. In between stoppages for rain and bad light, the Essex pace and seam attack dismissed Yorkshire for 220, the last wicket falling as news came through that Middlesex's match at Trent Bridge had been abandoned, thus confirming Essex as the 1983 champions. It was therefore immaterial that rain prevented them from attempting to score 137 for victory in 30 minutes and twenty overs.

Yorkshire

G. Boycott lbw b Lever	37	– lbw b Phillip	23
M. D. Moxon c McEwan b Lever	38	– b Turner	58
K. Sharp c Gooch b Lever	4	– c Turner b Lever	23
S. N. Hartley c Gooch b Pringle	0	– c D. E. East b Turner	18
J. D. Love b Phillip	55	– b Turner	20
†D. L. Bairstow c East b Lever	9	– lbw b Lever	12
P. Carrick b Lever	26	– b Lever	15
G. B. Stevenson b Lever	0	– b Turner	11
S. J. Dennis b Lever	0	– not out	11
S. D. Fletcher not out	1	– c Gooch b Lever	1
*R. Illingworth b Phillip	16	– b Phillip	3
B 7, l-b 7, w 2, n-b 2	18	B 6, l-b 14, w 5	25
	204		**220**

1/86 2/90 3/91 4/91   1/54 2/88 3/136 4/137
5/115 6/182 7/186 8/186 9/186   5/160 6/192 7/194 8/208 9/217

Bonus points – Yorkshire 2, Essex 4.

Bowling: *First Innings*—Lever 26–8–78–7; Phillip 13.2–2–53–2; Pringle 23–8–47–1; Turner 5–1–8–0. *Second Innings*—Lever 28–8–85–4; Phillip 17.3–3–43–2; Pringle 9–0–25–0; Acfield 5–0–11–0; Turner 9–3–31–4.

Essex

G. A. Gooch c Sharp b Dennis	111	†D. E. East c Hartley b Bairstow	40
C. Gladwin b Fletcher	31	J. K. Lever not out	10
B. R. Hardie b Dennis	10	D. L. Acfield c Hartley b Fletcher	0
*K. W. R. Fletcher b Stevenson	0		
K. S. McEwan c Bairstow b Dennis	9	B 9, l-b 16, n-b 7	32
D. R. Pringle b Fletcher	30		
N. Phillip lbw b Fletcher	4	1/31 2/32 3/56 4/58	**288**
S. Turner lbw b Stevenson	11	5/142 6/152 7/185 8/255 9/287	

Bonus points – Essex 3, Yorkshire 4.

Bowling: Dennis 17–2–69–3; Stevenson 14–3–53–2; Fletcher 16.4–2–71–4; Moxon 8–0–31–0; Carrick 4–0–12–0; Illingworth 1–0–2–0; Bairstow 4–1–18–1.

Umpires: P. J. Eele and R. Julian.

GLAMORGAN

President: His Honour Judge Rowe Harding
Chairman: O. S. Wheatley
Chairman, Cricket Committee: G. Craven
Secretary: P. G. Carling
  6 High Street, Cardiff CF1 2PW
  (Telephone: 0222-29956)
Captain: M. W. W. Selvey
Coach: A. Jones

In 1983 Glamorgan achieved a marginal improvement upon the previous season by moving up one place in the Schweppes County Championship table, from sixteenth to fifteenth. In the John Player League they remained in tenth position, which was disappointing after an impressive start, and in the other competitions they achieved little. They won only two Championship matches, though that was one more than in 1982.

There was no real change in performance or outlook, although there were changes in administration. The loss on the season was in excess of £100,000. It was the first season for a new captain, Mike Selvey, and a new secretary, Philip Carling. In 1984, by when they will both have settled in, a big effort will be needed on and off the field to improve the county's fortunes.

At the end of the 1983 season three well-known names disappeared from the first-team list: veteran opening batsman, Alan Jones, retired, Malcolm Nash was not re-engaged and wicket-keeper Eifion Jones has received a one-year contract and a testimonial, and will probably serve mainly in the Second team. One of the county's longest-serving and most able administrators, Richard Davies, also retired.

Alan Jones retired following magnificent service to Glamorgan. He made his début in 1957 and in 27 years amassed 34,056 runs in first-class cricket for the county, a Glamorgan record. His sense of loyalty and modesty made him a much-loved figure in Welsh cricket, which he will no doubt continue to be as coach. Nash required only nine more wickets to reach 1,000 in first-class cricket and Eifion Jones has had over 900 wicket-keeping victims in his 23-year career. At the end of October, the 37-year-old all-rounder formerly of Northamptonshire, John Steele, was signed from Leicestershire on a three-year contract. When Glamorgan take the field in 1984 it will be, therefore, with a new-look side, which will include Younis Ahmed, the 35-year-old Pakistani batsman signed at the end of the 1983 season on a three-year contract.

In 1983 four batsmen passed 1,000 runs – Alan Jones, Rodney Ontong, Alan Lewis Jones and John Hopkins, Ontong enjoying an especially good summer with both bat and ball. Alan Lewis Jones made strides and registered eight half-centuries. Stephen Henderson, the 1983 Cambridge captain, was a late acquisition – a forcing left-handed batsman who played with some success and enterprise in the last ten matches of the season, scoring a century against Warwickshire at Edgbaston.

Javed Miandad, partly through injuries and World Cup calls, played in only four Championship matches, scoring only 114 runs. Owing to the regulations concerning overseas players, Glamorgan were unable to play both Miandad and Winston Davis in the same match, a problem which was a constant worry.

The bowling was not strong, as a result of which the early grip achieved in many matches was sacrificed through a lack of variety and penetration. The long tradition of successful off-spin bowling, from which Glamorgan have derived so much success, was absent. Davis, though erratic, topped the averages, but he conceded in the region of 250 no-balls. Selvey had the satisfaction of being the leading wicket-taker, but he, too, was expensive.

Terry Davies took over the wicket-keeping duties from Eifion Jones in mid-season and performed ably, but, overall, the fielding was inconsistent. Membership remained stable, but gate receipts from three-day matches were poor. The Supporters Club continued to aid the club financially, though their contribution was less than in 1982 because of the acute economic position in the industrial areas of South Wales. There will be need of a curb in spending to meet the challenge of the future as the cost of maintaining first-class cricket increases with the passing of each season. – J.B.G.T.

GLAMORGAN 1983

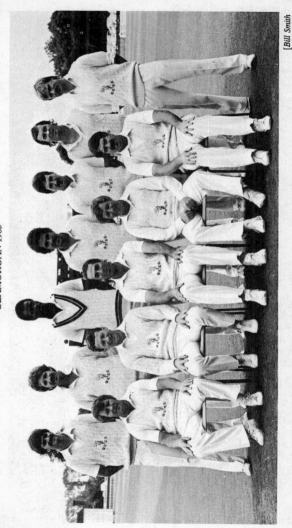

[*Bill Smith*]

Back row: G. C. Holmes, A. H. Wilkins, W. W. Davis, R. C. Ontong, A. L. Jones, C. J. C. Rowe, D. A. Francis. *Front row*: E. W. Jones, B. J. Lloyd, M. W. W. Selvey (*captain*), A. Jones, J. A. Hopkins.

GLAMORGAN RESULTS

All first-class matches – Played 26: Won 2, Lost 10, Drawn 14.

County Championship matches – Played 24: Won 2, Lost 10, Drawn 12.

Bonus points – Batting 45, Bowling 64.

Competition placings – Schweppes County Championship, 15th; NatWest Bank Trophy, 2nd round; Benson and Hedges Cup, 3rd in Group D; John Player League, 10th.

COUNTY CHAMPIONSHIP AVERAGES

BATTING

	Birthplace	M	I	NO	R	HI	Avge
R. C. Ontongᶜ	Johannesburg, SA	24	42	8	1,259	112	37.02
A. L. Jonesᶜ............	Alltwen	22	39	7	1,034	99	32.31
A. Jonesᶜ...............	Velindre	20	36	2	1,020	105	30.00
S. P. Henderson	Oxford	10	16	2	411	135*	29.35
G. C. Holmes	Newcastle-on-Tyne	3	6	2	116	46	29.00
J. A. Hopkinsᶜ........	Maesteg	23	42	2	1,087	116	27.17
D. A. Francisᶜ	Clydach	22	39	5	903	89*	26.55
J. Derrick..............	Cwmaman	4	4	2	48	24*	24.00
T. Davies	St Albans	11	15	4	260	69*	23.63
C. J. C. Roweᶜ	Hong Kong	20	32	2	682	82	22.73
H. Morris..............	Cardiff	8	14	3	228	34	20.72
E. W. Jonesᶜ...........	Velindre	13	18	5	256	39	19.69
Javed Miandadᶜ	Karachi, Pakistan	4	6	0	114	89	19.00
A. H. Wilkins	Cardiff	13	15	3	185	54	15.41
W. W. Davis...........	St Vincent, WI	15	18	9	135	39*	15.00
B. J. Lloydᶜ	Neath	12	12	2	135	38	13.50
J. G. Thomas..........	Garnswllt	7	9	1	96	23	12.00
M. W. W. Selveyᶜ ...	Chiswick	22	24	3	250	63	11.90
S. R. Barwick	Neath	7	7	4	31	22*	10.33

Also batted: M. A. Nashᶜ (*Abergavenny*) (4 matches) 27*, 2.

Signifies not out.   ᶜ Denotes county cap.

BOWLING

	O	M	R	W	Avge	BB
W. W. Davis...........	452.4	105	1,389	52	26.71	7–70
J. G. Thomas..........	129.5	28	472	15	31.46	5–78
M. W. W. Selvey.....	597.4	126	1,914	56	34.17	5–37
R. C. Ontong.........	611	122	1,978	54	36.62	6–64
C. J. C. Rowe........	455.4	85	1,528	37	41.29	4–29
B. J. Lloyd	261.5	36	842	18	46.77	4–93
S. R. Barwick	129.3	21	532	11	48.36	8–42
A. H. Wilkins	197	24	795	10	79.50	2–82

Also bowled: J. Derrick 8–1–31–0; D. A. Francis 4–0–25–0; S. P. Henderson 8–0–65–2; J. A. Hopkins 4–0–23–0; Javed Miandad 2–0–11–0; A. L. Jones 3–0–25–0; H. Morris 3.5–0–23–0; M. A. Nash 75–22–226–3.

The following played a total of seven three-figure innings for Glamorgan in County Championship matches – R. C. Ontong 3, J. A. Hopkins 2, S. P. Henderson 1, A. Jones 1.

At Cambridge, April 20, 21, 22. GLAMORGAN drew with CAMBRIDGE UNIVERSITY.

At Manchester, April 30, May 2, 3. GLAMORGAN drew with LANCASHIRE.

GLAMORGAN v ESSEX

At Cardiff, May 4, 5, 6. Drawn. Glamorgan 5 pts, Essex 6 pts. The first day, remarkable in such a wet May, provided a full day's cricket with Essex declaring with full bonus points and Glamorgan replying with 30 for one. Fletcher and McEwan, dropped at 26 and 60, provided 179 for the third wicket after the home seam bowlers had made early inroads. Glamorgan advanced to 62 for one on a curtailed second day, and on the third Miandad and new captain Selvey batted extremely well in a fourth-wicket stand of 124 to avert a crisis and to enable Glamorgan to achieve a third batting point. Selvey's 63 was his best Championship score, his previous highest, 57, having also been made against Essex.

Essex

G. A. Gooch c Miandad b Selvey	13	D. R. Pringle b Rowe	3
B. R. Hardie c Hopkins b Wilkins	0	N. Phillip c Ontong b Lloyd	25
*K. W. R. Fletcher not out	151	B 2, l-b 6, w 3, n-b 3	14
K. S. McEwan st E. W. Jones			
b Lloyd	107	1/2 2/20 3/199 (6 wkts dec.)	325
K. R. Pont lbw b Rowe	12	4/246 5/266 6/325	

†D. E. East, R. E. East, J. K. Lever and D. L. Acfield did not bat.

Bonus points – Essex 4, Glamorgan 2 (Score at 100 overs: 309-5).

Bowling: Thomas 6–1–33–0; Wilkins 15–4–40–1; Selvey 10–0–44–1; Ontong 30–6–72–0; Lloyd 28.5–4–81–2; Rowe 14–2–30–2; Miandad 2–0–11–0.

Glamorgan

A. Jones b Lever	13	R. C. Ontong not out	9
J. A. Hopkins c D. E. East b Lever	25		
*M. W. W. Selvey c Pringle b Lever	63	B 2, l-b 8, n-b 15	25
D. A. Francis lbw b Pringle	0		
Javed Miandad c Fletcher b Acfield	89	1/25 2/71 (5 wkts dec.)	255
C. J. C. Rowe not out	31	3/72 4/196 5/234	

B. J. Lloyd, J. G. Thomas, †E. W. Jones and A. H. Wilkins did not bat.

Bonus points – Glamorgan 3, Essex 2.

Bowling: Lever 28–9–61–3; Phillip 17–1–50–0; Pringle 12–2–22–1; Gooch 10–2–29–0; R. E. East 17–6–38–0; Acfield 10–0–31–1.

Umpires: W. E. Alley and K. E. Palmer.

At Oxford, May 11, 12, 13. GLAMORGAN drew with OXFORD UNIVERSITY.

At Lord's, May 25, 26, 27. GLAMORGAN lost to MIDDLESEX by an innings and 79 runs.

GLAMORGAN v GLOUCESTERSHIRE

At Swansea, May 28, 30, 31. Gloucestershire won by three wickets. Gloucestershire 18 pts, Glamorgan 3 pts. Only 56 overs were possible on the first day, when after being put in Glamorgan made steady progress to reach 151 without loss. Rain again curtailed play on the Monday, but not before Glamorgan were able to build on their best opening stand for five years and declare at 250 for five, to which Gloucestershire replied with an unbroken first-wicket stand of 125. Hopkins hit three 6s, a 5 and twelve 4s in his first century of the season. Gloucestershire's overnight declaration allowed Selvey to set them eventually 301 to win in two and a half hours plus twenty overs, and with Zaheer leading the way with fourteen 4s in his 116, they reached their target with four balls remaining.

Glamorgan

A. Jones c Childs b Shepherd	79	– b Bainbridge	8
J. A. Hopkins b Childs	116	– c Russell b Bainbridge	7
D. A. Francis run out	5	– b Bainbridge	66
Javed Miandad c Russell b Shepherd	0	– c Graveney b Dudleston	13
R. C. Ontong not out	19	– not out	31
A. L. Jones lbw b Shepherd	2	– st Russell b Dudleston	11
†E. W. Jones not out	9	– b Dudleston	0
M. A. Nash (did not bat)		– not out	27
L-b 14, w 2, n-b 4	20	L-b 6, w 4, n-b 2	12

1/160 2/219   (5 wkts dec.) 250   1/14 2/29 3/72   (6 wkts dec.) 175
3/219 4/219 5/229   4/108 5/135 6/135

*M. W. W. Selvey, B. J. Lloyd and A. H. Wilkins did not bat.

Bonus points – Glamorgan 3, Gloucestershire 2.

Bowling: *First Innings*—Sainsbury 15-1-46-0; Lawrence 11-1-43-0; Bainbridge 17-8-24-0; Shepherd 34-9-83-3; Childs 10.2-3-34-1. *Second Innings*—Shepherd 6-2-13-0; Bainbridge 23-6-67-3; Dudleston 17.5-3-83-3.

Gloucestershire

B. C. Broad not out	52	– lbw b Selvey	32
A. W. Stovold not out	69	– c Miandad b Ontong	39
Zaheer Abbas (did not bat)		– b Lloyd	116
P. Bainbridge (did not bat)		– c Miandad b Selvey	13
J. N. Shepherd (did not bat)		– c Lloyd b Selvey	20
*D. A. Graveney (did not bat)		– c Miandad b Selvey	35
B. Dudleston (did not bat)		– not out	35
†R. C. Russell (did not bat)		– c E. W. Jones b Lloyd	0
J. H. Childs (did not bat)		– not out	3
L-b 1, w 1, n-b 2	4	B 4, l-b 6, w 1	11

(no wkt dec.) 125   1/57 2/136 3/184   (7 wkts) 304
                         4/224 5/261 6/271 7/279

G. E. Sainsbury and D. V. Lawrence did not bat.

Bowling: *First Innings*—Nash 8-2-29-0; Selvey 5-1-21-0; Ontong 11-1-38-0; Wilkins 4-0-20-0; Lloyd 3.4-0-13-0. *Second Innings*—Nash 14-3-56-0; Selvey 24-2-125-4; Ontong 14-1-56-1; Wilkins 8-0-39-0; Lloyd 3.2-0-17-2.

Umpires: J. H. Harris and R. Palmer.

At Middlesbrough, June 4, 6, 7. GLAMORGAN drew with YORKSHIRE.

GLAMORGAN v WARWICKSHIRE

At Cardiff, June 11, 13, 14. Warwickshire won by five wickets. Warwickshire 18 pts, Glamorgan 2 pts. Glamorgan, having won the toss, batted for four overs and 6 runs before rain ended play. On the second day they continued to 202 for six before declaring, whereupon Warwickshire made 116 for one with a century second-wicket stand between David Smith and Amiss. After Warwickshire had declared overnight, Glamorgan batted for 57 overs to score 206 for two on an easy-paced wicket. This set Warwickshire 293 to win and it was agreed to cancel tea to help obtain a result. Lloyd and Smith got the visitors away to a good start, Humpage struck about him to good effect (he and Old put on 78 in eleven overs) and Warwickshire got home with 23 balls remaining.

Glamorgan

A. Jones b Hogg	3	– retired hurt	37
J. A. Hopkins run out	44	– b P. A. Smith	34
D. A. Francis lbw b Old	18	– c and b Asif Din	40
R. C. Ontong b Hogg	38	– not out	61
A. L. Jones lbw b Hogg	18	– not out	17
J. Derrick not out	24		
J. G. Thomas b Old	18		
†E. W. Jones not out	15		
L-b 10, w 1, n-b 13	24	L-b 8, w 1, n-b 8	17

1/8 2/40 3/113   (6 wkts dec.) 202   1/93 2/163   (2 wkts dec.) 206
4/135 5/147 6/183

*M. W. W. Selvey, B. J. Lloyd and S. R. Barwick did not bat.

Bonus points – Glamorgan 2, Warwickshire 2.

Bowling: *First Innings*—Hogg 20–5–28–2; Old 23–6–58–2; P. A. Smith 9–1–26–0; Ferreira 16–6–35–0; Gifford 9.3–2–31–0. *Second Innings*—Hogg 8–1–28–0; Old 5–3–5–0; Ferreira 7–1–24–0; P. A. Smith 6–0–23–1; Asif Din 15–0–52–1; Gifford 16–1–57–0.

Warwickshire

T. A. Lloyd b Thomas	5	– c Selvey b Lloyd	43
K. D. Smith not out	54	– c and b Lloyd	58
D. L. Amiss not out	54	– c Hopkins b Lloyd	15
G. W. Humpage (did not bat)		– b Thomas	79
Asif Din (did not bat)		– c E. W. Jones b Lloyd	40
C. M. Old (did not bat)		– not out	44
A. M. Ferreira (did not bat)		– not out	4
L-b 2, n-b 1	3	B 1, l-b 4, w 1, n-b 4	10

1/16   (1 wkt dec.) 116   1/87 2/112 3/123   (5 wkts) 293
                                             4/199 5/277

P. A. Smith, †G. A. Tedstone, *N. Gifford and W. Hogg did not bat.

Bowling: *First Innings*—Thomas 8–2–28–1; Barwick 6–2–15–0; Selvey 3–0–13–0; Lloyd 4–0–8–0; Ontong 9–0–35–0; Derrick 4–0–14–0. *Second Innings*—Thomas 11.1–0–62–1; Barwick 2–0–17–0; Ontong 15–0–78–0; Lloyd 21–3–93–4; Selvey 11–3–33–0.

Umpires: N. T. Plews and C. T. Spencer.

GLAMORGAN v SOMERSET

At Swansea, June 15, 16, 17. Drawn. Glamorgan 4 pts, Somerset 7 pts. Despite their weakened side, with six players away, Somerset batted all day to reach 323 for nine after Glamorgan had put them in. Rain delayed the start on the second day but Somerset declared at their overnight score and had Glamorgan in tatters at 141 for nine by the close, thanks mainly to the fast-medium bowling of seventeen-year-old Gary Palmer. Glamorgan followed on next day but easily saved the match through a fine first-wicket stand of 120 by Hopkins and A. L. Jones, who just failed to reach his first Championship century.

Somerset

R. L. Ollis lbw b Thomas	1	
*P. M. Roebuck c E. W. Jones b Nash..	40	
P. A. Slocombe c E. W. Jones b Ontong..	37	
P. W. Denning c Hopkins b Ontong....	2	
N. F. M. Popplewell c A. L. Jones b Thomas.	64	
J. W. Lloyds run out	34	
D. Breakwell not out	55	

G. V. Palmer b Thomas	0
†T. Gard lbw b Thomas	51
C. H. Dredge b Thomas	0
P. H. L. Wilson not out	0
B 5, l-b 13, w 4, n-b 17	39
	—
1/6 2/76 3/83 4/110 (9 wkts dec.)	323
5/186 6/223 7/223 8/323 9/323	

Bonus points – Somerset 3, Glamorgan 3 (Score at 100 overs: 274-7).

Bowling: Nash 28–10–69–1; Thomas 26–6–78–5; Barwick 27–5–85–0; Lloyd 2–1–5–0; Ontong 26–12–47–2.

Glamorgan

J. A. Hopkins c Gard b Palmer	12	– b Lloyds	65
A. L. Jones lbw b Palmer	0	– c Gard b Lloyds	99
D. A. Francis b Wilson	28	– c Lloyds b Breakwell	9
R. C. Ontong b Palmer	0	– not out	12
G. C. Holmes c Dredge b Popplewell	10	– not out	1
J. Derrick c Gard b Palmer	0		
J. G. Thomas lbw b Dredge	12		
†E. W. Jones st Gard b Lloyds	16		
*B. J. Lloyd b Wilson	38		
M. A. Nash c Wilson b Lloyds	2		
S. R. Barwick not out	22		
B 9, l-b 4, w 1	14	L-b 5, w 1, n-b 1	7

1/0 2/17 3/18 4/35	154	1/120 2/156 3/190 (3 wkts)	193
5/37 6/71 7/71 8/103 9/123			

Bonus points – Glamorgan 1, Somerset 4.

Bowling: *First Innings*—Wilson 13.4–4–25–2; Palmer 19–5–58–4; Dredge 23–10–38–1; Popplewell 5–3–6–1; Lloyds 13–8–13–2; Breakwell 1–1–0–0. *Second Innings*—Wilson 8–3–21–0; Palmer 11–3–27–0; Popplewell 16–3–32–0; Dredge 9–3–12–0; Lloyds 28–12–50–2; Breakwell 23–1–41–1; Slocombe 2–1–1–0; Ollis 1–0–2–0.

Umpires: N. T. Plews and C. T. Spencer.

GLAMORGAN v WORCESTERSHIRE

At Abergavenny, June 22, 23, 24. Drawn. Glamorgan 1 pt, Worcestershire 3 pts. After glorious sunshine on the first day, when over 400 runs were scored, rain on the second and third days allowed only nine and twelve overs respectively. This was unlucky for the local club, which was hosting its first Championship match. Worcestershire's large total was built around a hard-hitting century by Neale (three 6s, fifteen 4s) following an excellent first-wicket stand of 136 by Ormrod and Weston. Glamorgan, in their few periods of batting, were never happy against the pace of Warner and Ellcock.

Worcestershire

J. A. Ormrod lbw b Selvey	78	A. E. Warner lbw b Ontong	9
M. J. Weston run out	79		
*P. A. Neale c Nash b Ontong	135	B 1, l-b 3, w 1, n-b 5	10
D. N. Patel b Nash	7		
D. B. D'Oliveira c and b Ontong	42	1/136 2/190 3/207 (6 wkts dec.)	394
M. S. Scott not out	34	4/298 5/381 6/394	

†D. J. Humphries, R. K. Illingworth, R. M. Ellcock and A. P. Pridgeon did not bat.

Bonus points – Worcestershire 3, Glamorgan 1 (Score at 100 overs: 298-4).

Bowling: Nash 14–3–45–1; Selvey 27–6–70–1; Ontong 28–6–98–3; Rowe 24–3–95–0; Lloyd 26–4–76–0.

Glamorgan

J. A. Hopkins c Patel b Warner	8
A. L. Jones not out	31
D. A. Francis b Warner	7
H. Morris not out	7
B 4, l-b 3, w 3, n-b 13	23
1/18 2/61 (2 wkts)	76

C. J. C. Rowe, R. C. Ontong, J. Derrick, †E. W. Jones, *M. W. W. Selvey, B. J. Lloyd and M. A. Nash did not bat.

Bowling: Ellcock 12–2–26–0; Warner 12–4–25–2; Pridgeon 0.3–0–2–0.

Umpires: C. Cook and P. J. Eele.

At Hinckley, June 25, 27, 28. GLAMORGAN lost to LEICESTERSHIRE by 180 runs.

At Canterbury, July 2, 4, 5. GLAMORGAN drew with KENT.

GLAMORGAN v SUSSEX

At Cardiff, July 9, 11, 12. Drawn. Glamorgan 6 pts, Sussex 3 pts. Put in to bat, Glamorgan scored very slowly, Alan Jones reaching a painstaking century, but with the promising Morris he shared a fourth-wicket stand of 102. This was the pattern of a match dominated by medium-paced bowling and ending in inevitable stalemate.

Glamorgan

A. Jones c Imran b Waller	105	– c Reeve b le Roux	19
J. A. Hopkins b Reeve	22	– lbw b Reeve	6
R. C. Ontong b Pigott	24	– c Gould b le Roux	17
A. L. Jones b Pigott	0	– c and b Waller	5
H. Morris c and b Barclay	24	– run out	0
D. A. Francis c Wells b Barclay	6	– not out	46
C. J. C. Rowe c Gould b Pigott	16	– c Barclay b Reeve	52
†E. W. Jones c Waller b Pigott	18	– not out	21
*M. W. W. Selvey c Gould b le Roux	3		
A. H. Wilkins b le Roux	0		
W. W. Davis not out	0		
B 3, l-b 11, w 3, n-b 9	26	B 2, l-b 3, w 1, n-b 7	13
1/44 2/95 3/95 4/197	244	1/26 2/31 3/43 (6 wkts dec.)	179
5/199 6/206 7/234 8/242 9/244		4/50 5/52 6/118	

Bonus points – Glamorgan 2, Sussex 2 (Score at 100 overs: 220-6).

Bowling: *First Innings*—le Roux 20–3–57–2; Pigott 21.3–5–48–4; Reeve 17–4–29–1; Wells 6–4–2–0; Waller 28–10–44–1; Barclay 17–7–38–2. *Second Innings*—le Roux 13–4–27–2; Pigott 8–0–35–0; Waller 38–17–50–1; Reeve 21–10–28–2; Wells 8–0–26–0.

Sussex

G. D. Mendis c Wilkins b Selvey	9	– c Hopkins b Selvey	55
J. R. P. Heath lbw b Selvey	0	– (3) lbw b Davis	28
*J. R. T. Barclay c A. L. Jones b Davis	7	– (2) run out	35
Imran Khan c Hopkins b Selvey	23	– b Selvey	63
P. W. G. Parker c A. Jones b Davis	5	– b Ontong	1
C. M. Wells lbw b Davis	23	– lbw b Selvey	3
†I. J. Gould c Morris b Ontong	47	– not out	17
G. S. le Roux c and b Selvey	15	– c sub b Selvey	4
D. A. Reeve c A. L. Jones b Ontong	6	– not out	2
A. C. S. Pigott not out	5		
C. E. Waller b Selvey	0		
L-b 2, n-b 21	23	B 8, l-b 2, n-b 6	16

1/0 2/18 3/28 4/46   163   1/62 2/125 3/133   (7 wkts) 224
5/50 6/120 7/143 8/155 9/163   4/156 5/165 6/200 7/208

Bonus points – Sussex 1, Glamorgan 4.

Bowling: *First Innings*—Davis 19–7–41–3; Selvey 13.5–1–51–5; Ontong 15–5–45–2; Wilkins 1–0–3–0. *Second Innings*—Davis 16.4–1–48–1; Selvey 19–3–61–4; Wilkins 8–1–29–0; Ontong 20–5–70–1.

Umpires: A. Jepson and A. G. T. Whitehead.

GLAMORGAN v LANCASHIRE

At Swansea, July 13, 14, 15. Drawn. Glamorgan 6 pts, Lancashire 5 pts. Lancashire, put in, were in serious trouble before Simmons cracked a hard-hit century with two 6s and sixteen 4s. Lancashire reached 193 and in Glamorgan's reply of 243 Maynard held six catches behind the wicket. On the last day when Glamorgan were set to get 318 in 210 minutes he took his total to eight. The match ended with Francis defending stubbornly.

Lancashire

D. Lloyd c Hopkins b Davis	5	– c E. W. Jones b Davis	4
K. A. Hayes c A. L. Jones b Selvey	21	– lbw b Davis	32
F. C. Hayes c E. W. Jones b Davis	0	– c Hopkins b Ontong	30
*J. Abrahams c Morris b Selvey	6	– (5) c and b Lloyd	85
N. H. Fairbrother b Selvey	4	– (6) c Francis b Lloyd	40
I. Cockbain c A. L. Jones b Davis	14	– (4) c Ontong b Lloyd	22
†C. Maynard c Morris b Davis	6	– c A. L. Jones b Selvey	55
J. Simmons c E. W. Jones b Davis	104	– c E. W. Jones b Davis	22
M. Watkinson b Ontong	0	– not out	25
I. Folley b Selvey	10	– not out	15
L. L. McFarlane not out	7		
L-b 2, w 2, n-b 12	16	B 6, l-b 10, w 2, n-b 19	37

1/8 2/10 3/39 4/44   193   1/5 2/61 3/95 4/99   (8 wkts dec.) 367
5/51 6/64 7/71 8/74 9/135   5/199 6/292 7/308 8/331

Bonus points – Lancashire 1, Glamorgan 4.

Bowling: *First Innings*—Davis 22–9–64–5; Selvey 18–5–48–4; Ontong 11–5–24–1; Lloyd 14–2–41–0. *Second Innings*—Davis 25.5–5–82–3; Selvey 26–5–101–1; Ontong 24–4–65–1; Rowe 5–0–17–0; Lloyd 21–6–65–3.

Glamorgan

A. Jones c Folley b McFarlane	43	– c Maynard b McFarlane	0
J. A. Hopkins c Maynard b Watkinson	21	– c Abrahams b Simmons	23
R. C. Ontong c and b Simmons	20	– c K. A. Hayes b McFarlane	6
A. L. Jones c Maynard b Watkinson	23	– c Maynard b Simmons	31
H. Morris c Maynard b Watkinson	9	– c Cockbain b Simmons	4
B. J. Lloyd c Maynard b Watkinson	12		
D. A. Francis c Maynard b Watkinson	43	– (6) not out	45
C. J. C. Rowe c Abrahams b Simmons	8	– (7) c F. C. Hayes b Watkinson	43
†E. W. Jones c Lloyd b Abrahams	33	– (8) not out	37
*M. W. W. Selvey c Maynard b Watkinson	6		
W. W. Davis not out	0		
L-b 9, w 8, n-b 8	25	B 5, l-b 5, w 2, n-b 5	17

1/57 2/81 3/93 4/109   243   1/0 2/20 3/57   (6 wkts) 206
5/144 6/147 7/156 8/237 9/243   4/65 5/71 6/139

Bonus points – Glamorgan 2, Lancashire 4.

Bowling: *First Innings*—McFarlane 16–2–72–1; Watkinson 27.1–9–69–6; Folley 9–2–29–0; Simmons 24–15–39–2; Abrahams 8–4–8–1; Lloyd 3–2–1–0. *Second Innings*—McFarlane 14–2–59–2; Watkinson 14–3–47–1; Folley 3–0–18–0; Simmons 19.3–9–25–3; Lloyd 8–4–13–0; Abrahams 5–1–27–0.

Umpires: P. J. Eele and A. G. T. Whitehead.

At Southend, July 16, 18, 19. GLAMORGAN lost to ESSEX by an innings and 3 runs.

At Worcester, July 27, 28, 29. GLAMORGAN beat WORCESTERSHIRE by seven wickets.

GLAMORGAN v SURREY

At Swansea, July 30, August 1, 2. Glamorgan won by five wickets. Glamorgan 23 pts, Surrey 6 pts. Surrey scored 303 off 58.5 overs on the first day with Lynch striking five 6s in his 90 after they had been 99 for five. Glamorgan replied with 107 for one and on the second day reached 362 with most batsmen getting runs. Batting a second time, Surrey declared at 340 for four, Butcher scoring 128 in only 134 balls with two 6s and 21 4s. Glamorgan, with 282 to get in three hours, prospered through a fine century by Ontong (five 6s and twelve 4s) and a hard-hit 77 from A. L. Jones. Needing 134 in the last twenty overs, Glamorgan won with 22 deliveries remaining, their first home success of the Championship season.

Surrey

A. R. Butcher b Selvey	29	– b Rowe	128
A. Needham c Davies b Selvey	3	– lbw b Barwick	6
D. M. Smith c and b Selvey	35	– not out	131
*R. D. V. Knight c and b Ontong	17		
M. A. Lynch lbw b Rowe	90	– (4) c Jones b Henderson	18
†C. J. Richards c Henderson b Ontong	2	– not out	37
D. J. Thomas b Rowe	31	– (5) c Hopkins b Henderson	1
G. Monkhouse c Davies b Davis	46		
S. T. Clarke c Morris b Ontong	18		
P. I. Pocock not out	0		
I. J. Curtis lbw b Ontong	0		
B 2, l-b 12, w 6, n-b 12	32	B 4, l-b 3, w 1, n-b 11	19

1/35 2/52 3/97 4/97   303   1/58 2/180   (4 wkts dec.) 340
5/99 6/156 7/283 8/302 9/303   3/209 4/211

Bonus points – Surrey 4, Glamorgan 4.

Bowling: *First Innings*—Davis 15–5–56–1; Selvey 21–3–94–3; Barwick 7–1–38–0; Ontong 8.5–1–35–4; Rowe 7–0–48–2. *Second Innings*—Davis 11–1–66–0; Ontong 6–3–6–0; Selvey 10–3–41–0; Rowe 11–3–30–1; Barwick 4–0–34–1; Henderson 6–0–48–2; Jones 3–0–25–0; Morris 3.5–0–23–0; Francis 4–0–25–0; Hopkins 4–0–23–0.

Glamorgan

J. A. Hopkins c Clarke b Knight	27	– c Richards b Clarke	22
D. A. Francis b Richards b Clarke	41	– c Richards b Curtis	11
R. C. Ontong c Richards b Clarke	39	– st Richards b Needham	109
S. P. Henderson b Clarke	17	– c Thomas b Needham	32
H. Morris c Richards b Thomas	34	– (7) not out	21
C. J. C. Rowe b Monkhouse	32	– c Richards b Needham	0
A. L. Jones c Smith b Clarke	56	– (5) not out	77
†T. Davies not out	55		
*M. W. W. Selvey run out	0		
W. W. Davis c Smith b Clarke	15		
S. R. Barwick c Thomas b Monkhouse	0		
B 13, l-b 19, w 2, n-b 12	46	B 1, l-b 8, n-b 1	10

1/46 2/121 3/130 4/150   362   1/36 2/36 3/147   (5 wkts) 282
5/202 6/225 7/315 8/315 9/359   4/191 5/191

Bonus points – Glamorgan 3, Surrey 2 (Score at 100 overs: 278-6).

Bowling: *First Innings*—Clarke 35–10–82–5; Thomas 23–7–46–1; Monkhouse 16.5–4–71–2; Knight 10–1–30–1; Curtis 10–4–17–0; Pocock 9.5–5–11–0; Needham 23.1–11–59–0. *Second Innings*—Clarke 13–1–73–1; Thomas 4–0–10–1; Curtis 17–5–84–1; Pocock 10–3–41–0; Needham 8–0–63–3; Smith 0.2–0–1–0.

Umpires: P. J. Eele and R. Palmer.

At Cheltenham, August 6, 8, 9. GLAMORGAN lost to GLOUCESTERSHIRE by an innings and 9 runs.

GLAMORGAN v NOTTINGHAMSHIRE

At Ebbw Vale, August 10, 11, 12. Drawn. Glamorgan 5 pts, Nottinghamshire 6 pts. Glamorgan managed to avoid defeat on the third day in a match marked by the frequent no-balling of the West Indian fast bowler, Winston Davis, and splendid knocks by Randall and

A. L. Jones. An uneven surface assisted Davis on the first day when he claimed seven for 70 but delivered 31 no-balls and two wides. Left to get 345 in 285 minutes for victory, Glamorgan lost all hope of making them with the dismissal of Henderson.

Nottinghamshire

B. Hassan c Rowe b Davis	10	– b Selvey	44
R. T. Robinson c Davies b Selvey	4	– lbw b Davis	30
D. W. Randall c Davies b Selvey	10	– b Davis	70
*C. E. B. Rice b Davis	33	– c Ontong b Rowe	47
J. D. Birch b Ontong	88	– run out	35
†B. N. French b Davis	9	– lbw b Rowe	15
K. Saxelby c Ontong b Davis	7	– lbw b Rowe	6
K. E. Cooper b Davis	10	– (9) c Hopkins b Rowe	1
E. E. Hemmings b Davis	22	– (8) c Ontong b Barwick	12
M. Hendrick not out	14	– not out	7
P. M. Such b Davis	1		
B 2, l-b 1, w 3, n-b 31	37	B 1, l-b 5, n-b 13	19

1/19 2/31 3/40 4/119   245   1/71 2/124 3/182   (9 wkts dec.) 286
5/144 6/156 7/176 8/223 9/243   4/209 5/256 6/260 7/271 8/279 9/286

Bonus points – Nottinghamshire 2, Glamorgan 4.

Bowling: *First Innings*—Davis 22.5–4–70–7; Selvey 15–3–72–2; Ontong 15–2–38–1; Barwick 5–0–28–0. *Second Innings*—Davis 22–3–92–2; Barwick 20–3–59–1; Selvey 11–4–19–1; Ontong 14–0–68–0; Rowe 14–4–29–4.

Glamorgan

J. A. Hopkins c Robinson b Saxelby	29	– lbw b Hendrick	4
D. A. Francis b Saxelby	10	– c Hassan b Saxelby	33
R. C. Ontong lbw b Saxelby	4	– c Cooper b Such	12
C. J. C. Rowe c French b Saxelby	39	– lbw b Hemmings	61
H. Morris c French b Hemmings	26	– c Rice b Hemmings	7
A. L. Jones b Saxelby	12	– not out	84
S. P. Henderson c Birch b Cooper	36	– c French b Saxelby	40
†T. Davies c Hendrick b Cooper	12	– lbw b Saxelby	4
*M. W. W. Selvey run out	5	– c Hendrick b Cooper	0
W. W. Davis not out	5	– c Such b Hendrick	5
S. R. Barwick c French b Cooper	0	– not out	9
B 1, l-b 7, w 1	9	B 4, l-b 12, n-b 4	20

1/31 2/39 3/48 4/112   187   1/6 2/29 3/99 4/110   (9 wkts) 279
5/112 6/129 7/175 8/182 9/183   5/139 6/217 7/225 8/233 9/250

Bonus points – Glamorgan 1, Nottinghamshire 4.

Bowling: *First Innings*—Hendrick 18–4–43–0; Saxelby 23–7–52–5; Cooper 12.1–5–22–3; Hemmings 13–4–41–1; Such 7–2–20–0. *Second Innings*—Hendrick 17–6–55–2; Saxelby 17–3–45–3; Cooper 20–4–70–1; Such 9–0–38–1; Hemmings 18–7–51–2.

Umpires: C. Cook and R. Julian.

GLAMORGAN v KENT

At Cardiff, August 13, 15, 16. Kent won by seven wickets. Kent 20 pts, Glamorgan 5 pts. Batting first, Glamorgan made 336 for three, Ontong achieving an excellent century for the side to gain full batting points. The bat continued to hold the upper hand until Glamorgan, in their second innings, slumped to 124 for six at the close of the second day. Their recovery to 247 all out meant that Kent had four hours in which to score 283 to win. Thanks to Taylor's career-best 155 not out and a second good innings by Benson, they made them comfortably.

Glamorgan

A. Jones c Taylor b Johnson	60	– lbw b Ellison	7
D. A. Francis c Cowdrey b Johnson	63	– b Johnson	22
R. C. Ontong not out	105	– b Cowdrey	11
C. J. C. Rowe c Taylor b Johnson	82	– lbw b Johnson	13
A. L. Jones (did not bat)		– c Johnson b Cowdrey	1
H. Morris (did not bat)		– c Knott b Ellison	18
S. P. Henderson (did not bat)		– c Johnson b Ellison	26
†T. Davies (did not bat)		– not out	69
*M. W. W. Selvey (did not bat)		– c Johnson b Cowdrey	22
A. H. Wilkins (did not bat)		– b Underwood	45
W. W. Davis (did not bat)		– b Underwood	2
L-b 8, w 3, n-b 15	26	B 1, l-b 5, w 1, n-b 4	11

1/127 2/158 3/336 　　　　(3 wkts dec.) 336 　　1/15 2/31 3/46 4/47 　　　　247
　　　　　　　　　　　　　　　　　　　　　　5/56 6/85 7/129 8/179 9/243

Bonus points – Glamorgan 4 (Score at 100 overs: 333-2).

Bowling: *First Innings*—Jarvis 13–4–48–0; Ellison 22–6–59–0; Underwood 14–4–33–0; Baptiste 12–1–41–0; Cowdrey 4–0–8–0; Johnson 31.5–8–101–3; Aslett 4–0–20–0. *Second Innings*—Jarvis 10–0–45–0; Ellison 17–4–58–3; Underwood 7.1–6–2–2; Baptiste 13–2–33–0; Cowdrey 22–3–80–3; Johnson 15–9–18–2.

Kent

N. R. Taylor lbw b Wilkins	24	– not out	155
M. R. Benson b Ontong	111	– b Rowe	50
D. G. Aslett lbw b Selvey	0	– b Selvey	14
S. G. Hinks c Davies b Ontong	87	– b Ontong	41
*C. S. Cowdrey not out	58	– not out	15
E. A. E. Baptiste not out	4		
L-b 6, n-b 11	17	B 2, l-b 4, n-b 2	8

1/62 2/71 3/204 4/284 　　　　(4 wkts dec.) 301 　　1/115 2/146 3/252 　　　(3 wkts) 283

†A. P. E. Knott, G. W. Johnson, R. M. Ellison, D. L. Underwood and K. B. S. Jarvis did not bat.

Bonus points – Kent 4, Glamorgan 1.

Bowling: *First Innings*— Davis 11–3–32–0; Selvey 16–5–38–1; Rowe 19–2–67–0; Wilkins 8–0–34–1; Ontong 17.3–1–96–2; Henderson 2–0–17–0. *Second Innings*—Davis 11–0–50–0; Selvey 19–6–55–1; Rowe 22–4–77–1; Ontong 8.3–0–45–1; Wilkins 12–1–48–0.

Umpires: R. Julian and M. J. Kitchen.

GLAMORGAN v DERBYSHIRE

At Swansea, August 20, 22, 23. Derbyshire won by two wickets. Derbyshire 23 pts, Glamorgan 6 pts. After a delayed start on the first day Glamorgan, put in to bat, slumped to 50 for four before A. L. Jones and Ontong revived the situation. Derbyshire, in reply, lost five wickets for 89 runs before steady batting by Barnett and Fowler restored their fortunes. Holding then cracked Ontong for three 6s in an over to help Derbyshire to a 64-run lead. Although Hopkins carried his bat through the five and a half hours of Glamorgan's second innings, Derbyshire had 190 minutes in which to score 177 to win. They got them with two balls to spare.

Glamorgan

J. A. Hopkins c Barnett b Tunnicliffe	7	– not out 109
D. A. Francis c Anderson b Holding	2	– c Taylor b Mortensen 0
R. C. Ontong c Taylor b Mortensen	50	– c Taylor b Mortensen 6
A. Jones c Barnett b Tunnicliffe	18	– lbw b Mortensen........................ 0
C. J. C. Rowe c Anderson b Tunnicliffe	0	– run out 15
A. L. Jones lbw b Mortensen	57	– c Fowler b Miller..................... 53
S. P. Henderson lbw b Miller	27	– c Taylor b Tunnicliffe 5
†T. Davies lbw b Holding	12	– lbw b Tunnicliffe 0
A. H. Wilkins b Holding	17	– b Mortensen 2
*M. W. W. Selvey not out	1	– c Anderson b Tunnicliffe.......... 30
W. W. Davis (did not bat)		– b Tunnicliffe 4
B 5, l-b 15, w 2, n-b 8	30	B 4, l-b 1, w 1, n-b 10 16

1/4 2/26 3/50 4/50	(9 wkts dec.) 221	1/0 2/14 3/22 4/63 240
5/154 6/163 7/191 8/218 9/221		5/171 6/176 7/176 8/179 9/232

Bonus points – Glamorgan 2, Derbyshire 4.

Bowling: *First Innings*—Holding 18.3–3–41–3; Mortensen 17–4–43–2; Tunnicliffe 11–3–29–3; Finney 7–1–36–0; Miller 19–5–42–1. *Second Innings*—Holding 24–6–53–0; Mortensen 23–10–65–4; Tunnicliffe 18.5–7–48–4; Miller 21–5–49–1; Finney 4–1–9–0.

Derbyshire

†R. W. Taylor b Davis	5	– (9) c A. Jones b Ontong 3
I. S. Anderson c Davies b Rowe	19	– c Henderson b Rowe................ 39
*K. J. Barnett c Henderson b Selvey	67	– (1) c Davies b Davis............... 15
A. Hill c Davies b Wilkins	0	– (3) lbw b Selvey 10
J. H. Hampshire c Wilkins b Rowe	6	– (4) c A. L. Jones b Ontong 33
R. J. Finney c Hopkins b Selvey	6	– (5) c Henderson b Ontong 21
G. Miller b Ontong	22	– (6) not out 22
W. P. Fowler c A. L. Jones b Ontong	61	– (7) run out 3
C. J. Tunnicliffe c A. Jones b Rowe	10	– (8) run out 0
M. A. Holding b Davis	63	– not out 18
O. H. Mortensen not out	9	
B 4, l-b 4, w 1, n-b 8	17	L-b 7, w 1, n-b 5 13

1/13 2/65 3/66 4/75	285	1/24 2/63 3/77 4/124 (8 wkts) 177
5/89 6/131 7/151 8/183 9/228		5/136 6/141 7/151 8/154

Bonus points – Derbyshire 3, Glamorgan 4.

Bowling: *First Innings*—Davis 17.2–5–59–2; Selvey 18–3–58–2; Wilkins 10–1–35–1; Rowe 16–2–50–3; Ontong 13–3–66–2. *Second Innings*—Davis 6–1–25–1; Selvey 11–4–27–1; Rowe 20.4–0–89–1; Ontong 7–1–23–3.

Umpires: J. H. Harris and K. Ibadulla.

At Northampton, August 24, 25, 26. GLAMORGAN drew with NORTHAMPTONSHIRE.

At Taunton, August 27, 29, 30. GLAMORGAN lost to SOMERSET by three wickets.

GLAMORGAN v NORTHAMPTONSHIRE

At Cardiff, August 31, September 1, 2. Drawn. Glamorgan 4 pts, Northamptonshire 8 pts. Rain saved Glamorgan after they had put Northamptonshire in and seen them amass their largest total of the season at nearly six runs an over. Larkins, with a magnificent career-best 252, and Lamb put on 242 for the third wicket. Northamptonshire's was the highest total at Sophia Gardens. On the second day Glamorgan followed on, 366 behind, but rain on the third day prevented a finish. A. Jones reached 1,000 runs for the season for the 23rd consecutive time and passed 36,000 in first-class cricket.

Northamptonshire

*G. Cook b Davis	18	†G. Sharp lbw b Rowe	13
W. Larkins c Barwick b Rowe	252	N. A. Mallender not out	17
P. Willey c Francis b Barwick	13	J. A. Carse not out	16
A. J. Lamb c Ontong b Davis	119	L-b 7, n-b 26	33
R. G. Williams c Davies b Ontong	20		
R. J. Boyd-Moss c Davies b Rowe	21	1/46 2/106 3/348 (8 wkts dec.)	529
D. S. Steele c Hopkins b Wilkins	7	4/396 5/472 6/474 7/494 8/498	

B. J. Griffiths did not bat.

Bonus points – Northamptonshire 4, Glamorgan 3.

Bowling: Davis 17–1–93–2; Wilkins 16–3–90–1; Barwick 11–1–77–1; Rowe 23–0–123–3; Ontong 23–0–113–1.

Glamorgan

A. Jones c and b Griffiths	36	– not out	36
J. A. Hopkins b Carse	44	– c Cook b Mallender	1
D. A. Francis c Steele b Carse	11	– not out	11
*R. C. Ontong not out	21		
C. J. C. Rowe c Sharp b Carse	0		
A. L. Jones lbw b Carse	0		
S. P. Henderson c Larkins b Carse	0		
†T. Davies c Cook b Mallender	14		
A. H. Wilkins lbw b Mallender	4		
W. W. Davis b Mallender	8		
S. R. Barwick run out	0		
B 5, l-b 6, w 2, n-b 12	25	L-b 1, n-b 1	2
1/65 2/104 3/115 4/115	163	1/22 (1 wkt)	50
5/115 6/115 7/143 8/147 9/163			

Bonus points – Glamorgan 1, Northamptonshire 4.

Bowling: *First Innings*—Carse 17–4–43–5; Griffiths 19–3–44–1; Mallender 12–2–43–3; Steele 9–6–3–0; Williams 2–1–5–0. *Second Innings*—Mallender 6–2–16–1; Griffiths 6–1–27–0; Williams 4–3–2–0; Carse 5–3–3–0.

Umpires: D. J. Constant and K. Ibadulla.

At Birmingham, September 7, 8, 9. GLAMORGAN lost to WARWICKSHIRE by eight wickets.

At Southampton, September 10, 12, 13. GLAMORGAN drew with HAMPSHIRE.

GLOUCESTERSHIRE

Patron: The Duke of Beaufort
President: T. L. Robinson
Chairman: D. N. Perry
Chairman, Cricket Committee: D. G. Stone
Secretary/Manager: D. G. Collier
   Phoenix County Ground, Nevil Road,
   Bristol BS7 9EJ (Telephone: 0272-45216)
Captain: D. A. Graveney
Coach: G. G. Wiltshire

A top-class fast bowler and an off-spinner might well have made
Gloucestershire into a very useful side. As it was, lacking these two
weapons, they could do no more than progress from fifteenth to twelfth
in the Schweppes County Championship. None worked harder to try to
overcome bowling shortcomings than the new-ball pair, John Shepherd
and Gary Sainsbury.

Shepherd, in his 40th year, had a splendid season, doing the modern
equivalent of "the double" by claiming 67 wickets and scoring 1,025 runs.
He was always fit and ready to bowl, and he more than maintained the
high standards he has set himself throughout a long career. Sainsbury's
first full season of county cricket showed that his Essex apprenticeship
had enabled him to learn some valuable lessons from John Lever. After
a quiet start he took wickets regularly and should be an important
member of the side for years to come. Gloucestershire still hope that
David Lawrence may emerge as the fast bowler they so badly need. But
although showing some improvement under Shepherd's guidance, he was
still erratic and consequently expensive. Injury robbed him of the chance
of his first representative honour for Young England. Franklyn
Stephenson appeared in only two matches before a back injury and
Zaheer's return from the World Cup ruled him out of contention.

The batting exceeded expectations. There were seventeen Championship centuries as against eight in 1982, and six batsmen passed 1,000 runs,
Zaheer not being among them. The prolific Pakistani, having had a
month out of the team because of the World Cup, returned home after
the Cheltenham festival to help prepare his national side for a tour of
India. However, he played a key role in two of the Championship
victories, leading successful run chases against Glamorgan and Yorkshire
in majestic style. Zaheer was also seen at his best in Gloucestershire's
second-round NatWest Bank Trophy win over Leicestershire, when
Gloucestershire made 303 to win, and in a remarkable John Player
League victory over Middlesex at Lord's.

But batting honours for the season belonged to Andy Stovold, who
recalled C. J. Barnett in his heyday by the way he jousted with the fast
bowlers. He had his failures – this type of player always does – but he was
splendid to watch when in full flight and the later batsmen must have been

grateful to arrive so often and find the opposition on the defensive. Unfortunately Stovold will need a new opening partner in 1984. The committee took exception to a newspaper interview given by Chris Broad, concerning his ambition to play at the highest level and his relations with one or two of the senior players, and decided that in the interests of the team it would be better if he were not selected again. The news broke just after Broad had made a career-best 145 against Nottinghamshire, leaving supporters unhappy that the rift could not be healed.

Alastair Hignell announced his retirement to take up a teaching career at Sherborne School and will be much missed. Although not reaching the same eminence as a cricketer as he had as a rugby footballer, he was a valuable member of the side and played some typically boisterous innings in a successful last season. Gloucestershire's decision to give Paul Romaines a second chance to make a career as a county cricketer was amply justified. He had done well in club cricket in Sydney in the winter of 1982-83 and returned a more complete player, much readier to play his strokes. He succeeded as an opening batsman as well as in various positions lower in the order where Tony Wright again looked promising when given an opportunity.

More use could be made of the batting talent of the county's splendid young wicket-keeper, Jack Russell. He was second in the national wicket-keeper's table, won some glowing notices and seems certain to be a Test candidate if he continues to progress and is given the chance to score more runs. While many of the country's spin bowlers flourished, David Graveney and John Childs enjoyed only limited success, the captain making little use of his own bowling.

Gloucestershire headed their qualifying group in the Benson and Hedges Cup but then lost to Middlesex, the eventual winners, on the toss of a coin in the quarter-final, when rain prevented a result being obtained by legitimate means at Bristol. Both sides pleaded to be able to play some sort of a match at a later date but were over-ruled by the TCCB. The NatWest Bank Trophy win over Leicestershire took Gloucestershire to the quarter-finals of that competition too, but they lacked the bowling strength to trouble Hampshire.

With a little more good fortune in close finishes, Gloucestershire could have finished higher in the Championship. But the manner in which they were outclassed by Middlesex and Essex revealed a wide gulf to be bridged before Gloucestershire can be accounted a power in the land once more. – G.J.W.

389

GLOUCESTERSHIRE 1983

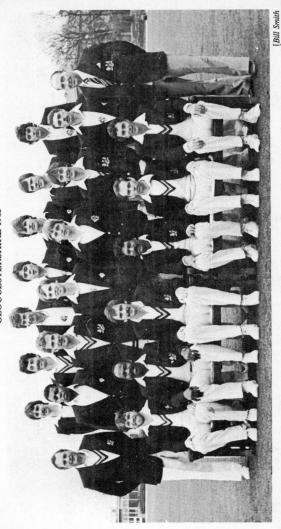

[*Bill Smith*

Back row: R. C. Russell, P. Bainbridge, E. J. Cunningham, A. J. Wright, R. J. Doughty, B. Dudleston, K. G. Rice. *Middle row:* G. M. Wiltshire (*coach*), D. V. Lawrence, B. C. Broad, G. E. Sainsbury, D. P. Simpkins, A. J. Brassington, P. W. Romaines, A. G. Avery (*scorer*). *Front row:* A. J. Hignell, J. N. Shepherd, D. A. Graveney (*captain*), Zaheer Abbas, A. W. Stovold, J. H. Childs.

GLOUCESTERSHIRE RESULTS

All first-class matches – Played 24: Won 3, Lost 8, Drawn 13.

County Championship matches – Played 23: Won 3, Lost 8, Drawn 12.

Bonus points – Batting 56, Bowling 61.

Competition placings – Schweppes County Championship, 12th eq; NatWest Bank Trophy, q-f; Benson and Hedges Cup, q-f; John Player League, 14th.

COUNTY CHAMPIONSHIP AVERAGES

BATTING

	Birthplace	M	I	NO	R	HI	Avge
Zaheer Abbasc	Sialkot, Pakistan	12	19	0	867	116	45.63
A. W. Stovoldc	Bristol	22	40	3	1,592	181	43.02
B. C. Broadc	Bristol	16	27	2	1,061	145	42.44
R. J. Doughty	Bridlington	6	9	6	123	32*	41.00
J. N. Shepherdc	St Andrew, Barbados	23	34	6	1,025	168	36.60
A. J. Hignellc	Cambridge	19	35	6	1,034	109*	35.65
P. W. Romainesc	Bishop Auckland	22	39	4	1,233	135	35.22
P. Bainbridgec	Stoke-on-Trent	23	41	2	1,068	99*	27.38
A. J. Wright	Stevenage	9	15	2	354	56*	27.23
R. C. Russell	Stroud	23	30	9	469	64*	22.33
D. A. Graveneyc	Bristol	21	26	7	397	94	20.89
E. J. Cunningham	Oxford	4	6	1	83	29*	16.60
J. H. Childsc	Plymouth	19	16	1	79	19	5.26
D. V. Lawrence	Gloucester	8	9	4	22	9	4.40
G. E. Sainsbury	Wanstead	22	21	7	61	13	4.35

Also batted: B. Dudleston (*Bebington*) (2 matches) 35*, 11, 12; F. D. Stephenson (*St James, Barbados*) (2 matches) 21.

*Signifies not out. c *Denotes county cap.*

BOWLING

	O	M	R	W	Avge	BB
F. D. Stephenson	52.4	13	140	11	12.72	5-56
J. N. Shepherd	776.1	209	2,047	67	30.55	7-50
G. E. Sainsbury	602.4	142	1,882	58	32.44	6-66
D. A. Graveney	498.1	153	1,160	35	33.14	6-88
J. H. Childs	647.5	194	1,691	48	35.22	6-81
P. Bainbridge	400.4	100	1,160	29	40.00	4-67

Also bowled: E. J. Cunningham 49–10–181–4; R. J. Doughty 76.5–11–285–5; B. Dudleston 27.5–4–164–4; A. J. Hignell 7–1–46–0; D. V. Lawrence 157–21–613–7; A. J. Wright 1–0–3–0; Zaheer Abbas 26–7–79–0.

The following played a total of seventeen three-figure innings for Gloucestershire in County Championship matches – A. W. Stovold 4, B. C. Broad 3, P. W. Romaines 3, Zaheer Abbas 3, A. J. Hignell 2, J. N. Shepherd 2.

At Derby, April 30, May 1, 2. GLOUCESTERSHIRE drew with DERBYSHIRE.

GLOUCESTERSHIRE v SURREY

At Bristol, May 4, 5, 6. Drawn. Gloucestershire 5 pts, Surrey 6 pts. On a sluggish pitch, the batsmen held the upper hand and the match was already heading for a draw when the third day was washed out. Bowlers of pace, handicapped by wet run-ups, were ineffective and only Pocock and Childs, who managed to extract some turn, needed careful watching. Stovold's second century in successive innings, coming out of 169 in 173 minutes, was the backbone of the Gloucestershire effort after they had been put in. Later there were lively contributions from Zaheer and Hignell as Pocock spun away willingly. The overnight loss of Butcher proved no hardship to Surrey, for whom Clinton marked his 30th birthday with the ninth century of his career. He and fellow-left-hander Smith put on 191, although Clinton was badly missed off Graveney when their partnership was worth no more than 58.

Gloucestershire

A. W. Stovold b Clarke	122	J. N. Shepherd c Knight b Pocock		5
B. C. Broad c Richards b Thomas	49	†R. C. Russell not out		9
P. Bainbridge b Clarke	11			
Zaheer Abbas c Smith b Pocock	44	B 6, l-b 6, w 2, n-b 16		30
P. W. Romaines c Smith b Pocock	4			
A. J. Hignell not out	50	1/143 2/197 3/208	(7 wkts dec.)	333
*D. A. Graveney c Richards b Pocock	9	4/249 5/256 6/283 7/291		

J. H. Childs and G. E. Sainsbury did not bat.

Bonus points – Gloucestershire 4, Surrey 3.

Bowling: Clarke 23–5–62–2; Thomas 17–3–78–1; Monkhouse 16–3–69–0; Pocock 32–10–70–4; Knight 10–4–24–0.

Surrey

A. R. Butcher st Russell b Childs	14	M. A. Lynch not out		9
G. S. Clinton c Bainbridge b Shepherd	105	B 3, l-b 8, w 1		12
D. M. Smith c Bainbridge b Childs	90			
G. P. Howarth not out	22	1/27 2/218	(4 wkts)	252
*R. D. V. Knight b Childs	0	3/234 4/238		

†C. J. Richards, D. J. Thomas, S. T. Clarke, G. Monkhouse and P. I. Pocock did not bat.

Bonus points – Surrey 3, Gloucestershire 1.

Bowling: Shepherd 25–3–77–1; Sainsbury 15–3–35–0; Childs 18–4–57–3; Graveney 19–4–38–0; Bainbridge 6–1–33–0.

Umpires: D. J. Constant and J. van Geloven.

GLOUCESTERSHIRE v SUSSEX

At Gloucester, May 11, 12, 13. Abandoned. The teams were not announced.

At Birmingham, May 25, 26, 27. GLOUCESTERSHIRE drew with WARWICKSHIRE.

At Swansea, May 28, 30, 31. GLOUCESTERSHIRE beat GLAMORGAN by three wickets.

GLOUCESTERSHIRE v SOMERSET

At Bristol, June 8, 9, 10. Drawn. Gloucestershire 8 pts, Somerset 6 pts. A much-weakened Somerset side, at one stage seriously threatened by the follow-on, recovered strongly to earn a draw. By the end of the first day Gloucestershire, launched by an innings of 84 in 78 minutes by Stovold, were firmly in control, their West Indian bowlers having sent back the first three Somerset batsmen for 23. On the second morning Somerset soon found themselves 74 for six against Stephenson's clever variations of pace, but then seventeen-year-old Palmer joined Denning in a stand of 124, dominating the rescue bid with some beautifully clean hitting which brought him a 6 and thirteen 4s. Although three wickets by Sainsbury regained a measure of control for Gloucestershire, Somerset's last pair, Dredge and Wilson, not only saved the follow-on but added 68 in an hour. With Stephenson nursing a back injury, Graveney set a stiff target of 330 in 217 minutes, and not surprisingly Roebuck and Ollis settled for batting practice, play continuing into the extra half-hour in a fruitless attempt to give Ollis the single he needed for a maiden century.

Gloucestershire

A. W. Stovold c Roebuck b Popplewell	84	– b Davis	35
B. C. Broad lbw b Davis	84	– c Gard b Dredge	92
P. Bainbridge c Palmer b Lloyds	37	– b Wilson	18
A. J. Hignell c Slocombe b Wilson	41	– (5) b Dredge	13
P. W. Romaines b Davis	73	– (6) not out	15
J. N. Shepherd lbw b Davis	14	– (7) not out	4
*D. A. Graveney b Palmer	4		
F. D. Stephenson b Dredge	21		
†R. C. Russell not out	1	– (4) c Ollis b Popplewell	44
B 6, l-b 4, w 5, n-b 1	16	B 4, l-b 4, n-b 2	10

1/112 2/176 3/234 4/267　　　(8 wkts dec.) 375　　1/66 2/114　　(5 wkts dec.) 231
5/287 6/302 7/371 8/375　　　　　　　　　　　　　　3/179 4/201 5/217

J. H. Childs and G. E. Sainsbury did not bat.

Bonus points – Gloucestershire 4, Somerset 3.

Bowling: *First Innings*—Wilson 14–2–64–1; Davis 15.4–2–62–3; Palmer 16–3–56–1; Popplewell 9–2–32–1; Dredge 14–1–59–1; Lloyds 23–7–86–1. *Second Innings*—Dredge 16–1–44–2; Wilson 12–3–43–1; Lloyds 10–5–32–0; Palmer 14–4–42–0; Davis 14–4–42–1; Popplewell 6.2–0–18–1.

Somerset

R. L. Ollis lbw b Shepherd	5	– not out	99
*P. M. Roebuck c and b Stephenson	4	– not out	74
P. A. Slocombe c Russell b Stephenson	5		
†T. Gard c Childs b Stephenson	13		
P. W. Denning c Russell b Sainsbury	73		
N. F. M. Popplewell lbw b Stephenson	6		
J. W. Lloyds run out	1		
G. V. Palmer c Stovold b Sainsbury	78		
C. H. Dredge not out	48		
M. R. Davis b Sainsbury	2		
P. H. L. Wilson b Graveney	25		
B 3, l-b 8, n-b 6	17	L-b 1	1

1/10 2/11 3/23 4/46　　　　　　277　　　　　　(no wkt) 174
5/60 6/74 7/198 8/199 9/209

Bonus points – Somerset 3, Gloucestershire 4.

Bowling: *First Innings*—Stephenson 27–4–74–4; Shepherd 27–10–67–1; Childs 10–4–32–0; Sainsbury 19–2–58–3; Graveney 5.3–0–29–1. *Second Innings*—Shepherd 10–3–16–0; Sainsbury 9–5–18–0; Graveney 16–7–28–0; Childs 16–3–55–0; Bainbridge 12–4–24–0; Hignell 6–1–32–0.

Umpires: W. E. Alley and J. D. Morley.

At Northampton, June 11, 13, 14. GLOUCESTERSHIRE lost to NORTHAMPTON-SHIRE by 141 runs.

At Leicester, June 15, 16, 17. GLOUCESTERSHIRE drew with LEICESTERSHIRE.

GLOUCESTERSHIRE v KENT

At Bristol, June 18, 20, 21. Drawn. Gloucestershire 6 pts, Kent 4 pts. Jarvis, Kent's last man, survived the final thirteen overs to deny Gloucestershire a victory their positive cricket would have merited. Shepherd, awarded his cap at the lunch interval on the Saturday, celebrated with a belligerent century against his former county, he and Romaines adding 221 for the fourth wicket before Underwood swept through the later batting. Kent, in troubled waters at 76 for five, were guided to safety by Knott with sensible assistance from Aslett and Ellison. Graveney declared on the third day, even though Bainbridge was on 99 for the second time in five days. He was on that score for seven deliveries before his partner, Hignell, was lbw. Kent were left 349 in 260 minutes, and with Knott and Cowdrey together and 143 needed from the last twenty overs they were still in the hunt. However, Shepherd took a hand again with three wickets in one over, leaving Jarvis, improbably, to keep Johnson company until the end.

Gloucestershire

A. W. Stovold c Cowdrey b Ellison	13	– c Baptiste b Ellison	57
B. C. Broad retired hurt	8		
P. Bainbridge c Johnson b Jarvis	43	– not out	99
A. J. Hignell b Baptiste	19	– (5) lbw b Ellison	35
P. W. Romaines b Johnson	135	– (2) c Benson b Jarvis	12
J. N. Shepherd c Aslett b Underwood	112		
*D. A. Graveney c Benson b Underwood	7		
†R. C. Russell not out	13	– (4) c Knott b Jarvis	2
J. H. Childs c Ellison b Underwood	3		
G. E. Sainsbury c Cowdrey b Underwood	0		
D. V. Lawrence lbw b Underwood	0		
L-b 7, n-b 10	17	L-b 8, n-b 17	25

1/17 2/55 3/102 4/323   370   1/31 2/126   (4 wkts dec.) 230
5/350 6/358 7/367 8/370 9/370   3/133 4/230

Bonus points – Gloucestershire 3, Kent 1 (Score at 100 overs: 279-3).

Bowling: *First Innings*—Jarvis 14–2–59–1; Ellison 19–7–53–1; Baptiste 7–1–22–1; Underwood 29.5–7–93–5; Cowdrey 15–5–47–0; Johnson 39–10–77–1; Potter 2–1–2–0. *Second Innings*—Jarvis 11–0–53–2; Ellison 18.1–2–63–2; Underwood 26–7–53–0; Cowdrey 7–1–36–0.

Kent

L. Potter c Shepherd b Lawrence	22	– st Russell b Graveney	50
N. R. Taylor lbw b Shepherd	16	– c Bainbridge b Shepherd	1
D. G. Aslett c Russell b Lawrence	52	– lbw b Sainsbury	34
M. R. Benson c and b Lawrence	8	– c and b Graveney	12
*C. S. Cowdrey b Sainsbury	6	– c Russell b Sainsbury	47
E. A. E. Baptiste lbw b Sainsbury	0	– c Hignell b Lawrence	32
†A. P. E. Knott b Childs	83	– c and b Shepherd	56
G. W. Johnson c and b Bainbridge	4	– not out	15
R. M. Ellison not out	40	– c Russell b Shepherd	0
D. L. Underwood not out	0	– lbw b Shepherd	0
K. B. S. Jarvis (did not bat)		– not out	9
B 1, l-b 5, w 1, n-b 14	21	B 4, l-b 5, w 5, n-b 2	16

1/46 2/46 3/65 4/74   (8 wkts dec.) 252   1/11 2/98 3/98 4/122   (9 wkts) 272
5/76 6/181 7/188 8/248   5/167 6/247 7/249 8/250 9/250

Bonus points – Kent 3, Gloucestershire 3.

Bowling: *First Innings*—Shepherd 23–8–54–1; Lawrence 16–0–62–3; Sainsbury 17.5–2–67–2; Childs 6–0–31–1; Bainbridge 5–0–17–1. *Second Innings*—Shepherd 20–5–42–4; Lawrence 22–4–84–1; Sainsbury 14–3–48–2; Graveney 16–2–61–2; Childs 2–0–21–0.

Umpires: K. Ibadulla and N. T. Plews.

At Bath, June 22, 23, 24. GLOUCESTERSHIRE drew with SOMERSET.

GLOUCESTERSHIRE v HAMPSHIRE

At Bristol, June 25, 27, 28. Hampshire won by 118 runs. Hampshire 22 pts, Gloucestershire 6 pts. Although three declarations were needed to bring about a result, Gloucestershire folded badly after being set 334 in 247 minutes. Hampshire were put in on a pitch showing traces of damp, but it played so easily that they lost only five wickets in gathering maximum batting points, Nicholas contributing a delightful hundred in three hours with nineteen boundaries. Gloucestershire, after some mid-innings problems, replied in spirited style through Hignell, whose second century in five days took only 135 minutes, and Graveney, who hurried to a half-century in 74 minutes before declaring 61 behind. Hampshire's third-innings effort centred around Robin Smith's third century in three weeks. He made 85 of the 132 scored on the last morning for the loss of four wickets. Gloucestershire began their chase with a will, but after Stovold's departure only Hignell maintained the required tempo. He fell to Cowley, all of whose eleven overs were maidens, and when Malone bowled Sainsbury Hampshire had 23 balls to spare.

Hampshire

V. P. Terry lbw b Shepherd	19	– c Zaheer b Childs	29
C. L. Smith c Russell b Sainsbury	68	– c Bainbridge b Sainsbury	42
M. C. J. Nicholas c Graveney b Doughty	110	– c Childs b Sainsbury	0
T. E. Jesty lbw b Sainsbury	40	– b Graveney	44
R. A. Smith lbw b Sainsbury	1	– c sub b Childs	100
*N. E. J. Pocock not out	50	– (7) b Doughty	9
N. G. Cowley c Bainbridge b Sainsbury	29	– (8) c and b Graveney	11
K. Stevenson c Romaines b Sainsbury	2	– (10) b Childs	1
T. M. Tremlett not out	11	– (9) not out	10
†R. J. Parks (did not bat)		– (6) b Childs	7
B 4, l-b 17, w 4, n-b 8	33	B 5, l-b 3, w 3, n-b 8	19

1/32 2/170 3/236   (7 wkts. dec.) 363   1/78 2/78 3/86   (9 wkts dec.) 272
4/237 5/257 6/331 7/333   4/136 5/162 6/178 7/254 8/267 9/272

S. J. Malone did not bat.

Bonus points – Hampshire 4, Gloucestershire 2 (Score at 100 overs: 312-5).

Bowling *First Innings*—Shepherd 19–4–70–1; Sainsbury 25–6–71–5; Childs 10–2–31–0; Graveney 18–7–43–0; Bainbridge 21–3–46–0; Doughty 17–3–69–1. *Second Innings*—Doughty 19–2–80–1; Sainsbury 14–2–73–2; Childs 33.1–9–66–4; Graveney 9–1–14–2; Bainbridge 4–0–20–0.

Gloucestershire

A. W. Stovold c Pocock b Stevenson	46	– b Tremlett	35
P. W. Romaines c Parks b Tremlett	40	– b Stevenson	23
P. Bainbridge c Jesty b Tremlett	3	– b Jesty	13
Zaheer Abbas b Tremlett	10	– c C. L. Smith b Tremlett	18
A. J. Hignell not out	109	– c R. A. Smith b Cowley	61
J. N. Shepherd lbw b Stevenson	23	– run out	8
*D. A. Graveney not out	57	– st Parks b Tremlett	14
R. J. Doughty (did not bat)		– not out	25
†R. C. Russell (did not bat)		– c Tremlett b C. L. Smith	5
J. H. Childs (did not bat)		– c sub b Cowley	3
G. E. Sainsbury (did not bat)		– b Malone	0
L-b 8, w 4, n-b 2	14	B 2, l-b 7, w 1	10

1/55 2/93   (5 wkts dec.) 302   1/54 2/77 3/79 4/108   215
3/107 4/114 5/172   5/126 6/176 7/183 8/196 9/199

Bonus points – Gloucestershire 4, Hampshire 2.

Bowling: *First Innings*—Malone 15–2–74–0; Stevenson 12–4–44–2; Tremlett 17–5–56–3; Jesty 14–4–50–0; Nicholas 8–0–36–0; Cowley 8–3–20–0; Pocock 1–0–8–0. *Second Innings*—Malone 11.1–4–31–1; Stevenson 8–0–41–1; Tremlett 16–2–47–3; Jesty 7–1–31–1; Cowley 11–11–0–2; Nicholas 1–0–1–0; C. L. Smith 13–3–54–1.

Umpires: D. O. Oslear and P. B. Wight.

At The Oval, July 2, 4. GLOUCESTERSHIRE lost to SURREY by an innings and 84 runs.

At Bristol, July 6, 7, 8. GLOUCESTERSHIRE drew with NEW ZEALANDERS (See New Zealand tour section).

GLOUCESTERSHIRE v DERBYSHIRE

At Bristol, July 9, 11, 12. Drawn. Gloucestershire 5 pts, Derbyshire 5 pts. Childs needed to do the hat-trick with the last three balls of the match to win the game for Gloucestershire, who had held control from the first afternoon when Shepherd rescued their faltering first innings. The left-arm spinner succeeded in removing Taylor and Moir with his first two balls but Mortensen nudged the final one to safety and Derbyshire survived, having been left 299 to win in 255 minutes – perhaps as generous a target as their slow cricket in heat-wave conditions had deserved. Gloucestershire's first-innings lead of 58 was attractively improved by Romaines and Hignell in a partnership of 142. Derbyshire then spent 26 overs making their first 51 runs in their second innings and never seemed sure whether a win or a draw was their objective. Childs slowly worked his way through but found the final challenge just beyond him.

Gloucestershire

A. W. Stovold b Mortensen	21	– lbw b Tunnicliffe	10
P. W. Romaines b Finney	13	– c and b Moir	71
P. Bainbridge c Miller b Finney	19	– c Taylor b Tunnicliffe	0
Zaheer Abbas c Moir b Finney	0	– (6) c Taylor b Moir	21
A. J. Hignell c Moir b Tunnicliffe	0	– (4) c Taylor b Moir	86
A. J. Wright c Taylor b Mortensen	23	– (5) run out	16
J. N. Shepherd b Tunnicliffe	80	– (8) c and b Moir	3
*D. A. Graveney c Moir b Mortensen	5		
†R. C. Russell b Mortensen	58	– (7) not out	25
J. H. Childs b Tunnicliffe	8		
G. E. Sainsbury not out	0		
B 2, l-b 1, n-b 6	9	L-b 6, n-b 2	8

1/32 2/44 3/44 4/49   236   1/15 2/15 3/157   (7 wkts dec.) 240
5/63 6/102 7/130 8/195 9/236   4/182 5/194 6/234 7/240

Bonus points – Gloucestershire 2, Derbyshire 4.

Bowling: *First Innings*—Mortensen 18.4–3–52–4; Tunnicliffe 23–5–66–3; Finney 14–1–54–3; Moir 9–2–30–0; Miller 7–0–25–0. *Second Innings*—Mortensen 17–3–47–0; Tunnicliffe 13–3–32–2; Finney 6–1–18–0; Moir 28–5–93–4; Miller 18–4–42–0.

Derbyshire

I. S. Anderson run out	10	– lbw b Childs	25
*K. J. Barnett c and b Bainbridge	21	– c Stovold b Bainbridge	36
A. Hill c Shepherd b Sainsbury	4	– c sub b Childs	64
J. H. Hampshire c Russell b Shepherd	10	– st Russell b Childs	23
R. J. Finney b Childs	29	– c sub b Childs	0
G. Miller lbw b Sainsbury	59	– run out	10
W. P. Fowler run out	4	– not out	7
C. J. Tunnicliffe c Wright b Childs	7	– c Russell b Shepherd	20
†R. W. Taylor c Russell b Shepherd	25	– c and b Childs	5
D. G Moir b Shepherd	3	– lbw b Childs	0
O. H. Mortensen not out	0	– not out	0
L-b 6	6	B 2	2

1/19 2/37 3/37 4/60   178   1/51 2/81 3/120   (9 wkts) 192
5/109 6/113 7/134 8/175 9/175   4/128 5/152 6/161 7/181 8/192 9/192

Bonus points – Derbyshire 1, Gloucestershire 3 (Score at 100 overs: 169-7).

Bowling: *First Innings*—Shepherd 25.5–4–52–3; Sainsbury 20–6–38–2; Bainbridge 8–3–12–1; Graveney 34–14–42–0; Childs 21–10–28–2. *Second Innings*—Shepherd 10–5–20–1; Sainsbury 6–2–16–0; Childs 35–11–81–6; Graveney 28–6–64–0; Bainbridge 3–0–9–1.

Umpires: J. Birkenshaw and R. Julian.

GLOUCESTERSHIRE v MIDDLESEX

At Bristol, July 13, 14, 15. Middlesex won by an innings and 69 runs. Middlesex 24 pts, Gloucestershire 3 pts. The Championship leaders had no trouble with Gloucestershire, for whom only Romaines looked equipped to handle the pace bowling of Daniel, Williams and Hughes. Hughes returned a career-best six for 32 in Gloucestershire's second innings. Barlow and Gatting also enjoyed themselves against a moderate Gloucestershire attack and although Butcher for once failed against them Downton and Williams built up the Middlesex lead with a seventh-wicket partnership of 101. Gloucestershire never looked capable of saving the innings defeat, Hughes emphasising the strength of the Middlesex reserve bowling.

Gloucestershire

A. W. Stovold c Downton b Daniel	15	– b Daniel	16
P. W. Romaines b Daniel	59	– lbw b Daniel	30
P. Bainbridge c Emburey b Daniel	19	– c Slack b Hughes	6
A. J. Hignell b Daniel	0	– c Emburey b Hughes	2
A. J. Wright c Gatting b Slack	23	– c Downton b Hughes	11
J. N. Shepherd lbw b Daniel	1	– c Butcher b Daniel	6
*D. A. Graveney c Downton b Daniel	6	– c Slack b Hughes	9
†R. C. Russell not out	21	– hit wkt b Hughes	14
J. H. Childs c Gatting b Williams	3	– b Slack	0
G. E. Sainsbury b Williams	1	– b Hughes	5
D. V. Lawrence c Downton b Daniel	9	– not out	5
L-b 6, n-b 13	19	B 1, l-b 2, w 1, n-b 21	25
	176		**129**

1/29 2/53 3/53 4/125   5/126 6/132 7/142 8/150 9/153

1/16 2/39 3/48 4/71   5/82 6/90 7/107 8/109 9/118

Bonus points – Gloucestershire 1, Middlesex 4.

Bowling: *First Innings*—Daniel 16.2–2–61–7; Williams 11–5–30–2; Hughes 7–0–39–0; Slack 8–5–10–1; Emburey 12–5–17–0. *Second Innings*—Daniel 14–3–46–3; Williams 7–3–13–0; Hughes 14.4–6–32–6; Emburey 7–4–5–0; Carr 3–1–7–0; Slack 2–1–1–1.

Middlesex

G. D. Barlow c Russell b Lawrence	90	J. D. Carr not out	9
W. N. Slack b Bainbridge	8	S. P. Hughes st Russell b Graveney	4
C. T. Radley run out	14	W. W. Daniel b Bainbridge	4
*M. W. Gatting c Stovold b Sainsbury	93	B 8, l-b 13, w 1, n-b 6	28
R. O. Butcher lbw b Shepherd	11		
J. E. Emburey b Sainsbury	13		**374**
†P. R. Downton c Russell b Bainbridge	58		
N. F. Williams lbw b Graveney	42		

1/36 2/92 3/182   4/210 5/252 6/255   7/356 8/360 9/369

Bonus points – Middlesex 4, Gloucestershire 2 (Score at 100 overs: 308-6).

Bowling: Shepherd 27–5–61–1; Lawrence 20–2–82–1; Sainsbury 21–3–66–2; Bainbridge 33–10–75–3; Childs 9–3–37–0; Graveney 14–3–25–2.

Umpires: R. Palmer and J. Birkenshaw.

At Southport, July 27, 28, 29. GLOUCESTERSHIRE lost to LANCASHIRE by five wickets.

At Portsmouth, July 30, August 1, 2. GLOUCESTERSHIRE drew with HAMPSHIRE.

GLOUCESTERSHIRE v GLAMORGAN

At Cheltenham, August 6, 8, 9. Gloucestershire won by an innings and 9 runs. Gloucestershire 23 pts, Glamorgan 4 pts. The pitch was reported as unfit after Gloucestershire's second victory of the season. Winning the toss proved vital and Graveney's decision to extend the innings into the second day was fully justified, the extra runs obtained enabling Gloucestershire to enforce the follow-on. Childs was mainly responsible for Glamorgan's dismissal the first time; then Shepherd took full advantage of a wearing pitch. Only Ontong, who had a good match, looked at all comfortable as some balls lifted and others kept low.

Gloucestershire

A. W. Stovold b Davis	83	†R. C. Russell b Davis		5
B. C. Broad c Francis b Davis	27	J. H. Childs c Davis b Ontong		2
P. Bainbridge c A. Jones b Selvey	21	G. E. Sainsbury b Selvey		13
Zaheer Abbas st Davies b Ontong	50	B 14, l-b 7, w 3		24
P. W. Romaines c and b Selvey	46			—
A. J. Hignell c Davis b Ontong	2	1/48 2/122 3/171		376
J. N. Shepherd not out	98	4/203 5/211 6/272		
*D. A. Graveney c Rowe b Lloyd	5	7/283 8/323 9/328		

Bonus points – Gloucestershire 3, Glamorgan 2 (Score at 100 overs: 269-5).

Bowling: Davis 34–5–112–3; Selvey 33.3–7–92–3; Ontong 32–11–70–3; Lloyd 25–5–51–1; Rowe 11–4–27–0.

Glamorgan

J. A. Hopkins c Graveney b Shepherd	15	– lbw b Shepherd	9
D. A. Francis c Zaheer b Sainsbury	13	– c Bainbridge b Shepherd	23
R. C. Ontong c Shepherd b Graveney	81	– c Russell b Childs	46
A. Jones c Stovold b Graveney	44	– c Stovold b Shepherd	0
C. J. C. Rowe c Russell b Childs	9	– lbw b Shepherd	20
S. P. Henderson b Childs	0	– c Russell b Shepherd	0
A. L. Jones c Graveney b Shepherd	30	– c Bainbridge b Shepherd	24
†T. Davies c Shepherd b Childs	2	– lbw b Graveney	0
B. J. Lloyd c Russell b Childs	1	– lbw b Shepherd	7
*M. W. W. Selvey not out	6	– lbw b Childs	24
W. W. Davis c Hignell b Childs	0	– not out	4
B 1, n-b 2	3	B 4, l-b 2	6

1/20 2/35 3/98 4/120	204	1/14 2/59 3/67 4/85	163
5/120 6/163 7/193 8/197 9/197		5/86 6/126 7/127 8/127 9/155	

Bonus points – Glamorgan 2, Gloucestershire 4.

Bowling: *First Innings*—Shepherd 23–9–56–2; Sainsbury 8–4–19–1; Childs 30.2–10–77–5; Zaheer 1–1–0–0; Graveney 17–5–49–2. *Second Innings*—Shepherd 32–10–64–7; Sainsbury 2–1–1–0; Childs 21.2–7–67–2; Bainbridge 4–1–11–0; Graveney 12–4–14–1.

Umpires: J. Birkenshaw and J. W. Holder.

GLOUCESTERSHIRE v WARWICKSHIRE

At Cheltenham, August 10, 11, 12. Warwickshire won by four wickets. Warwickshire 21 pts, Gloucestershire 7 pts. The College pitch at Cheltenham more than redeemed itself in a match of well over 1,100 runs, won by Warwickshire with a bye off the last ball. A heavy roller borrowed from the local council ironed out the square so effectively that batting was a joy after Gloucestershire had won the toss. Stovold was in five and a half hours for his unbeaten 164 and Zaheer's 50th century for his adopted county was as graceful as most of its predecessors. The contrast of styles made splendid entertainment while he and Stovold were adding 190. Smith's dogged 109 then steered Warwickshire out of early difficulties and enabled them to declare only 53 behind. Warwickshire finally had just over three hours to get 271. From the last twenty overs, they required 112 and Thorne and Asif Din scrambled the winning single when Russell could only parry a leg-side delivery from Sainsbury.

Gloucestershire

A. W. Stovold not out	164	– c Amiss b Gifford	38
B. C. Broad c Kallicharran b Hogg	4	– c Dyer b Kallicharran	39
P. Bainbridge lbw b Thorne	14	– c Amiss b Gifford	6
Zaheer Abbas c Gifford b Hogg	109	– c and b Gifford	42
P. W. Romaines lbw b Old	12	– c Thorne b Kallicharran	15
A. J. Hignell c Hogg b Kallicharran	11	– not out	51
J. N. Shepherd not out	16	– lbw b Gifford	10
*D. A. Graveney (did not bat)		– not out	12
B 11, l-b 11, n-b 4	26	B 1, n-b 3	4

1/6 2/74 3/264 4/290   (5 wkts dec.) 356   1/67 2/75 3/107   (6 wkts dec.) 217
5/320   4/139 5/143 6/160

†R. C. Russell, J. H. Childs and G. E. Sainsbury did not bat.

Bonus points – Gloucestershire 4, Warwickshire 2 (Score at 100 overs: 339-5).

Bowling: *First Innings*—Old 20–4–64–1; Hogg 15–1–53–2; Gifford 41–15–72–0; Thorne 10–0–59–1; Lethbridge 9–0–44–0; Kallicharran 11–1–38–1. *Second Innings*—Old 7–1–24–0; Hogg 7–3–16–0; Gifford 37.1–19–52–4; Thorne 2–0–12–0; Kallicharran 35–5–109–2.

Warwickshire

R. I. H. B. Dyer lbw b Sainsbury	9	– (6) c Stovold b Graveney	17
K. D. Smith c Stovold b Childs	109	– (1) c Graveney b Childs	66
C. Lethbridge b Sainsbury	1		
A. I. Kallicharran c Russell b Shepherd	16	– (3) c Graveney b Childs	48
D. L. Amiss c Russell b Sainsbury	52	– (4) c Graveney b Shepherd	31
†G. W. Humpage c Shepherd b Childs	6	– (2) b Graveney	31
Asif Din c Broad b Childs	15	– not out	28
C. M. Old c Russell b Shepherd	39	– (5) b Sainsbury	34
D. A. Thorne not out	23	– (8) not out	1
*N. Gifford c Romaines b Shepherd	13		
B 8, l-b 9, w 1, n-b 2	20	B 1, l-b 9, w 1, n-b 4	15

1/14 2/25 3/52 4/152   (9 wkts dec.) 303   1/77 2/131 3/172   (6 wkts) 271
5/163 6/214 7/224 8/283 9/303   4/218 5/223 6/261

W. Hogg did not bat.

Bonus points – Warwickshire 3, Gloucestershire 3 (Score at 100 overs: 277-7).

Bowling: *First Innings*—Shepherd 26.4–9–54–3; Sainsbury 33–10–101–3; Childs 27–9–69–3; Bainbridge 10–5–18–0; Graveney 10–0–41–0. *Second Innings*—Shepherd 13–2–56–1; Sainsbury 13–2–54–1; Childs 17–2–75–2; Graveney 17–0–71–2.

Umpires: J. Birkenshaw and B. J. Meyer.

GLOUCESTERSHIRE v YORKSHIRE

At Cheltenham, August 13, 15, 16. Gloucestershire won by five wickets. Gloucestershire 21 pts, Yorkshire 5 pts. Boycott batted throughout the first day for his unbeaten 140 which earned him a reprimand for slow scoring. Sharp's 121 was much more entertaining and it was no fault of his that Yorkshire missed a fourth batting point by 3 runs. Gloucestershire then slumped to 76 for five before Romaines and Shepherd added 171. Boycott, in far more sprightly mood, carried the Yorkshire second innings and it was a surprise when Graveney prised him out 3 short of a second century. Set 277 in 188 minutes, Gloucestershire paced their effort to perfection, winning with eleven balls to spare and so pushing Yorkshire to the bottom of the Championship table.

Yorkshire

G. Boycott not out	140	– c Stovold b Graveney 97
M. D. Moxon b Sainsbury	27	– c Russell b Shepherd 5
C. W. J. Athey lbw b Sainsbury	0	– b Sainsbury 36
K. Sharp run out	121	– c Romaines b Shepherd 2
G. B. Stevenson c Broad b Bainbridge	11	– (7) c Bainbridge b Childs 10
J. D. Love run out	22	– (5) c Hignell b Sainsbury.......... 14
†D. L. Bairstow not out	6	– (6) not out 40
P. Carrick (did not bat)		– st Russell b Graveney 4
S. J. Dennis (did not bat)		– c Hignell b Graveney................ 0
I. G. Swallow (did not bat)		– not out 4
B 8, l-b 8, w 1	17	B 13, l-b 11, n-b 3....... 27

1/50 2/50 3/274   (5 wkts dec.) 344   1/6 2/90 3/104   (8 wkts dec.) 239
4/294 5/334   4/135 5/195 6/212 7/226 8/226

*R. Illingworth did not bat.

Bonus points – Yorkshire 3, Gloucestershire 1 (Score at 100 overs: 297-4).

Bowling: *First Innings*—Shepherd 25–9–52–0; Sainsbury 25–5–86–2; Bainbridge 33–4–79–1; Childs 20–4–67–0; Graveney 12–0–43–0. *Second Innings*—Shepherd 18–6–34–2; Sainsbury 20–3–67–2; Childs 14–2–61–1; Graveney 18–4–45–3; Bainbridge 1–0–5–0.

Gloucestershire

A. W. Stovold b Dennis	37	– b Dennis 2
B. C. Broad b Stevenson	17	– c Carrick b Swallow 100
P. Bainbridge c Illingworth b Dennis	9	– c Athey b Illingworth 39
Zaheer Abbas c Illingworth b Stevenson	10	– c Stevenson b Carrick 75
P. W. Romaines not out	100	– (6) c Swallow b Dennis 16
A. J. Hignell lbw b Dennis	0	– (5) not out 24
J. N. Shepherd c Illingworth b Carrick	93	– not out 13
*D. A. Graveney not out	25	
B 1, l-b 9, n-b 6	16	B 4, l-b 4, w 1, n-b 2....... 11

1/27 2/41 3/72   (6 wkts dec.) 307   1/8 2/101 3/225   (5 wkts) 280
4/76 5/76 6/247   4/228 5/259

†R. C. Russell, J. H. Childs and G. E. Sainsbury did not bat.

Bonus points – Gloucestershire 4, Yorkshire 2.

Bowling: *First Innings*—Dennis 20–2–80–3; Stevenson 22–5–83–2; Carrick 33.4–10–76–1; Illingworth 12–5–17–0; Swallow 9–2–35–0. *Second Innings*—Dennis 9–2–36–2; Stevenson 10.1–2–43–0; Carrick 19–0–97–1; Illingworth 19–3–78–1; Swallow 2–1–15–1.

Umpires: J. H. Harris and B. J. Meyer.

At Colchester, August 20, 22. GLOUCESTERSHIRE lost to ESSEX by an innings and 37 runs.

At Scarborough, August 24, 25, 26. GLOUCESTERSHIRE drew with YORKSHIRE.

GLOUCESTERSHIRE v NOTTINGHAMSHIRE

At Bristol, August 27, 29, 30. Drawn. Gloucestershire 7 pts, Nottinghamshire 4 pts. A match containing three individual centuries ended tamely, but two of the century-makers had additional reasons for remembering it. Broad hit a career-best 145 for Gloucestershire on the second day, only to be told on the following afternoon that he would not be selected for the county again. This followed an interview in a local newspaper in which he said he wanted to leave to further his Test ambitions, charging that the selectors never watched Gloucestershire. He also cited differences with one or two senior players. Paul Johnson, only eighteen, hit an exhilarating maiden hundred in Nottinghamshire's second innings and Rice completed a more sedate hundred before leaving Gloucestershire 287 to win in three hours. Despite lively efforts by Broad and Hignell, also making his final appearance, steady bowling by Hemmings kept Gloucestershire behind the required rate. But on an easy pitch they had no difficulty in playing out time.

Nottinghamshire

P. Johnson c Broad b Sainsbury	52	– c Shepherd b Childs	125
R. T. Robinson lbw b Sainsbury	8	– c Russell b Shepherd	11
*C. E. B. Rice c Russell b Sainsbury	4	– not out	100
J. D. Birch run out	19	– st Russell b Cunningham	18
B. Hassan c Wright b Doughty	90	– run out	14
†B. N. French c Shepherd b Bainbridge	51	– not out	5
E. E. Hemmings c Wright b Childs	8		
K. Saxelby st Russell b Childs	23		
K. E. Cooper retired hurt	18		
M. K. Bore c Russell b Shepherd	20		
M. Hendrick c Cunningham b Doughty	5		
B 2, l-b 7, n-b 1	10	B 3, l-b 2	5

1/17 2/27 3/78 4/88   308   1/46 2/182   (4 wkts dec.) 278
5/197 6/212 7/248 8/299 9/299   3/235 4/265

Bonus points – Nottinghamshire 3, Gloucestershire 3 (Score at 100 overs: 250-7).

Bowling: *First Innings*—Sainsbury 29–7–76–3; Shepherd 24–7–78–1; Doughty 16.5–2–43–2; Childs 23–6–51–2; Cunningham 13–7–20–0; Bainbridge 12–2–30–1. *Second Innings*—Sainsbury 8–1–29–0; Shepherd 18–4–49–1; Childs 34–8–99–1; Cunningham 17–0–70–1; Doughty 7–0–26–0.

Gloucestershire

P. W. Romaines b Hemmings	46	– c French b Hemmings	6
B. C. Broad c French b Bore	145	– c French b Hemmings	43
P. Bainbridge st French b Hemmings	51	– c Hendrick b Hemmings	20
A. J. Wright not out	10	– not out	56
A. J. Hignell not out	31	– b Hemmings	40
E. J. Cunningham (did not bat)		– c Hassan b Hendrick	23
*J. N. Shepherd (did not bat)		– c Hassan b Hemmings	11
R. J. Doughty (did not bat)		– not out	2
B 1, l-b 13, n-b 3	17	B 5, n-b 2	7

1/137 2/251 3/257   (3 wkts dec.) 300   1/24 2/65 3/76   (6 wkts) 208
4/132 5/168 6/193

J. H. Childs, †R. C. Russell and G. E. Sainsbury did not bat.

Bonus points – Gloucestershire 4, Nottinghamshire 1.

Bowling: *First Innings*—Hendrick 9–2–27–0; Cooper 13–2–32–0; Saxelby 11–4–32–0; Bore 28–7–89–1; Hemmings 31.1–6–103–2. *Second Innings*—Hendrick 11–3–21–1; Cooper 2–0–13–0; Hemmings 24–5–102–5; Bore 16–4–65–0.

Umpires: R. Palmer and K. E. Palmer.

GLOUCESTERSHIRE v WORCESTERSHIRE

At Bristol, August 31, September 1, 2. Drawn. Gloucestershire 8 pts, Worcestershire 3 pts. Gales and rain came to Worcestershire's aid after they had lost three wickets for 14 runs when set 303 in 215 minutes. No Gloucestershire batsman failed as the Worcestershire bowlers took a first-day battering, Romaines thriving in his recently assumed role of opening batsman. A familiar early collapse by the young Worcestershire side was followed by a dour but successful fight-back, led by Curtis and D'Oliveira and rounded off by an adventurous half-century by Humphries. Russell, sent in as night-watchman, was unbeaten on 64 when Gloucestershire declared their second innings.

Gloucestershire

A. W. Stovold c Humphries b Inchmore	43	– c Weston b Pridgeon	38
P. W. Romaines c Illingworth b D'Oliveira	121	– c Humphries b Pridgeon	3
P. Bainbridge c Weston b Patel	56	– b Newport	50
A. J. Wright b Illingworth	56	– b Newport	5
E. J. Cunningham not out	29	– (6) lbw b Newport	0
R. J. Doughty not out	32	– (7) not out	31
†R. C. Russell (did not bat)	–	(5) not out	64
B 3, l-b 9, n-b 2	14	B 3, l-b 6, w 1, n-b 3	13

1/73 2/166 3/269   (4 wkts dec.) 351   1/22 2/54 3/69   (5 wkts dec.) 204
4/286   4/124 5/124

J. N. Shepherd, *D. A. Graveney, J. H. Childs and G. E. Sainsbury did not bat.

Bonus points – Gloucestershire 4, Worcestershire 1 (Score at 100 overs: 317-4).

Bowling: *First Innings*—Pridgeon 16–3–50–0; Inchmore 18–0–67–1; Newport 6–1–19–0; Illingworth 36–6–100–1; Patel 23–6–78–1; D'Oliveira 7–2–23–1. *Second Innings*—Pridgeon 16–2–46–2; Inchmore 15–4–59–0; Newport 14–2–40–3; Illingworth 6–0–22–0; Patel 8–0–24–0.

Worcestershire

M. S. A. McEvoy c Russell b Shepherd	22	– c Russell b Sainsbury	5
M. J. Weston lbw b Shepherd	13	– c Stovold b Shepherd	8
*P. A. Neale c Russell b Shepherd	4	– lbw b Shepherd	0
A. P. Pridgeon c Romaines b Shepherd	12		
D. N. Patel c Russell b Childs	38	– (4) not out	53
T. S. Curtis c Shepherd b Graveney	50	– (5) not out	9
D. B. D'Oliveira c Russell b Cunningham	42		
P. J. Newport c Stovold b Childs	2		
†D. J. Humphries not out	53		
R. K. Illingworth c Stovold b Graveney	0		
J. D. Inchmore b Sainsbury	11		
B 2, l-b 2, n-b 2	6	L-b 5, w 1	6

1/29 2/33 3/46 4/59   253   1/14 2/14 3/14   (3 wkts) 81
5/112 6/164 7/177 8/199 9/214

Bonus points – Worcestershire 2, Gloucestershire 4 (Score at 100 overs: 228-9).

Bowling: *First Innings*—Shepherd 25–6–76–4; Sainsbury 16.2–4–53–1; Bainbridge 9–2–29–0; Childs 31–10–52–2; Graveney 22–12–24–2; Cunningham 4–1–13–1. *Second Innings*—Shepherd 7–3–19–2; Sainsbury 6–2–12–1; Bainbridge 4–1–7–0; Childs 8–3–14–0; Cunningham 4–0–23–0.

Umpires: P. J. Eele and M. J. Kitchen.

At Worcester, September 7, 8, 9. GLOUCESTERSHIRE lost to WORCESTERSHIRE by 108 runs.

HAMPSHIRE

President: 1983 – R. Aird; 1984 – C. G. A. Paris
Chairman: G. Ford
Chairman, Cricket Committee: C. J. Knott
Secretary: A. K. James
  Northlands Road, Southampton SO9 2TY
  (Telephone: 0703-333788)
Captain: N. E. J. Pocock
Coach: P. J. Sainsbury

Hampshire could look back on the 1983 season with a sense of achievement and satisfaction, finishing third in the Schweppes County Championship and fifth in the John Player Sunday League, both identical positions to the previous year. However, 1983 was, if anything, the better performance, the World Cup depriving them for some weeks of the considerable talents of Gordon Greenidge, Malcolm Marshall and Trevor Jesty.

There were disappointments, however, in particular in the way Hampshire allowed winning positions to slip from their grasp against Kent at Canterbury, first in the quarter-final of the Benson and Hedges Cup and then in the semi-final of the NatWest Bank Trophy. Thus Hampshire still hold the unwelcome tag of being the only county not to have appeared in a Lord's final. This is something which rankles with their supporters, as it does with the captain, Nick Pocock. But those two defeats should not be allowed to cloud a season which saw much positive, attacking and entertaining cricket.

Hampshire won ten Championship matches and were beaten only twice. There is little doubt they would have finished with twelve victories but for the intervention of rain, which in an otherwise glorious August robbed them of success against Gloucestershire at Portsmouth and Somerset at Taunton. Getting the worst of the weather in two successive John Player League games in July could also be held responsible for the end of their challenge in that competition.

The highlight of the season came at Southend in July when Hampshire beat Essex, the eventual champions, by scoring over 400 runs in the fourth innings of the match. Hampshire were the first county to do this since 1939 and it was their own highest fourth-innings total in their 121-year history.

Hampshire's batting was in good order. Five players scored over 1,000 first-class runs and the strength in depth is shown by the fact that Marshall, who scored two centuries, batted at No. 7. Chris Smith, in his first season as a qualified "Englishman", was the leading run-getter; his consistency and application brought him six centuries in first-class cricket and earned him a place in the England side for the last two Test matches as well as selection for the winter tour.

Smith's younger brother, Robin, aged nineteen, who will be qualified for England in 1985, has already shown such great potential that he, too, could become a Test cricketer. His appearances in 1983 were restricted by the rules relating to overseas players, but he still managed to score three first-class centuries in his five matches. In addition to Chris Smith, Greenidge, who returned from the World Cup in splendid form, Mark Nicholas, who also made progress as a medium-paced bowler, Jesty and Paul Terry all scored 1,000 runs. The advance of Terry was especially gratifying for, besides having undoubted talent as a batsman, he is a superb fieldsman. After being brought into the side in early June, Terry held his place and completed three centuries in scoring 1,000 runs for the first time.

It is Hampshire's misfortune that their bowling does not contain the strength and depth of their batting, and problems were caused by the injuries and loss of form suffered by Kevin Emery and John Southern, the slow left-arm spinner who announced his retirement at the end of the season. In 1982 Emery took 83 first-class wickets and played for England B; in 1983 he took five. It is vital that he should recover his form and remain free from injury in 1984 when the West Indies tour is likely to deprive Hampshire of Marshall, their main strike bowler.

One of the game's finest fast bowlers, Marshall had another splendid season and finished second in the national bowling averages. He took 80 wickets at an average of 16.58 and would almost certainly have exceeded 100 for a second year running but for missing seven matches because of the World Cup. He was the one Hampshire bowler capable of winning a match himself, though there were gains to be found in the performances of others. Tim Tremlett, for one, had easily his best season and, under the right conditions, his seam bowling was excellent. His total of 63 first-class wickets almost doubled his tally of the previous summer. His advance earned him a county cap, as did Terry's batting. Behind only Marshall and Tremlett in wicket-taking was the whole-hearted Steve Malone, while Nigel Cowley bowled a tight line with his off-breaks and collected 41 wickets.

To build up the bowling generally is obviously a priority. If this can be done then Hampshire may look to the future with great confidence. The batting strength seems fairly secure, and the fielding and catching are good. Bob Parks again proved an efficient wicket-keeper, and Pocock was an enterprising captain who always put team above personal performance. The players responded well to his influence and quickly recovered from the disappointment of the NatWest Bank Trophy defeat to win matches at the tail end of a long and hard season. – B.H.

HAMPSHIRE 1983

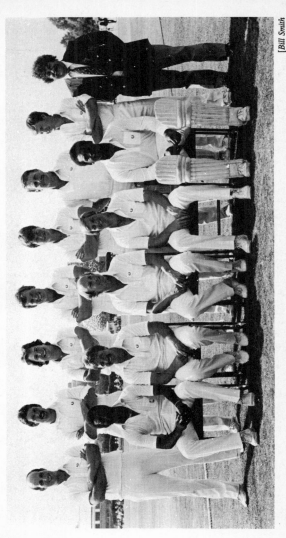

[*Bill Smith*]

Back row: K. Stevenson, S. J. Malone, M. C. J. Nicholas, T. M. Tremlett, V. P. Terry, C. L. Smith, R. J. Parks, V. Isaacs (*scorer*). *Front row:* M. D. Marshall, N. G. Cowley, N. E. J. Pocock (*captain*), T. E. Jesty, C. G. Greenidge.

HAMPSHIRE RESULTS

All first-class matches – Played 26: Won 11, Lost 3, Drawn 12.

County Championship matches – Played 24: Won 10, Lost 2, Drawn 12.

Bonus points – Batting 62, Bowling 71.

Competition placings – Schweppes County Championship, 3rd; NatWest Bank Trophy, s-f; Benson and Hedges Cup, q-f; John Player League, 5th.

COUNTY CHAMPIONSHIP AVERAGES

BATTING

	Birthplace	M	I	NO	R	HI	Avge
R. A. Smith............	Durban, SA	5	9	3	401	104*	66.83
C. G. Greenidge c	St Peter, Barbados	15	27	5	1,438	154	65.36
C. L. Smith c	Durban, SA	20	33	3	1,831	193	61.03
M. D. Marshall c	St Michael, Barbados	16	16	4	563	112	46.91
V. P. Terry c	Osnabruck, WG	18	29	6	1,039	115	45.17
T. E. Jesty c	Gosport	19	28	5	1,019	187	44.30
M. C. J. Nicholas c ...	London	24	39	5	1,192	110	35.05
D. R. Turner c	Chippenham	11	15	2	425	94*	32.69
N. E. J. Pocock c	Maracaibo, Venezuela	24	32	7	681	60*	27.24
T. M. Tremlett c	Wellington, Somerset	22	17	5	229	59	19.08
N. G. Cowley c	Shaftesbury	21	24	8	302	29	18.87
J. W. Southern c	King's Cross	14	13	5	146	45*	18.25
R. J. Parks c	Cuckfield	24	15	2	180	52	13.84
K. Stevenson c	Derby	6	7	3	51	25	12.75
S. J. Malone	Chelmsford	20	13	4	37	12	4.11

Also batted: K. St J. D. Emery (*Swindon*) (5 matches) 8.

*Signifies not out. c *Denotes county cap.*

BOWLING

	O	M	R	W	Avge	BB
M. D. Marshall	532.5	144	1,327	80	16.58	7-29
T. M. Tremlett........	557.2	177	1,285	58	22.15	6-82
N. G. Cowley	392.3	129	965	38	25.39	4-10
K. Stevenson	162.5	37	554	19	29.15	5-81
M. C. J. Nicholas	246.2	66	695	23	30.21	5-45
C. L. Smith	154	42	512	15	34.13	3-35
J. W. Southern	327.5	105	848	24	35.33	5-60
T. E. Jesty	256.5	70	804	21	38.28	3-48
S. J. Malone	481.1	104	1,620	41	39.51	4-39

Also bowled: K. St J. D. Emery 75–22–204–5; N. E. J. Pocock 18–3–87–1.

The following played a total of 21 three-figure innings for Hampshire in County Championship matches – C. L. Smith 6, C. G. Greenidge 4, R. A. Smith 3, V. P. Terry 3, M. D. Marshall 2, M. C. J. Nicholas 2, T. E. Jesty 1.

At Leicester, April 30, May 1, 2. HAMPSHIRE drew with LEICESTERSHIRE.

At Northampton, May 4, 5, 6. HAMPSHIRE drew with NORTHAMPTONSHIRE.

HAMPSHIRE v WARWICKSHIRE

At Southampton, May 11, 12, 13. Hampshire won by 9 runs. Hampshire 12 pts. After no play on the first two days, Hampshire won a one-innings match with two balls remaining. Having been put in, they were reduced to 56 for five, Old removing Pocock and Cowley with successive deliveries. However, Smith and Marshall added 158 in 113 minutes (34 overs) for the sixth wicket and Warwickshire were left a target of 217 in 160 minutes. They lost seven wickets for 86 before Lethbridge and Old put on 65 in eight overs, but Old, who hit two 6s, fell to Tremlett, Willis to Marshall, and Hogg was run out off the fourth ball of the final over to leave Lethbridge unbeaten.

Hampshire

D. R. Turner c Humpage b Willis	1	M. D. Marshall run out	79
C. L. Smith not out	81	J. W. Southern not out	0
M. C. J. Nicholas c Ferreira b Hogg	1	L-b 14, n-b 4	18
T. E. Jesty c Hogg b Ferreira	36		
*N. E. J. Pocock c Tedstone b Old	0	1/2 2/3 3/53	(6 wkts dec.) 216
N. G. Cowley c Tedstone b Old	0	4/56 5/56 6/214	

T. M. Tremlett, †R. J. Parks and S. J. Malone did not bat.

Bowling: Willis 11–1–50–1; Hogg 4–2–8–1; Ferreira 23–6–68–1; Old 10–0–37–2; Lethbridge 7–0–35–0.

Warwickshire

D. L. Amiss c Parks b Malone	4	C. M. Old c Southern b Tremlett	36
K. D. Smith lbw b Malone	10	*R. G. D. Willis c Tremlett b Marshall	2
A. I. Kallicharran c Southern b Jesty	53	W. Hogg run out	4
G. W. Humpage c Parks b Tremlett	1	B 3, l-b 14, w 1	18
Asif Din c Nicholas b Tremlett	1		
A. M. Ferreira c Parks b Tremlett	0	1/15 2/22 3/39 4/55	207
†G. A. Tedstone c Malone b Jesty	5	5/55 6/74 7/86 8/151 9/157	
C. Lethbridge not out	73		

Bowling: Marshall 19–4–61–1; Malone 12.4–5–36–2; Tremlett 9–0–53–4; Jesty 7–0–39–2.

Umpires: W. E. Alley and D. R. Shepherd.

HAMPSHIRE v WORCESTERSHIRE

At Southampton, May 25, 26, 27. Hampshire won by seven wickets. Hampshire 22 pts, Worcestershire 6 pts. Nicholas, moving the ball through the air and off the seam, returned career-best figures of five for 45 after Worcestershire had been put in. Hampshire's reply was 2 runs short, but the door to victory was opened by Marshall, who took six second-innings wickets, including four in twelve balls for 2 runs. Worcestershire's last seven wickets fell for 82 and Hampshire, chasing a target of 200, were steered to victory by Greenidge, whose 116 in 195 minutes contained two 6s, a 5 and eight 4s. After thundery rain had stopped play for nineteen minutes, Hampshire needed 11 runs from 3.5 overs and the target was achieved in nine deliveries to beat the weather.

Worcestershire

J. A. Ormrod b Nicholas	41	– c Parks b Marshall	4
M. J. Weston run out	38	– c Parks b Nicholas	15
*P. A. Neale c Marshall b Nicholas	38	– lbw b Marshall	49
D. N. Patel c Jesty b Nicholas	53	– c Parks b Malone	37
C. L. King c Greenidge b Nicholas	8	– (6) c Nicholas b Marshall	27
D. B. D'Oliveira c Tremlett b Nicholas	10	– (7) not out	30
†D. J. Humphries c Nicholas b Marshall	17	– (8) b Marshall	2
R. K. Illingworth c Parks b Marshall	8	– (9) c Parks b Marshall	0
A. E Warner lbw b Marshall	4	– (10) c and b Marshall	0
J. D. Inchmore not out	3	– (11) c Smith b Southern	21
A. P. Pridgeon lbw b Tremlett	4	– (5) c Marshall b Jesty	7
B 1, l-b 9, w 3	13	L-b 3, w 1, n-b 1	5

1/48 2/108 3/139 4/151   237   1/6 2/34 3/99 4/115   197
5/180 6/203 7/223 8/229 9/232   5/115 6/155 7/163 8/163 9/164

Bonus points – Worcestershire 2, Hampshire 4.

Bowling: *First Innings*—Marshall 21–6–39–3; Malone 20–6–58–0; Tremlett 22.3–9–41–1; Jesty 6–0–19–0; Southern 4–0–22–0; Nicholas 20–6–45–5. *Second Innings*—Marshall 24–7–58–6; Malone 16–5–39–1; Nicholas 10–0–39–1; Tremlett 7–3–12–0; Southern 2.3–1–10–1; Jesty 9–1–34–1.

Hampshire

C. G. Greenidge lbw b Inchmore	5	– c D'Oliveira b Patel	116
C. L. Smith c Weston b Pridgeon	37	– st Humphries b Patel	16
D. R. Turner b Inchmore	11	– st Humphries b Patel	13
T. E. Jesty c Humphries b Pridgeon	36	– not out	28
M. C. J. Nicholas lbw b Pridgeon	0	– not out	8
*N. E. J. Pocock not out	60		
M. D. Marshall c Ormrod b Inchmore	39		
T. M. Tremlett c D'Oliveira b Illingworth	15		
J. W. Southern c Humphries b Warner	5		
†R. J. Parks lbw b Warner	3		
S. J. Malone b Warner	0		
B 4, l-b 2, w 1, n-b 17	24	B 1, l-b 9, w 11	21

1/5 2/42 3/100 4/101   235   1/104 2/140 3/189   (3 wkts) 202
5/104 6/171 7/216 8/223 9/235

Bonus points – Hampshire 2, Worcestershire 4.

Bowling: *First Innings*—Pridgeon 23–8–61–3; Inchmore 23–3–59–3; Warner 19–3–52–3; Illingworth 8–2–26–1; King 7–1–13–0. *Second Innings*—Pridgeon 10–2–31–0; Inchmore 7–0–17–0; Warner 5–0–24–0; Patel 23–5–69–3; Illingworth 16.4–2–40–0.

Umpires: M. J. Kitchen and R. Palmer.

At Canterbury, May 28, 30, 31. HAMPSHIRE drew with KENT.

At Derby, June 4, 6, 7. HAMPSHIRE drew with DERBYSHIRE.

HAMPSHIRE v LANCASHIRE

At Bournemouth, June 8, 9, 10. Drawn. Hampshire 5 pts, Lancashire 5 pts. Hampshire's first innings was dominated by the South African-born Smith brothers, Chris and Robin, both of whom hit centuries on a placid wicket. Robin, on his Championship début, reached his century with a 4 off the last ball of the day, hitting two 6s and thirteen 4s in a stay of 142 minutes. A century by Abrahams, only his fourth in eleven years, helped Lancashire to maximum batting points and an immediate declaration, whereupon Terry hit a maiden hundred in Hampshire's second innings. Another declaration left Lancashire a target of 289 in 175 minutes, but the challenge was not taken up.

Hampshire

C. L. Smith c Cockbain b Nasir	100	– c Fairbrother b Simmons	61
V. P. Terry lbw b Jefferies	66	– st Maynard b Simmons	114
M. C. J. Nicholas run out	21	– b Folley	36
R. A. Smith not out	100	– not out	15
*N. E. J. Pocock not out	57		
L-b 6, w 1, n-b 6	13	L-b 3, w 1, n-b 2	6

1/158 2/196 3/211 (3 wkts dec.) 357   1/132 2/206 3/232 (3 wkts dec.) 232

N. G. Cowley, T. M. Tremlett, J. W. Southern, †R. J. Parks, K. St J. D. Emery and S. J. Malone did not bat.

Bonus points – Hampshire 3, Lancashire 1 (Score at 100 overs: 252-3).

Bowling: *First Innings*—Jefferies 33–10–87–1; Folley 26–7–54–0; O'Shaughnessy 20–5–93–0; Simmons 28–8–68–0; Nasir 17–5–42–1. *Second Innings*—Jefferies 24–3–76–0; Folley 28–7–67–1; O'Shaughnessy 5–1–19–0; Simmons 11.5–4–53–2; Nasir 2–0–11–0.

Lancashire

I. Cockbain c Terry b Emery	2	– c Pocock b Malone	31
S. J. O'Shaughnessy lbw b Tremlett	18	– c Cowley b Southern	28
F. C. Hayes c Southern b Emery	0	– (4) b Malone	13
D. P. Hughes c C. L. Smith b Emery	11	– (5) c Nicholas b Southern	0
*J. Abrahams not out	117	– (6) not out	4
N. H. Fairbrother c Southern b C. L. Smith	50		
J. Simmons b Tremlett	41		
S. T. Jefferies not out	37		
†C. Maynard (did not bat)		– (3) not out	36
B 9, l-b 9, w 2, n-b 5	25	L-b 4, w 1, n-b 5	10

1/11 2/11 3/38 (6 wkts dec.) 301   1/65 2/65 (4 wkts) 122
4/52 5/175 6/241   3/93 4/114

Nasir Zaidi and I. Folley did not bat.

Bonus points – Lancashire 4, Hampshire 2.

Bowling: *First Innings*—Malone 16–3–50–0; Emery 13–4–34–3; Tremlett 17.5–7–50–2; Cowley 24–7–62–0; Southern 11–3–42–0; Nicholas 8–3–18–0; C. L. Smith 7–5–20–1. *Second Innings*—Malone 10–3–42–2; Emery 13–6–24–0; C. L. Smith 7–2–18–0; Southern 16–8–19–2; Pocock 2–0–9–0.

Umpires: C. T. Spencer and R. A. White.

At Oxford, June 11, 13, 14. HAMPSHIRE beat OXFORD UNIVERSITY by eight wickets.

At Uxbridge, June 15, 16. HAMPSHIRE lost to MIDDLESEX by an innings and 64 runs.

HAMPSHIRE v YORKSHIRE

At Southampton, June 18, 20, 21. Yorkshire won by seven wickets. Yorkshire 23 pts, Hampshire 2 pts. Yorkshire laid the foundations for victory at the outset by dismissing Hampshire for a paltry 83 with Sidebottom the chief executioner, his five wickets costing just 6 runs. Yorkshire found batting altogether easier, especially Stevenson whose 52 came from 30 balls, as they built a lead of 349. Hampshire did not succumb so easily a second time, when there was some purposeful batting from the Smith brothers and Nicholas. Parks and Southern helped to avert an innings defeat, but Yorkshire, left to score 72 in fifteen overs, got home with four balls to spare.

Hampshire

V. P. Terry c Bairstow b Athey	22	– b Carrick 25
C. L. Smith lbw b Dennis	0	– b Carrick 75
M. C. J. Nicholas c Bairstow b Stevenson	5	– c Bairstow b Stevenson 97
R. A. Smith c Bairstow b Stevenson	3	– c Illingworth b Boycott 42
*N. E. J. Pocock c Love b Dennis	1	– c Athey b Sidebottom 23
N. G. Cowley c Bairstow b Sidebottom	10	– c Lumb b Stevenson 10
T. M. Tremlett b Sidebottom	3	– c Athey b Stevenson 0
†J. R. Parks b Sidebottom	0	– b Dennis 52
J. W. Southern not out	7	– not out 45
K. Stevenson c Bairstow b Sidebottom	25	– b Dennis 1
S. J. Malone c Love b Sidebottom	0	– b Sidebottom 12
B 1, l-b 1, w 2, n-b 3	7	B 4, l-b 9, w 4, n-b 21 38

1/1 2/15 3/28 4/29   83   1/68 2/135 3/248 4/266   420
5/46 6/46 7/46 8/83 9/83   5/297 6/297 7/297 8/386 9/388

Bonus points – Yorkshire 4.

Bowling: *First Innings*—Dennis 7–1–19–2; Stevenson 10–2–34–2; Sidebottom 8.5–6–6–5; Athey 5–1–17–1. *Second Innings*—Dennis 34–8–94–2; Stevenson 25–6–80–3; Carrick 51–22–78–2; Sidebottom 29.3–9–93–2; Illingworth 13–8–18–0; Athey 2–1–4–0; Boycott 9–4–15–1.

Yorkshire

G. Boycott c Nicholas b Tremlett	46	– run out 22
R. G. Lumb c Nicholas b Southern	60	– st Parks b Tremlett 19
C. W. J. Athey c Parks b Stevenson	90	– c Nicholas b Tremlett 15
S. N. Hartley c Nicholas b Cowley	23	– not out 2
S. J. Dennis c Malone b Southern	7	
G. B. Stevenson c Pocock b Stevenson	52	
J. D. Love c Terry b Stevenson	31	– (5) not out 9
†D. L. Bairstow not out	60	
P. Carrick not out	54	
B 1, l-b 6, w 1, n-b 1	9	B 1, l-b 3, w 1 5

1/91 2/131 3/190 4/199   (7 wkts dec.) 432   1/33 2/59 3/59   (3 wkts) 72
5/268 6/302 7/317

A. Sidebottom and *R. Illingworth did not bat.

Bonus points – Yorkshire 3, Hampshire 2 (Score at 100 overs: 272-5).

Bowling: *First Innings*—Stevenson 18–4–72–3; Malone 31–8–108–0; Nicholas 11–2–35–0; Tremlett 33–10–48–1; Southern 31–8–111–2; Cowley 13–3–49–1. *Second Innings*—Malone 7.2–1–32–0; Stevenson 1–0–9–0; Tremlett 6–0–26–2.

Umpires: J. H. Harris and J. van Geloven.

HAMPSHIRE v SUSSEX

At Basingstoke, June 22, 23, 24. Drawn. Hampshire 7 pts, Sussex 3 pts. A splendid effort by Mendis, eighth out at 188, stopped Sussex from complete collapse on a low, slow wicket. The humid atmosphere helped Stevenson's swing and his five for 81 was his best return for two years. Hampshire's reply was dominated by the Smith brothers, who put on 63 for the third wicket before Chris was caught at slip off Pigott. Robin went on to score an unbeaten century (two 6s, twelve 4s). Hampshire, who declared with a lead of 69, looked to have a chance of victory when Sussex lost three second-innings wickets for 62, but their hopes were dashed by Barclay, Parker and then le Roux's big hitting.

Sussex

G. D. Mendis c Nicholas b Tremlett	91	– c Pocock b Tremlett	29
J. R. P. Heath c Pocock b Malone	4	– c Malone b Stevenson	22
*J. R. T. Barclay c and b Stevenson	1	– c Nicholas b Tremlett	65
C. M. Wells c C. L. Smith b Stevenson	11	– lbw b Nicholas	0
P. W. G. Parker c Nicholas b Stevenson	4	– c Parks b Stevenson	58
A. P. Wells c Nicholas b Tremlett	12	– c Pocock b Tremlett	0
G. S. le Roux c Parks b Stevenson	29	– c Nicholas b C. L. Smith	80
D. A. Reeve b Malone	20	– not out	4
A. C. S. Pigott lbw b Tremlett	16	– not out	0
†D. J. Smith lbw b Stevenson	1		
C. E. Waller not out	17		
L-b 6, w 5, n-b 1	12	B 1, l-b 14, w 3	18

1/6 2/7 3/44 4/48   218   1/53 2/61 3/62   (7 wkts dec.) 276
5/70 6/122 7/170 8/188 9/189   4/184 5/188 6/197 7/274

Bonus points – Sussex 2, Hampshire 4.

Bowling: *First Innings*—Malone 14–3–52–2; Stevenson 25–5–81–5; Nicholas 17–6–28–0; Tremlett 21.2–7–39–3; Cowley 5–2–6–0. *Second Innings*—Malone 19–5–43–0; Stevenson 18–6–55–2; Tremlett 27–6–71–3; Nicholas 12–4–28–1; Cowley 8–4–41–0; C. L. Smith 4–1–20–1.

Hampshire

V. P. Terry c Smith b le Roux	6	N. G. Cowley not out	22
C. L. Smith c Heath b Pigott	83	B 1, l-b 6, w 2, n-b 5	14
M. C. J. Nicholas lbw b C. M. Wells	44		
R. A. Smith not out	104	1/10 2/115 (4 wkts dec.) 287
*N. E. J. Pocock c Smith b le Roux	14	3/178 4/224	

T. M. Tremlett, †R. J. Parks, J. W. Southern, K. Stevenson and S. J. Malone did not bat.

Bonus points – Hampshire 3, Sussex 1.

Bowling: le Roux 22–6–54–2; Pigott 13–0–67–1; Reeve 18–6–46–0; C. M. Wells 17–5–48–1; Waller 27–9–58–0.

Umpires: J. H. Harris and J. van Geloven.

At Bristol, June 25, 27, 28. HAMPSHIRE beat GLOUCESTERSHIRE by 118 runs.

At Liverpool, July 2, 4, 5. HAMPSHIRE drew with LANCASHIRE.

HAMPSHIRE v SURREY

At Southampton, July 9, 11, 12. Drawn. Hampshire 6 pts, Surrey 6 pts. Hampshire's opening stand of 134 soon made Surrey regret their decision to field. Greenidge was 17 short of his third successive Championship century when he was run out, but another Barbadian, Marshall, then made 100 in 112 minutes. Lynch and Richards dominated Surrey's reply, but when Hampshire went in again, Greenidge continued to reap a rich harvest of runs, hitting eight 6s and fourteen 4s in 168 minutes. Surrey, set a target of 342 in 240 minutes, lost half their wickets for 117, but Knight and Thomas ensured a draw.

Hampshire
C. G. Greenidge run out	83	– c Payne b Butcher 154
C. L. Smith c Butcher b Thomas	47	– c Richards b Butcher 26
M. C. J. Nicholas c Butcher b Clarke	23	– (4) c Richards b Butcher 34
T. E. Jesty c Payne b Clarke	12	
V. P. Terry c Thomas b Monkhouse	43	– not out 26
*N. E. J. Pocock c and b Pocock	30	– not out 17
M. D. Marshall not out	100	
J. W. Southern not out	13	
†R. J. Parks (did not bat)		– (3) c Knight b Butcher 29
L-b 7, w 4, n-b 9	20	B 7, l-b 7, w 4, n-b 5 23

1/134 2/135 3/174   (6 wkts dec.) 371   1/93 2/203   (4 wkts dec.) 309
4/176 5/220 6/311   3/250 4/277

T. M. Tremlett and S. J. Malone did not bat.

Bonus points – Hampshire 4, Surrey 2.

Bowling: *First Innings*—Clarke 23–6–67–2; Thomas 14–0–87–1; Monkhouse 17–5–59–1; Knight 14–2–50–0; Payne 12.5–3–46–0; Pocock 12–4–42–1. *Second Innings*—Clarke 6–1–20–0; Thomas 7–2–32–0; Payne 10–4–22–0; Pocock 23–6–89–0; Butcher 23–5–123–4.

Surrey
A. R. Butcher c Parks b Malone	19	– c sub b Smith 16
D. B. Pauline b Marshall	0	– lbw b Marshall 0
G. Monkhouse retired hurt	0	
D. M. Smith lbw b Marshall	18	– (3) c Marshall b Smith 24
*R. D. V. Knight b Tremlett	57	– not out 51
M. A. Lynch st Parks b Southern	119	– (4) c and b Smith 42
†C. J. Richards not out	85	– (6) b Southern 14
D. J. Thomas c Greenidge b Smith	24	– (7) not out 28
I. R. Payne not out	2	
B 2, l-b 6, w 1, n-b 6	15	L-b 2 2

1/1 2/25 3/53   (6 wkts dec.) 339   1/3 2/29 3/91   (5 wkts) 177
4/149 5/275 6/316   4/94 5/117

S. T. Clarke and P. I. Pocock did not bat.

Bonus points – Surrey 4, Hampshire 2.

Bowling: *First Innings*—Marshall 11–4–20–2; Malone 15–4–58–1; Jesty 8–2–15–0; Tremlett 11–3–25–1; Southern 20–2–91–1; Nicholas 8–2–24–0; Smith 10.5–0–76–1; Pocock 2–0–15–0. *Second Innings*—Marshall 10–4–25–1; Malone 9–3–22–0; Tremlett 3–3–0–0; Smith 21–7–70–3; Southern 21–7–52–1; Pocock 5–3–6–0.

Umpires: M. J. Kitchen and N. T. Plews.

At Southend, July 13, 14, 15. HAMPSHIRE beat ESSEX by four wickets.

HAMPSHIRE v NOTTINGHAMSHIRE

At Bournemouth, July 16, 18, 19. Hampshire won by eight wickets. Hampshire 24 pts, Nottinghamshire 4pts. Rice held Nottinghamshire together after they had been put in on a pitch that was sometimes uneven in bounce. In reply, Hampshire were always in command. For Nottinghamshire Hemmings bowled unchanged for 35 overs and had Terry dropped at 13, the batsman making no further mistake in an unbeaten century. Nottinghamshire resisted well in their second innings, which spanned five hours, but Hampshire needed only 68 for victory and these they achieved with 70 minutes to spare.

Nottinghamshire

B. Hassan c Greenidge b Marshall	3	– c Greenidge b Marshall	53
R. T. Robinson lbw b Nicholas	36	– b Southern	29
*C. E. B. Rice c Smith b Tremlett	79	– c Parks b Tremlett	68
J. D. Birch lbw b Tremlett	17	– c Tremlett b Southern	20
M. A. Fell run out	0	– b Southern	0
E. E. Hemmings lbw b Marshall	0	– b Tremlett	5
†B. N. French c Parks b Marshall	23	– c Nicholas b Southern	12
K. Saxelby c Tremlett b Marshall	34	– c Marshall b Southern	15
R. A. Pick not out	12	– b Marshall	14
M. K. Bore b Stevenson	4	– lbw b Marshall	8
M. Hendrick lbw b Stevenson	0	– not out	0
B 4, l-b 16, w 1, n-b 4	25	B 4, l-b 3, n-b 7	14

1/5 2/87 3/130 4/134   233   1/63 2/114 3/160 4/165   238
5/134 6/155 7/201 8/218 9/233   5/179 6/188 7/211 8/228 9/238

Bonus points – Nottinghamshire 2, Hampshire 4.

Bowling: *First Innings*—Marshall 31–10–70–4; Stevenson 18.5–6–67–2; Tremlett 23–15–12–2; Jesty 8–3–24–0; Nicholas 4–1–12–1; Southern 9–3–23–0. *Second Innings*—Marshall 20–4–46–3; Stevenson 11–2–30–0; Tremlett 17–9–21–2; Southern 29.2–8–75–5; Smith 6–2–21–0; Jesty 6–0–31–0.

Hampshire

C. G. Greenidge lbw b Hemmings	63	– not out	31
C. L. Smith c French b Hendrick	11	– b Hemmings	11
M. C. J. Nicholas c Hendrick b Bore	42	– c Hendrick b Bore	20
T. E. Jesty c Hendrick b Bore	86	– not out	6
V. P. Terry not out	106		
*N. E. J. Pocock c Rice b Bore	59		
M. D. Marshall c Bore b Hendrick	15		
K. Stevenson not out	10		
B 1, l-b 5, w 1	7		

1/33 2/111 3/121   (6 wkts dec.) 404   1/16 2/43   (2 wkts) 68
4/253 5/366 6/393

T. M. Tremlett, †R. J. Parks and J. W. Southern did not bat.

Bonus points – Hampshire 4, Nottinghamshire 2 (Score at 100 overs: 391-5).

Bowling: *First Innings*—Hendrick 16–5–36–2; Saxelby 8–0–42–0; Hemmings 37–6–129–1; Pick 20–3–101–0; Bore 21–4–89–3. *Second Innings*—Hendrick 4–2–6–0; Hemmings 10–4–31–1; Pick 2–0–13–0; Bore 4.3–1–18–1.

Umpires: J. Birkenshaw and C. T. Spencer.

HAMPSHIRE v DERBYSHIRE

At Portsmouth, July 27, 28, 29. Hampshire won by six wickets. Hampshire 23 pts, Derbyshire 5 pts. After losing three wickets cheaply, Derbyshire saw John Hampshire lead a splendid fight-back before the recovery was robustly completed by Tunnicliffe with his highest score in eleven years. Hampshire's Nicholas became their first English-born player to reach 1,000 runs for the season with an unbeaten century before his side declared 69 behind. Barnett batted attractively, but Derbyshire's last eight wickets fell for 103 as Tremlett returned career-best figures of six for 82. Needing to score 258 in 225 minutes, Hampshire made them with four overs to spare.

Derbyshire

*K. J. Barnett c Pocock b Emery	16	– c Parks b Tremlett	65
I. S. Anderson lbw b Marshall	1	– c Greenidge b Jesty	19
A. Hill c Tremlett b Marshall	0	– lbw b Tremlett	7
J. H. Hampshire c Pocock b Jesty	84	– c Cowley b Jesty	20
R. J. Finney c Smith b Tremlett	25	– c Smith b Tremlett	0
G. Miller c Smith b Cowley	40	– c Parks b Jesty	12
W. P. Fowler b Marshall	15	– c Jesty b Tremlett	41
C. J. Tunnicliffe c Greenidge b Tremlett	91	– c Greenidge b Marshall	12
S. Oldham b Marshall	15	– c and b Tremlett	0
†B. J. M. Maher c Smith b Cowley	2	– c Terry b Tremlett	0
O. H. Mortensen not out	0	– not out	5
B 4, l-b 16, w 6, n-b 4	30	L-b 6, n-b 1	7

1/17 2/17 3/20 4/59   319   1/67 2/85 3/114 4/114   188
5/181 6/195 7/230 8/276 9/319   5/116 6/160 7/176 8/178 9/178

Bonus points – Derbyshire 4, Hampshire 4.

Bowling: *First Innings*—Marshall 28–8–66–4; Emery 9–2–33–1; Tremlett 18–6–34–2; Jesty 18–6–47–1; Nicholas 4–0–23–0; Cowley 18.2–4–86–2. *Second Innings*—Marshall 14–2–47–1; Tremlett 27–5–82–6; Jesty 15–3–48–3; Smith 1–0–4–0.

Hampshire

C. G. Greenidge c and b Mortensen	72	– c Maher b Finney	57
C. L. Smith c Maher b Tunnicliffe	33	– b Mortensen	76
M. C. J. Nicholas not out	100	– c Mortensen b Tunnicliffe	29
T. E. Jesty lbw b Oldham	2	– lbw b Miller	43
V. P. Terry lbw b Tunnicliffe	33	– not out	38
*N. E. J. Pocock not out	9	– not out	11
L-b 1	1	B 1, l-b 2, w 1, n-b 2	6

1/82 2/122 3/133 4/230   (4 wkts dec.) 250   1/106 2/158   (4 wkts) 260
                                       3/195 4/223

M. D. Marshall, N. G. Cowley, T. M. Tremlett, †R. J. Parks and K. St J. D. Emery did not bat.

Bonus points – Hampshire 3, Derbyshire 1.

Bowling: *First Innings*—Mortensen 23–1–76–1; Oldham 22.5–6–56–1; Finney 14–3–40–0; Tunnicliffe 17–4–47–2; Miller 7–1–30–0. *Second Innings*—Mortensen 18–1–74–1; Tunnicliffe 15–1–85–1; Oldham 11–3–41–0; Finney 5–0–20–1; Miller 6–0–26–1; Anderson 1–0–8–0.

Umpires: W. E. Alley and A. Jepson.

HAMPSHIRE v GLOUCESTERSHIRE

At Portsmouth, July 30, August 1, 2. Drawn. Hampshire 8 pts, Gloucestershire 2 pts. Gloucestershire's decision to put Hampshire in was proved incorrect as Smith shared an opening partnership of 137 with Greenidge and went on to score his sixth first-class century of the season. After Gloucestershire had been made to follow on, Hampshire were thwarted by storms on the final day and the doggedness of Stovold. All but 25 minutes of two sessions were lost to the weather, while Stovold overcame a finger injury to be last out after batting for 219 minutes. Finally, needing 98 for victory, Hampshire did not attempt to get them when the umpires, with a questionable interpretation of the playing conditions, ruled that only five overs could be bowled. Hampshire believed it should have been eight.

Hampshire

C. G. Greenidge b Childs	71	V. P. Terry c and b Childs	22
C. L. Smith run out	125	*N. E. J. Pocock not out	10
M. C. J. Nicholas c Shepherd b Bainbridge	76	B 4, l-b 12, w 2, n-b 9	27
T. E. Jesty not out	31	1/137 2/278 3/305 4/336 (4 wkts dec.)	362

M. D. Marshall, N. G. Cowley, T. M. Tremlett, †R. J. Parks and S. J. Malone did not bat.

Bonus points – Hampshire 4, Gloucestershire 1.

Bowling: Lawrence 16–2–69–0; Sainsbury 16–3–39–0; Shepherd 20–1–69–0; Bainbridge 15–3–69–1; Childs 33–9–89–2.

Gloucestershire

A. W. Stovold c Terry b Tremlett	16	– (8) c Smith b Jesty	106
B. C. Broad lbw b Marshall	10	– (1) c Greenidge b Marshall	7
P. W. Romaines c Terry b Malone	6	– (2) run out	2
P. Bainbridge c Tremlett b Marshall	18	– (3) b Marshall	2
Zaheer Abbas b Marshall	25	– (4) c Parks b Malone	87
A. J. Hignell b Tremlett	10	– (5) c Nicholas b Tremlett	65
*J. N. Shepherd c Pocock b Jesty	10	– (6) c Parks b Malone	4
†R. C. Russell not out	34	– (7) b Jesty	1
J. H. Childs st Parks b Cowley	19	– c Cowley b Malone	14
G. E. Sainsbury b Cowley	0	– b Malone	3
D. V. Lawrence b Cowley	0	– not out	0
B 1, n-b 1	2	B 9, l-b 4, w 2	15
1/31 2/41 3/74 4/77	153	1/3 2/10 3/13 4/122	306
5/97 6/99 7/103 8/151 9/151		5/130 6/135 7/246 8/266 9/300	

Bonus points – Gloucestershire 1, Hampshire 4.

Bowling: *First Innings*—Marshall 12–4–29–3; Malone 11–0–61–1; Tremlett 14–5–30–2; Jesty 4–1–17–1; Cowley 4.3–1–14–3. *Second Innings*—Marshall 32–10–107–2; Malone 16–4–39–4; Tremlett 17–2–62–1; Jesty 14.3–2–62–2; Nicholas 2–0–16–0; Cowley 7–5–5–0.

Umpires: W. E. Alley and A. Jepson.

At Bournemouth, August 6, 7, 8. HAMPSHIRE lost to NEW ZEALANDERS by nine wickets (See New Zealand tour section).

At Eastbourne, August 10, 11, 12. HAMPSHIRE beat SUSSEX by three wickets.

At Nottingham, August 13, 15, 16. HAMPSHIRE drew with NOTTINGHAMSHIRE.

At Worcester, August 20, 22, 23. HAMPSHIRE beat WORCESTERSHIRE by an innings and 44 runs.

HAMPSHIRE v SOMERSET

At Bournemouth, August 24, 25. Hampshire won by ten wickets. Hampshire 22 pts, Somerset 4 pts. The fast bowling of Marshall and some fine catching saw Somerset put out for a paltry 76. Having taken seven for 29, Marshall, on a green wicket, then showed his skill as an all-rounder by scoring 50. Somerset fared better in their second innings, thanks to Richards, who took five 4s off an over from Jesty, and the resolute Denning, who battled for 147 minutes to remain undefeated. Hampshire needed only 39 for victory and Terry completed his 1,000 runs for the season as this simple target was achieved without loss on the second day.

Somerset

J. W. Lloyds c Jesty b Marshall	0	– c Nicholas b Malone	4
J. G. Wyatt c Greenidge b Tremlett	7	– c Parks b Jesty	17
R. L. Ollis c Parks b Marshall	13	– c Parks b Marshall	13
N. F. M. Popplewell c Jesty b Malone	15	– c Pocock b Jesty	7
*I. V. A. Richards c and b Tremlett	7	– c Greenidge b Marshall	44
P. W. Denning c Parks b Marshall	12	– not out	61
P. A. Slocombe b Marshall	0	– c Parks b Nicholas	4
†T. Gard c Turner b Marshall	5	– c Pocock b Malone	8
G. V. Palmer not out	5	– c Parks b Cowley	0
C. H. Dredge c Parks b Marshall	4	– c Tremlett b Cowley	2
S. C. Booth c Pocock b Marshall	0	– c Parks b Malone	4
L-b 2, n-b 6	8	B 5, l-b 1, n-b 3	9

1/0 2/19 3/35 4/41   76   1/5 2/35 3/35 4/74   173
5/49 6/53 7/67 8/68 9/72   5/93 6/115 7/150 8/151 9/161

Bonus points – Hampshire 4.

Bowling: *First Innings*—Marshall 13.3–4–29–7; Malone 7–2–17–1; Tremlett 11–3–18–2; Jesty 5–4–4–0. *Second Innings*—Marshall 17–4–49–2; Malone 15–1–42–3; Jesty 12–7–32–2; Tremlett 8–5–4–0; Nicholas 7–1–22–1; Cowley 9–3–15–2.

Hampshire

C. G. Greenidge c Slocombe b Popplewell	13	– not out	17
V. P. Terry lbw b Popplewell	25	– not out	18
M. C. J. Nicholas c Booth b Popplewell	14		
T. E. Jesty c Gard b Popplewell	31		
D. R. Turner lbw b Richards	3		
*N. E. J. Pocock c Gard b Booth	38		
M. D. Marshall c Denning b Lloyds	50		
N. G. Cowley lbw b Dredge	15		
T. M. Tremlett not out	9		
†R. J. Parks c Booth b Dredge	0		
S. J. Malone b Dredge	3		
B 4, l-b 4, w 1, n-b 1	10	L-b 1, w 2, n-b 1	4

1/32 2/51 3/58 4/73   211   (no wkt) 39
5/101 6/173 7/192 8/205 9/205

Bonus points – Hampshire 2, Somerset 4.

Bowling: *First Innings*—Dredge 15–5–23–3; Palmer 8–2–26–0; Popplewell 22–4–69–4; Richards 13–2–32–1; Booth 12–6–40–1; Lloyds 8–2–11–1. *Second Innings*—Dredge 4–0–11–0; Palmer 4–0–14–0; Popplewell 1.2–1–5–0; Richards 1–0–5–0.

Umpires: J. Birkenshaw and K. Ibadulla.

HAMPSHIRE v KENT

At Bournemouth, August 27, 29, 30. Hampshire won by eight wickets. Hampshire 24 pts, Kent 4 pts. Hampshire maintained their excellent form as they hustled Kent out for 162. Hampshire then lost half their wickets for 186 in reply, but were rallied by the aggressive Marshall, who scored his second century in England – 112 out of 148 in 147 minutes. Facing a deficit of 197, Kent batted with determination until their last five wickets went for 79.

Kent

R. A. Woolmer lbw b Nicholas	15	– lbw b Marshall	4
N. R. Taylor c Parks b Malone	29	– lbw b Jesty	15
D. G. Aslett c Pocock b Nicholas	3	– c Parks b Malone	42
M. R. Benson c Parks b Jesty	26	– b Nicholas	38
*C. S. Cowdrey b Tremlett	29	– b Malone	73
†A. P. E. Knott c Nicholas b Jesty	2	– c Terry b Marshall	64
G. W. Johnson c Terry b Marshall	6	– lbw b Marshall	32
G. R. Dilley run out	29	– b Malone	15
D. L. Underwood hit wkt b Marshall	0	– c Cowley b Malone	14
K. D. Masters c Greenidge b Marshall	0	– c Parks b Cowley	1
K. B. S. Jarvis not out	4	– not out	4
L-b 14, w 3, n-b 2	19	B 9, l-b 4, w 3, n-b 1	17

1/32 2/40 3/81 4/81   162   1/4 2/65 3/69 4/125   319
5/87 6/112 7/120 8/127 9/150   5/240 6/265 7/285 8/314 9/315

Bonus points – Kent 1, Hampshire 4.

Bowling: *First Innings*—Marshall 17–6–33–3; Malone 8–2–38–1; Jesty 7–3–15–2; Nicholas 6–1–23–2; Tremlett 15.5–6–34–1. *Second Innings*—Marshall 20–4–51–3; Malone 14–3–74–4; Jesty 17–0–89–1; Tremlett 8–0–38–0; Nicholas 4–2–22–1; Cowley 4.3–1–28–1.

Hampshire

C. G. Greenidge c Knott b Jarvis	9	– not out	48
V. P. Terry c Masters b Cowdrey	54	– lbw b Jarvis	4
M. C. J. Nicholas c Underwood b Woolmer	35	– c sub b Aslett	49
T. E. Jesty b Jarvis	35	– not out	15
D. R. Turner b Jarvis	38		
*N. E. J. Pocock b Underwood	9		
M. D. Marshall c Aslett b Underwood	112		
N. G. Cowley c Johnson b Underwood	4		
T. M. Tremlett not out	39		
†R. J. Parks c Cowdrey b Johnson	1		
S. J. Malone c Masters b Johnson	0		
B 2, l-b 13, w 3, n-b 5	23	L-b 1, n-b 8	9

1/38 2/105 3/105 4/175   359   1/6 2/105   (2 wkts) 125
5/186 6/194 7/204 8/350 9/359

Bonus points – Hampshire 4, Kent 3 (Score at 100 overs: 333-7).

Bowling: *First Innings*—Dilley 4–1–19–0; Jarvis 25–5–78–3; Masters 20–2–71–0; Woolmer 17–5–30–1; Cowdrey 9–2–28–1; Underwood 24–7–92–3; Johnson 6.3–2–16–2; Aslett 1–0–2–0. *Second Innings*—Jarvis 8–1–33–1; Masters 7–1–24–0; Underwood 10–6–23–0; Johnson 4–0–8–0; Aslett 6–1–28–1.

Umpires: J. Birkenshaw and K. Ibadulla.

At Taunton, August 31, September 1, 2. HAMPSHIRE drew with SOMERSET.

HAMPSHIRE v GLAMORGAN

At Southampton, September 10, 12, 13. Drawn. Hampshire 7 pts, Glamorgan 5 pts. After being put in, Glamorgan lost two wickets for 19 runs, including that of Alan Jones, who had announced his retirement before the game. Ontong led a recovery which extended into the second day. For Hampshire, Greenidge and Smith put on 159 in 50 overs, their sixth three-figure partnership of the season. Hampshire declared 1 run behind and the match looked poised for a good finish when rain ruled out any play on the final day.

Glamorgan

A. Jones c Nicholas b Stevenson	9	– b Marshall	4
J. A. Hopkins run out	3	– c Parks b Cowley	25
R. C. Ontong c Parks b Tremlett	50	– not out	38
D. A. Francis b Tremlett	29		
A. L. Jones c Pocock b Cowley	36		
C. J. C. Rowe c Jesty b Cowley	17		
S. P. Henderson c Greenidge b Smith	0		
†T. Davies c Tremlett b Smith	41		
A. H. Wilkins c Pocock b Smith	1	– (4) not out	0
*M. W. W. Selvey c Jesty b Marshall	8		
W. W. Davis not out	37		
B 6, l-b 9, w 6	21	L-b 9	9

1/11 2/19 3/106 4/119   252   1/12 2/74   (2 wkts) 76
5/152 6/157 7/165 8/169 9/191

Bonus points – Glamorgan 3, Hampshire 4.

Bowling: *First Innings*—Marshall 18–7–44–1; Stevenson 11–1–26–1; Tremlett 18–8–30–2; Nicholas 4–0–18–0; Jesty 6–2–13–0; Cowley 24–7–60–2; Smith 16.1–5–35–3; Pocock 1–0–5–0. *Second Innings*—Marshall 8–3–9–1; Stevenson 8–4–18–0; Tremlett 4–2–9–0; Cowley 10–5–11–1; Smith 6–3–20–0.

Hampshire

C. G. Greenidge c Davis b Rowe	77	M. D. Marshall lbw b Selvey	5
C. L. Smith c Ontong b Selvey	93	N. G. Cowley not out	13
M. C. J. Nicholas b Selvey	0	L-b 13, n-b 6	19
T. E. Jesty c Wilkins b Rowe	26		
V. P. Terry not out	9	1/159 2/166 3/193	(6 wkts dec.) 251
*N. E. J. Pocock b Rowe	9	4/211 5/224 6/235	

T. M. Tremlett, †R. J. Parks and K. Stevenson did not bat.

Bonus points – Hampshire 3, Glamorgan 2.

Bowling: Davis 7–1–13–0; Wilkins 5–1–22–0; Rowe 37–6–110–3; Selvey 35–4–87–3.

Umpires: D. R. Shepherd and D. J. Constant.

KENT

Patron: HRH The Duke of Kent
President: 1983 – F. O. A. G. Bennett;
    1984 – U. H. B. Alexander
Chairman: H. J. Pocock
Chairman, Cricket Committee: A. H. Phebey
Secretary: D. B. Dalby
    St Lawrence Ground, Old Dover Road,
    Canterbury, CT1 3NZ
    (Telephone: 0227-56886)
Cricket Manager: B. W. Luckhurst
Captain: C. J. Tavaré
Director of Youth Coaching: J. C. T. Page

Kent supporters are unlikely to forget the glory years of the 1970s; they could also remember 1983 as the season which launched a new-look team on the road back to better things. Certainly 1983 was a very satisfactory season for the new captain, Chris Tavaré, and for the county and its supporters in general.

The side returned to Lord's for a cup final for the first time since 1978. Although they lost the NatWest Bank Trophy to Somerset, they proved to themselves that the period of transition extending over the last few years could be nearing completion. Their Schweppes County Championship form was improved; they reached the semi-finals of the Benson and Hedges Cup, and a serious challenge was sustained for the John Player Sunday League.

The cricket manager, Brian Luckhurst, was quick to pay tribute to the contribution of the new captain. Certainly Tavaré, in his quiet but firm way, obtained the support of his players, old and young alike. He enjoys the considerable asset of being able to lead by example when at the crease. In Championship and limited-overs competitions he scored well off bowling of all types.

With four batsmen scoring 1,000 Championship runs – Derek Aslett, Mark Benson, Christopher Cowdrey and Neil Taylor – there was no shortage of runs. Bob Woolmer, who had a purple patch when runs flowed from his bat, would have joined them but for injuries, and his medium-paced bowling, when available, was a vital part of the side's all-round strength. The Championship form of Cowdrey was a revelation. He began the season with a century against Cambridge University, followed by four in the Championship, and sailed effortlessly past 1,000 first-class runs for the first time in his career. Cowdrey and Graham Johnson also lent admirable support to the new captain when they led the side in his absence.

In the early weeks of the season young players such as Aslett and the West Indian all-rounder, Eldine Baptiste, must have wondered if they would ever get a chance to establish themselves as the side remained unchanged. The calls of the World Cup and an injury to Woolmer provided them with the opportunities which could not have been more emphatically taken. Both played their first senior game at Hove in the second week of June, scoring a century apiece in a second-innings run-chase which brought victory. After that, neither looked back.

Baptiste and Aslett were awarded their county caps, as was the medium-paced Richard Ellison, and Baptiste's cup of joy overflowed when he was selected for the West Indies tour of India in 1983-84. Ellison, who is also a more-than-useful left-handed batsman, was in his first full season after completing his university studies. He settled into his role of first-change bowler to an opening attack of Graham Dilley and Kevin Jarvis and then handled the extra responsibility of having to take the new ball when Dilley was on England duty or injured and Jarvis suffered from loss of form.

Dilley, such an important factor in Kent's striking power, began the season well. He was then dogged by injury before returning to end the season with a fine spell of pace in the NatWest Bank Trophy final, which won him a place on England's winter tour. Johnson, in his benefit year, picked up over 50 wickets with his off-spin and proved his known usefulness with the bat as best one can in modern cricket when coming in at No. 8.

Fortunately for Kent, the man who has dominated their own attack, and opposing batsmen, for so many years continued to do so – Derek Underwood. In the Championship he bowled 919 overs – over 300 more than the next Kent bowler – and took 105 wickets. Four times in an innings he took seven wickets and his contribution towards Kent's re-emergence in 1983 as a force to be reckoned with in the four major competitions cannot be too highly stressed.

While Underwood, with another year of his contract to run, showed little sign of the advancing years, the same could also be said of Alan Knott, whose contract ended with the completion of the 1983 season. Batting first at No. 6 then dropping down to No. 7 when Baptiste established himself, he hit over 800 runs, averaging over 40, and kept wicket to the high standard which he demands of himself and which spectators take almost for granted. Kent have coped well with their period of transformation; but they will be hoping for providence to provide them with replacements for Underwood and Knott, two players who are, and have been for so many years, vitally important members of their side. – D.M.

KENT 1983

[*Bill Smith*]

Back row: S. Marsh, R. M. Ellison, C. Penn, D. G. Aslett. *Middle row*: C. Lewis (*scorer*), S. N. V. Waterton, S. G. Hinks, L. Potter, G. R. Dilley, N. R. Taylor, R. Chappell (*physiotherapist*). *Front row*: B. W. Luckhurst (*manager*), K. B. S. Jarvis, R. A. Woolmer, A. P. E. Knott, C. J. Tavaré (*captain*), G. W. Johnson, D. L. Underwood, C. S. Cowdrey, J. C. T. Page (*director of youth coaching*).

Kent in 1983

KENT RESULTS

All first-class matches – Played 25: Won 7, Lost 4, Drawn 14.

County Championship matches – Played 24: Won 7, Lost 4, Drawn 13.

Bonus points – Batting 68, Bowling 70.

Competition placings – Schweppes County Championship, 7th; NatWest Bank Trophy, r/u;
Benson and Hedges Cup, s-f; John Player League, 3rd.

COUNTY CHAMPIONSHIP AVERAGES

BATTING

	Birthplace	M	I	NO	R	HI	Avge
C. S. Cowdreyc	Farnborough	21	32	9	1,256	123	54.60
R. A. Woolmerc	Kanpur, India	13	20	1	969	129	51.00
C. J. Tavaréc	Orpington	10	14	0	633	94	45.21
D. G. Aslettc	Dover	20	36	3	1,437	168	43.54
M. R. Bensonc	Shoreham	22	36	3	1,410	152*	42.72
A. P. E. Knottc	Belvedere	22	29	8	806	92*	38.38
N. R. Taylorc	Orpington	22	38	6	1,161	155*	36.28
E. A. E. Baptistec ...	St John's, Antigua	17	26	5	755	136*	35.95
S. G. Hinks	Northfleet	6	10	0	253	87	25.30
R. M. Ellisonc	Ashford	21	21	7	343	63	24.50
G. W. Johnsonc	Beckenham	24	28	11	402	79*	23.64
L. Potter................	Bexleyheath	6	11	0	258	50	23.45
G. R. Dilleyc	Dartford	10	7	1	99	29	16.50
D. L. Underwoodc ..	Bromley	24	20	6	142	26*	10.14
K. B. S. Jarvisc	Dartford	20	13	5	43	9*	5.37
K. D. Masters........	Chatham	2	4	0	1	1	0.25

Also batted: S. Marsh (*Westminster*) (1 match) 5, 0; C. Penn (*Dover*) (2 matches) 24; S. N. V. Waterton (*Dartford*) (1 match) 8, 3.

*Signifies not out   cDenotes county cap.

BOWLING

	O	M	R	W	Avge	BB
D. L. Underwood....	919.3	349	2,024	105	19.27	7-55
G. R. Dilley...........	232.3	60	601	28	21.46	5-70
E. A. E. Baptiste	376.3	88	1,187	50	23.74	5-39
R. M. Ellison..........	580.4	161	1,455	49	26.69	5-73
G. W. Johnson........	616.1	160	1,617	51	31.70	7-76
K. B. S. Jarvis	485.5	93	1,545	29	53.27	3-32
C. S. Cowdrey	214.2	34	712	12	59.33	3-80

Also bowled: D. G. Aslett 37–5–218–3; M. R. Benson 5–1–16–0; K. D. Masters 33–4–121–2; C. Penn 35–8–116–2; L. Potter 6–2–14–0; C. J. Tavaré 3–0–3–0; N. R. Taylor 35–9–108–1; R. A. Woolmer 76–26–148–7.

The following played a total of twenty three-figure innings for Kent in County Championship matches – C. S. Cowdrey 4, N. R. Taylor 4, R. A. Woolmer 4, D. G. Aslett 3, M. R. Benson 3, E. A. E. Baptiste 2.

At The Oval, April 30, May 1, 2. KENT drew with SURREY.

At Cambridge, May 4, 5, 6. KENT drew with CAMBRIDGE UNIVERSITY.

At Chelmsford, May 11, 12, 13. KENT beat ESSEX by six wickets.

KENT v HAMPSHIRE

At Canterbury, May 28, 30, 31. Drawn. Kent 4 pts, Hampshire 2 pts. After the first day's play was washed out by rain Jesty, with 50 in 56 minutes, provided the best feature of the Hampshire innings. Kent forfeited their first innings and Hampshire set them 354 to win in five hours. Taylor and Tavaré added 73 off 22 overs for the second wicket, with Tavaré reaching 50 in 97 minutes with nine 4s. Kent needed 188 in two hours after tea but Marshall's return to bowl seven fiery, hostile overs for 6 runs ruined Kent's hopes and they ended 111 short with eleven overs left.

Hampshire

C. G. Greenidge c Tavaré b Underwood	68	– c Taylor b Ellison	4
C. L. Smith c Taylor b Jarvis	3	– retired hurt	4
D. R. Turner b Johnson	35	– not out	48
T. E. Jesty lbw b Dilley	50	– c Taylor b Ellison	14
M. C. J. Nicholas b Johnson	5	– not out	51
*N. E. J. Pocock b Ellison	29		
M. D. Marshall b Johnson	15		
N. G. Cowley c Knott b Ellison	8		
T. M. Tremlett lbw b Dilley	3		
†R. J. Parks not out	0		
S. J. Malone c Knott b Dilley	0		
B 1, l-b 6, n-b 5	12	L-b 3, w 1	4

1/10 2/87 3/162 4/168   **228**   1/12 2/31   (2 wkts dec.) **125**
5/180 6/212 7/218 8/228 9/228

Bonus points – Hampshire 2, Kent 4.

Bowling: *First Innings*—Dilley 15.3–8–27–3; Jarvis 12–2–37–1; Ellison 22–6–58–2; Underwood 21–5–37–1; Cowdrey 5–2–15–0; Johnson 14–2–42–3. *Second Innings*—Dilley 3–2–4–0; Jarvis 4–1–9–0; Ellison 7–2–15–2; Johnson 15–3–44–0; Underwood 7–1–20–0; Taylor 1–0–10–0; Cowdrey 3–0–19–0.

Kent

L. Potter (did not bat)		– lbw b Malone	29
N. R. Taylor (did not bat)		– st Parks b Tremlett	49
*C. J. Tavaré (did not bat)		– b Malone	70
M. R. Benson (did not bat)		– c Tremlett b Cowley	24
C. S. Cowdrey (did not bat)		– c Greenidge b Pocock	45
†A. P. E. Knott (did not bat)		– not out	7
G. W. Johnson (did not bat)		– not out	0
		B 5, l-b 8, w 2, n-b 4	19

1/46 2/119   (5 wkts) **243**
3/179 4/204 5/243

R. M. Ellison, G. R. Dilley, D. L. Underwood and K. B. S. Jarvis did not bat.

Bowling: Marshall 14–8–16–0; Malone 15–1–40–2; Nicholas 8–1–27–0; Tremlett 9–2–41–1; Jesty 11–5–30–0; Cowley 14–3–39–1; Pocock 4–0–31–1.

Kent forfeited their first innings.

Umpires: K. Ibadulla and A. G. T. Whitehead.

KENT v MIDDLESEX

At Dartford, June 4, 6, 7. Middlesex won by four wickets. Middlesex 21 pts, Kent 8 pts. A majestic century by Woolmer, who batted with a broken toe from the early seventies and hit a 6 and fourteen 4s in 185 minutes, gave Kent a fine start. Then Knott hit twelve 4s in his 147 minutes' innings. Butcher, with three 6s and fourteen 4s in his 131 minutes' century, enabled Middlesex to finish with a deficit of only 63, whereupon Embury and Edmonds hustled Kent out cheaply. Barlow and Gatting then defied all Underwood's determined efforts and Middlesex had come from behind to win on a wicket which had given help to spin bowlers throughout.

Kent

R. A. Woolmer b Williams	118	– (11) not out	0
N. R. Taylor c Downton b Cowans	0	– (1) c Barlow b Embury	29
*C. J. Tavaré c Downton b Edmonds	31	– lbw b Embury	5
M. R. Benson b Embury	4	– c Cowans b Edmonds	2
C. S. Cowdrey c Slack b Williams	28	– (10) c Butcher b Edmonds	2
†A. P. E. Knott not out	92	– c Radley b Edmonds	6
L. Potter c Cowans b Edmonds	33	– (2) c Barlow b Embury	14
G. W. Johnson not out	25	– (5) c Tomlins b Embury	0
D. L. Underwood (did not bat)		– (7) c Radley b Edmonds	15
K. B. S. Jarvis (did not bat)		– (8) c Slack b Embury	7
R. M. Ellison (did not bat)		– (9) b Embury	0
L-b 5, w 2, n-b 12	19	B 1, l-b 2, n-b 4	7

1/9 2/113 3/127 (6 wkts dec.) 350   1/47 2/50 3/53 4/55 87
4/188 5/205 6/308   5/56 6/64 7/79 8/85 9/85

Bonus points – Kent 4, Middlesex 2 (Score at 100 overs: 317-6).

Bowling: *First Innings*—Cowans 18–5–48–1; Williams 22–6–63–2; Edmonds 28.3–5–92–2; Embury 31–8–93–1; Gatting 6–1–35–0. *Second Innings*—Cowans 3–1–15–0; Williams 8–1–15–0; Edmonds 22.2–7–37–4; Embury 17–9–13–6.

Middlesex

G. D. Barlow c Knott b Underwood	41	– c sub b Underwood	53
W. N. Slack st Knott b Underwood	2	– st Knott b Underwood	1
C. T. Radley st Knott b Johnson	19	– lbw b Underwood	20
*M. W. Gatting c Tavaré b Jarvis	48	– c Tavaré b Underwood	41
R. O. Butcher lbw b Johnson	110	– c Ellison b Underwood	13
K. P. Tomlins c Cowdrey b Johnson	7	– not out	9
J. E. Embury c Benson b Underwood	40	– lbw b Underwood	1
†P. R. Downton c Knott b Jarvis	5	– not out	4
N. F. Williams lbw b Jarvis	1		
P. H. Edmonds lbw b Underwood	1		
N. G. Cowans not out	0		
B 4, l-b 7, n-b 2	13	L-b 5, w 2, n-b 5	12

1/6 2/52 3/88 4/144 287   1/3 2/60 3/101 (6 wkts) 154
5/191 6/259 7/284 8/285 9/287   4/134 5/138 6/140

Bonus points – Middlesex 3, Kent 4.

Bowling: *First Innings*—Jarvis 17–10–32–3; Ellison 14–3–69–1; Underwood 38.1–15–80–4; Johnson 30–11–93–2. *Second Innings*—Jarvis 6–3–9–0; Underwood 25–13–44–6; Johnson 25.3–6–82–0; Ellison 4–3–1–0; Potter 1–0–6–0.

Umpires: K. E. Palmer and D. O. Oslear.

At Hove, June 8, 9, 10. KENT beat SUSSEX by six wickets.

KENT v ESSEX

At Tunbridge Wells, June 11, 13, 14. Drawn. Kent 7 pts, Essex 6 pts. Pace and seam bowlers dominated a match in which batsmen, apart from McEwan, always found run-getting difficult. McEwan hit a 6 and nineteen 4s in his 269 minutes' innings which was almost completely responsible for Essex's getting to within 2 runs of Kent's total. Kent batted for 102 overs in their second innings, with Taylor reaching a five-hour century, and the eventual Essex target was 292 in 35 minutes plus the last twenty overs. The match ended, mercifully without any extra time, with both sides blaming each other's tactics. Whoever was right or wrong, there was no doubt that the crowd who paid to watch suffered most.

Kent

L. Potter c McEwan b Foster	19	– b Turner	19
N. R. Taylor c R. E. East b Gooch	64	– not out	116
D. G. Aslett c Gooch b Foster	47	– c R. E. East b Pont	39
M. R. Benson run out	72	– c D. E. East b Phillip	9
S. G. Hinks c Fletcher b Turner	11	– lbw b Pont	0
†A. P. E. Knott c Pont b Gooch	12	– lbw b Pont	11
E. A. E. Baptiste c Gooch b Phillip	2	– not out	61
*G. W. Johnson not out	25		
R. M. Ellison b Turner	0		
D. L. Underwood c McEwan b Phillip	2		
K. B. S. Jarvis c Hardie b Phillip	9		
L-b 14, w 4, n-b 6	24	B 2, l-b 23, w 1, n-b 8	34

1/34 2/105 3/157 4/184   287   1/55 2/146   (5 wkts dec.) 289
5/222 6/233 7/262 8/268 9/271   3/169 4/170 5/194

Bonus points – Kent 3, Essex 3 (Score at 100 overs: 268-8).

Bowling: *First Innings*—Foster 14–2–43–2; Phillip 18.5–6–44–3; Gooch 32–8–67–2; Turner 27–4–83–2; Acfield 10–4–18–0; R. E. East 1–0–8–0. *Second Innings*—Foster 23–6–81–0; Phillip 25–6–63–1; Turner 20–6–23–1; Pont 24–8–51–3; Gooch 5–0–17–0; McEwan 5–0–20–0.

Essex

G. A. Gooch c Johnson b Baptiste	38		
B. R. Hardie c Aslett b Ellison	13	– (1) not out	31
*K. W. R. Fletcher c Knott b Ellison	0		
K. S. McEwan c Knott b Baptiste	142		
K. R. Pont c Knott b Ellison	17		
N. Phillip c Aslett b Ellison	3		
S. Turner b Baptiste	12	– (3) b Baptiste	2
†D. E. East lbw b Baptiste	18	– (2) lbw b Jarvis	10
R. E. East c Hinks b Baptiste	1	– (4) not out	7
N. A. Foster not out	20		
D. L. Acfield b Jarvis	1		
L-b 9, w 2, n-b 9	20	L-b 1, n-b 3	4

1/31 2/31 3/92 4/145   285   1/28 2/41   (2 wkts) 54
5/161 6/191 7/224 8/231 9/274

Bonus points – Essex 3, Kent 4.

Bowling: *First Innings*—Jarvis 27.4–6–86–1; Ellison 28–13–58–4; Underwood 9–4–16–0; Baptiste 28–5–104–5; Johnson 1–0–1–0. *Second Innings*—Jarvis 6–0–19–1; Ellison 6–2–17–0; Baptiste 4–1–8–1; Potter 3–1–6–0.

Umpires: J. W. Holder and J. van Geloven.

KENT v SUSSEX

At Tunbridge Wells, June 15, 16, 17. Kent won by nine wickets. Kent 23 pts, Sussex 5 pts. Pace and seam again dominated, but in this match they effected a result. Kent were rallied by a fine innings from acting-captain Cowdrey and their lead of 72 became invaluable as Sussex lost four wickets in clearing it. For the second time in a week Ellison improved his career-best figures and Baptiste polished off the Sussex innings as they collapsed disastrously, taking his wickets for the season to 22 (for 258 runs) in his first three senior-team games. Kent, left with an easy task, were steered to victory in convincing style by Taylor.

Sussex

G. D. Mendis c Johnson b Ellison	1	– lbw b Ellison	6
A. M. Green c Aslett b Underwood	29	– c Cowdrey b Ellison	18
*J. R. T. Barclay c Benson b Baptiste	3	– c Johnson b Baptiste	14
C. M. Wells c Johnson b Jarvis	52	– c Johnson b Ellison	22
P. W. G. Parker c Ellison b Baptiste	58	– (6) c Knott b Baptiste	15
A. P. Wells c Potter b Baptiste	11	– (7) c Ellison b Jarvis	28
G. S. le Roux c Johnson b Underwood	15	– (8) c and b Baptiste	9
D. A. Reeve not out	9	– (9) not out	0
A. C. S. Pigott c and b Baptiste	1	– (10) c Cowdrey b Baptiste	0
†D. J. Smith c Knott b Ellison	0	– (5) c Cowdrey b Ellison	2
C. E. Waller lbw b Jarvis	1	– b Baptiste	0
L-b 1, w 2, n-b 8	11	L-b 6, w 1, n-b 11	18

1/7 2/18 3/83 4/92   191   1/27 2/32 3/62 4/72   132
5/125 6/169 7/180 8/187 9/190   5/79 6/122 7/123 8/132 9/132

Bonus points – Sussex 1, Kent 4.

Bowling: *First Innings*—Jarvis 25–7–54–2; Ellison 24–11–38–2; Baptiste 22–8–46–4; Underwood 12–7–24–2; Johnson 1–1–0–0; Cowdrey 9–1–18–0. *Second Innings*—Jarvis 18–7–36–1; Ellison 19–6–35–4; Baptiste 18.2–7–39–5; Cowdrey 5–3–4–0.

Kent

N. R. Taylor c Parker b le Roux	7	– not out	46
L. Potter b Pigott	17	– c Reeve b Green	11
D. G. Aslett b le Roux	25	– not out	3
D. L. Underwood c Smith b le Roux	16		
M. R. Benson c Pigott b Waller	56		
*C. S. Cowdrey lbw b Pigott	94		
E. A. E. Baptiste c Mendis b Pigott	12		
†A. P. E. Knott not out	24		
G. W. Johnson c Smith b Pigott	0		
R. M. Ellison b le Roux	3		
K. B. S. Jarvis c Pigott b le Roux	0		
L-b 7, w 1, n-b 1	9	L-b 2, n-b 1	3

1/20 2/36 3/64 4/74   263   1/54   (1 wkt) 63
5/207 6/232 7/238 8/252 9/263

Bonus points – Kent 3, Sussex 4.

Bowling: *First Innings*—le Roux 19.3–5–59–5; Pigott 28–4–73–4; Reeve 22–5–38–0; C. M. Wells 19–4–70–0; Waller 6–0–14–1. *Second Innings*—le Roux 6–2–12–0; Pigott 1–0–2–0; Reeve 3–0–19–0; C. M. Wells 5–1–12–0; Green 3.4–1–15–1.

Umpires: J. W. Holder and J. van Geloven.

At Bristol, June 18, 20, 21. KENT drew with GLOUCESTERSHIRE.

At Nottingham, June 22, 23, 24. KENT beat NOTTINGHAMSHIRE by six wickets.

KENT v GLAMORGAN

At Canterbury, July 2, 4, 5. Drawn. Kent 7 pts, Glamorgan 5 pts. A splendid innings by A. Jones, on one of his happiest hunting grounds, included two 6s and eleven 4s in 195 minutes, but consistent Kent batting enabled them to build a lead of 157. Woolmer batted 196 minutes, hitting twelve 4s, and Cowdrey raced to 50 out of 69 in 43 minutes. Glamorgan, batting to save the match, had A. L. Jones and Francis to thank for doing so, their unbroken fifth-wicket partnership being worth 125 in 135 minutes.

Glamorgan

A. Jones c Cowdrey b Baptiste	93	– c Ellison b Johnson	46
J. A. Hopkins c Tavaré b Ellison	1	– c Ellison b Johnson	24
R. C. Ontong run out	21	– c Johnson b Underwood	3
A. L. Jones c Woolmer b Dilley	16	– not out	58
C. J. C. Rowe c Woolmer b Cowdrey	26	– c Baptiste b Johnson	5
D. A. Francis c Woolmer b Johnson	23	– not out	50
†E. W. Jones c Knott b Ellison	15		
B. J. Lloyd lbw b Dilley	10		
*M. W. W. Selvey b Dilley	25		
A. H. Wilkins c Johnson b Dilley	15		
W. W. Davis not out	4		
B 2, l-b 3, n-b 11	16	B 2, l-b 12, w 1, n-b 15	30

1/14 2/77 3/119 4/149   265   1/70 2/83 3/86   (4 wkts) 216
5/186 6/190 7/203 8/225 9/260   4/91

Bonus points – Glamorgan 3, Kent 3 (Score at 100 overs: 254-8).

Bowling: *First Innings*—Dilley 21.1–6–52–4; Ellison 24–7–49–2; Underwood 18–10–28–0; Johnson 15–3–43–1; Baptiste 16–2–43–1; Cowdrey 10–0–34–1. *Second Innings* —Dilley 6–1–11–0; Baptiste 4–2–5–0; Underwood 30–9–57–1; Ellison 2–1–2–0; Johnson 32–10–85–3; Cowdrey 2–0–7–0; Aslett 6–2–12–0; Tavaré 3–0–3–0; Benson 1–0–4–0.

Kent

R. A. Woolmer lbw b Wilkins	97	R. M. Ellison not out	20
M. R. Benson c E. W. Jones b Selvey	39	G. R. Dilley b Rowe	13
*C. J. Tavaré b Davis	68	D. L. Underwood b Rowe	1
D. G. Aslett lbw b Davis	46	B 5, l-b 16, w 1, n-b 4	26
C. S. Cowdrey c Francis b Lloyd	50		—
E. A. E. Baptiste b Rowe	27	1/68 2/176 3/226	422
†A. P. E. Knott b Ontong	22	4/295 5/332 6/364	
G. W. Johnson c and b Rowe	13	7/366 8/380 9/416	

Bonus points – Kent 4, Glamorgan 2 (Score at 100 overs: 339-5).

Bowling: Davis 27–10–62–2; Selvey 18–1–76–1; Ontong 29–6–73–1; Rowe 23.2–6–64–4; Lloyd 23–2–87–1; Wilkins 9–2–34–1.

Umpires: A. Jepson and A. G. T. Whitehead.

KENT v LANCASHIRE

At Maidstone, July 9, 11, 12. Drawn. Kent 7 pts, Lancashire 5 pts. Woolmer and Aslett pulled Kent round with a third-wicket stand of 152 off 48 overs before Cowdrey reached his first century in the Championship since 1977, batting 132 minutes and hitting thirteen 4s. Lancashire had lost half their side for 97 after 31 overs, but Abrahams, with 105 in 256 minutes, rescued his side. Going for quick runs Kent were indebted to Woolmer again and to Tavaré, who thrashed nine 4s in a twenty-minute half-century. With Frank Hayes and Hughes adding 92 in 24 overs, Lancashire's final twenty-overs target was 135. Baptiste then raised Kent's hopes with three quick wickets, but Hughes ensured that Lancashire foiled the home side's victory bid.

Kent

R. A. Woolmer c Allott b Simmons	129	– c Hughes b Abrahams	92
N. R. Taylor lbw b McFarlane	3	– not out	67
*C. J. Tavaré c F. C. Hayes b Watkinson	0	– c Watkinson b Simmons	50
D. G. Aslett b Simmons	56	– c Fairbrother b Watkinson	0
C. S. Cowdrey not out	101	– not out	17
E. A. E. Baptiste lbw b Simmons	6		
†A. P. E. Knott c Maynard b Abrahams	26		
G. W. Johnson not out	14		
L-b 5, n-b 9	14	L-b 10	10

1/17 2/29 3/181 4/208 (6 wkts dec.) 349   1/129 2/187 3/190 (3 wkts dec.) 236
5/240 6/289

R. M. Ellison, D. L. Underwood and K. B. S. Jarvis did not bat.

Bonus points – Kent 4, Lancashire 2 (Score at 100 overs: 329-6).

Bowling: *First Innings*—Allott 24.2–2–74–0; McFarlane 17–2–67–1; Watkinson 24–2–83–1; Simmons 26–2–78–3; Hughes 4–0–14–0; Abrahams 7–1–19–1. *Second Innings* —Allott 11–3–28–0; McFarlane 13–1–64–0; Watkinson 11–1–40–1; Simmons 15–2–81–1; Abrahams 5–1–13–1.

Lancashire

G. Fowler c sub b Ellison	46	– c Johnson b Baptiste	23
K. A. Hayes c Taylor b Underwood	3	– c Knott b Underwood	20
M. Watkinson b Baptiste	6		
F. C. Hayes b Baptiste	4	– (3) b Underwood	52
D. P. Hughes lbw b Ellison	23	– (4) not out	75
*J. Abrahams c Aslett b Ellison	105	– (5) c Johnson b Baptiste	24
N. H. Fairbrother c Knott b Ellison	31	– (8) not out	4
†C. Maynard b Baptiste	2	– (6) c and b Baptiste	2
J. Simmons c Aslett b Cowdrey	9	– (7) lbw b Baptiste	0
P. J. W. Allott c Taylor b Ellison	41		
L. L. McFarlane not out	8		
B 4, l-b 13, w 6, n-b 9	32	L-b 3, n-b 1	4

1/8 2/21 3/27 4/89   310   1/37 2/49 3/141   (6 wkts) 204
5/97 6/155 7/167 8/209 9/286   4/184 5/190 6/190

Bonus points – Lancashire 3, Kent 3 (Score at 100 overs: 271-8).

Bowling: *First Innings*—Underwood 11–5–22–1; Jarvis 21–2–71–0; Baptiste 25–7–64–3; Ellison 31.5–8–73–5; Cowdrey 10–3–34–1; Johnson 9–5–14–0. *Second Innings*—Jarvis 7–0–30–0; Baptiste 10–3–38–4; Underwood 20.3–7–69–2; Ellison 8–1–27–0; Johnson 11–5–28–0; Aslett 1–0–8–0.

Umpires: D. J. Constant and R. A. White.

KENT v SOMERSET

At Maidstone, July 13, 14, 15. Kent won by three wickets. Kent 20 pts, Somerset 6 pts. A marathon innings by Roebuck, batting for 359 minutes, was boosted by Garner, who hit some of the longest 6s seen on the ground and helped in a ninth-wicket stand of 76 off 22 overs. Then Garner's pace destroyed Kent's first innings with only Woolmer preventing complete disaster. Apart from Richards, Somerset, batting again, struggled against the spin of Underwood and Johnson, whereupon Woolmer put Kent on the victory path with his second century of the week, made in 166 minutes. Benson assisted Woolmer in an important stand of 113 off 27 overs, the young left-hander staying to pilot Kent home.

Somerset

J. W. Lloyds c Taylor b Jarvis	0	– c and b Ellison	11
P. M. Roebuck c Ellison b Baptiste	99	– run out	9
*I. V. A. Richards c Taylor b Underwood	32	– c Cowdrey b Johnson	82
P. W. Denning c Taylor b Underwood	19	– b Johnson	3
N. F. M. Popplewell run out	2	– c Knott b Underwood	9
P. A. Slocombe c Ellison b Johnson	1	– b Underwood	0
N. A. Felton c Taylor b Johnson	9	– b Johnson	0
†T. Gard c Woolmer b Ellison	13	– c Woolmer b Johnson	0
C. H. Dredge st Knott b Johnson	16	– c Cowdrey b Underwood	11
J. Garner b Baptiste	44	– st Knott b Johnson	25
P. H. L. Wilson not out	0	– not out	0
B 1, l-b 7, w 1, n-b 12	21	L-b 6, w 1, n-b 16	23

1/0 2/51 3/84 4/89   256   1/29 2/44 3/54 4/97   173
5/93 6/109 7/149 8/180 9/256   5/97 6/99 7/99 8/141 9/150

Bonus points – Somerset 2, Kent 3 (Score at 100 overs: 230-8).

Bowling: *First Innings*—Jarvis 13–1–37–1; Baptiste 21.1–5–66–2; Underwood 26–11–35–2; Ellison 18–7–36–1; Johnson 28–9–56–3; Aslett 1–0–5–0. *Second Innings*—Jarvis 5–1–9–0; Baptiste 5–2–9–0; Ellison 6–2–11–1; Underwood 22–7–54–3; Johnson 17–2–67–5.

Kent

R. A. Woolmer c Popplewell b Richards	64	– c Gard b Wilson	110
N. R. Taylor lbw b Garner	8	– c Richards b Garner	3
D. G. Aslett lbw b Garner	3	– (4) lbw b Dredge	28
M. R. Benson lbw b Garner	0	– (5) not out	66
*C. S. Cowdrey b Popplewell	0	– (6) c Wilson b Dredge	25
E. A. E. Baptiste c Popplewell b Richards	37	– (7) c Popplewell b Lloyds	9
†A. P. E. Knott run out	9	– (8) b Lloyds	2
G. W. Johnson c Richards b Garner	3	– (9) not out	1
R. M. Ellison not out	18		
D. L. Underwood c Slocombe b Garner	5	– (3) c Popplewell b Wilson	13
K. B. S. Jarvis b Garner	0		
N-b 3	3	B 12, l-b 8, n-b 3	23

1/16 2/36 3/41 4/44	150	1/11 2/27 3/77	(7 wkts) 280
5/104 6/118 7/127 8/127 9/132		4/190 5/239 6/269 7/275	

Bonus points Kent 1, Somerset 4.

Bowling: *First Innings*—Garner 16.1–4–37–6; Dredge 9–1–27–0; Wilson 5–1–9–0; Popplewell 9–0–40–1; Richards 10–5–28–2; Lloyds 2–1–6–0. *Second Innings*—Garner 19–4–61–1; Dredge 15–1–37–2; Wilson 8–0–38–2; Popplewell 7–0–39–0; Richards 13–3–42–0; Lloyds 14–3–40–2.

Umpires: D. J. Constant and R. A. White.

At Sheffield, July 16, 18, 19. KENT drew with YORKSHIRE.

At Birmingham, July 27, 28, 29. KENT drew with WARWICKSHIRE.

At Chesterfield, July 30, August 1, 2. KENT drew with DERBYSHIRE.

KENT v WORCESTERSHIRE

At Canterbury, August 6, 8, 9. Drawn. Kent 5 pts, Worcestershire 6 pts. Worcestershire managed to foil Underwood's marathon spell thanks mainly to a stubborn sixth-wicket stand of 101 off 39 overs between Humphries and Curtis. The Kent-born Curtis batted 256 minutes and hit eight 4s. Tavaré held the Kent innings together, batting 261 minutes with eight 4s, though the spin of Illingworth was always threatening. Worcestershire struggled a second time against Underwood, who took his match return to fourteen for 158, and Kent were left 242 to win in 185 minutes. Benson, with his sixth 50 in eight innings, put them on schedule and 126 were needed off the last twenty overs. Against the off-spin of Patel this proved too many.

Worcestershire

J. A. Ormrod c Cowdrey b Underwood	46	– c Benson b Underwood	14
M. J. Weston b Baptiste	9	– c Aslett b Underwood	5
*P. A. Neale c Baptiste b Underwood	56	– c Knott b Underwood	38
D. N. Patel c Benson b Underwood	30	– b Underwood	32
D. B. D'Oliveira b Underwood	11	– (6) c Ellison b Johnson	0
T. S. Curtis b Johnson	84	– (7) c Johnson b Underwood	9
†D. J. Humphries st Knott b Underwood	59	– (5) c Benson b Underwood	2
R. K. Illingworth c Knott b Underwood	17	– b Johnson	1
J. D. Inchmore st Knott b Underwood	41	– c Knott b Underwood	0
R. M. Ellcock not out	0	– b Johnson	11
A. P. Pridgeon absent	0	– not out	1
L-b 9, w 2, n-b 12	23	B 7, l-b 11, w 10	28

1/23 2/110 3/121 4/153   376   1/9 2/48 3/74 4/77   141
5/163 6/264 7/304 8/374 9/376   5/78 6/122 7/123 8/123 9/129

Bonus points – Worcestershire 3, Kent 2 (Score at 100 overs: 286-6).

Bowling: *First Innings*—Jarvis 20–2–55–0; Ellison 11–1–30–0; Baptiste 18–0–88–1; Underwood 44.4–16–103–7; Johnson 27–6–73–1; Woolmer 3–2–4–0. *Second Innings*—Jarvis 2–0–6–0; Ellison 7–2–15–0; Underwood 22–6–55–7; Johnson 16.3–2–37–3.

Kent

R. A. Woolmer run out	5	– c D'Oliveira b Ellcock	3
M. R. Benson c Ormrod b Illingworth	53	– c Curtis b Patel	57
*C. J. Tavaré c Inchmore b Illingworth	93	– c Humphries b Pridgeon	13
D. G. Aslett b Illingworth	5	– c Patel b Pridgeon	43
C. S. Cowdrey b Ellcock	33	– not out	43
E. A. E. Baptiste b Inchmore	9	– st Humphries b Patel	13
†A. P. E. Knott lbw b Illingworth	21	– c D'Oliveira b Patel	1
G. W. Johnson c Patel b Inchmore	9	– st Humphries b Patel	9
R. M. Ellison not out	18	– not out	0
D. L. Underwood c Humphries b Inchmore	1		
K. B. S. Jarvis b Inchmore	0		
B 8, l-b 9, w 4, n-b 8	29	B 6, l-b 10, w 1	17

1/5 2/112 3/118 4/168   276   1/4 2/36 3/117 4/149   (7 wkts) 199
5/197 6/230 7/243 8/268 9/276   5/185 6/187 7/199

Bonus points – Kent 3, Worcestershire 3 (Score at 100 overs: 264-7).

Bowling: *First Innings*—Ellcock 13–3–37–1; Inchmore 11.5–3–32–4; Patel 39–14–86–0; Illingworth 39–7–86–4; Pridgeon 3–1–6–0. *Second Innings*—Ellcock 10–1–28–1; Pridgeon 10–2–30–2; Patel 23–3–88–4; Illingworth 14–3–36–0.

Umpires: H. D. Bird and R. A. Harris.

KENT v SURREY

At Canterbury, August 10, 11, 12. Surrey won by four wickets. Surrey 21 pts, Kent 6 pts. Surrey's pace and seam attack had Kent on the run until Woolmer and Baptiste added 177 off 47 overs. Woolmer reached his 100 in 210 minutes with twelve 4s; Baptiste batted 205 minutes and hit ten 4s. Not until the 102nd over did another batsman reach double figures. Surrey laboured so hard that between lunch and tea on the second day they managed only 70 runs off 39 overs. Kent failed badly in their second innings but declared leaving Surrey 232 to win in 208 minutes. They needed 125 off the last twenty overs with Pauline going well, but it was a furious onslaught from Lynch which clinched victory. With Richards helping him add 47 in seven overs, Surrey won with five balls to spare.

Kent

R. A. Woolmer c Lynch b Curtis	120	– c Monkhouse b Thomas	6
N. R. Taylor b Clarke	6	– c Richards b Monkhouse	16
D. G. Aslett b Monkhouse	8	– c Richards b Monkhouse	29
S. G. Hinks c and b Thomas	8	– c Richards b Clarke	16
*C. S. Cowdrey b Monkhouse	2	– not out	28
E. A. E. Baptiste c Richards b Clarke	91	– c Curtis b Monkhouse	6
†S. N. V. Waterton c Richards b Monkhouse	8	– c Knight b Pocock	3
G. W. Johnson not out	46	– b Curtis	1
R. M. Ellison b Clarke	29	– not out	8
D. L. Underwood not out	1		
B 1, l-b 16, n-b 7	24	B 4, l-b 2, n-b 2	8

1/13 2/34 3/46 4/52   (8 wkts dec.) 343   1/11 2/32 3/69   (7 wkts dec.) 121
5/229 6/259 7/272 8/336   4/69 5/81 6/99 7/112

K. B. S. Jarvis did not bat.

Bonus points – Kent 3, Surrey 3 (Score at 100 overs: 274-7).

Bowling: *First Innings*—Clarke 23–4–65–3; Thomas 13–3–35–1; Monkhouse 28–10–73–3; Knight 14–0–48–0; Pocock 15–4–48–0; Curtis 23–9–50–1. *Second Innings*—Clarke 13–3–38–1; Thomas 10–2–32–1; Monkhouse 10–4–24–3; Pocock 3–0–14–1; Curtis 2.2–1–5–1.

Surrey

A. R. Butcher b Woolmer	52	– c Waterton b Jarvis	6
D. B. Pauline b Ellison	14	– c Aslett b Underwood	60
A. J. Stewart c Waterton b Baptiste	20	– c sub b Johnson	25
*R. D. V. Knight c Cowdrey b Underwood	53	– c Baptiste b Underwood	16
M. A. Lynch lbw b Ellison	12	– not out	76
†C. J. Richards c Waterton b Baptiste	16	– (8) not out	19
D. J. Thomas c Baptiste b Jarvis	33	– c and b Ellison	14
G. Monkhouse c Cowdrey b Baptiste	7		
S. T. Clarke b Underwood	3	– (6) b Underwood	0
P. I. Pocock b Baptiste	0		
I. J. Curtis not out	0		
L-b 9, w 4, n-b 10	23	B 5, l-b 7, n-b 7	19

1/20 2/86 3/90 4/105   233   1/18 2/59 3/103   (6 wkts) 235
5/171 6/205 7/216 8/219 9/227   4/156 5/156 6/188

Bonus points – Surrey 2, Kent 3 (Score at 100 overs: 225-8).

Bowling: *First Innings*—Jarvis 18.1–3–32–1; Ellison 18–7–45–2; Underwood 20–10–28–2; Baptiste 25–10–73–4; Woolmer 8–5–9–1; Johnson 13–5–20–0; Cowdrey 2–0–3–0. *Second Innings*—Jarvis 7–2–23–1; Ellison 15.4–4–43–1; Underwood 24.1–5–84–3; Johnson 16–3–66–1.

Umpires: H. D. Bird and R. A. Harris.

At Cardiff, August 13, 15, 16. KENT beat GLAMORGAN by seven wickets.

KENT v WARWICKSHIRE

At Folkestone, August 20, 22, 23. Drawn. Kent 5 pts, Warwickshire 8 pts. Underwood was in the attack after only seven overs, but Kallicharran and Amiss, with a third-wicket stand of 133 off 41 overs, laid the foundations for a huge Warwickshire total. Kallicharran reached a chanceless century in 180 minutes, with one 6 and sixteen 4s, and on the second day Amiss moved past 150 in 349 minutes with two 6s and sixteen 4s. Gifford's persistence with spin and Old's with medium pace ensured that Kent would follow on, and but for an aggressive innings by Johnson, the arrears would have been higher. Kent were in desperate trouble when, batting again, they still needed 43 to avoid an innings defeat with half their side out, but Knott and Aslett, adding 149 off 35 overs, enabled them to set a token target.

Warwickshire

T. A. Lloyd c Taylor b Underwood	30	– not out	14
K. D. Smith c Cowdrey b Underwood	13	– not out	12
A. I. Kallicharran c Dilley b Underwood	111		
D. L. Amiss c Tavaré b Cowdrey	164		
†G. W. Humpage c Knott b Cowdrey	18		
R. I. H. B. Dyer c Aslett b Underwood	25		
C. M. Old c Knott b Underwood	16		
D. A. Thorne b Dilley	23		
C. Lethbridge not out	20		
B 4, l-b 12, n-b 34	50	L-b 3, n-b 2	5

1/19 2/84 3/217 4/247 (8 wkts dec.) 470 (no wkt) 31
5/332 6/353 7/429 8/470

N. Gifford and *R. G. D. Willis did not bat.

Bonus points – Warwickshire 4, Kent 2 (Score at 100 overs: 336-5).

Bowling: *First Innings*—Dilley 26–4–77–1; Ellison 20–1–60–0; Underwood 38–7–113–5; Johnson 21–7–61–0; Baptiste 13–2–72–0; Cowdrey 9.2–2–37–2. *Second Innings*—Dilley 5–2–5–0; Underwood 5–2–21–0; Johnson 1–1–0–0.

Kent

N. R. Taylor lbw b Willis	13	– c Humpage b Willis	3
M. R. Benson b Gifford	42	– b Old	52
*C. J. Tavaré lbw b Gifford	25	– b Gifford	62
D. G. Aslett c Smith b Gifford	1	– b Gifford	78
C. S. Cowdrey b Gifford	0	– st Humpage b Gifford	9
E. A. E. Baptiste b Old	38	– c Humpage b Old	12
†A. P. E. Knott c Lloyd b Old	27	– b Gifford	80
G. W. Johnson not out	79	– not out	20
R. M. Ellison lbw b Old	1	– b Old	10
G. R. Dilley c Old b Gifford	23	– not out	0
D. L. Underwood c Lloyd b Gifford	6		
B 3, l-b 1, n-b 9	13	B 2, l-b 2, n-b 14	18

1/31 2/73 3/83 4/83 268 1/5 2/114 3/126 (8 wkts dec.) 344
5/90 6/150 7/159 8/161 9/242 4/138 5/159 6/308 7/319 8/340

Bonus points – Kent 3, Warwickshire 4.

Bowling: *First Innings*—Willis 12–4–44–1; Old 21–3–107–3; Gifford 30.5–5–85–6; Lethbridge 2–0–19–0. *Second Innings*—Willis 17–4–44–1; Old 38–5–138–3; Gifford 42.3–12–111–4; Kallicharran 3–0–10–0; Thorne 5–0–23–0.

Umpires: D. G. L. Evans and P. B. Wight.

KENT v LEICESTERSHIRE

At Folkestone, August 24, 25, 26. Kent won by ten wickets. Kent 24 pts, Leicestershire 6 pts. A devastating spell by Baptiste, who then limped off with a pulled side muscle, led to a bad Leicestershire start from which Clift and Steele partially rescued them with a seventh-wicket stand of 91 off 36 overs. Benson and Cowdrey, adding 116 off 29 overs, ensured Kent a comfortable lead, with Cowdrey hitting his century in 152 minutes with one 6 and twelve 4s. Underwood then nearly bowled Leicestershire to defeat in two days with good support from Dilley. It still needed only 50 minutes for them to end Leicestershire's second innings on the final day, Underwood finishing with seven wickets in an innings for the fourth time in the season.

Leicestershire

J. C. Balderstone lbw b Baptiste	22	– b Underwood	16
I. P. Butcher c Dilley b Baptiste	29	– c Aslett b Underwood	24
N. E. Briers hit wkt b Baptiste	8	– lbw b Underwood	23
B. F. Davison b Cowdrey	4	– b Underwood	0
J. J. Whitaker c Benson b Dilley	15	– c Knott b Dilley	10
P. B. Clift not out	70	– (7) b Dilley	18
*†R. W. Tolchard run out	8	– (8) lbw b Dilley	1
J. F. Steele c Hinks b Underwood	26	– (9) not out	14
G. J. Parsons c and b Cowdrey	1	– (6) c Johnson b Underwood	4
J. P. Agnew c Benson b Dilley	5	– c Taylor b Underwood	13
G. J. F. Ferris lbw b Dilley	5	– c Knott b Underwood	0
L-b 7, w 2, n-b 4	13	B 8, l-b 9, n-b 12	29
	206		**152**

1/43 2/54 3/61 4/65 5/80 6/89 7/180 8/190 9/198

1/31 2/65 3/65 4/81 5/91 6/97 7/105 8/135 9/151

Bonus points – Leicestershire 2, Kent 4.

Bowling: *First Innings*—Dilley 18.5–3–53–3; Ellison 16–3–65–0; Baptiste 9.1–3–21–3; Underwood 18–12–18–1; Cowdrey 11–2–36–2. *Second Innings*—Dilley 21–7–41–3; Underwood 29–11–55–7; Johnson 1–0–3–0; Cowdrey 7–2–24–0.

Kent

N. R. Taylor b Clift	23	– not out	10
M. R. Benson c Briers b Steele	80	– not out	15
D. G. Aslett b Agnew	12		
S. G. Hinks c Briers b Agnew	16		
*C. S. Cowdrey st Tolchard b Steele	123		
†A. P. E. Knott c Steele b Ferris	19		
G. W. Johnson lbw b Parsons	23		
G. R. Dilley lbw b Parsons	1		
R. M. Ellison b Steele	12		
E. A. E. Baptiste b Parsons	3		
D. L. Underwood not out	0		
B 6, l-b 9, w 4, n-b 6	25		
	337	(no wkt)	**25**

1/36 2/61 3/93 4/209 5/252 6/317 7/317 8/323 9/335

Bonus points – Kent 4, Leicestershire 4.

Bowling: *First Innings*—Ferris 17–5–34–1; Parsons 21–4–67–3; Clift 20–0–72–1; Agnew 17–1–73–2; Steele 18.5–7–66–3. *Second Innings*—Clift 5–1–7–0; Davison 4.4–0–18–0.

Umpires: D. G. L. Evans and P. B. Wight.

At Bournemouth, August 27, 29, 30. KENT lost to HAMPSHIRE by eight wickets.

At Leicester, August 31, September 1, 2. KENT lost to LEICESTERSHIRE by eight wickets.

At Taunton, September 7, 8, 9. KENT drew with SOMERSET.

KENT v NORTHAMPTONSHIRE

At Canterbury, September 10, 12, 13. Drawn. Kent 6 pts, Northamptonshire 8 pts. A first century of the season by Cook, achieved in 128 minutes with ten 4s, paved the way for Northamptonshire's big total. He and Boyd-Moss added 170 off 55 overs for the second wicket. Tavaré and Aslett, who added 100 off 25 overs, paved the way for Kent to declare 24 behind, with Cowdrey hitting a half-century in 48 minutes. Johnson followed with a career-best bowling performance with his off-spin as Northamptonshire were bowled out cheaply, leaving Kent 192 to win in three hours. Kent lost two early wickets but were recovering when the chances of an interesting finish were spoiled by rain.

Northamptonshire

*G. Cook c and b Johnson	128	– c Cowdrey b Johnson	36
W. Larkins lbw b Underwood	22	– b Dilley	2
R. J. Boyd-Moss c and b Johnson	65	– c and b Johnson	37
A. J. Lamb b Johnson	15	– b Underwood	27
R. G. Williams c and b Cowdrey	31	– b Johnson	2
D. J. Capel c Dilley b Underwood	23	– lbw b Underwood	8
D. S. Steele not out	29	– b Johnson	3
†G. Sharp not out	15	– not out	22
N. A. Mallender (did not bat)		– b Johnson	8
A. Walker (did not bat)		– c Tavaré b Johnson	0
B. J. Griffiths (did not bat)		– c Dilley b Johnson	4
L-b 4, n-b 5	9	B 10, l-b 5, n-b 3	18

1/44 2/214 3/223 4/246   (6 wkts dec.) 337   1/5 2/80 3/107 4/117   167
5/283 6/304   5/125 6/125 7/134 8/150 9/150

Bonus points – Northamptonshire 4, Kent 2 (Score at 100 overs: 304-5).

Bowling: *First Innings*—Dilley 6–0–36–0; Jarvis 15–3–52–0; Underwood 31–12–60–2; Johnson 36–9–96–3; Cowdrey 19–0–68–1; Taylor 7–1–16–0. *Second Innings*—Dilley 5–0–13–1; Jarvis 2–0–10–0; Johnson 35.3–13–76–7; Underwood 33–17–50–2.

Kent

M. R. Benson c Lamb b Williams	44	– c Steele b Walker	2
N. R. Taylor c Capel b Walker	18	– not out	21
*C. J. Tavaré c sub b Walker	81	– c Sharp b Walker	0
D. G. Aslett b Williams	63	– not out	30
C. S. Cowdrey c Williams b Steele	53		
S. G. Hinks st Sharp b Williams	10		
G. W. Johnson c Lamb b Steele	9		
G. R. Dilley c Walker b Steele	18		
D. L. Underwood c Steele b Williams	3		
†A. P. E. Knott not out	8		
B 5, l-b 1	6	L-b 2, n-b 1	3

1/31 2/95 3/195 4/229   (9 wkts dec.) 313   1/3 2/6   (2 wkts) 56
5/271 6/272 7/288 8/295 9/313

K. B. S. Jarvis did not bat.

Bonus points – Kent 4, Northamptonshire 4.

Bowling: *First Innings*—Mallender 5–1–13–0; Walker 16–2–57–2; Williams 43–7–125–4; Griffiths 6–0–28–0; Steele 26.5–5–71–3; Capel 2–0–13–0. *Second Innings*—Griffiths 5–0–11–0; Walker 7–0–27–2; Steele 7–2–11–0; Williams 5–2–4–0.

Umpires: B. J. Meyer and R. Palmer.

LANCASHIRE

Patron: HM The Queen
President: Edwin Kay
Chairman: C. S. Rhoades
Secretary: C. D. Hassell
  County Cricket Ground, Old Trafford,
  Manchester M16 0PX
  (Telephone: 061-872 5533)
Cricket Manager: J. D. Bond
Captain: C. H. Lloyd
Coaches: J. S. Savage and P. Lever

Lancashire marked time in 1983, dropping one place in the Schweppes County Championship, rising two places in the John Player Sunday League, again reaching the semi-finals of the Benson and Hedges Cup, but being unable to get beyond the second round of the NatWest Bank Trophy. They lost fewer games than the champions, Essex, yet finished eleven positions and 159 points below them as they all too often settled for the draw.

There was not enough adventure in Lancashire's cricket and their position of twelfth in the Championship reflected their largely dour approach. The weather could hardly be blamed because by the beginning of June, from the same number of games, they were a position higher than Essex in the table. A sad moment in a disappointing season was the announcement of David Lloyd's retirement, only a year after he was Lancashire's leading run-scorer with nearly 2,000 in all competitions. He missed most of the first half of the season with a neck injury and soon after returning felt he was no longer a part of the club's plans for the future and decided to retire. He had the unusual experience of scoring a century in his last first-class match, at Northampton.

Lancashire's batting, which had been their strong point for several years, was like the curate's egg, with Graeme Fowler and John Abrahams the only ones to reach 1,000 runs. Clive Lloyd had his worst season for the county, and David Hughes went into decline after his outstanding performance of the previous year. Fowler showed he had learned from his experience in Australia in the winter and Abrahams thrived on the extra responsibility of the captaincy during Clive Lloyd's absence. Hughes started the season impressively with an innings of 153 against Glamorgan, then spent sixteen innings getting the next 153 as he struggled to reach 500 for the season. Frank Hayes made a welcome return to form after the bad injury of the previous year, and there was a most encouraging first season for Neil Fairbrother, who also played for Young England.

Fairbrother scored an unbeaten 94 in his first first-class innings, being denied a century only when Abrahams, captaining Lancashire for only the fifth time in a first-class match, stuck rigidly to an agreement with Warwickshire's captain, Willis, and declared at 250 for four. The nineteen-year-old batsman scored seven more fifties and impressed with his style and maturity. Jack Simmons showed at 42 that he still has a year or two of first-class cricket in him. He missed only one game because of injury, scored two centuries and equalled his highest number of wickets in a summer. In addition, he was the leading catcher after wicket-keeper Chris Maynard.

Another young player to make progress was Mike Watkinson, a 21-year-old medium-paced bowler who had two six-wicket returns, against Sussex and Glamorgan, in his 35 Championship wickets. Steve Jefferies, a rarity among South Africans in that he has no ambitions to play for England, impressed with his left-arm fast-medium bowling in his first season with Lancashire, and had the county's best return of the season when he took eight for 46 against Nottinghamshire at Trent Bridge. The law regarding overseas players debarred Jefferies from playing when Clive Lloyd was available and this, along with injury, restricted his appearances to only nine Championship matches. He gave the bowling much-needed penetration and Lancashire responded to his impressive all-round ability by offering him a contract for 1984 and 1985.

Paul Allott, overlooked by England for the previous winter's tour of Australia, must have been encouraged when he was chosen for the World Cup squad, yet disappointed with his 38 wickets from seventeen first-class matches, these including only one five-wicket return.

Lancashire took the unusual step of signing a leg-break and googly bowler in Nasir Zaidi, a Pakistani from the Lord's groundstaff. He played thirteen times but rarely bowled long spells, being handled with the care that befits a near extinct species. There was a touch of Abdul Qadir about his bowling, which, allied with competent batting and eager, alert fielding, made him an asset.

The left-arm medium-paced Ian Folley and all-rounder Steve O'Shaughnessy, both of whom made great strides forward in 1982, failed to make progress. Folley's seven wickets cost 74 runs each and O'Shaughnessy, despite surpassing his aggregate of the previous season, had a disappointing summer. Yet O'Shaughnessy stepped into history on the final day of the season by scoring a century in 35 minutes to equal P. G. H. Fender's 63-year-old record. His reaction, after being fed runs in the hope of a declaration, was, sadly but significantly, one of embarrassment. – B.B.

438

LANCASHIRE 1983

[Bill Smith]

Back row: L. L. McFarlane, S. J. O'Shaughnessy, G. J. Speak, M. Watkinson, C. Maynard, G. Fowler, N. H. Fairbrother. *Front row:* K. A. Hayes, J. Simmons, D. P. Hughes, J. Abrahams, F. C. Hayes, P. J. W. Allott, Nazir Zaidi. *Inset:* C. H. Lloyd (*captain*).

LANCASHIRE RESULTS

All first-class matches – Played 25: Won 3, Lost 4, Drawn 18.

County Championship matches – Played 24: Won 3, Lost 4, Drawn 17.

Bonus points – Batting 56, Bowling 61.

Competition placings – Schweppes County Championship, 12th eq; NatWest Bank Trophy, 2nd round; Benson and Hedges Cup, s-f; John Player League, 8th eq.

COUNTY CHAMPIONSHIP AVERAGES

BATTING

	Birthplace	M	I	NO	R	HI	Avge
G. Fowlerc	Accrington	15	25	2	1,253	156*	54.47
D. Lloydc	Accrington	9	14	2	485	123	40.41
J. Abrahamsc..........	Cape Town, SA	23	39	7	1,261	178	39.40
N. H. Fairbrother	Warrington	16	26	5	759	94*	36.14
L. L. McFarlane.....	Portland, Jamaica	9	9	8	35	12*	35.00
S. T. Jefferies	Cape Town, SA	9	12	4	260	75*	32.50
F. C. Hayesc	Preston	19	28	1	866	149	32.07
C. H. Lloydc	Georgetown, BG	11	16	1	447	86	29.80
S. J. O'Shaughnessy .	Bury	17	28	3	685	105	27.40
J. Simmonsc	Clayton-le-Moors	23	31	2	679	104	23.41
J. Stanworth	Oldham	3	6	2	90	31*	22.50
Nasir Zaidi	Karachi, Pakistan	12	16	6	215	51	21.50
I. Cockbain	Bootle	8	15	1	291	52	20.78
D. P. Huhgesc	Newton-le-Willows	18	28	2	522	153	20.07
I. Folley	Burnley	12	9	4	91	25	18.20
C. Maynard	Haslemere	21	27	3	417	61*	17.37
P. J. W. Allottc	Altrincham	17	18	4	225	41	16.07
K. A. Hayes	Thurnscoe	5	8	0	103	32	12.87
M. Watkinson	Westhoughton	15	20	4	168	29	10.50

Also batted: M. R. Chadwick (*Rochdale*) (1 match) 1, 1; N. V. Radford (*Luanshya, N. Rhodesia*) (1 match) 24, 27.

* *Signifies not out.*   c *Denotes county cap.*

BOWLING

	O	M	R	W	Avge	BB
D. Lloyd................	188	53	389	16	24.31	5-22
M. Watkinson	319.3	69	929	35	26.54	6-51
J. Simmons.............	744	214	1,807	68	26.57	7-73
S. T. Jefferies	256.5	60	782	27	28.96	8-46
P. J. W. Allott........	434.4	120	1,154	38	30.36	5-45
Nasir Zaidi	170.3	41	491	15	32.73	3-27
S. J. O'Shaughnessy .	227.2	40	816	22	37.09	4-73
L. L. McFarlane......	204.4	32	726	15	48.40	3-53
J. Abrahams	216	41	658	13	50.61	3-83

Also bowled: N. H. Fairbrother 3–2–1–0; I. Folley 191–49–522–7; G. Fowler 2–0–7–0; D. P. Hughes 60.5–8–218–2; N. V. Radford 25–2–99–0.

The following played a total of sixteen three-figure innings for Lancashire in County Championship matches – G. Fowler 4, J. Abrahams 3, F. C. Hayes 3, S. J. O'Shaughnessy 2, J. Simmons 2, D. P. Hughes 1, D. Lloyd 1.

At Oxford, April 23, 25, 26. LANCASHIRE drew with OXFORD UNIVERSITY.

LANCASHIRE v GLAMORGAN

At Manchester, April 30, May 2, 3. Drawn. Lancashire 7 pts, Glamorgan 3 pts. After the start had been delayed an hour Lancashire struggled through the 75 minutes to lunch, reached at 33 for two. Fowler and Hughes transformed the position with 192 runs between lunch and tea, taking their partnership to 245. The second day was washed out, and in a final day restricted to two hours Jefferies, in his Championship début, and Allott secured three bowling points.

Lancashire

G. Fowler b Selvey 133	J. Simmons b Thomas....................... 11
D. Lloyd c E. W. Jones b Thomas 0	S. T. Jefferies not out....................... 45
S. J. O'Shaughnessy c E. W. Jones	†C. Maynard b Thomas 3
b Nash. 1	B 4, l-b 13, w 2, n-b 13 32
D. P. Hughes c Nash b Thomas..........153	
F. C Hayes b Selvey........................ 12	1/0 2/19 (8 wkts dec.) 429
*J. Abrahams c E. W. Jones	3/264 4/295 5/366
b Thomas. 39	6/366 7/399 8/429

P. J. W. Allott and I. Folley did not bat.

Bonus points – Lancashire 4, Glamorgan 3.

Bowling: Thomas 24–7–103–5; Nash 11–4–27–1; Selvey 23–5–93–2; Rowe 11–6–34–0; Ontong 15–2–84–0; Lloyd 12–1–56–0.

Glamorgan

A. Jones c Hayes b Jefferies 2	B. J. Lloyd c Hughes b Jefferies 4
J. A. Hopkins not out 25	J. G. Thomas not out 5
D. A. Francis c Maynard b Allott....... 0	L-b 3, w 1, n-b 4 8
Javed Miandad b Jefferies 9	
C. J. C. Rowe lbw b Allott................ 1	1/8 2/11 (7 wkts dec.) 63
R. C. Ontong b Allott 0	3/27 4/29
†E. W. Jones c Maynard b Allott 9	5/29 6/49 7/54

M. A. Nash and *M. W. W. Selvey did not bat.

Bonus points – Lancashire 3.

Bowling: Allott 15.1–3–28–4; Jefferies 14–5–23–3; Folley 1–0–4–0.

Umpires: R. Julian and B. Leadbeater.

At Lord's, May 4, 5, 6. LANCASHIRE drew with MIDDLESEX.

At Chesterfield, May 11, 12, 13. LANCASHIRE drew with DERBYSHIRE.

At The Oval, May 25, 26, 27. LANCASHIRE drew with SURREY.

LANCASHIRE v YORKSHIRE

At Manchester, May 28, 30, 31. Drawn. Lancashire 8 pts, Yorkshire 3 pts. After the first day had been washed out Lancashire, put in to bat, took maximum batting points thanks to a second-wicket stand of 222 in 192 minutes between Fowler, whose career-best innings took his average for the season to 136, and Hayes. The temptation to forfeit innings was resisted and most of the final day was taken up with Yorkshire fighting off the threat of following on, finally achieved with three wickets standing after a partnership of 73 between Bairstow and Carrick.

Lancashire

G. Fowler not out	156		
I. Cockbain c Athey b Sidebottom	13	– (1) not out	6
F. C. Hayes b Stevenson	116		
D. P. Hughes b Sidebottom	6		
*J. Abrahams c Bairstow b Sidebottom	5	– (2) not out	16
S. J. O'Shaughnessy not out	1		
L-b 2, n-b 2	4	B 1, l-b 1	2

1/42 2/264 3/285 4/293   (4 wkts dec.) 301   (no wkt) 24

J. Simmons, †C. Maynard, M. Watkinson, P. J. W. Allott and I. Folley did not bat.

Bonus points – Lancashire 4, Yorkshire 1.

Bowling: *First Innings*—Ramage 6–0–18–0; Stevenson 20.4–2–72–1; Sidebottom 24–4–76–3; Love 5–1–18–0; Carrick 29–7–74–0; Illingworth 13–2–39–0. *Second Innings*—Bairstow 6–3–9–0; Love 3–0–11–0; Athey 2–1–2–0.

Yorkshire

G. Boycott lbw b Folley	18	G. B. Stevenson b O'Shaughnessy	9
R. G. Lumb c Maynard b Folley	8	*R. Illingworth c Hayes b Simmons	1
C. W. J. Athey c Maynard b Allott	2	A. Ramage not out	0
S. N. Hartley c Maynard b O'Shaughnessy	16		
J. D. Love lbw b Allott	36	B 2, l-b 3	5
†D. L. Bairstow b Watkinson	40		
P. Carrick b O'Shaughnessy	83	1/20 2/25 3/33	228
A. Sidebottom c Maynard b O'Shaughnessy	10	4/74 5/92 6/165	
		7/185 8/221 9/224	

Bonus points – Yorkshire 2, Lancashire 4.

Bowling: Allott 20–7–50–2; Folley 21–2–37–2; Watkinson 14–2–42–1; O'Shaughnessy 19.5–3–73–4: Simmons 10–3–21–1.

Umpires: D. J. Constant and D. O. Oslear.

At Birmingham, June 4, 6, 7. LANCASHIRE lost to WARWICKSHIRE by 93 runs.

At Bournemouth, June 8, 9, 10. LANCASHIRE drew with HAMPSHIRE.

LANCASHIRE v NOTTINGHAMSHIRE

At Manchester, June 11, 13, 14. Drawn. Lancashire 2 pts, Nottinghamshire 3 pts. Rain again washed out the opening day and also restricted the second to 49 overs. Both teams forfeited an innings on the final day, leaving Nottinghamshire to score 221 to win in 210 minutes. They needed 112 from the last sixteen overs when rain, accompanied by a gale which had blown over the sightscreens, ended play.

Lancashire

I. Cockbain c French b Hendrick	52	S. T. Jefferies c Fell b Cooper	8	
†C. Maynard b Saxelby	33	M. Watkinson not out	23	
F. C. Hayes b Hemmings	23	Nasir Zaidi not out	7	
D. P. Hughes c Hassan b Hemmings	23	L-b 5, w 1	6	
*J. Abrahams b Hendrick	0			
N. H. Fairbrother c Fell b Bore	42	1/51 2/94 3/113 4/113 (8 wkts dec.)	220	
J. Simmons b Saxelby	3	5/145 6/153 7/175 8/194		

I. Folley did not bat.

Bonus points – Lancashire 2, Nottinghamshire 3.

Bowling: Hendrick 22–9–38–2; Cooper 22–8–45–1; Saxelby 12–2–40–2; Bore 14–4–51–1; Hemmings 16–9–29–2; Fell 3–0–11–0.

Lancashire forfeited their second innings.

Nottinghamshire

R. T. Robinson (did not bat)	– not out	53	
B. Hassan (did not bat)	– c Nasir b Jefferies	9	
P. Johnson (did not bat)	– c Hughes b Jefferies	3	
M. A. Fell (did not bat)	– c Maynard b Nasir	4	
*J. D. Birch (did not bat)	– not out	35	
	B 2, l-b 3	5	
	1/14 2/24 3/32 (3 wkts)	109	

†B. N. French, E. E. Hemmings, K. Saxelby, K. E. Cooper, M. Hendrick and M. K. Bore did not bat.

Bowling: Jefferies 15–6–28–2; Folley 11–5–23–0; Watkinson 6–4–10–0; Simmons 11–1–37–0; Nasir 10–8–6–1.

Nottinghamshire forfeited their first innings.

Umpires: W. E. Alley and R. Julian.

LANCASHIRE v WARWICKSHIRE

At Manchester, June 15, 16, 17. Warwickshire won by six wickets. Warwickshire 23 pts, Lancashire 5 pts. Old made significant contributions towards Warwickshire's first-innings command with four inexpensive wickets and 62 runs, but it was Gifford, with a remarkable five for 31 in 35 overs, who set up Warwickshire's third successive Championship win, achieved with three balls to spare after a century opening stand by Smith and Lloyd.

Lancashire

I. Cockbain b Gifford	23	– c Old b Hogg	0
†C. Maynard lbw b Old	14	– b Ferreira	5
F. C. Hayes b Ferreira	6	– c Tedstone b Gifford	85
D. P. Hughes c Smith b Ferreira	5	– (5) c Tedstone b Old	3
*J. Abrahams b Old	45	– (6) c Amiss b Old	42
N. H. Fairbrother c Amiss b Old	40	– (7) c and b Gifford	68
J. Simmons lbw b Gifford	38	– (8) c and b Gifford	6
S. T. Jefferies b Old	7	– (9) c Tedstone b Gifford	4
M. Watkinson b Gifford	15	– (10) c Tedstone b Hogg	4
Nasir Zaidi b Ferreira	0	– (11) not out	0
I. Folley not out	4	– (4) c Old b Gifford	7
B 4, l-b 7, n-b 8	19	B 4, l-b 8, n-b 13	25

1/24 2/34 3/44 4/63   216   1/0 2/16 3/27 4/49   249
5/135 6/151 7/165 8/207 9/212   5/133 6/216 7/230 8/240 9/245

Bonus points – Lancashire 2, Warwickshire 4.

Bowling: *First Innings*—Hogg 15–5–48–0; Old 28–9–31–4; Ferreira 28–6–76–3; Gifford 24.3–8–42–3. *Second Innings*—Hogg 15.3–3–50–2; Old 17–6–29–2; Ferreira 17–3–40–1; Gifford 35–22–31–5; Asif Din 12–1–57–0; Kallicharran 4–0–17–0.

Warwickshire

K. D. Smith c Hayes b Jefferies	7	– b Watkinson	53
T. A. Lloyd c Maynard b Jefferies	12	– run out	45
A. I. Kallicharran c Fairbrother b Watkinson	30	– c Folley b Simmons	4
D. L. Amiss c Folley b Simmons	88	– b Simmons	16
G. W. Humpage lbw b Watkinson	17	– not out	6
Asif Din b Jefferies	65		
A. M. Ferreira lbw b Simmons	0		
†G. A. Tedstone lbw b Jefferies	11		
C. M. Old b Simmons	62	– (6) not out	6
*N. Gifford b Simmons	17		
W. Hogg not out	7		
B 3, l-b 1, n-b 3	12	L-b 8	8

1/9 2/50 3/50 4/75   328   1/105 2/106   (4 wkts) 138
5/218 6/219 7/225 8/264 9/314   3/114 4/130

Bonus points – Warwickshire 3, Lancashire 3 (Score at 100 overs: 263-7).

Bowling: *First Innings*—Jefferies 34–3–121–4; Folley 16–5–26–0; Watkinson 26–1–71–2; Simmons 25.5–5–71–4; Nasir 8–2–27–0. *Second Innings*—Jefferies 4–0–27–0; Watkinson 11–0–56–1; Folley 5–0–26–0; Simmons 5.3–0–21–2.

Umpires: W. E. Alley and R. Julian.

At Horsham, June 18, 20, 21. LANCASHIRE beat SUSSEX by 54 runs.

At Nottingham, June 25, 27, 28. LANCASHIRE lost to NOTTINGHAMSHIRE by 157 runs.

LANCASHIRE v HAMPSHIRE

At Liverpool, July 2, 4, 5. Drawn. Lancashire 6 pts, Hampshire 7 pts. Greenidge, who scored two centuries in the match and 162 not out in the John Player League on the Sunday, hit three in the four days to take his run tally to 366 for once out. When Hampshire closed their second innings Lancashire were left three hours to score 265. They only just saved the game after Marshall had taken five wickets, Allott and Nasir holding out for the final ten overs.

Hampshire

C. G. Greenidge c Abrahams b Simmons	104	– not out	100
C. L. Smith c Allott b Simmons	118	– c Maynard b O'Shaughnessy	42
M. C. J. Nicholas lbw b Allott	11	– not out	89
T. E. Jesty b Allott	16		
V. P. Terry lbw b Allott	4		
*N. E. J. Pocock run out	17		
M. D. Marshall not out	26		
N. G. Cowley not out	7		
B 3, l-b 15, n-b 2	20	B 4, l-b 8, n-b 3	15

1/191 2/220 3/238   (6 wkts dec.) 323   1/83   (1 wkt dec.) 246
4/246 5/270 6/296

T. M. Tremlett, †R. J. Parks and J. W. Southern did not bat.

Bonus points – Hampshire 4, Lancashire 2 (Score at 100 overs: 300-6).

Bowling: *First Innings*—Allott 23-9-41-3; Radford 22-2-79-0; O'Shaughnessy 12-1-54-0; Simmons 44-10-111-2; Nasir 5-0-18-0. *Second Innings*—Allott 20-5-58-0; Radford 3-0-20-0; O'Shaughnessy 12-2-51-1; Simmons 15-6-46-0; Nasir 4-1-16-0; Abrahams 11-1-40-0.

Lancashire

G. Fowler c and b Smith	73	– c Southern b Marshall	6
S. J. O'Shaughnessy b Marshall	11	– lbw b Tremlett	0
F. C. Hayes c Jesty b Cowley	66	– c Nicholas b Southern	13
D. P. Hughes c Terry b Cowley	19	– c Terry b Marshall	14
*J. Abrahams st Parks b Cowley	21	– c Greenidge b Marshall	14
†C. Maynard not out	61	– c Pocock b Marshall	5
J. Simmons lbw b Marshall	4	– lbw b Southern	35
N. V. Radford c Greenidge b Cowley	24	– c Parks b Marshall	27
Nasir Zaidi not out	3	– not out	13
P. J. W. Allott (did not bat)		– not out	5
B 7, l-b 13, n-b 3	23	B 3, l-b 1, w 1, n-b 1	6

1/56 2/102 3/147 4/200   (7 wkts dec.) 305   1/2 2/10 3/24 4/38   (8 wkts) 138
5/206 6/216 7/263   5/48 6/67 7/113 8/120

N. H. Fairbrother did not bat.

Bonus points – Lancashire 4, Hampshire 3.

Bowling: *First Innings*—Marshall 21-4-60-2; Tremlett 16-6-36-0; Jesty 8-2-24-0; Southern 27-7-69-0; Cowley 23-5-76-4; Smith 4-1-17-1. *Second Innings*—Marshall 22-3-64-5; Tremlett 5-1-11-1; Southern 21-7-47-2; Cowley 5-1-10-0.

Umpires: M. J. Kitchen and B. Leadbeater.

At Maidstone, July 9, 11, 12. LANCASHIRE drew with KENT.

At Swansea, July 13, 14, 15. LANCASHIRE drew with GLAMORGAN.

LANCASHIRE v WORCESTERSHIRE

At Manchester, July 16, 18, 19. Drawn. Lancashire 6 pts, Worcestershire 4 pts. Only Neale batted with any certainty in Worcestershire's first innings, dominating the scoring against an attack in which 73 of the overs were bowled by spinners. Abrahams shared in two century partnerships in his career-best innings as Lancashire batted on to a lead of 160. Worcestershire had no difficulty saving the match with Neale again leading the way.

Worcestershire

J. A. Ormrod lbw b D. Lloyd	40	– run out	22
M. J. Weston c Fairbrother b McFarlane	8	– b Allott	13
*P. A. Neale lbw b Allott	139	– lbw b McFarlane	64
D. N. Patel lbw b Watkinson	14	– st Maynard b Simmons	53
D. B. D'Oliveira c F. C. Hayes b D. Lloyd	10	– b Abrahams	18
D. A. Banks c Maynard b Simmons	24	– not out	40
R. K. Illingworth c F. C. Hayes b Simmons	6	– not out	13
J. D. Inchmore c C. H. Lloyd b D. Lloyd	6		
†P. Moores not out	21		
S. P. Perryman c C. H. Lloyd b Allott	0		
A. P. Pridgeon b Watkinson	12		
B 1, l-b 4, n-b 1	6	B 13, l-b 14, w 1, n-b 3	31

1/10 2/75 3/111 4/134   280   1/17 2/74 3/168   (5 wkts) 254
5/178 6/194 7/207 8/263 9/265   4/173 5/213

Bonus points – Worcestershire 3, Lancashire 3 (Score at 100 overs: 257-7).

Bowling: *First Innings*—Allott 11–4–28–2; McFarlane 8–5–10–1; Watkinson 16.1–4–41–2; Simmons 24–5–64–2; D. Lloyd 40–12–94–3; Abrahams 9–0–37–0. *Second Innings*—Allott 9–3–31–1; McFarlane 8–1–26–1; Watkinson 4–4–0–0; Simmons 31–4–80–1; D. Lloyd 24–8–51–0; Abrahams 13–4–34–1; Fairbrother 1–0–1–0.

Lancashire

K. A. Hayes c Inchmore b Pridgeon	11	M. Watkinson b Pridgeon	29
D. Lloyd c Ormrod b Patel	79	P. J. W. Allott c Patel b Pridgeon	17
F. C. Hayes c D'Oliveira b Patel	0	L. L. McFarlane not out	0
J. Abrahams run out	178		
*C. H. Lloyd lbw b Inchmore	76	B 14, l-b 19, w 2, n-b 14	49
N. H. Fairbrother b Inchmore	0		
†C. Maynard b Inchmore	1	1/37 2/40 3/155 4/305	440
J. Simmons run out	0	5/305 6/307 7/308 8/422 9/423	

Bonus points – Lancashire 3, Worcestershire 1 (Score at 100 overs: 264-3).

Bowling: Pridgeon 27.4–7–86–3; Inchmore 24–6–73–3; Patel 43–20–84–2; Perryman 15–2–38–0; D'Oliveira 22–6–64–0; Illingworth 10–1–46–0.

Umpires: K. E. Palmer and J. van Geloven.

LANCASHIRE v GLOUCESTERSHIRE

At Southport, July 27, 28, 29. Lancashire won by five wickets. Lancashire 23 pts, Gloucestershire 4 pts. Gloucestershire were put in to bat on a damp pitch and were bowled out by Simmons and Nasir. Lancashire lost three quick wickets but a partnership of 150 between Abrahams and Clive Lloyd, followed by a mature innings from Fairbrother, gave Lancashire control. Zaheer led Gloucestershire's second-innings resistance but Simmons, with twelve wickets in the match, took Lancashire to their second win of the season.

Gloucestershire

A. W. Stovold c Simmons b Folley	5	– c Nasir b Simmons	15
B. C. Broad lbw b O'Shaughnessy	35	– c Hughes b Simmons	19
P. W. Romaines c Hughes b Simmons	79	– lbw b McFarlane	27
Zaheer Abbas b Simmons	3	– (5) c Hughes b Simmons	112
P. Bainbridge c Nasir b Simmons	19	– (6) b Simmons	50
A. J. Hignell b Simmons	19	– (7) c and b Simmons	13
J. N. Shepherd lbw b Nasir	8	– (8) c O'Shaughnessy b Simmons.	3
*D. A. Graveney c C. H. Lloyd b Nasir	4	– (9) not out	0
†R. C. Russell c C. H. Lloyd b Simmons	9	– (4) b Abrahams	5
J. H. Childs c Simmons b Nasir	14	– c Hughes b Nasir	5
G. E. Sainsbury not out	0	– c Nasir b Simmons	1
B 4, l-b 2	6	L-b 1, n-b 4	5
	201		255

1/5 2/57 3/72 4/104   1/25 2/54 3/62 4/70
5/132 6/151 7/159 8/174 9/187   5/200 6/230 7/238 8/249 9/254

Bonus points – Gloucestershire 2, Lancashire 4.

Bowling: *First Innings*—McFarlane 8–1–23–0; Folley 6–2–18–1; Simmons 31–12–60–5; O'Shaughnessy 4–0–24–1; Hughes 6–1–18–0; Nasir 19.4–3–52–3. *Second Innings*—McFarlane 10–1–41–1; Folley 8–1–27–0; Simmons 26.5–6–73–7; O'Shaughnessy 8–0–23–0; Nasir 11–3–36–1; Abrahams 7–3–15–1; Hughes 13–3–35–0.

Lancashire

K. A. Hayes lbw b Sainsbury	6	– b Shepherd	2
S. J. O'Shaughnessy b Shepherd	2	– lbw b Sainsbury	4
J. Abrahams b Graveney	86	– c Bainbridge b Shepherd	4
D. P. Hughes c Bainbridge b Sainsbury	7	– (5) b Childs	2
*C. H. Lloyd b Russell b Childs	86	– (4) lbw b Childs	15
N. H. Fairbrother lbw b Shepherd	73	– not out	54
†C. Maynard c Broad b Shepherd	19	– not out	34
J. Simmons c Russell b Sainsbury	8		
Nasir Zaidi run out	8		
I. Folley st Russell b Childs	12		
L. L. McFarlane not out	6		
B 4, l-b 10, n-b 3	17	B 10, l-b 3, n-b 2	15
	330	(5 wkts)	130

1/9 2/11 3/22 4/172   1/6 2/10 3/11
5/225 6/271 7/297 8/309 9/312   4/22 5/37

Bonus points – Lancashire 3, Gloucestershire 2 (Score at 100 overs: 257-5).

Bowling: *First Innings*—Shepherd 33–5–77–3; Sainsbury 29–11–60–3; Childs 35.4–10–91–2; Graveney 21–8–50–1; Zaheer 13–4–35–0. *Second Innings*—Shepherd 15.5–2–50–2; Sainsbury 6–3–7–1; Childs 18–5–35–2; Zaheer 9–2–23–0.

Umpires: D. G. L. Evans and J. W. Holder.

LANCASHIRE v SOMERSET

At Manchester, July 30, August 1, 2. Lancashire won by an innings and 15 runs. Lancashire 22 pts, Somerset 3 pts. Simmons, with nine wickets in the match, took his tally to 21 in two games. David Lloyd, whose retirement at the end of the season was announced on the opening day, scored one of five half-centuries that carried Lancashire into a strong position with a first-innings lead of 170. Rain prevented a start until 2.15 on the final day when Somerset were 26 for one. Simmons took five of Somerset's first six second-innings wickets and Lloyd claimed the last four in completing his best return for four years.

Somerset

J. W. Lloyds c Maynard b Folley	12	– c sub b Simmons	21
P. M. Roebuck lbw b McFarlane	1	– (6) c Nasir b D. Lloyd	11
R. L. Ollis b McFarlane	38	– (4) b Simmons	17
N. F. M. Popplewell c Abrahams b McFarlane..	10	– (5) b D. Lloyd	6
*I. V. A. Richards c D. Lloyd b Simmons	37	– (7) c Nasir b Simmons	0
P. W. Denning c Abrahams b Simmons	15	– (2) lbw b Simmons	4
V. J. Marks b Simmons	14	– (8) c Nasir b D. Lloyd	44
†T. Gard c Fairbrother b Nasir	24	– (3) b Simmons	3
C. H. Dredge b Nasir	9	– c Nasir b D. Lloyd	2
J. Garner not out	21	– not out	17
S. C. Booth c D. Lloyd b Simmons	1	– c C. H. Lloyd b D. Lloyd	0
L-b 3	3	B 24, l-b 5, w 1	30
	185		**155**

1/13 2/13 3/24 4/63   1/25 2/26 3/31 4/50
5/103 6/117 7/133 8/155 9/170   5/58 6/58 7/130 8/132 9/135

Bonus points – Somerset 1, Lancashire 4.

Bowling: *First Innings*—McFarlane 14–3–53–3; Folley 8–3–23–1; Simmons 25.1–8–54–4; Nasir 13–3–29–2; Abrahams 5–0–18–0; D. Lloyd 2–0–5–0. *Second Innings*—McFarlane 11–2–25–0; Folley 2–0–3–0; Simmons 38–23–41–5; Nasir 12–5–34–0; D. Lloyd 18–6–22–5.

Lancashire

K. A. Hayes c Gard b Garner	8	Nasir Zaidi st Gard b Lloyds	51
D. Lloyd b Dredge	63	I. Folley st Gard b Booth	1
J. Abrahams c Richards b Garner	52	L. L. McFarlane not out	12
*C. H. Lloyd c Booth b Marks	6		
†C. Maynard c Roebuck b Dredge	16	B 3, l-b 10, n-b 7	20
N. H. Fairbrother lbw b Richards	50		
J. Simmons b Lloyds	75		**355**
D. P. Hughes c Gard b Garner	1		

1/33 2/109 3/122 4/141
5/153 6/243 7/244 8/324 9/343

Bonus points – Lancashire 2, Somerset 2 (Score at 100 overs: 218-5).

Bowling: Garner 26–10–52–3; Dredge 21–7–44–2; Marks 45–22–72–1; Richards 15–3–41–1; Booth 24.3–5–77–1; Lloyds 21–9–49–2.

Umpires: D. G. L. Evans and J. W. Holder.

At Leeds, August 6, 8, 9. LANCASHIRE drew with YORKSHIRE.

At Worcester, August 10, 11, 12. LANCASHIRE lost to WORCESTERSHIRE by five wickets.

LANCASHIRE v MIDDLESEX

At Manchester, August 13, 15, 16. Drawn. Lancashire 5 pts, Middlesex 4 pts. There was no play on the last day, rain denying the prospect of an interesting finish with Middlesex needing 234 more to win with all wickets in hand. Seventeen wickets had fallen on the opening day on an unreliable pitch, one being Brearley's on his return to the Middlesex team. Fowler and Clive Lloyd shared in a stand of 75 to build on Lancashire's first-innings lead of 73, but Emburey took four wickets in three overs without conceding a run as Lancashire's last seven wickets fell for 69 runs.

Lancashire

G. Fowler b Williams	20	– lbw b Emburey	59
D. Lloyd c Barlow b Daniel	6	– c Emburey b Daniel	14
S. J. O'Shaughnessy c Radley b Emburey	31	– lbw b Daniel	0
*C. H. Lloyd lbw b Williams	4	– run out	39
J. Abrahams c Downton b Slack	22	– b Emburey	25
N. H. Fairbrother b Williams	36	– c Slack b Sykes	1
†C. Maynard lbw b Emburey	28	– c Tomlins b Emburey	15
J. Simmons c and b Daniel	7	– b Emburey	0
Nasir Zaidi not out	16	– (10) c Downton b Emburey	0
M. Watkinson lbw b Daniel	0	– (9) c and b Williams	5
P. J. W. Allott b Daniel	7	– not out	15
L-b 2, w 1, n-b 13	16	B 5, l-b 4, n-b 11	20

1/8 2/46 3/58 4/79   193   1/49 2/49 3/124 4/124   193
5/107 6/159 7/159 8/183 9/183   5/125 6/167 7/167 8/169 9/169

Bonus points – Lancashire 1, Middlesex 4.

Bowling: *First Innings*—Williams 22–8–56–3; Daniel 9.2–1–37–4; Emburey 25–11–54–2; Sykes 8–1–22–0; Slack 4–2–8–1. *Second Innings*—Williams 11.2–1–45–1; Daniel 15–3–32–2; Emburey 33–16–64–5; Sykes 13–5–32–1.

Middlesex

W. N. Slack lbw b Allott	5	– not out	17
G. D. Barlow b Allott	50	– not out	16
C. T. Radley lbw b Allott	0		
K. P. Tomlins b Watkinson	0		
J. M. Brearley lbw b Watkinson	17		
R. G. P. Ellis lbw b Allott	2		
*J. E. Emburey c Maynard b Allott	4		
†P. R. Downton c Fowler b Watkinson	8		
N. F. Williams b O'Shaughnessy	20		
J. F. Sykes lbw b D. Lloyd	4		
W. W. Daniel not out	0		
B 4, l-b 1, n-b 5	10		

1/7 2/15 3/30 4/67   120   (no wkt) 33
5/69 6/79 7/84 8/99 9/109

Bonus points – Lancashire 4.

Bowling: *First Innings*—Allott 24–8–45–5; Watkinson 17–4–40–3; Simmons 8–3–9–0; D. Lloyd 5–2–3–1; O'Shaughnessy 4.1–1–13–1. *Second Innings*—Allott 4–0–18–0; Watkinson 5–1–12–0; Simmons 6–4–2–0; Abrahams 2–1–1–0.

Umpires: J. Birkenshaw and P. B. Wight.

At Northampton, August 20, 22, 23. LANCASHIRE drew with NORTHAMPTONSHIRE.

LANCASHIRE v DERBYSHIRE

At Blackpool, August 24, 25, 26. Drawn. Lancashire 5 pts, Derbyshire 6 pts. Simmons's second century of the season, the fifth of his career, helped Lancashire's last five wickets put on 165 runs. He was dropped at 66 and 96 whilst receiving staunch support from the tail, which included Stanworth, making his début as wicket-keeper. After Hill had scored his third century of the season for Derbyshire, Hayes hit a sparkling, unbeaten 127 in 218 minutes before Derbyshire, set to score 269 in 175 minutes, settled for a draw.

Lancashire

G. Fowler c Fowler b Miller	35	– b Tunnicliffe	14
S. J. O'Shaughnessy lbw b Finney	9	– st Maher b Moir	41
F. C. Hayes c Anderson b Miller	19	– not out	127
*C. H. Lloyd c Hampshire b Miller	4	– c Finney b Moir	20
J. Abrahams c and b Moir	37	– c Maher b Miller	4
N. H. Fairbrother c Anderson b Miller	55	– c Anderson b Moir	4
J. Simmons not out	101	– c Anderson b Moir	1
M. Watkinson c and b Fowler	14	– c Anderson b Miller	13
P. J. W. Allott run out	10	– run out	6
†J. Stanworth c Hampshire b Miller	14	– not out	8
L. L. McFarlane not out	0		
L-b 7, n-b 10	17	B 5, l-b 2, n-b 2	9

1/30 2/51 3/57 4/94   (9 wkts dec.) 315   1/19 2/120 3/152   (8 wkts dec.) 247
5/150 6/187 7/230 8/259 9/312   4/174 5/185 6/197 7/220 8/228

Bonus points – Lancashire 3, Derbyshire 3 (Score at 100 overs: 258-7).

Bowling: *First Innings*—Holding 17–4–55–0; Tunnicliffe 15–4–46–0; Finney 6–1–24–1; Miller 45–14–98–5; Moir 24–8–49–1; Fowler 11–2–26–1. *Second Innings*—Holding 8–3–21–0; Tunnicliffe 7–0–21–1; Moir 36–10–102–4; Miller 24.3–4–61–2; Fowler 11–2–33–0.

Derbyshire

†B. J. M. Maher lbw b Allott	8		
I. S. Anderson b Abrahams	68	– not out	54
*K. J. Barnett c Simmons b O'Shaughnessy	8	– (1) c Lloyd b Abrahams	34
A. Hill b Abrahams	106	– (3) run out	10
J. H. Hampshire b Abrahams	47	– (4) not out	13
G. Miller not out	8		
R. J. Finney c Fairbrother b Simmons	12		
W. P. Fowler not out	15		
B 6, l-b 12, w 1, n-b 3	22	B 4, l-b 2, n-b 2	8

1/21 2/40 3/136   (6 wkts dec.) 294   1/65 2/80   (2 wkts) 119
4/249 5/261 6/276

C. J. Tunnicliffe, M. A. Holding and D. G. Moir did not bat.

Bonus points – Derbyshire 3, Lancashire 2.

Bowling: *First Innings*—Allott 12–6–18–1; McFarlane 12–3–22–0; Watkinson 10–3–31–0; O'Shaughnessy 12–3–49–1; Simmons 28–5–69–1; Abrahams 26–5–83–3. *Second Innings*—Allott 3–2–2–0; McFarlane 4–0–12–0; Simmons 22–5–50–0; Abrahams 21–11–40–1; Fowler 2–0–7–0; Fairbrother 2–2–0–0.

Umpires: C. Cook and M. J. Kitchen.

LANCASHIRE v ESSEX

At Manchester, August 31, September 1, 2. Drawn. Lancashire 4 pts, Essex 6 pts. Eighteen wickets fell on the first day which ended with Essex 38 in front with two wickets in hand after Lever, who took the first four wickets, and Phillip had destroyed Lancashire. A late injury to Abrahams meant a last-minute summons for Hughes, who had gone to Preston to play in a second-team fixture. By the time Hughes was ready to bat, Lancashire were 57 for seven. Essex ended the second day poised for victory with Lancashire only 85 ahead and their last pair together. But Jefferies and Allott held out for 95 minutes and rain finally ended Essex's hopes of a victory that would virtually have secured them the Championship.

Lancashire

G. Fowler lbw b Lever	4	– c R. E. East b Phillip	5
M. R. Chadwick lbw b Lever	1	– lbw b Acfield	1
S. J. O'Shaughnessy b Lever	13	– c and b R. E. East	46
F. C. Hayes c D. E. East b Lever	2	– b Acfield	19
Nasir Zaidi b Phillip	4	– (7) b Acfield	2
S. T. Jefferies c and b Lever	16	– (8) not out	75
*J. Simmons c Fletcher b Phillip	5	– (6) c Gooch b Acfield	6
†J. Stanworth not out	31	– (9) b Acfield	4
D. P. Hughes c D. E. East b Phillip	13	– (5) c Lever b R. E. East	68
M. Watkinson c D. E. East b Phillip	0	– b Acfield	0
P. J. W. Allott c D. E. East b Phillip	22	– c McEwan b Acfield	35
B 1, l-b 4, w 1, n-b 5	11	B 1, l-b 16, w 1, n-b 5	23

1/5 2/18 3/19 4/23   122   1/5 2/7 3/45 4/109   284
5/30 6/34 7/57 8/84 9/88   5/122 6/146 7/170 8/203 9/207

Bonus points – Essex 4.

Bowling: *First Innings*—Lever 20–6–53–5; Phillip 23–7–54–5; Pringle 1–0–4–0; Acfield 2–2–0–0. *Second Innings*—Lever 18–2–60–0; Phillip 19–5–51–1; Acfield 49.2–14–100–7; R. E. East 29–13–50–2.

Essex

G. A. Gooch c Hughes b Jefferies	17	– c Stanworth b Allott	7
C. Gladwin lbw b Allott	31	– run out	38
B. R. Hardie c Jefferies b Watkinson	17	– c Hayes b Jefferies	0
K. S. McEwan c Allott b Watkinson	17	– b Watkinson	30
*K. W. R. Fletcher b Watkinson	8	– not out	1
D. R. Pringle b Simmons	18	– not out	7
N. Phillip c Chadwick b Jefferies	15		
†D. E. East c Stanworth b Nasir	61		
R. E. East b Simmons	0		
J. K. Lever c Simmons b Nasir	44		
D. L. Acfield not out	6		
L-b 6, n-b 5	11	L-b 6, n-b 2	8

1/39 2/51 3/86 4/87   245   1/9 2/10 3/78 4/79   (4 wkts) 91
5/99 6/112 7/156 8/160 9/218

Bonus points – Essex 2, Lancashire 4.

Bowling: *First Innings*—Jefferies 17–3–61–2; Allott 17–4–34–1; Watkinson 18–3–67–3; O'Shaughnessy 4–0–18–0; Simmons 14–5–22–2; Nasir 8.5–0–32–2. *Second Innings*—Jefferies 8–2–16–1; Allott 6–2–17–1; O'Shaughnessy 3–0–18–0; Watkinson 7–1–26–1; Simmons 5–3–6–0.

Umpires: W. E. Alley and D. O. Oslear.

LANCASHIRE v LEICESTERSHIRE

At Manchester, September 10, 12, 13. Drawn. Lancashire 3 pts, Leicestershire 5 pts. Just when the season looked to be drawing to a peaceful conclusion, a piece of history was created when O'Shaughnessy, in the last three hours of the season, equalled P. G. H. Fender's 63-year-old record of the fastest first-class century. After the first day and a half had been lost to rain Lancashire were put in to bat. Tolchard soon had his spinners operating to revive Leicestershire's flagging over-rate for the season. After taking four bowling points they needed one for batting to finish fourth in the Championship. Once this had been won Leicestershire declared, 86 behind, just before three o'clock on the last afternoon, whereupon Gower and Whitaker fed the Lancashire batsmen with long hops and full tosses in the hope of inducing a declaration. After a brief protest of blocking, Fowler and O'Shaughnessy hit 190 runs in the 35 minutes to tea, then took their stand to 201 in 43 minutes, the fastest first-class double-century partnership on record. O'Shaughnessy's century, in 35 minutes, included five 6s and seventeen 4s. Fowler's century, in 46 minutes, contained ten 6s and five 4s. Lancashire did not declare and the season ended in travesty.

Lancashire

G. Fowler b Steele	85	– b Balderstone	100
S. J. O'Shaughnessy c Steele b Cook	3	– st Tolchard b Balderstone	105
F. C. Hayes b Clift	11		
*C. H. Lloyd c Tolchard b Clift	24		
J. Abrahams c and b Clift	7	– (4) not out	3
D. P. Hughes c Cook b Clift	0		
N. H. Fairbrother c Davison b Cook	4	– (5) not out	1
J. Simmons b Clift	57		
†J. Stanworth c Balderstone b Cook	29	– (3) b Taylor	4
P. J. W. Allott c and b Taylor	4		
M. Watkinson not out	1		
B 9, l-b 1, n-b 1	11	W 1	1

1/31 2/97 3/103 4/136   236   1/201 2/206 3/213   (3 wkts) 214
5/136 6/139 7/145 8/224 9/231

Bonus points – Lancashire 2, Leicestershire 4.

Bowling: *First Innings*—Ferris 8–1–29–0; Taylor 4–0–14–1; Cook 28–10–74–3; Clift 31–5–73–5; Steele 16–3–35–1. *Second Innings*—Gower 9–0–102–0; Whitaker 8–1–87–0; Balderstone 4–0–10–2; Steele 5–2–13–0; Taylor 1.2–0–1–1.

Leicestershire

J. C. Balderstone c O'Shaughnessy b Simmons	33	J. J. Whitaker lbw b Simmons ... 24
I. P. Butcher lbw b Allott	4	P. B. Clift not out ... 26
D. I. Gower not out	56	N-b 5 ... 5
B. F. Davison c Lloyd b Watkinson	2	

1/31 2/46 3/51 4/114   (4 wkts dec.) 150

G. J. F. Ferris, *†R. W. Tolchard, J. F. Steele, N. G. B. Cook and L. B. Taylor did not bat.

Bonus points – Leicestershire 1, Lancashire 1.

Bowling: Allott 7–2–15–1; Watkinson 14–3–35–1; Simmons 15–3–51–2; Hughes 7.5–1–44–0.

Umpires: H. D. Bird and N. T. Plews.

LEICESTERSHIRE

President: W. Bentley
Chairman: C. H. Palmer
Chairman, Cricket Committee: J. J. Palmer
Secretary/Cricket Manager: F. M. Turner
    County Cricket Ground, Grace Road,
    Leicester LE2 8AD
    (Telephone: 0533-831880/832128)
Captain: 1983 – R. W. Tolchard; 1984 – D. I.
    Gower
Coach: K. Higgs

Leicestershire entered the 1983 season full of optimism, and at short odds for all four major trophies. In view of that, they fell a long way short of general, and indeed their own, expectations.

The biggest single factor in their failure to achieve any tangible success lay largely in their unhappy ability to play like princes one day and paupers the next. It was difficult to take issue with Roger Tolchard's post-mortem. While even the best sides have off days, he argued, Leicestershire had far too many to mount a realistic challenge in any of the competitions.

Things began to go wrong even before the season had begun. Les Taylor broke his right elbow in a freak gymnasium training accident, and Andy Roberts's World Cup commitments, plus the knee injury that finally culminated in an operation to have flaked bones removed, meant that a potentially destructive new-ball partnership was aborted. While Taylor did splendidly to end with 69 wickets from eighteen Schweppes County Championship games, Roberts's long absences meant that the pair took the field together on only four occasions.

In some ways this particular cloud had a silver lining, Roberts's unavailability paving the way for George Ferris's eventful entry into first-class cricket. Just eighteen, the Antiguan bowled with such genuine pace as to pick up 53 wickets in only thirteen games. The other major bowling gain was the form of Paddy Clift, after two virtually blank seasons because of injury. Clift took 83 wickets, scored nearly 850 runs, and achieved a maiden first-class century to justify thoroughly his award as Leicestershire's "Player of the Year". Jonathan Agnew again had limited opportunities, but Gordon Parsons had an especially disappointing season.

Almost all the front-line batsmen had good seasons, although the previously mentioned capacity to have bad days led far too often to first-innings totals low enough to preclude much chance of winning. A major success was the emergence of 21-year-old Ian Butcher, brother of Surrey's Alan, who forced his way into the side a third of the way through the season and came very close to scoring 1,000 runs. He made three centuries and formed a fine opening partnership with Chris Balderstone – who at the age of 42 came close to completing his most successful season with the bat.

Balderstone was controversially disciplined in mid-season when, after scoring an unbeaten century out of a total of 198 at Hereford and 63 in the second innings of a match that Leicestershire won, he was omitted from the following game at Lord's. His captain felt that he had not played sufficiently for the team at a crucial stage in the first innings. But while Balderstone accepted blame for the failure to capture an extra bonus point, he denied having been deliberately selfish, and spoke out forcibly against being dropped for one match.

Tolchard, for the most part, led the side intelligently, apart from the final afternoon of the season at Old Trafford when, in an attempt to contrive a result from a game already ruined by the weather, his tactics led to Steve O'Shaughnessy equalling the fastest-ever first-class century, in 35 minutes. David Gower and James Whitaker, used as "feed" bowlers, conceded 190 runs in seventeen overs of deliberate full-tosses and long-hops, many observers seeing it as a further erosion of old-style values.

Gower and Whitaker provided far more satisfaction with the bat. Gower's form for England made some of his county failures disappointing, but he ended the season with a flourish, and Whitaker looked every bit as good a discovery as Butcher. Nigel Briers played splendidly at No. 5 or, when Gower was absent, at No. 3. The form of Briers and Whitaker gave the club hope that the retirement of Brian Davison would be offset.

Davison, who only agreed to play in 1983 after a consortium of local businessmen supplemented, with £1,500 in cash, a wage he felt to be inadequate, scored 1,000 Championship runs for the thirteenth consecutive season. A magnificently aggressive cricketer, he announced his retirement in mid-season, to take up a position as player-coach with Tasmania.

By the end of 1983 Leicestershire were facing up to the fact that with Davison gone they also had to come to terms with the probability of missing another key player for long periods, along with Gower, because of Test calls. Nick Cook, despite having his least successful season with the county for three years, made a spectacular entry into Test cricket when, before the Lord's Test Match, Edmonds was forced to withdraw from the England side through injury.

Leicestershire, despite finishing fourth in the County Championship, failed to make an impact in any of the one-day competitions. They did not qualify for the Benson and Hedges Cup quarter-finals, largely thanks to the fact that the weather prevented them from bowling a ball against Scotland, and they won only five John Player Sunday League games. In the NatWest Bank Trophy they posted a first-innings total that no side had previously surpassed to win, only for Gloucestershire to eliminate them, thanks to a breathtaking innings of 158 from Zaheer. – M.J.

454

LEICESTERSHIRE 1983

[*Bill Smith*

Back row: N. E. Briers, I. P. Butcher, P. B. Clift, J. P. Agnew, G. J. F. Ferris, N. G. B. Cook, J. J. Whitaker. *Front row:* J. F. Steele, J. C. Balderstone, R. W. Tolchard (*captain*), L. B. Taylor, B. F. Davison. *Inset:* D. I. Gower, A. M. E. Roberts.

LEICESTERSHIRE RESULTS

All first-class matches – Played 26: Won 9, Lost 4, Drawn 13.

County Championship matches – Played 24: Won 9, Lost 3, Drawn 12.

Bonus points – Batting 52, Bowling 81.

Competition placings – Schweppes County Championship, 4th; NatWest Bank Trophy, 2nd round; Benson and Hedges Cup, 3rd in Group A; John Player League, 11th eq.

COUNTY CHAMPIONSHIP AVERAGES

BATTING

	Birthplace	M	I	NO	R	HI	Avge
J. C. Balderstonec ...	Huddersfield	23	38	4	1,443	112	42.44
N. E. Briersc	Leicester	23	35	6	1,206	201*	41.58
D. I. Gowerc..........	Tunbridge Wells	13	21	4	702	140	41.29
B. F. Davisonc.........	Bulawayo, Rhodesia	24	38	5	1,265	106	38.33
I. P. Butcher...........	Farnborough	17	30	1	973	139	33.55
P. B. Cliftc.............	Salisbury, Rhodesia	21	30	6	795	100*	33.12
R. W. Tolchardc	Torquay	24	32	6	671	80*	25.80
J. J. Whitaker	Skipton	10	16	4	305	56*	25.41
J. F. Steelec	Stafford	22	24	8	284	50	17.75
L. B. Taylorc..........	Earl Shilton	18	17	5	213	47	17.75
G. J. Parsons	Slough	13	15	3	207	56	17.25
R. A. Cobb	Leicester	7	9	0	98	28	10.88
N. G. B. Cookc	Leicester	21	19	5	150	32	10.71
J. P. Agnew...........	Macclesfield	8	4	0	24	13	6.00
G. J. F. Ferris........	Urlings Village, Antigua	13	12	4	38	11	4.75
T. J. Boon.............	Doncaster	4	7	0	18	5	2.57

Also batted: A. M. E. Roberts (*Urlings Village, Antigua*) (4 matches) 15, 3, 4.

* Signifies not out. c*Denotes county cap.*

BOWLING

	O	M	R	W	Avge	BB
A. M. E. Roberts	101.2	19	294	16	18.37	5-26
L. B. Taylor	509.5	143	1,338	69	19.39	7-73
P. B. Clift	573.3	152	1,481	71	20.85	5-73
G. J. F. Ferris	360	74	1,205	53	22.73	7-42
N. G. B. Cook	695.5	244	1,489	54	27.57	4-53
J. F. Steele	476.1	148	1,167	39	29.92	4-3
G. J. Parsons	241	65	732	26	28.15	5-51
J. P. Agnew	162	33	621	17	36.52	3-34

Also bowled: J. C. Balderstone 51–18–112–6; N. E. Briers 2–2–0–0; I. P. Butcher 2–0–2–1; B. F. Davison 4.4–0–18–0; D. I. Gower 9–0–102–0; J. J. Whitaker 10–2–88–0.

The following played a total of twelve three-figure innings for Leicestershire in County Championship matches – J. C. Balderstone 3, I. P. Butcher 3, B. F. Davison 2, D. I. Gower 2, N. E. Briers 1, P. B. Clift 1.

At Cambridge, April 23, 25, 26. LEICESTERSHIRE drew with CAMBRIDGE UNIVERSITY.

LEICESTERSHIRE v HAMPSHIRE

At Leicester, April 30, May 1, 2. Drawn. Leicestershire 2 pts, Hampshire 3 pts. A patient 129 from Smith, in 273 minutes, sustained Hampshire, who were put in. Turner, sharing a partnership of 113 in 141 minutes with Smith, batted urgently, but torrential rain on the second and third days forced an abandonment.

Hampshire

T. M. Tremlett c Tolchard b Agnew....	29	N. G. Cowley not out......................	6
C. L. Smith not out...........................	129		
M. C. J. Nicholas b Cook..................	1	L-b 11	11
T. E. Jesty c Tolchard b Clift.............	2		
D. R. Turner b Parsons	62	1/52 2/71　　　　　(5 wkts dec.) 252	
*N. E. J. Pocock c Briers b Parsons....	12	3/86 4/199 5/229	

J. W. Southern, †R. J. Parks, K. St J. D. Emery and S. J. Malone did not bat.

Bonus points – Hampshire 3, Leicestershire 2.

Bowling: Agnew 19–5–53–1; Parsons 23–6–71–2; Clift 15–5–43–1; Cook 26–12–36–1; Steele 11.3–2–38–0.

Leicestershire

J. C. Balderstone, R. A. Cobb, D. I. Gower, B. F. Davison, N. E. Briers, *†R. W. Tolchard, P. B. Clift, J. F. Steele, G. J. Parsons, J. P. Agnew and N. G. B. Cook.

Umpires: R. A. White and N. T. Plews.

LEICESTERSHIRE v DERBYSHIRE

At Leicester, May 4, 5, 6. Drawn. Leicestershire 7 pts, Derbyshire 4 pts. Gower and Davison were in splendid form, each hitting a 6 and eleven 4s as Leicestershire took maximum batting points off 76 overs. By the time Derbyshire continued their reply on the second day, from 7 without loss overnight, Wood had announced his resignation as captain, but on the field there was little further incident of note and rain washed out the final day.

Leicestershire

J. C. Balderstone c and b Moir	69	– not out	31
R. A. Cobb b Newman.............................	1	– lbw b Miller............................	14
D. I. Gower c Taylor b Newman...................	81	– not out	5
B. F. Davison not out....................................	84		
N. E. Briers not out....................................	45		
B 10, l-b 4, n-b 8................................	22	L-b 2, n-b 2..................	4

1/6 2/143 3/191　　　　(3 wkts dec.) 302	1/36　　　　(1 wkt) 54	

*†R. W. Tolchard, P. B. Clift, J. F. Steele, G. J. Parsons, J. P. Agnew and N. G. B. Cook did not bat.

Bonus points – Leicestershire 4, Derbyshire 1.

Bowling: *First Innings*—Oldham 20–2–66–0; Newman 14–2–71–2; Miller 5–1–10–0; Moir 15–2–50–1; Tunnicliffe 17–5–48–0; Wood 5–0–35–0. *Second Innings*—Oldham 6–1–15–0; Miller 4–2–4–1; Moir 6–2–14–0; Tunnicliffe 3–0–17–0.

Derbyshire

*B. Wood lbw b Agnew	18	C. J. Tunnicliffe st Tolchard b Cook	16
J. G. Wright c Balderstone b Clift	60	†R. W. Taylor not out	6
K. J. Barnett c Balderstone b Cook	20	D. G. Moir not out	13
J. H. Hampshire c Tolchard b Parsons	52	L-b 6, w 1, n-b 3	10
G. Miller b Steele	27		
A. Hill c Gower b Cook	31	1/44 2/95 3/103 4/180 (8 wkts dec.)	265
P. G. Newman c Steele b Agnew	12	5/185 6/213 7/244 8/245	

S. Oldham did not bat.

Bonus points – Derbyshire 3, Leicestershire 3.

Bowling: Agnew 23–5–90–2; Parsons 21–5–46–1; Cook 21–7–39–3; Clift 14–2–51–1; Steele 21–11–29–1.

Umpires: N. T. Plews and R. A. White.

At The Oval, May 11, 12, 13. LEICESTERSHIRE drew with SURREY.

LEICESTERSHIRE v ESSEX

At Leicester, May 25, 26, 27. Leicestershire won by four wickets. Leicestershire 24 pts, Essex 4 pts. Essex failed to capitalise on a lively opening partnership after being put in, and century partnerships between Balderstone and Gower, and Davison and Briers, emphasised the friendly nature of the wicket. McEwan's 151 in the second innings contained a 6 and 21 4s, and although Leicestershire met little resistance elsewhere, their chance seemed to have gone when Acfield, who scored just a single in a last-wicket stand of 66, and McEwan hung on for 100 minutes. However, a target of 214 in 140 minutes was achieved with five balls to spare, thanks to Balderstone and Briers who put on 117 in 22 overs for the third wicket.

Essex

G. A. Gooch lbw b Cook	37	– c Agnew b Roberts	13
B. R. Hardie c Cook b Roberts	62	– c and b Parsons	4
*K. W. R. Fletcher c Balderstone b Roberts	15	– (5) c Gower b Cook	25
K. S. McEwan c Tolchard b Roberts	1	– c Cook b Steele	151
K. R. Pont b Agnew	53	– (6) lbw b Cook	0
D. R. Pringle c Briers b Agnew	37	– (7) c Balderstone b Agnew	6
N. Phillip c Balderstone b Agnew	4	– (8) c and b Cook	4
†D. E. East c Davison b Cook	25	– (3) b Roberts	6
R. E. East c Parsons b Cook	25	– c Steele b Agnew	0
J. K. Lever b Cook	6	– lbw b Parsons	4
D. L. Acfield not out	4	– not out	1
L-b 7, w 1, n-b 6	14	B 4, l-b 7, n-b 5	16

1/96 2/108 3/111 4/137	283	1/6 2/23 3/25 4/72	230
5/207 6/220 7/221 8/266 9/278		5/76 6/114 7/139 8/141 9/164	

Bonus points – Essex 3, Leicestershire 4 (Score at 100 overs: 282-9).

Bowling: *First Innings*—Roberts 22–4–63–3; Agnew 18–5–61–3; Cook 28.2–12–53–4; Parsons 13–1–54–0; Steele 20–7–38–0. *Second Innings*—Roberts 16–3–37–2; Parsons 18–9–43–2; Cook 32–14–57–3; Agnew 19–4–75–2; Steele 3.2–1–2–1.

Leicestershire

J. C. Balderstone hit wkt b Lever	82	– not out	97
R. A. Cobb c D. E. East b Lever	14		
D. I. Gower c Gooch b Lever	74	– (2) b Phillip	12
B. F. Davison not out	82	– (3) st D. E. East b Acfield	2
N. E. Briers not out	38	– (4) c Gooch b R. E. East	55
A. M. E. Roberts (did not bat)	–	(5) lbw b Phillip	15
G. J. Parsons (did not bat)	–	(6) c sub b Acfield	1
*†R. W. Tolchard (did not bat)	–	(7) b R. E. East	10
J. F. Steele (did not bat)	–	(8) not out	2
B 2, l-b 4, w 1, n-b 3	10	B 4, l-b 14, w 1, n-b 1	20

1/33 2/154 3/181　　　　　　(3 wkts dec.) 300　　　1/19 2/32 3/149　　　　(6 wkts) 214
　　　　　　　　　　　　　　　　　　　　　　　　4/172 5/178 6/203

J. P. Agnew and N. G. B. Cook did not bat.

Bonus points – Leicestershire 4, Essex 1.

Bowling: *First Innings*— Lever 26–6–80–3; Phillip 17–3–64–0; Gooch 7–2–22–0; R. E. East 19–3–53–0; Acfield 20–1–71–0. *Second Innings*—Phillip 20–1–74–2; Gooch 1–0–10–0; Acfield 12–1–66–2; R. E. East 7.1–0–44–2.

Umpires: J. W. Holder and D. R. Shepherd.

At Northampton, May 28, 30, 31. LEICESTERSHIRE drew with NORTHAMPTON-SHIRE.

At Nottingham, June 4, 6, 7. LEICESTERSHIRE drew with NOTTINGHAMSHIRE.

LEICESTERSHIRE v YORKSHIRE

At Leicester, June 8, 9, 10. Drawn. Leicestershire 5 pts, Yorkshire 6 pts. Quite why sixteen wickets fell on the first day was not readily apparent, even allowing for a pitch of irregular bounce and occasionally offering slow spin. Clift and Steele rescued Leicestershire from 52 for six with a century partnership, and Love and Bairstow played with urgency in Yorkshire's second innings as bat regained supremacy over ball. Illingworth, returning to the scene of former captaincy triumphs, celebrated his 51st birthday on the opening day, but Leicestershire felt the target he left them, 307 in 220 minutes, was ungenerous and they showed no interest after Briers was fourth out at 138.

Yorkshire

G. Boycott c Davison b Cook	14	– c Steele b Cook	63
R. G. Lumb b Cook	32	– b Taylor	9
C. W. J. Athey c Steele b Taylor	58	– b Cook	7
S. N. Hartley c Tolchard b Clift	21	– lbw b Steele	17
J. D. Love c Steele b Clift	24	– lbw b Clift	53
†D. L. Bairstow c and b Steele	21	– st Tolchard b Cook	69
P. Carrick b Steele	3	– not out	45
A. Sidebottom c Tolchard b Taylor	12	– not out	7
G. B. Stevenson c Steele b Parsons	8		
*R. Illingworth b Cook	2		
S. J. Dennis not out	0		
B 1, l-b 5, w 1	7	B 8, l-b 1, w 1, n-b 1	11

1/24 2/91 3/111 4/150　　　　　　　　202　　1/26 2/35 3/82　　　(6 wkts dec.) 281
5/159 6/177 7/186 8/195 9/202　　　　　　　4/118 5/220 6/226

Bonus points – Yorkshire 2, Leicestershire 4.

Bowling: *First Innings*—Taylor 17.2–6–25–2; Parsons 9–6–14–1; Cook 31–13–63–3; Clift 16–4–47–2; Steele 17–7–46–2. *Second Innings*—Taylor 14–5–45–1; Parsons 9–4–25–0; Cook 50–16–100–3; Clift 12–8–15–1; Steele 32–8–85–1.

Leicestershire

J. C. Balderstone b Dennis	8	– st Bairstow b Illingworth	50
R. A. Cobb lbw b Sidebottom	22	– b Stevenson	2
T. J. Boon lbw b Stevenson	3	– (7) c Hartley b Carrick	2
B. F. Davison c Illingworth b Dennis	3	– not out	34
N. E. Briers b Sidebottom	7	– (3) b Carrick	63
*†R. W. Tolchard lbw b Carrick	3	– (5) b Carrick	5
P. B. Clift c Boycott b Stevenson	48	– (6) c Boycott b Carrick	10
J. F. Steele c Bairstow b Stevenson	50	– lbw b Carrick	0
G. J. Parsons lbw b Illingworth	5	– not out	11
N. G. B. Cook not out	8		
L. B. Taylor b Illingworth	4		
B 4, l-b 11, n-b 1	16	B 4, l-b 10, n-b 2	16

1/8 2/17 3/26 4/47   **177**   1/4 2/114 3/130 4/138   (7 wkts) **193**
5/52 6/52 7/158 8/159 9/165   5/171 6/177 7/177

Bonus points – Leicestershire 1, Yorkshire 4.

Bowling: *First Innings*—Dennis 11–1–42–2; Stevenson 14–3–33–3; Sidebottom 14–6–19–2; Carrick 31–17–39–1; Illingworth 19.3–8–28–2. *Second Innings*—Dennis 7–2–16–0; Stevenson 5–1–14–1; Carrick 33–10–69–5; Sidebottom 7–0–24–0; Illingworth 25–7–54–1.

Umpires: R. Julian and J. G. Langridge.

At Derby, June 11, 13, 14. LEICESTERSHIRE beat DERBYSHIRE by an innings and 4 runs.

LEICESTERSHIRE v GLOUCESTERSHIRE

At Leicester, June 15, 16, 17. Drawn. Leicestershire 4 pts, Gloucestershire 7 pts. Leicestershire's eighteen-year-old opener Butcher enjoyed a memorable first Championship appearance on the Grace Road ground, scoring a maiden century in the first innings and saving his side from defeat in the second with an unbeaten 76. All told, he saw fifteen partners come and go. Gloucestershire's Bainbridge also batted well to score 99 in 97 minutes before the third declaration of the match asked Leicestershire to make 299 in 220 minutes on a slow pitch. With the match apparently heading for a draw, Graveney took the first hat-trick of his career, but an earlier dropped catch when Butcher was 29 ultimately cost his side victory.

Gloucestershire

B. C. Broad c Parsons b Cook	32	– lbw b Parsons	20
A. W. Stovold c Balderstone b Cook	63	– b Parsons	15
P. Bainbridge c Briers b Steele	45	– c Balderstone b Steele	99
A. J. Hignell lbw b Clift	23	– b Balderstone	5
P. W. Romaines st Tolchard b Steele	23	– not out	25
A. J. Wright lbw b Parsons	17		
J. N. Shepherd not out	95		
†R. C. Russell c Tolchard b Clift	55		
L-b 10, n-b 3	13	B 4, l-b 10	14

1/85 2/122 3/152   (7 wkts dec.) **366**   1/33 2/44   (4 wkts dec.) **178**
4/179 5/192 6/238 7/366   3/79 4/178

*D. A. Graveney, F. D. Stephenson and J. H. Childs did not bat.

Bonus points – Gloucestershire 3, Leicestershire 2 (Score at 100 overs: 257-6).

Bowling: *First Innings*—Ferris 12–0–73–0; Parsons 15–1–64–1; Cook 44–11–117–2; Clift 18.5–4–38–2; Steele 34–11–61–2. *Second Innings*—Ferris 6–0–36–0; Parsons 8–1–28–2; Balderstone 10–3–26–1; Cook 11–2–43–0; Steele 5.1–0–31–1.

Leicestershire

J. C. Balderstone b Stephenson	0	b Stephenson	2
I. P. Butcher b Stephenson	103	not out	76
T. J. Boon b Stephenson	4	(5) b Graveney	1
B. F. Davison lbw b Shepherd	17	(4) c Russell b Shepherd	3
N. E. Briers c Graveney b Shepherd	68	(3) c and b Stephenson	9
*†R. W. Tolchard lbw b Shepherd	17	st Russell b Graveney	43
P. B. Clift c Bainbridge b Graveney	20	b Graveney	5
G. J. Parsons c Russell b Stephenson	1	(9) c Romaines b Graveney	0
J. F. Steele not out	5	(8) c Russell b Graveney	0
N. G. B. Cook b Stephenson	1	b Childs	12
G. J. F. Ferris (did not bat)	–	not out	0
L-b 7, n-b 3	10	B 2, l-b 4, w 1, n-b 3	10

1/0 2/4 3/30 4/160   (9 wkts dec.) 246   1/10 2/28 3/41 4/53   (9 wkts) 161
5/201 6/237 7/239 8/240 9/246   5/133 6/143 7/143 8/143 9/161

Bonus points – Leicestershire 2, Gloucestershire 4.

Bowling: *First Innings*—Stephenson 17.4–4–56–5; Shepherd 29–6–77–3; Childs 35–15–69–0; Graveney 17–4–34–1. *Second Innings*—Stephenson 8–5–10–2; Shepherd 15–5–46–1; Childs 26–13–47–1; Graveney 20–7–34–5; Hignell 1–0–14–0.

Umpires: A. Jepson and B. Leadbeater.

LEICESTERSHIRE v SURREY

At Leicester, June 22, 23, 24. Drawn. Leicestershire 8 pts, Surrey 4 pts. Leicestershire batted comfortably on a slow pitch after winning the toss, Tolchard and Clift adding 102 in 93 minutes for the fifth wicket. Clift and Cook then exploited uneven bounce well on the second day as Surrey, losing their last six wickets for 61, just avoided following on. However, with Surrey at 22 for two, chasing 280 on the final day, and Leicestershire well placed to win, rain and bad light intervened.

Leicestershire

J. C. Balderstone b Thomas	32	c Richards b Clarke	18
I. P. Butcher c and b Monkhouse	35	c Richards b Thomas	16
N. E. Briers b Clarke	27	(5) not out	36
B. F. Davison c Lynch b Knight	60	c Thomas b Monkhouse	10
*†R. W. Tolchard not out	80	(6) c Clarke b Monkhouse	0
P. B. Clift b Thomas	63	(7) c Richards b Clarke	20
J. J. Whitaker not out	22	(3) c Butcher b Thomas	17
J. F. Steele (did not bat)	–	not out	8
B 20, l-b 10	30	B 4, l-b 2, n-b 8	14

1/52 2/84 3/145 4/199   (5 wkts dec.) 349   1/32 2/54 3/60   (6 wkts dec.) 139
5/301   4/80 5/80 6/118

N. G. B. Cook, L. B. Taylor and G. J. F. Ferris did not bat.

Bonus points – Leicestershire 4, Surrey 2 (Score at 100 overs: 337-5).

Bowling: *First Innings*—Clarke 17.3–1–49–1; Thomas 15–1–73–2; Monkhouse 13.4–3–40–1; Curtis 31–9–70–0; Needham 17–2–64–0; Knight 8.2–2–23–1. *Second Innings*—Clarke 16–2–44–2; Thomas 16–7–27–2; Monkhouse 9–1–30–2; Curtis 10–2–24–0.

Surrey

A. R. Butcher c Tolchard b Ferris	21	– c Davison b Ferris	0
G. S. Clinton lbw b Ferris	5	– c Tolchard b Taylor	11
D. M. Smith not out	47		
*R. D. V. Knight c Steele b Balderstone	31	– (3) not out	6
M. A. Lynch c Tolchard b Taylor	33	– (4) not out	1
†C. J. Richards c Tolchard b Clift	24		
A. Needham b Cook	2		
D. J. Thomas lbw b Clift	13		
G. Monkhouse c Butcher b Cook	4		
S. T. Clarke c Tolchard b Clift	12		
I. J. Curtis c Balderstone b Cook	2		
B 5, l-b 3, w 1, n-b 6	15	B 4	4

1/30 2/31 3/101 4/148   209   1/5 2/15   (2 wkts) 22
5/153 6/176 7/181 8/193 9/193

Bonus points – Surrey 2, Leicestershire 4.

Bowling: *First Innings*—Taylor 21–5–67–1; Ferris 14–3–42–2; Clift 21–6–34–3; Cook 21.1–9–40–3; Balderstone 6–2–11–1. *Second Innings*—Taylor 5–2–9–1; Ferris 4–1–9–1.

Umpires: K. Ibadulla and C. T. Spencer.

LEICESTERSHIRE v GLAMORGAN

At Hinckley, June 25, 27, 28. Leicestershire won by 180 runs. Leicestershire 23 pts, Glamorgan 4 pts. Leicestershire's eighteen-year-old Antiguan fast bowler, Ferris, destroyed Glamorgan on the first evening, eventually taking seven for 42. Earlier Leicestershire had Davison to thank for a total of 253 which, with a damp patch on a seamer's length at one end, was better than it appeared. Gower's splendid second-innings hundred left Glamorgan with an impossible target.

Leicestershire

J. C. Balderstone lbw b Ontong	38	– b Selvey	20
I. P. Butcher c E. W. Jones b Selvey	17	– c Hopkins b Rowe	38
D. I. Gower c Selvey b Wilkins	26	– not out	108
B. F. Davison c E. W. Jones b Selvey	101	– c Thomas b Rowe	91
N. E. Briers c E. W. Jones b Wilkins	11		
P. B. Clift lbw b Ontong	11		
*†R. W. Tolchard c A. Jones b Ontong	7		
J. F. Steele lbw b Ontong	18		
N. G. B. Cook c E. W. Jones b Ontong	5		
L. B. Taylor c Rowe b Ontong	6		
G. J. F. Ferris not out	1		
B 2, l-b 9, n-b 1	12	L-b 6, n-b 3	9

1/47 2/80 3/120 4/151   253   1/35 2/93 3/266   (3 wkts dec.) 266
5/180 6/208 7/234 8/246 9/252

Bonus points – Leicestershire 3, Glamorgan 4.

Bowling: *First Innings*—Thomas 9–1–25–0; Selvey 21–6–68–2; Wilkins 19–0–82–2; Ontong 24.2–4–64–6; Lloyd 1–0–2–0. *Second Innings*—Thomas 4–1–10–0; Selvey 14–4–38–1; Ontong 12–1–52–0; Wilkins 10–1–56–0; Rowe 21.5–7–73–2; Lloyd 5–0–28–0.

Glamorgan

A. Jones c Tolchard b Taylor	3	– c Tolchard b Cook	38
J. A. Hopkins lbw b Ferris	1	– lbw b Ferris	0
D. A. Francis lbw b Ferris	6	– lbw b Ferris	6
A. L. Jones c Tolchard b Clift	37	– c Steele b Taylor	40
C. J. C. Rowe b Ferris	2	– c Balderstone b Clift	33
R. C. Ontong c Gower b Ferris	6	– lbw b Cook	27
†E. W. Jones b Ferris	4	– lbw b Cook	39
J. G. Thomas lbw b Ferris	13	– lbw b Clift	0
B. J. Lloyd lbw b Ferris	7	– not out	22
*M. W. W. Selvey c Gower b Taylor	11	– c Tolchard b Cook	2
A. H. Wilkins not out	0	– c Davison b Steele	6
B 6, l-b 6, n-b 7	19	B 7, l-b 7, n-b 3	17

1/5 2/5 3/20 4/27
5/36 6/40 7/71 8/86 9/109   **109**

1/8 2/27 3/62 4/121
5/138 6/169 7/178 8/217 9/219   **230**

Bonus points – Leicestershire 4.

Bowling: *First Innings*—Ferris 21–5–42–7; Taylor 20.5–5–47–2; Clift 3–2–1–1. *Second Innings*—Ferris 26–8–62–3; Taylor 17–3–66–1; Clift 20–6–40–2; Cook 19–8–40–3; Steele 4.5–2–5–1.

Umpires: K. Ibadulla and C. T. Spencer.

At Harrogate, July 2, 4, 5. LEICESTERSHIRE beat YORKSHIRE by 89 runs.

LEICESTERSHIRE v SOMERSET

At Leicester, July 9, 11, 12. Somerset won by an innings and 71 runs. Somerset 24 pts, Leicestershire 4 pts. After Leicestershire had batted poorly on a good pitch, Richards and Botham destroyed their attack in an eighth-wicket partnership of 172, a new Somerset record. Botham, batting at No. 9 because of a stomach upset, reached three figures in 101 deliveries and struck five 6s and eighteen 4s. Richards stroked one 6 and 26 4s in an innings of casual brilliance, and facing a mammoth deficit of 348, Leicestershire succumbed in their second innings to the off-spin of Marks, who took five of their last six wickets.

Leicestershire

J. C. Balderstone c Popplewell b Garner	52	– lbw b Dredge	25
I. P. Butcher c Gard b Botham	1	– c sub b Garner	5
D. I. Gower c Gard b Wilson	41	– b Richards	73
B. F. Davison b Botham	45	– c Gard b Dredge	26
N. E. Briers c Rose b Botham	11	– b Botham b Marks	11
*†R. W. Tolchard lbw b Garner	0	– b Richards	71
P. B. Clift retired hurt	11	– lbw b Marks	15
J. F. Steele c Richards b Botham	2	– not out	12
A. M. E. Roberts lbw b Botham	3	– (10) b Marks	4
N. G. B. Cook c Gard b Garner	1	– (9) c sub b Marks	3
L. B. Taylor not out	0	– c Wilson b Marks	22
B 2, l-b 6, n-b 5	13	B 1, l-b 2, n-b 7	10

1/3 2/67 3/137 4/145
5/145 6/174 7/178 8/179 9/180   **180**

1/13 2/77 3/117 4/137
5/153 6/212 7/240 8/243 9/247   **277**

Bonus points – Leicestershire 1, Somerset 4.

Bowling: *First Innings*—Garner 15.3–4–42–3; Botham 14–3–38–5; Dredge 4–1–25–0; Wilson 11–1–44–1; Marks 6–3–18–0. *Second Innings*—Garner 12–2–32–1; Wilson 6–1–7–0; Richards 29–13–75–2; Botham 3–2–9–0; Dredge 12–3–31–2; Marks 41.4–15–105–5; Popplewell 1–0–8–0.

Somerset

P. M. Roebuck lbw b Steele	51	I. T. Botham c Davison b Steele	152
*B. C. Rose c sub b Taylor	20	J. Garner c and b Taylor	5
I. V. A. Richards c Taylor b Roberts	216	P. H. L. Wilson not out	9
†T. Gard c Butcher b Roberts	10	B 1, l-b 13, w 3, n-b 7	24
P. W. Denning b Cook	14		
N. F. M. Popplewell c Tolchard b Cook	0	1/32 2/147 3/184	528
V. J. Marks b Clift	23	4/213 5/213 6/285	
C. H. Dredge c Butcher b Clift	4	7/289 8/461 9/478	

Bonus points – Somerset 4, Leicestershire 3 (Score at 100 overs: 332-7).

Bowling: Roberts 28–3–111–2; Taylor 34–5–115–2; Cook 42–6–143–2; Steele 20.5–3–90–2; Clift 13–2–45–2.

Umpires: C. Cook and P. B. Wight.

At Hereford, July 13, 14, 15. LEICESTERSHIRE beat WORCESTERSHIRE by five wickets.

At Lord's, July 16, 18, 19. LEICESTERSHIRE lost to MIDDLESEX by 180 runs.

LEICESTERSHIRE v SUSSEX

At Leicester, July 30, August 1. Leicestershire won by an innings and 103 runs. Leicestershire 24 pts, Sussex 2 pts. Sussex, without the injured le Roux and Greig, and with Imran able to bowl only a handful of overs because of a stress fracture to the shin, did not have the firepower to disturb Leicestershire after putting them in on a green pitch. Balderstone and Davison both struck eleven 4s. It was a vastly different story when Roberts was operating on the same pitch; he took Sussex's first five wickets at a personal cost of only 14 as they were bowled out in less than two hours. Following on 236 behind, Sussex subsided for a second time to Roberts, Taylor and Clift, the match ending before five o'clock on the second day.

Leicestershire

J. C. Balderstone c Gould b Waller	82	*†R. W. Tolchard not out	20
I. P. Butcher b Imran	59		
N. E. Briers c C. M. Wells b Pigott	20	B 2, l-b 8, w 3, n-b 10	23
B. F. Davison c C. M. Wells b Waller	85		
P. B. Clift c A. P. Wells b Pigott	34	1/137 2/161 (5 wkts dec.) 356
J. J. Whitaker not out	33	3/190 4/288 5/318	

A. M. E. Roberts, G. J. Parsons, L. B. Taylor and N. G. B. Cook did not bat.

Bonus points – Leicestershire 4, Sussex 2.

Bowling: Pigott 24–4–101–2; Jones 15–1–69–0; Waller 34–9–90–2; Cowan 5–1–24–0; Parker 2–0–16–0; Barclay 7–1–30–0; Imran 4–2–3–1.

Sussex

G. D. Mendis lbw b Roberts	12	– c Tolchard b Taylor	1
*J. R. T. Barclay c Parsons b Roberts	8	– c Tolchard b Taylor	5
P. W. G. Parker lbw b Roberts	0	– lbw b Roberts	4
Imran Khan lbw b Taylor	28	– b Cook	69
A. P. Wells b Roberts	0	– lbw b Taylor	7
R. S. Cowan b Roberts	1	– lbw b Clift	9
C. M. Wells b Clift	12	– b Clift	0
†I. J. Gould c Tolchard b Parsons	35	– lbw b Clift	26
A. C. S. Pigott lbw b Parsons	4	– lbw b Clift	4
C. E. Waller not out	5	– lbw b Roberts	1
A. N. Jones b Clift	3	– not out	4
B 5, l-b 4, n-b 3	12	L-b 1, n-b 2	3

1/22 2/22 3/43 4/47   120   1/5 2/10 3/16 4/36   133
5/53 6/57 7/103 8/105 9/117   5/73 6/75 7/109 8/114 9/129

Bonus points – Leicestershire 4.

Bowling: *First Innings*—Roberts 13–4–26–5; Taylor 13–1–60–1; Clift 5.4–1–9–2; Parsons 5–1–13–2. *Second Innings*—Roberts 10.2–2–26–2; Taylor 11–5–14–3; Clift 14–0–59–4; Parsons 6–1–22–0; Cook 4–2–9–1.

Umpires: C. Cook and B. Leadbeater.

LEICESTERSHIRE v NOTTINGHAMSHIRE

At Leicester, August 6, 8, 9. Leicestershire won by 50 runs. Leicestershire 22 pts, Nottinghamshire 6 pts. Leicestershire, put in on a grassy pitch, slid to 51 for five before they were rescued by Clift and Tolchard, putting on 74, and Parsons, scoring a maiden half-century. French's highest score of the season helped Nottinghamshire escape with a narrow first-innings deficit, but then Butcher's career-best score enabled Tolchard to set a target of 307 in 273 minutes. Randall's fluent 94 gave Nottinghamshire an unexpected glimpse of victory, but Taylor swung the game away from them, and Leicestershire won with seven of the final twenty overs remaining. Of the 38 wickets that fell in the match, Taylor and Hendrick took twenty between them.

Leicestershire

J. C. Balderstone c Rice b Hendrick	24	– c French b Saxelby	20
I. P. Butcher c French b Hendrick	9	– c Rice b Hendrick	139
D. I. Gower lbw b Hendrick	0	– lbw b Saxelby	0
B. F. Davison c Bore b Saxelby	10	– b Saxelby	4
N. E. Briers b Cooper	6	– b Hendrick	45
P. B. Clift c Rice b Cooper	49	– b Hendrick	8
*†R. W. Tolchard b Cooper	46	– not out	34
G. J. Parsons c Rice b Hendrick	56	– c Hemmings b Hendrick	9
N. G. B. Cook not out	12	– c Randall b Hendrick	1
L. B. Taylor b Bore	4	– not out	10
G. J. F. Ferris lbw b Bore	0		
B 1, l-b 6, w 2, n-b 1	10	B 2, l-b 11, w 5, n-b 4	22

1/17 2/17 3/34 4/48   226   1/66 2/70 3/74   (8 wkts. dec.)   292
5/51 6/125 7/176 8/211 9/222   4/217 5/231 6/242 7/268 8/278

Bonus points – Leicestershire 2, Nottinghamshire 4.

Bowling: *First Innings*—Hendrick 20–6–47–4; Cooper 21–6–59–3; Saxelby 11–1–57–1; Bore 16.5–4–53–2. *Second Innings*—Hendrick 19–9–25–5; Cooper 17–2–99–0; Hemmings 20–7–51–0; Saxelby 13–2–53–3; Bore 11–2–42–0.

Nottinghamshire

B. Hassan c Gower b Taylor	7	– lbw b Clift	24
R. T. Robinson lbw b Taylor	21	– c Tolchard b Taylor	8
P. Johnson b Clift	24	– (5) c Tolchard b Taylor	5
*C. E. B. Rice hit wkt b Ferris	9	– lbw b Taylor	7
D. W. Randall b Ferris	22	– (3) c Tolchard b Taylor	94
†B. N. French lbw b Clift	59	– lbw b Clift	18
E. E. Hemmings c Gower b Parsons	7	– b Ferris	33
K. Saxelby c Gower b Taylor	5	– lbw b Taylor	0
K. E. Cooper lbw b Clift	12	– c Briers b Taylor	15
M. K. Bore c Parsons b Taylor	1	– not out	15
M. Hendrick not out	0	– c Briers b Taylor	12
B 10, l-b 4, w 18, n-b 13	45	B 8, l-b 6, w 1, n-b 10	25

1/20 2/47 3/66 4/77   212   1/23 2/37 3/52 4/58   256
5/100 6/144 7/165 8/201 9/212   5/117 6/203 7/203 8/224 9/235

Bonus points – Nottinghamshire 2, Leicestershire 4.

Bowling: *First Innings*—Taylor 24.1–9–29–4; Ferris 17–2–69–2; Parsons 10–2–29–1; Clift 19–5–40–3. *Second Innings*—Ferris 13–3–40–1; Taylor 22.2–8–73–7; Clift 16–5–69–2; Cook 21–8–49–0.

Umpires: W. E. Alley and P. B. Wight.

At Chelmsford, August 10, 11, 12. LEICESTERSHIRE drew with ESSEX.

At Birmingham, August 13, 15, 16. LEICESTERSHIRE drew with WARWICKSHIRE.

At Leicester, August 20, 21, 22. LEICESTERSHIRE lost to NEW ZEALANDERS by eight wickets (See New Zealand tour section).

At Folkestone, August 24, 25, 26. LEICESTERSHIRE lost to KENT by ten wickets.

LEICESTERSHIRE v NORTHAMPTONSHIRE

At Leicester, August 27, 29, 30. Leicestershire won by five wickets. Leicestershire 24 pts, Northamptonshire 5 pts. Northamptonshire's decision to bat first on a green pitch looked justified when Williams and Capel put on 107 for the fifth wicket, but Steele dismissed both in quick succession and Ferris polished off the innings with his first hat-trick. Butcher's solid century and an unusually painstaking innings from Davison gave Leicestershire a big lead, but Boyd-Moss's century left the home side with a daunting target of 100 from thirteen overs. Davison, hitting four 4s in the eight balls he faced, gave the innings impetus, maintained by Briers and Clift, and Balderstone struck two 4s and one 6 in winning the game with ten deliveries to spare.

Northamptonshire

M. J. Bamber c Tolchard b Taylor	8	– c Butcher b Taylor	3
W. Larkins lbw b Clift	13	– b Taylor	47
P. Willey c Steele b Clift	11	– (4) lbw b Taylor	2
R. J. Boyd-Moss c Tolchard b Taylor	0	– (5) c Butcher b Taylor	101
R. G. Williams c Taylor b Steele	76	– (6) c Briers b Ferris	58
D. J. Capel c Davison b Steele	56	– (7) c Butcher b Ferris	0
D. S. Steele c Steele b Clift	12	– (8) c Tolchard b Ferris	7
*†G. Sharp b Ferris	16	– (9) not out	27
N. A. Mallender not out	6	– (3) b Taylor	1
J. A. Carse b Ferris	0	– b Clift	12
B. J. Griffiths c Taylor b Ferris	0	– lbw b Clift	0
B 4, l-b 4, w 6, n-b 7	21	L-b 4, w 1, n-b 16	21

1/32 2/36 3/43 4/44   219   1/8 2/16 3/25 4/100   279
5/151 6/196 7/201 8/219 9/219   5/212 6/215 7/231 8/240 9/279

Bonus points – Northamptonshire 2, Leicestershire 4.

Bowling: *First Innings*—Taylor 19–4–60–2; Ferris 15–5–44–3; Clift 24–9–51–3; Parsons 2–0–9–0; Steele 13–3–34–2. *Second Innings*—Taylor 27–10–59–5; Ferris 24–4–89–3; Steele 22–10–43–0; Clift 18–3–48–2; Parsons 4–1–19–0.

Leicestershire

J. C. Balderstone lbw b Mallender	5	– (6) not out	24
I. P. Butcher c Sharp b Griffiths	107	– c Williams b Griffiths	2
N. E. Briers c Bamber b Mallender	43	– c Steele b Carse	22
B. F. Davison c Bamber b Griffiths	67	– (1) c Sharp b Griffiths	18
J. J. Whitaker lbw b Steele	20	– c Bamber b Griffiths	2
P. B. Clift c Sharp b Griffiths	1	– (4) c Sharp b Carse	16
*†R. W. Tolchard c Sharp b Steele	2	– not out	1
J. F. Steele c Boyd-Moss b Steele	45		
G. J. Parsons b Carse	24		
L. B. Taylor not out	29		
G. J. F. Ferris b Steele	4		
B 7, l-b 16, w 7, n-b 22	52	L-b 12, n-b 3	15

1/21 2/143 3/228 4/267   399   1/19 2/30 3/66   (5 wkts) 100
5/273 6/276 7/294 8/358 9/385   4/67 5/72

Bonus points – Leicestershire 4, Northamptonshire 3 (Score at 100 overs: 310-7).

Bowling: *First Innings*—Carse 33–6–116–1; Mallender 28–6–77–2; Griffiths 32–5–85–3; Steele 27.5–10–59–4; Capel 4–0–10–0. *Second Innings*—Mallender 3–0–36–0; Griffiths 5.2–0–38–3; Carse 3–1–11–2.

Umpires: C. Cook and A. G. T. Whitehead.

LEICESTERSHIRE v KENT

At Leicester, August 31, September 1, 2. Leicestershire won by eight wickets. Leicestershire 24 pts, Kent 7 pts. Kent, missing several first-team regulars, owed their useful first-innings total, on a pitch which took spin from the first morning, to Taylor and Aslett. Taylor batted 199 minutes and hit sixteen 4s. Leicestershire's first innings followed a similar pattern, a collapse following a productive third-wicket partnership between Balderstone and Tolchard, who added 139 in 115 minutes. Kent had the misfortune to lose Woolmer who damaged his back when bowling, an injury which caused him to miss the NatWest Bank Trophy final two days later. The home spinners induced a spectacular second-innings collapse from 111 for four to 113 all out, and Leicestershire arrived at a comfortable victory by three o'clock on the third afternoon.

Kent

R. A. Woolmer b Taylor	22	– absent hurt	
N. R. Taylor c Davison b Steele	111	– b Cook	9
D. G. Aslett lbw b Cook	58	– c Whitaker b Steele	53
M. R. Benson st Tolchard b Cook	6	– (1) c Butcher b Taylor	0
S. G. Hinks b Cook	43	– st Tolchard b Clift	21
R. M. Ellison b Clift	10	– c Butcher b Steele	22
*G. W. Johnson c Butcher b Cook	1	– c Steele b Clift	0
†S. Marsh c Butcher b Clift	5	– (4) c Gower b Clift	0
D. L. Underwood not out	10	– (8) c Butcher b Clift	0
K. D. Masters b Clift	0	– (9) c Davison b Steele	0
K. B. S. Jarvis b Taylor	5	– (10) not out	0
B 4, l-b 9, w 1, n-b 4	18	B 6, l-b 2	8

1/38 2/147 3/167 4/229   289   1/0 2/16 3/16 4/51   113
5/241 6/252 7/267 8/277 9/278   5/111 6/112 7/113 8/113 9/113

Bonus points – Kent 3, Leicestershire 4 (Score at 100 overs: 289-9).

Bowling: First Innings—Taylor 11.3–7–17–2; Clift 17–6–48–3; Cook 39–12–94–4; Steele 24–5–73–1; Balderstone 9–1–39–0. *Second Innings*—Taylor 3–2–6–1; Cook 16–4–45–1; Steele 7.3–3–12–3; Clift 15–4–42–4.

Leicestershire

J. C. Balderstone lbw b Woolmer	112	– c Johnson b Underwood	29
I. P. Butcher lbw b Johnson	42	– c Taylor b Underwood	18
D. I. Gower b Underwood	4	– not out	30
*†R. W. Tolchard c Johnson b Jarvis	61	– not out	2
N. E. Briers b Underwood	5		
B. F. Davison c Aslett b Underwood	16		
J. J. Whitaker c Benson b Masters	10		
P. B. Clift c Benson b Underwood	1		
J. F. Steele b Underwood	0		
N. G. B. Cook not out	12		
L. B. Taylor c Taylor b Masters	18		
B 9, l-b 2, n-b 18	29	B 8, l-b 3, n-b 6	17

1/76 2/94 3/233 4/246   310   1/49 2/84   (2 wkts) 96
5/266 6/274 7/278 8/278 9/279

Bonus points – Leicestershire 4, Kent 4.

Bowling: First Innings—Jarvis 12–0–49–1; Ellison 14–3–43–0; Underwood 40–15–101–5; Johnson 19–4–48–1; Woolmer 8–4–14–1; Masters 6–1–26–2. *Second Innings*—Jarvis 1–1–0–0; Underwood 17–6–33–2; Johnson 13–2–31–0; Taylor 1–0–3–0; Benson 4–1–12–0.

Umpires: J. D. Morley and A. G. T. Whitehead.

At Hove, September 7, 8, 9. LEICESTERSHIRE drew with SUSSEX.

At Manchester, September 10, 12, 13. LEICESTERSHIRE drew with LANCASHIRE.

MIDDLESEX

Patron: HRH The Duke of Edinburgh
President: F. G. Mann
Chairman: F. G. Mann
Chairman, Cricket Committee: R. V. C. Robins
Secretary: 1983 – A. J. Wright; 1984 – T. M. Lamb
Lord's Cricket Ground, St John's Wood,
London NW8 8QN (Telephone: 01-289 1300)
Captain: M. W. Gatting
Coach: D. Bennett

If another season of high achievement ended in anticlimax through their being overtaken in the home straight of the Schweppes County Championship, Middlesex still had reason to look back on 1983 with satisfaction. Mike Gatting and John Emburey, who deputised as captain during the World Cup and the last two Tests, led the side so soundly that the retirement of Mike Brearley was absorbed with a minimum of difficulty. To finish second in the Championship, win the Benson and Hedges Cup, and be deprived of a second final only by a masterly 96 not out for Somerset by Ian Botham in the NatWest Bank Trophy semi-final, reflects a high level of consistency in view of the fact that they were constantly weakened by representative calls and injuries. Only in the John Player League, where they dropped six places, did they fail to leave their mark.

Inability to clinch the Championship, after establishing a commanding lead through six successive victories in June, was the major disappointment. One win in the last nine games suggests the team went off the boil. But the decline had to be measured against the increasing strain of having to make do without two main batsmen because of injury – Roland Butcher and Wilf Slack – in the last tense weeks. Retrospectively, it did Middlesex credit that they led from June 7 to August 23 despite fielding their full side in only the first match, against Essex, which rain and the marshy state of Lord's reduced to half a day. Through injuries, World Cup and Tests combined, Norman Cowans missed fourteen games, Butcher ten, Phil Edmonds nine, Gatting eight, and Slack and Wayne Daniel six each. Another, against Yorkshire, was washed out without a ball being bowled.

Butcher's was the season's gravest injury. Having beaten Kent and Derbyshire virtually off his own bat with innings of 110 and 179 in June, he looked to be emerging from a thinnish July when, helmetless as usual, he was hit by a bouncer missing a hook against Ferris, one of Leicestershire's West Indians. Butcher suffered multiple fractures to his left cheekbone, affecting the sight of the eye so badly that his vision was still blurred as the season ended. Butcher's absence gave Keith Tomlins a regular place at No. 5, and by making a hundred against Sussex, as well as three good NatWest Bank Trophy scores, he went on to win a county cap. Stylish batsman as he is, however, he could not make up for Butcher's ability to win a match through his rapid rate of scoring, and catching near the bat. Nothing painted a clearer picture of Butcher's value than that eight weeks after his withdrawal he was still the country's leading catcher. Slack, who needed a cartilage operation, was successfully replaced by another left-hander, twenty-year-old Oxford Blue, Andy Miller, who, in scoring 465 runs in eleven innings, revealed a pleasingly straight bat and as delicate a late-cut as could be seen in county cricket.

Naturally enough, however, it was the form of the older hands which gave the side its drive, none more so than Graham Barlow's. Initially given half-a-dozen games to establish himself in Brearley's place as opener, the 33-year-old left-hander started with 128 against Lancashire and never looked back. Self-confidence restored after a forlorn 1982, he batted with customary vigour and ever-increasing freedom to pass 1,500 for the first time in his career, making three more hundreds and two 90s.

Gatting, quick to take charge whether pressing home an advantage or consolidating an uncertain start, scored 216 against the New Zealanders – in 241 minutes – his first 200, and five hundreds in the Championship, of which four came in two hours or less. Inevitably in his first season at the helm he made some debatable decisions in the field, being sometimes slow to pair his spinners; but he was as positive and as obviously in charge as his celebrated predecessor. Emburey, rather more analytical, had the twin distinctions of taking 100 wickets for the first time and of winning his first four games as captain with a patched-up attack. In that he was hugely helped by Edmonds, the brilliance of whose left-arm spin bowling reached its peak during the World Cup. Seven games in June (one against Cambridge University) brought Edmonds 54 wickets at 13 each and won him back his Test place. But when his back played up again, keeping him out at Lord's, the golden seam dried up. Passed over for the England tour in favour of Leicestershire's Cook, he took only seven wickets in the last four games and fell eight short of a hundred.

The ascendancy of the spinners meant less work than usual for Daniel; but the fast bowler's wickets, though his fewest in seven seasons, were still economical and quick. Cowans did little, but in his first full season Neil Williams made an encouraging advance, his speed and out-swing producing many telling spells. Paul Downton, one of four ever-presents, kept wicket with his normal unobtrusive skill. Of the rest, Clive Radley endured his leanest season in the Championship since 1968. But he gave proof of his durability and temperament with a tenacious 89 not out that, by a hair's breadth, won Middlesex the Benson and Hedges Cup final. Overall, the team earned prizemoney of £29,610, over £3,000 more than Essex. Seam bowler Bill Merry and Rajesh Maru, the slow left-hander, were not retained. – J. D. T.

MIDDLESEX 1983

[Bill Smith]

Back row: C. P. Metson, N. F. Williams, W. G. Merry, N. G. Cowans, K. D. James, R. J. Maru, C. W. V. Robins. *Middle row:* H. P. Sharp (*scorer*), D. Bennett (*coach*), S. P. Hughes, K. P. Tomlins, C. R. Cook, P. R. Downton, A. G. Smith, K. R. Brown, J. Miller (*physiotherapist*). *Front row:* W. N. Slack, W. W. Daniel, P. H. Edmonds, M. W. Gatting (*captain*), J. E. Emburey, C. T. Radley, G. D. Barlow, R. O. Butcher.

MIDDLESEX RESULTS

All first-class matches – Played 25: Won 12, Lost 4, Drawn 9.

County Championship matches – Played 23: Won 11, Lost 5, Drawn 8.

Bonus points – Batting 60, Bowling 72.

Competition placings – Schweppes County Championship, 2nd; NatWest Bank Trophy, s-f;
Benson and Hedges Cup, winners; John Player League, 8th eq.

COUNTY CHAMPIONSHIP AVERAGES

BATTING

	Birthplace	M	I	NO	R	HI	Avge
M. W. Gattingᶜ........	Kingsbury	15	23	5	1,157	160	64.27
G. D. Barlowᶜ........	Folkestone	22	38	7	1,519	132	49.00
R. O. Butcherᶜ........	St Phillip, Barbados	13	17	2	646	179	43.06
A. J. T. Millerᶜ........	Chesham	6	11	0	465	86	42.27
W. N. Slack........	Troumaca, St Vincent	16	26	3	874	140	38.00
K. P. Tomlinsᶜ........	Kingston-upon-Thames	18	25	4	606	132*	28.85
J. E. Embureyᶜ........	Peckham	23	32	4	772	133	27.57
C. T. Radleyᶜ........	Hertford	23	36	6	748	67	24.93
K. D. James........	Lambeth	7	8	2	141	34	23.50
N. F. Williams........	Hope Well, St Vincent	23	25	7	407	63	22.61
P. R. Downtonᶜ........	Farnborough, Kent	23	30	7	508	87	22.08
P. H. Edmondsᶜ........	Lusaka, N. Rhodesia	15	16	3	145	65	11.15
R. G. P. Ellis........	Paddington	6	11	0	107	34	9.72
W. W. Daniel........	St Phillip, Barbados	16	13	2	88	18	8.00
N. G. Cowans........	Enfield St Mary, Jamaica	10	8	3	34	9	6.80
S. P. Hughesᶜ........	Kingston-upon-Thames	12	10	6	13	4*	3.25

Also batted: J. M. Brearleyᶜ (*Harrow*) (1 match) 17; J. D. Carr (*St John's Wood*) (3
matches) 9*, 12*, 1*; J. F. Sykes (*Shoreditch*) (1 match) 4.

*Signifies not out. ᶜ*Denotes county cap.*

BOWLING

	O	M	R	W	Avge	BB
J. E. Emburey........	833	289	1,677	96	17.46	6-13
P. H. Edmonds........	615.5	169	1,491	72	20.70	6-38
W. W. Daniel........	307.2	48	1,040	47	22.12	7-61
N. G. Cowans........	155	33	455	18	25.27	5-43
S. P. Hughes........	252.3	60	836	33	25.33	6-32
N. F. Williams........	503.2	107	1,571	62	25.33	5-77

Also bowled: G. D. Barlow 2–1–2–0; R. O. Butcher 1–1–0–0; J. D. Carr 15–4–31–0; M.
W. Gatting 81.2–25–209–5; K. D. James 69–12–178–6; C. T. Radley 1–0–4–0; W. N. Slack
36–18–71–5; J. F. Sykes 21–6–54–1; K. P. Tomlins 6–2–19–0.

The following played a total of fifteen three-figure innings for Middlesex in County
Championship matches – M. W. Gatting 5, G. D. Barlow 4, R. O. Butcher 2, W. N. Slack
2, J. E. Emburey 1, K. P. Tomlins 1.

At Lord's, April 27, 28, 29. MCC v MIDDLESEX. Abandoned.

MIDDLESEX v ESSEX

At Lord's, April 30, May 2, 3. Drawn. Essex 1 pt. Play was limited to two and a half hours on the first afternoon, though it was not until the third inspection on the last day that the match was finally abandoned. Gooch hit four 6s into the nearby Grandstand in his 72 not out, three of them off Edmonds in a fifteen-minute spell in which he moved from 30 to 60.

Essex

G. A. Gooch not out......................	72
B. R. Hardie c Barlow b Daniel.........	0
*K. W. R. Fletcher c Butcher b Emburey	37
K. S. McEwan not out.....................	40
L-b 7, w 1, n-b 3	11

1/2 2/74   (2 wkts) 160

K. R. Pont, N. Phillip, S. Turner, D. R. Pringle, †D. E. East, R. E. East and J. K. Lever did not bat.

Bonus points – Essex 1.

Bowling: Daniel 6–0–31–1; Cowans 8–2–16–0; Williams 12–0–56–0; Emburey 11–2–23–1; Edmonds 3–0–23–0.

Middlesex

G. D. Barlow, W. N. Slack, C. T. Radley, *M. W. Gatting, R. O. Butcher, J. E. Emburey, †P. R. Downton, P. H. Edmonds, N. F. Williams, N. G. Cowans and W. W. Daniel.

Umpires: K. Ibadulla and P. B. Wight.

MIDDLESEX v LANCASHIRE

At Lord's, May 4, 5, 6. Drawn. Middlesex 6 pts, Lancashire 2 pts. The second day produced the first full day's play of the Lord's season out of eight attempts; but with play limited to 25 minutes on the first day and little more than two hours on the last, there would have been no hope of progressing beyond the bonus-points stage even if Lancashire had matched Middlesex's anxiety to play. Contrarily, Abrahams put Middlesex in, subjecting his fielders to the soggy going, and Barlow responded with his first hundred since August 1981. He batted for 307 minutes, timing the ball well off his legs. On the last day Williams bowled effectively, rewarding Gatting for his patience in waiting four hours for the ground to dry while Lancashire wanted only to drive home.

Middlesex

G. D. Barlow run out......................128		J. E. Emburey b Abrahams...............	29
W. N. Slack lbw b Simmons	56	†P. R. Downton not out	4
C. T. Radley c sub b Simmons	33	B 4, l-b 6, w 1, n-b 5	16
*M. W. Gatting not out	64		
R. O. Butcher c Simmons b Allott......	0	1/119 2/203 3/235	(6 wkts dec.) 331
K. P. Tomlins lbw b Jefferies	1	4/235 5/238 6/310	

N. F. Williams, N. G. Cowans and W. W. Daniel did not bat.

Bonus points – Middlesex 3, Lancashire 2 (Score at 100 overs: 268-5).

Bowling: Allott 26–7–56–1; Jefferies 22–6–50–1; Simmons 31–7–73–2; Folley 13–3–55–0; O'Shaughnessy 8.4–0–30–0; Hughes 6–0–21–0; Lloyd 6–1–15–0; Abrahams 4–0–15–1.

Lancashire

D. Lloyd retired hurt	9	S. T. Jefferies c Tomlins b Williams	11
G. Fowler run out	7	P. J. W. Allott not out	16
S. J. O'Shaughnessy c Slack b Cowans	25	I. Folley not out	4
D. P. Hughes c Butcher b Cowans	15	L-b 1, n-b 4	5
F. C. Hayes b Williams	6		
*J. Abrahams c Downton b Williams	0	1/14 2/49 3/62 (7 wkts dec.) 98	
J. Simmons c Butcher b Williams	0	4/63 5/65 6/70 7/78	

†C. Maynard did not bat.

Bonus points – Middlesex 3.

Bowling: Daniel 5–1–7–0; Williams 15–4–47–4; Cowans 10–2–26–2; Emburey 4–2–6–0; Gatting 5–1–7–0; Slack 1–1–0–0.

Umpires: K. Ibadulla and P. B. Wight.

MIDDLESEX v YORKSHIRE

At Lord's, May 11, 12, 13. Abandoned.

MIDDLESEX v GLAMORGAN

At Lord's May 25, 26, 27. Middlesex won by an innings and 79 runs. Middlesex 24 pts, Glamorgan 2 pts. Dominating modest opposition in each of seven sessions, Middlesex swept to their fourth successive innings victory over Glamorgan at Lord's (and eleventh in succession home and away in the Championship) by lunch on the third day. Gatting, punching twelve 4s in 94 minutes, took full advantage of Slack's and Radley's spadework – their stand of 162 came off 48 overs. Jones and Hopkins offered Glamorgan hope with an untroubled opening at 3 an over, but subsequent resistance was unimpressive. Daniel, Williams and Cowans bowled with hostility on a slow pitch, Daniel doing most to influence the result by dismissing Javed Miandad first ball through a gloved catch to the wicket-keeper.

Middlesex

G. D. Barlow c E. W. Jones b Wilkins	30	R. O. Butcher not out	26
W. N. Slack c A. Jones b Rowe	140	B 4, l-b 15, n-b 8	27
C. T. Radley c Hopkins b Lloyd	59		
*M. W. Gatting c and b Rowe	94	1/60 2/222 3/290 4/376 (4 wkts dec.) 376	

K. P. Tomlins, J. E. Emburey, †P. R. Downton, N. F. Williams, N. G. Cowans and W. W. Daniel did not bat.

Bonus points – Middlesex 4, Glamorgan 1 (Score at 100 overs: 312-3).

Bowling: Selvey 25–2–76–0; Ontong 22–6–63–0; Wilkins 14–1–38–1; Lloyd 25–0–87–1; Rowe 23.2–3–85–2.

Glamorgan

A. Jones c Barlow b Daniel	57	– c Downton b Cowans 0
J. A. Hopkins b Emburey	34	– c Downton b Emburey 54
D. A. Francis c Emburey b Williams	9	– lbw b Emburey 19
Javed Miandad c Downton b Daniel	0	– c Gatting b Emburey 3
C. J. C. Rowe c Butcher b Daniel	6	– (11) absent hurt
R. C. Ontong lbw b Williams	3	– (5) c Butcher b Gatting 0
A. L. Jones c Daniel b Emburey	6	– (6) not out 21
†E. W. Jones c Tomlins b Williams	2	– (8) c Barlow b Daniel 0
*M. W. W. Selvey not out	8	– (9) b Cowans 6
B. J. Lloyd b Cowans	3	– (7) c Downton b Daniel 1
A. H. Wilkins c Slack b Emburey	1	– (10) c Slack b Daniel 20
B 6, l-b 6, w 1, n-b 12	25	B 9, l-b 3, n-b 7............ 19

1/91 2/111 3/111 4/125   154   1/0 2/67 3/81 4/84   143
5/125 6/136 7/136 8/138 9/149   5/84 6/90 7/90 8/103 9/143

Bonus points – Glamorgan 1, Middlesex 4.

Bowling: *First Innings*—Daniel 16–6–22–3; Williams 18–5–45–3; Emburey 18.3–10–22–3; Cowans 12–3–40–1. *Second Innings*—Daniel 13–3–27–3; Cowans 13–3–22–2; Williams 8–1–31–0; Emburey 21–8–29–3; Gatting 9–5–15–1.

Umpires: H. D. Bird and R. A. White.

MIDDLESEX v SUSSEX

At Lord's, May 28, 30, 31. Drawn. Middlesex 3 pts, Sussex 4 pts. After a blank first day – Middlesex's sixth complete washout in thirteen days of Championship cricket at Lord's – Gatting did his best to make up for lost time with an even-time hundred. But though that set the pattern of an enterprising match, Sussex responding by declaring 124 behind, a target of 239 in 170 minutes proved beyond the visitors on the last afternoon when wickets started falling in the second hour. However, they held on for a draw easily enough, Mendis's anchoring 86 being finished by Emburey just before the end.

Middlesex

G. D. Barlow c Barclay b Pigott	29	– b Greig 38
W. N. Slack c Gould b le Roux	11	– lbw b le Roux 3
C. T. Radley c A. P. Wells b Pigott	10	– b le Roux 4
*M. W. Gatting b Greig	118	– c Barclay b Greig............... 0
R. O. Butcher c Mendis b Jones	52	– c Barclay b Greig 7
K. P. Tomlins not out	30	– lbw b Greig 2
†P. R. Downton c Barclay b Pigott	4	– (8) not out 23
N. F. Williams lbw b Greig	6	
J. E. Emburey c Mendis b Jones	11	– (7) not out 35
L-b 4	4	L-b 1, w 1 2

1/27 2/49 3/54 4/169   (8 wkts dec.) 275   1/5 2/14 3/15   (6 wkts dec.) 114
5/228 6/243 7/258 8/275   4/23 5/29 6/64

N. G. Cowans and W. W. Daniel did not bat.

Bonus points – Middlesex 3, Sussex 3.

Bowling: *First Innings*—le Roux 13–5–39–1; Pigott 17–2–54–3; Greig 16–1–78–2; C. M. Wells 2–0–20–0; Jones 8.4–0–65–2; Barclay 2–0–15–0. *Second Innings*—le Roux 18–4–50–2; Pigott 13–4–20–0; Greig 18–4–42–4.

Sussex

G. D. Mendis b Emburey	38	– c Butcher b Emburey	86
A. M. Green run out	5	– c Downton b Williams	23
*J. R. T. Barclay not out	56	– (8) not out	4
C. M. Wells not out	37	– (3) run out	22
P. W. G. Parker (did not bat)	–	(4) c Butcher b Emburey	7
A. P. Wells (did not bat)	–	(5) c Radley b Emburey	12
†I. J. Gould (did not bat)	–	(6) not out	4
I. A. Greig (did not bat)	–	(7) c Downton b Cowans	1
L-b 2, n-b 13	15	L-b 6, n-b 3	9

1/20 2/76   (2 wkts dec.) 151   1/47 2/111 3/134   (6 wkts) 168
                                             4/159 5/162 6/164

G. S. le Roux, A. C. S. Pigott and A. N. Jones did not bat.

Bonus points – Sussex 1.

Bowling: *First Innings*—Daniel 8-0-40-0; Cowans 7-1-15-0; Emburey 12-5-24-1; Williams 12-3-34-0; Gatting 8-2-23-0. *Second Innings*—Daniel 9-0-45-0; Cowans 11-0-38-1; Emburey 13-4-34-3; Williams 9-1-33-1; Gatting 2-0-9-0; Tomlins 1-1-0-0; Butcher 1-1-0-0.

Umpires: H. D. Bird and R. A. White.

At Dartford, June 4, 6, 7. MIDDLESEX beat KENT by four wickets.

MIDDLESEX v DERBYSHIRE

At Uxbridge, June 8, 9, 10. Middlesex won by nine wickets. Middlesex 24 pts, Derbyshire 5 pts. Derbyshire seemed likely to have a say in the match when, thanks to the patient Hill, they scored 238 and dismissed Barlow cheaply before close of play. But on the second day Slack and Radley set the scene for a typically destructive assault by Butcher, who made full use of a pacey pitch and small, fast outfield by making 179 in three hours and a minute. He hit four 6s and 29 4s and scored his runs off only eighteen more balls than Slack needed for his 69: 171 to 153. Anderson played courageously in Derbyshire's second innings, returning at the fall of the eighth wicket after being hit in the mouth attempting to hook Williams; but time was on Middlesex's side thanks to Butcher and they won with a session unused.

Derbyshire

I. S. Anderson lbw b James	3	– (2) not out	76
J. E. Morris c Butcher b Edmonds	38	– (1) c Edmonds b Hughes	0
A. Hill b Emburey	89	– c Butcher b Edmonds	42
*K. J. Barnett c Butcher b Emburey	25	– (5) lbw b Williams	0
R. J. Finney c and b Edmonds	6	– (6) b Edmonds	55
G. Miller c Downton b Hughes	0	– (11) absent injured	
C. J. Tunnicliffe b Williams	1	– c Tomlins b Emburey	5
†R. W. Taylor b Williams	20	– c Slack b Williams	5
D. G. Moir c Butcher b Hughes	9	– (4) c Downton b Williams	6
S. Oldham c Hughes b Edmonds	19	– (9) c Butcher b James	37
O. H. Mortensen not out	7	– (10) lbw b Williams	0
L-b 9, w 1, n-b 11	21	B 10, l-b 9, n-b 11	30

1/23 2/70 3/119 4/136   238   1/6 2/97 3/123 4/127   256
5/145 6/162 7/192 8/212 9/212   5/132 6/142 7/219 8/222 9/256

Bonus points – Derbyshire 2, Middlesex 4.

Bowling: *First Innings*—Hughes 20-9-57-2; Williams 16-4-39-2; James 7-5-8-1; Emburey 28-12-53-2; Edmonds 22.5-7-60-3. *Second Innings*—Williams 23-6-67-4; Hughes 11-1-45-1; Edmonds 18.3-3-54-2; Emburey 16-4-40-1; Slack 3-2-2-0; James 8-1-18-1.

Middlesex

G. D. Barlow c Barnett b Oldham	7	– b Tunnicliffe	14
W. N. Slack c Miller b Moir	69	– not out	39
C. T. Radley lbw b Miller	46	– not out	17
R. O. Butcher b Finney	179		
K. P. Tomlins c Barnett b Moir	19		
*J. E. Emburey c Taylor b Tunnicliffe	2		
†P. R. Downton c Mortensen b Anderson	18		
K. D. James c Anderson b Finney	29		
N. F. Williams not out	11		
P. H. Edmonds not out	4		
B 8, l-b 17, w 2, n-b 8	35	B 2, l-b 1, n-b 6	9

1/8 2/124 3/149 4/228   (8 wkts dec.) 419   1/30   (1 wkt) 79
5/252 6/313 7/386 8/414

S. P. Hughes did not bat.

Bonus points – Middlesex 4, Derbyshire 3 (Score at 100 overs: 392-7).

Bowling: *First Innings*—Mortensen 18–5–48–0; Oldham 18–3–54–1; Tunnicliffe 16–4–75–1; Miller 16–6–34–1; Moir 27–4–110–2; Anderson 6–1–45–1; Finney 7–0–18–2. *Second Innings*—Mortensen 7–0–24–0; Tunnicliffe 9–2–29–1; Finney 3–0–13–0; Morris 2–2–0–0; Hill 1.2–1–4–0.

Umpires: J. W. Holder and A. Jepson.

At The Oval, June 11, 13, 14. MIDDLESEX beat SURREY by ten wickets.

MIDDLESEX v HAMPSHIRE

At Uxbridge, June 15, 16. Middlesex won by an innings and 64 runs. Middlesex 24 pts, Hampshire 4 pts. Middlesex were in charge throughout on a pitch with something in it for everyone, batsmen included – a characteristic they were coming to accept as normal at their suburban home from home. Hughes profited from its pace and bounce to take five of the last six wickets as Hampshire collapsed from 159 for four to 176 all out, whereupon Barlow, first with Slack and then Tomlins, firmly pushed home the advantage. By sharing stands of 81 and 103 they compensated for the absence of Radley, who had a toe broken by a drive from Pocock when fielding silly-point to Edmonds. Barlow batted for three hours, hitting seventeen 4s. Hampshire batted in the second innings like a beaten side and shortly before close of play on the second day they duly became Middlesex's fourth successive victims.

Hampshire

V. P. Terry c Butcher b Edmonds	61	– c Tomlins b Hughes	17
C. L. Smith c Tomlins b James	10	– c Downton b Hughes	22
M. C. J. Nicholas c Downton b James	1	– c Tomlins b Edmonds	5
R. A. Smith c Tomlins b James	10	– b Edmonds	26
*N. E. J. Pocock c Edmonds b Hughes	37	– b Emburey	19
N. G. Cowley c Downton b Hughes	22	– c Barlow b Edmonds	10
T. M. Tremlett b Hughes	0	– c Barlow b Edmonds	1
†R. J. Parks b Edmonds	8	– c Downton b Emburey	3
J. W. Southern c Tomlins b Hughes	0	– lbw b Emburey	0
K. Stevenson not out	5	– not out	7
S. J. Malone c Emburey b Hughes	1	– c Tomlins b Edmonds	4
L-b 13, n-b 8	21	L-b 3, n-b 4	7

1/41 2/48 3/64 4/117   176   1/36 2/48 3/48 4/89   121
5/159 6/159 7/166 8/170 9/170   5/97 6/102 7/105 8/105 9/113

Bonus points – Hampshire 1, Middlesex 4.

Bowling: *First Innings*—Williams 9–1–19–0; Hughes 18.2–5–48–5; James 9–1–14–3; Slack 1–0–8–0; Emburey 7–3–18–0; Edmonds 15–3–48–2. *Second Innings*—Williams 6–1–18–0; Hughes 13–5–32–2; Edmonds 22.5–6–42–5; Emburey 13–4–22–3.

Middlesex

G. D. Barlow lbw b Stevenson	105	N. F. Williams c C. L. Smith b Malone.. 39
W. N. Slack lbw b Tremlett	 27	S. P. Hughes b Tremlett 1
K. P. Tomlins b Southern	 77	C. T. Radley absent hurt
R. O. Butcher b Malone	 37	B 1, l-b 9, n-b 5...................... 15
*J. E. Emburey lbw b Malone	 0	
†P. R. Downton c Cowley b Stevenson.. 16		1/81 2/184 3/249 361
P. H. Edmonds c Parks b Stevenson.... 11		4/249 5/273 6/277
K. D. James not out	 33	7/288 8/356 9/361

Bonus points – Middlesex 4, Hampshire 3 (Score at 100 overs: 313-7).

Bowling: Stevenson 32–5–111–3; Malone 22–2–85–3; Tremlett 31.5–10–82–2; Cowley 2–0–14–0; Southern 18–5–53–1; Nicholas 2–1–1–0.

Umpires: C. Cook and R. A. White.

At Worcester, June 18, 20, 21. MIDDLESEX beat WORCESTERSHIRE by 75 runs.

At Cambridge, June 22, 23, 24. MIDDLESEX beat CAMBRIDGE UNIVERSITY by an innings and 30 runs.

At Chesterfield, June 25, 26. MIDDLESEX beat DERBYSHIRE by nine wickets.

At Birmingham, July 2, 4, 5. MIDDLESEX lost to WARWICKSHIRE by 167 runs.

At Lord's, July 9, 10, 11. MIDDLESEX drew with NEW ZEALANDERS (See New Zealand tour section).

At Bristol, July 13, 14, 15. MIDDLESEX beat GLOUCESTERSHIRE by an innings and 69 runs.

MIDDLESEX v LEICESTERSHIRE

At Lord's, July 16, 18, 19. Middlesex won by 180 runs. Middlesex 23 pts, Leicestershire 4 pts. Playing their first Championship match at Lord's for seven weeks, Middlesex were in command from the time Slack and Gatting added 93 for the third wicket either side of lunch on the first day. On a pitch without much pace, the accuracy of Cook and Steele, the slow left-armers, restricted Middlesex to three batting points in spite of Butcher's 62. Leicestershire were in danger of being forced to follow on until Clift and Taylor, helped by faulty catching, put on 53 for the ninth wicket, but Middlesex retained control. Despite an hour lost to a thunderstorm on the second evening, and a seven-minute delay while a helmetless Butcher was carried off *en route* to hospital after being hit in the face by a rising ball from Ferris, Gatting was able to leave his bowlers 322 minutes to win the match. Thanks to an incisive opening spell by Williams, who seamed the ball away from the bat at rapid pace, Leicestershire were quickly drained of hope and the match ended before tea. Emburey put up one of his best all-round performances, scoring 47 and 73 not out and taking eight for 22 in 21.2 overs.

Middlesex

G. D. Barlow c Cook b Taylor	10	– b Taylor	7
W. N. Slack b Cook	52	– lbw b Steele	55
C. T. Radley c Clift b Taylor	2	– lbw b Taylor	2
*M. W. Gatting c and b Steele	54	– lbw b Ferris	2
R. O. Butcher c Steele b Cook	62	– retired hurt	15
J. E. Emburey c Butcher b Clift	47	– not out	73
†P. R. Downton b Clift	25	– not out	19
N. F. Williams c Whitaker b Clift	6		
J. D. Carr not out	12		
S. P. Hughes b Ferris	1		
W. W. Daniel c Butcher b Ferris	4		
B 5, l-b 8, w 3, n-b 1	17	B 7, l-b 6, w 1, n-b 4	18

1/24 2/28 3/121 4/127   292   1/14 2/16 3/21   (4 wkts dec.) 191
5/215 6/251 7/260 8/274 9/277   4/119

Bonus points – Middlesex 3, Leicestershire 3 (Score at 100 overs: 276-8).

Bowling: *First Innings*—Taylor 15–2–48–2; Ferris 12–0–41–2; Clift 20–5–50–3; Cook 33–8–65–2; Steele 25–8–71–1. *Second Innings*—Taylor 11–1–39–2; Ferris 15–3–57–1; Cook 8–3–18–0; Clift 9–1–38–0; Steele 5–1–21–1.

Leicestershire

I. P. Butcher c Downton b Williams	16	– c Downton b Williams	16
J. F. Steele c Butcher b Emburey	5	– (8) c Barlow b Daniel	0
T. J. Boon b Emburey	5	– (7) b Daniel	3
N. E. Briers c Slack b Emburey	7	– (3) c Downton b Williams	2
B. F. Davison c Radley b Hughes	20	– (4) c Downton b Williams	12
J. J. Whitaker b Daniel	4	– (2) c Williams b Emburey	24
*†R. W. Tolchard lbw b Daniel	8	– (6) not out	41
P. B. Clift not out	44	– (5) lbw b Daniel	32
N. G. B. Cook lbw b Daniel	4	– lbw b Emburey	5
L. B. Taylor c Butcher b Daniel	21	– b Emburey	0
G. J. F. Ferris lbw b Emburey	6	– b Emburey	0
B 6, l-b 3, n-b 11	20	N-b 8	8

1/15 2/21 3/30 4/48   160   1/19 2/32 3/54 4/58   143
5/60 6/60 7/73 8/85 9/138   5/119 6/127 7/127 8/143 9/143

Bonus points – Leicestershire 1, Middlesex 4.

Bowling: *First Innings*—Daniel 14–2–50–4; Hughes 12–2–37–1; Emburey 12–8–8–4; Williams 13–1–45–1. *Second Innings*—Williams 14–2–58–3; Daniel 11–4–26–3; Emburey 9.2–3–14–4; Hughes 4–0–32–0; Gatting 3–1–5–0.

Umpires: D. J. Constant and R. Julian.

MIDDLESEX v WARWICKSHIRE

At Lord's, July 30, August 1, 2. Middlesex won by eight wickets. Middlesex 24 pts, Warwickshire 4 pts. Interruptions on the last day delayed Middlesex's victory until eight overs from the end. K. D. Smith held Warwickshire's first innings together after they had won the toss, but on a slow pitch he was unable to take control. On the second day the reigning champions imposed their authority. After the openers had put on 168, three quick wickets by Gifford briefly brought Warwickshire into the game; but after a tentative half hour, Gatting won back the initiative with typical gusto. He batted 150 minutes, hitting two 6s and twelve 4s, and adding 170 in 122 minutes with Emburey. On the third day, Kallicharran, and later Humpage, threatened to put victory out of Middlesex's reach, helped by intermittent showers. But Daniel struck three rapid blows to end resistance, and a target of 79 off twenty overs posed no problems.

Warwickshire

K. D. Smith c Gatting b Emburey	103	– (2) lbw b Emburey	18
T. A. Lloyd c Gatting b Williams	0	– (1) b Hughes	40
A. I. Kallicharran b Williams	7	– c Barlow b Emburey	55
D. L. Amiss c Downton b Daniel	5	– c Gatting b Williams	7
†G. W. Humpage lbw b Gatting	22	– b Hughes	25
R. I. H. B. Dyer c Downton b Daniel	3	– c Downton b Daniel	10
P. A. Smith c Barlow b Gatting	25	– b Emburey	5
A. M. Ferreira b Emburey	23	– lbw b Daniel	21
G. C. Small c and b Emburey	11	– not out	0
*N. Gifford not out	27	– c Emburey b Daniel	0
W. Hogg lbw b Emburey	0	– b Daniel	0
B 2, l-b 7, w 3, n-b 15	27	B 8, l-b 1, w 1, n-b 19	29
	253		**210**

1/10 2/19 3/24 4/74   253   1/51 2/76 3/95 4/166   210
5/95 6/132 7/174 8/194 9/251   5/169 6/180 7/201 8/210 9/210

Bonus points – Warwickshire 3, Middlesex 4.

Bowling: *First Innings*—Williams 12–3–38–2; Daniel 15–2–65–2; Emburey 26–12–48–4; Hughes 14–1–38–0; Gatting 16–7–28–2; Carr 4–2–7–0; Slack 3–2–2–0. *Second Innings*—Williams 12–1–56–1; Daniel 11.4–1–33–4; Emburey 23–11–42–3; Hughes 14–6–30–2; Gatting 1–0–3–0; Carr 8–1–17–0.

Middlesex

G. D. Barlow b Gifford	83	– b Small	6
W. N. Slack lbw b Ferreira	81	– b Hogg	14
C. T. Radley lbw b Gifford	4	– not out	31
*M. W. Gatting c Dyer b Small	116	– not out	20
K. P. Tomlins b Gifford	0		
J. E. Emburey b Hogg	61		
†P. R. Downton c Kallicharran b Small	6		
N. F. Williams not out	3		
W. W. Daniel b Hogg	0		
J. D. Carr not out	1		
B 5, l-b 20, w 1, n-b 4	30	L-b 6, w 1, n-b 3	10
	(8 wkts dec.) 385		**(2 wkts) 81**

1/168 2/176 3/189 4/191   (8 wkts dec.) 385   1/12 2/22   (2 wkts) 81
5/361 6/376 7/382 8/383

S. P. Hughes did not bat.

Bonus points – Middlesex 4, Warwickshire 1 (Score at 100 overs: 357-4).

Bowling: *First Innings*—Small 25–2–95–2; Hogg 20–4–69–2; Gifford 34–8–113–3; Ferreira 26–7–66–1; P. A. Smith 4–0–12–0. *Second Innings*—Small 1.5–0–5–1; Hogg 6–0–27–1; Ferreira 5.1–0–21–0; Gifford 2–0–10–0; P. A. Smith 1.2–0–8–0.

Umpires: J. H. Harris and J. van Geloven.

At Chelmsford, August 6, 8, 9. MIDDLESEX drew with ESSEX.

At Northampton, August 10, 11, 12. MIDDLESEX lost to NORTHAMPTONSHIRE by nine wickets.

At Manchester, August 13, 15, 16. MIDDLESEX drew with LANCASHIRE.

MIDDLESEX v SOMERSET

At Lord's, August 20, 22, 23. Somerset won by 33 runs. Somerset 22 pts, Middlesex 6 pts. After level first innings, distinguished by Gatting's third hundred of the month (162 minutes, two 6s and fifteen 4s), an electric storm on the second afternoon transformed what until then had been an unremarkable encounter. Lashed by almost cyclonic winds, the rain fell with such intensity that in twenty minutes it not only flooded the ground but the Long Room also. When the game continued after an early lunch on the third day, the spinners experienced the pleasure of bowling on a drying pitch for the first time since full covering was introduced in 1981. Somerset, 72 for one when they were so emphatically interrupted, were spun out for 47 more in 115 minutes. Needing 127 in 145 minutes against less skilful spinners, Middlesex were warm favourites when they reached tea at 15 for one. However, rain delayed the resumption for 40 minutes, and with 112 needed in 80 minutes the clock became a factor. When Booth, Somerset's nineteen-year-old left-arm spinner, bowled Daniel in the fifth last over, Middlesex, leaders of the Championship since June 7, had lost their place to Essex.

Somerset

J. W. Lloyds run out	21	– lbw b Emburey	32
P. M. Roebuck c Downton b Cowans	33	– retired hurt	10
R. L. Ollis c Radley b Emburey	21	– st Downton b Emburey	22
I. V. A. Richards b Emburey	35	– c Emburey b Edmonds	20
N. F. M. Popplewell c Gatting b Williams	25	– c Radley b Emburey	2
*I. T. Botham c Williams b Emburey	36	– b Edmonds	10
V. J. Marks c Williams b Emburey	7	– c Emburey b Edmonds	0
†T. Gard c Gatting b Emburey	23	– c Radley b Edmonds	0
M. R. Davis c Downton b Williams	2	– lbw b Edmonds	10
J. Garner c Emburey b Daniel	25	– c Downton b Emburey	2
S. C. Booth not out	1	– not out	0
B 4, l-b 4, w 1, n-b 11	20	B 3, l-b 3 n-b 5	11
	249		**119**

1/44 2/77 3/106 4/125   1/49 2/78 3/83 4/98
5/165 6/172 7/204 8/219 9/227   5/98 6/102 7/117 8/119 9/119

Bonus points – Somerset 2, Middlesex 4.

Bowling: *First Innings*—Daniel 13.1–2–30–1; Cowans 8–0–37–1; Williams 18–3–54–2; Edmonds 20–6–54–0; Emburey 21–8–54–4. *Second Innings*—Daniel 8–2–21–0; Cowans 5–1–18–0; Williams 7–2–21–0; Emburey 23–11–28–4; Edmonds 16.5–10–19–5; Gatting 1–0–1–0.

Middlesex

G. D. Barlow c Ollis b Davis	18	– b Lloyds	8
A. J. T. Miller lbw b Davis	6	– c Popplewell b Marks	3
K. P. Tomlins b Garner	4	– (5) c and b Booth	38
*M. W. Gatting b Marks	105	– run out	0
C. T. Radley lbw b Garner	11	– (3) c Gard b Garner	20
J. E. Emburey c Botham b Booth	63	– c sub b Marks	7
†P. R. Downton c and b Marks	1	– c Lloyds b Booth	0
N. F. Williams c sub b Booth	4	– (9) c Botham b Booth	0
P. H. Edmonds lbw b Booth	0	– (8) c Garner b Marks	0
W. W. Daniel not out	17	– b Booth	9
N. G. Cowans lbw b Marks	6	– not out	5
L-b 4, n-b 3	7	L-b 3	3
	242		**93**

1/18 2/25 3/35 4/91   1/7 2/15 3/16 4/39
5/193 6/195 7/208 8/210 9/219   5/79 6/79 7/79 8/79 9/79

Bonus points – Middlesex 2, Somerset 4.

Bowling: *First Innings*—Garner 15–4–63–2; Davis 13–3–69–2; Booth 12–2–21–3; Marks 16.5–2–59–3; Botham 6–1–23–0. *Second Innings*—Garner 7–1–27–1; Botham 1–0–2–0; Marks 6–3–17–3; Booth 7.4–2–26–4; Lloyds 6–2–18–1.

Umpires: J. W. Holder and R. Palmer.

MIDDLESEX v SURREY

At Lord's, August 24, 25, 26. Middlesex won by 103 runs. Middlesex 23 pts, Surrey 5 pts. Knight gave Middlesex first innings in the expectation that a pitch still damp from its flooding two days earlier would be of help to Clarke. But conditions proved deceptive and, following the loss of 70 minutes through bad light, Barlow and his new left-handed partner, Miller, built the foundations of what was to prove a useful score with a hard-earned stand of 91, Barlow's 113 coming in 250 minutes. After Surrey had batted poorly to concede a lead of 62, Miller, Radley and Tomlins pressed home Middlesex's advantage, setting up a declaration requiring 244 in 200 minutes. With the ball now turning, Emburey and Edmonds were soon in partnership, only Knight providing troublesome resistance as Surrey were bowled out with twenty minutes left for play.

Middlesex

G. D. Barlow c Butcher b Clarke	113	– c Payne b Clarke 2
A. J. T. Miller b Needham	43	– b Curtis 59
C. T. Radley lbw b Payne	27	– c Clarke b Pocock 45
K. P. Tomlins c Stewart b Payne	4	– c Knight b Curtis 45
R. G. P. Ellis c Stewart b Payne	27	– (6) c Lynch b Curtis 11
*J. E. Emburey c Clarke	11	– (5) st Stewart b Curtis 1
†P. R. Downton b Payne	1	– lbw b Knight 3
N. F. Williams c Curtis b Pocock	9	– not out 1
K. D. James not out	20	
W. W. Daniel b Clarke	18	
B 5, l-b 9, n-b 8	22	B 7, l-b 5, n-b 2 14

1/91 2/189 3/197 4/201 (9 wkts dec.) 295 1/2 2/89 3/146 (7 wkts dec.) 181
5/214 6/216 7/234 8/262 9/295   4/160 5/165 6/173 7/181

P. H. Edmonds did not bat.

Bonus points – Middlesex 3, Surrey 3 (Score at 100 overs: 253-7).

Bowling: *First Innings*—Clarke 27.1–5–83–3; Payne 24–7–56–4; Pocock 27–9–59–1; Curtis 9–0–28–0; Knight 9–3–26–0; Needham 12–4–21–1. *Second Innings*—Clarke 10–3–23–1; Payne 14–3–45–0; Pocock 15–5–34–1; Needham 6–0–30–0; Curtis 3.3–0–14–4; Knight 3–0–21–1.

Surrey

A. R. Butcher c Radley b Daniel	19	– c Radley b Williams 13
D. B. Pauline c Tomlins b Emburey	26	– c Emburey b Edmonds 20
A. J. Stewart c Radley b Emburey	31	– lbw b Williams 5
*R. D. V. Knight b Edmonds	7	– b Emburey 40
M. A. Lynch b Emburey	2	– c Tomlins b Edmonds 6
†C. J. Richards b Williams	24	– c Tomlins b Emburey 4
I. R. Payne not out	40	– b Emburey 13
A. Needham lbw b Williams	11	– (9) c Radley b Edmonds 3
S. T. Clarke run out	37	– (8) not out 18
P. I. Pocock lbw b Williams	0	– c Radley b Emburey 6
I. J. Curtis c Tomlins b Williams	1	– c Ellis b Emburey 4
B 7, l-b 7, w 2, n-b 19	35	L-b 2, n-b 6 8

1/28 2/76 3/89 4/92   233 1/21 2/35 3/61 4/76   140
5/101 6/128 7/177 8/221 9/222   5/92 6/99 7/110 8/117 9/124

Bonus points – Surrey 2, Middlesex 4.

Bowling: *First Innings*—Daniel 11–0–59–1; Williams 18–8–41–4; Edmonds 33–11–48–1; James 4–2–10–0; Emburey 28–12–40–3. *Second Innings*—Williams 9–1–25–2; Daniel 6–0–26–0; Emburey 22.1–2–38–5; Edmonds 21–9–42–3; James 1–0–1–0.

Umpires: J. W. Holder and R. Palmer.

At Hove, August 27, 29, 30. MIDDLESEX drew with SUSSEX.

At Leeds, August 31, September 1, 2. MIDDLESEX drew with YORKSHIRE.

MIDDLESEX v NORTHAMPTONSHIRE

At Lord's, September 7, 8, 9. Northamptonshire won by seven wickets. Northamptonshire 21 pts, Middlesex 6 pts. Middlesex looked to have won a valuable toss, but, following their highest opening stand of the season – 180 in 51 overs – they got into such a tangle that it was not until the fifth ball of the 100th over that they secured maximum batting points. On a slow, turning pitch, the champions had a glimpse of a much-needed victory when, after a brilliant 82 by Cook, Northamptonshire slumped to 140 for five on the second morning. But the loss of 215 minutes in the last two sessions, combined with a recovery by Lamb and Capel, cost them the initiative. Cook then threw Middlesex a life-line by declaring 128 behind on the third morning – a gamble vindicated by events. Northamptonshire were set 272 in 247 minutes. Larkins launched them with a powerful 100 in 143 minutes, and with rain threatening, Lamb assaulted Edmonds so vigorously that they galloped to the target in the tenth of the final twenty overs.

Middlesex

G. D. Barlow c Larkins b Mallender	99	– not out	89
A. J. T. Miller c Steele b Capel	74	– b Williams	44
C. T. Radley c Walker b Steele	54	– not out	5
*M. W. Gatting b Williams	25		
K. P. Tomlins b Williams	6		
J. E. Emburey c Walker b Steele	19		
†P. R. Downton c Griffiths b Williams	2		
P. H. Edmonds b Mallender	6		
N. F. Williams not out	35		
S. P. Hughes not out	0		
B 1, l-b 7, n-b 2	10	B 1, l-b 3, w 1	5

1/180 2/186 3/255 4/267   (8 wkts dec.) 330   1/118   (1 wkt dec.) 143
5/267 6/288 7/288 8/317

W. W. Daniel did not bat.

Bonus points – Middlesex 4, Northamptonshire 3 (Score at 100 overs: 305-7).

Bowling: *First Innings*—Mallender 16–2–53–2; Walker 17.4–2–64–0; Griffiths 13–4–32–0; Williams 25–3–77–3; Steele 23–6–73–2; Capel 11–5–21–1. *Second Innings*—Mallender 5–0–27–0; Griffiths 9–0–47–0; Walker 5–0–28–0; Williams 6–1–24–1; Steele 4.4–1–12–0.

Northamptonshire

*G. Cook c Barlow b Edmonds	82	– b Emburey	30
W. Larkins lbw b Edmonds	13	– c Edmonds b Daniel	100
N. A. Mallender b Daniel	21		
R. J. Boyd-Moss c Barlow b Emburey	6	– (3) c Downton b Emburey	13
A. J. Lamb not out	44	– (4) not out	79
R. G. Williams c Radley b Edmonds	6	– (5) not out	36
D. J. Capel not out	19		
L-b 5, n-b 6	11	B 2, l-b 5, n-b 10	17

1/20 2/120 3/133 4/133   (5 wkts dec.) 202   1/101 2/137 3/170   (3 wkts) 275
5/140

D. S. Steele, †G. Sharp, A. Walker and B. J. Griffiths did not bat.

Bonus points – Northamptonshire 2, Middlesex 2.

Bowling: *First Innings*—Daniel 7–2–26–1; Williams 4–0–29–0; Edmonds 26–4–76–3; Emburey 27.5–9–60–1. *Second Innings*—Daniel 9–0–33–1; Hughes 8–2–30–0; Edmonds 23.4–2–131–0; Emburey 23–6–64–2.

Umpires: W. E. Alley and M. J. Kitchen.

At Nottingham, September 10, 12, 13. MIDDLESEX drew with NOTTINGHAMSHIRE.

THE CRICKETER CUP WINNERS 1967-1983

Sponsored by *The Cricketer*

1967	REPTON PILGRIMS	beat Radley Rangers by 96 runs.

Final Sponsored by Champagne Mercier

1968	OLD MALVERNIANS	beat Harrow Wanderers by five wickets.
1969	OLD BRIGHTONIANS	beat Stowe Templers by 156 runs.
1970	OLD WYKEHAMISTS	beat Old Tonbridgians by 94 runs.

Final Sponsored by Moet & Chandon

1971	OLD TONBRIDGIANS	beat Charterhouse Friars on faster scoring-rate.
1972	OLD TONBRIDGIANS	beat Old Malvernians by 114 runs.
1973	RUGBY METEORS	beat Old Tonbridgians by five wickets.
1974	OLD WYKEHAMISTS	beat Old Alleynians on faster scoring-rate.
1975	OLD MALVERNIANS	beat Harrow Wanderers by 97 runs.
1976	OLD TONBRIDGIANS	beat Old Blundellians by 170 runs.
1977	SHREWSBURY SARACENS	beat Oundle Rovers by nine wickets.
1978	CHARTERHOUSE FRIARS	beat Oundle Rovers by nine wickets.
1979	OLD TONBRIDGIANS	beat Uppingham Rovers by 5 runs.
1980	MARLBOROUGH BLUES	beat Old Wellingtonians by 31 runs.
1981	CHARTERHOUSE FRIARS	beat Old Wykehamists by nine wickets.
1982	OLD WYKEHAMISTS	beat Old Malvernians on run rate.
1983	REPTON PILGRIMS	beat Haileybury Hermits by seven wickets.

All played at Burton Court, Chelsea.

NORTHAMPTONSHIRE

President: D. Brookes
Chairman: D. C. Lucas
Chairman, Cricket Committee: A. P. Arnold
Secretary: K. C. Turner
  County Ground, Wantage Road,
  Northampton NN1 4TJ
  (Telephone: 0604-32917)
Captain: G. Cook
Coach: B. L. Reynolds

Northamptonshire's season revolved round a series of improved Schweppes County Championship performances which earned sixth place in the table, their highest since 1976. They won seven matches, two more than in the previous season when four late victories had paved the way in confidence for continued progress in 1983. Washed-out third days also prevented two more likely successes when commanding situations had been achieved.

Geoff Cook, the captain, said progress was largely made because the batsmen scored quickly enough to give the bowlers time to dismiss the opposition. After expressing some disappointment with the bowling performances of the Indian captain, Kapil Dev, Cook said how well the other bowlers had done to gain 77 bonus points, a number exceeded only by Essex and Leicestershire.

The absence of a top-class strike bowler was the one department where Northamptonshire were lacking. Much was expected from Kapil Dev, who had made limited appearances in the two previous seasons. To cover his anticipated absence in the World Cup, the club engaged Jim Carse from Eastern Province. But things did not work out as hoped. In all Kapil Dev made just seven Championship appearances, taking sixteen wickets at 24.06. To make matters worse, Carse injured a rib and was out for a month over the World Cup period. He did, however, take an excellent five for 43 at Cardiff on his final appearance. The official comment on both these bowlers was that a decision would be deferred regarding an overseas player for 1984.

Nevertheless, for the most part the bowling force had one of its best recent seasons, aided by more helpful Northampton pitches. The 41-year-old David Steele was again the most successful with his orthodox left-arm spin, capably aided by the off-breaks of Richard Williams and Peter Willey. Jim Griffiths retained his consistency in the pace section, with Neil Mallender continuing to progress and Alan Walker, aged twenty, a recruit from Yorkshire, showing considerable promise. After playing intermittently Tim Lamb decided to retire after six years with the county.

Cook himself must take much credit for Northamptonshire's Championship improvement. Always striving for a result, he was ready to declare behind on the first innings and then lead a run-chase. His reliable batting brought 1,510 first-class runs. Strangely his only century came in the final match, yet he had eleven fifties. Cook also took 31 catches, and even kept wicket when George Sharp was injured. His opening partner, Wayne Larkins, had a remarkable season. Initially handicapped by three separate finger injuries on the same hand, he scored only 255 runs in May and June. He then hit a career-best 236 at Derby in July, and surpassed it with 252 at Cardiff at the end of August. In between he scored 187 against Lancashire when sharing a club record second-wicket stand of 342 with Willey. Scoring 816 runs in August, Larkins ended up as top scorer with 1,774. He also scored an unbeaten 172 against Warwickshire, a John Player League record until beaten a month later by Gooch.

Willey, however, created most discussion. First to 1,000 runs, he finished with 1,546 and was voted Northamptonshire's "Player of the Year" for the second season in succession. But he refused a new one-year contract, signing instead for Leicestershire for three years, which caused some public criticism of the committee. Willey had caused controversy in April by giving evidence, together with Larkins, at an Industrial Tribunal against the club on behalf of the dismissed groundsman, Les Bentley, who lost his appeal. Both players were then interviewed by the cricket committee. Although no details were revealed it was generally thought that Willey gave no assurances about his future attitude. His career spanned eighteen years with Northamptonshire and he played for England twenty times. One of the South African "rebels", Willey produced his most prolific run-getting since being banned for three years from Test cricket.

England calls limited Allan Lamb to 21 innings for the county, but he produced excellent batting to top the averages. Williams showed a welcome return to form after a couple of lean seasons. The Cambridge Blue, Robin Boyd-Moss, and David Capel gave more evidence of their potential. Although now down the order, Steele still proved a batsman of worth. Sharp, with 536 runs, also helped and was unfortunate to miss his first century by 2 runs in a vital rescue innings against Yorkshire.

But the story of Northamptonshire cricket in 1983 was entirely different in the one-day competitions. Although reaching the quarter-finals of the two knockouts, they were then heavily beaten by Lancashire in the Benson and Hedges Cup and by Middlesex in the NatWest Bank Trophy. A crumb of comfort was success in the Tilcon Trophy at Harrogate for the second year running.

The John Player League was also a failure, the county dropping from eighth place to fifteenth. Four wins came in an early-season spell, to raise hopes, but only one followed. In contrast to the Championship, the Sunday batting was mediocre and the run-rate one of the worst in the competition. Critics thought the attitude was not right, batsmen not applying themselves in the way they should, and that this was something to be sorted out by 1984. – F.S.

NORTHAMPTONSHIRE 1983

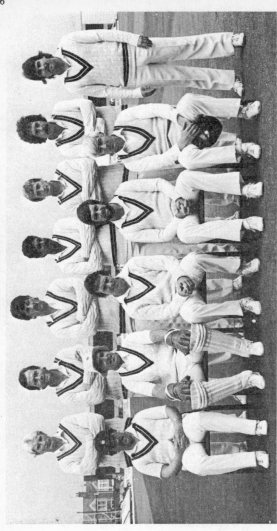

[*Bill Smith*]

Back row: N. A. Mallender, T. M. Lamb, B. J. Griffiths, Kapil Dev, D. J. Capel, W. Larkins, A. J. Lamb. *Front row*: R. G. Williams, G. Sharp, G. Cook (*captain*), P. Willey, D. S. Steele.

NORTHAMPTONSHIRE RESULTS

All first-class matches – Played 26: Won 8, Lost 4, Drawn 14.

County Championship matches – Played 24: Won 7, Lost 4, Drawn 13.

Bonus points – Batting 63, Bowling 77.

Competition placings – Schweppes County Championship, 6th; NatWest Bank Trophy, q-f;
Benson and Hedges Cup, q-f; John Player League, 15th eq.

COUNTY CHAMPIONSHIP AVERAGES

BATTING

	Birthplace	M	I	NO	R	HI	Avge
J. A. Carse..............	*Salisbury, S. Rhodesia*	10	10	8	129	36*	64.50
A. J. Lambc..............	*Langebaanweg, SA*	13	21	5	840	119	52.50
P. Willeyc..............	*Sedgefield*	22	38	7	1,483	175*	47.83
Kapil Dev	*Chandigarh, India*	7	10	2	349	120	43.62
W. Larkinsc.............	*Roxton*	24	41	0	1,739	252	42.41
G. Cookc..............	*Middlesbrough*	23	40	3	1,496	128	40.43
R. G. Williamsc.........	*Bangor*	24	37	8	1,161	104*	40.03
R. J. Boyd-Moss.....	*Hatton, Ceylon*	15	24	2	704	101	32.00
G. Sharpc..............	*West Hartlepool*	22	23	8	447	98	29.80
D. J. Capel	*Northampton*	16	22	4	470	109*	26.11
D. S. Steelec	*Stoke-on-Trent*	24	29	6	506	60	22.00
M. J. Bamber	*Cheam*	5	10	1	163	44	18.11
A. Walker	*Emley*	5	4	3	18	7*	18.00
N. A. Mallender.......	*Kirksandall*	21	25	7	238	24*	13.22
D. J. Wild	*Northampton*	3	5	0	64	29	12.80
T. M. Lambc..........	*Hartford*	7	9	1	36	21	4.50
B. J. Griffithsc.........	*Wellingborough*	22	13	2	27	15	2.45

Also batted: R. J. Bailey (*Stoke-on-Trent*) (1 match) 4.

*Signifies not out.   cDenotes county cap.

BOWLING

	O	M	R	W	Avge	BB
D. S. Steele.............	643.2	235	1,415	66	21.43	5-48
R. G. Williams........	363.3	109	906	42	21.57	4-18
T. M. Lamb.............	122.1	36	261	11	23.72	4-49
Kapil Dev	161	47	385	16	24.06	4-24
A. Walker	123.4	22	438	17	25.76	4-61
B. J. Griffiths.........	536.2	130	1,424	50	28.48	6-92
P. Willey.................	458.5	142	956	31	30.83	4-51
N. A. Mallender......	465.1	95	1,501	48	31.27	6-48
J. A. Carse.............	237	50	719	22	32.68	5-43

Also bowled: R. J. Boyd-Moss 11–5–15–1; D. J. Capel 57.5–12–194–4; G. Cook 11–3–43–0; A. J. Lamb 1–0–1–0; W. Larkins 25.4–3–67–5; D. J. Wild 23–7–72–2.

The following played a total of seventeen three-figure innings for Northamptonshire in County Championship matches – W. Larkins 5, P. Willey 4, A. J. Lamb 3, R. J. Boyd-Moss 1, D. J. Capel 1, G. Cook 1, Kapil Dev 1, R. G. Williams 1.

At Birmingham, April 30, May 2, 3. NORTHAMPTONSHIRE drew with WARWICK-SHIRE.

NORTHAMPTONSHIRE v HAMPSHIRE

At Northampton, May 4, 5, 6. Drawn. Northamptonshire 7 pts, Hampshire 4 pts. Hampshire must have regretted putting Northamptonshire in for, despite capable bowling by Malone, they were forced to follow on 169 behind. Their plans were upset by Willey, whose masterly unbeaten 175 included twenty 4s in 352 minutes. After promising early batting by Smith and Nicholas, Hampshire slumped against Northamptonshire's seam bowling. Rain, however, delayed play for an hour on the third morning and stubborn half-centuries by Tremlett and Jesty thwarted the home bid.

Northamptonshire

*G. Cook lbw b Malone	14	†G. Sharp c Cowley b Nicholas	11
W. Larkins lbw b Malone	27	N. A. Mallender b Malone	2
P. Willey not out	175	J. A. Carse not out	36
A. J. Lamb c Southern b Tremlett	14	B 9, l-b 9, w 1, n-b 15	34
R. G. Williams c Parks b Emery	6		
D. J. Capel c Parks b Malone	8	1/31 2/76 3/95 4/102 (8 wkts dec.) 346
D. S. Steele b Tremlett	19	5/157 6/198 7/243 8/264

B. J. Griffiths did not bat.

Bonus points – Northamptonshire 3, Hampshire 3 (Score at 100 overs: 283-8).

Bowling: Emery 22–3–87–1; Malone 27–6–93–4; Southern 15–9–12–0; Tremlett 20–10–29–2; Jesty 14–4–31–0; Cowley 11–0–30–0; Nicholas 6–0–30–1.

Hampshire

T. M. Tremlett c Sharp b Steele	9	– c Sharp b Steele	59
C. L. Smith c Sharp b Griffiths	55	– c Steele b Mallender	36
M. C. J. Nicholas c Larkins b Mallender	44	– lbw b Carse	5
T. E. Jesty b Carse	8	– not out	53
D. R. Turner b Griffiths	13	– c Sharp b Steele	18
*N. E. J. Pocock lbw b Mallender	4	– hit wkt b Steele	0
N. G. Cowley lbw b Carse	2	– not out	14
†R. J. Parks c Capel b Steele	15		
J. W. Southern lbw b Willey	7		
K. St J. D. Emery lbw b Carse	8		
S. J. Malone not out	0		
B 2, l-b 5, w 1, n-b 4	12	B 4, l-b 13, n-b 2	19

1/31 2/89 3/113 4/133   177   1/67 2/94 3/118   (5 wkts) 204
5/139 6/144 7/146 8/157 9/177   4/169 4/169

Bonus points – Hampshire 1, Northamptonshire 4.

Bowling: *First Innings*—Carse 18–2–54–3; Griffiths 17–6–28–2; Steele 17–11–21–2; Willey 14–5–26–1; Mallender 15–5–22–2; Williams 4–0–14–0. *Second Innings*—Carse 12–2–29–1; Griffiths 10–2–30–0; Willey 14–2–28–0; Williams 11–2–27–0; Steele 19–8–24–3; Mallender 9–3–25–1; Capel 4–0–17–0; Cook 1–0–4–0; Lamb 1–0–1–0.

Umpires: P. J. Eele and B. Leadbeater.

NORTHAMPTONSHIRE v NOTTINGHAMSHIRE

At Northampton, May 11, 12, 13. Drawn. Northamptonshire 1 pt. Only 68 overs were possible on the first day before rain prevented any play at all on the last two days. After Larkins had helped to put on 49 in thirteen overs, his partner, Cook, reached an excellent 71, containing eleven 4s. Willey and Lamb scored steadily against a visitors' attack that gained little aid from the pitch.

Northamptonshire

*G. Cook c Birch b Saxelby	71	
W. Larkins c Hassan b Hadlee	28	
P. Willey not out	52	
A. J. Lamb not out	43	
L-b 4	4	

1/49 2/113   (2 wkts) 198

R. G. Williams, D. J. Capel, D. S. Steele, †G. Sharp, N. A. Mallender, J. A. Carse and B. J. Griffiths did not bat.

Bonus points – Northamptonshire 1.

Bowling: Hadlee 10–3–40–1; Hendrick 6–2–10–0; Cooper 15–5–38–0; Saxelby 11–3–29–1; Hemmings 26–4–77–0.

Nottinghamshire

R. T. Robinson, B. Hassan, D. W. Randall, *C. E. B. Rice, J. D. Birch, R. J. Hadlee, †B. N. French, K. Saxelby, E. E. Hemmings, K. E. Cooper and M. Hendrick.

Umpires: H. D. Bird and A. Jepson.

At Bradford, May 25, 26, 27. NORTHAMPTONSHIRE drew with YORKSHIRE.

NORTHAMPTONSHIRE v LEICESTERSHIRE

At Northampton, May 28, 30, 31. Drawn. Northamptonshire 4 pts, Leicestershire 3 pts. After a blank first day both captains strove for a result. Put in on a seamers' wicket Leicestershire struggled against Griffiths and Tim Lamb, despite Balderstone's 132-minute half-century. Northamptonshire declared 145 runs behind, and in turn Tolchard set Northamptonshire to score 257 in 220 minutes. This final innings fluctuated sharply. Northamptonshire began aggressively, reaching 147 before the second wicket fell, but then Nick Cook and John Steele, aided by some erratic batting, effected a slump, and Sharp and Mallender had to cling on for a draw.

Leicestershire

J. C. Balderstone c Kapil Dev b T. M. Lamb....	51	– c and b Mallender....................	10
R. A. Cobb b Mallender.................................	7	– c A. J. Lamb b Steele..............	28
D. I. Gower c Sharp b T. M. Lamb	20	– c and b Kapil Dev....................	2
B. F. Davison b T. M. Lamb	37	– not out	39
N. E. Briers lbw b T. M. Lamb.....................	37		
*†R. W. Tolchard c Kapil Dev b Griffiths	20		
J. F. Steele b Griffiths	0		
G. J. Parsons b Kapil Dev	31	– (5) not out	28
N. G. B. Cook b Griffiths	11		
J. P. Agnew c Sharp b Griffiths....................	0		
L. B. Taylor not out.....................................	1		
L-b 2, n-b 2	4	L-b 4............................	4

1/28 2/59 3/117 4/122   219   1/13 2/16 3/78   (3 wkts dec.) 111
5/151 6/151 7/196 8/211 9/214

Bonus points – Leicestershire 2, Northamptonshire 4.

Bowling: *First Innings*—Kapil Dev 16–3–60–1; Mallender 18–4–60–1; T. M. Lamb 27–9–49–4; Griffiths 16.5–3–46–4; Steele 2–2–0–0. *Second Innings*—Kapil Dev 7–4–11–1; Mallender 7–2–12–1; Willey 15–3–43–0; Steele 14–3–41–1.

Northamptonshire

*G. Cook c Cobb b Taylor	28	– c Tolchard b Taylor.................	66
W. Larkins lbw b Parsons.............................	13	– c Balderstone b Parsons	52
P. Willey c Tolchard b Agnew.......................	8	– b Cook	41
A. J. Lamb not out	21	– c Briers b Taylor	8
T. M. Lamb not out	1	– (9) c Gower b Cook	0
Kapil Dev (did not bat)		– (5) b Cook	3
R. G. Williams (did not bat)...........................		– (6) c Taylor b Steele................	11
D. S. Steele (did not bat)..............................		– (7) c Davison b Steele	1
†G. Sharp (did not bat).................................		– (8) c Balderstone b Cook	14
N. A. Mallender (did not bat).........................		– (10) not out	24
L-b 1, n-b 2	3	B 4, l-b 1, n-b 2.............	7

1/24 2/45 3/64   (3 wkts dec.) 74   1/92 2/147 3/163 4/170   (9 wkts) 227
5/185 6/189 7/189 8/189 9/227

B. J. Griffiths did not bat.

Bonus points – Leicestershire 1.

Bowling: *First Innings*—Taylor 8–3–14–1; Parsons 5–1–22–1; Cook 6–2–14–0; Agnew 3–0–21–1. *Second Innings*—Taylor 13–1–44–2; Agnew 5–0–42–0; Cook 27–6–65–4; Steele 21–3–60–2; Parsons 4–1–9–1.

Umpires: R. Julian and D. R. Shepherd.

At Oxford, June 8, 9, 10. NORTHAMPTONSHIRE beat OXFORD UNIVERSITY by 281 runs.

NORTHAMPTONSHIRE v GLOUCESTERSHIRE

At Northampton, June 11, 13, 14. Northamptonshire won by 141 runs. Northamptonshire 22 pts, Gloucestershire 4 pts. Northamptonshire batted into the second day, amassing a big total that later proved too much for Gloucestershire on a pitch that helped the spinners. Cook led a consistent batting display, troubled only by Graveney. However, missed catches enabled Gloucestershire to avoid the follow-on. Cook and Willey hit freely 'n the second innings to set the visitors a target of 273 in 258 minutes which they never attempted, and despite a two-hour fourth-wicket stand of 64 by Bainbridge and Romaines, the spin of Williams, Steele and Willey gave Northamptonshire their first Championship win of the season.

Northamptonshire

*G. Cook st Russell b Bainbridge	59	– not out	77
W. Larkins c Graveney b Childs	48	– c Russell b Shepherd	0
P. Willey c Russell b Graveney	12	– not out	44
R. J. Boyd-Moss lbw b Graveney	7		
R. G. Williams c Stovold b Childs	35		
D. J. Capel b Graveney	52		
D. S. Steele st Russell b Graveney	60		
D. J. Wild c Shepherd b Childs	29		
†G. Sharp st Russell b Graveney	3		
N. A. Mallender not out	23		
T. M. Lamb c Romaines b Graveney	21		
B 6, l-b 11, w 1, n-b 4	22	L-b 2, n-b 2	4

1/93 2/124 3/128 4/152　　　　　　　371　1/1　　　　(1 wkt dec.) 125
5/178 6/277 7/288 8/310 9/328

Bonus points – Northamptonshire 2, Gloucestershire 2 (Score at 100 overs: 207-5).

Bowling: *First Innings*—Shepherd 25–5–68–0; Lawrence 9–3–27–0; Sainsbury 12–2–44–0; Bainbridge 6–1–18–1; Graveney 47.4–23–88–6; Childs 45–13–104–3. *Second Innings*— Shepherd 11–0–47–1; Lawrence 12–0–59–0; Sainsbury 2–0–15–0.

Gloucestershire

A. W. Stovold c Cook b Lamb	7	– c Sharp b Lamb	0
B. C. Broad lbw b Willey	32	– lbw b Lamb	14
P. Bainbridge c Wild b Steele	31	– b Willey	40
A. J. Hignell c Sharp b Willey	26	– c and b Steele	1
P. W. Romaines c Wild b Williams	19	– c Steele b Williams	29
J. N. Shepherd lbw b Willey	69	– lbw b Steele	3
*D. A. Graveney c Capel b Williams	7	– not out	11
†R. C. Russell c Cook b Williams	8	– c Sharp b Williams	6
J. H. Childs b Williams	0	– c Larkins b Williams	0
G. E. Sainsbury c Capel b Steele	5	– c Steele b Williams	0
D. V. Lawrence not out	7	– b Willey	0
L-b 6, w 1, n-b 6	13	B 10, l-b 11, n-b 6	27

1/16 2/55 3/100 4/102　　　　　　　224　1/0 2/21 3/25 4/89　　　　　131
5/165 6/179 7/212 8/212 9/213　　　　　5/103 6/107 7/120 8/126 9/126

Bonus points – Gloucestershire 2, Northamptonshire 4.

Bowling: *First Innings*—Mallender 5–0–15–0; Lamb 4–1–9–1; Willey 33–10–67–3; Steele 31–11–83–2; Williams 16–6–37–4. *Second Innings*—Lamb 13–6–18–2; Mallender 4–1–9–0; Willey 27.5–9–44–2; Steele 23–17–15–2; Williams 17–10–18–4; Cook 2–2–0–0.

Umpires: J. H. Harris and P. B. Wight.

At Cambridge, June 15, 16, 17. NORTHAMPTONSHIRE drew with CAMBRIDGE UNIVERSITY.

NORTHAMPTONSHIRE v WARWICKSHIRE

At Northampton, June 18, 20, 21. Warwickshire won by 166 runs. Warwickshire 23 pts, Northamptonshire 3 pts. Hit by the absence of three leading seam bowlers, plus a quick injury to medium-pace all-rounder Capel, Northamptonshire relied mainly on the spin of Williams and Steele. Lloyd dominated a fast-scoring opening stand, narrowly missing a deserved century, but the later batsmen played inconsistently, with Humpage the most aggressive. Warwickshire did not enforce the follow-on, but with the pace of Old and the spin of Gifford claiming sixteen wickets in all, they earned a comfortable victory. Championship débutant Bamber batted well in Northamptonshire's first innings, but they never threatened to reach a final target of 321 in 286 minutes and suffered their first defeat of the season.

Warwickshire

T. A. Lloyd c Steele b Mallender	97	– st Sharp b Wild	25
K. D. Smith c Larkins b Mallender	44	– lbw b Steele	30
A. I. Kallicharran c Cook b Williams	29	– b Wild	7
*D. L. Amiss c Sharp b Willey	1	– st Sharp b Steele	7
G. W. Humpage lbw b Williams	47	– b Williams	16
Asif Din b Steele	56	– not out	41
A. M. Ferreira lbw b Steele	1		
†G. A. Tedstone b Williams	36	– (7) c Cook b Williams	36
C. M. Old c and b Williams	1		
N. Gifford b Steele	20		
W. Hogg not out	0		
B 4, l-b 8, w 1, n-b 6	19	L-b 1, w 1, n-b 4	6

1/138 2/153 3/154 4/200   351   1/55 2/66 3/70   (6 wkts dec.) 168
5/243 6/247 7/318 8/323 9/334   4/79 5/91 6/168

Bonus points – Warwickshire 3, Northamptonshire 2 (Score at 100 overs: 278-6).

Bowling: *First Innings*—Mallender 26–4–104–2; Lamb 28.1–7–70–0; Larkins 4–0–16–0; Capel 2.5–0–16–0; Willey 32–6–73–1; Williams 12–2–30–4; Steele 12.4–5–23–3. *Second Innings*—Mallender 15–3–36–0; Lamb 8–1–27–0; Williams 6–4–23–2; Steele 14–9–14–2; Wild 20–5–62–2.

Northamptonshire

*G. Cook run out	29	– c Tedstone b Old	31
W. Larkins c Tedstone b Old	6	– b Old	6
P. Willey c Amiss b Ferreira	38	– c Tedstone b Hogg	4
D. J. Wild c Kallicharran b Gifford	19	– c Tedstone b Old	11
R. G. Williams st Tedstone b Gifford	0	– c Kallicharran b Ferreira	36
M. J. Bamber lbw b Old	44	– c Amiss b Gifford	2
D. S. Steele st Tedstone b Gifford	36	– lbw b Old	30
†G. Sharp b Old	0	– lbw b Gifford	18
D. J. Capel c Ferreira b Gifford	4	– c Asif Din b Gifford	3
N. A. Mallender not out	3	– not out	2
T. M. Lamb c Kallicharran b Old	6	– b Old	2
B 4, l-b 7, w 1, n-b 2	14	L-b 4, n-b 5	9

1/8 2/75 3/78 4/79   199   1/15 2/33 3/49 4/64   154
5/112 6/184 7/184 8/187 9/189   5/89 6/97 7/128 8/150 9/150

Bonus points – Northamptonshire 1, Warwickshire 4.

Bowling: *First Innings*—Hogg 7–2–10–0; Old 16.4–4–48–4; Ferreira 21–2–68–1; Gifford 27–8–53–4; Asif Din 1–0–6–0. *Second Innings*—Hogg 6–0–19–1; Old 17.4–4–50–5; Gifford 25–11–48–3; Ferreira 10–4–28–1.

Umpires: C. Cook and P. J. Eele.

At Ilford, June 22, 23, 24. NORTHAMPTONSHIRE lost to ESSEX by an innings and 51 runs.

At The Oval, June 25, 27, 28. NORTHAMPTONSHIRE drew with SURREY.

At Hove, July 2, 4, 5. NORTHAMPTONSHIRE beat SUSSEX by 119 runs.

NORTHAMPTONSHIRE v YORKSHIRE

At Northampton, July 9, 11, 12. Northamptonshire won by 81 runs. Northamptonshire 22 pts, Yorkshire 5 pts. Set to score 272 in 260 minutes, Yorkshire lost their last man to the fourth ball of the final over. When the last hour began Yorkshire were 171 for five, but in the end the left-arm spin of Steele prevailed. On the first day Northamptonshire were rescued by a career-best 98 from wicket-keeper Sharp. Despite brave middle-order batting Yorkshire then fell 35 behind. Before their declaration Northamptonshire's second innings was boosted by a brilliant century by Allan Lamb who hit one 6 and thirteen 4s.

Northamptonshire

*G. Cook c Boycott b Dennis	0	– c Bairstow b Dennis	51
W. Larkins c Love b Carrick	35	– lbw b Taylor	16
P. Willey lbw b Dennis	13	– c Boycott b Carrick	19
A. J. Lamb lbw b Sidebottom	24	– not out	107
R. G. Williams c Love b Carrick	0	– lbw b Sidebottom	27
R. J. Boyd-Moss c Moxon b Carrick	17	– not out	4
D. S. Steele c Carrick b Dennis	8		
†G. Sharp c Moxon b Taylor	98		
N. A. Mallender st Bairstow b Dennis	11		
T. M. Lamb c Boycott b Sidebottom	3		
B. J. Griffiths not out	1		
B 1, l-b 10, n-b 13	24	B 1, l-b 3, w 2, n-b 6	12

1/0 2/24 3/74 4/75   234   1/24 2/65 3/184   (4 wkts dec.) 236
5/87 6/105 7/117 8/184 9/209   4/227

Bonus points – Northamptonshire 2, Yorkshire 4.

Bowling: *First Innings*—Dennis 17–8–32–4; Taylor 13.5–5–33–1; Carrick 40–21–45–3; Sidebottom 20–1–73–2; Booth 6–0–27–0. *Second Innings*—Dennis 14–3–41–1; Taylor 15–3–59–1; Carrick 27.2–6–64–1; Sidebottom 7–0–37–1; Booth 11–3–23–0.

Yorkshire

G. Boycott c Sharp b Mallender	34	– run out	47
M. D. Moxon c Sharp b Steele	10	– lbw b Mallender	6
S. J. Dennis c and b Steele	0	– (9) not out	10
C. W. J. Athey lbw b Steele	8	– (3) c and b Steele	17
*S. N. Hartley c Cook b Mallender	1	– (4) lbw b Steele	0
J. D. Love c Cook b Willey	39	– (5) b Steele	0
†D. L. Bairstow lbw b Mallender	31	– (6) c Steele b Williams	80
P. Carrick not out	47	– (7) b Williams	20
A. Sidebottom run out	14	– (8) run out	0
P. A. Booth c Boyd-Moss b Williams	0	– lbw b Steele	0
N. S. Taylor lbw b Williams	0	– c A. J. Lamb b Steele	2
B 4, l-b 11	15	L-b 6, w 1, n-b 1	8

1/28 2/44 3/44 4/47   199   1/13 2/47 3/47 4/51   190
5/75 6/111 7/164 8/199 9/199   5/148 6/175 7/176 8/176 9/184

Bonus points – Yorkshire 1, Northamptonshire 4.

Bowling: *First Innings*—Griffiths 6–0–17–0; Mallender 18–5–41–3; Steele 41–19–56–3; Willey 22–6–50–1; Williams 8.4–3–20–2. *Second Innings*—Mallender 7–2–16–1; Griffiths 7–2–16–0; Steele 30.4–10–67–5; Willey 29–8–70–0; Williams 10–6–13–2.

Umpires: B. J. Meyer and J. W. Holder.

At Nottingham, July 13, 14. NORTHAMPTONSHIRE beat NOTTINGHAMSHIRE by an innings and 71 runs.

At Derby, July 16, 17, 18. NORTHAMPTONSHIRE drew with DERBYSHIRE.

NORTHAMPTONSHIRE v SOMERSET

At Northampton, July 27, 28, 29. Drawn. Northamptonshire 7 pts, Somerset 6 pts. Somerset's opening pair made no attempt to chase a final target of 273 in 160 minutes and a game containing several fine individual innings fizzled out. A maiden century from Capel, which included twenty 4s, helped to give Northamptonshire a good start. But Somerset were able to declare 1 run in front through magnificent hitting from Richards, whose century came off 95 balls, and Lloyds, who hit his third hundred in successive innings on the Northampton ground. Northamptonshire's advance to their second declaration featured fine batting by Cook and Boyd-Moss.

Northamptonshire

*G. Cook lbw b Garner	0	– c Popplewell b Dredge	82
W. Larkins c Dredge b Booth	50	– c Lloyds b Garner	24
P. Willey c Denning b Wilson	52	– b Garner	25
R. J. Boyd-Moss b Garner	2	– not out	90
R. G. Williams b Booth	35	– c Popplewell b Wilson	12
Kapil Dev b Booth	19	– b Richards	26
D. J. Capel not out	109	– not out	0
D. S. Steele b Garner	54		
†G. Sharp c Lloyds b Garner	0		
N. A. Mallender b Dredge	12		
B 1, l-b 2	3	B 4, l-b 6, n-b 4	14

1/0 2/84 3/89 4/116   (9 wkts dec.) 336   1/31 2/73 3/174   (5 wkts dec.) 273
5/135 6/170 7/319 8/319 9/336   4/208 5/263

B. J. Griffiths did not bat.

Bonus points – Northamptonshire 4, Somerset 2 (Score at 100 overs: 309-6).

Bowling: *First Innings*—Garner 18-2-58-4; Wilson 12-0-55-1; Popplewell 5-2-22-0; Dredge 17.1-7-56-1; Booth 37-12-93-3; Lloyds 7-3-26-0; Richards 11-4-23-0. *Second Innings*—Garner 16-5-34-2; Dredge 14-2-45-1; Booth 18-6-54-0; Wilson 14-2-64-1; Richards 18-0-56-1; Lloyds 4-1-6-0.

Somerset

J. W. Lloyds b Willey	100	– not out	38
P. M. Roebuck b Mallender	3	– not out	55
C. H. Dredge c Boyd-Moss b Griffiths	20		
R. L. Ollis c Steele b Griffiths	45		
N. F. M. Popplewell lbw b Williams	29		
*I. V. A. Richards not out	117		
P. W. Denning run out	2		
J. Garner c Capel b Steele	0		
P. H. L. Wilson not out	9		
L-b 10, w 2	12	B 9, l-b 3, w 5	17

1/22 2/58 3/170 4/172   (7 wkts dec.) 337   (no wkt) 110
5/268 6/281 7/283

†T. Gard and S. C. Booth did not bat.

Bonus points – Somerset 4, Northamptonshire 3 (Score at 100 overs: 315-7).

Bowling: *First Innings*—Kapil Dev 14–2–33–0; Mallender 19–5–47–1; Williams 16–0–65–1; Griffiths 18–4–55–2; Willey 18–3–49–1; Steele 16–2–76–1. *Second Innings*—Kapil Dev 7–3–16–0; Mallender 4–1–14–0; Steele 13–3–28–0; Willey 1–1–0–0; Griffiths 5–1–22–0; Williams 4–1–11–0; Boyd-Moss 3–1–2–0.

Umpires: R. Julian and H. D. Bird.

NORTHAMPTONSHIRE v WORCESTERSHIRE

At Northampton, July 30, August 1, 2. Northamptonshire won by seven wickets. Northamptonshire 22 pts, Worcestershire 5 pts. Northamptonshire reached a target of 299 in 160 minutes with eleven balls to spare. Larkins set the pace with 80 off 55 balls. Then Willey took over. Reaching his 1,000 runs for the season, he hit a century in 113 minutes, aided by Williams in an unbroken fourth-wicket stand of 134. Both teams' first innings had begun shakily, Worcestershire being rescued by excellent batting from Neale, and Northamptonshire owing their recovery to Williams and Capel. Cook declared the home innings 73 behind in a bid for a finish. Ormrod and Neale then produced half-centuries before the final declaration which intially seemed a safe one.

Worcestershire

M. J. Weston b Mallender	7	– st sub b Steele	24
M. S. A. McEvoy c Larkins b Mallender	8	– b Williams	38
J. A. Ormrod b Mallender	0	– not out	71
D. B. D'Oliveira lbw b Carse	31	– c Mallender b Steele	11
D. A. Banks lbw b Carse	15	– lbw b Steele	10
*P. A. Neale lbw b Carse	92	– not out	52
†P. Moores b Willey	30		
R. K. Illingworth c Sharp b Mallender	25		
J. D. Inchmore b Mallender	17		
S. P. Perryman not out	9		
A. P. Pridgeon c Cook b Mallender	13		
B 8, l-b 10, w 1, n-b 7	26	B 8, l-b 9, n-b 2	19

1/9 2/9 3/36 4/61   273   1/75 2/79 3/95   (4 wkts dec.) 225
5/71 6/161 7/209 8/242 9/243   4/131

Bonus points – Worcestershire 3, Northamptonshire 4 (Score at 100 overs: 272–9).

Bowling: *First Innings*—Carse 20–5–69–3; Mallender 24–7–48–6; Griffiths 22–8–43–0; Willey 19–5–48–1; Steele 12–3–32–0; Williams 5–2–7–0. *Second Innings*—Carse 7–1–23–0; Mallender 3–0–6–0; Griffiths 7–3–6–0; Williams 21–11–35–1; Steele 25–4–84–3; Cook 8–1–39–0; Capel 2–0–13–0.

Northamptonshire

*G. Cook c Moores b Pridgeon	23	– lbw b Pridgeon	18
W. Larkins c D'Oliveira b Pridgeon	9	– c McEvoy b D'Oliveira	80
P. Willey b Pridgeon	7	– not out	117
R. J. Boyd-Moss c Neale b Perryman	12	– b Illingworth	14
R. G. Williams b Pridgeon	85	– not out	51
D. J. Capel b Inchmore	48		
D. S. Steele not out	6		
†G. Sharp not out	3		
L-b 7	7	B 8, l-b 12	20

1/32 2/33 3/46 4/56   (6 wkts dec.) 200   1/52 2/137 3/166   (3 wkts) 300
5/181 6/188

N. A. Mallender, J. A. Carse and B. J. Griffiths did not bat.

Bonus points – Northamptonshire 2, Worcestershire 2.

Bowling: *First Innings*—Pridgeon 22–7–48–4; Inchmore 24–9–64–1; Perryman 22–6–61–1; Illingworth 8–1–20–0. *Second Innings*—Pridgeon 11.1–0–72–1; Inchmore 6–1–47–0; Perryman 3–0–16–0; Illingworth 15–0–69–1; D'Oliveira 13–1–76–1.

Umpires: H. D. Bird and R. Julian.

At Weston-super-Mare, August 6, 8, 9. NORTHAMPTONSHIRE drew with SOMERSET.

NORTHAMPTONSHIRE v MIDDLESEX

At Northampton, August 10, 11, 12. Northamptonshire won by nine wickets. Northamptonshire 24 pts, Middlesex 5 pts. Northamptonshire always had a grip after reducing Middlesex to 74 for five on the first morning. They took a first-innings lead of 109, despite sustained spin from Emburey. Middlesex, in their turn, had a long hard battle against the home spinners, although Downton scored a defiant 61, aided by Ellis and Williams in the later stages. Northamptonshire, however, only needed 102 and got them in 90 minutes.

Middlesex

G. D. Barlow c and b Kapil Dev	4	– c Kapil Dev b Williams	11
W. N. Slack c Kapil Dev b Mallender	5	– lbw b Kapil Dev	28
C. T. Radley c Steele b Capel	29	– c Capel b Williams	24
R. G. P. Ellis c Cook b Capel	14	– (5) b Willey	34
K. P. Tomlins lbw b Steele	49	– (4) c Kapil Dev b Steele	5
*J. E. Emburey st Sharp b Steele	4	– b Willey	0
†P. R. Downton b Steele	31	– lbw b Willey	61
N. F. Williams c Sharp b Steele	28	– c Larkins b Willey	23
K. D. James b Williams	34	– c Sharp b Williams	0
S. P. Hughes not out	4	– (11) not out	0
W. W. Daniel st Sharp b Williams	11	– (10) b Williams	8
B 1, l-b 6, n-b 3	10	B 3, l-b 4, w 1, n-b 8	16

1/5 2/14 3/54 4/69   **223**   1/18 2/74 3/74 4/83   **210**
5/74 6/138 7/145 8/188 9/209   5/93 6/139 7/187 8/202 9/202

Bonus points – Middlesex 2, Northamptonshire 4.

Bowling: *First Innings*—Kapil Dev 15–3–31–1; Mallender 20–8–46–1; Griffiths 17–9–27–0; Capel 11–1–35–2; Steele 23–7–46–4; Willey 8–3–22–0; Williams 1.2–0–6–2. *Second Innings*—Kapil Dev 7–3–12–1; Mallender 11–5–22–0; Williams 30.5–10–74–4; Steele 20–9–35–1; Willey 23–5–51–4.

Northamptonshire

*G. Cook lbw b Emburey	79	– not out	32
W. Larkins c James b Daniel	4	– c Tomlins b Emburey	34
P. Willey c Barlow b Emburey	52	– not out	26
R. J. Boyd-Moss c Radley b Slack	8		
R. G. Williams c Slack b Emburey	33		
Kapil Dev c Downton b Hughes	19		
D. J. Capel c Downton b Daniel	21		
D. S. Steele b Hughes	20		
†G. Sharp not out	55		
N. A. Mallender c Radley b Emburey	5		
B. J. Griffiths b Williams	2		
B 5, l-b 5, w 5, n-b 19	34	B 4, l-b 3, n-b 3	10

1/5 2/125 3/151 4/165   **332**   1/54   **(1 wkt) 102**
5/191 6/239 7/243 8/292 9/318

Bonus points – Northamptonshire 4, Middlesex 3 (Score at 100 overs: 301-8).

Bowling: *First Innings*—Daniel 21–4–68–2; Williams 12–2–42–1; Emburey 44–17–70–4; Hughes 25–4–83–2; Slack 10–3–35–1. *Second Innings*—Daniel 6–0–20–0; Emburey 11–1–32–1; Hughes 3–1–14–0; James 3–0–9–0; Tomlins 2–0–11–0; Barlow 2–1–2–0; Radley 1–0–4–0.

Umpires: K. Ibadulla and J. van Geloven.

NORTHAMPTONSHIRE v ESSEX

At Wellingborough, August 13, 15, 16. Essex won by 128 runs. Essex 22 pts, Northamptonshire 6 pts. Phillip finished the game dramatically with a hat-trick, Northamptonshire having faced a target of 272 in 180 minutes on an unhelpful pitch. There was also an eventful start when Northamptonshire's wicket-keeper, Sharp, injured his back in the game's opening over and took no further part. Cook substituted for him. After good early batting, particularly by Gooch, Essex fell, surprisingly, to Larkins. Lever caused Northamptonshire problems, but steady batting by Boyd-Moss, Steele and Capel enabled Cook to declare 35 behind in the hope of a finish. In the conditions the final target set by Fletcher was very stiff.

Essex

G. A. Gooch b Carse	60	– c Cook b Griffiths	5
C. Gladwin c Cook b Mallender	33	– c Steele b Griffiths	34
B. R. Hardie b Carse	37	– c Mallender b Steele	69
K. S. McEwan st Cook b Steele	37	– lbw b Griffiths	0
*K. W. R. Fletcher c Capel b Larkins	10	– c Mallender b Steele	71
N. Phillip b Mallender	29	– lbw b Williams	15
S. Turner c Capel b Larkins	16	– c Capel b Williams	8
†D. E. East lbw b Larkins	0	– not out	14
R. E. East lbw b Mallender	6	– not out	10
J. K. Lever not out	17		
D. L. Acfield c Steele b Larkins	9		
B 12, l-b 7, w 1, n-b 8	28	B 2, l-b 3, n-b 5	10

1/98 2/106 3/167 4/198   282   1/7 2/62 3/62   (7 wkts dec.) 236
5/198 6/237 7/237 8/250 9/251   4/176 5/203 6/205 7/212

Bonus points – Essex 3, Northamptonshire 4.

Bowling: *First Innings*—Carse 21–3–67–2; Mallender 19–2–78–3; Griffiths 19–5–56–0; Capel 7–2–18–0; Steele 2–0–5–1; Larkins 14.4–3–30–4. *Second Innings*—Mallender 9–1–36–0; Griffiths 22–6–69–3; Carse 11–5–32–0; Steele 9.2–3–41–2; Williams 12–0–48–2.

Northamptonshire

*G. Cook c D. E. East b Lever	21	– c R. E. East b Lever	22
W. Larkins c Gladwin b Lever	10	– b Lever	29
P. Willey c Gooch b Lever	27	– c D. E. East b Turner	1
R. J. Boyd-Moss c McEwan b Turner	60	– c D. E. East b Turner	2
R. G. Williams c Hardie b Turner	23	– c Gooch b Phillip	21
D. J. Capel c Gooch b Lever	31	– c Acfield b Lever	12
D. S. Steele not out	40	– c Gooch b Phillip	39
N. A. Mallender lbw b Lever	8	– c Hardie b Phillip	12
J. A. Carse not out	15	– not out	0
B. J. Griffiths (did not bat)		– b Phillip	0
†G. Sharp (did not bat)		– absent hurt	
B 4, l-b 4, w 1, n-b 3	12	L-b 2, n-b 3	5

1/16 2/40/ 3/90 4/147   (7 wkts dec.) 247   1/51 2/56 3/58 4/58   143
5/152 6/203 7/217   5/80 6/101 7/142 8/143 9/143

Bonus points – Northamptonshire 2, Essex 3 (Score at 100 overs: 231-7).

Bowling: *First Innings*—Lever 34–11–68–5; Phillip 13–1–48–0; Turner 22–7–47–2; Acfield 15–6–38–0; Gooch 8–4–5–0; R. E. East 15–3–29–0. *Second Innings*—Lever 17–9–48–3; Phillip 9.2–0–54–4; Turner 11–2–26–2; Acfield 7–2–10–0.

Umpires: D. O. Oslear and D. R Shepherd.

NORTHAMPTONSHIRE v LANCASHIRE

At Northampton, August 20, 22, 23. Drawn. Northamptonshire 4 pts, Lancashire 4 pts. A first-innings run harvest by both sides produced 712 runs for five wickets, four centuries and no bowling bonus points. Larkins and Willey established a new record partnership of 342 for Northamptonshire's second wicket, both hitting magnificently. David Lloyd and Fowler dominated the second day in Lancashire's best opening partnership of the season. Things changed in the second innings with spin bowlers coming more into their own. Northamptonshire needed a brave 78 from Boyd-Moss before setting a target of 264 in 165 minutes. Struggling on a turning pitch, Lancashire were indebted to resolute batting by Abrahams and, in the closing overs, by David Lloyd, who came in despite having broken a finger while fielding.

Northamptonshire

*†G. Cook lbw b Watkinson	29	– (7) b D. Lloyd	19
W. Larkins c Hayes b Allott	187	– lbw b Allott	7
P. Willey not out	147	– (8) not out	22
D. J. Capel (did not bat)		– (1) b McFarlane	12
A. J. Lamb (did not bat)		– (3) b McFarlane	13
R. J. Boyd-Moss (did not bat)		– (4) c and b D. Lloyd	78
N. A. Mallender (did not bat)		– (5) b D. Lloyd	21
R. G. Williams (did not bat)		– (6) c Maynard b D. Lloyd	14
D. S. Steele (did not bat)		– not out	13
B 2, l-b 8, n-b 8	18	B 8, l-b 5, n-b 1	14

1/39 2/381   (2 wkts dec.) 381   1/13 2/28 3/41   (7 wkts dec.) 213
                                                      4/114 5/140 6/163 7/178

J. A. Carse and B. J. Griffiths did not bat.

Bonus points – Northamptonshire 4 (Score at 100 overs: 326-1).

Bowling: *First Innings*—Allott 17.1–5–60–1; McFarlane 15–2–65–0; Watkinson 17–3–32–1; D. Lloyd 21–4–64–0; O'Shaughnessy 10–0–45–0; Abrahams 19–1–67–0; Nasir 9–2–30–0. *Second Innings*—Allott 11–2–23–1; McFarlane 13–2–41–2; Nasir 10–1–28–0; Watkinson 3–0–15–0; D. Lloyd 28–4–53–4; Abrahams 22–5–39–0.

Lancashire

D. Lloyd st Cook b Willey	123	– (9) not out	1
G. Fowler st Cook b Willey	107	– (1) b Williams	27
S. J. O'Shaughnessy c and b Steele	44	– (2) b Steele	17
*C. H. Lloyd not out	36	– c and b Steele	4
J. Abrahams not out	5	– (3) not out	39
F. C. Hayes (did not bat)		– (5) c Lamb b Steele	3
†C. Maynard (did not bat)		– (6) b Steele	0
Nasir Zaidi (did not bat)		– (7) b Boyd-Moss	15
M. Watkinson (did not bat)		– (8) c Capel b Williams	0
B 4, l-b 4, n-b 8	16	B 5, l-b 2, w 1, n-b 1	9

1/179 2/274 3/310   (3 wkts dec.) 331   1/46 2/50 3/56 4/70   (7 wkts) 115
                                                      5/70 6/96 7/97

P. J. W. Allott and L. L. McFarlane did not bat.

Bonus points – Lancashire 4 (Score at 100 overs: 302-2).

Bowling: *First Innings*—Mallender 2–0–2–0; Carse 11–0–62–0; Williams 27–9–90–0; Griffiths 6–1–19–0; Willey 40–14–74–2; Steele 26–4–68–1. *Second Innings*—Mallender 3–1–11–0; Carse 2–0–9–0; Steele 25–15–40–4; Williams 20.4–9–33–2; Boyd-Moss 8–4–13–1.

Umpires: D. J. Constant and P. J. Eele.

NORTHAMPTONSHIRE v GLAMORGAN

At Northampton, August 24, 25, 26. Drawn. Northamptonshire 6 pts, Glamorgan 7 pts. The game was dominated on the opening day by a masterly 145 from Larkins. After being 87 for four in reply, Glamorgan rallied and batted on for 117 overs which rather put a brake on the final day's tactics. Davis bowled so well when Northamptonshire batted again that their final declaration was delayed until tea on the last day. Set to score 203 in two hours, Glamorgan began briskly, Alan Jones and Hopkins putting on 73 in sixteen overs. But five wickets fell in six overs and Henderson and Holmes finished by fighting for survival.

Northamptonshire

M. J. Bamber b Davis	6	– c A. L. Jones b Ontong	14
W. Larkins c Rowe b Ontong	145	– lbw b Davis	26
P. Willey b Davis	2	– b Davis	10
R. J. Boyd-Moss lbw b Ontong	22	– lbw b Davis	22
R. G. Williams c Davis b Rowe	17	– not out	77
D. J. Capel c Davies b Davis	1	– c Henderson b Davis	26
*†G. Cook b Ontong	24	– (9) not out	21
D. S. Steele c Holmes b Rowe	3	– (7) b Davis	1
N. A. Mallender c Henderson b Ontong	20	– (8) lbw b Wilkins	0
J. A. Carse not out	28		
B. J. Griffiths c Rowe b Ontong	0		
B 2, l-b 5, w 1, n-b 8	16	B 7, l-b 16, w 1, n-b 8	32

1/24 2/42 3/85 4/131   **284**   1/44 2/50 3/72   (7 wkts dec.) **229**
5/136 6/228 7/231 8/241 9/277   4/83 5/152 6/154 7/163

Bonus points – Northamptonshire 3, Glamorgan 4.

Bowling: *First Innings*—Davis 24–6–56–3; Wilkins 8–1–46–0; Selvey 15–1–56–0; Ontong 18.5–6–52–5; Rowe 29–8–58–2. *Second Innings*—Davis 25–9–58–5; Wilkins 18–4–44–1; Ontong 27–6–49–1; Rowe 12–2–45–0; Selvey 1–0–1–0.

Glamorgan

J. A. Hopkins c Cook b Mallender	44	– b Willey	24
A. Jones b Willey	8	– c and b Steele	41
R. C. Ontong c Cook b Carse	0	– c Mallender b Willey	5
C. J. C. Rowe c Cook b Willey	43	– c Boyd-Moss b Willey	6
A. L. Jones c Willey b Mallender	2	– st sub b Williams	5
S. P. Henderson b Steele	61	– not out	6
G. C. Holmes lbw b Mallender	46	– not out	21
†T. Davies c and b Williams	3		
A. H. Wilkins b Mallender	54		
*M. W. W. Selvey b Willey	7		
W. W. Davis not out	0		
B 12, l-b 10, w 4, n-b 17	43	L-b 8, n-b 1	9

1/34 2/39 3/80 4/87   **311**   1/73 2/77 3/79   (5 wkts) **117**
5/150 6/188 7/199 8/300 9/311   4/84 5/90

Bonus points – Glamorgan 3, Northamptonshire 3 (Score at 100 overs: 261-7).

Bowling: *First Innings*—Carse 23–6–44–1; Mallender 19.4–3–62–4; Willey 24–6–64–3; Griffiths 5–0–17–0; Steele 33–16–56–1; Williams 12–4–25–1. *Second Innings*—Carse 3–0–13–0; Mallender 5–2–19–0; Griffiths 3–0–18–0; Willey 11–5–26–3; Steele 8–1–23–1; Williams 4–1–9–1.

Umpires: D. J. Constant and P. J. Eele.

At Leicester, August 27, 29, 30. NORTHAMPTONSHIRE lost to LEICESTERSHIRE by five wickets.

At Cardiff, August 31, September 1, 2. NORTHAMPTONSHIRE drew with GLAMORGAN.

At Lord's, September 7, 8, 9. NORTHAMPTONSHIRE beat MIDDLESEX by seven wickets.

At Canterbury, September 10, 12, 13. NORTHAMPTONSHIRE drew with KENT.

MCC TOUR

In May and June 1983, an MCC team paid a short visit to Holland and Denmark. Seven matches were played, of which two were won and five drawn. In the match at The Hague, arranged to celebrate the Centenary of the Dutch Cricket Federation, only 50 minutes' play was possible, owing to rain. Dermot Reeve, a member of the MCC Young Cricketers' staff, who made the tour as a last-minute replacement, headed both the bowling and batting averages. The team was: M. D. Mence (captain), J. A. F. Vallance (player/manager), J. P. B. Bell, K. G. Brooks, C. F. Brown, S. P. Coverdale, R. A. B. Ezekowitz, P. J. Graves, R. P. Hodson, M. E. Milton, D. A. Reeve and G. W. Sandrock.

NOTTINGHAMSHIRE

President: Dr J. B. Cochrane
Chairman: C. F. Ward
Chairman, Cricket Committee: R. T. Simpson
Secretary: B. Robson
   County Cricket Ground, Trent Bridge,
   Nottingham NG2 6AG
   (Telephone: 0602-821525)
Cricket Manager: K. A. Taylor
Captain: C. E. B. Rice

The summer of 1983 will not be remembered as one of great success or satisfaction for Nottinghamshire – but that hardly came as a surprise. The county went into the season with financial stringencies necessitating a cutback in the playing strength, which was to be further reduced by Test calls and injuries.

The loss of Richard Hadlee and Derek Randall for the World Cup and then the Test series between England and New Zealand was always going to provide the kind of handicap difficult to overcome. And if that were not enough, Nottinghamshire also lost the vital services of their captain, Clive Rice, following a hand operation. With one of the smallest pools of players in the country, they were forced to call on relatively untried, if promising, youngsters to fill the void.

Almost inevitably, the presence in the side of so much inexperience contributed to the uphill battle. It says much for the way the county has changed in substance that they were still able to produce more favourable performances than would have been at all likely in the same set of circumstances five or six years earlier. Even so, finishing fourteenth in the Schweppes County Championship, joint bottom of the John Player League and facing early elimination in both the Benson and Hedges Cup and the NatWest Bank Trophy represented overall failure. Within the framework of the season the encouragement came from individual performances suggesting that 1984 will be more prosperous.

No one acquitted himself better in this direction than Tim Robinson. The 25-year-old opening batsman had the considerable pleasure of being presented with his county cap on leaving the field after scoring 207 in the game against Warwickshire at Trent Bridge. Robinson, of whom so much was predicted, indeed expected, when he joined the staff in 1978, recovered from a season of uncertainty in 1982 to show that Nottinghamshire have unearthed a player capable of accruing big scores and high aggregates. He totalled 1,545 first-class runs and scored them in a confident and technically sound manner, hinting that with a little more maturity and variety of shots he could begin to figure in the thoughts of the Test selectors.

England calls so dominated Derek Randall's benefit season that he played little part in the fortunes of the county. Rice, because of injury and then a partial loss of form from his own imperious standards, only just managed to complete 1,000 runs in the final game against Middlesex

– a figure which John Birch reached earlier without the help of a century.

There was the usual whole-hearted approach of Basharat Hassan, but with Randall and Hadlee often missing the batting was vulnerable. Early experiments to promote wicket-keeper Bruce French in the order were abandoned.

However, the continuing emergence of Paul Johnson, who scored a maiden hundred against Gloucestershire, provided further evidence that his future holds more than promise. Johnson was one of three Nottinghamshire youngsters to be picked for the Young England side against Young Australia, the others being bowlers Andy Pick and Peter Such. Pick, in his first year on the staff, had to be drafted in when injuries left the manager, Ken Taylor, contemplating plucking a bowler out of club cricket. A brisk medium, Pick began by claiming Boycott's wicket in the Tilcon Trophy and showed undoubted potential. Such struggled to impose his youthful promise on the Trent Bridge scene and the fully-fledged off-spinner, Eddie Hemmings, perhaps suffered some after-effects from being rejected by England. He also played throughout the year with a troublesome shoulder injury.

Mike Hendrick, who is not unacquainted with injury worries, remained fit for a large part of the time and with 66 victims was the leading wicket-taker. He proved beyond doubt that he remains one of the country's most effective bowlers in conditions favourable to seam and swing bowling. Kevin Cooper, who like so many of the bowlers produced career-best figures during the summer, finished with 57 wickets and Kevin Saxelby with 50. Saxelby made definite strides towards establishing himself as a front-line bowler. The need for more variety in the attack left Nottinghamshire searching for a slow left-armer, and an indication of the desire to repeat the Championship success of 1981 came in the signing at the end of the season of Chris Broad from Gloucestershire.

With the possibility of further signings and the likelihood of having Hadlee available throughout the season, Nottinghamshire looked forward to better things in 1984. – J.L.

NOTTINGHAMSHIRE 1983

[*Bill Smith*]

Back row: P. Johnson, R. A. Pick, P. M. Such, R. T. Robinson, M. A. Fell, D. J. White, C. W. Scott. *Middle row:* E. E. Hemmings, N. J. B. Illingworth, K. Saxelby, M. J. Harris, K. E. Cooper, M. K. Bore, B. N. French. *Front row:* B. Hassan, R. J. Hadlee, C. E. B. Rice (*captain*), K. A. Taylor (*manager*), J. D. Birch, D. W. Randall, M. Hendrick.

NOTTINGHAMSHIRE RESULTS

All first-class matches – Played 26: Won 4, Lost 10, Drawn 12.

County Championship matches – Played 24: Won 3, Lost 10, Drawn 11.

Bonus points – Batting 39, Bowling 62.

Competition placings – Schweppes County Championship, 14th; NatWest Bank Trophy, 2nd round; Benson and Hedges Cup, 3rd in Group B; John Player League, 15th eq.

COUNTY CHAMPIONSHIP AVERAGES

BATTING

	Birthplace	M	I	NO	R	HI	Avge
R. T. Robinsonc	Sutton-in-Ashfield	24	39	3	1,464	207	40.66
C. E. B. Ricec	Johannesburg, SA	19	30	2	1,026	101*	36.64
R. J. Hadleec	Christchurch, NZ	5	4	0	119	103	29.75
J. D. Birch	Nottingham	23	36	2	1,007	95	29.61
D. W. Randallc	Retford	15	22	1	583	94	27.76
B. Hassanc	Nairobi, Kenya	21	34	1	890	112	26.96
P. Johnson	Newark	15	26	2	524	125	21.83
B. N. Frenchc	Warsop	23	36	4	589	91	18.40
R. A. Pick	Nottingham	6	8	2	84	25*	14.00
K. E. Cooperc	Hucknall	21	25	7	245	30*	13.61
E. E. Hemmingsc	Leamington Spa	23	32	3	377	38	13.00
M. K. Bore	Hull	12	15	4	134	24	12.18
K. Saxelby	Worksop	20	26	3	259	35	11.26
M. Hendrickc	Darley Dale	21	26	13	127	15*	9.76
N. J. B. Illingworth	Chesterfield	2	4	0	29	17	7.25
M. A. Fell	Newark	4	7	0	46	32	6.57
P. M. Such	Helensburgh	9	14	4	13	5	1.30

C. W. Scott (*Thorpe-on-the-Hill*) played in one match without batting.

*Signifies not out.   cDenotes county cap.

BOWLING

	O	M	R	W	Avge	BB
R. J. Hadlee	86.2	28	210	13	16.15	5-72
M. Hendrick	552.1	190	1,122	66	17.00	6-17
K. Saxelby	387.2	93	1,265	47	26.91	5-52
K. E. Cooper	545	149	1,530	50	30.60	7-33
E. E. Hemmings	710.4	195	2,000	59	33.89	7-23
P. M. Such	194	36	722	19	38.00	6-123
M. K. Bore	329.5	91	981	19	51.63	3-34

Also bowled: J. D. Birch 1–0–1–0; M. A. Fell 3–0–11–0; N. J. B. Illingworth 25–2–97–1; R. A. Pick 134.4–16–500–7; R. T. Robinson 1–0–1–0.

The following played a total of seven three-figure innings for Nottinghamshire in County Championship matches – C. E. B. Rice 2, R. T. Robinson 2, R. J. Hadlee 1, B. Hassan 1, P. Johnson 1.

NOTTINGHAMSHIRE v SOMERSET

At Nottingham, April 30, May 1, 2. Drawn. Nottinghamshire 1 pt, Somerset 2 pts. After a delayed start only 55 overs were played – all on the first day – before the game was washed out. The feature was a fourth-wicket stand between Rice and Birch, who added 74 in twenty overs, but they were out in quick succession and Somerset had taken the initiative by the time the weather took over.

Nottinghamshire

B. Hassan c Gard b Botham	22	†B. N. French not out	9
R. T. Robinson c Popplewell b Davis	43	E. E Hemmings not out	2
D. W. Randall lbw b Davis	8	B 1, l-b 3, n-b 2	6
*C. E. B. Rice b Popplewell	45		—
J. D. Birch c Slocombe b Dredge	45	1/42 2/64 3/91	(6 wkts) 181
R. J. Hadlee c sub b Wilson	1	4/165 5/169 6/177	

K. Saxelby, K. E. Cooper and M. Hendrick did not bat.

Bonus points – Nottinghamshire 1, Somerset 2.

Bowling: Botham 13–4–37–1; Wilson 15–6–30–1; Dredge 13–1–55–1; Davis 8–2–35–2; Popplewell 5–2–13–1; Marks 1–0–5–0.

Somerset

P. M. Roebuck, J. W. Lloyds, P. A. Slocombe, *B. C. Rose, I. T. Botham, N. F. M. Popplewell, V. J. Marks, †T. Gard, C. H. Dredge, M. R. Davis and P. H. L. Wilson.

Umpires: J. van Geloven and J. Birkenshaw.

At Hove, May 4, 5, 6. NOTTINGHAMSHIRE beat SUSSEX by an innings and 32 runs.

At Northampton, May 11, 12, 13. NOTTINGHAMSHIRE drew with NORTHAMPTON-SHIRE.

NOTTINGHAMSHIRE v DERBYSHIRE

At Nottingham, May 28, 30, 31. Derbyshire won by six wickets in match reduced to one innings per side after rain had washed out the first two days. Derbyshire 12 pts. Derbyshire produced a thrilling victory with only four balls to spare after being set to get 233 in 90 minutes plus twenty overs. Nottinghamshire, put in, had scored 232 for four, with Johnson, only eighteen, hitting an impressive career-best 65 not out. It looked a stiff target, but all Derbyshire's batsmen made significant contributions and Hill took control at the vital time to steer them to victory.

Nottinghamshire

B. Hassan c Oldham b Miller	43	P. Johnson not out	65
R. T. Robinson c Barnett b Moir	48	B 8, l-b 3, n-b 2	13
*J. D. Birch c Newman b Moir	2		—
R. J. Hadlee c and b Moir	9	1/96 2/98	(4 wkts dec.) 232
D. W. Randall not out	52	3/98 4/110	

E. E Hemmings, K. Saxelby, †C. W. Scott, K. E. Cooper and P. M. Such did not bat.

Bowling: Newman 11–4–28–0; Mortensen 7–2–24–0; Oldham 9–0–32–0; Moir 20–4–65–3; Miller 18–2–70–1.

Derbyshire

I. S. Anderson st Scott b Hemmings....	35	G. Miller not out............................	30
J. G Wright c Hassan b Hemmings	41	B 3, l-b 5, w 1, n-b 2...............	11
A. Hill not out.................................	57		
*K. J. Barnett b Such.......................	39	1/69 2/88	(4 wkts) 235
J. H. Hampshire c Hadlee b Saxelby...	22	3/152 4/178	

P. G. Newman, †R. W. Taylor, D. G. Moir, S. Oldham and O. H. Mortensen did not bat.

Bowling: Hadlee 12.2–2–37–0; Hemmings 17–1–68–2; Cooper 6–1–39–0; Such 5–0–30–1; Saxelby 7–0–50–1.

Umpires: D. G. L. Evans and B. Leadbeater.

NOTTINGHAMSHIRE v LEICESTERSHIRE

At Nottingham, June 4, 6, 7. Drawn. Nottinghamshire 6 pts, Leicestershire 4 pts. Leicestershire, having looked likely losers at the start of the final day, almost engineered an amazing victory. After Balderstone's five-hour century had seen them to safety, they left Nottinghamshire to get a virtually impossible 159 for victory in the last nineteen overs. Creditably, the home batsmen attempted to get the runs, but they soon ran into trouble against left-arm spinners Steele and Cook and were reduced to 31 for seven with more than six overs left. Nottinghamshire were saved the further embarrassment of defeat, for the addition of 1 run and the loss of another wicket, by the rearguard batting of their bowlers. Earlier Leicestershire had been the side in difficulty after four hours' play had been lost on the first day because of wet conditions. Hendrick's six for 17 – his best figures for Nottinghamshire – removed Leicestershire for 101, and Randall's 74 helped the home county to a healthy first-innings lead of 125.

Leicestershire

J. C. Balderstone c Birch b Hendrick	1	– (2) c Birch b Hemmings 108
R. A. Cobb c Randall b Saxelby.....................	0	– (1) lbw b Hendrick.................. 10
D. I. Gower c Birch b Saxelby	1	– b Hemmings 20
B. F. Davison c Johnson b Hendrick	28	– c Hassan b Hendrick 0
N. E. Briers c French b Hendrick	7	– b Cooper.............................. 60
*†R. W. Tolchard c Birch b Hendrick	0	– b Such................................ 18
J. F. Steele c Hemmings b Hendrick	0	– b Such................................ 10
P. B. Clift c French b Hendrick	25	– lbw b Hemmings..................... 31
G. J. Parsons c Hendrick b Saxelby................	15	– not out................................ 7
N. G. B. Cook not out	1	– b Hemmings 6
L. B. Taylor run out	19	
W 2, n-b 2	4	B 2, l-b 8, n-b 3............. 13

1/0 2/2 3/12 4/35	101	1/25 2/51 3/52	(9 wkts dec.) 283
5/35 6/35 7/43 8/73 9/82		4/187 5/219 6/223 7/268 8/268 9/283	

Bonus points – Nottinghamshire 4.

Bowling: *First Innings*—Hendrick 15.3–4–17–6; Saxelby 13–6–44–3; Cooper 11–3–36–0. *Second Innings*—Hendrick 18–4–49–2; Saxelby 13–3–43–0; Hemmings 44.5–18–85–4; Cooper 18–7–37–1; Such 16–5–56–2.

Nottinghamshire

B. Hassan run out	22	– (4) c Davison b Taylor	0
R. T. Robinson c Steele b Parsons	15	– (5) b Cook	4
D. W. Randall b Steele	74	– (1) lbw b Steele	8
P. Johnson c Gower b Clift	29	– (3) st Tolchard b Cook	8
*J. D. Birch c Clift b Cook	29	– (2) b Cook	2
†B. N. French b Cook	28	– c Cobb b Steele	0
E. E. Hemmings lbw b Steele	0	– c Cobb b Steele	4
K. Saxelby c Briers b Steele	11	– c Balderstone b Steele	0
K. E. Cooper c Cobb b Cook	4	– not out	0
M. Hendrick not out	3	– not out	0
P. M. Such run out	0		
B 6, l-b 5	11	B 4, w 1, n-b 1	6

1/37 2/37 3/94 4/165   226   1/6 2/18 3/19 4/28   (8 wkts) 32
5/193 6/195 7/205 8/215 9/225   5/28 6/30 7/31 8/32

Bonus points – Nottinghamshire 2, Leicestershire 4.

Bowling: *First Innings*—Taylor 13–5–33–0; Parsons 20–6–58–1; Clift 15–4–37–1; Cook 21–9–52–3; Steele 14.1–2–35–3. *Second Innings*—Taylor 3–0–16–1; Cook 9–5–7–3; Steele 7–5–3–4.

Umpires: J. H. Harris and B. J. Meyer.

At Chelmsford, June 8, 9, 10. NOTTINGHAMSHIRE lost to ESSEX by eight wickets.

At Manchester, June 11, 13, 14. NOTTINGHAMSHIRE drew with LANCASHIRE.

NOTTINGHAMSHIRE v SURREY

At Nottingham, June 15, 16, 17. Surrey won by ten wickets. Surrey 23 pts, Nottinghamshire 3 pts. A much weakened Nottinghamshire side were up against it from the start after inviting Surrey to bat. The visitors made slow progress but gradually moved into a position of strength with Clinton, Smith and Knight forming a base and Lynch accelerating the run-rate with 85, including three 6s and ten 4s, in 110 minutes. Cooper, taking six wickets for only the third time in his career, bowled superbly in attempting to curb Surrey's spree. Nottinghamshire, in their reply, looked comfortable for a time as Hassan held the innings together, but despite brave resistance from Cooper they failed by just 2 runs to avoid the follow-on. Robinson was the obstacle for the Surrey bowlers in the second innings, being ninth out for 94 after 237 minutes' defiance. When Pocock left the field injured, Needham stepped in with career-best figures of five for 52.

Surrey

A. R. Butcher c French b Cooper	13	– not out	7
G. S. Clinton c Bore b Such	57	– not out	5
D. M. Smith c Illingworth b Bore	68		
*R. D. V. Knight b Cooper	60		
M. A. Lynch c Bore b Cooper	85		
†C. J. Richards c French b Cooper	13		
A. Needham c Birch b Cooper	16		
D. J. Thomas not out	24		
S. T. Clarke b Cooper	21		
I. R. Payne not out	3		
B 1, l-b 6, w 1, n-b 1	9		

1/24 2/125 3/159 4/272   (8 wkts dec.) 369   (no wkt) 12
5/289 6/312 7/333 8/360

P. I. Pocock did not bat.

Bonus points – Surrey 3, Nottinghamshire 1 (Score at 100 overs: 264-3).

Bowling: *First Innings*—Hendrick 29–10–65–0; Cooper 32–9–89–6; Illingworth 16–1–46–0; Bore 26–6–62–1; Such 27–3–98–1. *Second Innings*—Such 2–1–4–0; Bore 2–1–8–0.

Nottinghamshire

B. Hassan lbw b Pocock	83	– lbw b Thomas	3
R. T. Robinson c Lynch b Clarke	16	– c Payne b Needham	94
†B. N. French c Lynch b Thomas	19	– c Knight b Needham	12
P. Johnson c Richards b Thomas	0	– b Clarke	1
*J. D. Birch c Clarke b Knight	27	– c Butcher b Needham	2
M. A. Fell c Butcher b Pocock	0	– b Thomas	6
N. J. B. Illingworth c Richards b Thomas	17	– lbw b Thomas	0
K. E. Cooper c Knight b Pocock	29	– c Smith b Thomas	7
M. K. Bore c Needham b Pocock	0	– c Knight b Needham	0
M. Hendrick c Payne b Clarke	7	– c Payne b Needham	12
P. M. Such not out	2	– not out	0
B 4, l-b 5, w 2, n-b 7	18	B 1, l-b 11, w 6, n-b 6	24
	218		**161**

1/54 2/95 3/95 4/153   1/12 2/55 3/56 4/67
5/154 6/157 7/206 8/207 9/207   5/79 6/83 7/105 8/146 9/149

Bonus points – Nottinghamshire 2, Surrey 4 (Score at 100 overs: 213-9).

Bowling: *First Innings*—Clarke 29.4–11–43–2; Thomas 20–5–50–3; Knight 9–2–29–1; Pocock 34–15–49–4; Needham 9–3–15–0; Payne 3–0–14–0. *Second Innings*—Clarke 17–6–37–1; Thomas 15–3–33–4; Payne 3–2–2–0; Pocock 5.4–2–5–0; Knight 5–3–8–0; Needham 21.2–5–52–5.

Umpires: D. J. Constant and J. H. Harris.

At Cambridge, June 18, 20, 21. NOTTINGHAMSHIRE beat CAMBRIDGE UNIVERSITY by 185 runs.

NOTTINGHAMSHIRE v KENT

At Nottingham, June 22, 23, 24. Kent won by six wickets. Kent 23 pts, Nottinghamshire 6 pts. Match figures of thirteen for 161 by Underwood tilted the game Kent's way on a pitch that always favoured the slow bowlers. Nottinghamshire, having won the toss, were in danger of collapse until Rice, back after five weeks' absence following a hand operation, held the innings together with 98, including fifteen 4s, in three hours. Nineteen-year-old off-spinner Such responded for Nottinghamshire by returning career-best figures of six for 123 as Kent were restricted to a first-innings lead of 22, but then Underwood got to work once more. And again only Rice looked capable of keeping him at bay for a lengthy period. With Kent needing 137 for victory, Such took the first three wickets to fall, but Aslett figured in partnerships with Cowdrey and Knott to see his side home.

Nottinghamshire

B. Hassan c Johnson b Penn	42	– lbw b Ellison	0
R. T. Robinson b Underwood	21	– b Underwood	25
†B. N. French c Cowdrey b Underwood	0	– c Johnson b Underwood	4
J. D. Birch c Taylor b Underwood	0	– c Aslett b Underwood	11
*C. E. B. Rice c Cowdrey b Underwood	98	– b Underwood	45
P. Johnson c Knott b Underwood	31	– c Knott b Johnson	6
E. E. Hemmings c Ellison b Underwood	7	– c and b Johnson	27
K. Saxelby c Penn b Underwood	18	– c Johnson b Underwood	13
K. E. Cooper b Johnson	2	– c Benson b Johnson	8
M. Hendrick not out	3	– c Aslett b Underwood	2
P. M. Such lbw b Johnson	0	– not out	3
L-b 3, w 1, n-b 12	16	B 3, n-b 11	14

1/53 2/64 3/67 4/67   238   1/0 2/16 3/37 4/79   158
5/154 6/173 7/216 8/220 9/234   5/90 6/118 7/126 8/142 9/147

Bonus points – Nottinghamshire 2, Kent 4.

Bowling: *First Innings*—Jarvis 7–0–44–0; Ellison 5–1–10–0; Underwood 38–12–88–7; Penn 9–2–18–1; Johnson 24.3–6–62–2. *Second Innings*—Ellison 8–3–18–1; Underwood 32–8–73–6; Johnson 24–3–53–3.

Kent

N. R. Taylor c Hassan b Such	29	– lbw b Such	13
M. R. Benson c Hassan b Hemmings	40	– c French b Such	7
C. Penn c Hendrick b Such	24		
D. G. Aslett c Cooper b Such	39	– (3) not out	45
E. A. Baptiste lbw b Hendrick	34	– (4) c French b Such	13
*C. S. Cowdrey c and b Hemmings	20	– (5) c Johnson b Hemmings	24
†A. P. E. Knott b Such	11	– (6) not out	28
G. W. Johnson lbw b Such	10		
R. M. Ellison b Hemmings	17		
D. L. Underwood not out	26		
K. B. S. Jarvis c Robinson b Such	0		
B 4, l-b 6	10	B 1, l-b 6	7

1/62 2/72 3/115 4/159   260   1/18 2/25   (4 wkts) 137
5/168 6/191 7/209 8/209 9/251   3/43 4/82

Bonus points – Kent 3, Nottinghamshire 4.

Bowling: *First Innings*—Hendrick 8–3–20–1; Saxelby 4–0–18–0; Cooper 4–0–6–0; Hemmings 29–6–83–3; Such 29.4–1–123–6. *Second Innings*—Hemmings 16.2–1–64–1; Such 16–2–66–3.

Umpires: B. Leadbeater and D. R. Shepherd.

NOTTINGHAMSHIRE v LANCASHIRE

At Nottingham, June 25, 27, 28. Nottinghamshire won by 157 runs. Nottinghamshire 20 pts, Lancashire 5 pts. Nottinghamshire, bowled out for 86 inside 28 overs on the opening morning, produced an amazing turnabout to win this game. Initially they had no answer to the swing and movement of the South African, Jefferies, who enjoyed career-best figures of eight for 46. A gritty half-century by Hayes gave Lancashire a lead of 72, despite some impressive bowling by Hendrick and Hemmings, and when Nottinghamshire lost half their side for 145 a Lancashire victory looked certain. However, when Jefferies had to leave the field with a shoulder injury, the game swung away from them. Birch, who richly deserved a hundred for batting with such application in testing conditions, made 95 in 207 minutes (thirteen 4s) to lift Nottinghamshire to a lead of 222, and before the close Hendrick opened the door by taking two quick wickets. On the third day Hemmings recorded Championship-best figures of seven for 23 as Lancashire lost their last seven wickets for just 10 runs.

Nottinghamshire

B. Hassan lbw b Jefferies	23	– lbw b Jefferies	51
R. T. Robinson lbw b Jefferies	3	– lbw b Jefferies	20
D. W. Randall lbw b Jefferies	31	– c Fowler b Jefferies	11
*C. E. B. Rice b Allott	6	– b Watkinson	36
J. D. Birch c Simmons b Jefferies	6	– c Simmons b Allott	95
P. Johnson lbw b Jefferies	0	– c Maynard b Watkinson	4
†B. N. French c Simmons b Allott	2	– c Hayes b Nasir	21
E. E. Hemmings c Watkinson b Jefferies	9	– c Simmons b Hughes	10
M. Hendrick b Jefferies	1	– (10) c Fowler b Allott	9
M. K. Bore not out	1	– (9) c Hughes b Watkinson	24
P. M. Such b Jefferies	0	– not out	0
L-b 3, n-b 1	4	L-b 9, n-b 4	13

1/4 2/55 3/62 4/68   86   1/50 2/73 3/88 4/141   294
5/68 6/71 7/77 8/84 9/86   5/145 6/212 7/251 8/262 9/294

Bonus points – Lancashire 4.

Bowling: *First Innings*—Allott 14–3–36–2; Jefferies 13.5–2–46–8. *Second Innings*—Allott 32–11–87–2; Jefferies 15–3–49–3; Nasir 10–1–34–1; Watkinson 17.1–4–59–3; Simmons 19–7–28–0; Hughes 8–2–24–1.

Lancashire

G. Fowler c Johnson b Hendrick	36	– c Such b Hemmings	36
†C. Maynard c Randall b Hendrick	0	– b Hendrick	2
F. C. Hayes c and b Hemmings	52	– c Such b Hendrick	12
D. P. Hughes c Randall b Hendrick	0	– (6) c Hassan b Hemmings	0
*J. Abrahams b Hemmings	15	– (7) c Hassan b Hemmings	1
N. H. Fairbrother c Rice b Hemmings	4	– (8) not out	2
J. Simmons c French b Hemmings	9	– (9) b Hemmings	0
S. T. Jefferies not out	28	– (11) c Birch b Hemmings	0
M. Watkinson c Hemmings b Hendrick	8	– (5) b Bore	3
Nasir Zaidi c Randall b Hendrick	0	– (4) c Rice b Hemmings	1
P. J. W. Allott b Hendrick	4	– (10) c Hassan b Hemmings	2
L-b 2	2	B 4, l-b 2	6

1/9 2/64 3/64 4/95   158   1/7 2/21 3/22 4/55   65
5/101 6/118 7/121 8/150 9/150   5/59 6/59 7/63 8/63 9/65

Bonus points – Lancashire 1, Nottinghamshire 4.

Bowling: *First Innings*—Hendrick 22.3–6–55–6; Bore 12–5–29–0; Hemmings 25–9–54–4; Such 3–0–18–0. *Second Innings*—Hendrick 14–4–31–2; Hemmings 25.3–15–23–7; Bore 9–6–4–1; Such 3–2–1–0.

Umpires: M. J. Kitchen and D. R. Shepherd.

NOTTINGHAMSHIRE v ESSEX

At Nottingham, July 2, 4, 5. Essex won by 201 runs. Essex 22 pts, Nottinghamshire 4 pts. Injury-hit Nottinghamshire had no answer to the all-round strength of an Essex team who improved their Championship chances with this emphatic victory. Although Nottinghamshire had them struggling on 124 for eight on the opening day, thanks largely to Ray East's 45, they were in the ascendancy. Nottinghamshire collapsed against Lever and Pringle, and some marvellous strokeplay from Gooch, Lilley, Fletcher, McEwan and Pont quickly made Essex's position impregnable. A target of 374 for victory was never really within Nottinghamshire's compass, and although Rice and Hemmings gave some resistance they only delayed the inevitable.

Essex

G. A. Gooch c Hendrick b Hemmings	21	– b Saxelby	73
A. W. Lilley c Birch b Hendrick	2	– c Robinson b Such	61
*K. W. R. Fletcher c French b Cooper	5	– c French b Saxelby	39
K. S. McEwan c Randall b Hendrick	31	– not out	81
K. R. Pont c and b Such	19	– not out	27
D. R. Pringle c French b Saxelby	36		
S. Turner c Birch b Saxelby	0		
†D. E. East run out	0		
R. E. East run out	45		
J. K. Lever c Randall b Saxelby	18		
N. A. Foster not out	25		
L-b 5, n-b 4	9	L-b 1, w 1, n-b 2	4

1/3 2/15 3/63 4/63   211   1/96   (3 wkts dec.) 285
5/112 6/112 7/112 8/124 9/178   2/158 3/185

Bonus points – Essex 2, Nottinghamshire 4 (Score at 100 overs: 211-9).

Bowling: *First Innings*—Hendrick 14–5–24–2; Cooper 30–15–39–1; Saxelby 18.2–3–56–3; Hemmings 15–3–31–1; Such 23–8–52–1. *Second Innings*—Hendrick 10–2–32–0; Cooper 22–3–81–0; Saxelby 18–1–67–2; Such 12–0–101–1.

Nottinghamshire

B. Hassan c Fletcher b Lever	25	– lbw b Lever	2
R. T. Robinson c Gooch b Foster	0	– c D. E. East b Lever	22
D. W. Randall c Pringle b Lever	16	– (4) b Turner	16
E. E. Hemmings c D. E. East b Lever	29	– (3) c D. E. East b Pringle	37
*C. E. B. Rice c McEwan b Foster	16	– b Pringle	47
J. D. Birch not out	23	– b Turner	5
†B. N. French c McEwan b Lever	0	– run out	8
K. Saxelby c D. E. East b Pringle	4	– c Lilley b R. E. East	0
K. E. Cooper c Fletcher b Pringle	1	– run out	0
M. Hendrick c Foster b Pringle	5	– not out	15
P. M. Such lbw b Pringle	1	– c Pringle b R. E. East	5
L-b 3	3	B 1, n-b 14	15

1/0 2/25 3/46 4/79   123   1/6 2/51 3/77 4/77   172
5/99 6/99 7/108 8/110 9/118   5/84 6/124 7/125 8/136 9/151

Bonus points – Essex 4.

Bowling: *First Innings*—Lever 19–3–65–4; Foster 12–0–42–2; Pringle 6.3–1–13–4. *Second Innings*—Lever 11–0–46–2; Foster 14–2–42–0; R. E. East 7–1–20–2; Pringle 10–1–43–2; Turner 8–4–6–2.

Umpires: H. D. Bird and P. J. Eele.

At Worcester, July 9, 11, 12. NOTTINGHAMSHIRE beat WORCESTERSHIRE by 215 runs.

NOTTINGHAMSHIRE v NORTHAMPTONSHIRE

At Nottingham, July 13, 14. Northamptonshire won by an innings and 71 runs. Northamptonshire 23 pts, Nottinghamshire 1 pt. Nottinghamshire were beaten in two days after two miserable batting performances. On a wicket helping the seamers on the first day they were bowled out by Kapil Dev, Griffiths and Walker. Northamptonshire were 117 for one by the close of the first day. On the second Willey, dropped by French off Hendrick before adding to his overnight 29, consolidated his side's position. He hit ten 4s in an innings that lasted 271 minutes. Nottinghamshire hit back well with the new ball to claim Northamptonshire's last six wickets for 30 runs, Saxelby finishing with a career-best five for 57. But only Hassan offered much resistance on a pitch still favouring the bowlers and Nottinghamshire, needing 169 to make Northamptonshire bat again, were once more dismissed cheaply.

Nottinghamshire

B. Hassan c Steele b Griffiths	6	– c Willey b Griffiths	25
R. T. Robinson lbw b Walker	22	– c Cook b Kapil Dev	18
*C. E. B. Rice c Sharp b Walker	36	– c Sharp b Walker	16
J. D. Birch c Cook b Walker	0	– lbw b Walker	0
P. Johnson c Larkins b Kapil Dev	21	– c Sharp b Walker	1
E. E. Hemmings lbw b Kapil Dev	9	– c Larkins b Willey	13
†B. N. French c Cook b Kapil Dev	3	– c Bailey b Willey	0
K. Saxelby lbw b Walker	0	– c Sharp b Griffiths	0
K. E. Cooper c Williams b Kapil Dev	15	– c Williams b Griffiths	12
M. K. Bore c Larkins b Griffiths	7	– c Steele b Griffiths	7
M. Hendrick not out	2	– not out	0
B 1, l-b 3, n-b 1	5	B 4, l-b 1, n-b 1	6
	124		98

1/7 2/31 3/31 4/71 5/99 6/99 7/102 8/102 9/114

1/22 2/48 3/48 4/50 5/79 6/79 7/79 8/79 9/87

Bonus points – Northamptonshire 4.

Bowling: *First Innings*—Kapil Dev 21.1–11–24–4; Griffiths 17–7–34–2; Walker 16–2–61–4; Willey 2–2–0–0. *Second Innings*—Kapil Dev 10–2–18–1; Griffiths 13.2–3–37–4; Williams 2–2–0–0; Walker 9–2–27–3; Willey 6–2–10–2.

Northamptonshire

*G. Cook c Birch b Saxelby	69	†G. Sharp c Rice b Hemmings	6
W. Larkins c Hendrick b Hemmings	43	A. Walker not out	7
P. Willey c Hendrick b Saxelby	108	B. J. Griffiths c French b Saxelby	0
R. J. Boyd-Moss c and b Bore	12		
Kapil Dev c Hendrick b Hemmings	8	B 2, l-b 7, w 1, n-b 6	16
R. G. Williams lbw b Saxelby	11		
R. J. Bailey lbw b Saxelby	4	1/75 2/183 3/223 4/236	293
D. S. Steele c Hendrick b Hemmings	9	5/263 6/269 7/274 8/286 9/289	

Bonus points – Northamptonshire 3, Nottinghamshire 1 (Score at 100 overs: 252-4).

Bowling: Hendrick 18–5–34–0; Cooper 19–6–35–0; Saxelby 23.2–8–57–5; Bore 23–4–54–1; Hemmings 35–6–97–4.

Umpires: J. W. Holder and C. T. Spencer.

At Bournemouth, July 16, 18, 19. NOTTINGHAMSHIRE lost to HAMPSHIRE by eight wickets.

At The Oval, July 27, 28, 29. NOTTINGHAMSHIRE lost to SURREY by nine wickets.

NOTTINGHAMSHIRE v YORKSHIRE

At Worksop, July 30, August 1, 2. Drawn. Nottinghamshire 2 pts, Yorkshire 5 pts. Rice had cause to regret his decision to invite Yorkshire to bat first as Boycott and Moxon shared an opening stand of 162. When Boycott went on to make a double-century, Yorkshire's large total ensured little chance of a positive result on a sound batting pitch. Robinson and Birch pointed Nottinghamshire towards an adequate reply and the match entered its final day with a draw inevitable.

Yorkshire

G. Boycott not out................214	– c Johnson b Bore................	16
M. D. Moxon c Hassan b Hemmings...... 68	– c Bore b Pick..................	50
J. D. Love c Robinson b Hemmings...... 4	– (6) not out..................	0
C. W. J. Athey c Bore b Saxelby...... 49	– (3) c Birch b Bore..........	27
G. B. Stevenson c Rice b Cooper 5		
K. Sharp c Birch b Hemmings...... 37	– (4) not out..................	15
†D. L. Bairstow not out.................. 24		
A. Ramage (did not bat)................	– (5) c Hassan b Bore..........	14
B 1, l-b 19, w 2, n-b 11 33	L-b 7, w 1, n-b 1	9

1/162 2/180 3/284 4/289   (5 wkts dec.) 434   1/38 2/52 3/110   (4 wkts dec.) 131
5/359   4/128

P. Carrick, *R. Illingworth and S. J. Dennis did not bat.

Bonus points – Yorkshire 3 (Score at 100 overs: 260-2).

Bowling: *First Innings*—Cooper 32–7–120–1; Saxelby 24–7–53–1; Pick 16–0–52–0; Hemmings 35–8–96–3; Bore 32–9–80–0. *Second Innings*—Cooper 12–4–19–0; Saxelby 8–3–16–0; Bore 22–11–34–3; Pick 5–0–21–1; Hemmings 14–3–30–0; Robinson 1–0–1–0; Birch 1–0–1–0.

Nottinghamshire

B. Hassan c Moxon b Stevenson........ 42	K. Saxelby lbw b Carrick	13
R. T. Robinson c Illingworth	R. A. Pick c Dennis b Illingworth.......	18
b Carrick. 56	K. E. Cooper not out	21
P. Johnson st Bairstow b Carrick 19	M. K. Bore c Dennis b Carrick	6
*C. E. B. Rice b Carrick.................. 17	B 8, l-b 10, w 1, n-b 17...........	36
J. D. Birch c Love b Dennis 60		
†B. N. French b Illingworth.............. 10	1/109 2/119 3/151 4/154	316
E. E. Hemmings lbw b Illingworth....... 18	5/182 6/244 7/263 8/286 9/292	

Bonus points – Nottinghamshire 2, Yorkshire 2 (Score at 100 overs: 247-6).

Bowling: Dennis 25–6–68–1; Stevenson 18–5–46–1; Ramage 7–1–28–0; Illingworth 32–13–69–3; Carrick 43.4–18–69–5.

Umpires: K. Ibadulla and A. G. T. Whitehead.

At Leicester, August 6, 8, 9. NOTTINGHAMSHIRE lost to LEICESTERSHIRE by 50 runs.

At Ebbw Vale, August 10, 11, 12. NOTTINGHAMSHIRE drew with GLAMORGAN.

NOTTINGHAMSHIRE v HAMPSHIRE

At Nottingham, August 13, 15, 16. Drawn. Nottinghamshire 6 pts, Hampshire 5 pts. Rain eventually denied Nottinghamshire after they had been set 199 to win in two hours. After winning the toss, Hampshire were in trouble until Turner provided stability with a sound 41. Robinson and the young Johnson then launched Nottinghamshire's innings with a century stand, but a middle-order collapse caused them to settle for a modest lead. After Hampshire, batting again, had been reduced to 104 for seven, Turner's unbeaten 94, then rain, put the game beyond Nottinghamshire's reach.

Hampshire

C. G. Greenidge b Pick	26	– c Birch b Saxelby	5
V. P. Terry b Pick	22	– lbw b Hendrick	25
M. C. J. Nicholas c French b Cooper	1	– c French b Saxelby	34
T. E. Jesty c Robinson b Saxelby	13	– c Hemmings b Saxelby	6
D. R. Turner c French b Hendrick	41	– (6) not out	94
*N. E. J. Pocock lbw b Saxelby	22	– (7) b Saxelby	1
M. D. Marshall c French b Cooper	17	– (8) c Hendrick b Cooper	19
N. G. Cowley c French b Saxelby	28	– (9) c Johnson b Hendrick	24
†R. J. Parks not out	14	– (5) c French b Hendrick	0
J. W. Southern run out	1	– c Birch b Pick	20
S. J. Malone b Cooper	2	– not out	4
L-b 3, n-b 4	7	L-b 1, w 1, n-b 9	11

1/40 2/41 3/54 4/63   194   1/11 2/58 3/73   (9 wkts dec.) 243
5/97 6/130 7/166 8/182 9/190   4/74 5/76 6/82 7/104 8/157 9/225

Bonus points – Hampshire 1, Nottinghamshire 4.

Bowling: *First Innings*—Hendrick 20–5–26–1; Saxelby 19–3–62–3; Cooper 18.5–5–38–3; Pick 19–4–50–2; Hemmings 5–0–11–0. *Second Innings*—Hendrick 25–10–50–3; Saxelby 20–7–49–4; Pick 15.2–2–53–1; Cooper 16–5–47–1; Hemmings 8–2–33–0.

Nottinghamshire

R. T. Robinson b Jesty	50	– not out	13
P. Johnson c Southern b Malone	47	– not out	11
D. W. Randall c Parks b Marshall	11		
*C. E. B. Rice c Parks b Jesty	0		
J. D. Birch lbw b Jesty	1		
†B. N. French lbw b Marshall	0		
E. E. Hemmings c Cowley b Malone	38		
K. Saxelby lbw b Cowley	23		
R. A. Pick c Turner b Cowley	4		
K. E. Cooper not out	30		
M. Hendrick lbw b Cowley	14		
L-b 16, n-b 5	21	W 4	4

1/100 2/104 3/113 4/114   239   (no wkt) 28
5/114 6/116 7/172 8/184 9/201

Bonus points – Nottinghamshire 2, Hampshire 4.

Bowling: *First Innings*—Marshall 25–5–55–2; Malone 19–3–51–2; Jesty 21–6–62–3; Nicholas 5–1–24–0; Cowley 14.4–4–26–3. *Second Innings*—Marshall 4–1–9–0; Malone 4–0–8–0; Jesty 2–0–6–0; Cowley 1–0–1–0.

Umpires: H. D. Bird and R. Palmer.

At Bradford, August 20, 22, 23. NOTTINGHAMSHIRE drew with YORKSHIRE.

At Bristol, August 27, 29, 30. NOTTINGHAMSHIRE drew with GLOUCESTERSHIRE.

NOTTINGHAMSHIRE v WARWICKSHIRE

At Nottingham, August 31, September 1, 2. Drawn. Nottinghamshire 8 pts, Warwickshire 2 pts. Only Lloyd and Lord, on his Championship début, mastered the Nottinghamshire seam attack as Warwickshire, who won the toss, were bowled out for 180. Nottinghamshire's reply was dominated by Robinson's first double-century. He reached 100 in 223 minutes and batted altogether for 406 minutes, hitting twenty boundaries. When Rice declared, Warwickshire needed 269 to avoid an innings defeat. Despite losing four wickets in the space of seven overs, half-centuries by Lloyd, Amiss and Paul Smith helped them to 256 for seven before bad light stopped play 75 minutes early.

Warwickshire

K. D. Smith c Hemmings b Hendrick	7	– (2) b Hemmings		14
T. A. Lloyd lbw b Cooper	70	– (1) c Hendrick b Saxelby		50
A. I. Kallicharran c Randall b Saxelby	5	– c Hendrick b Saxelby		5
D. L. Amiss c Birch b Cooper	1	– c French b Hemmings		60
†G. W. Humpage c French b Hendrick	10	– lbw b Hendrick		11
G. J. Lord c Robinson b Cooper	61	– run out		29
P. A. Smith c Rice b Hendrick	8	– not out		50
C. M. Old c Randall b Cooper	5	– c French b Hendrick		5
N. Gifford b Cooper	0	– not out		16
*R. G. D. Willis c French b Saxelby	4			
W. Hogg not out	3			
L-b 2, n-b 4	6	B 6, l-b 3, w 2, n-b 5		16

1/11 2/18 3/38 4/81   180   1/69 2/69 3/77 4/93   (7 wkts) 256
5/146 6/146 7/169 8/169 9/176   5/158 6/199 7/218

Bonus points – Warwickshire 1, Nottinghamshire 4.

Bowling: *First Innings*—Hendrick 18–3–49–3; Saxelby 16.1–5–37–2; Cooper 17–2–48–5; Hemmings 15–6–34–0; Bore 5–2–6–0. *Second Innings*—Hendrick 24–7–63–2; Saxelby 19.1–3–76–2; Cooper 13–2–48–0; Hemmings 29–18–45–2; Bore 3–1–8–0.

Nottinghamshire

B. Hassan lbw b Old	2	E. E. Hemmings c and b Kallicharran	2
R. T. Robinson c K. D. Smith b Gifford	207	K. Saxelby not out	13
D. W. Randall c Kallicharran b Old	47		
*C. E. B. Rice b P. A. Smith	22	L-b 9, n-b 21	30
J. D. Birch c Kallicharran b Gifford	90		
†B. N. French not out	36		

1/5 2/137 3/219 4/384   (6 wkts dec.) 449
5/408 6/410

K. E. Cooper, M. K. Bore and M. Hendrick did not bat.

Bonus points – Nottinghamshire 4, Warwickshire 1 (Score at 100 overs: 316-3).

Bowling: Willis 17–1–84–0; Old 26–4–67–2; Hogg 17–1–60–0; P. A. Smith 15–0–63–1; Gifford 43–13–99–2; Kallicharran 12–1–46–1.

Umpires: D. R. Shepherd and P. B. Wight.

At Derby, September 7, 8, 9. NOTTINGHAMSHIRE lost to DERBYSHIRE by 100 runs.

NOTTINGHAMSHIRE v MIDDLESEX

At Nottingham, September 10, 12, 13. Drawn. Nottinghamshire 7 pts, Middlesex 4 pts. Hadlee returned from New Zealand Test duty to influence the destiny of the Championship.

After the first day's play had been virtually washed out, he claimed five wickets as Middlesex were dismissed for 201. When Nottinghamshire made a solid start in reply, it left Rice in a quandary at the close of the second day. In normal circumstances, he would have declared in arrears and left the opposition to set a target, but to do so would have denied Middlesex the chance to claim the further bonus point they would have needed to win the Championship had they also won the match. Rice eventually batted on until lunch on the final day, and Middlesex had virtually conceded the Championship when rain closed the proceedings.

Middlesex

G. D. Barlow c Birch b Hadlee	1	– not out	15
A. G. T. Miller b Hadlee	70		
C. T. Radley c French b Hadlee	1		
*M. W. Gatting lbw b Cooper	13		
K. P. Tomlins b Pick	31		
J. E. Emburey c Randall b Hadlee	2	– (3) not out	38
N. F. Williams c Hadlee b Hendrick	32		
†P. R. Downton not out	19	– (2) lbw b Hendrick	0
P. H. Edmonds c French b Hendrick	0		
W. W. Daniel b Hadlee	7		
N. G. Cowans c French b Hendrick	9		
L-b 8, n-b 8	16	W 1	1

1/2 2/11 3/52 4/117   201   1/1   (1 wkt) 54
5/124 6/157 7/167 8/167 9/176

Bonus points – Middlesex 2, Nottinghamshire 4.

Bowling: *First Innings*—Hadlee 23–2–72–5; Hendrick 12.2–5–22–3; Hemmings 16–2–43–0; Cooper 14–5–36–1; Pick 6–1–12–1. *Second Innings*—Hadlee 2–1–5–0; Hendrick 7–4–12–1; Pick 5–0–21–0; Hemmings 3–0–15–0.

Nottinghamshire

P. Johnson b Cowans	0	†B. N. French c Williams b Cowans		6
R. T. Robinson b Cowans	56	E. E. Hemmings not out		11
D. W. Randall c Downton b Williams	23	B 1, l-b 4, w 1, n-b 14		20
*C. E. B. Rice not out	101			
J. D. Birch b Cowans	30	1/0 2/49 3/121 4/200	(6 wkts dec.)	253
R. J. Hadlee c Cowans	6	5/208 6/230		

R. A. Pick, K. E. Cooper and M. Hendrick did not bat.

Bonus points – Nottinghamshire 3, Middlesex 2.

Bowling: Cowans 15–3–43–5; Daniel 13–1–51–0; Williams 16–2–65–1; Gatting 8–3–17–0; Emburey 5–0–17–0; Edmonds 14.3–4–40–0.

Umpires: D. G. L. Evans and K. Ibadulla.

SOMERSET

President: C. R. M. Atkinson
Chairman: M. F. Hill
Chairman, Cricket Committee: 1983 – C. R. M.
  Atkinson
Secretary: A. S. Brown
  County Cricket Ground, St James's Street,
  Taunton TA1 1JT (Telephone: 0823-72946)
Captain: 1983 – B. C. Rose; 1984 – I. T. Botham
Coach: P. J. Robinson

Despite many difficulties, both expected and unforeseen, Somerset enjoyed another in their heartening sequence of successful seasons. Besides achieving record membership subscriptions and a healthy trading position, they won the NatWest Bank Trophy without the advantage of a single home tie, and again finished second in the John Player League. In such a closely fought competition as this, the Somerset record has been remarkable over the past ten years. They won it in 1979 and have been runners-up no fewer than six times, four of them when they have been equal on points with the winners.

These successes outweighed the disappointments of early removal from the Benson and Hedges Cup and one of the poorest Schweppes County Championship records of recent years. The World Cup took away four players (Botham and Marks of England, and Garner and Richards of West Indies) for an important period, while long-term injuries to Brian Rose, Hallam Moseley, and Hugh Wilson severely disrupted team plans. Furthermore, it was necessary to call on four captains – Rose, Peter Roebuck during the World Cup, and Vivian Richards during vice-captain Ian Botham's absences. However, these depredations forced young players to the fore, and here there were marked signs of hope for the future. Trevor Gard, having spent so much time in the wings, made a success of his first full season as wicket-keeper. Without a proved deputy, he steered clear of serious injury, played throughout, and his two fine stumpings in the NatWest Bank Trophy final rounded off a year of high accomplishment.

Stephen Booth, a nineteen-year-old slow left-armer from Yorkshire, made a promising start; twenty-year-old Julian Wyatt, opening against some high-class attacks in the last five games, displayed a splendid temperament and a sound technique; left-hander Richard Ollis emerged with considerable credit; and seventeen-year-old Gary Palmer did enough to suggest that development in physique and application will make him a valued member. Mark Davis, although demonstrating plenty of natural ability, was again plagued by minor injury, and so far unsolved problems with run-up and follow-through. Nigel Felton, who looked so good in 1982, was brought into the team before he was ready, but after a long period rebuilding his confidence, returned splendidly, compiling a highly satisfactory maiden century.

After Joel Garner's record-breaking winter with South Australia, his unhappy sequence of strains and lesser injuries militated against a serious Championship challenge. Significantly, his nine Championship appearances included all three Somerset victories. Vic Marks also played in these, while Richards and Botham played in two of them. Garner did play in all the one-day matches, often with important results. His fourteen for 90 in the NatWest Bank Trophy matches brooked no argument. Besides his normal quota of match-winning batting efforts, Richards also produced some very timely bowling spells. Botham and Marks also made their expected, indispensable contributions, particularly to the shorter matches. Colin Dredge returned to his usual reliable standards; Peter Denning had a splendid Sunday record; Jeremy Lloyds made many useful contributions; and, although unsuccessful overall, Philip Slocombe played three important one-day knocks.

Until his back injury, Wilson, the new recruit from Surrey, put in some lively, well-sustained spells, and when the team was especially hard pressed, the assistant coach, Dennis Breakwell, obliged with a few spirited performances. Two of the most improved players were Roebuck and Nigel Popplewell. Roebuck's thoughtful captaincy of weakened sides drew well-deserved praise, and his batting was rewarding, notably in the Sunday League when he and Denning eased the pressure on Richards. Popplewell's improved all-round application, coupled with some dazzling catches, found its high point in the five NatWest Bank Trophy matches. He was closely concerned in one of the great memories of the season, the great recovery in the semi-final against Middlesex, led unerringly by Botham.

Under Gordon Prosser, the ground-staff came through a series of devastating setbacks with flying colours. In a year which produced a cold, soggy winter, the wettest of Mays and a very hot July, completely relaid pitches at Bath and Weston-super-Mare of acceptable quality were outstanding achievements. After various Committee traumas during the winter, and the difficulties of the summer, Somerset could look back on 1983 with much satisfaction. – E.H.

SOMERSET 1983

[*Bill Smith*]

Back row: J. G. Wyatt, S. C. Booth, A. J. H. Dunning, T. Gard, N. A. Felton. *Middle row*: G. V. Palmer, J. W. Lloyds, C. H. Dredge, P. H. L. Wilson, M. R. Davis, R. L. Ollis, N. F. M. Popplewell. *Front row*: P. M. Roebuck, P. A. Slocombe, I. T. Botham, B. C. Rose (*captain*), I. V. A. Richards, P. W. Denning, V. J. Marks. *Inset*: J. Garner.

SOMERSET RESULTS

All first-class matches – Played 25: Won 3, Lost 7, Drawn 15.

County Championship matches – Played 24: Won 3, Lost 7, Drawn 14.

Bonus points – Batting 57, Bowling 75.

Competition placings – Schweppes County Championship, 10th; NatWest Bank Trophy, winners; Benson and Hedges Cup, 4th in Group C; John Player League, r/u.

COUNTY CHAMPIONSHIP AVERAGES

BATTING

	Birthplace	M	I	NO	R	HI	Avge
I. V. A. Richardsc ...	St John's, Antigua	12	20	4	1,204	216	75.25
I. T. Bothamc	Heswall	10	13	0	570	152	43.84
J. G. Wyatt	Paulton	5	10	2	338	82*	42.25
P. M. Roebuckc	Oxford	22	38	5	1,235	106*	37.42
N. A. Felton............	Guildford	7	12	1	376	173*	34.18
J. Garnerc	Barbados	9	14	6	223	44	27.87
J. W. Lloydsc	Penang, Malaya	20	33	2	803	100	25.90
N. F. M. Popplewellc	Chislehurst	23	37	3	879	143	25.85
R. L. Ollis	Clifton	13	22	2	517	99*	25.85
V. J. Marksc	Middle Chinnock	15	23	2	498	44*	23.71
P. W. Denningc	Chewton Mendip	20	34	3	659	85	21.25
B. C. Rosec.............	Dartford	7	7	0	138	52	19.71
T. Gardc	South Petherton	24	31	4	440	51	16.29
P. H. L. Wilson......	Guildford	10	9	6	45	25	15.00
C. H. Dredgec	Frome	21	26	5	296	50	14.09
P. A. Slocombec	Weston-super-Mare	10	15	2	145	37	11.15
G. V. Palmer..........	Taunton	10	13	2	119	78	10.81
M. R. Davis	Kilve	13	15	4	105	20	9.54
S. C. Booth	Leeds	10	12	5	24	9	3.42

Also batted: D. Breakwell (*Brierley Hill*) (2 matches) 55*, 4, 13; N. Russom (*Finchley*) (1 match) 8.

*Signifies not out.   c *Denotes county cap.*

BOWLING

	O	M	R	W	Avge	BB
J. Garner	256	67	659	34	19.38	6-37
C. H. Dredge..........	492.3	127	1,323	48	27.56	5-51
J. W. Lloyds...........	342.1	96	990	34	29.11	5-120
V. J. Marks	534.4	169	1,488	49	30.36	6-79
G. V. Palmer..........	208.3	39	630	20	31.50	5-38
N. F. M. Popplewell	225	37	736	23	32.00	4-69
I. T. Botham	119.3	28	388	12	32.33	5-38
M. R. Davis	212.4	40	746	23	32.43	4-34
P. H. L. Wilson......	213.3	37	717	21	34.14	4-77
I. V. A. Richards	188	61	462	12	38.50	3-56
S. C. Booth	296.2	85	849	21	40.42	4-26

Also bowled: D. Breakwell 49–17–121–4; T. Gard 0.2–0–8–0; R. L. Ollis 1–0–2–0; P. M. Roebuck 5–0–25–0; N. Russom 5–1–18–0; P. A. Slocombe 2–1–1–0.

The following played a total of eleven three-figure innings for Somerset in County Championship matches – I. V. A. Richards 5, I. T. Botham 2, N. A. Felton 1, J. W. Lloyds 1, N. F. M. Popplewell 1, P. M. Roebuck 1.

At Oxford, April 27, 28, 29. OXFORD UNIVERSITY v SOMERSET. Abandoned. A one-day match, played on April 29, was drawn.

At Nottingham, April 30, May 1, 2. SOMERSET drew with NOTTINGHAMSHIRE.

SOMERSET v WORCESTERSHIRE

At Taunton, May 4, 5, 6. Drawn. Somerset 7 pts, Worcestershire 5 pts. Over seven hours were lost after a solid Somerset first innings which featured an opening stand of 143 between Roebuck and Lloyds in 47 overs, a burst of four for 12 by Pridgeon, and bright batting later down the order. Between the showers Weston, at the crease for 61 overs, was well supported by the main Worcestershire batting before Younis ensured a third batting point ten minutes into extra time.

Somerset

J. W. Lloyds lbw b Pridgeon 58	V. J. Marks c McEvoy b Patel 32
P. M. Roebuck b Pridgeon 81	C. H. Dredge not out 30
P. A. Slocombe c Humphries	
b Pridgeon. 1	L-b 8, w 1, n-b 13 22
*B. C. Rose c Neale b Illingworth 40	
I. T. Botham c Ormrod b Pridgeon 24	1/143 2/151 (7 wkts dec.) 325
N. F. M. Popplewell c Humphries	3/164 4/190
b Pridgeon. 37	5/253 6/263 7/325

†T. Gard, M. R. Davis and P. H. L. Wilson did not bat.

Bonus points – Somerset 4, Worcestershire 2 (Score at 100 overs: 318-6).

Bowling: Pridgeon 29–6–58–5; Inchmore 24–5–68–0; Patel 15–1–59–1; Perryman 15–4–52–0; Illingworth 18–2–66–1.

Worcestershire

J. A Ormrod c Botham b Wilson 22	R. K. Illingworth lbw b Davis 1
M. J. Weston lbw b Dredge 92	J. D. Inchmore not out 5
*P. A. Neale c Lloyds b Dredge 40	B 2, l-b 5, w 1, n-b 10 18
D. N. Patel c Gard b Popplewell 31	
Younis Ahmed not out 35	1/39 2/160 (7 wkts) 253
M. S. A. McEvoy lbw b Popplewell 0	3/175 4/211
†D. J. Humphries b Popplewell 9	5/211 6/227 7/237

A. P. Pridgeon and S. P. Perryman did not bat.

Bonus points – Worcestershire 3, Somerset 3.

Bowling: Botham 7–3–11–0; Davis 15–2–51–1; Dredge 22–9–36–2; Wilson 12–0–52–1; Marks 19–7–49–0; Lloyds 3–0–10–0; Popplewell 7.1–1–26–3.

Umpires: R. Palmer and D. R. Shepherd.

At Worcester, May 11, 12, 13. SOMERSET drew with WORCESTERSHIRE.

SOMERSET v SUSSEX

At Taunton, May 25, 26, 27. Sussex won by ten wickets. Sussex 24 pts, Somerset 4 pts. A fourth-wicket stand of 103 in 24 overs between Parker (four 6s, seven 4s) and Colin Wells on a dry, bare pitch set Sussex on their way to a large total. Determined bowling completed the victory with 160 minutes to spare. Rose, for 49 overs, and Denning, for 40 overs, resisted firmly but Somerset followed on 184 behind. Following a partnership of 60 in sixteen overs between Richards and Lloyds, Barclay took three for 2 in seventeen balls, after which only Botham, with three 6s and seven 4s in a contrasting 43-over innings, and Gard, for a stout 26 overs, held up the advance.

Sussex

G. D. Mendis b Garner	65	– not out	8
A. M. Green c Marks b Garner	12	– not out	0
*J. R. T. Barclay c Botham b Marks	26		
C. M. Wells b Lloyds	63		
P. W. G. Parker lbw b Marks	79		
A. P. Wells not out	61		
I. A. Greig c Popplewell b Marks	59		
†I. J. Gould not out	33		
B 1, l-b 2, w 2, n-b 5	10		

1/28 2/96 3/132   (6 wkts dec.) 408   (no wkt) 8
4/235 5/261 6/343

G. S. le Roux, A. C. S. Pigott and C. E. Waller did not bat.

Bonus points – Sussex 4, Somerset 2 (Score at 100 overs: 337-5).

Bowling: *First Innings*—Garner 20–4–49–2; Dredge 11–1–44–0; Botham 6–0–25–0; Marks 37–9–112–3; Lloyds 27–6–108–1; Richards 12–4–32–0; Roebuck 2–0–15–0; Popplewell 6–0–13–0. *Second Innings*—Gard 0.2–0–8–0.

Somerset

J. W. Lloyds b Pigott	12	– c sub b le Roux	31
P. M. Roebuck st Gould b Barclay	19	– b Pigott	0
I. V. A. Richards c Gould b le Roux	2	– b Barclay	30
*B. C. Rose c Barclay b Pigott	52	– b Barclay	5
P. W. Denning c and b Waller	36	– c sub b Barclay	4
I. T. Botham c Pigott b Waller	27	– (7) c A. P. Wells b Pigott	81
N. F. M. Popplewell c and b Barclay	9	– (6) c Mendis b le Roux	3
V. J. Marks st Gould b Waller	26	– c Barclay b Pigott	3
†T. Gard run out	0	– c A. P. Wells b Greig	22
C. H. Dredge c A. P. Wells b le Roux	6	– c sub b Pigott	6
J. Garner not out	23	– not out	2
B 4, l-b 3, w 1, n-b 4	12	L-b 2, n-b 1	3

1/16 2/19 3/61 4/121   224   1/2 2/62 3/62 4/67   190
5/159 6/160 7/187 8/187 9/196   5/72 6/95 7/100 8/156 9/173

Bonus points – Somerset 2, Sussex 4.

Bowling: *First Innings*—le Roux 16–3–44–2; Pigott 20–3–55–2; Greig 5–0–15–0; Barclay 26–10–54–2; Waller 22–10–44–3. *Second Innings*—le Roux 22–5–80–2; Pigott 13.4–1–44–4; Greig 15–2–33–1; Barclay 14–8–30–3.

Umpires: D. G. L. Evans and A. G. T. Whitehead.

SOMERSET v ESSEX

At Taunton, June 4, 6, 7. Essex won by 141 runs. Essex 22 pts, Somerset 7 pts. A dry, bare pitch produced a well-balanced match for two and a half days. Gooch and Fletcher gave Essex a useful start, and McEwan led a recovery from some difficulties. Phillip quickly reduced Somerset to 19 for three but then Roebuck in 68 overs, Gard, Botham in sixteen balls, and Popplewell over a stout 54 overs checked the slump. Night-watchman David East, batting for 44 overs, established Essex's second innings, allowing Fletcher to set a target of 255 in 210 minutes. The spinners restricted Roebuck and Denning to a stand of 50 in 28 overs, so destroying any Somerset victory aspirations, and a remarkable final spell of five for 1 in thirteen balls by Acfield settled the match with 55 minutes to spare.

Essex

G. A. Gooch c Roebuck b Dredge	60	– b Marks	33
B. R. Hardie c Gard b Davis	4	– c sub b Botham	39
*K. W. R. Fletcher lbw b Popplewell	46	– (4) lbw b Dredge	12
K. S. McEwan c Lloyds b Marks	54	– (3) lbw b Marks	6
K. R. Pont c Popplewell b Dredge	1	– c Lloyds b Marks	22
D. R. Pringle run out	21		
N. Phillip c sub b Dredge	36	– c Denning b Botham	29
†D. E. East c Gard b Dredge	10	– (6) c Gard b Botham	77
R. E. East c Roebuck b Dredge	5	– (8) b Marks	16
N. A. Foster c sub b Marks	4	– (9) c Dredge b Botham	1
D. L. Acfield not out	4	– (10) not out	1
B 6, l-b 8, w 1, n-b 2	17	B 1, l-b 4, w 1	6

1/14 2/123 3/123 4/124   262   1/56 2/63 3/92   (9 wkts dec.) 242
5/174 6/219 7/241 8/250 9/257   4/98 5/146 6/219 7/226 8/240 9/242

Bonus points – Essex 3, Somerset 4.

Bowling: *First Innings*—Botham 17–3–61–0; Davis 17–2–55–1; Dredge 24.5–5–64–5; Marks 14–2–36–2; Popplewell 11–3–21–1; Lloyds 4–1–8–0. *Second Innings*—Botham 18–6–49–4; Davis 4–0–20–0; Marks 39.5–10–103–4; Dredge 15–5–35–1; Lloyds 11–2–29–0.

Somerset

J. W. Lloyds c D. E. East b Phillip	0	– c and b Phillip	0
P. M. Roebuck b Acfield	69	– lbw b R. E. East	41
P. A. Slocombe c D. E. East b Phillip	3	– c Gooch b Foster	10
P. W. Denning b Phillip	7	– lbw b Acfield	20
†T. Gard b Acfield	29	– (8) b Acfield	0
I. T. Botham st D. E. East b Acfield	34	– (5) lbw b Acfield	19
N. F. M. Popplewell not out	66	– (6) lbw b Acfield	8
V. J. Marks c Foster b Acfield	12	– (7) c Phillip b Acfield	8
M. R. Davis not out	16	– b Acfield	0
C. H. Dredge (did not bat)		– not out	1
*B. C. Rose (did not bat)		– absent injured	
B 4, l-b 6, n-b 4	14	L-b 3, n-b 3	6

1/0 2/10 3/19   (7 wkts dec.) 250   1/2 2/25 3/75 4/75   113
4/96 5/132 6/172 7/200   5/103 6/108 7/108 8/108 9/113

Bonus points – Somerset 3, Essex 3.

Bowling: *First Innings*—Phillip 14–5–24–3; Foster 19.3–3–49–0; Pringle 4–2–9–0; Acfield 34–6–106–4; R. E. East 27–7–48–0. *Second Innings*—Phillip 6–1–14–1; Foster 7–1–24–1; Acfield 18.3–5–34–6; R. E. East 17–4–35–1.

Umpires: A. G. T. Whitehead and J. Birkenshaw.

At Bristol, June 8, 9, 10. SOMERSET drew with GLOUCESTERSHIRE.

At Hove, June 11, 13, 14. SOMERSET lost to SUSSEX by seven wickets.

At Swansea, June 15, 16, 17. SOMERSET drew with GLAMORGAN.

SOMERSET v DERBYSHIRE

At Bath, June 18, 20, 21. Derbyshire won by 123 runs. Derbyshire 23 pts, Somerset 4 pts. Three cloudy mornings brought three collapses, but Derbyshire's recovery from 79 for five on the first day was the decisive factor. Miller, who batted for 62 overs, and Fowler added 124 in 33 overs and Tunnicliffe's 30-over half-century was valuable. Roebuck's fighting 42 overs led the Somerset attempt but only a ninth-wicket stand of 28 avoided the follow-on. Derbyshire built steadily on their lead of 148, helped by injury to two Somerset bowlers, and even a late collapse left Somerset needing 315 in 335 minutes. They immediately slumped, but Denning's heroic 66 overs and spirited resistance for twenty overs by Dredge gave Derbyshire an anxious period before they achieved victory with 93 minutes remaining.

Derbyshire

I. S. Anderson lbw b Davis	1	– b Lloyds	33
J. E. Morris lbw b Dredge	23	– c sub b Dredge	27
A. Hill c Gard b Davis	5	– run out	34
*K. J. Barnett b Davis	13	– c Denning b Breakwell	35
R. J. Finney c Denning b Popplewell	17	– st Gard b Breakwell	13
G. Miller b Palmer	84	– lbw b Popplewell	10
W. P. Fowler c Dredge b Lloyds	59	– lbw b Breakwell	2
C. J. Tunnicliffe c Palmer b Lloyds	51	– b Palmer	0
†R. W. Taylor c Roebuck b Lloyds	17	– not out	0
D. G. Moir c Palmer b Popplewell	4	– b Popplewell	0
O. H. Mortensen not out	0	– b Popplewell	0
B 1, l-b 12, w 2	15	B 2, l-b 7, w 1, n-b 2	12
	289		**166**

1/1 2/20 3/42 4/44 5/79 6/203 7/239 8/276 9/283

1/46 2/80 3/120 4/146 5/152 6/162 7/165 8/165 9/166

Bonus points – Derbyshire 3, Somerset 4.

Bowling: *First Innings*—Palmer 21–1–62–1; Davis 22–5–55–3; Lloyds 20.3–8–54–3; Popplewell 9–0–25–2; Breakwell 9–3–36–0; Dredge 18–7–42–1. *Second Innings*—Palmer 15–6–19–1; Dredge 8–3–11–1; Breakwell 16–3–44–3; Popplewell 19.4–3–54–3; Lloyds 13–3–26–1.

Somerset

*P. M. Roebuck lbw b Finney	44	– c Taylor b Mortensen	4
R. L. Ollis lbw b Mortensen	0	– b Tunnicliffe	1
N. A. Felton lbw b Mortensen	5	– lbw b Mortensen	1
P. W. Denning c Taylor b Tunnicliffe	9	– c Anderson b Miller	85
N. F. M. Popplewell lbw b Finney	19	– lbw b Finney	16
J. W. Lloyds lbw b Mortensen	19	– lbw b Finney	10
D. Breakwell c Moir b Finney	4	– (8) b Tunnicliffe	13
G. V. Palmer b Finney	0	– (9) c Fowler b Moir	4
†T. Gard not out	14	– (7) lbw b Miller	12
C. H. Dredge c Taylor b Mortensen	13	– b Tunnicliffe	35
M. R. Davis lbw b Mortensen	0	– not out	0
B 1, l-b 5, n-b 8	14	L-b 9, n-b 1	10
	141		**191**

1/0 2/14 3/36 4/73 5/91 6/96 7/113 8/113 9/141

1/1 2/4 3/13 4/52 5/70 6/83 7/115 8/123 9/179

Bonus points – Derbyshire 4.

Bowling: *First Innings*—Mortensen 22.1–9–43–5; Tunnicliffe 13–5–31–1; Miller 13–6–15–0; Moir 1–0–4–0; Finney 9–3–34–4. *Second Innings*—Mortensen 14–2–65–2; Tunnicliffe 18–4–41–3; Finney 12–0–49–2; Miller 18.4–9–20–2; Moir 8–6–6–1.

Umpires: W. E. Alley and R. A. White.

SOMERSET v GLOUCESTERSHIRE

At Bath, June 22, 23, 24. Drawn. Somerset 5 pts, Gloucestershire 6 pts. Lloyds, missed before scoring, rescued his side with a breezy 27-over innings after Shepherd had done the early damage. Wilson reduced Gloucestershire to 87 for five, but on a gloomy, dank Thursday only 34 overs were possible. Hignell batted splendidly for 43 overs, then on the final day Gloucestershire offered easy runs to promote a declaration which eventually set them 306 in 194 minutes. Popplewell took full advantage, reaching 100 in 41 minutes and finishing with 143 in 62 minutes off 40 scoring strokes, of which nine were 6s and seventeen 4s. Hignell and Romaines, putting on 93 in 22 overs, opened possibilities for a Gloucestershire victory, but Wilson's long exertions at last bore fruit and it needed Doughty and Russell to fight doggedly through all but three balls of the last fourteen overs to frustrate Somerset.

Somerset

*P. M. Roebuck c Russell b Shepherd	10	– b Dudleston	51
N. A. Felton lbw b Shepherd	11	– st Russell b Bainbridge	51
P. A. Slocombe lbw b Sainsbury	6	– (4) not out	20
P. W. Denning c Bainbridge b Shepherd	27	– (5) not out	21
R. L. Ollis b Shepherd	36		
N. F. M. Popplewell c Graveney b Shepherd	20	– (3) b Sainsbury	143
J. W. Lloyds b Sainsbury	81		
N. Russom lbw b Doughty	8		
†T. Gard not out	7		
G. V. Palmer c Romaines b Bainbridge	8		
P. H. L. Wilson b Bainbridge	1		
B 4, l-b 16, w 1, n-b 2	23	B 5, l-b 7, w 1	13

1/11 2/31 3/37 4/89   238   1/88   (3 wkts dec.) 299
5/100 6/171 7/212 8/212 9/228   2/235 3/263

Bonus points – Somerset 2, Gloucestershire 4.

Bowling: *First Innings*—Shepherd 27–7–80–5; Lawrence 19–5–52–0; Sainsbury 15–5–52–2; Bainbridge 5.5–2–10–2; Doughty 8–4–18–1; Graveney 5–3–3–0. *Second Innings*—Shepherd 7–7–0–0; Sainsbury 10.4–2–55–1; Graveney 17–2–85–0; Bainbridge 8–2–40–1; Dudleston 10–1–81–1; Doughty 5–0–25–0.

Gloucestershire

A. W. Stovold c Gard b Wilson	5	– lbw b Popplewell	6
P. W. Romaines lbw b Wilson	10	– b Popplewell	47
P. Bainbridge lbw b Palmer	5	– (4) c Gard b Palmer	27
A. J. Hignell c and b Lloyds	103	– (3) c Slocombe b Wilson	57
B. Dudleston c Lloyds b Wilson	11	– (7) b Wilson	12
†R. C. Russell c Gard b Wilson	0	– (9) b Lloyds	12
J. N. Shepherd c Felton b Palmer	22	– (5) b Wilson	4
*D. A. Graveney not out	49	– (6) run out	1
R. J. Doughty not out	8	– (8) not out	16
G. E. Sainsbury (did not bat)		– not out	0
B 4, l-b 10, w 2, n-b 3	19	B 5, l-b 10, w 1	16

1/10 2/20 3/26   (7 wkts dec.) 232   1/11 2/104 3/126 4/145   (8 wkts) 198
4/87 5/87 6/110 7/202   5/149 6/165 7/167 8/198

D. V. Lawrence did not bat.

Bonus points – Gloucestershire 2, Somerset 3.

Bowling: *First Innings*—Wilson 25–5–77–4; Palmer 20–1–94–2; Popplewell 7–0–33–0; Lloyds 5–1–9–1. *Second Innings*—Wilson 23–2–83–3; Popplewell 14–0–34–2; Palmer 9–1–27–1; Russom 5–1–18–0; Lloyds 5.5–2–14–1; Roebuck 2–0–6–0.

Umpires: R. A. White and W. E. Alley.

At Taunton, July 2, 3, 4. SOMERSET drew with NEW ZEALANDERS (See New Zealand tour section).

At Leicester, July 9, 11, 12. SOMERSET beat LEICESTERSHIRE by an innings and 71 runs.

At Maidstone, July 13, 14, 15. SOMERSET lost to KENT by three wickets.

SOMERSET v SURREY

At Taunton, July 16, 18, 19. Drawn. Somerset 8 pts, Surrey 5 pts. Two determined starts by Roebuck and Lloyds against a notably hostile Clarke opened the way for two splendid innings by Richards. In the first he batted 51 overs with three 6s and fifteen 4s and in the second set up a Somerset declaration with a dazzling 76 from 51 balls. Pocock took all seven wickets to fall on the last morning. Surrey's two innings followed a similar pattern, with Butcher, Knight and Lynch leading the way. The final target was 313 in 240 minutes, but when Knight's fine 64 ended only ten overs remained and the last pair successfully survived the final four overs.

Somerset

P. M. Roebuck c Richards b Thomas	58	– c Richards b Pocock	42
J. W. Lloyds b Pocock	41	– lbw b Pocock	48
N. A. Felton c Knight b Pocock	14	– (7) c and b Pocock	11
N. F. M. Popplewell c Richards b Clarke	46	– c Curtis b Pocock	8
*I. V. A. Richards not out	142	– (3) c Smith b Pocock	76
P. W. Denning c Knight b Clarke	2	– (5) not out	21
P. A. Slocombe c Richards b Clarke	22	– (6) c and b Pocock	0
G. V. Palmer (did not bat)	–	c Clarke b Pocock	2
B 5, l-b 5, w 1, n-b 6	17	B 5, l-b 2, w 6, n-b 2	15

1/82 2/114 3/123 4/242   (6 wkts dec.) 342   1/90 2/118 3/142   (7 wkts dec.) 223
5/248 6/342   4/195 5/195 6/221 7/223

†T. Gard, C. H. Dredge and J. Garner did not bat.

Bonus points – Somerset 4, Surrey 2 (Score at 100 overs: 309-5).

Bowling: *First Innings*—Clarke 19.3–1–53–3; Thomas 20–3–61–1; Mackintosh 15–2–47–0; Knight 9–1–32–0; Pocock 28–7–91–2; Curtis 16–4–41–0. *Second Innings*—Clarke 11–5–21–0; Thomas 9–0–42–0; Pocock 29.5–10–79–7; Curtis 20–3–66–0.

Surrey

A. R. Butcher c Palmer b Lloyds	40	– c Gard b Lloyds	45
G. S. Clinton c Richards b Garner	4	– c sub b Richards	19
D. M. Smith c Lloyds b Dredge	2	– c Richards b Lloyds	31
*R. D. V. Knight b Garner	52	– (5) st Gard b Lloyds	64
M. A. Lynch c Roebuck b Dredge	78	– (4) c Palmer b Dredge	34
†C. J. Richards st Gard b Lloyds	21	– (7) b Lloyds	14
D. J. Thomas c Garner b Richards	18	– (8) c Gard b Richards	25
K. S. Mackintosh not out	18	– (9) not out	5
S. T. Clarke c Garner b Richards	0	– (6) c Dredge b Lloyds	0
P. I. Pocock lbw b Garner	4	– c sub b Richards	1
I. J. Curtis c Denning b Lloyds	7	– not out	1
B 1, l-b 4, w 1, n-b 3	9	B 4, l-b 7, w 1, n-b 1	13

1/5 2/12 3/84 4/151   253   1/51 2/65 3/127   (9 wkts) 252
5/196 6/212 7/228 8/228 9/246   4/152 5/158 6/182 7/229 8/246 9/250

Bonus points – Surrey 3, Somerset 4.

Bowling: *First Innings*—Garner 19–7–41–3; Dredge 12–3–39–2; Palmer 10–1–46–0; Lloyds 28.5–8–89–3; Richards 14–6–29–2. *Second Innings*—Garner 19–5–43–0; Dredge 5–1–20–1; Lloyds 35–6–120–5; Richards 23–8–56–3.

Umpires: B. Leadbeater and D. O. Oslear.

At Northampton, July 27, 28, 29. SOMERSET drew with NORTHAMPTONSHIRE.

At Manchester, July 30, August 1, 2. SOMERSET lost to LANCASHIRE by an innings and 15 runs.

SOMERSET v NORTHAMPTONSHIRE

At Weston-super-Mare, August 6, 8, 9. Drawn. Somerset 4 pts, Northamptonshire 7 pts. Northamptonshire's first innings, based on a solid beginning and a lively innings from Kapil Dev, batting only 38 overs and hitting two 6s and sixteen 4s, kept them in charge for most of the match. Having earlier declared 138 behind, Somerset faced a final task of 321 in four hours. After an early collapse, Richards, batting late because of a stomach disorder and partnered by Marks, gave them a brief glimpse of victory, but when 80 were needed in ten overs with two wickets remaining, Richards changed from attack to strict defence and made sure Somerset saved the match. Richards's superb innings lasted 48 overs and included two 6s and 21 4s.

Northamptonshire

*G. Cook b Marks	43	– c Davis b Marks	43
W. Larkins lbw b Dredge	31	– c Gard b Davis	11
P. Willey b Booth	71	– c Botham b Booth	56
A. J. Lamb c Gard b Dredge	51	– c Davis b Marks	16
R. G. Williams not out	75	– not out	20
Kapil Dev b Booth	120	– not out	31
D. J. Capel not out	8		
L-b 2, w 4	6	L-b 5	5

1/56 2/107 3/189   (5 wkts dec.) 405   1/20 2/113 3/127   (4 wkts dec.) 182
4/209 5/381   4/137

D. S. Steele, †G. Sharp, N. A. Mallender and B. J. Griffiths did not bat.

Bonus points – Northamptonshire 4, Somerset 1 (Score at 100 overs: 331-4).

Bowling: *First Innings*—Botham 10–1–56–0; Davis 5–1–24–0; Richards 18–10–27–0; Dredge 18–10–40–2; Popplewell 3–0–22–0; Marks 33–9–123–1; Booth 38–4–107–2. *Second Innings*—Botham 6–0–22–0; Davis 7–2–29–1; Dredge 9–2–28–0; Marks 25–6–66–2; Booth 18–10–32–1.

Somerset

P. M. Roebuck c Sharp b Mallender	23	– c Kapil Dev b Steele	31
R. L. Ollis lbw b Kapil Dev	9	– lbw b Kapil Dev	14
P. W. Denning c Sharp b Mallender	10	– b Kapil Dev	15
I. V. A. Richards b Mallender	61	– (6) not out	128
*I. T. Botham b Mallender	40	– c Willey b Mallender	5
N. F. M. Popplewell c Kapil Dev b Williams	52	– (4) c Cook b Steele	10
V. J. Marks c Cook b Steele	15	– c Steele b Kapil Dev	42
†T. Gard not out	32	– c Cook b Kapil Dev	0
C. H. Dredge not out	0	– c Kapil Dev b Willey	8
M. R. Davis (did not bat)	–	– not out	6
B 6, l-b 10, n-b 9	25	B 9, l-b 5, n-b 5	19

1/38 2/42 3/67 4/139   (7 wkts dec.) 267   1/29 2/45 3/73 4/78   (8 wkts) 278
5/172 6/187 7/266   5/88 6/184 7/186 8/241

S. C. Booth did not bat.

Bonus points – Somerset 3, Northamptonshire 3.

Bowling: *First Innings*—Kapil Dev 18–5–45–1; Griffiths 24–6–49–0; Willey 9–2–17–0; Mallender 19–3–69–4; Capel 5–1–20–0; Steele 17–9–23–1; Williams 8–0–19–1. *Second Innings*—Kapil Dev 18.5–4–76–4; Mallender 11–0–55–1; Griffiths 7–0–25–0; Steele 16–4–67–2; Williams 15–5–29–0; Willey 6–2–7–1.

Umpires: C. T. Spencer and A. G. T. Whitehead.

SOMERSET v YORKSHIRE

At Weston-super-Mare, August 10, 11, 12. Drawn. Somerset 3 pts, Yorkshire 6 pts. Boycott, batting 71 overs, and Moxon began the match on a slow turning pitch with by far its highest partnership – 139 in 63 overs – before the bowlers took control. However, Stevenson, hitting four 6s and four 4s off seventeen balls, made progress. After his early bursts with the ball when Somerset replied, the Yorkshire spinners dominated Somerset. Davis caused the next collapse before Carrick, with a splendid innings, lasting 52 overs, set up a Yorkshire declaration. Family illness delayed Richards's entry, and Somerset, never in a position to attack the required 300 in 245 minutes, had to rely on Ollis for 50 overs and Richards for 29 to save the day.

Yorkshire

G. Boycott st Gard b Marks	83 – c Booth b Davis	0
M. D. Moxon run out	55 – lbw b Dredge	5
C. W. J. Athey st Gard b Marks	39 – b Davis	10
K. Sharp b Booth	4 – b Booth	37
J. D. Love b Marks	25 – c Gard b Davis	2
†D. L. Bairstow b Marks	0 – b Marks	10
P. Carrick c Popplewell b Marks	21 – c Popplewell b Booth	72
G. B. Stevenson b Dredge	44 – b Dredge	23
I. G. Swallow lbw Dredge	4 – not out	11
S. J. Dennis not out	4 – not out	0
*R. Illingworth c Popplewell b Marks	1	
L-b 5, n-b 1	6	B 3, l-b 4	7

1/139 2/143 3/148 4/185   286   1/0 2/8 3/32 4/40   (8 wkts dec.) 177
5/189 6/217 7/255 8/266 9/281   5/53 6/85 7/121 8/177

Bonus points – Yorkshire 2, Somerset 2 (Score at 100 overs: 201-5).

Bowling: *First Innings*—Davis 10–1–39–0; Dredge 10–5–25–2; Richards 10–3–12–0; Palmer 9–2–31–0; Marks 44.2–24–79–6; Booth 35–11–94–1. *Second Innings*—Davis 14–3–36–3; Dredge 16–2–33–2; Marks 22–8–61–1; Palmer 4–2–13–0; Richards 1–0–4–0; Booth 15–7–23–2.

Somerset

P. M. Roebuck lbw b Stevenson	4 – c Bairstow b Stevenson	0
R. L. Ollis b Stevenson	1 – (5) not out	27
P. W. Denning c Bairstow b Stevenson	27 – b Carrick	44
N. F. M. Popplewell lbw b Illingworth	29 – b Illingworth	26
*I. V. A. Richards b Illingworth	25 – (8) not out	27
V. J. Marks b Carrick	25 – c Athey b Carrick	3
†T. Gard c Bairstow b Carrick	5 – lbw b Illingworth	4
G. V. Palmer b Illingworth	1	
C. H. Dredge c Dennis b Illingworth	10 – (2) b Dennis	4
M. R. Davis c Bairstow b Swallow	20	
S. C. Booth not out	0	
B 8, l-b 7, n-b 2	17	B 7, l-b 4, w 6, n-b 1	18

1/4 2/25 3/36 4/73   164   1/5 2/5 3/89 4/89   (6 wkts) 153
5/103 6/124 7/128 8/131 9/158   5/96 6/109

Bonus points – Somerset 1, Yorkshire 4.

Bowling: *First Innings*—Dennis 9–4–22–0; Stevenson 10–4–32–3; Carrick 28–10–26–2; Illingworth 22–10–48–4; Swallow 10.4–2–19–1. *Second Innings*—Dennis 10–4–16–1; Stevenson 10–5–19–1; Illingworth 30–13–42–2; Carrick 28–13–45–2; Swallow 8–3–13–0.

Umpires: C. T. Spencer and A. G. T. Whitehead.

At Derby, August 13, 15, 16. SOMERSET drew with DERBYSHIRE.

At Lord's, August 20, 22, 23. SOMERSET beat MIDDLESEX by 33 runs.

At Bournemouth, August 24, 25. SOMERSET lost to HAMPSHIRE by ten wickets.

SOMERSET v GLAMORGAN

At Taunton, August 27, 29, 30. Somerset won by three wickets. Somerset 22 pts, Glamorgan 6 pts. The first three innings were distinguished mainly by a maiden half-century from the twenty-year-old Wyatt and a brisk opening stand of 103 in 28 overs by Alan Jones and Hopkins, which appeared to have put Glamorgan in control. However, they faded and Somerset, needing 241 in four hours, also slipped after a good start; but 47 in 25 overs from Popplewell, steadily supported, left Marks, who was batting well, and Garner to get 30 in the last five overs. Garner, with two huge 6s, and then Marks, ending with his fourth 4 of an invaluable innings, made it with three overs to spare.

Glamorgan

J. A. Hopkins lbw b Dredge	21	– c Garner b Marks	53
A. Jones lbw b Dredge	15	– c Popplewell b Lloyds	48
R. C. Ontong lbw b Marks	74	– b Lloyds	20
C. J. C. Rowe c Ollis b Marks	12	– (5) c Dredge b Booth	43
A. L. Jones b Booth	5	– (4) lbw b Garner	12
S. P. Henderson c Gard b Marks	17	– (7) run out	9
G. C. Holmes b Garner	18	– (8) c and b Marks	20
A. H. Wilkins not out	14	– (6) c Garner b Dredge	6
†T. Davies b Dredge	17	– not out	11
*M. W. W. Selvey c Garner b Dredge	0	– c Gard b Garner	3
W. W. Davis b Dredge	10	– run out	0
B 6, l-b 3, n-b 6	15	B 11	11

1/40 2/45 3/71 4/90   218   1/103 2/105 3/133 4/156   236
5/119 6/166 7/194 8/194 9/204   5/163 6/175 7/217 8/221 9/236

Bonus points – Glamorgan 2, Somerset 4.

Bowling: *First Innings*—Garner 14–5–2–1; Dredge 21.3–8–51–5; Popplewell 7–3–14–0; Booth 22–9–42–1; Marks 27–10–64–3; Lloyds 4–0–10–0. *Second Innings*—Dredge 15–2–31–1; Garner 15.5–2–51–2; Marks 21–9–52–2; Booth 13–2–44–1; Lloyds 17–2–47–2.

Somerset

J. G. Wyatt c A. L. Jones b Ontong	59	– c Davies b Davis	27
*P. M. Roebuck c Ontong b Selvey	34	– c Davies b Selvey	21
J. W. Lloyds c A. L. Jones b Rowe	0	– (7) c Hopkins b Rowe	9
R. L. Ollis lbw b Rowe	0	– st Davies b Rowe	21
N. F. M. Popplewell c and b Ontong	22	– (4) lbw b Ontong	47
P. W. Denning run out	6	– (3) lbw b Selvey	25
V. J. Marks lbw b Wilkins	30	– (6) not out	44
†T. Gard b Ontong	13	– b Davis	9
J. Garner c Hopkins b Ontong	31	– not out	18
C. H. Dredge c Davies b Ontong	8		
S. C. Booth not out	0		
B 2, l-b 3, n-b 6	11	B 3, l-b 9, n-b 8	20

1/83 2/84 3/86 4/118   214   1/51 2/68 3/99 4/140   (7 wkts) 241
5/130 6/133 7/168 8/200 9/207   5/170 6/194 7/211

Bonus points – Somerset 2, Glamorgan 4.

Bowling: *First Innings*—Davis 21–7–36–0; Selvey 11–5–21–1; Wilkins 12–3–32–1; Ontong 27.1–5–87–5; Rowe 10–2–27–2. *Second Innings*—Davis 19–5–48–2; Wilkins 6–0–33–0; Ontong 13–1–48–1; Selvey 10–3–20–2; Rowe 25–5–72–2.

Umpires: A. Jepson and J. W. Holder.

SOMERSET v HAMPSHIRE

At Taunton, August 31, September 1, 2. Drawn. Somerset 4 pts, Hampshire 5 pts. A steady batting performance led by Roebuck, who stayed for 74 overs, was answered by Hampshire after a delay for rain on the second day. Hampshire's brightest batting came from Jesty (four 6s and five 4s in 27 overs) before they declared 68 behind. Somerset slumped to 47 for three at the close of the second day and, after more delays, to 86 all out, Marshall dismissing Denning, Marks, Davis and Booth in five balls including the hat-trick. Hampshire needed 155 in 192 minutes before rain altered it to 155 in 88 minutes, and with 114 needed in nineteen overs the rain was conclusive. On the final day, gale force winds led to the abandonment of the bails, and the large sightscreen at the River End was blown down and rendered useless.

Somerset

J. W. Lloyds c Pocock b Malone	19	– c Terry b Marshall	18
J. G. Wyatt c Parks b Malone	44	– b Marshall	0
N. A. Felton c and b Nicholas	41	– st Parks b Cowley	18
*P. M. Roebuck not out	106	– c Terry b Cowley	20
N. F. M. Popplewell c Parks b Malone	0	– (7) not out	5
P. W. Denning run out	39	– c Smith b Marshall	17
V. J. Marks c Nicholas b Smith	21	– (8) c Greenidge b Marshall	0
†T. Gard not out	32	– (5) b Cowley	0
M. R. Davis (did not bat)		– b Marshall	0
S. C. Booth (did not bat)		– b Marshall	0
C. H. Dredge (did not bat)		– c Parks b Cowley	0
B 1, l-b 12, w 1, n-b 5	19	B 2, n-b 6	8

1/43 2/109 3/137 4/212   (6 wkts dec.) 321   1/7 2/40 3/47 4/53   86
5/212 6/253   5/75 6/81 7/81 8/81 9/81

Bonus points – Somerset 3, Hampshire 2 (Score at 100 overs: 259-6).

Bowling: *First Innings*—Marshall 7–0–31–0; Malone 22–5–64–3; Jesty 8–3–17–0; Nicholas 21–11–34–1; Cowley 26–2–77–0; Smith 32–3–79–1. *Second Innings*—Marshall 12–1–46–6; Malone 10–3–22–0; Cowley 15–10–10–4; Smith 1–1–0–0.

Hampshire

C. G. Greenidge c Marks b Lloyds	70	– not out	21
C. L. Smith b Lloyds	20	– c Gard b Dredge	17
M. C. J. Nicholas not out	83		
T. E. Jesty c Davis b Lloyds	61		
V. P. Terry not out	10		
B 1, l-b 7, n-b 1	9	L-b 3	3

1/71 2/98 3/212   (3 wkts dec.) 253   1/41   (1 wkt) 41

D. R. Turner, *N. E. J. Pocock, M. D. Marshall, N. G. Cowley, †R. J. Parks and S. J. Malone did not bat.

Bonus points – Hampshire 3, Somerset 1.

Bowling: *First Innings*—Dredge 13–5–22–0; Davis 8–1–35–0; Popplewell 10–4–24–0; Lloyds 17–2–72–3; Marks 13–4–40–0; Booth 15.1–6–51–0. *Second Innings*—Dredge 5–0–26–1; Popplewell 4–0–12–0.

Umpires: A. Jepson and R. Palmer.

SOMERSET v KENT

At Taunton, September 7, 8, 9. Drawn. Somerset 6 pts, Kent 7 pts. A match dominated by the bat and the weather ended quietly. Somerset's effort was based on a typical century in

42 overs by Richards and a patient, excellently disciplined maiden century by Felton, eventually batting 120 overs and hitting seventeen 4s. After rain Somerset batted on for 25 minutes on the second day. Kent were then sustained by Taylor, who was missed twice and batted for three hours, aided first by Tavaré and then Cowdrey, who reached 100 in 131 minutes. Kent declared 105 behind with two and a half hours left, reduced by further rain to half an hour, in which Taylor and Cowdrey, to boost Kent's over-rate for the season, bowled 33 overs.

Somerset

J. W. Lloyds c Underwood b Dilley	14	– not out	27
J. G. Wyatt c Tavaré b Dilley	8	– not out	25
N. A. Felton not out	173		
I. V. A. Richards c Dilley b Jarvis	103		
P. W. Denning c Aslett b Johnson	2		
*I. T. Botham run out	24		
V. J. Marks c Knott b Cowdrey	29		
†T. Gard c sub b Underwood	7		
M. R. Davis c Benson b Underwood	17		
C. H. Dredge b Underwood	50		
S. C. Booth c Cowdrey b Dilley	7		
B 6, l-b 11, w 1, n-b 10	28	W 2	2

1/15 2/36 3/204 4/209   462   (no wkt) 54
5/251 6/296 7/309 8/355 9/427

Bonus points – Somerset 4, Kent 3 (Score at 100 overs: 362-8).

Bowling: *First Innings*—Dilley 22.1–3–72–3; Jarvis 33–4–137–1; Cowdrey 24–0–90–1; Underwood 25–10–79–3; Johnson 20–1–56–1. *Second Innings*—Cowdrey 17–5–27–0; Taylor 16–6–25–0.

Kent

N. R. Taylor c Botham b Marks	104	†A. P. E. Knott c Dredge b Marks	38
M. R. Benson c Felton b Botham	8	G. W. Johnson not out	9
*C. J. Tavaré c Gard b Marks	41	B 8, l-b 2, n-b 3	13
D. G. Aslett c Booth b Marks	17		
C. S. Cowdrey not out	103	1/14 2/129 3/147	(6 wkts dec.) 357
E. A. E. Baptiste c Lloyds b Marks	24	4/219 5/259 6/312	

G. R. Dilley, D. L. Underwood and K. B. S. Jarvis did not bat.

Bonus points – Kent 4, Somerset 2.

Bowling: Botham 7–0–27–1; Davis 10–3–31–0; Dredge 8–0–36–0; Marks 31–7–134–5; Booth 18–1–105–0; Lloyds 3–0–11–0.

Umpires: D. O. Oslear and B. Leadbeater.

SOMERSET v WARWICKSHIRE

At Taunton, September 10, 12, 13. Drawn. Somerset 6 pts, Warwickshire 8 pts. Rain ruined the match, played on the same pitch as the Kent game. Wyatt, dropped before scoring and three more times, patiently batted 72 overs for his 69. Lloyd's splendid century in 39 overs and Humpage's 71 in 24 overs took Warwickshire well ahead at 270 for three before Palmer, taking three wickets in four balls and five in eighteen balls, achieved his best analysis. The declaration followed by bad light left Somerset only one over's batting on the Monday, then rain reduced the last day's play to 42.3 overs, in which Wyatt attacked briskly for his highest score off 135 balls.

Somerset

P. M. Roebuck c Lloyd b Old	2	– (3) not out	13
J. G. Wyatt c Amiss b P. A. Smith	69	– (1) not out	82
N. A. Felton c Amiss b P. A. Smith	42		
N. F. M. Popplewell c Amiss b P. A. Smith	0		
P. W. Denning c Lord b Gifford	12		
*I. T. Botham c Humpage b Gifford	11		
†T. Gard b Gifford	23		
V. J. Marks st Humpage b Gifford	26		
G. V. Palmer lbw b Lethbridge	11		
M. R. Davis c Humpage b Lethbridge	1		
S. C. Booth not out	2	– (2) lbw b Gifford	9
L-b 8, n-b 12	20	B 7, l-b 2, w 1, n-b 3	13

1/6 2/73 3/75 4/97   219   1/43   (1 wkt) 117
5/112 6/171 7/181 8/206 9/207

Bonus points – Somerset 2, Warwickshire 4.

Bowling: *First Innings*—Willis 16–6–20–0; Old 10–1–30–1; P. A. Smith 24–4–70–3; Gifford 32–11–64–4; Lethbridge 7.2–2–15–2. *Second Innings*—Willis 5.3–3–12–0; Gifford 21–8–45–1; Old 6–2–11–0; P. A. Smith 3–0–24–0; Lord 8–3–12–0.

Warwickshire

T. A. Lloyd b Booth	112
K. D. Smith c Booth b Marks	5
A. I. Kallicharran c and b Popplewell	30
D. L. Amiss lbw b Palmer	40
†G. W. Humpage c and b Palmer	71
G. J. Lord c Gard b Palmer	1
P. A. Smith c and b Palmer	4
C. Lethbridge lbw b Palmer	0
C. M. Old b Marks	16
N. Gifford not out	2
*R. G. D. Willis not out	2
B 2, l-b 6, w 3, n-b 6	17

1/79 2/149 3/157   (9 wkts dec.) 300
4/270 5/273 6/274
7/274 8/294 9/294

Bonus points – Warwickshire 4, Somerset 4.

Bowling: Palmer 12.3–2–38–5; Davis 9–0–48–0; Marks 27–3–105–2; Popplewell 11–0–52–1; Booth 11–2–40–1.

Umpires: B. Leadbeater and C. T. Spencer.

SURREY

Patron: HM The Queen
President: 1983-84 – M. R. Barton; 1984-85 – Sir
 Alexander Durie
Chairman: D. H. Newton
Chairman, Cricket Committee: J. C. Laker
Secretary: I. F. B. Scott-Browne
 Kennington Oval, London SE11 5SS
 (Telephone: 01-582 6660)
Cricket Manager: M. J. Stewart
Captain: 1983 – R. D. V. Knight; 1984 – G. P.
 Howarth
Coach: D. Gibson

Surrey suffered more than most from a wet May. They were unable to
bowl a ball in two of their first three Schweppes County Championship
games and did not bat or bowl in four of their first five Sunday League
matches. They were then hit by a "hurricane" at Chelmsford when Essex
bundled them out for 14, the lowest total in Surrey's history, and only 2
runs more than the lowest in the annals of the first-class game. Such a
happening could have knocked them sideways. Instead, Surrey answered
back immediately by beating Worcestershire for their first Championship
win, and although the final reading in the premier competition was not all
that pleasant, it could have been worse. Seven victories brought eighth
place in the table, which represented a very reasonable recovery.

Surrey's only victory in the Benson and Hedges Cup was against
Oxford and Cambridge Universities, and as soon as they came up against
opposition of any status in defence of the NatWest Bank Trophy, they
came a nasty cropper, beaten by nine wickets by Warwickshire at The
Oval. Four wins from sixteen John Player Sunday League games left them
in eleventh place, one better than in 1982.

It was the first time since Micky Stewart returned to The Oval in 1979,
to direct playing affairs, that Surrey had not had a say of any consequence
in the destination of the season's prizes. His feeling of optimism twelve
months earlier was not fulfilled. There were a number of reasons for this,
not least something that happened during the previous winter, namely
Robin Jackman's retirement. The absence of Geoff Howarth with New
Zealand limited the choice in batting, and injuries, particularly that
suffered by Kevin Mackintosh, who was expected to assume Jackman's
mantle, took their toll.

Sylvester Clarke, though his 79 wickets were bettered by only seven
bowlers in the country, took a long time getting into his stride, and
although Dave Thomas strove hard to fill the gap at the other end, he will
be best remembered in 1983 for his batting. He hit his maiden century
against Nottinghamshire in late July and then recorded another hundred
at Hove, which took him into the England party at Trent Bridge, though
in the event he was made twelfth man. Graham Monkhouse returned his
best figures, seven for 51, in the same game as Thomas reached three

figures for the first time, but he was soon to break a finger and, as Mackintosh was out virtually all the season with back trouble, support for Clarke was seriously limited. Pat Pocock bowled his off-breaks with customary skill, but too often he was in operation after only moderate penetration by the faster men.

To some extent, the batting followed a similar pattern. Alan Butcher and Grahame Clinton never settled to make the good starts of previous years, so that Monte Lynch, a stroke-maker who is seldom happy sitting on the splice, needed to restrain himself. To his credit, Lynch did that well, while still finding time to play some exciting innings on his way to 1,558 runs. Matters improved when Duncan Pauline, backed until then by a top first-class score of only 46 in 21 innings and four years with the club, replaced Clinton at the beginning of August. Pauline and Butcher immediately hit it off, opening against Warwickshire at The Oval with a partnership of 136, with Pauline registering his first first-class hundred, against Sussex, soon afterwards.

This heralded cricket more in keeping with the welcome change in the weather from mid-June. Like Pauline, Alec Stewart, son of the manager, did all that was expected of him in proving that his maiden century against Oxford University was not a one-off event, and Roger Knight, having made a rallying call during the closing days of July, saw it being answered. The captain responded to bad times by ordering extra nets and asking for a greater effort. The response was immediate and, in almost every aspect, satisfactory. The unhappy exception was made apparent on August 20 when Surrey accepted the resignation of David Smith, with the announcement: "The club appreciate Smith's cricket talent and potential but regret that he has not been able to maintain the standard of professional conduct expected of Surrey cricketers."

The statement spoke for itself, and many members were saddened that such a gifted and attractive player should depart under a cloud. Aged 27 and in his prime, he had been a considerable figure at The Oval since making his début ten years earlier when still a schoolboy. Surrey were without representation in the summer's Tests and with Paul Downton from across the river gaining preference over Jack Richards as standby wicket-keeper for Bob Taylor, they had no-one on England's winter tour either. – H.E.A.

SURREY 1983

[*Bill Smith*]

Back row: D. Gibson (*coach*), A. J. Stewart, I. R. Payne, A. Needham, R. G. L. Cheatle, I. J. Curtis, C. K. Bullen, M. A. Feltham, K. S. Mackintosh, D. B. Pauline, N. J. Falkner, G. Monkhouse, J. Hill (*scorer*). *Front row*: G. S. Clinton, C. J. Richards, G. P. Howarth, P. I. Pocock, M. J. Stewart (*manager*), R. D. V. Knight (*captain*), A. R. Butcher, D. M. Smith, D. J. Thomas, M. A. Lynch.

SURREY RESULTS

All first-class matches – Played 25: Won 8, Lost 4, Drawn 13.

County Championship matches – Played 24: Won 7, Lost 4, Drawn 13.

Bonus points – Batting 65, Bowling 70.

Competition placings – Schweppes County Championship, 8th; NatWest Bank Trophy, 2nd round; Benson and Hedges Cup, 4th in Group D; John Player League, 11th eq.

COUNTY CHAMPIONSHIP AVERAGES

BATTING

	Birthplace	M	I	NO	R	HI	Avge
M. A. Lynchc	Georgetown, BG	24	39	10	1,558	119	53.72
D. M. Smithc	Balham	13	20	4	748	131*	46.75
D. B. Pauline.......	Aberdeen	11	20	1	758	115	39.89
R. D. V. Knightc	Streatham	24	38	6	1,235	101*	38.59
D. J. Thomasc	Solihull	23	31	5	937	119	36.03
A. R. Butcherc	Croydon	24	43	3	1,341	128	33.52
A. J. Stewart	Merton	9	16	3	407	82	31.30
G. P. Howarthc.......	Auckland, NZ	4	5	1	123	66	30.75
C. J. Richardsc	Penzance	24	34	8	718	85*	27.61
I. R. Payne.............	Kennington	9	10	4	139	43	23.16
G. Monkhouse	Carlisle	17	18	5	291	46	22.38
G. S. Clintonc	Sidcup	12	21	3	371	105	20.61
S. T. Clarkec	Christ Church, Barbados	24	24	4	285	43	14.25
P. I. Pocockc	Bangor	23	19	7	110	23	9.16
A. Needham.............	Calow	8	13	1	88	18	7.33
I. J. Curtis.............	Purley	12	10	4	22	7	3.66

Also batted: K. S. Mackintosh (*Surbiton*) (1 match) 18*, 5*; P. A. Waterman (*Hendon*) (2 matches) 6*, 0.

*Signifies not out. c*Denotes county cap.*

BOWLING

	O	M	R	W	Avge	BB
G. Monkhouse	352.5	92	999	45	22.20	7-51
S. T. Clarke............	693.1	183	1,773	79	22.44	7-53
P. I. Pocock............	681.2	200	1,774	68	26.08	7-79
D. J. Thomas..........	547	113	1,781	57	31.24	4-22
I. R. Payne.............	150.5	38	435	12	36.25	5-13
A. Needham.............	123	29	409	10	40.90	5-52
R. D. V. Knight......	236	60	677	15	45.13	3-58
I. J. Curtis.............	239.5	65	647	11	58.81	4-14

Also bowled: A. R. Butcher 44.4–9–210–5; M. A. Lynch 7.3–0–47–0; K. S. Mackintosh 15–2–47–0; D. M. Smith 2.2–0–20–0; P. A. Waterman 39–7–151–1.

The following played a total of thirteen three-figure innings for Surrey in County Championship matches – A. R. Butcher 3, M. A. Lynch 3, D. M. Smith 2, D. J. Thomas 2, G. S. Clinton 1, R. D. V. Knight 1, D. B. Pauline 1.

SURREY v KENT

At The Oval, April 30, May 1, 2. Drawn. Kent 2 pts. Knight rescued Surrey from a start as unimpressive as the damp weather. With three out for 19, he nudged away on the leg side to keep the score moving and was becoming more adventurous past 50 when the rain came and washed out the Sunday and Monday. Play started at 2.45 on the Saturday, when the form of Dilley did much to please. A smoother approach to the wicket, developed during the winter in South Africa, helped him produce eighteen fiery overs of improved accuracy.

Surrey

A. R. Butcher c Cowdrey b Jarvis	1	†C. J. Richards c Johnson b Dilley	2
G. S. Clinton lbw b Dilley	0	D. J. Thomas not out	25
D. M. Smith lbw b Woolmer	10	L-b 4, n-b 2	6
G. P. Howarth c Cowdrey b Ellison	9		
*R. D. V. Knight not out	52	1/1 2/2 3/19	(6 wkts) 126
M. A. Lynch b Ellison	21	4/31 5/71 6/81	

G. Monkhouse, S. T. Clarke and P. I. Pocock did not bat.

Bonus points – Kent 2.

Bowling: Dilley 18–7–35–2; Jarvis 12–6–19–1; Ellison 11–2–24–2; Woolmer 9–3–13–1; Cowdrey 6–0–29–0; Underwood 1–1–0–0.

Kent

N. R. Taylor, R. A. Woolmer, *C. J. Tavaré, M. R. Benson, C. S. Cowdrey, †A. P. E. Knott, G. W. Johnson, R. M. Ellison, G. R. Dilley, D. L. Underwood and K. B. S. Jarvis.

Umpires: W. E. Alley and P. J. Eele.

At Bristol, May 4, 5, 6. SURREY drew with GLOUCESTERSHIRE.

SURREY v LEICESTERSHIRE

At The Oval, May 11, 12, 13. Drawn. Surrey 1 pt, Leicestershire 1 pt. Surrey recovered from the loss of Butcher and Clinton for 14 runs to reach a worthwhile 170 for four off 51 overs by the end of a first day cut to three hours. But with the next two days washed out completely by rain, it was all academic. Lynch scored his first 50 runs in 55 minutes.

Surrey

A. R. Butcher lbw b Parsons	9	M. A. Lynch not out	69
G. S. Clinton b Roberts	2	†C. J. Richards not out	21
G. P. Howarth c Tolchard b Parsons	20	L-b 6, w 1, n-b 2	9
*R. D. V. Knight c Tolchard			
b Roberts	40	1/10 2/14 3/60 4/127	(4 wkts) 170

I. J. Curtis, D. J. Thomas, G. Monkhouse, S. T. Clarke and P. I. Pocock did not bat.

Bonus points – Surrey 1, Leicestershire 1.

Bowling: Roberts 12–3–31–2; Parsons 21–5–63–2; Agnew 9–1–37–0; Cook 9–2–30–0.

Leicestershire

J. C Balderstone, R. A. Cobb, D. I. Gower, B. F. Davison, N. E. Briers, *†R. W. Tolchard, G. J. Parsons, A. M. E. Roberts, J. F. Steele, J. P. Agnew and N. G. B. Cook.

Umpires: J. H. Harris and K. E. Palmer.

SURREY v LANCASHIRE

At The Oval, May 25, 26, 27. Drawn. Surrey 8 pts, Lancashire 5 pts. Fowler was proving obstinate when Pocock opened wide the other end by dismissing Lloyd and Hughes, who had a king pair, with successive balls, so beckoning victory. But rained washed out the last 80 minutes. Two good batting performances played a big part in leaving Lancashire 133 adrift on the first innings and finally well short of their target of 317 in 280 minutes. Thomas stayed two hours for a career-best 76 before being run out at the striker's end when Simmons deflected a drive, and Butcher scored a century (one 6, thirteen 4s) in 198 minutes. There was something in the pitch for the bowlers most of the time.

Surrey

A. R. Butcher c Maynard b Allott	16	– c Abrahams b Simmons	100
G. S. Clinton c Lloyd b O'Shaughnessy	0	– c O'Shaughnessy b Simmons	23
D. M. Smith lbw b Hughes	32	– b O'Shaughnessy	2
G. P. Howarth c Hayes b Simmons	66	– (5) b Simmons	6
*R. D. V. Knight b Allott	28	– (7) not out	2
M. A. Lynch lbw b Allott	0	– not out	39
†C. J. Richards c Hayes b Abrahams	47		
D. J. Thomas run out	76		
S. T. Clarke c Fowler b Allott	11	– (4) c Hughes b O'Shaughnessy ..	0
G. Monkhouse c Hughes b Simmons	17		
P. I. Pocock not out	4		
L-b 8	8	B 1, l-b 9, w 1	11

1/16 2/16 3/89 4/139   305   1/67 2/78   (5 wkts dec.) 183
5/139 6/157 7/232 8/249 9/301   3/78 4/93 5/172

Bonus points – Surrey 4, Lancashire 4.

Bowling: *First Innings*—Allott 24–7–68–4; Folley 5–1–29–0; O'Shaughnessy 10–2–31–1; Simmons 27.1–6–62–2; Hughes 16–1–62–1; Abrahams 16–3–45–1. *Second Innings*—Allott 16–4–58–0; Folley 7–3–12–0; O'Shaughnessy 10–1–20–2; Simmons 19–4–69–3; Abrahams 3–0–13–0.

Lancashire

G. Fowler c Knight b Pocock	23	– not out	73
I. Cockbain b Pocock	4	– c Clarke b Monkhouse	19
I. Folley c Smith b Thomas	25		
F. C. Hayes c Butcher b Pocock	2	– (3) c Knight b Clarke	10
*C. H. Lloyd b Thomas	23	– (4) lbw b Pocock	18
D. P. Hughes c Richards b Thomas	0	– (5) b Pocock	0
J. Abrahams c Howarth b Pocock	4	– (6) not out	12
S. J. O'Shaughnessy c Butcher b Pocock	42		
J. Simmons b Clarke	28		
†C. Maynard c Richards b Thomas	4		
P. J. W. Allott not out	2		
L-b 9, n-b 6	15	B 1, l-b 4, w 1, n-b 4	10

1/12 2/55 3/62 4/81   172   1/55 2/78   (4 wkts) 142
5/81 6/90 7/90 8/149 9/160   3/119 4/119

Bonus points – Lancashire 1, Surrey 4.

Bowling: *First Innings*—Clarke 23–10–33–1; Thomas 16.4–4–41–4; Pocock 32–12–70–5; Knight 8–3–13–0. *Second Innings*—Clarke 10–1–40–1; Thomas 12.4–4–29–0; Pocock 23–10–30–2; Monkhouse 8–3–12–1; Butcher 2–0–9–0; Lynch 1.3–0–12–0.

Umpires: B. Leadbeater and B. J. Meyer.

At Chelmsford, May 28, 30, 31. SURREY drew with ESSEX.

At Worcester, June 8, 9, 10. SURREY beat WORCESTERSHIRE by ten wickets.

SURREY v MIDDLESEX

At The Oval, June 11, 13, 14. Middlesex won by ten wickets. Middlesex 24 pts, Surrey 6 pts. This overwhelming victory featured masterly spin bowling by Edmonds (ten for 161) and Emburey (six for 120) and a telling wicket when Roland Butcher threw out Thomas, which meant that Surrey went in a second time immediately 158 behind. Thomas and Monkhouse, the latter offered up for the last over of Saturday, did more than most recognised batsmen to worry Middlesex, who had compiled a substantial total through a solid century from Slack (one 6, nine 4s) and a dashing 81 (two 6s, ten 4s) from Butcher. These two were together in a stand of 127. In Surrey's second innings Smith hit an unbeaten 106 in 261 minutes, a patient effort, but he lacked support.

Middlesex

G. D. Barlow c Lynch b Thomas	9	– not out		54
W. N. Slack b Pocock	107	– not out		37
C. T. Radley lbw b Monkhouse	16			
R. O. Butcher b Monkhouse	81			
K. P. Tomlins b Pocock	38			
*J. E. Emburey st Richards b Pocock	42			
†P. R. Downton not out	27			
P. H. Edmonds c Richards b Monkhouse	12			
K. D. James lbw b Monkhouse	0			
N. F. Williams c Richards b Clarke	14			
S. P. Hughes not out	0			
B 11, l-b 13, n-b 2	26	L-b 1, w 1, n-b 4		6

1/23 2/50 3/177 4/252   (9 wkts dec.) 372   (no wkt) 97
5/312 6/325 7/340 8/340 9/370

Bonus points – Middlesex 4, Surrey 4 (Score at 100 overs: 370-9).

Bowling: *First Innings*—Clarke 18–2–55–1; Thomas 13–1–60–1; Monkhouse 26–7–59–4; Pocock 32.4–6–118–3; Knight 3–0–20–0; Needham 8–1–34–0. *Second Innings*—Clarke 3–0–6–0; Thomas 5–2–7–0; Pocock 11–1–28–0; Needham 9.3–1–50–0.

Surrey

G. Monkhouse c Emburey b Edmonds	35	– (9) b Edmonds		5
G. S. Clinton c Barlow b Edmonds	7	– c Downton b Williams		4
A. R. Butcher c Tomlins b Edmonds	14	– (1) c Butcher b Williams		14
D. M. Smith c Barlow b Edmonds	8	– (3) not out		106
*R. D. V. Knight c Butcher b Emburey	45	– c Butcher b Edmonds		10
M. A. Lynch b Emburey	0	– (4) c and b Edmonds		61
†C. J. Richards c Edmonds b Emburey	1	– (6) st Downton b Edmonds		3
A. Needham b Emburey	1	– (7) lbw b Emburey		0
D. J. Thomas run out	62	– (8) c Radley b Emburey		0
S. T. Clarke b Hughes	19	– b Edmonds		6
P. I. Pocock not out	0	– c and b Edmonds		23
B 9, l-b 3, n-b 6	18	B 10, l-b 6, n-b 6		22

1/11 2/52 3/66 4/82   214   1/9 2/23 3/154 4/180   254
5/83 6/87 7/105 8/156 9/196   5/196 6/197 7/197 8/206 9/212

Bonus points – Surrey 2, Middlesex 4.

Bowling: *First Innings*—Williams 6–0–19–0; Emburey 30–5–59–4; Edmonds 31.2–9–74–4; Hughes 11–3–44–1. *Second Innings*—Hughes 6–0–28–0; Williams 11–1–45–2; Emburey 31–11–61–2; Edmonds 34.3–7–87–6; James 5–0–11–0; Tomlins 1–1–0–0.

Umpires: A. Jepson and J. Morley.

At Nottingham, June 15, 16, 17. SURREY beat NOTTINGHAMSHIRE by ten wickets.

SURREY v OXFORD UNIVERSITY

At The Oval, June 18, 19. Surrey won by an innings and 98 runs. An Oxford side well under strength proved easy pickings for the county, whose manager, Mickey Stewart, had the satisfaction of seeing his son, twenty-year-old Alec, hit his maiden century (one 6, seventeen 4s) in 182 minutes. As twelfth man, father joined son on the field for a brief spell – the first time they had participated together in a first-class game. Spin bowlers Curtis, with a career best against his former University, and Needham each took six wickets in an innings.

Oxford University

*R. G. P. Ellis b Feltham	13	– b Curtis 34
A. G. T. Miller b Monkhouse	11	– c Monkhouse b Needham ... 22
P. J. Heseltine run out	5	– c Butcher b Needham ... 3
R. P. Moulding c Richards b Needham	16	– c Cheatle b Needham ... 0
J. G. Varey c Butcher b Needham	13	– c Butcher b Curtis ... 0
J. R. Chessher c and b Needham	0	– lbw b Curtis ... 11
†D. Harrison b Needham	1	– b Feltham ... 8
H. T. Rawlinson b Needham	21	– c Richards b Curtis ... 6
A. H. K. Smail b Needham	8	– not out ... 13
M. D. Petchey c Richards b Monkhouse	18	– lbw b Curtis ... 1
J. R. Turnbull not out	0	– b Curtis ... 0
B 3, l-b 3	6	B 3, l-b 2 ... 5

1/16 2/22 3/32 4/60   112   1/51 2/61 3/61 4/62   103
5/61 6/64 7/65 8/94 9/96   5/63 6/74 7/82 8/100 9/101

Bowling: *First Innings*—Feltham 11–4–25–1; Monkhouse 14.4–4–21–2; Needham 19–12–30–6; Payne 8–3–15–0; Curtis 7–4–15–0. *Second Innings*—Feltham 7–1–19–1; Monkhouse 6–1–20–0; Needham 22–9–31–3; Curtis 22.1–13–28–6.

Surrey

*A. R. Butcher c Turnbull b Petchey ..	8	D. B. Pauline not out ...	38
G. S. Clinton c Petchey b Rawlinson ...	68	B 8, l-b 2, w 2, n-b 8 ...	20
C. J. Richards c Harrison b Turnbull ...	33		
†A. J. Stewart not out ...	118	1/14 2/72	(4 wkts dec.) 313
I. R. Payne run out ...	28	3/176 4/240	

A. Needham, G. Monkhouse, R. G. L. Cheatle, M. A. Feltham and I. J. Curtis did not bat.

Bowling: Petchey 25–7–82–1; Rawlinson 21–6–63–1; Varey 18–3–73–0; Turnbull 14–3–59–1; Smail 5–1–16–0.

Umpires: B. Dudleston and J. D. Morley.

At Leicester, June 22, 23, 24. SURREY drew with LEICESTERSHIRE.

SURREY v NORTHAMPTONSHIRE

At The Oval, June 25, 27, 28. Drawn. Surrey 5 pts, Northamptonshire 7 pts. England's exit from the World Cup was Northamptonshire's gain as Lamb made up for his disappointment at being at The Oval instead of Lord's by hitting the Surrey bowlers for three 6s and fifteen

4s in a 137-minute century. Willey was his best ally in a stand of 126. Surrey, at 77 for seven in reply to 280, were given new life by tailenders Thomas, Monkhouse and Clarke with 136 runs between them. Thomas, dropped before scoring, made the most of his luck by good use of the long handle, hitting nine 4s in 52. A damaged hand kept Larkins from the crease subsequently and the game drifted to a draw.

Northamptonshire

*G. Cook b Monkhouse	8	– lbw b Clarke	35
W. Larkins lbw b Thomas	2		
P. Willey b Clarke	52	– c Clarke b Thomas	2
A. J. Lamb c Richards b Clarke	108	– st Richards b Monkhouse	39
R. G. Williams c Richards b Pocock	20	– lbw b Thomas	5
M. J. Bamber c Lynch b Monkhouse	4	– (2) lbw b Monkhouse	30
D. S. Steele not out	36	– (6) c Monkhouse b Clarke	30
†G. Sharp b Monkhouse	14	– (7) not out	21
N. A. Mallender c Richards b Clarke	1	– (8) c Knight b Monkhouse	4
A. Walker not out	5	– (9) not out	6
B 7, l-b 1, w 7, n-b 15	30	B 9, l-b 8, w 3, n-b 11	31

1/3 2/32 3/158 4/187   (8 wkts dec.) 280   1/63 2/66 3/87   (7 wkts dec.) 203
5/216 6/219 7/240 8/249   4/113 5/154 6/172 7/179

B. J. Griffiths did not bat.

Bonus points – Northamptonshire 3, Surrey 3.

Bowling: *First Innings*—Clarke 22–6–61–3; Thomas 15.2–3–36–1; Monkhouse 31–10–68–3; Knight 3.4–1–22–0; Pocock 22–6–63–1. *Second Innings*—Clarke 21–5–50–2; Thomas 19–3–56–2; Monkhouse 21–4–51–3; Pocock 6–0–15–0.

Surrey

A. R. Butcher lbw b Griffiths	10	– c Cook b Griffiths	12
G. S. Clinton c Bamber b Griffiths	9	– c Lamb b Mallender	17
A. J. Stewart lbw b Walker	25	– c Sharp b Griffiths	19
M. A. Lynch c Willey b Mallender	2	– c Mallender b Walker	6
*R. D. V. Knight c Williams b Willey	13	– lbw b Walker	38
†C. J. Richards c Sharp b Walker	0	– not out	44
A. Needham c Bamber b Mallender	8	– (8) not out	16
D. J. Thomas b Griffiths	52	– (7) lbw b Griffiths	0
G. Monkhouse b Griffiths	41		
S. T. Clarke b Mallender	43		
P. I. Pocock not out	0		
L-b 3, w 1, n-b 10	14	B 1, l-b 9, w 1	11

1/23 2/27 3/35 4/61   217   1/33 2/33 3/51 4/68   (6 wkts) 163
5/65 6/77 7/77 8/164 9/201   5/120 6/121

Bonus points – Surrey 2, Northamptonshire 4.

Bowling: *First Innings*—Mallender 17.5–6–65–3; Griffiths 25–11–66–4; Walker 15–1–62–2; Willey 7–4–10–1. *Second Innings*—Mallender 15–4–63–1; Griffiths 22–6–41–3; Walker 14–4–42–2; Willey 2–0–4–0; Williams 2–1–2–0.

Umpires: D. G. L. Evans and K. E. Palmer.

SURREY v GLOUCESTERSHIRE

At The Oval, July 2, 4. Surrey won by an innings and 84 runs. Surrey 24 pts, Gloucestershire 4 pts. Winning the toss and bowling first on a greenish pitch proved all-important. Clarke, in an early burst of three for 5, and later Monkhouse, with three for 4 in nineteen balls, had not only the Gloucestershire batsmen in trouble. Wicket-keeper Richards experienced unusual difficulty too, so that the extras at 32, including seventeen byes, in a total of 117 made the highest single contribution. Surrey, ahead for the loss of two wickets, had Lynch to bolster their advantage with twelve 4s in his 76. When the fourth Surrey bowler of any pace, Payne, then produced the best figures of his career, Gloucestershire were overwhelmed in two days.

Gloucestershire

A. W. Stovold b Clarke	0	– b Clarke		7
P. W. Romaines c Smith b Clarke	14	– lbw b Thomas		1
P. Bainbridge c Richards b Clarke	16	– b Clarke		1
A. J. Hignell lbw b Monkhouse	10	– c Thomas b Payne		46
Zaheer Abbas c Richards b Monkhouse	21	– c Butcher b Monkhouse		42
J. N. Shepherd c Lynch b Thomas	1	– (7) lbw b Payne		8
*D. A. Graveney c Payne b Monkhouse	1	– (8) c Monkhouse b Payne		4
R. J. Doughty c Clarke b Thomas	1	– (6) c Knight b Payne		8
†R. C. Russell c Monkhouse b Thomas	11	– c Richards b Thomas		2
G. E. Sainsbury b Thomas	10	– not out		4
D. V. Lawrence not out	0	– lbw b Payne		1
B 17, l-b 5, w 1, n-b 9	32	B 7, l-b 5, w 1, n-b 6		19

1/0 2/48 3/53 4/83   117   1/8 2/10 3/10 4/87   143
5/87 6/89 7/91 8/91 9/110   5/116 6/123 7/130 8/135 9/142

Bonus points – Surrey 4.

Bowling: *First Innings*—Clarke 14–10–14–3; Thomas 15.3–10–22–4; Monkhouse 14–3–27–3; Payne 9–3–22–0. *Second Innings*—Clarke 10–1–35–2; Thomas 10–2–43–2; Monkhouse 8–1–33–1; Payne 9–4–13–5.

Surrey

A. R. Butcher c Graveney b Shepherd	33	I. R. Payne lbw b Bainbridge	16
D. B. Pauline c Russell b Shepherd	19	G. Monkhouse lbw b Graveney	1
D. M. Smith c Stovold b Sainsbury	53	S. T. Clarke c Romaines b Graveney	12
*R. D. V. Knight c Russell b Sainsbury	32	P. I. Pocock b Shepherd	8
M. A. Lynch b Shepherd	76	B 6, l-b 13, w 1, n-b 1	21
†C. J. Richards c Romaines b Bainbridge	24		
D. J. Thomas not out	49		344

1/38 2/71 3/128 4/165
5/245 6/252 7/282 8/283 9/305

Bonus points – Surrey 4, Gloucestershire 4 (Score at 100 overs: 340-9).

Bowling: Shepherd 29.5–8–83–4; Lawrence 4–0–16–0; Sainsbury 24–6–70–2; Bainbridge 24–3–77–2; Doughty 4–0–24–0; Graveney 16–5–53–2.

Umpires: C. Cook and D. G. L. Evans.

At Southampton, July 9, 11, 12. SURREY drew with HAMPSHIRE.

At Taunton, July 16, 18, 19. SURREY drew with SOMERSET.

SURREY v NOTTINGHAMSHIRE

At The Oval, July 27, 28, 29. Surrey won by nine wickets. Surrey 24 pts, Nottinghamshire 5 pts. Three performances of particular merit helped Surrey complete a double over Nottinghamshire. Left-handed all-rounder Thomas hit his maiden century – 119 in 175 minutes, including two 6s and seventeen 4s – in between two fine spells of bowling. Monkhouse, with accurate medium pace, returned his best figures, seven for 51, and after Surrey had opened up a lead of 157, Pocock took six for 74. Robinson was Nottinghamshire's lone star, with scores of 92 and 82, the latter with the help of a runner. While fielding at silly-point he had been struck by a fierce cut from Smith, the ball rebounding to Hassan on the other side of the pitch for a clean catch.

Nottinghamshire

B. Hassan lbw b Monkhouse	19 – b Pocock	28
R. T. Robinson c Knight b Clarke	92 – c Smith b Curtis	82
*C. E. B. Rice b Monkhouse	39 – c and b Pocock	7
J. D. Birch st Richards b Monkhouse	11 – c Smith b Pocock	8
P. Johnson c Lynch b Monkhouse	6 – c Richards b Clarke	1
†B. N. French c Richards b Monkhouse	21 – c Knight b Pocock	22
E. E. Hemmings b Pocock	3 – c Thomas b Pocock	0
R. A. Pick b Pocock	7 – c Clarke b Pocock	4
N. J. B. Illingworth lbw b Monkhouse	8 – b Clarke	4
M. K. Bore not out	6 – not out	17
P. M. Such b Monkhouse	0 – lbw b Clarke	0
B 5, n-b 4	9	B 11, l-b 8, w 1, n-b 4 ... 24

1/32 2/103 3/115 4/128   221   1/77 2/91 3/105 4/119   197
5/195 6/200 7/206 8/207 9/221   5/162 6/162 7/176 8/176 9/191

Bonus points – Nottinghamshire 2, Surrey 4.

Bowling: *First Innings*—Clarke 21–4–50–1; Thomas 15–3–37–0; Monkhouse 21–5–51–7; Knight 10–3–21–0; Curtis 13–3–34–0; Pocock 17–6–19–2. *Second Innings*—Clarke 17.4–7–26–3; Monkhouse 6–3–16–0; Pocock 33–10–74–6; Thomas 5–3–10–0; Curtis 19–5–47–1.

Surrey

A. R. Butcher b Hemmings	40 – not out	23
G. S. Clinton lbw b Bore	3 – lbw b Such	0
D. M. Smith c Hassan b Hemmings	22 – not out	11
M. A. Lynch run out	67	
*R. D. V. Knight b Such	35	
†C. J. Richards lbw b Bore	1	
D. J. Thomas run out	119	
G. Monkhouse lbw b Bore	32	
S. T. Clarke c and b Illingworth	19	
P. I. Pocock not out	12	
I. J. Curtis not out	5	
B 3, l-b 17, w 1, n-b 2	23	B 4, l-b 3, n-b 1 ... 8

1/12 2/58 3/91 4/161   (9 wkts dec.) 378   1/8   (1 wkt) 42
5/171 6/188 7/299 8/332 9/365

Bonus points – Surrey 4, Nottinghamshire 3 (Score at 100 overs: 307-7).

Bowling: *First Innings*—Pick 24–4–70–0; Bore 33–13–80–3; Hemmings 28–4–104–2; Such 18.3–5–50–1; Illingworth 9–1–51–1. *Second Innings*—Pick 4–0–21–0; Such 3–0–13–1.

Umpires: J. Birkenshaw and B. Leadbeater.

At Swansea, July 30, August 1, 2. SURREY lost to GLAMORGAN by five wickets.

At The Oval, August 4. SURREY lost to NEW ZEALANDERS by 56 runs (See New Zealand tour section.).

SURREY v WARWICKSHIRE

At The Oval, August 6, 8, 9. Drawn. Surrey 7 pts, Warwickshire 5 pts. Although Clarke returned his best bowling figures, he could not get the better of Lloyd, who carried his bat in an innings lasting 338 minutes. Clarke finished with a spell of five for 23 in 30 balls. Despite Gifford's six for 94, Surrey led on first innings by 71, Pauline, who recorded his first fifty in the Championship, and Butcher opening with a stand of 136. Kallicharran, whose 173 in 220 minutes included one 6 and 30 4s, and Amiss put on 270 for the third wicket in Warwickshire's second innings, whereafter Surrey, set 253 in 135 minutes, played for a draw.

Warwickshire

T. A. Lloyd not out	124	– c Knight b Clarke 5
K. D. Smith b Thomas	4	– c Richards b Pocock 6
A. I. Kallicharran c Lynch b Clarke	1	– (4) not out 173
D. L. Amiss c Richards b Monkhouse	38	– (5) c Knight b Butcher 76
†G. W. Humpage b Clarke	13	– (6) not out 3
R. I. H. B. Dyer c Pauline b Clarke	17	
A. M. Ferreira b Clarke	4	– (3) retired hurt 20
C. M. Old c Smith b Knight	10	
*R. G. D. Willis b Clarke	0	
N. Gifford b Clarke	2	
W. Hogg b Clarke	0	
B 6, l-b 8, w 1, n-b 2	17	B 13, l-b 7, w 12, n-b 8 ... 40

1/15 2/26 3/117 4/142   230   1/23 2/25 3/295   (3 wkts dec.) 323
5/194 6/206 7/217 8/226 9/226

Bonus points – Warwickshire 2, Surrey 4.

Bowling: *First Innings*—Clarke 26–7–53–7; Thomas 17–2–52–1; Monkhouse 15–2–39–1; Knight 17–4–39–1; Pocock 14–5–21–0; Curtis 4–0–9–0. *Second Innings*—Clarke 15–6–26–1; Thomas 10–5–33–0; Pocock 18–5–44–1; Monkhouse 8–0–35–0; Curtis 13–1–55–0; Butcher 8.3–1–42–1; Lynch 5–0–29–0; Smith 2–0–19–0.

Surrey

A. R. Butcher c Dyer b Gifford	75	– c Lloyd b Gifford 9
D. B. Pauline c Gifford b Willis	52	– c Hogg b Gifford 37
D. M. Smith lbw b Hogg	0	– c Humpage b Old 43
*R. D. V. Knight lbw b Gifford	45	– (5) c Amiss b Old 16
M. A. Lynch lbw b Gifford	31	– (6) not out 59
†C. J. Richards st Humpage b Gifford	33	– (7) c Amiss b Gifford 8
D. J. Thomas b Gifford	16	– (4) c Kallicharran b Gifford 1
G. Monkhouse not out	8	– not out 4
S. T. Clarke c Dyer b Gifford	0	
P. I. Pocock c Amiss b Willis	15	
L-b 9, w 1, n-b 17	26	B 4, l-b 4, w 1, n-b 2 11

1/136 2/137 3/148 4/194   (9 wkts dec.) 301   1/24 2/95 3/96 4/96   (6 wkts) 188
5/243 6/268 7/279 8/281 9/301   5/123 6/138

I. J. Curtis did not bat.

Bonus points – Surrey 3, Warwickshire 3 (Score at 100 overs: 282-8).

Bowling: *First Innings*—Willis 14.5–4–35–2; Hogg 8–2–23–1; Old 18–5–57–0; Ferreira 27–6–66–0; Gifford 36–12–94–6. *Second Innings*—Willis 5–0–18–0; Hogg 2–1–2–0; Gifford 20–1–82–4; Old 14–1–54–2; Kallicharran 4–2–21–0.

Umpires: B. Dudleston and B. J. Meyer.

At Canterbury, August 10, 11, 12. SURREY beat KENT by four wickets.

SURREY v WORCESTERSHIRE

At Guildford, August 13, 15, 16. Surrey won by 227 runs. Surrey 24 pts, Worcestershire 5 pts. Two excellent partnerships, of 185 by Butcher and Stewart in the first innings and 141 by Butcher and Pauline in the second, enabled Surrey to take and maintain the initiative. Facing 363, Worcestershire had only Patel, with his first century of the summer, in 205 minutes with eleven 4s, and Neale to give an adequate response with a stand of 127 in 32 overs, and there was little in reply when, on the last day, Surrey set a target of 346 in just over four and a half hours. Butcher had batted 210 minutes, hitting one 6 and twenty 4s, in scoring 122 on the first day.

Surrey

A. R. Butcher b McEvoy b Illingworth	122	– c Neale b Perryman	85
D. B. Pauline lbw b Ellcock	17	– c Neale b Pridgeon	69
A. J. Stewart st Humphries b Illingworth	82	– (4) c sub b Ellcock	43
*R. D. V. Knight lbw b Illingworth	4	– (6) not out	20
M. A. Lynch lbw b Ellcock	25	– b Ellcock	9
†C. J. Richards b Ellcock	39	– (8) not out	8
D. J. Thomas c sub b Illingworth	32	– c Curtis b Pridgeon	3
G. Monkhouse not out	15	– (3) c Illingworth b Pridgeon	0
S. T. Clarke not out	9		
B 9, l-b 3, n-b 6	18	L-b 8, n-b 1	9

1/26 2/211 3/226 4/256   (7 wkts. dec.) 363   1/141 2/149 3/175   (6 wkts. dec.) 246
5/256 6/321 7/348   4/196 5/221 6/227

P. I. Pocock and I. J. Curtis did not bat.

Bonus points – Surrey 4, Worcestershire 2 (Score at 100 overs: 340-6).

Bowling: *First Innings*—Ellcock 16-6-53-3; Pridgeon 17-4-43-0; Perryman 23-1-92-0; Patel 22.5-2-76-0; Illingworth 25-9-76-4; D'Oliveira 1.1-0-5-0. *Second Innings*—Ellcock 17-1-100-2; Pridgeon 16-1-75-3; Illingworth 5-0-36-0; Perryman 5-1-26-1.

Worcestershire

J. A. Ormrod b Clarke	2	– b Thomas	28
M. S. A. McEvoy b Thomas	14	– c Pauline b Clarke	13
A. P. Pridgeon b Clarke	5	– (11) not out	0
*P. A. Neale c and b Pocock	58	– (3) b Thomas	7
D. N. Patel c Richards b Thomas	105	– (4) b Thomas	6
D. B. D'Oliveira c and b Monkhouse	22	– (5) b Thomas	10
T. S. Curtis c Butcher b Clarke	26	– (6) b Pocock	19
†D. J. Humphries c Clarke b Thomas	0	– (7) lbw b Pocock	13
R. K. Illingworth b Clarke	2	– (8) c Clarke b Pocock	2
R. M. Ellcock b Pocock	5	– (9) b Curtis	7
S. P. Perryman not out	2	– (10) c Thomas b Pocock	1
B 6, l-b 6, n-b 11	23	B 5, n-b 7	12

1/2 2/23 3/33 4/160   264   1/44 2/48 3/57 4/68   118
5/195 6/245 7/245 8/253 9/258   5/73 6/90 7/106 8/113 9/117

Bonus points – Worcestershire 3, Surrey 4.

Bowling: *First Innings*—Clarke 18-7-39-4; Thomas 15-1-48-3; Monkhouse 11-3-35-1; Pocock 21-5-63-2; Curtis 13-0-51-0; Butcher 5-3-5-0. *Second Innings*—Clarke 15-3-46-1; Thomas 14-5-33-4; Monkhouse 4-2-5-0; Pocock 16.4-9-13-4; Curtis 11-6-9-1.

Umpires: P. J. Eele and A. Jepson.

At Hove, August 20, 22, 23. SURREY drew with SUSSEX.

At Lord's, August 24, 25, 26. SURREY lost to MIDDLESEX by 103 runs.

SURREY v ESSEX

At The Oval, August 27, 29, 30. Surrey won by seven wickets. Surrey 24 pts, Essex 8 pts. Anxiety to maintain their place at the head of the Championship was reflected in Essex's performance. Their ninth-wicket pair were together before their strong batting line-up made sure of maximum bonus points and in their second innings Clarke ran through them, taking his match analysis to eleven for 111. This included a devastating spell of six for 17 in 13.1 overs on the last morning.

Essex

G. A. Gooch lbw b Payne	42	– c Knight b Thomas	4
C. Gladwin c Richards b Clarke	27	– b Thomas	5
B. R. Hardie lbw b Payne	28	– c Clarke b Payne	23
K. S. McEwan c Thomas b Clarke	72	– b Clarke	25
*K. W. R. Fletcher c Richards b Clarke	3	– c Knight b Clarke	12
D. R. Pringle c Knight b Thomas	7	– not out	33
N. Phillip c Clarke b Pocock	26	– c and b Clarke	5
†D. E. East c Pocock b Clarke	38	– c Payne b Clarke	2
R. E. East not out	31	– c Richards b Clarke	0
J. K. Lever c Knight b Clarke	5	– run out	2
D. L. Acfield not out	2	– c Butcher b Clarke	16
B 8, l-b 5, w 4, n-b 2	19	B 13, l-b 2, n-b 1	16

1/67 2/84 3/121 4/138   (9 wkts. dec.) 300   1/6 2/19 3/46 4/76   143
5/159 6/208 7/226 8/280 9/286   5/85 6/93 7/100 8/100 9/102

Bonus points – Essex 4, Surrey 4.

Bowling: *First Innings*—Clarke 18.1–5–63–5; Thomas 14–2–89–1; Payne 19–2–56–2; Knight 12–3–33–0; Pocock 9–1–23–1; Curtis 6–1–17–0. *Second Innings*—Clarke 24.1–10–48–6; Thomas 17–4–37–2; Payne 16–5–41–1; Pocock 3–2–1–0.

Surrey

A. R. Butcher c D. E. East b Lever	16	– lbw b Phillip	13
D. B. Pauline c D. E. East b Phillip	64	– lbw b Lever	9
A. J. Stewart c Gooch b Lever	20	– not out	52
*R. D. V. Knight b Lever	42	– c D. E. East b Acfield	46
M. A. Lynch b Gooch	13	– not out	0
†C. J. Richards c Hardie b Lever	43		
D. J. Thomas c Lever b Acfield	51		
I. R. Payne c Fletcher b Acfield	43		
S. T. Clarke not out	8		
P. I. Pocock c McEwan b R. E. East	0		
I. J. Curtis lbw b Acfield	2		
B 1, l-b 12, n-b 7	20	L-b 2, n-b 2	4

1/26 2/104 3/104 4/145   322   1/17 2/23 3/114   (3 wkts) 124
5/195 6/222 7/297 8/312 9/313

Bonus points – Surrey 4, Essex 4.

Bowling: *First Innings*—Lever 27–7–83–4; Phillip 18–4–45–1; R. E. East 11–3–47–1; Acfield 12.3–2–26–3; Gooch 20–1–65–1; Pringle 11–2–36–0. *Second Innings*—Lever 8–0–30–1; Phillip 8–0–19–1; Pringle 3–0–12–0; Acfield 8–4–20–1; R. E. East 2–0–12–0; Fletcher 3.3–0–27–0.

Umpires: B. Leadbeater and N. T. Plews.

SURREY v SUSSEX

At The Oval, August 31, September 1, 2. Sussex won by three wickets. Sussex 24 pts, Surrey 5 pts. A match in which 1,198 runs were scored for the loss of 22 wickets began with Pauline recording his first Championship century. His 115 in 52 overs included one 6 and 22 4s, but Imran matched that with four 6s and fourteen 4s in a chanceless 124 not out. After Butcher and Pauline had given Surrey another blistering start, which brought 129 runs in 73 minutes at the end of the second day, the Pakistani returned with another assault to win the match. Imran needed only 68 deliveries to plunder 78 from an attack minus Clarke, because of a pulled back muscle, and Sussex had 23 balls to spare in reaching a target of 296 in 200 minutes. Gould and Mendis hastened the end with 71 off ten overs.

Surrey

A. R. Butcher c Pigott b Reeve	18	– c sub b Waller	76
D. B. Pauline c Reeve b Green	115	– not out	79
A. J. Stewart c Wells b Pigott	8		
*R. D. V. Knight b Reeve	75		
M. A. Lynch c Wells b Reeve	53	– (3) not out	45
D. J. Thomas c and b Waller	41		
I. R. Payne c Barclay b Wells	0		
†C. J. Richards b Pigott	46		
S. T. Clarke c Standing b Waller	7		
P. I. Pocock st Gould b Waller	10		
P. A. Waterman not out	6		
L-b 4, n-b 5	9	B 4, l-b 4, n-b 1	9

1/59 2/93 3/207 4/254   388   1/134   (1 wkt dec.) 209
5/287 6/288 7/336 8/362 9/376

Bonus points – Surrey 4, Sussex 4.

Bowling: *First Innings*—Pigott 15.4–1–66–2; Reeve 17–5–46–3; Greig 18–1–85–0; Wells 10–0–60–1; Waller 24–5–66–3; Imran 3–2–5–0; Green 7–0–51–1. *Second Innings*—Pigott 14–0–75–0; Reeve 2–0–23–0; Greig 4–0–25–0; Waller 9–1–50–1; Green 2–0–13–0; Standing 1–0–5–0; Gould 2–0–9–0.

Sussex

G. D. Mendis retired hurt	53	– (8) not out	40
A. M. Green c Richards b Clarke	27	– (1) c Richards b Thomas	24
Imran Khan not out	124	– (4) c Clarke b Knight	78
C. M. Wells c and b Knight	26	– (3) c Knight b Pocock	39
D. K. Standing c Richards b Knight	10	– c Clarke b Pocock	37
I. A. Greig c Pauline b Pocock	38	– st Richards b Knight	19
†I. J. Gould not out	5	– b Knight	33
*J. R. T. Barclay (did not bat)		– (2) c Knight b Thomas	8
A. C. S. Pigott (did not bat)		– not out	0
B 1, l-b 13, w 1, n-b 4	19	B 5, l-b 10, n-b 6	21

1/87 2/150 3/170 4/281   (4 wkts dec.) 302   1/26 2/57 3/92 4/187   (7 wkts) 299
                                                  5/222 6/224 7/295

D. A. Reeve and C. E. Waller did not bat.

Bonus points – Sussex 4, Surrey 1.

Bowling: *First Innings*—Clarke 13–1–55–1; Thomas 16.1–3–54–0; Waterman 13–2–42–0; Pocock 17–3–50–1; Payne 12–4–45–0; Knight 13–4–37–2. *Second Innings*—Thomas 12–0–50–2; Waterman 8–0–45–0; Payne 3–0–18–0; Pocock 16–1–96–2; Knight 12–0–58–3; Butcher 1.1–0–11–0.

Umpires: J. H. Harris and N. T. Plews.

At Scarborough, September 7, 8, 9. SURREY drew with YORKSHIRE.

SURREY v DERBYSHIRE

At The Oval, September 10, 12, 13. Drawn. Surrey 4 pts, Derbyshire 8 pts. Before rain cut the match short, there had been two notable partnerships. Pauline and Butcher were involved in the first with a stand of 120, which made light of Barnett's decision to put Surrey in. Pauline completed his eighth fifty in eleven Championship games. Then Barnett and Hill shared Derbyshire's highest partnership of the summer, 198. Barnett went on to 121, his best score, in four hours, and Hill followed him to three figures. Fowler, in his first season, impressed while hitting 72 in 88 minutes. Stewart of Surrey suffered a fractured jaw, received when he ducked into a ball from Holding.

Surrey

A. R. Butcher c Newman b Miller	55	I. R. Payne not out	10
D. B. Pauline b Holding	75	S. T. Clarke b Holding	2
A. J. Stewart retired hurt	42	P. I. Pocock lbw b Newman	7
*R. D. V. Knight lbw b Mortensen	0	P. A. Waterman c Taylor b Newman	0
M. A. Lynch lbw b Holding	28	B 8, l-b 11	19
D. J. Thomas b Holding	0		
†C. J. Richards c Hampshire		1/120 2/157 3/158 4/207	244
b Holding.	6	5/207 6/223 7/229 8/244 9/244	

Bonus points – Surrey 2, Derbyshire 4.

Bowling: Holding 24–7–54–5; Mortensen 17–2–74–1; Newman 22.5–9–53–2; Finney 7–0–23–0; Miller 13–6–21–1.

Derbyshire

I. S. Anderson b Waterman	6	W. P. Fowler b Knight	72
*K. J. Barnett b Thomas	121	P. G. Newman b Clarke	0
A. Hill c Payne b Pocock	111	B 11, l-b 7, w 4, n-b 1	23
J. H. Hampshire b Thomas	6		
G. Miller not out	46	1/21 2/219 3/253 4/279 (7 wkts dec.)	385
R. J. Finney c Payne b Knight	0	5/280 6/384 7/385	

†R. W. Taylor, M. A. Holding and O. H. Mortensen did not bat.

Bonus points – Derbyshire 4, Surrey 2 (Score at 100 overs: 311-5).

Bowling: Clarke 12.2–2–27–1; Thomas 30–6–116–2; Waterman 18–5–64–1; Knight 23–11–44–2; Payne 8–1–37–0; Pocock 24–4–74–1.

Umpires: A. Jepson and A. G. T. Whitehead.

SUSSEX

President: A. M. Caffyn
Chairman: Dr D. Rice
Chairman, Cricket & Ground Sub-committee:
   D. J. Church
Secretary: 1983 – B. E. Simmonds;
   1984 – R. H. Renold
   County Ground, Eaton Road, Hove BN3 3AN
   (Telephone: 0273-732161)
Captain: J. R. T. Barclay
Coach: S. J. Storey

The season opened disastrously for Sussex with a home Championship defeat by Nottinghamshire, heavy reverses against Somerset in both the Benson and Hedges Cup and the John Player Sunday League, other matches washed out and a wait until mid-May before victory came.

This unfortunate opening set the general pattern for a season ranking with the worst in post-war years, a crop of injuries following and several players failing completely to produce anything like their best form. Ian Greig was first on the casualty list when he fell from his flat window, trying to gain entrance there after snapping his key in the lock. This was in early June, during a match with Kent at Hove; with Imran Khan unable to bowl until almost the end of the season, because of a stubborn stress fracture of the left shin, and Garth le Roux out of action from the start of August with a chronic groin condition, the pace battery was seriously depleted.

A great weight, therefore, rested on Tony Pigott, top wicket-taker in both Schweppes County Championship and Sunday League, Chris Waller, who bowled 752 overs, Colin Wells and a newcomer, Dermot Reeve, registered by the club shortly before Greig's mishap. Reeve's signing was a stroke of good fortune during a generally unfriendly campaign; after service on the Lord's groundstaff, he proved a consistent medium-pace bowler and a useful tail-end batsman.

Yet, despite the injuries to front-rank bowlers, it was the batting which gave most cause for concern. Time and again, a modest start was followed by half the wickets tumbling cheaply, with extra pressure on later batsmen to restore respectability. Gehan Mendis, opening the innings, did very well in such circumstances to record his highest aggregate for a season, with three centuries and eight half-centuries, but efforts to find him a satisfactory partner were not successful, hard as Allan Green, Jerry Heath and the captain, John Barclay, tried. In the one-day competitions the wicket-keeper, Ian Gould, gave Mendis belligerent support.

Holders of the John Player League title, Sussex battled hard to hold on to it, though having finally to settle for fourth place. The displays in the one-day competitions were, in fact, more confident than in the Championship where, at one time, twelve matches were played without a single win.

Barclay never wavered in his optimism or driving power, despite his own injury problem. Handicapped for much of the summer with a finger injury, he was unable to hold bat or ball comfortably. But he soldiered on uncomplainingly and waited until the season ended before having an operation. The captain remains hopeful that the club is getting the right balance of experience and youth.

Imran Khan strove almost impatiently to regain fitness and when eventually he resumed bowling, off a shortened run and at a far less fearsome pace than when in full cry, he produced one remarkable performance, against Warwickshire at Edgbaston. Although he said of himself that he was "only half a cricketer", he thrilled spectators with some brilliant batting and superb catches.

A young hopeful to take the eye was the locally born batsman, David Standing. He had earned his chance with consistent batting for the Second XI and took it well. In his début match, against Middlesex at Hove, he scored 56 not out and 37 not out at No. 3. It was an unusually lean Championship season for Paul Parker, the vice-captain, and he was rested at one stage. However, he headed the John Player League batting averages, a competition in which he played some typically dashing innings. His fielding remained at a very high level. Colin Wells, who was forced to become one of the club's main bowlers because of the injury crisis, was also disappointed with his batting. Towards the end of the season he was putting bat to ball more effectively, as well as taking wickets and completing sound spells, often opening the attack. His brother, Alan, played some hard-hitting innings, and his throwing from the deep was powerfully impressive. While finding the pressure of opening the innings an exacting one, Green held some fine close-to-the-wicket catches. After the rain of April and May there were glorious days on Horsham's attractive ground and the week at The Saffrons revived sun-drenched memories. There was some exciting play here at Eastbourne, with Reeve bowling the last decisive over in all three matches, twice successfully.

Sussex have a new secretary, Richard Renold, a Lancastrian business-man with a keen interest in cricket. The inn at the main gate, "The Sussex Cricketer" has been leased to a London firm, Sussex retaining the freehold. – J.A.

SUSSEX 1983

[Bill Smith]

Back row: D. J. Smith, D. A. Reeve, G. S. le Roux, A. P. Wells, C. M. Wells, A. M. Green. Front row: A. C. S. Pigott, G. D. Mendis, P. W. G. Parker, J. R. T. Barclay (captain), C. E. Waller, C. P. Phillipson. Inset: I. A. Greig, Imran Khan, I. J. Gould.

SUSSEX RESULTS

All first-class matches – Played 24: Won 3, Lost 10, Drawn 11.

County Championship matches – Played 23: Won 3, Lost 10, Drawn 10.

Bonus points – Batting 50, Bowling 72.

Competition placings – Schweppes County Championship, 11th; NatWest Bank Trophy, q-f; Benson and Hedges Cup, 3rd in Group C; John Player League, 4th.

COUNTY CHAMPIONSHIP AVERAGES

BATTING

	Birthplace	M	I	NO	R	HI	Avge
Imran Khanc	Lahore, Pakistan	13	25	3	1,260	124*	57.27
D. K. Standing	Brighton	4	8	3	240	60	48.00
G. D. Mendisc	Colombo, Ceylon	23	45	6	1,608	133*	41.23
I. J. Gould	Slough	17	22	6	473	59*	29.56
A. P. Wells	Newhaven	15	27	4	664	92	28.86
G. S. le Rouxc	Cape Town, SA	12	16	1	379	80	25.26
C. M. Wellsc	Newhaven	23	40	6	857	71	25.20
J. R. T. Barclayc	Bonn, WG	21	37	3	743	65	21.85
P. W. G. Parkerc	Bulawayo, Rhodesia	16	26	2	507	79	21.12
J. R. P. Heath	Turner's Hill	9	18	2	335	39	20.93
I. A. Greigc	Queenstown, SA	8	9	0	177	59	19.66
A. M. Green	Pulborough	15	29	2	519	53	19.22
A. C. S. Pigottc	London	22	28	8	381	63	19.05
R. S. Cowan	Hamlin, WG	5	10	0	154	50	15.40
D. A. Reeve	Hong Kong	17	20	5	192	42*	12.80
C. E. Wallerc	Guildford	21	22	11	98	21	8.90
D. J. Smith	Brighton	5	7	2	22	13	4.40
A. N. Jones	Woking	5	7	3	11	4*	2.75

Also batted: C. P. Phillipsonc (*Brindaban, India*) (1 match) 23, 28; A. Willows (*Portslade*) played in one match without batting.

*Signifies not out.   cDenotes county cap.

BOWLING

	O	M	R	W	Avge	BB
Imran Khan	46.2	12	86	12	7.16	6-6
G. S. le Roux	358.3	90	944	37	25.51	5-17
A. C. S. Pigott	577.5	98	1,879	72	26.09	6-22
D. A. Reeve	472.1	131	1,233	42	29.35	4-15
C. E. Waller	752	223	1,868	53	35.24	6-126
C. M. Wells	376.3	82	1,135	32	35.46	4-69
I. A. Greig	185	26	681	17	40.05	4-42
J. R. T. Barclay	231.3	59	774	17	45.52	3-30

Also bowled: R. S. Cowan 8-2-27-0; I. J. Gould 2-0-9-0; A. M. Green 53.4-9-248-6; J. R. P. Heath 8-0-58-0; A. N. Jones 81.4-10-358-6; P. W. G. Parker 4.2-1-30-0; D. K. Standing 4.3-0-32-0; A. Willows 8-3-11-0.

The following played a total of six three-figure innings for Sussex in County Championship matches – G. D. Mendis 4, Imran Khan 2.

At Oxford, April 30, May 2, 3. SUSSEX drew with OXFORD UNIVERSITY.

SUSSEX v NOTTINGHAMSHIRE

At Hove, May 4, 5, 6. Nottinghamshire won by an innings and 32 runs. Nottinghamshire 24 pts, Sussex 4 pts. An impressive display by the visitors revealed Hadlee to be in magnificent all-round form. His first-innings four for 25 was at one time four for 1 run as he and Hendrick began the match in quite a sensational manner by sending back five Sussex batsmen for only 5 runs on a lively wicket. Sussex were later eight down for 19, but the dependable Phillipson and fast bowler Pigott defied a strong attack to add 96, Pigott's 63 being a career best. The New Zealander then hit a brilliant century, generously sprinkled with boundaries, and finally hastened the Sussex defeat with three important wickets, the match finishing before tea on the final day.

Sussex

G. D. Mendis b Hadlee	0	– lbw b Hadlee	30
A. M. Green lbw b Hendrick	0	– (3) c Randall b Hendrick	6
*J. R. T. Barclay b Hadlee	0	– (2) b Cooper	36
P. W. G. Parker lbw b Hadlee	4	– lbw b Hadlee	20
C. M. Wells c French b Hendrick	6	– c Rice b Cooper	4
I. A. Greig b Hadlee	0	– lbw b Hadlee	1
†I. J. Gould c French b Hendrick	3	– c French b Hendrick	13
G. S. le Roux c Hemmings b Cooper	6	– c Birch b Saxelby	27
C. P. Phillipson c French b Cooper	23	– st French b Hemmings	28
A. C. S. Pigott b Hendrick	63	– c Hadlee b Hemmings	0
C. E. Waller not out	0	– not out	4
L-b 9, n-b 1	10	L-b 1, n-b 5	6
	115		**175**

1/0 2/0 3/0 4/5
5/5 6/8 7/17 8/19 9/115

1/53 2/61 3/80 4/99
5/99 6/100 7/127 8/147 9/152

Bonus points – Nottinghamshire 4.

Bowling: *First Innings*—Hadlee 20–11–25–4; Hendrick 19.5–10–28–4; Cooper 11–3–20–2; Saxelby 6–1–21–0; Hemmings 5–4–11–0. *Second Innings*—Hadlee 19–9–31–3; Hendrick 16–7–24–2; Hemmings 20.1–3–55–2; Cooper 12–5–28–2; Saxelby 9–3–31–1.

Nottinghamshire

B. Hassan c Green b Pigott	3	K. Saxelby not out	17
R. T. Robinson c Wells b le Roux	12	K. E. Cooper b Pigott	6
D. W. Randall b Pigott	43	M. Hendrick not out	1
*C. E. B. Rice b le Roux	37	B 10, w 2, n-b 6	18
J. D. Birch c Green b Waller	55		
R. J. Hadlee c Phillipson b Wells	103	1/11 2/18 3/84	(9 wkts dec.) 322
†B. N. French c Gould b Waller	16	4/135 5/213 6/268	
E. E. Hemmings c Gould b Waller	11	7/290 8/301 9/312	

Bonus points – Nottinghamshire 4, Sussex 4.

Bowling: le Roux 17–4–41–2; Pigott 20–4–81–3; Greig 18–1–68–0; Waller 31–10–60–3; Barclay 4–0–23–0; Wells 10–1–31–1.

Umpires: J. H. Harris and A. G. T. Whitehead.

At Gloucester, May 11, 12, 13. GLOUCESTERSHIRE v SUSSEX. Abandoned.

At Taunton, May 25, 26, 27. SUSSEX beat SOMERSET by ten wickets.

At Lord's, May 28, 30, 31. SUSSEX drew with MIDDLESEX.

SUSSEX v WORCESTERSHIRE

At Hove, June 4, 6, 7. Drawn. Sussex 8 pts, Worcestershire 3 pts. Sussex gained a first-innings lead of 113 following a splendid century by Mendis, who batted responsibly for 298 minutes and enjoyed a second-wicket stand with Barclay of 146 at a run a minute. On an easy-paced wicket Ormrod and Weston had given the visitors a sound start with an opening stand of 91, but Pigott ran through the later batting to finish with six for 74. An inconclusive final day's play belonged to the solid young opener, Weston, with a maiden century as he and Patel coasted through a partnership of 171 to ensure Worcestershire would not be beaten.

Worcestershire

J. A. Ormrod c Gould b C. M. Wells	50	– b le Roux	12
M. J. Weston c Gould b C. M. Wells	44	– b Green	115
*P. A. Neale lbw b Pigott	24	– lbw b Greig	7
D. N. Patel c A. P. Wells b Pigott	45	– c Gould b Greig	90
D. B. D'Oliveira le Roux	26	– c Pigott b Greig	8
M. S. A. McEvoy b C. M. Wells	6	– not out	16
†D. J. Humphries c le Roux b Pigott	11	– c C. M. Wells b Green	26
R. K. Illingworth not out	2	– not out	2
J. D. Inchmore b Pigott	0		
R. M. Ellcock c A. P. Wells b Pigott	0		
A. P. Pridgeon b Pigott	6		
B 1, l-b 7, n-b 1	9	B 5, l-b 7, w 1, n-b 2	15

1/91 2/114 3/132 4/173   223   1/34 2/62 3/233   (6 wkts) 291
5/204 6/204 7/215 8/215 9/215   4/242 5/247 6/287

Bonus points – Worcestershire 2, Sussex 4.

Bowling: *First Innings*—le Roux 21–6–38–1; Pigott 22–4–74–6; Greig 12–1–57–0; Barclay 4–1–8–0; C. M. Wells 16–4–28–3; Willows 5–2–9–0. *Second Innings*—Pigott 21–5–50–0; le Roux 18–4–41–1; Barclay 24–8–58–0; Greig 24–6–66–3; C. M. Wells 9–1–29–0; Willows 3–1–2–0; Green 11–3–30–2; Parker 1–1–0–0.

Sussex

G. D. Mendis run out	132	I. A. Greig run out	1
A. M. Green b Inchmore	48	L-b 12, n-b 12	24
*J. R. T. Barclay c Patel b Illingworth	64		
C. M. Wells not out	51	1/120 2/266 3/266 (5 wkts dec.) 336	
A. P. Wells lbw b Pridgeon	16	4/325 5/336	

P. W. G. Parker, †I. J. Gould, G. S. le Roux, A. C. S. Pigott and A. Willows did not bat.

Bonus points – Sussex 4, Worcestershire 1 (Score at 100 overs: 309-3).

Bowling: Ellcock 19–1–53–0; Pridgeon 21–4–79–1; Inchmore 18.1–3–52–1; Illingworth 28–7–85–1; Patel 21–7–43–0.

Umpires: P. J. Eele and P. B. Wight.

SUSSEX v KENT

At Hove, June 8, 9, 10. Kent won by six wickets. Kent 20 pts, Sussex 5 pts. The first two days were undistinguished, the batting of both sides being so pedestrian that not even the overcast conditions and a touch of Sussex sea fret could be offered as an excuse. The final day saw Kent successfully chase a target of 277 in 190 minutes, Aslett and Baptiste each making a century in a stand of 191 off 33 overs, although victory came with only three balls remaining. For Sussex, Alan Wells, 21-year-old younger brother of Colin, was top scorer in both innings with 92 and 60, as well as fielding very smartly.

Sussex

G. D. Mendis b Ellison	18	– c Underwood b Penn	29
A. M. Green b Baptiste	16	– (6) c Jarvis b Taylor	25
*J. R. T. Barclay b Baptiste	22	– (2) c Knott b Baptiste	33
C. M. Wells c Potter b Ellison	21	– (3) c Aslett b Underwood	25
P. W. G. Parker c Aslett b Jarvis	43	– (4) lbw b Baptiste	0
A. P. Wells c sub b Underwood	92	– (5) c Ellison b Aslett	60
I. A. Greig lbw b Baptiste	42		
G. S. le Roux c sub b Baptiste	4	– (7) not out	38
A. C. S. Pigott lbw b Jarvis	5	– (8) not out	5
†D. J. Smith not out	0		
C. E. Waller c and b Baptiste	0		
L-b 7, w 1, n-b 6	14	B 7, l-b 3	10

1/29 2/50 3/73 4/88   277   1/68 2/68 3/77   (6 wkts dec.) 225
5/194 6/267 7/272 8/277 9/277   4/116 5/151 6/207

Bonus points – Sussex 3, Kent 2 (Score at 100 overs: 270-6).

Bowling: *First Innings*—Jarvis 22–5–66–2; Ellison 22–12–32–2; Penn 19–4–74–0; Baptiste 17.3–5–45–5; Underwood 19–8–38–1; Johnson 3–0–8–0. *Second Innings*—Jarvis 11–3–33–0; Ellison 8–4–12–0; Penn 7–2–24–1; Baptiste 8–4–16–2; Underwood 7–3–14–1; Johnson 6–2–17–0; Aslett 10–0–69–1; Taylor 8–2–30–1.

Kent

K. B. S. Jarvis c Pigott b le Roux	0		
N. R. Taylor lbw b Waller	22	– (1) c Green b Pigott	22
L. Potter c Mendis b Waller	31	– (2) lbw b Pigott	13
D. G. Aslett run out	55	– (3) b Barclay	111
M. R. Benson lbw b C. M. Wells	20	– (4) c sub b Barclay	12
†A. P. E. Knott c Parker b Pigott	10	– not out	5
*G. W. Johnson not out	37		
R. M. Ellison not out	36		
E. A. E. Baptiste (did not bat)		– (5) not out	102
B 1, l-b 8, n-b 6	15	B 1, l-b 9, n-b 2	12

1/0 2/43 3/74 4/123   (6 wkts dec.) 226   1/31 2/47 3/80 4/271   (4 wkts) 277
5/140 6/149

C. Penn and D. L. Underwood did not bat.

Bonus points – Kent 2, Sussex 2.

Bowling: *First Innings*—le Roux 22–9–44–1; C. M. Wells 26–15–27–1; Pigott 20–4–67–1; Waller 25–9–52–2; Barclay 7–0–21–0. *Second Innings*—le Roux 8–0–43–0; C. M. Wells 8–0–33–0; Pigott 14–2–62–2; Waller 15.3–2–60–0; Barclay 12–0–67–2.

Umpires: P. J. Eele and P. B. Wight.

SUSSEX v SOMERSET

At Hove, June 11, 13, 14. Sussex won by seven wickets. Sussex 21 pts, Somerset 5 pts. In a low-scoring match on a lively wicket, the highest individual score was an efficient 67 by Ollis, and le Roux's five for 17 off fifteen overs was as hostile a performance as Somerset would want to experience for a long time. Sussex were finally required to grind their way to 116 for victory, the Somerset pacemen making them earn their second victory of the season over the West Country side.

Somerset

R. L. Ollis c Pigott b C. M. Wells	67	– b Reeve	17
P. M. Roebuck lbw b le Roux	2	– c Smith b Reeve	40
*B. C. Rose b C. M. Wells	11	– b le Roux	6
P. W. Denning c Smith b Reeve	6	– c Pigott b Barclay	3
N. F. M. Popplewell lbw b le Roux	27	– lbw b Pigott	9
J. W. Lloyds lbw b Reeve	0	– lbw b le Roux	20
G. V. Palmer b Reeve	3	– lbw b le Roux	1
†T. Gard b Barclay	24	– lbw b le Roux	7
C. H. Dredge c Waller b Pigott	9	– b le Roux	0
M. R. Davis b le Roux	19	– not out	5
P. H. L. Wilson not out	0	– b Pigott	1
B 2, l-b 7, w 1, n-b 3	13	L-b 1, n-b 2	3

1/10 2/38 3/53 4/103	181	1/34 2/41 3/50 4/65 5/94 112
5/113 6/121 7/123 8/137 9/181		6/98 7/106 8/106 9/111

Bonus points – Somerset 1, Sussex 4.

Bowling: *First Innings*—le Roux 20–9–28–3; Pigott 14–6–29–1; Reeve 25–9–48–3; C. M. Wells 7–4–37–2; Barclay 15.1–8–21–1; Waller 1–0–5–0. *Second Innings*—le Roux 15–7–17–5; Pigott 10.2–1–23–2; Reeve 15–3–42–2; Barclay 9–2–16–1; Waller 8–5–11–0.

Sussex

G. D. Mendis c Rose b Davis	31	– c Dredge b Palmer	20
A. M. Green c Dredge b Popplewell	10	– not out	37
*J. R. T. Barclay run out	6		
C. M. Wells c Davis b Dredge	37	– (3) c Popplewell b Palmer	26
P. W. G. Parker lbw b Dredge	6	– (4) lbw b Davis	20
A. P. Wells c Gard b Wilson	15	– (5) not out	11
G. S. le Roux lbw b Palmer	35		
A. C. S. Pigott lbw b Dredge	0		
D. A. Reeve lbw b Palmer	16		
†D. J. Smith c Gard b Wilson	13		
C. E. Waller not out	3		
L-b 5, n-b 1	6	L-b 3, n-b 1	4

1/34 2/48 3/48 4/60	178	1/28 2/75 3/105 (3 wkts) 118
5/87 6/137 7/137 8/147 9/162		

Bonus points – Sussex 1, Somerset 4.

Bowling: *First Innings*—Wilson 10.5–0–44–2; Dredge 17–7–42–3; Palmer 14–3–31–2; Popplewell 8–2–31–1; Davis 11–3–19–1; Lloyds 2–0–5–0. *Second Innings*—Wilson 15–7–21–0; Dredge 14–4–24–0; Palmer 10–3–18–2; Popplewell 3–1–12–0; Lloyds 1–0–10–0; Davis 6–1–25–1; Roebuck 1–0–4–0.

Umpires: C. Cook and R. A. White.

At Tunbridge Wells, June 15, 16, 17. SUSSEX lost to KENT by nine wickets.

SUSSEX v LANCASHIRE

At Horsham, June 18, 20, 21. Lancashire won by 54 runs. Lancashire 24 pts, Sussex 4 pts. An entertaining match, played in delightful weather, provided a fighting finish, with Sussex making a bold attempt to score 255 for victory in 185 minutes. A brilliant 149 by Hayes was the batting highlight, while veteran off-spinner Simmons checked a swashbuckling second-innings stand of 75 in 40 minutes between Parker and le Roux and polished off the tail. His five for 47 brought the game to an end with five overs to spare.

Lancashire

I. Cockbain lbw b C. M. Wells	21	– lbw b Pigott	20
†C. Maynard c Pigott b le Roux	4	– c Pigott b le Roux	2
F. C. Hayes c Smith b C. M. Wells	149	– c Green b Pigott	28
D. P. Hughes c Smith b C. M. Wells	53	– c Green b Pigott	0
*J. Abrahams c A. P. Wells b Reeve	49	– c A. P. Wells b Pigott	10
N. H. Fairbrother c Smith b le Roux	8	– lbw b Pigott	0
S. J. O'Shaughnessy not out	20	– c Barclay b Waller	19
Nasir Zaidi (did not bat)		– not out	47
J. Simmons (did not bat)		– c Parker b Barclay	35
S. T. Jefferies (did not bat)		– c Reeve b Barclay	5
M. Watkinson (did not bat)		– b Barclay	0
B 3, l-b 3, n-b 2	8	L-b 4, w 1, n-b 1	6

1/7 2/74 3/224 4/233   (6 wkts. dec.) 312   1/16 2/35 3/41 4/52 5/52   172
5/247 6/312   6/61 7/85 8/147 9/165

Bonus points – Lancashire 4, Sussex 2 (Score at 100 overs: 301-5).

Bowling: *First Innings*—le Roux 21–5–66–2; Pigott 16–2–63–0; Reeve 13.3–4–29–1; Waller 28–8–70–0; C. M. Wells 21–7–43–3; Barclay 4–0–33–0. *Second Innings*—le Roux 14–3–24–1; Pigott 18–2–55–5; Waller 26–16–30–1; C. M. Wells 12–1–21–0; Barclay 14.2–3–36–3.

Sussex

G. D. Mendis b Watkinson	4	– c Cockbain b O'Shaughnessy	17
*J. R. T. Barclay c Nasir b Watkinson	6	– b Nasir	23
†D. J. Smith lbw b Watkinson	6	– (11) not out	0
C. M. Wells c Abrahams b Watkinson	0	– (3) c Simmons b O'Shaughnessy	0
P. W. G. Parker lbw b Watkinson	4	– (4) c Fairbrother b Simmons	75
A. M. Green c Hayes b O'Shaughnessy	28	– (5) c Maynard b Nasir	0
A. P. Wells c Maynard b O'Shaughnessy	20	– (6) c Abrahams b Simmons	18
G. S. le Roux lbw b Watkinson	49	– (7) c Cockbain b Simmons	32
D. A. Reeve not out	42	– (8) lbw b Simmons	19
A. C. S. Pigott c Abrahams b Nasir	42	– (9) c Fairbrother b Simmons	4
C. E. Waller run out	2	– (10) b Nasir	0
B 4, l-b 9, w 2, n-b 12	27	B 1, l-b 6, n-b 5	12

1/8 2/17 3/17 4/23   230   1/24 2/26 3/60 4/60   200
5/38 6/83 7/92 8/153 9/213   5/92 6/167 7/186 8/200 9/200

Bonus points – Sussex 2, Lancashire 4.

Bowling: *First Innings*—Jefferies 23–8–56–0; Watkinson 25–12–51–6; O'Shaughnessy 19.4–4–46–2; Nasir 12–3–39–1; Simmons 7–2–11–0. *Second Innings*—Watkinson 12–0–45–0; Jefferies 7–1–34–0; O'Shaughnessy 9–1–35–2; Nasir 8–2–27–3; Simmons 12.2–3–47–5.

Umpires: J. W. Holder and C. T. Spencer.

At Basingstoke, June 22, 23, 24. SUSSEX drew with HAMPSHIRE.

At Ilford, June 25, 27. SUSSEX lost to ESSEX by nine wickets.

SUSSEX v NORTHAMPTONSHIRE

At Hove, July 2, 4, 5. Northamptonshire won by 119 runs. Northamptonshire 21 pts, Sussex 7 pts. Sussex never seriously threatened to make the 274 runs needed for victory in 220 minutes, Steele quickly snapping up three of their wickets for 18 runs in seven overs. Cook had a splendid match, scoring 58 and 67, making a magnificent catch, and leading his side skilfully. In Sussex's first innings Mendis showed that he can bat with justifiable caution.

Northamptonshire

*G. Cook c Parker b Jones	58	– c Mendis b Waller	67
W. Larkins b le Roux	93	– c Heath b Jones	0
P. Willey lbw b Reeve	39	– c le Roux b Waller	80
A. J. Lamb c Gould b Reeve	44	– st Gould b Waller	35
R. G. Williams c Gould b Reeve	0	– not out	26
R. J. Boyd-Moss c Gould b Wells	22	– st Gould b Waller	9
D. S. Steele lbw b Reeve	0	– not out	5
†G. Sharp b Wells	23		
N. A. Mallender b Wells	8		
J. A. Carse not out	6		
B. J. Griffiths b Wells	0		
B 1, l-b 3, w 1, n-b 2	7	W 1	1

1/124 2/169 3/236 4/236   300   1/4 2/114 3/167   (5 wkts dec.) 223
5/247 6/247 7/284 8/293 9/296   4/196 5/216

Bonus points – Northamptonshire 4, Sussex 4.

Bowling: *First Innings*—le Roux 19–4–49–1; Jones 13–3–57–1; Reeve 25–5–80–4; Wells 17.5–2–69–4; Waller 21–4–38–0. *Second Innings*—le Roux 9–0–37–0; Jones 6–0–37–1; Waller 29–6–58–4; Reeve 9–3–33–0; Wells 8–1–38–0; Barclay 5–0–19–0.

Sussex

G. D. Mendis not out	121	– c Sharp b Steele	18
J. R. P. Heath b Griffiths	39	– b Mallender	2
*J. R. T. Barclay c Sharp b Griffiths	16	– b Carse	41
Imran Khan c Lamb b Steele	17	– c Sharp b Carse	0
P. W. G. Parker not out	39	– c Cook b Steele	3
C. M. Wells (did not bat)	—	– c Lamb b Steele	0
†I. J. Gould (did not bat)	—	– b Griffiths	44
G. S. le Roux (did not bat)	—	– b Willey	11
D. A. Reeve (did not bat)	—	– b Willey	2
C. E. Waller (did not bat)	—	– b Griffiths	21
A. N. Jones (did not bat)	—	– not out	1
L-b 11, n-b 7	18	L-b 5, w 6	11

1/75 2/127 3/146   (3 wkts dec.) 250   1/10 2/35 3/56 4/63   154
                          5/63 6/93 7/124 8/132 9/136

Bonus points – Sussex 3, Northamptonshire 1.

Bowling: *First Innings*—Carse 17–3–59–0; Mallender 17–1–48–0; Griffiths 24–4–62–2; Willey 7–2–21–0; Steele 24.2–10–42–1. *Second Innings*—Mallender 5–0–23–1; Griffiths 8.5–0–45–2; Steele 7–3–18–3; Carse 9–0–43–2; Willey 6–2–14–2.

Umpires: R. Palmer and R. Julian.

At Cardiff, July 9, 11, 12. SUSSEX drew with GLAMORGAN.

At Leeds, July 13, 14, 15. SUSSEX drew with YORKSHIRE.

SUSSEX v ESSEX

At Hove, July 27, 28, 29. Essex won by an innings and 53 runs. Essex 24 pts, Sussex 5 pts. There were some splendid individual performances – notably magnificent batting by Gooch and Imran, whose dismissal in Sussex's second innings sparked off a bowling spell by Lever which demoralised the home side. Lever took six wickets, including Imran's, for 9 runs in a match-winning spell of 5.2 overs. East held nine catches behind the stumps for Essex and was unlucky to miss a maiden century.

Sussex

G. D. Mendis c Gooch b Pringle	18	– c D. E. East b Foster	14
*J. R. T. Barclay b Lever	21	– b Lever	9
C. M. Wells c D. E. East b Lever	7	– (6) lbw b Lever	0
Imran Khan c D. E. East b Lever	14	– c D. E. East b Lever	50
R. S. Cowan c Gooch b Foster	14	– (3) c D. E. East b Foster	2
A. P. Wells c D. E. East b Acfield	49	– (5) c D. E. East b Lever	45
†I. J. Gould not out	59	– c D. E. East b Lever	0
A. C. S. Pigott lbw b Pringle	4	– c Hardie b Lever	0
D. A. Reeve b Pringle	8	– c Pringle b Lever	0
C. E. Waller lbw b Lever	7	– c D. E. East b Foster	2
A. N. Jones c and b Lever	0	– not out	0
B 2, l-b 7, n-b 7	16	L-b 2, w 2, n-b 1	5

1/30 2/51 3/66 4/76   217   1/18 2/29 3/33 4/109   127
5/111 6/150 7/163 8/197 9/217   5/109 6/109 7/111 8/111 9/124

Bonus points – Sussex 2, Essex 4.

Bowling: *First Innings*—Lever 17.4–6–40–5; Foster 19–1–73–1; Turner 10–6–13–0; Pringle 19–3–68–3; Acfield 5–3–7–1. *Second Innings*—Lever 17.2–4–55–7; Foster 13–5–33–3; Pringle 2–0–21–0; Acfield 2–0–13–0.

Essex

G. A. Gooch lbw b Pigott	96	N. A. Foster st Gould b Waller	17
B. R. Hardie st Gould b Waller	56	J. K. Lever c Reeve b Waller	16
†D. E. East c C. M. Wells b Imran	91	D. L. Acfield not out	1
K. S. McEwan b Waller	5	B 4, l-b 4, n-b 18	26
*K. W. R. Fletcher b Reeve	10		
D. R. Pringle b Waller	46	1/133 2/262 3/267	397
K. R. Pont c Barclay b Jones	21	4/268 5/290 6/325	
S. Turner st Gould b Waller	12	7/361 8/372 9/396	

Bonus points – Essex 4, Sussex 3 (Score at 100 overs: 361-7).

Bowling: Pigott 11–1–56–1; Reeve 21–5–68–1; Jones 15–1–69–1; Waller 42.1–7 126–6; C. M. Wells 6.1–2–21–0; Barclay 6–2–12–0; Imran 4.5–0–16–1; Cowan 3–1–3–0.

Umpires: R. Palmer and P. B. Wight.

At Leicester, July 30, August 1. SUSSEX lost to LEICESTERSHIRE by an innings and 103 runs.

SUSSEX v DERBYSHIRE

At Eastbourne, August 6, 8, 9. Drawn. Sussex 8 pts, Derbyshire 5 pts. With healthy rings of spectators basking in the hot sunshine on all three days, the tempo of play was hardly more hectic than on the neighbouring croquet lawn – until the final hour of the match.

Derbyshire, set to score 250 in three hours, looked to be coasting to victory at 187 for two, but Pigott snatched four quick wickets and Taylor had to survive a desperate last over, bowled by Reeve, to save the game for his side.

Sussex

G. D. Mendis lbw b Tunnicliffe	59	– lbw b Finney	11
*J. R. T. Barclay lbw b Oldham	8	– c Barnett b Tunnicliffe	40
R. S. Cowan c Taylor b Finney	46	– lbw b Oldham	24
Imran Khan c Taylor b Mortensen	82	– b Tunnicliffe	5
J. R. P. Heath c Taylor b Oldham	23	– not out	38
A. P. Wells not out	54	– b Miller	6
C. M. Wells not out	31	– not out	49
B 1, l-b 11, w 2, n-b 3	17	L-b 8, n-b 5	13

1/21 2/93 3/160   (5 wkts dec.) 320   1/23 2/77 3/79   (5 wkts dec.) 186
4/225 5/234   4/105 5/119

†I. J. Gould, A. C. S. Pigott, D. A. Reeve and C. E. Waller did not bat.

Bonus points – Sussex 4, Derbyshire 2 (Score at 100 overs: 319-5).

Bowling: *First Innings*—Mortensen 27–5–89–1; Oldham 28–6–80–2; Finney 27–5–69–1; Tunnicliffe 19–2–65–1. *Second Innings*—Mortensen 14–6–29–0; Finney 6–2–19–1; Tunnicliffe 21–4–54–2; Miller 9–1–37–1; Oldham 13–5–34–1.

Derbyshire

*K. J. Barnett lbw b C. M. Wells	22	– c Barclay b Imran	51
I. S. Anderson c Gould b Pigott	87	– c Imran b Pigott	79
A. Hill lbw b C. M. Wells	19	– b Pigott	54
J. H. Hampshire c Barclay b C. M. Wells	8	– lbw b Pigott	9
R. J. Finney lbw b C. M. Wells	16	– b Pigott	4
G. Miller c Reeve b Waller	5	– c Gould b Reeve	1
W. P. Fowler b Pigott	40	– c A. P. Wells b Reeve	3
C. J. Tunnicliffe b Waller	40	– c Imran b Pigott	2
†R. W. Taylor st Gould b Waller	2	– not out	1
S. Oldham not out	3	– b Pigott	0
O. H. Mortensen b Waller	3	– not out	0
B 4, l-b 3, n-b 5	12	B 8, l-b 1, w 4, n-b 2	15

1/27 2/70 3/78 4/105   257   1/109 2/187 3/197   (9 wkts) 219
5/123 6/178 7/235   4/203 5/208 6/212
8/249 9/253   7/212 8/214 9/215

Bonus points – Derbyshire 3, Sussex 4.

Bowling: *First Innings*—Pigott 16–2–45–2; Reeve 17–3–49–0; C. M. Wells 24–4–72–4; Waller 35.2–18–60–4; Barclay 6–1–19–0. *Second Innings*—Pigott 11–2–22–6; Reeve 10–4–33–2; Waller 17–2–67–0; C. M. Wells 12–1–49–0; Imran 6–1–18–1; Barclay 2–0–15–0.

Umpires: D. R. Shepherd and J. van Geloven.

SUSSEX v HAMPSHIRE

At Eastbourne, August 10, 11, 12. Hampshire won by three wickets. Hampshire 23 pts, Sussex 5 pts. Hampshire won with one ball remaining, having accurately paced their target of 283, the highest total of the match. Terry's 115 laid the foundation for victory, while steady spin bowling by Waller and three superb catches in the deep by Imran kept the result in doubt until the end. The Saffrons' pitch, cause for such concern the previous season, was now greatly improved.

Sussex

†G. D. Mendis b Marshall	0	– b Nicholas	76
A. M. Green c Greenidge b Tremlett	19	– c Pocock b Tremlett	8
R. S. Cowan c Parks b Marshall	0	– lbw b Nicholas	50
Imran Khan b Jesty	101	– (5) c Jesty b Nicholas	55
J. R. P. Heath b Malone	1	– (6) c Malone b Cowley	27
A. P. Wells run out	3	– (7) c Greenidge b Jesty	18
C. M. Wells c Turner b Marshall	0	– (8) not out	6
*J. R. T. Barclay c Greenidge b Marshall	41		
A. C. S. Pigott lbw b Nicholas	63	– not out	16
D. A. Reeve lbw b Nicholas	9	– (4) c Nicholas b Malone	0
C. E. Waller not out	15		
L-b 7, w 2, n-b 2	11	L-b 9, w 2, n-b 2	13

1/0 2/0 3/56 4/57   263   1/41 2/124 3/129   (7 wkts dec.) 269
5/78 6/83 7/149 8/198 9/227   4/174 5/207 6/247 7/247

Bonus points – Sussex 3, Hampshire 4 (Score at 100 overs: 256-9).

Bowling: *First Innings*—Marshall 26–5–58–4; Malone 15–2–64–1; Tremlett 18–7–47–1; Nicholas 16.2–4–34–2; Jesty 8–3–12–1; Cowley 18–4–31–0; Pocock 1–0–6–0. *Second Innings*—Marshall 9–2–23–0; Malone 13–0–82–1; Tremlett 8–0–25–1; Jesty 15.2–6–33–1; Nicholas 18–4–50–3; Cowley 17–7–43–1.

Hampshire

C. G. Greenidge lbw b C. M. Wells	14	– b C. M. Wells	36
V. P. Terry run out	68	– c and b Waller	115
M. C. J. Nicholas b Reeve	8	– c Cowan b Waller	6
T. E. Jesty c A. P. Wells b Pigott	75	– c Imran b Waller	36
D. R. Turner c Cowan b Waller	27	– lbw b Waller	20
*N. E. J. Pocock c Mendis b Pigott	5	– c Imran b Barclay	11
M. D. Marshall not out	26	– c Imran b Waller	13
N. G. Cowley not out	14	– not out	25
T. M. Tremlett (did not bat)		– not out	12
B 2, l-b 8, w 2, n-b 1	13	B 7, l-b 3, n-b 1	11

1/47 2/58 3/165   (6 wkts dec.) 250   1/67 2/80 3/150   (7 wkts) 285
4/194 5/207 6/213   4/186 5/215 6/231 7/257

†R. J. Parks and S. J. Malone did not bat.

Bonus points – Hampshire 3, Sussex 2.

Bowling: *First Innings*—Pigott 19–6–53–2; Reeve 23–4–77–1; C. M. Wells 10–3–41–1; Imran 5–1–10–0; Waller 22–3–56–1. *Second Innings*—Pigott 11–0–59–0; Reeve 4.5–0–27–0; Waller 25–3–96–5; Barclay 10–0–60–1; C. M. Wells 5–2–15–1; Green 3–1–17–0.

Umpires: D. R. Shepherd and P. J. Eele.

SUSSEX v SURREY

At Hove, August 20, 22, 23. Drawn. Sussex 5 pts, Surrey 7 pts. Barclay declared Sussex's first innings 105 runs behind, but the daunting target of 304 set by Knight, with three hours remaining, led to a draw when early wickets fell.

Surrey

A. R. Butcher c Heath b Imran	40	– c Gould b Reeve	4
D. B. Pauline b Reeve	51	– c Gould b Reeve	5
A. J. Stewart lbw b Imran	0	– retired hurt	12
*R. D. V. Knight lbw b Reeve	57	– b Reeve	5
M. A. Lynch c Gould b Reeve	24	– not out	101
†C. J. Richards b Waller	23	– (8) not out	52
D. J. Thomas not out	103	– (6) st Gould b Waller	0
G. Monkhouse not out	39	– (7) c Gould b Wells	12
B 2, l-b 9, n-b 9	20	B 1, l-b 2, w 1, n-b 3	7

1/71 2/71 3/125   (6 wkts dec.) 357   1/10 2/13 3/25   (5 wkts dec.) 198
4/177 5/195 6/221   4/35 5/105

S. T. Clarke, P. I. Pocock and I. J. Curtis did not bat.

Bonus points – Surrey 4, Sussex 2 (Score at 100 overs: 351-6).

Bowling: *First Innings*—Pigott 19–7–66–0; Reeve 22–4–66–3; Wells 15–4–46–0; Waller 31–7–105–1; Imran 6–3–3–2; Heath 5–0–28–0; Barclay 3–0–23–0. *Second Innings*—Reeve 12–5–23–3; Wells 15–3–46–1; Waller 9–0–59–1; Imran 3–0–6–0; Barclay 6–0–27–0; Heath 3–0–30–0.

Sussex

G. D. Mendis c Stewart b Thomas	18	– b Pocock	35
A. M. Green b Knight	39	– c Knight b Thomas	0
R. S. Cowan lbw b Thomas	0	– lbw b Thomas	8
Imran Khan c and b Monkhouse	71	– lbw b Thomas	0
J. R. P. Heath c Pocock b Thomas	32	– lbw b Pocock	11
C. M. Wells c Knight b Clarke	45	– (7) not out	47
*J. R. T. Barclay c Stewart b Clarke	15	– (6) not out	12
†I. J. Gould not out	11		
A. C. S. Pigott not out	0		
B 5, l-b 3, w 8, n-b 5	21	B 4, l-b 2, n-b 1	7

1/44 2/48 3/96   (7 wkts dec.) 252   1/14 2/22 3/22   (5 wkts) 120
4/162 5/184 6/235 7/248   4/46 5/57

D. A. Reeve and C. E. Waller did not bat.

Bonus points – Sussex 3, Surrey 3.

Bowling: *First Innings*—Clarke 16–5–50–2; Thomas 16–3–52–3; Pocock 14–2–34–0; Monkhouse 14–3–57–1; Knight 8–1–23–1; Curtis 8–4–15–0. *Second Innings*—Clarke 10–6–13–0; Thomas 9–1–30–3; Monkhouse 5–2–6–0; Pocock 14–5–35–2; Curtis 9–8–3–0; Butcher 5–0–20–0; Lynch 1–0–6–0.

Umpires: J. Birkenshaw and R. A. White.

At Birmingham, August 24, 25, 26. SUSSEX lost to WARWICKSHIRE by 21 runs.

SUSSEX v MIDDLESEX

At Hove, August 27, 29, 30. Drawn. Sussex 7 pts, Middlesex 5 pts. Middlesex, urgently needing points to retain the Championship, and Sussex, having failed to win a single one of their previous fourteen matches, battled hard for a result on an easy-paced pitch. Faced with a target of 279 in 90 minutes plus twenty overs, Middlesex went for the runs with Tomlins leading the charge. But at 180 for six, with ten overs remaining, they "shut up shop". Standing, aged nineteen, made an encouraging début for Sussex.

Sussex

G. D. Mendis c Emburey b Hughes	105 – retired hurt		3
A. M. Green c Downton b Edmonds	38 – st Downton b Edmonds		53
*J. R. T. Barclay c Barlow b Williams	2 – c Downton b Hughes		6
Imran Khan c Emburey b Hughes	29 – c Barlow b James		62
C. M. Wells c Barlow b Emburey	65 – b Edmonds		10
D. K. Standing not out	56 – not out		37
A. P. Wells c Emburey b Hughes	56 – not out		15
†I. J. Gould c Emburey b Williams	1		
A. C. S. Pigott c and b Hughes	0		
B 3, l-b 6, w 2, n-b 20	31	B 4, l-b 2, n-b 5	11

1/87 2/109 3/163   (8 wkts dec.) 383   1/20 2/130 3/139   (4 wkts dec.) 197
4/214 5/280 6/376 7/382 8/383   4/146

D. A. Reeve and C. E. Waller did not bat.

Bonus points – Sussex 3, Middlesex 2 (Score at 100 overs: 290-5).

Bowling: *First Innings*—Williams 15–3–64–2; Hughes 19.3–4–69–4; James 15–3–41–0; Edmonds 45–7–106–1; Emburey 37–12–72–1. *Second Innings*—Hughes 9–1–27–1; Williams 8–0–16–0; Emburey 19–5–59–0; Edmonds 28–7–54–2; James 9–0–30–1.

Middlesex

G. D. Barlow c Gould b Pigott	0 – b Pigott		38
A. J. T. Miller b Pigott	86 – c Green b Waller		39
C. T. Radley b Waller	24 – c Green b Waller		37
K. P. Tomlins not out	132 – not out		54
R. G. P. Ellis c Green b Pigott	0 – (6) st Gould b Waller		1
*J. E. Emburey b Reeve	12 – (5) c Gould b Waller		6
†P. R. Downton b Waller	5 – st Gould b Green		0
K. D. James c sub b C. M. Wells	19		
N. F. Williams b C. M. Wells	4 – (8) not out		5
P. H. Edmonds c Reeve b Barclay	1		
S. P. Hughes not out	1		
L-b 12, n-b 6	18	B 5, l-b 6, w 1, n-b 3	15

1/0 2/60 3/175 4/185   (9 wkts dec.) 302   1/63 2/103 3/167   (6 wkts) 195
5/221 6/232 7/285 8/292 9/296   4/175 5/177 6/180

Bonus points – Middlesex 3, Sussex 4 (Score at 100 overs: 296-9).

Bowling: *First Innings*—Pigott 21–2–66–3; Reeve 21–5–62–1; C. M. Wells 10–2–26–2; Waller 34–12–70–2; Barclay 15–5–59–1; Green 1–0–1–0. *Second Innings*—Pigott 9–1–23–1; Reeve 7–0–30–0; Barclay 3–0–20–0; Waller 14–2–61–4; C. M. Wells 8–0–43–0; Green 1–0–3–1.

Umpires: R. Julian and D. G. L. Evans.

At The Oval, August 31, September 1, 2. SUSSEX beat SURREY by three wickets.

SUSSEX v LEICESTERSHIRE

At Hove, September 7, 8, 9. Drawn. Sussex 6 pts, Leicestershire 4 pts. Sussex gained a first-innings lead of 110, but a long delay through rain on the last day, when Gower batted skilfully for 140 and Clift used the long handle, caused a predictable draw. Clift's innings lasted only 50 minutes and included four 6s and thirteen 4s.

Leicestershire

J. C. Balderstone lbw b Greig	31	– lbw b Pigott	18
I. P. Butcher c Gould b Imran	43	– c Gould b Greig	17
D. I. Gower c Gould b Pigott	4	– c Greig b Green	140
N. E. Briers lbw b Greig	0	– retired hurt	42
B. F. Davison b Greig	17	– not out	36
P. B. Clift lbw b Wells	17	– not out	100
*†R. W. Tolchard b Reeve	22		
J. F. Steele not out	12		
N. G. B. Cook c Gould b Reeve	4		
L. B. Taylor b Pigott	6		
G. J. F. Ferris lbw b Waller	11		
L-b 5, n-b 3	8	B 4, l-b 4, w 2	10

1/62 2/72 3/82 4/97   175   1/36 2/36 3/242   (3 wkts dec.) 363
5/100 6/130 7/142 8/151 9/158

Bonus points – Leicestershire 1, Sussex 4.

Bowling: *First Innings*—Pigott 16–4–44–2; Reeve 16–5–46–2; Greig 15–4–58–3; Imran 5–1–11–1; Wells 6–2–8–1; Waller 0.3–0–0–1. *Second Innings*—Pigott 10–1–42–1; Reeve 16–2–44–0; Greig 7–0–50–1; Wells 7–1–38–0; Waller 26–3–104–0; Green 10–2–48–1; Standing 3.3–0–27–0.

Sussex

G. D. Mendis lbw b Taylor	84	– c sub b Taylor	30
A. M. Green lbw b Clift	11	– c Butcher b Cook	14
D. K. Standing c Steele b Taylor	18	– b Taylor	0
Imran Khan c and b Cook	73	– not out	17
*P. W. G. Parker c Steele b Taylor	1	– not out	1
C. M. Wells c Balderstone b Taylor	1		
I. A. Greig c and b Clift	16		
†I. J. Gould c Briers b Steele	23		
A. C. S. Pigott c Steele b Taylor	32		
D. A. Reeve c Steele b Ferris	12		
C. E. Waller not out	5		
B 1, l-b 3, w 1, n-b 4	9		

1/38 2/84 3/151 4/163   285   1/38 2/38 3/52   (3 wkts) 62
5/165 6/187 7/235 8/235 9/269

Bonus points – Sussex 2, Leicestershire 3 (Score at 100 overs: 247-8).

Bowling: *First Innings*—Taylor 28.2–5–80–5; Ferris 14–1–64–1; Clift 29–10–54–2; Cook 27–6–53–1; Steele 10–2–25–1. *Second Innings*—Taylor 11–2–27–2; Ferris 2–0–15–0; Cook 10–2–19–1; Clift 2–1–1–0; Steele 1–1–0–0.

Umpires: A. Jepson and B. J. Meyer.

At Worcester, September 10, 12, 13. SUSSEX drew with WORCESTERSHIRE.

WARWICKSHIRE

President: The Earl of Aylesford
Chairman: 1983 – C. C. Goodway;
   1984 – A. D. Steven
Chairman, Cricket Committee: R. E. Hitchcock
Secretary: A. C. Smith
   County Ground, Edgbaston,
   Birmingham B5 7QU
   (Telephone: 021-440 4292)
Cricket Manager: D. J. Brown
Captain: R. G. D. Willis
Coach: A. S. M. Oakman

Warwickshire's advance from seventeenth to fifth place in the Schweppes
County Championship, with ten wins compared to none in the previous
year, was due to the bowling performances of Norman Gifford and Chris
Old. These two newcomers to the side took 99 and 61 wickets
respectively, the number of overs they bowled giving Willis and
Warwickshire a control in the field they had not enjoyed for a decade.

Warwickshire, in fact, bowled 3,224 overs in the Championship.
Gifford and Old were responsible for 1,631.1 of these, in which they took
160 wickets at 25.03 apiece. In 1,592.5 overs the other bowlers between
them took 134 wickets at 37.77 apiece. In other words, the 1982 bowlers
were no more penetrative or economical than they were then, and only
eleven more bowling points were earned despite the extra two matches
played. The ten victories were the most since 1964, when 28 matches were
played, and the streak of seven successive wins in June and July was an
all-time club record for a season. Gifford was an inspiration to everyone.
His refusal to allow games to drift along was at least as important in the
development of the younger players as the scope afforded by his bowling
contribution. Old's performance off a permanently shortened run-up was
also particularly meritorious, many of his overs being bowled on
unresponsive pitches. He missed only three matches, which belied his
reputation for succumbing to minor injuries, and his batting contribution
was of value on several occasions.

The home win against Yorkshire was the most improbable of the
season. The pitch was an experimental, re-laid one, and deteriorated into
a dust heap. Set to score 299, comfortably the highest total of the match,
Warwickshire were 136 for six and then 181 for eight. Geoff Humpage
then took over to complete an unbeaten 141 which was a masterpiece of
sound defence and selective strokeplay. It was the innings of the season.
A win of only slightly less improbability was that against Glamorgan in
the last home match when a second-wicket stand of 308 in 71 overs
between Andy Lloyd and Alvin Kallicharran made such a nonsense of a
declaration setting a target of 414 that Warwickshire won by eight wickets
with nearly an hour to spare. Lloyd was called into the England party for
the Lord's Test, and although he did not play, his best Championship
season, including his first double-hundred which saved the match against

Gloucestershire, should ensure full recognition in the near future.

Kallicharran's follow-up to his record 1982 season was a good one, and he increased the number of double-hundreds he has scored to five, all of them since the West Indies Board banned him for coaching in South Africa. Dennis Amiss was as solid as ever. At No. 4, away from the new ball, his run-scoring ability showed no sign of diminishing. During the season he passed M. J. K. Smith's aggregate of runs for Warwickshire and now stands second only to W. G. Quaife.

Humpage had an inconsistent season but still topped 1,000 runs, and he decided to keep wicket again on a regular basis after a knee condition had given Geoff Tedstone ten matches at the start of the season. Anton Ferreira enjoyed his best all-round season until a broken thumb caused him to miss the last eight matches. He was the only bowler to give adequate support to Gifford and Old. Gladstone Small played in only five matches, owing to a recurring thigh injury, and Bob Willis's 247.2 overs produced only 21 wickets at a disappointingly high cost.

Of the younger players, Asif Din and Chris Lethbridge made little progress, but Paul Smith's all-round ability was full of promise. He is a clean striker of the ball, and in the last month of the season his bowling bordered on the genuinely fast. With David Thorne and Gordon Lord also making the most of their few chances to score some good runs, there will be plenty of competition in 1984 for middle-order places.

Warwickshire had a less good year in the three one-day competitions. In the John Player League their record over the last five years reads seventeenth, first, third, seventeenth and sixteenth. With wicket-keeper Humpage batting in the first five it should have been possible to pick a strong attack, but all the bowlers, including Gifford and Old, found containment difficult to achieve. After qualifying for the knockout stages of the Benson and Hedges Cup, Warwickshire went out in the quarter-final to Essex, their batsmen failing to cope with a not especially onerous task. Similarly, in their NatWest Bank Trophy quarter-final against Kent, the middle order lost its way at a crucial stage.

The explanation for Warwickshire's captain having played only half his side's Championship matches in the last four years is obviously that of Test calls. Less understandable is his record when he has appeared. In that period, his 44 matches have yielded only 85 wickets at 33 apiece.

Most unusually, Warwickshire were in conflict with the Test and County Cricket Board over the latter's handling of a breach of their regulations by Old. After Warwickshire had fined the player £1,000 following a series of unauthorised articles in the *Sun* newspaper, the TCCB imposed a further double punishment of £2,000 and twelve day's suspension.

Following a review by the Disciplinary sub-committee of the TCCB and an appeal by the Club to the Cricket Council, the fine was removed and the suspension reduced to three days. Warwickshire's Chairman, Mr Cyril Goodway, resigned, however, in protest at the Board's decision in the belief that the Club were unfairly penalised by having to lose the player's services for one match in 1984. Mr Goodway, who had been Chairman since 1971, is succeeded by Mr Tony Steven, a local insurance executive consultant. – J.D.B.

WARWICKSHIRE 1983

[Ken Kelly]

Back row: G. C. Small, P. A. Smith, W. Hogg, R. I. H. B. Dyer, A. M. Ferreira, C. M. Old, Asif Din, G. A. Tedstone. *Front row*: T. A. Lloyd, A. I. Kallicharran, N. Gifford, R. G. D. Willis (*captain*), D. L. Amiss, G. W. Humpage, K. D. Smith.

WARWICKSHIRE RESULTS

All first-class matches – Played 27: Won 10, Lost 4, Drawn 13.

County Championship matches – Played 24: Won 10, Lost 3, Drawn 11.

Bonus points – Batting 52, Bowling 64.

Competition placings – Schweppes County Championship, 5th; NatWest Bank Trophy, q-f; Benson and Hedges Cup, q-f; John Player League, 15th eq.

COUNTY CHAMPIONSHIP AVERAGES

BATTING

	Birthplace	M	I	NO	R	HI	Avge
A. I. Kallicharran c ..	Berbice, BG	22	34	4	1,637	243*	54.56
T. A. Lloyd c	Oswestry	22	39	4	1,659	208*	47.40
D. L. Amiss c	Birmingham	24	40	4	1,571	164	43.63
G. W. Humpage c ...	Birmingham	24	38	6	1,003	141*	31.34
P. A. Smith	Jesmond	11	14	3	335	65	30.45
K. D. Smith c	Jesmond	24	42	4	1,133	109	29.81
C. Lethbridge	Castleford	7	7	3	110	73*	27.50
Asif Din	Kampala, Uganda	12	18	2	361	65	22.56
A. M. Ferreira	Pretoria, SA	16	22	4	399	66	22.16
D. A. Thorne	Coventry	4	6	3	62	23*	20.66
C. M. Old	Middlesbrough	21	24	3	387	62	18.42
R. G. D. Willis c	Sunderland	12	12	7	79	20*	15.80
R. I. H. B. Dyer	Hertford	7	12	3	135	25	15.00
G. C. Small c	St George, Barbados	5	7	3	59	31	14.75
N. Gifford c	Ulverston	20	20	6	201	39	14.35
G. A. Tedstone	Southport	10	11	0	156	36	14.18
W. Hogg	Ulverston	20	16	6	59	27*	5.90

Also batted: G. J. Lord (*Birmingham*) (3 matches) 61, 29, 1.

*Signifies not out.   cDenotes county cap.

BOWLING

	O	M	R	W	Avge	BB
N. Gifford	991.4	336	2,220	99	22.42	6-22
C. M. Old	639.3	146	1,786	61	29.27	5-50
G. C. Small	89.5	12	299	10	29.90	3-13
A. M. Ferreira	485.4	128	1,237	39	31.71	5-19
W. Hogg	324.4	61	1,073	31	34.61	5-63
R. G. D. Willis	247.2	58	772	21	36.76	3-8
P. A. Smith	169	21	628	16	39.25	3-56

Also bowled: Asif Din 39.1–5–149–1; G. W. Humpage 3–0–13–0; A. I. Kallicharran 135–18–476–8; C. Lethbridge 69.1–11–264–6; T. A. Lloyd 1–0–24–0; G. J. Lord 8–3–12–0; D. A. Thorne 21–0–115–2.

The following played a total of eighteen three-figure innings for Warwickshire in County Championship matches – A. I. Kallicharran 6, T. A. Lloyd 5, D. L. Amiss 3, G. W. Humpage 2, K. D. Smith 2.

WARWICKSHIRE v NORTHAMPTONSHIRE

At Birmingham, April 30, May 2, 3. Drawn. Warwickshire 7 pts, Northamptonshire 5 pts. In a match reduced to two days because of rain, the home side were always in charge. Ferreira justified Amiss's decision to field with a fine spell, which was well supported by Warwickshire's all-seam attack. Only Willey and Sharp offered much resistance. The home team's reply was led by Smith and Humpage, with the former wicket-keeper hitting a belligerent 67. Rhodesian-born Carse showed impressive hostility, and his enthusiasm was not blunted by a typically slow-paced Edgbaston pitch.

Northamptonshire

*G. Cook c Lloyd b Small	25	
W. Larkins b Hogg	4	
P. Willey c Tedstone b Small	53	
A. J. Lamb b Ferreira	11	
R. G. Williams c Old b Ferreira	6	
D. J. Capel c Tedstone b Hogg	4	
D. J. Steele c Lloyd b Ferreira	9	
†G. Sharp c sub b Lethbridge	39	
N. A. Mallender c Tedstone b Ferreira	24 – (2) not out	1
J. A. Carse not out	8 – (1) not out	8
B. J. Griffiths c Hogg b Lethbridge	0	
L-b 3, w 1, n-b 6	10	

1/26 2/30 3/47 4/57   193   (no wkt) 9
5/88 6/104 7/143 8/170 9/186

Bonus points – Northamptonshire 1, Warwickshire 4.

Bowling: *First Innings*—Hogg 16–4–52–2; Small 11–3–28–2; Old 18–5–37–0; Ferreira 22–10–31–4; Lethbridge 9.5–2–35–2. *Second Innings*—Hogg 3–2–8–0; Lethbridge 2–1–1–0.

Warwickshire

K. D. Smith lbw b Carse	59	C. M. Old c Mallender b Griffiths	22
T. A. Lloyd c Willey b Griffiths	6	G. C. Small c Sharp b Carse	4
*D. L. Amiss lbw b Griffiths	37	W. Hogg not out	0
A. I. Kallicharran c Sharp b Mallender	28	B 17, l-b 5, w 6, n-b 6	34
G. W. Humpage b Steele b Mallender	67		
A. M. Ferreira c Williams b Steele	12	1/15 2/92 3/139	281
†G. A. Tedstone c Sharp b Steele	0	4/180 5/206 6/214	
C. Lethbridge c Lamb b Griffiths	12	7/238 8/277 9/281	

Bonus points – Warwickshire 3, Northamptonshire 4.

Bowling: Carse 25–9–42–2; Griffiths 23.1–7–55–4; Mallender 21–3–74–2; Capel 9–3–31–0; Steele 11–4–17–2; Willey 6–1–28–0.

Umpires: M. J. Kitchen and R. Palmer.

At Leeds, May 4, 5, 6. WARWICKSHIRE drew with YORKSHIRE.

At Southampton, May 11, 12, 13. WARWICKSHIRE lost to HAMPSHIRE by 9 runs.

WARWICKSHIRE v GLOUCESTERSHIRE

At Birmingham, May 25, 26, 27. Drawn. Warwickshire 5 pts, Gloucestershire 8 pts. Former Kent all-rounder John Shepherd had an astonishing match, following seven for 50 in Warwickshire's first innings (a career-best performance) with 168 to rescue Gloucestershire from 83 for five in reply to the home side's 213. Together with skipper Graveney he made the sixth-wicket stand worth 268 from 74 overs. Seam bowlers enjoyed movement from the well-grassed pitch for the first half of the match, justifying Graveney's decision to insert Warwickshire, but then Edgbaston's traditional docility asserted itself. Facing a deficit of 169, Warwickshire batted out the last day with Lloyd scoring a career-best unbeaten 208 and, together with Amiss, who in scoring 142 in 275 minutes hit his 83rd first-class century, adding 289 for the third wicket. Lloyd batted for 414 minutes, hitting one 6 and 35 4s.

Warwickshire

T. A. Lloyd b Shepherd	34	– not out	208
K. D. Smith c Broad b Lawrence	4	– c Shepherd b Sainsbury	34
A. I. Kallicharran c Zaheer b Lawrence	7		
D. L. Amiss c Russell b Shepherd	40	– (3) lbw b Sainsbury	142
G. W. Humpage c and b Shepherd	5	– (4) not out	13
A. M. Ferreira b Sainsbury	50		
†G. A. Tedstone c Stovold b Shepherd	7		
C. M. Old c Russell b Shepherd	2		
N. Gifford b Shepherd	15		
*R. G. D. Willis not out	20		
W. Hogg b Shepherd	13		
B 4, l-b 9, n-b 3	16	L-b 13, w 2, n-b 2	17

1/18 2/33 3/80 4/92   213   1/65 2/354   (2 wkts) 414
5/99 6/119 7/129 8/177 9/181

Bonus points – Warwickshire 2, Gloucestershire 4.

Bowling: First Innings—Sainsbury 26–6–81–1; Lawrence 11–2–41–2; Shepherd 28–12–50–7; Bainbridge 13–3–25–0. *Second Innings*—Lawrence 17–2–78–0; Sainsbury 31–7–108–2; Shepherd 19–6–47–0; Bainbridge 30–9–89–0; Graveney 23–7–51–0; Zaheer 3–0–21–0; Wright 1–0–3–0.

Gloucestershire

A. W. Stovold c Gifford b Old	47	†R. C. Russell c Willis b Hogg	13
B. C. Broad c Humpage b Willis	14	G. E. Sainsbury not out	1
P. Bainbridge c Humpage b Old	18	B 2, l-b 20, n-b 5	27
Zaheer Abbas c Tedstone b Old	0		
A. J. Wright b Ferreira	0	1/36 2/72 3/74 (8 wkts dec.) 382
J. N. Shepherd c Smith b Hogg	168	4/74 5/83 6/351
*D. A Graveney c Smith b Hogg	94	7/377 8/382

P. W. Romaines and D. V. Lawrence did not bat.

Bonus points – Gloucestershire 4, Warwickshire 3 (Score at 100 overs: 382-7).

Bowling: Willis 15–1–77–1; Hogg 8.1–3–31–3; Ferreira 33–8–88–1; Old 28–4–110–3; Gifford 16–6–49–0.

Umpires: D. J. Constant and A. Jepson.

At Worcester, May 28, 30, 31. WARWICKSHIRE drew with WORCESTERSHIRE.

WARWICKSHIRE v LANCASHIRE

At Birmingham, June 4, 6, 7. Warwickshire won by 93 runs. Warwickshire 21 pts, Lancashire 4 pts. An unusually early collusion between the captains produced Warwickshire's first Championship win at Edgbaston since August 1979. Lancashire's Neil Fairbrother was within 6 of a maiden century when Abrahams was forced to declare his first innings closed shortly after tea on the second day. Warwickshire's first innings was marked by Kallicharran's unbeaten 209 (two 6s, 34 4s) and 126 by Lloyd, the pair putting on 293 for the second wicket. Lancashire were set 344 to win, but despite good contributions from Fowler, Cockbain and Abrahams they never looked like getting the runs in the face of good spin bowling from Gifford, who turned in his best bowling performance since leaving Worcestershire.

Warwickshire

T. A. Lloyd c and b Abrahams	126	– b Jefferies		12
K. D. Smith lbw b Jefferies	1	– not out		68
A. I. Kallicharran not out	209			
D. L. Amiss run out	0	– (3) c Maynard b O'Shaughnessy		18
G. W. Humpage hit wkt b Abrahams	1	– not out		81
A. M. Ferreira not out	43			
†G. A. Tedstone (did not bat)		– (4) lbw b Folley		0
B 4, l-b 5, n-b 7	16	B 5, l-b 4, w 4, n-b 5		18

1/4 2/297 3/306 4/308   (4 wkts dec.) 396   1/31 2/66 3/67   (3 wkts dec.) 197

C. M. Old, N. Gifford, *R. G. D. Willis and W. Hogg did not bat.

Bonus points – Warwickshire 4, Lancashire 1 (Score at 100 overs: 318-4).

Bowling: *First Innings*—Allott 20–7–79–0; Jefferies 20–6–87–1; Simmons 40–13–81–0; O'Shaughnessy 12–0–54–0; Folley 7–3–24–0; Abrahams 15–0–55–2. *Second Innings*— Jefferies 7–2–21–1; Allott 4–0–15–0; O'Shaughnessy 11–2–34–1; Folley 9–1–39–1; Simmons 8–0–28–0; Abrahams 8–0–42–0.

Lancashire

G. Fowler c Tedstone b Hogg	23	– b Old		58
I. Cockbain lbw b Old	31	– c Humpage b Gifford		33
S. J. O'Shaughnessy lbw b Old	68	– c Willis b Gifford		23
*J. Abrahams lbw b Old	13	– c Old b Gifford		45
N. H. Fairbrother not out	94	– c Ferreira b Willis		17
J. Simmons not out	8	– lbw b Gifford		9
S. T. Jefferies (did not bat)		– b Gifford		24
†C. Maynard (did not bat)		– b Ferreira		8
P. J. W. Allott (did not bat)		– b Ferreira		0
F. C. Hayes (did not bat)		– c Amiss b Gifford		6
I. Folley (did not bat)		– not out		13
L-b 10, n-b 3	13	B 1, l-b 7, w 1, n-b 5		14

1/53 2/55 3/77 4/219   (4 wkts dec.) 250   1/87 2/109 3/166 4/170   250
                                                    5/194 6/198 7/231 8/231 9/232

Bonus points – Lancashire 3, Warwickshire 1.

Bowling: *First Innings*—Willis 12–3–20–0; Hogg 11–0–41–1; Old 26–7–43–3; Ferreira 20–6–42–0; Gifford 25.3–8–78–0; Humpage 3–0–13–0. *Second Innings*—Willis 11–3–43–1; Hogg 5–1–28–0; Ferreira 23–6–57–2; Old 13–5–16–1; Gifford 27.3–8–92–6.

Umpires: H. D. Bird and D. R. Shepherd.

At Cambridge, June 8, 9, 10. WARWICKSHIRE drew with CAMBRIDGE UNIVERSITY.

At Cardiff, June 11, 13, 14. WARWICKSHIRE beat GLAMORGAN by five wickets.

At Manchester, June 15, 16, 17. WARWICKSHIRE beat LANCASHIRE by six wickets.

At Northampton, June 18, 20, 21. WARWICKSHIRE beat NORTHAMPTONSHIRE by 166 runs.

WARWICKSHIRE v OXFORD UNIVERSITY

At Birmingham, June 22, 23, 24. Drawn. The third day was washed out after two days' play on a typically slow-paced Edgbaston batting wicket. For Oxford, Miller, Moulding and Edbrooke all played sound innings, the latter pair adding 140 for the fifth wicket. For Warwickshire Paul Smith (two 6s, thirteen 4s) and David Smith (unrelated) made their maiden first-class hundreds, sharing a stand for the eighth wicket of 155.

Oxford University

*R. G. P. Ellis lbw b Hogg	7	– c Tedstone b P. A. Smith	22
A. J. T. Miller c Tedstone b Hogg	76	– not out	20
P. J. Heseltine c Dyer b Sutcliffe	39	– not out	4
K. A. Hayes c Sutcliffe b P. A. Smith	3		
R. P. Moulding not out	80		
R. M. Edbrooke c and b D. M. Smith	71		
J. G. Varey not out	9		
B 13, l-b 10, w 2	25	W 1, n-b 1	2

1/8 2/116 3/136   (5 wkts dec.) 310   1/40   (1 wkt) 48
4/142 5/282

†M. R. Cullinan, H. T. Rawlinson, M. D. Petchey and J. R. Turnbull did not bat.

Bowling: *First Innings*—Hogg 14–2–32–2; P. A. Smith 19–4–68–1; Thorne 20–4–54–0; Sutcliffe 25–9–57–1; D. M. Smith 18–3–44–1; Asif Din 9–1–30–0. *Second Innings*—P. A. Smith 4–1–26–1; Thorne 4–1–20–0.

Warwickshire

*D. L. Amiss c Cullinan b Hayes	63	†G. A. Tedstone c Cullinan b Hayes	9
K. D. Smith b Petchey	7	D. M. Smith not out	100
R. I. H. B. Dyer c Cullinan b Petchey	7	W . Hogg not out	12
S. H. Wootton c Edbrooke b Hayes	34	B 14, l-b 8, w 2, n-b 4	28
Asif Din lbw b Hayes	14		
P. A. Smith c Cullinan b Hayes	114	1/11 2/31 3/117 4/131 (8 wkts dec.) 388
D. A. Thorne c Ellis b Hayes	0	5/142 6/142 7/168 8/323

S. P. Sutcliffe did not bat.

Bowling: Petchey 24–4–70–2; Rawlinson 17–2–74–0; Varey 16–1–74–0; Turnbull 19–7–63–0; Hayes 18–6–58–6; Ellis 1–0–8–0; Moulding 6.1–0–13–0.

Umpires: A. Jepson and J. W. Holder.

WARWICKSHIRE v YORKSHIRE

At Birmingham, June 25, 27, 28. Warwickshire won by one wicket. Warwickshire 20 pts, Yorkshire 6 pts. An experimental relaid pitch produced Warwickshire's fifth successive win – their best run since 1957 – thanks to a magnificent unbeaten 141 from Humpage. Batting became increasingly difficult as the match progressed, with most deliveries not bouncing at all. Seamers held sway through the first three innings when only Hartley, Love and Bairstow for Yorkshire, who had chosen to bat first, and Amiss and Ferreira for Warwickshire were able to apply themselves. Set 299 to win, Warwickshire slumped to 136 for six and 180 for eight, but Humpage led the lower order through progressively bigger partnerships of 42, 58 and 64 for the seventh, ninth and tenth wickets respectively. His innings included seventeen 4s and was chanceless against a Yorkshire attack in which skipper Illingworth bowled more overs than in any innings since his return to county cricket.

Yorkshire

G. Boycott c Asif Din b Willis	0	– lbw b Willis	28
R. G. Lumb c Kallicharran b Old	5	– lbw b Ferreira	13
C. W. J. Athey c Asif Din b Old	15	– st Tedstone b Ferreira	29
S. N. Hartley b Ferreira	69	– c Asif Din b Ferreira	11
J. D. Love c Amiss b Old	58	– lbw b Gifford	45
†D. L. Bairstow c Humpage b Old	45	– lbw b Gifford	11
P. Carrick b Gifford	6	– b Old	16
G. B. Stevenson c Humpage b Gifford	0	– b Old	5
*R. Illingworth lbw b Gifford	8		
S. J. Dennis b Ferreira	4	– (9) b Old	0
P. W. Jarvis not out	5	– (10) not out	1
B 7, l-b 7, n-b 10	24	B 3, l-b 19, n-b 3	25

1/0 2/20 3/35 4/160   239   1/33 2/53 3/87   (9 wkts dec.) 184
5/168 6/184 7/184 8/210 9/219   4/94 5/125 6/165 7/178 8/182 9/184

Bonus points – Yorkshire 2, Warwickshire 4 (Score at 100 overs: 233-9).

Bowling: *First Innings*—Willis 16–5–43–1; Old 26.1–7–63–4; Gifford 38–17–52–3; Ferreira 23–5–57–2. *Second Innings*—Willis 14–2–48–1; Old 13–3–26–3; Ferreira 17–4–41–2; Gifford 19.5–8–44–3.

Warwickshire

T. A. Lloyd b Dennis	11	– c Athey b Carrick	49
K. D. Smith b Dennis	0	– c Bairstow b Stevenson	2
A. I. Kallicharran c Bairstow b Stevenson	9	– b Illingworth	16
D. L. Amiss c Lumb b Stevenson	41	– lbw b Carrick	15
G. W. Humpage c Illingworth b Stevenson	0	– not out	141
Asif Din b Dennis	1	– b Illingworth	2
A. M. Ferreira lbw b Jarvis	36	– lbw b Illingworth	13
†G. A. Tedstone lbw b Illingworth	4	– lbw b Stevenson	8
C. M. Old c Bairstow b Stevenson	4	– run out	2
N. Gifford b Stevenson	4	– b Jarvis	14
*R. G. D. Willis not out	2	– not out	16
L-b 11, n-b 2	13	B 7, l-b 11, w 1, n-b 5	24

1/12 2/16 3/24 4/25   125   1/27 2/56 3/80 4/97   (9 wkts) 302
5/26 6/91 7/108 8/115 9/116   5/100 6/136 7/178 8/180 9/238

Bonus points – Yorkshire 4.

Bowling: *First Innings*—Dennis 10–5–24–3; Stevenson 13.2–2–35–5; Jarvis 9–3–28–1; Carrick 4–1–10–0; Illingworth 9–2–15–1. *Second Innings*—Dennis 13–4–46–0; Stevenson 20–2–54–2; Illingworth 37.3–13–71–3; Jarvis 13–4–43–1; Carrick 34–12–64–2.

Umpires: R. A. White and A. G. T. Whitehead.

WARWICKSHIRE v MIDDLESEX

At Birmingham, July 2, 4, 5. Warwickshire won by 167 runs. Warwickshire 20 pts, Middlesex 4 pts. An over-dry square gave a pitch which helped spin and seam bowlers alike, the ball starting to disturb the surface even on the first day when 23 wickets fell. Edmonds took five for 26 and only Amiss played him with any confidence. For Warwickshire Willis created the early breach with three lbws. Warwickshire's second innings contained another good innings by Amiss, well supported by Smith and night-watchman Gifford. Strangely, Gatting, captaining Middlesex, delayed using Emburey and Edmonds at the ends from which they had achieved their first-innings success. A target of 242 always looked beyond Middlesex, with Gifford returning his best figures for Warwickshire, who registered their sixth successive win.

Warwickshire

T. A. Lloyd c Gatting b Williams	19 – b Edmonds	1
K. D. Smith b Emburey	17 – c Butcher b Edmonds	32
A. I. Kallicharran b Williams	2 – lbw b Williams	3
D. L. Amiss b Edmonds	25 – (5) c Edmonds b Emburey	57
†G. W. Humpage c Tomlins b Emburey	0 – (6) c Butcher b Edmonds	24
Asif Din c Downton b Edmonds	10 – (7) c Tomlins b Emburey	9
A. M. Ferreira c Butcher b Edmonds	0 – (8) c Emburey b Edmonds	9
D. A. Thorne lbw b Emburey	8 – (9) not out	7
N. Gifford c Tomlins b Edmonds	0 – (4) c Downton b Williams	22
*R. G. D. Willis b Edmonds	12 – b Daniel	1
W. Hogg not out	1 – c and b Edmonds	3
B 11, l-b 5, n-b 3	19	B 9, l-b 21, n-b 8	38
	113		**206**

1/25 2/37 3/47 4/47   113   1/3 2/6 3/64 4/119   206
5/58 6/80 7/87 8/87 9/110   5/168 6/170 7/179 8/193 9/199

Bonus points – Middlesex 4.

Bowling: *First Innings*—Daniel 5–1–15–0; Cowans 2–0–14–0; Williams 8–0–24–2; Emburey 20–12–15–3; Edmonds 14.3–7–26–5. *Second Innings*—Williams 13–5–17–2; Cowans 3–2–9–0; Edmonds 35.3–16–46–5; Emburey 31–12–63–2; Daniel 9–1–33–1.

Middlesex

†P. R. Downton lbw b Willis	8 – (8) not out	5
K. P. Tomlins lbw b Willis	6 – (1) run out	13
C. T. Radley lbw b Willis	6 – lbw b Willis	10
*M. W. Gatting lbw b Gifford	15 – c Smith b Gifford	10
R. O. Butcher b Gifford	6 – (6) lbw b Willis	1
R. G. P. Ellis b Ferreira	0 – (2) b Gifford	13
J. E. Emburey lbw b Ferreira	23 – c Asif Din b Willis	0
P. H. Edmonds b Ferreira	0 – (9) b Gifford	0
N. F. Williams lbw b Ferreira	0 – (10) c Thorne b Gifford	0
W. W. Daniel b Ferreira	1 – (11) c Kallicharran b Gifford	7
N. G. Cowans not out	3 – (5) b Gifford	0
B 4, l-b 9, n-b 3	16	L-b 7, w 4, n-b 3	14
	78		**74**

1/9 2/10 3/17 4/26   78   1/29 2/43 3/48 4/49   74
5/37 6/41 7/46 8/46 9/63   5/50 6/52 7/64 8/64 9/66

Bonus points – Warwickshire 4.

Bowling: *First Innings*—Willis 10–5–8–3; Hogg 3–1–2–0; Gifford 22–12–33–2; Ferreira 15.1–9–19–5. *Second Innings*—Willis 14–5–14–3; Hogg 3–1–3–0; Gifford 24.3–11–22–6; Ferreira 14–6–21–0.

Umpires: D. R. Shepherd and C. T. Spencer.

WARWICKSHIRE v ESSEX

At Nuneaton, July 9, 11, 12. Warwickshire won by ten wickets. Warwickshire 24 pts, Essex 3 pts. Solid batting in Warwickshire's first innings, led by Amiss whose 111 in 214 minutes included one 6 and sixteen 4s and was his 84th first-class hundred, helped the home team win their second top-of-the-table clash within a week. Gifford took five for 2 to end the Essex first innings, all his wickets coming in eleven balls on a pitch taking spin. Following on, Essex lost both Hardie and Gooch in Old's first over, thus losing seven wickets in 23 deliveries. McEwan then played well for the second time in the match, but apart from Fletcher's 62 there was no other resistance until Phillip and Foster added 91 for the last wicket and so took the match into the third day. Again Gifford bowled well, the 43-year-old slow bowler's stamina under hot conditions being admirable. This was Warwickshire's seventh successive win.

Warwickshire
T. A. Lloyd c Foster b Phillip	89	– not out	20
K. D. Smith c McEwan b Phillip	10	– not out	13
A. I. Kallicharran c and b R. E. East	48		
D. L. Amiss c Phillip b R. E. East	111		
†G. W. Humpage lbw b Phillip	10		
Asif Din c Pringle b R. E. East	38		
A. M. Ferreira st D. E. East b R. E. East	4		
P. A. Smith c Hardie b Foster	34		
C. M. Old b Phillip	11		
N. Gifford not out	2		
*R. G. D. Willis not out	1		
B 2, l-b 5, w 2, n-b 12	21	N-b 3	3

1/30 2/104 3/214　　　　　　(9 wkts dec.) 379　　　　　　(no wkt) 36
4/242 5/303 6/314 7/333 8/371 9/375

Bonus points – Warwickshire 4, Essex 3 (Score at 100 overs: 333-7).

Bowling: *First Innings*—Foster 22–1–85–1; Phillip 18–0–80–4; Pringle 17–1–55–0; Turner 21–1–51–0; R. E. East 30–10–85–4; Pont 1–0–2–0. *Second Innings*—Foster 3–0–10–0; Pringle 3–1–18–0; Fletcher 1–0–5–0.

Essex
G. A. Gooch c Asif Din b Old	34	– c Humpage b Old	3
B. R. Hardie lbw b Old	26	– c Asif Din b Old	1
*K. W. R. Fletcher c Amiss b Willis	0	– c Amiss b Ferreira	62
K. S. McEwan b Gifford	28	– b Gifford	54
K. R. Pont c Humpage b Old	2	– lbw b Gifford	10
D. R. Pringle c Humpage b Ferreira	8	– c Humpage b Ferreira	7
N. Phillip st Humpage b Gifford	4	– st Humpage b Gifford	80
S. Turner lbw b Gifford	2	– b Ferreira	0
†D. E. East not out	5	– lbw b Willis	5
R. E. East c Old b Gifford	0	– c Amiss b Gifford	19
N. A. Foster b Gifford	0	– not out	40
B 1	1	B 2, l-b 16, n-b 2	20

1/53 2/58 3/76 4/78　　　　110　　1/4 2/5 3/94 4/124　　　301
5/87 6/102 7/103 8/106 9/106　　　　5/131 6/164 7/164 8/178 9/210

Bonus points – Warwickshire 4.

Bowling: *First Innings*—Willis 8–1–47–1; Old 14–4–40–3; Ferreira 12–5–20–1; Gifford 5.1–3–2–5. *Second Innings*—Willis 16–2–68–1; Old 10–1–46–2; Gifford 40.2–13–84–4; Ferreira 18–3–62–3; Asif Din 5–1–17–0; Kallicharran 2–1–4–0.

Umpires: J. H. Harris and B. Leadbeater.

WARWICKSHIRE v DERBYSHIRE

At Birmingham, July 13, 14, 15. Derbyshire won by ten wickets. Derbyshire 22 pts, Warwickshire 2 pts. On another slow, turning pitch Derbyshire's policy, after winning the toss, of crease occupation won them the match, although their batting time of eight hours for their first innings antagonised the home crowd. Hill took just over six hours for 121. With 52 overs, Gifford again carried the Warwickshire bowling. Warwickshire never looked like saving the follow-on, despite the first of two impressive innings by Paul Smith, a fine natural striker of the ball. The left-arm spinner, Moir, had good match figures and was well supported by the left-arm seamer, Finney.

Derbyshire

I. S. Anderson st Humpage b Gifford	39	– not out	16
J. E. Morris lbw b Old	15	– not out	21
A. Hill st Humpage b Gifford	121		
*K. J. Barnett c and b Gifford	53		
R. J. Finney b Ferreira	15		
†B. J. M. Maher b Gifford	24		
G. Miller not out	31		
W. P. Fowler c Asif Din b Old	6		
A. Watts b Gifford	6		
D. G. Moir st Humpage b Gifford	7		
S. Oldham b Ferreira	7		
L-b 24, w 7, n-b 10	41	B 4	4

1/17 2/114 3/206 4/249   365   (no wkt) 41
5/292 6/318 7/325 8/345 9/355

Bonus points – Derbyshire 2, Warwickshire 1 (Score at 100 overs: 215-3).

Bowling: *First Innings*—Hogg 12–1–45–0; Old 38–9–90–2; Ferreira 29.5–6–79–2; Gifford 52–25–77–6; P. A. Smith 8–1–20–0; Asif Din 6–3–13–0. *Second Innings*—Old 5–1–18–0; Gifford 5–1–15–0; Asif Din 0.1–0–4–0.

Warwickshire

T. A. Lloyd lbw b Oldham	13	– c and b Miller	14
K. D. Smith c Miller b Watts	9	– c Anderson b Oldham	7
A. I. Kallicharran c and b Oldham	4	– c Morris b Miller	14
D. L. Amiss c Barnett b Oldham	9	– b Moir	16
†G. W. Humpage c Maher b Moir	16	– c Anderson b Finney	24
Asif Din c Miller b Oldham	41	– c Morris b Moir	1
A. M. Ferreira c Morris b Moir	3	– lbw b Finney	66
P. A. Smith b Moir	57	– c Maher b Finney	65
C. M. Old c Hill b Moir	6	– c and b Finney	5
*N. Gifford not out	4	– not out	0
W. Hogg b Moir	1	– lbw b Finney	0
B 3, l-b 1, n-b 2	6	B 11, l-b 5, w 1, n-b 5	22

1/14 2/24 3/28 4/40   169   1/21 2/34 3/37 4/85   234
5/52 6/56 7/157 8/163 9/164   5/85 6/100 7/203 8/229 9/234

Bonus points – Warwickshire 1, Derbyshire 4.

Bowling: *First Innings*—Oldham 24–9–56–4; Watts 8–2–28–1; Moir 23.4–7–44–5; Miller 7–3–13–0; Fowler 7–3–11–0; Finney 8–4–10–0; Barnett 1–0–1–0; Hill 1–1–0–0. *Second Innings*—Oldham 13–3–44–1; Moir 25–8–63–2; Miller 4–2–9–2; Finney 16.3–1–58–5; Fowler 4–1–22–0; Watts 4–0–16–0.

Umpires: J. H. Harris and K. E. Palmer.

At Birmingham, July 23, 25, 26. WARWICKSHIRE lost to NEW ZEALANDERS by 172 runs (See New Zealand tour section).

WARWICKSHIRE v KENT

At Birmingham, July 27, 28, 29. Drawn. Warwickshire 7 pts, Kent 6 pts. Kent narrowly failed to win, Small, Warwickshire's last man, batting for 40 minutes for 2 runs in support of Amiss, whose 69 had defied Underwood when he seemed likely to decide the issue. For Kent, Benson scored a hundred in each innings, his partnership of 190 with Aslett in the second being instrumental in their setting a target of 305. Hogg registered his best bowling performance for Warwickshire, and Humpage scored a fine century in their first innings, when, on a slow, turning pitch, Underwood always posed the major threat.

Kent

R. A. Woolmer c Ferreira b Hogg	3	– c Humpage b Small	20
N. R. Taylor c and b Ferreira	51	– lbw b Hogg	1
D. G. Aslett b Hogg	2	– (4) b Ferreira	68
M. R. Benson c Small b Gifford	102	– (5) not out	152
*C. S. Cowdrey c P. A. Smith b Hogg	17	– (6) c Small b Ferreira	23
E. A. E. Baptiste c Ferreira b P. A. Smith	5	– (7) b P. A. Smith	2
†A. P. E. Knott b Hogg	92		
G. W. Johnson c Amiss b Ferreira	7		
R. M. Ellison run out	14	– (3) c Ferreira b Small	22
D. L. Underwood b Hogg	24		
K. B. S. Jarvis not out	5		
B 2, l-b 16, w 8, n-b 16	42	L-b 6, w 1, n-b 4	11

1/16 2/18 3/132 4/183   364   1/10 2/43 3/44   (6 wkts dec.) 299
5/192 6/264 7/291 8/315 9/351   4/234 5/288 6/299

Bonus points – Kent 4, Warwickshire 3 (Score at 100 overs: 320-8).

Bowling: *First Innings*—Small 18–1–62–0; Hogg 20.4–2–63–5; Ferreira 35–5–102–2; P. A. Smith 13–4–43–1; Gifford 18–3–52–1. *Second Innings*—Small 15–1–70–2; Hogg 10–1–55–1; Ferreira 16–1–90–2; Gifford 8–0–47–0; P. A. Smith 3.5–0–26–1.

Warwickshire

K. D. Smith b Underwood	35	– b Ellison	34
T. A. Lloyd c and b Underwood	41	– run out	23
A. I. Kallicharran c Knott b Jarvis	36	– c Knott b Jarvis	9
D. L. Amiss lbw b Baptiste	34	– not out	69
†G. W. Humpage c Benson b Jarvis	105	– lbw b Ellison	13
Asif Din b Underwood	6	– c Cowdrey b Underwood	0
P. A. Smith not out	35	– c Aslett b Underwood	0
A. M. Ferreira not out	38	– c Taylor b Underwood	0
*N. Gifford (did not bat)		– c Taylor b Underwood	0
G. C. Small (did not bat)		– not out	2
B 4, l-b 13, w 2, n-b 10	29	L-b 6, n-b 6	12

1/80 2/93 3/133 4/244   (6 wkts dec.) 359   1/49 2/63 3/100 4/125   (8 wkts) 162
5/272 6/282   5/135 6/141 7/141 8/144

W. Hogg did not bat.

Bonus points – Warwickshire 4, Kent 2 (Score at 100 overs: 342-6).

Bowling: *First Innings*—Jarvis 17–6–48–2; Baptiste 18–2–88–1; Ellison 16–4–49–0; Underwood 38–15–73–3; Johnson 10–0–47–0; Cowdrey 3–0–25–0. *Second Innings*—Jarvis 10–1–42–1; Baptiste 9–4–31–0; Underwood 22–11–30–4; Johnson 5.5–3–16–0; Ellison 5–0–23–2; Aslett 1–0–8–0.

Umpires: M. J. Kitchen and N. T. Plews.

At Lord's, July 30, August 1, 2. WARWICKSHIRE lost to MIDDLESEX by eight wickets.

At The Oval, August 6, 8, 9. WARWICKSHIRE drew with SURREY.

At Cheltenham, August 10, 11, 12. WARWICKSHIRE beat GLOUCESTERSHIRE by four wickets.

WARWICKSHIRE v LEICESTERSHIRE

At Birmingham, August 13, 15, 16. Drawn. Warwickshire 6 pts, Leicestershire 5 pts. On a good batting pitch, on which only one wicket fell to spin, the match petered out into a draw after Warwickshire had been set the difficult task of scoring 340 in approximately 60 overs. Rain prevented the final thirteen overs being bowled after Kallicharran had continued his good season with 88. After Warwickshire had earned a first-innings lead of 99, Briers hit a career-best 201 not out, including a 6 and 29 4s in a stay of nearly six hours. Balderstone, Davison and Whitaker shared in respective partnerships of 133, 132 and 133. For Warwickshire, Old claimed his 1,000th first-class wicket.

Leicestershire

J. C. Balderstone b Old	3	– lbw b Lethbridge	64
I. P. Butcher lbw b P. A. Smith	29	– b Old	13
N. E. Briers c Lloyd b Old	20	– not out	201
B. F. Davison lbw b Hogg	5	– c and b Kallicharran	66
J. J. Whitaker b P. A. Smith	22	– not out	56
P. B. Clift c Amiss b Lethbridge	11		
*†R. W. Tolchard c Lloyd b Old	22		
J. F. Steele c Kallicharran b Hogg	9		
G. J. Parsons lbw b Old	14		
J. P. Agnew lbw b Old	6		
L. B. Taylor not out	3		
B 1, l-b 2, n-b 3	6	B 2, l-b 18, n-b 18	38

1/8 2/30 3/43 4/71   150   1/40 2/173 3/305   (3 wkts dec.) 438
5/90 6/114 7/116 8/137 9/145

Bonus points – Leicestershire 1, Warwickshire 4.

Bowling: *First Innings*—Old 20–5–56–5; Hogg 14.2–6–39–2; P. A. Smith 7–3–32–2; Gifford 4–1–11–0; Lethbridge 2–1–6–1. *Second Innings*—Old 30–7–76–1; Hogg 15–1–65–0; P. A. Smith 9–1–40–0; Gifford 42–8–93–0; Lethbridge 21–3–89–1; Kallicharran 14–4–37–1.

Warwickshire

T. A. Lloyd c Tolchard b Parsons	75	– c Briers b Agnew	35
K. D. Smith c Tolchard b Taylor	38	– lbw b Parsons	10
A. I. Kallicharran lbw b Clift	3	– c Steele b Taylor	88
D. L. Amiss lbw b Agnew	4	– run out	18
†G. W. Humpage b Parsons	27	– c Davison b Taylor	9
R. I. H. B. Dyer lbw b Parsons	13	– not out	16
P. A. Smith b Parsons	0	– c Steele b Taylor	4
C. Lethbridge c Taylor b Parsons	4	– not out	0
C. M. Old b Taylor	0		
*N. Gifford c Clift b Taylor	39		
W. Hogg not out	27		
B 2, l-b 3, w 1, n-b 13	19	L-b 2, w 1, n-b 11	14

1/98 2/105 3/120 4/151   249   1/40 2/72 3/135 4/170   (6 wkts) 194
5/172 6/173 7/178 8/179 9/179   5/181 6/185

Bonus points – Warwickshire 2, Leicestershire 4.

Bowling: *First Innings*—Taylor 21.5–3–62–3; Agnew 12–2–44–1; Clift 24–9–59–1; Parsons 20–9–51–5; Steele 8–2–14–0. *Second Innings*—Taylor 12–3–35–3; Parsons 7–1–25–1; Agnew 6–1–31–1; Clift 11–2–48–0; Steele 12–4–41–0.

Umpires: J. van Geloven and J. W. Holder.

At Folkestone, August 20, 22, 23. WARWICKSHIRE drew with KENT.

WARWICKSHIRE v SUSSEX

At Birmingham, August 24, 25, 26. Warwickshire won by 21 runs. Warwickshire 23 pts, Sussex 5 pts. Warwickshire's ninth win of the season was notable for an exceptional individual performance for each side. For the first time in his career Kallicharran scored a hundred in each innings of a match, and Imran took six wickets in 23 balls, including a hat-trick, in Warwickshire's second innings. Despite needing only 219 to win, Sussex then collapsed, their batsmen, Imran excepted, being badly out of form. Kallicharran's 152 took 200 minutes and included 24 4s; his unbeaten 118 in the second innings held Warwickshire together and lasted for 157 minutes.

Warwickshire

T. A. Lloyd c Gould b Reeve	33	– c Green b C. M. Wells	17
K. D. Smith lbw b Pigott	36	– lbw b Pigott	4
A. I. Kallicharran c Green b Pigott	152	– (5) not out	118
D. L. Amiss b C. M. Wells	36	– lbw b C. M. Wells	54
†G. W. Humpage not out	20	– (6) b Imran	5
R. I. H. B. Dyer not out	6	– (3) c Gould b Pigott	0
D. A. Thorne (did not bat)		– b Imran	0
P. A. Smith (did not bat)		– lbw b Imran	0
C. M. Old (did not bat)		– b Imran	0
*N. Gifford (did not bat)		– b Imran	4
W. Hogg (did not bat)		– b Imran	0
B 1, l-b 5, w 5, n-b 6	17	B 9, l-b 3, w 1, n-b 3	16

1/59 2/90 3/225 4/286   (4 wkts dec.) 300   1/21 2/21 3/21 4/156   218
                                         5/173 6/176 7/176 8/176 9/204

Bonus points – Warwickshire 4, Sussex 1.

Bowling: *First Innings*—Pigott 19–4–54–2; Reeve 20–6–58–1; C. M. Wells 13–2–44–1; Waller 21.1–5–57–0; Barclay 5–2–31–0; Imran 5–1–8–0; Green 6–2–31–0. *Second Innings* —Pigott 7–1–29–2; Reeve 11–0–60–0; C. M. Wells 7–1–29–2; Waller 13–4–39–0; Green 9–0–39–0; Imran 4.3–1–6–6.

Sussex

G. D. Mendis lbw b P. A. Smith	41	– c Thorne b Old 2
A. M. Green c Humpage b Hogg	0	– lbw b Hogg 8
*J. R. T. Barclay c Humpage b Hogg	2	– c Lloyd b P. A. Smith 27
Imran Khan c Kallicharran b Thorne	94	– c K. D. Smith b Gifford 64
C. M. Wells lbw b P. A. Smith	71	– (6) lbw b Gifford 1
A. P. Wells b P. A. Smith	3	– (7) lbw b Gifford 19
†I. J. Gould c Kallicharran b Gifford	17	– (8) c Hogg b Gifford 22
J. R. P. Heath not out	31	– (5) c Humpage b Kallicharran ... 14
A. C. S. Pigott not out	22	– lbw b P. A. Smith 24
C. E. Waller (did not bat)		– not out 1
D. A. Reeve (did not bat)		– lbw b P. A. Smith 0
L-b 5, w 1, n-b 13	19	B 4, l-b 2, w 4, n-b 5 15

1/5 2/8 3/75 4/218   (7 wkts. dec.) 300   1/2 2/16 3/102 4/124   197
5/226 6/229 7/269   5/126 6/127 7/163 8/194 9/196

Bonus points – Sussex 4, Warwickshire 3.

Bowling: *First Innings*—Old 17–2–61–0; Hogg 12–2–46–2; P. A. Smith 18–2–59–3; Gifford 26.3–8–73–1; Thorne 4–0–21–1; Kallicharran 7–0–21–0. *Second Innings*—Old 15–3–46–1; Hogg 5–0–28–1; P. A. Smith 11.5–1–56–3; Gifford 24–11–33–4; Kallicharran 10–3–19–1.

Umpires: W. E. Alley and D. O. Oslear.

WARWICKSHIRE v WORCESTERSHIRE

At Birmingham, August 27, 29, 30. Drawn. Warwickshire 6 pts, Worcestershire 7 pts. A maiden hundred for Worcestershire by McEvoy, which took him nearly five and a half hours, and a more rapid one by Patel (135 minutes; four 6s and fifteen 4s) ensured that Worcestershire were never under pressure. For Warwickshire, Amiss led the way to full batting points. A stiff declaration by Neale finally left the home side to make 330 to win at a rate of more than five an over and the match drifted to a draw.

Worcestershire

J. A. Ormrod b Hogg	4	– c Lloyd b Old 3
M. S. A. McEvoy c sub b Gifford	103	– c Lloyd b Old 23
*P. A. Neale c Amiss b Gifford	40	– (4) not out 82
D. N. Patel c and b Gifford	112	– (5) b Kallicharran 80
T. S. Curtis lbw b P. A. Smith	5	– (6) lbw b Kallicharran 11
M. J. Weston c Amiss b Gifford	21	– (7) not out 3
P. J. Newport not out	41	
†D. J. Humphries not out	48	
A. P. Pridgeon (did not bat)		– (3) c Amiss b Gifford 20
B 4, l-b 16, w 1, n-b 7	28	B 1, l-b 1, w 1, n-b 5 8

1/5 2/92 3/256 4/271   (6 wkts. dec.) 402   1/18 2/47 3/53   (5 wkts. dec.) 230
5/289 6/305   4/196 5/220

R. K. Illingworth and J. D. Inchmore did not bat.

Bonus points – Worcestershire 4, Warwickshire 2 (Score at 100 overs: 305-6).

Bowling: *First Innings*—Small 8–1–26–0; Hogg 19–3–67–1; Old 25–8–71–0; P. A. Smith 21–1–76–1; Gifford 36–15–77–4; Kallicharran 10–0–57–0. *Second Innings*—Old 21–5–61–2; Hogg 3–0–9–0; Gifford 29.5–4–88–1; Kallicharran 13–0–64–2.

Warwickshire

T. A. Lloyd c Curtis b Pridgeon	13	– b Pridgeon	14
K. D. Smith c Humphries b Pridgeon	31	– c Humphries b Pridgeon	9
A. I. Kallicharran c Patel b Pridgeon	21	– c Pridgeon b Patel	53
D. L. Amiss b Pridgeon	84	– not out	59
†G. W. Humpage c and b Illingworth	28	– b Patel	18
R. I. H. B. Dyer b Patel	6	– not out	13
C. M. Old c Ormrod b Patel	46		
P. A. Smith not out	48		
G. C. Small not out	10		
B 3, l-b 12, w 1	16	L-b 7, n-b 1	8

1/18 2/69 3/74 4/126   (7 wkts dec.) 303   1/23 2/38 3/96 4/123   (4 wkts) 174
5/159 6/237 7/247

*N. Gifford and W. Hogg did not bat.

Bonus points – Warwickshire 4, Worcestershire 3.

Bowling: *First Innings*—Pridgeon 18–4–63–4; Inchmore 17–0–57–0; Newport 6–0–11–0; Illingworth 29–9–81–1; Patel 23.3–5–75–2. *Second Innings*—Pridgeon 8–2–29–2; Inchmore 10–2–40–0; Patel 19–1–63–2; Illingworth 15–4–28–0; Curtis 3–1–6–0.

Umpires: J. H. Harris and D. O. Oslear.

At Nottingham, August 31, September 1, 2. WARWICKSHIRE drew with NOTTINGHAMSHIRE.

WARWICKSHIRE v GLAMORGAN

At Birmingham, September 7, 8, 9. Warwickshire won by eight wickets. Warwickshire 18 pts, Glamorgan 3 pts. No play on the second day brought a forfeiture of Warwickshire's first innings and a remarkable third day's play. Glamorgan set a target of 414 in a full day, and thanks to a magnificent second-wicket stand of 308 in 71 overs between Lloyd and Kallicharran, Warwickshire won with nearly an hour to spare. Kallicharran's second double-hundred of the season and his fifth in two years occupied four and a half hours, while Lloyd's fourth hundred of the season came in an hour less. Glamorgan were handicapped by the absence of Davis for most of the last day. For Glamorgan, Henderson scored a powerful maiden Championship hundred and Francis batted for more overs than he scored runs.

Glamorgan

A. Jones b Willis	20			
J. A. Hopkins c Kallicharran b Gifford	32			
R. C. Ontong b Gifford	37			
C. J. C. Rowe b Gifford	3			
A. L. Jones b Gifford	44	– (1) not out	24	
D. A. Francis not out	89			
S. P. Henderson not out	135			
†T. Davies (did not bat)		– (2) not out	0	
L-b 20, w 1, n-b 8	29			

1/34 2/84 3/90 4/112   (5 wkts dec.) 389   (no wkt dec.) 24
5/179

*M. W. W. Selvey, A. H. Wilkins and W. W. Davis did not bat.

Bonus points – Glamorgan 3, Warwickshire 2 (Score at 100 overs: 260-5).

Bowling: *First Innings*—Willis 18–4–47–1; Old 30–6–94–0; Hogg 7–1–27–0; Gifford 51–18–109–4; P. A. Smith 15–3–50–0; Kallicharran 10–1–33–0. *Second Innings*—Lloyd 1–0–24–0.

Warwickshire

T. A. Lloyd (did not bat)		– lbw b Ontong	123
K. D. Smith (did not bat)		– lbw b Davis	1
A. I. Kallicharran (did not bat)		– not out	243
D. L. Amiss (did not bat)		– not out	33
		B 8, l-b 6, w 1, n-b 2	17

1/11 2/319   (2 wkts) 417

†G. W. Humpage, G. J. Lord, W. Hogg, P. A. Smith, C. M. Old, N. Gifford and *R. G. D. Willis did not bat.

Bowling: Davis 8–1–36–1; Wilkins 14–1–70–0; Rowe 40.3–8–139–0; Ontong 25–2–116–1; Selvey 10–1–39–0.

Warwickshire forfeited their first innings.

Umpires: J. van Geloven and R. A. White.

At Taunton, September 10, 12, 13. WARWICKSHIRE drew with SOMERSET.

WORCESTERSHIRE

President: 1983 – J. J. Roberts;
   1984 – J. C. Sellars
Chairman: Dr J. A. Burnett
Chairman, Cricket Committee: M. G. Jones
Secretary: M. D. Vockins
   County Ground, New Road, Worcester
   WR2 4QQ (Telephone: 0905-422694)
Captain: P. A. Neale
Coach: B. L. D'Oliveira

The irony of Worcestershire's least successful post-war campaign provided one of the imponderables of the 1983 season. How could a side, which individually hit many new heights, fashion no more than a handful of victories?

Phil Neale, the captain, and Dipak Patel both enjoyed their best seasons with the bat. Paul Pridgeon proved his point, after being offered his release at the end of the previous season, with his best haul of 72 first-class wickets. There were maiden centuries for Martin Weston, Damian D'Oliveira, Mike McEvoy and David Banks, and a string of career-best performances from the likes of Richard Illingworth, Alan Warner, Ricardo Ellcock and Tim Curtis. Yet a week from the end of the season Worcestershire were at the foot of both the Championship and the John Player Sunday League. They avoided their first Championship wooden spoon for half a century with a win over Gloucestershire in their penultimate match, and avoided bottom place in the Sunday League only by winning their last game against Sussex.

They were, in fact, a much better one-day side than their record suggests – a point underlined by their Sunday League victory over Somerset the day after they had lifted the NatWest Bank Trophy at Lord's. At one stage they had an unprecedented run of three successive Sunday ties – against Nottinghamshire, Lancashire and Warwickshire. But in the three-day game Worcestershire were usually found wanting. Their first Championship win came on August 12 against Lancashire, thus ending a sequence of nineteen Schweppes matches since their previous success, which was also against Lancashire in June 1982.

At one stage, when Worcestershire's fortunes hit rock bottom, their supporters had to endure a run of five Championship defeats on the trot, and no fewer than six successive home reverses against county opposition. The long, hot summer had, by this time, taken its toll on the now heavily compacted New Road square, which has since undergone major surgery. The pitch was twice reported – after the matches against Glamorgan and the New Zealanders. The unpredictable bounce began to undermine the confidence of the Worcestershire players, particularly the younger batsmen, and without a top-class fast bowler themselves they found visiting sides better equipped to exploit the conditions. Things might have been different but for two unfortunate set-backs which had a lot to do with Worcestershire's unsuccessful season.

Optimism in the camp was first undermined when the Australian bowler, Terry Alderman, who had accepted a one-year's contract, was unable to fulfil it owing to the shoulder injury sustained in the previous winter's Test series with England. Then, only a few weeks into the season, Worcestershire decided they had no alternative but to sack their leading batsman, Younis Ahmed, for placing a bet on Worcestershire to lose a John Player League game against Leicestershire in which he was due to play. In the event, the match was washed out by rain. Having already lost Glenn Turner from the previous season, Worcestershire were now without their main match-winner.

Younis's controversial departure created a void which D'Oliveira did his best to fill, initially with commendable success. He scored his maiden century against Middlesex, the defending champions rating it the best knock played against them in the first half of the season. With 972 first-class runs, D'Oliveira deserved his selection for a Whitbread Scholarship to New Zealand during the winter.

The West Indian all-rounder, Collis King, made only limited appearances owing to his Lancashire League commitments, though he hit his way into the record books with a spectacular 123 on his début against Somerset. The 22-year-old Banks created a little bit of history by becoming the youngest Worcestershire player to score a century on his first-class début, albeit against Oxford University.

Neale hit ten half-centuries in nineteen innings during one purple patch, and Patel finished with a flourish, hammering over 600 runs in a four-week period, which included centuries against Surrey, Warwickshire and Gloucestershire. At the end of the season Patel was only one wicket short of achieving the modern double of 50 wickets and 1,000 runs for the second season running. He could well become the next Worcestershire player to win an England cap. Results may not have gone Worcestershire's way in 1983, but their young players can only have benefited from their experiences. – C.M.

WORCESTERSHIRE 1983

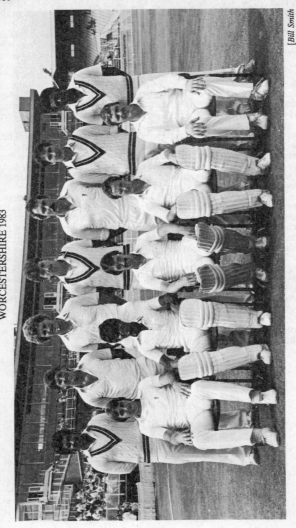

[*Bill Smith*]

Back row: D. B. D'Oliveira, S. P. Perryman, A. P. Pridgeon, D. A. Banks, J. D. Inchmore, R. K. Illingworth, A. E. Warner. *Front row*: M. J. Weston, D. N. Patel, P. A. Neale (*captain*), M. S. A. McEvoy, D. J. Humphries.

WORCESTERSHIRE RESULTS

All first-class matches – Played 27: Won 4, Lost 12, Drawn 11.

County Championship matches – Played 24: Won 2, Lost 11, Drawn 11.

Bonus points – Batting 43, Bowling 54.

Competition placings – Schweppes County Championship, 16th; NatWest Bank Trophy, 1st round; Benson and Hedges Cup, 4th in Group A; John Player League, 11th eq.

COUNTY CHAMPIONSHIP AVERAGES

BATTING

	Birthplace	M	I	NO	R	HI	Avge
P. A. Nealec	Scunthorpe	23	39	3	1,500	139	41.66
D. N. Patelc	Nairobi, Kenya	23	39	2	1,537	112	41.54
T. S. Curtis	Chislehurst	8	16	2	363	84	25.92
M. J. Weston..........	Worcester	19	33	1	823	115	25.71
D. B. D'Oliveira	Cape Town, SA	19	34	2	775	102	24.21
P. J. Newport	High Wycombe	4	4	1	72	41*	24.00
J. A. Ormrodc	Ramsbottom	23	40	3	883	78	23.86
M. S. Scott	Muswell Hill	5	9	2	155	57*	22.14
D. A. Banks...........	Pensnett	5	9	1	174	44	21.75
D. J. Humphriesc	Alveley	18	27	4	496	59	21.56
M. S. A. McEvoy ...	Jorhat Assam, India	15	24	1	491	103	21.34
J. D. Inchmorec	Ashington	17	22	3	330	51	17.36
P. Moores	Macclesfield	6	9	1	110	30	13.75
R. M. Ellcock........	Bridgetown, Barbados	12	18	4	154	36	11.00
R. K. Illingworth....	Bradford	22	30	5	238	55	9.52
A. P. Pridgeonc	Wall Heath	24	30	8	186	23	8.45
A. E. Warner	Birmingham	7	12	2	81	20*	8.10
S. P. Perryman........	Birmingham	10	13	6	54	22	7.71

Also batted: C. L. King (*Christ Church, Barbados*) (2 matches) 123, 8, 27; Younis Ahmed (*Jullundur, Pakistan*) (2 matches) 10*, 35*.

*Signifies not out.   c*Denotes county cap.*

BOWLING

	O	M	R	W	Avge	BB
A. E. Warner	168.4	26	501	21	23.85	4-72
A. P. Pridgeon	581.2	130	1,687	59	28.59	5-21
J. D. Inchmore........	384.2	75	1,107	32	34.59	5-45
R. M. Ellcock	244	39	931	25	37.24	4-70
D. N. Patel	638.4	185	1,709	45	37.97	5-52
R. K. Illingworth....	606.5	148	1,680	41	40.97	5-26
S. P. Perryman........	211.5	41	644	10	64.40	4-91

Also bowled: T. S. Curtis 3–1–6–0; D. B. D'Oliveira 65.1–13–250–3; C. L. King 15–2–39–1; P. J. Newport 41–3–118–3; M. J. Weston 14.2–3–69–2.

The following played a total of nine three-figure innings for Worcestershire in County Championship matches – D. N. Patel 3, P. A. Neale 2, D. B. D'Oliveira 1, C. L. King 1, M. S. A. McEvoy 1, M. J. Weston 1.

WORCESTERSHIRE v YORKSHIRE

At Worcester, April 30, May 1, 2. Drawn. Yorkshire 1 pt. The match was restricted to just 105 minutes' play on the first afternoon, in which time Sidebottom took three wickets in ten overs, including two in his first eight deliveries.

Worcestershire

J. A. Ormrod c Athey b Sidebottom ...	16	Younis Ahmed not out	10
M. J. Weston c Bairstow b Sidebottom ..	32	B 1, w 1, n-b 6	8
*P. A. Neale b Sidebottom................	2		—
D. N. Patel not out...........................	11	1/31 2/37 3/60	(3 wkts) 79

M. S. A. McEvoy, †D. J. Humphries, R. K. Illingworth, J. D. Inchmore, A. P. Pridgeon and S. P. Perryman did not bat.

Bonus points – Yorkshire 1.

Bowling: Dennis 13–2–30–0; Stevenson 6–3–11–0; Sidebottom 10–4–23–3; Carrick 3–1–7–0.

Yorkshire

G. Boycott, R. G. Lumb, C. W. J. Athey, S. N. Hartley, J. D. Love, †D. L. Bairstow, P. Carrick, G. B. Stevenson, A. Sidebottom, *R. Illingworth and S. J. Dennis.

Umpires: D. G. L. Evans and D. R. Shepherd.

At Taunton, May 4, 5, 6. WORCESTERSHIRE drew with SOMERSET.

WORCESTERSHIRE v SOMERSET

At Worcester, May 11, 12, 13. Drawn. Worcestershire 6 pts, Somerset 8 pts. Collis King marked his début for Worcestershire in spectacular style, smashing six 6s and twelve 4s in an innings of 123 out of 188 in 141 minutes. His second 50 came off 25 deliveries, with Wilson being hit for 17 off one over and Marks for 18 off another. It was the first time for 52 years a Worcestershire player had scored a century on his first-class début for the county. Worcestershire ended the first day at 329 for nine, despite losing the first two hours to rain, but only 26 overs were possible on the second day. On the final day Somerset slipped to 99 for four before Botham assured them of maximum batting points with his 21st first-class century. He moved off the mark by hitting Patel for 6 and hit three more to go with twelve 4s in his 107 out of 182 in 122 minutes.

Worcestershire

J. A. Ormrod c Lloyds b Marks	45	J. D. Inchmore c Gard b Dredge	0
M. J. Weston c Dredge b Palmer........	32	†P. Moores b Botham......................	19
*P. A. Neale c Popplewell b Marks.....	4	A. E. Warner not out......................	20
D. N. Patel c Palmer b Wilson...........	26	B 6, l-b 8	14
C. L. King c Popplewell b Dredge 123			—
M. S. A. McEvoy c Popplewell b Marks...	25	1/79 2/87 3/87 4/156	(9 wkts dec.) 329
R. K. Illingworth c Gard b Marks.......	21	5/253 6/275 7/276 8/292 9/329	

A. P. Pridgeon did not bat.

Bonus points – Worcestershire 4, Somerset 4.

Bowling: Botham 11.3–5–28–1; Dredge 20–2–90–2; Wilson 9–0–40–1; Marks 31–8–101–4; Palmer 12–0–28–1; Popplewell 4–0–28–0.

Somerset

J. W. Lloyds b Pridgeon	26	V. J. Marks not out	27
P. M Roebuck b Warner	23	G. V. Palmer not out	6
I. V. A. Richards c Pridgeon b King	20	B 5, l-b 11, w 1, n-b 13	30
*B. C. Rose c McEvoy b Warner	4		—
N. F. M. Popplewell retired hurt	58	1/67 2/78	(5 wkts dec.) 301
I. T. Botham c King b Weston	107	3/89 4/99 5/281	

C. H. Dredge, †T. Gard and P. H. L. Wilson did not bat.

Bonus points – Somerset 4, Worcestershire 2.

Bowling: Warner 16.4–3–54–2; Pridgeon 18.4–8–33–1; Inchmore 7.2–2–6–0; Illingworth 13–1–61–0; King 8–1–26–1; Patel 11–1–48–0; Weston 9–3–43–1.

Umpires: C. Cook and N. T. Plews.

At Southampton, May 25, 26, 27. WORCESTERSHIRE lost to HAMPSHIRE by seven wickets.

WORCESTERSHIRE v WARWICKSHIRE

At Worcester, May 28, 30, 31. Drawn. Worcestershire 4 pts, Warwickshire 5 pts. No play was possible on the first day, but a result still seemed likely when Ellcock, playing only his second Championship match, reduced Warwickshire to 45 for five in their first innings. The seventeen-year-old West Indian took four for 25 in his first seven overs before the Warwickshire middle order arrested the slide. Worcestershire at the close were precariously placed at 68 for seven, but Neale batted for all but four of their overs to prevent a complete collapse and so effectively ensure a stalemate.

Warwickshire

T. A. Lloyd b Ellcock	7	– lbw b Inchmore	4
K. D. Smith c Weston b Pridgeon	3	– c McEvoy b Illingworth	63
D. L. Amiss b Ellcock	3	– c McEvoy b Pridgeon	7
G. W. Humpage c Humphries b Ellcock	16	– c Patel b Pridgeon	4
Asif Din lbw b Ellcock	6	– b Inchmore	1
A. M. Ferreira c Humphries b Inchmore	38	– c McEvoy b Illingworth	14
†G. A. Tedstone c McEvoy b Pridgeon	17	– c D'Oliveira b Patel	32
C. M. Old run out	12	– not out	3
G. C. Small c Humphries b Pridgeon	31	– c Patel b Illingworth	1
*R. G. D. Willis not out	10	– not out	9
W. Hogg c Humphries b Pridgeon	0		
L-b 3, w 1, n-b 12	16	B 4, l-b 3, w 2, n-b 5	14
	—		—
1/7 2/13 3/15 4/37	159	1/13 2/32 3/38 4/42	(8 wkts) 152
5/45 6/79 7/92 8/138 9/155		5/64 6/135 7/137 8/140	

Bonus points – Warwickshire 1, Worcestershire 4.

Bowling: *First Innings*—Ellcock 15–2–70–4; Pridgeon 15.2–4–37–4; Inchmore 9–1–36–1; Patel 1–1–0–0. *Second Innings*—Ellcock 4–0–6–0; Pridgeon 17–4–30–2; Inchmore 12–5–19–2; Patel 26–10–55–1; Illingworth 25–12–28–3.

Worcestershire

J. A. Ormrod c Tedstone b Small	2	J. D. Inchmore c Tedstone b Willis	6
M. J. Weston c Tedstone b Willis	17	A. P. Pridgeon b Ferreira	3
*P. A. Neale lbw b Ferreira	47	R. M. Ellcock not out	1
D. N. Patel lbw b Willis	10	B 1, l-b 5, n-b 5	11
D. B. D'Oliveira lbw b Ferreira	12		—
M. S. A. McEvoy c Ferreira b Small	4	1/5 2/22 3/38	118
†D. J. Humphries c Asif Din b Small	4	4/56 5/61 6/66	
R. K. Illingworth c Lloyd b Ferreira	1	7/67 8/84 9/109	

Bonus points – Warwickshire 4.

Bowling: Willis 15–4–50–3; Small 11–4–13–3; Hogg 3–0–20–0; Ferreira 9.5–2–19–4; Old 1–0–5–0.

Umpires: K. E. Palmer and C. Cook.

At Hove, June 4, 6, 7. WORCESTERSHIRE drew with SUSSEX.

WORCESTERSHIRE v SURREY

At Worcester, June 8, 9, 10. Surrey won by ten wickets. Surrey 23 pts, Worcestershire 3 pts. Despite a career best from D'Oliveira, exactly nineteen years after his father, Basil, scored his first century at New Road, Surrey were left needing just 19 runs for their first Championship win of the season. D'Oliveira, in his sixth Championship game, held the Worcestershire second innings together for 184 minutes to help wipe out a deficit of 260, but only Inchmore provided any positive support. Lynch, with a 6 and sixteen 4s in his 112, and Butcher dominated the home attack in Surrey's first innings when only one of their batsmen failed to get into double figures.

Worcestershire

J. A. Ormrod lbw b Clarke	4	– c Smith b Monkhouse	24
M. J. Weston c Smith b Thomas	5	– (6) c Clarke b Thomas	18
*P. A. Neale c Richards b Clarke	52	– st Richards b Monkhouse	29
D. N. Patel b Clarke	6	– b Pocock	17
D. B. D'Oliveira b Pocock	29	– lbw b Monkhouse	82
M. S. A. McEvoy b Clarke	0	– (2) lbw b Monkhouse	7
†D. J. Humphries lbw b Clarke	25	– b Needham	17
R. K. Illingworth b Pocock	0	– c Knight b Pocock	15
J. D. Inchmore b Monkhouse	38	– c Lynch b Pocock	43
R. M. Ellcock not out	23	– not out	5
A. P. Pridgeon lbw b Monkhouse	0	– lbw b Pocock	0
L-b 4, n-b 5	9	B 7, l-b 4, n-b 10	21

1/4 2/20 3/37 4/94	191	1/16 2/40 3/65 4/105	278
5/98 6/108 7/112 8/156 9/179		5/161 6/212 7/216 8/272 9/278	

Bonus points – Worcestershire 1, Surrey 4.

Bowling: *First Innings*—Clarke 18–6–45–4; Thomas 16–3–43–1; Monkhouse 14.2–5–35–3; Knight 3–0–13–0; Pocock 19–8–45–2; Needham 2–1–1–0. *Second Innings*—Clarke 18–5–55–0; Thomas 11–3–36–1; Monkhouse 23–7–55–4; Pocock 29–8–83–4; Knight 6–4–8–0; Needham 7–1–20–1.

Surrey

A. R. Butcher b Inchmore	92	– not out	14
G. S. Clinton c Humphries b Patel	29	– not out	4
D. M. Smith lbw b Ellcock	15		
*R. D. V. Knight c Pridgeon b Illingworth	41		
M. A. Lynch c Weston b Pridgeon	112		
†C. J. Richards c Ormrod b Illingworth	6		
A. Needham lbw b Pridgeon	18		
D. J. Thomas c Ormrod b Weston	48		
G. Monkhouse lbw b Ellcock	23		
S. T. Clarke not out	24		
P. I. Pocock not out	16		
B 4, l-b 11, w 4, n-b 8	27	B 1	1

1/75 2/137 3/155 4/227   (9 wkts dec.) 451   (no wkt) 19
5/258 6/321 7/339 8/399 9/405

Bonus points – Surrey 3, Worcestershire 2 (Score at 100 overs: 280-5).

Bowling: *First Innings*—Ellcock 21–5–68–2; Pridgeon 18–1–79–2; Inchmore 21–5–55–1; Patel 43–16–110–1; Illingworth 23–6–79–2; Weston 3–0–15–1; D'Oliveira 2–0–18–0. *Second Innings*—Ellcock 2–1–4–0; Weston 2.2–0–11–0; D'Oliveira 1–0–3–0.

Umpires: W. L. Budd and K. Ibadulla.

At Oxford, June 15, 16, 17. WORCESTERSHIRE beat OXFORD UNIVERSITY by 148 runs.

WORCESTERSHIRE v MIDDLESEX

At Worcester, June 18, 20, 21. Middlesex won by 75 runs. Middlesex 24 pts, Worcestershire 6 pts. A maiden century from D'Oliveira, who put on 180 in 130 minutes with Patel, took Worcestershire to within 131 runs of victory before they lost their last seven wickets for 56, Edmonds taking five wickets for 10 with his last 23 balls. The pair came together after Williams had taken the first three Worcestershire wickets for 8 runs in seventeen balls. D'Oliveira's 102 in 173 minutes included eleven 4s. Downton, Edmonds and Williams, with a career-best 63, had rescued Middlesex on the opening day, adding 223 for the last four wickets.

Middlesex

G. D. Barlow retired hurt	2	– b Patel	58
W. N. Slack b Patel	50	– c Humphries b Warner	13
K. P. Tomlins b Humphries b Warner	9	– c Humphries b Ellcock	27
R. O. Butcher lbw b Pridgeon	1	– lbw b Warner	35
C. T. Radley lbw b Ellcock	2	– not out	32
*J. E. Emburey c Humphries b Warner	19	– lbw b Illingworth	31
†P. R. Downton lbw b Warner	87		
P. H. Edmonds c Patel b Illingworth	65	– (7) not out	7
K. D. James lbw b Patel	6		
N. F. Williams c D'Oliveira b Illingworth	63		
S. P. Hughes not out	0		
B 4, l-b 2, w 1, n-b 3	10	B 4, l-b 9, n-b 5	18

1/26 2/36 3/57 4/77   (9 wkts dec.) 314   1/26 2/89 3/137   (5 wkts dec.) 221
5/91 6/180 7/199 8/286 9/314   4/147 5/201

Bonus points – Middlesex 4, Worcestershire 4.

Bowling: *First Innings*—Ellcock 16–6–49–1; Warner 16.2–2–38–3; Pridgeon 16–3–48–1; Patel 25–3–91–2; Illingworth 26–7–78–2. *Second Innings*—Ellcock 11–1–54–1; Warner 12–0–43–2; Pridgeon 8–1–32–0; Patel 17–3–46–1; Illingworth 8–1–28–1.

Worcestershire

J. A. Ormrod c Downton b Hughes	12	– lbw b Williams	0
M. J. Weston c Butcher b Williams	32	– c Emburey b Williams	2
*P. A. Neale lbw b Hughes	55	– c Downton b Williams	3
D. N. Patel lbw b Emburey	24	– c and b Emburey	88
D. B. D'Oliveira c Edmonds b Slack	40	– c Butcher b Edmonds	102
M. S. Scott c Barlow b Edmonds	12	– c Butcher b Edmonds	8
†D. J. Humphries c Butcher b Edmonds	10	– c and b Emburey	1
R. K. Illingworth c Downton b Williams	7	– c Downton b Edmonds	0
A. E. Warner c Tomlins b Edmonds	5	– not out	14
R. M. Ellcock b Edmonds	1	– c Barlow b Edmonds	4
A. P. Pridgeon not out	0	– c Downton b Edmonds	1
B 1, l-b 7, n-b 10	18	B 4, l-b 8, w 1, n-b 8	21

1/49 2/51 3/110 4/150　　　　　　　　216　　1/0 2/5 3/8 4/188　　　　　244
5/186 6/189 7/204 8/214 9/216　　　　　　　5/221 6/222 7/222 8/226 9/233

Bonus points – Worcestershire 2, Middlesex 4.

Bowling: *First Innings*—Williams 20–3–53–2; Hughes 15–4–58–2; Emburey 9–0–34–1; James 5–0–19–0; Edmonds 13.1–4–29–4; Slack 2–0–5–1. *Second Innings*—Williams 12–3–43–3; Hughes 7–1–31–0; James 3–0–17–0; Edmonds 22–4–56–5; Emburey 23–4–76–2; Slack 1–1–0–0.

Umpires: A. Jepson and R. Julian.

At Abergavenny, June 22, 23, 24. WORCESTERSHIRE drew with GLAMORGAN.

WORCESTERSHIRE v CAMBRIDGE UNIVERSITY

At Worcester, June 25, 27, 28. Worcestershire won by an innings and 69 runs. Inchmore and Pridgeon exposed the university's brittle batting, dismissing them for 108 in their second innings when they needed 177 to avoid an innings defeat. Ormrod and Scott both compiled their highest scores of the season on the opening day, with D'Oliveira helping Ormrod add 98 for the fourth wicket. Cambridge lost sixteen wickets for 237 runs on the second day.

Worcestershire

J. A. Ormrod c Boyd-Moss b Doggart	84	R. K. Illingworth not out	19
M. J. Weston c and b Pollock	0	J. D. Inchmore c Hewitt b Pollock	18
*P. A. Neale b Pollock	21	A. E. Warner not out	8
D. N. Patel b Hodgson	24		
D. B. D'Oliveira c Henderson b Hodgson	58	L-b 8, w 3	11
M. S. Scott c Hewitt b Pollock	76	1/1 2/39 3/76 4/174　　(8 wkts dec.) 339
†D. J. Humphries c Hewitt b Pollock	20	5/211 6/292 7/294 8/314

A. P. Pridgeon did not bat.

Bowling: Pollock 28–6–107–5; Hodgson 24–4–82–2; Ellison 17–7–40–0; Cotterell 7–2–16–0; Doggart 21–7–60–1; Henderson 3–0–23–0.

Cambridge University

D. W. Varey b Illingworth	40	– c Weston b Pridgeon	7
T. S. Curtis b Pridgeon	8	– c sub b Inchmore	5
R. J. Boyd-Moss c Neale b Warner	5	– c Humphries b Pridgeon	0
*S. P. Henderson b Pridgeon	2	– retired hurt	25
G. Pathmanathan c Pridgeon b Warner	2	– run out	16
S. J. G. Doggart c and b Warner	19	– c Inchmore b Pridgeon	3
K. I. Hodgson b Inchmore	47	– c Inchmore	21
T. A. Cotterell st Humphries b Patel	22	– b Inchmore	5
C. C. Ellison c Ormrod b Patel	1	– not out	11
A. J. Pollock b Inchmore	3	– b Inchmore	0
†S. G. Hewitt not out	0	– lbw b Inchmore	0
B 6, l-b 2, w 1, n-b 4	13	L-b 3, w 5, n-b 7	15

1/23 2/34 3/37 4/41   162   1/10 2/14 3/18 4/50   108
5/81 6/93 7/154 8/155 9/162   5/85 6/89 7/93 8/108 9/108

Bowling: *First Innings*—Warner 17-4-46-3; Pridgeon 17-5-47-2; Inchmore 12-4-23-2; Weston 4-2-8-0; Illingworth 3-1-17-1; Patel 5.1-1-8-2. *Second Innings*—Pridgeon 16-9-28-3; Inchmore 18.1-4-47-5; Patel 6-4-5-0; Illingworth 7-5-13-0.

Umpires: D. J. Constant and R. Palmer.

At Derby, July 2, 4, 5. WORCESTERSHIRE lost to DERBYSHIRE by eight wickets.

WORCESTERSHIRE v NOTTINGHAMSHIRE

At Worcester, July 9, 11, 12. Nottinghamshire won by 215 runs. Nottinghamshire 21 pts, Worcestershire 4 pts. Career-best figures of seven for 33 by Cooper, followed, in their second innings, by a devastating spell of five wickets for no runs in nineteen balls by Hendrick, sentenced Worcestershire to their fourth defeat in five games. Twenty wickets tumbled on the first day, when Nottinghamshire recovered from 62 for six to reach 176, and Worcestershire were routed for 69, Cooper taking his first six wickets for 19 runs. Robinson, with 110 in 275 minutes, including fourteen 4s, led an opening stand of 112 with Hassan, which enabled Rice to set Worcestershire a hopeless task.

Nottinghamshire

B. Hassan lbw b Pridgeon	1	– b Patel	50
R. T. Robinson lbw b Inchmore	9	– c Illingworth b Patel	110
D. W. Randall lbw b Inchmore	10	– c and b Illingworth	29
*C. E. B. Rice lbw b Inchmore	15	– c Moores b Patel	3
J. D. Birch c Neale b Warner	12	– lbw b Inchmore	38
E. E. Hemmings c Moores b Inchmore	2	– c Moores b Warner	9
†B. N. French c Ormrod b Illingworth	46	– c Moores b Pridgeon	6
K. Saxelby run out	35	– c D'Oliveira b Illingworth	9
K. E. Cooper b Inchmore	5	– not out	16
M. K. Bore c D'Oliveira b Pridgeon	20		
M. Hendrick not out	2		
B 1, l-b 3, w 2, n-b 13	19	B 1, l-b 2, w 5, n-b 7	15

1/1 2/22 3/31 4/44   176   1/112 2/161 3/164 (8 wkts dec.) 285
5/47 6/62 7/136 8/145 9/160   4/209 5/234 6/253 7/260 8/285

Bonus points – Nottinghamshire 1, Worcestershire 4.

Bowling: *First Innings*—Warner 17-3-43-1; Pridgeon 21.4-9-38-2; Inchmore 23-5-45-5; Patel 4-1-11-0; Illingworth 9-2-20-1. *Second Innings*—Warner 14-0-57-1; Pridgeon 17-2-47-1; Inchmore 12-2-30-1; Patel 38-13-91-3; Illingworth 36-13-45-2.

Worcestershire

J. A. Ormrod c Rice b Cooper	3	– c Randall b Hemmings	30
M. J. Weston lbw b Cooper	3	– lbw b Saxelby	44
*P. A. Neale c Randall b Hendrick	11	– c Randall b Hendrick	32
D. N. Patel b Cooper	6	– c French b Hendrick	33
D. B. D'Oliveira c French b Cooper	6	– c Randall b Hendrick	0
M. S. Scott c French b Cooper	0	– c Randall b Hendrick	0
†P. Moores lbw b Hendrick	0	– lbw b Bore	2
J. D. Inchmore not out	33	– c Hassan b Hendrick	0
R. K. Illingworth c Hendrick b Cooper	1	– c French b Hemmings	13
A. E. Warner c Hemmings b Cooper	6	– c Cooper b Bore	12
A. P. Pridgeon lbw b Saxelby	0	– not out	9
		L-b 1, n-b 1	2

1/6 2/13 3/21 4/23	69	1/70 2/90 3/136 4/136	177
5/23 6/24 7/30 8/34 9/68		5/138 6/141 7/143 8/156 9/156	

Bonus points – Nottinghamshire 4.

Bowling: *First Innings*—Hendrick 9–2–17–2; Cooper 11–0–33–7; Saxelby 2.2–0–19–1. *Second Innings*—Hendrick 17–7–24–5; Cooper 11–4–25–0; Hemmings 31–10–85–2; Saxelby 5–1–18–1; Bore 10.3–4–23–2.

Umpires: W. E. Alley and K. Ibadulla.

WORCESTERSHIRE v LEICESTERSHIRE

At Hereford, July 13, 14, 15. Leicestershire won by five wickets. Leicestershire 21 pts, Worcestershire 6 pts. Leicestershire, set to score 236 in 196 minutes, won with five balls to spare. With an uninspiring first-innings century, Balderstone carried his bat for the second time in his career. In making 63 on the final afternoon, he showed another side to his game. Illingworth's career-best 55 on the opening day helped Worcestershire to add 101 off 306 balls for their last two wickets after they had slumped to 127 for eight. There was no such recovery in Worcestershire's second innings, when the loss of the last seven wickets for 67 runs gave Leicestershire their winning chance.

Worcestershire

J. A. Ormrod lbw b Ferris	0	– c Steele b Taylor	17
M. J. Weston b Clift	10	– lbw b Clift	11
*P. A. Neale lbw b Clift	33	– c Davison b Steele	50
D. N. Patel lbw b Ferris	0	– c Cook b Steele	54
D. B. D'Oliveira c Whitaker b Clift	30	– c Tolchard b Cook	5
D. A. Banks c Tolchard b Taylor	17	– run out	19
†P. Moores c Clift b Ferris	12	– lbw b Taylor	3
J. D. Inchmore c Tolchard b Taylor	19	– (9) b Ferris	22
R. K. Illingworth lbw b Cook	55	– (8) c Balderstone b Ferris	8
S. P. Perryman c Davison b Steele	22	– b Ferris	0
A. P. Pridgeon not out	16	– not out	1
L-b 9, w 1, n-b 4	14	B 5, l-b 5, w 2, n-b 3	15

1/1 2/41 3/42 4/52	228	1/32 2/40 3/138 4/145	205
5/81 6/97 7/123 8/127 9/189		5/151 6/165 7/173 8/200 9/204	

Bonus points – Worcestershire 2, Leicestershire 4.

Bowling: *First Innings*—Ferris 21–6–86–3; Taylor 27–10–53–2; Clift 18–3–41–3; Cook 15.2–7–18–1; Steele 14–5–16–1; Balderstone 1–1–0–0. *Second Innings*—Ferris 17.5–3–50–3; Taylor 12–6–13–2; Clift 11–3–36–1; Cook 27–13–43–1; Steele 25–11–48–2; Briers 1–1–0–0.

Leicestershire

J. C. Balderstone not out	100	– c Moores b Illingworth	63
I. P. Butcher b Inchmore	3	– lbw b Inchmore	0
N. E. Briers b Perryman	15	– b Patel	30
B. F. Davison c Moores b Inchmore	12	– st Moores b Illingworth	21
J. J. Whitaker lbw b Perryman	6	– (7) not out	40
*†R. W. Tolchard c Pridgeon b Patel	24	– (5) c Perryman b Illingworth	25
P. B. Clift b Patel	20	– (6) not out	34
J. F. Steele c Weston b Patel	0		
N. G. B. Cook c Banks b Patel	11		
L. B. Taylor c and b Patel	1		
G. J. F. Ferris b Illingworth	1		
L-b 4, n-b 1	5	B 12, l-b 13	25

1/9 2/50 3/65 4/72   198   1/2 2/84 3/116   (5 wkts) 238
5/118 6/156 7/160 8/192 9/195   4/156 5/163

Bonus points – Leicestershire 1, Worcestershire 4.

Bowling: *First Innings*—Pridgeon 11–4–19–0; Inchmore 15–4–33–2; Perryman 20–6–37–2; Patel 32–16–57–5; Illingworth 21.5–5–47–1. *Second Innings*—Pridgeon 5–1–10–0; Inchmore 5–1–13–1; Perryman 8–1–25–0; Patel 27–4–71–1; Illingworth 19.1–4–94–3.

Umpires: A. Jepson and W. E. Alley.

At Manchester, July 16, 18, 19. WORCESTERSHIRE drew with LANCASHIRE.

At Worcester, July 20, 21, 22. WORCESTERSHIRE lost to NEW ZEALANDERS by 100 runs (See New Zealand tour section).

WORCESTERSHIRE v GLAMORGAN

At Worcester, July 27, 28, 29. Glamorgan won by seven wickets. Glamorgan 22 pts, Worcestershire 2 pts. Worcestershire never recovered after Barwick had produced much the best return of his career to dismiss them in their first innings for 127 in only 44.3 overs. Neither county had won a Championship game, but Barwick set Glamorgan up for only their second victory in two years. Trailing by 131 on first innings, Worcestershire were given hope by a fourth-wicket stand of 112 between Neale and D'Oliveira. But from 204 for four they slumped to 234 all out in the next 45 minutes, Ontong taking four for 11 in 5.5 overs.

Worcestershire

J. A. Ormrod c Davies b Barwick	27	– lbw b Davis	22
M. J. Weston c Davies b Barwick	13	– lbw b Selvey	21
*P. A. Neale c Morris b Barwick	10	– lbw b Ontong	77
D. N. Patel c Ontong b Barwick	15	– b Selvey	10
D. B. D'Oliveira b Barwick	16	– b Davis	56
D. A. Banks c Davies b Barwick	0	– lbw b Davis	5
†D. J. Humphries c Davies b Davis	16	– (9) b Davis	15
J. D. Inchmore b Barwick	0	– (7) b Ontong	2
A. E. Warner b Davis	3	– (8) c A. L. Jones b Ontong	0
S. P. Perryman not out	4	– not out	6
A. P. Pridgeon c Hopkins b Barwick	5	– b Ontong	0
B 7, l-b 1, w 1, n-b 9	18	B 1, l-b 4, n-b 15	20

1/42 2/43 3/67 4/72   127   1/42 2/58 3/92 4/204   234
5/72 6/111 7/111 8/115 9/122   5/209 6/212 7/212 8/214 9/233

Bonus points – Glamorgan 4.

Bowling: *First Innings*—Davis 16–7–33–2; Selvey 12–5–30–0; Barwick 14.3–3–42–8; Ontong 2–1–4–0. *Second Innings*—Davis 25–5–76–4; Selvey 24–8–79–2; Barwick 6–1–28–0; Rowe 3–1–20–0; Ontong 5.5–2–11–4.

Glamorgan

J. A. Hopkins b Pridgeon	44	– lbw b Pridgeon 11
D. A. Francis c Ormrod b Perryman	36	– lbw b Warner 27
R. C. Ontong c Humphries b Inchmore	16	– c and b Warner 22
C. J. C. Rowe b Inchmore	5	– not out 23
H. Morris run out	27	– not out 9
A. Jones c Neale b Patel	1	
A. L. Jones lbw b Pridgeon	62	
†T. Davies b Inchmore	20	
*M. W. W. Selvey c sub b Pridgeon	9	
W. W. Davis c sub b Pridgeon	1	
S. R. Barwick not out	0	
B 10, l-b 23, n-b 4	37	B 2, l-b 6, w 4, n-b 2 14

1/65 2/93 3/109 4/109   258   1/21 2/68 3/71   (3 wkts) 106
5/114 6/207 7/222 8/256 9/258

Bonus points – Glamorgan 2, Worcestershire 2 (Score at 100 overs: 221-6).

Bowling: *First Innings*—Warner 16–2–44–0; Pridgeon 28–7–68–4; Inchmore 27.5–8–55–3; Perryman 26–11–41–1; Patel 15–10–13–1. *Second Innings*—Pridgeon 12–4–22–1; Inchmore 10–3–19–0; Warner 8–2–17–2; Perryman 9–0–22–0; Patel 3.5–2–12–0.

Umpires: C. Cook and J. H. Harris.

At Northampton, July 30, August 1, 2. WORCESTERSHIRE lost to NORTHAMPTON-SHIRE by seven wickets.

At Canterbury, August 6, 8, 9. WORCESTERSHIRE drew with KENT.

WORCESTERSHIRE v LANCASHIRE

At Worcester, August 10, 11, 12. Worcestershire won by five wickets. Worcestershire 21 pts, Lancashire 6 pts. Worcestershire achieved their first Championship win of the season in their seventeenth match, being steered home in dogged fashion by Ormrod, who batted 280 minutes in the final three sessions for a match-winning 72 not out. On a pitch which remained awkward to the end, Worcestershire's victory target of 207 was still a long way off as they stumbled to 110 for four, but Curtis helped Ormrod add 45 for the fifth wicket and Humphries cracked an unbeaten 32 to clinch their first home win for over a year.

Lancashire

D. Lloyd b Ellcock	11	– b Ellcock	78
S. J. O'Shaughnessy c Ellcock b Pridgeon	12	– lbw b Pridgeon	0
J. Abrahams c Neale b Patel	34	– b Patel	17
*C. H. Lloyd lbw b Patel	84	– c Pridgeon b Patel	0
D. P. Hughes b Patel	10	– c Curtis b Patel	0
N. H. Fairbrother lbw b Patel	26	– lbw b Patel	51
†C. Maynard c Humphries b Pridgeon	13	– b Ellcock	0
J. Simmons lbw b Pridgeon	2	– lbw b Ellcock	3
M. Watkinson c Patel b Pridgeon	3	– not out	19
P. J. W. Allott lbw b Pridgeon	0	– c Humphries b Pridgeon	13
L. L. McFarlane not out	1	– c Neale b Patel	0
B 4, l-b 8, n-b 1	13	B 1, l-b 10, n-b 4	15

1/16 2/41 3/77 4/110   209   1/1 2/83 3/91 4/91   196
5/179 6/202 7/205 8/206 9/208   5/119 6/119 7/129 8/168 9/191

Bonus points – Lancashire 2, Worcestershire 4.

Bowling: *First Innings*—Ellcock 12–3–32–1; Pridgeon 15.5–9–21–5; Perryman 8–1–28–0; Patel 27–11–54–4; Illingworth 13–3–43–0; D'Oliveira 5–1–18–0. *Second Innings*—Pridgeon 12–0–47–2; Ellcock 15–0–60–3; Patel 22.3–8–52–5; Perryman 6–1–22–0.

Worcestershire

J. A. Ormrod c O'Shaughnessy b D. Lloyd	30	– not out	72
M. S. A. McEvoy c D. Lloyd b Simmons	49	– c C. H. Lloyd b McFarlane	12
*P. A. Neale b Simmons	4	– c and b O'Shaughnessy	39
A. P. Pridgeon c Hughes b Allott	1		
D. N. Patel b Allott	24	– (4) b Watkinson	2
D. B. D'Oliveira c C. H. Lloyd b Allott	0	– (5) lbw b O'Shaughnessy	5
T. S. Curtis c D. Lloyd b Simmons	32	– (6) lbw b Allott	27
†D. J. Humphries c Simmons b D. Lloyd	32	– (7) not out	32
R. K. Illingworth b Simmons	7		
R. M. Ellcock lbw b Simmons	13		
S. P. Perryman not out	2		
B 5	5	B 8, l-b 5, n-b 5	18

1/74 2/84 3/84 4/98   199   1/14 2/102 3/104   (5 wkts) 207
5/98 6/115 7/169 8/173 9/190   4/110 5/155

Bonus points – Worcestershire 1, Lancashire 4.

Bowling: *First Innings*—Allott 18–4–51–3; McFarlane 7–0–45–0; O'Shaughnessy 3–1–13–0; Watkinson 1–0–8–0; Simmons 23.5–8–55–5; D. Lloyd 11–3–22–2. *Second Innings* —Allott 14–2–43–1; McFarlane 11–1–35–1; Simmons 15–4–30–0; Watkinson 15–4–37–1; D. Lloyd 7–2–11–0; O'Shaughnessy 6–2–21–2; Abrahams 3–0–12–0.

Umpires: B. Leadbeater and R. A. White.

At Guildford, August 13, 15, 16. WORCESTERSHIRE lost to SURREY by 227 runs.

WORCESTERSHIRE v HAMPSHIRE

At Worcester, August 20, 22, 23. Hampshire won by an innings and 44 runs. Hampshire 24 pts, Worcestershire 4 pts. Worcestershire suffered their seventh defeat in ten games after another very poor batting display. They lost their last seven first-innings wickets for 115 runs, and, after following on, their last eight second-innings wickets for just 90. The only stern resistance came from Curtis, who batted for 140 minutes in the first innings and 156 minutes in the second, though Ellcock hit four 6s of Smith's off-spin in a career-best 36. On the first day Greenidge hit a 6 and eleven 4s in his spectacular 95.

Hampshire

C. G. Greenidge st Humphries		
b Illingworth.	95	
C. L. Smith c McEvoy b Perryman	26	
M. C. J. Nicholas c Perryman		
b Illingworth.	27	
T. E. Jesty c D'Oliveira b Illingworth..	27	
V. P. Terry lbw b Perryman	17	
*N. E. J. Pocock st Humphries		
b Illingworth.	57	

M. D. Marshall c Ormrod b Perryman.	37
N. G. Cowley c and b Perryman.........	10
T. M. Tremlett lbw b Ellcock.............	10
†R. J. Parks lbw b Pridgeon	39
S. J. Malone not out	7
B 4, l-b 8, w 1........................	13
	365

1/44 2/131 3/158 4/191
5/203 6/274 7/300 8/306 9/330

Bonus points – Hampshire 4, Worcestershire 3 (Score at 100 overs: 313–8).

Bowling: Ellcock 19–5–80–1; Pridgeon 23.3–4–77–1; Perryman 32–6–91–4; Illingworth 35–7–104–4.

Worcestershire

J. A. Ormrod c Parks b Marshall....................	2	– lbw b Marshall	6
M. S. A. McEvoy c Pocock b Malone.............	4	– lbw b Marshall	22
*P. A. Neale retired hurt	10	– (7) lbw b Nicholas....................	2
D. N. Patel b Malone	12	– (3) c Tremlett b Marshall	21
T. S. Curtis c sub b Smith	46	– (4) not out	16
D. B. D'Oliveira b Cowley	11	– (5) c Pocock b Nicholas	19
†D. J. Humphries c Pocock b Smith	11	– (6) c Pocock b Nicholas	0
R. K. Illingworth not out	9	– c Tremlett b Cowley.................	9
R. M. Ellcock c Terry b Cowley	36	– lbw b Cowley	2
S. P. Perryman run out	0	– b Cowley................................	1
A. P. Pridgeon c Terry b Cowley....................	22	– st Parks b Cowley....................	23
B 3, l-b 5, n-b 4...................	12	B 16, l-b 4, w 3, n-b 2	25

1/2 2/20 3/60 4/83   175   1/15 2/56 3/61 4/93   146
5/101 6/104 7/147 8/147 9/175   5/93 6/95 7/108 8/112 9/118

Bonus points – Worcestershire 1, Hampshire 4.

Bowling: *First Innings*—Marshall 13–3–34–1; Malone 13–3–35–2; Tremlett 13–7–22–0; Cowley 22.5–11–26–3; Smith 11–5–39–2; Pocock 2–0–7–0. *Second Innings*—Marshall 19–10–24–3; Malone 11–6–23–0; Tremlett 5–1–16–0; Nicholas 14–8–20–3; Cowley 14.5–3–38–4.

Umpires: D. O. Oslear and R. Julian.

At Colchester, August 24, 25. WORCESTERSHIRE lost to ESSEX by an innings and 58 runs.

At Birmingham, August 27, 29, 30. WORCESTERSHIRE drew with WARWICKSHIRE.

At Bristol, August 31, September 1, 2. WORCESTERSHIRE drew with GLOUCESTER-SHIRE.

WORCESTERSHIRE v GLOUCESTERSHIRE

At Worcester, September 7, 8, 9. Worcestershire won by 108 runs. Worcestershire 18 pts, Gloucestershire 3 pts. With the second day washed out, it required two declarations to fashion a finish, with Worcestershire leaving their opponents to score 264 in 186 minutes. After reaching 109 for two they collapsed to the spin of Illingworth and Patel. Patel's 111 in Worcestershire's first innings was his third century at Worcester in eleven innings and boosted his aggregate in a month to 636.

Worcestershire

J. A. Ormrod lbw b Sainsbury	8	– b Cunningham	23
M. S. A. McEvoy lbw b Sainsbury	11	– c Cunningham b Bainbridge	51
*P. A. Neale c Russell b Sainsbury	14		
D. N. Patel c Cunningham b Graveney	111		
T. S. Curtis lbw b Sainsbury	25	– (3) lbw b Cunningham	0
D. B. D'Oliveira lbw b Childs	8	– (4) not out	43
P. J. Newport st Russell b Childs	25		
†D. J. Humphries c and b Graveney	12	– (5) not out	17
R. M. Ellcock lbw b Sainsbury	16		
R. K. Illingworth not out	3		
A. P. Pridgeon b Sainsbury	4		
B 1, l-b 9	10	B 1, l-b 2	3

1/11 2/25 3/40 4/116   247   1/59 2/71 3/75   (3 wkts dec.) 137
5/129 6/200 7/216 8/224 9/243

Bonus points – Worcestershire 2, Gloucestershire 3 (Score at 100 overs: 238-8).

Bowling: *First Innings*—Shepherd 13–6–33–0; Sainsbury 23.3–6–66–6; Graveney 30–15–47–2; Childs 36–18–64–2; Bainbridge 3–1–27–0. *Second Innings*—Sainsbury 6–1–14–0; Shepherd 5–1–16–0; Cunningham 11–2–55–2; Childs 4–1–6–0; Bainbridge 7–0–43–1.

Gloucestershire

A. W. Stovold not out	51	– c and b Illingworth	66
P. W. Romaines c McEvoy b Illingworth	25	– b Ellcock	0
P. Bainbridge not out	41	– b Ellcock	7
A. J. Wright (did not bat)		– st Humphries b Patel	27
E. J. Cunningham (did not bat)		– c Curtis b Illingworth	1
J. N. Shepherd (did not bat)		– b Illingworth	24
*D. A. Graveney (did not bat)		– b Patel	3
R. J. Doughty (did not bat)		– b Illingworth	0
†R. C. Russell (did not bat)		– not out	13
J. H. Childs (did not bat)		– b Patel	0
G. E. Sainsbury (did not bat)		– c Humphries b Illingworth	0
L-b 2, n-b 2	4	B 4, l-b 4, n-b 6	14

1/60   (1 wkt dec.) 121   1/1 2/27 3/109 4/109   155
                            5/120 6/141 7/141 8/147 9/155

Bowling: *First Innings*—Ellcock 5–0–27–0; Pridgeon 4–1–9–0; Patel 18–5–38–0; Illingworth 18–7–43–1. *Second Innings*—Ellcock 5–0–32–2; Pridgeon 6–1–29–0; Illingworth 20.1–11–26–5; Patel 19–6–42–3; D'Oliveira 5–2–12–0.

Umpires: A. G. T. Whitehead and P. B. Wight.

WORCESTERSHIRE v SUSSEX

At Worcester, September 10, 12, 13. Drawn. Worcestershire 2 pts, Sussex 6 pts. The weather wrecked Worcestershire's final game of the season, causing the loss of 260 minutes on the first two days and washing out the third. On the second afternoon Sussex bowled 67.2 overs to improve their season's over-rate.

Sussex

G. D. Mendis not out	133	– c McEvoy b Pridgeon	7
A. M. Green c Humphries b Pridgeon	16	– b Inchmore	5
D. K. Standing c McEvoy b Illingworth	60	– not out	22
Imran Khan (did not bat)		– not out	43
L-b 10, n-b 2	12	N-b 2	2

1/43 2/221   (2 wkts dec.) 221   1/12 2/17   (2 wkts) 79

*P. W. G. Parker, C. M. Wells, I. A. Greig, †I. J. Gould, A. C. S. Pigott, D. A. Reeve and C. E. Waller did not bat.

Bonus points – Sussex 2.

Bowling: *First Innings*—Pridgeon 24–6–54–1; Inchmore 20–1–68–0; Illingworth 20–5–40–1; Newport 11–0–28–0; Patel 9–2–19–0. *Second Innings*—Pridgeon 10–2–30–1; Inchmore 6.1–1–20–1; Illingworth 8–5–7–0; Newport 4–0–20–0.

Worcestershire

J. A. Ormrod c Pigott b Reeve	5	R. K. Illingworth lbw b Reeve	2
M. S. A. McEvoy c and b Greig	30	J. D. Inchmore c Gould b Waller	12
*P. A. Neale c Pigott b Reeve	3	A. P. Pridgeon not out	3
D. N. Patel b Greig	53	B 5, l-b 4, w 1, n-b 2	12
D. B. D'Oliveira b Waller	23		
D. A. Banks run out	44	1/9 2/21 3/90	221
P. J. Newport c Standing b Greig	4	4/103 5/133 6/154	
†D. J. Humphries c Pigott b Reeve	30	7/178 8/206 9/211	

Bonus points – Worcestershire 2, Sussex 4.

Bowling: Pigott 6–0–20–0; Reeve 14–6–15–4; Greig 33–6–104–3; Waller 38.2–17–70–2.

Umpires: M. J. Kitchen and D. O. Oslear.

WHITBREAD SCHOLARSHIPS

The Whitbread Brewery Scholarships, first awarded in 1976, were instituted to help young cricketers further their experience by playing for a season in Australia. Scholarships have been awarded to the following:

1976-77: C. W. J. Athey (Yorkshire), I. T. Botham (Somerset), M. W. Gatting (Middlesex), G. B. Stevenson (Yorkshire).

1977-78: C. S. Cowdrey (Kent), J. E. Emburey (Middlesex), J. A. Hopkins (Glamorgan), J. D. Love (Yorkshire).

1978-79: J. P. Agnew (Leicestershire), M. W. Gatting (Middlesex), W. Larkins (Northamptonshire), C. J. Tavaré (Kent).

1979-80: K. J. Barnett (Derbyshire), D. N. Patel (Worcestershire), A. C. S. Pigott (Sussex), R. G. Williams (Northamptonshire).

1980-81: N. G. B. Cook (Leicestershire), W. Hogg (Lancashire), D. M. Smith (Surrey).

1981-82: M. R. Benson (Kent), N. A. Foster (Essex), P. G. Newman (Derbyshire).

1982-83: D. J. Capel (Northamptonshire), R. K. Illingworth (Worcestershire), C. Penn (Kent), D. J. Thomas (Surrey).

1983-84: D. G. Aslett (Kent), D. B. D'Oliveira (Worcestershire).

ESSO SCHOLARSHIPS

The four young Australian cricketers who received Esso Scholarships to play in England in 1983 were: M. D. Haysman (South Australia, to Leicestershire), M. G. Hughes (Victoria, to Essex), R. B. Kerr (Queensland, to Nottinghamshire), G. R. J. Matthews (New South Wales, to Worcestershire).

YORKSHIRE

Patron: HRH The Duchess of Kent
President: N. W. D. Yardley
Chairman: M. G. Crawford
Secretary: J. Lister
   Headingley Cricket Ground, Leeds LS6 3BU
   (Telephone: 0532-787394)
Cricket Manager: R. Illingworth
Captain: 1983 – R. Illingworth; 1984 –
   D. L. Bairstow

Yorkshire's satisfaction at winning the John Player Sunday League, their first major trophy for fourteen years, was more than counterbalanced by the embarrassment of finishing at the foot of the Schweppes County Championship table and by the row which followed the sacking at the end of the season of Geoff Boycott.

The county's leading batsman was sacrificed to a youth policy which was the committee's answer to their drop from tenth place in the major competition, and the position was further complicated when Bill Athey refused a new contract and left to join Gloucestershire.

The pro-Boycott campaigners forced Yorkshire to reconsider their decision, made by eighteen committee votes to seven, but despite threats of action by members of the county club, a second committee meeting brought a comparable vote, thus setting the stage for what seemed likely to be a long and bitter winter.

The committee also made other significant moves, switching Ray Illingworth back to the role of manager and giving the captaincy to the enthusiastic David Bairstow. In the final analysis it was difficult to see how dispensing with Boycott, who, in any case, had been given a testimonial in 1984, could help to change a pattern of events which had brought Yorkshire a series of unwanted records.

Not since 1866 had they won only one Championship victory (as they did in 1983) and then, anyway, they completed only three fixtures. They also plumbed new depths by failing to win a home Championship match, and four consecutive defeats in mid-summer represented their worst run since 1947.

Additionally, Yorkshire failed miserably in the knockout competitions, being outplayed in the qualifying stages of the Benson and Hedges Cup and losing in the second round of the NatWest Bank Trophy after beating minor opposition in the first round. Basically, the bowlers carried the heavier responsibility for a depressing campaign. Usually, despite some dramatic batting collapses, there would have been sufficient runs to serve the purposes of an efficient team in the field.

The biggest disappointment was the fast bowler, Alan Ramage, who again broke down with injury and did not fulfil any of his obvious potential. Graham Stevenson struggled with a persistent back strain which limited his effectiveness and Arnie Sidebottom had sore shins. Among the younger medium-paced bowlers, the highly regarded Paul Jarvis suffered

similarly and lacked the accuracy which marked his work in 1982, while
Nick Taylor, son of Ken Taylor, the former Yorkshire player, fell short
of expectations through failing to find an effective rhythm.

In the circumstances, Simon Dennis emerged as the best of the quicker
bowlers. He was awarded his county cap. Even he, however, lacked the
extra yard of pace to be consistently dangerous. Thus, on a series of low,
slow pitches that made many games dull affairs, Yorkshire were not
equipped to bowl sides out, a state of affairs which made it difficult for
Illingworth to gamble with challenging declarations. Criticised for being
too cautious, Illingworth had to bear in mind his side's vulnerability under
pressure. Together with Phil Carrick, however, and even at 51, he formed
a steady spin partnership which contributed crucially to the winning of the
Sunday League. Indeed, the captain was comfortably the most successful
Sunday bowler, with twenty wickets for 259 runs in seventy-six overs. He
was fortunate with the toss on eleven Sundays out of fourteen – two
matches were abandoned without any play – and he pursued a policy of
containment by putting in the opposition. This worked pretty well,
although problems were highlighted when Boycott had to fill a key
bowling role.

Boycott also remained, in all cricket, much the most reliable batsman,
though as at Cheltenham, where he was reprimanded for it, he did not
always make his runs quickly enough. He and Athey were reminded of
the need to fit their innings into a satisfactory collective framework,
Boycott being left out of the side early in the Sunday programme in an
attempt to bring about more positive starts to the innings. This proved a
short-lived experiment.

Athey sought his release at the end of a poor season. He headed the
Sunday League averages, but scored only 758 Championship runs and did
not complete a century. Neither did Jim Love, despite topping 1,000 runs.
Bairstow was the most successful batsman after Boycott, becoming the
first specialist Yorkshire wicket-keeper to reach 1,000 runs twice.

Looking ahead, Martyn Moxon, who could not claim a place until July,
confirmed that he is a batsman of exceptional skill and a wide range of
strokes. His inclusion on a regular basis came at the expense of Richard
Lumb. Further competition is likely to be provided by Ashley Metcalfe.
A nineteen-year-old from Farsley in the Bradford League, Metcalfe
marked his first-class début with a Championship century against
Nottinghamshire and demonstrated a willingness to hit the ball hard. The
committee's plans to bring Neil Hartley gradually to the captaincy were
upset when he had to step back into the second team in a bid to find form
and confidence. He eventually gave way to Kevin Sharp, who overcame
some uncertainties to collect two centuries.

Any hope of a meaningful Yorkshire revival depends on their bowlers.
Stevenson has ability, Sidebottom is sometimes very hostile and Dennis
displays real persistence. It is unlikely, though, that this trio will become
a sufficiently destructive force to bring Yorkshire back to prominence. So
long as the club adheres to the estimable tradition of relying on players
born within the county they may find it difficult to challenge for the
Championship. – J.C.

YORKSHIRE 1983

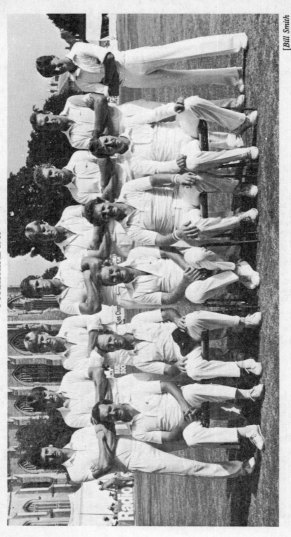

[Bill Smith

Back row: S. N. Hartley, M. D. Moxon, S. J. Dennis, N. S. Taylor, J. D. Love, K. Sharp, C. W. J. Athey, I. G. Swallow. Front row: P. Carrick, G. Boycott, R. Illingworth (captain), D. L. Bairstow, G. B. Stevenson.

YORKSHIRE RESULTS

All first-class matches – Played 23: Won 1, Lost 5, Drawn 17.

County Championship matches – Played 23: Won 1, Lost 5, Drawn 17.

Bonus points – Batting 45, Bowling 64.

Competition placings – Schweppes County Championship, 17th; NatWest Bank Trophy, 2nd round; Benson and Hedges Cup, 5th in Group B; John Player League, winners.

COUNTY CHAMPIONSHIP AVERAGES

BATTING

	Birthplace	M	I	NO	R	HI	Avge
G. Boycottc............	Fitzwilliam	23	40	5	1,941	214*	55.45
D. L. Bairstowc......	Bradford	23	35	6	1,102	100*	38.00
A. Sidebottomc.......	Barnsley	16	21	7	490	78	35.00
M. D. Moxon	Barnsley	12	23	0	780	153	33.91
J. D. Lovec............	Leeds	23	38	7	1,020	76*	32.90
K. Sharpc.............	Leeds	12	21	1	597	139	29.85
P. Carrickc............	Leeds	23	32	8	697	83	29.04
C. W. J. Atheyc......	Middlesbrough	20	32	1	758	90	24.45
R. G. Lumbc........	Doncaster	10	15	1	328	60	23.42
G. B. Stevensonc.....	Ackworth	20	25	1	396	52	16.50
S. N. Hartleyc........	Shipley	14	19	1	261	69	14.50
S. D. Fletcher	Keighley	3	4	2	14	12	7.00
R. Illingworthc.......	Pudsey	21	16	4	71	16	5.91
S. J. Dennisc	Scarborough	20	23	8	71	17	4.73
N. S. Taylor	Holmfirth	4	5	0	10	4	2.00

Also batted: P. A. Booth (*Huddersfield*) (1 match) 0, 0; P. W. Jarvis (*Redcar*) (2 matches) 5*, 1*, 11*; A. A. Metcalfe (*Horsforth*) (1 match) 122, 7; A. Ramage (*Guisborough*) (3 matches) 32, 0*, 14; I. G. Swallow (*Barnsley*) (2 matches) 4, 11*, 4*.

*Signifies not out.   cDenotes county cap.

BOWLING

	O	M	R	W	Avge	BB
G. B. Stevenson......	460.1	103	1,400	56	25.00	5-35
A. Sidebottom	361	81	1,080	39	27.69	5-6
P. Carrick	848.1	303	1,750	62	28.22	7-44
R. Illingworth	411.5	137	951	32	29.71	4-48
N. S. Taylor	111.1	23	427	14	30.50	5-49
S. J. Dennis............	525.2	119	1,600	52	30.76	4-32

Also bowled: C. W. J. Athey 38–8–110–3; D. L. Bairstow 10–4–27–1; P. A. Booth 17–3–50–0; G. Boycott 23–10–45–1; S. D. Fletcher 55.4–7–186–8; S. N. Hartley 15–4–40–1; P. W. Jarvis 44–8–155–3; J. D. Love 22–5–89–1; A. A. Metcalfe 2–0–6–0; M. D. Moxon 33–3–123–1; A. Ramage 39–4–145–2; I. G. Swallow 29.4–8–82–2.

The following played a total of twelve three-figure innings for Yorkshire in County Championship matches – G. Boycott 7, K. Sharp 2, D. L. Bairstow 1, A. A. Metcalfe 1, M. D. Moxon 1.

At Worcester, April 30, May 1, 2. YORKSHIRE drew with WORCESTERSHIRE.

YORKSHIRE v WARWICKSHIRE

At Leeds, May 4, 5, 6. Drawn. Only two and a quarter hours' play was possible on the second day and neither side had the chance to make a positive move as the game drifted along under threatening skies.

Yorkshire

G. Boycott b Ferreira	28
R. G. Lumb not out	29
G. B. Stevenson not out	0
L-b 3, n-b 1	4

1/55   (1 wkt) 61

C. W. J. Athey, J. D. Love, S. N. Hartley, †D. L. Bairstow, P. Carrick, A. Sidebottom, *R. Illingworth and S. J. Dennis did not bat.

Bowling: Hogg 4–2–3–0; Old 12–6–17–0; Ferreira 17.4–11–17–1; Lethbridge 9–2–20–0.

Warwickshire

T. A. Lloyd, K. D. Smith, *D. L. Amiss, A. I. Kallicharran, G. W. Humpage, A. M. Ferreira, †G. A. Tedstone, C. Lethbridge, C. M. Old, Asif Din and W. Hogg.

Umpires: H. D. Bird and R. Julian.

At Lord's, May 11, 12, 13. MIDDLESEX v YORKSHIRE. Abandoned.

YORKSHIRE v NORTHAMPTONSHIRE

At Bradford, May 25, 26, 27. Drawn. Yorkshire 5 pts, Northamptonshire 7 pts. A resourceful partnership of 127 from 31 overs between Williams and Kapil Dev rescued Northamptonshire on a slow wicket. Carrick bowled steadily but not so effectively as Steele, who found sufficient turn to confuse most of the Yorkshire batsmen. Sidebottom and Ramage put on 55 from seventeen overs for the last wicket to prevent total humiliation, and then Williams hit a 6 and sixteen 4s in a 166-minute century to put the visitors in total control before rain washed out the last day.

Northamptonshire

*G. Cook b Ramage	20	– lbw b Stevenson	9
W. Larkins c Sidebottom b Stevenson	13	– c Bairstow b Stevenson	6
P. Willey c Boycott b Ramage	5	– lbw b Illingworth	12
A. J. Lamb c Boycott b Sidebottom	7	– c Bairstow b Sidebottom	15
R. G. Williams c Lumb b Carrick	59	– not out	104
Kapil Dev c Bairstow b Carrick	81	– lbw b Stevenson	29
D. J. Capel c Boycott b Carrick	1	– st Bairstow b Carrick	24
D. S. Steele c Carrick	12	– b Illingworth	0
†G. Sharp b Illingworth	36	– not out	1
T. M. Lamb c Boycott b Carrick	3		
B. J. Griffiths not out	5		
B 1, l-b 7, w 1, n-b 6	15	B 3, l-b 4, w 6, n-b 5	18

1/33 2/37 3/46 4/61   257   1/19 2/22 3/48   (7 wkts) 218
5/188 6/196 7/197 8/218 9/232   4/93 5/126 6/203 7/212

Bonus points – Northamptonshire 3, Yorkshire 4.

Bowling: *First Innings*—Ramage 13–0–67–2; Stevenson 19–2–43–1; Sidebottom 22–4–70–1; Carrick 30–11–54–5; Illingworth 2.5–0–8–1. *Second Innings*—Stevenson 14–2–44–3; Ramage 13–3–32–0; Sidebottom 7–0–40–1; Carrick 19–11–32–1; Illingworth 16–7–38–2; Love 7–3–14–0.

Yorkshire

G. Boycott b Steele	7	A. Sidebottom not out	30
R. G. Lumb lbw b Kapil Dev	13	*R. Illingworth b Steele	5
C. W. J. Athey hit wkt b Steele	2	A. Ramage lbw b Steele	32
S. N. Hartley b Kapil Dev	0	B 4, l-b 2, n-b 3	9
J. D. Love c Cook b Griffiths	4		
†D. L. Bairstow lbw b Griffiths	30	1/18 2/22 3/25	157
G. B. Stevenson b Steele	19	4/26 5/37 6/66	
P. Carrick b Willey	6	7/88 8/90 9/102	

Bonus points – Yorkshire 1, Northamptonshire 4.

Bowling: Kapil Dev 19–6–33–2; Griffiths 17–5–34–2; Steele 24–6–48–5; Willey 13–6–33–1.

Umpires: C. T. Spencer and J. Birkenshaw.

At Manchester, May 28, 30, 31. YORKSHIRE drew with LANCASHIRE.

YORKSHIRE v GLAMORGAN

At Middlesbrough, June 4, 6, 7. Drawn. Yorkshire 2 pts, Glamorgan 6 pts. Ontong, badly missed by Boycott at slip when 33, dominated a slow first day. The pitch made strokeplay difficult but it did not account for a dreadful display by Yorkshire, who surrendered to straightforward length-and-line bowling by Selvey. A second-innings revival raised doubts as to whether Selvey had been wise to enforce the follow-on and Glamorgan, set a target of 245 in 160 minutes, had to struggle. Alan Jones played well and Derrick defied a leg injury to stand firm in the last hour.

Glamorgan

A. Jones b Dennis	18	– c Lumb b Carrick	87
J. A. Hopkins c Bairstow b Dennis	29	– c Bairstow b Stevenson	9
D. A. Francis c Bairstow b Sidebottom	11	– b Illingworth	17
A. L. Jones st Bairstow b Athey	3	– b Dennis	15
R. C. Ontong lbw b Dennis	112	– c Athey b Sidebottom	13
J. Derrick c Lumb b Illingworth	19	– (8) not out	5
J. G. Thomas b Dennis	23	– (6) run out	0
†E. W. Jones not out	32	– (7) c Bairstow b Stevenson	0
*M. W. W. Selvey c Bairstow b Stevenson	1		
B. J. Lloyd b Carrick	24	– (9) not out	6
S. R. Barwick not out	0		
B 1, l-b 5, n-b 11	17	B 4, l-b 1, n-b 5	10

1/30 2/50 3/53 4/93   (9 wkts dec.) 289   1/29 2/83 3/118 4/145   (7 wkts) 162
5/171 6/229 7/231 8/232 9/271   5/145 6/148 7/150

Bonus points – Glamorgan 2, Yorkshire 2 (Score at 100 overs: 209-5).

Bowling: *First Innings*—Dennis 25–10–54–4; Stevenson 23–9–43–1; Athey 12–4–25–1; Sidebottom 22–1–70–1; Carrick 30–12–59–1; Illingworth 12–4–21–1. *Second Innings*—Dennis 8–0–48–1; Stevenson 9–1–24–2; Sidebottom 14–4–48–1; Illingworth 10–4–27–1; Carrick 7–6–5–1.

Yorkshire

G. Boycott b Thomas	8	– c Derrick b Lloyd	69
R. G. Lumb b Thomas	9	– c Francis b Lloyd	56
C. W. J. Athey c E. W. Jones b Selvey	25	– c Francis b Lloyd	77
S. N. Hartley lbw b Selvey	0	– c Derrick b Lloyd	39
J. D. Love c E. W. Jones b Ontong	24	– not out	76
†D. L. Bairstow c Derrick b Selvey	0	– not out	75
P. Carrick run out	12		
A. Sidebottom b Selvey	40		
G. B. Stevenson c A. L. Jones b Ontong	0		
*R. Illingworth lbw b Selvey	1		
S. J. Dennis not out	0		
B 1, n-b 5	6	B 2, l-b 3, n-b 11	16

1/21 2/22 3/38 4/59　　　　　　　125　　1/127 2/134 3/219　(4 wkts dec.) 408
5/59 6/81 7/102 8/107 9/116　　　　　　4/274

Bonus points – Glamorgan 4.

Bowling: *First Innings*—Barwick 4–0–24–0; Thomas 10–2–25–2; Selvey 20–6–37–5; Ontong 19–7–33–2. *Second Innings*—Thomas 16.4–5–47–0; Ontong 19–6–37–0; Lloyd 47–8–132–4; Barwick 23–5–85–0; Selvey 29–9–74–0; Derrick 4–1–17–0.

Umpires: D. G. L. Evans and M. J. Kitchen.

At Leicester, June 8, 9, 10. YORKSHIRE drew with LEICESTERSHIRE.

At Southampton, June 18, 20, 21. YORKSHIRE beat HAMPSHIRE by four wickets.

YORKSHIRE v DERBYSHIRE

At Sheffield, June 22, 23, 24. Derbyshire won by 22 runs. Derbyshire 22 pts, Yorkshire 4 pts. Derbyshire gained their first victory over Yorkshire since 1957 by coping skilfully with a pitch reported as being sub-standard. Uneven bounce and considerable help for the spinners made batting difficult, but Barnett, hitting eleven boundaries, chanced his arm to notable effect. Yorkshire collapsed against hostile bowling from Mortensen, who made the ball lift unpleasantly, but their own seamers fared badly, bowling too short and wide. Morris hit out bravely and Yorkshire were set a formidable target. Boycott who carried his bat through a completed innings for the sixth time for Yorkshire, played brilliantly, making the most of some errors by Moir, who was not at his best, but the support was patchy and Boycott alone could not prevent defeat.

Derbyshire

I. S. Anderson c Lumb b Sidebottom	14	– (2) c Stevenson b Carrick	4
J. E. Morris c Bairstow b Stevenson	0	– (1) c Love b Carrick	58
A. Hill b Stevenson	12	– c Love b Stevenson	4
*K. J. Barnett b Carrick	95	– st Bairstow b Carrick	2
R. J. Finney c Boycott b Carrick	23	– (7) lbw b Carrick	14
G. Miller c Athey b Illingworth	4	– c Boycott b Carrick	2
W. P. Fowler c Bairstow b Stevenson	16	– (5) b Stevenson	8
C. J. Tunnicliffe c Bairstow b Carrick	18	– b Dennis	21
†R. W. Taylor not out	13	– not out	33
D. G. Moir c Athey b Carrick	0	– c Boycott b Carrick	0
O. H. Mortensen c and b Carrick	2	– c and b Carrick	0
B 3, l-b 13, w 6, n-b 6	28	L-b 2	2

1/1 2/28 3/50 4/141　　　　　　　225　　1/23 2/28 3/47 4/76　　　　　148
5/146 6/180 7/180 8/220 9/220　　　　5/79 6/90 7/94 8/145 9/146

Bonus points – Derbyshire 2, Yorkshire 4.

Bowling: *First Innings*—Dennis 10–3–24–0; Stevenson 15–5–44–3; Sidebottom 16–3–32–1; Carrick 23.4–8–45–5; Illingworth 14–2–52–1. *Second Innings*—Dennis 8–1–37–1; Stevenson 13–1–65–2; Carrick 18–7–44–7.

Yorkshire

G. Boycott c Anderson b Moir	33	– not out	112
R. G. Lumb lbw b Mortensen	28	– c Miller b Moir	0
C. W. J. Athey c Taylor b Moir	0	– st Taylor b Moir	12
S. N. Hartley c Moir b Mortensen	2	– lbw b Mortensen	4
J. D. Love c Taylor b Moir	3	– c Hill b Mortensen	8
S. J. Dennis c Taylor b Mortensen	0	– (11) c Fowler b Mortensen	17
†D. L. Bairstow c Taylor b Moir	4	– (6) b Moir	44
G. B. Stevenson c Taylor b Mortensen	3	– (9) c Fowler b Mortensen	3
P. Carrick b Mortensen	15	– (7) b Mortensen	1
A. Sidebottom c Taylor b Mortensen	7	– (8) b Moir	19
*R. Illingworth not out	12	– (10) b Moir	0
B 2, l-b 4, n-b 5	11	L-b 5, w 5, n-b 3	13
	118		**233**

1/63 2/63 3/69 4/72   1/9 2/21 3/34 4/52
5/72 6/76 7/78 8/79 9/91   5/142 6/157 7/192 8/197 9/198

Bonus points – Derbyshire 4.

Bowling: *First Innings*—Mortensen 16.4–5–27–6; Tunnicliffe 10–2–23–0; Moir 17–6–45–4; Fowler 3–0–12–0. *Second Innings*—Mortensen 24.1–3–62–5; Tunnicliffe 11–2–37–0; Moir 34–7–114–5; Miller 1–0–7–0.

Umpires: R. Julian and M. J. Kitchen.

At Birmingham, June 25, 27, 28. YORKSHIRE lost to WARWICKSHIRE by one wicket.

YORKSHIRE v LEICESTERSHIRE

At Harrogate, July 2, 4, 5. Leicestershire won by 89 runs. Leicestershire 23 pts, Yorkshire 4 pts. Leicestershire, who won in Yorkshire for the first time since 1948, dominated throughout on a pitch which gave a little assistance to the bowlers but was slow. A fast outfield, however, enabled the batsmen to maintain a reasonable rate, with Davison and Briers driving fluently. Yorkshire, batting badly, surrendered a substantial first-innings lead, and when Leicestershire batted a second time, only Dennis, who took three wickets for 16 in a fourteen-ball burst, held up their progress. A generous declaration set Yorkshire a target of 296 in 215 minutes and, although handicapped by a painful ankle injury, Ferris proved too much for the batsmen, who found various ways of getting out. Bairstow hit 50 in each innings of a Championship match for the first time but could not turn the tide.

Leicestershire

J. C. Balderstone lbw b Sidebottom	30	– run out	44
I. P. Butcher c Bairstow b Dennis	66	– b Dennis	44
D. I. Gower b Dennis	4	– c Boycott b Dennis	1
B. F. Davison c Bairstow b Dennis	81	– b Dennis	1
N. E. Briers b Stevenson	97	– not out	55
*†R. W. Tolchard c Illingworth b Sidebottom	3	– c Boycott b Sidebottom	27
P. B. Clift c Carrick b Illingworth	22		
J. F. Steele not out	15		
N. G. B. Cook not out	7		
B 8, l-b 7, w 3, n-b 9	27	L-b 9, w 2, n-b 11	22

1/92 2/103 3/112 4/245	(7 wkts dec.) 352	1/74 2/80 (5 wkts dec.) 194
5/258 6/303 7/341		3/88 4/130 5/194

G. J. F. Ferris and L. B. Taylor did not bat.

Bonus points – Leicestershire 4, Yorkshire 2 (Score at 100 overs: 322-6).

Bowling: *First Innings*—Dennis 30–6–92–3; Stevenson 21–4–63–1; Boycott 6–1–18–0; Sidebottom 25–3–73–2; Illingworth 10–2–38–1; Carrick 13–2–41–0. *Second Innings*—Stevenson 14–2–47–0; Dennis 18–2–66–3; Sidebottom 11.5–2–45–1; Carrick 7–1–14–0.

Yorkshire

G. Boycott c Tolchard b Taylor	16	– lbw b Clift	22
M. D. Moxon lbw b Clift	20	– run out	28
C. W. J. Athey lbw b Ferris	27	– c Gower b Clift	1
S. N. Hartley c Davison b Clift	2	– c Ferris b Clift	9
J. D. Love c Davison b Steele	53	– c Balderstone b Ferris	25
†D. L. Bairstow lbw b Taylor	50	– c Steele b Ferris	57
P. Carrick b Clift	15	– c Tolchard b Clift	26
A. Sidebottom not out	35	– lbw b Ferris	0
G. B. Stevenson c sub b Cook	16	– c Taylor b Ferris	27
S. J. Dennis c Gower b Taylor	1	– not out	0
*R. Illingworth absent ill		– absent ill	
B 1, l-b 11, n-b 4	16	B 1, l-b 4, w 2, n-b 4	11

1/26 2/55 3/59 4/100	251	1/48 2/54 3/63 4/66 206
5/134 6/170 7/209 8/235 9/251		5/137 6/154 7/154 8/200 9/206

Bonus points – Yorkshire 2, Leicestershire 3 (Score at 100 overs: 246-8).

Bowling: *First Innings*—Taylor 21.1–8–59–3; Ferris 19–6–61–1; Cook 33–18–35–1; Clift 21–2–52–3; Steele 8–3–28–1. *Second Innings*—Ferris 16.4–2–63–4; Taylor 6–1–16–0; Cook 17–10–29–0; Clift 18–4–84–4; Steele 6–3–3–0.

Umpires: D. O. Oslear and J. van Geloven.

At Northampton, July 9, 11, 12. YORKSHIRE lost to NORTHAMPTONSHIRE by 81 runs.

YORKSHIRE v SUSSEX

At Leeds, July 13, 14, 15. Drawn. Yorkshire 5 pts, Sussex 5 pts. Sussex, put in on a slow pitch, lost wickets to poor strokes, Taylor returning his best analysis. Pigott struck nine boundaries in an unbeaten 57 and then took five wickets as Yorkshire's batsmen also fell into unforced errors. Imran dominated the Sussex second innings but Yorkshire's target of 227 in 250 minutes seemed attainable. They collapsed badly, however, losing three wickets in 21 balls at one stage before settling for a draw. There were no fewer than fourteen lbw victims in the three days – a record for a Yorkshire match.

Sussex

*J. R. T. Barclay c Athey b Taylor	6	– (2) c Dennis b Carrick 17
G. D. Mendis c Athey b Sidebottom	22	– (1) c Boycott b Sidebottom 35
J. R. P. Heath lbw b Dennis	4	– c Athey b Taylor 9
Imran Khan lbw b Sidebottom	15	– c Bairstow b Sidebottom 83
P. W. G. Parker lbw b Dennis	2	– run out 19
C. M. Wells c Dennis b Taylor	9	– (7) c and b Carrick 8
†I. J. Gould c Sharp b Taylor	30	– (8) b Illingworth 5
D. A. Reeve lbw b Sidebottom	0	– (6) c Bairstow b Dennis 11
A. C. S. Pigott not out	57	– c Carrick b Illingworth........... 0
C. E. Waller c Illingworth b Taylor	3	– not out 11
A. N. Jones c and b Taylor	2	– b Sidebottom 1
B 1, l-b 13, w 4, n-b 17	35	B 9, l-b 10, w 6, n-b 14 ... 39

1/13 2/19 3/47 4/47   185   1/65 2/85 3/89 4/145   238
5/75 6/81 7/87 8/122 9/141   5/181 6/190 7/198 8/198 9/231

Bonus points – Sussex 1, Yorkshire 4.

Bowling: *First Innings*—Dennis 16–4–40–2; Taylor 15.4–3–49–5; Sidebottom 19–4–56–3; Athey 1–0–5–0. *Second Innings*—Dennis 20.3–3–47–1; Taylor 15.4–31–1; Boycott 6–4–3–0; Sidebottom 20.5–7–44–3; Carrick 33–15–62–2; Illingworth 4–1–12–2.

Yorkshire

G. Boycott lbw b Reeve	25	– lbw b Pigott 7
M. D. Moxon lbw b Reeve	20	– lbw b Waller 46
C. W. J. Athey c Gould b Wells	4	– lbw b Pigott 0
K. Sharp c Parker b Pigott	4	– b Reeve 17
J. D. Love lbw b Pigott	43	– lbw b Reeve 34
†D. L. Bairstow lbw b Pigott	2	– lbw b Reeve 10
P. Carrick lbw b Pigott	39	– c Gould b Wells 17
A. Sidebottom c Gould b Jones	23	– not out 5
S. J. Dennis c Heath b Pigott	3	– not out 4
*R. Illingworth not out	7	
N. S. Taylor b Reeve	4	
B 2, l-b 8, w 1, n-b 12	23	B 4, l-b 8, w 4, n-b 6 22

1/40 2/50 3/50 4/59   197   1/11 2/14 3/42 4/106   (7 wkts) 162
5/61 6/118 7/171 8/181 9/188   5/114 6/121 7/153

Bonus points – Yorkshire 1, Sussex 4.

Bowling: *First Innings*—Pigott 27–6–63–5; Jones 16–3–50–1; Reeve 29.5–14–34–3; Waller 2–0–5–0; Wells 11–2–22–1. *Second Innings*—Pigott 18.4–6–29–2; Jones 8–2–11–0; Reeve 20–9–36–3; Wells 4–0–11–1; Waller 19–7–38–1; Barclay 4–1–15–0.

Umpires: K. Ibadulla and J. van Geloven.

YORKSHIRE v KENT

At Sheffield, July 16, 18, 19. Drawn. Yorkshire 3 pts, Kent 8 pts. Against a weakened attack on a good batting pitch, Kent made their highest-ever total in Yorkshire, Cowdrey and Baptiste each hitting career-best scores. Despite a patient innings by Boycott, who by passing Hutton moved into second place behind Sutcliffe in the list of his county's century-makers, Yorkshire had to follow on. Dilley bowled very well, as did Ellison, but Cowdrey could with advantage have made more use of Underwood. Bad light finally allowed Yorkshire to escape with a draw.

Kent

R. A. Woolmer c Sharp b Jarvis......... 61	†A. P. E. Knott not out................... 9
N. S. Taylor lbw b Sidebottom........... 28	
D. G. Aslett b Taylor...................... 41	L-b 10, w 1, n-b 14 25
M. R. Benson c Athey b Taylor 11	
*C. S. Cowdrey c sub b Athey 113	1/63 2/134 3/156 (5 wkts dec.) 424
E. A. E. Baptiste not out..................136	4/161 5/389

G. W. Johnson, R. M. Ellison, G. R. Dilley and D. L. Underwood did not bat.

Bonus points – Kent 4, Yorkshire 1 (Score at 100 overs: 362-4).

Bowling: Taylor 20.5–5–105–2; Jarvis 22–1–84–1; Athey 9–1–34–1; Sidebottom 8–0–39–1; Carrick 39–7–106–0; Illingworth 8–1–31–0.

Yorkshire

G. Boycott c and b Ellison 101	– b Johnson................................ 34
M. D. Moxon c Knott b Dilley....................... 33	– c Knott b Dilley 0
C. W. J. Athey c Dilley b Baptiste.................. 2	– c Benson b Underwood 16
K. Sharp c Knott b Baptiste........................ 4	– b Baptiste................................ 30
J. D. Love c Cowdrey b Ellison..................... 10	– not out 26
†D. L. Bairstow c Dilley b Ellison 6	– c Johnson b Baptiste 0
P. Carrick c Knott b Woolmer 27	– lbw b Dilley 4
A. Sidebottom b Ellison............................ 44	– not out 3
N. S. Taylor b Woolmer 4	
P. W. Jarvis not out 11	
*R. Illingworth b Baptiste 9	
L-b 7, n-b 12................................ 19	L-b 2, w 2, n-b 4 8

1/87 2/117 3/122 4/149	270	1/3 2/41 3/75 4/101 (6 wkts) 121
5/163 6/170 7/241 8/247 9/249		5/101 6/115

Bonus points – Yorkshire 2, Kent 4 (Score at 100 overs: 249-9).

Bowling: *First Innings*—Dilley 26–8–66–1; Ellison 33–8–59–4; Underwood 3–3–0–0; Baptiste 28.2–3–72–3; Cowdrey 11–2–37–0; Woolmer 6–1–17–2. *Second Innings*—Dilley 13.1–5–20–2; Ellison 16–3–37–0; Underwood 12–9–9–1; Baptiste 16–8–21–2; Cowdrey 4–1–6–0; Woolmer 8–3–14–0; Johnson 3–2–6–1.

Umpires: A. Jepson and N. T. Plews.

At Worksop, July 30, August 1, 2. YORKSHIRE drew with NOTTINGHAMSHIRE.

YORKSHIRE v LANCASHIRE

At Leeds, August 6, 8, 9. Drawn. Yorkshire 7 pts, Lancashire 4 pts. Lancashire collapsed somewhat unexpectedly on a low, slow pitch, but Yorkshire were unable to press home their advantage against determined late resistance. Moxon led Yorkshire's reply with a career-best 153, which included one 6 and seventeen 4s and was highlighted by some splendid driving through the off side. Fowler, who had injured a leg muscle, then batted freely, scoring his first 50 from only 60 balls. But Lancashire were in no hurry to declare, finally setting a token target of 296 in two and a half hours after O'Shaughnessy had completed a maiden century in 220 minutes.

Lancashire

G. Fowler c Bairstow b Dennis	29	– (3) c Bairstow b Taylor	75
D. Lloyd lbw b Illingworth	73	– (1) c Bairstow b Stevenson	19
J. Abrahams c Bairstow b Dennis	26	– (4) c Carrick b Love	50
*C. H. Lloyd c Bairstow b Illingworth	8		
D. P. Hughes b Illingworth	12	– not out	9
S. J. O'Shaughnessy c Bairstow b Stevenson	2	– (2) not out	100
†C. Maynard b Carrick	49		
J. Simmons b Taylor	52		
Nasir Zaidi b Taylor	48		
P. J. W. Allott c Stevenson b Taylor	26		
L. L. McFarlane not out	1		
L-b 12, n-b 6	18	B 1, l-b 1, n-b 1	3

1/51 2/106 3/129 4/147   344   1/22 2/139 3/231   (3 wkts dec.) 256
5/158 6/158 7/234 8/289 9/334

Bonus points – Lancashire 3, Yorkshire 3 (Score at 100 overs: 261-7).

Bowling: *First Innings*—Dennis 27–6–88–2; Stevenson 18–6–38–1; Taylor 13.5–2–70–3; Illingworth 31–10–61–3; Carrick 26–7–60–1; Boycott 2–1–9–0. *Second Innings*—Dennis 10–1–39–0; Stevenson 7–0–24–1; Illingworth 13–5–23–0; Taylor 17–1–80–1; Carrick 15–7–18–0; Athey 7–0–23–0; Love 7–1–46–1.

Yorkshire

G. Boycott lbw b Allott	2	– c Simmons b McFarlane	1
M. D. Moxon c C. H. Lloyd b Allott	153	– c Simmons b O'Shaughnessy	39
C. W. J. Athey c Simmons b D. Lloyd	63	– b McFarlane	9
J. D. Love not out	67	– (7) not out	7
†D. L. Bairstow c Simmons b O'Shaughnessy	10	– (8) c sub b Simmons	18
P. Carrick not out	0	– (9) not out	0
K. Sharp (did not bat)		– (4) c Hughes b Simmons	6
N. S. Taylor (did not bat)		– (5) c Abrahams b O'Shaughnessy.	0
S. J. Dennis (did not bat)		– (6) lbw b O'Shaughnessy	0
B 1, l-b 5, n-b 4	10	B 4, l-b 4, w 1, n-b 1	10

1/6 2/137 3/279 4/300   (4 wkts dec.) 305   1/9 2/23 3/55 4/59   (7 wkts) 90
                                            5/60 6/60 7/84

G. B. Stevenson and *R. Illingworth did not bat.

Bonus points – Yorkshire 4, Lancashire 1.

Bowling: *First Innings*—Allott 15–1–53–2; McFarlane 13–2–40–0; Simmons 21–2–74–0; O'Shaughnessy 12–2–38–1; D. Lloyd 10–2–30–1; Nasir 9–1–25–0; Abrahams 7–0–35–0. *Second Innings*—Allott 8–2–22–0; McFarlane 10.4–2–26–2; D. Lloyd 5–3–5–0; O'Shaughnessy 11–8–14–3; Simmons 7–5–8–2; Nasir 2–1–5–0.

Umpires: R. Palmer and N. T. Plews.

At Weston-super-Mare, August 10, 11, 12. YORKSHIRE drew with SOMERSET.

At Cheltenham, August 13, 15, 16. YORKSHIRE lost to GLOUCESTERSHIRE by five wickets.

YORKSHIRE v NOTTINGHAMSHIRE

At Bradford, August 20, 22, 23. Drawn. Yorkshire 7 pts, Nottinghamshire 5 pts. Yorkshire, put in on a misty morning and another slow pitch, prospered against some less-than-accurate bowling. Metcalfe became the third and youngest Yorkshireman to mark his first-class début by scoring a century for the county. Having recovered from a poor start to claim maximum batting points, Nottinghamshire then allowed Yorkshire to score easy runs in the hope of a declaration. Boycott completed his second century of the match, adding 103 runs between the start and lunch, and Nottinghamshire were finally asked to score 297 for victory in 210 minutes, but they showed little interest despite some attacking gestures from Rice. Yorkshire's bowling had been weakened by their decision to bring in Hartley, as captain, in place of the injured Illingworth.

Yorkshire

G. Boycott c and b Hemmings	163	– not out	141
A. A. Metcalfe b Cooper	122	– c Hassan b Hemmings	7
G. B. Stevenson c French b Cooper	1		
C. W. J. Athey not out	17	– (3) c Saxelby b Hemmings	56
K. Sharp (did not bat)		– (4) lbw b Hemmings	0
J. D. Love (did not bat)		– (5) not out	75
B 5, l-b 4, w 1, n-b 3	13	B 1, l-b 1, n-b 2	4

1/248 2/251 3/316   (3 wkts dec.) 316   1/23 2/130 3/138   (3 wkts dec.) 283

*S. N. Hartley, †D. L. Bairstow, P. Carrick, A. Sidebottom and S. J. Dennis did not bat.

Bonus points – Yorkshire 4, Nottinghamshire 1.

Bowling: *First Innings*—Hendrick 16–8–22–0; Saxelby 15–5–57–0; Cooper 19–4–70–2; Hemmings 23.1–3–83–1; Bore 24–2–71–0. *Second Innings*—Hendrick 12–4–20–0; Saxelby 3–1–9–0; Hemmings 29–7–128–3; Cooper 4–2–7–0; Bore 17–1–115–0.

Nottinghamshire

B. Hassan lbw b Dennis	15	– retired hurt	6
R. T. Robinson c Boycott b Sidebottom	50	– not out	70
D. W. Randall c Stevenson b Sidebottom	1	– lbw b Stevenson	6
*C. E. B. Rice lbw b Stevenson	23	– c Metcalfe b Carrick	48
J. D. Birch c Sharp b Carrick	85	– b Carrick	5
†B. N. French c and b Carrick	91	– not out	5
E. E. Hemmings not out	12		
K. Saxelby c Bairstow b Carrick	0		
K. E. Cooper not out	10		
L-b 4, n-b 12	16	L-b 6, w 1, n-b 2	9

1/50 2/58 3/93 4/100   (7 wkts dec.) 303   1/30 2/129 3/143   (3 wkts) 149
5/262 6/286 7/286

M. K. Bore and M. Hendrick did not bat.

Bonus points – Nottinghamshire 4, Yorkshire 3.

Bowling: *First Innings*—Dennis 25–5–66–1; Stevenson 20–5–72–1; Sidebottom 16–5–39–2; Carrick 31.3–10–81–3; Hartley 6–1–24–0; Metcalfe 1–0–5–0. *Second Innings*—Dennis 11–2–36–0; Stevenson 9–1–30–1; Sidebottom 12–3–38–0; Carrick 18–10–35–2; Metcalfe 1–0–1–0.

Umpires: B. Dudleston and N. T. Plews.

YORKSHIRE v GLOUCESTERSHIRE

At Scarborough, August 24, 25, 26. Drawn. Yorkshire 6 pts, Gloucestershire 5 pts. Gloucestershire went into the match with only three front-line bowlers, but Yorkshire had to work hard for runs on a slow, low pitch that gave help to neither side. The pattern remained unchanged until the last afternoon, with the standard of cricket being disappointing. Gloucestershire were set a target of 266 in 185 minutes, but Stevenson took three wickets for 3 runs in fifteen balls to put them on the defensive. Finally Graveney, batting under the handicap of a badly bruised toe, and Shepherd, who hit two 6s and fourteen 4s in an unbeaten 73, which included spells of dogged defence as well as furious hitting, held Yorkshire at bay.

Yorkshire

G. Boycott c Russell b Sainsbury	28	– c Wright b Shepherd 43
M. D. Moxon lbw b Sainsbury	7	– c Shepherd b Bainbridge 22
C. W. J. Athey c Russell b Sainsbury	29	– c Broad b Bainbridge 16
K. Sharp lbw b Bainbridge	73	– b Sainsbury 19
J. D. Love c Cunningham b Bainbridge	9	– c Stovold b Sainsbury 31
†D. L. Bairstow run out	57	– c Wright b Bainbridge 35
G. B. Stevenson c Graveney b Bainbridge	38	– c Shepherd b Bainbridge 13
P. Carrick not out	24	– not out 4
A. Sidebottom b Shepherd	37	– not out 0
S. J. Dennis b Sainsbury	4	
*R. Illingworth b Sainsbury	2	
B 4, l-b 17, w 1, n-b 3	25	B 3, l-b 3, w 4 10

1/20 2/68 3/69 4/100   **333**   1/50 2/88 3/92   (7 wkts dec.) **193**
5/207 6/235 7/266 8/326 9/331   4/116 5/157 6/183 7/189

Bonus points – Yorkshire 3, Gloucestershire 3 (Score at 100 overs: 273-7).

Bowling: *First Innings*—Shepherd 28–9–79–1; Sainsbury 30–8–102–5; Bainbridge 39–15–79–3; Graveney 14–2–48–0. *Second Innings*—Sainsbury 17.2–4–68–2; Shepherd 20–5–48–1; Bainbridge 18–5–67–4.

Gloucestershire

B. C. Broad c Sidebottom b Carrick	44	– (2) b Stevenson 9
A. W. Stovold b Stevenson	6	– (1) c Athey b Stevenson 1
P. Bainbridge c Sharp b Carrick	26	– c Bairstow b Stevenson 2
P. W. Romaines c Bairstow b Sidebottom	36	– lbw b Dennis 1
A. J. Wright b Sidebottom	40	– c Bairstow b Sidebottom 19
A. J. Hignell c Dennis b Sidebottom	37	– lbw b Stevenson 37
E. J. Cunningham b Dennis	10	– c Moxon b Stevenson 20
J. N. Shepherd run out	1	– not out 73
*D. A. Graveney not out	26	– (10) run out 0
†R. C. Russell c Illingworth b Dennis	4	– (9) b Dennis 16
G. E. Sainsbury b Stevenson	4	– not out 4
B 4, l-b 9, w 2, n-b 12	27	B 5, l-b 1, n-b 8 14

1/15 2/69 3/90 4/170   **261**   1/3 2/10 3/15 4/15   (9 wkts) **196**
5/171 6/203 7/204 8/224 9/243   5/62 6/82 7/105 8/157 9/171

Bonus points – Gloucestershire 2, Yorkshire 3 (Score at 100 overs: 238-8).

Bowling: *First Innings*—Dennis 17–5–40–2; Stevenson 12.3–3–39–2; Sidebottom 21–9–43–3; Carrick 37–12–80–2; Illingworth 20–9–32–0. *Second Innings*—Dennis 14–5–42–2; Stevenson 13–3–47–5; Sidebottom 11–3–42–1; Carrick 15–5–41–0; Illingworth 4–1–10–0.

Umpires: J. van Geloven and A. G. T. Whitehead.

At Chesterfield, August 27, 29, 30. YORKSHIRE drew with DERBYSHIRE.

YORKSHIRE v MIDDLESEX

At Leeds, August 31, September 1, 2. Drawn. Yorkshire 4 pts, Middlesex 4 pts. Yorkshire batted slowly on an easy-paced pitch, but caution could not save Boycott, who failed by 16 to complete 1,000 runs in August. The rate was well below 2 an over until Bairstow and Sidebottom added 133 in 33 overs. Middlesex raced along in reply, with Gatting making his fifth century in six seasons against Yorkshire. He needed only 110 minutes and declared behind in the hope of winning the match on the last day in a run chase. Bairstow then became the first Yorkshire wicket-keeper to reach 1,000 runs in a season twice as he, too, raced to a century in 112 minutes. Middlesex were set a target of 340 in 225 minutes, but rain prevented a competitive finish.

Yorkshire

G. Boycott lbw b Williams	44	– c Edmonds b Daniel 2
R. G. Lumb b Hughes	15	– lbw b Embury 32
K. Sharp c Downton b Williams	24	– b Williams 10
J. D. Love c Williams b Emburey	21	– c Radley b Hughes 13
A. Sidebottom c Downton b Williams	78	– b Emburey 21
†D. L. Bairstow c and b Edmonds	86	– not out 100
P. Carrick b Gatting b Williams	9	– not out 59
G. B. Stevenson b Hughes	1	
S. J. Dennis c Gatting b Williams	0	
*R. Illingworth b Hughes	1	
S. D. Fletcher not out	0	
L-b 4, w 1, n-b 9	14	L-b 4, n-b 11 15

1/30 2/86 3/99 4/117   293   1/3 2/21 3/55   (5 wkts dec.) 252
5/250 6/271 7/276 8/283 9/286   4/78 5/91

Bonus points – Yorkshire 3, Middlesex 2 (Score at 100 overs: 257-5).

Bowling: *First Innings*—Daniel 9–3–31–0; Williams 21–4–77–5; Hughes 11–3–34–3; Edmonds 34–10–72–1; Emburey 34–10–65–1; Gatting 1–1–0–0. *Second Innings*—Daniel 10–3–41–1; Williams 10–3–25–1; Edmonds 24–5–72–0; Hughes 4–1–6–1; Emburey 16–1–58–2; Gatting 4.2–0–27–0; Tomlins 2–0–8–0.

Middlesex

G. D. Barlow b Stevenson	18	– c Bairstow b Stevenson 58
A. J. T. Miller b Dennis	5	– b Fletcher............................. 36
C. T. Radley b Fletcher	23	– (4) not out 12
*M. W. Gatting not out	100	– (3) not out 7
K. P. Tomlins lbw b Fletcher	0	
J. E. Emburey not out	44	
B 4, l-b 6, w 1, n-b 5	16	L-b 7, w 4, n-b 1 12

1/28 2/34 3/81 4/96   (4 wkts dec.) 206   1/102 2/104   (2 wkts) 125

†P. R. Downton, P. H. Edmonds, N. F. Williams, S. P. Hughes and W. W. Daniel did not bat.

Bonus points – Middlesex 2, Yorkshire 1.

Bowling: *First Innings*—Dennis 13–4–41–1; Stevenson 9.4–2–37–1; Carrick 5–1–32–0; Fletcher 9–0–26–2; Illingworth 8–1–54–0. *Second Innings*—Dennis 9–0–45–0; Stevenson 8.5–1–38–1; Illingworth 2–0–7–0; Fletcher 6–0–23–1.

Umpires: C. T. Spencer and R. A. White.

YORKSHIRE v SURREY

At Scarborough, September 7, 8, 9. Drawn. Yorkshire 8 pts, Surrey 5 pts. Surrey batted without much spirit on a slow pitch that allowed some movement off the seam. Sharp then produced a career-best innings highlighted by flashing strokeplay. Missed at 86 and 99, he ensured that Yorkshire obtained full batting bonus points for the first time in the season. Pocock found some turn which suggested Surrey might struggle again in their second innings, but with time lost to rain and bad light, a draw always seemed the most likely outcome.

Surrey

A. R. Butcher c Illingworth b Dennis	0	– lbw b Dennis	21
D. B. Pauline b Moxon	32	– c Bairstow b Stevenson	14
A. J. Stewart lbw b Dennis	17	– c Hartley b Dennis	6
*R. D. V. Knight c Bairstow b Hartley	33	– b Fletcher	1
M. A. Lynch c Hartley b Carrick	36	– not out	76
D. J. Thomas c Love b Stevenson	14	– run out	34
†C. J. Richards lbw b Illingworth	20	– not out	18
I. R. Payne c Sharp b Carrick	12		
S. T. Clarke c Bairstow b Illingworth	12		
P. I. Pocock lbw b Illingworth	0		
I. J. Curtis not out	0		
L-b 1, w 1	2	L-b 5, n-b 1	6

1/0 2/25 3/64 4/112   178   1/30 2/37 3/42   (5 wkts) 176
5/134 6/138 7/160 8/178 9/178   4/42 5/124

Bonus points – Surrey 1, Yorkshire 4.

Bowling: *First Innings*—Dennis 11–2–28–2; Stevenson 14–5–36–1; Fletcher 6–1–27–0; Moxon 7–1–25–1; Hartley 7–2–15–1; Carrick 14.2–5–29–2; Illingworth 5–3–16–3. *Second Innings*—Dennis 16–4–64–2; Stevenson 4–0–16–1; Fletcher 18–4–39–1; Moxon 6–1–24–0; Illingworth 6–1–11–0; Carrick 11–6–15–0; Hartley 2–1–1–0.

Yorkshire

G. Boycott lbw b Thomas	3	S. J. Dennis b Curtis	6
M. D. Moxon c Payne b Clarke	23	S. D. Fletcher c Lynch b Pocock	12
K. Sharp c Richards b Pocock	139	*R. Illingworth not out	0
S. N. Hartley b Pocock	27	B 12, l-b 19, w 1, n-b 7	39
J. D. Love lbw b Pocock	1		
†D. L. Bairstow c Richards b Thomas	13	1/3 2/92 3/159	329
P. Carrick st Richards b Pocock	20	4/172 5/234 6/246	
G. B. Stevenson c Pocock b Curtis	46	7/308 8/309 9/327	

Bonus points – Yorkshire 4, Surrey 4.

Bowling: Clarke 26–7–65–1; Thomas 21–2–83–2; Knight 9–2–22–0; Pocock 25.5–5–94–5; Payne 8–0–18–0; Curtis 2–0–8–2.

Umpires: H. D. Bird and J. Birkenshaw.

At Chelmsford, September 10, 12, 13. YORKSHIRE drew with ESSEX.

THE UNIVERSITIES IN 1983

OXFORD

President – LORD BLAKE
(The Queen's)

Hon. Treasurer – DR S. R. PORTER
(St Cross)

Captain – G. J. TOOGOOD
(North Bromsgrove HS and Lincoln)

Secretary – A. J. T. MILLER
(Haileybury and St Edmund Hall)

Captain for 1984 – K. A. HAYES
(Queen Elizabeth GS, Blackburn and Merton)

Secretary – J. D. CARR
(Repton and Worcester)

Oxford University suffered from one of the wettest of all seasons in The Parks. It resulted in every first-class match in April and May being affected, and the fixture between Oxford and Cambridge Universities and Glamorgan in the Benson and Hedges Cup competition had to be switched to Fenner's. More games were abandoned than completed, though an improvement in the weather in June made it possible for the last three matches to be played without serious interruption.

The frequent stoppages badly hindered the Dark Blues in their preparation for the University match, and in the event they did well to draw at Lord's. As in the previous year, Oxford's relative strength was their batting, even though Giles Toogood, the captain, and Kevin Hayes, because of exams, played in few matches. The two Haileyburians, Richard Ellis, who led the side in 1982, and Andrew Miller, developed into Oxford's best opening pair for many years. Both completed centuries in first-class matches – Ellis an unbeaten 103 against Glamorgan and Miller 127 not out against Hampshire. Roger Moulding, who created a small slice of cricket history by becoming the first player to play in six University matches, enjoyed his best season at Oxford. His consistency with the bat was invaluable, and in Toogood's absence he shared the captain's responsibilities with Ellis. Oxford were fortunate to have these two former captains regularly available.

Toogood's batting was a disappointment and Roger Edbrooke and Guy Franks both failed after extended trials. One of the places went to Philip Heseltine, who made a promising start in his first year in senior cricket, and John Carr, son of TCCB Secretary and former Oxford captain, Donald Carr, showed promise as an all-rounder. He was the only off-spinner in an attack which was even weaker than in the previous year. Mike Petchey and Harry Rawlinson emerged as the best new-ball bowlers, but neither was above a gentle medium pace and although no batsman scored a double-century against the University, as in 1982, Nicholas and Turner, who added 290 for Hampshire's second wicket, were two of five opposing batsmen recording centuries at The Parks. Oxford were well endowed with wicket-keepers, and Mark Cullinan, a South African freshman who had played for South African Universities, maintained a high standard throughout the season.

One major source of annoyance in The Parks was the failure to find anyone regularly to man the scoreboard. There were occasions when it was deserted, others when it was operated by the players themselves, or by boys so small that they had to stand on crates to reach the controls. Neither the local newspaper nor the local radio station was asked to help in the search for a regular operator, which was not good enough. It should not be allowed to happen again, being a discourtesy to visiting sides and unworthy of the University's first-class status. – P.F.

OXFORD UNIVERSITY RESULTS

First-class matches – Played 9: Lost 4, Drawn 5.

FIRST-CLASS AVERAGES – BATTING

	M	I	NO	R	HI	Avge
R. P. Moulding	8	13	3	448	80*	44.80
A. J. T. Miller	9	15	3	537	127*	44.75
R. G. P. Ellis	9	15	2	551	103*	42.38
J. G. Varey	6	10	3	187	69*	26.71
P. J. Heseltine	6	10	1	176	40	19.55
K. A. Hayes	3	4	0	62	45	15.50
J. G. Franks	5	7	0	98	29	14.00
H. T. Rawlinson	8	9	2	91	24	13.00
M. R. Cullinan	8	8	2	55	27	9.16
G. J. Toogood	5	6	0	48	18	8.00
J. D. Carr	6	7	1	45	18	7.50
A. H. K. Smail	6	6	1	24	13*	4.80
M. D. Petchey	6	6	0	21	18	3.50
J. R. Turnbull	7	7	4	5	5*	1.66

Played in two matches: R. M. Edbrooke 0, 71; R. P. Gibaut 7, 0. Played in one match: J. R. Chessher 0, 11; D. S. Harrison 1, 8; M. P. Lawrence did not bat.

* *Signifies not out.*

BOWLING

	O	M	R	W	Avge	BB
K. A. Hayes	33.5	10	124	8	15.50	6-58
J. R. Turnbull	130	34	424	12	35.33	4-51
A. H. K. Smail	70	18	222	5	44.40	3-49
H. T. Rawlinson	154.5	31	626	14	44.71	5-123
J. D. Carr	155	45	445	9	49.44	2-59
M. D. Petchey	206.2	36	804	12	67.00	2-70

Also bowled: R. G. P. Ellis 22–6–82–0; M. P. Lawrence 6–1–36–0; R. P. Moulding 9.4–0–22–0; J. G. Varey 77–10–316–3.

OXFORD UNIVERSITY 1983

[Bill Smith]

Back row: P. J. Heseltine, M. R. Cullinan, J. D. Carr, M. D. Petchey, H. T. Rawlinson, K. A. Hayes, W. R. Bristowe. *Front row:* J. G. Varey, A. J. T. Miller, G. J. Toogood (*captain*), R. P. Moulding, R. G. P. Ellis.

OXFORD UNIVERSITY v LANCASHIRE

At Oxford, April 23, 25, 26. Drawn. Oxford's opening match was badly hit by frequent thunderstorms which resulted in over eleven and a half hours of play being lost. Jefferies, a left-arm medium-pacer from South Africa, who played one game for Derbyshire in 1982, made a good start for Lancashire after they had won the toss and put Oxford in. On the third morning he took the last four wickets without conceding a run.

Oxford University

R. G. P. Ellis c Lloyd b O'Shaughnessy ..	26	†M. R. Cullinan not out...................	14
A. J. T. Miller c McFarlane b Nasir....	28	J. D. Carr lbw b Jefferies.................	0
R. M. Edbrooke c Allott		A. H. K. Smail b Jefferies................	0
b O'Shaughnessy.	0	R. P. Gibaut b Jefferies	7
K. A. Hayes lbw b O'Shaughnessy......	3	B 10, l-b 4............................	14
*G. J. Toogood c Lloyd b Jefferies	4		
J. G. Varey c Hughes b Lloyd............	8	1/56 2/56 3/66 4/66	145
R. P. Moulding lbw b Jefferies...........	41	5/72 6/98 7/133 8/133 9/133	

Bowling: Allott 23–11–24–0; Jefferies 21.2–14–15–5; Nasir 21–7–39–1; McFarlane 12–6–16–0; O'Shaughnessy 9–4–14–3; Lloyd 11–7–11–1; Hughes 7–1–12–0.

Lancashire

G. Fowler not out............................	16
D. Lloyd not out	22
W 1......................................	1

(no wkt) 39

S. J. O'Shaughnessy, F. C. Hayes, D. P. Hughes, *J. Abrahams, †C. Maynard, P. J. W. Allott, S. T. Jefferies, L. L. McFarlane and Nasir Zaidi did not bat.

Bowling: Varey 5–0–21–0; Smail 5–2–17–0.

Umpires: A. Jepson and B. Dudleston.

OXFORD UNIVERSITY v SOMERSET

At Oxford, April 29. Drawn. The three-day match against Somerset having been abandoned on the second day, owing to heavy rain, a limited-overs match was arranged for the last day, although that, too, was rain-affected. Oxford University 121 for eight (50 overs) (J. G. Varey 35; P. H. L. Wilson five for 25); Somerset 91 for six (34.2 overs) (J. G. Varey four for 43).

OXFORD UNIVERSITY v SUSSEX

At Oxford, April 30, May 2, 3. Drawn. Sussex, captained in Barclay's absence by Parker, were put in and by lunch were struggling at 69 for four. However, Greig, with an unbeaten 147 (two 6s, fourteen 4s), led a spirited recovery, putting on 101 for the eighth wicket with Pigott. Torrential rain over the week-end left the square under water and the match was abandoned after lunch on the second day.

Sussex

G. D. Mendis c Cullinan b Turnbull....	16	A. C. S. Pigott c Turnbull b Smail......	27
A. M. Green c Heseltine b Turnbull ...	33	C. E. Waller b Turnbull....................	2
*P. W. G. Parker c Cullinan b Smail....	5	C. M. Wells absent ill	
A. P. Wells b Smail	1	B 2, l-b 4, w 2........................	8
I. A. Greig not out	147		——
C. P. Phillipson c Ellis b Rawlinson ...	18	1/29 2/48 3/50	280
†I. J. Gould c Franks b Carr..............	1	4/57 5/120 6/123	
G. S. le Roux c Lawrence b Turnbull ..	22	7/174 8/275 9/280	

Bowling: Turnbull 22–5–51–4; Smail 20–8–49–3; Rawlinson 23–7–63–1; Carr 30–11–73–1; Lawrence 6–1–36–0.

Oxford University

R. G. P. Ellis not out......................	11		
A. J. T. Miller not out.....................	10		
	(no wkt) 21		

*G. J. Toogood, †M. R. Cullinan, J. R. Turnbull, P. J. Heseltine, A. H. K. Smail, J. G. Franks, J. D. Carr, H. T. Rawlinson and M. P. Lawrence did not bat.

Bowling: le Roux 4–2–6–0; Pigott 5–0–10–0; Waller 2–0–5–0.

Umpires: D. J. Constant and J. H. Harris.

OXFORD UNIVERSITY v GLAMORGAN

At Oxford, May 11, 12, 13. Drawn. Only three and a half hours' play was possible on the first day and after more heavy rain the match was abandoned before the scheduled start on the third. Oxford's opener, Ellis, was in excellent form and hit an unbeaten 103, which included sixteen boundaries, out of a meagre 163. Selvey's eighth over contained three wickets and as many no-balls.

Oxford University

R. G. P. Ellis not out......................	103	J. R. Turnbull c Ontong b Lloyd	0
A. J. T. Miller lbw b Selvey	6	A. H. K. Smail b Selvey....................	3
J. G. Franks lbw b Wilkins	15	R. P. Gibaut b Selvey......................	0
*G. J. Toogood b Selvey...................	1	B 8, l-b 1, w 4, n-b 9	22
R. P. Moulding lbw b Selvey	0		——
†M. R. Cullinan c Lloyd b Selvey	0	1/12 2/55 3/57	163
J. D. Carr b Wilkins......................	2	4/58 5/60 6/81	
H. T. Rawlinson c Miandad b Lloyd ...	11	7/122 8/122 9/159	

Bowling: Thomas 4–1–21–0; Selvey 20–8–47–6; Wilkins 8–0–25–2; Ontong 17–6–29–0; Lloyd 11–4–8–2; Rowe 2–1–11–0.

Glamorgan

A. Jones, J. A. Hopkins, D. A. Francis, Javed Miandad, C. J. C. Rowe, R. C. Ontong, †E. W. Jones, B. J. Lloyd, J. G. Thomas, *M. W. W. Selvey and A. H. Wilkins.

Umpires: D. G. L. Evans and P. B. Wight.

†At Oxford, May 25, 26, 27. Drawn. Oxford University 203 for nine dec. (A. J. T. Miller 56, J. D. Carr 52 not out) and 231; MCC 280 for four dec. (R. E. Hayward 102 not out, R. A. Hutton 75 not out).

†At Oxford, May 28, 29, 30. Oxford University won by four wickets. Free Foresters 124 (M. D. Petchey six for 36) and 252 (D. R. Worsley 76, S. J. Halliday 54); Oxford University 182 for six dec. (R. P. Moulding 55) and 196 for six (W. R. Bristow 74 not out).

†At Oxford, June 4, 6, 7. Drawn. Combined Services 113 and 317 for eight dec. (R. C. Moylan-Jones 106, E. C. Gordon-Lennox 64, C. R. Clark 56); Oxford University 196 for five dec. (A. J. T. Miller 115 not out) and 218 for nine (M. R. Cullinan 54).

OXFORD UNIVERSITY v NORTHAMPTONSHIRE

At Oxford, June 8, 9, 10. Northamptonshire won by 281 runs. Oxford University disappointed against Northamptonshire, whose opening bowler, Carse, broke down after completing less than two overs. Northamptonshire were further handicapped when Mallender was barred in Oxford's second innings for persistently running through on the pitch. Northamptonshire, who won the toss, lost six wickets for only 117, but their tail-enders rescued them. Oxford collapsed against Mallender and Lamb, Varey, with 69 not out, being the only batsman to resist. The follow-on was not enforced, Northamptonshire preferring to get batting practice before bowling Oxford out again.

Northamptonshire

D. S. Steele b Petchey	12	– c Carr b Turnbull	51
M. J. Bamber c Cullinan b Turnbull	17	– c Carr b Turnbull	44
R. G. Williams c Cullinan b Rawlinson	50		
D. J. Capel c Cullinan b Petchey	51	– (3) not out	51
D. J. Wild c Carr b Rawlinson	14	– (4) c Rawlinson b Carr	22
R. J. Bailey c Varey b Carr	4	– (5) not out	37
S. J. Lines c and b Turnbull	29		
*†G. Sharp b Carr	89		
N. A. Mallender not out	71		
T. M. Lamb c Turnbull b Rawlinson	34		
B 2, l-b 2, w 4, n-b 12	20	L-b 2, w 2, n-b 4	8

1/30 2/30 3/74 4/112 (9 wkts dec.) 353 1/90 2/99 3/140 (3 wkts dec.) 213
5/117 6/117 7/201 8/247 9/353

J. A. Carse did not bat.

Bowling: *First Innings*—Petchey 21–3–73–2; Turnbull 21–5–60–2; Varey 1–0–9–0; Rawlinson 18.5–3–90–3; Carr 25–7–71–2; Ellis 8–2–30–0. *Second Innings*—Petchey 9–1–36–0; Turnbull 13–3–46–2; Rawlinson 7–1–41–0; Carr 15–6–46–1; Ellis 10–2–36–0.

Oxford University

R. G. P. Ellis c Steele b Mallender	15	– lbw b Lamb	13
A. J. T. Miller lbw b Lamb	7	– b Lamb	4
J. G. Franks c Sharp b Lamb	4	– c Sharp b Williams	13
*G. J. Toogood lbw b Lamb	18	– lbw b Lamb	6
R. P. Moulding lbw b Lamb	3	– c Bailey b Mallender	35
J. G. Varey not out	69	– c Lines b Mallender	31
†M. R. Cullinan c Bailey b Steele	2	– run out	2
J. D. Carr run out	9	– c Capel b Steele	18
H. T. Rawlinson c Wild b Mallender	7	– lbw b Williams	4
M. D. Petchey b Mallender	2	– c Steele b Williams	0
J. R. Turnbull b Mallender	0	– not out	0
B 5, w 1, n-b 4	10	B 4, l-b 3, n-b 6	13

1/17 2/22 3/48 4/51 146 1/18 2/19 3/25 4/48 139
5/55 6/80 7/99 8/114 9/124 5/101 6/110 7/116 8/120 9/139

Bowling: *First Innings*—Carse 1.5–0–3–0; Mallender 21.3–7–41–4; Lamb 17.1–7–27–4; Capel 1–0–9–0; Williams 8–3–17–0; Steele 20–9–39–1. *Second Innings*—Mallender 13.4–6–31–2; Lamb 17–7–37–3; Capel 7–3–23–0; Williams 24–20–29–3; Steele 14.4–11–6–1.

Umpires: N. T. Plews and K. G. Suttle.

OXFORD UNIVERSITY v HAMPSHIRE

At Oxford, June 11, 13, 14. Hampshire won by eight wickets. Hampshire won a splendid match with 7.3 overs to spare after being set to score 301 in 105 minutes and twenty overs. They lost Terry in the first over but Turner and Nicholas all but won the match with a second-wicket partnership of 290. Nicholas, who had scored 369 runs for only once out in his previous four innings at The Parks, hit 158. The partnership overshadowed a maiden century by Miller, who went on to score an unbeaten 127 and share in an unbroken stand of 132 with Moulding in Oxford's second innings. The match had been given a whirlwind start by Ellis.

Oxford University

*R. G. P. Ellis c Parks b Malone	99	– c and b Tremlett	20
A. J. T. Miller lbw b Malone	26	– not out	127
P. J. Heseltine c Parks b Tremlett	36	– b Malone	4
J. G. Franks b Malone	21	– c Terry b Southern	11
R. P. Moulding c Pocock b Tremlett	34	– not out	58
H. T. Rawlinson c Parks b Tremlett	0		
J. D. Carr b Tremlett	0		
†M. R. Cullinan lbw b Southern	27		
A. H. K. Smail b Malone	0		
J. R. Turnbull not out	5		
M. D. Petchey c Tremlett b Southern	0		
L-b 4, w 1, n-b 5	20	L-b 1, w 4, n-b 5	10

1/127 2/134 3/172 4/230   268   1/36 2/58 3/98   (3 wkts dec.) 230
5/230 6/234 7/235 8/238 9/268

Bowling: *First Innings*—Malone 24–10–64–4; Emery 9–2–38–0; Tremlett 33–18–42–4; Nicholas 13–4–31–0; Southern 20–4–44–2; Cowley 12–3–29–0. *Second Innings*—Malone 13–3–40–1; Emery 10–4–20–0; Tremlett 6–2–12–1; Southern 22–6–74–1; Cowley 5–2–4–0; Pocock 11–0–51–0; Smith 2–0–19–0.

Hampshire

D. R. Turner c Ellis b Carr	51	– not out	122
V. P. Terry c and b Turnbull	36	– c Cullinan b Petchey	0
M. C. J. Nicholas c Franks b Turnbull	45	– c Moulding b Turnbull	158
R. A. Smith c Smail b Carr	14		
*N. E. J. Pocock not out	29		
N. G. Cowley not out	20		
S. J. Malone (did not bat)		– (4) not out	9
B 2, n-b 1	3	B 7, l-b 4, w 1	12

1/72 2/104 3/144 4/148   (4 wkts dec.) 198   1/0 2/290   (2 wkts) 301

T. M. Tremlett, J. W. Southern, †R. J. Parks and K. St J. D. Emery did not bat.

Bowling: *First Innings*—Petchey 20.1–8–62–0; Smail 10–2–34–0; Turnbull 22–10–40–2; Carr 21–7–59–2. *Second Innings*—Petchey 14–1–85–1; Smail 4–0–24–0; Turnbull 6–0–47–1; Carr 11–0–69–0; Rawlinson 6–0–49–0; Moulding 2.3–0–7–0; Ellis 1–0–8–0.

Umpires: B. Dudleston and K. G. Suttle.

OXFORD UNIVERSITY v WORCESTERSHIRE

At Oxford, June 15, 16, 17. Worcestershire won by 148 runs. Banks and Watkins both made promising débuts for Worcestershire, Banks reaching a maiden century in a little under two hours. Oxford replied with their highest score of the season before Banks and D'Oliveira dominated the county's second innings with a partnership of 100 in 54 minutes. Left to score 286 to win Oxford never recovered from the loss of early wickets.

Worcestershire

M. S. Scott c Cullinan b Smail	53	– b Varey	13
S. G. Watkins c Cullinan b Rawlinson	77	– b Rawlinson	28
*D. N. Patel c Petchey b Rawlinson	24	– c Cullinan b Rawlinson	22
M. J. Weston lbw b Rawlinson	14	– lbw b Petchey	15
D. B. D'Oliveira c Petchey b Rawlinson	10	– c Heseltine b Varey	52
D. A. Banks b Petchey	100	– run out	53
R. K. Illingworth c Miller b Rawlinson	4	– Rawlinson b Varey	1
†P. Moores c Heseltine b Petchey	27	– c Turnbull b Smail	17
A. E. Warner not out	26	– not out	16
J. D. Inchmore (did not bat)		– not out	1
L-b 3, w 1, n-b 3	7	B 1, l-b 5, w 2, n-b 2	10

1/122 2/144 3/163 4/176 (8 wkts dec.) 342 1/31 2/61 3/74 (8 wkts dec.) 228
5/199 6/205 7/301 8/342   4/84 5/184 6/191 7/193 8/222

A. P. Pridgeon did not bat.

Bowling: *First Innings*—Petchey 25.1–5–79–2; Varey 10–1–33–0; Turnbull 13–1–58–0; Rawlinson 30–7–123–5; Smail 17–4–42–1. *Second Innings*—Petchey 17–1–61–1; Varey 18–4–69–3; Ellis 2–2–0–0; Rawlinson 12–1–48–2; Smail 9–1–40–1.

Oxford University

*R. G. P. Ellis lbw b Pridgeon	61	– c Warner b Pridgeon	26
A. J. T. Miller st Moores b D'Oliveira	90	– lbw b Warner	0
P. J. Heseltine b Illingworth	40	– b Inchmore	3
J. G. Franks c Weston b Patel	5	– c Pridgeon b Illingworth	29
J. G. Varey c Banks b Illingworth	11	– (8) lbw b Illingworth	6
R. P. Moulding not out	53	– c Moores b Illingworth	35
†M. R. Cullinan c Illingworth b Patel	4	– (5) c Moores b Pridgeon	4
H. T. Rawlinson not out	0	– (7) c Moores b Warner	24
A. H. K. Smail (did not bat)		– lbw b Illingworth	0
M. D. Petchey (did not bat)		– b Warner	0
J. R. Turnbull (did not bat)		– not out	0
L-b 7, w 1, n-b 13	21	L-b 4, n-b 6	10

1/95 2/198 3/208 (6 wkts dec.) 285 1/6 2/26 3/36 4/43 137
4/223 5/236 6/276   5/103 6/105 7/129 8/137 9/137

Bowling: *First Innings*—Pridgeon 22–7–42–1; Inchmore 20–3–52–0; Illingworth 30–8–83–2; Warner 13.3–5–40–0; Patel 14–5–35–2; D'Oliveira 4–1–12–1. *Second Innings*—Pridgeon 13–1–26–2; Warner 11.2–4–21–3; Inchmore 9–2–27–1; Illingworth 18–10–37–4; Patel 12–7–16–0.

Umpires: M. J. Kitchen and J. D. Morley.

At The Oval, June 18, 19. OXFORD UNIVERSITY lost to SURREY by an innings and 98 runs.

At Birmingham, June 22, 23, 24. OXFORD UNIVERSITY drew with WARWICKSHIRE.

At Lord's, June 29, 30, July 1. OXFORD UNIVERSITY drew with CAMBRIDGE UNIVERSITY (See Other Matches at Lord's).

CAMBRIDGE

President – SIR JOHN BUTTERFIELD
(Downing)

Hon. Treasurer – PROFESSOR A. D. BUCKINGHAM
(Pembroke)

Captain – S. P. HENDERSON
(Downside and Magdalene)

Secretary – D. W. VAREY
(Birkenhead and Pembroke)

Captain for 1984 – A. J. POLLOCK
(Shrewsbury and Trinity)

Secretary – T. A. COTTERELL
(Downside and Peterhouse)

After the heights of the previous summer, when Lancashire and Oxford University were beaten, 1983 was a disappointing season for Cambridge. Despite the loss of Derek Pringle to county cricket, there had been high hopes that the progress made the previous year would be continued. But grey skies and slow pitches soon reduced the prospects for a side which had to rely heavily on its batting.

Although the worst of one of the wettest springs of the century avoided Cambridge, allowing play to continue when all had been lost elsewhere, the majority of the early games were still affected in some degree by rain. This accounted for the lack of early runs from a side full of batsmen who should have been capable of big scores, and for the first time in recent seasons no student made a first-class hundred in the short Fenner's season.

Robin Boyd-Moss, however, made a century in each innings in the University Match, the first player ever to do so. This also enabled him to set a new record aggregate of 489 runs for the series, bettering M. J. K. Smith's 477, made between 1954 and 1956. Boyd-Moss had also been closest to a Fenner's century, making 83 against Glamorgan in the first match and 97 against Northamptonshire.

Stephen Henderson, a popular and resourceful captain, who had scored well the previous season, could not quite recapture that form. Tim Curtis, a freshman from Worcestershire, was hindered by his role as reluctant opener and never made the runs that had been hoped for, while Gajan Pathmanathan,

CAMBRIDGE UNIVERSITY 1983

[*Bill Smith*]

Back row: B. Taylor (*coach*), T. S. Curtis, T. A. Cotterell, K. I. Hodgson, C. C. Ellison, S. G. P. Hewitt, G. Pathmanathan, C. R. Andrew. *Front row:* S. J. G. Doggart, D. W. Varey, S. P. Henderson (*captain*), A. J. Pollock, R. J. Boyd-Moss.

the latest in the line of players who have played for both Universities, often promised much, only to get himself out on pitches that were never as quick as he would have liked.

County batsmen found few problems against a University attack that rarely posed a serious threat. Angus Pollock took wickets, but expensively, while Paul Roebuck threatened occasionally, until injury ruled him out of contention for a Blue. Ian Hodgson failed to live up to his feats of 1982, although his batting did advance. The same could be said of Simon Doggart, who scored runs more readily than he took wickets with his off-spin.

With an abundance of seniors in the side, there were few encouraging pointers to the future, although, on occasions, the slow left-arm bowling of Archie Cotterell gave reason for some optimism. The inclusion of Cotterell and Steve Hewitt, the wicket-keeper, against Oxford brought two rare Blues to Peterhouse.

Despite their lack of success, Cambridge again owed a debt to the former Essex captain, Brian Taylor, who has proved such a source of help and encouragement as coach to the University. – D. G. H.

CAMBRIDGE UNIVERSITY RESULTS

First-class matches – Played 10: Lost 3, Drawn 7.

FIRST-CLASS AVERAGES – BATTING

	M	I	NO	R	HI	Avge
R. J. Boyd-Moss	10	19	0	733	139	38.57
T. S. Curtis	10	20	3	506	92	29.76
K. I. Hodgson	10	15	5	272	47	27.20
S. P. Henderson	10	19	3	409	90	25.56
S. J. G. Doggart	10	18	5	323	70	24.84
G. Pathmanathan	7	13	1	263	64	21.91
P. G. P. Roebuck	5	7	3	82	31*	20.50
D. W. Varey	10	20	1	342	65	18.00
C. C. Ellison	4	6	2	49	21	12.25
A. Odendaal	3	6	1	56	21*	11.20
T. A. Cotterell	10	12	3	81	22	9.00
A. J. Pollock	10	9	2	38	14*	5.42
S. G. P. Hewitt	6	7	2	9	6	1.80

Played in four matches: A. G. Davies 0, 0. Played in one match: R. W. M. Palmer 0.

* *Signifies not out.*

BOWLING

	O	M	R	W	Avge	BB
C. C. Ellison	56.4	17	153	7	21.85	4-36
R. J. Boyd-Moss	70	18	217	8	27.12	5-27
A. J. Pollock	230.2	49	750	21	35.71	5-107
T. A. Cotterell	273	67	758	17	44.58	5-89
P. G. P. Roebuck	75.5	17	269	6	44.83	2-44
S. J. G. Doggart	285.2	60	844	12	70.33	3-3
K. I. Hodgson	297	75	871	12	72.58	4-58

Also bowled: T. S. Curtis 40–6–144–3; S. P. Henderson 13–3–66–1; R. W. M. Palmer 12–0–75–1.

CAMBRIDGE UNIVERSITY v GLAMORGAN

At Cambridge, April 20, 21, 23. Drawn. The first day was lost to rain and play was delayed again on the third morning, allowing little time for any meaningful cricket. Boyd-Moss made 83 in under two hours before Cambridge declared. Glamorgan were in little difficulty on a slow pitch, taking the lead with four wickets down before Selvey, leading the county for the first time, declared.

Cambridge University

A. Odendaal c E. W. Jones b Thomas		1 – b Nash	0
D. W. Varey b Rowe	33	lbw b Thomas	10
R. J. Boyd-Moss c Nash b Ontong	83	c E. W. Jones b Thomas	3
*S. P. Henderson c and b Ontong	15	b Thomas	5
T. S. Curtis not out	24	not out	18
S. J. G. Doggart b Lloyd	3	not out	8
K. I. Hodgson not out	4		
B 4, l-b 2, w 1, n-b 10	17	N-b 4	4

1/3 2/115 3/137   (5 wkts dec.) 180   1/6 2/13 3/14   (4 wkts) 48
4/168 5/171   4/20

P. G. P. Roebuck, T. A. Cotterell, †A. G. Davies and A. J. Pollock did not bat.

Bowling: *First Innings*—Nash 6-2-12-0; Thomas 4-2-17-1; Selvey 12-4-42-0; Lloyd 9-3-21-1; Ontong 17-3-46-2; Rowe 11-2-25-1. *Second Innings*—Nash 10-5-12-1; Thomas 7-3-19-3; Lloyd 7-4-5-0; Rowe 5-3-8-0.

Glamorgan

A. Jones c Davies b Pollock	39	J. Derrick not out	4
J. A. Hopkins lbw b Pollock	36	B 4, l-b 4, w 3, n-b 2	13
A. L. Jones c Henderson b Pollock	2		
C. J. C. Rowe lbw b Curtis	39	1/75 2/79 3/87	(4 wkts dec.) 184
R. C. Ontong not out	51	4/164	

†E. W. Jones, J. G. Thomas, *M. W. W. Selvey, M. A. Nash and B. J. Lloyd did not bat.

Bowling: Roebuck 15-6-48-0; Hodgson 13-4-27-0; Doggart 9-2-25-0; Cotterell 16-2-39-0; Pollock 15-4-21-3; Curtis 2-0-11-1.

Umpires: B. J. Meyer and J. W. Holder.

CAMBRIDGE UNIVERSITY v LEICESTERSHIRE

At Cambridge, April 23, 25, 26. Drawn. Again rain washed out an entire day – the second. The start had been delayed by 90 minutes on the first morning before Cambridge batted sensibly with Boyd-Moss again the major run-maker. The university declared overnight, but it was not until the third morning that play could be resumed. The wait was worthwhile as Gower stroked the first century of the season with barely a blemish.

Cambridge University

T. S. Curtis c Briers b Parsons	33	– b Clift	38
D. W. Varey c Tolchard b Clift	11	– b Agnew	3
R. J. Boyd-Moss c Tolchard b Parsons	44	– lbw b Clift	48
*S. P. Henderson c Cobb b Cook	13	– lbw b Clift	0
A. Odendaal lbw b Clift	17	– lbw b Clift	10
S. J. G. Doggart lbw b Parsons	4	– b Clift	1
K. I. Hodgson b Clift	19	– not out	4
P. G. P. Roebuck not out	31	– not out	0
T. A. Cotterell not out	16		
L-b 4	4	N-b 1	1

1/32 2/47 3/103 4/107　　　(7 wkts dec.) 192　　1/11 2/83 3/83　　(6 wkts) 105
5/112 6/141 7/156　　　　　　　　　　　　　　4/90 5/96 6/105

†A. G. Davies and A. J. Pollock did not bat.

Bowling: *First Innings*—Agnew 19–4–61–0; Parsons 20–6–57–3; Clift 13–3–36–3; Cook 16–10–16–1; Steele 14–6–18–0. *Second Innings*—Agnew 8–1–39–1; Parsons 8–2–34–0; Clift 10–5–20–5; Cook 9–4–11–0.

Leicestershire

J. C. Balderstone run out	17	J. F. Steele not out	37
R. A. Cobb b Pollock	12	P. B. Clift not out	14
D. I. Gower c Curtis b Cotterell	124	B 1, l-b 3, w 2, n-b 2	8
B. F. Davison b Pollock	13		
N. E. Briers b Roebuck	24	1/25 2/36 3/63 4/125　　(6 wkts dec.) 310	
*†R. W. Tolchard c Davies b Cotterell	61	5/229 6/276	

N. G. B. Cook, G. J. Parsons and J. P. Agnew did not bat.

Bowling: Roebuck 8–1–29–1; Hodgson 16–4–55–0; Pollock 13–1–69–2; Doggart 16–2–48–0; Cotterell 23–5–73–2; Curtis 4–0–19–0; Henderson 4–1–9–0.

Umpires: B. J. Meyer and J. W. Holder.

CAMBRIDGE UNIVERSITY v ESSEX

At Cambridge, April 27, 28, 29. Drawn. Cambridge were grateful for the rain which came at a time when they were fighting to save a game dominated by the Essex batsmen. Gooch and Hardie made centuries in contrasting styles, Gooch scoring 174 in three hours while Hardie batted for five hours for 129. Cambridge lost a wicket on the first evening and only Curtis survived long as Lever destroyed their first innings. Fletcher did not enforce the follow-on, and when Essex declared for a second time, Cambridge needed 489 to win. Lever took a wicket with his second ball, but Henderson led a rearguard action before rain brought a premature end.

Essex

G. A. Gooch c Hodgson b Doggart	174		
B. R. Hardie b Roebuck	129		
K. S. McEwan b Roebuck	8	– (1) c Cotterell b Pollock	86
*K. W. R. Fletcher c Roebuck b Cotterell	34	– b Cotterell	17
K. R. Pont not out	16	– (3) b Cotterell	15
D. R. Pringle (did not bat)		– (2) c Doggart b Pollock	83
S. Turner (did not bat)		– (5) b Cotterell	16
†D. E. East (did not bat)		– (6) lbw b Cotterell	18
R. E. East (did not bat)		– (7) not out	23
J. K. Lever (did not bat)		– (8) c Curtis b Cotterell	4
D. L. Acfield (did not bat)		– (9) not out	8
B 3, l-b 10, n-b 1	14	B 3, l-b 3, w 1, n-b 1	8

1/263 2/280 3/349 4/375   (4 wkts dec.) 375   1/165 2/172 3/191 (7 wkts dec.) 278
                                                          4/217 5/226 6/241 7/248

Bowling: *First Innings*—Roebuck 18.5–2–74–2; Hodgson 22–6–81–0; Pollock 20–6–53–0; Doggart 32–2–109–1; Cotterell 10–0–44–1. *Second Innings*—Roebuck 9–1–42–0; Hodgson 33–12–71–0; Pollock 6–0–36–2; Cotterell 29–9–89–5; Doggart 10–3–27–0; Curtis 1–0–5–0.

Cambridge University

T. S. Curtis c Gooch b R. E. East	50	– lbw b Lever	0
D. W. Varey lbw b Lever	0	– b Turner	17
R. J. Boyd-Moss c D. E. East b Lever	15	– c Turner b Pringle	5
*S. P. Henderson b Lever	6	– lbw b Gooch	36
A. Odendaal lbw b Lever	7	– not out	21
P. G. P. Roebuck c Turner b Lever	19	– not out	11
K. I. Hodgson c Acfield b Lever	26		
S. J. G. Doggart not out	29		
T. A. Cotterell lbw b Lever	4		
†A. G. Davies c D. E. East b Turner	0		
A. J. Pollock b Turner	4		
L-b 2, n-b 3	5	L-b 1, n-b 2	3

1/1 2/45 3/57 4/80   165   1/0 2/11 3/43 4/72   (4 wkts) 93
5/86 6/128 7/133 8/144 9/145

Bowling: *First Innings*—Lever 22–9–63–7; Pringle 14–4–32–0; Turner 15–1–22–2; R. E. East 12–7–16–1; Acfield 15–8–21–0; Gooch 2–1–6–0. *Second Innings*—Lever 6–1–16–1; Pringle 7–2–24–1; Turner 7–2–19–1; R. E. East 10.4–4–15–0; Gooch 8–4–16–1.

Umpires: J. Birkenshaw and C. T. Spencer.

CAMBRIDGE UNIVERSITY v KENT

At Cambridge, May 4, 5, 6. Drawn. Rain again washed out much of the final day. Taylor, in three and a half hours, and Benson, in two and a half, scored centuries on the first day against an attack short of penetration. Pathmanathan scored 48 in the middle of the Cambridge reply which crumbled to the pace of Dilley. Kent did not enforce the follow-on, which allowed Cowdrey to score an attractive century in 110 minutes. Kent's overnight declaration became meaningless when play was delayed until 3.30 on the last afternoon, and the Cambridge openers batted out the final two hours.

Kent

N. R. Taylor c Boyd-Moss b Doggart	114			
R. A. Woolmer c Pathmanathan b Hodgson	21	– (1) c Boyd-Moss b Pollock	4
*C. J. Tavaré run out	23	– (2) b Cotterell	44
M. R. Benson b Roebuck	105			
C. S. Cowdrey lbw b Roebuck	5	– (3) not out	103
†A. P. E. Knott not out	42			
G. W. Johnson not out	7	– (4) not out	4
L-b 5, w 1, n-b 1	7	L-b 2	2

1/32 2/98 3/243 4/260   (5 wkts dec.) 324   1/4 2/119   (2 wkts dec.) 157
5/279

R. M. Ellison, G. R. Dilley, D. L. Underwood and K. B. S. Jarvis did not bat.

Bowling: *First Innings*—Pollock 31–6–74–0; Hodgson 28–5–85–1; Roebuck 13–3–44–2; Doggart 11–2–32–1; Cotterell 22–2–82–0. *Second Innings*—Pollock 12–4–35–1; Hodgson 19–5–57–0; Cotterell 12–1–46–1; Doggart 4–1–17–0.

Cambridge University

T. S. Curtis c and b Dilley	7	– not out	44
D. W. Varey c Knott b Underwood	19	– not out	28
R. J. Boyd-Moss c Knott b Ellison	3			
*S. P. Henderson lbw b Ellison	21			
G. Pathmanathan c Tavaré b Woolmer	48			
P. G. P. Roebuck lbw b Jarvis	12			
K. I. Hodgson c Knott b Woolmer	7			
S. J. G. Doggart b Woolmer	2			
T. A. Cotterell c Tavaré b Dilley	5			
A. J. Pollock not out	0			
†A. G. Davies b Dilley	0			
B 3, l-b 8, n-b 5	16	L-b 1, n-b 3	4

1/12 2/22 3/49 4/61   140   (no wkt) 76
5/111 6/119 7/130 8/139 9/139

Bowling: *First Innings*—Dilley 13–6–21–3; Jarvis 11–2–25–1; Ellison 13–3–31–2; Underwood 9–3–15–1; Johnson 9–3–19–0; Woolmer 7–3–13–3. *Second Innings*—Dilley 5–1–7–0; Jarvis 4–0–9–0; Underwood 8–6–5–0; Ellison 5–3–5–0; Cowdrey 6–0–21–0; Johnson 6–3–16–0; Woolmer 3–0–9–0.

Umpires: C. Cook and C. T. Spencer.

†At Cambridge, May 11, 12, 13. Drawn. Rain prevented any play on the second and third days. Cambridge University 337 for four dec. (S. P. Henderson 117, R. J. Compton-Burnett 77, R. J. Boyd-Moss 73); MCC 24 for two.

†At Cambridge, June 4. Sri Lankans won by 63 runs. Sri Lankans 218 for six (60 overs) (S. Wettimuny 70); Cambridge University 155 for seven (60 overs).

CAMBRIDGE UNIVERSITY v WARWICKSHIRE

At Cambridge, June 8, 9, 10. Drawn. Again county batsmen found the pitch and the Cambridge bowling to their liking as Dyer made 93 and Wootton completed a maiden century in 225 minutes. Both fell to Pollock, the pick of the Cambridge attack. Cambridge made a tentative reply before Henderson, assisted first by Boyd-Moss and then Pathmanathan, took them close to Warwickshire's first-innings total. After Gifford had declared a second time Hogg, taking a wicket in each of his first two overs, had Cambridge fighting a rearguard action.

Warwickshire

R. I. H. B. Dyer c Henderson b Pollock	93	– c Varey b Roebuck	7
K. D. Smith lbw b Pollock	4	– b Doggart	79
S. H. Wootton lbw b Pollock	104	– c Pathmanathan b Pollock	19
G. W. Humpage c Henderson b Doggart	63	– c Curtis b Doggart	24
Asif Din not out	36	– lbw b Pollock	0
†G. A. Tedstone not out	8	– not out	67
C. M. Old (did not bat)		– not out	9
B 2, l-b 4, w 1	7	B 5, w 2	7

1/6 2/192 3/209 4/294   (4 wkts dec.) 315   1/12 2/35 3/75   (5 wkts dec.) 212
                                                             4/79 5/187

C. Lethbridge, *N. Gifford, S. P. Sutcliffe and W. Hogg did not bat.

Bowling: *First Innings*—Pollock 19–5–69–3; Hodgson 18–8–35–0; Cotterell 30–10–85–0; Doggart 27–6–74–1; Boyd-Moss 9–1–28–0; Roebuck 2–1–8–0; Henderson 2–1–9–0. *Second Innings*—Pollock 18–4–44–2; Roebuck 10–3–24–1; Doggart 25–4–81–2; Cotterell 8–1–18–0; Boyd-Moss 9–2–38–0.

Cambridge University

D. W. Varey c Tedstone b Old	23	– b Hogg	0
P. G. P. Roebuck b Hogg	9	– lbw b Hogg	0
T. S. Curtis st Tedstone b Humpage	18	– c Humpage b Hogg	13
R. J. Boyd-Moss c Gifford b Asif Din	45	– c Tedstone b Sutcliffe	30
*S. P. Henderson c Tedstone b Hogg	90	– c Old b Sutcliffe	56
G. Pathmanathan c Asif Din b Gifford	53	– not out	18
S. J. G. Doggart lbw b Asif Din	17	– not out	1
T. A. Cotterell not out	10		
K. I. Hodgson not out	2		
B 3, l-b 15, n-b 2	20	L-b 1, n-b 2	3

1/18 2/34 3/74 4/121   (7 wkts dec.) 287   1/0 2/1 3/17 4/100   (5 wkts) 121
5/217 6/255 7/281   5/101

A. J. Pollock and †S. G. P. Hewitt did not bat.

Bowling: *First Innings*—Hogg 17–6–20–2; Old 14–5–35–1; Asif Din 24–5–77–2; Lethbridge 1–0–4–0; Humpage 13–1–38–1; Sutcliffe 28–3–84–0; Gifford 5–2–9–1. *Second Innings*—Hogg 6–1–17–3; Old 3–1–3–0; Sutcliffe 21–5–50–2; Asif Din 12–3–35–0; Gifford 6–1–13–0.

Umpires: J. van Geloven and R. A. Duckett.

CAMBRIDGE UNIVERSITY v NORTHAMPTONSHIRE

At Cambridge, June 15, 16, 17. Drawn. One of the university's better performances gave the county a fright before they batted out to draw the game. A century opening partnership between Varey and Curtis was built upon by Boyd-Moss and Doggart, enabling Cambridge to declare on the first evening. Northamptonshire's reply came at more than 4 an over until they declared after less than four hours' batting. Boyd-Moss dominated Cambridge's second innings before they set the county 292 to win. From 129 for two Northamptonshire lost their way and were in danger of defeat until Williams averted it.

Cambridge University

D. W. Varey c Larkins b Walker	65	– lbw b Walker	18
T. S. Curtis lbw b Lamb	92	– c Bailey b Mallender	5
R. J. Boyd-Moss lbw b Lamb	45	– c Bailey b Walker	97
*S. P. Henderson c Olley b Willey	4	– c Larkins b Walker	0
G. Pathmanathan c Larkins b Williams	10	– lbw b Mallender	13
S. J. G. Doggart not out	59	– b Lamb	28
K. I. Hodgson c Olley b Williams	14	– b Bailey	45
T. A. Cotterell (did not bat)		– c Olley b Walker	5
A. J. Pollock (did not bat)		– not out	14
R. W. M. Palmer (did not bat)		– c Cook b Bailey	0
†S. G. P. Hewitt (did not bat)		– lbw b Bailey	3
L-b 17, w 1	18	B 5, l-b 10, n-b 1	16

1/123 2/212 3/219 4/219   (6 wkts dec.) 307   1/8 2/77 3/77 4/101   244
5/249 6/307   5/149 6/198 7/220 8/226 9/231

Bowling: *First Innings*—Mallender 14–0–50–0; Walker 19–4–70–1; Lamb 20–6–47–2; Williams 21.4–8–53–2; Wild 13–3–56–0; Bailey 1–0–2–0; Willey 13–9–11–1. *Second Innings* —Mallender 11–4–19–2; Walker 23–4–70–4; Lamb 12–1–44–1; Williams 17–8–31–0; Bailey 14–5–33–3; Larkins 5–2–7–0; Willey 12–8–24–0.

Northamptonshire

M. J. Bamber c Hewitt b Hodgson	77	– c Palmer b Cotterell	59
D. J. Wild c Hewitt b Palmer	48	– (4) c Pollock b Doggart	14
R. J. Bailey c Boyd-Moss b Hodgson	32	– c Hodgson b Pollock	16
R. G. Williams not out	38	– (5) not out	56
P. Willey not out	52	– (7) lbw b Cotterell	11
W. Larkins (did not bat)		– (2) c Cotterell b Pollock	35
*G. Cook (did not bat)		– (6) st Hewitt b Cotterell	14
†M. Olley (did not bat)		– lbw b Doggart	8
N. A. Mallender (did not bat)		– not out	11
B 4, l-b 2, w 5, n-b 2	13	B 5, l-b 10, n-b 1	16

1/66 2/133 3/175   (3 wkts dec.) 260   1/49 2/100 3/129   (7 wkts) 240
                                             4/135 5/178 6/204 7/219

T. M. Lamb and A. Walker did not bat.

Bowling: *First Innings*—Pollock 11–2–38–0; Palmer 8–0–48–1; Hodgson 22–2–71–2; Cotterell 5–1–25–0; Doggart 12–3–53–0; Boyd-Moss 2–0–12–0. *Second Innings*—Palmer 4–0–27–0; Pollock 13–4–47–2; Hodgson 5–0–25–0; Doggart 31–4–69–2; Cotterell 23–6–48–3; Curtis 1–0–8–0.

Umpires: P. B. Wight and K. G. Suttle.

CAMBRIDGE UNIVERSITY v NOTTINGHAMSHIRE

At Cambridge, June 18, 20, 21. Nottinghamshire won by 185 runs. It was ironic that the university's first defeat should follow their best bowling performance. Unfortunately, after being dismissed for 127, Nottinghamshire, led by Birch, bowled Cambridge out for 97. In their second innings Nottinghamshire applied themselves more seriously and were able to leave the university the last day in which to score 378. This they were never in a position to do after losing their first five wickets for 50. Doggart improved matters, but he was able only to delay defeat.

Nottinghamshire

P. Johnson c Doggart b Hodgson	73	– c Henderson b Ellison	15
R. T. Robinson b Ellison	15	– c and b Curtis	66
B. N. French c and b Ellison	1	– c and b Curtis	40
M. A. Fell c Hewitt b Ellison	6	– lbw b Cotterell	41
*J. D. Birch b Hodgson	4	– c Varey b Henderson	75
†C. W. Scott c Henderson b Hodgson	2	– c Henderson b Ellison	78
K. Saxelby lbw b Doggart	11	– c Pollock b Ellison	4
N. J. B. Illingworth lbw b Doggart	5	– (9) not out	15
K. E. Cooper b Hodgson	5	– (8) c Henderson b Ellison	4
M. K. Bore not out	1		
P. M. Such c Curtis b Doggart	0		
L-b 3, w 1	4	L-b 5, w 2, n-b 2	9

1/36 2/40 3/55 4/74   127   1/41 2/120 3/125   (8 wkts dec.) 347
5/94 6/109 7/120 8/125 9/127   4/192 5/299 6/314 7/321 8/347

Bowling: *First Innings*—Pollock 8–2–27–0; Hodgson 28–13–58–4; Ellison 17–7–35–3; Doggart 4.2–2–3–3. *Second Innings*—Pollock 10–2–33–0; Hodgson 12–1–53–0; Ellison 8.4–0–36–4; Henderson 4–1–25–1; Doggart 21–6–66–0; Cotterell 29–14–42–1; Curtis 23–4–58–2; Boyd-Moss 9–2–25–0.

Cambridge University

D. W. Varey b Bore	14	– b Bore	12
T. S. Curtis c Scott b Saxelby	16	– lbw b Bore	5
R. J. Boyd-Moss c Fell b Saxelby	2	– c Scott b Cooper	4
*S. P. Henderson c Illingworth b Cooper	11	– (5) c Such b Cooper	16
G. Pathmanathan lbw b Saxelby	0	– (4) c Fell b Cooper	6
S. J. G. Doggart b Cooper	9	– lbw b Bore	70
K. I. Hodgson not out	26	– c Johnson b Such	28
A. J. Pollock lbw b Bore	4	– c Cooper	12
T. A. Cotterell run out	0	– not out	9
C. C. Ellison c Scott b Bore	1	– c Johnson b Cooper	21
†S. G. P. Hewitt lbw b Bore	6	– c Johnson b Bore	0
B 5, l-b 2, n-b 1	8	B 5, l-b 4	9

1/28 2/34 3/34 4/37   97   1/16 2/23 3/23 4/33   192
5/55 6/66 7/79 8/80 9/86   5/50 6/107 7/158 8/162 9/189

Bowling: *First Innings*—Cooper 12–5–27–2; Saxelby 12–1–28–3; Bore 14.2–4–29–4; Such 2–1–5–0. *Second Innings*—Saxelby 11–1–44–0; Bore 26–4–30–4; Cooper 22–10–53–5; Illingworth 12–4–16–0; Such 18–7–40–1.

Umpires: P. B. Wight and K. G. Suttle.

CAMBRIDGE UNIVERSITY v MIDDLESEX

At Cambridge, June 22, 23. Middlesex won by an innings and 30 runs. Middlesex won in two days after another indifferent batting display by the university in their last home game. James ran through the first innings as Cambridge crumbled after an encouraging start. The Middlesex reply was dominated by Slack, who hit one 6 and 25 4s in his 138 not out. Radley and Tomlins also enjoyed themselves before Edmonds and Emburey hurried their side to victory.

Cambridge University

D. W. Varey c Downton b Hughes	4	– b Hughes	0
T. S. Curtis run out	31	– b Edmonds	24
R. J. Boyd-Moss c Butcher b Hughes	20	– c and b Edmonds	21
*S. P. Henderson c Butcher b James	27	– c Slack b Emburey	23
G. Pathmanathan c Butcher b Edmonds	27	– b Edmonds	1
S. J. G. Doggart c Butcher b James	0	– c Downton b Emburey	21
K. I. Hodgson lbw b James	0	– b Edmonds	23
T. A. Cotterell lbw b James	0	– c Butcher b Edmonds	1
C. C. Ellison not out	15	– lbw b Edmonds	0
A. J. Pollock c Radley b Edmonds	1	– b Emburey	0
†S. G. P. Hewitt c Downton b James	0	– not out	0
B 5, l-b 1, w 3, n-b 12	21	B 8, l-b 5, n-b 6	19
	146		**133**

1/6 2/64 3/72 4/116   1/5 2/52 3/73 4/77
5/117 6/117 7/117 8/135 9/145   5/97 6/112 7/126 8/126 9/133

Bowling: *First Innings*—Williams 11–2–44–0; Hughes 8–0–51–2; James 15–7–28–5; Edmonds 9–7–2–2. *Second Innings*—Williams 7–3–9–0; Hughes 8–1–23–1; James 5–1–11–0; Emburey 29–17–22–3; Edmonds 25.3–7–49–6.

Middlesex

G. D. Barlow c Henderson b Pollock	26	K. P. Tomlins not out	55
W. N. Slack not out	138	L-b 4, w 2, n-b 2	8
C. T. Radley c Ellison b Cotterell	76		
R. O. Butcher b Boyd-Moss	6	1/59 2/210 3/221 (3 wkts dec.) 309

K. D. James, †P. R. Downton, P. H. Edmonds, *J. E. Emburey, N. F. Williams and S. P. Hughes did not bat.

Bowling: Pollock 15–1–67–1; Hodgson 16–4–46–0; Ellison 5–1–10–0; Cotterell 20–6–51–1; Doggart 13–2–58–0; Curtis 2–0–23–0; Boyd-Moss 9–0–46–1.

Umpires: K. E. Palmer and R. Palmer.

At Worcester, June 25, 27, 28. CAMBRIDGE UNIVERSITY lost to WORCESTERSHIRE by an innings and 69 runs.

At Lord's, June 29, 30, July 1. CAMBRIDGE UNIVERSITY drew with OXFORD UNIVERSITY (See Other Matches at Lord's).

OXFORD AND CAMBRIDGE BLUES

From 1946-1983, and some others

A full list of Blues from 1837 may be found in all *Wisdens* published between 1923 and 1939. Between 1948 and 1972 the list was confined to all those who had won Blues after 1880, plus some of "special interest for personal or family reasons." Between 1972 and 1982 the list was restricted to those who had won Blues since 1919. Such adjustments have been necessary owing to the exigencies of space.

OXFORD

Aamer Hameed (Central Model HS and Punjab U.) 1979
Abell, G. E. B. (Marlborough) 1924, 1926-27
Allan, J. M. (Edinburgh Academy) 1953-56
Allerton, J. W. O. (Stowe) 1969
Allison, D. F. (Greenmore Coll.) 1970
Altham, H. S. (Repton) 1911-12
Arenhold, J. A. (Diocesan Coll., SA) 1954

Baig, A. A. (Aliya and Osmania U., India) 1959-62
Baig, M. A. (Osmania U., India) 1962-64
Bailey, J. A. (Christ's Hospital) (Capt. in 1958) 1956-58
Barber, A. T. (Shrewsbury) (Capt. in 1929) 1927-29
Barker, A. H. (Charterhouse) 1964-65, 1967
Bartlett, J. H. (Chichester) 1946, 1951
Bettington, R. H. B. (The King's School, Parramatta) (Capt. in 1923) 1920-23
Bird, W. S. (Malvern) (Capt. in 1906) 1904-06
Birrell, H. B. (St Andrews, SA) 1953-54
Blake, P. D. S. (Eton) (Capt. in 1952) 1950-52
Bloy, N. C. F. (Dover) 1946-47
Boobbyer, B. (Uppingham) 1949-52
Bosanquet, B. J. T. (Eton) 1898-1900
Botton, N. D. (King Edward's, Bath) 1974
Bowman, R. C. (Fettes) 1957
Brettell, D. N. (Cheltenham) 1977
Brooks, R. A. (Quintin and Bristol U.) 1967
Burchnall, R. L. (Winchester) 1970-71
Burki, J. (St Mary's, Rawalpindi and Punjab U.) 1958-60
Burton, M. St J. W. (Umtali HS, Rhodesia and Rhodes U.) (Capt. in 1970) 1969-71
Bury, T. E. O. (Charterhouse) 1980
Bush, J. E. (Magdalen Coll. Sch.) 1952

Campbell, A. N. (Berkhamsted) 1970
Campbell, I. P. (Canford) 1949-50
Campbell, I. P. F. (Repton) (Capt. in 1913) 1911-13
Cantlay, C. P. T. (Radley) 1975
Carr, D. B. (Repton) (Capt. in 1950) 1949-51

Carr, J. D. (Repton) 1983
Carroll, P. R. (Newington Coll. and Sydney U.) 1971
Chalk, F. G. H. (Uppingham) (Capt. in 1934) 1931-34
Chesterton, G. H. (Malvern) 1949
Claughton, J. A. (King Edward's, Birmingham) (Capt. in 1978) 1976-79
Clements, S. M. (Ipswich) (Capt. in 1979) 1976, 1979
Clube, S. V. M. (St John's, Leatherhead) 1956
Corlett, S. C. (Worksop) 1971-72
Corran, A. J. (Gresham's) 1958-60
Coutts, I. D. F. (Dulwich) 1952
Cowan, R. S. (Lewes Priory CS) 1980-82
Cowdrey, M. C. (Tonbridge) (Capt. in 1954) 1952-54
Coxon, A. J. (Harrow CS) 1952
Crawley, A. M. (Harrow) 1927-30
Crutchley, G. E. V. (Harrow) 1912
Cullinan, M. R. (Hilton Coll., SA) 1983
Curtis, I. J. (Whitgift) 1980, 1982
Cushing, V. G. B. (KCS Wimbledon) 1973
Cuthbertson, J. L. (Rugby) 1962-63

Davidson, W. W. (Brighton) 1947-48
Davis, F. J. (Blundell's) 1963
Delisle, G. P. S. (Stonyhurst) 1955-56
de Saram, F. C. (Royal Coll., Colombo) 1934-35
Divecha, R. V. (Podar HS and Bombay U.) 1950-51
Dixon, E. J. H. (St Edward's, Oxford) (Capt. in 1939) 1937-39
Donnelly, M. P. (New Plymouth BHS and Canterbury U., NZ) (Capt. in 1947) 1946-47
Dowding, A. L. (St Peter's, Adelaide) (Capt. in 1953) 1952-53
Drybrough, C. D. (Highgate) (Capt. in 1961-62) 1960-62
Duff, A. R. (Radley) 1960-61
Dyer, A. W. (Mill Hill) 1965-66
Dyson, E. M. (QEGS, Wakefield) 1958

Eagar, M. A. (Rugby) 1956-59

Easter, J. N. C. (St Edward's, Oxford) 1967-68

Ellis, R. G. P. (Haileybury) (Capt. in 1982) 1981-83

Elviss, R. W. (Leeds GS) 1966-67

Ezekowitz, R. A. B. (Westville BHS, Durban and Cape Town U., SA) 1980-81

Faber, M. J. J. (Eton) 1972

Fane, F. L. (Charterhouse) 1897-98

Fasken, D. K. (Wellington) 1953-55

Fellows-Smith, J. P. (Durban HS, SA) 1953-55

Fillary, E. W. J. (St Lawrence) 1963-65

Findlay, W. (Eton) (Capt. in 1903) 1901-03

Fisher, P. B. (St Ignatius, Enfield) 1975-78

Foster, G. N. (Malvern) 1905-08

Foster, H. K. (Malvern) 1894-96

Foster, R. E. (Malvern) (Capt. in 1900) 1897-1900

Fry, C. A. (Repton) 1959-61

Fry, C. B. (Repton) (Capt. in 1894) 1892-95

Fursdon, E. D. (Sherborne) 1974-75

Gamble, N. W. (Stockport GS) 1967

Garofall, A. R. (Latymer Upper) 1967-68

Gibbs, P. J. K. (Hanley GS) 1964-66

Gibson, I. (Manchester GS) 1955-58

Gilliat, R. M. C. (Charterhouse) (Capt. in 1966) 1964-67

Gilligan, F. W. (Dulwich) (Capt. in 1920) 1919-20

Glover, T. R. (Lancaster RGS) (Capt. in 1975) 1973-75

Goldstein, F. S. (Falcon Coll., Bulawayo) (Capt. in 1968-69) 1966-69

Green, D. M. (Manchester GS) 1959-61

Grover, J. N. (Winchester) (Capt. in 1938) 1936-38

Groves, M. G. M. (Diocesan Coll., SA) 1964-66

Guest, M. R. J. (Rugby) 1964-66

Guise, J. L. (Winchester) (Capt. in 1925) 1924-25

Gurr, D. R. (Aylesbury GS) 1976-77

Halliday, S. J. (Downside) 1980

Hamblin, C. B. (King's, Canterbury) 1971-73

Hamilton, A. C. (Charterhouse) 1975

Harris, C. R. (Buckingham RLS) 1964

Harris, Hon. G. R. C. (Lord Harris) (Eton) 1871-72, 1874

Hayes, K. A. (QEGS, Blackburn) 1981-83

Heal, M. G. (St Brendan's, Bristol) 1970, 1972

Heard, H. (QE Hosp. Sch.) 1969-70

Henderson, D. (St Edward's, Oxford) 1950

Henley, D. F. (Harrow) 1947

Heseltine, P. G. (Holgate GS) 1983

Hiller, R. B. (Bec) 1966

Hobbs, J. A. D. (Liverpool Coll.) 1957

Hofmeyr, M. B. (Pretoria, SA) (Capt. in 1951) 1949-51

Holmes, E. R. T. (Malvern) (Capt. in 1927) 1925-27

Hone, B. W. (Adelaide U.) (Capt. in 1933) 1931-33

Howell, M. (Repton) (Capt. in 1919) 1914, 1919

Huxford, P. N. (Richard Hale) 1981

Imran Khan (Aitchison Coll., Lahore and Worcester RGS) (Capt. in 1974) 1973-75

Jakobson, T. R. (Charterhouse) 1961

Jardine, D. R. (Winchester) 1920-21, 1923

Jardine, M. R. (Fettes) (Capt. in 1891) 1889-92

Jarrett, D. W. (Wellington) 1975

Johns, R. L. (St Albans and Keele U.) 1970

Jones, A. K. C. (Solihull) (Capt. in 1973) 1971-73

Jones, P. C. H. (Milton HS, Rhodesia and Rhodes U.) (Capt. in 1972) 1971-72

Jose, A. D. (Adelaide U.) 1950-51

Jowett, D. C. P. R. (Sherborne) 1952-55

Jowett, R. L. (Bradford GS) 1957-59

Kamm, A. (Charterhouse) 1954

Kardar, A. H. (Islamia Coll. and Punjab U.) 1947-49

Kayum, D. A. (Selhurst GS and Chatham House GS) 1977-78

Keighley, W. G. (Eton) 1947-48

Kentish, E. S. M. (Cornwall Coll., Jamaica) 1956

Khan, A. J. (Aitchison Coll., Lahore and Punjab U.) 1968-69

Kingsley, P. G. T. (Winchester) (Capt. in 1930) 1928-30

Kinkead-Weekes, R. C. (Eton) 1972

Knight, D. J. (Malvern) 1914, 1919

Knight, J. M. (Oundle) 1979

Knott, C. H. (Tonbridge) (Capt. in 1924) 1922-24

Knott, F. H. (Tonbridge) (Capt. in 1914) 1912-14

Knox, F. P. (Dulwich) (Capt. in 1901) 1899-1901

Lamb, Hon. T. M. (Shrewsbury) 1973-74

Lee, R. J. (Church of England GS and Sydney U.) 1972-74

Legge, G. B. (Malvern) (Capt. in 1926) 1925-26

L'Estrange, M. G. (St Aloysius Coll. and Sydney U.) 1977, 1979

Leveson Gower, H. D. G. (Winchester) (Capt. in 1896) 1893-96

Lewis, D. J. (Cape Town U.) 1951

Lloyd, M. F. D. (Magdalen Coll. Sch.) 1974

Luddington, R. S. (KCS, Wimbledon) 1982

McCanlis, M. A. (Cranleigh) (Capt. in 1928) 1926-28
Macindoe, D. H. (Eton) (Capt. in 1946) 1937-39, 1946
McKinna, G. H. (Manchester GS) 1953
Majendie, N. L. (Winchester) 1962-63
Mallett, A. W. H. (Dulwich) 1947-48
Mallett, N. V. H. (St Andrew's Coll. and Cape Town U.) 1981
Manasseh, M. (Epsom) 1964
Marie, G. V. (Western Australia U. and Reading U.) (Capt. in 1979, but injury prevented him playing v Cambridge) 1978
Marks, V. J. (Blundell's) (Capt. in 1976-77) 1975-78
Marsden, R. (Merchant Taylors', Northwood) 1982
Marshall, J. C. (Rugby) 1953
Marsham, C. D. B. (Private) (Capt. in 1857-58) 1854-58
Marsham, C. H. B. (Eton) (Capt. in 1902) 1900-02
Marsham, C. J. B. (Private) 1851
Marsham, R. H. B. (Private) 1856
Marsland, G. P. (Rossall) 1954
Martin, J. D. (Magdalen Coll. Sch.) (Capt. in 1965) 1962-63, 1965
Maudsley, R. H. (Malvern) 1946-47
May, B. (Prince Edward's, Salisbury and Cape Town U.) (Capt. in 1971) 1970-72
Melville, A. (Michaelhouse, SA) (Capt. in 1931-32) 1930-33
Melville, C. D. M. (Michaelhouse, SA) 1957
Metcalfe, S. G. (Leeds GS) 1956
Millener, D. J. (Auckland GS and Auckland U.) 1969-70
Miller, A. J. T. (Haileybury) 1983
Minns, R. E. F. (King's, Canterbury) 1962-63
Mitchell, W. M. (Dulwich) 1951-52
Mitchell-Innes, N. S. (Sedbergh) (Capt. in 1936) 1934-37
Moore, D. N. (Shrewsbury) (Capt. in 1931, when he did not play v Cambridge owing to illness) 1930
Morgan, A. H. (Hastings GS) 1969
Morrill, N. D. (Sandown GS and Millfield) 1979
Moulding, R. P. (Haberdashers' Aske's) (Capt. in 1981) 1978-83
Mountford, P. N. G. (Bromsgrove) 1963

Neate, F. W. (St Paul's) 1961-62
Newton-Thompson, J. O. (Diocesan Coll., SA) 1946
Niven, R. A. (Berkhamsted) 1968-69, 1973

O'Brien, T. C. (St Charles' College, Notting-Hill) 1884-85
Orders, J. O. D. (Winchester) 1978-81
Owen-Smith, H. G. (Diocesan College, SA) 1931-33

Palairet, L. C. H. (Repton) (Capt. in 1892-93) 1890-93
Pataudi, Nawab of (Chief's College, Lahore) 1929-31
Pataudi, Nawab of (Winchester) (Capt. in 1961, when he did not play v Cambridge owing to a car accident and 1963) 1960, 1963
Pathmanathan, G. (Royal Coll., Colombo and Sri Lanka U.) 1975-78
Paver, R. G. L. (Fort Victoria HS and Rhodes U.) 1973-74
Pawson, A. C. (Winchester) 1903
Pawson, A. G. (Winchester) (Capt. in 1910) 1908-11
Pawson, H. A. (Winchester) (Capt. in 1948) 1947-48
Pearce, J. P. (Ampleforth) 1979
Peebles, I. A. R. (Glasgow Academy) 1930
Petchey, M. D. (Latymer Upper) 1983
Phillips, J. B. M. (King's, Canterbury) 1955
Piachaud, J. D. (St Thomas's, Colombo) 1958-61
Pithey, D. B. (Plumtree HS and Cape Town U.) 1961-62
Porter, S. R. (Peers School) 1973
Potter, I. C. (King's, Canterbury) 1961-62
Potts, H. J. (Stand GS) 1950
Price, V. R. (Bishop's Stortford) (Capt. in 1921) 1919-22
Pycroft, J. (Bath) 1836

Rawlinson, H. T. (Eton) 1983
Raybould, J. G. (Leeds GS) 1959
Ridge, S. P. (Dr Challenors) 1982
Ridley, G. N. S. (Milton HS, Rhodesia) (Capt. in 1967) 1965-68
Ridley, R. M. (Clifton) 1968-70
Robertson-Glasgow, R. C. (Charterhouse) 1920-23
Robinson, G. A. (Preston Cath. Coll.) 1971
Robinson, H. B. O. (North Shore Coll., Vancouver) 1947-48
Rogers, J. J. (Sedbergh) 1979-81
Ross, C. J. (Wanganui CS and Wellington U., NZ) (Capt. in 1980) 1978-80
Rudd, C. R. D. (Eton) 1949
Rumbold, J. S. (St Andrew's Coll., NZ) 1946

Sabine, P. N. B. (Marlborough) 1963
Sale, R. (Repton) 1910
Sale, R. (Repton) 1939, 1946
Sanderson, J. F. W. (Westminster) 1980
Saunders, C. J. (Lancing) 1964
Savage, R. Le Q. (Marlborough) 1976-78

Sayer, D. M. (Maidstone GS) 1958-60
Scott, M. D. (Winchester) 1957
Singleton, A. P. (Shrewsbury) (Capt. in 1937) 1934-37
Siviter, K. (Liverpool) 1976
Smith, A. C. (King Edward's, Birmingham) (Capt. in 1959-60) 1958-60
Smith, G. O. (Charterhouse) 1895-96
Smith, M. J. K. (Stamford) (Capt. in 1956) 1954-56
Stallibrass, M. J. D. (Lancing) 1974
Stevens, G. T. S. (UCS) (Capt. in 1922) 1920-23
Sutcliffe, S. P. (King George V GS, Southport) 1980-81
Sutton, M. A. (Ampleforth) 1946

Tavaré, C. J. (Sevenoaks) 1975-77
Taylor, C. H. (Westminster) 1923-26
Taylor, T. J. (Stockport GS) 1981-82
Thackeray, P. R. (St Edward's, Oxford and Exeter U.) 1974
Thomas, R. J. A. (Radley) 1965
Toft, D. P. (Tonbridge) 1966-67
Toogood, G. J. (N. Bromsgrove HS) (Capt. in 1983) 1982-83
Topham, R. D. N. (Shrewsbury and Australian National U., Canberra) 1976
Travers, B. H. (Sydney U.) 1946, 1948
Twining, R. H. (Eton) (Capt. in 1912) 1910-13

van der Bijl, P. G. (Diocesan Coll., SA) 1932
Van Ryneveld, C. B. (Diocesan Coll., SA) (Capt. in 1949) 1948-50
Varey, J. G. (Birkenhead) 1982-83

Wagstaffe, M. C. (Rossall and Exeter U.) 1972

Walford, M. M. (Rugby) 1936, 1938
Walker, D. F. (Uppingham) (Capt. in 1935) 1933-35
Waller, G. de W. (Hurstpierpoint) 1974
Walsh, D. R. (Marlborough) 1967-69
Walshe, A. P. (Milton HS, Rhodesia) 1953, 1955-56
Walton, A. C. (Radley) (Capt. in 1957) 1955-57
Ward, J. M. (Newcastle-u-Lyme HS) 1971-73
Warner, P. F. (Rugby) 1895-96
Watson, A. G. M. (St Lawrence) 1965-66, 1968
Webb, H. E. (Winchester) 1948
Webbe, A. J. (Harrow) (Capt. in 1877-78) 1875-78
Wellings, E. M. (Cheltenham) 1929, 1931
Westley, S. A. (Lancaster RGS) 1968-69
Wheatley, G. A. (Uppingham) 1946
Whitcombe, P. A. (Winchester) 1947-49
Whitcombe, P. J. (Worcester RGS) 1951-52
Wiley, W. G. A. (Diocesan Coll., SA) 1952
Williams, C. C. P. (Westminster) (Capt. in 1955) 1953-55
Wilson, P. R. B. (Milton HS, Rhodesia and Cape Town U.) 1968, 1970
Wilson, R. W. (Warwick) 1957
Wingfield Digby, A. R. (Sherborne) 1971, 1975-77
Winn, C. E. (KCS, Wimbledon) 1948-51
Woodcock, R. G. (Worcester RGS) 1957-58
Wookey, S. M. (Malvern and Cambridge U.) 1978
Wordsworth, Chas. (Harrow) (Capt. both years, first Oxford Capt.) 1827, 1829
Worsley, D. R. (Bolton) (Capt. in 1964) 1961-64
Wrigley, M. H. (Harrow) 1949

CAMBRIDGE

Acfield, D. L. (Brentwood) 1967-68
Aers, D. R. (Tonbridge) 1967
Aird, R. (Eton) 1923
Alexander, F. C. M. (Wolmer's Coll., Jamaica) 1952-53
Allbrook, M. E. (Tonbridge) 1975-78
Allen, G. O. (Eton) 1922-23
Allom, M. J. C. (Wellington) 1927-28
Ashton, C. T. (Winchester) (Capt. in 1923) 1921-23
Ashton, G. (Winchester) (Capt. in 1921) 1919-21
Ashton, H. (Winchester) (Capt. in 1922) 1920-22
Atkins, G. (Challenors GS) 1960
Aworth, C. J. (Tiffin) (Capt. in 1975) 1973-75

Bailey, T. E. (Dulwich) 1947-48

Baker, R. K. (Brentwood) 1973-74
Bannister, C. S. (Caterham) 1976
Barber, R. W. (Ruthin) 1956-57
Barford, M. T. (Eastbourne) 1970-71
Barrington, W. E. J. (Lancing) 1982
Bartlett, H. T. (Dulwich) (Capt. in 1936) 1934-36
Beaumont, D. J. (West Bridgford GS and Bramshill Coll.) 1978
Benke, A. F. (Cheltenham) 1962
Bennett, B. W. P. (Welbeck and RMA Sandhurst) 1979
Bennett, C. T. (Harrow) (Capt. in 1925) 1923, 1925
Bernard, J. R. (Clifton) 1958-60
Bhatia, A. N. (Doon School, India) 1969
Bligh, Hon. Ivo F. W. (Lord Darnley) (Eton) (Capt. in 1881) 1878-81

Hayward, W. I. D. (St Peter's Coll., Adelaide) 1950-51, 1953
Haywood, D. C. (Nottingham HS) 1968
Hazelrigg, A. G. (Eton) (Capt. in 1932) 1930-32
Henderson, S. P. (Downside and Durham U.) (Capt. in 1983) 1982-83
Hewitt, S. G. (Bradford GS) 1983
Hignell, A. J. (Denstone) (Capt. in 1977-78) 1975-78
Hobson, B. S. (Taunton) 1946
Hodgson, K. I. (Oundle) 1981-83
Hodson, R. P. (QEGS, Wakefield) 1972-73
Holliday, D. C. (Oundle) 1979-81
Howat, M. G. (Abingdon) 1977, 1980
Howland, C. B. (Dulwich) (Capt. in 1960) 1958-60
Hughes, G. (Cardiff HS) 1965
Hurd, A. (Chigwell) 1958-60
Hutton, R. A. (Repton) 1962-64
Huxter, R. J. A. (Magdalen Coll. Sch.) 1981

Insole, D. J. (Monoux, Walthamstow) (Capt. in 1949) 1947-49

Jackson, E. J. W. (Winchester) 1974-76
Jackson, F. S. (Harrow) (Capt. in 1892-93) 1890-93
Jahangir Khan (Lahore), 1933-36
James, R. M. (St John's, Leatherhead) 1956-58
Jameson, T. E. N. (Taunton and Durham U.) 1970
Jarrett, D. W. (Wellington and Oxford U.) 1976
Jefferson, R. I. (Winchester) 1961
Jenner, Herbert (Eton) (Capt. in 1827, First Cambridge Capt.) 1827
Jessop, G. L. (Cheltenham GS) (Capt. in 1899) 1896-99
Johnson, P. D. (Nottingham HS) 1970-72
Jones, A. O. (Bedford Modern) 1893
Jorden, A. M. (Monmouth) (Capt. in 1969-70) 1968-70

Kelland, P. A. (Repton) 1950
Kemp-Welch, G. D. (Charterhouse) (Capt. in 1931) 1929-31
Kendall, M. P. (Gillingham GS) 1972
Kenny, C. J. M. (Ampleforth) 1952
Kerslake, R. C. (Kingswood) 1963-64
Killick, E. T. (St Paul's) 1928-30
Kirby, D. (St Peter's, York) (Capt. in 1961) 1959-61
Kirkman, M. C. (Dulwich) 1963
Knight, R. D. V. (Dulwich) 1967-70
Knightley-Smith, W. (Highgate) 1953

Lacey, F. E. (Sherborne) 1882
Lacy-Scott, D. G. (Marlborough) 1946
Lewis, A. R. (Neath GS) (Capt. in 1962) 1960-62
Lewis, L. K. (Taunton) 1953
Littlewood, D. J. (Enfield GS) 1978
Lowry, T. C. (Christ's College, NZ) (Capt. in 1924) 1923-24
Lumsden, V. R. (Munro College, Jamaica) 1953-55
Lyttelton, 4th Lord (Eton) 1838
Lyttelton, Hon. Alfred (Eton) (Capt. in 1879) 1876-79
Lyttelton, Hon. C. F. (Eton) 1908-09
Lyttelton, Hon. C. G. (Lord Cobham) (Eton) 1861-64
Lyttelton, Hon. Edward (Eton) (Capt. in 1878) 1875-78
Lyttelton, Hon. G. W. S. (Eton) 1866-67

McAdam, K. P. W. J. (Prince of Wales, Nairobi and Millfield) 1965-66
MacBryan, J. C. W. (Exeter) 1920
McCarthy, C. N. (Maritzburg Coll., SA) 1952
McDowall, J. I. (Rugby) 1969
MacGregor, G. (Uppingham) (Capt. in 1891) 1888-91
McLachlan, A. A. (St Peter's, Adelaide) 1964-65
McLachlan, I. M. (St Peter's, Adelaide) 1957-58
Majid J. Khan (Aitchison Coll., Lahore and Punjab U.) (Capt. in 1971-72) 1970-72
Malalasekera, V. P. (Royal Coll., Colombo) 1966-67
Mann, E. W. (Harrow) (Capt. in 1905) 1903-05
Mann, F. G. (Eton) 1938-39
Mann, F. T. (Malvern) 1909-11
Marlar, R. G. (Harrow) (Capt. in 1953) 1951-53
Marriott, C. S. (St Columba's) 1920-21
Mathews, K. P. A. (Felsted) 1951
May, P. B. H. (Charterhouse) 1950-52
Melluish, M. E. L. (Rossall) (Capt. in 1956) 1954-56
Meyer, R. J. O. (Haileybury) 1924-26
Miller, M. E. (Prince Henry GS, Hohne, WG) 1963
Mills, J. M. (Oundle) (Capt. in 1948) 1946-48
Mills, J. P. C. (Oundle) (Capt. in 1982) 1979-82
Mischler, N. M. (St Paul's) 1946-47
Mitchell, F. (St Peter's, York) (Capt. in 1896) 1894-97
Morgan, J. T. (Charterhouse) (Capt. in 1930) 1928-30
Morgan, M. N. (Marlborough) 1954
Morris, R. J. (Blundell's) 1949

Morrison, J. S. F. (Charterhouse) (Capt. in 1919) 1912, 1914, 1919
Moses, G. H. (Ystalyfera GS) 1974
Moylan, A. C. D. (Clifton) 1977
Mubarak, A. M. (Royal Coll., Colombo and Sri Lanka U.) 1978-80
Murray, D. L. (Queen's RC, Trinidad) (Capt. in 1966) 1965-66
Murrills, T. J. (The Leys) (Capt. in 1976) 1973-74, 1976

Nevin, M. R. S. (Winchester) 1969
Norris, D. W. W. (Harrow) 1967-68

O'Brien, R. P. (Wellington) 1955-56
Odendaal, A. (Queen's Coll. and Stellenbosch U., SA) 1980
Owen-Thomas, D. R. (KCS, Wimbledon) 1969-72

Palfreman, A. B. (Nottingham HS) 1966
Palmer, R. W. M. (Bedford) 1982
Parker, G. W. (Crypt, Gloucester) (Capt. in 1935) 1934-35
Parker, P. W. G. (Collyer's GS) 1976-78
Parsons, A. B. D. (Brighton) 1954-55
Pathmanathan, G. (Royal Coll., Colombo, Sri Lanka U. and Oxford U.) 1982
Paull, R. K. (Millfield) 1967
Payne, M. W. (Wellington) (Capt. in 1907) 1904-07
Pearman, H. (King Alfred's and St Andrew's U.) 1969
Pearson, A. J. G. (Downside) 1961-63
Peck, I. G. (Bedford) (Capt. in 1980-81) 1980-81
Pepper, J. (The Leys) 1946-48
Pieris, P. I. (St Thomas's, Colombo) 1957-58
Pollock, A. J. (Shrewsbury) 1982-83
Ponniah, C. E. M. (St Thomas's, Colombo) 1967-69
Ponsonby, Hon. F. G. B. (Lord Bessborough) (Harrow) 1836
Popplewell, N. F. M. (Radley) 1977-79
Popplewell, O. B. (Charterhouse) 1949-51
Pretlove, J. F. (Alleyn's) 1954-56
Prideaux, R. M. (Tonbridge) 1958-60
Pringle, D. R. (Felsted) (Capt. in 1982, when he did not play v Oxford owing to Test selection) 1979-81
Pritchard, G. C. (King's, Canterbury) 1964
Pryer, B. J. K. (City of London) 1948
Pyemont, C. P. (Marlborough) 1967

Ranjitsinhji, K. S. (Rajkumar Coll., India) 1893
Ratcliffe, A. (Rydal) 1930-32
Reddy, N. S. K. (Doon School, India) 1959-61
Rimell, A. G. J. (Charterhouse) 1949-50
Robins, R. W. V. (Highgate) 1926-28

Roebuck, P. M. (Millfield) 1975-77
Roopnaraine, R. (Queen's RC, BG) 1965-66
Rose, M. H. (Pocklington) 1963-64
Ross, N. P. G. (Marlborough) 1969
Roundell, J. (Winchester) 1973
Russell, D. P. (West Park GS, St Helens) 1974-75
Russell, S. G. (Tiffin) (Capt. in 1967) 1965-67
Russom, N. (Huish's GS) 1980-81

Seabrook, F. J. (Haileybury) (Capt. in 1928) 1926-28
Seager, C. P. (Peterhouse, Rhodesia) 1971
Selvey, M. W. W. (Battersea GS and Manchester U.) 1971
Sheppard, D. S. (Sherborne) (Capt. in 1952) 1950-52
Short, R. L. (Denstone) 1969
Shuttleworth, G. M. (Blackburn GS) 1946-48
Silk, D. R. W. (Christ's Hospital) (Capt. in 1955) 1953-55
Singh, S. (Khalsa Coll. and Punjab U.) 1955-56
Sinker, N. D. (Winchester) 1966
Slack, J. K. E. (UCS) 1954
Smith, C. S. (William Hulme's GS) 1954-57
Smith, D. J. (Stockport GS) 1955-56
Smyth, R. I. (Sedbergh) 1973-75
Snowden, W. (Merchant Taylors', Crosby) (Capt. in 1974) 1972-75
Spencer, J. (Brighton and Hove GS) 1970-72
Steele, H. K. (King's Coll., NZ) 1971-72
Stevenson, M. H. (Rydal) 1949-52
Studd, C. T. (Eton) (Capt. in 1883) 1880-83
Studd, G. B. (Eton) (Capt. in 1882) 1879-82
Studd, J. E. K. (Eton) (Capt. in 1884) 1881-84
Studd, P. M. (Harrow) (Capt. in 1939) 1937-39
Studd, R. A. (Eton) 1895
Subba Row, R. (Whitgift) 1951-53
Surridge, D. (Richard Hale and Southampton U.) 1979
Swift, B. T. (St Peter's, Adelaide) 1957

Taylor, C. R. V. (Birkenhead) 1971-73
Thomson, R. H. (Bexhill) 1961-62
Thwaites, I. G. (Eastbourne) 1964
Tindall, M. (Harrow) (Capt. in 1937) 1935-37
Tordoff, G. G. (Normanton GS) 1952
Trapnell, B. M. W. (UCS) 1946
Turnbull, M. J. (Downside) (Capt. in 1929) 1926, 1928-29

Urquhart, J. R. (King Edward VI School, Chelmsford) 1948

Valentine, B. H. (Repton) 1929
Varey, D. W. (Birkenhead) 1982-83

Wait, O. J. (Dulwich) 1949, 1951
Warr, J. J. (Ealing County GS) (Capt. in 1951) 1949-52
Watts, H. E. (Downside) 1947
Webster, W. H. (Highgate) 1932
Weedon, M. J. H. (Harrow) 1962
Wells, T. U. (King's Coll., NZ) 1950
Wheatley, O. S. (King Edward's, Birmingham) 1957-58
Wheelhouse, A. (Nottingham HS) 1959
White, R. C. (Hilton Coll., SA) (Capt. in 1965) 1962-65
Wilcox, D. R. (Dulwich) (Capt. in 1933) 1931-33
Wilenkin, B. C. G. (Harrow) 1956

Wilkin, C. L. A. (St Kitts GS) 1970
Willard, M. J. L. (Judd) 1959-61
Willatt, G. L. (Repton) (Capt. in 1947) 1946-47
Windows, A. R. (Clifton) 1962-64
Wood, G. E. C. (Cheltenham) (Capt. in 1920) 1914, 1919-20
Wookey, S. M. (Malvern) 1975-76
Wooller, W. (Rydal) 1935-36
Wright, S. (Mill Hill) 1973

Yardley, N. W. D. (St Peter's, York) (Capt. in 1938) 1935-38
Young, R. A. (Repton) (Capt. in 1908) 1905-08

CRICKET ASSOCIATIONS AND SOCIETIES

AUSTRALIAN CRICKET SOCIETY: *Secretary* Christopher Harte, GPO Box 696, Adelaide, 5001, South Australia.
  ADELAIDE BRANCH: *Secretary* Michael Gandy, 28 Glenalvon Drive, Flagstaff Hill, South Australia 5159
  BRISBANE BRANCH: *Secretary* Robert Spence, GPO Box 1498, Brisbane 4001, Queensland.
  CANBERRA BRANCH: *Secretary* Julian Oakley, 38 Holden Crescent, Wanniassa, ACT 2903.
  MELBOURNE BRANCH: *Secretary* Alan Hart, PO Box 120, North Melbourne 3051.
  PERTH BRANCH: *Secretary* Kevin Collins, 11 Brindley Street, Belmont 6104, Western Australia.
  SYDNEY BRANCH: *Secretary* Ronald Cardwell, 24 New Street, Balgowlah Heights 2093, New South Wales.
BLACKLEY CRICKET SOCIETY: *Secretary* D. Butterfield, 7 Bayswater Terrace, West Yorkshire, HX3 0NB.
CAMBRIDGE UNIVERSITY CRICKET SOCIETY: *Secretary* G. K. Sankaran, Jesus College, Cambridge CB2 1TP.
CHESTERFIELD CRICKET LOVERS' SOCIETY: *Secretary* B. Holling, 24 Woodland Way, Old Tupton, Chesterfield, Derbyshire.
COUNCIL OF CRICKET SOCIETIES, THE: *Secretary* B. L. Mellis, The Old Vicarage, Church Hill, Bramhope, West Yorks LS16 9BA.
CRICKET SOCIETY, THE: *Secretary* E. C. R. Rice, 11 Clive Court, Babington Road, London SW16 6AL.
CRICKET STATISTICIANS, ASSOCIATION OF: *Secretary* P. Wynne-Thomas, The Bungalow, Haughton Mill, Retford, Nottinghamshire.
EAST RIDING CRICKET SOCIETY: *Secretary* H. K. Cooke, 104 Well Lane, Willerby, Kingston upon Hull, East Yorkshire.
ESSEX CRICKET SOCIETY: *Secretary* P. T. Roberts, 21 Hadrian Close, Lodge Park, Witham, Essex, CM8 1XA.
FYLDE COAST CRICKET SOCIETY: *Secretary* S. Kennedy, 36 Torquay Avenue, Marton, Blackpool, Lancashire.
HAMPSHIRE CRICKET SOCIETY: *Secretary* F. Bailey, 7 Lightfoot Grove, Basingstoke, Hampshire.
HEAVY WOOLLEN CRICKET SOCIETY: *Secretary* G. S. Cooper, 27 Milford Grove, Gomersal, Cleckheaton, West Yorkshire.

LANCASHIRE AND CHESHIRE CRICKET SOCIETY: *Secretary* H. W. Pardoe, Crantock, 117a Barlow Moor Road, Didsbury, Manchester, M20 8TS.

LIMITED-OVERS INFORMATION GROUP: *Secretary* T. Allcock, 57 Low Road, Rivelin, Sheffield, S6 5FY.

LINCOLNSHIRE CRICKET LOVERS' SOCIETY: *Secretary* C. Kennedy, ACP, 26 Eastwood Avenue, Grimsby, South Humberside, DN34 5BE.

NORTHERN CRICKET SOCIETY: *Secretary* B. L. Mellis, The Old Vicarage, Church Hill, Bramhope, West Yorks LS16 9BA.

NOTTINGHAM CRICKET SOCIETY: *Secretary* G. Blagdurn, 2 Inham Circus, Chilwell, Beeston, Nottinghamshire, NG9 4FN.

NUNTHORPE GRAMMAR SCHOOL CRICKET SOCIETY: *Secretary* H. J. George, 2 Braeside Gardens, Acomb, Yorks YO2 4EZ.

OXFORD UNIVERSITY CRICKET SOCIETY: *Secretary* Harriet Monkhouse, Corpus Christi College, Oxford.

PAKISTAN ASSOCIATION OF CRICKET STATISTICIANS: *Secretary* Abid Ali Kazi, 5-A, 11/1, Sunset Lane, Phase 11, Defence Housing Society, Karachi, Pakistan.

ROTHERHAM CRICKET SOCIETY: *Secretary* J. A. R. Atkin, 15 Gallow Tree Road, Rotherham, South Yorkshire, S65 3EE.

SCOTLAND, CRICKET SOCIETY OF: *Secretary* A. J. Robertson, 5 Riverside Road, Eaglesham, Glasgow, G76 0DA.

SOMERSET WYVERNS: *Secretary* M. Richards, "Wyvern", 3 Ash Road, Tring, Hertfordshire.

SOPHIANS, THE: *Secretary* A. K. Hignell, 79 Coed Glas Road, Llanishen, Cardiff.

STOURBRIDGE AND DISTRICT CRICKET SOCIETY: *Secretary* R. Barber, 6 Carlton Avenue, Stourbridge, DY9 9ED.

SUSSEX CRICKET SOCIETY: *Secretary* A. A. Dumbrell, 6 Southdown Avenue, Brighton, East Sussex, BN1 6EG.

SYDNEY BARNES CRICKET SOCIETY: *Secretary* J. D. Scholfield, 331 Turnhurst Road, Packmoor, Stoke-on-Trent, S77 4LA.

UPPINGHAM SCHOOL CRICKET SOCIETY: *Secretary* Dr E. J. R. Boston, The Common Room, Uppingham School, Rutland.

WALES, CRICKET SOCIETY OF: *Secretary* C. N. Fookes, 5 Melrose Close, St Mellons, Cardiff, CF3 9SW.

WEST LANCASHIRE CRICKET SOCIETY: *Secretary* D. H. Stringfellow, 36 Cardigan Road, Southport, Merseyside, PR8 4SF.

WOMBWELL CRICKET LOVERS' SOCIETY: *Secretary* J. Sokell, 42 Woodstock Road, Barnsley, South Yorkshire, S75 1DX.

ZIMBABWE, CRICKET SOCIETY OF: *Secretary* L. G. Morgenrood, 10 Elsworth Avenue, Balgravia, Harare, Zimbabwe.

OTHER MATCHES, 1983

THE TILCON TROPHY

The competition opened at the Harrogate Festival with Northamptonshire achieving a surprise win over Leicestershire when Larkins bowled Taylor with the second ball of the tense final over. On the second day Athey, who hit 76 off 100 balls, and acting-captain Hartley inspired an improbable win by Yorkshire over Nottinghamshire in an exciting high-scoring match. Northamptonshire then overwhelmed Yorkshire in the final to retain the Tilcon Trophy, despite Sidebottom's 79, which contained two 6s and seven 4s. They owed their victory to Larkins, who hit a punishing 104 off 80 balls (three 6s and fifteen 4s), having earlier taken four Yorkshire wickets, including three in four balls. His fourth victim was Bairstow, who, hit on the pad, leapt up to head the ball away from his wicket but landed on his stumps.

July 6. Northamptonshire won by 3 runs. Northamptonshire 171 for nine (55 overs) (R. G. Williams 43; G. J. F. Ferris four for 32); Leicestershire 168 (54.2 overs) (N. E. Briers 40; T. M. Lamb three for 36). *Man of the Match:* R. G. Williams.

July 7. Yorkshire won by four wickets. Nottinghamshire 265 for three (55 overs) (C. E. B. Rice 82 not out, R. T. Robinson 56, D. W. Randall 52, R. B. Kerr 36); Yorkshire 268 for six (53.4 overs) (C. W. J. Athey 76, S. N. Hartley 56 not out, D. L. Bairstow 36). *Man of the Match:* C. W. J. Athey.

July 8. Northamptonshire won by eight wickets. Yorkshire 178 (54.3 overs) (A. Sidebottom 79, P. Carrick 38; W. Larkins four for 20); Northamptonshire 182 for two (29.2 overs) (W. Larkins 104, P. Willey 64). *Man of the Match:* W. Larkins.

IRELAND v SCOTLAND

At Downpatrick, July 14, 15, 16. Ireland won by five wickets, to level the series at eighteen wins each. Scotland, playing at Downpatrick for the first time, elected to bat on a slow pitch in fine weather, which lasted throughout the match. Racionzer batted 256 minutes for his 115, which contained five 6s and thirteen 4s, his hundred coming in 234 minutes. When Ireland replied after Swan's declaration, Harrison came to within 14 runs of a century on his first-class début, and put on 93 for the seventh wicket with Prior. Scotland, batting again, could muster only 129 runs, leaving their opponents a target of 125, which they achieved comfortably.

Scotland

W. A. Donald lbw b Corlett	6	– c Dennison b Halliday	45
I. G. Kennedy b Harrison	3	– c Monteith b Corlett	12
T. B. Racionzer st Jackson b Halliday	115	– b Halliday	3
*R. G. Swan b Monteith	39	– c Short b Halliday	5
C. J. Warner c Jackson b Harrison	70	– c and b Monteith	11
A. B. M. Ker not out	27	– lbw b Corlett	20
†D. J. Haggo b Monteith	0	– lbw b Halliday	9
E. J. McIntyre not out	0	– b Corlett	1
W. A. Morton (did not bat)		– c Jackson b Corlett	5
J. E. Ker (did not bat)		– c Monteith b Corlett	0
W. A. McPate (did not bat)		– not out	5
B 5, l-b 8, w 2, n-b 2	17	B 4, l-b 1, n-b 8	13

1/11 2/18 3/108 4/203 (6 wkts dec.) 277   1/24 2/39 3/46 4/79 129
5/276 6/277   5/91 6/112 7/114 8/119 9/121

Bowling: *First Innings*—Corlett 22–6–53–1; Harrison 18–8–30–2; Monteith 37–10–88–2; Halliday 33–14–65–1; Prior 8–4–24–0. *Second Innings*—Corlett 23–8–40–5; Harrison 6–3–10–0; Monteith 14–5–22–1; Halliday 27–11–44–4.

Ireland

J. F. Short c A. B. M. Ker b Donald	30	– b McPate	10
D. Dennison b J. E. Ker	1	– lbw b Morton	16
S. J. S. Warke run out	63	– c and b Morton	45
R. T. Wills c and b Morton	1	– c J. E. Ker b Morton	3
R. I. Johnston c Haggo b Morton	2	– not out	14
J. A. Prior c Swan b J. E. Ker	55	– b Morton	0
*J. D. Monteith c and b Morton	0		
G. D. Harrison b Racionzer	86	– (7) not out	21
S. C. Corlett c Swan b Racionzer	14		
†P. B. Jackson b J. E. Ker	1		
M. Halliday not out	0		
B 10, l-b 4, n-b 15	29	B 15, l-b 3, n-b 1	19

1/3 2/86 3/87 4/89   282   1/15 2/33 3/57 4/99   (5 wkts) 128
5/128 6/135 7/228 8/268 9/277   5/99

Bowling: *First Innings*—J. E. Ker 18–3–45–3; McPate 13–3–37–0; Morton 27–6–94–3; Donald 19–6–46–1; McIntyre 4–2–20–0; Racionzer 1.2–0–11–2. *Second Innings*—J. E. Ker 5–1–18–0; McPate 4–3–8–1; Morton 18–6–40–4; Donald 3–1–3–0; McIntyre 1–0–4–0; Racionzer 15–7–36–0; Swan 0.4–0–0–0.

Umpires: J. A. Vaughan and P. Reith.

†At Titwood, Glasgow, August 17, 18, 19. Scotland won by five wickets. MCC 222 (O. Henry four for 67) and 73 (O. Henry four for 29); Scotland 200 (T. B. Racionzer 85) and 97 for five.

†At Neath, August 21, 22, 23. Drawn. Wales 190 (C. Elward 52, G. P. Ellis 43; J. D. Monteith seven for 67) and 193 for four dec. (N. Roberts 67 not out, C. Elward 44, G. P. Ellis 40 not out); Ireland 207 for seven dec. (G. D. Harrison 64, J. F. Short 50; G. Edwards four for 50) and 10 for one.

†At Swansea, August 24, 25, 26. Drawn. MCC 318 for five dec. (R. G. Lanchberry 108, J. P. Bell 60, M. G. Griffith 48) and 223 for nine dec. (P. J. Graves 88; P. J. Lawlor six for 67); Wales 265 (M. Davies 59, G. P. Ellis 56, R. Williams 54; D. W. Lewis four for 84) and 184 for seven (C. Elward 47; J. Spencer four for 50).

THE ASDA CHALLENGE

The first match of the 1983 ASDA Challenge, contested at the Scarborough Cricket Festival, was reduced by rain to 36 overs a side. Yorkshire, unable to build an innings after losing Boycott for 0, were comfortably beaten by Lancashire, for whom Clive Lloyd hit two big 6s and Fairbrother hastened victory with a rapid unbeaten 31. The second day saw Gladwin score his first century in senior cricket (one 6, thirteen 4s) but, with the last eight Essex batsmen failing to reach double figures and the last eight wickets falling for 46 runs, it was not enough to overtake Hampshire's total, which featured powerful hitting from Chris Smith (seven 4s), Greenidge and Tremlett (two 6s). The final featured an exciting finish when, with 17 needed off the last over, by Malone, Abrahams scored a single off the first ball, leaving the 42-year-old Simmons to take 2 off the second, duck a bouncer, pull the next two for 6 and scamper a single off the last ball to level the scores and bring Lancashire victory by virtue of losing fewer wickets.

September 4. Lancashire won by four wickets. Yorkshire 139 for nine (36 overs)

(J. D. Love 38; J. Simmons three for 38); Lancashire 141 for six (33 overs) (N. H. Fairbrother 31 not out). *Man of the Match:* N. H. Fairbrother.

September 5. Hampshire won by 10 runs. Hampshire 205 for nine (50 overs) (C. L. Smith 50, C. G. Greenidge 45; N. Phillip three for 31); Essex 195 (49 overs) (C. Gladwin 100, G. A. Gooch 32; T. E. Jesty three for 43). *Man of the Match:* C. Gladwin.

September 6. Lancashire won by virtue of losing fewer wickets. Hampshire 245 for seven (50 overs) (M. C. J. Nicholas 82, T. E. Jesty 61, N. E. J. Pocock 36); Lancashire 245 for five (50 overs) (J. Abrahams 69 not out, J. Simmons 57 not out, S. J. O'Shaughnessy 51, C. H. Lloyd 41). *Man of the Match:* J. Simmons.

I ZINGARI RESULTS, 1983

Matches – 28: Won 11, Lost 3, Tied 1, Drawn 6, Abandoned 7.

April 30	Charterhouse School	Drawn
May 7	Honourable Artillery Company	Abandoned
May 8	Staff College, Camberley	Won by 122 runs
May 14	Royal Military Academy	Won by 66 runs
May 15	Royal Artillery	Abandoned
May 21	Eton Ramblers	Abandoned
May 28	Eton College 1st XI	Abandoned
May 28	Eton College 2nd XI	Abandoned
June 4	Hurlingham CC	Abandoned
June 5	Lord Porchester's XI	Abandoned
June 11	Royal Regiment of Fusiliers	Won by 178 runs
June 14	Winchester College	Lost by 77 runs
June 18	Guards Brigade CC	Won by seven wickets
June 19	Lavinia, Duchess of Norfolk's XI	Won by five wickets
June 25	Harrow School	Drawn
July 2	Green Jackets Club	Won by four wickets
July 3	London New Zealand CC	Won by one wicket
July 10	Captain R. H. Hawkins's XI	Drawn
July 16	Bradfield Waifs	Drawn
July 17	Sir John Starkey's XI	Won by 82 runs
July 24	Royal Armoured Corps	Won by six wickets
July 30, 31	South Wales Hunts XI	Drawn
August 6	Band of Brothers	Drawn
August 7	R. Leigh-Pemberton's XI	Won by 175 runs
August 20	Hampshire Hogs	Tied
August 21	J. H. Pawle's XI	Lost by 62 runs
September 4	Rickling Green CC	Won by six wickets
September 10	J. H. Weatherby's XI	Lost by six wickets

NATWEST BANK TROPHY, 1983

Somerset, winners of the Gillette Cup in 1979, beat Kent at Lord's to become the third holders of the NatWest Bank Trophy. In addition to the trophy, they received a cheque for £13,000, while Kent received £6,500. The losing semi-finalists, Hampshire and Middlesex, each received £3,750, and Gloucestershire, Northamptonshire, Sussex and Warwickshire, the losing quarter-finalists, each received £2,000.

Vic Marks, of Somerset, received £500 as Man of the Match in the final. The Man of the Match in each semi-final received £250; in each quarter-final £175; and in each first and second round match £100.

FIRST ROUND

BERKSHIRE v YORKSHIRE

At Reading, June 29. Yorkshire won by seven wickets. Toss won by Yorkshire.
Man of the Match: G. B. Stevenson.

Berkshire

A. Dindar lbw b Dennis	0	†G. E. J. Child run out		5
M. Lickley lbw b Sidebottom	11	P. J. Lewington not out		3
J. A. Claughton st Bairstow b Boycott	9	J. H. Jones not out		0
G. R. J. Roope c Boycott b Stevenson	29	L-b 11, w 2, n-b 2		15
M. L. Simmons lbw b Stevenson	28			
*J. F. Harvey c Bairstow b Stevenson	8	1/0 2/23 3/25 (9 wkts, 60 overs)		128
S. Burrow c Boycott b Stevenson	14	4/80 5/88 6/101		
P. New c Sidebottom b Stevenson	6	7/112 8/120 9/124		

Bowling: Dennis 8–3–14–1; Stevenson 12–2–27–5; Sidebottom 12–5–11–1; Boycott 12–5–18–1; Athey 6–0–21–0; Illingworth 10–2–22–0.

Yorkshire

G. Boycott c Child b Jones	48	J. D. Love not out		8
C. W. J. Athey c Burrow b Lickley	34	B 4, l-b 2, w 7, n-b 3		16
K. Sharp not out	24			
S. N. Hartley b New	1	1/92 2/103 3/108 (3 wkts, 50.4 overs)		131

†D. L. Bairstow, P. Carrick, G. B. Stevenson, A. Sidebottom, *R. Illingworth and S. J. Dennis did not bat.

Bowling: Jones 10–3–32–1; New 10.4–3–25–0; Burrow 12–5–18–0; Lewington 12–5–23–0; Lickley 5–1–15–1; Dindar 1–0–2–0.

Umpires: R. Julian and P. S. G. Stevens.

CAMBRIDGESHIRE v MIDDLESEX

At Wisbech, June 29. Middlesex won by eight wickets. Toss won by Middlesex.
Man of the Match: N. T. Gadsby.

Cambridgeshire

G. V. Miller c Radley b Williams	0	†M. L. Saggers run out	6
N. T. Gadsby b Emburey	63	M. Brown b Daniel	0
D. C. Holliday c Butcher b Emburey	27	D. C. Wing b Daniel	0
D. R. Parry run out	21	B 5, l-b 9, n-b 2	16
*A. M. Ponder b Williams	8		
P. A. Redfarn b Edmonds	21	1/7 2/81 3/113 (58.4 overs) 172
P. J. Malkin run out	10	4/130 5/134 6/161
G. S. Rice lbw b Cowans	0	7/162 8/171 9/172

Bowling: Daniel 11.4–3–31–2; Williams 10–3–33–2; Cowans 12–3–22–1; Emburey 12–2–27–2; Edmonds 12–3–41–1; Gatting 1–0–2–0.

Middlesex

K. P. Tomlins c and b Rice	80
W. N. Slack c and b Brown	60
C. T. Radley not out	17
*M. W. Gatting not out	13
L-b 4	4

1/143 2/143   (2 wkts, 51 overs) 174

R. O. Butcher, †P. R. Downton, J. E. Emburey, P. H. Edmonds, N. F Williams, N. G. Cowans and W. W. Daniel did not bat.

Bowling: Brown 12–1–49–1; Rice 12–4–31–1; Parry 10–4–25–0; Wing 12–2–33–0; Malkin 4–1–25–0; Gadsby 1–0–7–0.

Umpires: B. Leadbeater and J. D. Morley.

DORSET v ESSEX

At Bournemouth, June 29. Essex won by seven wickets. Toss won by Essex.
Man of the Match: K. S. McEwan.

Dorset

R. V. Lewis c Pringle b R. E. East	28	D. R. Hayward lbw b Turner	7
A. Kennedy c Gooch b Foster	0	C. W. Allen b Foster	7
V. B. Lewis lbw b Lever	2	B. K. Shantry b Lever	3
S. J. Halliday c Gooch b Pringle	8	L-b 7, w 3, n-b 3	13
R. J. Scott b Pringle	0		
C. Stone b R. E. East	6	1/5 2/8 3/41 (59.4 overs) 111
*M. C. Wagstaffe not out	34	4/41 5/45 6/50
†D. A. Ridley c D. E. East b Foster	3	7/57 8/73 9/97

Bowling: Lever 11.4–2–27–2; Foster 12–4–19–3; Pringle 12–3–19–2; R. E. East 12–4–12–2; Turner 12–5–21–1.

Essex

G. A. Gooch c Wagstaffe b Hayward ..	14	K. R. Pont not out		20
A. W. Lilley c Halliday b Hayward	8	L-b 1, w 1		2
*K. W. R. Fletcher c Allen b Hayward ..	0			
K. S. McEwan not out	73	1/10 2/12 3/39	(3 wkts, 43.2 overs)	117

N. A. Foster, D. R. Pringle, S. Turner, †D. E. East, R. E. East and J. K. Lever did not bat.

Bowling: Shantry 11–1–32–0; Hayward 12–6–18–3; Stone 7–2–29–0; Allen 6–2–14–0; Kennedy 7–2–16–0; Wagstaffe 0.2–0–6–0.

Umpires: W. L. Budd and J. H. Harris.

DURHAM v LANCASHIRE

At Chester-le-Street, June 29. Lancashire won by 106 runs. Toss won by Durham. S. P. Davis's return of seven for 32 was the third-best ever recorded in the competition.
Man of the Match: S. P. Davis.

Lancashire

G. Fowler c Fothergill b Davis	31	N. V. Radford c Patel b Davis		14
†C. Maynard b Davis	0	M. Watkinson b Davis		0
F. C. Hayes b Greensword	18	P. J. W. Allott not out		6
D. P. Hughes c Kippax b Davis	71	B 1, l-b 11, w 4, n-b 3		19
*J. Abrahams not out	51			
J. Simmons c Lister b Davis	0	1/1 2/33 3/101	(8 wkts, 60 overs)	211
S. J. O'Shaughnessy c Patel b Davis	1	4/149 5/149 6/151 7/199 8/199		

I. Folley did not bat.

Bowling: Davis 12–4–32–7; Daniels 12–2–64–0; Johnston 12–2–35–0; Greensword 12–6–13–1; Kippax 12–0–48–0.

Durham

J. Lister c Maynard b O'Shaughnessy ..	4	†A. R. Fothergill c Radford b Simmons .		12
D. C. Jackson lbw b Allott	0	J. Johnston not out		8
P. J. Kippax b O'Shaughnessy	16	S. P. Davis c Hughes b Folley		10
S. Greensword c Simmons b Watkinson .	7	L-b 4, w 4, n-b 4		12
P. C. Birtwisle c Fowler b Folley	34			
A. S. Patel b Simmons	0	1/1 2/22 3/25	(46.3 overs)	105
*N. A. Riddell lbw b Simmons	1	4/47 5/48 6/61		
S. A. B. Daniels b Simmons	1	7/69 8/73 9/90		

Bowling: Allott 6–1–6–1; Radford 5–2–4–0; Folley 5.3–1–10–2; O'Shaughnessy 6–2–21–2; Watkinson 12–2–27–1; Simmons 12–4–25–4.

Umpires: J. van Geloven and C. T. Spencer.

GLOUCESTERSHIRE v SCOTLAND

At Bristol, June 29. Gloucestershire won by 88 runs. Toss won by Scotland.
Man of the Match: P. Bainbridge.

Gloucestershire

A. W. Stovold b Joseph	82
P. W. Romaines b Morton	28
P. Bainbridge b Joseph	75
Zaheer Abbas run out	39
A. J. Hignell c Swan b J. E. Ker	9
J. N. Shepherd lbw b Morton	7
*D. A. Graveney c Swan b Morton	23

D. V. Lawrence did not bat.

R. J. Doughty not out	5
†R. C. Russell st Brown b Morton	4
G. E. Sainsbury not out	2
B 5, l-b 5, w 7, n-b 6	23

1/92 2/151 3/236   (8 wkts, 60 overs) 297
4/252 5/256 6/280 7/291 8/295

Bowling: Joseph 12–0–65–2; J. E. Ker 12–1–61–1; Goddard 12–0–37–0; Morton 12–1–47–4; Johnston 9–0–51–0; Donald 3–0–13–0.

Scotland

T. B. Racionzer c Romaines b Zaheer	61
W. A. Donald c Hignell b Shepherd	10
*R. G. Swan c Doughty b Bainbridge	27
C. J. Warner lbw b Bainbridge	28
A. B. M. Ker not out	48
†A. Brown lbw b Bainbridge	0

G. F. Goddard, R. F. Joseph and J. E. Ker did not bat.

H. G. F. Johnston c Hignell b Doughty	4
W. A. Morton not out	11
L-b 14, w 4, n-b 2	20

1/19 2/76 3/120   (6 wkts, 60 overs) 209
4/175 5/181 6/188

Bowling: Lawrence 6–1–16–0; Sainsbury 6–4–4–0; Shepherd 12–5–25–1; Graveney 12–2–42–0; Bainbridge 12–2–49–3; Zaheer 6–0–25–1; Doughty 6–1–28–1.

Umpires: D. O. Oslear and P. B. Wight.

HERTFORDSHIRE v HAMPSHIRE

At Hitchin, June 29. Hampshire won by nine wickets. Toss won by Hertfordshire.
Man of the Match: F. E. Collyer.

Hertfordshire

W. M. Osman c Parks b Malone	32
B. G. Evans c Parks b Marshall	3
N. P. G. Wright run out	6
S. A. Dean lbw b Tremlett	6
C. Thomas run out	2
*†F. E. Collyer not out	58

R. L. Johns, R. J. Hailey and D. Surridge did not bat.

T. S. Smith b Malone	36
A. R. Garofall not out	0
B 5, l-b 9, w 2	16

1/8 2/37 3/44   (6 wkts, 60 overs) 159
4/50 5/62 6/154

Bowling: Marshall 12–2–23–1; Malone 12–4–40–2; Jesty 12–3–45–0; Tremlett 12–4–18–1; Cowley 12–7–17–0.

Hampshire

C. G. Greenidge lbw b Johns	55
C. L. Smith not out	66
M. C. J. Nicholas not out	37
B 2, l-b 1, w 1, n-b 1	5

1/94   (1 wkt, 48.2 overs) 163

T. E. Jesty, V. P. Terry, *N. E. J. Pocock, N. G. Cowley, M. D. Marshall, T. M. Tremlett, †R. J. Parks and S. J. Malone did not bat.

Bowling: Surridge 12–3–27–0; Smith 6–3–14–0; Hailey 12–0–46–0; Johns 12–1–39–1; Garofall 6.2–0–32–0.

Umpires: B. Dudleston and A. Jepson.

IRELAND v SUSSEX

At Dublin, June 29. Sussex won by 124 runs. Toss won by Ireland.
Man of the Match: M. A. Masood.

Sussex

G. D. Mendis c Warke b Harrison	11	C. P. Phillipson not out	40
*J. R. T. Barclay c Jackson b Halliday	48	D. A. Reeve not out	16
C. M. Wells b Harrison	11	B 1, l-b 6, w 9	16
P. W. G. Parker b Monteith	14		
Imran Khan b Johnston	41	1/19 2/37 (7 wkts, 60 overs) 265	
†I. J. Gould b Corlett	46	3/92 4/96	
G. S. le Roux c Prior b Harrison	22	5/182 6/190 7/221	

A. C. S. Pigott and C. E. Waller did not bat.

Bowling: Corlett 12–0–63–1; Harrison 11–2–42–3; Prior 12–2–40–0; Monteith 12–3–32–1; Halliday 10–0–47–1; Johnston 3–0–25–1.

Ireland

J. F. Short lbw b le Roux	2	S. C. Corlett c Pigott b Waller	5
M. A. Masood c Phillipson b Barclay	69	†P. B. Jackson b Reeve	4
R. T. Wills run out	10	M. Halliday not out	0
I. Johnston b Barclay	17	L-b 4, w 3, n-b 2	9
G. Harrison b Reeve	0		
S. J. Warke lbw b Reeve	0	1/6 2/50 3/94 (52.3 overs) 141	
J. A. Prior lbw b Barclay	3	4/95 5/97 6/106	
*J. D. Monteith b Phillipson	22	7/107 8/130 9/141	

Bowling: le Roux 6–3–11–1; Pigott 2–0–11–0; C. M. Wells 8–1–25–0; Waller 12–2–31–1; Barclay 12–1–28–3; Reeve 12–1–26–3; Phillipson 0.3–0–0–1.

Umpires: J. Birkenshaw and N. T. Plews.

KENT v CHESHIRE

At Canterbury, June 29. Kent won by 136 runs. Toss won by Cheshire.
Man of the Match: C. J. Tavaré.

Kent

R. A. Woolmer c Sutton b Mudassar	14	G. R. Dilley b Gemmell	2
M. R. Benson c Tipton b Gemmell	7	G. W. Johnson not out	22
C. J. Tavaré b Hitchmough	99	R. M. Ellison not out	4
D. G. Aslett st Pickup b Sutton	17	B 1, l-b 7, w 2	10
C. S. Cowdrey run out	52		
E. A. E. Baptiste b Sutton	6	1/14 2/37 3/97 (8 wkts, 60 overs) 237	
†A. P. E. Knott b Hitchmough	4	4/179 5/200 6/204 7/209 8/217	

D. L. Underwood did not bat.

Bowling: Gemmell 12–2–58–2; Hitchmough 12–1–52–2; O'Brien 12–2–34–0; Mudassar 12–4–33–1; Sutton 12–2–50–2.

Cheshire

Mudassar Nazar lbw b Woolmer	25	P. G. Wakefield lbw b Underwood	13
P. A. Tipton c Knott b Ellison	5	I. J. Gemmell c Dilley b Aslett	12
R. M. O. Cooke c Woolmer b Ellison	2	†J. K. Pickup not out	0
N. T. O'Brien b Dilley	16	B 5, l-b 3, w 2, n-b 5	15
D. Bailey c Woolmer b Ellison	0		
R. R. Simpson b Ellison	1	1/35 2/35 3/43	(57.5 overs) 101
*J. A. Sutton b Dilley	8	4/43 5/53 6/64	
J. Hitchmough b Dilley	4	7/65 8/69 9/101	

Bowling: Dilley 11–3–19–3; Baptiste 10–3–22–0; Ellison 12–3–19–4; Woolmer 12–7–11–1; Cowdrey 6–2–7–0; Underwood 6–3–8–1; Aslett 0.5–0–0–1.

Umpires: J. G. Langridge and K. G. Suttle.

LEICESTERSHIRE v DEVON

At Leicester, June 29. Leicestershire won by 132 runs. Toss won by Devon.
Man of the Match: R. W. Tolchard.

Leicestershire

J. C. Balderstone b Zahid	33	P. B. Clift b Goulding	24
I. P. Butcher lbw b Yeabsley	4	A. M. E. Roberts not out	32
D. I. Gower b Davey	25	L-b 4, w 6	10
B. F. Davison c Matthews b Davey	14		
N. E. Briers lbw b Yeabsley	40	1/10 2/44 3/69	(6 wkts, 60 overs) 253
*†R. W. Tolchard not out	71	4/85 5/172 6/216	

J. F. Steele, G. J. Parsons and N. G. B. Cook did not bat.

Bowling: Goulding 12–1–61–1; Yeabsley 12–2–73–2; Davey 12–3–45–2; Zahid 12–2–23–1; Allin 12–3–41–0.

Devon

Agha Zahid run out	22	J. Davey b Balderstone	1
J. G. Tolchard run out	24	M. J. Goulding run out	0
R. P. Tolchard c Gower b Parsons	0	D. I. Yeabsley b Balderstone	0
G. Wallen c Davison b Balderstone	33	B 4, l-b 3, w 6, n-b 2	15
A. Melhuish c Roberts b Steele	4		
*B. L. Matthews c and b Steele	0	1/50 2/50 3/54	(47.1 overs) 121
†R. M. Oliver not out	17	4/60 5/70 6/102	
A. W. Allin b Cook	5	7/108 8/113 9/113	

Bowling: Roberts 6–5–3–0; Clift 4–0–9–0; Steele 12–6–13–2; Cook 12–2–45–1; Balderstone 5.1–3–9–3.

Umpires: J. W. Holder and M. J. Kitchen.

LINCOLNSHIRE v SURREY

At Sleaford, June 29. Surrey won by 129 runs. Toss won by Lincolnshire. Richards, whose second fifty came in seventeen deliveries, including 24 off the last five balls of the innings, established a new seventh-wicket record of 160 for the competition with Payne.
Man of the Match: C. J. Richards.

Surrey

A. R. Butcher c Butler b Hacker	22	D. J. Thomas lbw b Estwick	5
G. S. Clinton b Estwick	6	I. R. Payne not out	56
D. M. Smith c Estwick b Marshall	19	B 1, l-b 20, w 15	36
*R. D. V. Knight b Hacker	26		
M. A. Lynch c and b Marshall	22	(6 wkts, 60 overs) 297	
†C. J. Richards not out	105	1/19 2/50 3/58	
		4/106 5/109 6/137	

G. Monkhouse, S. T. Clarke and P. I. Pocock did not bat.

Bowling: Estwick 12–2–76–2; Hacker 12–0–42–2; Marshall 12–1–34–2; Cope 12–7–12–0; Burton 9–0–74–0; Brooks 3–0–23–0.

Lincolnshire

*G. Robinson st Richards b Monkhouse	23	P. J. Hacker c Clarke b Lynch	5
H. Pougher st Richards b Butcher	30	G. A. Cope b Monkhouse	4
†N. Priestley c Knight b Payne	24	R. L. Burton not out	9
J. G. Franks b Payne	10	L-b 2, w 1	3
K. G. Brooks c Smith b Monkhouse	51		
P. R. Butler b Payne	4	1/30 2/77 3/79	(59.5 overs) 168
D. Marshall b Payne	0	4/115 5/133 6/133	
R. O. Estwick b Payne	5	7/139 8/144 9/155	

Bowling: Clarke 6–3–3–0; Thomas 4–1–16–0; Monkhouse 7.5–1–26–3; Pocock 12–4–14–0; Butcher 12–1–45–1; Payne 12–0–36–5; Lynch 6–1–25–1.

Umpires: H. D. Bird and R. H. Duckett.

NORFOLK v GLAMORGAN

At Norwich, June 29. Glamorgan won by 25 runs. Toss won by Norfolk.
Man of the Match: R. C. Ontong.

Glamorgan

A. Jones c Parvez Mir b Thomas	7	†E. W. Jones b Pilch	13
J. A. Hopkins lbw b Thomas	32	*M. W. W. Selvey not out	8
R. C. Ontong b Parvez Mir	45	W. W. Davis not out	1
A. L. Jones c Handley b Parvez Mir	26	L-b 2, w 2, n-b 8	12
C. J. C. Rowe c Innes b Plumb	19		
D. A. Francis lbw b Parvez Mir	24	1/9 2/75 3/116	(9 wkts, 60 overs) 202
J. G. Thomas c Ringwood b Pilch	15	4/123 5/151 6/176	
B. J. Lloyd c Handley b Pilch	0	7/180 8/180 9/199	

Bowling: Innes 11–1–34–0; Thomas 10–1–35–2; Agar 12–5–22–0; Plumb 11–3–41–1; Pilch 4–0–15–3; Parvez Mir 12–0–43–3.

Norfolk

*F. L. Q. Handley c A. L. Jones b Davis	11	†D. E. Mattocks b Ontong	1
S. G. Plumb c and b Rowe	33	A. C. Agar c Hopkins b Davis	3
R. D. Huggins c Davis b Lloyd	17	R. F. Innes not out	0
Parvez Mir lbw b Selvey	37	B 1, l-b 7, w 1, n-b 6	15
N. D. Cook c Francis b Ontong	30		
P. J. Ringwood b Ontong	19	1/28 2/68 3/72	(56.5 overs) 177
D. G. Pilch c and b Ontong	11	4/136 5/147 6/159	
P. W. Thomas b Davis	0	7/164 8/165 9/175	

Bowling: Davis 10.5–1–26–3; Selvey 12–5–20–1; Lloyd 12–7–17–1; Thomas 3–0–16–0; Ontong 9–1–49–4; Rowe 10–1–34–1.

Umpires: K. Ibadulla and K. E. Palmer.

SHROPSHIRE v SOMERSET

At Wellington, June 29, 30. Somerset won by 87 runs. Toss won by Shropshire.
Man of the Match: B. J. Perry.

Somerset

P. M. Roebuck b de Silva	37	†T. Gard b D. Perry	17
P. W. Denning b D. Perry	5	C. H. Dredge b B. J. Perry	7
I. V. A. Richards c Dawson b de Silva	74	J. Garner c Barnard b Dawson	3
P. A. Slocombe c Jones b B. J. Perry	16	P. H. L. Wilson not out	9
*I. T. Botham c Jones b B. J. Perry	16	B 4, l-b 6, w 6, n-b 3	19
N. F. M. Popplewell c Foster			
b B. J. Perry	14		246
V. J. Marks st Ashley b Dawson	29	1/12 2/115 3/135 4/157 (60 overs) 246	

1/12 2/115 3/135 4/157   (60 overs) 246
5/162 6/194 7/213 8/226 9/230

Bowling: Ogrizovic 6–0–33–0; D. Perry 8–1–30–2; Barnard 12–1–42–0; de Silva 12–4–30–2; Dawson 11–0–53–2; B. J. Perry 11–2–39–4.

Shropshire

J. Foster c Roebuck b Garner	2	†D. J. Ashley not out	6
J. A. Hulme c Garner b Marks	10	D. Perry run out	5
J. B. R. Jones c Marks b Garner	8	A. S. Barnard c Slocombe b Popplewell	0
C. N. Boyns b Garner	12	B 1, l-b 11, w 3, n-b 4	19
D. S. de Silva st Gard b Marks	24		
J. P. Dawson b Dredge	16	(55.2 overs) 159	
*B. J. Perry c Denning b Wilson	43	1/5 2/13 3/33	
S. Ogrizovic b Dredge	14	4/44 5/75 6/99	
		7/141 8/149 9/159	

1/5 2/13 3/33   (55.2 overs) 159
4/44 5/75 6/99
7/141 8/149 9/159

Bowling: Garner 9–2–19–3; Wilson 12–6–16–1; Popplewell 8.2–3–11–1; Marks 12–1–47–2; Dredge 12–2–34–2; Richards 2–0–13–0.

Umpires: D. R. Shepherd and G. C. Wilson.

SUFFOLK v DERBYSHIRE

At Bury St Edmunds, June 29, 30. Derbyshire won by six wickets. Toss won by Derbyshire.
Man of the Match: A. Hill.

Suffolk

J. W. Edrich c Miller b Mortensen	3	R. J. Robinson b Mortensen	17
P. D. Barker c Miller b Oldham	13	*C. Rutterford not out	8
S. M. Clements c Anderson b Mortensen	59	R. C. Green not out	8
R. F. Howlett c Finney b Miller	17	L-b 4, w 3, n-b 1	8
†S. A. Westley c Morris b Miller	2		
P. J. Caley c Mortensen b Miller	2	1/7 2/24 3/60 4/73 (8 wkts, 60 overs) 164	
R. J. Bond lbw b Oldham	27	5/79 6/128 7/140 8/150	

C. Graham did not bat.

1/7 2/24 3/60 4/73   (8 wkts, 60 overs) 164
5/79 6/128 7/140 8/150

Bowling: Mortensen 12–5–16–3; Finney 12–3–32–0; Oldham 12–1–47–2; Tunnicliffe 12–1–33–0; Miller 12–2–28–3.

Derbyshire

J. E. Morris b Green	7	G. Miller not out	1
I. S. Anderson c Edrich b Robinson	47	B 4, l-b 7	11
A. Hill c Westley b Caley	52		
*K. J. Barnett c and b Caley	35	1/20 2/88 (4 wkts, 56 overs) 167	
R. J. Finney not out	14	3/139 4/162	

1/20 2/88   (4 wkts, 56 overs) 167
3/139 4/162

W. P. Fowler, C. J. Tunnicliffe, †R. W. Taylor, S. Oldham and O. H. Mortensen did not bat.

Bowling: Green 12–4–14–1; Graham 11–2–41–0; Rutterford 12–0–36–0; Robinson 12–2–29–1; Clements 3–0–12–0; Caley 6–0–24–2.

Umpires: D. J. Dennis and C. T. Spencer.

WARWICKSHIRE v OXFORDSHIRE

At Birmingham, June 29. Warwickshire won by 18 runs. Toss won by Warwickshire.
Man of the Match: P. A. Fowler.

Warwickshire

K. D. Smith c Hobbins b Evans	60	A. M. Ferreira not out	8
T. A. Lloyd st Crossley b Evans	32	N. Gifford not out	4
A. I. Kallicharran c Busby b Porter	70	B 1, l-b 8, w 4, n-b 2	15
D. L. Amiss b Arnold	54		
†G. W. Humpage b Porter	0	1/67 2/144 (7 wkts, 60 overs) 274	
Asif Din c and b Garner	3	3/192 4/192	
C. M. Old b Arnold	28	5/195 6/246 7/270	

*R. G. D. Willis and W. Hogg did not bat.

Bowling: Busby 10–2–26–0; Hobbins 9–2–31–0; Arnold 9–0–55–2; Evans 12–5–35–2; Porter 12–1–54–2; Garner 8–0–58–1.

Oxfordshire

M. D. Nurton c Humpage b Hogg	58	R. N. Busby b Gifford	1
P. A. Fowler c and b Willis	119	P. J. Densham not out	6
*P. J. Garner lbw b Gifford	6	K. A. Arnold b Gifford	0
J. G. Manger c Kallicharran b Gifford	17	B 4, l-b 14, w 5, n-b 5	28
†A. Crossley b Willis	10		
S. R. Porter lbw b Ferreira	0	1/152 2/195 3/213 (58 overs) 256	
G. R. Hobbins b Willis	11	4/223 5/224 6/238	
R. A. Evans b Willis	0	7/238 8/243 9/245	

Bowling: Willis 11–0–25–4; Hogg 10–2–58–1; Old 2–0–16–0; Kallicharran 12–0–42–0; Ferreira 12–1–40–1; Gifford 11–0–47–4.

Umpires: R. A. White and A. G. T. Whitehead.

WILTSHIRE v NORTHAMPTONSHIRE

At Swindon, June 29. Northamptonshire won by 165 runs. Toss won by Wiltshire.
Man of the Match: A. J. Lamb.

Northamptonshire

*G. Cook c Newman b Gulliver	31	R. J. Bailey b Rice	21
W. Larkins b Thorn	65	D. S. Steele not out	5
P. Willey b Rice	32	B 2, l-b 4, w 7, n-b 2	15
A. J. Lamb st Meale b Bailey	75		
Kapil Dev b Barnes	18	1/44 2/89 3/214 (6 wkts, 60 overs) 285	
R. G. Williams not out	23	4/224 5/239 6/270	

†G. Sharp, N. A. Mallender and T. M. Lamb did not bat.

Bowling: Wilson 3–0–12–0; Barnes 11–1–62–1; Gulliver 12–2–42–1; Rice 10–0–57–2; Thorn 12–0–47–1; Bailey 12–1–50–1.

Wiltshire

J. Rice c A. J. Lamb b Kapil Dev	1	*R. J. Gulliver c Sharp b Williams	1
B. H. White lbw b Mallender	6	R. Wilson not out	9
P. Thorn c A. J. Lamb b Steele	15	T. Barnes c T. M. Lamb b Williams	13
R. C. Cooper b Steele	14	B 1, l-b 6	7
J. Newman st Sharp b Steele	4		
M. Bailey c Mallender b Williams	31	1/9 2/9 3/30	(45 overs) 120
D. Mercer st Sharp b Willey	0	4/43 5/60 6/69	
†G. E. Meale c Bailey b Kapil Dev	19	7/95 8/97 9/99	

Bowling: Kapil Dev 8–3–13–2; Mallender 6–0–22–1; Steele 12–4–31–3; Willey 12–3–31–1; Williams 7–3–16–3.

Umpires: W. E. Alley and P. J. Eele.

WORCESTERSHIRE v NOTTINGHAMSHIRE

At Worcester, June 29. Nottinghamshire won by 2 runs. Toss won by Worcestershire.
Man of the Match: D. B. D'Oliveira.

Nottinghamshire

B. Hassan b Ellcock	22	K. Saxelby b Ellcock	12
R. T. Robinson run out	26	K. E. Cooper b Ellcock	9
D. W. Randall st Humphries		M. K. Bore not out	3
b Illingworth	24	M. Hendrick run out	18
*C. E. B. Rice c Weston b Illingworth	0	B 3, l-b 8, w 1, n-b 6	18
J. D. Birch b D'Oliveira	11		
†B. N. French c Illingworth b D'Oliveira	11	1/29 2/79 3/79 4/80	(60 overs) 169
E. E. Hemmings c Humphries b Warner	15	5/101 6/106 7/137 8/147 9/147	

Bowling: Ellcock 10–2–49–3; Warner 8–0–38–1; Pridgeon 6–2–13–0; Patel 12–7–9–0; Illingworth 12–4–14–2; D'Oliveira 12–4–28–2.

Worcestershire

J. A. Ormrod lbw b Hendrick	0	R. K. Illingworth b Cooper	8
M. J. Weston b Hemmings	21	A. E. Warner b Saxelby	2
*P. A. Neale c French b Cooper	1	R. M. Ellcock c Robinson b Saxelby	6
D. N. Patel b Saxelby	24	A. P. Pridgeon not out	0
D. B. D'Oliveira c Randall b Cooper	48	B 4, l-b 15, w 1, n-b 4	24
M. S. Scott run out	23		
†D. J. Humphries c Robinson		1/5 2/6 3/44 4/70	(60 overs) 167
b Hendrick	10	5/127 6/142 7/149 8/156 9/163	

Bowling: Hendrick 12–3–31–2; Cooper 12–4–18–3; Hemmings 12–4–22–1; Saxelby 12–0–46–3; Bore 12–3–26–0.

Umpires: D. J. Constant and R. Palmer.

SECOND ROUND

DERBYSHIRE v MIDDLESEX

At Derby, July 20. Middlesex won by 30 runs. Toss won by Derbyshire.
Man of the Match: K. J. Barnett.

Middlesex

G. D. Barlow run out	62	P. H. Edmonds not out	18
W. N. Slack c Holding b Tunnicliffe	40	N. F. Williams c Taylor b Mortensen	1
C. T. Radley c Hill b Oldham	11	W. W. Daniel not out	4
*M. W. Gatting c Taylor b Oldham	3	B 1, l-b 11, w 2, n-b 1	15
K. P. Tomlins c Taylor b Holding	46		
J. E. Emburey c Taylor b Finney	28	1/113 2/115 3/122 (8 wkts, 60 overs) 240
†P. R. Downton c Anderson b Holding	12	4/139 5/182 6/215 7/226 8/227

N. G. Cowans did not bat.

Bowling: Holding 12–1–50–2; Finney 12–1–46–1; Mortensen 12–2–51–1; Tunnicliffe 12–1–46–1; Oldham 12–1–32–2.

Derbyshire

*K. J. Barnett c Cowans b Williams	88	S. Oldham b Daniel	6
I. S. Anderson c Downton b Daniel	28	M. A. Holding b Daniel	0
A. Hill b Cowans	8	O. H. Mortensen not out	2
J. H. Hampshire c Cowans b Edmonds	35	B 1, l-b 8, w 1, n-b 4	14
R. J. Finney c Slack b Williams	5		
W. P. Fowler b Williams	7	1/72 2/98 3/156 (58.2 overs) 210
C. J. Tunnicliffe c Edmonds b Williams	6	4/171 5/176 6/183
†R. W. Taylor run out	11	7/200 8/203 9/203

Bowling: Daniel 11.2–0–35–3; Cowans 10–0–41–1; Edmonds 12–2–38–1; Williams 9–1–36–4; Gatting 3–2–4–0; Emburey 12–1–36–0; Slack 1–0–6–0.

Umpires: K. Ibadulla and B. J. Meyer.

ESSEX v KENT

At Chelmsford, July 20. Kent won by 4 runs. Toss won by Kent.
Man of the Match: C. S. Cowdrey.

Kent

R. A. Woolmer b Turner	40	G. W. Johnson c D. E. East b Gooch	3
M. R. Benson lbw b Phillip	18	R. M. Ellison c D. E. East b Turner	10
*C. J. Tavaré b Foster	43	G. R. Dilley not out	7
D. G. Aslett b Phillip	0	B 1, l-b 11, w 5, n-b 7	24
C. S. Cowdrey not out	122		
E. A. E. Baptiste c D. E. East b Foster	7	1/48 2/70 3/75 (8 wkts, 60 overs) 274
†A. P. E. Knott b Foster	0	4/145 5/165 6/165 7/182 8/236

D. L. Underwood did not bat.

Bowling: Foster 12–0–44–3; Pringle 11–1–54–0; Phillip 10–1–43–2; Turner 10–1–56–2; R. E. East 5–0–23–0; Gooch 12–3–30–1.

Essex

G. A. Gooch c Knott b Baptiste.........122	S. Turner c Tavaré b Baptiste 0
B. R. Hardie b Woolmer 61	†D. E. East b Ellison 0
*K. W. R. Fletcher b Underwood....... 31	R. E. East not out 1
K. S. McEwan c Johnson b Underwood.. 17	L-b 7, w 1, n-b 1 9
D. R. Pringle b Ellison 19	
K. R. Pont b Ellison 0	1/147 2/210 3/233 (9 wkts, 60 overs) 270
N. Phillip c Tavaré b Ellison............. 10	4/240 5/240 6/262 7/267 8/269 9/270

N. A. Foster did not bat.

Bowling: Dilley 12–2–45–0; Ellison 12–3–54–4; Baptiste 12–0–70–2; Woolmer 12–0–52–1; Underwood 12–1–40–2.

Umpires: R. Julian and C. T. Spencer.

LEICESTERSHIRE v GLOUCESTERSHIRE

At Leicester, July 20. Gloucestershire won by four wickets. Their total, a competition record for a side batting second, was achieved thanks mainly to Zaheer, whose 158 was the second-highest score in the competition. Leicestershire, who won the toss, established a record for a side batting first and losing.

Man of the Match: Zaheer Abbas.

Leicestershire

J. C. Balderstone b Shepherd............. 24	P. B. Clift not out............................ 16
I. P. Butcher c Hignell b Lawrence 12	
D. I. Gower not out..........................138	B 4, l-b 12, w 3, n-b 5 24
B. F. Davison b Lawrence................. 68	
N. E. Briers c Graveney b Bainbridge . 4	1/25 2/62 (5 wkts, 60 overs) 302
*†R. W. Tolchard b Sainsbury 16	3/175 4/194 5/254

A. M. E. Roberts, G. J. Parsons, N. G. B. Cook and L. B. Taylor did not bat.

Bowling: Sainsbury 12–2–45–1; Lawrence 12–1–51–2; Shepherd 12–0–60–1; Childs 12–0–48–0; Graveney 1–0–8–0; Bainbridge 11–1–66–1.

Gloucestershire

A. W. Stovold c and b Taylor 9	*D. A. Graveney lbw b Roberts......... 0
P. W. Romaines c Gower b Taylor 9	†R. C. Russell not out..................... 14
P. Bainbridge lbw b Taylor............... 49	L-b 7, w 5, n-b 4 16
Zaheer Abbas st Tolchard b Cook 158	
A. J. Hignell lbw b Roberts............... 26	1/12 2/23 3/140 (6 wkts, 59.3 overs) 306
J. N. Shepherd not out 25	4/234 5/274 6/275

J. H. Childs, G. E. Sainsbury and D. V. Lawrence did not bat.

Bowling: Roberts 12–0–39–2; Taylor 12–1–45–3; Clift 11.3–0–69–0; Parsons 12–0–84–0; Cook 12–2–53–1.

Umpires: J. H. Harris and R. Palmer.

GLAMORGAN v HAMPSHIRE

At Swansea, July 7. Hampshire won by 156 runs. Toss won by Hampshire.
Man of the Match: C. G. Greenidge.

Hampshire

C. G. Greenidge c Hopkins b Rowe....108	M. D. Marshall not out...................... 15
C. L. Smith c Hopkins b Ontong........ 21	
M. C. J. Nicholas b Nash................. 19	L-b 9, w 5, n-b 8 22
T. E. Jesty b Davis 84	
V. P. Terry c Nash b Lloyd 5	1/46 2/115 3/199 (5 wkts, 60 overs) 294
*N. E. J. Pocock not out.................. 20	4/221 5/276

N. G. Cowley, T. M. Tremlett, †R. J. Parks and S. J. Malone did not bat.

Bowling: Nash 12–2–40–1; Davis 12–2–53–1; Ontong 12–3–58–1; Thomas 8–0–56–0;
Lloyd 11–1–33–1; Rowe 5–0–32–1.

Glamorgan

A. Jones st Parks b Cowley 22	*B. J. Lloyd b Cowley...................... 2
J. A. Hopkins c Pocock b Marshall 0	M. A. Nash not out 0
D. A. Francis c Malone b Jesty 12	W. W. Davis b Cowley...................... 0
R. C. Ontong c Parks b Jesty............. 23	
C. J. C. Rowe c Parks b Jesty 2	L-b 10, w 5............................ 15
A. L. Jones lbw b Malone 36	
J. G. Thomas b Tremlett.................... 24	1/1 2/42 3/49 4/54 (41.5 overs) 138
†E. W. Jones c Terry b Cowley 2	5/104 6/130 7/134 8/138 9/138

Bowling: Marshall 6–3–6–1; Malone 9–1–21–1; Jesty 11–2–46–3; Tremlett 7–1–29–1;
Cowley 8.5–4–21–4.

Umpires: W. E. Alley and D. J. Constant.

LANCASHIRE v SOMERSET

At Manchester, July 7. Somerset won by eight wickets. Toss won by Somerset.
Man of the Match: N. F. M. Popplewell.

Lancashire

G. Fowler b Richards 29	†C. Maynard c Botham b Garner........ 16
D. Lloyd lbw b Garner...................... 3	J. Simmons not out 6
F. C. Hayes c Slocombe b Dredge 16	B 3, l-b 10, w 1, n-b 3 17
*C. H. Lloyd c and b Richards........... 6	
J. Abrahams c Gard b Dredge 21	1/9 2/35 3/57 (6 wkts, 60 overs) 163
S. J. O'Shaughnessy not out 49	4/62 5/94 6/119

M. Watkinson, P. Lever and L. L. McFarlane did not bat.

Bowling: Garner 12–6–25–2; Botham 11–3–33–0; Marks 12–4–22–0; Dredge 11–1–30–2;
Richards 10–2–23–2; Popplewell 4–1–13–0.

Somerset

P. M. Roebuck not out...................... 43	N. F. M. Popplewell not out.............. 68
J. W. Lloyds c Simmons b McFarlane.. 5	B 1, l-b 9, w 3, n-b 3 16
I. V. A. Richards st Maynard	
b Simmons. 32	1/23 2/66 (2 wkts, 52.5 overs) 164

P. W. Denning, *I. T. Botham, P. A. Slocombe, V. J. Marks, †T. Gard, C. H. Dredge and
J. Garner did not bat.

Bowling: Lever 7.5–2–17–0; McFarlane 12–4–18–1; O'Shaughnessy 4–0–24–0; Simmons 12–0–32–1; D. Lloyd 7–0–18–0; Watkinson 8–0–20–0; Abrahams 2–0–19–0.

Umpires: J. van Geloven and J. W. Holder.

SURREY v WARWICKSHIRE

At The Oval, July 7. Warwickshire won by nine wickets. Toss won by Warwickshire.
Man of the Match: T. A. Lloyd.

Surrey

A. R. Butcher c Kallicharran b Willis..	1
G. S. Clinton run out	11
D. M. Smith lbw b Ferreira	20
*R. D. V. Knight c Kallicharran b Ferreira.	9
M. A. Lynch c Kallicharran b Lethbridge.	6
†C. J. Richards c Humpage b Lethbridge.	13
D. J. Thomas lbw b Gifford	37
I. R. Payne c Humpage b Willis	4
G. Monkhouse b Ferreira	7
S. T. Clarke c Smith b Willis	7
P. I. Pocock not out	0
L-b 12, w 1, n-b 10	23

1/3 2/37 3/42 4/52   (48.1 overs) 138
5/58 6/81 7/103 8/130 9/130

Bowling: Willis 10.1–3–23–3; Old 10–4–19–0; Lethbridge 10–3–26–2; Ferreira 8–1–25–3; Gifford 10–2–22–1.

Warwickshire

K. D. Smith c Richards b Payne	37
T. A. Lloyd not out	55
A. I. Kallicharran not out	44
L-b 1, w 2, n-b 4	7

1/81   (1 wkt, 42.5 overs) 143

D. L. Amiss, †G. W. Humpage, A. M. Ferreira, Asif Din, C. Lethbridge, C. M. Old, N. Gifford and *R. G. D. Willis did not bat.

Bowling: Clarke 10.5–1–32–0; Thomas 7–1–30–0; Monkhouse 5–1–33–0; Knight 7–1–13–0; Pocock 8–4–14–0; Payne 5–2–14–1.

Umpires: B. Leadbeater and D. R. Shepherd.

SUSSEX v NOTTINGHAMSHIRE

At Hove, July 7. Sussex won by 76 runs. Toss won by Sussex.
Man of the Match: Imran Khan.

Sussex

G. D. Mendis c French b Pick	8
*J. R. T. Barclay c Pick b Hemmings..	4
P. W. G. Parker c Hassan b Hemmings.	7
Imran Khan not out	114
C. M. Wells b Bore	28
†I. J. Gould c and b Hendrick	32
G. S. le Roux b Pick	12
A. P. Wells run out	8
B 1, l-b 7, w 4, n-b 2	14

1/11 2/22 3/29   (7 wkts, 60 overs) 227
4/101 5/168 6/200 7/227

A. C. S. Pigott, D. A. Reeve and C. E. Waller did not bat.

Bowling: Hendrick 12–4–35–1; Pick 12–2–60–2; Illingworth 12–5–40–0; Hemmings 12–5–24–2; Bore 12–2–54–1.

Nottinghamshire

B. Hassan b Reeve	3	R. A. Pick not out	34
R. T. Robinson lbw b Reeve	4	N. J. B. Illingworth c A. P. Wells	
D. W. Randall c A. P. Wells		b Parker.	2
b Barclay.	25	M. K. Bore not out	4
*C. E. B. Rice c le Roux b Waller	10		
J. D. Birch c Waller b C. M. Wells	28	B 2, l-b 4, w 14, n-b 1	21
E. E. Hemmings lbw b Barclay	9		
†B. N. French c A. P. Wells		1/17 2/18 3/36 4/85 (8 wkts, 60 overs) 151	
b Barclay.	11	5/86 6/101 7/113 8/132	

M. Hendrick did not bat.

Bowling: le Roux 7–3–15–0; Pigott 4–1–3–0; Reeve 12–3–17–2; Waller 12–3–19–1; Barclay 12–5–18–3; C. M. Wells 10–0–31–1; Imran 2–0–17–0; Parker 1–0–10–1.

Umpires: P. J. Eele and M. J. Kitchen.

YORKSHIRE v NORTHAMPTONSHIRE

At Leeds, July 20. Northamptonshire won by 46 runs. Toss won by Yorkshire.
Man of the Match: B. J. Griffiths.

Northamptonshire

*G. Cook b Dennis	2	†G. Sharp not out	41
W. Larkins c Stevenson b Carrick	39	N. A. Mallender not out	11
P. Willey c Bairstow b Ramage	0		
A. J. Lamb c and b Carrick	76	B 1, l-b 3, w 4, n-b 3	11
Kapil Dev c Illingworth b Carrick	0		
R. G. Williams run out	16	1/5 2/8 3/102 (7 wkts, 60 overs) 211	
D. J. Capel c Bairstow b Dennis	15	4/103 5/142 6/142 7/182	

T. M. Lamb and B. J. Griffiths did not bat.

Bowling: Dennis 10–1–45–2; Ramage 11–1–44–1; Stevenson 7–1–24–0; Boycott 8–2–19–0; Carrick 12–1–27–3; Illingworth 12–0–41–0.

Yorkshire

G. Boycott c Sharp b Griffiths	6	A. Ramage b Mallender	14
M. D. Moxon c Sharp b Mallender	0	S. P. Dennis c Griffiths b Kapil Dev	0
C. W. J. Athey lbw b Griffiths	54	*R. Illingworth not out	0
J. D. Love c Sharp b Griffiths	1		
S. N. Hartley c Larkins b Mallender	37	L-b 6, w 2	8
†D. L. Bairstow b Griffiths	11		
P. Carrick b Griffiths	0	1/0 2/19 3/21 (55.2 overs) 165	
G. B. Stevenson c Griffiths		4/100 5/114 6/115	
b Kapil Dev.	34	7/116 8/161 9/165	

Bowling: Kapil Dev 11.2–5–17–2; Mallender 12–1–34–3; Griffiths 10–4–33–5; T. M. Lamb 10–1–38–0; Larkins 8–0–18–0; Willey 4–0–17–0.

Umpires: A. Jepson and R. A. White.

QUARTER-FINALS

GLOUCESTERSHIRE v HAMPSHIRE

At Bristol, August 3. Hampshire won by six wickets. When, just before lunch, Gloucestershire were 149 for one, it seemed that they would be able to set a massive target.

But the departure of Romaines, after a splendid attacking innings, gave Hampshire their chance, and steady bowling restricted Gloucestershire to a total which was unlikely to be a match-winning one on a good batting pitch. Against a limited attack, Childs being unable to bowl because of a bruised hand, Hampshire overcame the early loss of Greenidge, Smith playing an admirable sheet-anchor role and not offering a chance until he was in the nineties. Nicholas and Jesty played vigorously and sensibly in support as Hampshire moved confidently towards their first semi-final appearance in the competition.

Man of the Match: C. L. Smith.

Gloucestershire

P. W. Romaines c Marshall b Tremlett.	82	*D. A. Graveney b Tremlett	3
B. C. Broad b Cowley	36	†R. C. Russell b Marshall	1
P. Bainbridge c Nicholas b Marshall	21	J. H. Childs not out	14
Zaheer Abbas b Stevenson	33	L-b 19, w 9	28
A. J. Hignell c Nicholas b Stevenson	28		
J. N. Shepherd b Cowley	6	1/95 2/149 3/155 (8 wkts, 60 overs) 252	
		4/193 5/208 6/215 7/220 8/252	

G. E. Sainsbury and D. V. Lawrence did not bat.

Bowling: Marshall 12–4–37–2; Stevenson 12–1–44–2; Jesty 12–0–65–0; Tremlett 12–1–47–2; Cowley 12–3–31–2.

Hampshire

C. G. Greenidge lbw b Sainsbury	9	*N. E. J. Pocock not out	8
C. L. Smith not out	101		
M. C. J. Nicholas c Hignell b Graveney.	51	B 1, l-b 6, w 8, n-b 2	17
T. E. Jesty b Lawrence	49	1/13 2/99 (4 wkts, 58.2 overs) 256	
V. P. Terry c Graveney b Shepherd	21	3/189 4/243	

M. D. Marshall, N. G. Cowley, T. M. Tremlett, †R. J. Parks and K. Stevenson did not bat.

Bowling: Lawrence 10.5–2–40–1; Sainsbury 12–3–51–1; Shepherd 11–0–58–1; Bainbridge 12–2–31–0; Graveney 12–0–54–1; Zaheer 0.3–0–5–0.

Umpires: D. G. L. Evans and C. T. Spencer.

KENT v WARWICKSHIRE

At Canterbury, August 3. Kent won by 105 runs. After the early loss of Woolmer, Kent again faltered as Ferreira dismissed Benson and Tavaré in successive overs. But Aslett and Cowdrey added 78 off twenty overs, Cowdrey reaching 56 in 72 minutes with a 6 and six 4s. Warwickshire were unable to get on terms with their target. Jarvis, back in the Kent attack in Dilley's absence, put them under pressure with two early wickets, and they lost half their side for 113 in 40 overs before Jarvis returned to take the last two wickets.

Man of the Match: K. B. S. Jarvis.

Kent

R. A. Woolmer c Ferreira b Willis	2	G. W. Johnson not out	26
M. R. Benson lbw b Ferreira	33	R. M. Ellison b Willis	11
*C. J. Tavaré b Ferreira	34	D. L. Underwood not out	2
D. G. Aslett b Gifford	29	B 4, l-b 11, w 1, n-b 7	23
C. S. Cowdrey b Ferreira	56		
E. A. E. Baptiste lbw b Gifford	22	1/2 2/69 3/78 4/156 (8 wkts, 60 overs) 251	
†A. P. E. Knott b Hogg	13	5/181 6/196 7/206 8/234	

K. B. S. Jarvis did not bat.

Bowling: Willis 12–1–44–2; Hogg 12–2–48–1; Old 12–0–38–0; Ferreira 12–0–43–3; Gifford 12–3–55–2.

Warwickshire

T. A. Lloyd lbw b Ellison	23		N. Gifford b Baptiste	5
K. D. Smith c Tavaré b Jarvis	5		*R. G. D. Willis c Cowdrey b Jarvis	3
A. I. Kallicharran c Johnson b Jarvis	8		W. Hogg b Jarvis	4
D. L. Amiss c Benson b Woolmer	21			
†G. W. Humpage c Tavaré b Baptiste	31		B 4, l-b 11, w 2, n-b 3	20
R. I. H. B. Dyer b Underwood	15			
C. M. Old c Knott b Underwood	5		1/14 2/24 3/52 4/75 (51.5 overs) 146	
A. M. Ferreira not out	6		5/113 6/125 7/125 8/132 9/137	

Bowling: Jarvis 7.5–2–19–4; Ellison 12–3–27–1; Woolmer 12–1–35–1; Underwood 12–5–20–2; Baptiste 8–1–25–2.

Umpires: J. van Geloven and P. B. Wight.

NORTHAMPTONSHIRE v MIDDLESEX

At Northampton, August 3. Middlesex won by seven wickets. Cook and Larkins began with 60 in fourteen overs for Northamptonshire, before the inspired introduction of Slack, as well as some wild shots, put Middlesex on top, Slack dismissing Larkins and Allan Lamb in three balls, plus Kapil Dev just after lunch. Willey promised a recovery until hitting adventurously at Gatting near the interval and thereafter only Williams and Capel stayed long. Middlesex quickly lost Slack through brilliant fielding by Kapil Dev, but Barlow and Radley methodically demolished the home attack in a capable stand of 149 in 40 overs, before Gatting and Ellis clinched the game in comfort.

Man of the Match: G. D. Barlow.

Northamptonshire

*G. Cook b Edmonds	29		†G. Sharp run out	14
W. Larkins c and b Slack	30		N. A. Mallender b Daniel	0
P. Willey c Radley b Gatting	41		T. M. Lamb not out	9
A. J. Lamb c Downton b Slack	0		L-b 6, w 2, n-b 5	13
R. G. Williams c Downton b Daniel	33			
Kapil Dev st Downton b Slack	2		1/60 2/72 3/72 4/117 (9 wkts, 60 overs) 198	
D. J. Capel b Daniel	27		5/128 6/157 7/184 8/184 9/198	

B. J. Griffiths did not bat.

Bowling: Daniel 12–2–42–3; Cowans 3–0–16–0; Williams 1–0–8–0; Slack 12–1–37–3; Edmonds 12–3–24–1; Emburey 12–4–25–0; Gatting 8–0–33–1.

Middlesex

G. D. Barlow b Mallender	77		R. G. P. Ellis not out	15
W. N. Slack run out	5		B 2, l-b 9	11
C. T. Radley b Mallender	63			
*M. W. Gatting not out	28		1/5 2/154 3/155 (3 wkts, 53.4 overs) 199	

J. E. Emburey, †P. R. Downton, P. H. Edmonds, N. F. Williams, W. W. Daniel and N. G. Cowans did not bat.

Bowling: Kapil Dev 9–4–21–0; Griffiths 8–0–32–0; T. M. Lamb 3–1–8–0; Mallender 12–1–37–2; Willey 11.4–1–53–0; Williams 10–0–37–0.

Umpires: H. D. Bird and A. G. T. Whitehead.

SUSSEX v SOMERSET

At Hove, August 3. Somerset won by seven wickets. Brilliant bowling by Garner (four for 8) and Botham (four for 20), as well as skilful wicket-keeping by Gard, who held five catches, resulted in Sussex being unceremoniously tumbled out for only 65. Without le Roux and Greig, and with Imran still unable to bowl, their attack proved ineffective, and the match was all over by mid-afternoon, to the disappointment of a 6,500 crowd in glorious sunshine.

Man of the Match: T. Gard.

Sussex

G. D. Mendis c Gard b Botham	4	C. P. Phillipson c Gard b Richards	13
*J. R. T. Barclay c Popplewell		A. C. S. Pigott b Garner	17
b Garner.	2	D. A. Reeve not out	6
A. P. Wells c Gard b Garner	9	C. E. Waller b Botham	0
Imran Khan c Gard b Botham	1	W 1, n-b 3	4
C. M. Wells lbw b Garner	0		—
†I. J. Gould b Botham	4	1/8 2/18 3/20 4/20 (40.4 overs) 65	
P. W. G. Parker c Gard b Dredge	5	5/24 6/26 7/36 8/54 9/64	

Bowling: Garner 11–7–8–4; Botham 9.4–4–20–4; Richards 11–1–21–1; Dredge 7–3–11–1; Marks 2–1–1–0.

Somerset

J. W. Lloyds retired hurt	28	P. A. Slocombe not out	1
P. M. Roebuck lbw b C. M. Wells	8		
I. V. A. Richards b Reeve	23	L-b 1, n-b 4	5
P. W. Denning lbw b Reeve	0		
N. F. M. Popplewell not out	4	1/37 2/60 3/64 (3 wkts, 23.5 overs) 69	

*I. T. Botham, V. J. Marks, †T. Gard, J. Garner and C. H. Dredge did not bat.

Bowling: Pigott 8–1–21–0; Reeve 8.5–4–28–2; C. M. Wells 7–2–15–1.

Umpires: C. Cook and D. R. Shepherd.

SEMI-FINALS

KENT v HAMPSHIRE

At Canterbury, August 17. Kent won by 71 runs. Kent, put in, were indebted to a solid innings from Tavaré who, with Aslett, added 73 off 22 overs. However, Tremlett and Marshall, who both had career-best bowling performances in the 60-overs competition, looked to have bowled their side into a winning position. Greenidge and Smith then added 41 in the first ten overs, but Hampshire ran into terrible trouble against the medium pace of Baptiste and Cowdrey. Both returned their best figures in the 60-overs competition and Hampshire collapsed so badly that they lost nine wickets for 61 runs in 30 overs.

Man of the Match: E. A. E. Baptiste.

Kent

N. R. Taylor c Parks b Marshall	0	R. M. Ellison c Pocock b Malone	0
M. R. Benson c Cowley b Tremlett	16	D. L. Underwood c Tremlett b Nicholas	5
*C. J. Tavaré c Parks b Tremlett	64	K. B. S. Jarvis not out	5
D. G. Aslett c Pocock b Marshall	42	B 1, l-b 5, w 5, n-b 2	13
C. S. Cowdrey c Pocock b Tremlett	5		—
E. A. E. Baptiste b Tremlett	6	1/0 2/39 3/112 (59.2 overs) 173	
†A. P. E. Knott c Parks b Marshall	7	4/123 5/141 6/144	
G. W. Johnson c Jesty b Marshall	10	7/155 8/158 9/161	

Bowling: Marshall 12–6–15–4; Malone 12–4–26–1; Jesty 12–2–34–0; Tremlett 12–1–38–4; Nicholas 5.2–0–25–1; Cowley 6–0–22–0.

Hampshire

C. G. Greenidge b Cowdrey	7	T. M. Tremlett c Knott b Baptiste		11
C. L. Smith c Taylor b Baptiste	25	†R. J. Parks c Aslett b Underwood		3
M. C. J. Nicholas c Tavaré b Cowdrey	28	S. J. Malone not out		4
T. E. Jesty b Baptiste	1	L-b 6, w 7, n-b 2		15
V. P. Terry lbw b Baptiste	0			
*N. E. J. Pocock b Baptiste	4	1/41 2/48 3/49	(39.4 overs)	102
M. D. Marshall c Johnson b Cowdrey	0	4/52 5/62 6/63		
N. G. Cowley c Johnson b Cowdrey	4	7/67 8/92 9/94		

Bowling: Jarvis 7–0–17–0; Ellison 5–0–11–0; Baptiste 12–5–20–5; Cowdrey 12–3–36–4; Underwood 3.4–1–3–1.

Umpires: K. E. Palmer and N. T. Plews.

MIDDLESEX v SOMERSET

At Lord's, August 17. Somerset won by virtue of losing fewer wickets with the scores level. A captain's innings lasting 205 minutes by Botham inched Somerset into their first 60-overs final for four years from an almost irretrievable position. Though Somerset, winning the toss on an overcast morning, would have expected, with Garner in their ranks, to take more than two wickets in the 40 overs they crammed into two and a quarter hours before lunch, Middlesex's 222 for nine looked well within reach in conditions which by afternoon had turned in favour of the bat. But Somerset were in trouble when Cowans dismissed Lloyds and Denning with successive balls in his second over. Worse followed. A disdainful Richards saw Daniel at mid-off reach behind him with a desperate left hand to clutch a checked on-drive, and when Roebuck edged a cut to second slip they were 52 for five. But Botham, communicating vast assurance and an unfamiliar air of calculation, inspired Popplewell and Marks in saving stands of 104 (in 33 overs) and 62 (in thirteen). In retrospect Gatting's decision to take Emburey out of the attack after being swept for 6 by Botham was questionable, although Slack's nine overs cost only 26 runs. The crowd was close to 20,000 and nobody who did not have to do so left before the end.

Man of the Match: I. T. Botham.

Middlesex

G. D. Barlow c Botham b Garner	8	P. H. Edmonds not out		7
W. N. Slack c Slocombe b Popplewell	57	W. W. Daniel run out		0
C. T. Radley b Marks	12	N. G. Cowans not out		0
*M. W. Gatting c Marks b Popplewell	49	L-b 11, w 5		16
K. P. Tomlins c Botham b Garner	58			
J. E. Emburey c Marks b Popplewell	1	1/16 2/55 3/117	(9 wkts, 60 overs)	222
†P. R. Downton b Garner	12	4/148 5/162 6/204		
N. F. Williams lbw b Botham	2	7/211 8/213 9/215		

Bowling: Garner 11–3–23–3; Botham 12–2–33–1; Dredge 9–0–48–0; Richards 12–3–23–0; Marks 8–0–45–1; Popplewell 8–0–34–3.

Somerset

J. W. Lloyds c Downton b Cowans	7	V. J. Marks c Emburey b Slack		21
P. M. Roebuck c Gatting b Cowans	7	J. Garner run out		0
P. W. Denning b Cowans	0	†T. Gard not out		0
I. V. A. Richards c Daniel b Williams	23	L-b 6, w 4, n-b 10		20
P. A. Slocombe c Downton b Williams	2			
*I. T. Botham not out	96	1/13 2/15 3/41	(8 wkts, 60 overs)	222
N. F. M. Popplewell c Downton b Daniel	46	4/43 5/52 6/156 7/218 8/221		

C. H. Dredge did not bat.

Bowling: Daniel 12–2–32–1; Cowans 12–2–48–3; Williams 12–0–54–2; Emburey 3–1–9–0; Edmonds 12–4–33–0; Slack 9–1–26–1.

Umpires: J. Birkenshaw and D. O. Oslear.

FINAL

KENT v SOMERSET

At Lord's, September 3. Somerset won by 24 runs. With the long spell of fine weather beginning to break up, the match began in poor light (the start was delayed by half an hour and the match reduced to 50 overs a side) and ended in the gloaming. By choosing to field upon winning the toss, Kent knew they were committing themselves to batting on a rapidly darkening evening unless they could bowl Somerset out cheaply, which they came quite near to doing.

When Richards was caught at the wicket for a dashing 51 off the last ball before lunch, Somerset were 95 for four, and soon afterwards Botham skied Cowdrey to square leg. Back in the Kent side after injury, Dilley bowled well in conditions which helped him move the ball about. His four for 29 clinched his place on England's winter tour. But Popplewell and Marks, batting sensibly, gave Somerset just enough runs for their bowlers to work with.

Kent, like Somerset, lost a wicket immediately, Benson being well caught at slip. Johnson and Tavaré then shared a partnership which had raised Kent's hopes to a high point when Marks, with slow off-spin, reduced them from 60 for one to 73 for four. When, at 88, Aslett went to a second smart leg-side stumping, Kent, now needing 106 in nineteen overs, were also behind the clock. Bravely though they tried after that to keep in the game, Knott's dismissal – he was caught at mid-on at 126 – and a blow on the knee for Ellison, which necessitated his having a runner, signalled the virtual end of Kent's chances. The attendance was 23,713, and Bob Willis, the England captain, made Marks Man of the Match.

Somerset

P. W. Denning lbw b Dilley	1	V. J. Marks c Benson b Cowdrey	29
P. M. Roebuck b Dilley	11	J. Garner run out	4
P. A. Slocombe c Johnson b Baptiste	20	C. H. Dredge not out	3
I. V. A. Richards c Knott b Dilley	51	B 1, l-b 17, w 2	20
*I. T. Botham c Johnson b Cowdrey	9		—
N. F. M. Popplewell c Cowdrey b Dilley	35	1/10 2/20 3/89 (9 wkts, 50 overs) 193	
J. W. Lloyds lbw b Jarvis	10	4/95 5/112 6/146 7/176 8/190 9/193	

†T. Gard did not bat.

Bowling: Dilley 10–1–29–4; Ellison 10–1–35–0; Jarvis 10–0–43–1; Baptiste 10–1–37–1; Cowdrey 10–2–29–2.

Kent

M. R. Benson c Lloyds b Garner	0	G. R. Dilley b Botham	19
G. W. Johnson b Marks	27	D. L. Underwood not out	5
*C. J. Tavaré c Roebuck b Marks	39	K. B. S. Jarvis c Botham b Dredge	3
D. G. Aslett st Gard b Richards	14	B 6, l-b 1, n-b 1	8
C. S. Cowdrey st Gard b Marks	0		
E. A. E. Baptiste b Botham	16	1/0 2/60 3/73 (47.1 overs) 169	
†A. P. E. Knott c Roebuck b Dredge	17	4/73 5/88 6/112	
R. M. Ellison b Garner	21	7/126 8/160 9/162	

Bowling: Garner 9–2–15–2; Botham 10–0–29–2; Dredge 8.1–0–50–2; Popplewell 1–0–9–0; Marks 10–0–30–3; Richards 9–1–28–1.

Umpires: D. J. Constant and D. G. L. Evans.

NATWEST BANK TROPHY RECORDS

(Including Gillette Cup, 1963-80)

Batting

Highest individual scores: 177, C. G. Greenidge, Hampshire v Glamorgan, Southampton, 1975; 158, Zaheer Abbas, Gloucestershire v Leicestershire, Leicester, 1983; 146, G. Boycott, Yorkshire v Surrey, Lord's, 1965; 145, P. W. Denning, Somerset v Glamorgan, Cardiff, 1978; 143 not out, B. L. Reed, Hampshire v Buckinghamshire, Chesham, 1970; 141 not out, G. D. Mendis, Sussex v Warwickshire, Hove, 1980; 141 not out, A. I. Kallicharran, Warwickshire v Somerset, Taunton, 1982; 140, R. E. Marshall, Hampshire v Bedfordshire, Goldington, 1968; 139 not out, I. V. A. Richards, Somerset v Warwickshire, Taunton, 1978; 138 not out, D. I. Gower, Leicestershire v Gloucestershire, Leicester, 1983; 135, D. L. Amiss, Warwickshire v Cambridgeshire, Birmingham, 1982. (93 hundreds were scored in the Gillette Cup; 20 hundreds have been scored in the NatWest Bank Trophy.)

Fastest hundred: R. E. Marshall in 77 minutes at Goldington, 1968.

Highest innings total: 371 for four wickets off 60 overs, Hampshire v Glamorgan, Southampton, 1975; 330 for four off 60 overs, Somerset v Glamorgan, Cardiff, 1978; 327 for seven off 60 overs, Gloucestershire v Berkshire, Reading, 1966; 326 for six off 60 overs, Leicestershire v Worcestershire, Leicester, 1979; 321 for four off 60 overs, Hampshire v Bedfordshire, Goldington, 1968; 317 for four off 60 overs, Yorkshire v Surrey (in the final), Lord's, 1965.
  The highest innings totals in the NatWest Bank Trophy are 306 for eight off 60 overs by Essex v Hertfordshire, Hitchin, 1981 and 306 for six off 59.3 overs by Gloucestershire v Leicestershire, Leicester, 1983.

Highest innings total by a minor county: 256 off 58 overs, Oxfordshire v Warwickshire, Birmingham, 1983.

Highest totals by a side batting second: 306 for six off 59.3 overs, Gloucestershire v Leicestershire, Leicester, 1983; 297 for four off 57.1 overs, Somerset v Warwickshire, Taunton, 1978; 290 for seven off 59.3 overs, Yorkshire v Worcestershire, Leeds, 1982; 287 for six off 59 overs, Warwickshire v Glamorgan, Birmingham, 1976; 287 off 60 overs, Essex v Somerset, Taunton, 1978; 282 for nine off 60 overs, Leicestershire v Gloucestershire, Leicester, 1975. Gloucestershire's 306 for six v Leicestershire, Leicester, 1983 was the highest by a side batting second and winning the match.

Highest innings by a side batting first and losing: 302 for five off 60 overs, Leicestershire v Gloucestershire, Leicester, 1983.

Lowest innings in the final at Lord's: 118 off 60 overs, Lancashire v Kent, 1974.

Lowest completed innings totals: 41 off 20 overs, Cambridgeshire v Buckinghamshire, Cambridge, 1972; 41 off 19.4 overs, Middlesex v Essex, Westcliff, 1972; 41 off 36.1 overs, Shropshire v Essex, Wellington, 1974.
  The lowest innings total in the NatWest Bank Trophy is 65 off 40.4 overs, Sussex v Somerset, Hove, 1983.

Lowest total by a side batting first and winning: 98 off 56.2 overs, Worcestershire v Durham, Chester-le-Street, 1968.

Shortest innings: 10.1 overs (60 for one), Worcestershire v Lancashire, Worcester, 1963.

Matches re-arranged on a reduced number of overs are excluded from the above.

Record partnerships for each wicket

227 for 1st	R. E. Marshall and B. L. Reed, Hampshire v Bedfordshire at Goldington..	1968
223 for 2nd	M. J. Smith and C. T. Radley, Middlesex v Hampshire at Lord's...	1977
160 for 3rd	B. Wood and F. C. Hayes, Lancashire v Warwickshire at Birmingham	1976
234* for 4th	D. Lloyd and C. H. Lloyd, Lancashire v Gloucestershire at Manchester	1978
166 for 5th	M. A. Lynch and G. R. J. Roope, Surrey v Durham at The Oval.	1982
105 for 6th	G. S. Sobers and R. A. White, Nottinghamshire v Worcestershire at Worcester...	1974
160* for 7th	C. J. Richards and I. R. Payne, Surrey v Lincolnshire at Sleaford..	1983
69 for 8th	S. J. Rouse and D. J. Brown, Warwickshire v Middlesex at Lord's	1977
87 for 9th	M. A. Nash and A. E. Cordle, Glamorgan v Lincolnshire at Swansea	1974
81 for 10th	S. Turner and R. E. East, Essex v Yorkshire at Leeds................	1982

The record partnership for any wicket in the NatWest Bank Trophy is:

184 for 1st	G. A. Gooch and B. R. Hardie, Essex v Hertfordshire at Hitchin..	1981

Bowling

Hat-tricks: J. D. F. Larter, Northamptonshire v Sussex, Northampton, 1963; D. A. D. Sydenham, Surrey v Cheshire, Hoylake, 1964; R. N. S. Hobbs, Essex v Middlesex, Lord's, 1968; N. M. McVicker, Warwickshire v Lincolnshire, Birmingham, 1971.

Four wickets in five balls: D. A. D. Sydenham, Surrey v Cheshire, Hoylake, 1964.

Best analyses: seven for 15, A. L. Dixon, Kent v Surrey, The Oval, 1967; seven for 30, P. J. Sainsbury, Hampshire v Norfolk, Southampton, 1965; seven for 32, S. P. Davis, Durham v Lancashire, Chester-le-Street, 1983; seven for 33, R. D. Jackman, Surrey v Yorkshire, Harrogate, 1970; six for 14, R. D. Healey, Devon v Hertfordshire, Stevenage, 1969; six for 14, J. A. Flavell, Worcestershire v Lancashire, Worcester, 1963; six for 15, F. S. Trueman, Yorkshire v Somerset, Taunton, 1965; six for 15, W. W. Daniel, Middlesex v Sussex, Hove, 1980; six for 18, T. J. P. Eyre, Derbyshire v Sussex, Chesterfield, 1969; six for 18, C. E. B. Rice, Nottinghamshire v Sussex, Hove, 1982.

Results

Largest victories in runs: Leicestershire by 214 runs v Staffordshire, Longton, 1975; Sussex by 200 runs v Durham, Hove, 1964; Essex by 191 runs v Hertfordshire, Hitchin, 1981; Surrey by 184 runs v Derbyshire, The Oval, 1967; and in the final by 175 runs, Yorkshire v Surrey, Lord's, 1965.

Quickest finishes: both at 2.20 p.m. Worcestershire beat Lancashire by nine wickets at Worcester, 1963; Essex beat Middlesex by eight wickets at Westcliff, 1972.

Scores level: Nottinghamshire 215, Somerset 215 for nine at Taunton, 1964; Surrey 196, Sussex 196 for eight at The Oval, 1970; Somerset 287 for six, Essex 287 at Taunton, 1978; Surrey 195 for seven, Essex 195 at Chelmsford, 1980; Essex 149, Derbyshire 149 for eight at Derby, 1981; Northamptonshire 235 for nine, Derbyshire 235 for six at Lord's, 1981; Middlesex 222 for nine, Somerset 222 for eight at Lord's, 1983. Under the rules the side which lost fewer wickets won.

Minor Counties: Durham became the first minor county to defeat a first-class county when they beat Yorkshire at Harrogate by five wickets in 1973. Lincolnshire became the second when they beat Glamorgan at Swansea by six wickets in 1974 and Hertfordshire the first minor county to reach the third round when they beat Essex at Hitchin by 33 runs in 1976. Cumberland is the only minor county that has not appeared in either competition.

PAST WINNERS

Gillette Cup

1963 SUSSEX beat Worcestershire by 14 runs.
1964 SUSSEX beat Warwickshire by eight wickets.
1965 YORKSHIRE beat Surrey by 175 runs.
1966 WARWICKSHIRE beat Worcestershire by five wickets.
1967 KENT beat Somerset by 32 runs.
1968 WARWICKSHIRE beat Sussex by four wickets.
1969 YORKSHIRE beat Derbyshire by 69 runs.
1970 LANCASHIRE beat Sussex by six wickets.
1971 LANCASHIRE beat Kent by 24 runs.
1972 LANCASHIRE beat Warwickshire by four wickets.
1973 GLOUCESTERSHIRE beat Sussex by 40 runs.
1974 KENT beat Lancashire by four wickets.
1975 LANCASHIRE beat Middlesex by seven wickets.
1976 NORTHAMPTONSHIRE beat Lancashire by four wickets.
1977 MIDDLESEX beat Glamorgan by five wickets.
1978 SUSSEX beat Somerset by five wickets.
1979 SOMERSET beat Northamptonshire by 45 runs.
1980 MIDDLESEX beat Surrey by seven wickets.

NatWest Bank Trophy

1981 DERBYSHIRE beat Northamptonshire by losing fewer wickets with the scores level.
1982 SURREY beat Warwickshire by nine wickets.
1983 SOMERSET beat Kent by 24 runs.

BENSON AND HEDGES CUP, 1983

Middlesex won the Benson and Hedges Cup for the first time when they beat Essex by 4 runs at Lord's in the twelfth final of the competition. In addition to the trophy, which they hold for a year, Middlesex received £13,000 in prizemoney. Essex received £6,500 as runners-up.

The losing semi-finalists, Kent and Lancashire, received £3,000 each, while Gloucestershire, Hampshire, Northamptonshire and Warwickshire, the losing quarter-finalists, received £1,750 each. The winners of the group matches each won £450.

C. T. Radley, nominated by L. E. G. Ames for the Gold Award in the final for his gallant, unbeaten 89, received £500. The Gold Award winners in the semi-finals each received £250; in the quarter-finals £175 each; and in the group matches £75 each.

Total prizemoney for the competition was £55,200, an increase of £12,800 over 1982. Benson and Hedges increased their total sponsorship to the TCCB for 1983 to £275,000.

FINAL GROUP TABLES

	Played	Won	Lost	No Result	Points
Group A					
GLOUCESTERSHIRE	4	3	0	1	7
NORTHAMPTONSHIRE	4	2	1	1	5
Leicestershire	4	1	1	2	4
Worcestershire	4	1	2	1	3
Scotland	4	0	3	1	1
Group B					
LANCASHIRE	4	2	0	2	6
WARWICKSHIRE	4	2	0	2	6
Nottinghamshire	4	2	1	1	5
Derbyshire	4	0	2	2	2
Yorkshire	4	0	3	1	1
Group C					
ESSEX	4	3	1	0	6
HAMPSHIRE	4	3	1	0	6
Sussex	4	2	2	0	4
Somerset	4	1	2	1	3
Minor Counties	4	0	3	1	1
Group D					
KENT	4	3	1	0	6
MIDDLESEX	4	2	0	2	6
Glamorgan	4	1	1	2	4
Surrey	4	1	2	1	3
Oxford & Cambridge Univs	4	0	3	1	1

The top two counties in each section qualified for the quarter-finals.
Where two counties finished with the same number of points, the position in the group was determined by their bowlers' striking-rate.

BOWLERS' STRIKING-RATES

Group A	Balls	Wickets	Striking-rate
GLOUCESTERSHIRE	877	26	33.73
NORTHAMPTONSHIRE	1,117	30	37.23
Leicestershire	636	13	48.92
Worcestershire	844	23	36.69
Scotland	761	15	50.73
Group B			
LANCASHIRE	484	13	37.23
WARWICKSHIRE	826	21	39.33
Nottinghamshire	879	22	39.95
Derbyshire	846	17	49.76
Yorkshire	913	19	48.05
Group C			
ESSEX	1,230	37	33.24
HAMPSHIRE	1,243	35	35.51
Sussex	1,286	28	45.92
Somerset	955	28	34.10
Minor Counties	825	10	82.50
Group D			
KENT	1,157	33	35.06
MIDDLESEX	450	9	50.00
Glamorgan	669	17	39.35
Surrey	988	24	41.16
Oxford & Cambridge Univs	956	22	43.45

GROUP A

LEICESTERSHIRE v WORCESTERSHIRE

At Worcester, May 7. Leicestershire won by 117 runs. Toss won by Worcestershire.
  Gold Award: J. F. Steele.

Leicestershire

J. C. Balderstone b Illingworth	35	J. F. Steele c Humphries b Warner	15
N. E. Briers b Warner	0	P. B. Clift lbw b Pridgeon	0
D. I. Gower b Patel	67	G. J. Parsons b Pridgeon	3
B. F. Davison st Humphries b Illingworth	32	J. P. Agnew not out	0
†M. A. Garnham lbw b Patel	2	B 1, l-b 11, n-b 5	17
*R. W. Tolchard c Humphries b Inchmore	27	1/5 2/108 3/108 (52.2 overs) 198	
A. M. E. Roberts b Illingworth	0	4/111 5/170 6/172	
		7/182 8/192 9/198	

  Bowling: Warner 9.2–0–40–2; Pridgeon 10–0–46–2; Inchmore 11–1–38–1; Patel 11–2–33–2; Illingworth 11–3–24–3.

Worcestershire

J. A. Ormrod b Parsons	5	R. K. Illingworth not out	11
M. J. Weston b Roberts	12	A. E. Warner b Steele	3
D. N. Patel lbw b Agnew	8	A. P. Pridgeon b Roberts	0
Younis Ahmed c Davison b Agnew	10	B 2, w 3	5
*P. A. Neale b Steele	5		—
M. S. A. McEvoy c and b Steele	15	1/11 2/19 3/35 (34.4 overs)	81
J. D. Inchmore b Steele	3	4/38 5/50 6/54	
†D. J. Humphries c Gower b Steele	4	7/60 8/74 9/80	

Bowling: Roberts 7.4–1–25–2; Parsons 7–3–10–1; Agnew 5–1–15–2; Steele 10–2–11–5; Clift 5–0–15–0.

Umpires: A. Jepson and W. E. Alley.

NORTHAMPTONSHIRE v GLOUCESTERSHIRE

At Northampton, May 7. Gloucestershire won by two wickets. Toss won by Gloucestershire.

Gold Award: P. Willey.

Northamptonshire

*G. Cook lbw b Bainbridge	33	J. A. Carse b Sainsbury	0
W. Larkins c Russell b Sainsbury	36	N. A. Mallender lbw b Shepherd	0
P. Willey lbw b Shepherd	71	B. J. Griffiths not out	1
A. J. Lamb c Childs b Bainbridge	14	B 1, l-b 9, w 1	11
R. G. Williams b Broad	16		—
D. J. Capel st Russell b Sainsbury	6	1/69 2/95 3/121 (54.4 overs)	191
†G. Sharp c Stovold b Sainsbury	3	4/160 5/182 6/187	
T. M. Lamb st Russell b Shepherd	0	7/188 8/188 9/188	

Bowling: Sainsbury 10.4–3–28–4; Doughty 3–0–20–0; Shepherd 10–1–42–3; Bainbridge 11–1–22–2; Childs 11–2–29–0; Graveney 4–0–13–0; Broad 5–0–26–1.

Gloucestershire

A. W. Stovold c A. J. Lamb b Griffiths	6	R. J. Doughty b Carse	0
B. C. Broad c Cook b T. M. Lamb	54	†R. C. Russell not out	10
P. Bainbridge b Willey	17	J. H. Childs not out	1
Zaheer Abbas lbw b T. M. Lamb	65	L-b 2, w 1, n-b 4	7
A. J. Hignell c Willey b Carse	17		—
J. N. Shepherd lbw b Mallender	2	1/7 2/37 3/123 (8 wkts, 55 overs)	192
*D. A. Graveney c Cook b Carse	28	4/134 5/148 6/154 7/155 8/191	

G. E. Sainsbury did not bat.

Bowling: Carse 11–1–38–3; Griffiths 10–1–46–1; Willey 11–1–26–1; T. M. Lamb 11–4–26–2; Williams 2–0–12–0; Mallender 10–0–37–1.

Umpires: P. J. Eele and B. Leadbeater.

GLOUCESTERSHIRE v LEICESTERSHIRE

At Gloucester, May 14, 15, 16. No result. Toss won by Leicestershire.

Gloucestershire

B. C. Broad not out		23
A. W. Stovold b Parsons		12
P. Bainbridge not out		14
L-b 6, w 2, n-b 2		10

1/17   (1 wkt, 27.2 overs) 59

Zaheer Abbas, A. J. Hignell, J. N. Shepherd, *D. A. Graveney, P. W. Romaines, †R. C. Russell, J. H. Childs and G. E. Sainsbury did not bat.

Bowling: Roberts 6–5–5–0; Parsons 6–3–8–1; Steele 8–3–21–0; Agnew 6–1–12–0; Cook 1.2–0–3–0.

Leicestershire

J. C. Balderstone, N. E. Briers, D. I. Gower, B. F. Davison, *R. W. Tolchard, J. F. Steele, †M. A. Garnham, G. J. Parsons, A. M. E. Roberts, N. G. B. Cook and J. P. Agnew.

Umpires: A. G. T. Whitehead and M. J. Kitchen.

SCOTLAND v WORCESTERSHIRE

At Aberdeen, May 14, 15. Worcestershire won by five wickets. Toss won by Worcestershire.
Gold Award: D. N. Patel.

Scotland

D. L. Haynes run out	21	D. De Neef not out	18
W. A. Donald c Ormrod b Warner	11	G. F. Goddard c Humphries	
*R. G. Swan c Illingworth b Patel	13	b D'Oliveira.	3
R. S. Weir lbw b Ellcock	13	W. A. Morton c Humphries b Warner	0
†A. Brown c and b Patel	0	L-b 2, w 2, n-b 2	6
G. D. Halliday lbw b Illingworth	2		
H. G. F. Johnston c Humphries		1/30 2/34 3/52 (52 overs) 105	
b D'Oliveira.	16	4/52 5/59 6/66	
D. L. Snodgrass c Ellcock b Illingworth	2	7/73 8/94 9/102	

Bowling: Pridgeon 5–0–15–0; Ellcock 7–1–17–1; Warner 11–0–26–2; Patel 11–4–13–2; Illingworth 11–4–15–2; D'Oliveira 7–2–13–2.

Worcestershire

J. A. Ormrod c Brown b Morton	8	D. B. D'Oliveira not out	0
M. J. Weston lbw b Haynes	56		
D. N. Patel c Brown b Morton	9	B 1, l-b 2	3
*P. A. Neale c Donald b Johnston	18		
†D. J. Humphries c Donald b Goddard	1	1/33 2/43 3/73 (5 wkts, 45.5 overs) 106	
M. S. A. McEvoy not out	11	4/74 5/103	

R. K. Illingworth, R. M. Ellcock, A. E. Warner and A. P. Pridgeon did not bat.

Bowling: De Neef 4–1–16–0; Snodgrass 2–1–6–0; Morton 11–5–29–2; Goddard 11–2–22–1; Johnston 10.5–4–17–1; Halliday 3–1–4–0; Haynes 4–0–9–1.

Umpires: C. Cook and N. T. Plews.

LEICESTERSHIRE v NORTHAMPTONSHIRE

At Leicester, May 17. Northamptonshire won by eight wickets. Toss won by Northamptonshire.
Gold Award: A. J. Lamb.

Leicestershire

J. C. Balderstone lbw b Capel	30	A. M. E. Roberts lbw b Capel	5
N. E. Briers c Sharp b T. M. Lamb	5	G. J. Parsons not out	29
D. I. Gower c Sharp b T. M. Lamb	13		
B. F. Davison b Griffiths	0	L-b 15, n-b 1	16
†M. A. Garnham c Sharp b Capel	19		
*R. W. Tolchard b T. M. Lamb	26	1/16 2/48 3/49　(7 wkts, 55 overs) 171	
J. F. Steele not out	28	4/65 5/88 6/114 7/119	

J. P. Agnew and N. G. B. Cook did not bat.

Bowling: Kapil Dev 11–3–31–0; Mallender 10–0–33–0; T. M. Lamb 11–3–28–3; Griffiths 11–3–35–1; Capel 11–2–24–3; Willey 1–0–4–0.

Northamptonshire

*G. Cook b Roberts	6
W. Larkins lbw b Parsons	4
P. Willey not out	54
A. J. Lamb not out	106
B 1, l-b 1, n-b 2	4

1/10 2/10　(2 wkts, 44 overs) 174

R. G. Williams, Kapil Dev, D. J. Capel, †G. Sharp, T. M. Lamb, N. A. Mallender and B. J. Griffiths did not bat.

Bowling: Roberts 10–1–28–1; Parsons 9–1–48–1; Agnew 7–1–32–0; Cook 11–1–32–0; Steele 7–2–30–0.

Umpires: K. Ibadulla and B. J. Meyer.

SCOTLAND v GLOUCESTERSHIRE

At West of Scotland Ground, Glasgow, May 17. Gloucestershire won by three wickets. Toss won by Gloucestershire.
Gold Award: R. C. Russell.

Scotland

D. L. Haynes b Shepherd	7	D. De Neef b Sainsbury	10
W. A. Donald st Russell b Bainbridge	12	G. F. Goddard c Bainbridge	
*R. G. Swan run out	3	b Shepherd	4
R. S. Weir c Russell b Bainbridge	6	W. A. Morton not out	11
†A. Brown b Sainsbury	22		
G. D. Halliday lbw b Graveney	1	B 1, l-b 8, w 1	10
H. G. F. Johnston c Stovold			
b Graveney	4	1/12 2/21 3/26 4/33　(54.3 overs) 90	
J. E. Ker b Graveney	0	5/39 6/55 7/58 8/61 9/74	

Bowling: Shepherd 10.3–2–22–2; Sainsbury 11–2–22–2; Childs 11–4–14–0; Bainbridge 11–3–9–2; Graveney 11–6–13–3.

Gloucestershire

A. W. Stovold c Morton b Ker	1	*D. A. Graveney b De Neef	13
B. C. Broad c Swan b De Neef	2	J. N. Shepherd not out	0
P. Bainbridge c Haynes b De Neef	4		
Zaheer Abbas c and b Morton	13	B 2, l-b 3, w 4	9
P. W. Romaines b Morton	9		
A. J. Hignell lbw b Morton	4	1/4 2/10 3/12 (7 wkts, 44.5 overs)	91
†R. C. Russell not out	36	4/33 5/37 6/45 7/87	

J. H. Childs and G. E. Sainsbury did not bat.

Bowling: Ker 9–4–11–1; De Neef 6–1–14–3; Haynes 11–3–18–0; Halliday 2–1–6–0; Morton 11–4–17–3; Johnston 2–0–8–0; Goddard 3.5–2–8–0.

Umpires: D. J. Constant and J. W. Holder.

LEICESTERSHIRE v SCOTLAND

At Leicester, May 19, 20. No result.

WORCESTERSHIRE v NORTHAMPTONSHIRE

At Worcester, May 19, 20. No result. Toss won by Northamptonshire.

Worcestershire

J. A. Ormrod b Kapil Dev	2	†D. J. Humphries not out	12
M. J. Weston lbw b Mallender	0		
D. N. Patel c Cook b Mallender	0	L-b 4, n-b 1	5
C. L. King b Kapil Dev	4		
*P. A. Neale not out	17	1/2 2/2 3/4 (5 wkts, 21.4 overs)	43
D. B. D'Oliveira c Sharp b Mallender	3	4/7 5/12	

R. K. Illingworth, A. E. Warner, J. D. Inchmore and A. P. Pridgeon did not bat.

Bowling: Kapil Dev 9–3–10–2; Mallender 7–2–12–3; Griffiths 3.4–2–10–0; Capel 2–1–6–0.

Northamptonshire

*G. Cook, W. Larkins, P. Willey, A. J. Lamb, R. G. Williams, Kapil Dev, D. J. Capel, †G. Sharp, N. A. Mallender, T. M. Lamb and B. J. Griffiths.

Umpires: B. J. Meyer and M. J. Kitchen.

GLOUCESTERSHIRE v WORCESTERSHIRE

At Bristol, May 21, 23. Gloucestershire won by seven wickets in a match reduced to 37 overs a side. Toss won by Gloucestershire.

Gold Award: Zaheer Abbas.

Worcestershire

M. S. A. McEvoy st Russell b Childs	24	†D. J. Humphries not out	17
M. J. Weston c Broad b Graveney	10	A. E. Warner not out	7
D. N. Patel st Russell b Childs	36		
C. L. King c Graveney b Sainsbury	51	B 2, l-b 12, w 1	15
*P. A. Neale run out	24		
D. B. D'Oliveira c Zaheer b Shepherd	13	1/25 2/54 3/106 (6 wkts, 37 overs)	197
		4/137 5/164 6/186	

R. K. Illingworth, J. D. Inchmore and A. P. Pridgeon did not bat.

Bowling: Shepherd 8–0–39–1; Sainsbury 8–2–30–1; Graveney 6–1–22–1; Bainbridge 5–0–32–0; Childs 7–0–32–2; Broad 3–0–27–0.

Gloucestershire

A. W. Stovold run out	32	A. J. Hignell not out	5
B. C. Broad b Patel	31	B 9, l-b 6, w 2, n-b 3	20
Zaheer Abbas c Patel b Pridgeon	70		
P. Bainbridge not out	40	1/69 2/85 3/180 (3 wkts, 36.2 overs) 198

P. W. Romaines, *D. A. Graveney, J. N. Shepherd, †R. C. Russell, J. H. Childs and G. E. Sainsbury did not bat.

Bowling: Warner 6–0–27–0; Pridgeon 7–1–37–1; Inchmore 4.2–0–23–0; Patel 8–1–36–1; Illingworth 8–0–37–0; King 3–0–18–0.

Umpires: K. E. Palmer and P. J. Eele.

NORTHAMPTONSHIRE v SCOTLAND

At Northampton, May 21, 23. Northamptonshire won by seven wickets. Toss won by Northamptonshire.
Gold Award: G. Cook.

Scotland

D. L. Haynes b Willey	44	W. A. Morton c Cook b Griffiths	5
W. A. Donald b Willey	13	D. De Neef c Williams b Griffiths	0
E. T. N. Pollock c Mallender b T. M. Lamb	6	J. E. Ker c A. J. Lamb b Kapil Dev	9
		G. F. Goddard not out	6
*R. G. Swan c Mallender b Griffiths	9	B 2, l-b 5, n-b 2	9
R. S. Weir b Steele	9		
†A. Brown lbw b Steele	4	1/29 2/40 3/73 4/81 (54.3 overs) 135
A. B. M. Ker b Steele	21	5/86 6/112 7/115 8/119 9/120

Bowling: Kapil Dev 5.3–3–6–1; Mallender 5–2–15–0; T. M. Lamb 6–1–23–1; Willey 11–3–18–2; Steele 11–4–23–3; Williams 5–2–13–0; Griffiths 11–2–28–3.

Northamptonshire

*G. Cook not out	63	Kapil Dev not out	18
W. Larkins c Haynes b Goddard	24	B 4, l-b 2, w 2	8
P. Willey c Weir b Morton	18		
A. J. Lamb c Pollock b Donald	10	1/44 2/79 3/98 (3 wkts, 36.1 overs) 141

R. G. Williams, D. S. Steele, †G. Sharp, T. M. Lamb, N. A. Mallender and B. J. Griffiths did not bat.

Bowling: J. E. Ker 4–1–7–0; De Neef 3–0–33–0; Morton 11–1–44–1; Goddard 9.1–2–31–1; Haynes 3–1–5–0; Donald 6–1–13–1.

Umpires: K. Ibadulla and B. Leadbeater.

GROUP B

DERBYSHIRE v YORKSHIRE

At Chesterfield, May 7, 9. No result.

LANCASHIRE v WARWICKSHIRE

At Manchester, May 7, 9. No result. Toss won by Warwickshire.

Lancashire

G. Fowler b Ferreira	45	J. Simmonds c Humpage b Hogg	0
S. J. O'Shaughnessy run out	0	†C. Maynard not out	0
F. C. Hayes lbw Ferreira	16	L-b 5, w 3, n-b 3	11
D. P. Hughes c and b Ferreira	19		
*C. H. Lloyd not out	20	1/3 2/63 3/74 (6 wkts, 41.4 overs)	127
J. Abrahams c Humpage b Lethbridge	16	4/96 5/126 6/127	

M. Watkinson, P. J. W. Allott and I. Folley did not bat.

Bowling: Willis 7–1–25–0; Hogg 7.4–2–22–1; Old 7–0–16–0; Ferreira 11–2–15–3; Lethbridge 9–1–38–1.

Warwickshire

K. D. Smith, T. A. Lloyd, A. I. Kallicharran, D. L. Amiss, †G. W. Humpage, Asif Din, A. M. Ferreira, C. Lethbridge, C. M. Old, *R. G. D. Willis and W. Hogg.

Umpires: B. J. Meyer and J. Birkenshaw.

WARWICKSHIRE v DERBYSHIRE

At Birmingham, May 14, 16. Warwickshire won by 61 runs. Toss won by Derbyshire.
Gold Award: R. G. D. Willis.

Warwickshire

K. D. Smith c Miller b Tunnicliffe	75	A. M. Ferreira not out	10
D. L. Amiss c Miller b Oldham	27	C. Lethbridge not out	4
A. I. Kallicharran run out	119	L-b 12, w 4, n-b 3	19
†G. W. Humpage c Taylor b Tunnicliffe	7	1/70 2/178 3/186 (5 wkts, 55 overs)	287
Asif Din c Tunnicliffe b Oldham	26	4/269 5/270	

C. M. Old, N. Gifford, *R. G. D. Willis and W. Hogg did not bat.

Bowling: Newman 11–1–56–0; Tunnicliffe 11–2–30–2; Oldham 11–0–58–2; Moir 3–1–21–0; Wood 11–0–59–0; Miller 8–0–44–0.

Derbyshire

J. G. Wright b Willis	0	P. G. Newman b Willis	4
B. Wood c and b Hogg	0	D. G. Moir c Willis b Ferreira	3
K. J. Barnett b Willis	30	S. Oldham c Humpage b Old	2
J. H. Hampshire lbw b Willis	83		
A. Hill c Humpage b Old	35	L-b 12, w 3, n-b 1	16
*G. Miller b Willis	41		
C. J. Tunnicliffe run out	2	1/0 2/7 3/64 4/123 (51 overs)	226
†R. W. Taylor not out	10	5/199 6/206 7/206 8/213 9/216	

Bowling: Willis 11–1–37–5; Hogg 11–0–40–1; Ferreira 10–1–42–1; Gifford 10–0–37–0; Old 9–0–54–2.

Umpires: J. Birkenshaw and J. van Geloven.

YORKSHIRE v NOTTINGHAMSHIRE

At Leeds, May 14, 16. Nottinghamshire won by 25 runs. Toss won by Yorkshire.
Gold Award: C. E. B. Rice.

Nottinghamshire

R. T. Robinson c Athey b Sidebottom .	18	E. E. Hemmings run out	19
B. Hassan hit wkt b Illingworth	36	K. Saxelby run out	0
D. W. Randall lbw b Illingworth	8		
*C. E. B. Rice not out	86	B 1, l-b 8, w 5, n-b 3	17
J. D. Birch c Love b Carrick	4		
R. J. Hadlee c Hartley b Sidebottom	6	1/36 2/57 3/72 4/91 (8 wkts, 55 overs) 195	
†B. N. French lbw b Sidebottom	1	5/117 6/121 7/195 8/195	

M. Hendrick and M. K. Bore did not bat.

Bowling: Stevenson 7–2–40–0; Dennis 10–1–37–0; Sidebottom 11–3–23–3; Boycott 6–0–16–0; Illingworth 11–2–18–2; Carrick 10–1–44–1.

Yorkshire

G. Boycott c Birch b Bore	12	A. Sidebottom c French b Hendrick	32
K. Sharp c Hassan b Hadlee	1	*R. Illingworth not out	9
C. W. J. Athey c Randall b Hadlee	18	S. J. Dennis c Bore b Hendrick	0
G. B. Stevenson b Hadlee	5		
S. N. Hartley c French b Saxelby	48	L-b 6, w 1, n-b 1	8
J. D. Love c French b Saxelby	37		
†D. L. Bairstow c French b Saxelby	0	1/3 2/29 3/33 4/38 (51 overs) 170	
P. Carrick c Randall b Hemmings	0	5/110 6/110 7/111 8/133 9/170	

Bowling: Hadlee 9–3–20–3; Bore 11–2–36–1; Hendrick 10–1–34–2; Hemmings 11–1–26–1; Saxelby 10–0–46–3.

Umpires: K. Ibadulla and R. Julian.

NOTTINGHAMSHIRE v DERBYSHIRE

At Nottingham, May 17. Nottinghamshire won by 51 runs. Toss won by Nottinghamshire.
Gold Award: R. J. Hadlee.

Nottinghamshire

B. Hassan c Taylor b Oldham	7	E. E. Hemmings c Hill b Newman	2
R. T. Robinson c Taylor b Newman	0	K. Saxelby not out	10
D. W. Randall c Tunnicliffe b Miller	27	M. K. Bore not out	0
*C. E. B. Rice c Taylor b Tunnicliffe	68	L-b 9, w 7	16
J. D. Birch b Newman	50		
R. J. Hadlee c Miller b Newman	37	1/5 2/13 3/82 4/123 (8 wkts, 55 overs) 226	
†B. N. French c Tunnicliffe b Oldham	9	5/185 6/209 7/210 8/224	

M. Hendrick did not bat.

Bowling: Newman 11–0–55–4; Oldham 11–2–53–2; Tunnicliffe 11–1–54–1; Wood 11–2–29–0; Miller 11–1–19–1.

Derbyshire

B. Wood run out	26	P. G. Newman not out	11
J. G. Wright run out	5	S. Oldham b Hadlee	0
I. S. Anderson c French b Saxelby	32	†R. W. Taylor not out	4
*K. J. Barnett run out	5	B 1, l-b 4, w 4, n-b 2	11
C. J. Tunnicliffe c Birch b Hemmings..	5		
G. Miller b Hemmings	16	1/5 2/55 3/72 4/73 (9 wkts, 55 overs) 175
A. Hill b Hadlee	39	5/90 6/102 7/147 8/171 9/171
R. J. Finney b Hadlee	21	

Bowling: Hadlee 11–3–25–3; Bore 11–2–36–0; Hendrick 11–1–33–0; Saxelby 11–0–44–1; Hemmings 11–1–26–2.

Umpires: B. Leadbeater and D. O. Oslear.

YORKSHIRE v LANCASHIRE

At Leeds, May 17, 18. Lancashire won on faster scoring-rate, no play being possible on the second day. Toss won by Yorkshire.
Gold Award: S. J. O'Shaughnessy.

Lancashire

G. Fowler c Dennis b Illingworth	31	J. Simmons b Ramage	1
S. J. O'Shaughnessy b Sidebottom	27	†C. Maynard not out	17
F. C. Hayes b Illingworth	37	B 4, l-b 16, w 6	26
D. P. Hughes c Love b Illingworth	28		
*C. H. Lloyd c Sharp b Ramage	18	1/57 2/77 3/140 (6 wkts, 55 overs) 222
J. Abrahams not out	37	4/150 5/175 6/185

P. J. W. Allott, M. Watkinson and I. Folley did not bat.

Bowling: Ramage 11–2–40–2; Dennis 11–2–52–0; Sidebottom 11–4–29–1; Stevenson 11–0–42–0; Illingworth 11–2–33–3.

Yorkshire

G. Boycott lbw b O'Shaughnessy	13	†D. L. Bairstow c Folley b Allott	4
K. Sharp lbw b Allott	8	G. B. Stevenson not out	1
C. W. J. Athey b Folley	5	L-b 6, w 2, n-b 1	9
S. N. Hartley not out	33		
J. D. Love b O'Shaughnessy	14	1/18 2/27 (5 wkts, 35.4 overs) 87
		3/37 4/69 5/77

A. Ramage, A. Sidebottom, *R. Illingworth and S. J. Dennis did not bat.

Bowling: Allott 7–1–14–2; Folley 11–3–27–1; O'Shaughnessy 11–4–14–2; Watkinson 5–0–15–0; Simmons 1.4–0–8–0.

Umpires: A. Jepson and J. van Geloven.

DERBYSHIRE v LANCASHIRE

At Derby, May 19, 20. No result. Toss won by Derbyshire.

Lancashire

G. Fowler run out	37	*C. H. Lloyd not out		1
S. J. O'Shaughnessy c Miller		J. Abrahams not out		0
b Oldham	5	L-b 2		2
F. C. Hayes c Hampshire b Wood	21			
D. P. Hughes lbw b Wood	2	1/12 2/65 3/65 4/68 (4 wkts, 31 overs)		68

J. Simmons, †C. Maynard, P. J. W. Allott, M. Watkinson and I. Folley did not bat.

Bowling: Newman 5–3–8–0; Oldham 5–3–4–1; Wood 11–2–26–2; Miller 10–1–28–0.

Derbyshire

B. Wood, J. H. Hampshire, *K. J. Barnett, A. Hill, G. Miller, I. S. Anderson, R. J. Finney, C. J. Tunnicliffe, P. G. Newman, †R. W. Taylor and S. Oldham.

Umpires: A. Jepson and R. A. White.

NOTTINGHAMSHIRE v WARWICKSHIRE

At Nottingham, May 19, 20. No result.

LANCASHIRE v NOTTINGHAMSHIRE

At Manchester, May 21, 23. Lancashire won by seven wickets in a match reduced by rain to 45 overs a side. Toss won by Lancashire.
Gold Award: G. Fowler.

Nottinghamshire

B. Hassan c Hughes b Watkinson	15	E. E. Hemmings b Watkinson		0
R. T. Robinson c Maynard b Allott	0	K. Saxelby not out		6
D. W. Randall b O'Shaughnessy	28	K. E. Cooper not out		25
*J. D. Birch c and b Folley	9			
R. J. Hadlee c Abrahams		B 5, l-b 8		13
b Watkinson	43			
P. Johnson b O'Shaughnessy	5	1/3 2/30 3/45 4/66 (8 wkts, 45 overs)		154
†B. N. French b Watkinson	10	5/90 6/116 7/121 8/122		

M. Hendrick did not bat.

Bowling: Allott 9–1–28–1; Folley 9–4–16–1; Watkinson 9–2–39–4; Simmons 9–0–28–0; O'Shaughnessy 9–3–30–2.

Lancashire

G. Fowler not out	59	D. P. Hughes not out		42
S. J. O'Shaughnessy lbw b Hadlee	5	B 9, n-b 2		11
F. C. Hayes b Hendrick	5			
*C. H. Lloyd run out	35	1/9 2/21 3/86 (3 wkts, 40.3 overs)		157

J. Abrahams, J. Simmons, †C. Maynard, M. Watkinson, P. J. W. Allott and I. Folley did not bat.

Bowling: Hadlee 8.3–2–16–1; Cooper 9–1–24–0; Hendrick 8–3–23–1; Saxelby 7–0–40–0; Hemmings 8–0–43–0.

Umpires: R. Palmer and C. T. Spencer.

WARWICKSHIRE v YORKSHIRE

At Birmingham, May 21, 23. Warwickshire won by five wickets, in a match reduced by rain to 45 overs a side. Toss won by Yorkshire.
Gold Award: C. W. J. Athey.

Yorkshire

G. Boycott c K. D. Smith b Willis	2	G. B. Stevenson not out	7
K. Sharp c Humpage b Hogg	20		
C. W. J. Athey not out	94	L-b 16, w 1, n-b 2	19
*S. N. Hartley c Humpage b Old	24		
J. D. Love b Willis	44	1/6 2/39 (5 wkts, 45 overs) 224	
†D. L. Bairstow b Willis	14	3/97 4/186 5/216	

A. Sidebottom, S. J. Dennis, P. Carrick and A. Ramage did not bat.

Bowling: Willis 9–1–37–3; Hogg 9–2–27–1; Ferreira 9–1–49–0; Old 9–0–45–1; Gifford 9–1–47–0.

Warwickshire

T. A. Lloyd b Sidebottom	43	A. M. Ferreira not out	0
K. D. Smith c Bairstow b Sidebottom	30		
A. I. Kallicharran lbw b Sidebottom	48	B 4, l-b 6, w 10, n-b 3	23
D. L. Amiss c Bairstow b Stevenson	64		
†G. W. Humpage b Ramage	4	1/84 2/91 (5 wkts, 42.1 overs) 225	
Asif Din not out	13	3/166 4/175 5/224	

C. M. Old, N. Gifford, *R. G. D. Willis and W. Hogg did not bat.

Bowling: Ramage 7.1–0–29–1; Dennis 9–1–46–0; Stevenson 8–0–56–1; Carrick 9–1–23–0; Sidebottom 9–0–48–3.

Umpires: D. O. Oslear and J. W. Holder.

GROUP C

HAMPSHIRE v ESSEX

At Southampton, May 7. Essex won by 113 runs. Toss won by Hampshire.
Gold Award: K. W. R. Fletcher.

Essex

G. A. Gooch c Emery b Nicholas	68	S. Turner st Parks b Tremlett	3
B. R. Hardie st Parks b Tremlett	34	D. R. Pringle not out	13
*K. W. R. Fletcher c Jesty b Tremlett	59	L-b 4, w 21, n-b 5	30
K. S. McEwan b Smith b Nicholas	28		
N. Phillip not out	20	1/73 2/164 3/215 (6 wkts, 55 overs) 260	
K. R. Pont c Cowley b Nicholas	5	4/221 5/233 6/238	

†D. E. East, R. E. East and J. K. Lever did not bat.

Bowling: Emery 8–0–32–0; Malone 6–0–25–0; Tremlett 11–1–45–3; Jesty 9–1–31–0; Cowley 11–1–46–0; Nicholas 10–0–51–3.

Hampshire

D. R. Turner c D. E. East b Pringle	... 28	†R. J. Parks c D. E. East		
V. P. Terry c D. E. East b Turner	 11		b R. E. East.	4
M. C. J. Nicholas c Hardie b Pringle	... 8	K. St J. D. Emery not out		6
T. E. Jesty c Fletcher b Phillip	 20	S. J. Malone c McEwan b Lever		16
R. A. Smith c Pringle b R. E. East	 9	L-b 12, w 1, n-b 1		14
*N. E. J. Pocock lbw b Turner	 17			
N. G. Cowley b Turner	 10	1/37 2/52 3/65 4/83	(48.3 overs)	147
T. M. Tremlett b R. E. East	 4	5/95 6/106 7/119 8/119 9/126		

Bowling: Lever 7.3–3–12–1; Phillip 10–0–27–1; Turner 11–2–33–3; Pringle 6–0–17–2; Gooch 3–0–11–0; R. E. East 11–0–33–3.

Umpires: D. J. Constant and A. G. T. Whitehead.

SOMERSET v SUSSEX

At Taunton, May 7, 9. Somerset won by 59 runs. Toss won by Sussex.
Gold Award: I. V. A. Richards.

Somerset

J. W. Lloyds c Pigott b Barclay	 51	C. H. Dredge not out	....	1
P. M. Roebuck c Green b Waller	 29	J. Garner not out	....	2
I. V. A. Richards c Pigott b Greig	 83			
*B. C. Rose run out	 25	B 1, l-b 8, n-b 1	....	10
I. T. Botham c Gould b Greig	 14			
N. F. M. Popplewell c Gould b Pigott . 18		1/81 2/91 3/157	(7 wkts, 55 overs)	251
V. J. Marks run out	 18	4/190 5/215 6/235 7/249		

†T. Gard and P. H. L. Wilson did not bat.

Bowling: le Roux 11–0–65–0; Pigott 11–0–52–1; Greig 11–1–54–2; Barclay 11–1–25–1; Waller 11–1–45–1.

Sussex

G. D. Mendis b Wilson	 11	G. S. le Roux c Marks b Botham	....	36
A. M. Green st Gard b Marks	 30	C. P. Phillipson run out	....	10
*J. R. T. Barclay c Rose b Marks	 18	A. C. S. Pigott lbw b Botham	....	4
P. W. G. Parker c Popplewell		C. E. Waller not out	....	4
b Marks.	11	L-b 9, w 2, n-b 2	....	13
C. M. Wells c Gard b Garner	 32			
†I. J. Gould c Botham b Wilson	 19	1/33 2/54 3/76 4/76	(51.2 overs)	192
I. A. Greig run out	 4	5/117 6/133 7/141 8/168 9/186		

Bowling: Garner 9–0–49–1; Botham 9.2–3–26–2; Wilson 11–2–30–2; Marks 11–0–38–3; Dredge 10–1–30–0; Richards 1–0–6–0.

Umpires: R. Palmer and D. R. Shepherd.

ESSEX v SOMERSET

At Chelmsford, May 14. Essex won by 53 runs. Toss won by Essex.
Gold Award: G. A. Gooch.

Essex

G. A. Gooch c Rose b Wilson 99	†D. E. East b Garner 3
B. R. Hardie c Gard b Dredge.......... 23	S. Turner c Gard b Botham 11
*K. W. R. Fletcher c Wilson b Marks.. 3	R. E. East not out 10
K. S. McEwan c Rose b Marks 1	B 4, l-b 6, n-b 2 12
K. R. Pont c and b Marks 13	
N. Phillip c Gard b Wilson 8	1/42 2/67 3/69 (8 wkts, 55 overs) 225
D. R. Pringle not out 42	4/92 5/111 6/176 7/202 8/209

J. K. Lever did not bat.

Bowling: Garner 11–2–47–1; Botham 10–1–51–1; Dredge 11–4–22–1; Marks 11–3–34–3; Wilson 9–0–40–2; Popplewell 3–0–19–0.

Somerset

J. W. Lloyds c Turner b Lever 10	J. Garner run out 6
P. M. Roebuck run out.................... 19	†T. Gard run out............................ 7
I. V. A. Richards b R. E. East 63	P. H. L. Wilson not out 0
*B. C. Rose b Gooch b Turner........... 0	B 2, l-b 8, w 2, n-b 2 14
I. T. Botham b R. E. East 1	
N. F. M. Popplewell lbw b Pringle..... 21	1/14 2/60 3/61 (46.3 overs) 172
V. J. Marks c R. E. East b Pringle 29	4/64 5/117 6/131
C. H. Dredge c D. E. East b Phillip.... 2	7/138 8/152 9/170

Bowling: Lever 7–0–16–1; Pringle 9.3–0–27–2; Turner 11–0–39–1; Phillip 8–1–36–1; R. E. East 11–0–40–2.

Umpires: D. O. Oslear and R. A. White.

SUSSEX v MINOR COUNTIES

At Hove, May 14. Sussex won by five wickets. Toss won by Sussex.
Gold Award: D. Bailey.

Minor Counties

A. Kennedy b Greig........................... 43	S. G. Plumb not out........................ 16
J. G. Tolchard c Phillipson b Greig..... 8	B 5, l-b 11, w 4 20
J. A. Claughton b Cowan.................. 40	
D. Bailey not out............................. 51	1/15 2/72 (4 wkts, 55 overs) 183
W. H. Osman c Barclay b le Roux...... 5	3/140 4/156

S. M. Clements, N. T. O'Brien, *†F. E. Collyer, I. L. Pont and D. Surridge did not bat.

Bowling: le Roux 11–0–38–1; Pigott 11–1–21–0; Greig 11–0–34–2; Wells 5–0–21–0; Barclay 11–4–28–0; Cowan 6–1–21–1.

Sussex

G. D. Mendis c Pont b O'Brien.......... 46	I. A. Greig not out 0
A. M. Green c Plumb b O'Brien 26	
*J. R. T. Barclay b Plumb................. 42	L-b 2, w 4, n-b 5 11
C. M. Wells run out 49	
P. W. G. Parker b Plumb.................. 8	1/73 2/80 (5 wkts, 48.3 overs) 184
†I. J. Gould not out 2	3/164 4/181 5/182

G. S. le Roux, C. P. Phillipson, A. C. S. Pigott and R. S. Cowan did not bat.

Bowling: Pont 9–3–22–0; Surridge 11–0–48–0; O'Brien 8–0–28–2; Kennedy 9–1–31–0; Clements 5–0–23–0; Bailey 3–0–18–0; Plumb 3.3–0–3–2.

Umpires: W. E. Alley and J. H. Harris.

MINOR COUNTIES v ESSEX

At Slough, May 17. Essex won by nine wickets. Toss won by Minor Counties.
Gold Award: K. W. R. Fletcher.

Minor Counties

A. Kennedy lbw b Pringle	2	*†F. E. Collyer c Fletcher b Lever	28
S. G. Plumb run out	13	I. L. Pont not out	13
D. Bailey c D. E. East b Turner	27	D. Surridge not out	0
R. V. Lewis c R. E. East b Turner	1	L-b 8, w 2, n-b 8	18
N. A. Riddell b Phillip	10		
W. M. Osman lbw b Pringle	11	1/9 2/30 3/34 (9 wkts, 55 overs)	140
S. Greensword lbw b Turner	0	4/63 5/63 6/63	
N. T. O'Brien b Lever	17	7/82 8/112 9/139	

Bowling: Lever 10–3–27–2; Pringle 11–3–26–2; Phillip 10–4–25–1; Turner 11–2–24–3; R. E. East 7–3–6–0; Gooch 6–2–14–0.

Essex

G. A. Gooch b O'Brien	38
B. R. Hardie not out	30
*K. W. R. Fletcher not out	62
B 1, l-b 9, w 1	11

1/55   (1 wkt, 41.1 overs) 141

K. S. McEwan, K. R. Pont, N. Phillip, D. R. Pringle, S. Turner, †D. E. East, R. E. East and J. K. Lever did not bat.

Bowling: Pont 8–1–37–0; Surridge 6–0–24–0; O'Brien 9–4–18–1; Plumb 11–3–22–0; Greensword 7–0–28–0; Kennedy 0.1–0–1–0.

Umpires: R. Julian and K. E. Palmer.

SOMERSET v HAMPSHIRE

At Taunton, May 17, 18. Hampshire won by 22 runs. Toss won by Somerset.
Gold Award: C. G. Greenidge.

Hampshire

C. G. Greenidge c Gard b Botham	45	T.M. Tremlett lbw b Dredge	6
C. L. Smith c Marks b Wilson	14	†R. J. Parks b Dredge	5
D. R. Turner c Botham b Marks	0	S. J. Malone not out	0
T. E. Jesty c Dredge b Marks	20	L-b 4, w 6, n-b 2	12
M. C. J. Nicholas c Gard b Botham	27		
*N. E. J. Pocock c Gard b Botham	0	1/46 2/47 3/72 (52.5 overs)	138
N. G. Cowley c Richards b Marks	0	4/112 5/112 6/112	
M. D. Marshall c Botham b Dredge	9	7/117 8/130 9/138	

Bowling: Garner 11–1–20–0; Botham 11–4–27–4; Dredge 8.5–2–26–3; Marks 11–2–21–2; Wilson 10–1–28–1; Richards 1–0–4–0.

Somerset

J. W. Lloyds c Turner b Marshall	8	†T. Gard c sub b Malone	10
P. M. Roebuck c Pocock b Jesty	21	J. Garner c Marshall b Malone	11
I. V. A. Richards c Pocock b Malone	16	P. H. L. Wilson not out	0
*B. C. Rose b Cowley	20	L-b 9, w 7, n-b 1	17
N. F. M. Popplewell c Parks b Jesty	5		—
I. T. Botham b Cowley	3	1/12 2/39 3/67	(44.1 overs) 116
V. J. Marks c Pocock b Marshall	5	4/77 5/82 6/88	
C. H. Dredge b Marshall	0	7/93 8/94 9/112	

Bowling: Marshall 11–2–22–3; Malone 8.1–2–24–3; Tremlett 5–1–18–0; Cowley 11–4–12–2; Jesty 9–2–23–2.

Umpires: C. T. Spencer and P. B. Wight.

ESSEX v SUSSEX

At Chelmsford, May 19, 20. Sussex won by 35 runs. Toss won by Sussex.
  Gold Award: I. J. Gould.

Sussex

G. D. Mendis c Gooch b Lever	9	G. S. le Roux lbw b Lever	6
A. M. Green run out	25	C. P. Phillipson not out	30
*J. R. T. Barclay c Fletcher b Turner	32	L-b 8, w 2, n-b 5	15
C. M. Wells lbw b Gooch	0		—
P. W. G. Parker b R. E. East	25	1/22 2/45	(8 wkts, 55 overs) 208
†I. J. Gould run out	55	3/45 4/93 5/114	
I. A. Greig c Fletcher b Turner	11	6/128 7/140 8/208	

A. C. S. Pigott and C. E. Waller did not bat.

Bowling: Lever 11–5–36–2; Pringle 11–1–57–0; Phillip 6–1–26–0; Gooch 9–0–23–1; R. E. East 10–1–25–1; Turner 8–1–26–2.

Essex

G. A. Gooch run out	6	†D. E. East run out	12
B. R. Hardie lbw b Greig	22	R. E. East not out	7
K. S. McEwan c Gould b Greig	25	J. K. Lever run out	0
*K. W. R. Fletcher lbw b Barclay	12	B 1, l-b 13, w 3, n-b 2	19
K. R. Pont run out	18		—
N. Phillip c Parker b Barclay	0	1/15 2/55 3/60	(50.3 overs) 173
D. R. Pringle c Wells b Pigott	49	4/76 5/76 6/107	
S. Turner c Waller b le Roux	3	7/111 8/156 9/173	

Bowling: le Roux 8.3–1–27–1; Pigott 9–1–33–1; Waller 11–1–31–0; Greig 11–1–30–2; Barclay 11–2–33–2.

Umpires: C. Cook and K. Ibadulla.

HAMPSHIRE v MINOR COUNTIES

At Bournemouth, May 19, 20. Hampshire won by six wickets. Toss won by Hampshire.
  Gold Award: T. E. Jesty.

Minor Counties

A. Kennedy c Pocock b Malone	7	I. L. Pont b Malone	5
S. G. Plumb b Marshall	6	S. P. Davis not out	7
R. V. Lewis c Marshall b Malone	0	D. Surridge not out	2
D. Bailey b Tremlett	5	B 1, l-b 16, w 16, n-b 1	34
S. Greensword st Parks b Tremlett	23		
W. M. Osman c Parks b Malone	36	1/11 2/11 3/13 (9 wkts, 55 overs) 168
N. A. Riddell run out	24	4/38 5/66 6/115
*†F. E. Collyer c Pocock b Marshall	19	7/139 8/148 9/162

Bowling: Marshall 11–1–38–2; Malone 11–2–25–4; Jesty 8–1–24–0; Tremlett 11–4–17–2; Cowley 11–2–22–0; Nicholas 3–0–8–0.

Hampshire

C. G. Greenidge b Davis	13	*N. E. J. Pocock not out	43
C. L. Smith c Collyer b Pont	0	L-b 3, w 1, n-b 4	8
D. R. Turner b Surridge	13		
T. E. Jesty not out	76	1/6 2/18 (4 wkts, 47.5 overs) 169
M. C. J. Nicholas b Plumb	16	3/42 4/76

M. D. Marshall, N. G. Cowley, †R. J. Parks, T. M. Tremlett and S. J. Malone did not bat.

Bowling: Davis 10–0–37–1; Pont 9.5–2–42–1; Surridge 10–3–30–1; Plumb 11–3–27–1; Greensword 6–1–18–0; Kennedy 1–0–7–0.

Umpires: D. G. L. Evans and J. H. Harris.

MINOR COUNTIES v SOMERSET

At Slough, May 21, 23. No result.

SUSSEX v HAMPSHIRE

At Hove, May 23. Hampshire won by three wickets. Toss won by Hampshire.
Gold Award: C. L. Smith.

Sussex

G. D. Mendis b Cowley	27	A. P. Wells run out	16
*J. R. T. Barclay c Pocock b Malone	5	A. C. S. Pigott lbw b Nicholas	4
C. M. Wells b Malone	43	C. E. Waller not out	3
P. W. G. Parker b Malone	20	B 1, l-b 13, w 3, n-b 1	18
†I. J. Gould c and b Nicholas	4		
I. A. Greig c Cowley b Tremlett	24	1/8 2/59 3/101 (53 overs) 171
G. S. le Roux run out	3	4/114 5/114 6/141
C. P. Phillipson c and b Tremlett	4	7/146 8/153 9/163

Bowling: Marshall 10–3–21–0; Malone 11–3–34–3; Tremlett 11–0–31–2; Cowley 11–2–34–1; Nicholas 10–0–33–2.

Hampshire

C. G. Greenidge lbw b le Roux	0	M. D. Marshall b le Roux	2
C. L. Smith not out	63	T. M. Tremlett not out	4
D. R. Turner c and b Barclay	17	L-b 9, w 6, n-b 1	16
T. E. Jesty c Parker b le Roux	37		
M. C. J. Nicholas c Mendis b Pigott	27	1/0 2/28 (7 wkts, 53.5 overs) 174
*N. E. J. Pocock b le Roux	6	3/91 4/143
N. G. Cowley lbw b Pigott	2	5/153 6/156 7/159

†R. J. Parks and S. J. Malone did not bat.

Bowling: le Roux 11–3–22–4; Pigott 11–1–29–2; Greig 11–1–41–0; Barclay 11–3–24–1; Waller 8.5–0–35–0; C. M. Wells 1–0–7–0.

Umpires: C. Cook and P. B. Wight.

GROUP D

OXFORD & CAMBRIDGE UNIVS v KENT

At Cambridge, May 7, 9. Kent won by 64 runs. Toss won by Kent.
Gold Award: N. R. Taylor.

Kent

N. R. Taylor c Ellis b Varey	100	G. R. Dilley b Hodgson	7
R. A. Woolmer lbw b Pollock	7	D. L. Underwood not out	2
*C. J. Tavaré b Varey	46	K. B. S. Jarvis not out	0
M. R. Benson c Cullinan b Henderson	17	B 4, l-b 9, w 12	25
C. S. Cowdrey run out	8		
†A. P. E. Knott c Henderson b Pollock	55	1/35 2/114 3/154	(9 wkts, 55 overs) 276
G. W. Johnson c sub b Hodgson	9	4/188 5/206 6/252	
R. M. Ellison c Cullinan b Hodgson	0	7/252 8/268 9/276	

Bowling: Pollock 11–2–50–2; Roebuck 7–1–25–0; Hodgson 11–3–52–3; Varey 11–2–58–2; Doggart 11–1–45–0; Henderson 4–1–21–1.

Oxford & Cambridge Univs

T. S. Curtis b Dilley	8	J. G. Varey not out	35
R. G. P. Ellis c Knott b Jarvis	16	†M. R. Cullinan b Dilley	0
R. J. Boyd-Moss c Woolmer b Dilley	0	A. J. Pollock b Dilley	2
*S. P. Henderson c Cowdrey b Johnson	82	B 5, l-b 18, w 5	28
G. Pathmanathan c Dilley b Ellison	4		
P. G. P. Roebuck run out	23	1/26 2/26 3/40	(54.4 overs) 212
K. I. Hodgson c Woolmer b Underwood	0	4/47 5/94 6/100	
S. J. G. Doggart b Underwood	14	7/143 8/198 9/198	

Bowling: Dilley 10.4–0–32–4; Jarvis 11–3–31–1; Ellison 9–1–41–1; Woolmer 11–0–47–0; Underwood 11–4–19–2; Johnson 2–0–14–1.

Umpires: C. T. Spencer and C. Cook.

SURREY v MIDDLESEX

At The Oval, May 7, 9. Middlesex won on faster scoring-rate, rain having ended play after Surrey had faced twenty overs. Toss won by Surrey.
Gold Award: R. O. Butcher.

Middlesex

G. D. Barlow c Knight b Payne	37	N. F. Williams not out	12
W. N. Slack c Smith b Knight	36	†P. R. Downton not out	11
C. T. Radley lbw b Knight	1	B 2, l-b 14, w 5, n-b 5	26
*M. W. Gatting c Payne b Thomas	53		
R. O. Butcher c Butcher b Thomas	85	1/74 2/81 3/85	(6 wkts, 55 overs) 273
J. E. Emburey c Smith b Thomas	12	4/206 5/246 6/257	

K. D. James, W. W. Daniel and N. G. Cowans did not bat.

Bowling: Clarke 11–0–52–0; Thomas 11–0–66–3; Monkhouse 4–0–24–0; Knight 11–2–32–2; Payne 11–0–44–1; Pocock 7–2–29–0.

Surrey

A. R. Butcher lbw b Cowans	6
G. S. Clinton st Downton b Emburey	18
D. M. Smith not out	26
*R. D. V. Knight not out	7
W 3, n-b 3	6

1/9 2/51   (2 wkts, 20 overs) 63

M. A. Lynch, †C. J. Richards, D. J. Thomas, I. R. Payne, G. Monkhouse, S. T. Clarke and P. I. Pocock did not bat.

Bowling: Daniel 3–0–10–0; Cowans 5–0–20–1; James 7–0–22–0; Emburey 5–1–5–1.

Umpires: M. J. Kitchen and J. van Geloven.

KENT v MIDDLESEX

At Canterbury, May 14. Middlesex won by five wickets. Toss won by Middlesex.
Gold Award: C. T. Radley.

Kent

N. R. Taylor c Downton b Williams	26	R. M. Ellison run out	12
R. A. Woolmer c Downton b Daniel	4	G. R. Dilley not out	16
*C. J. Tavaré c Radley b Daniel	2	L-b 3, w 6, n-b 3	12
M. R. Benson c Radley b James	3		
C. S. Cowdrey c Slack b James	0	1/14 2/24 (7 wkts, 55 overs) 190	
†A. P. E. Knott c Butcher b Cowans	43	3/36 4/41	
G. W. Johnson not out	72	5/43 6/114 7/151	

D. L. Underwood and K. B. S. Jarvis did not bat.

Bowling: Daniel 11–2–27–2; Cowans 7–0–34–1; Williams 7–2–17–1; James 11–3–31–2; Gatting 11–2–26–0; Emburey 8–0–43–0.

Middlesex

G. D. Barlow c Knott b Woolmer	15	J. E. Emburey not out	1
W. N. Slack c Knott b Jarvis	11		
C. T. Radley not out	88	B 1, l-b 10, n-b 5	16
*M. W. Gatting c and b Woolmer	7		
R. O. Butcher st Knott b Underwood	50	1/22 2/45 (5 wkts, 51.4 overs) 191	
K. D. James st Knott b Underwood	3	3/61 4/175 5/185	

†P. R. Downton, N. F. Williams, N. G. Cowans and W. W. Daniel did not bat.

Bowling: Dilley 10.4–1–31–0; Jarvis 10–1–34–1; Ellison 9–2–30–0; Woolmer 11–1–33–2; Underwood 10–2–38–2; Cowdrey 1–0–9–0.

Umpires: P. J. Eele and K. E. Palmer.

OXFORD & CAMBRIDGE UNIVS v GLAMORGAN

At Cambridge, May 14. Glamorgan won by 166 runs, Oxford & Cambridge Univs having recorded the second-lowest total in the competition. Toss won by Glamorgan.
Gold Award: Javed Miandad.

Glamorgan

A. Jones b Pollock	5	B. J. Lloyd c Pathmanathan b Hodgson	0
J. A. Hopkins c Ellis b Doggart	31	M. A. Nash c Henderson b Pollock	5
A. L. Jones c Hodgson b Roebuck	22	A. H. Wilkins not out	3
Javed Miandad b Hodgson	95	L-b 10, w 7, n-b 3	20
C. J. C. Rowe run out	6		
R. C. Ontong c Cullinan b Varey	0	1/23 2/60 3/75	(55 overs) 225
*M. W. W. Selvey c Henderson b Varey	0	4/89 5/91 6/91	
†E. W. Jones b Hodgson	38	7/208 8/208 9/217	

Bowling: Pollock 11–2–51–2; Varey 11–0–49–2; Hodgson 11–3–30–3; Roebuck 11–0–32–1; Doggart 11–1–43–1.

Oxford & Cambridge Univs

R. G. P. Ellis lbw b Selvey	8	S. J. G. Doggart c E. W. Jones b Ontong	32
T. S. Curtis lbw b Selvey	1	†M. R. Cullinan run out	8
R. J. Boyd-Moss c and b Selvey	0	A. J. Pollock not out	0
*S. P. Henderson lbw b Nash	0	L-b 2	2
G. Pathmanathan b Selvey	0		
P. G. P. Roebuck lbw b Nash	1	1/2 2/9 3/10	(34 overs) 59
J. G. Varey run out	4	4/10 5/12 6/12	
K. I. Hodgson b Nash	3	7/19 8/21 9/54	

Bowling: Selvey 11–6–10–4; Nash 11–7–9–3; Ontong 6–1–22–1; Wilkins 2–0–4–0; Lloyd 4–1–12–0.

Umpires: D. G. L. Evans and P. B. Wight.

KENT v SURREY

At Canterbury, May 17, 18. Kent won by 28 runs. Toss won by Surrey.
Gold Award: G. R. Dilley.

Kent

N. R. Taylor c Thomas b Knight	4	R. M. Ellison c Richards b Clarke	4
R. A. Woolmer c Richards b Knight	8	G. R. Dilley c Smith b Clarke	0
*C. J. Tavaré lbw b Knight	9	D. L. Underwood b Pocock	27
M. R. Benson b Monkhouse	10	K. B. S. Jarvis not out	1
C. S. Cowdrey c Richards b Pocock	49	L-b 7, w 3, n-b 2	12
†A. P. E. Knott c Howarth			
b Monkhouse	1	1/14 2/19 3/32 4/40	(54.4 overs) 150
G. W. Johnson c Smith b Pocock	25	5/46 6/106 7/118 8/118 9/122	

Bowling: Clarke 11–3–20–2; Thomas 10–3–34–0; Knight 11–1–26–3; Monkhouse 11–2–20–2; Pocock 9.4–4–21–3; Butcher 2–0–17–0.

Surrey

A. R. Butcher c Knott b Dilley	9	D. J. Thomas lbw b Dilley	1
G. S. Clinton c Knott b Jarvis	6	S. T. Clarke c Knott b Jarvis	2
D. M. Smith run out	14	G. Monkhouse run out	2
G. P. Howarth c Knott b Dilley	14	P. I. Pocock not out	0
*R. D. V. Knight c Tavaré		L-b 10, w 2, n-b 1	13
b Underwood	7		
M. A. Lynch c Johnson b Underwood	39	1/10 2/18 3/34 4/47	(47.3 overs) 122
†C. J. Richards c Woolmer b Dilley	15	5/60 6/114 7/118 8/118 9/122	

Bowling: Dilley 11–2–29–4; Jarvis 10.3–1–19–2; Ellison 11–0–30–0; Underwood 11–2–22–2; Woolmer 4–1–9–0.

Umpires: J. Birkenshaw and R. A. White.

MIDDLESEX v GLAMORGAN

At Uxbridge, May 17, 18. No result.

GLAMORGAN v SURREY

At Cardiff, May 19, 20. No result. Toss won by Surrey.

Surrey

A. R. Butcher lbw b Nash	20	†C. J. Richards not out	7
G. S. Clinton lbw b Selvey	0		
D. M. Smith lbw b Nash	14	L-b 12, w 3, n-b 1	16
G. P. Howarth not out	45		
*R. D. V. Knight c E. W. Jones b Rowe	10	1/1 2/25 (5 wkts, 44.4 overs) 142	
M. A. Lynch run out	30	3/49 4/68 5/133	

D. J. Thomas, G. Monkhouse, S. T. Clarke and P. I. Pocock did not bat.

Bowling: Selvey 8–2–18–1; Nash 11–2–21–2; Lloyd 9–0–31–0; Rowe 6–1–20–1; Ontong 5.4–0–26–0; Wilkins 5–0–10–0.

Glamorgan

A. Jones, J. A. Hopkins, A. L. Jones, Javed Miandad, C. J. C. Rowe, R. C. Ontong, †E. W. Jones, *M. W. W. Selvey, B. J. Lloyd, M. A. Nash and A. H. Wilkins.

Umpires: P. J. Eele and D. R. Shepherd.

MIDDLESEX v OXFORD & CAMBRIDGE UNIVS

At Lord's, May 19, 20. No result.

GLAMORGAN v KENT

At Swansea, May 21, 23. Kent won by eight wickets in a match reduced to 39 overs a side. Toss won by Glamorgan.
Gold Award: C. J. Tavaré.

Glamorgan

A. Jones run out	22	*M. W. W. Selvey b Woolmer	8
J. A. Hopkins b Woolmer	26	B. J. Lloyd c Ellison b Jarvis	18
Javed Miandad c Knott b Ellison	23	M. A. Nash not out	10
A. L. Jones run out	1	L-b 9, n-b 1	10
C. J. C. Rowe not out	25		
R. C. Ontong c Tavaré b Woolmer	5	1/40 2/73 3/76 (8 wkts, 39 overs) 148	
†E. W. Jones run out	0	4/76 5/87 6/89 7/100 8/134	

A. H. Wilkins did not bat.

Bowling: Dilley 8–2–33–0; Jarvis 8–1–29–1; Ellison 8–1–22–1; Woolmer 7–1–26–3; Underwood 8–2–28–0.

Kent

R. A. Woolmer c E. W. Jones b Selvey ..	6
N. R. Taylor lbw b Nash	17
*C. J. Tavaré not out	80
M. R. Benson not out	33
B 4, l-b 6, w 2, n-b 1	13

1/13 2/34   (2 wkts, 32.5 overs) 149

C. S. Cowdrey, †A. P. E. Knott, G. W. Johnson, R. M. Ellison, G. R. Dilley, D. L. Underwood and K. B. S. Jarvis did not bat.

Bowling: Selvey 8–1–29–1; Nash 8–1–33–1; Ontong 8–1–21–0; Lloyd 4–0–27–0; Wilkins 4.5–1–26–0.

Umpires: J. H. Harris and D. R. Shepherd.

SURREY v OXFORD & CAMBRIDGE UNIVS

At The Oval, May 21, 23. Surrey won by seven wickets. Toss won by Surrey.
Gold Award: S. T. Clarke.

Oxford & Cambridge Univs

R. G. P. Ellis c Richards b Clarke	5	J. D. Carr not out		42
T. S. Curtis b Clarke	2	A. J. Pollock run out		10
R. J. Boyd-Moss c Smith b Clarke	34	†A. G. Davies not out		1
*S. P. Henderson b Clarke	0	B 6, l-b 6, w 9, n-b 2		23
K. A. Hayes b Clarke	0			
P. G. P. Roebuck b Pocock	16	1/3 2/10 3/29 4/31 (8 wkts, 55 overs) 155		
S. J. G. Doggart b Monkhouse	22	5/59 6/84 7/111 8/150		

M. D. Petchey did not bat.

Bowling: Clarke 11–1–25–5; Thomas 11–2–25–0; Monkhouse 11–1–44–1; Pocock 11–5–15–1; Knight 11–3–23–0.

Surrey

A. R. Butcher c Curtis b Pollock	22	*R. D. V. Knight not out	9
G. S. Clinton c Petchey b Henderson ..	63	B 1, l-b 4, w 4	9
D. M. Smith lbw b Henderson	40		
G. P. Howarth not out	13	1/34 2/127 3/134 (3 wkts, 49.2 overs) 156

M. A. Lynch, †C. J. Richards, D. J. Thomas, G. Monkhouse, S. T. Clarke and P. I. Pocock did not bat.

Bowling: Pollock 11–2–25–1; Petchey 8–1–28–0; Doggart 11–3–20–0; Carr 11–4–34–0; Roebuck 5–0–20–0; Henderson 3–0–16–2; Curtis 0.2–0–4–0.

Umpires: N. T. Plews and A. G. T. Whitehead.

QUARTER-FINALS

ESSEX v WARWICKSHIRE

At Chelmsford, June 1, 2, 3. Essex won by 63 runs. When play started on Thursday, Fletcher, having won the toss, was in commanding form and shared in a stand of 150 in 37 overs with Gooch. Of the later batsmen, only Pringle showed any real authority, going on to destroy the early part of Warwickshire's innings before Phillip ended their challenge with four wickets in seven balls.
Gold Award: D. R. Pringle.

Essex

G. A. Gooch c Old b Gifford	67	S. Turner b Willis	9
A. W. Lilley c Humpage b Willis	0	†D. E. East c Lloyd b Ferreira	15
*K. W. R. Fletcher b Gifford	87	R. E. East not out	2
K. S. McEwan b Ferreira	3	B 1, l-b 11	12
K. R. Pont st Humpage b Gifford	4		
D. R. Pringle not out	31	1/3 2/153 3/164 (8 wkts, 55 overs) 231	
N. Phillip b Willis	1	4/165 5/174 6/175 7/199 8/224	

N. A. Foster did not bat.

Bowling: Willis 11–1–51–3; Small 11–3–30–0; Old 11–2–27–0; Ferreira 11–0–50–2; Gifford 11–0–61–3.

Warwickshire

T. A. Lloyd c D. E. East b Turner	25	G. C. Small c Lilley b Phillip	6
K. D. Smith c Gooch b Pringle	13	N. Gifford not out	1
A. I. Kallicharran lbw b Pringle	0	*R. G. D. Willis c D. E. East b Phillip	0
D. L. Amiss c Foster b Phillip	49	B 7, n-b 2	9
†G. W. Humpage c D. E. East b Pringle	8		
Asif Din c Foster b Foster	16	1/33 2/39 3/41 (50.3 overs) 168	
A. M. Ferreira b R. E. East	14	4/50 5/78 6/117	
C. M. Old c Foster b Phillip	27	7/158 8/158 9/168	

Bowling: Phillip 9.3–1–33–4; Foster 10–0–39–1; Turner 11–0–31–1; Pringle 9–2–14–3; R. E. East 7–0–27–1; Gooch 4–0–15–0.

Umpires: W. E. Alley and A. Jepson.

GLOUCESTERSHIRE v MIDDLESEX

At Bristol, June 1, 2, 3. Middlesex won on the toss of a coin, only four overs having been completed. Toss won by Middlesex.

Gloucestershire

B. C. Broad not out	1
A. W. Stovold not out	11
(no wkt, 4 overs)	12

P. Bainbridge, Zaheer Abbas, B. Dudleston, D. V. Lawrence, *D. A. Graveney, J. N. Shepherd, †R. C. Russell, J. H. Childs and G. E. Sainsbury did not bat.

Bowling: Cowans 2–1–3–0; Williams 2–0–9–0.

Middlesex

G. D. Barlow, W. N. Slack, C. T. Radley, *M. W. Gatting, R. O. Butcher, W. W. Daniel, J. E. Emburey, P. H. Edmonds, †P. R. Downton, N. F. Williams and N. G. Cowans.

Umpires: K. E. Palmer and R. Julian.

KENT v HAMPSHIRE

At Canterbury, June 1, 2. Kent won by 5 runs. A spell of three for 4 in six balls by Marshall had Kent reeling at 119 for seven in the 39th over, but Ellison and Dilley rescued the innings with 65 off fifteen overs. Greenidge and Terry shared an opening stand of 131 off 43 overs, but then, trying to increase the tempo, Hampshire lost nine wickets for 60 runs in twelve overs. With 9 needed off the last over to level the scores, Ellison bowled Marshall, Cowley and Parks with his first, third and fifth balls to deny them victory.

Gold Award: R. M. Ellison.

Kent

R. A. Woolmer c Terry b Marshall	7	G. R. Dilley not out	37
N. R. Taylor c Marshall b Cowley	47	D. L. Underwood run out	2
*C. J. Tavaré c Greenidge b Tremlett	18	K. B. S. Jarvis not out	0
M. R. Benson c Greenidge b Cowley	11	L-b 9, w 23	32
C. S. Cowdrey c Nicholas b Marshall	15		
†A. P. E. Knott c Parks b Marshall	1	1/16 2/67 3/98　　(9 wkts, 55 overs) 198
G. W. Johnson c Parks b Marshall	0	4/107 5/110 6/110
R. M. Ellison c Parks b Malone	28	7/119 8/184 9/196

Bowling: Marshall 11–4–26–4; Malone 8–1–28–1; Jesty 4–1–14–0; Tremlett 11–3–22–1; Nicholas 10–2–42–0; Cowley 11–3–34–2.

Hampshire

C. G. Greenidge c Cowdrey b Jarvis	60	N. G. Cowley b Ellison	0
V. P. Terry c Woolmer b Jarvis	72	T. M. Tremlett not out	1
T. E. Jesty c Ellison b Underwood	17	†R. J. Parks b Ellison	0
D. R. Turner c and b Cowdrey	4	S. J. Malone not out	2
M. C. J. Nicholas c Tavaré b Underwood	2	B 2, l-b 13, w 5, n-b 1	21
*N. E. J. Pocock c Tavaré b Jarvis	6	1/131 2/159 3/167　(9 wkts, 55 overs) 193
M. D. Marshall b Ellison	8	4/170 5/176 6/182 7/189 8/191 9/191

Bowling: Dilley 3–0–12–0; Jarvis 11–1–42–3; Ellison 11–3–22–3; Woolmer 11–0–27–0; Cowdrey 8–0–39–1; Underwood 11–2–30–2.

Umpires: H. D. Bird and J. Birkenshaw.

LANCASHIRE v NORTHAMPTONSHIRE

At Manchester, June 1, 2, 3. Lancashire won by 107 runs. The home side, put in, reached 186 for two at the close on Wednesday, after the start had been delayed by rain until 5.00. Thursday was completely washed out, but on Friday they took their total to a Lancashire record of 290, their last 104 runs coming in twelve overs as Lloyd and Hughes put on 87 in 38 overs for the fourth wicket, building on the foundation laid by Fowler – brilliantly caught by Tim Lamb just 3 short of his century – and Hayes. Northamptonshire, aware that a return of the threatening rain would require them to score 106 off twenty overs, were tied down by Folley, who removed Larkins and Williams before Cook and Allan Lamb were run out. Kapil Dev played freely, but when he went, all hope died and, despite a defiant innings from Steele, Lancashire cruised to victory in the gloom.

Gold Award: G. Fowler.

Lancashire

G. Fowler c and b T. M. Lamb	97	J. Simmons not out	4
S. J. O'Shaughnessy b Williams	8		
F. C. Hayes c A. J. Lamb b T. M. Lamb	75	B 3, l-b 4, w 4, n-b 3	14
*C. H. Lloyd c Steele b Kapil Dev	55		
D. P. Hughes not out	37	1/40 2/186　　(5 wkts, 55 overs) 290
J. Abrahams run out	0	3/194 4/281 5/281

†C. Maynard, M. Watkinson, P. J. W. Allott and I. Folley did not bat.

Bowling: Kapil Dev 9–0–47–1; Griffiths 11–0–55–0; Williams 11–1–41–1; T. M. Lamb 11–0–54–2; Steele 5–0–21–0; Mallender 8–0–58–0.

Northamptonshire

*G. Cook run out	25	T. M. Lamb b O'Shaughnessy		4
W. Larkins c O'Shaughnessy b Folley	18	N. A. Mallender b Allott		5
R. G. Williams c Maynard b Folley	0	B. J. Griffiths b Allott		3
A. J. Lamb run out	13	L-b 6		6
Kapil Dev c Fowler b Watkinson	49			
D. J. Capel b O'Shaughnessy	28	1/35 2/42 3/46	(47.1 overs)	183
†G. Sharp run out	16	4/47 5/119 6/141		
D. S. Steele not out	16	7/166 8/172 9/179		

Bowling: Allott 7.1–2–25–2; Folley 11–1–34–2; Watkinson 7–0–32–1; Simmons 11–1–40–0; O'Shaughnessy 11–0–46–2.

Umpires: D. O. Oslear and B. J. Meyer.

SEMI-FINALS

KENT v ESSEX

At Canterbury, July 6. Essex won by nine wickets. Put in to bat in overcast conditions, Kent struggled against accurate pace and seam bowling. Woolmer and Tavaré seemed on the way towards mastering the attack, but after the run-out of Woolmer, Kent had lost half their side for 84 in the 31st over as four wickets crashed for 22 runs in eight overs. The Essex bowlers were supported by brilliant catching and fielding with wicket-keeper David East in superb form. Essex made no mistake in reaching their modest target slowly but surely, Hardie returning to the side after sustaining a bad facial injury to lead the way.

Gold Award: S. Turner.

Kent

R. A. Woolmer run out	33	R. M. Ellison c Pringle b Lever		2
M. R. Benson b Lever	10	G. R. Dilley b Foster		5
*C. J. Tavaré lbw b Gooch	32	D. L. Underwood lbw b Pringle		0
D. G. Aslett c Gooch b Turner	6	L-b 5, w 8, n-b 4		17
C. S. Cowdrey c D. E. East b Gooch	5			
E. A. E. Baptiste c D. E. East b Turner	1	1/19 2/62 3/68	(51 overs)	128
†A. P. E. Knott c D. E. East b Lever	2	4/83 5/84 6/96		
G. W. Johnson not out	15	7/103 8/110 9/127		

Bowling: Lever 11–2–29–3; Foster 6–2–9–1; Pringle 7–1–22–1; Turner 11–5–15–2; R. E. East 5–0–11–0; Gooch 11–1–25–2.

Essex

G. A. Gooch c Knott b Ellison	18
B. R. Hardie not out	58
*K. W. R. Fletcher not out	33
B 1, l-b 4, w 5, n-b 11	21

1/44   (1 wkt, 46 overs) 130

K. S. McEwan, K. R. Pont, J. K. Lever, D. R. Pringle, S. Turner, †D. E. East, R. E. East and N. A. Foster did not bat.

Bowling: Dilley 11–1–35–0; Baptiste 11–2–28–0; Woolmer 4–2–5–0; Ellison 11–4–23–1; Underwood 6–1–12–0; Cowdrey 3–0–6–0.

Umpires: R. Palmer and A. G. T. Whitehead.

MIDDLESEX v LANCASHIRE

At Lord's, July 6. Middlesex won by six wickets. Cowans and Daniel took full advantage of a hard, fast pitch to wreck Lancashire's hopes with four wickets within eight overs. But their collapse for 90 – the lowest semi-final score in the competition's history – had more to do with inadequate batting than any terrors in the pitch, although on a hazy morning it was an important toss to win. Lancashire's ill-luck was compounded by the absence of Clive Lloyd, owing to a groin strain suffered during the World Cup final eleven days before. Fast as Cowans and Daniel bowled, however, all four early wickets stemmed from batting errors, the most far-reaching coming in the second over when Fowler, driving, edged Cowans to the wicket-keeper. Bad light and rain delayed Middlesex at 65 for three, but at 7.15 conditions improved enough for Radley to knock the runs off in the twilight.

Gold Award: N. G. Cowans.

Lancashire

G. Fowler c Downton b Cowans	1		M. Watkinson c Radley b Williams	3
S. J. O'Shaughnessy b Daniel	0		P. J. W. Allott b Daniel	0
F. C. Hayes b Cowans	3		I. Folley not out	1
D. P. Hughes c Downton b Gatting	27		L-b 1, w 2, n-b 8	11
*J. Abrahams c Butcher b Cowans	4			
†C. Maynard c Downton b Gatting	1		1/1 2/1 3/12 (31.5 overs)	90
J. Simmons c and b Cowans	25		4/23 5/39 6/54	
N. V. Radford b Daniel	14		7/84 8/85 9/85	

Bowling: Daniel 9–1–28–3; Cowans 11–4–33–4; Gatting 7–3–8–2; Williams 4.5–1–10–1.

Middlesex

K. P. Tomlins lbw b Allott	16		J. E. Emburey not out	0
W. N. Slack c Maynard b Allott	8		L-b 2, w 3	5
C. T. Radley not out	32			
*M. W. Gatting b Radford	18		1/24 2/33 (4 wkts, 30.2 overs)	91
R. O. Butcher c Maynard b Radford	12		3/65 4/77	

†P. R. Downton, P. H. Edmonds, N. F. Williams, N. G. Cowans and W. W. Daniel did not bat.

Bowling: Allott 11–3–23–2; Folley 3–0–7–0; Watkinson 7–2–14–0; O'Shaughnessy 5–1–15–0; Radford 4.2–0–27–2.

Umpires: B. Leadbeater and D. R. Shepherd.

FINAL

MIDDLESEX v ESSEX

At Lord's, July 23. Middlesex won by 4 runs. In a thrilling finish Middlesex saved themselves from what for most of the day had seemed like impending defeat. Owing to slight morning rain the match started 50 minutes late. Middlesex, having lost the toss, were put in, and with the ball moving around a good deal, both in the air and off the pitch, especially for Turner and Gooch, they had to work hard for their runs. In taking the first two wickets of the day, one with the help of a fine, low slip catch by Gooch, Foster created a favourable impression. For reaching 196 in their 55 overs, Middlesex were greatly indebted to Radley, whose adhesive qualities were never better demonstrated.

Batting was easier by the time Essex began their reply, soon after four o'clock. With Gooch in commanding form, he and Hardie raced to 79 with only eleven overs bowled. Cowans's first over cost 16 runs. In the twelfth over Gooch, driving at a wide off-side ball, was caught at the wicket, but by tea, taken as late as 6.20, Essex had reached 113 for one. Even after McEwan had gone to a diving catch in the covers and Fletcher to a bat and pad catch at silly-point, Essex, at 135 for three, looked to have plenty in hand.

But earlier in the same week, in similar circumstances, they had suffered a complete collapse against Kent, in the second round of the NatWest Bank Trophy, and they now lost their last seven wickets for 57 runs. Pont dropped his bat onto his stumps after being hit on the helmet by a short ball from Williams, and Hardie, whose early freedom had long deserted him, was caught at the wicket. When Pringle and Turner took the score to 185 for five, with four overs still left, it seemed that Essex would win after all. But with the light fading – the delay at the start made a difference here – and the tension rising, Middlesex, astutely led by Gatting, took Pringle's wicket in the 52nd over, Turner's in the 53rd, those of both Easts in the 54th and Foster's off the first ball of the 55th. John Carr, son of the secretary of the TCCB, held a good running catch at deep mid-on, having just come on as substitute for Williams; Gatting, at short mid-wicket, parried and then caught a firm pull by David East; Radley, from close in on the off side, threw out Ray East, who had been sent back after starting on a short single, and Cowans bowled Foster. The match, watched by 22,000 people, ended at 8.50. Middlesex had not previously won the competition.

Gold Award: C. T. Radley.

Middlesex

G. D. Barlow b Foster	14		P. H. Edmonds b Pringle	9
W. N. Slack c Gooch b Foster	1		N. F. Williams c and b Pringle	13
C. T. Radley not out	89		W. W. Daniel not out	2
*M. W. Gatting run out	22		B 3, l-b 9, w 4, n-b 3	19
K. P. Tomlins lbw b Gooch	0			—
J. E. Emburey c D. E. East b Lever	17		1/10 2/25 3/74 (8 wkts, 55 overs)	196
†P. R. Downton c Fletcher b Foster	10		4/74 5/123 6/141 7/171 8/191	

N. G. Cowans did not bat.

Bowling: Lever 11–1–52–1; Foster 11–2–26–3; Pringle 11–0–54–2; Turner 11–1–24–0; Gooch 11–2–21–1.

Essex

G. A. Gooch c Downton b Williams	46		R. E. East run out	0
B. R. Hardie c Downton b Cowans	49		N. A. Foster b Cowans	0
K. S. McEwan c Cowans b Edmonds	34		J. K. Lever not out	0
*K. W. R. Fletcher c Radley b Edmonds	3		L-b 12, w 3, n-b 8	23
K. R. Pont hit wkt b Williams	7			—
D. R. Pringle lbw b Daniel	16		1/79 2/127 3/135 (54.1 overs)	192
S. Turner c sub b Cowans	9		4/151 5/156 6/185	
†D. E. East c Gatting b Cowans	5		7/187 8/191 9/192	

Bowling: Daniel 11–2–34–1; Cowans 10.1–0–39–4; Williams 11–0–45–2; Emburey 11–3–17–0; Edmonds 11–3–34–2.

Umpires: H. D. Bird and B. J. Meyer.

BENSON AND HEDGES CUP RECORDS

Highest individual scores: 198 not out, G. A. Gooch, Essex v Sussex, Hove, 1982; 173 not out, C. G. Greenidge, Hampshire v Minor Counties (South), Amersham, 1973; 158 not out, B. F. Davison, Leicestershire v Warwickshire, Coventry, 1972. (97 hundreds have been scored in the competition.)

Highest totals in 55 overs: 350 for three, Essex v Oxford & Cambridge Univs, Chelmsford, 1979; 327 for four, Leicestershire v Warwickshire, Coventry, 1972; 327 for two, Essex v Sussex, Hove, 1982; 321 for one, Hampshire v Minor Counties (South), Amersham, 1973.

Highest match aggregate: 601 for thirteen wickets, Somerset (307 for six) v Gloucestershire (294 for seven), Taunton, 1982.

Lowest totals: 56 in 26.2 overs, Leicestershire v Minor Counties at Wellington, 1982; 59 in 34 overs, Oxford & Cambridge Univs v Glamorgan, Cambridge, 1983; 60 in 26 overs, Sussex v Middlesex, Hove, 1978; 62 in 26.5 overs, Gloucestershire v Hampshire, Bristol, 1975.

Best bowling: Seven for 12, W. W. Daniel, Middlesex v Minor Counties (East), Ipswich, 1978; seven for 22, J. R. Thomson, Middlesex v Hampshire, Lord's, 1981; seven for 32, R. G. D. Willis, Warwickshire v Yorkshire, Birmingham, 1981.

Hat-tricks: G. D. McKenzie, Leicestershire v Worcestershire, Worcester, 1972; K. Higgs, Leicestershire v Surrey in the final, Lord's, 1974; A. A. Jones, Middlesex v Essex, Lord's, 1977; M. J. Procter, Gloucestershire v Hampshire, Southampton, 1977; W. Larkins, Northamptonshire v Oxford & Cambridge Univs, Northampton, 1980; E. A. Moseley, Glamorgan v Kent, Cardiff, 1981.

Record partnerships for each wicket

241 for 1st	S. M. Gavaskar and B. C. Rose, Somerset v Kent at Canterbury...	1980
285* for 2nd	C. G. Greenidge and D. R. Turner, Hampshire v Minor Counties (South) at Amersham	1973
268* for 3rd	G. A. Gooch and K. W. R. Fletcher, Essex v Sussex at Hove	1982
184* for 4th	D. Lloyd and B. W. Reidy, Lancashire v Derbyshire at Chesterfield	1980
134 for 5th	M. Maslin and D. N. F. Slade, Minor Counties (East) v Nottinghamshire at Nottingham	1976
114 for 6th	Majid J. Khan and G. P. Ellis, Glamorgan v Gloucestershire at Bristol	1975
149* for 7th	J. D. Love and C. M. Old, Yorkshire v Scotland at Bradford	1981
109 for 8th	R. E. East and N. Smith, Essex v Northamptonshire at Chelmsford	1977
81 for 9th	J. N. Shepherd and D. L. Underwood, Kent v Middlesex at Lord's	1975
80* for 10th	D. L. Bairstow and M. Johnson, Yorkshire v Derbyshire at Derby	1981

WINNERS 1972–83

1972 LEICESTERSHIRE beat Yorkshire by five wickets.
1973 KENT beat Worcestershire by 39 runs.
1974 SURREY beat Leicestershire by 27 runs.
1975 LEICESTERSHIRE beat Middlesex by five wickets.
1976 KENT beat Worcestershire by 43 runs.
1977 GLOUCESTERSHIRE beat Kent by 64 runs.
1978 KENT beat Derbyshire by six wickets.
1979 ESSEX beat Surrey by 35 runs.
1980 NORTHAMPTONSHIRE beat Essex by 6 runs.
1981 SOMERSET beat Surrey by seven wickets.
1982 SOMERSET beat Nottinghamshire by nine wickets.
1983 MIDDLESEX beat Essex by 4 runs.

WINS BY OXFORD AND CAMBRIDGE UNIVERSITIES

1973 OXFORD beat Northamptonshire at Northampton by two wickets.
1975 OXFORD & CAMBRIDGE beat Worcestershire at Cambridge by 66 runs.
1975 OXFORD & CAMBRIDGE beat Northamptonshire at Oxford by three wickets.
1976 OXFORD & CAMBRIDGE beat Yorkshire at Barnsley by seven wickets.

WINS BY MINOR COUNTIES

1980 MINOR COUNTIES beat Gloucestershire at Chippenham by 3 runs.
1981 MINOR COUNTIES beat Hampshire at Southampton by 3 runs.
1982 MINOR COUNTIES beat Leicestershire at Wellington by 131 runs.

John Player
Special
League
Every Sunday
6th May – 9th September
DANGER: Government Health WARNING:
CIGARETTES CAN SERIOUSLY DAMAGE YOUR HEALTH

JOHN PLAYER LEAGUE, 1983

Yorkshire's victory was their first in any of the four major competitions for fourteen years and also their first in the John Player League. Sussex, the defending champions, were narrowly ahead of them half-way through the programme, but Yorkshire (sixteenth in 1982) took the lead on July 17, after which Somerset, with a match in hand, were the strongest threat to them.

With only two Sundays remaining, Somerset looked the likelier winners. Yorkshire, with one difficult match to play (away to Essex), had 44 points, while Somerset, faced by two seemingly easier games (away to Worcestershire and at home to Warwickshire), had 42 points. In the event, Yorkshire won despite not bowling another ball, Somerset surprisingly losing on a turning pitch at Worcester and Yorkshire's two points from their final match at Chelmsford being sufficient to give them the title. Yorkshire and Somerset both, in fact, finished with 46 points, but Yorkshire's superior away record (five wins to Somerset's three) was decisive.

Yorkshire's three defeats came from Somerset at Bradford, Glamorgan at Cardiff and Nottinghamshire at Trent Bridge; Somerset were beaten by Leicestershire at Leicester and Derbyshire at Heanor, as well as by Worcestershire. Both sides had three "no-results" owing to the rain, two fewer than Kent, Lancashire, Leicestershire and Surrey. Surrey lost no fewer than four of their first five matches to the weather, although with each of these worth two points to them they were still, even then, only four points behind Glamorgan, the early pacemakers.

Having badly damaged Somerset's chances on the penultimate Sunday, Worcestershire then beat Sussex, in a rain-affected match, the following week, by the smallest fraction of a run, thereby depriving Sussex of third place in the table. This went instead to Kent, who had finished fourth in 1982. Leicestershire declined from third place to joint eleventh and Nottinghamshire from fifth to joint fifteenth. Derbyshire, on the other hand, climbed from twelfth to joint sixth. Worcestershire tied three of their matches — against Lancashire, Nottinghamshire and Warwickshire.

Yorkshire's success brought a sharp rise in Sunday attendances within the county. Their eight home games attracted 46,700 people, despite one of them being a wash-out and only a single over being bowled in another. Their receipts of £33,793 were up by 78 per cent on 1982. Ray Illingworth, Yorkshire's captain and manager, had led Leicestershire to victory in the same competition in 1974 and 1977. Before the 1983 season started he had expressed the view, which proved well founded, that the Sunday League gave Yorkshire their best chance of winning their first prize of any importance since the County Championship in 1969.

Gordon Greenidge of Hampshire was the season's most prolific batsman with 661 runs at an average of 73.44. However, he lost the record for the highest individual score ever made in the competition, this passing to Graham Gooch when he hit 176 (one 6, 28 4s) for Essex against Glamorgan at Southend. Wayne Larkins also played a brilliant innings of 172 not out for Northamptonshire against Warwickshire at Luton, in which he hit six 6s and twelve 4s, and Trevor Jesty another of 166 not out (three 6s, eighteen 4s) for Hampshire against Surrey at Portsmouth. In his seven innings for Kent, Chris Tavaré hit four fifties and one century, and averaged 87.20.

The most economical bowler was Ray Illingworth with twenty wickets at 12.95 apiece. The most successful all-rounder was Vivian Richards with 445 runs and eighteen wickets for Somerset and the leading wicket-taker John Shepherd of Gloucestershire with 27 at 15.62 apiece. Kim Barnett (Derbyshire) with eight catches and Bobby Parks with 23 wicket-keeping victims (21 caught, two stumped) led the fielding tables, Parks for the second successive season.

FINAL TABLE

		P	W	L	T	NR	Pts	6s	4w
1	Yorkshire (16)	16	10	3	0	3	46	28	3
2	Somerset (9)	16	10	3	0	3	46	32	3
3	Kent (4)	16	8	3	0	5	42	16	4
4	Sussex (1)	16	9	5	0	2	40	33	1
5	Hampshire (5)	16	9	6	0	1	38	45	3
6	Derbyshire (12)	16	7	5	0	4	36	22	2
	Essex (5)	16	7	5	0	4	36	36	1
8	Lancashire (10)	16	5	5	1	5	32	32	1
	Middlesex (2)	16	7	7	0	2	32	40	3
10	Glamorgan (10)	16	6	8	0	2	28	24	3
11	Leicestershire (3)	16	4	7	0	5	26	16	2
	Surrey (12)	16	4	7	0	5	26	32	1
	Worcestershire (15)	16	4	7	3	2	26	25	3
14	Gloucestershire (14)	16	4	8	0	4	24	22	2
15	Northamptonshire (8)	16	5	10	0	1	22	28	3
	Nottinghamshire (5)	16	4	9	1	2	22	22	4
	Warwickshire (17)	16	4	9	1	2	22	37	2

1982 positions in brackets

Yorkshire finished in first place over Somerset by virtue of their greater number of away wins. This criteria applied only for the first four placings.

CHAMPIONS: 1969-83

1969	Lancashire	1977	Leicestershire
1970	Lancashire	1978	Hampshire
1971	Worcestershire	1979	Somerset
1972	Kent	1980	Warwickshire
1973	Kent	1981	Essex
1974	Leicestershire	1982	Sussex
1975	Hampshire	1983	Yorkshire
1976	Kent		

DISTRIBUTION OF PRIZE-MONEY

The total prize-money was £62,600

£13,000 and John Player Trophy: YORKSHIRE.
£6,500 to runners-up: SOMERSET.
£3,250 to third placing: KENT.
£1,750 to fourth placing: SUSSEX.
£275 each match to the winners – shared if tied or no result.

Batting award: £350 to C. G. Greenidge (Hampshire) who hit seventeen 6s in the season.

Other leading 6-hitters:

13 – M. A. Lynch (Surrey), I. V. A. Richards (Somerset).
12 – I. T. Botham (Somerset), T. E. Jesty (Hampshire).
11 – R. O. Butcher (Middlesex), M. W. Gatting (Middlesex), W. Larkins (Northamptonshire), C. H. Lloyd (Lancashire).
10 – C. L. King (Worcestershire), A. L. Jones (Glamorgan).
9 – G. W. Humpage (Warwickshire).
8 – G. A. Gooch (Essex).

Fastest televised match fifty

38 balls – T. A. Lloyd, Warwickshire v Northamptonshire, Luton, June 9.

Bowling award: £350 to J. G. Thomas (Glamorgan) who took four wickets or more in an innings on three occasions.

K. Saxelby (Nottinghamshire) and D. L. Underwood (Kent) each took four wickets in an innings twice; 34 players each took four wickets in an innings once.

DERBYSHIRE

At Manchester, May 8. LANCASHIRE v DERBYSHIRE. No result.

DERBYSHIRE v NORTHAMPTONSHIRE

At Derby, May 15. Derbyshire won by 78 runs. Toss won by Northamptonshire. Rain reduced the match to 39 overs a side.

Derbyshire

B. Wood c Sharp b T. M. Lamb	36	*G. Miller not out	26
J. G. Wright c and b Willey	67		
P. G. Newman lbw b Mallender	3	L-b 11, w 9, n-b 2	22
K. J. Barnett b Mallender	7		
J. H. Hampshire not out	36	1/104 2/111 (5 wkts, 39 overs) 201	
A. Hill c Sharp b Carse	4	3/121 4/131 5/147	

I. S. Anderson, C. J. Tunnicliffe, †R. W. Taylor and S. Oldham did not bat.

Bowling: Carse 7–1–15–1; Griffiths 6–0–22–0; Willey 8–0–36–1; T. M. Lamb 8–0–55–1; Steele 3–0–24–0; Mallender 7–0–27–2.

Northamptonshire

W. Larkins c Hampshire b Newman	3	J. A. Carse c Barnett b Anderson	4
P. Willey lbw b Newman	1	N. A. Mallender not out	4
A. J. Lamb lbw b Miller	10	B. J. Griffiths not out	0
R. G. Williams c Miller b Wood	20	L-b 3, w 2	5
*G. Cook c Newman b Miller	3		
†G. Sharp b Wood	22	1/4 2/9 3/27 (9 wkts, 39 overs) 123	
D. S. Steele c Taylor b Anderson	38	4/31 5/61 6/64	
T. M. Lamb b Wood	13	7/104 8/111 9/123	

Bowling: Oldham 8–1–16–0; Newman 8–3–15–2; Miller 8–0–19–2; Wood 8–0–35–3; Tunnicliffe 2–0–18–0; Anderson 5–1–15–2.

Umpires: J. Birkenshaw and J. van Geloven.

At Chelmsford, May 22. ESSEX v DERBYSHIRE. No result.

At Coventry, June 5. DERBYSHIRE beat WARWICKSHIRE by five wickets.

DERBYSHIRE v LEICESTERSHIRE

At Derby, June 12. Leicestershire won by five wickets. Toss won by Leicestershire.

Derbyshire

*K. J. Barnett c Steele b Parsons	0	†B. J. M. Maher b Steele	6
I. S. Anderson c and b Cook	35	S. Oldham lbw b Clift	4
A. Hill c Garnham b Cook	20	O. H. Mortensen not out	1
B. Wood c Parsons b Clift	17	L-b 7, w 2	9
J. E. Morris c Tolchard b Clift	21		
R. J. Finney st Garnham b Steele	7	1/0 2/46 3/77　　　(37.3 overs) 150	
W. P. Fowler b Clift	26	4/77 5/90 6/134	
C. J. Tunnicliffe c Clift b Taylor	4	7/135 8/142 9/149	

Bowling: Taylor 7–2–15–1; Parsons 8–1–29–1; Steele 8–0–49–2; Cook 8–0–28–2; Clift 6.3–1–20–4.

Leicestershire

N. E. Briers c Tunnicliffe b Wood	32	J. F. Steele not out	9
I. P. Butcher c Maher b Mortensen	9		
*R. W. Tolchard b Tunnicliffe	57	L-b 11, w 1, n-b 2	14
P. B. Clift b Fowler	25		
†M. A. Garnham c and b Fowler	2	1/28 2/84　　(5 wkts, 38.5 overs) 154	
T. J. Boon not out	6	3/127 4/130 5/143	

R. A. Cobb, G. J. Parsons, L. B. Taylor and N. G. B. Cook did not bat.

Bowling: Mortensen 8–0–15–1; Tunnicliffe 8–1–34–1; Wood 8–0–32–1; Oldham 8–0–29–0; Finney 3.5–0–28–0; Fowler 3–1–2–2.

Umpires: P. J. Eele and K. Ibadulla.

DERBYSHIRE v MIDDLESEX

At Chesterfield, June 26. Middlesex won by four wickets. Toss won by Middlesex. Rain restricted the match to 38 overs a side.

Derbyshire

I. S. Anderson lbw b James	7	†R. W. Taylor c Downton b Gatting	7
*K. J. Barnett run out	20	S. Oldham c Downton b Gatting	5
A. Hill b Williams	12	O. H. Mortensen not out	0
G. Miller c Gatting b Williams	0	L-b 3, n-b 2	5
J. E. Morris c Downton b Williams	61		
R. J. Finney c and b Edmonds	7	1/7 2/30 3/33　　　(34.5 overs) 160	
W. P. Fowler c Butcher b Williams	28	4/45 5/92 6/122	
C. J. Tunnicliffe run out	8	7/138 8/153 9/160	

Bowling: Cowans 8–1–29–0; James 8–1–23–1; Williams 8–1–40–4; Edmonds 6–0–35–1; Emburey 3–0–21–0; Gatting 1.5–0–7–2.

Middlesex

G. D. Barlow lbw b Mortensen	13	†P. R. Downton c Finney b Miller	35
W. N. Slack b Mortensen	28	P. H. Edmonds not out	15
C. T. Radley c Barnett b Tunnicliffe	27	L-b 4, w 3, n-b 3	10
*M. W. Gatting b Mortensen	0		
R. O. Butcher c Morris b Tunnicliffe	4	1/23 2/71 3/73 (6 wkts, 35.1 overs) 162	
J. E. Emburey not out	30	4/75 5/78 6/137	

N. F. Williams, N. G. Cowans and K. D. James did not bat.

Bowling: Finney 8–1–40–0; Mortensen 8–1–30–3; Tunnicliffe 8–0–24–2; Oldham 7–0–35–0; Miller 4.1–0–23–1.

Umpires: R. Julian and B. Leadbeater.

DERBYSHIRE v WORCESTERSHIRE

At Derby, July 3. Derbyshire won by four wickets. Toss won by Derbyshire.

Worcestershire

M. J. Weston c Barnett b Oldham	64	A. E. Warner run out	14
M. S. Scott b Mortensen	9	R. K. Illingworth not out	0
D. N. Patel b Finney	23	B 4, l-b 7, w 5, n-b 3	19
*P. A. Neale c Barnett b Oldham	47		
D. B. D'Oliveira b Mortensen	31	1/21 2/62 (7 wkts, 40 overs) 225	
D. A. Banks lbw b Mortensen	11	3/134 4/168	
J. D. Inchmore not out	7	5/199 6/207 7/225	

†P. Moores and A. P. Pridgeon did not bat.

Bowling: Finney 8–0–35–1; Mortensen 8–0–40–3; Miller 8–1–27–0; Tunnicliffe 8–0–38–0; Oldham 8–0–66–2.

Derbyshire

I. S. Anderson b Illingworth	39	W. P. Fowler run out	37
*K. J. Barnett b Inchmore	14	C. J. Tunnicliffe not out	33
A. Hill b D'Oliveira	30	B 1, l-b 10, w 6, n-b 5	22
G. Miller b D'Oliveira	2		
J. E. Morris st Moores b D'Oliveira	6	1/32 2/90 3/90 (6 wkts, 38.2 overs) 229	
R. J. Finney not out	46	4/101 5/102 6/162	

†R. W. Taylor, S. Oldham and O. H. Mortensen did not bat.

Bowling: Pridgeon 6–0–30–0; Warner 7.2–1–37–0; Patel 7–0–44–0; Inchmore 7–0–39–1; D'Oliveira 5–2–23–3; Illingworth 6–1–34–1.

Umpires: J. W. Holder and P. B. Wight.

At Bristol, July 10. DERBYSHIRE beat GLOUCESTERSHIRE by three wickets.

DERBYSHIRE v NOTTINGHAMSHIRE

At Derby, July 24. Derbyshire won by three wickets in a match reduced to seventeen overs following a thunderstorm when Nottinghamshire had faced 8.3 overs. Toss won by Derbyshire.

Nottinghamshire

B. Hassan c Taylor b Mortensen.........	24	
R. T. Robinson c and b Holding.........	34	
*C. E. B. Rice not out	4	
J. D. Birch not out	7	
B 2, l-b 4, w 11	17	

1/73 2/78   (2 wkts, 17 overs) 86

D. W. Randall, †B. N. French, R. A. Pick, E. E. Hemmings, P. M. Such, N. J. B. Illingworth and M. K. Bore did not bat.

Bowling: Finney 5–2–9–0; Holding 8–2–27–1; Mortensen 4–0–33–1.

Derbyshire

I. S. Anderson lbw b Bore	0	†R. W. Taylor b Bore	0
*K. J. Barnett b Bore......................	4	S. Oldham not out	2
A. Hill c Birch b Pick......................	26	L-b 6, n-b 1	7
J. H. Hampshire c Hassan b Hemmings.	15		
R. J. Finney c and b Hemmings	29	1/3 2/16 (7 wkts, 16.5 overs) 87	
W. P. Fowler b Bore	0	3/43 4/81	
C. J. Tunnicliffe not out...................	4	5/81 6/85 7/85	

M. A. Holding and O. H. Mortensen did not bat.

Bowling: Pick 8–0–38–1; Bore 7.5–0–38–4; Hemmings 1–0–4–2.

Umpires: A. Jepson and J. van Geloven.

DERBYSHIRE v KENT

At Chesterfield, July 31. No result. Toss won by Kent.

Derbyshire

*K. J. Barnett run out	29	R. J. Finney not out......................	31
I. S. Anderson c Cowdrey b Baptiste...	6	L-b 4, w 2	6
A. Hill c and b Baptiste...................	3		
G. Miller not out...........................	55	1/24 2/36 (4 wkts, 31.3 overs) 146	
J. E. Morris c and b Ellison...............	16	3/47 4/76	

W. P. Fowler, C. J. Tunnicliffe, †B. J. M. Maher, O. H. Mortensen and M. A. Holding did not bat.

Bowling: Jarvis 6–0–23–0; Baptiste 8–1–18–2; Woolmer 8–0–35–0; Ellison 4–0–20–1; Penn 3.3–0–27–0; Cowdrey 2–0–17–0.

Kent

R. A. Woolmer, C. Penn, D. G. Aslett, M. R. Benson, *C. S. Cowdrey, †A. P. E. Knott, G. W. Johnson, R. M. Ellison, E. A. E. Baptiste, D. L. Underwood and K. B. S. Jarvis.

Umpires: D. O. Oslear and D. R. Shepherd.

At Eastbourne, August 7. DERBYSHIRE lost to SUSSEX by 2 runs.

DERBYSHIRE v SOMERSET

At Heanor, August 14. Derbyshire won by eight wickets. Toss won by Derbyshire.

Somerset

P. M. Roebuck b Finney	32	J. Garner c Mortensen b Tunnicliffe	12
P. W. Denning b Finney	48	G. V. Palmer not out	13
*I. V. A. Richards c Maher b Finney	15	†T. Gard not out	14
N. F. M. Popplewell b Miller	3	B 3, l-b 9, w 7, n-b 1	20
J. W. Lloyds run out	17		
P. A. Slocombe lbw b Mortensen	7	1/86 2/103 3/104 (8 wkts, 40 overs) 219
V. J. Marks c Anderson b Tunnicliffe	38	4/116 5/127 6/144 7/163 8/194
C. H. Dredge did not bat.			

Bowling: Holding 8–3–32–0; Mortensen 8–0–19–1; Miller 8–1–49–1; Finney 8–1–37–3; Fowler 1–0–2–0; Tunnicliffe 7–0–60–2.

Derbyshire

*K. J. Barnett not out	100
I. S. Anderson lbw b Richards	54
A. Hill b Popplewell	19
G. Miller not out	30
L-b 11, w 4, n-b 2	17

1/105 2/152 (2 wkts, 37.2 overs) 220

J. E. Morris, R. J. Finney, W. P. Fowler, C. J. Tunnicliffe, †B. J. M. Maher, O. H. Mortensen and M. A. Holding did not bat.

Bowling: Garner 7–1–29–0; Dredge 6–0–35–0; Palmer 6–0–34–0; Marks 6–0–37–0; Richards 6.2–0–32–1; Popplewell 6–0–36–1.

Umpires: W. E. Alley and N. T. Plews.

At Swansea, August 21. DERBYSHIRE lost to GLAMORGAN by 22 runs.

At Bradford, August 28. DERBYSHIRE lost to YORKSHIRE by two wickets.

DERBYSHIRE v HAMPSHIRE

At Derby, September 4. Derbyshire won by 8 runs. Toss won by Hampshire.

Derbyshire

*K. J. Barnett b Cowley	5	†R. W. Taylor not out	13
I. S. Anderson b Tremlett	12	M. A. Holding c Cowley b Marshall	12
A. Hill c Terry b Tremlett	7	O. H. Mortensen not out	1
G. Miller b Cowley	14	B 3, l-b 8, w 5, n-b 1	17
J. E. Morris c Terry b Jesty	33		
R. J. Finney c Parks b Malone	11	1/23 2/23 3/36 (9 wkts, 40 overs) 143
W. P. Fowler c Greenidge b Malone	15	4/53 5/81 6/103
P. G. Newman c Parks b Nicholas	3	7/109 8/118 9/138

Bowling: Marshall 8–2–11–1; Malone 8–1–34–2; Tremlett 8–2–18–2; Cowley 8–1–26–2; Jesty 7–0–36–1; Nicholas 1–0–1–1.

Hampshire

C. G. Greenidge lbw b Finney	16	T. M. Tremlett b Newman	2
C. L. Smith lbw b Holding	2	†R. J. Parks b Holding	11
M. C. J. Nicholas lbw b Finney	11	S. J. Malone b Holding	0
*T. E. Jesty lbw b Finney	22	L-b 7, w 5	12
V. P. Terry not out	48		—
D. R. Turner b Newman	8	1/4 2/38 3/39	(38.4 overs) 135
M. D. Marshall lbw b Newman	0	4/68 5/79 6/85	
N. G. Cowley c Holding b Newman	3	7/95 8/101 9/135	

Bowling: Holding 7.4–1–19–3; Mortensen 7–2–17–0; Miller 8–1–39–0; Finney 8–0–27–3; Newman 8–2–21–4.

Umpires: A. Jepson and M. J. Kitchen.

At The Oval, September 11. SURREY v DERBYSHIRE. No result.

ESSEX

At Southampton, May 8. ESSEX lost to HAMPSHIRE by 15 runs.

ESSEX v LANCASHIRE

At Chelmsford, May 15. No result.

ESSEX v DERBYSHIRE

At Chelmsford, May 22. No result.

At Taunton, June 5. SOMERSET v ESSEX. No result.

ESSEX v KENT

At Chelmsford, June 12. Essex won by 53 runs. Toss won by Kent.

Essex

G. A. Gooch c Ellison b Cowdrey	58	K. R. Pont b Jarvis	7
B. R. Hardie c Taylor b Underwood	66	S. Turner not out	3
K. S. McEwan c Johnson b Cowdrey	13	L-b 13, w 3, n-b 3	19
N. Phillip b Ellison	35		—
*K. W. R. Fletcher not out	41	1/116 2/136 3/155	(6 wkts, 40 overs) 250
D. R. Pringle b Jarvis	8	4/205 5/224 6/236	

†D. E. East, R. E. East and J. K. Lever did not bat.

Bowling: Jarvis 8–1–56–2; Ellison 8–1–44–1; Cowdrey 8–0–39–2; Baptiste 8–0–39–0; Underwood 8–0–53–1.

Kent

L. Potter c McEwan b Phillip	1	R. M. Ellison not out	5
N. R. Taylor b Lever	17	D. L. Underwood c Fletcher b Phillip	0
D. G. Aslett c Gooch b Lever	2	K. B. S. Jarvis b Lever	2
M. R. Benson run out	21	L-b 6, w 9, n-b 1	16
*C. S. Cowdrey c Fletcher b R. E. East	52		
E. A. E. Baptiste c Pringle b Phillip	47	1/5 2/22 3/23 (38.2 overs)	197
†A. P. E. Knott c Phillip b Turner	1	4/84 5/115 6/118	
G. W. Johnson b Phillip	33	7/185 8/189 9/189	

Bowling: Lever 7.2–1–15–3; Phillip 7–0–24–4; Gooch 4–0–28–0; Pringle 8–0–36–0; Turner 8–0–52–1; R. E. East 4–0–26–1.

Umpires: J. W. Holder and J. van Geloven.

At Worcester, June 19. ESSEX lost to WORCESTERSHIRE by three wickets.

ESSEX v SUSSEX

At Ilford, June 26. Sussex won by four wickets. Toss won by Essex.

Essex

G. A. Gooch c Parker b Barclay	22	†D. E. East c C. M. Wells b Pigott	1
A. W. Lilley c Gould b C. M. Wells	28	J. K. Lever not out	7
K. S. McEwan c Mendis b Reeve	5	R. E. East not out	2
N. Phillip b Pigott	4	B 2, l-b 10, w 1, n-b 1	14
*K. W. R. Fletcher b le Roux	55		
B. R. Hardie c Barclay b le Roux	35	1/49 2/51 3/62 (9 wkts, 40 overs)	188
K. R. Pont c Imran b le Roux	6	4/62 5/146 6/167	
S. Turner c Phillipson b Pigott	9	7/169 8/179 9/179	

Bowling: C. M. Wells 8–0–21–1; le Roux 8–0–30–3; Barclay 8–0–49–1; Reeve 8–1–26–1; Pigott 8–0–48–3.

Sussex

G. D. Mendis c Lilley b Phillip	2	G. S. le Roux not out	46
P. W. G. Parker b R. E. East	11	C. P. Phillipson not out	23
C. M. Wells c and b R. E. East	23	L-b 12, w 2, n-b 1	15
Imran Khan c D. E. East b Gooch	24		
†I. J. Gould c Turner b Gooch	30	1/3 2/39 3/40 (6 wkts, 38.4 overs)	190
A. P. Wells b Lever	16	4/93 5/106 6/122	

*J. R. T. Barclay, A. C. S. Pigott and D. A. Reeve did not bat.

Bowling: Lever 7.4–0–39–1; Phillip 7–0–47–1; Gooch 8–2–17–2; Turner 8–0–30–0; R. E. East 8–0–42–2.

Umpires: J. Birkenshaw and N. T. Plews.

At Nottingham, July 3. ESSEX beat NOTTINGHAMSHIRE by 89 runs.

At Birmingham, July 10. ESSEX beat WARWICKSHIRE by 1 run.

ESSEX v GLAMORGAN

At Southend, July 17. Essex won by 56 runs, passing by 3 runs the previous record total after winning the toss. In scoring 176 in 126 minutes, with one 6 and 28 4s, Gooch established a new John Player League record and passed 3,000 Sunday League runs.

Essex

G. A. Gooch run out	176	*K. W. R. Fletcher not out	1
C. Gladwin c Selvey b Ontong	8		
K. S. McEwan b Derrick	32	B 2, l-b 7, n-b 1	10
N. Phillip lbw b Ontong	31		
D. R. Pringle not out	52	1/14 2/107 3/208 (5 wkts, 40 overs) 310	
S. Turner run out	0	4/281 5/282	

B. R. Hardie, †D. E. East, R. E. East and N. A. Foster did not bat.

Bowling: Selvey 7–0–56–0; Ontong 8–0–37–2; Lloyd 8–0–55–0; Derrick 8–0–64–1; Thomas 8–0–78–0; Rowe 1–0–10–0.

Glamorgan

J. A. Hopkins st D. E. East b R. E. East	27	J. G. Thomas not out	34
A. L. Jones lbw b Foster	13	B 1, l-b 13, w 2, n-b 7	23
Javed Miandad c R. E. East b Turner	68		
R. C. Ontong not out	73	1/27 2/73 (4 wkts, 40 overs) 254	
A. Jones c Gladwin b Pringle	16	3/157 4/192	

C. J. C. Rowe, †E. W. Jones, *M. W. W. Selvey, B. J. Lloyd and J. Derrick did not bat.

Bowling: Phillip 8–1–29–0; Foster 7–0–47–1; R. E. East 8–0–47–1; Turner 8–0–49–1; Pringle 8–0–54–1; Hardie 1–0–5–0.

Umpires: B. J. Meyer and D. R. Shepherd.

At Leicester, July 24. ESSEX beat LEICESTERSHIRE on faster scoring-rate.

ESSEX v MIDDLESEX

At Chelmsford, August 7. Middlesex won by four wickets. Toss won by Middlesex.

Essex

G. A. Gooch lbw b Daniel	18	S. Turner c Gatting b Cowans	7
C. Gladwin c Gatting b Daniel	1	†D. E. East run out	24
K. S. McEwan c Barlow b Edmonds	19	B 1, l-b 6, w 6, n-b 6	19
D. R. Pringle b Cowans	34		
N. Phillip c Daniel b Edmonds	5	1/4 2/25 (8 wkts, 40 overs) 184	
*K. W. R. Fletcher not out	55	3/55 4/77 5/91	
B. R. Hardie c Radley b Cowans	2	6/95 7/125 8/184	

R. E. East and J. K. Lever did not bat.

Bowling: Williams 7–0–22–0; Daniel 7–0–37–2; Slack 2–0–10–0; Edmonds 8–0–33–2; Emburey 8–0–27–0; Cowans 8–0–36–3.

Middlesex

G. D. Barlow st D. E. East b Turner ..	56	†P. R. Downton not out	35
W. N. Slack lbw b Phillip.................	0	P. H. Edmonds not out....................	5
C. T. Radley run out.....................	15	L-b 9, w 6, n-b 6	21
*M. W. Gatting lbw b Pringle	31		
R. G. P. Ellis run out....................	18	1/5 2/39 3/93 (6 wkts, 39 overs) 187	
J. E. Emburey c and b Lever.............	6	4/134 5/135 6/154	

N. F. Williams, W. W. Daniel and N. G. Cowans did not bat.

Bowling: Lever 8–0–33–1; Phillip 7–0–34–1; R. E. East 4–0–17–0; Turner 8–0–29–1; Pringle 8–1–27–1; Gooch 4–0–26–0.

Umpires: M. J. Kitchen and B. Leadbeater.

At Wellingborough, August 14. ESSEX beat NORTHAMPTONSHIRE by two wickets.

ESSEX v GLOUCESTERSHIRE

At Colchester, August 21. Essex won by 13 runs. Toss won by Gloucestershire.

Essex

G. A. Gooch b Shepherd.................	19	S. Turner c Stovold b Shepherd..........	33
C. Gladwin c Wright b Sainsbury........	7	†D. E. East c Childs b Shepherd	0
K. S. McEwan c Hignell b Graveney...	21	R. E. East not out...........................	1
N. Phillip c and b Sainsbury..............	95	B 1, l-b 5, n-b 1	7
*K. W. R. Fletcher b Graveney........	19		
B. R. Hardie run out.......................	25	1/26 2/31 3/62 (9 wkts, 40 overs) 233	
A. W. Lilley c Broad b Bainbridge	6	4/110 5/184 6/191 7/227 8/227 9/233	

J. K. Lever did not bat.

Bowling: Sainsbury 8–1–41–2; Shepherd 8–0–49–3; Bainbridge 8–0–58–1; Graveney 8–0–34–2; Childs 8–1–44–0.

Gloucestershire

A. W. Stovold b Lever	67	*D. A. Graveney not out.................	20
B. C. Broad c D. E. East b Gooch	10	†R. C. Russell not out....................	1
P. W. Romaines c D. E. East b Gooch ..	5	L-b 7, w 1, n-b 2	10
A. J. Hignell c Lever b R. E. East......	13		
P. Bainbridge c D. E. East b Phillip...	55	1/21 2/29 (7 wkts, 40 overs) 220	
A. J. Wright b Phillip b Lever............	23	3/52 4/136	
J. N. Shepherd c R. E. East b Lever...	16	5/179 6/182 7/204	

J. H. Childs and G. E. Sainsbury did not bat.

Bowling: Lever 8–1–42–3; Phillip 8–0–44–1; Gooch 8–0–46–2; R. E. East 8–0–52–1; Turner 8–0–26–0.

Umpires: W. E. Alley and C. T. Spencer.

At The Oval, August 28. ESSEX lost to SURREY by three wickets.

ESSEX v YORKSHIRE

At Chelmsford, September 11. No result.

GLAMORGAN

At Lord's, May 8. MIDDLESEX v GLAMORGAN. No result.

GLAMORGAN v WARWICKSHIRE

At Swansea, May 15. No result. Toss won by Warwickshire.

Glamorgan
A. Jones not out............................ 1
J. A. Hopkins not out 4
                                            ⎯
                    (no wkt, 1 over) 5

A. L. Jones, Javed Miandad, C. J. C. Rowe, R. C. Ontong, †E. W. Jones, B. J. Lloyd,
M. A. Nash, *M. W. W. Selvey and A. J. Wilkins did not bat.

Bowling: Willis 1–0–5–0.

Warwickshire
K. D. Smith, D. L. Amiss, A. I. Kallicharran, C. Lethbridge, †G. W. Humpage, Asif Din,
A. M. Ferreira, C. M. Old, N. Gifford, W. Hogg and *R. G. D. Willis.

Umpires: D. G. L. Evans and P. B. Wight.

GLAMORGAN v LANCASHIRE

At Swansea, May 29. Glamorgan won by 21 runs. Toss won by Lancashire.

Glamorgan
A. Jones lbw b Allott......................	13	D. A. Francis not out......................	4
J. A. Hopkins c Fowler b Watkinson...	76	B 1, l-b 9, w 3, n-b 2...............	15
A. L. Jones b Watkinson	49		⎯
Javed Miandad not out	61	1/36 2/144 (4 wkts, 40 overs) 253	
R. C. Ontong c Maynard b Allott.......	35	3/163 4/249	

†E. W. Jones, *M. W. W. Selvey, B. J. Lloyd, M. A. Nash and J. G. Thomas did not bat.

Bowling: Allott 8–0–48–2; Folley 8–1–35–0; Watkinson 8–0–46–2; Simmons 8–0–55–0;
O'Shaughnessy 8–0–54–0.

Lancashire
G. Fowler c Thomas b Selvey	27	†C. Maynard c E. W. Jones b Thomas.	13
F. C. Hayes b Ontong	72	M. Watkinson not out	15
*C. H. Lloyd c and b Ontong	21	P. J. W. Allott not out	5
D. P. Hughes b Lloyd	3	B 1, l-b 14, w 2, n-b 2	19
J. Abrahams c E. W. Jones b Thomas .	18		⎯
J. Simmons b Thomas......................	38	1/41 2/95 3/106 (8 wkts, 40 overs) 232	
S. J. O'Shaughnessy lbw b Thomas	1	4/139 5/157 6/158 7/190 8/214	

I. Folley did not bat.

Bowling: Nash 8–0–32–0; Selvey 8–0–56–1; Lloyd 8–0–33–1; Ontong 8–0–43–2; Thomas
8–0–49–4.

Umpires J. H. Harris and R. Palmer.

At Nottingham, June 5. GLAMORGAN beat NOTTINGHAMSHIRE by 11 runs.

GLAMORGAN v YORKSHIRE

At Cardiff, June 12. Glamorgan won by 12 runs. Toss won by Yorkshire.

Glamorgan

A. Jones lbw b Dennis	1	*M. W. W. Selvey not out		9
J. A. Hopkins run out	6	J. G. Thomas c Hartley b Stevenson	...	26
A. L. Jones b Sidebottom	49	M. A. Nash b Stevenson		0
D. A. Francis b Stevenson	25	L-b 7, w 4, n-b 1		12
R. C. Ontong b Jarvis	25			
J. Derrick run out	2	1/2 2/15 3/66	(40 overs)	167
†E. W. Jones run out	12	4/109 5/117 6/127		
B. J. Lloyd lbw b Stevenson	0	7/151 8/151 9/163		

Bowling: Dennis 8–2–19–1; Jarvis 8–1–25–1; Carrick 4–0–16–0; Illingworth 4–0–24–0; Stevenson 8–2–43–4; Sidebottom 8–1–28–1.

Yorkshire

K. Sharp c E. W. Jones b Nash	7	S. J. Dennis not out		16
C. W. J. Athey b Nash	12	P. W. Jarvis run out		3
S. N. Hartley b Thomas	20	*R. Illingworth not out		8
J. D. Love b Ontong	34	L-b 13, w 5, n-b 1		19
†D. L. Bairstow lbw b Thomas	1			
G. B. Stevenson c A. L. Jones b Thomas	27	1/9 2/30 3/49	(9 wkts, 40 overs)	155
P. Carrick b Thomas	3	4/54 5/102 6/105		
A. Sidebottom c Nash b Thomas	5	7/120 8/124 9/131		

Bowling: Selvey 8–3–16–0; Nash 8–2–19–2; Derrick 8–0–33–0; Thomas 8–0–38–5; Ontong 8–0–30–1.

Umpires: N. T. Plews and C. T. Spencer.

At Bath, June 19. GLAMORGAN lost to SOMERSET by five wickets.

At Leicester, June 26. GLAMORGAN lost to LEICESTERSHIRE by four wickets.

GLAMORGAN v SUSSEX

At Cardiff, July 10. Sussex won by five wickets. Toss won by Glamorgan.

Glamorgan

J. A. Hopkins lbw b Wells	0	†E. W. Jones c Barclay b Pigott	...	0
A. L. Jones b Wells	15	B. J. Lloyd not out		13
R. C. Ontong lbw b le Roux	8	*M. W. W. Selvey not out		2
Javed Miandad b Reeve	40	L-b 14, w 7, n-b 1		22
A. Jones b Reeve	38			
C. J. C. Rowe b Reeve	12	1/0 2/19 3/42	(8 wkts, 40 overs)	162
J. Derrick b Pigott	12	4/105 5/125 6/128 7/129 8/153		

A. H. Wilkins did not bat.

Bowling: Wells 8–1–21–2; le Roux 8–0–31–1; Barclay 4–0–19–0; Pigott 8–0–27–2; Reeve 8–0–25–3; Waller 4–0–17–0.

Sussex

G. D. Mendis c Hopkins b Lloyd	13	C. P. Phillipson not out		4
P. W. G. Parker c E. W. Jones b Ontong	1			
C. M. Wells c Selvey b Ontong	63	B 2, l-b 9, w 2, n-b 2		15
Imran Khan c A. L. Jones b Wilkins	8			
†I. J. Gould not out	39	1/2 2/35	(5 wkts, 35.3 overs)	164
G. S. le Roux b Wilkins	21	3/57 4/132 5/157		

C. E. Waller, *J. R. T. Barclay, D. A. Reeve and A. C. S. Pigott did not bat.

Bowling: Selvey 8–1–23–0; Ontong 8–1–36–2; Lloyd 7–0–32–1; Derrick 6.3–1–20–0; Wilkins 6–0–38–2.

Umpires: A. Jepson and A. G. T. Whitehead.

At Southend, July 17. GLAMORGAN lost to ESSEX by 56 runs.

At Northampton, July 24. GLAMORGAN lost to NORTHAMPTONSHIRE on faster scoring-rate.

GLAMORGAN v SURREY

At Swansea, July 31. Glamorgan won on faster scoring-rate, reaching their target of 118 with three overs to spare. Toss won by Surrey.

Surrey

A. R. Butcher c Davies b Barwick	5	I. R. Payne not out		33
†C. J. Richards c Davies b Selvey	8	G. Monkhouse not out		4
D. M. Smith c Davies b Derrick	37	L-b 9, w 1		10
M. A. Lynch c Jones b Lloyd	22			
D. J. Thomas b Ontong	72	1/13 2/17	(7 wkts, 26 overs)	204
S. T. Clarke b Selvey	9	3/62 4/109		
*R. D. V. Knight c Henderson b Selvey	4	5/127 6/148 7/182		

A. J. Stewart and A. Needham did not bat.

Bowling: Selvey 6–0–53–3; Barwick 6–0–29–1; Lloyd 6–0–37–1; Ontong 6–0–52–1; Derrick 2–0–23–1.

Glamorgan

J. A. Hopkins c Stewart b Thomas	1	S. P. Henderson not out		4
A. L. Jones not out	77	L-b 4, w 2		6
Javed Miandad c Smith b Thomas	1			
R. C. Ontong c Smith b Clarke	29	1/4 2/30 3/112	(3 wkts, 12 overs)	118

C. J. C. Rowe, †T. Davies, J. Derrick, B. J. Lloyd, *M. W. W. Selvey and S. R. Barwick did not bat.

Bowling: Clarke 5–0–22–1; Thomas 3–0–40–2; Knight 3–0–27–0; Monkhouse 1–0–23–0.

Umpires: P. J. Eele and R. Palmer.

At Cheltenham, August 7. GLAMORGAN lost to GLOUCESTERSHIRE by five wickets.

GLAMORGAN v KENT

At Cardiff, August 14. Kent won by 61 runs. Toss won by Glamorgan.

Kent

N. R. Taylor c Miandad b Selvey	67	R. M. Ellison not out	1
M. R. Benson c Davies b Selvey	29	G. R. Dilley not out	9
D. G. Aslett c Lloyd b Selvey	5	B 5, l-b 11	16
*C. S. Cowdrey c A. L. Jones b Ontong	46		
E. A. E. Baptiste st Davies b Ontong	42	1/65 2/107 (7 wkts, 40 overs)	230
†A. P. E. Knott run out	1	3/107 4/180	
G. W. Johnson c A. L. Jones b Ontong	14	5/183 6/207 7/220	

D. L. Underwood and K. B. S. Jarvis did not bat.

Bowling: Wilkins 8–0–40–0; Ontong 8–0–35–3; Holmes 8–0–46–0; Lloyd 8–0–37–0; Selvey 8–1–56–3.

Glamorgan

A. L. Jones c Knott b Baptiste	20	†T. Davies not out	46
D. A. Francis b Dilley	3	B. J. Lloyd not out	22
R. C. Ontong c Knott b Dilley	3	L-b 8, w 8, n-b 4	20
Javed Miandad c Taylor b Baptiste	22		
C. J. C. Rowe b Ellison	14	1/21 2/29 (7 wkts, 40 overs)	169
S. P. Henderson c Taylor b Ellison	15	3/40 4/67	
G. C. Holmes b Underwood	4	5/83 6/95 7/95	

*M. W. W. Selvey and A. H. Wilkins did not bat.

Bowling: Jarvis 8–1–42–0; Dilley 8–0–25–2; Baptiste 8–0–26–2; Ellison 8–0–32–2; Underwood 8–1–24–1.

Umpires: R. Julian and M. J. Kitchen.

GLAMORGAN v DERBYSHIRE

At Swansea, August 21. Glamorgan won by 22 runs in a match reduced to 25 overs a side. Toss won by Derbyshire.

Glamorgan

J. A. Hopkins c Hill b Tunnicliffe	52	†T. Davies b Holding	1
A. L. Jones c Holding b Miller	36	B. J. Lloyd lbw b Holding	0
R. C. Ontong b Tunnicliffe	23	L-b 9, w 3, n-b 1	13
S. P. Henderson run out	19		
J. G. Thomas c Holding b Tunnicliffe	3	1/71 2/99 3/122 (7 wkts, 25 overs)	155
G. C. Holmes not out	8	4/134 5/152 6/154 7/155	

A. H. Wilkins, *M. W. W. Selvey and W. W. Davis did not bat.

Bowling: Holding 5–0–21–2; Mortensen 5–0–27–0; Finney 5–0–45–0; Miller 5–0–19–1; Tunnicliffe 5–0–30–3.

Derbyshire

*K. J. Barnett c Wilkins b Lloyd	13	†R. W. Taylor c Davies b Davis	0
I. S. Anderson run out	1	M. A. Holding b Davis	7
A. Hill run out	25	O. H. Mortensen not out	3
G. Miller c Lloyd b Selvey	27	L-b 16, w 3, n-b 3	22
J. E. Morris c Hopkins b Selvey	6		
R. J. Finney not out	21	1/3 2/33 3/50 (9 wkts, 25 overs)	133
W. P. Fowler c Hopkins b Selvey	5	4/83 5/83 6/94	
C. J. Tunnicliffe c Holmes b Davis	3	7/103 8/106 9/118	

Bowling: Lloyd 5–0–18–1; Selvey 5–0–34–3; Wilkins 5–0–19–0; Davis 5–0–23–3; Ontong 5–0–17–0.

Umpires: J. H. Harris and K. Ibadulla.

GLAMORGAN v WORCESTERSHIRE

At Cardiff, August 28. Glamorgan won by 83 runs. Toss won by Worcestershire.

Glamorgan

J. A. Hopkins c Humphries b Patel	37	G. C. Holmes not out	23
A. L. Jones c and b Inchmore	30	†T. Davies not out	17
R. C. Ontong st Humphries b Illingworth	14	B 6, l-b 15, w 9, n-b 4	34
C. J. C. Rowe st Humphries b Illingworth	35	1/70 2/91 (5 wkts, 40 overs)	216
S. P. Henderson c Humphries b Warner	26	3/121 4/149 5/183	

B. J. Lloyd, A. H. Wilkins, *M. W. W. Selvey and W. W. Davis did not bat.

Bowling: Warner 8–0–27–1; Pridgeon 8–0–37–0; Inchmore 8–0–42–1; Patel 6–0–24–1; Weston 2–0–12–0; Illingworth 7–0–27–2; D'Oliveira 1–0–13–0.

Worcestershire

M. J. Weston c Jones b Wilkins	5	J. D. Inchmore c Davis b Selvey	12
M. S. A. McEvoy c Davis b Ontong	0	R. K. Illingworth st Davies b Lloyd	0
D. N. Patel c Lloyd b Ontong	1	A. P. Pridgeon lbw b Ontong	12
*P. A. Neale c Holmes b Wilkins	8	B 1, l-b 8, w 1, n-b 1	11
D. B. D'Oliveira c Selvey b Wilkins	29		
T. S. Curtis not out	32	1/0 2/6 3/9 (35.4 overs)	133
†D. J. Humphries b Davis	20	4/33 5/50 6/82	
A. E. Warner c Davies b Davis	3	7/86 8/114 9/115	

Bowling: Ontong 5.4–0–17–3; Wilkins 8–1–13–3; Selvey 8–0–37–1; Davis 6–0–29–2; Lloyd 8–0–26–1.

Umpires: W. E. Alley and P. B. Wight.

At Bournemouth, September 11. GLAMORGAN lost to HAMPSHIRE by one wicket.

GLOUCESTERSHIRE

GLOUCESTERSHIRE v LEICESTERSHIRE

At Gloucester, May 15. No result.

At Worcester, May 22. WORCESTERSHIRE v GLOUCESTERSHIRE. No result.

GLOUCESTERSHIRE v SURREY

At Bristol, June 5. No result.

At Northampton, June 12. GLOUCESTERSHIRE lost to NORTHAMPTONSHIRE by 17 runs.

GLOUCESTERSHIRE v KENT

At Bristol, June 19. Kent won by 55 runs. Toss won by Gloucestershire.

Kent

L. Potter c Sainsbury b Graveney	21	C. Penn b Shepherd	2
N. R. Taylor lbw b Shepherd	15	D. L. Underwood not out	0
D. G. Aslett b Doughty	56	K. B. S. Jarvis not out	1
M. R. Benson c Sainsbury b Shepherd	65	B 2, l-b 6, w 3	11
*C. S. Cowdrey c Childs b Shepherd	66		
E. A. E. Baptiste c Childs b Shepherd	4	1/25 2/42 3/144	(9 wkts, 39 overs) 244
†A. P. E. Knott c Graveney b Shepherd	1	4/174 5/193 6/199	
R. M. Ellison run out	2	7/224 8/243 9/243	

Bowling: Shepherd 8–0–52–6; Sainsbury 6–1–29–0; Graveney 6–0–26–1; Bainbridge 8–0–42–0; Childs 6–0–44–0; Doughty 5–0–40–1.

Gloucestershire

A. W. Stovold b Ellison	15	†R. C. Russell c Knott b Ellison	3
P. Bainbridge c Potter b Penn	24	J. H. Childs b Jarvis	5
A. J. Hignell b Penn	16	G. E. Sainsbury not out	1
P. W. Romaines run out	20	L-b 10, w 3	13
J. N. Shepherd c and b Baptiste	3		
A. J. Wright run out	1	1/27 2/53 3/60	(9 wkts, 39 overs) 189
*D. A. Graveney b Penn	38	4/81 5/83 6/91	
R. J. Doughty not out	50	7/153 8/172 9/189	

Bowling: Jarvis 8–1–29–1; Ellison 8–0–49–2; Baptiste 8–0–28–1; Penn 7–0–38–3; Underwood 8–0–32–0.

Umpires: K. Ibadulla and N. T. Plews.

At Bath, June 26. GLOUCESTERSHIRE lost to SOMERSET by 16 runs.

At Lord's, July 3. GLOUCESTERSHIRE beat MIDDLESEX by six wickets.

GLOUCESTERSHIRE v DERBYSHIRE

At Bristol, July 10. Derbyshire won by three wickets. Toss won by Derbyshire.

Gloucestershire

A. W. Stovold c Tunnicliffe b Miller ...	27	*D. A. Graveney c Miller b Oldham ...	26
P. W. Romaines c and b Miller	28	†R. C. Russell not out	1
Zaheer Abbas c Hill b Oldham	21	L-b 10, w 2	12
A. J. Hignell not out	41		
P. Bainbridge st Taylor b Tunnicliffe..	13	1/50 2/73 3/88 (6 wkts, 40 overs) 174	
J. N. Shepherd b Mortensen	5	4/110 5/118 6/162	

J. H. Childs, G. E. Sainsbury and D. V. Lawrence did not bat.

Bowling: Finney 8–1–30–0; Mortensen 8–0–47–1; Miller 8–2–12–2; Tunnicliffe 8–0–23–1; Oldham 8–0–50–2.

Derbyshire

I. S. Anderson lbw b Shepherd	0	C. J. Tunnicliffe not out	13
*K. J. Barnett b Childs	10	†R. W. Taylor not out	10
A. Hill c and b Graveney	30	L-b 10, w 2, n-b 1	13
G. Miller c Bainbridge b Lawrence	52		
J. E. Morris b Lawrence	22	1/0 2/32 (7 wkts, 39.5 overs) 176	
R. J. Finney c Romaines b Bainbridge.	2	3/66 4/115	
W. P. Fowler b Shepherd	24	5/122 6/136 7/156	

O. H. Mortensen and S. Oldham did not bat.

Bowling: Shepherd 8–0–29–2; Lawrence 8–0–26–2; Childs 5–0–21–1; Graveney 8–0–30–1; Sainsbury 7.5–0–39–0; Bainbridge 3–0–18–1.

Umpires: J. Birkenshaw and R. Julian.

GLOUCESTERSHIRE v WARWICKSHIRE

At Moreton-in-Marsh, July 17. Gloucestershire won by six wickets. Toss won by Gloucestershire.

Warwickshire

T. A. Lloyd c Lawrence b Shepherd....	15	D. A. Thorne c Stovold b Lawrence....	42
D. L. Amiss c Hignell b Childs	31	C. Lethbridge not out	8
A. I. Kallicharran c Hignell b Childs...	1	*N. Gifford not out........................	5
†G. W. Humpage b Childs	10	L-b 14, w 4, n-b 2	20
C. M. Old b Shepherd	5		
Asif Din c Romaines b Bainbridge	2	1/47 2/50 3/61 (9 wkts, 40 overs) 174	
A. M. Ferreira lbw b Shepherd	0	4/66 5/70 6/71	
P. A. Smith c Romaines b Lawrence ...	35	7/82 8/143 9/167	

Bowling: Lawrence 7–0–41–2; Sainsbury 7–0–31–0; Shepherd 8–0–24–3; Childs 8–5–11–3; Bainbridge 5–0–18–1; Graveney 5–0–29–0.

Gloucestershire

A. W. Stovold lbw b Gifford	30	J. N. Shepherd not out	11
P. W. Romaines c Humpage b Smith...	57	L-b 5, n-b 2	7
Zaheer Abbas not out	64		
A. J. Hignell c Humpage b Old..........	6	1/73 2/120 (4 wkts, 34.3 overs) 178	
P. Bainbridge run out	3	3/148 4/151	

*D. A. Graveney, †R. C. Russell, J. H. Childs, G. E. Sainsbury and D. V. Lawrence did not bat.

Bowling: Old 7–0–36–1; Thorne 4–0–32–0; Ferreira 8–0–19–0; Gifford 6–0–31–1; Lethbridge 7.3–0–34–0; Smith 2–0–19–1.

Umpires: B. Leadbeater and D. O. Oslear.

At Bournemouth, July 31. GLOUCESTERSHIRE beat HAMPSHIRE by eight wickets.

GLOUCESTERSHIRE v GLAMORGAN

At Cheltenham, August 7. Gloucestershire won by five wickets. Toss won by Gloucestershire.

Glamorgan

J. A. Hopkins c Broad b Shepherd	2	J. Derrick b Shepherd	4
A. L. Jones c Broad b Sainsbury	6	†T. Davies not out	2
R. C. Ontong st Russell b Graveney	27	B 5, l-b 8, w 2	15
Javed Miandad c Russell b Sainsbury	81		
C. J. C. Rowe st Russell b Graveney	2	1/7 2/13 3/72 (7 wkts, 40 overs) 187	
S. P. Henderson c and b Shepherd	48	4/78 5/165 6/182 7/187	

B. J. Lloyd, *M. W. W. Selvey and S. R. Barwick did not bat.

Bowling: Sainsbury 8–1–29–2; Shepherd 8–0–40–3; Childs 8–1–35–0; Graveney 8–0–37–2; Bainbridge 8–0–31–0.

Gloucestershire

A. W. Stovold st Davies b Rowe	29	J. N. Shepherd not out	13
B. C. Broad c Davies b Ontong	1		
Zaheer Abbas c Miandad b Ontong	80	L-b 5, w 4	9
P. W. Romaines c Davies b Rowe	24		
A. J. Hignell c Davies b Barwick	13	1/5 2/67 (5 wkts, 38.4 overs) 190	
P. Bainbridge not out	21	3/115 4/148 5/153	

*D. A. Graveney, †R. C. Russell, J. H. Childs and G. E. Sainsbury did not bat.

Bowling: Barwick 6.4–0–43–1; Ontong 7–0–30–2; Selvey 8–0–37–0; Rowe 8–1–42–2; Lloyd 8–1–20–0; Derrick 1–0–9–0.

Umpires: J. Birkenshaw and J. W. Holder.

GLOUCESTERSHIRE v YORKSHIRE

At Cheltenham, August 14. Yorkshire won by four wickets. Toss won by Yorkshire.

Gloucestershire

A. W. Stovold c and b Illingworth	47	P. Bainbridge not out	4
B. C. Broad b Dennis	96		
Zaheer Abbas c Hartley b Illingworth	8	L-b 4, w 1	5
P. W. Romaines c Athey b Dennis	36		
A. J. Hignell c Boycott b Dennis	26	1/80 2/98 (5 wkts, 40 overs) 233	
J. N. Shepherd not out	11	3/178 4/211 5/222	

*D. A. Graveney, †R. C. Russell, J. H. Childs and G. E. Sainsbury did not bat.

Bowling: Dennis 8–0–49–3; Boycott 8–0–38–0; Carrick 8–0–61–0; Illingworth 8–0–30–2; Stevenson 8–1–50–0.

Yorkshire

G. Boycott c and b Graveney	39	†D. L. Bairstow not out	18
C. W. J. Athey c Graveney b Bainbridge	42	P. Carrick not out	10
K. Sharp c Russell b Sainsbury	53	B 9, l-b 21, w 2	32
G. B. Stevenson st Russell b Graveney	18		
S. N. Hartley c Hignell b Zaheer	6	1/85 2/90 3/122 (6 wkts, 39.1 overs) 234	
J. D. Love run out	16	4/170 5/196 6/201	

M. D. Moxon, *R. Illingworth and S. J. Dennis did not bat.

Bowling: Sainsbury 8–0–32–1; Shepherd 7.1–0–43–0; Graveney 8–2–21–2; Childs 6–0–49–0; Bainbridge 8–0–46–1; Zaheer 2–0–11–1.

Umpires: B. J. Meyer and J. H. Harris.

At Colchester, August 21. GLOUCESTERSHIRE lost to ESSEX by 13 runs.

GLOUCESTERSHIRE v LANCASHIRE

At Bristol, August 28. Lancashire won by seven wickets. Toss won by Lancashire.

Gloucestershire

P. W. Romaines run out	31	R. J. Doughty b Watkinson	13
B. C. Broad c Chadwick b Abrahams	81	†R. C. Russell not out	9
P. Bainbridge b Watkinson	6		
A. J. Wright run out	1	L-b 6, w 1	7
A. J. Hignell c Stanworth b Allott	32		
E. J. Cunningham c Watkinson b Lloyd	4	1/43 2/68 (8 wkts, 40 overs) 187	
*J. N. Shepherd c Chadwick		3/71 4/141 5/151	
b Watkinson	3	6/161 7/164 8/187	

J. H. Childs and G. E. Sainsbury did not bat.

Bowling: Allott 8–0–40–1; Watkinson 8–0–34–3; O'Shaughnessy 8–0–41–0; Simmons 8–0–21–0; Abrahams 7–0–42–1; Lloyd 1–0–2–1.

Lancashire

G. Fowler lbw b Shepherd	18	J. Abrahams not out	65
M. R. Chadwick lbw b Shepherd	10	B 4, l-b 5, w 6	15
F. C. Hayes c sub b Shepherd	2		
*C. H. Lloyd not out	81	1/27 2/33 3/34 (3 wkts, 37.1 overs) 191	

S. J. O'Shaughnessy, †J. Stanworth, J. Simmons, M. Watkinson, N. H. Fairbrother and P. J. W. Allott did not bat.

Bowling: Sainsbury 7–0–33–0; Shepherd 8–1–18–3; Cunningham 8–0–35–0; Doughty 8–0–57–0; Childs 6.1–1–33–0.

Umpires: K. E. Palmer and R. Palmer.

At Hove, September 4. GLOUCESTERSHIRE lost to SUSSEX by seven wickets.

At Nottingham, September 11. NOTTINGHAMSHIRE v GLOUCESTERSHIRE. No result.

HAMPSHIRE

HAMPSHIRE v ESSEX

At Southampton, May 8. Hampshire won by 15 runs. Toss won by Essex.

Hampshire

V. P. Terry lbw b Phillip	2	M. D. Marshall not out	25
D. R. Turner c Lever b R. E. East	30	J. W. Southern not out	15
M. C. J. Nicholas c D. E. East b Lever	2	L-b 6, w 1, n-b 1	8
T. E. Jesty c R. E. East b Lever	100		
*N. E. J. Pocock b Turner	17	1/5 2/14 3/93 (6 wkts, 40 overs) 214	
N. G. Cowley c McEwan b Phillip	15	4/146 5/164 6/181	

T. M. Tremlett, †R. J. Parks and S. J. Malone did not bat.

Bowling: Lever 8–2–24–2; Phillip 8–0–53–2; Gooch 8–1–43–0; Turner 8–1–48–1; R. E. East 8–0–38–1.

Essex

G. A. Gooch c Nicholas b Malone	14	S. Turner c Pocock b Marshall	25
B. R. Hardie c and b Nicholas	51	†D. E. East not out	14
K. S. McEwan c Terry b Jesty	8	R. E. East not out	7
*K. W. R. Fletcher c and b Cowley	37	B 1, l-b 13, w 3	17
N. Phillip c Jesty b Cowley	1		
K. R. Pont c Cowley b Marshall	17	1/14 2/45 3/122 (8 wkts, 40 overs) 199	
A. W. Lilley lbw b Nicholas	8	4/124 5/124 6/135 7/176 8/176	

J. K. Lever did not bat.

Bowling: Marshall 8–2–22–2; Malone 4–0–21–1; Tremlett 5–0–34–0; Jesty 8–0–24–1; Cowley 8–0–38–2; Nicholas 7–0–43–2.

Umpires: D. J. Constant and A. G. T. Whitehead.

At Lord's, May 15. MIDDLESEX v HAMPSHIRE. No result.

HAMPSHIRE v NORTHAMPTONSHIRE

At Bournemouth, May 22. Hampshire won by seven wickets. Toss won by Northamptonshire.

Northamptonshire

W. Larkins c Cowley b Malone	30	†G. Sharp not out	7
P. Willey c Turner b Nicholas	67	T. M. Lamb not out	4
A. J. Lamb c Parks b Cowley	11	L-b 2, w 6	8
Kapil Dev c Greenidge b Jesty	1		
*G. Cook lbw b Nicholas	40	1/51 2/64 (7 wkts, 40 overs) 172	
R. G. Williams c Parks b Tremlett	0	3/68 4/145	
D. J. Capel b Tremlett	4	5/148 6/155 7/163	

N. A. Mallender and B. J. Griffiths did not bat.

Bowling: Marshall 8–0–17–0; Malone 8–0–36–1; Tremlett 8–0–31–2; Cowley 8–1–30–1; Jesty 4–1–19–1; Nicholas 4–0–31–2.

Hampshire

C. G. Greenidge b T. M. Lamb	34	M. C. J. Nicholas not out		10
C. L. Smith b Williams	44	L-b 9, w 1, n-b 2		12
D. R. Turner not out	56			
T. E. Jesty c Sharp b Griffiths	17	1/46 2/112 3/147	(3 wkts, 38 overs)	173

*N. E. J. Pocock, M. D. Marshall, N. G. Cowley, †R. J. Parks, T. M. Tremlett and S. J. Malone did not bat.

Bowling: Kapil Dev 4–0–11–0; Griffiths 7–1–38–1; Willey 8–0–24–0; T. M. Lamb 8–0–40–1; Mallender 4–0–15–0; Williams 7–1–33–1.

Umpires: C. Cook and P. B. Wight.

At Canterbury, May 29. HAMPSHIRE lost to KENT by 65 runs.

At Middlesbrough, June 5. HAMPSHIRE lost to YORKSHIRE by six wickets.

HAMPSHIRE v LEICESTERSHIRE

At Basingstoke, June 19. Hampshire won by nine wickets. Toss won by Leicestershire.

Leicestershire

I. P. Butcher b Nicholas	59	J. F. Steele not out		6
N. E. Briers b Nicholas	34	G. J. Parsons c Parks b Malone		0
B. F. Davison c Hardy b Nicholas	9	N. G. B. Cook not out		0
†M. A. Garnham c Hardy b Tremlett	10	L-b 8, n-b 1		9
*R. W. Tolchard c Parks b Malone	36			
P. B. Clift lbw b Stevenson	12	1/81 2/97 3/108	(8 wkts, 40 overs)	179
T. J. Boon run out	4	4/122 5/143 6/165 7/178 8/178		

L. B. Taylor did not bat.

Bowling: Stevenson 8–0–37–1; Malone 8–0–43–2; Cowley 8–0–34–0; Tremlett 8–3–24–1; Nicholas 8–0–32–3.

Hampshire

V. P. Terry not out	100			
C. L. Smith b Clift	55			
R. A. Smith not out	22			
L-b 2, w 1	3			
1/123	(1 wkt, 37.2 overs) 180			

M. C. J. Nicholas, J. J. E. Hardy, *N. E. J. Pocock, N. G. Cowley, T. M. Tremlett, †R. J. Parks, S. J. Malone and K. Stevenson did not bat.

Bowling: Taylor 7–2–28–0; Parsons 7–1–19–0; Clift 8–0–25–1; Cook 7.2–1–37–0; Steele 8–0–68–0.

Umpires: J. H. Harris and J. van Geloven.

At Birmingham, June 26. HAMPSHIRE lost to WARWICKSHIRE by 6 runs.

At Manchester, July 3. HAMPSHIRE beat LANCASHIRE by 58 runs.

HAMPSHIRE v SURREY

At Portsmouth, July 10. Hampshire won by 104 runs. Toss won by Surrey.

Hampshire
C. G. Greenidge not out 108
C. L. Smith b Thomas 5
T. E. Jesty not out 166
    L-b 5, w 1, n-b 7 13

1/23   (1 wkt, 40 overs) 292

V. P. Terry, M. C. J. Nicholas, *N. E. J. Pocock, N. G. Cowley, M. D. Marshall, T. M. Tremlett, †R. J. Parks and S. J. Malone did not bat.

Bowling: Thomas 7–0–47–1; Feltham 8–0–61–0; Knight 8–0–31–0; Clarke 8–0–57–0; Pocock 4–0–37–0; Payne 5–0–46–0.

Surrey
A. R. Butcher c Greenidge b Cowley .. 65
†C. J. Richards b Cowley 43
D. M. Smith st Parks b Cowley 20
M. A. Lynch c Terry b Malone 33
D. J. Thomas b Cowley 0
*R. D. V. Knight not out 11
I. R. Payne not out 5
    L-b 5, w 4, n-b 2 11

1/82 2/126 3/146   (5 wkts, 40 overs) 188
4/146 5/175

A. J. Stewart, S. T. Clarke, M. A. Feltham and P. I. Pocock did not bat.

Bowling: Marshall 7–2–14–0; Malone 7–0–26–1; Tremlett 8–0–39–0; Nicholas 8–0–51–0; Cowley 8–1–42–4; Greenidge 1–0–4–0; Pocock 1–0–1–0.

Umpires: M. J. Kitchen and N. T. Plews.

HAMPSHIRE v NOTTINGHAMSHIRE

At Portsmouth, July 17. Hampshire won by 56 runs. Toss won by Hampshire.

Hampshire
C. G. Greenidge c French b Hemmings . 80
C. L. Smith b Illingworth 43
T. E. Jesty c Birch b Hemmings 39
V. P. Terry c Bore b Saxelby 37
M. C. J. Nicholas b Pick 3
*N. E. J. Pocock c Fell b Saxelby 5
M. D. Marshall not out 27
N. G. Cowley not out 0
    L-b 8 8

1/89 2/141 3/172   (6 wkts, 40 overs) 242
4/176 5/189 6/239

T. M. Tremlett, †R. J. Parks and S. J. Malone did not bat.

Bowling: Saxelby 8–0–46–2; Bore 8–0–28–0; Pick 8–0–56–1; Illingworth 8–0–55–1; Hemmings 8–0–49–2.

Nottinghamshire
B. Hassan c Cowley b Jesty 39
R. T. Robinson b Malone 74
*C. E. B. Rice run out 11
J. D. Birch run out 12
M. A. Fell c Parks b Malone 5
E. E. Hemmings c Jesty b Malone 3
†B. N. French not out 17
K. Saxelby not out 5
    L-b 10, w 8, n-b 2 20

1/76 2/109 3/138   (6 wkts, 40 overs) 186
4/152 5/157 6/163

N. J. B. Illingworth, M. K. Bore and R. A. Pick did not bat.

Bowling: Malone 8–0–29–3; Marshall 6–0–15–0; Tremlett 8–0–35–0; Jesty 8–1–31–1; Cowley 8–0–49–0; Nicholas 2–0–7–0.

Umpires: J. Birkenshaw and C. T. Spencer.

At Taunton, July 24. HAMPSHIRE lost to SOMERSET by seven wickets.

HAMPSHIRE v GLOUCESTERSHIRE

At Bournemouth, July 31. Gloucestershire won by eight wickets in a match reduced by rain to twenty overs a side. Toss won by Hampshire.

Hampshire

C. G. Greenidge not out	....	52
C. L. Smith c Shepherd b Lawrence	....	56
T. E. Jesty c Broad b Lawrence	....	23
V. P. Terry not out	....	0
B 2, l-b 7, w 5	....	14

1/104 2/144   (2 wkts, 20 overs) 145

M. C. J. Nicholas, *N. E. J. Pocock, N. G. Cowley, M. D. Marshall, T. M. Tremlett, †R. J. Parks and S. J. Malone did not bat.

Bowling: Lawrence 7–0–54–2; Sainsbury 6–0–36–0; Shepherd 7-1-41–0.

Gloucestershire

B. C. Broad b Marshall	....	33
P. W. Romaines not out	....	80
Zaheer Abbas b Tremlett	....	1
A. J. Hignell not out	....	20
B 6, l-b 3, w 5	....	14

1/73 2/86   (2 wkts, 19.3 overs) 148

P. Bainbridge, J. N. Shepherd, *D. A. Graveney, †R. C. Russell, J. H. Childs, G. E. Sainsbury and D. V. Lawrence did not bat.

Bowling: Tremlett 8–0–63–1; Malone 4–0–36–0; Marshall 7.3–0–35–1.

Umpires: W. E. Alley and K. E. Palmer.

At Worcester, August 21. HAMPSHIRE beat WORCESTERSHIRE on faster scoring-rate.

HAMPSHIRE v SUSSEX

At Southampton, August 28. Hampshire won by four wickets. Toss won by Sussex.

Sussex

G. D. Mendis lbw b Malone	2
†I. J. Gould c Parks b Marshall	2
C. M. Wells c Pocock b Malone	6
Imran Khan c Terry b Malone	90
P. W. G. Parker c Marshall b Jesty	24
A. P. Wells c Parks b Marshall	38
I. A. Greig b Malone	4

C. P. Phillipson c Parks b Marshall	0
*J. R. T. Barclay not out	9
A. C. S. Pigott not out	3
L-b 6, w 8, n-b 1	15
	—
1/4 2/4 3/22 4/77 (8 wkts, 40 overs)	193
5/153 6/162 7/163 8/185	

D. A. Reeve did not bat.

Bowling: Malone 8–0–56–4; Marshall 8–2–19–3; Tremlett 8–0–28–0; Jesty 8–0–34–1; Cowley 8–0–41–0.

Hampshire

C. G. Greenidge c Gould b Reeve	15
V. P. Terry run out	26
T. E. Jesty b Imran	9
M. C. J. Nicholas run out	27
D. R. Turner not out	53
*N. E. J. Pocock lbw b Imran	4

M. D. Marshall lbw b Pigott	35
N. G. Cowley not out	5
B 2, l-b 10, w 8	20
	—
1/32 2/43 3/70 (6 wkts, 37.2 overs)	194
4/103 5/109 6/180	

T. M. Tremlett, †R. J. Parks and S. J. Malone did not bat.

Bowling: C. M. Wells 6.2–0–24–0; Reeve 8–0–45–1; Imran 8–0–37–2; Barclay 8–2–31–0; Pigott 7–0–37–1.

Umpires: J. Birkenshaw and K. Ibadulla.

At Derby, September 4. HAMPSHIRE lost to DERBYSHIRE by 8 runs.

HAMPSHIRE v GLAMORGAN

At Bournemouth, September 11. Hampshire won by one wicket. Toss won by Glamorgan.

Glamorgan

J. A. Hopkins c Parks b Cowley	13
A. Jones c Parks b Tremlett	12
A. L. Jones c Cowley b Jesty	45
S. P. Henderson b Cowley	0
C. J. C. Rowe c Greenidge b Jesty	22
D. A. Francis c Jesty b Malone	18
†T. Davies b Nicholas	7
B. J. Lloyd b Tremlett	12

A. H. Wilkins b Tremlett	5
*M. W. W. Selvey not out	5
W. W. Davis not out	2
B 2, l-b 10, w 5	17
	—
1/21 2/36 3/36 (9 wkts, 40 overs)	158
4/102 5/111 6/121	
7/141 8/151 9/151	

Bowling: Malone 6–0–19–1; Tremlett 8–0–25–3; Stevenson 6–0–26–0; Cowley 8–1–27–2; Nicholas 8–0–29–1; Jesty 4–0–15–2.

Hampshire

C. G. Greenidge b Selvey	33	†R. J. Parks not out		23
C. L. Smith b Selvey	10	K. Stevenson run out		1
*T. E. Jesty run out	3	S. J. Malone not out		8
V. P. Terry st Davies b Lloyd	7	B 4, l-b 13, w 5		22
D. R. Turner run out	18			
M. C. J. Nicholas b Lloyd	2	1/44 2/49 3/50	(9 wkts, 38.4 overs)	161
N. G. Cowley c Selvey b Rowe	34	4/64 5/76 6/89		
T. M. Tremlett run out	0	7/97 8/131 9/145		

Bowling: Davis 6–1–23–0; Wilkins 8–1–32–0; Selvey 8–1–24–2; Lloyd 8–3–14–2; Rowe 7–1–29–1; Henderson 1.4–0–17–0.

Umpires: D. J. Constant and D. R. Shepherd.

KENT

KENT v SURREY

At Canterbury, May 8. Kent won on faster scoring-rate, Surrey's target, after weather interference, having been reduced to 194 off 27 overs. Toss won by Surrey.

Kent

R. A. Woolmer c Payne b Thomas	19	G. W. Johnson c Knight b Monkhouse		7
N. R. Taylor c Clarke b Knight	36	R. M. Ellison not out		0
*C. J. Tavaré c Pocock b Thomas	82	B 1, l-b 7, n-b 1		9
M. R. Benson b Pocock	9			
C. S. Cowdrey not out	38	1/24 2/138 3/150	(6 wkts, 29 overs)	208
†A. P. E. Knott b Monkhouse	8	4/158 5/167 6/207		

G. R. Dilley, D. L. Underwood and K. B. S. Jarvis did not bat.

Bowling: Thomas 7–1–34–2; Monkhouse 6–0–40–2; Clarke 4–0–19–0; Knight 4–0–38–1; Payne 2–0–24–0; Pocock 6–0–44–1.

Surrey

A. R. Butcher c Woolmer b Dilley	14	I. R. Payne c Benson b Underwood		9
†C. J. Richards run out	6	G. Monkhouse not out		3
M. A. Lynch c Johnson b Woolmer	16	P. I. Pocock c Woolmer b Underwood		2
D. J. Thomas lbw b Jarvis	4	L-b 7, w 1, n-b 1		9
*R. D. V. Knight b Woolmer	9			
G. P. Howarth c Tavaré b Underwood	4	1/21 2/21 3/34	(20.4 overs)	80
G. S. Clinton c Jarvis b Underwood	4	4/54 5/55 6/60		
S. T. Clarke b Underwood	0	7/63 8/68 9/76		

Bowling: Dilley 5–1–22–1; Jarvis 5–0–24–1; Underwood 5.4–1–14–5; Woolmer 5–0–11–2.

Umpires: C. Cook and C. T. Spencer.

At Hove, May 15. SUSSEX v KENT. No result.

At Leicester, May 22. LEICESTERSHIRE v KENT. No result.

KENT v HAMPSHIRE

At Canterbury, May 29. Kent won by 65 runs, Ellison finishing off the Hampshire innings with a hat-trick. Toss won by Hampshire.

Kent
R. A. Woolmer b Nicholas	26	G. W. Johnson st Parks b Jesty		13
N. R. Taylor c Parks b Nicholas	32	R. M. Ellison not out		1
*C. J. Tavaré c Greenidge b Jesty	67	L-b 4, w 2, n-b 1		7
M. R. Benson c Parks b Nicholas	3			
C. S. Cowdrey c Tremlett b Jesty	17	1/56 2/61 3/66	(7 wkts, 40 overs)	198
†A. P. E. Knott c Parks b Malone	32	4/102 5/164 6/197 7/198		

G. R. Dilley, D. L. Underwood and K. B. S. Jarvis did not bat.

Bowling: Marshall 8–0–18–0; Malone 8–1–54–1; Tremlett 8–0–33–0; Nicholas 8–1–30–3; Jesty 6–0–37–3; Cowley 2–0–19–0.

Hampshire
C. G. Greenidge c Knott b Jarvis	22	N. G. Cowley c Johnson b Underwood		6
C. L. Smith c Knott b Underwood	31	T. M. Tremlett b Ellison		9
D. R. Turner b Ellison	3	†R. J. Parks c Knott b Ellison		0
T. E. Jesty c Johnson b Woolmer	4	S. J. Malone c Knott b Ellison		0
M. C. J. Nicholas c and b Cowdrey	7	L-b 3, w 2, n-b 3		8
*N. E. J. Pocock c Johnson				
b Underwood	16	1/44 2/53 3/61 4/65	(33.4 overs)	133
M. D. Marshall not out	27	5/86 6/98 7/110 8/133 9/133		

Bowling: Dilley 5–0–22–0; Jarvis 6–1–22–1; Ellison 4.4–0–15–4; Woolmer 4–1–11–1; Underwood 8–0–28–3; Cowdrey 6–0–27–1.

Umpires: K. Ibadulla and A. G. T. Whitehead.

At Chelmsford, June 12. KENT lost to ESSEX by 53 runs.

At Bristol, June 19. KENT beat GLOUCESTERSHIRE by 55 runs.

KENT v NOTTINGHAMSHIRE

At Canterbury, June 26. Kent won by 49 runs. Toss won by Kent.

Kent
R. A. Woolmer c sub b Saxelby	50	E. A. E. Baptiste not out		1
M. R. Benson b Hemmings	43	B 3, l-b 10, w 2, n-b 2		17
*C. J. Tavaré c and b Cooper	70			
D. G. Aslett b Hendrick	51	1/93 2/116	(4 wkts, 40 overs)	270
C. S. Cowdrey not out	38	3/210 4/261		

G. W. Johnson, †A. P. E. Knott, R. M. Ellison, G. R. Dilley and D. L. Underwood did not bat.

Bowling: Hendrick 8–1–59–1; Bore 8–0–48–0; Cooper 8–1–64–1; Hemmings 8–0–37–1; Saxelby 8–1–45–1.

Nottinghamshire

R. T. Robinson b Johnson	51	K. E. Cooper b Underwood	4	
B. Hassan c Aslett b Dilley	0	M. K. Bore b Baptiste	1	
*C. E. B. Rice b Underwood	97	M. Hendrick not out	4	
D. W. Randall lbw b Johnson	10	L-b 18, w 3, n-b 8	29	
J. D. Birch b Underwood	10			
†B. N. French run out	5	1/2 2/132 3/148 (9 wkts, 40 overs) 221		
K. Saxelby b Dilley	0	4/184 5/189 6/190		
E. E. Hemmings not out	10	7/203 8/210 9/216		

Bowling: Dilley 8–1–15–2; Ellison 5–0–23–0; Baptiste 5–0–30–1; Woolmer 6–0–38–0; Johnson 8–0–50–2; Underwood 8–0–36–3.

Umpires: D. G. L. Evans and K. E. Palmer.

KENT v LANCASHIRE

At Maidstone, July 10. Kent won by 63 runs. Toss won by Lancashire.

Kent

R. A. Woolmer b Watkinson	31	G. W. Johnson c O'Shaughnessy		
M. R. Benson run out	45	b Watkinson	3	
*C. J. Tavaré not out	59	R. M. Ellison not out	1	
D. G. Aslett b Simmons	38			
C. S. Cowdrey c Maynard b Allott	7	B 1, l-b 5, w 1, n-b 1	8	
E. A. E. Baptiste c Abrahams				
b Watkinson	24	1/58 2/99 3/152 (7 wkts, 40 overs) 217		
†A. P. E. Knott c and b Allott	1	4/166 5/201 6/203 7/206		

D. L. Underwood and G. R. Dilley did not bat.

Bowling: Allott 8–1–41–2; McFarlane 8–1–34–0; Watkinson 8–1–49–3; O'Shaughnessy 7–0–44–0; Simmons 8–0–31–1; Abrahams 1–0–10–0.

Lancashire

G. Fowler run out	42	M. Watkinson st Knott b Underwood	2	
F. C. Hayes c Knott b Dilley	0	P. J. W. Allott not out	1	
*J. Abrahams c Baptiste b Underwood	21	L. L. McFarlane b Underwood	0	
D. P. Hughes c Baptiste b Underwood	22	L-b 4, w 2, n-b 6	12	
†C. Maynard c Benson b Underwood	8			
N. R. Fairbrother run out	25	1/2 2/67 3/79 (39.5 overs) 154		
J. Simmons c Aslett b Baptiste	14	4/88 5/106 6/140		
S. J. O'Shaughnessy b Baptiste	7	7/150 8/150 9/154		

Bowling: Dilley 8–1–25–1; Baptiste 8–1–19–2; Ellison 6–0–18–0; Woolmer 4–0–26–0; Underwood 7.5–1–31–5; Cowdrey 6–0–23–0.

Umpires: D. J. Constant and R. A. White.

At Scarborough, July 17. YORKSHIRE v KENT. No result.

KENT v MIDDLESEX

At Canterbury, July 24. Middlesex won by 56 runs. Toss won by Kent.

Middlesex

C. T. Radley c Aslett b Underwood	31	J. E. Embury not out......................	21
W. N. Slack b Woolmer...................	35	L-b 12, w 2, n-b 1	15
*M. W. Gatting c Johnson b Dilley.....	69		
R. G. P. Ellis c Baptiste b Underwood..	1	1/70 2/74 3/85 (5 wkts, 40 overs)	227
K. P. Tomlins lbw b Ellison...............	55	4/167 5/227	

†P. R. Downton, P. H. Edmonds, K. D. James, W. W. Daniel and N. G. Cowans did not bat.

Bowling: Dilley 8–0–39–1; Ellison 8–0–33–1; Baptiste 8–0–44–0; Woolmer 8–1–33–1; Underwood 8–0–63–2.

Kent

R. A. Woolmer c Gatting b James......	20	G. R. Dilley b Slack	4
M. R. Benson c James b Emburey......	59	R. M. Ellison not out	2
*C. J. Tavaré c Downton b James.......	20	D. L. Underwood st Downton b Radley.	3
D. G. Aslett c and b Edmonds...........	19	B 1, l-b 5, w 1..................	7
C. S. Cowdrey c Cowans b Emburey ...	4		
E. A. E. Baptiste b Emburey.............	4	1/40 2/73 3/122 (38.4 overs)	171
†A. P. E. Knott c Slack b Daniel........	21	4/124 5/128 6/134	
G. W. Johnson b Daniel..................	8	7/156 8/165 9/166	

Bowling: James 8–0–29–2; Cowans 2–0–15–0; Daniel 6–0–26–2; Edmonds 8–1–38–1; Emburey 8–1–26–3; Slack 6–0–28–1; Radley 0.4–0–2–1.

Umpires: J. Birkenshaw and R. Palmer.

At Chesterfield, July 31. DERBYSHIRE v KENT. No result.

KENT v WORCESTERSHIRE

At Canterbury, August 7. Kent won by 108 runs. Toss won by Worcestershire.

Kent

R. A. Woolmer st Humphries b Patel..	22	G. W. Johnson b Ellcock	9
M. R. Benson c Humphries b Ellcock..	3	R. M. Ellison b Ellcock	0
*C. J. Tavaré c and b Patel	16	D. L. Underwood not out	0
D. G. Aslett st Humphries b Patel......	16	L-b 10, w 7...........................	17
C. S. Cowdrey c Pridgeon b Ellcock ...	95		
E. A. E. Baptiste b Pridgeon	27	1/20 2/47 3/50 (8 wkts, 40 overs)	228
†A. P. E. Knott not out....................	23	4/101 5/191 6/195 7/216 8/216	

K. B. S. Jarvis did not bat.

Bowling: Ellcock 8–0–43–4; Pridgeon 8–0–54–1; Inchmore 5–0–34–0; Illingworth 8–1–25–0; Patel 8–1–35–3; D'Oliveira 3–0–20–0.

Worcestershire

D. N. Patel c Woolmer b Ellison	15	R. K. Illingworth not out	11
S. G. Watkins c Knott b Woolmer	24	R. M. Ellcock c Knott b Jarvis	0
*P. A. Neale b Baptiste	11	A. P. Pridgeon b Jarvis	0
D. B. D'Oliveira lbw b Baptiste	1	L-b 4	4
M. J. Weston c Knott b Baptiste	5		
T. S. Curtis c Baptiste b Underwood	12	1/33 2/49 3/52 (32.4 overs) 120	
†D. J. Humphries c Jarvis b Baptiste	24	4/58 5/59 6/94	
J. D. Inchmore c Knott b Jarvis	13	7/99 8/114 9/114	

Bowling: Jarvis 5.4–0–20–3; Ellison 5–0–15–1; Woolmer 8–1–30–1; Baptiste 8–0–29–4; Underwood 6–0–22–1.

Umpires: H. D. Bird and J. H. Harris.

At Cardiff, August 14. KENT beat GLAMORGAN by 61 runs.

KENT v WARWICKSHIRE

At Folkestone, August 21. Kent won by 58 runs. Toss won by Kent.

Kent

N. R. Taylor c Humpage b Willis	0	†A. P. E. Knott not out	7
M. R. Benson c Amiss b Thorne	23		
*C. J. Tavaré not out	122	L-b 12, w 3, n-b 11	26
D. G. Aslett b Old	77		
C. S. Cowdrey b Willis	13	1/0 2/38 (5 wkts, 40 overs) 281	
E. A. E. Baptiste run out	13	3/208 4/241 5/272	

G. W. Johnson, R. M. Ellison, G. R. Dilley and D. L. Underwood did not bat.

Bowling: Willis 8–0–58–2; Old 8–0–58–1; Lethbridge 8–0–35–0; Thorne 8–1–37–1; Gifford 8–0–67–0.

Warwickshire

D. L. Amiss c Ellison b Cowdrey	17	D. A. Thorne run out	14
T. A. Lloyd c Baptiste b Underwood	62	C. Lethbridge lbw b Ellison	0
A. I. Kallicharran c Benson b Baptiste	8	N. Gifford not out	8
†G. W. Humpage c Johnson b Underwood	32	*R. G. D. Willis c Dilley b Ellison	7
C. M. Old c Dilley b Baptiste	10	B 2, l-b 11, w 5	18
R. I. H. B. Dyer run out	27		
Asif Din c Benson b Baptiste	20	1/48 2/68 3/114 4/140 (37.2 overs) 223	
		5/142 6/180 7/204 8/205 9/208	

Bowling: Dilley 7–0–30–0; Ellison 6.2–0–34–2; Cowdrey 8–0–39–1; Baptiste 8–0–52–3; Underwood 8–0–50–2.

Umpires: D. G. L. Evans and P. B. Wight.

At Taunton, August 28. KENT lost to SOMERSET by six wickets.

KENT v NORTHAMPTONSHIRE

At Canterbury, September 11. No result.

LANCASHIRE

LANCASHIRE v DERBYSHIRE

At Manchester, May 8. No result.

At Chelmsford, May 15. ESSEX v LANCASHIRE. No result.

At Birmingham, May 22. WARWICKSHIRE v LANCASHIRE. No result.

At Swansea, May 29. LANCASHIRE lost to GLAMORGAN by 21 runs.

LANCASHIRE v NORTHAMPTONSHIRE

At Manchester, June 5. Lancashire won by eight wickets. Toss won by Lancashire.

Northamptonshire

P. Willey b O'Shaughnessy	39	†G. Sharp run out 0
W. Larkins c Maynard b Allott	1	T. M. Lamb not out 13
A. J. Lamb c Lloyd b Allott	4	L-b 9, w 1 10
*G. Cook st Maynard b Simmons	26	
R. G. Williams b Watkinson	16	1/5 2/15 (7 wkts, 40 overs) 130
D. J. Capel c O'Shaughnessy b Simmons	1	3/65 4/81
D. J. Wild not out	20	5/82 6/105 7/107

B. J. Griffiths and J. A. Carse did not bat.

Bowling: Allott 8–0–20–2; Folley 8–0–16–0; O'Shaughnessy 8–0–27–1; Simmons 8–1–22–2; Watkinson 8–0–35–1.

Lancashire

G. Fowler c and b Willey	31
F. C. Hayes c Willey b Griffiths	2
*C. H. Lloyd not out	39
D. P. Hughes not out	50
L-b 5, w 1, n-b 3	9

1/20 2/45   (2 wkts, 35 overs) 131

J. Abrahams, J. Simmons, S. J. O'Shaughnessy, †C. Maynard, M. Watkinson, P. J. W. Allott and I. Folley did not bat.

Bowling: Carse 8–0–25–0; T. M. Lamb 7–1–25–0; Griffiths 7–0–26–1; Willey 8–2–22–1; Wild 4–0–18–0; Cook 1–0–6–0.

Umpires: D. J. Constant and B. Leadbeater.

LANCASHIRE v NOTTINGHAMSHIRE

At Manchester, June 12. Lancashire won by seven wickets. Toss won by Lancashire.

Nottinghamshire

R. T. Robinson c Abrahams b Folley ..	32	†B. N. French not out			21
B. Hassan lbw b Folley	38	B 1, l-b 9, w 4			14
*J. D. Birch not out	42				
P. Johnson lbw b Simmons	7	1/68 2/102 3/112	(3 wkts, 40 overs)		154

M. A. Fell, E. E. Hemmings, K. Saxelby, K. E. Cooper, M. Hendrick and M. K. Bore did not bat.

Bowling: Jefferies 8–2–29–0; Folley 8–0–26–2; Watkinson 8–1–21–0; O'Shaughnessy 8–0–37–0; Simmons 8–0–27–1.

Lancashire

I. Cockbain c Hendrick b Hemmings ...	25	S. T. Jefferies not out			37
F. C. Hayes c French b Bore	4	B 4, l-b 6, w 2			12
†C. Maynard c Saxelby b Hemmings ...	46				
D. P. Hughes not out	31	1/11 2/66 3/86	(3 wkts, 38.2 overs)		155

S. J. O'Shaughnessy, *J. Abrahams, N. H. Fairbrother, J. Simmons, M. Watkinson and I. Folley did not bat.

Bowling: Hendrick 7.2–0–22–0; Cooper 8–2–23–0; Bore 7–0–32–1; Saxelby 8–0–45–0; Hemmings 8–1–21–2.

Umpires: W. E. Alley and R. Julian.

At Horsham, June 19. LANCASHIRE lost to SUSSEX by 2 runs.

LANCASHIRE v HAMPSHIRE

At Manchester, July 3. Hampshire won by 58 runs. Toss won by Hampshire.

Hampshire

C. G. Greenidge not out	162	*N. E. J. Pocock not out			0
C. L. Smith run out	31	B 1, l-b 7, w 3, n-b 2			13
T. E. Jesty lbw b O'Shaughnessy	4				
V. P. Terry c Simmons b O'Shaughnessy.	34	1/57 2/69	(4 wkts, 40 overs)		268
M. C. J. Nicholas run out	24	3/196 4/267			

N. G. Cowley, M. D. Marshall, T. M. Tremlett, †R. J. Parks and S. J. Malone did not bat.

Bowling: Allott 8–1–51–0; Jefferies 8–0–34–0; Watkinson 8–1–52–0; O'Shaughnessy 8–0–53–2; Folley 3–0–20–0; Simmons 5–0–45–0.

Lancashire

G. Fowler b Jesty	22	M. Watkinson not out			27
I. Cockbain b Jesty	7	P. J. W. Allott lbw b Jesty			3
D. P. Hughes c Parks b Jesty	0	I. Folley not out			6
*J. Abrahams c Nicholas b Malone	65	L-b 7, w 18			25
S. T. Jefferies c Marshall b Tremlett ...	17				
J. Simmons c Parks b Jesty	13	1/35 2/35 3/40	(9 wkts, 40 overs)		210
†C. Maynard b Marshall	22	4/93 5/126 6/156			
S. J. O'Shaughnessy c Terry b Malone.	3	7/161 8/172 9/180			

Bowling: Malone 8–0–38–2; Marshall 8–0–22–1; Tremlett 8–0–33–1; Jesty 8–0–43–5; Cowley 8–0–49–0.

Umpires: M. J. Kitchen and B. Leadbeater.

At Maidstone, July 10. LANCASHIRE lost to KENT by 63 runs.

LANCASHIRE v WORCESTERSHIRE

At Manchester, July 17. Tied. Toss won by Worcestershire.

Lancashire

S. J. O'Shaughnessy c King b Inchmore	12	M. Watkinson not out	5
D. Lloyd b Pridgeon	8	N. H. Fairbrother run out	0
*C. H. Lloyd c D'Oliveira b Warner	52	B 4, l-b 10	14
J. Abrahams run out	10		
F. C. Hayes b Warner	23	1/13 2/39	(8 wkts, 19 overs) 142
J. Simmons b Patel	7	3/90 4/91 5/124	
†C. Maynard c Inchmore b Patel	11	6/126 7/142 8/142	

P. J. W. Allott and L. L. McFarlane did not bat.

Bowling: Warner 6–1–35–2; Pridgeon 7–0–45–1; Inchmore 3–0–23–1; Patel 3–0–25–2.

Worcestershire

M. J. Weston lbw b Allott	9	J. D. Inchmore not out	12
D. N. Patel b McFarlane	3		
C. L. King b Watkinson	16	B 2, l-b 8	10
*P. A. Neale c C. H. Lloyd b Allott	39		
D. B. D'Oliveira not out	51	1/10 2/14	(5 wkts, 19 overs) 142
D. A. Banks c Simmons b Allott	2	3/42 4/100 5/114	

†P. Moores, R. K. Illingworth, A. E. Warner and A. P. Pridgeon did not bat.

Bowling: Allott 8–1–42–3; McFarlane 6–0–50–1; Watkinson 4–0–27–1; Simmons 1–0–13–0.

Umpires: K. E. Palmer and J. van Geloven.

At The Oval, July 24. LANCASHIRE beat SURREY by four wickets.

LANCASHIRE v SOMERSET

At Manchester, July 31. No result. Toss won by Somerset.

Lancashire

D. Lloyd c Denning b Dredge	2	M. Watkinson lbw b Richards	0
S. J. O'Shaughnessy c Garner b Palmer	16	I. Folley not out	11
J. Abrahams c Garner b Palmer	8	L. L. McFarlane c Garner b Dredge	2
*C. H. Lloyd c Denning b Richards	46	B 1, l-b 11, w 4, n-b 1	17
D. P. Hughes c Popplewell b Richards	18		
N. H. Fairbrother b Richards	1	1/5 2/28 3/35	(38 overs) 132
†C. Maynard c Palmer b Richards	9	4/90 5/95 6/102	
J. Simmons c Gard b Richards	2	7/107 8/107 9/114	

Bowling: Garner 7–2–6–0; Dredge 5–1–8–2; Palmer 7–0–41–2; Marks 8–0–26–0; Richards 8–0–24–6; Popplewell 3–0–10–0.

Somerset

P. M. Roebuck not out	1
P. W. Denning not out	5
W 1	1

(no wkt, 1 over) 7

J. W. Lloyds, *I. V. A. Richards, P. A. Slocombe, N. F. M. Popplewell, C. H. Dredge, V. J. Marks, †T. Gard, J. Garner and G. V. Palmer did not bat.

Bowling: Folley 1–0–6–0.

Umpires: D. G. L. Evans and J. W. Holder.

At Leeds, August 7. LANCASHIRE lost to YORKSHIRE by six wickets.

LANCASHIRE v MIDDLESEX

At Manchester, August 14. Lancashire won by seven wickets. Toss won by Middlesex.

Middlesex

W. N. Slack b Allott	9	K. D. James c O'Shaughnessy		
G. D. Barlow run out	32		b Watkinson.	4
C. T. Radley b Allott	41	S. P. Hughes run out		9
†P. R. Downton c Maynard		J. F. Sykes not out		2
b Watkinson.	0	B 1, l-b 15, n-b 1		17
K. P. Tomlins c Maynard b Watkinson	4			
*J. E. Emburey st Maynard b D. Lloyd	15	1/17 2/59 3/60	(40 overs) 166	
R. G. P. Ellis b Allott	30	4/66 5/93 6/125		
N. F. Williams c Maynard b Allott	3	7/137 8/148 9/153		

Bowling: Allott 8–1–29–4; McFarlane 5–0–20–0; O'Shaughnessy 5–0–23–0; Watkinson 8–0–31–3; Simmons 8–1–26–0; D. Lloyd 6–0–20–1.

Lancashire

G. Fowler b Hughes	33	J. Abrahams not out		14
D. Lloyd c Ellis b Slack	50	B 1, l-b 5, w 1, n-b 3		10
S. J. O'Shaughnessy b Slack	31			
*C. H. Lloyd not out	29	1/57 2/114 3/136	(3 wkts, 38 overs) 167	

N. H. Fairbrother, †C. Maynard, J. Simmons, M. Watkinson L. L. McFarlane and P. J. W. Allott did not bat.

Bowling: Williams 7–1–32–0; James 8–0–20–0; Hughes 5–0–31–1; Sykes 2–0–11–0; Emburey 8–3–29–0; Slack 8–0–34–2.

Umpires: J. Birkenshaw and P. B. Wight.

At Bristol, August 28. LANCASHIRE beat GLOUCESTERSHIRE by seven wickets.

LANCASHIRE v LEICESTERSHIRE

At Manchester, September 11. No result.

LEICESTERSHIRE

LEICESTERSHIRE v WORCESTERSHIRE

At Leicester, May 8. No result.

At Gloucester, May 15. GLOUCESTERSHIRE v LEICESTERSHIRE. No result.

LEICESTERSHIRE v KENT

At Leicester, May 22. No result.

At Northampton, May 29. LEICESTERSHIRE lost to NORTHAMPTONSHIRE by four wickets.

At Derby, June 12. LEICESTERSHIRE beat DERBYSHIRE by five wickets.

At Basingstoke, June 19. LEICESTERSHIRE lost to HAMPSHIRE by nine wickets.

LEICESTERSHIRE v GLAMORGAN

At Leicester, June 26. Leicestershire won by four wickets. Toss won by Leicestershire.

Glamorgan

J. A. Hopkins c Parsons b Cook	46	*M. W. W. Selvey c Garnham b Taylor	4
H. Morris run out	5	B. J. Lloyd c Garnham b Taylor	5
A. L. Jones b Clift	19	W. W. Davis not out	0
D. A. Francis st Garnham b Cook	13	L-b 10, n-b 4	14
C. J. C. Rowe c Cook b Parsons	25		
R. C. Ontong c Garnham b Taylor	15	1/42 2/58 3/80	(39.5 overs) 156
J. G. Thomas c Clift b Taylor	3	4/114 5/122 6/134	
†E. W. Jones c Cook b Taylor	7	7/147 8/147 9/156	

Bowling: Roberts 8–2–20–0; Parsons 8–0–25–1; Taylor 7.5–0–41–5; Clift 8–1–21–1; Cook 8–0–35–2.

Leicestershire

D. I. Gower c A. L. Jones b Davis	0	†M. A. Garnham c Thomas b Davis	6
I. P. Butcher lbw b Thomas	5	A. M. E. Roberts not out	18
N. E. Briers b Thomas	24	L-b 16, w 3, n-b 3	22
B. F. Davison lbw b Ontong	25		
*R. W. Tolchard not out	33	1/0 2/7 3/60	(6 wkts, 37.4 overs) 157
P. B. Clift lbw b Rowe	24	4/64 5/111 6/132	

G. J. Parsons, N. G. B. Cook and L. B. Taylor did not bat.

Bowling: Davis 8–0–29–2; Thomas 8–0–27–2; Selvey 7–1–20–0; Ontong 6.4–0–29–1; Lloyd 3–0–17–0; Rowe 5–0–13–1.

Umpires: C. T. Spencer and K. Ibadulla.

At Scarborough, July 3. LEICESTERSHIRE lost to YORKSHIRE by seven wickets.

LEICESTERSHIRE v SOMERSET

At Leicester, July 10. Leicestershire won by eight wickets. Toss won by Leicestershire.

Somerset

P. M. Roebuck c Cook b Parsons	7	C. H. Dredge b Roberts	6
P. W. Denning c Briers b Clift	55	J. Garner not out	2
I. V. A. Richards b Cook	13	P. H. L. Wilson not out	1
I. T. Botham c Roberts b Parsons	64	B 5, l-b 6, w 3, n-b 2	16
*B. C. Rose c Gower b Parsons	3		
N. F. M. Popplewell c Cook b Clift	1	1/15 2/33 3/148　(9 wkts, 39 overs) 196	
V. J. Marks run out	20	4/149 5/153 6/154	
†T. Gard c Briers b Taylor	8	7/184 8/191 9/192	

Bowling: Roberts 8–2–17–1; Parsons 8–1–36–3; Cook 8–1–39–1; Taylor 7–1–47–1; Clift 8–2–41–2.

Leicestershire

D. I. Gower c Gard b Garner	12
I. P. Butcher c Gard b Dredge	43
N. E. Briers not out	77
B. F. Davison not out	46
B 4, l-b 11, w 2, n-b 2	19

1/16 2/105　　(2 wkts, 35.1 overs) 197

*R. W. Tolchard, †M. A. Garnham, P. B. Clift, G. J. Parsons, A. M. E. Roberts, N. G. B. Cook and L. B. Taylor did not bat.

Bowling: Garner 8–2–23–1; Botham 6–0–38–0; Wilson 6–0–38–0; Marks 8–0–30–0; Dredge 7–0–48–1; Richards 0.1–0–1–0.

Umpires: K. Higgs and P. B. Wight.

At Lord's, July 17. LEICESTERSHIRE lost to MIDDLESEX by 27 runs.

LEICESTERSHIRE v ESSEX

At Leicester, July 24. Essex won on faster scoring-rate, having been set a target of 64 off ten overs in a match previously reduced by rain to 21 overs a side. Toss won by Leicestershire.

Leicestershire

D. I. Gower c R. E. East b Phillip	16	†M. A. Garnham not out	1
I. P. Butcher b Pringle	4		
B. F. Davison b Gooch	5	L-b 6, w 1, n-b 1	8
N. E. Briers c D. E. East b Phillip	50		
*R. W. Tolchard b Turner	4	1/14 2/25　(5 wkts, 17.2 overs) 110	
P. B. Clift not out	22	3/59 4/74 5/100	

A. M. E. Roberts, G. J. Parsons, J. P. Agnew and N. G. B. Cook did not bat.

Bowling: Foster 2.2–0–13–0; Pringle 3–0–22–1; Phillip 3–0–16–2; Gooch 5–0–16–1; Turner 4–0–35–1.

Essex

G. A. Gooch not out........................	41
C. Gladwin c Garnham b Roberts.......	1
D. R. Pringle b Clift	15
N. Phillip not out.............................	6
L-b 1, w 2..............................	3

1/3 2/28   (2 wkts, 8.3 overs) 66

B. R. Hardie, P. J. Prichard, *K. W. R. Fletcher, S. Turner, †D. E. East, R. E. East and N. A. Foster did not bat.

Bowling: Roberts 4.3–0–24–1; Clift 3–0–26–1; Agnew 1–0–13–0.

Umpires: J. W. Holder and D. O. Oslear.

LEICESTERSHIRE v SUSSEX

At Leicester, July 31. No result. Toss won by Leicestershire.

Sussex

G. D. Mendis c Garnham b Taylor	2	*J. R. T. Barclay c Roberts b Steele ...	0
P. W. G. Parker b Roberts................	0	A. C. S. Pigott not out	1
C. M. Wells c Clift b Cook................	46	B 1, l-b 4	5
Imran Khan lbw b Roberts................	4		
†I. J. Gould c Taylor b Clift	14	1/1 2/7 (7 wkts, 34 overs) 105	
A. P. Wells c Briers b Steele	24	3/14 4/52	
R. S. Cowan not out	9	5/94 6/94 7/100	

D. A. Reeve and C. E. Waller did not bat.

Bowling: Roberts 7–2–11–2; Taylor 6–1–14–1; Clift 8–1–25–1; Parsons 1–0–9–0; Cook 8–0–34–1; Steele 4–0–7–2.

Leicestershire

I. P. Butcher not out........................	10
N. E. Briers not out.........................	0
B 2.......................................	2

(no wkt, 2.5 overs) 12

†M. A. Garnham, B. F. Davison, *R. W. Tolchard, P. B. Clift, A. M. E. Roberts, G. J. Parsons, J. F. Steele, N. G. B. Cook and L. B. Taylor did not bat.

Bowling: Imran 1.5–0–9–0; Reeve 1–0–1–0.

Umpires: B. Leadbeater and C. Cook.

LEICESTERSHIRE v NOTTINGHAMSHIRE

At Leicester, August 7. Leicestershire won by 26 runs. Toss won by Nottinghamshire.

Leicestershire

D. I. Gower c Johnson b Illingworth ...	57	P. B. Clift not out............................	31
I. P. Butcher lbw b Saxelby	8	B 4, l-b 10, w 1, n-b 1	16
N. E. Briers not out.........................	101		
J. J. Whitaker b Saxelby	27	1/43 2/102 3/170 (3 wkts, 40 overs) 240	

*†R. W. Tolchard, A. M. E. Roberts, G. J. Parsons, J. F. Steele, N. G. B. Cook and L. B. Taylor did not bat.

Bowling: Cooper 8–0–47–0; Bore 8–1–35–0; Saxelby 8–0–34–2; Hemmings 8–1–35–0; Illingworth 8–0–73–1.

Nottinghamshire

B. Hassan c Gower b Cook	14	E. E. Hemmings not out	23
R. T. Robinson c Taylor b Clift	68		
*C. E. B. Rice b Taylor	48	B 2, l-b 12, w 4, n-b 2	20
D. W. Randall c and b Steele	4		
P. Johnson not out	35	1/38 2/138 (5 wkts, 40 overs) 214	
†B. N. French c Steele b Parsons	2	3/143 4/159 5/162	

K. Saxelby, K. E. Cooper, N. J. B. Illingworth and M. K. Bore did not bat.

Bowling: Taylor 8–0–37–1; Parsons 3–0–11–1; Roberts 8–0–24–0; Cook 8–0–36–1; Clift 8–0–36–1; Steele 5–0–50–1.

Umpires: W. E. Alley and P. B. Wight.

At Birmingham, August 14. LEICESTERSHIRE lost to WARWICKSHIRE by eight wickets.

LEICESTERSHIRE v SURREY

At Leicester, September 4. Surrey won by 3 runs. Toss won by Leicestershire.

Surrey

A. R. Butcher c Whitaker b Briers	111	A. J. Stewart not out	5
D. B. Pauline lbw b Ferris	2	I. R. Payne not out	0
*R. D. V. Knight c Butcher b Agnew	65	B 5, l-b 3, n-b 6	14
M. A. Lynch c Clift b Agnew	43		
D. J. Thomas c Gower b Briers	4	1/3 2/190 3/191 (6 wkts, 40 overs) 261	
†C. J. Richards c Cook b Ferris	17	4/203 5/245 6/260	

P. A. Waterman, P. I. Pocock and I. J. Curtis did not bat.

Bowling: Ferris 8–0–38–2; Clift 8–0–47–0; Agnew 8–0–54–2; Cook 8–0–55–0; Steele 5–0–39–0; Briers 3–0–14–2.

Leicestershire

D. I. Gower b Knight	78	*†R. W. Tolchard not out	0
I. P. Butcher lbw b Knight	28		
N. E. Briers b Knight	14	L-b 12, w 4, n-b 2	18
P. B. Clift c Thomas b Knight	35		
J. J. Whitaker not out	65	1/93 2/113 (5 wkts, 40 overs) 258	
T. J. Boon c Lynch b Thomas	20	3/164 4/186 5/257	

J. F. Steele, N. G. B. Cook, G. J. F. Ferris and J. P. Agnew did not bat.

Bowling: Waterman 5–0–50–0; Payne 8–0–50–0; Thomas 8–0–49–1; Pocock 8–0–51–0; Knight 8–0–42–4; Curtis 3–0–29–0.

Umpires: D. G. L. Evans and D. O. Oslear.

At Manchester, September 11. LANCASHIRE v LEICESTERSHIRE. No result.

MIDDLESEX

MIDDLESEX v GLAMORGAN

At Lord's, May 8. No result.

MIDDLESEX v HAMPSHIRE

At Lord's, May 15. No result.

At Hull, May 22. MIDDLESEX lost to YORKSHIRE on faster scoring-rate.

MIDDLESEX v SUSSEX

At Lord's, May 29. Sussex won on faster scoring-rate after bad light had reduced their target to 98 off eighteen overs. Toss won by Sussex.

Middlesex

G. D. Barlow b le Roux	52	†P. R. Downton c and b Barclay	3
W. N. Slack run out	69	N. F. Williams not out	6
*M. W. Gatting b le Roux	9	B 15, w 2	17
R. O. Butcher c Mendis b Greig	31		
C. T. Radley not out	23	1/116 2/135 3/148 (6 wkts, 40 overs) 216
K. P. Tomlins c A. P. Wells b Greig	6	4/179 5/193 6/200

J. E. Emburey, K. D. James and W. W. Daniel did not bat.

Bowling: C. M. Wells 4–0–16–0; le Roux 8–1–32–2; Barclay 8–0–35–1; Greig 6–0–36–2; Pigott 8–0–46–0; Jones 6–1–34–0.

Sussex

G. D. Mendis c Barlow b Daniel	41	I. A. Greig not out	2
†I. J. Gould c Barlow b James	6	C. P. Phillipson not out	0
C. M. Wells c Downton b Williams	28	L-b 2, w 2, n-b 2	6
P. W. G. Parker run out	9		
A. P. Wells c Slack b Daniel	2	1/7 2/77 3/83 (6 wkts, 17.2 overs) 98
G. S. le Roux c Gatting b Emburey	4	4/91 5/96 6/96

*J. R. T. Barclay, A. C. S. Pigott and A. N. Jones did not bat.

Bowling: James 2–0–20–1; Williams 8–0–28–1; Daniel 6–0–38–2; Emburey 1.2–0–6–1.

Umpires: H. D. Bird and R. A. White.

MIDDLESEX v WORCESTERSHIRE

At Lord's, June 5. Middlesex won by seven wickets in a match reduced by rain to 33 overs a side. Toss won by Middlesex.

Worcestershire

M. S. Scott b Cowans	2	J. D. Inchmore c Barlow b Emburey	1
M. J. Weston c Tomlins b Cowans	23	R. M. Ellcock not out	5
D. N. Patel c Downton b Daniel	2	A. P. Pridgeon b Williams	0
*P. A. Neale c Downton b Daniel	2	L-b 7, w 6, n-b 1	14
D. B. D'Oliveira c Butcher b Gatting	19		—
M. S. A. McEvoy c Radley b Gatting	1	1/25 2/30 3/31	(31.3 overs) 89
†D. J. Humphries b Williams	20	4/37 5/46 6/65	
R. K. Illingworth c Downton b Gatting	0	7/69 8/72 9/89	

Bowling: Cowans 8–0–22–2; Williams 5.3–1–10–2; Daniel 6–0–15–2; Gatting 6–0–13–3; Slack 2–0–6–0; Emburey 4–2–9–1.

Middlesex

G. D. Barlow b Pridgeon	11	R. O. Butcher not out	1
W. N. Slack c Humphries b Ellcock	0	L-b 1, w 4, n-b 5	10
C. T. Radley not out	38		
*M. W. Gatting c D'Oliveira b Patel	30	1/1 2/20 3/87	(3 wkts, 25 overs) 90

J. E. Emburey, †P. R. Downton, K. P. Tomlins, N. F. Williams, N. G. Cowans and W. W. Daniel did not bat.

Bowling: Ellcock 7–0–14–1; Pridgeon 5–1–16–1; Illingworth 7–0–27–0; Inchmore 3–0–15–0; Patel 3–0–8–1.

Umpires: D. O. Oslear and K. E. Palmer.

At The Oval, June 12. MIDDLESEX lost to SURREY by 3 runs.

At Chesterfield, June 26. MIDDLESEX beat DERBYSHIRE by four wickets.

MIDDLESEX v GLOUCESTERSHIRE

At Lord's, July 3. Gloucestershire won by six wickets. Toss won by Gloucestershire.

Middlesex

K. P. Tomlins c Russell b Shepherd	0	†P. R. Downton not out	7
R. G. P. Ellis c Stovold b Shepherd	9		
C. T. Radley c and b Childs	18	B 1, l-b 10, w 2	13
*M. W. Gatting lbw b Shepherd	85		
R. O. Butcher b Sainsbury	100	1/0 2/12	(5 wkts, 40 overs) 270
J. E. Emburey not out	38	3/64 4/140 5/249	

P. H. Edmonds, N. F. Williams, N. G. Cowans and K. D. James did not bat.

Bowling: Shepherd 8–1–17–3; Sainsbury 8–1–36–1; Childs 8–1–36–1; Doughty 7–0–69–0; Bainbridge 4–0–54–0; Graveney 5–0–45–0.

Gloucestershire

A. W. Stovold b Edmonds	37	J. N. Shepherd not out	34
P. W. Romaines c Downton b Williams	30	B 2, l-b 8, w 4	14
Zaheer Abbas not out	106		
A. J. Hignell c Cowans b Emburey	47	1/53 2/87	(4 wkts, 39.2 overs) 272
P. Bainbridge c Butcher b James	4	3/200 4/208	

*D. A. Graveney, R. J. Doughty, †R. C. Russell, J. H. Childs and G. E. Sainsbury did not bat.

Bowling: James 8–0–68–1; Cowans 8–1–50–0; Williams 8–0–33–1; Edmonds 8–0–45–1; Gatting 1–0–13–0; Emburey 6.2–0–49–1.

Umpires: D. G. L. Evans and R. A. White.

MIDDLESEX v LEICESTERSHIRE

At Lord's, July 17. Middlesex won by 27 runs. Toss won by Middlesex.

Middlesex

W. N. Slack c Tolchard b Clift	19	†P. R. Downton not out	43
C. T. Radley c Tolchard b Clift	23		
*M. W. Gatting c Butcher b Taylor	56	L-b 12, w 1	13
R. O. Butcher c Steele b Taylor	37		
K. P. Tomlins c Butcher b Steele	0	1/33 2/65 (5 wkts, 40 overs)	231
J. E. Emburey not out	40	3/138 4/139 5/149	

N. F. Williams, K. D. James, W. G. Merry and S. P. Hughes did not bat.

Bowling: Roberts 8–1–42–0; Parsons 4–0–18–0; Cook 7–1–44–0; Clift 8–0–34–2; Taylor 7–0–45–2; Steele 6–0–35–1.

Leicestershire

I. P. Butcher st Downton b Emburey	43	G. J. Parsons c Downton b Merry	3
N. E. Briers b James	20	N. G. B. Cook c Briers b Slack	0
B. F. Davison b Slack	71	L. B. Taylor not out	1
M. A. Garnham c Downton b Williams	11	B 2, l-b 10, w 5, n-b 1	18
*†R. W. Tolchard c Downton b Williams	14		
P. B. Clift b Slack	14	1/35 2/147 3/147 (38.4 overs)	204
A. M. E. Roberts c Hughes b Slack	5	4/169 5/190 6/190	
J. F. Steele b Slack	4	7/196 8/202 9/202	

Bowling: James 6–0–29–1; Williams 8–0–31–2; Emburey 8–0–33–1; Hughes 7–1–36–0; Merry 3–0–25–1; Slack 6.4–0–32–5.

Umpires: D. J. Constant and R. Julian.

At Canterbury, July 24. MIDDLESEX beat KENT by 56 runs.

MIDDLESEX v WARWICKSHIRE

At Lord's, July 31. Middlesex won on faster scoring-rate when Warwickshire failed to reach a target of 92 off eighteen overs. Toss won by Warwickshire.

Middlesex

G. D. Barlow run out	2	N. F. Williams c and b Small	4
W. N. Slack run out	26	K. D. James not out	6
C. T. Radley b Ferreira	17	J. D. Carr not out	0
*M. W. Gatting b Hogg	47	B 1, l-b 10, w 4	15
R. G. P. Ellis b Small	18		
J. E. Emburey st Humpage b Gifford	8	1/9 2/39 3/77 4/110 (8 wkts, 32 overs)	163
†P. R. Downton c Amiss b Ferreira	20	5/123 6/143 7/153 8/157	

W. W. Daniel did not bat.

Bowling: Small 7–0–21–2; Hogg 5–0–15–1; Ferreira 5–0–22–2; Kallicharran 8–0–44–0; Gifford 7–0–46–1.

Warwickshire

T. A. Lloyd b Daniel	10	P. A. Smith st Downton b Emburey	2
D. L. Amiss c Downton b Slack	24	G. C. Small c James b Emburey	0
A. I. Kallicharran st Downton b Emburey.	7	*N. Gifford b Emburey	3
		W. Hogg not out	9
†G. W. Humpage c Carr b Williams	7	B 1, l-b 5	6
A. M. Ferreira c Radley b Daniel	8		
K. D. Smith run out	1	1/26 2/41 3/43 4/57 (17.5 overs) 82	
R. I. H. B. Dyer b Emburey	5	5/59 6/60 7/65 8/67 9/73	

Bowling: Daniel 8–0–29–2; Emburey 7.5–1–36–5; Slack 1–0–8–1; Williams 1–0–3–1.

Umpires: J. H. Harris and J. van Geloven.

At Chelmsford, August 7. MIDDLESEX beat ESSEX by four wickets.

At Manchester, August 14. MIDDLESEX lost to LANCASHIRE by seven wickets.

MIDDLESEX v SOMERSET

At Lord's, August 21. Somerset won by four wickets. Toss won by Middlesex.

Middlesex

G. D. Barlow b Dredge	19	†P. R. Downton c Denning b Botham	13
R. G. P. Ellis run out	19	N. F. Williams not out	13
*M. W. Gatting c Garner b Marks	28	K. D. James not out	7
C. T. Radley c Marks b Dredge	11	L-b 17, w 2, n-b 1	20
K. P. Tomlins c Popplewell b Richards	16		
C. R. Cook c Popplewell b Richards	6	1/40 2/49 3/77 4/99 (8 wkts, 40 overs) 158	
J. E. Emburey b Garner	6	5/107 6/115 7/118 8/145	

S. P. Hughes did not bat.

Bowling: Garner 8–0–17–1; Botham 8–0–34–1; Dredge 8–0–23–2; Marks 8–0–33–1; Richards 8–0–31–2.

Somerset

P. M. Roebuck run out	37	P. A. Slocombe not out	33
P. W. Denning c Downton b Gatting	15	V. J. Marks not out	6
I. V. A. Richards c James b Williams	30	L-b 3, w 2, n-b 3	8
N. F. M. Popplewell b Williams	3		
*I. T. Botham b Emburey	1	1/32 2/69 3/85 (6 wkts, 38.1 overs) 159	
J. W. Lloyds run out	26	4/91 5/91 6/153	

†T. Gard, C. H. Dredge and J. Garner did not bat.

Bowling: James 8–2–19–0; Hughes 7.1–1–28–0; Gatting 8–0–44–1; Emburey 8–0–13–1; Williams 7–0–47–2.

Umpires: J. W. Holder and R. Palmer.

At Milton Keynes, August 28. MIDDLESEX beat NORTHAMPTONSHIRE by eight wickets.

At Cleethorpes, September 4. MIDDLESEX lost to NOTTINGHAMSHIRE by four wickets.

NORTHAMPTONSHIRE

NORTHAMPTONSHIRE v NOTTINGHAMSHIRE

At Northampton, May 8. Nottinghamshire won on faster scoring-rate after rain had reduced their target to 74 runs off fourteen overs. Toss won by Nottinghamshire.

Northamptonshire

P. Willey c and b Hemmings	36	†G. Sharp not out	8
W. Larkins c Robinson b Hemmings	18	T. M. Lamb not out	0
A. J. Lamb c Robinson b Cooper	42	L-b 12, w 1, n-b 1	14
Kapil Dev lbw b Hendrick	66		
*G. Cook run out	20	(7 wkts, 40 overs) 210	
R. G. Williams run out	1	1/53 2/58	
D. J. Capel c Hassan b Cooper	5	3/167 4/169	
		5/180 6/196 7/202	

N. A. Mallender and B. J. Griffiths did not bat.

Bowling: Hadlee 8–3–29–0; Bore 8–1–55–0; Cooper 8–0–55–2; Hendrick 8–1–16–1; Hemmings 8–0–41–2.

Nottinghamshire

*C. E. B. Rice not out	45
R. J. Hadlee c Williams b Kapil Dev	17
J. D. Birch c and b T. M. Lamb	2
D. W. Randall not out	7
B 1, n-b 2	3

1/41 2/45   (2 wkts, 13.4 overs) 74

R. T. Robinson, B. Hassan, †B. N. French, M. K. Bore, E. E. Hemmings, K. E. Cooper and M. Hendrick did not bat.

Bowling: Kapil Dev 7–0–23–1; Mallender 1–0–7–0; T. M. Lamb 5.4–0–41–1.

Umpires: P. J. Eele and B. Leadbeater.

At Derby, May 15. NORTHAMPTONSHIRE lost to DERBYSHIRE by 78 runs.

At Bournemouth, May 22. NORTHAMPTONSHIRE lost to HAMPSHIRE by seven wickets.

NORTHAMPTONSHIRE v LEICESTERSHIRE

At Northampton, May 29. Northamptonshire won by four wickets. Toss won by Northamptonshire.

Leicestershire

D. I. Gower lbw b T. M. Lamb	5	P. B. Clift b Mallender	14
N. E. Briers c Larkins b Willey	29	G. J. Parsons not out	0
I. P. Butcher b T. M. Lamb	2	L. B. Taylor not out	1
B. F. Davison b T. M. Lamb	0	B 1, l-b 3, w 4	8
*R. W. Tolchard b T. M. Lamb	6		
†M. A. Garnham c and b Griffiths	0	(9 wkts, 40 overs) 103	
J. F. Steele st Sharp b Kapil Dev	29	1/10 2/16 3/16	
A. M. E. Roberts b Mallender	9	4/27 5/27 6/55	
		7/70 8/94 9/100	

Bowling: T. M. Lamb 8–2–9–4; Kapil Dev 8–1–24–1; Mallender 7–2–17–2; Griffiths 8–2–28–1; Capel 1–0–5–0; Willey 8–2–12–1.

Northamptonshire

W. Larkins c Gower b Taylor	1	D. J. Capel not out	11
P. Willey c Garnham b Taylor	2	†G. Sharp not out	0
A. J. Lamb c Tolchard b Roberts	33	B 5, l-b 3 w 1	9
Kapil Dev b Steele	28		
R. G. Williams b Steele	22	1/8 2/15 3/69　(6 wkts, 26.4 overs) 106
*G. Cook lbw b Steele	0	4/83 5/83 6/102

N. A. Mallender, T. M. Lamb and B. J. Griffiths did not bat.

Bowling: Roberts 8–0–31–1; Taylor 8–1–24–2; Clift 2.4–0–17–0; Steele 6–3–16–3; Parsons 2–0–9–0.

Umpires: R. Julian and D. R. Shepherd.

At Manchester, June 5. NORTHAMPTONSHIRE lost to LANCASHIRE by eight wickets.

NORTHAMPTONSHIRE v GLOUCESTERSHIRE

At Northampton, June 12. Northamptonshire won by 17 runs. Toss won by Gloucestershire.

Northamptonshire

W. Larkins c Hignell b Sainsbury	102	†G. Sharp not out	51
P. Willey c Childs b Shepherd	10	T. M. Lamb not out	0
*G. Cook c Hignell b Shepherd	13	L-b 7, w 5, n-b 2	14
R. G. Williams b Childs	2		
R. J. Boyd-Moss b Childs	2	1/34 2/52 3/55　(6 wkts, 40 overs) 198
D. J. Capel c Bainbridge b Childs	4	4/68 5/84 6/197

D. J. Wild, N. A. Mallender and B. J. Griffiths did not bat.

Bowling: Stephenson 8–1–51–0; Sainsbury 8–0–50–1; Shepherd 8–0–30–2; Childs 8–0–18–3; Bainbridge 8–0–35–0.

Gloucestershire

B. C. Broad c Lamb b Griffiths	30	*D. A. Graveney not out	27
A. W. Stovold c Sharp b Lamb	12	F. D. Stephenson not out	18
P. Bainbridge c Larkins b Willey	4	B 1, l-b 12, w 1, n-b 2	16
A. J. Hignell c Boyd-Moss b Mallender	70		
A. J. Wright b Willey	0	1/21 2/31 3/78　(6 wkts, 40 overs) 181
J. N. Shepherd b Willey	4	4/81 5/107 6/140

†R. C. Russell, J. H. Childs and G. E. Sainsbury did not bat.

Bowling: Lamb 8–0–58–1; Mallender 8–1–34–1; Willey 8–0–22–3; Williams 8–0–21–0; Griffiths 8–0–30–1.

Umpires: J. H. Harris and P. B. Wight.

NORTHAMPTONSHIRE v WARWICKSHIRE

At Luton, June 19. Northamptonshire won by 34 runs. Toss won by Northamptonshire. Larkins, with six 6s and twelve 4s, established a record highest score in the John Player League, while his second-wicket partnership with Willey was also a competition best. Neither record lasted the season.

Northamptonshire

R. J. Bailey c Ferreira b Gifford......... 27
W. Larkins not out 172
P. Willey b Gifford 84
*G. Cook not out 3
    L-b 9, n-b 3 12

1/64 2/277   (2 wkts, 40 overs) 298

R. G. Williams, R. J. Boyd-Moss, D. J. Wild, †G. Sharp, N. A. Mallender, T. M. Lamb and B. J. Griffiths did not bat.

  Bowling: Old 7–0–47–0; Hogg 6–0–55–0; Ferreira 8–0–44–0; P. A. Smith 6–0–62–0; Gifford 7–0–45–2; Kallicharran 6–0–33–0.

Warwickshire

T. A. Lloyd c sub b Williams............. 84	A. M. Ferreira c Williams b Mallender . 24	
K. D. Smith c Larkins b Willey 18	P. A. Smith not out 13	
A. I. Kallicharran c Cook b Williams .. 33	*N. Gifford not out........................ 32	
C. M. Old c Wild b Williams 11	L-b 11, w 1, n-b 2 14	
†G. W. Humpage c Mallender		
b Williams. 10	1/43 2/138 (8 wkts, 40 overs) 264	
D. L. Amiss c Lamb b Williams 6	3/154 4/157 5/172	
Asif Din c Lamb b Mallender 19	6/172 7/214 8/216	

W. Hogg did not bat.

  Bowling: Mallender 8–0–47–2; Griffiths 3–0–41–0; Willey 8–1–35–1; Bailey 5–0–49–0; Lamb 8–0–48–0; Williams 8–0–30–5.

Umpires: C. Cook and P. J. Eele.

At East Molesey, June 26. NORTHAMPTONSHIRE beat SURREY by five wickets.

At Hastings, July 3. NORTHAMPTONSHIRE lost to SUSSEX by 88 runs.

NORTHAMPTONSHIRE v YORKSHIRE

At Tring, July 10. Yorkshire won by ten wickets. Toss won by Yorkshire.

Northamptonshire

W. Larkins c Sharp b Stevenson 3	N. A. Mallender lbw b Sidebottom 14	
R. J. Bailey lbw b Stevenson 14	T. M. Lamb not out........................ 23	
P. Willey st Bairstow b Illingworth....... 11	A. Walker run out 13	
A. J. Lamb lbw b Illingworth............. 6	B 4, l-b 7, w 4, n-b 3 18	
*G. Cook c Illingworth b Dennis 26		
R. G. Williams c Boycott b Carrick..... 1	1/14 2/22 3/35 4/46 (9 wkts, 40 overs) 131	
†G. Sharp b Illingworth 2	5/49 6/55 7/82 8/95 9/131	

B. J. Griffiths did not bat.

Bowling: Dennis 8–1–31–1; Stevenson 5–0–14–2; Carrick 8–1–8–1; Illingworth 8–1–17–3; Boycott 4–0–15–0; Sidebottom 7–0–28–1.

Yorkshire

G. Boycott not out	64
C. W. J. Athey not out	63
L-b 4, n-b 1	5

(no wkt, 34.3 overs) 132

K. Sharp, S. N. Hartley, J. D. Love, †D. L. Bairstow, P. Carrick, A. Sidebottom, G. B. Stevenson, *R. Illingworth and S. J. Dennis did not bat.

Bowling: Griffiths 8–1–14–0; T. M. Lamb 7–0–30–0; Willey 8–0–24–0; Williams 8–1–28–0; Walker 2.3–0–24–0; Mallender 1–0–7–0.

Umpires: J. W. Holder and B. J. Meyer.

NORTHAMPTONSHIRE v GLAMORGAN

At Northampton, July 24. Northamptonshire won on faster scoring-rate, after rain had reduced Glamorgan's target to 168 off 34 overs. Toss won by Glamorgan.

Northamptonshire

P. Willey c Hopkins b Nash	0	D. J. Capel run out	0
W. Larkins c E. W. Jones b Ontong	18	†G. Sharp not out	34
A. J. Lamb lbw b Nash	22	B 2, l-b 11, w 7, n-b 5	25
Kapil Dev c Hopkins b Lloyd	22		
*G. Cook not out	59	1/0 2/39 3/51 (6 wkts, 40 overs) 196	
R. G. Williams c Francis b Derrick	16	4/67 5/89 6/99	

N. A. Mallender, T. M. Lamb and B. J. Griffiths did not bat.

Bowling: Nash 8–2–20–2; Barwick 6–0–39–0; Ontong 8–0–40–1; Derrick 8–1–29–1; Lloyd 8–1–26–1; Rowe 2–0–17–0.

Glamorgan

J. A. Hopkins c Willey b Kapil Dev	4	J. Derrick not out	18
A. L. Jones run out	24	*B. J. Lloyd run out	32
R. C. Ontong c Sharp b Mallender	37	M. A. Nash not out	0
Javed Miandad lbw b Griffiths	19	B 3, l-b 11	14
D. A. Francis lbw b Mallender	4		
C. J. C. Rowe c Sharp b Griffiths	10	1/4 2/59 3/86 4/94 (8 wkts, 34 overs) 162	
†E. W. Jones b Mallender	0	5/98 6/106 7/106 8/162	

S. R. Barwick did not bat.

Bowling: Kapil Dev 7–0–35–1; Mallender 8–0–27–3; T. M. Lamb 6–0–25–0; Willey 5–0–26–0; Griffiths 8–0–35–2.

Umpires: W. E. Alley and R. A. White.

At Worcester, July 31. NORTHAMPTONSHIRE lost to WORCESTERSHIRE on faster scoring-rate.

At Weston-super-Mare, August 7. NORTHAMPTONSHIRE lost to SOMERSET by ten wickets.

NORTHAMPTONSHIRE v ESSEX

At Wellingborough, August 14. Essex won by two wickets. Toss won by Northamptonshire.

Northamptonshire

R. G. Williams b Gooch	16	R. J. Boyd-Moss not out	6
W. Larkins lbw b Gooch	16		
P. Willey c Gooch b Phillip	62	L-b 3, w 1, n-b 5	9
Kapil Dev b R. E. East	1		
*†G. Cook b Gooch	29	1/33 2/38 (5 wkts, 40 overs)	158
D. J. Capel not out	19	3/45 4/126 5/140	

M. J. Bamber, N. A. Mallender, D. J. Wild and B. J. Griffiths did not bat.

Bowling: Lever 8–2–22–0; Phillip 8–0–18–1; R. E. East 8–1–23–1; Gooch 8–1–49–3; Turner 8–1–37–0.

Essex

G. A. Gooch lbw b Mallender	38	S. Turner not out	18
C. Gladwin b Willey	36	†D. E. East c Cook b Kapil Dev	0
K. S. McEwan b Wild	12	R. E. East not out	3
*K. W. R. Fletcher b Larkins	15	B 4, l-b 7	11
N. Phillip b Wild	9		
B. R. Hardie c Bamber b Kapil Dev	9	1/70 2/94 3/96 (8 wkts, 39.5 overs)	159
K. R. Pont b Kapil Dev	8	4/117 5/120 6/134 7/140 8/141	

J. K. Lever did not bat.

Bowling: Kapil Dev 8–2–23–3; Griffiths 3–0–19–0; Willey 8–1–23–1; Mallender 4.5–0–32–1; Wild 8–0–17–2; Larkins 8–0–34–1.

Umpires: D. O. Oslear and D. R. Shepherd.

NORTHAMPTONSHIRE v MIDDLESEX

At Milton Keynes, August 28. Middlesex won by eight wickets. Toss won by Northamptonshire.

Northamptonshire

W. Larkins c Embury b Merry	47	D. J. Wild c and b Hughes	6
M. J. Bamber b Emburey	13		
P. Willey run out	23	B 1, l-b 3, n-b 1	5
R. G. Williams b Hughes	47		
R. J. Boyd-Moss c Barlow b Emburey	25	1/40 2/65 3/106 (6 wkts, 40 overs)	182
D. J. Capel not out	16	4/162 5/182 6/182	

†*G. Sharp, A. Walker, N. A. Mallender and T. M. Lamb did not bat.

Bowling: Hughes 8–0–39–2; Rose 8–0–26–0; Emburey 8–3–27–2; James 8–0–48–0; Merry 8–0–37–1.

Middlesex

G. D. Barlow not out	68
C. T. Radley lbw b Mallender	1
R. G. P. Ellis b Wild	52
K. P. Tomlins not out	51
B 2, l-b 8, w 1	11

1/5 2/100 (2 wkts, 35.1 overs) 183

C. R. Cook, *J. E. Emburey, G. D. Rose, †C. P. Metson, K. D. James, W. G. Merry and S. P. Hughes did not bat.

Bowling: Mallender 5.1–1–22–1; Walker 6–0–25–0; Lamb 8–0–23–0; Williams 7–0–52–0; Wild 7–0–29–1; Capel 2–0–21–0 .

Umpires: C. Cook and A. G. T. Whitehead.

At Canterbury, September 11. KENT v NORTHAMPTONSHIRE. No result.

NOTTINGHAMSHIRE

At Northampton, May 8. NOTTINGHAMSHIRE beat NORTHAMPTONSHIRE on faster scoring-rate.

NOTTINGHAMSHIRE v SOMERSET

At Nottingham, May 15. Somerset won on faster scoring-rate, rain having ended play after eleven overs of Nottinghamshire's innings. Toss won by Nottinghamshire.

Somerset

J. W. Lloyds c Hadlee b Bore	22	*B. C. Rose not out 1
P. M. Roebuck c Robinson b Hemmings	46	B 2, l-b 5, n-b 1 8
I. V. A. Richards not out	117	
I. T. Botham c Rice b Hendrick	85	1/40 2/117 3/255 (3 wkts, 40 overs) 279

N. F. M. Popplewell, V. J. Marks, †T. Gard, J. Garner, C. H. Dredge and G. V. Palmer did not bat.

Bowling: Bore 8–2–31–1; Saxelby 8–0–42–0; Hadlee 8–0–48–0; Hendrick 8–0–62–1; Hemmings 8–0–88–1.

Nottinghamshire

B. Hassan c Palmer b Marks	7
R. T. Robinson not out	13
*C. E. B. Rice not out	11
L-b 1	1

1/16   (1 wkt, 11 overs) 32

D. W. Randall, J. D. Birch, R. J. Hadlee, †B. N. French, K. Saxelby, E. E. Hemmings, M. K. Bore and M. Hendrick did not bat.

Bowling: Garner 4–0–7–0; Botham 4–0–9–0; Marks 2–0–7–1; Dredge 1–0–8–0.

Umpires: A. Jepson and C. T. Spencer.

NOTTINGHAMSHIRE v SURREY

At Nottingham, May 29. No result. Toss won by Nottinghamshire.

NOTTINGHAMSHIRE v GLAMORGAN

At Nottingham, June 5. Glamorgan won by 11 runs. Toss won by Glamorgan.

Glamorgan

A. Jones c Randall b Cooper	34	†E. W. Jones not out	0
J. A. Hopkins lbw b Hendrick	23	B. J. Lloyd not out	1
Javed Miandad b Hadlee	62	L-b 10, w 4, n-b 2	16
A. L. Jones lbw b Cooper	0		
R. C. Ontong lbw b Cooper	12	1/54 2/71	(7 wkts, 39 overs) 200
D. A. Francis b Hemmings	15	3/72 4/96	
J. G. Thomas run out	37	5/116 6/199 7/199	

*M. W. W. Selvey and M. A. Nash did not bat.

Bowling: Hadlee 8–0–40–1; Bore 8–0–28–0; Hemmings 8–0–45–1; Hendrick 7–1–29–1; Cooper 8–0–42–3.

Nottinghamshire

B. Hassan lbw b Thomas	1	K. E. Cooper b Ontong	4
R. T. Robinson run out	28	M. K. Bore c Selvey b Thomas	1
D. W. Randall run out	75	M. Hendrick not out	0
R. J. Hadlee c Lloyd b Ontong	25	L-b 7, w 7, n-b 2	16
*J. D. Birch c Ontong b Lloyd	7		
P. Johnson c A. L. Jones b Thomas	26	1/2 2/49 3/101	(38.4 overs) 189
†B. N. French c Lloyd b Thomas	5	4/137 5/157 6/167	
E. E. Hemmings c Thomas b Ontong	1	7/173 8/181 9/189	

Bowling: Thomas 7.4–0–41–4; Nash 8–0–21–0; Selvey 7–0–37–0; Ontong 8–0–35–3; Lloyd 8–0–39–1.

Umpires: J. H. Harris and B. J. Meyer.

At Manchester, June 12. NOTTINGHAMSHIRE lost to LANCASHIRE by seven wickets.

At Canterbury, June 26. NOTTINGHAMSHIRE lost to KENT by 49 runs.

NOTTINGHAMSHIRE v ESSEX

At Nottingham, July 3. Essex won by 89 runs. Toss won by Essex. McEwan (seven 6s, seventeen 4s) and Gooch (three 6s, nine 4s) bettered the JPL record for the second wicket which had been established two weeks earlier by Larkins and Willey at Luton.

Essex

G. A. Gooch c Hassan b Cooper	116
A. W. Lilley b Saxelby	13
K. S. McEwan not out	162
N. Phillip not out	2
B 2, l-b 9, w 1, n-b 1	13

1/25 2/298 (2 wkts, 40 overs) 306

*K. W. R. Fletcher, K. R. Pont, D. R. Pringle, S. Turner, †D. E. East, R. E. East and N. A. Foster did not bat.

Bowling: Cooper 8–0–45–1; Saxelby 8–0–48–1; Hemmings 8–0–41–0; Such 7–0–66–0; Illingworth 7–0–65–0; Hassan 2–0–28–0.

Nottinghamshire

B. Hassan lbw b R. E. East	33	N. J. B. Illingworth st D. E. East b Lilley	2
R. T. Robinson run out	6	K. E. Cooper not out	0
*C. E. B. Rice c McEwan b Turner	2	P. M. Such not out	0
D. W. Randall c Pringle b Gooch	107	B 2, l-b 8, w 6, n-b 5	21
J. D. Birch b Phillip	1		
†B. N. French c D. E. East b Pringle	6	1/25 2/33 3/41	(9 wkts, 40 overs) 217
E. E. Hemmings c Gooch b Turner	34	4/55 5/72 6/163	
K. Saxelby run out	5	7/180 8/190 9/217	

Bowling: Phillip 6–0–19–1; Foster 4–0–9–0; Turner 8–0–50–2; R. E. East 5–0–10–1; Pringle 5–0–20–1; Pont 8–0–43–0; Lilley 2–0–19–1; Fletcher 1–0–26–0; Gooch 1–1–0–1.

Umpires: H. D. Bird and P. J. Eele.

At Hereford, July 10. NOTTINGHAMSHIRE tied with WORCESTERSHIRE.

At Portsmouth, July 17. NOTTINGHAMSHIRE lost to HAMPSHIRE by 56 runs.

At Derby, July 24. NOTTINGHAMSHIRE lost to DERBYSHIRE by three wickets.

NOTTINGHAMSHIRE v YORKSHIRE

At Nottingham, July 31. Nottinghamshire won by nine wickets in a match reduced to thirteen overs a side. Toss won by Nottinghamshire.

Yorkshire

G. Boycott b Bore	11	S. N. Hartley run out	1
C. W. J. Athey lbw b Bore	40		
G. B. Stevenson b Cooper	9	B 1, l-b 7, w 5	13
†D. L. Bairstow c Birch b Bore	24		
J. D. Love not out	0	1/19 2/36 3/96	(6 wkts, 13 overs) 106
K. Sharp run out	8	4/96 5/105 6/106	

A. Ramage, A. Sidebottom, *R. Illingworth and S. J. Dennis did not bat.

Bowling: Cooper 5–0–35–1; Bore 6–0–41–3; Saxelby 2–0–17–0.

Nottinghamshire

*C. E. B. Rice not out	66
J. D. Birch run out	26
R. T. Robinson not out	1
L-b 10, w 3, n-b 1	14

1/61   (1 wkt, 12.2 overs) 107

B. Hassan, P. Johnson, E. E. Hemmings, †B. N. French, R. A. Pick, K. E. Cooper, M. K. Bore and K. Saxelby did not bat.

Bowling: Dennis 6.2–0–31–0; Ramage 5–0–43–0; Sidebottom 1–0–19–0.

Umpires: K. Ibadulla and A. G. T. Whitehead.

At Leicester, August 7. NOTTINGHAMSHIRE lost to LEICESTERSHIRE by 26 runs.

NOTTINGHAMSHIRE v SUSSEX

At Nottingham, August 14. Nottinghamshire won by 33 runs. Toss won by Sussex.

Nottinghamshire

R. T. Robinson c Parker b C. M. Wells .	14	E. E. Hemmings not out	3
*C. E. B. Rice c and b Waller	9		
J. D. Birch c Barclay b Reeve	92	L-b 12, w 3, n-b 3	18
D. W. Randall c C. M. Wells b Greig .	40		
P. Johnson c C. M. Wells b Imran	6	1/26 2/40 3/119 (6 wkts, 40 overs) 197	
†B. N. French run out	15	4/130 5/177 6/197	

K. Saxelby, K. E. Cooper, R. A. Pick and N. J. B. Illingworth did not bat.

Bowling: C. M. Wells 4–0–15–1; Reeve 8–0–38–1; Imran 8–1–22–1; Waller 7–0–35–1; Pigott 8–0–41–0; Greig 5–0–28–1.

Sussex

G. D. Mendis c French b Pick	36	*J. R. T. Barclay c French b Saxelby	0
P. W. G. Parker c Robinson b Saxelby .	6	C. E. Waller b Cooper	1
C. M. Wells c French b Cooper	14	D. A. Reeve not out	0
Imran Khan c Hemmings b Saxelby	45	B 2, l-b 4, w 5, n-b 2	13
†I. J. Gould c Johnson b Pick	2		
A. P. Wells c Johnson b Cooper	23	1/9 2/24 3/94 (37.5 overs) 164	
I. A. Greig c Robinson b Cooper	18	4/97 5/116 6/153	
A. C. S. Pigott b Saxelby	6	7/162 8/162 9/162	

Bowling: Saxelby 8–0–37–4; Cooper 6.5–0–26–4; Illingworth 7–0–39–0; Pick 8–0–35–2; Hemmings 8–1–14–0.

Umpires: H. D. Bird and R. Palmer.

At Birmingham, August 28. NOTTINGHAMSHIRE lost to WARWICKSHIRE by 61 runs.

NOTTINGHAMSHIRE v MIDDLESEX

At Cleethorpes, September 4. Nottinghamshire won by four wickets. Toss won by Middlesex.

Middlesex

R. G. P. Ellis c Rice b Cooper	8	N. F. Williams not out	31
C. T. Radley c Birch b Hemmings	32	†P. R. Downton c Rice b Saxelby	2
K. P. Tomlins c French b Bore	12	G. D. Barlow not out	1
C. R. Cook c Randall b Saxelby	18	L-b 11, w 1	12
*M. W. Gatting c Robinson			
b Hemmings	7	1/20 2/41 (8 wkts, 40 overs) 181	
K. D. James c Birch b Hemmings	25	3/73 4/79 5/94	
G. D. Rose b Saxelby	33	6/120 7/169 8/179	

W. G. Merry did not bat.

Bowling: Cooper 8–2–31–1; Bore 8–1–37–1; Pick 8–0–21–0; Saxelby 8–0–29–3; Hemmings 8–0–51–3.

Nottinghamshire

P. Johnson c Rose b James	2	E. E. Hemmings not out	39	
R. T. Robinson b Gatting	0	K. Saxelby not out	23	
*C. E. B. Rice b Rose	48	L-b 7, w 9, n-b 7	23	
J. D. Birch c Cook b James	24			
D. W. Randall b Williams	23	1/1 2/6 3/46	(6 wkts, 39.2 overs) 186	
†B. N. French c Ellis b Williams	4	4/107 5/112 6/117		

K. E. Cooper, R. A. Pick and M. K. Bore did not bat.

Bowling: Gatting 8–1–25–1; James 7.2–0–25–2; Rose 8–0–41–1; Williams 8–0–48–2; Merry 8–0–24–0.

Umpires: C. T. Spencer and N. T. Plews.

NOTTINGHAMSHIRE v GLOUCESTERSHIRE

At Nottingham, September 11. No result.

SOMERSET

SOMERSET v SUSSEX

At Taunton, May 8. Somerset won by 89 runs. Toss won by Sussex.

Somerset

J. W. Lloyds c Pigott b C. M. Wells	2	V. J. Marks not out	10	
P. M. Roebuck c Phillipson b Pigott	50			
I. V. A. Richards not out	96			
I. T. Botham c Greig b Barclay	0	L-b 7, w 2, n-b 1	10	
*B. C. Rose b le Roux	42			
N. F. M. Popplewell c A. P. Wells		1/12 2/102	(5 wkts, 40 overs) 213	
b le Roux.	3	3/103 4/184 5/194		

†T. Gard, J. Garner, C. H. Dredge and G. V. Palmer did not bat.

Bowling: C. M. Wells 6–0–26–1; le Roux 8–0–45–2; Waller 3–0–25–0; Greig 7–0–37–0; Barclay 8–0–36–1; Pigott 8–0–34–1.

Sussex

G. D. Mendis run out	24	*J. R. T. Barclay not out	8	
†I. J. Gould c Garner b Marks	14	A. C. S. Pigott lbw b Botham	0	
C. M. Wells c Lloyds b Palmer	1	C. E. Waller c Dredge b Botham	2	
P. W. G. Parker c and b Richards	15	L-b 9, w 1, n-b 1	11	
G. S. le Roux c Rose b Dredge	16			
I. A. Greig c Dredge b Richards	33	1/42 2/49 3/49	(36.3 overs) 124	
C. P. Phillipson b Dredge	0	4/74 5/84 6/85		
A. P. Wells lbw b Dredge	0	7/85 8/119 9/119		

Bowling: Garner 5–0–12–0; Botham 5.3–0–14–2; Palmer 8–0–23–1; Marks 8–1–10–1; Dredge 4–0–22–3; Richards 6–1–32–2.

Umpires: R. Palmer and D. R. Shepherd.

At Nottingham, May 15. SOMERSET beat NOTTINGHAMSHIRE on faster scoring-rate.

At The Oval, May 22. SURREY v SOMERSET. No result.

At Bradford, May 29. SOMERSET beat YORKSHIRE on faster scoring-rate.

SOMERSET v ESSEX

At Taunton, June 5. No result.

SOMERSET v GLAMORGAN

At Bath, June 19. Somerset won by five wickets. Toss won by Glamorgan.

Glamorgan

J. A. Hopkins not out	130	R. C. Ontong not out	8
H. Morris run out	37	B 1, l-b 25, w 6	32
A. L. Jones c Gard b Dredge	17		
J. G. Thomas lbw b Dredge	0	1/135 2/167 (4 wkts, 40 overs) 235	
D. A. Francis b Wilson	11	3/167 4/202	

J. Derrick, †E. W. Jones, *M. W. W. Selvey, B. J. Lloyd and M. A. Nash did not bat.

Bowling: Wilson 8–0–40–1; Davis 4–0–23–0; Popplewell 7–1–38–0; Dredge 8–0–25–2; Breakwell 5–0–29–0; Palmer 8–0–48–0.

Somerset

P. W. Denning c and b Ontong	30	D. Breakwell b Derrick	0
R. L. Ollis lbw b Nash	0	C. H. Dredge not out	25
N. F. M. Popplewell st E. W. Jones b Derrick	84	B 1, l-b 11, w 9, n-b 1	22
P. A. Slocombe c Selvey b Lloyd	46	1/4 2/89 (5 wkts, 39 overs) 237	
*P. M. Roebuck not out	30	3/168 4/178 5/182	

G. V. Palmer, †T. Gard, M. R. Davis and P. H. L. Wilson did not bat.

Bowling: Selvey 8–1–27–0; Nash 5–0–23–1; Ontong 7–0–52–1; Lloyd 6–0–39–1; Thomas 5–0–42–0; Derrick 8–0–32–2.

Umpires: W. E. Alley and R. A. White.

SOMERSET v GLOUCESTERSHIRE

At Bath, June 26. Somerset won by 16 runs. Toss won by Gloucestershire.

Somerset

P. M. Roebuck c Russell b Lawrence	105	J. Garner not out	4
P. W. Denning c Russell b Lawrence	16		
I. V. A. Richards c Stovold b Lawrence	2	L-b 15, w 11	26
*I. T. Botham c Lawrence b Bainbridge	73		
N. F. M. Popplewell lbw b Bainbridge	7	1/34 2/43 3/170 (6 wkts, 40 overs) 254	
P. A. Slocombe b Lawrence	21	4/179 5/236 6/254	

V. J. Marks, †T. Gard, C. H. Dredge and P. H. L. Wilson did not bat.

Bowling: Sainsbury 8–0–41–0; Lawrence 8–0–41–4; Bainbridge 8–1–34–2; Shepherd 8–0–50–0; Doughty 8–0–62–0.

Gloucestershire

A. W. Stovold c Richards b Marks	57	*D. A. Graveney not out	7
P. W. Romaines b Dredge	30	R. J. Doughty not out	0
Zaheer Abbas c Slocombe b Richards	32	B 2, l-b 12, w 2	16
A. J. Hignell c Marks b Popplewell	8		
P. Bainbridge c Wilson b Popplewell	53	1/73 2/113 3/133 (6 wkts, 40 overs) 238	
J. N. Shepherd c Marks b Popplewell	35	4/133 5/221 6/238	

†R. C. Russell, D. V. Lawrence and G. E. Sainsbury did not bat.

Bowling: Garner 8–1–40–0; Wilson 6–0–49–0; Dredge 8–0–41–1; Marks 8–1–32–1; Richards 4–0–22–1; Popplewell 6–0–38–3.

Umpires: D. O. Oslear and P. B. Wight.

At Leicester, July 10. SOMERSET lost to LEICESTERSHIRE by eight wickets.

SOMERSET v HAMPSHIRE

At Taunton, July 24. Somerset won by seven wickets in a match reduced by rain to 21 overs a side. Toss won by Hampshire.

Hampshire

C. G. Greenidge c Gard b Dredge	29	N. G. Cowley run out	0
C. L. Smith c Gard b Botham	3	T. M. Tremlett not out	11
T. E. Jesty c Gard b Botham	10	B 1, l-b 8, w 1, n-b 1	11
V. P. Terry b Garner	11		
M. C. J. Nicholas c Denning b Botham	12	1/12 2/41 (7 wkts, 21 overs) 93	
M. D. Marshall b Botham	1	3/47 4/70	
*N. E. J. Pocock not out	5	5/74 6/74 7/76	

†R. J. Parks and S. J. Malone did not bat.

Bowling: Garner 8–0–30–1; Botham 8–2–22–4; Marks 1–0–3–0; Dredge 4–0–27–1.

Somerset

P. M. Roebuck c Parks b Marshall	0	N. F. M. Popplewell not out	5
P. W. Denning not out	37	W 2	2
I. V. A. Richards b Tremlett	28		
*I. T. Botham c Parks b Malone	25	1/1 2/45 3/79 (3 wkts, 12.4 overs) 97	

J. W. Lloyds, P. A. Slocombe, V. J. Marks, †T. Gard, C. H. Dredge and J. Garner did not bat.

Bowling: Marshall 6–0–35–1; Malone 2–0–32–1; Tremlett 4.4–0–28–1.

Umpires: C. Cook and D. R. Shepherd.

At Manchester, July 31. LANCASHIRE v SOMERSET. No result.

SOMERSET v NORTHAMPTONSHIRE

At Weston-super-Mare, August 7. Somerset won by ten wickets. Toss won by Somerset.

Northamptonshire

W. Larkins c Gard b Garner	0	†G. Sharp b Garner	22
P. Willey b Dredge	32	N. A. Mallender run out	22
A. J. Lamb b Garner	5	T. M. Lamb not out	2
Kapil Dev lbw b Garner	0	L-b 10, w 1, n-b 3	14
*G. Cook c Garner b Marks	16		
R. G. Williams c Ollis b Marks	9	1/5 2/18 3/19 4/54 (9 wkts, 40 overs) 123	
D. J. Capel c Gard b Richards	1	5/64 6/73 7/75 8/119 9/123	

B. J. Griffiths did not bat.

Bowling: Garner 8–3–22–4; Botham 8–1–27–0; Dredge 8–1–18–1; Marks 8–1–24–2; Richards 8–0–18–1.

Somerset

P. M. Roebuck not out	51
P. W. Denning not out	62
B 5, l-b 5, n-b 2	12

(no wkt, 33 overs) 125

R. L. Ollis, I. V. A. Richards, *I. T. Botham, N. F. M. Popplewell, P. A. Slocombe, V. J. Marks, J. Garner, †T. Gard and C. H. Dredge did not bat.

Bowling: Kapil Dev 4–1–13–0; Griffiths 8–2–31–0; Willey 4–0–17–0; Williams 5–1–18–0; Mallender 5–0–13–0; T. M. Lamb 7–1–21–0.

Umpires: C. T. Spencer and A. G. T. Whitehead.

At Heanor, August 14. SOMERSET lost to DERBYSHIRE by eight wickets.

At Lord's, August 21. SOMERSET beat MIDDLESEX by four wickets.

SOMERSET v KENT

At Taunton, August 28. Somerset won by six wickets. Toss won by Somerset.

Kent

N. R. Taylor c Richards b Palmer	47	G. W. Johnson not out	6
R. A. Woolmer c Popplewell b Palmer	21	R. M. Ellison not out	0
D. G. Aslett run out	100	B 2, l-b 7, w 3	12
M. R. Benson b Richards	5		
*C. S. Cowdrey c and b Richards	1	1/47 2/91 (7 wkts, 40 overs) 221	
E. A. E. Baptiste run out	25	3/115 4/127	
†A. P. E. Knott run out	4	5/187 6/202 7/219	

K. B. S. Jarvis and D. L. Underwood did not bat.

Bowling: Garner 8–0–42–0; Dredge 8–0–39–0; Marks 8–1–20–0; Palmer 8–0–58–2; Popplewell 4–0–35–0; Richards 4–0–15–2.

Somerset

P. M. Roebuck c Underwood b Ellison..	60	V. J. Marks not out	4
P. W. Denning b Woolmer................	50	B 4, l-b 5, w 1, n-b 1	11
*I. V. A. Richards c Woolmer b Ellison..	86		
N. F. M. Popplewell run out..............	13	1/99 2/182 (4 wkts, 38.3 overs)	224
J. Garner not out............................	0	3/216 4/220	

R. L. Ollis, P. A. Slocombe, G. V. Palmer, †T. Gard and C. H. Dredge did not bat.

Bowling: Jarvis 7.3–0–57–0; Ellison 7–0–27–2; Cowdrey 8–0–43–0; Woolmer 8–0–42–1; Underwood 8–0–44–0.

Umpires: J. W. Holder and A. E. Jepson.

At Worcester, September 4. SOMERSET lost to WORCESTERSHIRE by 55 runs.

SOMERSET v WARWICKSHIRE

At Taunton, September 11. Somerset won by three wickets. Toss won by Somerset.

Warwickshire

T. A. Lloyd b Marks	22	D. A. Thorne run out.......................	29
D. L. Amiss c Gard b Marks	28	C. Lethbridge not out	0
A. I. Kallicharran c Gard b Richards...	38		
†G. W. Humpage c Lloyds b Marks....	8	B 1, l-b 10, n-b 1	12
G. J. Lord b Richards	1		
Asif Din c Gard b Dredge	10	1/42 2/63 3/93 4/94 (7 wkts, 40 overs)	174
P. A. Smith not out	26	5/117 6/117 7/172	

N. Gifford and *R. G. D. Willis did not bat.

Bowling: Garner 8–0–27–0; Botham 8–0–42–0; Marks 8–1–23–3; Dredge 8–1–35–1; Richards 8–0–35–2.

Somerset

P. M. Roebuck b Smith	7	P. A. Slocombe run out	9
P. W. Denning c Humpage b Willis.....	5	J. Garner not out............................	14
I. V. A. Richards c Willis b Smith	4	J. W. Lloyds not out	2
N. F. M. Popplewell c Asif Din		B 9, l-b 6, w 2, n-b 1	18
b Thorne	23		
*I. T. Botham c Willis b Gifford.........	49	1/12 2/14 3/19 (7 wkts, 38.2 overs)	175
V. J. Marks c Lord b Willis	44	4/65 5/124 6/153 7/162	

†T. Gard and C. H. Dredge did not bat.

Bowling: Willis 7.2–2–19–2; Smith 8–1–32–2; Gifford 8–2–16–1; Thorne 8–0–49–1; Kallicharran 4–0–26–0; Lethbridge 3–0–15–0.

Umpires: B. Leadbeater and C. T. Spencer.

SURREY

At Canterbury, May 8. SURREY lost to KENT on faster scoring-rate.

At Leeds, May 15. YORKSHIRE v SURREY. No result.

SURREY v SOMERSET

At The Oval, May 22. No result.

At Nottingham, May 29. NOTTINGHAMSHIRE v SURREY. No result.

At Bristol, June 5. GLOUCESTERSHIRE v SURREY. No result.

SURREY v MIDDLESEX

At The Oval, June 12. Surrey won by 3 runs. Toss won by Surrey.

Surrey

A. R. Butcher c Slack b Emburey	46	S. T. Clarke b Hughes	8
†C. J. Richards b Hughes	19	I. R. Payne not out	5
D. M. Smith c Downton b Merry	28	L-b 5, w 2, n-b 1	8
M. A. Lynch c Downton b Emburey	7		
*R. D. V. Knight c Emburey b Merry	6	1/39 2/80 (7 wkts, 40 overs) 164	
A. Needham not out	25	3/91 4/105	
D. J. Thomas c Downton b Hughes	12	5/116 6/136 7/150	

G. Monkhouse and P. I. Pocock did not bat.

Bowling: Williams 8–1–38–0; James 8–0–31–0; Hughes 8–0–37–3; Emburey 8–0–21–2; Merry 8–0–29–2.

Middlesex

G. D. Barlow run out	35	K. D. James not out	11
W. N. Slack c Richards b Clarke	25	N. F. Williams not out	10
C. T. Radley c Richards b Clarke	4		
R. O. Butcher b Pocock	4	B 3, l-b 6, w 1	10
K. P. Tomlins c Smith b Thomas	31		
*J. E. Emburey c Monkhouse b Thomas	27	1/57 2/69 3/69 (7 wkts, 40 overs) 161	
†P. R. Downton b Clarke	4	4/86 5/131 6/137 7/137	

W. G. Merry and S. P. Hughes did not bat.

Bowling: Thomas 8–0–32–2; Monkhouse 8–0–31–0; Pocock 8–0–31–1; Clarke 8–1–21–3; Knight 5–0–24–0; Needham 3–0–12–0.

Umpires: J. Morley and B. J. Meyer.

SURREY v NORTHAMPTONSHIRE

At East Molesey, June 26. Northamptonshire won by five wickets. Toss won by Surrey.

Surrey

*A. R. Butcher c A. J. Lamb b Mallender	68	A. J. Stewart lbw b Mallender	0
†C. J. Richards c T. M. Lamb b Willey	26	A. Needham not out	0
		I. R. Payne not out	7
M. A. Lynch b Mallender	70	L-b 8, w 7	15
D. J. Thomas b Mallender	39	1/55 2/141 3/216 (6 wkts, 39 overs) 232	
S. T. Clarke b Walker	7	4/221 5/221 6/225	

G. S. Clinton, G. Monkhouse and P. I. Pocock did not bat.

Bowling: Griffiths 5–0–33–0; Walker 8–0–24–1; T. M. Lamb 8–0–64–0; Willey 8–1–34–1; Mallender 8–0–46–4; Williams 2–0–16–0.

Northamptonshire

R. J. Bailey c Stewart b Monkhouse....	19	D. J. Wild not out	0
M. J. Bamber c Pocock b Payne.........	71		
P. Willey c Richards b Monkhouse......	15	B 6, l-b 12, w 7	25
†A. J. Lamb c Clarke b Payne	72		
*G. Cook not out	29	1/40 2/81 3/190 (5 wkts, 37.3 overs) 234
R. G. Williams c Stewart b Payne.......	3	4/217 5/224	

A. Walker, N. A. Mallender, T. M. Lamb and B. J. Griffiths did not bat.

Bowling: Thomas 6.3–0–53–0; Monkhouse 8–0–26–2; Clarke 8–0–30–0; Pocock 7–0–54–0; Payne 8–0–46–3.

Umpires: M. J. Kitchen and D. R. Shepherd.

At Portsmouth, July 10. SURREY lost to HAMPSHIRE by 104 runs.

SURREY v LANCASHIRE

At The Oval, July 24. Lancashire won by four wickets. Toss won by Lancashire.

Surrey

A. R. Butcher c and b Abrahams	41	A. Needham lbw b McFarlane	19
†C. J. Richards c Fowler b McFarlane .	2	K. S. Mackintosh b Simmons.............	12
D. M. Smith c O'Shaughnessy		S. T. Clarke not out.........................	0
b Simmons.	41	G. Monkhouse b McFarlane	0
M. A. Lynch b O'Shaughnessy...........	26		
*R. D. V. Knight c Abrahams		L-b 13, w 1, n-b 2	16
b Simmons.	1		
D. J. Thomas run out.......................	12	1/11 2/82 3/100 4/101 (39.4 overs) 186
I. R. Payne b O'Shaughnessy	16	5/131 6/152 7/154 8/182 9/186	

Bowling: Folley 8–0–25–0; McFarlane 7.4–0–19–3; O'Shaughnessy 8–0–45–2; Simmons 8–0–37–3; Abrahams 8–0–44–1.

Lancashire

K. A. Hayes c Clarke b Monkhouse....	5	N. H. Fairbrother c Needham	
G. Fowler c Richards b Clarke	1	b Clarke.	44
S. J. O'Shaughnessy retired hurt.........	1	J. Simmons not out.........................	3
*C. H. Lloyd c Clarke b Thomas........	11	B 2, l-b 5, w 3, n-b 2..............	13
J. Abrahams b Thomas.....................	6		
D. P. Hughes not out.......................	87	1/2 2/9 3/26 (6 wkts, 38.4 overs) 187
†C. Maynard c Needham b Knight......	16	4/31 5/64 6/173	

I. Folley and L. L. McFarlane did not bat.

Bowling: Clarke 7–1–18–2; Monkhouse 8–1–17–1; Thomas 8–0–29–2; Knight 5–1–30–1; Payne 5–0–29–0; Mackintosh 5.4–0–51–0.

Umpires: A. G. T. Whitehead and P. B. Wight.

At Swansea, July 31. SURREY lost to GLAMORGAN on faster scoring-rate.

SURREY v WARWICKSHIRE

At The Oval, August 7. Warwickshire won by five wickets. Toss won by Warwickshire.

Surrey

*A. R. Butcher c Dyer b Willis	4	K. S. Mackintosh run out	12
D. B. Pauline b Lethbridge	35	S. T. Clarke b Thorne	22
†A. J. Stewart c Thorne b Lethbridge	8	I. J. Curtis not out	0
M. A. Lynch b Lethbridge	11		
D. J. Thomas b Gifford	13	L-b 10, w 5, n-b 1	16
I. R. Payne c Amiss b Ferreira	23		
A. Needham b Thorne	7	1/11 2/44 3/70 4/75 (38.5 overs) 157	
G. Monkhouse c Willis b Gifford	6	5/102 6/107 7/118 8/132 9/150	

Bowling: Willis 8–1–17–1; Ferreira 8–2–30–1; Lethbridge 8–1–27–3; Thorne 7.5–0–33–2; Gifford 7–0–34–2.

Warwickshire

T. A. Lloyd c Stewart b Clarke	11	Asif Din c Needham b Thomas	9
D. L. Amiss c Needham b Payne	60	A. M. Ferreira not out	5
A. I. Kallicharran c Butcher b Thomas	25		
		L-b 4, w 6	10
†G. W. Humpage c Mackintosh b Payne	15		
R. I. H. B. Dyer not out	25	1/23 2/67 3/96 (5 wkts, 37.3 overs) 160	
		4/139 5/154	

D. A. Thorne, C. Lethbridge, N. Gifford and *R. G. D. Willis did not bat.

Bowling: Monkhouse 5–1–21–0; Clarke 8–1–18–1; Mackintosh 5.3–0–26–0; Thomas 7–0–32–2; Payne 8–0–37–2; Curtis 4–0–16–0.

Umpires: B. J. Meyer and B. Dudleston.

SURREY v WORCESTERSHIRE

At Guildford, August 14. Surrey won by 28 runs. Toss won by Worcestershire.

Surrey

A. R. Butcher c King b Warner	1	†C. J. Richards b Pridgeon	6
D. B. Pauline b Warner	84	A. J. Stewart not out	5
*R. D. V. Knight c Neale b Patel	87	B 1, l-b 5, w 3, n-b 1	10
M. A. Lynch c King b Pridgeon	54		
D. J. Thomas c Ormrod b Pridgeon	3	1/2 2/147 3/229 (6 wkts, 37 overs) 270	
S. T. Clarke not out	20	4/236 5/243 6/262	

I. J. Curtis, G. Monkhouse and P. I. Pocock did not bat.

Bowling: Warner 8–0–32–2; Pridgeon 8–0–52–3; Perryman 6–0–44–0; King 8–0–51–0; Patel 5–0–53–1; Illingworth 2–0–28–0.

Worcestershire

J. A. Ormrod c and b Monkhouse	1	A. E. Warner c Stewart b Pocock	13
M. S. A. McEvoy c Richards b Thomas	17	R. K. Illingworth run out	1
D. N. Patel b Monkhouse	9	S. P. Perryman not out	8
C. L. King c Monkhouse b Clarke	127	A. P. Pridgeon b Thomas	3
*P. A. Neale c Richards b Pocock	21	L-b 11, w 3, n-b 4	18
D. B. D'Oliveira b Clarke	0		
†D. J. Humphries run out	24	1/10 2/31 3/33 4/112 (36.3 overs) 242	
		5/113 6/195 7/220 8/222 9/230	

Bowling: Thomas 6.3–0–43–2; Monkhouse 8–0–28–2; Knight 6–0–40–0; Clarke 8–0–54–2; Pocock 8–0–59–2.

Umpires: P. J. Eele and A. Jepson.

At Hove, August 21. SURREY lost to SUSSEX by 52 runs.

SURREY v ESSEX

At The Oval, August 28. Surrey won by three wickets. Toss won by Essex.

Essex

G. A. Gooch c Stewart b Knight	10	S. Turner c Pocock b Thomas	1
C. Gladwin b Payne	18	†D. E. East lbw b Pocock	1
K. S. McEwan b Waterman	8	R. E. East b Payne	8
D. R. Pringle c Stewart b Thomas	2	D. L. Acfield not out	9
N. Phillip c Lynch b Payne	21	B 2, l-b 5, w 4	11
*K. W. R. Fletcher c Waterman b Pocock	26		
		1/30 2/39 3/41 4/41 (39.4 overs)	127
B. R. Hardie c Lynch b Pocock	12	5/82 6/106 7/108 8/109 9/111	

Bowling: Waterman 8–1–25–1; Payne 6.4–0–33–3; Knight 8–1–15–1; Thomas 8–2–23–2; Pocock 8–1–18–3; Curtis 1–0–2–0.

Surrey

A. R. Butcher not out	63	I. R. Payne c Gooch b R. E. East	0
D. B. Pauline c Pringle b Turner	11	P. I. Pocock not out	12
*R. D. V. Knight b Acfield	5		
M. A. Lynch c R. E. East b Pringle	10	B 4, l-b 1, n-b 3	8
D. J. Thomas run out	8		
C. J. Richards b R. E. East	7	1/20 2/34 3/58 (7 wkts, 39 overs)	128
†A. J. Stewart lbw b Turner	4	4/75 5/96 6/101 7/102	

P. A. Waterman and I. J. Curtis did not bat.

Bowling: Phillip 4–1–13–0; Turner 7–1–30–2; Pringle 8–1–20–1; Acfield 8–3–14–1; R. E. East 8–1–20–2; Gooch 4–0–23–0.

Umpires: B. Leadbeater and N. T. Plews.

At Leicester, September 4. SURREY beat LEICESTERSHIRE by 3 runs.

SURREY v DERBYSHIRE

At The Oval, September 11. No result.

SUSSEX

At Taunton, May 8. SUSSEX lost to SOMERSET by 89 runs.

SUSSEX v KENT

At Hove, May 15. No result.

At Lord's, May 29. SUSSEX beat MIDDLESEX by four wickets.

SUSSEX v WARWICKSHIRE

At Hove, June 12. Sussex won by 52 runs. Toss won by Sussex.

Sussex

G. D. Mendis c Hogg b P. A. Smith ...	34	C. P. Phillipson not out	1
P. W. G. Parker b Ferreira................	104	B 4, l-b 9, n-b 7......................	20
C. M. Wells not out	104		
A. P. Wells lbw b Ferreira	0	1/73 2/262 3/262 (3 wkts, 40 overs)	263

G. S. le Roux, *J. R. T. Barclay, A. C. S. Pigott, †D. J. Smith, D. A. Reeve and
   C. E. Waller did not bat.

Bowling: Hogg 8–0–44–0; Old 8–0–61–0; P. A. Smith 8–0–38–1; Gifford 8–0–55–0;
Ferreira 8–0–45–2.

Warwickshire

K. D. Smith c Parker b Barclay..........	24	A. M. Ferreira c Pigott b le Roux.......	12
R. I. H. B. Dyer lbw b Barclay	43	P. A. Smith not out	10
D. L. Amiss c Parker b le Roux	35	*N. Gifford not out.........................	13
†G. W. Humpage c Barclay b Pigott ...	25	B 1, l-b 6, w 4......................	11
C. M. Old c C. M. Wells b le Roux ...	10		
Asif Din c A. P. Wells b Waller.........	10	1/53 2/84 3/122 (8 wkts, 40 overs)	211
S. H. Wootton run out	18	4/135 5/148 6/159 7/186 8/186	

W. Hogg did not bat.

Bowling: C. M. Wells 8–0–26–0; le Roux 8–0–45–3; Barclay 8–0–36–2; Reeve 6–0–31–0;
Pigott 8–0–45–1; Waller 2–0–17–1.

Umpires: C. Cook and R. A. White.

SUSSEX v LANCASHIRE

At Horsham, June 19. Sussex won by 2 runs. Toss won by Sussex.

Sussex

G. D. Mendis c Maynard b Jefferies....	25	*J. R. T. Barclay b Watkinson	11
P. W. G. Parker c Maynard b Folley...	52	A. C. S. Pigott not out	9
C. M. Wells run out	7	†D. J. Smith not out	5
A. P. Wells st Maynard b Simmons.....	38	B 1, l-b 15, w 5, n-b 1	22
C. P. Phillipson c Cockbain b Simmons .	15		
G. S. le Roux run out......................	16	1/51 2/63 3/131 (8 wkts, 40 overs)	202
D. A. Reeve run out........................	2	4/143 5/162 6/170 7/175 8/187	

C. E. Waller did not bat.

Bowling: Jefferies 8–1–40–1; Folley 8–0–39–1; Watkinson 8–0–25–1; O'Shaughnessy 8–1–35–0; Simmons 8–0–41–2.

Lancashire

F. C. Hayes c Smith b le Roux	1	M. Watkinson b Reeve	1
I. Cockbain lbw b le Roux	3	N. H. Fairbrother run out	19
†C. Maynard b Pigott	24	I. Folley run out	1
D. P. Hughes lbw b C. M. Wells	8	L-b 7, w 2	9
*J. Abrahams not out	79		
S. T. Jefferies lbw b Pigott	34	1/1 2/12 3/35	(39.5 overs) 200
S. J. O'Shaughnessy b le Roux	14	4/57 5/116 6/149	
J. Simmons b Pigott	7	7/160 8/169 9/199	

Bowling: C. M. Wells 8–0–28–1; le Roux 8–0–33–3; Pigott 8–0–31–3; Barclay 7.5–0–42–0; Reeve 8–1–57–1.

Umpires: J. W. Holder and C. T. Spencer.

At Ilford, June 26. SUSSEX beat ESSEX by four wickets.

SUSSEX v NORTHAMPTONSHIRE

At Hastings, July 3. Sussex won by 88 runs. Toss won by Sussex.

Sussex

G. D. Mendis c Williams b Mallender	11	G. S. le Roux not out	1
P. W. G. Parker not out	121	L-b 5, w 1, n-b 1	7
C. M. Wells c Cook b Griffiths	42		
Imran Khan c T. M. Lamb b Griffiths	49	1/25 2/115 3/227	(3 wkts, 40 overs) 231

A. P. Wells, †I. J. Gould, C. P. Phillipson, *J. R. T. Barclay, D. A. Reeve and A. C. S. Pigott did not bat.

Bowling: Carse 8–0–45–0; Mallender 8–1–34–1; T. M. Lamb 8–0–30–0; Willey 8–1–35–0; Griffiths 8–0–80–2.

Northamptonshire

R. J. Bailey run out	36	N. A. Mallender b Pigott	2
W. Larkins lbw b le Roux	3	T. M. Lamb lbw b Pigott	0
P. Willey lbw b le Roux	2	J. A. Carse not out	4
A. J. Lamb c le Roux b Barclay	12	B 1, l-b 6, w 1	8
*G. Cook b Barclay	2		
R. G. Williams not out	45	1/14 2/18 3/44 4/50	(8 wkts, 40 overs) 143
†G. Sharp b Pigott	29	5/62 6/122 7/130 8/130	

B. J. Griffiths did not bat.

Bowling: C. M. Wells 8–1–28–0; le Roux 8–0–36–2; Barclay 8–0–22–2; Reeve 8–1–26–0; Pigott 8–1–23–3.

Umpires: R. Julian and R. Palmer.

At Cardiff, July 10. SUSSEX beat GLAMORGAN by five wickets.

SUSSEX v YORKSHIRE

At Hove, July 24. Yorkshire won by six wickets. Toss won by Sussex.

Sussex

G. D. Mendis c Illingworth		C. P. Phillipson run out		1
b Sidebottom.	20	*J. R. T. Barclay c Athey		
P. W. G. Parker c Bairstow			b Stevenson.	5
b Sidebottom.	8	A. C. S. Pigott b Dennis		0
C. M. Wells b Illingworth	5	D. A. Reeve not out		1
Imran Khan lbw b Stevenson	28	L-b 7, n-b 3		10
†I. J. Gould c Dennis b Illingworth	9			
G. S. le Roux c Carrick b Stevenson	26	1/23 2/37 3/37 4/60 (39.3 overs)		135
A. P. Wells b Dennis	22	5/89 6/108 7/110 8/134 9/134		

Bowling: Dennis 7.3–0–31–2; Stevenson 8–0–35–3; Sidebottom 8–1–22–2; Illingworth 8–4–13–2; Carrick 8–0–24–0.

Yorkshire

G. Boycott not out	75	†D. L. Bairstow not out	2
C. W. J. Athey lbw b C. M. Wells	10	L-b 7, w 5, n-b 3	15
K. Sharp c Phillipson b Barclay	38		
S. N. Hartley c Phillipson b Pigott	0	1/29 2/122 3/126 (4 wkts, 38.2 overs)	141
J. D. Love c and b Reeve	1	4/129	

P. Carrick, A. Sidebottom, G. B. Stevenson, *R. Illingworth and S. J. Dennis did not bat.

Bowling: C. M. Wells 8–1–15–1; le Roux 8–1–19–0; Reeve 8–0–28–1; Barclay 5.2–0–32–1; Pigott 8–1–26–1; Parker 1–0–6–0.

Umpires: P. J. Eele and C. T. Spencer.

At Leicester, July 31. LEICESTERSHIRE v SUSSEX. No result.

SUSSEX v DERBYSHIRE

At Eastbourne, August 7. Sussex won by 2 runs. Toss won by Derbyshire.

Sussex

G. D. Mendis c Taylor b Miller	50	*J. R. T. Barclay not out		2
P. W. G. Parker c Hill b Oldham	46	A. C. S. Pigott c Barnett b Oldham		4
Imran Khan c Hampshire b Finney	11	D. A. Reeve c Taylor b Mortensen		0
C. M. Wells b Finney	0			
†I. J. Gould c Hill b Oldham	3	L-b 9, w 1		10
A. P. Wells b Oldham	3			
C. P. Phillipson b Mortensen	19	1/82 2/109 3/111 4/114 (38.3 overs)		148
I. A. Greig run out	0	5/121 6/136 7/137 8/142 9/147		

Bowling: Finney 8–1–20–2; Mortensen 7.3–0–33–2; Tunnicliffe 8–0–35–0; Miller 8–0–29–1; Oldham 7–1–21–4.

Derbyshire

*K. J. Barnett c Phillipson b C. M. Wells.	11	W. P. Fowler c Reeve b Greig	0
I. S. Anderson c Gould b Pigott	30	C. J. Tunnicliffe not out	18
J. H. Hampshire b Imran	21	†R. W. Taylor not out	1
G. Miller b Reeve	23	L-b 13, w 9, n-b 1	23
A. Hill b Pigott	13		
R. J. Finney b Greig	6	1/27 2/66 3/89 (7 wkts, 40 overs) 146
		4/106 5/120 6/120 7/120	

S. Oldham and O. H. Mortensen did not bat.

Bowling: C. M. Wells 8–0–22–1; Reeve 8–1–21–1; Imran 8–0–25–1; Greig 8–0–28–2; Pigott 8–0–27–2.

Umpires: D. R. Shepherd and J. van Geloven.

At Nottingham, August 14. SUSSEX lost to NOTTINGHAMSHIRE by 33 runs.

SUSSEX v SURREY

At Hove, August 21. Sussex won by 52 runs. Toss won by Sussex.

Sussex

G. D. Mendis b Pocock	52	R. S. Cowan c Stewart b Monkhouse	2
†I. J. Gould c Knight b Pocock	19	*J. R. T. Barclay not out	4
C. M. Wells run out	4		
Imran Khan c Butcher b Curtis	7	B 7, l-b 13, w 17, n-b 3	40
A. P. Wells lbw b Pocock	1		
I. A. Greig c Butcher b Monkhouse	35	1/69 2/86 3/103 (7 wkts, 40 overs) 196
C. P. Phillipson not out	32	4/104 5/105 6/161 7/168	

D. A. Reeve and C. E. Waller did not bat.

Bowling: Clarke 8–1–15–0; Monkhouse 8–0–38–2; Thomas 8–0–46–0; Pocock 8–1–22–3; Curtis 8–1–35–1.

Surrey

A. R. Butcher b Barclay	17	S. T. Clarke c Reeve b Greig	0
D. B. Pauline b Imran	32	P. I. Pocock c Imran b Greig	4
*R. D. V. Knight c Imran b Waller	11	I. J. Curtis not out	0
M. A. Lynch run out	1		
D. J. Thomas c Greig b Imran	9	B 1, l-b 3, w 2, n-b 1	7
†C. J. Richards run out	0		
A. J. Stewart c Gould b Imran	36	1/24 2/41 3/44 4/71 (37.2 overs) 144
G. Monkhouse c and b Reeve	27	5/73 6/73 7/136 8/140 9/144	

Bowling: C. M. Wells 3–0–16–0; Reeve 8–0–34–1; Barclay 8–0–23–1; Waller 8–0–24–1; Imran 6–1–13–3; Greig 4.2–0–27–2.

Umpires: J. Birkenshaw and R. A. White.

At Southampton, August 28. SUSSEX lost to HAMPSHIRE by four wickets.

SUSSEX v GLOUCESTERSHIRE

At Hove, September 4. Sussex won by seven wickets after rain had reduced the match to 27 overs a side. Toss won by Sussex.

Gloucestershire

A. W. Stovold c Gould b Reeve	13	R. J. Doughty not out	13
P. W. Romaines c Mendis		†R. C. Russell b Pigott	1
b C. M. Wells.	1	J. H. Childs run out	1
P. Bainbridge b Greig	39	G. E. Sainsbury not out	4
A. J. Wright c Gould b Greig	7	L-b 5, w 1	6
J. N. Shepherd c Reeve b Pigott	21		
E. J. Cunningham c Gould b Imran	7	1/6 2/28 3/60 4/69 (9 wkts, 27 overs) 115	
*D. A. Graveney c Gould b Reeve	2	5/78 6/93 7/95 8/103 9/104	

Bowling: Pigott 6–0–24–2; C. M. Wells 5–0–18–1; Reeve 5–0–21–2; Imran 6–1–16–1; Greig 5–0–30–2.

Sussex

G. D. Mendis c Russell b Shepherd	25	†I. J. Gould not out	44
P. W. G. Parker not out	35	B 1, l-b 8, w 2	11
C. M. Wells lbw b Doughty	0		
Imran Khan c Bainbridge b Shepherd	1	1/30 2/33 3/36 (3 wkts, 22.4 overs) 116	

A. P. Wells, I. A. Greig, C. P. Phillipson, *J. R. T. Barclay, D. A. Reeve and A. C. S. Pigott did not bat.

Bowling: Shepherd 6–0–29–2; Doughty 4.4–0–23–1; Wright 4–0–18–0; Sainsbury 4–0–24–0; Bainbridge 4–1–11–0.

Umpires: D. J. Constant and J. H. Harris.

At Worcester, September 11. SUSSEX lost to WORCESTERSHIRE on faster scoring-rate.

WARWICKSHIRE

WARWICKSHIRE v YORKSHIRE

At Birmingham, May 8. Yorkshire won by six wickets in a match reduced by rain to 24 overs a side. Toss won by Yorkshire.

Warwickshire

T. A. Lloyd b Stevenson	13	A. M. Ferreira not out	34
K. D. Smith c Boycott b Jarvis	16		
A. I. Kallicharran lbw b Jarvis	11	W 8	8
D. L. Amiss not out	55		
†G. W. Humpage b Jarvis	17	1/26 2/39 (5 wkts, 24 overs) 175	
Asif Din b Sidebottom	21	3/52 4/86 5/119	

C. M. Old, C. Lethbridge, *R. G. D. Willis and W. Hogg did not bat.

Bowling: Stevenson 8–1–39–1; Jarvis 8–0–39–3; Sidebottom 4–0–45–1; Athey 1–0–21–0; Carrick 3–0–23–0.

Yorkshire

K. Sharp b Old	17	S. N. Hartley not out	26
G. Boycott c Humpage b Old	18	L-b 17, w 1	18
C. W. J. Athey not out	72		
G. B. Stevenson run out	25	1/29 2/48 (4 wkts, 22.4 overs) 176	
†D. L. Bairstow b Ferreira	0	3/88 4/92	

J. D. Love, P. Carrick, A. Sidebottom, *R. Illingworth and P. W. Jarvis did not bat.

Bowling: Willis 7–0–48–0; Old 8–0–54–2; Ferreira 7.4–0–56–1.

Umpires: W. E. Alley and A. Jepson.

At Swansea, May 15. GLAMORGAN v WARWICKSHIRE. No result.

WARWICKSHIRE v LANCASHIRE

At Birmingham, May 22. No result. Toss won by Lancashire.

Warwickshire

K. D. Smith not out	2
D. L. Amiss not out	6
W 1, n-b 1	2

(no wkt, 3 overs) 10

A. I. Kallicharran, †G. W. Humpage, Asif Din, A. M. Ferreira, C. M. Old, C. Lethbridge, N. Gifford, *R. G. D. Willis and W. Hogg did not bat.

Bowling: Allott 2–1–3–0; Folley 1–0–5–0.

Lancashire

†G. Fowler, J. Abrahams, S. J. O'Shaughnessy, *C. H. Lloyd, D. P. Hughes, F. C. Hayes, I. Cockbain, J. Simmons, I. Folley, M. Watkinson and P. J. W. Allott.

Umpires: J. W. Holder and D. O. Oslear.

WARWICKSHIRE v DERBYSHIRE

At Coventry, June 5. Derbyshire won by five wickets. Toss won by Derbyshire.

Warwickshire

T. A. Lloyd c Barnett b Newman	10	C. M. Old not out	45
K. D. Smith c Barnett b Oldham	23	N. Gifford not out	0
A. I. Kallicharran c Wright b Wood	6	L-b 9, w 9, n-b 1	19
D. L. Amiss c Wright b Oldham	12		
†G. W. Humpage b Oldham	36	1/15 2/35 3/59 (7 wkts, 39 overs) 220	
Asif Din c Anderson b Newman	52	4/69 5/105	
A. M. Ferreira b Newman	17	6/158 7/219	

*R. G. D. Willis and W. Hogg did not bat.

Bowling: Newman 8–1–47–3; Mortensen 7–1–40–0; Tunnicliffe 8–0–34–0; Wood 8–3–29–1; Oldham 8–0–51–3.

Derbyshire

J. G. Wright lbw b Willis	108	C. J. Tunnicliffe not out	14
I. S. Anderson c Asif Din b Gifford	33		
*K. J. Barnett lbw b Old	11	B 5, l-b 10, w 1, n-b 1	17
A. Hill b Gifford	3		
B. Wood b Willis	10	1/113 2/140 (5 wkts, 38.3 overs) 223	
G. Miller not out	27	3/147 4/179 5/180	

P. G. Newman, †R. W. Taylor, O. H. Mortensen and S. Oldham did not bat.

Bowling: Willis 8–0–31–2; Hogg 7–0–49–0; Ferreira 8–0–35–0; Old 7.3–0–37–1; Gifford 8–0–54–2.

Umpires: H. D. Bird and D. R. Shepherd.

At Hove, June 12. WARWICKSHIRE lost to SUSSEX by 52 runs.

At Luton, June 19. WARWICKSHIRE lost to NORTHAMPTONSHIRE by 34 runs.

WARWICKSHIRE v HAMPSHIRE

At Birmingham, June 26. Warwickshire won by 6 runs. Toss won by Hampshire.

Warwickshire

T. A. Lloyd lbw b Malone	9	N. Gifford not out	19
K. D. Smith c Terry b Cowley	21	D. A. Thorne not out	10
A. I. Kallicharran c and b Nicholas	66	B 5, l-b 10, w 11	26
D. L. Amiss c Jesty b Nicholas	14		—
†G. W. Humpage c Pocock b Nicholas	11	1/21 2/63 (7 wkts, 40 overs)	241
Asif Din c Parks b Tremlett	13	3/116 4/136	
A. M. Ferreira c Nicholas b Malone	52	5/154 6/158 7/218	

*R. G. D. Willis and W. Hogg did not bat.

Bowling: Stevenson 8–0–56–0; Malone 8–0–55–2; Tremlett 8–1–29–1; Cowley 8–1–32–1; Nicholas 8–0–43–3.

Hampshire

V. P. Terry st Humpage b Gifford	37	T. M. Tremlett c Gifford b Kallicharran	8
C. L. Smith st Humpage b Kallicharran	62	K. Stevenson not out	4
T. E. Jesty b Willis	76	B 2, l-b 21, w 2	25
R. A. Smith b Gifford	13		—
*N. E. J. Pocock b Willis	2	1/98 2/126 (8 wkts, 40 overs)	235
M. C. J. Nicholas b Thorne	2	3/171 4/174 5/205	
N. G. Cowley run out	6	6/216 7/228 8/235	

†R. J. Parks and S. J. Malone did not bat.

Bowling: Willis 8–0–34–2; Hogg 8–1–26–0; Ferreira 7–0–37–0; Gifford 8–0–42–2; Kallicharran 6–0–34–2; Thorne 3–0–37–1.

Umpires: R. A. White and A. G. T. Whitehead.

WARWICKSHIRE v ESSEX

At Birmingham, July 10. Essex won by 1 run. Toss won by Warwickshire.

Essex

G. A. Gooch b Smith	38	D. R. Pringle c Willis b Hogg	47
A. W. Lilley c Humpage b Willis	7	K. R. Pont c Lethbridge b Willis	4
K. S. McEwan run out	7	B 1, l-b 8	9
N. Phillip c Willis b Hogg	51		—
*K. W. R. Fletcher not out	54	1/9 2/27 3/71 (7 wkts, 40 overs)	230
B. R. Hardie c Gifford b Ferreira	13	4/131 5/161 6/218 7/230	

†D. E. East, R. E. East and N. A. Foster did not bat.

Bowling: Willis 8–0–32–2; Hogg 7–0–64–2; Ferreira 8–0–22–1; Lethbridge 8–0–34–0; Smith 6–0–36–1; Gifford 3–0–33–0.

Warwickshire

T. A. Lloyd b Foster	9	N. Gifford b Phillip	7
D. L. Amiss c and b Gooch	30	*R. G. D. Willis not out	3
A. I. Kallicharran b Gooch	36	W. Hogg not out	7
†G. W. Humpage c Gooch b R. E. East	65	L-b 8, n-b 2	10
Asif Din st D. E. East b Pringle	15		
P. A. Smith c D. E. East b Pringle	41	1/15 2/60 3/90	(9 wkts, 40 overs) 229
A. M. Ferreira run out	5	4/140 5/175 6/208	
C. Lethbridge run out	1	7/210 8/218 9/218	

Bowling: Phillip 6–1–16–1; Foster 6–0–39–1; Pont 4–0–32–0; Gooch 8–0–36–2; Pringle 8–0–60–2; R. E. East 8–0–36–1.

Umpires: J. H. Harris and B. Leadbeater.

At Moreton-in-Marsh, July 17. WARWICKSHIRE lost to GLOUCESTERSHIRE by six wickets.

WARWICKSHIRE v WORCESTERSHIRE

At Birmingham, July 24. Tied on scoring-rate. Worcestershire figured in their third tie on successive Sundays – the first time a team has been involved in as many as three tied games in the John Player League in one season. Toss won by Warwickshire.

Worcestershire

M. S. A. McEvoy c Dyer b Smith	17	D. A. Banks b Ferreira	4
D. N. Patel b Old	34	J. D. Inchmore not out	1
*P. A. Neale c Amiss b Willis	83	A. E. Warner run out	1
D. B. D'Oliveira st Humpage b Kallicharran	11	B 4, l-b 8, w 1, n-b 2	15
M. J. Weston lbw b Willis	29		
†D. J. Humphries b Willis	13	1/31 2/115 3/133	(8 wkts, 40 overs) 208
		4/177 5/181 6/200 7/204 8/208	

R. K. Illingworth and A. P. Pridgeon did not bat.

Bowling: Willis 8–0–39–3; Old 8–0–31–1; Smith 6–0–40–1; Gifford 8–0–27–0; Ferreira 8–0–44–1; Kallicharran 2–0–12–1.

Warwickshire

T. A. Lloyd not out	19
D. L. Amiss not out	24
L-b 4, w 2, n-b 3	9

(no wkt, 10 overs) 52

R. I. H. B. Dyer, A. I. Kallicharran, †G. W. Humpage, Asif Din, A. M. Ferreira, C. M. Old, P. A. Smith, N. Gifford and *R. G. D. Willis did not bat.

Bowling: Warner 5–0–14–0; Pridgeon 5–0–29–0.

Umpires: M. J. Kitchen and N. T. Plews.

At Lord's, July 31. WARWICKSHIRE lost to MIDDLESEX on faster scoring-rate.

At The Oval, August 7. WARWICKSHIRE beat SURREY by five wickets.

WARWICKSHIRE v LEICESTERSHIRE

At Birmingham, August 14. Warwickshire won by eight wickets. Toss won by Warwickshire.

Leicestershire

J. C. Balderstone lbw b Lethbridge	45	A. M. E. Roberts b Old	10
N. E. Briers c Humpage b Old	10	J. F. Steele not out	22
*†R. W. Tolchard lbw b Lethbridge	12	L. B. Taylor not out	14
B. F. Davison b Gifford	25	B 2, l-b 7, w 1, n-b 2	12
P. B. Clift c Gifford b Kallicharran	7		
R. A. Cobb c Amiss b Kallicharran	12	1/17 2/40 3/94 4/104 (8 wkts, 40 overs) 179	
J. Addison run out	10	5/108 6/127 7/130 8/154	

J. P. Agnew did not bat.

Bowling: Old 7–1–22–2; Smith 8–0–32–0; Lethbridge 8–0–46–2; Thorne 3–0–25–0; Gifford 8–1–31–1; Kallicharran 6–2–11–2.

Warwickshire

T. A. Lloyd b Roberts	13
D. L. Amiss lbw b Roberts	4
A. I. Kallicharran not out	80
†G. W. Humpage not out	73
B 4, l-b 4, w 2, n-b 1	11
1/5 2/18 (2 wkts, 25.1 overs) 181	

R. I. H. B. Dyer, Asif Din, P. A. Smith, D. A. Thorne, C. Lethbridge, C. M. Old and *N. Gifford did not bat.

Bowling: Roberts 6–2–33–2; Taylor 4.1–0–25–0; Steele 6–0–44–0; Clift 6–0–33–0; Agnew 2–0–19–0; Addison 1–0–16–0.

Umpires: J. W. Holder and J. van Geloven.

At Folkestone, August 21. WARWICKSHIRE lost to KENT by 58 runs.

WARWICKSHIRE v NOTTINGHAMSHIRE

At Birmingham, August 28. Warwickshire won by 61 runs. Toss won by Nottinghamshire.

Warwickshire

T. A. Lloyd c Rice b Saxelby	57	D. A. Thorne b Saxelby	14
D. L. Amiss b Bore	29	P. A. Smith not out	6
A. I. Kallicharran c Johnson b Pick	26	B 1, l-b 14, w 1, n-b 1	17
†G. W. Humpage b Saxelby	3		
Asif Din b Saxelby	8	1/54 2/117 3/124 (7 wkts, 40 overs) 200	
G. J. Lord c Rice b Pick	40	4/131 5/145 6/177 7/200	

C. M. Old, *N. Gifford and W. Hogg did not bat.

Bowling: Cooper 8–1–43–0; Bore 8–0–31–1; Saxelby 8–0–29–4; Pick 8–0–43–2; Hemmings 8–0–37–0.

Nottinghamshire

B. Hassan b Smith	10	R. A. Pick b Old		4
R. T. Robinson b Smith	48	K. E. Cooper b Old		1
*C. E. B. Rice b Smith	0	M. K. Bore not out		0
J. D. Birch c Thorne b Smith	10	B 1, l-b 7, w 1, n-b 1		10
P. Johnson b Hogg	44			
†B. N. French b Old	7	1/18 2/18 3/32	(34.5 overs)	139
E. E. Hemmings lbw b Hogg	0	4/113 5/125 6/125		
K. Saxelby c and b Old	5	7/132 8/137 9/138		

Bowling: Old 5.5–1–14–4; Hogg 7–0–20–2; Smith 8–2–23–4; Thorne 6–0–36–0; Gifford 6–0–23–0; Kallicharran 2–0–13–0.

Umpires: J. H. Harris and D. O. Oslear.

At Taunton, September 11. WARWICKSHIRE lost to SOMERSET by three wickets.

WORCESTERSHIRE

At Leicester, May 8. LEICESTERSHIRE v WORCESTERSHIRE. No result.

WORCESTERSHIRE v GLOUCESTERSHIRE

At Worcester, May 22. No result.

At Lord's, June 5. WORCESTERSHIRE lost to MIDDLESEX by seven wickets.

WORCESTERSHIRE v ESSEX

At Worcester, June 19. Worcestershire won by three wickets. Toss won by Essex.

Essex

G. A. Gooch b Warner	20	†D. E. East c Pridgeon b Ellcock		5
B. R. Hardie b Pridgeon	25	S. Turner not out		0
K. S. McEwan b Pridgeon	65	L-b 10, w 7, n-b 1		18
*K. W. R. Fletcher b Pridgeon	30			
N. Phillip b Warner	25	1/31 2/67	(7 wkts, 40 overs)	207
D. R. Pringle lbw b Warner	11	3/148 4/160		
K. R. Pont not out	8	5/183 6/194 7/203		

R. E. East and J. K. Lever did not bat.

Bowling: Ellcock 7–1–25–1; Warner 8–1–26–3; Pridgeon 8–0–45–3; Weston 2–0–15–0; Illingworth 8–0–38–0; Patel 7–0–40–0.

Worcestershire

M. J. Weston c Pont b Turner	48	A. E. Warner lbw b Phillip		1
M. S. Scott b Turner	14	R. K. Illingworth not out		3
D. N. Patel c D. E. East b Pringle	14	B 1, l-b 11, w 2		14
*P. A. Neale not out	83			
D. B. D'Oliveira c R. E. East b Turner	26	1/34 2/62	(7 wkts, 40 overs)	208
D. A. Banks lbw b Phillip	0	3/107 4/168		
†D. J. Humphries run out	5	5/172 6/181 7/197		

R. M. Ellcock and A. P. Pridgeon did not bat.

Bowling: Lever 8–2–32–0; Phillip 8–0–33–2; Turner 8–0–48–3; R. E. East 8–0–28–0; Pringle 8–0–53–1.

Umpires: A. Jepson and R. Julian.

WORCESTERSHIRE v YORKSHIRE

At Worcester, June 26. Yorkshire won by four wickets in a match reduced by rain to 31 overs a side. Toss won by Yorkshire.

Worcestershire

M. J. Weston lbw b Illingworth	36	A. E. Warner c Hartley b Jarvis		1
M. S. Scott c and b Carrick	14	R. M. Ellcock not out		1
D. N. Patel b Illingworth	4	A. P. Pridgeon c Carrick b Stevenson		1
*P. A. Neale c Bairstow b Carrick	12	B 1, l-b 3, w 3		7
D. B. D'Oliveira c Jarvis b Carrick	1			
D. A. Banks c Boycott b Jarvis	18	1/36 2/43 3/66	(30.1 overs)	127
†D. J. Humphries c Love b Stevenson	32	4/69 5/70 6/107		
J. D. Inchmore b Stevenson	0	7/107 8/115 9/125		

Bowling: Dennis 6–1–13–0; Jarvis 6–0–30–2; Carrick 7–1–20–3; Illingworth 6–0–27–2; Stevenson 4.1–0–25–3; Boycott 1–0–5–0.

Yorkshire

G. Boycott c Weston b Patel	32	†D. L. Bairstow b Warner		8
C. W. J. Athey b Patel	18	P. Carrick not out		2
K. Sharp run out	16	B 5, l-b 3, w 3, n-b 4		15
G. B. Stevenson b Patel	10			
S. N. Hartley c Humphries b Inchmore	8	1/56 2/61 3/71	(6 wkts, 30.2 overs)	128
J. D. Love not out	19	4/91 5/98 6/126		

*R. Illingworth, S. J. Dennis and P. W. Jarvis did not bat.

Bowling: Ellcock 5.2–1–18–0; Warner 5–0–18–1; Pridgeon 4–0–18–0; Patel 7–1–28–3; D'Oliveira 6–0–23–0; Inchmore 3–0–8–1.

Umpires: D. J. Constant and R. Palmer.

At Derby, July 3. WORCESTERSHIRE lost to DERBYSHIRE by four wickets.

WORCESTERSHIRE v NOTTINGHAMSHIRE

At Hereford, July 10. Tied. Toss won by Worcestershire.

Nottinghamshire

B. Hassan c Illingworth b Warner		71
R. T. Robinson c Moores b Pridgeon		4
*C. E. B. Rice lbw b Inchmore		71
J. D. Birch b Warner		15
D. W. Randall not out		12
E. E. Hemmings not out		2
B 3, l-b 5, w 4, n-b 8		20
	(4 wkts, 40 overs)	195

1/14 2/126
3/177 4/191

†B. N. French, K. Saxelby, K. E. Cooper, M. K. Bore and M. Hendrick did not bat.

Bowling: Warner 8–0–40–2; Pridgeon 5–0–14–1; Inchmore 8–0–32–1; King 3–0–21–0; Illingworth 8–1–13–0; Patel 8–0–55–0.

Worcestershire

M. J. Weston lbw b Hendrick		9
D. N. Patel c Birch b Hemmings		44
*P. A. Neale run out		86
C. L. King b Bore		20
D. B. D'Oliveira lbw b Saxelby		3
J. D. Inchmore run out		2
M. S. Scott b Hendrick		0
A. E. Warner b Cooper		1
†P. Moores not out		10
A. P. Pridgeon run out		1
B 1, l-b 12, w 2, n-b 4		19
	(9 wkts, 40 overs)	195

1/21 2/73 3/122
4/131 5/172 6/172 7/175 8/191 9/195

R. K. Illingworth did not bat.

Bowling: Hendrick 8–0–39–2; Cooper 8–3–17–1; Hemmings 8–0–33–1; Saxelby 8–0–47–1; Bore 8–1–40–1.

Umpires: W. E. Alley and K. Ibadulla.

At Manchester, July 17. WORCESTERSHIRE tied with LANCASHIRE.

At Birmingham, July 24. WORCESTERSHIRE tied with WARWICKSHIRE on scoring-rate.

WORCESTERSHIRE v NORTHAMPTONSHIRE

At Worcester, July 31. Worcestershire won on faster scoring-rate, achieving their target of 96 with thirteen balls to spare. Toss won by Worcestershire.

Northamptonshire

D. J. Wild c McEvoy b Pridgeon		13
W. Larkins c Pridgeon b Patel		53
P. Willey b Patel		24
Kapil Dev st Humphries b Illingworth		12
*G. Cook b Patel		10
R. J. Boyd-Moss c and b Patel		6
†G. Sharp st Humphries b Illingworth		1
D. J. Capel c D'Oliveira b Illingworth		6
N. A. Mallender c Humphries b Patel		6
T. M. Lamb not out		1
B. J. Griffiths run out		0
L-b 9, w 6		15
	(33.4 overs)	147

1/35 2/97 3/114
4/117 5/130 6/133
7/137 8/141 9/146

Bowling: Ellcock 5–2–12–0; Pridgeon 5–0–18–1; Weston 5–0–27–0; Inchmore 5–1–21–0; Illingworth 7–0–27–3; Patel 6.4–0–27–5.

Worcestershire

M. S. A. McEvoy c Sharp b Kapil Dev ..	17	D. A. Banks not out	0
D. N. Patel c Larkins b Griffiths	52	L-b 10, w 3............................	13
*P. A. Neale c Sharp b Griffiths.........	0		
D. B. D'Oliveira c Wild b Griffiths.....	5	1/76 2/76 (4 wkts, 19.5 overs)	96
M. J. Weston not out	9	3/76 4/86	

†D. J. Humphries, R. K. Illingworth, J. D. Inchmore, A. P. Pridgeon and R. M. Ellcock did not bat.

Bowling: Kapil Dev 8–1–24–1; Mallender 3–0–17–0; Willey 2–0–21–0; Griffiths 4.5–0–18–3; Lamb 2–0–3–0.

Umpires: H. D. Bird and R. Julian.

At Canterbury, August 7. WORCESTERSHIRE lost to KENT by 108 runs.

At Guildford, August 14. WORCESTERSHIRE lost to SURREY by 28 runs.

WORCESTERSHIRE v HAMPSHIRE

At Worcester, August 21. Hampshire won on faster scoring-rate when rain ended play. Toss won by Worcestershire.

Hampshire

C. G. Greenidge c Perryman		M. D. Marshall c Curtis b Pridgeon	17
b Illingworth.	21	*N. E. J. Pocock not out..................	0
C. L. Smith c Ormrod b Warner.........	71	B 5, l-b 13, w 5, n-b 2	25
T. E. Jesty c Curtis b D'Oliveira	61		
V. P. Terry not out	39	1/45 2/150 (5 wkts, 37 overs)	239
M. C. J. Nicholas b Warner..............	5	3/186 4/206 5/239	

N. G. Cowley, T. M. Tremlett, †R. J. Parks and S. J. Malone did not bat.

Bowling: Warner 8–0–41–2; Pridgeon 8–0–51–1; Illingworth 7–0–46–1; Perryman 7–0–39–0; D'Oliveira 7–0–37–1.

Worcestershire

J. A. Ormrod c Smith b Malone	7
M. S. A. McEvoy not out	9
D. N. Patel b Tremlett	7
*P. A. Neale not out........................	0
L-b 2, w 3, n-b 1	6
1/17 2/29 (2 wkts, 11.2 overs)	29

D. B. D'Oliveira, T. S. Curtis, †D. J. Humphries, R. K. Illingworth, A. E. Warner, A. P. Pridgeon and S. P. Perryman did not bat.

Bowling: Malone 5–0–11–1; Marshall 4–1–6–0; Tremlett 1.2–0–3–1; Cowley 1–0–3–0.

Umpires: R. Julian and D. O. Oslear.

At Cardiff, August 28. WORCESTERSHIRE lost to GLAMORGAN by 83 runs.

WORCESTERSHIRE v SOMERSET

At Worcester, September 4. Worcestershire won by 55 runs. Toss won by Somerset.

Worcestershire

M. J. Weston b Marks	18	A. E. Warner lbw b Botham	1
T. S. Curtis c Garner b Marks	26	R. K. Illingworth run out	2
D. N. Patel b Richards	29	A. P. Pridgeon not out	4
C. L. King run out	48	L-b 7, w 1	8
*P. A. Neale c Botham b Dredge	11		
D. B. D'Oliveira not out	28	1/43 2/50 3/121 (9 wkts, 40 overs) 192
†D. J. Humphries b Botham	8	4/129 5/141 6/153
P. J. Newport b Botham	9	7/171 8/173 9/188

Bowling: Garner 8–0–41–0; Botham 8–0–29–3; Dredge 8–1–25–1; Marks 8–1–45–2; Richards 8–0–44–1.

Somerset

P. W. Denning c King b Newport	28	J. Garner c Curtis b Illingworth	9
P. M. Roebuck b Newport	23	J. W. Lloyds not out	4
I. V. A. Richards c King b Illingworth	20	†T. Gard b Patel	4
N. F. M. Popplewell c Illingworth b Patel	16	C. H. Dredge run out	4
		B 2, l-b 8, w 1	11
*I. T. Botham c Weston b Illingworth	16		
P. A. Slocombe b Illingworth	0	1/55 2/58 3/87 4/95 (35.3 overs) 137
V. J. Marks lbw b Illingworth	2	5/95 6/105 7/117 8/126 9/133

Bowling: Warner 4–0–8–0; Pridgeon 5–0–20–0; Newport 7–0–27–2; King 5–1–15–0; Patel 7.3–0–32–2; Illingworth 7–1–24–5.

Umpires: R. A. White and R. Julian.

WORCESTERSHIRE v SUSSEX

At Worcester, September 11. Worcestershire won on faster scoring-rate, when bad light ended play, having earlier restricted the match to twenty overs a side. Toss won by Worcestershire.

Sussex

G. D. Mendis b Newport	21	A. C. S. Pigott run out	3
P. W. G. Parker b Pridgeon	5	A. M. Green not out	3
Imran Khan c King b Patel	30	L-b 5, w 3, n-b 2	10
C. M. Wells b King	10		
†I. J. Gould b Patel	9	1/25 2/37 (8 wkts, 20 overs) 121
I. A. Greig b Warner	24	3/60 4/79 5/86
A. P. Wells st Humphries b Illingworth	6	6/108 7/116 8/121

*J. R. T. Barclay and D. A. Reeve did not bat.

Bowling: Warner 3–0–22–1; Pridgeon 2–0–13–1; King 4–0–18–1; Newport 4–0–16–1; Illingworth 4–0–14–1; Patel 3–0–28–2.

Worcestershire

M. J. Weston c Pigott b C. M. Wells...	16	P. J. Newport b Imran......................	4
T. S. Curtis lbw b C. M. Wells...........	5	A. E. Warner not out.......................	0
D. N. Patel lbw b C. M. Wells...........	9	L-b 5, w 2	7
C. L. King c Greig b C. M. Wells.......	5		
*P. A. Neale not out........................	1	1/20 2/31 (7 wkts, 10 overs)	64
D. B. D'Oliveira c Barclay b Pigott	14	3/34 4/39	
†D. J. Humphries run out	3	5/56 6/60 7/64	

R. K. Illingworth and A. P. Pridgeon did not bat.

Bowling: C. M. Wells 4–0–15–4; Reeve 1–0–11–0; Barclay 1–0–9–0; Imran 3–0–13–1; Pigott 1–0–9–1.

Umpires: M. J. Kitchen and D. O. Oslear.

YORKSHIRE

At Birmingham, May 8. YORKSHIRE beat WARWICKSHIRE by six wickets.

YORKSHIRE v SURREY

At Leeds, May 15. No result.

YORKSHIRE v MIDDLESEX

At Hull, May 22. Yorkshire won on faster scoring-rate, after rain had reduced their target to 80 off 25 overs. Toss won by Yorkshire.

Middlesex

*M. W. Gatting b Jarvis...................	13	N. F. Williams c Jarvis b Boycott	7
C. T. Radley b Illingworth	14	N. G. Cowans not out	2
R. O. Butcher b Jarvis.....................	0	W. W. Daniel b Stevenson	4
G. D. Barlow b Illingworth	11	B 2, l-b 5, w 2, n-b 1...............	10
W. N. Slack c Stevenson b Boycott	30		
J. E. Emburey c Boycott b Illingworth.	3	1/25 2/25 3/40 (39 overs)	127
P. H. Edmonds lbw b Illingworth	2	4/41 5/45 6/53	
†P. R. Downton b Hartley b Boycott....	31	7/105 8/119 9/119	

Bowling: Stevenson 8–0–28–1; Jarvis 8–0–37–2; Carrick 8–0–18–0; Illingworth 8–3–6–4; Sidebottom 3–0–13–0; Boycott 4–0–15–3.

Yorkshire

G. Boycott lbw b Emburey...............	6	†D. L. Bairstow not out....................	7
K. Sharp b Emburey	26	P. Carrick not out...........................	14
G. B. Stevenson c Slack b Daniel	3	B 3, l-b 1, w 1.........................	5
C. W. J. Athey c Barlow b Gatting.....	15		
S. N. Hartley c Emburey b Gatting.....	4	1/24 2/35 3/43 (6 wkts, 24 overs)	80
J. D. Love lbw b Emburey	0	4/52 5/58 6/62	

A. Sidebottom, *R. Illingworth and P. W. Jarvis did not bat.

Bowling: Daniel 8–0–17–1; Cowans 4–0–18–0; Emburey 8–2–19–3; Gatting 4–0–21–2.

Umpires: H. D. Bird and B. J. Meyer.

YORKSHIRE v SOMERSET

At Bradford, May 29. Somerset won on faster scoring-rate, bad light having stopped play. Toss won by Somerset.

Yorkshire

G. Boycott c Lloyds b Marks	32
K. Sharp c and b Popplewell	22
G. B. Stevenson c Lloyds b Marks	2
C. W. J. Athey c Roebuck b Popplewell	2
S. N. Hartley c Popplewell b Dredge	18
†D. L. Bairstow b Botham	25
A. Sidebottom b Garner	31

P. Carrick c Denning b Dredge	11
A. Ramage not out	2
P. W. Jarvis not out	8
L-b 7, w 2, n-b 2	11

1/48 2/58 3/58 4/61 (8 wkts, 40 overs) 164
5/97 6/112 7/152 8/155

*R. Illingworth did not bat.

Bowling: Garner 8–1–38–1; Botham 8–0–40–1; Popplewell 8–1–27–2; Marks 8–1–21–2; Dredge 8–0–27–2.

Somerset

J. W. Lloyds run out	14
P. M. Roebuck c and b Stevenson	7
I. V. A. Richards b Stevenson	34
I. T. Botham c Sharp b Illingworth	45
*B. C. Rose not out	33

N. F. M. Popplewell not out	0
L-b 6, w 2, n-b 6	14

1/31 2/37 (4 wkts, 32.1 overs) 147
3/74 4/146

V. J. Marks, †T. Gard, J. Garner, C. H. Dredge and P. W. Denning did not bat.

Bowling: Ramage 5–0–18–0; Jarvis 6–0–22–0; Stevenson 8–1–30–2; Sidebottom 8–2–23–0; Carrick 3.1–0–32–0; Illingworth 2–1–8–1.

Umpires: D. J. Constant and D. O. Oslear.

YORKSHIRE v HAMPSHIRE

At Middlesbrough, June 5. Yorkshire won by six wickets. Toss won by Yorkshire.

Hampshire

C. G. Greenidge c Love b Illingworth	89
V. P. Terry c Dennis b Stevenson	17
D. R. Turner b Stevenson	7
T. E. Jesty c Hartley b Jarvis	16
M. C. J. Nicholas run out	68
*N. E. J. Pocock b Illingworth	21
M. D. Marshall run out	18

N. G. Cowley b Sidebottom	4
T. M. Tremlett run out	1
†R. J. Parks not out	0
L-b 10, w 2, n-b 2	14

1/39 2/52 3/93 4/155 (9 wkts, 40 overs) 255
5/185 6/232 7/236 8/254 9/255

S. J. Malone did not bat.

Bowling: Jarvis 8–0–58–1; Dennis 8–0–38–0; Stevenson 8–2–57–2; Sidebottom 8–0–41–1; Illingworth 8–0–47–2.

Yorkshire

K. Sharp c Turner b Nicholas	40
G. Boycott c Greenidge b Cowley	8
C. W. J. Athey c Parks b Cowley	29
G. B. Stevenson c Jesty b Cowley	14
S. N. Hartley not out	67

J. D. Love not out	82
B 1, l-b 9, w 6, n-b 1	17

1/21 2/63 (4 wkts, 38.5 overs) 257
3/96 4/107

†D. L. Bairstow, S. J. Dennis, A. Sidebottom, *R. Illingworth and P. W. Jarvis did not bat.

Bowling: Marshall 8–0–23–0; Malone 7.5–0–41–0; Cowley 8–1–39–3; Nicholas 8–0–67–1; Tremlett 7–0–70–0.

Umpires: D. G. L. Evans and M. J. Kitchen.

At Cardiff, June 12. YORKSHIRE lost to GLAMORGAN by 12 runs.

At Worcester, June 26. YORKSHIRE beat WORCESTERSHIRE by four wickets.

YORKSHIRE v LEICESTERSHIRE

At Scarborough, July 3. Yorkshire won by seven wickets. Toss won by Yorkshire.

Leicestershire

D. I. Gower c Hartley b Illingworth	24	J. F. Steele b Sidebottom	0
I. P. Butcher run out	24	G. J. Parsons c Carrick b Stevenson	13
N. E. Briers st Bairstow b Carrick	4	L. B. Taylor not out	8
B. F. Davison c Bairstow b Sidebottom	35	L-b 7, w 5, n-b 3	15
*R. W. Tolchard lbw b Illingworth	5		
P. B. Clift lbw b Sidebottom	3	1/49 2/56 3/60 4/93 (8 wkts, 40 overs) 160	
†M. A. Garnham not out	29	5/99 6/118 7/118 8/141	

G. J. F. Ferris did not bat.

Bowling: Dennis 8–1–32–0; Stevenson 8–0–33–1; Illingworth 8–1–24–2; Carrick 8–0–23–1; Sidebottom 8–0–33–3.

Yorkshire

G. Boycott b Taylor	31	J. D. Love not out	12
C. W. J. Athey c Gower b Taylor	39	B 1, l-b 17, w 3, n-b 1	22
K. Sharp lbw b Clift	24		
S. N. Hartley not out	33	1/75 2/91 3/142 (3 wkts, 37.1 overs) 161	

†D. L. Bairstow, P. Carrick, A. Sidebottom, G. B. Stevenson, *R. Illingworth and S. J. Dennis did not bat.

Bowling: Ferris 8–0–23–0; Parsons 6.1–0–14–0; Steele 8–1–29–0; Clift 8–0–35–1; Taylor 7–0–38–2.

Umpires: D. O. Oslear and J. van Geloven.

At Tring, July 10. YORKSHIRE beat NORTHAMPTONSHIRE by ten wickets.

YORKSHIRE v KENT

At Scarborough, July 17. No result, rain having ended play after one over. Toss won by Yorkshire.

Kent

R. A. Woolmer not out	2
N. R. Taylor not out	5
W 1	1
(no wkt, 1 over)	8

C. Penn, M. R. Benson, *C. S. Cowdrey, †A. P. E. Knott, G. W. Johnson, R. M. Ellison, E. A. E. Baptiste, D. L. Underwood and G. R. Dilley did not bat.

Bowling: Dennis 1–0–7–0.

Yorkshire

G. Boycott, K. Sharp, C. W. J. Athey, S. N. Hartley, J. D. Love, †D. L. Bairstow, P. Carrick, S. J. Dennis, G. B. Stevenson, *R. Illingworth and P. W. Jarvis.

Umpires: A. Jepson and N. T. Plews.

At Hove, July 24. YORKSHIRE beat SUSSEX by six wickets.

At Nottingham, July 31. YORKSHIRE lost to NOTTINGHAMSHIRE by nine wickets.

YORKSHIRE v LANCASHIRE

At Leeds, August 7. Yorkshire won by four wickets. Toss won by Yorkshire.

Lancashire

D. Lloyd c and b Illingworth.............. 17	J. Simmons run out......................... 2
G. Fowler c Bairstow b Stevenson 16	M. Watkinson not out 8
D. P. Hughes b Stevenson................. 7	P. J. W. Allott not out 32
*C. H. Lloyd c Dennis b Moxon.......... 31	L-b 5, n-b 1 6
J. Abrahams run out 6	
†C. Maynard c Bairstow b Dennis....... 7	1/31 2/41 3/43 4/74 (8 wkts, 40 overs) 162
S. J. O'Shaughnessy c Hartley b Dennis . 30	5/85 6/98 7/108 8/123

L. L. McFarlane did not bat.

Bowling: Dennis 8–1–36–2; Boycott 4–0–15–0; Illingworth 8–0–36–1; Stevenson 8–1–35–2; Carrick 8–0–17–0; Moxon 4–0–17–1.

Yorkshire

G. Boycott run out 16	G. B. Stevenson b Watkinson 21
C. W. J. Athey lbw b Simmons 28	M. D. Moxon not out...................... 4
K. Sharp c Hughes b Simmons 38	L-b 11, w 4, n-b 2 17
S. N. Hartley c McFarlane b D. Lloyd. 15	
J. D. Love st Maynard b D. Lloyd...... 11	1/29 2/79 3/107 (6 wkts, 38.5 overs) 163
†D. L. Bairstow not out................... 13	4/123 5/126 6/152

P. Carrick, *R. Illingworth and S. J. Dennis did not bat.

Bowling: Allott 6–0–28–0; McFarlane 8–0–35–0; Watkinson 6.5–1–24–1; Simmons 8–0–21–2; O'Shaughnessy 6–1–23–0; D. Lloyd 4–0–15–2.

Umpires: R. Palmer and N. T. Plews.

At Cheltenham, August 14. YORKSHIRE beat GLOUCESTERSHIRE by four wickets.

YORKSHIRE v DERBYSHIRE

At Bradford, August 28. Yorkshire won by two wickets thanks to Athey who, injured in a car accident the previous evening and batting with a runner, rescued them from the brink of defeat. Toss won by Yorkshire.

Derbyshire

*K. J. Barnett c Athey b Illingworth ...	29	P. G. Newman c Athey b Stevenson.... 6
I. S. Anderson c Sidebottom b Carrick..	40	†B. J. M. Maher not out 13
A. Hill st Bairstow b Carrick	5	
G. Miller st Bairstow b Carrick	8	B 2, l-b 9, w 3, n-b 1 15
J. E. Morris st Bairstow b Carrick	3	—
R. J. Finney not out........................	41	1/72 2/84 3/91 4/95　(7 wkts, 40 overs) 168
W. P. Fowler c Bairstow b Boycott	8	5/96 6/109 7/126

O. H. Mortensen and M. A. Holding did not bat.

Bowling: Dennis 8–1–33–0; Boycott 6–0–32–1; Stevenson 6–0–28–1; Sidebottom 4–0–20–0; Illingworth 8–0–27–1; Carrick 8–1–13–4.

Yorkshire

G. Boycott c Maher b Mortensen	8	P. Carrick b Holding 5
C. W. J. Athey not out.....................	21	A. Sidebottom b Holding 5
K. Sharp run out	56	S. J. Dennis not out 16
S. N. Hartley c Maher b Mortensen	0	B 4, l-b 13, w 3, n-b 3 23
J. D. Love st Maher b Miller	19	—
G. B. Stevenson c Anderson b Miller ..	0	1/15 2/15 3/67　(8 wkts, 39.2 overs) 171
†D. L. Bairstow c Barnett b Holding...	18	4/67 5/120 6/123 7/131 8/150

*R. Illingworth did not bat.

Bowling: Holding 8–0–25–3; Mortensen 7.2–0–39–2; Newman 8–3–16–0; Miller 8–0–34–2; Fowler 6–0–24–0; Finney 2–0–10–0.

Umpires: D. R. Shepherd and R. A. White.

At Chelmsford, September 11. ESSEX v YORKSHIRE. No result.

JOHN PLAYER LEAGUE RECORDS

Batting

Highest score: 176 – G. A. Gooch, Essex v Glamorgan (Southend), 1983. (217 hundreds have been scored in the League.)

Most runs in a season: 814 – C. E. B. Rice (Nottinghamshire), 1977.

Most sixes in an innings: 10 – C. G. Greenidge, Hampshire v Warwickshire (Birmingham), 1979.

Most sixes by a team in an innings: 14 – Leicestershire v Somerset (Frome), 1970.

Most sixes in a season: 26 – I. V. A. Richards (Somerset), 1977.

Highest total: 310 for five – Essex v Glamorgan (Southend), 1983.

Highest total – batting second: 301 for six – Warwickshire v Essex (Colchester), 1982.

Highest match aggregate: 600 – Essex (299 for four) v Warwickshire (301 for six) (Colchester), 1982.

Lowest total: 23 – Middlesex v Yorkshire (Leeds), 1974.

Shortest completed innings: 16 overs – Northamptonshire 59 v Middlesex (Tring), 1974.

Shortest match: 2 hr 13 min (40.3 overs) – Essex v Northamptonshire (Ilford), 1971.

Biggest victories: 190 runs, Kent beat Northamptonshire (Brackley), 1973. There have been nineteen instances of victory by ten wickets – by Derbyshire, Essex, Glamorgan, Hampshire, Kent, Leicestershire (twice), Middlesex (twice), Somerset (twice), Surrey (twice), Warwickshire (twice), Worcestershire and Yorkshire (three times).

Ties: Nottinghamshire v Kent (Nottingham), 1969, in match reduced to 20 overs.
Gloucestershire v Hampshire (Bristol), 1972.
Gloucestershire v Northamptonshire (Bristol), 1972.
Surrey v Worcestershire (Byfleet), 1973.
Middlesex v Lancashire (Lord's), 1974.
Sussex v Leicestershire (Hove), 1974.
Lancashire v Worcestershire (Manchester), 1975.
Somerset v Glamorgan (Taunton), 1975.
Warwickshire v Kent (Birmingham), 1980.
Kent v Lancashire (Maidstone), 1981.
Yorkshire v Nottinghamshire (Hull), 1982.
Hampshire v Lancashire (Southampton), 1982.
Surrey v Hampshire (The Oval), 1982.
Worcestershire v Nottinghamshire (Hereford), 1983.
Lancashire v Worcestershire (Manchester), 1983 in match reduced to nineteen overs.
Warwickshire v Worcestershire (Birmingham), 1983, Warwickshire's innings having been reduced to ten overs.

Record Partnerships for each Wicket

224 for 1st	J. A. Ormrod and D. N. Patel, Worcestershire v Hampshire at Southampton	1982
273 for 2nd	G. A. Gooch and K. S. McEwan, Essex v Nottinghamshire at Nottingham	1983
215 for 3rd	W. Larkins and R. G. Williams, Northamptonshire v Worcestershire at Luton	1982
175* for 4th	M. J. K. Smith and D. L. Amiss, Warwickshire v Yorkshire at Birmingham	1970
179 for 5th	I. T. Botham and I. V. A. Richards, Somerset v Hampshire at Taunton	1981
121 for 6th	C. P. Wilkins and A. J. Borrington, Derbyshire v Warwickshire at Chesterfield	1972
101 for 7th	S. J. Windaybank and D. A. Graveney, Gloucestershire v Nottinghamshire at Nottingham	1981
95* for 8th	D. Breakwell and K. F. Jennings, Somerset v Nottinghamshire at Nottingham	1976
86 for 9th	D. P. Hughes and P. Lever, Lancashire v Essex at Leyton	1973
57 for 10th	D. A. Graveney and J. B. Mortimore, Gloucestershire v Lancashire at Tewkesbury	1973

Bowling

Best analyses: eight for 26, K. D. Boyce, Essex v Lancashire at Manchester, 1971; seven for 15, R. A. Hutton, Yorkshire v Worcestershire at Leeds, 1969; seven for 39, A. Hodgson, Northamptonshire v Somerset at Northampton, 1976; six for 6, R. W. Hooker, Middlesex v Surrey at Lord's, 1969; six for 7, M. Hendrick, Derbyshire v Nottinghamshire at Nottingham, 1972.

Four wickets in four balls: A. Ward, Derbyshire v Sussex at Derby, 1970.

Hat-tricks: A. Ward, Derbyshire v Sussex at Derby, 1970; R. Palmer, Somerset v Gloucestershire at Bristol, 1970; K. D. Boyce, Essex v Somerset at Westcliff, 1971; G. D. McKenzie, Leicestershire v Essex at Leicester, 1972; R. G. D. Willis, Warwickshire v Yorkshire at Birmingham, 1973; W. Blenkiron, Warwickshire v Derbyshire at Buxton, 1974; A. Buss, Sussex v Worcestershire at Hastings, 1974; J. M. Rice, Hampshire v Northamptonshire at Southampton, 1975; M. A. Nash, Glamorgan v Worcestershire at Worcester, 1975; A. Hodgson, Northamptonshire v Somerset at Northampton, 1976; A. E. Cordle, Glamorgan v Hampshire at Portsmouth, 1979; C. J. Tunnicliffe, Derbyshire v Worcestershire at Derby, 1979; M. D. Marshall, Hampshire v Surrey at Southampton, 1981; I. V. A. Richards, Somerset v Essex at Chelmsford, 1982; P. W. Jarvis, Yorkshire v Derbyshire at Derby, 1982; R. M. Ellison, Kent v Hampshire at Canterbury, 1983.

Most economical analysis: 8–8–0–0; B. A. Langford, Somerset v Essex at Yeovil, 1969.

Most expensive analysis: 8–0–88–1; E. E. Hemmings, Nottinghamshire v Somerset at Nottingham, 1983.

Most wickets in a season: 34 – R. J. Clapp (Somerset) 1974.

CRICKET IN THE SOUTH ATLANTIC

A soldier's report, written in January 1983

"During my visit I had time to ask questions about cricket on both the Falklands and Ascension. As far as the Falklands is concerned . . . cricket is not much played there. The only 'pitch' is the paddock in the grounds of Government House in Port Stanley, where there are at present two sets of goal posts. The only attempt made to play cricket there since the war was ended by a snowstorm. However, interest is not dead, and many of us from the General downwards (David Thorne, a very keen and competent club and service cricketer) awaited with bated breath the World Service sports news with the scores of the fourth and fifth Tests in Australia. The Royal Navy Flag Officer who took over from Admiral Sir 'Sandy' Woodward at the end of the war (Rear Admiral Ruffell) gave a trophy for an annual inter-service cricket competition – a broken wicket in wood. From what I saw there is enough flat ground at Ajax and Fitzroy Settlements to produce some sort of ground upon which cricket could be played – though I wouldn't answer for the state of the pitch – very low and slow because of the peaty soil. The only beach I saw which might have been fit for beach cricket was mined. There has been a game of cricket on Ascension between the Services and Cable & Wireless. The pitch there is matting on concrete and a composition ball was used in order to reduce the pace and height of bounce. The outfield is made of volcanic ash – there is no grass – which does not encourage clean ground fielding."

MINOR COUNTIES CHAMPIONSHIP, 1983

In 1983 the Minor Counties Championship, sponsored by the United Friendly Insurance Company, was contested in two divisions, each county playing every other county in its own division once and the leaders in each division – Hertfordshire (Eastern) and Buckinghamshire (Western) – meeting in a final play-off, which was won by Hertfordshire. There was also a knockout competition, sponsored by English Industrial Estates, which was won by Cheshire.

Bedfordshire, bottom of the Eastern Division and the only side with no wins, found consolation in reaching the final of the knockout competition. J. Kettleborough scored the side's only century – 127 against Staffordshire at Dunstable – and A. Fordham, still a schoolboy, batted well. S. E. Blott, making a welcome return after a year's absence, did the hat-trick against Suffolk at Southill Park.

With a good start to the season, **Berkshire** were disappointed to finish only sixth in the Western Division, ascribing their loss of form to the absence of two bowlers and careless fielding. G. R. J. Roope scored the most runs, albeit rather slowly, while P. J. Lewington, who bowled a third of the overs and was the top wicket-taker in Minor Counties cricket, took thirteen for 99 in the match against Cornwall at Truro.

Buckinghamshire, who comfortably headed the Western Division, only to be denied a ninth Championship win in the final, owed much to R. E. Hayward, whose return to the side after three years with Hampshire made a considerable impact. A. W. Lyon, C. E. Connor and M. E. Milton, who made 128 not out and took five for 33 against Devon at Torquay, bore the brunt of the bowling, which was enhanced by the late introduction of a West Indian fast bowler, M. Jean-Jacques.

Cambridgeshire were handicapped by the frequent absence of D. R. Parry, who took twelve for 70 and scored 122 in the match against Bedfordshire at Royston. N. T. Gadsby improved as a batsman and M. L. Saggers was a consistent wicket-keeper.

Cheshire batted soundly to gain first-innings points in six matches but, lacking the penetration to bring about victory, they finished a disappointing eighth in the Western Division. However, they won the knockout competition to take their first trophy since winning the Championship in 1967. Mudassar Nazar was again prolific and headed the Minor Counties batting averages.

In a disappointing season, **Cornwall** finished bottom of the Western Division. Their leading bowler, A. H. Watts, returned eight for 87 against Wiltshire at Wadebridge, while the Australian, S. F. Graf, who disappointed with the ball, did better than expected with the bat. Wicket-keeper T. L. Gall's 24 dismissals included eleven stumpings.

Bottom of the table in 1982, **Cumberland** responded to the new format by qualifying for the NatWest Bank Trophy for the first time ever. They owed their success to the batting of the former West Indian Test player, L. Baichan, R. O. Entwistle and the former Lancashire player, B. W. Reidy, who also took the most wickets, while S. Wall was a welcome newcomer.

A positive approach took **Devon** to third place in the Western Division. G. Wallen, who made 112 against Cheshire at Nantwich, batted consistently and was well supported by N. A. Folland, Agha Zahid and the Edwards brothers, J. H. and C. J. Injury kept D. I. Yeabsley out of the side for much of the season, but M. Taylor and P. A. Brown performed creditably with the new ball. A. W. Allin was the most successful spinner, with the veteran P. G. Considine doing well in his absence, with a return of twelve for 141 against Shropshire at Shrewsbury.

A promising start for **Dorset**, with a good victory over the eventual leaders, Buckinghamshire, was not maintained as they settled next to the bottom of the Western Division. Poor catching and the increasing inability to bat consistently prevented them from capitalising on the skills of R. V. Lewis and A. Kennedy with the bat, and C. Stone with the ball.

Durham were restricted by the frequent absence of P. J. Kippax and P. G. Lee from the attack, although S. P. Davis and S. Greensword bowled well, Greensword's match figures of thirteen for 65 against Lincolnshire at Lincoln including seven for 13 in the second innings. The match against Norfolk at Chester-le-Street was notable for J. W. Lister scoring his maiden century and R. Nanan taking a wicket with his first ball in Minor Counties cricket, and in the match against Staffordshire at Stone, wicket-keeper R. A. D. Mercer claimed six victims in an innings for the second time.

First winners of the Championship in its new form, **Hertfordshire** were ably led by F. E. Collyer. The attack was spearheaded by R. J. Hailey, who took the most wickets, including seven for 86 against Northumberland, and D. Surridge, who returned ten for 84 in the match against Cumberland in which W. M. Osman scored the side's only hundred.

Lincolnshire never recovered from a dismal start and finished next to the bottom of the Eastern Division. Two newcomers, N. Priestley, with 26 dismissals behind the stumps, and P. R. Butler performed well, as did H. Pougher, who retired at the end of the season with more than 5,000 runs to his credit, and G. A. Cope, who was the mainstay of the bowling.

Norfolk attributed much of their success to their captain, F. L. Q. Handley's, good fortune with the toss. Their bowling was less strong than their batting and their two victories followed fourth-innings run chases, with centuries from S. G. Plumb and Handley, the latter's coming in only 67 balls.

Undefeated, **Northumberland** considered themselves unlucky to finish only second in the Eastern Division. They owed much to Wasim Raja, who joined them after seven years with Durham; he made 115 not out against Suffolk at Mildenhall, and other three-figure innings came from G. D. Halliday (100 against Cambridgeshire) and K. Pearson (138 not out against Cumberland).

Oxfordshire, champions in 1982, often performed indifferently in 1983. Notable returns came from K. A. Arnold (seven for 59 against Shropshire), G. R. Hobbins (six for 50 against Cheshire) and S. R. Porter (eleven for 120 against Somerset II), while the best innings was P. A. Fowler's unbeaten 150 against Wiltshire.

A disappointing season for **Shropshire** followed a back injury to their captain and opening bat, J. S. Johnson, after the first match, B. J. Perry ably taking over the captaincy. The batting often failed, J. B. R. Jones having a lean spell in mid-season, but M. Davies proved a welcome newcomer. D. S. de Silva's leg-spin was less effective than in 1982, and S. Ogrizovic, a hostile opening bowler, missed the second half of the season owing to football commitments. However, P. N. Ranells did the hat-trick and J. P. Dawson took seven for 33 against Oxfordshire.

With many young players in the side, **Somerset II** were encouraged by their second place in the Western Division. Noteworthy features were the batting of J. G. Wyatt, the bowling of G. J. Hall, an off-spinner, and the useful all-round contribution of N. Russom.

Staffordshire qualified for the NatWest Bank Trophy for the first time since 1978. Their batting was strengthened by the return of P. N. Gill and the more frequent appearances of D. Cartledge and S. J. Dean, who shared first-wicket stands of 171 and 140 against Bedfordshire at Dunstable. Mushtaq Mohammad scored prolifically but was not retained, his bowling having proved expensive.

Suffolk shrugged off early setbacks to reach fifth place in the Eastern Division and to qualify for the NatWest Bank Trophy. Five centuries were scored and sound fielding backed up the attack in which notable returns came from R. C. Green – seven for 59 against Durham – and C. Rutterford, whose seven for 49 against Norfolk included the hat-trick. S. M. Clements (133) and P. D. Barker (100 not out) put on a record 222 for the third wicket against Staffordshire at Bury St Edmunds.

Wiltshire were strengthened by the inclusion of the all-rounder, J. M. Rice, from Hampshire and of an off-spinner, M. Bailey, who took eleven for 148 against Dorset at Salisbury. However, injury prevented the full side from appearing until the end of the season, and there was always an absence of a real pace attack.

UNITED FRIENDLY INSURANCE
MINOR COUNTIES CHAMPIONSHIP, 1983

Eastern Division	Played	Won	Lost	Drawn Won 1st Inns[1]	Drawn Lost 1st Inns[1]	Drawn Tied 1st Inns[1]	No Result	Points
Hertfordshire[NW]	9	4	1*	1	3	0	0	49
Northumberland[NW]	9	3	0	5	0	0	1	47
Durham[NW]	9	2	1*	3	2	0	1	36
Norfolk[NW]	9	2	1	4	2	0	0	34
Suffolk[NW]	9	2	3*	3	1	0	0	33
Cumberland[NW]	9	2	2	2	2	0	1	30
Staffordshire[NW]	9	2	1	1	5	0	0	28
Cambridgeshire	9	2	4*	1	2	0	0	28
Lincolnshire	9	1	3†	2	3	0	0	22
Bedfordshire	9	0	4*	1	3	0	1	11

Western Division	Played	Won	Lost	Drawn Won 1st Inns[1]	Drawn Lost 1st Inns[1]	Drawn Tied 1st Inns[1]	No Result	Points
Buckinghamshire[NW]	9	6	2	0	1	0	0	61
Somerset II	9	4	2*	0	2	1	0	47
Devon[NW]	9	3	1	4	1	0	0	43
Oxfordshire[NW]	9	3	2	2	2	0	0	38
Shropshire[NW]	9	2	3*	2	2	0	0	31
Berkshire[NW]	9	2	2	2	3	0	0	29
Wiltshire[NW]	9	2	2	2	3	0	0	29
Cheshire	9	1	1	5	1	1	0	28
Dorset	9	1	5†	1	2	0	0	19
Cornwall	9	1	5	1	2	0	0	15

[1] *After 55 overs completed.*
* *Denotes 1st-innings points in 1 match lost.*
† *Denotes tie on 1st innings in 2 matches lost.*
NW *Signifies qualified for NatWest Bank Trophy in 1984.*

FINAL PLAY-OFF

BUCKINGHAMSHIRE v HERTFORDSHIRE

At Worcester, September 18. Hertfordshire won by two wickets in a match reduced by overnight rain to 35 overs a side. After Buckinghamshire had won the toss, Milton, Gear and Hayward took them to a total which looked secure when Hertfordshire were 93 behind with six wickets down. Although T. S. Smith and Garofall revived the innings, 15 were still needed from the last over, bowled by Milton, but Smith needed only four balls to bring Hertfordshire the £2,000 prize.
Man of the Match: T. S. Smith

Buckinghamshire

M. E. Milton lbw b Garofall	34	*D. E. Smith not out	11
M. E. Gear lbw b Hailey	49	Extras	14
R. E. Hayward not out	60		
N. G. Hames c Osman b Collins	19	1/82 2/104	(4 wkts, 35 overs) 190
K. I. Hodgson run out	3	3/147 4/164	

†R. G. Humphrey, P. J. Newport, M. Jean-Jacques, A. W. Lyon and C. A. Connor did not bat.

Bowling: Surridge 7–1–41–0; Collins 7–1–39–1; Garofall 7–1–18–1; Smith 7–1–37–0; Hailey 7–1–41–1.

Hertfordshire

W. M. Osman b Newport	33
N. P. G. Wright b Connor	7
*†F. E. Collyer c Newport b Hodgson	29
S. Dean c Milton b Newport	10
T. S. Smith not out	59
J. D. Carr c Humphrey b Newport	0
C. Thomas c Humphrey b Hodgson	0

A. R. Garofall b Jean-Jacques	32
B. G. Collins b Jean-Jacques	0
D. Surridge not out	0
Extras	21

R. J. Hailey did not bat.

1/25 2/54 3/86   (8 wkts, 34.4 overs) 191
4/95 5/95 6/97 7/176 8/176

Bowling: Jean-Jacques 7–1–32–2; Connor 7–0–24–1; Newport 7–0–34–3; Hodgson 7–1–25–2; Milton 6.4–0–55–0.

Umpires: C. L. Head and C. Smith.

ENGLISH INDUSTRIAL ESTATES TROPHY

Rain affected the final stages of the English Industrial Estates Trophy, the semi-final between Bedfordshire and Cambridgeshire being decided on the toss of a coin, and the final being played two weeks later than planned, at a different venue, rather than the winners of that, too, being decided in the same way.

†At Macclesfield, September 24. Cheshire won by 36 runs and received £1,500. Cheshire 228 for six (50 overs) (I. Tansley 83, P. A. Tipton 67); Bedfordshire 192 (48.3 overs) (D. M. Daniels 70, S. J. Lines 33; R. A. Brown three for 23, N. T. O'Brien three for 37).

*In the averages that follow, * against a score signifies not out, * against a name signifies the captain, and † signifies wicket-keeper.*

BEDFORDSHIRE

Secretary – G. L. B. AUGUST, 24 Furzefield, Putnoe, Bedford

Matches 9: Lost – Durham, Hertfordshire, Northumberland, Staffordshire. Won on first innings – Cambridgeshire. Lost on first innings – Lincolnshire, Norfolk, Suffolk. No result – Cumberland.

Batting Averages

	I	NO	R	HI	Avge
G. N. Cederwall	9	2	264	55	37.71
A. Fordham	9	0	307	82	34.11
M. Morgan	14	2	398	75	33.16
A. R. Wagner	12	2	321	55	32.10
A. S. Pearson	10	0	264	57	26.40
S. J. Lines	10	0	250	96	25.00
C. A. Musson	7	2	125	45	25.00
K. V. Jones	16	5	246	50	22.36
J. Kettleborough	9	0	196	127	21.77
*D. M. Daniels	17	0	279	55	16.41
T. Thomas	11	0	142	49	12.90
J. R. Wake	10	2	86	40	10.75

Also batted: †P. G. M. August, S. E. Blott, F. R. Dethridge, K. V. Gentle, R. Loft, T. Patel, I. G. Peck, R. J. Plowman, †N. Randall.

Bowling Averages

	O	M	R	W	Avge
S. E. Blott..............	146.2	38	434	27	16.07
K. V. Jones.............	160.1	42	459	20	22.95
R. J. Plowman	51.5	7	199	7	28.42
A. R. Wagner.........	128	14	502	13	38.61
J. R. Wake.............	185	28	669	16	41.81
G. N. Cederwall......	128.4	25	421	9	46.77

Also bowled: F. R. Dethridge 34.2–8–112–3; J. Kettleborough 1–0–6–0; S. J. Lines 17–3–66–2; R. Loft 11–0–59–0; M. Morgan 5–0–35–0; A. S. Pearson 3–0–17–0.

BERKSHIRE

Secretary – C. F. V. MARTIN, Paradise Cottage, Paradise Road, Henley-on-Thames, Oxon RG9 1UB

Matches 9: Won – Cornwall, Wiltshire. Lost – Buckinghamshire, Somerset II. Won on first innings – Oxfordshire, Shropshire. Lost on first innings – Cheshire, Devon, Dorset.

Batting Averages

	I	NO	R	HI	Avge
G. R. J. Roope	13	6	541	79*	77.28
*J. F. Harvey..........	14	5	406	79*	45.11
J. A. Claughton.......	18	2	466	61	29.12
M. Lickley	18	1	432	73*	25.41
A. Dindar	18	0	414	76	23.00
M. L. Simmons	9	2	153	33*	21.85
S. Burrow	12	1	167	22	15.18

Also batted: P. Bradburn, †G. E. J. Child, M. Hinchcliffe, J. H. Jones, P. J. Lewington, P. New, A. Rollins, J. Woollhead.

Bowling Averages

	O	M	R	W	Avge
G. R. J. Roope	44	7	102	7	14.57
P. J. Lewington.......	332	117	741	46	16.10
P. New	117.4	46	256	14	18.28
P. Bradburn............	90	23	245	9	27.22
J. H. Jones.............	182	40	643	18	35.72
S. Burrow	144	37	396	9	44.00

Also bowled: G. E. J. Child 1–0–2–0; J. A. Claughton 0.2–0–5–0; A. Dindar 6–1–14–0; J. F. Harvey 3–1–8–0; M. Hinchcliffe 14–5–40–1; M. Lickley 0.1–0–4–0; A. Rollins 46–13–174–3; M. L. Simmons 16–6–60–2.

BUCKINGHAMSHIRE

Secretary – P. M. M. SLATTER, The White Cottage, Framewood Road, Stoke Poges SL2 4QR

Matches 9: Won – Berkshire, Cornwall, Devon, Oxfordshire, Shropshire, Somerset II. Lost – Dorset, Wiltshire. Lost on first innings – Cheshire.

Batting Averages

	I	NO	R	HI	Avge
R. E. Hayward........	16	5	853	108	77.54
†R. G. Humphrey....	12	3	479	129	53.22
M. E. Milton.........	15	2	558	128*	42.92
M. E. Gear..........	10	1	345	57	38.33
K. I. Hodgson......	11	5	199	74	33.16
N. G. Hames	9	2	232	58*	33.14
A. R. Harwood.......	5	1	124	46	31.00
S. A. Mehar...........	8	4	111	34	27.75
J. B. Turner	4	0	109	47	27.25
*D. E. Smith.........	15	3	195	40	16.25
M. J. J. Cox	6	1	77	37*	15.40
M. A. Murfin.........	5	1	61	24	15.25

Also batted: C. D. Booden, J. M. Coles, C. A. Connor, P. Dolphin, A. J. Herrington, A. W. Lyon, I. L. Pont, S. J. Renshaw, T. P. Russell.

Bowling Averages

	O	M	R	W	Avge
M. Jean-Jacques......	29	8	83	7	11.85
A. W. Lyon..........	282.4	89	785	42	18.69
M. E. Milton	257.1	83	627	32	19.59
C. A. Connor	185	35	498	23	21.65
K. I. Hodgson........	52.1	9	166	7	23.71
M. A. Murfin.........	80	23	254	5	50.80
S. A. Mehar...........	80.3	18	263	5	52.60

Also bowled: C. D. Booden 43–8–126–3; J. M. Coles 10–1–51–1; M. J. J. Cox 3–1–8–0; M. E. Gear 3–3–0–0; N. G. Hames 2–1–7–0; R. E. Hayward 1–0–3–0; I. L. Pont 15–2–62–2; D. E. Smith 5–0–23–1.

CAMBRIDGESHIRE

Secretary – P. W. GOODEN,
The Redlands, Oakington Road, Cottenham, Cambridge CB4 4TW

Matches 9: Won – Hertfordshire, Suffolk. Lost – Lincolnshire, Norfolk, Northumberland, Staffordshire. Won on first innings – Durham. Lost on first innings – Bedfordshire, Cumberland.

Batting Averages

	I	NO	R	HI	Avge
M. Afzal...............	10	2	243	71	30.37
N. T. Gadsby.........	18	2	446	89*	27.87
D. R. Parry	5	0	126	122	25.20
J. P. Mills	7	1	134	35	22.33
G. V. Miller	18	2	329	103*	20.56
G. I. Burgess	16	0	318	98	19.87
P. J. Malkin	14	4	196	43*	19.60
*A. M. Ponder........	14	0	234	48	16.71
†M. L. Saggers........	11	4	104	45*	14.85
M. Brown	11	5	75	24*	12.50

Also batted: S. Campin, G. Chapman, M. Gray, D. C. Holliday, J. Hulme, I. Reed, P. Redfarn, M. Stephenson, D. C. Wing.

Bowling Averages

	O	M	R	W	Avge
D. R. Parry	149	52	338	24	14.08
G. I. Burgess	193	46	556	20	27.80
M. Brown	237	55	778	26	29.92
P. J. Malkin	65	4	284	9	31.55
D. C. Wing	115	22	355	10	35.50

Also bowled: M. Afzal 16–3–54–1; G. Chapman 14–1–78–1; M. Gray 16–1–99–3; A. Guild 1–0–6–0; D. C. Holliday 22–0–122–2; N. Housden 29–8–128–1; J. Hulme 46.5–15–116–6; I. Reed 4–3–22–1; M. Stephenson 10.4–3–22–2.

CHESHIRE

Secretary – J. B. PICKUP,
2 Castle Street, Northwich, Cheshire CW8 1AB

Matches 9: Won – Dorset. Lost – Oxfordshire. Won on first innings – Berkshire, Buckinghamshire, Cornwall, Shropshire, Wiltshire. Tied on first innings – Somerset II. Lost on first innings – Devon.

Batting Averages

	I	NO	R	HI	Avge
Mudassar Nazar......	12	5	583	134*	83.28
R. M. O. Cooke......	13	7	301	105*	50.16
D. W. Varey.........	9	1	258	78	32.25
N. T. O'Brien.......	18	1	521	72	30.64
P. A. Tipton........	8	0	216	83	27.00
I. Tansley..........	6	0	148	69	24.66
S. C. Yates.........	12	1	250	62	22.72
D. Bailey...........	9	2	159	55*	22.71
R. R. Simpson	9	1	140	39	17.50
J. S. Hitchmough.....	15	1	191	38	13.64
J. A. Sutton........	11	2	120	37	13.33
P. G. Wakefield	8	4	43	24	10.75

Also batted: R. A. Brown, I. Cowap, I. J. Gemmell, †J. K. Pickup, S. C. Wundke.

Bowling Averages

	O	M	R	W	Avge
D. Bailey	80.3	32	188	15	12.53
J. A. Sutton............	164	50	393	23	17.08
J. S. Hitchmough.....	196	54	538	28	19.21
S. C. Wundke	46	14	103	5	20.60
P. G. Wakefield	90.1	19	354	17	20.82
I. J. Gemmell	99.2	20	312	11	28.36
N. T. O'Brien	153.1	41	381	13	29.30
R. A. Brown	59.5	8	243	8	30.37
R. M. O. Cooke	145	37	465	12	38.75

Also bowled: Mudassar Nazar 59–10–174–2; I. Tansley 2–2–0–0; P. A. Tipton 4–0–26–0; D. W. Varey 2–0–12–0; S. C. Yates 1–1–0–0.

CORNWALL

Secretary – T. D. MENEER, Falbridge, Penvale Cross, Penryn

Matches 9: Won – Dorset. Lost – Berkshire, Buckinghamshire, Shropshire, Somerset II, Wiltshire. Won on first innings – Devon. Lost on first innings – Cheshire, Oxfordshire.

Batting Averages

	I	NO	R	HI	Avge
S. F. Graf	13	4	405	62	45.00
*E. G. Willcock	16	1	496	76*	33.06
M. S. T. Dunstan	13	2	325	78*	29.54
J. M. H. Graham-Brown	7	0	198	61	28.28
C. P. Ollerenshaw....	11	1	212	65	21.20
T. J. Angove	16	1	298	62	19.86
†T. L. Gall.............	16	5	194	35*	17.63
M. C. Rowe	6	1	80	50	16.00
A. E. Snowdon	8	1	93	39	13.28
P. J. Stephens	12	0	155	49	12.91
D. A. Toseland	13	4	109	20	12.11
F. T. Willetts	10	0	121	37	12.10
A. H. Watts	10	2	85	33	10.62

Also batted: N. Cook, D. Jenkin, M. L. Roberts, P. Thomas, M. O. Trenwith, C. J. Trudgeon, G. G. Watts.

Bowling Averages

	O	M	R	W	Avge
A. H. Watts	271.1	71	926	43	21.53
J. M. H. Graham-Brown	24	2	119	5	23.80
D. A. Toseland	274.5	83	760	22	34.54
S. F. Graf	238.1	48	740	20	37.00
A. E. Snowdon	95.3	15	374	6	62.33

Also bowled: N. Cook 11–1–49–1; M. S. T. Dunstan 3–0–21–0; D. Jenkin 10–3–28–0; C. P. Ollerenshaw 4–1–12–0; M. O. Trenwith 12–5–25–1; G. G. Watts 4–1–23–0; E. G. Willcock 5.2–0–42–1; F. T. Willetts 5–1–34–0.

CUMBERLAND

Secretary – M. BEATY, 9 Abbey Drive, Natland, Kendal LA9 7QM

Matches 9: Won – Lincolnshire, Staffordshire. Lost – Hertfordshire, Norfolk. Won on first innings – Cambridgeshire, Suffolk. Lost on first innings – Durham, Northumberland. No result – Bedfordshire.

Batting Averages

	I	NO	R	HI	Avge
L. Baichan	17	7	727	108*	72.70
B. W. Reidy	14	3	572	84	52.00
R. O. Entwistle	17	1	524	76	32.75
I. Cooper	11	4	158	47	22.57
G. Fisher	8	2	131	36	21.83
J. R. Moyes............	7	2	108	31	21.60
*A. G. Wilson	5	1	81	40*	20.25
M. D. Woods...........	16	0	264	48	16.50
G. McMeekin	4	0	64	32	16.00

Also batted: D. L. Ash, †N. Boustead, H. Evans, D. Halliwell, D. J. Lupton, D. J. Parsons, K. Sample, D. Spruce, S. Wall, P. Wood.

Bowling Averages

	O	*M*	*R*	*W*	*Avge*
S. Wall	124.4	25	398	22	18.09
D. J. Lupton	26.5	6	75	4	18.75
B. W. Reidy	199.1	42	655	30	21.83
D. Halliwell	168.5	35	537	22	24.40
D. J. Parsons	38.3	12	111	4	27.75
K. Sample	110.3	23	383	12	31.91
M. Woods	154.3	28	482	11	43.81

Also bowled: D. L. Ash 29–10–78–0; H. Evans 42–14–155–3; R. Mowat 2–0–9–0.

DEVON

Secretary – Rev. K. J. WARREN,
49 Highfield, Lapford, Crediton, Devon EX17 6PY

Matches 9: Won – Dorset, Shropshire, Wiltshire. Lost – Buckinghamshire. Won on first innings – Berkshire, Cheshire, Oxfordshire, Somerset II. Lost on first innings – Cornwall.

Batting Averages

	I	*NO*	*R*	*HI*	*Avge*
G. Wallen	12	2	485	112	48.50
J. H. Edwards	9	1	314	70	39.25
N. A. Folland	13	2	359	89*	32.63
*B. L. Matthews	14	4	260	58*	26.00
Agha Zahid	14	1	332	102	25.53
C. J. Edwards	6	0	151	84	25.16
R. C. Tolchard	17	0	381	82	22.41
N. R. Gaywood	7	0	122	40	17.42
A. W. Allin	11	2	147	36	16.33
M. Taylor	10	5	66	21*	13.20
A. Thomas	14	2	153	47	12.75
†R. M. Oliver	8	2	54	28	9.00

Also batted: P. A. Brown, P. G. Considine, M. J. Goulding, C. A. Melhuish, I. F. Moore, †N. J. Mountford, B. Shaw, D. I. Yeabsley.

Bowling Averages

	O	*M*	*R*	*W*	*Avge*
P. G. Considine	85.5	20	260	16	16.25
D. I. Yeabsley	48	16	91	5	18.20
M. J. Goulding	80.5	19	233	12	19.41
A. W. Allin	267.1	84	720	30	24.00
M. Taylor	241.5	47	804	28	28.71
P. A. Brown	91	20	295	9	32.77
Agha Zahid	105	27	265	7	37.85

Also bowled: J. H. Edwards 3.4–0–40–1; N. A. Folland 14–0–86–3; N. R. Gaywood 11–2–34–2; M. Kingdon 34–13–67–0; I. F. Moore 4–1–16–1; A. Thomas 83–18–329–4; R. C. Tolchard 1–0–11–0; G. Wallen 7–1–39–0.

DORSET

Secretary – D. J. W. BRIDGE,
Long Acre, Tinney's Lane, Sherborne, Dorset DT9 3DY

Matches 9: Won – Buckinghamshire. Lost – Cheshire, Cornwall, Devon, Oxfordshire, Somerset II. Won on first innings – Berkshire. Lost on first innings – Shropshire, Wiltshire.

Batting Averages

	I	NO	R	HI	Avge
A. Kennedy............	16	2	548	89*	39.14
R. V. Lewis.............	16	1	504	108	33.60
S. J. Halliday..........	11	2	271	74*	30.11
C. Stone	15	3	271	63	22.58
V. B. Lewis.............	17	2	281	40	18.73
R. J. Scott..............	16	1	270	60	18.00
C. A. Graham.........	6	0	91	45	15.16
A. R. Wingfield Digby	10	1	124	30	13.77
D. A. Baty	4	0	53	22	13.25
*M. C. Wagstaffe	12	3	83	20*	9.22

Also batted: N. A. Ackland, C. W. Allen, J. F. Blackburn, R. V. J. Coombs, D. R. Hayward, G. R. Moakes, †D. A. Ridley, S. Sawney, D. K. Shantry.

Bowling Averages

	O	M	R	W	Avge
M. C. Wagstaffe......	39	7	127	6	21.16
C. Stone	308.4	87	802	35	22.91
B. K. Shantry	165	36	513	19	27.00
A. R. Wingfield Digby	113	26	379	14	27.07
A. Kennedy............	90	19	263	7	37.57
C. W. Allen............	110	19	398	9	44.22
R. V. J. Coombs	92.4	21	275	5	55.00

Also bowled: J. F. Blackburn 3–1–10–0; S. J. Halliday 3–0–6–0; D. R. Hayward 25–4–65–2; R. V. Lewis 10–1–53–0; S. Sawney 17–1–62–3; R. J. Scott 3–0–13–0.

DURHAM

Secretary – J. ILEY,
Roselea, Springwell Avenue, Durham City DH1 4LY

Matches 9: Won – Bedfordshire, Lincolnshire. Lost – Suffolk. Won on first innings – Cumberland, Hertfordshire, Staffordshire. Lost on first innings – Cambridgeshire, Norfolk. No result – Northumberland.

Batting Averages

	I	NO	R	HI	Avge
S. R. Atkinson........	13	3	517	130	51.70
J. W. Lister	14	2	506	104	42.16
D. C. Jackson	16	0	609	81	38.06
G. Hurst	8	1	255	58	36.42
A. S. Patel	15	4	388	91	35.27
S. Greensword	9	3	160	36*	26.66
*N. A. Riddell........	10	1	202	53*	22.44

Also batted: P. C. Birtwisle, P. J. Crane, S. P. Davis, †A. R. Fothergill, G. Johnson, J. Johnston, P. J. Kippax, P. G. Lee, †R. A. D. Mercer, R. Nanan, W. B. Parker, J. G. D. Smith. G. Forster played in one match but did not bat.

Bowling Averages

	O	M	R	W	Avge
J. Johnston.............	128.1	42	258	17	15.17
S. Greensword........	184.2	67	449	22	20.40
S. P. Davis.............	189.2	50	533	25	21.32
P. J. Kippax...........	90.3	27	224	10	22.40
P. G. Lee..............	159	33	473	16	29.56

Also bowled: S. R. Atkinson 4–0–34–0; P. C. Birtwisle 2–2–0–0; P. J. Crane 7–3–6–1; S. A. B. Daniels 10.1–3–23–2; G. Johnson 11–2–29–1; R. Nanan 61–16–169–4; A. S. Patel 57–19–166–5; N. A. Riddell 4–0–32–0; J. G. D. Smith 15–3–70–1.

HERTFORDSHIRE

Secretary – W. B. MORALEE,
Hermitage Cottage, Wareside, Hertfordshire

Matches 9: Won – Bedfordshire, Cumberland, Lincolnshire, Suffolk. Lost – Cambridgeshire. Won on first innings – Norfolk. Lost on first innings – Durham, Northumberland, Somerset II.

Batting Averages

	I	NO	R	HI	Avge
B. G. Evans...........	12	2	384	75	38.40
W. M. Osman.........	12	0	452	126	37.66
N. P. G. Wright......	14	2	432	73*	36.00
*†F. E. Collyer.......	13	3	311	78	31.10
C. Thomas.............	11	3	201	66	25.12
S. A. Dean.............	13	2	272	70	24.72
T. S. Smith............	13	4	222	40*	24.66
C. S. Bannister........	10	1	200	54	22.22
A. R. Garofall	6	2	59	41	14.75

Also batted: G. J. Andrews, M. Buzza, J. D. Carr, B. G. Collins, P. A. Driver, A. R. L. Emerton, N. Gilbert, R. J. Hailey, R. L. Johns, D. Surridge.

Bowling Averages

	O	M	R	W	Avge
J. D. Carr..............	36.2	5	103	7	14.71
D. Surridge	256.4	78	621	34	18.26
R. J. Hailey	235.4	65	649	35	18.54
T. S. Smith.............	217	81	484	22	22.00
A. R. Garofall	135.1	43	330	14	23.57
B. G. Collins	59	21	138	5	27.60
R. L. Johns	79	21	207	5	41.40

Also bowled: S. A. Dean 1.2–0–17–1; K. R. King 48–3–228–3; C. Thomas 20–4–82–2; J. D. W. Wright 21–3–69–1.

LINCOLNSHIRE

Secretary – C. H. WARMAN,
34 Aldrich Road, Cleethorpes, South Humberside

Matches 9: Won – Cambridgeshire. Lost – Cumberland, Durham, Hertfordshire. Won on first innings – Bedfordshire, Staffordshire. Lost on first innings – Norfolk, Northumberland, Suffolk.

Batting Averages

	I	NO	R	HI	Avge
P. R. Butler............	14	2	521	87	43.41
H. Pougher.............	14	1	507	113*	39.00
†N. Priestley............	16	1	490	70*	32.66
K. G. Brooks.........	14	3	335	55*	30.45
R. O. Estwick.........	7	2	136	55*	27.20
*G. Robinson	18	0	466	67	25.88
J. G. Franks	11	0	223	75	20.27
J. C. Munton	15	3	225	46	18.75
D. Marshall	10	5	73	24*	14.60
R. G. Draper..........	5	2	43	18*	14.33
P. W. Dykes...........	4	1	38	17*	12.66
G. A. Cope	8	3	38	19*	7.60

Also batted: R. L. Burton, A. Dolan, S. J. Mollin, A. Priestley, H. S. Stroud, J. C. Taylor, C. Wicks.

Bowling Averages

	O	M	R	W	Avge
G. A. Cope	293	88	815	42	19.40
R. O. Estwick.........	119.5	33	389	20	19.45
D. Marshall	196	38	657	18	36.50
S. J. Mollin	67	7	261	7	37.28
R. L. Burton	226	48	752	20	37.60

Also bowled: K. G. Brooks 47–11–147–1; P. R. Butler 8–3–32–2; P. W. Dykes 26–6–107–3; J. G. Franks 1–0–5–1; P. J. Hacker 20.5–4–79–3; G. Robinson 7.3–0–50–2.

NORFOLK

Secretary – D. J. M. ARMSTRONG, Thorpe Cottage, Mill Common, Ridlington, North Walsham NR28 9TY

Matches 9: Won – Cambridgeshire, Cumberland. Lost – Suffolk. Won on first innings – Bedfordshire, Durham, Lincolnshire, Staffordshire. Lost on first innings – Hertfordshire, Northumberland.

Batting Averages

	I	NO	R	HI	Avge
S. G. Plumb	16	2	776	122	55.42
R. D. Huggins	16	1	575	90*	38.33
Parvez Mir	14	0	421	86	30.07
P. J. Ringwood	8	1	160	89	22.85
R. F. Innes.............	8	3	109	32*	21.80
*F. L. Q. Handley ...	16	1	310	101*	20.66
N. D. Cook	10	2	156	56*	19.50
E. R. Hodson	10	2	142	29	17.75
†D. E. Mattocks......	11	4	113	29	16.14
D. G. Pilch	11	3	118	32	14.75

Also batted: A. C. Agar, D. N. Bassingthwaighte, B. A. Meigh, T. L. Powell, D. R. Thomas, P. W. Thomas, P. K. Whittaker.

Bowling Averages

	O	M	R	W	Avge
D. G. Pilch	46	7	196	10	19.60
Parvez Mir	303	88	855	32	26.71
P. W. Thomas.........	85.2	21	244	8	30.50
S. G. Plumb	261.3	55	870	21	41.42

Also bowled: A. C. Agar 49–14–156–4; D. N. Bassingthwaighte 33–4–157–1; N. D. Cook 2.5–0–24–1; F. L. Q. Handley 1–0–12–0; R. F. Innes 102–22–347–4; B. A. Meigh 101–17–302–3; P. J. Ringwood 8–0–22–0; D. R. Thomas 16.4–2–68–2; P. K. Whittaker 50–7–182–2.

NORTHUMBERLAND

Secretary – R. E. WOOD,
Osborne Avenue, Jesmond, Newcastle upon Tyne NE2 1JS

Matches 9: Won – Bedfordshire, Cambridgeshire, Suffolk. Won on first innings – Cumberland, Hertfordshire, Lincolnshire, Norfolk, Staffordshire. No result – Durham.

Batting Averages

	I	NO	R	HI	Avge
Wasim Raja.............	11	3	478	115*	59.75
K. Pearson	17	2	729	138*	48.60
*A. S. Thompson	14	3	486	97*	44.18
G. D. Halliday........	14	2	452	100*	37.66
R. D. Dodds...........	8	2	163	44	27.16
M. E. Younger.......	14	2	265	34*	22.08
J. S. Charleton........	5	1	77	27	19.25
S. G. Lishman.........	9	3	106	40	17.66
M. B. Anderson......	4	0	54	35	13.50
P. H. Twizell	8	3	35	13*	7.00

Also batted: R. Arrowsmith, †K. Corby, T. R. Etwaroo, J. N. Graham, A. Hardy, P. J. Pickworth, J. R. Purvis, J. Shotton. G. R. Morris played in one match but did not bat.

Bowling Averages

	O	M	R	W	Avge
J. N. Graham..........	189	60	496	26	19.07
R. Arrowsmith........	133.5	55	243	11	22.09
Wasim Raja.............	151.5	23	521	21	24.80
R. D. Dodds...........	88	18	304	12	25.33
P. H. Twizell	158.1	40	539	14	38.50
A. Hardy	41	10	159	4	39.75
M. E. Younger........	120	43	334	8	41.75

Also bowled: G. D. Halliday 12–1–49–1; S. G. Lishman 10–1–47–2; J. Shotton 14.1–2–61–2.

OXFORDSHIRE

Secretary – J. E. O. SMITH,
2 The Green, Horton-cum-Studley, Oxfordshire

Matches 9: Won – Cheshire, Dorset, Shropshire. Lost – Buckinghamshire, Somerset II. Won on first innings – Cornwall, Wiltshire. Lost on first innings – Berkshire, Devon.

Batting Averages

	I	NO	R	HI	Avge
P. A. Fowler............	14	2	474	150*	39.50
*P. J. Garner..........	18	2	458	90	28.62
G. Ford	10	1	243	62	27.00
D. Wise	12	3	228	76*	25.33
M. D. Nurton	16	0	354	121	22.12
†A. Crossley..........	15	4	238	59	21.63
J. G. Manger	7	1	125	77*	20.83
G. R. Hobbins........	8	1	119	38	17.00
S. R. Porter.............	14	3	167	39	15.18
K. A. Arnold..........	7	3	48	13*	12.00
P. J. Densham	12	0	115	22	9.58
R. N. Busby	7	2	41	15	8.20

Also batted: P. Bradbury, C. Clements, R. A. Evans, D. Gallop.

Bowling Averages

	O	M	R	W	Avge
P. J. Garner	60.2	13	149	10	14.90
K. A. Arnold..........	204	42	590	36	16.38
S. R. Porter............	231	61	700	34	20.58
G. R. Hobbins........	147	40	414	20	20.70
R. A. Evans	154	59	397	17	23.35
R. N. Busby	147	36	385	12	32.08

Also bowled: P. J. Densham 23–2–66–3; D. G. Gallop 19–3–60–1.

SHROPSHIRE

Secretary – H. BOTFIELD,
1 The Crescent, Much Wenlock

Matches 9: Won – Cornwall, Somerset II. Lost – Buckinghamshire, Devon, Oxfordshire. Won on first innings – Dorset, Wiltshire. Lost on first innings – Berkshire, Cheshire.

Batting Averages

	I	NO	R	HI	Avge
D. S. de Silva	12	1	390	97*	35.45
J. B. R. Jones.........	18	1	495	89	29.11
M. Davies	16	0	392	89	24.50
C. N. Boyns	12	1	237	49	21.54
J. Foster	16	1	269	62	17.93
†D. J. Ashley..........	11	4	124	26	17.71
*B. J. Perry...........	15	4	173	37	15.72
S. C. Gale	11	2	100	27*	11.11
J. P. Dawson	13	2	122	33	11.09
P. L. Ranells	10	1	94	29*	10.44
S. Ogrizovic............	6	1	47	16	9.40

Also batted: A. S. Barnard, W. Bott, C. R. Hemsley, J. A. Hulme, *J. S. Johnson, S. J. Mason, W. Moore, D. C. Perry, J. Roberts, J. A. Smith, D. Williamson.

Bowling Averages

	O	M	R	W	Avge
B. J. Perry	160.5	38	384	21	18.28
A. S. Barnard	162.1	46	444	24	18.50
J. P. Dawson	159.4	43	446	24	18.58
S. Ogrizovic............	72.3	16	190	10	19.00
J. Roberts	95.4	27	239	12	19.91
D. S. de Silva	207.4	56	584	24	24.33
P. L. Ranells	71	20	186	7	26.57
J. A. Smith..............	46.5	13	107	4	26.75

Also bowled: W. Bott 21–7–44–2; C. N. Boyns 15–5–36–2; J. B. R. Jones 4–0–11–0; D. C. Perry 24–7–74–2; D. Williamson 4–1–13–0.

SOMERSET SECOND ELEVEN

Secretary – A. S. BROWN,
County Cricket Ground, Taunton

Matches 9: Won – Berkshire, Cornwall, Dorset, Oxfordshire. Lost – Buckinghamshire, Shropshire. Tied on first innings – Cheshire. Lost on first innings – Devon, Wiltshire.

Batting Averages

	I	NO	R	HI	Avge
P. A. Slocombe	7	2	391	73*	78.20
J. G. Wyatt	14	2	572	100	47.66
N. Russom	13	1	420	56	35.00
N. A. Felton...........	16	2	422	100*	30.14
A. J. H. Dunning	13	1	299	61*	24.91
S. J. Turner	12	5	142	28	20.28
G. J. Hall	6	3	60	21	20.00
I. Cox....................	7	0	132	44	18.85
M. R. Davis	5	1	70	33	17.50
R. Harden..............	6	0	96	27	16.00
P. J. Robinson	6	3	42	25	14.00
S. C. Booth	6	3	21	6	7.00

Also batted: P. Bail, R. H. Copeland, M. D. Harman, G. S. Joyce, J. W. Lloyds, R. L. Ollis, G. V. Palmer, †M S. Turner, N. Williams, P. H. L. Wilson.

Bowling Averages

	O	M	R	W	Avge
G. J. Hall	234.4	70	586	33	17.75
N. Russom	209.4	59	544	23	23.65
S. C. Booth	160	29	493	18	27.38
M. D. Harman........	138	28	493	18	27.38
I. Cox....................	63	19	161	5	32.20
M. R. Davis	54	17	173	4	43.25

Also bowled: J. W. Lloyds 34.5–7–108–5; G. V. Palmer 44–3–207–4; P. J. Robinson 40.1–5–124–10; J. Thompson 34–8–79–7; M. S. Turner 27–5–76–4; P. H. L. Wilson 14–4–58–2.

STAFFORDSHIRE

Secretary – L. W. HANCOCK,
4 Kingsland Avenue, Oakhill, Stoke-on-Trent ST4 5LA

Matches 9: Won – Bedfordshire, Cambridgeshire. Lost – Cumberland. Won on first innings – Hertfordshire. Lost on first innings – Durham, Lincolnshire, Norfolk, Northumberland, Suffolk.

Batting Averages

	I	NO	R	HI	Avge
S. J. Dean..............	14	4	447	123	44.70
*P. N. Gill	14	2	502	79	41.83
Mushtaq Mohammad	16	2	501	77	35.78
G. S. Warner..........	18	5	392	63*	30.15
N. J. Archer	15	4	300	65	27.27
D. Cartledge...........	15	0	407	94	27.13
P. A. Marshall	9	3	122	52*	20.33
†A. Griffiths...........	10	3	136	37*	19.42
R. W. Flower..........	7	3	63	16	15.75
D. Blank...............	7	2	78	21	15.60
D. G. Nicholls	4	0	52	31	13.00

Also batted: M. E. W. Brooker, S. J. Dawson, D. A. Hancock, R. I. James.

Bowling Averages

	O	M	R	W	Avge
R. I. James..............	67.3	16	202	9	22.44
R. W. Flower..........	241.3	58	800	35	22.85
D. Cartledge...........	38.4	7	200	7	28.57
D. Blank...............	147	30	496	16	31.00
Mushtaq Mohammad	205.1	35	763	24	31.79
M. E. W. Brooker ...	105	22	348	9	38.66
D. G. Nicholls	103	20	317	5	63.40

Also bowled: N. J. Archer 5–0–35–2; R. P. Archer 6–2–17–0; S. J. Dean 3–0–29–1; P. N. Gill 2.4–0–27–0; P. A. Marshall 5–0–49–0; G. S. Warner 3–0–21–0.

SUFFOLK

Secretary – R. S. BARKER,
Harthill, 301 Henley Road, Ipswich IP1 6TB

Matches 9: Won – Durham, Norfolk. Lost – Cambridgeshire, Hertfordshire, Northumberland. Won on first innings – Bedfordshire, Lincolnshire, Staffordshire. Lost on first innings – Cumberland.

Batting Averages

	I	NO	R	HI	Avge
R. F. Howlett	10	2	272	79*	34.00
S. M. Clements	18	1	533	133	31.35
S. A. R. Ferguson ...	8	2	161	54*	26.83
P. D. Barker...........	18	2	423	107	26.43
J. W. Edrich...........	18	1	410	107*	24.11
R. J. Bond	14	3	264	57	24.00
R. J. Robinson........	10	2	182	78	22.75
P. J. Caley	18	1	319	125	18.76

	I	NO	R	HI	Avge
*C. Rutterford........	12	3	133	50*	14.77
M. D. Bailey..........	7	4	38	19*	12.66
K. P. Offord............	6	0	65	27	10.83
†S. A. Westley........	11	1	95	29	9.50
R. C. Green	11	5	49	16*	8.16

Also batted: K. J. Winder.

Bowling Averages

	O	M	R	W	Avge
C. Rutterford..........	236.4	62	576	34	16.94
R. C. Green	257.4	52	833	43	19.37
P. D. Barker...........	83	15	241	11	21.90
M. D. Bailey	100.3	21	328	9	36.44
R. J. Robinson........	88.1	19	265	7	37.85
P. J. Caley	142	19	467	11	42.45

Also bowled: S. M. Clements 7–0–21–0; S. A. R. Ferguson 7.2–0–42–1; R. F. Howlett 2–0–11–0; K. J. Winder 5–1–10–0.

WILTSHIRE

Secretary – J. C. GREENWOOD,
35 Rowden Hill, Chippenham, Wiltshire

Matches 9: Won – Buckinghamshire, Cornwall. Lost – Berkshire, Devon. Won on first innings – Dorset, Somerset II. Lost on first innings – Cheshire, Oxfordshire, Shropshire.

Batting Averages

	I	NO	R	HI	Avge
R. C. Cooper..........	9	1	519	137	64.87
J. M. Rice..............	13	0	539	121	41.46
D. Simpkins............	13	3	278	58*	27.80
P. L. Thorn	15	0	415	81	27.66
D. Crisp.................	10	4	154	60*	25.66
B. H. White	15	0	376	73	25.06
D. Mercer	10	0	243	75	24.30
†G. E. Meale..........	15	5	228	48*	22.80
M. Bailey...............	9	3	134	38	22.33
J. Newman	10	1	174	36	19.33

Also batted: T. H. Barnes, *R. J. Gulliver, A. J. Spencer.

Bowling Averages

	O	M	R	W	Avge
M. Bailey...............	154	36	537	29	18.51
J. M. Rice..............	68	19	208	10	20.80
P. L. Thorn	61	10	254	12	21.16
P. Meehan..............	45	13	141	6	23.50
T. H. Barnes	270	85	730	25	29.20
R. J. Gulliver	115	14	451	14	32.21
A. J. Spencer..........	84	15	324	8	40.50
D. Crisp.................	123	21	493	8	61.62

Also bowled: R. C. Cooper 24–8–81–3; D. Simpkins 7.3–0–29–0; B. H. White 5–2–27–0; R. Wilson 20–4–73–0.

LEADING MINOR COUNTIES AVERAGES – 1983

BATTING

(Qualification: 8 innings; average 40.00)

	I	NO	R	HI	Avge
Mudassar Nazar (*Cheshire*)	12	5	583	134*	83.28
R. E. Hayward (*Buckinghamshire*)	16	5	853	108	77.54
G. R. J. Roope (*Berkshire*)	13	6	541	79*	77.28
L. Baichan (*Cumberland*)	17	7	727	108*	72.70
R. C. Cooper (*Wiltshire*)	9	1	519	137	64.87
Wasim Raja (*Northumberland*)	11	3	478	115*	59.75
S. G. Plumb (*Norfolk*)	16	2	776	122	55.42
R. G. Humphrey (*Buckinghamshire*)	12	3	479	129	53.22
B. W. Reidy (*Cumberland*)	14	3	572	84	52.00
S. R. Atkinson (*Durham*)	13	3	517	130	51.70
R. M. O. Cooke (*Cheshire*)	13	7	301	105*	50.16
K. Pearson (*Northumberland*)	17	2	729	138*	48.60
G. Wallen (*Devon*)	12	2	485	112	48.50
J. G. Wyatt (*Somerset II*)	14	2	572	100	47.66
J. F. Harvey (*Berkshire*)	14	5	406	79*	45.11
S. F. Graf (*Cornwall*)	13	4	405	62	45.00
S. J. Dean (*Staffordshire*)	14	4	447	123	44.70
A. S. Thompson (*Northumberland*)	14	3	486	97*	44.18
P. R. Butler (*Lincolnshire*)	14	2	521	87	43.41
M. E. Milton (*Buckinghamshire*)	15	2	558	128*	42.92
J. W. Lister (*Durham*)	14	2	506	104	42.16
P. N. Gill (*Staffordshire*)	14	2	502	79	41.83
J. M. Rice (*Wiltshire*)	13	0	539	121	41.46

BOWLING

(Qualification: 20 wickets; average 20.00)

	O	M	R	W	Avge
D. R. Parry (*Cambridgeshire*)	149	52	338	24	14.08
S. E. Blott (*Bedfordshire*)	146.2	38	434	27	16.07
P. J. Lewington (*Berkshire*)	332	117	741	46	16.10
K. Arnold (*Oxfordshire*)	204	42	590	36	16.38
C. Rutterford (*Suffolk*)	236.4	62	576	34	16.94
J. A. Sutton (*Cheshire*)	164	50	393	23	17.08
G. J. Hall (*Somerset II*)	234.4	70	586	33	17.75
S. Wall (*Cumberland*)	124.4	25	398	22	18.09
D. Surridge (*Hertfordshire*)	256.4	78	621	34	18.26
B. J. Perry (*Shropshire*)	160.5	38	384	21	18.28
A. S. Barnard (*Shropshire*)	162.1	46	444	24	18.50
M. Bailey (*Wiltshire*)	154	36	537	29	18.51
R. J. Hailey (*Hertfordshire*)	235.4	65	649	35	18.54
J. P. Dawson (*Berkshire*)	159.4	43	446	24	18.58
A. W. Lyon (*Buckinghamshire*)	282.4	89	785	42	18.69
J. N. Graham (*Northumberland*)	189	60	496	26	19.07
J. S. Hitchmough (*Cheshire*)	196	54	538	28	19.21
R. C. Green (*Suffolk*)	257.4	52	833	43	19.37
G. A. Cope (*Lincolnshire*)	293	88	815	42	19.40
R. O. Estwick (*Lincolnshire*)	119.5	33	389	20	19.45
M. E. Milton (*Buckinghamshire*)	257.1	83	627	32	19.59

SECOND ELEVEN CHAMPIONSHIP, 1983

Derbyshire, with just one win, were again disappointing, only Barry Wood and William Fowler reaching three figures and the bowlers proving expensive, apart from Dallas Moir, who took the most wickets.

Although unbeaten until their last match, **Essex** managed only two wins. Owing to the absence through injury of Andrew Golding and Kevin Moye, the bowling lacked penetration, with the exception of Mervyn Hughes, on an Esso scholarship from Australia, whose 60 wickets included seven for 68 against Surrey at Southend and six for 80 against Northamptonshire. Michael Field-Buss, an off-spinner, scored his maiden century in any grade of cricket and he did it in style with 191 against Sussex.

In an improved season, **Glamorgan** raised themselves from the bottom of the table to take tenth place. Double-centuries came from Stephen Henderson – 218 not out against Gloucestershire at Bristol – and the West Indian, Linton Lewis, who made 211 against Somerset at Taunton. Mark Price, on trial from Bolton, took the most wickets, closely followed by Steve Barwick.

In a disappointing season for **Gloucestershire**, who managed no wins, notable performances came from Alastair Hignell, who made 217 in his only match – against Warwickshire at Bristol – and Chris Dale, a late recruit from Kent, who took eleven for 151 against Hampshire at Bristol.

For **Hampshire**, two centuries each came from Paul Terry and Robin Smith, the latter scoring by far the most runs. Keith Stevenson was the leading bowler, his 35 wickets including returns of six for 60 against Kent at Bournemouth and fourteen for 88 against Middlesex at Southgate.

At the beginning of the season, **Kent** were able to field an exceptionally strong side, but as players graduated to the first team, younger ones came to the fore. Kevin Masters had an outstanding season with his medium-fast deliveries, his 50 wickets including returns of seven for 103 against Essex at Eaton Manor and six for 51 against Hampshire at Bournemouth. He was ably assisted by Chris Penn, Chris Dale and Laurie Potter, who changed to orthodox left-arm spin, while Richard Pepper, Graham Cowdrey and Stephen Goldsmith took full advantage of their opportunities as batsmen.

Nine centuries were scored for **Lancashire**, four of them by Mark Chadwick. Notable bowling performances came from Ian Folley (eight for 15 against Yorkshire), Timothy Taylor (seven for 34 against Warwickshire), Steve Jefferies (seven for 55 against Somerset) and Ian Davidson (seven for 63 against Glamorgan).

Leicestershire, with six wins, comfortably headed the table. Eight centuries were scored, including John Whitaker's 190 not out against Worcestershire at Old Hill and his 186 against Nottinghamshire at Worksop. Gordon Parsons and James Addison were the leading bowlers; Parsons took eight for 70 against Lancashire at Manchester and thirteen for 122 in the match against Northampton at Market Harborough, and Addison eight for 80 against Derbyshire at Derby and seven for 24 against the same side at Leicester.

After the loss of three matches to rain, **Middlesex** had their worst season for some years, being top-heavy with bowlers and too dependent upon Colin Cook, Keith Brown and Andy Smith with the bat. Towards the end of the season they all lost form together, but Andrew Miller scored a magnificent unbeaten 201 against Kent. The bowlers often had too few runs to bowl at, the pick of the quicker bowlers being Bill Merry, although Jamie Sykes looked a promising off-spinner and Graham Rose a useful all-rounder.

For **Northamptonshire** Robert Bailey had an exceptionally good season, reaching three figures three times in his nine innings, the side's only other hundred coming from David Capel. Although Alan Walker and James Carse bowled well on occasions, the attack generally lacked penetration and variety.

Nottinghamshire, who called on a total of 34 players during the season, were not impressive. Their side was strengthened by two overseas players on scholarship – Robbie Kerr from Queensland, who was much the best batsman, his runs including a double-century against Derbyshire at Heanor, and a New Zealander, David White, who played some good innings once he had settled in. Paul Johnson, Peter Such and Chris Scott all improved during the season and did well in the first team.

Owing to World Cup commitments and injury in the first team, **Somerset** were rather depleted and sank to the bottom of the table. Julian Wyatt, in his first season, won a first-team place at the end of the season, while Steven Booth, a Yorkshireman from the Lord's ground-staff, bowled well. Neil Russom scored most runs and Phil Slocombe, with 274 runs in four innings, made 100 not out against Warwickshire at Coventry, Russom reaching 137 in the same match.

Surrey, for whom seven players made centuries, had a good season, with fine performances from many of their players. Injuries to Kevin Mackintosh and Mark Feltham gave opportunities to fast bowler Peter Waterman, while Andy Needham took the most wickets, and Brian Parkinson kept wicket commendably when Alec Stewart was playing for the first team.

For **Sussex**, David Standing had an outstanding first season and Alan Wells performed admirably throughout. David Wood made steady progress as a dogged opening batsman, and David Smith and Allan Green put on 231 runs for the first wicket in the second innings against Surrey at Guildford to win the match. Alan Willows took most wickets, including nine for 60 in the match against Essex at Chelmsford.

For **Warwickshire**, who, apart from Lancashire, played more matches than any other side, Robin Dyer passed 1,000 runs, including five centuries, and Gladstone Small's 232 runs included 146 against Lancashire. Asif Din continued to impress, David Thorne was effective with both bat and ball, and Gordon Lord, with hundreds against Gloucestershire and Middlesex, batted with great confidence. The bowlers, however, were disappointing, lacking the consistency to win matches.

Although **Worcestershire** failed to retain their title, they were the only side to remain unbeaten. The batting was again strong, Timothy Curtis scoring most runs, despite being available for only half the season, and Martin Weston making 308 in four innings. The side's bowling improved, with Greg Matthews, a New South Wales player on an Esso scholarship, collecting most wickets, as well as scoring a century against Somerset at Kidderminster, and Steve Perryman taking ten for 46 at Street, also against Somerset.

Yorkshire, who took second place, were encouraged by the performance of their younger players. Ashley Metcalfe scored the most runs while Ian Swallow showed promise as an off-spinner. Paul Booth, who took six for 78 against Lancashire, was a successful slow left-arm bowler. Against Nottinghamshire at Nottingham Simon Dennis took eight for 53 and Paul Robinson and Steven Rhodes each scored centuries.

SECOND ELEVEN CHAMPIONSHIP FINAL TABLE

	Played	Won	Lost	Drawn	Bonus Points Batting	Bonus Points Bowling	Total Points	Average
Leicestershire	10	6	1	3	35	30	161	16.1
Yorkshire	11	5	1	5	29	39	148	13.4
Surrey	13	5	3	5	35	40	155	11.9
Kent	11	4	4	3	27	35	126	11.4
Sussex	11	3	1	7	39	35	122	11.0
Lancashire	18	5	3	10	47	56	183	10.1
Warwickshire	17	4	5	8	48	52	164	9.6
Worcestershire	9	2	0	7	25	20	77	8.5
Northamptonshire	12	2	5	5	33	36	101	8.4
Glamorgan	13	2	3	8	38	34	104	8.0
Essex	12	2	1	9	31	30	93	7.7
Nottinghamshire	13	2	3	8	27	37	96	7.3
Hampshire	11	1	2	8	25	34	75	6.8
Derbyshire	9	1	3	5	17	25	58	6.4
Middlesex	11	1	5	5	25	22	63	5.7
Gloucestershire	7	0	3	4	13	21	34	4.8
Somerset	10	0	2	8	16	25	41	4.1

Notes: The averages to determine the positions in the Championship are worked to one, uncorrected decimal place.

The following matches were abandoned without a ball being bowled: Leicestershire v Middlesex, May 4, 5, 6; Sussex v Kent, Yorkshire v Surrey, both on May 11, 12, 13; Gloucestershire v Somerset, Northamptonshire v Middlesex, Yorkshire v Derbyshire, all on May 18, 19, 20; Lancashire v Nottinghamshire, Warwickshire v Middlesex, Worcestershire v Gloucestershire, Yorkshire v Glamorgan, all on June 1, 2, 3.

In the averages that follow, * against a score signifies not out, * against a name signifies the captain and † signifies the wicket-keeper.

DERBYSHIRE SECOND ELEVEN

Matches 9: Won – Northamptonshire. Lost – Lancashire, Leicestershire (twice). Drawn – Lancashire, Northamptonshire, Nottinghamshire (twice), Yorkshire.

Batting Averages

	I	NO	R	HI	Avge
B. Wood	9	1	419	165	52.37
W. P. Fowler	6	1	214	100*	42.80
B. Roberts	15	4	402	81*	36.54
N. Bradshaw	7	1	180	72	30.00
†B. J. M. Maher	14	1	378	82	29.07
G. J. Money	7	0	182	83	26.00
D. G. Moir	4	0	101	45	25.25
J. E. Morris	6	1	112	38*	22.40
K. G. Brooks	8	0	132	30	16.50
P. G. Newman	8	1	110	61*	15.71
A. M. Brown	7	1	81	41	13.50
C. Marples	5	1	49	30	12.25

Also batted: S. Bailey, I. Broome, A. H. Dyson, S. J. Farrell, R. J. Finney, A. Hill, D. Hopkinson, D. Kennedy, R. Merriman, F. Mitchell, A. Pierrepont, M. Pringle, P. E. Russell, R. Salmon, P. Taylor, A. Watts.

Bowling Averages

	O	M	R	W	Avge
D. G. Moir	129	47	229	20	11.45
A. M. Brown	17.5	6	83	5	16.60
A. Pierrepont	29	4	78	4	19.50
P. Taylor	86.5	21	260	13	20.00
W. P. Fowler	103	33	229	11	20.81
K. G. Brooks	52.4	17	147	7	21.00
B. Wood	94	40	137	6	22.83
S. J. Farrell	179	35	550	16	34.37
P. G. Newman	88.4	24	246	6	41.00
B. Roberts	110	14	365	8	45.62
I. Broome	66.4	13	247	5	49.40
A. Watts	229	54	713	12	59.41

Also bowled: A. H. Dyson 13–5–42–1; D. Eyre 41–11–101–1; R. J. Finney 16–6–27–0; A. Hill 5–3–4–0; D. Kennedy 5–0–22–0; F. Mitchell 12–1–66–0; J. E. Morris 4–0–24–0; O. H. Mortensen 38–3–74–3; S. Oldham 43–16–86–1; M. Pringle 0.3–0–0–0; P. E. Russell 10–6–9–0.

ESSEX SECOND ELEVEN

Matches 12: Won – Kent, Northamptonshire. Lost – Sussex.. Drawn – Hampshire, Kent, Middlesex (twice), Northamptonshire, Nottinghamshire, Surrey (twice), Sussex.

Batting Averages

	I	NO	R	HI	Avge
S. Ferguson	7	2	290	126*	58.00
R. J. Leiper............	22	6	809	148*	50.56
*M. H. Denness	10	6	192	39*	48.00
A. K. Golding.........	9	2	237	66	33.85
C. Gladwin	19	2	553	102	32.52
P. J. Prichard.........	19	2	513	78	30.17
M. R. Gouldstone....	15	3	351	71	29.25
A. W. Lilley	14	0	380	66	27.14
M. Field-Buss	21	1	496	191	24.80
M. Hughes	9	4	119	36	23.80
J. Stephenson.........	4	0	58	30	14.50
†N. D. Burns	13	2	94	25	8.54

Also batted: D. L. Acfield, C. Dale, T. Foley, N. A. Foster, N. King, S. Kippax, R. Miller, K. Moye, N. Phillip, I. L. Pont, K. R. Pont.

Bowling Averages

	O	M	R	W	Avge
M. Hughes	394.3	87	1,119	60	18.65
N. A. Foster...........	67	20	183	8	22.87
D. L. Acfield.........	64.2	18	115	5	23.00
G. Latner..............	28	1	119	4	29.75
A. W. Lilley...........	109.2	25	320	10	32.00
I. L. Pont.............	77	25	195	6	32.50
C. Gladwin............	137.1	47	341	9	37.88
A. K. Golding.........	173.2	47	523	12	43.58
R. Miller..............	93	13	369	8	46.12
K. Moye	152.3	36	461	9	51.22
M. Field-Buss	351.2	99	1,000	16	62.50

Also bowled: C. Dale 28–9–57–1; S. Ferguson 5–1–22–0; T. Foley 22–5–67–0; M. R. Gouldstone 2–0–6–0; S. Kippax 1–0–4–0; N. Phillip 6–2–15–1; K. R. Pont 7–1–20–0; J. Stephenson 7–4–22–1; S. Turner 5–1–5–0.

GLAMORGAN SECOND ELEVEN

Matches 13: Won – Gloucestershire, Somerset. Lost – Kent, Warwickshire, Yorkshire. Drawn – Gloucestershire, Hampshire, Lancashire (twice), Somerset, Warwickshire, Worcestershire (twice).

Batting Averages

	I	NO	R	HI	Avge
S. P. Henderson	5	2	392	218*	130.66
L. Lewis	9	0	570	211	63.33
†T. Davies	13	4	402	77*	44.66
M. Price	16	4	470	71	39.16
J. G. Thomas...........	4	0	152	117	38.00
G. C. Holmes	15	1	486	101*	34.71
H. Morris...............	6	0	207	83	34.50
A. Cottey...............	8	0	273	77	34.12
J. Derrick...............	18	2	522	133*	32.62
M. J. Cann.............	8	0	251	88	31.37
M. Cohen...............	14	0	373	79	26.64
E. W. Jones	9	2	183	98	26.14
A. L. Jones	6	1	103	42*	20.60
S. Maddock	8	3	101	32	20.20
B. J. Lloyd	5	0	81	43	16.20
K. J. Lyons	9	3	79	36*	13.16
S. R. Barwick	8	2	75	28	12.50
I. Smith	10	1	73	26	8.11
S. Watkins..............	8	4	31	8*	7.75

Also batted: R. Berry, T. Cartwright, C. Elward, D. A. Francis, J. A. Hopkins, C. Jones, P. Morris, M. A. Nash, P. North, N. Roberts, C. J. C. Rowe, C. Sargent, T. Topley, A. H. Wilkins, M. Williams. J. Cartwright played in one match but did not bat.

Bowling Averages

	O	M	R	W	Avge
J. G. Thomas...........	32.4	5	96	5	19.20
M. A. Nash	149	57	333	13	25.61
A. H. Wilkins	204	55	507	18	28.16
G. C. Holmes	201.1	57	609	19	32.05
J. Derrick...............	149.5	38	486	15	32.40
S. R. Barwick	241.2	50	778	24	32.41
S. Maddock	59	9	248	7	35.42
M. Price	338.3	112	978	29	33.72
B. J. Lloyd	135	30	382	8	47.75
S. Watkins..............	142.3	31	473	9	52.55

Also bowled: A. Cottey 2–2–0–0; K. J. Lyons 3.1–0–20–2; L. Lewis 4–0–14–0; P. North 14–5–35–0; C. J. C. Rowe 37–11–75–1; C. Sargent 8–1–49–1; I. Smith 68–15–229–3; T. Topley 25–8–72–1.

GLOUCESTERSHIRE SECOND ELEVEN

Matches 7: Lost – Glamorgan, Warwickshire (twice). Drawn – Glamorgan, Hampshire, Somerset, Worcestershire.

Batting Averages

	I	NO	R	HI	Avge
E. J. Cunningham....	10	2	367	175*	45.87
R. J. Doughty.........	9	0	363	145	40.33
A. J. Wright	7	0	276	88	39.42
J. E. Skinner	7	0	271	132	38.71
R. R. Savage	5	0	149	60	29.80
S. R. Tracy.............	6	2	111	56	27.75
*†A. J. Brassington..	9	4	89	39	17.80
D. P. Simpkins........	5	1	60	25	15.00
K. G. Rice	10	0	95	29	9.55

Also batted: G. Balmer, J. Benjamin, I. S. Bishop, P. R. Bishop, B. C. Broad, J. S. Brooks, P. Buchanan, J. H. Childs, C. Dale, T. Farnworth, N. A. Folland, M. Haswell, N. Hennessy, A. J. Hignell, D. V. Lawrence, R. Sharma, S. Sharp, L. Smith, W. M. Smith, B. Storie, D. Thomas, C. R. Trembath, A. Watts.

Bowling Averages

	O	M	R	W	Avge
C. Dale	73.5	25	151	11	13.72
J. H. Childs	41	10	93	5	18.60
S. R. Tracy	125.5	19	411	13	31.61
R. J. Doughty	150.3	28	506	13	38.92
E. J. Cunningham	158.1	46	442	8	55.25
D. P. Simpkins	92.4	14	336	6	56.00

Also bowled: G. Balmer 13–0–64–1; J. Benjamin 29–6–92–1; I. S. Bishop 23–6–88–1; P. Buchanan 27–6–87–1; T. Farnworth 59–10–235–4; A. J. Hignell 8.4–0–28–2; D. V. Lawrence 24–3–70–2; K. G. Rice 5–1–18–0; J. E. Skinner 31–6–96–1; W. M. Smith 21.5–5–51–3; B. Storie 26–5–95–1; D. Thomas 16–2–63–0; C. R. Trembath 18–5–48–1; A. Watts 39–10–109–3; A. J. Wright 28.3–5–92–2.

HAMPSHIRE SECOND ELEVEN

Matches 11: Won – Middlesex. Lost – Kent, Surrey. Drawn – Essex, Glamorgan, Gloucestershire, Somerset (twice), Surrey, Sussex (twice).

Batting Averages

	I	NO	R	HI	Avge
R. A. Smith	17	2	888	178	59.20
D. R. Turner	6	0	271	88	45.16
S. Cootes	6	2	142	58	35.50
R. Scott	14	4	333	121*	33.30
T. C. Middleton	19	1	502	63	27.88
J. E. Hardy	21	1	504	72	25.20
R. R. Savage	7	2	125	53*	25.00
R. Mason	8	1	160	80*	22.85
K. Stevenson	11	5	136	42*	22.66
M. Hussain	18	3	339	61	22.60
†C. F. E. Goldie	15	2	273	53	21.00
J. W. Southern	5	1	67	36*	16.75
S. J. Andrew	9	6	24	16*	8.00
K. St J. D. Emery	7	0	45	21	6.42

Also batted: J. Barnard, M. Bridal, I. Chivers, N. G. Cowley, S. Dutton, D. Hale, W. Jenner, A. Jones, S. Kimber, R. J. Maru, J. Newman, V. P. Terry, M. Wedderburn, A. Wright.

Bowling Averages

	O	M	R	W	Avge
M. Wedderburn	41	8	137	8	17.12
K. Stevenson	247.5	71	615	35	17.57
N. G. Cowley	31	10	91	5	18.20
J. W. Southern	185	64	460	19	24.21
R. Mason	73	22	230	9	25.55
K. St J. D. Emery	192.2	62	414	13	31.84
M. Hussain	271	64	866	21	41.23
S. J. Andrew	142.2	39	419	4	104.75

Also bowled: M. Bridal 13–1–54–1; I. Chivers 26–8–65–2; S. Cootes 27.3–3–100–3; S. Dutton 2–0–10–0; D. Hale 11–5–35–0; A. Jones 5–4–2–0; S. Kimber 19–2–65–0; R. J. Maru 34–10–80–1; T. C. Middleton 2.1–0–14–0; R. Scott 21.3–2–81–3; R. A. Smith 7–0–20–1; A. Wright 18–3–59–3.

KENT SECOND ELEVEN

Matches 11: Won – Glamorgan, Hampshire, Middlesex, Surrey. Lost – Essex, Middlesex, Surrey, Yorkshire. Drawn – Essex, Lancashire, Sussex.

Batting Averages

	I	NO	R	HI	Avge
R. M. Pepper	7	1	257	118*	42.83
G. R. Cowdrey	14	0	563	98	40.21
S. G. Hinks	15	0	534	120	35.60
R. Sharma	19	2	585	107	34.41
S. Goldsmith	10	0	298	81	29.80
L. Potter	18	2	420	105	26.25
C. Penn	14	1	335	89	25.76
†S. A. Marsh	16	2	335	62	23.92
†S. N. V. Waterton	10	2	176	55	22.00
M. Fleming	5	0	82	27	16.40
M. Maynard	13	0	195	49	15.00
C. Dale	15	1	162	38	11.57
K. D. Masters	13	6	62	26	8.85

Bowling Averages

	O	M	R	W	Avge
K. D. Masters	330	78	993	50	19.86
G. R. Cowdrey	69.2	21	200	10	20.00
L. Potter	242.5	83	518	21	24.66
C. Penn	232	67	615	20	30.75
C. Dale	340	104	827	26	31.80

LANCASHIRE SECOND ELEVEN

Matches 18: Won – Derbyshire, Northamptonshire, Surrey, Warwickshire, Yorkshire. Lost – Leicestershire (twice), Surrey. Drawn – Derbyshire, Glamorgan (twice), Kent, Northamptonshire, Nottinghamshire, Somerset, Warwickshire, Worcestershire, Yorkshire.

Batting Averages

	I	NO	R	HI	Avge
D. P. Hughes	6	2	269	111	67.25
H. Pilling	16	9	374	81	53.43
I. Cockbain	13	1	583	144	48.58
M. R. Chadwick	23	4	920	131*	48.42
N. H. Fairbrother	6	0	256	107	42.66
D. Lloyd	7	0	289	116	41.28
R. G. Watson	11	2	366	97*	40.66
S. J. O'Shaughnessy	5	1	160	56*	40.00
I. Folley	12	4	247	73	30.87
L. L. MacFarlane	7	4	92	46	30.66
K. A. Hayes	11	0	326	102	29.63
Nasir Zaidi	16	5	320	55*	29.09
S. T. Crawley	16	0	430	74	26.87
N. V. Radford	10	0	262	93	26.20
S. T. Jefferies	10	1	221	44	24.55
N. Speak	6	0	147	49	24.50
A. Settle	9	1	191	76*	23.87
D. Pearson	4	0	92	39	23.00
A. Wild	6	2	84	71	21.00
J. S. Hitchmough	12	1	207	52	18.81
A. Hayhurst	15	1	246	45	17.57
G. J. Speak	13	4	126	24	14.00
†M. A. Wallwork	5	0	69	24	13.80
†J. Stanworth	13	3	71	21	7.10

Also batted: R. Berry, G. Clarke, I. Davidson, M. Fallon, D. Fitton, †P. Gill, F. C. Hayes, W. Joyce, D. Makinson, A. Murphy, J. Pickard, A. Stevens, T. J. Taylor, S. Toogood, M. Watkinson, J. Whitehead.

Bowling Averages

	O	M	R	W	Avge
S. J. O'Shaughnessy .	38	10	109	7	15.57
D. Makinson............	90.1	16	270	16	16.87
I. Folley.................	193.2	60	433	22	19.68
S. T. Jefferies	191.4	55	493	25	19.72
N. V. Radford	166.5	57	414	20	20.70
T. J. Taylor............	169.4	57	460	20	23.00
L. L. MacFarlane	312.4	69	934	26	35.92
R. G. Watson	138	36	370	10	37.00
Nasir Zaidi	296	78	821	21	39.09
D. Lloyd................	162.3	51	316	8	39.50
I. Davidson	147.5	36	440	11	40.00
G. J. Speak	202.5	49	628	14	44.85

Also bowled: I. Cockbain 6–2–10–0; S. T. Crawley 27–10–81–3; N. H. Fairbrother 20–6–41–4; K. A. Hayes 11–3–30–1; A. Hayhurst 74.4–17–242–3; J. S. Hitchmough 1–0–12–0; D. P. Hughes 50–13–147–2; W. Joyce 2–1–1–0; A. Murphy 31–10–75–1; J. Pickard 16.4–40–2; H. Pilling 0.1–0–4–0; A. Settle 5–1–15–0; N. Speak 27–4–98–3; S. Toogood 1–0–5–0; M. Watkinson 64–19–122–2; A. Wild 72–17–187–4.

LEICESTERSHIRE SECOND ELEVEN

Matches 10: Won – Derbyshire (twice), Lancashire (twice), Northamptonshire, Nottingham-shire. Lost – Worcestershire. Drawn – Northamptonshire, Nottinghamshire, Warwickshire.

Batting Averages

	I	NO	R	HI	Avge
K. N. Foyle	8	6	329	79*	164.50
J. J. Whitaker	14	3	869	190*	79.00
I. P. Butcher	6	1	348	158*	69.60
T. J. Boon	17	4	756	101*	58.15
M. D. Haysman	10	2	455	145*	56.87
R. A. Cobb	20	3	730	108*	42.94
M. A. Garnham	15	3	483	84*	40.25
J. P. Addison	11	3	232	68	29.00

Also batted: J. P. Agnew, N. E. Briers, P. B. Clift, I. Cuthbertson, D. De Silva, D. Ellwood, G. J. F. Ferris, M. Gibson, A. Greasley, J. Harris, K. Higgs, P. Higgs, G. Inglis, K. Maguire, T. A. Munton, G. J. Parsons, A. Pearson, S. Schofield, R. Spiers, M. Whitmore.

Bowling Averages

	O	M	R	W	Avge
G. J. Parsons	200.3	49	660	38	17.36
G. J. F. Ferris........	33	7	100	5	20.00
J. P. Addison..........	297.5	109	737	36	20.47
J. P. Agnew............	164	28	509	22	23.13
K. Higgs	95.2	32	206	8	25.75
M. D. Haysman	203	54	536	17	31.52
T. J. Boon..............	40.3	4	200	5	40.00
G. Inglis...............	83	18	246	6	41.00

Also bowled: N. E. Briers 5–2–14–0; I. P. Butcher 28–7–139–4; R. A. Cobb 2–0–7–1; N. G. B. Cook 22.4–12–23–3; I. Cuthbertson 10–1–50–3; D. Ellwood 10–2–36–1; K. N. Foyle 40–15–149–3; M. A. Garnham 2–0–21–1; A. Greasley 62–21–126–3; J. Harris 6–1–19–1; K. Maguire 21–3–111–0; T. A. Munton 52–14–182–4; P. Higgs 22–5–85–0; R. Spiers 44–13–104–3; J. J. Whitaker 23–9–48–1.

MIDDLESEX SECOND ELEVEN

Matches 11: Won – Kent. Lost – Hampshire, Kent, Northamptonshire, Surrey, Warwickshire.
Drawn – Essex (twice), Surrey, Sussex (twice).

Batting Averages

	I	NO	R	HI	Avge
A. J. T. Miller	8	1	500	201*	71.42
M. Blackett	7	2	209	66*	41.80
C. R. Cook	21	1	707	151	35.35
K. D. James	11	1	337	69*	33.70
G. D. Rose	6	1	164	39	32.80
R. G. P. Ellis	8	0	241	79	30.12
K. R. Brown	21	0	585	92	27.85
G. A. Allen	4	0	83	34	20.75
C. W. V. Robins	18	3	294	90	19.60
S. P. Hughes	8	2	117	36	19.50
K. P. Tomlins	4	0	78	52	19.50
W. G. Merry	15	10	97	21	19.40
R. J. Maru	14	2	228	38	19.00
A. G. Smith	15	0	263	108	17.53
C. P. Metson	13	0	225	74	17.30
J. D. Carr	8	1	65	33	9.28
J. F. Sykes	11	2	72	23	8.00
G. D. Moss	6	2	29	20	7.25

Also batted: J. Bramble, G. K. Brown, D. S. English, K. T. Medlycott, P. Pradham.

Bowling Averages

	O	M	R	W	Avge
G. D. Rose	71.5	13	222	13	17.07
W. G. Merry	229.1	59	590	26	22.69
K. D. James	177.2	51	511	19	26.89
K. P. Tomlins	32	7	137	5	27.40
R. J. Maru	295.3	100	706	22	32.09
J. D. Carr	77	18	238	7	34.00
J. F. Sykes	299	82	816	20	40.80
G. D. Moss	115	22	421	10	42.10
C. W. V. Robins	132.2	41	390	8	48.75
S. P. Hughes	133.4	35	369	6	61.50

Also bowled: J. Bramble 6–0–10–2; G. K. Brown 25–7–102–4; K. R. Brown 10–2–43–10;
K. T. Medlycott 92–29–221–3.

NORTHAMPTONSHIRE SECOND ELEVEN

Matches 12: Won – Middlesex, Nottinghamshire. Lost – Derbyshire, Essex, Lancashire,
Leicestershire, Yorkshire. Drawn – Derbyshire, Essex, Lancashire, Leicestershire,
Nottinghamshire.

Batting Averages

	I	NO	R	HI	Avge
M. J. Bailey	9	0	687	193	76.33
T. J. Yardley	17	8	346	80*	38.44
D. Boyle	16	0	600	93	37.50
D. Ripley	12	3	303	65*	33.66
D. J. Wild	16	1	488	79	32.53
M. J. Bamber	12	0	382	85	31.83
M. R. Olley	6	2	123	37	30.75
D. J. Capel	6	0	179	121	29.83
S. J. Lines	20	2	450	91	25.00
R. Ashton	20	0	467	68	23.35
P. Oldham	8	0	167	50	20.87
T. M. Lamb	7	1	94	36*	15.66
A. Walker	13	6	100	23*	14.28
J. A. Carse	8	1	92	52	13.14
R. Bunting	9	3	71	22	11.83
S. Dean	5	0	58	25	11.60
C. Pickles	5	0	53	17	10.60

Also batted: I. Broome, N. Brough, J. Coles, G. Cook, P. Cooper, M. Cottam, H. Farrow, N. A. Mallender, J. Proud, M. A. Roseberry, T. Scriven, D. S. Steele, M. Wheeler.

Bowling Averages

	O	M	R	W	Avge
T. M. Lamb	109.2	41	181	16	11.31
J. Coles	21	7	61	4	15.25
J. A. Carse	150	31	442	18	24.55
A. Walker	239.1	68	732	28	26.14
D. J. Wild	123.4	34	321	11	29.18
R. Bunting	170.2	38	504	16	31.50
S. J. Lines	63.1	10	248	6	41.33
S. Dean	58	8	190	4	47.50
M. Wheeler	81	23	240	4	60.00
P. Oldham	91.4	18	309	5	61.80
R. Ashton	85	19	257	4	64.25
D. Boyle	107	19	387	5	77.40

Also bowled: M. J. Bailey 33–12–63–2; I. Broome 31–5–70–1; N. Brough 7–0–34–1; D. J. Capel 42–10–140–3; G. Cook 1.4–0–4–0; M. Cottam 7–2–22–0; N. A. Mallender 27–9–50–2; C. Pickles 1–0–1–0; J. Proud 8–0–43–0, T. Scriven 18–6–62–0; D. S. Steele 44–19–99–3.

NOTTINGHAMSHIRE SECOND ELEVEN

Matches 13: Won – Warwickshire (twice). Lost – Leicestershire, Northamptonshire, Yorkshire. Drawn – Derbyshire (twice), Essex, Lancashire, Leicestershire, Northamptonshire, Sussex, Yorkshire.

Batting Averages

	I	NO	R	HI	Avge
R. B. Kerr	12	2	839	212*	83.80
P. Johnson	8	1	375	181	53.57
M. J. Harris............	15	4	506	112	46.00
D. Saxelby	10	0	333	147	33.00
D. J. White	23	3	556	116	27.80
M. A. Fell...............	17	0	453	103	26.64
N. J. B. Illingworth..	16	1	375	47	23.80
C. W. Scott	21	3	426	50	23.66
R. A. Pick	11	3	98	17	12.25

Also batted: J. Bacon, M. Beck, D. Billington, M. Blatherwick, M. K. Bore, D. Borthwick, A. Bredin, M. Davidson, P. Delaney, R. Evans, P. Harvey, D. Lenge, R. J. Maru, S. R. Mee, M. Newell, R. O'Toole, G. W. Pym, P. Richardson, C. Stockdale, P. M. Such, D. Sutton, A. Varley.

Bowling Averages

	O	M	R	W	Avge
P. M. Such	149.5	51	348	15	23.20
M. K. Bore	223	80	443	18	24.61
A. Bredin...............	62	12	183	7	26.14
D. Sutton	77	15	240	9	26.66
R. J. Maru	61	12	226	8	28.25
S. R. Mee	129.1	20	420	14	30.00
A. Jessop	46	12	125	4	31.25
R. A. Pick	121.1	33	321	10	32.10
N. J. B. Illingworth..	310	54	958	25	38.32
M. Beck...............	55.2	10	156	4	39.00
D. J. White	221.5	52	728	17	42.82
P. Harvey..............	91	4	398	7	56.85

Also bowled: J. Bacon 19–2–62–0; M. Davidson 36–1–180–2; K. Evans 21–3–90–0; M. Harah 11–0–44–0; R. B. Kerr 4–2–16–0; D. Lenge 26–2–79–0; R. O'Toole 29–8–133–1; P. Richardson 4–0–18–0; C. Stockdale 6–0–43–0; A. Varley 13–2–88–0.

SOMERSET SECOND ELEVEN

Matches 10: Lost – Glamorgan, Worcestershire. Drawn – Glamorgan, Gloucestershire, Hampshire (twice), Lancashire, Warwickshire (twice), Worcestershire.

Batting Averages

	I	NO	R	HI	Avge
N. A. Felton...........	6	1	274	140*	54.80
N. Russom	12	2	471	137	47.10
M. R. Davis	6	1	228	64	45.60
G. J. Hall	14	5	314	54*	34.88
G. V. Palmer..........	8	2	188	54	31.33
R. L. Ollis	8	0	244	76	30.50
J. G. Wyatt	16	1	410	70	27.33
I. Cox.................	6	0	139	62	23.16
R. J. Greatorex........	4	0	83	48	20.75
S. C. Booth	9	2	124	47	17.71
*P. J. Robinson.......	7	2	79	41	15.80
I. R. Bussey	4	0	47	41	11.75
A. J. H. Dunning	8	0	90	51	11.25
R. J. Harden	4	0	35	14	8.75

Also batted: P. W. Denning, M. D. Harman, †G. S. Joyce, J. W. Lloyds, N. F. M. Popplewell, P. A. Slocombe, M. S. Turner.

Bowling Averages

	O	M	R	W	Avge
G. V. Palmer..........	112.5	24	356	16	22.25
N. Russom	143.4	44	351	13	27.00
S. C. Booth	262	69	701	22	31.86
P. J. Robinson	61	15	188	5	37.60
G. J. Hall	179	48	569	15	37.93
M. R. Davis	116	31	315	5	63.00

Also bowled: M. D. Harman 56–15–162–2; J. W. Lloyds 37–12–79–4; N. F. M. Popplewell 15–0–47–0; P. H. L. Wilson 19–9–38–3.

SURREY SECOND ELEVEN

Matches 13: Won – Hampshire, Kent, Lancashire, Middlesex, Sussex. Lost – Kent, Lancashire, Sussex. Drawn – Essex (twice), Hampshire, Middlesex, Yorkshire.

Batting Averages

	I	NO	R	HI	Avge
G. S. Clinton	10	1	588	177*	65.33
D. B. Pauline..........	14	1	616	158*	47.38
I. R. Payne.............	11	1	431	76	43.10
P. Marks.................	7	1	231	71	38.50
N. J. Falkner..........	23	3	761	129*	38.05
P. B. Taylor	10	1	322	101*	35.77
†A. J. Stewart..........	15	2	442	110	34.46
C. K. Bullen..........	22	3	563	108	29.63
†B. G. Parkinson.....	6	1	144	54	28.80
K. S. Mackintosh.....	17	2	359	82	23.93
A. Needham...........	16	0	358	140	22.37
D. M. Ward	9	0	174	54	19.33
*G. G. Arnold	14	5	156	70	17.33
R. G. L. Cheatle	14	4	166	50*	16.60
M. A. Feltham........	7	0	53	17	7.57

Also batted: A. M. Babington, H. Butler-Gallie, I. J. Curtis, P. D. Newman, I. G. Smith, J. A. Spalton, P. A. Waterman.

Bowling Averages

	O	M	R	W	Avge
N. J. W. Stewart	23	3	89	6	14.83
P. Marks.................	188.4	60	472	25	18.88
P. A. Waterman......	105.5	26	361	18	20.05
I. R. Payne.............	198.5	74	440	21	20.95
M. A. Feltham........	150	38	422	19	22.21
A. Needham...........	341.5	133	826	35	23.60
I. J. Curtis.............	226.5	75	615	22	27.95
K. S. Mackintosh.....	245.4	58	737	20	36.85
C. K. Bullen	120	32	341	9	37.88
R. G. L. Cheatle	140.5	40	403	9	44.77

Also bowled: G. G. Arnold 12–3–32–1; A. M. Babington 43–3–167–1; G. S. Clinton 3–2–1–1; P. D. Newman 12–3–28–0; D. B. Pauline 23–7–68–3; I. G. Smith 9.3–1–29–0.

SUSSEX SECOND ELEVEN

Matches 11: Won – Essex, Surrey, Warwickshire. Lost Surrey. Drawn – Essex (twice), Hampshire, Kent, Middlesex (twice), Nottinghamshire.

Batting Averages

	I	NO	R	HI	Avge
A. P. Wells	8	1	507	188*	72.42
D. K. Standing........	14	2	603	91	50.25
A. M. Green	11	1	493	160	49.30
J. R. P. Heath	18	3	663	112	44.20
C. Hartridge	6	1	213	49	42.60
D. Wood.................	17	3	578	77*	41.28
†D. J. Smith	11	4	248	97	35.42
M. Rushmere..........	8	1	225	109	32.14
R. S. Cowan	13	1	364	87	30.33
*C. P. Phillipson......	9	1	153	69	19.12
D. Briance	11	1	171	69	17.10
A. Willows	8	3	45	12*	9.00

Also batted: R. Carter, I. Cox, T. Dodd, I. A. Greig, S. Hull, A. N. Jones, H. Kasey, N. J. Lenham, P. W. G. Parker, D. A. Reeve, S. Ross, S. J. Storey, M. Taylor.

Bowling Averages

	O	M	R	W	Avge
D. A. Reeve...........	76	31	188	10	18.80
C. P. Phillipson	81	30	214	11	19.45
M. Taylor..............	52	16	148	7	21.14
D. K. Standing........	156	48	451	19	23.73
A. Willows	388	127	978	40	24.45
A. N. Jones	236	61	616	21	29.33
R. S. Cowan	168	38	531	18	29.50
C. Hartridge	176	34	639	21	30.42
J. R. P. Heath	85	23	232	6	38.66

Also bowled: C. Batchelor 22–4–87–0; T. Dodd 22–4–83–3; A. M. Green 78–13–269–4; I. A. Greig 18–2–79–2; S. Hull 3–0–24–1; P. W. G. Parker 11–1–21–0; S. Ross 29–8–71–2; S. J. Storey 8–1–24–0; A. P. Wells 6–0–31–0.

WARWICKSHIRE SECOND ELEVEN

Matches 17: Won – Glamorgan, Gloucestershire (twice), Middlesex. Lost – Lancashire, Nottinghamshire (twice), Sussex, Yorkshire. Drawn – Glamorgan, Lancashire, Leicestershire, Somerset (twice), Worcestershire (twice), Yorkshire.

Batting Averages

	I	NO	R	HI	Avge
R. I. H. B. Dyer	23	3	1,367	191	68.35
P. R. Oliver	11	1	487	111	48.70
P. A. Smith	8	2	281	161*	46.83
Asif Din.................	11	1	454	114*	45.40
W. P. Matthews	6	1	216	82	43.20
G. J. Lord.............	16	1	637	128	42.46
S. H. Wootton	23	2	772	90	36.76
D. M. Smith	24	10	441	55	31.50
D. A. Thorne	22	1	660	108	31.42
†G. A. Tedstone	19	3	453	78*	28.31
C. Lethbridge	5	0	138	32	27.60
*R. N. Abberley......	12	1	294	99	26.72
K. B. K. Ibadulla	25	5	441	80*	22.05
C. D. Mitchley.........	7	0	144	65	20.57
A. J. Moles	8	0	78	20	9.75
S. P. Sutcliffe	16	3	85	39	6.53

Also batted: G. Charlesworth, R. J. Grant, P. Higgs, D. S. Hoffman, W. Hogg, A. Hough, P. N. Hughes, W. Morton, A. J. Murphy, P. M. O'Reilly, G. Plimmer, J. A. Prior, J. Robinson, G. C. Small, G. P. Watson.

Bowling Averages

	O	M	R	W	Avge
P. A. Smith	152	37	506	23	22.00
Asif Din	44.5	7	177	7	25.28
S. P. Sutcliffe	559.3	174	1,317	50	26.34
D. A. Thorne	307.2	89	898	31	28.96
K. B. K. Ibadulla	118.4	16	388	13	29.84
D. M. Smith	446.1	87	1,440	48	30.00
P. M. O'Reilly	196	33	621	20	31.05
C. D. Mitchley	114.4	13	433	13	33.30
C. Lethbridge	120.2	20	350	10	35.00
D. S. Hoffman	145.4	32	536	10	53.60

Also bowled: R. I. H. B. Dyer 1–0–10–0; R. J. Grant 29–5–80–4; P. Higgs 28–9–104–0; W. Hogg 37–11–92–3; G. J. Lord 16.3–4–60–2; A. J. Moles 12–1–48–1; W. Morton 37.5–16–98–4; A. J. Murphy 21.2–3–71–3; G. C. Small 54–10–160–3.

WORCESTERSHIRE SECOND ELEVEN

Matches 9: Won – Leicestershire, Somerset. Drawn – Glamorgan (twice), Gloucestershire, Lancashire, Somerset, Warwickshire (twice).

Batting Averages

	I	NO	R	HI	Avge
*T. S. Curtis	8	1	519	105*	74.14
*M. S. Scott	6	0	381	140	63.50
†P. Moores	11	3	365	85	45.62
M. S. A. McEvoy	8	0	361	78	45.12
G. Matthews	10	1	360	121	40.00
D. A. Banks	10	0	318	174	31.80
S. G. Watkins	13	0	383	86	29.46
P. J. Newport	12	3	184	29*	20.44
D. J. Walker	6	0	110	78*	18.33

Also batted: D. B. D'Oliveira, R. M. Ellcock, D. J. Humphries, R. K. Illingworth, J. D. Inchmore, J. B. R. Jones, S. McEwan, I. McLaren, H. V. Patel, S. P. Perryman, M. Sedgley, A. E. Warner, M. J. Weston, N. Willetts, J. Wright.

Bowling Averages

	O	M	R	W	Avge
S. P. Perryman	103.3	40	175	14	12.50
G. Matthews	260.4	98	540	29	18.62
R. K. Illingworth	89.2	32	187	10	18.70
J. D. Inchmore	45	10	100	5	20.00
D. A. Banks	26.4	6	102	4	25.50
R. M. Ellcock	47	15	130	5	26.00
A. J. Webster	37	7	111	4	27.75
S. McEwan	53	6	127	4	31.75
P. J. Newport	179.5	35	572	16	35.75
D. J. Walker	65	19	188	4	47.00

Also bowled: S. Base 14–8–21–1; J. Benjamin 27–3–110–1; T. S. Curtis 23–0–95–0; D. B. D'Oliveira 16–3–52–0; M. Frost 24–2–98–1; A. Little 17–3–55–3; M. Sedgley 15–4–37–1; D. A. Slater 71–9–331–1; A. E. Warner 50–11–127–2; M. J. Weston 35–0–124–2; J. Wright 5–0–21–0.

YORKSHIRE SECOND ELEVEN

Matches 11: Won – Glamorgan, Kent, Northamptonshire, Nottinghamshire, Warwickshire. Lost – Lancashire. Drawn – Derbyshire, Lancashire, Nottinghamshire, Surrey, Warwickshire.

Batting Averages

	I	NO	R	HI	Avge
P. Robinson...........	8	0	483	233	60.37
K. Sharp...............	10	0	586	150	58.60
†S. J. Rhodes..........	13	4	507	140*	56.33
M. D. Moxon	11	1	467	116*	46.70
A. A. Metcalfe	16	1	614	117	40.93
A. P. Arundell.......	5	1	150	101	37.50
S. N. Hartley	9	1	262	69	32.75
*C. Johnson..........	14	2	381	102	31.75
R. G. Lumb	4	0	118	79	29.50
P. W. Jarvis............	8	5	68	25*	22.66
I. G. Swallow..........	16	2	285	44	20.35
N. S. Taylor	11	3	130	46	16.25
R. Blakey	7	0	89	46	12.71
A. Ramage.............	9	1	100	25	12.50
N. Nicholson..........	6	0	73	28	12.16
†J. Goldthorp	6	1	31	18	6.20
P. A. Booth	12	4	41	9	5.12

Also batted: N. Cowan, S. J. Dennis, S. D. Fletcher, J. Glendenen, M. Robinson, A. Sidebottom.

Bowling Averages

	O	M	R	W	Avge
A. Sidebottom	32	15	47	6	7.83
S. J. Dennis............	65.3	20	145	14	10.35
P. W. Jarvis............	208.3	52	582	28	20.78
I. G. Swallow..........	291	99	762	33	23.09
A. Ramage.............	104.1	32	272	11	24.72
P. A. Booth	384	148	858	32	26.81
*N. S. Taylor..........	195	45	630	23	27.39
S. D. Fletcher	162.5	45	516	18	28.66

Also bowled: A. P. Arundell 18–7–49–2; N. Cowan 18–8–38–2; S. N. Hartley 8–3–22–0; A. A. Metcalfe 8–1–19–0; M. Robinson 22–1–105–0.

WARWICK UNDER-25 COMPETITION, 1983

Zone A: This section was dominated by Derbyshire and Nottinghamshire who won, respectively, five and four of their six matches. Both counties had two convincing wins to start their programme, but when both met at the beginning of July, a devastating spell of bowling by Derbyshire's Paul Newman (8–4–7–6, including a hat-trick) meant that Nottinghamshire only managed 46 in 21.2 overs. Derbyshire reached that total for the loss of only one wicket. The following week, possibly still affected by that defeat, Nottinghamshire were beaten in a high-scoring match by Yorkshire. Having been put in to bat, a fine innings by Paul Johnson of 111 meant that Nottinghamshire scored 214 for five in 40 overs but their score was passed in the last over, thanks mainly to a good innings of 91 by Andrew Arundel. Nottinghamshire, however, did not falter again and won their remaining games, including a fine win in their return match against the eventual zonal winners, Derbyshire. Yorkshire and Lancashire had disappointing seasons, both winning only one match.

Zone B: Leicestershire won every match by a large margin. Their ability to score well over 200 runs when batting first, and to contain or bowl the opposition out when fielding first, ensured their progress to the later stages of the competition. An Australian, Mike Haysman, with Leicestershire on an Esso Scholarship, had a good season, scoring 91 not out against Northamptonshire and 112 not out and 79 not out against Middlesex, and then taking four for 26 against Middlesex. Leicestershire's main opposition came from Essex, who won three of the four matches they were able to play. Like many other counties, Essex suffered from abandoned matches in the early part of the season. They were involved in probably the most exciting match of the competition, against Middlesex, when they managed only 146 for eight in 40 overs. In reply, Middlesex were bowled out for 144 with the last ball of the match, Essex thus winning by 2 runs. Northamptonshire and Middlesex were both very disappointing.

Zone C: Kent, the holders, won what is always a competitive zone with another young side. Their first match against Hampshire was the only time they faltered. On a good Bournemouth pitch, Hampshire amassed 200 for three, with Robin Smith scoring an undefeated 93, and Kent managed only 161 for eight. On all other occasions, the all-round strength of the Kent side was too much for the opposition. Outstanding performances from Rajesh Sharma, Laurie Potter, Graham Cowdrey, Steven Marsh and Christopher Penn guaranteed a semi-final place. Sussex again were unable to perform consistently enough to challenge for a top place, while Surrey were very disappointing, losing all their matches.

Zone D: Eight matches in this group were abandoned owing to the inclement weather early in the season, but Worcestershire again edged ahead of the opposition by winning all their finished matches. Rain prevented any play in their opening two games, but emphatic wins over Gloucestershire, Glamorgan, Somerset and their closest rivals, Warwickshire, ensured their progress in the competition. Australian Esso Scholar, Greg Matthews, proved a valuable all-rounder, while Damian D'Oliveira, Martin Weston, Mark Scott and Tim Curtis all scored heavily. Warwickshire were also badly hit by abandoned matches, but consistent batting performances by Robin Dyer, Asif Din and Simon Wootton made them difficult to beat. The remaining teams in this zone lacked the consistency to challenge Worcestershire. The experience of Richard Ollis, Julian Wyatt and Neil Russom formed the backbone of a Somerset side that matured as the season progressed. Linton Lewis scored heavily for Glamorgan.

Semi-final: *Leicestershire v Derbyshire: at Leicester, August 14.* Leicestershire won by six wickets. Leicestershire put Derbyshire in on an easy-paced pitch and restricted the visitors to 161 for seven from their 40 overs. Leicestershire were soon in trouble when Newman dismissed both openers cheaply and Mike Garnham was run out. But Tim Boon and John Whitaker dominated the Derbyshire bowling with a mixture of power and elegance, adding 112 for the fourth wicket, and Leicestershire eased past the Derbyshire score with two overs remaining.

Derbyshire 161 for seven (40 overs); Leicestershire 165 for four (38 overs).

Semi-final: *Worcestershire v Kent: at Worcester, August 14.* Worcestershire won by six wickets. The powerful Kent batting performed indifferently, succumbing to the early pace of Philip Newport who took three for 32. Cowdrey was the only batsman to offer any resistance to the Worcestershire bowling. With Scott in fine form and Matthews making an unbeaten 37, Worcestershire reached the Kent total with 6.2 overs remaining.

Kent 149 for eight (40 overs); Worcestershire 152 for four (33.4 overs).

FINAL

LEICESTERSHIRE v WORCESTERSHIRE

At Birmingham, August 21. Leicestershire won by virtue of losing fewer wickets with the scores level on a dull day when rain threatened early. Thanks to an exciting fifth-wicket partnership of 81 in fifteen overs between Matthews and Hashad Patel, Worcestershire scored at nearly 5 an over. Leicestershire's reply fluctuated as wickets fell regularly. Garnham was magnificently caught by Scott, Ian Butcher was bowled for 38 and Whitaker fell second ball to a diving catch by Matthews. Only Boon dominated the Worcestershire bowling with some powerful and impressive strokeplay. The match was still in the balance with two overs remaining and 26 runs needed; but Richard Ellcock, who had until this point been economical, was hit for 14 in the penultimate over, and Boon levelled the scores off the last ball.

Worcestershire

*M. J. Weston run out	21	P. J. Newport not out		13
M. S. Scott b Wenlock	17	R. M. Ellcock c Higgs b Parsons		3
G. R. J. Matthews run out	54	A. J. Webster not out		4
D. A. Banks b Wenlock	1	L-b 10, w 6, n-b 5		21
S. G. Watkins c Garnham b Wenlock	11			—
H. V. Patel c Whitaker b Ferris	44	1/35 2/51 3/60	(8 wkts, 40 overs)	198
†P. Moores run out	9	4/74 5/155 6/166 7/178 8/189		

S. McEwan did not bat.

Bowling: Ferris 8-0-35-1; Munton 8-1-26-0; Wenlock 8-0-35-3; Higgs 8-0-34-0; Parsons 8-0-47-1.

Leicestershire

*†M. A. Garnham c Scott b Weston	17	G. J. Parsons not out		19
R. A. Cobb b Weston	7			
T. J. Boon not out	88	L-b 5, w 3, n-b 3		11
I. P. Butcher b Ellcock	38			—
J. J. Whitaker c Matthews b Ellcock	0	1/28 2/32	(5 wkts, 40 overs)	198
K. M. Foyle b Ellcock	18	3/93 4/93 5/169		

D. A. Wenlock, T. A. Munton, P. Higgs and G. J. F. Ferris did not bat.

Bowling: Ellcock 8-1-33-3; Webster 8-0-48-0; Weston 8-0-31-2; Newport 7-0-35-0; Matthews 8-0-30-0; McEwan 1-0-10-0.

Umpires: D. J. Constant and P. J. Eele.

UAU CHAMPIONSHIP, 1983

The preliminary stages of the UAU Championship were effectively washed out. But suddenly, in June, the weather lifted and there was a flurry of fixtures, the regional league matches being completed and the last three rounds of the competition hastily finished in five days of hectic activity.

The Championship followed its established pattern with virtually every English and Welsh University participating. Wherever possible matches were restricted to 60 overs, but no limit was set on the number of overs bowled by any one player. Initially the competition was restricted to small regional leagues and the leading contenders from each of these entered the knockout stage. However, one modification was introduced: to save time and travel costs, matches up to the semi-finals were also played within regions, a modification which proved particularly beneficial in view of the dismal weather.

The last eight in the competition included the four regulars – Durham, Exeter, Loughborough and Manchester, who were joined by Birmingham, Essex, Leeds and LSE. Manchester played host to Birmingham, but proved no match for their visitors. Batting first, Birmingham made 217 for eight, to which Greg Thrale contributed 53. In reply Manchester managed only 104, the wickets being divided between Richard Thorn (six for 37) and Steve Crawley (four for 40). LSE met Essex at New Malden where, although Essex scored 202, LSE's emphatic reply of 203 for three saw them safely into a semi-final match with Birmingham. In the other half of the competition Exeter visited Loughborough who batted first. Aided by an opening stand of 86 between Kevin Foyle and Rob Savage, the home team reached 205 for nine, Mathew Wheeler taking four for 44. Exeter started almost as well with a first-wicket partnership of 63 between Paul Taylor and Adrian Dunning, but a middle-order collapse saw them slump to 146 for six. Exeter's cause was saved by a spirited 82 not out from Nick Konig who steered his team safely home in the last over without further loss.

The match at the Racecourse between Durham and Leeds was also settled in the last over as Durham enhanced their reputation for living dangerously and unsuccessfully. Leeds chose to bat first and plodded steadily to a total of 173 in the 58th over. To this total Durham lavishly contributed 33 extras. Only Richard Keeble (six for 34) showed adequate control. Durham's cautious reply was well exploited by the experienced Bob Harriott, a post-graduate. Bowling off-spin from round the wicket, he pinned down Durham's uneasy batsmen, so that, despite a late scramble, they were left 2 short with one wicket remaining. Harriott's figures of 21–9–36–5 testify to his accuracy, and only Gordon Lord, with an accomplished innings of 64 as prelude to his move to Warwickshire, seemed up to the task.

In the semi-final at Bath, Leeds found Exeter a tougher prospect. Exeter batted first and used their 60 overs to reach 225 for eight. Opener Taylor (67) was top scorer, Konig (55) was again impressive, and captain Mike Wilcock was run out for 49. For Leeds David Standring (21–3–81–4) persisted valiantly, but they lacked the batting strength to meet the target, despite 49 from Neil Senior. LSE and Birmingham met the same day at Exeter in an equally one-sided contest. LSE were dismissed for 149, the wickets being shared by Thorn and Crawley. Birmingham passed this total for the loss of two wickets, Crawley dominating their innings with 82 not out.

The following day, June 22, the final at Bath University thus brought together Exeter and Birmingham. Although Exeter made a slow start, reaching 92 for three off 39 overs by lunch, a partnership of 142 between Taylor (127) and Konig (68) put Exeter in a strong position, so that they eventually made 232 for five. Birmingham never looked capable of meeting this target, and, in the face of accurate bowling by Wheeler, Martin Hall and Rob Combes, ably supported by good fielding, they succumbed for 158, leaving Exeter easy victors for the second year in succession.

Quarter-Finals

Leeds 173; Durham 171 for nine.
Birmingham 217 for eight; Manchester 104.
Essex 203; LSE 204 for three.
Loughborough 205 for nine; Exeter 206 for six.

Semi-Finals

LSE 149; Birmingham 150 for two.
Exeter 225 for eight; Leeds 148.

Final

At Bath University, June 22. Exeter 232 for five; Birmingham 158.

PREVIOUS WINNERS

1927	Manchester
1928	Manchester
1929	Nottingham
1930	Sheffield
1931	Liverpool
1932	Manchester
1933	Manchester
1934	Leeds
1935	Sheffield
1936	Sheffield
1937	Nottingham
1938	Durham
1939	Durham
1940-45	*No competition*
1946	*Not completed*
1947	Sheffield
1948	Leeds
1949	Leeds
1950	Manchester
1951	Manchester
1952	Loughboro Colleges
1953	Durham
1954	Manchester
1955	Birmingham
1956	*Null and void*
1957	Loughboro Colleges
1958	*Null and void*
1959	Liverpool
1960	Loughboro Colleges
1961	Loughboro Colleges
1962	Manchester
1963	Loughboro Colleges
1964	Loughboro Colleges
1965	Hull
1966	Southampton & Newcastle
1967	Manchester
1968	Southampton
1969	Southampton
1970	Southampton
1971	Loughboro Colleges
1972	Durham
1973	Loughboro Colleges & Leicester
1974	Durham
1975	Loughboro Colleges
1976	Loughborough
1977	Durham
1978	Manchester
1979	Manchester
1980	Exeter
1981	Durham
1982	Exeter
1983	Exeter

THE LANCASHIRE LEAGUES, 1983

By CHRIS ASPIN

Excellent batting, especially by the younger players, was the dominant feature of the Lancashire Leagues. Once the swamps of an appallingly wet spring had been replaced by the hard wickets of the summer, several new records were established. The scarcity of spin was again the main cause for regret. In this respect there was a lesson to be drawn from the fact that the Lancashire League bowling averages were headed by the oldest player, 51-year-old Brian Bowling of East Lancashire, who began his career when variety was considered an essential in any attack. His flighted leg-breaks earned him 31 wickets at 13.25 and the best striking-rate in the League.

Haslingden won the Lancashire League championship after a gap of 30 years, thanks to a powerful batting line-up and the lively bowling of their West Indian, Hartley Alleyne. For the first time in the club's history, three batsmen – Brian Knowles, Michael Ingham and Geoff Heaton – topped 600 runs. Knowles also hit the season's highest score – 143 not out against Todmorden – and joined the small group of players who have made a half-century both home and away against every other club. East Lancashire, runners-up in the championship, won the Martini knockout competition for the third time in four years, beating Ramsbottom in the final by four wickets. The fireworks were provided by Collis King, the Colne professional, who hit three centuries against Rishton, Rawtenstall and East Lancashire; his 123 at Rawtenstall included twelve 6s and his second 50 came off 21 balls.

The Lancashire League batting averages were headed by the New Zealander, Ross Ormiston (Bacup) with 910 runs (average 56.87). He was followed by a young Nelson amateur, Ian Clarkson, whose 888 runs (average 49.33) broke a club record which had stood since 1936. Other leading amateurs were Brian Knowles (633 runs), Michael Ingham (617), John Swanney (Rawtenstall, 615) and David Ainscough (Rishton, 600). While batsmen received £3,500 in collections, bowlers toiled for little more than £500. In one of their leanest seasons on record, only six professionals and one amateur took over 50 wickets. The amateur was Pat Calderbank of Nelson with 61 at 14.77. Jack Houldsworth, the Church seam bowler, became only the third player to take 1,000 championship wickets in the 91 years since the league was formed.

The Central Lancashire League competition was undecided until the closing minutes of the season. Three clubs finished with 80 points, but the title went to Littleborough, who had the most outright wins. Oldham, who challenged strongly for most of the season, had to be content with the Wood Cup. In the final, they beat Heywood, whose professional, Bob Cooke, made 111 not out, by two wickets.

Not for many years had the CLL been so rich in young talent. Perhaps the most promising was Mark Chadwick of Milnrow, who, at the age of 21, broke the League's amateur batting record, set up 70 years ago. In League and cup games, he made 1,267 runs (average 52.79) and comfortably topped the averages. Chadwick also played several fine innings for Lancashire Second Eleven and gained a first-team place at the end of the season. Another gifted batsman, Ian Tansley of Stockport, made 951 runs, and there were outstanding performances by John Whitehead (Norden, 872), Alan Howard (Rochdale,

864) and Andrew Wild (Werneth, 808). Littleborough owed much of their success to the fact that three young players – Leon Taylor, Chris Dearden and Phil Deakin – exceeded 700 runs. A noteworthy "double" was accomplished by seventeen-year-old Dexter Fitton, of Rochdale: with 599 runs and 52 wickets, he was the leading amateur all-rounder. The most successful amateur bowlers were Mel Whittle (Radcliffe) with 79 wickets at 16.32 apiece, Peter Davey (Middleton) with 68 at 16.12 and David Lees (Ashton) with 60 at 17.23.

In the professional ranks, Mohsin Khan (Walsden) and Cooke were the two players to score more than 1,000 runs. The West Indian Franklyn Stephenson (Oldham) was easily the most effective bowler, his 146 wickets costing only 8.73 runs each. Charles Alleyne (Milnrow) and Neil Phillips (Royton) also topped 100.

MATTHEW BROWN LANCASHIRE LEAGUE

	P	W	L	NR	Pts	Professional	Runs	Avge	Wkts	Avge
Haslingden......	26	18	3	5	80	H. L. Alleyne......	407	25.43	63	15.92
East Lancs......	26	15	6	5	73	I. W. Callen......	276	23.00	53	16.32
Burnley..........	26	13	7	6	63	Mudassar Nazar..	614	34.11	44	16.52
Lowerhouse	26	11	9	6	56	K. B. J. Azad....	757	44.52	37	16.91
Todmorden......	26	11	10	4	53	R. Estwick......	571	27.19	77	16.06
Bacup..........	26	11	10	3	52	R. W. Ormiston..	910	56.87	16	29.18
Ramsbottom	26	10	11	5	50	N. V. Radford....	522	27.47	77	16.25
Rishton	26	10	11	5	50	Kamal Singh.......	794	36.09	73	13.67
Colne..........	26	10	12	4	49	C. L. King......	847	44.57	45	21.84
Church..........	26	8	11	7	45	B. McArdle......	768	42.66	52	16.26
Rawtenstall	26	9	13	4	44	K. M. Curran.....	437	27.31	51	25.56
Nelson	26	8	14	4	41	G. R. J. Roope....	466	27.41	46	19.86
Enfield..........	26	7	13	6	35	B. R. Blair.........	882	49.00	16	33.31
Accrington......	26	5	16	5	25*	D. J. Parsons......	80	5.00	40	24.92

* *Four points deducted for playing unregistered professional.*

Note: One bonus point awarded for bowling out the opposition.

MARTINI CENTRAL LANCASHIRE LEAGUE

	P	W	L	D	Pts	Professional	Runs	Avge	Wkts	Avge
Littleborough ..	30	17	6	7	80	M. R. Whitney ...	150	9.38	88	12.82
Middleton..........	30	18	6	6	80	K. Boden........	926	31.93	70	19.09
Rochdale..........	30	18	6	6	80	S. Saunders.......	558	24.26	61	16.43
Oldham..........	30	17	7	6	79	F. D. Stephenson	621	23.00	146	8.73
Ashton..........	30	15	7	8*	74	G. N. Cederwall .	670	25.77	78	14.08
Milnrow..........	30	14	10	6*	71	C. C. Alleyne	120	7.06	120	13.32
Werneth..........	30	14	8	8	58	D. Schofield......	828	51.57	51	17.69
Heywood..........	30	12	12	6	56	R. M. O. Cooke..	1,005	41.88	57	14.86
Royton..........	30	8	12	10	50	N. Phillips	844	35.17	103	9.79
Norden..........	30	11	14	5	46	Anwar Khan	732	45.75	80	15.98
Crompton..........	30	8	14	8	42	S. T. Jefferies.....	214	23.78	35	11.49
Walsden..........	30	9	15	6	41	Mohsin Khan.....	1,067	56.16	45	22.62
Castleton Moor	30	8	17	5	39	B. Abrahams.....	869	31.04	51	21.94
Radcliffe	30	7	18	5	38	R. C. Haynes	589	22.65	63	21.21
Stockport........	30	7	17	6	35	G. Greenop	484	24.20	77	16.56
Hyde	30	4	17	4	26	J. C. Allen.......	790	32.92	38	24.95

**Includes 2 points for a tie.*

Note: Five points awarded for an outright win; three for a limited win.

AUSTRALIAN YOUNG CRICKETERS
IN ENGLAND, 1983

The Australian Young Cricketers arrived in time for the best weather of the season. They won the first two four-day "Tests", the first one-day international at Lord's and five games against representative sides. Two early matches were drawn, as was that against Young Scotland where there was some Edinburgh rain. The last three matches of the tour were lost – the second one-day international, an exciting match at Fenner's against the National Association of Young Cricketers and the third "Test" at Chelmsford, where the strongest of the three England teams was assembled.

As tourists the Young Australians were a happy and united party, well managed and well mannered; they made many friends while undertaking an intensive itinerary organised by the National Cricket Association in consultation with the Australian Cricket Board. There was no commercial sponsorship.

Western Australia's Darrin Ramshaw, at seventeen the youngest tourist, seemed the one most likely to succeed at higher, senior levels, but the outstanding performance of the series was by Tony Dodemaide. Fast bowler Craig McDermott strained muscles in his side during the Nottingham "Test" and was thereafter inoperative; Andrew Knight broke a finger early on and bowled only at Chelmsford. Dodemaide, although not always fully fit himself, carried the burden, bowling 140 overs for 22 "Test" wickets at a cost of 287 runs; Brett Mulder, off-spin, gave him most support. Michael Veletta, the captain, with previous experience of English conditions, handled his team well, and his 167 at Southampton was the highest individual innings of the tour. In the "Tests" Craig Bradley hit the only 100 for either side.

It was some time before the England selectors found a satisfactory blend. An impression existed that the honour of gaining a Young England "cap" may be under-valued in official quarters. Neil Lenham of Sussex was called to Scarborough as a replacement, but stayed on successfully. Neil Fairbrother, the Lancashire left-hander, looked the best of the English batsmen, together with Ashley Metcalfe of Yorkshire, who was not selected until he had made 122 on his first-class début. Nottinghamshire contributed three young players – the hard-hitting Paul Johnson, off-spinner Peter Such, and Andrew Pick, fast-medium. Hugh Morris of Glamorgan captained an ever-changing team with authority. A pleasing aspect of the series, in view of what happened to the contrary in 1982, was the unquestioning acceptance by both teams of umpiring decisions.

The tour party was: G. Murray (*manager*, Victoria), R. Bitmead (*assistant manager and coach*, Victoria), A. W. Walsh (*scorer*, Canberra), M. R. Veletta (*captain*, Western Australia), C. E. Bradley (*vice-captain*, South Australia), B. Djura, M. England, A. J. Knight, B. E. McNamara (all New South Wales), H. V. Hammelmann, I. A. Healy, C. J. McDermott (all Queensland), G. T. Connors, A. I. C. Dodemaide, D. P. Tindale (all Victoria), S. A. Henderson, B. Mulder, D. J. Ramshaw (all Western Australia).

RESULTS

Matches 14: Won 8, Lost 3, Drawn 3.

Note: None of the matches played was first-class.

v Surrey Cricket Association: at East Molesey, July 25. Australian YC won by four wickets. Surrey CA 114 (S. C. Goldsmith 30; S. A. Henderson three for 11); Australian YC 115 for six (D. J. Ramshaw 31).

v MCC Young Cricketers: at Ealing, July 26. Drawn. Australian YC 271 for five dec. (B. E. McNamara 76, C. E. Bradley 62, M. R. Veletta 60); MCC YC 98 for five (M. Blackett 43).

v Combined Services: at RAF Uxbridge, July 27. Australian YC won by seven wickets. Combined Services 214 for seven dec. (I. Izzard 68 not out, R. de Caires 41); Australian YC 216 for three (M. R. Veletta 78, A. I. C. Dodemaide 63, I. A. Healy 45 not out).

v Sussex Young Cricketers: at Horsham, July 29. Australian YC won by seven wickets. Sussex YC 237 for four dec. (R. Smith 64, M. Rose 63 not out, T. Bevan-Thomas 48); Australian YC 238 for three (D. P. Tindale 112, M. England 75).

v English Schools Cricket Association: at Southampton, July 30, 31, August 1. Drawn. Australian YC 352 for seven dec. (M. R. Veletta 167, D. P. Tindale 83, D. J. Ramshaw 33 not out) and 200 for five dec. (B. E. McNamara 52, D. P. Tindale 45, D. J. Ramshaw 38); ESCA 259 for seven dec. (N. J. Lenham 69, S. C. Goldsmith 63) and 121 for six (J. D. Stephenson 65 not out, R. M. Pepper 50 not out).

v Headmasters' Conference XI: at Charterhouse, August 2, 3. Australian YC won by eight wickets. HMC XI 92 (A. I. C. Dodemaide nine for 40) and 161 (R. W. S. Raper 37; B. Mulder three for 17, G. T. Connors three for 40); Australian YC 214 for seven dec. (M. R. Veletta 77, I. A. Healy 38 not out; N. C. W. Fenton three for 47) and 43 for two.

v England Young Cricketers – First One-day "International": at Lord's, August 5. Australian YC won by seven wickets. England YC 191 (53.1 overs) (J. E. Morris 42, G. V. Palmer 36; C. J. McDermott four for 33, G. T. Connors three for 37); Australian YC 192 for three (49.1 overs) (D. J. Ramshaw 64, B. E. McNamara 55 not out).

ENGLAND YOUNG CRICKETERS v AUSTRALIAN YOUNG CRICKETERS

First "Test" Match

At Nottingham, August 6, 7, 8. Australian Young Cricketers won by 84 runs. At the end of the first day, after Australia had chosen to bat, England were only 25 runs behind with five wickets in hand. However, Dodemaide began a personally successful series by taking four for 40 and holding England to a lead of 19. In Australia's second innings Veletta hit a determined 86, including twelve 4s, mainly from cuts and pulls and England, second-youngest member of the touring side, batted well to give Australia a lead of 252. Despite a swashbuckling innings, with three 6s, from Jarvis, the match ended in three days. In Australia's first innings Rhodes set a Young England wicket-keeping record with five dismissals.

Australian Young Cricketers

D. P. Tindale c Cowdrey b Pick	11 – lbw b Rose	13
*M. R. Veletta c Fairbrother b Such	26 – b Rose	86
C. E. Bradley c H. Morris b Pick	0 – c J. E. Morris b Such	26
D. J. Ramshaw c Rhodes b Palmer	15 – c sub b Pick	18
B. E. McNamara c Rhodes b Palmer	2 – lbw b Palmer	21
A. I. C. Dodemaide st Rhodes b Such	4 – lbw b Such	7
†B. Djura c Rhodes b Pick	14 – c H. Morris b Rose	7
M. England run out	49 – not out	43
C. J. McDermott c Rhodes b Pick	2 – c Palmer b Pick	9
B. Mulder c H. Morris b Jarvis	4 – b Rose	4
G. T. Connors not out	0 – lbw b Rose	10
L-b 7, w 1, n-b 2 ... 10	B 6, l-b 4, w 2, n-b 15 ... 27	

1/22 2/22 3/44 4/62   137   1/34 2/102 3/139 4/153   271
5/62 6/71 7/89 8/99 9/133   5/193 6/209 7/228 8/234 9/246

Bowling: *First Innings*—Jarvis 6–2–18–1; Pick 12–6–54–4; Rose 8–5–15–0; Palmer 7–4–10–2; Such 13.3–4–30–2. *Second Innings*—Pick 29–10–68–2; Rose 31.4–5–82–5; Palmer 19–4–48–1; Such 24–10–46–2.

England Young Cricketers

J. E. Morris (*Derby.*) c Djura b McDermott	0 – c Ramshaw b Connors	0
P. J. Prichard (*Essex*) b Dodemaide	23 – b Dodemaide	7
*H. Morris (*Glam.*) b Mulder	40 – c McNamara b England	21
N. H. Fairbrother (*Lancs.*) c Djura b Dodemaide	30 – c Ramshaw b England	25
G. R. Cowdrey (*Kent*) lbw b Mulder	0 – b England	9
G. D. Rose (*Middx*) b Dodemaide	14 – c Djura b Dodemaide	12
†S. J. Rhodes (*Yorks.*) run out	5 – c Bradley b Mulder	12
G. V. Palmer (*Somerset*) not out	18 – c sub b Dodemaide	4
P. W. Jarvis (*Yorks.*) b Dodemaide	2 – c sub b Dodemaide	55
R. A. Pick (*Notts.*) c Bradley b Connors	3 – b Mulder	5
P. M. Such (*Notts.*) c Connors b Mulder	4 – not out	1
L-b 13, w 1, n-b 3 ... 17	B 8, l-b 9 ... 17	

1/2 2/50 3/94 4/101   156   1/4 2/16 3/61 4/62   168
5/106 6/120 7/122 8/137 9/140   5/75 6/94 7/100 8/105 9/140

Bowling: *First Innings*—McDermott 12–2–44–1; Connors 14–6–28–1; England 6–2–14–0; Dodemaide 21–3–40–4; Mulder 11.4–6–13–3. *Second Innings*—Connors 8–2–19–1; Dodemaide 18–4–43–4; Mulder 22–8–57–2; England 12–3–32–3.

Umpires: A. Jepson and D. O. Oslear.

v Northumberland and Durham Young Cricketers: at Jesmond, August 11, 12. Australian YC won by an innings and 28 runs. Australian YC 357 for seven dec. (D. P. Tindale 118, D. J. Ramshaw 100 not out, I. A. Healy 42, B. E. McNamara 42); Northumberland and Durham YC 182 (R. Steele 53; S. A. Henderson four for 30, H. V. Hammelmann four for 36) and 147 (G. Cant 72 not out; G. T. Connors five for 28).

v Scotland Young Cricketers: at Edinburgh, August 14, 15. Drawn. Australian YC 294 for four dec. (I. A. Healy 94, C. E. Bradley 50, M. R. Veletta 48, D. P. Tindale 33) and 98 for six dec. (C. E. Bradley 37); Scotland YC 151 (M. England four for 14) and 81 for eight (G. T. Connors three for 7, M. England three for 31).

ENGLAND YOUNG CRICKETERS v
AUSTRALIAN YOUNG CRICKETERS

Second "Test" Match

At Scarborough, August 17, 18, 19, 20. Australian Young Cricketers won by six wickets and clinched the three-match series. Batting first, England soon took the two Morrises, but Lenham and Johnson took the score to 121 before Dodemaide struck, pitching the ball well up and swinging it away from tentative bats. Ramshaw saw Australia into a comfortable lead of 114 on first innings, but on the third day England fared so much better that victory on the fourth seemed on the cards. J. E. Morris batted 196 minutes for 31. Set to make 166 to win the series, Australia lost Tindale first ball before Veletta and Bradley put the result beyond doubt.

England Young Cricketers

J. E. Morris (*Derby.*) c Healy b Dodemaide	1 – c Tindale b Mulder	31
N. J. Lenham (*Sussex*) b Connors	72 – c and b Dodemaide	25
*H. Morris (*Glam.*) c Healy b Dodemaide	9 – c Bradley b Mulder	32
P. Johnson (*Notts.*) c Dodemaide b Mulder	50 – c and b England	15
N. H. Fairbrother (*Lancs.*) c Mulder		
b Dodemaide.	8 – c Mulder b Dodemaide	29
P. A. Smith (*Warw.*) c Tindale b Connors	16 – st Djura b Mulder.................	29
†S. J. Rhodes (*Yorks.*) c Djura b Dodemaide ...	6 – c Tindale b Mulder	0
G. D. Rose (*Middx*) c Djura b Dodemaide	12 – d Djura b Dodemaide............	39
K. T. Medlycott (*MCC*) lbw b Dodemaide	0 – c Healy b Mulder.................	24
R. A. Pick (*Notts.*) c Tindale b Mulder..........	4 – c McNamara b Mulder...........	19
P. M. Such (*Notts.*) not out	0 – not out	5
B 4, l-b 1	5	B 10, l-b 16, w 3, n-b 2 ...	31
	183		**279**

1/11 2/35 3/121 4/131   1/44 2/70 3/85 4/122
5/150 6/157 7/168 8/168 9/183   5/161 6/167 7/182 8/231 9/263

Bowling: *First Innings*—Connors 18–2–46–2; Dodemaide 22–7–54–6; England 9–1–33–0; Mulder 18.2–1–45–2. *Second Innings*—Dodemaide 38–20–69–3; Connors 25–9–52–0; Mulder 36.1–16–66–6; England 22–4–57–1; McNamara 3–1–4–0.

Australian Young Cricketers

D. P. Tindale lbw b Such	18 – lbw b Pick	0
*M. R. Veletta c H. Morris b Pick................	42 – lbw b Medlycott	56
C. E. Bradley b Smith	40 – c H. Morris b Medlycott	77
D. J. Ramshaw c Fairbrother b Rose............	82 – c Lenham b Medlycott.........	7
B. E. McNamara c H. Morris b Such	0 – not out	10
I. A. Healy lbw b Medlycott......................	12 – not out	6
A. I. C. Dodemaide b Rose	20	
M. England c Pick b Such	5	
†B. Djura c sub b Rose	45	
B. Mulder c Johnson b Pick.......................	8	
G. T. Connors not out	0	
B 6, l-b 9, w 8, n-b 2	25	B 4, l-b 4, n-b 3.............	11
	297		**167**

1/41 2/98 3/139 4/140   1/0 2/126   (4 wkts) 167
5/173 6/223 7/234 8/256 9/295   3/136 4/153

Bowling: *First Innings*—Pick 18–1–78–2; Rose 26.5–8–65–3; Such 34–12–54–3; Medlycott 17–4–49–1; Smith 8–2–26–1. *Second Innings*—Pick 8–0–35–1; Rose 4–2–10–0; Such 16.3–4–56–0; Medlycott 12–0–55–3.

Umpires: B. Leadbeater and D. R. Shepherd.

v England Young Cricketers – Second One-day "International": at Derby, August 22. England Young Cricketers won by three wickets. Australian YC 215 (54.2 overs) (D. J. Ramshaw 47, B. E. McNamara 46, M. R. Veletta 34; N. J. Lenham three for 34); England YC 216 for seven (47.4 overs) (P. Johnson 78, N. H. Fairbrother 56, P. A. Smith 32).

v National Association of Young Cricketers: at Cambridge, August 26, 27, 28. NAYC won by one wicket. Australian YC 175 (P. A. Booth three for 39) and 270 (M. R. Veletta 48, C. J. McDermott 47, M. England 46, D. P. Tindale 42; P. A. Booth four for 88, W. Smith three for 57); NAYC 228 (N. Hicks 64, R. N. Mason 56 not out, A. Harwood 53; S. A. Henderson six for 63, M. England four for 67) and 218 for nine (N. Hicks 51, A. Harwood 47, G. D. Rose 36, W. Smith 32 not out; A. J. Knight six for 48).

ENGLAND YOUNG CRICKETERS v AUSTRALIAN YOUNG CRICKETERS

Third "Test" Match

At Chelmsford, August 31, September 1, 2, 3. England won by 67 runs. Morris's decision to bat was justified when Metcalfe, first with Johnson, who retired ill, and then with Morris, opened for 109 for the first wicket. But, despite a solid innings from Lenham, England collapsed, losing their last nine wickets for 90 runs as Connors and Knight bowled straight and well up to the bat. On the second day Bradley proceeded from his overnight 58 to the only hundred of the series, but with Such's off-spin bringing him seven wickets for 72, the Australians were put out for 234. Fairbrother then showed some of his county form and with the England tail contributing well, Australia were left 300 to win. The final day started with Ramshaw unbeaten on 39 and England needing to take seven wickets for less than 205 runs. For a while Ramshaw fought well, but when he was sixth out the end was in sight.

England Young Cricketers

P. Johnson (*Notts.*) lbw b Connors	24	– lbw b Dodemaide	11
A. A. Metcalfe (*Yorks.*) c Bradley b England	54	– c Ramshaw b Dodemaide	4
*H. Morris (*Glam.*) c Djura b Connors	28	– b Knight	1
N. J. Lenham (*Sussex*) st Djura b England	48	– c McNamara b Dodemaide	3
N. H. Fairbrother (*Lancs.*) c Djura b Connors	2	– c sub b England	90
R. J. Bailey (*Northants*) lbw b Connors	8	– b Mulder	24
G. D. Rose (*Middx*) lbw b Knight	4	– c Dodemaide b Mulder	0
†S. J. Rhodes (*Yorks.*) b Knight	0	– not out	77
A. K. Golding (*Essex*) b Dodemaide	0	– c Djura b Dodemaide	11
R. A. Pick (*Notts.*) b Connors	8	– c sub b England	63
P. M. Such (*Notts.*) not out	5	– c sub b Mulder	24
B 1, l-b 13, n-b 4	18	L-b 17, w 2, n-b 7	26

1/109 2/128 3/130 4/132   199   1/16 2/17 3/19 4/30   334
5/140 6/154 7/154 8/155 9/191   5/85 6/108 7/146 8/168 9/290

Bowling: *First Innings*—Connors 12.2–0–33–5; Dodemaide 20–3–40–1; Knight 9–2–44–2; Mulder 15–4–50–0; England 13–7–14–2. *Second Innings*—Dodemaide 21–7–41–4; Knight 19–3–49–1; Connors 4–0–24–0; Mulder 30.4–9–69–3; England 28–8–73–2; McNamara 15–1–45–0; Veletta 2–0–7–0.

Australian Young Cricketers

A. I. C. Dodemaide c Fairbrother b Such	37	– lbw b Rose	11
*M. R. Veletta c Rhodes b Pick	5	– lbw b Pick	4
C. E. Bradley c Rhodes b Such	100	– c Rhodes b Rose	19
D. J. Ramshaw c Pick b Golding	6	– c Rose b Such	69
B. E. McNamara lbw b Such	0	– c Morris b Rose	10
I. A. Healy c Lenham b Such	0	– run out	16
M. England c Morris b Such	0	– c Fairbrother b Such	11
†B. Djura b Such	19	– c Morris b Golding	15
A. J. Knight not out	35	– run out	31
B. Mulder c Rhodes b Pick	14	– c Rose b Pick	15
G. T. Connors c Golding b Such	1	– not out	2
B 4, l-b 10, w 1, n-b 2	17	B 9, l-b 8, w 1, n-b 11	29

1/12 2/80 3/107 4/110	234	1/7 2/22 3/64 4/101	232
5/110 6/114 7/141 8/206 9/233		5/126 6/157 7/160 8/185 9/223	

Bowling: *First Innings*—Pick 8–1–34–2; Rose 10–0–42–0; Such 34.1–12–72–7; Golding 26–7–69–1. *Second Innings*—Pick 17.1–3–46–2; Rose 23–9–64–3; Fairbrother 2–0–8–0; Such 23–9–54–2; Golding 7–0–31–1.

Umpires: R. Julian and J. Birkenshaw.

UMPIRES FOR 1984

TEST MATCH UMPIRES

D. O. Oslear was restored to the panel of six umpires chosen to officiate in the Test matches in 1984 against West Indies and Sri Lanka. He stood in two Tests against Australia in 1981. The full Test panel is: H. D. Bird, D. J. Constant, D. G. L. Evans, B. J. Meyer and D. O. Oslear.

FIRST-CLASS UMPIRES

Two new umpires were added to the first-class list for 1984 – J. A. Jameson, the former Warwickshire and England batsman, and B. Dudleston, formerly of Leicestershire and more recently Gloucestershire's assistant coach. They replace C. T. Spencer and J. van Geloven. K. Ibadulla has retired to live in New Zealand. The full list is: W. E. Alley, H. D. Bird, J. Birkenshaw, D. J. Constant, C. Cook, B. Dudleston, P. J. Eele, D. G. L. Evans, J. H. Harris, J. W. Holder, J. A. Jameson, A. Jepson, R. Julian, M. J. Kitchen, B. Leadbeater, B. J. Meyer, D. O. Oslear, K. E. Palmer, R. Palmer, N. T. Plews, D. R. Shepherd, R. A. White, A. G. T. Whitehead and P. B. Wight.

MINOR COUNTIES UMPIRES

N. P. Atkins, F. Bingley, C. J. Chapman, D. C. Conners, Dr D. Fawkner-Corbett, D. J. Dennis, R. H. Duckett, D. J. A. Edwards, W. H. Gillingham, D. J. Halfyard, D. B. Harrison, C. L. Head, B. Knight, J. E. Lawton, S. Levison, T. Lynan, M. E. Manning, G. I. McLean, S. J. Noble, D. Norton, K. S. Shenton, C. Smith, P. S. G. Stevens, D. S. Thompsett, T. V. Wilkins, R. T. Wilson and T. G. Wilson.

SCHOOLS CRICKET IN 1983

Of the players "capped" in 1982, seven of whom went on to play first-class cricket in the following season, none was available in 1983, leaving ESCA with an inexperienced side. Selection problems were also compounded by the calls of NCA North and South teams for the International Youth Tournament in Holland, which coincided with three matches in the ESCA programme.

Their first game, in the Michael Gerard Trophy series, was against Welsh Schools at Bristol. After Wales had won the toss, J. P. Stephenson, aided somewhat by the fielders, dominated England's first innings with an unbeaten 157 out of 249 for four. Wales, struggling at 140 for six, added 70 in their last nine overs to finish 39 behind. England's rather belated declaration set Wales a target of 276 in just under two hours and twenty overs, and the match was drawn.

The three-day game against Australian Young Cricketers at Southampton proved a real test for the relatively inexperienced Schools side. Australia, electing to bat, amassed 352 for seven in ideal conditions, Veletta making 167, before England lost R. M. Pepper in their first over. However, N. J. Lenham and S. C. Goldsmith held the innings together, enabling them to declare at their overnight total of 259 for seven, in the hopes of being set a realistic target. Australia, though, mindful of their forthcoming "Test", were not so inclined and England were asked to score 294 at approximately 6 an over, towards which Pepper and Stephenson contributed an unbroken opening stand of 120.

Owing to injury and the calls of HMC Schools for their game against Australian Young Cricketers, five changes were made to the ESCA side for their final game at Glasgow against Scotland CU Colts, which had to be won for England to retain the Michael Gerard Trophy. M. A. Roseberry and D. Billington replaced Lenham and Stephenson, M. Roberts kept wicket in place of J. M. Robinson, with A. Dyson and D. Baines also coming into the side. Scotland were bowled out for 166, having collapsed from 122 for two, nine wickets falling to spin, six of them to K. T. Medlycott. England replied with 281 for five, achieving maximum bonus points, with fifties from Roseberry, M. Whitmore and P. A. Redfarn. Medlycott then took four for 41 as Scotland were bowled out again for 158, leaving England to score 44 runs in seventeen overs, of which they needed only 11.4, to bring victory by seven wickets and the Michael Gerard Trophy.

The side's batting was sound: centuries came from Pepper and Stephenson and the gifted Lenham was well supported by Whitmore and Redfarn. The brunt of the bowling was borne by Medlycott (slow left-arm) and W. M. Smith (off-spin), both of whom performed effectively. Medlycott twice took six wickets in an innings and returned ten for 102 against Scotland. The fielding was sound, especially that of Pepper, Goldsmith, Lenham and Whitmore, while Robinson was lively behind the stumps.

A notable performance in 1983 came from the Rendcombe College fast bowler, I. S. Bishop, who also played for NAYC against MCC. He took ten wickets in an innings for 5 runs against Marling GS, who were all out for 17 in reply to Rendcombe's 162 for six.

HMC SOUTHERN SCHOOLS v THE REST

At Eastbourne College, July 16, 17. The Rest won by eight wickets. The pick of the bowlers were Fenton, Barton and Allingham – all fast-medium and with the ability to achieve movement in the air and off the seam. Robinson was outstanding behind the stumps and the batting was dominated by Lenham and Stephenson, while Jenkins battled through sticky patches in both innings and Fell struck the ball cleanly.

HMC Southern Schools

N. J. Lenham (*Brighton*) b Allingham	51	– (7) c Burton b Allingham 105
*A. Fordham (*Bedford Modern*) b Burton	29	– (5) lbw b Fenton 0
†D. J. Jenkins (*Merchant Taylors', Northwood*) retired.	73	– (6) c Tyler b Willetts 39
I. C. D. Stuart (*King's, Bruton*) lbw b Kippax...	13	– (3) c Robinson b Allingham...... 14
R. M. C. Williams (*Epsom*) st Robinson b Raper.	9	– (2) b Allingham 18
†J. R. Ansell (*Epsom*) not out	25	– (1) b Fenton 0
R. J. Harden (*King's, Taunton*) c Robinson b Burton.	0	– (4) b Fenton 4
P. D. Newman (*Charterhouse*) c Stephenson b Kippax.	10	– (8) b Raper 7
W. M. Tebbit (*City of London*) not out	6	– (9) b Fenton 2
I. S. Bishop (*Rendcomb*) (did not bat).............		– c Fenton b Allingham.............. 0
P. G. Edwards (*Canford*) (did not bat)		– not out 3
Extras...	21	Extras.......................... 10

1/54 2/98 3/126 4/155   (6 wkts dec.) 237   1/0 2/27 3/36 4/40   202
5/211 6/222   5/44 6/129 7/159 8/182 9/185

Bowling: *First Innings*—Fenton 12–2–56–0; Burton 15–3–51–2; Allingham 9–4–25–1; Raper 11–4–26–1; Kippax 10–3–36–2; Mendes 5–0–42–0. *Second Innings*—Fenton 14–4–40–4; Allingham 13–0–46–4; Burton 8–4–12–0; Kippax 5–0–35–0; Raper 8–3–30–1; Willetts 5–1–29–1.

The Rest

J. P. Stephenson (*Felsted*) lbw b Bishop	6	– (2) retired 57
A. F. Tyler (*Leeds GS*) retired......................	57	
J. W. S. Raper (*Harrow*) c Tebbit b Edwards ...	17	– (1) c Ansell b Newman 36
N. A. Willetts (*KES, Birmingham*) c Jenkins b Stuart.	19	
M. J. de G. Allingham (*Strathallan*) not out	53	
D. J. Fell (*John Lyon*) not out......................	54	– (5) not out............................ 53
S. A. Mendes (*Magdalen College S*) (did not bat).		– (3) b Tebbit 28
*S. A. J. Kippax (*Woodhouse Grove*) (did not bat).		– (4) not out............................ 21
Extras...	15	Extras........................ 27

1/9 2/54 3/115   (3 wkts dec.) 221   1/77 2/135   (2 wkts) 222

†J. M. Robinson (*Solihull*), R. J. P. Burton (*Shrewsbury*) and N. C. W. Fenton (*Rugby*) did not bat.

Bowling: *First Innings*—Bishop 9–2–34–1; Newman 8–3–11–0; Tebbit 16–5–57–0; Edwards 16–6–36–1; Harden 8–1–35–0; Stuart 8–2–33–1. *Second Innings*—Newman 15–2–64–1; Bishop 4–0–30–0; Edwards 9–1–22–0; Tebbit 13–2–30–1; Lenham 9–1–28–0; Stuart 3–1–21–0.

HMC SCHOOLS v ESCA

At The Saffrons, Eastbourne, July 18, 19. HMC Schools won by seven wickets. ESCA, asked to bat, were restricted by defensive field placings to 171 for eight. They then allowed HMC Schools to recover from 108 for six to 201 for nine, before Pepper dominated their second innings with a sound century. Redfarn's declaration set HMC a target of 183 in two hours, which they comfortably achieved with 33 balls to spare.

ESCA

R. M. Pepper (*Dover GS and Kent*) c Lenham b Burton.	42	– lbw b Stephenson	108
M. A. Roseberry (*Durham S and Durham*) b Fenton.	6	– (6) lbw b Lenham	6
M. Whitmore (*Lutterworth GS and Cleveland*) c Robinson b Lenham.	33	– c Fell b Lenham	13
†*P. A. Redfarn (*Cambridge CAT and Cambridgeshire*) not out.	37	– b Burton	11
S. C. Goldsmith (*Simon Langton and Kent*) lbw b Burton.	0	– c Stephenson b Allingham	28
J. P. Barnard (*Richard Taunton and Hampshire*) run out.	8	– (2) b Fenton	3
K. T. Medlycott (*Wandsworth CS and London*) b Allingham.	8	– c Fell b Stephenson	24
W. M. Smith (*Colston's and Avon*) b Burton	9	– c Stephenson b Burton	5
J. N. Whitehouse (*Sir William Turner, Redcar and Cleveland*) b Allingham.	2	– not out	0
A. Dyson (*Derby and Derbyshire*) not out	3		
Extras	23	Extras	14

1/11 2/83 3/98 4/98 (8 wkts dec.) 171 1/14 2/49 3/93 (8 wkts dec.) 212
5/116 6/132 7/158 8/163 4/142 5/168 6/205 7/208 8/212

T. Ackland (*Somerset*) did not bat.

Bowling: *First Innings*—Fenton 9–2–27–1; Allingham 11–2–23–2; Burton 23–7–64–3; Lenham 11–3–15–1; Tebbit 6–1–19–0. *Second Innings*—Tebbit 17–6–53–0; Fenton 9–4–32–1; Allingham 12–0–42–1; Lenham 12–4–41–2; Burton 9–4–27–2; Stephenson 2–1–3–2.

HMC Schools

*N. J. Lenham (*Brighton*) c Pepper b Medlycott.	17	– (4) not out	66
J. P. Stephenson (*Felsted*) c Whitehouse b Smith ..	53	– b Ackland	17
A. F. Tyler (*Leeds GS*) b Medlycott	0		
A. Fordham (*Bedford Modern*) c Pepper b Smith.	7	– (1) lbw b Whitehouse	59
D. J. Jenkins (*Merchant Taylors', Northwood*) b Dyson.	71	– not out	10
D. J. Fell (*John Lyon*) c Ackland b Medlycott ..	4	– (3) lbw b Smith	21
M. J. de G. Allingham (*Strathallan*) b Medlycott.	4		
R. J. P. Burton (*Shrewsbury*) b Whitehouse	28		
†J. M. Robinson (*Solihull*) b Whitehouse	0		
W. M. Tebbit (*City of London*) not out	0		
Extras	17	Extras	13

1/41 2/49 3/72 4/91 (9 wkts dec.) 201 1/48 2/87 3/130 (3 wkts) 186
5/100 6/108 7/195 8/195 9/201

N. C. W. Fenton (*Rugby*) did not bat.

Bowling: *First Innings*—Whitehouse 7–1–21–2; Ackland 7–1–21–0; Medlycott 22–8–59–4; Smith 17–5–53–2; Dyson 4–1–30–1. *Second Innings*—Whitehouse 9–0–58–1; Ackland 5–0–30–1; Medlycott 8–0–52–0; Smith 2–0–20–1; Dyson 3–0–13–0.

Details of the match between MCC Schools and the National Association of Young Cricketers may be found in Other Matches at Lord's, 1983.

Reports from the Schools

Most schools were affected by the appalling weather early in the season, many losing the first six weeks to rain and suffering from lack of outdoor practice. For **Abingdon**, who beat

Brentwood, UCS Hampstead, Newbury and Pangbourne, the captain, S. J. Rushton, and the wicket-keeper, B. E. Woolley, were the leading batsmen, while T. D. Winter's medium-pace bowling brought him 41 wickets. The ability to bowl out their opponents brought **Aldenham**, who were unbeaten, their most successful record for many years, with wins v Mill Hill, Highgate, Liverpool College, King's School Chester and King William's College, Isle of Man. An inexperienced **Alleyn's** side were let down by brittle batting, too much depending on the captain, C. R. Preston. However, team spirit was excellent and the bowling tight, with C. W. B. Grigg (medium) taking wickets in every game, and left-arm spinners J. M. Nash and R. M. Antoniades proving a match-winning combination when the wickets became harder. Highlights for **Allhallows** were consecutive wins v MCC and Bradford GS, as well as a return of eight for 29 by E. R. M. Gard (right-arm fast-medium) against Sir Roger Manwood's.

Ampleforth, who finished the season with victories v Oundle, Blundell's and Uppingham, owed much to the swing bowling of J. N. Perry, who took seven for 13 v Bootham and seven for 40 v Uppingham, and the seam bowling of M. L. Roberts, who returned seven for 25 v Durham and seven for 33 v Sedbergh. The batting was led by C. P. Crossley, supported by R. P. Rigby, who scored the side's only hundred – v Denstone. An innings of 104 not out by A. J. Cardwell was a highlight for **Arnold School**, who beat RGS Lancaster, King's Macclesfield and Ipswich. Outstanding for **Ashville College**, who enjoyed a tour to Barbados in March and April, were left-hand bat and wicket-keeper J. C. Lister and left-armer I. D. Hopper, whose 53 wickets were more than twice as many as the next highest.

Bablake, unbeaten by a school for the fifth consecutive year, won the Birmingham and Warwickshire Schools Under-19 Knockout Cup, also for the fifth time running. Their captain, G. M. Charlesworth, later captained Warwickshire Schools Under-19 side. A. Glaznieks was the main bowler, with J. Desai's leg-breaks providing interesting contrast. A young **Bancroft's** side relied heavily on captain I. P. Debnam with both bat and ball, well supported by D. N. Thurston. The young J. P. Thomas opened the batting all season and made two hundreds, while W. J. Head excelled in the field and P. J. Savage proved a useful right-arm medium bowler. **Barnard Castle**, also with a young side, were encouraged by winning five matches against schools. **Bedford School's** season featured wins v Felsted, Campbell College, Belfast and Oundle. Their fielding was again excellent, as was the bowling of C. J. Bell.

Following a successful pre-season tour of Barbados, where five out of nine games were won, **Bedford Modern** were defeated only once, their seven wins including those v Bishop Vesey's GS, Oakham, Bedford, Oundle and Wolverhampton GS, against whom their leading bowler, P. A. Garratt (off-spin), took eight for 5. Fourteen-year-old A. D. McCartney (fastish right-arm) came into the side late in the season to finish top of the bowling averages and A. Fordham had another excellent season, scoring 133 not out against Stowe and passing 50 on six other occasions. He also appeared for Bedfordshire. In a season of rebuilding, **Berkhamsted** beat St Lawrence, Framlingham and RGS Colchester. The captain, P. L. Beard, hit a fine 131 not out against St Lawrence, P. A. Brown played some long innings and D. N. Jackson filled a sound supporting role. N. J. S. Cowley (fast medium) was the leading bowler, and the fifteen-year-old S. Hunt (slow medium) showed promise. **Birkenhead**, undefeated, were encouraged by the performance of another fifteen-year-old left-armer, E. N. Kitchen, while off-spinner S. McGowan bowled with admirable control of line and length. Outstanding with the bat were P. J. Sylvester and opener E. R. Hamilton.

The bowling of **Bishop's Stortford College**, who beat Stamford, relied heavily on G. L. Chapman and G. R. Marsh (both right-arm fast-medium), although they batted in depth and found P. Bashford, still a Colt, a good prospect behind the stumps. T. M. Cooper (fast-medium bowler and opening bat) dominated the averages for **Bloxham**, for whom E. J. MacLennan was a sound batsman-wicket-keeper and J. Rice an astute captain. **Blundell's** reported good wins v Downside, Plymouth College and Exeter School. Their captain, M. C. Coe, whose off-breaks brought him 46 wickets, was well supported by A. Kiloh (slow left-arm) with the ball and D. J. Dutton and C. Hunt with the bat. **Bradfield**, in their best season ever, were undefeated, with wins v Charterhouse, Eton, Wellington College, Winchester, Stowe, St Edward's and Westminster. They owed their success to H. J. Norman, the captain and wicket-keeper, as well as to the batting of J. M. Tremellen, who reached his 103 not out v Charterhouse with the winning hit, and the bowling of A. J. Straker (right-arm fast-medium), who took nine for 20 v St Edward's, the other batsman being run out.

A promising **Bradford GS** side were let down by poor fielding and an inability to bowl sides out. T. Welsh and A. M. Broadbent none the less both passed 40 wickets and I. J. McClay showed promise as a left-arm spin bowler. **Brighton**, who reported a successful tour to India at Christmas, won all ten of their matches against schools. N. J. Lenham, with five centuries and an unbeaten 93, was outstanding, his opening partnership of 249 against Eastbourne with A. J. Herbert being a highlight, as was his century before lunch v Cranleigh. In addition, he took the most wickets at medium pace, in a tight attack. **Bristol GS** were encouraged by exciting victories v Cotham GS and Queen's College, Taunton. In a closely fought season, **Bromsgrove** were let down by their lack of consistent batting, although P. J. Humphries (right-arm fast-medium and right-hand bat) proved a useful all-rounder and J. D. Hart's right-arm swing bowling was often accurate.

With wins v Blundell's and Taunton, **Canford** owed much to P. G. Edwards (slow left-arm) and D. G. LeSueur (right-arm fast-medium) for their dismissal of 94 out of a possible 100 opponents in ten matches. M. D. Smith scored nearly twice as many runs as the next batsman, including an unbeaten 137 to win the match v Royal Navy CC. A disappointing season for an experienced **Charterhouse** side featured wins v Tonbridge, Westminster and Rugby, against whom P. D. Newman (left-arm fast), took seven for 28. The advantage of a strong attack, though, was too often squandered by the middle-order batting. A similar weakness characterised the **Cheltenham** side in which the efforts of P. N. Richardson, S. P. E. Churchfield and R. P. W. Thompson, who made 137 not out v Haileybury, were often wasted, and the bowling was unspectacular. Outstanding for **Christ College, Brecon**, who were unbeaten, despite occasionally careless catching, was the captain, S. W. Harvey, who played the side's only three-figure innings and was well supported by two useful young players in N. P. Gibson and P. D. Thomas. In a season of steady improvement, **Christ's Hospital** recorded wins v Cranleigh and Whitgift. A highlight was the batting of T. A. P. Godfrey, who scored more than twice as many runs as anyone else.

Clifton were disappointed by the performance of their young side, for whom J. S. Matthews was consistent with the bat and P. A. Berry showed all-round promise. S. C. Hazlitt's lack of application rather restricted his undoubted talent. **Colfe's School** found satisfaction in wins v old rivals Trinity, Croydon and Emanuel, and in the all-round excellence of A. S. Byers, who achieved a "double" of 600 runs and 50 wickets. Also notable was the hard hitting of M. A. Saleemi, whose accurate right-arm seamers brought him seven for 23 v Trinity. K. J. Boxall (left-arm fast-medium) also bowled effectively, and fourteen-year-old C. Spencer showed potential as a batsman, coming into the side late in the season and scoring 101 not out v St Edmund's, Canterbury. With 723 runs in 1983, including a school record 142 v the XL Club, and 600 or more in four successive seasons, W. M. Smith of **Colston's School** achieved a record aggregate of 2,790.

A high point for **Dame Allan's School** was their victory in the Morpeth six-a-side competition. Brittle batting brought a depressing season for **Dauntsey's**, for whom J. Plumtree took eight for 21 v Wycliffe. **Dean Close** ascribed their success to a strong attack featuring P. M. Vincent (in-swing), R. N. Lindsay (right-arm fast) and M. C. A. Forster (left-arm spin). With an attack lacking penetration, despite the efforts of N. Baker (left-arm), A. T. Swales (left-arm chinaman) and R. C. F. Thompson (right-arm), **Denstone** were unable to capitalise on the batting of R. J. Robinson, who made 150 not out v Ampleforth and 96 v Barnard Castle. A tied match v Lancaster RGS and C. D. Chignell's unbeaten 105 v Free Foresters were highlights for **Downside**. With wins v Fettes, Giggleswick, Ashville, RGS Newcastle and St Bees, **Durham's** side was dominated by M. A. Roseberry, who averaged 75.09 with the bat and 8.45 with the ball and against St Bees reached 216 in two hours 40 minutes, a school record. During a summer tour to Barbados, three out of six schools matches were won.

Positive cricket was played by **Eastbourne**, for whom J. R. Prentis (right-arm fast-medium) collected 40 wickets and 811 runs, including 163 not out v The Hague. **Edinburgh Academy**, who beat Watson's, Merchiston Castle and Fettes, passed 200 runs on five consecutive occasions, with A. F. Gunn reaching three figures v Loretto and Denstone. Notable bowling performances came from the captain, G. R. Mawdsley (right-arm medium), who took seven for 20 v Watson's, and M. S. Watt (right-arm fast). For **Elizabeth College, Guernsey**, M. Read and C. Warlow consistently laid a solid foundation for the later batsmen, while J. Mattinson scored runs stylishly, as well as being the main strike bowler (left-arm fast-medium). An inexperienced **Ellesmere** side were encouraged to win their last three matches. The captain, R. T. Millinchip, took the most wickets (right-arm leg-break and googly). In another fine season, which left **Eltham** unbeaten and winners of the Kent Cup competition, their captain, M. J. Holcombe, set school records of over 2,600 runs and 132 wickets in four years. His brother, B. A. Holcombe, showed promise as an all-rounder, and with W. H. Wright fulfilling his potential, the side felt optimistic for 1984.

With a strong batting side, **Emanuel** won both the London and Surrey Schools knockout competitions for the fourth time in eight years, their victories including those v RGS Guildford, Kingston GS and Tiffin. Their leading batsman was F. Ahmed and the leading bowler T. J. Harmer, who returned nine for 19 v Westminster City School. Convincing wins v St Albans and RGS Colchester were highlights for **Enfield GS**, whose sound fielding and bowling, led by N. Jackett (slow left-arm) and R. Carter (right-arm medium), were let down by inconsistent batting, although R. Eustance scored two centuries. J. R. Ansell and R. M. C. Williams of **Epsom College** featured in two double-century and two century opening stands, Ansell bringing his aggregate for the school to 2,571 runs and Williams his to 2,015. **Eton**, whose seven victims included Charterhouse, Wellington College, Winchester and KCS Wimbledon, owed their batting strength to J. P. Berry and M. H. Brooks, whose 114 not out v Winchester brought victory in the last over. The attack was spearheaded by the two right-arm fast-medium bowlers, C. E. Pettifer and R. J. F. Luke, who together bowled out KCS Wimbledon for 35, Pettifer taking seven for 13, assisted by six slip catches. In a season of rebuilding, **Exeter** were encouraged by four victories and the promising off-spin bowling of I. D. Hayter.

Felsted achieved five of their six victories batting second, thanks largely to J. P. Stephenson, whose 913 runs included three centuries. A young **Fettes** side had a disappointing season, a tight attack often being frustrated by fragile batting. With wins v Hipperholme GS, Ashville and Loretto, **Giggleswick** owed much to the captaincy of N. C. Westhead, the all-round skills of B. L. Baldwin and the batting of R. M. White, who made 111 v MCC. Outstanding for **Glenalmond**, unbeaten by schools in Scotland, were all-rounder M. H. Alexander (slow left-arm and right-hand bat) and opening bowler J. F. Alexander (in-swing).

The **Haberdashers' Aske's, Elstree** side, carried mainly by all-rounders D. G. Price and A. P. Moulding, improved greatly during the season. A tour of Hong Kong and Singapore was planned for the winter. **Haileybury** were encouraged by the performances of N. R. Venning (left-hand bat) and J. T. Lumley (right-hand bat and right-arm fast-medium in-swing), who were expected to return for another two years. **Harrow**, unbeaten since 1980, achieved convincing wins v Radley and Wellington College, owing much to their captain and all-rounder, J. W. S. Raper. For a young **Hereford Cathedral School** side, promise was shown by P. J. Butler and N. R. Hales with the bat and by N. J. Startin with the ball (left-arm spin). An average season for **Highgate**, in which fifteen-year-old M. G. Griffiths (slow left-arm) took eight for 25 v Old Cholmelians, was followed by a tour to Holland, where three out of five matches were won. **Hurstpierpoint's** eight wins included those v Seaford, Cranleigh, The Hague, Bloxham, King's Taunton and Worksop. Right-armer J. R. C. Lamb led the attack with pace and hostility, and notable performances came from A. P. Subba Row (off-cutters) — seven for 48 v St George's, six for 38 v Bloxham and six for 37 v King's Taunton – and J. N. Rogers (off-spin).

In a mediocre season for **Ipswich**, a highlight was the fast-medium left-arm bowling of S. Priscott, whose 34 wickets included seven for 38 v Framlingham and six for 20 v Culford. Despite their inexperience, enthusiasm brought a young **Kelly College** side their most successful season for some years. Fragile batting was offset by outstanding ground fielding, notably from R. M. Summerell, and a strong attack, led by A. J. Carter and P. G. Shering (both right-arm fast), well supported by J. M. A. Stock, R. P. Edwards (right-arm medium) and off-spinner J. R. Parkhouse. Following a poor start, with eight batsmen failing to score v Stamford, strong team spirit brought success for **Kimbolton**, culminating in their winning the Cowall Cup v Berkhamsted, Framlingham and St Lawrence. Batsmen at **King Edward VI College, Stourbridge**, flourished once the pitches dried out, R. N. Tolley (667) and D. J. Shorter (634) both exceeding the record aggregate set in 1933 and scoring two centuries apiece, Shorter's 131 being a school record. He also captured the most wickets. D. J. Bullock returned nine for 27 on one occasion.

For **King Edward VI School, Southampton**, M. E. O'Connor's record aggregate of 889 runs was more than three times higher than the next. Unbeaten, **King Edward's School, Birmingham**, owed their success to a number of players, six of their side going on to play Young Amateur cricket for Warwickshire and Worcestershire. N. Willetts's 156 v Bablake included a hundred before lunch. Sixteen-year-old S. D. Heath led the attack with a haul of 58 wickets, ably supported behind the stumps by N. V. Subhedar, who took 23 catches and made twenty stumpings. The captain D. Sewell, who dominated the averages, was the outstanding cricketer for **King Henry VIII School, Coventry.** Although their attack lacked pace, the fourteen-year-old orthodox left-arm spinner, I. D. Harris, showed considerable promise.

The nine wins recorded by **King's College, Taunton,** included those v Wellington School, King's Bruton, Taunton, Allhallows, Blundell's, Worksop and Bloxham. Despite unimpressive fielding, the quicker bowlers did well, R. J. Harden (left-arm medium) taking most wickets as well as averaging over 40 with the bat. He was well supported by three right-arm fast-medium bowlers, A. J. Willson, H. D. Wordsworth and the fifteen-year-old G. K. Barber. Despite the efforts of P. S. Noble, lack of penetration brought a number of frustrating draws for **King's College School, Wimbledon,** for whom J. P. Feltham, aged fifteen, had a promising first season, in which he hit 100 not out v MCC and with his captain, J. H. Frost, who reached 134 not out, put on 193 for the second wicket v The Buccaneers. **King's School, Bruton,** owed their relative success to the leadership and all-round performance of I. C. D. Stuart, as well as to some good out-cricket, particularly the ground fielding of S. H. Maxwell, the slip-catching of D. J. M. Bruce and the wicket-keeping of J. C. Enderby.

In an entertaining season, **King's, Canterbury,** were unbeaten by schools. **King's School, Macclesfield,** however, won only their opening match – v King's School, Chester. For **King's School, Worcester,** R. Jones, J. Mackie and S. Preston all scored useful runs, K. Andrews (slow left-arm) was effective with the ball, and D. Rogers led the side well, his insistence on attacking cricket bringing a sequence of seven victories in eight days at the end of the season. Despite sound fielding, wayward bowling brought a mid-season slump for **King William's College, Isle of Man,** whose leading batsman, S. C. Watson, passed 80 on four occasions. Lack of penetrative bowling also hampered **Kingston GS,** who too often found themselves chasing large totals, despite the efforts of their captain, R. C. Marshall (left-arm seam). S. H. Clayson again dominated the batting, his two centuries including the side's first v MCC (102 not out), whom they beat. An enjoyable tour of Holland was undertaken in August.

In another successful season for **Lancing,** C. S. Mays was outstanding, passing 50 wickets for the second successive season, and scoring more than 600 runs, with 134 v Victoria College, Jersey, and 118 v The Hague, against whom he also took six for 53. **Leeds GS** were encouraged by the success of their young side for whom S. Joyce scored 101 not out v QEGS, Wakefield, and A. F. Tyler, who played for Yorkshire Senior Schools, topped the batting averages. Another pleasing aspect was the success of their spin-bowlers, A. Setia (off-breaks), who collected six for 4 v Bootham School, and G. R. Tyler (leg-breaks and googlies). Well led by C. A. J. Allan, a young and enthusiastic **Leighton Park** side collected six wins. P. D. R. Berridge was the most consistent batsman, although a fourteen-year-old, J. R. Wood, showed considerable promise. C. J. Pye-Smith, left-arm round the wicket and accurate, took the most wickets.

The Leys, who beat Fettes and St Paul's, benefited from the all-round skills of J. D. R. Benson, whose 757 runs included 201 not out v the Headmaster's XI. A disappointing season was reported by **Lord Wandsworth College,** whose leading batsman, A. M. Blows, was selected for the Bedfordshire Under-19 side. For **Lord Williams's School, Thame,** P. M. Jobson, an attacking batsman and right-arm medium bowler, made a significant all-round contribution. **Magdalen College School,** unbeaten, again relied heavily on the all-round talents of M. R. A. Barrow and their captain, S. A. Mendes, who have together scored 2,400 runs and taken 150 wickets in the past two years. Positive cricket, inspired by their captain, A. H. Lewis, brought **Malvern** an enjoyable, if not particularly successful season. R. A. F. Bache blossomed as an opener and N. R. C. Maclaurin could play a punishing innings, while R. G. Fleetwood bowled his out-swingers with enthusiasm and J. M. Davey's off-spin brought him 21 wickets in eight games. The bowlers were well served by athletic and eager fielding, with R. Wothers holding some excellent catches behind the stumps.

For **Manchester GS,** who were unbeaten, M. A. Crawley scored 135 not out v Leeds GS. **Marlborough's** strong batting side, featuring J. T. Burrell, who made 142 v St Edward's, were often frustrated by a wayward attack, in which the most consistent bowler was R. T. Thicknesse, whose orthodox left-arm spin brought him 35 wickets. Having won no matches in 1982, **Merchant Taylors', Crosby,** were encouraged to win four in 1983. Owing to a lack of application, their batting was disappointing, only I. M. Kerr passing 50, but the attack was more encouraging, with L. N. J. Heathcliff-Core (left-arm fast) bowling valiantly and

S. J. Weston (right-arm medium-fast) and S. R. Edgington (left-arm fast) emerging with promise.

Inspired by the example of left-hand opening bat and wicket-keeper D. J. Jenkins, **Merchant Taylors', Northwood**, batted aggressively and entertainingly to defeat Dulwich, Highgate, MCC, Westminster and a touring Under-19 side from Trinidad and Tobago. Owing to a back injury to their captain and fast bowler, A. M. Roberts, the attack lacked penetration, though, and they were beaten for the first time in three years – by RGS Colchester. The batting of **Merchiston Castle** was fragile, relying heavily on I. D. Rose and, later in the season, A. G. Young. The attack was accurate but expensive, although D. F. W. Burn showed promise. **Millfield** reported six wins, including those v Clifton, Downside and Blundell's, as well as narrow defeats by MCC and Sherborne. In a young side, captain P. A. C. Bail was the mainstay with both bat and ball, while J. C. M. Atkinson (also a useful bat) and J. A. Strachan formed a promising opening attack.

Mill Hill, another young side, also recorded six wins, the best being v Stowe, whose last nine wickets fell in 22 minutes, victory coming off the last ball of the match and R. S. W. Roberts returning six for 49. J. M. Cicale became the school's youngest centurian since W. Murray-Wood in 1933 when he scored 100 v Highgate. Left-handed opener A. P. Fussell showed promise for **Monkton Combe**, whose batsmen scored freely but whose attack lacked penetration. **Monmouth**, winners of the Barclays Bank/ESCA Under-17 tournament, owed their success to depth in batting in which S. P. James, captain of the Welsh Under-15 side, scored the most runs. The attack was spearheaded by two slow bowlers, A. J. Kear and D. W. Joseph.

Three-figure innings were played for **Norwich** by N. J. E. Foster and P. D. C. Nicholls, the latter, with 127 not out, being responsible for the victory v Trent College, and leading the attack with J. A. Cooper. Following an uncertain start to the season, **Nottingham HS** achieved six victories, including those v Worksop, William Hulme's GS and Plymouth. A highlight for **Oakham** was M. Steans's, innings of 178 in one hour 47 minutes before lunch v the XL Club. A disappointing **Oundle** side did not live up to expectations, being easily beaten by Felsted, Rugby and Bedford, although victories came v Stowe, Uppingham and Blundell's.

For **The Perse School**, the prolific J. M. C. Stenner played several fine innings, including 138 not out v RGS Newcastle and 134 not out v The Leys. He was well supported by W. R. Graham, M. Melzer and C. P. Wass, who also bowled aggressively, with R. Hanka, and was missed when injury or illness prevented him playing a full part in some matches. Positive, enjoyable cricket was played by **Pocklington**, for whom R. V. Henderson amassed a school record of 515 runs and 51 wickets. **Plymouth College** had a mediocre season in which J. Chislett captained the side with authority, and A. Dowling and S. Woodward performed usefully with the ball. For **Queen Elizabeth GS, Wakefield**, whose lack of bowling brought eight drawn games, notable débuts were made by J. Swain, who scored two centuries and made 390 runs in nine days, and the fourteen-year-old S. Wood. Lack of consistent batting was a problem for **Queen's College, Taunton**, although with most of a young side returning in 1984, prospects are good.

Radley's strong batting side featured R. C. H. Reed, who scored 111 v St Edward's and topped the averages, with E. J. B. Popplewell, brother of N. F. M., who scored the most runs and did well behind the stumps with 30 dismissals. Although a brisk pace brought R. B. Lagden 42 wickets, the attack often struggled. Outstanding fielding, notably that of all-rounder P. W. Tarimo, and steady bowling for **Ratcliffe College** tended to be let down by brittle batting, although an experienced side had an above-average season. A highlight was C. R. Merriman's 121 not out v Mount St Marys. Excellent team spirit brought an enjoyable season for **Reading School**. The batting of D. G. Purslow was noteworthy, especially his 121 v Abingdon, and captain E. P. O'Leary was competent with both bat and ball (off-spin), scoring 82 and taking five for 50 in the same match v Shiplake.

Reed's School were frustrated by inconsistent batting, several opportunities for victory being missed. A highlight was the defeat of MCC, who lost eight of their wickets for 52 to R. Saddleton (right-arm fast-medium). An inexperienced **Reigate GS** side struggled to find consistency, although they recorded good wins v Emanuel and King Edward VI, Southampton, whom they beat by six wickets, chasing 243 for nine. D. G. C. Downman and the captain, D. R. Cawthrow, both made centuries, and mature performances in tight situations came from a young all-rounder, P. A. Rowlinson. **Repton**, with nine wins, owed their success to a well-balanced attack, excellent fielding and the consistent left-handed batting of S. W. Lovell, who averaged more than 100 in his last seven innings. Highlights for **Rossall** were a century by N. V. Salvi v the Old Rossallians, and his stand of 161 with R. I. Kanhai in the same match. **Royal GS, Guildford,** with eight wins, were defeated only once. Notable performances came from J. Perrin, whose 40 wickets included an analysis of seven for 34 v Wimbledon College, and from J. Figuera, a reliable wicket-keeper, who held five catches in the match v Trinity, Croydon. **Royal GS, Newcastle,** owed much to the wicket-keeping of D. Archer, the batting of L. D. Anderson, who made 92 not out and 109 not out in successive matches, and the development of M. Bailey whose thoughtful approach enabled him to build a useful innings and produced a dangerous mixture of right-arm swing and seam bowling. The left-arm spin of R. S. Wise was effective, but the off-spin of the injured S. J. Gill was missed.

With only one defeat by a school and thirteen wins, including the side's first v Bedford Modern, **Royal GS, Worcester,** owed much to the batting of P. Bent, whose 926 runs at an average of 57.87 included three hundreds. The strength of **Rugby's** experienced side was the attack, spearheaded by N. C. W. Fenton – who headed the averages with fast and penetrative bowling, and D. J. Cleverly (right-arm fast-medium), who took the most wickets and also batted usefully. D. P. W. Umbers played an outstanding innings v Oundle, making an unbeaten 181 out of 236 for five. A successful **Rydal** side, who won their first five matches, relied heavily for their runs on C. Robinson and left-hander J. T. Owen, while the attack was led by R. Williams (right-arm medium) and J. M. Sherrington (slow left-arm).

With strong teamwork, a balanced attack and pride in their fielding, **St Dunstan's** won five matches in succession v Colfe's, Sutton Valence, Judd, Highgate and the XL Club. Their most successful player was S. J. Cross, who headed both batting and bowling averages. Their middle order being prone to collapse, **St Edward's, Oxford,** relied heavily on D. A. Soper, who made 100 not out v Oundle. He also provided valuable support (right-arm medium) for R. N. C. Franklin (left-arm chinamen and googlies), whose 47 wickets included a match-winning return of seven for 63 v Cheltenham. In a strong **St George's, Weybridge,** side, T. J. O'Gorman equalled a 50-year-old record of five centuries, while J. W. P. Jones and R. Garland formed an effective opening partnership. Keen fielding backed up varied and accurate bowling, which featured A. J. Woodhead (slow left-arm), P. J. Davis (fast-medium) and A. P. Jansen (medium). A valuable contribution from each member of the side brought success to **St John's, Leatherhead,** who were unbeaten.

St Lawrence, Ramsgate, depended for their batting on P. R. Hobcraft, with S. W. Cook and N. A. Crush, who scored the side's only century. G. G. Philpott, aged fifteen, and J. M. G. Barber shared most of the bowling, but the efforts of the captain, Hobcraft, were often let down by poor catching. The all-round strength of **St Peter's, York,** was epitomized by their captain, S. R. Gorman (opening bat and off-spinner), A. Forman (fast) and S. P. A. Burdass (left-hand bat and wicket-keeper). They were unbeaten, as were **Sedbergh,** whose sound team-work brought victories in Stonyhurst, Rossall, RGS Newcastle and William Hulme's GS. Sedbergh's high standard of fielding was maintained, J. E. K. Wilson excelling behind the stumps.

A disappointing season for **Sevenoaks,** who none the less beat King's, Rochester and Caterham, was brightened by the emergence of the sixteen-year-old J. D. Mitchell as wicket-keeper-batsman, and the right-arm fast-medium bowling of A. J. Preston, as well as by a return of six for 38 v Maidstone GS by A. J. Bell. Discipline and determination as well as a high standard of fielding characterised the cricket played by **Sherborne,** who were beaten only by Radley, their seven wins including convincing defeats of Cheltenham and Haileybury during their end-of-term festival. Never bowled out, yet dismissing the opposition on twelve occasions, **Shrewsbury** won thirteen matches and lost none. R. J. P. Burton, an outstanding captain, became the first Salopian to achieve a school career "double" of 1,000 runs and 100 wickets. I. J. F. Hutchinson scored three centuries and was well supported by A. D. Hobson and D. J. Pollock, while R. P. Holt collected 51 wickets, backed up by excellent fielding.

Highlights for **Sir Roger Manwood's** were a tied match v St Edmund's, Canterbury, when M. I. A. Howell took seven for 25, and the all-round excellence of G. W. Laslett (right-arm medium). Following a tour to Australia at Christmas, **Stamford** were encouraged to beat Kimbolton, Deacon's, Peterborough and Bishop's Stortford. In the match v an MCC side containing G. Boycott, a stand of 201 between G. M. Canham and N. J. Tyers brought victory with an over to spare. R. P. Alston (right-arm seam) and Tyers (left-arm spin) took most wickets in an otherwise disappointing attack. **Stowe** were let down by weak middle-order batting, although the young attack looked promising. **Strathallan,** unbeaten by schools, owed much to captain M. J. de G. Allingham whose 551 runs at 91.83 included three hundreds. An inexperienced **Sutton Valence** side, frustrated by fragile batting, owed much to captain R. D. Coate, who bowled quite quickly to take the most wickets, and also scored the most runs.

For **Taunton School,** who recorded convincing wins v King's Bruton, Blundell's and Queen's Taunton, three players reached three figures and J. C. Pike did the hat-trick v MCC. In the absence of fast bowlers, **Tiffin** did well to win six matches, owing much to their orthodox left-arm spinners, M. R. Coote and W. Shermer. No batsman was outstanding, but useful contributions were made right down the order and the captain, N. A. Legg, made the most of his slender resources. Following an early loss to Charterhouse, **Tonbridge** beat Sevenoaks, Lancing, Wellington College and Clifton. Their strength came from depth in batting and the development of their captain, A. D. H. Grimes, into a penetrating opening bowler. With 901 runs, N. W. F. Redwood was the leading batsman for **Trinity School, Croydon,** who won eight matches and were beaten by only one school. Other batsmen lacked consistency, although P. J. Smith made 112 not out v St Benedict's. Of the bowlers P. D. Bone (right-arm) and B. S. Lees (right-arm leg-spin) took most wickets, with Redwood's leg-spin also proving effective. In a season of mixed fortunes, **Truro** benefited from the all-round contribution of their captain, D. C. Aldwinckle, well supported by the opening batsmen, T. W. R. Scott and left-hander A. J. Jones. **Uppingham,** in a season of rebuilding, achieved wins v Oakham, Rugby, Blundell's and Oundle.

Victoria College, Jersey, owed their success to a strong batting line-up, headed by their captain, W. Jenner, who passed 1,000 runs for the second season, including four centuries. Other three-figure innings came from P. L. Lalor (two) and D. A. Oliver. An opening partnership of 197 v Elizabeth College between Jenner and A. J. Sugden was a school record. Inability to bowl out the opposition brought ten drawn games for a young **Warwick** side, who were none the less unbeaten, with wins v MCC and Solihull. N. C. B. Robinson was an astute captain and the mainstay of the batting, which had depth but lacked quality. S. J. Holdsworth developed promisingly as a right-arm out-swing bowler. Inconsistent batting hindered **Wellingborough,** who beat Alleyn's and Lord Williams's School, with M. Griffiths the leading bowler. A young **Wellington College** side, who beat Stowe, Bedford and Haileybury, were encouraged by the promise of the young G. D. Reynolds, who came into the side in mid-season and topped the batting averages. For **Wellington School,** who played only six matches, no batsman totalled 100 runs.

Early batting disasters unsettled the batsmen of **Westminster,** until the end of the season when R. J. Levy made an aggressive century v Free Foresters. However, the bowling and fielding were always good, with the leading bowler, T. E. Lunn, proving a competent captain. Inconsistent batting brought a mediocre season for **Whitgift,** for whom S. Talbot (right-arm fast-medium) bowled effectively. Despite some erratic performances, a young **William Hulme's GS** side beat Hulme GS, Oldham and Loughborough GS, against whom the leg-spinner, N. R. Fairfax, returned seven for 58, while I. D. Thorpe (right-arm fast) took six for 28 v Stockport GS. Of the batsmen, A. G. Cleary (left-hand) opened competently and P. T. Fearnley showed promise, putting on 150 for the second wicket with his captain, J. D. Sealy, who showed great skill in the field.

Sound team performances brought **Winchester** nine wins, including those v Charterhouse, Felsted, Eastbourne, Clifton and the Hampshire Schools, to equal the record of the Nawab of Pataudi's side in 1959. Left-arm spinner J. D. Dean took 58 wickets and I. L. M. Henry made a valuable all-round contribution. C. N. N. Smith and the captain, W. E. J. Holland, scored plenty of runs. **Woodbridge,** beaten by only one school, were encouraged by the emergence of promising young players S. Bacon and M. Whitehead (off-spin). In their best season ever, **Woodhouse Grove** were unbeaten with eight wins, including those v Leeds GS, Bradford GS, Hipperholme GS and Giggleswick. Their strength lay in the all-round ability of their captain, S. A. J. Kippax (leg-spin), and the brothers Percy, A. G. averaging a remarkable 4.93 with the ball.

Despite their youth, **Wrekin** recorded three wins and were encouraged by the success of their captain, R. P. Mitchell (right-arm fast), with the ball in the second half of the season. Weak middle-order batting brought **Wycliffe** their first defeats by schools – Dean Close and Dauntsey's – since 1980. The exception was J. R. Bodington's innings of 116 in 74 minutes v Hereford Cathedral School. The attack was strong, slow left-armer S. L. Thomas being potentially very good, R. B. Hair (seam) showing admirable control and R. J. Boulton, Bodington and S. J. Shorthose all making useful contributions.

THE SCHOOLS

(Qualification: Batting 100 runs; Bowling 10 wickets)

* On name indicates captain.   ** On figures indicates not out.*

Note: The line for batting reads Innings–Not Outs–Runs–Highest Innings–Average; that for bowling reads Overs–Maidens–Runs–Wickets–Average.

ABINGDON SCHOOL

Played 16: Won 7, Lost 3, Drawn 6. Abandoned 2

Master i/c: N. H. Payne

Batting—M. T. Boobbyer 13–1–358–75*–29.83; B. E. Woolley 16–1–437–54–29.13; *S. J. Rushton 16–1–406–64–27.06; R. M. R. Suggate 14–3–229–52–20.81; D. R. Newman 16–3–208–51*–16.00; M. C. Cox 11–1–152–26–15.20; M. A. Wiles 11–1–126–27*–12.60.

Bowling—M. A. Marsden 54–15–113–14–8.07; M. C. Day 94.5–17–249–26–9.57; T. D. Winter 216.2–42–624–41–15.21; M. C. Cox 96.2–19–356–18–19.77; M. A. Surridge 121–18–371–14–26.50.

ALDENHAM SCHOOL

Played 11: Won 8, Lost 0, Drawn 3

Master i/c: P. K. Smith

Batting—*P. A. Stenning 11–3–419–83*–52.37; C. R. D. Bateson 10–1–303–75–33.66; N. T. Robson 9–5–121–61*–30.25; S. P. Radin 8–1–178–51*–25.42; S. W. H. Vickers 8–0–158–58–19.75; N. J. Davies 9–1–145–45–18.12.

Bowling—P. A. Stenning 142–37–362–32–11.31; S. W. H. Vickers 156–48–363–28–12.96; A. R. Kentish 99–27–225–16–14.06.

ALLEYN'S SCHOOL

Played 15: Won 3, Lost 5, Drawn 7. Abandoned 2

Master i/c: J. F. C. Nash

Batting—*C. R. Preston 16–0–348–68–21.75; J. M. Nash 14–6–154–31*–19.25; J. M. Bridgeman 16–2–203–37–14.50; J. C. Wareham 14–0–203–54–14.50; C. W. B. Grigg 16–2–151–50*–10.78; J. P. Cockett 13–1–117–32–9.75; R. M. Antoniades 14–0–121–26–8.64.

Bowling—C. W. B. Grigg 202–49–602–38–15.84; R. M. Antoniades 72–21–227–14–16.21; J. M. Nash 96.3–20–351–20–17.55; H. Webber 142.5–35–452–24–18.83; J. D. Spence 121–24–438–11–39.81.

ALLHALLOWS SCHOOL

Played 16: Won 5, Lost 7, Drawn 4. Abandoned 3

Master i/c: P. L. Petherbridge

Batting—P. N. Fisher 15–1–290–67*–20.71; W. H. P. Ferguson 15–2–235–52*–18.07; G. P. Spark 16–2–229–49–16.35; *P. M. B. Zealey 16–1–231–50*–15.40; R. J. White 15–0–206–45–13.73; S. M. Turner 11–1–132–50–13.20; A. H. D. Harvey-Kelly 12–3–108–52*–12.00.

Bowling—E. R. M. Gard 180–59–397–31–12.80; P. M. B. Zealey 159.4–43–358–26–13.76; W. H. P. Ferguson 110.2–21–342–20–17.10; G. E. C. Rigby 79–14–294–12–24.50.

AMPLEFORTH COLLEGE

Played 16: Won 5, Lost 3, Drawn 8. Abandoned 1

Master i/c: J. G. Willcox

Batting—C. P. Crossley 16–3–470–73–36.15; J. S. Kennedy 13–3–257–81*–25.70; R. P. Rigby 16–0–360–100–22.50; M. L. Roberts 14–4–161–25*–16.10; J. N. Perry 15–1–222–51–15.85; N. J. Read 13–1–174–31–14.50; D. S. Mitchell 13–2–127–39–11.54; *M. T. Kennedy 14–2–104–24–8.66.

Bowling—R. P. Rigby 47–16–128–10–12.80; M. L. Roberts 188.1–51–500–33–15.15; J. N. Perry 212.4–55–570–34–16.76; J. G. Porter 79.5–24–191–10–19.10; N. J. Read 68–12–233–12–19.41; S. J. Evans 172–60–453–13–34.84.

ARDINGLY COLLEGE

Played 10: Won 2, Lost 4, Drawn 4. Abandoned 1

Master i/c: N. D. Duncan

Batting—*S. A. Jacobsen 11–3–600–167–75.00; R. F. Mitchell 10–1–267–125–29.66; M. D. Spicer 10–2–155–61–19.37; H. C. B. Teague 8–1–111–56*–15.85; R. D. Calvert-Lee 11–0–125–29–11.36.

Bowling—G. R. Emmerson 138.2–42–338–23–14.69; G. L. Calvert-Lee 115.1–34–309–20–15.45.

ARNOLD SCHOOL

Played 14: Won 6, Lost 2, Drawn 6. Abandoned 7

Master i/c: S. T. Godfrey

Batting—A. J. Cardwell 13–3–472–104*–47.20; *R. Southern 13–1–385–89–32.08; S. M. Beckwith 13–2–328–89–29.81; J. R. C. Lyon 13–2–248–69*–27.55; J. F. Nicholson 12–1–290–55–26.36; S. E. Davies 13–0–263–54–20.23.

Bowling—A. J. Cardwell 51.3–10–188–13–14.46; T. P. Phillips 103.4–35–260–17–15.29; R. Southern 102.1–28–324–18–18.00; J. C. Cassidy 109–24–362–17–21.29.

ASHVILLE COLLEGE

Played 22: Won 8, Lost 5, Drawn 9

Master i/c: J. M. Bromley

Batting—*J. C. Lister 19–1–514–105–28.55; D. A. Kindon 15–3–329–84–27.41; A. D. Reaks 12–1–291–55–26.45; A. Perkins 18–4–216–42*–15.42; A. A. Bradwell 17–4–198–32–15.23; T. L. Holgate 18–0–250–72–13.88; N. M. Rogers 12–2–105–24–10.50; S. J. Ashman 13–1–113–20*–9.41.

Bowling—C. M. Booth 21.1–3–118–10–11.80; I. D. Hopper 178.1–25–634–53–11.96; E. J. London 135–14–500–23–21.73; A. D. Reaks 89–19–273–11–24.81; A. Perkins 198.2–37–704–24–29.33.

BABLAKE SCHOOL

Played 14: Won 9, Lost 1, Drawn 4. Abandoned 2

Master i/c: B. J. Sutton

Batting—*G. M. Charlesworth 13–2–555–102*–50.45; E. T. Milburn 8–2–264–58–44.00; M. B. Twigger 10–3–238–72*–34.00; S. J. Pilbin 10–5–124–40–24.80; D. C. Percival 12–2–231–50–23.10; A. Glaznieks 11–3–155–45*–19.37; A. M. J. Kearns 10–2–150–33–18.75.

Bowling—J. Desai 99.2–20–182–15–12.13; E. T. Milburn 65–13–183–14–13.07; A. Glaznieks 118.4–38–296–21–14.09; D. C. Percival 70–18–187–12–15.58; R. T. Cassidy 94–19–285–18–15.83.

BANCROFT'S SCHOOL

Played 20: Won 4, Lost 9, Drawn 7. Abandoned 4

Master i/c: J. G. Bromfield

Batting—J. P. Thomas 20–0–530–106–26.50; S. W. Gant 5–1–100–56–25.00; W. J. Head 21–1–454–66–22.70; *I. P. Debnam 21–1–400–58–20.00; S. P. Laiker 20–0–349–59–17.45; D. N. Thurston 15–8–103–20–14.71; S. J. Linney 15–2–122–40–9.38; N. P. Bingle 17–4–117–19–9.00; K. R. Gold 19–0–141–23–7.42.

Bowling—M. G. de Jode 42–9–101–10–10.10; I. P. Debnam 161–20–556–34–16.35; S. W. Gant 55.2–9–173–10–17.30; P. J. Savage 123–25–443–24–18.45; D. N. Thurston 167–47–473–22–21.50; W. J. Head 97–16–355–16–22.18; R. S. Patel 128.2–23–391–16–24.43.

BARNARD CASTLE SCHOOL

Played 16: Won 5, Lost 4, Drawn 7

Master i/c: R. T. Mardon

Batting—J. Ashman 16–3–447–127*–34.38; G. Underwood 16–3–443–135*–34.07; S. Foster 13–2–233–71–21.18; *T. Blackburn 16–0–311–63–19.43; K. Clapham 11–5–114–30*–19.00; A. Wilkie 15–0–253–44–16.86; R. Pettit 14–1–215–59–16.53; S. Crowther 10–1–142–40–15.77.

Bowling—S. Crowther 124–35–249–19–13.10; K. Clapham 107–15–404–28–14.42; R. Blamire 173–46–553–30–18.43; E. Seery 124–14–498–19–26.21; S. Foster 135–22–414–10–41.40.

BEDFORD SCHOOL

Played 18: Won 6, Lost 5, Drawn 7. Abandoned 2

Master i/c: P. D. Briggs   Cricket professional: R. G. Caple

Batting—*M. C. Nutt 19–2–456–84*–26.82; C. J. Bell 19–2–409–64*–24.05; M. P. N. Waterfield 16–5–254–52*–23.09; E. H. Castenskiold 17–1–345–76*–21.56; G. A. Buchanan 19–1–345–72–19.16; D. W. A. Stroud 10–4–113–39–18.83; T. J. Campbell-Gray 11–1–171–49–17.10; D. W. M. Mitchell 12–0–127–28–10.58; N. J. Young 17–1–168–25–10.50.

Bowling—C. J. Bell 292.1–98–586–50–11.72; M. P. N. Waterfield 193.4–49–482–32–15.06; D. W. A. Stroud 233.1–82–548–29–18.89; E. H. Castenskiold 180.5–70–346–18–19.22; C. W. Blackie 133.4–45–288–12–24.00.

BEDFORD MODERN SCHOOL

Played 17: Won 7, Lost 1, Drawn 9. Abandoned 5

Master i/c: A. D. Curtis

Batting—*A. Fordham 16–4–731–133*–60.91; T. M. Lord 17–3–537–77*–38.35; S. D. Crowther 14–3–271–64*–24.63; P. A. Garratt 12–3–198–51*–22.00; D. F. Fishwick 12–4–150–33–18.75; N. A. Stanley 11–0–132–34–12.00.

Bowling—A. D. McCartney 109.3–32–243–25–9.72; P. A. Garratt 274.2–105–522–41–12.73; J. D. Webb 143.5–56–309–21–14.71; D. F. Fishwick 123.1–19–368–14–26.28.

BERKHAMSTED SCHOOL

Played 9: Won 5, Lost 3, Drawn 1. Abandoned 7

Master i/c: F. J. Davis   Cricket professional: M. Herring

Batting—*P. L. Beard 9–1–358–131*–44.75; P. A. Brown 9–0–317–87–35.22; D. N. Jackson 8–2–208–53–34.66; A. J. Hunt 8–1–121–34–17.28.

Bowling—D. J. G. Smith 53–5–193–12–16.08; N. J. S. Cowley 142–24–380–22–17.27; S. Hunt 108–39–248–14–17.71.

BIRKENHEAD SCHOOL

Played 15: Won 6, Lost 0, Drawn 9. Abandoned 2

Master i/c: M. H. Bowyer

Batting—E. R. Hamilton 14–5–443–100*–49.22; *P. J. Sylvester 10–3–310–97–44.28; D. R. K. Windler 9–2–175–65*–25.00; M. C. Juniper 13–2–267–43–24.27; J. M. Harrison 11–3–153–45–19.12.

Bowling—S. McGowan 126–39–293–32–9.15; E. N. Kitchen 102–21–253–22–11.50; E. R. Hamilton 57–12–188–10–18.80.

BISHOP'S STORTFORD COLLEGE

Played 12: Won 1, Lost 3, Drawn 8. Abandoned 4

Master i/c: D. A. Hopper   Cricket professional: E. G. Witherden

Batting—M. C. Dodshon 6–3–106–75*–35.33; G. L. Chapman 12–2–277–52–27.70; S. E. Kok 12–0–286–80–23.83; *G. R. Marsh 11–0–243–74–22.09; R. J. Wilkinson 11–0–230–65–20.90; D. G. E. Wilde 12–0–198–52–16.50; L. S. P. Fishpool 12–0–182–33–15.16.

Bowling—G. L. Chapman 200.4–40–554–28–19.78; G. R. Marsh 188.2–56–457–21–21.76.

BLOXHAM SCHOOL

Played 14: Won 6, Lost 3, Drawn 5. Abandoned 2

Master i/c: A. L. Bateman   Cricket professional: N. C. W. Furley

Batting—T. M. Cooper 11–1–448–93–44.80; E. J. MacLennan 13–2–319–61–29.00; E. S. Gurney 10–2–183–60*–22.87; S. D. Janes 14–2–206–50–17.16.

Bowling—T. M. Cooper 202–61–506–43–11.76; I. R. Davies 91–15–306–19–16.10; P. M. G. Rozée 105–19–317–14–22.64.

BLUNDELL'S SCHOOL

Played 16: Won 5, Lost 8, Drawn 3

Master i/c: E. D. Fursdon   Cricket professional: E. Steele

Batting—D. J. Dutton 16–4–381–79–31.75; J. C. Hunt 16–1–432–55–28.80; *M. C. Coe 16–0–376–88–23.50; R. C. Lowe 13–2–232–39–21.09; R. Hughes 13–0–251–63–19.30; J. E. M. Hunt 15–6–133–68–14.77.

Bowling—M. C. Coe 204.5–59–577–46–12.54; A. Kiloh 158.4–36–483–28–17.25; P. Byrne 83–23–232–11–21.09; J. D. Hollands 101.5–26–274–12–22.83.

BRADFIELD COLLEGE

Played 11: Won 7, Lost 0, Drawn 4. Abandoned 3

Master i/c: R. A. Brooks   Cricket professional: J. F. Harvey

Batting—*H. J. Norman 9–1–246–70*–30.75; J. M. Tremellen 11–1–249–103*–24.90; R. M. Layton 11–1–233–77*–23.30; M. E. Wills 11–1–204–44*–20.40; J. S. C. Bathurst 11–3–141–39*–17.62.

Bowling—A. S. Gilbert 111–38–228–17–13.41; A. J. Straker 179–46–418–31–13.48; R. M. Layton 145–41–322–19–16.94; P. M. Last 98–29–265–14–18.92.

BRADFORD GRAMMAR SCHOOL

Played 21: Won 5, Lost 4, Drawn 12. Abandoned 6

Master i/c: A. G. Smith   Cricket professional: G. A. Cope

Batting—A. A. D. Gillgrass 17–4–508–104*–39.07; J. B. Gray 21–2–688–87*–36.21; C. E. Nichols 17–1–533–93*–33.31; *S. T. Firth 17–0–347–62–20.41; R. M. Nichols 9–2–138–36–19.71; G. M. Bentley 18–5–226–80*–17.38; P. A. Greenwood 8–0–110–71–13.75; N. J. Rhodes 10–2–101–32–12.62; A. M. Broadbent 12–2–115–34–11.50.

Bowling—A. M. Broadbent 243.2–63–695–49–14.18; T. Welsh 224.4–62–645–40–16.12; G. M. Bentley 63.4–16–253–12–21.08; I. J. McClay 119–33–367–16–22.93; R. G. Jamieson 64–16–232–10–23.20.

BRENTWOOD SCHOOL

Played 14: Won 2, Lost 8, Drawn 4. Abandoned 1

Master i/c: A. G. Guyver   Cricket professional: K. C. Preston

Batting—*P. Lindley 14–1–360–60*–27.69; P. Smaje 15–2–328–66–25.23; S. Smith 11–5–142–30–23.66; R. Loughland 14–0–313–48–22.35; S. Koka 9–1–161–44–20.12; S. Moore 7–1–100–34*–16.66; R. Newman 14–1–159–30–12.23; C. Jarvis 13–0–148–32–11.38.

Bowling—P. Braund 130.3–32–332–21–15.80; R. Newman 178.4–41–505–27–18.70; S. Smith 152.3–38–489–24–20.37; P. Walker 84–14–307–11–27.90.

BRIGHTON COLLEGE

Played 14: Won 11, Lost 0, Drawn 3. Abandoned 3

Master i/c: J. Spencer

Batting—N. J. Lenham 15–3–981–164–81.75; M. G. Simmonds 14–4–384–67–38.40; D. G. Shaw 13–4–257–55*–28.55; J. G. Appleton 15–2–359–113*–27.61; M. A. Bewick 8–2–155–66*–25.83; A. J. Herbert 10–1–191–71–21.22.

Bowling—D. J. Panto 79.1–22–214–21–10.19; G. Bradshaw 71–24–140–10–14.00; *J. A. Gorton 164.1–39–412–27–15.25; N. J. Lenham 172–44–479–28–17.10; M. A. Bewick 103–29–270–14–19.28.

BRISTOL GRAMMAR SCHOOL

Played 11: Won 2, Lost 3, Drawn 6. Abandoned 4

Master i/c: A. J. Booth

Batting—J. R. Fraser 7–4–153–36*–51.00; *R. P. Yelland 7–2–173–69–34.60; T. M. Evans 10–1–194–55–21.55; W. J. Richardson 8–0–123–55–15.37; I. F. Rice 9–1–114–42–14.25.

Bowling—A. Henson 71–18–202–15–13.46; R. P. Yelland 86.1–23–204–15–13.60; T. M. Evans 65.1–9–216–10–21.60; J. G. Beale 93.5–16–278–11–25.27.

BROMSGROVE SCHOOL

Played 13: Won 2, Lost 5, Drawn 6. Abandoned 3

Master i/c: P. R. Sawtell

Batting—P. J. Humphries 10–1–196–63*–21.77; M. R. Thomas 13–0–256–48–19.69; M. R. Dudley 13–0–242–56–18.61; A. J. Morgan 13–0–211–55–16.23; P. J. B. Ingle 9–1–117–34*–14.62; O. F. Page 11–2–110–34–12.22.

Bowling—J. D. Hart 128.1–40–341–36–9.47; P. J. Humphries 138.5–39–328–26–12.61; K. B. Eyre 79–11–259–14–18.50; M. G. M. Harris 98.2–28–210–11–19.09.

BRYANSTON SCHOOL

Played 10: Won 4, Lost 2, Drawn 4. Abandoned 1

Master i/c: M. C. Wagstaffe

Batting—G. Binns 11–1–451–106–45.10; M. Guymer 10–3–311–64–44.42; J. Morton 10–1–244–38–27.11; N. Davis 7–3–111–44*–27.75; R. Stanbrook 6–1–108–45–21.60; C. Phillips 10–3–143–49*–20.42.

Bowling—P. Partridge 88.6–27–230–24–9.58; M. Guymer 107.2–28–275–23–11.95; N. Davis 59.2–26–230–11–20.90; C. Phillips 112.6–26–325–13–25.00; J. Quinn 94–19–293–11–26.63.

CANFORD SCHOOL

Played 10: Won 3, Lost 2, Drawn 5. Abandoned 4

Master i/c: H. A. Jarvis   Cricket professional: D. Shackleton

Batting—*M. D. Smith 10–2–339–137*–42.37; T. R. McLaughlin 8–3–175–58–35.00; K. J. Harris 10–0–191–44–19.10; J. R. Doble 10–2–143–39*–17.87.

Bowling—P. G. Edwards 189.2–55–402–41–9.80; D. G. LeSueur 190.5–52–426–31–13.74.

CHARTERHOUSE

Played 19: Won 5, Lost 8, Drawn 6

Master i/c: M. F. D. Lloyd   Cricket professional: R. V. Lewis

Batting—J. D. Reid 16–4–294–64–24.50; A. G. Proctor 13–1–283–57–23.58; R. C. Thompson 18–1–354–50–20.82; T. J. Stilwell 18–0–365–84–20.27; P. R. Durnford 19–2–324–74–19.05; N. T. Kingston 15–5–187–37–18.70; M. Z. A. Dudhia 17–1–279–49–17.43; P. D. Newman 15–1–222–59–15.85; J. Griffiths 7–0–107–36–15.28; J. C. Davis 14–1–175–27–13.46; C. J. L. Bayman 16–1–161–41–10.73.

Bowling—R. C. Thompson 66.3–20–142–11–12.90; P. D. Newman 226.5–57–646–42–15.38; N. T. Kingston 141.2–29–579–31–18.67; *R. J. Rogers 249–73–744–28–26.57; J. D. Reid 234–48–774–26–29.76.

CHELTENHAM COLLEGE
Played 16: Won 3, Lost 4, Drawn 9. Abandoned 5

Master i/c: R. D. Knight   Cricket professional: G. A. Edrich

Batting—*R. P. W. Thompson 15–2–472–137*–36.30; P. N. Richardson 12–1–395–66–35.90; S. P. E. Churchfield 14–0–367–79–26.21; P. D. Richardson 11–2–182–72–20.22; A. J. Brettell 10–1–163–34*–18.11; C. J. Edwards 13–1–190–48–15.83; C. M. Tollerfield 13–2–164–34–14.90.

Bowling—M. W. B. G. Dyer 73–20–201–16–12.56; J. le M. Lawrence 194.5–46–494–26–19.00; B. D. J. Kent 107.5–23–312–16–19.50; R. P. W. Thompson 136.3–23–545–25–21.80; C. M. Tollerfield 116.3–22–447–15–29.80.

CHIGWELL SCHOOL, ESSEX
Played 8: Won 3, Lost 1, Drawn 4. Abandoned 6

Master i/c: D. N. Morrison

Batting—*J. W. Yates 6–1–187–60–37.40; D. Rogers 8–1–209–72–29.85; J. R. Maskey 8–0–117–25–14.62; R. O. Noble 8–1–102–50–14.57.

Bowling—J. R. Maskey 109–22–265–32–8.28; R. O. Noble 59–23–154–14–11.00; J. W. Yates 73–13–236–12–19.66.

CHRIST COLLEGE, BRECON
Played 11: Won 7, Lost 0, Drawn 4. Abandoned 8

Master i/c: C. W. Kleiser

Batting—*S. W. Harvey 11–3–464–114–58.00; J. W. Lewis 10–2–181–46*–22.62; N. P. Gibson 9–2–130–52*–18.57; K. Noble 8–1–111–38–15.85; K. M. Towell 11–0–136–42–12.36; P. S. Burgess 11–0–115–35–10.45.

Bowling—J. W. Lewis 86.4–25–215–26–8.26; S. W. Harvey 66.3–20–153–16–9.56; J. W. Thomas 38.4–7–123–10–12.30; N. P. Gibson 76.3–16–224–17–13.17; P. D. Thomas 109.5–35–247–17–14.52.

CHRIST'S HOSPITAL
Played 14: Won 3, Lost 5, Drawn 6. Abandoned 1

Master i/c: G. M. Baldwin

Batting—*T. A. P. Godfrey 14–4–601–135*–60.10; T. I. Chrishop 9–2–252–51*–36.00; P. J. Goodwin 12–1–208–48–18.90; S. G. M. Shepard 12–1–202–35–18.36; S. C. Wilson 14–0–252–48–18.00; J. D. Brown 11–5–103–46*–17.16; P. J. English 13–1–142–33–11.83; J. O. J. Bennett 13–2–111–36–10.09.

Bowling—P. J. Goodwin 109.4–24–260–20–13.00; R. L. Turner 154.5–43–378–24–15.75; J. A. T. Pritchard 113–19–311–10–31.10; T. I. Chrishop 179–39–537–12–44.75.

CITY OF LONDON SCHOOL
Played 7: Won 3, Lost 2, Drawn 2

Master i/c: L. M. Smith

Batting—W. A. Saunders 5–2–140–57*–46.66; S. B. Zamet 6–2–119–64–29.75; W. M. Tebbit 7–1–173–67*–28.83; J. S. Statham 6–1–116–34*–23.20.

Bowling—W. M. Tebbit 73–17–215–13–16.53.

CLIFTON COLLEGE

Played 15: Won 1, Lost 8, Drawn 6. Abandoned 2

Master i/c: D. C. Henderson   Cricket professional: F. J. Andrew

Batting—J. S. Matthews 13–1–408–88*–34.00; S. C. Hazlitt 14–0–355–94–25.35; P. A. Berry 9–2–155–68*–22.14; A. H. Fairhurst 13–2–213–44*–19.36; J. M. Braybrooke 8–0–113–39–14.12; C. T. J. Manners 12–2–137–25*–13.70; J. D. Lee 11–0–143–25–13.00.

Bowling—P. A. Berry 158–25–520–22–23.63; M. C. H. Jones 181–36–549–19–28.89; S. C. Hazlitt 212–38–693–16–43.31.

COLFE'S SCHOOL

Played 19: Won 9, Lost 4, Drawn 6

Masters i/c: M. L. Taylor and R. J. Evans

Batting—*A. S. Byers 19–6–624–72*–48.00; C. Spencer 10–3–222–101*–31.71; M. A. Saleemi 12–2–310–69*–31.00; G. C. Tomkins 14–2–192–77–16.00; K. P. Weir 14–0–200–51–14.28; J. Waddell 19–1–161–25–8.94.

Bowling—R. Keen 51–14–153–15–10.20; K. J. Boxall 171.5–56–382–36–10.61; A. S. Byers 212.1–54–638–52–12.26; M. A. Saleemi 186.4–55–486–39–12.46; M. P. Davies 119.1–26–394–21–18.76.

COLSTON'S SCHOOL

Played 16: Won 6, Lost 2, Drawn 8. Abandoned 4

Master i/c: M. P. B. Tayler   Cricket professional: R. A. Sinfield

Batting—W. M. Smith 15–3–723–142–60.25; J. N. Stutt 16–4–521–103*–43.41; *L. M. Roll 15–1–339–68–24.21; J. N. Gleeson 7–1–101–35–16.83; D. C. Kettlewell 13–2–159–34–14.45.

Bowling—S. Luxton 148–53–363–26–13.96; W. M. Smith 56.2–8–195–12–16.25; D. J. Pope 116.4–29–390–20–19.50; R. Lawrence 61.1–7–318–14–22.71; L. M. Roll 97–21–301–11–27.36.

CRANBROOK SCHOOL

Played 11: Won 1, Lost 3, Drawn 7

Masters i/c: T. K. Gunn and J. Furminger

Batting—R. Fry 8–2–175–83*–29.16; J. Tatt 11–2–218–83*–24.22; J. Brown 11–0–241–98–21.90; H. Youngman 11–0–240–69–21.81; M. Rayfield 11–2–177–72–19.66; J. Gurney 8–2–108–57–18.00; G. Watson 11–0–143–37–13.00.

Bowling—D. Spriggs 33–7–141–12–11.75; S. Rubin 96.2–23–284–15–18.93; C. Brotherton 89–17–284–13–21.84; R. Wall 108.2–30–345–14–24.64; R. Fry 79–12–311–10–31.10.

DAME ALLAN'S SCHOOL

Played 10: Won 1, Lost 4, Drawn 5. Abandoned 5

Master i/c: P. Balmer

Batting—P. G. Clark 10–3–205–60–29.28; S. N. Walton 10–2–165–53–20.62; S. J. Russell 9–0–114–38–12.66.

Bowling—S. J. Nichols 49–12–121–14–8.64; S. J. Russell 54.1–8–196–19–10.31; I. Dodds 50–5–186–10–18.60.

DAUNTSEY'S SCHOOL

Played 12: Won 6, Lost 5, Drawn 1

Master i/c: M. K. F. Johnson   Cricket professional: P. Hough

Batting—A. Brooks 5–1–103–50*–25.75; P. G. Clarke 11–0–174–69–15.81; J. R. Parker 12–0–177–49–14.75.

Bowling—J. Plumtree 84–8–288–20–14.40; P. J. Coffey 78–29–181–12–15.08.

DEAN CLOSE SCHOOL

Played 9: Won 6, Lost 2, Drawn 1. Abandoned 5

Master i/c: C. M. Kenyon   Cricket professional: D. Walker

Batting—P. M. Vincent 9–3–254–61*–42.33; R. N. Lindsay 6–1–108–38–21.60; K. B. Hemshall 8–1–141–58*–20.14; H. M. Davies-Thomas 9–0–180–56–20.00; A. Carroll 8–0–159–58–19.87; C. R. Torrens 6–0–107–46–17.83; D. R. Friend 8–1–119–52–17.00.

Bowling—M. C. A. Forster 67.1–21–179–17–10.52; P. M. Vincent 122–39–259–23–11.26; R. N. Lindsay 98.2–30–212–16–13.25; K. B. Hemshall 70.1–19–173–12–14.41.

DENSTONE COLLEGE

Played 16: Won 4, Lost 2, Drawn 10. Abandoned 3

Master i/c: D. Dexter   Cricket professional: H. J. Rhodes

Batting—R. J. Robinson 16–1–649–150*–43.26; T. A. Venner 9–0–236–82–26.22; J. C. G. Moss 14–2–237–42–19.75; A. T. Swales 11–2–172–34–19.11; D. J. North 14–0–264–52–18.85; J. V. Collier 17–4–242–48–18.61; N. D. Baker 13–5–142–32–17.75; *M. J. Underwood 17–0–279–44–16.41; J. C. Davison 12–2–140–33–14.00.

Bowling—A. T. Swales 128.5–34–375–25–15.00; N. D. Baker 217.3–67–478–30–15.93; R. J. Robinson 93–25–235–12–19.58; M. J. Underwood 118–30–337–17–19.82; R. C. F. Thompson 161.1–53–454–21–21.61.

DOVER COLLEGE

Played 15: Won 6, Lost 6, Drawn 3

Master i/c: R. Quinton-Jones   Cricket professional: A. H. Drake

Batting—*J. Corbett 13–4–403–81–44.77; P. Wijegooneratna 8–1–149–65–21.28; D. Carrion 11–1–163–43–16.30; P. Radford 15–1–216–51–15.42.

Bowling—D. Carrion 254–66–660–53–12.45; A Iliasu 210–60–572–33–17.33; J. Masters 57–6–243–14–17.35; S. Carrion 76–14–250–10–25.00.

DOWNSIDE SCHOOL
Played 12: Won 3, Lost 4, Drawn 4, Tied 1. Abandoned 3

Master i/c: D. Baty

Batting—C. D. Chignell 9–3–318–105*–53.00; *N. R. J. Mackenzie 12–1–299–65*–27.18; A. P. Smerdon 10–0–203–51–20.30; T. L. Colston 10–1–158–63*–17.55; J. R. D. Anton 10–0–126–30–12.60; C. D. C. Brown 11–1–108–27–10.80.

Bowling—C. D. C. Brown 130.1–30–433–21–20.61; T. J. Nesbitt 110–27–380–13–29.23; D. H. Chisholm 105.3–28–307–10–30.70; H. F. G. Cordey 100.4–22–340–11–30.90.

DULWICH COLLEGE
Played 17: Won 7, Lost 5, Drawn 5. Abandoned 2

Master i/c: N. D. Cousins   Cricket professional: W. A. Smith

Batting—*P. J. Hulston 17–1–517–89–32.31; C. J. Webb 15–1–323–56–23.07; I. D. Waters 16–1–303–62–20.20; N. D. Martin Clark 16–1–287–59–19.13; J. R. Hearn 15–2–246–73*–18.92; A. A. McKee 15–2–211–44–16.23; J. S. Lennox 13–3–161–41–16.10; N. P. King 12–1–108–23–9.81.

Bowling—N. P. Rutherford 113–31–262–27–9.70; R. J. Dove 256–73–728–47–15.48; C. J. Webb 61.2–11–194–10–19.40; J. R. Hearn 168–43–456–19–24.00; J. A. Swinney 111.1–18–460–13–35.38.

DURHAM SCHOOL
Played 14: Won 7, Lost 1, Drawn 6. Abandoned 5

Master i/c: W. J. R. Allen   Cricket professional: M. Hirsch

Batting—M. A. Roseberry 13–2–826–216–75.09; J. N. Whitfield 12–4–221–44–27.62; J. M. Alderson 9–2–178–83–25.42; *C. R. Mayes 13–4–184–44–20.44; C. D. Ive 11–1–190–54–19.00; B. M. Hume 10–2–115–38–14.37; S. C. Hussain 14–0–175–38–12.50.

Bowling—M. A. Roseberry 178.3–70–406–48–8.45; J. M. Alderson 159–55–303–21–14.42; R. A. Sowerby 127–36–379–22–17.22; C. D. Ive 64–17–240–12–20.00.

EASTBOURNE COLLEGE
Played 18: Won 6, Lost 4, Drawn 8

Master i/c: N. L. Wheeler   Cricket professional: A. E. James

Batting—J. R. Prentis 18–3–811–163*–54.06; M. H. Edwardes-Evans 18–3–625–86*–41.66; J. C. Wallace 17–3–470–86–33.57; S. M. Wheeler 14–5–207–47–23.00; S. H. C. Cosstick 18–2–356–42–22.25; S. J. N. Gray 12–4–124–50*–15.50; *S. K. Kiley-Worthington 14–4–137–33*–13.70.

Bowling—J. R. Prentis 235.3–57–688–40–17.20; J. C. Wallace 133.5–25–456–22–20.72; R. J. W. Anstey 153.4–35–495–19–26.05; P. D. Hole 227–59–733–25–29.32.

THE EDINBURGH ACADEMY
Played 16: Won 6, Lost 6, Drawn 4

Master i/c: A. R. Dyer

Batting—A. F. Gunn 17–1–473–107*–29.56; J. D. Kudianavala 17–2–373–86–24.86; *G. R. Mawdsley 14–0–325–47–23.21; D. J. Zuill 14–4–185–57*–18.50; J. McGlynn 16–2–194–62–13.85; B. J. Hay-Smith 14–2–166–33*–13.83; M. S. Watt 16–4–161–40*–13.41; R. A. Mawdsley 14–0–164–48–11.71.

Bowling—J. D. Kudianavala 85.3–20–215–18–11.94; G. R. Mawdsley 106.2–43–204–17–12.00; M. S. Watt 217.4–54–577–39–14.79; I. S. Wilmshurst 121.2–28–388–22–17.63; B. J. M. Clube 224–68–536–29–18.48.

ELIZABETH COLLEGE, GUERNSEY

Played 17: Won 3, Lost 4, Drawn 10

Master i/c: M. E. Kinder

Batting—T. Wheadon 13–3–350–73–35.00; M. Read 14–2–416–90–34.66; C. Warlow 17–3–291–46–20.78; J. Mattinson 12–3–159–43*–17.66; T. Belton 15–2–189–46–14.53; N. Mechem 11–1–122–29–12.20.

Bowling—J. Crocker 47.3–8–183–10–18.30; J. Mattinson 155.3–32–524–20–26.20; N. Ravenscroft 113–21–371–13–28.53; N. Mechem 116.5–33–380–13–29.23; R. Gipp 112–24–373–10–37.30.

ELLESMERE COLLEGE

Played 13: Won 3, Lost 3, Drawn 7. Abandoned 4

Master i/c: R. K. Sethi

Batting—D. M. P. Maisey 12–2–322–63–32.20; *R. T. Millinchip 13–1–326–95*–27.16; J. Holmes 11–3–153–45*–19.12; S. M. Carter 12–1–113–23–10.27.

Bowling—S. J. W. Taylor 38.5–6–113–13–8.69; R. T. Millinchip 73–11–288–23–12.52; D. V. Millward-Hopkins 147.2–38–332–21–15.80; D. M. P. Maisey 118.1–45–280–14–20.00.

ELTHAM COLLEGE

Played 21: Won 11, Lost 0, Drawn 10. Abandoned 2

Masters i/c: B. M. Withecombe and P. C. McCartney

Batting—*M. J. Holcombe 20–4–749–124–46.81; B. A. Holcombe 13–3–370–78*–37.00; W. H. Wright 21–4–593–73–34.88; I. N. Whalley 13–6–198–47*–28.28; J. R. S. Brown 7–3–113–89*–28.25; M. G. Pratt 17–5–332–72*–27.66; N. D. A. Baxter 13–7–152–94–25.33; A. Baidya 11–6–122–29–24.40.

Bowling—B. A. Holcombe 210–58–474–39–12.15; W. H. Wright 160.1–44–363–26–13.96; I. N. Whalley 42.1–8–150–10–15.00; M. G. Pratt 88.4–17–332–20–16.60; M. J. Holcombe 189.5–52–546–32–17.06.

EMANUEL SCHOOL

Played 24: Won 14, Lost 6, Drawn 4. Abandoned 4

Master i/c: M. J. Stewart

Batting—F. Ahmed 24–0–706–100–29.41; I. M. Carrick 19–3–456–70–28.50; *S. Sharma 20–1–466–67–24.52; G. P. Piddington 20–8–178–41*–14.83; T. P. Wignall 22–2–290–49–14.50; C. E. Noble 22–1–297–49–14.14; T. J. Harmer 23–3–276–40–13.80; S. J. Park 23–2–284–73–13.52; N. A. Fraser 12–0–142–26–11.83; J. Goodson 22–2–210–29–10.50.

Bowling—T. J. Harmer 216–70–481–41–11.73; G. M. Sizeland 76–13–310–25–12.40; I. M. Carrick 109.4–23–356–23–15.47; T. P. Wignall 139.1–20–497–29–17.13; G. P. Piddington 148–32–428–20–21.40; C. E. Noble 86.5–11–296–13–22.76.

ENFIELD GRAMMAR SCHOOL

Played 17: Won 8, Lost 3, Drawn 6. Abandoned 4

Master i/c: J. J. Conroy

Batting—G. Allen 17–3–566–80*–40.42; R. Eustance 16–1–460–117–30.66; N. Jackett 13–3–287–57*–28.70; M. Taylor 12–4–195–59*–24.37; R. Carter 15–4–254–50*–23.09; P. Pemberton 9–1–163–53*–20.37; G. Jardine 10–1–125–36–13.88.

Bowling—N. Jackett 180–43–441–44–10.02; T. Andrews 72.5–18–163–13–12.53; D. Allen 109.3–22–329–24–13.70; R. Carter 178–45–432–31–13.93; M. Taylor 126.3–26–354–16–22.12.

EPSOM COLLEGE

Played 15: Won 3, Lost 4, Drawn 8. Abandoned 1

Master i/c: J. T. J. Houlson

Batting—*J. R. Ansell 15–3–944–150*–78.66; R. M. C. Williams 15–2–415–108*–31.92; G. R. J. Corcoran 7–2–113–55*–22.60; J. A. Baldwin 9–4–110–43*–22.00; P. R. Hedge 14–2–253–63*–21.08; M. B. Finnigan 12–0–162–39–13.50.

Bowling—W. M. May 121.1–35–323–23–14.04; D. G. Henwood 185.2–45–525–31–16.93; J. N. Barnardo 69–14–217–12–18.08; G. R. J. Corcoran 86.5–16–337–17–19.82; J. A. Baldwin 125–33–377–18–20.94.

ETON COLLEGE

Played 13: Won 7, Lost 1, Drawn 5. Abandoned 3

Master i/c: P. R. Thackeray   Cricket professional: V. H. D. Cannings

Batting—M. H. Brooks 15–2–466–114*–35.84; J. P. Berry 15–3–423–107*–35.25; R. V. Watson 8–1–192–100*–27.42; F. P. E. Marsland 14–0–235–49–16.78; C. E. Pettifer 13–5–128–25*–16.00; *W. A. B. Russell 13–1–128–30*–10.66.

Bowling—C. E. Pettifer 292–88–676–47–14.38; R. J. F. Luke 143.3–39–392–25–15.68.

EXETER SCHOOL

Played 10: Won 4, Lost 3, Drawn 3. Abandoned 3

Master i/c: T. J. Dewes

Batting—*T. N. H. Nash 5–1–113–53*–28.25; R. J. Hudson 6–1–119–52*–23.80; M. F. Gunter 9–1–164–66–20.50; D. M. Clune 10–1–154–37–17.11; M. F. Booth 9–0–102–33–11.33.

Bowling—M. P. Liversage 84–35–168–14–12.00; I. R. Hutcheson 99–34–222–14–15.85; I. D. Hayter 123–34–361–22–16.40.

FELSTED SCHOOL

Played 14: Won 6, Lost 2, Drawn 6. Abandoned 5

Master i/c: M. Surridge

Batting—J. P. Stephenson 15–1–913–157–65.21; D. C. Banner 13–4–263–51*–29.22; R. J. Carr 15–1–379–100–27.07; N. R. W. Down 11–4–178–39*–25.42; P. C. C. Savage 7–2–110–51*–22.00; S. S. J. Miller 15–2–247–59*–19.00; G. M. Martin 8–1–107–37–15.28.

Bowling—G. A. Lambert 240–76–574–41–14.00; S. S. J. Miller 48–9–161–11–14.63; J. P. Stephenson 148–41–388–18–21.55; A. J. Haynes 156–44–423–15–28.20; I. J. Woodward 104–19–345–11–31.36.

FETTES COLLEGE

Played 14: Won 1, Lost 7, Drawn 6. Abandoned 1

Master i/c: V. G. B. Cushing

Batting—B. Wilson 15–1–530–133–37.85; N. Ferguson 11–1–189–51*–18.90; A. Lockhart 13–0–192–42–14.76; G. Lawrie 13–2–143–32–13.00; I. Jack 13–1–130–36–10.83; R. Peacock 15–1–148–31–10.57; *R. Barker 15–1–107–23–7.64.

Bowling—A. Lockhart 136–30–410–22–18.63; G. Macleod 141–34–355–19–18.68; I. Ramsey 147–42–361–19–19.00; R. Barker 139–23–476–20–23.80.

FRAMLINGHAM COLLEGE

Played 16: Won 8, Lost 5, Drawn 3

Master i/c: S. A. Westley   Cricket professional: C. Rutterford

Batting—R. D. O. Earl 16–6–503–100*–50.30; *N. C. J. Holmes 16–1–377–70–25.13; C. E. Wright 12–3–217–53*–24.11; M. R. Brearey 16–3–297–52–22.84; A. C. Pulham 12–1–214–62*–19.45; R. F. Clement 14–3–208–41–18.90.

Bowling—P. M. Hunter 211.5–55–472–42–11.23; J. R. Gubbins 139.2–29–349–25–13.96; R. D. O. Earl 133–38–393–24–16.37; C. E. Wright 133–39—339–19–17.84; N. C. J. Holmes 144–47–312–13–24.00.

GIGGLESWICK SCHOOL

Played 13: Won 4, Lost 4, Drawn 5. Abandoned 4

Master i/c: J. Mayall   Cricket professional: I. W. Callen

Batting—R. M. White 12–0–369–111–30.75; J. T. Hopkinson 10–4–128–36–21.33; *N. C. Westhead 13–1–245–66–20.41; M. T. Haward 11–0–143–41–13.00; J. P. Manduell 11–2–114–52*–12.66; B. L. Baldwin 12–1–138–61–12.54.

Bowling—A. J. Fowler 132.2–44–262–26–10.07; B. L. Baldwin 131–44–235–22–10.68; M. J. R. Stewart 58–14–142–11–12.90; N. C. Westhead 40.2–6–156–11–14.18; C. A. Chapman 111–19–376–12–31.33.

GLENALMOND

Played 13: Won 3, Lost 4, Drawn 6. Abandoned 4

Master i/c: Alwyn James   Cricket professional: W. J. Dennis

Batting—M. H. Alexander 11–1–297–53*–29.70; D. A. Walker 13–2–223–65*–20.27; *J. Sutton 13–0–257–76–19.76; A. M. Stevenson 13–1–225–67–18.75; G. M. Sommerville 13–0–165–66–12.69; G. J. Harley 12–1–127–26*–11.54.

Bowling—M. H. Alexander 135–6–271–18–15.05; J. F. Alexander 143–34–400–24–16.66; W. Paterson-Brown 132.4–29–422–17–24.82; A. E. Kennedy 112–21–390–11–35.45.

HABERDASHERS' ASKE'S SCHOOL

Played 15: Won 6, Lost 2, Drawn 7. Abandoned 5

Master i/c: D. I. Yeabsley

Batting—*A. P. Moulding 15–3–598–136–49.83; R. Bate 15–0–521–74–34.73; D. G. Price 15–2–440–84*–33.84; E. Addy 12–1–233–72–21.18; D. Griffiths 13–2–154–35–14.00; M. Whitmore 11–1–104–40–10.40.

Bowling—A. P. Moulding 207.5–55–518–27–19.18; D. G. Price 165.5–21–597–29–20.58.

HAILEYBURY

Played 14: Won 1, Lost 2, Drawn 11. Abandoned 5

Master i/c: M. S. Seymour   Cricket professional: P. M. Ellis

Batting—N. R. Venning 15–1–480–124*–34.28; *S. L. Feast 15–6–279–58*–31.00; J. T. Lumley 11–4–174–73*–24.85; M. J. Churchill 15–0–309–58–20.60; S. D. Matthews 15–0–246–93–16.40; R. K. Seecharan 11–0–154–65–14.00.

Bowling—R. J. G. Madden 80–33–193–15–12.86; J. T. Lumley 244–83–493–33–14.93; E. P. Okumu 114–32–229–12–19.08; J. W. S. Meacock 259–60–713–31–23.00; T. R. Symonds 104–32–299–10–29.90.

HARROW SCHOOL

Played 11: Won 2, Lost 0, Drawn 9. Abandoned 3

Master i/c: G. M. Attenborough   Cricket professional: P. Davis

Batting—A. T. C. Lloyd-Jones 7–2–254–61–50.80; *J. W. S. Raper 12–0–503–106–41.90; J. M. H. Ford 12–1–418–89–38.00; D. J. Nirmalalingam 9–1–299–101*–37.37; W. D. Peel-Yates 9–1–260–49*–32.50; S. A. James 12–3–171–42–19.00; R. G. Robinson 10–2–104–35–13.00.

Bowling—S. A. James 57–4–121–13–9.30; J. W. S. Raper 129–38–322–26–12.38; J. E. J. Booth 76–19–193–12–16.08.

HEREFORD CATHEDRAL SCHOOL

Played 8: Won 1, Lost 3, Drawn 4. Abandoned 5

Master i/c: M. V. Howlett

Batting—N. R. Hales 8–1–246–57–35.14; P. J. Butler 8–0–216–61–27.00; L. H. L. Shutler 8–1–114–39–16.28.

Bowling—D. M. T. Owens 88.1–16–280–18–15.55; N. J. Startin 74–15–271–13–20.84.

HIGHGATE SCHOOL

Played 16: Won 5, Lost 7, Drawn 4. Abandoned 4

Master i/c: R. W. Halstead

Batting—*A. Walton 15–1–317–59–22.64; N. K. F. Banks 11–1–213–99–21.30; N. Rathbone 15–1–279–58–19.92; M. E. Lyon 11–2–154–45*–17.11; O. Bull 14–2–194–78–16.16; A. D. Ferrari 15–0–204–53–13.60.

Bowling—M. G. Griffiths 111–27–358–22–16.27; D. J. Wright 68–24–174–10–17.40; P. J. Haynes 176.2–39–485–19–25.52; A. Walton 140.1–37–418–16–26.12; C. W. J. Wawn 84–11–264–10–26.40.

HURSTPIERPOINT COLLEGE

Played 19: Won 8, Lost 4, Drawn 7. Abandoned 2

Master i/c: M. E. Allbrook   Cricket professional: D. J. Semmence

Batting—M. D. Foulds 16–2–379–71–27.07; M. P. Speight 19–4–403–54*–26.86; *T. J. Thorne 16–1–319–60*–21.26; J. P. Graham 18–0–349–72–19.38; J. N. Rogers 18–4–254–56–18.14; A. J. L. Sawers 7–1–103–31*–17.16; J. P. Terry 9–2–105–25–15.00; G. J. M. McMillan 13–4–126–30–14.00.

Bowling—A. P. Subba Row 76.1–21–181–22–8.22; J. N. Rogers 168–43–489–27–18.11; J. R. C. Lamb 226.4–51–617–28–22.03.

IPSWICH SCHOOL

Played 14: Won 1, Lost 5, Drawn 8

Master i/c: P. M. Rees   Cricket professional: K. Winder

Batting—P. Finch 7–1–146–50*–24.33; J. Nicholls 12–0–279–53–23.25; T. Rollett 13–0–250–65–19.23; D. Patient 11–3–139–37*–17.37; E. Downie 11–0–123–27–11.18; *S. Priscott 12–0–131–37–10.91; J. Bryden 12–1–120–37–10.90.

Bowling—S. Priscott 217.5–70–492–34–14.47; D. Lilley 64–20–180–10–18.00; D. Patient 111–29–280–11–25.45; J. Nicholls 143–23–512–17–30.11.

KELLY COLLEGE, TAVISTOCK

Played 12: Won 7, Lost 1, Drawn 4. Abandoned 5

Master i/c: T. Ryder

Batting—R. A. Saxon 11–1–213–46–21.30; S. J. B. Aylwin 12–1–215–67–19.54; J. R. Parkhouse 12–0–213–73–17.75; P. G. Shering 11–3–128–79*–16.00; *J. M. A. Stock 12–1–125–43*–11.36; R. M. Summerell 11–0–100–22–9.09.

Bowling—A. J. Carter 101–33–228–22–10.36; J. M. A. Stock 104.2–26–270–26–10.38; J. R. Parkhouse 40–12–119–10–11.90; P. G. Shering 114–34–273–22–12.40; R. P. Edwards 45–8–145–10–14.50.

KIMBOLTON SCHOOL

Played 14: Won 7, Lost 2, Drawn 5

Master i/c: I. J. Burton   Cricket professional: J. W. Hart

Batting—R. A. Johnson 14–1–521–89–40.07; G. J. Kerr 14–1–390–77–30.00; P. D. Shorrick 12–4–171–53*–21.37; *S. A. Sharpe 14–2–234–80–19.50; P. R. F. D. Aylott 14–0–235–38–16.78; A. W. Caswell 12–0–151–42–12.58; R. Hall 12–2–114–24–11.40.

Bowling—A. W. Caswell 118.3–41–312–23–13.56; S. A. Sharpe 223.3–61–585–40–14.62; P. R. F. D. Aylott 60–10–178–10–17.80; R. A. Johnson 140–35–412–13–31.69; P. A. J. Brittain 168–16–351–11–31.90.

KING EDWARD VI COLLEGE, STOURBRIDGE

Played 18: Won 6, Lost 2, Drawn 10. Abandoned 6

Master i/c: M. L. Ryan

Batting—R. N. Tolley 18–4–667–110*–47.64; D. J. Shorter 16–1–634–131–42.26; M. W. Fisher 9–2–269–69–38.42; N. A. Barrett 15–3–314–88–26.16; M. J. Price 12–3–162–32–18.00; *D. J. Bullock 13–4–156–33*–17.33; S. J. Baker 10–3–108–32*–15.42.

Bowling—D. J. Bullock 144.5–40–328–32–10.25; M. J. Price 132.2–47–272–19–14.31; S. J. Baker 114–27–278–17–16.35; D. J. Shorter 242–73–598–35–17.08; N. A. Barrett 90.3–17–312–15–20.80.

KING EDWARD VI SCHOOL, SOUTHAMPTON

Played 20: Won 6, Lost 4, Drawn 10

Master i/c: M. H. May

Batting—M. E. O'Connor 20–2–889–102–49.38; G. Irish 12–3–196–51*–21.77; *S. P. Arnold 18–1–332–87–19.52; R. M. A. Metcalfe 17–3–266–38*–19.00; R. Hambly 19–4–273–71*–18.20; M. G. Hickman 10–3–111–56–15.85; J. Sealy 14–1–184–51–14.15.

Bowling—M. E. O'Connor 95.3–20–382–17–22.47; J. Donaldson 86.5–14–327–14–23.35; R. T. Minns 135–29–519–22–23.59; M. G. Hickman 103–29–334–14–23.85; R. J. Cross 104.5–24–412–16–25.75; P. J. May 99.5–5–513–19–27.00.

KING EDWARD'S SCHOOL, BIRMINGHAM

Played 19: Won 7, Lost 0, Drawn 12. Abandoned 7

Master i/c: D. H. Benson   Cricket professional: G. P. Thomas

Batting—M. K. S. Hughes 17–2–806–116*–53.73; N. A. Willetts 14–2–596–156–49.66; C. Ibbetson 17–1–690–107–43.12; S. D. Heath 11–5–191–56–31.83; J. S. Crawford 12–4–160–24*–20.00; J. R. Bishop 17–3–249–87*–17.78; E. J. Tann 14–5–155–27–17.22; N. V. Subhedar 14–1–129–33–9.92.

Bowling—S. D. Heath 251.2–76–682–58–11.75; P. W. Nienow 86.1–22–220–16–13.75; *A. N. Marshall 129.2–39–367–24–15.29; N. A. Willetts 94.2–28–245–16–15.31; M. K. S. Hughes 74–22–194–12–16.16; C. Ibbetson 167–47–391–23–17.00.

KING HENRY VIII SCHOOL, COVENTRY

Played 16: Won 6, Lost 3, Drawn 7. Abandoned 5

Master i/c: G. P. C. Courtois

Batting—*D. R. Sewell 15–0–534–85–35.60; A. R. Nicholson 14–8–208–41*–34.66; P. M. Smith 16–1–346–50–23.06; E. A. Ansari 15–2–244–57–18.76; A. C. Wallbridge 11–3–142–46*–17.75; J. C. Ockenden 13–1–194–51*–16.16.

Bowling—D. R. Sewell 96–22–277–19–14.57; E. A. Ansari 67–6–220–12–18.33; R. F. Stokes 56.3–11–208–11–18.90; R. Smith 166.1–41–510–24–21.25; I. D. Harris 141.3–27–478–19–25.15.

KING'S COLLEGE, TAUNTON

Played 15: Won 9, Lost 2, Drawn 4. Abandoned 3

Master i/c: P. A. Dossett   Cricket professional: R. E. Marshall

Batting—*R. J. Harden 8–3–229–61*–45.80; R. G. Twose 14–4–281–100*–28.10; G. R. N. Drayton 14–1–351–76–27.00; N. D. Everest 16–1–362–90–24.13; S. J. Kaye 16–2–288–85–20.57; J. P. Brunt 12–3–185–65*–20.55.

Bowling—R. J. Harden 115.4–47–185–29–6.37; H. D. Wordsworth 159.3–47–361–27–13.37; A. J. Willson 151.4–39–371–26–14.26; G. K. Barber 118.2–27–327–20–16.35; G. R. N. Drayton 95.2–16–308–17–18.11.

KING'S COLLEGE SCHOOL, WIMBLEDON

Played 15: Won 3, Lost 2, Drawn 10. Abandoned 2

Master i/c: A. G. P. Lang   Cricket professional: R. A. Dare

Batting—J. P. Feltham 14–2–460–100*–38.33; P. J. Graham 12–0–377–84–31.41; *J. H. Frost 14–1–381–134*–29.30; M. Woolnough 11–3–230–125*–28.75; P. S. Noble 11–3–191–38–23.87; P. R. Endean 13–4–209–46–23.22; C. J. Mills 12–0–171–51–14.25.

Bowling—D. R. G. Hains 58.1–14–152–10–15.20; N. J. W. Penser 78–22–237–14–16.92; P. S. Noble 210.3–46–599–35–17.11; J. P. Feltham 145.3–40–436–18–24.22.

KING'S SCHOOL, BRUTON

Played 13: Won 5, Lost 4, Drawn 4

Master i/c: A. S. Linney

Batting—S. H. Maxwell 10–3–284–102*–40.57; *I. C. D. Stuart 10–1–343–90*–38.11; C. R. B. Campbell-Stanway 9–2–189–78*–27.00; J. Cassell 9–0–232–88–25.77; D. Spenser 5–0–125–51–25.00; D. J. M. Bruce 10–1–110–22–12.22.

Bowling—R. C. Gainher 112–23–254–25–10.16; G. R. Tillyard 82–27–254–21–12.09; I. C. D. Stuart 127–39–270–17–15.88; D. J. M. Bruce 69.1–8–288–12–24.00.

THE KING'S SCHOOL, CANTERBURY

Played 15: Won 7, Lost 1, Drawn 7

Master i/c: A. W. Dyer   Cricket professional: D. V. P. Wright

Batting—J. H. Tattersfield 11–8–128–26*–42.66; J. H. A. Albin 16–0–519–93–32.43; *D. J. Pritchard 16–2–345–50*–24.64; R. W. G. Oliver 16–0–351–70–21.93; S. C. Hodgson 16–5–189–50*–17.18; J. E. S. Weston 16–1–247–51*–16.46; A. W. H Whittlesea 12–3–136–43*–15.11; S. J. S. Lark 15–0–207–70–13.80; N. D. Ratcliff 14–3–108–25–9.81.

Bowling—G. M. J. Dawson 153.5–44–340–24–14.16; D. J. Pritchard 191.3–50–499–34–14.67; J. H. Tattersfield 164.5–55–370–25–14.80; R. W. G. Oliver 141.1–23–522–26–20.07.

THE KING'S SCHOOL, CHESTER

Played 16: Won 1, Lost 6, Drawn 9. Abandoned 5

Master i/c: A. Neeves

Batting—R. S. G. Whittle 16–0–403–82–25.18; T. Jones 7–1–144–44–24.00; D. Jones 16–1–218–51*–14.53; D. Thorley 15–0–140–37–9.33; A. Jones 14–1–120–28–9.23; P. McLoughlin 12–0–107–27–8.91.

Bowling—D. Parr 109.2–40–160–19–8.42; S. Tonks 80–27–247–20–12.35; R. Morgan-Jones 121–47–289–18–16.05; R. S. G. Whittle 171.4–22–538–26–20.69.

THE KING'S SCHOOL, MACCLESFIELD

Played 23: Won 1, Lost 10, Drawn 12. Abandoned 3

Master i/c: D. M. Harbord

Batting—C. J. R. Eccles 19–3–420–82–26.25; *T. I. Moore 22–0–560–71–25.45; C. J. Belfield 21–1–424–72*–21.20; R. A. D. Laughton 20–4–251–37–15.68; D. B. Rousham 16–1–234–46–15.60; D. G. Walker 16–5–101–21–9.18; S. R. Greenfield 16–1–129–41–8.60; N. E. J. Hampson 19–0–160–26–8.42.

Bowling—R. A. D. Laughton 293–81–754–52–14.50; C. J. Belfield 131.2–33–402–20–20.10; D. G. Walker 138.3–36–474–18–26.33; J. C. Sandford 152–31–496–13–38.15.

KING'S SCHOOL, ROCHESTER

Played 17: Won 7, Lost 3, Drawn 7. Abandoned 2

Master i/c: J. S. Irvine

Batting—T. W. Collard 16–3–422–64*–32.46; R. P. Mernagh 15–2–419–169*–32.23; *R. D. Barrett 17–0–521–86–30.64; N. C. Heaver 10–1–227–72–25.22; A. S. Brown 13–3–244–58–24.40; R. K. Mellor 13–2–261–61*–23.72; R. A. Hargraves 11–2–132–38–14.66.

Bowling—N. Q. Miller 163.4–37–517–37–13.97; M. E. Rowe 154.1–37–479–27–17.74; F. E. E. Dyediran 127.2–24–418–20–20.90; R. P. Mernagh 154.3–46–477–22–21.68.

KING'S SCHOOL, WORCESTER

Played 14: Won 9, Lost 3, Drawn 2. Abandoned 8

Master i/c: P. Iddon

Batting—S. Preston 9–2–245–96*–35.00; R. Jones 14–1–389–66–29.92; J. Mackie 13–2–326–67–29.63; S. Evans 11–2–183–44*–20.33; *D. Rogers 11–2–168–50–18.66; D. Bishop 14–0–200–47–14.28; M. Morgan 12–2–128–25*–12.80.

Bowling—N. Fisher 111.1–30–339–26–13.03; K. Andrews 203.3–50–607–36–16.86; J. Hodgson 116–20–357–20–17.85; A. Suckling 94.2–17–358–15–23.86.

KING WILLIAM'S COLLEGE, ISLE OF MAN

Played 16: Won 3, Lost 4, Drawn 9. Abandoned 2

Master i/c: A. Q. Bashforth   Cricket professional: D. Mark

Batting—S. C. Watson 16–0–628–96–39.25; G. R. Murray 9–2–237–41–33.85; T. S. Glover 17–0–394–69–23.17; D. A. J. Butterfield 15–2–266–62–20.46; N. R. J. Cowley 12–5–102–39*–14.57; S. R. Dane 15–2–172–50–13.23; A. J. A. Turnbull 16–2–162–29–11.57; *R. K. Corkill 16–1–134–26–8.93.

Bowling—A. J. A. Turnbull 249.2–94–516–36–14.33; A. A. M. Cooper 236–91–507–29–17.48; D. A. J. Butterfield 176.4–31–486–19–25.57.

KINGSTON GRAMMAR SCHOOL

Played 18: Won 3, Lost 9, Drawn 6. Abandoned 4

Master i/c: R. J. Sturgeon

Batting—S. H. Clayson 17–2–727–114*–48.46; J. P. Molloy 16–1–376–94–25.06; A. S. K. Ghauri 17–1–388–102*–24.25; S. C. R. Cox 17–0–330–70–19.41; D. G. S. Gordon 14–4–169–39–16.90; R. J. Gornall 9–0–116–33–12.88; G. B. Foreman 16–1–174–36–11.60; A. D. Harding 13–3–109–28*–10.90.

Bowling—*R. C. Marshall 199.3–51–610–29–21.03; A. D. Harding 141.3–22–640–18–35.55; J. P. Molloy 141.5–32–472–12–39.33.

KINGSWOOD SCHOOL, BATH

Played 11: Won 0, Lost 4, Drawn 7

Master i/c: G. Mobley

Batting—C. E. Rogers 9–3–152–31–25.33; R. J. Lloyd-Williams 10–2–198–75*–24.75; A. C. Hymer 9–0–199–46–22.11; S. J. Lowe 8–0–156–58–19.50; S. W. Abbott 11–0–153–50–13.90; *C. J. Huxtable 11–0–131–30–11.90; J. F. Ducker 11–0–104–28–9.45.

Bowling—T. S. Hammond 91–17–290–20–14.50; A. C. Hymer 129.4–25–373–22–16.95; A. C. Halaby 56–10–211–10–21.10.

LANCING COLLEGE

Played 18: Won 8, Lost 3, Drawn 7. Abandoned 2

Master i/c: E. A. Evans-Jones   Cricket professional: D. V. Smith

Batting—C. S. Mays 18–0–619–134–34.38; J. D. Robinson 18–1–474–82–27.88; P. G. Sealey 17–1–384–84–24.00; J. N. P. Davies 10–4–120–29*–20.00; J. G. Wills 16–1–251–58–16.73; M. D. Erskine 12–3–143–32–15.88; A. P. Miller 12–5–104–21–14.85; *I. C. Martin 16–1–185–56–12.33.

Bowling—C. S. Mays 302.1–85–497–57–8.71; A. N. McPherson 79.2–23–134–15–8.93; P. G. Sealey 143.2–47–364–25–14.56; J. N. P. Davies 120–35–264–15–17.60.

LEEDS GRAMMAR SCHOOL

Played 16: Won 3, Lost 5, Drawn 8. Abandoned 6

Master i/c: I. R. Briars

Batting—*A. F. Tyler 15–2–581–109–44.69; S. Joyce 13–2–340–101*–30.90; D. A. Smith 13–3–203–51–20.30; J. R. Clark 12–2–203–49–20.30; A. Setia 13–1–236–43–19.66; J. A. Verity 11–1–166–45–16.60; S. R. Bowman 12–1–105–21–9.54.

Bowling—A. Setia 100.4–28–329–22–14.95; G. R. Tyler 106.5–31–337–22–15.31; D. C. Barker 165.1–39–511–29–17.62; A. M. Watson 115–30–283–12–23.58; D. A. Smith 115.3–30–481–17–28.29.

LEIGHTON PARK SCHOOL

Played 10: Won 6, Lost 3, Drawn 1. Abandoned 3

Master i/c: G. C. Shaw

Batting—J. R. Wood 4–0–161–62–40.25; P. D. R. Berridge 9–2–232–68–33.14; *C. A. J. Allan 9–0–169–64–18.77; D. Doraisamy 10–0–180–49–18.00.

Bowling—C. J. Pye-Smith 43–6–139–16–8.68; D. Doraisamy 90–29–203–15–13.53; E. P. Salisbury 76.5–11–244–13–18.76.

THE LEYS SCHOOL

Played 17: Won 7, Lost 2, Drawn 8. Abandoned 1

Master i/c: P. R. Chamberlain

Batting—J. D. R. Benson 17–1–757–201*–47.31; M. P. Fernandez 15–2–343–93*–26.38; S. J. W. Hamilton 18–2–380–57–23.75; J. S. Kerkham 6–1–101–35*–20.20; M. R. K. Nesbitt 18–1–321–61–18.88; D. O. Omitowoju 15–5–188–47*–18.80; S. J. Arnold 12–3–143–29–15.88; A. J. B. Symes 16–2–159–21–11.35.

Bowling—T. C. Bent 48–10–156–11–14.18; J. D. R. Benson 201–49–577–34–16.97; J. S. Kerkham 124–27–403–22–18.31; *M. Gardner 170–43–506–27–18.74; T. W. Gray 67–13–234–11–21.27; M. P. Fernandez 104–16–388–18–21.55.

LIVERPOOL COLLEGE

Played 9: Won 1, Lost 4, Drawn 4. Abandoned 7

Master i/c: J. R. H. Robertson   Cricket professional: W. J. Clutterbuck

Batting—P. D. Williams 9–1–278–70*–34.75; M. Llewellyn 6–0–114–43–19.00; A. N. Hughes 9–1–118–34*–14.75; *D. M. Fletcher 10–0–144–29–14.40; D. N. Young 9–1–113–30*–14.12; S. R. Downes 9–0–123–30–13.66.

Bowling—J. A. Brown 98–23–246–16–15.37; A. P. Hanson 104.4–28–271–12–22.58.

LLANDOVERY COLLEGE

Played 11: Won 2, Lost 4, Drawn 5. Abandoned 3

Master i/c: T. G. Marks

Batting—S. Meredith 10–0–201–47–20.10; N. Whiskerd 10–0–172–39–17.20; B. D. Evans 11–0–161–46–14.63; D. A. Williams 9–0–118–43–13.11.

Bowling—*G. E. Owen 177–65–352–40–8.80; E. Clancy 63–16–154–11–14.00; J. Mosely 105–23–299–17–17.58.

LORD WANDSWORTH COLLEGE

Played 10: Won 1, Lost 3, Drawn 6

Masters i/c: S. R. Davidson and A. G. Whibley

Batting—A. M. Blows 10–2–374–86*–46.75; S. B. Talbot 8–0–119–59–14.87.

Bowling—J. Ingledew 52–10–173–14–12.35; S. G. Saunders 81–16–223–13–17.15; D. S. Morris 84–15–302–11–27.45.

LORD WILLIAMS'S SCHOOL, THAME

Played 12: Won 2, Lost 6, Drawn 4. Abandoned 4

Masters i/c: G. M. D. Howat and A. M. Brannan

Batting—C. M. Payne 8–1–222–74*–31.71; A. J. Deans 10–1–254–75*–28.22; *S. J. Lewis 7–0–189–57–27.00; G. A. Westlake 6–0–100–52–16.66; P. M. Jobson 7–0–114–67–16.28.

Bowling—P. M. Jobson 81–14–238–20–11.90; R. B. Travers 62.2–21–179–12–14.91.

LORETTO SCHOOL

Played 15: Won 3, Lost 3, Drawn 9. Abandoned 3

Master i/c: R. G. Selley   Cricket professional: W. Heathcoat

Batting—*P. D. Stevenson 15–1–348–71–24.85; S. E. Maguire 15–2–300–73*–23.07; T. D. Smith 13–3–165–31–16.50; A. G. D. Aitchison 17–2–234–54–15.60; J. A. Hodgson 16–3–195–32–15.00.

Bowling—A. G. D. Aitchison 280–83–707–53–13.33; I. R. Sinclair 79.5–17–236–16–14.75; T. D. Smith 165.2–26–566–24–23.58; E. K. R. Foy 140–35–453–13–34.84.

MAGDALEN COLLEGE SCHOOL

Played 13: Won 7, Lost 0, Drawn 6. Abandoned 5

Master i/c: E. P. L. Sandbach

Batting—*S. A. Mendes 13–3–552–101–55.20; M. R. A. Barrow 13–0–419–91–32.23; J. F. Atkins 11–2–205–72–22.77; P. A. Witts 12–0–223–56–18.58; S. M. Kilgour 11–3–126–40–15.75; M. Mackinlay 13–3–145–57–14.50.

Bowling—M. Mackinlay 45.3–12–122–14–8.71; M. R. A Barrow 203.3–76–481–34–14.14; G. Adams 77.3–22–220–15–14.66; S. A. Mendes 192.3–42–605–37–16.35.

MALVERN COLLEGE

Played 15: Won 1, Lost 5, Drawn 9. Abandoned 4

Master i/c: A. J. Murtagh   Cricket professional: G. D. Morton

Batting—R. A. F. Bache 15–0–507–106–33.80; N. R. C Maclaurin 15–1–464–103–33.14; S. J. Creffield 13–1–261–81*–21.75; E. H. Gilbert 13–0–277–78–21.30; M. C. J. Smith 13–2–221–37–20.09; *A. H. Lewis 14–3–191–44–17.36.

Bowling—J. M. Davey 125–31–363–21–17.28; R. G. Fleetwood 148–29–441–25–17.64; R. F. Young 105.3–18–371–16–23.18; T. J. Young 116.4–23–390–15–26.00.

MANCHESTER GRAMMAR SCHOOL

Played 17: Won 4, Lost 0, Drawn 13. Abandoned 5

Master i/c: D. Moss

Batting—M. A. Atherton 14–6–539–91–67.37; M. A. Crawley 16–6–538–135*–53.80; G. Yates 13–3–189–52*–27.00; C. D. James 17–2–384–77*–25.60; R. E. Johnston 13–0–327–61–25.15; *S. C. Corbett 7–2–115–40–23.00.

Bowling—M. A. P. Jefferson 244.4–57–631–37–17.05; S. C. Corbett 117.1–26–359–17–21.11; G. Yates 173–28–597–26–22.96; M. A. Atherton 146.3–38–433–17–25.47; I. D. Botterill 155–48–392–13–30.15.

MARLBOROUGH COLLEGE

Played 12: Won 1, Lost 3, Drawn 8. Abandoned 4

Master i/c: P. J. Lough

Batting—J. T. Burrell 15–1–591–142–42.21; R. J. P. Young 14–3–325–90–29.54; R. T. Thicknesse 14–3–309–61–28.09; R. Nath 12–3–249–50*–27.66; *A. W. Woodhouse 13–2–276–88*–25.09; J. E. J. Morris 13–1–267–58–22.25; C. A. L. Hill 15–0–260–32–17.33; C. Whittaker 9–2–112–23–16.00.

Bowling—R. T. Thicknesse 272.3–93–719–35–20.54; A. J. P. Busk 169.1–33–483–20–24.15; R. O. Stafford 211–42–627–25–25.08.

MERCHANT TAYLORS' SCHOOL, CROSBY

Played 15: Won 4, Lost 7, Drawn 4

Master i/c: Rev. D. A. Smith

Batting—*D. H. Cooke 15–4–190–42–17.27; L. N. J. Heathcliff-Core 14–3–180–41–16.36; I. M. Kerr 15–0–240–51–16.00; M. J. Cooke 16–0–204–46–12.75; D. R. Drury 13–2–130–37–11.81; A. Walmsley 13–3–101–44–10.10.

Bowling—L. N. J. Heathcliff-Core 246.1–72–597–46–12.97; D. R. Drury 78–11–290–19–15.26; D. H. Cooke 96–24–298–11–27.09; M. J. Clinton 99.3–29–317–10–31.70.

MERCHANT TAYLORS' SCHOOL, NORTHWOOD

Played 12: Won 5, Lost 1, Drawn 6. Abandoned 3

Master i/c: W. M. B. Ritchie

Batting—D. J. Jenkins 12–1–479–138*–43.54; J. H. Armstrong 12–3–377–65*–41.88; S. R. C. Mee 11–3–332–93*–41.50; I. P. R. Collins 12–0–220–60–18.33; M. A. St C. Stewart 10–2–139–44–17.37; H. L. Thompson 8–1–112–33–16.00; P. J. Trussell 7–0–110–55–15.71.

Bowling—A. J. Cornish 140.1–35–382–25–15.28; D. J. Hannam 122.5–35–356–22–16.18; J. H. Armstrong 74–21–220–11–20.00; *A. M. Roberts 115.3–9–428–11–38.90.

MERCHISTON CASTLE SCHOOL

Played 9: Won 1, Lost 1, Drawn 7. Abandoned 5

Master i/c: M. C. L. Gill   Cricket professional: R. M. Ratcliffe

Batting—I. D. Rose 9–3–347–83*–57.83; *D. A. G. Watson 6–0–159–70–26.50; A. G. Young 9–0–186–66–20.66.

Bowling—D. F. W. Burn 110.5–20–350–23–15.21; I. D. Rose 93.3–25–259–14–18.50; J. P. Winpenny 99.5–30–224–12–18.66.

MILLFIELD SCHOOL

Played 15: Won 6, Lost 2, Drawn 7. Abandoned 6

Master i/c: F. N. Fenner   Cricket professional: G. Wilson

Batting—R. A. Hawes 10–5–188–45*–37.60; R. W. Hill 11–5–220–81–36.66; J. C. M. Atkinson 16–2–443–57*–31.64; R. M. Cooper 7–0–206–55–29.42; *P. A. C. Bail 16–0–451–91–28.18; M. D. C. Partington 11–2–225–70–25.00; A. C. H. Seymour 10–2–182–73*–22.75; E. M. Greenwood 15–0–317–46–21.13.

Bowling—P. A. C. Bail 130.5–39–341–33–10.33; J. C. M. . Atkinson 117.5–28–329–18–18.27; M. D. C. Partington 71–13–240–10–24.00; A. T. Brooker 62–11–261–10–26.10; J. A. Strachan 106–28–363–13–27.92.

MILL HILL SCHOOL

Played 16: Won 6, Lost 6, Drawn 4. Abandoned 6

Master i/c: C. Dean   Cricket professional: R. E. Hayward

Batting—*R. S. W. Roberts 10–0–408–104–40.80; M. J. Swinn 9–1–185–93–23.12; J. M. Cicale 15–2–274–100–21.07; P. B. Mensah 7–0–146–67–20.85; *I. A. O. Adebayo 15–1–279–87–19.92; C. E. Dawson 12–2–192–69–19.20; J. A. Robin 14–2–183–57–15.25; S. Premadasa 9–0–122–50–13.55.

Bowling—R. S. W. Roberts 136.2–33–392–24–16.33; J. A. Robin 193.1–43–592–32–18.50; D. A. Weddell 118.2–26–348–18–19.33; C. E. Dawson 78.1–17–221–11–20.09; A. J. Veal 90.2–22–225–11–20.45.

MILTON ABBEY SCHOOL
Played 10: Won 3, Lost 6, Drawn 1. Abandoned 4

Master i/c: S. T. Smail

Batting—C. D. Mesquita 10–3–168–28–24.00; *C. W. Moyle 10–1–189–45–21.00; C. G. Bevan 9–0–153–70–17.00; J. M. Hopkins 10–0–156–55–15.60.

Bowling—D. A. C. Meredith 49.2–13–144–15–9.60; C. D. Lindsay 68.3–13–236–18–13.11; C. W. Moyle 74.3–9–300–18–16.66.

MONKTON COMBE SCHOOL
Played 11: Won 1, Lost 4, Drawn 6

Master i/c: P. C. Sibley

Batting—A. P. Fussell 11–3–265–68*–33.12; A. G. Bristow 9–4–162–43*–32.40; I. G. Osborne 11–2–271–50*–30.11; D. J. Knight 7–0–154–48–22.00; *J. J. A. Beales 10–0–176–70–17.60.

Bowling—A. D. W. Kenworthy 89.3–29–195–12–16.25; I. G. Osborne 99–14–366–13–28.15.

MONMOUTH SCHOOL
Played 10: Won 4, Lost 1, Drawn 5. Abandoned 7

Masters i/c: P. Dennis-Jones and P. D. R. Anthony   Cricket professional: G. I. Burgess

Batting—S. P. James 10–3–297–72*–42.42; *R. S. Kear 8–3–164–55–32.80; A. C. Olney 9–2–200–52–28.57; M. J. Tremlett 6–1–105–36–21.00.

Bowling—A. J. Kear 110.5–27–260–20–13.00; D. W. Joseph 170.2–52–324–21–15.42; B. T. B. Kantolinna 83–17–243–15–16.20; G. A. Davies 111.4–28–299–13–23.00.

NORWICH SCHOOL
Played 19: Won 4, Lost 8, Drawn 7. Abandoned 1

Master i/c: P. J. Henderson

Batting—*S. P. Bowling 18–3–622–126*–41.46; N. J. E. Foster 17–1–538–100*–33.62; P. D. C. Nicholls 16–2–460–127*–32.85; J. A. Cooper 12–2–200–57–20.00; G. Morgan-Hughes 16–2–235–47–16.78; A. G. Clarke 12–2–131–46*–13.10.

Bowling—P. D. C. Nicholls 167–45–414–31–13.35; J. A. Cooper 138.2–24–430–31–13.87; N. J. E. Foster 173.4–34–647–25–25.88; D. Orr 88.3–15–355–11–32.27.

NOTTINGHAM HIGH SCHOOL
Played 21: Won 6, Lost 4, Drawn 10, Tied 1. Abandoned 4

Master i/c: P. G. Morris   Cricket professional: H. Latchman

Batting—J. A. Pitman 20–4–369–62*–23.06; *R. C. Elgie 18–2–337–76*–21.06; M. D. Hyland 9–1–142–35*–17.75; T. D. Jackman 12–4–134–29*–16.75; W. E. C. Browne 12–3–147–58*–16.33; J. G. Morris 16–2–201–58–14.35; S. D. Wilkins 18–2–200–37–12.50.

Bowling—A. J. Reeves 50–19–104–12–8.66; M. Saxelby 61.2–18–151–12–12.58; G. D. Harding 134.5–25–420–29–14.48; J. P. Heather 167.2–57–416–22–18.90; T. D. Jackman 99.3–13–350–18–19.44; P. J. Hall 137–33–450–21–21.42; S. D. Wilkins 220.3–71–568–22–25.81.

OAKHAM SCHOOL
Played 18: Won 4, Lost 5, Drawn 9

Master i/c: J. Wills   Cricket professional: I. H. S. Balfour

Batting—A. Douglass 16–4–564–107*–47.00; *M. Steans 17–0–588–178–34.58; S. Ratcliffe
18–1–427–69–25.11; S. Stephenson 13–5–141–43–17.62; C. Welch 16–1–201–42–13.40; T.
Shaw 16–1–199–41*–13.26; J. Wratten 16–1–111–14–7.40.

Bowling—S. Stephenson 102.5–31–298–17–17.52; D. Lewis 214.4–60–617–31–19.90; A.
Douglass 241.4–64–667–33–20.21; J. Wratten 206–57–566–21–26.95.

OUNDLE SCHOOL
Played 16: Won 3, Lost 7, Drawn 6. Abandoned 3

Master i/c: M. J. Goatly   Cricket professional: A. Watkins

Batting—A. S. A. Townsend 10–1–334–100–37.11; J. A. MacMillan 14–1–320–87–24.61;
J. B. W. Taylor 13–0–226–50–17.38; T. Chater 14–1–226–67–17.38; R. J. F. Bronks
13–0–218–33–16.76; J. H. D. Andrews 10–2–118–36*–14.75; J. R. Waters
12–1–161–49–14.63; H. J. K. Asquith 12–1–145–33–13.18; J. S. Carr 15–1–155–31–11.07.

Bowling—P. J. Williamson 116.2–29–352–18–19.55; J. A. MacMillan
140.2–23–460–23–20.00; M. I. W. Russell 133.3–23–415–16–25.93; J. S. Carr
192.1–40–616–22–28.00.

THE PERSE SCHOOL
Played 15: Won 4, Lost 4, Drawn 7

Master i/c: A. W. Billinghurst

Batting—*J. M. C. Stenner 14–3–723–138*–65.72; C. P. Wass 14–3–246–40–22.36; W. R.
Graham 14–0–254–54–18.14; M. Melzer 14–1–214–74*–16.46; C. A. Riley
10–3–112–25–16.00.

Bowling—R. Hanka 162–52–355–29–12.24; J. M. C. Stenner 116–26–350–20–17.50; C. P.
Wass 160–46–389–20–19.45.

POCKLINGTON SCHOOL
Played 25: Won 9, Lost 6, Drawn 10

Master i/c: D. Nuttall

Batting—R. V. Henderson 23–5–515–65*–28.61; *S. J. Hall 24–3–579–69*–27.57; R. T.
Nuttall 25–1–654–101*–27.25; J. J. Mansfield 20–5–304–60–20.26; R. M. Picknett
23–1–432–77–19.63; D. Ellinor 21–1–299–57–14.95; S. D. R. Beynon 21–8–184–27*–14.15;
A. M. Billington 23–0–270–56–11.73.

Bowling—R. V. Henderson 285.2–68–804–51–15.76; P. Buckley 243–68–623–39–15.97; D.
Ellinor 70–20–182–11–16.54; N. C. Pickard 183–40–546–27–20.22; S. J. Hall
245–71–712–28–25.42.

PLYMOUTH COLLEGE

Played 13: Won 6, Lost 3, Drawn 4. Abandoned 7

Master i/c: T. J. Stevens

Batting—*J. Chislett 12–3–298–67–33.11; S. Crawford 13–1–318–59–26.50; N. Trobridge 12–1–264–77–24.00; C. Stevens 13–0–309–58–23.76; C. Chipman 7–1–128–78–21.33; C. Norsworthy 13–0–233–59–17.92.

Bowling—S. Woodward 70–16–222–15–14.80; A. Dowling 122–35–356–23–15.47; S. Crawford 80–17–264–15–17.60; A. Luffman 126–18–411–19–21.63.

QUEEN ELIZABETH GRAMMAR SCHOOL, WAKEFIELD

Played 12: Won 3, Lost 1, Drawn 8. Abandoned 3

Master i/c: C. W. M. Furniss

Batting—J. Swain 10–2–464–103*–58.00; S. P. Jubb 10–3–285–57–40.71; S. S. K. Das 9–2–176–47–25.14; A. M. Taylor 8–1–116–34–16.57; A. K. Das 11–1–100–61–10.00.

Bowling—*P. Heseltine 157–33–388–29–13.37; S. Wood 144–46–345–24–14.37; S. Atkinson 56–9–213–10–21.30.

QUEEN'S COLLEGE, TAUNTON

Played 13: Won 1, Lost 3, Drawn 9. Abandoned 6

Master i/c: J. W. Davies

Batting—A. Free 13–0–284–62–21.84; N. Brown 13–0–271–55–20.84; M. Jones 13–1–188–37–15.56; J. Wilson 13–3–160–42*–16.00; A. Tanner 13–0–152–32–11.69.

Bowling—G. Hawkins 116.2–35–282–20–14.10; A. Essien 138–29–329–19–17.31; R. Veillard 128–18–466–22–21.18; A. Tanner 117–37–328–15–21.86.

RADLEY COLLEGE

Played 15: Won 4, Lost 2, Drawn 9. Abandoned 1

Master i/c: C. H. Hirst　　　　　　　　　　　Cricket professional: A. G. Robinson

Batting—R. C. H. Reed 12–2–496–111–49.60; E. J. B. Popplewell 14–1–571–97–43.92; J. R. L. Ballantyne 12–3–221–49–24.55; J. A. G. Fawcett 13–0–291–65–22.38; R. G. Butler 13–1–238–48–19.83; B. D. Robertson 9–2–118–34–16.85; *C. C. H. Phillips 10–2–122–22*–15.25.

Bowling—R. B. Lagden 213.4–64–453–42–10.78; R. G. Butler 79–22–232–16–14.50; S. N. A. Leefe 213.1–49–587–35–16.77; J. A. G. Fawcett 167.4–65–385–21–18.33.

RATCLIFFE COLLEGE

Played 13: Won 4, Lost 4, Drawn 5. Abandoned 7

Master i/c: C. W. Swan

Batting—C. R. Merriman 9–1–293–121*–36.62; P. W. Tarimo 9–1–193–62–24.12; *J. A. Foulds 12–0–185–52–15.41; D. M. Prior 11–2–111–39*–12.33.

Bowling—P. W. Tarimo 100–39–196–21–9.33; A. H. Relton 78–27–170–15–11.33; D. M. Prior 93–31–233–18–12.94; D. H. Mestecky 94–39–230–17–13.52; J. D. Sill 55–17–150–10–15.00.

READING SCHOOL

Played 14: Won 3, Lost 1, Drawn 9, Tied 1. Abandoned 2

Master i/c: R. G. Owen   Cricket professional: A. Dindar

Batting—D. G. Purslow 14–0–615–121–43.92; *E. P. O'Leary 13–0–474–87–36.46; A. D. Beckett 13–3–272–53–27.20; R. I. West 13–4–194–46–21.55; M. W. Allen 13–0–263–50–20.23; P. C. Nicholls 12–1–204–44–18.54; K. W. Seymour 13–1–219–41–18.25.

Bowling—N. Heppel 68–15–169–13–13.00; P. C. Nicholls 117–30–371–26–14.26; A. D. Beckett 117–22–398–23–17.30; E. P. O'Leary 158–33–512–22–23.27; A. N. S. Hampton 84–21–300–10–30.00.

REED'S SCHOOL

Played 11: Won 3, Lost 3, Drawn 5. Abandoned 4

Master i/c: G. R. Martin

Batting—A. P. Shiells 11–2–343–85*–38.11; D. Jaksic 7–2–168–37*–33.60; A. H. Bailey 11–2–300–70–33.33; *A. M. J. Glass 10–0–320–90–32.00; J. M. A. Price 9–1–151–50–18.87; W. M. Pendered 9–0–147–44–16.33.

Bowling—R. Saddleton 165.5–48–449–30–14.96; A. P. Shiells 95.1–25–305–19–16.05; L. M. T. Peart 153–59–335–18–18.61; C. R. Hartley 94–17–347–11–31.54.

REIGATE GRAMMAR SCHOOL

Played 15: Won 4, Lost 4, Drawn 7. Abandoned 6

Master i/c: D. C. R. Jones   Cricket professional: H. Newton

Batting—D. G. C. Downman 15–2–399–125*–30.69; *D. R. Cawthrow 13–0–362–100–27.84; P. A. Rowlinson 13–7–160–33–26.66; S. A. Bedell 12–2–251–73*–25.10; J. D. Morgan 9–1–137–38–17.12; D. McG. Gilbertson 9–0–120–29–13.33.

Bowling—M. J. Chenery 106.1–28–257–20–12.85; M. Peckham 72–20–193–15–12.86; A. C. Bradley 167.3–52–458–28–16.35; D. G. C. Downman 119.3–25–326–18–18.11.

REPTON SCHOOL

Played 16: Won 9, Lost 2, Drawn 5. Abandoned 6

Master i/c: J. F. M. Walker   Cricket professional: M. Kettle

Batting—*S. W. Lovell 15–6–567–102*–63.00; C. Benn 13–2–400–94*–36.36; A. S. J. Pass 16–3–401–100*–30.84; M. W. Robinson 10–3–139–34–19.85; S. E. J. Whitehouse 15–0–292–68–19.46; J. C. Gibbon 14–1–235–48–18.07.

Bowling—G. P. J. Emmerson 186.2–49–495–37–13.37; M. S. H. Smith 184.2–48–465–34–13.67; S. M. R. R. de Silva 209–45–670–35–19.14; N. F. Slater 188–52–497–22–22.59.

ROSSALL SCHOOL

Played 7: Won 3, Lost 2, Drawn 2. Abandoned 6

Master i/c: R. J. Clapp

Batting—N. V. Salvi 7–2–257–100*–51.40; *R. I. Kanhai 7–4–143–77*–47.66; T. D. Garner 7–1–126–32*–21.00.

Bowling—R. I. Kanhai 84.4–28–182–14–13.00; K. C. Stiles 129.2–36–225–16–14.06; C. J. D. Lees 68–20–179–10–17.90.

ROYAL GRAMMAR SCHOOL, GUILDFORD
Played 11: Won 8, Lost 1, Drawn 2. Abandoned 1

Master i/c: M. D. Chisholm

Batting—M. Newman 11–2–231–55*–25.66; R. Taylor 11–3–166–99–20.75; H. Millar 11–1–184–35–18.40; C. Livingston 10–1–140–28–15.55; N. Bowman 8–0–105–31–13.12.

Bowling—*J. Perrin 126.1–43–267–40–6.67; J. Bigg 103–44–210–26–8.07; W. Duckworth 112.1–48–184–19–9.68.

ROYAL GRAMMAR SCHOOL, NEWCASTLE
Played 15: Won 7, Lost 5, Drawn 3. Abandoned 5

Master i/c: D. W. Smith   Cricket professional: J. N. Graham

Batting—L. D. Anderson 13–2–354–109*–32.18; M. Bailey 12–3–240–44*–26.66; *S. D. Pyle 13–2–283–57*–25.72; M. A. Reed 12–1–254–72*–23.09; S. J. Sill 7–1–105–44–17.50; I. D. Lumley 12–0–158–50–13.16; G. R. G. Terrett 10–0–100–34–10.00; P. W. Morton 12–0–109–34–9.08.

Bowling—M. Bailey 151.1–54–376–26–14.46; R. S. Wise 101.2–18–245–15–16.33; P. W. Morton 130–44–312–18–17.33; M. L. Elliott 94–37–254–14–18.14; I. D. Lumley 96.3–29–275–10–27.50.

ROYAL GRAMMAR SCHOOL, WORCESTER
Played 21: Won 13, Lost 2, Drawn 6. Abandoned 4

Master i/c: B. M. Rees

Batting—P. Bent 20–4–926–121–57.87; *S. D. Cairney 20–6–563–73*–40.21; J. S. Phillips 17–1–431–77–26.93; D. C. Richmond 18–2–342–122–21.37; M. Pearce 9–2–144–63–20.57; J. D. Powell 10–3–127–42–18.14; N. A. D. Austin 14–4–140–43–14.00; C. A. Carter 11–3–107–56*–13.37.

Bowling—I. G. Jinks 144.3–34–406–31–13.09; D. C. Richmond 45.1–15–136–10–13.60; A. R. Hill 254.1–70–654–45–14.53; P. Bent 169–47–389–24–16.20; J. S. Phillips 193–81–419–22–19.04; J. B. Phillips 182.1–40–569–25–22.76.

RUGBY SCHOOL
Played 15: Won 4, Lost 6, Drawn 5. Abandoned 1

Master i/c: K. Siviter   Cricket professional: W. J. Stewart

Batting—D. P. W. Umbers 16–2–565–181*–40.35; J. R. B. Stoddart 16–1–363–69–24.20; D. J. Cleverly 16–0–341–64–21.31; A. C. M. Brown 9–2–105–36*–15.00; A. J. Stewart 16–2–192–45–13.71; *P. J. Leaver 16–0–189–31–11.81; J. G. A. Squire 14–0–160–35–11.42.

Bowling—N. C. W. Fenton 165–39–342–32–10.68; D. J. Cleverly 213.1–59–581–42–13.83; R. J. Leaver 100–24–322–19–16.94.

RYDAL SCHOOL

Played 9: Won 5, Lost 1, Drawn 3. Abandoned 4

Master i/c: M. H. Stevenson   Cricket professional: R. W. C. Pitman

Batting—C. Robinson 8–3–179–62*–35.80; J. T. Owen 8–1–120–39*–17.14.

Bowling—R. Williams 127–31–290–28–10–35; J. M. Sherrington 108–28–335–25–13.40.

ST ALBANS SCHOOL

Played 16: Won 5, Lost 4, Drawn 7

Master i/c: R. J. K. Hughes

Batting—*W. Dean 15–2–376–103–28.92; P. Williams 15–0–380–77–25.33; M. Lynes 16–0–399–88–24.93; N. Roper 15–0–278–47–18.53; A. McCree 13–1–177–41–14.75.

Bowling—W. Dean 250–60–679–44–15.43; J. Tillbrook 85–21–212–11–19.27; K. Levell 128–24–447–22–20.31; H. Ross 85–13–285–14–20.35.

ST DUNSTAN'S COLLEGE

Played 11: Won 5, Lost 3, Drawn 3. Abandoned 2

Master i/c: C. Matten

Batting—S. J. Cross 12–1–359–91*–32.63; P. M. Slade 12–0–379–67–31.58; D. C. Edwards 12–0–261–43–21.75; A. W. Rouse 12–0–229–37–19.08; A. R. Colley 11–1–167–51–16.70.

Bowling—S. J. Cross 140–44–390–31–12.58; W. G. Beavington 93–25–233–13–17.92; G. Pointer 149–52–322–12–26.83; K. Norman 104–26–345–11–31.36.

ST EDWARD'S SCHOOL, OXFORD

Played 14: Won 2, Lost 4, Drawn 8. Abandoned 1

Master i/c: P. G. Badger   Cricket professional: B. R. Edrich

Batting—D. A. Soper 14–2–581–100*–48.41; D. A. Cane 14–0–358–96–25.57; A. E. G. Lewis 13–1–192–34–16.00; N. R. E. Telfer 14–1–100–38–7.69.

Bowling—R. N. C. Franklin 236.3–54–679–47–14.44; D. A. Soper 158.5–33–437–22–19.86; T. J. C. Rayne 91–16–294–10–29.40; R. W. Sadler 129.4–27–418–11–38.00.

ST GEORGE'S, WEYBRIDGE

Played 17: Won 6, Lost 1, Drawn 10. Abandoned 1

Master i/c: B. V. O'Gorman

Batting—T. J. O'Gorman 17–5–799–111*–66.58; R. Garland 17–1–522–63–32.62; J. W. P. Jones 17–0–522–95–30.70; A. J. Woodhead 9–2–175–37–25.00; D. A. Creber 11–2–190–49–21.11; A. B. High 10–3–135–39*–19.28; A. P. Jansen 15–2–238–67–18.30; P. E. Jansen 10–1–127–40–14.11.

Bowling—A. J. Woodhead 230.2–101–383–37–10.35; A. P. Jansen 140.4–43–349–27–12.92; *P. J. Davis 185.5–65–462–29–15.93; P. J. Segal 141–58–315–14–22.50; T. J. O'Gorman 120.1–31–404–18–22.44.

ST JOHN'S SCHOOL, LEATHERHEAD

Played 14: Won 3, Lost 0, Drawn 11

Master i/c: A. B. Gale   Cricket professional: E. Sheppard

Batting—P. J. Warren 11–1–325–58–32.50; P. M. Richardson 14–4–306–69*–30.60; P. J. Tiley 14–2–314–90*–26.16; *J. M. Downing 14–1–277–75–21.30; G. C. Blows 14–0–244–70–17.42; T. G. Mawdsley 10–1–113–32–12.55.

Bowling—D. B. Millard 126–45–303–26–11.65; J. M. Downing 178.3–44–521–18–28.94; K. C. Bance 119.4–24–440–14–31.42; T. G. Mawdsley 130–33–413–12–34.41.

ST LAWRENCE COLLEGE

Played 14: Won 3, Lost 7, Drawn 4. Abandoned 2

Master i/c: N. O. S. Jones

Batting—*P. R. Hobcraft 14–2–373–71–31.08; T. A. Adebayo 8–3–118–35*–23.60; N. A. Crush 13–1–281–112–23.41; S. W. Cook 14–1–288–41–22.15; S. El Fadil 12–0–187–59–15.58; G. G. Philpott 11–4–104–30*–14.85; J. L. Binfield 10–1–102–30–11.33.

Bowling—G. G. Philpott 191.5–45–607–39–15.56; P. R. Hobcraft 153.2–23–473–23–20.56; J. M. G. Barber 197.4–51–590–26–22.69.

ST PAUL'S SCHOOL

Played 11: Won 1, Lost 5, Drawn 5. Abandoned 6

Master i/c: G. Hughes   Cricket professional: E. W. Whitfield

Batting—*N. H. D. Macklin 11–0–363–81–33.00; M. M. Camilleri 5–0–126–51–25.20; O. F. Paish 11–0–223–59–20.27; T. J. K. Evans 11–0–172–60–15.63; C. J. Manson 10–2–104–22–13.00; C. A. S. Malir 11–2–101–36–11.22.

Bowling—J. M. Webber 118.4–35–337–20–16.85; P. A. McGuinness 94–21–251–10–25.10; C. A. S. Malir 90.5–17–329–11–29.90.

ST PETER'S SCHOOL, YORK

Played 12: Won 7, Lost 0, Drawn 5. Abandoned 4

Master i/c: D. Kirby   Cricket professional: K. Mohan

Batting—J. P. Atkinson 10–6–204–55*–51.00; J. L. Barrett 5–1–171–101*–42.75; S. P. A. Burdass 11–3–311–71*–38.87; A. Forman 8–4–148–44–37.00; *S. R. Gorman 13–2–349–64–31.72; A. J. Stubbs 13–2–275–59–25.00; G. Y. Taylor 8–2–103–27–17.16.

Bowling—A. Forman 193–63–426–38–11.21; S. R. Gorman 143–44–409–34–12.02; G. Y. Taylor 91–20–320–14–22.85; D. W. Thomas 117.3–30–324–11–29.45.

SEDBERGH SCHOOL

Played 11: Won 5, Lost 0, Drawn 6. Abandoned 4

Master i/c: M. J. Morris

Batting—M. R. de W. Rogers 9–3–241–65*–40.16; W. D. C. Carling 8–1–227–98–32.42; J. P. Cheetham 9–0–280–76–31.11; J. Roberts 11–1–292–72–29.20; J. B. Coulthard 11–1–260–100*–26.00; M. T. Alban 10–0–234–65–23.40.

Bowling—*M. G. Burgess 146–64–226–37–6.10; S. R. Mewburn 96–37–201–16–12.56; J. P. Cheetham 131.4–34–319–21–15.19.

SEVENOAKS SCHOOL

Played 13: Won 3, Lost 5, Drawn 4. Tied 1. Abandoned 2

Master i/c: I. J. B. Walker

Batting—J. D. Mitchell 9–2–436–87*–62.28; *J. Hodder-Williams 11–1–216–55–21.60; N. B. Turk 8–1–134–42–19.14; R. P. Roberts 9–1–139–45–17.37; N. J. Polkinhorne 12–0–187–62–15.58.

Bowling—A. J. Preston 59.1–13–185–15–12.33; A. J. Bell 93–23–307–17–18.05; R. P. Roberts 137.5–28–441–24–18.37; H. Bhatti 89–22–226–12–18.83.

SHERBORNE SCHOOL

Played 15: Won 7, Lost 1, Drawn 7

Master i/c: D. F. Gibbs   Cricket professional: C. Stone

Batting—D. W. Thorne 13–3–431–100*–43.10; M. B. Bryant 13–2–423–91*–38.45; *R. A. Rydon 14–3–320–65–29.09; P. S. A. Cockerham 14–2–343–55*–28.58; R. A. B. Spink 11–1–243–37–24.30; S. W. S. Millar 9–4–109–25–21.80; R. A. Mathews 11–5–103–26*–17.16; R. W. Lloyd 9–0–127–45–14.11.

Bowling—I. P. M. Sharpe 75.5–14–201–18–11.16; J. D. Quinlan 206.5–66–421–36–11.69; J. R. P. Gilshenan 136.4–29–346–20–17.30; R. A. Rydon 155–46–401–23–17.43.

SHREWSBURY SCHOOL

Played 19: Won 13, Lost 0, Drawn 6. Abandoned 4

Master i/c: C. M. B. Williams   Cricket professional: P. H. Bromley

Batting—A. D. Hobson 16–3–721–95–55.46; I. J. F. Hutchinson 15–3–659–160*–54.91; I. M. Garrard 6–3–130–62*–43.33; D. J. Pollock 17–4–559–65*–43.00; J. O. Cadwallader 11–4–242–93*–34.57; *R. J. P. Burton 12–3–298–61*–33.11.

Bowling—E. L. Home 60–15–192–14–9.42; J. M. Eaton 38.5–6–105–10–10.50; R. P. Holt 294–92–655–51–12.84; A. D. Hobson 56.4–11–218–13–16.76; J. E. Reakes-Williams 174.2–44–475–24–19.79; R. J. P. Burton 208.5–64–496–24–20.66; R. L. Harvey 143–22–406–17–23.88.

SIMON LANGTON GRAMMAR SCHOOL

Played 12: Won 6, Lost 2, Drawn 4. Abandoned 9

Master i/c: I. M. Gillespie

Batting—S. C. Goldsmith 11–1–452–102–45.20; *R. I. James 11–1–253–49–25.30; G. Wiskar 12–1–277–43–25.18; M. Lewns 11–0–211–80–19.18; I. M. Scoones 7–1–106–28–17.66.

Bowling—R. I. James 80–26–198–17–11.64; S. Sloman 97.3–20–277–21–13.19; G. Sullivan 87.3–15–323–18–17.94; S. C. Goldsmith 126–32–347–19–18.26; A. Hawkes 90–28–244–11–22.18.

SIR ROGER MANWOOD'S SCHOOL

Played 12: Won 2, Lost 5, Drawn 4. Tied 1

Master i/c: P. W. Kullman

Batting—G. W. Laslett 12–0–245–49–20.41; V. C. Marsh 12–2–166–59*–16.60; *S. F. L. Danilewicz 11–1–105–22–10.50; C. R. E. Clarke 11–1–101–33–10.10; M. I. A. Howell 12–0–121–46–10.08.

Bowling—G. W. Laslett 80.2–20–219–21–10.42; M. I. A. Howell 167.3–42–429–29–14.79; V. C. Marsh 114–29–245–13–18.84.

STAMFORD SCHOOL, LINCOLNSHIRE

Played 13: Won 4, Lost 3, Drawn 6. Abandoned 6

Master i/c: H. K. Bell

Batting—N. J. Tyers 11–1–411–96–41.10; G. M. Canham 12–0–360–116–30.00; R. P. Alston 12–1–323–60–29.36; M. G. Cope 11–1–226–62–22.60; R. C. Hibbitt 11–2–107–26–11.88.

Bowling—P. N. Bell 52–9–195–15–13.00; R. P. Alston 123.3–30–353–19–18.57; N. J. Tyers 123.3–22–419–17–24.64; M. A. Welch 149–41–380–14–27.14.

STOCKPORT GRAMMAR SCHOOL

Played 15: Won 4, Lost 5, Drawn 6. Abandoned 4

Master i/c: L. Kynaston

Batting—*T. P. R. Reeman 16–2–355–66–25.35; N. Samarji 11–2–180–53*–20.00; J. A. Bailey 8–1–128–57–18.28; T. A. Ambler 19–7–216–60*–18.00; T. Firth 11–2–137–30–15.22; I. Hall 16–1–193–39–12.86; L. T. Tittle 12–1–139–30*–12.63.

Bowling—T. P. R. Reeman 98–22–268–18–14.88; T. Firth 200–60–537–33–16.27; R. Samarji 144–49–352–20–17.60; E. F. Aspinall 163–26–438–17–25.76.

STOWE SCHOOL

Played 18: Won 3, Lost 9, Drawn 6. Abandoned 3

Master i/c: L. E. Weston   Cricket professional: I. L. Pont

Batting—*D. A. Steward 18–1–454–72–26.70; J. H. M. Claydon 6–0–116–46–19.33; J. G. Stocks 10–1–170–41–18.88; D. M. W. Thomas 10–0–188–46–18.80; C. J. Rotheroe 8–1–120–34–17.14; C. M. Ruddock 17–1–223–47–13.93; C. J. Stopford 17–0–208–41–12.23; M. S. Riley 13–0–113–23–8.69.

Bowling—D. M. W. Thomas 59.2–16–161–12–13.41; P. A. Campbell 139–33–359–20–17.95; C. Whitmore 194–46–524–28–18.71; C. M. Ruddock 194–45–533–27–19.74; J. G. Stocks 112–23–336–16–21.00; D. A. Steward 118–20–364–14–26.00.

STRATHALLAN SCHOOL

Played 11: Won 4, Lost 1, Drawn 6. Abandoned 3

Master i/c: R. J. W. Proctor

Batting—*M. J. de G. Allingham 10–4–551–108*–91.83; N. H. McKee 11–5–336–118*–56.00; G. S. B. Corbett 11–2–411–78*–45.66; R. W. N. Kilpatrick 11–1–421–114*–42.10; G. E. McClung 8–3–160–54*–32.00.

Bowling—N. H. McKee 69–16–169–13–13.00; M. J. De G. Allingham 180.5–72–366–28–13.07; R. W. N. Kilpatrick 93–33–208–14–14.85.

SUTTON VALENCE SCHOOL

Played 14: Won 1, Lost 9, Drawn 4. Abandoned 5

Master i/c: G. G. Able

Batting—B. W. Gedney 13–4–197–30–21.88; *R. D. Coate 14–0–286–77–20.42; J. P. Sunnucks 14–0–202–34–14.42; R. Morton 14–0–186–49–13.28; R. J. H. Thomas 14–0–179–40–12.78; D. G. Curtis 14–0–162–35–11.57.

Bowling—R. D. Coate 177.3–55–390–36–10.83; J. P. Sunnucks 123.5–28–336–20–16.80; B. H. Saint 149–36–363–20–18.15; R. J. H. Thomas 117.4–15–392–20–19.60.

TAUNTON SCHOOL

Played 12: Won 3, Lost 3, Drawn 6. Abandoned 2

Master i/c: R. P. Smith

Batting—N. J. Waters 12–1–451–105*–41.00; *A. N. Challacombe 12–0–479–139–39.91; N. J. Pringle 12–1–395–101*–35.90; R. J. Bartlett 12–3–247–63*–27.44; M. E. Masters 10–2–163–34–20.37; J. C. Pike 10–2–129–24–16.12.

Bowling—J. C. Pike 162–51–371–28–13.25; P. H. Gibb 88–24–208–13–16.00.

TIFFIN SCHOOL

Played 18: Won 6, Lost 7, Drawn 5. Abandoned 2

Master i/c: M. J. Williams

Batting—M. J. Campbell 16–1–389–89–25.93; *N. A. Legg 15–0–345–58–23.00; A. M. Morley-Brown 16–0–361–93–22.56; D. R. Hickman 15–2–228–63–17.53; D. F. Godfrey 15–0–204–36–13.60; G. D. Coxhead 14–4–125–41–12.50.

Bowling:—M. R. Coote 214.2–67–580–41–14.14; W. Shermer 226.3–58–687–40–17.17; N. M. Williams 109.2–18–379–10–37.90.

TONBRIDGE SCHOOL

Played 16: Won 6, Lost 3, Drawn 7. Abandoned 1

Master i/c: D. R. Walsh   Cricket professional: H. J. Mutton

Batting—C. M. Millerd 6–3–178–100*–59.33; J. N. C. Budden 15–2–410–78–31.53; B. P. Ward 11–2–278–82–30.88; M. A. Hardcastle 10–5–153–36–30.60; A. M. Spurling 12–2–213–53–21.30; J. B. Coburn 8–1–140–40–20.00; E. M. Wesson 14–2–217–61–18.08; R. Owen-Browne 11–1–178–43–17.80.

Bowling—*A. D. H. Grimes 228–81–481–39–12.33; A. M. Spurling 142–57–312–25–12.48; R. Owen-Browne 182–66–325–21–15.47; M. A. Hardcastle 130–34–330–12–27.50; R. J. Butler 92–30–295–10–29.50.

TRINITY SCHOOL

Played 25: Won 8, Lost 4, Drawn 13. Abandoned 2

Master i/c: B. Widger

Batting—*N. W. F. Redwood 24–4–901–91–45.05; D. H. Cooper 24–5–516–66–27.15; J. A. J. Warburton 19–6–342–56*–26.30; P. J. Smith 23–1–473–112*–21.50; P. D. Bone 14–7–140–35*–20.00; M. P. Cuin 17–1–319–73–19.93; A. P. Williams 13–4–136–30–15.11; A. J. Holder 15–1–209–33–14.92; C. J. Holder 13–6–101–25*–14.42.

Bowling—B. S. Lees 196.3–34–706–46–15.34; C. J. Holder 156–55–361–23–15.69; P. D. Bone 278.2–70–724–40–18.10; M. J. Steele 193.5–61–454–23–19.73; N. W. F. Redwood–227.1–54–668–28–23.85.

TRURO SCHOOL

Played 14: Won 6, Lost 4, Drawn 4. Abandoned 3

Master i/c: A. J. D. Aldwinckle

Batting—T. W. R. Scott 13–1–326–79*–27.16; *D. C. Aldwinckle 14–2–302–51–25.16; A. H. Jones 12–0–298–80–24.83; M. J. Blomfield 12–0–140–39–11.66.

Bowling—T. J. Horne 38–11–84–10–8.40; D. C. Aldwinckle 156–49–333–34–9.79; A. C. Bailey 122–31–256–17–15.05; R. J. Heath 58–1–212–12–17.66.

UPPINGHAM SCHOOL

Played 11: Won 4, Lost 3, Drawn 4. Abandoned 3

Master i/c: G. A. Wheatley   Cricket professional: M. R. Hallam

Batting—*J. S. Williams 12–2–453–88*–45.30; D. J. Kennedy 12–2–323–88*–32.30; A. G. Lewin 11–1–164–40–16.40; R. M. Sunderland 12–0–150–52–12.50.

Bowling—J. S. Williams 132–48–304–19–16.00; C. R. J. Timm 149–33–419–24–17.45; M. A. F. Riddington 185–66–480–25–19.20; P. C. A. Turton 80–22–219–11–19.90; A. H. Riddington 87–33–216–10–21.60.

VICTORIA COLLEGE, JERSEY

Played 20: Won 7, Lost 2, Drawn 11. Abandoned 6

Master i/c: D. A. R. Ferguson

Batting—*W. Jenner 17–4–1,010–112–77.69; P. L. Lalor 16–6–527–129–52.70; D. A. Oliver 16–4–474–100–39.50; C. M. Graham 11–2–286–57–31.77; A. J. Sugden 15–1–416–83–29.71; E. B. Gothard 7–1–159–55–26.50; J. W. Kellett 7–3–100–41–25.00; R. G. W. Breton 8–1–135–41–19.28.

Bowling—D. V. Carnegie 98–17–376–21–17.90; D. A. Oliver 77–15–235–13–18.07; T. V. R. Hanson 105–33–328–18–18.22; J. M. W. Giles 230–66–659–35–18.82; A. D. Brown 118–21–414–19–21.78; C. M. Graham 97–23–296–11–26.90.

WARWICK SCHOOL

Played 13: Won 3, Lost 0, Drawn 10. Abandoned 2

Master i/c: I. B. Moffatt   Cricket professional: N. Horner

Batting—J. T. R. Pollard 4–1–141–105*–47.00; *N. C. B. Robinson 13–1–469–100–39.08; N. Haynes 10–0–303–68–30.30; G. M. Robinson 10–3–147–73–21.00; D. W. Hancock 13–2–227–38–20.63; A. Woodcock 7–1–108–38–18.00; R. J. Dillon 11–1–172–41–17.20; N. M. K. Smith 13–0–191–72–14.69.

Bowling—S. J. Holdsworth 184–44–513–31–16.54; D. W. Hancock 131–32–375–20–18.75; N. C. B. Robinson 80–15–340–13–26.15; N. M. K. Smith 103–23–282–10–28.20.

WELLINGBOROUGH SCHOOL

Played 15: Won 2, Lost 3, Drawn 10. Abandoned 6

Master i/c: C. J. Ford   Cricket professional: J. C. J. Dye

Batting—P. Wilson 12–6–171–67–28.50; R. Gane 14–0–327–92–23.35; *R. Woodhall 15–2–210–47–16.15; A. Mabbutt 15–0–202–42–13.46; R. Harston 12–1–148–64*–13.45; M. Griffiths 15–3–152–38*–12.66; I. Tinson 15–0–183–43–12.20; C. Smith 12–3–103–25*–11.44.

Bowling—R. Harston 94–21–258–23–11.21; M. Griffiths 132–35–372–27–13.77; A. Cross 68–7–204–10–20.40; C. Smith 111–27–307–10–30.70; R. Woodhall 116–28–405–12–33.75.

WELLINGTON COLLEGE, BERKS

Played 14: Won 5, Lost 4, Drawn 5. Abandoned 3

Master i/c: D. J. Mordaunt   Cricket professional: P. J. Lewington

Batting—G. D. Reynolds 10–3–387–71–55.28; B. A. M. Wessely 16–3–431–113–33.15; *G. R. L. Spackman 15–0–380–113–25.33; D. S. C. Mallinson 16–2–279–85–19.92; J. T. E. Illingworth 15–2–242–81–18.61; G. I. G. Sharp 15–1–219–57–15.64; T. M. R. Lord 13–0–168–45–12.92.

Bowling—A. J. L. Hunter 191–51–453–29–15.62; B. A. M. Wessely 242.1–71–620–38–16.31; C. E. D'Oyly 138–47–361–19–19.00; T. M. R. Lord 119–31–292–13–22.46.

WELLINGTON SCHOOL, SOMERSET

Played 6: Won 1, Lost 5, Drawn 0. Abandoned 5

Master i/c: I. F. Loudon

Batting—No qualifiers.

Bowling—R. J. Milton 48–20–79–12–6.58; N. C. Hall-Palmer 41.5–8–104–10–10.40; N. D. Macdonald 52–13–133–10–13.30; B. W. Loudon 39.1–6–147–11–13.36.

WESTMINSTER SCHOOL

Played 11: Won 0, Lost 8, Drawn 3. Abandoned 2

Master i/c: J. A. Cogan   Cricket professional: R. Gilson

Batting—R. J. Levy 11–1–341–104*–34.10; W. Cash 11–0–337–84–30.63; O. C. Pennant-Jones 10–1–113–39–12.55; C. J. A. Morrell 11–0–122–53–11.09.

Bowling—*T. E. Lunn 145–40–412–24–17.16; N. Coleman 70.2–15–227–12–18.91; M. D. F. Pennington 74.2–14–321–14–22.92; C. J. A. Morrell 108–14–422–17–24.82.

WHITGIFT SCHOOL

Played 15: Won 4, Lost 5, Drawn 6. Abandoned 3

Master i/c: P. C. Fladgate   Cricket professional: A. Long

Batting—R. B. Weller 13–1–339–75–28.25; R. I. Taylor 14–2–321–60*–26.75; *P. W. J. Ellingham 13–2–294–50*–26.72; J. M. Rose 15–0–359–72–23.93; A. D. H. Marshall 14–2–257–49*–21.41; R. G. R. Heber 11–3–139–37*–17.37.

Bowling—R. P. James 145.5–46–359–21–17.09; S. Talbot 186.3–48–471–26–18.11; D. N. Drinkwater 181–40–637–22–28.95; S. M. Conn 109–23–349–11–31.72; R. B. Weller 135.1–38–396–10–39.60.

WILLIAM HULME'S GRAMMAR SCHOOL
Played 20: Won 6, Lost 8, Drawn 6. Abandoned 1

Master i/c: I. J. Shaw

Batting—A. G. Cleary 20–1–381–85–20.05; J. D. Braddock 19–0–330–57–17.36; S. M. Kennedy 16–8–134–30–16.75; M. L. Jackson 12–1–162–32–14.72; P. T. Fearnley 20–1–275–77–14.47; *J. D . Sealy 20–0–271–72–13.55.

Bowling—I. D. Thorpe 180–45–537–32–16.78; S. G. McLoughlin 180–44–494–27–18.29; N. R. Fairfax 201–39–494–33–14.96; M. I. Cross 134–35–460–17–27.05.

WINCHESTER COLLEGE
Played 18: Won 9, Lost 2, Drawn 7. Abandoned 1

Master i/c: J. F. X. Miller   Cricket professional: V. Broderick

Batting—I. L. M. Henry 19–1–592–95–32.88; C. N. N. Smith 18–1–551–96–32.41; *W. E. J. Holland 18–2–489–100*–30.56; C. E. R. M. Hall 17–3–366–46–26.14; T. G. M. Adshead 16–4–222–51*–18.50; R. B. M. Heyworth 19–1–276–45–15.33; J. F. Thornycroft 13–4–117–25*–13.00.

Bowling—J. D. Dean 332.3–91–843–58–14.53; I. L. M. Henry 127.3–32–337–16–21.06; C. E. R. M. Hall 175.2–43–546–23–23.73; C. H. M. Ridley 112.3–29–336–14–24.00; S. J. H. Whitehead 237.4–45–641–26–24.65.

WOODBRIDGE SCHOOL
Played 18: Won 10, Lost 3, Drawn 5

Master i/c: J. Bidwell   Cricket professional: J. Pugh

Batting—S. Bacon 17–2–420–100*–28.00; J. Speedman 11–4–167–45–23.85; E. Griffiths 19–0–360–70–18.94; S. Beresford 16–1–277–56–18.46; M. Fox 12–3–164–39–18.22; R. Toye 10–0–166–29–16.66; *D. Kemsley 18–4–231–54–16.50.

Bowling—M. Whitehead 85.5–23–269–29–9.27; J. Speedman 112–43–230–24–9.58; R. Jack 165–42–428–29–14.75; S. Reeve 158.1–47–398–26–15.30.

WOODHOUSE GROVE SCHOOL
Played 10: Won 8, Lost 0, Drawn 2. Abandoned 4

Master i/c: J. F. Clay   Cricket professional: P. J. Kippax

Batting—*S. A. J. Kippax 7–2–259–96–51.80; B. S. Percy 10–2–356–65*–44.50; A. G. Percy 9–1–265–67–33.12; N. A. Ledgard 8–1–177–62–25.28; I. W. Stott 10–0–213–61–21.30.

Bowling—A. G. Percy 38.5–10–74–15–4.93; S. A. J. Kippax 65–21–169–20–8.45; B. S. Percy 122–38–312–24–13.00; R. L. Halstead 71.3–20–161–10–16.10.

WREKIN COLLEGE
Played 16: Won 3, Lost 9, Drawn 4. Abandoned 6

Master i/c: E. C. Gower

Batting—C. S. Joyner 16–0–307–96–19.18; *R. P. Mitchell 17–0–301–41–17.70; A. W. Hartley 16–0–275–56–17.18; O. C. Davies 16–0–222–52–13.87; P. R. Richardson 16–1–208–43–13.86.

Bowling—R. P. Mitchell 194–56–426–28–15.21; O. C. Davies 115–35–269–16–16.81; P. R. Richardson 179–40–481–28–17.17; A. W. Hartley 136–25–381–21–18.14.

WYCLIFFE COLLEGE

Played 10: Won 2, Lost 3, Drawn 5. Abandoned 7

Master i/c: H. W. Scott

Batting—P. J. Rowley 9–1–185–47*–23.12; *S. J. Shorthose 8–2–135–38–22.50; J. R. Bodington 9–1–158–116–19.75.

Bowling—S. L. Thomas 64.3–11–195–18–10.83; R. B. Hair 97–38–170–13–13.07; R. J. Boulton 72–22–164–11–14.90; J. R. Bodington 82.3–17–170–11–15.45; S. J. Shorthose 57.5–14–161–10–16.10.

WYGGESTON & QUEEN ELIZABETH I SIXTH FORM COLLEGE

Played 9: Won 3, Lost 2, Drawn 3, Tied 1. Abandoned 6

Master i/c: G. G. Wells

Batting—*N. Patel 6–1–175–80–35.00; S. G. Holyland 8–1–136–47*–19.42.

Bowling—M. Wadhwana 61.5–23–105–17–6.17; A. Jones 64.1–28–91–11–8.27; D. A. Silver 45.5–12–94–10–9.40.

IRISH CRICKET IN 1983

By DEREK SCOTT

As has been customary in recent years, Ireland played seven matches in 1983, with a total of thirteen days' cricket spread over eleven weeks. There was only one victory, but it was the sweetest of all – over Scotland, who had beaten Ireland in 1982.

Worcestershire brought their best team for two one-day matches over a weekend in mid-June at Rathmines, Dublin. As a substitute bowler, the youngest of the Harrison brothers, Garfield, made his début in these matches. Four Harrison brothers have now played for Ireland, emulating the Quinns. Ireland lost easily in the first match, their 155 for nine (R. T. Wills 59) being nothing like enough, but the next day was different, S. C. Corlett and M. Halliday reducing Worcestershire to 56 for seven. A. E. Warner, however, arrived at No. 9 and made 97 not out in 80 minutes. I. J. Anderson (37) and Harrison (36) did their best for Ireland, but the match was lost by 42 runs.

Clontarf, Dublin was the venue for the NatWest Bank Trophy match against Sussex. Anderson's inability to play was a blow. Nevertheless, as has become usual in these matches, Ireland had a good phase. They put Sussex in and took four of their wickets for 96. Then Imran Khan, I. J. Gould and C. P. Phillipson all made 40s in a final Sussex score of 265 for seven. Again a difficult but vital catch was missed, Imran surviving a chance when he was 14. M. A. Masood became Ireland's first Man of the Match when he made 69 in 128 minutes on his last appearance in 1983, but Ireland slumped from 94 for two to 141 all out. Aer Lingus gave generous assistance to the match.

The one-day programme behind them, Ireland settled down to "proper" cricket and beat Scotland by five wickets in mid-July at Downpatrick, where youth was to the fore, featuring S. S. J. Warke (63), J. A. Prior (55) and Harrison (86), all in their early twenties. Indeed the latter, who batted for only 92 minutes, almost wrote himself into the record books in his first first-class match. Halliday, in his 50th match for Ireland, claimed four second-innings wickets but it was Corlett's four for 5 on the third morning which gave Ireland their quite simple target of 125 to win. It was J. D. Monteith's ninth win in his 29 matches as captain, both records which he has taken from A. J. O'Riordan.

The international season ended in August with an Allied Irish Banks tour. It began at Bristol with a three-day match against Gloucestershire, who fielded a mixture of their first and second teams. Over 1,000 runs were scored in an entertaining match. For Gloucestershire A. J. Wright and P. Bainbridge were century-makers, while the tireless Corlett took six wickets in the match and Monteith five. Ireland, with 254, were only 6 behind on the first innings with six batsmen doing well but only the reliable R. T. Wills (62) passing 50. Then, with 276 needed to win in 258 minutes plus twenty overs, all seemed lost at 209 for eight. But Monteith played his finest innings for Ireland, aided splendidly by Halliday, who indulged in a form of French cricket, and together they put on 59. Now only 8 were needed, but having made 91 in 103 minutes Monteith was out to a good catch and the match was lost by 7 runs.

Neath came next and a three-day match against Wales in which a draw followed the loss of the first day to rain. Wales made 190 after being put in, Monteith's seven for 67 including his 300th wicket for Ireland. He finished the season with 305, two short of J. C. Boucher's record. Ireland took 75 overs to make 208 for seven and this was too slow, taking into account the lost day. J. F. Short, in his 50th match, scored exactly 50 and Harrison hit 64 in 67 minutes. Wales then declared at 193 for four, whereupon Ireland played out time. G. A. Kirwan (Clontarf Cricket Club) made his début for Ireland in this match, aged 41. He is a medium-paced left-arm swing bowler and did well.

The final match of the tour was over two days, against MCC at the Bank of England ground at Roehampton. This was the first time Ireland had ever played their away match with MCC anywhere but at Lord's. A damp green wicket greeted them and they were short of seam bowling to exploit it. MCC made 220 for two (R. E. Hayward 100 not out, R. T. Hart 84 not out) and then bowled the Irish out for 49, A. J. Pollock, the Cambridge Blue, taking six for 18. The follow-on was inevitable and at 19 for four another disaster looked imminent. But Wills made 100 in 206 minutes and, with Harrison, Monteith and P. B. Jackson also making runs, MCC at least had to bat a second time.

The best feature of the season was the win over Scotland and the success of some of the younger batsmen. The bowling remained a major problem. New caps were awarded during the season to G. D. Harrison, D. Dennison, J. W. Kirkwood (already a hockey International) and G. A. Kirwan. Harrison proved a real find. This 22-year-old left-handed bat scored 322 runs in his first season (average 35.77), having come in as a substitute bowler. Wills averaged 29.50 for 295 runs. Monteith took most wickets (eighteen) and Corlett, as usual, had the best average, his sixteen wickets costing 22.43. Of the eight players of under 23 who played, only one, P. M. O'Reilly, could be described as a front-line bowler and he is contracted to Warwickshire.

Ulster Town regained the Guinness Cup by winning all their five matches. Since mid-1979 they have now played 21 matches without defeat. Wills, Warke and R. I. Johnston all made runs and only 21 wickets were lost. Corlett took 28 wickets (a season's record) at 11.14 each and R. Haire, a slow left-armer, took thirteen. The Guinness Cup format was changed for 1983: a draw is not now possible. For North Leinster against South Leinster Masood made 196 not out, the highest score ever in this competition.

Holland was the venue for the Under-19 International Tournament. The first two matches were lost and the remaining four won. Run-rate alone squeezed Ireland out of the final.

The Schools International against Wales at Pontardulais was won for the third successive year, though no fewer than 382 runs were required in the fourth innings. In the three-day match 1,267 runs were scored while only 29 wickets fell. The Under-19 Trophy went to North Leinster.

The National club tournament for the Schweppes Cup was won by Waringstown, the strongest club in Ireland. They beat North of Ireland

Cricket Club, last year's winners, in the final in Belfast. Waringstown also won the John Player Cup in their region while the Benson and Hedges League went to Downpatrick.

In the North West, Sion Mills (Cup) and Brigade (League) won the trophies. Wanderers dominated in Munster, winning both Shield and League. Church of Ireland won the Cup, all three competitions being sponsored by the Bank of Ireland. In Dublin Phoenix lost only one match during the season – to Pembroke in the Sportsgear/Parliament Cup semi-final. Pembroke went on to win the Cup. Phoenix won both the Belvedere Bond and Wiggins Teape League. For them M. A. Masood made 1,218 runs, breaking all records, while C. M. Kuggeleijn, a professional from New Zealand, scored 1,086 runs and took 53 wickets for Pembroke.

SCOTTISH CRICKET IN 1983

By WATSON BLAIR

Despite the imaginative decision by the Scottish Cricket Union to engage Desmond Haynes, the West Indian opening batsman, Scotland again failed in the zonal round of the Benson and Hedges Cup. After four seasons in the competition, their record shows fifteen defeats and one "no result". In 1983 rain interfered with every match during a hectic ten-day programme. Haynes's contribution to Scotland's aggregate of 331 runs in their three matches was 72, double the runs scored by the first native Scot, Willie Donald (Aberdeenshire). In bowling, Willie Morton caught the eye with six wickets for 87 runs and, like his predecessor, Dallas Moir, the Stirling county left-arm slow bowler, he has been lured away from the Scottish scene to join the Warwickshire staff.

The initial appearance of Scotland in the NatWest Bank Trophy created much interest and speculation. Haynes being unable to play, owing to a hand injury, the SCU called in Ray Joseph, a young West Indian fast bowler in his second season as professional at Kirkcaldy. Against Gloucestershire Joseph impressed with his pace, but his length was erratic. Recalled to the side, after a two-year absence, Terry Racionzer (Clydesdale), formerly of Sussex, exhibited a wide range of strokes, and notwithstanding Scotland's ultimate defeat, their total of 209 for six was the highest by any of the "minor" teams in the first round of the competition.

For the 64th match between Scotland and Ireland, on July 14, 15 and 16, the SCU had to cope with numerous unforeseen problems. No fewer than five of the anticipated team were unavailable and two new "caps", David Haggo (Ayr) and Billy McPate (Drumpellier), were given their baptism at Downpatrick. This was the first time since 1971 that Scotland had played in Northern Ireland. The temperature was in the 80s when Scotland opened their innings. Donald and Ian Kennedy were dismissed early and it was Racionzer who retrieved the situation, batting superbly for 256 minutes, during which he hit five 6s and thirteen 4s, to make 115, his fifth century for Scotland and his first against Ireland. When Ireland batted Racionzer, introduced into a rather weak attack, dismissed Corlett and Harrison in eight balls to restrict Ireland to 282. The final day, though, proved disastrous for Scotland. In 45 minutes their last five second-innings wickets fell for the addition of only 17 runs. Two quick wickets to Morton staggered the Irish when they went in again, but a fierce onslaught by Harrison (five boundaries) saw Ireland home.

Success finally came Scotland's way on August 17, 18 and 19 when at Titwood, Glasgow, MCC were beaten by five wickets. In their second innings MCC were skittled out for 73, the lowest score ever by an MCC side against Scotland. The two previous low scores were 76 in 1874 and 95 in 1961. The occasion saw the retirement of George Goddard (Heriots FP) from representative cricket. Apart from the Benson and Hedges Cup matches Goddard, from 1960 to 1983, had played 63 times for Scotland, scoring 1,033 runs and capturing 154 wickets. He captained Scotland for ten successive years and was awarded the MBE for his services to cricket.

The only other representative game in 1983 was between Scotland B and a powerful Durham University side at Nunholm, Dumfries, on June 15, 16 and 17. Durham fielded nine players contracted to English counties. An opening stand of 144 by Mike Arnold (76) and Graham Cowdrey (75) enabled the students to declare at 287 for five. Scotland just saved the follow-on, scoring 146, of which Kennedy contributed a steady 40. Eager to score quick runs, Durham lost wickets at regular intervals in their second innings. Apart from Kennedy (44), Scotland B never looked like scoring the 286 required to win and were all out for 159 to give Durham University their first success against Scotland's B side.

Young Scotland failed to make any impression on the Young Australian Cricketers at Myreside, Edinburgh, on August 14 and 15. The match was drawn with the Australians taking the honours. Had they enforced the follow-on they might well have won.

On the domestic front the West District qualified for the final of the NCA County Championship for the British Reserve Insurance Trophy. Victories over Cumbria CA at Titwood and Essex CA at Southport took the West to Tunbridge Wells for the final against Nottinghamshire CA on September 8. This was the first time that any Scottish team had reached the final of a national tournament. But the outcome of a long and tiring trip was disappointing. While the Scottish representation had been advised to make provisions for a possible stay over until the following day, the opposition were unable to comply. In consequence the West's innings was curtailed. Nottinghamshire CA had favourable conditions for their innings before heavy rain halted progress after only two overs of the West's innings. After that, in deteriorating conditions and bad light, the West had no chance of achieving success by scoring at a faster rate.

In the Ryden and Partners East League, Heriots FP became champions for the seventh successive season. Since the East League was formed in 1953, Heriots have won the title nine times. Stenhousemuir, Carlton and Watsonians were next in line. All four clubs were in contention right up to the final Saturday of the season when Heriots FP demolished Leith Franklin to clinch the title. Morison Zuill not only reached 1,000 runs in all matches for Stenhousemuir but topped the 25,000 run aggregate in his career. The Chairman of the SCU selectors also featured in a new club record partnership. Against Cupar, Zuill and Eddie Pollock scored 234 off 32.5 overs for Stenhousemir's second wicket.

The extension of Division One in the East League to ten clubs in 1984 saved Fauldhouse and Cupar from relegation. The clubs promoted from Division Two were Kirkcaldy and Royal High. There was also an extension to the Scottish Counties Championship from eight to ten clubs. Prestwick and Strathmore from the Glasgow and District League and Strathmore Union respectively are the new county sides. The 1983 Beneagles Scottish Counties Title was regained by Aberdeenshire with Forfarshire and Perthshire in second and third positions.

The D. M. Hall Western Union also had an exciting climax. Ayr were ahead with one match to play with Poloc, Drumpellier and Ferguslie all handily placed to usurp the title. Poloc surged through to success over Kelburne while Ayr's match against Greenock was nullified because of rain and bad light. Poloc's title win was due in no small way to the prowess of Omar Henry. The Western Province player established a new batting record, his final aggregate of 1,012 runs in the Union beating his own 945 in 1981. Ayr, Drumpellier and Ferguslie, by virtue of their final placings, qualify for the 1984 Knight Frank & Rutley Scottish Cup. Fifth-placed Greenock also qualify as Ferguslie won the 1983 Cup Final at the expense of Watsonians.

The new concept of the Knight Frank & Rutley Scottish Cup introduced in 1983 proved successful. Twenty clubs from the major competitions in Scotland were placed in four groups of five clubs with the winners and runners-up in each group progressing to the knockout stages. All the group winners were eliminated in the first round of the knockout section. In the final at Hamilton Crescent, Watsonians recovered from a bad start to finish with 174 for seven. Only a determined unbeaten 57 by H. Muzammill enabled Ferguslie to win the trophy in the second-last over with 176 for six. Huntly equalled a north record by winning the Macallan North of Scotland League for the seventeenth time. Nairn County and Northern Counties are the other two clubs with a similar record. Northern Counties were runners-up.

At the other end of the country, "dark horses" St Boswells carried off the Border league title, with Kelso in second place. The Sondico Strathmore Union Championship went to Strathmore, who won the first of their twenty titles in 1946. In second position were Aberdeen GSFP, who pipped Meigle, winners of the Three Counties Cup. Prestwick again won the Abbey Life Glasgow and District League title with Kelvinside Academicals as runners-up.

Escalating costs have considerably reduced the number of professionals playing in the various leagues throughout Scotland. The presence of a professional certainly enhances any team's prospects; in the major leagues only Heriots FP succeeded without one.

At the beginning of the season the SCU appointed a full-time administrator in Robin Prentice, an Uddingston stalwart for many years. In recent years the SCU have developed a more positive approach to matters and are endeavouring to make further advances by the introduction of sub-committees to deal more adequately with the many facets of the game. Brian Adair (Watsonians), President of the SCU, was to the forefront of a lot of the forward thinking in 1983. His successor, Billy Mann (Glasgow Academicals), is of a similar mould.

OVERSEAS CRICKET, 1982-83

Note: Throughout this section, matches not first-class are denoted by the use of a dagger.

ENGLAND IN AUSTRALIA AND NEW ZEALAND, 1982-83

England's tour of Australia and, very briefly, New Zealand in the winter of 1982-83 had, for them, two redeeming features: one of the most exciting Test matches ever played, at Melbourne immediately after Christmas, resulted in an English victory, and despite some transparently poor umpiring England played the game in a good spirit. The Ashes, which England had held since 1977, were surrendered, Australia winning the Test series by two victories to one, and, in competition with Australia and New Zealand, England failed, really rather abjectly, to reach the final stages of the Benson and Hedges World Series Cup.

With those players who, against the wishes of the Test and County Cricket Board, had been to South Africa in the spring of 1982 being barred from Test cricket, England flew to Brisbane on October 13 some way below full strength. Of the "outcasts" none was missed more than Graham Gooch. Without him England were practically never given a good start to an innings. Against his inclinations, Chris Tavaré was obliged to open in four of the five Test matches. Of his partners, Geoff Cook, though he did quite well against the states, proved easy prey for Australia's opening bowlers in the Test matches, while Graeme Fowler, after a dreadful start to the tour, suffered a broken bone in his foot in the fourth Test match, just when he was beginning to play with some assurance. Eight times in ten Test innings England lost their first wicket before 15 runs were on the board.

With the last five and a half weeks of the tour being set aside for one-day cricket, the five Test matches had to be finished by January 7. This allowed little time for acclimatisation and none for up-country matches. It also meant that the players who were not in the Test team had hopelessly little first-class cricket. Robin Jackman, Vic Marks and the reserve wicket-keeper, Ian Gould, all had to wait until the one-day games before making any sort of an impact. Another snag proceeding from the itinerary was that England, after being eliminated from the World Series Cup on February 6, had eleven days to kill, without cricket, before going on to New Zealand for a series of three one-day matches. On their way home from New Zealand, where their form and fortunes were abysmal, England broke fresh ground when eleven of them played an unofficial one-day match against a strong Pakistan XI in Dubai.

Once again fast bowling proved the decisive factor in the Test series. Although Dennis Lillee and Terry Alderman were injured in the first Test match and unable to play in the last four, Australia were still able to field much the stronger pace attack, Geoff Lawson, Jeff Thomson and Rodney Hogg all being faster and more consistently hostile than anything England could muster. England lost the second and third Tests easily enough to go to Melbourne for the fourth, which they won, in some disarray. Victory there was a great tonic, not only for Bob Willis and his side but for everyone associated with English cricket. Had John Dyson, one of Australia's opening batsmen, been given run out, as he palpably should have been, in the first over of the fifth Test match, the series might even have been saved and the Ashes retained, though had that happened it would not have reflected Australia's undoubted superiority.

Willis was the first specialist fast bowler, in modern times, to captain England on tour. G. O. Allen, when he led England in Australia in 1936-37, though a fast bowler was also no mean batsman. Tenacious by nature, Willis was at his best off the field where he adhered, often despite extreme provocation, to his pre-tour resolution never to be critical of the umpires, whose job was made barely tolerable by the constant use, on television, of slow-motion action replays. During the tour the introduction of a third 'arbiter', with access to these replays, was widely canvassed. On the field Willis left much to the other senior members of his side – David Gower, his vice-captain, Ian Botham and Bob Taylor. Willis seemed unable to put everything into his own bowling, while applying himself, simultaneously, to tactical requirements.

In retrospect Willis may have felt that more could and should have been made of Norman Cowans's bowling. But what, more than anything, upset England's calculations was the fact that Botham, their match-winner, failed to win them any matches. Never, by contemporary standards, particularly fit (back trouble hindered his pivot, and he grew very heavy), he failed to produce, either with bat or ball, a single devastating piece of cricket. In 32 innings, in all kinds of cricket, his top score was 65. He left behind in Australia many past cricketers and present judges who have yet to be convinced that he is a great all-rounder. For all that, Botham held more catches in the Test matches than anyone else on either side, many of them of the utmost brilliance, and his eighteen wickets, though expensive, were exceeded in the Test series by no other Englishman.

In Gower England had the outstanding batsman of the Australian season. His elegant style, powered by fine timing, was much admired. His consistency improved as soon as he started to take greater care when playing the ball off his legs, a stroke which got him into trouble in the early part of the tour. As Botham's stock declined so Gower's went up. Allan Lamb, visiting Australia for the first time, also created a good impression. When he made runs he did so in a sturdy, pugnacious, uncompromising way. The third batsman to pull his weight was Derek Randall, whose two innings of 78 and 115 in the first Test ensured England a draw. Randall had a much lower failure-rate than when he had been in Australia on England's previous tour. He was also, of course, England's outstanding all-round fielder, as he would have been in sides that fielded better than Willis's.

Although Tavaré scored 147 against New South Wales and twice made 89 in the Test matches, he was too often non-plussed by the pace and the bounce of Australian pitches. If he is ever to be really successful overseas he may need to quicken up his footwork, especially when going in first. By the end of the tour he was fortunate still to be in what was considered the best side. However, to many who had thought of him only as a stonewaller, his first innings in the Melbourne Test match came as a revelation.

England's bowling, though seldom if ever inspired, was not wholly collared until towards the end of the one-day matches. It happened then with increasing regularity, and by the time they got to New Zealand the attack was barely second-rate. Willis reached his peak in the first innings of the second Test match. After that, having had problems with his run-up and follow-through in the second innings of the same match, he was reliable but rarely threatening. Plucked out of county cricket as a raw 21-year-old, with fewer than 50 first-class wickets to his credit, Cowans, for some weeks, cut a somewhat lonely figure. He was virtually ignored for long stretches of the second Test, and left out of the third, before bowling like a hero in the fourth. By dint of hard practice he improved his accuracy as the tour went on, and he could bowl the occasional very fast ball.

Through some long weeks of idleness and lack of success Jackman's enthusiasm was never seen to wane. The three off-spinners – two would have been ample – had changing fortunes. Geoff Miller played in all five Tests, not without success, and Marks, a bystander for nearly three months, finished by being the most economical of all the bowlers. Having had a good run-up to the first Test match, Eddie Hemmings was left out of it, and when in the last in Sydney he had the chance to bowl on a turning pitch he failed to make the most of it. But he was by no means a failure, bowling one long and admirably steady spell in perfect batting conditions in the Adelaide Test and making 95 on the last day of the series, an innings that was by way of being a major windfall.

Derek Pringle was given three Test matches, more as an extra seam bowler than as an all-rounder, though he did make two Test 40s, the second of them at an important time in England's Melbourne victory. At times he made the ball lift more than England's other bowlers, but he bowled far too many no-balls and gave the impression generally of needing time to mature. Pringle was as lucky to be chosen for the tour as Trevor Jesty, Phil Edmonds, Mike Gatting and David Bairstow were unlucky to be left behind. When, in fact, Jesty was sent for, just before Christmas, after Randall had suffered a nasty injury in Tasmania, he soon won a place in the one-day team. This was mainly as a batsman, though in his first over in Australia, under the Sydney lights, he dismissed Kim Hughes for 0 and had Hookes dropped, first ball, off a difficult chance.

As always, Taylor was utterly dependable behind the stumps. Gould, because of his potentially livelier batting, was eventually preferred to Taylor in the one-day games. Until then Gould had been mainly a wholehearted spectator, and the highlight of his tour remained the moment when, fielding as substitute for Fowler, he held a spectacular catch to dismiss Greg Chappell in the Melbourne Test.

The tour was a huge financial success. The five Tests were watched by 554,142 people, the seventeen one-day games by 451,098. Of Melbourne's three one-day games, two attracted crowds of 84,153 and 71,393. It was soon obvious that the winning of the Ashes means as much to the Australian players and public as it ever did; with the help of a good deal of brain-washing on television, the Benson and Hedges World Series Cup also attracted great interest. The Australian players shared, all told, just over £100,000 in prize-money. Strengthened by the introduction of the naturalised South African, Kepler Wessels, and with David Hookes showing real signs of fulfilling his outstanding promise, and Hughes having a fine Test series with the bat, Chappell making two hundreds in his first five Test innings, and Allan Border overcoming a poor start to the series, and with Thomson, Hogg and Lawson replacing Lillee and Alderman so effectively, Australia played at times like a distinctly good side. In going down to them by only the odd Test match in five,

England, despite their many shortcomings, did a lot better than they might have. If they were unlucky to be deprived by the weather in Perth of reaching the finals of the World Series Cup, which was won eventually by Australia, they had only themselves to blame for not having made sure of doing so long before. Once against New Zealand, and once against Australia, England were run ragged in the one-day games, and seldom did a match of any kind go by without their suffering a batting collapse. They were a side with too few players good enough to be representing England in Australia and too many batsmen without a sound basic technique.

There were times during the World Series Cup when the game that was being played bore little resemblance to the more sophisticated and skilful form of cricket which had preceded it in the Ashes series. To gratify PBL Marketing Ltd, who now promote cricket in Australia, all the one-day games were played in coloured clothing and with a white ball. Fired by chauvinism and the exaggerated gestures of some of the Australian players, as well as the frantic nature of much of the cricket, the atmosphere seemed at times more like that of the Colosseum than a cricket ground. There were days when gimmickry reigned supreme, a development which not only the most conservative of watchers viewed with some anxiety.

The England team were quietly and efficiently managed by D. J. Insole, whose experience will be of value to him in his capacity as Chairman of the Cricket Committee of the Test and County Cricket Board. Norman Gifford, of Worcestershire until 1982, was assistant manager, and the physiotherapist for the eleventh successive tour was Bernard Thomas of Warwickshire, who kept muscles finely tuned, if not every waistline slim. – J.W.

ENGLAND TOUR RESULTS

In Australia

Test matches—Played 5: Won 1, Lost 2, Drawn 2.

First-class matches—Played 11: Won 4, Lost 3, Drawn 4.

Wins—Australia, New South Wales, Tasmania, Western Australia.

Losses—Australia (2), Queensland.

Draws—Australia (2), South Australia, Victoria.

Non first-class matches—Played 12: Won 6, Lost 6. *Wins*—Australia (2), New Zealand (2), Northern New South Wales, Tasmania. *Losses*—Australia (3), New Zealand (3).

In New Zealand

Non first-class matches—Played 3: Lost 3. *Losses*—New Zealand (3).

TEST MATCH AVERAGES

AUSTRALIA v ENGLAND

AUSTRALIA – BATTING

	T	*I*	*NO*	*R*	*HI*	*100s*	*Avge*
K. J. Hughes	5	8	1	469	137	1	67.00
D. W. Hookes	5	8	1	344	68	0	49.14
G. S. Chappell	5	10	2	389	117	2	48.62
K. C. Wessels	4	8	0	386	162	1	48.25
A. R. Border	5	9	2	317	89	0	45.28
J. Dyson	5	10	2	283	79	0	35.37
B. Yardley	5	7	0	141	53	0	20.14
R. W. Marsh	5	7	0	124	53	0	17.71
G. F. Lawson..........	5	8	1	98	50	0	14.00
R. M. Hogg.............	3	5	3	26	14*	0	13.00
J. R. Thomson	4	6	1	42	21	0	8.40

Played in one Test: T. M. Alderman did not bat; D. K. Lillee 2*; C. G. Rackemann 4; G. M. Wood 29, 0.

* *Signifies not out.*

BOWLING

	O	*M*	*R*	*W*	*Avge*	*BB*
J. R. Thomson	128.4	22	411	22	18.68	5-50
G. F. Lawson..........	230.4	51	687	34	20.20	6-47
R. M. Hogg.............	107.3	26	302	11	27.45	4-69
B. Yardley	292.2	91	793	22	36.04	5-107
D. K. Lillee.............	71	25	185	4	46.25	3-96

Also bowled: T. M. Alderman 43–15–84–1; A. R. Border 31–7–71–0; G. S. Chappell 14.3–3–44–1; D. W. Hookes 8–2–20–0; C. G. Rackemann 33.2–11–96–2.

ENGLAND – BATTING

	T	*I*	*NO*	*R*	*HI*	*100s*	*Avge*
D. W. Randall	4	8	0	365	115	1	45.62
D. I. Gower	5	10	0	441	114	1	44.10
A. J. Lamb.............	5	10	0	414	83	0	41.40
G. Fowler	3	6	0	207	83	0	34.50
E. E. Hemmings	3	6	1	157	95	0	31.40
I. T. Botham..........	5	10	0	270	58	0	27.00
D. R. Pringle..........	3	6	2	108	47	0	27.00
C. J. Tavaré	5	10	0	218	89	0	21.80
G. Miller	5	10	1	193	60	0	21.44
R. W. Taylor	5	10	3	135	37	0	19.28
N. G. Cowans	4	7	1	68	36	0	11.33
R. G. D. Willis	5	9	3	63	26	0	10.50
G. Cook	3	6	0	54	26	0	9.00

* *Signifies not out.*

BOWLING

	O	M	R	W	Avge	BB
R. G. D. Willis	166.3	28	486	18	27.00	5–66
G. Miller	171	50	397	13	30.53	4–70
N. G. Cowans	107	14	396	11	36.00	6–77
I. T. Botham	213.5	35	729	18	40.50	4–75
E. E. Hemmings......	188.3	59	409	9	45.44	3–68
D. R. Pringle	73.5	12	214	4	53.50	2–97

Also bowled: G. Cook 6–3–23–0; A. J. Lamb 1–1–0–0.

ENGLAND AVERAGES – FIRST-CLASS MATCHES

BATTING

	M	I	NO	R	HI	100s	Avge
A. J. Lamb.............	9	18	0	852	117	2	47.33
D. W. Randall	9	17	1	732	115	1	45.75
D. I. Gower	10	19	1	821	114	2	45.61
E. E. Hemmings......	5	9	3	228	95	0	38.00
G. Cook	7	14	1	428	99	0	32.92
I. J. Gould	4	5	0	164	73	0	32.80
G. Miller	10	19	4	465	83	0	31.00
R. D. Jackman........	4	5	2	88	50*	0	29.33
C. J. Tavaré	10	19	0	489	147	1	25.73
G. Fowler	9	18	0	445	83	0	24.72
I. T. Botham	9	18	0	434	65	0	24.11
R. W. Taylor	7	14	5	188	37	0	20.88
D. R. Pringle	9	16	5	207	47*	0	18.81
R. G. D. Willis	7	13	5	65	26	0	8.12
V. J. Marks	4	6	0	41	13	0	6.83
N. G. Cowans	8	13	2	70	36	0	6.36

* *Signifies not out.*

BOWLING

	O	M	R	W	Avge	BB
G. Cook	56	12	178	8	22.25	3–47
R. G. D. Willis	225	41	656	28	23.42	5–66
G. Miller	325	96	761	27	28.18	4–63
N. G. Cowans	223.4	38	745	26	28.65	6–77
D. R. Pringle	263.3	53	739	22	33.59	4–66
E. E. Hemmings......	323	84	789	23	34.30	5–101
I. T. Botham	319.4	63	1,033	29	35.62	4–43
R. D. Jackman........	88.5	15	272	3	90.66	2–37
V. J. Marks	107	26	351	3	117.00	1–39

Also bowled: G. Fowler 6–0–43–2; A. J. Lamb 1–1–0–0.

FIELDING

R. W. Taylor 18 (17ct, 1st); I. T. Botham 17; D. W. Randall 11; I. J. Gould 10 (9ct, 1st); D. I. Gower 9; R. G. D. Willis 7; G. Fowler 6, A. J. Lamb 6, D. R. Pringle 6; N. G. Cowans 5, V. J. Marks 5, G. Miller 5; G. Cook 4, C. J. Tavaré 4; E. E. Hemmings 3; R. D. Jackman 2.

QUEENSLAND v AN ENGLAND XI

At Brisbane, October 22, 23, 24, 25. Queensland won by 171 runs. Although England were still adjusting to local conditions, the state deserved their first win against an England side since they beat A. H. H. Gilligan's 1929-30 MCC team. Queensland, without their three Test players (who were still on tour in Pakistan), outplayed England on the last two days on a good pitch. Chanceless hundreds by Gower and Lamb in an otherwise uneven England first innings left Queensland trailing by 75 runs. Dropped catches and the need to give their spinners extended practice then prevented England consolidating their advantage. Wessels, missed when 18, and Chappell, dropped three times, became more and more dominant. England, set to make 361 in 306 minutes, always struggled after Fowler and Gower were out in the left-arm Frei's first two overs. Frei, aged 31, had a successful début, having reached his 50 in Queensland's first innings from only 24 balls, 38 of them from two overs by Marks. Taylor made his 1,528th dismissal in first-class cricket when he stumped Broad on the third day, thus passing J. T. Murray's world record for a wicket-keeper.

Queensland

K. C. Wessels c Taylor b Willis	14	– c Pringle b Miller	103
R. B. Kerr c and b Botham	7	– c Cowans b Marks	65
W. R. Broad c Miller b Willis	20	– st Taylor b Miller	45
*G. S. Chappell c Lamb b Willis	40	– b Botham	126
A. B. Henschell c Marks b Miller	50	– c Gower b Willis	54
R. J. Lawrence c and b Pringle	1	– not out	6
T. V. Hohns c Botham b Marks	17		
†R. B. Phillips not out	55	– (7) not out	5
H. Frei b Cowans	57		
C. G. Rackemann lbw b Miller	11		
J. N. Maguire not out	10		
L-b 3, w 1, n-b 11	15	B 4, l-b 7, w 1, n-b 19	31

1/22 2/22 3/82 4/105   (9 wkts dec.) 297   1/152 2/222   (5 wkts dec.) 435
5/120 6/163 7/164 8/239 9/277   3/256 4/421 5/427

Bowling: *First Innings*—Botham 18-7-46-1; Willis 13-6-43-3; Pringle 19-6-44-1; Cowans 14-3-47-1; Miller 15-1-63-2; Marks 3-0-39-1. *Second Innings*—Botham 14-3-44-1; Willis 12-2-45-1; Pringle 16-1-49-0; Cowans 16-3-58-0; Miller 27-5-66-2; Marks 40-6-142-1.

An England XI

G. Cook lbw b Rackemann	0	– c Chappell b Henschell	39
G. Fowler c Broad b Frei	9	– b Frei	0
D. I. Gower c Chappell b Frei	100	– c Lawrence b Frei	1
A. J. Lamb c Broad b Henschell	117	– c Chappell b Maguire	42
I. T. Botham c Kerr b Henschell	32	– c Phillips b Maguire	0
G. Miller c Chappell b Henschell	4	– lbw b Henschell	46
V. J. Marks c Henschell b Rackemann	3	– c Kerr b Frei	13
D. R. Pringle c and b Henschell	24	– not out	15
†R. W. Taylor c Kerr b Maguire	37	– c Broad b Henschell	9
N. G. Cowans c Chappell b Maguire	0	– c Frei b Henschell	1
*R. G. D. Willis not out	0	– c Broad b Henschell	0
B 9, l-b 20, w 1, n-b 16	46	B 6, l-b 8, w 2, n-b 7	23

1/0 2/48 3/187 4/281   372   1/2 2/4 3/75 4/77   189
5/281 6/284 7/288 8/369 9/372   5/130 6/165 7/171 8/180 9/184

Bowling: *First Innings*—Rackemann 20-6-61-2; Frei 19-4-76-2; Maguire 20-6-48-2; Hohns 28-5-90-0; Henschell 12.2-3-51-4. *Second Innings*—Rackemann 12-5-35-0; Frei 15-7-31-3; Maguire 12-5-28-2; Henschell 18.1-2-60-5; Chappell 6-1-12-0.

Umpires: M. W. Johnson and J. T. C. Taylor.

†At Newcastle, October 27, 28, 29. An England XI won by ten wickets. Northern New South Wales 163 (R. B. McCosker 53, G. Arms 35; E. E Hemmings five for 38, N. G. Cowans four for 46) and 166 (G. Arms 53; E. E. Hemmings four for 30, N. G. Cowans three for 30); An England XI 305 (C. J. Tavaré 157, D. I. Gower 56; S. Hatherall five for 37) and 27 for no wkt.

SOUTH AUSTRALIA v AN ENGLAND XI

At Adelaide, October 31, November 1, 2, 3. Drawn. On a docile pitch, which helped spin only towards the end, the game brought disquieting features for England. Their main batsmen tended to get themselves out, primarily against the spinners, and their attack lacked penetration. Botham, who led the side, was given out obstructing the field in his second innings but was recalled by Hookes with the umpires' permission. Botham was uncertain where the ball had gone after trying to sweep Harms, an off-spinner. It flew from a top edge above the head of Botham, who unintentionally impeded Wright, the wicket-keeper, as he went to make a catch. Miller batted confidently in England's first innings and Hemmings and Jackman shared an unfinished tenth-wicket stand of 112. Fowler's sequence of low scores continued when he was unluckily run out in the second innings, the bowler deflecting a return hit into the stumps. Hookes underlined his greater maturity in both innings and Hilditch drove strongly after the state had been left to make 375 in four hours.

An England XI

C. J. Tavaré b Harms	29	– (2) c Wright b Harms	38
G. Fowler b Christensen	10	– (1) run out	12
G. Cook c sub b Sleep	58	– lbw b Sleep	5
A. J. Lamb c Zadow b Sleep	78	– (5) b Sleep	17
*I. T. Botham c Christensen b Dolman	18	– (7) st Wright b Harms	24
D. W. Randall b Sleep	31	– (4) c and b Sleep	47
G. Miller c Sleep b Hookes	83	– (8) not out	25
†I. J. Gould c Zadow b Dolman	45	– (9) c and b Sleep	14
D. R. Pringle c Sincock b Hookes	16	– (10) not out	9
E. E. Hemmings not out	60		
R. D. Jackman not out	50	– (6) st Wright b Harms	29
B 8, l-b 6	14	B 3, l-b 2, n-b 1	6

1/13 2/80 3/112 4/148   (9 wkts dec.) 492   1/41 2/47 3/65   (8 wkts dec.) 226
5/227 6/236 7/339 8/379 9/380   4/90 5/152 6/152 7/180 8/208

Bowling: *First Innings*—Christensen 27–6–84–1; Sincock 30–4–105–0; Hookes 12–2–33–2; Sleep 34–9–89–3; Harms 32–11–79–1; Dolman 15–3–72–2; Hilditch 3–2–4–0; Darling 2–0–12–0. *Second Innings*—Christensen 6–1–15–0; Sincock 7–2–22–0; Hookes 1–0–1–0; Sleep 29–11–86–4; Harms 28–6–96–3.

South Australia

W. M. Darling b Pringle	39	– c Tavaré b Cook	23
W. B Phillips lbw b Botham	5	– b Hemmings	5
A. M. J. Hilditch c Randall b Hemmings	38	– c and b Cook	79
R. J. Zadow b Hemmings	11	– (6) c Randall b Hemmings	8
*D. W. Hookes c Randall b Hemmings	74	– (4) b Cook	39
P. R. Sleep c Botham b Cook	51	– (5) st Gould b Hemmings	9
†K. J. Wright not out	65	– run out	38
C. L. Harms c Fowler b Cook	22	– not out	46
R. C. Christensen lbw b Pringle	3	– c sub b Pringle	2
A. T. Sincock c Botham b Cook	24	– not out	6
M. C. Dolman c Cook b Hemmings	0		
B 4, l-b 4, n-b 4	12	B 8, l-b 6, w 1, n-b 1	16

1/9 2/71 3/90 4/105   344   1/26 2/42 3/151 4/164   (8 wkts) 271
5/210 6/241 7/280 8/284 9/341   5/164 6/185 7/246 8/255

Bowling: *First Innings*—Botham 5–1–18–1; Pringle 17–3–60–2; Jackman 10–0–26–0; Hemmings 44.3–12–102–4; Miller 16–1–79–0; Cook 17–4–47–3. *Second Innings*—Botham 1–0–9–0; Pringle 9–1–37–1; Jackman 3–0–14–0; Hemmings 31–6–110–3; Cook 25–4–85–3.

Umpires: B. E. Martin and A. R. Crafter.

WESTERN AUSTRALIA v AN ENGLAND XI

At Perth, November 5, 6, 7, 8. An England XI won by one wicket. A low-scoring match reached an exciting climax with England 5 runs short of victory when their last pair came together. The cracks which developed on an infrequently used pitch did not account for further injudicious strokes by several England batsmen. Quicker bowlers always dominated. Cowans took four for 6 in 25 balls, which did much to wreck Western Australia's first innings after they had been put in. Lillee, with early successes in both innings, and Alderman, who took ten wickets in the match, also scored psychological points on the eve of the Test series. England, needing 209 to win, slumped to 82 for five before Randall, dropped at long-leg off Lillee when 9, and Pringle stood firm. With 41 still needed on the final morning England gathered runs calmly until Alderman took four of the five remaining wickets for 7 runs in twenty balls. Willis, now partnering Taylor, played and missed several times before pushing the winning single into the covers.

Western Australia

G. M. Wood lbw b Cowans	31	– (2) c Taylor b Willis	25
B. M. Laird c Willis b Pringle	11	– (1) c Randall b Botham	1
G. Shipperd c Randall b Cowans	20	– c Taylor b Cowans	39
*K. J. Hughes b Willis	20	– c Cowans b Willis	37
G. R. Marsh c Botham b Cowans	0	– lbw b Willis	21
K. H. MacLeay lbw b Cowans	2	– c Fowler b Cowans	28
†R. W. Marsh c Tavaré b Botham	25	– c Willis b Botham	29
B. Yardley c Botham b Willis	8	– c Botham b Cowans	0
T. G. Hogan c Willis b Botham	15	– c Gower b Botham	1
D. K. Lillee c Pringle b Willis	26	– b Botham	1
T. M. Alderman not out	0	– not out	1
B 1, l-b 5, n-b 3	9	L-b 5, w 1, n-b 8	14

1/32 2/58 3/64 4/64   167   1/11 2/56 3/82 4/128   197
5/76 6/103 7/120 8/123 9/166   5/136 6/177 7/177 8/181 9/193

Bowling: *First Innings*—Willis 16.3–1–52–3; Botham 18–5–48–2; Pringle 11–3–25–1; Cowans 13–4–33–4. *Second Innings*—Willis 17–4–30–3; Botham 20–7–43–4; Pringle 16–5–44–0; Cowans 19.4–3–66–3.

An England XI

C. J. Tavaré c R. W. Marsh b Lillee	0	– c R. W. Marsh b Lillee	0
G. Fowler b Lillee	14	– c Hogan b Lillee	2
D. I. Gower c Laird b Alderman	7	– c Shipperd b Lillee	33
A. J. Lamb lbw b Lillee	8	– b Alderman	28
I. T. Botham lbw b Alderman	65	– c Hogan b MacLeay	8
D. W. Randall c Hogan b Alderman	14	– c R. W. Marsh b Alderman	92
G. Miller retired hurt	39	– (9) c Yardley b Alderman	6
D. R. Pringle b Alderman	2	– (7) c Wood b Alderman	24
†R. W. Taylor not out	2	– (8) not out	5
N. G. Cowans lbw b Alderman	0	– lbw b Alderman	1
*R. G. D. Willis c Laird b Hogan	1	– not out	1
L-b 3, w 1	4	L-b 4, w 4, n-b 1	9

1/4 2/13 3/30 4/31   156   1/0 2/7 3/59 4/72   (9 wkts) 209
5/60 6/151 7/155 8/155 9/156   5/82 6/187 7/201 8/202 9/204

Bowling: *First Innings*—Lillee 20–7–53–3; Alderman 24–6–63–5; MacLeay 9–3–23–0; Yardley 4–0–13–0; Hogan 1.1–1–0–1. *Second Innings*—Lillee 22–5–64–3; Alderman 22.2–3–67–5; MacLeay 12–1–42–1; Yardley 7–1–27–0.

Umpires: P. G. McConnell and C. Bezant.

AUSTRALIA v ENGLAND

First Test Match

At Perth, November 12, 13, 14, 16, 17. Drawn. Ugly crowd scenes marred an otherwise good match, Alderman, on the second afternoon, becoming the first player to be badly hurt in Test cricket after a field invasion. In the fighting that followed on the terraced side of the ground 26 arrests were made.

A pitch that lasted better than expected helped foil the bowlers of both sides, though Lawson gave Australia a clear advantage when he took early wickets in England's second innings. On the last day a hundred by Randall, a typical mixture of effervescence and resolution, was needed to put the match beyond Australia's reach. Botham, in his 55th game for England, became the first man to pass 3,000 runs and 250 wickets in Test history.

Chappell put England in after winning the toss, but Australia bowled with insufficient accuracy to take advantage of what early moisture the pitch held. Lillee became increasingly churlish as several raucous appeals were rejected. Tavaré, concentrating solely on survival, was the cornerstone of England's innings. At the end of the first day he had made 66 out of England's 242 for four. He survived chances at 31 and 41, to second slip off Lawson and forward short-leg off Yardley, but otherwise gave the Australian bowlers little hope. Gower played in his best vein before falling to a brilliant diving catch at short square leg by Dyson. Botham was given out in unusual circumstances. He played forward to Lawson, who alone appealed as Marsh took the ball low down. When this appeal was rejected Lawson turned to umpire Johnson, standing not at square leg but on the off side of the wicket, who confirmed a catch. Botham walked immediately, after indicating, while the umpires were conferring, that the ball had struck his pad.

On Saturday Tavaré and Randall were not separated until shortly before lunch when Tavaré was brilliantly caught at leg slip, trying to sweep. Tavaré batted seven and threequarter hours, hitting nine 4s. Randall became Yardley's 100th Test victim, caught at short leg, before England's innings was usefully, if streakily, extended by Taylor and Willis. It was when these two took the total past the 400 mark that about fifteen spectators, some carrying Union Jacks, ran on to the field and the troubles began.

One intruder, coming from behind, cuffed Alderman round the head. Giving chase, Alderman dislocated his right shoulder as he brought his man down with a rugby tackle, Lillee and Border joining in before the offender was led away in handcuffs and Alderman carried off on a stretcher. Although Alderman's shoulder was soon put back, the injury effectively ended his season, at great personal cost. With the incident causing numerous fights to break out between rival English and Australian factions, and other spectators bursting over the boundary fence, Chappell led the Australians from the field. The game was resumed after an interruption of fourteen minutes, whereupon England's innings soon ended. Wood and Dyson came safely through the day's last 52 minutes.

At 123 for three the next day Chappell and Hughes averted the threat of an Australian collapse with some exhilarating batting. They added 141 in 34 overs, both driving and pulling splendidly against bowling which, Willis apart, looked very ordinary. Cowans, on his Test début, bowled too short. Hughes, after two hours of delightful batting, was caught at deep mid-off, but Chappell went on to reach his 21st Test hundred and his eighth against England.

Willis was finally rewarded after taking the new ball, Chappell deflecting a rising ball high over the slips and Lamb holding a good low catch at deep third man. Chappell had batted for four and a quarter hours and hit two 6s and eleven 4s. After the rest day Australia added a further 91, mainly through forceful strokes from Hookes and Lawson, before declaring at lunch with a lead of 13 and only the injured Alderman to bat.

With Australia reduced to three front-line bowlers, the situation brought forth the best in Lawson and also Lillee, until he wrenched his troublesome right knee in a loose foothold and was reduced to a shortened run. These two alternated at one end while Yardley, flighting the ball well, bowled from the other. With some loose strokes contributing to the loss of their first five second-innings wickets, England ended the penultimate day only 150 runs ahead and in danger of defeat.

Australia's hopes of victory declined on the final morning when they were unable to dismiss Taylor, England's night-watchman, for a further 90 minutes. With Lawson looking tired, and Lillee struggling, the Australians were unable to summon the zest and penetration they had shown the previous day. Taylor was bowled off his pads after a vital 77 had been added in 25 overs; Miller then failed, but Pringle hung on with Randall after Australia had taken a new ball just before lunch.

Randall completed his third century against Australia, all made in Australia and when England had their backs to the wall. When, at last, he chopped Lawson into his stumps, he had been in for four and a half hours and hit thirteen 4s, mostly from sweeps and sparkling drives. England's lead at this point was 279, and with Pringle and Cowans lasting together for 65 minutes, Australia were left with the impossible task of scoring 346 in two hours. The total attendance for the match was 60,252.

England

G. Cook c Dyson b Lillee	1	– c Border b Lawson	7
C. J. Tavaré c Hughes b Yardley	89	– c Chappell b Yardley	9
D. I. Gower c Dyson b Alderman	72	– lbw b Lillee	28
A. J. Lamb c Marsh b Yardley	46	– c Marsh b Lawson	56
I. T. Botham c Marsh b Lawson	12	– b Lawson	0
D. W. Randall c Wood b Yardley	78	– b Lawson	115
G. Miller c Marsh b Lillee	30	– (8) c Marsh b Yardley	0
†R. W. Taylor not out	29	– (7) b Yardley	31
*R. G. D. Willis c Lillee b Yardley	26	– b Lawson	0
N. G. Cowans b Yardley	4	– lbw b Chappell	36
B 7, l-b 9, w 2, n-b 6	24	B 5, l-b 11, w 2, n-b 11	29

1/14 2/109 3/189 4/204   411   1/10 2/51 3/77 4/80   358
5/304 6/323 7/342 8/357 9/406   5/151 6/229 7/242 8/292 9/292

Bowling: *First Innings*—Lillee 38–13–96–3; Alderman 43–15–84–1; Lawson 29–6–89–1; Chappell 3–0–11–0; Yardley 42.4–15–107–5. *Second Innings*—Lillee 33–12–89–1; Lawson 32–5–108–5; Chappell 2.3–1–8–1; Yardley 41–10–101–3; Border 7–2–21–0; Hookes 1–0–2–0.

Australia

G. M. Wood c and b Willis	29	– c Taylor b Willis	0
J. Dyson lbw b Miller	52	– c Cowans b Willis	12
A. R. Border c Taylor b Botham	8	– not out	32
*G. S. Chappell c Lamb b Willis	117	– not out	22
K. J. Hughes c Willis b Miller	62		
D. W. Hookes lbw b Miller	56		
†R. W. Marsh c Cook b Botham	0		
G. F. Lawson b Miller	50		
B. Yardley c Lamb b Willis	17		
D. K. Lillee not out	2		
B 4, l-b 1, w 1, n-b 25	31	L-b 1, n-b 6	7

1/63 2/76 3/123 4/264   (9 wkts dec.) 424   1/2 2/22   (2 wkts) 73
5/311 6/311 7/374 8/414 9/424

T. M. Alderman did not bat.

Bowling: *First Innings*—Willis 31.5–4–95–3; Botham 40–10–121–2; Cowans 13–2–54–0; Pringle 10–1–37–0; Miller 33–11–70–4; Cook 4–2–16–0. *Second Innings*—Willis 6–1–23–2; Botham 6–1–17–0; Cowans 3–1–15–0; Pringle 2–0–3–0; Miller 4–3–8–0; Lamb 1–1–0–0.

Umpires: A. R. Crafter and M. W. Johnson.

NEW SOUTH WALES v AN ENGLAND XI

At Sydney, November 20, 21, 22, 23. An England XI won by 26 runs. On a slow pitch this was an evenly contested match, which went into the last twenty overs. Hemmings's off-spin was the decisive factor in the later stages after Chappell and Toohey had been mainly responsible for keeping the hopes of New South Wales, needing 333 to win, alive. England's batting was again uneven, though Cook, with scores of 99 and 77, found his best form for the first time on the tour. Gould hit a brisk 73 in the first innings, but later he damaged a thumb at net practice and on the final day Taylor was allowed to keep wicket as a substitute. Tavaré made an accomplished 147 in the second innings, though it took him nearly six hours. Lawson strained his right arm in the field on the first day and did not bowl again. Smith played some good strokes in the state's first innings, and Bennett, slow left-arm, also hinted at a promising future.

An England XI

C. J. Tavaré c Dyson b Whitney	3 – c Smith b Bennett	147
G. Fowler b Chappell	12 – b Whitney	14
G. Cook c Holland b Bennett	99 – c Wellham b Bennett	77
*D. I. Gower c Dyson b Chappell	0 – c Smith b Bennett	13
D. W. Randall c Wellham b Bennett	11 – c McCosker b Whitney	48
D. R. Pringle b Bennett	1 – st Rixon b Bennett	1
V. J. Marks c Rixon b Lawson	1 – (8) c Rixon b Whitney	9
†I. J. Gould b Chappell	73 – (7) lbw b Whitney	8
E. E. Hemmings st Rixon b Bennett	4 – not out	7
R. D. Jackman b Chappell	6 – c McCosker b Bennett	3
N. G. Cowans not out	0 – run out	0
B 5, l-b 13, n-b 12	30 B 7, l-b 4, w 2, n-b 2	15

1/6 2/60 3/80 4/109   240   1/32 2/167 3/191 4/309   342
5/111 6/125 7/168   5/309 6/319 7/319
8/221 9/235   8/339 9/342

Bowling: *First Innings*—Lawson 15–4–30–1; Whitney 19–4–73–1; Chappell 8.1–1–23–4; Holland 7–3–19–0; Bennett 21–5–65–4. *Second Innings*—Whitney 27.3–6–60–4; Chappell 11–3–21–0; Holland 38–8–123–0; Bennett 44–13–123–5.

New South Wales

*R. B. McCosker c Gould b Cowans	3 – (2) b Cowans	1
J. Dyson c Randall b Jackman	43 – (1) c sub b Pringle	59
T. M. Chappell b Jackman	1 – (4) c Jackman b Marks	61
D. M. Wellham c Gould b Pringle	23 – (5) b Hemmings	38
S. B. Smith c Gould b Cowans	50 – (6) lbw b Hemmings	3
P. M. Toohey c Hemmings b Cowans	17 – (7) c Gower b Hemmings	69
†S. J. Rixon not out	57 – (3) lbw b Cowans	7
M. J. Bennett c Gould b Pringle	10 – b Hemmings	29
G. F. Lawson c Fowler b Hemmings	22 – c Randall b Hemmings	1
R. G. Holland c Pringle b Hemmings	0 – not out	17
M. R. Whitney not out	5 – lbw b Pringle	7
L-b 7, n-b 12	19 L-b 10, n-b 4	14

1/6 2/7 3/51 4/117   (9 wkts. dec.) 250   1/2 2/25 3/115 4/165   306
5/144 6/157 7/177   5/177 6/187 7/260
8/213 9/228   8/266 9/283

Bowling: *First Innings*—Cowans 5–2–44–3; Jackman 17–5–37–2; Pringle 17–1–61–2; Hemmings 28–4–67–2; Marks 9–2–22–0. *Second Innings*—Cowans 11–3–29–2; Jackman 14–3–38–0; Pringle 14.1–1–38–2; Hemmings 31–3–101–5; Marks 26–7–86–1.

Umpires: M. Jay and R. A. French.

AUSTRALIA v ENGLAND

Second Test Match

At Brisbane, November 26, 27, 28, 30, December 1. Australia won by seven wickets. Batting failures in their first innings, which could not be blamed on the pitch, coupled with some wayward fast bowling, always left England struggling in a match full of incident. Australia, in spite of dropping eight catches in England's second innings, deserved their success, owing much to Wessels, who made a remarkable début, and to Lawson, who finished with eleven wickets. Other features included a warning to Thomson for intimidatory bowling, and to Willis, Lawson (twice) and Cowans for running through on to the pitch. Crumbling footholds, especially at the Vulture Street end, were partially blamed for this, as they were for the 84 no-balls bowled in the match, this figure including those that were scored off.

Australia included the South African-born Wessels for Wood, Thomson for the injured Alderman and Rackemann for Lillee who, although in the original twelve, had had to have a knee operation. Ritchie was again made twelfth man. England included Hemmings for Pringle and Fowler for Cook, the latter having cracked a rib at practice the day before. Chappell again put England in, but a greenish pitch seldom provided the early assistance expected.

Lawson, bowling with the wind, soon put Australia in control, helped at this stage by some brilliant catching. Fowler and Tavaré went cheaply and Gower, having survived one chance to backward short leg, was held in the same place just before lunch. Lamb and Botham found little wrong with the pitch as they added 78 in thirteen overs before Botham sliced a drive to deep backward point. With three more wickets falling before tea, England were in deep trouble. A spectacular left-handed leg-side catch by Marsh ended Lamb's stay and gave the Australian wicket-keeper his 300th catch in his 88th Test match. When bad light brought the first day's play to a close, 65 minutes early, England were 219 for nine. Cowans was out first ball next morning.

Australia, like England, made a poor start, but they were rescued by a solid innings from the left-handed Wessels, who had taken up residence in Australia in 1978, specifically to become eligible for Test cricket. Wessels gathered runs steadily in an arc between cover point and third man, with occasional hits to the leg side. One of his few mistakes came when he was 15, a hard chance being put down in the gully off Botham. Willis bowled with determination; Botham, after starting well, and Cowans were both costly.

Australia were 130 for five after Chappell, when playing well, had badly misjudged a single to Miller at cover point and Hughes and Hookes had both gone cheaply. Marsh lingered for 78 minutes and Yardley stayed with Wessels as he inched his way towards his century. At 97 Wessels might have been stumped off Hemmings – the ball bounced awkwardly for Taylor – and by close of play Australia were 246 for six, Wessels having just become the thirteenth Australian to make a hundred in his first Test.

Australia's innings lasted until ten minutes before lunch on the third day, Wessels being the last man out after batting for seven and threequarter hours and hitting seventeen 4s. Towards the end of his innings he showed some freedom.

England, going in again 122 runs behind, were given a torrid time by the Australian fast bowlers. Tavaré was dropped twice before being caught at the wicket for 13, trying to leg-glance, and at tea England were 65 for one with Fowler in all sorts of trouble. The light deteriorated during the interval, and, one ball afterwards, a bouncer from Thomson was enough to bring a stoppage. An hour later, when fifteen more balls were bowled, Thomson was given an official warning by umpire Bailhache for under-pitching and Gower survived a chance in the gully. When bad light finally stopped play Chappell stayed in the middle to discuss with the umpires what, in their opinion, constituted intimidatory bowling.

There was no let-up for England after the rest day when Thomson, bowling to a slightly fuller length and with fine control, swung the game Australia's way, England's batsmen being tempted into rash leg-side strokes. Rackemann went off after half an hour with a groin strain, which meant that for the second successive Test Australia had a depleted attack. But Yardley was kept one end tight, and Thomson, bowling with pace and lift, took five for 12 in 47 balls, spread over three spells, to wreck the England innings. Fowler rode his luck outside the off stump for almost six hours, but there was little other resistance until Miller and Hemmings held out against a tiring attack through the last 100 minutes.

England thus went into the final day 157 runs ahead, with three wickets standing. Lawson collected the remaining wickets at a personal cost of 21 runs, leaving Australia 188 to win in five hours on a pitch with rough patches outside the left-handers' off stump. With England's new-ball bowlers in wayward form and Wessels being badly missed at cover point before he had scored, Australia raced to 60 in an hour, despite losing Dyson, hit on the shoulder by Willis. There was some excitement in the afternoon when Australia lost three quick wickets and Hemmings bowled well. But Hughes and Hookes batted carefully and, eventually, freely. The match ended in the second of the last twenty overs, having been watched by a total of 55,028 people. The nineteen catches which Australia held in the match constituted a world Test record.

England

C. J. Tavaré c Hughes b Lawson	1	– c Marsh b Lawson 13
G. Fowler c Yardley b Lawson	7	– c Marsh b Thomson 83
D. I. Gower c Wessels b Lawson	18	– c Marsh b Thomson 34
A. J. Lamb c Marsh b Lawson	72	– c Wessels b Thomson 12
I. T. Botham c Rackemann b Yardley	40	– (6) c Marsh b Thomson 15
D. W. Randall c Lawson b Rackemann	37	– (5) c Yardley b Thomson 4
G. Miller c Marsh b Lawson	0	– c Marsh b Lawson 60
†R. W. Taylor c Lawson b Rackemann	1	– c Hookes b Lawson 3
E. E. Hemmings not out	15	– b Lawson 18
*R. G. D. Willis c Thomson b Yardley	1	– not out 10
N. G. Cowans c Marsh b Lawson	10	– c Marsh b Lawson 5
L-b 2, w 1, n-b 14	17	B 8, l-b 8, w 1, n-b 35 52

1/8 2/13 3/63 4/141   219   1/54 2/144 3/165 4/169   309
5/152 6/152 7/178 8/191 9/195   5/194 6/201 7/226 8/285 9/295

Bowling: *First Innings*—Lawson 18.3–4–47–6; Rackemann 21–8–61–2; Thomson 8–0–43–0; Yardley 17–5–51–2. *Second Innings*—Lawson 35.3–11–87–5; Rackemann 12.2–3–35–0; Thomson 31–6–73–5; Yardley 40.4–21–50–0; Chappell 6–2–8–0; Hookes 2–0–4–0.

Australia

K. C. Wessels b Willis	162	– b Hemmings 46
J. Dyson b Botham	1	– retired hurt 4
A. R. Border c Randall b Willis	0	– c Botham b Hemmings 15
*G. S. Chappell run out	53	– c Lamb b Cowans 8
K. J. Hughes c Taylor b Botham	0	– not out 39
D. W. Hookes c Taylor b Miller	28	– not out 66
†R. W. Marsh c Taylor b Botham	11	
B. Yardley c Tavaré b Willis	53	
G. F. Lawson c Hemmings b Willis	6	
C. G. Rackemann b Willis	4	
J. R. Thomson not out	5	
B 2, l-b 8, n-b 8	18	B 2, l-b 5, n-b 5 12

1/4 2/11 3/94 4/99   341   1/60 2/77 3/83   (3 wkts) 190
5/130 6/171 7/271 8/310 9/332

Bowling: *First Innings*—Willis 29.4–3–66–5; Botham 22–1–105–3; Cowans 6–0–36–0; Hemmings 33.3–6–81–0; Miller 19.3–4–35–1. *Second Innings*—Willis 4–1–24–0; Botham 15.5–1–70–0; Cowans 9–1–31–1; Hemmings 29–9–43–2; Miller 3–0–10–0.

Umpires: R. C Bailhache and M. W. Johnson.

VICTORIA v AN ENGLAND XI

At Melbourne, December 4, 5, 6, 7. Drawn. Apart from the batting of Gower and Lamb, England failed to show the improvement they sought from a game which seldom caught the imagination. This was the first cricket played on the much-criticised square since the previous season, though it took place on that part of it which had not been relaid. Unlike some of its predecessors, it did not deteriorate, but it lost what early bounce it had and became too slow to help either batsmen or bowlers. Gower, who scored 88 in each innings, batted with fluent aggression on the first day. He and Lamb, who made his second century of the tour, added 189 in 54 overs in the second innings. No-one else did himself justice. Yallop and Wiener looked confident in Victoria's first innings, but the state were never in a position to accept the challenge of making 305 to win in four and a half hours on the last day. A large new electronic scoreboard, which also showed televised replays of the fall of wickets and carried much advertising, was used for cricket for the first time.

An England XI

C. J. Tavaré c Whatmore b Bright	18	– (2) b McCurdy	35
G. Fowler c Templeton b Balcam	5	– (1) b McCurdy	31
*D. J. Gower c Bright b Callen	88	– b Wiener	88
A. J. Lamb c Yallop b Bright	40	– st Templeton b Bright	108
I. T. Botham c Richardson b Callen	10	– (6) lbw b McCurdy	7
D. W. Randall c Wiener b Balcam	30	– (7) b McCurdy	4
G. Miller c Templeton b Bright	22	– (8) not out	17
D. R. Pringle st Templeton b Bright	0	– (9) not out	7
†I. J. Gould c Yallop b Bright	24		
V. J. Marks c Taylor b Balcam	9	– (5) c Bright b Callen	6
R. D. Jackman not out	0		
B 8, l-b 3, n-b 18	29	B 2, l-b 2, w 1, n-b 16	21

1/19 2/99 3/157 4/173   275   1/52 2/79 3/268   (7 wkts dec.) 324
5/188 6/230 7/232 8/249 9/275   4/283 5/295 6/299 7/301

Bowling: *First Innings*—Callen 20–8–53–2; Balcam 21.5–7–50–3; McCurdy 10–1–58–0; Bright 30–7–81–5; Wiener 1–0–4–0. *Second Innings*—Callen 26–9–71–1; Balcam 16–4–50–0; McCurdy 20–3–70–4; Bright 27–4–83–1; Wiener 8–2–29–1.

Victoria

J. M. Wiener c Marks b Pringle	49	– (2) lbw b Pringle	8
G. F. Richardson lbw b Miller	31	– (1) b Miller	27
D. F. Whatmore c Gould b Pringle	0	– (4) c and b Miller	2
*G. N. Yallop c Pringle b Miller	69	– (6) not out	24
M. D. Taylor c Gould b Botham	2	– (3) not out	56
D. M. Jones c Gould b Jackman	36	– (5) c Botham b Miller	0
R. J. Bright b Pringle	36		
L. F. Balcam lbw b Miller	5		
†R. I. Templeton c Fowler b Pringle	40		
I. W. Callen not out	3		
R. J. McCurdy c Marks b Botham	0		
B 8, l-b 5, n-b 11	24	B 3, l-b 1, n-b 1	5

1/77 2/78 3/96 4/107   295   1/14 2/57   (4 wkts) 122
5/203 6/207 7/217 8/283 9/294   3/63 4/63

Bowling: *First Innings*—Botham 22.5–4–78–2; Jackman 21–4–70–1; Pringle 21–4–66–4; Miller 28–15–35–3; Marks 8–3–22–0. *Second Innings*—Botham 7–1–18–0; Jackman 0.5–0–1–0; Pringle 13–3–33–1; Miller 20–6–36–3; Marks 13–4–29–0.

Umpires: R. C. Isherwood and R. V. Whitehead.

AUSTRALIA v ENGLAND

Third Test Match

At Adelaide, December 10, 11, 12, 14, 15. Australia won by eight wickets. For the second time in a fortnight England could find no adequate answer to the Australian fast bowling. With Rackemann not recovered from the groin strain which he suffered in the second Test, and Lillee and Alderman still unfit, Lawson and Thomson were partnered now by Hogg, playing in his first Test match for nearly eighteen months. Hogg's speed and hostility, no less than Lawson's and Thomson's, came as a nasty shock to England's batsmen. Between them these three took seventeen wickets in the match, Lawson bringing his tally from the first three Tests to 26.

Hogg for Rackemann was Australia's only change. England preferred Pringle to Cowans and, upon winning the toss, took the major gamble of putting Australia in. The pitch, though damp the day before the match, looked a beauty by the time Willis chose to field. He was, he said, well aware of the disasters which had attended previous England captains who had done the same thing in Australia (eight defeats and only one victory) but felt the first morning provided his bowlers with the best chance of "getting back into the series". In the event, it was an hour before a ball got past the bat, and Australia, by the close of the first day, were 265 for three. Chappell's second hundred of the series, his 22nd for Australia and first in Adelaide, was smoothly and chancelessly compiled. It contained nineteen 4s and was ended, ten minutes before stumps, only by a blinding catch in the gully by Gower.

England's one good day of the match was the second when, by accurate bowling and keen fielding, and with the pitch playing at its very best, they claimed Australia's last seven first-innings wickets for the addition of 173 runs. Gower held another brilliant catch, this time at cover point, and Botham two, one at second slip, the other at deep square leg. Hemmings, despite a sore shoulder, played an important part by pinning the batsmen down with his excellent control. Pringle's no-balls, eighteen on the first day, were fewer on the second. With Lamb and Gower gaining confidence after the early loss of Tavaré and Fowler, England, in their first innings, were 66 for two at the end of the second day and 140 for two at lunch on the third.

Their collapse on the third afternoon was one of the worst they have ever suffered in Australia. When Gower was third out in the first over after lunch, caught at the wicket off a ball of steep bounce, England needed only 99 to save the follow-on. It seemed they had nothing to worry about. Yet by tea they were padding up again, having lost their last seven wickets for 76 runs, the last six of them for 35. If Lamb was unlucky to be given out, caught at the wicket down the leg side for a well-made 82, what happened owed no more than that to chance. Things only began to look really ominous for England when Randall and Miller went in quick succession, Randall yorked second ball. Botham was still there, playing carefully, but at 213 he was eighth out, caught at short mid-wicket off the first ball of a new spell by Thomson, who then finished off the innings, with England still 23 runs short of saving the follow-on. With the rest day to come, Chappell had no hesitation in enforcing it.

When, in the third over of England's second innings, Thomson had Tavaré caught at short leg, he had taken four wickets in 22 balls for 6 runs, the last three in the first innings and the first in the second. No wicket had fallen in the morning of this third day, none fell in the last 110 minutes (England were 90 for one at the close: Fowler 37, Gower 43); between 1.42 and 4.10 nine went down. Until affected by the heat, in the last hour or so, Lawson, Thomson and Hogg made a fast and awkward trio, pitching short enough though not, in Willis's opinion, excessively so.

England began the fourth day still 132 behind and knowing that they would need to bat for four full sessions, probably more, to save the match. Only when Gower and Botham were adding 118 for the fourth wicket (during this second innings Botham passed 1,000 Test runs for 1982) did they look remotely like managing it. Gower was eventually fifth out at 247, and there were still 50 minutes of the fourth day left when Australia went in again, needing only 83 to win. Gower's splendidly staunch 100 was his fifth for England, though his first for 38 Test innings. The increasingly uneven bounce of the ball added to its merit. Australia cantered to victory on the last morning.

The total attendance of 75,678 was considered satisfactory in view of the timing of the match. Previously the Adelaide Test had benefited from being played over the Australia Day weekend in late January.

Australia

K. C. Wessels c Taylor b Botham	44	– (2) c Taylor b Botham	1
J. Dyson c Taylor b Botham	44	– (1) not out	37
*G. S. Chappell c Gower b Willis	115	– (4) not out	26
K. J. Hughes run out	88		
G. F. Lawson c Botham b Willis	2	– (3) c Randall b Willis	14
A. R. Border c Taylor b Pringle	26		
D. W. Hookes c Botham b Hemmings	37		
†R. W. Marsh c Hemmings b Pringle	3		
B. Yardley c Gower b Botham	38		
R. M. Hogg not out	14		
J. R. Thomson c and b Botham	3		
L-b 6, n-b 18	24	N-b 5	5

1/76 2/138 3/264 4/270   438   1/3 2/37   (2 wkts) 83
5/315 6/355 7/359 8/391 9/430

Bowling: *First Innings*—Willis 25–6–76–2; Botham 36.5–5–112–4; Pringle 33–5–97–2; Miller 14–2–33–0; Hemmings 48–17–96–1. *Second Innings*—Willis 8–1–17–1; Botham 10–2–45–1; Pringle 1.5–0–11–0; Hemmings 4–1–5–0.

England

C. J. Tavaré c Marsh b Hogg	1	– c Wessels b Thomson	0
G. Fowler c Marsh b Lawson	11	– c Marsh b Lawson	37
D. I. Gower c Marsh b Lawson	60	– b Hogg	114
A. J. Lamb c Marsh b Lawson	82	– c Chappell b Yardley	8
I. T. Botham c Wessels b Thomson	35	– c Dyson b Yardley	58
D. W. Randall b Lawson	0	– c Marsh b Lawson	17
G. Miller c Yardley b Hogg	7	– lbw b Lawson	17
†R. W. Taylor c Chappell b Yardley	2	– (9) not out	3
D. R. Pringle not out	1	– (8) c Marsh b Thomson	9
E. E. Hemmings b Thomson	0	– c Wessels b Lawson	0
*R. G. D. Willis b Thomson	1	– c Marsh b Lawson	10
L-b 5, n-b 11	16	B 7, l-b 6, w 3, n-b 15	31

1/1 2/21 3/140 4/181   216   1/11 2/90 3/118 4/236   304
5/181 6/194 7/199 8/213 9/213   5/247 6/272 7/277 8/289 9/290

Bowling: *First Innings*—Lawson 18–4–56–4; Hogg 14–2–41–2; Thomson 14.5–3–51–3; Yardley 21–7–52–1. *Second Innings*—Lawson 24–6–66–5; Hogg 19–5–53–1; Thomson 13–3–41–2; Yardley 37–12–90–2; Border 8–2–14–0; Hookes 3–1–9–0.

Umpires: R. A. French and M. W. Johnson.

TASMANIA v AN ENGLAND XI

At Hobart, December 18, 19, 20. An England XI won by six wickets. Once Tasmania had batted until lunchtime on the second day for their first-innings total of 273, Gower opted for a game of declarations, which began with an hour to go on the second evening, after Cook and Fowler had enjoyed the best opening partnership of the tour, and ended with England being left to score 264 to win in three hours plus twenty overs. This they managed comfortably, despite occasional brief stoppages for rain. For the last two days the weather was bitterly cold and very windy. A partnership between the promising Saunders and the left-handed Reid held England up on the first day. On the last, Fowler, Randall and Gower took full advantage of a fairly mild attack. Holding, the West Indian Test player, was seldom at full pace. Miller bowled with admirable control on the first day, and Pringle well but unluckily, while Cowans, given every chance to win back his Test place, was again erratic. Small crowds watched the match on Hobart's old-fashioned but scenic ground.

Tasmania

D. A. Smith c Gould b Cowans	5	– not out	52
I. R. Beven c Fowler b Miller	26	– b Pringle	28
D. C. Boon b Miller	46	– st Gould b Cook	16
P. J. Mancell c Jackman b Miller	1		
R. O. Butcher c Marks b Miller	0	– (4) c Gower b Fowler	7
S. J. Reid lbw b Pringle	79		
*†R. D. Woolley run out	14	– not out	3
S. L. Saunders c Cook b Cowans	53	– (6) b Fowler	7
P. A. Blizzard c Gower b Pringle	31	– (5) c Pringle b Cook	13
M. A. Holding c Randall b Pringle	6		
P. M. Clough not out	1		
B 5, l-b 2, n-b 4	11	B 1, l-b 3, n-b 1	5

1/8 2/51 3/57 4/59   273   1/40 2/63   (5 wkts dec.) 131
5/89 6/123 7/211 8/256 9/265   3/74 4/87 5/118

Bowling: *First Innings*—Cowans 24–6–55–2; Pringle 29.3–9–58–3; Jackman 20–3–75–0; Miller 39–16–63–4; Marks 8–4–11–0. *Second Innings*—Cowans 4–0–17–0; Pringle 7–4–10–1; Jackman 3–0–11–0; Miller 9–2–22–0; Cook 8–1–23–2; Fowler 6–0–43–2.

An England XI

G. Cook not out	73	– (3) c Woolley b Mancell	23
G. Fowler c Reid b Clough	63	– c Beven b Saunders	66
C. J. Tavaré (did not bat)		– (1) lbw b Clough	1
D. W. Randall (did not bat)		– not out	90
G. Miller (did not bat)		– c Woolley b Clough	30
*D. I. Gower (did not bat)		– not out	50
B 3, l-b 2	5	B 3, w 1	4

1/141   (1 wkt dec.) 141   1/23 2/81 3/97 4/165   (4 wkts) 264

†I. J. Gould, V. J. Marks, D. R. Pringle, N. G. Cowans and R. D. Jackman did not bat.

Bowling: *First Innings*—Holding 12–2–19–0; Blizzard 13–2–56–0; Clough 9.5–2–24–1; Mancell 7–1–35–0; Saunders 1–0–2–0. *Second Innings*—Holding 9–2–24–0; Blizzard 9–2–33–0; Clough 15–2–87–2; Mancell 7–1–33–1; Saunders 14–1–76–1; Reid 1–0–3–0; Smith 3–0–4–0.

Umpires: R. J. Marshall and S. G. Randell.

†At Launceston, December 22. An England XI won by four wickets. Tasmania 112 (42.5 overs) (V. J. Marks three for 13, R. D. Jackman three for 17); An England XI 113 for six (23.4 overs) (I. T. Botham 56).

AUSTRALIA v ENGLAND
Fourth Test Match

At Melbourne, December 26, 27, 28, 29, 30. England won by 3 runs. A magnificent Test match, to be ranked among the best ever played, produced a finish of such protracted excitement that it had the whole of Australia by the ears. Needing 292 to win, Australia were 218 for nine when Border and Thomson embarked on a last-wicket partnership of epic proportions. At close of play on the fourth day they had taken the score to 255 for nine, leaving another 37 runs to be found on the last morning for Australia, there and then, to regain the Ashes.

Although, on this last day, the match could have been over within moments, 18,000 spectators, admitted free of charge, went to the Melbourne Cricket Ground in the hope of seeing Border and Thomson achieve their improbable goal. All things considered, among them a new ball taken at 259 for nine, Thomson was rarely in trouble; Border never was. By the time Botham began the eighteenth over of the morning Australia were within 4 runs of victory. His first ball was short of a length and wide of the off stump. Thomson, sparring at it, edged a none-too-difficult catch to Tavaré, the second of Botham's two slips. Tavaré managed only to parry it, the ball bouncing away behind him but within reach of Miller, fielding at first slip, deeper than Tavaré. With a couple of quick strides Miller reached the catch and completed it, the ball still some eighteen inches off the ground.

No-one who played in the game or watched it, or who saw it on television, or who listened to it on the radio, many of them from halfway across the world, could have been left unmoved. In terms of runs, the only closer Test match ever played was the Brisbane tie between Australia and West Indies in 1960-61. In 1902, at Old Trafford, the margin between England and Australia was also 3 runs, on that occasion in Australia's favour.

England made two changes from the side that had lost the third Test in Adelaide, one optional, the other not. Randall, having been hit in the face by a short ball from Holding during England's one-day match in Launceston, was unfit, his place being taken by Cook. Cowans was preferred to Hemmings. Australia were unchanged. For the fourth time in the series the captain winning the toss chose to field. With the match being played on a pitch that had been laid only nine months before, Chappell took a calculated gamble when he committed Australia to batting last. In the event the pitch lasted surprisingly well and was, as Chappell expected, damp enough on the first day for England to be in early trouble. When Gower was third out, immediately after lunch, they were 56 for three. The innings was saved by a brilliant fourth-wicket partnership of 161 in only 32 overs by Tavaré and Lamb.

With Cook and Fowler going in first, Tavaré was able to bat at number three, which he much prefers to opening. After his usual slow start Tavaré began to attack the bowling, especially Yardley's, with unaccustomed vigour. By the time he was very well caught in the gully, England had fairly galloped to 217. But Lamb soon followed Tavaré, a fine innings ending a little unworthily when he got himself out to Yardley, and by close of play England, having fallen right away, were all out for 284. Cook, when first out, had given Chappell, at slip, his 111th Test catch, a new Australian record.

Each of the first three days saw one full innings completed. On the second Australia were bowled out in their first innings for 287, on the third England, in their second innings, for 294. By taking the wickets of Dyson and Chappell with successive balls in Australia's first innings, Cowans made his first impact on a match from which he was to emerge as a hero. Chappell hooked the first ball he received to deep square leg, where Lamb had just been carefully stationed. In the end Australia owed their narrow first-innings lead to Hughes's application, Hookes's good fortune laced with strokes of fine timing, and Marsh's belligerence. By now the umpiring of Rex Whitehead was becoming an irritant. On the second day, when they were in the field, and on the third, when they were batting, England were in danger of allowing it to undermine their resolve. After the match it was forgotten, all else being dwarfed by the climax, but it was undoubtedly erratic.

At 45 for three in their second innings England faced their next crisis. This time, however, after Botham had made 46 in 46 balls, their last five wickets made a vital contribution. Pringle and Taylor added 61 together, every run of some concern to Australia, faced by the prospect of batting last. Fowler, too, until hit on the foot by Thomson and forced to have a runner (the injury was to put him out of the next Test match) had played much his best innings of the tour. When Lawson found the edge of Pringle's bat Marsh claimed his 27th victim of the series, a new record for Test cricket.

Although the occasional ball was keeping very low, Australia's final target of 292, on an uncommonly fast Melbourne outfield (a prolonged and serious drought had restricted the watering of the ground), was eminently attainable. The equality of the four totals – 284, 287, 294 and 288 – tells of the unyielding nature of the match, with first one side, then the other, holding the advantage. When, as in Australia's first innings, Chappell fell cheaply to Cowans, splendidly caught low down in the covers by Gould (fielding as substitute for Fowler) off a hard slash from a short ball, England were in front, Wessels having already been bowled off his pads by Cowans. When, at 71, Dyson was beautifully caught at slip, by Tavaré off Botham, it remained that way. Hughes and Hookes then added 100, which gave Australia the initiative. Hughes's departure to a tumbling catch by Taylor off Miller, followed quickly by Hookes's, restored it to England. With Cowans, inspired by his successes over Chappell and generously encouraged by the crowd, claiming Australia's fifth (Hookes), sixth (Marsh), seventh (Yardley) and ninth (Hogg) wickets for 19 runs in seven overs, England had all but won when Thomson, his hair dyed platinum blond, joined Border.

As Thomson took root and Border switched to the attack, Willis adopted tactics which, though they brought final victory, were much criticised at the time. When Border had the strike Willis placed all his fielders in a far-flung ring, which meant that if England were to win they would almost certainly have to get Thomson out. Even for the last two overs of the fourth day, after a brief stoppage for rain, Border was allowed to bat unharassed by close fielders. It was the same next morning, even when England took the new ball.

Thus flattered, Border, whose previous fifteen Test innings had brought him only 245 runs, was now at his fighting best. Thomson, growing in confidence, occasionally pierced England's off-side field, his feet spreadeagled. As Australia slowly closed the gap, every run was cheered to the echo. England, in their fielding, showed understandable signs of panic. Cowans, though he continued to bowl well, failed to find quite his best rhythm; Willis, though admirably accurate, lacked his old pace. In the end, all hope for England almost gone, Botham, their great all-rounder, produced the ball that not only won the match but revived the tour. Botham's dismissal of Thomson made him only the second Englishman, Wilfred Rhodes being the other, to have scored 1,000 runs and taken 100 wickets against Australia.

For the first time in a Test match, Melbourne's huge video scoreboard was in operation, the screen being used to show action replays and advertisements as well as the score and other sundry details. It was, on the whole, well received, although Willis remarked after the match that there had been occasions when, needing to know the score, he found himself looking instead at a picture of a motor car or a meat pie. The first day's crowd of 64,051 might have reached 80,000 but for poor organisation. Thousands of would-be spectators turned back when they saw that it was taking up to 90 minutes to get into the ground. Even so, the total attendance, including the last day's approximate figure of 18,000, was 214,861.

England

G. Cook c Chappell b Thomson	10	– c Yardley b Thomson	26
G. Fowler c Chappell b Hogg	4	– b Hogg	65
C. J. Tavaré c Yardley b Thomson	89	– b Hogg	0
D. I. Gower c Marsh b Hogg	18	– c Marsh b Lawson	3
A. J. Lamb c Dyson b Yardley	83	– c Marsh b Hogg	26
I. T. Botham c Wessels b Yardley	27	– c Chappell b Thomson	46
G. Miller c Border b Yardley	10	– lbw b Lawson	14
D. R. Pringle c Wessels b Hogg	9	– c Marsh b Lawson	42
†R. W. Taylor c Marsh b Yardley	1	– lbw b Thomson	37
*R. G. D. Willis not out	6	– not out	8
N. G. Cowans c Lawson b Hogg	3	– b Lawson	10
B 3, l-b 6, w 3, n-b 12	24	B 2, l-b 9, n-b 6	17

1/11 2/25 3/56 4/217   284   1/40 2/41 3/45 4/128   294
5/227 6/259 7/262 8/268 9/278   5/129 6/160 7/201 8/262 9/282

Bowling: *First Innings*—Lawson 17–6–48–0; Hogg 23.3–6–69–4; Yardley 27–9–89–4; Thomson 13–2–49–2; Chappell 1–0–5–0. *Second Innings*—Lawson 21.4–6–66–4; Hogg 22–5–64–3; Yardley 15–2–67–0; Thomson 21–3–74–3; Chappell 1–0–6–0.

Australia

K. C. Wessels b Willis	47	– b Cowans	14
J. Dyson lbw b Cowans	21	– c Tavaré b Botham	31
*G. S. Chappell c Lamb b Cowans	0	– c sub b Cowans	2
K. J. Hughes b Willis	66	– c Taylor b Miller	48
A. R. Border b Botham	2	– (6) not out	62
D. W. Hookes c Taylor b Pringle	53	– (5) c Willis b Cowans	68
†R. W. Marsh b Willis	53	– lbw b Cowans	13
B. Yardley b Miller	9	– b Cowans	0
G. F. Lawson c Fowler b Miller	0	– c Cowans b Pringle	7
R. M. Hogg not out	8	– lbw b Cowans	4
J. R. Thomson b Miller	1	– c Miller b Botham	21
L-b 8, n-b 19	27	B 5, l-b 9, w 1, n-b 3	18
	287		**288**

1/55 2/55 3/83 4/89   287 1/37 2/39 3/71 4/171   288
5/180 6/261 7/276 8/276 9/278   5/173 6/190 7/190 8/202 9/218

Bowling: *First Innings*—Willis 15–2–38–3; Botham 18–3–69–1; Cowans 16–0–69–2; Pringle 15–2–40–1; Miller 15–5–44–3. *Second Innings*—Willis 17–0–57–0; Botham 25.1–4–80–2; Cowans 26–6–77–6; Pringle 12–4–26–1; Miller 16–6–30–1.

Umpires: A. R. Crafter and R. V. Whitehead.

AUSTRALIA v ENGLAND

Fifth Test Match

At Sydney, January 2, 3, 4, 6, 7. Drawn. Australia achieved, without too much trouble, a result which was enough to make sure they regained the Ashes, held by England since 1977. Although Australia had also beaten England in Australia in 1979-80, that was a three-match series, arranged at short notice, in which the Ashes were not at stake. After this victory in Sydney, Greg Chappell stood down from the Australian captaincy for the series of one-day matches that was to start in Melbourne two days later, Hughes being appointed in his place. The match won, Chappell also produced a silver cup, presented by an Australian supporter, which he said contained the ashes of one of the bails used at Sydney and which, in future, would be kept in the offices of the Australian Cricket Board in Melbourne. "Who said the Ashes never come back to Australia?" commented Chappell, a reference to the fact that the original urn is permanently housed at Lord's.

Australia fielded the side that had just lost in Melbourne. England made two changes, Hemmings being preferred to Pringle, because of bare patches on the pitch, and Randall coming in for Fowler, whose toe, hit by a ball from Thomson in Melbourne, was found to be chipped. With the ball expected to turn appreciably later in the match, Chappell, on winning the toss, chose to bat. Off the last ball of the first over, without a run on the board, Willis, off his own bowling, looked to throw out Dyson, who had answered Wessels's call for a sharp single. Although shown on film to have been a good eighteen inches short of his ground, Dyson was given not out by umpire Johnson, who said afterwards that he had given Dyson the benefit of the doubt, being unsure whether he was six inches in or six inches out. No-one could do more than speculate as to the significance, not least from a psychological viewpoint, of this unhappy decision. England had to wait for another hour before they took a wicket; Dyson went on to make 79, and Australia, by close of play on the first day, were 138 for two, nearly three hours having been lost to rain. For totalling 314 Australia had to thank Border, who, after a shaky start (he survived a difficult chance to silly point off Hemmings when he was 15), played very well. Botham held four splendid catches in the match, the first of them at slip, in Australia's first innings, when he clung to a flash from Hookes off Hemmings.

Left with two and a half hours' batting on the second evening England made their customary poor start, soon being 24 for three. Gower and Randall, continuing into the third morning, then added 122 with some rousing strokeplay. Until Gower was sixth out, brilliantly caught at slip by Chappell, diving to his left, it looked as though England might do better than the 237 with which they finished. In the end, though, only a partnership of 50 for the eighth wicket between Taylor and Hemmings enabled them to get even as far as that.

With the ball starting to turn, Australia were glad of a first-innings lead of 77. In the closing stages of the third day and for the first hour of the fourth (which followed the rest day), their batsmen were under pressure from England's spinners. Had Hughes been given out, caught at short leg off Hemmings, as England were convinced he was, Australia would have been 88 for four in their second innings, a lead of 165 with their last two specialist batsmen together. Instead, Miller and Hemmings, given every chance, took time to settle into a length, and with Hughes going on to make a superb 137, his third hundred against England and eighth for Australia, and Border, another fine player of spin, helping him to add 149 for the fifth wicket, England's chances of winning had virtually gone by the middle of the fourth afternoon. Border, by then, was well clear of the bad run he had had for much of 1982.

With 460 needed in 375 minutes – scarcely more than an academic proposition – England's hopes for the last day were concentrated on putting up a spirited resistance, which, for the most part, they did. Led by Hemmings, who had gone in as a night-watchman on the fourth evening and came within 5 runs of scoring an improbable hundred, England managed to save the game without boring the crowd. With an hour of the match left, and faced by a possible eleven overs of a new ball, England, at 293 for seven, became finally safe from defeat only when Miller and Taylor dug their toes in. Australia's catching for most of the series had been very good. Chappell claimed he had never played in a series in which more good catches were held. Of these, none was better than Hookes's on the last day when, at extra cover, he dived for a skier from Gower which had looked as though it would drop far over his shoulder. Marsh's 28 catches in the five Test matches surpassed by two the previous record for a Test series. The total attendance of 148,323 was the best for a Sydney Test match since the middle seventies.

Australia

K. C. Wessels c Willis b Botham	19	– (2) lbw b Botham	53
J. Dyson c Taylor b Hemmings	79	– (1) c Gower b Willis	2
*G. S. Chappell lbw b Willis	35	– c Randall b Hemmings	11
K. J. Hughes c Cowans b Botham	29	– c Botham b Hemmings	137
D. W. Hookes c Botham b Hemmings	17	– lbw b Miller	19
A. R. Border c Miller b Hemmings	89	– c Botham b Cowans	83
†R. W. Marsh c and b Miller	3	– c Taylor b Miller	41
B. Yardley b Cowans	24	– c Botham b Hemmings	0
G. F. Lawson c and b Botham	6	– not out	13
J. R. Thomson c Lamb b Botham	0	– c Gower b Miller	12
R. M. Hogg not out	0	– run out	0
B 3, l-b 8, w 2	13	L-b 7, n-b 4	11

1/39 2/96 3/150 4/173	314	1/23 2/38 3/82 4/113	382
5/210 6/219 7/262 8/283 9/291		5/262 6/350 7/357 8/358 9/382	

Bowling: *First Innings*—Willis 20–6–57–1; Cowans 21–3–67–1; Botham 30–8–75–4; Hemmings 27–10–68–3; Miller 17–7–34–1. *Second Innings*—Willis 10–2–33–1; Cowans 13–1–47–1; Botham 10–0–35–1; Hemmings 47–16–116–3; Miller 49.3–12–133–3; Cook 2–1–7–0.

England

G. Cook c Chappell b Hogg	8	– lbw b Lawson	2
C. J. Tavaré b Lawson	0	– lbw b Yardley	16
D. I. Gower c Chappell b Lawson	70	– (4) c Hookes b Yardley	24
A. J. Lamb b Lawson	0	– (5) c and b Yardley	29
D. W. Randall b Thomson	70	– (6) b Thomson	44
I. T. Botham c Wessels b Thomson	5	– (7) lbw b Thomson	32
G. Miller lbw b Thomson	34	– (8) not out	21
†R. W. Taylor lbw b Thomson	0	– (9) not out	28
E. E. Hemmings c Border b Yardley	29	– (3) c Marsh b Yardley	95
*R. G. D. Willis c Border b Thomson	1		
N. G. Cowans not out	0		
B 4, l-b 3, n-b 13	20	B 1, l-b 10, w 1, n-b 11	23

1/8 2/23 3/24 4/146   237   1/3 2/55 3/104   (7 wkts) 314
5/163 6/169 7/170 8/220 9/232   4/155 5/196 6/260 7/261

Bowling: *First Innings*—Lawson 20–2–70–3; Hogg 16–2–50–1; Thomson 14.5–2–50–5; Yardley 14–4–47–1. *Second Innings*—Lawson 15–1–50–1; Hogg 13–6–25–0; Thomson 13–3–30–2; Yardley 37–6–139–4; Border 16–3–36–0; Chappell 1–0–6–0; Hookes 2–1–5–0.

Umpires: R. A. French and M. W. Johnson.

England's matches v Australia and New Zealand in the Benson and Hedges World Series Cup may be found in that section.

†NEW ZEALAND v ENGLAND

First One-day International

At Auckland, February 19. New Zealand won by six wickets. On a dry pitch, of low and awkward bounce, Willis chose to bat and England, although New Zealand were without Hadlee, soon showed the effects of having had no cricket for a fortnight. Even Gower, dropped twice, found freedom hard to achieve, his 84 containing no fewer than 40 singles. The match-winning innings was played for New Zealand by Turner, who scored the first 50 of his 88 in 54 balls. With Edgar making him a good opening partner (New Zealand were also without Wright), and Cairns contributing a brief but explosive 19, New Zealand won with 21 balls to spare.

Man of the Match: G. M. Turner.   *Attendance:* 41,000.

England

C. J. Tavaré b Cairns	11	V. J. Marks not out	23
I. T. Botham c Morrison b Chatfield	12	R. D. Jackman b Cairns	4
D. I. Gower c Morrison b Snedden	84	*R. G. D. Willis not out	1
A. J. Lamb run out	0	L-b 10, w 2	12
D. W. Randall b Chatfield	30		
T. E. Jesty c Coney b Chatfield	1	1/17 2/40 3/40 (9 wkts, 50 overs) 184
†I. J. Gould lbw b Cairns	3	4/104 5/106 6/110
G. Miller lbw b Morrison	3	7/115 8/168 9/176

Bowling: Webb 10–0–30–0; Cairns 10–2–28–3; Snedden 8–1–35–1; Chatfield 10–0–27–3; Coney 2–0–17–0; Morrison 10–1–35–1.

New Zealand

G. M. Turner c sub b Willis	88	*G. P. Howarth not out	14
B. A. Edgar c Jackman b Miller	35	B 1, l-b 4, n-b 2	7
B. L. Cairns c Lamb b Botham	19		
J. J. Crowe lbw b Botham	15	1/101 2/129	(4 wkts, 46.3 overs) 187
J. V. Coney not out	9	3/164 4/166	

J. F. M. Morrison, †W. K. Lees, M. C. Snedden, E. J. Chatfield and R. J. Webb did not bat.

Bowling: Willis 10–1–39–1; Jackman 8.3–0–38–0; Botham 8–0–40–2; Miller 10–0–33–1; Marks 10–0–30–0.

Umpires: F. R. Goodall and D. A. Kinsella.

†NEW ZEALAND v ENGLAND

Second One-day International

At Wellington, February 23. New Zealand won by 103 runs. By beating England for a second time running, even more convincingly than in Auckland, New Zealand made sure of winning the trophy provided by the Rothmans Foundation. Having been put in, New Zealand were given a fine start by Turner and Edgar, with a partnership of 152 in 29 overs. Turner was in prime form, scoring 94 in 94 balls. England, in reply, were never in the hunt, their first five wickets falling for only 83 runs. A very good return catch by Chatfield accounted for Gower. In defeat, Willis described his side's performance as "dismal".
Man of the Match: G. M. Turner.   *Attendance:* 15,000

New Zealand

G. M. Turner b Willis	94	J. F. M. Morrison b Botham	8
B. A. Edgar run out	60	†W. K. Lees not out	3
B. L. Cairns b Willis	44	L-b 9, w 4, n-b 2	15
J. G. Wright b Miller	30		
J. V. Coney not out	31	1/152 2/193 3/214	(6 wkts, 50 overs) 295
*G. P. Howarth c Botham b Jackman	10	4/250 5/275 6/287	

M. C. Snedden, E. J. Chatfield and R. J. Webb did not bat.

Bowling: Willis 9–0–54–2; Jackman 10–2–38–1; Pringle 7–0–57–0; Miller 10–0–51–1; Marks 7–0–34–0; Botham 7–0–46–1.

England

C. J. Tavaré c Howarth b Chatfield	32	D. R. Pringle b Webb	11
I. T. Botham c Lees b Cairns	15	R. D. Jackman b Cairns	9
D. I. Gower c and b Chatfield	2	*R. G. D. Willis not out	2
A. J. Lamb b Coney	7		
D. W. Randall c Howarth b Morrison	16	L-b 6, w 5	11
†I. J. Gould c Wright b Coney	14		
G. Miller b Cairns	46	1/20 2/37 3/52 4/60	(44.5 overs) 192
V. J. Marks c Snedden b Webb	27	5/83 6/106 7/162 8/170 9/182	

Bowling: Snedden 10–1–37–0; Cairns 10–0–38–3; Webb 7.5–0–27–2; Chatfield 7–1–28–2; Coney 5–0–17–2; Morrison 5–0–34–1.

Umpires: S. C. Cowman and S. J. Woodward.

†NEW ZEALAND v ENGLAND

Third One-day International

At Christchurch, February 26. New Zealand won by 84 runs. England suffered their ninth defeat in thirteen matches since the protracted one-day programme began in Melbourne on January 9. The result gave New Zealand a clean sweep in their short series with England and confirmed the low state to which the England side had sunk. New Zealand, winning the toss and taking first use of a poor pitch, were given another good start by Turner and Edgar, and when, after a middle-order collapse, they were short of runs Morrison and Snedden rallied them. The only English batsmen not to fail were Lamb and Gower, who added 86 for the third wicket and ended the tour as they had started it – by overshadowing England's other batsmen. Although Gower was unsettled by field invasions, the predominant reason for England's defeat was their poor and colourless cricket.

Man of the Match: M. C. Snedden.   *Attendance:* 31,750, a record for Lancaster Park.

New Zealand

G. M. Turner lbw b Botham	34		J. F. M. Morrison not out	24
B. A. Edgar b Marks	32		†W. K. Lees c Botham b Cowans	2
J. G. Wright st Gould b Marks	2		M. C. Snedden not out	31
B. L. Cairns c Marks b Jackman	21		L-b 5, w 3, n-b 1	9
J. J. Crowe lbw b Jackman	18			
J. V. Coney run out	30		1/64 2/70 3/93 4/103 (8 wkts, 50 overs)	211
*G. P. Howarth lbw b Miller	8		5/126 6/152 7/153 8/156	

E. J. Chatfield did not bat.

Bowling: Willis 10–1–35–0; Cowans 10–2–55–1; Jackman 8–1–32–2; Botham 5–1–17–1; Miller 7–1–32–1; Marks 10–2–31–2.

England

†I. J. Gould c Turner b Snedden	0		V. J. Marks b Cairns	1
C. J. Tavaré b Snedden	4		R. D Jackman b Cairns	5
D. I. Gower c Wright b Chatfield	53		*R. G. D. Willis c Coney b Morrison	6
A. J. Lamb c Chatfield b Morrison	37		N. G. Cowans not out	1
I. T. Botham c and b Morrison	3		L-b 6, w 1, n-b 1	8
D. W. Randall b Coney	2			
G. Miller c and b Chatfield	7		1/0 2/8 3/94 4/103 (40.1 overs)	127
			5/105 6/114 7/114 8/116 9/125	

Bowling: Snedden 7–3–14–2; Cairns 7–0–13–2; Chatfield 8–2–26–2; Coney 10–0–42–1; Morrison 8.1–0–24–3.

Umpires: F. R. Goodall and I. C. Higginson.

THE AUSTRALIANS IN PAKISTAN, 1982-83

By PHIL WILKINS

The premonitions before the Australian team's six-week campaign in Pakistan proved well founded. Despite the unavailability of Greg Chappell, Dennis Lillee and Len Pascoe for personal and business reasons, and the late arrival, through the illness of a son, of Rodney Marsh, it seemed that Kim Hughes had a strong and well-balanced team under his command. In the event they failed to win a single one of their nine games. They lost all three Tests comprehensively, the two limited-overs internationals which were completed – the third was abandoned because of spectator disruptions – and drew the three three-day first-class matches against Invitation XIs.

The Australians proved ill equipped to cope with a Pakistan side beginning to exert its international authority under the leadership of Imran Khan. The timing of the tour was a liability. The Australians left for the Indian sub-continent when most football competitions were reaching their climax in Australia. The last Test the players had engaged in was in New Zealand six months before. Pre-season net practice and a brief training camp in Perth left them at a disadvantage against a Pakistan side fresh from a hard Test series in England. Despite claiming he was in need of a rest, Imran Khan proved a major force, with eight wickets in the Lahore Test and many judicious spells of genuinely fast bowling.

At the start of the tour, both Hughes and Imran made pleas for pitches which were evenly grassed and fair to each team. For the most part their appeals were heeded. The major Test centres of Karachi and Lahore provided excellent conditions, and it was sad that so much good could be undone by a few rabble-rousers in the two games at the National Stadium in Karachi.

The triumph of the dominant personality of the series, leg-spinner Abdul Qadir, deserved high tribute. Although his selection for the first Test in Karachi was criticised in some quarters, by the end of the series the thick-set wrist-spinner had so frustrated and bewildered the Australians that he had established a new record of 22 wickets for a series against Australia. His remarkable dexterity, variety and accuracy, usually exploited from round the wicket, to find boot marks at the other end, caused the Australians such difficulties that it made his absence from the team which had visited Australia the previous summer all the more inexplicable. His success was achieved, moreover, against batsmen who prided themselves on their ability to cope with the ball tossed into the air and turning from leg. Qadir's ability to turn the ball sharply in both directions eroded the Australians' patience and confidence and frustrated their desires to advance down the pitch to get the better of him.

If, in all aspects of the series, Pakistan were the better side, the tourists' anger was understandable at the interference by spectators during the first Test and third limited-overs international in Karachi and, to a lesser extent, during the games in Hyderabad and Sialkot. Hughes threatened to end the tour and return to Australia if any of his players was hurt by the stone-throwing from the uncovered grandstand – mostly occupied at reduced rates by university students – at the National Stadium in Karachi, which led to two walk-offs during the first Test. He said: "When a player cannot field on the boundary without being hit, then something serious has to be done to make spectators realise it is wrong. People do not deserve to see international cricket when they behave like this."

After less than an hour's play in the final limited-overs international in Karachi, by which time Geoff Lawson, Ian Callen and Greg Ritchie had been struck on the body and legs by missiles, Hughes led his players off and returned to the team's hotel. It was a sad end to the tour. These spectator disruptions, usually politically motivated, seem likely to remain part and parcel of cricket in Pakistan.

But difficulties and frustrations aside – and all members of the party sooner or later had some illness or other, stemming from the food or water, despite the presence of an accompanying doctor and physiotherapist – there was no denying that for Pakistan it was the country's finest cricketing hour. Their three-nil Test victory was unprecedented in a short series there.

Even without Sarfraz Nawaz, whose injury in England and leanings towards retirement prevented him from taking any part in the tour, Pakistan were able to field a versatile and consistent attack, although none of the three specialist pacemen considered to partner Imran Khan – Tahir Naqqash, Jalal-ud-Din and Sikander Bakht – advanced sufficiently to suggest that he would adequately replace Sarfraz in the immediate future. Even so, together with the medium-paced Mudassar Nazar, they all provided moments of perplexity for the Australians, as the scores indicate. It was in spin, though, that Pakistan found themselves with an embarrassment of riches. Qadir and his left-arm orthodox spin partner, Iqbal Qasim, took 30 of the 56 Australian wickets to fall to bowlers in the three Tests. The off-spinner, Tauseef Ahmed, became an indispensable member of the limited-overs side, and was unfortunate not to play in the Tests. The slow left-arm orthodox spinner, Amin Lakhani, appeared of Test potential, and Iqbal Sikander displayed enough leg-spinning talent to remain on the selectors' short-list for a touring side.

Pakistan also had a much greater depth in batting than Australia, with Mohsin Khan and Mudassar Nazar often providing a substantial start. Few of the Australians would have disputed that these two were, as a partnership, the equal of West Indies' Haynes and Greenidge. Mohsin showed remarkable improvement from his brief tour of Australia, when he appeared there as a reinforcement. His century in the Lahore Test caused Hughes to consider him worthy of a position in a World XI. Zaheer Abbas was employed profitably in the middle order. The Australians were convinced of his vulnerability against the new ball, but the superiority of the earlier Pakistan batsmen invariably prevented them from cornering him. Dropped catches, offered by Zaheer, also proved disastrous for the Australians. Mansoor Akhtar, some ten years younger than Zaheer, occupied the No. 3 position so adequately that he hit his maiden Test century in Faisalabad. Javed Miandad also grew further in stature as an international batsman, his youthful audacity now being supplanted by a technical competence and insatiable appetite for runs.

Australia's heroes were few. Openers Graeme Wood and Bruce Laird provided some sound starts, but it was John Dyson, in more forthright mood than on previous tours, who was the most consistent and valued batsman. Greg Ritchie and Wayne Phillips were two young batsmen introduced to international cricket on the tour, Ritchie displaying talent and a good temperament in a crisis, as evidenced by his century in the Faisalabad Test. Hughes began with a century in the first match, but he and Allan Border failed to provide the long partnerships that had been hoped for from them.

Lawson was the outstanding Australian. Starting as the third-string paceman behind Jeff Thomson and Terry Alderman, he bowled with such speed and bounce on the clay pitch at Multan that he went automatically into the Test side ahead of Alderman. His spirit was undaunted by the failures of his fellow players, and he remained the one bowler to trouble the Pakistanis in all conditions throughout the series. Australia's trio of spinners took only six wickets in the Test series between them, an indication of their failure when compared with Qadir and Qasim. Coupled with the Australians' dropping of fifteen catches in the Tests, it all amounted to a tour to rank among the most dismal ever made by an Australian side. The team's manager, Col Egar, the former Test umpire, said he would recommend that future Australian sides visited the Indian sub-continent at a less inappropriate time of year, delaying their departure at least until November when the climate was cooler and the players had had some domestic preparation. But as Hughes pointed out, it is equally important to make psychological adjustments on visiting Pakistan.

AUSTRALIAN TOUR RESULTS

Test matches – Played 3: Lost 3.
First-class matches – Played 6: Lost 3, Drawn 3.
Losses – Pakistan (3).
Draws – BCCP Patron's XI, Pakistan Cricket Board XI, BCCP Invitation XI.
Non first-class matches – Played 3: Lost 2, Abandoned 1 (owing to crowd disruptions).
Losses – Pakistan (2). *Abandoned* – Pakistan.

TEST MATCH AVERAGES
PAKISTAN – BATTING

	T	I	NO	R	HI	100s	Avge
Zaheer Abbas.............	3	3	0	269	126	1	89.66
Mohsin Khan..............	3	5	1	297	135	1	74.25
Mudassar Nazar.........	3	5	2	198	79	0	66.00
Imran Khan	3	3	2	64	39*	0	64.00
Mansoor Akhtar	3	5	2	183	111	1	61.00
Javed Miandad	3	5	0	176	138	1	58.66
Haroon Rashid	3	3	0	148	82	0	49.33
Tahir Naqqash...........	3	3	2	37	15*	0	37.00
Abdul Qadir...............	3	2	0	30	29	0	15.00

Played in three Tests: Wasim Bari 0. Played in two Tests: Iqbal Qasim 2*. Jalal-ud-Din played in one Test but did not bat.

* *Signifies not out.*

BOWLING

	O	M	R	W	Avge	BB
Imran Khan	103.2	35	171	13	13.15	4–35
Jalal-ud-Din	35	12	92	5	18.40	3–77
Abdul Qadir...............	212.2	48	562	22	25.54	7–142
Iqbal Qasim	118.5	45	228	8	28.50	2–28
Tahir Naqqash............	81	18	228	7	32.57	4–61
Mudassar Nazar...........	37	6	89	1	89.00	1–8

Also bowled: Javed Miandad 1–0–2–0; Zaheer Abbas 6–0–8–0.

AUSTRALIA – BATTING

	T	I	NO	R	HI	100s	Avge
G. M. Ritchie..............	3	6	1	206	106*	1	41.20
J. Dyson.....................	3	6	0	220	87	0	36.66
G. M. Wood.................	3	6	0	203	85	0	33.83
K. J. Hughes...............	3	6	0	154	54	0	25.66
A. R. Border...............	3	6	1	118	55*	0	23.60
B. M. Laird.................	3	6	0	137	60	0	22.83
G. F. Lawson	3	6	1	90	57*	0	18.00
B. Yardley..................	2	4	0	61	40	0	15.25
P. R. Sleep	1	2	0	29	29	0	14.50
J. R. Thomson.............	3	6	2	49	18	0	12.25
R. W. Marsh................	3	6	0	72	32	0	12.00
R. J. Bright.................	2	4	1	34	32*	0	11.33

Played in one Test: T. M. Alderman 7, 0.

Signifies not out.

BOWLING

	O	M	R	W	Avge	BB
A. R. Border	16	4	63	2	31.50	1–12
G. F. Lawson	114	21	301	9	33.44	4–96
R. J. Bright.................	82	23	217	3	72.33	3–96
T. M. Alderman	37	4	154	2	77.00	2–144
J. R. Thomson.............	79	12	295	3	98.33	1–16

Also bowled: K. J. Hughes 0.1–0–6–0; P. R. Sleep 36–3–159–1; B. Yardley 53–9–209–2.

AUSTRALIAN AVERAGES – FIRST-CLASS MATCHES

	M	I	NO	R	HI	100s	Avge
G. M. Ritchie..............	5	9	2	294	106*	1	42.00
J. Dyson.....................	6	10	1	361	87	0	40.11
K. J. Hughes...............	6	11	1	396	101*	1	39.60
W. B. Phillips..............	2	3	0	118	92	0	39.33
G. M. Wood.................	6	10	1	343	85	0	38.11
A. R. Border	6	11	1	259	59	0	25.90
B. M. Laird	5	10	0	258	60	0	25.80
G. F. Lawson	4	7	1	106	57*	0	17.66
B. Yardley..................	5	7	0	111	40	0	15.85
J. R. Thomson.............	4	8	3	67	18	0	13.40
R. W. Marsh................	4	7	0	83	32	0	11.85
R. J. Bright.................	5	7	2	55	32*	0	11.00
P. R. Sleep	3	5	1	38	29	0	9.50
T. M. Alderman	3	2	0	7	7	0	3.50

Played in two matches: I. W. Callen 1*.

Signifies not out.

BOWLING

	O	M	R	W	Avge	BB
I. W. Callen	20	3	60	4	15.00	2-15
A. R. Border	28	9	77	4	19.25	2-14
G. F. Lawson	134.3	23	364	15	24.26	5-32
R. J. Bright	137	43	363	12	30.25	5-40
T. M. Alderman	68	12	260	4	65.00	2-144
B. Yardley	119	26	443	5	88.60	2-136

Also bowled: K. J. Hughes 0.1–0–6–0; P. R. Sleep 56.2–7–247–1; J. R. Thomson 89–13–352–3.

FIELDING

R. W. Marsh 7 (5ct, 2st), A. R. Border 6, B. M. Laird 6, W. B. Phillips 2 (1ct, 1st), K. J. Hughes 2, G. M. Ritchie 2, G. M. Wood 2, B. Yardley 2, T. M. Alderman 1, R. J. Bright 1, J. R. Thomson 1.

BCCP PATRON'S XI v AUSTRALIANS

At Rawalpindi, September 12, 13, 14. Drawn. Coming out of an Australian winter, the tourists quickly showed their need for intensive match practice with an unconvincing performance against a strong combined side. Wood and Laird made a watchful 91, after Hughes won the toss, against a capable opening attack, and the first day finished encouragingly with a Border half-century and Hughes's drive over extra cover to the library roof for a century in 142 minutes with three 6s and eleven 4s. Reality, however, set in the next day as Masood Anwar and Mansoor Akhtar put on 189 for the second wicket in 153 minutes, Mansoor giving the younger Masood 53 runs start and beating him to the first century of the tour against the Australians. Haroon Rashid followed with a punishing 94, allowing Iqbal Qasim to declare 97 runs ahead. After the Australians in their second innings had declined to 82 for five, only John Dyson's vigour allowed them to escape with a draw.

Australians

G. M. Wood c Mansoor b Sikander	50	– (2) c Iqbal b Sikander 0
B. M. Laird c Ijaz b Qasim	48	– (1) c Mansoor b Iqbal 22
A. R. Border b Sikander	59	– c Yousuf b Sikander 21
*K. J. Hughes not out	101	– c Yousuf b Ijaz 19
J. Dyson c Salim b Qasim	2	– run out 47
P. R. Sleep b Qasim	7	– c Masood b Iqbal 0
†W. B. Phillips lbw b Ijaz	4	– c Shoaib b Iqbal 22
B. Yardley b Iqbal	24	– b Iqbal 12
R. J. Bright c Yousuf b Iqbal	5	– not out 1
J. R. Thomson c Sikander b Iqbal	11	– not out 7
B 7, l-b 5, n-b 4	16	B 4, l-b 2, n-b 9 15

1/91 2/163 3/175 4/195	(9 wkts dec.) 327	1/3 2/33 3/62 4/80 (8 wkts) 166
5/206 6/213 7/267 8/279 9/327		5/82 6/132 7/156 8/156

T. M. Alderman did not bat.

Bowling: *First Innings*—Sikander 13–1–45–2; Zakir 7–1–50–0; Ijaz 24–7–62–1; Iqbal 16–2–82–3; Qasim 34–11–72–3. *Second Innings*—Sikander 11–1–36–2; Zakir 3–0–11–0; Ijaz 18–7–32–1; Iqbal 22–5–52–4; Qasim 12–4–20–0.

BCCP Patron's XI

Shoaib Mohammad c Wood b Yardley . 21	Ijaz Faqih not out 6
Masood Anwar c Thomson b Border ...125	B 11, l-b 3, n-b 7 21
Mansoor Akhtar st Phillips b Border ...130	
Haroon Rashid b Alderman............... 94	1/82 2/271 3/328 (5 wkts. dec.) 424
Salim Malik c Wood b Yardley........... 27	4/388 5/424

†Salim Yousuf, Sikander Bakht, Zakir Khan, Iqbal Sikandar and *Iqbal Qasim did not bat.

Bowling: Thomson 10–1–57–0; Alderman 16–3–64–1; Bright 16–2–71–0; Yardley 28–5–136–2; Border 10–3–14–2; Sleep 15–3–61–0.

Umpires: Khizar Hayat and Javed Akhtar.

PAKISTAN CRICKET BOARD XI v AUSTRALIANS

At Multan, September 16, 17, 18. Drawn. Lawson and Ritchie, given their first opportunities, did well enough to become automatic choices for the first Test. Hughes again won the toss and batted on a newly laid clay pitch. Despite its lack of pace Jalal-ud-Din was able to move the ball effectively, and clever spin bowling by Amin Lakhani and Ilyas Khan helped the BCCP XI to restrict the Australians to 277. Lawson's speed disrupted the home side after an opening stand of 96, leaving the BCCP XI trailing by 101 runs. Hughes opened his team's second innings in a bid for victory, closing at 124 for three, but despite the early successes of Lawson and Callen in the BCCP XI's second innings, Salim Malik and Rameez Raja barred the tourists' path.

Australians

G. M. Wood b Lakhani	52		
B. M. Laird c Agha b Jalal...........................	28	– c Rashid b Ilyas.......................	23
A. R. Border st Ashraf b Ilyas.....................	6	– lbw b Rashid	38
*K. J. Hughes b Lakhani	50	– (1) c Jalal b Lakhani	43
G. M. Ritchie c Lakhani b Jalal	59	– (4) not out...........................	15
J. Dyson lbw b Rashid................................	21		
†R. W. Marsh lbw b Rashid	11		
B. Yardley c Ashraf b Jalal	14		
R. J. Bright c Ashraf b Jalal	15		
G. F. Lawson c Ashraf b Jalal......................	16		
I. W. Callen not out....................................	1		
B 2, l-b 1, n-b 1..................................	4	B 1, l-b 1, n-b 3.............	5

1/42 2/55 3/122 4/147	277	1/71 2/72	(3 wkts. dec.) 124
5/174 6/198 7/226 8/259 9/264		3/124	

Bowling: *First Innings*—Jalal 18.5–5–70–5; Rashid 22–5–55–2; Ilyas 19–2–55–1; Lakhani 32–7–93–2. *Second Innings*—Jalal 10–2–29–0; Rashid 9.4–1–30–1; Ilyas 9–4–19–1; Lakhani 9–1–31–1; Anwarul 3–1–10–0.

Pakistan Cricket Board XI

Agha Zahid b Lawson	64	– (3) lbw b Callen	4
*Taslim Arif c Border b Bright	51	– (1) c Laird b Lawson	10
Anwarul Haq c Border b Bright	0	– (2) b Callen	0
Salim Malik c Laird b Bright	4	– c Ritchie b Bright	34
Rameez Raja c Border b Bright	3	– not out	11
Nasir Valika c Marsh b Lawson	10	– not out	0
†Ashraf Ali c Border b Lawson	2		
Ilyas Khan st Marsh b Bright	7		
Rashid Khan not out	4		
Jalal-ud-Din c Marsh b Lawson	9		
Amin Lakhani b Lawson	0		
B 14, l-b 6, n-b 2	22	B 5, l-b 2, n-b 1	8

1/96 2/96 3/108 4/128   176   1/10 2/14   (4 wkts) 67
5/152 6/156 7/157 8/167 9/176   3/17 4/61

Bowling: *First Innings*—Lawson 13.3–2–32–5; Callen 6–1–24–0; Yardley 20–5–58–0; Bright 23–10–40–5. *Second Innings*—Lawson 7–0–31–1; Callen 5–0–21–2; Bright 7–4–7–1; Border 2–2–0–0.

Umpires: Ghafoor Butt and Iqbal Ather.

†PAKISTAN v AUSTRALIA

First One-day International

At Hyderabad, September 20. Pakistan won by 59 runs. Pakistan were led by Zaheer Abbas in the absence of Imran Khan, who was unwilling to risk a recurrence of a thigh muscle strain so soon after the tour to England. Jalal-ud-Din, Imran's replacement, took the first hat-trick in a one-day international against Australia. With the fourth, fifth and sixth balls of his seventh over, he bowled Marsh, had Yardley caught at the wicket and bowled Lawson. Hughes put Pakistan in on a greenish pitch which proved gentle in pace, and Mohsin Khan hit fifteen boundaries in his 165-minute stay. Wood and Laird began with a run-a-minute partnership of 104 in 23 overs, but Tauseef Ahmed claimed three wickets in quick succession and Jalal-ud-Din hammered home the advantage. There were so many spectator intrusions during Pakistan's innings that Hughes and manager Egar demanded police action to prevent them. The Australians' collapse from 104 for one to 170 for nine was indicative of looming batting difficulties.

Man of the Match: Mohsin Khan.

Pakistan

Mudassar Nazar c Marsh b Alderman	28	Tahir Naqqash c and b Alderman	8
Mohsin Khan c Dyson b Lawson	104	†Wasim Bari not out	5
*Zaheer Abbas c Wood b Yardley	26	B 1, l-b 6, n-b 8	15
Javed Miandad not out	31		
Mansoor Akhtar c Laird b Thomson	8	1/82 2/160 3/169 (6 wkts, 40 overs) 229
Haroon Rashid b Callen	4	4/180 5/191 6/202

Sikander Bakht, Jalal-ud-Din and Tauseef Ahmed did not bat.

Bowling: Lawson 8–0–29–1; Alderman 8–0–63–2; Callen 8–0–32–1; Thomson 8–0–48–1; Yardley 8–1–42–1.

Australia

B. M. Laird b Tauseef	44	I. W. Callen b Sikander	0
G. M. Wood c Jalal b Tauseef	52	J. R. Thomson c Zaheer b Mohsin	1
*K. J. Hughes c Haroon b Tauseef	2	T. M. Alderman not out	1
A. R. Border c Bari b Jalal	24	L-b 6, w 8, n-b 1	15
J. Dyson not out	30		
†R. W. Marsh b Jalal	1	1/104 2/106 3/109 (9 wkts, 40 overs) 170	
B. Yardley c Bari b Jalal	0	4/157 5/162 6/162	
G. F. Lawson b Jalal	0	7/162 8/164 9/169	

Bowling: Sikander 7–0–24–1; Tahir 7–0–20–0; Jalal 8–1–32–4; Mudassar 8–0–38–0; Tauseef 8–0–38–3; Mohsin 1–0–2–1; Mansoor 1–0–1–0.

Umpires: Khizar Hayat and Mahboob Shah.

PAKISTAN v AUSTRALIA

First Test Match

At Karachi, September 22, 23, 24, 26, 27. Pakistan won by nine wickets. Australia won the toss and batted on a fair, true pitch. They began poorly, losing Wood in Imran's second over, trying to withdraw his bat from an in-swinger. Laird was run out just before lunch and although Dyson drove and square cut powerfully, Australia's 218 for five at the close of the first day was inadequate considering the excellent conditions. Tahir Naqqash then demolished the innings by taking four wickets in eight balls the next morning. When Pakistan batted, umpire Mahboob Shah's rejection of a catch at the wicket from Mohsin Khan at 33 drew an angry response from the Australians, and the day ended in unusual fashion with Mohsin being given out "handled the ball". Playing a ball from Lawson, which fell behind him, he instinctively brushed it away from his wicket with his hand. Haroon Rashid and Zaheer Abbas had moments of good fortune, but their punishing hitting enabled Pakistan to take a substantial lead. Zaheer was dropped three times, twice by Border and once by Bright, and the Australians never overcame these flaws. Mudassar Nazar, batting at No. 6 because of an ankle injury, provided an unbeaten half-century.

On the first day there had been a hint of mischief to come when a marquee was set alight. On the third day the gradually increasing practice of rocks, vegetables and other missiles being thrown at the Australian fieldsmen caused Hughes to take his side off the field on two separate occasions. Fourteen minutes were lost before lunch and another 25 before tea. Political agitation, drawing attention to the military involvement in government, was suggested as being the root cause of the trouble.

Imran's confidence in Qadir – he had pressed hard for his inclusion – proved more than justified when, with the pitch still hard and true, he mesmerised the Australians in their second innings with a superb display of bowling. He claimed five for 19 in 78 minutes after Imran made his usual early breakthrough, and Pakistan cruised to victory on the last day.

Australia

G. M. Wood c Bari b Imran	0	– c sub (Salim Malik) b Qadir	17
B. M. Laird run out	32	– c Mansoor b Imran	3
J. Dyson b Qasim	87	– b Qadir	6
*K. J. Hughes c Bari b Qasim	54	– (5) c Bari b Qadir	14
A. R. Border not out	55	– (4) c sub (Salim Malik) b Qadir	8
G. M. Ritchie c Haroon b Qadir	4	– b Qasim	17
†R. W. Marsh b Tahir	19	– lbw b Imran	32
B. Yardley c Miandad b Tahir	0	– lbw b Qadir	0
R. J. Bright c Haroon b Tahir	2	– not out	32
G. F. Lawson b Tahir	0	– run out	11
J. R. Thomson st Bari b Qadir	14	– c Bari b Qasim	18
B 4, l-b 10, w 1, n-b 2	17	B 2, l-b 19	21

1/0 2/71 3/169 4/202   284   1/10 2/10 3/32 4/45   179
5/211 6/249 7/249 8/255 9/255   5/72 6/72 7/73 8/137 9/160

Bowling: *First Innings*—Imran 23–3–38–1; Tahir 16–3–61–4; Mudassar 13–0–33–0; Qadir 21.4–1–80–2; Qasim 26–10–55–2. *Second Innings*—Imran 12–5–17–2; Tahir 7–3–17–0; Qadir 26–7–76–5; Qasim 21.5–6–48–2.

Pakistan

Mohsin Khan handled the ball	58	– not out	14
Mansoor Akhtar c Bright b Thomson	32	– (3) not out	26
Haroon Rashid c Laird b Yardley	82		
Javed Miandad b Lawson	32		
Zaheer Abbas c Marsh b Lawson	91		
Mudassar Nazar not out	52	– (2) c Border b Thomson	5
*Imran Khan c Yardley b Bright	1		
Tahir Naqqash st Marsh b Bright	15		
†Wasim Bari b Bright	0		
Abdul Qadir run out	29		
Iqbal Qasim not out	2		
B 4, l-b 8, w 1, n-b 12	25	N-b 2	2

1/43 2/168 3/188 4/277   (9 wkts dec.) 419   1/5   (1 wkt) 47
5/328 6/329 7/351 8/353 9/404

Bowling: *First Innings*—Thomson 29–5–103–1; Lawson 39–10–93–2; Bright 36–8–96–3; Yardley 23–2–98–1; Border 1–0–4–0. *Second Innings*—Thomson 3–1–16–1; Bright 5–0–14–0; Yardley 3–1–9–0; Hughes 0.1–0–6–0.

Umpires: Khizar Hayat and Mahboob Shah.

PAKISTAN v AUSTRALIA

Second Test Match

At Faisalabad, September 30, October 1, 2, 4, 5. Pakistan won by an innings and 3 runs. Although it had been announced that Javed Akhtar and Shakoor Rana would umpire the second Test, at the request of the Australians the umpires from the Karachi Test were retained. Australia made one change, Sleep replacing Yardley who was ill.

So stultifying did the Australians find the pitch that well before stumps on the first day, Pakistan having chosen to bat, Lawson and Thomson were bowling without a slip or gully. Mudassar and Mohsin began with a partnership of 123, Mohsin passing 1,000 Test runs. Mansoor and Zaheer added 155 in 174 minutes for the fourth wicket, with Mansoor poised on 99 for 25 minutes before cover driving Border to the boundary for his maiden Test century in his ninth Test. Zaheer, dropped when 57 and 119, hit three 6s and twelve 4s in his 337-minute innings, including 19 runs from one over by Sleep. Lawson's four for 96 from 33 overs was an effort of sustained pace and fortitude.

Two days in the field had the expected effect on the Australians. With the pitch extremely dry and containing only dead grass, Imran introduced his spinners within an hour of their first innings beginning. Qadir deceived Laird with a top-spinner in his third over and by stumps Australia were up against it. Wood provided genuine resistance, but it was Ritchie who displayed most character in the closing stages of the match. After defying Pakistan's bowlers for almost three hours before being run out in the first innings, when Australia followed on he continued calmly, judiciously and much more aggressively to make his maiden century – an unbeaten 106. Ritchie hit three 6s and nine 4s in his 295-minute innings, adding 56 with Sleep in 45 minutes as they attempted to punish Qadir. The latter, who took eleven wickets in the match, and seven in an innings for the first time, received clever assistance from his spin-bowling partner, Iqbal Qasim.

Pakistan

Mohsin Khan c Marsh b Lawson	76	*Imran Khan not out	24
Mudassar Nazar c Hughes b Border	79	Tahir Naqqash not out	15
Mansoor Akhtar c Marsh b Lawson	111	B 4, l-b 1, n-b 8	13
Javed Miandad c Laird b Lawson	6		
Zaheer Abbas b Sleep	126	1/123 2/181 3/201 (6 wkts dec.) 501	
Haroon Rashid c Laird b Lawson	51	4/356 5/428 6/482	

†Wasim Bari, Abdul Qadir and Iqbal Qasim did not bat.

Bowling: Thomson 23–5–79–0; Lawson 33–6–96–4; Sleep 36–3–159–1; Bright 41–5–107–0; Border 11–3–47–1.

Australia

B. M. Laird lbw b Qadir	8	– c Mudassar b Qadir	60
G. M. Wood c Bari b Mudassar	49	– (7) c Bari b Qasim	22
J. Dyson c Mudassar b Qasim	23	– (2) c Qasim b Qadir	43
A. R. Border c Miandad b Imran	9	– (3) c Haroon b Qadir	31
*K. J. Hughes c Imran b Qadir	11	– (4) lbw b Qadir	7
G. M. Ritchie run out	34	– (5) not out	106
P. R. Sleep lbw b Imran	0	– (6) c Mohsin b Qadir	29
†R. W. Marsh b Qadir	0	– run out	8
R. J. Bright c Haroon b Qadir	0	– c sub (Salim Malik) b Qasim	0
G. F. Lawson c Zaheer b Qasim	14	– lbw b Qadir	0
J. R. Thomson not out	1	– st Bari b Qadir	11
B 8, l-b 6, w 2, n-b 3	19	L-b 7, w 1, n-b 5	13

1/20 2/82 3/96 4/113	168	1/73 2/125 3/133 4/162 330
5/123 6/123 7/124 8/124 9/167		5/218 6/290 7/309 8/309 9/310

Bowling: *First Innings*—Imran 14–6–16–2; Tahir 15–4–21–0; Qadir 42–14–76–4; Qasim 25–11–28–2; Mudassar 7–2–8–1. *Second Innings*—Imran 10–5–20–0; Tahir 9–1–25–0; Qadir 50.4–12–142–7; Qasim 46–18–97–2; Mudassar 9–3–26–0; Zaheer 3–0–5–0; Miandad 1–0–2–0.

Umpires: Khizar Hayat and Mahboob Shah.

†PAKISTAN v AUSTRALIA

Second One-day International

At Lahore, October 8. Pakistan won by 28 runs. Zaheer's successes continued after Pakistan were put in to bat on a green but true pitch. He struck the ball with such assurance and beautiful timing that his 109 came in 139 minutes with two 6s and twelve 4s. Miandad provided excellent support, and there was almost an inevitability about Pakistan's advance to victory, despite the temporary abandonment of the antiquated scoreboard by the scorers and a stand of 117 between Laird and Hughes in 74 minutes. Hughes's splendid 64 was ended by an acrobatic catch by Mudassar. Laird was three hours making 91 not out when Australia desperately needed more positive strokeplay.

Man of the Match: Zaheer Abbas.

Pakistan

Mohsin Khan run out	17	*Imran Khan not out	29	
Mudassar Nazar lbw b Thomson	7	B 1, l-b 6, w 1, n-b 3	11	
Zaheer Abbas st Marsh b Border	109			
Javed Miandad not out	61	1/17 2/52 3/171	(3 wkts, 40 overs) 234	

Mansoor Akhtar, Haroon Rashid, †Wasim Bari, Tahir Naqqash, Jalal-ud-Din and Tauseef Ahmed did not bat.

Bowling: Thomson 8–0–41–1; Lawson 8–0–47–0; Alderman 8–1–29–0; Callen 8–1–50–0; Border 8–1–56–1.

Australia

B. M. Laird not out	91	G. M. Ritchie not out	4	
G. M. Wood b Jalal	21	L-b 10, w 4, n-b 1	15	
J. Dyson c Imran b Jalal	11			
A. R. Border b Tauseef	0	1/37 2/73 3/73	(4 wkts, 40 overs) 206	
*K. J. Hughes c Mudassar b Imran	64	4/190		

†R. W. Marsh, T. M. Alderman, G. F. Lawson, J. R. Thomson and I. W. Callen did not bat.

Bowling: Imran 8–1–38–1; Tahir 8–0–28–0; Jalal 8–1–33–2; Tauseef 8–0–40–1; Mudassar 6–0–40–0; Zaheer 2–0–12–0.

Umpires: Shakoor Rana and Amanullah Khan.

BCCP INVITATION XI v AUSTRALIANS

At Sialkot, October 10, 11, 12. Drawn. A rain-damaged pitch prevented any play on the first day and cost the first two hours of the second. Making only his second appearance of the tour, Phillips, the Australians' reserve wicket-keeper, showed splendid enterprise in an opening stand with Wood. Driving and pulling the ball strongly for a 6 and thirteen 4s, Phillips made 92 while his more eminent partner made 38 before retiring with a cramp. Callen, another who had few opportunities on the tour, took the wickets of Masood Anwar and Majid in his first over, but a dogged half-century by Rizwan-uz-Zaman and some punishing hitting by the discarded Test all-rounder, Wasim Raja, with three 6s and eight 4s, saw the Invitation XI prevent a first-innings loss. Hughes led the Australians off the Jinnah Park Stadium an over early on the last day when Wood was struck several times by stones thrown by spectators. Again, it seemed that no malice was intended to the players.

Australians

G. M. Wood retired hurt	38	G. M. Ritchie b Mohsin	14	
†W. B. Phillips c Raja b Sikander	92	P. R. Sleep not out	2	
J. Dyson not out	71	B 8, l-b 3, w 3, n-b 6	20	
A. R. Border c Aamer b Raja	17			
*K. J. Hughes b Rizwan	29	1/142 2/168 3/231 4/261	(4 wkts dec.) 283	

B. Yardley, R. J. Bright, I. W. Callen and T. M. Alderman did not bat.

Bowling: Sikander 14–2–62–1; Mohsin 13–1–44–1; Hasan 15–3–52–0; Fayyaz 15–2–45–0; Raja 12–1–43–1; Rizwan 3–1–4–1; Aamer 3–0–13–0.

BCCP Invitation XI

Rizwan-uz-Zaman b Yardley	53		†Anil Dalpat not out	17
Masood Anwar c Alderman b Callen	0		Mian Fayyaz not out	6
*Majid J. Khan c Border b Callen	0			
Wasim Raja b Bright	66		B 8, l-b 5, w 1, n-b 3	17
Aamer Malik lbw b Alderman	8			
Feroze Mehdi c Phillips b Bright	2		1/0 2/0 3/109 4/130 (7 wkts)	169
Hasan Jamil b Bright	0		5/143 6/143 7/146	

Sikander Bakht and Mohsin Kamal did not bat.

Bowling: Alderman 15–5–42–1; Callen 9–2–15–2; Bright 9–4–28–3; Sleep 5.2–1–27–0; Yardley 18–7–40–1.

Umpires: Amanullah Khan and Mohammad Shakeel Khan.

PAKISTAN v AUSTRALIA

Third Test Match

At Lahore, October 14, 15, 16, 18, 19. Pakistan won by nine wickets. In the belief that the well-grassed pitch would be fast, Imran put Australia in, and once again the touring side's middle order failed lamentably. Imran and the new Test cap, Jalal-ud-Din – preferred in the conditions to Iqbal Qasim – took seven wickets between them as Australia were dismissed for 316, which looked like being fewer until Lawson, Yardley and Alderman made late runs. Yardley and Alderman were preferred to the spinners, Bright and Sleep. Lawson's growing stature as a late-order batsman was seen as he hit a 6 and nine 4s in his 57 not out in 102 minutes.

Mohsin and Mudassar provided another fine start to Pakistan's first innings, and although Pakistan were uneasy at 119 for three, Mohsin and Miandad rallied them with centuries and a 150-run partnership in 191 minutes. Mohsin's third Test century was achieved in his sixteenth Test, Miandad's eighth in his 46th. After Alderman, one of the most reliable of fieldsmen, failed to hold a catch at slip when Miandad was only 9, Miandad became restricted in his bid to reach his century, staying on 96 for almost an hour as Thomson, in particular, bowled with considerable hostility. Miandad was dropped three times during his innings, so continuing the Australians' series of costly mistakes. Thomson's aggression was inadequately rewarded, and in an untypical action he kicked down the stumps on the second day after umpire Shakoor Rana had no-balled him. The umpire spoke to the bowler and then to Hughes. After several more no-balls had upset Thomson, he was taken out of the attack.

Imran closed Pakistan's first innings 151 runs ahead, and by stumps on the fourth day Australia were in a grim position at 66 for three. Dyson made 51 in dogged fashion and Hughes took three hours over 39. But Australia were incapable of resisting the Pakistan advance, Imran again being among the wickets. Pakistan needed only 64 runs in their second innings and achieved a third successive victory in the last hour of the game. Qadir's 22 wickets in the series constituted a new record for Pakistan against Australia.

Australia

G. M. Wood c Miandad b Qadir	85	– (2) c Mudassar b Jalal	30
B. M. Laird lbw b Qadir	28	– (1) lbw b Tahir	6
J. Dyson b Jalal	10	– lbw b Tahir	51
A. R. Border lbw b Imran	9	– st Bari b Qadir	6
*K. J. Hughes b Tahir	29	– st Bari b Qadir	39
G. M. Ritchie lbw b Imran	26	– lbw b Imran	19
†R. W. Marsh c sub (Iqbal Sikandar) b Imran	1	– c Mudassar b Jalal	12
B. Yardley c Haroon b Jalal	40	– b Imran	21
G. F. Lawson not out	57	– c sub (Iqbal Sikandar) b Imran	8
J. R. Thomson lbw b Jalal	0	– not out	5
T. M. Alderman b Imran	7	– c Zaheer b Imran	0
B 5, l-b 13, w 1, n-b 5	24	B 4, l-b 5, n-b 8	17

1/85 2/120 3/140 4/140   316   1/21 2/55 3/64 4/138   214
5/197 6/202 7/203 8/264 9/264   5/157 6/170 7/189 8/203 9/203

Bowling: *First Innings*—Imran 24.2–10–45–4; Tahir 18–4–65–1; Mudassar 6–1–17–0; Jalal 19–4–77–3; Qadir 37–7–86–2; Zaheer 2–0–2–0. *Second Innings*—Imran 20–6–35–4; Tahir 16–3–39–2; Mudassar 2–0–5–0; Jalal 16–8–15–2; Qadir 35–7–102–2; Zaheer 1–0–1–0.

Pakistan

Mohsin Khan b Border	135	– lbw b Lawson	14
Mudassar Nazar lbw b Lawson	23	– not out	39
Abdul Qadir c Laird b Yardley	1		
Mansoor Akhtar lbw b Lawson	12	– (3) not out	2
Javed Miandad c Hughes b Alderman	138		
Zaheer Abbas c Yardley b Alderman	52		
Haroon Rashid c Ritchie b Thomson	15		
*Imran Khan not out	39		
Tahir Naqqash not out	7		
B 3, l-b 13, w 2, n-b 27	45	B 4, l-b 5	9

1/92 2/93 3/119 4/269   (7 wkts dec.) 467   1/55   (1 wkt) 64
5/392 6/402 7/442

†Wasim Bari and Jalal-ud-Din did not bat.

Bowling: *First Innings*—Thomson 19–1–73–1; Lawson 35–4–91–2; Alderman 34–4–144–2; Yardley 27–6–102–1; Border 4–1–12–1. *Second Innings*—Thomson 5–0–24–0; Lawson 7–1–21–1; Alderman 3–0–10–0.

Umpires: Shakoor Rana and Javed Akhtar.

†PAKISTAN v AUSTRALIA

Third One-day International

At Karachi, October 22. Abandoned. The Australians' unhappy tour ended bitterly at the National Stadium following two disruptions by missile-throwing spectators in the crowd of 30,000. Imran won the toss and batted in ideal conditions, short-lived though the game proved to be. After sixteen minutes Lawson threw back a missile from his position at fine leg, whereupon Hughes spoke to him and also conferred with umpire Shakoor Rana and the Australian manager. Seven minutes later, after Lawson had been struck on the leg and with other fieldsmen under fire, Hughes led the Australians from the field with Pakistan 39 for one. The players were off the field for 55 minutes before, upon the wishes of their manager, they returned. Trouble immediately flared again and with the game only twelve overs old, the players left the ground for the last time. When it was announced that the game had been abandoned and that the players were no longer on the ground, violence erupted inside and outside the stadium.

Pakistan

Mohsin Khan not out	25
Mudassar Nazar b Alderman	8
Zaheer Abbas not out	5
B 1, l-b 2, w 2, n-b 1	6

1/23   (1 wkt, 12 overs) 44

Javed Miandad, Mansoor Akhtar, *Imran Khan, Wasim Raja, †Wasim Bari, Tahir Naqqash, Jalal-ud-Din and Tauseef Ahmed did not bat.

Bowling: Thomson 4–2–9–0; Lawson 2–0–7–0; Alderman 6–2–22–1.

Australia

W. B. Phillips, G. M. Wood, *K. J. Hughes, A. R. Border, G. M. Ritchie, J. Dyson, †R. W. Marsh, G. F. Lawson, I. W. Callen, J. R Thomson and T. M. Alderman.

Umpires: Shakoor Rana and Amanullah Khan.

INDIA v PAKISTAN, 1983-84

At Bangalore, September 14, 15, 17, 18, 19. Drawn. India 275 (R. M. H. Binny 83, Madan Lal 74, S. M. Gavaskar 42; Tahir Naqqash five for 76) and 176 for no wkt (S. M. Gavaskar 103 not out, A. D. Gaekwad 66); Pakistan 288 (Javed Miandad 99, Wasim Bari 64; Kapil Dev five for 68).

At Jullundur, September 24, 25, 26, 28, 29. Drawn. Pakistan 337 (Wasim Raja 125, Javed Miandad 66, Zaheer Abbas 49; Kapil Dev four for 80) and 16 for no wkt; India 374 (A. D. Gaekwad 201, R. M. H. Binny 54; Wasim Raja four for 50).

At Nagpur, October 5, 6, 8, 9, 10. Drawn. India 245 (R. J. Shastri 52, S. M. Gavaskar 50; Azeem Hafeez four for 58) and 262 for eight dec. (S. M. Gavaskar 64, D. B. Vengsarkar 40; Mohammad Nazir five for 72); Pakistan 322 (Zaheer Abbas 85, Javed Miandad 60, Mohsin Khan 44; R. J. Shastri five for 75) and 42 for no wkt.

THE SRI LANKANS IN INDIA, 1982-83

By P. N. SUNDARESAN

Sri Lanka lost all three one-day internationals during their first official tour of India, in September 1982. However, they drew the one Test match, in Madras, and won a one-day limited-overs match against Delhi, the Ranji Trophy champions.

The Sri Lankan side consisted of C. Shaffter (manager), A. Polonovita (assistant manager), Bandula Warnapura (captain), Duleep Mendis (vice-captain), Ashantha de Mel, Ajith de Silva, Somachandra de Silva, Roy Dias, Mahes Goonatillake, Vinodhan John, Ranjan Madugalle, Bernard Perera, Anura Ranasinghe, Arjuna Ranatunga, Ravi Ratnayeke and Sidath Wettimuny. Rumesh Ratnayake, a medium-paced bowler, was flown in on the eve of the Madras Test, when there was some doubt about de Mel's fitness.

It was Krishnamachari Srikkanth who upset Sri Lanka's plans in the one-day internationals, his personal scoring-rate of 1.3 runs a ball (244 runs off 195 balls) having a telling effect. Dias, his successful counterpart in the Sri Lanka team, made 39, 102 and 121 in the three matches. Dias was a more cultured stroke-player than Srikkanth but what mattered in these matches was the latter's better scoring-rate.

Sri Lanka ended all speculation about their ability to stand up to India in a five-day Test match by achieving an honourable draw. Their adventurous approach to batting, which won them many admirers, was reflected in the way Dias and Mendis rescued them from a poor start in both innings. Mendis, who batted with masterly efficiency to become the first Sri Lankan batsman to score a century in each innings of a Test, and Dias, who played dazzling front-foot drives, exposed the Indian attack's vulnerability under pressure. Sri Lanka's fielding, with Dias outstanding in the covers, was good, but their bowling set few problems for the Indian batting, Sunil Gavaskar and Sandip Patil scoring centuries. Gavaskar, nursing an injured foot, withdrew from the one-day internationals.

†INDIA v SRI LANKA

First One-day International

At Amritsar, September 12. India won by 78 runs. When India were put in to bat Srikkanth set the pace with a sparkling knock of 57 off 43 balls. His strokes all round the wicket included a 6 and ten 4s. Malhotra followed with a sound 40 while skipper Kapil Dev raced to 49, with a 6 and three 4s. Sri Lanka were never in the chase, being unable to shake off a slow start of 27 in their first ten overs.

India

R. M. H. Binny lbw b de Mel	16	Yashpal Sharma not out	37
K. Srikkanth c John b Warnapura	57	M. Amarnath c Wettimuny b John	13
D. B. Vengsarkar c Ratnayeke b de Silva	23		
A. Malhotra b Warnapura	40	L-b 4, w 11, n-b 4	19
S. M. Patil lbw b Ranasinghe	15	1/62 2/95 3/129 (7 wkts, 46 overs) 269	
*Kapil Dev st Goonatillake b de Silva	49	4/162 5/173 6/241 7/269	

†S. M. H. Kirmani, Madan Lal and D. R. Doshi did not bat.

Bowling: de Mel 7–0–58–1; John 9–1–44–1; Ratnayeke 7–1–37–0; Warnapura 10–1–41–2; de Silva 10–0–49–2; Ranasinghe 3–0–21–1.

Sri Lanka

*B. Warnapura b Madan Lal	0	D. S. de Silva b Kapil Dev	9
S. Wettimuny b Amarnath	43	†H. M. Goonatillake not out	14
R. L. Dias c Yashpal b Doshi	39	J. R. Ratnayeke not out	6
L. R. D. Mendis c Kapil Dev b Doshi	33		
R. S. Madugalle c Madan Lal b Doshi	1	B 1, l-b 5, w 2, n-b 2	10
A. N. Ranasinghe c Binny			
b Amarnath	35	1/8 2/67 3/95 4/98 (8 wkts, 46 overs) 191
A. L. F. de Mel c Madan Lal b Doshi	1	5/155 6/158 7/166 8/175

V. B. John did not bat.

Bowling: Kapil Dev 8–6–9–1; Madan Lal 8–2–24–1; Binny 6–0–33–0; Doshi 10–0–44–4; Amarnath 9–0–50–2; Patil 3–0–17–0; Vengsarkar 1–0–4–0; Malhotra 1–1–0–0.

Umpires: P. R. Punjabi and Rajan Mehra.

†At Delhi, September 14. Sri Lankans won by 12 runs. Sri Lankans 241 for seven (48 overs) (R. L. Dias 89, B. Warnapura 51, J. R. Ratnayeke 30; R. Peter three for 55); Delhi 229 for seven (48 overs) (K. B. J. Azad 41, M. Amarnath 40, C. P. S. Chauhan 37, R. Lamba 35).

†INDIA v SRI LANKA

Second One-day International

At New Delhi, September 15. India won by six wickets, covering a target of 279 runs in 40.5 overs with 9.1 overs to spare. A 15,000 crowd was kept on its toes by the brilliant strokeplay of Dias, who scored 102 for Sri Lanka, and Srikkanth, who missed his century for India by 5 runs. Excelling in front-foot strokes, Dias faced 114 balls and hit eight 4s. With Wettimuny he added 170 runs for the second wicket. Dias offered return catches to Doshi and Yashpal at 44 and 63 but these could not detract from the high merit of his knock. Srikkanth's scoring-rate of 95 runs off 66 balls (one 6 and thirteen 4s) had a shattering effect on Sri Lanka's bowlers. With Vengsarkar he added 134 runs for the second wicket.

Sri Lanka

*B. Warnapura lbw b Kapil Dev	4	A. L. F. de Mel run out	28
S. Wettimuny c Srikkanth b Binny	74	†H. M. Goonatillake not out	4
R. L. Dias c Doshi b Binny	102	G. R. A. de Silva not out	6
L. R. D. Mendis c Srikkanth b Binny	10		
A. N. Ranasinghe b Kapil Dev	20	B 2, l-b 18	20
J. R. Ratnayeke st Kirmani			
b Madan Lal	2	1/10 2/180 3/198 (8 wkts, 50 overs) 277
R. S. Madugalle c Kirmani		4/218 5/229 6/229
b Madan Lal	7	7/240 8/269

V. B. John did not bat.

Bowling: Kapil Dev 10–0–41–2; Madan Lal 10–0–51–2; Binny 7–0–39–3; Patil 4–0–24–0; Amarnath 10–0–52–0; Doshi 5–0–34–0; Yashpal 4–0–16–0.

India

R. M. H. Binny lbw b John	10	*Kapil Dev not out	1
K. Srikkanth c Mendis b Warnapura	95		
D. B. Vengsarkar c Warnapura		B 5, l-b 8, n-b 1	14
b Ratnayeke.	53		
A. Malhotra not out	44	(4 wkts, 40.5 overs)	281
S. M. Patil c Dias b de Silva	64	1/26 2/160 3/168 4/278	

M. Amarnath, Yashpal Sharma, Madan Lal, †S. M. H. Kirmani and D. R. Doshi did not bat.

Bowling: de Mel 2–0–23–0; John 5–0–44–1; Ratnayeke 8–0–48–1; de Silva 5.5–0–36–1; Ranasinghe 10–0–78–0; Warnapura 10–1–38–1.

Umpires: S. N. Hanumantha Rao and B. Ganguli.

INDIA v SRI LANKA

Inaugural Test Match

At Madras, September 17, 18, 19, 21, 22. Drawn. Mendis celebrated his country's first Test match against India with a century in each innings, a feat achieved previously against India only by Sir Donald Bradman and Everton Weekes. On a true pitch batsmen dominated the match, with Sri Lanka exhibiting the more positive approach. The match, which provided excellent entertainment (347 runs were scored on the fourth day), deserved a much better attendance than the 45,000 who watched it.

Deprived of their opening batsman, Wettimuny, owing to illness, Sri Lanka, who won the toss, were soon 11 for two. But Dias, missed at the wicket off Kapil Dev before he had scored, and Mendis retrieved the situation in the grand manner, adding 153 in 140 minutes. Shortly before falling leg-before to Doshi, Mendis reached his 100 with a 6 to long-on. He batted for 179 minutes and 123 balls, hitting one 6 and seventeen 4s. Doshi, who took his 100th Test wicket when he dismissed Ranatunga, reduced Sri Lanka to 204 for six before they rallied to reach 346.

By the close of the second day India were strongly placed at 251 for one, Gavaskar, who was going well, having reached his 25th Test century and added 156 with his new opening partner, Arun Lal. Next day India had 329 on the board before losing their second wicket, this after the resumption had been delayed for 165 minutes. Vengsarkar scored 90 (199 minutes, eight 4s) before being run out. Gavaskar's 155 came in 399 minutes off 293 balls and included one 6 and 24 4s. India declared on the fourth afternoon after Patil had completed a hard-hit century in 216 minutes.

Sri Lanka, 220 behind, started their second innings as badly as their first, Kapil Dev dismissing both opening batsmen for 6 runs each. But as on the opening day Dias and Mendis enterprisingly retrieved the position. Dias scattered the Indian attack, reaching his 50 in 53 minutes with twelve 4s. Although he slowed down as he neared his 100, his 97 took only 117 minutes and contained eighteen 4s. Having added 110 in better than even time with Dias, Mendis went on to complete his second century of the match (105 in 236 minutes) in the company of Ranasinghe, who made an aggressive 77.

With the two de Silvas and de Mel all scoring useful runs late in the Sri Lankan innings, India were left to make 175 to win in 53 minutes plus the mandatory twenty overs. Their hopes of getting them were high while Patil and Kapil Dev were together for the third wicket, but the attempt fizzled out after these two went in quick succession. The match aggregate of 1,441 runs was a new record for a Test in India.

Sri Lanka

*B. Warnapura c Yashpal b Madan Lal	4	– c Yashpal b Kapil Dev	6
†H. M. Goonatillake c Patil b Kapil Dev	7	– (10) c sub (K. Srikkanth) b Kapil Dev	0
R. L. Dias c Arun Lal b Doshi	60	– c Gavaskar b Shukla	97
L. R. D. Mendis lbw b Doshi	105	– b Shukla	105
A. Ranatunga c Vengsarkar b Doshi	25	– c Kirmani b Doshi	15
R. S. Madugalle c Madan Lal b Doshi	46	– c Patil b Doshi	4
A. N. Ranasinghe c Arun Lal b Doshi	0	– b Kapil Dev	77
D. S. de Silva c Gavaskar b Madan Lal	49	– not out	46
J. R. Ratnayeke lbw b Kapil Dev	23	– (2) c Yashpal b Kapil Dev	6
A. L. F. de Mel not out	18	– (9) b Doshi	12
G. R. A. de Silva c Viswanath b Kapil Dev	0	– b Kapil Dev	14
L-b 4, n-b 5	9	B 4, l-b 5, w 1, n-b 2	12

1/11 2/11 3/164 4/203   346   1/6 2/47 3/157 4/198   394
5/204 6/204 7/281 8/304 9/346   5/202 6/291 7/340 8/361 9/362

Bowling: *First Innings*—Kapil Dev 22.5–2–97–3; Madan Lal 16–1–72–2; Doshi 30–8–85–5; Patil 2–0–13–0; Shukla 22–4–70–0. *Second Innings*—Kapil Dev 24.3–3–110–5; Madan Lal 7–1–43–0; Doshi 38–4–147–3; Shukla 27–5–82–2.

India

*S. M. Gavaskar c de Mel b D. S. de Silva	155	– (9) not out	4
Arun Lal b de Mel	63	– c Dias b de Mel	1
D. B. Vengsarkar run out	90	– (1) c and b de Mel	5
G. R. Viswanath c Warnapura b D. S. de Silva	7	– (6) lbw b de Mel	2
S. M. Patil not out	114	– (3) run out	46
Yashpal Sharma c Goonatillake b de Mel	17	– (5) not out	31
Kapil Dev c Goonatillake b Ratnayeke	31	– (4) c Goonatillake b de Mel	30
Madan Lal not out	37	– (7) c and b D. S. de Silva	9
†S. M. H. Kirmani (did not bat)		– (8) b de Mel	5
B 11, l-b 8, w 2, n-b 29	50	N-b 2	2

1/156 2/329 3/347   (6 wkts dec.) 566   1/3 2/16 3/78   (7 wkts) 135
4/363 5/403 6/488   4/90 5/94 6/125 7/130

R. C. Shukla and D. R. Doshi did not bat.

Bowling: *First Innings*—de Mel 28–2–133–2; Ratnayeke 19–1–75–1; G. R. A. de Silva 17–2–78–0; Warnapura 9–3–27–0; D. S. de Silva 48–4–162–2; Ranasinghe 7–0–29–0; Ranatunga 1–0–12–0. *Second Innings*—de Mel 14–0–68–5; Ratnayeke 5–0–36–0; D. S de Silva 9–1–29–1.

Umpires: M. V. Gothaskar and Swaroop Kishen.

†INDIA v SRI LANKA

Third One-day International

At Bangalore, September 26. India won by six wickets to make a clean sweep of the one-day series. Sri Lanka's innings was sustained by another century from Dias, a sparkling effort of 121 off 144 balls with eleven 4s. But the dazzling batsmanship of Srikkanth paved the way for an easy Indian win with 10.4 overs to spare. Srikkanth's partnership of 119 runs in 18.3 overs with Vengsarkar for the second wicket overran the Sri Lankan attack.

Sri Lanka

*B. Warnapura lbw b Kapil Dev	1	D. S. de Silva lbw b Madan Lal	3
S. Wettimuny lbw b Binny	18	†H. M. Goonatillake not out	8
R. L. Dias c Doshi b Kapil Dev	121	R. J. Ratnayake not out	6
L. R. D. Mendis b Doshi	23	B 1, l-b 3, n-b 5	9
R. S. Madugalle run out	18		
A. L. F. de Mel b Doshi	25	1/2 2/48 3/106 4/157 (8 wkts, 50 overs) 233	
J. R. Ratnayeke b Madan Lal	1	5/193 6/198 7/208 8/222	

V. B. John did not bat.

Bowling: Kapil Dev 10-2-41-2; Madan Lal 10-0-41-2; Amarnath 10-0-53-0; Binny 10-0-54-1; Doshi 10-0-35-2.

India

R. M. H. Binny run out	15	Yashpal Sharma not out	30
K. Srikkanth b de Silva	92	B 7, l-b 1, w 3, n-b 2	13
D. B. Vengsarkar c Dias b de Mel	42		
A. Malhotra not out	27	1/34 2/153 3/160 (4 wkts, 39.2 overs) 234	
*Kapil Dev c Ratnayeke b de Mel	15	4/177	

Madan Lal, M. Amarnath, S. M. Patil, †S. M. H. Kirmani and D. R. Doshi did not bat.

Bowling: de Mel 8-1-58-2; John 9-0-33-0; Warnapura 2-0-15-0; Ratnayake 7-0-38-0; Ratnayeke 3-0-25-0; de Silva 10-1-51-1; Dias 0.2-0-1-0.

Umpires: D. N. Dotiwala and K. B. Ramaswamy.

INDIA v WEST INDIES, 1983-84

At Kanpur, October 21, 22, 23, 25. West Indies won by an innings and 83 runs. West Indies 454 (C. G. Greenidge 194, M. D. Marshall 92, P. J. Dujon 81; Kapil Dev four for 99); India 207 (Madan Lal 63 not out; M. D. Marshall four for 19) and 164 (D. B. Vengsarkar 65, R. J. Shastri 46; M. D. Marshall four for 47).

At Delhi, October 29, 30, November 1, 2, 3. Drawn. India 464 (D. B. Vengsarkar 159, S. M. Gavaskar 121, R. M. H. Binny 52; M. A. Holding four for 107) and 233 (D. B. Vengsarkar 63); West Indies 384 (C. H. Lloyd 103, I. V. A. Richards 67, A. L. Logie 63; Kapil Dev six for 77) and 120 for two (C. G. Greenidge 72 not out).

At Ahmedabad, November 12, 13, 14, 16. West Indies won by 138 runs. West Indies 281 (P. J. Dujon 98, C. H. Lloyd 68; Maninder Singh four for 85) and 201 (M. A. Holding 58; Kapil Dev nine for 89); India 241 (S. M. Gavaskar 90; W. W. Daniel five for 39) and 103 (M. A. Holding four for 30).

At Bombay, November 24, 26, 27, 28, 29. Drawn. India 463 (D. B. Vengsarkar 100, R. J. Shastri 77, R. M. H. Binny 65, A. D. Gaekwad 48, S. M. H. Kirmani 43 not out; M. A. Holding five for 105) and 173 for five dec. (A. Malhotra 72 not out); West Indies 393 (I. V. A. Richards 120, P. J. Dujon 84, C. H. Lloyd 67, D. L. Haynes 55; N. S. Yadav five for 131) and 104 for four.

At Calcutta, December 10, 11, 12, 14. West Indies won by an innings and 46 runs. India 241 (Kapil Dev 69, S. M. H. Kirmani 49, R. M. H. Binny 44) and 90 (M. D. Marshall six for 37); West Indies 377 (C. H. Lloyd 161 not out, A. M. E. Roberts 68, M. D. Marshall 54; Kapil Dev four for 91).

At Madras, December 24, 26, 27, 28, 29. Drawn. West Indies 313 (P. J. Dujon 62) and 64 for one; India 451 for eight dec. (S. M. Gavaskar 236 not out, R. J. Shastri 72, S. M. H. Kirmani 63 not out; M. D. Marshall five for 72).

Note: In accordance with playing conditions for the series, no-balls and wides are debited to bowlers' analyses.

THE INDIANS IN PAKISTAN, 1982-83

By QAMAR AHMED

In a one-sided series Pakistan beat India by three Tests to none, their victories at Karachi, Hyderabad and Faisalabad all being achieved by large margins. They also won the series of one-day internationals. Imran Khan's team plundered the mild Indian attack almost to their hearts' content, breaking record after record as the season progressed. The consistency and scoring feats of Zaheer Abbas, Mudassar Nazar, Javed Miandad, and to a slightly lesser extent Mohsin Khan, destroyed the Indian bowlers.

Mudassar scored four Test centuries and Zaheer three, both players also performing outstandingly in the one-day internationals. Added together Mudassar's 761 runs, Zaheer's 650 and Miandad's 594 constituted a record for the three top batsmen in any Test series. Miandad and Mudassar created a new world Test record for the third wicket at Hyderabad, their partnership of 451 also equalling the all-time record for any Test wicket, set up by D. G. Bradman and W. H. Ponsford.

Imran, who became the first Pakistan bowler to take 200 Test wickets, bowled with such venom and fire that no Indian batsman other than Mohinder Amarnath faced him with any confidence. Sarfraz was also still a force to be reckoned with.

India's poor showing was due mainly to patchy batting and weak fielding. Many catches were dropped at crucial moments. In addition, except for Kapil Dev, none of their bowlers posed any real threat to the home batsmen. Madan Lal had to return to India because of a badly bruised heel. India relied principally on their three left-arm spinners, of whom Dilip Doshi, the most experienced of them, did not show his best form after the first Test. Ravi Shastri, another of them, had injury problems, and the turbaned Maninder Singh did not enjoy the best of luck.

An umpiring controversy in the middle of the six-Test series, when the manager of the Indian team, the Maharaja of Baroda, was critical of local standards, blew over with the release of a statement by Sunil Gavaskar, the Indian captain, expressing his confidence in the umpires of Pakistan. Although, yet again, politically motivated rioting marred the last Test in Karachi, the series was played, on the whole, in a cordial atmosphere.

INDIAN TOUR RESULTS

Test matches – Played 6: Lost 3, Drawn 3.

First-class matches – Played 10: Won 1, Lost 3, Drawn 6.

Win – NWFP Governor's XI.

Losses – Pakistan (3).

Draws – Pakistan (3), BCCP XI, BCCP Patron's XI, Punjab Governor's XI.

Non first-class matches – Played 5: Won 2, Lost 3. *Wins* – Pakistan, Baluchistan Governor's XI. *Losses* – Pakistan (3).

TEST MATCH AVERAGES

PAKISTAN – BATTING

	T	I	NO	R	HI	100s	Avge
Zaheer Abbas	6	6	1	650	215	3	130.00
Mudassar Nazar	6	8	2	761	231	4	126.83
Javed Miandad	6	6	1	594	280*	2	118.80
Imran Khan	6	5	1	247	117	1	61.75
Mohsin Khan	6	8	2	341	101*	1	56.83
Salim Malik	6	4	0	122	107	1	30.50
Abdul Qadir	5	3	1	38	38	0	19.00
Sarfraz Nawaz	6	5	1	67	26	0	16.75
Wasim Bari	6	5	0	68	30	0	13.60
Mansoor Akhtar	3	4	1	40	23	0	13.33

Played in two Tests: Iqbal Qasim 0; Jalal-ud-Din 0*, 1*; Tahir Naqqash 20. Played in one Test: Haroon Rashid 0; Majid J. Khan 0; Sikander Bakht 9; Wasim Raja 10.

* *Signifies not out.*

BOWLING

	O	M	R	W	Avge	BB
Imran Khan	223.1	69	558	40	13.95	8-60
Sarfraz Nawaz	241.1	62	633	19	33.31	4-63
Iqbal Qasim	52	15	125	3	41.66	2-58
Abdul Qadir	151.3	23	526	11	47.81	4-67
Mudassar Nazar	52	11	147	3	49.00	2-39

Also bowled: Jalal-ud-Din 51–14–152–2; Javed Miandad 2–0–11–0; Majid J. Khan 1–0–4–0; Mohsin Khan 1–0–3–0; Sikander Bakht 22–4–107–1; Tahir Naqqash 61–14–211–2; Wasim Raja 6–2–13–0; Zaheer Abbas 8–0–24–0.

INDIA – BATTING

	T	I	NO	R	HI	100s	Avge
Yashpal Sharma	2	3	2	91	63*	0	91.00
M. Amarnath	6	10	2	584	120	3	73.00
B. S. Sandhu	3	3	1	115	71	0	57.50
R. J. Shastri	2	3	0	152	128	1	50.66
S. M. Gavaskar	6	10	1	434	127*	1	48.22
Madan Lal	3	5	2	126	54	0	42.00
D. B. Vengsarkar	6	9	2	241	89	0	34.42
S. M. Patil	4	7	0	173	85	0	24.71
Kapil Dev	6	8	0	178	73	0	22.25
Arun Lal	3	5	0	100	51	0	20.00
G. R. Viswanath	6	8	0	134	53	0	16.75
S. M. H. Kirmani	6	8	0	113	66	0	14.12
K. Srikkanth	2	3	0	28	21	0	9.33
Maninder Singh	5	6	1	24	12*	0	4.80
D. R. Doshi	4	7	1	21	14	0	3.50

Played in two Tests: T. A. Sekhar 0*.

* *Signifies not out.*

BOWLING

	O	M	R	W	Avge	BB
Kapil Dev	205.2	22	831	24	34.62	8-85
Madan Lal	83	9	349	8	43.62	3-101
D. R. Doshi	135.5	20	488	8	61.00	5-91
B. S. Sandhu	82.2	13	250	4	62.50	2-87

Also bowled: M. Amarnath 78–9–281–1; Arun Lal 1.1–0–6–0; S. M. Gavaskar 3–1–10–0; Maninder Singh 150–25–444–3; T. A. Sekhar 34–3–129–0; R. J. Shastri 58–5–176–1.

INDIAN AVERAGES – FIRST-CLASS MATCHES

BATTING

	M	I	NO	R	HI	100s	Avge
M. Amarnath	9	14	4	738	120	3	73.80
D. B. Vengsarkar	9	14	6	499	100*	2	62.37
R. J. Shastri	4	4	0	245	128	1	61.25
S. M. Gavaskar	8	13	2	579	127*	1	52.63
S. M. Patil	6	10	0	413	137	1	41.30
K. Srikkanth	6	10	0	357	135	1	35.70
Madan Lal	4	6	2	129	54	0	32.25
B. S. Sandhu	6	6	1	133	71	0	26.60
Yashpal Sharma	5	7	2	131	63*	0	26.20
Arun Lal	7	12	0	299	84	0	24.91
Kapil Dev	7	8	0	178	73	0	22.25
L. Sivaramakrishnan	4	2	1	22	21*	0	22.00
G. R. Viswanath	10	14	3	238	53	0	21.63
S. M. H. Kirmani	8	9	0	140	66	0	15.55
Maninder Singh	9	6	1	24	12*	0	4.80
D. R. Doshi	6	8	2	26	14	0	4.33

Also batted: T. A. Sekhar 0*

BOWLING

	O	M	R	W	Avge	BB
Kapil Dev	216.2	23	879	25	35.16	8-85
Madan Lal	102	16	393	11	35.72	3-37
Maninder Singh	316	64	861	16	53.81	6-35
D. R. Doshi	190	26	651	12	54.25	5-91
R. J. Shastri	142	26	335	6	55.83	4-80
B. S. Sandhu	150.2	29	466	8	58.25	2-87
L. Sivaramakrishnan	94.2	12	348	4	87.00	4-46
M. Amarnath	108	19	389	2	194.50	1-3

Also bowled: Arun Lal 6.1–0–29–0; S. M. Gavaskar 3–1–10–0; T. A. Sekhar 34–3–129–0; K. Srikkanth 13–1–11–0; D. B. Vengsarkar 6–0–25–0; G. R. Viswanath 2–0–12–0.

FIELDING

S. M. H. Kirmani 17 (15ct, 2st), S. M. Gavaskar 8, M. Amarnath 6, Arun Lal 5, Maninder Singh 4, G. R. Viswanath 3, Kapil Dev 2, Madan Lal 2, Yashpal Sharma 2, D. R. Doshi 1, R. J. Shastri 1, L. Sivaramakrishnan 1, K. Srikkanth 1, D. B. Vengsarkar 1.

†At Quetta, November 27. Indians won by four wickets. Baluchistan Governor's XI 170 for seven (35 overs) (Mohsin Khan 71, Mudassar Nazar 37); Indians 174 for six (34.2 overs) (M. Amarnath 43 not out, S. M. Gavaskar 36, Yashpal Sharma 34 not out).

BCCP XI v INDIANS

At Sahiwal, November 29, 30, December 1. Drawn. Set 245 to win in 80 minutes and twenty overs, the Indians played for a draw after losing three early wickets. The BCCP XI were 32 for three, only 65 ahead, when the final day began, but a century by their captain, Ijaz, enabled them to declare. On the first day, after a bad start, the BCCP XI had recovered well, thanks to Malik. The feature of the Indian batting was an unbeaten century by Vengsarkar.

BCCP XI

Rizwan-uz-Zaman lbw b Madan Lal	13	– c Kapil Dev b Shastri	12
Qasim Omar b Madan Lal	7	– b Shastri	15
Salim Malik not out	124	– b Shastri	1
Rameez Raza c and b Kapil Dev	1	– not out	73
Azhar Khan b Madan Lal	1	– c Kirmani b Shastri	8
*Ijaz Faqih b Shastri	51	– not out	100
†Ashraf Ali not out	66		
B 7, l-b 5, w 4, n-b 3	19	L-b 2	2

1/14 2/21 3/22   (5 wkts dec.) 282   1/20 2/27 3/32   (4 wkts dec.) 211
4/25 5/141   4/42

Amin Lakhani, Rashid Khan, Tahir Naqqash and Mansoor Elahi did not bat.

Bowling: *First Innings*— Kapil Dev 11–1–48–1; Madan Lal 15–6–37–3; Amarnath 4–1–15–0; Maninder 19–2–63–0; Shastri 29–9–33–1; Sivaramakrishnan 13–0–67–0. *Second Innings*—Madan Lal 4–1–7–0; Amarnath 2–0–10–0; Maninder 26–8–47–0; Shastri 29–6–80–4; Sivaramakrishnan 14–2–59–0; Srikkanth 1–0–6–0.

Indians

K. Srikkanth lbw b Rashid	33	– lbw b Tahir	20
Arun Lal c Tahir b Ijaz	76	– run out	6
D. B. Vengsarkar not out	100	– (5) not out	28
G. R. Viswanath not out	25		
M. Amarnath (did not bat)		– (3) not out	23
Madan Lal (did not bat)		– (4) c Ashraf b Rashid	3
L-b 5, n-b 10	15	B 2, l-b 2, w 1, n-b 1	6

1/48 2/162   (2 wkts dec.) 249   1/26 2/27 3/35   (3 wkts) 86

*Kapil Dev, †S. M. H. Kirmani, R. J. Shastri, L. Sivaramakrishnan and Maninder Singh did not bat.

Bowling: *First Innings*—Tahir 12–0–61–0; Rashid 13–0–50–1; Lakhani 16.4–3–49–0; Mansoor 5–0–20–0; Ijaz 19–2–43–1; Malik 1–0–6–0; Rizwan 1–0–5–0. *Second Innings*—Tahir 9–1–33–1; Rashid 6–1–14–1; Lakhani 2–1–7–0; Mansoor 7–0–26–0; Malik 1–1–0–0; Azhar 1–1–0–0; Qasim 1–1–0–0.

Umpires: Shakoor Rana and Khizar Hayat.

†PAKISTAN v INDIA

First One-day International

At Gujranwala, December 3. Pakistan won by 14 runs. After India had put Pakistan in, Miandad scored a brilliant century in 114 minutes with one 6 and twelve 4s. A fourth-wicket stand of 111 between him and Imran wrecked India's hope of dismissing Pakistan cheaply. After the early dismissal of India's openers, Vengsarkar and Amarnath added 71 for the third wicket. But that was not enough as Jalal struck twice in the same over, getting rid of Kapil Dev and Amarnath.

Pakistan

Mohsin Khan b Madan Lal	5	Mansoor Akhtar not out	21
Mudassar Nazar run out	20	B 1, l-b 6, w 6	13
Zaheer Abbas c Kapil Dev b Madan Lal	10		—
Javed Miandad not out	106	1/5 2/25 (4 wkts, 40 overs)	224
*Imran Khan b Kapil Dev	49	3/49 4/160	

Wasim Raja, Ijaz Faqih, †Wasim Bari, Tahir Naqqash and Jalal-ud-Din did not bat.

Bowling: Kapil Dev 8–1–42–1; Madan Lal 8–0–39–2; Amarnath 8–1–20–0; Sandhu 8–0–55–0; Shastri 6–0–41–0; Patil 2–0–14–0.

India

*S. M. Gavaskar lbw b Imran	1	Yashpal Sharma not out	56
K. Srikkanth c Bari b Imran	6	†S. M. H. Kirmani not out	27
D. B. Vengsarkar run out	39	B 1, l-b 3, w 2, n-b 5	11
M. Amarnath c Tahir b Jalal	51		—
S. M. Patil c Mohsin b Mudassar	4	1/2 2/13 3/84 (6 wkts, 40 overs)	210
Kapil Dev c Mansoor b Jalal	15	4/100 5/120 6/121	

Madan Lal, R. J. Shastri and B. S. Sandhu did not bat.

Bowling: Imran 8–0–38–2; Jalal 8–2–36–2; Tahir 8–0–31–0; Ijaz 8–0–38–0; Mudassar 7–0–50–1; Zaheer 1–0–6–0.

Umpires: Amanullah Khan and Shakeel Khan.

BCCP PATRON'S XI v INDIANS

At Rawalpindi, December 5, 6, 7. Drawn. When the match was abandoned owing to bad light, the Patron's XI had scored 8 for two when chasing 241 to win. On the first day the Indians scored 255 for three and the home side 23 for one. Zaheer scored his 99th first-class century on the second day, when, leading the Patron's XI, he hit five 6s and nine 4s in his 108. For the Indians, Srikkanth scored a scintillating century which included five 6s and seventeen 4s.

Indians

K. Srikkanth lbw b Tahir	8	– c Tauseef b Ijaz	135
Arun Lal b Raja	84	– c Malik b Tahir	17
*S. M. Gavaskar c Zaheer b Tauseef	84	– (6) not out	11
G. R. Viswanath not out	50	– (7) c Zaheer b Masood	5
S. M. Patil (did not bat)		– (3) c and b Raja	70
†Yashpal Sharma (did not bat)		– (4) c Zaheer b Masood	25
M. Amarnath (did not bat)		– st Yousuf b Masood	20
B. S. Sandhu (did not bat)		– c Sikander b Malik	6
L. Sivaramakrishnan (did not bat)		– c Malik b Tauseef	1
D. R. Doshi (did not bat)		– not out	5
B 9, l-b 10, w 4, n-b 6	29	B 2, l-b 3, n-b 7	12

1/13 2/165 3/255   (3 wkts dec.) 255   1/25 2/230 3/230   (8 wkts dec.) 307
4/274 5/277 6/283 7/290 8/298

Maninder Singh did not bat.

Bowling: *First Innings*—Sarfraz 13–2–52–0; Tahir 10–0–41–1; Sikander 10–1–25–0; Tauseef 20–4–58–1; Raja 11.3–3–36–1; Ijaz 9–2–14–0. *Second Innings*—Sarfraz 12–2–62–0; Tahir 6–0–25–1; Sikander 5–1–25–0; Tauseef 13–2–55–1; Raja 14–3–60–1; Ijaz 9–2–38–1; Masood 9–3–11–3; Mansoor 5–1–13–0; Malik 3–0–6–1.

Patron's XI

Mansoor Akhtar lbw b Maninder	39	– b Sandhu	4
Masood Anwar c Gavaskar b Maninder	8	– lbw b Amarnath	0
Salim Malik c Viswanath b Sandhu	105		
Wasim Raja c Arun Lal b Doshi	34	– (3) not out	3
*Zaheer Abbas c Yashpal b Doshi	108		
Ijaz Faqih not out	12	– (4) not out	0
B 9, l-b 6, n-b 1	16	L-b 1	1

1/23 2/86 3/137   (5 wkts dec.) 322   1/4 2/8   (2 wkts) 8
4/250 5/322

†Salim Yousuf, Tauseef Ahmed, Sarfraz Nawaz, Tahir Naqqash and Sikander Bakht did not bat.

Bowling: *First Innings*—Sandhu 12–4–44–1; Amarnath 8–2–36–0; Maninder 21–2–85–2; Doshi 18–0–71–2; Sivaramakrishnan 11–0–70–0. *Second Innings*—Sandhu 3–1–4–1; Amarnath 2–1–3–1.

Umpires: Mahboob Shah and Javed Akhtar.

PAKISTAN v INDIA

First Test Match

At Lahore, December 10, 11, 12, 14, 15. Drawn. The match, though rain-affected, was a statistician's delight. Pakistan thrashed the Indian attack to the tune of 485 after Gavaskar had put them in. Zaheer's 215 was his 100th first-class century – he became the twentieth batsman to have achieved this great feat – and his ninth for Pakistan. He batted for five and a half hours, hitting two 6s and 23 4s. Mohsin became the first Pakistani to complete 1,000 Test runs in a calendar year, his century being his fourth in Test matches, three of them at the Gaddafi Stadium, Lahore in 1982. Sarfraz took four for 63 in India's innings, having changed his mind about retiring. For India, Amarnath made his third Test century, reached in 383 minutes, and Gavaskar passed 7,000 runs in Tests, a feat achieved only by Boycott, Cowdrey, Hammond and Sobers. A draw became virtually inevitable after rain and bad light had accounted for a total of 235 minutes on the first and third days.

Pakistan

Mohsin Khan c Amarnath b Madan Lal	94	– not out	101
Mudassar Nazar c Gavaskar b Kapil Dev	50	– c Arun Lal b Doshi	17
Mansoor Akhtar c Gavaskar b Kapil Dev	3	– not out	14
Javed Miandad c Gavaskar b Madan Lal	17		
Zaheer Abbas b Doshi	215		
Salim Malik b Madan Lal	6		
*Imran Khan c Madan Lal b Doshi	45		
†Wasim Bari c Arun Lal b Doshi	12		
Tahir Naqqash st Kirmani b Doshi	20		
Sarfraz Nawaz c Amarnath b Doshi	18		
Jalal-ud-Din not out	1		
L-b 3, n-b 1	4	L-b 3	3

1/85 2/100 3/126 4/238   485 1/55   (1 wkt) 135
5/250 6/367 7/438 8/447 9/478

Bowling: *First Innings*—Kapil Dev 39–3–149–2; Madan Lal 27–2–101–3; Amarnath 23–5–60–0; Doshi 32.5–6–90–5; Shastri 22–3–81–0. *Second Innings*—Kapil Dev 8–2–27–0; Madan Lal 5–1–10–0; Amarnath 3–1–5–0; Doshi 15–2–57–1; Shastri 14–1–33–0; Gavaskar 1–1–0–0.

India

*S. M. Gavaskar c Bari b Sarfraz	83
Arun Lal c Mudassar b Imran	51
D. B. Vengsarkar c Mudassar b Imran	3
G. R. Viswanath c Bari b Imran	1
M. Amarnath not out	109
S. M. Patil run out	68
Kapil Dev c Bari b Sarfraz	9
R. J. Shastri lbw b Jalal	7
†S. M. H. Kirmani c Bari b Jalal	10
Madan Lal c Malik b Sarfraz	7
D. R. Doshi b Sarfraz	0
B 2, l-b 11, n-b 18	31

1/105 2/111 3/123   379
4/188 5/294 6/305
7/322 8/348 9/375

Bowling: Imran 27–8–68–3; Sarfraz 31.5–11–63–4; Jalal 34–10–93–2; Tahir 29–6–114–0; Mudassar 3–1–10–0.

Umpires: Amanullah Khan and Mahboob Shah.

†PAKISTAN v INDIA

Second One-day International

At Multan, December 17. Pakistan won by 37 runs. After Pakistan had won the toss, magnificent centuries by Zaheer and Mohsin helped them to a two-nil lead in the one-day series. They shared a record stand of 205 in 27 overs, the highest for any wicket in one-day internationals, surpassing the previous best of 182 between McCosker and Turner for Australia against Sri Lanka in the 1975 World Cup. Despite Patil's 84 and his fourth-wicket partnership of 109 with Vengsarkar, India's reply, though spirited, was inadequate.

Pakistan

Mohsin Khan not out	117
Mudassar Nazar run out	12
Zaheer Abbas b Kapil Dev	118
Javed Miandad not out	3
B 1, l-b 10, w 2	13

1/41 2/246   (2 wkts, 40 overs) 263

Mansoor Akhtar, *Imran Khan, Wasim Raja, †Wasim Bari, Jalal-ud-Din, Ijaz Faqih and Sikander Bakht did not bat.

Bowling: Kapil Dev 8–0–42–1; Sandhu 8–0–28–0; Amarnath 6–0–46–0; Doshi 8–1–58–0; Shastri 4–0–31–0; Yashpal 6–0–45–0.

India

K. Srikkanth b Jalal	8	†S. M. H. Kirmani not out	16
Arun Lal b Jalal	6	R. J. Shastri not out	3
*D. B. Vengsarkar c Sikander b Zaheer.	37	L-b 10, w 3, n-b 2	15
M. Amarnath c Mansoor b Ijaz	6		
S. M. Patil c Miandad b Zaheer	84	1/14 2/17	(7 wkts, 40 overs) 226
Kapil Dev b Mudassar	35	3/34 4/143	
Yashpal Sharma b Mudassar	16	5/162 6/190 7/205	

D. R. Doshi and B. S. Sandhu did not bat.

Bowling: Imran 8–4–14–0; Jalal 4–0–21–2; Ijaz 8–0–50–1; Mudassar 7–0–40–2; Mansoor 1–0–3–0; Sikander 8–1–50–0; Zaheer 4–0–33–2.

Umpires: Shakoor Rana and Khizar Hayat.

PUNJAB GOVERNOR'S XI v INDIANS

At Multan, December 18, 19, 20. Drawn. A prolific scorer in first-class cricket, Qasim Omar shared a first-wicket stand of 208 in the Governor's XI's second innings with Shoaib Mohammad, son of Hanif. Facing a deficit of 196, Qasim and Shoaib batted for most of the final day to gain a draw. Spinners had revelled on a turning wicket as fourteen wickets fell on the opening day, all of the Governor's XI to Maninder Singh and Sivaramakrishnan.

Governor's XI

Qasim Omar c and b Maninder	55	– c Arun Lal b Maninder	120
Shoaib Mohammad c Gavaskar b Maninder	25	– c Vengsarkar b Maninder	82
Aamer Malik c Sivaramakrishnan b Maninder	2	– (4) b Maninder	0
Mohammad Javed b Maninder	17	– (3) not out	5
*Wasim Raja c Viswanath b Sivaramakrishnan	4		
Zafar Ahmed b Sivaramakrishnan	17	– (5) c Kirmani b Maninder	1
Iqbal Sikandar c Shastri b Sivaramakrishnan	4		
†Anil Dalpat st Kirmani b Maninder	1	– (6) not out	0
Shahid Mahboob c Gavaskar b Maninder	0		
Iqbal Qasim b Sivaramakrishnan	1		
Azeem Hafeez not out	1		
L-b 4, w 1	5	L-b 6, w 1	7

1/82 2/87 3/90 4/108   132   1/208 2/209   (4 wkts) 215
5/108 6/121 7/122 8/124 9/127   3/209 4/211

Bowling: *First Innings*—Sandhu 12–2–27–0; Srikkanth 5–1–19–0; Maninder 24–7–35–6; Sivaramakrishnan 20.2–5–46–4. *Second Innings*—Sandhu 12–2–36–0; Srikkanth 2–0–3–0; Maninder 33–14–49–4; Sivaramakrishnan 28–5–62–0; Shastri 26–6–46–0; Viswanath 2–0–12–0.

Indians

K. Srikkanth st Anil b Iqbal	64	†S. M. H. Kirmani c Omar b Shahid	27
Arun Lal c Raja b Azeem	10	B. S. Sandhu c Zafar b Iqbal	7
D. B. Vengsarkar b Qasim	4	L. Sivaramakrishnan not out	0
G. R. Viswanath run out	16	B 16, l-b 4, w 9, n-b 7	36
Yashpal Sharma b Qasim	0		
*S. M. Gavaskar st Anil b Iqbal	50	1/33 2/74 3/84 4/95	(9 wkts dec.) 328
R. J. Shastri c Anil b Iqbal	93	5/117 6/194 7/255 8/282 9/328	

Maninder Singh did not bat.

Bowling: Shahid 13–2–47–1; Azeem 21–3–94–1; Iqbal 29.3–7–72–4; Qasim 25–9–46–2; Raja 12–0–33–0.

Umpires: Agha Saadat and Mian Aslam.

PAKISTAN v INDIA

Second Test Match

At Karachi, December 23, 24, 25, 27. Pakistan won by an innings and 86 runs. This was Pakistan's biggest-ever victory over India, erasing the previous largest – by an innings and 43 runs at Lucknow in 1952-53. Pakistan put India in and bowled them out for 169, the only real resistance coming from Kapil Dev. In reply Pakistan piled up another huge total. Zaheer and Mudassar added 213 for the fifth wicket, Mudassar passing 1,500 runs in Tests. Pakistan's victory was achieved with a day to spare, Imran finishing with match figures of eleven for 79, which took him past 200 wickets in Tests. India's dramatic collapse in their second innings sealed their fate, when they crashed from 102 for one to 114 for seven, Imran's blistering pace being altogether too much for them.

India

*S. M. Gavaskar run out	8	– b Imran	42
Arun Lal lbw b Sarfraz	35	– lbw b Qadir	11
D. B. Vengsarkar c Mohsin b Imran	0	– c Bari b Imran	79
G. R. Viswanath c Bari b Qadir	24	– b Imran	0
M. Amarnath lbw b Imran	5	– lbw b Imran	3
S. M. Patil c Miandad b Qadir	4	– b Imran	0
Kapil Dev c and b Sarfraz	73	– (8) b Imran	1
†S. M. H. Kirmani c Mohsin b Qadir	11	– (7) c Malik b Qadir	1
Madan Lal not out	3	– not out	52
Maninder Singh lbw b Qadir	0	– lbw b Imran	0
D. R. Doshi b Imran	0	– b Imran	0
L-b 4, n-b 2	6	B 1, l-b 3, w 1, n-b 3	8

1/10 2/10 3/48 4/55   169   1/28 2/102 3/108 4/112   197
5/70 6/130 7/165 8/168 9/168   5/112 6/113 7/114 8/197 9/197

Bowling: *First Innings*—Imran 12.1–6–19–3; Jalal 10–2–28–0; Sarfraz 16–2–49–2; Qadir 15–3–67–4. *Second Innings*—Imran 20.1–4–60–8; Jalal 7–2–31–0; Sarfraz 10–2–23–0; Qadir 23–3–75–2.

Pakistan

Mohsin Khan c Amarnath b Madan Lal .. 12	†Wasim Bari c Arun Lal b Doshi 30
Mansoor Akhtar c Kirmani b Madan Lal. 0	Abdul Qadir b Kapil Dev 0
Salim Malik c Kirmani b Madan Lal.... 3	Sarfraz Nawaz lbw b Kapil Dev.......... 13
Javed Miandad b Amarnath............... 39	Jalal-ud-Din not out 0
Zaheer Abbas lbw b Kapil Dev 186	B 2, l-b 6, w 2, n-b 7 17
Mudassar Nazar c Kirmani b Kapil Dev .119	
*Imran Khan c Amarnath b Kapil Dev.. 33	1/6 2/15 3/18 4/128 452
	5/341 6/397 7/427 8/427 9/452

Bowling: Kapil Dev 28.5–3–102–5; Madan Lal 23–1–129–3; Maninder 23–2–67–0; Amarnath 17–1–69–1; Doshi 18–1–68–1.

Umpires: Khizar Hayat and Shakoor Ahmed.

†PAKISTAN v INDIA

Third One-day International

At Lahore, December 31. India won on faster scoring-rate (7.14 runs per over to 6.48) after bad light had stopped play, India having scored 193 for four in 27 overs in reply to Pakistan's 252 for three in 33. The result was calculated on Pakistan's score (175 for two) after 27 overs. The number of overs had already been reduced by seven after the start had been delayed by 45 minutes. Imran won the toss, whereupon Zaheer (one 6 and seven 4s) scored his fifth century in one-day internationals and Miandad (one 6 and eight 4s) made a hurricane 119.

Pakistan

Mohsin Khan c and b Kapil Dev.........	0	Wasim Raja not out....................... 1
Mudassar Nazar c and b Shastri..........	24	L-b 1, w 2 3
Zaheer Abbas c Srikkanth b Amarnath	.105	
Javed Miandad not out.....................	119	1/1 2/70 3/228 (3 wkts, 33 overs) 252

Mansoor Akhtar, *Imran Khan, Ijaz Faqih, †Wasim Bari, Shahid Mahboob and Tahir Naqqash did not bat.

Bowling: Kapil Dev 7–0–73–1; Madan Lal 7–0–35–0; Sandhu 7–0–52–0; Shastri 7–0–39–1; Amarnath 5–0–50–1.

India

*S. M. Gavaskar c Mansoor b Tahir....	69	M. Amarnath not out...................... 1
K. Srikkanth c Zaheer b Shahid	39	L-b 7, w 12, n-b 2................. 21
S. M. Patil c Raja b Mudassar.............	51	
Kapil Dev lbw b Mudassar	6	1/57 2/172 (4 wkts, 27 overs) 193
Yashpal Sharma not out...................	6	3/185 4/192

D. B. Vengsarkar, †S. M. H. Kirmani, R. J. Shastri, Madan Lal and B. S. Sandhu did not bat.

Bowling: Imran 5–2–23–0; Tahir 6–0–42–1; Shahid 7–0–55–1; Ijaz 7–0–39–0; Mudassar 2–0–13–2.

Umpires: Shakoor Rana and Khizar Hayat.

PAKISTAN v INDIA

Third Test Match

At Faisalabad, January 3, 4, 5, 7, 8. Pakistan won by ten wickets. For India the one consolation in defeat was Gavaskar's 26th Test century, the same number as Gary Sobers and only three fewer than D. G. Bradman's world record. He also became the first Indian to carry his bat through a completed Test innings, batting for more than seven hours.

Pakistan's victory was another personal triumph for Imran, who, by following his century and six wickets in India's first innings with five more in the second, became only the second player to have scored a century and taken ten wickets in the same Test match, the other being England's Ian Botham at Bombay in 1980. Four centuries in their first innings – by Miandad, Zaheer, Malik and Imran – reflected Pakistan's vast superiority and took them to their highest score against India.

India

*S. M. Gavaskar c Malik b Imran	12	– not out 127
Arun Lal b Sarfraz.....................	0	– c Zaheer b Sarfraz................. 3
D. B. Vengsarkar lbw b Imran..................	6	– lbw b Imran.................... 1
G. R. Viswanath b Mudassar..................	53	– c Miandad b Sarfraz............ 9
M. Amarnath b Mudassar.................	22	– lbw b Imran.................... 78
S. M. Patil c Bari b Imran...........	85	– b Imran........................ 6
Kapil Dev lbw b Imran.................	41	– c Sikander b Sarfraz............ 16
†S. M. H. Kirmani b Imran............	66	– c Bari b Sikander............... 6
Madan Lal c Malik b Imran...........	54	– lbw b Sarfraz 10
Maninder Singh c Mohsin b Qadir	6	– lbw b Imran.................... 2
D. R. Doshi not out...............	2	– b Imran........................ 4
B 6, l-b 7, w 4, n-b 8................	25	B 1, l-b 9, n-b 14.......... 24

1/6 2/17 3/22 4/82	373	1/27 2/28 3/48 4/193	286
5/122 6/220 7/235 8/357 9/370		5/201 6/227 7/236 8/261 9/282	

Bowling: *First Innings*—Imran 25–3–99–6; Sarfraz 23–4–95–1; Sikander 13–1–66–0; Mudassar 12–2–39–2; Qadir 12.3–1–48–1. *Second Innings*—Imran 30.5–12–82–5; Sarfraz 33–11–79–4; Sikander 9–3–41–1; Mudassar 11–3–27–0; Qadir 11–1–33–0.

Pakistan

Mohsin Khan c Kirmani b Kapil Dev..............	4	– not out 8
Mudassar Nazar c Kirmani b Kapil Dev...........	38	– not out 2
Mansoor Akhtar c Kirmani b Kapil Dev	23	
Javed Miandad c Gavaskar b Madan Lal.........126		
Zaheer Abbas c Kirmani b Madan Lal.............168		
Salim Malik b Kapil Dev....................107		
*Imran Khan c Madan Lal b Maninder 117		
†Wasim Bari c Kirmani b Kapil Dev	6	
Sarfraz Nawaz c Gavaskar b Kapil Dev............	4	
Abdul Qadir not out	38	
Sikander Bakht b Kapil Dev	9	
L-b 10, n-b 2...................................	12	

1/4 2/66 3/79 4/366	652	(no wkt) 10
5/367 6/574 7/595 8/599 9/612		

Bowling: *First Innings*—Kapil Dev 38.4–3–220–7; Madan Lal 28–5–109–2; Doshi 29–2–130–0; Amarnath 16–1–68–0; Maninder 29–3–103–1; Gavaskar 2–0–10–0. *Second Innings*—Arun Lal 1.1–0–6–0; Vengsarkar 1–0–4–0.

Umpires: Mahboob Shah and Shakil Ahmed.

NWFP GOVERNOR'S XI v INDIANS

At Peshawar, January 10, 11, 12. Indians won by four wickets. Chasing a target of 250 in 83 minutes and twenty overs, the Indians stormed to victory in brilliant fashion. Haroon, leading the Governor's XI, declared 55 minutes before stumps on the first day, having scored 133 himself, and the Indians were 15 for three at the close. At the end of the second day the home side, 37 behind on the first innings, were 65 for one. On the final day Haroon's second declaration came after Raja and Ijaz had each made centuries.

Governor's XI

Mansoor Akhtar c Maninder b Sandhu	15	– c and b Doshi	47
Shoaib Mohammad lbw b Doshi	71	– lbw b Sandhu	19
*Haroon Rashid b Maninder	133		
Wasim Raja not out	6	– (3) not out	102
Ijaz Faqih not out	7	– (4) not out	100
B 10, l-b 11, n-b 2	23	B 4, l-b 9, n-b 5	18

1/22 2/242 3/242   (3 wkts dec.) 255   1/29 2/80   (2 wkts dec.) 286

Nasir Abbas, †Masood Iqbal, Anwar Zeb, Afzaal Butt, Zakir Khan and Farrukh Zaman did not bat.

Bowling: *First Innings*—Sandhu 14–4–58–1; Amarnath 7–4–21–0; Srikkanth 1–0–5–0; Maninder 17–1–51–1; Doshi 22–5–53–1; Sivaramakrishnan 8–0–44–0. *Second Innings*—Sandhu 15–3–47–1; Amarnath 7–2–23–0; Srikkanth 4–0–28–0; Maninder 26–5–87–0; Doshi 15–1–39–1; Arun Lal 5–0–23–0; Vengsarkar 5–0–21–0.

Indians

K. Srikkanth b Zakir	2	– (2) b Afzaal	67
Arun Lal run out	0	– (1) c Raja b Afzaal	6
D. B. Vengsarkar not out	100	– (7) not out	26
†Yashpal Sharma run out	2	– (3) b Afzaal	13
*G. R. Viswanath c Masood b Afzaal	4	– (8) not out	4
S. M. Patil b Ijaz	137	– (5) b Zakir	33
M. Amarnath not out	27	– (4) c Ijaz b Shoaib	84
B. S. Sandhu (did not bat)	–	(6) run out	5
B 11, l-b 4, n-b 5	20	B 1, l-b 12, n-b 2	15

1/0 2/2 3/12 4/15   (5 wkts dec.) 292   1/40 2/80 3/97 4/171   (6 wkts) 253
5/227   5/205 6/245

L. Sivaramakrishnan, Maninder Singh and D. R. Doshi did not bat.

Bowling: *First Innings*—Afzaal 12–5–29–1; Zakir 12–2–44–1; Nasir 8–1–51–0; Farrukh 6–0–34–0; Ijaz 16–1–63–1; Raja 16–2–49–0; Anwar 2.1–1–2–0. *Second Innings*—Afzaal 13–0–79–3; Zakir 12–0–85–1; Ijaz 5–0–41–0; Anwar 2–0–10–0; Mansoor 1–0–10–0; Shoaib 1–0–9–1; Haroon 0.1–0–4–0.

Umpires: Amanullah Khan and Masroor Ali.

PAKISTAN v INDIA

Fourth Test Match

At Hyderabad, January 14, 15, 16, 18, 19. Pakistan won by an innings and 119 runs, an even more sweeping victory than in Karachi. After winning the toss Pakistan scored 581 for three in two days. The feature of the innings was the third-wicket stand of 451 between Mudassar and Miandad, which equalled the world Test record for any wicket. Both batsmen made their highest Test score. India, again hopelessly outplayed, were all out for the first time for 189 on the third day, Sandhu, on his Test début, contributing a defiant 71. Forced to follow on, they suffered another disastrous collapse on the final morning, when their last seven wickets fell for only 72 runs. Viswanath equalled Sobers's world record of 85 consecutive Test appearances.

Pakistan

Mohsin Khan lbw b Sandhu	24	Zaheer Abbas not out		25
Mudassar Nazar c Maninder b Doshi	231	B 9, l-b 12		21
Haroon Rashid b Sandhu	0			
Javed Miandad not out	280	1/60 2/60 3/511	(3 wkts dec.)	581

Salim Malik, *Imran Khan, †Wasim Bari, Sarfraz Nawaz, Abdul Qadir and Iqbal Qasim did not bat.

Bowling: *First Innings*—Kapil Dev 27–2–111–0; Sandhu 33–7–107–2; Amarnath 15–0–64–0; Maninder 50–10–135–0; Doshi 41–9–143–1.

India

*S. M. Gavaskar c Bari b Imran	17	– c and b Qasim		60
K. Srikkanth lbw b Sarfraz	2	– c Malik b Imran		5
M. Amarnath st Bari b Imran	61	– c Imran b Qasim		64
G. R. Viswanath lbw b Imran	0	– lbw b Sarfraz		37
D. B. Vengsarkar c Bari b Imran	4	– not out		58
Kapil Dev b Imran	3	– b Sarfraz		2
†S. M. H. Kirmani b Imran	1	– lbw b Sarfraz		0
S. M. Patil c Imran b Sarfraz	2	– c Imran b Qadir		9
B. S. Sandhu b Sarfraz	71	– c Imran b Qadir		12
Maninder Singh not out	12	– lbw b Sarfraz		4
D. R. Doshi lbw b Imran	1	– b Imran		14
B 1, l-b 7, n-b 7	15	B 1, l-b 1, n-b 6		8

1/3 2/44 3/44 4/52	189	1/8 2/133 3/134 4/201	273
5/61 6/65 7/72 8/131 9/184		5/203 6/203 7/223 8/249 9/254

Bowling: *First Innings*—Imran 17.2–3–35–6; Sarfraz 19–5–56–3; Qadir 11–2–35–0; Qasim 9–3–48–1. *Second Innings*—Imran 24.4–14–45–2; Sarfraz 30–4–85–4; Qadir 26–7–77–2; Qasim 31–9–58–2.

Umpires: Javed Akhtar and Khizar Hayat.

†PAKISTAN v INDIA

Fourth One-day International

At Karachi, January 21. Pakistan won by eight wickets to clinch the four-match series by a three-one margin. Zaheer's seventh hundred against the tourists included three 6s and eleven 4s. He received 99 balls and with Mudassar added 170 for the second wicket. After India had won the toss and managed no more than 197 for six, it was virtually inevitable that Pakistan would have little difficulty knocking off the runs.

India

K. Srikkanth c Tahir b Ijaz	48	D. B. Vengsarkar not out		22
Arun Lal b Sarfraz	16	†S. M. H. Kirmani not out		1
M. Amarnath b Sarfraz	8	L-b 12, w 16, n-b 4		32
Yashpal Sharma c Imran b Sarfraz	27			
Kapil Dev c Mansoor b Imran	20	1/41 2/54 3/120	(6 wkts, 40 overs)	197
*S. M. Gavaskar c Raja b Imran	23	4/124 5/162 6/192		

T. A. Sekhar, B. S. Sandhu and Maninder Singh did not bat.

Bowling: Imran 8–3–15–2; Tahir 8–1–38–0; Mudassar 8–1–30–0; Sarfraz 8–1–31–3; Ijaz 8–0–51–1.

Pakistan

Mohsin Khan lbw b Sandhu	5
Mudassar Nazar not out	61
Zaheer Abbas c Amarnath b Sandhu	113
Javed Miandad not out	6
L-b 9, w 4	13

1/9 2/179   (2 wkts, 35 overs) 198

Mansoor Akhtar, Wasim Raja, *Imran Khan, Ijaz Faqih, †Wasim Bari, Sarfraz Nawaz and Tahir Naqqash did not bat.

Bowling: Kapil Dev 5–1–11–0; Sandhu 7–0–38–2; Sekhar 4–0–19–0; Srikkanth 2–0–27–0; Yashpal 8–0–39–0; Maninder 8–0–47–0; Gavaskar 1–0–4–0.

Umpires: Mahboob Shah and Khizar Hayat.

PAKISTAN v INDIA

Fifth Test Match

At Lahore, January 23, 24, 25, 27, 28. Drawn. The fourth and fifth days' play was washed out by heavy and unseasonable thunderstorms. Although India had lost the series at Hyderabad, their display in this fifth Test provided some consolation. Amarnath scored another century, establishing a new third-wicket record for India against Pakistan of 190, with Yashpal, and there was an outstanding performance by Kapil Dev, who claimed the last three wickets in Pakistan's innings in five balls and finished with eight for 85, his best Test figures. However, this time it was a Pakistani, Mudassar, who carried his bat through an innings, thus emulating, with his 152 not out, his father, Nazar Mohammad, who did the same against India in Lucknow in 1952-53.

Pakistan

Mohsin Khan c Srikkanth b Kapil Dev	7	Sarfraz Nawaz c Yashpal b Kapil Dev	26
Mudassar Nazar not out	152	Abdul Qadir b Kapil Dev	0
Majid J. Khan c Kirmani b Kapil Dev	0	Iqbal Qasim lbw b Kapil Dev	0
Javed Miandad c Viswanath b Maninder	85	L-b 6	6
Zaheer Abbas c Kirmani b Kapil Dev	13		
Salim Malik b Maninder	6	1/22 2/26 3/178	323
*Imran Khan c Kirmani b Kapil Dev	20	4/191 5/202 6/244	
†Wasim Bari c Amarnath b Kapil Dev	8	7/276 8/323 9/323	

Bowling: Kapil Dev 30.5–7–85–8; Sandhu 21–2–56–0; Sekhar 20–2–86–0; Maninder 32–7–90–2.

India

*S. M. Gavaskar lbw b Imran	13	D. B. Vengsarkar not out	1
K. Srikkanth b Qadir	21	B 6, l-b 5, w 1, n-b 5	17
M. Amarnath c Bari b Imran	120		
Yashpal Sharma not out	63	1/29 2/41 3/231 (3 wkts) 235	

G. R. Viswanath, Kapil Dev, †S. M. H. Kirmani, B. S. Sandhu, Maninder Singh and T. A. Sekhar did not bat.

Bowling: Imran 18–5–45–2; Sarfraz 23.2–9–46–0; Qadir 16–1–63–1; Majid 1–0–4–0; Mudassar 11–1–41–0; Qasim 12–3–19–0.

Umpires: Javed Akhtar and Khizar Hayat.

PAKISTAN v INDIA

Sixth Test Match

At Karachi, January 30, 31, February 1, 3, 4. Drawn. Crowd demonstrations, thought to have been prompted by students protesting against arrests made at a University campus brawl, and high scores made this a typical Karachi Test. The fourth day's play had to be abandoned after lunch, because of the rioting. In completing his sixth Test century Mudassar passed 2,000 runs for Pakistan, and Wasim Bari became only the fourth wicket-keeper to claim 200 Test victims. For India Amarnath made his fifth Test hundred and his third of the series, reached in 238 minutes in the last hour of the last day. He and Kirmani also reached 2,000 Test runs. Shastri's maiden century for India, which he scored as a stop-gap opener, was an outstanding achievement.

India

*S. M. Gavaskar c Bari b Tahir	5	– b Imran	67
R. J. Shastri st Bari b Qadir	128	– c Bari b Imran	17
M. Amarnath c Bari b Imran	19	– not out	103
Yashpal Sharma c Bari b Imran	9	– not out	19
D. B. Vengsarkar c and b Tahir	89		
G. R. Viswanath b Mudassar	10		
†S. M. H. Kirmani c Zaheer b Sarfraz	18		
Kapil Dev lbw b Imran	33		
B. S. Sandhu not out	32		
T. A. Sekhar not out	0		
B 13, l-b 9, n-b 28	50	B 10, w 3, n-b 5	18

1/47 2/86 3/109 4/178   (8 wkts dec.) 393   1/43 2/150   (2 wkts) 224
5/218 6/267 7/316 8/393

Maninder Singh did not bat.

Bowling: *First Innings*—Imran 32–11–65–3; Sarfraz 41–10–92–1; Tahir 24–7–69–2; Qadir 13–3–86–1; Mudassar 15–4–30–1; Raja 1–0–1–0. *Second Innings*—Imran 16–3–41–2; Sarfraz 14–4–45–0; Tahir 8–1–28–0; Qadir 14–2–42–0; Raja 5–2–12–0; Zaheer 8–2–24–0; Mohsin 1–0–3–0; Miandad 2–0–11–0.

Pakistan

Mohsin Khan lbw b Kapil Dev	91	†Wasim Bari c Kirmani b Sandhu	12
Mudassar Nazar lbw b Kapil Dev	152	Sarfraz Nawaz not out	6
Javed Miandad c Kirmani b Sandhu	47	B 5, l-b 12, w 1, n-b 9	27
Zaheer Abbas c Amarnath b Shastri	43		
Wasim Raja run out	10	1/157 2/269 3/342 (6 wkts dec.) 420	
*Imran Khan not out	32	4/362 5/371 6/411	

Salim Malik, Abdul Qadir and Tahir Naqqash did not bat.

Bowling: Kapil Dev 33–2–137–2; Sandhu 28.2–4–87–2; Sekhar 14–1–43–0; Maninder 16–3–49–0; Shastri 22–1–62–1; Amarnath 5–1–15–0.

Umpires: Javed Akhtar and Khizar Hayat.

THE NEW ZEALANDERS IN AUSTRALIA, 1982-83

By way of preparation for the Benson and Hedges World Series Cup, which started on January 9, the New Zealanders spent two and a half weeks in Australia before Christmas, which they had at home. In this time they played two first-class matches and two one-day games. They were thoughtfully captained on their two-part tour by Geoff Howarth and reinforced for the first time for six years by Glenn Turner.

Their WSC matches against Australia, though not those against England, followed the somewhat acrimonious pattern of recent years, with the Australian players, more often than not, being the aggressors. Until he pulled a hamstring Richard Hadlee, both as batsman and bowler, did as much as anyone to enable New Zealand to head the WSC qualifying table. Turner batted well until the finals, John Wright scored quite consistently and Lance Cairns made some dangerous sorties with the bat. With Ewen Chatfield, Cairns and Martin Snedden all bowling steadily, New Zealand acquitted themselves well, until being heavily beaten by Australia in the one-day finals.

†At Horsham, December 8. New Zealanders won by seven wickets and batted on. Victorian Country XI 146 for eight (50 overs) (G. K. Robertson three for 43); New Zealanders 186 for five (50 overs) (M. D. Crowe 77, B. A. Edgar 44, B. R. Blair 38).

VICTORIA v NEW ZEALANDERS

At Melbourne, December 10, 11, 12, 13. Tied. This was the first first-class match in Australia to end in a tie since 1976-77 and the first in Melbourne since 1956-57. Left with 246 to win in 100 minutes plus the last twenty overs, Victoria, at 174 for three and up with the clock, looked like doing it. In the end, though, they needed 6 from the last over, with their last pair together, and 1 to win with two balls to go, whereupon Callen was bowled, middle stump, by Snedden. Fewer than 100 people watched the finish, which came at the end of a final day's play which produced 419 runs. The relaid Melbourne pitch, being used for the first time, played well enough for a result never to be likely without the help of declarations.

New Zealanders

B. A. Edgar run out	66	– (2) c Watts b Bright	45
M. D. Crowe c Watts b Balcam	27	– (1) c Miles b McCurdy	13
*G. P. Howarth c Whatmore b McCurdy	102		
J. V. Coney c Miles b McCurdy	10	– not out	18
J. F. Reid c Watts b Bright	2	– (3) b Balcam	58
J. F. M. Morrison not out	32	– (5) not out	25
†W. K. Lees c Balcam b Bright	2		
M. C. Snedden b Callen	3		
G. K. Robertson c Green b Balcam	14		
G. B. Troup c Yallop b Balcam	1		
B 4, l-b 10, w 3, n-b 25	42	B 1, l-b 10, n-b 4	15

1/64 2/170 3/234 4/239   (9 wkts dec.) 301   1/20 2/130   (3 wkts dec.) 174
5/245 6/252 7/262 8/297 9/301   3/132

E. J. Chatfield did not bat.

Bowling: First Innings—Callen 20–6–50–1; McCurdy 28–13–52–2; Bright 34–10–89–2; Balcam 17.2–1–53–3; Green 8–4–15–0; Yallop 1–1–0–0. *Second Innings*—Callen 8–1–21–0; McCurdy 9–0–29–1; Bright 16–2–56–1; Balcam 13–1–41–1; Green 4–0–12–0.

Victoria

J. M. Wiener c Lees b Troup	3	– (2) st Lees b Morrison	75
G. M. Watts lbw b Howarth	45	– (1) c Howarth b Robertson	25
*G. N. Yallop c Morrison b Troup	38	– c Lees b Troup	33
D. F. Whatmore c Coney b Morrison	81	– b Chatfield	13
M. D. Taylor not out	34	– c Crowe b Morrison	38
B. C. Green b Robertson	1	– c Reid b Morrison	5
†G. J. Miles not out	15	– (10) run out	0
L. F. Balcam (did not bat)		– (7) b Snedden	0
I. W. Callen (did not bat)		– (8) b Snedden	21
R. J. McCurdy (did not bat)		– (9) b Morrison	15
R. J. Bright (did not bat)		– not out	0
L-b 5, n-b 8	13	B 10, l-b 8, n-b 2	20

1/5 2/52	(5 wkts dec.) 230	1/53 2/106 3/127 4/195 245
3/151 4/195 5/196		5/203 6/207 7/209 8/240 9/241

Bowling: First Innings—Troup 8–0–30–2; Snedden 14–5–53–0; Chatfield 17–6–40–0; Robertson 10–1–26–1; Morrison 17–5–39–1; Howarth 8–2–21–1; Crowe 3–1–8–0. *Second Innings*—Troup 8–0–33–1; Snedden 7.5–0–28–2; Chatfield 9–0–46–1; Robertson 5–0–30–1; Morrison 9–0–62–4; Coney 5–0–26–0.

Umpires: R. C. Bailhache and A. Nicosia.

†At Sydney, December 16. New South Wales won by 16 runs. New South Wales 239 for eight (50 overs) (T. M. Chappell 89, J. Dyson 44); New Zealanders 223 for seven (50 overs) (J. F. M. Morrison 63, G. P. Howarth 32; G. R. J. Matthews three for 41).

QUEENSLAND v NEW ZEALANDERS

At Salter Oval, Bundaberg, December 18, 19, 20, 21. Drawn. This was the first first-class match to be played anywhere in Queensland other than at Brisbane. With 6,649 spectators paying to watch, it was considered a successful departure and one that could in future be extended to take in the Sheffield Shield. After Queensland's first innings of 403 for three declared, in which Wessels, Border and Kerr all made hundreds, the New Zealanders were at different times in danger of defeat. They were saved from it in the end by Morrison, at 35 their oldest player, who made 78 not out on the last day after the New Zealanders had been left 358 to win and lost wickets steadily. Ray Phillips, the Queensland wicket-keeper, claimed nine victims in the match, seven of them in the first innings.

Queensland

*K. C. Wessels b Robertson	129	– (7) c Lees b Chatfield	16
W. B. Kerr c Troup b Carrington	102	– (6) run out	33
A. R. Border not out	104	– (8) not out	30
G. M. Ritchie b Morrison	24	– run out	9
A. B. Courtice not out	21	– (1) c and b Chatfield	37
T. V. Hohns (did not bat)		– (2) c Lees b Carrington	28
†R. B. Phillips (did not bat)		– (3) c Lees b Troup	61
A. B. Henschell (did not bat)		– (5) c Reid b Coney	1
H. Frei (did not bat)		– c Crowe b Robertson	14
M. S. Mainhardt (did not bat)		– run out	5
C. G. Rackemann (did not bat)		– c Carrington b Troup	3
B 7, l-b 2, n-b 14	23	B 3, l-b 8, w 1, n-b 9	21

1/232 2/251   (3 wkts dec.) 403   1/52 2/109 3/128 4/140   258
3/303   5/155 6/197 7/204 8/247 9/252

Bowling: *First Innings*—Troup 16-3-54-0; Carrington 16-2-82-1; Robertson 15-0-94-1; Chatfield 18-7-43-0; Howarth 6-0-30-0; Coney 18-5-34-0; Morrison 15-4-43-1. *Second Innings*—Troup 13.5-1-41-2; Carrington 10-0-51-1; Robertson 13-2-56-1; Chatfield 14-3-31-2; Coney 12-5-29-1; Crowe 10-1-29-0.

New Zealanders

M. D. Crowe c Border b Rackemann	9	– c Phillips b Frei	0
*G. P. Howarth c Phillips b Henschell	138	– c Kerr b Rackemann	13
J. F. Reid c Phillips b Rackemann	0	– lbw b Rackemann	43
J. V. Coney c Border b Mainhardt	0	– c Ritchie b Rackemann	0
B. R. Blair c Phillips b Frei	27	– c Phillips b Mainhardt	19
J. F. M. Morrison c Courtice b Hohns	62	– not out	78
†W. K. Lees c Phillips b Rackemann	1	– c Kerr b Hohns	19
G. K. Robertson c Phillips b Rackemann	0	– c Border b Hohns	18
G. B. Troup c Phillips b Rackemann	21	– not out	1
M. S. Carrington st Phillips b Hohns	10		
E. J. Chatfield not out	0		
B 1, l-b 7, n-b 18	26	B 8, l-b 5, w 2, n-b 15	30

1/11 2/23 3/52 4/126   304   1/5 2/33 3/33   (7 wkts) 221
5/248 6/250 7/250 8/285 9/304   4/68 5/138 6/174 7/210

Bowling: *First Innings*—Rackemann 20-6-47-5; Frei 19-2-59-1; Mainhardt 12-2-44-1; Hohns 17.2-2-70-2; Henschell 16-2-58-1; Border 1-1-0-0. *Second Innings*—Rackemann 21.3-8-40-3; Frei 20-7-44-1; Mainhardt 8-0-20-1; Hohns 22-8-60-2; Henschell 13-4-27-0.

Umpires: C. D. Timmins and M. W. Johnson.

†At Geelong, January 7. New Zealanders won by 99 runs. New Zealanders 292 (50 overs) (R. J. Hadlee 117, J. G. Wright 62); Geelong 193 for five (50 overs) (C. Lynch 54, P. Oxlade 49, G. Anderton 31).

†At Canberra, January 24. New Zealanders won by 97 runs. New Zealanders 271 for six (50 overs) (J. J. Crowe 90, P. N. Webb 52, J. V. Coney 34 not out, J. F. M. Morrison 34; B. Hannam three for 56); Australian Capital Territory 174 (44.5 overs) (G. Irvine 43; J. V. Coney four for 32).

†At Canberra, January 25. New Zealanders won by six wickets. Australian Capital Territory 168 (48.3 overs) (C. P. Gulbransen 39, K. Stone 30; G. B. Troup three for 24); New Zealanders 169 for four (42.2 overs) (J. V Coney 60 not out, J. G. Wright 47; R. P. Done three for 28).

†At Canberra, January 26. New Zealanders won on faster scoring-rate. New Zealanders 189 (40 overs) (B. A. Edgar 42; G. Irvine four for 23); Australian Capital Territory 48 for six (23 overs) (B. L. Cairns three for 10).

†At Northam, February 2. New Zealanders won by 58 runs. New Zealanders 221 for five (40 overs) (B. A. Edgar 62, J. F. M. Morrison 57, P. N. Webb 55); Western Australian Country XI 163 for four (40 overs) (M. Crook 41).

New Zealand's matches v Australia and England in the Benson and Hedges World Series Cup may be found in that section.

FUTURE TOURS

1984   Indians to Sri Lanka
       New Zealanders to Sri Lanka
       Australians to West Indies
       West Indians to England
       Sri Lankans to England
       New Zealanders to Pakistan

1984-85 England to India and Sri Lanka
        West Indians and Sri Lankans to
          Australia
        Pakistanis to New Zealand

1985   New Zealanders to West Indies
       Sri Lankans to Pakistan (and visit
         returned)
       Australians to England
       Indians to Pakistan

1985-86 Pakistanis to West Indies
        Indians and New Zealanders to
          Australia
        England to West Indies

1986   Australians to New Zealand
       Indians to Sri Lanka
       Indians to England
       New Zealanders to England
       Australians to India
       West Indians to Pakistan
       New Zealanders to India and
         Sri Lanka

1986-87 England and West Indians to
          Australia
        Pakistanis to Sri Lanka
        West Indians to New Zealand
          (Provisional)

1987   World Cup
       Pakistanis to England
       Sri Lankans to England
         (if no World Cup in England)
       Sri Lankans to Pakistan
       West Indians to India

1987-88 England to Pakistan and
          New Zealand
        New Zealanders and Sri Lankans
          to Australia

1988   Australians to West Indies
       West Indians to England
       Sri Lankans to England
       Australians to Pakistan

1988-89 England to India and Sri Lanka
        West Indians and Pakistanis to
          Australia
        Pakistanis to New Zealand

THE SRI LANKANS IN AUSTRALIA AND NEW ZEALAND, 1982-83

By R. T. BRITTENDEN

As part of an ambitious five-month programme, aimed at widening their experience and culminating with the Prudential World Cup in England in June 1983, Sri Lanka arranged a seven-week tour of Australia and New Zealand, their first to either country. They played two three-day first-class matches and three non first-class matches in Australia, followed by nine matches in New Zealand, including two Tests and three one-day internationals.

In Australia they drew with New South Wales, in poor weather, and also with Tasmania, holding their own quite well in both matches. In New Zealand their lack of success was attributable in equal measure to inexperience and misfortune, as well as to a lack of any fast, as distinct from medium-paced, bowling. Their only victory came in a limited-overs match at New Plymouth against a New Zealand Minor Associations XI. They lost the one-day international series three-nil, and were heavily defeated in both Test matches.

As usual, the pitches in New Zealand allowed seam bowlers to move the ball about, and the Sri Lankans showed a fatal fascination for the ball leaving the bat. In the two Tests, something like 70 per cent of the wickets which fell to the New Zealand bowlers went to catches at the wicket, in the slips or at gully. The New Zealand wicket-keeper, Warren Lees, was able to break a New Zealand Test record by taking eight catches at Wellington, five of them in Sri Lanka's second innings.

There was evidence of inexperience, too, in Sri Lanka's performance in the field. In both Tests the tourists won promising positions before letting them slip through a lack of sustained application. For all that, they made a good impression with their positive methods, lively over-rates and friendly ways. Only once did they fall from grace, when, in the second Test match, a bat-pad catch appeal was turned down and they were demonstrative in their displeasure. The manager, Mr Abu Fuard, chose this moment to express concern with the umpiring in forthright terms. It was the only sour note during a short but pleasant tour.

The Sri Lankans were very unlucky to lose Duleep Mendis in the opening match. He broke a finger in the game with Canterbury and played again, even then with difficulty, only in the two one-day internationals with which the tour ended. Their other leading batsman, Roy Dias, was hurt while fielding at Wanganui – in only the third fixture – and did not play again on the tour. It was also unfortunate for the tourists that their veteran leg-spinner, Somachandra de Silva, never found a pitch which allowed him to give full expression to his talents.

Among the batsmen none made a better impression than Ranjan Madugalle, whose free stroke-making was delightful: he had a tour average of 39.20. Ashantha de Mel, a good medium-paced bowler, was another whose tour was restricted by injury, but Vinodhan John bowled with skill and spirit. The star fieldsman was Yohan Gunasekera, whose catching in the gully was outstanding.

New Zealand's clean sweep against Sri Lanka, following three successive victories over England in one-day internationals, afforded them an unprecedented run of success. Although there had been tremendous public interest in the games with England, dismal weather contributed towards a substantial financial loss on the Sri Lankans' visit.

SRI LANKAN TOUR RESULTS

Test matches – Played 2: Lost 2.

First-class matches – Played 6: Lost 3, Drawn 3.

Losses – New Zealand (2), Canterbury.

Draws – New South Wales, Tasmania, Auckland.

Non first-class matches – Played 8: Won 2, Lost 5, Drawn 1. *Wins* – Australian Capital Territory, New Zealand Minor Associations XI. *Losses* – Victoria, New Zealand (3), New Zealand Minor Associations XI. *Draw* – Victoria.

TEST MATCH AVERAGES

NEW ZEALAND – BATTING

	T	I	NO	R	HI	Avge
B. A. Edgar	2	3	1	96	47*	48.00
W. K. Lees	2	2	0	89	89	44.50
J. V. Coney	2	3	0	103	84	34.33
R. J. Hadlee	2	3	1	59	30	29.50
B. L. Cairns	2	2	0	48	45	24.00
G. M. Turner	2	3	0	71	32	23.66
J. J. Crowe	2	3	0	59	36	19.66
J. G. Wright	2	2	0	27	14	13.50
M. C. Snedden	2	2	0	27	22	13.50
G. P. Howarth	2	3	0	37	36	12.33

Played in two Tests: E. J. Chatfield 10*, 2*.

* *Signifies not out.*

BOWLING

	O	M	R	W	Avge	BB
E. J. Chatfield	70.4	19	141	10	14.10	4-66
R. J. Hadlee	77.3	27	141	10	14.10	4-33
B. L. Cairns	62	20	157	9	17.44	4-47
M. C. Snedden	74	19	155	8	19.37	3-21

Also bowled: J. V. Coney 5–2–11–0.

SRI LANKA – BATTING

	T	I	NO	R	HI	Avge
R. S. Madugalle	2	4	0	149	79	37.25
D. S. de Silva	2	4	0	120	61	30.00
S. Wettimuny	2	4	1	87	63*	29.00

	T	I	NO	R	HI	Avge
E. R. N. S. Fernando	2	4	0	70	46	17.50
J. R. Ratnayeke...........................	2	4	1	48	29*	16.00
Y. Gunasekera	2	4	0	48	23	12.00
M. D. Wettimuny.........................	2	4	0	28	17	7.00
V. B. John..................................	2	4	2	11	8*	5.50
S. Jeganathan	2	4	0	19	8	4.75
R. J. Ratnayake..........................	2	4	0	14	12	3.50

Played in one Test: R. G. de Alwis 0, 3; S. A. R. Silva 8, 0.

Signifies not out.

BOWLING

	O	M	R	W	Avge	BB
V. B. John......................	45.2	13	143	8	17.87	5-60
D. S. de Silva..................	37.5	16	72	3	24.00	1-13
R. J. Ratnayake................	70	13	252	7	36.00	4-81
J. R. Ratnayeke................	53.1	16	149	4	37.25	3-93

Also bowled: S. Jeganathan 5–2–12–0.

SRI LANKAN AVERAGES – FIRST-CLASS MATCHES

BATTING

	M	I	NO	R	HI	100s	Avge
R. S. Madugalle..............	6	10	0	392	81	0	39.20
D. S. de Silva.................	5	8	1	243	65	0	34.71
S. Wettimuny	5	8	1	231	105	1	33.00
J. R. Ratnayeke...............	5	9	3	174	64*	0	29.00
E. R. N. S. Fernando	4	7	0	188	72	0	26.85
R. L. Dias	3	5	0	112	40	0	22.40
S. Jeganathan	6	10	1	170	74	0	18.88
L. R. D. Mendis	2	2	1	15	15	0	15.00
Y. Gunasekera	4	7	0	89	27	0	12.71
M. D. Wettimuny.............	6	10	0	126	31	0	12.60
A. L. F. de Mel..............	2	2	1	12	12	0	12.00
R. G. de Alwis	3	5	0	53	42	0	10.60
S. A. R. Silva................	3	5	0	51	43	0	10.20
V. B. John....................	6	7	3	20	8*	0	5.00
R. J. Ratnayake..............	5	7	0	14	12	0	2.00

Played in one match: R. G. C. E. Wijesuriya 1.

BOWLING

	O	M	R	W	Avge	BB
R. J. Ratnayake.................	163	42	524	22	23.81	5-50
J. R. Ratnayeke.................	92.1	22	255	10	25.50	4-34
V. B. John......................	135.3	31	421	16	26.31	5-60
D. S. de Silva..................	128.5	41	311	8	38.87	2-44
A. L. F. de Mel................	40	10	122	3	40.66	2-36
S. Jeganathan	99	26	243	3	81.00	2-58

Also bowled: Y. Gunasekera 16–3–33–1; M. D. Wettimuny 11–5–24–0; R. G. C. E. Wijesuriya 5–1–20–0.

FIELDING

Y. Gunasekera 8, S. A. R. Silva 7 (all ct), R. G. de Alwis 6 (all ct), D. S. de Silva 3, S. Jeganathan 3, J. R. Ratnayeke 3, A. L. F. de Mel 2, R. S. Madugalle 2, M. D. Wettimuny 2, E. R. N. S. Fernando 1, V. B. John 1, S. Wettimuny 1, R. G. C. E. Wijesuriya 1.

†At Melbourne, February 3, 4. Drawn. Victoria 220 for six dec. (G. F. Richardson 90) and 336 for four (G. M. Watts 164, M. D. Taylor 93); Sri Lankans 295 for seven dec. (L. R. D. Mendis 141, D. S. de Silva 39 not out).

†At Melbourne, February 6. Victoria won by six wickets. Sri Lankans 211 for nine (48 overs); Victoria 213 for four (44.3 overs) (G. F. Richardson 80 not out).

†At Canberra, February 8. Sri Lankans won by 59 runs. Sri Lankans 212 for six (50 overs) (S. Wettimuny 50); Australian Capital Territory 153 (V. B. John five for 24).

NEW SOUTH WALES v SRI LANKANS

At Sydney, February 10, 11, 12. Drawn. Rain and poor light on all three days frustrated the captains' combined efforts to achieve a result by declarations. By the end of the first day the Sri Lankans were 15 for two in reply to the state side's slowly made 253 for five declared. By the close of the second day the Sri Lankans were 170 for seven. The match, sparsely attended all through, was ended early on the third day. New South Wales included nine Test players in their side.

New South Wales

*R. B. McCosker b de Mel	8	– not out		45
J. Dyson b Jeganathan	52			
I. C. Davis c de Mel b John	14			
D. M. Wellham c and b Jeganathan	35			
P. M. Toohey c de Mel b de Silva	58	– not out		2
T. M. Chappell not out	40	– (3) c and b Ratnayeke		2
G. R. J. Matthews not out	26			
M. J. Bennett (did not bat)		– (2) c de Alwis b Ratnayeke		24
†S. J. Rixon (did not bat)		– (4) c de Silva b John		14
B 2, l-b 2, n-b 16	20	L-b 1, w 2, n-b 14		17

1/19 2/51 3/120   (5 wkts dec.) 253   1/66 2/74 3/101   (3 wkts) 104
4/127 5/205

L. S. Pascoe and M. R. Whitney did not bat.

Bowling: *First Innings*—de Mel 12–1–49–1; John 14–1–41–1; Ratnayeke 6–1–12–0; de Silva 22–3–70–1; Jeganathan 22–5–58–2; M. D. Wettimuny 1–0–3–0. *Second Innings*—de Mel 6–0–24–0; John 12–2–27–1; Ratnayeke 6–1–20–2; Jeganathan 10–3–16–0.

Sri Lankans

S. Wettimuny c Rixon b Whitney	9	J. R. Ratnayeke c McCosker		
M. D. Wettimuny c Bennett			b Matthews.	5
	b Whitney.	0	S. Jeganathan c McCosker b Pascoe	10
†R. G. de Alwis c and b Pascoe	42	A. L. F. de Mel not out		0
R. L. Dias c Matthews b Pascoe	15	L-b 1, n-b 10		11
*L. R. D. Mendis b Chappell	15			
R. S. Madugalle c Rixon b Bennett	35	1/9 2/14 3/48 4/82 (9 wkts dec.) 207		
D. S. de Silva c Dyson b Bennett	65	5/89 6/146 7/167 8/207 9/207		

V. B. John did not bat.

Bowling: Pascoe 19–1–66–3; Whitney 15–0–54–2; Chappell 10–3–20–1; Bennett 14.3–3–42–2; Matthews 6–1–14–1.

Umpires: R. Emerson and R. G. Harris.

TASMANIA v SRI LANKANS

At Devonport, February 14, 15, 16. Drawn. After the first two innings of the match had been declared – Tasmania closed theirs when still 22 behind – the Sri Lankans, at 89 for seven on the last day, were in some danger of defeat. However, Ratnayeke and Jeganathan added 140 for the eighth wicket and Dias could have afforded to be more generous than he was in the target he set. The Tasmanians expressed disappointment that he was not.

Sri Lankans

M. D. Wettimuny c Reid b Allanby	31	– c Woolley b Kirkman		24
E. R. N. S. Fernando c Ray b Saunders	72	– c Woolley b Faulkner		19
Y. Gunasekera c Woolley b Allanby	27	– c Butcher b Faulkner		7
*R. L. Dias c Woolley b Clough	27	– c Saunders b Kirkman		25
R. S. Madugalle lbw b Saunders	24	– (6) c Woolley b Faulkner		9
†S. A. R. Silva c Woolley b Clough	0	– (7) c Woolley b Faulkner		0
J. R. Ratnayeke not out	0	– (8) not out		64
S. Jeganathan b Kirkman	14	– (9) b Smith b Kirkman		74
R. G. C. E. Wijesuriya (did not bat)		– (5) c Ray b Kirkman		1
L-b 4	4	B 2, 1-b 3, w 1		6

1/60 2/114 3/142 4/164   (7 wkts dec.) 221   1/30 2/40 3/71   (8 wkts dec.) 229
5/170 6/190 7/221   4/76 5/77 6/82 7/89 8/229

R. J. Ratnayake and V. B. John did not bat.

Bowling: *First Innings*—Clough 16–4–41–2; Kirkman 16–3–52–1; Faulkner 12–1–35–0; Allanby 16–6–38–2; Saunders 20–5–50–2; Reid 1–0–1–0. *Second Innings*—Clough 11–2–23–0; Kirkman 19–6–44–4; Faulkner 23–5–55–4; Allanby 10–2–37–0; Saunders 16–7–35–0; Reid 1–0–6–0; Smith 5–1–14–0; Butcher 4–1–9–0.

Tasmania

D. A. Smith c Silva b Ratnayake	25	– b John		3
M. Ray c Gunasekera b Ratnayeke	14	– c Wijesuriya b Ratnayeke		25
D. C. Boon c Gunasekera b Ratnayeke	31			
N. J. Allanby c Fernando b Ratnayeke	18	– not out		19
P. Faulkner c Ratnayeke b Gunasekera	32			
W. Kirkman c Silva b Ratnayeke	0			
R. O. Butcher c Jeganathan b Ratnayeke	13	– (3) c Ratnayeke b John		40
*†R. D. Woolley not out	53			
S. J. Reid not out	9	– (5) not out		19
L-b 3, n-b 1	4	L-b 2, n-b 2		4

1/40 2/41 3/91 4/92   (7 wkts dec.) 199   1/5 2/57 3/71   (3 wkts) 110
5/94 6/110 7/176

S. L. Saunders and P. M. Clough did not bat.

Bowling: *First Innings*—Ratnayake 19–12–34–2; Ratnayeke 16–3–34–4; Gunasekera 4–0–17–1; John 15–4–52–0; Jeganathan 16–4–38–0; Wijesuriya 5–1–20–0. *Second Innings* —Ratnayake 10–4–39–1; Ratnayeke 4–0–13–0; John 12–2–37–2; Jeganathan 6–2–11–0; Wettimuny 5–3–6–0.

Umpires: S. G. Randell and J. H. Hinds.

CANTERBURY v SRI LANKANS

At Christchurch, February 18, 19, 20. Canterbury won by eight wickets. In achieving only their third victory over an international team Canterbury owed most to the former Test bowler, Dayle Hadlee, who scored his maiden century in first-class cricket. Sri Lanka failed against some lively seam bowling from the broad-shouldered Thiele. Then Hadlee and his young captain, Leggat, scored 186 together for Canterbury's seventh wicket. On the last day Madugalle batted superbly for 81, but this time another medium-pacer, Bateman, had a career-best return. In his last 38 balls Bateman took four wickets for 7 runs.

Sri Lankans

S. Wettimuny c Hart b Thiele	8	– lbw b Thiele	22
M. D. Wettimuny c Stead b Hadlee	16	– c Hart b Bateman	18
R. L. Dias c Hart b Hadlee	40	– (4) b Thiele	5
*L. R. D. Mendis retired hurt	0	– absent hurt	
R. S. Madugalle lbw b Thiele	30	– c Leggat b Bateman	81
D. S. de Silva b Thiele	26	– c Hart b Hadlee	17
J. R. Ratnayeke b Bateman	9	– c Gully b Bateman	26
†R. G. de Alwis c Stead b Thiele	0	– (3) c Gully b Bateman	8
S. Jeganathan c Hart b Thiele	12	– (8) not out	14
R. J. Ratnayake c Hart b Thiele	0	– (9) b Bateman	0
V. B. John not out	6	– (10) c and b Bateman	3
B 9, l-b 5, w 1, n-b 5	20	B 8, l-b 4, n-b 8	20

1/18 2/48 3/93 4/128   167   1/45 2/45 3/56 4/73   214
5/139 6/139 7/149 8/156 9/167   5/130 6/188 7/204 8/210 9/214

Bowling: *First Innings*—Thiele 17.5–5–45–6; Bateman 24–5–71–1; Hadlee 12–6–17–2; Dempsey 5.2–5–14–0. *Second Innings*—Thiele 14–1–56–2; Bateman 19.2–2–66–6; Hadlee 11–4–19–1; Dempsey 12–6–27–0; Stead 9–3–26–0.

Canterbury

J. Gully c de Alwis b Ratnayake	22	– c Madugalle b Ratnayake	0
D. A. Dempsey lbw b John	0	– not out	22
P. J. Rattray c de Alwis b de Silva	62	– c de Alwis b Ratnayake	12
P. E. McEwan c de Alwis b John	6	– not out	2
D. J. Boyle lbw b Ratnayake	0		
D. W. Stead run out	14		
*R. I. Leggat b Ratnayake	83		
D. R. Hadlee not out	109		
†A. W. Hart b Ratnayake	12		
B 2, l-b 12, w 5, n-b 17	36	L-b 1, n-b 1	2

1/4 2/31 3/50 4/53   (8 wkts dec.) 344   1/3 2/27   (2 wkts) 38
5/102 6/128 7/314 8/344

G. C. Bateman and C. H. Thiele did not bat.

Bowling: *First Innings*—John 14–3–55–2; Ratnayake 29–2–101–4; Ratnayeke 7–1–27–0; de Silva 25–9–80–1; Jeganathan 19–6–45–0. *Second Innings*—John 3.1–0–20–0; Ratnayake 4–0–16–2.

Umpires: B. L. Aldridge and R. L. McHarg.

†At New Plymouth, February 23. Sri Lankans won by five wickets. New Zealand Minor Associations 184 for nine (50 overs) (J. M. Parker 81; A. L. F. de Mel three for 20); Sri Lankans 187 for five (47.3 overs) (R. S. Madugalle 64 not out).

†At Wanganui, February 24. New Zealand Minor Associations won by five wickets. Sri Lankans 216 (44.4 overs) (R. L. Dias 50, R. S. Madugalle 42); New Zealand Minor Associations 220 for five (49 overs) (J. M. Parker 91 not out, S. J. Gill 64).

AUCKLAND v SRI LANKANS

At Auckland, February 26, 27, 28. Drawn. Auckland gave an unconvincing display in their first innings, taking 77 overs to score 198. The Sri Lankan schoolboy, Rumesh Ratnayake, bowled accurately in taking five for 50. Sidath Wettimuny then batted very competently to make 105, and there was some spectacular strokeplay from Madugalle. Auckland, however, although 140 behind on the first innings, saved the game comfortably.

Auckland

A. E. W. Parsons c Silva b Ratnayake	42	– c and b Jeganathan	11
M. J. Greatbatch c Silva b Ratnayake	4	– lbw b de Silva	36
J. G. Bracewell c Silva b de Mel	3	– c Madugalle b de Silva	29
M. D. Crowe b de Mel	0	– not out	70
A. J. Hunt lbw b John	15	– lbw b Ratnayake	16
A. T. R. Hellaby b Ratnayake	62	– b John	8
I. Fisher run out	6	– not out	10
†P. J. Kelly b de Silva	0		
*J. M. McIntyre not out	31		
J. A. Cushen c Silva b Ratnayake	17		
G. B. Troup b Ratnayake	0		
B 2, l-b 9, w 3, n-b 4	18	B 2, l-b 4	6

1/18 2/21 3/24 4/24   198   1/29 2/78 3/83   (5 wkts) 186
5/127 6/144 7/144 8/145 9/163   4/120 5/158

Bowling: *First Innings*—Ratnayake 23–10–50–5; de Mel 17–9–36–2; John 11–3–15–1; de Silva 17–5–45–1; Jeganathan 8–2–28–0; M. D. Wettimuny 1–0–6–0. *Second Innings*—Ratnayake 8–1–32–1; de Mel 5–0–13–0; John 9–3–31–1; de Silva 27–8–44–2; Jeganathan 13–2–35–1; M. D. Wettimuny 4–2–9–0; Gunasekera 12–3–16–0.

Sri Lankans

S. Wettimuny c Kelly b Fisher	105	R. J. Ratnayake c Hellaby	
E. R. N. S. Fernando c Kelly b Troup	27	b Bracewell	0
M. D. Wettimuny lbw b Crowe	9	*D. S. de Silva not out	15
Y. Gunasekera b Bracewell	7	V. B. John lbw b Bracewell	0
R. S. Madugalle c Kelly b Troup	64		
†S. A. R. Silva c McIntyre		B 11, l-b 13, n-b 5	29
b Bracewell	43		
A. L. F. de Mel b Cushen	12	1/56 2/112 3/128 4/213	338
S. Jeganathan b Troup	27	5/231 6/254 7/305 8/310 9/338	

Bowling: Troup 28–8–53–3; Cushen 20–2–57–1; Crowe 9–2–32–1; Bracewell 22.4–7–56–4; McIntyre 17–8–28–0; Hellaby 7–3–15–0; Fisher 18–5–45–1; Hunt 12–5–23–0.

Umpires: J. B. R. Hastie and T. A. McCall.

†NEW ZEALAND v SRI LANKA

First One-day International

At Dunedin, March 2. New Zealand won by 65 runs. Although accurate Sri Lankan bowling, on a pitch of variable bounce, confined New Zealand to 183 for eight wickets, this was a total Sri Lanka never looked like overhauling. Their calling and running between wickets were poor throughout the tour: on this occasion they suffered three run-outs. These costly errors, and two accurate and lively spells by Hadlee, wrapped up the Sri Lankan innings in cold and murky conditions.

Man of the Match: J. G. Wright.

New Zealand

G. M. Turner b John	18	
B. A. Edgar c de Alwis b de Mel	3	
J. G. Wright lbw b Ratnayake	45	
J. J. Crowe lbw b Ratnayeke	5	
J. V. Coney b Ratnayake	15	
*G. P. Howarth b Ratnayeke	11	
B. L. Cairns b John	37	

R. J. Hadlee b John 11
M. C. Snedden not out 13
†W. K. Lees not out 7
L-b 10, w 4, n-b 4 18

1/26 2/26 3/50 4/99 (8 wkts, 50 overs) 183
5/113 6/124 7/150 8/165

E. J. Chatfield did not bat.

Bowling: de Mel 9.3–2–36–1; John 10–4–28–3; Ratnayake 10–0–30–3; Ratnayeke 10–0–45–1; de Silva 10–1–20–0; S. Wettimuny 0.3–0–6–0.

Sri Lanka

S. Wettimuny run out 15
E. R. N. S. Fernando c Turner
    b Hadlee. 0
M. D. Wettimuny b Hadlee 2
Y. Gunasekera run out 23
R. S. Madugalle run out 3
*D. S. de Silva b Chatfield 18
A. L. F. de Mel lbw b Hadlee 1

J. R. Ratnayeke c Snedden b Coney ... 14
†R. G. de Alwis not out 13
R. J. Ratnayeke c Coney b Howarth ... 15

B 2, l-b 10, w 2 14

1/1 2/7 3/39 4/46 (9 wkts, 50 overs) 118
5/62 6/65 7/85 8/85 9/118

V. B. John did not bat.

Bowling: Hadlee 8–3–9–3; Cairns 10–6–10–0; Snedden 9–1–25–0; Chatfield 10–4–8–1; Coney 10–1–42–1; Howarth 2–0–10–1; Wright 1–1–0–0.

Umpires: S. C. Cowman and I. C. Higginson.

NEW ZEALAND v SRI LANKA

First Test Match

At Christchurch, March 4, 5, 6. New Zealand won by an innings and 25 runs. The first day, when the start was delayed by two and a half hours and New Zealand were sent in, was the only one which the Sri Lankans could view with satisfaction. At the end of it New Zealand had struggled to 217 for seven.

New Zealand started well enough, Turner marking his return to Test cricket after six years with a stream of well-timed shots. The early bowling was loose, New Zealand taking 32 from the opening five overs. But at 171 for seven New Zealand were in trouble. Lees finished with 89, the only time he had passed 50 in a Test except when making 152 against Pakistan at Karachi in 1976. But at 171 for seven New Zealand were in trouble. Coney and Lees, however, saw the first day out and were in fine form next morning. Coney's 84 was his highest Test score. Sri Lanka's grip was further loosened by partnerships between Lees and Snedden and then Lees and Chatfield. Lees finished with 89, the only time he had passed 50 in a Test except when making 152 against Pakistan at Karachi in 1976.

Sri Lanka's first innings consisted almost entirely of Sidath Wettimuny, who carried his bat (210 minutes) for 63. There was also an attractive 34 in 52 minutes from Madugalle. Wettimuny made little effort late in the innings to protect his less able partners and Sri Lanka failed by only 1 run to save the follow-on. Their second innings was hardly happier. Fighting qualities were shown by de Silva, who survived 150 minutes despite needing a runner, and there was some resolution from Fernando, but little else. It was only the second time New Zealand had won a Test by an innings.

New Zealand

G. M. Turner c de Alwis b John	32	†W. K. Lees b de Silva	89
B. A. Edgar c M. D. Wettimuny		M. C. Snedden c sub (S. A. R. Silva)	
b Ratnayeke.	39	b Ratnayeke.	22
J. G. Wright b Ratnayake	13	E. J. Chatfield not out	10
*G. P. Howarth c Gunasekera			
b Ratnayeke.	0		
J. J. Crowe run out	12	L-b 14, w 2, n-b 12	28
J. V. Coney run out	84		
R. J. Hadlee b John	12	1/59 2/93 3/93	344
B. L. Cairns c M. D. Wettimuny		4/93 5/137 6/159	
b Ratnayeke.	3	7/171 8/250 9/292	

Bowling: Ratnayake 31–8–125–2; John 12–2–45–2; Ratnayeke 31–9–93–3; de Silva 22.5–10–41–1; Jeganathan 5–2–12–0.

Sri Lanka

S. Wettimuny not out	63	– lbw b Cairns	7
M. D. Wettimuny c Lees b Cairns	17	– c Lees b Snedden	5
E. R. N. S. Fernando b Cairns	0	– b Cairns	46
Y. Gunasekera c Lees b Cairns	4	– c Turner b Cairns	8
R. S. Madugalle run out	34	– c Lees b Snedden	23
*D. S. de Silva c Lees b Hadlee	7	– b Chatfield	52
J. R. Ratnayeke run out	0	– lbw b Cairns	7
†R. G. de Alwis c Turner b Hadlee	0	– c Hadlee b Snedden	3
S. Jeganathan lbw b Cairns	6	– b Chatfield	8
R. J. Ratnayake c Coney b Hadlee	1	– c Howarth b Chatfield	0
V. B. John lbw b Hadlee	0	– not out	3
B 2, l-b 7, n-b 3	12	B 2, l-b 5, w 5, n-b 1	13

1/49 2/49 3/55 4/104	144	1/14 2/26 3/46 4/95	175
5/121 6/129 7/133 8/141 9/144		5/100 6/124 7/133 8/168 9/170	

Bowling: *First Innings*—Hadlee 13.3–1–33–4; Snedden 10–1–30–0; Cairns 15–6–49–4; Chatfield 15–4–20–0. *Second Innings*—Hadlee 22–12–27–0; Snedden 23–6–48–3; Cairns 20–7–47–4; Chatfield 16.5–3–40–3.

Umpires: F. R. Goodall and D. A. Kinsella.

NEW ZEALAND v SRI LANKA

Second Test Match

At Wellington, March 11, 12, 13, 14, 15. New Zealand won by six wickets. Although there was some play on each of the five days, the match lasted for only a little over eighteen hours. When it started at 4.45 on the first day, after rain, only some 200 people were in attendance. Sent in, Sri Lanka were 34 for two at the close and slumped to 48 for four on the second morning. Then came a splendid stand of 130 between Madugalle and de Silva. Madugalle played many graceful attacking strokes and this time the adhesive de Silva saw it out for

226 minutes. Later there was some handsome driving by the tall left-hander, Ratnayeke.

In reply to Sri Lanka's 240, New Zealand, at 169 for nine, were on the run, but again the visitors lost their advantage. On a pitch which favoured seam bowling, John was most effective. Crowe, in his second Test, stayed for two hours, and Howarth for three hours and a quarter, but John and Ratnayake enjoyed consistent success. In the end, though, Sri Lanka's fielding, then their batting, let them down. Towards the end of New Zealand's first innings Hadlee, dropped when 0, scored a brisk 30, and Cairns, also missed before scoring, hit 45 in 50 balls, adding 32 for the last wicket with Chatfield. So New Zealand's deficit was reduced to 39. Early in their innings Wright's nose had been broken by a bouncer from Ratnayake, although he returned later to hit 4 more runs, enough to take his Test aggregate past 1,000.

Batting again, Sri Lanka failed to handle a difficult situation. There was occasional lift in the pitch and regular movement off the seam, and the batsmen chased the wide ball with fatal results, five of them falling to catches at the wicket. Left with only 133 to win, New Zealand were 62 for the loss of Turner at the end of the fourth day. On the last morning Sri Lanka took two more consolation wickets before Hadlee won the match, 48 minutes before lunch, with a huge 6 off Ratnayeke.

Sri Lanka

S. Wettimuny c Cairns b Hadlee	8	– c Coney b Hadlee	9
M. D. Wettimuny c Coney b Snedden	6	– c Cairns b Snedden	0
E. R. N. S. Fernando c Wright b Hadlee	12	– c Lees b Snedden	12
Y. Gunasekera c Lees b Cairns	13	– (5) c Lees b Chatfield	23
R. S. Madugalle run out	79	– (6) c Lees b Hadlee	13
*D. S. de Silva lbw b Chatfield	61	– (7) c Lees b Chatfield	0
†S. A. R. Silva c Lees b Chatfield	8	– (4) c Crowe b Hadlee	0
J. R. Ratnayeke not out	29	– b Hadlee	12
S. Jeganathan c Lees b Chatfield	5	– c Lees b Chatfield	0
R. J. Ratnayake b Snedden	12	– c sub (de Alwis) b Chatfield	1
V. B. John c Wright b Chatfield	0	– not out	8
B 1, l-b 5, n-b 1	7	B 5, l-b 10	15

1/14 2/14 3/34 4/48   240   1/0 2/12 3/12 4/57   93
5/178 6/191 7/220 8/239 9/240   5/61 6/61 7/78 8/81 9/83

Bowling: *First Innings*—Hadlee 25-9-47-2; Snedden 24-5-56-2; Chatfield 26.5-7-66-4; Cairns 20-5-53-1; Coney 5-2-11-0. *Second Innings*—Hadlee 17-5-34-4; Snedden 17-7-21-3; Chatfield 12-5-15-3; Cairns 7-2-8-0.

New Zealand

G. M. Turner c Gunasekera b John	10	– b Ratnayeke	29
B. A. Edgar c John b Ratnayeke	10	– not out	47
J. G. Wright c de Silva b Ratnayeke	14		
*G. P. Howarth c S. Wettimuny b de Silva	36	– (3) c Silva b John	1
J. J. Crowe c Silva b Ratnayeke	36	– (4) b Ratnayeke	11
J. V. Coney c Gunasekera b John	2	– (5) c Gunasekera b de Silva	17
R. J. Hadlee c Gunasekera b John	30	– (6) not out	17
†W. K. Lees c Gunasekera b John	0		
B. L. Cairns c de Silva b John	45		
M. C. Snedden lbw b Ratnayeke	5		
E. J. Chatfield not out	2		
B 4, l-b 3, w 3, n-b 1	11	L-b 11, n-b 1	12

1/12 2/33 3/104 4/107   201   1/59 2/62 3/81 4/116   (4 wkts) 134
5/141 6/141 7/145 8/163 9/169

Bowling: *First Innings*—Ratnayake 24-5-81-4; John 25.2-9-60-5; Ratnayeke 14-3-36-0; de Silva 9-5-13-1. *Second Innings*—Ratnayake 15-0-46-1; John 8-2-38-1; Ratnayeke 8.1-4-20-1; de Silva 6-1-18-1.

Umpires: I. C. Higginson and S. J. Woodward.

†NEW ZEALAND v SRI LANKA

Second One-day International

At Napier, March 19. New Zealand won by seven wickets. Fresh from a victory over Australia in a one-day match played in Sydney in aid of a bushfire appeal, New Zealand won very easily. The tourists totalled 167 for eight, many of these coming from a late stand between Ratnayeke and de Silva. For New Zealand the Crowe brothers, Jeff and Martin, shared an unbroken partnership of 87, the first 50 of them coming in 38 minutes.

Man of the Match: M. D. Crowe.

Sri Lanka

S. Wettimuny b M. D. Crowe	20	J. R. Ratnayeke c M. D. Crowe
E. R. N. S. Fernando run out	0	b Snedden. 27
†R. G. de Alwis b Cairns	12	D. S. de Silva not out 37
Y. Gunasekera c Turner		R. J. Ratnayake not out 1
b M. D. Crowe.	11	B 10, l-b 11, n-b 1 22
*L. R. D. Mendis c Hadlee b Chatfield	11	—
R. S. Madugalle b Cairns	7	1/5 2/35 3/51 4/51　(8 wkts, 50 overs) 167
A. L. F. de Mel c Coney b Chatfield	19	5/63 6/76 7/105 8/161

V. B. John did not bat.

Bowling: Hadlee 10-3–22–0; Snedden 10-2–25–1; Cairns 10-2–25–2; Chatfield 10-2–43–2; M. D. Crowe 10-2–30–2.

New Zealand

G. M. Turner c Ratnayake b John	25	M. D. Crowe not out 43
B. A. Edgar c Madugalle b Ratnayeke.	8	B 1, l-b 4, w 3, n-b 7 15
*J. G. Wright hit wkt b de Silva	31	—
J. J. Crowe not out	46	1/32 2/56 3/81　(3 wkts, 36.4 overs) 168

B. L. Cairns, R. J. Hadlee, J. V. Coney, M. C. Snedden, E. J. Chatfield and †W. K. Lees did not bat.

Bowling: de Mel 4–0–27–0; John 10–4–31–1; Ratnayake 6.4–0–17–0; Ratnayeke 7–0–39–1; de Silva 6–1–28–1; Gunasekera 3–0–11–0.

Umpires: I. C. Higginson and S. J. Woodward.

†NEW ZEALAND v SRI LANKA

Third One-day International

At Auckland, March 20. New Zealand won by 116 runs. There was a brilliant innings by Turner, who, after being dropped when 6, shared an opening stand of 132 in 112 minutes with Edgar and reached his century in 138 minutes. New Zealand, taking 99 runs from the final ten overs, passed 300 for the first time in a limited-overs international. Sri Lanka, starting slowly, never looked capable of matching such furious scoring. For them it was a disappointing end to their tour.

Man of the Match: G. M. Turner.

New Zealand

G. M. Turner c Ratnayeke b Ratnayake.	140
B. A. Edgar c de Mel b Gunasekera	52
B. L. Cairns b Ratnayake	18
J. G. Wright b Wettimuny	45
R. J. Hadlee c Raynayeke b de Mel	9
J. J. Crowe not out	17
M. D. Crowe not out	7
B 3, l-b 10, w 3	16
1/132 2/158 3/230 (5 wkts, 50 overs)	304
4/267 5/279	

M. C. Snedden, E. J. Chatfield, *G. P. Howarth and †W. K. Lees did not bat.

Bowling: de Mel 10–1–65–1; Ratnayake 10–0–50–2; Ratnayake 5–0–41–0; de Silva 10–0–46–0; Jeganathan 10–0–49–0; Gunasekera 3–0–24–1; Wettimuny 2–0–13–1.

Sri Lanka

S. Wettimuny run out	31
E. R. N. S. Fernando b Cairns	36
Y. Gunasekera c Turner b Cairns	35
*L. R. D. Mendis c Wright b Cairns	7
R. S. Madugalle not out	30
D. S. de Silva b Cairns	1
A. L. F. de Mel c Hadlee b M. D. Crowe	16
J. R. Ratnayeke not out	13
B 4, l-b 9, w 5, n-b 1	19
1/55 2/110 3/111 (6 wkts, 50 overs)	188
4/118 5/123 6/165	

R. J. Ratnayake, S. Jeganathan and †R. G. de Alwis did not bat.

Bowling: Hadlee 7–2–18–0; Snedden 7–0–22–0; Cairns 10–2–23–4; M. D. Crowe 10–1–51–1; Chatfield 10–0–47–0; Wright 2–0–2–0; Edgar 2–0–5–0; J. J. Crowe 1–0–1–0; Turner 1–1–0–0.

Umpires: F. R. Goodall and D. A. Kinsella.

A CASE FOR CORNHILL

A woman walked on to the County Ground at Southampton last season to demand an apology from Robin Smith, who, while batting for Hampshire Second XI, had hit a ball through a window of her flat. Mrs Iris Clarke, aged 62, refused to return the ball. Hampshire, in their turn, advised her to refer the matter to her insurance company.

THE INDIANS IN WEST INDIES, 1982-83

By TONY COZIER

For a combination of reasons, India's fifth Test series in the West Indies fell disappointingly short of the hard-fought drama of the previous two, in 1971 and 1976. Rain, which affected every Test in varying degrees, made the third meaningless. West Indies won two of the other four and had the better of the two drawn matches. At no stage of any match were India in a position to win, although the West Indian bowling often lacked the penetration which has become its hallmark.

India arrived direct from a trying series in Pakistan, in which they had been badly beaten. The consequence of their defeat was the replacement of their long-standing captain, Sunil Gavaskar, by the dynamic all-rounder, Kapil Dev, besides a number of other critical team changes, notably the exclusion of Gundappa Viswanath, after 89 Tests, and the left-arm spinner Dilip Doshi.

The new formula made little difference. West Indies won the first Test, following a thrilling final session in which India lost their last four wickets for 6 runs and West Indies then reached the 172 runs they needed in the last over of the match. India's spirits were revived by a courageous second-innings battle which saved the second Test, an unexpected victory in the second of the three one-day internationals and a return to form of Gavaskar, who compiled his 27th Test century in the truncated third Test.

Gavaskar's performance, however, was only a temporary reminder of what he had achieved on his two previous tours, and the series was decided with a massive West Indies victory in the fourth Test in Bridgetown where conditions were ideally suited to the West Indian fast bowlers. The Indian captain and manager complained after that Test of intimidatory bowling, a charge which did have some merit although the umpires had not felt obliged to intervene. The umpires' attitude may have been conditioned by the magnificence of Mohinder Amarnath, who, far from being intimidated, hooked and cut with certainty.

Amarnath had returned to the Indian team for the series against Pakistan, after three years out of Test cricket. The fine form he showed there continued with centuries at Port-of-Spain and Antigua, two vital innings of 91 and 80 when all others around him were falling in Bridgetown and a final aggregate of 598 Test runs (average 66.44). His choice as Benson and Hedges Man of the Series was obligatory. No other Indian passed 300 for the series, Gavaskar being the major disappointment with no score above 40 except for his Georgetown century. Six times in his nine Test innings he was caught behind the wicket, although he was not alone in this, the West Indian wicket-keeper and slips being kept busy throughout.

India's bowling was limited. While Kapil Dev was never less than the quality fast-medium bowler he was known to be, in West Indian conditions the medium-paced swing of Balwinder Sandhu and Madan Lal was inadequate support once the ball had lost its shine. Srinivasaraghavan Venkataraghavan, the veteran off-spinner brought back at age 38 for his experience, bowled steadily on his third West Indian tour, as did the two orthodox left-arm spinners, Ravi Shastri and Maninder Singh. Shastri developed as a batsman, scoring a century in the final Test.

India's wicket-keeper, Syed Kirmani, dropped catches at critical stages in the second and fifth Tests, helping West Indies to total 394, 470, 486 and 550 in successive innings. The first seven in the West Indian order all scored centuries. One of these was the only new batsman introduced by West Indies in the series, Augustine Logie, a stroke-playing right-hander from Trinidad. He was badly missed when 7 in the course of his 130 in Bridgetown and managed only 37 in his five other innings.

With the exception of Lloyd and the fluent wicket-keeper-batsman, Jeffrey Dujon, no West Indian batsman was at his best throughout the series. Nor were two of the leading bowlers, Michael Holding and Joel Garner, both of whom were obviously feeling the effects of demanding seasons in Australia, where Holding, still not recovered from the effects of a knee operation the previous year, played for Tasmania and Garner for South Australia. Holding only occasionally reached his fastest, while the giant Garner, who complained of fatigue, eventually lost his Test place. It was left to Marshall, generating tremendous pace and hostility mainly from round the wicket, to spearhead the West Indian attack. The 32-year-old Andy Roberts, with clever change of pace, made an ideal foil. As India batted comfortably to draws in the second and fifth Tests on slow pitches, the West Indian policy of concentrating purely on fast bowling to the exclusion of specialist spin was again brought into question.

Outside the Tests, the Indians were unbeaten, though this was more a reflection of the weakness of their territorial opponents than their own strengths. Although the West Indies Cricket Board of Control estimated another loss on the tour, that was principally because of the playing days washed out by rain. The Indians proved popular wherever they went, particularly in Trinidad and Guyana where large sections of the the population are of Indian descent. Their public relations, under the astute management of the former Test batsman, Hanumant Singh, gained them many friends.

INDIAN TOUR RESULTS

Test matches – Played 5: Lost 2, Drawn 3.

First-class matches – Played 10: Won 3, Lost 2, Drawn 5.

Wins – Trinidad & Tobago, Windward Islands, Leeward Islands.

Losses – West Indies (2).

Draws – West Indies (3), Jamaica, Barbados.

Non first-class matches – Played 4: Won 1 Lost 2, Drawn 1. *Win* – West Indies. *Losses* – West Indies (2). *Draw* – Guyana.

TEST MATCH AVERAGES

WEST INDIES – BATTING

	T	I	NO	R	HI	100s	Avge
C. G. Greenidge	5	7	2	393	154*	1	78.60
C. H. Lloyd	5	6	0	407	143	2	67.83
D. L. Haynes	5	7	1	333	136	1	55.50
P. J. Dujon	5	6	1	259	110	1	51.80
I. V. A. Richards	5	6	0	282	109	1	47.00
H. A. Gomes	5	5	0	178	123	1	35.60
A. L. Logie	5	6	0	167	130	1	27.83
A. M. E. Roberts	5	6	1	84	36	0	16.80
M. D. Marshall	5	6	1	74	27	0	14.80
M. A. Holding	5	5	0	27	24	0	5.40

Played in four Tests: J. Garner 0*, 21*, 1*, 2*. Played in one Test: W. W. Davis 14.

* *Signifies not out.*

BOWLING

	O	M	R	W	Avge	BB
A. M. E. Roberts	187.5	36	545	24	22.70	5-39
M. D. Marshall	174.2	39	495	21	23.57	5-37
M. A. Holding	162	23	500	12	41.66	2-36
J. Garner	113	35	301	7	43.00	2-41
W. W. Davis	52	5	175	4	43.75	2-54
H. A. Gomes	84	20	203	3	67.66	1-9

Also bowled: I. V. A. Richards 36–9–89–1.

INDIA – BATTING

	T	I	NO	R	HI	100s	Avge
M. Amarnath	5	9	0	598	117	2	66.44
Kapil Dev	5	8	2	254	100*	1	42.33
R. J. Shastri	5	8	2	236	102	1	39.33
Yashpal Sharma	5	9	2	242	63	0	34.57
D. B. Vengsarkar	5	9	0	279	94	0	31.00
S. M. Gavaskar	5	9	1	240	147*	1	30.00
B. S. Sandhu	4	6	2	91	68	0	22.75
A. D. Gaekwad	5	9	0	200	72	0	22.22
Madan Lal	2	3	1	41	35*	0	20.50
S. M. H. Kirmani	5	7	0	98	33	0	14.00
Maninder Singh	3	3	1	6	3*	0	3.00
S. Venkataraghavan	5	6	1	6	5	0	1.20

Played in one Test: L. Sivaramakrishnan 17.

* *Signifies not out.*

INDIA – BOWLING

	O	M	R	W	Avge	BB
Kapil Dev	154	32	424	17	24.94	4-45
Madan Lal	62	9	201	5	40.20	3-105
B. S. Sandhu	63.4	12	229	5	45.80	3-87
R. J. Shastri	163.4	31	472	10	47.20	4-43
S. Venkataraghavan	190	27	586	10	58.60	3-146

Also bowled: M. Amarnath 2.2–0–34–2; A. D. Gaekwad 2–1–3–0; S. M. H. Kirmani 0.0–0–0–0; Maninder Singh 84.3–16–192–2; L. Sivaramakrishnan 25–1–95–0; Yashpal Sharma 1–0–6–1.

INDIAN AVERAGES – FIRST-CLASS MATCHES

BATTING

	M	I	NO	R	HI	100s	Avge
M. Amarnath	8	14	1	959	117	4	73.76
Madal Lal	6	9	2	290	97	0	41.42
R. J. Shastri	9	14	3	422	102	1	38.36
D. B. Vengsarkar	8	14	0	502	94	0	35.85
Kapil Dev	7	11	2	315	100*	1	35.00
Yashpal Sharma	9	16	2	478	63	0	34.14
K. More	3	4	2	66	31	0	33.00
S. M. Gavaskar	6	10	1	245	147*	1	27.22
A. Malhotra	4	7	1	157	59	0	26.16
A. D. Gaekwad	9	16	0	414	89	0	25.87
Arun Lal	5	9	1	170	77	0	21.25
Gursharan Singh	4	6	0	123	89	0	20.50
B. S. Sandhu	5	8	2	110	68	0	18.33
L. Sivaramakrishnan	5	7	1	109	32	0	18.16
S. M. H. Kirmani	8	12	1	199	33	0	18.09
Maninder Singh	6	7	4	40	14	0	13.33
S. Venkataraghavan	8	10	1	32	14	0	3.55

* *Signifies not out.*

BOWLING

	O	M	R	W	Avge	BB
M. Amarnath	35.2	8	142	7	20.28	4-26
Kapil Dev	197	42	539	25	21.56	4-45
Madan Lal	145.2	14	504	20	25.20	5-68
Maninder Singh	189.4	39	464	18	25.77	7-47
A. D. Gaekwad	63	17	188	6	31.33	2-48
S. Venkataraghavan	291.2	60	768	21	36.57	4-5
R. J. Shastri	272.1	51	734	18	40.77	4-43
B. S. Sandhu	87.4	19	293	7	41.85	3-87
L. Sivaramakrishnan	118	15	400	9	44.44	3-105

Also bowled: S. M. H. Kirmani 0.0–0–0–0; Yashpal Sharma 22–4–68–2.

Kirmani's only delivery was a no-ball.

FIELDING

S. M. H. Kirmani 12 (10ct, 2st), K. More 10 (5ct, 5st), S. Venkataraghavan 9, Gursharan Singh 7, Yashpal Sharma 6, Arun Lal 5, Kapil Dev 5, M. Amarnath 4, A. D. Gaekwad 4, S. M. Gavaskar 4, Madan Lal 3, Maninder Singh 3, D. B. Vengsarkar 3, R. J. Shastri 2, B. S. Sandhu 1, L. Sivaramakrishnan 1.

JAMAICA v INDIANS

At Sabina Park, Kingston, February 17, 18, 19, 20. Drawn. Feeling their way in their first match of the tour after arriving less than three days earlier, the Indians were bowled out just after tea on the first day by an inexperienced Jamaican team. An aggressive 75 from the left-handed Powell and a polished century from the captain, Dujon, with one 6 and seven 4s in just under four hours' batting, yielded a lead of 121 for the home team, but the Indian batsmen found their form in the second innings in which the Jamaican fast bowler, Patterson, was injured after six overs.

Indians

A. D. Gaekwad c Francis b Patterson	12	– c Neita b Daley	89
Arun Lal c Davidson b Walsh	1	– b Neita	77
M. Amarnath b Walsh	3	– c and b Wilson	82
D. B. Vengsarkar c Francis b Daley	42	– (5) c sub b Wilson	82
Yashpal Sharma b Daley	17	– (6) c Peters b Neita	24
R. J. Shastri b Wilson	35	– (7) not out	3
*Kapil Dev c Dujon b Wilson	23		
†S. M. H. Kirmani c Fletcher b Daley	0	– not out	1
L. Sivaramakrishnan not out	21		
B. S. Sandhu c Fletcher b Walsh	13	– lbw b Daley	6
S. Venkataraghavan b Walsh	0		
B 1, l-b 1, w 12, n-b 4	18	B 6, l-b 6, w 18, n-b 1	31

1/3 2/12 3/49 4/86   185   1/61 2/205 3/222   (6 wkts dec.) 395
5/89 6/123 7/126 8/167 9/184   4/352 5/383 6/391

Bowling: *First Innings*—Walsh 12–2–31–4; Patterson 10–1–24–1; Daley 20–2–66–3; Wilson 22–6–46–2. *Second Innings*—Walsh 22–6–63–0; Patterson 6–0–26–0; Daley 30–3–101–2; Wilson 40–8–95–2; Neita 21–6–43–2; Davidson 3–0–9–0; Fletcher 8–1–27–0.

Jamaica

C. W. Fletcher lbw b Kapil Dev	28	– not out	32
O. W. Peters b Sandhu	11	– lbw b Sandhu	8
G. Powell c Yashpal b Amarnath	75	– (5) c Arun Lal b Shastri	18
*†P. J. Dujon b Amarnath	104	– (4) not out	6
M. C. Neita c and b Venkataraghavan	15	– (3) b Kapil Dev	1
C. A. Davidson lbw b Kapil Dev	22	– (4) lbw b Kapil Dev	0
P. A. Francis c Kirmani b Kapil Dev	2		
A. G. Daley lbw b Amarnath	18		
C. A. Walsh b Amarnath	6		
P. Patterson c Vengsarkar b Venkataraghavan	3		
E. Wilson not out	2		
B 4, l-b 6, n-b 10	20	L-b 6	6

1/29 2/81 3/163 4/212   306   1/16 2/19   (4 wkts) 71
5/263 6/269 7/281 8/292 9/302   3/19 4/58

Bowling: *First Innings*—Kapil Dev 18–2–57–3; Sandhu 16–5–39–1; Venkataraghavan 34.5–7–75–2; Shastri 30–4–82–0; Sivaramakrishnan 3–1–5–0; Amarnath 10–2–26–4; Gaekwad 1–0–2–0. *Second Innings*—Kapil Dev 8–3–11–2; Sandhu 8–2–25–1; Venkataraghavan 5–2–8–0; Shastri 7–3–11–1; Amarnath 3–1–10–0.

Umpires: A. Gaynor and W. Malcolm.

WEST INDIES v INDIA

First Test Match

At Sabina Park, Kingston, February 23, 24, 26, 27, 28. West Indies won by four wickets, in a frenzied finish with four balls of the final twenty overs remaining. At tea on the final day, after the first heavy rain in Kingston for two years had washed out the fourth day, a draw appeared inevitable as India, 168 for six, were 165 in the lead with four wickets standing. Roberts then dramatically changed the course of the match by dismissing Kirmani, Sandhu and Venkataraghavan in his first over on resumption and completing the rout with the last man, Maninder, in his fourth over.

Even then, West Indies needed to score 172 off what turned out to be 26 overs to secure the lead in the series. Haynes set them on their way with a delightful 34 off 21 deliveries, but it required batting of exceptional brilliance from Richards for the target to be reached. His appearance delayed to one position below his accustomed No. 3 because of a painful shoulder, Richards's first scoring stroke was the first of four huge 6s, and, off 35 deliveries, he attacked mercilessly for 61. When he was out at 156 for five, West Indies required 16 off two and a half overs and, with 6s from Logie – off his first ball – and Dujon, over square leg off Amarnath, West Indies won amidst scenes of great excitement.

The final session of the match had been in complete contrast to what had gone before, when batsmen on both sides struggled to assert themselves on an easy-paced pitch which offered bounce as its only encouragement to the bowlers.

Sent in after Lloyd had won the toss in his 50th Test as captain, India were floundering at 127 for seven midway through the first day to the four opposing fast bowlers. Then Yashpal, batting four and a half hours before he was last out for 63, and the turbanned and helmeted Sandhu revived the innings with an eighth-wicket partnership of 107, a record for India against West Indies.

West Indies also made hard work of their reply, only just managing to squeeze a first-innings lead of 3 runs. Greenidge laboured five hours, twenty minutes for his top score of 70 and no one else passed 30 against steady bowling. Kapil Dev, who ended the innings with three of the last four wickets after lunch on the second day, and the tall left-arm spinner, Shastri, each claimed four wickets.

The loss of the experienced Gavaskar, first ball, bowled leg stump by Holding, was an immediate second-innings setback for India, who ended the third day at 81 for three. Because of the rain, play was not resumed until an hour into the fifth and final day and, although three more Indian wickets fell by tea, this hardly seemed enough to cause their eventual defeat until Roberts, who bowled superbly in both innings, and Richards so dramatically altered the situation.

India

S. M. Gavaskar c Dujon b Marshall	20	– b Holding	0
A. D. Gaekwad c Dujon b Holding	1	– c Greenidge b Marshall	23
M. Amarnath c Dujon b Garner	29	– c Garner b Marshall	40
D. B. Vengsarkar c Richards b Roberts	30	– c Garner b Marshall	20
Yashpal Sharma c Haynes b Garner	63	– c Gomes b Holding	24
R. J. Shastri c Dujon b Holding	1	– not out	25
*Kapil Dev c Marshall b Roberts	5	– c Dujon b Roberts	12
†S. M. H. Kirmani c Dujon b Marshall	5	– c Haynes b Roberts	10
B. S. Sandhu c Garner b Roberts	68	– c Garner b Roberts	0
S. Venkataraghavan b Roberts	0	– c Greenidge b Roberts	0
Maninder Singh not out	3	– c Holding b Roberts	2
B 1, l-b 15, n-b 10	26	B 2, l-b 4, w 1, n-b 11	18
	251		**174**

1/10 2/58 3/66 4/98   5/99 6/104 7/127 8/234 9/238

1/0 2/68 3/69 4/112   5/118 6/136 7/168 8/168 9/168

Bowling: *First Innings*—Holding 24–5–57–2; Roberts 22–4–61–4; Garner 15.4–4–41–2; Marshall 16–4–35–2; Gomes 9–0–31–0; Richards 1–1–0–0. *Second Innings*—Holding 17–4–36–2; Roberts 24.3–9–39–5; Garner 13–6–16–0; Marshall 24–6–56–3; Gomes 7–2–9–0.

West Indies

C. G. Greenidge c Venkataraghavan b Shastri ..	70	– b Kapil Dev	42
D. L. Haynes c Amarnath b Kapil Dev	25	– b Kapil Dev	34
I. V. A. Richards c Venkataraghavan b Shastri .	29	– (4) c Kapil Dev b Amarnath	61
H. A. Gomes c Yashpal b Shastri	4		
A. L. Logie run out	13	– (7) lbw b Kapil Dev	10
*C. H. Lloyd b Venkataraghavan	24	– (3) c Amarnath b Kapil Dev	3
†P. J. Dujon lbw b Kapil Dev	29	– (6) not out	17
M. D. Marshall c Yashpal b Kapil Dev	23	– not out	0
A. M. E. Roberts c Sandhu b Shastri	17	– (5) c Kirmani b Amarnath	1
M. A. Holding c Kirmani b Kapil Dev	1		
J. Garner not out	0		
B 1, l-b 8, n-b 10	19	N-b 5	5

1/36 2/83 3/91 4/114   254   1/47 2/65 3/131   (6 wkts) 173
5/157 6/186 7/228 8/244 9/254   4/132 5/156 6/161

Bowling: *First Innings*—Kapil Dev 25.3–6–45–4; Sandhu 11–4–30–0; Venkataraghavan 25–3–66–1; Maninder 31–6–51–0; Shastri 24–8–43–4. *Second Innings*—Kapil Dev 13–0–73–4; Sandhu 3–0–22–0; Venkataraghavan 7–0–39–0; Amarnath 2.2–0–34–2.

Umpires: D. M. Archer and W. Malcolm.

TRINIDAD & TOBAGO v INDIANS

At Pointe-á-Pierre, Trinidad, March 3, 4, 5. Indians won by an innings and 69 runs with a day to spare, following two inept batting performances by the home team. The eighteen-year-old left-arm spinner, Maninder, took twelve wickets for 95 in the match, his seven for 47 in the second innings causing the collapse of Trinidad and Tobago's last eight wickets for 44 runs. The only worthwhile innings for the home team was played by Simmonds, a tall, nineteen-year-old opener, who batted stubbornly for 81, surviving four chances. Gavaskar, hitting out to every delivery he faced, fell to a catch at mid-on in the second over of the Indians' innings, but a century by Amarnath and positive batting by Gaekwad, Malhotra, Kirmani and Madan Lal provided the Indians with a winning lead. The leg-spinner, Mahabir, was the best of a local attack based on spin.

Trinidad & Tobago

R. S. Gabriel c More b Amarnath	10	– c Maninder b Madan Lal	30
P. V. Simmonds lbw b Maninder	81	– b Maninder	22
A. L. Logie c Shastri b Madan Lal	7	– (4) lbw b Maninder	13
*H. A. Gomes c Arun Lal b Gaekwad	22	– (3) c and b Maninder	27
K. G. d'Heurieux c and b Maninder	18	– c Amarnath b Maninder	0
†T. Cuffy b Maninder	2	– b Gaekwad	2
R. Nanan lbw b Gaekwad	18	– lbw b Maninder	5
R. Ramparrass c sub b Maninder	3	– c Madan Lal b Maninder	5
P. Ramnath b Maninder	1	– not out	11
G. S. Antoine not out	7	– st More b Maninder	0
G. Mahabir c sub b Madan Lal	13	– run out	8
B 2, l-b 3, n-b 6	11	B 5, l-b 12, n-b 1	18

1/23 2/36 3/84 4/113   193   1/38 2/69 3/97 4/97   141
5/117 6/152 7/157 8/164 9/171   5/100 6/110 7/112 8/113 9/117

Bowling: *First Innings*—Madan Lal 14.1–0–44–2; Amarnath 11–2–42–1; Maninder 21–7–48–5; Gaekwad 16–2–48–2. *Second Innings*—Madan Lal 4–1–28–1; Amarnath 3–0–16–0; Maninder 19.2–2–47–7; Gaekwad 18–4–32–1.

Indians

S. M. Gavaskar c Mahabir b d'Heurieux.	5	*S. M. H. Kirmani lbw b Mahabir	74
A. D. Gaekwad c Ramparrass b Gomes.	81	Madan Lal c Antoine b Mahabir	45
M. Amarnath c Ramparrass b d'Heurieux.	114	†K. More not out	1
		Maninder Singh c Simmonds b Nanan..	14
A. Malhotra c Simmonds b Mahabir....	59	R. J. Shastri absent hurt	
Arun Lal lbw b Mahabir	0	B 4, l-b 6	10
Gursharan Singh lbw b Nanan	0		—
		1/5 2/146 3/254 4/254	403
		5/255 6/279 7/387 8/388 9/403	

Bowling: Antoine 20–1–82–0; d'Heurieux 11–0–44–2; Nanan 41–13–78–2; Mahabir 27–5–71–4; Ramnath 14–3–56–0; Gomes 18–2–51–1; Simmonds 4–0–11–0.

Umpires: Sadiq Mohammad and C. Shaffrali.

†WEST INDIES v INDIA

First One-day International

At Port-of-Spain, March 9. West Indies won by 52 runs. The match was reduced to 39 overs a side as excessive sweating under the covers had left the pitch too damp for a prompt start. The West Indian openers did well to survive an early, difficult period and put on 125. Greenidge was in commanding form, with four 6s, while Haynes seemed to have a century for the taking before being caught at square leg. India never got on terms with the run-rate and the main excitement for a massive crowd estimated at 30,000 was a sharp but brief earth tremor in mid-afternoon which sent spectators scampering and left a dozen slightly injured.

West Indies

C. G. Greenidge c Madan Lal b Maninder.	66	*C. H. Lloyd c Kirmani b Kapil Dev...	3
D. L. Haynes c Yashpal b Kapil Dev ..	97	B 4, l-b 5, w 1, n-b 1	11
I. V. A. Richards c Gaekwad b Amarnath.	32		—
A. L. Logie not out	6	1/125 2/198 3/207 (4 wkts, 38.5 overs) 215	
		4/215	

H. A. Gomes, †P. J. Dujon, M. D. Marshall, A. M. E. Roberts, M. A. Holding and J. Garner did not bat.

Bowling: Kapil Dev 6.5–0–21–2; Madan Lal 7–0–34–0; Venkataraghavan 9–0–48–0; Amarnath 7–0–39–1; Maninder 9–0–62–1.

India

S. M. Gavaskar c Roberts b Garner	25	†S. M. H. Kirmani not out	13
A. D. Gaekwad b Gomes	22	Madan Lal not out	13
M. Amarnath run out	27		
D. B. Vengsarkar c Logie b Roberts	27	B 1, l-b 3, w 5, n-b 4	13
*Kapil Dev lbw b Roberts	0		—
Yashpal Sharma c Haynes b Gomes	2	1/55 2/59 3/110 (7 wkts, 39 overs) 163	
A. Malhotra c Holding b Gomes	21	4/110 5/115 6/117 7/140	

Maninder Singh and S. Venkataraghavan did not bat.

Bowling: Holding 5–1–8–0; Roberts 7–2–27–2; Marshall 8–0–25–0; Garner 9–1–39–1; Gomes 9–0–50–3; Logie 1–0–1–0.

Umpires: A. Weekes and P. Narine.

WEST INDIES v INDIA

Second Test Match

At Port-of-Spain, March 11, 12, 13, 15, 16. Drawn. Forced to bat first, when the pitch contained moisture which made batting difficult, India recovered from a worrying first-innings total to earn a commendable draw. To do so, they needed to bat ten hours, twenty minutes in their second innings, in which they recorded their highest-ever total in a Test in West Indies.

Rain on the eve of the match and on the first day affected the preparation of the pitch, the ball moving in the heavy atmosphere and off the well-grassed surface throughout a greatly reduced first day. India scored 44 for three and Yashpal retired hurt. They might well have lost more wickets with better bowling and a little less luck, especially after Gaekwad had been run out off the third ball answering Gavaskar's call for an impossible single.

For the rest of the match, the weather remained warm and sunny and the pitch became better and better. India's first-innings 175 was based on a stand of 103 between Amarnath and Shastri for the fourth wicket after which the last six wickets fell for 44, four going to Marshall, whose five for 37 were his best Test figures.

There was an astonishing start to the West Indian innings in which both openers fell to Sandhu's medium-paced swing without scoring and Richards was caught behind down the leg side off Kapil Dev for 1. Never in Test history had West Indies lost their first three wickets so cheaply and they might not have recovered had wicket-keeper Kirmani not missed a straightforward catch from Gomes off Venkataraghavan when 21 and a barely acceptable one down the leg side from Lloyd off Sandhu when 10. As it was, the two left-handers rebuilt the innings in their contrasting styles by adding 237 for the fourth wicket. Lloyd's 143 included two 6s and thirteen 4s and was his fifteenth Test century. Gomes, less assured than his captain, batted seven and threequarter hours for his fifth Test century and his first on his home ground. The lower order extended West Indies' lead to 219, the rest of the innings including Kapil Dev's 200th Test wicket when he bowled Roberts with the second ball of the fourth day. He had passed 2,000 runs in the previous Test.

India were left with just over five sessions to bat for a draw, and the loss of Gavaskar, completely out of sorts, put the pressure on the other batsmen. By now, however, the pitch was placid and, with the exception of the hostile Marshall, no West Indian bowler could strike life from it.

Amarnath led the way for India with a flawless 117, his fourth century in eight Tests since his triumphant return in the previous series in Pakistan. Amarnath, often battered and bruised during his defiant five and threequarter hours at the wicket, eventually fell lbw to a gentle off-break from Richards, whereupon the quick loss of Yashpal and Shastri raised West Indian hopes. But Kapil Dev, batting with characteristic abandon, scotched any thoughts of an Indian collapse similar to that of the first Test, and, Lloyd having sportingly claimed the last half hour, he reached an explosive 100 with three 6s and thirteen 4s.

India

S. M. Gavaskar c Dujon b Holding		1 – c Dujon b Garner	32
A. D. Gaekwad run out	0	– c sub (S. F. A. Bacchus) b Gomes	35
M. Amarnath c Lloyd b Roberts	58	– lbw b Richards	117
D. B. Vengsarkar c Holding b Marshall	7	– c Dujon b Roberts	45
Yashpal Sharma not out	11	– b Roberts	50
R. J. Shastri c Gomes b Marshall	42	– lbw b Holding	9
*Kapil Dev c Haynes b Marshall	13	– not out	100
†S. M. H. Kirmani b Roberts	7	– run out	30
B. S. Sandhu c Richards b Marshall	11	– not out	0
S. Venkataraghavan c Richards b Roberts	1		
Maninder Singh c Dujon b Marshall	1		
B 5, l-b 1, w 3, nb 14	23	B 10, l-b 20, n-b 21	51

1/1 2/5 3/28 4/131   175   1/63 2/132 3/206   (7 wkts) 469
5/146 6/147 7/164 8/166 9/171   4/312 5/325 6/329 7/463

Bowling: *First Innings*—Holding 13–2–24–1; Roberts 22–5–72–3; Marshall 19.2–5–37–5; Garner 10–5–17–0; Gomes 2–1–2–0. *Second Innings*—Holding 31–2–104–1; Roberts 25–3–100–2; Marshall 27.1–8–72–0; Garner 30–7–81–1; Gomes 19–7–45–1; Richards 7–4–16–1.

West Indies

C. G. Greenidge b Sandhu	0	M. D. Marshall lbw b Shastri	14
D. L. Haynes c Kirmani b Sandhu	0	A. M. E. Roberts b Kapil Dev	9
I. V. A. Richards c Kirmani b Kapil Dev.	1	M. A. Holding c Vengsarkar b Maninder.	24
H. A. Gomes c Gavaskar b Venkataraghavan.	123	J. Garner not out	21
*C. H. Lloyd st Kirmani b Shastri	143	B 4, l-b 7, w 1, n-b 3	15
A. L. Logie c Kapil Dev b Venkataraghavan.	13	1/0 2/1 3/1 4/238	394
†P. J. Dujon lbw b Kapil Dev	31	5/255 6/316 7/324 8/340 9/346	

Bowling: Kapil Dev 31–6–91–3; Sandhu 19–2–69–2; Venkataraghavan 41–13–97–2; Shastri 21–2–71–2; Maninder 26.3–7–51–1.

Umpires: Sadiq Mohammad and S. E. Parris.

WINDWARD ISLANDS v INDIANS

At St George's, Grenada, March 18, 19, 20, 21. Indians won by 129 runs. Neither team held the advantage in a tense, low-scoring match, until the final day when the Indian spin bowlers routed the Windwards' batsmen. The Indians, batting first, struggled to score 182 and the Windwards were made to fight equally hard for runs, the left-handed Slack batting four and a half hours, with only six 4s, guiding them to a lead of 35 with his highest score in the West Indies. Shastri batted well at the start of India's second innings but with the score 159 for six at lunch on the final day, the Windwards held the initiative until Yashpal, with support from Kapil Dev and Madan Lal, eventually set the islanders a challenging target which they never seemed likely to reach.

Indians

Arun Lal b Williams	21	– c Cadette b Williams	5
R. J. Shastri c Cadette b Davis	17	– c Cadette b Davis	73
A. Malhotra c Slack b Williams	21	– c Kentish b Phillip	12
D. B. Vengsarkar lbw b Phillip	4	– (5) b Williams	40
Yashpal Sharma b Davis	23	– (6) b Davis	57
Gursharan Singh b Phillip	4	– (3) b Williams	0
*Kapil Dev b Phillip	2	– (8) c Cadette b Davis	36
Madan Lal c and b Phillip	4	– (9) not out	37
L. Sivaramakrishnan c sub b Davis	32	– (10) lbw b Davis	6
†K. More not out	23	– (4) run out	11
S. Venkataraghavan c Thorpe b Phillip	12	– b Davis	0
B 7, n-b 12	19	L-b 3, n-b 7	10
1/24 2/54 3/70 4/80	182	1/38 2/60 3/89 4/118	287
5/90 6/105 7/109 8/126 9/155		5/154 6/155 7/210 8/273 9/287	

Bowling: *First Innings*—Davis 22–4–43–3; Phillip 16–3–56–5; Williams 12.2–3–44–2; Kentish 10–4–14–0; Charles 1–0–6–0. *Second Innings*—Davis 23.5–4–84–5; Phillip 19–4–52–1; Williams 21–3–84–3; Kentish 22–6–51–0; Slack 2–1–3–0; Thorpe 3–1–3–0.

Windward Islands

L. C. Sebastien c More b Kapil Dev	0	– b Shastri	10
L. D. John b Kapil Dev	4	– c Arun Lal b Madan Lal	7
S. W. Julien lbw b Madan Lal	37	– c More b Kapil Dev	0
W. N. Slack b Venkataraghavan	97	– st More b Venkataraghavan	32
F. Thorpe c Vengsarkar b Sivaramakrishnan	22	– c Gursharan b Shastri	14
J. D. Charles st More b Sivaramakrishnan	20	– c Gursharan b Shastri	13
*N. Phillip st More b Venkataraghavan	1	– c Gursharan b Shastri	9
†I. Cadette run out	0	– c Gursharan b Sivaramakrishnan	15
N. F. Williams c Arun Lal b Venkataraghavan	13	– c Gursharan b Sivaramakrishnan	1
T. Kentish run out	16	– not out	15
W. W. Davis not out	0	– c Kapil Dev b Shastri	3
B 3, l-b 3, n-b 1	7	B 1, n-b 3	4

1/0 2/11 3/59 4/105   217   1/14 2/14 3/63 4/65   123
5/140 6/146 7/147 8/192 9/217   5/68 6/73 7/92 8/93 9/108

Bowling: *First Innings*—Kapil Dev 7–3–18–2; Madan Lal 11–0–47–1; Venkataraghavan 20.1–5–34–3; Shastri 25–5–47–0; Sivaramakrishnan 20–1–64–2. *Second Innings*—Kapil Dev 10–2–29–1; Madan Lal 9–1–18–1; Venkataraghavan 14–6–16–1; Shastri 18.3–3–22–5; Sivaramakrishnan 11–2–34–2.

Umpires: G. Johnson and S. Rock.

GUYANA v INDIANS

At Georgetown, March 24, 25, 26, 27. Abandoned.

†At Georgetown, March 26, 27. Drawn. Indians 286 for three dec. (M. Amarnath 121, R. J. Shastri 75, S. M. Gavaskar 36 not out, D. B. Vengsarkar 34 not out); Guyana 119 for six (T. R. Etwaroo 53).

†WEST INDIES v INDIA

Second One-day International

At Berbice, Guyana, March 29. India won by 27 runs, achieving the highest total ever recorded against West Indies in a limited-overs international at a rate of 5.4 an over. Gavaskar, in his first innings of note on the tour, and Shastri led the way by contributing 93 at 5 an over, but Kapil Dev provided the real momentum by lashing three 6s and seven 4s off 38 deliveries. The West Indian bowling and fielding were unusually slack, and the early loss of Greenidge, Haynes and Lloyd virtually sealed the match in India's favour. A crowd of 15,000 watched the match in the heart of Guyana's sugar area.

India

S. M. Gavaskar run out	90	A. Malhotra not out	1
R. J. Shastri c Dujon b Marshall	30		
M. Amarnath b Richards	30	B 1, l-b 9, w 4, n-b 4	18
*Kapil Dev b Roberts	72		
Yashpal Sharma c Greenidge b Davis	23	1/93 2/152 (5 wkts, 47 overs) 282	
D. B. Vengsarkar not out	18	3/224 4/246 5/277	

Madan Lal, †S. M. H. Kirmani, B. S. Sandhu and S. Venkataraghavan did not bat.

Bowling: Holding 7–0–49–0; Roberts 9–0–44–1; Davis 8–0–40–1; Marshall 7–0–23–1; Gomes 10–0–64–0; Richards 6–0–44–1.

West Indies

C. G. Greenidge c and b Kapil Dev	16	A. M. E. Roberts b Kapil Dev	12
D. L. Haynes lbw b Sandhu	2	M. A. Holding c Malhotra b Sandhu	2
I. V. A. Richards b Madan Lal	64	W. W. Davis not out	7
*C. H. Lloyd c Amarnath b Madan Lal	8	L-b 6, w 1, n-b 1	8
S. F. A. Bacchus c Yashpal b Shastri	52		
H. A. Gomes c Kapil Dev b Shastri	26	1/6 2/22 3/62 (9 wkts, 47 overs)	255
†P. J. Dujon not out	53	4/98 5/154 6/181	
M. D. Marshall c Sandhu b Shastri	5	7/192 8/228 9/232	

Bowling: Shastri 8–0–48–3; Venkataraghavan 10–0–63–0; Madan Lal 9–0–65–2; Kapil Dev 10–0–33–2; Sandhu 10–0–38–2.

Umpires: D. M. Archer and M. Baksh.

WEST INDIES v INDIA

Third Test Match

At Georgetown, March 31, April 2, 3, 4, 5. Drawn. Yet again, the Guyanese public had to endure a Test match spoiled by the weather. Heavy overnight and early-morning rain prevented any play on the sodden ground on the second and fourth days and before lunch on the third. In the event, on a typically beautiful batting pitch, only thirteen wickets fell while over 750 runs were scored.

For the third time in the series, Lloyd won the toss but this time decided to bat first and, by the end of the first day, West Indies were 259 for five after the late loss of three quick wickets. Richards was then 97 and had to wait through the rest day, Good Friday, the rained-out Saturday and until after lunch on the Sunday before he could resume to complete his fourteenth Test century and his first on the ground, with two 6s and nine 4s.

India were left with two days to bat for a draw and, when rain reduced this by half, the last day was of no more than academic interest. Gavaskar used the occasion to pass Sobers's tally of 26 Test centuries on the ground where, twelve years earlier, he had scored his first. He offered a direct catch to second slip off Marshall when 44, but that was his only mistake in five and a half hours, in which he hit one 6 and seventeen 4s, passing 7,500 Test runs.

West Indies

C. G. Greenidge c Kirmani b Maninder	70	†P. J. Dujon c and b Venkataraghavan	47
D. L. Haynes c Yashpal b Venkataraghavan	46	M. D. Marshall lbw b Kapil Dev	27
		A. M. E. Roberts c Gavaskar b Sandhu	36
I. V. A Richards c Venkataraghavan b Sandhu	109	J. Garner not out	1
H. A. Gomes c Gaekwad b Kapil Dev	36	B 1, l-b 14, w 1, n-b 1	17
M. A. Holding run out	0		
A. L. Logie c Kirmani b Sandhu	0	1/89 2/157 3/252	470
*C. H. Lloyd c Kirmani b Shastri	81	4/253 5/256 6/299	
		7/387 8/417 9/460	

Bowling: Kapil Dev 30–7–68–2; Sandhu 25.4–5–87–3; Shastri 22–3–84–1; Maninder 27–3–90–1; Venkataraghavan 38–4–124–2.

India

S. M. Gavaskar not out	147	Yashpal Sharma not out	35
A. D. Gaekwad c Dujon b Holding	8	B 1, l-b 3, n-b 15	19
M. Amarnath c Richards b Marshall	13		
D. B. Vengsarkar c Richards b Garner	62	1/24 2/68 3/160 (3 wkts)	284

R. J. Shastri, *Kapil Dev, †S. M. H. Kirmani, B. S. Sandhu, Maninder Singh and S. Venkataraghavan did not bat.

Bowling: Roberts 15–2–38–0; Holding 16–1–72–1; Garner 17–4–57–1; Marshall 13–2–39–1; Gomes 14–5–35–0; Richards 4–0–24–0.

Umpires: D. M. Archer and D. Narine.

†WEST INDIES v INDIA

Third One-day International

At St George's, Grenada, April 7. West Indies won by seven wickets, thus clinching the three-match series. A public holiday was declared for the first international match played in Grenada and over 10,000 spectators crowded the picturesque ground overlooking St George's harbour. With the exception of Vengsarkar, the Indian batsmen could not find the inspiration they did in the previous one-day match, their total of 166 proving quite inadequate.

India

S. M. Gavaskar c Richards b Roberts..	3	†S. M. H. Kirmani run out	3
R. J. Shastri c Dujon b Marshall	17	B. S. Sandhu not out	16
M. Amarnath b Gomes	11	S. Venkataraghavan b Holding	3
D. B. Vengsarkar c Richards b Gomes .	54	B 5, l-b 7, w 5, n-b 3	20
A. Malhotra c Richards b Gomes	7		
Yashpal Sharma b Holding	25	1/9 2/36 3/47 (44.4 overs) 166	
*Kapil Dev lbw b Roberts	1	4/74 5/109 6/114	
Madan Lal b Gomes	6	7/127 8/138 9/153	

Bowling: Holding 8.4–2–15–2; Roberts 9–0–38–2; Garner 10–1–30–0; Marshall 7–2–25–1; Gomes 10–0–38–4.

West Indies

C. G. Greenidge c Sandhu b Shastri....	64	S. F. A. Bacchus not out	26
D. L. Haynes c Venkataraghavan		†P. J. Dujon not out	20
b Amarnath.	19	L-b 7, w 3	10
I. V. A. Richards c Shastri			
b Venkataraghavan.	28	1/61 2/106 3/132 (3 wkts, 40.2 overs) 167	

*C. H. Lloyd, H. A. Gomes, M. D. Marshall, A. M. E. Roberts, M. A. Holding and J. Garner did not bat.

Bowling: Kapil Dev 6–2–21–0; Sandhu 8–2–30–0; Madan Lal 7–1–37–0; Amarnath 4–0–23–1; Venkataraghavan 8–0–24–1; Shastri 5–1–10–1; Yashpal 2.2–0–12–0.

Umpires: S. E. Parris and P. Whyte.

BARBADOS v INDIANS

At Bridgetown, April 9, 10, 11, 12. Drawn. Barbados outplayed the Indians throughout, but just failed to improve upon their record of three consecutive victories over Indian touring teams as Gursharan, in his best innings of the tour, and the consistent Amarnath, batting at No. 9 because of illness, defied them with an eighth-wicket stand of 163 in the second innings. Despite half-centuries by Amarnath and Yashpal, who shared a century partnership, and Shastri, India's 246 after being sent in was unsatisfactory. In their turn, Barbados were struggling at 134 for four before the captain, Greenidge, with his highest score in the West Indies and the first double-century by a Barbados batsman since 1967 (three 6s and 22 4s), shared century partnerships with the all-rounder Linton and the new wicket-keeper Worrell. When Greenidge was out after batting for eight and a quarter hours without a chance, the tailenders lashed seven 6s whilst adding 72 in half an hour. The Indians declined to 223 for seven just after lunch on the final day and another defeat to Barbados looked certain before the steady Gursharan and the confident Amarnath, whose fourth century of the tour took only three hours and included eleven 4s, saved the day.

Indians

A. D. Gaekwad c Worrell b Garner	4	– c Payne b Alleyne 28
Arun Lal lbw b Alleyne	5	– c Worrell b Linton 31
M. Amarnath c Reifer b Alleyne	61	– (9) not out 101
A. Malhotra c Worrell b Garner	0	– (3) c Worrell b Garner 55
Yashpal Sharma c Worrell b Phillips	59	– (6) c Garner b Phillips 11
Gursharan Singh c Best b Phillips	15	– (7) c Worrell b Garner 89
R. J. Shastri lbw b Garner	58	– (5) lbw b Garner 0
*†S. M. H. Kirmani c Garner b Phillips	4	– (4) b Garner 22
Madan Lal c Haynes b Linton	13	– (8) c Garner b Linton 53
L. Sivaramakrishnan c Best b Linton	4	– lbw b Garner 0
Maninder Singh not out	6	– not out 1
L-b 3, w 3, n-b 11	17	B 6, l-b 2, n-b 4 12

1/8 2/12 3/12 4/140   246   1/34 2/95 3/132 4/132   (9 wkts) 403
5/140 6/164 7/182 8/200 9/212   5/148 6/160 7/223 8/386 9/389

Bowling: *First Innings*—Garner 16.1–3–52–3; Alleyne 19–4–47–2; Phillips 13–3–50–3; Estwick 14–4–47–0; Linton 10–3–33–2. *Second Innings*—Garner 33–4–127–5; Alleyne 24–1–106–1; Phillips 13–2–41–1; Estwick 16–4–46–0; Linton 16–3–52–2; Reifer 2–0–8–0; Haynes 2–0–11–0.

Barbados

D. L. Haynes b Sivaramakrishnan	25	N. A. Phillips c sub b Sivaramakrishnan . 51
C. A. Best lbw b Madan Lal	6	R. O. Estwick st Kirmani b Gaekwad .. 11
T. R. O. Payne c Madan Lal b Sivaramakrishnan.	26	J. Garner b Maninder 17
*C. G. Greenidge c Arun Lal b Gaekwad.	237	H. L. Alleyne not out 15
G. N. Reifer c sub b Maninder	32	B 4, l-b 11 15
G. N. Linton c Kirmani b Madan Lal ..	66	1/11 2/60 3/61 542
†M. C. Worrell c Gursharan b Shastri .	41	4/134 5/330 6/442
		7/470 8/510 9/510

Bowling: Madan Lal 24–1–71–2; Amarnath 6–3–14–0; Sivaramakrishnan 31–7–105–3; Maninder 41.5–6–121–2; Gaekwad 22–9–94–2; Shastri 28–5–100–1; Yashpal 7–2–22–0.

Umpires: L. Barker and S. E. Parris.

WEST INDIES v INDIA

Fourth Test Match

At Bridgetown, April 15, 16, 17, 19, 20. West Indies won by ten wickets, their fourth victory in five Tests against India at the ground, the other being drawn. On a fast, true pitch, with encouraging bounce for their fast bowlers, they encountered defiant opposition from only one Indian batsman, the magnificent Amarnath. While his team-mates capitulated to a diet of short-pitched bowling, which later brought complaints of intimidation from the Indian manager and captain, Amarnath, batting for a combined total of six and a half hours, met the challenge with courage, hooking with certainty, despite a blow on the mouth which caused his temporary retirement in the second innings.

Unseasonal rain delayed the start until half an hour before lunch on the first day and then another torrential downpour during the interval prevented any further play. By then, India had been sent in and were 13 for the loss of their opening batsmen. Amarnath led a recovery on the second day, hooking Roberts, Holding and Garner for 6s in the first session, but after he and Kapil Dev fell to successive deliveries from Marshall, India's 172 for four became 209 all out.

Haynes, at pains to provide the sheet anchor for the West Indian reply, put on 98 for the first wicket with Greenidge and 122 for the second with Richards. West Indies went into the lead with only one wicket down, but the spinners then dismissed Richards, Gomes and Haynes – whose 92 took him six and a quarter hours – in the space of 32 runs. Had Venkataraghavan not dropped Logie at slip off Shastri – a gentle, lobbed catch off the glove – when the batsman was 7, India might have limited the eventual West Indian advantage. As it was, the little Trinidadian right-hander gradually overcame his early nerves, reached 72 by the end of the second day and went on to his maiden Test century with growing confidence. His 130, ended as he was forcing the pace, included two 6s and twelve 4s. Lloyd reached his third consecutive half-century and India, 277 behind, needed to bat through the final day and a half to save the match.

They had done so in the second Test but now the pitch remained hard and fast and only Amarnath, his innings divided into two parts by his injury, caused when he missed a hook off Marshall, and Gaekwad delayed the West Indian victory. An innings defeat was just avoided and a no-ball from the wicket-keeper, Kirmani, was the run which put the home team two ahead in the series. Roberts, who took eight wickets in the match, passed Wes Hall's record of 192 wickets taken by a West Indian fast bowler.

India

S. M. Gavaskar c Dujon b Holding	2	– c Roberts b Garner	19
A. D. Gaekwad c Marshall b Roberts	3	– b Holding	55
M. Amarnath c Dujon b Marshall	91	– c Dujon b Roberts	80
D. B. Vengsarkar c Marshall b Holding	15	– lbw b Holding	6
Yashpal Sharma c Richards b Roberts	24	– c Greenidge b Roberts	12
R. J. Shastri c Richards b Roberts	29	– c Lloyd b Marshall	19
*Kapil Dev c Lloyd b Marshall	0	– (8) c Lloyd b Marshall	26
†S. M. H. Kirmani c Haynes b Roberts	11	– (9) run out	33
Madan Lal c Holding b Garner	6	– (10) lbw b Roberts	0
B. S. Sandhu not out	8	– (7) lbw b Roberts	4
S. Venkataraghavan c Dujon b Garner	5	– not out	0
L-b 1, n-b 14	15	B 5, l-b 2, n-b 16	23

1/2 2/10 3/39 4/91   209   1/61 2/108 3/109 4/132   277
5/172 6/172 7/180 8/196 9/200   5/139 6/155 7/214 8/276 9/276

Bowling: *First Innings*—Holding 14–4–46–2; Roberts 16–4–48–4; Marshall 13–1–56–2; Garner 12.2–5–41–2; Gomes 2–1–3–0. *Second Innings*—Holding 21–2–75–2; Roberts 19.2–3–31–4; Marshall 16–1–80–2; Garner 15–4–48–1; Gomes 8–3–20–0.

West Indies

C. G. Greenidge c Gavaskar b Madan Lal	57	– not out	0
D. L. Haynes c Kapil Dev b Shastri	92	– not out	0
I. V. A. Richards c Gavaskar b Venkataraghavan	80		
H. A. Gomes c sub (L. Sivaramakrishnan) b Venkataraghavan	6		
A. L. Logie c Amarnath b Shastri	130		
*C. H. Lloyd c sub (L. Sivaramakrishnan) b Venkataraghavan	50		
†P. J. Dujon c Vengsarkar b Kapil Dev	25		
M. D. Marshall c Venkataraghavan b Kapil Dev	8		
A. M. E. Roberts c Kapil Dev b Madan Lal	20		
M. A. Holding c Kirmani b Kapil Dev	2		
J. Garner not out	2		
B 1, l-b 11, n-b 2	14	N-b 1	1

1/98 2/220 3/230 4/262   486   (no wkt) 1
5/395 6/454 7/458 8/481 9/483

Bowling: *First Innings*—Kapil Dev 32.3–7–76–3; Sandhu 5–1–21–0; Madan Lal 27–2–96–2; Shastri 50–13–133–2; Venkataraghavan 43–6–146–3; Gaekwad 1–1–0–0. *Second Innings*—Kirmani 0.0–0–0–0.

Umpires: D. M. Archer and S. E. Parris.

LEEWARD ISLANDS v INDIANS

At St Kitts, April 22, 23, 24. Indians won by nine wickets with a day to spare, the Leewards, without their Test players, Richards and Roberts, being completely outplayed. They started well enough when West Indies' youth team's fast bowler, Merrick, took the first four wickets cheaply as the Indians faltered at 138 for five. However, a boisterous 97 from Madan Lal, and important assistance from the tailenders boosted that to 362. Madan Lal and Venkataraghavan then skittled the home team for 103 in 27.2 overs between the two intervals on the second day. Following on 259 behind, the Leewards showed more fight in their second innings, especially from the experienced Eddy, who batted for three and threequarter hours without a mistake. Madan Lal completed an excellent all-round match by taking the last three wickets at a personal cost of 1 run with the second new ball.

Indians

*A. D. Gaekwad b Merrick	0	– c Baptiste b Merrick	0
Arun Lal lbw b Merrick	29	– not out	1
A. Malhotra c Baptiste b Merrick	9	– not out	1
D. B. Vengsarkar c Sargeant b Merrick	55		
Gursharan Singh st Sargeant b Willett	15		
Yashpal Sharma b Baptiste	45		
Madan Lal c Baptiste b Merrick	97		
†K. More c Richardson b Baptiste	31		
L. Sivaramakrishnan b Newton	29		
S. Venkataraghavan c Richardson b Newton	14		
Maninder Singh not out	13		
B 5, l-b 8, w 4, n-b 8	25	L-b 4	4

1/0 2/12 3/91 4/98   362   1/0   (1 wkt) 6
5/138 6/212 7/290 8/321 9/337

Bowling: *First Innings*—Merrick 28–5–68–5; White 17–4–56–0; Baptiste 23–5–61–2; Willett 41–14–87–1; Newton 29.3–13–45–2; Eddy 4–0–20–0. *Second Innings*—Merrick 1–0–2–1; White 0.2–0–0–0.

Leeward Islands

*A. L. Kelly c More b Madan Lal	5	– c Venkataraghavan b Gaekwad	54
R. B. Richardson b Madan Lal	4	– st More b Maninder	10
R. S. Otto c Gursharan b Madan Lal	5	– b Maninder	17
V. A. Eddy c and b Yashpal	1	– not out	91
S. Liburd b Venkataraghavan	41	– c Venkataraghavan b Sivaramakrishnan	6
E. A. E. Baptiste c More b Madan Lal	9	– c Madan Lal b Sivaramakrishnan	20
†E. Sergeant lbw b Madan Lal	9	– b Venkataraghavan	12
A. C. M. White c Gursharan b Venkataraghavan	0	– run out	6
A. Merrick c Gaekwad b Venkataraghavan	10	– c Sivaramakrishnan b Madan Lal	30
E. T. Willett not out	6	– lbw b Madan Lal	0
V. C. Newton lbw b Venkataraghavan	9	– b Madan Lal	1
L-b 1, n-b 3	4	B 4, l-b 10, n-b 3	17

1/9 2/10 3/11 4/32   103   1/46 2/56 3/99 4/120   264
5/51 6/73 7/77 8/79 9/88   5/153 6/178 7/193 8/257 9/257

Bowling: *First Innings*—Madan Lal 14–0–68–5; Yashpal 9–1–26–1; Venkataraghavan 4.2–2–5–4. *Second Innings*—Madan Lal 7.1–2–27–3; Yashpal 5–1–14–0; Venkataraghavan 23–11–44–1; Maninder 23–8–56–2; Sivaramakrishnan 28–3–97–2; Gaekwad 4–1–9–1.

Umpires: A. Weekes and P. White.

N. Jones stood in for White on the final day.

WEST INDIES v INDIA

Fifth Test Match

At St John's, Antigua, April 28, 29, 30, May 1, 3. Drawn. Batsmen enjoyed themselves on a true, easy-paced pitch to such an extent that six of them scored centuries, two others were out in the nineties and 1,254 runs were scored for 25 wickets. In the circumstances, it was a difficult initiation to Test cricket for the two new players introduced, one by each team – Davis, a fast bowler from St Vincent, and Sivaramakrishnan, a leg-spinner who became the youngest Indian Test cricketer at the age of seventeen years and 118 days.

The adverse weather which had affected each preceding Test again attended the first day of this one, bad light and rain causing the loss of two hours. An aggressive 94 by Vengsarkar led India to 188 for four at the end of it and two innings of differing moods by Shastri and Kapil Dev, who added 156 for the fifth wicket, ensured India of a big first-innings total. Shastri, strong off his legs and relying mainly on timing and deflections, just passed his century in five and a quarter hours before being stumped down the leg side off Gomes. Kapil Dev, who dominated the stand with powerful hitting, took two and a half hours to score 98.

By the time India were all out in the closing stages of the second day, a commanding first-innings total had been achieved. However, for the remainder of that day and almost right through the next, Greenidge and Haynes made sure West Indies would face no embarrassment with a new first-wicket record against all countries of 296. Greenidge's 154 was his first century in Tests since 1977 and Haynes's his first since 1980. A stiff neck restricted Kapil Dev to four overs on the third day, and India did not claim a wicket until the final five minutes when Yashpal, given the new ball in his captain's absence, had Haynes caught at long-leg after an innings lasting six hours, ten minutes and including one 6 and ten 4s. As soon as Greenidge left the ground, having hit a 6 and fourteen 4s, he flew to his native Barbados to be with his ailing two-year-old daughter, who died two days after the match ended.

Richards, the local hero, resumed in Greenidge's place but his was the first of four wickets to fall for 31 runs to the swing of Kapil Dev and Madan Lal early on the fourth morning. However, Kirmani dropped Dujon off Madan Lal when he was 7 and India's chance of breaking through to the tail was wasted, Dujon and Lloyd restoring the innings with another double-century partnership. Dujon's 110 (fourteen 4s) was his first century in Tests, Lloyd's 106 (one 6 and ten 4s) was his sixteenth. It was only the fifth time in Test cricket that four or more batsmen had passed three figures in a single innings.

Only just over a day remained when India began their second innings and, after Davis caused an early stir by dismissing Gavaskar in his first over, Gaekwad and Amarnath settled the issue with yet another double-century partnership. Already hampered by the absence of a spinner, West Indies' attack was further reduced by foot soreness which kept Holding off the field for all of the final day. Amarnath's fifth century of the tour carried him past 1,000 runs in all matches and was another impeccable innings. Not surprisingly, he was named Man of the Series.

India

S. M. Gavaskar c Dujon b Marshall	18	– c Dujon b Davis 1
A. D. Gaekwad c Richards b Roberts	3	– lbw b Marshall 72
M. Amarnath c Lloyds b Davis	54	– c Logie b Davis 116
D. B. Vengsarkar c Davis b Marshall	94	– c Dujon b Marshall 0
Yashpal Sharma c Gomes b Roberts	3	– c sub (S. F. A. Bacchus)
		b Gomes. 20
R. J. Shastri st Dujon b Gomes	102	– not out 9
*Kapil Dev lbw b Holding	98	– not out 0
†S. M. H. Kirmani c Greenidge b Davis	2	
Madan Lal not out	35	
L. Sivaramakrishnan c sub (S. F. A. Bacchus)		
b Marshall.	17	
S. Venkataraghavan b Marshall	0	
B 14, l-b 7, w 1, n-b 9	31	B 8, l-b 11, n-b 10.......... 29

1/5 2/28 3/119 4/181   457   1/1 2/201 3/201   (5 wkts dec.) 247
5/337 6/372 7/376 8/419 9/457   4/234 5/245

Bowling: *First Innings*—Roberts 29–3–110–2; Holding 26–3–86–1; Marshall 27.5–5–87–4; Davis 29–1–121–2; Richards 11–3–13–0; Gomes 4–1–9–1. *Second Innings*—Roberts 15–3–46–0; Marshall 18–7–33–2; Davis 23–4–54–2; Richards 13–1–36–0; Gomes 19–0–49–1.

West Indies

C. G. Greenidge retired not out 154	*C. H. Lloyd c Yashpal b Shastri........106
D. L. Haynes c Shastri b Yashpal 136	M. D. Marshall b Venkataraghavan 2
W. W. Davis b Madan Lal 14	A. M. E. Roberts not out 1
I. V. A. Richards c Gaekwad	M. A. Holding run out 0
b Madan Lal. 2	
H. A. Gomes lbw b Madan Lal 9	B 6, l-b 5, n-b 4..................... 15
A. L. Logie hit wkt b Kapil Dev 1	
†P. J. Dujon c Gaekwad	1/296 2/303 3/323 4/324 550
b Venkataraghavan.110	5/334 6/541 7/547 8/549 9/550

Bowling: Kapil Dev 22–6–71–1; Madan Lal 35–7–105–3; Sivaramakrishnan 25–1–95–0; Shastri 46.4–5–141–1; Venkataraghavan 36–1–114–2; Gaekwad 1–0–3–0; Yashpal 1–0–6–1.

Umpires: D. M. Archer and R. Weeks.

THE CHINESE YEAR OF THE CRICKET

Following a short three-match tour to the People's Republic of China, undertaken in August, 1983, by the St George's Cricket Club of Hong Kong, it is hoped that the All China Sports Federation may set up a team of indigenous cricketers. A fair crowd, including a sprinkling of bemused Chinese, watched the matches between the St George's Club and teams composed mainly of diplomats, ex-patriate businessmen, journalists and students from the United Kingdom, Australia, India, Pakistan, New Zealand and Africa. The Beijing Cricket Club, c/o The British Embassy, The People's Republic of China, would be pleased to hear from would-be visiting sides.

THE AUSTRALIANS IN SRI LANKA, 1982-83

By GEOFFREY SAULEZ

Australia made a short tour of Sri Lanka in April 1983, playing one Test match, one three-day match and four one-day internationals, two at each end of the visit. Kim Hughes, Rodney Marsh, Jeff Thomson and Geoff Lawson were unavailable, Greg Chappell returning to the captaincy with David Hookes as his vice-captain. In Marsh's absence, the selectors chose Roger Woolley, who thus became the first Tasmanian to appear for Australia, while still a Tasmanian player, since L. J. Nash in 1931-32.

Australia won the Test match by an innings, with a day and a half to spare, after Chappell had won a toss which gave his side first use of a pitch that soon took spin. Sri Lanka won the first two one-day internationals, the first played only a day after the Australians had arrived; rain in the last two ruined the Australians' chances of levelling the series. The three-day match against the Board President's XI was drawn, the President's XI containing many young players, of whom one played in the Test match and three others were selected for the 1983 World Cup team.

The most successful Australian batsman was Graham Yallop. Consistent throughout, he made at least 30 every time he batted. In the Test match, only six were required to bat, and of these all but Graeme Wood made a significant contribution. Curiously, of these six all except Chappell were left-handers.

The slow pitches meant that spin was the main weapon, to the advantage of Tom Hogan, on his first tour, and Bruce Yardley. Dennis Lillee, after missing much of the Australian season through injury, passed a stringent fitness test before the tour, and in unhelpful conditions had his successes, notably making an early breakthrough in each innings of the Test match. John Maguire's bowling was restricted to 49 balls in the first one-day international, the early abandonment of the last two matches, in which he played, giving him no chance to bowl.

Sri Lanka picked an unbalanced attack for the Test match, including two leg-spinners, and, batting against a large Australian total, could not afford failures by four of the first six batsmen in each innings. Especially disappointing was the double failure of Roy Dias, who had batted so successfully in previous Test matches but was troubled now by a hand injury suffered in New Zealand. Arjuna Ranatunga, the young left-hander who missed that tour, made a successful return.

The tour was managed by Mr H. W. H. Rigg, a former player for Western Australia.

AUSTRALIAN TOUR RESULTS

Test matches – Played 1: Won 1.

First-class matches – Played 2: Won 1, Drawn 1.

Win – Sri Lanka.

Draw – Board President's XI.

Non first-class matches – Played 4: Lost 2, Drawn 2. *Losses* – Sri Lanka (2). *Draws* – Sri Lanka (2).

†SRI LANKA v AUSTRALIA

First One-day International

At Saravanamuttu Stadium, Colombo, April 13. Sri Lanka won by two wickets. Batting first after winning the toss, Australia soon lost Smith, but Wood and Yallop added 72 in seventeen overs before Wood was bowled, offering no stroke. Chappell was brilliantly caught wide on the leg side, one of five catches by wicket-keeper de Alwis, during a middle-order collapse when four wickets fell for 15 runs. Wettimuny and Fernando opened confidently, but then Chappell, Lillee and Hogan (who turned the ball considerably) slowed the run-rate. When Smith, running 30 yards from third man, brilliantly caught Madugalle, 57 were still needed in 10.3 overs. However, an aggressive de Mel, supported by de Silva, brought victory with five balls to spare.

Man of the Match: R. G. de Alwis.

Australia

G. M. Wood b de Silva	50	T. G. Hogan c Ratnayake b de Mel	27
S. B. Smith c de Alwis b John	1	D. K. Lillee run out	5
G. N. Yallop c de Alwis b Ranatunga	39	R. M. Hogg not out	0
*G. S. Chappell c de Alwis b John	11	L-b 7, w 2	9
D. W. Hookes c de Alwis b Ranatunga	0		
A. R. Border b de Silva	10	1/15 2/87 3/103 (9 wkts, 45 overs) 168	
†R. D. Woolley c de Alwis b de Mel	16	4/107 5/109 6/118 7/144 8/167 9/168	

J. N. Maguire did not bat.

Bowling: de Mel 9-2-35-2; John 9-1-33-2; Ratnayake 9-1-44-0; Ranatunga 9-1-26-2; de Silva 9-0-21-2.

Sri Lanka

S. Wettimuny b Hogan	37	D. S. de Silva not out	15
E. R. N. S. Fernando st Woolley b Hogan	31	†R. G. de Alwis b Hogg	6
R. L. Dias lbw b Chappell	5	R. J. Ratnayake not out	0
*L. R. D. Mendis b Hogan	16	L-b 5, w 5, n-b 3	13
R. S. Madugalle c Smith b Maguire	9		
A. Ranatunga c Hogan b Hogg	10	1/71 2/82 (8 wkts, 44.1 overs) 169	
A. L. F. de Mel c Woolley b Maguire	27	3/82 4/102 5/112	
		6/139 7/157 8/168	

V. B. John did not bat.

Bowling: Hogg 9-1-40-2; Maguire 8.1-0-43-2; Lillee 9-0-25-0; Chappell 9-2-21-1; Hogan 9-1-27-3.

Umpires: C. E. B. Anthony and P. W. Vidamagamage.

†SRI LANKA v AUSTRALIA

Second One-day International

At Saravanamuttu Stadium, Colombo, April 16. Sri Lanka won by four wickets. A fine innings by Ranatunga, who hit three 6s and three 4s in his 39 balls, brought victory with ten balls to spare after Sri Lanka had needed 90 off the last twelve overs. Sri Lanka's openers had made a solid start with 101 before both were out in the 29th over, and Dias and Mendis followed two overs later, Yardley taking three of the wickets in ten balls. Earlier Australia, put in, made steady progress with Yallop scoring freely with one 6 and six 4s, off 63 balls.

Man of the Match: A. Ranatunga.

Australia

G. M. Wood lbw b Ratnayake	9	†R. D. Woolley not out	3
K. C. Wessels b Ratnayake	39		
G. N. Yallop c Mendis b Ranatunga	59	L-b 8, n-b 2	10
*G. S. Chappell not out	54		
D. W. Hookes run out	27	1/34 2/77 (5 wkts, 45 overs) 207	
A. R. Border c Dias b John	6	3/136 4/195 5/201	

B. Yardley, T. G. Hogan, D. K. Lillee and R. M. Hogg did not bat.

Bowling: de Mel 9–1–29–0; John 9–0–33–1; Ratnayake 9–0–38–2; Ranatunga 9–0–45–1; de Silva 9–0–52–0.

Sri Lanka

S. Wettimuny b Yardley	56	A. L. F. de Mel c Wood b Border	1
E. R. N. S. Fernando run out	34	D. S. de Silva not out	7
R. L. Dias c Wood b Yardley	2	B 2, l-b 14, n-b 3	19
*L. R. D. Mendis b Yardley	2		
A. Ranatunga not out	55	1/101 2/101 3/107 (6 wkts, 43.2 overs) 213	
R. S. Madugalle b Hogan	37	4/108 5/177 6/178	

†R. G. de Alwis, R. J. Ratnayake and V. B. John did not bat.

Bowling: Hogg 7–1–18–0; Lillee 9–0–30–0; Chappell 6.2–0–37–0; Hogan 9–0–62–1; Yardley 9–1–28–3; Border 2–0–10–1; Yallop 1–0–9–0.

Umpires: D. Buultjens and H. C. Felsinger.

BOARD PRESIDENT'S XI v AUSTRALIANS

At Moratuwa, April 17, 18, 19. Drawn. In a consistent Australian innings, Yallop again played fluently, while de Silva (medium pace), Weerasinghe (off-spin) and Gunaratne (leg-spin) bowled impressively, Weerasinghe taking his last three wickets for 12 runs in 25 balls on the second morning. After Hogan had run through the Board President's XI's middle order, taking three wickets without cost in thirteen balls, Ratnayeke, with the later batsmen, avoided the follow-on. The Australians had useful batting practice before a lunch-time declaration on the last day left the President's XI to score 244 in 150 minutes plus twenty overs. Although Warnakulasuriya and Kuruppu, as in the first innings, batted well, the batsmen were always behind the clock.

Australians

K. C. Wessels b Gunaratne	28	– c Abeynaike b de Silva	30
G. M. Wood c Silva b Samarasekera	13	– b de Silva	14
G. N. Yallop c Abeynaike b de Silva	43	– (4) not out	30
G. S. Chappell c Weerasinghe b Gunaratne	26		
*D. W. Hookes c Mendis b de Silva	20		
S. B. Smith lbw b Weerasinghe	21	– (3) not out	33
†R. D. Woolley c Warnakulasuriya b Weerasinghe	57		
T. G. Hogan lbw b de Silva	10		
B. Yardley st Silva b Weerasinghe	14		
D. K. Lillee not out	12		
R. M. Hogg c and b Weerasinghe	0		
B 4, l-b 4, w 5, n-b 2	15	L-b 7, n-b 1	8

1/48 2/50 3/115 4/143   259   1/43 2/48   (2 wkts dec.) 115
5/143 6/188 7/233 8/235 9/255

Bowling: *First Innings*—de Silva 17–2–51–3; Ratnayeke 13–1–36–0; Samarasekera 5–1–18–1; Gunaratne 19–3–66–2; Abeynaike 11–2–26–0; Weerasinghe 13.4–2–47–4. *Second Innings*—de Silva 12–2–36–2; Ratnayeke 10–2–21–0; Gunaratne 1–0–8–0; Weerasinghe 7–1–24–0; Abeynaike 4–0–18–0.

Board President's XI

M. A. R. Samarasekera b Lillee	0	– lbw b Lillee	11
C. P. Senanayeke c Woolley b Hogg	0	– c Woolley b Hogg	4
S. Warnakulasuriya b Yardley	32	– c Wessels b Yardley	31
D. S. B. Kuruppu c Woolley b Hogan	21	– lbw b Hogg	25
B. H. P. Mendis b Hogan	1	– c Hookes b Hogan	30
*R. G. Abeynaike c Hookes b Hogan	0	– c Hookes b Hogan	34
†S. A. R. Silva c Hookes b Yardley	18	– (8) c Hogg b Wessels	28
J. R. Ratnayeke lbw b Lillee	32	– (7) c Wood b Hogan	5
H. P. O. Weerasinghe lbw b Hogg	9	– not out	4
R. P. W. Gunaratne not out	7	– not out	0
G. N. de Silva b Lillee	4		
B 7	7	B 10, l-b 2	12

1/0 2/6 3/42 4/44   131   1/10 2/26 3/70 4/72   (8 wkts) 184
5/52 6/77 7/80 8/103 9/123   5/139 6/140 7/173 8/184

Bowling: *First Innings*—Lillee 10.2–2–26–3; Hogg 9–2–17–2; Hogan 15–5–37–3; Yardley 17–6–44–2. *Second Innings*—Lillee 12–4–46–1; Hogg 7–1–26–2; Yardley 15–1–51–1; Hogan 16–3–42–3; Yallop 3–1–7–0; Wessels 1–1–0–1.

Umpires: K. T. Francis and E. Seneviratne.

SRI LANKA v AUSTRALIA

Inaugural Test Match

At Kandy, April 22, 23, 24, 26. Australia won by an innings and 38 runs. After Chappell had won the toss, Wessels dominated an opening partnership which ended when Wood was caught at long-leg off Ranatunga's first ball. Strong in cutting and driving and quick to punish the loose ball, Wessels reached his hundred in 173 minutes and had added 170 in 195 minutes with Yallop before pulling a short ball from de Silva to mid-wicket. Chappell stayed with Yallop until the close, but next morning de Mel, with the new ball, dismissed Yallop 2 short of his hundred. Hookes and Border punished tiring bowlers during the afternoon session, adding 155, of which Hookes scored 106, in 145 minutes. Hookes reached his first Test century in 156 minutes, his innings including two 6s and seventeen 4s; he scored 100 between lunch and tea.

After Chappell's tea-time declaration, Lillee took two wickets in his first over and, with Hogg dismissing Fernando, Sri Lanka were 9 for three. Mendis started aggressively and with Ranatunga added 96 in 92 minutes before mistiming a drive to mid-off. The spinners came in for punishment, ten overs at one stage costing 73 runs, and Ranatunga hit fourteen 4s while moving from 12 to 76. After lunch Yardley broke through, and, despite an aggressive innings by de Mel, Chappell was able to enforce the follow-on. Sri Lanka's second innings was destroyed when five wickets, including that of Wettimuny who batted for three hours, fell for 13 runs either side of lunch on the fourth day, bringing Australia victory with a day and a half to spare.

The attendance in the four days was approximately 30,000.

Australia

K. C. Wessels c Dias b de Silva	141	A. R. Border not out	47
G. M. Wood c Ratnayeke b Ranatunga	4	L-b 11, w 1, n-b 3	15
G. N. Yallop lbw b de Mel	98		
*G. S. Chappell lbw b de Mel	66	1/43 2/213 (4 wkts dec.) 514	
D. W. Hookes not out	143	3/290 4/359	

†R. D. Woolley, T. G. Hogan, B. Yardley, D. K. Lillee and R. M. Hogg did not bat.

Bowling: de Mel 23–3–113–2; Ratnayake 28–4–108–0; Ranatunga 19–2–72–1; de Silva 44–7–122–1; Gunaratne 17–1–84–0.

Sri Lanka

S. Wettimuny c Woolley b Lillee	0	– b Hogan	96
E. R. N. S. Fernando c Woolley b Hogg	0	– c Woolley b Lillee	3
R. L. Dias c Border b Lillee	4	– b Hogan	10
*L. R. D. Mendis c Hookes b Yardley	74	– (5) c Border b Yardley	6
R. S. Madugalle c and b Yardley	9	– (6) b Yardley	0
A. Ranatunga c Lillee b Yardley	90	– (7) b Hogan	32
D. S. de Silva c Hogan b Yardley	26	– (8) c Woolley b Hogan	5
A. L. F. de Mel c Hookes b Hogan	29	– (9) c Yallop b Hogan	0
†R. G. de Alwis c Border b Yardley	3	– (10) run out	9
R. J. Ratnayake c Woolley b Border	14	– (4) run out	30
R. P. W. Gunaratne not out	0	– not out	0
B 4, l-b 5, w 1, n-b 12	22	B 6, l-b 7, n-b 1	14

1/1 2/5 3/9 4/46   271   1/17 2/59 3/120 4/151   205
5/142 6/220 7/224 8/247 9/270   5/155 6/155 7/162 8/164 9/191

Bowling: *First Innings*—Lillee 19–3–67–2; Hogg 12–4–31–1; Chappell 1–0–2–0; Yardley 25–7–88–5; Hogan 11–1–50–1; Border 4.5–0–11–1. *Second Innings*—Lillee 11–3–40–1; Hogg 3–2–7–0; Yardley 26–6–78–2; Hogan 25.2–6–66–5.

Umpires: C. E. B. Anthony and H. C. Felsinger.

†SRI LANKA v AUSTRALIA

Third One-day International

At SSC Ground, Colombo, April 29. Drawn. A storm which flooded the ground caused the match to be abandoned after Australia, who were sent in, had batted for 39.2 overs. Yallop, dropped when 1, continued his good form, scoring 51 off 55 balls.

Australia

G. M. Wood b Ranatunga	35	†R. D. Woolley not out	12
K. C. Wessels c Dias b de Silva	43		
G. N. Yallop c de Alwis b de Silva	51	L-b 8, w 1, n-b 2	11
D. W. Hookes c de Alwis b John	23		
A. R. Border b de Mel	10	1/60 2/105 (5 wkts, 39.2 overs) 194
*G. S. Chappell not out	9	3/151 4/172 5/172

T. G. Hogan, B. Yardley, R. M. Hogg and J. N. Maguire did not bat.

Bowling: de Mel 9–0–44–1; John 6.2–1–23–1; Ranatunga 9–0–42–1; Ratnayake 6–0–23–0; de Silva 9–0–51–2.

Sri Lanka

S. Wettimuny, E. R. N. S. Fernando, R. L. Dias, *L. R. D. Mendis, R. S. Madugalle, A. Ranatunga, D. S. de Silva, A. L. F. de Mel, †R. G. de Alwis, R. J. Ratnayake and V. B. John.

Umpires: K. T. Francis and P. W. Vidamagamage.

†SRI LANKA v AUSTRALIA

Fourth One-day International

At SSC Ground, Colombo, April 30. Drawn. Overnight rain delayed the start, causing a reduction to a 30-overs match, and further rain caused the match to be abandoned after Australia, who won the toss, had batted for 19.2 overs.

Australia

K. C. Wessels b de Mel	6	S. B. Smith not out	0
G. M. Wood b de Mel	2	B 2, l-b 4, w 1	7
G. N. Yallop not out	60		
D. W. Hookes b Ratnayeke	49	1/3 2/12 3/124 (3 wkts, 19.2 overs)	124

*G. S. Chappell, A. R. Border, †R. D. Woolley, B. Yardley, R. M. Hogg and J. N. Maguire did not bat.

Bowling: de Mel 4–0–9–2; John 5–0–15–0; de Silva 4–0–21–0; Ranatunga 3–0–35–0; Ratnayeke 2.2–0–16–1; Wettimuny 1–0–21–0.

Sri Lanka

S. Wettimuny, E. R. N. S. Fernando, R. L. Dias, *L. R. D. Mendis, R. S. Madugalle, A. Ranatunga, †D. S. B. Kuruppu, A. L. F. de Mel, J. R. Ratnayeke, V. B. John and G. N. de Silva.

Umpires: D. Buultjens and S. Ponnadurai.

ALL TEN WICKETS FOR MALAYSIA

Playing for Malaysia in the Saudara Cup match against Singapore, at Kuala Lumpur in December 1983, K. Saker, bowling at medium pace, took ten wickets for 25 runs in Singapore's first innings. Malaysia won the match by ten wickets. The Saudara Cup series was inaugurated in 1970. Of the fourteen matches played, each side has won three and eight have been drawn.

NINE CATCHES IN AN INNINGS

Les Andrews, keeping wicket in a first-grade match in Sydney, for Bankstown-Canterbury against Sydney University in November 1982, held nine catches during Sydney's innings of 236. So far as is known this constitutes a world record. The tenth wicket fell to a run-out at the bowler's end.

BENSON AND HEDGES WORLD SERIES CUP, 1982-83

†AUSTRALIA v NEW ZEALAND

At Melbourne, January 9. Australia won by eight wickets. New Zealand fell away badly after making a lively start. Hughes, captaining Australia for the first time at home (Chappell had stood down at the end of the Test series), put New Zealand in, and when Wright was first out, in the sixteenth over, the score was already 84. But with Turner resting a sprained knee and the middle order failing, New Zealand were all out with 5.1 of their 50 overs still unused. After a cautious start, Wessels and Dyson, opening for Australia, made 154 together in 40 overs and put the result beyond doubt.

Man of the Match: J. Dyson.   *Attendance:* 45,259.

New Zealand

J. G. Wright c Dyson b Rackemann	 54	R. J. Hadlee run out	24
B. A. Edgar lbw b Rackemann	 38	B. L. Cairns c Hookes b Lawson	7
*G. P. Howarth c and b Rackemann	... 5	M. C. Snedden c Marsh b Hogg	2
J. J. Crowe c Lawson b Chappell	 7	E. J. Chatfield not out	0
J. V. Coney c Marsh b Rackemann	 4	L-b 9, w 7, n-b 5	21
J. F. M. Morrison c Marsh			
b Thomson	10	1/84 2/89 3/98 4/114 (44.5 overs) 181	
†P. N. Webb b Lawson	 9	5/128 6/134 7/167 8/173 9/181	

Bowling: Lawson 7.5–1–28–2; Thomson 9–1–39–1; Hogg 8–0–32–1; Rackemann 10–1–39–4; Chappell 10–1–22–1.

Australia

K. C. Wessels b Snedden	79
J. Dyson not out	78
G. S. Chappell c and b Snedden	3
*K. J. Hughes not out	7
B 1, l-b 11, w 3	15

1/154 2/168   (2 wkts, 46.4 overs) 182

A. R. Border, D. W. Hookes, †R. W. Marsh, G. F. Lawson, J. R. Thomson, R. M. Hogg and C. G. Rackemann did not bat.

Bowling: Hadlee 9.4–2–36–0; Chatfield 10–4–18–0; Snedden 10–1–47–2; Cairns 8–1–30–0; Coney 9–1–36–0.

Umpires: A. R. Crafter and R. V. Whitehead.

†AUSTRALIA v ENGLAND

At Sydney, January 11. Australia won by 31 runs. In the first day-night match of the competition England put Australia in, thereby committing themselves to batting under lights, which five of their side had previously done only in practice. Against an England attack containing two off-spinners, Miller and Marks, who shared five wickets between them, and Jesty, making his first appearance of the tour, Australia were reduced to 132 for seven, several wild strokes being played. Lawson's 33, made from No. 8, proved important. Needing 181 to win, England batted poorly in front of a large, loud and partisan crowd. Even with the help of 35 extras they were bowled out for 149, only Lamb making over 20. Although not the truest of pitches, it was certainly not a bad one. Australia relied on speed, Lawson, Thomson, Hogg and Rackemann making a testing quartet. Dyson missed a simple catch when he was blinded by one of the six nests of lights, a much rarer occurrence at Sydney than might be expected.

Man of the Match: C. G. Rackemann.   *Attendance:* 42,030.

Australia

J. Dyson c Randall b Marks	49	J. R. Thomson b Miller	8
K. C. Wessels b Cowans	18	R. M. Hogg c and b Cowans	8
G. S. Chappell c Marks b Botham	3	C. G. Rackemann b Willis	0
*K. J. Hughes c Taylor b Jesty	0		
D. W. Hookes b Marks	11	L-b 13, w 8	21
A. R. Border b Miller	22		
†R. W. Marsh c Taylor b Miller	7	1/26 2/33 3/36 4/77 (46.4 overs) 180	
G. F. Lawson not out	33	5/118 6/124 7/132 8/158 9/175	

Bowling: Willis 6.4–1–20–1; Cowans 7–0–20–2; Botham 7–1–41–1; Jesty 6–0–23–1; Marks 10–1–27–2; Miller 10–0–28–3.

England

D. I. Gower c Hookes b Thomson	9	†R. W. Taylor lbw b Chappell	2
C. J. Tavaré c Border b Rackemann	6	*R. G. D. Willis c Marsh b Chappell	0
A. J. Lamb b Thomson	49	N. G. Cowans b Chappell	4
D. W. Randall b Rackemann	5		
I. T. Botham b Rackemann	18	L-b 12, w 17, n-b 6	35
T. E. Jesty run out	12		
G. Miller lbw b Hogg	2	1/11 2/44 3/53 4/95 (41.1 overs) 149	
V. J. Marks not out	7	5/131 6/131 7/135 8/142 9/142	

Bowling: Lawson 8–1–33–0; Thomson 10–4–21–2; Hogg 10–1–15–1; Rackemann 8–1–28–3; Chappell 5.1–0–17–3.

Umpires: R. A. French and M. W. Johnson.

†ENGLAND v NEW ZEALAND

At Melbourne, January 13. New Zealand won by 2 runs. England again lost a match they had looked like winning. Needing 240 they were 190 for four with ten overs remaining. Botham had just been caught at long-on, but Gower was past his hundred and batting very well. Support then dried up for Gower, and when, at 223, he pulled Hadlee hard and straight to short mid-wicket, Marks and Taylor found the job of scoring 17 from the last three overs, on a slow pitch, beyond them. Marks had to hit 3 off the last ball to win and 2 to tie, but it bowled him. Only two of the England side passed 20. New Zealand, after being put in, had batted much more consistently. Wright and Edgar gave them a good start; Cairns, promoted to No. 3 to attack the England spinners, scored 36 off 26 balls by doing just that; Turner marked his return to the international scene with a useful 38, and Hadlee made a rapid 24.

Man of the Match: D. I. Gower.   *Attendance:* 11,266.

New Zealand

J. G. Wright run out	55	R. J. Hadlee c Botham b Willis	24
B. A. Edgar c Randall b Marks	30	J. V. Coney not out	13
B. L. Cairns c Miller b Botham	36	†W. K. Lees run out	3
G. M. Turner b Willis	38	B 1, l-b 10, w 5	16
*G. P. Howarth c Willis b Botham	13		
J. F. M. Morrison c Randall		1/87 2/100 3/137 (8 wkts, 50 overs) 239	
b Botham	11	4/164 5/188 6/205 7/231 8/239	

E. J. Chatfield and M. C. Snedden did not bat.

Bowling: Willis 8–1–29–2; Cowans 10–0–50–0; Jesty 3–0–11–0; Botham 10–0–40–3; Marks 9–0–47–1; Miller 10–0–46–0.

England

D. I. Gower c Turner b Hadlee	122	V. J. Marks b Snedden	5
C. J. Tavaré run out	16	†R. W. Taylor not out	5
A. J. Lamb st Lees b Coney	15		
T. E. Jesty c Wright b Coney	5	L-b 14, w 3, n-b 1	18
I. T. Botham c Cairns b Snedden	41		
D. W. Randall c Snedden c Coney	8	1/42 2/80 3/92 4/190 (8 wkts, 50 overs) 237	
G. Miller c Turner b Chatfield	2	5/205 6/221 7/223 8/237	

*R. G. D. Willis and N. G. Cowans did not bat.

Bowling: Snedden 10–0–34–2; Chatfield 10–0–38–1; Cairns 10–1–64–0; Hadlee 10–1–37–1; Coney 10–0–46–3.

Umpires: M. W. Johnson and B. E. Martin.

†ENGLAND v NEW ZEALAND

At Brisbane, January 15. England won by 54 runs. A magnificent innings by Gower set England on the road to their first victory in the competition. Coming in in the ninth over, after England had been sent in to bat, Gower was out off the last ball of the innings, having made a chanceless 158, the highest individual score since the World Series Cup started in 1979-80. Previously, Richards's 153 for West Indies against Australia in Melbourne was the best. Gower hit four 6s and eighteen 4s and received 118 balls in a brilliant exhibition of relaxed strokeplay. His most effective partner was Randall, who helped to add 113 for the fifth wicket. New Zealand fell away after a promising start, Marks taking three good wickets in his ten overs. Gould, having been preferred to Taylor, made a lively opening partner for Tavaré, held two catches and made a stumping.

Man of the Match: D. I. Gower.   *Attendance:* 12,585.

England

C. J. Tavaré b Cairns	24	T. E. Jesty not out	4
†I. J. Gould c Howarth b Troup	15		
D. I. Gower c sub b Snedden	158	L-b 9, w 9, n-b 1	19
A. J. Lamb c Cairns b Hadlee	13		
I. T. Botham c Webb b Hadlee	0	1/26 2/89 3/114 (6 wkts, 50 overs) 267	
D. W. Randall run out	34	4/116 5/229 6/267	

V. J. Marks, G. Miller, N. G. Cowans and †R. G. D. Willis did not bat.

Bowling: Hadlee 10–1–44–2; Chatfield 10–3–44–0; Snedden 10–0–76–1; Troup 7–1–38–1; Cairns 10–0–29–1; Coney 3–0–17–0.

New Zealand

J. G. Wright c Randall b Cowans	30	M. C. Snedden run out	0
B. A. Edgar c Gould b Botham	40	G. B. Troup c Botham b Willis	39
*G. P. Howarth c Jesty b Marks	13	E. J. Chatfield not out	0
B. L. Cairns c Gould b Marks	12		
G. M. Turner c Jesty b Botham	29	L-b 6, w 6	12
J. V. Coney st Gould b Marks	13		
†P. N. Webb c Cowans b Botham	4	1/43 2/75 3/100 4/100 (48.2 overs) 213	
R. J. Hadlee b Willis	21	5/148 6/148 7/150 8/150 9/213	

Bowling: Willis 9.2–1–30–2; Cowans 10–0–52–1; Botham 9–2–47–3; Marks 10–2–30–3; Miller 10–1–42–0.

Umpires: R. A. French and B. E. Martin.

†AUSTRALIA v ENGLAND

At Brisbane, January 16. Australia won by seven wickets. Having been put in, on a good morning for bowling, England were dismissed for 182 and easily beaten. Losing Gould, run out, in the second over, and Cook, brilliantly caught at second slip at 10, England were soon looking to Gower to save them again. This time he went for 22, bowled off the inside edge by Hogg. Randall and Botham added 57 for the fifth wicket, giving England some hope of a total in excess of 200, but Botham could not contain himself and Randall, when playing well, threw away his wicket, so that at 178 for nine England had seven overs left and no-one to take advantage of them. Thomson, being wild, was responsible for more than his share of the 37 extras. A capacity crowd (tickets for the match had been sold out for a fortnight) saw Australia win with nine overs to spare, Hookes finishing the match with a fine flourish, scoring the last 22 runs in an over from Willis.

Man of the Match: D. W. Hookes.   *Attendance:* 22,174.

England

G. Cook c Hookes b Lawson	2	V. J. Marks b Thomson	3
†I. J. Gould run out	2	*R. G. D. Willis not out	7
D. I. Gower b Hogg	22	N. G. Cowans c Lawson	
A. J. Lamb c Marsh b Thomson	19	b Rackemann	0
I. T. Botham c Hookes b Rackemann	29	B 4, l-b 12, w 13, n-b 8	37
D. W. Randall b Lawson	57		—
T. E. Jesty c Marsh b Rackemann	0	1/2 2/10 3/54 4/71 (46.4 overs)	182
G. Miller run out	4	5/128 6/138 7/143 8/165 9/178	

Bowling: Lawson 10–2–23–2; Thomson 10–0–32–2; Hogg 9–1–29–1; Rackemann 8.4–1–28–3; Chappell 9–1–33–0.

Australia

K. C. Wessels c Gould b Botham	19	A. R. Border not out	30
J. Dyson c Marks b Botham	40	L-b 9, w 2	11
G. S. Chappell c Jesty b Botham	30		—
D. W. Hookes not out	54	1/41 2/95 3/98 (3 wkts, 41 overs)	184

*K. J. Hughes, †R. W. Marsh, G. F. Lawson, J. R. Thomson, C. G. Rackemann and R. M. Hogg did not bat.

Bowling: Willis 7–1–31–0; Cowans 9–1–35–0; Botham 8–1–29–3; Miller 6–0–25–0; Marks 10–0–46–0; Jesty 1–0–7–0.

Umpires: M. W. Johnson and P. J. McConnell.

†AUSTRALIA v NEW ZEALAND

At Sydney, January 18. New Zealand won by 47 runs. Australia's first defeat of the 1982-83 World Series Cup came after they had put New Zealand in and pinned them down, in the first 25 overs of the match, to 87 for the loss of Wright and Howarth. Turner (55 in 21 overs) and Crowe (56 in 27 overs), with Coney and Webb in useful supporting roles, turned this into a winning total of 226 for eight, the last six overs producing 63 runs, 17 of them off Rackemann's last, which included two no-balls. When coasting along in reply Australia suddenly lost Dyson, Chappell and Hughes in successive overs, and with twenty overs left they still needed 140. Eight overs later they were chasing hard, with Hookes in brilliant form until, as the non-striker, he was unluckily run out, Coney, the bowler, deflecting a drive by Wessels into the stumps. After that Australia, hitting at everything, lost their last six wickets for 34 runs.

Man of the Match: D. W. Hookes.   *Attendance:* 31,461.

New Zealand

J. G. Wright c Marsh b Hogg	1	B. L. Cairns c Border b Hogg		2
B. A. Edgar b Chappell	32	†P. N. Webb not out		10
*G. P. Howarth c Marsh b Chappell	29			
G. M. Turner b Thomson	55	B 7, l-b 10, w 6		23
J. J. Crowe run out	56			
R. J. Hadlee c Chappell b Thomson	5	1/7 2/65 3/93 4/159 (8 wkts, 50 overs) 226		
J. V. Coney c Marsh b Lawson	13	5/167 6/191 7/194 8/226		

M. C. Snedden and E. J. Chatfield did not bat.

Bowling: Lawson 10–3–33–1; Hogg 10–2–32–2; Thomson 10–0–42–2; Rackemann 10–0–59–0; Chappell 10–0–37–2.

Australia

J. Dyson run out	11	J. R. Thomson b Cairns		0
K. C. Wessels c Cairns b Snedden	58	R. M. Hogg not out		3
G. S. Chappell c Webb b Snedden	1	C. G. Rackemann lbw b Hadlee		2
*K. J. Hughes c and b Cairns	1			
D. W. Hookes run out	68	B 4, l-b 9, w 5		18
A. R. Border c Hadlee b Cairns	11			
†R. W. Marsh b Cairns	6	1/27 2/28 3/29 4/145 (45.3 overs) 179		
G. F. Lawson run out	0	5/163 6/169 7/169 8/169 9/176		

Bowling: Chatfield 10–1–47–0; Hadlee 8.3–2–19–1; Snedden 8–2–24–2; Cairns 10–4–16–4; Coney 9–0–55–0.

Umpires: M. W. Johnson and P. J. McConnell.

†ENGLAND v NEW ZEALAND

At Sydney, January 20. England won by eight wickets. After their success against Australia on the same ground two days earlier, New Zealand were now fancied to beat England. Instead they were heavily beaten, mainly because of a superb partnership of 190 between Tavaré and Lamb, who came together when England, needing 200 to win, were 10 for two. Starting slowly, against some testing overs from Chatfield and particularly Hadlee, they had taken the score only to 47 for two after twenty overs. The remaining runs then came at the rate of very nearly 8 an over, with Lamb storming to a brilliant hundred, scored off 104 balls, in the over in which England won. For Tavaré, his innings of 83 not out marked a spectacular return to form, after being dropped by England in their previous match. New Zealand had also lost two early wickets, those of Wright and Howarth, before Edgar and Turner added 81. After 40 overs New Zealand were 156 for five, but their final attack rather petered out. Several fine catches were made for England, notably by Gower, Randall and Miller.

Man of the Match: A. J. Lamb.   *Attendance:* 13,416.

New Zealand

J. G. Wright c Randall b Willis	9	J. V. Coney c Miller b Willis		6
B. A. Edgar c Willis b Cowans	74	M. C. Snedden not out		2
*G. P. Howarth c Miller b Willis	1	E. J. Chatfield lbw b Botham		0
G. M. Turner c Gower b Marks	37			
B. L. Cairns c Gower b Miller	11	L-b 17, w 3		20
†W. K. Lees b Botham	12			
J. J. Crowe run out	12	1/14 2/20 3/101 4/118 (47.2 overs) 199		
R. J. Hadlee c Lamb b Willis	15	5/152 6/171 7/178 8/197 9/197		

Bowling: Willis 9–0–23–4; Cowans 10–1–26–1; Botham 8.2–0–30–2; Marks 10–0–49–1; Miller 10–0–51–1.

England

G. Fowler c sub b Chatfield		0
C. J. Tavaré not out		83
D. I. Gower b Hadlee		0
A. J. Lamb not out		108
B 1, l-b 5, w 3		9

1/10 2/10   (2 wkts, 42.4 overs) 200

D. W. Randall, †I. J. Gould, I. T. Botham, G. Miller, V. J. Marks, N. G. Cowans and *R. G. D. Willis did not bat.

Bowling: Hadlee 9–2–37–1; Chatfield 10–2–25–1; Cairns 8–2–31–0; Snedden 8.4–0–61–0; Coney 7–0–37–0.

Umpires: A. R. Crafter and R. A. French.

†AUSTRALIA v NEW ZEALAND

At Melbourne, January 22. New Zealand won by 58 runs, outplaying Australia for the second time in five days. After being put in by Hughes, on a hot and cloudless day, New Zealand, building on an opening partnership of 83 between Wright and Edgar, reached 246 for six. Australia, whose catching had been a feature of earlier matches, missed Turner when 18 and Wright when 59. When Australia batted they threatened their target only during a fourth-wicket partnership of 63 between Wessels and Chappell, ended when Chappell pulled Troup to deep square leg. Wessels, sixth out at 151, batted for 38 overs. The match was much affected by injuries. Lawson left the field with a groin strain after bowling his ten overs; Thomson, suffering from chest congestion, bowled in short spells; Howarth, with a pinched nerve in his back, had to leave the captaincy to Wright soon after New Zealand had taken the field; Hogg needed eleven stitches in his left ear after being hit by a rising ball from Hadlee, and, also in the field, Turner pulled a hamstring. Australia objected to Turner being allowed a substitute on the grounds that he had entered the match with the same injury. Only later, during an interval for drinks, when the New Zealand physiotherapist persuaded the umpires that this was not so, was he allowed a replacement.
Man of the Match: J. G. Wright.   *Attendance:* 31,378.

New Zealand

J. G. Wright c Dyson b Rackemann	84		B. L. Cairns c Border b Lawson	0
B. A. Edgar c Marsh b Rackemann	32		†W. K. Lees not out	5
G. M. Turner lbw b Thomson	31		B 4, l-b 13, w 4, n-b 2	23
R. J. Hadlee c Wessels b Rackemann	21			
*G. P. Howarth run out	30		1/83 2/151 3/184 (6 wkts, 50 overs) 246	
J. J. Crowe not out	20		4/198 5/236 6/236	

M. C. Snedden, G. B. Troup and E. J. Chatfield did not bat.

Bowling: Lawson 10–2–27–1; Hogg 10–1–40–0; Rackemann 10–0–52–3; Thomson 10–0–52–1; Chappell 10–0–52–0.

Australia

K. C. Wessels c sub b Troup	62		R. M. Hogg retired hurt	0
J. Dyson c Wright b Snedden	21		J. R. Thomson c Crowe b Chatfield	4
D. W. Hookes c Hadlee b Cairns	1		C. G. Rackemann not out	0
*K. J. Hughes c Hadlee b Troup	12			
G. S. Chappell c Snedden b Troup	37		L-b 11, w 1, n-b 2	14
A. R. Border c and b Troup	5			
†R. W. Marsh c sub b Snedden	32		1/41 2/43 3/66 4/129 (44.1 overs) 188	
G. F. Lawson lbw b Hadlee	0		5/142 6/151 7/155 8/155 9/188	

Bowling: Hadlee 8–2–21–1; Chatfield 9–1–38–1; Snedden 7.1–1–12–2; Troup 10–0–54–4; Cairns 10–0–49–1.

Umpires: R. A. French and R. V. Whitehead.

†AUSTRALIA v ENGLAND

At Melbourne, January 23. Australia won by five wickets. The attendance record for one-day cricket, set up at the corresponding match a year earlier when Australia were playing West Indies, was beaten, 84,153 seeing Australia win a game reduced by morning rain to 37 overs a side. Put in in overcast weather, England made only modest progress until Lamb and Randall, coming together at 66 for three, added 139 in 23 overs. Lamb's 94 was a magnificent exhibition of aggressive, all-round strokeplay. Australia were without Thomson (bronchitis) and Lawson (groin strain). Just over two months since having a knee operation Lillee returned to their attack, which was completed by Maguire, who had been taken out of a Sheffield Shield match in Brisbane to make his first representative appearance for Australia. Border, promoted to open with Dyson, got Australia off to a flying start. From 41 for no wicket after four overs, they always had something in hand.

Man of the Match: A. J. Lamb.   *Attendance:* 84,153.

England

C. J. Tavaré c Lillee b Rackemann	.....	20	T. E. Jesty not out..........................	1
I. T. Botham b Lillee	....	19		
D. I. Gower c Marsh b Rackemann	......	6	L-b 10, w 5, n-b 4	19
A. J. Lamb c sub b Lillee	....	94		
D. W. Randall not out	....	51	1/32 2/50 3/66 (5 wkts, 37 overs) 213	
†I. J. Gould b Hogg	....	3	4/205 5/209	

D. R. Pringle, G. Miller, N. G. Cowans and †R. G. D. Willis did not bat.

Bowling: Hogg 7–0–36–1; Lillee 8–2–50–2; Rackemann 8–0–41–2; Maguire 7–0–34–0; Chappell 7–0–33–0.

Australia

A. R. Border run out	....	54	K. C. Wessels not out.....................	5
J. Dyson run out	....	54		
D. W. Hookes c Gower b Cowans	......	50	L-b 5, w 2, n-b 1	8
*K. J. Hughes c Miller b Cowans	....	6		
G. S. Chappell not out	....	32	1/85 2/157 3/167 (5 wkts, 34.4 overs) 217	
†R. W. Marsh run out	....	8	4/176 5/190	

D. K. Lillee, R. M. Hogg, J. N. Maguire and C. G. Rackemann did not bat.

Bowling: Willis 6.4–1–29–0; Cowans 6–0–46–2; Botham 7–1–45–0; Pringle 7–0–47–0; Miller 8–0–42–0.

Umpires: A. R. Crafter and P. J. McConnell.

†AUSTRALIA v ENGLAND

At Sydney, January 26. England won by 98 runs. Australia's first defeat by England came on Australia Day in a match reduced to 41 overs a side by afternoon rain. It was their second-line players who carried the day for England, Jackman, having his first game since before Christmas and lost their first four wickets for 47 runs. Randall played another useful innings, his partnership of 54 with Jesty being the first to hold Australia up. With 24 in their first two overs, bowled by Willis and Jackman, it looked as though Australia might repeat their performance of three days before when they punished the England bowlers unmercifully. But Willis steadied things, and when Jackman found a length, on a pitch not entirely unhelpful to him, he removed Hughes, Chappell and Wessels in seven balls. Australia lost their last eight wickets for 37 runs.

Man of the Match: R. D. Jackman. *Attendance:* 41,048.

England

C. J. Tavaré c Marsh b Thomson	14	E. E. Hemmings run out		3
I. T. Botham c Wessels b Hogg	0	R. D. Jackman b Hogg		0
D. I. Gower b Lillee	25	*R. G. D. Willis not out		5
A. J. Lamb lbw b Lillee	0			
D. W. Randall run out	47	B 2, l-b 4, w 9, n-b 4		19
T. E. Jesty b Maguire	30			
†I. J. Gould c Wessels b Hogg	42	1/8 2/45 3/47 4/47	(41 overs)	207
V. J. Marks c and b Lillee	22	5/101 6/157 7/197 8/201 9/201		

Bowling: Hogg 10–1–44–3; Maguire 8–0–42–1; Lillee 8–0–34–3; Thomson 8–0–40–1; Chappell 7–0–28–0.

Australia

A. R. Border c and b Willis	31	J. R. Thomson b Marks		7
J. Dyson c Randall b Botham	23	R. M. Hogg not out		0
D. W. Hookes b Marks	32	J. N. Maguire c Lamb b Hemmings		2
*K. J. Hughes c Gould b Jackman	0			
G. S. Chappell b Jackman	0	B 2, l-b 2, w 3, n-b 2		9
K. C. Wessels b Jackman	1			
†R. W. Marsh b Hemmings	1	1/40 2/72 3/73 4/73	(27.3 overs)	109
D. K. Lillee b Hemmings	3	5/77 6/96 7/99 8/106 9/106		

Bowling: Willis 6–1–23–1; Jackman 10–1–41–3; Botham 2–0–13–1; Marks 6–0–12–2; Hemmings 3.3–0–11–3.

Umpires: R. A. French and B. E. Martin.

†ENGLAND v NEW ZEALAND

At Adelaide, January 29. New Zealand won by four wickets. A match which produced 593 runs from 98.5 overs saw New Zealand bring off a remarkable victory. England's 296 for five, a record for the competition, seemed secure from assault, especially when New Zealand, after twenty overs, were only 79 for two. But from then on New Zealand scored at more than 7 an over, Cairns making 49 in 24 balls, Hadlee 79 in 64 balls and Coney 47 not out in 51 balls after Crowe and Wright, benefiting from poor English catching, had first raised the tempo. On a perfect pitch and in great heat England, with Botham bowling under the handicap of a strained side, lost all control, Coney making the winning hit with seven balls remaining. England's own run-spree had been launched by Botham with several huge hits and continued by Gower, whose third hundred in four one-day games against New Zealand took 85 balls.

Man of the Match: R. J. Hadlee. *Attendance:* 12,724.

England

I. T. Botham b Chatfield	65	†I. J. Gould not out		1
C. J. Tavaré c Crowe b Chatfield	16	L-b 1, w 1, n-b 1		3
A. J. Lamb run out	19			
D. W. Randall c Wright b Snedden	31	1/75 2/86 3/121	(5 wkts, 50 overs)	296
D. I. Gower c Coney b Troup	109	4/204 5/278		
T. E. Jesty not out	52			

E. E. Hemmings, V. J. Marks, *R. G. D. Willis and R. D. Jackman did not bat.

Bowling: Hadlee 10–1–36–0; Cairns 10–1–45–0; Chatfield 10–2–64–2; Snedden 10–0–72–1; Troup 10–0–76–1.

New Zealand

G. M. Turner b Willis	23	J. V. Coney not out	47
*G. P. Howarth b Jackman	3	†W. K. Lees not out	1
J. G. Wright run out	30	B 2, l-b 7, n-b 6	15
J. J. Crowe c Willis b Botham	50		
B. L. Cairns c Gower b Botham	49	1/26 2/33 3/96 (6 wkts, 48.5 overs) 297	
R. J. Hadlee c Jesty b Jackman	79	4/166 5/166 6/287	

G. B. Troup, E. J. Chatfield and M. C. Snedden did not bat.

Bowling: Willis 9.5-2-43-1; Jackman 10-1-49-2; Jesty 8-0-52-0; Hemmings 6-0-49-0; Botham 8-0-61-2; Marks 7-1-28-0.

Umpires: A. R. Crafter and R. A. French.

†AUSTRALIA v ENGLAND

At Adelaide, January 30. England won by 14 runs. By succeeding where they had failed the previous day, England kept alive their hopes of reaching the finals of the competition. Choosing to bat first they lost Botham, Lamb and Tavaré in the first nineteen overs before Gower and Randall added 106, Gower again appearing unruffled by the atmosphere generated by a large and enthusiastic crowd. In great heat Australia, plagued by wides and no-balls, bowled only 47 of their 50 overs in the three and a half hours allotted to them. For this they were fined approximately £170 per player. In trying to make 229 to win at 4.87 an over Australia lost Border at 27, in the eighth over, and were not well served by Dyson, who took 26 overs to score 17. Hookes, hit on the ankle in a club match the day before, was the best of the Australians until Jesty, running in from deep mid-wicket, caught him off Jackman. All tickets for the match were sold in advance.

Man of the Match: D. I. Gower.   *Attendance:* 34,897.

England

C. J. Tavaré b Hogg	18	†I. J. Gould c Lillee b Lawson	9
I. T. Botham b Lawson	14	V. J. Marks not out	10
D. I. Gower c Lillee b Thomson	77	B 1, l-b 14, w 6, n-b 6	27
A. J. Lamb b Hogg	2		
D. W. Randall c and b Lawson	49	1/25 2/62 3/70 (6 wkts, 47 overs) 228	
T. E. Jesty not out	22	4/176 5/178 6/200	

E. E. Hemmings, *R. G. D. Willis and R. D. Jackman did not bat.

Bowling: Lawson 10-0-27-3; Lillee 10-0-50-0; Hogg 9-1-25-2; Thomson 9-0-38-1; Chappell 7-0-45-0; Hookes 2-0-16-0.

Australia

A. R. Border c Randall b Willis	19	G. F. Lawson not out	28
J. Dyson c Lamb b Hemmings	17	J. R. Thomson not out	12
*K. J. Hughes c Gower b Marks	4		
D. W. Hookes c Jesty b Jackman	76	B 6, l-b 5	11
†R. W. Marsh c Jackman b Botham	7		
G. S. Chappell c Gower b Jackman	33	1/27 2/89 3/97 4/149 (7 wkts, 47 overs) 214	
K. C. Wessels b Botham	7	5/161 6/167 7/189	

R. M. Hogg and D. K. Lillee did not bat.

Bowling: Willis 10-1-40-1; Jackman 10-3-36-2; Botham 7-0-49-2; Hemmings 10-0-40-1; Marks 10-1-38-1.

Umpires: M. W. Johnson and P. J. McConnell.

†AUSTRALIA v NEW ZEALAND

At Adelaide, January 31. New Zealand won by 46 runs. In temperatures which rose to 107.6 degrees in the shade Australia lost again, their fifth defeat in six matches. New Zealand thus made their appearance in the finals virtually certain, if only on their scoring-rate which was much superior to Australia's who could now only equal New Zealand's points total. Australia brought in MacLeay, an all-rounder of medium pace, and Hogan, an orthodox left-arm spinner, in place of Lillee (dropped for the first time in his international career) and Wessels. New Zealand chose to bat and Turner, despite being troubled by the heat, made 84 in 34 overs, the innings which decided the match. Although five other New Zealanders reached double figures, none passed 20. At 100 for two, with twenty overs left and Hookes not out, Australia seemed to have the match in hand. But Hughes and Chappell went cheaply, Marsh was well caught near the sightscreen, Hookes was caught at the wicket, and when Thomson was yorked Australia had lost their last seven wickets for 50 runs.
Man of the Match: G. M. Turner.   *Attendance:* 27,328.

New Zealand
J. G. Wright c Border b Thomson	15	†W. K. Lees b Hogg	9
B. A. Edgar b MacLeay	18	M. C. Snedden not out	16
G. M. Turner c Hookes b Thomson	84	E. J. Chatfield not out	2
J. J. Crowe c and b Hogan	14		
B. L. Cairns c MacLeay b Hogan	0	L-b 8, w 2, n-b 3	13
*G. P. Howarth c Hughes b Chappell	15		
R. J. Hadlee run out	8	1/23 2/64 3/95 4/95 (9 wkts, 50 overs) 199
J. V. Coney c Marsh b Thomson	5	5/144 6/156 7/170 8/171 9/195	

Bowling: Lawson 10–3–20–0; Hogg 9–0–32–1; Thomson 5–0–27–3; MacLeay 10–0–39–1; Hogan 10–0–42–2; Chappell 6–0–26–1.

Australia
J. Dyson c Coney b Chatfield	24	T. G. Hogan run out	4
A. R. Border c Snedden b Chatfield	41	J. R. Thomson b Cairns	3
D. W. Hookes c Lees b Hadlee	27	R. M. Hogg not out	1
*K. J. Hughes c Wright b Coney	6	L-b 13, w 2	15
G. S. Chappell c Lees b Cairns	7		
K. H. MacLeay lbw b Hadlee	3	1/64 2/73 3/103 4/112 (44 overs) 153
†R. W. Marsh c Hadlee b Coney	15	5/116 6/116 7/141 8/148 9/149	
G. F. Lawson b Coney	7		

Bowling: Hadlee 7–1–15–2; Cairns 10–0–41–2; Snedden 7–1–16–0; Chatfield 10–1–26–2; Coney 10–0–40–3.

Umpires: A. R. Crafter and R. A. French.

†ENGLAND v NEW ZEALAND

At Perth, February 5. New Zealand won by seven wickets. Heavy rain, rare for the time of year, reduced the match to one of 23 overs a side. With the pitch starting damp and allowing the bowlers undue assistance, winning the toss gave New Zealand a decisive advantage. In the 70 minutes before the storm broke, England struggled to 45 for three in 17.3 overs, Hadlee being well-nigh unplayable. Upon the resumption (a helicopter was brought in to help dry the flooded outfield) there was time for England to receive only another 6.3 overs in which to try and raise their scoring-rate. In this time, for the loss of four more wickets, they slogged 43 runs, Gower making 27 of them. Despite losing Turner and Wright for 12 runs between them in their first seven overs and Crowe at 47 in the thirteenth, New Zealand had fifteen balls to spare when Howarth made the winning hit. England's defeat opened the way for Australia to reach the finals by beating New Zealand next day.
Man of the Match: R. J. Hadlee.   *Attendance:* 16,501.

England

C. J. Tavaré c Lees b Hadlee	0	V. J. Marks b Hadlee		2
I. T. Botham c Lees b Hadlee	19	R. D. Jackman not out		0
D. I. Gower not out	35			
A. J. Lamb c Crowe b Snedden	7	B 3, l-b 10		13
D. W. Randall c Howarth b Snedden	12			
T. E. Jesty run out	0	1/18 2/23 3/37	(7 wkts, 23 overs)	88
†I. J. Gould b Snedden	0	4/66 5/66 6/82 7/87		

N. G. Cowans and *R. G. D. Willis did not bat.

Bowling: Hadlee 8–2–15–3; Cairns 5–0–21–0; Snedden 6–1–25–3; Chatfield 4–1–14–0.

New Zealand

J. G. Wright c Tavaré b Willis	12	*G. P. Howarth not out		26
G. M. Turner c Jackman b Willis	0	L-b 1, w 3		4
J. J. Crowe c Botham b Cowans	18			
J. V. Coney not out	29	1/5 2/20 3/47	(3 wkts, 20.3 overs)	89

†W. K. Lees, J. F. M. Morrison, B. L. Cairns, R. J. Hadlee, M. C. Snedden and E. J. Chatfield did not bat.

Bowling: Willis 6.3–1–28–2; Cowans 8–0–32–1; Jackman 2–0–16–0; Botham 4–0–9–0.

Umpires: R. A. French and P. J. McConnell.

†AUSTRALIA v NEW ZEALAND

At Perth, February 6. Australia won by 27 runs. Australia's victory assured them of second position in the WSC qualifying table and so a place in the finals. They were given a good start, after being put in, by the new opening pair of Wood and Smith. Smith, a 21-year-old New South Welshman, was playing in his first representative match. On a pitch helpful to seam bowlers, runs were always hard to come by, the top score for either side being Wright's 33, other than the 35 extras which New Zealand conceded. Hadlee, much New Zealand's best bowler, retired with hamstring trouble after bowling only five of his ten overs. Morrison, slow left-arm, took three wickets in his first bowl of the competition. While Wright and Turner were adding 52 for New Zealand's second wicket an Australian defeat looked possible; but at 61 Lillee bowled Turner and Crowe with successive balls, after which only Morrison and Snedden, in a ninth-wicket partnership of 37, threatened Australia. After the match Marsh admitted to having deliberately kicked the ball away while taking a quick single, to avoid being run out. The New Zealanders had appealed, unsuccessfully, against him for "obstructing the field".

Man of the Match: R. W. Marsh.   *Attendance:* 25,000.

Australia

G. M. Wood c Wright b Chatfield	25	J. R. Thomson b Morrison		4
S. B. Smith c Webb b Chatfield	28	R. M. Hogg not out		1
*K. J. Hughes b Morrison	21	D. K. Lillee not out		0
A. R. Border c and b Coney	2	B 9, l-b 19, w 7		35
D. W. Hookes b Hadlee	12			
G. S. Chappell b Snedden	24	1/65 2/74 3/77	(9 wkts, 50 overs)	191
†R. W. Marsh c Snedden b Morrison	31	4/110 5/118 6/159		
G. F. Lawson b Snedden	8	7/183 8/188 9/191		

Bowling: Hadlee 5–2–7–1; Cairns 6–0–20–0; Snedden 10–1–41–2; Chatfield 10–2–30–2; Coney 10–0–22–1; Morrison 9–0–36–3.

New Zealand

*G. P. Howarth b Hogg	8	B. L. Cairns run out	1
J. G. Wright c Marsh b Chappell	33	M. C. Snedden c Thomson b Lawson	25
G. M. Turner c Marsh b Lillee	30	E. J. Chatfield b Lawson	0
J. J. Crowe c Marsh b Lillee	0	B 2, l-b 6, w 8, n-b 4	20
J. V. Coney c Thomson b Chappell	10		
†P. N. Webb c Border b Chappell	7	1/9 2/61 3/61 (44.5 overs) 164	
J. F. M. Morrison not out	25	4/61 5/92 6/108	
R. J. Hadlee c Marsh b Hogg	5	7/123 8/125 9/162	

Bowling: Lawson 9.5–0–24–2; Hogg 9–0–37–2; Lillee 10–2–24–2; Thomson 8–0–24–0; Chappell 8–0–35–3.

Umpires: A. R. Crafter and M. W. Johnson.

QUALIFYING TABLE

	P	W	L	Pts
New Zealand	10	6	4	12
Australia	10	5	5	10
England	10	4	6	8

FINAL MATCHES

†AUSTRALIA v NEW ZEALAND

First Final Match

At Sydney, February 9. Australia won by six wickets. New Zealand were without Hadlee, who had pulled a hamstring in Perth, a handicap they were unable to overcome. After winning the toss and batting they struggled against some accurate Australian bowling, their score after 30 overs being 81 for four. Coney and Morrison then brought the match to life with a rousing partnership of 85 in fifteen overs. Australia, replying to 193 for seven (49 overs), had Hughes back in form and never lost touch with their target, which was reduced by a shower to 150 from 38 overs and reached with 4.5 overs to spare. A brilliant catch by Coney, diving to his left behind the square-leg umpire, accounted for Hughes. Although they had bowled only 49 overs in their three and a half hours – they were required to bowl 50 – Australia were not fined for it, as they could and should have been.

Attendance: 30,527.

New Zealand

J. G. Wright c Chappell b Lawson	36	B. L. Cairns c Lillee b Hogg	9
B. A. Edgar b Thomson	12	M. C. Snedden not out	2
G. M. Turner lbw b Lillee	4		
*G. P. Howarth c Marsh b Chappell	9	L-b 15, w 11, n-b 1	27
J. V. Coney not out	58		
J. F. M. Morrison b Lillee	35	1/44 2/57 3/77 (7 wkts, 49 overs) 193	
†W. K. Lees c Marsh b Lawson	2	4/81 5/166 6/171 7/190	

E. J. Chatfield and G. B. Troup did not bat.

Bowling: Lawson 10–4–28–2; Hogg 10–2–24–1; Lillee 10–1–35–2; Thomson 10–0–42–1; Chappell 9–0–37–1.

Australia

G. M. Wood b Chatfield	12	G. S. Chappell not out	21
S. B. Smith b Cairns	10	B 4, l-b 16	20
*K. J. Hughes c Coney b Chatfield	63		
A. R. Border c sub b Chatfield	9	1/14 2/59 (4 wkts, 33.1 overs) 155	
D. W. Hookes not out	20	3/83 4/119	

†R. W. Marsh, G. F. Lawson, D. K. Lillee, J. R. Thomson and R. M. Hogg did not bat.

Bowling: Troup 5–0–30–0; Cairns 8.1–0–27–1; Snedden 9–0–45–0; Chatfield 10–1–27–3; Coney 1–0–6–0.

Umpires: R. A. French and M. W. Johnson.

†AUSTRALIA v NEW ZEALAND

Second Final Match

At Melbourne, February 13. Australia won by 149 runs. Without the least difficulty Australia won the second of the finals and the World Series Cup with it. Having won the toss they were given a flying start by Wood and Smith, whose scoring-rate in an opening partnership of 140 was never below 5 an over. Wood, first out, scored 91 off 84 balls; Smith went on to make his first representative hundred, his deft cutting and strong driving being features of his innings. New Zealand badly missed Hadlee, whose hamstring had been slow to heal. Richard Webb, flown across from Dunedin the previous day, took Hadlee's place and finished with the best figures of the New Zealand bowlers. Australia preferred MacLeay to Thomson. Australia's 302 for eight was a new record for the competition. When New Zealand batted they were soon beyond recovery. Only Cairns, coming in at 44 for six, and some charitable bowling from Chappell and Hookes kept the game going. In a brief but remarkable display of hitting Cairns reached 50 in 21 balls, including six 6s.

Man of the Finals: K. J. Hughes.   *Attendance:* 71,393.
International Cricketer of the Year: D. I. Gower.

Australia

G. M. Wood b Coney	91	†R. W. Marsh not out	3
S. B. Smith b Webb	117	G. F. Lawson run out	3
*K. J. Hughes c Lees b Chatfield	12	B 1, l-b 7	8
A. R. Border c and b Chatfield	11		
D. W. Hookes c Wright b Webb	40	1/140 2/167 (8 wkts, 50 overs) 302	
G. S. Chappell c Wright b Cairns	7	3/205 4/261 5/280	
K. H. MacLeay run out	10	6/285 7/299 8/302	

D. K. Lillee and R. M. Hogg did not bat.

Bowling: Webb 9–1–47–2; Cairns 8–0–56–1; Chatfield 10–0–54–2; Snedden 7–0–47–0; Morrison 7–0–39–0; Coney 9–0–51–1.

New Zealand

J. G. Wright c Marsh b Hogg	3	M. C. Snedden c Marsh b Hookes	35
G. M. Turner b Marsh b Lawson	1	E. J. Chatfield lbw b Chappell	10
*G. P. Howarth b Lawson	3	R. J. Webb not out	6
J. J. Crowe lbw b MacLeay	27	L-b 6, w 2, n-b 1	9
J. V. Coney b Lillee	2		
J. F. M. Morrison b Lillee	2	1/8 2/8 3/13 (39.5 overs) 153	
†W. K. Lees run out	3	4/23 5/42 6/44	
B. L. Cairns c Smith b Lawson	52	7/92 8/103 9/144	

Bowling: Lawson 8–3–11–3; Hogg 10–1–31–1; Lillee 7–3–29–2; MacLeay 8–0–56–1; Chappell 5–1–15–1; Hookes 1.5–0–2–1.

Umpires: A. R. Crafter and P. J. McConnell.

CRICKET IN AUSTRALIA, 1982-83

By PETER MACKINNON

For the first time, the Sheffield Shield was decided by means of a final played between the teams finishing first and second in the table. With Tasmania participating as a full member of the competition for the first time, each state played ten games. Although those well endowed with representative players sometimes found themselves without their star performers, the programme was organised in such a way as to ensure that the Test players were more often available for Shield cricket than in 1981-82.

Three of the states had a chance of winning the Shield until towards the end of the season, but despite this crowds were again sparse. Even the five-day final, a tightly fought game from start to finish, attracted a total of only 16,443. On the assumption that city crowds are now satiated with international cricket, either live or on television, the next experiment may involve taking Shield cricket more often to the country centres.

The Shield was won by New South Wales for the first time since 1965-66. It was a well-deserved triumph and a fitting reward for Rick McCosker, who had captained the side through several "near misses" in previous seasons. If there was criticism of McCosker's somewhat defensive leadership, there was none of his batting. His main batting support came from Dirk Wellham, who recovered the form that he had lost the year before. Steve Smith continued to play exciting cricket, but after a marathon innings of 263 in Melbourne, lost form late in the season. When available, Geoff Lawson was the spearhead of the attack; Michael Whitney showed greater consistency than before and the left-arm spin of Murray Bennett was a valuable help to the balance of the side. Steve Rixon was a reliable wicket-keeper, and Trevor Chappell, although a controversial choice early in the season, ended it by taking important wickets and making vital runs.

Western Australia will look back on the season with some disappointment, not just because of their indifferent performance in the final. Although a talented side with greater depth of reserve strength than most other states, they too often played below their best. This was especially the case with the batsmen, whose approach tended to be too defensive. Kim Hughes, who should be excepted from this criticism, seldom failed. Geoff Marsh did best of the younger batsmen. The bowling, which lacked genuine pace, was weakened by Terry Alderman's absence through injury, and with Dennis Lillee also frequently unavailable, the brunt of the new-ball bowling was borne by Wayne Clark. Ken MacLeay developed his all-round skills usefully; and with Bruce Yardley and Tom Hogan enjoying considerable success, the spin bowling was usually of high standard.

The most exciting team in the competition was South Australia, whom David Hookes led by example. In an outstandingly successful summer, Hookes frequently exhibited a capacity to turn a game in a single session. Wayne Phillips at his best was capable of almost similar deeds. The evergreen John Inverarity provided the side with middle-order stability and in Mike Haysman South Australia had the batting find of the year. Andrew Hilditch had reasonable success in a summer interrupted by injury while Kevin Wright, apart from keeping wicket with quiet efficiency, also made useful runs. The side was less strong in bowling than in batting for, although possessing in Joel Garner, the West Indian, and a rejuvenated Rodney Hogg the best opening attack in the country, there were deficiencies in the spin-bowling department. Peter Sleep had a disappointing summer with both bat and ball and Inverarity was less effective than in 1981-82.

From their first full season of Shield cricket, Tasmania had cause for satisfaction, particularly when their lack of resources is taken into account. Especially gratifying to them was their outright victory over New South Wales in Sydney and a win on first innings in the return encounter in Hobart. The batting depended heavily for its success upon David Boon and Roger Woolley. Of the remainder, Stuart Saunders made more runs than might have been expected of one batting so low in the order, but as his batting flourished so his leg-break bowling fell away. Tasmania's two imported players experienced varying fortunes. While Roland Butcher from Middlesex had a wretched summer, Michael Holding, the Jamaican, was a great success. Holding's presence was of much benefit to his fellow fast bowlers, Peter Clough and Philip Blizzard.

Queensland had a disappointing summer, even allowing for the fact that they suffered more than most sides from the calls of the national selectors. Allan Border and Kepler Wessels usually scored heavily, but Greg Chappell's achievements were modest. The players regularly available mostly lacked consistency, although Robert Kerr was a notable exception. Alan Henschell had one memorable match but was otherwise disappointing and Greg Ritchie, after a successful tour in Pakistan, lost form. John Maguire was the mainstay of the attack, but once the injury-prone Carl Rackemann had left the scene there was no-one else capable of destructive bursts.

The wooden spoon was won for the second successive summer by Victoria, for whom very little went right. Persistent debate about the leadership and composition of the team must have been unsettling for the players and, in the circumstances, it was remarkable that Graeme Yallop should have batted with such consistent success. Frequently the Victorians assured themselves of defeat by inept batting in their first innings; from then on it could be only a battle for survival. What satisfaction there was for Victoria came from the promise of a number of the younger players, notably Dean Jones, Michael Taylor and Rod McCurdy.

At the end of the season, Hughes won approximately £1,150 as Sheffield Shield "Player of the Year". This award was decided on the votes of the umpires in each match: Hughes, who scored nineteen points from six matches, won narrowly from McCosker and Hookes.

Several senior players were disciplined or fined for misdemeanours during the summer. Hughes, Border, Lillee and Marsh were fined for breaches of the Australian Cricket Board's player-writer rules and Lillee received a suspended £600 fine for using abusive language towards spectators in the Shield match between Western Australia and South Australia in Adelaide in February. In the Sheffield Shield final in Perth, Whitney incurred a small fine for aggressive behaviour towards Rodney Marsh during Western Australia's first innings. Another New South Wales player, Peter Toohey, missed one Shield match following a disagreement with the umpires in a grade match in Sydney.

Esso Scholarships were awarded to Michael Haysman (South Australia), Greg Matthews (New South Wales), Mervyn Hughes (Victoria) and Robert

Kerr (Queensland) to enable them to further their cricketing education in England during the 1983 season.

FIRST-CLASS AVERAGES, 1982-83

BATTING

(Qualification: 300 runs)

	M	I	NO	R	HI	100s	Avge
A. R. Border (*Qld*)	11	20	5	1,081	165	2	72.06
G. N. Yallop (*Vic*)	12	22	1	1,418	246	4	67.52
D. M. Wellham (*NSW*)	13	23	5	1,205	136*	2	66.94
D. W. Hookes (*SA*)	13	23	1	1,424	193	4	64.72
K. J. Hughes (*WA*)	13	21	1	1,280	137	4	64.00
K. C. Wessels (*Qld*)	12	23	0	1,325	249	5	57.60
M. D. Haysman (*SA*).......	7	14	2	684	153	2	57.00
R. B. McCosker (*NSW*) ...	13	25	4	1,153	124	3	54.90
D. M. Jones (*Vic*)	7	11	0	603	199	2	54.81
G. R. J. Matthews (*NSW*)	7	11	4	343	81*	0	49.00
M. D. Taylor (*Vic*)	11	19	3	771	144	1	48.18
G. Shipperd (*WA*)...........	12	19	1	816	166	2	45.33
R. J. Inverarity (*SA*)........	10	19	3	699	126	2	43.68
R. D. Woolley (*Tas*)........	12	16	3	551	111*	1	42.38
S. L. Saunders (*Tas*)........	12	15	3	498	79*	0	41.50
D. C. Boon (*Tas*)	12	19	2	682	115	2	40.11
R. B. Kerr (*Qld*).............	12	22	0	876	132	3	39.81
G. S. Chappell (*Qld*)	11	20	2	703	126	1	39.05
S. B. Smith (*NSW*)	11	21	1	762	263	2	38.10
W. B. Phillips (*SA*)	9	18	0	680	161	2	37.77
B. M. Laird (*WA*)...........	11	18	1	622	99	0	36.58
G. M. Wood (*WA*)	11	18	1	610	138	2	35.88
J. Dyson (*NSW*).............	12	23	3	688	79	0	34.40
A. M. J. Hilditch (*SA*)	9	17	1	546	109	1	34.12
P. M. Toohey (*NSW*).......	11	19	2	568	104	1	33.41
M. J. Bennett (*NSW*).......	13	18	7	356	59*	0	32.36
K. J. Wright (*SA*)	11	19	4	455	65*	0	30.33
A. B. Henschell (*Qld*)......	12	19	1	543	162	1	30.16
D. F. Whatmore (*Vic*)......	8	15	1	410	81	0	29.28
T. V. Hohns (*Qld*)	12	19	5	376	66	0	28.92
T. M. Chappell (*NSW*)	13	24	2	633	132	1	28.77
G. R. Marsh (*WA*)	11	18	0	511	54	0	28.38
W. R. Broad (*Qld*)...........	6	11	0	310	89	0	28.18
S. J. Reid (*Tas*)	9	13	2	309	79	0	28.09
R. B. Phillips (*Qld*)	12	20	6	391	61	0	27.92
J. M. Wiener (*Vic*)	10	19	0	530	75	0	27.89
D. A. Smith (*Tas*)...........	12	20	1	527	81	0	27.73
R. W. Marsh (*WA*)	13	20	0	538	110	1	26.90
R. O. Butcher (*Tas*)	12	19	2	423	53	0	24.88
G. M. Watts (*Vic*)...........	7	13	0	321	61	0	24.69
K. H. MacLeay (*WA*)	12	18	1	407	100	1	23.94
G. M. Ritchie (*Qld*)	9	16	0	382	67	0	23.87
B. Yardley (*WA*)	14	20	3	400	65	0	23.52
M. Ray (*Tas*)	9	15	1	327	39	0	23.35
S. J. Rixon (*NSW*)	13	20	3	393	57*	0	23.11

* *Signifies not out.*

BOWLING

(Qualification: 15 wickets)

	O	M	R	W	Avge
C. G. Rackemann (*Qld*) .	239.5	75	553	35	15.80
J. Garner (*SA*)..............	403.1	131	976	55	17.74
T. M. Chappell (*NSW*) ...	192.5	52	482	27	17.85
T. M. Alderman (*WA*) ...	137.2	36	353	18	19.61
G. F. Lawson (*NSW*)	495.4	110	1,368	65	21.04
J. R. Thomson (*Qld*)......	254.4	50	766	34	22.52
R. M. Hogg (*SA*)	400.2	85	1,120	49	22.85
W. M. Clark (*WA*)	339.2	89	801	31	25.83
M. A. Holding (*Tas*)	371.4	93	946	36	26.27
P. M. Clough (*Tas*)	414.1	91	1,089	41	26.56
T. G. Hogan (*WA*)	415.2	133	939	35	26.82
D. K. Lillee (*WA*)	343	103	907	32	28.34
M. J. Bennett (*NSW*)	507.5	203	1,102	38	29.00
B. Yardley (*WA*)...........	705	237	1,782	61	29.21
M. R. Whitney (*NSW*).....	422.5	85	1,323	45	29.40
R. J. McCurdy (*Vic*)	345.1	56	1,327	45	29.48
L. S. Pascoe (*NSW*)	264.1	41	878	27	32.51
P. R. Sleep (*SA*)	206.4	48	689	21	32.80
A. B. Henschell (*Qld*)	321.5	90	832	24	34.66
K. H. MacLeay (*WA*)	349.3	90	912	26	35.07
P. A. Blizzard (*Tas*)	275.4	60	842	24	35.08
J. N. Maguire (*Qld*)	370	86	1,019	28	36.39
H. Frei (*Qld*)................	355.5	93	985	27	36.48
R. J. Inverarity (*SA*)	291.5	80	733	19	38.57
R. J. Bright (*Vic*)	465	125	1,199	31	38.67
I. W. Callen (*Vic*)..........	267	57	823	21	39.19
T. V. Hohns (*Qld*).........	388.4	114	978	21	46.57
A. T. Sincock (*SA*)	201	42	721	15	48.06
A. G. Holland (*NSW*)	370.4	134	833	16	52.06
S. L. Saunders (*Tas*)	285.2	67	875	15	58.33

WICKET-KEEPING

R. W. Marsh (*WA*) 62 (62ct); R. D. Woolley (*Tas*) 42 (40ct, 2st); K. J. Wright (*SA*) 40 (36ct, 4st); R. B. Phillips (*Qld*) 37 (35ct, 2st); S. J. Rixon (*NSW*) 37 (27ct, 10st); G. J. Miles (*Vic*) 26 (24ct, 2st).

SHEFFIELD SHIELD, 1982-83

	P	W	L	Drawn Won on 1st inns	Lost on 1st inns	Pts
Western Australia	10	3	1	3	3	64
New South Wales	10	3	2	4	1	60
South Australia	10	3	1	3	3	60
Tasmania	10	1	1	4	4	32
Queensland	10	1	4	3	2	28
Victoria	10	0	2	2	6	8

Points: Win = 12; lead on first innings = 4.

Note: Western Australia received 4 points for leading New South Wales on first innings when beaten outright at Sydney.

New South Wales received only 12 points for their outright win over Western Australia after trailing on first innings at Sydney.

QUEENSLAND v SOUTH AUSTRALIA

At Brisbane, October 15, 16, 17. South Australia won by 146 runs. South Australia 16 pts. On a sub-standard pitch which drew critical comment from both captains, the bowlers were well on top. For Queensland, Rackemann, who had missed much of the previous season through injury, made an encouraging comeback; in South Australia's first innings he achieved a career-best seven for 49. Garner was largely responsible for Queensland's first-innings collapse in which the last nine wickets fell for only 46 runs.

South Australia

W. M. Darling c Lawrence b Rackemann	26	– c Phillips b Rackemann	5
K. P. Harris b Rackemann	1	– lbw b Maguire	1
A. M. J. Hilditch c Chappell b Rackemann	7	– c Hohns b Maguire	8
R. J. Inverarity c Chappell b Maguire	63	– c Phillips b Rackemann	2
*D. W. Hookes b Hohns	53	– c Phillips b Rackemann	87
R. J. Zadow lbw b Rackemann	4	– c Henschell b Gallagher	87
†K. J. Wright c Henschell b Gallagher	9	– c Chappell b Henschell	4
C. L. Harms b Rackemann	23	– c Phillips b Henschell	4
J. Garner c Phillips b Rackemann	14	– b Maguire	0
R. M. Hogg c Chappell b Rackemann	7	– c Kerr b Rackemann	7
A. T. Sincock not out	4	– not out	4
L-b 8, n-b 16	24	L-b 5, w 1, n-b 9	15

1/7 2/32 3/36 4/135   235   1/7 2/7 3/12 4/53   224
5/147 6/171 7/175 8/219 9/222   5/142 6/152 7/185 8/198 9/212

Bowling: *First Innings*—Rackemann 23–8–49–7; Maguire 24–2–78–1; Chappell 5–0–13–0; Hohns 14–7–24–1; Gallagher 8–2–30–1; Broad 7–1–17–0. *Second Innings*—Rackemann 24.3–7–58–4; Maguire 21–5–50–3; Chappell 6–3–8–0; Hohns 13–4–31–0; Gallagher 15–4–33–1; Henschell 6–0–29–2.

Queensland

K. C. Wessels b Hogg	39	– c Wright b Garner	12
R. B. Kerr lbw b Garner	48	– b Garner	8
W. R. Broad c and b Harms	36	– c Wright b Hogg	8
*G. S. Chappell c and b Harms	1	– c Hookes b Inverarity	5
A. B. Henschell lbw b Garner	0	– c Harris b Inverarity	25
R. J. Lawrence st Wright b Inverarity	19	– c Sincock b Harms	48
T. V. Hohns b Hogg	4	– b Inverarity	2
†R. B. Phillips c Wright b Garner	14	– lbw b Hogg	13
I. N. Gallagher b Garner	3	– c Hookes b Inverarity	3
C. G. Rackemann c Wright b Garner	0	– b Inverarity	8
J. N. Maguire not out	1	– not out	0
B 1, l-b 3, n-b 9	13	N-b 3	3

1/64 2/132 3/136 4/137   178   1/19 2/25 3/29 4/46   135
5/140 6/148 7/170 8/174 9/174   5/65 6/67 7/86 8/109 9/135

Bowling: *First Innings*—Hogg 19–7–44–2; Garner 24.1–12–32–5; Harms 14–5–27–2; Inverarity 9–1–26–1; Sincock 8–1–36–0. *Second Innings*—Hogg 13–6–27–2; Garner 13–4–32–2; Harms 4.1–0–17–1; Inverarity 14–4–56–5.

Umpires: M. W. Johnson and C. D. Timmins.

WESTERN AUSTRALIA v NEW SOUTH WALES

At Perth, October 15, 16, 17, 18. Drawn. New South Wales 4 pts. Winning the toss, the visitors were given a solid start by McCosker and Davis, and later Toohey dealt severely with the bowling of the half-fit Lillee. Wellham also showed a welcome return to form with a chanceless and painstaking effort which lasted almost six hours. From the start of their innings Western Australia were content to play for a draw, which was not entirely surprising considering that six of their best players were still in Pakistan with the Australian team. Shipperd's marathon innings lasted ten hours and covered six sessions of play. With Zoehrer, Rodney Marsh's substitute, he added 206 for the seventh wicket, a record for Western Australia. Zoehrer's century was his first in any class of cricket.

New South Wales

*R. B. McCosker c Zoehrer b MacLeay	84	– lbw b MacLeay	59
I. C. Davis c Zoehrer b MacLeay	56	– c sub b Lillee	17
T. M. Chappell c Wolfe b Lillee	16	– not out	30
S. B. Smith c Zoehrer b Clark	52	– not out	21
D. M. Wellham not out	136		
P. M. Toohey c Clements b Lillee	75		
†S. J. Rixon b Mann	27		
M. J. Bennett not out	30		
B 3, l-b 12, w 1, n-b 10	26	B 1, l-b 1	2

1/148 2/159 3/183 4/314   (6 wkts dec.) 502   1/95 2/98   (2 wkts) 129
5/362 6/426

L. S. Pascoe, A. J. Skilbeck and M. R. Whitney did not bat.

Bowling: *First Innings*—Lillee 37–11–118–2; Clark 36–10–91–1; Thomson 20–2–117–0; MacLeay 40–16–85–2; Mann 27–9–65–1. *Second Innings*—Lillee 9–1–42–1; Clark 6–1–22–0; Thomson 7–1–33–0; MacLeay 9–3–20–1; Wolfe 1–0–6–0; Marsh 1–0–4–0.

Western Australia

G. R. Marsh b Chappell	33	D. K. Lillee c Wellham b McCosker	0
S. C. Clements c Bennett b Pascoe	30	W. M. Clark not out	19
G. Shipperd c Rixon b Pascoe	166	G. D. Thomson c Toohey b Pascoe	0
M. F. Wolfe lbw b Skilbeck	39	B 5, l-b 3, n-b 22	30
*C. S. Serjeant st Rixon b Bennett	2		
K. H. MacLeay c Davis b Skilbeck	5	1/57 2/76 3/163 4/166	428
A. L. Mann c Davis b Bennett	0	5/179 6/180 7/386 8/394 9/427	
†T. J. Zoehrer c and b McCosker	104		

Bowling: Pascoe 39.4–11–109–3; Skilbeck 35–11–87–2; Whitney 29–6–74–0; Chappell 15–6–26–1; Bennett 52–25–74–2; McCosker 14–4–28–2.

Umpires: P. J. McConnell and A. Claydon.

SOUTH AUSTRALIA v VICTORIA

At Adelaide, October 22, 23, 24, 25. Drawn. South Australia 4 pts. Notwithstanding some fine batting by Yallop for Victoria and a first South Australian innings which was rescued by the experience of Inverarity and Hookes, the climax to the game overshadowed all else. An ungenerous declaration had left South Australia with the seemingly impossible task of scoring 272 in approximately 30 overs. Opening the innings, Hookes scored the fastest century ever made by an Australian in first-class cricket. It took him 43 minutes (34 balls) and contained three 6s and seventeen 4s. When dismissed, he had batted for 55 minutes, and after ten overs the score was 128. But it was too good to last, and another five wickets having fallen in failing light, the chase was called off and play halted with six overs remaining and Victoria only three wickets from victory.

Victoria

J. M. Wiener c Hookes b Garner	2 – b Garner	73
G. M. Watts c Hilditch b Garner	0 – c Wright b Hogg	0
*G. N. Yallop c Darling b Sincock	28 – c and b Sincock	151
P. J. Davies c Garner b Hookes	29 – b Garner	27
B. C. Green c Wright b Garner	14 – c Harris b Inverarity	70
P. J. Cox c Hogg b Garner	20 – c and b Harms	47
S. F. Graf c Garner b Harms	48 – c Wright b Inverarity	18
†P. G. Sacristani c Garner b Sincock	55 – lbw b Harms	2
P. D. King c Wright b Hogg	54 – not out	15
R. J. McCurdy not out	5 – lbw b Inverarity	9
J. D. Higgs b Hogg	0 – not out	1
B 1, l-b 1, n-b 3	5	L-b 3, n-b 4	7

1/1 2/2 3/39 4/63   260   1/0 2/141 3/220   (9 wkts dec.) 420
5/95 6/109 7/168 8/248 9/256   4/261 5/373 6/373 7/380 8/404 9/418

Bowling: *First Innings*—Garner 28–5–73–4; Hogg 20.1–4–38–2; Sincock 18–9–50–2; Harms 14–4–38–1; Hookes 3–1–8–1; Inverarity 14–5–48–0. *Second Innings*—Garner 30–9–81–2; Hogg 21–6–62–1; Sincock 18–3–77–1; Harms 29–9–71–2; Hookes 2–1–6–0; Inverarity 41–7–116–3.

South Australia

W. M. Darling c McCurdy b King	10 – c Sacristani b McCurdy	11
K. P. Harris c Sacristani b McCurdy	9 – (8) lbw b Graf	0
A. M. J. Hilditch b Graf	42 – (9) not out	0
R. J. Inverarity lbw b McCurdy	126 – (7) not out	15
*D. W. Hookes c Sacristani b Cox	137 – (2) c Green b McCurdy	107
R. J. Zadow c Wiener b King	5 – lbw b McCurdy	8
†K. J. Wright c Davies b King	33 – (3) b McCurdy	30
C. L. Harms c Wiener b Green	21 – (5) c Sacristani b McCurdy	3
J. Garner c Sacristani b King	7 – (4) b Graf	19
R. M. Hogg c Wiener b King	0	
A. T. Sincock not out	8	
L-b 6, w 1, n-b 4	11	B 5, l-b 7, w 1	13

1/16 2/28 3/76 4/288   409   1/122 2/128 3/154 4/159 (7 wkts) 206
5/301 6/367 7/373 8/386 9/390   5/184 6/203 7/204

Bowling: *First Innings*—McCurdy 23–2–95–2; King 28–5–88–5; Graf 23–5–74–1; Cox 25–3–69–1; Higgs 10–1–46–0; Green 4.3–1–16–1; Yallop 5–2–10–0. *Second Innings*—McCurdy 12–0–88–5; King 2–0–38–0; Graf 10–0–67–2.

Umpires: A. R. Crafter and B. E. Martin.

NEW SOUTH WALES v TASMANIA

At Sydney, October 22, 23, 24, 25. Tasmania won by seven wickets. Tasmania 16 pts. Playing for the first time as full members of the Sheffield Shield, Tasmania achieved a famous victory after Woolley won the toss and elected to bat. Against some moderate bowling and lacklustre fielding, he looked the best of the Tasmanian batsmen, though good support came from Saunders, with whom he added 111 for the seventh wicket. New South Wales never recovered from a calamitous start to their first innings and were forced to follow on. Holding was playing his first game since a serious knee operation in February. In the second New South Wales innings two run-outs accounted for Rixon and O'Neill when they were playing well, and the visitors were left with the reasonably simple task of scoring 94 in twenty minutes and twenty overs.

Tasmania

D. A. Smith c and b Bennett	52	– b Holland	27
M. Ray c Wellham b Pascoe	3	– c O'Neill b Pascoe	23
D. C. Boon c Davis b Holland	27	– lbw b Pascoe	5
S. M. Small c Toohey b Bennett	44	– not out	13
R. O. Butcher lbw b Pascoe	29	– not out	21
*†R. D. Woolley c McCosker b Holland	88		
P. J. Mancell c Toohey b Bennett	0		
S. L. Saunders b Holland	59		
M. A. Holding c Chappell b Holland	16		
P. A. Blizzard c McCosker b Bennett	13		
P. M. Clough not out	0		
B 6, l-b 8, w 1, n-b 5	20	L-b 4, n-b 1	5

1/15 2/88 3/88 4/143   351   1/53 2/59 3/61   (3 wkts) 94
5/188 6/188 7/299 8/317 9/351

Bowling: *First Innings*—Pascoe 33–8–112–2; Skilbeck 14–1–47–0; Holland 54–22–100–4; Chappell 8–2–17–0; Bennett 40.1–22–55–4. *Second Innings*—Pascoe 10.2–0–45–2; Skilbeck 3–0–11–0; Holland 7–0–33–1.

New South Wales

*R. B. McCosker lbw b Holding	1	– c Woolley b Clough	69
I. C. Davis b Holding	0	– c Butcher b Clough	14
T. M. Chappell c Blizzard b Clough	1	– st Woolley b Saunders	16
D. M. Wellham c and b Ray	37	– c Blizzard b Ray	16
P. M. Toohey lbw b Clough	14	– lbw b Saunders	21
M. D. O'Neill lbw b Saunders	36	– (7) run out	65
†S. J. Rixon c Woolley b Holding	11	– (6) run out	46
M. J. Bennett not out	21	– c Woolley b Clough	23
A. J. Skilbeck c Blizzard b Mancell	0	– b Holding	0
L. S. Pascoe lbw b Holding	2	– c Small b Saunders	15
R. G. Holland b Clough	3	– not out	9
L-b 3, w 1, n-b 3	7	B 7, l-b 3, n-b 7	17

1/1 2/2 3/2 4/24   133   1/16 2/65 3/102 4/128   311
5/84 6/106 7/108 8/108 9/117   5/164 6/212 7/266 8/266 9/292

Bowling: *First Innings*—Holding 24–5–43–4; Clough 9.1–2–19–3; Blizzard 4–1–8–0; Saunders 21–5–51–1; Mancell 6–4–4–1; Ray 4–3–1–1. *Second Innings*—Holding 24–6–54–1; Clough 23–7–41–3; Blizzard 4–0–8–0; Saunders 46.2–12–115–3; Mancell 31–7–57–0; Ray 19–8–19–1.

Umpires: R. A. French and M. Jay.

WESTERN AUSTRALIA v VICTORIA

At Perth, October 29, 30, 31, November 1. Drawn. Western Australia 4 pts. Western Australia, put in by Yallop, made a poor start and would have fared even worse had Hughes not been dropped three times in making 67. In reply Victoria began well, but fine bowling by Alderman and MacLeay brought about a collapse, the last seven wickets falling for only 38 runs. Western Australia's second innings was a pedestrian affair until Hughes raised the tempo to allow a declaration, but even with the benefit of five dropped catches, Victoria's target proved well beyond them.

Western Australia

B. M. Laird c Bright b Graf	2	– lbw b King	99
G. M. Wood b Graf	11	– c Yallop b Graf	4
G. Shipperd c Graf b Callen	0	– (4) b Callen	20
*K. J. Hughes c Graf b Callen	67	– (5) c Sacristani b Graf	130
G. R. Marsh c Watts b Bright	39	– (6) c and b Graf	42
K. H. MacLeay st Sacristani b Bright	23		
†R. W. Marsh c King b Graf	3	– (7) c Davies b Graf	23
B. Yardley not out	47	– (8) not out	9
T. G. Hogan c Sacristani b Callen	14	– (3) c Sacristani b Graf	17
D. K. Lillee c Sacristani b Bright	5		
T. M. Alderman c Taylor b Bright	4		
B 1, l-b 7, n-b 9	17	B 3, l-b 6, w 2, n-b 3	14

1/9 2/18 3/23 4/114   232   1/4 2/32 3/98   (7 wkts dec.) 358
5/142 6/145 7/163 8/202 9/221   4/216 5/310 6/328 7/358

Bowling: *First Innings*—Callen 21–3–69–3; Graf 23–9–53–4; King 9–2–44–0; Bright 28.5–12–43–3; Green 4–1–6–0. *Second Innings*—Callen 19–5–71–1; Graf 34.2–8–95–5; King 11–0–47–1; Bright 32–9–97–0; Green 4–0–17–0; Yallop 3–0–17–0.

Victoria

J. M. Wiener lbw b Alderman	35	– c Laird b Yardley	44
G. M. Watts b Alderman	25	– c R. W. Marsh b Alderman	56
*G. N. Yallop c Lillee b Alderman	84	– c Alderman b Yardley	58
P. J. Davies c R. W. Marsh b Alderman	3	– b Lillee	38
B. C. Green lbw b Alderman	10	– c Wood b Yardley	2
M. D. Taylor c R. W. Marsh b MacLeay	5	– not out	69
S. F. Graf c Alderman b MacLeay	9	– (8) c MacLeay b Alderman	24
R. J. Bright c R. W. Marsh b MacLeay	11	– (9) not out	6
†P. G. Sacristani not out	2	– (7) c Hogan b Yardley	6
P. D. King c R. W. Marsh b MacLeay	0		
I. W. Callen b MacLeay	0		
B 2, l-b 5, w 2, n-b 1	10	B 4, l-b 10, w 1, n-b 1	16

1/54 2/62 3/86 4/156   194   1/82 2/124 3/193 4/201   (7 wkts) 319
5/164 6/180 7/185 8/191 9/194   5/233 6/251 7/307

Bowling: *First Innings*—Lillee 20–10–29–0; Alderman 26–9–65–5; Yardley 13–2–42–0; MacLeay 15.5–5–26–5; Hogan 7–0–22–0. *Second Innings*—Lillee 27–6–88–1; Alderman 22–3–74–2; Yardley 28–10–75–4; MacLeay 21–5–51–0; Hogan 2–0–15–0.

Umpires: P. J. McConnell and D. G. Weser.

TASMANIA v QUEENSLAND

At Launceston, October 29, 30, 31, November 1. Drawn. Queensland 4 pts. With part of the first day lost to rain, it was not until late on the second that Chappell closed the Queensland innings. All Queensland's batsmen got a start, but only Border, Ritchie, Kerr and Wessels built reasonable scores. A full toss accounted for Wessels when he was staking a claim for a place in the Australian team. Tasmania's reply was a dogged effort which owed much to Smith and Woolley until Saunders led a rearguard action which only narrowly failed to bring them a first-innings lead.

Queensland

K. C. Wessels c Holding b Saunders	65	– b Blizzard	12
R. B. Kerr c Blizzard b Holding	59	– c Boon b Clough	12
*G. S. Chappell c Saunders b Holding	30		
A. R. Border b Blizzard	93	– not out	79
†R. B. Phillips c Smith b Mancell	15		
G. M. Ritchie c Woolley b Blizzard	67	– (3) b Mancell	46
H. Frei c Small b Blizzard	16		
A. B. Henschell st Woolley b Saunders	21	– (5) not out	0
T. V. Hohns not out	11		
C. G. Rackemann not out	16		
B 1, l-b 5, n-b 1	7	L-b 3	3

1/95 2/155 3/156 4/211   (8 wkts dec.) 400   1/15 2/27 3/152   (3 wkts) 152
5/318 6/339 7/357 8/377

J. N. Maguire did not bat.

Bowling: *First Innings*—Holding 33–9–93–2; Clough 31–5–83–0; Blizzard 17–2–75–3; Ray 5–0–23–0; Mancell 13–3–14–1; Saunders 30–4–105–2. *Second Innings*—Holding 4–0–12–0; Clough 13–1–33–1; Blizzard 9–2–24–1; Ray 13–0–51–0; Mancell 8–1–29–1.

Tasmania

D. A. Smith c Phillips b Rackemann	81	
M. Ray c Phillips b Rackemann	33	
D. C. Boon c Chappell b Henschell	16	
S. M. Small c Border b Henschell	0	
R. O. Butcher c Ritchie b Henschell	17	
*†R. D. Woolley c Border b Rackemann	80	
P. J. Mancell b Maguire	23	
S. L. Saunders not out	79	
M. A. Holding lbw b Rackemann	11	
P. A. Blizzard c Ritchie b Henschell	31	
P. M. Clough c Chappell b Henschell	4	
L-b 7, n-b 14	21	

1/58 2/98 3/98 4/124   396
5/208 6/248 7/286 8/312 9/367

Bowling: Rackemann 39–13–86–4; Frei 16–3–42–0; Maguire 33–11–73–1; Hohns 35–12–78–0; Henschell 34.2–10–82–5; Border 3–1–12–0; Chappell 4–3–2–0.

Umpires: M. Hull and S. G. Randell.

SOUTH AUSTRALIA v NEW SOUTH WALES

At Adelaide, November 6, 7, 8, 9. Drawn. New South Wales 4 pts. The game opened brightly with Darling playing fluently and Hookes making 65 from only 52 balls, an innings in which he was particularly severe on the leg-spin of Holland. South Australia's later batsmen fell to Lawson and Whitney, who made good use of the second new ball. McCosker's hundred, his first in Adelaide, was the foundation of the New South Wales reply, and Bennett shared with Whitney a last-wicket partnership of 45, which steered his side to a narrow first-innings lead. The remainder of the game was an anticlimax. Garner had remarkable match figures of 58–15–170–11.

South Australia

W. M. Darling c and b Whitney	98	– c Rixon b Whitney	5
W. B. Phillips c Smith b Lawson	8	– c McCosker b Lawson	15
A. M. J. Hilditch c Bennett b Lawson	59	– st Rixon b Holland	45
R. J. Inverarity lbw b Whitney	77	– c and b Holland	21
*D. W. Hookes lbw b Chappell	65	– c Bennett b Lawson	60
P. R. Sleep c McCosker b Lawson	52	– c Rixon b Whitney	7
†K. J. Wright b Whitney	0	– not out	49
C. L. Harms b Whitney	28	– c Chappell b Holland	11
J. Garner c Smith b Whitney	10	– not out	8
R. M. Hogg not out	3		
A. T. Sincock c Rixon b Lawson	8		
B 2, l-b 3, n-b 5	10	B 5, l-b 5, n-b 4	14

1/11 2/141 3/179 4/264   418   1/11 2/29 3/94   (7 wkts dec.) 235
5/365 6/366 7/372 8/396 9/407   4/101 5/130 6/192 7/225

Bowling: *First Innings*—Lawson 29.4–7–77–4; Whitney 32–3–133–5; Chappell 16–5–52–1; Holland 22–4–86–0; Bennett 18–7–60–0. *Second Innings*—Lawson 25–5–58–2; Whitney 21–7–62–2; Chappell 4–0–14–0; Holland 34–10–65–3; Bennett 4–1–22–0.

New South Wales

*R. B. McCosker c Harmes b Garner	116	– b Garner	30
J. Dyson c Hookes b Sincock	15	– not out	55
T. M. Chappell lbw b Garner	92	– lbw b Garner	0
S. B. Smith c Inverarity b Garner	2	– lbw b Garner	13
D. M. Wellham lbw b Sincock	75	– not out	6
P. M. Toohey c Hookes b Garner	24	– c Wright b Garner	16
†S. J. Rixon lbw b Garner	0		
M. J. Bennett not out	59		
G. F. Lawson lbw b Garner	0		
R. G. Holland c Inverarity b Garner	10		
M. R. Whitney b Inverarity	10		
B 2, l-b 8, w 1, n-b 11	22	L-b 2, n-b 1	3

1/69 2/184 3/186 4/317   425   1/65 2/65 3/89 4/105   (4 wkts) 123
5/329 6/341 7/356 8/356 9/380

Bowling: *First Innings*—Hogg 20–1–73–0; Garner 46–14–113–7; Sincock 21–3–69–2; Sleep 12–3–30–0; Inverarity 25.5–6–65–1; Harms 8–1–28–0; Hookes 7–0–25–0. *Second Innings*—Hogg 9–2–29–0; Garner 12–1–57–4; Sincock 1–0–13–0; Sleep 6–1–20–0; Inverarity 1–1–0–0; Darling 1–0–1–0.

Umpires: A. R. Crafter and B. E. Martin.

VICTORIA v TASMANIA

At St Kilda, Melbourne, November 12, 13, 14, 15. Drawn. Victoria 4 pts. Despite being troubled by a sore knee, Holding wrecked Victoria's first innings with a fine display of pace bowling. Tasmania, in reply, capitulated to McCurdy and Bright in undistinguished fashion. Victoria's second innings opened brightly, but once Yallop was dismissed it lost momentum, only Whatmore and Taylor providing any resistance. Although Tasmania were left eventually to score 344 in 373 minutes, rain caused most of the final day to be lost – a fitting conclusion perhaps to a contest in which each captain accused the other of "disgracefully slow play".

Victoria

J. M. Wiener c Small b Holding	4	– c Small b Clough 28
G. M. Watts c Faulkner b Holding	61	– c Woolley b Holding 2
*G. N. Yallop b Holding	8	– b Clough 47
D. F. Whatmore c Woolley b Holding	37	– c Ray b Mancell 74
M. D. Taylor c Woolley b Holding	13	– c Small b Holding 85
B. C. Green c Woolley b Mancell	45	– run out 7
S. F. Graf c Small b Mancell	22	– c Faulkner b Mancell 5
R. J. Bright c Butcher b Faulkner	9	– (9) not out 2
†P. G. Sacristani not out	18	
R. J. McCurdy b Mancell	0	– (8) c Woolley b Clough 6
I. W. Callen b Holding	8	– (10) not out 1
B 1, l-b 1, n-b 1	3	B 6, l-b 6, n-b 3 15

1/6 2/16 3/84 4/123	228	1/6 2/73 3/91	(8 wkts dec.) 272
5/124 6/177 7/197 8/203 9/211		4/245 5/250 6/260 7/261 8/268	

Bowling: *First Innings*—Holding 26.5–5–66–6; Clough 17–5–45–0; Faulkner 13–0–36–1; Saunders 13–4–38–0; Mancell 18–7–40–3; Ray 1–1–0–0. *Second Innings*—Holding 34–11–70–2; Clough 21–7–44–3; Faulkner 13–0–53–0; Saunders 12–0–30–0; Mancell 25–3–60–2.

Tasmania

D. A. Smith c Yallop b Bright	37	– c Yallop b Bright 19
M. Ray c Watts b Bright	33	– not out 12
D. C. Boon c Yallop b McCurdy	29	– not out 0
S. M. Small c Watts b Callen	2	
R. O. Butcher c Yallop b McCurdy	11	
*†R. D. Woolley c sub b McCurdy	7	
S. L. Saunders c Yallop b McCurdy	2	
P. Faulkner b Bright	2	
P. J. Mancell b Bright	5	
M. A. Holding b Bright	9	
P. M. Clough not out	1	
B 5, l-b 6, w 4, n-b 4	19	B 7, n-b 2 9

1/75 2/89 3/96 4/120	157	1/40	(1 wkt) 40
5/132 6/136 7/140 8/144 9/154			

Bowling: *First Innings*—Callen 17–2–34–1; McCurdy 22–7–52–4; Bright 28.5–12–38–5; Graf 10–2–14–0. *Second Innings*—Callen 6–1–21–0; McCurdy 5–1–10–0; Bright 0.4–0–0–1.

Umpires: R. V. Whitehead and R. C. Bailhache.

NEW SOUTH WALES v WESTERN AUSTRALIA

At Sydney, November 12, 13, 14, 15. New South Wales won by four wickets. New South Wales 12 pts, Western Australia 4 pts. Spin bowlers dominated a game in which batsmen seldom aspired to do much more than occupy the crease. On the first day Western Australia scored 240 for eight after 103 overs, a tempo which set the pattern for the game. Except for McCosker and Wellham, New South Wales showed little more enterprise when it came to their turn. Western Australia's second innings was no better than their first, so that New South Wales were left with ample time to score the 230 needed to win, and after a middle-order collapse had provided some anxious moments, Toohey steered them home.

Western Australia

B. M. Laird c Whitney b Bennett	55	– c Gordon b Bennett	13
S. C. Clements c McCosker b Gordon	20	– c Wellham b Bennett	45
G. Shipperd c Holland b Gordon	12	– c Gordon b Bennett	18
G. R. Marsh b Matthews	37	– b Matthews	17
*C. S. Serjeant st Rixon b Holland	16	– c Rixon b Chappell	18
K. H. MacLeay c Matthews b Bennett	26	– c Chappell b Bennett	26
A. L. Mann c Rixon b Whitney	34	– (8) b Whitney	8
†T. J. Zoehrer b Whitney	17	– (9) not out	27
T. G. Hogan not out	72	– (10) c Chappell b Bennett	6
D. L. Boyd st Rixon b Holland	21	– (11) b Holland	0
W. M. Clark c McCosker b Bennett	5	– (7) c McCosker b Matthews	0
L-b 5, w 2, n-b 5	12	B 8, l-b 7, n-b 4	19
	327		**197**

1/38 2/71 3/119 4/137   1/49 2/65 3/84 4/114
5/148 6/202 7/219 8/226 9/307   5/124 6/128 7/149 8/169 9/194

Bowling: *First Innings*—Whitney 27–7–68–2; Gordon 17–2–53–2; Chappell 5–1–12–0; Bennett 29.2–16–47–3; Holland 35–12–98–2; Matthews 22–8–37–1. *Second Innings*—Whitney 8–3–27–1; Gordon 6–3–16–0; Chappell 4–1–10–1; Bennett 36–23–39–5; Holland 44.4–22–59–1; Matthews 13–7–27–2.

New South Wales

*R. B. McCosker c Shipperd b Hogan	60	– lbw b Hogan	21
T. M. Chappell c Clements b Hogan	15	– c Zoehrer b Hogan	42
D. M. Wellham b Hogan	81	– c Laird b Mann	42
S. B. Smith lbw b Mann	1	– b Clark	40
P. M. Toohey run out	11	– not out	46
G. R. J. Matthews c Serjeant b Mann	4	– c Clements b Hogan	1
†S. J. Rixon c Serjeant b Hogan	19	– lbw b Clark	0
M. J. Bennett c Serjeant b Hogan	20	– not out	21
E. S. Gordon c Boyd b Hogan	1		
R. G. Holland lbw b Boyd	40		
M. R. Whitney not out	28		
B 5, l-b 3, w 1, n-b 6	15	B 2, l-b 7, n-b 8	17
	295	(6 wkts)	**230**

1/53 2/118 3/124 4/152   1/47 2/109 3/142 4/181
5/157 6/196 7/205 8/215 9/225   5/182 6/183

Bowling: *First Innings*—Boyd 9.3–1–43–1; MacLeay 15–3–29–0; Clark 3–0–10–0; Hogan 46–14–91–6; Mann 37–8–107–2. *Second Innings*—Boyd 5–1–14–0; MacLeay 11–2–34–0; Clark 9.4–0–38–2; Hogan 23–5–71–3; Mann 12–1–56–1.

Umpires: M. Jay and A. G. Marshall.

QUEENSLAND v VICTORIA

At Brisbane, November 19, 20, 21, 22. Queensland won by ten wickets. Queensland 16 pts. Victoria went to Brisbane having not won there for seventeen years, and a woeful start ensured that this unsuccessful sequence would continue. Rackemann crashed through their batting and, by the end of the first day, Queensland were almost ahead of them without the loss of a wicket. On the second day, Kerr, Wessels, Ritchie and Border built up a massive lead, whereafter the only question was whether or not Victoria could save the game. While Yallop and Wiener were together there was some chance that they would, but once they were separated the end was inevitable, with the leg-spinner, Hohns, joining forces with Rackemann to bowl them out.

Victoria

J. M. Wiener c Chappell b Rackemann	11	– c Kerr b Thomson	67
G. M. Watts c Border b Frei	16	– c Phillips b Frei	2
*G. N. Yallop c Phillips b Rackemann	20	– c Frei b Thomson	73
D. F. Whatmore c Hohns b Rackemann	26	– b Hohns	43
M. D. Taylor c Ritchie b Rackemann	2	– c Hohns b Rackemann	66
B. C. Green not out	37	– c Wessels b Frei	14
S. F. Graf b Thomson	5	– b Hohns	12
R. J. Bright b Rackemann	6	– c Phillips b Rackemann	0
†R. I. Templeton st Phillips b Henschell	0	– c Wessels b Rackemann	0
I. W. Callen run out	1	– not out	12
R. J. McCurdy run out	4	– c Border b Hohns	4
B 1, l-b 5, w 2, n-b 15	23	B 3, l-b 11, w 3, n-b 16	33

1/30 2/34 3/55 4/58   151   1/13 2/151 3/156 4/237   326
5/102 6/110 7/116 8/121 9/145   5/273 6/295 7/299 8/305 9/322

Bowling: *First Innings*—Thomson 13–6–24–1; Frei 8–2–30–1; Rackemann 17.3–5–38–5; Chappell 1–0–12–0; Henschell 7–3–24–1. *Second Innings*—Thomson 21–1–74–2; Frei 19–9–25–2; Rackemann 28–6–43–3; Chappell 7–1–23–0; Henschell 10–3–39–0; Hohns 32.3–10–89–3.

Queensland

K. C. Wessels c Templeton b Callen	86		
R. B. Kerr c Green b Bright	112		
G. M. Ritchie c Templeton b Bright	55		
*G. S. Chappell b Green	19		
A. B. Henschell c Green b Bright	6		
A. R. Border c Templeton b Wiener	99		
T. V. Hohns c Templeton b Callen	30	– (1) not out	10
†R. B. Phillips not out	5	– (2) not out	19
H. Frei b Wiener	0		
C. G. Rackemann not out	2		
L-b 12, w 5, n-b 18	35	L-b 2, w 1	3

1/160 2/241 3/270 4/287   (8 wkts dec.) 449   (no wkt) 32
5/296 6/425 7/447 8/447

J. R. Thomson did not bat.

Bowling: *First Innings*—Callen 28–6–105–2; McCurdy 25–3–93–0; Graf 26–6–77–0; Bright 39–11–102–3; Green 12–5–18–1; Wiener 3–0–19–2. *Second Innings*—Callen 2–0–13–0; Graf 2–0–9–0; Watts 1–0–3–0; Taylor 0.5–0–4–0.

Umpires: C. D. Timmins and J. T. C. Taylor.

TASMANIA v WESTERN AUSTRALIA

At Devonport, November 20, 21, 22, 23. Western Australia won by an innings and 119 runs. Western Australia 16 pts. With Western Australia near full strength, Tasmania were outplayed. Western Australia's batting proved to be far too strong, Hughes displaying his most scintillating style and Rodney Marsh recapturing form seldom seen in recent summers. The only batting successes for the home team were Saunders and Blizzard, who shared in a Tasmanian record eighth-wicket stand of 96 in the first innings, and Boon, who was unlucky to miss a century when Tasmania followed on.

Western Australia

G. M. Wood b Blizzard	20	
B. M. Laird b Holding	25	
G. Shipperd b Mancell	39	
*K. J. Hughes c Butcher b Clough	129	
†R. W. Marsh c Blizzard b Mancell	110	
G. R. Marsh c Boon b Mancell	37	
K. H. MacLeay not out	49	
B. Yardley b Blizzard	48	

D. L. Boyd run out	7
T. G. Hogan lbw b Holding	1
D. K. Lillee not out	22
B 5, l-b 10, w 2	17

1/29 2/58 3/173   (9 wkts dec.) 504
4/233 5/355 6/377
7/452 8/460 9/463

Bowling: Holding 43–12–114–2; Clough 29–3–85–1; Blizzard 35–6–118–2; Saunders 16–6–55–0; Mancell 21–2–78–3; Ray 13–3–37–0.

Tasmania

D. A. Smith c R. W. Marsh b Lillee	2	– run out	11
M. Ray lbw b Lillee	1	– b Hogan	17
D. C. Boon c R. W. Marsh b Boyd	4	– c Wood b Yardley	99
R. O. Butcher c Laird b Yardley	35	– c Laird b Hogan	4
S. J. Reid c R. W. Marsh b Yardley	10	– (6) c Wood b Yardley	0
*†R. D. Woolley c Shipperd b Yardley	20	– (7) c and b MacLeay	33
P. J. Mancell c R. W. Marsh b Yardley	6	– (9) run out	1
S. L. Saunders b MacLeay	58	– c Wood b Yardley	4
P. A. Blizzard lbw b Boyd	51	– (10) not out	2
M. A. Holding b Yardley	8	– (11) c Hogan b Yardley	0
P. M. Clough not out	0	– (5) c Wood b Yardley	2
W 1, n-b 5	6	B 3, l-b 4, n-b 4	11

1/2 2/8 3/12 4/53   201   1/29 2/35 3/54 4/97   184
5/58 6/82 7/93 8/189 9/193   5/97 6/169 7/179 8/180 9/182

Bowling: *First Innings*—Lillee 7–0–13–2; Boyd 19–2–64–2; MacLeay 18–5–48–1; Yardley 31.4–15–41–5; Hogan 23–12–29–0; Laird 1–1–0–0. *Second Innings*—Boyd 6–2–11–0; MacLeay 18–6–29–1; Yardley 44–24–68–5; Hogan 32–14–65–2.

Umpires: R. J. Marshall and S. G. Randell.

SOUTH AUSTRALIA v QUEENSLAND

At Adelaide, November 26, 27, 28, 29. Drawn. South Australia 4 pts. In one of the season's most exciting matches victory could easily have gone to either side. Both were below full strength, Queensland being without four Test players and South Australia, for much of the time, lacking Darling and Hilditch, who were both injured during the game. Fortunes fluctuated until South Australia were left with a final target of 176 runs to win, which, but for two run-outs, they might have achieved. As it was, they finished with their last pair together, still 18 runs short. Hilditch, nursing a broken jaw, had made a brave but unavailing return; Darling was absent in hospital. Hogg returned to his best bowling form, Haysman made a highly promising début, and Henschell scored a large proportion of Queensland's runs.

Queensland

R. B. Kerr c Inverarity b Hogg	16	– c Phillips b Hogg	48
A. B. Courtice c Wright b Hogg	25	– c Sleep b Hogg	0
W. R. Broad c Phillips b Hogg	32	– c Wright b Hogg	14
C. B. Smart st Wright b Sleep	34	– lbw b Hogg	0
A. B. Henschell c Haysman b Garner	71	– c Inverarity b Garner	162
R. J. Lawrence lbw b Garner	11	– lbw b Hogg	1
*T. V. Hohns b Garner	18	– c and b Harms	21
†R. B. Phillips lbw b Hogg	8	– c Sleep b Garner	50
H. Frei c Hogg b Garner	13	– b Hogg	2
S. Beattie not out	10	– lbw b Hogg	0
J. N. Maguire lbw b Hogg	2	– not out	0
B 10, l-b 9, n-b 8	27	B 1, l-b 3, n-b 7	11

1/35 2/84 3/91 4/169   267   1/0 2/24 3/24 4/181   309
5/206 6/214 7/232 8/249 9/260   5/189 6/214 7/302 8/307 9/309

Bowling: *First Innings*—Hogg 27.2–7–51–5; Garner 31–4–79–4; Johnston 7–1–26–0; Inverarity 16–4–38–0; Sleep 12–1–38–1; Harms 11–7–8–0. *Second Innings*—Hogg 18–3–53–7; Garner 23.4–5–63–2; Johnston 6–2–14–0; Inverarity 11–2–33–0; Sleep 21–3–89–0; Harms 12–2–46–1.

South Australia

W. M. Darling retired hurt	17		
W. B. Phillips c and b Hohns	92	– c Phillips b Maguire	30
R. J. Inverarity b Frei	8	– lbw b Frei	20
M. D. Haysman c Phillips b Hohns	126	– lbw b Maguire	9
P. R. Sleep c Henschell b Frei	23	– run out	18
*†K. J. Wright b Frei	52	– (1) c Broad b Maguire	0
C. L. Harms b Maguire	12	– (6) run out	42
D. A. Johnston c and b Hohns	43	– not out	15
J. Garner b Frei	12	– (7) c Smart b Maguire	13
R. M. Hogg not out	1	– not out	0
A. M. J. Hilditch absent injured	–	– (9) c Phillips b Broad	4
B 2, l-b 2, n-b 11	15	B 1, l-b 5, n-b 1	7

1/115 2/129 3/190 4/270   401   1/0 2/44 3/60 4/63   (8 wkts) 158
5/289 6/384 7/389 8/401   5/107 6/136 7/143 8/158

Bowling: *First Innings*—Maguire 39–11–127–1; Frei 35.1–8–106–4; Broad 4–0–17–0; Beattie 7–0–39–0; Hohns 27–6–51–3; Henschell 16–2–46–0. *Second Innings*—Maguire 28–5–70–4; Frei 21–4–64–1; Broad 7–2–17–1.

Umpires: A. R. Crafter and M. G. O'Connell.

WESTERN AUSTRALIA v QUEENSLAND

At Perth, December 3, 4, 5. Western Australia won by an innings and 93 runs. Western Australia 16 pts. Despite their four Test players being restored to the side, Queensland crumbled to a Western Australian attack which was without Lillee and Alderman. After Wessels had been out to the third ball of the game, Clark and MacLeay ran through the rest of the innings, Queensland being all out shortly after lunch for their second-lowest Shield score ever. To show that the pitch was not to blame for this, Laird and Wood then made 134 in 202 minutes. Wood's 138 took him eight hours. In their second innings Queensland again played ineptly, with the notable exception of Wessels.

Queensland

K. C. Wessels c R. W. Marsh b Boyd	0	– c Laird b Hogan	128
R. B. Kerr c Laird b Clark	7	– c MacLeay b Boyd	13
A. R. Border c R. W. Marsh b Clark	1	– c Shipperd b Yardley	23
*G. S. Chappell c Hogan b MacLeay	19	– c Shipperd b MacLeay	28
G. M. Ritchie c R. W. Marsh b Clark	5	– c Laird b MacLeay	5
A. B. Henschell c R. W. Marsh b MacLeay	1	– (9) c Hughes b Hogan	0
T. V. Hohns not out	10	– (6) c and b Yardley	5
†R. B. Phillips b MacLeay	1	– (7) c R. W. Marsh b Clark	1
H. Frei c R. W. Marsh b Clark	4	– (8) c G. R. Marsh b Hogan	18
J. R. Thomson b MacLeay	0	– c MacLeay b Hogan	22
J. N. Maguire c Boyd b MacLeay	0	– not out	7
L-b 1, n-b 3	4	L-b 6, n-b 5	11

1/0 2/6 3/21 4/34   52   1/32 2/77 3/133 4/141   261
5/36 6/42 7/44 8/51 9/52   5/162 6/169 7/219 8/227 9/232

Bowling: *First Innings*—Boyd 8–4–15–1; Clark 14–7–21–4; MacLeay 6.4–1–12–5. *Second Innings*—Boyd 12–0–44–1; Clark 12–2–34–1; MacLeay 18–5–55–2; Yardley 32–8–93–2; Hogan 11–2–24–4.

Western Australia

B. M. Laird c Henschell b Hohns	84	T. G. Hogan c Frei b Thomson	7
G. M. Wood c Phillips b Chappell	138	D. L. Boyd c Ritchie b Frei	3
G. Shipperd c Phillips b Frei	44	W. M. Clark not out	4
*K. J. Hughes c Henschell b Maguire	29	B 2, l-b 5, n-b 6	13
G. R. Marsh c Phillips b Chappell	45		
†R. W. Marsh c sub b Chappell	8	1/134 2/217 3/273	406
B. Yardley c Wessels b Frei	27	4/336 5/360 6/361	
K. H. MacLeay b Frei	4	7/388 8/399 9/401	

Bowling: Thomson 24–6–76–1; Frei 29.1–5–69–4; Maguire 19–3–46–1; Chappell 15–3–31–3; Hohns 49–16–122–1; Henschell 35–18–49–0.

Umpires: P. J. McConnell and D. G. Weser.

NEW SOUTH WALES v SOUTH AUSTRALIA

At Sydney, December 3, 4, 5, 6. South Australia won by 107 runs. South Australia 16 pts. Whereas spin bowlers had dominated the previous game at the Sydney Cricket Ground, this time the wicket favoured pace, with Hogg and Garner of South Australia marginally more effective than Pascoe and Whitney. For South Australia, Phillips was in his most dashing form, while Inverarity's patient hundred, the 26th of his career, was several times prolonged by poor catching.

South Australia

I. R. McLean c McCosker b Pascoe	0	– c Toohey b Pascoe	5
W. B. Phillips c Bennett b Pascoe	112	– c and b Whitney	54
P. R. Sleep c Rixon b Pascoe	2	– c Rixon b Whitney	13
R. J. Inverarity c McCosker b Bennett	104	– (6) not out	46
*D. W. Hookes b Whitney	35	– (4) c Toohey b Whitney	42
†K. J. Wright c Bennett b Whitney	0	– (7) not out	49
M. D. Haysman c Chappell b Pascoe	45	– (5) b Whitney	6
C. L. Harms b Pascoe	3		
J. Garner c Smith b Bennett	22		
D. A. Johnston not out	0		
L-b 4, n-b 8	12	B 2, n-b 6	8

1/1 2/16 3/161 4/209   (9 wkts dec.) 335   1/54 2/67 3/78   (5 wkts dec.) 223
5/209 6/291 7/301 8/327 9/335   4/110 5/125

R. M. Hogg did not bat.

Bowling: *First Innings*—Pascoe 28–5–99–5; Whitney 25–3–92–2; Spring 33–9–76–0; Bennett 10.5–6–34–2; Holland 11–7–16–0; Chappell 2–1–6–0. *Second Innings*—Pascoe 12–3–44–1; Whitney 20–6–70–4; Spring 6–1–23–0; Bennett 7–0–27–0; Holland 22–4–51–0.

New South Wales

*R. B. McCosker c Hookes b Johnston	67	– lbw b Hogg	5
T. M. Chappell c Hookes b Garner	37	– lbw b Garner	5
D. M. Wellham c Wright b Garner	55	– run out	11
P. M. Toohey c Hookes b Garner	0	– c Johnston b Garner	14
S. B. Smith c Inverarity b Hogg	65	– b Sleep	32
G. Spring c Haysman b Hogg	1	– (7) c Haysman b Garner	10
†S. J. Rixon c Haysman b Hogg	11	– (8) c Hookes b Garner	52
M. J. Bennett lbw b Garner	31	– (6) c Phillips b Garner	6
L. S. Pascoe c Wright b Hogg	5	– c Hookes b Hogg	5
R. G. Holland b Sleep	1	– b Garner	0
M. R. Whitney not out	0	– not out	0
B 2, l-b 9, n-b 13	24	B 8, l-b 1, w 1, n-b 4	14

1/77 2/148 3/154 4/223   297   1/11 2/13 3/47 4/50   154
5/241 6/249 7/260 8/280 9/293   5/86 6/86 7/131 8/140 9/149

Bowling: *First Innings*—Hogg 32–6–90–4; Garner 39–18–61–4; Johnston 26–8–47–1; Sleep 12–2–34–1; Harms 5–1–13–0; Inverarity 12–2–28–0. *Second Innings*—Hogg 15–4–42–2; Garner 20.1–7–70–6; Sleep 5–1–16–1; Hookes 1–0–12–0.

Umpires: R. A. French and A. G. Marshall.

QUEENSLAND v TASMANIA

At Brisbane, December 10, 11, 12, 13. Drawn. Tasmania 4 pts. In a rain-affected game Tasmania did well to take first-innings points, even allowing for the fact that Queensland were without their Test men. In their first innings Tasmania were rescued by sensible batting from Boon and Reid and the big hitting of Holding. Apart from Ritchie and Hohns, Queensland's batsmen found it hard going against the pace of Holding and of Clough, who was warned for over-use of the bouncer. When Tasmania batted a second time, Boon was heading for his second hundred in the match when rain brought an early finish.

Tasmania

I. R. Beven b Frei	1	– b Broad	39
D. A. Smith c Frei b Maguire	1	– c Broad b Maguire	6
D. C. Boon c Broad b Maguire	115	– not out	57
R. O. Butcher c Mainhardt b Maguire	15	– not out	21
S. J. Reid b Hohns	54		
*†R. D. Woolley c Gaskell b Hohns	7		
S. L. Saunders b Frei	17		
P. J. Mancell c Phillips b Maguire	8		
P. A. Blizzard b Henschell	7		
M. A. Holding not out	47		
P. M. Clough c Phillips b Hohns	4		
B 3, l-b 5, w 2, n-b 10	20	W 1, n-b 3	4

1/3 2/5 3/33 4/125   296   1/11 2/95   (2 wkts) 127
5/133 6/172 7/206 8/232 9/247

Bowling: *First Innings*—Maguire 34–10–93–4; Frei 28–7–66–2; Mainhardt 13–2–40–0; Henschell 17–6–51–1; Hohns 26.1–15–26–3. *Second Innings*—Maguire 6–1–12–1; Frei 10–5–25–0; Mainhardt 13–2–38–0; Henschell 16–6–26–0; Broad 10–2–22–1.

Queensland

R. B. Kerr c Boon b Blizzard	0	H. Frei c Clough b Beven	41
A. B. Courtice c Beven b Holding	9	J. N. Maguire b Blizzard	10
W. R. Broad c Butcher b Blizzard	16	M. S. Mainhardt not out	0
G. M. Ritchie run out	60		
*T. V. Hohns b Holding	66	B 1, l-b 9, w 2, n-b 2	14
M. A. Gaskell c Woolley b Clough	10		
A. B. Henschell c Woolley b Holding	10	1/0 2/26 3/28 4/61	242
†R. B. Phillips b Saunders	6	5/85 6/140 7/156 8/217 9/242	

Bowling: Holding 25–8–56–3; Blizzard 18.1–6–48–3; Clough 17–2–42–1; Mancell 8–3–10–0; Saunders 19–5–60–1; Beven 3–1–12–1.

Umpires: C. D. Timmins and A. Fulwood.

WESTERN AUSTRALIA v SOUTH AUSTRALIA

At Perth, December 17, 18, 19, 20. Drawn. Western Australia 4 pts. After much good cricket earlier in the match, Western Australia made little effort to score the 352 they were set to make in five hours. When bad light halted play, with eight overs remaining, they had no chance of victory and South Australia were being held up by Laird, who had batted 269 minutes for his 88 not out. The slow tempo of the final day was in marked contrast to much that had gone before. For the third time in the season Hookes scored a century in a session of play, his 146 coming off only 140 balls. It was an innings played in 37°C heat and, with Harris, he added 215 runs in only 148 minutes. Lillee returned to Western Australia's side, a fact all the more remarkable considering it was only 24 days after an operation on his right knee. Hughes contributed another fine century and, with Geoff Marsh and Yardley, was instrumental in securing a first-innings lead for Western Australia.

South Australia

K. P. Harris c Yardley b Hogan	22	– lbw b Clark	74
W. B. Phillips lbw b Lillee	58	– c R. W. Marsh b Clark	10
R. J. Inverarity lbw b Lillee	8	– c R. W. Marsh b Clark	0
*D. W. Hookes c Clark b Lillee	10	– c Hogan b MacLeay	146
M. D. Haysman c Shipperd b Clark	71	– c R. W. Marsh b Clark	53
G. A. Bishop c R. W. Marsh b Yardley	9	– c R. W. Marsh b Clark	31
†K. J. Wright c R. W. Marsh b Lillee	64	– c and b MacLeay	22
C. L. Harms c R. W. Marsh b Clark	14	– not out	30
D. A. Johnston c MacLeay b Clark	2	– not out	2
J. Garner c and b Clark	6		
R. M. Hogg not out	0		
B 5, l-b 4, w 2, n-b 13	24	L-b 10, w 3, n-b 6	19

1/56 2/97 3/102 4/111   288   1/17 2/17 3/232   (7 wkts dec.) 387
5/120 6/225 7/266 8/270 9/281   4/253 5/327 6/330 7/383

Bowling: First Innings—Lillee 25–6–72–4; Clark 22.4–4–47–4; MacLeay 15–4–56–0; Hogan 25–9–48–1; Yardley 26–15–41–1. *Second Innings*—Lillee 12–0–58–0; Clark 33–2–125–5; MacLeay 13–2–82–2; Hogan 35–2–103–0.

Western Australia

G. M. Wood c Phillips b Garner	0	– lbw b Hogg	4
B. M. Laird c Phillips b Johnston	13	– not out	88
G. Shipperd c Wright b Garner	9	– b Garner	5
*K. J. Hughes c Wright b Hogg	123	– c Hookes b Inverarity	38
G. R. Marsh c Wright b Hogg	54	– c Wright b Garner	25
K. H. MacLeay c Wright b Hogg	0	– c Wright b Garner	0
†R. W. Marsh c Haysman b Johnston	8	– c Phillips b Garner	28
T. G. Hogan c Wright b Hogg	3	– not out	8
B. Yardley b Garner	65		
W. M. Clark c Wright b Hogg	9		
D. K. Lillee not out	4		
B 9, l-b 17, n-b 10	36	L-b 9, w 1, n-b 3	13

1/1 2/20 3/48 4/156   324   1/9 2/22 3/86   (6 wkts) 209
5/168 6/195 7/300 8/304 9/307   4/147 5/147 6/198

Bowling: First Innings—Garner 32–11–87–3; Hogg 25.5–4–88–5; Johnston 21–3–72–2; Inverarity 10–3–16–0; Harms 4–0–25–0. *Second Innings*—Garner 23–11–43–4; Hogg 10–1–27–1; Johnston 8–3–13–0; Inverarity 31–11–72–1; Harms 9–4–23–0; Hookes 3–0–18–0.

Umpires: P. J. McConnell and A. Claydon.

NEW SOUTH WALES v VICTORIA

At Newcastle, December 18, 19, 20, 21. Drawn. New South Wales 4 pts. In their first innings New South Wales again owed much to McCosker and Wellham, who added 181 together for the third wicket out of a total that was to prove more than adequate when Victoria could make nothing of the bowling of Lawson and Bennett. Not since 1906-07 had Victoria been bowled out for as few as 90 by New South Wales. When they followed on, their batting showed remarkable improvement and they quite comfortably saved the game. The form of their relatively inexperienced middle-order players, Taylor, Jones and Miles, was encouraging.

New South Wales

*R. B. McCosker c McCurdy b Bright	124	– not out		66
J. Dyson c Wiener b McCurdy	4	– lbw b McCurdy		18
T. M. Chappell b Callen	7			
D. M. Wellham run out	88	– b Callen		9
S. B. Smith c Miles b Balcam	0	– st Miles b Bright		14
P. M. Toohey c Miles b Callen	28	– (3) b Callen		0
†S. J. Rixon b Callen	20	– (6) not out		25
M. J. Bennett c Miles b Balcam	4			
G. F. Lawson not out	16			
L. S. Pascoe c Miles b Balcam	0			
B 3, l-b 5, w 3, n-b 14	25	B 4, l-b 6, n-b 8		18

1/16 2/48 3/229 4/238   (9 wkts dec.) 316   1/29 2/35 3/51   (4 wkts) 150
5/248 6/287 7/293 8/309   4/95

M. R. Whitney did not bat.

Bowling: *First Innings*—Callen 28–5–81–3; McCurdy 17–1–56–1; Balcam 23–5–59–3; Bright 26–2–74–1; Wiener 1–0–4–0; Jones 5–1–17–0. *Second Innings*—Callen 11–0–36–2; McCurdy 3–0–26–1; Balcam 7–2–26–0; Bright 9–4–22–1; Wiener 3–0–7–0; Yallop 1–0–10–0; Whatmore 1–0–1–0; Taylor 1–0–4–0.

Victoria

J. M. Wiener c and b Pascoe	5	– c Rixon b Lawson		26
G. F. Richardson b Lawson	3	– c and b Chappell		46
*G. N. Yallop b Whitney	15	– c Lawson b Chappell		38
D. F. Whatmore c and b Bennett	16	– c McCosker b Bennett		22
M. D. Taylor c Smith b Bennett	21	– lbw b Lawson		94
D. M. Jones c McCosker b Bennett	8	– c Chappell b Bennett		94
†G. J. Miles c and b Lawson	7	– lbw b Lawson		75
R. J. Bright b Lawson	5	– not out		64
L. F. Balcam b Bennett	3	– not out		1
I. W. Callen not out	0			
R. J. McCurdy c Dyson b Lawson	0			
L-b 1, w 5, n-b 1	7	B 1, l-b 12, w 1, n-b 5		19

1/8 2/16 3/40 4/58   90   1/45 2/110 3/113   (7 wkts dec.) 479
5/72 6/75 7/87 8/90 9/90   4/160 5/284 6/396 7/430

Bowling: *First Innings*—Lawson 15.2–6–36–4; Pascoe 9–2–16–1; Whitney 8–2–22–1; Bennett 14–10–9–4. *Second Innings*—Lawson 40–5–120–3; Pascoe 34–3–123–0; Whitney 24–6–94–0; Bennett 47–18–97–2; Chappell 10–3–17–2; McCosker 2–0–9–0.

Umpires: R. A. French and A. G. Marshall.

TASMANIA v SOUTH AUSTRALIA

At Launceston, December 31, January 1, 2, 3. Drawn. South Australia 4 pts. Rain spoilt a match in which first-innings points were won by South Australia because, in the conditions, they had the more effective West Indian fast bowler. Garner's figures were his best in an excellent season.

South Australia

K. P. Harris c Boon b Holding	5	– not out	20
W. B. Phillips c Woolley b Clough	53	– c Butcher b Holding	13
A. M. J. Hilditch c Saunders b Beven	59	– c Woolley b Blizzard	26
R. J. Inverarity lbw b Blizzard	66		
M. D. Haysman c sub b Beven	29	– (4) not out	14
G. A. Bishop run out	55		
P. R. Sleep b Blizzard	13		
*†K. J. Wright not out	31		
D. A. Johnston b Blizzard	0		
J. Garner b Blizzard	0		
R. C. Christensen b Holding	0		
B 5, l-b 9, w 1, n-b 4	19	B 4, w 1	5

1/34 2/81 3/135 4/185   330   1/17 2/58   (2 wkts) 78
5/275 6/283 7/310 8/326 9/328

Bowling: *First Innings*—Holding 31–10–82–2; Blizzard 23–8–62–4; Clough 16–3–55–1; Saunders 12–0–63–0; Beven 27–14–49–2. *Second Innings*—Holding 7–1–25–1; Blizzard 12–2–34–1; Clough 2–0–5–0; Saunders 3–0–9–0.

Tasmania

D. A. Smith c Hilditch b Garner	40	S. L. Saunders b Garner		11
I. R. Beven c Harris b Garner	0	P. A. Blizzard c Hilditch b Garner		2
D. C. Boon c Wright b Garner	28	M. A. Holding c Bishop b Garner		0
S. M. Small c Johnston b Inverarity	36	P. M. Clough not out		2
R. O. Butcher b Inverarity	51	L-b 5, n-b 9		14
S. J. Reid c Wright b Christensen	55			
*†R. D. Woolley c Inverarity				
b Garner	27	1/0 2/76 3/81 4/159		266

5/182 6/216 7/234 8/264 9/264

Bowling: Christensen 14–3–37–1; Garner 33.1–16–78–7; Johnston 16–3–56–0; Inverarity 23–8–51–2; Sleep 3–0–30–0.

Umpires: R. J. Marshall and S. G. Randell.

QUEENSLAND v WESTERN AUSTRALIA

At Brisbane, January 8, 9, 10, 11. Drawn. Queensland 4 pts. The objective of neither side seemed to extend much beyond winning first-innings points. The fourth day began with this issue still in doubt. Queensland took more than nine hours to compile 394, Broad batting for almost five hours for 89. Western Australia's innings was played at an even more pedestrian tempo: Wood grafted for four hours for 74, Shipperd even longer for 64. Eventually Western Australia finished 18 behind on first innings. There were no fewer than 115 maiden overs in the match, virtually a full day of scoreless cricket.

Queensland

R. B. Kerr b Hogan	36	– c Mann b Clark	12
A. B. Courtice b Hogan	39	– b Hogan	22
G. M. Ritchie lbw b Hogan	12	– b Hogan	0
A. B. Henschell c Zoehrer b Boyd	44		
W. R. Broad lbw b Clark	89	– (4) st Zoehrer b Hogan	37
G. S. Trimble c Hogan b MacLeay	48	– (5) not out	5
*T. V. Hohns b Mann	21		
H. Frei c Wood b Mann	26		
†R. B. Phillips st Zoehrer b Hogan	56	– (6) not out	12
P. W. Twible not out	4		
J. N. Maguire c Wood b Hogan	3		
B 1, l-b 8, w 5, n-b 2	16	B 2, l-b 2	4

1/64 2/93 3/133 4/215   394   1/16 2/68 3/68 4/85   (4 wkts) 92
5/255 6/296 7/325 8/364 9/390

Bowling: *First Innings*—Boyd 19–3–75–1; Clark 35–11–76–1; MacLeay 33–6–72–1; Hogan 42.3–18–74–5; Mann 20–1–81–2. *Second Innings*—Boyd 8–1–26–0; Clark 7–4–8–1; Hogan 15–6–27–3; Mann 10–3–22–0; Clements 4–2–5–0.

Western Australia

*B. M. Laird c Phillips b Twible	26	T. G. Hogan lbw b Henschell		1
S. C. Clements c Ritchie b Frei	28	D. L. Boyd b Twible		12
G. M. Wood c Ritchie b Henschell	74	W. M. Clark not out		2
G. R. Marsh b Twible	28			
K. H. MacLeay c Trimble b Maguire	15	B 8, l-b 10, n-b 16		34
G. Shipperd b Henschell	64			
†T. J. Zoehrer b Henschell	36	1/59 2/60 3/140 4/172		376
A. L. Mann c Henschell b Frei	56	5/197 6/262 7/344 8/349 9/372		

Bowling: Maguire 29–8–66–1; Frei 37–16–75–2; Twible 31.4–10–82–3; Henschell 47–16–76–4; Hohns 24–10–43–0.

Umpires: C. D. Timmins and A. Fulwood.

TASMANIA v VICTORIA

At Devonport, January 8, 9, 10, 11. Drawn. Tasmania 4 pts. Holding, who had earlier taken eight Victorian wickets in Melbourne, now achieved even more spectacular results as, in their first innings, he brushed them aside. For a while Tasmania made little better progress when they batted, but, aided by an uncharacteristically patient innings from Clough (23 in 221 minutes), some good batting from Saunders, and Holding's aggression, their lead was eventually a useful 109. Victoria were making a better fist of their second innings when the weather intervened.

Victoria

J. M. Wiener b Blizzard	33	– lbw b Holding		6
G. F. Richardson c Boon b Holding	0	– not out		74
*G. N. Yallop c Woolley b Holding	23	– (4) c Saunders b Clough		13
D. F. Whatmore c Holding b Clough	24	– (5) not out		39
M. D. Taylor lbw b Blizzard	1			
D. M. Jones lbw b Holding	20			
†G. J. Miles b Holding	6	– (3) c Butcher b Holding		14
S. F. Graf c Ray b Holding	7			
R. J. Bright c Butcher b Holding	27			
I. W. Callen c Woolley b Holding	2			
R. J. McCurdy not out	4			
B 4, l-b 2	6	B 4, l-b 4		8
1/3 2/45 3/60 4/64	153	1/16 2/41 3/74	(3 wkts)	154
5/97 6/109 7/109 8/134 9/140				

Bowling: *First Innings*—Holding 22.5–5–59–7; Blizzard 15–3–46–2; Clough 14–3–42–1. *Second Innings*—Holding 29–7–79–2; Blizzard 14–6–17–0; Clough 19–6–35–1; Saunders 10–7–15–0; Ray 3–3–0–0.

Tasmania

D. A. Smith c Whatmore b Callen	0	S. L. Saunders not out		79
M. Ray c Miles b McCurdy	24	P. A. Blizzard c Miles b McCurdy		0
D. C. Boon c Whatmore b Callen	7	M. A. Holding c Richardson		
S. M. Small c Whatmore b Callen	31	b McCurdy		39
R. O. Butcher c Bright b McCurdy	31	B 4, l-b 5, w 1, n-b 12		22
S. J. Reid c Miles b McCurdy	2			
*†R. D. Woolley c Whatmore b Graf	35	1/1 2/20 3/23 4/68		262
P. M. Clough c Jones b Wiener	23	5/72 6/77 7/126 8/201 9/201		

Bowling: Callen 29–6–83–3; McCurdy 24.1–3–98–5; Graf 19–5–30–1; Bright 22–12–18–0; Wiener 6–3–11–1.

Umpires: R. J. Marshall and S. G. Randell.

VICTORIA v WESTERN AUSTRALIA

At Melbourne, January 14, 15, 16, 17. Drawn. Victoria 4 pts. Victoria's batting displayed new-found determination, so that an indifferent start was transformed into a very large total. The chief architect of recovery was Jones who, playing in only his fifth Shield game, batted for five and a half hours, hit 27 boundaries and was unlucky to be run out when going for his 200th run. Western Australia also started inauspiciously and, although MacLeay and Shipperd improved matters with a partnership of 155 for the fifth wicket, the follow-on was not avoided. MacLeay's century was his first in first-class cricket. Western Australia's second innings was little more than an exercise in playing out time, and it allowed Shipperd his second hundred of the season. Victoria's improvement was particularly timely in view of much local criticism of the team and of Yallop's leadership.

Victoria

J. M. Wiener c Wood b Hogan	60	R. J. Bright not out	44
G. F. Richardson c Zoehrer b Clark	1	I. W. Callen st Zoehrer b Mann	16
*G. N. Yallop c Laird b Clark	69	R. J. McCurdy not out	13
D. F. Whatmore c Marsh b Yardley	11	B 2, l-b 11, n-b 8	21
M. D. Taylor c MacLeay b Yardley	5		
D. M. Jones run out	199	1/5 2/121 3/145 4/151 (8 wkts dec.) 500	
†G. J. Miles c Shipperd b Yardley	61	5/151 6/367 7/448 8/482	

M. G. Hughes did not bat.

Bowling: Clark 48–15–113–2; MacLeay 23–6–64–0; Yardley 51–18–132–3; Hogan 40–12–102–1; Mann 15–0–63–1; Clements 1–0–5–0.

Western Australia

*B. M. Laird c Miles b McCurdy	30	– c Hughes b Bright	37
S. C. Clements c Whatmore b McCurdy	2	– c Miles b Hughes	33
G. M. Wood c McCurdy b Callen	30	– run out	28
G. R. Marsh b McCurdy	12	– lbw b Hughes	0
K. H. MacLeay c Miles b McCurdy	100	– b Bright	0
G. A. Shipperd c Callen b Bright	79	– c Miles b McCurdy	107
†T. J. Zoehrer c Jones b Bright	31	– not out	24
A. L. Mann c Miles b Callen	4	– not out	15
B. Yardley b McCurdy	11		
T. G. Hogan b Bright	30		
W. M. Clark not out	0		
B 1, l-b 8, w 1, n-b 9	19	L-b 5, w 1, n-b 3	9

1/14 2/72 3/72 4/73	336	1/49 2/96 3/166 4/169 (6 wkts) 265
5/228 6/270 7/278 8/289 9/333		5/221 6/231

Bowling: *First Innings*—Callen 27–4–87–2; McCurdy 28–5–94–5; Hughes 19–2–60–0; Bright 22.4–6–58–3; Wiener 7–1–18–0. *Second Innings*—Callen 5–1–28–0; McCurdy 21–4–72–1; Hughes 21–4–68–2; Bright 35–16–37–2; Wiener 13–5–23–0; Yallop 2–0–11–0; Jones 5–1–10–0; Whatmore 2–2–0–0; Taylor 2–0–7–0.

Umpires: R. V. Whitehead and A. Nicosia.

QUEENSLAND v NEW SOUTH WALES

At Brisbane, January 21, 22, 23, 24. New South Wales won by an innings and 5 runs. New South Wales 16 pts. Queensland were all out shortly after lunch on the first day, with only Kerr and Hohns saving them from a complete rout. By the close New South Wales were 148 for no wicket and well on the way to outright victory. Next day McCosker and Smith both made hundreds and, with Wellham and Matthews also making useful contributions, the declaration was made with a lead of 296. Although Queensland's innings was an improvement on their first, they failed to avoid an innings defeat early on the last day.

Queensland

R. B. Kerr b Matthews	49	– b Matthews	28
A. B. Courtice c Rixon b Skilbeck	0	– c Rixon b Whitney	74
W. R. Broad c Bennett b Whitney	9	– c McCosker b Matthews	4
G. M. Ritchie c Wellham b Whitney	0	– c Chappell b Matthews	1
A. B. Henschell c McCosker b Chappell	3	– run out	53
G. R. Trimble b Chappell	1	– c Holland b Whitney	10
*T. V. Hohns not out	31	– not out	54
†R. B. Phillips st Rixon b Holland	9	– lbw b Whitney	11
H. Frei c Skilbeck b Holland	1	– c Rixon b Whitney	20
P. W. Twible c McCosker b Holland	0	– c Rixon b Whitney	11
J. N. Maguire c Matthews b Whitney	5	– on international duty	
M. G. Maranta		– b Chappell	11
L-b 1, w 1	2	B 5, l-b 7, n-b 2	14

1/2 2/29 3/29 4/49	110	1/46 2/52 3/54 4/137	291
5/57 6/74 7/83 8/87 9/96		5/171 6/176 7/202 8/225 9/259	

Bowling: *First Innings*—Whitney 10.3–0–33–3; Skilbeck 7–1–21–1; Chappell 5–1–21–2; Matthews 13–7–17–1; Holland 11–6–16–3. *Second Innings*—Whitney 39–11–93–5; Skilbeck 6–1–16–0; Chappell 11.4–4–17–1; Matthews 29–8–65–3; Holland 37–17–53–0; Bennett 14–6–33–0.

New South Wales

*R. B. McCosker c Phillips b Maguire	112	G. R. J. Matthews not out	49
S. B. Smith c Frei b Henschell	119	L-b 10, w 1, n-b 3	14
T. M. Chappell b Frei	16		
D. M. Wellham c Phillips b Frei	93	1/218 2/255	(5 wkts dec.) 406
P. M. Toohey c Broad b Maguire	3	3/267 4/273 5/406	

†S. J. Rixon, M. J. Bennett, M. R. Whitney, A. J. Skilbeck and R. G. Holland did not bat.

Bowling: Maguire 29–5–80–2; Frei 30.2–5–98–2; Twible 20–4–73–0; Henschell 27–10–66–1; Hohns 28–4–70–0; Broad 2–0–5–0.

Maranta was permitted by the ACB to bat in Queensland's second innings in place of Maguire, who was selected mid-match to represent Australia in a one-day International.

Umpires: C. D. Timmins and A. Fulwood.

SOUTH AUSTRALIA v TASMANIA

At Adelaide, January 21, 22, 23, 24. Drawn. Tasmania 4 pts. In a game of fluctuating fortunes, Tasmania seemed comfortably in control for the first two days but were fighting to avoid defeat at the finish. After Clough and Holding had dismissed South Australia for only 148, Tasmania carefully built a useful lead, thanks largely to Boon and Butcher, who gave a glimpse of the form that eluded him for most of the season. When South Australia went in a second time 188 runs behind, Phillips and Hilditch soon knocked off the arrears. Phillips, in superb form, scored 161 off only 224 balls, while Hilditch, only recently recovered from a broken jaw, provided invaluable support. Wright's declaration left

Tasmania with 260 to make in 65 overs. After a promising start they were halted by Sleep, who produced his best bowling of the season.

South Australia

K. P. Harris c Woolley b Clough	21	– c Woolley b Blizzard	17
W. B. Phillips c Woolley b Holding	7	– c Clough b Saunders	161
A. M. J. Hilditch c Boon b Holding	0	– b Holding	109
R. J. Inverarity c Woolley b Clough	21	– (5) c Ray b Clough	51
M. D. Haysman c Woolley b Clough	21	– (6) lbw b Ray	54
G. A. Bishop lbw b Clough	19	– (4) run out	9
P. R. Sleep not out	28	– (8) not out	10
*†K. J. Wright c Ray b Clough	0	– (7) c Reid b Clough	10
J. Garner c and b Blizzard	17		
A. T. Sincock c Holding b Clough	2		
S. D. H. Parkinson b Holding	7		
B 3, w 1, n-b 1	5	B 3, l-b 19, n-b 4	26

1/10 2/10 3/47 4/66   **148**   1/59 2/257 3/284   (7 wkts dec.) **447**
5/77 6/102 7/102 8/129 9/135   4/323 5/410 6/429 7/447

Bowling: *First Innings*—Holding 16–3–52–3; Blizzard 9–0–38–1; Clough 16–3–53–6. *Second Innings*—Holding 31–7–98–1; Blizzard 26–8–70–1; Clough 30.3–1–107–2; Ray 22–3–70–1; Saunders 23–3–73–1; Reid 1–0–3–0.

Tasmania

D. A. Smith c and b Sincock	23	– c Wright b Sleep	72
M. Ray c Hilditch b Inverarity	36	– c and b Sleep	39
D. C. Boon lbw b Sincock	109	– (4) lbw b Inverarity	15
P. M. Clough run out	6		
S. M. Small c and b Sleep	27	– c Hilditch b Sleep	12
R. O. Butcher c Haysman b Sincock	53	– (3) c Phillips b Garner	3
S. J. Reid c Bishop b Inverarity	17	– (9) b Sleep	0
S. L. Saunders c Hilditch b Sincock	1	– (7) not out	27
*†R. D. Woolley lbw b Sincock	16	– b Inverarity	21
P. A. Blizzard c Inverarity b Sleep	9	– not out	0
M. A. Holding not out	16	– (8) c Bishop b Sleep	35
B 1, l-b 5, w 1, n-b 16	23	B 4, l-b 8, n-b 3	15

1/48 2/91 3/114 4/198   **336**   1/111 2/118 3/130   (8 wkts) **239**
5/250 6/275 7/277 8/310 9/310   4/146 5/170 6/182 7/227 8/230

Bowling: *First Innings*—Garner 23–10–44–0; Parkinson 21–4–58–0; Sincock 31–8–96–5; Inverarity 32–13–51–2; Sleep 20.4–5–64–2. *Second Innings*—Garner 25–4–63–1; Parkinson 6–0–25–0; Sincock 8–0–41–0; Inverarity 6–0–18–2; Sleep 20–4–77–5.

Umpires: M. G. O'Connell and B. E. Martin.

VICTORIA v NEW SOUTH WALES

At Melbourne, January 28, 29, 30, 31. Drawn. New South Wales 4 pts. A well-timed declaration by McCosker and some spirited batting by Yallop, Taylor and Jones enabled both sides to come close to victory. On the first day Smith and Toohey added 251 in only 179 minutes for New South Wales's fourth wicket, Smith scoring 116 in the final two-hour session. Even Toohey, in his best form, was overshadowed by the 21-year-old Smith. In reply to New South Wales's huge first-innings total, Victoria achieved respectability thanks to Yallop – who batted superbly despite being hampered by a torn calf muscle – and Taylor. McCosker did not enforce the follow-on, preferring to bat again and set Victoria 333 in 231 minutes and twenty overs for victory. It was to Victoria's credit that their run-chase was kept going until the second-last over of the match. On the final day Pascoe had to return to Sydney, owing to a family illness.

New South Wales

*R. B. McCosker c Miles b Hughes	6	– not out	66
S. B. Smith c Miles b Wiener	263	– b McCurdy	1
T. M. Chappell c Taylor b Graf	8	– c Bright b Hughes	22
D. M. Wellham b Hughes	56	– not out	72
P. M. Toohey c Miles b McCurdy	104		
G. R. J. Matthews not out	81		
†S. J. Rixon c Miles b Yallop	1		
M. J. Bennett c Miles b Yallop	4		
R. G. Holland not out	5		
B 11, l-b 14, n-b 9	34	L-b 1, w 1, n-b 3	5

1/11 2/37 3/160 4/411 (7 wkts dec.) 562 1/13 2/48 (2 wkts dec.) 166
5/509 6/528 7/540

L. S. Pascoe and M. R. Whitney did not bat.

Bowling: *First Innings*—McCurdy 20–2–88–1; Hughes 35–5–136–2; Bright 35–6–141–0; Jones 8–0–43–0; Graf 4–3–8–1; Wiener 17–3–66–1; Yallop 8–0–36–2; Whatmore 2–0–10–0. *Second Innings*—McCurdy 17–2–87–1; Hughes 13–1–51–1; Bright 4–0–20–0; Jones 1–0–3–0.

Victoria

J. M. Wiener b Whitney	1	– b Whitney	0
G. F. Richardson b Pascoe	5	– c Rixon b Holland	22
*G. N. Yallop c Holland b Pascoe	109	– b Bennett	86
D. F. Whatmore lbw b Pascoe	15	– c Whitney b Holland	7
M. D. Taylor run out	144	– c Whitney b Chappell	88
D. M. Jones c Pascoe b Bennett	37	– b Bennett	69
†G. J. Miles c and b Chappell	48	– lbw b Chappell	3
R. J. Bright c Rixon b Whitney	2	– lbw b Chappell	5
R. J. McCurdy c Whitney b Chappell	2	– not out	10
S. F. Graf b Chappell	4	– not out	1
M. G. Hughes not out	0		
B 8, l-b 11, n-b 10	29	B 10, l-b 12, w 1	23

1/1 2/41 3/89 4/185 396 1/1 2/42 3/74 4/176 (8 wkts) 314
5/301 6/375 7/379 8/391 9/394 5/274 6/291 7/291 8/299

Bowling: *First Innings*—Pascoe 28–3–98–3; Whitney 23–2–98–2; Chappell 17.1–5–40–3; Bennett 19–8–31–1; Matthews 18–3–60–0; Holland 23–14–40–0. *Second Innings*—Whitney 7–2–14–1; Chappell 21–3–87–3; Bennett 31–6–102–2; Matthews 4–0–14–0; Holland 23–5–74–2.

Umpires: R. C. Bailhache and R. C. Isherwood.

VICTORIA v SOUTH AUSTRALIA

At St Kilda, Melbourne, February 18, 19, 20. South Australia won by seven wickets. South Australia 16 pts. Once again Victoria surrendered all hope of victory with an inept batting performance in their first innings. South Australia were without Garner, but Hogg and Sleep bowled Victoria out for 132, 22 of which were extras. South Australia also fared badly until Hookes and Haysman added 264 for the fifth wicket and virtually settled the match. Hookes scored his runs in better than even time and did not seem inconvenienced by a broken thumb. Struggling to avoid outright defeat, the Victorian openers gave their side a sound start, but after that Yallop, in superlative form, fought a lone hand.

Victoria

G. M. Watts c Haysman b Hogg	13	– c Hookes b Hogg	57
G. F. Richardson c Wright b Hogg	7	– lbw b Inverarity	48
*G. N. Yallop b Sincock	18	– c Wright b Parkinson	168
M. D. Taylor c Wright b Sleep	15	– c Wright b Parkinson	13
D. M. Jones b Sleep	17	– run out	7
D. Shepherd c Hookes b Parkinson	17	– b Sincock	2
†G. J. Miles c Wright b Hogg	4	– c Wright b Sincock	8
R. J. Bright c Sincock b Hogg	16	– c Inverarity b Sincock	11
R. J. McCurdy c Hookes b Sleep	3	– c Wright b Hogg	4
M. G. Hughes not out	0	– not out	14
J. D. Higgs c and b Sleep	0	– c Wright b Parkinson	0
B 1, l-b 13, n-b 8	22	B 4, l-b 13, w 1, n-b 9	27

1/17 2/40 3/49 4/78   **132**   1/101 2/122 3/148 4/170   **359**
5/105 6/105 7/128 8/132 9/132   5/181 6/253 7/273 8/336 9/342

Bowling: *First Innings*—Hogg 12–2–31–4; Sincock 7–1–35–1; Sleep 10–3–29–4; Parkinson 5–1–15–1. *Second Innings*—Hogg 21–4–67–2; Sincock 21–4–73–3; Sleep 19–4–75–0; Parkinson 16.5–2–79–3; Inverarity 14–5–38–1.

South Australia

W. M. Darling c Bright b McCurdy	15	– c Jones b McCurdy	4
W. B. Phillips b Hughes	4	– b McCurdy	1
A. M. J. Hilditch c Watts b Hughes	2	– c Miles b Hughes	6
R. J. Inverarity lbw b McCurdy	0	– not out	15
*D. W. Hookes c Bright b McCurdy	193		
M. D. Haysman c Miles b Yallop	153	– (5) not out	10
P. R. Sleep c Jones b Bright	0		
†K. J. Wright b McCurdy	8		
A. T. Sincock not out	40		
R. M. Hogg b McCurdy	13		
S. D. H. Parkinson c Watts b McCurdy	0		
L-b 8, n-b 9	17	B 7, l-b 1, w 1, n-b 2	11

1/10 2/21 3/22 4/48   **445**   1/8 2/12 3/23   **(3 wkts) 47**
5/312 6/315 7/328 8/421 9/445

Bowling: *First Innings*—McCurdy 18.3–3–73–6; Hughes 16–0–98–2; Bright 27–1–102–1; Higgs 18–0–115–0; Yallop 11–1–40–1. *Second Innings*—McCurdy 6.3–1–21–2; Hughes 6–0–15–1.

Umpires: R. C. Bailhache and B. Guy.

NEW SOUTH WALES v QUEENSLAND

At Sydney, February 18, 19, 20, 21. New South Wales won by four wickets. New South Wales 16 pts. In an exciting finish, New South Wales won with fourteen balls to spare. They had been set 193 runs to make in 209 minutes and it was largely thanks to some mature cricket from Wellham that they succeeded. Earlier, Queensland's batting had been disappointingly uneven. Kerr played well in their first innings but it was really Border who enabled them to extend New South Wales until late on the fourth day. Wellham and Chappell added 253 for the fourth wicket in the first New South Wales innings and made useful runs again in the second.

Queensland

K. C. Wessels c and b Lawson	25	– c Rixon b Whitney	39
R. B. Kerr st Rixon b Bennett	72	– c Rixon b Pascoe	15
*G. S. Chappell c Dyson b Matthews	17	– c Lawson b Pascoe	29
A. R. Border b Pascoe	165	– c Bennett b Pascoe	47
G. M. Ritchie c and b Bennett	0	– c Rixon b Lawson	3
A. B. Henschell c Rixon b Lawson	10	– c Rixon b Whitney	4
T. V. Hohns b Lawson	38	– c Matthews b Lawson	4
†R. B. Phillips run out	23	– c Dyson b Matthews	9
H. Frei c Chappell b Lawson	1	– b Lawson	30
J. R. Thomson b Matthews	13	– b Lawson	0
J. N. Maguire not out	7	– not out	0
B 3, l-b 10, w 18	31	B 1, l-b 2, w 2, n-b 10	15

1/46 2/94 3/170 4/172   402   1/17 2/59 3/61 4/119   195
5/193 6/276 7/322 8/324 9/379   5/130 6/145 7/153 8/195 9/195

Bowling: *First Innings*—Lawson 36–6–102–4; Pascoe 17.3–1–60–1; Whitney 9–1–30–0; Matthews 25–5–63–2; Bennett 37–7–108–2; Chappell 4–2–8–0. *Second Innings*—Lawson 19–2–59–4; Pascoe 10.4–1–32–3; Whitney 16–4–40–2; Matthews 18–4–49–1.

New South Wales

*R. B. McCosker c Kerr b Thomson	8	– lbw b Maguire	9
J. Dyson c Ritchie b Hohns	35	– c Frei b Thomson	21
S. B. Smith c Kerr b Maguire	15	– c Ritchie b Thomson	18
D. M. Wellham c Phillips b Maguire	124	– not out	50
T. M. Chappell c Phillips b Maguire	132	– c Phillips b Thomson	35
G. R. J. Matthews not out	40	– c Phillips b Frei	15
†S. J. Rixon c Thomson b Hohns	18	– c Wessels b Maguire	10
M. J. Bennett not out	6	– not out	6
B 1, l-b 3, n-b 23	27	B 5, l-b 7, w 3, n-b 14	29

1/25 2/51 3/81   (6 wkts dec.) 405   1/28 2/65 3/65   (6 wkts) 193
4/334 5/341 6/379   4/131 5/170 6/184

G. F. Lawson, M. R. Whitney and L. S. Pascoe did not bat.

Bowling: *First Innings*—Thomson 25–7–70–1; Frei 23–5–61–0; Maguire 30–8–93–3; Chappell 1–0–1–0; Henschell 12–1–43–0; Hohns 32–8–101–2; Border 3–0–9–0. *Second Innings*—Thomson 11–4–26–3; Frei 7–0–28–1; Maguire 17–4–51–2; Chappell 9–1–43–0; Henschell 2–0–16–0.

Umpires: R. A. French and A. G. Marshall.

WESTERN AUSTRALIA v TASMANIA

At Perth, February 19, 20, 21, 22. Drawn. Western Australia 4 pts. A match which contained much very slow batting and, particularly in the second Tasmanian innings, some costly fielding lapses, none the less had a thrilling finish. At 115 for six, chasing 312, Tasmania's cause seemed lost. However, their later batsmen produced unexpected resistance. Only five overs were left when their ninth wicket fell and there was much excitement as Lillee bowled the last over to Clough. The fourth ball was snicked to Laird at slip but the catch was dropped and Tasmania survived. Of the game's 390 overs, 120 were maidens.

Western Australia

G. R. Marsh c Woolley b Clough	40	– c Woolley b Clough	30
B. M. Laird run out	21	– b Blizzard	72
G. M. Wood c Reid b Faulkner	7	– not out	53
*K. J. Hughes c Woolley b Blizzard	22	– b Blizzard	4
K. H. MacLeay c Ray b Faulkner	96	– c and b Blizzard	7
G. Shipperd c Woolley b Faulkner	47	– not out	33
†R. W. Marsh c Boon b Clough	52	– c Small b Blizzard	7
B. Yardley b Faulkner	4	– c Woolley b Clough	17
T. G. Hogan c Woolley b Blizzard	20		
D. K. Lillee c Woolley b Clough	5		
W. M. Clark not out	0		
B 1, l-b 5, w 1, n-b 8	15	B 1, l-b 11, w 5, n-b 2	19

1/55 2/67 3/84 4/112   329   1/74 2/125 3/134   (6 wkts dec.) 242
5/240 6/243 7/252 8/316 9/329   4/141 5/144 6/149

Bowling: *First Innings*—Clough 25–10–53–3; Blizzard 19.3–4–66–2; Faulkner 25–4–86–4; Ray 21–7–56–0; Saunders 11–2–53–0. *Second Innings*—Clough 18–5–49–2; Blizzard 27–5–70–4; Faulkner 10–0–56–0; Ray 19–2–48–0.

Tasmania

D. A. Smith lbw b Lillee	0	– c Hughes b Yardley	15
M. Ray c MacLeay b Clark	11	– lbw b Hogan	32
D. C. Boon c Wood b Yardley	59	– lbw b Lillee	11
S. M. Small c Hughes b Clark	2	– c and b Yardley	0
R. O. Butcher c MacLeay b Hogan	52	– c Hogan b Yardley	0
S. J. Reid c Laird b Yardley	8	– c MacLeay b Yardley	42
*†R. D. Woolley b Lillee	18	– b Lillee	18
S. L. Saunders b Yardley	47	– c R. W. Marsh b Clark	50
P. Faulkner c R. W. Marsh b Lillee	25	– c Hogan b Yardley	47
P. A. Blizzard c Laird b Hogan	4	– not out	46
P. M. Clough not out	0	– not out	0
B 9, l-b 9, n-b 16	34	B 3, l-b 5, w 1, n-b 3	12

1/4 2/49 3/67 4/112   260   1/25 2/59 3/64 4/114   (9 wkts) 273
5/157 6/177 7/177 8/242 9/260   5/114 6/115 7/163 8/181 9/268

Bowling: *First Innings*—Lillee 26–7–57–3; Clark 24–10–42–2; MacLeay 12–0–44–0; Yardley 31–18–34–3; Hogan 20–7–49–2. *Second Innings*—Lillee 27–13–45–2; Clark 14–5–37–1; MacLeay 6–3–8–0; Yardley 39–11–117–5; Hogan 16–7–54–1.

Umpires: P. J. McConnell and D. G. Weser.

VICTORIA v QUEENSLAND

At St Kilda, Melbourne, February 25, 26, 27, 28. Drawn. Queensland 4 pts. The game saw a succession of records established, but no prospect of an outright result. The bowlers would mostly prefer to forget it, only Thomson emerging with much credit. After the visitors had been sent in to bat, the first record to fall was that for Queensland's first wicket, Wessels and Kerr putting on 388, which was also a record for any Queensland wicket since they were admitted to the Sheffield Shield in 1927-28. Wessels scored 249 in 340 minutes off 285 balls (36 4s); Kerr hit 132 in 323 minutes off 252 balls (fifteen 4s). Border and Ritchie continued the demolition of the Victorian attack until the declaration was made at 536 for four. Victoria's innings was again dominated by Yallop, though on this occasion he received excellent support from Jones. Their even-time fifth-wicket partnership of 270 was only 1 short of the Victorian record. In making 246 Yallop batted for 495 minutes (27 4s) and in the course of his innings overtook W. H. Ponsford's record Shield aggregate established in 1927-28.

Queensland

K. C. Wessels c Jones b Yallop	249	– c Watts b Hughes	22
R. B. Kerr c Taylor b McCurdy	132	– c Miles b McCurdy	2
A. R. Border c Taylor b Hughes	80	– b Higgs	43
G. M. Ritchie b Hughes	58	– st Miles b Bright	37
A. B. Courtice not out	5	– c Miles b McCurdy	2
A. B. Henschell (did not bat)		– c Miles b Bright	28
*T. V. Hohns (did not bat)		– c Yallop b Higgs	6
†R. B. Phillips (did not bat)		– not out	18
H. Frei (did not bat)		– c Bright b McCurdy	15
J. N. Maguire (did not bat)		– not out	1
L-b 7, n-b 5	12	B 6, l-b 2, w 1, n-b 5	14

1/388 2/394 3/519 4/536　　　　　(4 wkts dec.) 536　　1/10 2/31 3/42 4/99　　(8 wkts) 188
　　　　　　　　　　　　　　　　　　　　　　　　5/112 6/147 7/154 8/176

J. R. Thomson did not bat.

Bowling: *First Innings*—McCurdy 20-1-127-1; Hughes 31.1-1-132-2; Higgs 20-2-90-0; Bright 26-5-77-0; Yallop 11-0-44-1; Green 7-0-35-0; Jones 4-0-19-0. *Second Innings*—McCurdy 16-4-37-3; Hughes 18-7-43-1; Higgs 10-1-24-2; Bright 22-6-61-2; Yallop 2-1-3-0; Watts 2-1-6-0.

Victoria

G. M. Watts c Frei b Thomson	19	M. G. Hughes c and b Hohns	0
G. F. Richardson c Phillips b Frei	9	R. J. McCurdy c and b Hohns	25
*G. N. Yallop c Ritchie b Thomson	246	J. D. Higgs c Wessels b Hohns	0
B. C. Green c Wessels b Thomson	22	L-b 6, n-b 17	23
M. C. Taylor c Ritchie b Thomson	20		
D. M. Jones run out	116	1/28 2/36 3/87	510
†G. J. Miles c and b Hohns	5	4/160 5/430 6/458	
R. J. Bright not out	25	7/462 8/462 9/510	

Bowling: Thomson 33-4-85-4; Maguire 29-4-104-0; Frei 19-4-86-1; Hohns 40.4-7-123-4; Henschell 33-4-89-0.

Umpires: R. C. Isherwood and A. Nicosia.

TASMANIA v NEW SOUTH WALES

At Hobart, February 25, 26, 27, 28. Drawn. Tasmania 4 pts. When the game began, it was thought necessary for New South Wales to win at least first-innings points if they were to reach the Sheffield Shield final. There was therefore considerable excitement as, with one wicket to spare, Tasmania denied the visitors this lead. Later it was discovered that under the new Shield rules New South Wales had already qualified for the final. Wellham, a model of reliability throughout the season, was again the most successful of the New South Wales batsmen. An unbeaten century by Woolley and a brave last-wicket partnership of 48 between him and Clough provided Tasmania with a first-innings lead of 21. Before bad light brought the game to a premature end, a hat-trick by Clough, involving Dyson, Smith and Chappell, was the highlight of New South Wales's second innings.

New South Wales

*R. B. McCosker c Saunders b Clough	13	– not out	65
J. Dyson c Woolley b Clough	22	– c Boon b Clough	14
S. B. Smith b Faulkner	3	– c Woolley b Clough	0
D. M. Wellham b Clough	76	– not out	6
T. M. Chappell c Reid b Saunders	12	– c Woolley b Clough	0
G. R. J. Matthews c Butcher b Allanby	24	– c Clough b Saunders	45
†S. J. Rixon c Butcher b Faulkner	28	– lbw b Saunders	17
M. J. Bennett not out	43		
L. S. Pascoe c Butcher b Saunders	15		
G. F. Lawson c Butcher b Clough	44		
M. R. Whitney b Clough	0		
L-b 13, w 5, n-b 3	21	B 5, l-b 4, n-b 8	17

1/20 2/41 3/102 4/147   311   1/38 2/38 3/40 4/128   (5 wkts) 164
5/170 6/204 7/206 8/265 9/310   5/156

Bowling: *First Innings*—Clough 37.4–10–80–5; Blizzard 21–3–68–0; Faulkner 27–5–78–2; Ray 16–4–32–0; Saunders 5–2–15–2; Allanby 6–1–17–1. *Second Innings*—Clough 24–8–43–3; Faulkner 17–5–37–0; Ray 4–1–4–0; Saunders 13–4–30–2; Allanby 9–2–33–0.

Tasmania

D. A. Smith b Lawson	56	P. Faulkner b Whitney	16
M. Ray c Rixon b Whitney	24	P. A. Blizzard c and b Pascoe	18
D. C. Boon c McCosker b Pascoe	8	P. M. Clough c Bennett b Whitney	10
N. J. Allanby b Matthews	32	L-b 8, w 1, n-b 10	19
R. O. Butcher c Dyson b Lawson	20		
S. L. Saunders b Pascoe	4	1/44 2/59 3/122	332
*†R. D. Woolley not out	111	4/130 5/145 6/165	
S. J. Reid c Lawson b Chappell	14	7/193 8/239 9/284	

Bowling: Lawson 35–8–89–2; Pascoe 23–3–74–3; Whitney 19.3–4–74–3; Chappell 4–0–14–1; Bennett 18–6–45–0; Matthews 8–4–17–1.

Umpires: R. J. Marshall and S. G. Randell.

SOUTH AUSTRALIA v WESTERN AUSTRALIA

At Adelaide, February 25, 26, 27, 28. Western Australia won by an innings and 17 runs. Western Australia 16 pts. The result proved crucial in deciding the finalists of the Shield competition. After playing much attractive cricket through the summer, South Australia now played very poorly. Western Australia's first innings of 430 virtually made them safe from defeat. Without Garner, back in the West Indies, the South Australian attack looked less menacing than usual. Parkinson, in only his second Shield game of the summer, was easily their most successful bowler. Having failed to avert the follow-on, South Australia did little better in their second innings. The game ended on a sour note when complaints were laid against Lillee for using abusive language as he left the ground. The Western Australian players rejected the report on the incident, whereupon the South Australian officials, in their turn, appealed. Ultimately Lillee received a fourteen-month suspended fine of £600.

Western Australia

B. M. Laird lbw b Hogg	6	T. G. Hogan c Wright b Parkinson	31
G. M. Wood c Hookes b Inverarity	111	D. K. Lillee c Wright b Parkinson	19
G. Shipperd lbw b Parkinson	56	W. M. Clark not out	4
*K. J. Hughes lbw b Parkinson	91	B 9, l-b 9, w 8, n-b 5	31
K. H. MacLeay lbw b Sincock	1		
W. Andrews c Wright b Parkinson	48	1/12 2/154 3/213	430
B. Yardley c Haysman b Parkinson	5	4/222 5/322 6/329	
†R. W. Marsh c Hogg b Parkinson	27	7/351 8/403 9/405	

Bowling: Hogg 31–2–96–1; Parkinson 27.5–3–98–7; Sincock 31–7–104–1; Inverarity 32–8–77–1; Sleep 3–1–12–0; Haysman 5–2–12–0.

South Australia

K. P. Harris lbw b Lillee	0	– c Wood b Yardley	17
W. B. Phillips c Wood b Yardley	42	– b Clark	10
A. M. J. Hilditch c Andrews b Hogan	20	– c Clark b Yardley	42
*D. W. Hookes b Hogan	32	– b Yardley	0
R. J. Inverarity b Yardley	37	– lbw b Lillee	18
M. D. Haysman c and b Lillee	34	– lbw b Lillee	59
P. R. Sleep lbw b Lillee	6	– c Shipperd b MacLeay	40
†K. J. Wright c Marsh b Yardley	1	– b Lillee	0
A. T. Sincock b Hogan	5	– lbw b Lillee	5
R. M. Hogg not out	17	– c sub b MacLeay	9
S. D. H. Parkinson c Laird b Hogan	0	– not out	3
B 3, l-b 3	6	B 3, l-b 6, w 1	10

1/0 2/35 3/93 4/134   200   1/14 2/45 3/84 4/88   213
5/134 6/144 7/149 8/158 9/199   5/106 6/192 7/192 8/201 9/204

Bowling: *First Innings*—Lillee 21–2–54–3; Clark 7–0–11–0; Hogan 14–4–59–4; Yardley 24–8–62–3; MacLeay 8–3–18–0. *Second Innings*—Lillee 19–10–29–4; Clark 19–6–36–1; Hogan 29–11–55–0; Yardley 25–3–71–3; MacLeay 3–1–5–2; Andrews 1–0–7–0.

Umpires: A. R. Crafter and B. E. Martin.

SHEFFIELD SHIELD FINAL

WESTERN AUSTRALIA v NEW SOUTH WALES

At Perth, March 4, 5, 6, 7, 8. New South Wales won by 54 runs. The inaugural Sheffield Shield final was played in Perth, where New South Wales had not won a game since 1965. It was a closely contested match in which the bowlers usually held the upper hand, and the late withdrawal of Lillee damaged Western Australia's chances. McCosker, who won the toss, and Dyson gave New South Wales an excellent start with an opening partnership of 110, easily the highest stand of the game. Thereafter, only Toohey looked likely to master a steady attack. Western Australia's chance of securing a first-innings lead disappeared when Hughes was bowled by Lawson. In a game mostly free from incident, an altercation between Rodney Marsh and Whitney led to the latter being fined £30 for "unseemly conduct". Batting a second time with a meagre lead, most of the New South Wales batsmen got a reasonable start but only Wellham passed 50. Western Australia needed 293 to win, and although Hughes and Rodney Marsh appeared at one stage to have given them a good chance of victory, their last six wickets fell for only 52 runs. Chappell's all-round form had as much as anything to do with his side's victory.

New South Wales

*R. B. McCosker c Boyd b Yardley	71	– lbw b MacLeay	44
J. Dyson c Shipperd b Yardley	57	– c R. W. Marsh b Yardley	10
S. B. Smith c Hughes b Yardley	3	– (6) c R. W. Marsh b Boyd	37
D. M. Wellham c Laird b MacLeay	6	– c R. W. Marsh b MacLeay	70
P. M. Toohey lbw b Clark	40	– c MacLeay b Clark	26
T. M. Chappell c Laird b Hogan	10	– (3) run out	33
G. R. J. Matthews lbw b Hogan	34	– c MacLeay b Boyd	24
M. J. Bennett c Wood b Yardley	10	– c R. W. Marsh b Clark	9
†S. J. Rixon c R. W. Marsh b Clark	20	– not out	10
G. F. Lawson not out	7	– b Clark	2
M. R. Whitney c G. R. Marsh b Clark	0	– run out	0
B 3, l-b 8, n-b 2	13	B 8, l-b 5, n-b 2	15

1/110 2/125 3/142 4/149   271   1/32 2/84 3/101 4/155   280
5/188 6/216 7/237 8/243 9/271   5/218 6/252 7/265 8/273 9/275

Bowling: *First Innings*—Boyd 12–3–51–0; Clark 24–4–42–3; MacLeay 22–7–45–1; Yardley 29–8–92–4; Hogan 16–7–28–2. *Second Innings*—Boyd 13.2–3–39–2; Clark 25–8–48–3; MacLeay 21–3–64–2; Yardley 28–5–81–1; Hogan 12–2–33–0.

Western Australia

G. M. Wood c Toohey b Whitney	45	– c Chappell b Lawson	0
B. M. Laird run out	24	– lbw b Whitney	15
G. Shipperd lbw b Lawson	10	– c Toohey b Lawson	48
*K. J. Hughes b Lawson	66	– c Toohey b Lawson	55
G. R. Marsh c Rixon b Chappell	32	– c Dyson b Chappell	18
†R. W. Marsh c Smith b Whitney	36	– b Dyson b Lawson	58
D. L. Boyd lbw b Whitney	16	– (10) not out	9
K. H. MacLeay c Rixon b Chappell	1	– (7) c Matthews b Chappell	24
B. Yardley not out	14	– (8) c Rixon b Chappell	4
T. G. Hogan lbw b Chappell	2	– (9) lbw b Lawson	0
W. M. Clark b Whitney	3	– c Whitney b Chappell	0
B 2, l-b 5, w 3	10	B 5, l-b 1, n-b 1	7

1/70 2/76 3/105 4/183   259   1/3 2/40 3/67 4/125   238
5/200 6/234 7/235 8/247 9/256   5/186 6/206 7/222 8/229 9/229

Bowling: *First Innings*—Lawson 22–6–58–2; Whitney 25.2–4–67–4; Chappell 16–5–32–3; Bennett 29–12–50–0; Matthews 20–9–42–0. *Second Innings*—Lawson 28–10–52–5; Whitney 18–4–45–1; Chappell 20.5–6–45–4; Bennett 22–9–39–0; Matthews 18–4–50–0.

Umpires: R. A. French and P. J. McConnell.

SHEFFIELD SHIELD WINNERS

1892-93	Victoria	1926-27	South Australia
1893-94	South Australia	1927-28	Victoria
1894-95	Victoria	1928-29	New South Wales
1895-96	New South Wales	1929-30	Victoria
1896-97	New South Wales	1930-31	Victoria
1897-98	Victoria	1931-32	New South Wales
1898-99	Victoria	1932-33	New South Wales
1899-1900	New South Wales	1933-34	Victoria
1900-01	Victoria	1934-35	Victoria
1901-02	New South Wales	1935-36	South Australia
1902-03	New South Wales	1936-37	Victoria
1903-04	New South Wales	1937-38	New South Wales
1904-05	New South Wales	1938-39	South Australia
1905-06	New South Wales	1939-40	New South Wales
1906-07	New South Wales	1940-46	No competition
1907-08	Victoria	1946-47	Victoria
1908-09	New South Wales	1947-48	Western Australia
1909-10	South Australia	1948-49	New South Wales
1910-11	New South Wales	1949-50	New South Wales
1911-12	New South Wales	1950-51	Victoria
1912-13	South Australia	1951-52	New South Wales
1913-14	New South Wales	1952-53	South Australia
1914-15	Victoria	1953-54	New South Wales
1915-19	No competition	1954-55	New South Wales
1919-20	New South Wales	1955-56	New South Wales
1920-21	New South Wales	1956-57	New South Wales
1921-22	Victoria	1957-58	New South Wales
1922-23	New South Wales	1958-59	New South Wales
1923-24	Victoria	1959-60	New South Wales
1924-25	Victoria	1960-61	New South Wales
1925-26	New South Wales	1961-62	New South Wales

1962-63	Victoria	1973-74	Victoria
1963-64	South Australia	1974-75	Western Australia
1964-65	New South Wales	1975-76	South Australia
1965-66	New South Wales	1976-77	Western Australia
1966-67	Victoria	1977-78	Western Australia
1967-68	Western Australia	1978-79	Victoria
1968-69	South Australia	1979-80	Victoria
1969-70	Victoria	1980-81	Western Australia
1970-71	South Australia	1981-82	South Australia
1971-72	Western Australia	1982-83	New South Wales
1972-73	Western Australia		

New South Wales have won the Shield 37 times, Victoria 24, South Australia 12, Western Australia 8, Queensland 0, Tasmania 0.

†McDONALD'S CUP, 1982-83

At Hobart, November 6. Queensland won by seven wickets. Tasmania 147 (D. C. Boon 53, R. D. Woolley 35; J. N. Maguire three for 26); Queensland 151 for three (K. C. Wessels 57, A. R. Border 56 not out).

At Hobart, November 7. Victoria won by 103 runs. Victoria 272 for two (J. M. Wiener 94, G. M. Watts 85, G. N. Yallop 42 not out); Tasmania 169 for seven (D. C. Boon 49, S. L. Saunders 43).

At Sydney, November 18. Western Australia won by six wickets. New South Wales 166 (S. J. Rixon 33; K. H. MacLeay four for 15, D. L. Boyd three for 23); Western Australia 167 for four (K. J. Hughes 36; T. M. Chappell three for 25).

At Sydney, December 8. New South Wales won by eight wickets. South Australia 195 for nine (P. R. Sleep 61, I. R. McLean 35, G. A. Bishop 32); New South Wales 197 for two (T. M. Chappell 75 not out, R. B. McCosker 58).

At Perth, December 22. Western Australia won by two wickets. South Australia 157 (D. W. Hookes 30; K. H. MacLeay three for 23, T. G. Hogan three for 25); Western Australia 158 for eight (B. M. Laird 58, R. W. Marsh 30; D. A. Johnston three for 35).

At Melbourne, January 1. Queensland won by 13 runs. Queensland 270 for five (A. B. Courtice 105, R. B. Kerr 86); Victoria 257 (J. M. Wiener 51, D. M. Jones 40, G. J. Miles 39; W. R. Broad three for 71).

Semi-Finals

At Perth, March 12. Western Australia won by three wickets. Victoria 112 (D. L. Boyd five for 15); Western Australia 115 for seven (R. W. Marsh 35 not out; S. F. Graf four for 15, I. W. Callen three for 28).

At Brisbane, March 13. New South Wales won by two wickets. Queensland 205 for nine (G. S. Chappell 71, G. M. Ritchie 69); New South Wales 206 for eight (S. B. Smith 59 not out, R. B. McCosker 40, S. J. Rixon 31; G. S. Chappell four for 35).

FINAL

Owing to rain, the final between New South Wales and Western Australia, which was to have been played in Sydney on March 20, was postponed until October 8, when it was played at Perth. Western Australia won by four wickets.
Man of the Match: K. J. Hughes.

New South Wales

*R. B. McCosker c Marsh b Boyd	21	†S. J. Rixon c Marsh b Clark	9
J. Dyson c Andrews b MacLeay	42	G. F. Lawson not out	5
T. M. Chappell c sub b Boyd	0	B 3, l-b 4, w 8, n-b 3	18
D. M. Wellham not out	65		
S. B. Smith c and b Hogan	11	1/50 2/56 3/91 (6 wkts, 50 overs)	195
P. M. Toohey c Laird b Hogan	24	4/118 5/158 6/172	

G. Spring, M. J. Bennett and M. R. Whitney did not bat.

Bowling: Lillee 10–1–38–0; Clark 10–0–36–1; Boyd 10–2–29–2; MacLeay 10–0–33–1; Hogan 10–1–41–2.

Western Australia

B. M. Laird c Spring b Lawson	10	K. H. MacLeay run out	0
G. M. Wood c Rixon b Bennett	30	D. L. Boyd not out	0
G. Shipperd lbw b Whitney	54	L-b 3, w 5	8
*K. J. Hughes b Lawson	61		
W. Andrews not out	22	1/13 2/68 3/133 (6 wkts, 49.1 overs)	198
†R. W. Marsh b Whitney	13	4/172 5/187 6/194	

T. G. Hogan, W. M. Clark and D. K. Lillee did not bat.

Bowling: Lawson 10–2–27–2; Spring 10–2–26–0; Whitney 9.1–0–35–2; Chappell 10–0–39–0; Bennett 10–0–63–1.

Umpires: P. J. McConnell and D. G. Weser.

KNOCKOUT COMPETITION WINNERS

Australasian Knockout

1969-70	New Zealand
1970-71	Western Australia
1971-72	Victoria
1972-73	New Zealand

McDonald's Cup

1979-80	Victoria
1980-81	Queensland
1981-82	Queensland
1982-83	Western Australia

Gillette Cup

1973-74	Western Australia
1974-75	New Zealand
1975-76	Queensland
1976-77	Western Australia
1977-78	Western Australia
1978-79	Tasmania

CRICKET IN SOUTH AFRICA, 1982-83

By PETER SICHEL

The South African season closed later than usual on account of two unscheduled tours. Firstly, a Sri Lankan side arrived in October for a hastily arranged tour embracing four Provincial games, which were given first-class status, and two unofficial "Tests". The tourists were by no means a powerful combination, lacking a bowler of anything above quite gentle medium-pace and also being short of reliable spinners with the ability to bowl tightly over long periods. To the full South African side they offered only token resistance.

The West Indian side, which followed the Sri Lankans, also had psychological problems to contend with by way of reprisal threats for having gone to South Africa. They, however, had enough players of Test experience to put up a show, and whilst not performing as well as they might have done they produced one or two good performances. The value of really fast bowling was demonstrated by Sylvester Clarke, whose five for 66 and seven for 34 in the Wanderers "Test", which Lawrence Rowe's side won, must have been one of the best exhibitions of its kind seen on the ground. Of the West Indian batsmen Collis King was the most exciting, his hundred in Johannesburg being the individual highlight of a tour which did much to stir enthusiasm for the game in the black townships.

Of the South Africans who played for their representative side, Jim Cook was outstanding, especially against the Sri Lankans off whom he scored at will. Graeme Pollock and Barry Richards played well against the West Indian fast bowling. Clive Rice and Peter Kirsten, however, were disappointing. Alan Kourie, although troubled by a groin injury, bowled his orthodox left-arm spin consistently accurately and also batted resolutely enough to be considered as perhaps South Africa's best current all-rounder. Vintcent van der Bijl, as usual, commanded respect, whilst Ray Jennings kept wicket well.

Domestically Transvaal swept all before them. Not only did they win the SAB Currie Cup, they did it most comprehensively. They also picked up all the main limited-overs competitions. The only competition they did not win was the SAB Bowl, in which their B team takes part. In this they were runners-up to Western Province. Transvaal were seldom under pressure, the exceptions being on the first day at Newlands over the New Year, when Western Province put them out for less than 200, and at the Wanderers when a premature declaration by Eastern Province let them off the hook. They also allowed Western Province to recover from a bad start at the Wanderers. For the rest, they had things all their own way.

Special mention should be made of Henry Fotheringham, who started the season in the Transvaal B side and earned promotion with two fine innings in his first match. From there he never looked back, finishing the season at the top of the national batting averages. It used to be said that he was a bad starter, but no evidence of this was discernible and he made his runs most attractively. Alvin Kallicharran and Kevin McKenzie also enjoyed good seasons. Such was McKenzie's success that he won a Springbok "cap" against the West Indies XI. Pollock had a poor Currie Cup season, averaging only 27.08 with the bat.

Western Province experienced mixed fortunes. There were times when they looked very good, others when they played poorly. Graham Gooch of Essex had a season of ups and downs and made two good hundreds. Laurence Seeff, technically sound, scored heavily against the Sri Lankans but fell away towards the end of the season. Kirsten, captaining the side, while not enjoying one of his better seasons did score a notable 168 in the Currie Cup Challenge Match against Transvaal. Western Province's younger players rose more than once to the occasion, especially Roy Pienaar and Paul Rayner. Richie Ryall was a promising wicket-keeper. Back trouble kept Garth le Roux out of several matches.

Natal, with so much talent, disappointed, recording only one outright victory during the season. In the Smith brothers, Chris and Robin, together with Brian Whitfield, they have three young batsmen of high potential. Barry Richards, in what was thought might be his last season, showed occasional glimpses of his best form. Mike Procter missed the greater part of the season through injury, though he had one great all-round match against Northern Transvaal. Most of all Natal missed the bowling of van der Bijl, their spearhead for so many seasons.

Both Northern Transvaal and Eastern Province remain enigmas. Often they appeared to be putting a good performance together, only to let things fall apart. Neither of them recorded a first-class victory. For Eastern Province, the two Northamptonshire players who had been in South Africa the previous season with the SAB English XI – Peter Willey and Wayne Larkins – averaged only 24 and 25 respectively. Robbie Armitage was again the sheet-anchor of the side. Dave Richardson, the Eastern Province wicket-keeper, besides his good form behind the stumps showed marked improvement as a batsman.

Over the season as a whole the bat dominated the ball, so much so that no fewer than 23 batsmen totalled over 500 runs and only two bowlers took ten wickets in a match. One disturbing aspect was the vast difference in strength between Transvaal and Western Province on the one hand and the three other sides in the Currie Cup. A wider spread of talent would make for a better competition.

FIRST-CLASS AVERAGES, 1982-83

BATTING

(Qualification: 500 runs, average 35)

	M	I	NO	R	HI	100s	Avge
H. R. Fotheringham (*Transvaal/Tvl B*).....	9	15	3	935	159*	2	77.91
K. Sharp (*Griqualand West*)...................	6	12	0	760	125	2	63.33
S. J. Cook (*Transvaal*).........................	13	21	2	1,142	201*	4	60.10
A. I. Kallicharran (*Transvaal*)................	11	17	1	822	151	2	51.37
K. A. McKenzie (*Transvaal*)..................	11	16	2	675	164*	1	48.21
R. G. Pollock (*Transvaal*).....................	13	19	2	818	197	2	48.11
K. S. McEwan (*W. Province*)..................	10	15	1	654	149	4	46.71
M. S. Venter (*Transvaal/Tvl B*)	8	15	3	556	132*	3	46.33
R. M. Bentley (*Natal/Natal B*).................	9	16	2	639	151	1	45.64
P. N. Kirsten (*W. Province*)...................	14	23	4	837	168	1	44.05
P. H. Rayner (*W. Province/W. Province B*)..	10	16	3	561	162	1	43.15
L. Seeff (*W. Province*)	10	19	3	671	188	2	41.93
D. Bestall (*Natal*)...............................	9	15	2	540	80*	0	41.53

	M	I	NO	R	HI	100s	Avge
B. J. Whitfield (*N. Transvaal/Natal*)	8	15	0	608	117	1	40.53
C. E. B. Rice (*Transvaal*)......................	14	19	3	644	104	1	40.25
G. A. Gooch (*W. Province*)	9	18	3	597	126	2	39.80
C. L. Smith (*Natal/Natal B*)	9	17	1	628	154	1	39.25
M. Yachad (*Transvaal B/N. Transvaal*)	8	15	1	531	102*	1	37.92
R. F. Pienaar (*W. Province/W. Province B*) .	12	18	1	633	112	2	37.23
B. A. Richards (*Natal*)...........................	11	17	1	590	123	1	36.87
D. J. Richardson (*E. Province*)...............	10	19	1	635	134	1	35.27

Signifies not out.

BOWLING

(Qualification: 25 wickets, average 30)

	R	W	Avge	5 W/i	BB
T. H. Parrymore (*Transvaal/Tvl B*)...............	420	26	16.15	0	4-8
G. M. Gower (*Border*)...........................	487	26	18.73	1	6-44
V. A. P. van der Bijl (*Transvaal*).................	976	52	18.76	1	7-42
T. G. Shaw (*E. Province/E. Province B*)	512	27	18.96	2	5-59
G. S. le Roux (*W. Province*)	907	46	19.71	3	6-55
E. J. Hodkinson (*Natal/Natal B*)	624	31	20.12	1	5-40
O. Henry (*W. Province/W. Province B*)..........	866	41	21.12	4	6-19
J. E. Emburey (*W. Province*)	785	36	21.80	3	6-33
R. W. Hanley (*Transvaal*)........................	671	30	22.36	2	5-41
A. J. Kourie (*Transvaal*)	1,501	63	23.82	5	7-79
S. T. Jefferies (*W. Province*)	1,386	58	23.89	3	6-91
W. K. Watson (*E. Province*)	770	32	24.06	2	7-50
C. D. Mitchley (*Transvaal/Tvl B*)................	690	28	24.64	1	5-39
L. B. Taylor (*Natal*)...............................	828	29	28.55	1	6-68
K. R. Cooper (*Natal*).............................	774	27	28.66	2	6-36

SPRINGBOK CAPS

The following players were awarded Springbok caps for representing South Africa in the two four-day matches against Arosa Sri Lanka: S. J. Cook (2), D. L. Hobson, S. T. Jefferies (2), R. V. Jennings (2), P. N. Kirsten (2), A. J. Kourie (2), A. P. Kuiper (2), G. S. le Roux (2), R. G. Pollock (2), C. E. B. Rice (2), B. A. Richards, L. Seeff, V. A. P. van der Bijl.

The following players were awarded Springbok caps for representing South Africa in the two four-day matches against the West Indies XI: S. J. Cook (2), S. T. Jefferies (2), R. V. Jennings (2), P. N. Kirsten (2), A. J. Kourie (2), G. S. le Roux (2), K. A. McKenzie (2), R. G. Pollock (2), C. E. B. Rice (2), B. A. Richards (2), V. A. P. van der Bijl (2).

SAB CURRIE CUP, 1982-83

	Played	Won	Lost	Drawn	Bonus Points Batting	Bonus Points Bowling	Total Points
Transvaal...........................	8	5	0	3	43	34	137
Western Province	8	5	1	3	30	35	115
Natal	8	1	2	5	28	31	69
Northern Transvaal.............	8	0	5	3	14	34	48
Eastern Province................	8	0	4	4	15	24	39

Transvaal and Western Province drew the Currie Cup Final at Johannesburg.

NORTHERN TRANSVAAL v NATAL

At Berea Park, Pretoria, November 12, 13, 15. Drawn. Northern Transvaal 6 pts, Natal 6 pts.

Northern Transvaal

B. J. Whitfield c Procter b Daniels	69	– c Daniels b Taylor	51
V. F. du Preez c A. J. S. Smith b Cooper	14	– lbw b Taylor	12
*L. J. Barnard b Taylor	6	– lbw b Cooper	12
C. S. Stirk c Richards b Lever	32	– c A. J. S. Smith b Taylor	7
†N. T. Day b Daniels	36	– not out	61
A. M. Ferreira c A. J. S. Smith b Taylor	49	– c and b Daniels	48
P. J. A. Visagie run out	0	– not out	23
P. Carrick lbw b Cooper	21		
G. E. McMillan not out	7		
F. E. Joubert b Taylor	0		
S. P. Hughes c Procter b Cooper	0		
L-b 7, w 1, n-b 2	10	B 2, l-b 9	11

1/33 2/49 3/118 4/150	244	1/44 2/62 3/84 (5 wkts dec.) 225
5/179 6/184 7/227 8/241 9/241		4/85 5/172

Bowling: *First Innings*—Taylor 29–6–74–3; Lever 25–7–48–1; Cooper 27.5–7–61–3; Procter 10–1–21–0; Daniels 10–2–30–2. *Second Innings*—Taylor 24–6–46–3; Lever 20–6–32–0; Cooper 17–3–48–1; Procter 2–1–1–0; Daniels 30–7–87–1.

Natal

C. L. Smith lbw b Ferreira	35	– (2) b Hughes	5
B. A. Richards c Barnard b Joubert	19		
R. M. Bentley lbw b Carrick	62	– not out	17
D. Bestall run out	46		
R. A. Smith c Joubert b Carrick	7	– (1) not out	30
*M. J. Procter c McMillan b Carrick	26		
N. P. Daniels c and b Ferreira	2		
†A. J. S. Smith not out	5		
K. R. Cooper b Ferreira	11		
B 4, l-b 6, n-b 25	35	B 6, l-b 3, w 1, n-b 2	12

1/27 2/103 3/166 4/194 (8 wkts dec.) 248	1/16	(1 wkt) 64
5/221 6/230 7/231 8/248		

L. B. Taylor and J. K. Lever did not bat.

Bowling: *First Innings*—Hughes 23–5–55–0; Joubert 15–2–43–1; McMillan 9–0–30–0; Carrick 16–6–38–3; Ferreira 22–7–47–3. *Second Innings*—Hughes 7–2–19–1; Joubert 5–1–18–0; McMillan 3–1–7–0; Ferreira 1–0–8–0.

Umpires: C. J. Mitchley and G. Baker.

NORTHERN TRANSVAAL v TRANSVAAL

At Berea Park, Pretoria, November 26, 27, 29. Transvaal won by ten wickets. Transvaal 22 pts, Northern Transvaal 4 pts.

Transvaal

S. J. Cook c Ferreira b Carrick	92		
M. S. Venter c Whitfield b Joubert	4	– not out	10
A. I. Kallicharran c McMillan b Ferreira	44		
R. G. Pollock c Day b Hughes	50		
*C. E. B. Rice c Day b Barnard	37		
K. A. McKenzie c du Preez b Ferreira	51		
†R. V. Jennings c du Preez b Ferreira	18	– not out	8
A. J. Kourie c Day b Hughes	11		
N. V. Radford b Hughes	21		
V. A. P. van der Bijl c Day b Carrick	14		
R. W. Hanley not out	0		
L-b 12, n-b 13	25	L-b 4	4

1/15 2/80 3/188 4/206   367   (no wkt) 22
5/293 6/294 7/325 8/330 9/362

Bowling: *First Innings*—Hughes 22–3–93–3; Joubert 18–4–77–1; Ferreira 27–5–74–3; McMillan 5–0–36–0; Carrick 23–9–47–2; Barnard 2–0–15–1. *Second Innings*—Joubert 3.4–1–4–0; McMillan 3–0–14–0.

Northern Transvaal

B. J. Whitfield c Kourie b Hanley	3	– c Jennings b van der Bijl	23
V. F. du Preez c Jennings b Hanley	11	– c Jennings b Kourie	13
*L. J. Barnard c Kourie b van der Bijl	19	– c Pollock b Hanley	27
P. Carrick c McKenzie b Hanley	8	– c McKenzie b Hanley	1
C. S. Stirk lbw b van der Bijl	68	– c McKenzie b van der Bijl	0
†N. T. Day lbw b Hanley	0	– b Kourie	69
A. M. Ferreira b Kourie	11	– c Jennings b Kourie	19
P. J. A. Visagie c Rice b Kourie	26	– lbw b Radford	42
G. E. McMillan c Jennings b Hanley	12	– run out	7
F. E. Joubert c Cook b Kourie	0	– c Venter b Radford	3
S. P. Hughes not out	2	– not out	2
L-b 2, n-b 7	9	L-b 7, n-b 6	13

1/11 2/22 3/38 4/46   169   1/38 2/44 3/44 4/107   219
5/51 6/94 7/144 8/160 9/162   5/146 6/167 7/184 8/199 9/203

Bowling: *First Innings*—van der Bijl 22–7–36–2; Hanley 19.3–4–53–5; Radford 7–0–47–0; Kourie 22–13–24–3. *Second Innings*—van der Bijl 14–2–44–2; Hanley 17–5–47–2; Radford 13–5–24–2; Kourie 36–14–91–3.

Umpires: G. Hawkins and D. D. Schoof.

EASTERN PROVINCE v NORTHERN TRANSVAAL

At St Georges Park, Port Elizabeth, December 4, 5, 6. Drawn. Eastern Province 6 pts, Northern Transvaal 4 pts.

Eastern Province

S. J. Bezuidenhout c Whitfield b Old	17	– not out	60
W. Larkins c Whitfield b Old	3	– lbw b Old	0
R. L. S. Armitage run out	77	– c Day b Old	24
†D. J. Richardson c Day b Joubert	17	– not out	7
P. Willey c Day b Ferreira	5		
R. G. Fensham lbw b Carrick	54		
M. B. Billson c Ferreira b Joubert	9		
*G. S. Cowley c Joubert b Barnard	12		
D. J. Brickett c Old b Barnard	68		
W. K. Watson not out	99		
J. A. Carse run out	0		
L-b 5, w 1, n-b 6	12	B 1, l-b 4, n-b 11	16

1/11 2/24 3/64 4/91　　　　　　　373　1/1 2/61　　　(2 wkts dec.) 107
5/168 6/183 7/205 8/205 9/356

Bowling: *First Innings*—Old 24.2–9–75–2; Joubert 21–5–72–2; Ferreira 23–6–69–1; Carrick 31–5–91–1; Barnard 9–1–54–2. *Second Innings*—Old 19–2–48–2; Joubert 4–0–21–0; Ferreira 14–7–22–0.

Northern Transvaal

B. J. Whitfield c Billson b Willey	59	– c Richardson b Brickett	53
J. W. Furstenburg c Bezuidenhout b Carse	2	– (9) not out	2
P. J. A. Visagie c Richardson b Carse	8	– (2) b Carse	20
V. F. du Preez lbw b Watson	32	– (3) not out	52
*L. J. Barnard c Carse b Watson	47	– (4) b Brickett	0
C. S. Stirk c Watson b Cowley	23	– (5) c Willey b Brickett	8
†N. T. Day b Carse	12	– (8) c Billson b Willey	1
A. M. Ferreira not out	13	– (6) run out	0
P. Carrick not out	14		
C. M. Old (did not bat)		– (7) c Armitage b Brickett	2
B 2, l-b 14, n-b 4	20	B 4, l-b 3, w 1	8

1/4 2/14 3/108 4/110　　　(7 wkts dec.) 230　1/47 2/102 3/102　　　(7 wkts) 146
5/162 6/187 7/204　　　　　　　　　　　4/118 5/126 6/134 7/138

F. E. Joubert did not bat.

Bowling: *First Innings*—Carse 23.2–2–82–3; Watson 20–7–47–2; Brickett 18–5–40–0; Armitage 11–5–6–0; Cowley 8–1–18–1; Willey 17–9–17–1. *Second Innings*—Carse 9–4–25–1; Watson 6–1–24–0; Brickett 16–3–48–4; Armitage 4–2–6–0; Willey 23–10–35–1; Larkins 1–1–0–0.

Umpires: D. H. Bezuidenhout and T. Pole.

NATAL v WESTERN PROVINCE

At Kingsmead, Durban, December 4, 5, 6. Drawn. Natal 9 pts, Western Province 3 pts.

Natal

C. L. Smith c Hobson b le Roux	18	– c McEwan b Jefferies	7
C. P. Wilkins c McEwan b le Roux	0	– c Gooch b le Roux	5
R. M. Bentley c Emburey b le Roux	47	– c McEwan b le Roux	1
D. Bestall run out	69	– c McEwan b Emburey	12
R. A. Smith c Bruce b Hobson	39	– c Pienaar b Emburey	33
B. A. Richards c Seeff b Emburey	16	– c Pienaar b Emburey	9
*N. P. Daniels c McEwan b le Roux	49	– c Pienaar b Emburey	0
†A. J. S. Smith c Kirsten b le Roux	22	– b Jefferies	2
K. R. Cooper c McEwan b Jefferies	2	– lbw b Emburey	9
J. K. Lever run out	19	– c le Roux b Emburey	13
L. B. Taylor not out	20	– not out	21
B 1, l-b 11, w 2, n-b 9	23	L-b 5, n-b 7	12

1/1 2/64 3/78 4/143   324   1/10 2/14 3/14 4/56   124
5/166 6/226 7/270 8/275 9/292   5/56 6/61 7/73 8/74 9/89

Bowling: *First Innings*—le Roux 28.5–1–88–5; Jefferies 25–7–76–1; Pienaar 3–0–13–0; Emburey 32–10–71–1; Hobson 10–1–45–1; Kuiper 3–0–8–0. *Second Innings*—le Roux 19–7–37–2; Jefferies 16–6–31–2; Pienaar 3–3–0–0; Emburey 17.5–7–36–6; Kuiper 5–2–8–0.

Western Province

G. A. Gooch c A. J. S. Smith b Cooper	11	– b Taylor	87
L. Seeff c A. J. S. Smith b Taylor	7	– c Richards b Lever	47
*P. N. Kirsten c Daniels b Lever	19	– run out	44
K. S. McEwan c A. J. S. Smith b Cooper	4	– c R. A. Smith b Lever	35
A. P. Kuiper lbw b Cooper	0	– not out	1
R. F. Pienaar lbw b Cooper	27		
†S. D. Bruce run out	10		
G. S. le Roux c Bestall b Cooper	5	– not out	17
S. T. Jefferies c R. A. Smith b Taylor	15		
J. E. Emburey not out	7		
D. L. Hobson c A. J. S. Smith b Taylor	3		
B 4, l-b 2, n-b 7	13	B 2, l-b 10, n-b 4	16

1/23 2/31 3/46 4/50   121   1/111 2/165 3/217   (4 wkts) 247
5/50 6/64 7/85 8/98 9/115   4/241

Bowling: *First Innings*—Taylor 21.1–8–35–3; Lever 20–7–32–1; Cooper 22–9–25–5; Wilkins 8–3–16–0; Daniels 1–1–0–0. *Second Innings*—Taylor 22–7–60–1; Lever 17.4–2–70–2; Cooper 16–5–78–0; Daniels 6–1–23–0.

Umpires: B. C. Smith and D. A. Sansom.

EASTERN PROVINCE v WESTERN PROVINCE

At St Georges Park, Port Elizabeth, December 26, 27, 28. Western Province won by nine wickets. Western Province 21 pts, Eastern Province 5 pts.

Western Province

G. A. Gooch b Carse	19	– c Williams b Watson	3
L. Seeff c Richardson b Brickett	13	– not out	4
*P. N. Kirsten c Larkins b Carse	81	– not out	0
K. S. McEwan c Williams b Willey	106		
A. P. Kuiper c Williams b Cowley	71		
R. F. Pienaar b Brickett	12		
†S. D. Bruce not out	74		
G. S. le Roux not out	51		
B 1, l-b 3, w 5, n-b 8	17	L-b 1	1

1/29 2/42 3/194 4/284 5/307 6/325   (6 wkts dec.) 444   1/7   (1 wkt) 8

S. T. Jefferies, J. E. Emburey and D. L. Hobson did not bat.

Bowling: *First Innings*—Watson 23–5–109–0; Carse 21–3–78–2; Brickett 26–5–57–2; Cowley 18–2–92–1; Larkins 7–1–23–0; Armitage 8–1–31–0; Willey 6–1–37–1. *Second Innings*—Watson 3–1–3–1; Carse 3.1–1–4–0.

Eastern Province

†D. J. Richardson c Bruce b le Roux	18	– c McEwan b Pienaar	6
W. Larkins c McEwan b le Roux	40	– c Emburey b Pienaar	7
R. L. S. Armitage c Bruce b Jefferies	4	– c Gooch b le Roux	25
R. G. Fensham c Hobson b Pienaar	35	– c Pienaar b Hobson	58
P. Willey b Pienaar	1	– c Kirsten b Jefferies	46
R. J. D. Whyte c Bruce b Jefferies	6	– c Gooch b Emburey	34
P. H. Williams c Emburey b Kuiper	21	– c Bruce b Jefferies	24
*G. S. Cowley not out	64	– c Bruce b Jefferies	3
D. J. Brickett c Pienaar b Emburey	4	– not out	7
W. K. Watson c Gooch b Emburey	1	– c McEwan b Jefferies	2
J. A. Carse run out	0	– b Jefferies	1
L-b 15, w 3, n-b 6	24	B 9, l-b 4, w 3, n-b 4	20

1/41 2/51 3/101 4/105   218   1/12 2/21 3/113 4/120   233
5/113 6/120 7/185 8/189 9/195   5/173 6/211 7/218 8/229 9/231

Bowling: *First Innings*—le Roux 16–6–25–2; Jefferies 18–3–45–2; Kuiper 8–1–45–1; Pienaar 10–3–28–2; Emburey 11–3–26–2; Hobson 7–3–25–0. *Second Innings*—le Roux 23–7–39–1; Jefferies 20–3–56–5; Kuiper 1–0–9–0; Pienaar 9–2–23–2; Emburey 22–6–35–1; Hobson 25–9–51–1.

Umpires: S. G. Moore and P. R. Hurwitz.

TRANSVAAL v NATAL

At Wanderers, Johannesburg, December 26, 27, 28. Drawn. Transvaal 11 pts, Natal 9 pts.

Transvaal

S. J. Cook c A. J. S. Smith b Taylor	121	– lbw b Lever	69
A. J. Kourie c Richards b Cooper	22	– b Clare	57
A. I. Kallicharran lbw b Taylor	60	– lbw b Clare	34
R. G. Pollock c A. J. S. Smith b Cooper	0	– not out	45
*C. E. B. Rice c A. J. S. Smith b Taylor	37	– not out	26
K. A. McKenzie c A. J. S. Smith b Taylor	2		
†R. V. Jennings lbw b Taylor	0		
I. F. N. Weideman not out	30		
N. V. Radford c Bestall b Taylor	2		
T. H. Parrymore not out	4		
B 4, l-b 13, w 3, n-b 3	23	B 2, l-b 24, w 3, n-b 1	30

1/63 2/204 3/205 4/221 (8 wkts dec.) 301 1/109 2/167 3/178 (3 wkts dec.) 261
5/229 6/229 7/286 8/296

R. W. Hanley did not bat.

Bowling: First Innings—Taylor 25–5–68–6; Lever 23.3–4–85–0; Cooper 21–6–58–2; Clare 15–1–67–0. *Second Innings*—Taylor 19–1–70–0; Lever 18–3–67–1; Cooper 18–5–64–0; Clare 9–3–30–2.

Natal

C. L. Smith c Jennings b Kourie	28	– b Hanley	1
B. A. Richards b Radford	21	– b Hanley	16
R. M. Bentley b Radford	6	– lbw b Kourie	25
*D. Bestall c Jennings b Hanley	71	– c Jennings b Radford	22
R. A. Smith c McKenzie b Parrymore	26	– c Cook b Kourie	2
T. R. Madsen c Rice b Kourie	57	– c and b Weideman	62
†A. J. S. Smith not out	45	– c Kallicharran b Kourie	16
J. K. Lever c Pollock b Kourie	3	– b Kourie	4
K. R. Cooper c Jennings b Hanley	11	– not out	6
L. B. Taylor b Hanley	0	– b Kourie	4
M. D. Clare st Jennings b Kourie	0		
B 4, l-b 2, n-b 1	7	L-b 5, w 2, n-b 6	13

1/45 2/55 3/61 4/117 275 1/8 2/19 3/44 4/54 (9 wkts) 171
5/200 6/224 7/229 8/250 9/250 5/82 6/144 7/157 8/167 9/171

Bowling: First Innings—Hanley 22–6–64–3; Radford 18–4–64–2; Weideman 12–2–26–0; Kourie 24.5–6–88–4; Parrymore 7–0–26–1. *Second Innings*—Hanley 21–10–40–2; Radford 16–4–51–1; Weideman 7–3–8–1; Kourie 26–12–50–5; Parrymore 3–2–9–0.

Umpires: D. Lee and A. J. Norton.

WESTERN PROVINCE v TRANSVAAL

At Newlands, Cape Town, December 31, January 1, 3. Transvaal won by 122 runs. Transvaal 16 pts, Western Province 7 pts.

Transvaal

S. J. Cook c Kuiper b Emburey	13	– lbw b le Roux	6
H. R. Fotheringham c Seeff b Emburey	61	– c Bruce b Emburey	61
A. I. Kallicharran b Jefferies	1	– b Emburey	29
R. G. Pollock lbw b le Roux	13	– b Hobson	22
*C. E. B. Rice run out	43	– c Bruce b Jefferies	62
K. A. McKenzie c Seeff b Emburey	43	– c Bruce b Jefferies	70
A. J. Kourie c Seeff b Emburey	1	– not out	19
†R. V. Jennings not out	5	– not out	28
N. V. Radford c Kuiper b Emburey	0		
V. A. P. van der Bijl c Bruce b Hobson	2		
R. W. Hanley run out	1		
B 2, l-b 7, w 1, n-b 3	13	L-b 26, w 2, n-b 3	31

1/32 2/37 3/70 4/113   196   1/7 2/87 3/121   (6 wkts dec.) 328
5/173 6/186 7/190 8/192 9/195   4/137 5/276 6/277

Bowling: *First Innings*—le Roux 13–3–36–1; Jefferies 19–6–35–1; Emburey 28.2–12–53–5; Hobson 17–3–44–1; Pienaar 5–1–15–0. *Second Innings*—le Roux 20–4–65–1; Jefferies 22–5–65–2; Emburey 36–5–99–2; Hobson 16–2–51–1; Pienaar 9–3–16–0; Kirsten 3–2–1–0.

Western Province

G. A. Gooch b van der Bijl	4	– c and b Kourie	10
L. Seeff c Jennings b Radford	14	– lbw b Kourie	21
*P. N. Kirsten c Rice b Kallicharran	65	– b Kourie	2
K. S. McEwan c Rice b Kallicharran	29	– b Kourie	28
A. P. Kuiper c and b Kourie	0	– c Radford b Kourie	0
†S. D. Bruce b Kallicharran	14	– lbw b Kallicharran	9
R. F. Pienaar st Jennings b Kourie	25	– lbw b van der Bijl	28
G. S. le Roux c Fotheringham b Kallicharran	8	– c Jennings b Kourie	18
S. T. Jefferies lbw b van der Bijl	25	– c McKenzie b Kourie	2
J. E. Emburey lbw b Kallicharran	2	– c Fotheringham b van der Bijl	42
D. L. Hobson not out	9	– not out	35
B 4, l-b 3	7	B 4, l-b 1	5

1/4 2/32 3/112 4/113   202   1/27 2/33 3/52 4/52   200
5/117 6/133 7/141 8/180 9/183   5/75 6/75 7/115 8/117 9/125

Bowling: *First Innings*—van der Bijl 22–8–42–2; Hanley 4–1–10–0; Radford 6–0–18–1; Kourie 25.2–6–80–2; Kallicharran 19–4–45–5. *Second Innings*—van der Bijl 12.4–4–36–2; Hanley 3–1–8–0; Radford 1–0–4–0; Kourie 32–8–79–7; Kallicharran 22–4–67–1; Fotheringham 1–0–1–0.

Umpires: B. C. Smith and B. J. Meyer.

NATAL v EASTERN PROVINCE

At Kingsmead, Durban, January 1, 2, 3. Drawn. Natal 4 pts, Eastern Province 6 pts.

Natal

B. J. Whitfield c Carse b Armitage	8	– st Richardson b Willey	30
C. L. Smith b Brickett	31	– c Richardson b Cowley	12
R. M. Bentley c Carse b Watson	55	– c Richardson b Armitage	18
*D. Bestall b Watson	11	– lbw b Armitage	1
B. A. Richards lbw b Watson	61		
R. A. Smith c Richardson b Brickett	2	– (5) not out	75
†A. J. S. Smith c Brickett b Watson	27	– (6) not out	47
J. K. Lever b Watson	6		
K. R. Cooper b Watson	3		
L. B. Taylor b Watson	20		
M. D. Clare not out	3		
B 1, l–b 12, w 2, n-b 3	18	L-b 3, n-b 6	9

1/21 2/86 3/105 4/124   245   1/22 2/51   (4 wkts) 192
5/127 6/205 7/210 8/217 9/230   3/77 4/78

Bowling: *First Innings*—Watson 24.1–4–50–7; Brickett 27–9–51–2; Willey 17–6–30–0; Armitage 15–7–25–1; Carse 18–7–48–0; Cowley 5–1–23–0. *Second Innings*—Watson 11–4–21–0; Willey 24–7–56–1; Armitage 18–5–36–2; Carse 6–3–19–0; Cowley 10–1–30–1; Williams 8–1–21–0; Larkins 0.2–0–0–0.

Eastern Province

†D. J. Richardson c A. J. S. Smith b Clare.	69	R. J. D. Whyte not out	45
W. Larkins lbw b Clare	32	P. H. Williams not out	14
R. L. S. Armitage lbw b Cooper	17	L-b 8, w 2, n-b 11	21
R. G. Fensham b Clare	13	1/77 2/111 3/145 (5 wkts dec.) 225	
P. Willey c A. J. S. Smith b Lever	14	4/148 5/194	

*G. S. Cowley, D. J. Brickett, W. K. Watson and J. A. Carse did not bat.

Bowling: Taylor 18–8–44–0; Lever 23–6–48–1; Cooper 21–6–59–1; Clare 19–4–45–3; C. L. Smith 2–1–8–0.

Umpires: D. D. Schoof and K. E. Liebenberg.

EASTERN PROVINCE v NATAL

At St Georges Park, Port Elizabeth, January 15, 16, 17. Drawn. Eastern Province 7 pts, Natal 7 pts.

Eastern Province

†D. J. Richardson c A. J. S. Smith b Lever	5	– c Whitfield b Cooper	59
W. Larkins b Lever	29	– c Bestall b Procter	86
R. L. S. Armitage lbw b Procter	79	– b Lever	81
P. Willey c Cooper b Lever	11	– b Clare	34
R. G. Fensham b Taylor	66	– not out	36
R. J. D. Whyte c Madsen b Clare	12	– not out	17
P. H. Williams lbw b Cooper	12		
*G. S. Cowley c Cooper b Lever	33		
D. J. Brickett c and b Cooper	27		
W. K. Watson b Lever	0		
M. K. van Vuuren not out	0		
L-b 5, w 2, n-b 2	9	B 3, l-b 4, n-b 1	8

1/35 2/36 3/52 4/176   283   1/125 2/154   (4 wkts dec.) 321
5/206 6/214 7/225 8/279 9/283   3/214 4/290

Bowling: *First Innings*—Taylor 18–4–75–1; Lever 24–5–79–5; Cooper 22.3–7–36–2; Clare 16–6–56–1; Procter 18–4–28–1. *Second Innings*—Taylor 20–5–53–0; Lever 15.3–1–63–1; Cooper 12–0–50–1; Clare 16–2–81–1; Procter 23–2–62–1; C. L. Smith 2–0–4–0.

Natal

B. J. Whitfield run out	27	– b van Vuuren	117
C. L. Smith c Willey b Armitage	40	– c Richardson b Brickett	77
R. A. Smith run out	51	– c Richardson b Brickett	19
D. Bestall b Watson	70	– c Armitage b Brickett	41
T. R. Madsen c sub b Watson	17	– (7) c sub b Watson	4
*M. J. Procter c Whyte b Watson	0	– (5) run out	1
†A. J. S. Smith not out	12	– (6) c Larkins b Watson	30
K. R. Cooper c Willey b Watson	21	– (9) lbw b Watson	2
J. K. Lever not out	2	– (8) c Willey b Watson	10
L. B. Taylor (did not bat)		– not out	2
M. B. Clare (did not bat)		– not out	0
B 5, l-b 2, w 1, n-b 5	13	B 4, l-b 18, w 1, n-b 3	26

1/64 2/86 3/175 4/210   (7 wkts dec.) 253   1/131 2/167 3/237 4/245 (9 wkts) 329
5/213 6/218 7/246   5/290 6/296 7/318 8/327 9/327

Bowling: *First Innings*—Watson 18–4–48–4; van Vuuren 16.2–5–54–0; Armitage 28–6–82–1; Willey 12–6–26–0; Cowley 6–2–15–0; Brickett 3–0–13–0; Larkins 1–0–2–0. *Second Innings*—Watson 15–4–58–4; van Vuuren 14–2–51–1; Armitage 13–3–49–0; Willey 14–0–50–0; Brickett 18–0–95–3.

Umpires: C. J. Mitchley and B. J. Meyer.

TRANSVAAL v NORTHERN TRANSVAAL

At Wanderers, Johannesburg, January 15, 16, 17. Transvaal won by 111 runs. Transvaal 18 pts, Northern Transvaal 5 pts.

Transvaal

S. J. Cook c Day b Robinson	18	– c Ferreira b Robinson	8
H. R. Fotheringham lbw b Robinson	64	– c Carrick b Old	16
A. I. Kallicharran b Robinson	11	– b Old	35
R. G. Pollock lbw b Old	25	– c sub b Joubert	40
*C. E. B. Rice c Carrick b Old	16	– not out	35
K. A. McKenzie c Stirk b Carrick	52	– c Yachad b Robinson	5
A. J. Kourie not out	40	– not out	17
†R. V. Jennings c Old b Carrick	0		
I. F. N. Weideman c Robinson b Carrick	0		
N. V. Radford lbw b Ferreira	1		
V. A. P. van der Bijl c Day b Ferreira	2		
B 4, l-b 13, w 1, n-b 2	20	L-b 6	6

1/35 2/57 3/111 4/148   249   1/25 2/25 3/87   (5 wkts dec.) 162
5/164 6/229 7/229 8/237 9/239   4/120 5/125

Bowling: *First Innings*—Old 19–4–65–2; Robinson 17–1–57–3; Ferreira 24.4–10–44–2; Joubert 11–2–45–0; Carrick 11–3–18–3. *Second Innings*—Old 15–1–57–0; Robinson 13–4–35–2; Ferreira 12–2–40–0; Joubert 11–4–24–1.

Northern Transvaal

M. Yachad c Kourie b Weideman	32	– lbw b Radford	42
V. F. du Preez b Weideman	3	– c Rice b Radford	52
*L. J. Barnard c Kourie b Weideman	24	– lbw b Weideman	24
C. S. Stirk lbw b Radford	2	– c McKenzie b Weideman	4
†N. T. Day c Pollock b van der Bijl	48	– c Rice b van der Bijl	4
A. M. Ferreira c McKenzie b Weideman	6	– b Kourie	2
P. J. A. Visagie c Jennings b Radford	9	– c Kourie b van der Bijl	1
P. Carrick c Jennings b Radford	4	– c Jennings b van der Bijl	0
C. M. Old c Jennings b Radford	4	– c Kallicharran b Radford	11
P. A. Robinson b Radford	0	– c Cook b Radford	8
F. E. Joubert not out	1	– not out	3
L-b 9	9	L-b 4, n-b 3	7

1/24 2/37 3/42 4/93   142   1/69 2/119 3/125 4/130   158
5/109 6/132 7/132 8/136 9/136   5/133 6/134 7/134 8/142 9/147

Bowling: *First Innings*—van der Bijl 23–5–43–1; Radford 19.1–5–39–5; Weideman 17–5–29–4; Kourie 12–4–22–0. *Second Innings*—van der Bijl 26–8–50–3; Radford 15.2–0–66–4; Weideman 13–4–21–2; Kourie 6–2–14–1.

Umpires: J. W. Peacock and D. H. Bezuidenhout.

NATAL v NORTHERN TRANSVAAL

At Kingsmead, Durban, February 26, 27, 28. Natal won by an innings and 84 runs. Natal 24 pts, Northern Transvaal 6 pts.

Northern Transvaal

V. F. du Preez c Bestall b Procter	9	– c Bestall b Procter	32
P. J. A. Visagie c Madsen b Taylor	0	– c Whitfield b Lever	21
*L. J. Barnard c A. J. S. Smith b Taylor	8	– lbw b Lever	33
†N. T. Day c Whitfield b Procter	23	– c Madsen b Procter	9
C. S. Stirk c Richards b Procter	19	– c Richards b Taylor	12
K. D. Verdoorn st A. J. S. Smith b Makin	81	– c Taylor b Procter	7
A. M. Ferreira b Makin	96	– c Whitfield b Procter	35
P. Carrick b Taylor	10	– b Procter	18
G. E. McMillan not out	10	– c Lever b Procter	1
P. A. Robinson lbw b Taylor	0	– lbw b Makin	12
S. P. Hughes c R. A. Smith b Procter	2	– not out	1
B 1, l-b 7, w 1	9	B 8, l-b 4, w 3, n-b 1	16

1/1 2/15 3/27 4/59   267   1/28 2/71 3/93 4/101   197
5/62 6/214 7/255 8/255 9/259   5/120 6/129 7/154 8/163 9/183

Bowling: *First Innings*—Taylor 16–2–45–4; Lever 16–6–36–0; Cooper 9–1–47–0; Procter 27.2–5–83–4; Makin 19–3–47–2. *Second Innings*—Taylor 12–1–44–1; Lever 17–5–46–2; Cooper 4–0–12–0; Procter 30.1–14–52–6; Makin 8–1–27–1.

Natal

B. J. Whitfield run out	50	†A. J. S. Smith c du Preez b Ferreira	97
B. A. Richards c Hughes b Carrick	123	L-b 16, n-b 15	31
T. R. Madsen c Robinson b Ferreira	87		
D. Bestall c Verdoorn b Carrick	9	1/156 2/217	(6 wkts dec.) 548
*M. J. Procter b McMillan	99	3/246 4/384	
R. A. Smith not out	52	5/391 6/548	

J. K. Lever, M. D. Makin, K. R. Cooper and L. B. Taylor did not bat.

Bowling: Hughes 21–4–84–0; Robinson 15–1–75–0; Ferreira 16.5–0–87–2; McMillan 18–3–64–1; Carrick 32–4–127–2; Barnard 15–2–61–0; du Preez 3–0–19–0.

Umpires: B. J. Meyer and S. G. Moore.

WESTERN PROVINCE v EASTERN PROVINCE

At Newlands, Cape Town, February 26, 27, 28. Western Province won by ten wickets. Western Province 21 pts, Eastern Province 2 pts.

Eastern Province

†D. J. Richardson c During b Emburey	40 – c Gooch b Hobson	68
W. Larkins c McEwan b Emburey	17 – lbw b Kuiper	4
R. L. S. Armitage lbw b Emburey	0 – c Gooch b Hobson	26
P. Willey c Henry b Emburey	35 – c Henry b Hobson	4
R. G. Fensham c and b Emburey	12 – c Pienaar b Emburey	4
P. H. Williams c Ryall b Pienaar	9 – c Ryall b Hobson	0
D. H. Howell run out	5 – lbw b Emburey	37
T. G. Shaw lbw b Hobson	1 – c Henry b Hobson	2
*G. S. Cowley b Hobson	0 – not out	16
D. J. Brickett not out	18 – c Kirsten b Hobson	28
W. K. Watson c Pienaar b Emburey	14 – b Emburey	21
B 8, l-b 8, w 3	19	B 8, l-b 4, n-b 1	13
	170		**223**

1/38 2/50 3/89 4/112
5/113 6/134 7/135 8/137 9/137

1/21 2/70 3/127 4/130
5/139 6/139 7/147 8/192 9/220

Bowling: *First Innings*—Kuiper 6–1–19–0; Pienaar 14–3–34–1; Emburey 24.5–12–33–6; During 7–2–15–0; Henry 7–1–17–0; Hobson 12–3–33–2. *Second Innings*—Kuiper 11–3–25–1; Pienaar 4–2–5–0; Emburey 44–20–62–3; During 6–1–7–0; Henry 16–2–38–0; Hobson 33.4–12–73–6.

Western Province

G. A. Gooch c Richardson b Watson	38 – not out	7
L. Seeff lbw b Watson	32 – not out	11
*P. N. Kirsten lbw b Cowley	69	
K. S. McEwan c Shaw b Willey	33	
R. F. Pienaar b Watson	112	
A. P. Kuiper c Shaw b Watson	66	
O. Henry b Watson	10	
J. During c Brickett b Willey	3	
J. E. Emburey c Shaw b Watson	0	
†R. J. Ryall run out	0	
D. L. Hobson not out	2	
L-b 7, n-b 5	12	L-b 1, w 1	2
	377	(no wkt)	**20**

1/73 2/76 3/130 4/201
5/335 6/349 7/368 8/369 9/373

Bowling: *First Innings*—Watson 28.3–8–87–6; Brickett 17–4–70–0; Cowley 14–5–43–1; Armitage 13–1–54–0; Shaw 12–1–62–0; Willey 16–1–49–2. *Second Innings*—Watson 4–3–4–0; Shaw 2.4–1–9–0; Larkins 6–4–5–0.

Umpires: H. R. Martin and D. H. Bezuidenhout.

NORTHERN TRANSVAAL v EASTERN PROVINCE

At Berea Park, Pretoria, March 4, 5, 7. Drawn. Northern Transvaal 7 pts, Eastern Province 5 pts.

Northern Transvaal

M. Yachad c and b Brickett	22	– c Brickett b Carse	24
V. F. du Preez c Richardson b Carse	22	– lbw b Brickett	14
*L. J. Barnard b van Vuuren	17	– c Armitage b Brickett	2
†N. T. Day lbw b Carse	0	– c Larkins b Brickett	84
C. S. Stirk c Armitage b van Vuuren	10	– run out	93
K. D. Verdoorn b van Vuuren	0	– not out	3
A. M. Ferreira b van Vuuren	75	– c Richardson b Willey	20
P. Carrick b Brickett	13		
G. L. Ackermann b van Vuuren	25		
P. A. Robinson c Armitage b Carse	11		
S. P. Hughes not out	4		
B 2, l-b 13, w 1, n-b 5	21	L-b 13, w 2	15

1/27 2/58 3/58 4/73   220   1/32 2/42 3/45   (6 wkts dec.) 255
5/73 6/84 7/134 8/193 9/206   4/194 5/239 6/255

Bowling: *First Innings*—Watson 14–4–41–0; Carse 20.5–5–61–3; Brickett 15–6–20–2; Willey 18–4–29–0; van Vuuren 17–5–47–5; Armitage 1–0–1–0. *Second Innings*—Watson 10–3–24–0; Carse 19–4–62–1; Brickett 15–2–56–3; Willey 7.2–2–22–1; van Vuuren 13–3–53–0; Armitage 7–0–23–0.

Eastern Province

†D. J. Richardson b Robinson	9	– lbw b Robinson	0
W. Larkins c Yachad b Ferreira	21	– c Verdoorn b Hughes	5
R. L. S. Armitage c Day b Hughes	20	– not out	97
*P. Willey c Verdoorn b Ackermann	37	– not out	57
R. G. Fensham c Robinson b Hughes	0		
D. H. Howell c Barnard b Robinson	15		
P. H. Williams b Ackermann	21		
D. J. Brickett c Ferreira b Hughes	9		
W. K. Watson c Day b Hughes	2		
M. K. van Vuuren b Ackermann	11		
J. A. Carse not out	0		
L-b 10, w 2, n-b 5	17	B 7, l-b 1, w 4, n-b 5	17

1/19 2/48 3/64 4/81   162   1/3 2/15   (2 wkts) 176
5/102 6/114 7/149 8/149 9/162

Bowling: *First Innings*—Robinson 19–8–32–2; Ackermann 11–3–35–3; Ferreira 19–6–28–1; Hughes 15.1–4–45–4; Carrick 4–2–5–0. *Second Innings*—Robinson 10–1–34–1; Ackermann 3–2–5–0; Ferreira 17–5–40–0; Hughes 16–4–39–1; Carrick 7–3–17–0; Barnard 3–0–12–0; du Preez 5–1–12–0.

Umpires: E. A. Carter and B. C. Smith.

TRANSVAAL v WESTERN PROVINCE

At Wanderers, Johannesburg, March 4, 5, 6. Drawn. Transvaal 9 pts, Western Province 7 pts.

Western Province

G. A. Gooch b Hanley	5	– c and b Radford	104
L. Seeff b van der Bijl	0	– lbw b Radford	42
*P. N. Kirsten c Cook b van der Bijl	55		
K. S. McEwan lbw b van der Bijl	6	– st Jennings b Kourie	13
R. F. Pienaar b Kourie	61	– c Jennings b Radford	12
A. P. Kuiper c Fotheringham b Kourie	7	– c Kallicharran b Radford	39
P. H. Rayner not out	121	– not out	5
J. E. Emburey run out	5	– b van der Bijl	1
S. T. Jefferies c Kourie b Radford	39	– c sub b Radford	31
J. During b Radford	31		
†R. J. Ryall not out	1		
B 3, l-b 10, n-b 5	18	L-b 12, n-b 1	13

1/5 2/5 3/23 4/86 (9 wkts dec.) 349 1/98 2/144 3/173 (7 wkts dec.) 260
5/103 6/158 7/168 8/235 9/347 4/188 5/246 6/254 7/260

Bowling: *First Innings*—van der Bijl 26–10–45–3; Hanley 8–4–16–1; Radford 25–4–96–2; Kourie 46–13–133–2; Kallicharran 8–1–41–0. *Second Innings*—van der Bijl 30.2–9–68–1; Radford 24–3–116–5; Kourie 15–1–63–1.

Transvaal

S. J. Cook lbw b Jefferies	5	– not out	51
H. R. Fotheringham b During	45	– not out	43
†R. V. Jennings lbw b Jefferies	0		
A. I. Kallicharran c Gooch b Jefferies	5		
R. G. Pollock b Emburey	41		
*C. E. B. Rice c Ryall b Jefferies	24		
K. A. McKenzie lbw b Jefferies	38		
A. J. Kourie not out	72		
N. V. Radford c Emburey b During	8		
V. A. P. van der Bijl b Jefferies	30		
R. W. Hanley c Seeff b Pienaar	1		
L-b 7, w 3, n-b 7	17	B 1, l-b 4, w 1, n-b 1	7

1/8 2/8 3/18 4/76 286 (no wkt) 101
5/126 6/136 7/205 8/219 9/285

Bowling: *First Innings*—Jefferies 34–3–91–6; Kuiper 6–0–30–0; Emburey 22–4–82–1; Pienaar 10.1–1–30–1; During 15–5–36–2. *Second Innings*—Jefferies 8–2–26–0; Emburey 12–5–18–0; Pienaar 8–0–34–0; During 5–0–15–0; Seeff 1–0–1–0.

Umpires: B. J. Meyer and O. R. Schoof.

TRANSVAAL v EASTERN PROVINCE

At Wanderers, Johannesburg, March 12, 13, 14. Transvaal won by an innings and 104 runs. Transvaal 21 pts, Eastern Province 4 pts.

Eastern Province

†D. J. Richardson c Cook b Kourie	56	– c McKenzie b Hanley	30
W. Larkins c Hanley b Kourie	64	– absent hurt	
R. L. S. Armitage lbw b van der Bijl	48	– lbw b van der Bijl	2
P. Willey c Jennings b Weideman	31	– c Fotheringham b Hanley	14
R. G. Fensham lbw b van der Bijl	0	– c Cook b Hanley	18
D. H. Howell not out	64	– c Cook b Hanley	13
*G. S. Cowley lbw b Kourie	56	– b van der Bijl	8
D. J. Brickett (did not bat)		– c Hanley b Kourie	0
W. K. Watson (did not bat)		– c McKenzie b van der Bijl	17
M. K. van Vuuren (did not bat)		– c Rice b van der Bijl	2
J. A. Carse (did not bat)		– not out	0
L-b 7, w 2	9	B 7, l-b 1, n-b 2	10

1/101 2/142 3/203   (6 wkts dec.) 328   1/10 2/41 3/48 4/69   114
4/207 5/208 6/328   5/77 6/78 7/108 8/108 9/114

Bowling: *First Innings*—van der Bijl 32–12–69–2; Hanley 20–4–61–0; Weideman 24–6–97–1; Kourie 38–10–87–3; Kallicharran 2–0–5–0. *Second Innings*—van der Bijl 15.1–4–24–4; Hanley 15–4–42–4; Weideman 5–1–17–0; Kourie 13–2–21–1.

Transvaal

S. J. Cook b Watson	58	†R. V. Jennings not out	49
H. R. Fotheringham c Willey		I. F. N. Weideman lbw b Carse	0
b van Vuuren	116	V. A. P. van der Bijl not out	10
A. I. Kallicharran c Richardson b Carse	139	B 1, l-b 15, w 7, n-b 6	29
R. G. Pollock b Carse	14		
*C. E. B. Rice c Brickett b Carse	104	1/118 2/248 (8 wkts dec.) 546	
K. A. McKenzie c Richardson b Carse	4	3/300 4/382 5/390	
A. J. Kourie c Richardson b van Vuuren	23	6/444 7/510 8/510	

R. W. Hanley did not bat.

Bowling: Watson 28–2–94–1; Carse 27–3–140–5; Brickett 21–4–92–0; van Vuuren 18–2–104–2; Armitage 21–4–68–0; Willey 3–0–19–0.

Umpires: B. C. Smith and B. M. P. Alistoun.

WESTERN PROVINCE v NORTHERN TRANSVAAL

At Newlands, Cape Town, March 11, 12, 14. Western Province won by nine wickets. Western Province 20 pts, Northern Transvaal 8 pts.

Northern Transvaal

M. Yachad c Gooch b Pienaar	24	– lbw b le Roux	4
V. F. du Preez c Ryall b Jefferies	3	– c Pienaar b le Roux	17
K. D. Verdoorn c Ryall b le Roux	50	– c Pienaar b Jefferies	9
†N. T. Day c Ryall b Jefferies	23	– lbw b Jefferies	15
C. S. Stirk run out	7	– c Rayner b Emburey	0
*L. J. Barnard c Kuiper b Jefferies	1	– not out	46
A. M. Ferreira c Ryall b Hobson	25	– c le Roux b Emburey	2
P. J. A. Visagie lbw b Jefferies	72	– c Ryall b Jefferies	4
P. Carrick lbw b Jefferies	12	– b Hobson	2
P. A. Robinson c Kuiper b Emburey	3	– c Rayner b Hobson	10
S. P. Hughes not out	0	– c Pienaar b Emburey	5
L-b 14, w 1, n-b 2	17	B 1, l-b 1, w 1	3

1/15 2/41 3/104 4/110   237   1/12 2/25 3/44 4/44   117
5/118 6/118 7/184 8/219 9/237   5/46 6/59 7/74 8/81 9/106

Bowling: *First Innings*—le Roux 19–6–47–1; Jefferies 26–6–85–5; Pienaar 8–2–22–1; Emburey 24.1–7–34–1; Hobson 8–1–32–1. *Second Innings*—le Roux 14–2–25–2; Jefferies 15–3–38–3; Pienaar 3–1–6–0; Emburey 11.4–2–28–3; Hobson 7–2–17–2.

Western Province

G. A. Gooch run out	126	– not out	26
A. P. Kuiper c Day b Robinson	12	– c Yachad b Hughes	4
*P. N. Kirsten c Barnard b Hughes	16	– not out	22
K. S. McEwan b Ferreira	2		
J. E. Emburey c Barnard b Carrick	25		
R. F. Pienaar c and b Carrick	15		
P. H. Rayner c Day b Ferreira	14		
S. T. Jefferies c Day b Ferreira	60		
G. S. le Roux run out	9		
D. L. Hobson c Visagie b Hughes	6		
†R. J. Ryall not out	0		
B 2, l-b 3, w 2, n-b 3	10	B 2, l-b 2, w 3, n-b 1	8

1/29 2/67 3/80 4/157   295   1/11   (1 wkt) 60
5/192 6/206 7/239 8/280 9/295

Bowling: *First Innings*—Robinson 19–2–61–1; Hughes 19.2–4–60–2; Ferreira 26–9–89–3; Carrick 15–2–60–2; du Preez 1–0–4–0; Barnard 4–1–11–0. *Second Innings*—Robinson 9.4–2–19–0; Hughes 3–0–13–1; Ferreira 7–1–20–0.

Umpires: A. T. Maasch and O. R. Schoof.

EASTERN PROVINCE v TRANSVAAL

At St Georges Park, Port Elizabeth, March 20, 21, 22. Transvaal won by an innings and 89 runs. Transvaal 22 pts, Eastern Province 4 pts.

Eastern Province

†D. J. Richardson c Jennings b van der Bijl	14	– c Fotheringham b van der Bijl	31
P. Willey c Kourie b Mitchley	20	– b Radford	5
R. L. S. Armitage b Kourie	10	– c Radford b van der Bijl	5
R. G. Fensham c Jennings b Radford	15	– c Jennings b Mitchley	10
D. H. Howell c Fotheringham b Kourie	2	– c McKenzie b Kourie	5
P. H. Williams c Jennings b Radford	9	– b van der Bijl	17
*G. S. Cowley c Jennings b van der Bijl	45	– b van der Bijl	6
J. D. Ogilvie c McKenzie b Kourie	14	– c Rice b van der Bijl	0
W. K. Watson c and b Kourie	29	– c Jennings b van der Bijl	27
J. A. Carse not out	21	– c Jennings b van der Bijl	0
M. K. van Vuuren c Fotheringham b Radford	11	– not out	0
B 2, l-b 7, n-b 2	11	B 6, n-b 2	8

1/24 2/36 3/59 4/61   201   1/22 2/31 3/43 4/54   114
5/66 6/96 7/136 8/136 9/180   5/75 6/75 7/80 8/81 9/81

Bowling: *First Innings*—van der Bijl 22–9–45–2; Radford 22.1–8–63–3; Mitchley 8–2–36–1; Kourie 28–10–46–4. *Second Innings*—van der Bijl 16.1–4–42–7; Radford 7–2–26–1; Mitchley 4–0–27–1; Kourie 5–2–11–1.

Transvaal

S. J. Cook not out	201	K. A. McKenzie lbw b van Vuuren.....	2
H. R. Fotheringham c Richardson		A. J. Kourie not out	17
	b Cowley. 27	L-b 9, n-b 3	12
A. I. Kallicharran c van Vuuren b Carse. 95			
R. G. Pollock c Richardson b Cowley..	8	1/64 2/259	(5 wkts dec.) 404
*C. E. B. Rice c Cowley b Watson	42	3/275 4/362 5/365	

†R. V. Jennings, C. D. Mitchley, N. V. Radford and V. A. P. van der Bijl did not bat.

Bowling: Watson 22–3–65–1; Carse 17–1–76–1; van Vuuren 20–3–84–1; Cowley 10–2–33–2; Ogilvie 12–3–47–0; Willey 15–4–53–0; Armitage 9–1–34–0.

Umpires: H. R. Martin and T. Pole.

WESTERN PROVINCE v NATAL

At Newlands, Cape Town, March 20, 21, 22. Western Province won by nine wickets. Western Province 19 pts, Natal 5 pts.

Natal

B. J. Whitfield c Ryall b le Roux..................	10 – run out	17
C. L. Smith b Jefferies...........................	2 – lbw b le Roux	8
R. M. Bentley c Seeff b le Roux..................	19 – c le Roux b Jefferies...............	41
B. A. Richards c Ryall b Embury.................	46 – (6) c and b Embury	26
D. Bestall c Seeff b Pienaar.....................	16 – b Jefferies	8
*M. J. Procter c Ryall b Pienaar.................	0 – absent	
T. R. Madsen b le Roux.........................	18 – (4) c Gooch b Hobson	28
†A. J. S. Smith b Jefferies.......................	0 – not out	37
J. K. Lever c Ryall b le Roux....................	2 – (8) b Hobson	1
K. R. Cooper not out............................	6 – c Kirsten b Hobson	10
L. B. Taylor b le Roux...........................	4 – b Jefferies	0
L-b 2, w 2, n-b 7	11	L-b 7, w 2, n-b 4	13

1/15 2/25 3/46 4/103   134   1/20 2/36 3/91 4/109   189
5/103 6/103 7/107 8/123 9/124   5/113 6/154 7/175 8/186 9/189

Bowling: *First Innings*—le Roux 13–3–34–5; Jefferies 15–3–45–2; Pienaar 7–1–30–2; Emburey 4–1–14–1. *Second Innings*—le Roux 10–3–34–1; Jefferies 21.4–4–51–3; Pienaar 2–0–10–0; Emburey 9–4–24–1; Hobson 18–3–57–3.

Western Province

G. A. Gooch b Taylor...........................	41 – not out	31
L. Seeff c Whitfield b Taylor	63 – lbw b Cooper...........................	21
*P. N. Kirsten b Madsen b Taylor...............	70 – not out	10
J. E. Emburey b Taylor.........................	9	
K. S. McEwan c Whitfield b Lever..............	10	
R. F. Pienaar lbw b Cooper.....................	1	
P. H. Rayner b Lever...........................	5	
S. T. Jefferies b Lever..........................	22	
G. S. le Roux b Cooper.........................	9	
†R. J. Ryall c Whitfield b Cooper...............	4	
D. L. Hobson not out...........................	2	
B 5, l-b 9, w 1, n-b 5	20	B 4, n-b 2	6

1/88 2/118 3/140 4/181   256   1/47   (1 wkt) 68
5/192 6/216 7/216 8/242 9/254

Bowling: *First Innings*—Taylor 24–4–59–4; Lever 34–9–105–3; Cooper 26.2–5–65–3; Richards 1–0–7–0. *Second Innings*—Taylor 7–1–23–0; Lever 2–0–15–0; Cooper 8–3–13–1; A. J. S. Smith 1.2–0–7–0; C. L. Smith 1–0–4–0.

Umpires: D. D. Schoof and B. Glass.

NORTHERN TRANSVAAL v WESTERN PROVINCE

At Berea Park, Pretoria, March 25, 26, 28. Western Province won by four wickets. Western Province 17 pts, Northern Transvaal 8 pts.

Northern Transvaal

M. Yachad c Ryall b Kuiper	6	– lbw b Kuiper	15
V. F. du Preez c Ryall b Kuiper	78	– c Ryall b Pienaar	37
K. D. Verdoorn lbw b Kuiper	9	– c Ryall b Pienaar	22
†N. T. Day c Rayner b Jefferies	9	– b Jefferies	26
*L. J. Barnard run out	39	– c Ryall b Gooch	33
A. M. Ferreira c Gooch b Hobson	32	– c Gooch b Jefferies	9
P. J. A. Visagie c and b Jefferies	6	– b Gooch	1
G. E. McMillan c Hobson b Kirsten	50	– lbw b Gooch	9
G. L. Ackermann not out	18	– not out	11
P. A. Robinson not out	3	– c sub b Jefferies	4
B. Proctor (did not bat)		– c Ryall b Gooch	1
B 10, l-b 8, w 4, n-b 12	34	B 2, l-b 11, w 5, n-b 5	23

1/21 2/35 3/49 4/114   (8 wkts dec.) 284   1/23 2/76 3/87 4/150   191
5/125 6/208 7/231 8/274   5/160 6/162 7/162 8/179 9/187

Bowling: *First Innings*—le Roux 3–0–12–0; Jefferies 30–5–80–2; Kuiper 23–4–55–3; Pienaar 15–3–50–0; Gooch 5–2–8–0; Hobson 26–11–35–1; Kirsten 4–1–10–1. *Second Innings* Jefferies 31–6–64–3; Kuiper 13–4–22–1; Pienaar 13–3–34–2; Gooch 21.2–15–15–4; Hobson 13–2–33–0.

Western Province

G. A. Gooch b Robinson	4	– lbw b Robinson	34
L. Seeff b McMillan	12	– lbw b Ferreira	13
†R. J. Ryall c Day b Ferreira	42		
*P. N. Kirsten c Proctor b Ferreira	18	– (3) b Ferreira	1
K. S. McEwan c Proctor b McMillan	100	– (4) c Day b Ferreira	0
R. F. Pienaar lbw b Proctor	9	– (5) not out	67
P. H. Rayner c Day b Ferreira	18	– (6) c Barnard b Robinson	47
A. P. Kuiper c du Preez b Ferreira	15	– (7) run out	5
S. T. Jefferies c du Preez b Robinson	49	– (8) not out	0
D. L. Hobson c Day b McMillan	0		
G. S. le Roux not out	24		
B 2, l-b 5, w 4, n-b 2	13	B 2, l-b 6	8

1/4 2/34 3/70 4/91   304   1/41 2/51 3/51 4/52   (6 wkts) 175
5/116 6/170 7/202 8/234 9/234   5/166 6/171

Bowling: *First Innings*—Robinson 20.4–1–51–2; McMillan 22–8–64–3; Ferreira 25–8–63–4; Ackermann 10–0–55–0; Proctor 12–4–40–1; Barnard 7–2–18–0. *Second Innings* —Robinson 12–4–55–2; McMillan 7–1–31–0; Ferreira 14.1–0–62–3; du Preez 3–0–19–0.

Umpires: S. G. Moore and P. L. Van der Merwe.

NATAL v TRANSVAAL

At Kingsmead, Durban, March 26, 27, 28. Transvaal won by 39 runs. Transvaal 18 pts, Natal 5 pts.

Transvaal

S. J. Cook c Madsen b Clare	31	– c A. J. S. Smith b Taylor	7
H. R. Fotheringham c A. J. S. Smith b Lever	45	– lbw b Lever	4
K. A. McKenzie lbw b Lever	95	– not out	164
R. G. Pollock run out	20	– b Lever	30
*C. E. B. Rice c A. J. S. Smith b Lever	24	– not out	51
A. J. Kourie b Lever	11		
†R. V. Jennings b Taylor	14		
N. V. Radford c Cooper b Taylor	45		
C. D. Mitchley not out	25		
K. J. Kerr not out	9		
B 1, l-b 9, w 2	12	B 1, l-b 4	5

1/51 2/111 3/192 (8 wkts dec.) 331   1/10 2/22 3/113 (3 wkts dec.) 261
4/206 5/235 6/238 7/284 8/307

V. A. P. van der Bijl did not bat.

Bowling: *First Innings*—Taylor 26–7–70–2; Lever 37–5–124–4; Cooper 21–5–76–0; Clare 12–3–49–1. *Second Innings*—Taylor 17–1–62–1; Lever 22–1–91–2; Cooper 10–0–42–0; Clare 7–0–61–0.

Natal

B. J. Whitfield c Jennings b Radford	8	– c and b Kerr	83
R. A. Smith c Pollock b van der Bijl	75	– (4) c Kourie b Kerr	21
R. M. Bentley c Jennings b Mitchley	45	– b Kourie	13
D. Bestall not out	80	– (6) not out	52
T. R. Madsen lbw b van der Bijl	13	– c Cook b Kerr	4
*B. A. Richards st Jennings b Kerr	3	– (2) c McKenzie b Kerr	82
†A. J. S. Smith b Mitchley	19	– c sub b Kourie	19
M. D. Clare c Cook b Mitchley	0	– (10) c Jennings b Kourie	2
J. K. Lever run out	5	– b Kourie	2
K. R. Cooper c Cook b Radford	1	– (8) c Jennings b Radford	0
L. B. Taylor c Jennings b van der Bijl	2	– c Radford b Kourie	0
B 2, w 1, n-b 10	13	L-b 10, n-b 1	11

1/30 2/125 3/152 4/172 264   1/156 2/178 3/190 4/200 289
5/177 6/218 7/225 8/251 9/259   5/222 6/262 7/263 8/270 9/279

Bowling: *First Innings*—van der Bijl 28.3–13–37–3; Radford 26–7–68–2; Kourie 16–4–54–0; Mitchley 12–1–46–3; Kerr 20–4–46–1. *Second Innings*—van der Bijl 5–3–2–0; Radford 16–2–50–1; Kourie 36–6–111–5; Mitchley 4–0–23–0; Kerr 25–4–92–4.

Umpires: D. D. Schoof and K. E. Liebenberg.

TRANSVAAL v WESTERN PROVINCE

Currie Cup Challenge Match

At Wanderers, Johannesburg, April 2, 3, 4, 5. Drawn.

Transvaal

S. J. Cook c and b Henry	49	– lbw b Emburey	26
H. R. Fotheringham c Pienaar b Jefferies	89	– not out	44
A. I. Kallicharran c Ryall b Jefferies	151	– not out	23
R. G. Pollock c Ryall b Gooch	17		
*C. E. B. Rice c Henry b Emburey	15		
K. A. McKenzie c Seeff b Henry	92		
A. J. Kourie b Jefferies	11		
†R. V. Jennings not out	28		
N. V. Radford c Emburey b Henry	7		
V. A. P. van der Bijl b Henry	5		
R. W. Hanley b Emburey	3		
L-b 5, w 1, n-b 2	8	B 4	4

1/106 2/214 3/248 4/299 　　　　　　475　1/47　　　　　　(1 wkt) 97
5/362 6/380 7/440 8/450 9/470

Bowling: *First Innings*—Jefferies 32–2–161–3; Kuiper 5–2–16–0; Gooch 27–5–63–1; Emburey 40.5–6–137–2; Henry 16–2–48–4; Pienaar 11–2–42–0. *Second Innings*—Jefferies 10–0–31–0; Emburey 16–5–33–1; Henry 7–4–24–0; Kirsten 1–0–5–0.

Western Province

G. A. Gooch b van der Bijl	11	– lbw b Kourie	36
L. Seeff c Jennings b van der Bijl	7	– lbw b van der Bijl	71
*P. N. Kirsten b Hanley	19	– b van der Bijl	168
K. S. McEwan c Rice b Radford	9	– not out	130
R. F. Pienaar b Radford	51	– c Jennings b Radford	19
P. H. Rayner c and b Kourie	13	– c Jennings b van der Bijl	8
A. P. Kuiper b Radford	4	– not out	23
S. T. Jefferies c Fotheringham b Kourie	38	– c Jennings b van der Bijl	10
O. Henry c Kourie b Hanley	50	– c Jennings b Radford	1
J. E. Emburey lbw b van der Bijl	0		
†R. J. Ryall not out	12		
B 3, l-b 7, n-b 4	14	B 1, l-b 16, n-b 7	24

1/18 2/21 3/35 4/75 　　　　　　228　1/53 2/190 3/371　(7 wkts dec.) 490
5/112 6/124 7/124 8/204 9/207 　　　　　4/407 5/428 6/440 7/441

Bowling: *First Innings*—Hanley 18.1–3–55–2; van der Bijl 21–13–23–3; Kourie 28–14–63–2; Radford 11–0–68–3; Kallicharran 2–0–5–0. *Second Innings*—Hanley 21–2–107–0; van der Bijl 35–5–109–4; Kourie 24–2–84–1; Radford 30–3–143–2; Kallicharran 3–0–23–0.

Umpires: D. D. Schoof and B. J. Meyer.

SAB BOWL, 1982-83

					Bonus Points		Total
	Played	Won	Lost	Drawn	Batting	Bowling	Points
Western Province B	6	5	0	1	19	23	92
Transvaal B	6	3	2	1	16	27	73
Natal B	6	3	3	0	14	26	70
Orange Free State	6	2	3	1	13	24	57
Border	6	2	0	4	10	26	56
Boland	6	1	2	3	13	24	47
Eastern Province B	6	0	1	5	23	22	45
Northern Transvaal B	6	1	4	1	9	24	43
Griqualand West	6	1	3	2	12	18	40

SAB BOWL, 1982-83

At Ramblers, Bloemfontein, November 4, 5, 6. Western Province B won by ten wickets. Orange Free State 346 for seven dec. (R. A. le Roux 144, S. N. Hartley 61, R. J. East 52) and 70 (O. Henry six for 19, J. D. du Toit four for 21); Western Province B 416 (R. F. Pienaar 109, W. G. Kruger 80, J. Seeff 68, O. Henry 49) and 1 for no wkt. *Western Province B 17 pts, Orange Free State 7 pts.*

At De Beers Country Club, Kimberley, November 6, 7, 8. Griqualand West won by six wickets. Northern Transvaal B 271 (W. F. Morris 51, C. P. L. de Lange 48, N. Rynners 42, J. W. Furstenburg 42; P. McLaren four for 76) and 304 for seven dec. (K. D. Verdoorn 50, J. W. Furstenburg 45, G. W. Jones 43 not out, C. P. L. de Lange 41); Griqualand West 319 (K. Sharp 82, P. L. Symcox 47; H. W. Raath four for 82) and 257 for four (K. Sharp 125, M. D. Moxon 53, A. P. Beukes 40 not out). *Griqualand West 19 pts, Northern Transvaal B 7 pts.*

At Constantia, Cape Town, November 12, 13, 14. Western Province B won by eight wickets. Natal B 200 (T. R. Madsen 68, M. D. Tramontino 45) and 181 (C. P. Wilkins 40; R. R. Lawrenson four for 45); Western Province B 248 (W. G. Kruger 51, M. D. Mellor 50; M. D. Clare five for 61) and 134 for two (J. P. Ackermann 70 not out, M. D. Mellor 50). *Western Province B 16 pts, Natal B 3 pts.*

At Willowmore Park, Benoni, November 12, 13, 15. Orange Free State won by 101 runs. Orange Free State 175 (D. P. le Roux 57; T. H. D. Wheelwright four for 83) and 340 (R. A. le Roux 75, R. J. East 73, S. Curren 46 not out); Northern Transvaal B 200 (J. W. Furstenburg 76; S. Dennis five for 54) and 214 (J. W. Furstenburg 41; G. Grobler five for 59). *Orange Free State 16 pts, Northern Transvaal B 7 pts.*

At Oude Libertas, Stellenbosch, November 26, 27, 29. Boland won by 101 runs. Boland 315 (E. J. Barlow 153, A. du Toit 65) and 193 for eight dec. (E. J. Barlow 47, K. J. Barnett 47); Orange Free State 221 (D. P. le Roux 108, R. J. East 44) and 186 (D. Traut four for 83). *Boland 18 pts, Orange Free State 3 pts.*

At Wanderers, Johannesburg, November 27, 28, 29. Transvaal B won by 114 runs. Transvaal B 284 for nine dec. (H. R. Fotheringham 70, I. F. N. Weideman 47 not out, C. D. Mitchley 44; W. J. Wilson four for 40) and 246 for four dec. (H. R. Fotheringham 91, M. Yachad 65, W. Kirsh 64); Griqualand West 228 (K. Sharp 113; T. H. Parrymore four for 59, I. F. N. Weideman four for 80) and 188 (P. L. Symcox 44, H. J. Liebenberg 42; C. D. Mitchley five for 39). *Transvaal B 19 pts, Griqualand West 6 pts.*

At UPE Ground, Port Elizabeth, December 2, 3, 4. Drawn. Eastern Province B 322 (R. J. D. Whyte 176) and 249 for nine dec. (N. Mandy 45, I. K. Daniell 40); Boland 238 (K. J. Barnett 79, S. S. Barnard 57 not out; M. K. van Vuuren five for 53) and 194 for eight (K. J. Barnett 82 not out, E. J. Barlow 63; I. L. Howell four for 65). *Eastern Province B 10 pts, Boland 8 pts.*

At Oude Libertas, Stellenbosch, December 27, 28, 29. Western Province B won by 77 runs. Western Province B 227 (P. H. Rayner 64, W. G. Kruger 58, J. Seeff 53; S. A. Jones four for 22) and 150 (P. Anker four for 48); Boland 199 (K. J. Barnett 91; O. Henry five for 58) and 101 (O. Henry six for 32). *Western Province B 15 pts, Boland 2 pts.*

At UCC Ground, Uitenhage, January 1, 2, 3. Western Province B won by five wickets. Eastern Province B 245 (D. H. Howell 59, T. G. Shaw 57, G. Emslie 48) and 265 (I. K. Daniell 96); Western Province B 385 (P. H. Rayner 162, R. J. Ryall 51; T. G. Shaw four for 86, G. L. Long four for 94) and 127 for five. *Western Province B 18 pts, Eastern Province B 6 pts.*

At Jan Smuts Ground, East London, January 1, 2, 3. Border won by two wickets. Natal B 211 (G. M. Smith 47, M. D. Logan 43; G. M. Gower six for 44) and 180 (M. D. Logan 42; R. C. Ontong six for 61); Border 176 (G. C. G. Fraser 40; E. J. Hodkinson four for 40) and 216 for eight (E. T. Laughlin 53, G. C. G. Fraser 43 not out). *Border 15 pts, Natal B 6 pts.*

At George Lea Park, Sandton, Johannesburg, January 1, 3, 4. Transvaal B won by four wickets. Transvaal B 324 for eight dec. (M. S. Venter 127, M. Yachad 82, A Barrow 40) and 108 for six; Orange Free State 123 (K. J. Kerr four for 32) and 305 (J. J. Strydom 104, C. J. van Heerden 65, S. N. Hartley 54; B. Roberts four for 32). *Transvaal B 21 pts, Orange Free State 4 pts.*

At De Beers Country Club, Kimberley, February 3, 4, 5. Drawn. Griqualand West 174 (G. L. Hayes four for 13) and 279 (M. D. Moxon 119 not out, K. Sharp 53; I. Foulkes five for 64); Border 304 (I. Foulkes 110, R. C. Ontong 67) and 138 for eight (G. M. Gower 40; A. P. Beukes four for 32). *Border 6 pts, Griqualand West 2 pts.*

At Pietersburg, January 14, 15, 17. Northern Transvaal B won by 66 runs. Northern Transvaal B 87 and 276 (C. P. L. de Lange 82; C. D. Mitchley four for 84); Transvaal B 156 (W. Kirsh 46; G. E. McMillan five for 28) and 141 (A. Barrow 43; B. Proctor five for 30, G. E. McMillan four for 52). *Northern Transvaal B 15 pts, Transvaal B 5 pts.*

At Jan Smuts Stadium, Pietermaritzburg, January 15, 17, 18. Natal B won by six wickets. Boland 70 (E. J. Hodkinson four for 21) and 139 (S. A. Jones 46; P. de V. Geyer five for 31); Natal B 152 (H. Mansell 69; P. D. Swart four for 31) and 59 for four. *Natal B 15 pts, Boland 5 pts.*

At Ramblers, Bloemfontein, January 15, 17, 18. Drawn. Eastern Province B 293 (D. H. Howell 109, J. D. Ogilvie 54 not out) and 307 for nine dec. (D. H. Howell 114, M. B. Billson 41; R. A. le Roux four for 43, W. M. van der Merwe four for 63); Orange Free State 320 (R. J. East 69, W. M. van der Merwe 42 not out; B. de K. Robey four for 56) and 151 (R. A. le Roux 46; T. G. Shaw four for 33). *Orange Free State 9 pts, Eastern Province B 9 pts.*

At Jan Smuts Ground, East London, January 20, 21, 22. Drawn. Border 280 for five dec. (G. C. G. Fraser 105 not out, G. L. Hayes 68 not out, E. T. Laughlin 60) and 227 for seven (G. L. Hayes 80, G. C. G. Fraser 71; S. A. Jones four for 34); Boland 377 (K. J. Barnett 90, E. J. Barlow 82; R. C. Ontong six for 108). *Boland 7 pts, Border 6 pts.*

At Country Club, Kimberley, January 20, 21, 22. Drawn. Eastern Province B 264 (M. B. Billson 73) and 260 for nine dec. (V. G. Cresswell 55, D. H. Howell 54, D. G. Emslie 54, M. B. Billson 41; A. P. Beukes four for 50); Griqualand West 200 (K. Sharp 66; J. D Ogilvie four for 58) and 282 for nine (P. L. Symcox 80, K. Sharp 61, M. D. Moxon 57; T. G. Shaw five for 59). *Eastern Province B 8 pts, Griqualand West 5 pts.*

At Jan Smuts Ground, East London, January 27, 28, 29. Border won by four wickets. Northern Transvaal B 182 (D. N. Edwards 40; G. L. Hayes six for 57) and 176 (C. P. L. de Lange 40); Border 223 (H. W. Raath four for 56) and 136 for six (E. T. Laughlin 44, R. C. Ontong 40 not out). *Border 16 pts, Northern Transvaal 5 pts.*

At Berea Park, Pretoria, February 3, 4, 5. Drawn. Eastern Province B 262 (D. G. Emslie 78, G. L. Long 59, V. G. Cresswell 43; B. Proctor six for 74) and 266 for seven dec. (I. K. Daniell 101, T. G. Shaw 43, V. G. Cresswell 40); Northern Transvaal B 245 for nine dec. (S. Vercueil 71 not out; T. G. Shaw four for 51) and 189 for five (C. S. Stirk 79 not out). *Eastern Province B 7 pts, Northern Transvaal B 4 pts.*

At Constantia, Cape Town, February 4, 5, 6. Western Province B won by an innings and 81 runs. Western Province B 434 for eight dec. (S. D. Bruce 176, J. D. du Toit 63, M. D. Mellor 53; K. J. Kerr four for 125); Transvaal B 166 (O. Henry five for 63) and 187 (O. Henry four for 50). *Western Province B 18 pts, Transvaal B 3 pts.*

At Ramblers, Bloemfontein, February 15, 16, 17. Orange Free State won by nine wickets. Griqualand West 200 (K. Sharp 78; W. M. van der Merwe five for 49) and 198 (K. Sharp 52, G. P. van Rensburg 46; C. J. van Heerden five for 56); Orange Free State 360 (S. N. Hartley 79, R. A. le Roux 68, W. M. van der Merwe 42) and 41 for one. *Orange Free State 18 pts, Griqualand West 5 pts.*

At Prospect Ground, Grahamstown, February 25, 26, 27. Drawn. Eastern Province B 271 (J. D. Ogilvie 54, I. L. Howell 44, I. K. Daniell 43; I. Foulkes five for 73) and 65 for one; Border 379 for seven dec. (I. Foulkes 135 not out, M. R. Ballantyne 86, R. C. Ontong 56). *Border 7 pts, Eastern Province B 5 pts.*

At Wanderers, Johannesburg, February 26, 27, 28. Transvaal B won by 121 runs. Transvaal B 328 (B. Roberts 70 not out, A. Barrow 70; D. K. Pearse four for 50) and 241 for three dec. (M. S. Venter 100, A. Barrow 91); Natal B 201 (D. K. Pearse 47) and 247 (C. L. Smith 66, M. D. Tramontino 44; B. Roberts four for 56). *Transvaal B 21 pts, Natal B 7 pts.*

At Oude Libertas, Stellenbosch, March 4, 5, 7. Drawn. Boland 244 (E. J. Barlow 82) and 209 for seven dec. (A. du Toit 40); Transvaal B 136 (P. Anker four for 39) and 23 for two. *Boland 7 pts, Transvaal B 4 pts.*

At Jan Smuts Stadium, Pietermaritzburg, March 5, 6, 7. Natal B won by six wickets. Natal B 382 for eight dec. (C. L. Smith 88, R. M. Bentley 76, S. M. Hedley 54, G. N. Lister-James 51 not out, D. K. Pearse 40) and 89 for four; Griqualand West 209 (P. L. Symcox 53, K. Sharp 42, M. D. Moxon 40; E. J. Hodkinson four for 50) and 261 (F. W. Swarbrook 70, H. J. Liebenberg 61, K. Sharp 45; E. J. Hodkinson five for 40). *Natal B 17 pts, Griqualand West 3 pts.*

At Newlands, Cape Town, March 5, 6, 7. Drawn. Western Province B 242 (T. A. Clarke 68) and 258 (O. Henry 54, S. D. Bruce 43; G. M. Gower four for 64); Border 191 (W. du Plessis 52, L. Pearson 48; E. O. Simons four for 56) and 1 for no wkt. *Western Province B 8 pts, Border 6 pts.*

At Kingsmead, Durban, March 12, 13, 14. Natal B won by ten wickets. Northern Transvaal B 243 (S. Vercueil 67) and 315 (M. B. Logan 90, G. E. McMillan 66, C. P. L. de Lange 41); Natal B 441 (C. L. Smith 154, R. M. Bentley 151, S M. Hedley 51; G. L. Ackermann four for 87) and 121 for no wkt (M. D. Tramontino 71 not out). *Natal B 22 pts, Northern Transvaal B 5 pts.*

OTHER FIRST-CLASS MATCH

At Potchefstroom, December 13, 14, 15. Drawn. Transvaal 275 (M. S. Venter 80; T. G. Shaw five for 73) and 160 for two (M. Yachad 102 not out); South African Universities 101 (T. H. Parrymore four for 8) and 398 (M. D. Logan 129, T. G. Shaw 76, D. J. Richardson 50).

†DATSUN SHIELD

The Datsun Shield was again very popular. Before a large crowd Transvaal beat Western Province in the final.

At The Wanderers, Johannesburg, February 19. Transvaal won by 109 runs. Transvaal 303 for five (53 overs) (A. I. Kallicharran 74, S. J. Cook 70, H. R. Fotheringham 67, R. G. Pollock 55); Western Province 194 (48.1 overs) (K. S. McEwan 57, R. F. Pienaar 36; N. V. Radford three for 40).

THE AROSA SRI LANKANS IN SOUTH AFRICA, 1982-83

†At Berea Park, Pretoria, October 26, 27, 28. Combined Transvaal XI won by six wickets. Arosa Sri Lanka 315 for nine dec. (A. N. Ranasinghe 80, G. J. A. F. Aponso 68, J. B. N. Perera 65 not out, N. D. P. Hettiaratchi 32; H. A. Page four for 75) and 123 (B. de Silva 61); Combined Transvaal XI 313 for four dec. (B. J. Whitfield 77, V. F. du Preez 71, R. G. Pollock 66, N. T. Day 47 not out, H. R. Fotheringham 39) and 127 for four (A. M. Ferreira 32 not out, Y. Rubidge 32).

WESTERN PROVINCE v AROSA SRI LANKA

At Newlands, Cape Town, October 30, 31, November 1. Drawn.

Arosa Sri Lanka

N. D. P. Hettiaratchi c Bruce b le Roux	37 – lbw b le Roux	2
†H. H. Devapriya c Henry b Pienaar	24 – b le Roux	0
B. de Silva c Kirsten b Kuiper	15 – c Hobson b Kuiper	29
G. J. A. F. Aponso run out	1 – c Bruce b Kuiper	92
*B. Warnapura c Bruce b Henry	18 – (6) c Seeff b Hobson	14
A. N. Ranasinghe c Bruce b le Roux	0 – (7) c sub b Kuiper	52
J. B. N. Perera run out	69 – (5) c Hobson b du Toit	47
J. F. Woutersz c Kuiper b du Toit	4 – not out	42
L. W. Kaluperuma c McEwan b le Roux	67 – c Henry b Kuiper	17
A. R. Opatha lbw b le Roux	15 – b Kuiper	0
G. R. A. de Silva not out	10 – c McEwan b Henry	2
B 3, l-b 11, n-b 1	15	B 3, l-b 4, w 2, n-b 1	10

1/32 2/66 3/73 4/92   275   1/1 2/4 3/53 4/116   307
5/92 6/115 7/141 8/221 9/255   5/171 6/214 7/254 8/276 9/291

Bowling: *First Innings*—le Roux 20.5–5–31–4; Pienaar 10–2–50–1; Kuiper 10–1–42–1; du Toit 19–4–54–1; Hobson 23–7–43–0; Henry 15–4–34–1; Kirsten 1–0–6–0. *Second Innings* —le Roux 12–3–18–2; Pienaar 10–4–11–0; Kuiper 19–3–60–5; du Toit 18–6–30–1; Hobson 21–5–62–1; Henry 24.3–10–60–1; Kirsten 14–1–37–0; Clarke 3–0–19–0.

Western Province

K. S. McEwan c and b G. R. A. de Silva	149	
L. Seeff c and b Ranasinghe	105 – (8) not out	0
*P. N. Kirsten not out	70	
A. P. Kuiper b Ranasinghe	0 – (2) c Kaluperuma b Warnapura	11
†S. D. Bruce c Perera b Ranasinghe	24 – (6) b Opatha	13
T. A. Clarke b Opatha	7 – (5) c Aponso b Opatha	6
R. F. Pienaar c Devapriya b Opatha	0 – (1) c Woutersz b Opatha	37
G. S. le Roux c Kaluperuma b Warnapura	26	
O. Henry not out	8 – (4) run out	5
J. D. du Toit (did not bat)	– (3) b Opatha	13
D. L. Hobson (did not bat)	– (7) not out	16
B 5, l-b 6	11	L-b 3, w 2	5

1/235 2/276 3/276 4/316   (7 wkts dec.) 400   1/24 2/58 3/65   (6 wkts) 106
5/329 6/329 7/381   4/69 5/88 6/89

Bowling: *First Innings*—Opatha 34–6–85–2; Warnapura 17–5–42–1; Woutersz 6–0–34–0; Kaluperuma 11–1–54–0; G. R. A. de Silva 6–0–59–1; Ranasinghe 23–0–115–3. *Second Innings*—Opatha 5–0–49–4; Warnapura 4–0–37–1; Woutersz 1–0–15–0.

Umpires: B. Glass and H. R. Martin.

---

†At Oude Libertas, Stellenbosch, November 3, 4. Boland won by five wickets. Arosa Sri Lanka 208 (N. D. P. Hettiaratchi 56; P. Anker seven for 66) and 79 (D. Traut four for 32); Boland 141 (A. du Toit 54; L. W. Kaluperuma six for 38) and 149 for five (P. D. Swart 59).

---

†At Wanderers, Johannesburg, November 6 (First one-day International). South Africa won by 189 runs. South Africa 291 for four (S. J. Cook 120, R. G. Pollock 76 not out, B. A. Richards 71); Arosa Sri Lanka 102.

†At Berea Park, Pretoria, November 8 (Second one-day International). South Africa won by 107 runs. South Africa 281 for five (S. J. Cook 131, P. N. Kirsten 77, A. P. Kuiper 46 not out); Arosa Sri Lanka 174 for five (N. D. P. Hettiaratchi 50).

EASTERN PROVINCE v AROSA SRI LANKA

At St Georges Park, Port Elizabeth, November 13, 14, 15. Drawn.

Arosa Sri Lanka

N. D. P. Hettiaratchi c Cowley b Armitage	22	– c Brickett b Watson	1
B. de Silva lbw b Watson	7	– c Richardson b Williams	73
†H. M. Goonatillake b Brickett	9	– c Richardson b Carse	34
G. J. A. F. Aponso c Richardson b Brickett	9	– c and b Armitage	20
J. B. N. Perera c Brickett b Armitage	1	– b Brickett	96
*J. F. Woutersz c Richardson b Carse	76	– lbw b Howell	11
A. N. Ranasinghe b Watson	32	– c Carse b Watson	64
P. L. J. Fernando c Richardson b Brickett	19	– c Williams b Watson	1
A. R. Opatha b Carse	35	– not out	6
L. W. Kaluperuma not out	2	– not out	0
G. R. A. de Silva b Watson	3		
B 2, l-b 2, w 3, n-b 1	8	B 5, l-b 7, n-b 3	15

1/13 2/41 3/41 4/42   223   1/2 2/54 3/93   (8 wkts dec.) 321
5/63 6/113 7/153 8/209 9/218   4/210 5/229 6/306 7/313 8/315

Bowling: *First Innings*—Watson 18–7–29–3; Carse 11–2–35–2; Cowley 10–2–27–0; Armitage 23–8–52–2; Brickett 17–4–42–3; Howell 11–3–30–0. *Second Innings*—Watson 15–1–66–3; Carse 18–5–55–1; Cowley 3–1–8–0; Armitage 21–6–53–1; Brickett 13–5–35–1; Howell 17–4–46–1; Williams 7–1–43–1.

Eastern Province

†D. J. Richardson c Fernando b Woutersz	134	– c Woutersz b Opatha	19
R. L. S. Armitage c Goonatillake b Fernando	14	– (3) run out	5
R. J. D. Whyte b Fernando	0	– (4) b Opatha	34
R. G. Fensham run out	42	– (6) lbw b Fernando	6
M. B. Billson lbw b Opatha	69	– (2) c Ranasinghe b Opatha	0
P. H. Williams not out	8	– (7) c Aponso b Woutersz	29
*G. S. Cowley not out	2	– (8) not out	17
I. L. Howell (did not bat)		– (10) not out	0
D. J. Brickett (did not bat)		– (5) c Aponso b Fernando	29
W. K. Watson (did not bat)		– (9) st Goonatillake b Woutersz	0
B 1, l-b 7, n-b 10	18	B 1, l-b 14, n-b 8	23

1/36 2/36 3/153   (5 wkts dec.) 287   1/1 2/21 3/32 4/87   (8 wkts) 162
4/248 5/285   5/104 6/118 7/160 8/161

J. A. Carse did not bat.

Bowling: *First Innings*—Opatha 17–3–51–1; Fernando 13–2–63–2; Woutersz 19–1–84–1; G. R. A. de Silva 2–0–16–0; Ranasinghe 6–0–32–0; Kaluperuma 7–1–23–0. *Second Innings*—Opatha 17–1–72–3; Fernando 14–1–61–2; Woutersz 2–0–6–2.

Umpires: C. M. P. Coetzee and P. R. Hurwitz.

†At Kingsmead, Durban, November 17 (Third one-day International). South Africa won by eight wickets. Arosa Sri Lanka 140 (V. A. P. van der Bijl four for 12); South Africa 143 for two (B. A. Richards 74).

SOUTH AFRICA v AROSA SRI LANKA

At Wanderers, Johannesburg, November 19, 20, 22, 23. South Africa won by an innings and 24 runs.

Arosa Sri Lanka

N. D. P. Hettiaratchi c Jennings b le Roux	1	– lbw b le Roux	1
B. de Silva c Jennings b Jefferies	70	– c and b Kourie	3
*B. Warnapura lbw b Jefferies	15	– c Jennings b Jefferies	31
G. J. A. F. Aponso lbw b le Roux	12	– c Jefferies b Kirsten	44
J. B. N. Perera c Jennings b Kuiper	2	– c Pollock b Jefferies	0
J. F. Woutersz lbw b le Roux	51	– c Kuiper b Kourie	0
P. L. J. Fernando c Rice b van der Bijl	21	– absent hurt	
L. W. Kaluperuma c Rice b le Roux	2	– (7) c Richards b Kourie	39
†H. M. Goonatillake not out	15	– (8) b Kourie	2
A. R. Opatha c Jennings b le Roux	9	– (9) c and b Kourie	4
G. R. A. de Silva c Jennings b le Roux	0	– (10) not out	8
L-b 5, w 9, n-b 1	15	B 4, l-b 3, w 2	9

1/10 2/34 3/73 4/76	213	1/6 2/46 3/46 4/49	141
5/134 6/176 7/179 8/193 9/213		5/51 6/103 7/123 8/131 9/141	

Bowling: *First Innings*—le Roux 18.3–1–55–6; van der Bijl 21–4–51–1; Jefferies 14–3–44–2; Kourie 15–2–42–0; Kuiper 4–0–6–1. *Second Innings*—le Roux 8–1–22–1; van der Bijl 14–8–22–0; Jefferies 14–4–29–2; Kourie 22–6–54–5; Kirsten 4.1–2–5–1.

South Africa

S. J. Cook b Perera	169	A. J. Kourie lbw b Opatha	11
B. A. Richards b Opatha	1	†R. V. Jennings lbw b Kaluperuma	2
S. T. Jefferies c Fernando b Kaluperuma	45	G. S. le Roux c Kaluperuma b Perera	6
		V. A. P. van der Bijl not out	4
*P. N. Kirsten c Goonatillake b Opatha	3		
R. G. Pollock c and b Kaluperuma	79	B 6, l-b 3, w 16, n-b 3	28
C. E. B. Rice b Kaluperuma	19		
A. P. Kuiper c Opatha b Kaluperuma	11		378

1/4 2/93 3/96 4/261 5/291 6/317 7/348 8/357 9/373

Bowling: Opatha 29–4–111–3; Fernando 7–1–24–0; Woutersz 2–0–11–0; Kaluperuma 45–7–123–5; G. R. A. de Silva 5–0–33–0; Perera 18.5–2–48–2.

Umpires: C. J. Mitchley and O. R. Schoof.

NATAL v AROSA SRI LANKA

At Kingsmead, Durban, November 27, 28, 29. Natal won by an innings and 95 runs.

Arosa Sri Lanka

N. D. P. Hettiaratchi c Smith b Clare	9	– c sub b Hodkinson	0
B. de Silva b Cooper	13	– lbw b Clare	0
*B. Warnapura c Bestall b Cooper	12	– c Wilkins b Clare	1
G. J. A. F. Aponso c Smith b Cooper	16	– c Madsen b Clare	8
A. N. Ranasinghe b Wilkins	13	– b Cooper	50
J. B. N. Perera not out	39	– b Hodkinson	3
H. H. Devapriya c Bestall b Cooper	4	– b Clare	27
L. W. Kaluperuma c Smith b Cooper	0	– b Cooper	4
†H. M. Goonatillake c Smith b Cooper	0	– lbw b Clare	0
S. Karunaratne lbw b Hodkinson	16	– c Daniels b Clare	1
G. R. A. de Silva c Cooper b Hodkinson	3	– not out	5
W 1, n-b 3	4	L-b 3, n-b 2	5

1/24 2/24 3/45 4/61   129   1/0 2/1 3/9 4/24   104
5/68 6/73 7/77 8/77 9/113   5/27 6/88 7/94 8/94 9/96

Bowling: *First Innings*—Hodkinson 9.4–1–33–2; Clare 12–6–23–1; Cooper 20–10–36–6; Daniels 3–1–5–0; Wilkins 14–3–28–1. *Second Innings*—Hodkinson 9–1–46–2; Clare 11–1–49–6; Cooper 3–1–4–2; Daniels 1–1–0–0.

Natal

M. B. Logan c Goonatillake b Karunaratne.	28	T. R. Madsen b Perera	58
C. P. Wilkins lbw b Karunaratne	26	K. R. Cooper c Kaluperuma b Ranasinghe.	9
R. M. Bentley c Aponso b Kaluperuma.	35	E. J. Hodkinson c Kaluperuma b Ranasinghe.	3
D. Bestall c Aponso b Kaluperuma	32	M. D. Clare not out	0
N. P. Daniels b Perera	19	B 3, l-b 6	9
*B. A. Richards retired ill	52		
†A. J. S. Smith c Aponso b Ranasinghe.	57	1/69 2/96 3/99 4/141 328	
		5/143 6/274 7/304 8/319 9/328	

Bowling: Karunaratne 29–8–72–2; Ranasinghe 39–8–123–3; Warnapura 3–0–9–0; Kaluperuma 19–4–62–2; Perera 22.1–5–53–2.

Umpires: B. C. Smith and D. H. Bezuidenhout.

†At St Georges Park, Port Elizabeth, December 1 (Fourth one-day International). South Africa won by six wickets. Arosa Sri Lanka 276 for nine (A. N. Ranasinghe 100, G. J. A. F. Aponso 48, H. H. Devapriya 44). South Africa 278 for four (L. Seeff 142, P. N. Kirsten 100).

TRANSVAAL v AROSA SRI LANKA

At Wanderers, Johannesburg, December 4, 5, 6. Transvaal won by an innings and 40 runs.

Arosa Sri Lanka

H. H. Devapriya c Jennings b Hanley	2	– c Jennings b Radford	7
B. de Silva c Radford b Hanley	0	– c Jennings b Radford	31
*B. Warnapura b Mitchley	8	– c Jennings b Hanley	10
G. J. A. F. Aponso c Jennings b Parrymore	7	– c Jennings b Parrymore	18
J. B. N. Perera c Fotheringham b Weideman	50	– b Mitchley	28
J. F. Woutersz c Jennings b Weideman	10	– c Jennings b Weideman	12
P. L. J. Fernando c Fotheringham b Parrymore	0	– b Weideman	17
L. W. Kaluperuma c Jennings b Parrymore	9	– c Jennings b Parrymore	15
†H. M. Goonatillake c Yachad b Hanley	15	– c Yachad b Radford	20
S. Karunaratne not out	6	– b Radford	6
G. R. A. de Silva b Hanley	5	– not out	23
L-b 4, w 1, n-b 5	10	B 7, l-b 3, w 3	13

1/2 2/3 3/21 4/21   122   1/9 2/22 3/67 4/71   200
5/48 6/50 7/62 8/83 9/87   5/100 6/130 7/132 8/155 9/173

Bowling: *First Innings*—Hanley 12.2–4–41–5; Radford 11–2–24–0; Mitchley 5–1–14–1; Parrymore 8–3–22–2; Weideman 4–2–11–2. *Second Innings*—Hanley 13–1–25–1; Radford 12.5–1–56–4; Mitchley 6–1–24–1; Parrymore 11–4–49–2; Weideman 9–1–33–2.

Transvaal

M. Yachad b G. R. A. de Silva	50
M. S. Venter not out	132
H. R. Fotheringham not out	159
B 9, l-b 7, w 3, n-b 2	21

1/97   (1 wkt dec.) 362

*C. E. B. Rice, †R. V. Jennings, C. D. Mitchley, N. V. Radford, I. F. N. Weideman, K. J. Kerr, T. H. Parrymore and R. W. Hanley did not bat.

Bowling: Karunaratne 18–4–57–0; Fernando 8–1–41–0; Warnapura 6–1–22–0; Woutersz 3–0–11–0; G. R. A. de Silva 31–3–133–1; Kaluperuma 14–3–55–0; Perera 5–0–22–0.

Umpires: A. J. Norton and B. M. P. Alistoun.

SOUTH AFRICA v AROSA SRI LANKA

At Newlands, Cape Town, December 9, 10, 11, 13. South Africa won by an innings and 100 runs.

Arosa Sri Lanka

N. D. P. Hettiaratchi c Jennings b le Roux	4	– (3) b Hobson	10
H. H. Devapriya c Seeff b Kuiper	29	– st Jennings b Hobson	53
*B. Warnapura c Pollock b Kuiper	21	– (1) b Jefferies	14
G. J. A. F. Aponso c sub b Kirsten	81	– b Kuiper	7
A. N. Ranasinghe c Hobson b Jefferies	54	– b Kuiper	9
J. B. N. Perera c Seeff b Hobson	13	– c Rice b Jefferies	102
J. F. Woutersz c Jennings b le Roux	31	– c Jefferies b Hobson	32
†H. M. Goonatillake b Jefferies	19	– c Pollock b le Roux	10
L. W. Kaluperuma b Jefferies	9	– (10) not out	1
A. R. Opatha not out	5	– (9) lbw b Jefferies	20
G. R. A. de Silva b le Roux	0	– st Jennings b Kirsten	0
L-b 6, w 4, n-b 6	16	L-b 15, w 4, n-b 4	23

1/4 2/47 3/77 4/150   282   1/48 2/83 3/90 4/102   281
5/174 6/229 7/268 8/268 9/281   5/109 6/186 7/236 8/271 9/280

Bowling: *First Innings*—le Roux 18.5–5–69–3; Jefferies 18–5–43–3; Kuiper 13–3–37–2; Kourie 6–0–12–0; Hobson 25–2–77–1; Kirsten 10–1–28–1. *Second Innings*—le Roux 12–3–39–1; Jefferies 19–6–76–3; Kuiper 12–3–33–2; Hobson 34–9–87–3; Kirsten 4.2–0–23–1.

South Africa

S. J. Cook b Ranasinghe	112	†R. V. Jennings not out	11
L. Seeff c Woutersz b Perera	188		
*P. N. Kirsten run out	27	B 2, l-b 12, w 2, n-b 9	25
R. G. Pollock c Goonatillake b Perera	197		
C. E. B. Rice c Perera b Opatha	37	(6 wkts dec.) 663	
A. P. Kuiper st Goonatillake		1/250 2/328	
b Woutersz.	66	3/344 4/449	
		5/623 6/663	

G. S. le Roux, S. T. Jefferies, A. J. Kourie and D. L. Hobson did not bat.

Bowling: Opatha 42–5–150–1; Ranasinghe 36–3–123–1; de Silva 7–0–41–0; Kaluperuma 16–0–110–0; Perera 42.3–3–154–2; Woutersz 16–0–60–1.

Umpires: B. C. Smith and D. D. Schoof.

WEST INDIES TEAM IN SOUTH AFRICA, 1982-83

†At Newlands, Cape Town, January 15. West Indies XI won by 21 runs. West Indies XI 204 for nine (50 overs) (C. L. King 79 not out, L. G. Rowe 66; S. T. Jefferies four for 31); Western Province 183 (49.4 overs) (G. A. Gooch 64, K. S. McEwan 37; E. A. Moseley four for 23).

†At Jan Smuts Ground, East London, January 17. West Indies XI won by seven wickets. Border 100 for eight (50 overs); West Indies XI 101 for three (22.5 overs) (C. L. King 56 not out).

†At St Georges Park, Port Elizabeth, January 19. West Indies XI won by 85 runs. West Indies XI 243 (49.2 overs) (C. L. King 71, A. I. Kallicharran 65, L. G. Rowe 41; J. A. Carse four for 31); Eastern Province 158 (44.2 overs) (R. L. S. Armitage 58, P. Willey 40; F. D. Stephenson five for 20).

SOUTH AFRICA v WEST INDIES XI

At Newlands, Cape Town, January 21, 22, 24. 25. South Africa won by five wickets.

South Africa

S. J. Cook c Murray b Stephenson	73	– c Rowe b Moseley	6
B. A. Richards c Rowe b Moseley	49	– c Parry b Clarke	7
*P. N. Kirsten lbw b Parry	2	– b Parry	13
R. G. Pollock b Moseley	100	– not out	43
C. E. B. Rice lbw b Parry	16	– lbw b Clarke	6
K. A. McKenzie lbw b Parry	4	– lbw b Parry	0
A. J. Kourie c Murray b Moseley	69	– not out	12
†R. V. Jennings b Parry	15		
G. S. le Roux c and b Stephenson	30		
V. A. P. van der Bijl c Stephenson b Parry	10		
S. T. Jefferies not out	40		
B 18, l-b 13, w 2, n-b 8	41	B 8, l-b 5, w 5, n-b 3	21

1/85 2/98 3/201 4/264	449	1/14 2/18 3/65 (5 wkts) 108
5/270 6/276 7/351 8/371 9/382		4/82 5/85

Bowling: *First Innings*—Clarke 34–9–88–0; Moseley 25–3–87–3; Stephenson 23.4–0–93–2; Parry 43–10–117–5; Austin 7–1–23–0. *Second Innings*—Clarke 15–4–22–2; Moseley 8–1–25–1; Parry 7–1–40–2.

West Indies XI

R. A. Austin c Jennings b van der Bijl	93	– b Kourie	23
A. T. Greenidge b Jefferies	4	– lbw b le Roux	23
E. H. Mattis lbw b le Roux	0	– c Jennings b le Roux	19
A. I. Kallicharran b van der Bijl	21	– st Jennings b Kourie	89
*L. G. Rowe c Kourie b van der Bijl	9	– lbw b Jefferies	26
C. L. King c Jennings b van der Bijl	19	– b Jefferies	13
†D. A. Murray b Kourie	3	– c Jennings b le Roux	27
D. R. Parry b Kourie	18	– lbw b Jefferies	29
F. D. Stephenson run out	56	– b Jefferies	16
E. A. Moseley st Jennings b Kourie	8	– c Kirsten b van der Bijl	25
S. T. Clarke not out	5	– not out	0
B 1, l-b 7, n-b 2	10	B 3, l-b 9, w 3, n-b 4	19
	246		**309**

1/8 2/9 3/46 4/66   1/43 2/70 3/73 4/127
5/86 6/89 7/129 8/212 9/232   5/177 6/198 7/253 8/280 9/308

Bowling: *First Innings*—le Roux 17–4–56–1; Jefferies 9–4–28–1; van der Bijl 20–6–44–4; Kourie 28–6–101–3; Kirsten 1–0–7–0. *Second Innings*—le Roux 21–5–71–3; Jefferies 35.4–17–58–4; van der Bijl 22–4–46–1; Kourie 31–4–94–2; Kirsten 13–3–21–0.

Umpires: B. C. Smith and O. R. Schoof.

SOUTH AFRICA v WEST INDIES XI

At Wanderers, Johannesburg, January 28, 29, 31, February 1. West Indies XI won by 29 runs.

West Indies XI

R. A. Austin c Pollock b van der Bijl	4	– c McKenzie b van der Bijl	14
A. T. Greenidge not out	42	– c Jennings b le Roux	48
E. H. Mattis lbw b le Roux	3	– b Jefferies	21
A. I. Kallicharran b Kourie	37	– b van der Bijl	13
*L. G. Rowe b van der Bijl	0	– b Jefferies	0
C. L. King lbw b Kourie	101	– lbw b Kourie	39
†D. A. Murray c Pollock b van der Bijl	8	– c Cook b Jefferies	4
D. R. Parry b Kourie	20	– b van der Bijl	15
F. D. Stephenson c Pollock b Kourie	0	– c Pollock b le Roux	4
S. T. Clarke c Rice b Kourie	25	– c Kourie b le Roux	0
R. A. Wynter b Kourie	9	– not out	0
L-b 9, w 2, n-b 7	18	B 4, l-b 4, w 5, n-b 5	18
	267		**176**

1/13 2/16 3/39 4/104   1/33 2/56 3/56 4/57
5/164 6/185 7/185 8/222 9/233   5/65 6/70 7/70 8/105 9/176

Bowling: *First Innings*—le Roux 17–2–58–1; Jefferies 16–3–62–0; van der Bijl 16–3–74–3; Kourie 29–9–55–6. *Second Innings*—le Roux 15.1–3–46–3; Jefferies 22–8–66–3; van der Bijl 16–7–24–2; Kourie 9–2–22–2.

South Africa

S. J. Cook c Wynter b Stephenson	0	– c King b Clarke	27
B. A. Richards c Kallicharran b Clarke	0	– b Parry	59
†R. V. Jennings c Parry b Clarke	0	– c Murray b Clarke	0
*P. N. Kirsten b Clarke	56	– b Clarke	7
R. G. Pollock b Stephenson	73	– c King b Clarke	1
C. E. B. Rice c Austin b Parry	38	– c Austin b Clarke	12
K. A. McKenzie c Rowe b Wynter	27	– not out	26
A. J. Kourie lbw b Clarke	17	– c Murray b Clarke	5
G. S. le Roux lbw b Wynter	0	– lbw b King	2
S. T. Jefferies b Clarke	11	– run out	31
V. A. P. van der Bijl not out	1	– b Clarke	2
L-b 7, w 1, n-b 2	10	B 1, l-b 4, w 1, n-b 3	9

1/1 2/1 3/8 4/122   233   1/87 2/97 3/97 4/100   181
5/151 6/199 7/203 8/204 9/230   5/111 6/117 7/119 8/124 9/179

Bowling: *First Innings*—Clarke 23.3–4–66–5; Wynter 11–3–26–2; Stephenson 18–1–68–2; King 7–2–29–0; Parry 17–5–25–1; Austin 2–0–9–0. *Second Innings*—Clarke 22.2–10–34–7; Wynter 9–0–33–0; Stephenson 18–3–47–0; King 1–0–3–1; Parry 20–3–51–1; Austin 1–0–4–0.

Umpires: D. D. Schoof and C. J. Mitchley.

†At Kingsmead, Durban, February 3. A Natal XI won by 84 runs. Natal 202 for eight (50 overs) (B. A. Richards 53, M. D. Tramontino 50; F. D. Stephenson four for 46); West Indies XI 118 (38.3 overs) (C. E. H. Croft 33, H. S. Chang 30; K. R. Cooper three for 26).

†At St Georges Park, Port Elizabeth, February 5 (First one-day International). South Africa won by 91 runs. South Africa 250 for seven (50 overs) (B. A. Richards 102, R. G. Pollock 66 not out, S. J. Cook 40); West Indies XI 159 (44.3 overs) (A. T. Greenidge 32; A. J. Kourie three for 24).

†At Newlands, Cape Town, February 7 (Second one-day International). South Africa won by 43 runs. South Africa 194 for eight (50 overs) (K. S. McEwan 61, P. N. Kirsten 50, G. S. le Roux 34 not out; B. D. Julien three for 17); West Indies XI 151 (42.4 overs) (E. N. Trotman 46, S. T. Clarke 31; S. T. Jefferies three for 21, A. J. Kourie three for 39).

†At Berea Park, Pretoria, February 9 (Third one-day International). South Africa won by 12 runs. South Africa 179 for nine (50 overs) (K. S. McEwan 38, A. J. Kourie 37; E. A. Moseley four for 27); West Indies XI 167 (47 overs) (F. D. Stephenson 35, L. G. Rowe 33; V. A. P. van der Bijl three for 21).

†At Wanderers, Johannesburg, February 11 (Fourth one-day International). West Indies XI won by seven wickets. South Africa 139 (42.1 overs) (F. D. Stephenson three for 30); West Indies XI 141 for three (38.4 overs) (L. G. Rowe 34 not out, H. S. Chang 33).

†At Wanderers, Johannesburg, February 12 (Fifth one-day International). South Africa won by 57 runs. South Africa 228 for six (50 overs) (R. L. S. Armitage 46, K. S. McEwan 40, C. E. B. Rice 35); West Indies XI 171 (41.3 overs) (L. G. Rowe 71, A. I. Kallicharran 53; R. W. Hanley four for 25).

†At Kingsmead, Durban, February 13 (Sixth one-day International). West Indies XI won by 84 runs. West Indies XI 155 (36.5 overs) (C. L. King 60); South Africa 71 (25.5 overs) (F. D. Stephenson six for 9).

CRICKET IN WEST INDIES, 1982-83

By TONY COZIER

In becoming the first team ever to win the Shell Shield and the Geddes Grant/ Harrison Line Trophy in the same season, Guyana achieved an astonishing transformation of fortunes. Since last clinching the Shield in 1975, they had endured seven depressing seasons. In that time, they won only a single Shield match and lost ten; they had been bottom of the table four times and one from the bottom twice. Yet now they won four of their five Shield matches by convincing margins, while drawing the other against defending champions Barbados, and they were never seriously challenged in the limited-overs tournament, beating Jamaica by 128 runs in the final.

The Guyanese owed their success to many factors, the most influential, without doubt, being the leadership of the West Indies captain, Clive Lloyd. Owing to international commitments, Lloyd had last led them in the Shield in 1975, the year, significantly, when they last won it. His presence and stature helped remove the self-doubt which had afflicted their cricket. With another experienced cricketer, the former West Indies opening batsman, Roy Fredericks, as player/manager, a confident team spirit emerged. Lloyd himself scored two centuries, while Fredericks, returning to the team after an absence of two seasons at the age of 40 and as a junior minister responsible for sport in the government of Guyana, made 103 and 217 in his only two innings.

Guyana's younger players also contributed much to their triumph. The aggressive opening bat, Andrew Lyght, finally confirmed the potential he had shown for some years, scoring 493 Shield runs at an average of 61.62, while the spin trio of Roger Harper and Clive Butts (both off-spin) and Derek Kallicharran (leg-spin), brother of the former Test player, Alvin, claimed 65 wickets between them. Derek Kallicharran's left-handed batting also made him one of the season's leading all-rounders. Leslaine Lambert, big and strong, bowled with speed and hostility and took twenty wickets.

The season was overshadowed, however, by the furore over the unauthorised tour of South Africa by a team of seventeen West Indians under the captaincy of Lawrence Rowe. The controversy was intense, although the public at large expressed some sympathy for the players' positions in view of the fees they were earning. The venture brought automatic life bans on all who went and considerably weakened the Barbados and Jamaica teams. Eight of those who were in the Barbados team which won the Shell Shield in 1982 headed for South Africa, and it was a tribute to the standard of cricket on that small island that reserves of sufficient strength could be found to complete victories over the Leeward Islands, Jamaica and Trinidad & Tobago. Jamaica lost four of its most experienced batsmen and found it impossible to replace them, failing to win a single match and finishing last of the six teams.

The Windward Islands, unaffected by defections to South Africa, embarrassed those who claimed their performance the previous year, when they were runners-up, was a flash in the pan. Victories over Barbados, Trinidad & Tobago and the Leewards, the last in a dramatic finish by 1 run, again placed them second, their fast bowler, Winston Davis, creating a Shield record for the number of wickets in a season (33) and finding a place in the Test team.

Two batsmen passed 500 runs in the Shield – the little Trinidadian, Augustine Logie, who scored 540 at 60 an innings in a weak side and earned his Test cap against India, and the left-handed Barbadian, Thelston Payne, another diminutive player who might hardly have played at all but for the exodus to South Africa. Payne seized his opportunity with three centuries and 517 runs at 73.85, which placed him top of the overall averages.

The established fast bowlers – Andy Roberts, Malcolm Marshall and Wayne Daniel – more than held their own, but there were also young bowlers, of every variety, who enhanced reputations. Butts and Harper were the leading spinners, and Ganesh Mahabir, bowling leg-breaks, impressed in his first season for Trinidad & Tobago. Eldine Baptiste, at a lively fast-medium pace and with an impressive action, never failed to take a wicket, his 26 for the Leewards at under twenty each suggesting that he could be a Test player of the near future.

The Barbadian fast bowler, Hartley Alleyne, who had been called for throwing three seasons earlier, was again no-balled for his action, once in Jamaica and twice in Trinidad. The Windward Islands player, Wilfred Slack, while deputising as captain in the match against Jamaica, was given a one-game suspension by the West Indies Board for an incident in the field.

An international team, led by the New Zealander, John Wright, played against a West Indies team in the second Jamaica Festival in September, during which the England off-spinner, Eddie Hemmings, created a record for West Indies first-class cricket by taking all ten wickets in a four-day match. Lancashire and Essex undertook unofficial tours of Barbados, where they played against club opposition. Night cricket continued to flourish in Barbados where an island team, led by Sir Gary Sobers, played two matches against an international eleven. In January Bermuda toured Jamaica.

FIRST-CLASS AVERAGES, 1982-83

BATTING

(Qualification: 150 runs, average 35.00)

	M	I	NO	R	HI	Avge
T. R. O. Payne (*Barbados*)	6	10	2	543	123	67.87
C. H. Lloyd (*Guyana*)	10	14	1	819	143	63.00
A. A. Lyght (*Guyana*).............	5	9	1	493	112	61.62
V. A. Eddy (*Leeward I*)	5	9	2	429	124	61.28
P. J. Dujon (*Jamaica*).............	11	17	3	762	110	54.42
C. G. Greenidge (*Barbados*).....	11	18	3	785	237	52.33
S. I. Williams (*Leeward I*)........	3	5	0	255	120	51.00
L. C. Sebastien (*Windward I*) ...	6	12	1	480	122	43.63
S. F. A. Bacchus (*Guyana*).......	5	8	0	349	143	43.62
A. L. Logie (*T & T*)	11	18	1	727	138	42.76
D. L. Haynes (*Barbados*)..........	11	18	1	725	136	42.64
I. V. A. Richards (*Leeward I*)...	6	8	0	327	109	40.87
C. W. Fletcher (*Jamaica*)	6	11	1	393	99	39.30
S. W. Julien (*Windward I*)	6	12	0	462	123	38.50
O. W. Peters (*Jamaica*)............	6	11	0	419	89	38.09
H. A. Gomes (*T & T*)	6	7	0	252	123	36.00
P. V. Simmonds (*T & T*)	6	12	0	428	106	35.66
D. I. Kallicharran (*Guyana*)	5	8	1	248	57	35.42

BOWLING

(Qualification: 15 wickets)

	O	*M*	*R*	*W*	*Avge*
W. W. Davis (*Windward I*).............	324	63	802	45	17.82
L. A. Lambert (*Guyana*).................	112.2	21	358	20	17.90
C. Butts (*Guyana*)	209.3	59	458	25	18.32
W. W. Daniel (*Barbados*)	109.3	11	409	22	18.59
E. A. E. Baptiste (*Leeward I*).........	177.4	36	569	28	20.32
A. M. E. Roberts (*Leeward I*)	350	65	1,059	52	20.36
R. A. Harper (*Guyana*)	233	66	492	24	20.50
N. F. Williams (*Windward I*)	94.2	22	367	17	21.58
H. L. Alleyne (*Barbados*)	123.2	25	398	18	22.11
G. N. Linton (*Barbados*)................	127.2	25	344	15	22.93
M. D. Marshall (*Barbados*)	370.4	85	1,020	41	24.87
G. Mahabir (*T & T*)......................	267.1	59	707	27	26.18
N. Phillip (*Windward I*)	149.2	18	498	19	26.21
D. I. Kallicharran (*Guyana*)	161.5	44	427	16	26.68
N. A. Phillips (*Barbados*)...............	145.5	28	467	17	27.47
R. Nanan (*T & T*)	378.3	82	869	26	33.42
M. A. Holding (*Jamaica*)	196.2	30	639	15	42.60

Note: Matches taken into account are Shell Shield and those against the Indian touring side.

SHELL SHIELD, 1982-83

	Won	*Lost*	*Drawn*	*1st Inns lead*	*1st Inns arrears*	*Pts*
Guyana	4	0	1	0	2†	68
Windward Islands............	3	1	1	2*	1†	61
Barbados	3	1	1	1	0	56
Leeward Islands	1	3	1	2*	0	29
Trinidad & Tobago..........	0	3	2	1*	2	13
Jamaica	0	3	2	1	1	12

* *First-innings lead on one match lost outright.*
† *First-innings arrears on one match won outright.*

Win = 16 pts; first-innings win in match lost outright = 5 pts; first-innings lead in drawn match = 8 pts; first-innings arrears in drawn match = 4 pts.

JAMAICA v TRINIDAD & TOBAGO

At Sabina Park, Kingston, January 21, 22, 23, 24. Drawn. Trinidad & Tobago 4 pts, Jamaica 8 pts. Toss won by Jamaica.

Jamaica

G. Powell b Williams	0	– run out	49
O. W. Peters c Williams b Mahabir	82	– run out	79
C. W. Fletcher c Lyon b Williams	27	– b Nanan	0
H. S. Chang c Mahabir b Nanan	64	– (6) c Cuffy b Antoine	22
M. C. Neita lbw b Mahabir	74	– (5) c sub b Nanan	1
*†P. J. Dujon c and b Williams	49	– (4) run out	34
M. A. Tucker c Simmonds b Nanan	12	– (8) not out	0
C. Gordon c Cuffy b Mahabir	15		
J. A. Williams c Gabriel b Mahabir	0		
C. U. Thompson not out	28	– (7) b Antoine	2
C. A. Walsh lbw b Mahabir	16		
B 12, l-b 10, n-b 1	23	L-b 3, n-b 1	4

1/0 2/42 3/176 4/186   390   1/95 2/96 3/150   (7 wkts dec.) 191
5/296 6/317 7/329 8/333 9/361   4/155 5/188 6/188 7/191

Bowling: First Innings—Williams 18–0–78–3; Antoine 19–3–66–0; Nanan 50–11–103–2; d'Heurieux 1–0–7–0; Mahabir 43.1–8–113–5. *2nd Innings*—Williams 4.2–0–31–0; Antoine 12–1–51–2; Nanan 20–3–55–2; Mahabir 2–0–13–0; d'Heurieux 9–1–37–0.

Trinidad & Tobago

R. S. Gabriel b Walsh	71	– lbw b Williams	96
P. V. Simmonds run out	6	– c Dujon b Gordon	31
A. L. Logie c Neita b Williams	5	– (6) not out	36
K. G. d'Heurieux run out	59	– (3) lbw b Thompson	44
S. A. Gomes c Peters b Gordon	50	– (4) b Williams	16
*T. Cuffy lbw b Walsh	12	– (5) b Walsh	6
R. Nanan c Thompson b Gordon	33	– lbw b Gordon	19
†J. R. Lyon c Walsh b Gordon	0	– not out	4
G. S. Antoine c Powell b Gordon	6		
G. Mahabir run out	0		
K. A. Williams not out	2		
L-b 5, n-b 13	18	B 1, l-b 2, n-b 4	7

1/13 2/23 3/147 4/152   262   1/47 2/142 3/191   (6 wkts) 259
5/171 6/237 7/243 8/254 9/254   4/192 5/207 6/250

Bowling: First Innings—Williams 17–7–33–1; Walsh 25–7–79–2; Gordon 15–2–46–4; Thompson 14–3–54–0; Tucker 16–6–32–0. *Second Innings*—Williams 13–3–34–2; Walsh 19–5–49–1; Gordon 17–2–67–2; Tucker 21–1–65–0; Thompson 11–0–37–1.

Umpires: R. Bell and J. Gayle.

BARBADOS v LEEWARD ISLANDS

At Kensington Oval, Bridgetown, January 21, 22, 23, 24. Barbados won by 56 runs. Barbados 16 pts, Leeward Islands 5 pts. Toss won by Leeward Islands.

Barbados

*C. G. Greenidge c Richardson b Ferris	8	– (6) c Richards b Baptiste.......... 0
D. L. Haynes c Allen b Baptiste....................	97	– (1) c Richards b Baptiste.......... 38
C. A. Best b Ferris	14	– (2) c Sergeant b Roberts 4
T. R. O. Payne lbw b Baptiste	71	– (3) c Richardson b Roberts....... 0
L. N. Reifer run out....................................	0	– (4) c Sergeant b Roberts 0
†R. L. Skeete st Sergeant b Guishard	17	– (5) c Kelly b Ferris.................... 48
M. D. Marshall b Baptiste............................	3	– b Baptiste................................ 71
G. N. Linton c Richardson b Guishard	9	– c Guishard b Baptiste 1
N. A. Phillips c Sergeant b Roberts................	11	– c Sergeant b Roberts 18
H. L. Alleyne b Guishard	0	– (11) c Lewis b Guishard 24
W. W. Daniel not out..................................	0	– (10) not out 28
L-b 3, w 1, n-b 8	12	B 1, l-b 7, w 2, n-b 14 24

1/11 2/44 3/184 4/187   242   1/18 2/23 3/23 4/82   256
5/216 6/219 7/220 8/240 9/242   5/83 6/114 7/117 8/164 9/226

Bowling: *First Innings*—Roberts 14–6–35–1; Ferris 7–1–34–2; White 7–0–43–0; Baptiste 18–4–64–3; Guishard 23.1–3–54–3. *Second Innings*—Roberts 15–5–55–4; Ferris 10–0–50–1; White 4–0–19–0; Baptiste 16–4–51–4; Guishard 16.3–4–57–1.

Leeward Islands

A. L. Kelly lbw b Marshall..............................	7	– c Skeete b Phillips.................... 55
R. B. Richardson c Haynes b Daniel	102	– c Marshall b Daniel.................. 15
E. E. Lewis c Skeete b Daniel	40	– c Skeete b Daniel 1
*I. V. A. Richards b Daniel	0	– c Skeete b Phillips.................... 45
J. C. Allen c Linton b Daniel..........................	19	– lbw b Daniel 21
†E. Sergeant c Marshall b Phillips..................	28	– c Greenidge b Linton 7
E. A. E. Baptiste lbw b Phillips	16	– c Skeete b Daniel 5
A. C. M. White c Skeete b Daniel..................	8	– b Daniel.................................. 0
A. M. E. Roberts not out	14	– c Greenidge b Linton 9
N. C. Guishard c Payne c Daniel....................	3	– run out 15
G. J. F. Ferris c Marshall b Daniel	1	– not out 0
B 3, l-b 3, w 1, n-b 8	15	L-b 4, w 1, n-b 11 16

1/8 2/84 3/84 4/130   253   1/48 2/54 3/125 4/128   189
5/189 6/218 7/234 8/236 9/240   5/156 6/162 7/162 8/162 9/189

Bowling: *First Innings*—Marshall 16–2–57–1; Alleyne 12–2–43–0; Daniel 13.1–2–55–7; Linton 13–3–36–1; Phillips 16–4–47–1. *Second Innings*—Marshall 17–5–36–0; Alleyne 8–1–35–0; Daniel 10–2–33–5; Phillips 17–5–45–2; Linton 3.4–0–24–2.

Umpires: N. Harrison and D. M. Archer.

WINDWARD ISLANDS v GUYANA

At Windsor Park, Dominica, January 21, 22, 23, 24. Guyana won by 108 runs. Guyana 16 pts, Windward Islands 5 pts. Toss won by Windward Islands.

Guyana

A. A. Lyght lbw b Kentish	56	– c Slack b Davis	23
T. R. Etwaroo run out	37	– c Slack b Davis	46
M. A. Lynch c Kentish b Davis	1	– c Slack b Phillip	11
S. F. A. Bacchus c Cadette b Davis	1	– c Elwin b Davis	143
*C. H. Lloyd b Davis	28	– run out	1
†M. R. Pydanna lbw b Davis	18	– lbw b Hinds	34
R. A. Harper c Cadette b Davis	4	– lbw b Phillip	16
D. I. Kallicharran c Cadette b Davis	0	– c Kentish b Phillip	4
C. Butts lbw b Phillip	7	– lbw b Davis	13
L. A. Lambert not out	4	– not out	9
R. F. Joseph b Phillip	2	– b Phillip	0
B 3, l-b 1	4	B 21, l-b 11, n-b 2	34

1/73 2/74 3/76 4/120   162   1/39 2/54 3/116 4/120   334
5/135 6/139 7/147 8/148 9/158   5/240 6/303 7/309 8/311 9/323

Bowling: *First Innings*—Davis 18–1–54–6; Phillip 8.4–0–33–2; Slack 2–1–4–0; Kentish 18–3–47–1; Hinds 7–1–20–0. *Second Innings*—Davis 30–5–78–4; Phillip 21.1–2–77–4; Hinds 32–5–87–1; Kentish 19–1–57–0; Sebastien 1–0–1–0.

Windward Islands

L. C. Sebastien c Harper b Butts	88	– lbw b Joseph	12
L. D. John c Lyght b Kallicharran	56	– c Pydanna b Lambert	1
C. A. Elwin b Lambert	16	– lbw b Lambert	30
W. N. Slack c and b Butts	11	– b Harper	20
S. W. Julien c Kallicharran b Butts	13	– c Bacchus b Butts	14
A. D. Texeira b Harper	0	– lbw b Harper	18
*N. Phillip b Harper	30	– c Kallicharran b Butts	17
†I. Cadette lbw b Kallicharran	11	– c Lynch b Harper	1
T. Kentish c Pydanna b Butts	0	– (10) c and b Harper	0
S. J. Hinds c Bacchus b Butts	15	– (9) c Kallicharran b Harper	2
W. W. Davis not out	0	– not out	1
B 7, l-b 7, n-b 4	18	B 7, l-b 4, n-b 3	14

1/122 2/149 3/168 4/188   258   1/13 2/22 3/67 4/75   130
5/188 6/198 7/225 8/226 9/258   5/93 6/125 7/127 8/127 9/127

Bowling: *First Innings*—Lambert 9–1–26–1; Joseph 2–0–11–0; Harper 35–10–62–2; Butts 47.1–16–81–5; Kallicharran 22–7–60–2. *Second Innings*—Lambert 8–1–22–2; Joseph 7–3–8–1; Harper 24.1–10–33–5; Butts 20–7–30–2; Kallicharran 11–3–23–0.

Umpires: N. Thomas and T. J. Baptiste.

JAMAICA v BARBADOS

At Sabina Park, Kingston, January 28, 29, 30, 31. Barbados won by nine wickets. Barbados 16 pts. Toss won by Jamaica.

Jamaica

G. Powell c Alleyne b Marshall	38	– (5) c Reifer b Linton	67
O. W. Peters c Greenidge b Marshall	19	– (2) lbw b Marshall	31
C. W. Fletcher lbw b Marshall	0	– (1) c Skeete b Marshall	24
C. Baugh lbw b Alleyne	32	– (4) c Marshall b Phillips	21
M. C. Neita c Reifer b Daniel	0	– (6) b Daniel	33
*†P. J. Dujon not out	96	– (7) c Skeete b Alleyne	30
M. A. Tucker c Greenidge b Alleyne	3	– (8) lbw b Daniel	0
R. C. Haynes c Skeete b Alleyne	4	– (3) c Daniel b Marshall	0
C. Gordon lbw b Alleyne	2	– c Skeete b Alleyne	13
J. A. Williams b Phillips	4	– c Greenidge b Alleyne	20
C. A. Walsh b Marshall	18	– not out	1
B 2, l-b 1, w 5, n-b 10	18	B 4, l-b 5, w 1, n-b 5	15

1/11 2/33 3/38 4/75   234   1/54 2/54 3/63 4/119   255
5/79 6/97 7/99 8/114 9/161   5/170 6/196 7/202 8/225 9/250

Bowling: *First Innings*—Marshall 17.2–4–49–4; Daniel 14–0–55–1; Alleyne 13–3–46–4; Phillips 9–4–26–1; Linton 8–1–40–0. *Second Innings*—Marshall 18–4–46–3; Daniel 14.2–2–53–2; Phillips 15–1–43–1; Alleyne 13.4–3–37–3; Linton 21–5–61–1.

Powell retired hurt at 11 and resumed at 161.

Barbados

*C. G. Greenidge c and b Fletcher	38	– not out	20
D. L. Haynes lbw b Fletcher	50	– c Peters b Tucker	18
C. A. Best b Gordon	84	– not out	17
T. R. O. Payne lbw b Walsh	123		
L. N. Reifer c sub b Gordon	27		
†R. L. Skeete c Tucker b Gordon	3		
M. D. Marshall st Dujon b Tucker	35		
G. N. Linton not out	43		
N. A. Phillips c Neita b Tucker	7		
W. W. Daniel not out	4		
B 2, l-b 10, w 1, n-b 8	21		

1/79 2/114 3/261 4/317   (8 wkts dec.) 435   1/27   (1 wkt) 55
5/321 6/372 7/420 8/420

H. L. Alleyne did not bat.

Bowling: *First Innings*—Williams 18–3–44–0; Walsh 23–2–53–1; Haynes 19–5–45–0; Tucker 28–6–71–2; Fletcher 41–9–84–2; Gordon 33–6–114–3; Neita 1–0–3–0. *Second Innings* —Williams 3–0–18–0; Walsh 7–1–20–0; Tucker 4.3–0–17–1.

Umpires: J. Gayle and W. Malcolm.

LEEWARD ISLANDS v GUYANA

At Grove Park, Nevis, January 28, 29, 30. Guyana won by 173 runs. Guyana 16 pts. Toss won by Leeward Islands.

Guyana

A. A. Lyght lbw b Roberts	94	– c Ferris b Willett	100
T. R. Etwaroo c Kelly b Willett	4	– b Roberts	0
M. A. Lynch c Lewis b Guishard	6	– run out	2
S. F. A. Bacchus c Roberts b Eddy	25	– c Eddy b Baptiste	56
*C. H. Lloyd c and b Guishard	12	– (9) not out	40
†M. R. Pydanna lbw b Willett	5	– (5) c Eddy b Willett	2
R. A. Harper c Sergeant b Baptiste	20	– (6) c Sergeant b Baptiste	21
D. I. Kallicharran c Baptiste b Guishard	20	– (7) c and b Willett	69
G. E. Charles b Guishard	0	– (8) lbw b Baptiste	10
C. Butts lbw b Baptiste	7	– run out	0
L. A. Lambert not out	4	– c Kelly b Baptiste	4
L-b 12, n-b 4	16	B 3, l-b 9, n-b 2	14

1/30 2/41 3/105 4/151   213   1/9 2/21 3/139 4/151   318
5/151 6/162 7/200 8/200 9/208   5/173 6/188 7/218 8/302 9/303

Bowling: *First Innings*—Roberts 7–2–20–1; Ferris 5–1–14–0; Baptiste 9.3–2–22–2; Willett 26–9–47–2; Guishard 29–6–79–4; Eddy 3–0–15–1. *Second Innings*—Roberts 14–1–43–1; Ferris 3–0–12–0; Baptiste 13.5–2–46–4; Willett 37–11–82–3; Guishard 25–4–92–0; Eddy 3–0–29–0.

Leeward Islands

A. L. Kelly lbw b Charles	1	– c Lyght b Butts	56
R. B. Richardson b Lambert	5	– c Butts b Harper	28
E. E. Lewis run out	31	– c and b Lambert	7
J. C. Allen c Pydanna b Lambert	4	– c Lloyd b Harper	8
V. A. Eddy c Lloyd b Butts	4	– c Charles b Kallicharran	58
†E. Sergeant c Lambert b Butts	5	– c Lyght b Butts	14
N. C. Guishard c Bacchus b Butts	17	– (9) c and b Harper	13
E. A. E. Baptiste c Lloyd b Kallicharran	8	– (7) c Charles b Harper	37
*A. M. E. Roberts c Lynch b Butts	8	– (8) c and b Harper	0
E. T. Willett c Lyght b Butts	1	– not out	7
G. J. F. Ferris not out	2	– c Pydanna b Butts	26
B 1, n-b 4	5	B 3, l-b 4, n-b 3	13

1/7 2/9 3/13 4/31   91   1/72 2/83 3/98 4/130   267
5/47 6/63 7/80 8/80 9/89   5/165 6/192 7/194 8/229 9/231

Bowling: *First Innings*—Lambert 7–3–18–2; Charles 3–1–4–1; Harper 6–3–11–0; Butts 12.5–4–23–5; Kallicharran 10–2–30–1. *Second Innings*—Lambert 12–3–39–1; Charles 8–5–9–0; Kallicharran 25–9–49–1; Butts 24.2–8–62–3; Harper 34–6–95–5.

Umpires: A. Weekes and L. Joseph.

TRINIDAD & TOBAGO v WINDWARD ISLANDS

At Queen's Park Oval, Port-of-Spain, January 28, 29, 30, 31. Windward Islands won by two wickets. Windward Islands 16 pts, Trinidad & Tobago 5 pts. Toss won by Trinidad & Tobago.

Trinidad & Tobago

R. S. Gabriel c Davis b Kentish	37	– lbw b Davis	0
P. V. Simmonds c Slack b Phillip	10	– c Sebastien b Davis	75
A. L. Logie c Cadette b Davis	138	– c and b Kentish	79
A. T. Rajah c Cadette b Hinds	27	– c Phillip b Kentish	15
S. A. Gomes c and b Hinds	16	– c Sebastien b Kentish	7
*T. Cuffy c sub b Kentish	36	– not out	13
R. Sampath c Cadette b Davis	4	– not out	17
R. Nanan c Cadette b Davis	21		
†J. R. Lyon not out	22		
G. Mahabir c Elwin b Phillip	17		
K. A. Williams run out	0		
B 2, l-b 3, n-b 20	25	B 10, l-b 14, n-b 7	31

1/10 2/79 3/131 4/151   **353**   1/0 2/164 3/171   (5 wkts dec.) **237**
5/240 6/264 7/311 8/320 9/353   4/193 5/194

Bowling: *First Innings*—Davis 29–6–98–3; Phillip 25.5–2–79–2; Slack 4–1–14–0; Kentish 26–4–81–2; Hinds 21–6–56–2. *Second Innings*—Davis 15–1–57–2; Phillip 5–1–26–0; Hinds 24–6–52–0; Kentish 22–1–71–3.

Windward Islands

L. C. Sebastien run out	5	– st Lyon b Nanan	122
L. D. John c Gomes b Mahabir	20	– c Rajah b Nanan	42
S. W. Julien lbw b Mahabir	15	– lbw b Williams	123
W. N. Slack lbw b Nanan	10	– (5) lbw b Williams	27
C. A. Elwin c Sampath b Mahabir	7	– (7) b Williams	10
A. D. Texeira lbw b Nanan	39	– (8) lbw b Williams	4
*N. Phillip b Nanan	45	– (4) c sub b Nanan	5
†I. Cadette run out	7	– (9) not out	6
S. J. Hinds not out	49	– (6) b Williams	0
T. Kentish c Lyon b Simmonds	18	– not out	13
W. W. Davis run out	0		
B 2, l-b 6	8	B 3, l-b 15, n-b 1	19

1/12 2/37 3/44 4/52   **223**   1/99 2/284 3/295   (8 wkts) **371**
5/66 6/120 7/149 8/157 9/221   4/306 5/337 6/337 7/344 8/355

Bowling: *First Innings*—Williams 16–3–38–0; Sampath 8–1–19–0; Nanan 35–7–64–3; Mahabir 41–10–91–3; Simmonds 2.1–1–3–1. *Second Innings*—Williams 23–3–98–5; Sampath 4–1–13–0; Nanan 36.4–2–142–3; Simmonds 12–1–44–0; Mahabir 20–4–55–0.

Umpires: A. Shafrall and Z. Macuum.

JAMAICA v WINDWARD ISLANDS

At Sabina Park, Kingston, February 4, 5, 6, 7. Drawn. Jamaica 4 pts, Windward Islands 8 pts. Toss won by Windward Islands.

Windward Islands

L. C. Sebastien c Fletcher b J. A. Gordon	73	– c and b C. Gordon	77
L. D. John lbw b Thompson	80	– c and b C. Gordon	19
S. W. Julien c Dujon b Thompson	88	– c Peters b C. Gordon	50
*W. N. Slack lbw b Thompson	66		
A. D. Texeira c Dujon b Williams	25	– (4) not out	48
J. D. Charles c Dujon b Thompson	0	– (5) run out	0
†I. Cadette c Dujon b Thompson	22	– (6) c Davidson b Baugh	7
N. F. Williams not out	51	– (7) run out	3
S. J. Hinds run out	0		
T. Kentish c Davidson b Fletcher	8	– (8) not out	1
W. W. Davis c Dujon b C. Gordon	0		
L-b 6, n-b 22	28	L-b 2, n-b 4	6

1/142 2/221 3/299 4/342   441   1/36 2/127 3/161   (6 wkts) 211
5/347 6/349 7/377 8/379 9/440   4/169 5/196 6/208

Bowling: *First Innings*—Williams 29-3-86-1; Thompson 41-7-114-5; J. A. Gordon 27-2-121-1; C. Gordon 4.2-0-23-1; Fletcher 30-8-60-1; Neita 6-2-9-0. *Second Innings*—Williams 9-1-26-0; Thompson 8-1-28-0; C. Gordon 22-3-106-3; Fletcher 13-3-28-0; Davidson 7-3-8-0; Baugh 4-0-9-1; Neita 1-1-0-0.

Jamaica

C. W. Fletcher c and b Kentish	99	C. Gordon b Davis	21
O. W. Peters b Kentish	27	J. A. Williams c and b Davis	9
G. Powell c Cadette b Davis	11	C. U. Thompson not out	8
*†P. J. Dujon c Texeira b Davis	102	B 1, l-b 12, n-b 26	39
M. C. Neita c Texeira b Sebestien	75		
C. Baugh b Hinds	22		
C. A. Davidson run out	26	1/34 2/65 3/218 4/245	440
J. A. Gordon b Davis	1	5/278 6/343 7/346 8/407 9/422	

Bowling: *First Innings*—Davis 48.5-15-98-5; Williams 17-2-76-0; Kentish 38-13-67-2; Hinds 38-10-82-1; Charles 20-3-48-0; Sebestien 11-2-30-1.

Umpires: W. Malcolm and L. Bell.

BARBADOS v GUYANA

At Kensington Oval, Bridgetown, February 4, 5, 6, 7. Drawn. Barbados 8 pts, Guyana 4 pts. Toss won by Barbados.

Guyana

A. A. Lyght c Best b Linton	112	– c Best b Broomes	53
T. R. Etwaroo c Reifer b Marshall	0	– c Payne b Estwick	2
M. A. Lynch c Linton b Estwick	47	– st Skeete b Linton	75
S. F. A. Bacchus c Skeete b Marshall	2	– (5) c Skeete b Estwick	37
*C. H. Lloyd c and b Phillips	27	– (4) c Broomes b Phillips	104
†M. R. Pydanna b Linton	11	– not out	72
R. A. Harper c Haynes b Linton	2	– (8) b Estwick	1
D. I. Kallicharran c Skeete b Linton	4	– (9) c Skeete b Phillips	57
C. Butts run out	4	– (7) b Estwick	0
L. A. Lambert st Skeete b Linton	9	– lbw b Marshall	1
R. F. Joseph not out	2	– c Best b Marshall	1
B 2, l-b 5, w 1, n-b 2	10	L-b 5, w 6, n-b 6	17

1/5 2/86 3/154 4/174   230   1/2 2/69 3/180 4/266   420
5/201 6/205 7/211 8/218 9/219   5/286 6/286 7/292 8/379 9/412

Bowling: *First Innings*—Marshall 15–3–51–2; Phillips 14–3–53–1; Estwick 4–0–31–1; Linton 9.4–2–35–5; Broomes 20–6–50–0. *Second Innings*—Marshall 26.4–5–86–2; Estwick 19–0–89–4; Broomes 22–3–73–1; Linton 14–1–81–1; Phillips 16–0–74–2.

Bacchus retired hurt at 86 and resumed at 154.

Barbados

*C. G. Greenidge c Kallicharran b Lambert	3	– c Lynch b Harper	15
D. L. Haynes c Pydanna b Harper	79	– c Lyght b Lambert	9
C. A. Best b Kallicharran	47	– c Lyght b Lambert	12
T. R. O. Payne c Pydanna b Joseph	107	– not out	37
L. N. Reifer c Kallicharran b Harper	0	– c sub b Butts	32
†R. L. Skeete b Harper	0	– not out	15
M. D. Marshall c Lyght b Lambert	34		
G. N. Linton b Joseph	66		
N. A. Phillips lbw b Lambert	5		
N. da C. Broomes not out	11		
R. O. Estwick st Pydanna b Harper	19		
B 4, l-b 6, w 6, n-b 16	32	B 3, l-b 3, w 1, n-b 5	12

1/18 2/118 3/151 4/155 　　　　　　　403　1/31 2/31 3/45　　　(4 wkts) 132
5/155 6/240 7/359 8/369 9/372　　　　　　4/115

Bowling: *First Innings*—Lambert 28–5–103–3; Joseph 18–4–58–2; Harper 41.5–18–89–4; Kallicharran 22–8–65–1; Butts 25–7–49–0; Lynch 3–1–7–0. *Second Innings*—Lambert 6–0–27–2; Joseph 5–1–12–0; Harper 18–4–43–1; Butts 12–2–34–1; Lynch 1–0–4–0.

Umpires: S. E. Parris and L. Barker.

TRINIDAD & TOBAGO v LEEWARD ISLANDS

At Guaracara Park, Pointe-á-Pierre, February 4, 5, 6, 7. Drawn. Trinidad & Tobago 4 pts, Leeward Islands 8 pts. Toss won by Leeward Islands.

Leeward Islands

A. L. Kelly c sub b Mahabir	38	– b d'Heurieux	18
R. B. Richardson c d'Heurieux b Williams	8	– c Logie b d'Heurieux	0
E. E. Lewis run out	19	– b Mahabir	138
J. C. Allen lbw b Simmonds	50	– (5) c Nanan b Mahabir	4
R. S. Otto c Mahabir b Nanan	4	– (4) c and b Mahabir	22
V. A. Eddy run out	124	– c sub b Nanan	0
†S. I. Williams lbw b Nanan	120	– c Rajah b Daniel	31
E. A. E. Baptiste c Nanan b Mahabir	44	– lbw b Nanan	5
*A. M. E. Roberts c Cuffy b Mahabir	0	– (10) not out	4
N. C. Guishard b Nanan	30	– (9) lbw b Nanan	19
E. T. Willett not out	6		
B 4, l-b 8, w 1, n-b 3	16	B 4, l-b 2	6

1/20 2/68 3/69 4/81　　　　　　　459　1/14 2/27 3/107　　(9 wkts dec.) 247
5/164 6/322 7/388 8/388 9/444　　　　　4/128 5/131 6/206 7/219 8/227 9/247

Bowling: *First Innings*—Williams 5–0–26–1; d'Heurieux 16–0–78–0; Nanan 54.3–15–116–3; Mahabir 37–12–98–3; Daniel 10–3–50–0; Simmonds 26–2–75–1. *Second Innings*—d'Heurieux 14–3–34–2; Simmonds 5–0–24–0; Nanan 33.4–7–71–3; Mahabir 23–3–74–3; Daniel 11–3–38–1.

Trinidad & Tobago

R. S. Gabriel c Richardson b Guishard	32		
P. V. Simmonds run out	106	– (1) lbw b Baptiste	15
A. L. Logie st Williams b Willett	46	– not out	43
K. G. d'Heurieux c Guishard b Roberts	0	– not out	33
A. T. Rajah c and b Guishard	9	– (2) b Baptiste	0
*T. Cuffy c Otto b Baptiste	38		
R. Nanan c Eddy b Willett	125		
†D. Williams c Baptiste b Guishard	2		
A. E. Daniel lbw b Baptiste	0		
G. Mahabir c Willett b Roberts	8		
K. A. Williams not out	0		
B 2, l-b 8, w 1, n-b 6	17	B 5, w 1, n-b 3	9
	383	(2 wkts)	**100**

1/85 2/173 3/178 4/198   1/11 2/35
5/200 6/321 7/330 8/332 9/375

Bowling: *First Innings*—Roberts 28–3–99–2; Baptiste 16–2–68–2; Guishard 37–9–85–3; Willett 41.3–8–106–2; Eddy 2–0–8–0. *Second Innings*—Roberts 7–1–34–0; Baptiste 10–2–23–2; Allen 3–1–6–0; Guishard 4–1–3–0; Willett 4–1–13–0; Kelly 1–0–1–0; Otto 2–1–9–0; Richardson 3–1–2–0.

Umpires: Sadiq Mohammad and Mohammad Hosein.

LEEWARD ISLANDS v JAMAICA

At Sturge Park, Montserrat, February 11, 12, 13, 14. Leeward Islands won by eight wickets. Leeward Islands 16 pts. Toss won by Leeward Islands.

Jamaica

C. W. Fletcher c Williams b Baptiste	33	– c Williams b Baptiste	70
O. W. Peters b Baptiste	35	– c Merrick b Willett	23
G. Powell c Williams b Merrick	2	– b Willett	6
*†P. J. Dujon b Merrick	5	– c Lewis b Baptiste	55
M. C. Neita c Roberts b Willett	48	– b Roberts	22
C. Baugh c Williams b Baptiste	1	– c Richardson b Roberts	5
R. L. Haynes b Willett	62	– not out	27
M. A. Holding c Williams b Willett	16	– c Williams b Roberts	6
C. Gordon not out	11	– lbw b Roberts	16
C. A. Walsh b Merrick	0	– c Lewis b Roberts	1
P. Patterson c Williams b Merrick	0	– b Roberts	3
L-b 1, w 2, n-b 8	11	B 6, l-b 6, w 3, n-b 15	30
	224		**264**

1/52 2/67 3/72 4/78   1/39 2/51 3/143 4/194
5/80 6/165 7/206 8/213 9/214   5/200 6/210 7/220 8/254 9/260

Bowling: *First Innings*—Roberts 14–1–49–0; Merrick 19.5–2–76–4; Baptiste 16–3–38–3; Willett 15–5–32–3; Guishard 5–1–18–0. *Second Innings*—Roberts 25.5–3–65–6; Merrick 5–1–19–0; Willett 20–11–27–2; Guishard 18–5–26–0; Baptiste 25–8–88–2; Eddy 4–1–9–0.

Leeward Islands

A. L. Kelly lbw b Patterson	18	– c Fletcher b Patterson	20
R. B. Richardson c Dujon b Walsh	156	– c Dujon b Patterson	26
N. C. Guishard run out	14		
E. Lewis lbw b Walsh	26	– (3) not out	12
J. C. Allen lbw b Holding	42	– (4) not out	2
V. A. Eddy not out	80		
†S. I. Williams c Holding b Fletcher	18		
E. A. E. Baptiste c Walsh b Holding	32		
*A. M. E. Roberts c Patterson b Haynes	6		
A. Merrick c Walsh b Haynes	2		
E. T. Willett b Holding	4		
B 7, l-b 3, n-b 14	24	B 6, l-b 1	7

1/39 2/71 3/124 4/221   422   1/43 2/54   (2 wkts) 67
5/298 6/327 7/380 8/409 9/413

Bowling: *First Innings*—Holding 32.2–7–128–3; Patterson 17–4–53–1; Walsh 17–0–70–2; Haynes 30–11–63–2; Gordon 21–5–60–0; Fletcher 6–1–24–1. *Second Innings*—Holding 2–0–11–0; Patterson 5–0–26–2; Walsh 4–1–23–0.

Umpires: P. Bramble and A. Weekes.

WINDWARD ISLANDS v BARBADOS

At Arnos Vale, St Vincent, February 11, 12, 13, 14. Windward Islands won by four wickets. Windward Islands 16 pts. Toss won by Barbados.

Barbados

*C. G. Greenidge lbw b Phillip	6	– lbw b Phillip	15
D. L. Haynes b Phillip	27	– c Williams b Phillip	18
C. A. Best lbw b Davis	20	– b Hinds	37
T. R. O. Payne not out	107	– lbw b Phillip	2
G. N. Reifer lbw b Phillip	26	– lbw b Williams	10
†R. L. Skeete b Williams	15	– (7) c Cadette b Williams	0
M. D. Marshall c John b Williams	2	– (8) lbw b Williams	36
G. N. Linton b Hinds	6	– (9) lbw b Davis	12
N. A. Phillips c Cadette b Hinds	2	– (10) c Slack b Davis	25
W. W. Daniel b Williams	1	– (11) not out	1
N. da C. Broomes lbw b Davis	7	– (6) c Sebastien b Williams	18
B 7, l-b 4, n-b 13	24	B 3, l-b 6, n-b 13	22

1/11 2/42 3/89 4/153   243   1/31 2/45 3/48 4/70   196
5/184 6/186 7/200 8/219 9/220   5/102 6/103 7/137 8/157 9/187

Bowling: *First Innings*—Davis 17–4–69–2; Phillip 17–2–49–3; Williams 18–3–53–3; Kentish 11–2–21–0; Hinds 15–6–27–2. *Second Innings*—Davis 26.1–8–49–2; Phillip 21–4–39–3; Williams 22–6–38–4; Hinds 21–9–30–1; Kentish 21–8–18–0.

Windward Islands

L. C. Sebastien c Skeete b Daniel	11	– (4) not out	29
L. D. John b Phillips	110	– (1) b Marshall	21
S. W. Julien c Phillips b Linton	41	– c Skeete b Marshall	13
W. N. Slack lbw b Phillips	20	– (2) c Skeete b Marshall	12
A. D. Texeira c Payne b Marshall	12	– run out	12
*N. Phillip b Daniel	12	– c Reifer b Phillips	0
†I. Cadette c Haynes b Daniel	14	– b Phillips	39
N. F. Williams c Best b Daniel	15		
S. J. Hinds c Haynes b Phillips	24	– (8) not out	2
T. Kentish lbw b Broomes	18		
W. W. Davis not out	0		
B 15, l-b 18, n-b 7	40	L-b 4, w 2	6

1/17 2/93 3/140 4/147   307   1/25 2/40 3/55 4/62   (6 wkts) 134
5/182 6/218 7/243 8/283 9/293   5/62 6/130

Bowling: *First Innings*—Marshall 30–9–68–1; Daniel 26–3–73–4; Linton 19–2–50–1; Broomes 15.5–5–23–1; Phillips 25–6–53–3. *Second Innings*— Marshall 13–0–58–3; Daniel 7–0–35–0; Phillips 7.5–0–35–2.

Umpires: S. Rock and J. Simon.

GUYANA v TRINIDAD & TOBAGO

At Albion, Berbice, February 10, 11, 12, 13. Guyana won by nine wickets. Guyana 16 pts. Toss won by Trinidad & Tobago.

Trinidad & Tobago

P. V. Simmonds b Lambert	13	– c and b Harper	13
W. Debissette c Pydanna b Lambert	2	– b Harper	28
A. L. Logie c Fredericks b Lambert	117	– b Lambert	62
K. G. d'Heurieux c Harper b Butts	16	– c sub b Butts	5
P. Moosai c Harper b Butts	29	– b Kallicharran	7
*T. Cuffy lbw b Charles	24	– c sub b Kallicharran	14
R. Nanan c Kallicharran b Lambert	16	– lbw b Lambert	8
†D. Williams not out	13	– not out	2
S. Jumadeen b Lambert	1	– absent ill	
G. S. Antoine c and b Lambert	0	– (9) run out	1
G. Mahabir lbw b Lambert	0	– (10) run out	0
L-b 4, n-b 8	12	B 12, l-b 2, w 1, n-b 4	19

1/15 2/16 3/49 4/158   243   1/35 2/58 3/79 4/111   159
5/211 6/211 7/238 8/240 9/243   5/129 6/149 7/152 8/159 9/159

Bowling: *First Innings*—Lambert 23.3–7–59–7; Charles 10–1–31–1; Harper 12–1–38–0; Kallicharran 14–3–31–0; Butts 25–6–56–2; Lynch 6–1–16–0. *Second Innings*—Lambert 6.5–0–16–2; Charles 3–0–15–0; Butts 15–2–51–1; Harper 14–3–30–2; Kallicharran 10–3–23–2; Lynch 3–1–5–0.

Guyana

A. A. Lyght b d'Heurieux	14	– not out	5
R. C. Fredericks c Nanan b Antoine	103		
M. A. Lynch c Moosai b d'Heurieux	4	– not out	3
S. F. A. Bacchus c Moosai b Nanan	28		
*C. H. Lloyd c Nanan b Antoine	136		
†M. R. Pydanna run out	0	– (2) c Mahabir b Antoine	1
D. I. Kallicharran b Antoine	44		
R. A. Harper run out	29		
G. E. Charles not out	11		
L. A. Lambert c and b Nanan	14		
C. Butts not out	2		
B 4, l-b 6	10		

1/43 2/47 3/100 4/263   (9 wkts dec.) 395   1/6   (1 wkt) 9
5/271 6/298 7/359 8/368 9/391

Bowling: *First Innings*—Antoine 25–3–112–3; d'Heurieux 8–0–26–2; Nanan 54–12–118–2; Jumadeen 20–2–59–0; Mahabir 18–3–66–0; Simmonds 1–0–4–0. *Second Innings*—Antoine 1.3–0–9–1; Nanan 1–1–0–0.

Umpires: M. Baksh and C. Vyfhuis.

GUYANA v JAMAICA

At Bourda Oval, Georgetown, March 3, 4, 5, 6. Guyana won by an innings and 101 runs. Guyana 16 pts. Toss won by Jamaica.

Jamaica

C. W. Fletcher st Pydanna b Kallicharran	44	– c Lynch b Harper	36
O. W. Peters c Bacchus b Harper	15	– c Charles b Butts	89
G. Powell b Harper	37	– c Harper b Butts	6
M. C. Neita c Pydanna b Kallicharran	2	– (5) c Bacchus b Kallicharran	60
*P. J. Dujon lbw b Butts	4	– (4) c Lambert b Butts	8
C. A. Davidson st Pydanna b Kallicharran	13	– c and b Harper	9
R. C. Haynes c Bacchus b Harper	0	– lbw b Kallicharran	26
†P. A. Francis not out	11	– c Kallicharran b Butts	7
A. G. Daley c and b Kallicharran	4	– c sub b Kallicharran	5
C. A. Walsh c Pydanna b Kallicharran	6	– c sub b Butts	1
E. L. Wilson c Bacchus b Kallicharran	0	– not out	0
B 4, l-b 1, w 1, n-b 7	13	B 3, l-b 14, w 1, n-b 2	20

1/49 2/94 3/104 4/114   149   1/97 2/131 3/138 4/154   267
5/117 6/117 7/132 8/143 9/149   5/183 6/242 7/260 8/260 9/265

Bowling: *First Innings*—Lambert 5–0–15–0; Charles 4–0–14–0; Harper 17–7–29–3; Kallicharran 21.5–5–60–6; Butts 10–5–18–1. *Second Innings*—Lambert 7–1–33–0; Charles 2–0–12–0; Harper 21–4–62–2; Kallicharran 26–4–86–3; Butts 18.1–3–54–5.

Guyana

A. A. Lyght c Neita b Wilson	36		D. I. Kallicharran not out	50
R. C. Fredericks c Davidson b Walsh	217		G. E. Charles run out	13
R. A. Harper c Fletcher b Haynes	0		C. Butts not out	0
M. A. Lynch c Francis b Walsh	20		B 16, l-b 10, n-b 6	32
S. F. A. Bacchus c Haynes b Wilson	57			
*C. H. Lloyd c Dujon b Davidson	64		1/94 2/104 3/149 4/286 (8 wkts dec.) 517	
†M. R. Pydanna run out	28		5/416 6/424 7/499 8/516	

L. A. Lambert did not bat.

Bowling: Walsh 22–5–57–2; Daley 22–2–112–0; Fletcher 1–0–6–0; Wilson 51.4–7–152–2; Haynes 16–1–69–1; Davidson 7–1–18–1; Neita 16–0–71–0.

Umpires: R. Haynes and C. Vyfhuis.

LEEWARD ISLANDS v WINDWARD ISLANDS

At Warner Park, St Kitts, March 3, 4, 5, 6. Windward Islands won by 1 run. Windward Islands 16 pts. Toss won by Leeward Islands.

Windward Islands

L. C. Sebastien lbw b Baptiste	44	– b Roberts 9
L. D. John c Williams b Roberts	1	– c Kelly b Roberts 15
S. W. Julien lbw b Roberts	68	– c Richardson b Roberts 0
A. D. Texeira c Kelly b Willett	6	– b Roberts 16
C. A. Elwin c Eddy b Roberts	12	– c Kelly b Roberts 0
*N. Phillip c Guishard b Baptiste	25	– (7) c Kelly b Roberts 49
†I. Cadette c Merrick b Baptiste	35	– (6) run out 2
N. F. Williams c and b Guishard	32	– c Richardson b Roberts 19
S. J. Hinds b Roberts	12	– lbw b Roberts 20
T. Kentish b Roberts	2	– not out 17
W. W. Davis not out	0	– b Baptiste 11
B 1, l-b 7, n-b 11	19	B 12, l-b 5, n-b 7 24
	256	**182**

1/9 2/86 3/117 4/140 5/151 6/187 7/216 8/252 9/256
1/26 2/26 3/48 4/49 5/51 6/60 7/127 8/142 9/166

Bowling: *First Innings*—Roberts 17.2–1–52–5; Merrick 12–1–46–0; Baptiste 17–2–56–3; Willett 17–1–61–1; Guishard 11–1–22–1. *Second Innings*—Roberts 20–6–62–8; Baptiste 13.2–2–52–1; Merrick 4–0–20–0; Willett 6–2–4–0; Guishard 7–0–20–0.

Leeward Islands

A. L. Kelly lbw b Davis	14	– c Elwin b Hinds 41
R. B. Richardson c Cadette b Williams	17	– b Williams 39
E. E. Lewis c Kentish b Davis	12	– c Texeira b Williams 1
N. C. Guishard lbw b Davis	3	– (9) lbw b Davis 0
J. C. Allen c Sebastien b Williams	14	– (4) lbw b Williams 7
V. A. Eddy lbw b Kentish	36	– (5) b Davis 35
†S. I. Williams b Davis	52	– (6) c sub b Davis 34
E. A. E. Baptiste lbw b Davis	20	– (7) lbw b Davis 4
*A. M. E. Roberts c Williams b Kentish	5	– (8) lbw b Kentish 16
A. Merrick not out	24	– lbw b Kentish 2
E. T. Willett c Julien b Kentish	12	– not out 4
B 5, l-b 9, n-b 11	25	B 3, l-b 8, n-b 9 20
	234	**203**

1/34 2/48 3/57 4/59 5/80 6/156 7/183 8/188 9/192
1/63 2/67 3/85 4/111 5/147 6/153 7/185 8/191 9/194

Bowling: *First Innings*—Davis 24–7–60–5; Phillip 14–1–49–0; Williams 11–3–32–2; Hinds 5–0–24–0; Kentish 16.1–5–32–3; Sebastien 1–0–12–0. *Second Innings*—Davis 18.1–2–57–4; Phillip 4–0–18–0; Kentish 30–8–53–2; Williams 13–2–40–3; Hinds 7–1–15–1.

Umpires: P. White and A. Weekes.

TRINIDAD & TOBAGO v BARBADOS

At Queen's Park Oval, Port-of-Spain, March 19, 20, 21, 22. Barbados won by 19 runs. Barbados 16 pts. Toss won by Trinidad & Tobago.

Barbados

*C. G. Greenidge lbw b Mahabir	44	– lbw b Mahabir	6
D. L. Haynes b K. A. Williams	0	– c Moosai b Nanan	31
C. A. Best b Simmonds	16	– c Mahabir b Jumadeen	16
T. R. O. Payne c and b Nanan	55	– b Mahabir	15
G. N. Reifer c Moosai b Nanan	1	– lbw b Jumadeen	36
†R. L. Skeete lbw b Mahabir	2	– c D. Williams b Mahabir	14
M. D. Marshall b Mahabir	0	– b Mahabir	28
G. N. Linton run out	45	– b Mahabir	3
W. W. Daniel b Nanan	42	– c Moosai b Nanan	29
R. O. Estwick not out	0	– lbw b Mahabir	18
H. L. Alleyne lbw b Nanan	0	– not out	0
L-b 7	7	L-b 8	8
	212		**204**

1/7 2/34 3/89 4/110
5/117 6/117 7/133 8/210 9/212

1/29 2/48 3/60 4/82
5/120 6/126 7/131 8/174 9/204

Bowling: *First Innings*—K. A. Williams 11-0-58-1; Simmonds 6-2-10-1; Nanan 21.1-5-46-4; Jumadeen 6-1-33-0; Mahabir 18-5-58-3. *Second Innings*—K. A. Williams 5-1-9-0; Simmonds 2-1-8-0; Mahabir 38-9-68-6; Nanan 31.3-6-76-2; Jumadeen 14-5-27-2; Gomes 2-0-8-0.

Trinidad & Tobago

R. S. Gabriel c Skeete b Daniel	22	– lbw b Estwick	30
P. V. Simmonds lbw b Estwick	26	– lbw b Alleyne	30
A. L. Logie c Greenidge b Estwick	14	– (4) b Alleyne	0
W. Debissette c Skeete b Estwick	1	– (6) b Alleyne	23
*H. A. Gomes c Skeete b Alleyne	7	– (3) c Skeete b Alleyne	67
P. Moosai c Best b Alleyne	11	– (5) b Alleyne	37
†D. Williams c Best b Marshall	7	– (8) b Marshall	0
R. Nanan c Payne b Daniel	0	– (7) lbw b Alleyne	12
S. Jumadeen c Linton b Daniel	18	– b Marshall	0
G. Mahabir c Best b Marshall	17	– run out	0
K. A. Williams not out	18	– not out	7
B 1, l-b 1, n-b 10	12	B 5, l-b 6, w 7, n-b 20	38
	153		**244**

1/39 2/42 3/69 4/76
5/77 6/91 7/93 8/114 9/125

1/63 2/81 3/81 4/174
5/212 6/223 7/224 8/224 9/226

Bowling: *First Innings*—Marshall 13.2-4-22-2; Daniel 10-0-62-3; Estwick 8-0-29-3; Alleyne 6-0-21-2; Linton 1-0-7-0. *Second Innings*—Marshall 30-10-52-2; Daniel 15-2-43-0; Estwick 7-3-23-1; Alleyne 28-11-63-6; Linton 12-5-25-0.

Umpires: Mohammad Hosein and Zainool Mohammad.

SHELL SHIELD WINNERS

1965-66	Barbados	1975-76	Trinidad / Barbados
1966-67	Barbados	1976-77	Barbados
1968-69	Jamaica	1977-78	Barbados
1969-70	Trinidad	1978-79	Barbados
1970-71	Trinidad	1979-80	Barbados
1971-72	Barbados	1980-81	Combined Islands
1972-73	Guyana	1981-82	Barbados
1973-74	Barbados	1982-83	Guyana
1974-75	Guyana		

OTHER FIRST-CLASS MATCHES

WEST INDIES XI v INTERNATIONAL XI

At Kingston, September 25, 26, 27, 28. Drawn.

International XI

G. D. Mendis c Lloyd b Clarke	20	P. J. W. Allott b Clarke	7
G. Fowler lbw b Roberts	63	K. D. Ghavri c Powell b R. C. Haynes	21
A. R. Butcher lbw b Roberts	2	K. B. S. Jarvis not out	14
R. O. Butcher c Dujon b Marshall	15	B 12, l-b 7, w 1, n-b 6	26
*J. G. Wright c and b R. C. Haynes	2		
T. E. Jesty c Dujon b Clarke	30		262
†C. J. Richards c Dujon b Clarke	62	1/82 2/97 3/98	
E. E. Hemmings lbw b Clarke	0	4/111 5/131 6/184	
		7/190 8/202 9/229	

Bowling: Clarke 21–9–26–5; Roberts 7–3–44–2; Holding 14–5–33–0; Marshall 15–3–25–1; R. C. Haynes 23.3–4–91–2; Powell 4–0–8–0; Rowe 1–0–9–0.

West Indies XI

C. G. Greenidge c Ghavri b Hemmings	43	A. M. E. Roberts st Richards b Hemmings	34
D. L. Haynes c A. R. Butcher b Hemmings	96	S. T. Clarke b Hemmings	6
G. Powell c Richards b Hemmings	16	M. A. Holding not out	3
L. G. Rowe c sub b Hemmings	47	B 18, l-b 11, w 1, n-b 10	40
†P. J. Dujon c Jesty b Hemmings	19		
*C. H. Lloyd c Jesty b Hemmings	60		419
M. D. Marshall c sub b Hemmings	40	1/98 2/137 3/198	
R. C. Haynes c Wright b Hemmings	15	4/254 5/261 6/353	
		7/359 8/400 9/414	

Bowling: Allott 24–6–70–0; Ghavri 17–1–70–0; Hemmings 49.3–14–175–10; Jarvis 16–2–45–0; Jesty 7–1–19–0.

Umpires: D. Sang Hue and L. Bell.

JONES CUP, 1982-83

BERBICE v DEMERARA

At Albion, Berbice, October 22, 23, 24, 25. Drawn. Toss won by Demerara.

Berbice

*L. Baichan run out	132	– not out	101
T. R. Etwaroo c Lynch b Gordon	5	– c and b R. A. Harper	61
A. Ramcharitar c White b Maxwell	10	– b Butts	4
†M. R. Pydanna c White b Maxwell	5	– (6) c R. A. Harper b Butts	6
K. Singh c M. A. Harper b Maxwell	0	– (4) b Butts	0
S. Persaud c sub b Butts	54	– (5) b Butts	0
D. I. Kallicharran c Lynch b White	56	– (8) c Seeram b R. A. Harper	54
S. Ganouri c Seeram b Butts	22	– (9) b R. A. Harper	4
J. Angus c White b Butts	2	– (7) c R. A. Harper b Butts	0
L. A. Lambert c Lynch b Butts	0	– b Butts	7
R. F. Joseph not out	2	– lbw b Butts	0
B 3, l-b 3, w 1, n-b 12	19	B 8, l-b 8, n-b 4	20

1/5 2/20 3/28 4/29	307	1/106 2/111 3/111 4/111	257
5/119 6/236 7/274 8/283 9/286		5/137 6/137 7/228 8/241 9/250	

Bowling: *First Innings*—Gordon 17–4–53–1; Maxwell 14–4–47–3; Butts 45–19–76–4; Solomon 13–0–60–0; R. A. Harper 10–0–44–0; White 7–2–8–1. *Second Innings*—Maxwell 8–0–27–0; Gordon 10–0–33–0; White 9–0–21–0; Butts 51–23–56–7; Solomon 16–0–47–0; R. A. Harper 14–0–53–3.

Demerara

A. A. Lyght c Persaud b Angus	87	– lbw b Joseph	18
R. Seeram c Pydanna b Singh	17	– not out	19
*M. A. Harper lbw b Kallicharran	60	– st Pydanna b Ganouri	16
M. A. Lynch lbw b Lambert	52		
W. White b Kallicharran	13		
C. Butts c Kallicharran b Lambert	38		
†S. Bamfield b Lambert	2	– (4) not out	7
R. A. Harper c Pydanna b Lambert	26		
V. Solomon not out	2		
O. Gordon b Lambert	0		
K. Maxwell b Lambert	0		
B 24, l-b 7, w 2, n-b 7	40	B 2, l-b 1, w 5, n-b 5	13

1/61 2/156 3/198 4/237   337   1/27 2/53   (2 wkts) 73
5/264 6/269 7/330 8/337 9/337

Bowling: *First Innings*—Lambert 16.5–0–60–6; Joseph 7–0–39–0; Kallicharran 26–3–95–2; Singh 15–5–40–1; Ganouri 15–1–32–0; Angus 8–0–30–1; Persaud 2–0–1–0. *Second Innings* —Lambert 6–1–24–0; Joseph 5–1–13–1; Ganouri 6–1–8–1; Angus 6–0–15–0.

Umpires: R. Haynes and C. Vyfhuis.

BEAUMONT CUP

NORTH AND EAST v SOUTH AND CENTRAL

At Pointe-á-Pierre, Trinidad, January 7, 8, 9. Drawn.

North and East

R. S. Gabriel lbw b Antoine	103	– c Debisette b Antoine	2
P. V. Simmonds c Sagram b Jumadeen	24	– c and b Ramnath	20
D. C. Furlonge lbw b Jumadeen	0		
A. T. Rajah run out	9	– not out	109
S. A. Gomes c McLeod b Ramnath	24	– not out	64
K. G. d'Heurieux lbw b Antoine	0		
P. Moosai b Antoine	4	– (3) run out	33
D. E. Audain b Antoine	6		
*†J. R. Lyon c McLeod b Ramnath	2		
G. Mahabir not out	3		
B 2, w 1, n-b 2	5	B 5, l-b 2, n-b 4	11

1/62 2/68 3/92 4/163   (9 wkts dec.) 180   1/2 2/30 3/76   (3 wkts dec.) 239
5/163 6/168 7/172 8/176 9/180

K. C. Williams did not bat.

Bowling: *First Innings*—Antoine 12–1–42–4; Sampath 3–1–15–0; Singh 3–0–11–0; Jumadeen 17–2–36–2; Ramnath 22.4–4–57–2; McLeod 8–1–14–0. *Second Innings*—Antoine 21–5–53–1; Sampath 3–1–6–0; Singh 7–0–34–0; Jumadeen 21–3–58–0; Ramnath 21–5–60–1; McLeod 6–0–17–0.

South and Central

B. Sagram c Moosai b Williams	0	– c Moosai b Williams	10
D. Paul c Furlonge b Williams	11	– lbw b Mahabir	29
W. Debisette c Audain b Mahabir	53	– c Williams b Mahabir	7
*T. Cuffy lbw b Mahabir	31	– run out	49
R. Sampath c Gomes b Williams	22	– c and b d'Heurieux	62
D. McLeod st Lyon b Mahabir	0	– (7) c Mahabir b Williams	16
R. Singh b Williams	0	– (8) b Mahabir	13
†R. Ramparass b Mahabir	0	– (6) lbw b Mahabir	1
P. Ramnath b d'Heurieux	1	– not out	1
S. Jumadeen lbw b Mahabir	0	– not out	10
G. S. Antoine not out	6		
L-b 7, n-b 2	9	B 5, l-b 1, n-b 2	8

1/1 2/26 3/101 4/105   133   1/25 2/44 3/71 4/159   (8 wkts) 206
5/111 6/118 7/119 8/125 9/126   5/166 6/166 7/187 8/196

Bowling: *First Innings*—Williams 17–3–38–4; Audain 6–3–8–0; Mahabir 18–5–52–5; d'Heurieux 7.3–3–26–1. *Second Innings*—Williams 16–2–64–2; Audain 6–1–23–0; Mahabir 22–6–66–4; d'Heurieux 9–2–24–1; Gomes 3–0–12–0; Simmonds 1–0–9–0.

LORD'S (1809-1813) WASN'T SO FAVOURED

Epping Foresters Cricket Club made a successful application for a conservation order to be placed on its ground, which lay on the projected route of the M25 motorway. A 300-yard tunnel is being dug under the ground and surrounding woodlands at a cost of £12 million, and a special clause in the City of London Various Powers Act states that the pitch, pavilion and other facilities shall be left in as good a condition as before the laying of London's orbital road.

CRICKET IN NEW ZEALAND, 1982-83

By C. R. BUTTERY

Wellington repeated their achievement of the previous year by finishing the season clear winners of the Shell Trophy. Following victories in their second and third matches they became competition leaders and had little difficulty retaining their position until the final match, when only an outright loss to Central Districts could have threatened them. Despite a valiant effort by Central Districts, who had Wellington struggling throughout, this decisive match was drawn.

Much of Wellington's success was attributable to the visiting Sussex professional, Tony Pigott, who took 33 wickets, a higher number than any other bowler. Pigott's lively medium pace frequently forced an early breakthrough on which the other bowlers were able to capitalise, leaving Wellington, in most cases, a moderate total to chase. They were, in fact, headed on the first innings in only two of their eight games. This was remarkable considering that their three leading batsmen, Bruce Edgar, John Morrison and Jeremy Coney, were on tour in Australia with the representative New Zealand side for much of the season. However, Robert Vance and Ross Ormiston rose to the occasion, while Evan Gray's all-round ability proved invaluable. Special mention should be made of Ervin McSweeney: in addition to keeping wicket and captaining the side during Morrison's absence, he averaged 52.33 with the bat.

Bottom of the table in 1981-82, Central Districts recorded three outright wins and in finishing runners-up to Wellington came closer than ever before to winning the Shell Trophy. Wicket-keeper Ian Smith emulated his Wellington counterpart by having an excellent season with the bat, scoring 446 runs at an average of 55.75. It is difficult to recall when two wicket-keepers last featured so prominently in the batting averages. David O'Sullivan was the side's leading bowler with 30 somewhat costly wickets.

Otago suffered from a lack of depth in batting. Bruce Blair enjoyed a highly satisfactory season, scoring 680 runs including two centuries, but none of the other batsmen came up to expectations. The bowlers, on the other hand, performed well, Stephen Boock taking 30 wickets at a low cost and the pace attack of Richard Webb and Brendon Bracewell being the best Otago had produced for a long while. Bracewell, who improved steadily as the season progressed, looked like justifying the promise he showed when he was eighteen, five years earlier. Kassim Ibadulla, son of the former Pakistan Test player, Billy Ibadulla, played his first games for Otago as a young all-rounder.

Northern Districts had quite an impressive batting line-up, but their bowling lacked penetration. On several occasions the side accumulated what should have been match-winning totals, only to see their opponents bat their way out of trouble. While not scoring as freely as in the previous season John Parker still batted well. His best support came from Andy Roberts and Michael Wright.

Auckland began the season on a promising note, winning their first two matches. At that point, however, their opening bowlers, Gary Troup and Martin Snedden, departed for Australia with the New Zealand side, and they struggled for the rest of the season. For all that, their batting was strong. Trevor Franklin and Martin Crowe each scored three centuries. Crowe was also a useful medium-paced bowler and John Bracewell had a good all-round record – 27 wickets and 409 runs in Shell Trophy matches.

The once-proud cricketing province of Canterbury had another disappointing season. Their lack of success over the last two years must be giving the national selectors cause for concern. The problem lay mainly with the batting. After six matches, only David Stead and Vaughan Brown had scored an innings of more than 50. These two players were also the best of the bowlers. Stead's leg-breaks brought him 22 wickets, while Brown obtained 30 wickets with economical off-spin. It was Brown who was mainly responsible for the highlight of Canterbury's season, their victory by ten wickets over Wellington.

The New Zealand Cricket Council made one major change to the rules governing the points system. Batting and bowling bonus points were replaced by points for a first-innings lead, similar to the Sheffield Shield format in Australia. This removed some of the pressure on middle-order batsmen to take unreasonable risks and was greeted with enthusiasm by the players.

FIRST-CLASS AVERAGES, 1982-83

BATTING

(Qualification: 5 complete innings; average 35.00)

	I	NO	R	HI	Avge
I. D. S. Smith (*Central Districts*)	8	0	446	145	55.75
M. D. Crowe (*Auckland*)	16	2	736	119	52.57
E. B. McSweeney (*Wellington*)	9	3	314	130	52.33
B. R. Blair (*Otago*)	13	0	680	143	52.30
T. J. Franklin (*Auckland*)	15	2	664	136	51.07
R. W. Ormiston (*Wellington*)	13	2	502	179	45.63
D. J. White (*Northern Districts*)	7	2	227	66	45.40
J. M. Parker (*Northern Districts*)	14	1	560	91	43.07
R. H. Vance (*Wellington*)	12	1	462	112	42.00
M. H. Toynbee (*Central Districts*)	9	2	293	100	41.85
A. D. G. Roberts (*Northern Districts*)	14	3	453	79*	41.18
M. J. E. Wright (*Northern Districts*)	14	1	486	115	37.38
R. Hart (*Central Districts*)	7	0	260	54	37.14
P. S. Briasco (*Central Districts*)	15	1	519	95	37.07
W. K. Lees (*Otago*)	6	0	214	89	35.66
S. J. Gill (*Central Districts*)	10	2	282	107	35.25

* Signifies not out.

BOWLING

(Qualification: 20 wickets)

	O	M	R	W	Avge
R. J. Hadlee (*Canterbury*)	152.5	52	277	23	12.04
V. R. Brown (*Canterbury*)	202.2	64	452	30	15.06
M. C. Snedden (*Auckland*)	149.2	38	372	24	15.50
E. J. Chatfield (*Wellington*)	190.5	66	389	25	15.56
A. C. S. Pigott (*Wellington*)	196.4	56	581	33	17.60
R. J. Webb (*Otago*)	166	50	397	22	18.04

	O	M	R	W	Avge
S. L. Boock (*Otago*)	290	127	604	30	20.13
D. A. Stirling (*Central Districts*)	203.3	55	552	25	22.08
D. W. Stead (*Canterbury*)	228.3	74	509	22	23.13
C. H. Thiele (*Canterbury*)	196	39	580	23	25.21
E. J. Gray (*Wellington*)	241.5	95	596	22	27.09
B. P. Bracewell (*Otago*)	224	56	603	22	27.40
G. K. Robertson (*Central Districts*)	234	47	720	25	28.80
L. W. Stott (*Auckland*)	386.3	101	760	26	29.23
J. G. Bracewell (*Auckland*)	400.2	126	964	31	31.09
D. R. O'Sullivan (*Central Districts*)	403	120	950	30	31.66
C. W. Dickeson (*Northern Districts*)	260.4	80	748	23	32.52

SHELL TROPHY

	Played	Won	Lost	Drawn	Points Outright win	Points 1st inns lead	Total
Wellington	8	4	1	3	48	24	71*
Central Districts	8	3	2	3	36	24	59*
Otago	8	2	4	2	24	20	44
Northern Districts	8	2	1	5	24	12	35*
Auckland	8	2	2	4	24	8	31*
Canterbury	8	2	5	1	24	8	31*

* *Wellington, Central Districts, Northern Districts, Auckland and Canterbury were each penalised one point.*

CANTERBURY v CENTRAL DISTRICTS

At Christchurch, December 27, 28, 29. Central Districts won by 23 runs. Central Districts 16 pts.

Central Districts

I. R. Snook c Rutledge b Hadlee	33	– lbw b Stead	14
R. A. Pierce c Bateman b Hadlee	6	– lbw b Bateman	6
P. S. Briasco c Latham b Bateman	4	– c Rutledge b Hadlee	32
*J. R. Wiltshire lbw b Thiele	6	– c Hadlee b Bateman	2
A. E. Blain c Hadlee b Stead	7	– c Rutledge b Hadlee	4
S. J. Gill c Rutledge b Hadlee	0	– b Hadlee	2
†I. D. S. Smith c Hadlee b Stead	34	– lbw b Hadlee	0
G. K. Robertson b Bateman	32	– b Hadlee	7
D. C. Aberhart not out	40	– b Hadlee	29
D. R. O'Sullivan c Rutledge b Hadlee	20	– c Hadlee b Thiele	42
D. A. Stirling lbw b Thiele	13	– not out	3
L-b 10, n-b 7	17	L-b 3	3
	212		144

1/14 2/29 3/36 4/63
5/63 6/67 7/135 8/139 9/181

1/20 2/22 3/29 4/43
5/51 6/51 7/59 8/83 9/132

Bowling: *First Innings*—Hadlee 23–8–40–4; Thiele 19.1–4–50–2; Bateman 18–5–52–2; Carter 6–2–9–0; Stead 15–5–40–2; Brown 4–2–4–0. *Second Innings*—Hadlee 25–6–43–6; Thiele 11–1–27–1; Bateman 13–0–26–2; Stead 16–5–39–1; Brown 7–5–6–0.

Canterbury

D. A. Dempsey c Snook b Stirling	2	– c Pierce b Stirling	11
D. W. Stead c sub b O'Sullivan	2	– lbw b Robertson	23
V. R. Brown c Aberhart b O'Sullivan	33	– b O'Sullivan	14
R. M. Carter b O'Sullivan	6	– c Smith b Robertson	3
R. T. Latham c Pierce b Stirling	5	– c Robertson b O'Sullivan	0
P. J. Rattray c Aberhart b Robertson	47	– c Smith b O'Sullivan	7
R. I. Leggat lbw b Stirling	45	– lbw b O'Sullivan	36
*R. J. Hadlee c Snook b Aberhart	21	– c Blain b Stirling	26
S. N. Bateman c Smith b Gill	7	– lbw b Aberhart	0
†P. D. Rutledge c Pierce b Stirling	0	– c and b O'Sullivan	0
C. H. Thiele not out	2	– not out	0
B 4, l-b 15, n-b 13	32	B 3, l-b 5, n-b 3	11

1/4 2/13 3/30 4/54   202   1/21 2/46 3/50 4/52   131
5/58 6/143 7/178 8/195 9/195   5/77 6/109 7/126 8/131 9/131

Bowling: *First Innings*—Stirling 19–5–34–4; O'Sullivan 36–15–55–3; Robertson 14–1–50–1; Aberhart 16–8–21–1; Gill 7–3–8–1; Snook 2–0–2–0. *Second Innings*—Stirling 11–1–34–2; O'Sullivan 32–10–64–5; Robertson 16–7–14–2; Aberhart 4.3–1–8–1.

Umpires: B. L. Aldridge and R. L. McHarg.

WELLINGTON v NORTHERN DISTRICTS

At Wellington, December 27, 28, 29. Drawn. Wellington 3 pts, Northern Districts minus 1 pt.

Northern Districts

L. M. Crocker c McSweeney b Pigott	48	– lbw b Pigott	0
J. G. Wright c Vance b Maguiness	20	– b Maguiness	43
*G. P. Howarth c Cederwall b Maguiness	45	– c Vance b Maguiness	9
B. G. Cooper b Chatfield	16	– c Maguiness b Cederwall	2
J. M. Parker lbw b Chatfield	12	– c McSweeney b Chatfield	3
A. D. G. Roberts c Ormiston b Chatfield	15	– not out	79
†M. J. E. Wright c Ormiston b Pigott	23	– b Coney	20
B. L. Cairns c Coney b Chatfield	0	– not out	77
S. R. Gillespie c and b Chatfield	59	– c Coney b Pigott	10
S. M. Carrington c McSweeney b Chatfield	8		
K. Treiber not out	1		
B 1, l-b 13, n-b 5	19	B 6, l-b 5, n-b 4	15

1/42 2/96 3/138 4/138   266   1/1 2/35 3/52 4/67 (7 wkts dec.) 258
5/165 6/166 7/166 8/219 9/245   5/89 6/92 7/146

Bowling: *First Innings*—Pigott 25–6–70–2; Chatfield 31.1–9–76–6; Maguiness 29–12–60–2; Gray 11–6–20–0; Cederwall 5–1–21–0; Coney 1–1–0–0. *Second Innings*—Pigott 6–2–23–2; Chatfield 34–15–61–1; Maguiness 17–3–56–2; Gray 1–0–17–0; Cederwall 13–3–39–1; Coney 4–0–20–1; Morrison 4–1–27–0.

Wellington

R. H. Vance c Howarth b Gillespie	26	– not out	3
B. A. Edgar c J. G. Wright b Treiber	146	– not out	4
R. W. Ormiston run out	44		
E. J. Gray not out	35		
*J. F. M. Morrison not out	10		
L-b 4, n-b 2	6	W 2, n-b 1	3

1/48 2/187 3/256   (3 wkts dec.) 267   (no wkt) 10

J. V. Coney, †E. B. McSweeney, B. W. Cederwall, S. J. Maguiness, A. C. S. Pigott and E. J. Chatfield did not bat.

Bowling: *First Innings*—Carrington 22–7–50–0; Cairns 26–5–54–0; Treiber 20–5–44–1; Gillespie 19–2–75–1; Roberts 11–3–21–0; Howarth 5–2–17–0. *Second Innings*—Carrington 5–2–5–0; Cairns 1.3–1–0–0; Treiber 3–2–2–0.

Umpires: S. C. Cowman and G. E. Reardon.

AUCKLAND v OTAGO

At Auckland, December 27, 28, 29. Auckland won by eight wickets. Auckland 11 pts, Otago 4 pts.

Otago

I. A. Rutherford c Webb b Troup	9	– lbw b Snedden	18
*G. M. Turner c J. J. Crowe b Stott	55	– b Snedden	7
B. R. Blair c Hellaby b Troup	61	– c M. D. Crowe b Snedden	0
W. L. Blair c Bracewell b Snedden	6	– c Snedden b Bracewell	27
R. N. Hoskin c sub b Bracewell	55	– c sub b Bracewell	10
G. J. Dawson c Bracewell b Troup	11	– c Reid b Bracewell	12
†W. K. Lees c Scott b Stott	50	– run out	22
B. Abernathy c Reid b Stott	3	– c J. J. Crowe b Snedden	2
S. L. Boock not out	3	– b Bracewell	14
B. P. Bracewell c Reid b Bracewell	9	– lbw b Snedden	8
R. J. Webb b Bracewell	0	– not out	5
B 2, l-b 13, n-b 8	23	B 9, l-b 4, n-b 2	15

1/42 2/74 3/116 4/149   285   1/29 2/38 3/38 4/54   140
5/165 6/254 7/268 8/268 9/285   5/64 6/101 7/109 8/119 9/126

Bowling: *First Innings*—Troup 17–4–56–3; Snedden 20–2–68–1; Stott 22–6–77–3; Bracewell 19.2–7–29–3; Hellaby 6–2–17–0; M. D. Crowe 5–0–15–0. *Second Innings*—Troup 9–3–27–0; Snedden 19.1–6–50–5; Stott 3–2–6–0; Bracewell 23–11–37–4; M. D. Crowe 2–1–5–0.

Auckland

T. J. Franklin b Webb	17	– b Webb	0
P. N. Webb c Lees b Boock	59	– not out	76
*J. F. Reid b Webb	2	– c Bracewell b Boock	38
J. J. Crowe run out	4	– not out	34
M. D. Crowe c Dawson b Boock	119		
J. G. Bracewell c Turner b Boock	4		
M. C. Snedden b B. R. Blair	29		
A. T. R. Hellaby c Turner b Bracewell	34		
L. W. Stott c and b Boock	0		
G. B. Troup not out	4		
†N. A. Scott b Boock	0		
L-b 2, w 2, n-b 1	5	L-b 1, n-b 3	4

1/34 2/36 3/41 4/130   277   1/0 2/66   (2 wkts) 152
5/134 6/208 7/271 8/273 9/273

Bowling: *First Innings*—Webb 26–11–33–2; Bracewell 36–10–94–1; Abernathy 19–6–45–0; Boock 37.5–16–79–5; B. R. Blair 9–3–21–1. *Second Innings*—Webb 8–1–26–1; Bracewell 16–4–37–0; Abernathy 7–3–20–0; Boock 15–6–44–1; B. R. Blair 4–0–12–0; Hoskin 1–0–1–0; Rutherford 1–0–1–0; W. L. Blair 0.2–0–5–0; Dawson 1–0–2–0.

Umpires: N. W. Stoupe and T. A. McCall.

AUCKLAND v CANTERBURY

At Auckland, January 1, 2, 3. Auckland won by ten wickets. Auckland 16 pts.

Canterbury

D. A. Dempsey c Franklin b Troup	19	– c Snedden b Bracewell	14
D. W. Stead c Reid b Stott	9	– c J. J. Crowe b Stott	21
V. R. Brown c Hellaby b Snedden	15	– c M. D. Crowe b Bracewell	28
R. M. Carter c Hellaby b Snedden	4	– b Snedden	17
R. T. Latham c Kelly b Snedden	0	– c Webb b Bracewell	29
P. J. Rattray b Snedden	28	– st Kelly b Bracewell	1
R. I. Leggat c Kelly b Snedden	0	– b Snedden	1
*R. J. Hadlee b Troup	46	– c Reid b Snedden	19
S. N. Bateman c Kelly b Snedden	14	– c Snedden b Stott	14
†A. W. Hart not out	8	– not out	0
C. H. Thiele c Kelly b Snedden	0	– run out	1
L-b 10, n-b 12	22	B 3, l-b 1, n-b 1	5

1/25 2/44 3/54 4/54   165   1/29 2/43 3/79 4/91   150
5/55 6/55 7/108 8/152 9/165   5/92 6/93 7/129 8/139 9/149

Bowling: *First Innings*—Troup 12–3–33–2; Snedden 24.1–9–49–7; Stott 17–6–40–1; Bracewell 11–6–21–0. *Second Innings*—Troup 6–1–23–0; Snedden 12–2–50–3; Stott 15–6–25–2; Bracewell 25.1–13–40–4; Reid 1–0–7–0.

Auckland

T. J. Franklin lbw b Thiele	66	– not out	22
P. N. Webb lbw b Bateman	17	– not out	10
*J. F. Reid lbw b Stead	10		
J. J. Crowe b Hadlee	23		
M. C. Snedden b Hadlee	32		
M. D. Crowe c Hart b Thiele	6		
A. T. R. Hellaby b Brown	39		
J. G. Bracewell c Thiele b Brown	61		
†P. J. Kelly c Latham b Stead	9		
L. W. Stott not out	9		
G. B. Troup c Hart b Hadlee	0		
L-b 3, n-b 6	9	B 1, l-b 1	2

1/28 2/52 3/115 4/153   282   (no wkt) 34
5/159 6/171 7/211 8/236 9/278

Bowling: *First Innings*—Hadlee 27.2–11–53–3; Thiele 20–6–65–2; Carter 4–1–13–0; Bateman 13–3–66–1; Stead 23–4–55–2; Brown 9–1–21–2. *Second Innings*—Brown 4–1–7–0; Leggat 4–0–22–0; Latham 1–0–2–0; Rattray 0.5–0–1–0.

Umpires: I. C. Higginson and T. A. McCall.

NORTHERN DISTRICTS v OTAGO

At Tauranga, January 1, 2, 3. Northern Districts won by an innings and 34 runs. Northern Districts 16 pts.

Otago

I. A. Rutherford c Parker b Carrington	0	c M. J. E. Wright b Carrington	18
C. R. Dickel c Crocker b Carrington	1	b Dickeson	56
B. R. Blair c Cooper b Carrington	3	c Cooper b Cairns	21
W. L. Blair c Harris b Cairns	19	b Cooper	16
R. N. Hoskin lbw b Carrington	0	c Howarth b Cooper	39
G. J. Dawson not out	28	c Howarth b Cooper	10
†W. K. Lees c Carrington b Roberts	21	b Cooper	32
B. Abernathy c M. J. E. Wright b Gillespie	2	c and b Cairns	32
P. W. Hills b Cairns	3	c Carrington b Dickeson	1
B. P. Bracewell c Parker b Gillespie	1	not out	0
*S. L. Boock b Cairns	0	c and b Cooper	6
B 3, l-b 3, w 1, n-b 5	12	B 7, l-b 3, n-b 5	15

1/0 2/1 3/4 4/12   90   1/33 2/71 3/118 4/118   246
5/37 6/58 7/69 8/78 9/83   5/137 6/205 7/206 8/218 9/229

Bowling: *First Innings*—Carrington 7–6–3–4; Gillespie 12–3–24–2; Cairns 9.5–0–39–3; Roberts 4–2–12–1. *Second Innings*—Carrington 15–5–36–1; Gillespie 8–1–35–0; Cairns 17.2–8–39–2; Roberts 2–0–8–0; Dickeson 29–10–67–2; Howarth 2–0–6–0; Cooper 24–11–40–5.

Northern Districts

J. G. Wright c Abernathy b Boock	35	B. L. Cairns c Hoskin b Boock	58
L. M. Crocker c Lees b Boock	32	C. W. Dickeson c Lees b Abernathy	1
*G. P. Howarth c Dickel b Boock	19	S. M. Carrington c W. L. Blair b Boock	16
B. G. Cooper c Hills b Dickel	9		
J. M. Parker c Lees b Dickel	78	B 2, l-b 5, n-b 4	11
A. D. G. Roberts lbw b B. R. Blair	38		
†M. J. E. Wright not out	72	1/62 2/78 3/91 4/103	370
S. R. Gillespie c Lees b Bracewell	1	5/186 6/235 7/244 8/325 9/335	

Bowling: Bracewell 15–1–51–1; Hills 16–2–36–0; Abernathy 10–2–32–1; Boock 45.3–20–99–5; Dickel 31–4–104–2; B. R. Blair 6–0–37–1.

Umpires: F. R. Goodall and J. B. R. Hastie.

CENTRAL DISTRICTS v WELLINGTON

At New Plymouth, January 1, 2, 3. Wellington won by ten wickets. Wellington 16 pts.

Central Districts

I. R. Snook c McSweeney b Holland	28	c Coney b Chatfield	1
R. A. Pierce lbw b James	7	lbw b Chatfield	13
P. S. Briasco b Coney	20	c and b Gray	59
*J. R. Wiltshire c Cederwall b Gray	41	c James b Chatfield	41
†A. E. Blain lbw b Maguiness	29	b Cederwall	4
M. H. Toynbee c Edgar b Gray	5	c Morrison b Chatfield	35
S. J. Gill b Chatfield	53	c McSweeney b Cederwall	0
G. K. Robertson not out	22	c McSweeney b Cederwall	8
D. C. Aberhart b James	0	c Maguiness b Gray	1
D. R. O'Sullivan c Coney b Chatfield	0	c Morrison b Chatfield	23
D. A. Stirling c McSweeney b Chatfield	1	not out	1
B 6, l-b 5, w 1	12	B 6, l-b 7, w 1, n-b 3	17

1/16 2/43 3/82 4/104   218   1/4 2/25 3/108 4/139   209
5/116 6/193 7/193 8/201 9/202   5/139 6/139 7/159 8/160 9/194

Bowling: *First Innings*—Chatfield 27.3–14–42–3; Maguiness 15–7–29–1; James 8–1–30–2; Gray 28–13–58–2; Holland 11–5–23–1; Coney 12–6–20–1; Morrison 1–0–4–0. *Second Innings* —Chatfield 27.3–9–69–5; Maguiness 8–5–6–0; James 7–3–13–0; Gray 26–15–51–2; Holland 2–0–10–0; Coney 8–4–18–0; Cederwall 10–4–25–3.

Wellington

B. A. Edgar lbw b Aberhart	17	– not out	0
P. J. Holland c Blain b Robertson	52	– not out	4
R. W. Ormiston c Aberhart b Pierce	179		
B. W. Cederwall st Blain b Aberhart	26		
E. J. Gray run out	25		
*J. F. M. Morrison c Blain b Aberhart	0		
J. V. Coney run out	93		
†E. B. McSweeney not out	4		
K. D. James not out	0		
B 3, l-b 8, n-b 17	28		

1/29 2/82 3/152 4/211   (7 wkts. dec.) 424   (no wkt) 4
5/216 6/419 7/419

S. J. Maguiness and E. J. Chatfield did not bat.

Bowling: *First Innings*—Stirling 17–5–31–0; Robertson 22–4–76–1; Aberhart 25–8–69–3; O'Sullivan 29–9–68–0; Toynbee 16–1–64–0; Briasco 10–2–39–0; Gill 15–3–41–0; Pierce 4–1–8–1. *Second Innings*—Stirling 0.2–0–4–0.

Umpires: R. G. Hoskin and S. J. Woodward.

CENTRAL DISTRICTS v AUCKLAND

At Napier, January 6, 7, 8. Central Districts won by 8 runs. Central Districts 15 pts.

Central Districts

I. R. Snook c Hunt b Bracewell	28	– lbw b Stott	10
R. A. Pierce b Tracy	3	– c and b McIntyre	94
P. S. Briasco c Bracewell b Crowe	8	– not out	49
*J. R. Wiltshire b Crowe	1		
A. E. Blain c Franklin b Bracewell	19		
M. H. Toynbee c Parsons b Crowe	100		
†I. D. S. Smith c and b Crowe	145		
D. C. Aberhart c Parsons b Crowe	1	– lbw b Stott	14
D. R. O'Sullivan lbw b Hellaby	1		
G. K. Robertson not out	32		
D. A. Stirling c Tracy b Bracewell	7		
B 9, l-b 4, w 1, n-b 4	18	B 4, l-b 6, w 1, n-b 1	12

1/5 2/15 3/17 4/71   363   1/17 2/57 3/173   (3 wkts. dec.) 179
5/88 6/308 7/312 8/319 9/329

Bowling: *First Innings*—Tracy 19–4–69–1; Stott 23–7–48–0; Crowe 23–3–69–5; Hellaby 14–3–41–1; Bracewell 29–3–81–3; McIntyre 32–6–37–0. *Second Innings*—Tracy 7–0–31–0; Stott 29–11–46–2; Crowe 2–1–4–0; Bracewell 9–0–41–0; McIntyre 29–11–45–1.

Auckland

T. J. Franklin c sub b Robertson	107	– b Aberhart	23
A. E. W. Parsons c Smith b Stirling	0	– st Smith b O'Sullivan	29
*J. F. Reid lbw b Aberhart	67	– run out	54
M. D. Crowe lbw b O'Sullivan	33	– lbw b Stirling	57
A. J. Hunt c Blain b O'Sullivan	25	– lbw b Aberhart	61
A. T. R. Hellaby lbw b Robertson	0	– run out	4
J. G. Bracewell c Blain b O'Sullivan	3	– c Robertson b Aberhart	16
J. M. McIntyre not out	1	– not out	4
L. W. Stott run out	2	– lbw b Aberhart	0
†P. J. Kelly c Blain b O'Sullivan	8	– c Robertson b Aberhart	19
S. R. Tracy b O'Sullivan	0	– lbw b Aberhart	1
B 3, l-b 3, n-b 7	13	L-b 9, w 1, n-b 1	11

1/1 2/146 3/203 4/242   259   1/28 2/90 3/120 4/201   275
5/246 6/249 7/249 8/251 9/259   5/208 6/238 7/269 8/273 9/275

Bowling: *First Innings*—Stirling 14–3–37–1; Robertson 17–3–52–2; Aberhart 16–4–36–1; O'Sullivan 44.3–15–82–5; Briasco 7–1–15–0; Pierce 8–1–24–0. *Second Innings*—Stirling 13–1–61–1; Robertson 13–0–67–0; Aberhart 15.2–0–55–6; O'Sullivan 13–0–73–1; Toynbee 1–0–8–0.

Umpires: D. A. Kinsella and S. C. Cowman.

NORTHERN DISTRICTS v CANTERBURY

At Hamilton, January 6, 7, 8. Drawn. Northern Districts 4 pts.

Canterbury

P. J. Rattray c Kuggeleijn b Dickeson	4	– c Carrington b Dickeson	41
R. M. Carter c Crocker b Dickeson	28	– b Gillespie	45
D. J. Boyle c Gillespie b Carrington	2	– lbw b Dickeson	7
V. R. Brown b Carrington	6	– not out	118
R. T. Latham c Cooper b Carrington	49	– c Dickeson b Cooper	20
D. W. Stead lbw b Carrington	16	– c Kuggeleijn b Carrington	45
*R. I. Leggat c Wright b Gillespie	17	– c Crocker b Roberts	16
S. N. Bateman c Parker b Dickeson	7	– not out	0
†A. W. Hart c Crocker b Gillespie	10		
A. J. Nuttall lbw b Dickeson	3		
C. H. Thiele not out	1		
B 2, l-b 4, n-b 1	7	B 8, l-b 11, w 1, n-b 1	21

1/2 2/20 3/71 4/101   150   1/77 2/104 3/104 4/158   (6 wkts) 313
5/110 6/110 7/136 8/139 9/146   5/268 6/297

Bowling: *First Innings*—Carrington 14–6–23–4; Treiber 8–1–25–0; Gillespie 17–3–36–2; Roberts 4–1–4–0; Dickeson 22.3–8–49–4; Cooper 1–0–6–0. *Second Innings*—Carrington 23–2–70–1; Treiber 18.4–3–59–0; Gillespie 21–4–48–1; Roberts 5–3–5–1; Dickeson 27–7–74–2; Cooper 13–4–22–1; Kuggeleijn 4–1–14–0.

Northern Districts

L. M. Crocker lbw b Stead	33	S. R. Gillespie run out	0
C. M. Kuggeleijn c Hart b Thiele	85	C. W. Dickeson c Boyle b Brown	0
K. Treiber b Bateman	31	S. M. Carrington not out	0
R. D. Broughton b Leggat	1	B 5, l-b 3, n-b 5	13
B. G. Cooper b Nuttall	21		
*J. M. Parker st Hart b Brown	57	1/71 2/159 3/160	273
A. D. G. Roberts c Hart b Bateman	7	4/162 5/192 6/215	
†M. J. E. Wright c Carter b Brown	25	7/269 8/269 9/272	

Bowling: Bateman 26–9–35–2; Thiele 23–4–63–1; Carter 10–3–25–0; Nuttall 21–9–45–1; Stead 27–6–47–1; Brown 17.1–5–31–3; Leggat 6–1–14–1.

Umpires: G. I. S. Cowan and J. B. R. Hastie.

OTAGO v WELLINGTON

At Alexandra, January 6, 7, 8. Wellington won by seven wickets. Wellington 16 pts.

Wellington

R. H. Vance lbw b Dickel	112		
P. J. Holland c Milburn b Webb	4		
R. W. Ormiston c Milburn b Abernathy	25	– c Milburn b Webb	0
E. J. Gray lbw b B. R. Blair	69	– b Webb	6
B. W. Cederwall lbw b Bracewell	28	– not out	15
*†E. B. McSweeney c Milburn b Bracewell	47		
S. B. Cater b Webb	12		
R. J. Pither c Boock b Abernathy	14	– not out	13
G. N. Cederwall c and b Abernathy	11	– c Rutherford b Dickel	28
A. C. S. Pigott b Webb	35		
S. J. Maguiness not out	7		
L-b 12, n-b 4	16	B 2, l-b 3, w 1, n-b 2	8

1/12 2/96 3/163 4/225   380   1/1 2/11 3/53   (3 wkts) 70
5/281 6/300 7/308 8/331 9/342

Bowling: *First Innings*—Bracewell 29–3–85–2; Abernathy 29–6–90–3; Webb 26.3–3–82–3; B. R. Blair 9–3–19–1; Boock 38–18–73–0; Dickel 11–1–15–1. *Second Innings*—Bracewell 3–0–15–0; Abernathy 1–0–2–0; Webb 9–2–30–2; Boock 3–0–12–0; Dickel 3–1–3–1.

Otago

I. A. Rutherford c sub b Pigott	4	– c McSweeney b Pigott	4
C. R. Dickel b Gray	16	– c McSweeney b Pigott	8
R. P. Jones c G. N. Cederwall b Pigott	4	– c G. N. Cederwall b Pigott	45
W. L. Blair c McSweeney b Gray	46	– run out	21
B. R. Blair c and b Pigott	27	– c Maguiness b Pigott	106
G. J. Dawson c McSweeney b Maguiness	16	– run out	28
A. Abernathy c Ormiston b Gray	0	– c Maguiness b B. W. Cederwall	4
*†B. D. Milburn c McSweeney b Pigott	1	– c B. W. Cederwall b Gray	18
S. L. Boock c B. W. Cederwall b Pigott	6	– c B. W. Cederwall b Pigott	2
B. P. Bracewell run out	17	– not out	36
R. J. Webb not out	1	– lbw b Gray	5
L-b 3, w 1, n-b 18	22	B 3, w 1, n-b 5	9

1/23 2/31 3/33 4/63   160   1/7 2/14 3/64 4/92   286
5/135 6/135 7/135 8/142 9/145   5/108 6/197 7/202 8/228 9/253

Bowling: *First Innings*—Pigott 17.4–8–47–5; Maguiness 12–8–18–1; Gray 17–7–37–3; G. N. Cederwall 8–1–20–0; Cater 9–3–16–0. *Second Innings*—Pigott 21–4–93–5; Maguiness 26–11–40–0; Gray 26.5–4–84–2; G. N. Cederwall 3–1–12–0; B. W. Cederwall 9–3–27–1; Pither 10–2–21–0.

Umpires: G. C. Morris and N. F. Tapper.

NORTHERN DISTRICTS v AUCKLAND

At Gisborne, January 13, 14, 15. Drawn. Auckland 4 pts.

Auckland

T. J. Franklin c Wright b Presland	136		
A. E. W. Parsons c Parker b Carrington	3	– c Dickeson b Carrington	19
*J. F. Reid c Wright b Presland	68	– c Dickeson b Pollock	7
M. D. Crowe c Roberts b Pollock	6	– st Wright b Dickeson	108
A. J. Hunt c and b Presland	33	– c Kuggeleijn b Dickeson	26
A. T. R. Hellaby lbw b Pollock	41	– not out	9
J. G. Bracewell not out	54	– c Cooper b Pollock	36
†P. J. Kelly not out	10		
L-b 11, w 1, n-b 2	14	B 5, l-b 7, n-b 2	14

1/3 2/101 3/136   (6 wkts dec.) 365   1/40 2/62 3/79   (5 wkts dec.) 219
4/188 5/290 6/306   4/174 5/219

J. M. McIntyre, L. W. Stott and S. R. Tracy did not bat.

Bowling: *First Innings*—Carrington 24–5–70–1; Pollock 24–2–98–2; Presland 29.3–8–96–3; Roberts 4–1–11–0; Dickeson 18–5–53–0; Cooper 9–2–23–0. *Second Innings*—Carrington 6–0–32–1; Pollock 10–3–38–2; Dickeson 12.1–1–55–2; Cooper 7–0–20–0; Broughton 4–0–28–0; Wright 4–0–32–0.

Northern Districts

L. M. Crocker c Hellaby b Crowe	39	– lbw b Tracy	19
C. M. Kuggeleijn c Kelly b Crowe	9	– c Kelly b Tracy	2
A. D. G. Roberts c Kelly b Crowe	1	– b Bracewell	79
*J. M. Parker c Stott b McIntyre	91	– c and b Stott	8
B. G. Cooper c Franklin b Tracy	14	– c Kelly b McIntyre	4
†M. J. E. Wright c Reid b Tracy	6	– c Kelly b Stott	24
R. D. Broughton c Hunt b Stott	8	– b McIntyre	26
C. M. Presland c Franklin b Stott	6	– not out	60
C. W. Dickeson b Tracy	18	– not out	7
S. M. Carrington c and b Bracewell	20		
N. D. Pollock not out	0		
B 4, n-b 2	6	B 5, l-b 6, n-b 1	12

1/40 2/45 3/48 4/64   218   1/2 2/35 3/51 4/60   (7 wkts) 241
5/76 6/87 7/101 8/184 9/204   5/75 6/134 7/207

Bowling: *First Innings*—Tracy 14–4–54–3; Stott 22–6–48–2; Crowe 20–8–45–3; Bracewell 10.3–1–46–1; McIntyre 6–1–19–1. *Second Innings*—Tracy 15–2–42–2; Stott 17–6–31–2; Crowe 5–2–19–0; Bracewell 23–3–77–1; McIntyre 26–9–46–2; Reid 4–1–14–0.

Umpires: G. I. S. Cowan and S. J. Woodward.

CANTERBURY v WELLINGTON

At Christchurch, January 13, 14, 15. Canterbury won by ten wickets. Canterbury 16 pts.

Canterbury

P. J. Rattray b James	20	– not out	19
R. M. Carter lbw b Cater	12	– not out	1
V. R. Brown c McSweeney b Maguiness	34		
P. E. McEwan c Gray b Cater	1		
R. T. Latham lbw b Cater	18		
D. W. Stead c McSweeney b James	81		
*R. I. Leggat lbw b Maguiness	27		
S. N. Bateman c sub b Maguiness	0		
A. J. Nuttall c G. N. Cederwall b B. W. Cederwall	32		
†P. D. Rutledge not out	8		
C. H. Thiele c McSweeney b James	2		
L-b 5, w 1, n-b 14	20		
	255		**(no wkt) 20**

1/22 2/59 3/65 4/77
5/103 6/166 7/166 8/230 9/255

Bowling: *First Innings*—James 16.5–3–52–3; Maguiness 35–13–62–3; Cater 19–5–44–3; Gray 6–1–18–0; Pither 4–3–1–0; B. W. Cederwall 10–2–17–1; G. N. Cederwall 12–3–41–0. *Second Innings*—Gray 5–1–13–0; Pither 5.1–3–7–0.

Wellington

J. G. Boyle c Brown b Thiele	8	– c and b Stead	7
R. J. Pither b Brown	9	– c Latham b Brown	4
R. H. Vance c and b Brown	32	– lbw b Brown	41
R. W. Ormiston c and b Brown	0	– lbw b Bateman	30
E. J. Gray c Latham b Brown	8	– c Nuttall b Stead	17
*†E. B. McSweeney lbw b Carter	5	– c Nuttall b Stead	8
B. W. Cederwall b Brown	0	– c McEwan b Brown	1
G. N. Cederwall c Latham b Brown	3	– c Latham b Bateman	0
K. D. James c Rattray b Stead	11	– not out	16
S. J. Maguiness lbw b Brown	11	– c Thiele b Bateman	4
S. B. Cater not out	3	– c Thiele b Brown	20
B 11, l-b 3	14	B 14, l-b 3, w 1, n-b 1	19
	104		**167**

1/9 2/56 3/56 4/61   1/46 2/58 3/85 4/102
5/70 6/70 7/70 8/90 9/90   5/103 6/111 7/134 8/134 9/141

Bowling: *First Innings*—Bateman 12–7–28–0; Brown 18.2–12–28–7; Stead 4–3–3–1; Thiele 10–3–19–1; Carter 7–3–12–1. *Second Innings*—Bateman 10–5–23–3; Brown 13.5–5–28–4; Stead 21–7–40–3; Thiele 10–1–35–0; Nuttall 14–8–22–0.

Umpires: B. L. Aldridge and I. C. Higginson.

OTAGO v CENTRAL DISTRICTS

At Dunedin, January 13, 14, 15. Drawn. Otago 4 pts.

Otago

I. A. Rutherford c Smith b Stirling	62	C. R. Dickel not out	5
W. L. Blair c Snook b Aberhart	35	B 4, l-b 15, w 7, n-b 15	41
R. N. Hoskin b O'Sullivan	38		
B. R. Blair c Wiltshire b Robertson	143	1/72 2/143	**(6 wkts dec.) 396**
G. J. Dawson b Gill	67	3/175 4/375	
B. P. Bracewell lbw b Gill	5	5/381 6/396	

*†B. D. Milburn, S. L. Boock, K. B. K. Ibadulla and R. J. Webb did not bat.

Bowling: Stirling 16–5–67–1; Robertson 17–6–46–1; Aberhart 19–7–54–1; O'Sullivan 25–3–88–1; Gill 13–1–66–2; Toynbee 3–1–9–0; Briasco 9–3–25–0.

Central Districts

I. R. Snook c Milburn b Bracewell	2	– b Boock	37
P. S. Briasco b Webb	0	– c Rutherford b Boock	57
R. A. Pierce b Webb	29	– c Milburn b B. R. Blair	7
*J. R. Wiltshire c Rutherford b Webb	11	– not out	10
M. H. Toynbee c Milburn b Bracewell	43	– not out	7
†I. D. S. Smith lbw b Dickel	11		
S. J. Gill b Boock	107		
D. C. Aberhart c Milburn b Bracewell	1		
D. R. O'Sullivan b Boock	23		
G. K. Robertson c Ibadulla b Boock	6		
D. A. Stirling not out	0		
L-b 4, n-b 7	11	B 1, l-b 6, n-b 3	10

1/0 2/4 3/21 4/54   244   1/31 2/94 3/112   (3 wkts) 128
5/88 6/123 7/131 8/237 9/243

Bowling: *First Innings*—Webb 18–4–49–3; Bracewell 15–2–62–3; B. R. Blair 10–3–23–0; Boock 10.5–4–40–3; Dickel 11–3–38–1; Ibadulla 6–1–21–0. *Second Innings*—Webb 3–1–13–0; Bracewell 8–3–21–0; B. R. Blair 4–2–10–1; Boock 28–16–40–2; Dickel 11–5–22–0; Ibadulla 6–2–12–0.

Umpires: F. R. Goodall and R. L. McHarg.

CANTERBURY v OTAGO

At Christchurch, January 20, 21. Otago won by an innings and 40 runs. Otago 16 pts, Canterbury minus 1 pt.

Canterbury

P. J. Rattray c Milburn b Webb	11	– c Milburn b Webb	0
R. M. Carter c Milburn b Webb	1	– c Bracewell b Webb	10
D. J. Boyle lbw b Bracewell	4	– lbw b Dickel	7
V. R. Brown c Bracewell b Abernathy	1	– lbw b Dickel	31
P. E. McEwan c Bracewell b Abernathy	24	– lbw b Boock	19
D. W. Stead c Dawson b Abernathy	18	– c and b Bracewell	14
*R. I. Leggat lbw b Bracewell	2	– not out	12
S. N. Bateman not out	5	– lbw b Boock	
A. J. Nuttall c Milburn b Abernathy	3	– c Milburn b Dickel	3
†P. D. Rutledge c Hoskin b Webb	1	– c Rutherford b Boock	11
C. H. Thiele b Webb	17	– c Boock b Dickel	0
B 5, l-b 1, w 2, n-b 4	12	B 1, l-b 5, w 1, n-b 3	10

1/5 2/12 3/19 4/19   99   1/1 2/12 3/26 4/72   117
5/65 6/65 7/67 8/77 9/78   5/80 6/95 7/95 8/101 9/112

Bowling: *First Innings*—Webb 13.5–4–33–4; Bracewell 12–2–27–3; Abernathy 15–6–27–3. *Second Innings*—Webb 12–6–20–2; Bracewell 12–2–37–1; Abernathy 2–0–5–0; B. R. Blair 1–0–3–0; Boock 14–5–20–2; Dickel 10.5–5–22–5.

Otago

I. A. Rutherford c Thiele b Brown	39	B. P. Bracewell st Rutledge b Stead	25
W. L. Blair c Rutledge b Thiele	29	S. L. Boock c Bateman b Brown	0
R. N. Hoskin c Rattray b Brown	5	R. J. Webb not out	0
B. R. Blair c Stead b Brown	70	B 5, l-b 8, w 1, n-b 4	18
G. J. Dawson c Carter b Stead	17		
C. R. Dickel run out	11	1/72 2/82 3/92	256
B. Abernathy lbw b Brown	40	4/133 5/155 6/211	
*†B. D. Milburn c Stead b Brown	2	7/215 8/254 9/254	

Bowling: Thiele 19–3–63–1; Bateman 18–3–58–0; Carter 4–1–15–0; Brown 20–6–55–6; Stead 15.4–4–41–2; Nuttall 7–2–6–0.

Umpires: F. R. Goodall and R. G. Hoskin.

CENTRAL DISTRICTS v NORTHERN DISTRICTS

At Palmerston North, January 21, 22, 23. Northern Districts won by four wickets. Northern Districts 12 pts, Central Districts 4 pts.

Central Districts

I. R. Snook b Carrington	4	– c Scott b Presland	21
R. T. Hart c Parker b Presland	0	– c Broughton b White	51
P. S. Briasco c Crocker b Scott	53	– c Wright b Roberts	52
R. A. Pierce lbw b Carrington	2	– c sub b Roberts	46
*J. R. Wiltshire c Crocker b Roberts	12	– not out	0
M. H. Toynbee c Scott b Dickeson	8		
†I. D. S. Smith b Cooper	111		
G. K. Robertson c and b Presland	24	– c sub b Scott	15
D. R. O'Sullivan c Broughton b Roberts	36		
D. C. Aberhart not out	14		
D. A. Stirling c Broughton b Cooper	4	– c sub b Roberts	37
B 8, l-b 12, w 1, n-b 6	27	B 4, l-b 12, n-b 1	17

1/4 2/4 3/11 4/61   295   1/39 2/112 3/144   (6 wkts dec.) 239
5/80 6/107 7/148 8/240 9/287   4/219 5/237 6/239

Bowling: *First Innings*—Carrington 10–1–37–2; Presland 16–4–53–2; Roberts 17–3–50–2; Scott 20–6–59–1; Dickeson 12–4–43–1; White 1–0–4–0; Cooper 8.2–3–22–2. *Second Innings* —Presland 24–4–62–1; Roberts 14–3–30–2; Scott 16.3–5–53–1; Dickeson 22–11–48–0; White 2–1–2–1; Cooper 13–4–27–0.

Northern Districts

L. M. Crocker lbw b Robertson	10	– c Smith b Stirling	10
†M. J. E. Wright c Smith b Stirling	13	– c Hart b Aberhart	1
R. D. Broughton c Smith b Robertson	1	– c Hart b O'Sullivan	122
*J. M. Parker c O'Sullivan b Aberhart	3	– c Smith b Aberhart	69
B. G. Cooper c sub b O'Sullivan	55	– lbw b O'Sullivan	18
A. D. G. Roberts c Smith b Stirling	39	– not out	49
D. J. White not out	54	– b Robertson	34
C. M. Presland c Pierce b Robertson	0		
C. W. Dickeson b Stirling	20	– not out	4
S. J. Scott c Wiltshire b Pierce	5		
S. M. Carrington b Robertson	0		
L-b 5, w 1, n-b 8	14	L-b 8, w 1, n-b 6	15

1/24 2/24 3/27 4/35   214   1/12 2/17 3/156 4/215   (6 wkts) 322
5/129 6/139 7/139 8/180 9/211   5/230 6/314

Bowling:*First Innings*—Stirling 19–5–67–3; Robertson 23–7–57–4; Aberhart 13–4–26–1; O'Sullivan 20–7–48–1; Pierce 2–1–2–1. *Second Innings*—Stirling 6–3–11–1; Robertson 16–2–42–1; Aberhart 18–9–40–2; O'Sullivan 41–8–125–2; Toynbee 21–5–89–0.

Umpires: G. I. S. Cowan and D. A. Kinsella.

WELLINGTON v AUCKLAND

At Wellington, January 21, 22, 23. Wellington won by an innings and 59 runs. Wellington 16 pts.

Auckland

T. J. Franklin c Vance b Rule	5	– c McSweeney b Pigott	34	
A. E. W. Parsons c Pigott b Maguiness	40	– b Maguiness	17	
*J. F. Reid c Ormiston b Maguiness	4	– c Vance b Rule	21	
M. D. Crowe c McSweeney b Maguiness	27	– c Cederwall b Maguiness	19	
A. J. Hunt c McSweeney b Cederwall	2	– c Gray b Rule	4	
A. T. R. Hellaby c McSweeney b Pigott	0	– b Pigott	21	
J. G. Bracewell not out	60	– c sub b Gray	44	
†P. J. Kelly c Boyle b Rule	2	– b Pigott	0	
J. M. McIntyre b Pigott	4	– c Cederwall b Gray	5	
L. W. Stott b Maguiness	1	– not out	2	
S. R. Tracy c Gray b Pigott	4	– c Ritchie b Gray	3	
B 1, n-b 3	4	L-b 8	8	
	153		178	

1/17 2/39 3/64 4/80
5/80 6/104 7/112 8/127 9/128

1/40 2/59 3/92 4/92
5/97 6/148 7/156 8/164 9/172

Bowling: *First Innings*—Pigott 16.4–2–51–3; Rule 11–3–36–2; Maguiness 17–7–28–4; Cederwall 7–1–20–1; Gray 2–0–14–0. *Second Innings*—Pigott 24–8–53–3; Rule 11–3–32–2; Maguiness 20–8–36–2; Cederwall 6–4–7–0; Gray 9.5–1–42–3.

Wellington

R. H. Vance lbw b Crowe	61	A. C. S. Pigott c sub b McIntyre	24
J. G. Boyle c Kelly b Tracy	1	S. J. Maguiness c Tracy b Stott	6
P. J. Holland st Kelly b Bracewell	56	B. Rule not out	0
R. W. Ormiston b Crowe	26		
E. J. Gray b Bracewell	24	B 15, l-b 4, n-b 5	24
T. D. Ritchie b Crowe	4		
*†E. B. McSweeney lbw b Stott	130	1/9 2/93 3/104 4/110	390
B. W. Cederwall c Kelly b McIntyre	34	5/153 6/279 7/355 8/365 9/388	

Bowling: Tracy 28–6–80–1; Stott 49–18–105–2; Crowe 14–5–31–3; Hellaby 12–3–41–0; Bracewell 27–9–72–2; McIntyre 17–7–37–2.

Umpires: G. E. Reardon and S. J. Woodward.

OTAGO v CANTERBURY

At Invercargill, January 28, 29. Otago won by an innings and 87 runs. Otago 16 pts.

Otago

I. A. Rutherford c and b Stead	96	*†B. D. Milburn c Farrant b Leggat	9
W. L. Blair c Brown b Stead	13	B. P. Bracewell lbw b Stead	0
R. N. Hoskin lbw b Stead	57	S. L. Boock st Rutledge b Stead	21
B. R. Blair b Stead	0		
G. J. Dawson c Rutledge b Bateman	28	B 16, l-b 2	18
C. R. Dickel c Brown b Stead	10		
B. Abernathy lbw b Bateman	0	1/57 2/156 3/156 4/189	282
K. B. K. Ibadulla not out	30	5/215 6/216 7/217 8/248 9/248	

Bowling: Bateman 19–7–33–2; Farrant 12–5–18–0; Dempsey 6–3–14–0; Brown 40–12–72–0; Stead 48.1–17–99–7; Leggat 11–3–28–1.

Canterbury

J. Gully c Milburn b Ibadulla	20	– b Boock	6
D. A. Dempsey c Hoskin b Abernathy	11	– c Ibadulla b Abernathy	0
R. M. Carter c Abernathy b Boock	8	– lbw b Boock	38
V. R. Brown c Milburn b Ibadulla	0	– c Dawson b Boock	2
P. E. McEwan c Milburn b Boock	44	– c B. R. Blair b Ibadulla	2
D. W. Stead c Dickel b Boock	5	– c B. R. Blair b Ibadulla	0
P. J. Rattray c Dawson b Boock	0	– b Ibadulla	1
*R. I. Leggat b Dickel	0	– not out	5
S. N. Bateman c sub b Dickel	0	– c Dawson b Ibadulla	0
A. J. Farrant b Dickel	7	– c Abernathy b Boock	18
†P. D. Rutledge not out	0	– c Boock b Ibadulla	3
B 5, l-b 4, n-b 2	11	B 6, l-b 8	14

1/32 2/45 3/45 4/51   **106**   1/4 2/22 3/35 4/55   **89**
5/56 6/63 7/95 8/95 9/104   5/55 6/55 7/63 8/63 9/68

Bowling: *First Innings*—Bracewell 4-1-14-0; Abernathy 7-1-17-1; Boock 19-11-34-4; Ibadulla 11-1-30-2; Dickel 4.2-4-0-3. *Second Innings*—Bracewell 4-3-1-0; Abernathy 6-4-7-1; Boock 20-8-45-4; Ibadulla 7.2-7-22-5.

Umpires: G. C. Morris and N. F. Tapper.

AUCKLAND v WELLINGTON

At Auckland, January 29, 30, 31. Drawn. Wellington 4 pts.

Wellington

R. H. Vance b Tracy	14	– c McIntyre b Bracewell	31
J. G. Boyle b Cushen	0	– c Hunt b Stott	26
P. J. Holland c Hunt b Tracy	45	– c Tracy b Bracewell	29
R. W. Ormiston c Hunt b Bracewell	45	– lbw b Tracy	26
E. J. Gray c Kelly b McIntyre	45	– not out	53
T. D. Ritchie c and b Bracewell	8	– lbw b McIntyre	24
*†E. B. McSweeney c Crowe b Bracewell	27	– not out	61
B. W. Cederwall c Reid b Stott	20		
A. C. S. Pigott lbw b Stott	21		
S. J. Maguiness c Tracy b Stott	0		
B. Rule not out	4		
B 3, l-b 5, n-b 1	9	B 10, l-b 6, n-b 3	19

1/5 2/38 3/95 4/125   **238**   1/58 2/70 3/121   (5 wkts dec.) **269**
5/137 6/169 7/201 8/230 9/230   4/129 5/161

Bowling: *First Innings*—Tracy 17-3-66-2; Cushen 21-11-26-1; Bracewell 32-7-97-3; Stott 9.3-4-16-3; McIntyre 18-8-21-1; Reid 1-0-3-0. *Second Innings*—Tracy 16-3-64-1; Cushen 6-1-17-0; Bracewell 40-16-89-2; McIntyre 23-15-17-1; Stott 13-4-27-1; Reid 4-1-11-0; Hunt 6-1-15-0; Franklin 3-1-10-0.

Auckland

T. J. Franklin c Cederwall b Gray	50	– b Cederwall	35
M. J. Greatbatch b Gray	28	– b Maguiness	28
J. A. Cushen not out	30		
*J. F. Reid c Ritchie b Maguiness	1	– not out	22
M. D. Crowe c Ritchie b Pigott	100	– b Ormiston	30
A. J. Hunt lbw b Pigott	0	– lbw b Gray	27
J. G. Bracewell c Ormiston b Pigott	0	– c Boyle b Holland	7
†P. J. Kelly c Holland b Pigott	0	– not out	9
J. M. McIntyre lbw b Gray	1		
L. W. Stott st McSweeney b Gray	2		
S. R. Tracy run out	5		
L-b 5, w 1, n-b 1	7	N-b 1	1

1/77 2/86 3/89 4/202	224	1/51 2/65 3/95 (5 wkts) 159
5/202 6/202 7/204 8/205 9/209		4/100 5/140

Bowling: *First Innings*—Pigott 19–7–38–4; Rule 3–0–16–0; Gray 50.5–20–100–4; Maguiness 20–9–34–1; Holland 8–1–17–0; Cederwall 9–5–12–0. *Second Innings*—Pigott 7–1–30–0; Rule 2–0–15–0; Gray 7–3–16–1; Maguiness 6–1–23–1; Holland 7–1–19–1; Cederwall 4–0–10–1; Ormiston 6–0–26–1; Boyle 2–0–19–0; Vance 1–1–0–0.

Umpires: N. W. Stoupe and S. C. Cowman.

NORTHERN DISTRICTS v CENTRAL DISTRICTS

At Hamilton, January 29, 30, 31. Drawn. Central Districts 4 pts.

Central Districts

R. A. Pierce c Crocker b Presland	0	– lbw b Dickeson	31
R. T. Hart lbw b Carrington	8	– c and b White	54
P. S. Briasco c Parker b Dickeson	52	– c Roberts b White	9
R. Hayward b Carrington	0	– b Dickeson	24
*J. R. Wiltshire c Carrington b Presland	8	– not out	29
M. H. Toynbee c Crocker b White	27		
†I. D. S. Smith b Scott	143		
S. J. Gill c Roberts b Dickeson	0	– not out	22
G. K. Robertson c Broughton b Dickeson	96	– c Carrington b White	5
D. R. O'Sullivan c Broughton b Dickeson	33		
D. A. Stirling not out	1	– st Wright b White	33
B 3, l-b 19, w 1, n-b 1	24	B 3, l-b 6, w 1, n-b 1	11

1/1 2/19 3/23 4/46	392	1/43 2/96 3/123 (6 wkts dec.) 218
5/97 6/117 7/117 8/290 9/352		4/139 5/169 6/180

Bowling: *First Innings*—Carrington 15–4–41–2; Presland 14–6–62–2; Scott 25.3–6–80–1; Roberts 13–5–42–0; Dickeson 28–12–84–4; White 8–3–35–1; Cooper 3–0–24–0. *Second Innings*—Carrington 5–1–17–0; Presland 6–1–9–0; Scott 5–2–5–0; Dickeson 27.3–9–87–2; White 24–4–89–4.

Northern Districts

L. M. Crocker lbw b Robertson	15	– b Gill	8
†M. J. E. Wright c Toynbee b O'Sullivan	37	– c Smith b Stirling	31
R. D. Broughton c Smith b O'Sullivan	37	– c Hayward b Stirling	22
*J. M. Parker c Gill b O'Sullivan	39	– c Smith b O'Sullivan	27
B. G. Cooper run out	0	– c Briasco b O'Sullivan	29
A. D. G. Roberts b Gill	65	– run out	11
D. J. White lbw b Stirling	66	– c Smith b Stirling	13
C. M. Presland b Robertson	0	– not out	46
S. J. Scott b Stirling	4	– b Robertson	5
S. M. Carrington run out	1	– not out	5
C. W. Dickeson not out	15	– lbw b Stirling	0
B 2, l-b 10, w 1	13	B 1, l-b 3, n-b 1	5

1/43 2/73 3/127 4/127   292   1/9 2/56 3/67 4/100   (9 wkts) 202
5/149 6/234 7/235 8/285 9/289   5/129 6/130 7/177 8/177 9/193

Bowling: *First Innings*—Stirling 20–4–63–2; O'Sullivan 38.3–11–83–3; Toynbee 14–3–29–0; Gill 13–3–40–1; Robertson 17–3–52–2; Pierce 2–0–4–0; Hayward 1–1–0–0; Briasco 2–0–8–0. *Second Innings*—Stirling 9–4–23–4; O'Sullivan 29–16–37–2; Toynbee 21–8–44–0; Gill 13–4–28–1; Robertson 13–3–33–1; Pierce 4–2–12–0; Briasco 6–2–8–0; Hart 1–0–12–0.

Umpires: B. L. Aldridge and J. B. R. Hastie.

AUCKLAND v NORTHERN DISTRICTS

At Auckland, February 2, 3, 4. Drawn. Northern Districts 4 pts.

Northern Districts

L. M. Crocker c Stott b Cushen	8	– b Tracy	12
†M. J. E. Wright c Kelly b Tracy	115	– c and b Stott	45
R. D. Broughton c Bracewell b Stott	40	– lbw b Stott	49
*J. M. Parker b Hellaby	71	– not out	56
B. G. Cooper c Tracy b Reid	10	– c Kelly b Stott	9
A. D. G. Roberts c Kelly b Cushen	29	– not out	19
D. J. White c Kelly b Cushen	15		
C. M. Presland c Reid b Bracewell	17		
C. W. Dickeson not out	21		
S. J. Scott not out	5	– c Crowe b Bracewell	12
B 8, l-b 5, n-b 8	21	B 3, l-b 9, n-b 5	17

1/13 2/99 3/230 4/245   (8 wkts dec.) 352   1/23 2/113 3/114   (5 wkts dec.) 219
5/277 6/308 7/310 8/333   4/129 5/158

K. Treiber did not bat.

Bowling: *First Innings*—Tracy 15–4–53–1; Cushen 22–7–76–3; Stott 33–13–81–1; Hellaby 14–4–42–1; Bracewell 25–9–58–1; Hunt 6–1–16–0; Reid 4–2–5–1. *Second Innings*—Tracy 9–0–37–1; Cushen 4–0–10–0; Stott 33–8–84–3; Bracewell 30–8–71–1.

Auckland

T. J. Franklin c Scott b Presland	57	– b Treiber	5
M. J. Greatbatch b Treiber	8	– c Wright b Presland	80
*J. F. Reid b Presland	33	– not out	11
M. D. Crowe lbw b Dickeson	46	– c sub b Dickeson	35
A. J. Hunt not out	68	– c Presland b Dickeson	41
J. G. Bracewell c Crocker b Treiber	40	– c Scott b Cooper	20
A. T. R. Hellaby run out	0	– c Crocker b Cooper	16
†P. J. Kelly c and b Dickeson	12	– run out	36
J. A. Cushen not out	0	– c Wright b Dickeson	5
L. W. Stott (did not bat)	– run out		5
S. R. Tracy (did not bat)	– not out		0
B 9, l-b 8, w 3, n-b 3	23	B 1, l-b 10, w 1, n-b 6	18

1/19 2/97 3/127 4/177   (7 wkts dec.) 287   1/8 2/106 3/156 4/183   (9 wkts) 272
5/254 6/254 7/280   5/191 6/238 7/251 8/251 9/266

Bowling: *First Innings*—Treiber 20–3–58–2; Presland 20–3–67–2; Scott 17–5–47–0; Roberts 11–7–7–0; Dickeson 21–4–58–2; White 6–1–27–0. *Second Innings*—Treiber 4–0–15–1; Presland 9–4–26–1; Scott 4–2–8–0; Dickeson 28–3–99–3; White 11–1–64–0; Cooper 9–1–42–2.

Umpires: T. A. McCall and R. L. McHarg.

CENTRAL DISTRICTS v CANTERBURY

At Nelson, February 2, 3, 4. Central Districts won by 37 runs. Central Districts 16 pts.

Central Districts

R. A. Pierce c Gully b Stead	89	– c Bateman b Dempsey	29
R. T. Hart c Dempsey b Brown	53	– b Thiele	42
P. S. Briasco c McEwan b Thiele	95	– c Leggat b Thiele	12
R. Hayward c and b Leggat	0	– not out	33
*J. R. Wiltshire c McEwan b Brown	52	– c Rutledge b Thiele	0
M. H. Toynbee not out	66		
†I. D. S. Smith c Brown b Thiele	2		
S. J. Gill not out	37	– c McEwan b Brown	10
G. K. Robertson (did not bat)	– not out		9
B 4, l-b 14, n-b 5	23	L-b 7, n-b 1	8

1/132 2/178 3/181   (6 wkts dec.) 417   1/52 2/76 3/103   (5 wkts dec.) 143
4/279 5/330 6/332   4/114 5/120

D. R. O'Sullivan and D. A. Stirling did not bat.

Bowling: *First Innings*—Thiele 13–3–37–2; Bateman 10–1–63–0; Farrant 19–5–57–0; Brown 34–8–107–2; Stead 40–18–91–1; Leggat 13–2–39–1. *Second Innings*—Thiele 15–3–46–3; Bateman 7–0–29–0; Brown 7–0–31–1; Dempsey 9–2–29–1.

Canterbury

J. Gully c Smith b Robertson	0	– b Robertson 5
D. A. Dempsey c Hart b Robertson	23	– lbw b Gill 42
V. R. Brown c Gill b Robertson	12	– c Gill b Toynbee 44
P. E. McEwan c Wiltshire b Stirling	22	– c Toynbee b Robertson 50
D. W. Stead c Pierce b O'Sullivan	81	– b Gill 13
P. J. Rattray run out	2	– c Briasco b O'Sullivan 133
*R. I. Leggat c Robertson b O'Sullivan	15	– lbw b Gill 18
S. N. Bateman c Smith b O'Sullivan	0	– run out 0
†P. D. Rutledge b O'Sullivan	10	– c Smith b Gill 0
A. J. Farrant c Smith b Stirling	6	– run out 0
C. H. Thiele not out	4	– not out 0
B 11, l-b 3, w 1, n-b 9	24	B 9, l-b 8, n-b 2 19

1/0 2/29 3/39 4/74   199   1/15 2/98 3/190   324
5/88 6/163 7/169 8/186 9/187

Bowling: *First Innings*—Robertson 14–1–56–3; O'Sullivan 29–9–57–4; Stirling 11.4–5–28–2; Gill 7–3–17–0; Toynbee 9–1–17–0; Hayward 2–2–0–0. *Second Innings*—Robertson 17–3–76–2; O'Sullivan 35–6–111–1; Stirling 17–4–38–0; Gill 12.4–3–28–4; Toynbee 9–1–47–1; Pierce 1–0–5–0.

Umpires: I. C. Higginson and D. A. Kinsella.

WELLINGTON v OTAGO

At Wellington, February 4, 5, 6. Wellington won by six wickets. Wellington 16 pts.

Otago

I. A. Rutherford b Pigott	6	– c McSweeney b Pigott 2
W. L. Blair c Gray b Cederwall	2	– c McSweeney b Cederwall 22
R. N. Hoskin b Pigott	4	– b Pigott 77
B. R. Blair b Gray	90	– c Vance b Cederwall 39
G. J. Dawson c Ormiston b Cederwall	54	– c McSweeney b Pigott 16
C. R. Dickel lbw b Cederwall	0	– not out 21
B. Abernathy c Gray b Cederwall	8	– run out 0
*†B. D. Milburn run out	1	– c Pigott b Cederwall 1
B. P. Bracewell c Vance b Gray	8	– st McSweeney b Gray 5
S. L. Boock not out	2	– c McSweeney b Pigott 3
R. J. Webb c Ritchie b Gray	0	– run out 2
B 3, l-b 1, n-b 2	6	B 2, l-b 5, n-b 2 9

1/2 2/9 3/20 4/144   181   1/2 2/35 3/101 4/160   197
5/146 6/168 7/168 8/177 9/177   5/173 6/180 7/187 8/192 9/195

Bowling: *First Innings*—Pigott 18–5–65–2; Cederwall 16–8–34–4; Maguiness 13–6–31–0; Rule 4–0–22–0; Gray 10.2–4–23–3. *Second Innings*—Pigott 18–8–47–4; Cederwall 16–8–40–3; Maguiness 15–5–26–0; Rule 8–3–10–0; Gray 21–11–53–1; Holland 12–6–12–0.

Wellington

R. H. Vance b Boock	42	– lbw b Bracewell	33
J. G. Boyle c Rutherford b Dickel	76	– b Boock	27
P. J. Holland c Hoskin b Dickel	1	– c Milburn b Bracewell	7
R. W. Ormiston run out	20	– not out	42
E. J. Gray c Abernathy b Bracewell	33	– c Dawson b Bracewell	7
T. D. Ritchie lbw b Bracewell	6	– not out	26
*†E. B. McSweeney c Milburn b Bracewell	0		
B. W. Cederwall lbw b Dickel	18		
A. C. S. Pigott b Bracewell	1		
S. J. Maguiness not out	7		
B. Rule b Webb	0		
B 2, l-b 8, w 1, n-b 9	20	B 2, l-b 4, n-b 7	13

1/75 2/98 3/143 4/150   224   1/39 2/70 3/73   (4 wkts) 155
5/170 6/170 7/203 8/208 9/220   4/86

Bowling: *First Innings*—Webb 18.2–4–50–1; Abernathy 15–5–44–0; Bracewell 19–7–44–4; Boock 11–5–26–1; Dickel 23–10–40–3. *Second Innings*—Webb 10.2–3–25–0; Abernathy 7–3–14–0; Bracewell 15–5–36–3; Boock 24–9–38–1; Dickel 11–2–28–0; W. L. Blair 2–1–1–0.

Umpires: G. E. Reardon and S. J. Woodward.

CANTERBURY v NORTHERN DISTRICTS

At Christchurch, February 10, 11, 12. Canterbury won by three wickets. Canterbury 16 pts.

Northern Districts

L. M. Crocker lbw b Thiele	0	– c Hart b Bateman	20
†M. J. E. Wright lbw b Thiele	1	– c McEwan b Dempsey	73
R. D. Broughton c McEwan b Bateman	18	– c Thiele b Stead	11
*J. M. Parker b Bateman	1	– c Carter b Dempsey	45
B. G. Cooper c Hart b Brown	25	– lbw b Dempsey	0
A. D. G. Roberts lbw b Hadlee	0	– c Hart b Brown	22
D. J. White not out	33	– c Rattray b Brown	12
C. M. Presland c McEwan b Hadlee	52	– c Dempsey b Brown	7
C. W. Dickeson lbw b Hadlee	0	– b Brown	1
S. J. Scott b Bateman	0	– not out	44
S. M. Carrington c and b Hadlee	23	– c Carter b Stead	15
B 3, l-b 7, w 2, n-b 10	22	B 7, l-b 4, w 2, n-b 6	19

1/0 2/7 3/11 4/37   175   1/45 2/75 3/147 4/167   269
5/40 6/79 7/129 8/129 9/130   5/173 6/182 7/190 8/200 9/232

Bowling: *First Innings*—Thiele 10–2–33–2; Bateman 20–6–50–3; Hadlee 19.2–6–58–4; Brown 4–0–12–1. *Second Innings*—Thiele 14–3–41–0; Bateman 8–2–23–1; Hadlee 12–1–41–0; Brown 24–7–50–4; Stead 9.4–2–28–2; Dempsey 21–6–67–3.

Canterbury

D. A. Dempsey c Broughton b Scott	30	– c and b Presland 5
R. M. Carter c Cooper b Presland	11	– c Crocker b Presland 0
P. J. Rattray c Dickeson b Presland	3	– c Scott b Roberts 63
V. R. Brown c Wright b Dickeson	16	– c Parker b Roberts 21
P. E. McEwan c Wright b Scott	9	– lbw b Roberts 39
D. W. Stead lbw b Scott	51	– lbw b Roberts 24
*R. I. Leggat c Crocker b Presland	22	– not out 16
D. R. Hadlee lbw b Presland	43	– lbw b Scott 11
†A. W. Hart c Scott b Carrington	25	– not out 1
G. C. Bateman b Scott	13	
C. H. Thiele not out	1	
L-b 24, w 3, n-b 4	31	B 3, l-b 4, w 2, n-b 1 10

1/41 2/44 3/51 4/65   255   1/1 2/12 3/83   (7 wkts) 190
5/107 6/145 7/180 8/233 9/238   4/112 5/151 6/163 7/189

Bowling: *First Innings*—Carrington 22–2–66–1; Presland 29–12–47–4; Scott 30.1–7–66–4; Roberts 12–4–22–0; Dickeson 8–2–23–1. *Second Innings*—Carrington 3–0–6–0; Presland 23–4–75–2; Scott 13–2–46–1; Roberts 21–8–45–4; Dickeson 6–4–8–0.

Umpires: F. R. Goodall and R. G. Hoskin.

OTAGO v AUCKLAND

At Dunedin, February 10, 11, 12. Drawn. Otago 4 pts.

Otago

I. A. Rutherford b Cushen	12	– lbw b Stott 15
W. L. Blair c Adams b Bracewell	20	– not out 65
R. N. Hoskin c Kelly b Cushen	33	– lbw b Stott 3
B. R. Blair run out	72	– c Hunt b Stott 48
K. R. Rutherford b Cushen	17	– c Kelly b Stott 13
G. J. Dawson not out	31	– lbw b Bracewell 39
K. B. K. Ibadulla lbw b Cushen	1	
B. P. Bracewell c Adams b McIntyre	22	– not out 10
S. L. Boock not out	18	
L-b 8	8	B 4, l-b 11, n-b 3 18

1/14 2/40 3/110 4/152   (7 wkts dec.) 234   1/27 2/36 3/135   (5 wkts dec.) 211
5/152 6/161 7/185   4/153 5/200

*†B. D. Milburn and R. J. Webb did not bat.

Bowling: *First Innings*—Cushen 26–7–67–4; Stott 26–6–51–0; Bracewell 25–8–74–1; Adams 3–0–11–0; Hellaby 2–0–2–0; McIntyre 4–0–21–1. *Second Innings*—Cushen 8–1–18–0; Stott 49–2–75–4; Bracewell 49–18–75–1; McIntyre 7–2–25–0.

Auckland

T. J. Franklin c Milburn b Bracewell	6	– not out	101
J. G. Bracewell b Webb	18	– c Milburn b Bracewell	46
M. J. Greatbatch c K. R. Rutherford b Boock	11	– c W. L. Blair b Bracewell	10
M. D. Crowe b Webb	55	– not out	25
A. J. Hunt c Milburn b Bracewell	5		
S. Adams retired hurt	7		
A. T. R. Hellaby c Milburn b Webb	2		
†P. J. Kelly c Ibadulla b Webb	0		
J. A. Cushen c and b K. R. Rutherford	4		
*J. M. McIntyre c Hoskin b Boock	23		
L. W. Stott not out	6		
B 8, l-b 10, n-b 4	22	B 5, l-b 8, n-b 3	16

1/24 2/28 3/62 4/101   159   1/31 2/126   (2 wkts) 198
5/107 6/119 7/119 8/133 9/159

Bowling: *First Innings*—Webb 21–11–36–4; Bracewell 21–9–36–2; Ibadulla 10–3–16–0; Boock 18.5–7–36–2; K. R. Rutherford 7–1–13–1. *Second Innings*—Bracewell 15–4–43–2; Ibadulla 4–0–26–0; Boock 5–2–18–0; Abernathy 19–5–72–0; B. R. Blair 6–0–23–0.

Umpires: G. C. Morris and N. F. Tapper.

WELLINGTON v CENTRAL DISTRICTS

At Wellington, February 11, 12, 13. Drawn. Central Districts 4 pts.

Wellington

R. H. Vance c Pierce b Robertson	15	– c Toynbee b Robertson	52
J. G. Boyle lbw b Gill	11	– c Briasco b O'Sullivan	67
P. J. Holland c Wiltshire b Pierce	17	– c Robertson b O'Sullivan	4
R. W. Ormiston c Smith b Robertson	5	– not out	60
E. J. Gray b Robertson	1	– c Robertson b Stirling	10
T. D. Ritchie c Stirling b Pierce	8	– not out	16
*†E. B. McSweeney not out	32		
B. W. Cederwall c Pierce b Stirling	3		
A. C. S. Pigott c Stirling	7		
G. N. Cederwall lbw b Robertson	6		
S. J. Maguiness c Robertson b Stirling	5		
B 8, l-b 6, n-b 5	19	B 5, l-b 6, w 3, n-b 4	18

1/30 2/42 3/62 4/63   129   1/112 2/128   (4 wkts) 227
5/64 6/80 7/86 8/98 9/121   3/142

Bowling: *First Innings*—Robertson 17–5–42–4; Gill 14–5–31–1; Stirling 11.3–3–26–3; Pierce 10–5–8–2; O'Sullivan 4–2–3–0. *Second Innings*—Robertson 18–2–57–1; Gill 16–6–28–0; Stirling 19–7–28–1; Pierce 3–0–11–0; O'Sullivan 27–9–56–2; Toynbee 10–3–25–0; Hayward 3–1–4–0.

Central Districts

R. A. Pierce lbw b Pigott	20	†I. D. S. Smith c McSweeney b G. N. Cederwall	0
R. T. Hart lbw b G. N. Cederwall	52	S. J. Gill b B. W. Cederwall	51
P. S. Briasco c G. N. Cederwall b Gray	17	G. K. Robertson b Pigott	2
R. Hayward c McSweeney b G. N. Cederwall	10	D. R. O'Sullivan not out	0
*J. R. Wiltshire b G. N. Cederwall	33	B 5, l-b 5, w 3, n-b 12	25
M. H. Toynbee c Holland b Pigott	2		
D. A. Stirling c Vance b B. W. Cederwall	47	1/29 2/86 3/98 4/118	259
		5/120 6/164 7/172 8/255 9/259	

Bowling: *First Innings*—Pigott 24.2–5–64–3; G. N. Cederwall 20–5–47–4; Maguiness 14–6–20–0; Gray 20–9–50–1; B. W. Cederwall 12–4–32–2; Holland 3–0–21–0.

Umpires: S. C. Cowman and D. A. Kinsella.

ERRATA IN WISDEN, 1983

Page 109	Majid Khan's 100 in 74 balls was omitted from the list of fastest Test centuries.
Pages 145 and 271	S. Amarnath had played in ten Tests, including three v New Zealand in 1975.
Page 148	R. J. Shastri had played in twelve Tests, including three v New Zealand in 1980.
Page 152	R. W. Marsh (83) had made the most appearances for Australia.
Page 156	G. M. Turner's 311 not out was made in 1982.
Page 175	Highest Batting Averages in an English Season – add: Mudassar Nazar, 1982, 16 innings, 6 not out, 825 runs, highest innings 211*, 4 hundreds, average 82.50.
Page 206	D. L. Underwood's entry should read: 86 Tests, 21,862 balls, 7,674 runs, 287 wickets, average 25.83, 5 w/i 17, 10 w/m 6.
Page 208	Iqbal Qasim's entry should read: 32 Tests, 8,269 balls, 3,073 runs, 104 wickets, average 29.54, 5 w/i 4, 10 w/m 2.
Page 211	Most Dismissals in a Career – add: R. W. Taylor (England), 42 Tests, 131 ct, 7 st, total 138.
Page 212	Most Catches in a Test Career – add: G. S. Chappell (Australia), 106 in 76 matches.
Page 214	Youngest Test Players – add: A. Ranatunga, 18 years 78 days, Sri Lanka v England at Colombo, 1981-82.
Page 281	Hundred Before Lunch – add: Mansoor Akhtar, Pakistanis v Somerset at Taunton (1st day).
Page 283	Eight or More Dismissals in a Match by a Wicket-keeper – add: Nine, C. Maynard, 7 ct, 2 st.
Page 297	Six wickets in an Innings – add: S. C. Corlett, 7-82, Ireland v Scotland, Edinburgh.
Page 659	G. M. Turner's 239 not out was not a career best. His highest score at that point was 259.
Page 849	P. G. C. Harvey's maiden century was scored at Chesham, not Ipswich.
Page 974	In their second innings England scored 171 for three.
Page 1011	In Australia's innings B. P. Bracewell bowled 10.4 overs (not 11), G. K. Robertson bowled 25.2 (not 26) and E. J. Gray bowled 23 (not 22). The umpires were S. C. Cowman (not F. R. Goodall) and I. C. Higginson.

WISDEN, 1979

Page 113	F. E. Woolley's 172 for Kent against Essex in 1934 was scored at Brentwood, not Gravesend.

CRICKET IN INDIA, 1982-83

By P. N. SUNDARESAN

The 1982-83 season in India was confined to domestic engagements, except for a brief visit by Sri Lanka in September to play their first official Test against India. However, India's tour to Pakistan, at the start of the season, and to West Indies towards its close, meant that some of the teams, particularly Bombay and Delhi, were deprived of the services of top players.

Karnataka won the final of the Ranji Trophy by virtue of their first-innings lead against Bombay. This was Karnataka's third triumph in ten years. The final was almost a replica of the epic contest between Karnataka and Delhi in the previous season. Interest in the match did not cease as soon as Karnataka took their first-innings lead late on the afternoon of the fourth and penultimate day. A blistering innings of 121 not out, off 96 balls, by Sandeep Patil enabled Ashok Mankad to declare Bombay's second innings at lunch on the final day, and set Karnataka a target of 197 runs for outright victory. Initially Karnataka accepted the challenge and were only 46 runs away from victory at the start of the last twenty overs. But, after the fall of Gundappa Viswanath's wicket at 161 for five, Brijesh Patel, the captain, who was at the crease, switched to total defence. While Patel's acceptance of a victory based on first-innings lead was understandable, his tactics came in for sharp criticism.

Karnataka and Tamil Nadu from the South Zone, Orissa and Bengal from the East Zone, Baroda and Bombay from the West Zone, Uttar Pradesh and Rajasthan from the Central Zone and Haryana and Delhi from the North Zone qualified for the knockout rounds. For Orissa, who had been working hard in recent years under the captaincy of Paramjit Singh, this was their first entry into the knockout as well as their first triumph in the East Zone league, in which they headed the table.

Another noteworthy, if not historic, event was the first outright victory in more than two decades by Jammu and Kashmir, achieved in the North Zone league. They beat Services by four wickets, owing largely to the bowling of their captain Mehboob Iqbal, a seam bowler, and left-arm spinner Ashinder Kaul. Kaul had an excellent season, taking seven for 54 against Delhi and five for 74 against Punjab. Iqbal became the first Jammu and Kashmir bowler to take 100 wickets in the Ranji Trophy.

Ashok Malhotra of Haryana and Anshuman Gaekwad of Baroda gathered 859 runs each in first-class matches in the season. But the outstanding batsman was Mohinder Amarnath. Though he did not play in the Ranji Trophy matches, he touched peak form in the Irani and Duleep Trophy matches, scoring 537 runs and topping the first-class averages with 107.40. The national selectors could not deny him a place in the Indian team to Pakistan. Both there, and later in West Indies, he was India's leading batsman.

Karnataka's left-arm spinner Raghuram Bhat headed the season's wicket-takers with 43, while the performances of leg-spinner Sanjay Hazare of Baroda, and Chetan Sharma, medium-paced seamer of Haryana, were also striking. Each of them took 27 wickets in his first first-class season. Two other striking bowling efforts were by Roger Binny of Karnataka and T. A. Sekhar of Tamil Nadu, both medium-paced. Binny took eight wickets for 22 runs against Haryana in the semi-final of the Ranji Trophy, while Sekhar claimed nine wickets in Kerala's second innings in the South Zone league. In this match, Tamil Nadu's wicket-keeper, A. Bharat Reddy, took eight catches, six of them in Kerala's second innings.

For the first time in its history, the Duleep Trophy zonal championship was held at one centre, Bombay. The Wankhede Stadium, currently the venue for Tests there, and the Brabourne Stadium, formerly scene of many famous Tests, were used to stage the matches. North Zone won the Trophy.

The Irani Trophy match was held at Delhi after the conclusion of the Duleep Trophy matches and was won by the Rest of India, who defeated Delhi, the Ranji Trophy champions. Rest of India were able to beat a target of 421 runs in four hours and twenty overs, thanks to a dazzling 110 by Krishnamachari Srikkanth. He batted 90 balls and 99 minutes and hit fourteen 4s and one 6.

FIRST-CLASS AVERAGES, 1982-83

BATTING

(Qualification: 500 runs)

	I	NO	R	HI	100s	Avge
M. Amarnath (*Delhi*)	6	1	537	207	2	107.40
A. Malhotra (*Haryana*)	9	1	859	228	4	107.37
A. D. Gaekwad (*Baroda*)	10	1	859	225	4	95.44
A. V. Mankad (*Bombay*)	10	3	526	150*	2	75.14
S. S. Hattangadi (*Bombay*)	11	2	554	141	1	61.55
K. B. J. Azad (*Delhi*)	14	3	668	186	2	60.72
R. M. H. Binny (*Karnataka*)	15	3	635	115	1	52.91
R. C. Shukla (*Delhi*)	13	1	506	163*	1	42.16

* *Signifies not out.*

BOWLING

(Qualification: 25 wickets)

	O	M	R	W	Avge
D. V. Pardeshi (*Baroda*)	201.2	117	403	31	13.00
S. Talwar (*Haryana*)	247.5	55	535	37	14.45
B. Vijayakrishna (*Karnataka*)	216.3	84	530	30	17.66
R. V. Kulkarni (*Bombay*)	193.4	43	540	30	18.00
A. Raghuram Bhat (*Karnataka*)	338.5	107	798	43	18.55
S. S. Hazare (*Baroda*)	165.1	32	501	27	18.55
R. M. H. Binny (*Karnataka*)	185.5	40	518	25	20.72
R. Thakkar (*Bombay*)	327.1	100	724	34	21.29
R. Goel (*Haryana*)	314.4	110	558	26	21.46
R. S. Hans (*Uttar Pradesh*)	247.5	64	577	26	22.19
Chetan Sharma (*Haryana*)	158.1	27	618	27	22.88
Maninder Singh (*Delhi*)	215.2	58	612	26	23.53
K. B. J. Azad (*Delhi*)	300.4	55	731	30	24.36
T. A. Sekhar (*Tamil Nadu*)	199	28	667	27	24.70
R. C. Shukla (*Delhi*)	300.5	59	774	30	25.80

Note: Matches taken into account are Ranji Trophy, Irani Trophy, Duleep Trophy matches and the Test match against Sri Lanka.

RANJI TROPHY, 1982-83

*In the following scores, (M) indicates that a match was played on coir matting, (T) that it was played on turf, and * by the name of the team indicates that they won the toss.*

Central Zone

At Nagpur (T), November 20, 21, 22. Uttar Pradesh won by nine wickets. Vidarbha* 296 (R. Pankule 72, J. Bhatt 48, V. Gawate 40; R. S. Hans five for 66, V. Dutt four for 68) and 148 (J. Rathod 43; A. Mathur three for 40, R. S. Hans three for 53); Uttar Pradesh 384 (A. Bambi 109 not out, V. Chopra 91; R. Pankule three for 23, H. Wasu three for 86) and 61 for one. *Uttar Pradesh 8 pts.*

At Bhopal (M), November 27, 28, 29. Madhya Pradesh won by 202 runs. Madhya Pradesh* 304 (S. Ansari 56, Gulrez Ali 50, A. Gupta 46 not out; V. Gawate three for 95) and 256 for six dec. (Sanjeeva Rao 105, S. Joshi 50, S. Jagdale 47; R. Pankule five for 61); Vidarbha 160 (J. Rathod 73; Gopal Rao three for 42, A. Patel three for 46) and 198 (S. Phadkar 62, R. Pankule 45; A. Patel five for 64). *Madhya Pradesh 8 pts.*

At Gorakhpur (T), December 3, 4, 5. Railways won by five wickets. Vidarbha 170 (Aslam Ali four for 22, A. Mathur four for 37) and 318 (V. Telang 155, S. Phadkar 40; P. Banerjee four for 85); Railways* 291 (A. Burrows 91, P. Vedraj 51; H. Wasu three for 56, R. Pankule three for 63) and 200 for five (R. Vats 65, P. A. Khan 41). *Railways 9 pts including 1 bonus point.*

At Sagar (M), December 4, 5, 6. Drawn. Madhya Pradesh* 256 (Sanjeeva Rao 139 not out; Vivek Bhan Singh three for 31, P. Sunderam three for 95) and 271 for six (M. Hassan 79 not out, S. Deshmukh 60, Sanjeeva Rao 40; Vivek Bhan Singh four for 43); Rajasthan 409 for nine dec. (K. R. Gattani 100, P. Sharma 55, Suresh Shastri 48; Gulrez Ali four for 89). *Rajasthan 5 pts, Madhya Pradesh 3 pts.*

At Hinganghat (M), December 9, 10, 11. Rajasthan won by five wickets. Vidarbha* 153 (K. R. Gattani four for 38, P. Sharma three for 45) and 212 (V. Telang 64, S. Hedaoo 52 not out; Vivek Bhan Singh eight for 64); Rajasthan 221 (Padam Shastri 120; S. Takle five for 46, R. Pankule three for 24) and 150 for five (D. Mahan 47 not out, Padam Shastri 42 not out). *Rajasthan 8 pts.*

At Delhi (T), December 9, 10, 11. Drawn. Railways 196 (A. Burrows 62; Gulrez Ali four for 54, N. Bagtheria three for 50) and 342 for two dec. (N. Churi 178 not out, R. Vats 88, A. Burrows 68); Madhya Pradesh* 135 for nine (Hyder Ali three for 27, Aslam Ali three for 32) and 274 for nine (R. Talwar 74, Gopal Rao 54 not out, M. Hassan 48; Hyder Ali four for 49, A. Mathur three for 38). *Railways 5 pts, Madhya Pradesh 3 pts.*

At Agra (T), December 14, 15, 16. Uttar Pradesh won by nine wickets. Madhya Pradesh* 195 (S. Deshmukh five for 54) and 257 (M. Hassan 85, A. Gupta 58; S. Mehrotra four for 62, G. Sharma three for 41); Uttar Pradesh 385 for seven dec. (Shekar Anand 120 not out, G. Sharma 76, A. Mathur 40) and 68 for one. *Uttar Pradesh 8 pts.*

At Jaipur (T), December 14, 15, 16. Drawn. Rajasthan* 377 (P. Sharma 115, D Mahan 55, S. Joshi 53, Padam Shastri 51, Suresh Shastri 50); Railways 139 (N. Churi 41; Suresh Shastri three for 28) and 168 for three (R. Vats 85). *Rajasthan 5 pts, Railways 3 pts.*

At Allahabad (T), December 19, 20, 21. Drawn. Uttar Pradesh 504 for seven dec. (A. Mathur 201 not out, Shekar Anand 114, S. S. Khandkar 46; Aslam Ali four for 105); Railways* 318 (M. I. Ansari 82, U. Dastane 62, Aslam Ali 55; V. Dutt four for 82, R. S. Hans three for 70) and 232 for seven (U. Dastane 78 not out, Hyder Ali 52 not out; A. Mathur three for 41). *Uttar Pradesh 6 pts including 1 bonus point, Railways 3 pts.*

At Udaipur (M), December 25, 26, 27. Drawn. Uttar Pradesh 158 (Charanjit Singh 44; K. R. Gattani four for 36) and 293 for five (A. Bambi 128, G. Sharma 57 not out, V. Chopra 46); Rajasthan* 246 (D. Mahan 53, Vivek Bhan Singh 48; G. Sharma three for 53). *Rajasthan 5 pts, Uttar Pradesh 3 pts.*

Uttar Pradesh 25 pts, Rajasthan 23 pts, Railways 20 pts, Madhya Pradesh 14 pts, Vidarbha 0 pts. Uttar Pradesh and Rajasthan qualified for the knockout stage.

East Zone

At Dibrugarh (T), December 4, 5, 6. Drawn. Assam* 196 (M. Kakoti 57; M. R. Bhalla four for 42, R. Venkatram four for 71) and 108 for four (S. Dutta 47); Bihar 260 for two dec. (S. Das 129, H. Gidwani 89 not out). *Bihar 6 pts including 1 bonus point, Assam 3 pts.*

At Dibrugarh (T), December 10, 11, 12. Orissa won by ten wickets. Assam* 100 (H. Praharaj three for 8, S. Sahu three for 16, Paramjit Singh three for 21) and 154 (R. Haque 47; H. Praharaj six for 29, A. Bharadwaj three for 30); Orissa 184 (C. Biswal 51; U. Bhattacharya three for 42) and 71 for no wkt (K. Dubey 40 not out). *Orissa 8 pts.*

At Krishnanagar (T), December 11, 12, 13. Drawn. Bihar* 138 (M. Ghosh four for 33, S. Bhattacharjee three for 59) and 193 for eight (S. Roy 83 not out; M. Ghosh six for 64); Bengal 323 for six dec. (P. Roy 109, Raja Venkat 60, P. Chail 58 not out, Palash Nandy 44). *Bengal 5 pts, Bihar 3 pts.*

At Patna (T), December 17, 18, 19. Drawn. Bihar 334 (D. Augustus 110, S. S. Karim 70, H. Gidwani 49; S. Sahu six for 121); Orissa* 262 for seven (A. Jayaprakash 73 not out, M. Mahalik 58, K. Dubey 54; M. R. Bhalla three for 81). *Bihar 2 pts, Orissa 2 pts.*

At Dibrugarh (T), December 17, 18, 19. Drawn. Bengal 248 for two dec. (Palash Nandy 140, P. Roy 75); Assam* 122 (P. Kalita 46; A. Bhattacharya four for 44) and 28 for five (A. Bhattacharya three for six). *Bengal 6 pts including 1 bonus point, Assam 3 pts.*

At Asansol (T), December 23, 24, 25. Drawn. Orissa 271 (B. K. R. Patnaik 96, H. Praharaj 74; A. Bhattacharya five for 75, S. Bhattacharya three for 37) and 205 (A. Bharadwaj 48; A. Bhattacharya four for 62, M. Ghosh three for 52); Bengal* 231 (Raja Venkat 44, A. Bhattacharya 42; Paramjit Singh four for 59, A. Jayaprakash three for 33, S. Sahu three for 75) and 26 for no wkt. *Orissa 5 pts, Bengal 3 pts.*

Orissa 15 pts, Bengal 14 pts, Bihar 11 pts, Assam 6 pts. Orissa and Bengal qualified for the knockout stage.

North Zone

At Srinagar (T), October 14, 15, 16. Haryana won by nine wickets. Jammu and Kashmir 129 (S. Talwar five for 21, R. Goel four for 43) and 135 (M. Akthar Ajaj 49; S. Talwar five for 51, R. Goel three for 32); Haryana* 246 (Deepak Sharma 102, R. Chadda 50; M. Iqbal four for 76, Ashinder Kaul four for 100) and 19 for one. *Haryana 8 pts.*

At Srinagar (T), October 20, 21, 22. Punjab won by an innings and 36 runs. Punjab 273 (R. Handa 117, Y. Dutta 40; Ashinder Kaul five for 74, F. Buchh four for 84); Jammu and Kashmir* 97 (D. Chopra seven for 32) and 140 (Akthar Ajaj 59; D. Chopra seven for 52). *Punjab 8 pts.*

At Chandigarh (T), December 5, 6, 7. Drawn. Haryana* 301 (A. Malhotra 155; M. Prabhakar five for 88, S. Valson four for 62) and 64 for no wkt (Deepak Sharma 41 not out); Delhi 366 (R. C. Shukla 163 not out, K. B. J. Azad 44; R. Goel four for 71, Chetan Sharma three for 155). *Delhi 5 pts, Haryana 3 pts.*

At Delhi (T), December 5, 6, 7. Drawn. Punjab* 386 (R. Handa 72, Y. Dutta 66, R. S. Ghai 44; V. Chavan three for 79, A. Jha three for 86) and 128 for five (Y. Dutta 55; A. Jha three for 46); Services 291 (B. Ghosh 134, R. Das 43; D. Chopra three for 63, Umesh Kumar three for 76). *Punjab 5 pts, Services 3 pts.*

At Delhi (T), December 9, 10, 11. Drawn. Delhi* 180 (R. S. Ghai four for 50, Yograj three for 30) and 209 for two (R. Lamba 107 not out, C. P. S. Chauhan 76); Punjab 313 (Y. Dutta 104, Yograj 46; R. C. Shukla five for 75, S. Valson three for 75). *Punjab 5 pts, Delhi 3 pts.*

At Delhi (T), December 10, 11, 12. Haryana won by an innings and 27 runs. Haryana* 481 for five dec. (A. Malhotra 228, Aman Kumar 100 not out, S. Ahmed 46 not out; V. Chavan three for 111); Services 160 (Sudhakar Rao 43; S. Talwar three for 21, Chetan Sharma three for 70) and 294 (Sudhakar Rao 88, R. Das 59, A. Jha 53, A. K. Seth 41; Chetan Sharma five for 59, R. Goel three for 108). *Haryana 9 pts including 1 bonus point.*

At Delhi (T), December 15, 16, 17. Delhi won by nine wickets. Services* 164 (A. K. Seth 57; K. B. J. Azad five for 47) and 221 (P. Sur 110; K. B. J. Azad four for 68); Delhi 297 (Gusharan Singh 60, R. C. Shukla 53, Tilakraj 47, C. P. S. Chauhan 41; B. Ghosh three for 29, A. Jha three for 92, V. Chavan three for 116) and 89 for one. *Delhi 8 pts.*

At Chandigarh (T), December 18, 19, 20. Drawn. Punjab* 208 (Balkar Singh 74, Y. Dutta 43, R. S. Ghai 41; Chetan Sharma three for 39) and 250 for eight dec. (K. P. Amarjeet 120 not out, D. Chopra 45; S. Talwar five for 85, Chetan Sharma three for 62); Haryana 313 (R. Jolly 88 not out, Aman Kumar 65, A. Malhotra 60; Satish Kumar four for 35, Yograj four for 97). *Haryana 5 pts, Punjab 3 pts.*

At Jammu (T), December 19, 20, 21. Delhi won by seven wickets. Jammu and Kashmir 132 (Ashok Singh 48; A. Khurana four for 33, K. B. J. Azad four for 37) and 80 (K. B. J. Azad three for 17, A. Khurana three for 18); Delhi* 150 (Ashinder Kaul seven for 54, M. Iqbal three for 49) and 67 for three. *Delhi 8 pts.*

At Udhampur (T), December 24, 25, 26. Jammu and Kashmir won by four wickets. Services 81 (M. Iqbal six for 35, Z. Butt three for 29) and 320 (Chander Vijay 98, R. Das 51; Ashinder Kaul five for 110); Jammu and Kashmir* 326 (Vinod Sharma 92, P. Akhtar 55, F. Mirza 48; A. Jha five for 115, P. Sumnat four for 41) and 73 for six (A. K. Seth three for 19). *Jammu and Kashmir 9 pts including 1 bonus point.*

Haryana 25 pts, Delhi 24 pts, Punjab 21 pts, Jammu and Kashmir 9 pts, Services 3 pts. Haryana and Delhi qualified for the knockout stage.

South Zone

At Secunderabad (T), December 4, 5, 6. Drawn. Tamil Nadu* 373 (P. S. Moses 120, R. Madhavan 96, A. Bharat Reddy 53; N. S. Yadav six for 111) and 50 for three; Hyderabad 469 (T. Vijay Paul 156 not out, K. A. Qayyum 135, V. Mohanraj 44). *Hyderabad 5 pts, Tamil Nadu 3 pts.*

At Bangalore (T), December 4, 5, 6. Karnataka won by 117 runs. Karnataka 377 for eight dec. (M. R. Srinivasaprasad 106, R. Sudhakar Rao 56, J. Abhiram 52 not out, B. Vijayakrishna 51, B. P. Patel 42; D. Meher Baba three for 61); and 155 for five dec. (B. P. Patel 47; D. Meher Baba three for 61); Andhra* 274 (K. B. Ramamurthy 106, M. N. Ravikumar 45; B. Vijayakrishna seven for 85) and 141 (B. Vijayakrishna five for 28, A. Raghuram Bhat four for 47). *Karnataka 9 pts including 1 bonus point.*

At Kothagudem (M), December 10, 11, 12. Hyderabad won by an innings and 14 runs. Hyderabad 347 for four dec. (V. Mohanraj 122, T. Vijay Paul 67 not out, M. V. Narasimha Rao 57, Shahid Akbar 49); Kerala* 112 (C. Sridhar five for 41, A. B. Wahab three for 41) and 221 (V. Hariharan 56; N. S. Yadav six for 49). *Hyderabad 9 pts including 1 bonus point.*

At Venkatagiri (M), December 14, 15, 16. Andhra won by an innings and 127 runs. Andhra* 362 (G. A. Pratapkumar 68, K. V. S. D. Kamaraju 59, V. Chamundeswarnath 41, M. N. Ravikumar 40; P. T. Godwin four for 96); Kerala 133 (K. Chandasekhar Rao three for 15, K. B. Ramamurthy three for 26, V. S. Prasad three for 40) and 102 (K. Chandrasekhar Rao six for 28). *Andhra 8 pts.*

At Madras (T), December 18, 19, 20. Tamil Nadu won by an innings and 98 runs. Tamil Nadu 398 for nine dec. (V. Sivaramakrishnan 104, P. Vijayakumar 101 not out, A. Jabbar 66); Andhra* 144 (S. Venkataraghavan seven for 44) and 156 (D. Meher Baba 45; R. Madhavan five for 32). *Tamil Nadu 9 pts including 1 bonus point.*

At Bangalore (T), December 18, 19, 20. Drawn. Karnataka* 217 (J. Abhiram 70; N. S. Yadav four for 69, Arshad Ayub three for 14) and 203 for three dec. (R. M. H. Binny 111 not out, M. R. Srinivasaprasad 41); Hyderabad 156 (M. V. Narasimha Rao 44; A. Raghuram Bhat six for 55) and 119 for six (A. Raghuram Bhat three for 61). *Karnataka 5 pts, Hyderabad 3 pts.*

At Madras (T), December 24, 25, 26. Drawn. Karnataka* 186 (S. Viswanath 55; S. Vasudevan three for 33, T. A. Sekhar three for 55, S. Venkataraghavan three for 59) and 231 for two (R. M. H. Binny 69, S. Viswanath 67 not out, M. R. Srinivasaprasad 59); Tamil Nadu 376 for nine dec. (C. S. Sureshkumar 146, P. Vijayakumar 57, V. Sivaramakrishnan 52; R. Sudhakar Rao three for 45). *Tamil Nadu 5 pts, Karnataka 3 pts.*

At Palghat (M), January 8, 9, 10. Tamil Nadu won by ten wickets. Kerala 211 (S. Ramesh 53, S. Rajesh 40; B. Arun four for 43, T. A. Sekhar three for 41) and 136 (T. A. Sekhar nine for 54); Tamil Nadu* 343 for four dec. (C. S. Sureshkumar 162, A. Jabbar 83, V. Sivaramakrishnan 61; T. S. Mahadevan four for 103) and four for no wkt. *Tamil Nadu 9 pts including 1 bonus point.*

At Calicut (M), January 21, 22, 23. Karnataka won by ten wickets. Kerala 126 (R. M. H. Binny four for 29, A. Raghuram Bhat three for 39) and 135 (R. M. H. Binny five for 52, A. Raghuram Bhat three for 16); Karnataka* 213 for six dec. (R. M. H. Binny 62, S. Viswanath 46 not out, R. Sudhakar Rao 41; S. Ramesh four for 58) and 41 for no wkt. *Karnataka 9 pts including 1 bonus point.*

At Guntur (M), January 22, 23, 24. Hyderabad won by eight wickets. Andhra 164 (V. Janakiram 41 not out, J. K. Ghiya 41; M. V. Narasimha Rao five for 46, C. Sridhar three for 27) and 213 for nine dec. (M. V. Ravikumar 87, P. Prasannakumar 81; M. V. Narasimha Rao five for 71); Hyderabad* 321 for seven dec. (T. Vijay Paul 86, K. A. Qayyum 58, Azhar-ud-Din 55, M. V. Narasimha Rao 51; J. K. Ghiya three for 48) and 57 for two. *Hyderabad 9 pts including 1 bonus point.*

Karnataka 26 pts, Tamil Nadu 26 pts, Hyderabad 26 pts, Andhra 8 pts, Kerala 0 pts. Karnataka and Tamil Nadu qualified for the knockout stage because of their better quotient, Karnataka's being 1.81, Tamil Nadu's 1.75 and Hyderabad's 1.29.

West Zone

At Kolhapur (T), November 20, 21, 22. Drawn. Bombay 370 (K. D. Mokashi 80, S. S. Hattangadi 69, C. S. Pandit 44, R. Thakkar 44; S. Gudge three for 99, R. Daniel three for 122) and 145 for three dec. (G. A. Parkar 51 not out); Maharashtra* 279 (M. D. Gunjal 77; R. Thakkar eight for 102) and 112 for four (S. Nimbalkar 69). *Bombay 5 pts, Maharashtra 3 pts.*

At Baroda (T), November 20, 21, 22. Baroda won by an innings and 44 runs. Gujarat 184 (P. Desai 58, A. Shroff 47; S. S. Hazare five for 47) and 162 (J. Bakrania 71; S. S. Hazare six for 46); Baroda* 390 for six dec. (A. D. Gaekwad 225, R. V. Hazare 53). *Baroda 9 pts including 1 bonus point.*

At Surat (M), November 28, 29, 30. Saurashtra won by three wickets. Gujarat 146 (K. Brahmbhatt 59; S. Keshwala five for 48) and 259 (J. Bakrania 100, B. Mistry 64, P. Desai 46; A. Patel four for 26); Saurashtra* 225 (S. Keshwala 62, A. Patel 59; J. Pandya three for 36, R. Desai three for 56) and 184 for seven (L. Chauhan 51, S. Keshwala 40; J. Pandya five for 47). *Saurashtra 9 pts including 1 bonus point.*

At Baroda (T), November 27, 28, 29. Baroda won by nine wickets. Maharashtra* 180 (M. D. Gunjal 59, K. Fakih 42; D. V. Pardeshi three for 30, V. Patel three for 53) and 187 (R. B. Bhalekar 65 not out, R. Poonawala 52; S. S. Hazare four for 49); Baroda 253 (A. D. Gaekwad 64, K. More 43; R. Daniel four for 38, S. Gudge three for 80) and 115 for one (A. D. Gaekwad 81). *Baroda 8 pts.*

At Thane (T), December 4, 5, 6. Drawn. Bombay* 243 (G. A. Parkar 52; S. S. Hazare five for 29) and 101 for no wkt (L. S. Rajput 64 not out); Baroda 337 for seven dec. (A. D. Gaekwad 144, R. V. Hazare 77, R. V. Deshmukh 51; K. D. Mokashi three for 69). *Baroda 5 pts, Bombay 3 pts.*

At Surendranagar (M), December 4, 5, 6. Maharashtra won by five wickets. Saurashtra 262 (K. Chauhan 79, K. D. Ghavri 58; R. Daniel six for 60) and 158 (R. Daniel three for 52); Maharashtra* 223 (R. Poonawala 40; D. D. Parsana four for 55, N. Parsana three for 44) and 198 for five (R. B. Bhalekar 83 not out). *Maharashtra 8 pts.*

At Bombay (T), December 11, 12, 13. Bombay won by an innings and 66 runs. Gujarat 101 (R. Thakkar six for 25) and 196 (P. Desai 55, J. Bakrania 51; S. Shetty four for 50); Bombay* 363 for two dec. (R. V. Mankad 138 not out, A. V. Mankad 121 not out, L. S. Rajput 54). *Bombay 9 pts including 1 bonus point.*

At Baroda (T), December 11, 12, 13. Drawn. Saurashtra* 233 (K. Chauhan 45, K. D. Ghavri 40; D. V. Pardeshi four for 42, S. S. Hazare three for 67) and 118 for two (S. Keshwala 63 not out); Baroda 401 (A. D. Gaekwad 135, A. Bhansali 100 not out, S. Parikh 52, K. More 44; H. Joshi four for 81, A. Patel three for 90). *Baroda 5 pts, Saurashtra 3 pts.*

At Jamnagar (M), December 18, 19, 20. Drawn. Bombay 388 for seven dec. (A. V. Mankad 74, R. V. Mankad 72, S. V. Nayak 65, S. S. Hattangadi 52; D. D. Parsana four for 58) and 107 for no wkt (S. S. Hattangadi 59 not out, L. S. Rajput 45 not out); Saurashtra* 353 (H. Joshi 67, B. Jadeja 56, N. Jadeja 52, A. Pandya 43; R. V. Kulkarni five for 99). *Bombay 5 pts, Saurashtra 3 pts.*

At Nasik (M), December 18, 19, 20. Drawn. Gujarat 337 (K. Brahmbhatt 100, B. Mistry 70, J. Saigal 42; G. DeMonte three for 76, R. Daniel three for 83) and 171 for four (J. Desai 67); Maharashtra* 462 for six dec. (R. B. Bhalekar 126, P. Pradhan 110, M. D. Gunjal 77, M. Dixit 50, K. Fakih 47 not out). *Maharashtra 5 pts, Gujarat 3 pts.*

Baroda 27 pts, Bombay 22 pts, Maharashtra 16 pts, Saurashtra 15 pts, Gujarat 3 pts. Baroda and Bombay qualified for the knockout stage.

KNOCKOUT STAGES

TAMIL NADU v UTTAR PRADESH

At Madras (T), January 29, 30, 31, February 1. Tamil Nadu won by four wickets. Toss won by Uttar Pradesh.

Uttar Pradesh

S. Chaturvedi c Vijayakumar b Venkataraghavan	34	– c Jabbar b Venkataraghavan 11
S. S. Khandkar c Bharat Reddy b Arun 191		– lbw b Venkataraghavan............ 76
†V. Chopra c Prasad b Venkataraghavan	2	– c Arun b Prasad 39
Yusuf Ali Khan c and b Vasudevan................	42	– run out 16
A. Bambi lbw b Venkataraghavan	5	– c Jabbar b Prasad 0
S. Anand c Sivaramakrishnan b Vasudevan	14	– c Sivaramakrishnan b Venkataraghavan. 13
*A. G. Mathur c Jabbar b Vasudevan	0	– not out 56
G. Sharma c and b Vasudevan	7	– b Prasad 28
S. Mehrotra c Madhavan b Venkataraghavan	17	– b Venkataraghavan 3
R. S. Hans not out	15	– run out 6
V. Dutt c Sureshkumar b Venkataraghavan	11	– c Arun b Venkataraghavan 4
B 5, l-b 5, w 3	13	B 12, l-b 3, n-b 2 17

1/63 2/70 3/196 4/225   351   1/37 2/131 3/137 4/137   269
5/257 6/257 7/271 8/310 9/331   5/156 6/162 7/217 8/220 9/241

Bowling: *First Innings*—Arun 19–2–73–1; Sivaramakrishnan 7–1–17–0; Venkataraghavan 48.2–9–134–5; Vasudevan 41–7–93–4; Prasad 3–0–16–0; Jabbar 1–0–5–0. *Second Innings*—Arun 4–0–10–0; Sivaramakrishnan 2–0–16–0; Venkataraghavan 35.4–6–110–5; Vasudevan 20–5–62–0; Jabbar 2–0–6–0; Prasad 14–1–48–3.

Tamil Nadu

V. Sivaramakrishnan c and b Sharma	54	– c Mathur b Hans	18
C. S. Sureshkumar c Chopra b Mathur	15	– b Hans	21
S. Srinivasan not out	148	– c Khandkar b Hans	27
A. Jabbar lbw b Hans	16	– not out	40
N. P. Madhavan b Hans	125	– c sub b Sharma	13
P. Vijayakumar c Mathur b Hans	16	– st Chaturvedi b Hans	15
V. Prasad c Chopra b Hans	0		
S. Vasudevan c and b Mehrotra	28		
†A. Bharat Reddy st Chopra b Hans	23	– st Chaturvedi b Mathur	27
*S. Venkataraghavan c sub b Hans	12	– not out	1
B. Arun st Chopra b Mehrotra	0		
B 4, l-b 1, w 1, n-b 6	12	B 6, l-b 4	10

1/60 2/72 3/115 4/327   449   1/23 2/64 3/81 4/116   (6 wkts) 172
5/353 6/353 7/403 8/435 9/448   5/131 6/170

Bowling: *First Innings*—Dutt 8–0–59–0; Mathur 12–1–48–1; Sharma 51–8–124–1; Hans 56–18–125–6; Mehrotra 27.3–2–81–2. *Second Innings*—Dutt 3–1–2–0; Mathur 4–2–3–1; Sharma 23–3–76–1; Hans 25–7–54–4; Mehrotra 4–0–26–0; Khandkar 0.1–0–1–0.

Umpires: M. V. Gothaskar and R. R. Kadam.

BARODA v RAJASTHAN

At Baroda (T), January 29, 30, 31, February 1. Drawn. Baroda declared winners by virtue of their first-innings lead. Toss won by Baroda.

Rajasthan

K. Mathur b Patel	3	– b Pardeshi	14
Vivek Bhan Singh c Pardeshi b Satham	36	– not out	104
Padam Shastri c More b Wadkar	8	– c and b Pardeshi	3
S. Mudkavi c Satham b S. S. Hazare	20	– c More b R. V. Hazare	52
*P. Sharma c Deshmukh b Pardeshi	44		
D. Mahan lbw b Pardeshi	18	– c Deshumukh b R. V. Hazare	9
K. R. Gattani lbw b Patel	41	– not out	22
Suresh Shastri run out	37	– c More b R. V. Hazare	7
S. Joshi b Pardeshi	36	– c Satham b R. V. Hazare	4
†S. Kaushik not out	12		
P. Sunderam b Pardeshi	3		
B 4, l-b 11, n-b 8	23	B 3, l-b 4, w 1, n-b 7	15

1/7 2/21 3/72 4/87   281   1/28 2/34 3/138 4/160   (6 wkts) 230
5/141 6/148 7/219 8/236 9/273   5/180 6/186

Bowling: *First Innings*—Wadkar 7–1–17–1; Patel 17–1–62–2; Satham 25–4–63–1; Pardeshi 29.3–13–42–4; S. S. Hazare 20–3–68–1; Gaekwad 1–0–6–0. *Second Innings*—Wadkar 12–3–40–0; Patel 4–1–11–0; Pardeshi 29–9–52–2; S. S. Hazare 14–3–32–0; R. V. Hazare 25–3–78–4; Deshmukh 1–0–2–0.

Baroda

R. Y. Deshmukh c Kaushik		V. S. Wadkar c Kaushik	
b Sunderam.	46	b Vivek Bhan Singh.	7
S. Parikh lbw b Sunderam	18	S. S. Hazare c Kaushik	
*A. D. Gaekwad b Padam Shastri	82	b Vivek Bhan Singh.	22
R. V. Hazare c Kaushik		D. V. Pardeshi b Vivek Bhan Singh	0
b Padam Shastri.	49	V. Patel b Vivek Bhan Singh	0
A. Bhansali lbw b Vivek Bhan Singh	116	B 29, l-b 7, w 2, n-b 2,	40
N. Y. Satham lbw b Vivek			
Bhan Singh	131	1/70 2/83 3/203 4/226	558
†K. More not out	47	5/475 6/484 7/496 8/542 9/542	

Bowling: Sunderam 48–7–165–2; Joshi 9–1–29–0; Suresh Shastri 39–9–96–0; Sharma 7–2–11–0; Gattani 12–2–23–0; Vivek Bhan Singh 21.5–2–45–6; Mudkavi 21–3–53–0; Padam Shastri 38–10–96–2.

Umpires: B. R. Keshavamurthy and S. Banerjee.

QUARTER-FINALS

DELHI v TAMIL NADU

At Delhi (T), February 11, 12, 13, 14. Drawn. Delhi declared winners by virtue of their first-innings lead. Toss won by Delhi.

Tamil Nadu

K. Srikkanth c Khanna b Susilkumar	58	– c Khanna b Prabhakar	14
V. Sivaramakrishnan b Valson	21	– c sub b Azad	9
C. S. Sureshkumar b Valson	8	– c and b Azad	110
S. Srinivasan b Prabhakar	13	– c Rajinder b Shukla	67
A. Jabbar not out	87		
P. Vijayakumar b Susilkumar	20	– c Lamba b Azad	2
N. P. Madhavan c Sethi b Shukla	5	– lbw b Skukla	15
W. V. Raman c Khanna b Shukla	3	– not out	23
*†A. Bharat Reddy c Rajinder b Shukla	1	– b Susilkumar	38
T. A. Sekhar b Shukla	2	– c Valson b Azad	2
M. Santoshkumar b Shukla	0	– not out	6
B 2, l-b 5, w 2, n-b 2	11	B 3, l-b 9, n-b 8	20

1/55 2/78 3/107 4/111	229	1/26 2/207 3/213 4/220 (8 wkts) 306
5/175 6/197 7/201 8/215 9/225		5/226 6/256 7/284 8/294

Bowling: *First Innings*—Valson 18–4–51–2; Prabhakar 23–8–58–1; Peter 6–5–8–0; Susilkumar 16–2–32–2; Shukla 11.4–3–24–5; Azad 17–3–45–0. *Second Innings*—Valson 10–3–30–0; Prabhakar 9–3–24–1; Peter 4–0–17–0; Susilkumar 15–4–51–1; Rajinder 3–0–10–0; Azad 36–4–83–4; Shukla 28–5–71–2.

Delhi

R. Sethi c Bharat Reddy b Sekhar	33	R. Peter run out	6
R. Lamba c Srinivasan b Raman	52	Susilkumar not out	7
Rajinder Singh lbw b Jabbar	74	S. Valson c sub b Santoshkumar	8
K. B. J. Azad st Bharat Reddy			
b Santoshkumar.	186	B 4, l-b 3, w 2, n-b 10	19
*C. P. S. Chauhan			
lbw b Sivaramakrishnan.	27		547
R. C. Shukla c Sekhar		Penalty for 3 overs short	12
b Santoshkumar.	57		
†S. C. Khanna b Raman	77	1/85 2/101 3/218 4/309	559
M. Prabhakar lbw b Raman	1	5/428 6/455 7/462 8/523 9/528	

Bowling: Sekhar 27–4–131–1; Sivaramakrishnan 12–7–35–1; Santoshkumar 48.5–7–201–3; Raman 33–5–110–3; Jabbar 10–4–14–1; Srikkanth 7–1–37–0.

Umpires: M. V. Gothaskar and S. Das.

HARYANA v BENGAL

At Faridaba (T), February 11, 12, 13, 14. Haryana won by 71 runs. Toss won by Bengal.

Haryana

Deepak Sharma c Banerjee b Bhattacharya	30	– c Porel b Ghosh 50
V. Agarwal b Bhattacharya	18	– lbw b Ghosh 0
Ashwan Kumar c Porel b Bhattacharya	44	– b Bhattacharya 66
Aman Kumar lbw b Bhattacharya	46	– c and b Doshi 3
*R. Chadda hit wkt b Mukherjee	12	– run out 4
N. P. Singh lbw b Mukherjee	21	– lbw b Doshi 0
†Salim Ahmed not out	46	– c and b Doshi 8
R. Jolly c Roy b Bhattacharya	0	– c Porel b Doshi 0
Chetan Sharma run out	13	– b Doshi 40
S. Talwar lbw b Doshi	25	– c Mukherjee b Doshi 5
R. Goel run out	3	– not out 2
B 1, l-b 14, n-b 6	21	L-b 6, n-b 6 12
	279	**190**

1/31 2/72 3/123 4/150
5/178 6/185 7/185 8/213 9/266

1/0 2/70 3/77 4/82
5/91 6/110 7/110 8/166 9/176

Bowling: *First Innings*—Ghosh 7–2–26–0; Porel 15.3–8–22–0; Doshi 46–15–97–1; Bhattacharya 34–11–67–5; Mukherjee 13–1–46–2. *Second Innings*—Porel 5–1–12–0; Ghosh 25–12–33–2; Bhattacharya 16–2–37–1; Doshi 36.4–9–78–6; Mukherjee 6–3–13–0; Pronab Nandy 1–0–5–0.

Bengal

P. Roy b Chetan Sharma	9	– b Talwar 40
Palash Nandy b Chetan Sharma	16	– b Goel 38
Raja Venkat b Chetan Sharma	2	– c Salim Ahmed b Goel 73
Pronab Nandy b Chetan Sharma	0	– lbw b Goel 27
P. Chail c Deepak Sharma b Talwar	13	– c Chadda b Talwar 7
A. Bhattacharya c Ashwan Kumar b Chetan Sharma	40	– c sub b Talwar 13
†S. Banerjee b Talwar	31	– not out 21
S. Mukherjee c Agarwal b Talwar	11	– lbw b Talwar 4
*D. R. Doshi b Singh b Talwar	9	– c Chadda b Talwar 3
M. Ghosh c Deepak Sharma b Talwar	7	– b Goel 17
S. Porel not out	0	– c Ashwan Kumar b Talwar 0
B 1, l-b 2, n-b 4	7	B 3, l-b 2, n-b 5 10
	145	**253**

1/21 2/23 3/25 4/32
5/82 6/82 7/122 8/129 9/140

1/62 2/98 3/143 4/178
5/203 6/217 7/221 8/227 9/252

Bowling: *First Innings*—Chetan Sharma 17–5–70–5; Jolly 6–1–18–0; Singh 4–1–11–0; Goel 6–1–10–0; Talwar 12.2–2–29–5. *Second Innings*—Chetan Sharma 10–0–41–0; Jolly 3–0–14–0; Singh 5–1–12–0; Goel 49–17–73–4; Talwar 45.3–9–96–6; Deepak Sharma 2–0–7–0.

Umpires: K. B. Ramaswamy and M. G. Subramaniam.

BARODA v KARNATAKA

At Baroda (T), February 11, 12, 13, 14. Karnataka won by 114 runs. Toss won by Karnataka.

Karnataka

R. M. H. Binny b V. Patel	3	– b Satham	17
M. R. Srinivasaprasad lbw b Pardeshi	22	– run out	21
A. V. Jayaprakash c R. V. Hazare b Pardeshi	13	– c Bhansali b Pardeshi	1
G. R. Viswanath c S. S. Hazare b Pardeshi	4	– st M. S. Patel b Pardeshi	19
*B. P. Patel c M. S. Patel b Pardeshi	22	– b Petiwale	10
R. Sudhakar Rao lbw b Petiwale	32	– c R. V. Hazare b S. S. Hazare	30
B. Vijayakrishna b Pardeshi	1	– run out	42
J. Abhiram c R. V. Hazare b Petiwale	11	– st M. S. Patel b Pardeshi	11
†S. Viswanath b Pardeshi	0	– b Petiwale	12
R. Khanvilkar st M. S. Patel b Pardeshi	7	– not out	0
A. Raghuram Bhat not out	7	– c Deshmukh b Pardeshi	1
B 4, l-b 2	6	B 5, l-b 9, w 1	15

1/4 2/28 3/41 4/52   128   1/41 2/41 3/64 4/64   179
5/89 6/91 7/111 8/114 9/114   5/74 6/123 7/147 8/170 9/170

Bowling: *First Innings*—V. Patel 11–2–42–1; Satham 6–1–13–0; Pardeshi 25.1–7–33–7; Petiwale 16–5–26–2; S. S. Hazare 1–0–8–0. *Second Innings*—Satham 7–0–30–1; V. Patel 3–0–11–0; Pardeshi 18.3–5–47–4; Petiwale 10–1–44–2; S. S. Hazare 3–0–22–1; Panchasara 2–0–10–0.

Baroda

R. Y. Deshmukh b Bhat	7	– c S. Viswanath b Vijayakrishna	7
S. Parikh c G. R. Viswanath b Vijayakrishna	8	– c Srinivasaprasad b Bhat	29
B. J. Panchasara c Khanvilkar b Bhat	0	– c G. R. Viswanath b Bhat	13
R. V. Hazare c Binny b Vijayakrishna	3	– c S. Viswanath b Bhat	2
A. Bhansali c S. Viswanath b Vijayakrishna	17	– b Bhat	23
*N. Y. Satham not out	15	– b Sudhakar Rao	19
S. S. Hazare lbw b Vijayakrishna	0	– c Khanvilkar b Bhat	22
D. V. Pardeshi run out	0	– c Jayaprakash b Bhat	0
V. Patel b Bhat	10	– c Srinivasaprasad b Vijayakrishna	2
†M. S. Patel b Vijayakrishna	0	– c Vijayakrishna b Bhat	0
A. Petiwale c Abhiram b Vijayakrishna	0	– not out	0
B 1, l-b 1, n-b 1	3	B 6, l-b 7	13

1/15 2/15 3/18 4/35   63   1/16 2/26 3/26 4/30   130
5/44 6/44 7/50 8/62 9/63   5/65 6/77 7/123 8/130 9/130

Bowling: *First Innings*—Binny 6–1–15–0; Abhiram 2–1–1–0; Vijayakrishna 15–8–17–6; Bhat 18.1–3–27–3. *Second Innings*—Binny 5–4–4–0; Khanvilkar 3–1–3–0; Bhat 36–16–57–7; Vijayakrishna 34.1–13–51–2; Sudhakar Rao 5–3–2–1.

Umpires: Rajan Mehra and S. K. Ghosh.

BOMBAY v ORISSA

At Bombay (T), February 11, 12, 13, 14. Bombay won by an innings and 255 runs. Toss won by Bombay.

Bombay

S. S. Hattangadi c and b Praharaj	141	R. V. Kulkarni c Mahalik b Praharaj	0
J. Sanghani c Patnaik b Sahu	11	H. Contractor c Nag b Paramjit	0
R. V. Mankad lbw b Sahu	52	†Z. A. Parkar c and b Praharaj	0
S. M. Patil c and b Bharadwaj	39	R. Thakkar not out	3
G. A. Parkar c Jayaprakash b Bharadwaj	0	B 3, l-b 3, w 2, n-b 6	14
*A. V. Mankad not out	150	1/23 2/151/ 3/226 4/226 (9 wkts dec.) 500
S. V. Nayak c Nag b Praharaj	90	5/267 6/457 7/457 8/477 9/480

Bowling: Sahu 36–5–101–2; Praharaj 25–4–94–4; Paramjit 40–6–127–1; Sabir Hussain 30–3–93–0; Bharadwaj 17–2–62–2; Jayaprakash 1–0–6–0; Dubey 1–0–3–0.

Orissa

K. Dubey c Z. A. Parkar b Contractor	26	– c Z. A. Parkar b Thakkar	34
B. K. R. Patnaik c Z. A. Parkar b Kulkarni	0	– c Z. A. Parkar b A. V. Mankad.	43
A. Jayaprakash c Nayak b Kulkarni	0	– c Z. A. Parkar b Contractor	25
A. Bharadwaj lbw b Nayak	1	– lbw b Kulkarni	4
H. Praharaj not out	28	– b Kulkarni	0
S. Mahalik lbw b Contractor	4	– lbw b Kulkarni	0
R. Panda c Z. A. Parkar b Nayak	4	– c G. A. Parkar b Thakkar	11
S. Sahu c R. V. Mankad b Thakkar	12	– c G. A. Parkar b Thakkar	5
†G. Nag run out	2	– not out	21
*Paramjit Singh lbw b Kulkarni	2	– c Z. A. Parkar b Thakkar	0
Sabir Hussain lbw b Kulkarni	0	– b Thakkar	0
L–b 1, w 1, n–b 7	9	B 2, l–b 1, n–b 7	10
	88		**153**

Penalty for 1 over short 4

1/10 2/14 3/15 4/35   92   1/74 2/85 3/94 4/94
5/40 6/61 7/79 8/85 9/88   5/94 6/109 7/123 8/146 9/153

Bowling: *First Innings*—Kulkarni 13.5–4–21–4; Contractor 14–5–26–2; Nayak 11–4–23–2; Thakkar 10–6–8–1; Patil 2–1–1–0. *Second Innings*—Kulkarni 16–8–39–3; Contractor 9–1–38–1; Nayak 4–2–6–0; Thakkar 25.5–10–34–5; A. V. Mankad 11–3–26–1.

Umpires: R. B. Gupta and R. G. Rathore.

SEMI-FINALS

HARYANA v KARNATAKA

At Faridabad (T), February 25, 26, 27, 28. Karnataka won by an innings and 27 runs. Toss won by Haryana.

Haryana

Deepak Sharma c S. Viswanath b Binny	0	– lbw b Binny	11
Ashwan Kumar c Sudhakar Rao b Khanvilkar	7	– c Khanvilkar b Bhat	29
†Salim Ahmed c S. Viswanath b Binny	2	– lbw b Bhat	20
Aman Kumar c S. Viswanath b Binny	7	– b Sudhakar Rao	30
*R. Chadda c S. Viswanath b Binny	0	– c S. Viswanath b Bhat	15
N. P. Singh c Vijayakrishna b Binny	0	– b Bhat	12
M. Arya c Binny b Abhiram	8	– run out	2
R. Jolly c S. Viswanath b Binny	26	– c Khanvilkar b Bhat	0
Chetan Sharma b Binny	8	– b Bhat	1
S. Talwar c Vijayakrishna b Binny	0	– c Sudhakar Rao b Bhat	0
R. Goel not out	0	– not out	1
B 1, l–b 1, n–b 2	4	B 1, n–b 3	4
	62		**125**

Penalty for 4 overs short 16

1/0 2/2 3/17 4/17   78   1/22 2/36 3/77 4/105
5/17 6/18 7/44 8/57 9/57   5/106 6/108 7/117 8/119 9/124

Bowling: *First Innings*—Binny 13–6–22–8; Khanvilkar 7–4–8–1; Abhiram 4–0–23–1; Bhat 1–0–5–0. *Second Innings*—Binny 12–1–27–1; Khanvilkar 9–3–21–0; Bhat 23–11–24–7; Vijayakrishna 14–2–22–0; Sudhakar Rao 9–2–27–1.

Karnataka

†S. Viswanath lbw b Goel	8	J. Abhiram lbw b Goel	12
M. R. Srinivasaprasad c Singh		B. Vijayakrishna c Chetan Sharma	
b Chetan Sharma.	32	b Goel.	36
R. M. H. Binny c Salim Ahmed		R. Khanvilkar not out	8
b Chetan Sharma.	54	A. Raghuram Bhat run out	0
A. V. Jayaprakash b Goel	19		
G. R. Viswanath c Salim Ahmed			
b Chetan Sharma.	4	B 4, l-b 8	12
*B. P. Patel b Talwar	42		
R. Sudhakar Rao b Talwar	3	1/19 2/79 3/106 4/112	230
		5/142 6/174 7/175 8/213 9/226	

Bowling: Chetan Sharma 20–2–65–3; Jolly 1–0–4–0; Goel 26.5–10–73–4; Singh 8–1–40–0; Talwar 16–1–36–2.

Umpires: P. D. Reporter and D. N. Dotiwala.

DELHI v BOMBAY

At Delhi (T), February 25, 26, 27, 28. Drawn. Bombay declared winners by virtue of their first-innings lead. Toss won by Bombay.

Bombay

S. S. Hattangadi b Susilkumar	92	S. V. Nayak c Rajinder b Susilkumar ..	14
J. Sanghani c Mohanty b Shukla	37	R. V. Kulkarni c Rajinder b Shukla	8
R. V. Mankad c Rajinder		K. D. Mokashi not out	5
b Prabhakar.	76	R. Thakkar c and b Shukla	5
S. M. Patil c Valson b Azad	7	B 3, l-b 19, w 3, n-b 7	32
G. A. Parkar st Khanna b Shukla	141		
†C. S. Pandit lbw b Valson	12	1/101 2/190 3/207 4/244	494
*A. V. Mankad lbw b Azad	65	5/261 6/389 7/426 8/463 9/468	

Bowling: Valson 35–7–97–1; Prabhakar 38–11–95–1; Lamba 3–1–6–0; Azad 43–3–114–2; Shukla 26.3–5–72–4; Susilkumar 40–14–78–2.

Delhi

R. Sethi b Kulkarni	12		
R. Lamba c Pandit b Kulkarni	15	– b Thakkar	10
Rajinder Singh c A. V. Mankad b Thakkar	16	– c Pandit b Kulkarni	3
K. B. J. Azad c Pandit b Kulkarni	30	– b Thakkar	75
Tilakraj c and b Mokashi	16	– c Kulkarni b Thakkar	12
*R. C. Shukla c Parkar b Kulkarni	47	– c A. V. Mankad b Thakkar	1
†S. C. Khanna c and b Kulkarni	143	– not out	16
D. Mohanty c Pandit b Kulkarni	2	– not out	5
M. Prabhakar c Pandit b Kulkarni	37	– c Pandit b Thakkar	86
Susilkumar c Hattangadi b Kulkarni	1		
S. Valson not out	10		
B 5, l-b 2, n-b 2	9	B 5, l-b 2, n-b 1	8

1/26 2/40 3/59 4/90	338	1/26 2/36 3/66 4/176	(6 wkts) 216
5/92 6/240 7/248 8/321 9/323		5/186 6/208	

Bowling: *First Innings*—Kulkarni 34.1–3–111–8; Nayak 21–5–56–0; Thakkar 40–14–71–1; Mokashi 29–5–81–1; Patil 2–0–10–0. *Second Innings*—Kulkarni 7–2–11–1; Nayak 10–3–25–0; Patil 6–0–30–0; Thakkar 31–12–53–5; Mokashi 20–4–54–0; R. V. Mankad 7–1–13–0; A. V. Mankad 1–0–8–0; Parkar 1–0–1–0; Sanghani 4–0–13–0.

Umpires: B. Ganguli and I. R. Rao.

FINAL

BOMBAY v KARNATAKA

At Bombay (T), March 11, 12, 13, 14, 15. Drawn. Karnataka declared winners by virtue of their first-innings lead. Patel surprised everyone by putting Bombay in to bat on the Wankhede Stadium pitch, and Bombay showed their appreciation of the gesture by running up a score of 534 runs. Chandrakant Pandit, in his first season, having replaced Zulfiqar Parkar as wicket-keeper, was mainly responsible for this comfortable position. He showed patience and discipline in scoring 157 runs and was involved in partnerships with Ghulam Parkar and Suru Nayak, adding 112 for the fifth wicket and 133 for the seventh respectively. Pandit was at the crease for 332 minutes and hit nineteen 4s.

A. V. Jayaprakash, a lanky, elegant striker of the ball, gave the clarion call for victory when Karnataka went in for their reply. He scored a classic 89 and found in wicket-keeper-batsman Sadanand Viswanath an ideal partner, who did not hesitate to attack the Bombay bowling. The pair added 174 runs, but more than the runs it was the tone of their batting that set Karnataka's stride to victory. Though Gundappa Viswanath, Patel and Sudhakar Rao were dismissed cheaply, Roger Binny took charge of the situation and while notching up a very competent 115, took his side close to Bombay's score; left-hander Vijayakrishna, Ranjit Khanvilkar and Raghuram Bhat followed up to overhaul Bombay's total by a run, which, incidentally, was through a leg-bye. This lead eventually rose by another 16 runs awarded as penalty for Bombay's failure to maintain the prescribed 15-an-hour over-rate. Then came Patil's electrifying knock, all his 121 runs coming before lunch on the final day, as with Pandit he added 136 runs during their unbroken fifth-wicket stand. Mankad's declaration at 213 for four was followed by an anticlimax as Karnataka, after a challenging run for victory, pulled back and settled for a draw. A feature of the match was the poor catching, at least a dozen catches being floored on either side.

Bombay

S. S. Hattangadi c Sudhakar Rao b Binny	13	– c Binny b Abhiram	3
J. Sanghani c Jayaprakash b Binny	78	– c Sudhakar Rao b Khanvilkar	0
R. V. Mankad c Srinivasaprasad b Abhiram	14	– c S. Viswanath b Khanvilkar	23
S. M. Patil b Vijayakrishna	48	– not out	121
G. A. Parkar c S. Viswanath b Bhat	60	– c S. Viswanath b Abhiram	7
†C. S. Pandit c S. Viswanath b Khanvilkar	157	– not out	33
*A. V. Mankad c Srinivasaprasad b Binny	13		
S. V. Nayak c Srinivasaprasad b Bhat	67		
R. Kulkarni c G. R. Viswanath b Bhat	40		
S. Shetty not out	22		
R. Thakkar c S. Viswanath b Bhat	0		
B 3, l-b 7, w 2, n-b 10	22	L-b 4, n-b 2	6
	534	**(4 wkts dec.)**	**193**
		Penalty for 5 overs short	20

1/27 2/57 3/138 4/186
5/298 6/329 7/462 8/493 9/534

1/4 2/4 3/36 4/57   213

Bowling: *First Innings*—Binny 43–12–119–3; Khanvilkar 34–4–116–1; Jayaprakash 5–2–8–0; Abhiram 11–1–43–1; Vijayakrishna 37–5–86–1; Raghuram Bhat 52.4–15–121–4; Sudhakar Rao 10–2–19–0. *Second Innings*—Khanvilkar 11–3–51–2; Abhiram 8–0–48–2; Vijayakrishna 4–1–39–0; Raghuram Bhat 4–0–49–0.

Karnataka

M. R. Srinivasaprasad lbw b Kulkarni	29	– c Pandit b Kulkarni	2
†S. Viswanath c Pandit b Shetty	92	– b Shetty	77
A. V. Jayaprakash c and b Thakkar	89	– lbw b Shetty	10
R. M. H. Binny c Hattangadi b Thakkar	115	– c Sanghani b Thakkar	45
G. R. Viswanath lbw b Shetty	3	– c Pandit b Shetty	20
*B. P. Patel c Pandit b Kulkarni	18	– not out	4
R. Sudhakar Rao c Parkar b Kulkarni	9		
J. Abhiram c A. V. Mankad b Nayak	69	– not out	11
R. Khanvilkar b Kulkarni	32		
B. Vijayakrishna lbw b Kulkarni	42		
A. Raghuram Bhat not out	0		
B 10, l-b 19, w 1, n-b 7	37	L-b 6, n-b 4	10
	535	**(5 wkts)**	**179**
Penalty for 4 overs short	16		

1/51 2/225 3/227 4/237   **551**   1/6 2/39 3/124 4/149
5/273 6/293 7/447 8/470 9/526   5/161

Bowling: *First Innings*—Kulkarni 40.4–4–157–5; Nayak 27–8–58–1; Shetty 26–4–75–2; Patil 2–0–16–0; Thakkar 49–6–167–2; A. V. Mankad 9–1–25–0. *Second Innings*—Kulkarni 19–6–57–1; Thakkar 25–9–54–1; Nayak 7–3–24–0; Shetty 19–7–34–3.

Umpires: Swaroop Kishen and S. R. Bose.

DULEEP TROPHY, 1982-83

NORTH ZONE v CENTRAL ZONE

At Brabourne Stadium, Bombay (T), October 2, 3, 4. North Zone won by an innings and 101 runs. Toss won by Central Zone.

Central Zone

S. S. Khandkar b Maninder	26	– b Maninder	54
*Sanjeeva Rao st Khanna b Maninder	20	– c Kapil Dev b Azad	45
S. Chaturvedi lbw b Madan Lal	12	– c Chauhan b Maninder	17
A. Burrows b Shukla	14	– run out	15
S. Mudkavi run out	10	– c sub b Azad	4
†P. Vedraj st Khanna b Shukla	13	– b Azad	0
A. Mathur c Kapil Dev b Azad	18	– c Chauhan b Maninder	1
G. Sharma st Khanna b Maninder	51	– b Azad	7
V. Dutt c Chauhan b Maninder	0	– c Gursharan b Maninder	2
P. Banerjee run out	0	– c sub b Maninder	0
R. S. Hans not out	6	– not out	0
L-b 2	2	B 4, l-b 2, n-b 1	7
	172		**152**

1/37 2/58 3/58 4/80   **172**   1/71 2/102 3/133 4/137   **152**
5/86 6/98 7/153 8/154 9/156   5/141 6/142 7/147 8/148 9/148

Bowling: *First Innings*—Kapil Dev 5–0–19–0; Madan Lal 11–4–16–1; Amarnath 6–1–20–0; Maninder 33.1–11–66–4; Shukla 19–3–45–2; Azad 7–2–4–1. *Second Innings*—Madan Lal 5–1–26–0; Amarnath 2–0–8–0; Maninder 26.5–11–48–5; Shukla 9–1–24–0; Azad 18–4–39–4.

North Zone

C. P. S. Chauhan lbw b Dutt	8	Madan Lal b Banerjee	15
†S. C. Khanna c Mudkavi b Sharma	64	R. C. Shukla c Khandekar b Hans	7
M. Amarnath b Mathur	4	Maninder Singh not out	0
A. Malhotra run out	0		
Yashpal Sharma c sub b Sharma	134	B 3, l-b 3, n-b 1	7
K. B. J. Azad c sub b Hans	25		
Gursharan Singh b Sharma	72	1/12 2/21 3/34 4/102	425
*Kapil Dev st Chaturvedi b Hans	89	5/152 6/294 7/327 8/379 9/420	

Bowling: Dutt 22–5–83–1; Mathur 10–2–36–1; Hans 39.4–10–77–3; Sharma 36–5–105–3; Banerjee 16–1–61–1; Mudkavi 17–1–56–0.

Umpires: S. R. Bose and M. I. Mohammad Ghouse.

SEMI-FINALS
WEST ZONE v SOUTH ZONE

At Wankhede Stadium, Bombay (T), October 8, 9, 10, 11. Drawn. West Zone declared winners by virtue of their first-innings lead. Toss won by West Zone.

West Zone

A. D. Gaekwad c Kirmani b Binny	..	1 – c Viswanath b L. Sivaramakrishnan	21
G. A. Parkar c V. Sivaramakrishnan b Sekhar	..	4 – b Bhat	26
*S. M. Gavaskar b Binny	17	lbw b L. Sivaramakrishnan	23
R. B. Bhalekar c Kirmani b Srikkanth	2	c Kirmani b L. Sivaramakrishnan	12
M. D. Gunjal run out	16	retired hurt	69
R. J. Shastri c Viswanath b Sekhar	51	c L. Sivaramakrishnan b Sekhar	21
R. G. Borde c Kirmani b Sekhar	89	b L. Sivaramakrishnan	13
†Z. A. Parkar lbw b Sekhar	10	b L. Sivaramakrishnan	11
S. Keshwala not out	56	c Yadav b Sekhar	11
U. C. Joshi b Sekhar	0	not out	0
B. S. Sandhu c V. Sivaramakrishnan b Binny	56	not out	17
B 3, l-b 2, n-b 6	11	B 2, l-b 2, n-b 3	7

1/2 2/13 3/29 4/29	313	1/47 2/47 3/69 (8 wkts dec.) 231
5/47 6/174 7/186 8/201 9/201		4/97 5/136 6/183 7/205 8/231

Bowling: *First Innings*—Sekhar 25–4–66–5; Binny 21.5–2–69–3; Srikkanth 3–2–1–1; Bhat 33–14–49–0; L. Sivaramakrishnan 22–4–43–0; Yadav 16.1–3–51–0; Narasimha Rao 7–0–23–0. *Second Innings*—Sekhar 16–0–42–2; Binny 13–0–52–0; L. Sivaramakrishnan 31–3–63–5; Bhat 24–6–43–1; Yadav 10–0–22–0; Narasimha Rao 1–0–2–0.

South Zone

R. M. H. Binny c Z. A. Parkar b Sandhu	12	not out	53
K. Srikkanth c Gaekwad b Sandhu	23	b Sandhu	0
V. Sivaramakrishnan c G. A. Parkar b Borde	48	c Gavaskar b Keshwala	10
*G. R. Viswanath c Bhalekar b Shastri	56		
M. V. Narasimha Rao c Z. A. Parkar b Sandhu	22	c Keshwala b Sandhu	4
†S. M. H. Kirmani c Bhalekar b Keshwala	19		
A. Jabbar c Gaekwad b Shastri	52	not out	17
L. Sivaramakrishnan c Gavaskar b Sandhu	7		
N. S. Yadav c Shastri b Sandhu	10		
A. Raghuram Bhat c Z. A. Parkar b Sandhu	0		
T. A. Sekhar not out	19		
B 4, l-b 3, w 1	8	L-b 2	2

1/29 2/38 3/129 4/157	273	1/0 2/6 3/46 (3 wkts) 86
5/172 6/190 7/206 8/222 9/222		

Bowling: *First Innings*—Sandhu 33–8–86–6; Keshwala 15–1–49–1; Bhalekar 5–1–10–0; Shastri 29.1–8–50–2; Joshi 23–7–47–0; Borde 15–4–17–1; Gunjal 2–0–6–0. *Second Innings* —Sandhu 9–1–27–2; Keshwala 6–1–22–1; Bhalekar 5–1–10–0; Joshi 7–2–11–0; Borde 5–1–7–0; Gaekwad 3–1–7–0.

Umpires: R. B. Gupta and P. G. Pandit.

NORTH ZONE v EAST ZONE

At Brabourne Stadium, Bombay (T), October 8, 9, 10, 11. North Zone won by an innings and 302 runs. Toss won by North Zone.

North Zone

R. C. Shukla b Paramjit		77
†S. C. Khanna b Doshi		27
A. Malhotra b Burman		139
M. Amarnath c Randhir b Burman		207
K. B. J. Azad b Paramjit		156
Gursharan Singh not out		26
B 5, l-b 8, n-b 7		20

(5 wkts dec.) 652

Penalty for 3 overs short 12

1/54 2/149 3/323 4/596 5/652   664

Yashpal Sharma, *Kapil Dev, Madan Lal, S. Valson and Maninder Singh did not bat.

Bowling: Randhir 32–3–122–0; Burman 21.1–0–126–2; Doshi 27–5–96–1; Paramjit 37–7–135–2; Palash Nandy 30–3–129–0; Gidwani 3–0–13–0; Pronab Nandy 3–0–11–0.

East Zone

Palash Nandy c Khanna b Valson		17 – lbw b Valson	22
Arun Lal lbw b Madan Lal		3 – b Madan Lal	68
H. Gidwani c Khanna b Maninder	54	– c Amarnath b Madan Lal	58
K. Dubey c Azad b Maninder	41	– c Yashpal b Maninder	2
R. Venkatram c Valson b Maninder	11	– c Madan Lal b Maninder	16
Pronab Nandy c Shukla b Maninder	7	– c Amarnath b Maninder	9
†S. Banerjee c Valson b Shukla	2	– c Gursharan b Maninder	2
B. Burman c Madan Lal b Shukla	4	– c sub b Maninder	10
*D. R. Doshi c Malhotra b Shukla	11	– run out	2
Paramjit Singh b Shukla	2	– c Valson b Azad	2
Randhir Singh not out	5	– not out	0
B 2, l-b 1, n-b 1	4	B 6, l-b 3, n-b 1	10

1/8 2/28 3/118 4/121   161   1/43 2/154 3/157 4/159   201
5/134 6/139 7/143 8/143 9/156   5/176 6/181 7/188 8/199 9/199

Bowling: *First Innings*—Valson 11–0–29–1; Kapil Dev 3–1–6–0; Madan Lal 11–1–19–1; Maninder 28–7–48–4; Shukla 22.4–10–31–4; Azad 13–2–20–0; Gursharan 1–0–4–0. *Second Innings*—Madan Lal 16–5–34–2; Valson 9–0–38–1; Maninder 39–11–53–5; Shukla 16–2–36–0; Azad 14.4–3–30–1.

Umpires: A. L. Narasimhan and V. K. Ramaswamy.

FINAL

NORTH ZONE v WEST ZONE

At Wankhede Stadium, Bombay (T), October 13, 14, 15, 16, 17. North Zone won by eight wickets. Toss won by West Zone.

West Zone

A. D. Gaekwad lbw b Madan Lal	2	– c Yashpal b Madan Lal	104
G. A. Parkar c Azad b Madan Lal	26	– c Shukla b Madan Lal	11
*S. M. Gavaskar c Azad b Kapil Dev	1	– c Azad b Madan Lal	67
A. V. Mankad b Kapil Dev	44	– b Madan Lal	1
D. B. Vengsarkar c Azad b Madan Lal	1	– c Chauhan b Kapil Dev	50
R. J. Shastri b Madan Lal	5	– run out	30
R. G. Borde lbw b Madan Lal	3	– run out	0
S. Keshwala lbw b Madan Lal	0	– c Yashpal b Madan Lal	5
B. S. Sandhu c and b Amarnath	10	– b Kapil Dev	13
S. Gudge c and b Valson	37	– not out	4
†Z. A. Parkar not out	20	– c Amarnath b Kapil Dev	0
B 7, l-b 5, n-b 3	15	B 13, l-b 10, n-b 6	29

	164		314
Penalty for 1 over short	4	Penalty for 4 overs short	16

1/14 2/15 3/65 4/72   168   1/43 2/123 3/237 4/272   330
5/84 6/86 7/87 8/96 9/113   5/273 6/291 7/291 8/314 9/314

Bowling: *First Innings*—Kapil Dev 18–6–37–2; Madan Lal 25–9–59–6; Valson 12.2–3–24–1; Amarnath 7–1–18–1; Maninder 5–1–6–0; Shukla 3–1–5–0. *Second Innings*—Kapil Dev 31.5–4–97–3; Madan Lal 25–7–63–5; Valson 9–1–37–0; Maninder 17–4–45–0; Shukla 6–1–14–0; Azad 8–0–29–0.

North Zone

C. P. S. Chauhan c Gaekwad b Sandhu	0	– not out	63
R. C. Shukla c Gaekwad b Shastri	31	– b Shastri	19
A. Malhotra c and b Shastri	76	– c Z. A. Parkar b Shastri	18
M. Amarnath run out	80	– not out	67
†Yashpal Sharma c Borde b Shastri	83		
K. B. J. Azad b Shastri	4		
Gursharan Singh lbw b Shastri	0		
*Kapil Dev c Keshwala b Shastri	39		
Madan Lal c Keshwala b Gudge	8		
S. Valson c Borde b Shastri	0		
Maninder Singh not out	0		
B 2, l-b 3, n-b 3	8	B 2, l-b 1	3

1/0 2/70 3/143 4/232   329   1/25 2/49   (2 wkts) 170
5/239 6/243 7/299 8/311 9/328

Bowling: *First Innings*—Sandhu 35–11–76–1; Keshwala 20–5–56–0; Shastri 49.3–10–105–7; Gudge 22–6–52–1; Borde 5–1–7–0; Mankad 9–3–25–0. *Second Innings*—Sandhu 13–5–18–0; Keshwala 2–1–5–0; Shastri 20–7–37–2; Mankad 7–1–14–0; Gudge 14–2–60–0; Borde 8–0–29–0; Gavaskar 1–0–4–0.

Umpires: P. G. Pandit and R. Mrutyanjayan.

IRANI TROPHY, 1982-83

RANJI TROPHY CHAMPIONS (DELHI) v REST OF INDIA

At Delhi (T), October 21, 22, 23, 24. Rest of India won by five wickets.

Delhi

C. P. S. Chauhan c Parkar b Sandhu	8	– lbw b Sandhu	26
R. Lamba b Doshi	93	– b Sandhu	46
Gursharan Singh b Shastri	94	– st Parkar b Sivaramakrishnan	18
*M. Amarnath c Malhotra b Doshi	127	– c Gavaskar b Shastri	52
K. B. J. Azad c Shastri b Sandhu	32	– st Parkar b Shastri	46
R. C. Shukla lbw b Sandhu	29	– c Parkar b Sivaramakrishnan	5
Madan Lal c Parkar b Sandhu	12	– c Arun Lal b Shastri	0
†S. C. Khanna b Sandhu	0	– c and b Sivaramakrishnan	0
R. Peter c Srikkanth b Doshi	3	– st Parkar b Doshi	46
S. Valson c Srikkanth b Doshi	14	– lbw b Sivaramakrishnan	2
Maninder Singh not out	1	– not out	5
B 1, l-b 10, n-b 5	16	B 5, l-b 4, n-b 3	12

1/32 2/172 3/268 4/337   429   1/67 2/78 3/124 4/187   258
5/384 6/400 7/404 8/407 9/415   5/187 6/194 7/194 8/202 9/209

Bowling: *First Innings*—Sekhar 24–3–74–0; Sandhu 30–8–110–5; Srikkanth 1–0–4–0; Doshi 29.2–11–66–4; Sivaramakrishnan 22–1–97–0; Shastri 21–6–62–1. *Second Innings*—Sekhar 11–1–27–0; Sandhu 11–3–34–2; Doshi 13.1–4–31–1; Sivaramakrishnan 30–3–127–4; Shastri 23–12–27–3.

Rest of India

K. Srikkanth st Khanna b Maninder	83	– c Maninder b Valson	110
Arun Lal lbw b Valson	5	– st Khanna b Maninder	82
A. Malhotra lbw b Maninder	67	– not out	116
S. M. Patil c Amarnath b Maninder	0	– b Azad	41
*S. M. Gavaskar b Maninder	0	– c Lamba b Maninder	28
R. J. Shastri lbw b Shukla	29	– st Khanna b Amarnath	26
B. S. Sandhu st Khanna b Maninder	20	– not out	0
T. A. Sekhar c Chauhan b Shukla	12		
L. Sivaramakrishnan not out	20		
†Z. A. Parkar c Chauhan b Maninder	0		
D. R. Doshi c Maninder b Shukla	11		
B 16, l-b 2, n-b 2	20	B 13, l-b 7, n-b 1	21

1/16 2/123 3/125 4/125   267   1/143 2/143 3/192   (5 wkts) 424
5/199 6/203 7/220 8/240 9/240   4/359 5/418

Bowling: *First Innings*—Madan Lal 8–3–44–0; Valson 13–1–56–1; Amarnath 4–0–15–0; Peter 2–0–8–0; Maninder 28–10–66–6; Shukla 16–1–44–3; Azad 9–4–14–0. *Second Innings* —Madan Lal 7–4–10–0; Valson 5–0–52–1; Maninder 38.2–3–180–2; Shukla 14–0–70–0; Azad 3–2–51–1; Amarnath 6–0–40–1.

Umpires: P. D. Reporter and V. Vikaramraju.

CRICKET IN PAKISTAN, 1982-83

By QAMAR AHMED

Pakistan's premier domestic tournament, the Quaid-e-Azam Trophy, was won by United Bank, who so regained the Trophy they had lost the previous year. The competition, in which Pakistan's top ten teams participate, was highly exciting. National Bank finished second, and Railways, who had a fine season, third, as they did in the PACO Cup, which was won by Habib Bank. Pakistan's Automobile Corporation (PACO) won the Patron's Trophy and, along with the runners-up, House Building Finance Corporation (HBFC), earned the right to compete in the 1983-84 Quaid-e-Azam Trophy.

For the first time in 25 years the Quaid-e-Azam tournament was sponsored, Fujicolor putting up prizemoney of £35,000. Muslim Commercial Bank's Nairobi-born opening batsman, Qasim Omar, became the first player in the Trophy's history to score more than 1,000 runs with a total of 1,078. His record aggregate included five centuries. Twice he hit double-centuries and twice he scored a century in each innings of a match. Zaheer Abbas, Salim Malik and Majid Khan also scored two centuries in a match. PIA's Rashid Khan, with 55 wickets, was another major recipient of the awards, while Mohammad Nazir was another bowler to take over 50 wickets in the Quaid-e-Azam Trophy. Habib Bank's leg-spinner, Abdul Qadir, finished at the top of the Trophy bowling averages with 44 wickets at 14.97 apiece from only four matches. He twice captured nine wickets in an innings.

Kamal Najamuddin, Karachi's wicket-keeper, equalled the Pakistan record of ten dismissals in a first-class match. Iqbal Qasim achieved the only hat-trick of the tournament, for National Bank against Allied Bank. The most unusual match was between Lahore and Habib Bank in Lahore. Rain prevented play until the last day, when by mutual consent the teams decided to play for bonus points. In 102 overs no fewer than twenty wickets fell and 595 runs were scored, a record for a day in Pakistan, eight bonus points thus going to each team.

Habib Bank retained the PACO Cup, United Bank being among their victims. They won three of their four matches outright, the other being washed out. The best batsman of the tournament was Agha Zahid, whose 552 runs included three centuries. The best bowlers were Abdul Qadir and Shahid Butt. Qadir took 26 wickets in the competition and became the first Pakistan bowler ever to capture 100 wickets in a home season.

The 1982-83 season saw a record number of 72 first-class matches. A PACO league fixture, which had to be abandoned owing to riots in Karachi, was retained in the list of first-class matches for statistical purposes. Crowd trouble plagued the season, especially in Karachi where a one-day international against Australia had to be abandoned. The two Karachi Tests against India were also disrupted several times. All in all, however, the season was one of great success, highlighted by famous victories over Australia and India.

For the 1983-84 season it was agreed that the rules of domestic cricket would be changed, with the Quaid-e-Azam Trophy being played on a league-cum-knockout basis. In future, the teams will be divided into two groups, with the top two teams from each group going forward to the semi-finals, while the teams finishing at the bottom of the table in the Quaid-e-Azam will be relegated to the Patron's Trophy.

FIRST-CLASS AVERAGES, 1982-83

BATTING

(Qualification: 600 runs, average 35)

	M	I	NO	R	HI	Avge
Zaheer Abbas (*PIA*)	13	15	1	1,371	215	97.92
Qasim Omar (*MCB*)	9	18	4	1,275	210*	91.07
Mudassar Nazar (*United Bank*)	11	17	4	1,110	231	85.38
Javed Miandad (*Habib Bank*)	14	16	2	1,124	280*	80.28
Zafar Ahmed (*Karachi*)	10	18	7	800	140	72.72
Agha Zahid (*Habib Bank*)	14	23	2	1,220	175	58.09
Majid J. Khan (*Lahore*)	8	13	2	629	128*	57.18
Mohsin Khan (*Habib Bank*)	12	18	4	797	135	56.92
Ashraf Ali (*United Bank*)	14	20	7	719	111*	55.30
Shafiq Ahmad (*National Bank*)	13	23	3	1,104	118	55.20
Rizwan-uz-Zaman (*PIA*)	14	25	0	1,352	152	54.08
Nasir Valika (*United Bank*)	14	24	9	806	103*	53.73
Sadiq Mohammad (*United Bank*)	11	21	2	1,009	157	53.10
Saadat Ali (*Railways*)	12	22	2	1,013	206*	50.65
Saleem Pervez (*National Bank*)	14	27	3	1,136	102*	47.33
Feroze Najamuddin (*Karachi*)	9	17	2	710	144	47.33
Salim Malik (*Habib Bank*)	18	23	1	1,013	124*	46.04
Sultan Rana (*Habib Bank*)	13	17	3	633	127	45.21
Haroon Rashid (*United Bank*)	12	17	2	671	133	44.73
Ali Zia (*National Bank*)	14	24	5	785	83	41.31
Masood Anwar (*Rawalpindi*)	11	20	2	701	125	38.94
Taslim Arif (*National Bank*)	12	19	0	728	111	38.31
Arshad Pervez (*Habib Bank*)	12	18	2	613	109	38.31
Shoaib Mohammad (*PIA*)	14	24	3	792	109*	37.71

    * *Signifies not out.*

BOWLING

(Qualification: 30 wickets)

	O	M	R	W	Avge
Imran Khan (*Pakistan*)	326.4	103	729	53	13.75
Khatib Rizwan (*Rawalpindi*)	181.1	28	568	31	18.32
Shahid Mahboob (*Allied Bank*)	293	50	800	43	18.60
Jalal-ud-Din (*Allied Bank*)	284	77	784	41	19.12
Tauseef Ahmed (*United Bank*)	365.4	77	956	48	19.91
Mohammad Nazir (*Railways*)	841.1	269	1,451	70	20.72
Adbul Wahab (*Rawalpindi*)	232	40	652	31	21.03
Iqbal Qasim (*National Bank*)	578.5	161	1,477	65	22.72
Khurshid Akhtar (*United Bank*)	393.1	91	1,011	44	22.97
Abdul Qadir (*Habib Bank*)	827.2	184	2,367	103	22.98
Abdul Raqeeb (*Habib Bank*)	485.4	102	1,398	59	23.69
Shahid Butt (*Railways*)	508.4	121	1,431	60	23.85
Ilyas Khan (*MCB*)	304.4	53	860	34	25.29
Rashid Khan (*PIA*)	514.5	95	1,772	70	25.31
Iqbal Sikandar (*PIA*)	496.4	110	1,362	53	25.69
Ehtesham-ud-Din (*United Bank*)	314	59	978	38	25.73
Mohinder Kumar (*Karachi*)	265.2	32	940	36	26.11
Afzaal Butt (*National Bank*)	400.1	78	1,349	49	27.53
Sikander Bakht (*United Bank*)	291.4	51	1,051	36	29.19

Note: Matches taken into account are Quaid-e-Azam Trophy, PACO Cup and first-class matches against Australia and India.

QUAID-E-AZAM TROPHY WINNERS

1953-54	Bahawalpur	1970-71	Karachi Blues
1954-55	Karachi	1972-73	Railways
1956-57	Punjab	1973-74	Railways
1957-58	Bahawalpur	1974-75	Punjab A
1958-59	Karachi	1975-76	National Bank
1959-60	Karachi	1976-77	United Bank
1961-62	Karachi B	1977-78	Habib Bank
1962-63	Karachi A	1978-79	National Bank
1963-64	Karachi Blues	1979-80	PIA
1964-65	Karachi Blues	1980-81	United Bank
1966-67	Karachi	1981-82	National Bank
1968-69	Lahore	1982-83	United Bank
1969-70	PIA		

QUAID-E-AZAM TROPHY, 1982-83

The tournament was contested on a league basis between Pakistan's top ten teams. Ten points were awarded for a win. Four bonus points for batting and four bonus points for bowling were also available.

	Played	Won	Drawn	Lost	Bonus Points Batting	Bonus Points Bowling	Total Points
United Bank	9	5	4	0	31	25	106
National Bank	9	4	4	1	25	26	91
Railways	9	3	3	3	27	29	86
Habib Bank	9	2	7	0	31	31	82
PIA	9	2	5	2	30	32	82
MCB	9	2	5	2	27	28	75
Allied Bank	9	2	4	3	22	28	70
Karachi	9	1	4	4	30	22	62
Rawalpindi	9	2	2	5	16	24	60
Lahore	9	0	6	3	20	31	51

Note: First innings closed at 85 overs.

At National Stadium, Karachi, October 10, 11, 12, 13. Drawn. Habib Bank 274 for eight (Agha Zahid 98, Azhar Khan 52; Shoaib Habib three for 50, Shahid Mahboob three for 59) and 259 for eight dec. (Sultan Rana 78, Azhar Khan 68, Agha Zahid 61; Shahid Mahboob six for 107); Allied Bank 275 (Iqtidar Ali 99, Salim Yousuf 30) and 152 for three (Iqtidar Ali 56, Salim Yousuf 41, Salman Qizalbash 39). *Habib Bank 8 pts, Allied Bank 6 pts.*

At Iqbal Stadium, Faisalabad, October 10, 11, 12, 13. MCB won by ten wickets. Rawalpindi 179 for nine dec. (Maqsood Kundi 46, Azmat Jalil 41; Farrukh Zaman five for 54) and 222 (Mohammad Riaz 70, Raja Afaq 62; Nadeem Yousuf three for 31); MCB 391 for four dec. (Azmat Rana 113 not out, Ijaz Faqih 107, Babar Basharat 77, Qasim Omar 47; Mohammad Riaz three for 137) and 12 for no wkt. *MCB 17 pts, Rawalpindi 2 pts.*

At Karachi, October 16, 17, 18, 19. United Bank won by 154 runs. United Bank 260 for seven (Sadiq Mohammad 109, Nasir Valika 47; Tariq Nazar five for 94) and 346 for six dec. (Sadiq Mohammad 115, Nasir Valika 65, Siddiq Patni 62, Ashraf Ali 50 not out; Tanvir Ali three for 89); Karachi 315 for four (Feroze Najamuddin 92 not out, Umar Rashid 72, Sajid Ali 54) and 137 (Feroze Najamuddin 36; Sikander Bakht five for 38, Tauseef Ahmed four for 28). *United Bank 15 pts, Karachi 6 pts.*

At Karachi, October 16, 17, 18, 19. Drawn. PIA 235 for nine dec. (Rizwan-uz-Zaman 112; Azhar Khan four for 45, Agha Zahid three for 66) and 195 (Zahid Ahmed 62; Raees Ahmad four for 90, Liaqat Ali three for 22); Habib Bank 120 (Salim Malik 51; Rashid Khan seven for 72) and 279 for eight (Salim Malik 78, Sultan Rana 46, Aslam Qureshi 44). *PIA 7 pts, Habib Bank 3 pts.*

At Rawalpindi, October 16, 17, 18. Allied Bank won by seven wickets. Rawalpindi 107 for eight dec. (Shahid Mahboob six for 28) and 191 (Raja Sarfraz 43, Raja Afaq 40; Shoaib Habib six for 70); Allied Bank 217 for nine dec. (Salim Yousuf 145 not out; Raja Afaq three for 83) and 86 for three (Mohammad Riaz three for 17). *Allied Bank 14 pts, Rawalpindi 3 pts.*

At Lahore, October 16, 17, 18, 19. Drawn. MCB 212 (Ijaz Faqih 73; Mohammad Nazir three for 37, Musleh-ud-Din three for 63) and 365 for two (Qasim Omar 203 not out, Anwarul Haq 115); Railways 315 for seven (Talat Mirza 96, Ejaz Ahmad 66, Shahid Pervez 50; Ilyas Khan four for 82). *Railways 8 pts, MCB 4 pts.*

At Karachi, October 22, 23, 24, 25. Habib Bank won by ten wickets. Karachi 219 (Kamal Najamuddin 58, Zafar Ahmed 44 not out; Abdul Qadir five for 79, Abdul Raqeeb three for 59) and 164 (Feroze Najamuddin 67; Abdul Qadir nine for 82); Habib Bank 326 for four (Arshad Pervez 109, Agha Zahid 79, Azhar Khan 58 not out; Afzaal Ahmed three for 50) and 58 for no wkt. *Habib Bank 18 pts, Karachi 3 pts.*

At Lahore, October 22, 23, 24, 25. MCB won by 27 runs. MCB 282 for eight dec. (Qasim Omar 89, Azmat Rana 81, Babar Basharat 46) and 198 (Babar Basharat 60; Shahid Mahboob seven for 65); Allied Bank 243 (Shoaib Habib 54, Salman Qizalbash 53, Zafar Mehdi 44 not out; Ijaz Faqih six for 107) and 210 (Salim Yousuf 64; Ijaz Faqih five for 57). *MCB 18 pts, Allied Bank 5 pts.*

At Karachi, October 29, 30, 31, November 1. Drawn. PIA 370 for five dec. (Zaheer Abbas 125 retired, Rizwan-uz-Zaman 121, Zahid Ahmed 40 not out; Mohinder Kumar three for 95) and 267 for six dec. (Zaheer Abbas 101, Aftab Baloch 69); Karachi 302 for nine (Afzaal Ahmed 98, Umar Rashid 65, Zafar Ahmed 50; Rashid Khan four for 53, Iqbal Sikandar three for 128) and 273 for eight (Afzaal Ahmed 58, Umar Rashid 50, Zafar Ahmed 39; Rashid Khan five for 83). *PIA 7 pts, Karachi 5 pts.*

At Lahore, October 29, 30, 31, November 1. Drawn. MCB 356 for six dec. (Qasim Omar 210 not out, Tahir Naqqash 39) and 271 for five dec. (Qasim Omar 110, Asif Ali 67 not out; Mohsin Kamal three for 70); Lahore 297 for seven (Saleem Taj 85, Rameez Raja 84; Tahir Naqqash three for 68) and 161 for three (Majid J. Khan 76 not out, Tahir Shah 54). *MCB 6 pts, Lahore 6 pts.*

At Lahore, October 29, 30, 31. Allied Bank won by 81 runs. Allied Bank 98 for eight dec. (Mohammad Nazir four for 15) and 216 (Iqtidar Ali 66, Salman Qizalbash 52; Mohammad Nazir seven for 74); Railways 60 for nine dec. (Shahid Mahboob five for 30, Jalal-ud-Din four for 25) and 173 (Mohammad Nazir 39, Talat Mirza 36; Jalal-ud-Din six for 61). *Allied Bank 13 pts, Railways 2pts.*

At Karachi, November 4, 5, 6, 7. Drawn. United Bank 308 for seven (Sadiq Mohammad 110, Mudassar Nazar 81) and 257 for six dec. (Ashraf Ali 75 not out, Mudassar Nazar 54, Sikander Bakht 35 not out; Afzaal Butt four for 78); National Bank 261 for four (Saleem Pervez 74, Ali Zia 72 not out, Taslim Arif 46; Tauseef Ahmed three for 73) and 159 for three (Saleem Pervez 102 not out). *National Bank 6 pts, United Bank 5 pts.*

At Hyderabad, November 4, 5, 6, 7. Drawn. Habib Bank 250 for eight dec. (Salim Malik 103, Arshad Pervez 43; Zaigham Burki three for 55) and 307 for seven dec. (Salim Malik 107, Agha Zahid 51, Arshad Pervez 50); MCB 270 for four (Salah-ud-Din 100 not out, Babar Basharat 41; Abdul Qadir seven for 151) and 175 for four (Asif Ali 49, Salah-ud-Din 48 not out). *Habib Bank 6 pts, MCB 6 pts.*

At Lahore, November 4, 5, 6, 7. Drawn. Lahore 189 (Rameez Raja 48, Mohammad Naeem 38; Jalal-ud-Din six for 45) and 329 for eight dec. (Majid J. Khan 101, Parvez Mir 52, Rameez Raja 40; Amin Lakhani four for 44); Allied Bank 291 (Shahid Mahboob 110, Shoaib Habib 46, Salman Qizalbash 44, Iqtidar Ali 41; Sarfraz Nawaz four for 73) and 89 for two (Salman Qizalbash 45 not out). *Allied Bank 8 pts, Lahore 5 pts.*

At Lahore, November 4, 5, 6, 7. PIA won by four wickets. Railways 356 for seven (Saadat Ali 206 not out, Ejaz Ahmad 51; Rashid Khan four for 103) and 248 for nine dec. (Asad Rauf 84, Mohammad Nazir 48, Musleh-ud-Din 34; Iqbal Sikandar five for 91, Rizwan-uz-Zaman three for 26); PIA 265 for five (Rizwan-uz-Zaman 152, Shoaib Mohammad 69; Mohammad Nazir four for 74) and 341 for six (Rizwan-uz-Zaman 99, Shoaib Mohammad 69, Zaheer Abbas 57). *PIA 16 pts, Railways 5 pts.*

At Karachi, November 10, 11, 12, 13. National Bank won by eight wickets. Karachi 352 for seven dec. (Afzaal Ahmed 105, Umar Rasheed 61, Kamal Najamuddin 54, Zafar Ahmed 50 not out; Iqbal Qasim five for 133) and 294 for nine dec. (Feroze Najamuddin 100 not out, Mohiuddin Khan 51; Iqbal Qasim four for 101, Shafiq Ahmad three for 66); National Bank 339 (Mohammad Jamil 77 not out, Iqbal Qasim 58; Atiq-ur-Rehman five for 142) and 308 for two (Shafiq Ahmad 104 not out, Saleem Pervez 75, Ali Zia 56 not out, Taslim Arif 56). *National Bank 16 pts, Karachi 8 pts.*

At Bahawalpur, November 10, 11, 12, 13. United Bank won by seven wickets. Railways 135 (Naveed Anjam 43; Ehtesham-ud-Din six for 48, Sikander Bakht three for 58) and 373 (Abdul Sami 78, Naveed Anjam 54, Musleh-ud-Din 54, Saadat Ali 45; Tauseef Ahmed four for 69, Kurshid Akhtar four for 71); United Bank 347 for six (Farooq Shera 91, Sadiq Mohammad 65, Haroon Rashid 64 retired, Nasir Valika 56) and 162 for three (Mansoor Akhtar 76, Sadiq Mohammad 52). *United Bank 18 pts, Railways 2 pts.*

At Lahore, November 10, 11, 12, 13. Drawn. PIA 252 (Naeem Ahmad 63, Zaheer Abbas 57; Shahid Mahboob five for 95, Jalal-ud-Din three for 45) and 182 (Rizwan-uz-Zaman 45, Zahid Ahmad 39; Jalal-ud-Din four for 41, Azeem Hafeez four for 41); Allied Bank 175 (Zafar Mehdi 55 not out; Rashid Khan seven for 77) and 178 for seven (Iqtidar Ali 56, Zafar Mehdi 33; Rashid Khan three for 57). *PIA 8 pts, Allied Bank 5 pts.*

At Rawalpindi, November 11, 12. Habib Bank won by an innings and 60 runs. Habib Bank 276 for eight (Javed Miandad 96, Azhar Khan 50; Abdul Wahab three for 83, Raja Afaq three for 84); Rawalpindi 125 (Masood Anwar 29; Abdul Qadir nine for 49) and 91 (Abdul Qadir four for 27, Izhar Khan three for 15). *Habib Bank 18 pts, Rawalpindi 2 pts.*

At Karachi, November 16, 17, 18. National Bank won owing to MCB's refusal to appear following crowd disturbances on the third day. MCB 225 (Anwarul Haq 54, Qasim Omar 53; Iqbal Qasim six for 99, Wasim Raja four for 76) and 125 for nine (Wasim Raja six for 66, Iqbal Qasim three for 33); National Bank 273 (Taslim Arif 73, Shafiq Ahmad 51; Ilyas Khan seven for 90, Ijaz Faqih three for 90). *National Bank 18 pts, MCB 7 pts.*

At Karachi, November 16, 17, 18, 19. Drawn. Railways 239 (Munawar Javed 58, Naveed Anjam 46, Ejaz Ahmad 45; Mohinder Kumar four for 81, Tariq Nazar three for 34) and 329 (Asad Rauf 106, Munawar Javed 64, Naveed Anjam 47; Tanvir Ali five for 131, Tariq Nazar four for 97); Karachi 236 (Zafar Ahmed 42, Feroze Najamuddin 35; Mohammad Nazir six for 62) and 209 for five (Feroze Najamuddin 52, Sajid Ali 48, Afzaal Ahmed 40; Mohammad Nazir three for 67). *Railways 7 pts, Karachi 7 pts.*

At Karachi, November 22, 23, 24, 25. Drawn. Karachi 246 (Zafar Ahmed 72, Khalid Alvi 58; Ijaz Faqih six for 88) and 417 (Feroze Najamuddin 144, Zafar Ahmed 140; Ilyas Khan five for 88, Farrukh Zaman four for 80); MCB 334 for seven (Qasim Omar 174, Anwarul Haq 43, Ijaz Faqih 34; Tanvir Ali five for 118) and 207 for one (Qasim Omar 110 not out, Anwarul Haq 95). *MCB 8 pts, Karachi 5 pts.*

At Hyderabad, November 22, 23, 24, 25. Railways won by seven wickets. National Bank 257 (Taslim Arif 64, Shafiq Ahmad 43; Shahid Butt six for 110) and 213 (Shafiq Ahmad 79; Mohammad Nazir four for 52, Shahid Butt four for 81); Railways 279 (Naveed Anjam 53, Saadat Ali 40; Taslim Arif four for 46) and 195 for three (Saadat Ali 92 not out). *Railways 18 pts, National Bank 8 pts.*

At Lahore, November 22, 23, 24. United Bank won by seven wickets. Allied Bank 255 for eight dec. (Iqtidar Ali 86, Shahid Mahboob 58; Ehtesham-ud-Din three for 76) and 90 (Ehtesham-ud-Din seven for 43); United Bank 295 for nine (Siddiq Patni 60, Sadiq Mohammad 53, Nasir Valika 46, Ashraf Ali 46) and 52 for three. *United Bank 16 pts, Allied Bank 7 pts.*

At Rawalpindi, November 22, 23, 24, 25. PIA won by 108 runs. PIA 239 (Aftab Baloch 74, Shahid Mohammad 54; Khatib Rizwan six for 66) and 276 (Rizwan-uz-Zaman 142, Zahid Ahmad 30; Abdul Wahab seven for 74); Rawalpindi 220 (Qazi Khalid 67, Maqsood Kundi 34; Iqbal Sikandar six for 60) and 187 (Mohammad Riaz 39; Iqbal Sikandar six for 56). *PIA 17 pts, Rawalpindi 6 pts.*

At Lahore, November 28, 29, 30, December 1. Drawn. Lahore 248 for nine (Majid J. Khan 69, Parvez Mir 45; Raja Akbar five for 79, Iqbal Sikandar three for 80) and 275 for five (Aamer Malik 91, Mansoor Rana 62, Majid J. Khan 58); PIA 281 for seven (Aftab Baloch 73, Shoaib Mohammad 56; Sarfraz Nawaz four for 81). *PIA 7 pts, Lahore 5 pts.*

At Rawalpindi, November 28, 29, 30, December 1. Drawn. United Bank 318 for eight (Nasir Valika 95, Mahmood Rasheed 85, Farooq Shera 64; Abdul Wahab four for 104) and 313 for six (Sadiq Mohammad 157, Farooq Shera 50; Abdul Wahab four for 79); Rawalpindi 231 (Maqsood Kundi 59, Raja Afaq 47, Azmat Jalil 46; Shahid Aziz four for 40) and 92 for five (Shahid Gulraiz 43; Ehtesham-ud-Din four for 31). *United Bank 8 pts, Rawalpindi 5 pts.*

At Bahawalpur, December 4, 5, 6, 8. Drawn. Karachi 262 (Munir-ul-Haq 88 not out, Zafar Ahmed 30; Amin Lakhani five for 57) and 313 for four (Munir-ul-Haq 135 not out, Zafar Ahmed 73 not out, Afzaal Ahmed 41); Allied Bank 275 for eight (Talat Masood 89, Moin-ud-Din 61, Zafar Mehdi 42; Mohinder Kumar six for 70) and 124 for five (Iqtidar Ali 31; Tanvir Ali three for 29). *Allied Bank 8 pts, Karachi 6 pts.*

At Lahore, December 4, 5, 6, 8. Drawn. Railways 250 (Musleh-ud-Din 72, Saadat Ali 71; Raees Ahmad three for 56) and 242 for six (Adbul Sami 97 not out, Asad Rauf 62); Habib Bank 233 (Anwar Miandad 97, Agha Zahid 42; Musleh-ud-Din three for 67). *Railways 8 pts, Habib Bank 7 pts.*

At Lahore, December 4, 5, 6, 8. Drawn. Lahore 301 (Majid J. Khan 101, Rameez Raja 76, Mohammad Naeem 51; Sadiq Mohammad six for 84) and 285 for five (Majid J. Khan 128 not out, Aamer Malik 120); United Bank 294 for nine (Ashraf Ali 111 not out, Nasir Valika 38; Nasir Abbas three for 90, Ali Ahmad three for 100). *United Bank 8 pts, Lahore 7 pts.*

At Rawalpindi, December 11, 12, 13. Railways won by five wickets. Rawalpindi 268 (Azmat Jalil 62, Qazi Khalid 57, Masood Anwar 54, Shahid Gulraiz 42; Mohammad Nazir five for 90, Shahid Butt four for 103) and 56 (Musleh-ud-Din six for 23, Mohammad Nazir four for 12); Railways 278 (Abdul Sami 78; Raja Afaq six for 97, Abdul Wahab three for 77) and 48 for five (Khatib Rizwan three for 14). *Railways 18 pts, Rawalpindi 8 pts.*

At Lahore, December 11, 12, 13, 14. Drawn. National Bank 196 (Wasim Raja 66, Taslim Arif 35; Athar Khan three for 45, Ali Ahmad three for 52) and 154 for five (Shafiq Ahmad 56, Ali Zia 51); Lahore 273 (Ali Ahmad 61 not out, Mohammad Naeem 46; Jehanzeb Khan three for 45). *Lahore 8 pts, National Bank 5 pts.*

At Lahore, December 11, 12, 13, 14. Drawn. United Bank 278 for seven (Sadiq Mohammad 59, Mahmood Rashid 58, Mahmood Ahmad 48; Liaqat Ali four for 92) and 64 for one; Habib Bank 252 for five dec. (Sultan Rana 57 not out, Agha Zahid 47, Azhar Khan 44; Farooq Shera five for 87). *Habib Bank 6 pts, United Bank 5 pts.*

At Lahore, December 17, 18, 19, 20. Drawn. Habib Bank 348 for three (Tehsin Javed 100, Arshad Pervez 87, Agha Zahid 80, Azhar Khan 54 not out) and 82 for three dec.; National Bank 183 (Saleem Pervez 49, Taslim Arif 48; Abdul Raqeeb seven for 77, Abdul Qadir three for 79) and 428 for nine (Shafiq Ahmad 118, Saleem Pervez 92, Taslim Arif 69, Saleem Anwar 55; Abdul Qadir five for 125). *Habib Bank 8 pts, National Bank 2 pts.*

At Rawalpindi, December 17, 18, 19, 20. Rawalpindi won by ten wickets. Lahore 95 for eight dec. (Abdul Wahab five for 16, Raja Afaq three for 28) and 346 (Rameez Raja 108, Parvez Mir 90, Mansoor Rana 87, Athar Khan 73 not out; Abdul Wahab four for 84, Mohammad Sabir three for 121); Rawalpindi 220 (Masood Anwar 99, Raja Afaq 71; Parvez Mir six for 31, Ali Ahmad three for 50) and 223 for no wkt (Masood Anwar 108 not out, Azmat Jalil 107 not out). *Rawalpindi 14 pts, Lahore 4 pts.*

At Lahore, December 18, 19, 20, 21. Drawn. MCB 221 (Asif Ali 39; Rashid Khan five for 105, Naeem Ahmad four for 32) and 263 (Azmat Rana 89; Rashid Khan five for 117); PIA 317 for nine (Naeem Ahmad 61, Feroze Mehdi 55, Rizwan-uz-Zaman 52; Zaigham Burki four for 116) and 100 for seven (Aftab Baloch 30; Zaigham Burki five for 48). *PIA 8 pts, MCB 5 pts.*

At Lahore, December 23, 24, 25. Railways won by an innings and 21 runs. Railways 313 (Asad Rauf 92, Talat Mirza 61; Nasir Abbas five for 108); Lahore 138 (Mansoor Rana 50 not out; Shahid Butt five for 60, Mohammad Nazir four for 31) and 154 (Mansoor Rana 38; Shahid Butt seven for 60). *Railways 18 pts, Lahore 4 pts.*

At Lahore, December 23, 24, 25, 26. National Bank won by seven wickets. PIA 315 for four (Shoaib Mohammad 109 not out, Asif Mohammad 57, Zahid Ahmed 53 not out, Iqbal Sikandar 52) and 120 (Afzaal Butt nine for 41); National Bank 234 (Wasim Raja 55, Saleem Pervez 54, Mohammad Shafiq 41; Rashid Khan five for 105, Iqbal Sikandar three for 42) and 204 for three (Saleem Pervez 95, Shafiq Ahmad 55, Ali Zia 44 not out). *National Bank 14 pts, PIA 8 pts.*

At Bahawalpur, December 29, 30, 31. United Bank won by seven wickets. MCB 147 (Babar Basharat 70, Nadeem Yousuf 46; Sikander Bakht six for 38) and 123 (Azmat Rana 59; Tauseef Ahmed four for 30, Khurshid Akhtar three for 29); United Bank 176 (Sadiq Mohammad 58; Ilyas Khan six for 51) and 98 for three (Ashraf Ali 38 not out). *United Bank 15 pts, MCB 4 pts.*

At Multan, December 30, 31, January 1, 2. Rawalpindi won by seven wickets. Karachi 212 for eight dec. (Zafar Ahmed 60 not out, Umar Rasheed 58; Khatib Rizwan three for 30, Sabih Azhar three for 67) and 65 (Khatib Rizwan six for 19, Mohammad Sabir three for 11); Rawalpindi 137 for eight dec. (Masood Anwar 61; Mohinder Kumar six for 28) and 142 for three (Masood Anwar 70 not out, Sohail Kiani 56). *Rawalpindi 12 pts, Karachi 4 pts.*

At Lahore, December 30, 31, January 1, 2. National Bank won by eight wickets. Allied Bank 118 (Talat Masood 50; Afzaal Butt five for 44, Iqbal Qasim five for 48) and 127 (Farooq Rashid 38, Salim Yousuf 35; Iqbal Qasim five for 26, Afzaal Butt three for 64); National Bank 162 (Taslim Arif 49; Azeem Hafeez seven for 68) and 87 for two (Saleem Pervez 51 not out). *National Bank 14 pts, Allied Bank 4 pts.*

At Lahore, December 30, 31, January 1, 2. Drawn. Habib Bank 255 (Agha Zahid 82, Azhar Khan 76; Ali Ahmad five for 64); Lahore 340 (Parvez Mir 73, Aamer Malik 53, Khalid Niazi 45 not out, Mansoor Rana 45; Abdul Raqeeb eight for 80). *Lahore 8 pts, Habib Bank 8 pts.*

At Karachi, January 3, 4, 5, 6. United Bank won by three wickets. PIA 120 (Khurshid Akhtar six for 45) and 259 (Aftab Baloch 123 not out, Rizwan-uz-Zaman 58; Khurshid Akhtar five for 73); United Bank 243 (Mahmood Rashid 65, Siddiq Patni 60; Iqbal Sikandar three for 104) and 137 for seven (Nasir Valika 30; Rashid Khan four for 57). *United Bank 17 pts, PIA 4 pts.*

At Multan, January 4, 5, 6. Karachi won by ten wickets. Lahore 168 (Tariq Mansoor 36; Mohinder Kumar five for 53, Tanvir Ali three for 17) and 178 (Ali Ahmad 47, Tariq Mansoor 42; Mohinder Kumar seven for 73); Karachi 316 (Zafar Ahmed 100, Feroze Najamuddin 73, Mohiuddin Khan 44; Ali Ahmad five for 122) and 33 for no wkt. *Karachi 18 pts, Lahore 4 pts.*

At Rawalpindi January 4, 5, 6, 7. Drawn. Rawalpindi 288 (Sohail Kiani 103, Mohammad Riaz 56; Wasim Raja six for 106, Shafiq Ahmad three for 63) and 430 (Mohammad Riaz 134, Azmat Jalil 129; Wasim Raja five for 154); National Bank 427 (Shafiq Ahmad 112, Taslim Arif 111, Ali Zia 74; Khatib Rizwan five for 78, Mohammad Riaz five for 109) and 68 for two. *National Bank 8 pts, Rawalpindi 8 pts.*

PACO CUP, 1982-83

The pentangular tournament, sponsored by Pakistan Automobile Corporation, was played on a league basis, with the trophy decided on points. The five leading sides in the Quaid-e-Azam Trophy tournament qualify to compete for the PACO Cup.

	Played	Won	Drawn	Lost	Bonus Points Batting	Bonus Points Bowling	Total Points
Habib Bank	4	3	1	0	16	13	59
United Bank	4	2	1	1	12	11	43
Railways	4	1	2	1	13	11	34
National Bank	4	0	2	2	9	14	23
PIA	4	0	2	2	11	9	20

Note: First innings closed at 85 overs.

RAILWAYS v UNITED BANK

At LCCA Ground, Lahore, January 17, 18, 19, 20. Drawn. Railways 5 pts, United Bank 6 pts. Toss won by United Bank.

United Bank

Sadiq Mohammad c Talat b Shahid Butt	33	– c Shahid Butt b Nazir 19
Siddiq Patni st Zulqarnain b Nazir	18	– lbw b Naveed 4
Khalid Irtiza c Nazir b Shahid Butt	11	– b Shahid Butt 15
*Nasir Valika c Shahid Pervez b Shahid Butt	78	– not out 103
†Ashraf Ali c Shahid Pervez b Nazir	0	– b Shahid Butt 30
Mahmood Rashid c Sami b Shahid Pervez	23	– c Zulqarnain b Nazir 47
Kamal Merchant b Nazir	38	– c and b Shahid Butt 12
Sikander Bakht c Naveed b Shahid Butt	14	– c Musleh b Shahid Butt 29
Tauseef Ahmed not out	0	– not out 20
B 10, l-b 3, n-b 3	16	B 4, l-b 7, n-b 4 15

1/46 2/63 3/66 4/71   (8 wkts dec.) 231   1/5 2/44 3/44 4/89   (7 wkts dec.) 294
5/132 6/199 7/229 8/231   5/177 6/196 7/251

Khurshid Akhtar and Ehtesham-ud-Din did not bat.

Bowling: *First Innings*—Musleh 7–2–24–0; Naveed 3–1–13–0; Shahid Pervez 19–7–26–1; Nazir 35–7–86–3; Shahid Butt 19.4–2–66–4. *Second Innings*—Musleh 5–0–21–0; Naveed 4–1–9–1; Nazir 79–39–90–2; Shahid Butt 69–19–129–4; Sami 1–0–4–0; Asad 8–2–24–0; Saadat 2–0–2–0.

Railways

Abdul Sami c Ashraf b Khurshid	40	– c Ashraf b Ehtesham 27
Saadat Ali c Sadiq b Tauseef	39	– c Sadiq b Khurshid 47
Talat Mirza c Mahmood b Tauseef	3	– c Mahmood b Khurshid 22
Naveed Anjam c Khalid b Tauseef	11	– b Nasir b Khurshid 24
Asad Rauf c Khalid b Tauseef	14	– c Mahmood b Khurshid 47
Ejaz Ahmad c Kamal b Tauseef	61	– not out 41
Musleh-ud-Din c Ashraf b Khurshid	13	– (8) c Ashraf b Khurshid 1
Shahid Pervez c Khalid b Khurshid	3	– (9) c and b Kamal 2
*Mohammad Nazir b Ehtesham	31	– (7) c Sadiq b Khurshid 26
†Zulqarnain not out	4	– (11) not out 0
Shahid Butt (did not bat)	–	– (10) c Sikander b Khurshid 6
L-b 17, n-b 3	20	B 1, l-b 17, w 1, n-b 5 24

1/79 2/85 3/89 4/108   (9 wkts dec.) 239   1/35 2/90 3/126 4/160   (9 wkts) 267
5/117 6/140 7/148 8/212 9/239   5/215 6/249 7/253 8/258 9/267

Bowling: *First Innings*—Sikander 5–0–28–0; Khurshid 27–6–94–3; Tauseef 23.2–6–77–5; Ehtesham 10–1–20–1. *Second Innings*—Sikander 10–0–64–0; Ehtesham 10–2–37–1; Khurshid 21.4–3–101–7; Tauseef 3–0–10–0; Kamal 7–0–31–1.

Umpires: Amanullah Khan and Nasir Butt.

NATIONAL BANK v UNITED BANK

At Punjab University Ground, Lahore, January 22, 23, 24. United Bank won by nine wickets. United Bank 15 pts, National Bank 4 pts. Toss won by United Bank.

National Bank

†Taslim Arif b Ehtesham	0	– (2) lbw b Sikander	0
Saleem Pervez c Farooq b Sikander	3	– (1) st Ashraf b Tauseef	102
*Shafiq Ahmad c Ashraf b Tauseef	13	– b Sikander	0
Ali Zia lbw b Tauseef	40	– lbw b Tauseef	70
Mohammad Shafiq c Khalid b Ehtesham	4	– lbw b Sikander	5
Anwar Khan not out	3	– c sub b Tauseef	4
Afzno Butt lbw b Ehtesham	2	– b Tauseef	2
Jehanzeb Khan b Tauseef	2	– (9) c Sikander b Tauseef	7
Iqbal Butt c Mahmood b Tauseef	0	– (8) st Ashraf b Tauseef	6
Irshadullah (did not bat)		– not out	0
Wasim Raja (did not bat)		– absent	
B 1, l-b 1, n-b 5	7	B 5, l-b 15, w 1, n-b 7	28

1/4 2/7 3/40 4/66   (8 wkts dec.) 74   1/15 2/15 3/179 4/188   224
5/66 6/71 7/74 8/74   5/197 6/202 7/204 8/218 9/224

Bowling: *First Innings*—Sikander 8–5–9–1; Ehtesham 14–0–39–3; Khurshid 1–0–1–0; Tauseef 7.4–2–18–4. *Second Innings*—Sikander 19–3–77–3; Ehtesham 3–0–22–0; Farooq 3–0–25–0; Tauseef 20.1–3–49–6; Khurshid 7–0–23–0.

United Bank

Sadiq Mohammad lbw b Jehanzeb	31	– not out	29
Siddiq Patni c Wasim b Jehanzeb	27	– c Iqbal b Jehanzeb	0
Khalid Irtiza c Taslim b Jehanzeb	15	– not out	18
*Nasir Valika c Taslim b Afzal	15		
Tauseef Ahmed b Afzaal	1		
Farooq Shera c Taslim b Afzaal	46		
Mahmood Rashid c sub b Jehanzeb	1		
†Ashraf Ali not out	61		
Sikander Bakht run out	18		
Ehtesham-ud-Din b Afzaal	3		
Khurshid Akhtar run out	3		
B 1, l-b 7, w 7, n-b 13	28	B 1, w 2, n-b 1	4

1/62 2/71 3/97 4/99   249   1/7   (1 wkt) 51
5/115 6/123 7/193 8/238 9/246

Bowling: *First Innings*—Afzaal 29–6–70–4; Jehanzeb 26.4–4–95–4; Anwar 5–1–21–0; Iqbal 10–3–34–0; Irshadullah 1–0–1–0. *Second Innings*—Afzaal 5–0–17–0; Jehanzeb 5–1–25–1; Ali Zia 0.2–0–5–0.

Umpires: Shakoor Rana and Nasir Butt.

RAILWAYS v PIA

At LCCA Ground, Lahore, January 22, 23, 24, 25. Railways won by eight wickets. Railways 16 pts, PIA 5 pts. Toss won by PIA.

PIA

Rizwan-uz-Zaman st Zulqarnain b Shahid	37	– c Shahid b Nazir 41
Feroze Mehdi b Nazir	24	– lbw b Shahid 4
Asif Mohammad c and b Shahid	37	– (8) not out 31
Shahid Mohammad c Zulqarnain b Shahid	3	– (9) lbw b Nazir 7
Aftab Baloch c and b Shahid	54	– c Sami b Shahid 27
Zahid Ahmad not out	27	– c Ejaz b Shahid 6
*Naeem Ahmad c Nazir b Shahid	1	– c Zulqarnain b Nazir 25
†Anil Dalpat c Sami b Nazir	5	– (3) c Zulqarnain b Shahid 6
Rashid Khan c Munawwar b Shahid	11	– (10) c Zulqarnain b Shahid 1
Hasan Jamil not out	2	– (4) st Zulqarnain b Shahid 93
Raja Akbar (did not bat)		– c Munawwar b Nazir 11
B 4, l-b 4	8	B 4, l-b 4, n-b 1 9

1/59 2/75 3/79 4/138   (8 wkts) 209   1/10 2/26 3/125 4/163   261
5/185 6/186 7/188 8/199   5/179 6/188 7/230 8/244 9/245

Bowling: *First Innings*—Musleh 5–0–22–0; Naveed 5–0–10–0; Nazir 38–10–79–2; Shahid 37–10–90–6. *Second Innings*—Musleh 2–0–2–0; Naveed 2–1–1–0; Nazir 62.2–28–112–4; Shahid 55–17–127–6; Saadat 6–1–10–0.

Railways

Abdul Sami lbw b Rashid	0	– c Feroze b Akbar 4
Saadat Ali c Rizwan b Naeem	170	– lbw b Zahid 18
Talat Mirza b Naeem	20	– not out 15
Naveed Anjam c Anil b Zahid	81	– not out 26
Asad Rauf b Zahid	4	
Ejaz Ahmad c Anil b Zahid	10	
Munawwar Javed c Anil b Rizwan	24	
*Mohammad Nazir b Rizwan	31	
Musleh-ud-Din b Zahid	12	
Shahid Butt not out	24	
†Zulqarnain not out	0	
L-b 15, w 1, n-b 8	24	B 4, l-b 2, n-b 3 9

1/0 2/47 3/222 4/244   (9 wkts) 400   1/10 2/39   (2 wkts) 72
5/278 6/308 7/335 8/364 9/376

Bowling: *First Innings*—Rashid 9–2–45–1; Hasan 3–1–9–0; Naeem 17–1–73–2; Aftab 23–0–101–0; Akbar 3–1–11–0; Zahid 23–1–114–4; Rizwan 7–2–23–2. *Second Innings*—Rashid 6–2–14–0; Akbar 7–1–15–1; Zahid 2.5–1–30–1; Rizwan 1–0–4–0.

Umpires: Amanullah Khan and Shakeel Khan.

PIA v NATIONAL BANK

At National Stadium, Karachi, February 20, 21, 22. Toss won by National Bank. Owing to riot and curfew in Karachi, the match was abandoned at lunchtime on the third day, and was replayed in Lahore on March 27, 28, 29, 30.

National Bank

Taslim Arif c Anil b Rashid	14		
Saleem Pervez c Feroze b Rashid	6	– (1) lbw b Rashid	0
†Mohammad Jamil lbw b Rashid	11	– (2) c Asif b Naeem	13
Ali Zia st Anil b Iqbal	83	– not out	2
Wasim Raja c Rashid b Akbar	17		
Ijaz Ahmad c Iqbal b Rizwan	74	– (3) not out	59
Saleem Anwar c Rashid b Iqbal	5		
Anwar Khan run out	19		
*Iqbal Qasim not out	20		
Afzaal Butt b Iqbal	3		
Jehanzeb Khan c Akbar b Iqbal	0		
B 4, l-b 5, n-b 5	14	B 5, l-b 1	6

1/12 2/22 3/53 4/86   266   1/0 2/72   (2 wkts) 80
5/161 6/170 7/231 8/256 9/264

Bowling: *First Innings*—Rashid 22–4–86–3; Akbar 16–1–48–1; Naeem 3–0–6–0; Aftab 10–2–31–0; Iqbal 23.4–7–63–4; Rizwan 10–1–18–1. *Second Innings*—Rashid 5–0–38–1; Akbar 7–2–21–0; Iqbal 4–1–10–0; Naeem 2–1–5–1.

PIA

Rizwan-uz-Zaman b Qasim	39	†Anil Dalpat c Jamil b Raja	49
Shoaib Mohammad c Anwar b Afzaal	9	Rashid Khan lbw b Raja	0
Asif Mohammad c Taslim b Afzaal	16	Raja Akbar not out	0
Feroze Mehdi c Taslim b Jehanzeb	32	B 6, l-b 3, n-b 8	17
Aftab Baloch c Taslim b Jehanzeb	40		
*Naeem Ahmad not out	84	1/24 2/66 3/79	(9 wkts) 292
Zahid Ahmad c Qasim b Jehanzeb	0	4/142 5/158 6/162	
Iqbal Sikandar lbw b Qasim	6	7/180 8/282 9/282	

Bowling: Afzaal 17–2–80–2; Jehanzeb 18–5–36–3; Anwar 17–4–55–0; Qasim 23–3–67–2; Ijaz 1–0–4–0; Raja 9–1–33–2.

Umpires: Shakeel Khan and Feroze Butt.

HABIB BANK v RAILWAYS

At Gaddafi Stadium, Lahore, February 20, 21, 22. Habib Bank won by 184 runs. Habib Bank 18 pts, Railways 8 pts. Toss won by Habib Bank.

Habib Bank

Mohsin Khan c Saadat b Naveed	15	– (6) not out	101
Agha Zahid c Zulqarnain b Shahid Butt	102	– (1) c Musleh b Naveed	119
Salim Malik b Nazir	24	– (2) c Zulqarnain b Shahid Butt	14
*Javed Miandad b Shahid Butt	38		
Anwar Miandad c Zulqarnain b Saadat	40	– (7) not out	30
Sultan Rana c Zulqarnain b Saadat	19	– (3) st Zulqarnain b Shahid Butt	127
Azhar Khan st Zulqarnain b Saadat	16		
†Zaheer Ahmed c Naveed b Saadat	0		
Abdul Qadir c and b Shahid Butt	0		
Abdul Raqeeb c and b Shahid Butt	2	– (4) b Shahid Butt	3
Liaqat Ali not out	4	– (5) st Zulqarnain b Shahid Butt	8
B 4, l-b 4, n-b 4	12	B 3, l-b 8, n-b 3	14

1/40 2/104 3/179 4/199   272   1/20 2/271 3/276   (5 wkts dec.) 416
5/238 6/249 7/249 8/261 9/262   4/286 5/287

Bowling: *First Innings*—Musleh 10–0–32–0; Naveed 8–0–31–1; Shahid Butt 30–3–94–4; Nazir 24–3–78–1; Saadat 5–1–25–4. *Second Innings*—Naveed 5–2–17–1; Shahid Pervez 5–0–20–0; Sami 5–0–31–0; Shahid Butt 34–3–177–4; Saadat 19–1–99–0; Asad 11–0–58–0.

Railways

Saadat Ali st Zaheer b Raqeeb	107	– (2) c sub b Qadir 34
Abdul Sami c Zaheer b Mohsin	1	– (4) c sub b Qadir 2
Naveed Anjam c Anwar b Mohsin	8	– (1) c Qadir b Raqeeb 50
Asad Rauf c Sultan b Raqeeb	41	– (3) c Salim b Raqeeb 35
*Mohammad Nazir c Zaheer b Raqeeb	6	– (8) c Qadir b Anwar........ 50
Munawwar Javed st Zaheer b Qadir	30	– (5) c Salim b Raqeeb 15
Musleh-ud-Din st Zaheer b Raqeeb	0	– c Zaheer b Qadir 2
Shahid Pervez c sub b Qadir	25	– (6) lbw b Raqeeb 38
Shahid Butt c Sultan b Qadir	5	– c Javed Miandad b Raqeeb....... 0
†Zulqarnain c sub b Raqeeb	22	– (11) not out 5
Ejaz Ahmad not out	0	– (10) run out 2
B 14, l-b 8, n-b 1	23	L-b 3 3

1/38 2/54 3/146 4/152	268	1/69 2/103 3/121 4/123 236
5/167 6/167 7/211 8/219 9/268		5/157 6/176 7/178 8/178 9/221

Bowling: *First Innings*—Liaqat 7–5–10–0; Salim 6–4–6–0; Qadir 16–6–73–3; Raqeeb 14–5–74–5; Azhar 8–2–34–0; Mohsin 5–3–13–2; Anwar 3–1–10–0; Sultan 4–2–25–0. *Second Innings*—Liaqat 3–0–10–0; Javed Miandad 3–1–10–0; Qadir 20–1–108–3; Raqeeb 18–2–94–5; Anwar 1.1–0–11–1.

Umpires: Amanullah Khan and Mian Aslam.

HABIB BANK v PIA

At Gaddafi Stadium, Lahore, March 17, 18, 19, 20. Drawn. Habib Bank 6 pts, PIA 5 pts. Toss won by Habib Bank.

Habib Bank

Agha Zahid c Shoaib b Akbar	175	†Masood Iqbal not out 7
Arshad Pervez c Hasan b Akbar	79	
*Javed Miandad run out	53	B 6, l-b 13, w 2, n-b 2 23
Salim Malik c Shoaib b Akbar	48	
Sultan Rana not out	14	1/157 2/279 3/375 4/390 (4 wkts) 399

Anwar Miandad, Azhar Khan, Abdul Qadir, Abdul Raqeeb and Liaqat Ali did not bat.

Bowling: Rashid 21–0–119–0; Hasan 10–4–24–0; Akbar 25–3–101–3; Iqbal 16–2–65–0; Naeem 7–1–33–0; Aftab 6–0–34–0.

PIA

Shoaib Mohammad not out	101	Iqbal Sikandar st Masood b Raqeeb 20
Rizwan-uz-Zaman c Arshad b Raqeeb	41	
Feroze Mehdi c Sultan b Raqeeb	5	B 10, l-b 6, n-b 4 20
Hasan Jamil c Azhar b Raqeeb	30	
Aftab Baloch b Qadir	7	1/82 2/99 3/159 (6 wkts) 254
Zahid Ahmad c Javed b Raqeeb	30	4/172 5/228 6/254

*Naeem Ahmad, †Anil Dalpat, Rashid Khan and Raja Akbar did not bat.

Bowling: Liaqat 6–1–10–0; Salim 2–0–8–0; Qadir 36–6–108–1; Raqeeb 36–7–93–5; Javed 2–0–9–0; Azhar 3–0–6–0.

Umpires: Khizar Hayat and Mian Aslam.

NATIONAL BANK v RAILWAYS

At LCCA Ground, Lahore, March 17, 18, 19, 20. Drawn. National Bank 8 pts, Railways 5 pts. Toss won by National Bank.

National Bank

Afzaal Ahmad c and b Nazir	21	– c Nazir b Shahid Butt	29
Saleem Pervez b Nazir	49	– not out	45
Shafiq Ahmad b Nazir	92	– not out	6
Ali Zia c Zulqarnain b Saadat	52		
Mohammad Shafiq b Nazir	5		
Saleem Anwar c Musleh b Nazir	12		
Shahid Tanvir c Saadat b Nazir	15		
†Mohammad Jamil not out	5		
Anwar Khan c Ejaz b Nazir	0		
Afzaal Butt c Zulqarnain b Shahid Butt	1		
L-b 5, n-b 4	9	L-b 1	1

1/50 2/83 3/178 4/191   (9 wkts dec.) 261   1/10   (1 wkt) 81
5/220 6/249 7/258 8/258 9/261

*Iqbal Qasim did not bat.

Bowling: *First Innings*—Musleh 3–0–12–0; Naveed 2–0–25–0; Shahid Butt 27.2–2–106–1; Nazir 36–5–75–7; Saadat 10–0–34–1. *Second Innings*—Musleh 4–0–16–0; Naveed 3–0–23–0; Nazir 13–6–12–0; Shahid Butt 13–6–29–1.

Railways

Saadat Ali lbw b Anwar	22	Shahid Pervez lbw b Qasim	1
Abdul Sami st Jamil b Qasim	47	†Zulqarnain c Anwar b Qasim	0
Talat Mirza lbw b Qasim	24	Shahid Butt c Saleem Anwar b Qasim	1
Naveed Anjam c Shafiq b Qasim	35		
Ejaz Ahmed c Afzaal Butt b Qasim	15	B 5, l-b 3, w 7, n-b 4	19
Munawwar Javed lbw b Afzaal Butt	23		
*Mohammad Nazir b Afzaal Butt	13	1/42 2/81 3/118 4/136	212
Musleh-ud-Din not out	12	5/165 6/192 7/203 8/203 9/204	

Bowling: Afzaal Butt 23–5–64–2; Anwar 25–11–51–1; Qasim 25.2–7–78–7.

Umpires: Amanullah Khan and Javed Akhtar.

HABIB BANK v NATIONAL BANK

At Gaddafi Stadium, Lahore, March 22, 23, 24. Habib Bank won by eight wickets. Habib Bank 18 pts, National Bank 3 pts. Toss won by Habib Bank.

Habib Bank

Agha Zahid lbw b Qasim	41	– not out	40
Arshad Pervez c Shahid b Qasim	24	– run out	29
Salim Malik c and b Qasim	11	– st Jamil b Qasim	0
*Javed Miandad c Afzaal Butt b Anwar	115	– not out	9
Anwar Miandad c Ali Zia b Qasim	7		
Sultan Rana run out	110		
Azhar Khan not out	30		
†Zaheer Ahmed c Saleem Anwar b Qasim	27		
Abdul Qadir not out	5		
B 4, l-b 14, n-b 3	21		

1/73 2/84 3/89 4/103   (7 wkts) 391   1/62 2/63   (2 wkts) 78
5/316 6/331 7/382

Abdul Raqeeb and Liaqat Ali did not bat.

Bowling: *First Innings*—Afzaal Butt 20–5–72–0; Anwar 23–5–97–1; Qasim 28–3–115–5; Ali Zia 4–0–29–0; Shahid 10–0–57–0. *Second Innings*—Anwar 5–0–29–0; Ali Zia 5–0–26–0; Qasim 3–0–17–1; Shahid 2–0–6–0.

National Bank

Saleem Pervez c Azhar b Qadir	53	– (2) c Salim b Raqeeb	74
Afzaal Ahmad c and b Salim	6	– (1) lbw b Qadir	1
Shafiq Ahmad c Liaqat b Raqeeb	43	– lbw b Raqeeb	84
Mohammad Shafiq b Qadir	4	– (7) lbw b Qadir	32
Ali Zia c Arshad b Raqeeb	28	– (4) b Qadir	4
†Mohammad Jamil st Zaheer b Qadir	1	– c Liaqat b Qadir	43
Saleem Anwar c Azhar b Qadir	4	– (5) c Sultan b Qadir	2
Shahid Tanvir c Arshad b Raqeeb	14	– not out	22
Anwar Khan c Salim b Raqeeb	10	– lbw b Raqeeb	4
*Iqbal Qasim not out	0	– (11) c Azhar b Qadir	2
Afzaal Butt run out	1	– (10) c Zahid b Qadir	2
B 5, l-b 1, w 4, n-b 3	13	B 12, n-b 8	20

1/20 2/93 3/106 4/137   177   1/3 2/156 3/177 4/177   290
5/148 6/148 7/148 8/173 9/175   5/203 6/251 7/265 8/282 9/285

Bowling: *First Innings*—Liaqat 3–1–6–0; Salim 7–2–13–1; Qadir 24–5–89–4; Raqeeb 19.2–4–56–4. *Second Innings*—Liaqat 6–3–14–0; Salim 8–1–12–0; Qadir 31.3–5–91–7; Raqeeb 29–4–109–3; Azhar 3–0–6–0; Anwar 13–5–38–0.

Umpires: Javed Akhtar and Iftikhar Malik.

PIA v UNITED BANK

At LCCA Ground, Lahore, March 22, 23, 24, 25. United Bank won by eight wickets. United Bank 18 pts, PIA 4 pts. Toss won by United Bank.

PIA

Rizwan-uz-Zaman c Ashraf b Shahid	61	– c Nasir Shah b Shahid	69
Feroze Mehdi b Shahid	51	– lbw b Farooq	0
Shahid Mohammad not out	29	– b Shahid	29
*Hasan Jamil b Shahid	0	– (7) c Nasir Shah b Tauseef	25
Aftab Baloch c Haroon b Sikander	8	– c Mahmood b Tauseef	16
Iqbal Sikandar c Ashraf b Sikander	0	– (4) c Mansoor b Khurshid	4
Zahid Ahmad c Ashraf b Sikander	4	– (6) st Ashraf b Shahid	5
†Anil Dalpat c Mahmood b Tauseef	3	– lbw b Khurshid	14
Rashid Khan b Tauseef	19	– c Mansoor b Shahid	32
Kamran Rasheed st Ashraf b Shahid	5	– b Tauseef	2
Raja Akbar c Mansoor b Khurshid	0	– not out	1
B 2, l-b 3, w 4, n-b 6	15	B 11, l-b 4, w 1, n-b 3	19

1/116 2/117 3/117 4/135   195   1/11 2/69 3/83 4/128   216
5/135 6/144 7/153 8/182 9/190   5/134 6/137 7/175 8/181 9/202

Bowling: *First Innings*—Sikander 13–2–49–3; Farooq 4–2–7–0; Khurshid 16.2–7–25–1; Tauseef 27–7–61–2; Shahid 17–3–38–4. *Second Innings*—Sikander 9–2–15–0; Farooq 4–0–14–1; Shahid 26–4–87–4; Khurshid 15–1–46–2; Tauseef 20–3–35–3.

United Bank

Mansoor Akhtar lbw b Rashid	6	– c Anil b Iqbal	12
Nasir Shah c Anil b Rashid	17	– c Rashid b Aftab	32
*Haroon Rashid lbw b Rashid	29	– not out	61
Nasir Valika c Zahid b Rashid	6	– not out	30
Mahmood Rashid c Rizwan b Iqbal	21		
†Ashraf Ali c Shahid b Aftab	90		
Farooq Shera c Rashid b Iqbal	11		
Sikander Bakht run out	67		
Tauseef Ahmed b Aftab	7		
Shahid Aziz not out	1		
B 10, l-b 4	14	B 6, l-b 5, w 1	12

1/12 2/31 3/45 4/64   (9 wkts dec.) 269   1/24 2/56   (2 wkts) 147
5/82 6/102 7/249 8/268 9/269

Khurshid Akhtar did not bat.

Bowling: *First Innings*—Rashid 26–8–63–4; Hasan 2–0–10–0; Iqbal 24–7–68–2; Akbar 8–2–26–0; Zahid 14–4–30–0; Rizwan 3–1–22–0; Aftab 11–3–24–2; Kamran 2–0–12–0. *Second Innings*—Rashid 4–0–17–0; Akbar 2–0–10–0; Iqbal 10–1–38–1; Aftab 5–0–13–1; Rizwan 3.1–0–12–0; Zahid 5–0–18–0; Kamran 7–1–27–0.

Umpires: Shakoor Rana and Khizar Hayat.

NATIONAL BANK v PIA

At LCCA Ground, Lahore, March 27, 28, 29, 30. Drawn. National Bank 8 pts, PIA 6 pts. Toss won by National Bank.

National Bank

Saleem Pervez lbw b Rashid Khan	0	– c Naeem b Ameer	86
†Mohammad Jamil c and Rizwan	139	– c Shoaib b Ameer	4
Shafiq Ahmad c Anil b Aftab	70	– (4) c Rashid Khan b Naeem	60
Ali Zia run out	10	– (5) st Anil b Naeem	36
Ijaz Ahmad c Feroze b Shoaib	41	– (3) st Anil b Naeem	137
Shahid Tanvir c and b Rizwan	38	– b Rizwan	6
Mohammad Shafiq not out	34	– lbw b Ameer	54
Saleem Anwar lbw b Rizwan	18	– c Shahid b Naeem	1
*Iqbal Qasim not out	3		
Anwar Khan (did not bat)		– (9) not out	4
Afzaal Butt (did not bat)		– (10) not out	5
L-b 3, w 1, n-b 5	9	B 5, l-b 7, n-b 2	14

1/0 2/154 3/165 4/246　　　　　　　(7 wkts) 362　　1/20 2/176 3/274　　(8 wkts dec.) 407
5/296 6/311 7/341　　　　　　　　　　　　　　　　　4/303 5/312 6/361 7/365 8/401

Bowling: *First Innings*—Rashid Khan 7-0-43-1; Ameer 12-0-58-0; Iftikhar 10-0-53-0; Naeem 15-3-34-0; Aftab 15-1-54-1; Rizwan 15-0-55-3; Shoaib 11-1-56-1. *Second Innings* —Rashid Khan 6-0-42-0; Ameer 26-5-94-3; Iftikhar 15-0-72-0; Rizwan 18-2-49-1; Shoaib 9-0-38-0; Naeem 20-3-66-4; Aftab 9-1-21-0; Shahid 2-0-11-0.

PIA

Rizwan-uz-Zaman lbw b Afzaal	38	– c Jamil b Saleem Anwar	89
Shoaib Mohammad lbw b Qasim	24	– not out	33
Feroze Mehdi b Afzaal	1		
Rashid Israr lbw b Afzaal	4		
Aftab Baloch c Jamil b Qasim	59	– (4) not out	6
Shahid Mohammad c Saleem Pervez b Qasim	0		
*Naeem Ahmad b Qasim	16		
†Anil Dalpat c and b Ali Zia	50		
Rashid Khan b Ali Zia	53	– (3) b Qasim	25
S. M. Iftikhar not out	6		
Ameer Khan run out	1	– (5) st Ali Zia b Shahid	9
B 15, l-b 4, w 3, n-b 3	25	B 4, l-b 2, w 5, n-b 4	15

1/47 2/49 3/70 4/82　　　　　　　　277　　1/124 2/155 3/163　　(3 wkts) 177
5/82 6/162 7/189 8/263 9/276

Bowling: *First Innings*—Afzaal 20-2-69-3; Anwar 10-2-26-0; Qasim 26-1-111-4; Shahid 10-1-40-0; Ali Zia 2.5-0-6-2. *Second Innings*—Afzaal 9-2-37-0; Ali Zia 12-1-50-0; Qasim 9-2-18-1; Shahid 8-0-29-1; Saleem Anwar 5-0-21-1; Anwar 2-0-4-0; Jamil 1-0-3-0.

Umpires: Shakoor Rana and Iftikhar Malik.

HABIB BANK v UNITED BANK

At Gaddafi Stadium, Lahore, March 27, 28, 29, 30. Habib Bank won by 108 runs. Habib Bank 17 pts, United Bank 4 pts. Toss won by Habib Bank.

Habib Bank

Agha Zahid lbw b Sikander	75	– lbw b Ehtesham	0
Arshad Pervez b Ehtesham	17	– lbw b Sikander	22
Salim Malik c Mansoor b Tauseef	119	– lbw b Sikander	16
*Javed Miandad run out	41	– c Ashraf b Sikander	2
Sultan Rana not out	25	– c Mahmood b Sikander	15
Anwar Miandad run out	13	– c Ashraf b Sikander	10
Azhar Khan c and b Tauseef	0	– c Mahmood b Shahid	18
†Zaheer Ahmed c sub b Tauseef	4	– run out	11
Abdul Qadir lbw b Sikander	1	– b Tauseef	28
Abdul Raqeeb (did not bat)		– lbw b Tauseef	5
Liaqat Ali (did not bat)		– not out	3
B 2, l-b 4, w 2, n-b 2	10	B 1, l-b 3, w 1, n-b 16	21

1/21 2/171 3/258 4/259   (8 wkts dec.) 305   1/3 2/41 3/46 4/48   151
5/292 6/301 7/303 8/305   5/71 6/85 7/100 8/136 9/148

Bowling: *First Innings*—Sikander 20.4–3–96–2; Ehtesham 14–3–31–1; Shahid 32–6–101–0; Tauseef 17–0–67–3. *Second Innings*—Sikander 18–4–58–5; Ehtesham 15–2–37–1; Shahid 11–3–19–1; Tauseef 4–0–16–2.

United Bank

Siddiq Patni c Azhar b Qadir	4	– b Qadir	3
Nasir Shah c Javed b Qadir	34	– c Zaheer b Liaqat	12
Mansoor Akhtar st Zaheer b Qadir	25	– b Raqeeb	35
*Haroon Rashid c Azhar b Qadir	5	– st Zaheer b Raqeeb	24
Nasir Valika not out	70	– (6) c Saleem b Qadir	10
†Ashraf Ali c Zaheer b Raqeeb	32	– (7) lbw b Raqeeb	7
Mahmood Rashid b Raqeeb	22	– (8) not out	19
Sikander Bakht lbw b Qadir	1	– (9) c sub b Raqeeb	3
Tauseef Ahmed run out	5	– (5) lbw b Liaqat	2
Shahid Aziz c Azhar b Raqeeb	8	– c Azhar b Qadir	5
Ehtesham-ud-Din (did not bat)		– run out	0
B 8, l-b 1, n-b 6	15	B 1, l-b 2, w 2, n-b 2	7

1/19 2/64 3/78 4/83   (9 wkts dec.) 221   1/17 2/17 3/63 4/67   127
5/146 6/147 7/181 8/202 9/221   5/82 6/97 7/98 8/108 9/124

Bowling: *First Innings*—Liaqat 6–0–15–0; Salim 3–2–12–0; Qadir 38–11–91–5; Raqeeb 36–8–88–3. *Second Innings*—Liaqat 8–1–31–2; Qadir 24.1–6–60–3; Raqeeb 16–5–29–4.

Umpires: Shakeel Khan and B. K. Tahir.

A BLOW ON THE BOX

A protest group in Pakistan attempted unsuccessfully to have cricket banned from television, claiming that attendances at mosques fell away sharply when the Test series between Pakistan and India was being televised. A spokesman for the group, which petitioned the President, asserted that the media's main purpose should be "to implement and propagate Islam and not give mileage to a game more British than Asian".

CRICKET IN SRI LANKA, 1982-83

By GERRY VAIDYASEKERA

The name of the premier cricket tournament, the P. Saravaramuttu Trophy, instituted in 1950, was changed to the Lakspray Trophy, at the request of its sponsors. Bloomfield, last winners of the Saravaramuttu Trophy, became the first winners of the re-named competition, the championship being decided on a late protest by Bloomfield and a further scrutiny of points. After some years, the Tamil Union met with success and were declared runners-up. The Burgher Recreation Club, without a trophy for 25 years, won the Raheman-Hathy Trophy.

The highest team total in Trophy cricket was exceeded twice during the season. The Colombo Cricket Club, formed by European merchants in 1863 and now comprising mostly Lankans, registered 583 for seven declared against Saracens at Maitland Place. They scored 400 for four on the first day – another record in club cricket. The total was exceeded a few days later when Bloomfield thrashed the bowling of this same Colombo Cricket Club, at Bloomfield, to the tune of 602 for nine declared. To this latter total, Sunil Jayasinghe contributed 283 runs, the highest individual score in club cricket. He batted for ten hours, 26 minutes in the longest innings in all kinds of cricket in Lanka. A wicket-keeper-batsman, Jayasinghe toured England for the World Cup in 1979. He shared in a second-wicket partnership of 272 with S. Kaluperuma (124), a new Sri Lankan club record.

After nineteen seasons of club cricket, the tall left-arm spin bowler, Daya Sahabandu, captured his 1,000th wicket, his figures being: 241 matches, 6,430.2 overs, 1,805 maidens, 14,160 runs, 1,000 wickets, average 14.16. W. T. Greswell of Repton and Somerset fame, captured 1,016 wickets for 8.72 runs each between 1909 and 1923, although he was away from the island for three of these years, and Tommy Kelaart, a great Ceylon bowler between 1889 and 1905, also captured over 1,000 wickets.

A Cricket Secretariat and a Cricket Foundation were established under the guidance of Mr Gamini Dissanayaka, a senior cabinet minister and President of the Sri Lankan Board of Control. Its main duty is to lay out turf pitches in the main cities and supply cricket gear and implements to deserving clubs. Already a new stadium and turf pitch have been provided in the southern port of Galle.

SRI LANKA BOARD PRESIDENT'S XI v TAMIL NADU

M. J. Gopalan Trophy Match

At Colombo, January 22, 23, 24. Drawn. Sri Lanka retained the Gopalan Trophy by virtue of their first-innings lead of 192. Mendis batted 335 minutes for his 189, hitting one 6 and 22 4s.

Sri Lanka Board President's XI

M. D. Wettimuny c Vasan			J. R. Ratnayeke lbw b Arun	24
b Vasudevan.	26		S. Jeganathan b Santoshkumar	43
E. R. N. S. Fernando c Jabbar			A. L. F. de Mel not out	100
b Bharatkumar.	4		†R. G. de Alwis st Reddy b Jabbar	0
R. L. Dias b Bharatkumar	0		R. J. Ratnayeke b Santoshkumar	7
*L. R. D. Mendis c Sivaramakrishnan			B 3, l-b 3, n-b 1	7
b Bharatkumar.	189			
R. S. Madugalle b Bharatkumar	3		1/27 2/27 3/57 4/60	450
D. S. de Silva run out	47		5/209 6/272 7/307 8/430 9/431	

Bowling: Bharatkumar 21–3–106–4; Arun 15–0–71–1; Vasudevan 34–5–104–1; Santoshkumar 29.3–1–128–2; Jabbar 24–4–34–1.

Tamil Nadu

S. Sivaramakrishnan c Mendis b Jeganathan	74	– not out		58
C. S. Sureshkumar lbw b de Silva	20	– c and b Ratnayeke		2
N. P. Madhavan c de Silva b Ratnayeke	10			
A. Jabbar c Mendis b de Silva	2			
B. Arun c Jeganathan b Ratnayeke	21	– c Dias b Ratnayeke		5
P. Vijaykumar not out	61			
R. Vasan c Mendis b de Silva	8	– b Ratnayeke		0
S. Vasudevan b Jeganathan	8	– not out		4
*†A. Bharat Reddy c Wettimuny b de Mel	26			
K. Bharatkumar lbw b de Mel	6			
M. Santoshkumar b de Mel	0			
B 12, l-b 3, w 2, n-b 5	22	B 4, w 1, n-b 1		6
1/94 2/94 3/96 4/126	258	1/30 2/50 3/60	(3 wkts)	75
5/141 6/169 7/188 8/232 9/258				

Bowling: *First Innings*—de Mel 15.5–2–54–3; Ratnayake 18–3–53–1; Ratnayeke 10–4–25–1; de Silva 15–4–55–3; Jeganathan 21–9–49–2. *Second Innings*—de Mel 8–1–23–0; Ratnayake 11–2–18–2; Jeganathan 4–1–15–0; Ratnayeke 4–1–12–1; Wettimuny 1–0–1–0.

Umpires: H. Felsinger and E. Senewiratne.

ASIAN CRICKET CONFERENCE

The Asian Cricket Conference held its inaugural meeting in Delhi in September 1983, the founder members being Bangladesh, India, Malaysia, Pakistan, Singapore and Sri Lanka. N. K. P. Salve and A. W. Kanmadikar, President and Secretary respectively of the Board of Control for Cricket in India, were elected to fill the corresponding posts in the Conference for the first two years. The United Arab Emirates were admitted as associate members and asked to stage the first Asian Cup in Sharjah in April 1984.

CRICKET IN ZIMBABWE, 1982-83

By ALWYN PICHANICK

The national team of Sri Lanka visited Zimbabwe in November 1982 for a three-week tour, during which they played two four-day "Tests" and two one-day "Internationals" against Zimbabwe, together with three other one-day matches against other teams. In the one-day "International" series, each team won one match, while in the four-day series, the first match played was drawn but in the second Zimbabwe triumphed by an innings with a day and a half to spare. Zimbabwe's outstanding performers were Andy Pycroft with the bat and Peter Rawson with the ball. Pycroft scored a century and 81 in the first and 96 in the return encounter. Rawson bowled admirably in all matches played against the visitors, and Vincent Hogg returned an outstanding analysis in the second innings in Harare. Kevin Curran also shone as an all-rounder.

In December and January an official English international schoolboy team made a comprehensive and successful tour of the country. Included in their fixtures were two three-day "Internationals" against the Zimbabwe national school team. The visitors won the first game and the second was drawn.

Towards the end of the season, an Australian Under-25 Team played one four-day, one three-day and three one-day matches against Zimbabwe, as well as three other one-day matches. After being outclassed by the Australians in the four-day encounter at the commencement of the tour, Zimbabwe beat the Australians in the three-day game. The Australians were a strong combination, and provided the Zimbabwean players with an ideal preparation for the forthcoming Prudential World Cup in England. The highlights of the tour from the Zimbabwean point of view were the continued development of Rawson, who captured thirteen wickets during the three-day fixture which Zimbabwe won, and a magnificent innings by Duncan Fletcher during the one-day "International" played in Bulawayo. Ali Shah made an impressive début by scoring consistently in the one-day series. He also had the distinction of recording a maiden century in his second first-class game.

Fletcher again led Zimbabwe well, while David Houghton progressed both as a wicket-keeper and a batsman and John Traicos continued to bowl with great consistency.

SRI LANKA IN ZIMBABWE

†At Harare South, October 27. Sri Lankans won by seven wickets. Zimbabwe Country Districts 213 for nine (50 overs) (I. P. Butchart 66, R. D. Brown 65); Sri Lankans 214 for three (44 overs) (R. L. Dias 102*, L. R. D. Mendis 50).

†At Harare, October 30 (First one-day International). Sri Lanka won by three wickets. Zimbabwe 196 for six (50 overs) (K. M. Curran 59); Sri Lanka 197 for seven (45.5 overs) (L. R. D. Mendis 53).

†At Harare, October 31 (Second one-day International). Zimbabwe won by six wickets. Sri Lanka 161 (48.5 overs); Zimbabwe 162 for four (43 overs) (D. A. G. Fletcher 60 not out, A. J. Pycroft 50).

†At Mutare, November 3. Sri Lankans won by 166 runs. Sri Lankans 284 for six (50 overs) (L. R. D. Mendis 87); Zimbabwe Select XI 118 (38.4 overs).

ZIMBABWE v SRI LANKA

At Bulawayo, November 5, 6, 7, 8. Drawn.

Zimbabwe

†D. L. Houghton c Jeganathan b Ratnayake	45	– c Mendis b John 77
J. G. Heron lbw b John	3	– c de Alwis b de Mel 10
K. M. Curran b Jeganathan	96	– b de Silva 18
A. J. Pycroft c de Mel b Ratnayake	128	– c de Mel b John 81
C. Robertson c M. D. Wettimuny b de Silva	9	– lbw b Jeganathan 0
C. A. T. Hodgson b de Mel	40	– not out 7
I. P. Butchart c Madugalle b Ratnayake	15	– st de Alwis b Jeganathan .. 22
P. W. E. Rawson c M. D. Wettimuny b Jeganathan	1	
*A. J. Traicos not out	32	
E. J. Hough st de Alwis b Jeganathan	9	
V. R. Hogg lbw b Ratnayake	1	
B 5, l-b 16, w 1, n-b 15	37	L-b 1, w 1, n-b 4 6
	416	**(6 wkts dec.) 221**

1/9 2/94 3/238 4/267   1/23 2/53 3/190   (6 wkts dec.)
5/334 6/366 7/368 8/368 9/409   4/191 5/193 6/221

Bowling: *First Innings*—de Mel 20–6–59–1; John 20–5–60–1; Ratnayake 29–7–79–4; de Silva 29–3–109–1; Jeganathan 33–9–72–3. *Second Innings*—de Mel 4–0–29–1; John 8–1–29–2; Ratnayake 9–1–34–0; de Silva 9–2–75–1; Jeganathan 20.5–5–48–2.

Sri Lanka

S. Wettimuny lbw b Hogg	2	– c Houghton b Rawson 12
M. D. Wettimuny run out	55	– c and b Traicos 18
R. L. Dias c Houghton b Rawson	85	– not out 61
*L. R. D. Mendis b Rawson	42	– not out 25
R. S. Madugalle b Rawson	19	
S. Jeganathan st Houghton b Traicos	21	
D. S. de Silva c Houghton b Curran	11	
A. L. F. de Mel b Rawson	35	
†R. G. de Alwis b Rawson	40	
R. J. Ratnayake not out	2	
V. B. John b Rawson	1	
B 2, l-b 12, w 3, n-b 5	22	B 1, l-b 2, n-b 7 10
	335	**(2 wkts) 126**

1/10 2/127 3/163 4/203   1/33 2/39   (2 wkts)
5/226 6/246 7/246 8/324 9/331

Bowling: *First Innings*—Hogg 16–5–51–1; Hough 12–3–47–0; Rawson 27.5–5–82–6; Traicos 27–6–63–1; Curran 13–2–61–1; Butchart 5–2–9–0. *Second Innings*—Hogg 5–1–12–0; Hough 5–2–7–0; Rawson 9–3–11–1; Traicos 16–5–37–1; Curran 5–0–25–0; Butchart 3–0–21–0; Hodgson 1–0–3–0.

†At Triangle, November 10. Sri Lankans won by five wickets. Zimbabwe Select XI 165 for nine (50 overs); Sri Lankans 169 for five (46.3 overs).

ZIMBABWE v SRI LANKA

At Harare, November 12, 13, 14. Zimbabwe won by an innings and 40 runs.

Zimbabwe

†D. L. Houghton c M. D. Wettimuny	I. P. Butchart c de Silva b Jeganathan.. 0
b de Silva.. 50	P. W. E. Rawson not out.................. 63
J. G. Heron lbw b de Silva............... 72	A. J. Traicos c de Alwis b Ratnayake.. 2
K. M. Curran c sub b de Silva........... 26	V. R. Hogg b John..................... 0
A. J. Pycroft c M. D. Wettimuny b John.. 96	L-b 13, w 4, n-b 8.............. 25
*D. A. G. Fletcher c sub b de Silva.... 14	
C. A. T. Hodgson c Mendis	1/106 2/145 3/170 365
b Jeganathan.. 5	4/190 5/202 6/238
C. Robertson c and b Jeganathan 12	7/238 8/338 9/346

Bowling: John 10.3–2–42–2; Ratnayeke 4–2–26–0; Ratnayake 13–1–53–1; Jeganathan 42–10–74–3; de Silva 35–3–145–4.

Sri Lanka

S. Wettimuny lbw b Hogg................	5 – c Pycroft b Hogg....................	0
M. D. Wettimuny c Pycroft b Fletcher....	5 – c Robertson b Hogg.................	38
R. L. Dias c and b Fletcher.............	10 – c Hodgson b Rawson...............	18
A. Ranatunga c Houghton b Fletcher......	0 – (6) c Heron b Hogg.................	0
*L. R. D. Mendis c Houghton b Hogg......	14 – (4) c Hodgson b Hogg..............	67
S. Jeganathan b Curran.................	13 – (7) c Hodgson b Hogg..............	4
D. S. de Silva c Traicos b Rawson........	19 – (8) not out......................	37
†R. G. de Alwis c Fletcher b Curran......	4 – (9) c sub b Curran.................	3
J. R. Ratnayeke c Heron b Curran........	20 – (5) c Houghton b Hogg.............	0
R. J. Ratnayake c Fletcher b Curran......	12 – c Pycroft b Traicos...............	47
V. B. John not out.....................	2 – c Butchart b Curran...............	0
		B 1, l-b 5, n-b 1..............	7

1/6 2/20 3/20 4/34	104	1/0 2/22 3/117 4/121 221
5/34 6/58 7/62 8/90 9/102		5/121 6/130 7/133 8/141 9/221

Bowling: *First Innings*—Hogg 9–3–34–2; Fletcher 7–2–30–3; Traicos 1–1–0–0; Curran 7.2–1–24–4; Rawson 5–2–16–1. *Second Innings*—Hogg 15–4–26–6; Fletcher 8–5–17–0; Traicos 16–2–64–1; Curran 10.2–3–25–2; Rawson 25–7–57–1; Butchart 3–0–25–0.

YOUNG AUSTRALIA IN ZIMBABWE

†At Harare, March 30. Young Australia won by 121 runs. Zimbabwe 43 (R. J. McCurdy three for 4, K. H. MacLeay three for 10); Young Australia 164 (G. Shipperd 75 not out).

ZIMBABWE v YOUNG AUSTRALIA

At Harare, April 1, 2, 3, 4. Young Australia won by an innings and 55 runs.

Young Australia

R. B. Kerr c Butchart b Rawson 23	S. L. Saunders b Traicos................ 17
†W. B. Phillips c Fletcher b Traicos 58	R. J. McCurdy lbw b Traicos........... 1
G. Shipperd lbw b Rawson.............. 11	M. R. Whitney not out................. 2
*D. M. Wellham c Butchart b Rawson.... 0	Extras................................ 24
D. C. Boon st Houghton b Shah.........148	
G. M. Ritchie c Houghton b Rawson .. 69	1/36 2/60 3/62 408
K. H. MacLeay c Shah b Traicos........ 31	4/117 5/269 6/320
M. J. Bennett c Shah b Traicos.......... 24	7/374 8/394 9/395

Bowling: Hogg 26–11–48–1; Traicos 44.1–9–103–5; Rawson 41–11–92–3; Fletcher 15–5–34–0; Butchart 10–3–18–0; Curran 13–2–51–0; Shah 11–1–38–1.

Zimbabwe

J. G. Heron lbw b McCurdy	0	– b Whitney	2
A. Shah run out	42	– c Kerr b Whitney	55
R. D. Brown c Ritchie b Whitney	7	– b Saunders	22
A. J. Pycroft lbw b McCurdy	33	– c Kerr b Whitney	6
†D. L. Houghton c Ritchie b MacLeay	17	– c Shipperd b McCurdy	55
*D. A. G. Fletcher c Boon b Saunders	0	– b Whitney	1
K. M. Curran c Shipperd b McCurdy	4	– lbw b MacLeay	7
I. P. Butchart c MacLeay b McCurdy	1	– c sub b Bennett	7
P. W. E. Rawson c Phillips b Whitney	4	– lbw b Bennett	2
A. J. Traicos not out	23	– not out	4
V. R. Hogg c Kerr b Saunders	9	– b Whitney	10
Extras	24	Extras	19

1/0 2/22 3/77 4/110   164   1/6 2/48 3/77 4/96   190
5/117 6/121 7/121 8/126 9/138   5/100 6/119 7/139 8/153 9/177

Bowling: *First Innings*—McCurdy 19–6–40–4; Whitney 18–6–32–2; MacLeay 14–6–28–1; Saunders 17.4–6–30–2; Bennett 11–8–10–0. *Second Innings*—McCurdy 16–3–43–1; Whitney 23.4–11–29–5; MacLeay 20–10–18–1; Bennett 16–5–39–2; Saunders 18–4–42–1.

Umpires: A. Wilmot and I. Robinson.

†At Mutare, April 6. Young Australia won by 22 runs. Young Australia 236 for five (D. M. Jones 66, G. Shipperd 49); Zimbabwe 214 (G. A. Paterson 47, K. M. Curran 46).

†At Bulawayo, April 9. Zimbabwe won by 12 runs. Zimbabwe 234 for eight (D. A. G. Fletcher 79); Young Australia 222 for six (W. B. Phillips 75, D. C. Boon 65 not out).

†At Harare South, April 12. Young Australia won by 137 runs. Young Australia 242 for five (G. Shipperd 67, R. B. Kerr 58, D. C. Boon 53); Zimbabwe Country Districts 105 (M. Seager 31; P. A. Blizzard four for 7, M. J. Bennett four for 15).

ZIMBABWE v YOUNG AUSTRALIA

At Harare, April 14, 15, 16. Zimbabwe won by 93 runs.

Zimbabwe

A. Shah c Phillips b McCurdy	13	– (2) c Phillips b Bennett	105
R. D. Brown b McCurdy	2	– (1) b Whitney	3
J. G. Heron c and b McCurdy	10	– c Bennett b Whitney	16
A. J. Pycroft c Kerr b Bennett	6	– c Boon b McCurdy	35
†D. L. Houghton lbw b McCurdy	27	– c Phillips b Whitney	14
*D. A. G. Fletcher b Whitney	44	– b McCurdy	56
C. A. P. Hodgson c Haysman b MacLeay	9	– c Boon b Bennett	5
I. P. Butchart c Haysman b Whitney	1	– (9) not out	48
P. W. E. Rawson c Bennett b MacLeay	1	– (10) lbw b McCurdy	2
A. J. Traicos not out	4	– (8) c MacLeay b McCurdy	0
V. R. Hogg c Bennett b MacLeay	0	– not out	5
Extras	10	Extras	19

1/6 2/25 3/35 4/52   127   1/3 2/33 3/128   (9 wkts dec.) 308
5/75 6/107 7/108 8/123 9/123   4/160 5/239 6/247 7/251 8/252 9/275

Bowling: *First Innings*—Whitney 17–4–39–2; McCurdy 13–4–37–4; Bennett 6–4–14–1; MacLeay 14.1–6–27–3. *Second Innings*—McCurdy 23–4–75–4; Whitney 23–5–62–3; MacLeay 21–6–68–0; Bennett 20–7–50–2; Saunders 7–0–34–0.

Young Australia

R. B. Kerr c Houghton b Rawson	2	– (2) c Hodgson b Rawson	12
G. Shipperd c Houghton b Rawson	16	– (3) lbw b Rawson	5
*D. M. Wellham c and b Rawson	8	– (4) c Fletcher b Traicos	16
D. C. Boon lbw b Traicos	18	– (5) c Houghton b Fletcher	108
M. D. Haysman c Traicos b Rawson	8	– (6) c Brown b Rawson	4
†W. B. Phillips b Rawson	20	– (1) c Hodgson b Rawson	4
K. H. MacLeay c Fletcher b Traicos	1	– c Pycroft b Traicos	4
M. J. Bennett c Traicos b Rawson	21	– lbw b Rawson	35
S. L. Saunders c Heron b Traicos	1	– not out	17
R. J. McCurdy not out	20	– c Houghton b Rawson	0
M. R. Whitney c Pycroft b Rawson	2	– b Traicos	1
Extras	9	Extras	10

1/17 2/20 3/29 4/39   126   1/8 2/17 3/24 4/50   216
5/73 6/75 7/84 8/85 9/118   5/61 6/70 7/195 8/197 9/197

Bowling: *First Innings*—Hogg 13–5–26–0; Rawson 18.3–5–55–7; Traicos 11–5–22–3; Butchart 5–1–14–0. *Second Innings*—Hogg 14–2–34–0; Rawson 28–5–88–6; Traicos 21.5–5–44–3; Fletcher 10–2–21–1; Shah 5–1–16–0; Butchart 1–0–3–0.

Umpires: A. Wilmot and K. Kanjee.

†At Harare, April 17. Young Australia won by six wickets. Zimbabwe 242 for seven (J. G. Heron 82, A. Shah 68; K. H. MacLeay four for 53); Young Australia 246 for four (W. B. Phillips 135).

CRICKET IN JAPAN

The cameras of three television channels, together with several newspaper reporters, were present when, after lapsing for eighteen years, the "Interport" fixture between the Kobe Regatta and Athletic Club and the Yokohama Country and Athletic Club was revived. Professor Makoto Yamada of Kobe University, who has done much in recent years to stimulate an interest in cricket among his students, preceded the game by attempting to explain it to quite an eager Japanese public.

CRICKET IN CANADA

By KENNETH R. BULLOCK

After a year such as 1982, in which Canada and other Associate Members of ICC played for the ICC Trophy in England, there is usually a let-down in activities. However, it is encouraging to report that in 1983 the Canadian Cricket Association carried out a programme that gave every support to younger cricketers. A particular effort was made by the selection committee to reduce the average age of the national side.

Holland were hosts, for the second time, to the fifth International Youth Festival. Again, the participants were Bermuda, Canada, Denmark, England North, England South, Holland and Ireland. The tournament was won by Denmark, who lost only one match in the round-robin and defeated Holland in the play-off championship match. Bermuda, as in 1981, finished last, with the rest being evenly matched. Canada won two and lost four matches, but came close to winning at least two more.

Vancouver played host to the fifteenth National Senior Tournament from July 23 to 29. The weather was excellent, and all seven provinces participated, with Alberta the defending champions from 1981. Ontario won the tournament with five victories and a draw in their one rained-out match against Alberta, the runners-up. O. Dipchand of Manitoba was the leading scorer with 308 runs and C. Nibbs of Ontario took the bowling honours with thirteen wickets. Gary Smee of British Columbia won the fielding award.

The John Ross Robertson Trophy for club sides continued in the same format as in the past few years, in which Western Canada and Eastern Canada declare champions. This year the Sportsmen Cricket Club of Edmonton won the Western Canada play-off and Defence Cricket Club of Ottawa won the Eastern play-off.

Coaching and umpiring received continued support by national committees. In particular, the number of certified umpires rose to over 200 in 1983. The Canadian Cricket Association held its semi-annual meeting in Toronto and its Annual General Meeting in Montreal. Mr Jack Kyle was re-elected President for a sixth year. 1983 also marked the return of competition for the K. Auty Trophy between the United States and Canada after a lapse of two years. It was successfully played in Los Angeles on September 3 and 4, Canada winning by an innings and 28 runs.

Plans for 1984 include a tour to Jamaica by a national senior side, an Under-18 tournament in Ontario, and an Under-25 tournament also in Ontario. Cricket continues to grow in Canada, there being 248 teams in competition, 137 of them in Ontario.

USA v CANADA

At Woodley Park, Los Angeles. September 3, 4. Canada won the 62nd match between the two countries by an innings and 28 runs. USA won the toss and batted on a well-prepared, green-topped turf wicket. This may have been their downfall, Abraham of

Saskatchewan and B. Singh of Ontario quickly capturing four wickets for only 17 runs. By lunch seven wickets were down and an hour afterwards USA were all out. After Canada had made a shaky start, Prashad and Dipchand rallied them with a stand of 82. Dipchand then provided Lance Gibbs of West Indian fame with the first of his two wickets. The day ended with Canada 244 for seven. USA eventually needed 171 to force Canada to bat a second time. Again the openers failed and three early wickets were lost, with Oscar Durity, formerly of Trinidad, getting his second duck of the match. For Canada B. Singh took his match figures to seven for 55. The match was a victory for youth, Canada's team having an average age of only 25.

USA

N. Lashkari c Naicken b Abraham	13	– c Kirmani b Hakim 16
J. Reid lbw b Abraham	7	– c Naicken b B. Singh 16
†H. Mirza c Naicken b B. Singh	1	– (7) lbw b B. Singh 15
*O. Durity c Bhudoo b B. Singh	0	– (3) b B. Singh 0
K. Venkersammy b B. Singh	2	– (6) c Prashad b D. Singh 39
K. Khan c Prashad b Melaram	26	– (5) lbw b Melaram 25
S. Shivnarine b Abraham	0	– (4) b B. Singh 7
A. Jaleel c and b Hakim	2	– (11) not out 0
H. Khan c Kirmani b Hakim	20	– (9) b Prashad 2
R. Menon c Abraham b Hakim	20	– (8) c Hakim b D. Singh 3
L. R. Gibbs not out	8	– (10) b D. Singh 4
Extras	9	Extras......................... 16

1/14 2/15 3/15 4/17   108   1/25 2/27 3/36 4/63   143
5/33 6/33 7/57 8/73 9/85   5/73 6/109 7/129 8/136 9/140

Bowling: *First Innings*—Abraham 20–6–26–3; B. Singh 12–5–14–3; Melaram 10–3–29–1; Hakim 13.5–4–26–3; Prashad 1–0–4–0. *Second Innings*—Abraham 15–8–21–0; B. Singh 18–4–41–4; Hakim 15–3–24–1; Melaram 8–3–25–1; D. Singh 5.5–2–11–3; Prashad 3–0–5–1.

Canada

G. Smee c Durity b H. Khan	2	B. Melaram lbw b Menon 23
O. Dipchand c sub b Gibbs	59	†S. Naicken b Menon 12
*F. Kirmani c Mirza b Menon	3	A. Hakim not out............................ 2
G. Budhoo lbw b K. Khan	0	Extras............................ 30
M. Prashad c Reid b Gibbs	73	
D. Singh b K. Khan	1	1/10 2/20 3/27 279
B. Singh c H. Khan b K. Khan	25	4/109 5/114 6/154
D. Abraham c Reid b Menon	49	7/185 8/252 9/271

Bowling: H. Khan 15–6–29–1; Menon 18.5–4–49–4; K. Khan 16–2–49–3; Gibbs 22–2–71–2; Shivnarine 13–2–32–0; Durity 2–0–9–0; Venkersammy 1–0–10–0.

WOMEN'S CRICKET, 1983

By NETTA RHEINBERG

It is not possible to present a cheerful overall picture of the state of affairs in women's cricket in 1983, though there is perhaps some consolation in the fact that many of the smaller sports associations are also suffering from similar symptoms. Nevertheless, despite the difficulties, women cricketers soldier on in the hope that better times will come and encouraged by knowing that the game for women is flourishing in other parts of the world.

Dwindling membership, too few volunteers for secretarial and committee work, lack of financial support in the way of sponsorship, and a dearth of leadership are the main problems. In days gone by, schoolgirls and young women had the choice of two summer games, tennis or cricket, and cricket, then a novelty, presented a challenge which was immensely popular. Great and sustained efforts were made to achieve the recognition of cricket as a normal activity for women and many battles were fought and won against strong opposition. That recognition has come about and the Women's Cricket Association is now a universally recognised and established body under whose authority hundreds of girls and women are given the opportunity to enjoy the game. Familiarity, however, breeds contempt and the choice of sports now open to women has widened considerably, with emphasis on individual activities such as athletics and swimming. It is therefore vital that young women are encouraged to play cricket and given the right coaching facilities. The game, however, is not included in the syllabus in the majority of physical education colleges, and only a fraction of secondary schools provide the chance to play it. But the news is not all gloomy. Although the editor of the WCA Bulletin, a useful house magazine, has tendered her resignation after seven years of hard work, a replacement has already volunteered to continue a long run of editorial work, started by Marjorie Pollard with *Women's Cricket* in 1930.

Proof that the Women's Cricket Association is a force to be contended with came in February with the sudden cancellation, less than a week before departure, of a representative tour to West Indies, a decision made by the Caribbean Women's Cricket Federation for political reasons. The tour was cancelled when it became known that five members of the English team had visited South Africa on a private tour four years previously.

This considerable disappointment had its effect on the 1983 season, which started with an unusually wet spring. Nevertheless the subsequent sunshine allowed a good deal of cricket to be played and resulted in an enjoyable domestic season. Twelve teams attended the annual Cricket Week at Colwall, Worcestershire, which took place under cloudless skies. Five of the County Associations – Kent, Lancashire, Middlesex, Nottinghamshire and Surrey – celebrated their Golden Jubilees, all in their different ways, at the end of the season. All were founded in 1933, at the height of the women's cricket boom, when any county having three active clubs in its area was permitted to form its own Association.

The search for sponsorship, not only for tour purposes but also to sustain the valuable junior programme, continues unabated and there are grounds for hope, modest though the sums expected may be. The Co-operative Insurance

Society, who sponsored the juniors, has opted out, but the Lord's Taverners have replaced them with a generous donation.

The much overdue invitation to New Zealand for a tour of this country is in the last stages of ratification. In the absence of a major sponsor, hospitality will be for the most part private, and each area staging a match will administer its own, helped by whatever local sponsorship can be obtained. The England team will not be selected until the spring. Should Jan Southgate be re-appointed captain, it will help soften the blow of the cancelled West Indies tour and give her the much needed chance to show her capabilities.

An invitation was received from Australia for a tour of that country in 1983-84, to mark the celebration of the Golden Jubilee of the Australian Women's Cricket Council. Women's cricket in the Antipodes is currently on the crest of a wave and enjoying excellent administration. The tour was to include five four-day Tests at Perth, Adelaide, Brisbane, Sydney and Melbourne, as well as two one-day internationals, and a two-day match against each state, including Tasmania.

ANOTHER BASTION FALLS

Women are to be admitted as full members of the Melbourne Cricket Club. A postal ballot of the 19,800 present members resulted in a 2-1 majority in favour of female admission. With a waiting list already in excess of 50,000, it has been calculated that the first woman is unlikely to become a member for 26 years, without the introduction of some form of associate membership.

BIRTHS AND DEATHS OF CRICKETERS

The qualifications are as follows:

1. All players who have appeared in a Test match.

2. Players who have appeared in 50 or more first-class matches during their career and, if dead, were still living ten years ago.

3. Players who appeared in fifteen or more first-class matches in the 1983 English season.

4. English county captains, county caps and captains of Oxford and Cambridge Universities who, if dead, were still living ten years ago.

5. Oxford and Cambridge Blues of the last ten years. Earlier Blues may be found in previous *Wisdens*.

6. All players chosen as *Wisden* Cricketers of the Year, including the Public Schoolboys chosen for the 1918 and 1919 Almanacks. Cricketers of the Year are identified by the italic notation *CY* and year of appearance.

7. Players or personalities not otherwise qualified who are thought to be of sufficient interest to merit inclusion.

Although the country is given for most overseas players, it is omitted for England Test cricketers. There is a full list of Test Cricketers from page 83.

Aamer Hameed (Oxford U.) b Oct. 18, 1954

Abberley, R. N. (Warw.) b April 22, 1944

A'Beckett, E. L. (Australia) b Aug. 11, 1907

Abdul Kadir (Pakistan) b May 5, 1944

Abdul Qadir Khan (Pakistan) b Sept. 15, 1955

Abel, R. (Surrey; *CY 1890*) b Nov. 30, 1857, d Dec. 10, 1936

Abell, Sir G. E. B. (Oxford U., Worcs. and N. India) b June 22, 1904

Aberdare, 3rd Lord (*see* Bruce, Hon. C. N.)

Abid Ali, S. (India) b Sept. 9, 1941

Abrahams, J. (Lancs.) b July 21, 1952

Absolom, C. A. (Camb. U. and Kent) b June 7, 1846, d July 30, 1889

Acfield D. L. (Camb. U. and Essex) b July 24, 1947

Achong, E. (W. Indies) b Feb. 16, 1904

Ackerman, H. M. (Border, NE Transvaal, Northants, Natal and W. Province) b April 28, 1947

A'Court, D. G. (Glos.) b July 27, 1937

Adam, Sir Ronald, 2nd Bt (Pres. MCC 1946-47) b Oct. 30, 1885, d Dec. 26, 1982

Adams, P. W. (Cheltenham and Sussex; *CY 1919*) b 1900, d Feb. 28, 1962

Adcock, N. A. T. (S. Africa; *CY 1961*) b March 8, 1931

Adhikari, Col. H. R. (India) b July 31, 1919

Afaq Hussain (Pakistan) b Dec. 31, 1939

Aftab Baloch (Pakistan) b April 1, 1953

Aftab Gul (Pakistan) b March 31, 1946

Agha Saadat Ali (Pakistan) b June 21, 1929

Agha Zahid (Pakistan) b Jan. 7, 1953

Agnew, J. P. (Leics.) b April 4, 1960

Ainsworth, Lt-Cdr M. L. Y. (Worcs.) b May 13, 1922, d Aug. 28, 1978

Aird, R. (Camb. U. and Hants; Sec. MCC 1953-62, Pres. MCC 1968-69) b May 4, 1902

Aitchison, Rev. J. K. (Scotland) b May 26, 1920

Alabaster, G. D. (Canterbury, N. Districts and Otago) b Dec. 10, 1933

Alabaster, J. C. (N. Zealand) b July 11, 1930

Alcock, C. W. (Sec. Surrey CCC 1872-1907, Editor *Cricket* 1882-1907) b Dec. 2, 1842, d Feb. 26, 1907

Alderman, A. E. (Derby.) b Oct. 30, 1907

Alderman, T. M. (Australia; *CY 1982*) b June 12, 1956

Aldridge, K. J. (Worcs. and Tasmania) b March 13, 1935

Alexander of Tunis, 1st Lord (Pres. MCC 1955-56) b Dec. 10, 1891, d June 16, 1969

Alexander, F. C. M. (Camb. U. and W. Indies) b Nov. 2, 1928

Alexander, G. (Australia) b April 22, 1851, d Nov. 6, 1930

Alexander, H. H. (Australia) b June 9, 1905

Alim-ud-Din (Pakistan) b Dec. 15, 1930

Allan, D. W. (W. Indies) b Nov. 5, 1937

Allan, F. E. (Australia) b Dec. 2, 1849, d Feb. 9, 1917

Allan, J. M. (Oxford U., Kent, Warw. and Scotland) b April 2, 1932

Allan, P. J. (Australia) b Dec. 31, 1935

Allbrook, M. E. (Camb. U., Kent and Notts.) b Nov. 15, 1954

Allcott, C. F. W. (N. Zealand) b Oct. 7, 1896, d Nov. 21, 1973

Allen, A. W. (Camb. U. and Northants) b Dec. 22, 1912

Allen, B. O. (Camb. U. and Glos.) b Oct. 13, 1911, d May 1, 1981

Allen, D. A. (Glos.) b Oct. 29, 1935

Allen, G. O. (Camb. U. and Middx; Pres. MCC 1963-64) b Sydney July 31, 1902

Allen, J. C. (Leeward I.) b Aug. 18, 1951

Allen, M. H. J. (Northants and Derby.) b Jan. 7, 1933

Allen, R. C. (Australia) b July 2, 1858, d May 2, 1952

Alletson, E. B. (Notts.) b March 6, 1884, d July 5, 1963

Alley, W. E. (NSW and Somerset; CY 1962) b Feb. 3, 1919

Allom, M. J. C. (Camb. U. and Surrey; Pres. MCC 1969-70) b March 23, 1906

Allott, P. J. W. (Lancs.) b Sept. 14, 1956

Altham, H. S. (Oxford U., Surrey and Hants; Pres. MCC 1959-60) b Nov. 30, 1888, d March 11, 1965

Amarnath, Lala (India) b Sept. 11, 1911

Amarnath, M. (India; CY 1984) b Sept. 24, 1950

Amarnath, S. (India) b Dec. 30, 1948

Amar Singh, L. (India) b Dec. 4, 1910, d May 20, 1940

Ames, L. E. G. (Kent; CY 1929) b Dec. 3, 1905

Amir Elahi (India and Pakistan) b Sept. 1, 1908, d Dec. 28, 1980

Amiss, D. L. (Warw.; CY 1975) b April 7, 1943

Anderson, I. S. (Derby.) b April 24, 1960

Anderson, J. H. (S. Africa) b April 26, 1874, d March 11, 1926

Anderson, R. W. (N. Zealand) b Oct. 2, 1948

Anderson, W. McD. (N. Zealand) b Oct. 8, 1919, d Dec. 21, 1979

Andrew, K. V. (Northants) b Dec. 15, 1929

Andrews, B. (N. Zealand) b April 4, 1945

Andrews, T. J. E. (Australia) b Aug. 26, 1890, d Jan. 28, 1970

Andrews, W. H. R. (Somerset) b April 14, 1908

Angell, F. L. (Somerset) b June 29, 1922

Anwar Hussain (Pakistan) b July 16, 1920

Anwar Khan (Pakistan) b Dec. 24, 1955

Appleyard, R. (Yorks.; CY 1952) b June 27, 1924

Apte, A. L. (India) b Sept. 29, 1934

Apte, M. L. (India) b Oct. 5, 1932

Archer, A. G. (Worcs.) b Dec. 6, 1871, d July 15, 1935

Archer, K. A. (Australia) b Jan. 18, 1928

Archer, R. G. (Australia) b Oct. 25, 1933

Arif Butt (Pakistan) b May 17, 1944

Arlott, John, (Writer and Broadcaster) b Feb. 25, 1914

Armitage, R. L. S. (E. Province and N. Transvaal) b July 9, 1955

Armitage, T. (Yorks.) b April 25, 1848, d Sept. 21, 1922

Armstrong, N. F. (Leics.) b Dec. 22, 1892

Armstrong, T. R. (Derby.) b Oct. 13, 1909

Armstrong, W. W. (Australia; CY 1903) b May 22, 1879, d July 13, 1947

Arnold, E. G. (Worcs.) b Nov. 7, 1876, d Oct. 25, 1942

Arnold, G. G. (Surrey and Sussex; CY 1972) b Sept. 3, 1944

Arnold, J. (Hants) b Nov. 30, 1907

Arnold, P. (Canterbury and Northants) b Oct. 16, 1926

Arnott, T. (Glam.) b Feb. 16, 1902, d Feb. 2, 1975

Arun Lal, J. (India) b Aug. 1, 1955

Asgarali, N. (W. Indies) b Dec. 12, 1922

Ashdown, W. H. (Kent) b Dec. 27, 1898, d Sept. 15, 1979

Ashley, W. H. (S. Africa) b Feb. 10, 1862, d July 14, 1930

Ashraf Ali (Pakistan) b April 22, 1958

Ashton, Sqdn-Ldr C. T. (Camb. U. and Essex) b Feb. 19, 1901, d Oct. 31, 1942

Ashton, G. (Camb. U. and Worcs.) b Sept. 27, 1896, d Feb. 6, 1981

Ashton, Sir H. (Camb. U. and Essex; CY 1922; Pres. MCC 1960-61) b Feb. 13, 1898, d June 17, 1979

Asif Din. M. (Warw.) b Sept. 21, 1960

Asif Iqbal (Kent and Pakistan; CY 1968) b June 6, 1943

Asif Masood, S. (Pakistan) b Jan. 23, 1946

Aslett, D. G. (Kent) b Feb. 12, 1958

Aspinall, R. (Yorks.) b Nov. 27, 1918

Astill, W. E. (Leics.; CY 1933) b March 1, 1888, d Feb. 10, 1948

Athey, C. W. J. (Yorks.) b Sept. 27, 1957

Atkinson, C. R. M. (Somerset) b July 23, 1931

Atkinson, D. St E. (W. Indies) b Aug. 9, 1926

Atkinson, E. St E. (W. Indies) b Nov. 6, 1927

Atkinson, G. (Somerset and Lancs.) b March 29, 1938

Atkinson, T. (Notts.) b Sept. 27, 1930

Attenborough, G. R. (S. Australia) b Jan. 17, 1951

Attewell, W. (Notts.; *CY 1892*) b June 12, 1861, d June 11, 1927

Austin, Sir H. B. G. (Barbados) b July 15, 1877, d July 27, 1943

Austin, R. A. (W. Indies) b Sept. 5, 1954

Avery, A. V. (Essex) b Dec. 19, 1914

Aworth, C. J. (Camb. U. and Surrey) b Feb. 19, 1953

Aylward, J. (Hants and All-England) b 1741, d Dec. 27, 1827

Azad, K. B. J. (India) b Jan. 2, 1959

Azhar Khan (Pakistan) b Sept. 7, 1955

Azmat Rana (Pakistan) b Nov. 3, 1951

Bacchus, S. F. A. (W. Indies) b Jan. 31, 1954

Bacher, Dr A. (S. Africa) b May 24, 1942

Badcock, C. L. (Australia) b April 10, 1914, d Dec. 13, 1982

Badcock, F. T. (N. Zealand) b Aug. 9, 1898, d Sept. 19, 1982

Baggallay, R. R. C. (Derby.) b May 4, 1884, d Dec. 12, 1975

Bagnall, H. F. (Camb. U. and Northants) b Feb. 18, 1904, d Sept. 2, 1974

Baichan, L. (W. Indies) b May 12, 1946

Baig, A. A. (Oxford U., Somerset and India) b March 19, 1939

Bailey, Sir Derrick (D. T. L.) (Glos.) b August 5, 1918

Bailey, J. (Hants) b April 6, 1908

Bailey, J. A. (Essex and Oxford U.; Sec. MCC 1974-   ) b June 22, 1930

Bailey, T. E. (Essex and Camb. U.; *CY 1950*) b Dec. 3, 1923

Bainbridge, P. (Glos.) b April 16, 1958

Bairstow, D. L. (Yorks. and Griqualand W.) b Sept. 1, 1951

Baker, C. S. (Warw.) b Jan. 5, 1883, d Dec. 16 1976

Baker, R. K. (Camb. U. and Essex) b April 28, 1952

Baker, R. P. (Surrey) b April 9, 1954

Bakewell, A. H. (Northants; *CY 1934*) b Nov. 2, 1908, d Jan. 23, 1983

Balaskas, X. C. (S. Africa) b Oct. 15, 1910

Balderstone, J. C. (Yorks. and Leics.) b Nov. 16, 1940

Baldry, D. O. (Middx and Hants) b Dec. 26, 1931

Baldwin, H. G. (Surrey; Umpire) b March 16, 1893, d March 7, 1969

Banerjee, S. A. (India) b Nov. 1, 1919

Banerjee, S. N. (India) b Oct. 3, 1913, d Oct. 14, 1980

Bannerman, A. C. (Australia) b March 21, 1854, d Sept. 19, 1924

Bannerman, Charles (Australia) b Woolwich, Kent July 23, 1851, d Aug. 20, 1930

Bannister, C. S. (Camb. U.) b May 22, 1956

Bannister, J. D. (Warw.) b Aug. 23, 1930

Baptiste, E. A. E. (Kent and Leeward I.) b March 12, 1960

Barber, A. T. (Oxford U. and Yorks.) b June 17, 1905

Barber, R. T. (N. Zealand) b June 23, 1925

Barber, R. W. (Lancs., Camb. U. and Warw.; *CY 1967*) b Sept. 26, 1935

Barber, W. (Yorks.) b April 18, 1901, d Sept. 10, 1968

Barclay, J. R. T. (Sussex and Orange Free State) b Jan. 22, 1954

Bardsley, W. (Australia; *CY 1910*) b Dec. 7, 1882, d Jan. 20, 1954

Baring, A. E. G. (Hants) b Jan. 21, 1910

Barker, G. (Essex) b July 6, 1931

Barling, T. H. (Surrey) b Sept. 1, 1906

Barlow, A. (Lancs.) b Aug. 31, 1915, d May 9, 1983

Barlow, E. A. (Oxford U. and Lancs.) b Feb. 24, 1912, d June 27, 1980

Barlow, E. J. (Derby. and S. Africa) b Aug. 12, 1940

Barlow, G. D. (Middx) b March 26, 1950

Barlow, R. G. (Lancs.) b May 28, 1851, d July 31, 1919

Barnard, H. M. (Hants) b July 18, 1933

Barnard, L. J. (Transvaal and N. Transvaal) b Jan. 5, 1956

Barnes, A. R. (Sec. Australian Cricket Board 1960-81) b Sept. 12, 1916

Barnes, S. F. (Warw. and Lancs.; *CY 1910*) b April 19, 1873, d Dec. 26, 1967

Barnes, S. G. (Australia) b June 5, 1916, d Dec. 16, 1973

Barnes, W. (Notts.; *CY 1890*) b May 27, 1852, d March 24, 1899

Barnett, B. A. (Australia) b March 23, 1908, d June 29, 1979

Barnett, C. J. (Glos.; *CY 1937*) b July 3, 1910

Barnett, K. J. (Derby. and Boland) b July 17, 1960

Barnwell, C. J. P. (Somerset) b June 23, 1914

Baroda, Maharaja of (Manager, India in England, 1959) b April 2, 1930

Barratt, Fred (Notts.) b April 12, 1894, d Jan. 29, 1947

Barratt, R. J. (Leics.) b May 3, 1942

Barrett, A. G. (W. Indies) b Jan. 4, 1944

Barrett, J. E. (Australia) b Oct. 15, 1866, d Feb. 9, 1916

Barrick, D. W. (Northants) b April 28, 1926

Barrington, K. F. (Surrey; *CY 1960*) b Nov. 24, 1930, d March 14, 1981

Barrington, W. E. J. (Camb. U.) b Jan. 4, 1960

Barron, W. (Lancs. and Northants) b Oct. 26, 1917

Barrow, A. (Natal) b Jan. 23, 1955

Barrow, I. (W. Indies) b Jan. 6, 1911, d April 2, 1979

Bartholomew, P. C. S. (Trinidad) b Oct. 9, 1939

Bartlett, E. L. (W. Indies) b March 18, 1906, d Dec. 21, 1976

Bartlett, G. A. (N. Zealand) b Feb. 3, 1941

Bartlett, H. T. (Camb. U., Surrey and Sussex; *CY 1939*) b Oct. 7, 1914

Bartley, T. J. (Umpire) b March 19, 1908, d April 2, 1964

Barton, M. R. (Oxford U. and Surrey) b Oct. 14, 1914

Barton, P. T. (N. Zealand) b Oct. 9, 1935

Barton, V. A. (Kent and Hants) b Oct. 6, 1867, d March 23, 1906

Bates, D. L. (Sussex) b May 10, 1933

Bates, W. (Yorks.) b Nov. 19, 1855, d Jan. 8, 1900

Bath, B. F. (Transvaal) b Jan. 16, 1947

Baumgartner, H. V. (S. Africa) b Nov. 17, 1883, d April 8, 1938

Baxter, A. D. (Devon, Lancs., Middx and Scotland) b Jan. 20, 1910

Bean, G. (Notts. and Sussex) b March 7, 1864, d March 16, 1923

Bear, M. J. (Essex and Canterbury) b Feb. 23, 1934

Beard, D. D. (N. Zealand) b Jan. 14, 1920, d July 15, 1982

Beard, G. R. (Australia) b Aug. 19, 1950

Beauclerk, Lord Frederick (Middx, Surrey and MCC) b May 8, 1773, d April 22, 1850

Beaufort, 10th Duke of (Pres. MCC 1952-53) b April 4, 1900

Beaumont, D. J. (Camb. U.) b Sept. 1, 1944

Beaumont, R. (S. Africa) b Feb. 4, 1884, d May 25, 1958

Beck, J. E. F. (N. Zealand) b Aug. 1, 1934

Bedford, P. I. (Middx) b Feb. 11, 1930, d Sept. 18, 1966

Bedi, B. S. (Northants and India) b Sept. 25, 1946

Bedser, A. V. (Surrey; *CY 1947*) b July 4, 1918

Bedser, E. A. (Surrey) b July 4, 1918

Beet, G. (Derby.; Umpire) b April 24, 1886, d Dec. 13, 1946

Begbie, D. W. (S. Africa) b Dec. 12, 1914

Beldham, W. (Hambledon and Surrey) b Feb. 5, 1766, d Feb. 20, 1862

Bell, A. J. (S. Africa) b April 15, 1906

Bell, J. T. (Yorks. and Glam.) b June 16, 1896, d Aug. 8, 1974

Bell, R. V. (Middx and Sussex) b Jan. 7, 1931

Bell, W. (N. Zealand) b Sept. 5, 1931

Bellamy, B. W. (Northants) b April 22, 1891

Benaud, J. (Australia) b May 11, 1944

Benaud, R. (Australia; *CY 1962*) b Oct. 6, 1930

Bennett, B. W. P. (Camb. U.) b Feb. 6, 1955

Bennett, C. T. (Camb. U., Surrey and Middx) b Aug. 10, 1902, d Feb. 3, 1978

Bennett, D. (Middx) b Dec. 18, 1933

Bennett, G. M. (Somerset) b Dec. 17, 1909, d July 26, 1982

Bennett, N. H. (Surrey) b Sept. 23, 1912

Bennett, R. (Lancs.) b June 16, 1940

Benson, M. R. (Kent) b July 6, 1958

Bensted, E. C. (Queensland) b Feb. 11, 1901, d Jan. 21, 1980

Bernard, Dr J. R. (Camb. U. and Glos.) b Dec. 7, 1938

Berry, L. G. [G. L.] (Leics.) b April 28, 1906

Berry, R. (Lancs., Worcs. and Derby.) b Jan. 29, 1926

Beslee, G. P. (Kent) b March 27, 1904

Bessant, J. G. (Glos.) b Nov. 11, 1892, d Jan. 18, 1982

Bestall, D. (N. Transvaal, Natal and E. Province) b May 28, 1952

Betancourt, N. (W. Indies) b June 4, 1887, d Oct. 12, 1947

Bezuidenhout, S. J. (E. Province) b July 11, 1946

Bhandari, P. (India) b Nov. 27, 1935

Bick, D. A. (Middx) b Feb. 22, 1936

Bickmore, A. F. (Oxford U. and Kent) b May 19, 1899, d March 18, 1979

Biddulph, K. D. (Somerset) b May 29, 1932

Biggs, A. L. (E. Province) b April 26, 1946

Bilby, G. P. (N. Zealand) b May 7, 1941

Binks, J. G. (Yorks.; *CY 1969*) b Oct. 15, 1935

Binny, R. M. H. (India) b July 19, 1955

Binns, A. P. (W. Indies) b July 24, 1929

Birch, J. D. (Notts.) b June 18, 1955

Bird, H. D. (Yorks. and Leics.; umpire) b April 19, 1933

Bird, M. C. (Lancs. and Surrey) b March 25, 1888, d Dec. 9, 1933

Bird, R. E. (Worcs.) b April 4, 1915

Birkenshaw, J. (Yorks., Leics. and Worcs.) b Nov. 13, 1940

Birkett, L. S. (W. Indies) b April 14, 1904

Birrell, H. B. (E. Province, Rhodesia and Oxford U.) b Dec. 1, 1927

Bisset, Sir Murray (S. Africa) b April 14, 1876, d Oct. 24, 1931

Bissett, G. F. (S. Africa) b Nov. 5, 1905, d Nov. 14, 1965

Bissex, M. (Glos.) b Sept. 28, 1944

Blackham, J. McC. (Australia; *CY 1891*) b May 11, 1853, d Dec. 27, 1932

Blackie, D. D. (Australia) b April 5, 1882, d April 18, 1955

Blackledge, J. F. (Lancs.) b April 15, 1928

Blair, B. R. (Otago) b Dec. 27, 1957

Blair, R. W. (N. Zealand) b June 23, 1932

Blair, W. L. (Otago) b May 11, 1948

Blake, D. E. (Hants) b April 27, 1925

Blake, Rev. P. D. S. (Oxford U. and Sussex) b May 23, 1927

Blanckenberg, J. M. (S. Africa) b Dec. 31, 1893, 'presumed dead'

Bland, K. C. (S. Africa; *CY 1966*) b April 5, 1938

Blenkiron, W. (Warw.) b July 21, 1942

Bligh, Hon. Ivo (*see* 8th Earl of Darnley)

Block, S. A. (Camb. U. and Surrey) b July 15, 1908, d Oct. 7, 1979

Blofeld, H. C. (Camb. U.; Writer and Broadcaster) b Sept. 23, 1939

Blundell, Sir E. D. (Camb. U. and N. Zealand) b May 29, 1907

Blunt, R. C. (N. Zealand; *CY 1928*) b Durham, England Nov. 3, 1900, d London June 22, 1966

Blythe, C. (Kent; *CY 1904*) b May 30, 1879, d Nov. 8, 1917

Board, J. H. (Glos.) b Feb. 23, 1867, d at sea April 16, 1924

Bock, E. G. (S. Africa) b Sept. 17, 1908, d Sept. 5, 1961

Boddington, R. A. (Lancs.) b June 30, 1892, d Aug. 5, 1977

Bodkin, P. E. (Camb. U.) b Sept. 15, 1924

Bolton, B. A. (N. Zealand) b May 31, 1935

Bolus, J. B. (Yorks., Notts. and Derby.) b Jan. 31, 1934

Bond, G. E. (S. Africa) b April 5, 1909, d Aug. 27, 1965

Bond, J. D. (Lancs. and Notts.; *CY 1971*) b May 6, 1932

Bonnor, G. J. (Australia) b Feb. 25, 1855, d June 27, 1912

Boock, S. L. (N. Zealand) b Sept. 20, 1951

Booth, A. (Yorks.) b Nov. 3, 1902, d Aug. 17, 1974

Booth, B. C. (Australia) b Oct. 19, 1933

Booth, B. J. (Lancs. and Leics.) b Dec. 3, 1935

Booth, F. S. (Lancs.) b Feb. 12, 1907, d Jan. 21, 1980

Booth, M. W. (Yorks.; *CY 1914*) b Dec. 10, 1886, d July 1, 1916

Booth, P. (Leics.) b Nov. 2, 1952

Booth, R. (Yorks. and Worcs.) b Oct. 1, 1926

Borde, C. G. (India) b July 21, 1934

Border, A. R. (Glos. and Australia; *CY 1982*) b July 27, 1955

Bore, M. K. (Yorks. and Notts.) b June 2, 1947

Borrington, A. J. (Derby.) b Dec. 8, 1948

Bosanquet, B. J. T. (Oxford U. and Middx; *CY 1905*) b Oct. 13, 1877, d Oct. 12, 1936

Boshier, B. S. (Leics.) b March 6, 1932

Botham, I. T. (Somerset; *CY 1978*) b Nov. 24, 1955

Botten, J. T. (S. Africa) b June 21, 1938

Botton, N. D. (Oxford U.) b June 21, 1954

Boucher, J. C. (Ireland) b Dec. 22, 1910

Bourne, W. A. (Barbados and Warw.) b Nov. 15, 1952

Bowden, M. P. (Surrey and Transvaal) b Nov. 1, 1865, d Feb. 19, 1892

Bowditch, M. H. (W. Province) b Aug. 30, 1945

Bowes, W. E. (Yorks.; *CY 1932*) b July 25, 1908

Bowley, E. H. (Sussex and Auckland; *CY 1930*) b June 6, 1890, d July 9, 1974

Bowley, F. L. (Worcs.) b Nov. 9, 1873, d May 31, 1943

Bowman, R. (Oxford U. and Lancs.) b Jan. 26, 1934

Box, T. (Sussex) b Feb. 7, 1808, d July 12, 1876

Boyce, K. D. (Essex and W. Indies; *CY 1974*) b Oct. 11, 1943

Boycott, G. (Yorks. and N. Transvaal; *CY 1965*) b Oct. 21, 1940

Boyd-Moss, R. J. (Camb. U. and Northants) b Dec. 16, 1959

Boyes, G. S. (Hants) b March 31, 1899, d Feb. 11, 1973

Boyle, H. F. (Australia) b Dec. 10, 1847, d Nov. 21, 1907

Bracewell, B. P. (N. Zealand) b Sept. 14, 1959

Bracewell, J. G. (N. Zealand) b April 15, 1958

Bradburn, W. P. (N. Zealand) b Nov. 24, 1938

Bradley, W. M. (Kent) b Jan. 2, 1875, d June 19, 1944

Bradman, Sir D. G. (Australia; *CY 1931*) b Aug. 27, 1908

Bradshaw, J. C. (Leics.) b Jan. 25, 1902

Brain, B. M. (Worcs. and Glos.) b Sept. 13, 1940

Brann, W. H. (S. Africa) b April 4, 1899, d Sept. 22, 1953

Brassington, A. J. (Glos.) b Aug. 9, 1954

Bratchford, J. D. (Queensland) b Feb. 2, 1929

Braund, L. C. (Surrey and Somerset; *CY 1902*) b Oct. 18, 1875, d Dec. 22, 1955

Bray, C. (Essex) b April 6, 1898

Brayshaw, I. J. (W. Australia) b Jan. 14, 1942

Brazier, A. F. (Surrey and Kent) b Dec. 7, 1924

Breakwell, D. (Northants and Somerset) b July 2, 1948

Brearley, J. M. (Camb. U. and Middx; *CY 1977*) b April 28, 1942

Brearley, W. (Lancs.; *CY 1909*) b March 11, 1876, d Jan. 30, 1937

Brennan, D. V. (Yorks.) b Feb. 10, 1920

Brettell, D. N. (Oxford U.) b March 10, 1956

Brickett, D. J. (E. Province) b Dec. 9, 1950

Bridge, W. B. (Warw.) b May 29, 1938

Bridger, Rev. J. R. (Hants) b April 8, 1920

Brierley, T. L. (Glam. and Lancs.) b June 15, 1910

Briers, N. E. (Leics.) b Jan. 15, 1955

Briggs, John (Lancs.; *CY 1889*) b Oct. 3, 1862, d Jan. 11, 1902

Bright, R. J. (Australia) b July 13, 1954

Briscoe, A. W. (S. Africa) b Feb. 6, 1911, d April 22, 1941

Broad, B. C. (Glos.) b Sept. 29, 1957

Broadbent, R. G. (Worcs.) b June 21, 1924

Brocklebank, Sir J. M. Bt (Camb. U. and Lancs.) b Sept. 3, 1915, d Sept. 13, 1974

Brocklehurst, B. G. (Somerset) b Feb. 18, 1922

Brockwell, W. (Kimberley and Surrey; *CY 1895*) b Jan. 21, 1865, d July 1, 1935

Broderick, V. (Northants) b Aug. 17, 1920

Brodhurst, A. H. (Camb. U. and Glos.) b July 21, 1916

Bromfield, H. D. (S. Africa) b June 26, 1932

Bromley, E. H. (Australia) b Sept. 2, 1912, d Feb. 1, 1967

Bromley-Davenport, H. R. (Camb. U., Cheshire and Middx) b Aug. 18, 1870, d May 23, 1954

Brooker, M. E. W. (Camb. U.) b March 24, 1954

Brookes, D. (Northants; *CY 1957*) b Oct. 29, 1915

Brookes, W. H. (Editor of *Wisden* 1936-39) b Dec. 5, 1894, d May 28, 1955

Brooks, E. W. J. (Surrey) b July 6, 1898, d Feb. 10, 1960

Brooks, R. A. (Oxford U. and Somerset) b June 14, 1943

Brown, A. (Kent) b Oct. 17, 1935

Brown, A. S. (Glos.) b June 24, 1936

Brown, D. J. (Warw.) b Jan. 30, 1942

Brown, D. W. J. (Glos.) b Feb. 26, 1942

Brown, E. (Warw.) b Nov. 27, 1911

Brown, F. R. (Camb. U., Surrey and Northants; *CY 1933*; Pres. MCC 1971-72) b Lima, Peru Dec. 16, 1910

Brown, George (Sussex and England) b April 27, 1783, d June 25, 1857

Brown, G. (Hants) b Oct. 6, 1887, d Dec. 3, 1964

Brown, J. (Scotland) b Sept. 24, 1931

Brown, J. T. (Yorks.; *CY 1895*) b Aug. 20, 1869, d Nov. 4, 1904

Brown, L. S. (S. Africa) b Nov. 24, 1910, d Sept. 1, 1983

Brown, S. M. (Middx) b Dec. 8, 1917

Brown, W. A. (Australia; *CY 1939*) b July 31, 1912

Brown, W. C. (Northants) b Nov. 13, 1900

Browne, C. R. (W. Indies) b Oct. 8, 1890, d Jan. 12, 1964

Bruce, Hon. C. N. (3rd Lord Aberdare) (Oxford U. and Middx) b Aug. 2, 1885, d Oct. 4, 1957

Bruce, S. D. (W. Province and Orange Free State) b Jan. 11, 1954

Bruce, W. (Australia) b May 22, 1864, d Aug. 3, 1925

Bruyns, A. (W. Province and Natal) b Sept. 19, 1946

Bryan, Brig. G. J. (Kent) b Dec. 29, 1902

Bryan, J. L. (Camb. U. and Kent; *CY 1922*) b May 26, 1896

Bryan, R. T. (Kent) b July 30, 1898, d July 27, 1970

Buckenham, C. P. (Essex) b Jan. 16, 1876, d Feb. 23, 1937

Buckingham, J. (Warw.) b Jan. 21, 1903

Buckston, R. H. R. (Derby.) b Oct. 10, 1908, d May 16, 1967

Budd, E. H. (Middx and All-England) b Feb. 23, 1785, d March 29, 1875

Budd, W. L. (Hants) b Oct. 25, 1913

Buggins, B. L. (W. Australia) b Jan. 29, 1935

Bull, C. L. (Canterbury) b Aug. 19, 1946

Bull, D. F. E. (Queensland) b Aug. 13, 1935

Bull, F. G. (Essex; *CY 1898*) b April 2, 1875, d Sept. 16, 1910

Buller, J. S. (Yorks. and Worcs.) b Aug. 23, 1909, d Aug. 7, 1970

Burden, M. D. (Hants) b Oct. 4, 1930

Burge, P. J. (Australia; *CY 1965*) b May 17, 1932

Burger, C. G. de V. (S. Africa) b July 12, 1935

Burgess, G. I. (Somerset) b May 5, 1943

Burgess, M. G. (N. Zealand) b July 17, 1944

Burke, C. (N. Zealand) b March 22, 1914

Burke, J. W. (Australia; *CY 1957*) b June 12, 1930, d Feb. 2, 1979

Burke, S. F. (S. Africa) b March 11, 1934

Burki, Javed (Oxford U. and Pakistan) b May 8, 1938

Burn, K. E. (Australia) b Sept. 17, 1862, d July 20, 1956

Burnet, J. R. (Yorks.) b Oct. 11, 1918

Burnup, C. J. (Camb. U. and Kent; *CY 1903*) b Nov. 21, 1875, d April 5, 1960

Burrough, H. D. (Somerset) b Feb. 6, 1909

Burrow, B. W. (Griqualand W.) b Feb. 8, 1940

Burton, D. C. F. (Yorks.) b Sept. 13, 1887, d Sept. 24, 1971

Burton, F. J. (Australia) b 1866, d Aug. 25, 1929

Burtt, J. W. (C. Districts) b June 11, 1944

Burtt, T. B. (N. Zealand) b Jan. 22, 1915

Bury, T. E. O. (Oxford U.) b May 14, 1958

Buse, H. T. F. (Somerset) b Aug. 5, 1910

Bushby, M. H. (Camb. U.) b July 29, 1931

Buss, A. (Sussex) b Sept. 1, 1939

Buss, M. A. (Sussex and Orange Free State) b Jan. 24, 1944

Buswell, J. E. (Northants) b July 3, 1909

Butcher, A. R. (Surrey) b Jan. 7, 1954

Butcher, B. F. (W. Indies; *CY 1970*) b Sept. 3, 1933

Butcher, I. P. (Leics.) b July 1, 1962

Butcher, R. O. (Middx, Barbados and Tasmania) b Oct. 14, 1953

Butler, H. J. (Notts.) b March 12, 1913

Butler, L. C. (Wellington) b Sept. 2, 1934

Butler, L. S. (W. Indies) b Feb. 9, 1929

Butt, H. R. (Sussex) b Dec. 27, 1865, d Dec. 21, 1928

Butterfield, L. A. (N. Zealand) b Aug. 29, 1913

Buxton, I. R. (Derby.) b April 17, 1938

Buys, I. D. (S. Africa) b Feb. 3, 1895, dead

Bynoe, M. R. (W. Indies) b Feb. 21, 1941

Caccia, Lord (Pres. MCC 1973-74) b Dec. 21, 1905

Caesar, Julius (Surrey and All-England) b March 25, 1830, d March 6, 1878

Caffyn, W. (Surrey and NSW) b Feb. 2, 1828, d Aug. 28, 1919

Caine, C. Stewart (Editor of *Wisden* 1926-33) b Oct. 28, 1861, d April 15, 1933

Cairns, B. L. (N. Zealand) b Oct. 10, 1949

Calder, H. L. (Cranleigh; *CY 1918*) b 1900

Callaway, S. T. (Australia) b Feb. 6, 1868, d Nov. 25, 1923

Callen, I. W. (Australia) b May 2, 1955

Calthorpe, Hon. F. S. Gough- (Camb. U., Sussex and Warw.) b May 27, 1892, d Nov. 19, 1935

Camacho, G. S. (W. Indies) b Oct. 15, 1945

Cameron, F. J. (W. Indies) b June 22, 1923

Cameron, F. J. (N. Zealand) b June 1, 1932

Cameron, H. B. (S. Africa; *CY 1936*) b July 5, 1905, d Nov. 2, 1935

Cameron, J. H. (Camb. U., Somerset and W. Indies) b April 8, 1914

Campbell, K. O. (Otago) b March 20, 1943

Campbell, T. S. (S. Africa) b Feb. 9, 1882, d Oct. 5, 1924

Cannings, V. H. D. (Warw. and Hants) b April 3, 1919

Capel, D. J. (Northants) b Feb. 6, 1963

Caple, R. G. (Middx and Hants) b Dec. 8, 1939

Cardus, Sir Neville (Cricket Writer) b April 2, 1889, d Feb. 27, 1975

Carew, G. McD. (W. Indies) b 1910, d Dec. 9, 1974

Carew, M. C. (W. Indies) b Sept. 15, 1937

Carkeek, W. (Australia) b Oct. 17, 1878, d Feb. 20, 1937

Carlson, P. H. (Australia) b Aug. 8, 1951

Carlstein, P. R. (S. Africa) b Oct. 28, 1938

Carmody, D. K. (NSW and W. Australia) b Feb. 16, 1919, d Oct. 21, 1977

Carpenter, D. (Glos.) b Sept. 12, 1935

Carpenter, R. (Cambs. and Utd England XI) b Nov. 18, 1830, d July 13, 1901

Carr, A. W. (Notts.; *CY 1923*) b May 21, 1893, d Feb. 7, 1963

Carr, D. B. (Oxford U. and Derby.; *CY 1960*; Sec. TCCB 1974-) b Dec. 28, 1926

Carr, D. W. (Kent; *CY 1910*) b March 17, 1872, d March 23, 1950

Carr, J. D. (Oxford U. and Middx) b June 15, 1963

Carrick, P. (Yorks. and E. Province) b July 16, 1952

Carrigan, A. H. (Queensland) b Aug. 26, 1917

Carrington, E. (Derby.) b March 25, 1914

Carter, C. P. (S. Africa) b April 23, 1881, d Nov. 8, 1952

Carter, H. (Australia) b Halifax, Yorks. March 15, 1878, d June 8, 1948

Carter, R. G. (Warw.) b April 14, 1933

Carter, R. G. M. (Worcs.) b July 11, 1937

Carter, R. M. (Northants and Canterbury) b May 25, 1960

Carter, W. (Derby.) b May 14, 1896, d Nov. 1, 1975

Cartwright, H. (Derby.) b May 12, 1951

Cartwright, T. W. (Warw., Somerset and Glam.) b July 22, 1935

Carty, R. A. (Hants) b July 28, 1922

Cass, G. R. (Essex and Worcs.) b April 23, 1940

Castell, A. T. (Hants) b Aug. 6, 1943

Castle, F. (Somerset) b April 9, 1909

Catt, A. W. (Kent and W. Province) b Oct. 2, 1933

Catterall, R. H. (S. Africa; *CY 1925*) b July 10, 1900, d Jan. 2, 1961

Causby, J. P. (S. Australia) b Oct. 27, 1942

Cave, H. B. (N. Zealand) b Oct. 10, 1922

Cederwall, B. W. (Wellington) b Feb. 24, 1952

Chadwick, D. (W. Australia) b March 29, 1941

Chalk, F. G. H. (Oxford U. and Kent) b Sept. 7, 1910, d Feb. 20, 1943

Challenor, G. (W. Indies) b June 28, 1888, d July 30, 1947

Chandrasekhar, B. S. (India; *CY 1972*) b May 18, 1945

Chang, H. S. (W. Indies) b July 22, 1952

Chapman, A. P. F. (Uppingham, Camb. U. and Kent; *CY 1919*) b Sept. 3, 1900, d Sept. 16, 1961

Chapman, H. W. (S. Africa) b June 30, 1890, d Dec. 1, 1941

Chapman, T. A. (Leics. and Rhodesia) b May 14, 1919, d Feb. 19, 1979

Chappell, G. S. (Somerset and Australia; *CY 1973*) b Aug. 7, 1948

Chappell, I. M. (Lancs. and Australia; *CY 1976*) b Sept. 26, 1943

Chappell, T. M. (Australia) b Oct. 12, 1952

Chapple, M. E. (N. Zealand) b July 25, 1930

Charlton, P. C. (Australia) b April 9, 1867, d Sept. 30, 1954

Charlwood, H. R. J. (Sussex) b Dec. 19, 1846, d June 6, 1888

Chatfield, E. J. (N. Zealand) b July 3, 1950

Chatterton, W. (Derby.) b Dec. 27, 1861, d March 19, 1913

Chauhan, C. P. S. (India) b July 21, 1947

Cheatle, R. G. L. (Sussex and Surrey) b July 31, 1953

Cheetham, J. E. (S. Africa) b May 26, 1920, d Aug. 21, 1980

Chester, F. (Worcs.; Umpire) b Jan. 20, 1895, d April 8, 1957

Chesterton, G. H. (Oxford U. and Worcs.) b July 15, 1922

Chevalier, G. A. (S. Africa) b March 9, 1937

Childs, J. H. (Glos.) b Aug. 15, 1951

Childs-Clarke, A. W. (Middx and Northants) b May 13, 1905, d Feb. 19, 1980

Chipperfield, A. G. (Australia) b Nov. 17, 1905

Chisholm, R. H. E. (Scotland) b May 22, 1927

Chowdhury, N. R. (India) b May 23, 1923, d Dec. 14, 1979

Christiani, C. M. (W. Indies) b Oct. 28, 1913, d April 4, 1938

Christiani, R. J. (W. Indies) b July 19, 1920

Christopherson, S. (Kent; Pres. MCC 1939-45) b Nov. 11, 1861, d April 6, 1949

Christy, J. A. J. (Queensland and S. Africa) b Dec. 12, 1904, d Feb. 1, 1971

Chubb, G. W. A. (S. Africa) b April 12, 1911, d Aug. 28, 1982

Clark, D. G. (Kent; Pres. MCC 1977-78) b Jan. 27, 1919

Clark, E. A. (Middx) b April 15, 1937

Clark, E. W. (Northants) b Aug. 9, 1902, d April 28, 1982

Clark, L. S. (Essex) b March 6, 1914

Clark, T. H. (Surrey) b Oct. 4, 1924, d June 15, 1981

Clark, W. M. (Australia) b Sept. 19, 1953

Clarke, Dr C. B. (Northants, Essex and W. Indies) b April 7, 1918

Clarke, R. W. (Northants) b April 22, 1924, d Aug. 3, 1981

Clarke, S. T. (Barbados, Surrey and W. Indies) b Dec. 11, 1954

Clarke, William (Notts.; founded All-England XI and Trent Bridge ground) b Dec. 24, 1798, d Aug. 25, 1856

Clarkson, A. (Yorks. and Somerset) b Sept. 5, 1939

Claughton, J. A. (Oxford U. and Warw.) b Sept. 17, 1956

Clay, J. C. (Glam.) b March 18, 1898, d Aug. 12, 1973

Clay, J. D. (Notts.) b Oct. 15, 1924

Clayton, G. (Lancs. and Somerset) b Feb. 3, 1938

Clements, S. M. (Oxford U.) b April 19, 1956

Cleverley, D. C. (N. Zealand) b Dec. 23, 1909

Clift, Patrick B. (Rhodesia, Leics. and Natal) b July 14, 1953

Clift, Philip B. (Glam.) b Sept. 3, 1918

Clinton, G. S. (Kent, Surrey and Zimbabwe-Rhodesia) b May 5, 1953

Close, D. B. (Yorks. and Somerset; *CY 1964*) b Feb. 24, 1931

Cobb, R. A. (Leics.) b May 18, 1961

Cobden, F. C. (Camb. U.) b Oct. 14, 1849, d Dec. 7, 1932

Cobham, 10th Visct (Hon. C. J. Lyttelton) (Worcs.; Pres. MCC 1954) b Aug. 8, 1909, d March 20, 1977

Cochrane, J. A. K. (S. Africa) b July 15, 1909

Cockbain, I. (Lancs.) b April 19, 1958

Coen, S. K. (S. Africa) b Oct. 14, 1902, d Jan. 28, 1967

Colah, S. M. H. (India) b Sept. 22, 1902, d Sept. 11, 1950

Colchin, Robert ("Long Robin") (Kent and All-England) b Nov. 1713, d April 1750

Coldwell, L. J. (Worcs.) b Jan. 10, 1933

Coleman, C. A. R. (Leics.) b July 7, 1906, d June 14, 1978

Colley, D. J. (Australia) b March 15, 1947

Collin, T. (Warw.) b April 7, 1911

Collinge, R. O. (N. Zealand) b April 2, 1946

Collins, H. L. (Australia) b Jan. 21, 1889, d May 28, 1959

Collins, R. (Lancs.) b March 10, 1934

Colquhoun, I. A. (N. Zealand) b June 8, 1924

Comber, J. T. H. (Camb. U.) b Feb. 26, 1911, d May 3, 1976

Commaille, J. M. M. (S. Africa) b Feb. 21, 1883, d July 27, 1956

Compton, D. C. S. (Middx; *CY 1939*) b May 23, 1918

Compton, L. H. (Middx) b Sept. 12, 1912

Coney, J. V. (N. Zealand; *CY 1984*) b June 21, 1952

Congdon, B. E. (N. Zealand; *CY 1974*) b Feb. 11, 1938

Coningham, A. (Australia) b July 4, 1863, d July 13, 1939

Connolly, A. N. (Middx and Australia) b June 29, 1939

Constable, B. (Surrey) b Feb. 19, 1921

Constant, D. J. (Kent and Leics.; Umpire) b Nov. 9, 1941

Constantine, Lord L. N. (W. Indies; *CY 1940*) b Sept. 21, 1902, d July 1, 1971

Constantine, L. S. (Trinidad) b May 25, 1874, d Jan. 5, 1942

Contractor, N. J. (India) b March 7, 1934

Conyngham, D. P. (S. Africa) b May 10, 1897

Cook, C. (Glos.) b Aug. 23, 1921

Cook, F. J. (S. Africa) b 1870, dead

Cook, G. (Northants and E. Province) b Oct. 9, 1951

Cook, G. G. (Queensland) b June 29, 1910, d Sept. 12, 1982

Cook, N. G. B. (Leics.) b June 17, 1956

Cook, S. J. (Transvaal) b July 31, 1953

Cook, T. E. (Sussex) b Feb. 5, 1901, d Jan. 15, 1950

Coope, M. (Somerset) b Nov. 28, 1917, d July 5, 1974

Cooper, A. H. C. (S. Africa) b Sept. 2, 1893, d July 18, 1963

Cooper, B. B. (Middx, Kent and Australia) b March 15, 1844, d Aug. 7, 1914

Cooper, F. S. Ashley- (Cricket Historian) b March 17, 1877, d Jan. 31, 1932

Cooper, G. C. (Sussex) b Sept. 2, 1936

Cooper, H. P. (Yorks. and N. Transvaal) b April 17, 1949

Cooper, K. E. (Notts.) b Dec. 27, 1957

Cooper, K. R. (Natal) b April 1, 1954

Cooper, N. H. C. (Glos. and Camb. U.) b Oct. 14, 1953

Cooper, W. H. (Australia) b Sept. 11, 1849, d April 5, 1939

Cope, G. A. (Yorks.) b Feb. 23, 1947

Copson, W. H. (Derby.; *CY 1937*) b April 27, 1908, d Sept. 14, 1971

Cordle, A. E. (Glam.) b Sept. 21, 1940

Corling, G. E. (Australia) b July 13, 1941

Cornford, J. H. (Sussex) b Dec. 9, 1911

Cornford, W. L. (Sussex) b Dec. 25, 1900, d Feb. 6, 1963

Cornwallis, Capt. Hon. W. S. (2nd Lord Cornwallis) (Kent) b March 14, 1892, d Jan. 4, 1982

Corrall, P. (Leics.) b July 16, 1906

Corran, A. J. (Oxford U. and Notts.) b Nov. 25, 1936

Cosh, N. J. (Camb. U. and Surrey) b Aug. 6, 1946

Cosier, G. J. (Australia) b April 25, 1953

Cottam, J. T. (Australia) b Sept. 5, 1867, d Jan. 30, 1897

Cottam, R. M. H. (Hants and Northants) b Oct. 16, 1944

Cotter, A. (Australia) b Dec. 3, 1884, d Oct. 31, 1917

Cotterell, T. A. (Camb. U.) b May 12, 1963

Cotton, J. (Notts. and Leics.) b Nov. 7, 1940

Cottrell, G. A. (Camb. U.) b March 23, 1945

Cottrell, P. R. (Camb. U.) b May 22, 1957

Coulson, S. S. (Leics.) b Oct. 17, 1898, d Oct. 3, 1981

Coulthard, G. (Australia) b Aug. 1, 1856, d Oct. 22, 1883

Coventry, Hon. C. J. (Worcs.) b Feb. 26, 1867, d June 2, 1929

Coverdale, S. P. (Camb. U. and Yorks.) b Nov. 20, 1954

Cowan, M. J. (Yorks.) b June 10, 1933

Cowan, R. S. (Oxford U. and Sussex) b March 30, 1960

Cowans, N. G. (Middx) b April 17, 1961

Cowdrey, C. S. (Kent) b Oct. 20, 1957

Cowdrey, M. C. (Oxford U. and Kent; *CY 1956*) b. Dec. 24, 1932

Cowie, J. (N. Zealand) b March 30, 1912

Cowley, G. S. (E. Province) b March 1, 1953

Cowley, N. G. (Hants) b March 1, 1953

Cowper, R. M. (Australia) b Oct. 5, 1940

Cox, A. L. (Northants) b July 22, 1907

Cox, G., jun. (Sussex) b Aug. 23, 1911

Cox, G. R. (Sussex) b Nov. 29, 1873, d March 24, 1949

Cox, J. L. (S. Africa) b June 28, 1886, d July 4, 1971

Coxon, A. (Yorks.) b Jan. 18, 1916

Crabtree, H. P. (Essex) b April 30, 1906, d May 28, 1982

Craig, E. J. (Camb. U. and Lancs.) b March 26, 1942

Craig, I. D. (Australia) b June 12, 1935

Cranfield, L. M. (Glos.) b Aug. 29, 1909

Cranmer, P. (Warw.) b Sept. 10, 1914

Cranston, J. (Glos.) b Jan. 9, 1859, d Dec. 10, 1904

Cranston, K. (Lancs.) b Oct. 20, 1917

Crapp, J. F. (Glos.) b Oct. 14, 1912, d Feb. 15, 1981

Crawford, J. N. (Surrey, S. Australia, Wellington and Otago; *CY 1907*) b Dec. 1, 1886, d May 2, 1963

Crawford, N. C. (Camb. U.) b Nov. 26, 1958

Crawford, W. P. A. (Australia) b Aug. 3, 1933

Crawley, A. M. (Oxford U. and Kent; Pres. MCC 1972-73) b April 10, 1908

Crawley, L. G. (Camb. U., Worcs. and Essex) b July 26, 1903, d July 9, 1981

Cray, S. J. (Essex) b May 29, 1921

Creese, W. L. C. (Hants) b Dec. 28, 1907, d March 9, 1974

Cresswell, G. F. (N. Zealand) b March 22, 1915, d Jan. 10, 1966

Cripps, G. (S. Africa) b Oct. 19, 1865, d July 27, 1943

Crisp, R. J. (Worcs. and S. Africa) b May 28, 1911

Croft, C. E. H. (Lancs. and W. Indies) b March 15, 1953

Cromb, I. B. (N. Zealand) b June 25, 1905

Crookes, N. S. (Natal) b Nov. 15, 1935

Cross, G. F. (Leics.) b Nov. 15, 1943

Crowe, J. J. (N. Zealand) b Sept. 14, 1958

Crowe, M. D. (N. Zealand) b Sept. 22, 1962

Crump, B. S. (Northants) b April 25, 1938

Crush, E. (Kent) b April 25, 1917

Cuffy, T. (Trinidad) b Nov. 9, 1949

Cumbes, J. (Lancs., Surrey, Worcs. and Warw.) b May 4, 1944

Cunis, R. S. (N. Zealand) b Jan. 5, 1941

Cunningham, K. G. (S. Australia) b July 26, 1939

Curnow, S. H. (S. Africa) b Dec. 16, 1907

Curtis, I. J. (Oxford U.) b May 13, 1959

Curtis, T. S. (Worcs. and Camb. U.) b Jan. 15, 1960

Cuthbertson, G. B. (Middx, Sussex and Northants) b March 28, 1901

Cutmore, J. A. (Essex) b Dec. 28, 1898

Cuttell, W. R. (Lancs.; *CY 1898*) b Sept. 13, 1864, d Dec. 9, 1929

Da Costa, O. C. (W. Indies) b Sept. 11, 1907, d Oct. 1, 1936

Dacre, C. C. (Auckland and Glos.) b May 15, 1899, d Nov. 2, 1975

Daer, A. G. (Essex) b Nov. 22, 1906

Daft, Richard (Notts. and All-England) b Nov. 2, 1835, d July 18, 1900

Dakin, G. F. (E. Province) b Aug. 13, 1935

Dalmeny, Lord (6th Earl of Rosebery) (Middx and Surrey) b Jan. 8, 1882, d May 30, 1974

Dalton, E. L. (S. Africa) b Dec. 2, 1906, d June 3, 1981

Dani, H. T. (India) b May 24, 1933

Daniel, W. W. (Barbados, Middx, W. Australia and W. Indies) b Jan. 16, 1956

Dansie, H. N. (S. Australia) b July 2, 1928

D'Arcy, J. W. (N. Zealand) b April 23, 1936

Dare, R. (Hants) b Nov. 26, 1921

Darling, J. (Australia; *CY 1900*) b Nov. 21, 1870, d Jan. 2, 1946

Darling, L. S. (Australia) b Aug. 14, 1909

Darling, W. M. (Australia) b May 1, 1957

Darnley, 8th Earl of (Hon. Ivo Bligh) (Camb. U. and Kent; Pres. MCC 1900) b March 13, 1859, d April 10, 1927

Davey, J. (Glos.) b Sept. 4, 1944

Davidson, A. K. (Australia; *CY 1962*) b June 14, 1929

Davies, Dai (Glam.) b Aug. 26, 1896, d July 16, 1976

Davies, Emrys (Glam.) b June 27, 1904, d Nov. 10, 1975

Davies, E. Q. (S. Africa) b Aug. 26, 1909, d Nov. 11, 1976

Davies, G. R. (NSW) b July 22, 1946

Davies, H. D. (Glam.) b July 23, 1932

Davies, H. G. (Glam.) b April 23, 1913

Davies, J. G. W. (Camb. U. and Kent) b Sept. 10, 1911

Davis, B. A. (Glam. and W. Indies) b May 2, 1940

Davis, C. A. (W. Indies) b Jan. 1, 1944

Davis, E. (Northants) b March 8, 1922

Davis, I. C. (Australia) b June 25, 1953

Davis, P. C. (Northants) b May 24, 1915

Davis, R. C. (Glam.) b Jan. 1, 1946

Davis, W. W. (Glam. and W. Indies) b Sept. 18, 1958

Davison, B. F. (Rhodesia, Leics. and Tasmania) b Dec. 21, 1946

Davison, I. (Notts.) b Oct. 4, 1937

Dawkes, G. O. (Leics. and Derby.) b July 19, 1920

Dawson, E. W. (Camb. U. and Leics.) b Feb. 13, 1904, d June 4, 1979

Dawson, O. C. (S. Africa) b Sept. 1, 1919

Day, A. P. (Kent; *CY 1910*) b April 10, 1885, d Jan. 22, 1969

Day, H. L. V. (Hants) b Aug. 12, 1898, d June 15, 1972

Day, N. T. (Transvaal) b Dec. 31, 1953

de Alwis, R. G. (Sri Lanka) b Feb. 15, 1960

Dean, H. (Lancs.) b Aug. 13, 1884, d March 12, 1957

Deane, H. G. (S. Africa) b July 21, 1895, d Oct. 21, 1939

De Caires, F. I. (W. Indies) b May 12, 1909, d Feb. 2, 1959

De Courcy, J. H. (Australia) b April 18, 1927

Deed, J. A. (Kent) b Sept. 12, 1901, d Oct. 19, 1980

Delisle, G. P. S. (Middx and Oxford U.) b Dec. 25, 1934

Dell, A. R. (Australia) b Lymington, Hants Aug. 10, 1947

de Mel, A. L. F. (Sri Lanka) b May 9, 1959

Dempster, C. S. (Leics., Warw. and N. Zealand; *CY 1932*) b Nov. 15, 1903, d Feb. 14, 1974

Dempster, E. W. (N. Zealand) b Jan. 25, 1925

Denness, M. H. (Scotland, Kent and Essex; *CY 1975*) b Dec. 1, 1940

Dennett, E. G. (Glos.) b April 27, 1880, d Sept. 14, 1937

Denning, P. W. (Somerset) b Dec. 16, 1949

Dennis, F. (Yorks.) b June 11, 1907

Dennis, S. J. (Yorks. and Orange Free State) b Oct. 18, 1960

Denton, D. (Yorks.; *CY 1906*) b July 4, 1874, d Feb. 17, 1950

Denton, J. S. (Northants) b Nov. 2, 1890, d April 9, 1971

Denton, W. H. (Northants) b Nov. 2, 1890, d April 23, 1979

Depeiaza, C. C. (W. Indies) b Oct. 10, 1927

Desai, R. B. (India) b June 29, 1939

De Saram, F. C. (Oxford U. and Ceylon) b Sept. 5, 1912, d April 11, 1983

de Schmidt, R. (W. Province; oldest surviving Currie Cup player) b Nov. 24, 1883

de Silva, D. S. (Sri Lanka) b June 11, 1941

de Silva, G. R. A. (Sri Lanka) b Dec. 12, 1952

De Vaal, P. D. (Transvaal) b Dec. 3, 1945

Devereux, L. N. (Middx, Worcs. and Glam.) b Oct. 20, 1931

Dewdney, C. T. (W. Indies) b Oct. 23, 1933

Dewes, A. R. (Camb. U.) b June 2, 1957

Dewes, J. G. (Camb. U. and Middx) b Oct. 11, 1926

Dews, G. (Worcs.) b June 5, 1921

Dexter, E. R. (Camb. U. and Sussex; *CY 1961*) b May 15, 1935

Dias, R. L. (Sri Lanka) b Oct. 18, 1952

Dibbs, A. H. A. (Pres. MCC 1983-84) b Dec. 9, 1918

Dick, A. E. (N. Zealand) b Oct. 10, 1936

Dickeson, C. W. (N. Districts) b March 26, 1955

Dickinson, G. R. (N. Zealand) b March 11, 1903, d March 17, 1978

Dilley, G. R. (Kent) b May 18, 1959

Diment, R. A. (Glos. and Leics.) b Feb. 9, 1927

Dipper, A. E. (Glos.) b Nov. 9, 1885, d Nov. 7, 1945

Divecha, R. V. (Oxford U., Northants and India) b Oct. 18, 1927

Diver, A. J. D. (Cambs., Middx, Notts. and All-England) b June 6, 1824, d March 25, 1876

Dixon, A. L. (Kent) b Nov. 27, 1933

Dixon, C. D. (S. Africa) b Feb. 12, 1891, d Sept. 9, 1969

Dodds, T. C. (Essex) b May 29, 1919

Doggart, A. G. (Camb. U., Durham and Middx) b June 2, 1897, d June 7, 1963

Doggart, G. H. G. (Camb. U. and Sussex; Pres. MCC 1981-82) b July 18, 1925

Doggart, S. J. G. (Camb. U.) b Feb. 8, 1961

Doherty, M. J. D. (Griqualand W.) b March 14, 1947

D'Oliveira, B. L. (Worcs.; *CY 1967*) b Oct. 4, 1931

D'Oliveira, D. B. (Worcs.) b Oct. 19, 1960

Dollery, H. E. (Warw. and Wellington; *CY 1952*) b Oct. 14, 1914

Dollery, K. R. (Queensland, Auckland, Tasmania and Warw.) b Dec. 9, 1924

Dolphin, A. (Yorks.) b Dec. 24, 1885, d Oct. 24, 1942

Donnan, H. (Australia) b Nov. 12, 1864, d Aug. 13, 1956

Donnelly, M. P. (Middx, Warw., Oxford U. and N. Zealand; *CY 1948*) b Oct. 17, 1917

Dooland, B. (Notts. and Australia; *CY 1955*) b Nov. 1, 1923, d Sept. 8, 1980

Dorrinton, W. (Kent and All-England) b April 29, 1809, d Nov. 8, 1848

Dorset, 3rd Duke of (Kent) b March 24, 1745, d July 19, 1799

Doshi, D. R. (Notts., Warw. and India) b Dec. 22, 1947

Douglas, J. W. H. T. (Essex; *CY 1915*) b Sept. 3, 1882, d Dec. 19, 1930

Dovey, R. R. (Kent) b July 18, 1920, d Dec. 27, 1974

Dowding, A. L. (Oxford U.) b April 4, 1929

Dowe, U. G. (W. Indies) b March 29, 1949

Dower, R. R. (S. Africa) b June 4, 1876, d Sept. 15, 1964

Dowling, D. F. (Border, NE Transvaal and Natal) b July 25, 1914

Dowling, G. T. (N. Zealand) b March 4, 1937

Downton, P. R. (Kent and Middx) b April 4, 1957

Draper, E. J. (E. Province and Griqualand W.) b Sept. 27, 1934

Draper, R. G. (S. Africa) b Dec. 24, 1926

Dredge, C. H. (Somerset) b Aug. 4, 1954

Druce, N. F. (Camb. U. and Surrey; *CY 1898*) b Jan. 1, 1875, d Oct. 27, 1954

Drybrough, C. D. (Oxford U. and Middx) b Aug. 31, 1938

D'Souza, Antao (Pakistan) b Jan. 1, 1938

Ducat, A. (Surrey; *CY 1920*) b Feb. 16, 1886, d July 23, 1942

Duckworth, C. A. R. (S. Africa) b March 22, 1933

Duckworth, G. (Lancs.; *CY 1929*) b May 9, 1901, d Jan. 5, 1966

Dudleston, B. (Leics., Glos. and Rhodesia) b July 16, 1945

Duff, R. A. (Australia) b Aug. 17, 1878, d Dec. 13, 1911

Dujon, P. J. (W. Indies) b May 28, 1956

Duleepsinhji, K. S. (Camb. U. and Sussex; *CY 1930*) b June 13, 1905, d Dec. 5, 1959

Dumbrill, R. (S. Africa) b London Nov. 19, 1938

Duminy, J. P. (Oxford U. and S. Africa) b Dec. 16, 1897, d Jan. 31, 1980

Duncan, J. R. F. (Australia) b March 25, 1944

Dunell, O. R. (S. Africa) b July 15, 1856, d Oct. 21, 1929

Dunning B. (N. Districts) b March 20, 1940

Dunning, J. A. (Oxford U. and N. Zealand) b Feb. 6, 1903, d June 24, 1971

Du Preez, J. H. (S. Africa) b Nov. 14, 1942

Durani, S. A. (India) b Dec. 11, 1934

Durose, A. J. (Northants) b Oct. 10, 1944

Durston, F. J. (Middx) b July 11, 1893, d April 8, 1965

Du Toit, J. F. (S. Africa) b April 5, 1868, d July 10, 1909

Dye, J. C. J. (Kent, Northants and E. Province) b July 24, 1942

Dyer, D. D. (Natal and Transvaal) b Dec. 3, 1946

Dyer, D. V. (S. Africa) b April 2, 1914

Dymock, G. (Australia) b July 21, 1946

Dyson, A. H. (Glam.) b July 10, 1905, d June 7, 1978

Dyson, J. (Lancs.) b July 8, 1934

Dyson, John (Australia) b June 11, 1954

Eady, C. J. (Australia) b Oct. 29, 1870, d Dec. 20, 1945

Eagar, E. D. R. (Oxford U., Glos. and Hants) b Dec. 8, 1917, d Sept. 13, 1977

Eagar, M. A. (Oxford U. and Glos.) b March 20, 1934

Eaglestone, J. T. (Middx and Glam.) b July 24, 1923

Ealham, A. G. E. (Kent) b Aug. 30, 1944

East, D. E. (Essex) b July 27, 1959

East, R. E. (Essex) b June 20, 1947

East, R. J. (Orange Free State) b March 31, 1953

Eastman, G. F. (Essex) b April 7, 1903

Eastman, L. C. (Essex and Otago) b June 3, 1897, d April 17, 1941

Eastwood, K. H. (Australia) b Nov. 23, 1935

Ebeling, H. I. (Australia) b Jan. 1, 1905, d Jan. 12, 1980

Eckersley, P. T. (Lancs.) b July 2, 1904, d Aug. 13, 1940

Edgar, B. A. (N. Zealand) b Nov. 23, 1956

Edinburgh, HRH Duke of (Pres. MCC 1948-49, 1974-75) b June 10, 1921

Edmeades, B. E. A. (Essex) b Sept. 17, 1941

Edmonds, P. H. (Camb. U., Middx and E. Province) b March 8, 1951

Edmonds, R. B. (Warw.) b March 2, 1941

Edrich, B. R. (Kent and Glam.) b Aug. 18, 1922

Edrich, E. H. (Lancs.) b March 27, 1914

Edrich, G. A. (Lancs.) b July 13, 1918

Edrich, J. H. (Surrey; *CY 1966*) b June 21, 1937

Edrich, W. J. (Middx; *CY 1940*) b March 26, 1916

Edwards, F. (Surrey) b May 23, 1885, d July 10, 1970

Edwards, G. N. (N. Zealand) b May 27, 1955

Edwards, J. D. (Australia) b June 12, 1862, d July 31, 1911

Edwards, M. J. (Camb. U. and Surrey) b March 1, 1940

Edwards, R. (Australia) b Dec. 1, 1942

Edwards, R. M. (W. Indies) b June 3, 1940

Edwards, T. D. W. (Camb. U.) b Dec. 6, 1958

Edwards, W. J. (Australia) b Dec. 23, 1949

Eele, P. J. (Somerset) b Jan. 27, 1935

Eggar, J. D. (Oxford U., Hants and Derby.) b Dec. 1, 1916, d May 3, 1983

Ehtesham-ud-Din (Pakistan) b Sept. 4, 1950

Elgie, M. K. (S. Africa) b March 6, 1933

Elliott, C. S. (Derby.) b April 24, 1912

Elliott, H. (Derby.) b Nov. 2, 1891, d Feb. 2, 1976

Elliott, Harold (Lancs.; Umpire) b June 15, 1904

Ellis, G. P. (Glam.) b May 24, 1950

Ellis, J. L. (Victoria) b May 9, 1890, d Jan. 26, 1974

Ellis, R. G. P. (Oxford U. and Middx) b Oct. 20, 1960

Ellison, C. C. (Camb. U.) b Feb. 11, 1962

Ellison, R. M. (Kent) b Sept. 21, 1959

Elms, R. B. (Kent and Hants) b April 5, 1949

Emburey, J. E. (Middx and W. Province; *CY 1984*) b Aug. 20, 1952

Emery, R. W. G. (N. Zealand) b March 28, 1915, d Dec. 18, 1982

Emery, S. H. (Australia) b Oct. 16, 1885, d Jan. 7, 1967

Emmett, G. M. (Glos.) b Dec. 2, 1912, d Dec. 18, 1976

Emmett, T. (Yorks.) b Sept. 3, 1841, d June 29, 1904

Endean, W. R. (S. Africa) b May 31, 1924

Engineer, F. M. (Lancs. and India) b Feb. 25, 1938

Enthoven, H. J. (Camb. U. and Middx) b June 4, 1903, d June 29, 1975

Evans, A. J. (Oxford U., Hants and Kent) b May 1, 1889, d Sept. 18, 1960

Evans, D. G. L. (Glam.; Umpire) b July 27, 1933

Evans, E. (Australia) b March 6, 1849, d July 2, 1921

Evans, G. (Oxford U., Glam. and Leics.) b Aug. 13, 1915

Evans, J. B. (Glam.) b Nov. 9, 1936

Evans, T. G. (Kent; *CY1951*) b Aug. 18, 1920

Evans, V. J. (Essex) b March 4, 1912, d March 28, 1975

Every, T. (Glam.) b Dec. 19, 1909

Eyre, T. J. P. (Derby.) b Oct. 17, 1939

Ezekowitz, R. A. B. (Oxford U.) b Jan. 19, 1954

Faber, M. J. J. (Oxford U. and Sussex) b Aug. 15, 1950

Fagg, A. E. (Kent) b June 18, 1915, d Sept. 13, 1977

Fairbairn, A. (Middx) b Jan. 25, 1923

Fairbairn, G. A. (Camb. U. and Middx) b June 26, 1892, d Nov. 5, 1973

Fairbrother, N. H. (Lancs.) b Sept. 9, 1963

Fairfax, A. G. (Australia) b June 16, 1906, d May 17, 1955

Fairservice, C. (Kent and Middx) b Aug. 21, 1909

Fairservice, W. J. (Kent) b May 16, 1881, d June 26, 1971

Falcon, M. (Camb. U.) b July 21, 1888, d Feb. 27, 1976

Fallows, J. A. (Lancs.) b July 25, 1907, d Jan. 20, 1974

Fane, F. L. (Oxford U. and Essex) b April 27, 1875, d Nov. 27, 1960

Fantham, W. E. (Warw.) b May 14, 1918

Farnes, K. (Camb. U. and Essex; *CY 1939*) b July 8, 1911, d Oct. 20, 1941

Farooq Hamid (Pakistan) b March 3, 1945

Farrer, W. S. (S. Africa) b Dec. 8, 1936

Farrimond, W. (Lancs.) b May 23, 1903, d Nov. 14, 1979

Farrukh Zaman (Pakistan) b April 2, 1956

Faulkner, G. A. (S. Africa) b Dec. 17, 1881, d Sept. 10, 1930

Favell, L. E. (Australia) b Oct. 6, 1929

Fazal Mahmood (Pakistan; *CY 1955*) b Feb. 18, 1927

Fearnley, C. D. (Worcs.) b April 12, 1940

Featherstone, N. G. (Transvaal, N. Transvaal, Middx and Glam.) b Aug. 20, 1949

'Felix', N. (Wanostrocht) (Kent, Surrey and All-England) b Oct. 4, 1804, d Sept. 3, 1876

Fellows-Smith, J. P. (Oxford U., Northants and S. Africa) b Feb. 3, 1932

Fender, P. G. H. (Sussex and Surrey; *CY 1915*) b Aug. 22, 1892

Fenley, S. (Surrey and Hants) b Jan. 4, 1896, d Sept. 2, 1972

Fenner, D. (Border) b March 27, 1929

Ferguson, W. (W. Indies) b Dec. 14, 1917, d Feb. 23, 1961

Fernandes, M. P. (W. Indies) b Aug. 12, 1897, d May 8, 1981

Fernando, E. R. N. S. (Sri Lanka) b Dec. 19, 1955

Ferrandi, J. H. (W. Province) b April 3, 1930

Ferreira, A. M. (N. Transvaal and Warw.) b April 13, 1955

Ferris, J. J. (Glos., Australia and England; *CY 1889*) b May 21, 1867, d Nov. 21, 1900

Fichardt, C. G. (S. Africa) b March 20, 1870, d May 30, 1923

Fiddian-Green, C. A. F. (Camb. U., Warw. and Worcs.) b Dec. 22, 1898, d Sept. 5, 1976

Fiddling, K. (Yorks. and Northants) b Oct. 13, 1917

Field, M. N. (Camb. U. and Warw.) b March 23, 1950

Fielder, A. (Kent; *CY 1907*) b July 19, 1877, d Aug. 30, 1949

Findlay, T. M. (W. Indies) b Oct. 19, 1943

Findlay, W. (Oxford U. and Lancs.; Sec. Surrey CCC, Sec. MCC 1926-36) b June 22, 1880, d June 19, 1953

Fingleton, J. H. (Australia) b April 28, 1908, d Nov. 22, 1981

Finlason, C. E. (S. Africa) b Feb. 19, 1860, d July 31, 1917

Finney, R. J. (Derby.) b Aug. 2, 1960

Firth, J. (Yorks. and Leics.) b June 27, 1918, d Sept. 6, 1981

Firth, Rev. Canon J. D'E. E. (Winchester, Oxford U. and Notts.; *CY 1918*) b Jan. 21, 1900, d Sept. 21, 1957

Fisher, B. (Queensland) b Jan. 20, 1934, d April 6, 1980

Fisher, F. E. (N. Zealand) b July 28, 1924

Fisher, P. B. (Oxford U., Middx and Worcs.) b Dec. 19, 1954

Fishlock, L. B. (Surrey; *CY 1947*) b Jan. 2, 1907

Fitzroy-Newdegate, Cdr. Hon. J. M. (Northants) b March 20, 1897, d May 7, 1976

Flanagan, J. P. D. (Transvaal) b Sept. 20, 1947

Flavell, J. A. (Worcs.; *CY 1965*) b May 15, 1929

Fleetwood-Smith, L. O'B. (Australia) b March 30, 1910, d March 16, 1971

Fletcher, D. A. G. (Rhodesia, Zimbabwe) b Sept. 27, 1948

Fletcher, D. G. W. (Surrey) b July 6, 1924

Fletcher, K. W. R. (Essex; *CY 1974*) b May 20, 1944

Floquet, C. E. (S. Africa) b Nov. 3, 1884, d Nov. 22, 1963

Flowers, W. (Notts.) b Dec. 7, 1856, d Nov. 1, 1926

Foat, J. C. (Glos.) b Nov. 21, 1952

Foley, H. (N. Zealand) b Jan. 28, 1906, d Oct. 16, 1948

Folley, I. (Lancs.) b Jan. 9, 1963

Foord, C. W. (Yorks.) b June 11, 1924

Forbes, C. (Notts.) b Aug. 9, 1936

Ford, D. A. (NSW) b Dec. 12, 1930

Ford, F. G. J. (Camb. U. and Middx) b Dec. 14, 1866, d Feb. 7, 1940

Ford, N. M. (Oxford U., Derby. and Middx) b Nov. 18, 1906

Ford, R. G. (Glos.) b March 3, 1907, d Oct. 1981

Foreman, D. J. (W. Province and Sussex) b Feb. 1, 1933

Fosh, M. K. (Camb. U. and Essex) b Sept. 26, 1957

Foster, D. G. (Warw.) b March 19, 1907, d Oct. 13, 1980

Foster, F. R. (Warw.; *CY 1912*) b Jan. 31, 1889, d May 3, 1958

Foster, G. N. (Oxford U., Worcs. and Kent) b Oct. 16, 1884, d Aug. 11, 1971

Foster, H. K. (Oxford U. and Worcs.; *CY 1911*) b Oct. 30, 1873, d June 23, 1950

Foster, M. K. (Worcs.) b Jan. 1, 1889, d Dec. 3, 1940

Foster, M. L. C. (W. Indies) b May 9, 1943

Foster, N. A. (Essex) b May 6, 1962

Foster, P. G. (Kent) b Oct. 9, 1916

Foster, R. E. (Oxford U. and Worcs.; *CY 1901*) b April 16, 1878, d May 13, 1914

Fothergill, A. J. (Somerset) b Aug. 26, 1854, d Aug. 1, 1932

Fotheringham, H. R. (Natal and Transvaal) b April 4, 1953

Foulkes, I. (Border and Orange Free State) b Feb. 22, 1955

Fowler, A. J. B. (Middx) b April 1, 1891, d May 7, 1977

Fowler, G. (Lancs.) b April 20, 1957

Fowler, W. P. (Derby., N. Districts and Auckland) b March 13, 1959

Francis, B. C. (Essex and Australia) b Feb. 18, 1948

Francis, D. A. (Glam.) b Nov. 29, 1953

Francis, G. N. (W. Indies) b Dec. 7, 1897, d Jan. 12, 1942

Francis, H. H. (S. Africa) b May 26, 1868, d Jan. 7, 1936

Francke, F. M. (Sri Lanka and Queensland) b March 29, 1941

Francois, C. M. (S. Africa) b June 20, 1897, d May 26, 1944

Frank, C. N. (S. Africa) b Jan. 27, 1891, d Dec. 26, 1961

Frank, W. H. B. (S. Africa) b Nov. 23, 1872, d Feb. 16, 1945

Franklin, H. W. F. (Oxford U., Surrey and Essex) b June 30, 1901

Franklin, T. J. (N. Zealand) b March 18, 1962

Frederick, M. C. (Derby. and W. Indies) b May 6, 1927

Fredericks, R. C. (Glam. and W. Indies; *CY 1974*) b Nov. 11, 1942

Freeman, A. P. (Kent; *CY 1923*) b May 17, 1888, d Jan. 28, 1965

Freeman, D. L. (N. Zealand) b Sept. 8, 1914

Freeman, E. W. (Australia) b July 13, 1944

Freer, F. W. (Australia) b Dec. 4, 1915

French, B. N. (Notts.) b Aug. 13, 1959

Frost, G. (Notts.) b Jan. 15, 1947

Fry, C. A. (Oxford U., Hants and Northants) b Jan. 14, 1940

Fry, C. B. (Oxford U., Sussex and Hants; *CY 1895*) b April 25, 1872, d Sept. 7, 1956

Fuller, E. R. H. (S. Africa) b Aug. 2, 1931

Fuller, R. L. (W. Indies) b Jan. 30, 1913

Fullerton, G. M. (S. Africa) b Dec. 8, 1922

Funston, G. K. (NE Transvaal and Griqualand W.) b Nov. 21, 1948

Funston, K. J. (S. Africa) b Dec. 3, 1925

Furlonge, H. A. (W. Indies) b June 19, 1934

Fursdon, E. D. (Oxford U.) b Dec. 20, 1952

Gabriel, R. S. (Trinidad) b June 5, 1952

Gadkari, C. V. (India) b Feb. 3, 1928

Gaekwad, A. D. (India) b Sept. 23, 1952

Gaekwad, D. K. (India) b Oct. 27, 1928

Gaekwad, H. G. (India) b Aug. 29, 1923

Gale, R. A. (Middx) b Dec. 10, 1933

Gallichan, N. (N. Zealand) b June 3, 1906, d March 25, 1969

Gamsy, D. (S. Africa) b Feb. 17, 1940

Gandotra, A. (India) b Nov. 24, 1948

Gannon, J. B. (Australia) b Feb. 2, 1947

Ganteaume, A. G. (W. Indies) b Jan. 22, 1921

Gard, T. (Somerset) b June 2, 1957

Gardiner, H. A. B. (Rhodesia) b Jan. 3, 1944

Gardiner, S. J. C. (Camb. U.) b March 19, 1947

Gardner, F. C. (Warw.) b June 4, 1922, d Jan. 13, 1979

Gardner, L. R. (Leics.) b Feb. 23, 1934

Garland-Wells, H. M. (Oxford U. and Surrey) b Nov. 14, 1907

Garlick, R. G. (Lancs. and Northants) b April 11, 1917

Garner, J. (Somerset and W. Indies; *CY 1980*) b Dec. 16, 1952

Garrett, T. W. (Australia) b July 26, 1858, d Aug. 6, 1943

Gaskin, B. M. (Manager, W. Indies in England, 1963) b March 21, 1908, d May 2, 1979

Gatting, M. W. (Middx; *CY 1984*) b June 6, 1957

Gaunt, R. A. (Australia) b Feb. 26, 1934

Gavaskar, S. M. (Somerset and India; *CY 1980*) b July 10, 1949

Gay, L. H. (Camb. U., Hants and Somerset) b March 24, 1871, d Nov. 1, 1949

Geary, A. C. T. (Surrey) b Sept. 11, 1900

Geary, G. (Leics.; *CY 1927*) b July 9, 1893, d March 6, 1981

Gedye, S. G. (N. Zealand) b May 2, 1929

Gehrs, D. R. A. (Australia) b Nov. 29, 1880, d June 25, 1953

Ghavri, K. D. (India) b Feb. 28, 1951

Ghazali, Mohammad E. Z. (Pakistan) b June 15, 1924

Ghorpade, J. M. (India) b Oct. 2, 1930, d March 29, 1978

Ghulam Abbas (Pakistan) b May 1, 1947

Ghulam Ahmed (India) b July 4, 1922

Gibb, P. A. (Camb. U., Scotland, Yorks. and Essex) b July 11, 1913, d Dec. 7, 1977

Gibbons, H. H. (Worcs.) b Oct. 10, 1904, d Feb. 16, 1973

Gibbs, G. L. (W. Indies) b Dec. 27, 1925, d Feb. 21, 1979

Gibbs, L. R. (Warw., S. Australia and W. Indies; *CY 1972*) b Sept. 29, 1934

Gibbs, P. J. K. (Oxford U. and Derby.) b Aug. 17, 1944

Gibson, C. H. (Eton, Camb. U. and Sussex; *CY 1918*) b Aug. 23, 1900, d Dec. 31, 1976

Gibson, D. (Surrey) b May 1, 1936

Gibson, J. G. (N. Districts and Auckland) b Nov. 12, 1948

Giffen, G. (Australia; *CY 1894*) b March 27, 1859, d Nov. 29, 1927

Giffen, W. F. (Australia) b Sept. 10, 1863, d June 29, 1949

Gifford, N. (Worcs. and Warw.; *CY 1975*) b March 30, 1940

Gilchrist, R. (Jamaica, Hyderabad and W. Indies) b June 28, 1934

Giles, R. J. (Notts.) b Oct. 17, 1919

Gill, A. (Notts.) b Aug. 4, 1940

Gilhouley, K. (Yorks. and Notts.) b Aug. 8, 1934

Gilliat, R. M. C. (Oxford U. and Hants) b May 20, 1944

Gilligan, A. E. R. (Camb. U., Surrey and Sussex; *CY 1924*; Pres. MCC 1967-68) b Dec. 23, 1894, d Sept. 5, 1976

Gilligan, A. H. H. (Sussex) b June 29, 1896, d May 5, 1978

Gilligan, F. W. (Oxford U. and Essex) b Sept. 20, 1893, d May 4, 1960

Gilmour, G. J. (Australia) b June 26, 1951

Gimblett, H. (Somerset; *CY 1953*) b Oct. 19, 1914, d March 30, 1978

Gladstone, G. (W. Indies) (*see* Marais, G. G.)

Gladwin, C. (Derby.) b April 3, 1916

Gleeson, J. W. (E. Province and Australia) b March 14, 1938

Gleeson, R. A. (S. Africa) b Dec. 6, 1873, d Sept. 27, 1919

Glover, G. K. (S. Africa) b May 13, 1870, d Nov. 15, 1938

Glover, T. R. (Oxford U.) b Nov. 26, 1951

Goddard, G. F. (Scotland) b May 19, 1938

Goddard, J. D. C. (W. Indies) b April 21, 1919

Goddard, T. L. (S. Africa) b Aug. 1, 1931

Goddard, T. W. (Glos.; *CY 1938*) b Oct. 1, 1900, d May 22, 1966

Goldie, C. F. E. (Camb. U. and Hants) b Nov. 20, 1960

Goldsmith, F. S. (Oxford U., Northants, Transvaal and W. Province) b Oct. 14, 1944

Gomes, H. A. (Middx and W. Indies) b July 13, 1953

Gomes, S. A. (Trinidad) b Oct. 18, 1950

Gomez, G. E. (W. Indies) b Oct. 10, 1919

Gooch, G. A. (Essex; *CY 1980*) b July 23, 1953

Goodway, C. C. (Warw.) b July 10, 1909

Goodwin, K. (Lancs.) b June 25, 1938

Goodwin, T. J. (Leics.) b Jan. 22, 1929

Goonatillake, H. M. (Sri Lanka) b Aug. 16, 1952

Goonesena, G. (Ceylon, Notts., Camb. U. and NSW) b Feb. 16, 1931

Gopalan, M. J. (India) b June 6, 1909

Gopinath, C. D. (India) b March 1, 1930

Gordon, N. (S. Africa) b Aug. 6, 1911

Gore, A. C. (Eton and Army; *CY 1919*) b May 14, 1900

Gothard, E. J. (Derby.) b Oct. 1, 1904, d Jan. 17, 1979

Gould, I. J. (Middx, Auckland and Sussex) b Aug. 19, 1957

Gover, A. R. (Surrey; *CY 1937*) b Feb. 29, 1908

Gower, D. I. (Leics.; *CY 1979*) b April 1, 1957

Gowrie, 1st Lord (Pres. MCC 1948-49) b July 6, 1872, d May 2, 1955

Grace, Dr Alfred b May 17, 1840, d May 24, 1916

Grace, Dr Alfred H. (Glos.) b March 10, 1866, d Sept. 16, 1929

Grace, C. B. (Clifton) b March 1882, d June 6, 1938

Grace, Dr E. M. (Glos.) b Nov. 28, 1841, d May 20, 1911

Grace, Dr Edgar M. (MCC) (son of E. M. Grace) b Oct. 6, 1886, d Nov. 24, 1974

Grace, G. F. (Glos.) b Dec. 13, 1850, d Sept. 22, 1880

Grace, Dr Henry (Glos.) b Jan. 31, 1833, d Nov. 15, 1895

Grace, Dr H. M. (father of W. G., E. M. and G. F.) b Feb. 21, 1808, d Dec. 23, 1871

Grace, Mrs H. M. (mother of W. G., E. M. and G. F.) b July 18, 1812, d July 25, 1884

Grace, Dr W. G. (Glos.; *CY 1896*) b July 18, 1848, d Oct. 23, 1915

Grace, W. G., jun. (Camb. U. and Glos.) b July 6, 1874, d March 2, 1905

Graham, H. (Australia) b Nov. 29, 1870, d Feb. 7, 1911

Graham, J. N. (Kent) b May 8, 1943

Graham, R. (S. Africa) b Sept. 16, 1877, d April 21, 1946

Grant, G. C. (Camb. U., Rhodesia and W. Indies) b May 9, 1907, d Oct. 26, 1978

Grant, R. S. (Camb. U. and W. Indies) b Dec. 15, 1909, d Oct. 18, 1977

Graveney, D. A. (Glos.) b Jan. 21, 1953

Graveney, J. K. (Glos.) b Dec. 16, 1924

Graveney, T. W. (Glos., Worcs. and Queensland; *CY 1953*) b June 16, 1927

Graves, P. J. (Sussex and Orange Free State) b May 19, 1946

Gray, E. J. (New Zealand) b Nov. 18, 1954

Gray, J. R. (Hants) b May 19, 1926

Gray, L. H. (Middx) b Dec. 16, 1915, d Jan. 3, 1983

Greasley, D. G. (Northants) b Jan. 20, 1926

Green, A. M. (Sussex) b May 28, 1960

Green, D. J. (Derby. and Camb. U.) b Dec. 18, 1935

Green, D. M. (Oxford U., Lancs. and Glos.; *CY 1969*) b Nov. 10, 1939

Green, Brig. M. A. (Glos. and Essex; Manager MCC in S. Africa 1948-49, MCC in Australia 1950-51) b Oct. 3, 1891, d Dec. 28, 1971

Greenhough, T. (Lancs.) b Nov. 9, 1931

Greenidge, A. E. (W. Indies) b Aug. 20, 1956

Greenidge, C. G. (Hants and W. Indies; *CY 1977*) b May 1, 1951

Greenidge, G. A. (Sussex and W. Indies) b May 26, 1948

Greensmith, W. T. (Essex) b Aug. 16, 1930

Greenwood, A. (Yorks.) b Aug. 20, 1847, d Feb. 12, 1889

Greenwood, F. E. (Yorks.) b Sept. 28, 1905, d July 30, 1963

Greenwood, H. W. (Sussex and Northants) b Sept. 4, 1909, d Oct. 16, 1983

Greenwood, P. (Lancs.) b Sept. 11, 1924

Greetham, C. M. H. (Somerset) b Aug. 28, 1936

Gregory, David W. (Australia; first Australian captain) b April 15, 1845, d Aug. 4, 1919

Gregory, E. J. (Australia) b May 29, 1839, d April 22, 1899

Gregory, J. M. (Australia; *CY 1922*) b Aug. 14, 1895, d Aug. 7, 1973

Gregory, R. G. (Australia) b Feb. 26, 1916, d June 10, 1942

Gregory, R. J. (Surrey) b Aug. 26, 1902, d Oct. 6, 1973

Gregory, S. E. (Australia; *CY 1897*) b April 14, 1870, d July 31, 1929

Greig, A. W. (Border, E. Province and Sussex; *CY 1975*) b Oct. 6, 1946

Greig, I. A. (Camb. U., Border and Sussex) b Dec. 8, 1955

Grell, M. G. (W. Indies) b Dec. 18, 1899, d Jan. 11, 1976

Greswell, W. T. (Somerset and Ceylon) b Oct. 15, 1889, d Feb. 12, 1971

Grieve, B. A. F. (England) b May 28, 1864, d Nov. 19, 1917

Grieves, K. J. (NSW and Lancs.) b Aug. 27, 1925

Grieveson, R. E. (S. Africa) b Aug. 24, 1909

Griffin, G. M. (S. Africa) b June 12, 1939

Griffith, C. C. (W. Indies; *CY 1964*) b Dec. 14, 1938

Griffith, G. ("Ben") (Surrey and Utd England XI) b Dec. 20, 1833, d May 3, 1879

Griffith, H. C. (W. Indies) b Dec. 1, 1893, d March 18, 1980

Griffith, K. (Worcs.) b Jan. 17, 1950

Griffith, M. G. (Camb. U. and Sussex) b Nov. 25, 1943

Griffith, S. C. (Camb. U., Surrey and Sussex; Sec. MCC 1962-74; Pres. MCC 1979-80) b June 16, 1914

Griffiths, B. J. (Northants) b June 13, 1949

Griffiths, Sir W. H. (Camb. U. and Glam.) b Sept. 26, 1923

Grimmett, C. V. (Wellington and Australia; *CY 1931*) b Dec. 25, 1891, d May 2, 1980

Grimshaw, N. (Northants) b May 5, 1911

Gripper, R. A. (Rhodesia) b July 7, 1938

Groube, T. U. (Australia) b Sept. 2, 1857, d Aug. 5, 1927

Grout, A. T. W. (Australia) b March 30, 1927, d Nov. 9, 1968

Grove, C. W. (Warw. and Worcs.) b Dec. 16, 1912, d Feb. 15, 1982

Grover, J. N. (Oxford U.) b Oct. 15, 1915

Groves, B. S. (Border and Natal) b March 1, 1947

Groves, M. G. M. (Oxford U., Somerset and W. Province) b Jan. 14, 1943

Grundy, J. (Notts. and Utd England XI) b March 5, 1824, d Nov. 24, 1873

Guard, G. M. (India) b Dec. 12, 1925, d March 13, 1978

Guest, C. E. J. (Australia) b Oct. 7, 1937

Guha, S. (India) b Jan. 31, 1946

Guillen, S. C. (W. Indies and N. Zealand) b Sept. 24, 1924

Guise, J. L. (Oxford U. and Middx) b Nov. 25, 1903

Gul Mahomed (Pakistan and India) b Oct. 15, 1921

Gunasekera, Y. (Sri Lanka) b Nov. 8, 1957

Guneratne, R. P. W. (Sri Lanka) b Jan. 26, 1962

Gunn, G. (Notts.; *CY 1914*) b June 13, 1879, d June 28, 1958

Gunn, G. V. (Notts.) b June 21, 1905, d Oct. 14, 1957

Gunn, J. (Notts.; *CY 1904*) b July 19, 1876, d Aug. 21, 1963

Gunn, T. (Sussex) b Sept. 27, 1935

Gunn, William (Notts.; *CY 1890*) b Dec. 4, 1858, d Jan. 29, 1921

Gupte, B. P. (India) b Aug. 30, 1934

Gupte, S. P. (India) b Dec. 11, 1929

Gurr, D. R. (Oxford U. and Somerset) b March 27, 1956

Guy, J. W. (Northants and N. Zealand) b Aug. 29, 1934

Hacker, P. J. (Notts., Derby. and Orange Free State) b July 16, 1952

Hadlee, B. G. (Canterbury) b Dec. 14, 1941

Hadlee, D. R. (N. Zealand) b Jan. 6, 1948

Hadlee, R. J. (Notts. and N. Zealand; *CY 1982*) b July 3, 1951

Hadlee, W. A. (N. Zealand) b June 4, 1915

Hafeez, A. (*see* Kardar)

Haig, N. E. (Middx) b Dec. 12, 1887, d Oct. 27, 1966

Haigh, S. (Yorks.; *CY 1901*) b March 19, 1871, d Feb. 27, 1921

Halfyard, D. J. (Kent and Notts.) b April 3, 1931

Hall, A. E. (S. Africa) b Jan. 23, 1896, d Jan. 1, 1964

Hall, G. G. (S. Africa) b May 24, 1938

Hall, I. W. (Derby.) b Dec. 27, 1939

Hall, Louis (Yorks.; *CY 1890*) b Nov. 1, 1852, d Nov. 19, 1915

Hall, T. A. (Derby. and Somerset) b Aug. 19, 1930

Hall, W. W. (Queensland and W. Indies) b Sept. 12, 1937

Hallam, A. W. (Lancs. and Notts.; *CY 1908*) b Nov. 12, 1869, d July 24, 1940

Hallam, M. R. (Leics.) b Sept. 10, 1931

Halliday, S. J. (Oxford U.) b July 13, 1960

Halliwell, E. A. (Middx and S. Africa; *CY 1905*) b Sept. 7, 1864, d Oct. 2, 1919

Hallows, C. (Lancs.; *CY 1928*) b April 4, 1895, d Nov. 10 1972

Hallows, J. (Lancs.; *CY 1905*) b Nov. 14, 1873, d May 20, 1910

Halse, C. G. (S. Africa) b Feb. 28, 1935

Hamence, R. A. (Australia) b Nov. 25, 1915

Hamer, A. (Yorks. and Derby.) b Dec. 8, 1916

Hamilton, A. C. (Oxford U.) b Sept. 23, 1953

Hammond, H. E. (Sussex) b Nov. 7, 1907

Hammond, J. R. (Australia) b April 19, 1950

Hammond, W. R. (Glos.; *CY 1928*) b June 19, 1903, d July 2, 1965

Hampshire, J. H. (Yorks., Derby. and Tasmania) b Feb. 10, 1941

Hands, P. A. M. (S. Africa) b March 18, 1890, d April 27, 1951

Hands, R. H. M. (S. Africa) b July 26, 1888, d April 20, 1918

Hands, W. C. (Warw.) b Dec. 20, 1886, d Aug. 31, 1974

Hanif Mohammad (Pakistan; *CY 1968*) b Dec. 21, 1934

Hanley, M. A. (S. Africa) b Nov. 10, 1918

Hanley, R. W. (E. Province, Orange Free State and Transvaal) b Jan. 29, 1952

Hanumant Singh (India) b March 29, 1939

Hardie, B. R. (Scotland and Essex) b Jan. 14, 1950

Hardikar, M. S. (India) b Feb. 8, 1936

Hardinge, H. T. W. (Kent; *CY 1915*) b Feb. 25, 1886, d May 8, 1965

Hardstaff, J. (Notts.) b Nov. 9, 1882, d April 2, 1947

Hardstaff, J., jun. (Notts. and Auckland; *CY 1938*) b July 3, 1911

Harfield, L. (Hants) b Aug. 16, 1905

Harford, N. S. (N. Zealand) b Aug. 30, 1930, d March 30, 1981

Harford, R. I. (N. Zealand) b May 30, 1936

Harman, R. (Surrey) b Dec. 28, 1941

Haroon Rashid (Pakistan) b March 25, 1953

Harris, 4th Lord (Oxford U. and Kent; Pres. MCC 1895) b Trinidad Feb. 3, 1851, d March 24, 1932

Harris, David (Hants and All-England) b 1755, d May 19, 1803

Harris, C. B. (Notts.) b Dec. 6, 1907, d Aug. 8, 1954

Harris, M. J. (Middx, Notts., E. Province and Wellington) b May 25, 1944

Harris, P. G. Z. (N. Zealand) b July 18, 1927

Harris, R. M. (N. Zealand) b July 27, 1933

Harris, T. A. (S. Africa) b Aug. 27, 1916

Harrison, L. (Hants) b June 8, 1922

Harry, J. (Australia) b Aug. 1, 1857, d Oct. 27, 1919

Hart, G. E. (Middx) b Jan. 13, 1902

Hartigan, G. P. D. (S. Africa) b Dec. 30, 1884, d Jan. 7, 1955

Hartigan, R. J. (Australia) b Dec. 12, 1879, d June 7, 1958

Hartkopf, A. E. V. (Australia) b Dec. 28, 1889, d May 20, 1968

Hartley, A. (Lancs.; *CY 1911*) b April 11, 1879, d Oct. 1918

Hartley, J. C. (Oxford U. and Sussex) b Nov. 15, 1874, d March 8, 1963

Hartley, S. N. (Yorks. and Orange Free State) b March 18, 1956

Harty, I. D. (Border) b May 7, 1941

Harvey, J. F. (Derby.) b Sept. 27, 1939

Harvey, M. R. (Australia) b April 29, 1918

Harvey, P. F. (Notts.) b Jan. 15, 1923

Harvey, R. L. (S. Africa) b Sept. 14, 1911

Harvey, R. N. (Australia; *CY 1954*) b Oct. 8, 1928

Harvey-Walker, A. J. (Derby.) b July 21, 1944

Haseeb Ahsan (Pakistan) b July 15, 1939

Hassan, B. (Notts.) b March 24, 1944

Hassett, A. L. (Australia; *CY 1949*) b Aug. 28, 1913

Hastings, B. F. (N. Zealand) b March 23, 1940

Hathorn, C. M. H. (S. Africa) b April 7, 1878, d May 17, 1920

Hawke, 7th Lord (Camb. U. and Yorks.; *CY 1909*; Pres. MCC 1914-18) b Aug. 16, 1860, d Oct. 10, 1938

Hawke, N. J. N. (Australia) b June 27, 1939

Hawker, Sir Cyril (Essex; Pres. MCC 1970-71) b July 21, 1900

Hawkins, D. G. (Glos.) b May 18, 1935

Hawtin, A. P. R. (Northants) b Feb. 1, 1883, d Jan. 15, 1975

Hayes, E. G. (Surrey and Leics.; *CY 1907*) b Nov. 6, 1876, d Dec. 2, 1953

Hayes, F. C. (Lancs.) b Dec. 6, 1946

Hayes, J. A. (N. Zealand) b Jan. 11, 1927

Hayes, K. A. (Oxford U. and Lancs.) b Sept. 26, 1962

Hayes, P. J. (Camb. U.) b May 20, 1954

Haygarth, A. (Sussex; Historian) b Aug. 4, 1825, d May 1, 1903

Haynes, D. L. (W. Indies) b Feb. 15, 1956

Haynes, R. W. (Glos.) b Aug. 27, 1913, d Oct. 16, 1976

Hayward, T. (Cambs. and All-England) b March 21, 1835, d July 21, 1876

Hayward, T. W. (Surrey; *CY 1895*) b March 29, 1871, d July 19, 1939

Haywood, P. R. (Leics.) b March 30, 1947

Hazare, V. S. (India) b March 11, 1915

Hazell, H. L. (Somerset) b Sept. 30, 1909

Hazlerigg, Lord, formerly Hon. A. G. (Camb. U. and Leics.) b Feb. 24, 1910

Hazlitt, G. R. (Australia) b Sept. 4, 1888, d Oct. 30, 1915

Headley, G. A. (W. Indies; *CY 1934*) b Panama May 30, 1909, d Nov. 30, 1983

Headley, R. G. A. (Worcs. and W. Indies) b June 29, 1939

Heane, G. F. H. (Notts.) b Jan. 2, 1904, d Oct. 24, 1969

Hearn, P. (Kent) b Nov. 18, 1925

Hearne, Alec (Kent; *CY 1894*) b July 22, 1863, d May 16, 1952

Hearne, Frank (Kent, England and S. Africa) b Nov. 23, 1858, d July 14, 1949

Hearne, G. A. L. (S. Africa) b March 27, 1888, d Nov. 13, 1978

Hearne, George G. (Kent) b July 7, 1856, d Feb. 13, 1932

Hearne, J. T. (Middx; *CY 1892*) b May 3, 1867, d April 17, 1944

Hearne, J. W. (Middx; *CY 1912*) b Feb. 11, 1891, d Sept. 13, 1965

Hearne, Thos. (Middx) b Sept. 4, 1826, d May 13, 1900

Hearne, Thos., jun. (Lord's Ground Superintendent) b Dec. 29, 1849, d Jan. 29, 1910

Heath, G. E. M. (Hants) b Feb. 20, 1913

Heath, M. (Hants) b March 9, 1934

Hedges, B. (Glam.) b Nov. 10, 1927

Hedges, L. P. (Tonbridge, Oxford U., Kent and Glos.; *CY 1919*) b July 13, 1900, d Jan. 12, 1933

Heine, P. S. (S. Africa) b June 28, 1928

Hemmings, E. E. (Warw. and Notts.) b Feb. 20, 1949

Hemsley, E. J. O. (Worcs.) b Sept. 1, 1943

Henderson, M. (N. Zealand) b Aug. 2, 1895, d June 17, 1970

Henderson, R. (Surrey; *CY 1890*) b March 30, 1865, d Jan. 29, 1931

Henderson, S. P. (Camb. U., Worcs. and Glam.) b Sept. 24, 1958

Hendren, E. H. (Middx; *CY 1920*) b Feb. 5, 1889, d Oct. 4, 1962

Hendrick, M. (Derby. and Notts.; *CY 1978*) b Oct. 22, 1948

Hendriks, J. L. (W. Indies) b Dec. 21, 1933

Hendry, H. L. (Australia) b May 24, 1895

Henwood, P. P. (Orange Free State and Natal) b May 22, 1946

Herman, O. W. (Hants) b Sept. 18, 1907

Herman, R. S. (Middx, Border, Griqualand W. and Hants) b Nov. 30, 1946

Heron, J. G. (Zimbabwe) b Nov. 8, 1948

Heseltine, C. (Hants) b Nov. 26, 1869, d June 13, 1944

Heseltine, P. J. (Oxford U.) b June 21, 1960

Hever, N. G. (Middx and Glam.) b Dec. 17, 1924

Hewetson, E. P. (Oxford U. and Warw.) b May 27, 1902, d Dec. 26, 1977

Hewett, H. T. (Oxford U. and Somerset; *CY 1893*) b May 25, 1864, d March 4, 1921

Hewitt, S. G. P. (Camb. U.) b April 6, 1963

Hibbert, P. A. (Australia) b July 23, 1952

Higgins, H. L. (Worcs.) b Feb. 24, 1894, d Sept. 15, 1979

Higgs, J. D. (Australia) b July 11, 1950

Higgs, K. (Lancs. and Leics.; *CY 1968*) b Jan. 14, 1937

Hignell, A. J. (Camb. U. and Glos.) b Sept. 4, 1955

Hilditch, A. M. J. (Australia) b May 20, 1956

Hill, Alan (Derby. and Orange Free State) b June 29, 1950

Hill, Allen (Yorks.) b Nov. 14, 1843, d Aug. 29, 1910

Hill, A. J. L. (Camb. U. and Hants) b July 26, 1871, d Sept. 6, 1950

Hill, Clement (Australia; *CY 1900*) b March 18, 1877, d Sept. 5, 1945

Hill, E. (Somerset) b July 9, 1923

Hill, G. (Hants) b April 15, 1913

Hill, J. C. (Australia) b June 25, 1923, d Aug, 11. 1974

Hill, L. W. (Glam.) b April 14, 1942

Hill, M. (Notts., Derby. and Somerset) b Sept. 14, 1935

Hill, N. W. (Notts.) b Aug. 22, 1935

Hill, W. A. (Warw.) b April 27, 1910

Hills, J. J. (Glam.; Umpire) b Oct. 14, 1897, d Oct. 1969

Hills, R. W. (Kent) b Jan. 8, 1951

Hill-Wood, C. K. B. H. (Oxford U. and Derby.) b June 5, 1907

Hill-Wood, Sir W. W. H. (Camb. U. and Derby.) b Sept. 8, 1901, d Oct. 10, 1980

Hilton, C. (Lancs. and Essex) b Sept. 26, 1937

Hilton, J. (Lancs. and Somerset) b Dec. 29, 1930

Hilton, M. J. (Lancs.; *CY 1957*) b Aug. 2, 1928

Hime, C. F. W. (S. Africa) b Oct. 24, 1869, d Dec. 6, 1940

Hindlekar, D. D. (India) b Jan. 1, 1909, d March 30, 1949

Hirst, G. H. (Yorks.; *CY 1901*) b Sept. 7, 1871, d May 10, 1954

Hitch, J. W. (Surrey; *CY 1914*) b May 7, 1886, d July 7, 1965

Hitchcock, R. E. (Canterbury and Warw.) b Nov. 28, 1929

Hoad, E. L. G. (W. Indies) b Jan. 29, 1896

Hoare, D. E. (Australia) b Oct. 19, 1934

Hobbs, Sir J. B. (Surrey; *CY 1909, special portrait 1926*) b Dec. 16, 1882, d Dec. 21, 1963

Hobbs, R. N. S. (Essex and Glam.) b May 8, 1942

Hobson, D. L. (E. Province and W. Province) b Sept. 3, 1951

Hodges, J. H. (Australia) b July 31, 1856, d Jan. 17, 1933

Hodgkinson, G. F. (Derby.) b Feb. 19, 1914

Hodgson, A. (Northants) b Oct. 27, 1951

Hodgson, K. I. (Camb. U.) b Feb. 24, 1960

Hofmeyr, M. B. (Oxford U. and NE Transvaal) b Dec. 9, 1925

Hogan, T. G. (Australia) b Sept. 23, 1956

Hogg, R. M. (Australia) b March 5, 1951

Hogg, W. (Lancs. and Warw.) b July 12, 1955

Hohns, T. V. (Queensland) b Jan. 23, 1954

Holder, V. A. (Worcs. and W. Indies) b Oct. 8, 1945

Holding, M. A. (Lancs., Derby., Tasmania and W. Indies: *CY 1977*) b Feb. 16, 1954

Holdsworth, R. L. (Oxford U., Warw. and Sussex) b Feb. 25, 1899, d June 20, 1976

Hole, G. B. (Australia) b Jan. 6, 1931

Holford, D. A. J. (W. Indies) b April 16, 1940

Holliday, D. C. (Camb. U.) b Dec. 20, 1958

Hollies, W. E. (Warw.; *CY 1955*) b June 5, 1912, d April 16, 1981

Hollingdale, R. A. (Sussex) b March 6, 1906

Holmes, A. J. (Sussex) b June 30, 1899, d May 21, 1950

Holmes, E. R. T. (Oxford U. and Surrey; *CY 1936*) b Aug. 21, 1905, d Aug. 16, 1960

Holmes, G. C. (Glam.) b Sept. 16, 1958

Holmes, Percy (Yorks.; *CY 1920*) b Nov. 25, 1886, d Sept. 3, 1971

Holt, A. G. (Hants) b April 8, 1911

Holt, J. K., jun. (W. Indies) b Aug. 12, 1923

Home of the Hirsel, Lord (Middx; Pres. MCC 1966-67) b July 2, 1903

Hone, Sir B. W. (S. Australia and Oxford U.) b July 1, 1907, d May 28, 1978

Hone, L. (MCC) b Jan. 30, 1853, d Dec. 31, 1896

Hooker, J. E. H. (NSW) b March 6, 1898, d Feb. 12, 1982

Hooker, R. W. (Middx) b Feb. 22, 1935

Hookes, D. W. (Australia) b May 3, 1955

Hopkins, A. J. Y. (Australia) b May 4, 1874, d April 25, 1931

Hopkins, J. A. (Glam.) b June 16, 1953

Hopkins, V. (Glos.) b Jan. 21, 1911

Hopwood, J. L. (Lancs.) b Oct. 30, 1903

Horan, T. P. (Australia) b March 8, 1854, d April 16, 1916

Hordern, H. V. (Australia) b Feb. 10, 1883, d June 17, 1938

Hornby, A. N. (Lancs.) b Feb. 10, 1847, d Dec. 17, 1925

Horner, N. F. (Yorks. and Warw.) b May 10, 1926

Hornibrook, P. M. (Australia) b July 27, 1899, d Aug. 25, 1976

Horsfall, R. (Essex and Glam.) b June 26, 1920, d Aug. 25, 1981

Horsley, J. (Notts. and Derby.) b Jan. 4, 1890, d Feb. 13, 1976

Horton, H. (Worcs. and Hants) b April 18, 1923

Horton, J. (Worcs.) b Aug. 12, 1916

Horton, M. J. (Worcs. and N. Districts) b April 21, 1934

Hossell, J. J. (Warw.) b May 25, 1914

Hough, K. W. (N. Zealand) b Oct. 24, 1928

Howard, A. B. (W. Indies) b Aug. 27, 1946

Howard, A. H. (Glam.) b Dec. 11, 1910

Howard, B. J. (Lancs.) b May 21, 1926

Howard, K. (Lancs.) b June 29, 1941

Howard, N. D. (Lancs.) b May 18, 1925, d May 31, 1979

Howard, Major R. (Lancs.; MCC Team Manager) b April 17, 1890, d Sept. 10, 1967

Howarth, G. P. (Surrey and N. Zealand) b March 29, 1951

Howarth, H. J. (N. Zealand) b Dec. 25, 1943

Howat, M. G. (Camb. U.) b March 2, 1958

Howell, H. (Warw.) b Nov. 29, 1890, d July 9, 1932

Howell, M. (Oxford U. and Surrey) b Sept. 9, 1893, d Feb. 23, 1976

Howell, W. P. (Australia) b Dec. 29, 1869, d July 14, 1940

Howland, C. B. (Camb. U., Sussex and Kent) b Feb. 6, 1936

Howorth, R. (Worcs.) b April 26, 1909, d April 2, 1980

Hughes, D. P. (Lancs. and Tasmania) b May 13, 1947

Hughes, K. J. (Australia; *CY 1981*) b Jan. 26, 1954

Hughes, S. P. (Middx and N. Transvaal) b Dec. 20, 1959

Huish, F. H. (Kent) b Nov. 15, 1869, d March 16, 1957

Hulme, J. H. A. (Middx) b Aug. 26, 1904

Human, J. H. (Camb. U. and Middx) b Jan. 13, 1912

Humpage, G. W. (Warw. and Orange Free State) b April 24, 1954

Humphries, D. J. (Leics. and Worcs.) b Aug. 6, 1953

Humphries, J. (Derby.) b May 17, 1876, d May 8, 1946

Hunt, A. V. (Scotland and Bermuda) b Oct. 1, 1910

Hunt, W. A. (Australia) b Aug. 26, 1908

Hunte, C. C. (W. Indies; *CY 1964*) b May 9, 1932

Hunte, E. A. C. (W. Indies) b Oct. 3, 1905, d Aug. 1967

Hunter, David (Yorks.) b Feb. 23, 1860, d Jan. 11, 1927

Hunter, Joseph (Yorks.) b Aug. 3, 1855, d Jan. 4, 1891

Hurd, A. (Camb. U. and Essex) b Sept. 7, 1937

Hurst, A. G. (Australia) b July 15, 1950

Hurst, R. J. (Middx) b Dec. 29, 1933

Hurwood, A. (Australia) b June 17, 1902, d Sept. 26, 1982

Hussain, M. Dilawar (India) b March 19, 1907, d Aug. 26, 1967

Hutchings, K. L. (Kent; *CY 1907*) b Dec. 7, 1882, d Sept. 3, 1916

Hutchinson, J. M. (Derby.) b Nov. 29, 1896

Hutchinson, P. (S. Africa) b Jan. 26, 1862, d Sept. 30, 1925

Hutton, Sir Leonard (Yorks.; *CY 1938*) b June 23, 1916

Hutton, R. A. (Camb. U., Yorks. and Transvaal) b Sept. 6, 1942

Huxford, P. N. (Oxford U.) b Feb. 17, 1960

Huxter, R. J. A. (Camb. U.) b Oct. 3, 1959

Hylton, L. G. (W. Indies) b March 29, 1905, d May 17, 1955

Ibadulla, K. (Warw., Tasmania, Otago and Pakistan) b Dec. 20, 1935

Ibrahim, K. C. (India) b Jan. 26, 1919

Iddon, J. (Lancs.) b Jan. 8, 1902, d April 17, 1946

Ijaz Butt (Pakistan) b March 10, 1938

Ijaz Faqih (Pakistan) b March 24, 1956

Ikin, J. T. (Lancs.) b March 7, 1918

Illingworth, R. (Yorks. and Leics.; *CY 1960*) b June 8, 1932

Illingworth, R. K. (Worcs.) b Aug. 23, 1963

Imran Khan Niazi (Oxford U., Worcs., Sussex and Pakistan; *CY 1983*) b Nov. 25, 1952

Imtiaz Ahmed (Pakistan) b Jan. 5, 1928

Imtiaz Ali (W. Indies) b July 28, 1954

Inchmore, J. D. (Worcs. and N. Transvaal) b Feb. 22, 1949

Indrajitsinhji, K. S. (India) b June 15, 1937

Ingle, R. A. (Somerset) b Nov. 5, 1903

Ingleby-Mackenzie, A. C. D. (Hants) b Sept. 15, 1933

Inman, C. C. (Ceylon and Leics.) b Jan. 29, 1936

Innes, G. A. S. (W. Province and Transvaal) b Nov. 16, 1931, d July 19, 1982

Inshan Ali (W. Indies) b Sept. 25, 1949

Insole, D. J. (Camb. U. and Essex; *CY 1956*) b April 18, 1926

Intikhab Alam Khan (Surrey and Pakistan) b Dec. 28, 1941

Inverarity, R. J. (Australia) b Jan. 31, 1944

Iqbal Qasim (Pakistan) b Aug. 6, 1953

Irani, J. K. (India) b Aug. 18, 1923

Iredale, F. A. (Australia) b June 19, 1867, d April 15, 1926

Iremonger, J. (Notts.; *CY 1903*) b March 5, 1876, d March 25, 1956

Ironmonger, H. (Australia) b April 7, 1882, d May 31, 1971

Ironside, D. E. J. (S. Africa) b May 2, 1925

Irvine, B. L. (Natal, Essex and Transvaal) b March 9, 1944

Israr Ali (Pakistan) b May 1, 1927

Iverson, J. B. (Australia) b July 27, 1915, d Oct. 24, 1973

Jackman, R. D. (Surrey, W. Province and Rhodesia; *CY 1981*) b Aug. 13, 1945
Jackson, A. (Australia) b Scotland Sept. 5, 1909, d Feb. 16, 1933
Jackson, A. B. (Derby.) b Aug. 21, 1933
Jackson, Sir A. H. M. (Derby.) b Nov. 9, 1899, d Oct. 11, 1983
Jackson, E. J. W. (Camb. U.) b March 26, 1955
Jackson, Rt Hon. Sir F. S. (Camb. U. and Yorks.; *CY 1894*; Pres. MCC 1921) b Nov. 21, 1870, d March 9, 1947
Jackson, G. R. (Derby.) b June 23, 1896, d Feb. 21, 1966
Jackson, H. L. (Derby.; *CY 1959*) b April 5, 1921
Jackson, John (Notts. and All-England) b May 21, 1833, d Nov. 4, 1901
Jackson, P. F. (Worcs.) b May 11, 1911
Jacques, T. A. (Yorks.) b Feb. 19, 1905
Jahangir Khan, Dr (Camb. U. and India) b Feb. 1, 1910
Jai, L. P. (India) b April 1, 1902, d Jan. 29, 1968
Jaisimha, M. L. (India) b March 3, 1939
Jakeman, F. (Yorks. and Northants) b Jan. 10, 1920
Jalal-ud-Din (Pakistan) b June 12, 1959
James, A. E. (Sussex) b Aug. 7, 1924
James, K. C. (Northants and N. Zealand) b March 12, 1904, d Aug. 21, 1976
James, R. M. (Camb. U. and Wellington) b Oct. 2, 1934
Jameson, J. A. (Warw.) b June 30, 1941
Jamshedji, R. J. D. (India) b Nov. 18, 1892, d April 5, 1976
Jardine, D. R. (Oxford U. and Surrey; *CY 1928*) b Oct. 23, 1900, d June 18, 1958
Jardine, M. R. (Oxford U. and Middx) b June 8, 1869, d Jan. 16, 1947
Jarman, B. N. (Australia) b Feb. 17, 1936
Jarrett, D. W. (Oxford U. and Cambridge U.) b April 19, 1952
Jarvis, A. H. (Australia) b Oct. 19, 1860, d Nov. 15, 1933
Jarvis, K. B. S. (Kent) b April 23, 1953
Jarvis, T. W. (N. Zealand) b July 29, 1944
Javed Akhtar (Pakistan) b Nov. 21, 1940
Javed Miandad Khan (Sussex, Glam. and Pakistan; *CY 1982*) b June 12, 1957
Jayantilal, K. (India) b Jan. 13, 1948
Jayasekera, R. S. A. (Sri Lanka) b Dec. 7, 1957
Jayasinghe, S. (Ceylon and Leics.) b Jan. 19, 1931
Jefferson, R. I. (Camb. U. and Surrey) b Aug. 15, 1941
Jeganathan, S. (Sri Lanka) b July 11, 1951

Jenkins, R. O. (Worcs.; *CY 1950*) b Nov. 24, 1918
Jenkins, V. G. J. (Oxford U. and Glam.) b Nov. 2, 1911
Jenner, T. J. (Australia) b Sept. 8, 1944
Jennings, C. B. (Australia) b June 5, 1884, d June 20, 1950
Jennings, K. F. (Somerset) b Oct. 5, 1953
Jennings, R. V. (Transvaal) b Aug. 9, 1954
Jepson, A. (Notts.) b July 12, 1915
Jessop, G. L. (Camb. U. and Glos.; *CY 1898*) b May 19, 1874, d May 11, 1955
Jesty, T. E. (Hants, Border and Griqualand W; *CY 1983*) b June 2, 1948
Jewell, Major M. F. S. (Sussex and Worcs.) b Sept. 15, 1885, d May 28, 1978
Jilani, M. Baga Khan (India) b July 20, 1911, d July 2, 1941
John, V. B. (Sri Lanka) b June 27, 1960
Johnson, C. (Yorks.) b Sept. 5, 1947
Johnson, C. L. (S. Africa) b 1871, d May 31, 1908
Johnson, G. W. (Kent and Transvaal) b Nov. 8, 1946
Johnson, H. H. H. (W. Indies) b July 17, 1910
Johnson, H. L. (Derby.) b Nov. 8, 1927
Johnson, I. W. (Australia) b Dec. 8, 1918
Johnson, L. A. (Surrey and Northants) b Aug. 12, 1936
Johnson, L. J. (Australia) b March 18, 1919, d April 20, 1977
Johnson, P. (Notts.) b April 24, 1965
Johnson, P. D. (Camb. U. and Notts.) b Nov. 12, 1949
Johnson, T. F. (W. Indies) b Jan. 10, 1917
Johnston, W. A. (Australia; *CY 1949*) b Feb. 26, 1922
Johnstone, C. P. (Camb. U., Kent and Madras) b Aug. 19, 1895, d June 23, 1974
Jones, A. (Glam., W. Australia, N. Transvaal and Natal; *CY 1978*) b Nov. 4, 1938
Jones, A. A. (Sussex, Somerset, Middx, Glam., N. Transvaal and Orange Free State) b Dec. 9, 1947
Jones, A. L. (Glam.) b June 1, 1957
Jones, A. O. (Notts. and Camb. U.; *CY 1900*) b Aug. 16, 1872, d Dec. 21, 1914
Jones, B. J. R. (Worcs.) b Nov. 2, 1955
Jones, C. M. (W. Indies) details not known
Jones, Ernest (Australia) b Sept. 30, 1869, d Nov. 23, 1943
Jones, E. C. (Glam.) b Dec. 14, 1912
Jones, E. W. (Glam.) b June 25, 1942
Jones, I. J. (Glam.) b Dec. 10, 1941
Jones, K. V. (Middx) b March 28, 1942
Jones, P. E. (W. Indies) b June 6, 1917
Jones, P. H. (Kent) b June 19, 1935
Jones, S. P. (Auckland and Australia) b Aug. 1, 1861, d July 14, 1951
Jones, W. E. (Glam.) b Oct. 31, 1916

Jordan, A. B. (C. Districts) b Sept. 5, 1949

Jordan, J. M. (Lancs.) b Feb. 7, 1932

Jorden, A. M. (Camb. U. and Essex) b Jan. 28, 1947

Jordon, R. C. (Victoria) b Feb. 17, 1937

Joshi, P. G. (India) b Oct. 27, 1926

Joshi, U. C. (Gujerat and Sussex) b Dec. 23, 1944

Joslin, L. R. (Australia) b Dec. 13, 1947

Jowett, D. C. P. R. (Oxford U.) b June 24, 1931

Judd, A. K. (Camb. U. and Hants) b Jan. 1, 1904

Judge, P. F. (Middx, Glam. and Bengal) b May 23, 1916

Julian, R. (Leics.) b Aug. 23, 1936

Julien, B. D. (Kent and W. Indies) b March 13, 1950

Jumadeen, R. R. (W. Indies) b April 12, 1948

Jupp, H. (Surrey) b Nov. 19, 1841, d April 8, 1889

Jupp, V. W. C. (Sussex and Northants; *CY 1928*) b March 27, 1891, d July 9, 1960

Kallicharran, A. I. (Warw., Queensland and W. Indies; *CY 1983*) b March 21, 1949

Kaluperuma, L. W. (Sri Lanka) b June 25, 1949

Kanhai, R. B. (Warw., W. Australia, Tasmania and W. Indies; *CY 1964*) b Dec. 26, 1935

Kanitkar, H. S. (India) b Dec. 8, 1942

Kapil Dev (Northants and India; *CY 1983*) b Jan. 6, 1959

Kaplan, C. J. (Orange Free State) b Jan. 26, 1909

Kardar, A. H. (formerly Abdul Hafeez) (Oxford U., Warw., India and Pakistan) b Jan. 17, 1925

Katz, G. A. (Natal) b Feb. 9, 1947

Kayum, D. A. (Oxford U.) b Oct. 13, 1955

Keeton, W. W. (Notts.; *CY 1940*) b April 30, 1905, d Oct. 9, 1980

Keighley, W. G. (Oxford U. and Yorks.) b Jan. 10, 1925

Keith, G. L. (Somerset, W. Province and Hants) b Nov. 19, 1937, d Dec. 26, 1975

Keith, H. J. (S. Africa) b Oct. 25, 1927

Kelleher, H. R. A. (Surrey and Northants) b March 3, 1929

Kelleway, C. (Australia) b April 25, 1886, d Nov. 16, 1944

Kelly, J. (Notts.) b Sept. 15, 1930

Kelly, J. J. (Australia; *CY 1903*) b May 10, 1867, d Aug. 14, 1938

Kelly, J. M. (Lancs. and Derby.) b March 19, 1922, d Nov. 13, 1979

Kelly, T. J. D. (Australia) b Ireland May 3, 1844, d July 20, 1893

Kempis, G. A. (S. Africa) b Aug. 4, 1865, d May 19, 1890

Kendall, T. (Australia) b Bedford, England Aug. 24, 1851, d Aug. 17, 1924

Kennedy, A. (Lancs.) b Nov. 4, 1949

Kennedy, A. S. (Hants; *CY 1933*) b Jan. 24, 1891, d Nov. 15, 1959

Kenny, R. B. (India) b Sept. 29, 1930

Kent, M. F. (Australia) b Nov. 23, 1953

Kentish, E. S. M. (Oxford U. and W. Indies) b Nov. 21, 1916

Kenyon, D. (Worcs.; *CY 1963*) b May 15, 1924

Kerr, J. L. (N. Zealand) b Dec. 28, 1910

Kerslake, R. C. (Camb. U. and Somerset) b Dec. 26, 1942

Kettle, M. K. (Northants) b March 18, 1944

Khalid Hassan (Pakistan) b July 14, 1937

Khalid Ibadulla, (*see* Ibadulla, K.)

Khalid Wazir Ali (Pakistan) b April 27, 1936

Khan Mohammad (Somerset and Pakistan) b Jan. 1, 1928

Kidd, E. L. (Camb. U. and Middx; oldest living County Championship player) b Oct. 18, 1889

Killick, Rev. E. T. (Camb. U. and Middx) b May 9, 1907, d May 18, 1953

Kilner, Norman (Yorks. and Warw.) b July 21, 1895, d April 28, 1979

Kilner, Roy (Yorks.; *CY 1924*) b Oct. 17, 1890, d April 5, 1928

Kimpton, R. C. M. (Oxford U. and Worcs.) b Sept. 21, 1916

King, C. L. (Glam., Worcs. and W. Indies) b June 11, 1951

King, F. McD. (W. Indies) b Dec. 14, 1926

King, I. M. (Warw. and Essex) b Nov. 10, 1931

King, J. B. (Philadelphia) b Oct. 19, 1873, d Oct. 17, 1965

King, J. H. (Leics.) b April 16, 1871, d Nov. 20, 1946

King, L. A. (Jamaica, Bengal and W. Indies) b Feb. 27, 1939

Kingsley, Sir Patrick (PGT) (Oxford U.) b May 26, 1908

Kinneir, S. P. (Warw.; *CY 1912*) b May 13, 1871, d Oct. 16, 1928

Kippax, A. F. (Australia) b May 25, 1897, d Sept. 5, 1972

Kirby, D. (Camb. U. and Leics.) b Jan. 18, 1939

Kirmani, S. M. H. (India) b Dec. 29, 1949

Kirsten, P. N. (W. Province, Sussex and Derby.) b May 14, 1955

Kirton, K. N. (Border and E. Province) b Feb. 24, 1928

Kischenchand, G. (India) b April 14, 1925

Kitchen, M. J. (Somerset) b Aug. 1, 1940

Kline, L. F. (Australia) b Sept. 29, 1934

Knight, A. E. (Leics.; *CY 1904*) b Oct. 8, 1872, d April 25, 1946

Knight, B. R. (Essex and Leics.) b Feb. 18, 1938

Knight, D. J. (Oxford U. and Surrey; *CY 1915*) b May 12, 1894, d Jan. 5, 1960

Knight, J. M. (Oxford U.) b March 16, 1958

Knight, R. D. V. (Camb. U., Surrey, Glos. and Sussex) b Sept. 6, 1946

Knight, W. H. (Editor of *Wisden* 1870-79) b Nov. 29, 1812, d Aug. 16, 1879

Knott, A. P. E. (Kent and Tasmania; *CY 1970*) b April 9, 1946

Knott, C. H. (Oxford U. and Kent) b March 20, 1901

Knott, C. J. (Hants) b Nov. 26, 1914

Knowles, J. (Notts.) b March 25, 1910

Knox, G. (Lancs.) b April 22, 1937

Knox, N. A. (Surrey; *CY 1907*) b Oct. 10, 1884, d March 3, 1935

Kortright, C. J. (Essex) b Jan. 9, 1871, d Dec. 12, 1952

Kotze, J. J. (S. Africa) b Aug. 7, 1879, d July 7, 1931

Kourie, A. J. (Transvaal) b July 30, 1951

Kripal Singh, A. G. (India) b Aug. 6, 1933

Krishnamurthy, P. (India) b July 12, 1947

Kulkarni, U. N. (India) b March 7, 1942

Kumar, V. V. (India) b June 22, 1935

Kunderan, B. K. (India) b Oct. 2, 1939

Kuys, F. (S. Africa) b March 21, 1870, d Sept. 12, 1953

Lacey, Sir F. E. (Camb. U. and Hants; Sec. MCC 1898-1926) b Oct. 19, 1859, d May 26, 1946

Laird, B. M. (Australia) b Nov. 21, 1951

Laker, J. C. (Surrey, Auckland and Essex; *CY 1952*) b Feb. 9, 1922

Lall Singh (India) b Dec. 12, 1909

Lamb, A. J. (W. Province and Northants; *CY 1981*) b June 20, 1954

Lamb, T. M. (Oxford U., Middx and Northants) b March 24, 1953

Lambert, G. E. E. (Glos. and Somerset) b May 11, 1919

Lambert, R. H. (Ireland) b July 18, 1874, d March 24, 1956

Lambert, Wm (Surrey) b 1779, d April 19, 1851

Lampard, A. W. (Victoria and AIF, oldest living Sheffield Shield player) b July 3, 1885

Lance, H. R. (S. Africa) b June 6, 1940

Langdon, C. W. (W. Australia) b July 4, 1922

Langdale, G. R. (Derby. and Somerset) b March 11, 1916

Langford, B. A. (Somerset) b Dec. 17, 1935

Langley, G. R. A. (Australia; *CY 1957*) b Sept. 19, 1919

Langridge, James (Sussex; *CY 1932*) b July 10, 1906, d Sept. 10, 1966

Langridge, J. G. (Sussex; *CY 1950*) b Feb. 10, 1910

Langridge, R. J. (Sussex) b April 13, 1939

Langton, A. B. C. (S. Africa) b March 2, 1912, d Nov. 27, 1942

Larkins, W. (Northants and E. Province) b Nov. 22, 1953

Larter, J. D. F. (Northants) b April 24, 1940

Larwood, H. (Notts.; *CY 1927*) b Nov. 14, 1904

Lashley, P. D. (W. Indies) b Feb. 11, 1937

Latchman, A. H. (Middx and Notts.) b July 26, 1943

Laughlin, T. J. (Australia) b Jan. 30, 1951

Laver, F. (Australia) b Dec. 7, 1869, d Sept. 24, 1919

Lawrence, G. B. (S. Africa) b March 31, 1932

Lawrence, J. (Somerset) b March 29, 1914

Lawry, W. M. (Australia; *CY 1962*) b Feb. 11, 1937

Lawson, G. F. (Lancs. and Australia) b Dec. 7, 1957

Leadbeater, B. (Yorks.) b Aug. 14, 1943

Leadbeater, E. (Yorks. and Warw.) b Aug. 15, 1927

Leary, S. E. (Kent) b April 30, 1933

Lee, C. (Yorks. and Derby.) b March 17, 1924

Lee, F. S. (Middx and Somerset) b July 24, 1905, d March 30, 1982

Lee, G. M. (Notts. and Derby.) b June 7, 1887, d Feb. 29, 1976

Lee, H. W. (Middx) b Oct. 26, 1890, d April 21, 1981

Lee, I. S. (Victoria) b March 24, 1914

Lee, J. W. (Middx and Somerset) b Feb. 1, 1904, d June 20, 1944

Lee, P. G. (Northants and Lancs.; *CY 1976*) b Aug. 27, 1945

Lee, P. K. (Australia) b Sept. 15, 1904, d Aug. 9, 1980

Lee, R. J. (Oxford U.) b March 6, 1950

Lees, W. K. (N. Zealand) b March 19, 1952

Lees, W. S. (Surrey; *CY 1906*) b Dec. 25, 1875, d Sept. 10, 1924

Leese, Sir Oliver W. H., 3rd Bt (Pres. MCC 1965-66) b Oct. 27, 1894, d Jan. 20, 1978

Legall, R. A. (W. Indies) b Dec. 1, 1925

Legard, E. (Warw.) b Aug. 23, 1935

Leggat, I. B. (N. Zealand) b June 7, 1930

Leggat, J. G. (N. Zealand) b May 27, 1926, d March 8, 1973

Lenham, L. J. (Sussex) b May 24, 1936

le Roux, F. L. (S. Africa) b Feb. 5, 1882, d Sept. 22, 1963

le Roux, G. S. (W. Province and Sussex) b Sept. 4, 1955

le Roux, R. A. (Orange Free State) b May 27, 1950

Leslie, C. F. H. (Oxford U. and Middx) b Dec. 8, 1861, d Feb. 12, 1921

Lester, E. I. (Yorks.) b Feb. 18, 1923

Lester, G. (Leics.) b Dec. 27, 1915

Lester, Dr J. A. (Philadelphia) b Cumberland, England Aug. 1, 1871, d Sept. 3, 1969

L'Estrange, M. G. (Oxford U.) b Oct. 12, 1952

Lever, J. K. (Essex and Natal; *CY 1979*) b Feb. 24, 1949

Lever, P. (Lancs. and Tasmania) b Sept. 17, 1940

Leveson Gower, Sir H. D. G. (Oxford U. and Surrey) b May 8, 1873, d Feb. 1, 1954

Levett, W. H. V. (Kent) b Jan. 25, 1908

Lewington, P. J. (Warw.) b Jan. 30, 1950

Lewis, A. R. (Camb. U. and Glam.) b July 6, 1938

Lewis, C. (Kent) b July 27, 1908

Lewis, D. J. (Oxford U. and Rhodesia) b July 27, 1927

Lewis, D. M. (W. Indies) b Feb. 21, 1946

Lewis, E. B. (Warw.) b Jan. 5, 1918, d Oct. 19, 1983

Lewis, E. J. (Glam. and Sussex) b Jan. 31, 1942

Lewis, P. T. (S. Africa) b Oct. 2, 1884, d Jan. 30, 1976

Lewis, R. V. (Hants) b Aug. 6, 1947

Leyland, M. (Yorks.; *CY 1929*) b July 20, 1900, d Jan. 1, 1967

Liaqat Ali Khan (Pakistan) b May 21, 1955

Liddicutt, A. E. (Victoria) b Oct. 17, 1891, d April 8, 1983

Lightfoot, A. (Northants) b Jan. 8, 1936

Lill, J. C. (S. Australia) b Dec. 7, 1933

Lillee, D. K. (Australia; *CY 1973*) b July 18, 1949

Lilley, A. A. (Warw.; *CY 1897*) b Nov. 28, 1866, d Nov. 17, 1929

Lilley, B. (Notts.) b Feb. 11, 1895, d Aug. 4, 1950

Lillywhite, Fred (Sussex; Editor of *Lillywhite's Guide to Cricketers*) b July 23, 1829, d Sept. 15, 1866

Lillywhite, F. W. ("William") (Sussex) b June 13, 1792, d Aug. 21, 1854

Lillywhite, James, jun. (Sussex) b Feb. 23, 1842, d Oct. 25, 1929

Lindsay, D. T. (S. Africa) b Sept. 4, 1939

Lindsay, J. D. (S. Africa) b Sept. 8, 1909

Lindsay, N. V. (S. Africa) b July 30, 1886, d Feb. 2, 1976

Lindwall, R. R. (Australia; *CY 1949*) b Oct. 3, 1921

Ling, W. V. S. (S. Africa) b Oct. 3, 1891, d Sept. 26, 1960

Lissette, A. F. (N. Zealand) b Nov. 6, 1919, d Jan. 24, 1973

Lister, J. (Yorks. and Worcs.) b May 14, 1930

Lister, W. H. L. (Lancs.) b Oct. 7, 1911

Littlewood, D. J. (Cambridge U.) b Oct. 28, 1955

Livingston, L. (NSW and Northants) b May 3, 1920

Livingstone, D. A. (Hants) b Sept. 21, 1933

Livsey, W. H. (Hants) b Sept. 23, 1893, d Sept. 12, 1978

Llewellyn, C. B. (Hants and S. Africa; *CY 1911*) b Sept. 26, 1876, d June 7, 1964

Llewellyn, M. J. (Glam.) b Nov. 27, 1953

Lloyd, B. J. (Glam.) b Sept. 6, 1953

Lloyd, C. H. (W. Indies and Lancs.; *CY 1971*) b Aug. 31, 1944

Lloyd, D. (Lancs.) b March 18, 1947

Lloyd, T. A. (Warw. and Orange Free State) b Nov. 5, 1956

Lloyds, J. W. (Somerset) b Nov. 17, 1954

Loader, P. J. (Surrey and W. Australia; *CY 1958*) b Oct. 25, 1929

Lobb, B. (Warw. and Somerset) b Jan. 11, 1931

Lock, G. A. R. (Surrey, Leics. and W. Australia; *CY 1954*) b July 5, 1929

Lock, H. C. (Surrey) b May 8, 1903, d May 18, 1978

Lockwood, Ephraim (Yorks.) b April 4, 1845, d Dec. 19, 1921

Lockwood, W. H. (Notts. and Surrey; *CY 1899*) b March 25, 1868, d April 26, 1932

Lockyer, T. (Surrey and All-England) b Nov. 1, 1826, d Dec. 22, 1869

Logan, J. D. (S. Africa) b June 24, 1880, d Jan. 3, 1960

Logie, A. L. (W. Indies) b Sept. 28, 1960

Lohmann, G. A. (Surrey, W. Province and Transvaal; *CY 1889*) b June 2, 1865, d Dec. 1, 1901

Lomax, J. G. (Lancs. and Somerset) b May 5, 1925

Long, A. (Surrey and Sussex) b Dec. 18, 1940

Longfield, T. C. (Camb. U. and Kent) b May 12, 1906, d Dec. 21, 1981

Longrigg, E. F. (Camb. U. and Somerset) b April 16, 1906, d July 23, 1974

Lord, Thomas (Middx; founder of Lord's) b Nov. 23, 1755, d Jan. 13, 1832

Love, H. S. B. (Australia) b Aug. 10, 1895, d July 22, 1969

Love, J. D. (Yorks.) b April 22, 1955

Lowndes, W. G. L. F. (Oxford U. and Hants) b Jan. 24, 1898, d May 23, 1982

Lowry, T. C. (Camb. U., Somerset and N. Zealand) b Feb. 17, 1898, d July 20, 1976

Lowson, F. A. (Yorks.) b July 1, 1925

Loxton, S. J. E. (Australia) b March 29, 1921

Lucas, A. P. (Camb. U., Surrey, Middx and Essex) b Feb. 20, 1857, d Oct. 12, 1923

Luckes, W. T. (Somerset) b Jan. 1, 1901, d Oct. 27, 1982

Luckhurst, B. W. (Kent; *CY 1971*) b Feb. 5, 1939

Luddington, R. S. (Oxford U.) b April 8, 1960

Lumb, R. G. (Yorks.) b Feb. 27, 1950

Lundie, E. B. (S. Africa) b March 15, 1888, d Sept. 12, 1917

Lynch, M. A. (Surrey and Guyana) b May 21, 1958

Lyon, B. H. (Oxford U. and Glos.; *CY 1931*) b Jan. 19, 1902, d June 22, 1970

Lyon, J. (Lancs.) b May 17, 1951

Lyon, M. D. (Cambridge U. and Somerset) b April 22, 1898, d Feb. 17, 1964

Lyons, J. J. (Australia) b May 21, 1863, d July 21, 1927

Lyons, K. J. (Glam.) b Dec. 18, 1946

Lyttelton, Rt Hon. Alfred (Camb. U. and Middx; Pres. MCC 1898) b Feb. 7, 1857, d July 5, 1913

Lyttelton, Rev. Hon. C. F. (Camb. U. and Worcs.) b Jan. 26, 1887, d Oct. 3, 1931

Lyttelton, Hon. C. J. (*see* 10th Visct Cobham)

Lyttelton, Hon. R. H. (Eton) b Jan. 18, 1854, d Nov. 7, 1939

McAlister, P. A. (Australia) b July 11, 1869, d May 10, 1938

Macartney, C. G. (Australia; *CY 1922*) b June 27, 1886, d Sept. 9, 1958

Macaulay, G. G. (Yorks.; *CY 1924*) b Dec. 7, 1897, d Dec. 14, 1940

Macaulay, M. J. (S. Africa) b April 19, 1939

MacBryan, J. C. W. (Camb. U. and Somerset; *CY 1925*) b July 22, 1892, d July 15, 1983

McCabe, S. J. (Australia; *CY 1935*) b July 16, 1910, d Aug. 25, 1968

McCanlis, M. A. (Oxford U., Surrey and Glos.) b June 17, 1906

McCarthy, C. N. (Camb. U. and S. Africa) b March 24, 1929

McConnon, J. (Glam.) b June 21, 1922

McCool, C. L. (Somerset and Australia) b Dec. 9, 1915

McCorkell, N. T. (Hants) b March 23, 1912

McCormick, E. L. (Australia) b May 16, 1906

McCosker, R. B. (Australia; *CY 1976*) b Dec. 11, 1946

McDonald, C. C. (Australia) b Nov. 17, 1928

McDonald, E. A. (Lancs. and Australia; *CY 1922*) b Jan. 6, 1891, d July 22, 1937

McDonnell, P. S. (Australia) b London Nov. 13, 1858, d Sept. 24, 1896

McEvoy, M. S. A. (Essex and Worcs.) b Jan. 25, 1956

McEwan, K. S. (E. Province, W. Province, Essex and W. Australia; *CY 1978*) b July 16, 1952

McEwan, P. E. (N. Zealand) b Dec. 19, 1953

McGahey, C. P. (Essex; *CY 1902*) b Feb. 12, 1871, d Jan. 10, 1935

MacGibbon, A. R. (N. Zealand) b Aug. 28, 1924

McGirr, H. M. (N. Zealand) b Nov. 5, 1891, d April 14, 1964

McGlew, D. J. (S. Africa; *CY 1956*) b March 11, 1929

MacGregor, G. (Camb. U. and Middx; *CY 1891*) b Aug. 31, 1869, d Aug. 20, 1919

McGregor, S. N. (N. Zealand) b Dec. 18, 1931

McHugh, F. P. (Yorks. and Glos.) b Nov. 15, 1925

McIlwraith, J. (Australia) b Sept. 7, 1857, d July 5, 1938

Macindoe, D. H. (Oxford U.) b Sept. 1, 1917

McIntyre, A. J. W. (Surrey; *CY 1958*) b May 14, 1918

McIntyre, J. M. (Auckland and Canterbury) b July 4, 1944

Mackay, K. D. (Australia) b Oct. 24, 1925, d June 13, 1982

McKay-Coghill, D. (Transvaal) b Nov. 4, 1941

McKenzie, G. D. (Leics. and Australia; *CY 1965*) b June 24, 1941

McKenzie, K. A. (NE Transvaal and Transvaal) b July 16, 1948

McKibbin, T. R. (Australia) b Dec. 10, 1870, d Dec. 15, 1939

McKinnon, A. H. (S. Africa) b Aug. 20, 1932, d Dec. 2, 1983

MacKinnon, F. A. (Camb. U. and Kent) b April 9, 1848, d Feb. 27, 1947

McLachlan, I. M. (Camb. U. and S. Australia) b Oct. 2, 1936

MacLaren, A. C. (Lancs.; *CY 1895*) b Dec. 1, 1871, d Nov. 17, 1944

McLaren, J. W. (Australia) b Dec. 24, 1887, d Nov. 17, 1921

McLaughlin, J. J. (Queensland) b Feb. 18, 1930

Maclean, J. A. (Australia) b April 27, 1946

McLean, R. A. (S. Africa; *CY 1961*) b July 9, 1930

McLeod, C. E. (Australia) b Oct. 24, 1869, d Nov. 26, 1918

McLeod, E. G. (N. Zealand) b Oct. 14, 1900

McLeod, R. W. (Australia) b Jan. 19, 1868, d June 15, 1907

McMahon, J. W. (Surrey and Somerset) b Dec. 28, 1919

McMahon, T. G. (N. Zealand) b Nov. 8, 1929

McMaster, J. E. P. (England) b March 16, 1861, d June 7, 1929

McMillan, Q. (S. Africa) b June 23, 1904, d July 3, 1948

McMorris, E. D. A. (W. Indies) b April 4, 1935

McNally, J. P. (Griqualand W.) b Nov. 27, 1907

McRae, D. A. N. (N. Zealand) b Dec. 25, 1912

McShane, P. G. (Australia) b 1857, d Dec. 11, 1903

McVicker, N. M. (Warw. and Leics.) b Nov. 4, 1940

McWatt, C. A. (W. Indies) b Feb. 1, 1922

Madan Lal (India) b March 20, 1951

Maddocks, L. V. (Australia) b May 24, 1926

Madray, I. S. (W. Indies) b July 2, 1934

Madson, M. B. (Natal) b Sept. 29, 1949

Madugalle, R. S. (Sri Lanka) b April 22, 1959

Mahmood Hussain (Pakistan) b April 2, 1932

Mailey, A. A. (Australia) b Jan. 3, 1886, d Dec. 31, 1967

Majid J. Khan (Camb. U., Glam., Queensland and Pakistan; *CY 1970*) b Sept. 28, 1946

Maka, E. S. (India) b March 5, 1922

Makepeace, H. (Lancs.) b Aug. 22, 1881, d Dec. 19, 1952

Malhotra, A. (India) b June 26, 1957

Mallender, N. A. (Northants) b Aug. 13, 1961

Mallett, A. A. (Australia) b July 13, 1945

Mallett, A. W. H. (Oxford U. and Kent) b Aug. 29, 1924

Mallett, N. V. H. (Oxford U.) b Oct. 30, 1956

Malone, M. F. (Australia and Lancs.) b Oct. 9, 1950

Malone, S. J. (Essex and Hants) b Oct. 19, 1953

Manjrekar, V. L. (India) b Sept. 26, 1931, d Oct. 18, 1983

Mankad, A. V. (India) b Oct. 12, 1946

Mankad, V. (M. H.) (India; *CY 1947*) b April 12, 1917, d Aug. 21, 1978

Mann, A. L. (Australia) b Nov. 8, 1945

Mann, F. G. (Camb. U. and Middx) b Sept. 6, 1917

Mann, F. T. (Camb. U. and Middx) b March 3, 1888, d Oct. 6, 1964

Mann, J. P. (Middx) b June 13, 1919

Mann, N. B. F. (S. Africa) b Dec. 28, 1920, d July 31, 1952

Manning, J. S. (S. Australia and Northants) b June 11, 1924

Manning, T. E. S. (Northants) b Sept. 2, 1884, d Nov. 22, 1975

Mansell, P. N. F. (S. Africa) b Shropshire March 16, 1920

Mansoor Akhtar (Pakistan) b Dec. 25, 1956

Mantri, M. K. (India) b Sept. 1, 1921

Maqsood Ahmed (Pakistan) b March 26, 1925

Marais, G. G. ("G. Gladstone") (W. Indies) b Jan. 14, 1901, d May 19, 1978

Marie, G. V. (Oxford U.) b Feb. 17, 1945

Markham, L. A. (S. Africa) b Sept. 12, 1924

Marks, V. J. (Oxford U. and Somerset) b June 25, 1955

Marlar, R. G. (Camb. U. and Sussex) b Jan. 2, 1931

Marlow, W. H. (Leics.) b Feb. 13, 1900, d Dec. 16, 1975

Marner, P. T. (Lancs. and Leics.) b March 31, 1936

Marr, A. P. (Australia) b March 28, 1862, d March 15, 1940

Marriott, C. S. (Camb. U., Lancs. and Kent) b Sept. 14, 1895, d Oct. 13, 1966

Marsden, R. (Oxford U.) b April 2, 1959

Marsden, Tom (England) b 1805, d Feb. 27, 1843

Marsh, F. E. (Derby.) b July 7, 1920

Marsh, R. W. (Australia; *CY 1982*) b Nov. 4, 1947

Marshal, Alan (Queensland and Surrey; *CY 1909*) b June 12, 1883, d July 23, 1915

Marshall, J. M. A. (Warw.) b Oct. 26, 1916

Marshall, M. D. (Hants and W. Indies; *CY 1983*) b April 18, 1958

Marshall, N. E. (W. Indies) b Feb. 27, 1924

Marshall, R. E. (Hants and W. Indies; *CY 1959*) b April 25, 1930

Martin, E. J. (Notts.) b Aug. 17, 1925

Martin, F. (Kent; *CY 1892*) b Oct. 12, 1861, d Dec. 13, 1921

Martin, F. R. (W. Indies) b Oct. 12, 1893, d Nov. 23, 1967

Martin, J. D. (Oxford U. and Somerset) b Dec. 23, 1941

Martin, J. W. (Australia) b July 28, 1931

Martin, J. W. (Kent) b Feb. 16, 1917

Martin, S. H. (Worcs., Natal and Rhodesia) b Jan. 11, 1909

Martindale, E. A. (W. Indies) b Nov. 25, 1909, d March 17, 1972

Marx, W. F. E. (S. Africa) b July 4, 1895, d June 2, 1974

Mason, J. R. (Kent; *CY 1898*) b March 26, 1874, d Oct. 15, 1958

Massie, H. H. (Australia) b April 11, 1854, d Oct. 12, 1938

Massie, R. A. L. (Australia; *CY 1973*) b April 14, 1947

Matheson, A. M. (N. Zealand) b Feb. 27, 1906

Mathias, Wallis (Pakistan) b Feb. 4, 1935

Matthews, A. D. G. (Northants and Glam.) b May 3, 1904, d July 29, 1977

Matthews, C. S. (Notts.) b Oct. 17, 1929

Matthews, T. J. (Australia) b April 3, 1884, d Oct. 14, 1943

Mattis, E. H. (W. Indies) b April 11, 1957

Maudsley, R. H. (Oxford U. and Warw.) b April 8, 1918, d Sept. 29, 1981

May, P. B. H. (Camb. U. and Surrey; *CY 1952*; Pres. MCC 1980-81) b Dec. 31, 1929

Mayer, J. H. (Warw.) b March 2, 1902, d Sept. 6, 1981

Mayes, R. (Kent) b Oct. 7, 1921

Maynard, C. (Warw. and Lancs.) b April 8, 1958

Mayne, E. R. (Australia) b July 2, 1882, d Oct. 26, 1961

Mayne, L. C. (Australia) b Jan. 26, 1942

Mead, C. P. (Hants; *CY 1912*) b March 9, 1887, d March 26, 1958

Mead, W. (Essex; *CY 1904*) b March 25, 1868, d March 18, 1954

Meads, E. A. (Notts.) b Aug. 17, 1916

Meale, T. (N. Zealand) b Nov. 11, 1928

Meckiff, I. (Australia) b Jan. 6, 1935

Meher-Homji, K. R. (India) b Aug. 9, 1911, d Feb. 10, 1982

Mehra, V. L. (India) b March 12, 1938

Meintjes, D. J. (S. Africa) b June 9, 1890, d July 17, 1979

Melle, M. G. (S. Africa) b June 3, 1930

Melluish, M. E. L. (Camb. U. and Middx) b June 13, 1932

Melville, A. (Oxford U., Sussex and S. Africa; *CY 1948*) b May 19, 1910, d April 18, 1983

Mence, M. D. (Warw. and Glos.) b April 30, 1944

Mendis, G. D. (Sussex) b April 20, 1955

Mendis, L. R. D. (Sri Lanka) b Aug. 25, 1952

Mendonca, I. L. (W. Indies) b July 13, 1934

Mercer, J. (Sussex, Glam. and Northants; *CY 1927*) b April 22, 1895

Merchant, V. M. (India; *CY 1937*) b Oct. 12, 1911

Merritt, W. E. (Northants and N. Zealand) b Aug. 18, 1908, d June 9, 1977

Merry, C. A. (W. Indies) b Jan. 20, 1911, d April 19, 1964

Meuleman, K. D. (Australia) b Sept. 5, 1923

Meuli, E. M. (N. Zealand) b Feb. 20, 1926

Meyer, B. J. (Glos.) b Aug. 21, 1932

Meyer, R. J. O. (Camb. U., Somerset and W. India) b March 15, 1905

Mian Mohammad Saaed (Pakistan's first captain) b Aug. 31, 1910, d Aug. 23, 1979

Middleton, J. (S. Africa) b Sept. 30, 1865, d Dec. 23, 1913

Midwinter, W. E. (Victoria, Glos., Australia and England) b Forest of Dean, England June 19, 1851, d Dec. 3, 1890

Milburn, B. D. (N. Zealand) b Nov. 24, 1943

Milburn, C. (Northants and W. Australia; *CY 1967*) b Oct. 23, 1941

Milkha Singh, A. G. (India) b Dec. 31, 1941

Miller, A. J. T. (Oxford U. and Middx) b May 30, 1963

Miller, A. M. (England) b Oct. 19, 1869, d June 26, 1959

Miller, G. (Derby.) b Sept. 8, 1952

Miller, K. R. (Notts. and Australia; *CY 1954*) b Nov. 28, 1919

Miller, L. S. M. (N. Zealand) b March 31, 1923

Miller, R. (Warw.) b Jan. 6, 1941

Miller, R. C. (W. Indies) b Dec. 24, 1924

Milligan, F. W. (Yorks.) b March 19, 1870, d March 31, 1900

Millman, G. (Notts.) b Oct. 2, 1934

Mills, C. H. (Surrey and S. Africa) b Nov. 26, 1867, d July 26, 1948

Mills, G. H. (Otago) b Aug. 1, 1916

Mills, J. E. (N. Zealand) b Sept. 3, 1905, d Dec. 11, 1972

Mills, J. M. (Camb. U. and Warw.) b July 27, 1921

Mills, J. P. C. (Camb. U. and Northants) b Dec. 6, 1958

Milner, J. (Essex) b Aug. 22, 1937

Milton, C. A. (Glos.; *CY 1959*) b March 10, 1928

Milton, W. H. (S. Africa) b Dec. 3, 1854, d March 6, 1930

Minnett, R. B. (Australia) b June 13, 1888, d Oct. 21, 1955

"Minshull", John (scorer of first recorded century) b *circa* 1741, d Oct. 1793

Miran Bux, M. (Pakistan) b April 20, 1907

Misson, F. M. (Australia) b Nov. 19, 1938

Mitchell, A. (Yorks.) b Sept. 13, 1902, d Dec. 25, 1976

Mitchell, B. (S. Africa; *CY 1936*) b Jan. 8, 1909

Mitchell, C. G. (Somerset) b Jan. 27, 1929

Mitchell, F. (Camb. U., Yorks., England and S. Africa; *CY 1902*) b Aug. 13, 1872, d Oct. 11, 1935

Mitchell, T. B. (Derby.) b Sept. 4, 1902

Mitchell-Innes, N. S. (Oxford U. and Somerset) b Sept. 7, 1914

Mobey, G. S. (Surrey) b March 5, 1904

Modi, R. S. (India) b Nov. 11, 1924

Mohammad Aslam (Pakistan) b Jan. 5, 1920

Mohammad Farooq (Pakistan) b April 8, 1938

Mohammad Ilyas (Pakistan) b March 19, 1946

Mohammad Munaf (Pakistan) b Nov. 2, 1935

Mohammad Nazir (Pakistan) b March 8, 1946

Mohinder Singh (India) b June 13, 1963

Mohsin Khan (Pakistan) b March 15, 1955

Moir, A. McK. (N. Zealand) b July 17, 1919

Moir, D. G. (Derby. and Scotland) b April 13, 1957

Mold, A. W. (Lancs.; *CY 1892*) b May 27, 1863, d April 29, 1921

Moloney, D. A. R. (N. Zealand) b Aug. 11, 1910, d July 15, 1942

Monckton of Brenchley, 1st Lord (Pres. MCC 1956-57) b Jan. 17, 1891, d Jan. 9, 1965

Monkhouse, G. (Surrey) b April 26, 1954

Monks, C. I. (Glos.) b March 4, 1912, d Jan. 23, 1974

Moodie, G. H. (W. Indies) b Nov. 25, 1915

Moon, L. J. (Camb. U. and Middx) b Feb. 9, 1878, d Nov. 23, 1916

Mooney, F. L. H. (N. Zealand) b May 26, 1921

Moore, D. N. (Oxford U. and Glos.) b Sept. 26, 1910

Moore, H. I. (Notts.) b Feb. 28, 1941

Moore, R. H. (Hants) b Nov. 14, 1913

Morgan, D. C. (Derby.) b Feb. 26, 1929

Morgan, J. T. (Camb. U. and Glam.) b May 7, 1907, d Dec. 18, 1976

Morgan, M. (Notts.) b May 21, 1936

Morgan, R. W. (N. Zealand) b Feb. 12, 1941

Morkel, D. P. B. (S. Africa) b Jan. 25, 1906, d Oct. 6, 1980

Morley, F. (Notts.) b Dec. 16, 1850, d Sept. 28, 1884

Morley, J. D. (Sussex) b Oct. 20, 1950

Moroney, J. R. (Australia) b Oct. 10, 1917

Morrill, N. D. (Oxford U.) b Dec. 9, 1957

Morris, A. R. (Australia; *CY 1949*) b Jan. 19, 1922

Morris, H. M. (Camb. U. and Essex) b April 16, 1898

Morris, R. E. T. (W. Province) b Jan. 28, 1947

Morris, S. (Australia) b June 22, 1855, d Sept. 20, 1931

Morrisby, R. O. G. (Tasmania) b Jan. 12, 1915

Morrison, B. D. (N. Zealand) b Dec. 17, 1933

Morrison, J. F. M. (N. Zealand) b Aug. 27, 1947

Mortensen, O. H. (Denmark and Derby.) b Jan. 29, 1958

Mortimore, J. B. (Glos.) b May 14, 1933

Mortlock, W. (Surrey and Utd England XI) b July 18, 1832, d Jan. 23, 1884

Moseley, H. R. (Somerset) b May 28, 1948

Moses, G. H. (Camb. U.) b Sept. 24, 1952

Moses, H. (Australia) b Feb. 13, 1858, d Dec. 7, 1938

Moss, A. E. (Middx) b Nov. 14, 1930

Moss, J. K. (Australia) b June 29, 1947

Motz, R. C. (N. Zealand; *CY 1966*) b Jan. 12, 1940

Moulding, R. P. (Oxford U. and Middx) b Jan. 3, 1958

Moule, W. H. (Australia) b Jan. 31, 1858, d Aug. 24, 1939

Moylan, A. C. D. (Camb. U.) b June 26, 1955

Mubarak, A. M. (Camb. U.) b July 4, 1951

Mudassar Nazar (Pakistan) b April 6, 1956

Muddiah, V. M. (India) b June 8, 1929

Mufasir-ul-Haq (Pakistan) b Aug. 16, 1944, d. July 27, 1983

Muncer, B. L. (Middx and Glam.) b Oct. 23, 1913, d Jan. 18, 1982

Munden, V. S. (Leics.) b Jan. 2, 1928

Munir Malik (Pakistan) b July 10, 1934

Murdoch, W. L. (Sussex, Australia and England) b Oct. 18, 1854, d Feb. 18, 1911

Murray, A. R. A. (S. Africa) b April 30, 1922

Murray, B. A. G. (N. Zealand) b Sept. 18, 1940

Murray, D. A. (W. Indies) b May 29, 1950

Murray, D. L. (Camb. U., Notts., Warw. and W. Indies) b May 20, 1943

Murray, J. T. (Middx; *CY 1967*) b April 1, 1935

Murray-Willis, P. E. (Worcs. and Northants) b July 14, 1910

Murray-Wood, W. (Oxford U. and Kent) b June 30, 1917, d Dec. 21, 1968

Murrell, H. R. (Kent and Middx) b Nov. 19, 1879, d Aug. 15, 1952

Murrills, T. J. (Camb. U.) b Dec. 22, 1953

Musgrove, H. (Australia) b Nov. 27, 1860, d Nov. 2, 1931

Mushtaq Ali, S. (India) b Dec. 17, 1914

Mushtaq Mohammad (Northants and Pakistan; *CY 1963*) b Nov. 22, 1943

Muzzell, R. K. (W. Province, Transvaal and E. Province) b Dec. 23, 1945

Mynn, Alfred (Kent and All-England) b Jan. 19, 1807, d Oct. 31, 1861

Nadkarni, R. G. (India) b April 4, 1932

Nagel, L. E. (Australia) b March 6, 1905, d Nov. 23, 1971

Naik, S. S. (India) b Feb. 21, 1945

Nanan, R. (W. Indies) b May 29, 1953

Naoomal Jaoomal, M. (India) b April 17, 1904, d July 18, 1980

Narasimha Rao, M. V. (India) b Aug. 11, 1954

Nash, J. E. (S. Australia) b April 16, 1950

Nash, L. J. (Australia) b May 2, 1910

Nash, M. A. (Glam.) b May 9, 1945

Nasim-ul-Ghani (Pakistan) b May 14, 1941

Naushad Ali (Pakistan) b Oct. 1, 1943

Navle, J. G. (India) b Dec. 7, 1902, d Sept. 7, 1979

Nayak, S. V. (India) b Oct. 20, 1954

Nayudu, Col. C. K. (India; *CY 1933*) b Oct. 31, 1895, d Nov. 14, 1967

Nayudu, C. S. (India) b April 18, 1914

Nazar Mohammad (Pakistan) b Aug. 5, 1921

Nazir Ali, S. (Sussex and India) b June 8, 1906, d Feb. 1975

Neale, P. A. (Worcs.) b June 5, 1954

Neblett, J. M. (W. Indies) b Nov. 13, 1901, assumed dead

Neilson, D. R. (Transvaal) b Dec. 17, 1948

Nel, J. D. (S. Africa) b July 10, 1928

Nelson, G. W. (Border) b Nov. 14, 1941

Nelson, R. P. (Camb. U. and Northants) b Aug. 7, 1912, d Oct. 29, 1940

Nevell, W. T. (Middx, Surrey and Northants) b June 13, 1916

Newberry, C. (S. Africa) b 1889, d Aug. 1, 1916

Newdick, G. A. (Wellington) b Jan. 11, 1949

Newham, W. (Sussex) b Dec. 12, 1860, d June 26, 1944

Newland, Richard (Sussex) b *circa* 1718, d May 29, 1791

Newman, G. C. (Oxford U. and Middx) b April 26, 1904, d Oct. 13, 1982

Newman, J. (N. Zealand) b July 3, 1902

Newman, J. A. (Hants and Canterbury) b Nov. 12, 1884, d Dec. 21, 1973

Newsom, E. S. (S. Africa) b Dec. 2, 1910

Newstead, J. T. (Yorks.; *CY 1909*) b Sept. 8, 1877, d March 25, 1952

Niaz Ahmed (Pakistan) b Nov. 11, 1945

Nicholas, M. C. J. (Hants) b Sept. 29, 1957

Nicholls, D. (Kent) b Dec. 8, 1943

Nicholls, R. B. (Glos.) b Dec. 4, 1933

Nichols, M. S. (Essex; *CY 1934*) b Oct. 6, 1900, d Jan. 26, 1961

Nicholson, A. G. (Yorks.) b June 25, 1938

Nicholson, F. (S. Africa) b Sept. 17, 1909, d July 30, 1982

Nicolson, J. F. W. (S. Africa) b July 19, 1899, d Dec. 13, 1935

Nissar, Mahomed (India) b Aug. 1, 1910, d March 11, 1963

Nitschke, H. C. (Australia) b April 14, 1905, d Sept. 29, 1982

Noble, M. A. (Australia; *CY 1900*) b Jan. 28, 1873, d June 21, 1940

Noblet, G. (Australia) b Sept. 14, 1916

Noreiga, J. M. (W. Indies) b April 15, 1936

Norfolk, 16th Duke of (Pres. MCC 1957-58) b May 30, 1908, d Jan. 31, 1975

Norman, M. E. J. C. (Northants and Leics.) b Jan. 19, 1933

Norton, N. O. (S. Africa) b May 11, 1881, d June 27, 1968

Nothling, O. E. (Australia) b Aug. 1, 1900, d Sept. 26, 1965

Nourse, A. D. ("Dudley") (S. Africa; *CY 1948*) b Nov. 12, 1910, d Aug. 14, 1981

Nourse, A. W. ("Dave") (S. Africa) b Croydon, Surrey Jan. 26, 1878, d July 8, 1948

Nugent, 1st Lord (Pres. MCC 1962-63) b Aug. 11, 1895, d April 27, 1973

Nunes, R. K. (W. Indies) b June 7, 1894, d July 22, 1958

Nupen, E. P. (S. Africa) b Jan. 1, 1902, d Jan. 29, 1977

Nurse, S. M. (W. Indies; *CY 1967*) b Nov. 10, 1933

Nutter, A. E. (Lancs. and Northants) b June 28, 1913

Nyalchand, S. (India) b Sept. 14, 1919

Nye, J. K. (Sussex) b May 23, 1914

Nyren, John (Hants) b Dec. 15, 1764, d June 28, 1837

Nyren, Richard (Hants and Sussex) b 1734, d April 25, 1797

Oakes, C. (Sussex) b Aug. 10, 1912

Oakes, J. (Sussex) b March 3, 1916

Oakman, A. S. M. (Sussex) b April 20, 1930

Oates, T. W. (Notts.) b Aug. 9, 1875, d June 18, 1949

Oates, W. F. (Yorks. and Derby.) b June 11, 1929

O'Brien, F. P. (Canterbury and Northants) b Feb. 11, 1911

O'Brien, L. P. J. (Australia) b July 2, 1907

O'Brien, Sir T. C. (Oxford U. and Middx) b Nov. 5, 1861, d Dec. 9, 1948

Ochse, A. E. (S. Africa) b March 11, 1870, d April 11, 1918

Ochse, A. L. (S. Africa) b Oct. 11, 1899, d May 6, 1949

O'Connor, J. (Essex) b Nov. 6, 1897, d Feb. 22, 1977

O'Connor, J. D. A. (Australia) b Sept. 9, 1875, d Aug. 23, 1941

Odendaal, A. (Camb. U. and Boland) b May 4, 1954

Ogilvie, A. D. (Australia) b June 3, 1951

O'Keeffe, K. J. (Somerset and Australia) b Nov. 25, 1949

Old, C. M. (Yorks., Warw. and N. Transvaal; *CY 1979*) b Dec. 22, 1948

Oldfield, N. (Lancs. and Northants) b May 5, 1911

Oldfield, W. A. (Australia; *CY 1927*) b Sept. 9, 1894, d Aug. 10, 1976

Oldham, S. (Yorks. and Derby.) b July 26, 1948

Oldroyd, E. (Yorks.) b Oct. 1, 1888, d Dec. 27, 1964

O'Linn, S. (Kent and S. Africa) b May 5, 1927

Oliver, P. R. (Warw.) b May 9, 1956

O'Neill, N. C. (Australia; *CY 1962*) b Feb. 19, 1937

Ontong, R. C. (Border, Transvaal, N. Transvaal and Glam.) b Sept. 9, 1955

Ord, J. S. (Warw.) b July 12, 1912

Orders, J. O. D. (Oxford U.) b Aug. 12, 1957

O'Reilly, W. J. (Australia; *CY 1935*) b Dec. 20, 1905

O'Riordan, A. J. (Ireland) b July 20, 1940

Ormrod, J. A. (Worcs.) b Dec. 22, 1942

O'Shaughnessy, S. J. (Lancs.) b Sept. 9, 1961

Oslear, D. O. (Umpire) b March 3, 1929

O'Sullivan, D. R. (Hants and N. Zealand) b Nov. 16, 1944

Outschoorn, L. (Worcs.) b Sept. 26, 1918

Overton, G. W. F. (N. Zealand) b June 8, 1919

Owen-Smith, H. G. O. (Oxford U., Middx and S. Africa; *CY 1930*) b Feb. 18, 1909

Owen-Thomas, D. R. (Camb. U. and Surrey) b Sept. 20, 1948

Oxenham, R. K. (Australia) b July 28, 1891, d Aug. 16, 1939

Packe, M. St J. (Leics.) b Aug. 21, 1916, d Dec. 20, 1978

Padgett, D. E. V. (Yorks.) b July 20, 1934

Padmore, A. L. (W. Indies) b Dec. 17, 1946

Page, J. C. T. (Kent) b May 20, 1930

Page, M. H. (Derby.) b June 17, 1941

Page, M. L. (N. Zealand) b May 8, 1902

Pai, A. M. (India) b April 28, 1945

Paine, G. A. E. (Middx and Warw.; *CY 1935*) b June 11, 1908, d March 30, 1978

Pairaudeau, B. H. (N. Districts and W. Indies) b April 14, 1931

Palairet, L. C. H. (Oxford U. and Somerset; *CY 1893*) b May 27, 1870, d March 27, 1933

Palairet, R. C. N. (Oxford U. and Somerset; Joint-Manager MCC in Australia 1932-33) b June 25, 1871, d Feb. 11, 1955

Palia, P. E. (India) b Sept. 5, 1910, d Sept. 9, 1981

Palm, A. W. (S. Africa) b June 8, 1901, d Aug. 17, 1966

Palmer, C. H. (Worcs. and Leics.; Pres. MCC 1978-79) b May 15, 1919

Palmer, G. E. (Australia) b Feb. 22, 1860, d Aug. 22, 1910

Palmer, K. E. (Somerset) b April 22, 1937

Palmer, R. (Somerset) b July 12, 1942

Palmer, R. W. M. (Camb. U.) b June 4, 1960

Pardon, Charles Frederick (Editor of *Wisden* 1887-90) b March 28, 1850, d April 18, 1890

Pardon, Edgar S. (12 years associated with *Wisden*) b Sept. 28, 1859, d July 16, 1898

Pardon, Sydney H. (Editor of *Wisden* 1891-1925) b Sept. 23, 1855, d Nov. 20, 1925

Parfitt, P. H. (Middx; *CY 1963*) b Dec. 8, 1936

Paris, C. G. A. (Hants; Pres. MCC 1975-76) b Aug. 20, 1911

Parish, R. J. (Aust. Administrator) b May 7, 1916

Park, R. L. (Australia) b July 30, 1892, d Jan. 23, 1947

Parkar, G. A. (India) b Oct. 24, 1955

Parkar, R. D. (India) b Oct. 31, 1946

Parker, C. W. L. (Glos.; *CY 1923*) b Oct. 14, 1882, d July 11, 1959

Parker, E. F. (Rhodesia and Griqualand W.) b April 26, 1939

Parker, G. M. (S. Africa) b May 27, 1899, d May 1, 1969

Parker, G. W. (Camb. U. and Glos.) b Feb. 11, 1912

Parker, J. F. (Surrey) b April 23, 1913, d Jan. 27, 1983

Parker, J. M. (Worcs. and N. Zealand) b Feb. 21, 1951

Parker, J. P. (Hants) b Nov. 29, 1902

Parker, N. M. (N. Zealand) b Aug. 28, 1948

Parker, P. W. G. (Camb. U., Sussex and Natal) b Jan. 15, 1956

Parkhouse, W. G. A. (Glam.) b Oct. 12, 1925

Parkin, C. H. (Yorks. and Lancs.; *CY 1924*) b Feb. 18, 1886, d June 15, 1943

Parkin, D. C. (S. Africa) b Feb. 18, 1870, d March 20, 1936

Parks, H. W. (Sussex) b July 18, 1906

Parks, J. H. (Sussex and Canterbury; *CY 1938*) b May 12, 1903, d Nov. 21, 1980

Parks, J. M. (Sussex and Somerset; *CY 1968*) b Oct. 21, 1931

Parks, R. J. (Hants) b June 15, 1959

Parr, F. D. (Lancs.) b June 1, 1928

Parr, George (Notts. and All-England) b May 22, 1826, d June 23, 1891

Parry, D. R. (W. Indies) b Dec. 22, 1954

Parsana, D. D. (India) b Dec. 2, 1947

Parsons, A. B. D. (Camb. U. and Surrey) b Sept. 20, 1933

Parsons, A. E. W. (Auckland and Sussex) b Glasgow Jan. 9, 1949

Parsons, G. J. (Leics.) b Oct. 17, 1959

Parsons, Canon J. H. (Warw.) b May 30, 1890, d Feb. 2, 1981

Partridge, J. T. (S. Africa) b Dec. 9, 1932

Partridge, N. E. (Malvern, Camb. U. and Warw.; *CY 1919*) b Aug. 10, 1900, d March 10, 1982

Partridge, R. J. (Northants) b Feb. 11, 1912

Pascoe, L. S. (Australia) b Feb. 13, 1950

Passailaigue, C. C. (W. Indies) b Aug. 1902, d Jan. 7, 1972

Patankar, C. T. (India) b Nov. 24, 1930

Pataudi, Iftikhar Ali, Nawab of (Oxford U., Worcs., England and India; *CY 1932*) b March 16, 1910, d Jan. 5, 1952

Pataudi, Mansur Ali, Nawab of (Oxford U., Sussex and India; *CY 1968*) b Jan. 5, 1941

Patel, B. P. (India) b Nov. 24, 1952

Patel, D. N. (Worcs.) b Oct. 25, 1958

Patel, J. M. (India) b Nov. 26, 1924

Paterson, R. F. T. (Essex) b Sept. 8, 1916, d May 29, 1980

Pathmanathan, G. (Oxford U., Camb. U. and Sri Lanka) b Jan. 23, 1954

Patiala, Yuvraj of (India) b Jan. 17, 1913

Patil, S. M. (India) b Aug. 18, 1956

Patil, S. R. (India) b Oct. 10, 1933

Paulsen, R. G. (Queensland and W. Australia) b Oct. 18, 1947

Paver, R. G. L. (Oxford U.) b April 4, 1950

Pawson, A. G. (Oxford U. and Worcs.; oldest living Blue) b May 30, 1888

Pawson, H. A. (Oxford U. and Kent) b Aug. 22, 1921

Payn, L. W. (Natal) b May 6, 1915

Paynter, E. (Lancs.; *CY 1938*) b Nov. 5, 1901, d Feb. 5, 1979

Payton, D. H. (C. Districts) b Feb. 19, 1945

Payton, W. R. D. (Notts.) b Feb. 13, 1882, d May 2, 1943

Pearce, G. (Sussex) b Oct. 27, 1908

Pearce, J. P. (Oxford U.) b April 18, 1957

Pearce, T. A. (Kent) b Dec. 18, 1910, d Aug. 11, 1982

Pearce, T. N. (Essex) b Nov. 3, 1905

Pearse, C. O. C. (S. Africa) b Oct. 10, 1884, d May 7, 1953

Pearson, D. B. (Worcs.) b March 29, 1937

Peate, E. (Yorks.) b March 2, 1856, d March 11, 1900

Peck I. G. (Camb. U. and Northants) b Oct. 18, 1957

Peebles, I. A. R. (Oxford U., Middx and Scotland; *CY 1931*) b Jan. 20, 1908, d Feb. 28, 1980

Peel, R. (Yorks.; *CY 1889*) b Feb. 12, 1857, d Aug. 12, 1941

Pegler, S. J. (S. Africa) b July 28, 1888, d Sept. 10, 1972

Pellew, C. E. (Australia) b Sept. 21, 1893, d May 9, 1981

Penn, F. (Kent) b March 7, 1851, d Dec. 26, 1916

Pepper, C. G. (NSW and Aust. Services; Umpire) b Sept. 15, 1918

Perkins, C. G. (Northants) b June 4, 1911

Perks, R. T. D. (Worcs.) b Oct. 4, 1911, d Nov. 22, 1977

Perrin, P. A. (Essex; *CY 1905*) b May 26, 1876, d Nov. 20, 1945

Perryman, S. P. (Warw. and Worcs.) b Oct. 22, 1955

Pervez Sajjad (Pakistan) b Aug. 30, 1942

Petchey, M. D. (Oxford U.) b Dec. 16, 1958

Petherick, P. J. (N. Zealand) b Sept. 25, 1942

Petrie, E. C. (N. Zealand) b May 22, 1927

Pfuhl, G. P. (W. Province) b Aug. 27, 1947

Phadkar, D. G. (India) b Dec. 12, 1925

Phebey, A. H. (Kent) b Oct. 1, 1924

Phelan, P. J. (Essex) b Feb. 9, 1938

Philipson, H. (Oxford U. and Middx) b June 8, 1866, d Dec. 4, 1935

Phillip, N. (Essex and W. Indies) b June 22, 1949

Phillipps, J. H. (N. Zealand Manager 1949, 1958; Manager MCC in N. Zealand 1960-61) b Jan. 1, 1898, d June 8, 1977

Phillipson, C. P. (Sussex) b Feb. 10, 1952

Phillipson, W. E. (Lancs.) b Dec. 3, 1910

Philpott, P. I. (Australia) b Nov. 21, 1934

Piachaud, J. D. (Oxford U., Hants and Ceylon) b March 1, 1937

Pickles, L. (Somerset) b Sept. 17, 1932

Pierre, L. R. (W. Indies) b June 5, 1921

Pigott, A. C. S. (Sussex) b June 4, 1958

Pilch, Fuller (Norfolk and Kent) b March 17, 1804, d May 1, 1870

Pilling, H. (Lancs.) b Feb. 23, 1943

Pilling, R. (Lancs.; *CY 1891*) b July 5, 1855, d March 28, 1891

Pinch, C. J. (NSW and S. Australia) b June 23, 1921

Pithey, A. J. (S. Africa) b July 17, 1933

Pithey, D. B. (Oxford U., Northants and S. Africa) b Oct. 10, 1936

Pitman, R. W. C. (Hants) b Feb. 21, 1933

Place, W. (Lancs.) b Dec. 7, 1914

Platt, R. K. (Yorks. and Northants) b Dec. 21, 1932

Playle, W. R. (W. Australia and N. Zealand) b Dec. 1, 1938

Pleass, J. E. (Glam.) b May 21, 1923

Plimsoll, J. B. (S. Africa) b Oct. 27, 1917

Pocock, N. E. J. (Hants) b Dec. 15, 1951

Pocock, P. I. (Surrey and N. Transvaal) b Sept. 24, 1946

Pollard, R. (Lancs.) b June 19, 1912

Pollard, V. (N. Zealand) b Burnley Sept. 7, 1945

Pollock, A. J. (Camb. U.) b April 19, 1962

Pollock, P. M. (S. Africa; *CY 1966*) b June 30, 1941

Pollock, R. G. (S. Africa; *CY 1966*) b Feb. 27. 1944

Ponsford, W. H. (Australia; *CY 1935*) b Oct. 19, 1900

Pont, K. R. (Essex) b Jan. 16, 1953

Poole, C. J. (Notts.) b March 13, 1921

Pooley, E. (Surrey and first England tour) b Feb. 13, 1838, d July 18, 1907

Poore, M. B. (N. Zealand) b June 1, 1930

Poore, Brig-Gen. R. M. (Hants and S. Africa; *CY 1900*) b March 20, 1866, d July 14, 1938

Pope, A. V. (Derby.) b Aug. 15, 1909

Pope, G. H. (Derby.) b Jan. 27, 1911

Pope, R. J. (Australia) b Feb. 18, 1864, d July 27, 1952

Popplewell, N. F. M. (Camb. U. and Somerset) b Aug. 8, 1957

Portal of Hungerford, 1st Lord (Pres. MCC 1958-59) b May 21, 1893, d April 22, 1971

Porter, A. (Glam.) b March 25, 1914

Porter, G. D. (W. Australia) b March 18, 1955

Pothecary, E. A. (Hants) b March 1, 1906

Pothecary, J. E. (S. Africa) b Dec. 6, 1933

Potter, G. (Sussex) b Oct. 26, 1931

Potter, J. (Victoria) b April 13, 1938

Pougher, A. D. (Leics.) b April 19, 1865, d May 20, 1926

Pountain, F. R. (Sussex) b April 23, 1941

Powell, A. G. (Camb. U. and Essex) b Aug. 17, 1912, d June 7, 1982

Powell, A. W. (S. Africa) b July 18, 1873, d Sept. 11, 1948

Prasanna, E. A. S. (India) b May 22, 1940

Pratt, R. C. E. (Surrey) b May 5, 1928, d June 7, 1977

Pratt, R. L. (Leics.) b Nov. 15, 1938

Preece, C. R. (Worcs.) b Dec. 15, 1888, d Feb. 5, 1976

Prentice, F. T. (Leics.) b April 22, 1912, d July 10, 1978

Pressdee, J. S. (Glam. and N. E. Transvaal) b June 19, 1933

Preston, Hubert (Editor of *Wisden* 1944-51) b Dec. 16, 1868, d Aug. 6, 1960

Preston, K. C. (Essex) b Aug. 22, 1925

Preston, Norman (Editor of *Wisden* 1951-80) b March 18, 1903, d March 6, 1980

Pretlove, J. F. (Camb. U. and Kent) b Nov. 23, 1932

Price, E. J. (Lancs. and Essex) b Oct. 27, 1918

Price, J. S. E. (Middx) b July 22, 1937

Price, W. F. F. (Middx) b April 25, 1902, d Jan. 12, 1969

Prideaux, R. M. (Camb. U., Kent, Northants, Sussex and Orange Free State) b July 31, 1939

Pridgeon, A. P. (Worcs.) b Feb. 22, 1954

Prince, C. F. H. (S. Africa) b Sept. 11, 1874, d March 5, 1948

Pringle, D. R. (Camb. U. and Essex) b Sept. 18, 1958

Pritchard, T. L. (Wellington, Warw. and Kent) b March 10, 1917

Procter, M. J. (Glos. and S. Africa; *CY 1970*) b Sept. 15, 1946

Prodger, J. M. (Kent) b Sept. 1, 1935

Promnitz, H. L. E. (S. Africa) b Feb. 23, 1904, d Sept. 7, 1983

Prouton, R. O. (Hants) b March 1, 1926

Puckett, C. W. (W. Australia) b Feb. 21, 1911

Pugh, C. T. M. (Glos.) b March 13, 1937

Pullan, D. A. (Notts.) b May 1, 1944

Pullar, G. (Lancs. and Glos.; *CY 1960*) b Aug. 1, 1935

Pullinger, G. R. (Essex) b March 14, 1920

Puna, N. (N. Zealand) b Oct. 28, 1929

Punjabi, P. H. (India) b Sept. 20, 1921

Pydanna, M. (Guyana) b Jan. 27, 1950

Quaife, B. W. (Warw. and Worcs.) b Nov. 24, 1899

Quaife, William ("W. G.") (Warw. and Griqualand W.; *CY 1902*) b March 17, 1872, d Oct. 13, 1951

Quick, I. W. (Victoria) b. Nov. 5, 1933

Quinn, N. A. (S. Africa) b Feb. 21, 1908, d Aug. 5, 1934

Rabone, G. O. (N. Zealand) b Nov. 6, 1921

Rackemann, C. G. (Australia) b June 3, 1960

Radford, N. V. (Lancs. and Transvaal) b June 7, 1957

Radley, C. T. (Middx; *CY 1979*) b May 13, 1944

Rae, A. F. (W. Indies) b Sept. 30, 1922

Rai Singh, K. (India) b Feb. 24, 1922

Rait Kerr, Col. R. S. (Sec. MCC 1936-52) b April 13, 1891, d April 2, 1961

Rajindernath, V. (India) b Jan. 7, 1928

Rajinder Pal (India) b Nov. 18, 1937

Ralph, L. H. R. (Essex) b May 22, 1920

Ramadhin, S. (Lancs. and W. Indies; *CY 1951*) b May 1, 1929

Ramaswami, C. (India) b June 18, 1896

Ramchand, G. S. (India) b July 26, 1927

Ramji, L. (India) b 1900, d Dec. 20, 1948

Ramsamooj, D. (Trinidad and Northants) b July 5, 1932

Ranasinghe, A. N. (Sri Lanka) b Oct. 13, 1956

Ranatunga, A. (Sri Lanka) b Dec. 1, 1963

Randall, D. W. (Notts.; *CY 1980*) b Feb. 24, 1951

Randhir Singh (Bihar and Indian tourist) b Aug. 16, 1957

Rangachari, C. R. (India) b April 14, 1916

Rangnekar, K. M. (India) b June 27, 1917

Ranjane, V. B. (India) b July 22, 1937

Ranjitsinhji, Kumar Shri, afterwards H. H. the Jam Saheb of Nawanagar (Camb. U. and Sussex; *CY 1897*) b Sept. 10, 1872, d April 2, 1933

Ransford, V. S. (Australia; *CY 1910*) b March 20, 1885, d March 19, 1958

Ransom, V. J. (Hants and Surrey) b March 17, 1918

Rashid Khan (Pakistan) b Dec. 15, 1959

Ratcliffe, R. M. (Lancs.) b Nov. 29, 1951

Ratnayake, R. J. (Sri Lanka) b Jan. 2, 1964

Ratnayeke, J. R. (Sri Lanka) b May 2, 1960

Rawlinson, H. T. (Oxford U.) b Jan. 21, 1963

Rayment, A. W. H. (Hants) b May 29, 1928

Raymer, V. N. (Queensland) b May 4, 1918

Read, H. D. (Surrey and Essex) b Jan. 28, 1910

Read, J. M. (Surrey; *CY 1890*) b Feb. 9, 1859, d Feb. 17, 1929

Read, W. W. (Surrey; *CY 1893*) b Nov. 23, 1855, d Jan. 6, 1907

Reddick, T. B. (Middx, Notts. and W. Province) b Feb. 17, 1912, d June 1, 1982

Reddy, B. (India) b Nov. 12, 1954

Redman, J. (Somerset) b March 1, 1926, d Sept. 19, 1981

Redmond, R. E. (N. Zealand) b Dec. 29, 1944

Redpath, I. R. (Australia) b May 11, 1941

Reed, B. L. (Hants) b Sept. 9, 1937

Reedman, J. C. (Australia) b Oct. 9, 1865, d March 25, 1924

Rees, A. (Glam.) b Feb. 17, 1938

Reeve, D. A. (Sussex) b April 2, 1963

Reeves, W. (Umpire) b Jan. 22, 1875, d March 22, 1944

Rege, M. R. (India) b March 18, 1924

Rehman, S. F. (Pakistan) b June 11, 1935

Reid, J. F. (N. Zealand) b March 3, 1956

Reid, J. R. (N. Zealand; *CY 1959*) b June 3, 1928

Reid, K. P. (E. Province and Northants) b July 24, 1951

Reid, N. (S. Africa) b Dec. 26, 1890, d June 10, 1947

Reidy, B. W. (Lancs.) b Sept. 18, 1953

Relf, A. E. (Sussex and Auckland; *CY 1914*) b June 26, 1874, d March 26, 1937

Renneburg, D. A. (Australia) b Sept. 23, 1942

Revill, A. C. (Derby. and Leics.) b March 27, 1923

Reynolds, B. L. (Northants) b June 10, 1932

Reynolds, G. R. (Queensland) b Aug. 24 1936

Rhodes, A. E. G. (Derby.) b Oct. 10, 1916, d. Oct. 18, 1983

Rhodes, H. J. (Derby.) b July 22, 1936

Rhodes, S. D. (Notts.) b March 24, 1910

Rhodes, Wilfred (Yorks.; *CY 1899*) b Oct. 29, 1877, d July 8, 1973

Rice, C. E. B. (Transvaal and Notts.; *CY 1981*) b July 23, 1949

Rice, J. M. (Hants) b Oct. 23, 1949

Richards, A. R. (S. Africa) b 1868, d Jan. 9, 1904

Richards, B. A. (Glos., Hants, S. Australia and S. Africa; *CY 1969*) b July 21, 1945

Richards, C. J. (Surrey) b Aug. 10, 1958

Richards G. (Glam.) b Nov. 29, 1951

Richards, I. V. A. (Somerset, Queensland and W. Indies; *CY 1977*) b March 7, 1952

Richards, W. H. M. (S. Africa) b Aug. 1862, d Jan. 4, 1903

Richardson, A. J. (Australia) b July 24, 1888, d Dec. 23, 1973

Richardson, A. W. (Derby.) b March 4, 1907, d July 29, 1983

Richardson, D. W. (Worcs.) b Nov. 3, 1934

Richardson, G. W. (Derby.) b April 26, 1938

Richardson, P. E. (Worcs. and Kent; *CY 1957*) b July 4, 1931

Richardson, T. (Surrey and Somerset: *CY 1897*) b Aug. 11, 1870, d July 2, 1912

Richardson, V. Y. (Australia) b Sept. 7, 1894, d Oct. 29, 1969

Riches, N. V. H. (Glam.) b June 9, 1883, d Nov. 6 1975

Richmond, T. L. (Notts.) b June 23, 1890, d Dec. 29, 1957

Rickards, K. R. (Essex and W. Indies) b Aug. 23, 1923

Riddington, A. (Leics.) b Dec. 22, 1911

Ridge, S. P. (Oxford U.) b Nov. 23, 1961

Ridgway, F. (Kent) b Aug. 10, 1923

Ridings, P. L. (S. Australia) b Oct. 2, 1917

Rigg, K. E. (Australia) b May 21, 1906

Riley, H. (Leics.) b Oct. 3, 1902

Ring, D. T. (Australia) b Oct. 14, 1918

Rist, F. H. (Essex) b March 30, 1914

Ritchie, G. G. (Transvaal) b Sept. 16, 1933

Ritchie, G. M. (Australia) b Jan. 23, 1960

Rixon, S. J. (Australia) b Feb. 25, 1954

Rizwan-uz-Zaman (Pakistan) b Sept. 4, 1962

Roach, C. A. (W. Indies) b March 13, 1904

Roberts, A. D. G. (N. Zealand) b May 6, 1947

Roberts, A. M. E. (Hants, Leics., NSW and W. Indies; *CY 1975*) b Jan. 29, 1951

Roberts, A. T. (W. Indies) b Sept. 18, 1937

Roberts, A. W. (N. Zealand) b Aug. 20, 1909, d May 13, 1978

Roberts, Pascal (Trinidad) b Dec. 15, 1937

Roberts, W. B. (Lancs. and Victory Tests) b Sept. 27, 1914, d Aug. 24, 1951

Robertson, J. B. (S. Africa) b June 5, 1906

Robertson, J. D. (Middx; *CY 1948*) b Feb. 22, 1917

Robertson, S. D. (Rhodesia) b May 1, 1947

Robertson, W. R. (Australia) b Oct. 6, 1861, d June 24, 1938

Robertson-Glasgow, R. C. (Oxford U. and Somerset) b July 15, 1901, d March 4, 1965

Robins, R. V. C. (Middx) b March 13, 1935

Robins, R. W. V. (Camb. U. and Middx; *CY 1930*) b June 3, 1906, d Dec. 12, 1968

Robinson, A. L. (Yorks.) b Aug. 17, 1946

Robinson, Emmott (Yorks.) b Nov. 16, 1883, d Nov. 17, 1969

Robinson, Ellis P. (Yorks. and Somerset) b Aug. 10, 1911

Robinson, H. B. O. (Oxford U. and Canada) b March 3, 1919

Robinson, M. (Glam. and Warw.) b July 16, 1921

Robinson, P. J. (Worcs. and Somerset) b Feb. 9, 1943

Robinson, Ray (Writer) b July 8, 1908, d July 6, 1982

Robinson, R. D. (Australia) b June 8, 1946

Robinson, R. H. (Australia) b March 26, 1914, d Aug. 10, 1965

Robinson, R. T. (Notts.) b Nov. 21, 1958

Robson, E. (Somerset) b May 1, 1870, d May 23, 1924

Rochford, P. (Glos.) b Aug. 27, 1928

Rodriguez, W. V. (W. Indies) b June 25, 1934

Roe, B. (Somerset) b Jan. 27, 1939

Roebuck, P. M. (Camb. U. and Somerset) b March 6, 1956

Rogers, J. J. (Oxford U.) b Aug. 20, 1958

Rogers, N. H. (Hants) b March 9, 1918

Rogers, R. E. (Queensland) b Aug. 24, 1916

Romaines, P. W. (Northants and Glos.) b Dec. 25, 1955

Roope, G. R. J. (Surrey and Griqualand W.) b July 12, 1946

Root, C. F. (Derby. and Worcs.) b April 16, 1890, d Jan. 20, 1954

Rorke, G. F. (Australia) b June 27, 1938

Rose, B. C. (Somerset; *CY 1980*) b June 4, 1950

Rosebery, 6th Earl of (*see* Dalmeny, Lord)

Rose-Innes, A. (S. Africa) b Feb. 16, 1868, d Nov. 22, 1946

Rosendorff, N. (OFS) b Jan. 22, 1945

Ross, C. J. (Wellington and Oxford U.) b June 24, 1954

Rotherham, G. A. (Rugby, Camb. U., Warw. and Wellington; *CY 1918*) b May 28, 1899

Rouse, S. J. (Warw.) b Jan. 20, 1949

Routledge, R. (Middx) b July 7, 1920

Routledge, T. W. (S. Africa) b April 18, 1867, d May 9, 1927

Rowan, A. M. B. (S. Africa) b Feb. 7, 1921

Rowan, E. A. B. (S. Africa; *CY 1952*) b July 20, 1909

Rowe, C. G. (N. Zealand) b June 30, 1915

Rowe, C. J. C. (Kent) b May 5, 1953

Rowe, E. J. (Notts.) b July 21, 1920

Rowe, G. A. (S. Africa) b June 15, 1874, d Jan. 8, 1950

Rowe, L. G. (Derby. and W. Indies) b Jan. 8, 1949

Roy, A. (India) b June 5, 1945

Roy, Pankaj (India) b May 31, 1928

Roy, Pranab (India) b Feb. 10, 1957

Royle, Rev. V. P. F. A. (Oxford U. and Lancs.) b Jan. 29, 1854, d May 20, 1929

Rumsey, F. E. (Worcs., Somerset and Derby.) b Dec. 4, 1935

Russell, A. C. [C. A. G.] (Essex; *CY 1923*) b Oct. 7, 1887, d March 23, 1961

Russell, D. P. (Camb. U.) b June 4, 1951

Russell, P. E. (Derby.) b May 9, 1944

Russell, R. C. (Glos.) b Aug. 15, 1963

Russell, S. E. J. (Middx and Glos.) b Oct. 4, 1937

Russell, W. E. (Middx) b July 3, 1936

Russom, N. (Camb. U. and Somerset) b Dec. 3, 1958

Rutherford, I. A. (Worcs. and Otago) b June 30, 1957

Rutherford, J. W. (Australia) b Sept. 25, 1929

Ryan, M. (Yorks.) b June 23, 1933

Ryan, M. L. (Canterbury) b June 7, 1943

Ryder, J. (Australia) b Aug. 8, 1889, d April 3, 1977

Sadiq Mohammad (Tasmania, Glos., Essex and Pakistan) b May 3, 1945

Sadler, W. C. H. (Surrey) b Sept. 24, 1896

Saeed Ahmed (Pakistan) b Oct. 1, 1937

Saggers, R. A. (Australia) b May 15, 1917

Sainsbury, G. E. (Essex and Glos.) b Jan. 17, 1958

Sainsbury, P. J. (Hants; *CY 1974*) b June 13, 1934

St Hill, E. L. (W. Indies) b March 9, 1904, d May 21, 1957

St Hill, W. H. (W. Indies) b July 6, 1893, d 1957

Salah-ud-Din (Pakistan) b Feb. 14, 1947

Sale, R. (Oxford U. and Derby.) b June 21, 1889, d Sept. 7, 1970

Sale, R. jun. (Oxford U., Warw. and Derby.) b Oct. 4 1919

Saleem Altaf (Pakistan) b March 23, 1944

Salim Malik (Pakistan) b April 16, 1963

Salim Yousuf (Pakistan) b Dec. 7, 1959

Sampson, H. (Yorkshire and All-England) b March 13, 1813, d March 29, 1885

Samuelson, S. V. (S. Africa) b Nov. 21, 1883, d Nov. 18, 1958

Sanderson, J. F. W. (Oxford U.) b Sept. 10, 1954

Sandham, A. (Surrey; *CY 1923*) b July 6, 1890, d April 20, 1982

Sandhu, B. S. (India) b March 1, 1956

Sandman, D. McK. (Canterbury) b Nov. 3, 1889, d Jan. 29, 1973

Sardesai, D. N. (India) b Aug. 8, 1940

Sarfraz Nawaz (Northants and Pakistan) b Dec. 1, 1948

Sarwate, C. T. (India) b June 22, 1920

Saunders, J. V. (Australia) b Feb. 3, 1876, d Dec. 21, 1927

Savage, J. S. (Leics. and Lancs.) b March 3, 1929

Savage, R. Le Q. (Oxford U. and Warw.) b Dec. 10, 1955

Savill, L. A. (Essex) b June 30, 1935

Saville, G. J. (Essex) b Feb. 5, 1944

Saxelby, K. (Notts.) b Feb. 23, 1959

Saxena, R. C. (India) b Sept. 20, 1944

Sayer, D. M. (Oxford U. and Kent) b Sept. 19, 1936

Scarlett, R. O. (W. Indies) b Aug. 15, 1934

Schmidt, E. (E. Province and Orange Free State) b Sept. 21, 1950

Schofield, R. M. (C. Districts) b Nov. 6, 1939

Scholes, W. J. (Victoria) b Feb. 5, 1950

Schonegevel, D. J. (Orange Free State and Griqualand W.) b Oct. 9, 1934

Schultz, S. S. (Camb. U. and Lancs.) b Aug. 29, 1857, d Dec. 17, 1937

Schwarz, R. O. (Middx and S. Africa; *CY 1908*) b Lee, Kent May 4, 1875, d Nov. 18, 1918

Scott, A. P. H. (W. Indies) b July 29, 1934

Scott, Christopher J. (Lancs.) b Sept. 16, 1959

Scott, Colin J. (Glos.) b May 1, 1919

Scott, H. J. H. (Australia) b Dec. 26. 1858, d Sept. 23, 1910

Scott, M. E. (Northants) b May 8, 1936

Scott, O. C. (W. Indies) b Aug. 25, 1893, d June 16, 1961

Scott, R. H. (N. Zealand) b March 6, 1917

Scott, R. S. G. (Oxford U. and Sussex) b April 26, 1909, d Aug. 26, 1957

Scott, S. W. (Middx; *CY 1893*) b March 24, 1854, d Dec. 8, 1933

Scott, V. J. (N. Zealand) b July 31, 1916, d Aug. 2, 1980

Scotton, W. H. (Notts.) b Jan. 15, 1856, d July 9, 1893

Seabrook, F. J. (Camb. U. and Glos.) b Jan. 9, 1899, d Aug. 7, 1979

Sealey, B. J. (W. Indies) b Aug. 12, 1899, d Sept. 12, 1963

Sealy, J. E. D. (W. Indies) b Sept. 11, 1912, d Jan. 3, 1982

Seamer, J. W. (Somerset and Oxford U.) b June 23, 1913

Sebastian, L. C. (Windwards) b Oct. 31, 1955

Seccull, A. W. (S. Africa) b Sept. 14, 1868, d July 20, 1945

Sekar, T. A. (India) b May 25, 1955

Selby, J. (Notts.) b July 1, 1849, d March 11, 1894

Sellers, A. B. (Yorks.; *CY 1940*) b March 5, 1907, d Feb. 20, 1981

Sellers, R. H. D. (Australia) b Aug. 20, 1940

Selvey, M. W. W. (Camb. U., Surrey, Middx, Glam. and Orange Free State) b April 25, 1948

Sen, P. (India) b May 31, 1926, d Jan. 27, 1970

Sen Gupta, A. K. (India) b Aug. 3, 1939

Serjeant, C. S. (Australia) b Nov. 1, 1951

Seymour, James (Kent) b Oct. 25, 1879, d Sept. 30, 1930

Seymour, M. A. (S. Africa) b June 5, 1936

Shackleton, D. (Hants; *CY 1959*) b Aug. 12, 1924

Shafiq Ahmad (Pakistan) b March 28, 1949

Shafqat Rana (Pakistan) b Aug. 10, 1943

Shahid Israr (Pakistan) b March 1, 1950

Shahid Mahmoud (Pakistan) b March 13, 1939

Shalders, W. A. (S. Africa) b Feb. 12, 1880, d March 18, 1917

Sharma, P. (India) b Jan. 5, 1948

Sharp, G. (Northants) b March 12, 1950

Sharp, H. P. H. (Middx) b Oct. 6, 1917

Sharp, J. (Lancs.) b Feb. 15, 1878, d Jan. 27, 1938

Sharp, K. (Yorks. and Griqualand W.) b April 6, 1959

Sharpe, D. (Pakistan) b Aug. 3, 1937

Sharpe, J. W. (Surrey and Notts.; *CY 1892*) b Dec. 9, 1866, d June 19, 1936

Sharpe, P. J. (Yorks. and Derby.; *CY 1963*) b Dec. 27, 1936

Shastri, R. J. (India) b May 27, 1962

Shaw, Alfred (Notts. and Sussex) b Aug. 29, 1842, d Jan. 16, 1907

Shaw, J. H. (Victoria) b Oct. 18, 1932

Sheahan, A. P. (Australia) b Sept. 30, 1946

Sheffield, J. R. (Essex and Wellington) b Nov. 19, 1906

Shepherd, B. K. (Australia) b April 23, 1938

Shepherd, D. J. (Glam.; *CY 1970*) b Aug. 12, 1927

Shepherd, D. R. Glos.) b Dec. 27, 1940

Shepherd, J. N. (Kent, Glos., Rhodesia and W. Indies; *CY 1979*) b Nov. 9, 1943

Shepherd, T. F. (Surrey) b Dec. 5, 1889, d Feb. 13, 1957

Sheppard, Rt Rev. D. S. (Bishop of Liverpool) (Camb. U. and Sussex; *CY 1953*) b March 6, 1929

Shepstone, G. H. (S. Africa) b April 8, 1876, d July 3, 1940

Sherwell, P. W. (S. Africa) b Aug. 17, 1880, d April 17, 1948

Sherwin, M. (Notts.; *CY 1891*) b Feb. 26, 1851, d July 1910

Shillingford, G. C. (W. Indies) b Sept. 25, 1944

Shillingford, I. T. (W. Indies) b April 18, 1944

Shinde, S. G. (India) b Aug. 18, 1923, d June 22, 1955

Shipman, A. W. (Leics.) b March 7, 1901, d Dec. 12, 1979

Shirreff, A. C. (Camb. U., Hants, Kent and Somerset) b Feb. 12, 1919

Shivnarine, S. (W. Indies) b May 13, 1952

Shodhan, R. H. (India) b Oct. 18, 1928

Short, A. M. (Natal) b Sept. 27, 1947

Shrewsbury, Arthur (Notts.; *CY 1890*) b April 11, 1856, d May 19, 1903

Shrimpton, M. J. F. (N. Zealand) b June 23, 1940

Shuja-ud-Din, Col. (Pakistan) b April 10, 1930

Shukla, R. C. (India) b Feb. 4, 1948

Shuter, J. (Kent and Surrey) b Feb. 9, 1855, d July 5, 1920

Shuttleworth, K. (Lancs. and Leics.) b Nov. 13, 1944

Sidebottom, A. (Yorks. and Orange Free State) b April 1, 1954

Siedle, I. J. (S. Africa) b Jan. 11, 1903, d Aug. 24, 1982

Sievers, M. W. (Australia) b April 13, 1912, d May 10, 1968

Sikander Bakht (Pakistan) b Aug. 25, 1957

Silk, D. R. W. (Camb. U. and Somerset) b Oct. 8, 1931

Silva, S. A. R. (Sri Lanka) b Dec. 12, 1960

Sime, W. A. (Notts.) b Feb. 8, 1909, d May 5, 1972

Simmons, J. (Lancs. and Tasmania) b March 28, 1941

Simpson, R. B. (Australia; *CY 1965*) b Feb. 3, 1936

Simpson, R. T. (Notts. and Sind; *CY 1950*) b Feb. 27, 1920

Simpson-Hayward, G. H. (Worcs.) b June 7, 1875, d Oct. 2, 1936

Sims, Sir Arthur (Canterbury) b July 22, 1877, d April 27, 1969

Sims, J. M. (Middx) b May 13, 1903, d April 27, 1973

Sinclair, B. W. (N. Zealand) b Oct. 23, 1936

Sinclair, I. McK. (N. Zealand) b June 1, 1933

Sinclair, J. H. (S. Africa) b Oct. 16, 1876, d Feb. 23, 1913

Sincock, D. J. (Australia) b Feb. 1, 1942

Sinfield, R. A. (Glos.) b Dec. 24, 1900

Singh, Charan K. (West Indies) b 1938

Singh, Maninder (India) b June 13, 1965

Singh, Swaranjit (Camb. U., Warw., E. Punjab and Bengal) b July 18, 1931

Singleton, A. P. (Oxford U., Worcs. and Rhodesia) b Aug. 5, 1914

Sivaramakrishnan, L. (India) b Dec. 31, 1965

Siviter, K. (Oxford U.) b Dec. 10, 1953

Skeet, C. H. L. (Oxford U. and Middx) b Aug. 17, 1895, d April 20, 1978

Skelding, Alec (Leics.) b Sept. 5, 1886, d April 17, 1960

Skinner, A. F. (Derby. and Northants) b April 22, 1913, d Feb. 28, 1982

Skinner, D. A. (Derby.) b March 22, 1920

Skinner, L. E. (Surrey and Guyana) b Sept. 7, 1950

Slack, W. N. (Middx and Windward Islands) b Dec. 12, 1954

Slade, D. N. F. (Worcs.) b Aug. 24, 1940

Slade, W. D. (Glam.) b Sept. 27, 1941

Slater, K. N. (Australia) b March 12, 1935

Sleep, P. R. (Australia) b May 4, 1957

Slight, J. (Australia) b Oct. 20, 1855, d Dec. 9, 1930

Slocombe, P. A. (Somerset) b Sept. 6, 1954

Smailes, T. F. (Yorks.) b March 27, 1910, d Dec. 1, 1970

Smales, K. (Yorks. and Notts.) b Sept. 15, 1927

Small, G. C. (Warw.) b Oct. 18, 1961

Small, John, sen. (Hants and All-England) b April 19, 1737, d Dec. 31, 1826

Small, J. A. (W. Indies) b Nov. 3, 1892, d April 26, 1958

Smart, C. C. (Warw. and Glam.) b July 23, 1898, d May 21, 1975

Smart, J. A. (Warw.) b April 12, 1891, d Oct. 3, 1979

Smedley, M. J. (Notts.) b Oct. 28, 1941

Smith, A. C. (Oxford U. and Warw.) b Oct. 25, 1936

Smith, A. J. S. (Natal) b Feb. 8, 1951

Smith, Sir C. Aubrey (Camb. U., Sussex and Transvaal) b July 21, 1863, d Dec. 20, 1948

Smith, C. I. J. (Middx; *CY 1935*) b Aug. 25, 1906, d Feb. 8, 1979

Smith, C. J. E. (S. Africa) b Dec. 25, 1872, d March 27, 1947

Smith, C. L. (Natal, Glam. and Hants; *CY 1984*) b Oct. 15, 1958

Smith, C. S. (Camb. U. and Lancs.) b Oct. 1, 1932

Smith, C. W. (W. Indies) b July 29, 1933

Smith, Denis (Derby.; *CY 1936*) b Jan. 24, 1907, d Sept. 12, 1979

Smith, D. B. M. (Australia) b Sept. 14, 1884, d July 29, 1963

Smith, D. H. K. (Derby. and Orange Free State) b June 29, 1940

Smith, D. M. (Surrey) b Jan. 9, 1956

Smith, D. R. (Glos.) b Oct. 5, 1934

Smith, D. V. (Sussex) b June 14, 1923

Smith, Edwin (Derby.) b Jan. 2, 1934

Smith, E. J. (Warw.) b Feb. 6, 1886, d Aug. 31, 1979

Smith, F. B. (N. Zealand) b March 13, 1922

Smith, F. W. (S. Africa) No details of birth or death known

Smith, G. (Kent) b Nov. 30, 1925

Smith, G. J. (Essex) b April 2, 1935

Smith, Harry (Glos.) b May 21, 1890, d Nov. 12, 1937

Smith, H. D. (N. Zealand) b Jan. 8, 1913

Smith, I. D. S. (N. Zealand) b Feb. 28, 1957

Smith, K. D. (Warw.) b July 9, 1956

Smith, L. D. (Otago) b Dec. 23, 1914

Smith, M. J. (Middx) b Jan. 4, 1942

Smith, M. J. K. (Oxford U., Leics. and Warw.; *CY 1960*) b June 30, 1933

Smith, N. (Yorks. and Essex) b April 1, 1949

Smith, O. G. (W. Indies; *CY 1958*) b May 5, 1933, d Sept. 9, 1959

Smith, Ray (Essex) b Aug. 10, 1914

Smith, Roy (Somerset) b April 14, 1930

Smith, R. C. (Leics.) b Aug. 3, 1935

Smith, Sydney (Manager Australians in England 1921 and 1926) b March 1, 1880, d April 11, 1972

Smith, S. G. (Trinidad, Northants and Auckland; *CY 1915*) b Jan. 15, 1881, d Oct. 25, 1963

Smith, T. P. B. (Essex; *CY 1947*) b Oct. 30, 1908, d Aug. 4, 1967

Smith, V. I. (S. Africa) b Feb. 23, 1925

Smith, W. A. (Surrey) b Sept. 15, 1937

Smith, W. C. (Surrey; *CY 1911*) b Oct. 4, 1877, d July 16, 1946

Smithson, G. A. (Yorks. and Leics.) b Nov. 1, 1926, d Sept. 6, 1970

Smythe, R. I. (Camb. U.) b Nov. 19, 1951

Snedden, C. A. (N. Zealand) b Jan. 7, 1918

Snedden, M. C. (N. Zealand) b Nov. 23, 1958

Snellgrove, K. L. (Lancs.) b Nov. 12, 1941

Snooke, S. D. (S. Africa) b Nov. 11, 1878, d April 4, 1959

Snooke, S. J. (S. Africa) b Feb. 1, 1881, d Aug. 14, 1966

Snow, J. A. (Sussex; *CY 1973*) b Oct. 13, 1941

Snowden, A. W. (Northants) b Aug. 15, 1913, d May 7, 1981

Snowden, W. (Camb. U.) b Sept. 27, 1952

Sobers, Sir G. St A. (Notts., S. Australia and W. Indies; *CY 1964*) b June 28, 1936

Sohoni, S. W. (India) b March 5, 1918

Solanky, J. W. (E. Africa and Glam.) b June 30, 1942

Solkar, E. D. (Sussex and India) b March 18, 1948

Solomon, J. S. (W. Indies) b Aug. 26, 1930

Solomon, W. R. T. (S. Africa) b April 23, 1872, d July 12, 1964

Sood, M. M. (India) b July 6, 1939

Southern, J. W. (Hants) b Sept. 2, 1952

Southerton, James (Surrey, Hants and Sussex) b Nov. 16, 1827, d June 16, 1880

Southerton, S. J. (Editor of *Wisden* 1934-35) b July 7, 1874, d March 12, 1935

Sparling, J. T. (N. Zealand) b July 24, 1938

Spencer, C. T. (Leics.) b Aug. 18, 1931

Spencer, J. (Camb. U. and Sussex) b Oct. 6, 1949

Spencer, T. W. (Kent) b March 22, 1914

Sperry, J. (Leics.) b March 19, 1910

Spofforth, F. R. (Australia) b Sept. 9, 1853, d June 4, 1926

Spooner, R. H. (Lancs.; *CY 1905*) b Oct. 21, 1880, d Oct. 2, 1961

Spooner, R. T. (Warw.) b Dec. 30, 1919

Springall, J. D. (Notts.) b Sept. 19, 1932

Squires, H. S. (Surrey) b Feb. 22, 1909, d Jan. 24, 1950

Srikkanth, K. (India) b Dec. 21, 1959

Srinivasan, T. E. (India) b Oct. 26, 1950

Stackpole, K. R. (Australia; *CY 1973*) b July 10, 1940

Stallibrass, M. J. D. (Oxford U.) b June 28, 1951

Standen, J. A. (Worcs.) b May 30, 1935

Stanyforth, Lt-Col. R. T. (Yorks.) b May 30, 1892, d Feb. 20, 1964

Staples, S. J. (Notts.; *CY 1929*) b Sept. 18, 1892, d June 4, 1950

Starkie, S. (Northants) b April 4, 1926

Statham, J. B. (Lancs.; *CY 1955*) b June 16, 1930

Stayers, S. C. (Guyana, Bombay and W. Indies) b June 9, 1937

Stead, B. (Yorks., Essex, Notts. and N. Transvaal) b June 21, 1939, d April 15, 1980

Stead, D. W. (Canterbury) b May 26, 1947

Steel, A. G. (Camb. U. and Lancs.; Pres. MCC 1902) b Sept. 24, 1858, d June 15, 1914

Steele, D. S. (Northants and Derby.; *CY 1976*) b Sept. 29, 1941

Steele, J. F. (Leics. and Natal) b July 23, 1946

Stephens, E. J. (Glos.) b March 23, 1910

Stephenson, G. R. (Derby. and Hants) b Nov. 19, 1942

Stephenson, H. H. (Surrey and All-England) b May 3, 1832, d Dec. 17, 1896

Stephenson, H. W. (Somerset) b July 18, 1920

Stephenson, Lt-Col. J. W. A. (Essex and Worcs.) b Aug. 1, 1907, d May 20, 1982

Stevens, Edward ("Lumpy") (Hants) b *circa* 1735, d Sept. 7, 1819

Stevens, G. B. (Australia) b Feb. 29, 1932

Stevens, G. T. S. (UCS, Oxford U. and Middx; *CY 1918*) b Jan. 7, 1901, d Sept. 19, 1970

Stevenson, G. B. (Yorks.) b Dec. 16, 1955

Stevenson, K. (Derby. and Hants) b Oct. 6, 1950

Stevenson, M. H. (Camb. U. and Derby.) b June 13, 1927

Stewart, M. J. (Surrey; *CY 1958*) b Sept. 16, 1932

Stewart, R. B. (S. Africa) b Sept. 3, 1856, d Sept. 12, 1913

Stewart, R. W. (Glos. and Middx) b Feb. 28, 1945

Stewart, W. J. (Warw. and Northants) b Aug. 31, 1934

Stocks, F. W. (Notts.) b Nov. 6, 1917

Stoddart, A. E. (Middx; *CY 1893*) b March 11, 1863, d April 3, 1915

Stollmeyer, J. B. (W. Indies) b April 11, 1921

Stollmeyer, V. H. (W. Indies) b Jan. 24, 1916

Storer, W. (Derby.; *CY 1899*) b Jan. 25, 1867, d March 5, 1912

Storey, S. J. (Surrey and Sussex) b Jan. 6, 1941

Stott, L. W. (Auckland) b Dec. 8, 1946

Stott, W. B. (Yorks.) b July 18, 1934

Stovold, A. W. (Glos. and Orange Free State) b March 19, 1953

Street, G. B. (Sussex) b Dec. 6, 1889, d April 24, 1924

Stricker, L. A. (S. Africa) b May 26, 1884, d Feb. 5, 1960

Stringer, P. M. (Yorks. and Leics.) b Feb. 23, 1943

Strudwick, H. (Surrey; *CY 1912*) b Jan. 28, 1880, d Feb. 13, 1970

Strydom, W. T. (Orange Free State) b March 21, 1942

Studd, C. T. (Camb. U. and Middx) b Dec. 2, 1860, d July 16, 1931

Studd, G. B. (Camb. U. and Middx) b Oct. 20, 1859, d Feb. 13, 1945

Studd, Sir Peter M. (Camb. U.) b Sept. 15, 1916

Sturt, M. O. C. (Middx) b Sept. 12, 1940

Subba Row, R. (Camb. U., Surrey and Northants; *CY 1961*) b Jan. 29, 1932

Subramanya, V. (India) b July 16, 1936

Sueter, T. (Hants and Surrey) b *circa* 1749, d Feb. 17, 1827

Sugg, F. H. (Yorks., Derby. and Lancs.; *CY 1890*) b Jan. 11, 1862, d May 29, 1933

Sullivan, J. (Lancs.) b Feb. 5, 1945

Sully, H. (Somerset and Northants) b Nov. 1, 1939

Sunderram, G. R. (India) b March 29, 1930

Sunnucks, P. R. (Kent) b June 22, 1916

Surendranath, R. (India) b Jan. 4, 1937

Surridge, D. (Camb. U. and Glos.) b Jan. 6, 1956

Surridge, W. S. (Surrey; *CY 1953*) b Sept. 3, 1917

Surti, R. F. (Queensland and India) b May 25, 1936

Susskind, M. J. (Middx and S. Africa) b June 8, 1891, d July 9, 1957

Sutcliffe, B. (N. Zealand; *CY 1950*) b Nov. 17, 1923

Sutcliffe, H. (Yorks.; *CY 1920*) b Nov. 24, 1894, d Jan. 22, 1978

Sutcliffe, S. P. (Oxford U. and Warw.) b May 22, 1960

Sutcliffe, W. H. H. (Yorks.) b Oct. 10, 1926

Suttle, K. G. (Sussex) b Aug. 25, 1928

Sutton, R. E. (Auckland) b May 30, 1940

Swamy, V. N. (India) b May 23, 1924, d May 1, 1983

Swanton, E. W. (Middx; Writer) b Feb. 11, 1907

Swarbrook, F. W. (Derby., Griqualand W. and Orange Free State) b Dec. 17, 1950

Swart, P. D. (Rhodesia, W. Province, Glam. and Boland) b April 27, 1946

Swetman, R. (Surrey, Notts. and Glos.) b Oct. 25, 1933

Sydenham, D. A. D. (Surrey) b April 6, 1934

Symington, S. J. (Leics.) b Sept. 16, 1926

Taber, H. B. (Australia) b April 29, 1940

Taberer, H. M. (S. Africa) b Oct. 7, 1870, d June 5, 1932

Tahir Naqqash (Pakistan) b June 28, 1959

Tait, A. (Northants and Glos.) b Dec. 27, 1953

Talat Ali (Pakistan) b May 29, 1950

Talbot, R. O. (Canterbury and Otago) b Nov. 26, 1903, d Jan. 5, 1983

Tallon, D. (Australia; *CY 1949*) b Feb. 17, 1916

Tamhane, N. S. (India) b Aug. 4, 1931

Tancred, A. B. (S. Africa) b Aug. 20, 1865, d Nov. 23, 1911

Tancred, L. J. (S. Africa) b Oct. 7, 1876, d July 28, 1934

Tancred, V. M. (S. Africa) b 1875, d June 3, 1904

Tapscott, G. L. (S. Africa) b Nov. 7, 1889, d Dec. 13, 1940

Tapscott, L. E. (S. Africa) b March 18, 1894, d July 7, 1934

Tarapore, K. K. (India) b Dec. 17, 1910

Tarbox, C. V. (Worcs.) b July 2, 1891, d June 15, 1978

Tarrant, F. A. (Victoria and Middx; *CY 1908*) b Dec. 11, 1880, d Jan. 29, 1951

Tarrant, George F. (Cambs. and All-England) b Dec. 7, 1838, d July 2, 1870

Taslim Arif (Pakistan) b May 1, 1954

Tate, F. W. (Sussex) b July 24, 1867, d Feb. 24, 1943

Tate, M. W. (Sussex; *CY 1924*) b May 30, 1895, d May 18, 1956

Tattersall, R. (Lancs.) b Aug. 17, 1922

Tauseef Ahmed (Pakistan) b May 10, 1960

Tavaré, C. J. (Oxford U. and Kent) b Oct. 27, 1954

Tayfield, A. (Natal, Transvaal and NE Transvaal) b June 21, 1931

Tayfield, H. J. (S. Africa; *CY 1956*) b Jan. 30, 1929

Taylor, A. I. (S. Africa) b July 25, 1925

Taylor, B. (Essex; *CY 1972*) b June 19, 1932

Taylor, B. R. (N. Zealand) b July 12, 1943

Taylor, Daniel (S. Africa) b Jan. 9, 1887, d Jan. 24, 1957

Taylor, D. D. (Warw. and N. Zealand) b March 2, 1923, d Dec. 5, 1980

Taylor, D. J. S. (Surrey, Somerset and Griqualand W.) b Nov. 12, 1942

Taylor, G. R. (Hants) b Nov. 25, 1909

Taylor, H. W. (S. Africa; *CY 1925*) b May 5, 1889, d Feb. 8, 1973

Taylor, J. M. (Australia) b Oct. 10, 1895, d May 12, 1971

Taylor, J. O. (W. Indies) b Jan. 3, 1932

Taylor, K. (Yorks. and Auckland) b Aug. 21, 1935

Taylor, K. A. (Warw.) b Sept. 29, 1916

Taylor, L. B. (Leics. and Natal) b Oct. 25, 1953

Taylor, M. L. (Lancs.) b July 16, 1904, d March 14, 1978

Taylor, M. N. S. (Notts. and Hants) b Nov. 12, 1942

Taylor, N. R. (Kent) b July 21, 1959

Taylor, R. M. (Essex) b Nov. 30, 1909

Taylor, R. W. (Derby.; *CY 1977*) b July 17, 1941

Taylor, T. J. (Oxford U. and Lancs.) b March 28, 1961

Taylor, T. L. (Camb. U. and Yorks.; *CY 1901*) b May 25, 1878, d March 16, 1960

Taylor, W. (Notts.) b Jan. 24, 1947

Tennekoon, A. P. B. (Sri Lanka) b Oct. 29, 1946

Tennyson, 3rd Lord (Hon. L. H.) (Hants; *CY 1914*) b Nov. 7, 1889, d June 6, 1951

Terry, V. P. (Hants) b Jan. 14, 1959

Thackaray, P. R. (Oxford U.) b Sept. 26, 1950

Theunissen, N. H. (S. Africa) b May 4, 1867, d Nov. 9, 1929

Thomas, D. J. (Surrey and N. Transvaal) b June 30, 1959

Thomas, G. (Australia) b March 21, 1938

Thompson, A. W. (Middx) b April 17, 1916

Thompson, G. J. (Northants; *CY 1906*) b Oct. 27, 1877, d March 3, 1943

Thompson, J. R. (Camb. U. and Warw.) b May 10, 1918

Thompson, Nathaniel (Australia) b Birmingham, England April 21, 1838, d Sept. 2, 1896

Thompson, P. M. (Orange Free State and W. Province) b April 25, 1948

Thompson, R. G. (Warw.) b Sept. 26, 1932

Thoms, G. R. (Australia) b March 22, 1927

Thomson, A. L. (Australia) b Dec. 2, 1945

Thomson, J. R. (Middx and Australia) b Aug. 16, 1950

Thomson, K. (N. Zealand) b Feb. 26, 1941

Thomson, N. I. (Sussex) b Jan. 23, 1929

Thornton, C. I. (Camb. U., Kent and Middx) b March 20, 1850, d Dec. 10, 1929

Thornton, P. G. (Yorks., Middx and S. Africa) b Dec. 24, 1867, d Jan. 31, 1939

Thurlow, H. M. (Australia) b Jan. 10, 1902, d Dec. 3, 1975

Tilly, H. W. (Middx) b May 25, 1932

Timms, B. S. V. (Hants and Warw.) b Dec. 17, 1940

Timms, J. E. (Northants) b Nov. 3, 1906, d May 18, 1980

Timms, W. W. (Northants) b Sept. 28, 1902

Tindall, M. (Camb. U. and Middx) b March 31, 1914

Tindall, R. A. E. (Surrey) b Sept. 23, 1935

Tindill, E. W. T. (N. Zealand) b Dec. 18, 1910

Titmus, F. J. (Middx, Surrey and Orange Free State; *CY 1963*) b Nov. 24, 1932

Todd, L. J. (Kent) b June 19, 1907, d Aug. 20, 1967

Todd, P. A. (Notts.) b March 12, 1953

Tolchard, J. G. (Leics.) b March 17, 1944

Tolchard, R. W. (Leics.) b June 15, 1946

Tomlins, K. P. (Middx) b Oct. 23, 1957

Tomlinson, D. S. (S. Africa) b Sept. 4, 1910

Tompkin, M. (Leics.) b Feb. 17, 1919, d Sept. 27, 1956

Toogood, G. J. (Oxford U.) b Nov. 19, 1961

Toohey, P. M. (Australia) b April 20, 1954

Topham, R. D. N. (Oxford U.) b July 17, 1952

Tordoff, G. G. (Camb. U. and Somerset) b Dec. 6, 1929

Toshack, E. R. H. (Australia) b Dec. 15, 1914

Townsend, A. (Warw.) b Aug. 26, 1921

Townsend, A. F. (Derby.) b March 29, 1912

Townsend, C. L. (Glos.; *CY 1899*) b Nov. 7, 1876, d Oct. 17, 1958

Townsend, D. C. H. (Oxford U.) b April 20, 1912

Townsend, L. F. (Derby.; *CY 1934*) b June 8, 1903

Traicos, A. J. (S. Africa) b May 17, 1947

Travers, J. P. F. (Australia) b Jan. 10, 1871, d Sept. 15, 1942

Tremlett, M. F. (Somerset and C. Districts) b July 5, 1923

Tremlett, T. M. (Hants) b July 26, 1956

Tribe, G. E. (Northants and Australia; *CY 1955*) b Oct. 4, 1920

Trim, J. (W. Indies) b Jan. 24, 1915, d Nov. 12, 1960

Trimble, S. C. (Queensland) b Aug. 16, 1934

Trimborn, P. H. J. (S. Africa) b May 18, 1940

Trott, A. E. (Middx, Australia and England; *CY 1899*) b Feb. 6, 1873, d July 30, 1914

Trott, G. H. S. (Australia; *CY 1894*) b Aug. 5, 1866, d Nov. 10, 1917

Troup, G. B. (N. Zealand) b Oct. 3, 1952

Trueman, F. S. (Yorks.; *CY 1953*) b Feb. 6, 1931

Trumble, H. (Australia; *CY 1897*) b May 12, 1867, d Aug. 14, 1938

Trumble, J. W. (Australia) b Sept. 16, 1863, d Aug. 17, 1944

Trumper, V. T. (Australia; *CY 1903*) b Nov. 2, 1877, d June 28, 1915

Truscott, P. B. (N. Zealand) b Aug. 14, 1941

Tuckett, L. (S. Africa) b Feb. 6, 1919

Tuckett, L. R. (S. Africa) b April 19, 1885, d April 8, 1963

Tufnell, N. C. (Camb. U. and Surrey) b June 13, 1887, d Aug. 3, 1951

Tuke, Sir Anthony (Pres. MCC 1982-83) b Aug. 22, 1920

Tunnicliffe, C. J. (Derby.) b Aug. 11, 1951

Tunnicliffe, H. T. (Notts.) b March 4, 1950

Tunnicliffe, J. (Yorks.; *CY 1901*) b Aug. 26, 1866, d July 11, 1948

Turnbull, M. J. (Camb. U. and Glam.; *CY 1931*) b March 16, 1906, d Aug. 5, 1944

Turner, A. (Australia) b July 23, 1950

Turner, C. T. B. (Australia; *CY 1889*) b Nov. 16, 1862, d Jan. 1, 1944

Turner, D. R. (Hants and W. Province) b Feb. 5, 1949

Turner, F. M. (Leics.) b Aug. 8, 1934

Turner, G. M. (Worcs. and N. Zealand; *CY 1971*) b May 26, 1947

Turner, S. (Essex and Natal) b July 18, 1943

Twentyman-Jones, P. S. (S. Africa) b Sept. 13, 1876, d March 8, 1954

Twining, R. H. (Oxford U. and Middx; Pres. MCC 1964-65) b Nov. 3, 1889, d Jan. 3, 1979

Tyldesley, E. (Lancs.; *CY 1920*) b Feb. 5, 1889, d May 5, 1962

Tyldesley, J. T. (Lancs.; *CY 1902*) b Nov. 22, 1873, d Nov. 27, 1930

Tyldesley, R. K. (Lancs.; *CY 1925*) b March 11, 1897, d Sept. 17, 1943

Tylecote, E. F. S. (Oxford U. and Kent) b June 23, 1849, d March 15, 1938

Tyler, E. J. (Somerset) b Oct. 13, 1864, d Jan. 21, 1917

Tyson, F. H. (Northants; *CY 1956*) b June 6, 1930

Ufton, D. G. (Kent) b May 31, 1928

Ulyett, G. (Yorks.) b Oct. 21, 1851, d June 18, 1898

Umrigar, P. R. (India) b March 28, 1926

Underwood, D. L. (Kent; *CY 1969*) b June 8, 1945

Unwin, F. St G. (Essex) b April 23, 1911

Valentine, A. L. (W. Indies; *CY 1951*) b April 29, 1930

Valentine, B. H. (Camb. U. and Kent) b Jan. 17, 1908, d Feb. 2, 1983

Valentine, V. A. (W. Indies) b April 4, 1908, believed dead

Vance, R. H. (Wellington) b March 31, 1955

van der Bijl, P. G. V. (S. Africa) b Oct. 21, 1907, d Feb. 16, 1973

van der Bijl, V. A. P. (Natal and Middx; *CY 1981*) b March 19, 1948

Van der Gucht, P. I. (Glos.) b Nov. 2, 1911

Van der Merwe, E. A. (S. Africa) b Nov. 9, 1904, d Feb. 28, 1971

Van der Merwe, P. L. (S. Africa) b March 14, 1937

van Geloven, J. (Yorks. and Leics.) b Jan. 4, 1934

Van Ryneveld, C. B. (Oxford U. and S. Africa) b March 19, 1928

Varachia, R. (First Pres. S. African Cricket Union) b Oct. 12, 1915, d Dec. 11, 1981

Varey, D. W. (Camb. U.) b Oct. 15, 1961

Varey, J. G. (Oxford U.) b Oct. 15, 1961

Varnals, G. D. (S. Africa) b July 24, 1935

Vaulkhard, P. (Notts. and Derby.) b Sept. 15, 1911

Vengsarkar, D. B. (India) b April 6, 1956

Veivers, T. R. (Australia) b April 6, 1937

Venkataraghavan, S. (Derby. and India) b April 21, 1946

Verity, Capt. H. (Yorks.; *CY 1932*) b May 18, 1905, d July 31, 1943

Vernon, G. F. (Middx) b June 20, 1856, d Aug. 10, 1902

Vernon, M. T. (W. Australia) b Feb. 9, 1937

Vials, G. A. T. (Northants) b March 18, 1887, d April 26, 1974

Vigar, F. H. (Essex) b July 7, 1917

Viljoen, K. G. (S. Africa) b May 14, 1910, d Jan. 21, 1974

Vincent, C. L. (S. Africa) b Feb. 16, 1902, d Aug. 24, 1968

Vine, J. (Sussex; *CY 1906*) b May 15, 1875, d April 25, 1946

Vintcent, C. H. (S. Africa) b Sept. 2, 1866, d Sept. 28, 1943

Virgin, R. T. (Somerset and Northants; *CY 1971*) b Aug. 26, 1939

Viswanath, G. R. (India) b Feb. 12, 1949

Vivian, G. E. (N. Zealand) b Feb. 28, 1946

Vivian, H. G. (N. Zealand) b Nov. 4, 1912, d Aug. 12, 1983

Voce, W. (Notts.; *CY 1933*) b Aug. 8, 1909

Vogler, A. E. E. (Middx and S. Africa; *CY 1908*) b Nov. 28, 1876, d Aug. 9, 1946

Vizianagram, Maharaj Sir Vijaya of (India) b Dec. 28, 1905, d Dec. 2, 1965

Waddington, A. (Yorks.) b Feb. 4, 1893, d Oct. 27, 1959

Waddington, J. E. (Griqualand W.) b Dec. 30, 1918

Wade, H. F. (S. Africa) b Sept. 14, 1905, d Nov. 22, 1980

Wade, T. H. (Essex) b Nov. 24, 1910

Wade, W. W. (S. Africa) b June 18, 1914

Wadekar, A. L. (India) b April 1, 1941

Wadsworth, K. J. (N. Zealand) b Nov. 30, 1946, d Aug. 19, 1976

Wainwright, E. (Yorks.; *CY 1894*) b April 8, 1865, d Oct. 26, 1919

Waite, J. H. B. (S. Africa) b Jan. 19, 1930

Waite, M. G. (Australia) b Jan. 7, 1911

Walcott, C. L. (W. Indies; *CY 1958*) b Jan. 17, 1926

Walcott, L. A. (W. Indies) b Jan. 18, 1894

Walden, F. I. (Northants; Umpire) b March 1, 1888, d May 3, 1949

Walford, M. M. (Oxford U. and Somerset) b Nov. 27, 1915

Walker, A. K. (NSW and Notts.) b Oct. 4, 1925

Walker, C. (Yorks. and Hants) b June 27, 1920

Walker, C. W. (S. Australia) b Feb. 19, 1909, d Dec. 21, 1942

Walker, I. D. (Middx) b Jan. 8, 1844, d July 6, 1898

Walker, M. H. N. (Australia) b Sept. 12, 1948

Walker, P. M. (Glam., Transvaal and W. Province) b Feb. 17, 1936

Walker, W. (Notts.) b Nov. 24, 1892

Wall, T. W. (Australia) b May 13, 1904, d March 26, 1981

Wallace, W. M. (N. Zealand) b Dec. 19, 1916

Waller, C. E. (Surrey and Sussex) b Oct. 3, 1948

Waller, G. de W. (Oxford U.) b Feb. 10, 1950

Walsh, J. E. (NSW and Leics.) b Dec. 4, 1912, d May 20, 1980

Walter, K. A. (S. Africa) b Nov. 5, 1939

Walters, C. F. (Glam. and Worcs.; *CY 1934*) b Aug. 28, 1905

Walters, F. H. (Australia) b Feb. 9, 1860, d June 1922

Walters, J. (Derby.) b Aug. 7, 1949

Walters, K. D. (Australia) b Dec. 21, 1945

Walton, A. C. (Oxford U. and Middx) b Sept. 26, 1933

Waqar Hassan (Pakistan) b Sept. 12, 1932

Ward, Alan (Derby., Leics. and Border) b Aug. 10, 1947

Ward, Albert (Yorks. and Lancs.; *CY 1890*) b Nov. 21, 1865, d Jan. 6, 1939

Ward, B. (Essex) b Feb. 28, 1944

Ward, D. (Glam.) b Aug. 30, 1934

Ward, F. A. (Australia) b Feb. 23, 1909, d March 25, 1974

Ward, J. T. (N. Zealand) b March 11, 1937

Ward, T. A. (S. Africa) b Aug. 2, 1887, d Feb. 16, 1936

Ward, William (MCC and Hants) b July 24, 1787, d June 30, 1849

Wardle, J. H. (Yorks.; *CY 1954*) b Jan. 8, 1923

Warnapura, B. (Sri Lanka) b March 1, 1953

Warne, F. B. (Worcs., Victoria and Transvaal) b Oct. 3, 1906

Warner, Sir Pelham (Oxford U. and Middx; *CY 1904, special portrait 1921*) b Oct. 2, 1873, d Jan. 30, 1963

Warr, J. J. (Camb. U. and Middx) b July 16, 1927

Warren, A. (Derby.) b April 2, 1875, d Sept. 3, 1951

Washbrook, C. (Lancs.; *CY 1947*) b Dec. 6, 1914

Wasim Bari (Pakistan) b March 23, 1948

Wasim Raja (Pakistan) b July 3, 1952

Wass, T. G. (Notts.; *CY 1908*) b Dec. 26, 1873, d Oct. 27, 1953

Wassell, A. (Hants) b April 15, 1940

Watkins, A. J. (Glam.) b April 21, 1922

Watkins, J. C. (S. Africa) b April 10, 1923

Watkins, J. R. (Australia) b April 16, 1943

Watson, C. (Jamaica, Delhi and W. Indies) b July 1, 1938

Watson, F. B. (Lancs.) b Sept. 17, 1898, d Feb. 1, 1976

Watson, G. D. (Australia) b March 8, 1945

Watson, G. G. (NSW and Worcs.) b Jan. 29, 1955

Watson, G. S. (Kent and Leics.) b April 10, 1907, d April 1, 1974

Watson, W. (Yorks. and Leics.; *CY 1954*) b March 7, 1920

Watson, W. (Australia) b Jan. 31, 1931

Watson, W. K. (Border, N. Transvaal, E. Province and Notts.) b May 21, 1955

Watt, A. E. (Kent) b June 19, 1907, d Feb. 3, 1974

Watt, L. (N. Zealand) b Sept. 17, 1924

Watts, E. A. (Surrey) b Aug. 1, 1911, d May 2, 1982

Watts, H. E. (Camb. U. and Somerset) b March 4, 1922

Watts, P. D. (Northants and Notts.) b March 31, 1938

Watts, P. J. (Northants) b June 16, 1940

Wazir Ali, S. (India) b Sept. 15, 1903, d June 17, 1950

Wazir Mohammad (Pakistan) b Dec. 22, 1929

Webb, M. G. (N. Zealand) b June 22, 1947

Webb, P. N. (N. Zealand) b July 14, 1957

Webb, R. T. (Sussex) b July 11, 1922

Webb, S. G. (Manager Australians in England 1961) b Jan. 31, 1900, d Aug. 5, 1976

Webbe, A. J. (Oxford U. and Middx) b Jan. 16, 1855, d Feb. 19, 1941

Webster, J. (Camb. U. and Northants) b Oct. 28, 1917

Webster, Dr R. V. (Warw. and Otago) b June 10, 1939

Webster, W. H. (Camb. U. and Middx; Pres. MCC 1976-77) b Feb. 22, 1910

Weekes, E. D. (W. Indies; *CY 1951*) b Feb. 26, 1925

Weekes, K. H. (W. Indies) b Jan. 24, 1912

Weeks, R. T. (Warw.) b April 30, 1930

Weir, G. L. (N. Zealand) b June 2, 1908

Wellard, A. W. (Somerset; *CY 1936*) b April 8, 1902, d Dec. 31, 1980

Wellham, D. M. (Australia) b March 13, 1959

Wellings, E. M. (Oxford U. and Surrey) b April 6, 1909

Wells, A. P. (Sussex) b March 3, 1960

Wells, B. D. (Glos. and Notts.) b July 27, 1930

Wells, C. M. (Sussex and Border) b March 3, 1960

Wenman, E. G. (Kent and England) b Aug. 18, 1803, d Dec. 31, 1879

Wensley, A. F. (Sussex) b May 23, 1898, d June 17, 1970

Wesley, C. (S. Africa) b Sept. 5, 1937

Wessels, K. C. (Orange Free State, W. Province, N. Transvaal, Sussex and Australia) b Sept. 14, 1957

West, G. H. (Editor of *Wisden* 1880-86) b 1851, d Oct. 6, 1896

Westcott, R. J. (S. Africa) b Sept. 19, 1927

Weston, M. J. (Worcs.) b April 8, 1959

Wettimuny, M. D. (Sri Lanka) b June 11, 1951

Wettimuny, S. (Sri Lanka) b Aug. 12, 1956

Wharton, A. (Lancs. and Leics.) b April 30, 1923

Whatmore, D. F. (Australia) b March 16, 1954

Wheatley, K. J. (Hants) b Jan. 20, 1946

Wheatley, O. S. (Camb. U., Warw. and Glam.; *CY 1969*) b May 28, 1935

Whitaker, Haddon (Editor of *Wisden* 1940-43) b Aug. 30, 1908, d Jan. 5, 1982

Whitcombe, P. A. (Oxford U. and Middx) b April 23, 1923

White, A. F. T. (Camb. U., Warw. and Worcs.) b Sept. 5, 1915

White, D. W. (Hants and Glam.) b Dec. 14, 1935

White, E. C. S. (NSW) b July 14, 1913

White, G. C. (S. Africa) b Feb. 5, 1882, d Oct. 17, 1918

White, J. C. (Somerset; *CY 1929*) b Feb. 19, 1891, d May 2, 1961

White, Hon. L. R. (5th Lord Annaly) (Middx and Victory Test) b March 15, 1927

White, R. A. (Middx and Notts.) b Oct. 6, 1936

White, R. C. (Camb. U., Glos. and Transvaal) b Jan. 29, 1941

White, W. A. (W. Indies) b Nov. 20, 1938

Whitehead, J. P. (Yorks. and Worcs.) b Sept. 3, 1925

Whitehouse, J. (Warw.) b April 8, 1949

Whitelaw, P. E. (N. Zealand) b Feb. 10, 1910

Whitfield, E. W. (Surrey and Northants) b May 31, 1911

Whiting, N. H. (Worcs.) b Oct. 2, 1920

Whitington, R. S. (S. Australia and Victory Tests; Writer) b June 30, 1912

Whitney, M. R. (Glos. and Australia) b Feb. 24, 1959

Whittaker, G. J. (Surrey) b May 29, 1916

Whittingham, N. B. (Notts.) b Oct. 22, 1940

Whitty, W. J. (Australia) b Aug. 15, 1886, d Jan. 30, 1974

Whysall, W. W. (Notts.; *CY 1925*) b Oct. 31, 1887, d Nov. 11, 1930

Wiener, J. M. (Australia) b May 1, 1955

Wight, C. V. (W. Indies) b July 28, 1902, d 1969

Wight, G. L. (W. Indies) b May 28, 1929

Wight, P. B. (B. Guiana, Somerset and Canterbury) b June 25, 1930

Wijesuriya, R. G. C. E. (Sri Lanka) b Feb. 18, 1960

Wilcox, D. R. (Camb. U. and Essex) b June 4, 1910, d Feb. 6, 1953

Wiles, C. A. (W. Indies) b Aug. 11, 1892

Wilkins, A. H. (Glam., Glos. and N. Transvaal) b Aug. 22, 1953

Wilkins, C. P. (Derby., E. Province and Natal) b July 31, 1944

Wilkinson, C. T. A. (Surrey) b Oct. 4, 1884, d Dec. 16, 1970

Wilkinson, L. L. (Lancs.) b Nov. 5, 1916

Wilkinson, P. A. (Notts.) b Aug. 23, 1951

Wilkinson, Col. W. A. C. (Oxford U.) b Dec. 6, 1892, d Sept. 19, 1983

Willatt, G. L. (Camb. U., Notts. and Derby.) b May 7, 1918

Willett, E. T. (W. Indies) b May 1, 1953

Willett, M. D. (Surrey) b April 21, 1933

Willey, P. (Northants and E. Province) b Dec. 6, 1949

Williams, A. B. (W. Indies) b Nov. 21, 1949

Williams, C. B. (Barbados) b March 8, 1926

Williams, C. C. P. (Oxford U. and Essex) b Feb. 9, 1933

Williams, D. L. (Glam.) b Nov. 20, 1946

Williams, E. A. V. (W. Indies) b April 10, 1914

Williams, N. F. (Middx) b July 2, 1962

Williams, R. G. (Northants) b Aug. 10, 1957

Williams, R. J. (S. Africa) b April 12, 1912

Williamson, J. G. (Northants) b April 4, 1936

Willis, R. G. D. (Surrey, Warw. and N. Transvaal; *CY 1978*) b May 30, 1949

Willoughby, J. T. (S. Africa) b Nov. 7, 1874, d *circa* 1955

Willsher, E. (Kent and All-England) b Nov. 22, 1828, d Oct. 7, 1885

Wilmot, A. L. (E. Province) b June 1, 1943

Wilmot, K. (Warw.) b April 3, 1911

Wilson, A. (Lancs.) b April 24, 1921

Wilson, A. E. (Middx and Glos.) b May 5, 1912

Wilson, Rev. C. E. M. (Camb. U. and Yorks.) b May 15, 1875, d Feb. 8, 1944

Wilson, D. (Yorks. and MCC) b Aug. 7, 1937

Wilson, E. F. (Surrey) b June 24, 1907, d March 3, 1981

Wilson, E. R. (Camb. U. and Yorks.) b March 25, 1879, d July 21, 1957

Wilson, J. V. (Yorks.; *CY 1961*) b Jan. 17, 1921

Wilson, J. W. (Australia) b Aug. 20, 1921

Wilson, P. H. L. (Surrey, Somerset and N. Transvaal) b Aug. 17, 1958

Wilson, R. C. (Kent) b Feb. 18, 1928

Wimble, C. S. (S. Africa) b Jan. 9, 1864, d Jan. 28, 1930

Windows, A. R. (Glos. and Camb. U.) b Sept. 25, 1942

Winfield, H. M. (Notts.) b June 13, 1933

Wingfield Digby, A. R. (Oxford U.) b July 25, 1950

Winlaw, Sqn Ldr R. de W. K. (Camb. U. and Surrey) b March 28, 1912, d Oct. 31, 1942

Winn, C. E. (Oxford U. and Sussex) b Nov. 13, 1926

Winslow, P. L. (Sussex and S. Africa) b May 21, 1929

Wisden John (Sussex; founder John Wisden and Co. and *Wisden's Cricketers' Almanack*) b Sept. 5, 1826, d April 5, 1884

Wishart, K. L. (W. Indies) b Nov. 28, 1908, d Oct. 18, 1972

Wolton, A. V. G. (Warw.) b June 12, 1919

Wood, A. (Yorks.; *CY 1939*) b Aug. 25, 1898, d April 1, 1973

Wood, B. (Yorks., Lancs., Derby. and E. Province) b Dec. 26, 1942

Wood, C. J. B. (Leics.) b Nov. 21, 1875, d June 5, 1960

Wood, D. J. (Sussex) b May 19, 1914

Wood, G. E. C. (Camb. U. and Kent) b Aug. 22, 1893, d March 18, 1971

Wood, G. M. (Australia) b Nov. 6, 1956

Wood, H. (Kent and Surrey; *CY 1891*) b Dec. 14, 1854, d April 30, 1919

Wood, R. (Lancs. and Victoria) b March 7, 1860, d Jan. 6, 1915

Woodcock, A. J. (Australia) b Feb. 27, 1948

Woodfull, W. M. (Australia; *CY 1927*) b Aug. 22, 1897, d Aug. 11, 1965

Woodhead, F. G. (Notts.) b Oct. 30, 1912

Woodhouse, G. E. S. (Somerset) b Feb. 15, 1924

Woods, S. M. J. (Camb. U., Somerset, Australia and England; *CY 1889*) b April 14, 1867, d April 30, 1931

Wookey, S. M. (Camb. U. and Oxford U.) b Sept. 2, 1954

Wooler, C. R. D. (Leics. and Rhodesia) b June 30, 1930

Wooller, W. (Camb. U. and Glam.) b Nov. 20, 1912

Woolley, C. N. (Glos. and Northants) b May 5, 1886, d Nov. 3, 1962

Woolley, F. E. (Kent; *CY 1911*) b May 27, 1887, d Oct. 18, 1978

Woolley, R. D. (Australia) b Sept. 16, 1954

Woolmer, R. A. (Kent, Natal and W. Province; *CY 1976*) b May 14, 1948

Worrall, J. (Australia) b May 12, 1863, d Nov. 17, 1937

Worrell, Sir F. M. M. (W. Indies; *CY 1951*) b Aug. 1, 1924, d March 13, 1967

Worsley, D. R. (Oxford U. and Lancs.) b July 18, 1941

Worsley, Sir W. A. 4th Bt. (Yorks.; Pres. MCC 1961-62) b April 5, 1890, d Dec. 4, 1973

Worthington, T. S. (Derby.; *CY 1937*) b Aug. 21, 1905, d Aug. 31, 1973

Wright, A. (Warw.) b Aug. 25, 1941

Wright, C. W. (Camb. U. and Notts.) b May 27, 1863, d Jan. 10, 1936

Wright, D. V. P. (Kent; *CY 1940*) b Aug. 21, 1914

Wright, J. G. (Derby. and N. Zealand) b July 5, 1954

Wright, K. J. (Australia) b Dec. 27, 1953

Wright, L. G. (Derby.; *CY 1906*) b June 15, 1862, d Jan. 11, 1953

Wright, M. J. E. (N. Districts) b Jan. 17, 1950

Wyatt, R. E. S. (Warw. and Worcs.; *CY 1930*) b May 2, 1901

Wynne, O. E. (S. Africa) b June 1, 1919, d July 13, 1975

Wynyard, E. G. (Hants) b April 1, 1861, d Oct. 30, 1936

Yadav, N. S. (India) b Jan. 26, 1957

Yajurvindra Singh, (India) b Aug. 1, 1952

Yallop, G. N. (Australia) b Oct. 7, 1952

Yardley, B. (Australia) b Sept. 7, 1947

Yardley, N. W. D. (Camb. U. and Yorks.; *CY 1948*) b March 19, 1915

Yardley, T. J. (Worcs. and Northants) b Oct. 27, 1946

Yarnold, H. (Worcs.) b July 6, 1917, d Aug. 13, 1974

Yashpal Sharma (India) b Aug. 11, 1954

Yawar Saeed (Somerset and Punjab) b Jan. 22, 1935

Yograj Singh (India) b March 25, 1958

Young, D. M. (Worcs. and Glos.) b April 15, 1924

Young, H. I. (Essex) b Feb. 5, 1876, d Dec. 12, 1964

Young, J. A. (Middx) b Oct. 14, 1912

Young, R. A. (Camb. U. and Sussex) b Sept. 16, 1885, d July 1, 1968

Younis Ahmed, M. (Surrey, Worcs., S. Australia and Pakistan) b Oct. 21, 1947

Yuile, B. W. (N. Zealand) b Oct. 29, 1941

Zaheer Abbas (Glos. and Pakistan; *CY 1972*) b July 24, 1947

Zulch, J. W. (S. Africa) b Jan. 2, 1886, d May 19, 1924

Zulfiqar Ahmed (Pakistan) b Nov. 22, 1926

OBITUARIES

ALVA, B. CHANDRAHASA, who died at Bangalore on November 6, 1982, at the age of 59, was a competent all-rounder, a sound right-hand batsman and a reliable medium-paced bowler. He played for Madras and Mysore in the Ranji Trophy between 1944 and 1959, captaining both teams. He scored 1,082 runs at an average of 30.33 and took 57 wickets at 23.71 apiece. In 1950-51 he played in two unofficial "Tests" against the Commonwealth team which toured India. An engineer by profession, Alva occupied influential positions in the Mysore, later Karnataka, state service.

AUSTEN, DR ERNEST THOMAS, who died in Melbourne on June 21, 1983, aged 82, played twice for Victoria in 1928-29. He might have thought that once would have been enough, for at Melbourne in his first match, having fielded through a New South Wales innings of 713 for six declared, he became, in Victoria's second innings, one of Hooker's four victims in successive balls.

BADCOCK, CLAYVEL LINDSAY ("JACK"), who died at his birthplace, Exton, Tasmania, on December 13, 1982, aged 68, was something of an infant prodigy, making his début for Tasmania in 1929 when still under sixteen. A right-handed batsman, Badcock was sturdily built and a punishing driver. He was also a fine cutter of the ball, especially square of the wicket. He played nineteen matches for Tasmania before transferring to South Australia for whom he played until his early retirement, owing to lumbago, in 1941. He had an insatiable appetite for runs. Playing for South Australia against Victoria at Adelaide in 1936 he made 325, his highest score. He also scored 271 not out for South Australia against New South Wales in 1938-39 and 236 against Queensland in 1939-40. His highest score for Tasmania was 274 against Victoria at Launceston in 1933-34.

For such a prolific scorer in Sheffield Shield cricket Badcock had a disappointing Test record, scoring only 160 runs in twelve innings, despite making 118 against England in only his third Test, at Melbourne in 1936-37. He toured England in 1938 and enjoyed considerable success outside the Test matches, his aggregate of 1,604 runs (average 45.82) being inferior only to those of Bradman and Brown. Self-effacing and immensely popular, he scored 7,571 runs in first-class cricket at an average of 51.54 and hit 26 centuries.

BADCOCK, FREDERICK THEODORE, who died in Perth, Western Australia, on September 19, 1982, aged 84, played seven times for New Zealand between 1929-30 and 1932-33, though he was born in India and educated at Wellington College, Berkshire. Tall, dark and handsome, he bowled at a good medium pace, was a brilliant fielder and a good enough batsman to score 64 and 53 in successive Tests against South Africa in 1931-32. His first Test, against England at Wellington, was also New Zealand's first, and he made a "pair" in it, as well as being one of M. J. C. Allom's four victims in five balls. He ended his Test career, barely three years later, bowling to Hammond while he was scoring 227 and 336 not out in the only two Test matches which England played in New Zealand in 1932-33. Badcock's peripatetic life included a spell in England during the Second World War, when he played occasionally for Northamptonshire, some coaching in Ceylon and retirement in Western Australia. In all first-class cricket he scored 2,356 runs (average 26.47), including four centuries, and took 214 wickets at 23 apiece.

BADHAM, PETER HENRY CHRISTOPHER, died at Upton, near Poole, on April 10, 1983, aged 72. After a humble record in the Winchester XI in 1930, he made such rapid progress as an all-rounder that he had several trials for Oxford and in 1933 played for Leicestershire, for whom he had a birth qualification, against the University. He also played with some success for Buckinghamshire and later for Dorset. He was a fast-medium right-hand opening bowler with a high action.

BAKEWELL, ALFRED HARRY (FRED), who died at Westbourne, Bournemouth, on January 23, 1983, aged 74, was, from the spectator's point of view, one of the most exciting batsmen of his generation and the car smash which ended his career was as disastrous as that which finished Milburn's years later. While, as the vicissitudes of some of our modern Test match batsmen demonstrate, it is impossible to exaggerate the importance of a sound orthodox method, it is salutary that just now and again a player emerges who can defy some of what are normally considered the cardinal principles and yet completely confound the critics. Bakewell's stance was one of the most two-eyed ever seen, with the right shoulder so far round that it seemed almost to be facing mid-on: it was not helped by a slight crouch and he gripped the bat throughout with one hand at the top and the other at the bottom of the handle. Seeing this for the first time, one would have diagnosed a dull and ugly player who would score, if at all, by nudges and deflections. Yet there was in him some natural genius which enabled him to be one of the most brilliant drivers and cutters in the world, nor did he have any difficulty in getting right down the pitch to hit the ball. Naturally he was also strong on the leg side and, if in his early years his defence was a trifle suspect, especially on his off stump, he soon improved it.

If ever a batsman was a law unto himself, he was. In 1933 he scored 246 for Northamptonshire against Nottinghamshire at Northampton in just under six hours. In order to keep him quiet, Sam Staples, one of the most accurate off-spinners in England, bowled at the stumps with a packed leg side. To cut an off-break is generally a recipe for trouble: to cut an off-break on the middle stump is suicidal. Yet Bakewell, standing well clear of his leg stump, in the intervals of jumping out and driving him for 4 past the place where extra-cover might have been, constantly cut him. In 30 overs Staples conceded 177 runs. The innings was regarded by many as the finest they had ever seen on the ground and was a record for the county. It did not stay a record for long. In the next match Bakewell beat it with 257 against Glamorgan at Swansea. By contrast, opening for England against West Indies at The Oval later that summer, he was faced with a score-board reading 68 for four, Walters, Hammond, Wyatt and Turnbull all being out. His answer was to make 107 out of 194 in three hours, 50 minutes, a sensible, controlled innings which was just what the situation called for and which saved the side.

Born at Walsall, Bakewell learned his cricket at St John's School, Tiffield, and later received further coaching in Oxford under the scheme organised by J. R. F. Turner. He made his first appearance for Northamptonshire in June, 1928, and immediately made his place secure not only with some useful innings, but by his brilliant fielding at short-leg. In 1929 he got his 1,000 runs and did so every season for the rest of his career. Having played his first innings of 200 in 1930, 204 against Somerset at Bath, he was picked in 1931 for the Players at Lord's and also to open the innings for England against New Zealand at Lord's and The Oval. At The Oval he made 40 and was batting well when he allowed himself to be run out rather than Sutcliffe. In 1933 his aggregate of 1,952 runs for the county was a record and in all matches he exceeded 2,000 runs, the first Northamptonshire man ever to do so. That winter he went to India with Jardine's side and was only moderately successful and in 1934, being doubtless stale, failed to get a place against the Australians. Back in form in 1935, he played in two Tests against South Africa without much success, but made 1,719 runs for the county, including a remarkable innings against Yorkshire at Harrogate. Those were the days when D. R. Jardine, if he wished to know how good a cricketer was, always asked, "What has he done against Yorkshire?" On this occasion someone remarked to Bakewell that he had never taken a hundred off Yorkshire: he replied, "I will do so today". The Yorkshire bowling was opened by Smailes and off his first over Bakewell hit five 4s, followed by three more three overs later. In two hours he had reached 96 when Sellers just reached, one-handed at full stretch over his head at mid-off, a tremendous drive and held it. In 1936 Bakewell had another good season and ended it and his career with a great innings. At Chesterfield Northamptonshire were 65 runs down on the first innings to Derbyshire, the champions. Going in again Bakewell batted over six hours for 241 not out before his captain declared, leaving Derbyshire 347 to get. At the close they were 173 for seven. On the return journey the car in which R. P. Northway and Bakewell were travelling overturned. Northway was killed outright and Bakewell's right arm was so badly broken that he could never play county cricket again.

In all first-class matches he had scored 14,570 runs with an average of 33.98, besides being a great short-leg. It is sometimes suggested, surely somewhat harshly, that he should, even in his short career, have achieved more than he did, but it must be remembered that he was throughout playing for a very weak county. During his nine seasons Northamptonshire won only 31 matches and lost 119: five times they were bottom of the table. So let the last word lie with his old captain, W. C. Brown: "During an all-too-short first-class career his approach to life in general may have seemed somewhat lackadaisical. Out in the middle, though, he was a splendid chap to have on the side and, when a change in the field involving someone in a long trek between overs became necessary, Fred was always the first to call out, 'I'll go skipper'."

BARLOW, ALFRED, who died on May 9, 1983, aged 67, kept wicket very neatly for Lancashire in 74 matches between 1947 and 1951. He was capped in 1950, a year in which Lancashire shared the Championship with Surrey, and in the winter of 1950-51 he toured India with a strong Commonwealth side. All told he made 104 catches and 46 stumpings, most of the stumpings coming off Tattersall and Hilton. Quite a useful tail-end batsman, he was prominent in the tied match between Lancashire and Hampshire at Bournemouth in 1947. When Hill of Hampshire began the final over Lancashire's last pair, Ikin and Barlow, were together, with the scores level. In trying a sharp single Barlow was run out.

BEESON, F. EDWARD, who died on April 10, 1982, was a hard-hitting batsman who played occasionally for Buckinghamshire. For some years he was groundsman at High Wycombe Grammar School.

BLUNDELL, NEIL, who died in Adelaide on September 24, 1983, aged 53, was Assistant Secretary of the South Australian Cricket Association from 1970 until 1978 and Secretary from 1978 until 1980. He had been a cricket umpire and a linesman with Davis Cup experience.

BROWN, LENNOX SIDNEY, who died in Durban on September 1, 1983, aged 72, toured Australia and New Zealand with H. B. Cameron's South African side in 1931-32, playing one Test in each country. Against Australia he took one for 100 and against New Zealand at Wellington two for 89. He could bowl effectively at two paces – medium and slow. On his first-class début, for Transvaal against MCC at Johannesburg in 1930-31, he took seven wickets in the match, including Hammond's twice, and he had played only one more first-class game when, at the age of twenty, he was chosen for the Australasian tour. In the Currie Cup he played first for Transvaal and later for North-Eastern Transvaal, for whom, against his former province in 1937-38, he took ten wickets in the match. He finished his career with Rhodesia, having also played Lancashire League cricket for Church and professional football for Huddersfield Town and Oldham Athletic. Altogether he took 147 first-class wickets. His top score was 75, for North-Eastern Transvaal against the 1938-39 MCC side.

BUCKLE, FRANK ("SANDY"), who died in Sydney on June 4, 1982, aged 90, was, at the time of his death, the oldest surviving New South Wales player. A right-hand bat, he played one game for the state in 1913, in which he scored 10.

CARLISLE, KENNETH RALPH MALCOLM, who died on July 23, 1983, aged 75, was in the Harrow XI in 1925, 1926 and 1927. In 1925 he made 45 at Lord's, in 1926 62 and in 1927, playing for Sussex in their last match against Essex at Hove, made 34, top score, in the second innings. Making 108 in the Freshmen's Match at Oxford next year, he received two invitations to play for the University: the first he had to refuse through injury, the second did not reach him in time. Meanwhile his substitute had made runs in each match and his own chance was gone. He did not make runs later that year for Sussex, nor in a trial or two for the University in 1929. He was an aggressive batsman, an attractive off-side player, with a good straight drive, who could also score well off his legs. His father captained Oxford in 1905.

COLLINSON, JOHN, who died at Hove on August 29, 1979, aged 67, appeared in two matches for Middlesex in 1939 and in his first innings for the county, against Gloucestershire at Cheltenham, was second-highest scorer with 34. In 1946, having gone as a master to Malvern, where for some years he ran the cricket, he played one match for Worcestershire. He had a solid defence, but was a very slow scorer.

COOMBES, MAXWELL JAMES, who died at Longley, Tasmania, on March 10, 1983, aged 71, was a right-hand bat who played ten times for Tasmania between 1932-33 and 1938-39. He scored 361 runs for them at an average of 24.06. He had a brother, G. A., who also played for Tasmania.

COOK, GEOFFREY GLOVER, who died on September 12, 1982, aged 72, was a right-hand bat and medium-pace bowler who played 68 matches for Queensland between 1931 and 1947. He made 3,453 runs (average 29.76), took 125 wickets (average 35.50) and held 33 catches. His highest score, 169 not out, was made in 1946-47 against W. R. Hammond's MCC team. In 1938-39 he had helped W. A. Brown make 265 for Queensland's first wicket against New South Wales in Sydney. This remained a Queensland record until 1983. Cook, who scored three first-class centuries, was the son of Barney Cook, himself a former Queensland player.

CORBETT, LEONARD JAMES, died on January 26, 1983, aged 85. Better known as one of the great rugger three-quarters of his day, who had sixteen international caps and twice captained England, he was also a good cricketer, who, in nine matches for Gloucestershire between 1920 and 1925, made 373 runs with an average of 20.72, his highest score being 55 in the August Bank Holiday match against Somerset in 1923 at a time when the side was doing very badly. Perhaps one who well remembers fielding in a club match while he made a hundred may be allowed to say that if he had had the opportunity to play regularly he would have been invaluable to the county. Moving with all the ease of a natural games player, he had beautiful strokes and made batting look very simple; moreover he was, as one would expect, a superb field. In later life he wrote well both on rugger and cricket for the *Sunday Times*.

COY, ARTHUR H., OBE, who died at Port Elizabeth on May 15, 1983, was a prominent member of the South African Cricket Association during the days of strictly segregated cricket, being its President from 1953 to 1955 and again from 1957 to 1959. He had captained Eastern Province before the Second World War, in which he served with the Royal Engineers, and was much in the news at the time of the D'Oliveira affair in 1968.

CROLE-REES, ANTONY, who died suddenly at Hove on October 8, 1983, aged 58, was for 24 years on the Sussex Committee and for seven years its Chairman. He had been in the Charterhouse XI and was a useful all-round games-player until crippled by arthritis.

DE SARAM, FREDERICK CECIL (DERRICK), died in Colombo on April 11, 1983, aged 70. Strange things happened in the world of cricket at Oxford in the 30s, few stranger than that De Saram, one of the finest bats at either University between the wars, should have had only one trial in The Parks in his first two years. Coming up from Royal College, Colombo, he played in the Freshmen's Match in 1932 without success and was not seen again until the Seniors' Match in 1934, when he probably owed his place to a fine record for Hertfordshire the season before. Making 64 in this match, he was picked for the University's opening fixture against Gloucestershire, in which, on his first-class début in England, he made 176 in three hours. A few weeks later he scored 128 against the Australians, treating Grimmett with a disrespect of which few Test batsmen had shown themselves capable: the Oxford total was 216 and the next highest score 16. In all for Oxford that summer he scored 1,119 runs with an average of 50.86, his highest score being 208 against a weak bowling side of H. D. G. Leveson Gower at Eastbourne. Like some other outstanding batsmen, he failed against Cambridge. In 1935 Schools prevented him from playing regularly or getting into form, but in the first innings at Lord's, when things were going badly, he got 85 in two and a half hours, easily top score in a total of 221, and, when he was out, he received an ovation. That was the end of his first-class cricket in England, but for Hertfordshire in the vacation he had an aggregate of 904 runs and an average of 90.40, figures believed at that time to be a record for Minor County cricket. He continued to play with great success in Ceylon, whom he captained from 1949 to 1954: indeed in 1954 he made 43 against MCC on their way to Australia. He also did much for the game off the field as an administrator and selector. A complete batsman with lovely wrists, all the strokes and at the same time a strong defence, he was a fierce competitor who, had he been born 50 years later, would have been a godsend to the present Sri Lankan side – unless politics had intervened. In 1962, as formidable in public life as on the cricket field or lawn tennis court (a game at which he also represented Oxford), he was sentenced to a long term of imprisonment for conspiring against the Government of the day.

DEWFALL, ERNEST GEORGE, who died in November 1982, aged 72, played two matches for Gloucestershire in 1938 as a fast bowler without much success.

EDGSON, CHARLES LESLIE, died suddenly in hospital on June 28, 1983, aged 67. A heavy scorer at Stamford School, he played occasionally for Leicestershire from 1933 to 1939 and against Derbyshire at Chesterfield in 1934, when only nineteen, played two invaluable innings of 49 and 43. Going up to Oxford he made 57 in the Freshmen's Match in 1936, but did not get a trial for the University. Altogether for Leicestershire he scored 321 runs with an average of 13.38. Later he was for years a master at Brentwood School, where he was in charge of the cricket.

EGGAR, JOHN DRENNAN, who died aged 66 on May 3, 1983, while playing lawn tennis, was three years in the Winchester XI and captain in 1935, but neither then, nor in his first two years at Oxford, did he do anything outstanding, though his friends knew him to be a good player. However, in 1938 he followed a hundred in the Seniors' Match with 51 not out early in May out of a total of 117 against the Australians. As he had Schools that summer, he could not play again for the University until the match against Lancashire in The Parks six weeks later, when an innings of 125 made it clear that he must be in the side, even though it meant relegating to twelfth man E. D. R. Eagar, who had a good record. At Lord's Eggar, who had meanwhile made 98 against Sussex, justified his selection: a stubborn second innings of 29 ensured that Oxford saved a match that they could easily have lost. Later that summer he appeared twice for Hampshire, but after the war, being a master at Repton, he played for Derbyshire in the summer holidays, regularly until 1950 and occasionally until 1954. His record of 1,385 runs with an average of 31.48 shows how valuable he was. In 1947 he and C. S. Elliott put on 349 for the second wicket against Nottinghamshire at Trent Bridge, still the highest partnership ever made for the county. He was essentially a sound player, whose bat in defence could look unnaturally broad, but he did not lack strokes, and, though the highest of his three centuries for the county, 219 against Yorkshire at Bradford in 1949, took over seven hours, it included 27 4s. On that occasion he was battling in vain to save his side from defeat. Well-taught at Winchester by H. S. Altham and E. R. Wilson, he was himself a successful coach at Repton. Later he was for sixteen years Headmaster of Shiplake College, where he was greatly respected and achieved a considerable success, more than trebling the numbers of what, when he went there, was a school with an uncertain future.

EMERY, RAYMOND WILLIAM GEORGE, who died in Auckland on December 18, 1982, aged 67, played twice for New Zealand as a right-hand opening bat in their inaugural series against West Indies, in 1951-52. He was already 36 when he did so, though it was during his best season (433 runs at 72.16 for Canterbury in the Plunket Shield). He also bowled, at medium pace, and in a West Indian total of 546 for six in the second Test at Auckland took the wickets of Worrell and Walcott. In all first-class cricket he scored 1,177 runs (average 29.42), including three centuries, and took 22 wickets at 34.27 apiece.

GAUNT, THE REV. CANON HOWARD CHARLES ADIE, who died at Winchester on February 1, 1983, aged 80, was a successful bat at Tonbridge, but did not obtain a Blue at Cambridge. However, he played in eleven matches for Warwickshire between 1919 and 1922, his highest score being 32 against Somerset at Edgbaston in 1922. From 1937 to 1953 he was Headmaster of Malvern and once, batting for Free Foresters, won the admiration of Arthur Povey, the much-loved pro at Tonbridge, who exclaimed, "He may be a Headmaster, but he can hit them to square leg all right!" He represented Cambridge at hockey and lawn tennis.

GILBERT, ALAN, who died early in 1983, aged 67, was educated at Manchester Grammar School and kept wicket for Cheshire occasionally in the 1950s.

GORNALL, CAPTAIN JAMES PARRINGTON, DSO, RN (Retd), who died at Lower Froyle, Hampshire, on November 13, 1983, aged 84, was a good club batsman who played several times for the Navy and made one appearance for Hampshire in 1923.

GOULDING, SIR WILLIAM BASIL, BT, died in Dublin on January 16, 1982, aged 71. Educated at Winchester, where he was not in the XI, he was a wicket-keeper and right-hand bat who played two matches for Ireland in 1934, the year in which his father was President of the Irish Cricket Union. He also played squash for Ireland and captained Oxford University at soccer.

GRAY, LAURENCE HERBERT, died at Langdon Hills, Essex, after a long illness, on January 3, 1983, aged 67. Born at Tottenham, he was that comparative rarity, a Middlesex cricketer with a birth qualification. After a few matches in 1934 and 1935, he began to make his mark as a fast bowler in 1936, when he and Jim Smith bowled out Nottinghamshire at Lord's in the second innings for 41, his own share being four for 26. From then until 1949 he was a regular and valuable member of a side which depended largely on slow spin, the other quick bowlers being Jim Smith (until the war), Edrich and G. O. Allen, when available. It was a glorious period in the county's history: in those eight seasons they won the Championship twice, were second five times and third once. To this impressive record Gray made a considerable contribution, though after doing much good work in 1937 and 1938 he fell off sadly in 1939. At this period he was apt to lose his length and bowl short, faults which were less evident after the war. In 1946 he took for Middlesex 95 wickets at 19.06 and in all matches, for the only time, exceeded 100 wickets, while in 1947 his record for the county was 92 at 22.46. He continued to bowl with some success for two more years, but, losing a regular place in 1950, played his last match in 1951. An arthritic hip shortened his career. In 1946, when he took eleven for 34 against Hampshire at Lord's, he appeared for the Players at Lord's and in a Test trial. It will be seen that the war robbed him of six seasons when he might reasonably have expected to be in his prime. Even so it may be doubted whether he would ever have been more than a good county bowler. He had not quite the physique or the speed to attain greatness. In all first-class matches he took 637 wickets for 25.14. A batting average for his career of 7.38, with a highest score of 35 not out, suggests no great ability in that line, but he played at least one memorable innings. Against Essex at Lord's in 1939 he helped Denis Compton to put on 83 in three-quarters of an hour for the last wicket, his own share being 1 not out. To Compton he later owed a great debt. As the senior of the two, Compton was due for his benefit in 1948, but waived his claim in Gray's favour. Gray's benefit raised over £6,000, a sum which, low though it may seem by modern standards, had then only once been exceeded. From 1953 to 1970 Gray was a first-class umpire, standing in four Test matches.

GREENWOOD, HENRY WILLIAM, who died in hospital in Horsham on October 16, 1983, aged 74, was a batsman who just failed to make the grade in first-class cricket. A short, stocky man, he was not a natural stroke-player, but had limitless patience and a strong defence and could cut well. After playing a few games for Sussex in 1933 and 1934, he helped John Langridge to put on 101 for their first wicket against Oxford in 1935, going on to make 77, and a few weeks later the two shared in an opening partnership of 305 in four hours against Essex at Hove, to which he contributed 115. For the county that season he scored 404 runs with an average of 36.72, but even so failed to get a regular place and next year did not play in a single Championship match. Perhaps his fielding did not help as, though an adequate slip, he was a slow mover elsewhere. Moreover, the Sussex batting was strong at the time. So he left the county and on his own initiative qualified for Northamptonshire, then the weakest side in the competition, playing meanwhile first for Forfarshire and then for Stoke. In 1938 he was available for Northamptonshire only in mid-week, but did fairly well, scoring 573 runs with an average of 26.04. However, in 1939 he was disappointing, though he made his highest score for the county, 94 against Warwickshire at Edgbaston. After serving in the RAF in the war, he returned to the side in 1946, but had a poor season, not helped by being required to act as wicket-keeper in the absence of anyone better. This concluded his first-class career.

GRIFFITH, BERNIE, who died in Wellington on September 29, 1982, aged 72, played as a leg-break and googly bowler for New Zealand in the last two unofficial Tests against E. R. T. Holmes's MCC side in 1935, having earlier helped Wellington to a famous victory over the tourists by 14 runs. In fourteen first-class matches he took 50 wickets at 26.88 apiece.

HALL, DEREK, who was killed in a car crash in Canada in late April, 1983, played for Derbyshire from 1955 to 1958. Standing well over six feet, he had a good trial in 1955 and, without any notable performance, showed promise, taking 24 wickets at 26.41. Given another good trial in 1956, he was disappointing and after a match or two in 1957 and 1958 he left the county. Altogether he took 48 wickets at 28.88. As a batsman he did not contribute much, his highest score in twenty matches being 10 not out.

HARDY, MAJOR RICHARD SOMERS ANGUS, died at Harlaston on June 23, 1983, aged 78. Captain of Stonyhurst, where he had been for four years in the XI, he later played occasionally for Staffordshire as a batsman.

HARPER, HERBERT, who died at Birmingham on August 6, 1983, aged 94, made one appearance for Worcestershire, against Yorkshire, as a batsman, without success.

HEADLEY, GEORGE ALPHONSO, MBE, who died in Jamaica on November 30, 1983, aged 74, was the first of the great black batsmen to emerge from the West Indies. Between the wars, when the West Indies batting was often vulnerable and impulsive, Headley's scoring feats led to his being dubbed "the black Bradman". His devoted admirers responded by calling Bradman "the white Headley" – a pardonable exaggeration. In 22 Tests, when the innings could stand or fall on his performance, Headley scored 2,190 runs, including ten centuries – eight against England – with an average of 60.83. He was the first to score a century in each innings of a Test at Lord's, in 1939, and it was a measure of his ability that from 1929 to 1939 he did not have a single bad Test series. By the start of the Second World War he had totalled 9,532 runs in first-class cricket with an average of 72.21. Afterwards, though not the power that he had been, he extended his aggregate to 9,921 runs, with 33 centuries and an average of 69.86.

Born in Panama, where his father had helped to build the Canal, Headley was taken to Jamaica at the age of ten to perfect his English - Spanish had been his first tongue – and to prepare to study dentistry in America. At school he fell in love with cricket, but he might still have been lost to the game had there not been a delay in getting his passport for the United States. While he was waiting, Headley was chosen to play against a visiting English team captained by the Hon. L. H. Tennyson.

Though not yet nineteen, he had innings of 78 in the first match and 211 in the second, and dentistry lost a student. Surprisingly he was not chosen for the 1928 tour of England immediately afterwards, but in the home series against England in 1929-30 he scored 703 runs in eight Test innings, averaging 87.80. His scores included 21 and 176 in his first Test, 114 and 112 in the third and 223 in the fourth. In 1930-31 in Australia he scored two more Test centuries and ended the tour with 1,066 runs. Clarrie Grimmett described him as the strongest on-side player he had ever bowled against. In 1932, in a single month, he hit 344 not out (his highest-ever score), 84, 155 not out and 140 against another English side to visit Jamaica. Against sterner opposition and in more difficult conditions in England in the following year, he averaged 66 for the tour, scoring a century on his first appearance at Lord's and taking 224 not out off Somerset. In the second Test at Manchester he made 169 not out, a score he improved upon with 270 not out at Kingston in the 1934-35 series.

Headley was of medium build, compact, balanced and light on his feet. Like most great batsmen he was a superb back-foot player and seldom made a hurried shot. Sir Leonard Hutton, who saw him at his best in 1939, declares he has never seen a batsman play the ball later. It was hard to set a field for him, such was his genius for collecting runs with his precise placement of the ball. In League cricket in England Headley also excelled. At every level of the game, in fact, he scored an avalanche of runs with a style and brilliance few of any age have matched. His contribution to the strength and power of modern West Indies teams cannot be exaggerated.

One of his sons, R. G. A., an opening batsman for Worcestershire and Derbyshire, played twice for West Indies in England in 1973.

HILL, CHARLES MERRIN, who died in Dublin in July 1982, eleven days before his 79th birthday, was a member of the Leinster club and played once for Ireland against Scotland as a right-hand bat in 1927, scoring 5.

HILLYARD, MAJOR JACK MONTAGU, who died on February 16, 1983, aged 92, was in the Harrow XI in 1909 and 1910. A son of G. W. Hillyard, who, besides bowling fast for Middlesex and Leicestershire, was a first-class lawn tennis player and golfer, he had inherited much of his father's ability and was a fine natural games player. In 1910 at Lord's, in "Fowler's Match", he made 62 very well in the first innings, which was top score, and also took five wickets.

HUNT, ROBERT NORMAN, died in hospital at Chichester on October 13, 1983, aged 80. A good bat and a useful fast-medium right-hand bowler he was for years a prominent member of the Ealing side and between 1926 and 1928 made a few appearances for Middlesex. Though his total record was only 138 runs with an average of 19.71 he had one good performance, scoring 81 not out against Worcestershire at Lord's in 1926.

HURWOOD, ALEXANDER, who died in Brisbane on September 26, 1982, aged 80, was a right-hand bowler, who could spin the ball appreciably at near medium pace, and a fine slip fielder. He played eighteen matches for Queensland between 1925-26 and 1931-32 and won two caps for Australia against West Indies in 1930-31. In January 1930 he took six for 179 for Queensland against New South Wales in Sydney in the innings in which Bradman made the then world record individual score of 452 not out. When Bradman had made 80, Hurwood bowled a ball which hit Bradman's wicket without dislodging a bail. He toured England in 1930 with W. M. Woodfull's side, but without appearing in a Test match. He took 28 wickets on the tour and had a top score of 61 against Sussex. After taking eleven wickets in the first two Tests against West Indies in 1930-31 he somewhat unluckily lost his place. All told he scored 575 runs in first-class cricket (average 11.27) and took 113 wickets (average 27.62).

JACK, KEITH MAYALL, who died in Queensland in November 1982, aged 55, played 25 times for that state, as a batsman, between 1948 and 1952. He scored 1,104 first-class runs at an average of 26.92.

JACKSON, ALFRED LOUIS STUART, who died on July 23, 1982, aged 79, was captain of Cheltenham in 1922, when he headed the batting averages and played for the Lord's Schools. Going out to South America, he played for both Chile and the Argentine and was a member of the South American side which toured England in 1932 and played a number of first-class matches. He himself came out top of the batting averages, making 674 with an average of 39.64. Against a strong side of Sir Julien Cahn's he and D. Ayling put on 102 and 113 for the first wicket, the second of these partnerships taking only 65 minutes. Jackson's scores were 62 and 78. The touring side, facing a total of 413, won by five wickets. He was a younger brother of J. A. S. Jackson of Somerset.

JAMES, RONALD VICTOR, who died on April 28, 1983, aged 62, was a right-hand batsman and agile field who played 33 Sheffield Shield games – twenty for New South Wales and thirteen for South Australia. For South Australia he scored 85 against W. R. Hammond's MCC team in 1946-47 and in the following season made his best score, 210, for South Australia against Queensland. In 1949-50, by when he had returned to Sydney, he took over the captaincy of New South Wales from Keith Miller who had been called to reinforce the Australian team then in South Africa. New South Wales won the Shield. At the end of a career in which he scored 2,582 runs (average 40.34), James became a New South Wales selector.

JARRETT, HAROLD HARVEY, died on March 17, 1983, aged 75. A leg-break and googly bowler, who took a longer run than most of his type, he came out for Warwickshire at the beginning of August 1932 and, playing in their last seven matches, took 36 wickets for an average of 29.63, showing distinct promise. On his first appearance he also played a valuable innings of 45. Next year his chances were limited by the rapid rise of Eric Hollies and his career for the county ended. Moving to South Wales, he later edited the *South Wales Cricketers' Magazine* and in 1938 made an appearance for Glamorgan. In his first-class career he took 51 wickets at 32.35. His son represented Wales at rugger as a full-back and also played cricket for Glamorgan II.

JAYAWICKREME, S. S. ("SARGO"), MBE, who has died at the age of 72, was one of Sri Lanka's leading batsmen in the days when, as Ceylon, they were taking their first tentative steps beyond their own shores. As a member of C. H. Gunasekera's side to India in 1932-33 he scored the first century (130) on the Ferosha Kotla in New Delhi, the ground being inaugurated with an unofficial "Test" between the two countries. In 1940-41, as captain of the second Ceylon side to visit India, he scored 138 against an Indian XI in Calcutta. Jayawickreme made many runs for the Sinhalese Sports Club and is the only Sri Lankan cricketer to have been decorated for his services to the game in the island.

LEE, HIS HONOUR JUDGE ARTHUR MICHAEL, DSO, died in hospital at Midhurst on January 14, 1983, aged 69. A useful bat and slow spinner, he was captain of Winchester in 1932 and had a trial for Hampshire in 1933. His father, an Oxford Blue, had also played for the county.

LEWIS, ESMOND BURMAN, who died at Dorridge on October 19, 1983, aged 71, created a Warwickshire record on his first appearance for the county, against Oxford University at Edgbaston in 1949, catching eight batsmen and stumping one. He continued to keep occasionally for the county until 1958, but his opportunities were limited because the regular wicket-keeper, Spooner, was a far better batsman and so Lewis only kept in 43 matches in all. In 1957 he was picked for the Gentlemen at Lord's and kept very well. His highest score was 51 against the Combined Services in 1949.

LIDDICUT, ARTHUR EDWARD, who died in Melbourne on April 8, 1983, aged 91, toured New Zealand with Vernon Ransford's Australian team in 1920-21. An all-rounder, who often opened the bowling at right-arm medium-pace and went in usually at No. 8 or 9 in a strong Victorian batting side, he started his first-class career in 1911-12 and retired in 1932. He scored three centuries and achieved his best bowling figures of seven for 40 for Victoria against Tasmania at the age of 39. Against A. C. MacLaren's MCC team in 1922-23 he was one of four Victorians to score a century in a total of 617 for six declared. In the same match he took four for 16 in MCC's first innings. In 62 first-class games he took 133 wickets (average 27.56) and scored 2,503 runs (average 31.28). On his retirement from active cricket Liddicut was for many years a delegate to the Victorian Cricket Association.

LONEY, ESCOTT FRITH, who died in Toronto on June 19, 1982, aged 78, played for Derbyshire between 1925 and 1927, scoring 511 runs (average 17.03) and taking twenty wickets at 32.50 apiece.

LOVELOCK, OSWALD H., who died in Perth on August 1, 1981, was a wicket-keeper and middle-order batsman who played twenty matches for Western Australia between 1932 and 1940, scoring 731 runs (average 27.07) and claiming 33 victims behind the stumps.

MacBRYAN, JOHN CRAWFORD WILLIAM, who died on July 14, 1983, a few days before his 91st birthday, was England's oldest surviving Test cricketer. Captain of cricket at Exeter School, he was in the XI at the RMC Sandhurst when he played for Somerset in their last two matches in 1911 and against Surrey at The Oval was second-top scorer with 20 in a total of 97. In the next three years he made a few appearances for the county and in 1914 scored 61 against Gloucestershire. But in August that year he was wounded in the right arm at Le Cateau and spent the rest of the war as a prisoner, latterly in Holland, where he was able to play plenty of cricket. In 1919 he was up at Cambridge, but, though he scored 90 against the Navy, was only twelfth man at Lord's. However, he topped the Somerset averages and indeed did so in six of the eight seasons 1919–26. He duly got his Blue in 1920. His two best years for Somerset were 1923, when he made 1,507 runs for them with an average of 37.67, and 1924, when his aggregate was 1,355 and his average 43.70. By now he was near the England side. In 1923 he made top score, 80, for the Rest against England in the Test trial at Lord's and in 1924 he was picked for the Gentlemen at Lord's, and again made runs in a Test trial. As a result he was selected for the fourth Test against South Africa at Old Trafford, but the match was ruined by rain and he did not bat. Many expected him to be in the side for Australia, but his chance was probably lost when the doctors passed J. W. Hearne as fit. In any case, the team was overweighted with openers: in addition to Hobbs and Sutcliffe, there were Sandham, Whysall and J. L. Bryan. Instead MacBryan went with the Hon. L. H. Tennyson's unofficial side to South Africa, where he was only moderately successful. Two more seasons for Somerset virtually concluded his career. Though he continued to play occasionally until 1931, he was never after 1926 in sufficient practice to do himself justice, and so, like many other amateurs, he dropped out just when he was at his best. Short but strongly built, he was primarily a back-foot player and a fine cutter and hooker. He also played well off his legs and was a far better bat on a turning wicket than most amateurs. Moreover, lack of inches did not stop him countering Tate at his best by playing forward and getting well over the ball. In all his movements he was neat and elegant. In the field his wounded arm prevented him throwing far, but he was good near the wicket, especially at short-leg. A rich character, he was in his element in a side captained by John Daniell and containing R. C. Robertson-Glasgow, G. F. Earle and J. C. White, with the great Sam Woods, to whom he acknowledged a special debt for teaching him to play Tate, in support off the field. In all first-class cricket he scored 10,322 runs with an average of 29.50, including eighteen centuries, the highest of them 164 against Leicestershire at Taunton in 1922.

McKINNON, ATHOLL HENRY, who died in Durban on December 2, 1983, aged 51, played eight times for South Africa between 1960 and 1967, taking 26 Test wickets at 35.57 apiece. As portly as he was affable, he belonged to the classical school of slow orthodox left-arm bowlers, length, line and flight playing at least as much a part as spin. Born at Port Elizabeth and educated, like the Pollock brothers, at Grey High School, McKinnon began his first-class career, in 1952-53, with Eastern Province and ended it, in 1967-68, with Transvaal. He toured England twice, in 1960 and 1965, being the only member of the 1965 team to have also been in the previous side. In 1964-65, when England were last in South Africa, McKinnon was brought into the South African side for the fourth Test. His four for 128 in 51 overs in England's first innings and three for 44 in 35 overs in the second showed him at his best, his control being excellent, his line off stump and outside. In South Africa in 1966-67 when, amid nation-wide excitement, the home side won a series against Australia for the first time, he played in the first two Tests. He was a burly tail-ender, who batted right-handed and had a top score of 62. After retiring he was a patient and popular cricket coach. His death, from a heart attack, came when he was managing the unofficial West Indian team touring South Africa. All told he took 470 first-class wickets (average 21.14) and scored 1,687 runs (average 15.06).

MacLEOD, ALASTAIR, who died at Broomfield, near Colchester, on April 24, 1982, aged 87, made twelve appearances for Hampshire between 1914 and 1938. Four years in the Felsted XI, he came into the county side the month after leaving and crowned several useful scores with a fine innings of 87 in two hours against Essex at Bournemouth. He played a couple of matches in 1920 and made 48, top score, against Sussex at Brighton and, had he been able to play more frequently, would probably have been valuable. However, his next appearance was not till 1935 and a few matches in 1938 concluded his first-class career. A fine driver, he made altogether 271 runs with an average of 15.05. From 1936 to 1939 he was Secretary of the Hampshire County Cricket Club.

MANJREKAR, VIJAY LAXMAN, who died in Madras, where he had gone for a sportsmen's gathering, on October 18, 1983, aged 52, was a conspicuously good player of fast bowling in an era when India had few of them. Having played in the first of his 55 Tests in 1951-52, against England at Calcutta, he soon showed his quality by making 133 in his first Test in England (at Headingley) in June, 1952, when only twenty. Coming in at 42 for three on the first morning, with Trueman and Bedser on the warpath (and Laker to follow), he and his captain, Hazare, rescued India's innings with a fourth-wicket partnership of 222, which still stands as a record between the two countries. If, as the years passed, problems of weight slowed him down, he had sufficiently nimble footwork and enough natural ability always to be a dangerous opponent and often a joy to watch. Like many of the best Indian batsmen, he was small and a fine cutter and hooker. Within nine months of his 133 at Headingley he scored 118 against West Indies at Kingston, sharing on that occasion a record second-wicket partnership with Pankaj Roy. His two best Test series were against New Zealand in India in 1955-56 (386 runs, average 77.20) and against England in India in 1961-62 (586 runs, average 83.71). He made seven Test centuries, the highest his 189 against England at Delhi in 1961-62 and the last of them in his final Test innings, against New Zealand at Madras in February 1965. At Bombay in 1964-65 his two innings of 59 and 39 were invaluable contributions towards India's first Test victory over Australia. An occasional off-spinner, a serviceable wicket-keeper and in his early days a fine cover fielder, he played at different times for no fewer than six sides in the Ranji Trophy – Bombay, Bengal, Andhra, Uttar Pradesh, Rajasthan and Maharashtra. In Test matches he scored 3,208 runs (average 39.12), took one wicket, held nineteen catches and made two stumpings. In the Ranji Trophy he scored 3,734 runs (average 57.44) and hit twelve hundreds.

MATHER-JACKSON, SIR ANTHONY HENRY, BT, who died suddenly on October 11, 1983, aged 83, was in the Harrow XI in 1916 and 1917: in 1917 he took six for 43 in the one-day match against Eton at Eton. Between 1920 and 1927 he played fairly frequently for Derbyshire, but only in 1922 was he able to appear regularly. In that season he made 580 runs with an average of 18.12 and played a number of useful innings, including 75 against Leicestershire, his highest score in first-class cricket, and 69 against Worcestershire. He was an attacking batsman and a good field and bowled fast-medium swingers. In all for the county he scored 1,199 runs with an average of 14.80 and took 44 wickets at 30.89. He was a cousin of G. R. Jackson, the Derbyshire captain.

MAYES, DR ALEXANDER DUNBAR AITKEN, who died on February 8, 1983, aged 81, played ten times for Queensland between 1924 and 1927, taking 21 wickets and scoring 297 runs.

MEHRA, RAMPRAKASH, who died in Delhi on March 7, 1983, aged 65, was a batsman of more than average ability who became closely associated with the growth of cricket in Delhi and was President of the Board of Control for Cricket in India in 1975-76 and 1976-77. For Northern India and Delhi, in the early days of the Ranji Trophy, he scored 1,202 runs with an average of 30.82, many of them with a flourish. In 1940-41 he scored 209 against Maharashtra.

MELVILLE, ALAN, who died in the Kruger National Park on April 18, 1983, aged 72, was arguably the most elegant batsman of his generation. Those who were lucky enough to see it still remember after 50 years his innings of 114 in two and a half hours for Sussex against the West Indians at Hove in 1933. It was the summer after the body-line tour and the fast bowlers, Griffith and Martindale, assailed him with vicious bouncers. They might have been serving up by request something to amuse him and the spectators. They were mercilessly hooked and, if they pitched the ball up, they were driven. Even granted the placid Hove wicket, it was a remarkable display. Years afterwards, meeting him at Lord's at a time when short-pitched fast bowling was being constantly discussed, I asked him if he had ever ducked to it. He smiled sweetly and said, "I don't think so. I think either I hit them or they hit me!" From what I saw of him I doubt if he was ever hit by anything that rose high enough to be hooked.

Standing six feet two inches and slightly built, he was a wonderful timer of the ball; his methods were a model for the young cricketer and reduced every risk to a minimum. The drive, the hook and the cut all seemed to come equally easily to him and he was, besides, a good player off his legs. Moreover he was a fine field anywhere and in his younger days a serviceable change bowler, first with leg-breaks and later with off-breaks and swingers.

Picked for Natal at seventeen, while still a boy at Michaelhouse, he scored a century next season in a trial to select the 1929 side to England and his father was asked whether he would allow him to go. But he was anxious to follow his elder brother, Colin (also a stylish batsman who had a trial for the University), to Trinity, Oxford, and it was thought wiser to refuse. In the Freshmen's Match in 1930 he made 132 not out and took eight for 72. Naturally he was picked for the first match, against Kent, in which he scored 78 and put on 148 with N. M. Ford for the fourth wicket before being run out. In the next match he made 118 against Yorkshire. These innings were the more remarkable as he had had little experience of playing on grass. Unfortunately in the 'Varsity match he was hampered by a knee so weak that it was only a few minutes before the start that it was decided to play him and he did nothing. In 1931 D. N. Moore fell ill and Melville was appointed captain in his place. In 1932 he was captain in his own right, but missed much of the season owing to a collar-bone broken by a collision while batting. In 1933, when he played a fourth time, he had to stand out of many matches in order to work. Although his cricket for Oxford during these years left no-one in any doubt about his class, he was, like some other notable 'Varsity bats, a disappointment in the match at Lord's: his highest score was 47 and his six innings produced an average of 16 only. As Oxford had Peebles in 1930 and Owen-Smith for the next three years, comparatively little use was made of his leg-breaks, but in 1932 he did the hat-trick against Leveson Gower's XI at Eastbourne and headed the averages.

He had been playing for Sussex since 1932 and continued to do so with great success until 1936, captaining them in 1934 and 1935. In 1935 and 1936 he headed their batting averages and in 1935 the bowling averages too, though he took only twelve wickets. It will not surprise the friends of so charming and modest a man that he was criticised for not bowling himself more. In 1935, though suffering from a very sore thumb, he made 101 in 90 minutes against Larwood, then admittedly past his best, and Voce at Hove, and his last innings for the county, against All India in September 1936, was the highest he ever played for them, 152, including a hundred before lunch on the second morning.

Returning home at the end of that season and joining a firm of stockbrokers in Johannesburg, he became captain of the Transvaal side and then captained South Africa in 1938-39 against England. He did little himself in the first two Tests, but in the third promoted himself to open and shared in stands of 108 and 131 for the first wicket, and in the notorious timeless Test which concluded the tour scored 78 and 103, though he was handicapped throughout these three matches by a bad leg which finally forced him to move himself down the order.

Not physically very strong, he had never fully recovered from a back injury sustained in a car smash before he went up to Oxford, and a fall while training with the South African forces in the war caused a recurrence of the trouble. For nearly a year he was in a steel jacket and it was feared that his career was at an end. Luckily the fears proved false and by 1947, after various vicissitudes, he was fit to undertake the captaincy of the South African side in England. The earlier part of the tour was a personal triumph for him, culminating in innings of 189 and 104 not out in the first Test at Nottingham, followed by 117 in the first innings of the Lord's Test. He thus became the first batsman to score four consecutive hundreds against England in Tests. Moreover at Nottingham his stand of 319 with Nourse, made in exactly four hours, was at the time the highest for the third wicket in any Test. After this and in view of his inspiring captaincy, it was disappointing that his side should lose three of the Tests and draw two. He himself was, not surprisingly, completely worn out by the end of June: he had lost a lot of weight and the food rationing still in force did not help him. After a brave 59 in the second innings of the third Test, he accomplished, by the high standards he had set himself, comparatively little, though an innings of 114 not out against his own county at Hove must have given him much pleasure. At the end of the tour he announced his retirement from first-class cricket. However, in the autumn of 1948 he was persuaded to reappear and an innings of 92 for Transvaal against F. G. Mann's MCC side brought him an invitation to play in the first Test. This he had to refuse owing to an injured wrist, but played in the third Test, in which he ended his international career with two useful innings. Later he was for many years a South African selector.

MILLS, GEORGE THOMAS, sometime Headmaster of Bromsgrove High School, died at Bromsgrove on September 15, 1983, aged 60. He kept wicket for Worcestershire in two matches in 1963, catching five and stumping four. His club cricket was mainly for Stourbridge.

MUFASIR-UL-HAQ, who died in Karachi on July 27, 1983, aged 38, played his one Test match, for Pakistan against New Zealand, at Christchurch in February 1965, taking three wickets and scoring 8 not out. A left-arm medium-paced bowler, he played for Karachi, PWD and National Bank in first-class cricket. He was only the second Pakistani Test cricketer to die, the first being Amir Elahi.

MURPHY, DESMOND J., who died in Dublin in January 1981, was a right-hand bat and leg-break bowler who played for Ireland against Scotland in 1920, obtaining a pair and taking nought for 49. He believed that only his fielding was of the required class. For many years he was Headmaster of St Gerard's, a lay Catholic preparatory school in Co. Wicklow.

ORMEROD, MAJOR SIR CYRIL BERKELY, who died on November 1, 1983, aged 86, was in the XI at St Paul's School and later represented both the Army and Oxfordshire. He was a fast-medium right-hand bowler. In 1924 he was Army Golf champion.

PARKER, JOHN FREDERICK, who died on January 26, 1983, aged 69, played for Surrey from 1932 to 1952, his career spanning the last days of Jack Hobbs to the early days of Peter May. For years he was an essential member of the side, a consistent bat and a fine driver whose instinct was to attack and many of whose best innings were played in a crisis, a medium-paced bowler who could open if required and who, without many sensational performances, was always getting wickets, and a safe catcher in the slips. A tall man, he would have done even better but for a troublesome back. He was almost solely a county player and, though he had been picked for the tour of India in 1939 which never took place, one may doubt if he would have established himself in Test cricket. It is, however, fair to point out that the war deprived him of his cricket between the ages of 26 and 33, when he might have expected to be at his best. He had a good trial in 1932 and 1933 and, without doing anything exceptional, showed promise, but then came a setback: in 1934 he lost his place and did little more till 1937, when he scored 915 runs with an average of 27.72 and took 65 wickets at 28.36. In 1938 came his first century and in 1939 he surpassed anything he had done before with 1,549 runs and an average of 37.78 and 56 wickets at 22.83. This improvement was partly due to health, while in bowling he concentrated more on length and on always aiming at the stumps. But on the whole his best years were after the war. In 1946, despite further trouble with his health, he headed the bowling averages with 56 wickets at 15.58 and followed in 1947 by heading the batting. In 1949 he made the highest score of his career, 255 against the New Zealanders, made out of 568 in six and a half hours, and he continued to be a valuable member of the Surrey side until 1952, when, although he was unable to bowl, he still got his 1,000 runs as usual, but retired at the end of the season, having had the satisfaction of playing in the first Surrey team to win the Championship since 1914. He had had a benefit in 1951. In all first-class cricket he scored 14,272 runs with an average of 31.58, including twenty centuries, took 543 wickets at 28.87 and caught 331 catches.

PERCIVAL, JOHN DOUGLAS, died in hospital at Roehampton on March 5, 1983, aged 80. After heading the Radley batting averages in 1918, when he was under sixteen, he was in the Westminster XI in the next three years and captain in 1921. With a good defence and strong on the leg side, he seemed to have a bright future. However, at Oxford, though he had a trial for the University and played for Gloucestershire against them in 1923, he was never seriously in the running for a Blue. His batting style and even his mannerisms were modelled closely on D. J. Knight, from whom he had learnt much of his cricket.

PRAGG, SHERVAN, who died in Trinidad on November 26, 1982, aged twenty, as the result of injuries sustained in a road accident, had not long returned home from a successful tour of England with the West Indies Young Cricketers. As a left-arm bowler of googlies and chinamen he had shown the highest promise.

PRATT, RICHARD, who died on October 10, 1982, aged 86, had a few trials for Derbyshire as a batsman in 1923 and 1924, but met with no success. He could also keep wicket.

PRITCHARD, DAVID EDWARD, who died on July 4, 1983, aged 90, scored six centuries for South Australia, including 119 against the 1928-29 MCC team. For nearly 50 years his 327 not out for Port Adelaide against Sturt stood as the highest individual score in Adelaide district cricket.

PROCTOR, SIR PHILIP DENNIS, KCB, who died at Lewes on August 30, 1983, aged 77, was a member of the Harrow XI in 1924. He was an outstanding school wicket-keeper, who kept particularly well at Lord's.

PROMNITZ, HENRY LOUIS ERNEST, who died at King William's Town on September 7, 1983, aged 79, played twice for South Africa, against England in 1927-28. Like bowlers of more modern times, such as Iverson of Australia and the West Indian, Ramadhin, his spin was difficult to fathom, the off- and leg-breaks being frequently misread. Also like Iverson and Ramadhin, he was a poor fielder, which may have accounted for his playing in only two Test matches. In the first of them, at Johannesburg, he finished England's first innings with five for 58 in 37 overs after the score at one time had been 230 for one. In his second Test, at Cape Town, he took three for 56 in 30 overs in England's second innings. His eight Test wickets included Hammond, Sutcliffe, Ernest Tyldesley, Wyatt and Stevens. Between 1924-25 and 1936-37 he played at different times for Border, Griqualand West and Orange Free State, taking 150 first-class wickets at 23.80.

PYE-SMITH, DR EDWARD JOHN, who died at Bishop Monkton, near Harrogate, on March 6, 1983, aged 80, was captain of Cheltenham in 1920, when he made a fine hundred against Haileybury at Lord's. A strong, determined batsman, he did not get a Blue at Cambridge, but played for Yorkshire Second XI.

RAWLENCE, COL JOHN ROOKE, OBE, who died in hospital at Ascot on January 17, 1983, aged 67, played two matches for Hampshire in 1934 and in the second, against Nottinghamshire at Southampton, made 38 and helped Creese put on 60 for the seventh wicket in just over half an hour. He had headed the Wellington College averages in 1933. Later he played for the Army.

RHODES, ALBERT ENNION GROCOTT ("DUSTY"), died at his home at Barlow, near Chesterfield, on October 18, 1983, aged 67. Born in Cheshire, he came into the Derbyshire side in 1937 and showed great promise as an all-rounder, scoring 363 runs with an average of 21.35 and taking 25 wickets at 27.72. Originally a leg-spinner, he was now bowling fast-medium out-swingers with a long run which put an undue strain on a slight physique. Indeed, his record throughout his career suggests that he was never sufficiently robust to be a genuine all-rounder: in the seasons in which he scored runs his bowling usually suffered and vice versa. Thus in 1938, while he made 916 runs at an average of 27.75, he took only eighteen wickets and in 1939, when his batting was disappointing his bowling was less expensive: in any case the county's bowling was then so strong that he was only used as a change. By 1946 things were very different: most of the pre-war bowlers had gone and Rhodes was used freely both as an opener and a leg-spinner. Not surprisingly his bowling in this dual role was expensive, his 75 wickets being obtained at 29.90 and not surprisingly, too, he met with little success as a bat. Thereafter he concentrated on leg-breaks and googlies, but though he had considerable powers of spin and might at any time take valuable wickets, he never attained consistent accuracy. However, he performed the hat-trick five times, a number which only three bowlers have exceeded. By far his best season with the ball was 1950, when he took 130 wickets at 22.19. In 1951 he was very expensive but none the less was selected for the MCC tour of India and Pakistan that winter. The opening matches showed that his spin, though costly, might be valuable and it was a blow to the side when he had to return home before the first Test for an operation. In 1952 he had a good season, taking 83 wickets at 24.95. This was almost the end of his career, though he played in a few matches in 1953 and 1954. Since the war he had been regarded largely as a bowler, but in 1949 he again showed what a good bat he could be, scoring 1,156 runs with an average of 25.68. Significantly that year his 66 wickets cost 38.62 each. In all he made in first-class cricket 7,363 runs with an average of 18.98, including four centuries, and took 661 wickets at 28.83. A determined batsman, he had a sound defence but was also a powerful off-side player and could score fast. Against Nottinghamshire at Ilkeston in 1949 he made a hundred before lunch. His highest score was 127 against Somerset at Taunton in the same season. From 1959 to 1979 he was a first-class umpire and stood in eight Tests. He had also coached at both Oxford and Cambridge. He was father of Harold Rhodes, the England fast bowler.

RICHARDSON, ARTHUR WALKER, who died in a nursing home at Ednaston on July 29, 1983, will be remembered as the captain under whom Derbyshire won the Championship in 1936, at a time when this was regarded as the prerogative of the 'Big six'. After many vicissitudes, including a period when they were relegated to second-class status, Derbyshire had reached rock bottom in 1920 when they suffered the indignity of losing all their matches except one in which not a ball was bowled. For the change in their fortunes in the next sixteen years they owed much to successive captains, G. M. Buckston for one season in 1921, G. R. Jackson for nine and then, for the last six, Richardson. He had a side rich in bowling, which he managed shrewdly, among other things seeing to it that Copson, who was to mean so much to the team in the future, was not overbowled at the start of his career. He did much also by his own enthusiasm and warm personality. A solid and slightly ungainly batsman, he scored mainly on the leg, but by determination and courage and keeping sensibly within his own limitations, he played many useful innings. By far his best season was 1932, when he scored 1,258 runs with an average of 29.95 and made the highest score of his career, 90 against Nottinghamshire at Ilkeston. In all, between 1928 and 1936, he made 3,982 runs with an average of 19.05. He was also a good mid-off. He had been in the Winchester XI in 1925 and had played an innings of 117 against Harrow, putting on 295 for the second wicket with E. Snell. His son, G. W. Richardson, later represented Derbyshire with some success.

RICHARDSON, LESLIE WALTER, who died in Hobart on November 1, 1981, aged 70, was one of seven members of the same family who played for Tasmania, the others being his four brothers, his father and an uncle.

SHANMUGANATHAN, THIAGARAJAH, who died in September 1982, aged 52, was one of the best leg-break bowlers produced by Sri Lanka.

SIME, HIS HONOUR WILLIAM ARNOLD, CMG, MBE, died at Wymeswold, Leicestershire, on May 5, 1983, aged 74. Four years in the XI at Bedford School, in 1928, when he was captain, he made two centuries for Bedfordshire. He did not get a Blue at Oxford, but continued to play with success for Bedfordshire and captained them in 1934. In 1935 he transferred to Nottinghamshire, but made only occasional appearances until 1947 when he was appointed captain, a position he held until 1950. He proved a useful member of the side and made in all 2,328 runs with an average of 19.98, besides taking occasional wickets as a slow left-hander: he was also a good field. His outstanding performance and his only century was an innings of 176 not out against Sussex at Hove in 1948. This took him six hours, a contrast to his usual methods, but it secured a victory for his side, who had lost three for 33 when he went in in the first innings. More typical perhaps was his 58 not out against Surrey at Trent Bridge in 1949, made in 37 minutes and including three 6s: Nottinghamshire, set to get 206 in two hours, got them in 97 minutes. It may be noted that in this time Surrey bowled 36.3 overs. Sime was also a first-class rugger player, who appeared in an England trial, and a good golfer. Later he was Recorder of Grantham and in 1972 was appointed a Circuit Judge. However he did not lose touch with cricket, being President of Nottinghamshire in 1975-77 and lately President of the XL Club.

SMITH, ANDREW EDWIN, who died on May 18, 1983, aged 93, scored 774 runs (average 33.65) and took seventeen wickets (average 48.76) for South Australia.

STANLEY-CLARKE, BRIG. ARTHUR CHRISTOPHER LANCELOT, CB, DSO, MC, who died at Shiel, Bailey, Dublin, on January 8, 1983, aged 96, was in the Winchester XI in 1905, when he scored 82 not out in the second innings against Eton and headed the batting averages. A solid opening bat, he later played for the Army. At the time of his death he was the oldest living member of I Zingari and, as far as is known, the oldest living English first-class cricketer.

SUMMERS, GERALD FRANK, who died at Harrogate on August 12, 1983, aged 78, played for Surrey II for some years with considerable success, and from 1930 to 1939 was a regular member of Sir Julien Cahn's side. For them he scored 13,289 runs with an average of 42.05, his highest score being 246 against Bedfordshire in 1934, a season in which he scored over 2,000 runs. On that occasion he put on 404 for the third wicket with D. P. B. Morkel, the highest stand ever made for the side for any wicket. He was a very hard-hitting bat, a useful change bowler and a fine field.

SWAMY, V. N., who died at Dehra Dun on May 1, 1983, was a medium-paced bowler who played in one Test match against New Zealand at Hyderabad in 1955-56. He opened the bowling, without taking a wicket, and did not bat. Swamy played for Services in the Ranji Trophy, taking 58 wickets at 19.98 apiece. His best performance was six for 29 against East Punjab in 1954-55.

TALBOT, RONALD OSMAN, who died in Auckland on January 5, 1983, at the age of 79, toured with the New Zealand team to England in 1931 as a forceful right-handed batsman and a medium-paced bowler. In his best innings of the tour – 66 against MCC at Lord's (his country's first appearance there) – he made one of the biggest straight drives, high onto the pavilion, seen on the ground. The first of his three first-class hundreds was in his début match – for Otago against Canterbury at Dunedin in 1922-23. An all-round sportsman, he excelled at squash, golf, bowls and athletics, and he played rugby for Canterbury.

THORN, HUBERT WETHERED, died at Colchester on May 20, 1982, aged 73. In 1928 he made one appearance as an all-rounder for Essex.

THORNLEY, BILL, who has died at the age of 76, was a valued friend of Nottinghamshire cricket, being for the last few years of his life their trusty scorer. Although he never played county cricket he was a useful club cricketer in the High Peak league.

TOWNLEY, REGINALD COLIN, who died in Hobart on May 3, 1982, aged 76, was a well-known Tasmanian cricketer who later became a member of the Tasmanian House of Assembly and, for six years, Leader of the Opposition. A right-handed batsman and leg-spin bowler, he played sixteen times for Tasmania between 1926-27 and 1935-36, scoring only 175 runs but taking 36 wickets at an average of 35.42. His last match for Tasmania was against South Australia, when in twenty overs he took three for 169, including the wicket of Bradman, caught and bowled for 369.

TREMLETT, MAJOR-GENERAL ERROLL ARTHUR EDWIN, who died on December 24, 1982, aged 89, played in first-class matches for MCC, but the most remarkable thing about him was that he was still doing his full share of bowling, medium-pace, in good-class club cricket, largely for the Devon Dumplings, until he was 80 and, what is more, taking wickets.

VALENTINE, BRYAN HERBERT, MC, who died on February 2, 1983, aged 75, was a gifted athlete to whom most games came naturally. At Repton he won the public schools lawn tennis with the great H. W. Austin; at Cambridge he got a soccer Blue as a brilliant forward and later he became a scratch golfer. But, happily, it was to cricket that he really devoted himself and he never made the mistake, which so many talented players have made, of being satisfied with what he could achieve without study and effort. He was three years in the Repton XI, but after a splendid season in 1925, his last was spoilt by illness and injury. After a year spent in duels with the examiners, he made 114 (retired) in 75 minutes in the Freshmen's Match at Cambridge in 1928, but it was not until 1929 that he got a Blue and even then his place was in doubt until the last match at Fenner's, when, against an unusually strong Free Foresters bowling side, which included M. J. C. Allom, R. J. O. Meyer, C. S. Marriott, M. Falcon and A. G. Doggart, he scored 101 in 85 minutes. Meanwhile he had been playing for Kent since 1927, but with only moderate success, and it was not until 1931 that he made his place secure. At this period he was just a promising county cricketer with beautiful strokes, capable of playing a brilliant innings and stronger on the leg than most of his type, but distinctly suspect in defence. By the mid-thirties he had become far sounder, had learned to watch the turning ball and was a potential England player, and this without curbing his instinct to attack. His average rate of scoring throughout his career is said to have been some 50 runs an hour. He was particularly adept at on-driving, with a full swing of the bat, the numerous off-spinners and in-swingers encouraged by the new lbw law. However, English batting was strong at this time and his Test cricket was confined to the tours of India in 1933-34 and South Africa in 1938-39. In India he came third in the batting, and at Bombay in the first Test made 136 in under three hours. In South Africa consistent batting brought him an average of 45.38 and in the second Test, at Cape Town, he made 112 in two hours, 40 minutes. In the previous summer he had made the highest score of his career, 242 for Kent against Leicestershire at Oakham.

After serving in the war, winning the MC and being severely wounded, he returned to captain the county from 1946 to 1948, when he retired from first-class cricket. He had already captained frequently in the absence of A. P. F. Chapman and in 1937 had shared the captaincy with R. T. Bryan. A post-war England captain, who played under Valentine, whom he had not previously met, on an MCC side years after his retirement, said regretfully, "What fun county cricket must have been when men like that were captain!" And of course he was right. Valentine took his cricket seriously enough, as the story of his career shows, and was as keen as anyone to win, but he never forgot that cricket is a game and as such he enjoyed it himself and did all he could to see that others enjoyed it too, including the spectators. In a friendship of over 50 years I myself never saw him anything but cheerful and usually laughing. His own account of his mild away-swingers is typical. He used to say that Chapman had occasionally given him the new ball "because no-one else ever gets the shine off so quickly for 'Tich'". As a fieldsman he was in the top class, equally good on the boundary or close to the wicket. President of Kent in 1967 and for many years on the Committee, he remained in close touch with the county and will be widely missed. In all first-class cricket he scored 18,306 runs with an average of 30.15 and made 35 centuries.

VAN MANEN, HUGO, who died on January 2, 1983, captained Holland between the wars and again after the Second World War, being the most prolific Dutch batsman of his day. From 1945 to 1955 he was President of the Netherlands Cricket Association.

VIVIAN, HENRY GIFFORD, who died in Auckland on August 12, 1983, aged 70, was only eighteen years 267 days when, as a left-handed all-rounder of much natural ability, he played in the first of his seven Tests for New Zealand. That was at The Oval in 1931, and, besides taking the wickets of Sutcliffe and Ames, he was top scorer, in New Zealand's second innings, with 51. His record on that tour (1,002 runs and 64 wickets) included centuries against Oxford University and Yorkshire. At Wellington in 1931-32, against South Africa, he scored 100 (his only Test century) and 73, the highest score in each innings. On his second tour to England, in 1937, he opened New Zealand's innings in the three Test matches, three times reaching 50. A charming person and welcoming host, he had been only 22 when appointed to the captaincy of Auckland. By the time a back injury ended his first-class career and confined him to the game's administration – he did not play after the Second

World War – he had scored 4,443 runs (average 34.71), including six centuries, the highest of them 165 for Auckland against Wellington in 1931-32, and taken 223 wickets. He also played with success in the late 30s for Sir Julien Cahn's XI. His son, Graham, played five times for New Zealand between 1964 and 1972.

WATKINS, BERT THOMAS LEWIS, died in December 1982, aged 80. In 1932 he had a good trial for Gloucestershire, who were trying to find a replacement for H. Smith as wicket-keeper and in 1937 again came into the side when Smith's successor, Hopkins, a far better bat than Watkins, broke a finger. He made his last appearance for the county in 1938. Unfortunately he was slightly uncertain in taking the spinners, in whom much of the bowling strength of the side lay at that period.

WESTBROOK, KEITH RAYMOND, who died in Tasmania on January 20, 1982, aged 94, was at that time the second-oldest surviving Australian first-class cricketer. Two of his great-uncles played in the first first-class match ever played in Australia. A right-handed batsman he scored 35 and 25 in his one game for Tasmania, against Victoria in 1910.

WILKINSON, COLONEL WILLIAM ALEXANDER CAMAC, DSO, MC, GM, who died at Storrington on September 19, 1983, aged 90, was a soldier of great gallantry in two wars and a cricketer who overcame a serious handicap to become one of the most consistent batsmen of his day in a high class of club cricket and indeed, when the opportunity offered, in first-class cricket. A legendary character whose outspokenness knew no close season, he was no respecter of persons; yet he is seldom mentioned by anyone who knew him without genuine affection. Leaving Eton too young to have been in the XI and finishing his school education in Australia, where his father, an old Middlesex cricketer, was in practice as a doctor, he went up to Oxford and got his Blue in his third year, 1913, largely on the strength of an innings of 129 in an hour and a half against MCC, in which, *Wisden* says, "he hit with delightful freedom all round the wicket". In 1914 he had a poor season and lost his place. He had also represented Oxford twice in the hurdles. In the war he was shot through the right hand and narrowly avoided amputation. As it was, though he could put his hand on the bat it had little strength. His beautiful cutting, however, remained as much a feature of his play as his skill on the leg. Despite his handicap he was not a slow scorer. Almost as remarkable as his batting was his fielding. Though much of the work on his right side had to be done back-handed by his left hand, he was never reckoned a liability in the field.

For years he was a regular member of the Army side, which he often captained, and most of his other cricket was played for the Household Brigade, Eton Ramblers, I Zingari, Harlequins, Free Foresters and other clubs. He never played for a first-class county, though he appeared for Sussex II before the Great War, but he was constantly to be found in first-class matches for MCC or Free Foresters and played too in the Folkestone Festival and for the Gentlemen at The Oval. His scoring in these matches right up to 1939 suggested that he would not have been out of place in county cricket. More solid evidence was provided when he went as a member of A. C. MacLaren's side to Australia and New Zealand in 1922-23. On this tour he scored 689 runs with an average of 28.70, his highest score being 102 against Canterbury. On this occasion he added 282 with A. P. F. Chapman in two and a quarter hours. Even after the Second World War he continued to make runs in club cricket and he himself believed that the century which he made in his last innings was the 100th of his career. In any case it was a fitting finale to the career of a brave and determined man.

WILLIAMS, RICHARD HARRY, died in December 1982, aged 81. A left-hander who often went in first, he played for Worcestershire from 1923 to 1932. A record of 713 runs with an average of 11.14 does not look much, but he played some useful innings. The highest, 81 against Nottinghamshire at Trent Bridge in 1926, was made largely off change bowlers when the match was dead, but in the corresponding match the year before he had scored 56 going in first, the highest score in a total of 161, and in 1928 against Yorkshire at Worcester he made 76 not out. True, the total was 402, but there were no easy runs in those days against the Yorkshire bowling.

WILLIAMS, TREVOR CHRISTOPHER, who died in Dublin in August 1982, was an outstanding all-rounder for the Pembroke club. However, in his four matches for Ireland he achieved nothing of note. His brother, Michael, also played for Ireland.

WINSER, LEGH, who died in Australia on December 20, 1983, aged 99, was at the time the oldest living Sheffield Shield cricketer. Born in Cheshire and educated at Oundle, he played for Staffordshire from 1906 to 1908, keeping wicket to S. F. Barnes, at the time perhaps the world's deadliest bowler. Emigrating to South Australia in 1909, Winser was soon keeping wicket for that state. By 1913 he had become a strong candidate for a place in the Australian team to South Africa, a tour that was, in fact, cancelled because of the onset of war. After giving up cricket he achieved eminence as an amateur golfer, winning the Championship of South Australia eight times and the Australian Amateur Championship once. At the time of the Bodyline tour, in 1932-33, he was secretary to the Governor of South Australia, Sir Alexander Hore-Ruthven (afterwards the Earl of Gowrie). Hore-Ruthven being in England at the time, Winser was intimately concerned with the exchange of cables between the Australian Board of Control and MCC when, after ugly scenes in the Adelaide Test match, the future of the tour, indeed of the special relationship between the United Kingdom and Australia, were put in jeopardy. In his later years, spent at Barwon Heads, near Geelong in Victoria, he regularly beat his age at golf, on one occasion by no fewer than eleven strokes: when 87 he played the eighteen holes of the Barwon Heads links in 76 strokes.

WISE, NORMAN, who died in Workington on March 23, 1983, was a great servant of the Cumberland County Cricket Club, being Secretary from its reconstitution in 1948 until his death.

YORKE, GERALD JOSEPH, who died on April 29, 1983, aged 81, was in the Eton XI in 1918 and 1919 and in 1920 played against Winchester, but did not play at Lord's. A strong hitter, he made one appearance for Gloucestershire in 1925. His father had also played for the county.

A mistake has been pointed out in *Wisden* for 1965, where it states in the obituaries that M. D. Lyon's last appearance for Somerset was in 1935. In fact, having returned to England, he played throughout the season of 1938, though, not surprisingly after so long an absence from regular first-class cricket, he was a shadow of his former self. He did however play a valuable innings of 122 not out against Northamptonshire at Frome. His figures for his career should read 7,294 runs with an average of 29.18, and he made fourteen hundreds.

THE LAWS OF CRICKET

(1980 CODE)

World copyright of MCC and reprinted by permission of MCC. Copies of the "Laws of Cricket" may be obtained from Lord's Cricket Ground.

INDEX TO THE LAWS

LAW 1.   THE PLAYERS

1. Number of Players and Captain

A match is played between two sides each of eleven players, one of whom shall be captain. In the event of the captain not being available at any time, a deputy shall act for him.

2. Nomination of Players

Before the toss for innings, the captain shall nominate his players, who may not thereafter be changed without the consent of the opposing captain.

Note

(a) **More or Less than Eleven Players a Side**
A match may be played by agreement between sides of more or less than eleven players, but not more than eleven players may field.

LAW 2.   SUBSTITUTES AND RUNNERS: BATSMAN OR FIELDSMAN LEAVING THE FIELD: BATSMAN RETIRING: BATSMAN COMMENCING INNINGS

1. Substitutes

Substitutes shall be allowed by right to field for any player who, during the match, is incapacitated by illness or injury. The consent of the opposing captain must be obtained for the use of a substitute if any player is prevented from fielding for any other reason.

2. Objection to Substitutes

The opposing captain shall have no right of objection to any player acting as substitute in the field, nor as to where he shall field, although he may object to the substitute acting as wicket-keeper.

3. Substitute not to Bat or Bowl

A substitute shall not be allowed to bat or bowl.

4. A Player for whom a Substitute has Acted

A player may bat, bowl or field even though a substitute has acted for him.

5. Runner

A runner shall be allowed for a batsman who, during the match, is incapacitated by illness or injury. The person acting as runner shall be a member of the batting side and shall, if possible, have already batted in that innings.

6. Runner's Equipment

The person acting as runner for an injured batsman shall wear batting gloves and pads if the injured batsman is so equipped.

7. Transgression of the Laws by an Injured Batsman or Runner

An injured batsman may be out should his runner break any one of Laws 33 (Handled the Ball), 37 (Obstructing the Field) or 38 (Run Out). As striker he remains himself subject to the Laws. Furthermore, should he be out of his ground for any purpose and the wicket at the wicket-keeper's end be put down he shall be out under Law 38 (Run Out) or Law 39 (Stumped), irrespective of the position of the other batsman or the runner, and no runs shall be scored.

When not the striker, the injured batsman is out of the game and shall stand where he does not interfere with the play. Should he bring himself into the game in any way, then he shall suffer the penalties that any transgression of the Laws demands.

8. Fieldsman Leaving the Field

No fieldsman shall leave the field or return during a session of play without the consent of the umpire at the bowler's end. The umpire's consent is also necessary if a substitute is required for a fieldsman, when his side returns to the field after an interval. If a member of the fielding side leaves the field or fails to return after an interval and is absent from the field for longer than fifteen minutes, he shall not be permitted to bowl after his return until he has been on the field for at least that length of playing time for which he was absent. This restriction shall not apply at the start of a new day's play.

9. Batsman Leaving the Field or Retiring

A batsman may leave the field or retire at any time owing to illness, injury or other unavoidable cause, having previously notified the umpire at the bowler's end. He may resume his innings at the fall of a wicket, which for the purposes of this Law shall include the retirement of another batsman.

If he leaves the field or retires for any other reason he may resume his innings only with the consent of the opposing captain.

When a batsman has left the field or retired and is unable to return owing to illness, injury or other unavoidable cause, his innings is to be recorded as "retired, not out". Otherwise it is to be recorded as "retired, out".

10. Commencement of a Batsman's Innings

A batsman shall be considered to have commenced his innings once he has stepped on to the field of play.

Note

(a) Substitutes and Runners
For the purpose of these Laws, allowable illnesses or injuries are those which occur at any time after the nomination by the captains of their teams.

LAW 3.   THE UMPIRES

1. Appointment

Before the toss for innings, two umpires shall be appointed, one for each end, to control the game with absolute impartiality as required by the Laws.

2. Change of Umpires

No umpire shall be changed during a match without the consent of both captains.

3. Special Conditions

Before the toss for innings, the umpires shall agree with both captains on any special conditions affecting the conduct of the match.

4. The Wickets

The umpires shall satisfy themselves before the start of the match that the wickets are properly pitched.

5. Clock or Watch

The umpires shall agree between themselves and inform both captains before the start of the match on the watch or clock to be followed during the match.

6. Conduct and Implements

Before and during a match the umpires shall ensure that the conduct of the game and the implements used are strictly in accordance with the Laws.

7. Fair and Unfair Play

The umpires shall be the sole judges of fair and unfair play.

8. Fitness of Ground, Weather and Light

(a) The umpires shall be the sole judges of the fitness of the ground, weather and light for play.

   (i) However, before deciding to suspend play, or not to start play, or not to resume play after an interval or stoppage, the umpires shall establish whether both captains (the batsmen at the wicket may deputise for their captain) wish to commence or to continue in the prevailing conditions; if so, their wishes shall be met.

   (ii) In addition, if during play the umpires decide that the light is unfit, only the batting side shall have the option of continuing play. After agreeing to continue to play in unfit light conditions, the captain of the batting side (or a batsman at the wicket) may appeal against the light to the umpires, who shall uphold the appeal only if, in their opinion, the light has deteriorated since the agreement to continue was made.

(b) After any suspension of play, the umpires, unaccompanied by any of the players or officials, shall, on their own initiative, carry out an inspection immediately the conditions improve and shall continue to inspect at intervals. Immediately the umpires decide that play is possible they shall call upon the players to resume the game.

9. Exceptional Circumstances

In exceptional circumstances, other than those of weather, ground or light, the umpires may decide to suspend or abandon play. Before making such a decision the umpires shall establish, if the circumstances allow, whether both captains (the batsmen at the wicket may deputise for their captain) wish to continue in the prevailing conditions; if so, their wishes shall be met.

10. Position of Umpires

The umpires shall stand where they can best see any act upon which their decision may be required.

Subject to this over-riding consideration, the umpire at the bowler's end shall stand where he does not interfere with either the bowler's run-up or the striker's view.

The umpire at the striker's end may elect to stand on the off instead of the leg side of the pitch, provided he informs the captain of the fielding side and the striker of his intention to do so.

11. Umpires Changing Ends

The umpires shall change ends after each side has had one innings.

12. Disputes

All disputes shall be determined by the umpires, and if they disagree the actual state of things shall continue.

13. Signals

The following code of signals shall be used by umpires who will wait until a signal has been answered by a scorer before allowing the game to proceed.

Boundary   – by waving the arm from side to side.
Boundary 6   – by raising both arms above the head.
Bye   – by raising an open hand above the head.
Dead Ball   – by crossing and re-crossing the wrists below the waist.
Leg-bye   – by touching a raised knee with the hand.
No-ball   – by extending one arm horizontally.
Out   – by raising the index finger above the head. If not out, the umpire shall call "not out".
Short run   – by bending the arm upwards and by touching the nearer shoulder with the tips of the fingers.
Wide   – by extending both arms horizontally.

14. Correctness of Scores

The umpires shall be responsible for satisfying themselves on the correctness of the scores throughout and at the conclusion of the match. See Law 21.6 (Correctness of Result).

Notes

(a) Attendance of Umpires
The umpires should be present on the ground and report to the ground executive or the equivalent at least thirty minutes before the start of a day's play.

(b) Consultation between Umpires and Scorers
Consultation between umpires and scorers over doubtful points is essential.

(c) Fitness of Ground
The umpires shall consider the ground as unfit for play when it is so wet or slippery as to deprive the bowlers of a reasonable foothold, the fieldsmen, other than the deep-fielders, of the power of free movement, or the batsmen of the ability to play their strokes or to run between the wickets. Play should not be suspended merely because the grass and the ball are wet and slippery.

(d) Fitness of Weather and Light
The umpires should suspend play only when they consider that the conditions are so bad that it is unreasonable or dangerous to continue.

LAW 4. THE SCORERS

1. Recording Runs

All runs scored shall be recorded by scorers appointed for the purpose. Where there are two scorers they shall frequently check to ensure that the score sheets agree.

2. Acknowledging Signals

The scorers shall accept and immediately acknowledge all instructions and signals given to them by the umpires.

LAW 5.   THE BALL

1. Weight and Size

The ball, when new, shall weigh not less than 5½ ounces/155.9g, nor more than 5¾ ounces/163g; and shall measure not less than 8$\frac{13}{16}$ inches/22.4cm, nor more than 9 inches/22.9cm in circumference.

2. Approval of Balls

All balls used in matches shall be approved by the umpires and captains before the start of the match.

3. New Ball

Subject to agreement to the contrary, having been made before the toss, either captain may demand a new ball at the start of each innings.

4. New Ball in Match of Three or More Days' Duration

In a match of three or more days' duration, the captain of the fielding side may demand a new ball after the prescribed number of overs has been bowled with the old one. The governing body for cricket in the country concerned shall decide the number of overs applicable in that country, which shall be not less than 75 six-ball overs (55 eight-ball overs).

5. Ball Lost or Becoming Unfit for Play

In the event of a ball during play being lost or, in the opinion of the umpires, becoming unfit for play, the umpires shall allow it to be replaced by one that in their opinion has had a similar amount of wear. If a ball is to be replaced, the umpires shall inform the batsman.

Note

  (a) **Specifications**
  The specifications, as described in 1 above, shall apply to top-grade balls only. The following degrees of tolerance will be acceptable for other grades of ball.
     (i) *Men's Grades 2–4*
          Weight: 5$\frac{5}{16}$ ounces/150g to 5$\frac{13}{16}$ ounces/165g.
          Size: 8$\frac{11}{16}$ inches/22.0cm to 9$\frac{1}{16}$ inches/23.00cm.
    (ii) *Women's*
          Weight: 4$\frac{15}{16}$ ounces/140g to 5$\frac{5}{16}$ ounces/150g.
          Size: 8¼ inches/21.0cm to 8$\frac{6}{8}$ inches/22.5cm.
   (iii) *Junior*
          Weight: 4$\frac{11}{16}$ ounces/133g to 5$\frac{1}{16}$ ounces/143g.
          Size: 8$\frac{1}{16}$ inches/20.5cm to 8$\frac{11}{16}$ inches/22.0cm.

LAW 6.   THE BAT

1. Width and Length

The bat overall shall not be more than 38 inches/96.5cm in length; the blade of the bat shall be made of wood and shall not exceed 4¼ inches/10.8cm at the widest part.

Note

  (a) The blade of the bat may be covered with material for protection, strengthening or repair. Such material shall not exceed $\frac{1}{16}$ inch/1.56mm in thickness.

LAW 7.   THE PITCH

1. Area of Pitch

The pitch is the area between the bowling creases – see Law 9 (The Bowling and Popping Creases). It shall measure 5ft/1.52m in width on either side of a line joining the centre of the middle stumps of the wickets – see Law 8 (The Wickets).

2. Selection and Preparation

Before the toss for innings, the executive of the ground shall be responsible for the selection and preparation of the pitch; thereafter the umpires shall control its use and maintenance.

3. Changing Pitch

The pitch shall not be changed during a match unless it becomes unfit for play, and then only with the consent of both captains.

4. Non-Turf Pitches

In the event of a non-turf pitch being used, the following shall apply:

    (a) Length: That of the playing surface to a minimum of 58ft/17.68m.
    (b) Width: That of the playing surface to a minimum of 6ft/1.83m.

See Law 10 (Rolling, Sweeping, Mowing, Watering the Pitch and Re-marking of Creases) Note (a).

LAW 8.   THE WICKETS

1. Width and Pitching

Two sets of wickets, each 9 inches/22.86cm wide, and consisting of three wooden stumps with two wooden bails upon the top, shall be pitched opposite and parallel to each other at a distance of 22 yards/20.12m between the centres of the two middle stumps.

2. Size of Stumps

The stumps shall be of equal and sufficient size to prevent the ball from passing between them. Their tops shall be 28 inches/71.1cm above the ground, and shall be dome-shaped except for the bail grooves.

3. Size of Bails

The bails shall be each 4⅜ inches/11.1cm in length and when in position on the top of the stumps shall not project more than ½ inch/1.3cm above them.

Notes

    (a) **Dispensing with Bails**
    In a high wind the umpires may decide to dispense with the use of bails.
    (b) **Junior Cricket**
    For junior cricket, as defined by the local governing body, the following measurements for the wickets shall apply:
        Width   – 8 inches/20.32cm.
        Pitched – 21 yards/19.20m.
        Height   – 27 inches/68.58cm.
        Bails   – each 3⅞ inches/9.84cm in length and should not project more than ½ inch/1.3cm above the stumps.

LAW 9.   THE BOWLING, POPPING AND RETURN CREASES

1. The Bowling Crease

The bowling crease shall be marked in line with the stumps at each end and shall be 8 feet 8 inches/2.64m in length, with the stumps in the centre.

2. The Popping Crease

The popping crease, which is the back edge of the crease marking, shall be in front of and parallel with the bowling crease. It shall have the back edge of the crease marking 4 feet/ 1.22m from the centre of the stumps and shall extend to a minimum of 6 feet/1.83m on either side of the line of the wicket.

The popping crease shall be considered to be unlimited in length.

3. The Return Crease

The return crease marking, of which the inside edge is the crease, shall be at each end of the bowling crease and at right angles to it. The return crease shall be marked to a minimum of 4 feet/1.22m behind the wicket and shall be considered to be unlimited in length. A forward extension shall be marked to the popping crease.

LAW 10.   ROLLING, SWEEPING, MOWING, WATERING THE PITCH AND RE-MARKING OF CREASES

1. Rolling

During the match the pitch may be rolled at the request of the captain of the batting side, for a period of not more than seven minutes before the start of each innings, other than the first innings of the match, and before the start of each day's play. In addition, if, after the toss and before the first innings of the match, the start is delayed, the captain of the batting side shall have the right to have the pitch rolled for not more than seven minutes.

The pitch shall not otherwise be rolled during the match.

The seven minutes' rolling permitted before the start of a day's play shall take place not earlier than half an hour before the start of play and the captain of the batting side may delay such rolling until ten minutes before the start of play should he so desire.

If a captain declares an innings closed less than fifteen minutes before the resumption of play, and the other captain is thereby prevented from exercising his option of seven minutes' rolling or if he is so prevented for any other reason, the time for rolling shall be taken out of the normal playing time.

2. Sweeping

Such sweeping of the pitch as is necessary during the match shall be done so that the seven minutes allowed for rolling the pitch, provided for in 1 above, is not affected.

3. Mowing

(a) Responsibilities of Ground Authority and of Umpires

All mowings which are carried out before the toss for innings shall be the responsibility of the ground authority; thereafter they shall be carried out under the supervision of the umpires. See Law 7.2 (Selection and Preparation).

(b) Initial Mowing

The pitch shall be mown before play begins on the day the match is scheduled to start, or in the case of a delayed start on the day the match is expected to start. See 3(a) above (Responsibilities of Ground Authority and of Umpires).

(c) Subsequent Mowings in a Match of Two or More Days' Duration

In a match of two or more days' duration, the pitch shall be mown daily before play begins. Should this mowing not take place because of weather conditions, rest days or other reasons, the pitch shall be mown on the first day on which the match is resumed.

(d) Mowing of the Outfield in a Match of Two or More Days' Duration

In order to ensure that conditions are as similar as possible for both sides, the outfield shall normally be mown before the commencement of play on each day of the match, if ground and weather conditions allow. See Note (b) to this Law.

4. Watering

The pitch shall not be watered during a match.

5. Re-marking Creases

Whenever possible the creases shall be re-marked.

6. Maintenance of Foot-holes

In wet weather, the umpires shall ensure that the holes made by the bowlers and batsmen are cleaned out and dried whenever necessary to facilitate play. In matches of two or more days' duration, the umpires shall allow, if necessary, the re-turfing of foot-holes made by the bowler in his delivery stride, or the use of quick-setting fillings for the same purpose, before the start of each day's play.

7. Securing of Footholds and Maintenance of Pitch

During play, the umpires shall allow either batsman to beat the pitch with his bat and players to secure their footholds by the use of sawdust, provided that no damage to the pitch is so caused, and Law 42 (Unfair Play) is not contravened.

Notes

(a) Non-turf Pitches

The above Law 10 applies to turf pitches.

The game is played on non-turf pitches in many countries at various levels. Whilst the conduct of the game on these surfaces should always be in accordance with the Laws of Cricket, it is recognised that it may sometimes be necessary for governing bodies to lay down special playing conditions to suit the type of non-turf pitch used in their country.

In matches played against touring teams, any special playing conditions should be agreed in advance by both parties.

(b) Mowing of the Outfield in a Match of Two or More Days' Duration

If, for reasons other than ground and weather conditions, daily and complete mowing is not possible, the ground authority shall notify the captains and umpires, before the toss for innings, of the procedure to be adopted for such mowing during the match.

(c) Choice of Roller

If there is more than one roller available, the captain of the batting side shall have a choice.

LAW 11. COVERING THE PITCH

1. Before the Start of a Match

Before the start of a match, complete covering of the pitch shall be allowed.

2. During a Match

The pitch shall not be completely covered during a match unless prior arrangement or regulations so provide.

3. Covering Bowlers' Run-up

Whenever possible, the bowlers' run-up shall be covered, but the covers so used shall not extend further than 4 feet/1.22m in front of the popping crease.

Note

(a) **Removal of Covers**
The covers should be removed as promptly as possible whenever the weather permits.

LAW 12.   INNINGS

1. Number of Innings

A match shall be of one or two innings of each side according to agreement reached before the start of play.

2. Alternate Innings

In a two-innings match each side shall take their innings alternately except in the case provided for in Law 13 (The Follow-on).

3. The Toss

The captains shall toss for the choice of innings on the field of play not later than fifteen minutes before the time scheduled for the match to start, or before the time agreed upon for play to start.

4. Choice of Innings

The winner of the toss shall notify his decision to bat or to field to the opposing captain not later than ten minutes before the time scheduled for the match to start, or before the time agreed upon for play to start. The decision shall not thereafter be altered.

5. Continuation after One Innings of Each Side

Despite the terms of 1 above, in a one-innings match, when a result has been reached on the first innings, the captains may agree to the continuation of play if, in their opinion, there is a prospect of carrying the game to a further issue in the time left. See Law 21 (Result).

Notes

(a) **Limited Innings – One-innings Match**
In a one-innings match, each innings may, by agreement, be limited by a number of overs or by a period of time.

(b) **Limited Innings – Two-innings Match**
In a two-innings match, the first innings of each side may, by agreement, be limited to a number of overs or by a period of time.

LAW 13.   THE FOLLOW-ON

1. Lead on First Innings

In a two-innings match the side which bats first and leads by 200 runs in a match of five days or more, by 150 runs in a three-day or four-day match, by 100 runs in a two-day match, or by 75 runs in a one-day match, shall have the option of requiring the other side to follow their innings.

2. Day's Play Lost

If no play takes place on the first day of a match of two or more days' duration, 1 above shall apply in accordance with the number of days' play remaining from the actual start of the match.

LAW 14.   DECLARATIONS

1. Time of Declaration

The captain of the batting side may declare an innings closed at any time during a match, irrespective of its duration.

2. Forfeiture of Second Innings

A captain may forfeit his second innings, provided his decision to do so is notified to the opposing captain and umpires in sufficient time to allow seven minutes' rolling of the pitch. See Law 10 (Rolling, Sweeping, Mowing, Watering the Pitch and Re-marking of Creases). The normal ten-minute interval between innings shall be applied.

LAW 15.   START OF PLAY

1. Call of Play

At the start of each innings and of each day's play, and on the resumption of play after any interval or interruption, the umpire at the bowler's end shall call "play".

2. Practice on the Field

At no time on any day of the match shall there be any bowling or batting practice on the pitch.

No practice may take place on the field if, in the opinion of the umpires, it could result in a waste of time.

3. Trial Run-up

No bowler shall have a trial run-up after "play" has been called in any session of play, except at the fall of a wicket when an umpire may allow such a trial run-up if he is satisfied that it will not cause any waste of time.

LAW 16.   INTERVALS

1. Length

The umpire shall allow such intervals as have been agreed upon for meals, and ten minutes between each innings.

2. Luncheon Interval – Innings Ending or Stoppage within Ten Minutes of Interval

If an innings ends or there is a stoppage caused by weather or bad light within ten minutes of the agreed time for the luncheon interval, the interval shall be taken immediately.

The time remaining in the session of play shall be added to the agreed length of the interval but no extra allowance shall be made for the ten-minute interval between innings.

3. Tea Interval – Innings Ending or Stoppage within Thirty Minutes of Interval

If an innings ends or there is a stoppage caused by weather or bad light within thirty minutes of the agreed time for the tea interval, the interval shall be taken immediately.

The interval shall be of the agreed length and, if applicable, shall include the ten-minute interval between innings.

4. Tea Interval – Continuation of Play

If, at the agreed time for the tea interval, nine wickets are down, play shall continue for a period not exceeding thirty minutes or until the innings is concluded.

5. Tea Interval – Agreement to Forgo

At any time during the match, the captains may agree to forgo a tea interval.

6. Intervals for Drinks

If both captains agree before the start of a match that intervals for drinks may be taken, the option to take such intervals shall be available to either side. These intervals shall be restricted to one per session, shall be kept as short as possible, shall not be taken in the last hour of the match, and in any case shall not exceed five minutes.

The agreed times for these intervals shall be strictly adhered to, except that if a wicket falls within five minutes of the agreed time then drinks shall be taken out immediately.

If an innings ends or there is a stoppage caused by weather or bad light within thirty minutes of the agreed time for a drinks interval, there will be no interval for drinks in that session.

At any time during the match the captains may agree to forgo any such drinks interval.

Notes

(a) **Tea Interval – One-day Match**

In a one-day match, a specific time for the tea interval need not necessarily be arranged, and it may be agreed to take this interval between the innings of a one-innings match.

(b) **Changing the Agreed Time of Intervals**

In the event of the ground, weather or light conditions causing a suspension of play, the umpires, after consultation with the captains, may decide in the interests of time-saving to bring forward the time of the luncheon or tea interval.

LAW 17.   CESSATION OF PLAY

1. Call of Time

The umpire at the bowler's end shall call "time" on the cessation of play before any interval or interruption of play, at the end of each day's play, and at the conclusion of the match. See Law 27 (Appeals).

2. Removal of Bails

After the call of "time", the umpires shall remove the bails from both wickets.

3. Starting a Last Over

The last over before an interval or the close of play shall be started provided the umpire, after walking at his normal pace, has arrived at his position behind the stumps at the bowler's end before time has been reached.

4. Completion of the Last Over of a Session

The last over before an interval or the close of play shall be completed unless a batsman is out or retires during that over within two minutes of the interval or the close of play or unless the players have occasion to leave the field.

5. Completion of the Last Over of a Match

An over in progress at the close of play on the final day of a match shall be completed at the request of either captain, even if a wicket falls after time has been reached.

If, during the last over, the players have occasion to leave the field, the umpires shall call "time" and there shall be no resumption of play and the match shall be at an end.

6. Last Hour of Match – Number of Overs

The umpires shall indicate when one hour of playing time of the match remains according to the agreed hours of play. The next over after that moment shall be the first of a minimum of 20 six-ball overs (15 eight-ball overs), provided a result is not reached earlier or there is no interval or interruption of play.

7. Last Hour of Match – Intervals between Innings and Interruptions of Play

If, at the commencement of the last hour of the match, an interval or interruption of play is in progress or if, during the last hour, there is an interval between innings or an interruption of play, the minimum number of overs to be bowled on the resumption of play shall be reduced in proportion to the duration, within the last hour of the match, of any such interval or interruption.

The minimum number of overs to be bowled after the resumption of play shall be calculated as follows:

(a) In the case of an interval or interruption of play being in progress at the commencement of the last hour of the match, or in the case of a first interval or interruption, a deduction shall be made from the minimum of 20 six-ball overs (or 15 eight-ball overs).

(b) If there is a later interval or interruption, a further deduction shall be made from the minimum number of overs which should have been bowled following the last resumption of play.

(c) These deductions shall be based on the following factors:

  (i) The number of overs already bowled in the last hour of the match or, in the case of a later interval or interruption, in the last session of play.

  (ii) The number of overs lost as a result of the interval or interruption allowing one six-ball over for every full three minutes (or one eight-ball over for every full four minutes) of interval or interruption.

  (iii) Any over left uncompleted at the end of an innings to be excluded from these calculations.

  (iv) Any over left uncompleted at the start of an interruption of play to be completed when play is resumed and to count as one over bowled.

  (v) An interval to start with the end of an innings and to end ten minutes later; an interruption to start on the call of "time" and to end on the call of "play".

(d) In the event of an innings being completed and a new innings commencing during the last hour of the match, the number of overs to be bowled in the new innings shall be calculated on the basis of one six-ball over for every three minutes or part thereof remaining for play (or one eight-ball over for every four minutes or part thereof remaining for play); or alternatively on the basis that sufficient overs to be bowled to enable the full minimum quota of overs to be completed under circumstances governed by (a), (b) and (c) above. In all such cases the alternative which allows the greater number of overs shall be employed.

8. Bowler Unable to Complete an Over during Last Hour of the Match

If, for any reason, a bowler is unable to complete an over during the period of play referred to in 6 above, Law 22.7 (Bowler Incapacitated or Suspended during an Over) shall apply.

LAW 18. SCORING

1. A Run

The score shall be reckoned by runs. A run is scored:

    (a) So often as the batsmen, after a hit or at any time while the ball is in play, shall have crossed and made good their ground from end to end.

    (b) When a boundary is scored. See Law 19 (Boundaries).

    (c) When penalty runs are awarded. See 6 below.

2. Short Runs

    (a) If either batsman runs a short run, the umpire shall call and signal "one short" as soon as the ball becomes dead and that run shall not be scored. A run is short if a batsman fails to make good his ground on turning for a further run.

    (b) Although a short run shortens the succeeding one, the latter, if completed, shall count.

    (c) If either or both batsmen deliberately run short the umpire shall, as soon as he sees that the fielding side have no chance of dismissing either batsman, call and signal "dead ball" and disallow any runs attempted or previously scored. The batsmen shall return to their original ends.

    (d) If both batsmen run short in one and the same run, only one run shall be deducted.

    (e) Only if 3 or more runs are attempted can more than one be short and then, subject to (c) and (d) above, all runs so called shall be disallowed. If there has been more than one short run the umpires shall instruct the scorers as to the number of runs disallowed.

3. Striker Caught

If the striker is caught, no run shall be scored.

4. Batsman Run Out

If a batsman is run out, only that run which was being attempted shall not be scored. If, however, an injured striker himself is run out, no runs shall be scored. See Law 2.7 (Transgression of the Laws by an Injured Batsman or Runner).

5. Batsman Obstructing the Field

If a batsman is out Obstructing the Field, any runs completed before the obstruction occurs shall be scored unless such obstruction prevents a catch being made, in which case no runs shall be scored.

6. Runs Scored for Penalties

Runs shall be scored for penalties under Laws 20 (Lost Ball), 24 (No-ball), 25 (Wide-ball), 41.1 (Fielding the Ball) and for boundary allowances under Law 19 (Boundaries).

7. Batsman Returning to Wicket he has Left

If, while the ball is in play, the batsmen have crossed in running, neither shall return to the wicket he has left, even though a short run has been called or no run has been scored as in the case of a catch. Batsmen, however, shall return to the wickets they originally left in the cases of a boundary and of any disallowance of runs and of an injured batsman being, himself, run out. See Law 2.7 (Transgression by an Injured Batsman or Runner).

Note

    (a) Short Run

    A striker taking stance in front of his popping crease may run from that point without penalty.

LAW 19.   BOUNDARIES

1. The Boundary of the Playing Area

Before the toss for innings, the umpires shall agree with both captains on the boundary of the playing area. The boundary shall, if possible, be marked by a white line, a rope laid on the ground, or a fence. If flags or posts only are used to mark a boundary, the imaginary line joining such points shall be regarded as the boundary. An obstacle, or person, within the playing area shall not be regarded as a boundary unless so decided by the umpires before the toss for innings. Sightscreens within, or partially within, the playing area shall be regarded as the boundary and when the ball strikes or passes within or under or directly over any part of the screen, a boundary shall be scored.

2. Runs Scored for Boundaries

Before the toss for innings, the umpires shall agree with both captains the runs to be allowed for boundaries, and in deciding the allowance for them, the umpires and captains shall be guided by the prevailing custom of the ground. The allowance for a boundary shall normally be 4 runs, and 6 runs for all hits pitching over and clear of the boundary line or fence, even though the ball has been previously touched by a fieldsman. 6 runs shall also be scored if a fieldsman, after catching a ball, carries it over the boundary. See Law 32 (Caught) Note (a). 6 runs shall not be scored when a ball struck by the striker hits a sightscreen full pitch if the screen is within, or partially within, the playing area, but if the ball is struck directly over a sightscreen so situated, 6 runs shall be scored.

3. A Boundary

A boundary shall be scored and signalled by the umpire at the bowler's end whenever, in his opinion:

(a) A ball in play touches or crosses the boundary, however marked.

(b) A fieldsman with ball in hand touches or grounds any part of his person on or over a boundary line.

(c) A fieldsman with ball in hand grounds any part of his person over a boundary fence or board. This allows the fieldsman to touch or lean on or over a boundary fence or board in preventing a boundary.

4. Runs Exceeding Boundary Allowance

The runs completed at the instant the ball reaches the boundary shall count if they exceed the boundary allowance.

5. Overthrows or Wilful Act of a Fieldsman

If the boundary results from an overthrow or from the wilful act of a fieldsman, any runs already completed and the allowance shall be added to the score. The run in progress shall count provided that the batsmen have crossed at the instant of the throw or act.

Note

(a) **Position of Sightscreens**
Sightscreens should, if possible, be positioned wholly outside the playing area, as near as possible to the boundary line.

LAW 20.   LOST BALL

1. Runs Scored

If a ball in play cannot be found or recovered, any fieldsman may call "lost ball" when 6 runs shall be added to the score; but if more than 6 have been run before "lost ball" is called, as many runs as have been completed shall be scored. The run in progress shall count provided that the batsmen have crossed at the instant of the call of "lost ball".

2. How Scored

The runs shall be added to the score of the striker if the ball has been struck, but otherwise to the score of byes, leg-byes, no-balls or wides as the case may be.

LAW 21.   THE RESULT

1. A Win – Two-innings Matches

The side which has scored a total of runs in excess of that scored by the opposing side in its two completed innings shall be the winners.

2. A Win – One-innings Matches

(a) One-innings matches, unless played out as in 1 above, shall be decided on the first innings, but see Law 12.5 (Continuation after One Innings of Each Side).

(b) If the captains agree to continue play after the completion of one innings of each side in accordance with Law 12.5 (Continuation after One Innings of Each Side) and a result is not achieved on the second innings, the first innings result shall stand.

3. Umpires Awarding a Match

(a) A match shall be lost by a side which, during the match, (i) refuses to play, or (ii) concedes defeat, and the umpires shall award the match to the other side.

(b) Should both batsmen at the wickets or the fielding side leave the field at any time without the agreement of the umpires, this shall constitute a refusal to play and, on appeal, the umpires shall award the match to the other side in accordance with (a) above.

4. A Tie

The result of a match shall be a tie when the scores are equal at the conclusion of play, but only if the side batting last has completed its innings.

If the scores of the completed first innings of a one-day match are equal, it shall be a tie but only if the match has not been played out to a further conclusion.

5. A Draw

A match not determined in any of the ways as in 1, 2, 3 and 4 above shall count as a draw.

6. Correctness of Result

Any decision as to the correctness of the scores shall be the responsibility of the umpires. See Law 3.14 (Correctness of Scores).

If, after the umpires and players have left the field in the belief that the match has been concluded, the umpires decide that a mistake in scoring has occurred, which affects the result, and provided time has not been reached, they shall order play to resume and to continue until the agreed finishing time unless a result is reached earlier.

If the umpires decide that a mistake has occurred and time has been reached, the umpires shall immediately inform both captains of the necessary corrections to the scores and, if applicable, to the result.

7. Acceptance of Result

In accepting the scores as notified by the scorers and agreed by the umpires, the captains of both sides thereby accept the result.

Notes

(a) Statement of Results
The result of a finished match is stated as a win by runs, except in the case of a win by the side batting last when it is by the number of wickets still then to fall.

(b) Winning Hit or Extras

As soon as the side has won, see 1 and 2 above, the umpire shall call "time", the match is finished, and nothing that happens thereafter other than as a result of a mistake in scoring (see 6 above) shall be regarded as part of the match.

However, if a boundary constitutes the winning hit – or extras – and the boundary allowance exceeds the number of runs required to win the match, such runs scored shall be credited to the side's total and, in the case of a hit, to the striker's score.

LAW 22.   THE OVER

1. Number of Balls

The ball shall be bowled from each wicket alternately in overs of either six or eight balls according to agreement before the match.

2. Call of "Over"

When the agreed number of balls has been bowled, and as the ball becomes dead or when it becomes clear to the umpire at the bowler's end that both the fielding side and the batsmen at the wicket have ceased to regard the ball as in play, the umpire shall call "over" before leaving the wicket.

3. No-ball or Wide-ball

Neither a no-ball nor a wide-ball shall be reckoned as one of the over.

4. Umpire Miscounting

If an umpire miscounts the number of balls, the over as counted by the umpire shall stand.

5. Bowler Changing Ends

A bowler shall be allowed to change ends as often as desired, provided only that he does not bowl two overs consecutively in an innings.

6. The Bowler Finishing an Over

A bowler shall finish an over in progress unless he be incapacitated or be suspended under Law 42.8 (The Bowling of Fast Short-pitched Balls), 9 (The Bowling of Fast High Full Pitches), 10 (Time Wasting) and 11 (Players Damaging the Pitch). If an over is left incomplete for any reason at the start of an interval or interruption of play, it shall be finished on the resumption of play.

7. Bowler Incapacitated or Suspended during an Over

If, for any reason, a bowler is incapacitated while running up to bowl the first ball of an over, or is incapacitated or suspended during an over, the umpire shall call and signal "dead ball" and another bowler shall be allowed to bowl or complete the over from the same end, provided only that he shall not bowl two overs, or part thereof, consecutively in one innings.

8. Position of Non-striker

The batsman at the bowler's end shall normally stand on the opposite side of the wicket to that from which the ball is being delivered, unless a request to do otherwise is granted by the umpire.

LAW 23.   DEAD BALL

1. The Ball Becomes Dead

When:

(a) It is finally settled in the hands of the wicket-keeper or the bowler.

(b) It reaches or pitches over the boundary.

(c) A batsman is out.

(d) Whether played or not, it lodges in the clothing or equipment of a batsman or the clothing of an umpire.

(e) A ball lodges in a protective helmet worn by a member of the fielding side.

(f) A penalty is awarded under Law 20 (Lost Ball) or Law 41.1 (Fielding the Ball).

(g) The umpire calls "over" or "time".

2. Either Umpire Shall Call and Signal "Dead Ball"

When:

(a) He intervenes in a case of unfair play.

(b) A serious injury to a player or umpire occurs.

(c) He is satisfied that, for an adequate reason, the striker is not ready to receive the ball and makes no attempt to play it.

(d) The bowler drops the ball accidentally before delivery, or the ball does not leave his hand for any reason.

(e) One or both bails fall from the striker's wicket before he receives delivery.

(f) He leaves his normal position for consultation.

(g) He is required to do so under Law 26.3 (Disallowance of Leg-byes).

3. The Ball Ceases to be Dead

When:

(a) The bowler starts his run-up or bowling action.

4. The Ball is Not Dead

When:

(a) It strikes an umpire (unless it lodges in his dress).

(b) The wicket is broken or struck down (unless a batsman is out thereby).

(c) A unsuccessful appeal is made.

(d) The wicket is broken accidentally either by the bowler during his delivery or by a batsman in running.

(e) The umpire has called "no-ball" or "wide".

Notes

(a) Ball Finally Settled
Whether the ball is finally settled or not – see 1(a) above – must be a question for the umpires alone to decide.

(b) Action on Call of "Dead Ball"
(i) If "dead ball" is called prior to the striker receiving a delivery, the bowler shall be allowed an additional ball.

(ii) If "dead ball" is called after the striker receives a delivery, the bowler shall not be allowed an additional ball, unless a "no-ball" or "wide" has been called.

LAW 24. NO-BALL

1. Mode of Delivery

The umpire shall indicate to the striker whether the bowler intends to bowl over or round the wicket, overarm or underarm, right- or left-handed. Failure on the part of the bowler to indicate in advance a change in his mode of delivery is unfair and the umpire shall call and signal "no-ball".

2. Fair Delivery – The Arm

For a delivery to be fair the ball must be bowled, not thrown – see Note (a) below. If either umpire is not entirely satisfied with the absolute fairness of a delivery in this respect he shall call and signal "no-ball" instantly upon delivery.

3. Fair Delivery – The Feet

The umpire at the bowler's wicket shall call and signal "no-ball" if he is not satisfied that in the delivery stride:

(a) The bowler's back foot has landed within and not touching the return crease or its forward extension; or

(b) Some part of the front foot whether grounded or raised was behind the popping crease.

4. Bowler Throwing at Striker's Wicket before Delivery

If the bowler, before delivering the ball, throws it at the striker's wicket in an attempt to run him out, the umpire shall call and signal "no-ball". See Law 42.12 (Batsman Unfairly Stealing a Run) and Law 38 (Run Out).

5. Bowler Attempting to Run Out Non-striker before Delivery

If the bowler, before delivering the ball, attempts to run out the non-striker, any runs which result shall be allowed and shall be scored as no-balls. Such an attempt shall not count as a ball in the over. The umpire shall not call "no-ball". See Law 42.12 (Batsman Unfairly Stealing a Run).

6. Infringement of Laws by a Wicket-keeper or a Fieldsman

The umpire shall call and signal "no-ball" in the event of the wicket-keeper infringing Law 40.1 (Position of Wicket-keeper) or a fieldsman infringing Law 41.2 (Limitation of On-side Fieldsmen) or Law 41.3 (Position of Fieldsmen).

7. Revoking a Call

An umpire shall revoke the call "no-ball" if the ball does not leave the bowler's hand for any reason. See Law 23.2 (Either Umpire Shall Call and Signal "Dead Ball").

8. Penalty

A penalty of 1 run for a no-ball shall be scored if no runs are made otherwise.

9. Runs from a No-ball

The striker may hit a no-ball and whatever runs result shall be added to his score. Runs made otherwise from a no-ball shall be scored no-balls.

10. Out from a No-ball

The striker shall be out from a no-ball if he breaks Law 34 (Hit the Ball Twice) and either batsman may be run out or shall be given out if either breaks Law 33 (Handled the Ball) or Law 37 (Obstructing the Field).

11. Batsman Given Out off a No-ball

Should a batsman be given out off a no-ball the penalty for bowling it shall stand unless runs are otherwise scored.

Notes

(a) **Definition of a Throw**

A ball shall be deemed to have been thrown if, in the opinion of either umpire, the process of straightening the bowling arm, whether it be partial or complete, takes place during that part of the delivery swing which directly precedes the ball leaving the hand. This definition shall not debar a bowler from the use of the wrist in the delivery swing.

(b) **No-ball Not Counting in Over**

A no-ball shall not be reckoned as one of the over. See Law 22.3 (No-ball or Wide-ball).

LAW 25.   WIDE-BALL

1. Judging a Wide

If the bowler bowls the ball so high over or so wide of the wicket that, in the opinion of the umpire, it passes out of the reach of the striker, standing in a normal guard position, the umpire shall call and signal "wide-ball" as soon as it has passed the line of the striker's wicket.

The umpire shall not adjudge a ball as being wide if:

(a) The striker, by moving from his guard position, causes the ball to pass out of his reach.

(b) The striker moves and thus brings the ball within his reach.

2. Penalty

A penalty of 1 run for a wide shall be scored if no runs are made otherwise.

3. Ball Coming to Rest in Front of the Striker

If a ball which the umpire considers to have been delivered comes to rest in front of the line of the striker's wicket, "wide" shall not be called. The striker has a right, without interference from the fielding side, to make one attempt to hit the ball. If the fielding side interfere, the umpire shall replace the ball where it came to rest and shall order the fieldsmen to resume the places they occupied in the field before the ball was delivered.

The umpire shall call and signal "dead ball" as soon as it is clear that the striker does not intend to hit the ball, or after the striker has made an unsuccessful attempt to hit the ball.

4. Revoking a Call

The umpire shall revoke the call if the striker hits a ball which has been called "wide".

5. Ball Not Dead

The ball does not become dead on the call of "wide-ball" – see Law 23.4 (The Ball is Not Dead).

6. Runs Resulting from a Wide

All runs which are run or result from a wide-ball which is not a no-ball shall be scored wide-balls, or if no runs are made 1 shall be scored.

7. Out from a Wide

The striker shall be out from a wide-ball if he breaks Law 35 (Hit Wicket), or Law 39 (Stumped). Either batsman may be run out and shall be out if he breaks Law 33 (Handled the Ball), or Law 37 (Obstructing the Field).

8. Batsman Given Out off a Wide

Should a batsman be given out off a wide, the penalty for bowling it shall stand unless runs are otherwise made.

Note

    (a) Wide-ball Not Counting in Over
    A wide-ball shall not be reckoned as one of the over – see Law 22.3 (No-ball or Wide-ball).

LAW 26.   BYE AND LEG-BYE

1. Byes

If the ball, not having been called "wide" or "no-ball", passes the striker without touching his bat or person, and any runs are obtained, the umpire shall signal "bye" and the run or runs shall be credited as such to the batting side.

2. Leg-byes

If the ball, not having been called "wide" or "no-ball", is unintentionally deflected by the striker's dress or person, except a hand holding the bat, and any runs are obtained the umpire shall signal "leg-bye" and the run or runs so scored shall be credited as such to the batting side.

    Such leg-byes shall be scored only if, in the opinion of the umpire, the striker has:

        (a) Attempted to play the ball with his bat; or

        (b) Tried to avoid being hit by the ball.

3. Disallowance of Leg-byes

In the case of a deflection by the striker's person, other than in 2(a) and (b) above, the umpire shall call and signal "dead ball" as soon as 1 run has been completed or when it is clear that a run is not being attempted, or the ball has reached the boundary.

    On the call and signal of "dead ball" the batsmen shall return to their original ends and no runs shall be allowed.

LAW 27.   APPEALS

1. Time of Appeals

The umpires shall not give a batsman out unless appealed to by the other side which shall be done prior to the bowler beginning his run-up or bowling action to deliver the next ball. Under Law 23.1 (f) (The Ball Becomes Dead), the ball is dead on "over" being called; this does not, however, invalidate an appeal made prior to the first ball of the following over provided "time" has not been called – see Law 17.1 (Call of Time).

2. An Appeal "How's That?"

An appeal "How's That?" shall cover all ways of being out.

3. Answering Appeals

The umpire at the bowler's wicket shall answer appeals before the other umpire in all cases except those arising out of Law 35 (Hit Wicket) or Law 39 (Stumped) or Law 38 (Run Out) when this occurs at the striker's wicket.

When either umpire has given a batsman not out, the other umpire shall, within his jurisdiction, answer the appeal on a further appeal, provided it is made in time in accordance with 1 above (Time of Appeals).

4. Consultation by Umpires

An umpire may consult with the other umpire on a point of fact which the latter may have been in a better position to see and shall then give his decision. If, after consultation, there is still doubt remaining the decision shall be in favour of the batsman.

5. Batsman Leaving his Wicket under a Misapprehension

The umpires shall intervene if satisfied that a batsman, not having been given out, has left his wicket under a misapprehension that he has been dismissed.

6. Umpire's Decision

The umpire's decision is final. He may alter his decision, provided that such alteration is made promptly.

7. Withdrawal of an Appeal

In exceptional circumstances the captain of the fielding side may seek permission of the umpire to withdraw an appeal provided the outgoing batsman has not left the playing area. If this is allowed, the umpire shall cancel his decision.

LAW 28.   THE WICKET IS DOWN

1. Wicket Down

The wicket is down if:

(a) Either the ball or the striker's bat or person completely removes either bail from the top of the stumps. A disturbance of a bail, whether temporary or not, shall not constitute a complete removal, but the wicket is down if a bail in falling lodges between two of the stumps.

(b) Any player completely removes with his hand or arm a bail from the top of the stumps, provided that the ball is held in that hand or in the hand of the arm so used.

(c) When both bails are off, a stump is struck out of the ground by the ball, or a player strikes or pulls a stump out of the ground, provided that the ball is held in the hand(s) or in the hand of the arm so used.

2. One Bail Off

If one bail is off, it shall be sufficient for the purpose of putting the wicket down to remove the remaining bail, or to strike or pull any of the three stumps out of the ground in any of the ways stated in 1 above.

3. All the Stumps Out of the Ground

If all the stumps are out of the ground, the fielding side shall be allowed to put back one or more stumps in order to have an opportunity of putting the wicket down.

4. Dispensing with Bails

If owing to the strength of the wind, it has been agreed to dispense with the bails in accordance with Law 8, Note (a) (Dispensing with Bails), the decision as to when the wicket is down is one for the umpires to decide on the facts before them. In such circumstances and if the umpires so decide, the wicket shall be held to be down even though a stump has not been struck out of the ground.

Note

> **(a) Remaking the Wicket**
> If the wicket is broken while the ball is in play, it is not the umpire's duty to remake the wicket until the ball has become dead – see Law 23 (Dead Ball). A member of the fielding side, however, may remake the wicket in such circumstances.

LAW 29.   BATSMAN OUT OF HIS GROUND

1. When out of his Ground

A batsman shall be considered to be out of his ground unless some part of his bat in his hand or of his person is grounded behind the line of the popping crease.

LAW 30.   BOWLED

1. Out Bowled

The striker shall be out *Bowled* if:

> (a) His wicket is bowled down, even if the ball first touches his bat or person.
>
> (b) He breaks his wicket by hitting or kicking the ball on to it before the completion of a stroke, or as a result of attempting to guard his wicket. See Law 34.1 (Out Hit the Ball Twice).

Note

> **(a) Out Bowled – Not lbw**
> The striker is out bowled if the ball is deflected on to his wicket even though a decision against him would be justified under Law 36 (lbw).

LAW 31.   TIMED OUT

1. Out Timed Out

An incoming batsman shall be out *Timed Out* if he wilfully takes more than two minutes to come in – the two minutes being timed from the moment a wicket falls until the new batsman steps on to the field of play.

If this is not complied with and if the umpire is satisfied that the delay was wilful and if an appeal is made, the new batsman shall be given out by the umpire at the bowler's end.

2. Time to be Added

The time taken by the umpires to investigate the cause of the delay shall be added at the normal close of play.

Notes

> **(a) Entry in Scorebook**
> The correct entry in the scorebook when a batsman is given out under this Law is "timed out", and the bowler does not get credit for the wicket.
>
> **(b) Batsmen Crossing on the Field of Play**
> It is an essential duty of the captains to ensure that the in-going batsman passes the out-going one before the latter leaves the field of play.

LAW 32. CAUGHT

1. Out Caught

The striker shall be out *Caught* if the ball touches his bat or if it touches below the wrist his hand or glove, holding the bat, and is subsequently held by a fieldsman before it touches the ground.

2. A Fair Catch

A catch shall be considered to have been fairly made if:
  (a) The fieldsman is within the field of play throughout the act of making the catch.

    (i) The act of making the catch shall start from the time when the fieldsman first handles the ball and shall end when he both retains complete control over the further disposal of the ball and remains within the field of play.

    (ii) In order to be within the field of play, the fieldsman may not touch or ground any part of his person on or over a boundary line. When the boundary is marked by a fence or board the fieldsman may not ground any part of his person over the boundary fence or board, but may touch or lean over the boundary fence or board in completing the catch.

  (b) The ball is hugged to the body of the catcher or accidentally lodges in his dress or, in the case of the wicket-keeper, in his pads. However, a striker may not be caught if a ball lodges in a protective helmet worn by a fieldsman, in which case the umpire shall call and signal "dead ball". See Law 23 (Dead Ball).

  (c) The ball does not touch the ground even though a hand holding it does so in effecting the catch.

  (d) A fieldsman catches the ball, after it has been lawfully played a second time by the striker, but only if the ball has not touched the ground since being first struck.

  (e) A fieldsman catches the ball after it has touched an umpire, another fieldsman or the other batsman. However, a striker may not be caught if a ball has touched a protective helmet worn by a fieldsman.

  (f) The ball is caught off an obstruction within the boundary provided it has not previously been agreed to regard the obstruction as a boundary.

3. Scoring of Runs

If a striker is caught, no run shall be scored.

Notes

(a) Scoring from an Attempted Catch
When a fieldsman carrying the ball touches or grounds any part of his person on or over a boundary marked by a line, 6 runs shall be scored.

(b) Ball Still in Play
If a fieldsman releases the ball before he crosses the boundary, the ball will be considered to be still in play and it may be caught by another fieldsman. However, if the original fieldsman returns to the field of play and handles the ball, a catch may not be made.

LAW 33. HANDLED THE BALL

1. Out Handled the Ball

Either batsman on appeal shall be out *Handled the Ball* if he wilfully touches the ball while in play with the hand not holding the bat unless he does so with the consent of the opposite side.

Note

(a) Entry in Scorebook
The correct entry in the scorebook when a batsman is given out under this Law is "handled the ball", and the bowler does not get credit for the wicket.

LAW 34.   HIT THE BALL TWICE

1. Out Hit the Ball Twice

The striker, on appeal, shall be out *Hit the Ball Twice* if, after the ball is struck or is stopped by any part of his person, he wilfully strikes it again with his bat or person except for the sole purpose of guarding his wicket: this he may do with his bat or any part of his person other than his hands, but see Law 37.2 (Obstructing a Ball From Being Caught).

For the purpose of this Law, a hand holding the bat shall be regarded as part of the bat.

2. Returning the Ball to a Fieldsman

The striker, on appeal, shall be out under this Law if, without the consent of the opposite side, he uses his bat or person to return the ball to any of the fielding side.

3. Runs from Ball Lawfully Struck Twice

No runs except those which result from an overthrow or penalty – see Law 41 (The Fieldsman) – shall be scored from a ball lawfully struck twice.

Notes

(a) Entry in Scorebook
The correct entry in the scorebook when the striker is given out under this Law is "hit the ball twice", and the bowler does not get credit for the wicket.

(b) Runs Credited to the Batsman
Any runs awarded under 3 above as a result of an overthrow or penalty shall be credited to the striker, provided the ball in the first instance has touched the bat, or, if otherwise, as extras.

LAW 35.   HIT WICKET

1. Out Hit Wicket

The striker shall be out *Hit Wicket* if, while the ball is in play:

(a) His wicket is broken with any part of his person, dress, or equipment as a result of any action taken by him in preparing to receive or in receiving a delivery, or in setting off for his first run, immediately after playing, or playing at, the ball.

(b) He hits down his wicket whilst lawfully making a second stroke for the purpose of guarding his wicket within the provisions of Law 34.1 (Out Hit the Ball Twice).

Notes

(a) Not Out Hit Wicket
A batsman is not out under this Law should his wicket be broken in any of the ways referred to in 1(a) above if:
(i) It occurs while he is in the act of running, other than in setting off for his first run immediately after playing at the ball, or while he is avoiding being run out or stumped.
(ii) The bowler after starting his run-up or bowling action does not deliver the ball; in which case the umpire shall immediately call and signal "dead ball".
(iii) It occurs whilst he is avoiding a throw-in at any time.

LAW 36. LEG BEFORE WICKET

1. Out lbw

The striker shall be out *lbw* in the circumstances set out below:

(a) Striker Attempting to Play the Ball
The striker shall be out lbw if he first intercepts with any part of his person, dress or equipment a fair ball which would have hit the wicket and which has not previously touched his bat or a hand holding the bat, provided that:

(i) The ball pitched in a straight line between wicket and wicket or on the off side of the striker's wicket, or in the case of a ball intercepted full pitch would have pitched in a straight line between wicket and wicket; and

(ii) The point of impact is in a straight line between wicket and wicket, even if above the level of the bails.

(b) Striker Making No Attempt to Play the Ball
The striker shall be out lbw even if the ball is intercepted outside the line of the off stump if, in the opinion of the umpire, he has made no genuine attempt to play the ball with his bat, but has intercepted the ball with some part of his person and if the circumstances set out in (a) above apply.

LAW 37. OBSTRUCTING THE FIELD

1. Wilful Obstruction

Either batsman, on appeal, shall be out *Obstructing the Field* if he wilfully obstructs the opposite side by word or action.

2. Obstructing a Ball From Being Caught

The striker, on appeal, shall be out should wilful obstruction by either batsman prevent a catch being made.

This shall apply even though the striker causes the obstruction in lawfully guarding his wicket under the provisions of Law 34. See Law 34.1 (Out Hit the Ball Twice).

Notes

(a) Accidental Obstruction
The umpires must decide whether the obstruction was wilful or not. The accidental interception of a throw-in by a batsman while running does not break this Law.

(b) Entry in Scorebook
The correct entry in the scorebook when a batsman is given out under this Law is "obstructing the field", and the bowler does not get credit for the wicket.

LAW 38. RUN OUT

1. Out Run Out

Either batsman shall be out *Run Out* if in running or at any time while the ball is in play – except in the circumstances described in Law 39 (Stumped) – he is out of his ground and his wicket is put down by the opposite side. If, however, a batsman in running makes good his ground he shall not be out run out if he subsequently leaves his ground, in order to avoid injury, and the wicket is put down.

2. "No-ball" Called

If a no-ball has been called, the striker shall not be given run out unless he attempts to run.

3. Which Batsman Is Out

If the batsmen have crossed in running, he who runs for the wicket which is put down shall be out; if they have not crossed, he who has left the wicket which is put down shall be out. If a batsman remains in his ground or returns to his ground and the other batsman joins him there, the latter shall be out if his wicket is put down.

4. Scoring of Runs

If a batsman is run out, only that run which is being attempted shall not be scored. If, however, an injured striker himself is run out, no runs shall be scored. See Law 2.7 (Transgression of the Laws by an Injured Batsman or Runner).

Notes

(a) Ball Played on to Opposite Wicket
If the ball is played on to the opposite wicket, neither batsman is liable to be run out unless the ball has been touched by a fieldsman before the wicket is broken.

(b) Entry in Scorebook
The correct entry in the scorebook when a batsman is given out under this Law is "run out", and the bowler does not get credit for the wicket.

LAW 39.   STUMPED

1. Out Stumped

The striker shall be out *Stumped* if, in receiving the ball, not being a no-ball, he is out of his ground otherwise than in attempting a run and the wicket is put down by the wicket-keeper without the intervention of another fieldsman.

2. Action by the Wicket-keeper

The wicket-keeper may take the ball in front of the wicket in an attempt to stump the striker only if the ball has touched the bat or person of the striker.

Note

(a) Ball Rebounding from Wicket-keeper's Person
The striker may be out stumped if, in the circumstances stated in 1 above, the wicket is broken by a ball rebounding from the wicket-keeper's person or equipment or is kicked or thrown by the wicket-keeper on to the wicket.

LAW 40.   THE WICKET-KEEPER

1. Position of Wicket-keeper

The wicket-keeper shall remain wholly behind the wicket until a ball delivered by the bowler touches the bat or person of the striker, or passes the wicket, or until the striker attempts a run.

In the event of the wicket-keeper contravening this Law, the umpire at the striker's end shall call and signal "no ball" at the instant of delivery or as soon as possible thereafter.

2. Restriction on Actions of the Wicket-keeper

If the wicket-keeper interferes with the striker's right to play the ball and to guard his wicket, the striker shall not be out except under Laws 33 (Handled the Ball), 34 (Hit the Ball Twice), 37 (Obstructing the Field), 38 (Run Out).

3. Interference with the Wicket-keeper by the Striker

If in the legitimate defence of his wicket, the striker interferes with the wicket-keeper, he shall not be out, except as provided for in Law 37.2 (Obstructing a Ball From Being Caught).

LAW 41.   THE FIELDSMAN

1. Fielding the Ball

The fieldsman may stop the ball with any part of his person, but if he wilfully stops it otherwise, 5 runs shall be added to the run or runs already scored; if no run has been scored 5 penalty runs shall be awarded. The run in progress shall count provided that the batsmen have crossed at the instant of the act. If the ball has been struck, the penalty shall be added to the score of the striker, but otherwise to the scores of byes, leg-byes, no-balls or wides as the case may be.

2. Limitation of On-side Fieldsmen

The number of on-side fieldsmen behind the popping crease at the instant of the bowler's delivery shall not exceed two. In the event of infringement by the fielding side the umpire at the striker's end shall call and signal "no-ball" at the instant of delivery or as soon as possible thereafter.

3. Position of Fieldsmen

Whilst the ball is in play and until the ball has made contact with the bat or the striker's person or has passed his bat, no fieldsman, other than the bowler, may stand on or have any part of his person extended over the pitch (measuring 22 yards/20.12m × 10 feet/3.05m). In the event of a fieldsman contravening this Law, the umpire at the bowler's end shall call and signal "no-ball" at the instant of delivery or as soon as possible thereafter. See Law 40.1 (Position of Wicket-keeper).

Note

> (a) **Batsmen Changing Ends**
> The 5 runs referred to in 1 above are a penalty and the batsmen do not change ends solely by reason of this penalty.

LAW 42.   UNFAIR PLAY

1. Responsibility of Captains

The captains are responsible at all times for ensuring that play is conducted within the spirit of the game as well as within the Laws.

2. Responsibility of Umpires

The umpires are the sole judges of fair and unfair play.

3. Intervention by the Umpire

The umpires shall intervene without appeal by calling and signalling "dead ball" in the case of unfair play, but should not otherwise interfere with the progress of the game except as required to do so by the Laws.

4. Lifting the Seam

A player shall not lift the seam of the ball for any reason. Should this be done, the umpires shall change the ball for one of similar condition to that in use prior to the contravention. See Note (a).

5. Changing the Condition of the Ball

Any member of the fielding side may polish the ball provided that such polishing wastes no time and that no artificial substance is used. No-one shall rub the ball on the ground or use any artificial substance or take any other action to alter the condition of the ball.

In the event of a contravention of this Law, the umpires, after consultation, shall change the ball for one of similar condition to that in use prior to the contravention.

This Law does not prevent a member of the fielding side from drying a wet ball, or removing mud from the ball. See Note (b).

6. Incommoding the Striker

An umpire is justified in intervening under this Law and shall call and signal "dead ball" if, in his opinion, any player of the fielding side incommodes the striker by any noise or action while he is receiving the ball.

7. Obstruction of a Batsman in Running

It shall be considered unfair if any fieldsman wilfully obstructs a batsman in running. In these circumstances the umpire shall call and signal "dead ball" and allow any completed runs and the run in progress, or alternatively any boundary scored.

8. The Bowling of Fast Short-pitched Balls

The bowling of fast short-pitched balls is unfair if, in the opinion of the umpire at the bowler's end, it constitutes an attempt to intimidate the striker. See Note (d).

Umpires shall consider intimidation to be the deliberate bowling of fast short-pitched balls which by their length, height and direction are intended or likely to inflict physical injury on the striker. The relative skill of the striker shall also be taken into consideration.

In the event of such unfair bowling, the umpire at the bowler's end shall adopt the following procedure:

(a) In the first instance the umpire shall call and signal "no-ball", caution the bowler and inform the other umpire, the captain of the fielding side and the batsmen of what has occurred.

(b) If this caution is ineffective, he shall repeat the above procedure and indicate to the bowler that this is a final warning.

(c) Both the above caution and final warning shall continue to apply even though the bowler may later change ends.

(d) Should the above warnings prove ineffective the umpire at the bowler's end shall:

(i) At the first repetition call and signal "no-ball" and when the ball is dead direct the captain to take the bowler off forthwith and to complete the over with another bowler, provided that the bowler does not bowl two overs or part thereof consecutively. See Law 22.7 (Bowler Incapacitated or Suspended during an Over).

(ii) Not allow the bowler, thus taken off, to bowl again in the same innings.

(iii) Report the occurrence to the captain of the batting side as soon as the players leave the field for an interval.

(iv) Report the occurrence to the executive of the fielding side and to any governing body responsible for the match, who shall take any further action which is considered to be appropriate against the bowler concerned.

9. The Bowling of Fast High Full Pitches

The bowling of fast high full pitches is unfair. See Note (e).

In the event of such unfair bowling the umpire at the bowler's end shall adopt the procedures of caution, final warnings, action against the bowler and reporting as set out in 8 above.

10. Time Wasting

Any form of time wasting is unfair.

(a) In the event of the captain of the fielding side wasting time or allowing any member of his side to waste time, the umpire at the bowler's end shall adopt the following procedure:

    (i) In the first instance he shall caution the captain of the fielding side and inform the other umpire of what has occurred.

    (ii) If this caution is ineffective he shall repeat the above procedure and indicate to the captain that this is a final warning.

    (iii) The umpire shall report the occurrence to the captain of the batting side as soon as the players leave the field for an interval.

    (iv) Should the above procedure prove ineffective the umpire shall report the occurrence to the executive of the fielding side and to any governing body responsible for that match, who shall take appropriate action against the captain and the players concerned.

(b) In the event of a bowler taking unnecessarily long to bowl an over the umpire at the bowler's end shall adopt the procedures, other than the calling of "no-ball", of caution, final warning, action against the bowler and reporting.

(c) In the event of a batsman wasting time (See Note (f)) other than in the manner described in Law 31 (Timed Out), the umpire at the bowler's end shall adopt the following procedure:

    (i) In the first instance he shall caution the batsman and inform the other umpire at once, and the captain of the batting side, as soon as the players leave the field for an interval, of what has occurred.

    (ii) If this proves ineffective, he shall repeat the caution, indicate to the batsman that this is a final warning and inform the other umpire.

    (iii) The umpire shall report the occurrence to both captains as soon as the players leave the field for an interval.

    (iv) Should the above procedure prove ineffective, the umpire shall report the occurrence to the executive of the batting side and to any governing body responsible for that match, who shall take appropriate action against the player concerned.

11. Players Damaging the Pitch

The umpires shall intervene and prevent players from causing damage to the pitch which may assist the bowlers of either side. See Note (c).

(a) In the event of any member of the fielding side damaging the pitch, the umpire shall follow the procedure of caution, final warning, and reporting as set out in 10(a) above.

(b) In the event of a bowler contravening this Law by running down the pitch after delivering the ball, the umpire at the bowler's end shall first caution the bowler. If this caution is ineffective the umpire shall adopt the procedures as set out in 8 above other than the calling and signalling of "no-ball".

(c) In the event of a batsman damaging the pitch the umpire at the bowler's end shall follow the procedures of caution, final warning and reporting as set out in 10(c) above.

12. Batsman Unfairly Stealing a Run

Any attempt by the batsman to steal a run during the bowler's run-up is unfair. Unless the bowler attempts to run out either batsman – see Law 24.4 (Bowler Throwing at Striker's Wicket before Delivery) and Law 24.5 (Bowler Attempting to Run Out Non-striker before Delivery) – the umpire shall call and signal "dead ball" as soon as the batsmen cross in any such attempt to run. The batsmen shall then return to their original wickets.

13. Player's Conduct

In the event of a player failing to comply with the instructions of an umpire, criticising his decisions by word or action, or showing dissent, or generally behaving in a manner which might bring the game into disrepute, the umpire concerned shall, in the first place, report the matter to the other umpire and to the player's captain requesting the latter to take action. If this proves ineffective, the umpire shall report the incident as soon as possible to the executive of the player's team and to any governing body responsible for the match, who shall take any further action which is considered appropriate against the player or players concerned.

Notes

(a) The Condition of the Ball
Umpires shall make frequent and irregular inspections of the condition of the ball.

(b) Drying of a Wet Ball
A wet ball may be dried on a towel or with sawdust.

(c) Danger Area
The danger area on the pitch, which must be protected from damage by a bowler, shall be regarded by the umpires as the area contained by an imaginary line 4 feet/1.22m from the popping crease, and parallel to it, and within two imaginary and parallel lines drawn down the pitch from points on that line 1 foot/30.48cm on either side of the middle stump.

(d) Fast Short-pitched Balls
As a guide, a fast short-pitched ball is one which pitches short and passes, or would have passed, above the shoulder height of the striker standing in a normal batting stance at the crease.

(e) The Bowling of Fast Full Pitches
The bowling of one fast, high full pitch shall be considered to be unfair if, in the opinion of the umpire, it is deliberate, bowled at the striker, and if it passes or would have passed above the shoulder height of the striker when standing in a normal batting stance at the crease.

(f) Time Wasting by Batsmen
Other than in exceptional circumstances, the batsman should always be ready to take strike when the bowler is ready to start his run-up.

INTERNATIONAL CRICKET CONFERENCE

On June 15, 1909, representatives of cricket in England, Australia and South Africa met at Lord's and founded the Imperial Cricket Conference. Membership was confined to the governing bodies of cricket in countries within the British Commonwealth where Test cricket was played. India, New Zealand and West Indies were elected as members on May 31, 1926, Pakistan on July 21, 1953, and Sri Lanka on July 21, 1981. South Africa ceased to be a member of the ICC on leaving the British Commonwealth in May, 1961.

On July 15, 1965, the Conference was renamed the International Cricket Conference and new rules were adopted to permit the election of countries from outside the British Commonwealth.

CONSTITUTION

Chairman: The President of MCC for the time being or his nominee.
Secretary: The Secretary of MCC.
Foundation members: United Kingdom and Australia.
Full members: India, New Zealand, West Indies, Pakistan and Sri Lanka.
Associate members*: Argentina (1974), Bangladesh (1977), Bermuda (1966), Canada (1968), Denmark (1966), East Africa (1966), Fiji (1965), Gibraltar (1969), Hong Kong (1969), Israel (1974), Kenya (1981), Malaysia (1967), Netherlands (1966), Papua New Guinea (1973), Singapore (1974), USA (1965), West Africa (1976) and Zimbabwe (1981).
* *Year of election shown in parentheses.*

MEMBERSHIP

The following governing bodies for cricket shall be eligible for election.

Foundation Members: The governing bodies for cricket in the United Kingdom and Australia are known as Foundation Members, and while being Full Members of the Conference such governing bodies have certain additional rights as set out in the rules of the Conference.

Full Members: The governing body for cricket recognised by the Conference of a country, or countries associated for cricket purposes, of which the representative teams are accepted as qualified to play official Test matches.

Associate Members: The governing body for cricket recognised by the Conference of a country, or countries associated for cricket purposes, not qualifying as Full Members but where cricket is firmly established and organised.

Chairman: P. A. Snow (Fiji). *Deputy Chairman:* J. Buzaglo (Gibraltar). *Hon. Treasurer:* G. Davis (Israel).

TEST MATCHES

1. Duration of Test Matches

Within a maximum of 30 hours' playing time, the duration of Test matches shall be a matter for negotiation and agreement between the two countries in any particular series of Test matches.

When agreeing the Playing Conditions prior to the commencement of a Test series, the participating countries may:

(a) Extend the playing hours of the last Test beyond the limit of 30 hours, in a series in which, at the conclusion of the penultimate match, one side does not hold a lead of more than one match.

(b) Allow an extension of play by one hour on any of the first four days of a Test match, in the event of play being suspended for one hour or more on that day, owing to weather interference.

(c) Play on the rest day, conditions and circumstances permitting, should a full day's play be lost on either the second or third scheduled days of play.

(d) Make up time lost in excess of five minutes in each day's play owing to circumstances outside the game, other than acts of God.

Note. The umpires shall determine when such time shall be made up. This could, if conditions and circumstances permit, include the following day.

2. Qualification Rules

A cricketer is qualified to play in a Test match either by birth or residence.

(a) Qualification by birth. A cricketer, unless debarred by the Conference, is always eligible to play for the country of his birth.

(b) Qualification by residence. A cricketer, unless debarred by the Conference, shall be eligible to play for any country in which he is residing and has been residing during the four immediately preceding years, provided that he has not played for the country of his birth during that period.

Note. Notwithstanding anything hereinbefore contained, any player who has once played in a Test match for any country shall not afterwards be eligible to play in a Test match against that country, without the consent of its governing body.

FIRST-CLASS MATCHES

1. Definitions

(a) A match of three or more days' duration between two sides of eleven players officially adjudged first-class shall be regarded as a first-class fixture.

(b) In the following Rules the term "governing body" is restricted to Foundation Members, Full Members and Associate Members of the conference.

2. Rules

(a) Foundation and Full Members of the ICC shall decide the status of matches of three or more days' duration played in their countries.

(b) In matches of three or more days' duration played in countries which are not Foundation Members or Full Members of the ICC:

    (i) If the visiting team comes from a country which is a Foundation or Full Member of the ICC, that country shall decide the status of matches.

    (ii) If the visiting team does not come from a country which is a Foundation or Full Member of the ICC, or is a Commonwealth team composed of players from different countries, the ICC shall decide the status of matches.

Notes

(a) Governing bodies agree that the interest of first-class cricket will be served by ensuring that first-class status is *not* accorded to any match in which one or other of the teams taking part cannot on a strict interpretation of the definition be adjudged first-class.

(b) In case of any disputes arising from these Rules, the Secretary of the ICC shall refer the matter for decision to the Conference, failing unanimous agreement by postal communication being reached.

3. First-class Status

The following matches shall be regarded as first-class, subject to the provisions of Definitions (a) being completely complied with:

(a) In the British Isles and Eire

The following matches of three or more days' duration shall automatically be considered first-class:

    (i) County Championship matches.

    (ii) Official representative tourist matches from Full Member countries unless specifically excluded.

    (iii) MCC v any first-class county.

    (iv) Oxford v Cambridge and either University against first-class counties.

    (v) Scotland v Ireland.

(b) In Australia

    (i) Sheffield Shield matches.

    (ii) Matches played by teams representing states of the Commonwealth of Australia between each other or against opponents adjudged first-class.

(c) In India

    (i) Ranji Trophy matches.

    (ii) Duleep Trophy matches.

    (iii) Irani Trophy matches.

    (iv) Matches played by teams representing state or regional associations affiliated to the Board of Control between each other or against opponents adjudged first-class.

    (v) All three-day matches played against representative visiting sides.

(d) In New Zealand

    (i) Shell Trophy matches.

    (ii) Matches played by teams representing provinces or the North or South Islands between each other or against opponents adjudged first-class.

(e) In Pakistan

    (i) Matches played by teams representing divisional associations affiliated to the Board of Control, between each other or against teams adjudged first-class.

    (ii) Matches between the divisional associations and the Universities past and present XI.

    (iii) Quaid-e-Azam Trophy matches.

    (iv) BCCP Trophy Tournament matches.

    (v) Pentangular Trophy Tournament matches.

(f) In Sri Lanka

    (i) Matches of three days or more against touring sides adjudged first-class.

    At the time of going to press details of domestic competitions with first-class status were not available.

(g) In West Indies

    (i) Matches played by teams representing Barbados, Guyana, Jamaica, Trinidad, the Windward Islands and the Leeward Islands, either for the Shell Shield or against other opponents adjudged first-class.

    (ii) The final of the inter-county tournament for the Jones Cup in Guyana between Berbice, Demerara and Essequibo.

(h) In all Foundation (including South Africa) and Full Member countries represented on the Conference

    (i) Test matches and matches against teams adjudged first-class played by official touring teams.

    (ii) Official Test Trial matches.

    (iii) Special matches between teams adjudged first-class by the governing body or bodies concerned.

MAIN RULES AND PLAYING CONDITIONS OF LIMITED-OVERS COMPETITIONS

The following rules, playing conditions and variations of the Laws of Cricket are common to all three county competitions – the Benson and Hedges Cup (55 overs a side), the NatWest Bank Trophy (60 overs) and the John Player League (40 overs):

Status of Matches

Matches shall not be considered first-class.

Declarations

No declarations may be made at any time.

Restriction on Placement of Fieldsmen

At the instant of delivery a minimum of four fieldsmen (plus the bowler and wicket-keeper) must be within an area bounded by two semi-circles centred on each middle stump (each with a radius of 30 yards) and joined by a parallel line on each side of the pitch. In the event of an infringement, the square-leg umpire shall call "No-ball". The fielding circle should be marked by painted white "dots" at five-yard intervals.

Fieldsman Leaving the Field

In addition to Law 2.8, a player who suffers an injury caused by an external blow (e.g. not a pulled muscle) and has to leave the field for medical attention may bowl immediately on his return.

Mode of Delivery

No bowler may deliver the ball under-arm.

Limitation of Overs by Any One Bowler

No bowler may deliver more than one fifth of the allocated overs.

Wide-ball – Judging a Wide

Umpires are instructed to apply a very strict and consistent interpretation in regard to the Law in order to prevent negative bowling wide of the wicket or over the batsman's head.

The following criteria should be adopted as a guide to umpires:

1. If the ball passes either side of the wicket sufficiently wide to make it virtually impossible for the striker to play a "normal cricket stroke" both from where he is standing and from where he should normally be standing at the crease, the umpire shall call and signal "Wide".

2. If the ball passes over head-height of the striker standing upright at the crease, the umpire shall call and signal "Wide".

Note: The above provisions do not apply if the striker makes contact with the ball.

RULES COMMON TO THE BENSON AND HEDGES CUP AND THE NATWEST BANK TROPHY

The Result

1. A Tie.

In the event of a tie, the following shall apply:
    (i) The side taking the greater number of wickets shall be the winner.

(ii) If both sides are all out, the side with the higher overall scoring-rate shall be the winner.

(iii) If the result cannot be decided by either of the first two methods, the winner shall be the side with the higher rate after 30 overs or, if still equal, after twenty or, if still equal, after ten.

2. Unfinished Match

If a match remains unfinished after the allocated number of days, the winner shall be the side which has scored the faster in runs per over throughout the innings, provided that at least twenty overs have been bowled at the side batting second. If the scoring-rate is the same, the side losing fewer wickets in the first twenty overs of each innings shall be the winner.

If, however, at any time on the last day the umpires are satisfied that there is insufficient time remaining to achieve a definite result or, where applicable, for the side batting second to complete its 60 overs, they shall order a new match to be started, allowing an equal number of overs per side (minimum ten overs per side) bearing in mind the time remaining for play until scheduled close of play. In this event, team selection for the new match will be restricted to the eleven players and twelfth man originally chosen, unless authorised otherwise in advance by the Secretary of the Board.

In the event of no result being obtained within this rule, and the captains being unable to reach agreement on an alternative method of achieving a result, other than re-arranging the match, it shall be decided by the toss of a coin, except in a Benson and Hedges zonal match which shall be declared to have "No Result".

RULES AND PLAYING CONDITIONS APPLYING ONLY TO THE BENSON AND HEDGES CUP

Duration of Play

The matches, of 55 overs per side, will be completed in one day, if possible, but two days will be allocated for zonal league matches and three days for knockout matches in case of weather interference. Matches started on Saturday but not completed may only be continued on Sunday with the approval of the Board.

Normal hours will be 11 a.m. to 7.30 p.m. (start at 2 p.m. on Sundays). The umpires may order extra time if they consider a finish can be obtained on any day, or in order to give the team batting second an opportunity to complete twenty overs.

Intervals

Lunch 1.15-1.55. The tea interval in an uninterrupted match will be taken at 4.30 or after 25 overs of the innings of the side batting second, whichever is the later. In a match which has had a delayed start or which is unlikely to be finished in a day, the tea interval will be at 4.30.

Qualification of Players

The University qualification will take precedence in respect of those players who are also qualified for county clubs and no cricketer may play for more than one team in the same year's competition.

Scoring System

In the zonal league matches the winning team scores two points. In a "no result" match each side scores one point.

If two or more teams in any zone finish with an equal number of points, their position in the table shall be based on the faster rate of taking wickets in all zonal league matches. This is calculated by total balls bowled, divided by wickets taken.

RULES AND PLAYING CONDITIONS APPLYING ONLY TO THE NATWEST BANK TROPHY

Duration and hours of play

The matches, of 60 overs per side, will be completed in one day, if possible, but three days (four days, if Sunday play is scheduled) will be allocated in case of weather interference.

Cup Final only: If the match starts not less than half an hour late, owing to weather or the state of the ground, and not more than one and a half hours late, each innings shall be limited to 50 overs. If, however, the start is delayed for more than one and a half hours, the 60-over limit shall apply.

Normal hours will be 10.30-7.30. The umpires may order extra time if, in their opinion, a finish can be obtained on any day or in order to give the team batting second an opportunity to complete twenty overs.

The captains of the teams in the final shall be warned that heavy shadows may move across the pitch towards the end of the day and that no appeal against the light will be considered in such circumstances.

RULES AND PLAYING CONDITIONS APPLYING ONLY TO THE JOHN PLAYER LEAGUE

Hours of play

All matches shall commence at 2 p.m. with a tea interval of fifteen minutes at the end of the over in progress at 4.15, or between innings, whichever is the earlier. The duration and time of the tea interval can be varied in the case of an interrupted match. Close of play shall normally be at 6.45 p.m. but play may continue after that time if, in the opinion of the umpires, the overs remaining can be completed by 7 p.m.

Length of Innings

(i) In an uninterrupted match:
    (a) Each side shall bat for 40 overs unless all out earlier.
    (b) If the side fielding first fails to bowl 40 overs by 4.15 p.m., the over shall be completed and the side batting second shall receive the same number of overs as their opponents.
    (c) If the team batting first is all out within two minutes of the scheduled time for the tea interval, the innings of the side batting second shall be limited to the same number of overs as their opponents have received, the over in which the last wicket falls to count as a complete over.
(ii) In matches where the start is delayed or play is suspended:
    (a) The object shall be to rearrange the number of overs so that both teams may receive the same number of overs (minimum ten each). The calculation of the overs to be bowled shall be based on an average rate of eighteen overs per hour (one over per 3⅓ minutes or part thereof) in the time remaining before 6.45 p.m.
    (b) If the start is delayed by not more than an hour and the match is thereby reduced to no fewer than 31 overs a side, the time of the close of the first innings shall be fixed allowing 3⅓ minutes for each over.
    (c) If, owing to a suspension of play during the innings of the team batting second, it is not possible for that team to have the opportunity of batting for the same number of overs as their opponents, they will bat for a number of overs to be calculated as above. The team batting second shall not bat for a greater number of overs than their opponents unless the latter have been all out in fewer than the agreed number of overs.

The Result

(i) A result can only be achieved if both teams have batted for at least ten overs, unless one team has been all out in fewer than ten overs or unless the team batting second scores enough runs to win in fewer than ten overs.
(ii) Where both sides have had the opportunity to bat for the same number of overs and the scores are level, the result is a tie, no account being taken of the number of wickets which have fallen.

(iii) If, owing to suspension of play, the number of overs in the innings of the side batting second has to be revised, their target score, which they must exceed to win the match, shall be calculated by multiplying the revised number of overs by the average runs per over scored by the side batting first. If the target score involves a fraction, the final scores cannot be equal and the result cannot be a tie.

(iv) If a match is abandoned before the side batting second has received its allotted number of overs, the result shall be decided on the average run-rate throughout both innings.

(v) If the team batting first has been all out without using its full quota of overs, the calculation of the run-rate shall be based on the full quota of overs to which it was entitled.

Scoring of points

(i) The team winning a match to score four points.
(ii) In a "tie" each team to score two points.
(iii) In a "No Result" match each team to score two points.
(iv) If two or more teams finish with an equal number of points, their final positions will be decided by:
(a) The most wins or, if still equal
(b) The most away wins or, if still equal
(c) The higher run-rate throughout the season.

CAREER FIGURES OF PLAYERS RETIRING OR NOT RETAINED

BATTING

	M	I	NO	R	HI	100s	Avge	1,000 r in season
B. F. Davison ...	415	680	64	24,608	189	47	33.94	13
A. J. Hignell	170	289	36	7,459	149*	1	29.48	3
A. Jones	645	1,168	72	36,049	204*	56	32.89	23
T. M. Lamb......	160	163	61	1,274	77	–	12.49	–
D. Lloyd..........	407	652	74	19,269	241*	38	33.33	11
S. Oldham........	119	90	37	555	50	–	10.47	–
P. R. Oliver	89	128	20	2,679	171*	2	24.80	–
S. P. Perryman..	156	162	68	872	43	–	9.27	–
J. W. Southern..	164	179	71	1,653	61*	–	15.30	–
R. W. Tolchard.	483	680	189	15,288	126*	12	31.31	–
C. J. Tunnicliffe	150	176	30	2,092	91	–	14.32	–
B. Wood..........	357	591	75	17,453	198	30	33.82	8

BOWLING AND FIELDING

	R	W	Avge	BB	5 W/i	10 W/m	Ct	St
B. F. Davison ...	2,635	82	32.13	5–32	1	–	312	–
A. J. Hignell	230	3	76.66	2–13	–	–	150	–
A. Jones	333	3	111.00	1–24	–	–	288	–
T. M. Lamb......	10,459	361	28.97	7–56	10	–	40	–
D. Lloyd..........	7,172	237	30.26	7–38	–	–	334	–
S. Oldham........	8,114	251	32.32	7–78	4	–	32	–
P. R. Oliver	2,115	27	78.33	2–28	–	–	46	–
S. P. Perryman..	11,337	358	31.66	7–49	19	3	58	–
J. W. Southern..	12,283	412	29.81	6–46	17	–	59	–
R. W. Tolchard.	34	1	34.00	1–4	–	–	913	125
C. J. Tunnicliffe	10,265	319	32.17	7–36	6	–	65	–
B. Wood..........	9,160	298	30.73	7–52	8	–	283	–

Note: Although B. F. Davison will no longer play county cricket, he hopes to continue playing in the Sheffield Shield.

MEETINGS IN 1983

TCCB SPRING MEETING

At their Spring Meeting, held at Lord's on March 8, the TCCB accepted the recommendation of the cricket sub-committee that there should be a voluntary code of conduct relating to appealing, to apply in all English domestic first-class cricket. Concern had been growing at the level of appealing and the extra pressure which this placed upon umpires. Although no sanctions were to be imposed, players would be expected in 1983 to observe the following formula: for catches at the wicket and lbws only the bowler and the wicket-keeper would be expected to appeal; for other close catches only the bowler, the wicket-keeper and the catcher concerned; for run-outs only the fielder involved and others with a clear view of the incident. The measure had the support of the players themselves through the Cricketers Association. (On April 15 the idea was abandoned, following the normal pre-season meeting of county captains, who considered that it would be very difficult to implement and was also unnecessary.)

It was announced that New Zealand, having hinted previously that they would be agreeable to a minimum of 100 overs in a day's play in the Test series in England in 1983, had declined in the end to accept a figure of more than 96. The two countries had agreed to a limit, in the same series, of one bouncer an over. Counties were reminded that all groundsmen must aim to produce pitches that were "completely dry, firm and true, providing pace and an even bounce throughout a match". Interference with a groundsman's pitch preparation would not be tolerated. The Board selectors for 1983 would be P. B. H. May (chairman), A. V. Bedser, P. J. Sharpe and A. C. Smith. Sharpe replaced N. Gifford, who was not available. F. G. Mann's successor as chairman of the TCCB, to take over in October, would be C. H. Palmer (nominated by Nottinghamshire), who was elected after a ballot in which R. Subba Row (proposed by Surrey) was the other candidate.

INTERNATIONAL CRICKET CONFERENCE

As in 1982, no hearing was given to the delegates of the South African Cricket Union, who were in London at the time, when the International Cricket Conference held their annual meeting at Lord's on June 29 and 30. The SACU had applied for readmission to the Conference, if only as "non-playing" members. The South African Cricket Board, a splinter group from the SACU with a membership mainly of Indian and Cape Coloured cricketers, also had an application for a hearing turned down. To such an extent did the question of South Africa, and of past and future "rebel" tours to that country, dominate the Conference that the atmosphere surrounding it was more that of a political convention than a cricket meeting. Mr J. A. Bailey, secretary of the ICC, spoke afterwards of attitudes having, if anything, "hardened" towards South Africa.

A move to ban under-arm bowling was rejected, as was a proposal by the United Kingdom that bouncers in Test cricket should be limited to one an over. The idea that a code of conduct should apply in Test cricket was accepted, but only in so far as it should be something for each country to enforce unilaterally. The 1983 Prudential World Cup having just been successfully completed, tenders were sought from member countries wishing to stage the next such competition. These were called for by the end of 1983. In future a batsman's runner must wear exactly the same equipment as the batsman himself, a helmet included. More far-reachingly, it was proposed, and is likely to be accepted at the Conference's next meeting, that bowlers should be debited with the wides and no-balls they bowl. This means that a bowler, rather than being able to bowl a maiden over in which there might be several no-balls or wides, would in future have these charged to his analysis.

TCCB SPECIAL GENERAL MEETING

On November 9 the Board met in an unsuccessful attempt to revise the qualification regulations relating to players from overseas. The regulation, agreed in 1978 and aimed at reducing all counties within a reasonably short time to one such player, was considered to be taking effect too slowly. But all proposals were heavily defeated and the matter was deferred to the main winter meeting. The Board's executive committee suggested a restriction to one overseas player per county from 1985, with the exception of Somerset, who had I. V. A. Richards and J. Garner under contract until 1986. This proposal fell a long way short of receiving the required two-thirds majority. Kent's proposal, along Board executive lines but without the Somerset clause, came closer to success. Glamorgan and Gloucestershire proposed an earlier restriction to one overseas player, starting either immediately or, at the latest, at the end of the 1984 season. Warwickshire and Hampshire moved that long-serving overseas players be exempt from any new legislation. Support for both amendments was inadequate, and the balance of overseas players among the counties was enough to show why agreement is unlikely. Seven counties could play two such men, while the others were restricted to one, though Yorkshire, by tradition, chose to have none.

TCCB WINTER MEETING

At the Board's Winter Meeting, held at Lord's on December 13, it was decided to end the experimental rule, which had applied in domestic first-class cricket in England since 1979, that only one bouncer an over be allowed. England's Test batsmen felt that this was handicapping them when they played in Australia and West Indies where short-pitched bowling abounds. Before the start of the 1984 season umpires would be instructed that the law as it relates to intent and intimidation must be strictly enforced. Rather than the system of fines (see page 337) for slow over-rates, which had been introduced into the County Championship in 1978, it was agreed that a minimum of 117 overs (eighteen an hour) must in future be bowled in an uninterrupted day's play. County captains had been in favour of this. In 1984 West Indies would be asked to agree to a minimum of 96 overs a day (sixteen an hour) in the Test series against England. A further abortive attempt was made to bring forward the time when no county shall be allowed to include in the same side more than one player not qualified for England. The Board's executive committee proposed this time that 1985 should be the last season when two such players could appear in the same county side. Although ten of the counties were in favour of this and only seven against, that did not amount to the two-thirds majority required. It was decided to ask the TCCB's registration committee to reappraise the rules governing qualification for England, with special reference to players born and brought up in South Africa. The case of the Guyana-born Surrey batsman, M. A. Lynch, who was currently in South Africa with an unofficial West Indian side, was considered, with particular regard to his status as an England-qualified player. Although, having sought legal advice, the Board accepted that his status would be unaffected, he was to be asked to appear before them on his return from South Africa.

The County Championship, under the recently acquired sponsorship of the Britannic Assurance Company, would be played under an unchanged format (24 three-day matches), anyway until the end of the 1985 season. There might be changes in 1986. These could conceivably involve a system of promotion and relegation, with the Championship being divided into two halves. Northumberland and Durham (jointly) and Shropshire had made approaches about joining the Championship and been asked to conduct "feasibility studies". In theory, the idea was well received. A proposal that in the Benson and Hedges Cup three bowlers should be allowed fifteen overs each and that in a full innings of 55 overs only four bowlers, rather than five, need bowl, was turned down. However, in both the Benson and Hedges Cup and the NatWest Bank Trophy counties were to be urged to bowl their overs more expeditiously, so as to reduce the chances of the side batting second being handicapped by fading light. It was announced that in 1985 two of the six Test matches against Australia, rather than the traditional one, would be played at Lord's, owing to the revenue factor.

CRICKET BOOKS, 1983

The 79 titles sent for review in this year included an impressive proportion of the authoritative and the distinguished, the original and the valuable. Over the years since these surveys began, in the Almanack for 1950, the advance has not been made only on the highest plane. Most convincingly there has been a lifting of the popular level of cricket books quite remarkable within a span of 30 years.

There have been previous attempts, at book length and within wider studies, to make some evaluation of cricket art. In the past, though, they have been by writers whose particular field was cricket rather than art. Now, however, in *The Art of Cricket* (Secker & Warburg; £15) Robin Simon, formerly lecturer in the History of Art at Nottingham University, and Professor Alastair Smart of the Edinburgh College of Art and the Institute of Fine Arts in New York, but both cricket enthusiasts, have collaborated in a study based on expert knowledge of the artistic side of the subject.

This evaluation has two important aspects. In the first place, it points out that some of the best-known cricket works, including several at Lord's, are either copies or simple fakes. Then, on that side it proceeds to trace the development of cricket art from medieval stained glass, by way of the "conversation" pieces, J. M. W. Turner and Camille Pissaro, to the present-day Lawrence Toynbee.

The 145 illustrations (32 in colour) include much that will be fresh to the general cricket follower who has had little opportunity to see cricket pictures in any number except in the major pavilions, especially Lord's, the Hutchinson exhibition (many of its items later went to Lord's) and the collection in the Piccadilly pub called "The Yorker" which seems now, disappointingly, to have disappeared. The reproductions here, gathered from general and private collections, make a most illuminating display.

If the work is to be faulted it is for its scant attention to the work in lithography of J. C. Anderson and C. J. Basébé, as well as the Staffordshire figures of the same period, which represent the best of popular art in cricket. Otherwise the authors have worked thoroughly in their chosen field. The book does, though, prompt the idea of a study of cricket photography.

Australian Cricket (Hodder & Stoughton; £15.95) by Jack Pollard fills one of the few remaining major gaps in cricket literature. A. G. Moyes's *Australian Cricket* (1959) emphasised the need for a more detailed history of cricket there. Now Jack Pollard, after his preliminary studies in compiling *Six and Out*, has produced a definitive history in a form which will allow convenient expansion to keep it up to date. The method is alphabetical – from "Abandoned Matches" to "Zimbulis, Anthony George" – but with major sections on England *versus* Australia, West Indies *versus* Australia, and so on. The method is particularly valuable in handling the wealth of biographical material, including generous portrait illustration and the – perhaps unnecessary – inclusion of players' nicknames. The statistics are careful, so far as can be ascertained, accurate, and illuminate – but do not overwhelm – the rest of the information. The book runs to 1,162 pages and sticks admirably and economically to its subject except, perhaps, in reprinting the Laws of Cricket complete. That, though, is a minor flaw in what now takes its place as one of the two or three major works of cricket reference.

Also outstanding, though in a different style, is *Patrons, Players and the Crowd* (Orient Longman; available from the author: School of History, University of NSW, Kensington, NSW 2033, Australia; 194pp, \$A20 airmail, \$A16 surface mail) by Richard Cashman, which is sub-titled "The Phenomenon of Indian Cricket". Dr Cashman is an Australian; researcher and teacher of modern Indian history at the University of New South Wales; while, as a cricketer, he has played for Elphinstone College, Bombay, and for New South Wales. His book is not a study of cricket which looks no further than the playing of the game. He begins his preface with the essential basis of the work: "Cricket enjoys, and has enjoyed for some time, a unique status in Indian society. This book explores some of the groups who have had a stake in the game and who have developed the cricketing tradition of the country." That tradition, of course, is quite different from that of English, Australian or, indeed, of any other country's cricket. Most significantly, a major chapter – 33 pages – is devoted to "The Crowd" which has been such an important formative factor there. The result is a work of considerable social significance which will prove unusually illuminating to non-Indians and, one may suspect, to many Indians also.

Vijay Merchant, as knowledgeable as any on Indian cricket, and not given to extravagance, makes it clear in his foreword that he believes Dr Cashman has succeeded in both his examination and exposition. The research has obviously been extremely thorough; and the facts are illuminated by a true sympathy with the Indian mind. It is significant that the University of New South Wales provided some financial backing for the publication, for it is an important contribution to international understanding on a theme which occupies the interest and attention of so many members of the Commonwealth. Dr Cashman's study is entitled to a place in even the smallest and most selective cricket library.

The Pakistan Book of Test Cricket (from Abid Ali Kazi, 5A 11/1, Sunset Lane, Phase II, Defence Housing Society, Karachi, Pakistan; 45 rupees) by Abid Ali Kazi and Masood Hamid is a complete statistical record. It contains scoresheets and reports for the 123 Test matches played by Pakistan between the fixture with India at Delhi in October 1952 and that with England at Headingley in August 1982. There is a substantial – 67 page – appendix which includes the main records and individual career figures.

One of the most important advances in cricket writing since 1945 has undoubtedly been made in the field of statistics. *The Guinness Book of Cricket Facts and Feats* (Guinness Superlatives; £8.95) by Bill Frindall is an indication of that progress. Mr Frindall is the author of *The Wisden Book of Cricket Records* and of *The Wisden Book of Test Cricket*, yet his acknowledgements of those who checked his figures in this book emphasises his enduring concern with accuracy. As indication of his thoroughness, the index includes the birth and death dates, where ascertainable, of the cricketers mentioned. This is not quite like any other book of cricket statistics. Divided into sections on Test cricket; first-class play in Britain, Australia, South Africa, West Indies, New Zealand, India and Pakistan; first-class career records; women's cricket; limited-overs play, and minor cricket, it is, quite unusually in its kind, compellingly readable; to check on a single fact is to read on for page after page, diverted as well as informed. Without departing from his purpose, Mr Frindall drops in such intriguing facts as the only animal to be accorded an

obituary entry in *Wisden* and the only Test cricketer to climb Mount Kilimanjaro – twice.

The Hamlyn A-Z of Cricket Records (Hamlyn; £7.95) is by another established cricket statistician, Peter Wynne-Thomas. His alphabetically arranged material, complete to September 1981, includes potted scores of all Test matches; County Championship and Sheffield Shield tables; winners of other domestic competitions, and the major English leagues; statistical histories of the counties, figures for the limited-overs competitions. It is a most solid work of reference.

In *The Book of One-Day Internationals* (Stanley Paul; £7.95) the diligent David Lemmon provides scores and notes on the 157 matches to August 31, 1982, and summarised scores of the further 27 played to March 21, 1983; i.e. all to the commencement of the 1983 World Cup. The first limited-overs competition between sides of first-class standing (Gillette Cup) began only in 1963; the first at international level in 1971.

The indefatigable R. S. Whitington has compiled *Australians Abroad* (Five Mile Press; distributed by William Collins; $A16.95), a record of all the overseas Test matches played by Australia up to April 1983. Within 476 pages, he has included the complete scorecard and an account of every one of those matches; averages for each series; and, at the end, the career Test averages, home and away, of all the Australian cricketers concerned.

All in a Day (Robin Clark; £8.95) by Mihir Bose, is an historical survey of the limited-overs game. It traces its development from the early broadcasts of the International Cavaliers matches, through the growth of the English one-day competitions and the international "World Series" promotions of the Packer organisation, to its eventual establishment acceptance in the form of the World Cup. Conscientiously researched, well set out, and smoothly narrated, it is a worthwhile exercise; and, as well as relevant illustrations, he has provided an excellent statistical appendix.

It must appear a truism that most cricket books are written by cricket writers. From time to time, however, authors with reputations outside the game enter its relatively limited field. In 1979, Geoffrey Moorhouse published *The Best Loved Game*, a survey of cricket at all levels in England, which won the Cricket Society's Literary Award. His wider – and considerable – reputation depends upon his analysis of places and institutions, and the rare capacity to set them in true perspective. He has brought precisely that capacity to *Lord's* (Hodder & Stoughton; £9.95), a study, in some depth, of MCC, the great Test ground, Middlesex County Club, and the entire pattern of the government and economy of cricket. He was characteristically determined not to write without adequate access to the information needed. Required to appear before the General Purposes Committee of MCC with his request, as a result, he relates, he "spent a couple of years, on and off, enjoying the facilities and pleasures of Lord's to a degree that no complete outsider will have done before". He had undertaken to submit his manuscript for examination; and accepted the – helpful – official correction of errors of fact. He felt unable, however, to suppress a passage – the accuracy of which was not questioned – in order to spare MCC embarrassment. As a by-product of his book he was clearly left with an impression of the fairness and dignity of the club. His book is the best examination of the subject ever written; a model of its kind, which ought to be compulsory reading for all concerned

with the administration of the game, and all who wish to understand it.

The Way to Lord's (Collins Willow; £8.95), selected and introduced by Marcus Williams, is a quite different, but nevertheless absorbing, study. It is a collection of letters to *The Times* on cricket – which produces more correspondence to the paper than all other sports put together. As John Woodcock points out in his foreword, if a team were picked from all the correspondents – who include sixteen England captains – and W. G. Grace were to open the innings, there would be a choice from twelve other England opening batsmen to go in with him. The choice of letters represents various views on the cancelled South African tour, overseas players, the "new" lbw law, one-day cricket, over-rates, intimidatory bowling, the Packer affair and most of the other controversies the game has known. There are, too, splendid dashes of humour, some true illumination of cricket history, and astute pieces of argument. Not all the contributors, though, are eminent in the game; for instance, the names of "A Grandmother" and the sage "X.Y.Z." are not revealed; while Lewis Carroll, who can hardly rank as a player, is quoted as saying that, having been put on to bowl, he delivered a ball which "I was told, had it gone far enough, would have been a wide".

As I Said at the Time (Collins Willow; £14.95) by E. W. Swanton is, in effect, a history of post-1945 cricket as seen by the well-known and respected correspondent of *The Daily Telegraph*. Widely experienced – he covered 270 Test matches in England and overseas – since his "retirement" in 1975 he has observed, and commented on, the cricket scene as editorial director of *The Cricketer*. He was always an utterly conscientious watcher and reporter of any match. His standards were always high; he explains here that he has deliberately excluded mention of two Australian cricketers – "the reader must draw his own conclusions as to my reasons". Even at 542 pages, this collection represents only a fraction of his journalistic output. Apart from its soundness and thoroughness, it is impressive for the fact that he has, clearly, never lost his enthusiasm for his subject.

Gloucestershire Road (Pelham Books; £8.95) is a history of that club, written by Grahame Parker. He is a Gloucestershire man who played for the county between 1932 and 1950 and was their secretary/manager from 1968 to 1976. Thus he grew up in the atmosphere and traditions of Gloucestershire cricket, picking up the lore of the game there from men whose memories reached back to the Grace brothers, knowing the players of another 70 or 80 years personally. Thus this is as informed, sound and sympathetic a county history as could be wished; written with all the knowledge, care, accuracy and warmth one would expect from the author.

Hampshire Cricketers 1800-1982 (Association of Cricket Statisticians; 127, Davenport Drive, Cleethorpes, S Humberside; £1.50) by Victor Isaacs and Philip Thorn is yet another – the fifteenth – in the Association's series of biographical notes on the players of various counties, states and countries. It maintains the usual high standards of concentration and thoroughness.

Milestones of Hampshire Cricket (Hampshire Cricket Society; 34, Porteous Crescent, Chandler's Ford, Eastleigh, Hampshire SO5 2DH; 80p) by Alan Edwards is a sound, nineteen-page, octavo, chronological listing of the main events and records in the county's history.

Victoria versus Western Australia; a Statistical Survey (from Roger Page, 55 Tarcoola Drive, Yallambie, Victoria, Australia; $A5.50; in the UK from E. K.

Brown, Bevois Mount, Church Street, Liskeard, Cornwall) is a duplicated 32-page folio covering the period 1892-93 to 1982-83. Like the author's *Queensland versus Western Australia* of 1982, it is published in a limited edition of 100 copies signed by the author.

That meticulous researcher, James D. Coldham, has gathered together the relatively thin information available on the subject in *German Cricket: a Brief History* (limited edition of 125 copies, 100 of which are for sale signed by the author, from E. K. Brown, Bevois Mount, Church Street, Liskeard, Cornwall; £5.75). The story runs from the formation by some English and American residents of Berlin CC in 1858. It deals with the Berlin League; the German cricketers' only tour to England, in 1930; visits to Leicester, Dartford, Gentlemen of Worcestershire and Somerset Wanderers, all before 1939. Since 1945 there have been many visits by English clubs to BAOR: cricketers of many nationalities have played in Germany, and there have been frequent fixtures between Germany and Denmark. The father figure of the game there and former player, Kurt Rietz, still hopes that another German team may yet visit England.

Once more the crop of club histories seems to call for a separate collection, or at least a bibliography, of them. This year six are offered for review, and they are listed alphabetically.

One Hundred and Fifty Years of Cricket and Sport in County Carlow (from N. D. McMillan, Carlow Regional Technical College, Kilkenny Road, Carlow, Ireland; £2, plus 50p postage) by N. D. McMillan and D. Foot is subtitled "An illustrated social history of conflict and sport". A 60-page quarto, meticulously researched and documented, it chronicles the progress and problems of what the authors describe as "Ireland's Premier Team".

Sides and Squares (Clifton Cricket Club, Cribb's Causeway, Henbury, Bristol; £3) is an 84-page octavo history of Clifton Cricket Club 1819-1983, edited by J. F. Burrell. Described as one of the oldest of cricket clubs and founded on Clifton Downs, its playing members have included W. G. Grace, C. L. Townsend, Walter Hammond, Barry Richards and more than a hundred other Test and county cricketers. The story is impressive and readable.

Durham School Cricket Club (from Durham School, Durham, DH1 4SZ; no price given) is a 40-page octavo. It marks a remarkable twelvemonth in which the school team reached the final of the National Schools Competition, made a trip to Holland, a tour of Barbados and met a Warwickshire county XI in a benefit match for the former Warwickshire player, now the school professional and groundsman, Tom Collin.

Hertfordshire Cricket Club; One Hundred Years of Cricket at Balls Park (Hertford CC, 7, Sadlers Way, Hertford; 75p) by Lawrie Wright is a 35-page octavo. As evidence of the current health of the club, the foreword indicates that, in 1946 "the club struggled to run two elevens a week, and the average age was slightly over forty. Today the club runs as many as eight elevens a week and the average age is probably below twenty – and this does not include our colts fixtures".

100 Years at Bankfield 1883-1983 (Kirkheaton Cricket Club, Kirkheaton, Yorkshire; £1) by D. Alan Stephenson is a 64-page octavo. It is the centenary history of the club immortalised in the old Yorkshire saw – "Who is the world's greatest all round cricketer? Nobody knows except that he batted right-hand, bowled left; and played for Kirkheaton." It was the club of George

Henry Hirst and Wilfred Rhodes, both of whom feature, and are quoted, in the history.

About Twenty-five Years of Cricket (from the author, Department of Agricultural Economics, University of Reading, Whiteknights, Reading, RG6 2AA; £5.50 including postage) by Tony Giles is a 185-page octavo. It is a painstakingly recorded history of the Reading University Academic Staff Cricket Club.

If some think that the England tour of Australia in 1932-33 has been – and continues to be – flogged to death, there must always be gratitude for any study which sheds fresh and unbiased light on a matter which has engendered so much, and such distorted and heated, argument. Therefore it is reassuring to find *The Bodyline Controversy* (Secker & Warburg; £9.95) by Laurence Le Quesne commended by G. O. Allen in his foreword and containing much considered and fresh first-hand testimony from Bob Wyatt, Bill Bowes and Leslie Ames. It must be difficult to decide the best qualifications for a writer on this subject. This author, however, has been a history teacher at Shrewsbury School, spent two periods as a university lecturer in Australia, has long had "a passionate armchair interest in cricket" and has published studies of Francis Kilvert and Thomas Carlyle. That would seem a sound balance of interests, and he maintains an admirable objectivity. It remains surprising that none of the writers on this subject has referred to the known instances of the employment of fast-leg theory, not only by Bill Voce, but also by Harold Larwood, in the English county season of 1932. Nevertheless this is a valuable contribution to an over-laboured theme.

Cricket's Biggest Mystery: The Ashes (Lutterworth Press; £6.95) by Ronald Willis, a Yorkshireman now settled in Australia, offers another likelihood of a balanced story. In this instance, though, there is no real dispute nor partisan feeling. It would be difficult to agree that this is, in fact, the game's biggest mystery, or, for that matter, that its solution is of any great historic importance. Further, it would be difficult for anyone to argue that Mr Willis solves such mystery as does exist. Nevertheless this is a carefully researched, thoroughly documented, readable, and well-constructed period piece about the second stage of the story of "The Ashes".

The Wisden Book of Cricket Quotations (Queen Anne Press; £9.95) by David Lemmon represents much faithful study and selection by one who describes himself as "an avid reader of the game". Mr Lemmon has obviously ranged far, wide and deeply in the literature of cricket. Some readers may argue with his choice; justifiably, in part, because the literature of the sport is so rich that much of it demands inclusion in such a book. It might be suggested, though, that if selection is on a strictly literary basis, then Sir Neville Cardus is entitled not only to more, but to far more, than any other writer. Nevertheless this is an enthusiastic, well-arranged, ponderable and diverting selection.

A Question of Cricket (Unwin Paperbacks; £1.75) is a collection of quiz questions by Derek Lodge who won the Council of Cricket Societies quiz for three years running. It comprises 420 questions as diverting to the reader who can answer them as to the one who cannot. Fortunately for everyone's peace of mind, the answers are appended.

Summer of Speed (Collins; £6.95) is a photographic record by Patrick Eagar, with commentary by Alan Ross, on the Australia-England Test series of

1982-83. As Patrick Eagar grows older he grows also in wisdom. He has always had an all but uncannily brilliant knack of taking his photographs at the precise moment of relevant event. He has, too, developed a parallel dimension of human perception which illuminates the players as well as the play. This collection demonstrates that extra dimension: and establishes him firmly at the top of his tree, not merely as a specialist cricket photographer, but as an all-round creative artist with a camera.

Botham Down Under (Collins; £7.95) by Ian Botham, with the assistance of Ian Jarrett, deals with the same Test series. The account is never more convincing than on the final phases of the fourth – Melbourne – Test, when Botham recalls that bowling to Thomson he was "scared stiff for about the first time on a cricket pitch". About the entire series, and his own cricket and future in particular, Botham is revealingly frank.

Decision Against England (Methuen; £7.95) by Robin Marlar also deals with England in Australia 1982-83. Mr Marlar has a considerable background of cricket experience, a quick mind, something of a taste for controversy and a lively writing style. Here he recounts the playing side of the tour thoroughly enough; but he is also concerned with the general scene. The values, stresses, setting, and ideas of present-day cricket differ vastly from those of former times. Mr Marlar examines them in characteristic style in his chapters on "Packaged Cricket; Australian Style"; "Codes of Behaviour"; "Electronic Aids"; "The Great Umpire Controversy"; and "Australia off the Field"; and he quotes the script of the TV Test commercial. This is an immensely readable and thought-provoking book.

The Fight for the Ashes 1982-83 (from the author, GPO Box 696, Adelaide 5001, South Australia; £4), by Chris Harte, is a 253-foolscap-page, cyclostyled account of that series, published in a limited edition of 400 copies. Mr Harte, who is editor of the Australian Cricket Society journal, has written an enthusiastic, painstaking and detailed account of the Tests, with illuminating background material. Printing and illustration, too, are of unusually high standard for the method.

Cricket World Cup '83 (Unwin Paperbacks; £1.95) edited by Derek Hodgson is a 48-page quarto, brought out with commendable speed, with results, full scores, averages and accounts of that entire competition. The report of the final, in which India prevented West Indies from achieving a third win, is engrossing. So are several other match reports; some of them amazing. The appendix of records is adequate; the illustrations good and varied.

In *Kiwis and Indians* (Collins; £6.95) Patrick Eagar illustrates, with a commentary by Alan Ross, the main interests of the English season of 1983; World Cup, Test series with New Zealand, Benson and Hedges Cup, NatWest Bank Trophy and, finally, Yorkshire's win in the John Player League – which provides a picture of human rather than player interest. Once again, Alan Ross, poet, cricketer, cricket correspondent of *The Observer* and, subsequently, reporter for *The Times*, provides an economic, perceptive and polished commentary. The combination of photographer and writer has proved most effective.

Tea for Twenty-two (from the author, The Coach House, Ponsonby, Seascale, Cumbria, CA20 1BX; £6.95) is the tireless and cheerful Nico Craven's latest – seventeenth – annual act of Gloucestershire piety from Cumbria. His 131 infallibly chatty pages have a wrapper and frontispiece by

Frank Fisher, a foreword by Paul Fitzpatrick and a few intrusions of non-Gloucestershire matches.

Probably the greatest of all the advances in cricket writing during the past 30 years has been in the field of biography, autobiography and "autobiography". The "ghost" has been replaced by the acknowledgement and acceptance of responsibility by the writer or assistant. In addition, there are now, as a determinable trend, fewer books on lesser, currently, but often briefly, successful players and more on past cricketers of genuine importance.

The Centurions (Dent; £8.95) by Patrick Murphy is further evidence of the author's advance into maturity. It is subtitled "Profiles of the 20 batsmen who have scored a hundred 100s – from Grace to Zaheer". Mr Murphy has obviously gone as near as possible to source, and to first-hand evidence, for his material. The result is a series of essays which blend history, technical analysis, character study and anecdote in a satisfying and pleasingly readable fashion.

Vintage Cricketers (Allen & Unwin; £9.95) is a series of studies and opinions of cricketers by E. M. Wellings who was, for 36 years, cricket correspondent of the London *Evening News*, for whom he made nine tours of Australia. The time range is wide but pre-1939 players receive most attention and produce the best anecdotes, especially in the chapter on "Survivors of the Golden Age".

Bradman; the Illustrated Biography (Macmillan, Australia; £14.95) by Michael Page is a weighty volume in the best sense of the word. It is also large; 376 quarto pages with 300 illustrations, all of which are strictly relevant and many of which are here published for the first time. The wrapper and the title page note that this biography has been compiled "using the private possessions of Sir Donald Bradman" which, as the author's introduction, "A Note of Thanks", makes clear, may be taken to mean also that Sir Donald provided personal information and, where necessary, guidance. Michael Page, who is English born, settled in Australia in 1952 and is an experienced author of fiction, travel, and, most notably, studies of Australian history and social life. He was invited to prepare this book after Sir Donald had declared himself unable to accept Macmillan's request to write his autobiography, but agreed to make his personal records available to Mr Page if he would undertake a biography. He notes that his subject has "a formidable memory, apparently capable of recalling every ball of every significant match"; as a result he is "able to feel that the narrative is a totally accurate interpretation of Sir Donald's story and of his attitude towards life".

His final words of gratitude to Sir Donald are "for the privilege of knowing one of the great men of our time". This is not, however, a fulsome book. Indeed, it deliberately avoids sensationalism or extravagance. There have been eleven previous biographical studies of Bradman; those of A. G. Moyes and Irving Rosenwater of appreciable value; while Sir Donald himself has published four books of an autobiographical nature. None, though, is of this stature. It is not an easy read, but it is as near complete as may be; and, in its way, a model of its kind. Would indeed that there existed comparably subject-assisted studies of, especially, W. G. Grace, F. R. Spofforth and S. F. Barnes; how much more profound the understanding and knowledge of cricket would be if such information were available.

Johnny Won't Hit Today (Allen & Unwin; £8.95) by David Lemmon is, of course, a biography of J. W. H. T. Douglas, which was one of the few

remaining major gaps in player studies. The author, a loyal supporter of Essex, has much worthwhile material to his hand. Although Douglas grew up into the Edwardian age he was more of a modern in his sternly competitive approach. Never a lucky cricketer, he was fearless, a man of inflexible integrity; an unusually talented all-round athlete; Olympic gold medallist as a boxer; English amateur international footballer; an immensely determined batsman and, in the opinion of Sir Jack Hobbs, the finest fast-medium bowler he ever faced. The Rev. Frank Gillingham said of him "If I had my back to the wall and was in trouble, I would rather have John Douglas alongside me than any other man". Surely enough, he died heroically. There is no need to say more than that Mr Lemmon has done his subject justice.

A Funny Turn (Allen & Unwin; £5.95) is the autobiography of Ray East, the slow left-arm bowler of Essex, written "in association with Ralph Dellor" and embellished with drawings by the effervescent Bill Tidy. Ray East is a genuinely and naturally funny man. He tells a good story, writes and jokes entirely without malice, and has produced a happy, amusing, readable – and often wise – book.

Captain's Innings; An Autobiography (Stanley Paul; £6.95) by Keith Fletcher with almost invisible acknowledgement to Alan Lee is, at 156 pages and without index, physically slight. That said, it must be recognised as being as honest, revealing, sincere, and even moving, a story as any cricketer has told these many years. Fletcher's treatment by the crowd at Headingley – which obliquely explains many of Yorkshire's current cricketing problems – Pakistan 1969 ("the worst tour ever?" he asks); and his handling by Mr Peter May, are related as simply and convincingly as could be asked. Mr Fletcher has never been an extrovert figure; and, utterly averse to public speaking, has not always made his case clear. Here, though – and Mr Lee's work in this respect is unobtrusively skilful – he speaks from the heart. Many reading this book will find new sympathy with him, and appreciate the admiration of other county dressing rooms for his captaincy. This is not "the gnome" but the captain the Essex players know, respect and have followed to success.

Heroes and Contemporaries (Collins; £5.95) by David Gower – with Derek Hodgson – is an evaluation of some of the major cricketers the author has played with and against. His judgements are often technically perceptive, humanly astute, well illustrated by anecdote, and infallibly free of rancour, even where that might so easily occur. These eighteen studies are followed by an essay on David Gower which Derek Hodgson obviously enjoyed writing.

The Heart of Cricket (Arthur Barker; £7.50) by Tom Graveney comes from a publisher with a most happy record of cricket books. It is a spontaneous piece of writing from a man who was a spontaneous cricketer, naturally relaxed. Competitive, at need, he had always an ease which was as apparent in the unhurried elegance of his stroke-making as it now is in his observant but sympathetic broadcasting on the game. It will be read with the same warmth and pleasure with which it was written.

Family Argument (Allen & Unwin; £6.95) by John Hampshire "in association with Don Mosey" is subtitled "My 20 years in Yorkshire cricket". In 1982 John Hampshire left Yorkshire and "went to Derbyshire to see if it was possible once more to find joy and pleasure and laughter in playing cricket". Although it has its phase of violence – Charlie Griffith – his book shows at every page how deep was his loyalty to, and preoccupation with, Yorkshire

cricket; and it emphasises the extent of the trauma that caused him to leave. This is a piece of Yorkshire cricket history, with at least a half-happy ending.

Although Lord Harris had written two volumes of autobiography (*A Century of Yeoman Service* of 1899 and *A Few Short Runs*, 1921) there had never been a serious attempt at a biographical examination of this most considerable figure in cricket history, until now, with James D. Coldham's *Lord Harris* (Allen & Unwin; £10.95). It was the lack of any appreciable objective information about him that prompted that tireless and impeccable researcher, James Coldham, to embark on this study; and it has proved most illuminating. He is persuaded to greater personal admiration than others have evinced, but then his studies may well have enabled him to understand his subject better than they. Another significant gap in the cricket bookshelf has now been filled.

Ranji: Prince of Cricketers (Collins; £10.95) by Alan Ross is a biography of a quite remarkable cricketer by one of the most accomplished writers modern cricket has had. Mr Ross has accomplished the necessary bridge of understanding. He has much picturesque material, notably from the cricket field, but also in the social world, where his subject "introduced the motor car to Connemara", and his place in international affairs as Chancellor of the Chamber of Princes and India's representative at the League of Nations. He quotes Gilbert Jessop on Ranji, "he was indisputably the greatest genius who ever stepped on to a cricket field, the most brilliant figure in what, I believe, was cricket's most brilliant period". He quotes, also, Anthony de Mello, a major administrator of Indian cricket: "Ranji did absolutely nothing for Indian sport and sportsmen. To all our requests for aid, encouragement and advice Ranji gave but one answer; 'Duleep and I are English cricketers'." Alan Ross, at the end of a compelling story, writes: "Ranji never attempted to fuse the English cricketer and the Indian prince. England was his glorious past, not India, which represented a present and future fraught with problems and frustrations."

Everything Under the Sun (Stanley Paul; £8.95) by Jeff Stollmeyer is subtitled "My Life in West Indies Cricket". It is the story of the man who, as batsman, member of the breakthrough team of 1950, captain, administrator and, eventually, president of the West Indies Board of Control, aided, counselled and helped to lead his country's cricket to its present position of eminence. A successful and astute businessman, he did much to steer the game there through the Packer turmoil; and he ends on a note of caution, that it still walks an economic and, therefore, political tightrope. Essentially, though, it is the book of an observant, happy, and humorous cricketer with a knack of making friends.

Glenn Turner's Century of Centuries (Hodder & Stoughton; £9.95) by Ray Cairns, a New Zealand journalist, and Glenn Turner himself is, in effect, a phase of autobiography written partly in the third person. It lists those centuries one by one, relating each to the match situation, describing them technically, and reflecting, sometimes deliberately, sometimes unconsciously, the development of the skills and the personality of one of the more humanly complex characters among modern cricketers. So, far from the repetitive method becoming monotonous, it remains immensely readable.

The Captain's Diary (Collins Willow; £8.95) by Bob Willis, in conjunction with the diligent Alan Lee and with a foreword by Greg Chappell, is a running account of England's tour in Australia and New Zealand 1982-83. Despite their

defeat and the captain's disappointments, it is a good-tempered book; and full of interesting information, without being sensationalist. The illustrations are good, and the Frindall scoresheets as revealing as ever.

Zed; Zaheer Abbas (World's Work; £6.95) is an autobiographical study written "with David Foot" who also provides a substantial introductory profile. It is a revealing picture. To take two examples: of his work for his BA degree, "I have studied hard by my standard and, for a number of years, hardly picked up a bat. It was the responsibility of a son to his parents". (By the age of 34 he had completed one hundred centuries.) Or "70 per cent of my fan mail comes from India (which) no doubt emanates from the very successful series I had against India in 1978 when I finished with an average of 194". It is an interesting but cool look at the cricket – county and international – of our time by one of its most successful run scorers.

Test Match Special 2 (Queen Anne Press; £9.95) edited by Peter Baxter, is an all-but-complete re-write of the first *Test Match Special*; devoting most of its space to the 1981, 1982, 1983 seasons both at home and overseas. There are, too, some fresh stories – or as fresh as the programme's traditions allow. Familiar, often funny, profoundly friendly, it does not disturb the pattern.

Playfair Cricket Annual 1983 (Queen Anne Press; £1.25) edited by Gordon Ross, with statistics by Barry McCaully, Brian Heald and Brian Croudy, is the 36th edition of this useful pocket-sized annual. Much of its value lies in the concise biographies. There is, though, a well-arranged series of statistics, including career records of contemporary players.

Daily Telegraph Cricket Year Book '84 (The Daily Telegraph; £4.95), edited by Norman Barrett, has Michael Melford as consultant editor and Bill Frindall contributing statistics. Once more, in its second year, it has succeeded in appearing in mid-November with records of the cricket year and, therefore, the English season complete to September 1983. Surveys by Michael Melford, E. W. Swanton and the relative newcomer, David Green, are followed by the facts of tours by and to England; the home Championship; limited-overs competitions; and the representative cricket of the other seven Test-playing countries. It ends a highly professional editorial and production operation with fixtures for, and a look forward to, the English season of 1984.

Benson and Hedges Cricket Year: Second Edition (Pelham Books; £10.95) edited by David Lemmon, with Tony Lewis as associate editor and Victor Isaacs as credited statistician, covers the period September 1982 to September 1983, thus rounding off at the end of the English season. An extremely ambitious venture, it, too, achieved publication by mid-November. Its 544 pages are 65 more than the previous issue and it deals thoroughly with the cricket, domestic and representative, of full members of the ICC and the visits to Zimbabwe. Its statistics, even of limited-overs matches are exhaustive; the reviews – by Frank Tyson, Robin Marlar, Don Cameron, Tony Lewis and the editor – are both ample and "a good read" as the saying is, while illustration (with plenty of colour pictures) and production are generous.

The 1982 Shell Cricket Almanack of New Zealand (available in the UK from E. K. Brown, Bevois Mount, Church Street, Liskeard, Cornwall; £5), edited by the late Arthur H. Carman, was the 35th issue, all having been produced by the diligent Mr Carman. It is as immaculate as ever in presentation and content. As well as providing thorough coverage of the 1981-82 season there, it reports the 1981-82 Australian tour of New Zealand; and the Women's

World Cup, staged in New Zealand in January–February 1982 and won by Australia, who beat England in the final. The Batsman of the Year is J. G. Wright; the Bowler of the Year M. C. Snedden. This and the previous 34 almanacks make an unspectacular but enduring memorial to the man who created and sustained it.

Indian Cricket 1982 (Kasturi; available in the UK from E. K. Brown, Bevois Mount, Church Street, Liskeard, Cornwall; £3) compiled by S. Thyagarajan, is the 36th issue. At 616 pages it is both wide in coverage and remarkably good money's-worth. It covers the domestic competitions, England in India 1981-82 and India in England 1982. The Four Cricketers of the Year are I. T. Botham, G. Boycott, Maninder Singh and Raghuram Bhat.

Indian Cricket 1983 (Kasturi; available in the UK from Appleby's Books, 29 Millcroft, Carlisle, Cumbria, CA3 0HX; £3.25 post free) compiled by S. Thyagarajan is the 37th edition. As well as reports and records of domestic competitions, it covers India in West Indies 1983, and in Pakistan 1982-83; and Sri Lanka in India 1982. The Cricketers of the Year are M. Amarnath, L. R. D. Mendis, R. M. H. Binny, S. Khandkar and B. S. Sandhu; and there is an enthusiastic appreciation of Salim Durrani.

The 1982 Protea Cricket Annual of South Africa (available in the UK from E. K. Brown, Bevois Mount, Church Street, Liskeard, Cornwall; £5 including post), published with the co-operation of the South African Cricket Union, is "Volume 29" of the series. It was the first issue to be edited by Eric Litchfield, but he never saw the completed work. Previously sports editor of *The Cape Times*, he had been appointed to editorship of the annual only a few months before, and had almost completed preparation of the copy for print when he died from a heart attack. So his obituary is one of several in this Annual; others are of I. J. Siedle, Tom Reddick, Geoff Chubb, Frank Nicholson and Gerald Innes. In his editor's notes Mr Litchfield wrote of the "sanctions-busting operation" of Graham Gooch's team; and his choice of Cricketers of the Year fell on R. L. S. Armitage, A. P. Kuiper, V. F. du Preez and S. T. Jefferies. The 386 well-printed-and-produced pages are strong on statistics and deal with all levels of white South African cricket, including the schools.

Hampshire Handbook 1983 (Hampshire CCC, County Ground, Southampton; £1.50) edited by Peter Marshall and Tony Mitchener, contains a number of feature articles. They are by David Frith, Imogen Grosberg, Nick Pocock, David Kenny, Kevin Emery, Patrick Symes and Victor Isaacs.

Middlesex County Club Review 1982/83 (Middlesex CCC, Lord's Ground, London NW8 8QN; £2.95) edited by A. D. Seth-Smith, marks another year of success in which the county won the Championship. The review contains articles by Mike Brearley (on "Developing a Winning Team"), Michael Melford, Derek Lodge, Bill Tucker and Barry Norman; and many well-reproduced photographs.

Surrey County Cricket Club Yearbook 1983 (Surrey CCC, Kennington Oval, London SE11 5SS; £2.95), edited by C. H. Burgess, is a well-produced booklet. There are features about Roger Knight and Robin Jackman, articles by Micky Stewart, Alex Bannister and Raman Subba Row, records and statistics by George Russ.

The Irish Cricket Union Yearbook, 1983 (Irish Cricket Union, 45 Foxrock Park, Foxrock, Dublin 18, Ireland; 80p including postage) covers the Union's doings at all levels.

Cricket '83 (TCCB, Lord's Ground, London NW8 8QN; £1) edited by Reg Hayter, is the official public relations annual of the TCCB. It is an attractive and entertaining compilation with feature articles by Frank Keating, John Warr, Benny Green, Ian Wooldridge, Dudley Doust, Robin Marlar, Tony Lewis, Peter Smith, Mike Brearley, Paul Parker, Alex Bannister, Frank Tyson, Phil Sharpe, Scyld Berry, Colin Cowdrey and Peter Roebuck; and generous illustrations, many of them in colour.

The periodicals seem in a healthy state. *The Cricketer International Quarterly* (The Cricketer, Beech Hanger, Ashurst, Tunbridge Wells, Kent; four issues annually; £1.05 each), edited by Gordon Ross and subtitled *Facts and Figures*, reached ten years of publication with the Spring issue of 1983. It is most valuable in maintaining full scores of Test series and international tours, the Sheffield Shield and West Indian Shell Shield, potted scores of other national competitions, together with career records, and the unofficial tours of South Africa. The statistical team is composed of Barry McCaully, Bill Frindall, Brian Heald and Brian Croudy. Mr Heald's county "Who's Who" is admirably complemented by Mr Frindall's "Meet the Newcomers", which affords early information on players making first appearances in the first-class or county game.

Cricketer International (The Cricketer, Beech Hanger, Ashurst, Tunbridge Wells, Kent, TN3 9ST; monthly 85p), now in its 64th volume, is edited by Christopher Martin-Jenkins. Among its regular contributors are its editorial director, E. W. Swanton, Tony Cozier, Michael Melford, Alan Gibson, Alan Lee (the County Scene), Andrew Longmore and the editor. Production is good – including colour – and presentation attractive.

Wisden Cricket Monthly (Wisden Cricket Magazines; Punch Distribution Services, 23-27 Tudor Street, London EC4 0HR; monthly 75p), edited by David Frith, is now in its fifth year. Regular contributors are Keith Andrew, Bob Willis, Jim Laker, Ted Dexter, Derek Lodge, Jack Bannister, David Gower, Patrick Eagar, John Arlott and the editor. The magazine has a considerable pictorial bias and reputation, reflected in the "Picture Gallery" feature, cricket film nights, and the occasional use of colour photography.

Cricketer (Newpress, 603-611 Little Lonsdale Street, Melbourne 3000, Victoria, Australia, five magazines, December–April, and two "tour specials" [seven publications in all]; $A16.50), edited by Ken Piesse, has endured strongly into its eleventh volume. It covers about 70 pages an issue, and its contributors include Ian Brayshaw, Phil Wilkins, "Dick" Whitington, Frank Tyson, Bill Lawry, Ashley Mallett and Richard Cashman. Interesting occasional use is made of colour illustrations, but its main strength lies in its news, separate state reports, and feature coverage.

Australian Cricket (Federal Publishing Co., 140 Joynton Avenue, Waterloo, NSW 2017, Australia; eight fortnightly issues October–February; $A1.75 each) appears in tabloid newspaper form and makes considerable use of colour illustration in a "pop", WSC star, approach.

The Cricket Player (Marlborough House, PO Box 28-280 Remuera, Auckland, New Zealand; eight issues, September to April, annually; subscription $NZ9.75) is now edited by Richard Becht with Robin Craze as managing editor. Contributors include Dick Brittenden, Don Cameron, and Martin Horton, who is the national director of coaching. This remains a sound magazine, affording a unique coverage of New Zealand cricket.

An unusually large number of seven fiction titles ranges widely in approach and quality. *Thomas Winsden's Cricket Almanack* (Severn House; £5.95) is a 122-page octavo. As its title and yellow wrapper indicate, it is intended to be a take-off of *Wisden*. No-one can speak with certainty of other people's sense of humour. Some people may find it funny.

Run Out in the Country (Macmillan; £5.95) by Richard Digance is a 203-page story including statistics, written by an author who does not allow his biographical blurb to be serious, or important. Solicitor's clerk Winston Waites takes his team of West Indians from the decaying streets of East London to Little Dow in Buckinghamshire. "The air filled with cockney rhyming slang and pleasurable prittle-prattlings as the two sides mingled before the game. But enough of the old 'rabbit' me old china, your presence is required at Lord Smythe's meadow." Who should be there but Slogger Stevenson whose strokeplay was "about as subtle as a road accident". The glossary is necessary as it gradually becomes more laboured and more murky than funny.

The Guide to Real Village Cricket (Harrap; £4.95) is written by Robert Holles, illustrated by Roy Raymonde, and has an appreciative foreword by Trevor Bailey. Both the text and the illustrations are unforcedly funny; but there is a genuine undercurrent of truth, never stronger than on the subject of "Commuter Takeovers". It is a cricketer's book.

Pulpit Cricket and Other Stories (Collins Willow; £7.95) by Fergus McKendrick is worthwhile for the rules of "Pulpit Cricket" alone. There are, though, other pleasures in a collection based on the author's experience of "cricket at all levels where competence is not a prerequisite".

Horton's Test (Rotabook; £5.95) by David Petri describes itself as: "A cliffhanging novel by the king of descriptive action. The background is a dynamic and nailbiting cricket story." By coincidence, Michael Horton was biting his nails on the verandah outside the England changing room while Sir Maurice Kerr stood in Bebington's office watching the Australian Fleetfoot-Jones bowling to Porthead. A famous cricket critic is credited with describing this as "A highly inventive tale which cricket addicts will find hard to resist". Those with longer memories will find it a souped up *Boy's Realm*.

The Brigadier Down Under (Macmillan; £4.95) by Peter Tinniswood follows not only the Brigadier, but also his lady wife, to Australia. The Brigadier does not find the territory pleasing: "The vile sun blazed down shamelessly from a smug and disgustingly blue sky." Despite his Tony Greig medal for supreme patriotism, which he displays on his hip pocket, he has problems getting into the Melbourne ground, although Innersoles has assured him that, if the lady wife – whom they have adopted as a mascot – does not attend, the England team will refuse to play. Even "the worldly, debonair, sophisticated Lord Henry Blofeld had to rattle his sabre most fearsomely before he was let in, disguised as Mrs Bill Frindall". The brigadier was not so badly off as Naunton, who was threatened with "the ultimate deterrent known to Australian jurisprudence – two days' solitary confinement with Ian Chappell". For those anxious about his welfare it may be stated that he returns safely to the mythology of Witney Scrotum.

Bodyline (Faber; £7.95) by Paul Wheeler is subtitled "The Novel" and is a fictional presentation of the unquenchable story of the 1932-33 Australian-England Test series. It has been skilfully written; and is to be made into a film by David Puttnam, which is in itself a considerable commendation. Yet it is difficult to resist the impression that the reading of the main characters, by one who never knew them, does not justify the course of the plot. Perhaps the label of fiction is never more justified than in locating the love interest with Freddie Brown.

Cathedral End (Adelaide Branch of the Australian Cricket Society, GPO Box 696, Adelaide 5001, South Australia; apparently three issues a year gratis to members, or $A2.00 per issue), edited by Christopher Harte, has entered its fourth year. A cyclostyled foolscap of unnumbered pages it has a wide range and enthusiastic approach.

The Cricket Diary 1984 (from the editor, 18, Ashley Avenue, Lower Weston, Bath, BA1 3DS; £2.95) is edited by John Dixon, who a few years ago used to open the bowling for Gloucestershire. It is a good working diary, embellished with an historical chart, a number of illustrations, and quotations from a wide range of sources. There are, too, a number of useful addresses and telephone numbers, as well as some illuminating statistics.

The last item to arrive in time for inclusion in this notice was *The Cricket Year* (Peter Isaacson Publications, 46, Porter Street, Pahran 3181, Victoria, Australia; $A9.95), edited by Ken Piesse; a 176-page quarto annual of Australian cricket. Generously illustrated, both lively and thorough in treatment, it reviews the Australian season of 1982-83, and covers the tours of England, New Zealand and Sri Lanka in Australia; Australia in Sri Lanka, and the Australian Under-25 side in Zimbabwe. The Who's Who section of 170 Australian players is particularly valuable. There is an eight-page picture supplement, largely by Patrick Eagar and Garry Sparke; and the five cricketers of the year are David Gower, Geoff Lawson, Graham Yallop, Kepler Wessels and Kim Hughes – J. A.

★   ★   ★   ★   ★

The reviewer wrote one book himself, *How to Watch Cricket* (Collins Willow; £6.95), and another, *A Word from Arlott* (Pelham; £9.95), bore his name. John Arlott published *How to Watch Cricket* in 1948 and again in 1949. His latest book employs the same title; but, as the text indicates, the game itself and, because of television, watching it have changed so much in the interim that it has been completely rewritten. The author introduces the game, describes the basics, establishes definitions and differentiates between first-class and other cricket. There is additional information on England's six Test grounds and profiles of the seventeen first-class counties.

A Word from Arlott is a selection of Mr Arlott's work made by David Rayvern Allen, who worked closely at the BBC with his subject. Besides cricket commentaries there are pieces on enough other topics to give some idea of the remarkable breadth of Mr Arlott's knowledge. As one reads the extracts it is as though that inimitable voice can be clearly heard. This is a well-earned tribute to one whose brilliant broadcasting provided as much pleasure to the cricketing fraternity as the batting of many a famous player.

FIXTURES, 1984

* Indicates Sunday play.   *† Not first-class.*

Wednesday, April 18

Cambridge	Univ. v Leics.

Saturday, April 21

Cambridge	Univ. v Essex
Oxford	Univ. v Notts.

Wednesday, April 25

Lord's	MCC v Essex
Cambridge	Univ. v Hants
Oxford	Univ. v Glam.

Saturday, April 28

Chesterfield	Derby. v Leics.
Bristol*	Glos. v Kent
Southampton*	Hants v Essex
Lord's	Middx v Glam.
Nottingham*	Notts. v Surrey
Taunton*	Somerset v Yorks.
Birmingham*	Warw. v Northants
Worcester*	Worcs. v Sussex
Oxford	Univ. v Lancs.

Wednesday, May 2

Canterbury	Kent v Essex
Manchester	Lancs. v Derby.
Nottingham	Notts. v Leics.
The Oval	Surrey v Northants
Worcester	Worcs. v Glam.
Cambridge	Univ. v Sussex
Oxford	Univ. v Somerset

Saturday, May 5

Birmingham	Warw. v Surrey

†Benson and Hedges Cup (1 day)

Chelmsford	Essex v Glos.
Swansea	Glam. v Somerset
Southampton	Hants v Oxford & Cam. U.
Lord's	Middx v Kent
Bowdon	Minor Counties v Lancs.
Northampton	Northants v Scotland
Nottingham	Notts. v Worcs.
Leeds	Yorks. v Leics.

Wednesday, May 9

Derby	Derby. v Glam.
Southampton	Hants v Glos.
Manchester	Lancs. v Kent
Leicester	Leics. v Worcs.
Northampton	Northants v Essex
Hove	Sussex v Surrey

Leeds	Yorks. v Notts.
Cambridge	Univ. v Warw.
Oxford	Univ. v Middx

Saturday, May 12

† Benson and Hedges Cup (1 day)

Bristol	Glos. v Hants
Canterbury	Kent v Glam.
Manchester	Lancs. v Notts.
Leicester	Leics. v Warw.
Oxford	Oxford & Cam. U. v Surrey
Perth	Scotland v Yorks.
Taunton	Somerset v Sussex
Worcester	Worcs. v Derby.

Tuesday, May 15

† Benson and Hedges Cup (1 day)

Derby	Derby. v Notts.
Chelmsford	Essex v Surrey
Bristol	Glos. v Oxford & Cam. U.
Canterbury	Kent v Somerset
Leicester	Leics. v Northants
Lord's	Middx v Sussex
Birmingham	Warw. v Yorks.
Worcester	Worcs. v Minor Counties

Thursday, May 17

† Benson and Hedges Cup (1 day)

Manchester	Lancs. v Worcs.
Shrewsbury	Minor Counties v Derby.
Northampton	Northants v Warw.
Cambridge	Oxford & Cam. U. v Essex
Taunton	Somerset v Middx
The Oval	Surrey v Hants
Hove	Sussex v Glam.
Glasgow (Hamilton Cres.)	Scotland v Leics.

Saturday, May 19

Worcester*	Worcs. v West Indians
Leicester	Leics. v Somerset
Oxford	†Univ. v MCC

† Benson and Hedges Cup (1 day)

Derby	Derby. v Lancs.
Cardiff	Glam. v Middx
Southampton	Hants v Essex
Nottingham	Notts. v Minor Counties
The Oval	Surrey v Glos.
Hove	Sussex v Kent
Birmingham	Warw. v Scotland
Bradford	Yorks. v Northants

Wednesday, May 23

Taunton	Somerset v West Indians
Chesterfield	Derby. v Surrey
Chelmsford	Essex v Notts.
Cardiff	Glam. v Glos.
Lord's	Middx v Northants
Hove	Sussex v Hants
Nuneaton (Griff and Coton)	Warw. v Lancs.
Worcester	Worcs. v Leics.

Saturday, May 26

Swansea*	Glam. v West Indians
Derby	Derby. v Notts.
Chelmsford	Essex v Surrey
Canterbury	Kent v Hants
Leicester	Leics. v Northants
Lord's	Middx v Sussex
Taunton	Somerset v Glos.
Birmingham	Warw. v Worcs.
Leeds*	Yorks. v Lancs.
Oxford	†Univ. v Free Foresters

Tuesday, May 29

Liverpool	†Lancs. v West Indians (1 day)

Wednesday, May 30

Southampton	Hants v Somerset
Dartford	Kent v Middx
Northampton	Northants v Lancs.
The Oval	Surrey v Glam.
Birmingham	Warw. v Notts.
Worcester	Worcs. v Essex
Sheffield	Yorks. v Sussex
Oxford	Univ. v Glos.

Thursday, May 31

Manchester	†ENGLAND v WEST INDIES (1st 1-day Texaco Trophy)

Saturday, June 2

Nottingham	†ENGLAND v WEST INDIES (2nd 1-day Texaco Trophy)
Derby	Derby. v Middx
Swansea	Glam. v Worcs.
Bournemouth	Hants v Notts.
Canterbury	Kent v Glos.
Manchester	Lancs. v Surrey
Hinckley	Leics. v Essex
Horsham	Sussex v Northants
Middlesbrough	Yorks. v Somerset
Belfast (Ormeau)*	†Ireland v MCC

Monday, June 4

Lord's	†ENGLAND v WEST INDIES (3rd 1-day Texaco Trophy)

Wednesday, June 6

†**Benson and Hedges Cup – Quarter-Finals**
(1 day)

Thursday, June 7

Oxford	†Oxford & Cam. U. v West Indians (2 days)

Saturday, June 9

Milton Keynes*	Northants v West Indians
Ilford	Essex v Warw.
Gloucester	Glos. v Derby.
Tunbridge Wells	Kent v Yorks.
Manchester	Lancs. v Sussex
Nottingham	Notts. v Glam.
Bath	Somerset v Middx
The Oval	Surrey v Leics.
Worcester	Worcs. v Hants

Wednesday, June 13

Ilford	Essex v Derby.
Gloucester	Glos. v Worcs.
Basingstoke	Hants v Yorks.
Tunbridge Wells	Kent v Sussex
Leicester	Leics. v Warw.
Lord's	Middx v Surrey
Bath	Somerset v Lancs.
Cambridge	Univ. v Glam.

Thursday, June 14

Birmingham	ENGLAND v WEST INDIES (1st Cornhill Test, 5 days)

Saturday, June 16

Chelmsford	Essex v Northants
Cardiff	Glam. v Lancs.
Southampton	Hants v Leics.
Lord's	Middx v Warw.
Nottingham	Notts. v Glos.
Guildford	Surrey v Sussex
Harrogate	Yorks. v Derby.
Worcester	Worcs. v Cambridge U.
Oxford	Univ. v Kent

Wednesday, June 20

†**Benson and Hedges Cup – Semi-Finals**
(1 day)

Harrogate	†Tilcon Trophy (3 days)

Thursday, June 21

Dublin   †Ireland v West Indians
(Rathmines)   (2 days)

Saturday, June 23

Chelmsford*	Essex v West Indians
Derby	Derby. v Kent
Bristol	Glos. v Hants
Manchester	Lancs. v Worcs.
Leicester	Leics. v Notts.
Northampton	Northants v Yorks.
The Oval	Surrey v Middx
Hove	Sussex v Glam.
Birmingham	Warw. v Somerset

Wednesday, June 27

Chesterfield	Derby. v Essex
Swansea	Glam. v Middx
Bournemouth	Hants v Sussex
Manchester	Lancs. v Glos.
Northampton	Northants v Warw.
Nottingham	Notts. v Yorks.
Taunton	Somerset v Leics.
Hereford	Worcs. v Kent
The Oval	Surrey v Cambridge U.

Thursday, June 28

Lord's   ENGLAND v
             WEST INDIES
             (2nd Cornhill Test,
             5 days)

Saturday, June 30

Swansea	Glam. v Leics.
Liverpool	Lancs. v Middx
Northampton	Northants v Somerset
The Oval	Surrey v Hants
Hastings	Sussex v Kent
Birmingham	Warw. v Glos.
Worcester	Worcs. v Derby.
Leeds	Yorks. v Essex
Nottingham	Notts. v Cambridge U.
Portsmouth*	†Combined Services v Oxford U.

Wednesday, July 4

Lord's   Oxford v Cambridge

†NatWest Bank Trophy – First Round
(1 day)

Kendal (Netherfield)	Cumb. v Derby.
Darlington (Feethams)	Durham v Northants
Chelmsford	Essex v Scotland
Swansea	Glam. v Notts.
St Albans	Herts. v Somerset
Canterbury	Kent v Berks.
Manchester	Lancs. v Bucks.

Norwich (Lakenham)	Norfolk v Hants
Jesmond	Northumb. v Middx
Telford (St Georges)	Salop. v Yorks.
Stone	Staffs. v Glos.
The Oval	Surrey v Ireland
Hove	Sussex v Devon
Birmingham	Warw. v Oxon.
Swindon (County Ground)	Wilts. v Leics.
Worcester	Worcs. v Suffolk

Thursday, July 5

Colwyn Bay   †League Cricket
             Conference v West
             Indians (2 days)

Saturday, July 7

Leicester*	Leics. v West Indians
Chesterfield	Derby. v Warw.
Southend	Essex v Glam.
Maidstone	Kent v Lancs.
Uxbridge	Middx v Worcs.
Northampton	Northants v Surrey
Nottingham	Notts. v Sussex
Taunton	Somerset v Hants
Bradford	Yorks. v Glos.

Wednesday, July 11

Southend	Essex v Lancs.
Cardiff	Glam. v Yorks.
Southampton	Hants v Northants
Maidstone	Kent v Derby.
Leicester	Leics. v Sussex
Uxbridge	Middx v Glos.
Nottingham	Notts. v Somerset
Worcester	Worcs. v Warw.

Thursday, July 12

Leeds   ENGLAND v WEST
            INDIES (3rd Cornhill
            Test, 5 days)

Saturday, July 14

Cardiff	Glam. v Somerset
Bristol	Glos. v Essex
Portsmouth	Hants v Lancs.
Lord's	Middx v Yorks.
Northampton	Northants v Kent
Nottingham	Notts. v Worcs.
The Oval	Surrey v Derby.
Birmingham	Warw. v Sussex

Sunday, July 15

Dublin   †Ireland v Wales
(Malahide)

Wednesday, July 18
†NatWest Bank Trophy – Second Round
(1 day)

Chester-le-Street or Northampton	Durham or Northants v Worcs. or Suffolk
Chelmsford or Glasgow (Titwood)	Essex or Scotland v Surrey or Ireland
Cardiff or Nottingham	Glam. or Notts. v Northumb. or Middx
Norwich (Lakenham) or Southampton	Norfolk or Hants v Kent or Berks.
Stone or Bristol	Staffs. or Glos. v Lancs. or Bucks.
Hove or Torquay	Sussex or Devon v Herts. or Somerset
Birmingham or Oxford (Morris Motors)	Warw. or Oxon. v Salop. or Yorks.
Swindon (County Ground) or Leicester	Wiltshire or Leics. v Cumb. or Derby.

Thursday, July 19

West Bromwich (Dartmouth)	†Minor Counties v West Indies (2 days)

Saturday, July 21

Lord's	†BENSON & HEDGES CUP FINAL (1 day)
Derby*	Derby v West Indies (or Warw. if Derby in B & H Cup Final)

Wednesday, July 25

Cleethorpes	Notts. v Sri Lankans
Buxton	Derby. v Lancs.
Bristol	Glos. v Leics.
Northampton	Northants v Middx
Taunton	Somerset v Glam.
The Oval	Surrey v Kent
Birmingham	Warw. v Hants
Scarborough	Yorks. v Worcs.

Thursday, July 26

Manchester	ENGLAND v WEST INDIES (4th Cornhill Test, 5 days)

Saturday, July 28

The Oval*	Surrey v Sri Lankans
Chelmsford	Essex v Worcs.
Swansea	Glam. v Derby.
Bristol	Glos. v Northants

Lord's	Middx v Hants
Nottingham	Notts. v Lancs.
Hove	Sussex v Somerset
Birmingham	Warw. v Kent
Sheffield	Yorks. v Leics.

Wednesday, August 1

Nottingham	Notts. v West Indies (if Notts. not in NatWest Bank Trophy quarter-finals)

†NatWest Bank Trophy – Quarter-Finals
(1 day)

Saturday, August 4

Lord's*	Middx v West Indies
Cheltenham	Glos. v Sri Lankans
Southampton	Hants v Warw.
Canterbury	Kent v Leics.
Manchester	Lancs. v Yorks.
Northampton	Northants v Derby.
Weston-super-Mare	Somerset v Surrey
Eastbourne	Sussex v Essex
Worcester	Worcs. v Notts.

Sunday, August 5
†Warwick Under-25
Semi-Finals (1 day)
(or Sunday, August 12)

Wednesday, August 8

Southampton	Hants v Sri Lankans
Cheltenham	Glos. v Glam.
Canterbury	Kent v Surrey
Southport	Lancs. v Northants
Leicester	Leics. v Yorks.
Lord's	Middx v Essex
Nottingham	Notts. v Derby.
Weston-super-Mare	Somerset v Worcs.
Eastbourne	Sussex v Warw.

Thursday, August 9

The Oval	ENGLAND v WEST INDIES (5th Cornhill Test, 5 days)

Saturday, August 11

Canterbury*	Kent v Sri Lankans
Derby	Derby. v Sussex
Chelmsford	Essex v Somerset
Cardiff	Glam. v Hants
Cheltenham	Glos. v Surrey
Leicester	Leics. v Lancs.
Lord's	Middx v Notts.
Wellingborough School	Northants v Worcs.
Leeds	Yorks. v Warw.

Sunday, August 12

†Warwick Under-25
Semi-Finals (1 day)
(if not played on
Sunday, August 5)

Wednesday, August 15
†NatWest Bank Trophy – Semi-Finals

Saturday, August 18

Hove*	Sussex v Sri Lankans
Colchester	Essex v Hants
Swansea	Glam. v Northants
Folkestone	Kent v Notts.
Manchester	Lancs. v Warw.
Leicester	Leics. v Middx
Taunton	Somerset v Derby.
The Oval	Surrey v Yorks.
Worcester	Worcs. v Glos.

Wednesday, August 22

Chesterfield	Derby. v Yorks.
Colchester	Essex v Kent
Bournemouth	Hants v Middx
Blackpool	Lancs. v Notts.
Leicester	Leics. v Glos.
Northampton	Northants v Sussex
The Oval	Surrey v Somerset
Birmingham	Warw. v Glam.
Glasgow (Titwood)	Scotland v Ireland

Thursday, August 23

Lord's	ENGLAND v SRI LANKA (Cornhill Test, 5 days)

Saturday, August 25

Bristol	Glos. v Lancs.
Bournemouth	Hants v Kent
Northampton	Northants v Leics.
Nottingham	Notts. v Warw.
The Oval	Surrey v Essex
Hove	Sussex v Middx
Worcester	Worcs. v Somerset
Bradford	Yorks. v Glam.

Sunday, August 26

Birmingham	†Warwick Under-25 Final (1 day)

Wednesday, August 29

Birmingham	Warw. v Sri Lankans
Chelmsford	Essex v Middx
Swansea	Glam. v Surrey
Nottingham	Notts. v Northants
Taunton	Somerset v Kent
Hove	Sussex v Glos.
Scarborough	†Derby. v Yorks. (1 day, ASDA Cricket Challenge)

Thursday, August 30

Scarborough	†Hants v Lancs. (1 day, ASDA Cricket Challenge)

Friday, August 31

Scarborough	†ASDA Cricket Challenge Final (1 day)

Saturday, September 1

Lord's	†NATWEST BANK TROPHY FINAL (1 day)

Sunday, September 2

Scarborough	DB Close's International XI v Sri Lankans

Wednesday, September 5

Cardiff	Glam. v Warw.
Bristol	Glos. v Somerset
Leicester	Leics. v Derby.
Lord's	Middx v Kent
Hove	Sussex v Notts.
Worcester	Worcs. v Northants
Scarborough	Yorks. v Hants

Saturday, September 8

Derby	Derby. v Hants
Bristol	Glos. v Middx
Canterbury	Kent v Glam.
Manchester	Lancs. v Essex
Taunton	Somerset v Notts.
The Oval	Surrey v Worcs.
Hove	Sussex v Yorks.
Birmingham	Warw. v Leics.

WEST INDIAN TOUR, 1984

MAY

19 Worcester	v Worcs.
23 Taunton	v Somerset
26 Swansea	v Glam.
29 Liverpool	†v Lancs. (1 day)
31 Manchester	†v ENGLAND (1-day Texaco Trophy)

JUNE

2 Nottingham	†v ENGLAND (1-day Texaco Trophy)
4 Lord's	†v ENGLAND (1-day Texaco Trophy)

7 Oxford	†v Oxford & Cam. U. (2 days)	19 West Bromwich (Dartmouth)	†v Minor Counties (2 days)
9 Milton Keynes*	v Northants	21 Derby	v Derby. (or v Warw. if Derby. in B & H Cup Final)
14 Birmingham	v ENGLAND (1st Cornhill Test, 5 days)		
21 Dublin (Rathmines)	†v Ireland (2 days)	26 Manchester	v ENGLAND (4th Cornhill Test, 5 days)
23 Chelmsford*	v Essex		
28 Lord's	v ENGLAND (2nd Cornhill Test, 5 days)		

AUGUST

JULY

5 Colwyn Bay	†v League Cricket Conference (2 days)	1 Nottingham	v Notts. (or v another county if Notts. in NatWest Bank Trophy quarter-finals)
7 Leicester*	v Leics.		
12 Leeds	v ENGLAND (3rd Cornhill Test, 5 days)	4 Lord's*	v Middx
		9 The Oval	v ENGLAND (5th Cornhill Test, 5 days)

SRI LANKAN TOUR, 1984

JULY

25 Cleethorpes	v Notts.	18 Hove*	v Sussex
28 The Oval*	v Surrey	23 Lord's	v ENGLAND (Cornhill Test, 5 days)
		29 Birmingham	v Warw.

AUGUST

4 Cheltenham*	v Glos.
8 Southampton	v Hants
11 Canterbury	v Kent

SEPTEMBER

2 Scarborough	v DB Close's International XI

†JOHN PLAYER SUNDAY LEAGUE, 1984

APRIL

29 – Leics. v Derby. (Leicester)

MAY

6 – Essex v Notts. (Chelmsford); Glam. v Glos. (Swansea); Hants v Sussex (Southampton); Middx v Kent (Lord's); Warw. v Surrey (Birmingham); Yorks. v Worcs. (Bradford).

13 – Lancs. v Northants (Manchester); Middx v Essex (Lord's); Somerset v Hants (Taunton); Surrey v Glam. (The Oval); Worcs. v Notts. (Worcester).

20 – Derby. v Lancs. (Derby); Glam. v Middx (Cardiff); Kent v Surrey (Canterbury); Leics. v Somerset (Leicester); Northants v Warw. (Northampton); Sussex v Glos. (Hove); Yorks. v Notts. (Hull).

27 – Essex v Surrey (Chelmsford); Glos. v Somerset (Bristol); Leics. v Sussex (Leicester); Middx v Northants (Lord's); Notts. v Derby. (Nottingham); Warw. v Worcs. (Birmingham).

JUNE

3 – Derby. v Middx (Derby); Hants v Notts. (Southampton); Kent v Glos. (Canterbury); Lancs. v Surrey (Manchester); Leics. v Essex (Hinckley); Sussex v Northants (Horsham); Worcs. v Glam. (Worcester); Yorks. v Somerset (Middlesbrough).

10 – Essex v Warw. (Ilford); Glos. v Derby. (Gloucester); Kent v Yorks. (Canterbury); Lancs. v Sussex (Manchester); Notts. v Glam. (Nottingham); Somerset v Middx (Bath); Surrey v Leics. (The Oval); Worcs. v Hants (Worcester).

17 – Derby. v Yorks. (Chesterfield); Essex v Northants (Chelmsford); Glam. v Lancs. (Cardiff); Hants v Leics. (Basingstoke); Middx v Warw. (Lord's); Notts. v Glos. (Nottingham); Somerset v Kent (Bath); Surrey v Sussex (Guildford).

24 – Derby. v Kent (Derby); Glos. v Hants (Bristol); Lancs. v Worcs. (Manchester); Leics. v Notts. (Nottingham); Northants v Yorks. (Luton); Surrey v Middx (The Oval); Sussex v Glam. (Hove); Warw. v Somerset (Birmingham).

JULY

1 – Glam. v Leics. (Swansea); Lancs. v Middx (Manchester); Northants v Somerset (Northampton); Surrey v Hants (The Oval); Sussex v Kent (Hastings); Warw. v Glos. (Birmingham); Worcs. v Derby. (Worcester); Yorks. v Essex (Leeds).

8 – Derby. v Warw. (Derby); Essex v Glam. (Southend); Kent v Lancs. (Maidstone); Middx v Worcs. (Lord's); Northants v Surrey (Northampton); Notts. v Sussex (Nottingham); Yorks. v Glos. (Scarborough).

15 – Glam. v Somerset (Cardiff); Glos. v Essex (Bristol); Hants v Lancs. (Portsmouth); Middx v Yorks. (Lord's); Northants v Kent (Tring); Surrey v Derby. (Imber Court, East Molesey); Warw. v Sussex (Birmingham); Worcs. v Leics. (Worcester).

22 – Hants v Yorks. (Bournemouth); Kent v Essex (Canterbury); Leics. v Glos. (Leicester); Notts. v Northants (Nottingham); Somerset v Lancs. (Taunton); Worcs. v Sussex (Worcester).

29 – Essex v Worcs. (Chelmsford); Glam. v Derby. (Ebbw Vale); Glos. v Northants (Bristol); Middx v Hants (Lord's); Notts. v Lancs. (Nottingham); Sussex v Somerset (Hove); Warw. v Kent (Birmingham); Yorks. v Leics. (Bradford).

AUGUST

5 – Hants v Warw. (Portsmouth); Kent v Leics. (Canterbury); Lancs. v Yorks. (Manchester); Northants v Derby. (Northampton); Somerset v Surrey (Weston-super-Mare); Sussex v Essex (Eastbourne).

12 – Derby. v Sussex (Heanor); Essex v Somerset (Chelmsford); Glam. v Hants (Cardiff); Glos. v Surrey (Cheltenham); Leics. v Lancs. (Leicester); Middx v Notts. (Lord's); Northants v Worcs. (Wellingborough School); Yorks. v Warw. (Scarborough).

19 – Essex v Hants (Colchester); Glam. v Northants (Swansea); Kent v Notts. (Folkestone); Lancs. v Warw. (Manchester); Leics. v Middx (Leicester); Somerset v Derby. (Taunton); Surrey v Yorks. (The Oval); Worcs. v Glos. (Worcester).

26 – Glos. v Lancs. (Moreton-in-Marsh); Hants v Kent (Bournemouth); Northants v Leics. (Northampton); Notts. v Warw. (Nottingham); Somerset v Worcs. (Taunton); Sussex v Middx (Hove); Yorks. v Glam. (Leeds).

SEPTEMBER

2 – Derby. v Essex (Derby); Hants v Northants (Southampton); Notts. v Surrey (Nottingham); Warw. v Glam. (Birmingham); Worcs. v Kent (Worcester).

9 – Derby. v Hants (Derby); Glos. v Middx (Bristol); Kent v Glam. (Canterbury); Lancs. v Essex (Manchester); Somerset v Notts. (Taunton); Surrey v Worcs. (The Oval); Sussex v Yorks. (Hove); Warw. v Leics. (Birmingham).

MINOR COUNTIES CHAMPIONSHIP, 1984

Sponsored by United Friendly Insurance

All matches are of two days' duration.

MAY

27 – Lincs. v Staffs. (Sleaford); Northumb. v Herts. (Jesmond).

29 – Cumb. v Herts. (Carlisle).

JUNE

6 – Cambs. v Herts. (Wisbech).

10 – Ches. v Salop. (Oxton); Cumb. v Northumb. (Barrow); Lincs. v Beds. (Cleethorpes).

12 – Durham v Beds. (Durham City).

13 – Herts. v Staffs. (to be arranged).

19 – Herts. v Lincs. (to be arranged).

24 – Beds. v Cambs. (Henlow); Cornwall v Ches. (Falmouth); Durham v Cumb. (Hartlepool).

26 – Somerset II v Ches. (Westlands, Yeovil).

27 – Staffs. v Beds. (Leek).

JULY

8 – Ches. v Bucks. (Broughton Hall, Chester); Cornwall v Somerset II (Falmouth); Cumb. v Norfolk (Kendal); Lincs. v Cambs. (Stamford); Northumb. v Durham (Jesmond).

10 – Salop. v Bucks. (Bridgnorth); Staffs. v Norfolk (Brewood).

16 – Ches. v Oxon. (Toft).

18 – Cambs. v Suffolk (Fenner's); Devon v Cornwall (Exmouth); Salop. v Oxon. (Wellington).

21 – Beds. v Herts. (Bedford School); Berks. v Bucks. (Finchampstead).

22 – Durham v Lincs. (Stockton-on-Tees); Oxon. v Somerset II (Morris Motors); Staffs. v Cumb. (Knypersley).

23 – Beds. v Northumb. (Wardown Park, Luton); Cornwall v Salop. (Truro); Herts. v Suffolk (to be arranged).

24 – Dorset v Wilts. (Weymouth).

25 – Devon v Salop. (Newton Abbot); Cambs. v Northumb. (Peterborough).

26 – Berks. v Oxon. (Bradfield College).

29 – Ches. v Berks. (Nantwich); Cornwall v Dorset (St Austell); Somerset II v Wilts. (Taunton).

31 – Norfolk v Lincs. (Lakenham); Salop. v Berks. (Shrewsbury); Suffolk v Durham (GRE, Ipswich); Wilts. v Devon, (Bemerton, Salisbury).

AUGUST

2 – Dorset v Devon (Bournemouth Sports Club); Norfolk v Cambs. (Lakenham).

5 – Beds. v Cumb. (to be arranged); Bucks. v Somerset II (Slough); Dorset v Ches. (Sherborne School); Lincs. v Northumb. (Lincoln Lindum); Oxon. v Cornwall (St Edward's School).

6 – Staffs. v Suffolk (Walsall).

7 – Berks. v Somerset II (Kidmore End); Cambs. v Cumb. (March); Devon v Ches. (Torquay); Norfolk v Northumb. (Lakenham); Wilts. v Cornwall (Chippenham).

9 – Norfolk v Durham (Lakenham).

12 – Dorset v Berks. (Dean Park, Bournemouth); Oxon. v Devon (Christchurch).

13 – Durham v Cambs. (Chester-le-Street); Herts. v Norfolk (to be arranged); Northumb. v Staffs. (Jesmond); Somerset II v Salop. (Westlands, Weston-super-Mare); Suffolk v Lincs. (Mildenhall).

14 – Berks. v Devon (Reading School); Wilts. v Bucks. (Devizes).

15 – Dorset v Salop. (Bournemouth Sports Club); Durham v Staffs. (Gateshead Fell); Suffolk v Norfolk (Ransomes, Ipswich).

16 – Bucks. v Devon (Marlow); Oxon. v Wilts. (Banbury Twenty Club).

19 – Beds. v Norfolk (Goldington Bury, Bedford); Bucks. v Cornwall (High Wycombe); Ches. v Wilts. (Bowdon); Cumb. v Lincs. (Millom); Northumb. v Suffolk (Jesmond); Oxon. v Dorset (Christchurch).

20 – Devon v Somerset II (Bovey Tracey); Herts. v Durham (to be arranged).

21 – Berks. v Cornwall (Reading CC); Bucks. v Dorset (Monks Risborough); Cumb. v Suffolk (Netherfield, Kendal); Salop. v Wilts. (Oakengates, St Georges).

22 – Cambs. v Staffs. (Fenner's).

26 – Bucks. v Oxon. (Amersham); Somerset II v Dorset (Millfield School, Street); Suffolk v Beds. (Bury St Edmunds).

27 – Wilts. v Berks. (County Ground, Trowbridge).

SEPTEMBER

8 – Final Play-off.

The composition of the Eastern and Western Divisions may be found on page 785.

†MINOR COUNTIES KNOCKOUT COMPETITION, 1984

English Industrial Estates Trophy

Qualifying Round

May 20 Berks. v Bucks. (Courage, Reading); Ches. v Cumb. (Neston); Norfolk v Suffolk (Pinebanks, Norwich).

First Round

June 3 Ches. v Cumb. or Durham (Winnington Park, Northwich or to be arranged); Devon v Cornwall (Sidmouth); Dorset v Wilts. (Sherborne School); Herts. v Cambs. (to be arranged); Lincs. v Northumb. (Long Sutton); Norfolk or Suffolk v Beds. (Pinebanks or to be arranged); Oxon. v Staffs. (Christchurch, Oxford); Salop. v Berks. or Bucks. (Newport, Salop.).

Quarter-Finals to be played on June 17.

Semi-Finals to be played on July 1.

Final to be played at Fenner's, Cambridge, on July 15.

†SECOND ELEVEN CHAMPIONSHIP, 1984

All matches are of three days' duration.

APRIL

25 – Glos. v Warw. (Bristol).

MAY

2 – Derby. v Lancs. (Derby), Leics. v Warw. (Leicester), Notts. v Glam. (Caythorpe).

9 – Essex v Kent (Eton Manor, Leyton), Lancs. v Northants (Blackburn), Notts. v Yorks. (Nottingham), Somerset v Warw. (Taunton), Sussex v Surrey (Eastbourne).

16 – Derby. v Yorks. (Chesterfield), Glam. v Notts. (Neath), Hants v Somerset (Bournemouth), Kent v Surrey (Maidstone), Leics. v Northants (Market Harborough), Warw. v Glos. (Stratford-upon-Avon).

23 – Lancs. v Kent (Manchester), Middx v Sussex (Southgate), Northants v Derby. (Northampton), Notts. v Leics. (Worksop), Somerset v Hants (Imperial, Bristol), Surrey v Essex (The Oval), Yorks. v Warw. (Harrogate).

30 – Derby. v Leics. (Bass, Burton upon Trent), Glam. v Lancs. (Cardiff), Middx v Kent (Lensbury, Teddington), Notts. v Warw. (Collingham), Somerset v Worcs. (Taunton).

JUNE

6 – Glos. v Glam. (Bristol), Hants v Essex (Southampton), Northants v Middx (Finedon), Notts. v Lancs. (Worthington Simpson, Newark), Sussex v Kent (Hastings), Yorks. v Surrey (Bradford).

13 – Derby. v Notts. (Derby), Northants v Lancs. (Northampton), Surrey v Middx (The Oval), Sussex v Essex (Hove), Warw. v Somerset (Knowle and Dorridge), Worcs. v Leics. (Worcester), Yorks. v Kent (Elland).

20 – Hants v Kent (Bournemouth), Lancs. v Derby. (Blackpool), Northants v Essex (Horton), Sussex v Middx (Eastbourne), Warw. v Notts. (Leamington), Worcs. v Somerset (Ombersley), Yorks. v Glam. (Marske-by-Sea).

27 – Essex v Sussex (Chelmsford), Glam. v Glos. (Usk), Leics. v Lancs. (Leicester), Surrey v Hants (Banstead), Warw. v Worcs. (Olton), Yorks. v Notts. (Bradford).

JULY

4 – Glam. v Hants (Cardiff), Kent v Essex (Dartford), Lancs. v Yorks. (Liverpool), Leics. v Notts. (Lutterworth), Middx v Northants (Harefield), Surrey v Sussex (Guildford), Worcs. v Warw. (Old Hill).

11 – Kent v Lancs. (Canterbury), Northants v Yorks. (Milton Keynes), Notts. v Derby. (Steetley), Somerset v Glam. (Taunton), Sussex v Hants (Hove), Warw. v Leics. (Griff & Coton, Nuneaton).

18 – Derby. v Northants (Heanor), Glam. v Worcs. (Swansea), Kent v Hants (Folkestone), Leics. v Middx (Hinckley), Somerset v Glos. (Taunton), Surrey v Yorks. (The Oval), Sussex v Notts. (Eastbourne), Warw. v Lancs. (Moseley).

25 – Essex v Northants (Southchurch Park, Southend), Glam. v Yorks. (Gorseinon), Leics. v Derby. (Leicester), Middx v Warw. (Harrow), Surrey v Lancs. (Barclays Bank, Norbury), Worcs. v Glos. (Worcester).

AUGUST

1 – Essex v Middx (Westcliff-on-Sea), Glam. v Somerset (Llanarth), Glos. v Worcs. (Bristol), Hants v Surrey (Bournemouth), Kent v Sussex (Gore Court, Sittingbourne), Lancs. v Warw. (Middleton), Northants v Notts. (Peterborough).

8 – Essex v Notts. (Chelmsford), Northants v Leics. (Northampton), Surrey v Kent (Purley), Warw. v Middx (Birmingham), Worcs. v Glam. (Worcester), Yorks. v Lancs. (York).

15 – Derby. v Worcs. (Shipley Hall), Glos. v Somerset (Bristol), Kent v Middx (Dover), Lancs. v Surrey (Southport), Warw. v Glam. (Moseley).

22 – Glam. v Warw. (Pontardulais), Glos. v Essex (Bristol), Hants v Sussex (Southampton), Lancs. v Somerset (Preston), Middx v Surrey (Enfield), Notts. v Northants (Southwell), Yorks. v Derby. (Barnsley).

29 – Glam. v Kent (Usk), Hants v Glos. (Southampton), Lancs. v Notts. (Heywood), Leics. v Worcs. (Leicester), Middx v Essex (South Hampstead), Sussex v Warw. (Eastbourne), Yorks. v Northants (Leeds).

SEPTEMBER

5 – Essex v Surrey (Chelmsford), Hants v Middx (Southampton), Lancs. v Glam. (Manchester), Warw. v Yorks. (Birmingham).